Drama

Drama

Drama

Jeffrey D. Hoeper

Arkansas State University

James H. Pickering

University of Houston

Deborah K. Chappel

Arkansas State University

Macmillan Publishing Company
New York

Editor: D. Anthony English
Production Supervisor: Jane O'Neill
Production Manager: Francesca Drago
Text Designer: Anne Flanagan
Cover Designer: Tom Mack
Cover illustration: Francis Hayman, "Wrestling Scene," Tate Gallery, London. Cover
art photographed by John Webb.

This book was set in New Baskerville by Americomp and was printed and bound by
Rand McNally and Co. The cover was printed by New England Book Components,
Inc.

Acknowledgments appear on pages 1467–1469, which constitute an extension of the
copyright page.

Macmillan Publishing Company
866 Third Avenue, New York, New York 10022

Macmillan Publishing Company is part of
the Maxwell Communication Group of Companies.

Maxwell Macmillan Canada, Inc.
1200 Eglinton Avenue East
Suite 200
Don Mills, Ontario M3C 3N1

Library of Congress Cataloging-in-Publication Data
Drama / [compiled by] Jeffrey D. Hoeper, James H. Pickering, Deborah
   K. Chappel.
       p.   cm.
   An anthology of twenty-nine theatrical works, with critical
commentary.
   ISBN 0-02-355601-3
   1. Plays—Collections.   I. Hoeper, Jeffrey D.   II. Pickering,
James H.   III. Chappel, Deborah K.
PN6111.D68   1994
808.2—dc20   92-43806
                    CIP

Printing: 1   2   3   4   5   6   7   Year: 4   5   6   7   8   9   0

Preface

Between the covers of this book twenty-nine plays wait to be brought to life by a new generation of students. Many of the plays have been widely considered classics for centuries; others have won their places in the past hundred years; still others are among today's contenders for a place in the literary canon. The most recent authors range from men such as Nigerian Nobel prizewinner Wole Soyinka and American cult figure Sam Shepard to such ground-breaking women dramatists as Susan Glaspell and Alice Childress. Although this collection includes the plays most often taught by professors and most often demanded by students, our principal criterion in selection was to include plays that would be sure to provoke classroom discussion while illustrating the historical development of drama. Despite the twenty-four hundred years that separate *Agamemnon* from *Am I Blue?*, Aeschylus and Beth Henley are of the same creative lineage. The reader's understanding will be richer for comprehending the work of both artists and what stands chronologically between them.

Because it is an anthology of theatrical works, this book could have been called *Plays,* but a play is a solid fact: a set structure of plot, characters, dialogue, and stage directions. "Drama" is not only the play itself but the atmosphere the play creates—the different effect every stage production of the play has on every different audience, the intellectual stimulation it produces in every different reader, the entire spectrum of emotional responses it elicits. Therefore this book is entitled *Drama.* It is not just a generous collection of plays but an introduction to the critical reading of them. It provides a brief review of the elements of drama and the critical vocabulary necessary for discussing the experience of seeing or reading a play. But it goes beyond these fundamentals: it encourages the reader to recognize and explore the many different angles of appreciation from which a play can be viewed as a performance or read as a work.

The introductory chapters in *Drama* lay the groundwork for critical approaches and supply some basic tools. The critical commentary that follows each play offers at least one practical opening for critical interpretation, although not by any means the only interpretation or even the best interpretation. It is the reader's duty to argue with each such commentary and to

weigh alternatives. To help the reader do so, each play is also followed by a
selective bibliography for further reading. The critical commentary for three
of the plays—*King Oedipus, Othello,* and *The Glass Menagerie*—is augmented
with extracts from a variety of critical essays to illustrate how professional
scholars use critical strategies and to demonstrate how such professional
conclusions often differ widely from each other. These tools, models, and
approaches will help readers discover their own routes for critical interpretation.

Drama is the result of several years' hard work and many vigorous, although friendly, disputes. We found our own advice to quarrel with particular interpretations and approaches almost too easy to follow. Fortunately,
our debates were enlightened by many recommendations from numerous
colleagues who commented candidly on our proposed selections and our
editorial analysis. To the following we offer our sincere thanks for their
advice and assistance: Professor Richard T. Brucher, University of Maine;
Nancy E. Carrick, Ph.D., University of Redlands; Ralph G. Dille, Ph.D.,
University of Southern Colorado; Professor Bernard Einbond, Lehman
College of the City University of New York; Professor Leona W. Fisher,
Georgetown University; Professor Graham Hayes, Housatonic Community
College; Professor Peter Heinegg, Union College; Professor Morgan Y.
Himelstein, Adelphi University; Professor Robert E. Hoover, Iowa State Uni-
versity; Professor Kathleen Hulley, New York University; Professor Emeritus
William Hunter, The University of Houston; Professor Jascha Kessler, Uni-
versity of California, Los Angeles; Professor Stanely Kozikowski, Bryant Col-
lege; Professor Naomi C. Lieber, Montclair State College; Michael A. Miller,
Ph.D., Longview Community College; Professor Emeritus George Muldrow,
Western Washington University; Professor Georgeann Murphy, Centre Col-
lege; Professor Roger W. Oliver, New York University; Professor Harold
Orel, The University of Kansas; Professor Margaret B. Racin, West Virginia
University; Professor Leah Richards, Alderson-Broaddus College; Professor
Gabrielle Robinson, Indiana University, South Bend; Professor Maureen
Des Roches, Marygrove College; Professor Leo Rockas, University of Hart-
ford; Professor Susan Smith, University of Pittsburgh; Professor Robert
Todd, Worcester State College; Professor Hari Vishwanadha, Santa Monica
College; Professor Emeritus James E. White, Rhode Island College; Profes-
sor Elaine Wise, University of Louisville; and Professor Roy S. Wolper, Tem-
ple University.

In addition, we are particularly grateful to Tony English, our editor at
Macmillan, whose willingness to provide guidance and assistance has done
much to mold the text into its final form.

Whatever merits *Drama* may have are owed in large part to these individuals. Whatever faults or errors have slipped into the text are unfortunately
our own doing.

JDH

JHP

DKC

Contents

1   SEEING AND "READING" DRAMA   1

2   THE NATURE OF DRAMA   5

Drama and Poetry   6
Drama and Fiction   8
The Actors   9
The Audience   14
The Theater   17

3   THE ELEMENTS OF DRAMA   35

Dialogue   35
Story   41
Character   46
Action   49

4   THE CLASSIFICATIONS OF DRAMA   53

Tragedy   53
Comedy   55

5   LITERARY CRITICISM   59

The Nature of Literary Criticism   59
Reading Literary Criticism   61
Critical Strategies for Reading Drama   62
    Formalist Criticism   62
    Psychoanalytical Criticism   64
    Historical Criticism   66

Anthropological and Myth Criticism   69
Structuralist and Deconstructionist Criticism   70
Multicultural Criticism   72

6   ANALYZING AND EVALUATING DRAMA   77

Questions to Ask About Drama   78
Questions to Ask About Literary Criticism   80

7   PLAYS   81

Aeschylus, *Agamemnon*   83
     Critical Commentary on *Agamemnon*   122
     A Selective Bibliography on *Agamemnon*   124
Sophocles, *Antigonê*   127
     Critical Commentary on *Antigonê*   155
     A Selective Bibliography on *Antigonê*   158
Sophocles, *King Oedipus*   161
     Critical Commentary on *King Oedipus*   182
     A Collection of Critical Interpretations   184
     A Selective Bibliography on *King Oedipus*   192
Euripides, *Hippolytus*   195
     Critical Commentary on *Hippolytus*   232
     A Selective Bibliography on *Hippolytus*   235
Aristophanes, *Lysistrata*   237
     Critical Commentary on *Lysistrata*   294
     A Selective Bibliography on *Lysistrata*   296
[anon.], *The Second Shepherd's Play*   297
     Critical Commentary on *The Second Shepherd's Play*
       316
     A Selective Bibliography on *The Second Shepherd's
       Play*   317
[anon.], *Everyman*   319
     Critical Commentary on *Everyman*   339
     A Selective Bibliography on *Everyman*   341
Christopher Marlowe, *Dr. Faustus*   343
     Critical Commentary on *Dr. Faustus*   398
     A Selective Bibliography on *Dr. Faustus*   401
William Shakespeare, *A Midsummer Night's Dream*   403
     Critical Commentary on *A Midsummer Night's Dream*
       455
     A Selective Bibliography on *A Midsummer Night's
       Dream*   457
William Shakespeare, *Othello*   461
     Critical Commentary on *Othello*   539
     A Collection of Critical Interpretations   542

A Selective Bibliography on *Othello*   566
Ben Jonson, *Volpone*   571
    Critical Commentary on *Volpone*   668
    A Selective Bibliography on *Volpone*   670
Molière (Jean-Baptiste Poquelin), *Tartuffe*   673
    Critical Commentary on *Tartuffe*   711
    A Selective Bibliography on *Tartuffe*   713
Henrik Ibsen, *A Doll's House*   715
    Critical Commentary on *A Doll's House*   765
    A Selective Bibliography on *A Doll's House*   767
August Strindberg, *Miss Julia*   769
    Critical Commentary on *Miss Julia*   797
    A Selective Bibliography on *Miss Julia*   798
Henrik Ibsen, *Hedda Gabler*   801
    Critical Commentary on *Hedda Gabler*   858
    A Selective Bibliography on *Hedda Gabler*   860
George Bernard Shaw, *Mrs Warren's Profession*   863
    Critical Commentary on *Mrs Warren's Profession*   909
    A Selective Bibliography on *Mrs Warren's Profession*
      911
Anton Pavlovich Chekhov, *The Cherry Orchard*   913
    Critical Commentary on *The Cherry Orchard*   951
    A Selective Bibliography on *The Cherry Orchard*   953
Susan Glaspell, *Trifles*   955
    Critical Commentary on *Trifles*   964
    A Selective Bibliography on *Trifles*   967
Luigi Pirandello, *Six Characters in Search of an Author*   969
    Critical Commentary on *Six Characters*   1015
    A Selective Bibliography on *Six Characters*   1018
Eugene O'Neill, *Desire Under the Elms*   1021
    Critical Commentary on *Desire Under the Elms*   1060
    A Selective Bibliography on *Desire Under the Elms*
      1062
Tennessee Williams, *The Glass Menagerie*   1065
    Critical Commentary on *The Glass Menagerie*   1114
    The Life of Tennessee Williams   1117
    A Collection of Critical Interpretations   1120
    A Selective Bibliography on *The Glass Menagerie*   1133
Samuel Beckett, *All That Fall*   1135
    Critical Commentary on *All That Fall*   1155
    A Selective Bibliography on *All That Fall*   1157
Lorraine Hansberry, *A Raisin in the Sun*   1159
    Critical Commentary on *A Raisin in the Sun*   1219
    A Selective Bibliography on *A Raisin in the Sun*   1220
Wole Soyinka, *The Strong Breed*   1223
    Critical Commentary on *The Strong Breed*   1247

A Selective Bibliography on *The Strong Breed*   1250
Tom Stoppard, *The Real Inspector Hound*   1253
     Critical Commentary on *The Real Inspector Hound*
        1280
     A Selective Bibliography on *The Real Inspector Hound*
        1283
Alice Childress, *Wine in the Wilderness*   1285
     Critical Commentary on *Wine in the Wilderness*   1309
     A Selective Bibliography on *Wine in the Wilderness*
        1311
Peter Shaffer, *Amadeus*   1313
     Critical Commentary on *Amadeus*   1377
     A Selective Bibliography on *Amadeus*   1380
Samuel Shepard, *True West*   1381
     Critical Commentary on *True West*   1422
     A Selective Bibliography on *True West*   1425
Beth Henley, *Am I Blue?*   1427
     Critical Commentary on *Am I Blue?*   1441

GLOSSARY   1445

Drama

Drama

CHAPTER ONE

❊ ❊ ❊ ❊ ❊ ❊ ❊

Seeing and "Reading" Drama

Seeing a play is quite different from reading it—even if both experiences grow out of a classroom assignment. There is a pleasurable anticipation about going to a live performance of a play. It is an *event,* not something that you do every day. You will probably attend the play in the company of friends, and you may wear your best clothes for the occasion. If it is a good play—and well produced—the stage spectacle will fully engage your senses. When the curtain rises or the stage lights brighten, you will, quite literally, see and hear the characters "come to life." The three dimensional sets and the physical presence of the actors may combine to make this the most "realistic" esthetic experience you have ever had. At the same time you are apt to be quite conscious that what you see is not real at all. It takes place, after all, on a modern stage observed by rustling, coughing spectators and not in the privacy of Desdemona's bedchamber or in ancient Thebes at the palace of Oedipus. If you sit close enough to the stage, you may see the stone wall of the palace tremble a bit as a slammed door shakes the painted cloth.

In contrast, reading a play is usually a solitary procedure, perhaps occurring at a desk in your bedroom or a table in the library. Instead of awakening the senses, it awakens the imagination as you try to visualize the characters, picture the settings, and reconstruct the tones of voice, gestures, and facial expressions that accompany the words. Often these imaginings are somewhat sketchy and ill-defined, like characters seen in silhouette instead of sunlight, but the imaginative activity is always there.

If you are reading carefully, you will also make an effort to "read" the play in a second sense. When we speak of reading someone's mind, reading a map, or reading the clues at the scene of a crime, we use *reading* to mean analyzing or interpreting. A good reading of a play always involves some movement toward critical interpretation. In such a reading one looks for character development, indications of theme, and obvious symbols. Note, however, that this method of reading a play is quite often shared by both the readers of the text and the members of audience at the theater, who rise from their seats after the final curtain eager to discuss what they have just seen. Very likely, they will discuss not only the production itself, but also the characters, action, and ideas in the play. Indeed, this process of critical reading is almost certainly shared by the director and the actors, who must analyze and interpret the play (or their part in it) before attempting to stage it. Critical reading is thus a very natural and necessary activity even though it is sometimes undertaken casually and without deliberation.

This book is an introduction to the critical reading of drama. In the pages that follow, you will find a brief introduction to the elements of drama and the critical vocabulary that enables a discussion of the esthetic experience of seeing or reading a play. But one of the primary goals of this text—a goal that sets it apart from many other texts—is that we want you to recognize the many different angles of vision one can take in seeing a play—or reading it.

As theater-goers, we see plays in a variety of circumstances with a variety of expectations. Sometimes we are seeing a play for the first time, without having read it or any other work by its author. At the other extreme we may attend a performance of a play that we have studied for years and seen in other productions. We may know much—or nothing—about the actors and director. We may know much—or nothing—about the critical interpretation of drama or the technicalities of play production. The characters and action in the play may be strikingly similar to events in the life of one member of the audience while simultaneously so remote from the experiences of the person in the very next seat as to be almost completely unbelievable. A person sitting in the first row may be so close to the actors that she sees every bead of sweat and hears the tap of fingers on a table top; meanwhile, a person sitting in the deepest recess of the balcony may have trouble seeing and hearing at all. On any given night all members of the audience see the same performance, but it is probably fair to say that it is a somewhat different play for each member of the audience. In essence, when we see a play, we bring to it all of our knowledge and experience and interpret the play within the context of what we know. In other words, when we see a play, we also "read" it, but each of us will have something slightly different to read and will read it differently.

The same thing is true of the scholar in her office or the student at his desk. Each will read the play from a different—perhaps even unique—angle of vision. As you learn more about the process of critical interpretation, you will discover that every great play can be approached from many directions. What one sees in the text is heavily influenced by the critical assumptions one makes in choosing an angle of vision. When Sigmund Freud read *King Oedipus*, he saw it as a textbook illustration of the clinical symptoms of arrested sexual development. But when literary critic Francis Fergusson read the same play, he saw it (in part at least) as the first great mystery story in Western literary history. Critics have approached *King Oedipus* from dozens of different angles; each angle of vision may involve quite different critical strategies and spring from very different assumptions about the text. Yet just as one sees something different and revealing by looking at Michelangelo's sculpture of *David* from a different position in the courtyard, so too each well-reasoned interpretation of a play adds useful and revealing insights.

To argue that any great play can be approached from a variety of perspectives is not the same thing, however, as saying that all critical interpretations are equally valid or useful. Just as there may be a great many "right" things that remain to be said about *Oedipus*, so too there are countless "wrong" things that may be said. It is no easy task to distinguish between good interpretations and bad ones, but communicating a shared response is the first obligation of sound criticism. No matter what angle of vision a critic takes, the basic goal should always be the same: to articulate an understanding of the play that grows out of the text or performance and that somehow clarifies the nature of the play.

By introducing you to a variety of critical strategies that you can use in studying individual plays, we hope to put your hands on the levers of power that too often are seen as the exclusive possessions of grey-haired, myopic professors at the most exclusive universities. Surely, you have experienced the vexation of reading a difficult play and feeling absolutely mired in mud, unable to take a single squishy step toward the high ground of a solid critical interpretation. Then your professor explains the play, or you read a thorough critical commentary about it in your textbook. As if by magic, you find yourself on high ground, but you were towed there by a force mightier than your own. And if you are asked to write or say something new about the play, you are in almost the same fix as before, perched on your one mound of high ground with quicksand all around you. By learning some of the basic premises and methods of different critical strategies, we hope to provide you with the intellectual equivalent of four-wheel drive.

The introductory chapters on the elements of drama and the strategies for the study of drama should give you a critical tune-up and a set of sturdy mud tires. The critical commentary that follows each play offers at least one secure spot of high ground, and the selective bibliography for each play is the equivalent of a map to other routes out of the mire. For three major plays—*King Oedipus, Othello,* and *The Glass Menagerie*—we have provided extracts from a variety of critical essays to illustrate how critical strategies are employed by professional scholars. We hope that with these tools and these models you will eventually feel secure enough to venture out on your own journeys of critical exploration.

CHAPTER TWO

❖ ❖ ❖ ❖ ❖ ❖ ❖ ❖

The Nature of Drama

The word *drama* comes from the Greek verb *dran,* meaning "to perform." **When we speak of a drama, we mean a story in dialogue performed by actors, on a stage, before an audience—in other words, a *play*. We also use the term *drama* in a more general sense to refer to the literary genre that encompasses all written plays and to the profession of writing, producing, and performing plays.***

Because drama presupposes performance, it is not a purely literary genre. It combines the use of language with representational arts involving scenery, costuming, and the actors' physical appearance. It also makes use of vocal emphasis and tone of voice, along with such nonverbal forms of expression as physical gesture, facial expression, and sometimes music and dance. Thus, a drama only becomes a complete work of art when it is seen on the stage, and the written text of a play is only its skeletal frame—lacking flesh, blood, and a life of its own. This skeletal script is, however, the only permanent part of a play. The rest is ephemeral: it changes to some degree with each night's performance and, to a considerable extent, with each new production. Presentations of Greek tragedy, for example, have ranged from stately, historically accurate productions to loose, avant-garde adaptations. In one production of Euripides's *The Bacchae* (ca. 405 B.C.) we watch "larger than life" actors struggle to speak clearly while costumed in oversized masks, padded clothing, and sandals with thick platform soles. And in another production of the same play (renamed *Dionysus in 69*), we find naked women splashing their way through oceans of stage blood, engaging in simulated sex, and writhing through a savage "birth ritual."

Such extremes serve to remind us that the script is the only part of the play over which the author has complete control; the rest is the collaborative creation of many different artists, some of whom may misunderstand and therefore misrepresent what the author intended. Because we can never

---

* NOTE: Throughout these introductory chapters, terms that are commonly used in the study of drama are emphasized by boldface italics. Definitions of those terms are set in bold print. When full definitions are not formally marked in the text, they will be found in the glossary.

know exactly how Sophocles, Shakespeare, Molière, and other early drama-tists staged their plays, we can never reproduce exactly the work of art they intended. But in reading the words of the play, we *can* share in the imagi-native experience that—even more than success on the stage—is responsible for the survival and enduring popularity of great drama. We know, for ex-ample, that the plays of Euripides (ca. 480–407 B.C.) were not popular with the audience when first presented in ancient Greece. Yet Euripides' plays have survived through the ages, and those of his more popular contempo-raries are all but forgotten. Apparently, Euripides' intense, introverted style and penetrating character analyses appealed to the readers who commis-sioned and preserved manuscripts of his plays. In contrast, the record for the longest continuous run for a single play is held by Agatha Christie's *The Mousetrap,* which, whatever its merit as drama, as of 1992 had been on stage for 40 years and more than 16,650 performances. Christie's play will not, of course, continue its run forever. Someday the show will close, and thereafter its survival will depend on readers. Only if the demand by the play-reading public is sufficient to keep a play in print, and only if the play in its written form appeals to a succession of producers and directors, can we expect that it will truly become a stage classic.

This is precisely what has happened in the case of Euripides, Shakespeare, and other great classic and modern dramatists, whose readers have almost always outnumbered their viewers. Even today, when the average citizen has an unparalleled opportunity to see outstanding theater on stage (or in ad-aptations for television or film), copies of printed scripts continue to be sold in ever-increasing numbers. Although most lovers of the theater insist upon *seeing* great drama performed, they insist equally upon owning, reading, and studying the plays they love.

The reason for this phenomenon is clear enough: when we study drama as literature—that is, when we study the text of the play, apart from its stag-ing—we may not see the entire work intended by the author, but we do see the words exactly as the playwright wrote them, or as they have been trans-lated, without any cutting, rearranging, or rewriting by the director and without the interpretive assistance (or hindrance) of the actors. The written script may be skeletal compared to a stage presentation, but that limitation can help us to concentrate on the play's structure and on those elements of drama that fall directly under the author's control.

DRAMA AND POETRY

As soon as we think of drama as a form of literature, we begin to notice that a play shares many similarities with a long narrative poem. In fact, from the days of ancient Greece through the first half of the nineteenth century, most plays were written in verse. The dramatic works of Aeschylus, Sophocles, Euripides, Aristophanes, Marlowe, Shakespeare, Jonson, Molière, Racine, Corneille, and many others are largely or entirely poetic. Even Ibsen, who probably did more than any other dramatist to make prose acceptable in tragedy, wrote two of his most famous plays, *Brand* (1866) and *Peer Gynt* (1867), in verse.

The reasons for the historical predominance of verse in drama are not difficult to discover. Drama, like poetry, is meant to be heard. As a result, like poetry, it sometimes makes use of the aural qualities of rhythm and rhyme. Furthermore, because Greek drama originally grew out of choral songs, it was only natural that the musical elements in the songs should be preserved in the plays; and because Greek drama served as a model for most subsequent generations, verse remained an integral part of most playwriting until a growing preoccupation with realism near the end of the nineteenth century made the contrivance of dialogue in verse undesirable. Finally, many of the stages used for drama were relatively barren, and the playwright was forced to evoke through poetic language any characteristics of the setting that he or she wished the audience to envision. Thus, poetic diction, imagery, and techniques of versification became thoroughly integrated into the drama.

One cannot conclude, however, that drama is inevitably a form of poetry. Indeed, in the last century new poetic dramas have rarely been successful on the stage. Popular taste has changed, and audiences now demand realism instead of poetic flourishes. Of course, many of these realistic plays—especially those of Tennessee Williams and Eugene O'Neill—are written in prose which is so imagistic and suggestive that it may be studied as a form of free verse, but even if we confine this discussion to plays more obviously written in verse, we will find some differences between poetry and drama. In the first place, a poem is usually meant for only one speaker; a play for two or more. Similarly, a poem can be written in virtually any verse form, while a play (in English) is limited by tradition to blank verse, heroic couplets, or prose. Finally, most poems are quite short, while most plays are comparatively long. When we speak of the poetry in Shakespeare's plays, we ordinarily refer to only a few well-known passages: the descriptions of Cleopatra's barge or her death in *Antony and Cleopatra*, Marc Anthony's oration in *Julius Caesar*, Portia's speech on mercy in *The Merchant of Venice*, Othello's last words, Hamlet's soliloquies, and so on. Such passages, and others like them, are memorized and anthologized almost as if they were separate poems, while the rest of each play, whether it is truly poetic or not, is read, performed, and analyzed in much the same way as if it were prose. Shakespeare, after all, was human and like other men was apt to put in an occasional dull day at his desk. Take, for example, the following brief scene from *Othello*:

SCENE 2: *A room in the castle. Enter* OTHELLO, IAGO, *and* GENTLEMEN.

OTHELLO.   These letters give, Iago, to the pilot,
   And by him do my duties to the Senate.
   That done, I will be walking on the works.
   Repair there to me.
IAGO.   Well, my good lord, I'll do 't.
OTHELLO.   This fortification, gentlemen, shall we see 't?
GENTLEMEN.   We'll wait upon your lordship.

[*Exeunt.*]

—From *Othello*, act 3, scene 2,
William Shakespeare [1604]

Even if this scene of only six lines served some dramatic function, it would be uninspired writing. Othello's letters to the Senate have no further significance, nor does his inspection of the fortifications. The scene is an encounter of no substance that serves only to waste a little stage time, allowing Cassio to begin the interview with Desdemona that was promised in the preceding scene and that we join in progress in the subsequent one.

The same kind of mechanical drama is even more common in the works of lesser dramatists. The quantity of true poetry in a play is always slight when compared with the larger body of dialogue that is necessary to move the characters around and push the action forward. Indeed, the preponderance of prosaic and merely competent lines in a play helps to make the poetic moments stand out more clearly, so that they seem (to quote Shakespeare) "as the spots of heaven, / More fiery by the night's blackness."

DRAMA AND FICTION

If we take it as axiomatic that the best of a play approaches the level of poetry while the bulk of it remains prosaic, then it follows that most drama is closer to fiction than to poetry. Plays are fictitious both in the literal sense that their plots are generally untrue and in the figurative sense that they intend to convey general truths. Like a novel, a play always tells a story. It cannot be purely lyric, descriptive, or argumentative—although each of these modes of expression has a place in drama. Instead, a play begins like a typical short story with an introduction to the characters, the situation, and the setting. It rapidly develops some conflict among the characters that typically reaches a crisis in the fourth act and finds its resolution in the fifth. And in presenting its action, a play manipulates many of the elements found in a short story. Aristotle, the first theoretician of drama, identified six basic elements in the genre: setting, character, plot, language, theme, and music. All but the last are also elements of fiction, and music is no longer requisite or even common in modern drama.

Despite these similarities, a play clearly differs from a short story and drama differs from fiction. Some of the main differences between genres emerge in the handling of point of view, time, and structure. Unlike a short story, which can present the action from many different points of view, a play is obliged to present its story dramatically. The characters speak directly to one another, and the audience observes their actions without the assistance of a narrator to fill in background information, draw conclusions, and generally serve as a guide to the significance of unfolding events.[1] The playwright cannot pry into the minds of the characters as an omniscient narrator might, and the audience can have no knowledge of a character's thoughts, emotions, or past unless these emerge through dialogue, physical action, or the use of soliloquy.

Because of its dramatic point of view, a play takes place in the perpetual present tense. Where the short story or the novel always implicitly begins, "Once upon a time . . . ," a play both begins and proceeds with "now . . . now . . . now!" The audience always knows what the characters *are*

---

[1] *Our Town* (1938) by Thornton Wilder, *The Glass Menagerie* (1944) by Tennessee Williams, *After the Fall* (1964) by Arthur Miller and a number of other modern plays use a narrator to introduce and control the action, but even in these plays the narrator must eventually step aside and allow the events to unfold objectively and dramatically.

doing while they are onstage, but the playwright has no unobtrusive means of showing what they *have done* either before the curtain rises or while they are offstage. The confidant, who is made privy to another's past, and the messenger, who reports offstage activities, are obvious and sometimes inadequate substitutes for fictional omniscience. Indeed, the author's desire to supply characters with a past helps us to understand why many plays focus on heroes whose exploits are already known to the audience through history or legend.

Another way of stating the difference between fiction and drama is to observe that **a play is structured around a succession of** *scenes*. **A new scene is needed whenever there is a change of setting or time.** (In many French and a few English dramas, a new scene also begins with the entrance or exit of any major character.) **The scenes are often then grouped into** *acts*, **which indicate the major units in the development of the plot.** The formal division of plays into acts and scenes represents a major difference between the structure of drama and that of fiction. In the latter, the plot *may* unfold as a chronological series of scenes, but there is nothing to keep an author from reminiscing within a scene. Thus, fiction may present a convoluted series of stories within stories—*The Arabian Nights* provides many examples—but drama is obliged to present only those plots that can be developed continuously and chronologically.[2]

In the following pages, as we examine the influence of the actors, the audience, and the stage, we will discover other ways in which drama differs from poetry and fiction; it should now be clear, however, that the major elements of drama are also the major elements of poetry and fiction. If you have studied fiction and poetry in the past, you will find that you are already familiar with much of the critical vocabulary for the study of drama.

THE ACTORS

Because drama is primarily designed for performance, we can expect that the greatest plays will encourage and successfully incorporate the creative potential of the actors. A dramatist writes with the knowledge that the play will be presented on stage in a way that emphasizes tonal implications and fulfills the incidents suggested by the dialogue. But while a professional playwright seeks to encourage the actors to interpret their lines creatively, he or she may wish to be sure that the larger thematic impact of the play remains unchanged by different acting styles. By writing their plays for specific stage companies, some dramatists are able to retain a greater measure of control over the initial stage production. Not only can these dramatists conceive the play and write the first draft with the strengths and limitations of key actors and actresses already in mind, but they can also supervise the rehearsals and revise the parts of the play that seem ill-suited to the actors. In many cases, therefore, the text of the play that emerges is the result of some form of collaboration between the playwright and the actors.

Because a playwright must assume that the roles in the script will be

---

[2] There are, to be sure, exceptions, as usual. In *Our Town*, to cite Wilder's play again, the action returns to the past in the last act.

played by real people, with real idiosyncrasies in personality and appearance, there is no need to describe any character's external appearance. The audience can see for itself what Ibsen's Hedda Gabler looks like, and a description of Hedda's appearance, such as one might find in a novel, becomes redundant and unnecessary in the dialogue of a play. Of course, the author's parenthetic stage directions sometimes do include a description of the characters. Hedda, for example, is introduced as

> a woman of nine-and-twenty. Her face and figure show refinement and distinction. Her complexion is pale and opaque. Her steel-gray eyes express a cold, unruffled repose. Her hair is of an agreeable medium brown but not particularly abundant. She is dressed in a tasteful, somewhat loose-fitting morning gown.
>
> —From *Hedda Gabler,* act 1,
> Henrik Ibsen [1890]

But such comments are directed at readers, not viewers. They underscore the fact that a playwright often writes simultaneously for two audiences: one in the theater and the other in the armchair.

In writing for the theater, the dramatist has in the actors a great advantage over the novelist, for the characters in a play *are* real. They live and breathe, stand up and sit down, sigh and smile, enter and exit—all with greater realism than even the most competent novelist can create. The actions and expressions of several characters can be conveyed on stage in a matter of seconds, whereas a novelist might have to devote several pages to a description of the same incidents. As a result, drama has an immediate impact that fiction and poetry can never equal. The illusion of reality in some plays or films is as close as art can ever come to bringing its fictional incidents to life.

But although the playwright is relieved from describing the physical appearance or actions of the characters at length, he or she *cannot* analyze their personalities and motives directly and concisely. An omniscient inquiry into how and why a character speaks, moves, and thinks as he or she does is both desirable and entertaining in a novel by Dickens, but it is not easy to present through dialogue on a stage. Instead, a dramatist individualizes the characters by giving them distinctive habits or quirks of speech and by allowing them to express their personalities through action. Soon after Hedda Gabler first appears on stage, for example, we see her impatience with any references to her femininity or possible pregnancy:

TESMAN.   . . . Auntie, take a good look at Hedda before you go! See how handsome she is!

MISS TESMAN.   Oh, my dear boy, there's nothing new in that. Hedda was always lovely. [*She nods and goes toward the right.*]

TESMAN [*following*].   Yes, but have you noticed what splendid condition she is in? How she has filled out on the journey?

HEDDA [*crossing the room*].   Oh, do be quiet!

MISS TESMAN [*who has stopped and turned*].   Filled out?

TESMAN.   Of course you don't notice it so much now that she has that dress on. But I, who can see—

HEDDA [*at the glass door, impatient*].   Oh, you can't see anything.

TESMAN. It must be the mountain air in the Tyrol—

HEDDA [*curtly interrupting*]. I am exactly as I was when I started.

TESMAN. So you insist, but I'm quite certain you are not. Don't you agree with me, Auntie?

MISS TESMAN [*who has been gazing at her with folded hands*]. Hedda is lovely— lovely—lovely. [*Goes up to her, takes her head between both hands, draws it downward and kisses her hair.*] God bless and preserve Hedda Tesman—for George's sake.

HEDDA [*gently freeing herself*]. Oh! Let me go.

MISS TESMAN [*in quiet emotion*]. I shall not let a day pass without coming to see you.

TESMAN. No, you won't, will you, Auntie? Eh?

MISS TESMAN. Good-by—good-by! [*She goes out by the hall door.* TESMAN *accompanies her. The door remains half open.* TESMAN *can be heard repeating his message to Aunt Rina and his thanks for the slippers. In the meantime* HEDDA *walks about the room raising her arms and clenching her hands as if in desperation. Then she flings back the curtains from the glass door and stands there looking out.*]

—From *Hedda Gabler*, act 1,
Henrik Ibsen [1890]

Even here the superiority of fictional omniscience in describing motives and emotions is obvious. Ibsen's parenthetic stage directions succinctly and unambiguously inform the reader about the attitudes of the characters. Where these describe actions ("She nods and goes toward the right"), there is no problem presenting them on stage. Where they describe a tone of voice ("HEDDA [at the glass door, impatient]") they can be a challenge to acting skills but are still likely to be understood by the audience. When, however, they indicate a state of mind more than a tone of voice, the reader is apt to fare very much better than the viewer. How, for example, is Miss Tesman's "quiet emotion" to be conveyed in her final comment to Hedda?

Usually, Ibsen avoids vague instructions about an actor's tone of voice and strives instead to bring out his characters' attitudes through their words and actions. Hedda, for example, is frustrated by the timid and retiring role that nineteenth-century women were expected to play. Like many other women of the day, she feels imprisoned by the one-sided decorum imposed by her male-dominated society. To dramatize this, Ibsen never allows her to leave her own constricting household during the play's four acts. Through her conversations with Eilert Lövborg and Judge Brack, we discover that she wishes she could participate in the excitement and dissipations of masculine life, but is hindered by a dread of scandal. Thus, although she tries to satisfy her adventurous urges by manipulating the lives of others—particularly Tesman and Eilert—her repressed passions continually break out. These aspects of her personality are given dramatic form by her actions in the brief scene quoted here. She grows irritated at the allusions to her pregnancy, clenches her fists, restlessly paces to and from the windows of the parlor, and a few moments later begins to toy with guns. Using these and other dramatic indications of Hedda's underlying turmoil, Ibsen is able to expose the hidden core of her personality without access to the novelist's omniscient narration.

While writing into the script words and actions that help to define the characters, a playwright must also allow some room for the actors' interpretation and self-expression. In other words, a successful play will stimulate and inspire the actors to use their talents creatively in presenting the play before an audience. In practice, the meaning of the play and the vital intellectual substance that animates each character should be suggested in the script but not rigidly imposed on it. Thus, Ibsen wisely leaves it unclear whether Hedda truly wishes she were a man or is simply rebelling against the traditionally subdued role of her sex. Part of the pleasure of the theater for habitual playgoers derives from this artistic ambiguity. In successive productions of established classics, those who follow the theater closely are able to see how different actresses and actors interpret their roles and are able to compare those interpretations with perceptions based on a study of the text.

But while a dramatist must allow some flexibility in the characterizations to accommodate the actors' differences in physical appearance as well as their need for creative self-expression, he or she must not allow these freedoms to get out of hand. A play, like most other literary works, ordinarily presents an ethical point or some thematic statement about the world and our place in it that the playwright feels to be both relevant and significant. Because drama is a collaborative art—drawing on the talents of the actors, director, musicians, stagehands, scenic artists, and others—a playwright must learn to sketch theme and plot in simple, vigorous, and bold strokes, to be certain that the "message" will come through to the audience. Good drama implies the successive unfolding of the implications of one overarching idea: Hedda's desire to control a human destiny, Tartuffe's hypocrisy, Othello's jealousy, Oedipus's false pride. In each case the central idea is traced by the course of seemingly inevitable events. It is not in the power of the actors to change the concept of the play, just as it is not in the power of an engineer to change the downhill flow of a river. The natural path may be momentarily blocked, but its ultimate course cannot be stopped or stayed.

A careful and single-minded plot development is but one means by which playwrights sometimes seek to control the influence of the cast on the impact of a play. As already noted, many dramatists have composed their plays with the specific abilities of specific actors in mind in an effort to minimize the risk of parts being misplayed. The parts in Shakespeare's plays, for example, were often carefully tailored to suit his fellow members of the Lord Chamberlain's Men (later the King's Men), a professional acting company with which Shakespeare was associated throughout his career. Thus, we find that while Will Kempe was with the company, Shakespeare wrote into his plays a part for a boisterous and farcical clown; but when Kempe was replaced by Robert Armin, the role of the clown became more subtle and witty. Similarly, Shakespeare could confidently create the demanding roles of Hamlet, Lear, and Othello because he knew that in Richard Burbage the company had an actor capable of playing such diverse parts. One of the many contemporary tributes to Burbage's skill describes him as follows:

> His stature small, but every thought and mood
> Might thoroughly from the face be understood
> And his whole action he could change with ease
> From ancient Lear to youthful Pericles.

Shakespeare himself is said to have specialized in playing old men—the old servant Adam in *As You Like It*, the ghost in *Hamlet*, and so on.

In addition to writing specific roles for specific actors, Shakespeare and other Renaissance playwrights had to write all the female parts in such a way that they could be played by preadolescent boys. (Up until about 1660, acting was considered a profession too depraved for women. Men played all the women's parts, even in ancient Greece and Rome.) Naturally, the nude scenes that now abound in films and on the stage would have been out of the question in Shakespeare's day—for reasons other than moral decorum. Indeed, demonstrations of physical passion are comparatively rare in Shakespearean drama because too much kissing and clutching between characters whom the audience knows full well to be a man and a boy might break down the dramatic illusion and become either ludicrous or offensive. In all of *Othello*, a play about sexual conduct and misconduct, there are only four kisses. Three are mere courtesy kisses given to Desdemona in public by Cassio and Othello after she has survived a fierce storm at sea. The only kiss in private is the one Othello gives the sleeping Desdemona just before he suffocates her. Similarly, the height of the balcony in *Romeo and Juliet* keeps the lovers apart during their most passionate moments, and in *Antony and Cleopatra* there is but one embrace before the death scene.

The influence of the actors on the script of a play is not unique to Shakespearean drama. All playwrights must work within the limitations imposed by the medium. Dramatists are, for example, obviously limited in the number of characters they can use. Even though Aristophanes in *Lysistrata* (411 B.C.) wanted to show the effects of a sex strike by the entire female population of Greece, he actually used only three Athenians and one Spartan in speaking roles—with perhaps a score of nonspeaking women to stand for all the rest. Apart from the fact that only a limited number of actors can fit on a stage, the number of speaking roles in a play must be few enough so that the director can round up (and pay) enough accomplished actors and few enough so that the audience can remember who they all are. By convention, as well as by economic and practical necessity, Greek dramatists limited themselves to three speakers and a chorus. This does not mean that there were only three parts in a play, but rather that only three speaking characters could be on stage at any one time. Because the same actors might play several roles (changing masks and costumes offstage), the number of speaking roles could range anywhere from two to twenty, but the dramatist had at all times to balance the requirements of his story with the practical concerns of allowing the actors sufficient time to change costume and of matching the physical and vocal demands of the roles to those of the actors available to play them. It would not do, for example, to send an actor playing a husky, deep-voiced king offstage and then to bring him back as a petite princess. The same character would be physically unable to play both parts. These restrictions are less stringent in plays written after the golden age of Greek drama (ca. 480–380 B.C.), but accomplished playwrights have always manipulated their plots to allow some doubling up of parts and have always been aware that the physical size of the stage itself does not allow them to portray the assembled masses of contending armies. Hence, in the prologue to *Henry the Fifth*, Shakespeare asks the audience to

Suppose within the girdle of these walls
Are now confined two mighty monarchies,
. . . .
Into a thousand parts divide one man;
And make imaginary puissance;
Think, when we talk of horses, that you see them
Printing their proud hoofs i' th' receiving earth.
For 'tis your thoughts that now must deck our kings.

—From *Henry the Fifth*, "Prologue,"
William Shakespeare [1599]

One final way in which the actors influence the drama deserves mention: plays are sometimes conceived, and often revised, as a result of the advice of the actors and the director. Indeed, contemporary plays normally open "out of town" to allow time for revision before risking an expensive production— and facing the critics—in the heart of New York. A similar process has operated throughout history of the theater, and Shakespeare's plays, in this sense at least, are probably much the better for having remained unpublished until long experience on the stage had taught the members of his company which lines played well and which were in need of revision.

THE AUDIENCE

A few plays are intended only to be read and therefore are known as *closet dramas* (*Samson Agonistes* by Milton, *Cain* by Byron, and *Prometheus Unbound* by Shelley are notable examples); but most plays make an effort to please an audience massed in a theater. Playwrights who compose for the stage have learned by experience the truth of Samuel Johnson's eighteenth-century dictum that

The drama's laws the drama's patrons give,
And we who live to please, must please to live.

The goal of a playwright is to fill the theater and to keep on filling it for as long as possible. A play must have popular appeal, and the quest for it naturally influences the choice and treatment of dramatic subjects.

Alexander Dumas (the elder) once claimed that all he needed for success on the stage was "four boards, two actors, and a passion." Dumas knew, as all of us now do, that the ingredients for a popular play (and certainly for popular TV) usually include sex and violence—the two principal motives for passionate dialogue. As the tragedian in Tom Stoppard's *Rosencrantz and Guildenstern Are Dead* put it, well-liked plays are of the "blood, love, and rhetoric school":

. . . I can do you blood and love without the rhetoric, and I can do you blood and rhetoric without the love, and I can do you all three concurrent or consecutive, but I can't do you love and rhetoric without the blood. Blood is compulsory—they're all blood [in tragedy], you see.

—From *Rosencrantz and Guildenstern Are Dead*, act 1,
Tom Stoppard [1967]

The plots of most plays do in fact focus on one of the violent passions (anger, jealousy, revenge, lust, treachery) or on some form of love (love of woman, love of home, love of country, love of justice). Aristophanes' *Lysistrata,* for example, cleverly combines love of woman, love of country, and simple lust; *Othello* builds on jealousy; and much of the plot of *Hedda Gabler* revolves on Hedda's envy of Thea. Other plays examine the effects of less violent, but still powerful, passions: pride in *King Oedipus,* zealotry in *Tartuffe,* and prudery in *Mrs. Warren's Profession.*

Plays do differ, however, as John Dryden once observed, because of the historical differences in the play-going audience:

> They who have best succeeded on the stage
> Have still conformed their genius to the age.

Greek dramas were presented before huge audiences drawn from all levels of society, from poor to rich and from illiterate to sophisticated. Attendance was viewed as a religious duty. As a result, the tragedies dealt with simple and well-known stories that all members of the audience could understand; but they did have to deal with the play's subject in a way that underscored the necessity of reverence for the gods and their decrees. Elizabethan dramas were also aimed at an audience drawn from all levels of society, but by then the connection of the theater with religion had been severed. Thus, Shakespeare's plays contained enough blood and love to keep the illiterate mob in the pit entertained and enough lofty rhetoric to please the lords and ladies in the box seats, but they did not seek to inculcate any particular religious or philosophic views.

By the late nineteenth century, the price of a theater ticket exceeded the means of the laboring classes, and therefore plays like *Hedda Gabler* (1890) portray the problems and conditions of life in the upper and middle classes. There is occasionally a bit of genteel poverty in the plays of this period, but the degrading and impoverished conditions of factory labor are almost entirely ignored. More recently, the technological revolution of the twentieth century has meant that people can often find their entertainment at home on television or at the local movie theater. Most of the people who attend plays today do so because they want to combine culture with entertainment. As a result, much contemporary drama tends to be intellectual and allusive, as in the witty manipulations of *Hamlet* in Tom Stoppard's *Rosencrantz and Guildenstern Are Dead* (1967) or in the parody of Agatha Christie's *Mousetrap* in Stoppard's *The Real Inspector Hound* (1968).

Even in modern drama, however, the plot usually makes an appeal to mass psychology. The playwright must cling first to those elemental passions and emotions common to all humanity and only secondarily, if at all, stimulate the qualities of intellect, in which people differ. The audience in a theater is, after all, a crowd and therefore "less intellectual and more emotional than the individuals that compose it. It is less reasonable, less judicious, less disinterested, more credulous, more primitive, more partisan."[3] In a theater, the sophisticated responses of the few are outnumbered by the instinctive

---

[3] Clayton Hamilton, as quoted by Brander Matthews, *A Study of the Drama* (New York: Houghton Mifflin, 1910), p. 88.

responses of the many. As a result, the dramatist writes for a live audience that is spontaneous and unreflective in both its approval and disapproval.

Because most members of the audience can be expected to see the play once and only once, a successful play must be clearly plotted, easy to understand, and both familiar and acceptable in its theme. Playwrights satisfy the tastes of the times, but they rarely guide them. A novel may survive, even if its initial acclaim is slight, so long as those who first read and understand it are able to influence subsequent intellectual and literary thinking. But a play that fails in its first performance is unlikely to be published at all. Even if a few enthusiasts keep it from sinking immediately into oblivion, one costly failure on Broadway is usually sufficient to scare away future producers. The financial risks in producing plays are more clear-cut than those in publishing novels. If a new play proves to be unpopular, the initial costs involved in scenery, costuming, and rehearsal are not recouped, and the debts mount every day that actors play before a half-filled house. In contrast, if a new novel at first seems unpopular, the cost of storing a few thousand copies will scarcely distress the publisher as long as the demand is constant and seems likely to grow. Thus, a play, unlike a novel, must please upon first acquaintance; and if it is to have durable literary value, it must continue to please during successive viewings or readings. The challenge in writing drama is, thus, to be at once popular *and* intellectually stimulating. Comparatively few playwrights have succeeded at being both.

There are a number of good reasons for the frequent failures in the theater. Even if a playwright chooses a popular subject and develops the plot with simplicity and grace, he or she cannot be confident of pleasing an audience unless the structure of the play is carefully crafted to meet the physical needs of spectators: the duration of scenes and the mixture of dialogue and action, for example, must be adapted to the audience's attention span. A play, like other forms of literature, is principally composed of words, but too much talk and too little action may produce a result about as exciting as a town council meeting. Conversely, actions that remain uninterpreted by dialogue quickly become chaotic. A sword fight on stage may show the physical agility of the actors and the conflict between characters; but if it is continued too long, it threatens to turn the drama into a gladiatorial exhibition, in which most of the interest is drained by the recognition that the swords are wooden, the blood is artificial, and each thrust or parry has been carefully choreographed in advance.

In some ways, of course, the playwright has a tremendous amount of control. Once the theater is darkened and the play begins, the audience is captive: the seats all face the stage, the only well lit part of the theater. When the curtain rises, any lingering conversations are "shushed." The closely packed patrons watch and listen attentively because they have paid to do so, because there is little else they *can* do in a dark theater, and because the seating arrangement makes it difficult to leave before the intermission.

These theatrical conditions directly influence the structure of the play. As much as dramatists may lust after the novelist's right to a leisurely introduction, they must resign themselves to the bald fact that, because no audience can sit still for more than an hour at a time, the play must be at its intriguing best by the intermission. Similarly, a play that begins at 8:00 P.M. must certainly end by 11:00 P.M., lest all the teenagers with curfews, all the parents with babysitters, and all the young couples with romantic plans leave *en masse* before the final curtain.

THE THEATER

In writing a play, a dramatist is always aware of the physical conditions of the theater. These conditions often govern the actions and settings that can be presented, as well as the way in which the scenes are developed. The size of the theater, the proximity of the audience to the stage, and the characteristics of the stage itself influence the scenery, the costuming, and the actors' methods.

As we will see, the conditions for staging Greek drama were unlike those for Elizabethan drama, Elizabethan unlike neoclassical, and neoclassical unlike modern. Nonetheless, each stage provides an arena within which the words and actions of the performers are observed by an audience of substantial size. It follows that some actions are too minute and others too grand to be staged effectively. In Shakespeare's *Othello,* for example, Desdemona's handkerchief is a vital element in the plot, but this piece of cloth, which is too small to bind Othello's forehead, is also too small to be seen clearly by the most distant members of the audience. Thus, Shakespeare takes care to identify it in the dialogue whenever he introduces it on stage. For example, when Bianca flings the handkerchief back to Cassio in act 4, scene 1, Othello, who is watching from a distance, says, "By heaven, that should be my handkerchief!" And then, to clear up any possible confusion, Iago, who has had a closer vantage point, drives home the identification:

IAGO. And did you see the handkerchief?
OTHELLO. Was that mine?
IAGO. Yours, by this hand. And to see how he prizes the foolish woman your
    wife! She gave it him, and he hath given it his whore.

Large events can be even more difficult to present on stage. In the second act of *Othello,* Shakespeare wishes to describe the arrival at Cyprus of Cassio, Desdemona, and Othello after they have been separated by a storm at sea. Naturally it is difficult to depict either the turbulent sea or the arrival of the shattered flotilla. Instead Shakespeare introduces three minor characters whose primary function is to help us imagine the setting and events offstage:

SCENE 1: *A seaport in Cyprus. An open place near the wharf. Enter* MONTANO *and* TWO GENTLEMEN.

MONTANO. What from the cape can you discern at sea?

FIRST GENTLEMAN. Nothing at all. It is a high-wrought flood.
   I cannot 'twixt the heaven and the main
   Descry° a sail.   *see*
MONTANO. Methinks the wind hath spoke aloud at land,
   A fuller blast ne'er shook our battlements.
   If it hath ruffianed° so upon the sea   *raged*
   What ribs of oak, when mountains melt on them,
   Can hold the mortise? What shall we hear of this?

SECOND GENTLEMAN.   A segration° of the Turkish fleet.   *dispersal*
   For do but stand upon the foaming shore,
   The chidden billow seems to pelt the clouds;
   The wind-shaked surge, with high and monstrous mane,
   Seems to cast water on the burning bear,°   *a constellation*
   And quench the guards of the ever-fixed pole.
   I never did like molestation° view   *disruption*
   On the enchafed flood.°   *raging sea*
MONTANO.   If that the Turkish fleet
   Be not ensheltered and embayed, they are drowned.
   It is impossible to bear it out.
   [*Enter a* THIRD GENTLEMAN.]
THIRD GENTLEMAN.   News, lads! Our wars are done.
   The desperate tempest hath so banged the Turks
   That their designment° halts. A noble ship of Venice   *plan*
   Hath seen a grievous wreck and sufferance°   *suffering*
   On most part of their fleet.
MONTANO.   How! Is this true?
THIRD GENTLEMAN.   The ship is here put in,
   A Veronesa. Michael Cassio,
   Lieutenant to the warlike Moor Othello,
   Is come on shore, the Moor himself at sea,
   And is in full commission here for Cyprus.

—From *Othello,* act 2, scene 1,
William Shakespeare [1604]

Presumably the first gentleman is standing at one edge of the stage looking into the distance as though out to sea. He shouts back to the others that he sees nothing but enormous waves. The second gentleman, who has recently stood on the shore, gives a fuller and more poetic account of the storm. Then the third gentleman, having just come from the wharf, brings news of the destruction of the Turkish fleet and the arrival of Cassio's ship. Thus, events that Shakespeare would have had difficulty portraying on stage are made vivid and convincing through the dramatic accounts of three different reporters.

Just as the actions in a drama are limited by the size of the stage and its distance from the audience, so, too, the settings are influenced by the practical problems associated with a visual presentation. Some scenes are next to impossible to stage. Act 2 of Lord Byron's *Cain* (1822), for example, opens in "the Abyss of Space" and a stage direction in act 3 (which is set outside of Eden) reads: "The fire upon the altar of Abel kindles into a column of the brightest flame, and ascends to heaven; while a whirlwind throws down the altar of Cain, and scatters the fruits abroad upon the earth."

As a closet drama, Byron's play was never intended to be staged, but similar difficulties sometimes present themselves in conventional plays. Shortly after Byron's death, in fact, his poem "Mazeppa" was dramatized. We can only pity the poor director who was asked in one scene to show the hero "strapped to the back of a wild horse, while birds peck at his eyes, lightning destroys a tree on stage, and wolves pursue the horse."

During the late nineteenth century, in response to a demand for greater realism, playwrights began to specify the arrangement of furniture in a room, the number of pictures on the walls, and sometimes even the thickness of the butter on a piece of stage toast. Here is the first stage direction in Ibsen's *Hedda Gabler:*

SCENE: *A spacious, handsome and tastefully furnished drawing room, decorated in dark colors. In the back a wide doorway with curtains drawn back, leading into a smaller room decorated in the same style as the drawing room. In the right-hand wall of the front room a folding door leading out to the hall. In the opposite wall, on the left, a glass door, also with curtains drawn back. Through the panes can be seen part of a veranda outside and trees covered with autumn foliage. An oval table, with a cover on it and surrounded by chairs, stands well forward. In front, by the wall on the right, a wide stove of dark porcelain, a high-backed armchair, a cushioned footrest and two footstools. A settee with a small round table in front of it fills the upper right-hand corner. In front, on the left, a little way from the wall, a sofa. Further back than the glass door a piano. On either side of the doorway at the back a whatnot with terra-cotta and majolica ornaments. Against the back wall of the inner room a sofa, with a table, and one or two chairs. Over the sofa hangs the portrait of a handsome elderly man in a general's uniform. Over the table, a hanging lamp with an opal glass shade. A number of bouquets are arranged about the drawing room in vases and glasses. Others lie upon the tables. The floors in both rooms are covered with thick carpets. Morning light. The sun shines in through the glass door.*

—From Hedda Gabler, act 1,
Henrik Ibsen [1890]

Clearly, a setting as complex as this cannot be changed for every new scene. As it happens, all of the action in *Hedda Gabler* takes place in the same two rooms. Similarly, the entire action of *King Oedipus* takes place in front of the royal palace at Thebes, that of *Lysistrata* before the Acropolis, and that of *Tartuffe* in Orgon's house. In a fair number of plays, however, the scene changes with every act, and in a few, like *Othello*, it changes for virtually every scene. Yet, even in *Othello*, a stage with half-dozen different acting areas and a few moveable props can be made to convey the whole range of settings.

Unlike the novelist or the film-maker, the playwright cannot allow the plot to flow freely across unlimited fields of action. If the scenery is to be at all realistic, very few settings can be used unless the playwright is prepared to have the work produced only in the few modern theaters with "revolving stages," on which several realistic sets can be erected and alternately used. Even if the scenery is only suggestive, the playwright is much more limited by the genre than other narrative artists. In general, the action of a play takes place in only one or two locales. These may be quite narrowly and specifically defined in realistic drama (Hedda's drawing room, for example) or broadly conceived in more imaginative works (Venice and Cyprus in *Othello*), but a play that uses too many settings risks confusing the audience and consequently failing in the theater. Shakespeare's *Antony and Cleopatra*, for example, is a poetic masterpiece, but it has rarely been successful on the stage because its forty-two scenes skip bewilderingly around the Roman Empire, and the action spans years rather than days. Ordinarily, it is only through the devices of a film-maker or a novelist that such action can be presented clearly and convincingly.

Thus far, we have been discussing the general effects of any theater on the scenes and actions of drama, but different theaters in different historical periods have had quite different impacts on the drama. A play like *Othello* is written for the intimate Elizabethan stage. The subtle and insinuating facial expressions necessary for a convincing portrayal of Iago's manipulation of Othello would have been lost in the vast amphitheaters of ancient Greece. Similarly, the stark plots and grand rhetoric of Greek tragedy might seem histrionic and ridiculous in the confines of a small modern theater. In order to understand a play, in short, we must know something about the stage for which it was written. In the past, most masterpieces of the drama have been produced in one of four basic theaters: the classical Greek theater, the Elizabethan theater, the neoclassical French theater, and the realistic "box set." Modern drama, however, has moved toward a more flexible theater that can easily be adapted to suit the specific needs of each new play.

The Classical Greek Theater (ca. 480–380 B.C.)

Greek Drama grew out of the primitive rituals performed in conjunction with the three annual festivals dedicated to Dionysus (or Bacchus), the god of fertility, regeneration, and wine. Indeed, the very names for the three forms of Greek drama—tragedy, comedy, and satyr play—derive from the worship of Dionysus. The word *tragedy* means "goat song," probably referring to the goat-skinned satyrs; the derivation of the term *satyr play* is obvious; and the word *comedy* comes from *comos*, Greek for "revelry." In time, such rituals evolved into the drama of Aeschylus, Euripides, Sophocles, and Aristophanes as the uninhibited revels of Dionysus were exchanged for more dignified role playing within a formal theatrical setting. Nonetheless, the classic drama of the ancient Greeks retained, however loosely, its original ties with religion. It continued to be performed only three times a year and then in massive doses of four or five plays a day—circumstances that had an important impact on the audience, the content, and the structure of Greek drama.

In the first place, the audience in a Greek theater was enormous. Everyone who wanted to see a play had only a few opportunities each year to do so, and the idea of attending was all the more attractive because of the sporting element inherent in the prizes awarded for the best tragedies and comedies. The theater of Dionysus at Athens (see Figures 1 and 2), which was used in the first productions of all the great fifth-century Greek plays, probably seated about 17,000. The theater at Epidaurus, built a century later, seated 20,000; and the theater at Ephesus held more than 50,000. Because no existing building was large enough to accommodate so vast a crowd, the plays were performed outdoors in the natural basin formed where two hills met.

During the life of Sophocles (495–406 B.C.) the audience sat on wooden benches that ascended the hillside, more than half encircling an *orchestra* or "dancing place" some 78 feet in diameter. A wooden building called the *skene* (from which we derive the term *scene*) closed off the second half of the amphitheater. It served as an acoustical wall (reflecting the voices of the actors back into the audience), a scenic background (representing any building central to the action), and a convenient place for the three principal

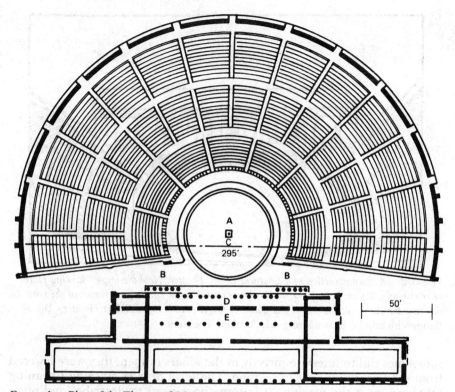

FIGURE 1.   *Plan of the Theater of Dionysus at Athens. A.* orchestra; *B.* chorus entrance;
C. altar to Dionysus; *D.* proskenion; *E.* skene.

actors to change masks and costumes. The narrow space between the *skene*
and the *orchestra* was known as the *proskenion* and served as the main acting
area.[4] **The *proscenium*, in modern stagecraft, is the forward part of the
stage between the curtain and the orchestra. The arch from which the
curtain hangs is the *proscenium arch*.**

The chorus normally remained in the *orchestra*, while the major characters
moved from the *proskenion* to the *orchestra* and back again, according to the
script. The chorus and any processions entered and exited along the edge of
the stands to the far right or left of the *skene*. Although the major characters
used these aisles when the plot called for an outside entrance, at times they
also emerged from, or retreated into, one of the three doors of the *skene* as
if from a temple, palace, or some other building. Action on a balcony or a
cliff could be staged on top of the *skene*, and when the gods appeared, as they

---

[4] There is much confusion over what the Greeks actually meant by the term *proskenion*. Some
scholars think that it referred to the wall of the *skene*; others that it referred to a row of columns
that supported the roof of a porch extending out from the *skene*; and still others agree with our
interpretation. Literally, the word means "before" (*pro-*) "the skene" (*skenion*).

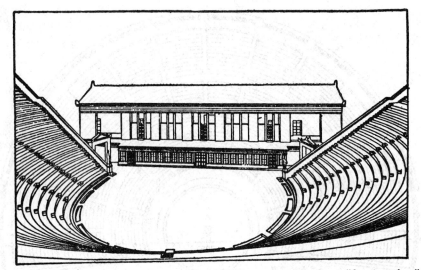

FIGURE 2. *A Reconstruction of a Classical Greek Theater. Note the large "dancing place" or* orchestra, *the encircling tiers of benches, and the scene building or* skene *at the rear. In this case the* skene *includes a raised platform stage. (From Ernst Robert Fiechter's* Die Baugeschichtliche Entwicklung des Antiken Theaters.)

sometimes did to interfere directly in the affairs of men, they were lowered from the top of the *skene* by a crane. **The term *deus ex machina* (meaning "the god from the machine") is sometimes used to describe (and often deride) such divine interventions.**

This massive open-air arena naturally imposed special conditions on the plays performed in it. First of all, there was no curtain to rise at the beginning, fall at the end, and separate the various scenes. As a result, the chorus had to march on stage early in the play (the *parados*) and off stage at the end (the *exodos*). The continuous presence of the chorus during the intervening period encouraged a constant setting throughout the play and a close correspondence between the period of time covered by the play and the amount of real time that elapsed during the actual on-stage presence of the chorus. As a result, Greek drama tended to concentrate on a single complex situation.[5] The typical Greek tragedy begins only a matter of hours before its catastrophe is to occur. The characters stand on the brink of disaster, and the playwright swiftly tells us how they got there, using a formal prologue or a series of interviews with messengers, nurses, and other minor characters. In the first moments of *King Oedipus,* for example, we learn that a plague afflicts Thebes because the murder of the former king, Laius, has not been punished. Oedipus immediately vows to find the killer and drive him from the land. The remainder of the play works out the consequences of this impet-

---

[5] The unity of place, time, and action demanded in the neoclassical drama of the seventeenth and eighteenth centuries was an outgrowth of these tendencies. Greek playwrights did not, however, formally require adherence to these three unities.

uous vow by revealing that Oedipus himself is the killer, that Laius was his father, and therefore that Laius's wife, Jocasta, is actually Oedipus's mother as well as his wife and the mother of his children.

The four scenes, or *episodes*, during which Oedipus discovers the tragedy of his past are separated from one another not by the fall of a curtain but by a series of choral interludes called odes. Each *ode* (or *stasimon*) was accompanied by music and the choreographed dancing of the chorus. During these odes the chorus was able to provide essential background information, reflect on past actions, or anticipate future ones. Often, too, the responses of the chorus represent those of an ideal audience or provide a lyric respite from the intense emotions of the episodes. In addition these interludes may symbolize the passage of time necessary to send for a character or accomplish some other offstage action.

Because the theater was unenclosed and the plays were performed during the daytime, the action of Greek drama normally also took place during the daytime, out-of-doors. However, some events in Greek drama did require an interior setting—Jocasta's suicide is an example—and, accordingly, Greeks were forced to improvise. One frequently used technique was to have a messenger, or some other character, come outside and describe in detail what had taken place within. This is exactly how Sophocles handled the death of Jocasta:

CHORUS.   Alas, miserable woman, how did she die?
SECOND MESSENGER.   By her own hand. It cannot be as terrible to you as to one that saw it with his eyes, yet so far as words can serve, you shall see it. When she had come into the vestibule, she ran half crazed towards her marriage-bed, clutching at her hair with the fingers of both hands, and once within the chamber dashed the doors together behind her. Then called upon the name of Laius, long since dead, remembering that son who killed the father and upon the mother begot an accursed race. And wailed because of that marriage wherein she had borne a two-fold race—husband by husband, children by her child. Then Oedipus with a shriek burst in and running here and there asked for a sword, asked where he would find the wife that was no wife but a mother who had borne his children and himself. Nobody answered him, we all stood dumb; but supernatural power helped him, for, with a dreadful shriek, as though beckoned, he sprang at the double doors, drove them in, burst the bolts out of their sockets, and ran into the room. There we saw the woman hanging in a swinging halter, and with a terrible cry he loosened the halter from her neck.

—From *King Oedipus*,
Sophocles [430 B.C.]

A second possibility was simply to throw open the doors of the *skene* and allow the audience to peer inside. Although this technique later worked in the smaller Elizabethan theater, the size of the Greek theater and the unavoidable obscurity of the interior of the *skene* rendered this approach unsatisfactory. To overcome this obstacle, the Greeks constructed a platform on wheels (the *eccyclema*) that could be rolled out of the *skene* as required. This device became the accepted convention for portraying an interior scene or tableau.

The size of the Greek theater had still other effects on the nature of Greek drama. The actors wore large masks, padded clothing, and platform sandals in order to increase their stature and expressiveness for the viewers at the rear of the amphitheater. Although those costumes must have significantly restricted mobility and made physical actions awkward, the masks were designed to function like primitive megaphones and improved the carrying power of the actors' voices. As such, it is little wonder that Greek drama came to be made up of words rather than actions. This verbal emphasis complements the Greek dramatist's preoccupation with motive and character rather than plot, for the state of mind and feelings of an individual can only be fully explained and analyzed using words. The excellence of Greek tragedy came about in part because it was a drama of the mind and not the body.

Then, as now, the audience exerted its influence on both the structure and the content of the plays presented. Because Greek audiences remained in the theater all day, lapses of attention, and periods of jostling, munching, joking, and dozing were inevitable. It was nevertheless essential that all the members of the audience understand the key turning points of the action if the play were to succeed at all; as a result, playwrights preferred to present bold, simple stories that were either familiar to the audience (for example, the story of Oedipus) or, in the case of comedy, predicated on a simple, straightforward hypothesis (in *Lysistrata* that sexual denial can put an end to war). Not surprisingly, given the religious traditions associated with drama and the stylization imposed by the use of masks, many tragic plots were drawn from mythology. The comedies, on the other hand, sought a similar ease of understanding by burlesquing contemporary personalities and events.

The Elizabethan Theater (ca. 1550–1620)

The decline of the Roman Empire brought an end to the Greek theater, and for nearly a thousand years Europe produced little drama of significant literary merit. It is true that the Catholic church, in about the tenth century, began to encourage the production of plays filled with moral or religious instruction, but these anonymous creations are more important as historical curiosities than as dramatic achievements. As a result, when the rediscovery of Greek and Roman literature first spread through Europe to England, few people had any idea what a theater ought to look like. Plays were put on wherever a stage could be erected or a crowd could gather. Amateur groups performing at a university and professionals performing at an inn found that the courtyard provided a ready-made theater. A fairly large stage could be easily set up at one end, and the audience could watch the play from the surrounding yard or balconies. The balcony immediately above the stage, in turn, could be conveniently used by the actors for playing scenes that called for a hill, a cliff, an upstairs window, or any other high place.

No doubt innkeepers found that an afternoon play stimulated business. Those standing in the courtyard watching the play could take their minds off their aching feet by calling for more beer, and the surrounding bedchambers encouraged other forms of trade—so much so that the municipal officials of London (who were staunch puritans) soon began to regulate the production of plays, denouncing the "evil practices of incontinency in great Inns having chambers and secret places adjoining to their open stages and galleries, inveigling and allurement of maidens." As a result of these regulations, several of the theatrical companies decided to build their own playhouses just outside of the city limits. It is hardly surprising that when they did so, beginning in about 1576, they patterned their theaters on the very courtyards to which they had become accustomed.

The existing evidence about the size, shape, and structure of the Elizabethan stage and theater is scanty, but it does allow us to state some facts positively and to make other educated guesses. From a contract for the construction of the Fortune Theater (see Figures 3 and 4) we know that the building was square and relatively small, measuring 80 feet on each side. (The Globe Theater, where Shakespeare's plays were performed, was about the same size, but octagonal or even round.) The pit, or inner yard, of the Fortune measured 55 feet per side, and the stage, which was 43 feet wide, projected halfway (exactly 27½ feet) into the yard. Three galleries were partitioned into "two-penny rooms" and "convenient divisions for gentlemen's rooms"—presumably the equivalent of box seats. When filled to capacity, the theater probably held a crowd of about 1500, with the common folk pressed elbow to elbow around three sides of the stage.

Because the stage intruded so far into the middle of the audience, most spectators sat or stood within thirty feet of the actors, and even the distant corners of the third balcony were but sixty feet away. As a result, the Elizabethan theater fostered a sense of intimacy utterly foreign to its predecessor. *Asides* and *soliloquies*, which would seem contrived if the actor had to strain visibly to make his stage whisper carry to a distant audience, here seemed natural and unaffected. **An *aside* is a brief comment, that a character makes in the presence of others, intending only some of them—or none of them—to hear it. A *soliloquy* is a speech delivered by a character alone on stage.** Because of the intimacy of the Elizabethan theater, Elizabethan plays came to be filled with lines intended for the audience alone. In the third act of *Othello*, where Iago comes *downstage* toward the audience with Desdemona's handkerchief in his hand, he is so near the audience that his low reflections are delivered almost conspiratorially into their ears:

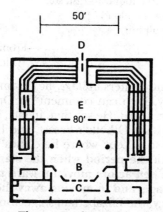

FIGURE 3.   *Plan of the Fortune Theater, London. A.* front stage; *B.* back stage; *C.* inner stage; *D.* entrance; *E.* courtyard.

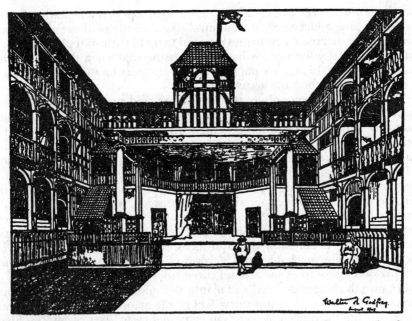

FIGURE 4.   *A Reconstruction of the Fortune Theater by Walter H. Godfrey. Note the platform stage projecting into the "pit," the curtained inner stage, the two side entrances, the balcony, the "crow's nest," and the three rows of galleries for spectators. (From Shakespeare's Theatre by Ashley H. Thorndike.)*

I will in Cassio's lodging lose this napkin,
And let him find it. Trifles light as air
Are to the jealous confirmations strong
As proofs of Holy Writ. This may do something.
The Moor already changes with my poison.
Dangerous conceits are in their natures poisons,
Which at the first are scarce found to distaste,
But with a little act upon the blood
Burn like the mines of sulphur.

                                  —From *Othello*, act 3, scene 3,
                                      William Shakespeare [1604]

When Othello subsequently enters *upstage*, he is some forty to fifty feet away from Iago; consequently, Iago can comment on Othello's visible agitation without fear of being overheard. He see that, in fact, jealousy does "burn like the mines of sulphur" within Othello's breast, and he addresses the spectators directly: "I did say so. / Look where he comes!" **The terms *downstage* and *upstage* derive from the period when the stage was raked, or tilted, toward the audience. When actors moved toward the audience they literally moved down the stage, and in moving away they climbed slightly up.**

In addition to intimacy, the Elizabethan stage also had versatility. It probably contained at least three different acting areas (see Figure 4). The main one was, of course, the 27½- by 43-foot platform. In this large neutral area, characters could meet and interact without raising any question in the minds of an Elizabethan audience about the exact setting. In the original text of *Othello,* for example, there are only three directions for setting, and all of them are quite indefinite: two calls for the use of an inner chamber or curtained area and one for an upstairs window. If, for some reason, a specific setting *was* important, the characters themselves would describe it, as in the seaport scene quoted earlier (pp. 17–18).

An inner stage behind the main platform may have been used to represent the interior of a council chamber, a bedroom, a tent, a tomb, a throne room, and so on. Act 1, scene 3 of *Othello* seems to require that this inner stage be screened by curtains that can be drawn to reveal "the Duke and Senators set at a table." Similarly, act 5, scene 2 opens on "Desdemona in bed." Because every other scene in the play calls for each character to enter, speak his lines, and then exit, only these two scenes need to be staged in the curtained chamber.

According to the records available to us, some form of upper stage or balcony apparently extended above the inner stage. In act 1, scene 1 of *Othello,* Roderigo and Iago converse in the street before calling up to Brabantio who "appears above, at a window." Similarly, Juliet appears at a window in her first balcony scene. Such stage directions, together with the "convenient windows" called for in the contract for the Fortune Theater, imply that these areas were either shuttered or curtained so that the characters could suddenly "appear." But the balcony must also on occasion have provided a fairly large area in which several characters could meet, as indicated by such stage directions as "Enter Cleopatra and her maids aloft."

Although there may also have been an even higher balcony for the musicians (or for action taking place in a tower or in the crow's nest of a ship), few scenes—none in *Othello*—were staged very far above the crowd assembled in the yard. In fact, the vast majority of the scenes in Elizabethan drama were presented on the main stage, so that the audience was able to see and hear clearly.

Because the audience stood around three sides of the main stage, it was impossible to use a curtain to separate scenes. And because the public theaters were unenclosed and plays were performed during the daytime, it was impossible to throw the stage into darkness during a change of scene. Hence, a scene would start with the entrance of one or more characters, and the locale would remain the same until all of the characters left the stage—or were carted off, if dead ("Exeunt severally; Hamlet dragging in [i.e., offstage] Polonius"). Action in a new locale would then commence with a new set of entrances. We know that at least two doors could be used for entrances and exits because of such stage directions as the following: ("Enter Pompey at one door, with drum and trumpet: at another, Caesar, Lepidus, Antony, Maecenas, Agrippa, with soldiers marching").

The different settings in an Elizabethan play were rarely indicated by any change in props or scenery. *Othello* contains fifteen different scenes, and if the suggested stage directions of modern editions are followed, a production would require at least eleven different settings. Obviously, such changes were impossible on an open stage. Indeed, if the list of properties owned by the Fortune Theater is indicative of the period, scenery was used mainly to adorn the inner stage and even there only sparingly. Among the bulkiest were:

i rock, i cage, i tomb, i Hell mouth.
i tomb of Guido, i tomb of Dido, i bedstead.
viii lances, i pair of stairs for Phaeton.
i golden fleece; ii rackets; i bay tree.
Iris head, & rainbow; i little altar.
ii fanes of feathers; Bellendon stable; i tree of golden
    apples; Tantalus' tree; ix iron targets.
i copper target, & xvii foils.
i wheel and frame in the Siege of London.
i cauldron for the Jew.

For the most part, Elizabethans relied on words rather than props to give a sense of locale.

All of this means that the Elizabethan theater, with its multiple acting areas and its imaginary settings, was well suited to plays with rapidly shifting scenes and continuous action. It gave rise to a form of drama entirely unlike that of ancient Greece. Instead of the play starting a few fictional hours before the crisis (as in *Oedipus*), the Renaissance play starts at the beginning of a story and skips from time to time and place to place until the crisis is reached. Act 1 of *Othello*, for example, begins in Venice on the night of Othello and Desdemona's marriage. Then act 2 skips more than a week ahead to a period when all of the principals arrive in Cyprus, and there the action requires two more nights and a day. Because Elizabethan plays range freely in time and setting, all of the most dramatic moments in a story are presented on stage. Thus, if *King Oedipus* had been written by Shakespeare, the audience might have seen and heard events that Sophocles included only as reminiscences—particularly, the original prophecies of the oracle to Oedipus, Oedipus's flight from Corinth, and his murder of Laius at the place where three roads meet. Scenes of violence, which occur offstage in Greek tragedy (like the death of Jocasta) were physically enacted before the Elizabethan audience. *Othello* includes several sword fights, three murders, and a suicide—all on stage. And this carnage is only moderate by Renaissance standards. (Note that despite its general paucity of props, the Fortune Theater inventoried *seventeen* foils!) The audience standing in the yard demanded action, and the versatile Elizabethan stage made this demand easy to fulfill.

The Neoclassical French Theater (ca. 1660–1800)

The early acting companies of France, like those of England, toured the countryside, playing wherever they could. As luck would have it, tennis had been popular in France during the fifteenth century, and many noblemen had erected indoor tennis courts, some of which were transformed during the next two centuries into primitive theaters. A temporary stage would be erected on one half of the court; ordinary folk would stand or sit on wooden benches in the other half, and the nobles would be seated in the galleries overlooking the playing area. It was in such converted quarters that Corneille and Molière, two of the greatest of the neoclassical playwrights, saw their first plays produced.

Thus, early French theaters evolved in a direction that differed radically from their Elizabethan counterparts. The single most significant change was the increased separation of the actors from the audience. Whereas the Elizabethan audience had nearly encircled the actors, the seventeenth-century French audience sat along one side of the stage and looked in on the action, as if peering through an invisible wall (see Figures 5 and 6). This arrangement eventually led to the use of a front curtain to conceal the stage between acts and made possible elaborate changes of scenery.

Because all members of the audience watched the play from a similar vantage point, **the setting could be vividly depicted on huge flat canvases, using the devices of perspective developed by the painters of the Italian Renaissance** (see Figure 6). **These** *flats* **could easily be replaced, providing the opportunity for changes in setting.** The curtain concealed the scene before the start of the play, but thereafter any changes in scenery were made mechanically in full view of the audience, as a form of special effect. In his prologues Molière himself was not beyond using fountains, aerial chariots, the descent of a god in a cloud, or a maiden emerging from a sea shell to bring the crowd to its feet and to delight the king.

It is almost axiomatic in theater that whenever innovations in staging begin to turn drama into spectacle, the quality of the writing in plays declines. However, at least three factors kept seventeenth-century French drama from degenerating into exhibitionistic extravaganzas. First, **neoclassical scholars and critics imposed their standards on the age by requiring that every play fulfill the three unities:** *unity of time* **mandated that the play's action should be confined to a single day;** *unity of action* **forbade subplots and irrelevant or incongruous episodes; and** *unity of place* **required that all of the action take place in a single setting or vicinity.** The exclusion of digressions and the limitation on settings greatly constricted the use that French playwrights could make of their curtained stage. Molière's *Tartuffe* (1664), for example, takes place in fewer than twelve hours, in a single setting that has a simple dinner table as its most elaborate prop. Those plays by Molière that do include spectacular stage effects usually confine

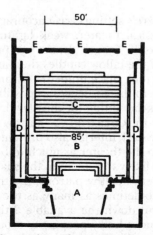

FIGURE 5.   *Plan of the Richelieu-Molière Theater, Paris. A.* stage; *B.* parterre; *C.* seats; *D.* galleries; *E.* entrances.

Figure 6.   *A Neoclassical Theater in Strasburg (1655). Note the flat wings representing rows of buildings, the painted backdrop showing the continuation of the street, and the actors at the forefront of the stage beneath the chandeliers. (From* Wiener Szenische Kunst *by Joseph Gregor.)*

them to a prologue or epilogue, so that formal adherence to the unities is preserved.

The simplicity of Molière's settings was encouraged by two physical characteristics of the neoclassical theater: weak lighting and the presence of spectators on the stage itself. French drama was performed indoors, often under artificial light, and the tallow candles then in use burned dimly. As a result, most of the acting took place immediately under the chandeliers and as far downstage (as close to the audience) as possible. Thus, the elaborately painted flats served less as the setting for the play than as a general backdrop to the action, which often took place on the narrow strip or *apron* in front of the proscenium arch. The dark interior also presented problems for the fops and dandies who came to the theater as much to be seen as to see the play itself. The box seats were likely to remain in the shadows, and because many of those vain creatures were wealthy patrons, the theater owners accommodated them with seats (sometimes as many as two hundred) on the stage. Naturally, such seating cut down the available acting area and limited the ability of stagehands to move bulky properties around.

As a result of the seating, the lighting, and the neoclassical rules of composition, most of the plays in this period were set in a single place of general resort—a courtyard, a street, a drawing room. The plots developed scenes of emotional intensity, but because decorum and probability were required by unity of action, they rarely erupted into the violent activity that so often left the Elizabethan stage littered with bodies. The drama of the period is witty, intellectual, and refined. Characteristically, it depicts highly idealized and artificial conversations among men and women (female parts were now actually performed by women) representing broad human types—classical heroes or gods in tragedy, contemporary scoundrels or buffoons in comedy. It is an intentionally stylized drama based on the premise that fixed rules of structure are necessary in refined literature.

The Development of the Box Set (ca. 1830–1920)

In 1642 Oliver Cromwell and his Puritan followers closed down all the playhouses in England, and by the time they were reopened in 1660, the Elizabethan theater was dead. Not surprisingly, given the predilection of Charles II and his court for all things French, the English drama that succeeded the Restoration was heavily influenced by the neoclassical conventions of the French theater—an influence that persisted throughout most of the eighteenth century. In the nineteenth century, however, the situation changed. A series of important technical innovations encouraged dramatists to abandon neoclassicism in favor of a drama characterized by realistic (mimetic) plots performed within equally realistic settings.

The first of these changes was the introduction, between 1820 and 1840, of gas lighting. Not only were gas lights brighter than the candles and oil lamps that had hitherto served, but now all the lights in the house could be controlled from a single instrument panel. For the first time, a director could focus the audience's attention on the lighted stage by leaving the rest of the auditorium in total darkness; this increased control over stage lights allowed playwrights to switch their scenes from day to night without recourse to cumbersome passages of dialogue calling attention to the fact. The improved lighting also allowed the actors to move more or less freely about the setting, instead of forcing them to remain out in front of the proscenium arch. Such maneuverability naturally called greater attention to the setting, which could now become a functional, rather than simply an ornamental, feature of the play. As a consequence, directors began to eliminate the backdrops and the artificial perspective of movable flats.

Soon after 1830, the *box set* was introduced in England. In its ultimate development, the box set is identical to a real room with one wall removed. Even though the audience can peer through this "invisible" fourth wall to eavesdrop on the action taking place within, the actors pretend that the invisible wall exists. Thus, asides directed to the audience can no longer occur and soliloquies must be strictly limited to those emotional moments during which a character might logically be overheard talking to himself. Nineteenth-century producers understandably relished these innovations and some went so far as to boast in their advertisements of having sets with real ceilings, real doors, and working locks. The description of the set for *Hedda Gabler* is a typical example of the meticulous care with which late nineteenth-century playwrights envisioned the locale of their plays.

At about the same time that candlelight was being replaced by gas, directors also discovered ways to focus spotlights on single characters. This was first achieved by burning small chunks of lime and reflecting the light off of curved mirrors onto the leading man or leading lady (who was then, quite literally, "in the limelight"). Most directors, understandably, became enamored with the technique, and throughout the nineteenth century talented actors and actresses often held to the limelight to the detriment of the play as a whole. A particularly fine speech by Edmund Kean or Sarah Kemble Siddons, for example, might bring the audience to its feet in midscene. And if the applause were long and loud enough, Mr. Kean or Mrs. Siddons would simply recite the speech again as an encore. The inevitable effect of such an emphasis was to encourage dramatists to concentrate on writing good parts for the leading roles without giving equal attention to plot, structure, and theme.

A further development in nineteenth-century stagecraft was the increasing use made of the curtain spanning the proscenium arch. Until about 1875, the curtain was used only to screen the stage before the start of the play; once raised, it did not fall again until the end of the last act. The intention, of course, was to startle and delight the spectators when the curtain first rose on the fanciful world of the theater and then to entertain them by magically transforming that world before their eyes. So long as the scenery was mainly composed of paintings on flats that could be slid off stage mechanically and replaced by others, such changes of scene could occur swiftly and smoothly. But the advent of the realistic box set inevitably brought with it an increasing number of unwieldy props. The stage became cluttered with footstools, sofas, armchairs, end tables, vases, and portraits that stagehands were required to cart off or rearrange during any change of scene. The whole process soon became more frantic than magical and more distracting than entertaining. Furthermore, to effect such changes before the eyes of the audience only served to break down the illusion of reality. In order to sustain the illusion, directors and playwrights began to use the curtain between acts and even between scenes.

This had an immediate and important influence on the text of plays written in the final quarter of the nineteenth century. Before then a scene or an act necessarily began with a set of entrances and concluded with some pretext calling for the characters to exit—usually a variant of "Come! Let's be off to dine [or drink, or dance, or what have you]." The increased use of the curtain freed the dramatist from such constrictions. The emphasis changed from finding a way of getting the characters offstage to finding a way of building dramatic tension and emphasizing basic themes at the end of acts or scenes. The resulting *curtain line* (**a moment of high drama at the very end of an act or scene**) is perhaps the most distinctive feature of modern drama. Ibsen was among the first to employ the curtain line, and in *Hedda Gabler* he honed it to perfection. Each act ends on a note of high drama, but for the purpose of illustration, we will look at the conclusion to the third act:

LÖVBORG.   Good-by, Mrs. Tesman. And give George Tesman my love. [*He is on the point of going.*]

HEDDA.   No, wait! I must give you a memento to take with you. [*She goes to the writing table and opens the drawer and the pistol case, then returns to* LÖVBORG *with one of the pistols.*]

LÖVBORG [*looks at her*].   This? Is this the memento?
HEDDA [*nodding slowly*].   Do you recognize it? It was aimed at you once.
Lövborg.   You should have used it then.
HEDDA.   Take it—and do you use it now.
LÖVBORG   [*puts the pistol in his breast pocket*]. Thanks!
HEDDA.   And beautifully, Eilert Lövborg. Promise me that!
Lövborg.   Good-by, Hedda Gabler. [*He goes out by the hall door.*]

[HEDDA *listens for a moment at the door. Then she goes up to the writing table, takes out the packet of manuscript, peeps under the cover, draws a few of the sheets half out and looks at them. Next she goes over and seats herself in the armchair beside the stove, with the packet in her lap. Presently she opens the stove door and then the packet.*]

HEDDA [*throws one of the quires into the fire and whispers to herself*].   Now I am burning your child, Thea! Burning it, curlylocks! [*Throwing one or two more quires into the stove.*] Your child and Eilert Lövborg's. [*Throws the rest in.*] I am burning—I am burning your child.

—From *Hedda Gabler*, act 3,
Henrik Ibsen [1890]

With growing horror, we realize not only that Hedda is encouraging Eilert to kill himself, but also that she could have prevented his death by returning the manuscript. She burns the only copy of Eilert's book because she is insanely jealous that Thea, "that pretty little fool" as Hedda thinks of her, should after all have had "her fingers in a man's destiny." The curtain drops just as Hedda reaches her deepest and most chilling insight into her own actions: "I am burning—I am burning your child."

The Modern Theater

Twentieth-century stagecraft has been characterized by flexibility. An improved understanding of the past has allowed us to stage the plays of Sophocles, Shakespeare, Molière, and others with greater fidelity to the original intentions of the author. Furthermore, modern critical principles encourage playwrights and directors to put aside their *a priori* notions about staging and recognize that each play requires and deserves a separate approach. Continuing technical developments in the twentieth century have facilitated this flexibility both through further refinements in lighting and through machinery that can easily manipulate the sets and sometimes even the seating arrangement in the theater.

Although most modern theaters retain the proscenium arch and a clear division between the audience and the actors, many small theaters (especially temporary ones) have experimented with other structures. The most innovative of these have tried to recreate the intimacy and versatility of the Elizabethan stage either in small semicircular amphitheaters or in arena theaters. **Arena staging or theater-in-the-round has emerged as the most distinctive twentieth-century contribution to stagecraft. The audience totally surrounds the stage and is therefore as close to the action of the play as is physically possible. Entrances and exits are made through the aisles normally used by the spectators and in some cases these become secondary acting areas, as well.** Inevitably, however, the actors cannot simultaneously face all members of the audience. So long as the play focuses on the conflict between at least two characters, this presents no problem. When the two square off, all members of the audience will have at least a frontal view of one character or a profile of both. When the dramatic interest is focused totally on one character, however, as it is in the final moments of *Othello,* one fourth of the audience is apt to feel frustrated at being unable to see his face and hear his climactic speech clearly. For this reason, arena staging is less successful than other approaches for plays with one dominant role.

Most of the major playhouses in America were built long before arena staging became widely accepted, but they, too, have adapted to the twentieth-century demand for flexibility. Modern set designs have been transformed by a consensus that their primary purpose is to provide three-dimensional areas for acting. The movable flats that were used well into the twentieth century to create perspective in outdoor settings have now been all but eliminated. Playwrights and directors seem to agree that everything depicted on stage should be functional and esthetically pleasing but not necessarily realistic. The sets should draw no attention to themselves or away from the acting. The general trend has been toward a simple, almost architectural stage, with platforms at various levels linked by stairways and ramps. The modern set strives to be suggestive and intellectually stimulating instead of purely pictorial, and this aim is facilitated by modern electrical lighting, which can actually create moods by "drawing" on the stage with shadows and prismatic colors to transform a single set into a constantly changing environment.

The trends in the modern theater have imposed no new conditions on playwrights; instead, they have been freed from many of the old limitations of the stage. This flexibility is best illustrated by the range of settings used in the classics of modern drama. Eugene O'Neill's *Desire Under the Elms* (1924), for example, takes place in, and immediately outside of, the Cabot farmhouse. O'Neill's own sketches show the exterior of the farmhouse, with various sections of the wall removed as the action shifts from one room to another. In effect, it is a stage with multiple box sets. Arthur Miller's *Death of a Salesman* (1949) also calls for the interior of a house, but in this case all of the walls are invisible and the house itself becomes a large, skeletal structure of various platforms for acting and observing actions. Finally, Tom Stoppard's *Rosencrantz and Guildenstern Are Dead* (1967) is set on a barren stage, "a place without any visible character"; it requires only a platform with two different levels and a few simple properties.

The causes of the modern trend toward flexibility, suggestivity, and simplicity of setting are complex, but certainly television and the movies have had something to do with it. Before films became popular, there had been an ever-increasing trend toward spectacle in the theater. Although crowds once flocked to playhouses to see a theatrical railroad engine steaming along toward the bound heroine or baying bloodhounds pursuing the bleeding hero, they soon found that the movies—through close-ups, cuts, and editing—could present those thrills more realistically while indulging in the additional expensive luxuries of having the train explode or the hero slog through miles of snake-infested swamp. Within a few years, therefore, playhouses ceased to stage spectacular extravaganzas, and drama once again became the verbal and intellectual experience previously enjoyed by the Elizabethans and the Greeks.

CHAPTER THREE

※ ※ ※ ※ ※ ※ ※

The Elements of Drama

For the most part, the elements of drama are identical to those of fiction and poetry. Plays have plots, themes, characters, and settings and make use of the many devices of poetic diction. Thus, many of the steps in the analysis of a play should parallel those used for a poem or a short story. At the same time, however, drama is a different literary genre and it imposes its own constraints on the playwright's use of certain elements of literature. These unique aspects of dramatic writing are our present concern.

Every play unfolds a story through the dialogue and actions of its characters. An understanding of these four elements—story, dialogue, action, and character—is therefore crucial to the appreciation of drama.

DIALOGUE

Tom Stoppard's *Rosencrantz and Guildenstern Are Dead* has no story apart from that already told in *Hamlet;* its principal characters are notable mainly because no one can distinguish between them; and the most significant action in the play is prolonged waiting. Part of the fun of Stoppard's work is that he has nearly stripped drama to its one indispensible element, dialogue.

A theatrical production without dialogue can be a mime or a ballet, but it is never a play. As Stoppard himself might have put it: a play can give you talk and characters without much action. And a play can give you talk and action without strong characters. But a play cannot give you characters and action without talk. It is all talk in drama.

Dramatic dialogue, however, is very different from the kind of dialogue that makes up so much of our ordinary lives. Actual conversation is full of hesitations, pauses, fragments, misunderstandings, and repetitions. The communication itself is often as much a product of inflections, gestures, and facial expressions as it is of the spoken word. It depends so much on innuendo and allusions to previous conversations that an outsider is often unable to determine the exact meaning of a discussion heard out of context. This in fact was Richard Nixon's contention when he protested in July and August 1973 against the release of the transcripts of his conversations about the Watergate break-in. The following selection from the Nixon tapes may have been one of the most important moments in the history of the United States presidency; its release shocked the nation and eventually led to Nixon's resignation in August 1974. As we will see, however, it is far from being good drama:

THE SETTING.   *March 21, 1973, 10:12 A.M. The Oval Office*
THE PARTICIPANTS.   *Richard Nixon and John Dean*
THE SITUATION.   *Dean has just reviewed the history of the Watergate cover-up, calling it a "cancer" close to the presidency. Having described the continual demands for hush money by the Watergate burglars, he continues:*

DEAN.   . . . It will cost money. It is dangerous. People around here are not pros at this sort of thing. This is the sort of thing Mafia people can do: washing money, getting clean money, and things like that. We just don't know about those things, because we are not criminals and not used to dealing in that business.
NIXON.   That's right.
DEAN.   It is a tough thing to know how to do.
NIXON.   Maybe it takes a gang to do that.
DEAN.   That's right. There is a real problem as to whether we could even do it. Plus there is a real problem in raising money. Mitchell has been working on raising some money. He is one of the ones with the most to lose. But there is no denying the fact that the White House, in Ehrlichman, Haldeman, and Dean, are involved in some of the early money decisions.
NIXON.   How much money do you need?
DEAN.   I would say these people are going to cost a million dollars over the next two years.
NIXON.   We could get that. On the money, if you need the money you could get that. You could get a million dollars. You could get it in cash. I know where it could be gotten. It is not easy, but it could be done. But the question is who the hell would handle it? Any ideas on that?
DEAN.   That's right. Well, I think that is something that Mitchell ought to be charged with.
NIXON.   I would think so too.
DEAN.   And get some pros to help him.

—From *Submission of Recorded
Presidential Conversations,*
April 30, 1974

It is clear enough that the president and his chief counsel are discussing obstruction of justice, acquiescence in blackmail, and involvement with professional criminals. The very topics of conversation are momentous and appalling. Yet the passage is stylistically weak and grammatically inept. The conversation redundantly returns to the difficulty of raising the money and the need for "pros" to handle the payoffs; and when Dean digresses into a discussion of the White House involvement, the president brings him back to the point by asking, "How much money do you need?" The sentences are choppy and inelegant, and the participants do not come to a clear decision until many exchanges later. Even then the discussion does not end. It meanders along for at least another hour, with the participants drifting away from the central issue and then darting back to it like minnows chasing a spinner.

In contrast, important conversations in drama slash past trivial details and strike the lure with vigor and directness. A play necessarily packs a story of significance into two or three hours of stage time. As a result, each sentence is hard and muscular—made up of concrete nouns and active verbs. The dialogue continuously and clearly builds toward its point, eliminating irrelevancies and unnecessary repetitions. When trimmed to its dramatic core, a real conversation, like the one between Richard Nixon and John Dean, might well be cut by half.

Dramatic dialogue ordinarily carries with it still another burden: it must include sufficient background information to fix the time, place, and circumstances of the action firmly in the mind of the audience. Nixon and Dean, after all, knew each other well and also knew the circumstances surrounding the issues described in their conversation; the playwright, however, must introduce the characters and provide background information before the audience can really understand what is going on. Although some playwrights prefer to have a narrator set the scene in a formal prologue—as, for example, in Williams's *The Glass Menagerie* or Wilder's *Our Town*—most try to bring out the background information gradually during the play's first act. Ibsen was a master of the gradual introduction, as illustrated in the first few moments of *Hedda Gabler:*

MISS JULIANA TESMAN, *with her bonnet on and carrying a parasol, comes in from the hall, followed by* BERTA, *who carries a bouquet wrapped in paper.* MISS TESMAN *is a comely and pleasant-looking lady of about sixty-five. She is nicely but simply dressed in a gray walking costume.* BERTA *is a middle-aged woman of plain and rather countrified appearance.*

MISS TESMAN [*stops close to the door, listens and says softly*].   Upon my word, I don't believe they are stirring yet!

BERTA [*also softly*].   I told you so, miss. Remember how late the steamboat got in last night. And then, when they got home!—good lord, what a lot the young mistress had to unpack before she could get to bed.

MISS TESMAN.   Well, well—let them have their sleep out. But let us see that they get a good breath of the fresh morning air when they do appear. [*She goes to the glass door and throws it open.*]

BERTA [*beside table, at a loss what to do with the bouquet in her hand*].   I declare, there isn't a bit of room left. I think I'll put it down here, miss. [*She places it on the piano.*]

MISS TESMAN.   So you've got a new mistress now, my dear Berta. Heaven knows it was a wrench to me to part with you.

BERTA [*on the point of weeping*].   And do you think it wasn't hard for me too, miss? After all the blessed years I've been with you and Miss Rina.

MISS TESMAN.   We must make the best of it, Berta. There was nothing else to be done. George can't do without you, you see—he absolutely can't. He has had you to look after him ever since he was a little boy.

BERTA.   Ah, but, Miss Julia, I can't help thinking of Miss Rina lying helpless at home there, poor thing. And with only that new girl too! She'll never learn to take proper care of an invalid.

MISS TESMAN.   Oh, I shall manage to train her. And of course, you know, I shall

take most of it upon myself. You needn't be uneasy about my poor sister, my
dear Berta.

BERTA.   Well, but there's another thing, miss. I'm so mortally afraid I shan't be
able to suit the young mistress.

MISS TESMAN.   Oh well—just at first there may be one or two things—

BERTA.   Most like she'll be terrible grand in her ways.

MISS TESMAN.   Well, you can't wonder at that—General Gabler's daughter!
Think of the sort of life she was accustomed to in her father's time. Don't you
remember how we used to see her riding down the road along with the
general? In that long black habit—and with feathers in her hat?

BERTA.   Yes, indeed—I remember well enough! But, good lord, I should never
have dreamt in those days that she and Master George would make a match
of it.

MISS TESMAN.   Nor I. But by-the-bye, Berta—while I think of it: in future you
mustn't say Master George. You must say Doctor Tesman.

BERTA.   Yes, the young mistress spoke of that too—last night—the moment
they set foot in the house. Is it true then, miss?

MISS TESMAN.   Yes, indeed it is. Only think, Berta—some foreign university has
made him a doctor—while he has been abroad, you understand. I hadn't
heard a word about it until he told me himself upon the pier.

BERTA.   Well, well, he's clever enough for anything, he is. But I didn't think
he'd have gone in for doctoring people too.

MISS TESMAN.   No, no, it's not that sort of doctor he is. [*Nods significantly.*] But
let me tell you, we may have to call him something still grander before long.

BERTA.   You don't say so! What can that be, miss?

MISS TESMAN [*smiling*].   H'm—wouldn't you like to know!

—From *Hedda Gabler,*
Henrik Ibsen [1890]

Everything in this conversation is natural and unstrained, yet it tells us all
that we immediately need to know about the main characters and their
relationships with one another. We learn that George Tesman and his new
wife have just returned from their honeymoon, that no one had ever dreamt
the two would wed, that prior to his marriage George had lived with his two
aunts and the maid Berta, and that George had recently been awarded a
doctorate by "some foreign university." These few facts give us our bearings
and prepare us for the entrance of George and Hedda. They also hint at
Hedda's romantic past and George's professional ambitions, thus preparing
us for the entrance of Eilert Lövborg, who is about to compete for George's
academic position as he had once competed for Hedda's affections.

But we learn even more. Ibsen is so economical a craftsman that these few
lines of dialogue also contribute to the characterization of George, Hedda,
and Aunt Julia. We learn, for example, that George is helpless and relies on
others to provide him with the comforts of life. When Aunt Julia must choose
whether Berta should stay with Aunt Rina or go with George, she decides that
her invalid sister is more self-sufficient than her nephew. We also learn that
George is not the elegant sort of man one would expect to marry a general's
daughter, although his aunts and Berta are genuinely fond of him. Thus,
when we first see Tesman on stage we have been prepared, subtly, for his

kindly, methodical, sentimental, and slightly incompetent approach to life.

Hedda, on the other hand, is a far more formidable character. She is mentioned by Berta and Julia with anxiety. Because Hedda is so "grand in her ways," Berta fears that she "shan't be able to suit the young mistress" and Aunt Julia agrees that "at first there may be one or two things." Aunt Julia's reminiscences about how Hedda used to ride in a long black habit with feathers in her hat prepare us for a woman of aristocratic and romantic disposition. And Hedda's insistence that her husband be called Doctor Tesman hints at her desire for a dignified and proper place in society. These few introductory remarks, then, indicate that Hedda is likely to be emotionally unsuited to a drab life with Tesman and suggest that her romantic predilections may eventually come into conflict with her equally strong desire for propriety.

Finally, the lines indirectly characterize Aunt Julia. She is a fussy, meddling, and kindly woman who habitually thinks of others first. She listens carefully to find out if the newlyweds are stirring, throws open the glass door to give them plenty of air, and gives up her own maid to be sure they will be well served. Berta's mistaken assumption that George has become a medical doctor apparently triggers one of the preoccupations of Aunt Julia's prying mind. The allusion to a medial doctor in the context of George's marriage evidently arouses her hope that the household may soon need an obstetrical physician and that George will become a father as well as a doctor of philosophy. She nods significantly and says mysteriously, "we may have to call him something still grander [than doctor] before long."

Yet another function of the dialogue in this introductory scene is to foreshadow themes of later importance. The oblique allusion to Hedda's possible pregnancy is but one such example. In a more overt and pragmatic way, the opening dialogue and accompanying actions often help to initiate events that are further developed as the play progresses. The bouquet that is in Berta's hand as the play opens carries a card promising a visit from Thea Elvsted, a visit that will develop into a competition between Hedda and Thea for control over Eilert Lövborg. Similarly, Aunt Julia's well-intentioned opening of the glass doors will later irritate Hedda, who prefers a "softer light" and complains, "Oh—there the servant has gone and opened the veranda door and let in a whole flood of sunshine." From that point on, Hedda maliciously seeks opportunities to goad Aunt Julia and to prevent any attempt to create a tight family circle that will include George's aunts. As the play unfolds, the expressed anxieties of Aunt Julia and Berta that "there may be one or two" points of conflict between them and Hedda are amply confirmed.

In summary, the dialogue in Ibsen's plays, as in most other plays, serves many simultaneous functions. It is used to provide necessary factual information, to reminisce, to characterize, to speculate, and to foreshadow. Such dialogue may take the form of discussion (as in the quoted scene), argument, or inquiry. It may accompany and clarify actions or simply reveal attitudes and opinions. In short, good dialogue is a very flexible narrative tool.

Dialogue is not, however, an easy tool to use. A playwright, unlike a novelist, cannot simply halt proceedings to introduce formal character sketches or to set a scene; nor can a playwright exert the same direct control over the "story." A fictional "yarn" is spun out of a voice that the author, as narrator, can fully control. But the dramatist has no voice of his or her own. When the curtain rises, the fabric of the plot must emerge naturally from interwoven and independent threads of conversation.

When we argue that the plot of a play must emerge naturally from its dialogue, we do not mean that the dialogue itself must inevitably be "natural" or "realistic." As the Watergate tapes demonstrate, the real words of real people often seem awkward and unnatural in transcript. But art is not life. We hold art to a higher standard of probability, eloquence, and organization; therefore, nearly all dramatic dialogue is more rhetorical—more poetic, if you will—than real dialogue. Even so, however, there is an enormous range between the dialogue of *Hedda Gabler*, for example, and that of *Othello*. Part of the difference results from the fact that the former is written in prose, the latter in verse; and verse is almost always much richer than prose in sound, rhythm, and imagery.

There is, however, also the matter of level of style. The language of *Othello* is often lofty and formal; the language of *Hedda Gabler*, by contrast, is colloquial and informal. Listen to the reflections of Othello as he looks upon Desdemona by candlelight before mercilessly slaying her:

> If I quench thee, thou flaming minister,
> I can thy former light restore,
> Should I repent me: but once put out thy light,
> Thou cunning'st pattern of excelling nature,
> I know not where is that Promethean heat
> That can thy light relume. When I have plucked the rose,
> I cannot give it vital growth again,
> It must needs wither: I'll smell it on the tree.
>   [*Kissing her.*]
> Ah, balmy breath, that dost almost persuade
> Justice to break her sword! One more, one more.
> Be thus when thou art dead, and I will kill thee,
> And love thee after.
>
>   —From *Othello*, act 5, scene 2,
>   William Shakespeare [1604]

Even in this moment of aroused emotion Othello's thoughts roll forth in grammatically complete and relatively complex sentences. His fevered and fertile imagination leads him to express himself through a series of poetic devices. First he compares snuffing a candle with snuffing Desdemona's life; then he alludes to the Greek myth of Prometheus, a Titan who originally gave fire to mankind; next he compares the beauty of Desdemona with that of the rose that "must needs wither" when plucked; and finally, after bending to "smell it on the tree," he uses personification in claiming that Desdemona's "balmy breath" could "almost persuade / Justice to break her sword." Plays like *Othello*, which make use of careful syntax and copious poetic devices, are said to be written in the *high style*.

The language of *Hedda Gabler* is, of course, far different. Notice, for example, the casual and conversational tone. Phrases are inserted to capture the flavor of everyday speech ("upon my word," "good lord," "well, well," "I declare"[1]). Grammatical relationships, too, are informal: the dialogue is sprinkled with dashes to indicate incomplete thoughts or sudden changes in direction. And Ibsen makes no attempt to use poetical devices. Playwrights occasionally carry this colloquial, *low style* even further and use ungrammatical and dialectical speech as a tool of characterization. The back-country accents and diction of the Cabots, for example, help Eugene O'Neill explore crude and elemental passions in *Desire Under the Elms*. Similarly, Stanley Kowalski's inarticulate speech in Tennessee Williams's *A Streetcar Named Desire* underscores his assertive, uneducated, and violent character. And even in *Othello* Iago's worldly and profane speech helps to identify him as a villain.

Dramatic theory during the classical and neoclassical periods held that tragedy should be written in the high style and that the colloquial, or low, style was appropriate only to comedy. In practice, however, as the plays of Shakespeare amply demonstrate, such a distinction need not be rigidly observed, and in more modern times it has been all but abandoned. Most drama is mixed in style, rising to eloquence or falling to informality according to the inherent demands of the dramatic situation.

STORY

People come to the theater because they wish to be entertained. Although they may be willing to admire fine writing or to tolerate moral instruction, they demand an engrossing story. An audience is, after all, a crowd, and the principal desire of a crowd is to find out "what happens next." Drama, however, would emphasize story even if it were not demanded by the audience, for the dramatic point of view necessitates a fundamentally chronological development of action. Reminiscences can be, and often are, used to precipitate the action, but once the play has begun, the events on the stage inevitably unfold according to the simple time sequence of a story.

Dramatic actions as they unfold upon the stage do not, of course, simply "happen"; they are premeditated and artistically arranged by the playwright to yield a dramatic plot. The ability to understand the story (the "what happens") may satisfy our basic desire as theatergoers to be entertained, but as literary critics we also need to understand not only "what happens" but "why"—a question that invariably forces us to consider the dynamics of plot.

Like a typical short story, the plot of nearly every play contains five structural elements: *exposition, complication, crisis, falling action,* **and** *resolution.* The principal difference between fictional and dramatic plots is that the latter are more regular in their use of these five elements, as is illustrated in the following paragraphs.

---

[1] If these expressions seem too stilted to qualify as "everyday speech," remember that *Hedda Gabler* was written nearly 100 years ago and has been translated into English from the original Norwegian. It is always well to bear such factors in mind when considering the language of a play.

Exposition

The *exposition* **provides essential background information, introduces the cast, begins the characterization, and initiates the action.** Some exposition is always provided in the first scene, and all of the essential background material is usually provided by the end of the first act. Sometimes a formal prologue or introduction by a narrator helps to set the scene, but more often there is no sharp division between the exposition and the complication that follows. In fact, **most plays begin** *in medias res* **(in the middle of things), just after some event has taken place that will eventually lead to the crisis.**

Examples of the Situation at the Commencement of Dramatic Action

King Oedipus. A plague afflicts Thebes because the murderer of King Laius has never been punished.

Othello. Othello and Desdemona have secretly married; and Cassio, rather than Iago, has been made Othello's lieutenant.

Tartuffe. To be nearer to his religious adviser, Orgon has installed Tartuffe in his home.

Hedda Gabler. After their honeymoon, Hedda and George have returned to town, as has Eilert Lövborg, who is seeking to publish a new book. Rumor has it that George's faculty appointment must await the outcome of a competition with Eilert.

The situation at the outset of a play usually gives us important clues to its direction and meaning. We do not, for example, see Oedipus at his moment of early triumph over the Sphinx; instead we first see him as he proudly promises that he will discover Laius's killer just as he once discovered the meaning of the Sphinx's riddle. The play explores the consequences of this rash promise. Similarly, *Othello* does not begin with a scene showing Othello's wedding ceremony, but rather with the conspiracy between Roderigo and Iago, in order to focus the audience's attention immediately on Iago's thirst for revenge.

Complication

The *complication* **introduces and develops the conflict. It commences when one or more of the main characters first become aware of an impending difficulty or when their relationships first begin to change.**

Examples of Initial Complication

King Oedipus. Tiresias alleges that Oedipus has murdered Laius.

Othello. Iago recognizes that Cassio's courteous attentions to Desdemona can be used to make Othello jealous (act 2, scene 2).

Tartuffe. Orgon reveals his decision that Mariane must marry Tartuffe instead of Valère, whom she loves (act 2, scene 1).

Hedda Gabler. Thea informs Hedda that Eilert Lövborg is in town and that he is still preoccupied by the memory of an unknown woman (act 1).

It is not always possible to identify the precise point at which the complication of the plot begins. The plot of *Othello*, for example, obviously turns on

Iago's ability to make Othello suspect Desdemona of infidelity. But how does this suspicion originate? Does it begin as a scheme in Iago's brain when, having seen Cassio take Desdemona by the hand (act 2, scene 2), he whispers slyly, "With as little a web as this will I ensnare as great a fly as Cassio"? Or does it begin somewhat later (act 3, scene 3), when (as Cassio parts from Desdemona) Iago says to Othello, "Ha! I like not that"? Or did Othello's jealousy start as early as act 1, scene 3, when Brabantio exclaimed, "Look to her, Moor, if thou has eyes to see. She has deceived her father, and may thee"? In a sense it begins at each place. It was foreshadowed in act 1, scene 3; first plotted by Iago in act 2, scene 2; and first felt by Othello in act 3, scene 3. From relatively small beginnings, Othello's jealousy grows until it dominates his entire personality. Much of the impact of the play results from the fact that the tragedy that ultimately destroys Othello has its roots in such small and indefinite beginnings.

In other plays, however, the conflict and its thematic significance are immediately clear. Oedipus's pride and impetuosity are implicit in his very first speech, but they only take on the aspect of tragic flaws when he refuses to check the accuracy of the prophesies reported by Tiresias and rashly concludes that the priest has joined with Creon in conspiring to usurp his throne. Similarly, Orgon's excessive faith in Tartuffe is clear throughout the first act, but only becomes dangerous and destructive when it leads him to break his promise that Valère shall marry Mariane. In both plays, the tensions that dramatically affect the protagonist's subsequent conduct are implicit in the opening scenes.

Crisis

The *crisis*, or turning point of the play, occurs at the moment of peak emotional intensity and usually involves a decision, a decisive action, or an open conflict between the protagonist and antagonist. It is often called the *obligatory scene* because the audience demands to *see* such moments acted out on stage.

Examples of the Crisis

King Oedipus. The shepherd's information about Oedipus's birth finally convinces the king that he has murdered his father and married his mother. Meanwhile Jocasta has gone into the palace to kill herself.

Othello. Through the machinations of Iago, Othello sees Desdemona's handkerchief in the hand of Cassio and concludes that she must die for her infidelity (act 4, scene 1).

Tartuffe. While hidden under a table, Orgon hears Tartuffe trying to seduce his wife and finally recognizes Tartuffe's hypocrisy for what it is (act 4, scene 5).

Hedda Gabler. Instead of returning Eilert's manuscript, Hedda encourages him to believe it is lost and gives him a pistol with which to commit suicide. After he has left, she burns the manuscript (act 3).

Just as it is sometimes difficult to determine where the conflict originates, it is sometimes also difficult to determine when the crisis takes place. Once Othello has seen Cassio with Desdemona's handkerchief, he is convinced of her guilt and the tragic conclusion of the play is foreordained. The scene, then, marks an important turning point in the characterization of Othello. But the dramatic tension continues to mount until the confrontation between Othello and Desdemona in her bed chamber (act 5, scene 2). We do not *know* that Othello will actually kill Desdemona until he does so. And only when he does so in spite of Desdemona's moving pleas and his own obvious reluctance, do we recognize the extent to which his jealousy has blinded him. Clearly, this scene, too, is a crisis in the plot and another turning point in the characterization of Othello. A hundred lines further into the scene we find yet another crisis and another turning point when Emilia tells Othello that Desdemona could not have given the handkerchief to Cassio for she, Emilia, had found it and given it to Iago. This revelation is the turning point in Iago's fortunes; it finally shows Othello how mistaken he has been all along. In the few remaining moments of the play, Othello rises again to the dignity and nobility that had first characterized him.

It is a mistake, therefore, in plays like *Othello* always to seek the crisis within a single moment of emotional intensity. Great literature is never bound by formula. Instead, as critics we must learn to look carefully at each moment of high drama in an effort to determine what we can learn from it about the play, its characters, and their relationship to the playwright's overall intention.

Falling Action and Resolution

As the consequences of the crisis accumulate, events develop a momentum of their own. Especially in tragedy, the *falling action* of the play results from the protagonist's loss of control and a final catastrophe often appears inevitable. The plot of a comedy, however, frequently includes some unexpected twist (for example, the intervention of the king or the revelation of the hero's true parents). This twist cuts sharply through all difficulties and allows the play to end on a happy note. In both tragedy and comedy, the *resolution* brings to an end the conflict that has been implicit (or explicit) since the play's opening scenes. When the curtain falls, the relationships among the characters have once more stabilized.

Examples of the Falling Action and Resolution

King Oedipus. Oedipus blinds himself in sorrow and then is banished by the new king, Creon.

Othello. After smothering Desdemona, Othello learns of her innocence and slays himself.

Tartuffe. Using a deed that Orgon had foolishly signed, Tartuffe attempts to expel Orgon and his family from their own home. At the last moment, Tartuffe is arrested and imprisoned by order of the king.

Hedda Gabler. After Eilert's death, George and Thea set to work reproducing the lost manuscript. Hedda, whom George has commended to Judge Brack's attention, finds herself in Brack's power when he threatens to reveal information that would involve her in scandal. Rather than become Brack's mistress or tolerate scandal, Hedda shoots herself.

The resolution, or *dénouement*, merits special attention because it is the author's last chance to get the point across. Thus, it is not surprising that

**the resolution often contains a clear statement (or restatement) of the
theme and a full revelation of character.** In the last lines of *Hedda Gabler,* for
example, Hedda realizes that Thea will indeed inspire Tesman just as she
had Eilert Lövborg, while she, Hedda, can do "nothing in the world to help
them." And Othello, in his last lines, begs that, when relating his story,
Lodovico and Gratiano will speak

> Of one that loved not wisely but too well,
> Of one not easily jealous, but, being wrought,
> Perplexed in the extreme, of one whose hand,
> Like the base Indian, threw a pearl away
> Richer than all his tribe—of one whose subdued eyes,
> Albeit unused to the melting mood,
> Drop tears as fast as the Arabian trees
> Their medicinal gum.
>
> —From *Othello,* act 5, scene 2,
> William Shakespeare [1604]

In the last lines of *Tartuffe,* the officer presents Molière's conception of the
ideal man:

> We live under a king who is an enemy to fraud, a king whose eyes look into the
> depths of all hearts, and who cannot be deceived by the most artful imposter.
> Gifted with a fine discernment, his lofty soul at all times sees things in the right
> light. He is never betrayed into exaggeration, and his sound judgment never
> falls into any excess. He confers an everlasting glory upon men of worth; but
> this zeal does not radiate blindly: his esteem for the sincere does not close his
> heart to the horror aroused by those who are treacherous.
>
> —From *Tartuffe,* act 5, scene 7,
> Molière [1664]

And finally, the chorus pronounces a telling judgment upon Oedipus, as that
play closes:

> CHORUS.   Make way for Oedipus. All people said,
>   "That is a fortunate man;"
> And now what storms are beating on his head!
>   "That is a fortunate man,"
> Call no man fortunate that is not dead.
> The dead are free from pain.
>
> —From *King Oedipus,*
> Sophocles [430 B.C.]

In each case the lines are so crucial and so clearly a summary of what the
author finds most important that literary critics often use them as keys to
unlock the riches of each play.

Although virtually all plays include an exposition, complication, crisis,
falling action, and resolution, and most take approximately the same amount
of time to perform, they differ drastically in the amount of fictional time
covered by the action shown on stage. In plays like *King Oedipus, Tartuffe,* and
Hedda Gabler, the action begins just a few hours before the crisis. This allows

the drama to unfold before the spectators' eyes, much as if they were looking in on real events. But because nearly any plot of significance builds to a crisis that caps a series of events dating back months or years, these *unfolding plots* necessarily make use of reminiscences introduced via the testimony of elderly step-parents, conversations between friends and servants, or other similar strategies. The manipulation of these reminiscences requires considerable ingenuity in order to avoid a sense of obvious contrivance. One alternative is to present the action episodically, skipping weeks, months, or years between scenes as the chief events leading up to the crisis are acted out on stage. *Othello* and most other Elizabethan plays employ such *episodic plots.*

Whether a plot is unfolding or episodic, it ought to be tightly structured and pruned of unnecessary characters, actions, speeches, and scenes. The term *well-made play,* or *"pièce bien faite,"* was coined by Eugène Scribe, a French playwright (1791–1861), to describe such plots—especially when they proceed logically from cause to effect in building toward a climatic scene in which the hero triumphs by revealing some adeptly foreshadowed secret. Although the formula prescribed by Scribe is now out-of-date, the craftsmanship he advocated will never be. It is, and always has been, an unmistakable sign of good drama. The first truly well-made plays were not written by Scribe or Ibsen, but by Aeschylus and Sophocles. And the latter's *King Oedipus* probably conforms more closely than any later drama to the description of the well-made play first given in Aristotle's *Poetics*:

> The plot, being an imitation of an action must imitate one action and that a whole, the structural union of the parts being such that, if any one of them is displaced or removed, the whole will be disjointed and disturbed.[2]

CHARACTER

For many of us, an interest in literature is an outgrowth of our interest in people and their personalities. Drama is particularly satisfying in this respect, for plays are inevitably and immediately concerned with the human beings who are impersonated by live actors and actresses on the stage. The terms used to describe characters in drama are, for the most part, the same as those used for fiction. In fact, some of these terms were originally borrowed from drama to describe fictional qualities. **The *dramatis personae* (or characters) of a play usually include a** *protagonist* **(the play's central character) and an opposing** *antagonist* **or an antagonistic force. (The protagonist in a tragedy, however, is often called the** *tragic hero.***)** Othello and Oedipus are clearly protagonists; Iago is Othello's antagonist; and the will of the gods is the antagonistic force opposing Oedipus. A great many plays also include a *confidant* (*confidante* if female) **to whom a major character "confides" his or her most private thoughts and feelings.** Emilia, for example, serves as Desdemona's confidante in *Othello,* just as Dorine is Mariane's confidante in *Tartuffe.* **A** *foil* **is a minor figure whose contrasting personality in some ways clarifies that of a major character,** as Cléante's moderation

---

[2] *The Poetics of Aristotle,* 3rd ed., trans. by S. H. Butcher (New York: Macmillan Publishing Company, 1902), p. 35.

serves as a foil for Orgon's zealotry in *Tartuffe* and as Shakespeare's Laertes becomes a foil for Hamlet while both are seeking to revenge their fathers' death. **A *caricature* is a character with a habit or trait that is carried to a ridiculous extreme.** In *Hedda Gabler* George Tesman, who has spent his honeymoon researching a book on "the domestic industries of Brabant during the Middle Ages" is a caricature of the scholarly temperament. And nearly everyone in *Tartuffe* is a caricature of some aspect of seventeenth-century French society.

This terminology underscores the obvious difference between *major* **and** *minor characters.* **The parts of the protagonist and antagonist are major, whereas those of the confidant and foil are often (but not always) minor.** Because it is only reasonable to assume that most of a playwright's attention will be focused on his major characters, one of our first steps in the analysis of a play should be to identify the characters who have leading roles. The most obvious clue is the number of lines spoken by each character: major characters have many, and minor characters few. But more importantly, major characters are usually individualized and given both complex motives and a past, while minor characters often have no past at all and sometimes represent no more than a common character type. One has said nearly all that need be said about the characters of the messenger and the shepherd in *King Oedipus* as soon as their titles are mentioned. They have few individual traits and serve primarily to convey information to Oedipus and the audience. Similarly, Judge Brack in *Hedda Gabler* is a middle-aged rake whose single motive is to establish a comfortable triangular friendship in which Hedda becomes his mistress while George remains his friend. No such simple statements, however, can accurately describe the personalities of major characters like Oedipus, Othello, and Hedda. In order to understand these individuals, we must look carefully at the various means of characterization used to bring them to life.

Characterizing details in drama come to us from many different sources. We immediately learn something from the *name and physical appearance* of each character—although this information is often unreliable. The characters in *Othello,* for example, so often use the adjective *honest* when they refer to Iago that it seems (ironically) a part of his name, and they mistakenly take his coarse manner and military bearing as signs of simplicity and firmness. A second method of characterization is through an individual's *patterns of action* over the course of the play. Hedda Gabler's pacing, for example, is an indication of her sense of suffocating confinement in her role as a woman. Much characterization, however, is accomplished through dialogue in one of four ways. A character can reveal his or her personality and motives, as Iago often does, through *asides and soliloquies.* There may also be self-revelation in *the way a character speaks* because dialect, word choice, and grammar all provide clues to a person's background and intelligence. Othello's "perfect soul" is partially revealed through his eloquence, while Iago's idiomatic slang marks him as a "profane wretch" (according to Brabantio) in the very first scene of the play. *The way a character responds* to others is also important. Adversity seems at first only to make Othello more self-confident. When swords on both sides are drawn as Brabantio seeks to arrest Othello, the latter averts a crisis with composure: "Good signior, you shall more command with years / Than with your weapons." Yet the violent temper of this eminent soldier eventually surfaces, and he himself recognizes that he is one not easily made jealous or moved to anger, "but, being wrought, / Perplexed in the extreme." Finally, *what others say about a character* can help us to understand him or her. As we have seen, the conversation between Aunt Julia and Berta is packed with observations, speculations, reminiscences, and judgments about Hedda and Tesman. These characterizing details come at us in fragmentary glimpses during the normal ebb and flow of the conversation. Occasionally, however, an author may provide a more concentrated sketch of a character's actions or personality—usually in the form of such *hidden narration* as the messenger's account of Oedipus's rage after learning his true parentage (see p. 23).

The process of understanding drama is very closely linked to our ability to understand the personalities and motives of the major characters. As we read and study a play, we inevitably raise a host of questions: Why does Iago dedicate himself to tormenting Othello? Why is Othello so susceptible to Iago's manipulations? What makes the lost handkerchief so important to Othello? Why does Desdemona lie about the handkerchief? What stops Othello and Desdemona from talking about their misunderstanding openly and fully? Is Othello thoroughly noble or is his character seriously flawed in some way? These questions, and others like them, are concerned with fundamental character traits and express our expectation that the actions of the characters should be plausible, consistent, and adequately motivated. In attempting to answer them, we continually compare what is said by or about a character with the way in which that character acts on stage, searching for the thread of unity that creates a convincing personality.

At the same time, however, characters who are too consistent generally seem unrealistic. Conventional wisdom tells us that real people are full of surprises and so, in literature, we tend to demand characters who are capable of surprising us in a convincing way. Their motives should be complex and even competing, as Othello's obvious love for Desdemona competes with his injured pride when he thinks that she has been unfaithful to him. Moreover, those characters who most interest us usually undergo a process of growth and change during the course of the play. Othello fascinates us as he sinks from his initial nobility to an all-consuming jealousy, before rising again in the tragic self-knowledge of his last speech. Similarly, Oedipus's blind complacency and self-satisfaction break down as the unfolding events force him to see the criminal actions of his past. At the end of the play, this banished and self-blinded man realizes that, although his eyes once were clear, he has had "neither sight nor knowledge."

We must be careful, however, not to push too far the demand for growth and change in character. Many fine plays, including *Tartuffe* and *Hedda Gabler*, present personalities or dilemmas without even hinting at the possibility of moral improvement or permanent solutions. Apparently Molière felt that a man like Tartuffe can be imprisoned but rarely improved, and that Orgon is as naturally impetuous in desiring Tartuffe's punishment as he had earlier been in praising him. Similarly, *Hedda Gabler* is a bleak study of a fundamentally pathological personality. The value of such drama is not that it creates characters just like our next-door neighbors, but rather that it shows how only slight distortions in personality can destabilize the whole structure of ordinary social relationships.

ACTION

John Wilmot, the Earl of Rochester, once criticized Charles II as a king who "never said a foolish thing / Nor ever did a wise one." Many a dramatist, after seeing his plays poorly acted, must have sympathized with the response of Charles II: "This is very true: for my words are my own, and my actions are my ministers'." The playwright must live with the parallel and sometimes melancholy realization that, while his words are his own, his actions are the actors'. Fortunately for the play-going public, actors are much more successful at putting the words of a play into action than bureaucrats are at implementing those of heads of government.

Although the actions in a play may sometimes be indicated or suggested in the script, they are just as often the inevitable by-products of the performance. When Berta and Aunt Julia are talking in the first scene of *Hedda Gabler* (see p. 37), we should not assume that they face each other motionlessly throughout their conversation. Ibsen himself directs them to perform a few actions— close the front door, open the door to the veranda, put down the bouquet, and so on—but twelve consecutive exchanges take place without a single stage direction. What do these women do with their hands during these exchanges? Do they remain motionless or move about the room? Do they face each other, the audience, or neither? Ibsen doesn't say, but surely some actions must take place—if only an averted glance here and a penetrating look there. Although the lines must be spoken, the director is free to present them as he wishes, and this presentation will affect both the characterization of the speakers and the degree of dramatic emphasis given to their words.

As readers of drama, we may attempt to be our own director, moving the characters about an imaginary stage and endowing them with gestures and expressions suitable to the dialogue. Most of us, however, are content to concentrate on the words in the play and leave the accompanying actions vague, except where they are demanded by the script. In either approach, however, we must be very sensitive to actions implied in the dialogue. This is especially true when we read plays written before the middle of the nineteenth century. Thereafter the techniques of the novel began to infiltrate drama and the playwright's stage directions became more frequent and more detailed. But early playwrights kept their stage directions to an absolute minimum. Here, for example, is part of a scene from Shakespeare's *Othello* as it was published in the famous *First Folio* (1623):

[*Enter* LODOVICO, DESDEMONA, *and* ATTENDANTS]

LODOVICO.   Save you worthy General!
OTHELLO.   With all my heart, sir.
LODOVICO.   The Duke and Senators of Venice greet you.
OTHELLO.   I kiss the instrument of their pleasures.
DESDEMONA.   And what's the news, good Cousin Lodovico?
IAGO.   I am very glad to see you, signior.
   Welcome to Cyprus.
LODOVICO.   I thank you. How does Lieutenant Cassio?
IAGO.   Lives, sir.
DESDEMONA.   Cousin, there's fall'n between him and my lord
   An unkind breach, but you shall make all well.

OTHELLO.   Are you sure of that?

DESDEMONA.   My lord?

OTHELLO.   "This fail you not to do, as you will—"

LODOVICO.   He did not call, he's busy in the paper.
    Is there division 'twixt my lord and Cassio?

DESDEMONA.   A most unhappy one. I would do much
    To atone them, for the love I bear to Cassio.

OTHELLO.   Fire and brimstone!

DESDEMONA.   My lord?

OTHELLO.   Are you wise?

DESDEMONA.   What, is he angry?

LODOVICO.   Maybe the letter moved him,
    For, as I think, they do command him home,
    Deputing Cassio in his government.

DESDEMONA.   By my troth, I am glad on 't.

OTHELLO.   Indeed!

DESDEMONA.   My lord?

OTHELLO.   I am glad to see you mad.

DESDEMONA.   Why, sweet Othello?

OTHELLO.   Devil!

DESDEMONA.   I have not deserved this.

LODOVICO.   My lord, this would not be believed in Venice.
    Though I should swear I saw 't. 'Tis very much.
    Make her amends, she weeps.

OTHELLO.   O devil, devil!
    If that the earth could teem with a woman's tears,
    Each drop she falls would prove a crocodile.
    Out of my sight!

DESDEMONA.   I will not stay to offend you.

LODOVICO.   Truly, an obedient lady.
    I do beseech your lordship, call her back.

                            —From *Othello*, act 4, scene 1,
                                 William Shakespeare [1604]

The only stage direction is that calling for the entrance of Lodovico, Desdemona, and attendants. But if we read the lines with care, we realize that Lodovico has brought a letter from Venice that he gives to Othello at line 3, and that Othello refers to this letter when he says, "I kiss the instrument of their pleasures." Presumably, Othello does kiss the letter, and he must open it before line 14, when he pretends to be deeply engrossed in his reading. We can also conclude that Othello slaps Desdemona when he calls her a devil in line 31, for Lodovico later exclaims to Iago, "What, strike his wife!" And we know that Desdemona must start to leave the stage after saying, "I will not stay to offend you" (line 40), because Lodovico asks Othello to call her back in line 42.

All of these actions are implicit in the dialogue, and most modern texts of the play formally incorporate them into editorial stage directions. Even so, however, the questions, counterquestions, exclamations, and asides in the rapid exchanges between lines 8 and 31 presume many additional actions and interactions. As readers we may not pause to speculate on the exact nature of this interplay, but we should realize that here, as in all drama, the script itself is only a partial guide to the dramatic action, as any glance at a director's prompt book would quickly prove. Both the formal stage directions and the creative contributions of the actors and director are designed either to emphasize the themes and character traits introduced in the dialogue or to stimulate further dialogue. The relationship between dialogue and dramatic action is like that between a diamond and its setting in a ring: in both cases the latter enhances and emphasizes the value and clarity of the former.

CHAPTER FOUR

The Classifications of Drama

No one denies that ***tragedy*** and ***comedy*** are the major subgenres of drama, but the debate over their precise meaning has persisted through at least one hundred generations of philosophers and literary critics. Can this immense investment of intellectual energy have been worthwhile? The ability to classify plays may not help us in any important way to understand what a playwright has done, why he or she has done it, or what makes the play interesting. Yet these are the questions with which we must always deal in order to understand literature. Moreover, making a simple distinction between tragedy and comedy is about as easy as determining whether we more often sorrow or smile in reading or viewing a particular play. It is only when we demand precision in defining the kinds of plot, character, and action that create tragic or comic emotions that the issue becomes complex and irresolvable.

Most playwrights have been indifferent to these matters of classification, preferring simply to write their plays and let others worry about categorizing them. Plato tells us that Socrates once cornered Agathon, a respected tragic playwright, and Aristophanes, the greatest comic playwright, at the end of a party in Athens. In his enthusiasm for philosophy, Socrates began to lecture them on his theory that the genius of comedy is the same as that of tragedy. Being drowsy and half drunk, both poets agreed, shared another cup of wine, and promptly dozed off, leaving Socrates to peddle his theory elsewhere.

If the responses of Agathon and Aristophanes were universal, we would not need to discuss tragedy and comedy any further. However, some playwrights do write plays according to some theory of the formal principles for each subgenre, and therefore we need to have at least rudimentary knowledge of the theories behind tragedy and comedy.

TRAGEDY

The first, and most influential, literary theorist was Aristotle (384–322 B.C.) whose famous definition of tragedy remains the cornerstone upon which all discussions of the subject must build. *Tragedy,* Aristotle contended, is an imitation of an action of high importance, complete and of some amplitude; in language enhanced by distinct and varying beauties; acted not narrated; by means of pity and fear effecting its purgation of these emotions.[1]

This definition puts much of its emphasis on the tragic action, or story, which Aristotle thought should be serious, complex, and tightly structured. Tragedy does not need to show events that have happened, but only those that would happen, given a certain set of circumstances. The events must be arranged in a causal progression, so that no action in the play can be eliminated or displaced without damaging the whole structure. Ideally the plot should include both irony and a surprising disclosure, each evolving naturally out of the story. In *King Oedipus*, for example, the arrival of the messenger is ironic because the news of Polybus's death might be expected to release Oedipus from any fear of murdering his father, but instead it leads directly to the disclosure of his incest and parricide. Thus, the plot interweaves the irony with the fatal disclosure.

The requirement that the action of a tragedy be of "high importance" led Aristotle to demand that the protagonist be nobly born and more admirable than ordinary men. He cannot, however, be morally perfect because the best plots arise when his downfall is the inevitable consequence of some defect in character (or *tragic flaw*). The spectacle of a good man dragged to destruction by a single error arouses in the audience both pity and fear, leading to a *catharsis*, a psychological state through which those emotions are purged; the audience leaves the theater relieved, or even exalted, rather than depressed.

This Aristotelian definition accurately reflects the goal of most Greek, Roman, and neoclassical tragedy, but it is too narrow to include many serious and important plays written during other periods. Richard III, Macbeth, and Hedda Gabler, for example, are certainly *less* virtuous than ordinary men and women; it is debatable whether Romeo, Juliet, Hamlet, and Othello have tragic flaws; and very few of the characters in modern drama are nobly born. A definition of tragedy that excludes most of the work of Shakespeare and all of Ibsen—not to mention that of more recent playwrights—cannot be complete.

A more modern view is that there are at least three variations of the tragic situation or tragic emotion.[2] **Some plays ask us to look on the sufferings of the tragic hero as a human sacrifice that is necessary to cleanse society.** The fall of Oedipus, for example, is necessary to purge Thebes of hidden crime and to free the city from a plague imposed by the gods. Similarly, Richard III, Iago, and Macbeth can all be viewed as warped personalities who must perish before ordinary and stable social relationships can reassert themselves. As these examples suggest, the plots of sacrificial tragedies take one of two forms. The tragic hero suffers either through the will of the gods (like Oedipus) or through a rejection by society (like Macbeth). And in either form the protagonist may merit his suffering, as Oedipus and Macbeth do, or he may be an innocent victim of forces beyond his control, as are Romeo and Juliet.

---

[1] Aristotle on *The Art of Fiction*, trans. by L. J. Potts (Cambridge, England: Cambridge University Press, 1962), p. 24.

[2] See E. M. W. Tillyard, *Shakespeare's Problem Plays* (Toronto: University of Toronto Press, 1949), pp. 14–17.

A second tragic pattern arises from the paradox of the fortunate fall. As plots of this kind unfold, we realize that the hero's destruction is necessary if he is to rise to a higher level of personal awareness and development. Othello, for example, must be brought to recognize his responsibility for Desdemona's death if he is to change from a man who once spoke smugly of his "perfect soul" into a tragic figure who accepts himself as one who "Like the base Indian, threw away a pearl/Richer than all his tribe." Oedipus must be blinded before he can truly see. And King Lear must be stripped of his regal pride and forced to "hovel . . . with swine and rogues forlorn in short and musty straw" before he can find his humanity. Tragedies of this second kind reaffirm our human capacity to learn from our experiences; they extend to us the reassurance that even in defeat we can rise above our limitations to an immortal grandeur.

A third tragic pattern involves the simple spectacle of sufferings that greatly exceed normal bounds. The tragic characters struggle helplessly to survive in an environment weighted against them. Like small insects entangled in a web, their futile flutterings express their surprise, regret, and bewilderment at the difference between their own fate and that of other men. Such plays usually include an inquiry by the characters and the playwright into the purpose (or futility) of the tragic individual's sufferings and the role of all human suffering in the scheme of the universe. If Tom Stoppard's *Rosencrantz and Guildenstern Are Dead* is a tragedy at all, it is a tragedy of inexplicable suffering. From the first scene to the last, the characters question the reasons for their involvement in the action and the nature of the world into which they are unwillingly cast. Ultimately their plight becomes a symbol of our plight, and Stoppard persuades us that the death they experience is not simply a variant of the tragedian's phoney "deaths for all ages and occasions," but rather, like real death, "the endless time of never coming back . . . a gap you can't see, and when the wind blows through it, it makes no sound. . . ."

Should we, however, define *Rosencrantz and Guildenstern Are Dead* as a tragedy? It is tragic in the sense that the main characters are victims of forces beyond their control; it is tragic in the sense that the protagonists are destroyed; and, moreover, it is tragic in the sense that the plot deals with issues of high importance, such as reality, fate, and death. But from start to finish, the dialogue is hilarious. If comedy has anything to do with humor, then surely this play qualifies as comic. The situation of Stoppard's characters, and by extension that of all human beings, is absurd—both macabre and wildly funny. It is senseless, silly, and sobering, all at the same time. In contemporary theater, we call this mixture of tragedy and comedy the **theater of the absurd;** its very existence reminds us that there need be no sharp distinction between the frowning mask of tragedy and the smiling mask of comedy.

COMEDY

Horace Walpole, the eighteenth-century man of letters, once observed that "the world is a comedy to those that think, a tragedy to those who feel." Walpole's comparison is as good a guide as any to the key differences between these two modes of drama. The tragic hero is closely examined and portrayed as an individual; the comic character is viewed intellectually from a distance and represents a broad human "type"—a young lover, a hypocrite, an elegant fop, and so on. The tragic mode asks us to sympathize with the hero and imagine ourselves in his position; the comic mode suggests that we step back from life and look with amusement on the humorous predicament of others. The subject matter of comedy is often as serious as that of tragedy, but the comic playwright consciously distorts events and personalities in order to remind the audience that the play deals with fantasy and not fact. The plots of comedy are usually convoluted exercises in authorial imagination; the plots of tragedy are sobering relevations of our emotional and psychological core.

A lighthearted but intellectual approach to comedy has prevailed from the very beginning. The extant plays of Aristophanes (called **Old Comedy**) are carefully structured explorations of a bizarre intellectual hypothesis. What would happen, he asks in *Lysistrata* (411 B.C.), if all Greek women refused to participate in sexual relations until the Peloponnesian War was brought to an end? Suppose (in *The Birds*) that one could found an empire in the air and starve the gods by intercepting the smoke from earthly sacrifices. Imagine (in *The Clouds*) that a farmer attends the school of Socrates in hopes of learning how to avoid paying his debts. In each case the idea and background of the situation are presented in the prologue. The merits and deficiencies of the hypothesis are then formally explored in an *agon*, or debate. The application of the debate is then illustrated in a series of episodes that concludes with a final song and a scene of merriment. In addition, each play contains a number of elements that apparently were required by convention: the entrance of a wildly costumed chorus, an elaborately structured song (*parabasis*) in which the playwright lectures the audience and satirizes the society, and a host of meticulous rules ranging from a required form of *agon* to the necessity of reciting the *pignos* or "choking song" in only one breath.

Within this highly structured form, Aristophanes continually sought to satirize the society at large and its most prominent individuals. He repeatedly attacked the Peloponnesian War and decadent innovations in religion, education, and poetry. He created ridiculous caricatures of Socrates, Euripides, Aeschylus, the politicians of Athens, and even the Greek gods. And throughout it all he continually explored and distorted the implications of his initial intellectual hypothesis.

Few modern comedies have been influenced by the Aristophanic tradition because the hypothetical postulate with which Old Comedy begins tends to favor a rather limiting form of social satire. The plays of Aristophanes are so filled with topical and personal allusions that many parts of them are now unintelligible. In order to survive as a literary form, comedy had to begin using plots and characters that could be universally understood and enjoyed.

By the time Aristophanes wrote his last comedy, *Plutus*, in 388 B.C., he had already evolved beyond the conventions of Old Comedy. The **New Comedy** that ensued has proven to be remarkably durable. Even today most comedies continue to follow the same plot structure:

> What normally happens is that a young man wants a young woman, that his desire is resisted by some opposition, usually paternal, and that near the end of the play some twist in the plot enables the hero to have his will. . . . The movement of comedy is usually a movement from one kind of society to another. At the beginning of the play the obstructing characters are in charge of the play's society, and the audience recognizes that they are usurpers. At the

end of the play the device in the plot that brings the hero and heroine together causes a new society to crystallize around the hero. . . .

The appearance of this new society is frequently signalized by some kind of party or festive ritual, which either appears at the end of the play or is assumed to take place immediately afterward.[3]

Northrop Frye, the critic cited here, has also identified most of the other conventional elements of comedy. He argues that the form appeals most directly to the young men and women in the audience, who identify with the hero and heroine precisely because these protagonists are unindividualized representatives of youth in whom each member of the audience can find his or her own traits. The antagonist who blocks the hero's wishes is either a father or a father-figure and is often made ridiculous by the exaggeration of a single character trait. Molière's Tartuffe and Orgon are typical blocking figures, just as Mariane and Valère are the nondescript protagonists. The plot itself usually overflows with complications that place all of the characters in ticklish situations, and these complications are often resolved by an unexpected twist in the plot, such as the miraculous intervention of the king at the end of *Tartuffe*. At the beginning of *Tartuffe*, hypocrisy dominates the play's society, but by the end a more sensible and honest social structure has emerged that will be celebrated through the marriage of Valère and Mariane.

When the main sources of humor in a play are the ludicrous complications of love, the play is called a *romantic comedy*. **When the emphasis is on the ridiculous foibles or characteristics of the blocking figures, it is called a** *comedy of humours*. (This term derives from the medieval physiological theory of the "four humours," four identifiable elements believed to determine and control individual temperament and personality; an imbalance was thought to result in a lopsided, eccentric personality who became a natural object for comic treatment.) **When the play makes fun of the affectations, manners, and conventions of human behavior, it is called a** *comedy of manners*. **And when it achieves its effects through buffoonery, horseplay, and crude jokes, it is called a** *farce*.

Minute subcategories such as those defined in the preceding paragraph can be compounded almost indefinitely by considering that broad middle ground between tragedy and comedy. The players who performed before the court in *Hamlet* were supposed to be capable of acting "tragedy, comedy, history, pastoral, pastoral-comical, historical-pastoral, tragical-historical, tragical-comical-historical-pastoral, scene individable, or poem unlimited." Shakespeare's mockery of such generic hair splitting is implicit in the exaggerations of the list and in his satire of Polonius, who utters it. Contemporary drama criticism may have moved away from pastoral, historical, and the various hyphenated couplings, but it has developed a myriad of other terms to describe minor classifications of the tone and structure of drama. The most significant of these (*domestic tragedy, melodrama, naturalism, realism, revenge tragedy, thesis play*, etc.) are defined in the glossary appended to this text.

---

[3] Northrop Frye, *Anatomy of Criticism: Four Essays* (Princeton: Princeton University Press, 1957), p. 163.

CHAPTER FIVE

❊ ❊ ❊ ❊ ❊ ❊ ❊

Literary Criticism

THE NATURE OF LITERARY CRITICISM

At some point in our classroom study of literature, most of us have had the experience of being asked to answer the question, "What is the theme of this work?" This question seems to assume that a given literary text has one dominant theme about which everyone should be able to agree. But we all recognize intuitively that any literary work has many themes and that the dominant theme is always a matter of individual perception. If we read Shakespeare's *Othello* primarily as a love story, we might say that the theme of the play is jealousy. If we read the play while undergoing a power struggle at work we might identify power as the dominant theme, and if we read it in the context of the 1992 Los Angeles riots, we might see race as most significant. In fact, the meaning of the play is not entirely stable and unchanging; it is influenced by the interaction of the text and our own experience. That interaction is what produces literary criticism.

Traditionally, literary criticism requires the coming together of three key elements—an author, a literary text, and a reader. Each element (author, text, and reader) can also be regarded as the basis for claims about what a text means.

Surely you have had the experience of discussing a literary work in a classroom only to hear someone say, "But is that what the author intended this to mean?" This person is assuming that the primary site of textual meaning is the author's intention. For this person, the best way to study a literary work is to understand the period in which the author wrote and to read the author's biography, correspondence, and comments about the text. Any interpretation of the text which did not seem consistent with the author's history and presumed intention would be seen as invalid.

On the other hand, another student in that same class might insistently break into the class discussion to say, "But I don't see where you got that interpretation! Show me in the text where it says that." This student sees the text itself as the primary site of meaning. For this student, the best way to study a text is to concentrate on the words on the page, on word choice, structure, and metaphor, the meanings of which are seen as stable. Any interpretation derived by going outside the text itself would be suspect.

In fact, most of our study of literature has probably focused on the author and text, which is why we've spent so much class time taking notes about the author's life and times and closely explicating lines of poetry to unfold their meaning. But if all the meaning of a text can be located in the text itself or in what the author intended, how do we explain the fact that a text can mean different things to different readers, or even that a book we read in childhood may seem quite different to us when we read it today? If the meaning of a text is fixed by the author's original intention, or even by the text itself, both of which do not change over time, why does *Romeo and Juliet* seem so different when we read it as an adult than it did when we read it as adolescents? Almost everyone has reread a novel only to find that because the reader has changed, the novel itself seems different, but we may never have thought about why this is so or how this challenges our most basic assumptions about literature.

A third site for investigating what a text means, therefore, is the reader of the text, and the student who says (or, more likely, thinks), "I don't see how the teacher comes up with all this symbolic stuff—that's not what it means to me!" is also expressing an assumption about the primary site of literary meaning. For this student, the best way to study literature is to investigate the subjective experience of reading and compare our reading with the reading of others.

In fact, when we come together in the classroom to study literature, we bring with us all of our different assumptions about what literature means. We are already predisposed to value those methods of literary study which seem most familiar and obvious to us, and we often seem irrevocably locked within our own interpretations. Because students often feel unable to identify the bases from which claims about meaning are made, they are timid about suggesting alternate interpretations. Too often, a single interpretation (usually the teacher's) is accepted as the only interpretation, even though the teacher and students would have welcomed the stimulus of new ideas.

All three elements of the aesthetic triangle (author, text, and reader) suggest useful methods for the study of literature and for determining a work's meaning. If you think that an author's intention is the best way to understand what a text means, you will no doubt be fascinated by a discussion of the author's life and times, but you are probably wise enough to realize that close textual analysis is necessary if you are to understand fully the indications of intention in the text, and you will probably also take a keen interest in the way other readers have perceived the author's intentions. If you think that the text itself is all that really counts, you should nonetheless recognize that all great authors have a personal style which is more fully understood through a study of the life experiences that contributed to that style. Moreover, the most interesting elements of a text are often amorphous ones involving large patterns, symbols, and metaphors—the meaning of which can sometimes only be deduced through an examination of their effect on readers. Finally, if you think that literature is important only because of its effects on readers, you will still acknowledge that the words of the text help create those effects and that a knowledge of history frequently helps us resolve much that is puzzling in our responses. In short, good literary criticism may begin with a primary interest in author, text, or reader, but it is unwise to ignore any of these key elements in determining literary meaning.

Part of the pleasure of reading and interpreting literature is that, through study and discussion, our understanding continuously grows richer and more varied. Once we have mastered the Freudian interpretation of *Oedipus*, we may go on to the play's image patterns of sight and blindness or to its historical bearing on the Greek conception of fate and divinity. It is for this reason that great scholars have sometimes devoted their entire lives to studying the works of a single author.

The way literature resists all our attempts to finally solve the question of meaning is probably what makes literary study most valuable. Discussions about how differences in interpretation arise should provide a context in which alternate interpretations enrich our understanding of literature rather than threatening the validity of our individual positions. Certainly, the author's intentions, the text itself, and the reading experience all place limits on how we can reasonably interpret a literary work, but the dynamic of all three elements is what makes meaning possible.

READING LITERARY CRITICISM

Reading literary criticism is a little like being a child when the adults are talking about sex. You know something important is going on, but you can't figure out what, and you probably can't get anyone to explain it to you.

Students are often confused when asked to write a paper incorporating scholarly criticism because they have little context for the kinds of arguments being made. They often do not know who the critics are, what theories they are identified with, or what such theories assume that the reader will know. For the beleaguered student, reading literary criticism is a bit like coming in to an unfamiliar play during the fourth act. Characters on stage mention other characters by name, but the latecomer has absolutely no idea who anyone is.

The following section on critical strategies is a bit like a plot summary for the latecomer to the theater or like a sex manual for the inquisitive child of our first paragraph. In each case, the summary provided in a few pages is no substitute for first-hand experience. Although this introduction to critical strategies can't take the place of a course in critical theory, it should at least provide students with enough context to understand many essays in literary criticism now being published.

Each of the critical methods discussed in the following sections is still influential today. Besides a general description and overview of the methods, each section outlines criticisms that have been leveled against that approach, ways in which students can use the approach, and names of scholars most associated with that particular body of theory. Finally, each section points the reader to specific essays (some of them reprinted in this anthology) which can serve as examples.

The editors of this anthology assume in offering these tools to the student that the more critical approaches a student can understand and use, the more equipped that student will be to analyze literature and literary criticism. Some approaches are more difficult than others. Just as we all have individual tastes in literature and individual preferences for ways of analyzing literature, so students may find some approaches more exciting and approachable than others. No critic is a master of every theory. When you discover which theories seem to make the most sense to you, we encourage you to explore those theories more fully through reading books and articles by some of the theorists whose names are associated with that approach.

CRITICAL STRATEGIES FOR READING DRAMA

Formalist Criticism

Formalism is a method of approaching literature that emphasizes intrinsic elements of a literary work, including language, structure, and repetition of images and symbols that occur within a text. In the preceding chapter titled "The Elements of Drama," we identified the formal elements of drama as story, dialogue, action, and character, and we devoted a separate section to explaining and exploring each of these elements. A formalist analysis of a play might focus on one or more of these elements or on other textual matters such as patterns of rhythm, imagery, or symbolism. Each of these elements having to do with language and structure can be analyzed without going outside the play itself. What the formalist critic is asking us to do is to change our angle of vision on the play from a broad focus on the drama as a whole to a narrower perspective on some particular feature of the text.

The process is rather like a good photographer looking at an important event. The photographer sees a panorama, a confusing jumble of sensory impressions. The cover photo which results is likely to be a close-up which captures the essence of the photographer's experience in a way the wide-angle lens could not. We all remember, for example, the famous picture of a Chinese student facing down a tank in Tiennamen Square. That photograph focused on a small moment in the crisis as a way of conveying to others how the character of the protesters affected the photographer.

We might think generally about the process of formalist criticism in this way: when you enter a room, you gain an overall impression of color, atmosphere, and use of space. You might say, "This room is decorated in warm colors and seems very cozy and comfortable." If you wanted to understand how that overall impression is achieved, you might look at the room again, more carefully and at greater length, and analyze one or more elements individually. For instance, you might look only at the use of color, or lighting, or the placement of furniture. By understanding one or more of these elements, you would change your angle of vision but you would also understand more about why you first experienced the room as warm, cozy, and comfortable.

This is what formalist analysis can do—sharpen and narrow the focus on a particular element in order to help us better understand the work as a whole. This is the method of literary analysis with which students are most familiar and the foundation from which students can develop maturity and flexibility in critical analysis. Most other methods of literary criticism are dependent on formal analysis of the text; therefore, formalism is perhaps the most basic and requisite of literary tools.

Like many terms in literature, though, formalism has more than one meaning. At one time formalism was synonymous with the more specific term, **New Criticism, in which critics study a literary work as having autonomous and stable meaning, without reference to the author's intention,**

the effect of the work on a reader, or the historical period in which the work was written. The New Critics, who included such prominent figures as Cleanth Brooks, John Crowe Ransom, Maynard Mack, Allen Tate, and William K. Wimsatt, dominated the field of literary criticism during the post-World War II 1940s and 1950s. Many of the teachers in high schools and colleges today were taught by New Critics, so you have probably been influenced by New Criticism even if you've never heard the term.

New Criticism is more than a formalist method of literary study; it is a philosophy which holds that literature differs from ordinary prose in one fundamental way: in literature, meaning grows out of form; in practical prose, form is subordinate to meaning. A New Critic would point out that the structure of a textbook on anatomy, for example, is entirely governed by its subject. In contrast, the subject of a poem is often defined only by its unique structure or form. Thus, the New Critic sees the text (the novel, poem, or play) as the primary source of literary meaning. For the New Critic, paying attention to the reader's response to the text could lead a critic into committing the *affective fallacy*, which New Critics saw as **the mistake of confusing what the text *is* with what the text *does*.** In addition, paying attention to the author's intentions in writing a literary work may lead a critic into committing the *intentional fallacy*, which New Critics saw as **the mistake of confusing what is actually in a text with what an author intended to put there.** Thus, New Critics are defined not just by the formalist methods of analysis they employed but by the forms of analysis they excluded. New Critics believed that a literary work can only be explained by the internal features of that literary work, since it exists autonomously as an artistic object, outside of history, social forces, the reader's subjective experience, and even the author's intentions.

There is quite clearly something rather extreme about trying to exclude from consideration all of our knowledge about the author, the times, and the psychological impact of a work on its readers. Few contemporary formalists now accept the rigid theoretical premises of the New Critics. Formalist methods, however, are still widely practiced and important to both students and scholars. When faced with the daunting task of saying something new about literature, looking to the formal elements of the text—its language, structure, and symbols—is often an excellent and even necessary place to begin.

Here is a brief example of how formalism is often used among scholars today: When reading Shakespeare's *Othello*, you might notice that white and black are frequently used as symbols, especially since the main characters are a fair Venetian woman and a dark Moorish man. You might, therefore, reread the play looking only for references to black and white and write an essay showing exactly how these terms are used within the play. Such an exploration would almost inevitably lead you to a consideration of racial conflict and racial preconceptions within *Othello*, for Shakespeare clearly links this imagery with matters of race. So far, your work would all be confined to the text. But then what? Does the imagery in *Othello* reflect racial conflicts in Shakespeare's England? Does it explore ideas that are still relevant in the racially charged politics of modern America? Does Shakespeare accurately reveal the psychology of racism through Iago's manipulations of Brabantio and Othello? To answer such questions, you must take up the critical tools described in the succeeding pages of this introduction.

For an example of a recent article that begins with formal analysis of *Othello* and then incorporates a variety of other critical methods, including historical approaches to race and gender, see Karen Newman's " 'And wash the Ethiop white': Femininity and the monstrous in *Othello*" in the selection of critical essays following *Othello* in this anthology.

For examples of more sustained formalist approaches, see Diane Elizabeth Dreher's character study of Desdemona in the section of critical essays on *Othello* and Sam Bluefarb's study of Tennessee Williams's *The Glass Menagerie*.

PSYCHOANALYTICAL CRITICISM

Perhaps no thinker has influenced twentieth-century thought more than Sigmund Freud. Terms such as the unconscious, id, ego, and the Oedipus complex have become part of our common vocabulary, familiar to millions of people who have never read a single word of Freud's writings. So perhaps it's inevitable that Freud's influence has been felt not just in the field of psychoanalysis but in the analysis of literature as well, especially since literature reflects, after all, human dreams and desires, and our responses to literature are inevitably governed by our psychological processes.

When we discuss *Freudian interpretations* of literature, we should first distinguish this enterprise from that of psychoanalysis and explain Freud's place in both these fields. Psychoanalysis is the clinical practice of treating mental disorders by bringing to light the patient's unconscious, often repressed motivation. Freud is the most important single influence in psychoanalysis, but few practitioners today would identify themselves as Freudian. Many concepts attributed to Freud were actually introduced by predecessors whose names are less well known today, and when we discuss modern Freudian thought we are actually dealing with a long line of theorists and therapists who have further developed and articulated Freud's ideas. We still read Freud, but not as a practical guide to modern psychoanalysis. Even in the field of literary criticism, we are more likely to read someone interpreting Freud than we are to read Freud's often contradictory and somewhat diffuse writings.

What has made Freudian psychoanalysis so appealing to literary scholars is Freud's emphasis on the unconscious as the source for powerful human desires and fears. First and foremost, *psychoanalytical criticism* of literature is **engaged in uncovering the mostly unconscious motives of characters, authors, and readers.** Thus, psychological readings of literature can be text-based when focusing on literary characters, historical when focusing on the motivations of the author, or reader-response oriented when focusing on the unconscious thought processes of a reader.

Although Freudian criticism can certainly be complex and we cannot hope to acquaint students with it adequately in these few paragraphs, a brief discussion of some key Freudian terms may help students to interpret psychoanalytic criticism and to use some psychoanalytic concepts in their own analysis.

First, Freud saw the human mind as composed of three parts: the *id*, the *ego*, and the *superego*. The *id* is **that part of ourselves that desires pleasure and avoids pain. The id is unconscious, irrational, and most easily under-**

stood as the infantile part of ourselves that wants what it wants when it wants it and is unable to recognize any desires but its own. The *ego* is the Freudian term for what we usually imagine as the "I," that part of ourselves that is conscious, rational, and orderly. The third part of the psyche is the *superego*, which can be understood as a mediator between the id and the ego. The superego often seems to stand outside the ego, helping us make moral judgments even when such judgments run counter to our own interests. The superego represents not the unconscious or the "I" but the composite voice of moral authority acquired through culture (i.e., our parents, our churches, our schools, our laws). Desires that are taboo or forbidden by the ego and superego are repressed or pushed back into the id or unconscious mind, where they exert powerful influence over our actions.

Freud claimed that much of the repressed desire in the unconscious mind is sexual and relates to an individual's movement to sexual maturity through psychosexual stages of development. In early infancy, human desire is what Freud called "polymorphously perverse" in that the infant willingly takes pleasure wherever it finds it, but pleasure quickly begins to be organized around the mouth (the oral stage, the first stage of infantile development, when desires for food and sexual pleasure overlap), the anus (the anal stage, when defecating is experienced as powerful and pleasurable), the urethra, the genitals, and, finally, the fifth stage of psychosexual development, the Oedipal conflict.

The *Oedipal conflict* is a stage encountered by both boys and girls in which sexual desire for the parent of the opposite sex leads to a desire to kill the same-sex parent. Freud named this fifth stage of individual human development the Oedipal stage because of the Greek tragedy of *King Oedipus*, reprinted in this anthology, which Freud saw as reflecting the common unconscious desire of a boy to kill his father in order to take his father's place in the mother's affections. The Oedipal crisis places the child in conflict with cultural taboos against incest and fratricide or matricide; thus, during this stage of development Oedipal desires are pushed back into the unconscious where they may remain unresolved and affect all of the child's future relationships. Freud believed that during these five stages of psychosexual development, the child could become fixated or stopped at any point in the process and unable to proceed to "normal" adult sexuality. Thus, Freudian analysis refers to "anal fixation" as the inability to let go and, more commonly, a literary analysis might look at how a work that links images of food, speech, and sexual desire reflects tensions unresolved in the oral stage of development.

For Freud, normal adult sexuality is organized around the penis. Having discovered that the penis is linked to power in the world, boys fear castration and experience castration anxiety. Girls also associate the penis with the power of the father and the freedom of the outside world, away from the holding mother in the home. Having discovered that they do not possess penises, Freud argued that girls commonly experience penis envy. These powerful fears and desires are so deeply threatening that they, too, are repressed into the unconscious, but they resurface in our literature through phallic symbols (representations of the power of the penis; common examples are guns, knives, even the Washington Monument) and that frequently recurring literary character, the castrating or phallic woman.

There are, of course, other important concepts in Freudian thought, but the foregoing introduction should help acquaint students with some key terms. A word or two of caution may be in order: nothing is more irritating to many English professors than a student's overly simplistic Freudian analysis of a literary work. Phallic symbols, oral fixations, Oedipal complexes— all can be powerful tools for understanding human motivations, but these concepts must be handled judiciously in literary analysis. Not every pointed object is a phallic symbol; not every strong woman is a castrating mother. A clear pattern of sexual imagery is probably the best indication that a Freudian approach is worth considering.

Students should also be aware of the major criticisms leveled against Freud and the reasons his methods have been rejected by many literary scholars in our own time. First, Freud's emphasis on the penis as the locus of meaning has caused many women to regard Freudian theory as misogynist (reflecting a hatred of women). Second, Freud's tendency to see his own theories as ahistorical (existing outside of history) and universal (experienced by all humans in all cultures) has made his ideas unpalatable to many literary scholars who see history and culture as central in determining the meaning of a text. Third, a few literary scholars reject any Freudian analysis of literature unless it meets a certain litmus test: the text being analyzed must have been written after Freud's ideas became widely known and the author must have been influenced by Freud's theories. Hence, some scholars would say, we can apply Freud's theories to Eugene O'Neill's *Desire Under the Elms* but not to Shakespeare's *Othello* or even Sophocles' *Oedipus*.

Today, students will still encounter very powerful psychoanalytical criticism of literature, but it is most likely to quote post-Freudians like Jacques Lacan. Lacanian analysis focuses on language as phallic and representative of "the law of the fathers." For Lacanians, the structure of language reveals much about the structure of the unconscious, and at the center of the unconscious (and, therefore, at the center of the language) is the lack or absence of a highly desired object.

Other theorists who are currently associated with psychoanalytical thought or criticism are Jessica Benjamin, Juliet Mitchell, Norman Holland, Bernard Paris, Harold Bloom, Bruno Bettelheim, Geoffrey Hartman, Nancy Chodorow, Carol Gilligan, and Julia Kristeva. Frequent quotation of any of these scholars is a good indication that a scholarly article is taking a psychoanalytical approach.

Freud's analysis of Sophocles' *Oedipus the King*, from which Freud formulated his theory of the Oedipus complex, is included in the critical material following the play in this anthology. For an example of more contemporary psychoanalytical literary criticism, see Madelon Gohlke Sprengnether's essay on Shakespeare's *Othello*.

HISTORICAL CRITICISM

Just as there are many types of and occasions for psychoanalytical literary criticism, historical analysis of literature occurs in many different forms. Scholars analyze literature using historical methods that are as old as literature itself and as radically new as tomorrow's headlines. Many students are attracted to historical approaches to literature partly because these methods are, like formalism, familiar through prior classroom experience. Brief biographies of writers and facts about the historical period in which a work was written are often used by teachers to introduce a literary work, so students are already accustomed to incorporating biography and history in their understanding of literary meaning.

Some of the forms of historical literary study that students are likely to encounter are authors' biographies, works which recover lost allusions or inform us about the period in which a work was written, textual histories that trace the changes in a literary work through the record of its publications (often in an effort to establish a standard or definitive edition), and accounts of how literary works have influenced history (for example, how various stage productions of Harriet Beecher Stowe's *Uncle Tom's Cabin* helped fuel abolitionist sympathies). Among the most common historical approaches to drama are accounts of how dramatic works have been staged in other times and how certain plays reflect the influence of other texts and writers.

While the appeal and relevance of historical approaches should be obvious, historical analysis can also be dangerous. Students should beware of making broad claims based on isolated biographical or historical knowledge; good analysis requires a solid historical framework. Another pitfall for the unwary student is that he or she may end up simply reporting on what other scholars have written and not be able to say anything new or provocative. What could you say about the Globe Theater, after all, except to quote from authorities in the field? Though students are unlikely to have access to unpublished primary materials, they can still produce solid historical criticism if they consider how to use history to say something interesting about a text. Sometimes it's a matter of luck; perhaps your university manuscript department houses a collection of unpublished letters from Tennessee Williams. Or perhaps your great-grandfather had a part in one of the plays William Faulkner wrote while he was a student at the University of Mississippi and left you his old playbook and notes. Such good fortune is rare for undergraduates these days, however, so you'll most likely find yourself reading somebody else's historical article and trying to make a connection that that scholar did not make.

In the excerpt included in this anthology in the critical essays following *The Glass Menagerie*, Nancy Tischler predicates her analysis of setting on historical information about Williams's study of expressionism. Charles Kligerman concludes his psychoanalytical study of Pirandello's *Six Characters in Search of an Author* with a confirming historical anecdote obtained through an interview with Pirandello's daughter. You can find Kligerman's article and many other helpful historical studies by using the selected bibliographies following each play in this collection.

One of the most intriguing developments in literary criticism is the advent of **New Historicism**, which, like other historical approaches to literature, **assumes that a text is not independent of history but deeply embedded within it. New Historicism significantly broadens the application of historical methods through two bold claims: history and literature are not distinct from each other, and neither is ever completely neutral or objective.**

First, New Historians blur the distinction between literature and history; for New Historians, literature is viewed as history, and vice versa, and both literature and history can be studied in the broader category of "writing." Literary critics use New Historical methods today to analyze primary documents such as postal records, legal and medical textbooks and pamphlets, subscription records, marginalia and flyleaf dedications in books, as well as traditional literary texts. Thus, a New Historicist might consider issues such as how local theaters actually advertised plays and, through their actions, thereby helped determine who saw plays and indirectly set limits on the subject matter and style of successful productions. Such an analysis might include not just the text of the play, but also the billboards and flyers which promoted it, and would emphasize how variables such as social class, gender, and race helped shape the text of the advertisements and, thus, the play's stage history. Michael Neill's New Historicist essay on *Othello*, for example, which is included in this anthology, claims that the engravings on the covers of eighteenth- and nineteenth-century editions of the play show an underlying illicit anxiety about the marriage bed as a site of racial transgression.

The second bold claim of New Historicism is that history is never entirely objective or neutral but is always a selective account of human experience. Whereas earlier generations of literary critics saw history as a set of facts one must know to be able to understand and appreciate a literary text, New Historicism goes much deeper to destabilize our perception of history as fact and truth. New Historicism not only reminds us that Shakespeare's historical plays are written from the perspective of a white male of middle-class origins embroiled in the politics of the Elizabethan court; a New Historicist also reminds us that the scholar writes from his or her perspective as well, and further that no one reads a literary text or a scholarly article except through the lens of his or her individual experience and assumptions. For New Historicists, what we see as fact is a fictionalized product of a series of reading experiences, each experience embedded within the next like Chinese nesting boxes. For example, Shakespeare took the premise of *Othello* from his reading of Giraldi Cinthio's *Hecatommithi*, but he also "read" the politics of the Elizabethan court to shape Othello's story into a play that would appeal to his contemporaries, especially those with political power. The critic then "reads" Shakespeare's *Othello* from the critic's own limited and self-interested perspective, and your reading of that critic's work is also a product of your own angle of vision. The complicated relationships between all of these perspectives is what the New Historicist explores, often with fascinating and insightful results.

Some literary fields (for instance, Renaissance drama) have been more attractive to New Historicists than others, but this critical approach has so far had much less impact on fields such as classical and modern drama.

New Historicism is an especially useful critical development for the student because it relies less on the accidental discovery of a historical document, or on specialized knowledge of literary periods, than it does on reanalyzing the relationships between authors, texts, readers, and histories with an eye to uncovering limits in the perspectives of each. New Historians continuously remind us (and themselves) that we cannot easily separate ourselves or our study of literature from our own social and political concerns. Once students understand the assumptions of New Historical approaches to literature, many students find this approach interesting and relatively easy to appropriate.

From the preceding discussion, students should be able to recognize New Historicism when they see it, but this process may be easier if students recognize some of the important New Historicist critics apt to be frequently quoted. These names include Jerome McGann, Stephen Greenblatt, Annabel Patterson, Jonathan Dollimore, and Jonathan Goldberg, many of whom will frequently quote French theorist Michel Foucault, who, while not a New Historicist himself, deeply influenced proponents of this approach.

For examples of New Historicist essays on drama, see Karen Newman's and Michael Neill's essays on *Othello* in this anthology.

ANTHROPOLOGICAL AND MYTH CRITICISM

Anthropological and *myth criticism* often intersect with historical and psychoanalytic approaches. Many New Historicists quote the anthropological work of Clifford Geertz, and myth criticism's exploration of archetypes is in large part the result of Carl Jung's break with his mentor, Sigmund Freud. Although myth critical approaches may intersect with psychology and history, there are philosophical differences between all of these approaches. Simply stated, anthropologists and myth critics may use historical facts in their studies, but their emphasis is on uncovering symbols and patterns that transcend specific historic context. **Anthropological and myth critics wish to get beyond history to what they see as more important, especially those images and patterns that reoccur across historical periods and cultures and can thus be seen as universal and archetypal, part of our collective human unconscious.** Myth criticism differs sharply from psychoanalysis as well in that Freud focused on the unconscious of the individual in order to cure "abnormal" behavior, but Jung focused on those unconscious fears and images which large groups of human beings share.

Myth criticism has recently been attacked for its frequent failure to account for historical, cultural, and individual differences. Because myth critics look for commonalities in human experience, they often make assertions that are seen as ahistorical (seeing myth as operating outside of history), trans-historical (seeing myth as larger than history), or universalist (falsely claiming universality). As contemporary scholarship has become increasingly interdisciplinary and multicultural, scholars have become more aware of their own assumptions about what is real and more suspicious of claims of universal truth.

In the field of drama, however, myth criticism remains one of the most powerful and widely published approaches. Perhaps because drama is aimed primarily at rather homogeneous groups instead of at individual readers, myth criticism and drama seem like comfortable bedfellows. After all, drama is by nature a collective and ritual spectacle, whether it is staged in an elementary school cafeteria or on a hillside in ancient Greece.

Myth criticism has been used to theorize about the use of space on the stage, certainly one of the most concrete, practical matters for everyone who enjoys and studies drama. This approach has also been used to help us understand the impact of conventional symbols such as color and the seasons, as well as the reasons some stories (such as cycles of birth and death, quest narratives, and rituals of sacrificial cleansing) appeal to readers and viewers from different times and cultures.

Some of the important anthropologists, myth critics, and religious historians who are apt to be quoted in myth critical literary analysis are Sir James Frazer, Maud Bodkin, Joseph Campbell, Northrop Frye, Claude Levi-Strauss, Clifford Geertz, and Mircea Eliade. Anthropologist Victor Turner is arguably the most influential myth critic writing today, especially for the field of drama. Turner explores how social dramas (from trial marriages to Presidential inaugurations to Native American peyote hunts to productions of *Othello*) invoke ritualized forms of authority to heal individual and social breeches. If the drama is successful in healing these wounds, Turner claims, then the status quo is restored. While Turner concentrated on ceremonial life, drama scholars such as Richard Schechner have applied Turner's theories to other dramatic events as well.

For an example of anthropological or myth critical approaches to drama, see Judith Thompson's article on *The Glass Menagerie* included in this anthology.

STRUCTURALIST AND DECONSTRUCTIONIST CRITICISM

During the first decades of the twentieth century, Russian formalists such as Roman Jakobson and Mikhail Bakhtin were prominent in European literary theory. When the theories of these scholars intersected with those of Ferdinand de Saussure, the result was the creation of a new and more powerful field of study, that of *semiotics* (**an attempt to make the study of language scientific**), a field that has profoundly influenced almost every discipline in the humanities.

As Freud is the founder of psychoanalysis, so Saussure (especially lectures given to his students in Geneva between 1906 and 1911) established the field of semiotics, or structural linguistics. Saussure's *Course in General Linguistics* was not published until after his death and only gained widespread recognition in the 1930s and 1940s. Still influential today, semiotics is a very complex critical method which cannot be mastered without intense study. Students may encounter references to Saussure and structural linguistics when reading literary criticism, and in that regard being able to place the name is at least helpful, but the average undergraduate would be unwise to try this method. Like deconstruction, structural linguistics is an endeavor best left to those literary theorists who have the training and inclination to practice it. For the rest of us, what we are likely to need to know about Saussure's theories is his contention that language is a system of signs from which meaning is made. **Signs, like words, are arbitrary and not meaningful in themselves; they acquire meaning only through their relation to other signs and to the system of signs we call language.** The sign is divided into the *signifier* (**the unit of language itself, such as a word**) and the *signified* (**what the unit of language stands for**). The relationship between signifier and signified is arbitrary; thus, Saussure claimed that, instead of concentrating on the etymology or history of words, linguists should study how we make meaning of language and communicate that meaning to one another.

Deconstruction and its relatives, structural linguistics and post-structuralism, have a much-deserved reputation for density, self-referentiality, and elusiveness. For many theorists and scholars, deconstruction is not a tool for understanding literature so much as it is a philosophy or way of life. You as a student are unlikely to read these few pages and have a firm enough grasp of deconstruction to apply it to one of the plays in this anthology. You may, however, find these pages will help you in reading literary criticism (deconstructive as well as much feminist, New Historicist, and reader-response criticism, since all of these approaches incorporate insights from deconstruction) and some of the concepts may prove useful in your own analysis of drama as well.

Deconstruction began as a reaction against structuralism, briefly described in the preceding section. **Structuralism** is **a theoretical system that focuses on the structure of language rather than on the stories language conveys.** Structuralism seemed to promise many scholars in the middle decades of this century that semiotics, an attempt to make the study of language scientific, could uncover fixed laws for the way humans make meaning through signs. Thus, structuralists hoped to be able to explain through language and myth how humans produce and texts reflect finite, stable meanings.

Jacques Derrida, the theorist most associated with deconstruction, re-jected structuralists' scientific study of language as the site of universal mean-ing. He denied the claims of structuralist Noam Chomsky that the study of language can yield principles that guide us to "linguistic competence," or one right way to read a literary text. Indeed, Derrida rejected the very notion that any text can ever be completely understood.

Derrida proposed a different way of seeing language and structure which emphasizes contingency and variability. Derrida claims that language is structured according to binary oppositions; the term "man" gets its meaning by being distinguished from its excluded opposite, "woman." Not only are these terms polarized or separated, but they are hierarchized. In other words, one term (in this case, "man") comes to be viewed by the culture as superior to its binary opposite (in this case, "woman"). Thus, the term itself, "man," has for many years been accepted as meaning all of humanity, while the less-valued term, "woman," is almost never used in this way. As long as the terms "man" and "woman" can be seen as opposites, the system continues to function. The meaning of "man" is thus contingent on maintaining its sep-arateness from "woman," but, of course, these terms actually overlap. An individual man is sometimes said to have "feminine" qualities, for example, and men and women have much more in common with one another than they do with algae or birds. In order to see woman as opposite, man has had to avoid acknowledging his similarities to woman. The need to police the boundaries between such binary oppositions (remember, the system depends on maintaining the view that "man" and "woman" are absolutely distinct) creates tension which spills over into our language and our narratives. This tension then creates ruptures in the text, internal contradictions which the deconstructive critic explores to destabilize the text's apparent meaning.

Derridean analysis doesn't concentrate on the stable structures of lan-guage and narrative or on the need to show that the binary oppositions are false; rather, this approach focuses on rupture, on seemingly inconsequential disturbances in the smooth surface of a text—a footnote, a flaw, something which doesn't seem to fit—and uses it as a thread to unravel the assumption of stable binary meaning. For example, a deconstructive reader might look at a text like Henrik Ibsen's *A Doll's House*, which seems to present very

distinct views of man and woman, and show how internal contradictions in
the text reveal the effort expended in keeping two overlapping categories,
male and female, separate. Thus, what the analysis would produce is a breaking down of the original opposition of man and woman.

Deconstruction is a term caught between destruction and construction,
and it is this sense that Derrida pursues in his analysis. In the process of
constructing meaning, texts are simultaneously contradicting the very
meanings they seem to create. In J. Hillis Miller's well-known description,
"deconstruction is not a dismantling of the structure of a text but a demonstration that it has already dismantled itself."

Deconstruction has gone beyond a rejection of structuralism to a more
generalized critique of Western logic and culture. For this reason, deconstruction has been seen as dangerous and radical, a threat to American
education's mission to pass on Western traditions. Other critics, including
M. H. Abrams, have claimed that deconstruction is "parasitical," a method
that could not exist by itself but can only be used to unravel the meaning
someone else has already produced. The prose in deconstructive criticism is
often described as "thick" and "turgid," and many literary critics have regarded deconstruction as a kind of siren, luring the unwary critic away from
the study of literature and into the murky, rarefied world of high theory.
Many have seen deconstruction as elitist because of the difficulty of the
theory, and many feel that playing the theory game (for deconstruction is
often playful and irreverent, which also helps explain its appeal) leads critics
into abandoning discussion of real-world social problems. While all these
criticisms are at least partially warranted, Derrida galvanized a generation of
literary scholars and changed the practice of literary criticism. Because of
Derrida's impact, we live in a poststructuralist age suspicious of stable categories of meaning.

Deconstruction is less popular today as a philosophy than it was a decade
ago, but it is still a valuable tool for dismantling old ideas to make room for
new ones and its assumptions are woven into the very fabric of current
literary theory. Other poststructuralist approaches, such as the psychological
theories of Jacques Lacan and many influential theories in feminist and race
studies, are heavily indebted to Derrida's work. Indeed, while deconstruction
does not hold the power today which it did a decade ago, most influential
theorists today arrived at their positions through the work of Jacques Derrida.

Some of the names students may see quoted in deconstructive essays are
Jacques Derrida, Paul de Man, J. Hillis Miller, and Jonathan Culler.

MULTICULTURAL CRITICISM

We all recognize that we are biologically and culturally different from other
people and that the ways in which we are different give us our sense of
personal identity. No one is just a man or woman. No one is just black or
white. No single factor affecting identity is able to determine that identity
completely; all African-Americans, for example, are not identical. Rather,
individual identity is shaped by a complex matrix of variables. If a person is
white, female, Italian-American, currently middle class but from a working
class family, heterosexual, and living in the Midwest, each of these charac-

teristics is important to her identity but still doesn't totally explain who she is. Change just one variable, and you subtly change all the rest. The impact these differences have on this woman, and the relationship among all these variables, profoundly shape this woman's perception of herself.

Scholars have found that narrowing the focus on a literary work to look at just one of these variables is an important critical tool which can change the way we interpret a text. Another strategy for looking at difference is to study how a literary work reflects the intersection of race, class, gender, and other variables. For example, in Margaret Mitchell's *Gone With the Wind*, Scarlett's understanding of what it means to be a woman is not the same as the prostitute Belle Watling's because of their differences in social class. Scarlett's African-American slaves, Mammy and Prissy, would offer still different accounts of the meaning of being female. An Orthodox Jewish man in New York would explain masculinity in very different terms than would a logger in the Pacific Northwest, a cotton farmer in Mississippi, or a homosexual pharmacist in Indianapolis.

Approaches that focus on difference ask us to analyze what seems most obvious—our own perspectives—and show how that perspective is not obvious (i.e., natural and unconstructed) at all. For instance, race studies tell us that no view of the world is ever race-neutral, even when we'd like it to be. Most of us would agree that minority groups such as African-American, Hispanic, and Asian-American see the world differently from whites and from one another. When we read literature written by a minority writer, we almost always acknowledge that author's race. We refer to Lorraine Hansberry as an African-American playwright rather than simply as an American playwright because we assume that her experience will alter her perspective and provide an alternative to mainstream thought. We would be unlikely, however, to refer to Tennessee Williams as a white playwright because we assume that as a member of the majority race, his views do not reflect racial difference. Of course, a white playwright is seeing through the limited lens of his own Caucasian eyes just as surely as any minority writer. Tennessee Williams did not write just as a man, but as a gay white man from the South. The critical essays on *Othello* by Karen Newman and Michael Neill, included in this anthology, use insights from race studies to illustrate how in this play sexuality and femininity are made grotesque through their link with racial images. Such insights from race studies highlight the ways in which meaning is always determined by the racial perspectives and experiences of writers, characters, audiences, and readers.

Scholars who focus on social class often appropriate Marxist terms such as bourgeoisie, alienation of labor, and material means of production, but not all scholars who use these terms advocate the overthrow of capitalism. Many are "materialist" critics, who see economic forces as having the most profound impact on identity and, thus, on characterization in literature and the circumstances of readers. Materialist literary criticism considers questions such as who owned the theaters and printing presses, who could afford the price of tickets, how did actors' attitudes toward work influence play productions, and how did the social classes of authors, actors, and audiences interact.

Louis Althusser, an influential Marxist critic, wrote about ideology, the system of beliefs which supports the state and the political and economic status quo. To some extent ideology is taught through state apparatuses such as schools, churches, families, and courts. Without that ideology, Althusser claims, the capitalist state could not survive since its interests do not coincide with those of most of its people. Marxist literary critics such as Terry Eagleton and Fredric Jameson study how literature reflects the state's interest in ideology. For instance, Eagleton claims that the rise of the novel as a literary form in England was fuelled by a rise in power of the middle class; thus, these novels became popular because they reinforced those values which helped the middle class to gain power and maintain the status quo. Marxist and materialist literary critics such as Edward Said also study how the literature of the United States and Western Europe reflects imperialist assumptions and, further, how Western imperialism created the clash of cultures portrayed in the literature of colonized groups.

Marxist and materialist critics have sometimes been criticized for subordinating race, gender, and even human emotions to economic forces. Other critics have attacked Marxist and materialist critics as, ironically, elitist, especially in the assumption that the working class is easily manipulated by ideologues. Still, most of us see economic forces and social class as major factors influencing human identity, particularly in countries such as Great Britain which still maintains vestiges of a strong class system, and Marxist or materialist literary criticism is still a powerful approach to literature.

Critics such as Werner Sollors study how ethnic identity is invented and maintained, and how ethnicity is reflected in literature. Lesbian scholars such as Adrienne Rich claim that heterosexuality is "compulsory," so pervasive in our culture and its literature that it seems obvious and universal and thus is forced instead of consciously chosen. Writers such as Eve Sedgwick look at how fear of homosexuality structures the way masculinity is presented in male-authored literature.

This discussion makes apparent that almost any difference in perspective can be explored in literary criticism, but none has been so influential as that of gender. Feminist scholarship is a product of the Women's Movement of the late 1960s and early 1970s and of the Women's Studies programs that have been opening in major universities since then. The amount of feminist literary criticism is staggering, so it is helpful to first break this field down into three historic periods.

The first stage in American feminist scholarship was initiated by Kate Millett's book in 1970 titled *Sexual Politics*, in which Millett argued that literature by male authors such as Henry Miller, D. H. Lawrence, and Norman Mailer reflected widespread misogyny or hatred of women. The first stage of feminist scholarship in America, therefore, was one in which women critics pointed to a gender bias in male writers, critics, and characters, and, indeed, in the culture at large.

The second stage of feminist scholarship in this country, often called *gynocriticism*, reflected scholars' search for female writers to reflect a woman's perspective and a female aesthetic. This project, which began in the 1970s with critics such as Elaine Showalter and Sandra Gilbert, continues today as scholars study women's writing and theorize about what makes women's writing different from that of men.

Gender studies, the third and most recent stage of feminist criticism, began in the 1980s when some men began calling themselves feminist, some women began realizing that woman-authored texts didn't always reflect feminist politics, and many critics began to recognize that masculinity had for too long been seen as natural, obvious, and unconstructed. Approaches that saw man and woman as distinct categories no longer seemed appropriate. Influenced by deconstruction, scholars began to demonstrate how these categories break down. **Gender studies does not rely on distinctions between male and female so much as it examines gender as a system;** instead of being mutually exclusive, the terms "masculinity" and "femininity" overlap and press against one another. Most gender theorists don't regard gender differences as biological but as culturally produced. They emphasize the artificiality and permeability of gender constructions. What distinguishes gender study from feminist criticism is that gender approaches encompass both men's studies and women's studies. Many feminist critics object to gender studies because they claim it blunts the political edge of women's studies and diverts scarce resources from the long-neglected study of women. Gender critics include Peter Schwenger, Jane Tompkins, and Deborah Tannen, all of whom have written on the language of men.

These three stages in American feminist criticism only begin to characterize the range of gender theory and criticism. We have not even mentioned British feminist criticism, which tends to pay more attention to Marxist and materialist issues, or European feminist criticism, which is heavily influenced by French theorists such as Helen Cixous and Julia Kristeva. In recent years, American feminist criticism, spurred by complaints that women's studies only reflects the views of white, middle-class women, has tried to incorporate a broader range of perspectives to include more women of color, working-class women, and lesbians. But today, the major issue dividing feminist critics is the meaning of the category "woman." Cultural feminists claim that, even if "woman" is so much a product of culture that the term has little meaning, the category of woman is strategically necessary to maintain a feminist politics. How can you argue that Ibsen's Hedda Gabler and Nora Helmer are oppressed if you don't base that argument on the recognition of "women" as a group? Poststructural feminists, influenced by Derrida and Lacan, see "woman's literature" and, indeed, "woman" itself, as empty signs, terms without stable meaning. Poststructural feminists do not argue for "women's writing" or a "female aesthetic," because they claim such arguments are essentialist. The debate is an old one—are there essential female qualities, female ways of thinking and behaving in the world? If so, are these produced by culture (in which case altering culture would also alter what it means to be female) or are they biologically determined (in which case change would be more difficult to achieve)? Poststructural feminists argue that gender is not constituted by fixed categories of male and female but is, instead, more fluid. An individual man or woman can assume a feminine or a masculine position and can move from one to another. Thus, for poststructuralist feminists the boundaries between men and women are culturally produced, permeable, and unstable.

For an example of feminist analysis of drama, see Madelon Sprengnether's essay on *Othello* in this anthology.

If we look at critical approaches focusing on difference, it's easy to see how students can appropriate these methods and incorporate them into their own essays. As with formalist methods, all the student need do is narrow his or her focus. The careless student can, however, fall into traps. For instance, ventriloquism is the term given to white critics who try to speak for minority groups. But such traps can be avoided if the student always remembers to consider his or her own perspective when constructing an argument based on difference. If you want to write about race in Hansberry's *A Raisin in the Sun,* for example, be sure to acknowledge your own racial perspective and to think about how that affects your analysis.

Multicultural criticism may seem diffuse, but it **is united by a common assumption that literary criticism is a political act. Whether it focuses on race, class, ethnicity, sexual orientation, gender, or some other variable, political criticism attempts to expose differences in perspective** in order to advance the goals of civil rights, feminism, and equality. It is precisely the political nature of multicultural criticism that has made it the target of so much criticism in recent years, especially from educators and critics who want to maintain the separation between politics and literature and between politics and the classroom.

Analyzing and Evaluating Drama

It's all very well to talk about reading drama and even about reading critical work on drama. But when you receive your first assignment to write about drama, that's something else entirely.

Just about all of us who have studied literature recognize the panic of knowing that we have to write on a literary work about which we feel we have nothing interesting to say. The student may understand the literal plot and be interested in class discussion of the work, but when it comes to finding his or her unique angle of vision, everything seems too obvious.

Sometimes reading literary criticism can help you construct an interesting and original literary analysis. A scholarly essay may show you that your ideas about the text aren't obvious after all; you may find when reading critical treatments that what you assumed was too commonplace to write about is, in fact, the subject of a hotly contested debate. You may even find that your ideas about the work have never been discussed by critics. If either of these situations occurs, this is good news for the struggling student writer. You have something new to say about the literature, and your main concern now is with making sure that you can adequately support your claims.

Quite often, however, reading literary criticism only seems to make your panic worse. What the scholars are debating may seem obscure or peripheral; it may not immediately suggest good directions for writing. Even worse, you may encounter a scholarly article that seems so conclusive and engaging that you are left muttering to yourself, "It has all been said. There's nothing left to say!"

No one can truthfully say that moving from reading literature to writing about literature is easy, but there are techniques that can make this process easier. The first technique is to take a deep breath and remind yourself that when it comes to a literary work, no one ever said all there is to say. There's always room for your own perspective.

The first step in writing literary criticism is to be sure you understand the assignment. Does your instructor want a subjective account of your own reading experience? A summary of critical viewpoints? More commonly, what your instructor wants is your own original thesis about the work, supported by details from the text, quotes from critical sources, or both.

The second step in constructing your essay is to read the literary text very carefully, noting passages that interest you or seem important and recording your ideas as you go. The following lists of questions may help you to focus on the formal elements of drama.

QUESTIONS TO ASK ABOUT DRAMA

Plot

1. Describe the plot in terms of its *exposition, complication, crisis, falling action,* and *conclusion.* Is the plot unified? Do the individual acts and scenes seem logically related to each other? Are there any scenes that seem to be unnecessary?
2. What is the essential problem or conflict on which the plot turns? Where does the turning point seem to occur? How is the plot resolved? Does the resolution seem to be an appropriate and satisfactory one?
3. Compare the end of the play with its beginning. What are the major changes that have taken place?
4. Describe the function of each act and scene. Do certain scenes seem to be linked in some way in order to contrast with or reinforce one another? Do any of the scenes seem to present a microcosm, condensation, or metaphor of the play as a whole?
5. In what ways does the opening act or scene serve the purpose of exposition, and how is this exposition achieved? What important events have taken place before the play opens? In what ways does the exposition serve to introduce or *foreshadow* the major problems or conflicts of the plot?
6. Does the play contain one or more *subplots*? If so, what is their relationship to the main plot of the play? Are they, for example, intended to reinforce, contrast, or parody the main action?

Character

1. Who is the *protagonist* of the play, and who is the *antagonist?*
2. What is the function of the play's other major characters? What is their relationship to the protagonist and antagonist and to each other?
3. What is the function of the play's minor characters? Is their role mainly one of exposition or interpretation, or are they used as *foils* to oppose, contrast, or caricature certain of the major characters?
4. What methods does the playwright employ to establish and reveal the characters?
5. Are the actions of the characters properly motivated, consistent, and plausible?
6. Do any of the characters serve *symbolic* or *allegorical* functions?
7. To what extent does the playwright rely on the reader's or audience's prior knowledge of one or more of the characters? (Remember that many of the major figures of Greek tragedy were well known in advance to their audiences.)

Dialogue

1. Is the dialogue written in *high style, low style,* or some combination of the two?
2. How does the dialogue of the characters differ? How do such differences serve as an aid in characterization?

3. What stylistic devices contribute most to the play's dialogue? (Consider, for example, the use the playwright makes of patterns of poetic rhythm and sound, repetition, puns or word play, comparison, allusion, imagery, irony, symbolism, etc.)
4. Does the playwright make use of certain key words or phrases that gain a cumulative effect and added significance through repetition in a succession of contexts?

Setting

1. What is the play's setting in time and space?
2. To what extent does the setting functionally serve to aid in characterization, establish and sustain atmosphere, and/or influence plot?
3. What is the relationship of the setting to the play's action? Does it serve to reinforce the action, or is the relationship one of contrast?
4. Does the setting have symbolic overtones?

Theme

1. What is the play's theme or controlling idea?
2. How is the theme presented? Is it explicitly stated by one or more of the characters or is it merely implied by the action? What specific passages of dialogue or action contribute most clearly to the revelation or presentation of theme? To what extent do such moments occur at or near the ends of acts or scenes as a way of building dramatic tension?
3. What is the value or significance of the play's theme? Is it topical or universal in its application?

Other Aspects of Drama

1. *Title.* Consider the play's title. What clues does it provide, if any, in identifying the playwright's emphasis?
2. *Dramatic conventions.* To what extent does the playwright make use of such dramatic conventions as *asides, soliloquies,* a *chorus,* or the *three unities* of time, place, and action? What function or functions do these conventions serve? To what extent do these conventions reflect the kind of theater in which the play was originally staged?
3. *Actions and stage directions.* Identify the major physical actions of the play and explain their significance.
4. What help, if any, do the author's stage directions provide in helping the reader to understand the play?
5. *Classification.* Is the play a *tragedy,* a *comedy,* or some hybrid of two or more types? (Be prepared to explain your answer by making reference to the discussion in the text.)
6. *Audience appeal.* To what extent is the appeal of the play topical (that is, to what extent does it contain certain elements that reflect the manners, customs, attitudes, and beliefs of the society for which it was originally written)? To what extent is its appeal permanent and universal?

Evaluating the Whole

1. How well do you think the playwright has managed to achieve a total integration of his or her materials?
2. What is *your* reaction to the play? Do you like the play? If so, why? If not, why not?

Once you have read the work carefully and examined its formal qualities, you may want or need to consider critical sources. Literary criticism is, above all, a conversation among scholars and students of literature about what literature means. When you write literary criticism, you are taking part in that conversation. As in any other conversation, it is crucial to identify those who are speaking and understand their comments not in isolation but as a response to the comments of other critics or an intervention in an ongoing debate. To understand a critical essay, you must be able to answer the question, "How does this critic want to change the way we see this piece of literature, and why?" When reading a critical argument, you can admire a scholar's knowledge or virtuosity without being overpowered by it. Instead, look always to your own understanding of a literary work and judge the article by how useful it will be to you in forming your own arguments.

The following is a list of questions that may help you understand critical articles and how to use them.

QUESTIONS TO ASK ABOUT LITERARY CRITICISM

1. What are the author's critical approaches, and what assumptions do such approaches bring with them?
2. Does the essay help you understand your own assumptions about the text? Once you have uncovered these assumptions and examined them, do you still agree with them?
3. What argument is the critic making and why? Is the essay a response to another argument, and if so, why and in what way?
4. What language does the critic use in making his or her argument? Does the language used coincide with what is said or seem to contradict it?
5. How does the essay reflect the critic's perspective? Does the critic seem aware of the limits of his or her perspective? What assumptions are being made about race, class, gender, region, and ethnicity?
6. If you like the argument a critic has made, can you use that scholar's approach in a different context? For example, if a scholar analyzes the use of time in *King Oedipus* as a way of sharpening our understanding of the plot, can you show how that emphasis on time could also produce new readings of character?

CHAPTER SEVEN

Plays

Aeschylus (ca. 525–456 B.C.)

AGAMEMNON

Translation and Notes by Douglas Young

CHARACTERS

WATCHMAN
CHORUS OF ARGIVE ELDERS
CLYTEMNESTRA, *wife of* AGAMEMNON
HERALD
AGAMEMNON, *King of Argos*

CASSANDRA, *daughter of Priam and*
slave of AGAMEMNON
AEGISTHUS, *son of Thyestes, cousin of*
AGAMEMNON
Servants, Attendants, Soldiers

SCENE: *The background is the east front of the palace of the sons of Atreus at Argos,*
a pillared main front with a broad double doorway and pillared side wings with
smaller doors. Below the pillars a few shallow steps lead downward to the dance area
(orchestra). There are statues of deities facing east.

On the flat palace roof is a WATCHMAN, *lying on his forearms on a couch. He is*
facing east toward Mount Arachnaeon and the final beacon in a system of signals
arranged from Mount Ida near Troy, a city which the Greeks have been besieging for
over nine years under the leadership of the sons of Atreus, AGAMEMNON *and his brother*
Menelaus, who in this play are assumed to live jointly in the Argos palace. It is a dark
November night.

WATCHMAN.   O Gods, I pray for riddance from these troubles,
   my year's assignment to this outlook post.
      Lying like a dog on the Atreids' palace roof,
   I know the muster of the stars by night
   and those bright dynasts shining through the ether,
   the stars that bring to men summer and winter
   at their setting times. Yes, and I know their risings.
      Now here's me watching for this beacon signal,
   a glow of fire bringing from Troy a message,
10   news of its capture. That's the woman's orders.
   Man-minded she is, and she's expecting something.
      Every night in the restless couch I've got,
   where dew drops in, but dreams don't pay me visits—
   Fear, not Sleep, is my comrade in the ranks—
   so I cannot shut my eyes to sleep securely—
   whenever I take a notion to sing or hum,
   with a dose of tune as antidote to sleep,
   then I feel sad. I mourn the state of this household,
   no longer properly run like the good old days.
20   I pray for a joyful riddance from these troubles
   by a show of fire through the dark to bring good news.
      Hullo! Hullo! Welcome, you torch in the night,

flashing like daybreak. There'll be dancing today
all over Argos to celebrate this event.
      Hey! Hey you! Hey!
I'm shouting a message to Agamemnon's wife
to get out of bed at once and tell the household
to cry aloud, "Oh! Glory! Sing for triumph"
because of this flare, now that the city of Troy
30   has been captured, as the beacon clearly announces.
      I'll do a bit of a solo dance for prelude.
For I shall assume our master's luck is in,
and for me this beacon-watch has thrown three sixes.
      Heaven grant that, when the king comes home to the palace,
I'll get a chance to shake the dear man's hand.
I say no more. A mighty ox has trodden
on my tongue. But if the house itself got a voice
it could tell a most plain tale. But where I can choose,
with folk in the know I speak: with the rest—I forget.

[*Exit the* WATCHMAN. *Sounds are heard offstage, of horns blowing, cymbals clashing, shouts of joy. Servants come and kindle fires on altars. Dawn begins to show in the east. Enter in procession the* CHORUS *of Argive Privy Councilors, twelve elderly noblemen of military bearing, wearing swords and carrying staves. Accompanied by a piper, they chant in anapaestic rhythm as they march into the choral dance area below the stage.*]

40 CHORUS.   We are now in the tenth year since against Priam,
      his mighty opponent in legal attack,
      Menelaus the king, and the king Agamemnon,
      the Atreid yoke-pair, holding from Zeus
      their royal rights, twin-throned, twin-sceptred,
      launched out from this land with a thousand ships
      the armada of Argives, a militant aid,
      with heartfelt anger invoking great Ares[1]
      in the manner of vultures,
50   who, in extravagant grief for their children,
      wheel away from the nest, round and round, up on high,
      rowing with oarlike strokes of their wings
      after losing the labor they had
      in guarding their chicks in the nest.
      But on high, hearing the woeful shrill yelps
      of the birds that are resident aliens in Heaven,
      Apollo maybe, or Pan, or Zeus
      dispatches a Fury[2] to punish the guilty
      with the penalty due sooner or later.
60   So Zeus, the protector of hospitality,
      Zeus the supreme sends against Paris,

---

[1] Ares was the Greek god of war, equivalent to the Roman Mars.
[2] One of the vengeful Greek goddesses who punish human crimes against divine law or will (JDH).

that treacherous Trojan, the sons of Atreus
for the sake of Helen, that much-wooed wife.
    That mission of Zeus was to cause to the Greeks
and the Trojans likewise many a struggle,
weighing down men's limbs, with the knee
pressed in the dust, and the spearshaft split
in the rites that precede final revenge.
Things are as they are now, and all in the end
will be done as is fated. No man shall ever,
by burning a victim or pouring libations,
70 nor yet by weeping, appease the Wrath-Fiends[3]
intent upon unburned victims.
    We now are old, and contribute nothing;
exempt from that draft, we remain behind
in a second childhood, walking with staves;
and the boys that have marrow growing in their chests
are as yet no stronger than we old men.
No warlike vigor is left in the land,
where, with its foliage withered and grey,
80 old age with a staff walks three-footed ways,
and, as weak as a boy, goes wandering on
like a dream that appears in the daylight.

[*The* Chorus *now turns toward Queen* Clytemnestra, *who has come on stage close
to the central door of the palace, giving orders to servants to take gifts to altars.*]

May it please Your Majesty, Queen Clytemnestra,
daughter of Tyndareus, we beg to ask.
What has happened? What news? What have you learned?
What report are you trusting that keeps you so busy
sending round to make ritual offerings?
    Now all the gods that dwell in our city,
gods both over and under the earth,
90 heavenly gods and gods of the market,
all have their altars flaming with gifts.
From here and from yonder to heaven's height
flares reach up,
medicined with genuine gentle
persuasions of purest unction,
a royal mixture from treasury stores.
    Vouchsafe to inform us, as far as you can,
and as far as is right;
and cure our constant turmoil of mind,
100 which at one time seems a malignant growth,
and then through the offerings that you display,
hope wards off my insatiable worry,
the soul-devouring pain of my heart.

---

[3] Wrath-Fiends are repeatedly said to be lurking in the palace at Argos to exact vengeance
for former victims.

[CLYTEMNESTRA *does not answer the questions of the* CHORUS *and exits, back into the palace. The* CHORUS *then sings its first nonprocessional ode, with six pairs of corresponding stanzas (strophe and antistrophe), and one noncorresponsive section (mesode, 140–159). They start in a lyrical dactylic rhythm similar to the epic narrative verse of Homer.*]

[STROPHE 1]

I can expound the well-omened command of the
    warrior manhood,
when they set out in their prime, for the years I count in my lifetime
still can inspire divinely persuasion, the strength of my songs:
110   how the Achaeans' twin-throned command, the concordant
leadership of the manhood of Hellas, was ordered
forth with spear and exacting hand to Troyland,
urged by a vehement omen of birds—two eagles,
kings of the birds, to the kings of the fleet appearing,
one bird totally black, and a part-white younger one, perching
near the halls, on the right, the spear-wielding right hand.
There the two eagles perched, in a place to be seen by all men,
120   and they guzzled a pregnant hare, with her young, cut off from her
    coursing.
Woe, sing *woe,* sing *woe,* but may the good be triumphant.

[ANTISTROPHE 1]

Calchas, true seer of the army, observed that the two sons of Atreus,
generals different in temper, were symbolized by the eagles
eating the hare. Then this way he told what the omen must mean:
"One day this host now journeying captures the city,
Priam's city; and all of the ramparts' possessions,
confiscated for our whole people's sharing,
130   Fate shall remove and apportion by strength and violence.
Only I pray that there come not some heaven-sent Ruin
overclouding the bridle of Troy, strong forged by the army.
Holy Artemis[4] grudges the house its triumph,
hating the winged hounds' dinner, the eagles of Zeus her father,
sacrificing that wretched hare and her unborn young to their own
    selves."
Woe, sing *woe,* sing *woe,* but may the good be triumphant.

[*The* CHORUS *turns toward the statue of Artemis.*]

[MESODE]

140   "Fair goddess, who are so greatly kind
to the infant cubs of ravening lions,
and who give joy to the suckling young
of all wild creatures that roam the fields,
you are prayed to confirm the omens of yonder birds,
favorable omens, that yet have a taint of blame."

---

[4] Artemis, goddess of wild animals and protectress of childbirth, was known to the audience from Homer to have been pro-Trojan. The pregnant hare symbolizes the doomed city of Troy and its occupants.

[*The* Chorus *turns toward the statue of Apollo.*]

"And I call on Apollo, the Healer, brother of Artemis:
150   let her not hinder for long the fleet of the Greeks from sailing,
sending adverse winds, in her urge for another sacrifice,
songless and feastless, maker of strife among kindred,
not man-fearing. There lies in wait a frightful, recurrent,
treacherous, mindful Wrath, home-keeping and offspring-avenging."
    Such were the fated events, commingled with mighty blessings,
Calchas foretold for the royal house from those ominous eagles,
right at the start; so, in harmony with them
woe, sing *woe,* sing *woe,* but may the good be triumphant.

[STROPHE 2]

160   Zeus, whoever he may be,
if that be the name he likes,
by that name I call on him.
I have nothing to compare,
weighing all things thoroughly—
only Zeus, if I truly shall cast off my burden,
thoughts that vainly weigh me down.

[ANTISTROPHE 2]

He[5] that formerly was great,
bold, and fit for any fight,
170   shall no more be spoken of.
He that next was born has gone,
three times floored in wrestling falls.
Only he that cries heartily, "Zeus is the winner!"
hits the mark of wisdom square—

[STROPHE 3]

Zeus, whose guidance makes us mortals wise,
fixing as a valid law,
"Knowledge comes by suffering."
When one sleeps, there drips before the heart
180   agony, recalling pain.[6] To men
wisdom comes against their wills—
gift of grace, I think, that comes with force
from the gods on high who steer the world.

[ANTISTROPHE 3]

That time too the elder sovereign,
Agamemnon, did not blame
Calchas for his prophecy.
He complied with Fortune's sudden blasts,
when the Achaean host was weather-stayed,
lacking food and sore distressed,

---

   [5] Uranus, god of the sky, was overthrown by his son Cronus, who in turn was overthrown by his son Zeus, whom Aeschylus believed to be the supreme god for the foreseeable future and the operator of a system of more or less rough justice in human affairs sooner or later.

   [6] Most Greeks of the fifth century thought that the heart was the seat of sensation, perception, memory, intelligence, and other functions that we locate in the brain.

190   opposite to Chalcis on the shore
       where the Aulis currents rush.

                                                                [STROPHE 4]

       North winds came, blowing from the Strymon,
       and made men stray;
       they wasted hulls of ships and tackle alike,
       making delay just doubly long;
       wore down and ruined the flower of the Argives.
       Then prophet Calchas told the chieftains
       of another remedy, more grievous,
200   for the bitter tempest,
       bringing the name of Artemis forward:
       so that the sons of Atreus smote
       the ground with their sceptres, and could not keep
       their tears from flowing.

                                                                [ANTISTROPHE 4]

       The elder king spoke, Agamemnon:
       "A heavy visitation, disobedience,
       and heavy too
       if I shall slay my daughter, pride of my house,
       fouling a father's hands with blood
210   poured from a maiden slain at the altar.
       What choice have I that is free of evil?
       To desert the fleet? How could I do it,
       and betray the alliance?
       Now they desire a wind-stopping victim,
       blood of a maiden sacrificed.
       And righteous it is that they so desire,
       May all go well then."

                                                                [STROPHE 5]

       He set his neck under the yoke of compulsion,
       and the wind of his mind veered, his temper altered,
220   unholy now, impure, and impious,
       resolved to venture extremes of horror.
       Men grow bold on deciding for shameful deeds,
       wretched derangement, the first cause of disaster.
       He brought himself to sacrifice
       his daughter as an aid to warfare
       waged for vengeance for a woman,
       a magic act to free the fleet.

                                                                [ANTISTROPHE 5]

       Her prayers, her outcries of "Father! Father!"
       and her virginal life—all were counted nothing
230   by those fight-loving arbitrators.
       She still was clutching his robes in anguish
       while he prayed. Then he signed to the acolytes,
       so that they lifted her, face down, like a she-goat,
       above the altar, bound and gagged.
       They gagged her lovely lips to silence,

lest some inauspicious outcry
might bring a curse upon the house.

[STROPHE 6]

That way her pretty mouth was curbed to silence.
But from her eyes she shot piteous glances
240   at all who helped in her sacrificing.
Her saffron dress flowed down in folds.
She looked as in a picture, striving
to speak to each: for often she,
at banquets in her father's palace,
had sung, and with her chaste girl's voice
lovingly praised, at the pouring of wine to Zeus,
her loving father's happy life.

[ANTISTROPHE 6]

I neither saw nor tell what happened later.
The arts of Calchas, that trusty prophet,
250   lack not fulfillment. But Justice weighs out,
to those who suffer, understanding.
One hears the future when it happens.
Till then, let it fare well—or ill.
True news will come with homing sailors.
Hereafter Heaven grant us joy!
Such is the wish of our Regent, the present aid
that guards alone our Argive land.

[*Enter* CLYTEMNESTRA *from the palace central door on stage. The* CHORUS LEADER
addresses her in normal dialogue meter (iambic trimeters).]

CHORUS LEADER.   Queen Clytemnestra, I revere Your Majesty.
   For, when a throne is empty of its king,
260   his royal consort should be paid due honor.
   Now, whether you have learned good news or not
   but sacrifice in hopes to learn good news,
   I would in loyalty hear but grudge not silence.
CLYTEMNESTRA.   Daughters are like their mothers: so this night
   of good news ought to bear a dawn of good news.
   You will learn a joy greater than expectation.
   Our Argive men have captured Priam's city.
CHORUS LEADER.   I cannot grasp your meaning. It's incredible.
CLYTEMNESTRA.   The Achaeans now have Troy. Do I speak clearly?
270 CHORUS LEADER.   I am overcome. I am shedding tears for joy.
CLYTEMNESTRA.   Yes, I can see your face proclaims your gladness.
CHORUS LEADER.   But what is your proof? And can you demonstrate it?
CLYTEMNESTRA.   Of course I have proof, unless a god deceives me.
CHORUS LEADER.   Visions in dreams do you regard as cogent?
CLYTEMNESTRA.   I would not accept the fancy of a mind asleep.
CHORUS LEADER.   Then has some premonition cheered your spirit?
CLYTEMNESTRA.   You criticize my judgment like a girl's.
CHORUS LEADER.   Well then, since when has Troy been devastated?

CLYTEMNESTRA.   During this night that now gives birth to dawn.
280 CHORUS LEADER.   What messenger could come with so much speed?
CLYTEMNESTRA.   Hephaestus,[7] sending forth bright light from Ida.
   And beacon sent out beacon all the way here
   from the courier fire:—Ida to Hermes' crag
   on Lemnos; then Mount Athos, height of Zeus,
   received a third great flare from Lemnos' island;
   and rising high, to skim the back of the sea,
   the strength of the traveler torch right joyfully
   informed Macistus' lookouts, passing on,
   just like a sun, the golden-gleaming radiance;
290   he too did not neglect his turn as messenger,
   not dallying, nor slackly sunk in sleep;
   but far beyond Euripus' streams he showed
   Messapion's guards the beacon light's arrival.
   They answered with a fire and signaled forward,
   kindling a heap of old and withered heather.
   The strong and lusty flare, not yet made dim,
   leaping Asopus' plain like a bright moon,
   traversed Boeotia to Cithaeron's cliff
   and roused a fresh relay of the envoy fire.
300   That post did not refuse the far-sent light,
   burning a mass far bigger than was ordered.
   Over the grim-eyed gulf the light sloped down,
   reaching Mount Aegiplanctus, in the Megarid,
   and roused that station to be lavish of fire.
   They, with ungrudging power, kindled and sent
   a mighty beard of flame; the peak flung it forward
   even beyond the mirror of the Saronic Strait,
   flaming. Then it sloped down. Then it reached
   Mount Arachnaeon, the watchpost near our city;
310   and next, it slopes down here to the Atreids' palace,
   this light descended from the fire on Ida.
      Such were my distributions of torchbearers,
   each from the next successively supplied.
   The winner, who ran first and last, is Fire.
   Such is the proof and signal that I tell you,
   my husband having signaled me from Troy.
   CHORUS LEADER.   My prayers to the gods shortly I shall renew.
   But now, My Lady, I would hear in full
   and marvel at your tale, as you repeat it.
320 CLYTEMNESTRA.   This very day the Achaeans have got Troy.
   I think unmixable cries are heard in the city.
   If you pour oil and vinegar in one dish,
   you would call them bitter enemies, standing apart.
   Equally opposed are the cries that one may hear
   of vanquished and victors in this twofold event.

---

[7] Hephaestus, god of fire and metallurgy, is the Greek equivalent of the Roman Vulcan.

Some fall around the bodies of their husbands,
or brothers; children clutch their aged parents,
who nursed their infancy, and mourn the doom
of near and dear ones, now enslaved themselves.
330   The victors, worn from a night of shifting battle,
sit down famished to whatever the city offers
by way of breakfast, in no regular order,
but just as each man drew his lot from Fortune.
They are housed already in captured Trojan homes,
rid of the frost and dew in the open air.
Poor wretches, what a miserable time they had had!
With no guards posted, they will sleep all night.
    If they show piety to the city's gods,
who hold the conquered land, and the gods' shrines,
340   the conquerors would not in turn be conquered.
But may no passion fall upon the army
to plunder what they ought not, yielding to greed.
They still must finish the last lap of the journey
to make a safe return back to their homes.
And if the army, without offense to the gods,
were to come back, then the woe of the dead would be wakeful,
unless some unexpected evils should happen.
You have heard me say what a mere woman thinks.
May the good prevail, to be seen unwaveringly.
350   I choose to enjoy all our many blessings.
  CHORUS LEADER.   Excellently reasoned, Madam, like a wise man.
Now, after hearing your convincing proofs,
I make ready to thank and glorify the gods:
for the favor they have wrought is worth the trouble.
  CHORUS [*in an anapaestic prelude*].   Hail, sovereign Zeus! Hail, kindly Night!
grandly adorned with great possessions,
you threw a close-confining net
over the towers of Troy, that no one,
old or young, could overleap,
360   a dredging net that drags in all to slavery.
Zeus, who protects the rights of host and guest,
we now adore. This vengeance has been wrought
by Zeus, the god of hospitality.
He stretched his bow with long and careful aim
at Paris of Troy, not falling short of the target
nor striking uselessly far beyond the stars.

                                       [STROPHE 1]

"Zeus struck this blow that the Trojans suffer."
We may proclaim this, and we can trace it,
how Zeus performed, and how he finished.
370   There was a man who said that the gods
never concern themselves with men that trample
the grace of holy things. That man was impious.
The ruin of foolhardy men has been seen making haste,
the ruin of men puffed up beyond all justice,

the ruin of houses that had enormous wealth
beyond whatever is best. Let holiness be unharmed,
380   that deeds possessed of wisdom may suffice.
For there is no defense
for a man who in wealth and wantonness
gives mighty kicks to the altar of Justice
on the way to perdition.

[ANTISTROPHE 1]

But vile Persuasion assails the doer,
the irresistible child of Ruin,
planning beforehand. Cures are useless.
With dreadful glare the menace is seen.
390   Brought to the test of Justice, Trojan Paris
is shown up counterfeit like plated copper
that loses its gold veneer when it gets worn and knocked.
As boys chase flying birds and cannot catch them,
the chances of Paris were hopeless, once he caused
that dire affliction for Troy. No deity hears his prayers.
The man that does such things some god destroys.
Paris had come as guest
400   to the home of the Atreids, gallantly;
then brought disgrace on his host and the palace
by the theft of its mistress.

[STROPHE 2]

Then Helen, leaving to our townsmen
turmoil of shield and spearpoint
and fitting of gear for ships,
and taking to Troy destruction for her dowry,
went off gaily through the doorway,
daring a deed that none should dare. Then loudly
the household spokesmen lamenting cried:
410   "Oh woe for the house, for the house and its master!
Woe for the bed and the traces of married love!
Menelaus is here in silence, dishonored but unreproachful,
least angry-looking of husbands whose wives have left them.
With yearning for Helen, gone over the sea,
he will seem but a phantom lord of the house.
The grace of the shapely life-size statues of Helen
grows hateful now to her husband;
their charm has gone, now that his eyes
are starved of her.

[ANTISTROPHE 2]

420   "But in his dreaming there keep coming
visions of Helen mournful
that bring him an empty joy.
Whenever he looks to grasp the apparition,
through his arms the shining phantom
lightly goes off, elusively, that instant,
on wings that follow the paths of Sleep."
    Such then are the woes at the hearth of the palace:
yes, and the palace has other woes worse than these.

There is general mourning also for all who set off from Hellas;
430   some sign is seen in the home of each absent soldier,
when suffering spirits give way to their grief;
there is many a sorrow piercing the heart.
For everyone knows the men who waved them good-bye then;
but now, instead of the persons,
at each man's house nothing arrives
but urns and ash.

[STROPHE 3]

The war god sets up his scales, like a money-changer,
right in the thick of battle, with bodies to trade for coins;
440   from Troy he sends home well-fired dust—
a heavy weight for dear ones, watered with tears—
filling urns with ash,
a man's worth in each,
of ash easily packed.
The people at home lament and praise
one man as "a good soldier,"
the next as "dying a hero's death"—
"all for the sake of someone else's wife."
But that they growl under their breath.
450   Grief and resentment swell up in them
against the Atreidai, champions of Justice.
Others yonder, around the wall,
possess now graves of the Trojan earth,
handsome men; and the enemy land
hides its possessors.

[ANTISTROPHE 3]

When fired with anger, the citizens' voice is dreadful:
some one must pay the debt of a curse that the people brew.
And therefore now my anxious thought
460   still waits to hear of something hidden in night.
Men that cause much death
the gods duly mark.
The dark Furies in time
seize any man that unjustly wins
brief gain. Then, with dimmed luster
his fortune dwindles beyond all aid,
vanished among the souls lost hopelessly.
And danger lies in too much praise,
glory, and power. Upon how many
470   have thunderbolts fallen! Zeus may be jealous.
I choose fortune that brings no grudge.
A city-sacker I would not be
nor see life as a prisoner of war,
conquered by others.

[EPODE]

[*Spoken by three individual chorusmen.*]

FIRST.   Caused by the good news beacon,
    rumor ran swift through the city.

But if it be true, who knows?
It is either a heaven-sent truth or a mere fiction.
SECOND.   Who is so childish or maimed in his wits,
480   that first his heart goes on fire at the novel message
brought by the flame and later
grows faint at the change of rumor?
THIRD.   It suits a woman's eagerness to approve
the giving of thanks before the truth is shown.
The boundary of a woman's credulous mind
is soon encroached upon by a speedy movement.
And speedy is the death a rumor dies
when women's tongues have talked it into life.
CLYTEMNESTRA.   Soon we shall know the truth of these transmissions
490   by torches bearing light, by beacons, and by fire,
whether they are really true, or our wits were cheated
in the fashion of dreams by this light that came with joy.
I see a herald coming from the shore
with an olive wreath for victory. Thirsty dust,
sister and neighbor of mud, kicked up as he moves,
bears witness he will not be a voiceless messenger
kindling up mountain wood and signaling you smoke.
Either his tale will command greater rejoicing,
or else—But I am out of love with the contrary.
500   May he add happily to the happy sight of the beacon.
CHORUS LEADER.   In this if any prays otherwise for the state,
may he reap himself the crop of his mind's error!

[*Enter a* HERALD *with olive wreath and herald's staff. He kisses the earth, then salutes the statues of deities.*]

HERALD.   I greet you, ancestral soil of the land of Argos.
This is the tenth year's light in which I come home,
attaining this single hope out of many hopes wrecked.
I never thought that here in this land of Argos
I would share when I die in burial with my dear ones.
Hail! Land of Argos! Hail! O light of the sun,
and Zeus, supreme in the land, and the Lord of Delphi!
510   —No more may he shoot arrows from his bow against us.
Beside Scamander[8] they came in plenty to plague us—
But now in turn become our Savior and Healer,
O Lord Apollo. All the gods in assembly
I call upon, and especially my own patron,
Hermes, dear herald, whom we heralds worship,
and the heroes who sent us forth. Now graciously
receive the army that has survived the fighting.
Hail, palace of our kings, beloved halls

---

[8] Beside Scamander, the chief river of the Trojan plain, Apollo, with volleys of arrows, caused a plague for the Greeks and their animals to punish Agamemnon for refusing to ransom Chryseis, captured daughter of a priest of Apollo.

and seats of state! You gods that face the sun,
520 if ever in time past, now with shining eyes
receive the king in state after long time.
For Agamemnon the king has come and brings
light in the dark to you and all here in common.
 Then welcome him right well, for so it is fitting,
the man who demolished Troy with the crowbar of Zeus,
the bringer of justice, and thoroughly worked its ground.
The altars and shrines of the gods have utterly vanished,
and the seed of the whole land is eradicated.
Such is the yoke of subjection forced upon Troy
530 by the senior Atreid king, a heaven-blest man,
Agamemnon, who now comes most worthy of honor
of all men living. Neither Paris nor Troy,
which shared his liability, can boast
that what they did was less than what they suffered.
Found guilty in this case of rape and thieving,
Paris both lost the property he took
and mowed his country down to the barest stubble.
Thus Priam's race paid doubly for these crimes.
CLYTEMNESTRA. Herald of the Achaeans from the army, fare you well!

[*Exit* CLYTEMNESTRA *into the palace to prepare* AGAMEMNON's *reception.*]

540 HERALD. I do fare well. I have nothing better to live for.
CHORUS LEADER. Were you all worked up with passion for our country?
HERALD. Yes. And I actually weep with tears of joy.
CHORUS LEADER. Then realize you suffered from a pleasant sickness.
HERALD. How do you mean? Do you call homesickness pleasant?
CHORUS LEADER. Yes, for the folk at home shared in your yearning.
HERALD. So the country longed for the army that longed for it?
CHORUS LEADER. The country often mourned with gloomy spirit.
HERALD. But why such gloom? The army had the gloom.
CHORUS LEADER. I have long believed silence the cure for mischief.
HERALD. How? Had you any to fear when the kings were absent?
550 CHORUS LEADER. Of that—no more now. I would gladly die.
HERALD. With these achievements we have nothing better to live for.
They took a long time, though. Some things one might praise
for turning out nicely; others left room for complaint.
Who but the gods has a whole life free of troubles?
Suppose I told you of our hardships and hard lodgings,
narrow half-decks, causing nasty bruises . . . ,
us doing nothing but groan . . . , not a scrap of rug!
And then on land—even more disgusting!
Because our bivouacs were near the enemy walls . . . ,
560 because the meadow dews from the sky and the ground
bespattered us, spoiling our clothes continually,
making our hair and beards beastly and lousy.
 And the winter—what if I told how it killed the birds
with blizzards of snow sweeping from off Mount Ida?

And then the heat of summer, when the Hellespont
took its midday siesta in a flat calm!
   But why do I mourn all that? The trouble is past.
It is past too for the dead. They need not worry—
not even about the problem of getting up again!
570   They were expended. So why count them?
Must the living feel pain at their malignant fortune?
I think it right to enjoy the result vastly.
For us, the survivors of the Argives' army,
profit is the winner. Loss cannot outweigh it.
   Therefore this day it is reasonable to boast,
with winged words soaring over sea and land:
"The armada of Argives, after taking Troy,
hung up these trophies for the gods of Hellas,
to become a traditional glory of their temples."
580   And men that hear such boasts must praise the country
and our generals too. And the favor of Zeus shall be honored,
that brought this to pass. You have the whole of my speech.
CHORUS LEADER.   I do not refuse to be conquered by your reasons.
Old men have youth enough to learn correctly.
This chiefly concerns the palace and the Queen
to reward your message, but I must share the rewarding.

[*Each member of the* CHORUS *gives the* HERALD *a gift. Enter* CLYTEMNESTRA *with
attendants, one of whom gives to the* HERALD *the customary reward of bringers of good
news.*]

CLYTEMNESTRA.   I raised the song of triumph long ago,
when the first night-time messenger of fire
came telling Troy was taken and overthrown.
590   One of my critics asked, "Do you rely
on beacons for your belief that Troy has been sacked?
How like a woman to let her heart go soaring!"
With such remarks, it was thought my wits were wandering.
Yet I started sacrificing; and through the city
at shrines of the gods, men, in our women's fashion,
piously cried, "Praise be, praise be!" as they lulled with wine
the fragrant flames, fed with incense and victims.
Now why should *you* tell *me* the further details?
From the king's own lips I shall learn the whole story.
600   I shall study to receive in the best way possible
my respected husband when he comes home again.
For a wife what day is sweeter to behold than this,
the opening of doors when heaven brings her husband
home from campaigning? Take my husband this message:
let him come with all speed, the darling of the country;
and on reaching home may he find his wife faithful,
just as he left her, the watchdog of the household,
good to him yonder, hostile to malignants,
in all unchanged, not having broken any

610   of the seals she had to guard through all these years.
Pleasure from another man, or improper proposals,
I know no more of than—how to stain steel!

[CLYTEMNESTRA *turns away but does not re-enter the palace.*]

HERALD.   Boasting in such a style, being full of truth,
is most honorable for a noble wife to utter.
CHORUS LEADER.   Your understanding of her speech was fair,
as seems to us, who can interpret clearly.
But, Herald, say—I ask about Menelaus,
if he is safe, and will come home again,
dear sovereign of this land, along with you.
620 HERALD.   I could not make untruths sound well by my telling,
so that my friends could enjoy their sound for long.
CLYTEMNESTRA.   How then with good news may you hit the truth?
Severance of good and true is not easily hidden.
HERALD.   Menelaus vanished from the Greek armada,
himself and his ship. I am telling you no untruths.
CLYTEMNESTRA.   After you saw him launch from Troy? Or was he
snatched from the fleet by a storm that oppressed you all?
HERALD.   You have hit the target like an expert archer.
You have briefly put in words a huge disaster.
630 CLYTEMNESTRA.   What were the rumors running through the fleet?
Was Menelaus reckoned alive or dead?
HERALD.   Nobody knows enough for a plain report,
except the sun that fosters life on earth.
CLYTEMNESTRA.   How do you say the storm began for the fleet?
And how did it end, with the immortal gods' anger?
HERALD.   On this auspicious day one should honor the gods,
and not befoul it with talk of evil happenings.
When a grimfaced messenger reports to a city
abominable disasters of a fallen army—
640   that one single common wound has struck the country,
and many men from many homes as victims
driven by the two-pronged goad the war god loves—
a Ruin that wields two spears, a murderous pair—
when such disasters have been piled upon one,
it is right to chant this paean of the Furies.
    But when one brings good news of safe deliverance
to a city that rejoices in prosperity—
Oh, how am I to mix any good with the evil that happened
when I tell of the storm on the Greeks that the gods' wrath brought?
650   For fire and sea, which had been foes before,
conspired together and gave proof of their compact
by destroying the unhappy armada of the Argives.
    By night mischief arose with swelling waves,
for winds from Thrace began to rend the ships
against one another. Violently rammed and battered
with the typhoon's blast and the squall of thunder-rain,
they strayed and vanished, ill-shepherded by the whirlwind.

And after the shining light of the sun came up
we saw the Aegean Sea flowering with corpses,
660   of men of the Achaeans, and wreckage of ships and tackle.
        Ourselves and our ship, with her hull still undamaged,
some god had stolen away, or else begged off,
grasping the steering-gear. No man could have done it.
Savior Fortune chose to settle on our ship,
that the squall might not get her, at anchor from the waves,
nor drive her ashore where rocks would break her back.
        After we had escaped from death at sea,
in the white daylight, not believing our fortune,
we tended a new suffering in our thoughts,
670   with the armada fallen sick and badly smitten.
And now, if any of them is still alive,
they speak of us as perished. Why, of course.
And we suppose that they have the same fate.

[Exit CLYTEMNESTRA.]

        May it all turn out for the best! As for Menelaus—
first and best, assume that he reached the shore.
At least, if any ray of the sun observes him
alive and seeing the light, by the plans of Zeus,
not yet consenting to have his breed expended,
there is hope that he will come to his home later.
680   Having heard all this, be assured you heard the truth.

[Exit the HERALD.]

[STROPHE 1]

CHORUS.   Who named Helen by that name
        altogether truthfully?[9]
        Was it some Unknown One, who,
        knowing beforehand what was fated,
        aimed his tongue successfully,
        naming *Helen* that bride disputed, with spears for her in-laws?
        Helen was Hell indeed for ships and men and cities,
690   when from her delicate, costly curtains
        she sailed with the breeze of the earthborn west wind,
        and squadrons of hunters carrying shields set sail
        to follow the vanished track of the oars
        of those that had beached on the leafy banks of Simois,[10]
        through Eris,[11] the goddess of strife.

[ANTISTROPHE 1]

        Wife and Strife combined in one,
700   Helen entered into Troy,

---

[9] The mention of Menelaus reminds the Chorus of Helen, and they sing of the significance of her name, which to a Greek ear conveys the idea of conquest and subjection.

[10] Simois is the second river of the Trojan plain.

[11] Eris, at the marriage of Peleus and Thetis started a beauty contest among the goddesses, which Paris judged. Aphrodite, goddess of sex, bribed him by offering the world's most beautiful woman, Helen: the elopement of Helen with Paris caused the Greek attack on Troy.

driven by a Wrath that knew
how to carry out its purpose,
Wrath exacting afterwards
retribution for hospitality Paris dishonored,
impious to Zeus. Those who paid that retribution
were in-laws of Helen who loudly chanted
the bridal refrain for the couple's honor.

710 But Priam's city learns a new tune, a dirge;
and *fatally mated Paris* is cursed.
With dirges unique the pathetic deaths of citizens
Troy now laments in the depth of grief.

[STROPHE 2]

There once was a man who reared in his home
a ravager lion cub, giving no milk
but loving the breast.

720 At the start of its life it was tame,
the children's darling,
the old folk's joy.
Held in their arms like a new-weaned child,
it swallowed tasty titbits in plenty,
with bright glad gaze at the hand that fed it,
fawning as hunger seized it.

[ANTISTROPHE 2]

But when it grew up, maturing with time,
it showed the ancestral ways of its breed.
As thanks to its hosts,
730 in a frenzy of slaughtering sheep
it made a banquet,
an unbidden guest,
fouling the house with the blood all through.
And none could fight the murderous monster.
Some god had reared it to serve the household,
serve it as priest of Ruin.

[STROPHE 3]

What came to Troy at the start
one might call a temper of windless calm,
740 and a gentle delight of wealth,
or a delicate shaft of the eyes,
a soul-biting flower of passion.
But, swerving aside, she accomplished
a bitter completion of marriage,
ill to sit with, ill to consort with,
in her onrush on the sons of King Priam,
sent by Zeus, the god of friendship,
a Fury bewailed by their wives.

[ANTISTROPHE 3]

750 An ancient doctrine is held,
that a person's happiness, grown full great,
will get children before it dies,
and the misery born from good luck
infests later generations.

But I disagree with the others;
I argue a view of my own here:
I think only impious actions
760   will produce impious actions hereafter;
but the righteous family's fortune
bears always a beautiful breed.

[STROPHE 4]

Among the wicked of mankind
an old crime breeds a younger crime,
sooner or later, when the appointed day
comes for the new crime to be born—
a Wrath, a Demon of the house,
unfightable, unwarrable on, unholy,
770   a bold, black Ruin for the household—
truebred to its ancestral type.

[ANTISTROPHE 4]

But Justice shines in smoky homes,
and honors righteous, humble lives.
Leaving with eyes averted the gilded halls,
where there is guilt fouling men's hands,
she seeks the holy and the pure,
not reverencing the power and prestige of riches,
780   the false coin spurious praise forges.
She guides each act to its just end.

[*Enter King* AGAMEMNON, *standing on a chariot, escorted by a bodyguard of twenty men from his ship, some sounding trumpets. The chariot is followed by a covered wagon, like that of King Xerxes* (Persae 1000), *containing, among other spoils of war, the prophetess* CASSANDRA, *hidden by the hood of the wagon. Enter* CLYTEMNESTRA *from the palace.*]

CHORUS.   Come now, O King, sacker of Troy, son of King Atreus,
how am I to greet you, how am I to worship you,
not overshooting nor falling short
of the true mark of honor, gratitude, and grace?
Many men honor appearances in preference
to genuine reality, violating justice.
790   Everyone is ready, for anyone unfortunate,
to heave a sigh of sympathy, but their display of grief
does not reach the heart at all.
Just in the same way they share in rejoicing,
forcing their unsmiling faces to smile.
But the trueborn ruler, the shepherd of his people,
can tell from a man's eyes whether he is loyal
or fawns with a watery love that is not from the heart.
Ten years ago, when you took the expedition out
800   all because of Helen—I must freely speak my mind—
I did not like the look of you; I thought you were not wise,
at cost of men's lives bringing back a willful wanton woman.
But now I declare with heartfelt affection,

"Joyful is the toil that men finish with joy."
In time you will ask, and in time you will learn,
who did his duty in guiding affairs here
and who proved rather troublesome.

810 AGAMEMNON [*still standing in the chariot*]. This land of Argos first I must
salute
and the gods of the country jointly responsible
for my return and the justice I exacted
from Priam's city. The gods heard the pleadings,
not told with tongues but by men's deaths, and cast
their votes unwaveringly into the bloodstained urn
for Troy's destruction. In the urn of acquittal
nothing was there but Hope. No hand threw a vote in.
    The captured city still sends fine smoke signals.
820 The squalls of Ruin are lively, and, joining in death,
the embers puff forth plenteous wafts of wealth.
For that we must pay mindful thanks to the gods:
for we made our hunting nets exceeding cruel,
and for a woman's sake the Argive beast,
the horse's chick,[12] the folk that twirl the shield
at the Pleiads' autumn setting rushed with a leap,
and, jumping the tower, a raw-devouring lion[13]
licked up his fill of princely Trojan blood.
    I say this much to the gods by way of prelude.
830 As for your sentiments, I remember them.
I say the same; I share your advocacy.
Few among men are born with the habit of mind
to honor a friend's good fortune without jealousies;
malignant poison, which besets his heart,
doubles the burden for one who has got that disease.
The jealous man is burdened by his own troubles
and mourns when he sees an outsider's happiness.
I have met and studied men, as in a looking glass.
From knowledge I would call mere shadows of images
840 those who pretend strong loyalty to me.
Only Odysseus, who joined against his will,
once harnessed, proved an eager trace horse for me.
I cannot say now if he is alive or dead.
    For the rest, as regards the citizens and the gods,
we shall hold general gatherings and deliberate
in full assembly. That which is well disposed—
we must take counsel for its long continuance.
But where there is some need for healing remedies
by cautery or surgery, expertly,
850 we shall make trial of the sore, to rout the disease.

---

[12] Aeschylus alludes to the legend that the Greeks took Troy by hiding picked warriors
inside a large wooden horse, which the Trojans unaccountably dragged inside their walls.
[13] The lion seems to have been a heraldic emblem of the Pelopid dynasty of Argos, as seen
over the gateway of their castle at Mycenae.

Now I shall enter the palace, my hearth and home,
and first salute the gods with my right hand raised,
the gods who sent me out and brought me back.
Victory is with us. May she stay forever!

[*Before* AGAMEMNON *can descend from the chariot,* CLYTEMNESTRA *descends the steps to the choral area and places herself at the back of the chariot to block his descent. She then addresses the* CHORUS.]

CLYTEMNESTRA.   Honorable citizens, My Lords of the Privy Council,
I shall not be ashamed to declare to you
how much I love my husband. Lapse of time
makes shyness dwindle. From my own experience,
not hearsay, I shall tell how ill to bear
860   my life was all that time this man was at Troy.
First, for a wife to sit at home deserted,
apart from her man, is enormously distressing,
hearing much talk of his unpleasant pleasures;
distressing too to have one man after another
come crying woe to the household, each worse than the last.
If as many wounds were inflicted on this man
as the flow of reports that was channeled into the house,
he has far more wounds to count than a net has holes.
And if he had died as multiple reports said,
870   then triple-bodied, like a second Geryon,[14]
he could boast of getting a threefold cloak of earth,
plenty on top and incalculable below,
having died and been buried once for every body.
And so, because of such unpleasant rumors,
many a noose gripped my neck from above;
but people forcibly loosened them when I was caught.
That is why our son is not here in the ranks
as he ought to have been, Orestes, who keeps safe
the pledges of our pact as man and wife.
880   But do not wonder. He is well looked after
by Strophius of Phocis, a kind host, who warned me
of double menaces—your dangers at Troy
and the prospect that lawless clamor of the people
might overthrow the good counsel of this council,
as humans naturally kick a man when he is down.
This excuse that I have made has no guile in it.
My gushing springs of tears are all dried up;
no single drop is left to weep for joy;
my eyes are sore with watching late at night
890   and weeping that the beacons were not kindled,
set ready for news of you. And in my dreams

---

[14] Geryon, a cattle rancher in the Far West of Europe, was a triple-bodied monster, whom Heracles slew.

I was often roused by a mosquito trumpeting
in airy zigzags, while I dreamed of disasters
befalling you, too many for the time I slept.
Now, freed from grief after all these sufferings,
I would call this man the watchdog of the homestead,
the forestay that saves the ship, the firm-based pillar
of the lofty roof, the father's only child,
and land appearing to sailors beyond all hope.
900 Most lovely it is to see daylight out of storm,
for a thirsty traveler to see a stream from a spring;
and pleasant it is to escape from all constraint.
    With such addresses, then, I express my esteem.
But may jealousy keep away. For the evils in the past
that we endured were many. But come now, darling,
step down from this chariot. But do not set on the ground
Your Majesty's foot, the devastator of Troy.
    Slave-girls, what are you waiting for? You had orders
to spread with cloths the ground that he must tread.
910 So make at once a crimson-carpeted path,
that Justice may lead him to his place unhoped for.
And the rest will be arranged with vigilant purpose,
justly, according to the gods' destined plan.

[*The female attendants give ritual cries of Glory be! Oh, glory! and crouch on their knees, beating the ground with their foreheads in Oriental style.* CLYTEMNESTRA *does so too.*]

AGAMEMNON [*from the chariot, to* CLYTEMNESTRA].   Daughter of Leda,
    guardian of my palace,
the speech you have made was fitting to my absence—
lengthy. But as for proper commendation—
such a reward ought to proceed from others.
    For the rest, do not pamper me with womanish fashions.
It is most un-Greek to stage this kind of kowtowing,
920 to grovel on the ground and yell and gape to welcome me.
Do not bring down heaven's jealousy on my path
by spreading cloths. Such honors should be kept for gods.
For me, as a mortal, there would be great danger
in treading upon such beautiful embroideries.
I bid you show me reverence as a man, not a god.
My fame, without footwipers and embroideries,
makes itself heard. The greatest gift of heaven
is to be wise, not foolish. One should call happy
a man who lives to the end with lovely Prosperity.
930 Could I do all things thus, I should be confident.
CLYTEMNESTRA.   Tell me now, not contrary to your true judgment—
AGAMEMNON.   My true judgment, I assure you, I shall not corrupt.
CLYTEMNESTRA.   Through fear, perhaps, you vowed to the gods to act thus?
AGAMEMNON.   In announcing this aim I had knowledge, as good as any
    man's.

CLYTEMNESTRA.   What would Priam have done, do you think, had he been
  victor?
AGAMEMNON.   I certainly think he would have walked on embroideries.
CLYTEMNESTRA [*coaxing him, with gestures, to step down onto the crimson and
  purple and embroidered cloths*].   As victor by God's grace you should
  scorn men's criticisms.
AGAMEMNON.   But the force of public opinion is most powerful.
CLYTEMNESTRA (*tugging* AGAMEMNON *by the arm*).   A man who is not envied is
  not admirable.
940 AGAMEMNON.   It is most improper for a woman to spoil for a fight.
CLYTEMNESTRA (*continuing to tug* AGAMEMNON *downward*).   Happy victors must
  take their turn to submit.
AGAMEMNON (*adopting a rigid attitude of resistance*).   Do you really set store
  by winning in this struggle?
CLYTEMNESTRA (*still tugging him with all her force*).   Please do as I say. Relax
  your toughness for my sake.
AGAMEMNON (*giving in, with a shrug of his shoulders*).   Oh well, if it pleases
  you. Quickly, somebody,
    take off my boots, downtrodden slaves of my feet.
    And as I walk on the gods' sea-purples here,
    may no jealous Evil Eye strike me from afar.
    Great shame it is to spoil a husband's body,
    while he spoils wealth, textiles bought with silver.

[*Attendants lower the hood of the wagon, revealing* CASSANDRA *in the insignia of a
prophetess seated among Priam's treasures.*]

950 AGAMEMNON.   Enough of that. This stranger lady here—
    receive her with kindness. Those that use power gently
    the deity views from afar with gracious eye.
    No one willingly bears the yoke of slavery.
    This lady accompanied me as the army's gift,
    a choice flower chosen from among great treasures.
    Now, since I am conquered by you and forced to obey,
    I shall enter the halls of the palace trampling on purples.
CLYTEMNESTRA.   The sea exists—and who shall dry it up?—
    breeding abundant purple, secreted fresh,
960   worth its weight in silver, as dyes for cloths.
    We have a roomful of such to choose from, Your Majesty,
    thanks to the gods. This house knows nothing of poverty.
    I would have vowed trampling of many cloths,
    had that been ordained in oracles to the house,
    when devising means to bring this man back safe.
    While the vinestock lives, foliage comes to the house,
    stretching a shade over it against the dog star.
    And as you return here to your household hearth,
    warmth in winter you signify by your coming.
970   And whenever Zeus makes wine from the sour grape
    in the height of summer, there is coolness in the house,
    as the perfect husband goes about his home.

O Zeus, perfector of all, perfect my vows.
It is your concern, whatever you plan to perfect.

[*As* AGAMEMNON *walks up the steps, over the crimson and purple embroideries,*
CLYTEMNESTRA *raises the ritual cry with which women hail a sacrifice.* AGAMEMNON'S
bodyguard march off to the palace kitchens, except for those guarding the treasure-wagon containing CASSANDRA.]

[STROPHE 1]

CHORUS.   Why does this manifestation hover around me,
obsessing my heart as it watches for omens?
And a chant, unbidden, unhired, sounds in my ears
980   a prophetic refrain of "Woe. Sing woe."
I spit it away, like an evil, ambiguous nightmare;
and yet cheering confidence will not come
to rest at home in my heart.
Calchas foretold a stay of nine full years
for the Greek armada, beached on the sandy coast.
Surely the prophesied Ruin has passed its peak
when the host from the ships moved forward
into the city of Troy and sacked it.

[ANTISTROPHE 1]

Now I have news from my eyes, and witness in person
our soldiers' returning. Yet still I am haunted
990   by the hymn my spirit within endlessly chants,
not invited, not harping, "Woe. Sing woe,"
self-taught and repetitive, sounding the dirge of the Fury,
with no cheering confidence, born of hope.
My inward feelings forebode,
not like a foolish witness, while my mind
is engaged in righteous judgment. My heart responds,
moved with the rhythms of the cycles that fulfill.
But I pray that my fears prove figments.
1000   Off with forebodings, to nonfulfillment!

[STROPHE 2]

Great good health has a boundary line
likely to keep out a surfeit of health;
for disease keeps house next door,
a pushing and troublesome neighbor.
In a lengthy course of plain sailing
a man's destiny suddenly
may go crash upon some hidden reef.
To save the rest of the merchandise
caution jettisons part of the cargo,
1010   balancing well its derrick's load,
so the family's whole ship does not sink
into disaster through overloading,
and keeps its hull afloat.
Or again, a cure may come for famine,

with some great gift from Zeus, the god of weather,
abounding out of this year's croplands.

[ANTISTROPHE 2]

But dark blood that has fallen to the ground,
fallen from in front of a man that is slain,
1020   tell me who there is that knows
a chant or a charm to recall it.
With a stroke of lightning Zeus punished
that old doctor Aesculapius,
who revived Hippolytus when dead.
The gods have given our heart and tongue
different duties as separate organs;
neither can snatch the other's rights.
If not, my heart would outrun my tongue
telling the tale of its dire forebodings.
1030   Now plunged in gloom it sees
and is grieved, perplexed, but never hoping
to ravel out and end all opportunely,
while my whole bosom burns with anguish.

[Enter CLYTEMNESTRA, speaking from the palace doorway.]

CLYTEMNESTRA.   Now come inside, you too. I mean Cassandra.
Since Zeus in his mercy placed you in our household
to share our worship, standing with many slaves
by the altar of Zeus, the god who grants possessions,
step down from this wagon. Do not be too proud.
1040   For even Heracles, they say, was sold
and forced to endure the humble food of slaves.[15]
Well, if the balance should tilt to such a destiny,
one should be thankful for masters whose wealth is ancient.
The *nouveaux riches* have really no idea
how to treat servants—cheeseparing skinflints.
You get from us the right and proper treatment.
CHORUS LEADER.   She has finished the plain statement she was making.
[*To* CASSANDRA.] Caught in the nets of Fate, you would obey
if you were obedient. But perhaps you would disobey.
1050 CLYTEMNESTRA.   Well, unless the language she has inside herself
is some unknown non-Greek twittering, like a swallow's,
what I am saying is reasonable and should persuade her.
CHORUS LEADER.   Go with her. She says what is best in the circumstances.
So leave this wagon seat and be obedient.
CLYTEMNESTRA [*impatiently, turning to go inside again*].
I have not all day to wear away this doorframe.
For the victims due to the central fire of Hestia,
the hearth-goddess, are placed ready for slaughter
by worshipers who never expected this favor.

---

[15] To raise blood money for his slaughter of Iphitus, Heracles was sold as a slave to Omphale, Queen of Lydia, for a term of penal servitude of a year, or three years.

If you are to share in the ritual, do not delay.
1060   But, if you do not understand what I tell you—
[*To the* CHORUS LEADER.] Well, you explain to the foreigner with gestures.
CHORUS LEADER.   The stranger lady seems to need an interpreter.
She is bewildered, like a wild animal newly taken.
CLYTEMNESTRA.   The fact is—she is mad, subject to mental disorder,
arriving like this from a city newly taken,
like a horse that has not learned to wear the bit
before exhausting its strength in bloody froth.
I will waste no more words, to be treated with contempt.

[*Exit* CLYTEMNESTRA.]

CHORUS LEADER.   And I, for I pity her, shall not get angry.
1070   Come, my poor lady, leave your seat and willingly
try to adapt yourself to the yoke, as is fated.

[CASSANDRA *steps from the wagon, wearing her insignia as prophetess of Apollo, and runs to clasp the stone pillar of Apollo Aguiatis ("of the Ways") by the palace steps. She cries out in short lines of verse, punctuated by brutal howls, sometimes speaking, sometimes singing.*]

[STROPHE 1]

CASSANDRA.   Otototototoi popoi da.
O Apollo! O Apollo!
CHORUS LEADER.   What makes you shriek Apollo's name so shrilly?
The god of healing should not hear a dirge.

[ANTISTROPHE 1]

CASSANDRA.   Otototototoi popoi da.
O Apollo! O Apollo!
CHORUS LEADER.   Again she calls, with that ill-omened cry,
a god who is not concerned to support laments.

[STROPHE 2]

1080 CASSANDRA.   Apollo! Apollo!
God of the Ways! My appalling destroyer!
You have ruined me a second time most easily.
CHORUS LEADER.   It seems she will prophesy some woes of her own.
Although enslaved, she keeps her god-given powers.

[ANTISTROPHE 2]

CASSANDRA.   God of the Ways! My appalling destroyer!
Oh, where have you brought me? What sort of house is this?
CHORUS LEADER.   The house of the sons of Atreus. I tell you this,
if you do not know it. You will not call this fiction.

[STROPHE 3]

1090 CASSANDRA.   Ah! Ah! A house hating the gods, conscious of many
murders of kinsmen, yet unpurged,
a human slaughterhouse, with its floor blood-sprinkled.
CHORUS LEADER.   The stranger is keen-scented like a hound
and tracks the gore of those whom she may find.

[ANTISTROPHE 3]

CASSANDRA.   Yes, there are proofs here that convince me—
  children that weep their slaughtering
  and roasted flesh consumed by their own dear father.
CHORUS LEADER.   Truly we knew your fame as a prophetess.
  This is so plain we do not seek interpreters.

[STROPHE 4]

1100 CASSANDRA.   Io popoi! What ever is being plotted?
  What is this new and monstrous woe?
  A monstrous crime is plotted in this palace,
  intolerable to near and dear, incurable.
  And help stands far away.
CHORUS LEADER.   These later prophecies I have no knowledge of.
  I knew the earlier. The whole country shouts them.

[ANTISTROPHE 4]

CASSANDRA.   Ah, wretch! Is this what you do?
  Washing in a bathtub the husband
  who shares her bed—how shall I tell the finish?
1110 It will come soon. She stretches out
  hand after hand, reaching.
CHORUS LEADER.   Not yet have I understood. Through her riddles
  I am now perplexed by these obscure prophecies.

[STROPHE 5]

CASSANDRA.   Eh eh, papai papai! What is appearing here?
  Some sort of net of death.
  But the snare is his bedmate, accomplice in murder.
  Now let the insatiable pack raise for the family
  the hue and cry for a sacrifice that deserves stoning.
CHORUS LEADER [*in agitated dochmiac meter, a sort of Sprechgesang*].   What
    Fury is this you summon to howl
1120 for the house of Pelops? Your words dismay me.
  A thrill of yellow fear runs to my heart
  like the stroke of a Dorian knife in sacrifice.
  With the setting rays of my life some Ruin
  reaches its end with a final spurt.

[ANTISTROPHE 5]

CASSANDRA.   Ah, ah, look out, look out! Keep from the cow the bull!
  She catches him in folds
  of a robe that enwraps and a dark-horned contrivance.
  And now she is striking. He falls, down in the water.
  A cunning crime in a bath I tell of, a sly murder.
1130 CHORUS LEADER.   I should not boast of expert judgment
  in prophecies, but this means mischief
  for someone. Does there ever come from prophecies
  tidings of good for mortals? Through misfortunes
  the wordy arts of prophetic chanters
  bring to us knowledge of fear on fear.

[STROPHE 6]

CASSANDRA.   Oh, how wretched I am, how ill-fated!
In this lament I pour my own suffering now.
Oh, why did you bring me here in misery?
For nothing else but to be joined in death.

1140 CHORUS LEADER.   Now you are raving, possessed by the god,
lamenting your own fate
with a tuneless tune like the warbling nightingale,
Procne, insatiably crying, with piteous emotion,
"Oh, Itys, my son Itys!"
mourning her life that abounded in evils.[16]

[ANTISTROPHE 6]

CASSANDRA.   Oh, the nightingale's doom, the clear singer!
On her the gods put feathers to fly and escape
and gave her struggle a pleasant, tearless ending.
My prospect is cleaving with a two-edged spearhead.

1150 CHORUS LEADER.   Whence comes this rushing of futile laments
possessed by the godhead?
You are moulding into a song these fearful deeds,
mixing in shouts of ill omen and lyrical high notes.
And why, within those limits
must you proceed on this ominous song track?

[STROPHE 7]

CASSANDRA.   Woe for the marriage, the marriage of Paris,
destructive of dear ones.
O river Scamander, drunk by more forebears,
in time gone by I was bred beside you;
I grew up along your shores.

1160 But now, it seems, I shall soon utter my prophecies
in Hades by the streams of Wailing and Woe.
CHORUS LEADER.   What is this that you say all too plain?
A mere child could understand it.
I am stricken deep by a murderous bite,
as you cry, complaining of your painful fate,
shattering for me to be hearing.

[ANTISTROPHE 7]

CASSANDRA.   Woe for the troubles, the troubles of Troyland,
destroyed altogether.
O victims uncounted, slain by my father,
in sacrifice for the ramparts' safety.

1170 They did not effect a cure
to prevent the city's suffering the way it has.

---

[16] The Athenian princess Procne married Tereus, a Thracian king, who later, asserting that she was dead, had sent out to him her sister, Philomela, whom he raped and then made dumb by cutting out her tongue. Philomela embroidered her story on a cloth and sent it to Procne, who thereupon killed her son Itys and served up portions to his father Tereus. When Tereus began to chase the sisters, the gods changed him into a hoopoe, Procne into a nightingale, and Philomela to a swallow.

And I, the hothead, soon shall hit on the ground.

CHORUS LEADER.   You have spoken again, as before:
for some harsh, malignant spirit
is obsessing you and compels you to sing
of these grievous sufferings that lead to death.
What will be the finish I know not.

CASSANDRA.   But now my prophecy no longer shall be looking
obscurely out through veils, like a new-wed bride.

1180   But clear and brisk like a wind that blows to the sunrise,
surely it will come surging up like a wave
and sweep to the light a woe far greater than this woe.
   I will no longer teach you through such riddles,
but you must keep abreast and bear me witness
as I snuff the spoor of crimes done long ago.
   This palace here is haunted by a chorus
in uneuphonious unison, evil-speaking;
and, drunk with human blood, for greater boldness,
a rout of revelers still outstay their welcome,

1190   hard to put out, the Furies of slain kinsmen.
Besetting the house here, they are chanting a chant.
Precentor and choir, they denounce a ruinous sin,
loathing the man that seduced his brother's wife.[17]
   Did I miss? Or am I watching my shot like an archer?
Am I a false prophet, a door-to-door quack?
Then testify on oath that I knew by hearsay
the ancient crimes committed in this palace.

CHORUS LEADER.   And how would an oath, a trap splendidly set,
do any good?[18] I am astonished that you,

1200   bred overseas, should hit the mark when you speak
of a foreign city as if you had been present.

CASSANDRA.   The prophet Apollo appointed me to this task.

CHORUS LEADER.   God that he is, was he smitten with desire for you?

CASSANDRA.   Till now I was too modest to speak of this.

CHORUS LEADER.   The overfortunate are always overdelicate.

CASSANDRA.   He wrestled with me, and breathed his charm upon me.

CHORUS LEADER.   Did the pair of you come to the usual business of
   children?

CASSANDRA.   I gave my consent to Apollo, and then I cheated.

CHORUS LEADER.   When already possessed by the arts of divine prophecy?

1210 CASSANDRA.   Already foretelling to the citizens all their sufferings.

CHORUS LEADER.   How so? Were you brought to justice by Apollo's wrath?

CASSANDRA.   I convinced no one of anything, after my fault.

CHORUS LEADER.   You convince us at least of what you prophesy.

CASSANDRA.   Eeoo, eeoo! Oh, Oh, what crimes!

---

[17] The reference is to Thyestes' seduction of Aerope, wife of his brother Atreus, the start, by Aeschylus' account, of the "tragedy of Pelops' line."

[18] By the Greek conception, an oath can never do good, but only harm: for it only comes into operation in order to harm him that breaks it. Therefore it is compared to an elaborate trap.

Again the terrible agony of true prophecy
drives me wild with its prelude. Sitting yonder
do you see them—the children sitting yonder,
besieging the house, like shapes in dreams?
Children who died, it seems, by the act of near ones,
1220 they are seen holding handfuls of meat, their own
flesh that their father fed on, a pathetic load,
heart, innards, and guts, which their own father tasted.[19]
    Therefore, I say, someone is plotting revenge,
a cowardly lion, making free in a bed,
watching at home—alas—for the homecomer—
my master—for I must bear the yoke of slavery.
    The commander in chief of the fleet, overthrower of Troy,
does not know what a tongue the hateful bitch has.
Speaking and killing lightheartedly she will effect
1230 the justice of a secret Ruin, with an ill success.
Such audacity! A female killer of a male!
She is—what hateful monster should I call her
to hit the mark? A double-headed viper?[20]
A Scylla living in rocks, the plague of sailors?
A mother seething with death? A truceless Curse-Fiend
blasting her dear ones? How she yelled in triumph,
all-daring, as at some turning point of a battle!
She pretended to be rejoicing at his safe return.
    It is all the same whether or not I convince you.
1240 What is to be will come. And shortly you
will call me, pityingly, too true a prophet.
CHORUS LEADER.   Thyestes' feasting on his children's flesh
   I understood and shuddered at. I am terrified
   at hearing the facts so truly represented.
   The rest of what I heard I have lost the track of.
CASSANDRA.   I say that you will see Agamemnon's doom.
CHORUS LEADER.   Hush, my poor lady. Say nothing so ill-omened.
CASSANDRA.   This speech has not a savior god for patron.
CHORUS LEADER.   None, if the doom is to happen. I pray it may not.
1250 CASSANDRA.   You are praying. Their business is slaying.
CHORUS LEADER.   Who is the man that plans this calamity?
CASSANDRA.   You failed to see correctly the curse in my prophecies.
CHORUS LEADER.   I have not grasped the perpetrator's scheme.
CASSANDRA.   I spoke plain Greek. Too well I understand it.
CHORUS LEADER.   So does the Delphic oracle. Yet it is puzzling.
CASSANDRA.   Papai! What a bright fire! It comes upon me!
   Ototoi! Wolf-killer[21] Apollo! Woe is me!

---

[19] The reference is to the twelve elder children of Thyestes, killed and cooked by their paternal uncle Atreus.

[20] A double-headed viper meant for the Greeks one with a head at each end of it.

[21] "Wolf-killer" is one possible interpretation of the epithet *Lukeios* used of Apollo, and is specially relevant to this context, in which Clytemnestra's paramour Aegisthus is referred to as a wolf.

That lioness with two feet who sleeps with a wolf
in the noble lion's absence will kill me miserably.

1260   As if brewing a poison, she will add to her wrath
an item for payment by him on my account.
As she whets the blade for her man, she vows to exact
slaughter as her revenge for his bringing me here.

Oh why do I keep these trappings that make a mock of me—
prophetic wands, and garlands around my neck?

[CASSANDRA *breaks her ceremonial staff.*]

You I shall break before my own doom comes.

[*She throws down her garlands in front of Apollo's statute.*]

Lie there and be damned. Thus I give you back.
Enrich some other Ruin instead of me.

[*She throws off her robe in front of Apollo's statute, turning so that the statue's hands seem to take it.*]

But look! Apollo himself stripping me
1270   of my prophetess's robe! In these insignia
he watched me being mocked by friend and foe
with mockery that never wavered—all in vain.
They called me "a wander-witted sort of revivalist,"
"a wretched starveling beggar." And I endured it.
And now the prophet god who made me a prophetess
has haled me off into such deadly happenings.
There awaits me no family altar, but a chopping block,
red with my hot blood, stabbed as a funeral victim.

And yet our death shall be revenged by the gods.
1280   Another shall come in turn as avenger of us,
a son that slays his mother, his father's avenger.
An exile, wandering far from this land, he will come
to cause the culmination of woes for the family;
his outstretched father's supplication will bring him.

But why do I, the incomer, thus lament?
Since first of all I saw the city of Troy
faring as it did fare, and those who held the city
came off that way in the judgment of the gods,
I shall go and fare as I must. I shall suffer death.
1290   For Fate is fixed by a mighty oath of the gods.

As the gates of Hades I now address these gates.
And I pray for a mortal blow at the right spot,
that I may close my eyes with never a struggle,
as my lifeblood ebbs away in an easy death.

CHORUS LEADER.   Lady of great misfortunes and great talents,
we have heard your long address. But if in truth
you know your doom, why do you walk with confidence
as a heifer dedicated to a god goes to an altar?

CASSANDRA. There is no escape, my friend. My time is up.
1300 CHORUS LEADER. The last of time receives the greatest honor.
CASSANDRA. The day is here. I shall gain little by flight.
CHORUS LEADER. Your steadfast conduct springs from a confident spirit.
CASSANDRA. No one among the happy hears that said.
CHORUS LEADER. It is surely a grace for a mortal to die gloriously.
CASSANDRA. Alas, father, for you and your noble children!

[*From the palace door* CASSANDRA *turns back with a start.*]

CHORUS LEADER. What is it? What fearsome object turns you back?
CASSANDRA. Oh woe! Oh woe!
CHORUS LEADER. What makes you cry woe? Some horror in your mind?
CASSANDRA. The house breathes out a terror of dripping blood.
1310 CHORUS LEADER. How so? This smell is of victims slain at the hearth.
CASSANDRA. The atmosphere has a reek as from out of a tomb.
CHORUS LEADER. Surely you mean the incense burnt in the palace?
CASSANDRA. Yet I shall go to bewail even in the house
Agamemnon's doom and mine. Enough of life!

[CASSANDRA *suddenly turns again from the palace doors and utters the regular cry for help from the general public.*]

Hi! Help me, friends!
My cry is not from fear like a bird at a trap;
but that you may bear me witness after my death,
when a woman dies in return for me, a woman,
and a man falls in return for an ill-wived man.
1320 On the point of death I claim this gift of friendship.

CHORUS LEADER. Unhappy lady, I pity your prophesied doom.
CASSANDRA. Another speech I make, or rather a dirge,
my own for myself. I make my prayer to the sun,
on my last day of light, that my enemies may pay
together to my avengers for my slaughter,
my death in slavery, an easy conquest.
Alas for human concerns! In better fortune
a mere shadow might spoil them. In ill fortune
the strokes of a damp sponge wipe out the picture.
1330 I am sorrier far for the wretched than for the prosperous.

[*Exit* CASSANDRA *into the palace.*]

CHORUS. Mortals can never get too much
of prosperity. Nobody points
a warning finger and cries, "Keep out.
Do not come to this house any more."
The gods granted to Agamemnon
the conquest of Priam's city.
Honored by heaven he reaches home.
But now, if he pays for the bloodshed of past generations

and effects for the dead by his death retribution for other deaths,
1340   who among mortals, on hearing of this,
       would claim to be born with a destiny free from harm?
AGAMEMNON [*from inside the palace*].   Oh, oh! I have been hit—a killing
       blow.
CHORUS LEADER.   Silence! Who was that that shouted he was hit a killing
       blow?
AGAMEMNON.   Oh, oh! I am hit again—a second blow.

[*Inarticulate groans are heard from inside the palace. The* CHORUS LEADER *consults the councilors in turn.*]

CHORUS LEADER.   Now the deed is done, it seems. I hear the king's
       expiring moans.
       Let us share our counsels freely. Some proposal may prove safe.
FIRST COUNCILOR.   My Lords, I offer this advice to you,
       to raise a cry for help and summon the citizens.
1350 SECOND COUNCILOR.   My opinion is, we should break in at once
       and prove the deed, while still the sword is dripping.
THIRD COUNCILOR.   I also am a sharer of such a view.
       I vote to do something. It is high time to make haste.
FOURTH COUNCILOR.   One can easily see. The prelude they perform
       shows signs that they plan a tyranny for the country.
FIFTH COUNCILOR.   Yes, we are wasting time. They do not sleep,
       but act, and spurn the Siren "Wait and see."
SIXTH COUNCILOR.   I have not hit on any plan to propose.
       The doer has the initiative in planning.
1360 SEVENTH COUNCILOR.   I too am of such an opinion. I see no means
       to make the dead man rise again by talking.
EIGHTH COUNCILOR.   Shall we make life unlivable by submitting
       to the rule of these outragers of the palace?
NINTH COUNCILOR.   That is intolerable. It is better to die,
       a milder dispensation than dictatorship.
TENTH COUNCILOR.   How do we know he is dead? Are we all prophets?
       We have no evidence yet but a few groans.
ELEVENTH COUNCILOR.   We need to know for certain before we discuss.
       Guessing is very far from knowing for certain.

[*There is a general nodding of heads in agreement.*]

1370 CHORUS LEADER.   From every side I receive a majority of votes
       to know for sure and determine how Agamemnon—

[*The* CHORUS LEADER *breaks off his sentence as the palace doors are opened, and* CLYTEMNESTRA *is seen, standing over a silver-sided bathtub, with the corpse of* AG-AMEMNON *wrapped in a robe with animal designs, and the corpse of* CASSANDRA.]

CLYTEMNESTRA.   Till now I have made many time-serving speeches:
       henceforth I shall not be ashamed to state the contrary.

For, plotting hostile acts against a foe
pretending friendship, how could one set the nets
of injury so high he could not leap out?
    This struggle of mine, long premeditated,
starting from an ancient quarrel, has been fought at last.
I stand where I struck the blows, with the deeds done.

1380   I acted in such a way—I shall not deny it—
that he could not escape nor ward off his doom.
    An endless wrap-around, like a fishing net,
I fix about him, an evil wealth of cloth,
and I strike him twice. In the space of a couple of groans
his limbs went slack. And there, as he lay fallen,
I hit him a third time—three is a lucky number—
in thanks for a vow to Death, the savior of—corpses!²²
    Thus fallen, he gasps his soul away in rushes;
and blowing forth a sharp wound of blood

1390   he hits me with a dark shower of crimson dew,
while I rejoiced, as a crop grows bright with rain
that comes to swell the grain growing in the corn ear.
    All this being so, My Lords of the Privy Council,
you could rejoice if you would, but I am boasting.
Were it fitting to pour reproaches over a corpse,
them one might justly pour, and more than justly.
Such a bowl of cursed evils he mixed for the family
and now has come home and himself drunk it off.
  CHORUS LEADER.   We are amazed at the audacity of your speech,

1400   uttering a boast like this about your husband.
  CLYTEMNESTRA.   You test me out, as an irresponsible wife.
But with unflinching heart I declare—and you know it—
it is all the same whether you approve or censure—
this is Agamemnon, my husband, and my corpse,
a product of the work of this right hand of mine,
a craftsman that makes things even. That is how it is.

                                        [STROPHE 1]

  CHORUS.   Ah, lady, what virulent poison
have you eaten, some earth-reared edible,
or a poison sprung from the wrinkled brine,
to bring on yourself this sacrifice
and the curses the people utter?

1410   You threw him down; you butchered him. You will be banished,
an object of mighty hate to the citizens.
  CLYTEMNESTRA.   You sentence me to banishment from the country,
with the citizens' hate and the curses the people utter,
though you passed no such sentence against this man here,

---

²² At drinking parties in Greece the third of three formal libations of wine was to Zeus the Savior. Here the god of death, Hades, is conceived as a Zeus below the earth, and by a grim joke, as the Savior of corpses.

when, heeding it no more than the doom of a sheep,
with plenty of sheep among his well-fleeced flocks,
he sacrificed his own daughter, my dearest child,
by way of a charm against the winds of Thrace.
Surely you ought to have banished him from the land,
1420   as penalty for pollution? Yet when you hear
of my actions you pass a heavy sentence.
        Realize, when you threaten, that I am ready to accept
the rule of the winner in a fair and equal fight.
If a god fulfill the contrary, you shall learn,
by a lesson late in life, what sound sense is.

[ANTISTROPHE 1]

CHORUS.   How grandly you plan your ambition!
And how subtly you speak! How arrogantly!
But your mind is crazed by the deeds of blood;
the bloodshot glitter that shines so clear on your eyes
is a sign of madness.
Yet, even so, bereft of friends, you shall be punished
1430   and pay for a wound, a wound as a penalty.
CLYTEMNESTRA.   This too I declare to you and duly swear it:
I swear by the perfect Justice of my daughter,
by the Ruin and the Fury to whom I sacrificed him,
that no foreboding of fear enters my house
so long as fire is kindled on my hearth
by Aegisthus, loyal to me still, as in the past.
For in him we have a strong shield of confidence.
Here lies the man who outraged me as a wife,
the darling of every golden girl round Troy.[23]
1440   And the prisoner of war here, the watcher for omens,
who shared his bed, the teller of prophecies,
his trusty concubine, a filthy whore
of the lower decks. . . . But the pair are not without honor:
he lies in a robe of state; and she, like a swan,
having sung her last lament at the point of death,
lies lovingly beside him. The robe of my pride
brought me this tasty fish too from his spawning bed.

[STROPHE 2]

CHORUS.   Oh, oh! I pray for a fate that would swiftly,
with no long sickness, painlessly visit us,
1450   bringing among us all here the sleep
that lasts forever and knows no waking,
now that our kind and much-enduring guardian
has been brought low for a woman's sake,
and by the hands of a woman he perished.

[REFRAIN 1]

---

[23] "every golden girl" represents original "Chryseises," i.e., "women like Chryseis," the
captured girl whom Homer's Agamemnon announced to be much preferable to Clytemnestra.
The name suggests *chrusos*, gold.

Oh, criminal Helen, breaking the law,
you alone destroyed the many,
the countless souls slain at Troy;
and finally now you adorned yourself
1460   with long-remembered clamor for unpurged bloodshed.
Truly there was then in the house
an irresistible Strife, a husband's woe.
CLYTEMNESTRA. Do not pray for a fate of death,
through grieving at this;
and do not turn your anger on Helen
as a murderess, the sole destroyer of many
souls of the men of Greece
and causer of pain incurable.

[ANTISTROPHE 2]

CHORUS. O Demon, ever haunting this palace
and our two kings descended from Tantalus,
1470   now you are wielding, to my distress,
a power equal in soul through women,
Helen and Clytemnestra. She is standing
like a dread raven above his corpse
and boasts her chanting is righteous and lawful.
CLYTEMNESTRA. Now you have got correct the judgment you pronounce,
when you summon the thrice-fatted[24]
Demon of this family.
For from him a blood-licking lust
swims and flows and grows—before the old ache ceases,
1480   fresh festering pus.

[STROPHE 3]

CHORUS. Truly, mighty and heavy in wrath
for Pelops' house is the Demon you speak of.
Woe, woe, what an evil plague
of a ruinous fortune, insatiable!
Woe, woe, by the will of Zeus,
causer of all, worker of all.
For what is done for mortals on earth without Zeus?
Of all this is there anything not wrought by gods?

[REFRAIN 2]

O my king, my king,
1490   how shall I weep for you?
From my loving heart what shall I say?
You lie in this web like a spider's,
having breathed your life away in an impious death—
Oh, woe is me!—on a lowly couch, ignobly,
brought down by a treacherous doom, by a wife's hand
with a two-edged weapon.

---

[24] The Demon was "thrice-fatted" by (1) the twelve elder children of Thyestes, (2) Iphigenia, (3) Agamemnon.

CLYTEMNESTRA.   You are asserting that I did this deed.
    Do not even think that I
    am the consort of King Agamemnon.
1500   For, taking the form of the dead man's wife,
    the ancient cruel Spirit exacting vengeance
    for Atreus, that harsh banqueter,
    paid this man out, and sacrificed
    a perfect full-grown victim for Thyestes' children.

[ANTISTROPHE 3]

CHORUS.   Who will testify, taking an oath,
    that you are free from the guilt of this murder?
    How so? But perhaps you had
    as accomplice his father's punisher.
    Now, forcing his way through blood,
1510   pouring in streams shed by the kin,
    the swarthy god of Slaughter is dealing justice
    to those children devoured, and their chill clotted gore.

[REFRAIN 2]

    O my king, my king,
    how shall I weep for you?
    From my loving heart what shall I say?
    You lie in this web like a spider's,
    having breathed your life away in an impious death—
    Oh, woe is me!—on a lowly couch, ignobly,
    brought down by a treacherous doom, by a wife's hand
1520   with a two-edged weapon.
CLYTEMNESTRA.   Not ignoble, to my thinking,
    was the death that this man died.
    And, as for treachery, did not he
    by treachery cause ruinous loss for the family?
    My child, and his, whom I reared and mourn for, Iphigenia,
    he treated unjustly, and justly he suffers.
    In Hades' house let him not boast,
    having paid for what he started
    with a death caused by a sword.

[STROPHE 4]

1530 CHORUS.   I know not where to turn, bereft
    of reason's resourceful thoughts,
    as the Pelopid dynasty crumbles and falls.
    I dread the thunder rain that tumbles the house
    in blood and ruins. For now the small drops cease,
    and Fate is sharpening Justice on other whetstones
    to cause another act of damage.

[REFRAIN 3]

    O earth, would you had buried me first,
    before I saw him laid so low,
1540   here in a silver-sided bathtub!
    Who will bury him? Who will mourn him?
    Truly will you have the heart to do this,

to bewail your husband after slaying him
and perform unjustly for his soul
a favor that is no favor, in return for mighty deeds?
Who at his tomb, sending forth with tears
a eulogy of the marvelous man,
1550 will labor in truthfulness of mind?
CLYTEMNESTRA. It is no concern of yours
to trouble about this matter. By our hands
he fell, he died, and we shall bury him,
not with shedding of tears by the household.
But Iphigenia, his daughter,
welcomingly as is proper,
will go to meet her father
at the swift ferry of Charon on the river of woes,
and put an arm about him and kiss him.

[ANTISTROPHE 4]

1560 CHORUS. Reproach comes answering reproach.
I struggle in vain to judge.
For the spoiler is spoiled, and the slayer must pay.
While Zeus abides this law abides, that in time
the doer suffers—a fundamental law.
Ah, would that someone would drive the accursed seed out!
The race is welded firm to Ruin.
CLYTEMNESTRA. Your mention of that divinely stated law
was truthful and realistic. I am ready
to swear a pact with the Demon of the Pleisthenid house
1560 to accept this situation,
hard as it is to endure. But for the future
let him leave this house and oppress some other family
with deaths caused by kinsmen.
To offer the Demon a share of our wealth
is little to me, who possess it all.
Sufficient for me if I drive out of the house
these frenzies of mutual slaughter.

[*Enter* AEGISTHUS *alone from a door in a wing of the palace.*]

AEGISTHUS. O kindly light of the day that brought justice,
now I would say that gods from above the earth
supervise mortals' woes with vengeful eye,
1580 when I see lying in the woven robes of the Furies
this man here, dead, well disposed to my thinking,
paying in full what his father's hands contrived.
    For Atreus, ruler of this land, father of him here,
expelled from home and country my father Thyestes,
his own brother—let me expound it clearly—
being challenged by him in his title to sovereignty.
Then, coming back as a suppliant at his hearth,
unhappy Thyestes gained immunity,
so as not to die on the spot and redden with blood

1590   his ancestral floor. But by way of guest gifts, Atreus,
impious father of him here, in welcoming my father
more eagerly than kindly, pretended to offer heartily
a choice meat dinner, and served him—the flesh of his children.
     The joints of the feet and the finger joints of the hands
he scattered in pieces over kindled charcoal;
and indistinguishable parts he took in ignorance
and ate—a ruinous meal, you see, for the family.
Then, recognizing the crime that had been committed,
he groaned, and fell back from the butcherwork, vomiting,

1600   and cursed the house of Pelops with a doom unbearable,
kicking over the dinner to supplement his curse,
that thus might perish the whole race of Pleisthenes.
     So that is why you can see him fallen here,
and I justify my plotting of this slaughter.
For I, the thirteenth child of my luckless father,
was banished with him, as a baby in swaddling clothes.
Now, grown to manhood, Justice brought me home.
And, while still abroad, I got a grip on this man here,
fixing every link in the hostile plot.

1610   So my triumph is complete. I could die happy
now I have seen him caught in the nets of Justice.
  CHORUS LEADER. Aegisthus, I disapprove of insult in misfortune.
Do you state that you killed this man of your own free will,
and that you alone plotted this pitiful murder?
I say that in justice your head will not escape,
be sure of it, the curses and stones the people will hurl.
  AEGISTHUS. Is that what you say, as you sit at the oar below,
while the officers on deck have command of the ship?
Old man as you are, you shall learn how nasty it is

1620   to be taught at your age, when the set task is wisdom.
Imprisonment and old age and the pangs of hunger
are excellent physicians for teaching the mind,
quite magically. Do you not see when you see these?

                           [AEGISTHUS *points to the two corpses.*]

Do not kick at the goads. If you hit them, you will be sorry.

  CHORUS LEADER [*incoherently to* CLYTEMNESTRA, *who stays silent*]. Woman, the
men new come from battle . . . you . . . a homekeeper sharing your
husband's bed all the time . . .
against your husband, the commander, did you plot this doom?
  AEGISTHUS. These phrases too are founding a family of laments.
Your tongue is just the opposite of Orpheus's.

1630   He carried off everything by the joy of his song.
But you exasperate with your dulcet—yappings!
You will be carried off, and tamed by the force of a master.
  CHORUS LEADER. I suppose you are to be the dictator of Argos,
though, after you had plotted this man's doom,
you had not the guts to do the killing yourself.

AEGISTHUS.　The trickery, of course, was clearly a job for the wife.
　　For I was a born enemy, long suspected.
　　　Using the wealth of him here, I shall try
　　to rule the citizens. Any who disobeys me
1640　I shall yoke with a heavy yoke, like a beast of burden,
　　not a pampered trace horse.[25] Hunger, that ill companion
　　as a roommate for Anger, will see him soften up.
CHORUS LEADER.　You, with your cowardly soul, why did you not
　　slay this man yourself, but let your accomplice,
　　that woman, his wife, kill him to pollute the country
　　and the country's gods? Orestes—is he living somewhere,
　　to come home here, with Fortune favoring him,
　　to become the omnipotent killer of the pair of you?
AEGISTHUS [*signing to his bodyguard in the palace*].　Well, since you resolve to
　　　act and talk like that,
　　you'll shortly learn . . . .

[AEGISTHUS' *bodyguard, twenty in number* (*cf. Odyssey 4.530*), *file onto the stage from
a wing of the palace.*]

CHORUS LEADER.　Ho! there, double up, dear guardsmen!
1650　Here's a job for you to do!

[AGAMEMNON's *bodyguard run round a wing of the palace into the choral area.*]

　Ho! there, men, get set for action! Hand on swordhilt! Ready, now!

[*The two bodyguards stand with their swords drawn.*]

AEGISTHUS.　I too stand here at the ready. I do not refuse to die.
CHORUS LEADER.　How we welcome what you say about your dying. Omens
　　good!
CLYTEMNESTRA.　Stop, oh stop, my darling man, now. Let us cause no more
　　distress.
　　Here we have a wretched harvest, long and sore to reap and bind.
　　Do not start again. Our woes are plenty. We are soaked in blood.
　　March off home, you old men, now, wherever Fate has set your
　　　homes,
　　lest the doer suffer. We must tie the threads that I have worked.
　　If an end should come of all these troubles, we would cling to it,
1660　smitten by the Demon's heavy talon most disastrously.
　　That is how a woman reasons, if it please you to attend.
AEGISTHUS.　But to think that they should flourish foolish insults in my
　　face!
　　Pelting me with vile aspersions, trusting in their cursed luck!
　　Damn their insubordination, not accepting me as boss!
CHORUS LEADER.　This is not an Argive habit, truckling to a yellow rat.

---

[25] A trace horse was an especially strong horse harnessed by a trace on the right side of the
yoked pair of horses in a chariot team to give extra power in pulling the chariot smartly leftward
round the turning point of the course.

CLYTEMNESTRA.   Just you wait! The time is coming when I shall get after
    you.
CHORUS LEADER.   Not if heaven guides Orestes back to his own homeland
    here.
AEGISTHUS.   Men in exile, well I know it, get their bellyful of hopes.
CHORUS LEADER.   Get to work, get fat, polluting Justice, while you have the
    chance.
1670 AEGISTHUS.   Now get this. I'll make you pay for all this nonsense through
    the nose.
CHORUS LEADER.   Crow away, you bantam cockerel, with that hen you love
    to peck.
CLYTEMNESTRA.   Darling, pay no heed to all that silly yapping. I and you,
    ruling from this royal palace, soon will fix things as we wish.

                                                    [*Exeunt Omnes.*]

                                                    [458 B.C.]

Critical Commentary on *Agamemnon*

Aeschylus's *Agamemnon* is the first play of the *Oresteia*, the only trilogy whose
plays have been handed down to us from ancient Greece. It was first produced in the Theater of Dionysus close by the Acropolis in Athens in 458 B.C.,
winning first prize in that year's competition. The *Oresteia* dramatizes the
tragic history of the House of Atreus and its ultimate redemption through
suffering and pain. The trilogy takes its name from Orestes, Agamemnon's
son, who is the chief character in the second and third plays (*The Libation-
Bearers* and *The Eumenides*).

   The events of *Agamemnon*, like those of all Greek tragedies, are rooted in
the widely shared legends of Greece's past—in this case, in the story of King
Atreus of Argos and his descendants. According to legend, Atreus had a long
and bitter quarrel with his exiled younger brother Thyestes, who had seduced Atreus's wife, Aerope, and contested his right to the throne. In retaliation, Atreus killed Thyestes's sons and then served them to Thyestes in a
stew during a banquet ostensibly given by Atreus as a demonstration of his
"forgiveness." Forced to flee once again into exile, Thyestes responded by
laying a curse on the House of Atreus. It is this curse that, in turn, is inherited
by Atreus's two sons, Agamemnon and Menelaus.

   Agamemnon and Menelaus married sisters (Clytemnestra and Helen);
and when Helen (the most beautiful woman in the world) fled to Troy with
her lover, Paris, it became Agamemnon's duty as the strongest king in Greece
to go after her. The expedition set sail for Troy, but unfavorable winds sent
by Artemis stalled his fleet at Aulis until Agamemnon reluctantly sacrificed
his daughter Iphigenia to appease the goddess. (Artemis was angry with
Agamemnon because he had boasted that his skill at archery was superior to
her own.) Then followed the ten long years of the Trojan War, at the conclusion of which the victorious Agamemnon murdered the aged King Priam,
sacked the city, enslaved its citizens, destroyed its temples, and abducted and
dishonored the priestess of Apollo, Cassandra.

Agamemnon is the story of the tragedy that follows this long war. At the very moment of his victorious return to Argos, Agamemnon is murdered in his own palace by his wife Clytemnestra, who simultaneously usurps the throne and installs in his place her paramour, Aegisthus (the sole surviving son of Atreus). *Agamemnon* thus continues the deeds of pride, arrogance, and violence that are the legacy of Atreus. Only in *The Eumenides*, the concluding play of the trilogy, is the cycle of sin and retribution broken when Orestes is tried by the goddess Athena and a jury of twelve Athenians and is declared free from the curse of his ancestral blood. As a result a clearer, more understandable contract of justice is established between the gods and humanity—one that simultaneously gives divine sanction to Athenian democracy.

Aeschylus's *Agamemnon* is particularly noted for its masterful characterizations of Agamemnon, Clytemnestra, Cassandra, and Aegisthus, for the simplicity and intensity of its central conflict, and for the powerful, suspenseful, and indeed spectacular, dramatic rendering of many of its scenes (the opening tableau with the watchman; the entrance and first speeches of the cold, sinister, and calculating Clytemnestra; Clytemnestra's hypocritical and effusive welcome upon the return of Agamemnon; the famous tapestry scene; the scene in which the pathetic Cassandra throws off Apollo's prophetic insignia; the murder tableau in which Clytemnestra stands over the bodies of her two victims, Agamemnon and Cassandra; the introduction of the boastful and cowardly Aegisthus). All of these scenes gain added weight by being set off against the unseen but imaginatively felt mountaintop beacons which flash the news of the fall of Troy through the darkness and across the Aegean from Mount Ida.

The character of Agamemnon, to whom the audience is instinctively drawn despite his errors, has all the requisites of the tragic hero. He is a noble warrior and a good ruler, loved by his people, doomed from birth as a member of the House of Atreus, whose curse he nonetheless merits through his overweening arrogance and pride. Agamemnon's initial error is the automatic assumption that, in H. D. F. Kitto's words, "a war for a wanton woman is a proper thing." This misguided assumption leads inevitably to the long, protracted, and debilitating war with Troy. In the process, as the chorus reminds him, he abdicates his responsibilities as a ruler at home and thus makes possible the trap which will ultimately ensnare and destroy him.

Agamemnon, in short, is blind to everything but the fact of his own greatness. This blindness extends to his misunderstanding of Clytemnestra, whose bold intelligence and ferocity of purpose he either discounts or simply fails to see. He adds insult to injury by thrusting his new concubine, Cassandra, into his wife's presence without the slightest concern for her thoughts or feelings.

The strong, ingenuous, and shrewd Clytemnestra is, by contrast, the most impressive character of the play, and indeed one of the most impressive in all of Greek drama. Her motives partake of a dynamic and complex mixture of love, hate, jealousy, pride, and willfulness. It is the very complexity of these motives that gives her ruthless and cunning character much of its fascination. To what extent, we find ourselves asking, is her conduct to be explained by her personal hatred of Agamemnon? By a mother's need to avenge the murder of her daughter? By the strength of her illicit passion for Aegisthus, with whom she has conducted an adulterous relationship during her husband's long absence? By the jealousy she feels in the presence of Cassandra? By her own ambitions to wield the reins of power?

Whatever the precise motivation, hatred and revenge guide her conduct in the course of the play. Whereas Agamemnon's words, however arrogant, are spoken without deceit, Clytemnestra's are filled with hypocrisy—a fact that underscores and heightens the differences between them, and, in turn, keys the audience's response. Note how easily and skillfully she overcomes Agamemnon's initial resistance and maneuvers him into a position of self-condemnation by persuading him to walk on the tapestries as if he were a god, an act which once again reveals his hubris. The scene is potent with symbolic overtones: from this point on few would doubt that Agamemnon, for all his reputation for astuteness, is firmly within Clytemnestra's power.

The dominant rhythm and mood of the play (and indeed the entire trilogy) are established in the opening scene of *Agamemnon* where the weary watchman, stationed on a roof of the city, warily scans the night sky for the beacon signaling both Agamemnon's final victory at Troy and alerting Clytemnestra that the hour of revenge is at hand. Despite the imminent victory, the watchman's anxious and apprehensive mood (what one scholar refers to as his "futile cheerfulness") wavers between joy and fear as he warns us with his own premonitions of still greater troubles to come. The scene thus provides the play with a kind of cosmic framework and establishes a tension that the play itself intensifies and will not relieve. It also introduces the contrasting images of light and darkness that will recur as a form of refrain.

Greek tragedies, almost by definition, deal with the fundamental and unchanging aspects of the eternal human condition. As such, they retain their relevancy and their power to move contemporary audiences. This is particularly true of the *Oresteian* trilogy, which deals not only with the consequences of human pride, but also with the choices that human beings make and with our capacity to endure and, ultimately, to learn through suffering.

A Selective Bibliography on *Agamemnon*

Conacher, D. J. *Aeschylus' Oresteia*. Toronto: U of Toronto P, 1987. 3–101.

Counts, J. Wilma. "Cassandra: An Approach to Aeschylus' *Agamemnon*." *English Journal* 62 (1973): 33–36.

Dover, Kenneth J. "Some Neglected Aspects of Agamemnon's Dilemma." *Journal of Hellenistic Studies* 93 (1973): 58–69.

Edwards, Mark W. "Agamemnon's Decision: Freedom and Folly in Aeschylus." *California Studies in Classical Antiquity* 10 (1977): 17–37.

Ferguson, John. *A Companion to Greek Tragedy*. Austin: U of Texas P, 1972. 74–89.

Furley, William D. "Motivation in the Parados of Aeschylus' Agamemnon," *Classical Philology* 81 (1986): 109–21.

Gantz, Timothy. "The Chorus of Aeschylus' *Agamemnon*." *Harvard Studies in Classical Philology* 87 (1983): 65–86.

Gargarin, Michael. *Aeschylean Drama*. Berkeley: U of California P, 1976. 57–114.

Goldhill, Simon. *Language, Sexuality, Narrative: The Orestia*. Cambridge, Eng.: Cambridge UP, 1984.

Herington, John. *Aeschylus*. New Haven: Yale UP, 1986. 111–24.

Hogan, James C. *A Commentary on the Complete Greek Tragedies: Aeschylus.* Chicago: U of Chicago P, 1984. 30–105.

Kitto, H. D. F. *Greek Tragedy: A Literary Study.* London: Methuen, 1968. 64–78.

Lebeck, Anne. *The Oresteia: A Study in Language and Structure.* Cambridge, Harvard UP, 1971. 7–58.

Lloyd-Jones, Hugh. "The Guilt of Agamemnon." *Classical Quarterly* 12 (1962): 187–99.

———. "Introduction." *Oresteia: Agamemnon.* London: Duckworth, 1982. i–xxii.

Murray, Gilbert. *Aeschylus: The Creator of Tragedy.* Oxford: Clarendon P, 1940. 185–234.

Olson, Elder. *Tragedy and the Theory of Drama.* Detroit: Wayne State UP, 1961. 171–94.

Otis, Brooks. *Cosmos & Tragedy: An Essay on the Meaning of Aeschylus.* Chapel Hill: U of North Carolina P, 1981. 12–65.

Podlecki, Anthony J. *The Political Background of Aeschylean Tragedy.* Ann Arbor: U of Michigan P, 1966. 63–100.

Pool, E. H. "Clytemnestra's First Encounter in Aeschylus' *Agamemnon:* Analysis of a Controversy." *Mnemosyne* 36 (1983): 71–116.

Pope, Maurice. "Merciful Heavens? A Question in Aeschylus' *Agamemnon.*" *Journal of Hellenistic Studies* 94 (1974): 100–13.

Rosenmeyer, Thomas G. *The Art of Aeschylus.* Berkeley: U of California P, 1982.

Smethurst, M. J. "The Authority of the Elders: The *Agamemnon,*" *Classical Philology* 67 (1972): 89–93.

Smyth, Herbert Weir. *Aeschylean Tragedy.* New York: Biblo & Tannen, 1969. 151–78.

Taplin, Oliver. *The Stagecraft of Aeschylus: The Dramatic Use of Exits and Entrances in Greek Tragedy.* Oxford: Clarendon P, 1977. 276–332.

Vellacott, Philip. *The Logic of Tragedy: Morals and Integrity in Aeschylus' Oresteia.* Durham: Duke UP, 1984.

Sophocles (ca. 496–406 B.C.)

ANTIGONÊ

Translated by Dudley Fitts and Robert Fitzgerald

CHARACTERS

ANTIGONÊ, *daughter of Oedipus, the former king*
ISMENÊ, *daughter of Oedipus*
CREON, *the King of Thebes and Antigonê's uncle.*
HAIMON, *Creon's son and Antigonê's fiancée*

TEIRESIAS, *a blind prophet*
A SENTRY
A MESSENGER
CHORUS

SCENE: *Before the palace of Creon, King of Thebes. A central double door, and two lateral doors. A platform extends the length of the façade, and from this platform three steps lead down into the "orchestra," or chorus-ground.*

   Time: Dawn of the day after the repulse of the Argive army from the assault on Thebes.[1]

PROLOGUE

[ANTIGONÊ *and* ISMENÊ *enter from the central door of the palace.*]

ANTIGONÊ.   Ismenê, dear sister,
   You would think that we had already suffered enough
   For the curse on Oedipus.[2]
   I cannot imagine any grief
   That you and I have not gone through. And now—
   Have they told you of the new decree of our King Creon?
ISMENÊ.   I have heard nothing: I know
   That two sisters lost two brothers, a double death
   In a single hour; and I know that the Argive army
10   Fled in the night; but beyond this, nothing.
ANTIGONÊ.   I thought so. And that is why I wanted you
   To come out here with me. There is something we must do.

---

[1] After Oedipus blinded and banished himself, his two sons, Eteoclês and Polyneicês, initially agreed to rule Thebes in alternate years. Eteoclês first assumed the throne and at the end of his year he refused to hand over power to Polyneicês. As a result, Polyneicês raised an army among the sympathetic Argives and laid siege to Thebes. At length Eteoclês and Polyneicês slew each other in single combat, the Argive army was vanquished, and Creon assumed the throne. At this point the action of the play begins.
[2] From the day of his birth Oedipus was fated to murder his father and marry his mother.

ISMENÊ.   Why do you speak so strangely?
ANTIGONÊ.   Listen, Ismenê:
Creon buried our brother Eteoclês
With military honors, gave him a soldier's funeral,
And it was right that he should; but Polyneicês,
Who fought as bravely and died as miserably,—
They say that Creon has sworn
20   No one shall bury him, no one mourn for him,
But his body must lie in the fields, a sweet treasure
For carrion birds to find as they search for food.
That is what they say, and our good Creon is coming here
To announce it publicly; and the penalty—
Stoning to death in the public square!

                             There it is,
And now you can prove what you are:
A true sister, or a traitor to your family.
ISMENÊ.   Antigonê, you are mad! What could I possibly do?
ANTIGONÊ.   You must decide whether you will help me or not.
30   ISMENÊ.   I do not understand you. Help you in what?
ANTIGONÊ.   Ismenê, I am going to bury him. Will you come?
ISMENÊ.   Bury him! You have just said the new law forbids it.
ANTIGONÊ.   He is my brother. And he is your brother, too.
ISMENÊ.   But think of the danger! Think what Creon will do!
ANTIGONÊ.   Creon is not strong enough to stand in my way.
ISMENÊ.   Ah sister!
Oedipus died, everyone hating him.
For what his own search brought to light, his eyes
Ripped out by his own hand; and Iocastê died,
40   His mother and wife at once: she twisted the cords
That strangled her life; and our two brothers died,
Each killed by the other's sword. And we are left:
But oh, Antigonê,
Think how much more terrible than these
Our own death would be if we should go against Creon
And do what he has forbidden! We are only women,
We cannot fight with men, Antigonê!
The law is strong, we must give in to the law
In this thing, and in worse. I beg the Dead
50   To forgive me, but I am helpless: I must yield
To those in authority. And I think it is dangerous business
To be always meddling.
ANTIGONÊ.   If that is what you think,
I should not want you, even if you asked to come.
You have made your choice, you can be what you want to be.
But I will bury him; and if I must die,
I say that this crime is holy: I shall lie down
With him in death, and I shall be as dear
To him as he to me.
                    It is the dead,

60   Not the living, who make the longest demands:
     We die for ever . . .
                        You may do as you like,
     Since apparently the laws of the gods mean nothing to you.
ISMENÊ.   They mean a great deal to me; but I have no strength
     To break laws that were made for the public good.
ANTIGONÊ.   That must be your excuse, I suppose. But as for me,
     I will bury the brother I love.
ISMENÊ.   Antigonê,
     I am so afraid for you!
ANTIGONÊ.   You need not be:
     You have yourself to consider, after all.
70 ISMENÊ.   But no one must hear of this, you must tell no one!
     I will keep it a secret, I promise!
ANTIGONÊ.   O tell it! Tell everyone!
     Think how they'll hate you when it all comes out
     If they learn that you knew about it all the time!
ISMENÊ.   So fiery! You should be cold with fear.
ANTIGONÊ.   Perhaps. But I am doing only what I must.
ISMENÊ.   But can you do it? I say that you cannot.
ANTIGONÊ.   Very well: when my strength gives out,
     I shall do no more.
ISMENÊ.   Impossible things should not be tried at all.
ANTIGONÊ.   Go away, Ismenê:
80   I shall be hating you soon, and the dead will too,
     For your words are hateful. Leave me my foolish plan:
     I am not afraid of the danger; if it means death,
     It will not be the worst of deaths—death without honor.
ISMENÊ.   Go then, if you feel that you must.
     You are unwise,
     But a loyal friend indeed to those who love you.

[Exit into the palace. ANTIGONÊ *goes off, left. Enter the* CHORUS.]

PARODOS[3]

[STROPHE 1]

CHORUS.   Now the long blade of the sun, lying
     Level east to west, touches with glory
90   Thebes of the Seven Gates. Open, unlidded
     Eye of golden day! O marching light
     Across the eddy and rush of Dircê's stream,[4]
     Striking the white shields of the enemy
     Thrown headlong backward from the blaze of morning!

---

[3] The *parodos* is sung by the chorus as it first comes on stage. The *exodus* is sung on leaving at the play's end. The various songs, or odes, of the chorus are divided into *strophe* and *antistrophe,* each with similar (but opposite) dance steps.
[4] A stream near Thebes.

CHORAGOS.[5]   Polyneicês their commander
  Roused them with windy phrases,
  He the wild eagle screaming
  Insults above our land,
  His wings their shields of snow,
100   His crest their marshalled helms.

[ANTISTROPHE 1]

CHORUS.   Against our seven gates in a yawning ring
  The famished spears came onward in the night;
  But before his jaws were sated with our blood,
  Or pinefire took the garland of our towers,
  He was thrown back; and as he turned, great Thebes—
  No tender victim for his noisy power—
  Rose like a dragon behind him, shouting war.
CHORAGOS.   For God hates utterly
  The bray of bragging tongues;
110   And when he beheld their smiling,
  Their swagger of golden helms,
  The frown of his thunder blasted
  Their first man from our walls.[6]

[STROPHE 2]

CHORUS.   We heard his shout of triumph high in the air
  Turn to a scream; far out in a flaming arc
  He fell with his windy torch, and the earth struck him.
  And others storming in fury no less than his
  Found shock of death in the dusty joy of battle.
CHORAGOS.   Seven captains at seven gates
120   Yielded their clanging arms to the god
  That bends the battle-line and breaks it.
  These two only, brothers in blood,
  Face to face in matchless rage,
  Mirroring each the other's death,
  Clashed in long combat.

[ANTISTROPHE 2]

CHORUS.   But now in the beautiful morning of victory
  Let Thebes of the many chariots sing for joy!
  With hearts for dancing we'll take leave of war:
  Our temples shall be sweet with hymns of praise,
130   And the long nights shall echo with our chorus.

SCENE I

CHORAGOS.   But now at last our new King is coming:
  Creon of Thebes, Menoikeus' son.

---

[5] The title used in Greek plays for the leader of the chorus.
[6] Polyneicês' ally, Capaneus, mounted a siege ladder, declaring that he would force his way into Thebes despite the opposition of Jove himself. For this impiety, Jove blasted him from the ladder with a thunderbolt.

In this auspicious dawn of his reign
What are the new complexities
That shifting Fate has woven for him?
What is his counsel? Why has he summoned
The old men to hear him?

[*Enter* CREON *from the palace, center. He addresses the* CHORUS *from the top step.*]

CREON.   Gentlemen: I have the honor to inform you that our Ship of
State, which recent storms have threatened to destroy, has come safely
140   to harbor at last, guided by the merciful wisdom of Heaven. I have
summoned you here this morning because I know that I can depend
upon you: your devotion to King Laïos was absolute; you never
hesitated in your duty to our late ruler Oedipus; and when Oedipus
died, your loyalty was transferred to his children. Unfortunately, as you
know, his two sons, the princes Eteoclês and Polyneicês, have killed
each other in battle; and I, as the next in blood, have succeeded to the
full power of the throne.
    I am aware, of course, that no Ruler can expect complete loyalty
from his subjects until he has been tested in office. Nevertheless, I say
150   to you at the very outset that I have nothing but contempt for the kind
of Governor who is afraid, for whatever reason, to follow the course
that he knows is best for the State; and as for the man who sets private
friendship above the public welfare,—I have no use for him, either. I
call God to witness that if I saw my country headed for ruin, I should
not be afraid to speak out plainly; and I need hardly remind you that I
would never have any dealings with an enemy of the people. No one
values friendship more highly than I; but we must remember that
friends made at the risk of wrecking our Ship are not real friends at all.
    These are my principles, at any rate, and that is why I have made the
160   following decision concerning the sons of Oedipus: Eteoclês, who died
as a man should die, fighting for his country, is to be buried with full
military honors, with all the ceremony that is usual when the greatest
heroes die; but his brother Polyneicês, who broke his exile to come
back with fire and sword against his native city and the shrines of his
fathers' gods, whose one idea was to spill the blood of his blood and
sell his own people into slavery—Polyneicês, I say, is to have no burial:
no man is to touch him or say the least prayer for him; he shall lie on
the plain, unburied; and the birds and the scavenging dogs can do with
him whatever they like.
170   This is my command, and you can see the wisdom behind it. As long
as I am King, no traitor is going to be honored with the loyal man. But
whoever shows by word and deed that he is on the side of the
State,—he shall have my respect while he is living and my reverence
when he is dead.
CHORAGOS.   If that is your will, Creon son of Menoikeus,
   You have the right to enforce it: we are yours.
CREON.   That is my will. Take care that you do your part.
CHORAGOS.   We are old men: let the younger ones carry it out.
CREON.   I do not mean that: the sentries have been appointed.

CHORAGOS.   Then what is it that you would have us do?
CREON.   You will give no support to whoever breaks this law.
CHORAGOS.   Only a crazy man is in love with death!
180 CREON.   And death it is; yet money talks, and the wisest
Have sometimes been known to count a few coins too many.

[Enter SENTRY *from left.]*

SENTRY.   I'll not say that I'm out of breath from running, King, because
every time I stopped to think about what I have to tell you, I felt like
going back. And all the time a voice kept saying, "You fool, don't you
know you're walking straight into trouble?"; and then another voice:
"Yes, but if you let somebody else get the news to Creon first, it will be
even worse than that for you!" But good sense won out, at least I hope
it was good sense, and here I am with a story that makes no sense at
all; but I'll tell it anyhow, because, as they say, what's going to happen's
going to happen and—
190 CREON.   Come to the point. What have you to say?
SENTRY.   I did not do it. I did not see who did it. You must not punish me
for what someone else has done.
CREON.   A comprehensive defense! More effective, perhaps,
If I knew its purpose. Come: what is it?
SENTRY.   A dreadful thing . . . I don't know how to put it—
CREON.   Out with it!
SENTRY.   Well, then;
The dead man—
              Polyneicês—

[Pause. The SENTRY *is overcome, fumbles for words.* CREON *waits impassively.]*

                    out there—
                              someone,—
New dust on the slimy flesh!

[Pause. No sign from CREON.*]*

200   Someone has given it burial that way, and
Gone . . .

[Long pause. CREON *finally speaks with deadly control.]*

CREON.   And the man who dared do this?
SENTRY.   I swear I
Do not know! You must believe me!
                              Listen:
The ground was dry, not a sign of digging, no,
Not a wheeltrack in the dust, no trace of anyone.
It was when they relieved us this morning: and one of them,
The Corporal, pointed to it.
                        There it was,
The strangest—
            Look:

210   The body, just mounded over with light dust: you see?
Not buried really, but as if they'd covered it
Just enough for the ghost's peace. And no sign
Of dogs or any wild animal that had been there.

And then what a scene there was!! Every man of us
Accusing the other: we all proved the other man did it,
We all had proof that we could not have done it.
We were ready to take hot iron in our hands,
Walk through fire, swear by all the gods,
It was not I!
220   *I do not know who it was, but it was not I!*

[CREON's *rage has been mounting steadily, but the* SENTRY *is too intent upon his story to notice it.*]

And then, when this came to nothing, someone said
A thing that silenced us and made us stare
Down at the ground: you had to be told the news,
And one of us had to do it! We threw the dice,
And the bad luck fell to me. So here I am,
No happier to be here than you are to have me:
Nobody likes the man who brings bad news.

CHORAGOS.   I have been wondering, King: can it be that the gods have
     done this?
230 CREON [*furiously*]. Stop!
Must you doddering wrecks
Go out of your heads entirely? "The gods"!
Intolerable!
The gods favor this corpse? Why? How had he served them?
Tried to loot their temples, burn their images,
Yes, and the whole State, and its laws with it!
Is it your senile opinion that the gods love to honor bad men?
A pious thought—
                  No, from the very beginning
240   There have been those who have whispered together,
Stiff-necked anarchists, putting their heads together,
Scheming against me in alleys. These are the men.
And they have bribed my own guard to do this thing.
[*Sententiously.*] Money!
There's nothing in the world so demoralizing as money.
Down go your cities,
Homes gone, men gone, honest hearts corrupted,
Crookedness of all kinds and all for money!
[*To Sentry.*]   But you—
I swear by God and by the throne of God,
250   The man who has done this thing shall pay for it!
Find that man, bring him here to me, or your death
Will be the least of your problems: I'll string you up
Alive, and there will be certain ways to make you

Discover your employer before you die;
And the process may teach you a lesson you seem to have missed:
The dearest profit is sometimes all too dear:
That depends on the source. Do you understand me?
A fortune won is often misfortune.

SENTRY.   King, may I speak?

260 CREON.   Your very voice distresses me.

SENTRY.   Are you sure that it is my voice, and not your conscience?

CREON.   By God, he wants to analyze me now!

SENTRY.   It is not what I say, but what has been done, that hurts you.

CREON.   You talk too much.

SENTRY.   Maybe; but I've done nothing.

CREON.   Sold your soul for some silver: that's all you've done.

SENTRY.   How dreadful it is when the right judge judges wrong!

CREON.   Your figures of speech
May entertain you now; but unless you bring me the man,

270   You will get little profit from them in the end.

[*Exit* CREON *into the palace.*]

SENTRY.   "Bring me the man"—!
I'd like nothing better than bringing him the man!
But bring him or not, you have seen the last of me here.
At any rate, I am safe!

[*Exit* SENTRY.]

ODE I

[STROPHE 1]

CHORUS.   Numberless are the world's wonders, but none
More wonderful than man; the stormgray sea
Yields to his prows, the huge crests bear him high;
Earth, holy and inexhaustible, is graven
With shining furrows where his plows have gone

280   Year after year, the timeless labor of stallions.

[ANTISTROPHE 1]

The lightboned birds and beasts that cling to cover,
The lithe fish lighting their reaches of dim water,
All are taken, tamed in the net of his mind;
The lion on the hill, the wild horse windy-maned,
Resign to him; and his blunt yoke has broken
The sultry shoulders of the mountain bull.

[STROPHE 2]

Words also, and thought as rapid as air,
He fashions to his good use; statecraft is his,
And his the skill that deflects the arrows of snow,

290   The spears of winter rain: from every wind
He has made himself secure—from all but one:
In the late wind of death he cannot stand.

O clear intelligence, force beyond all measure!
O fate of man, working both good and evil!
When the laws are kept, how proudly his city stands!
When the laws are broken, what of his city then?
Never may the anarchic man find rest at my hearth,
Never be it said that my thoughts are his thoughts.

SCENE II

[*Reenter* SENTRY *leading* ANTIGONÊ.]

CHORAGOS.   What does this mean? Surely this captive woman
300   Is the Princess, Antigonê. Why should she be taken?
SENTRY.   Here is the one who did it! We caught her
   In the very act of burying him.—Where is Creon?
CHORAGOS.   Just coming from the house.

[*Enter* CREON *center.*]

CREON.   What has happened?
   Why have you come back so soon?
SENTRY [*expansively*].   O King,
   A man should never be too sure of anything:
   I would have sworn
   That you'd not see me here again: your anger
   Frightened me so, and the things you threatened me with;
   But how could I tell then
310   That I'd be able to solve the case so soon?
   No dice-throwing this time: I was only too glad to come!
   Here is this woman. She is the guilty one:
   We found her trying to bury him.
   Take her, then; question her; judge her as you will.
   I am through with the whole thing now, and glad of it.
   CREON.   But this is Antigonê! Why have you brought her here?
   SENTRY.   She was burying him, I tell you!
   CREON [*severely*].   Is this the truth?
   SENTRY.   I saw her with my own eyes. Can I say more?
   CREON.   The details: come, tell me quickly!
320 SENTRY.   It was like this:
   After those terrible threats of yours, King,
   We went back and brushed the dust away from the body.
   The flesh was soft by now, and stinking,
   So we sat on a hill to windward and kept guard.
   No napping this time! We kept each other awake.
   But nothing happened until the white round sun
   Whirled in the center of the round sky over us:
   Then, suddenly,
   A storm of dust roared up from the earth, and the sky

330   Went out, the plain vanished with all its trees
In the stinging dark. We closed our eyes and endured it.
The whirlwind lasted a long time, but it passed;
And then we looked, and there was Antigonê!
I have seen
A mother bird come back to a stripped nest, heard
Her crying bitterly a broken note or two
For the young ones stolen. Just so, when this girl
Found the bare corpse, and all her love's work wasted,
She wept, and cried on heaven to damn the hands
That had done this thing.

340   And then she brought more dust
And sprinkled wine three times for her brother's ghost.

We ran and took her at once. She was not afraid,
Not even when we charged her with what she had done.
She denied nothing.
                                And this was a comfort to me,
And some uneasiness: for it is a good thing
To escape from death, but it is no great pleasure
To bring death to a friend.
                                Yet I always say
There is nothing so comfortable as your own safe skin!
CREON [*slowly, dangerously*].   And you, Antigonê,
350   You with her head hanging,—do you confess this thing?
ANTIGONÊ.   I do. I deny nothing.
CREON [*to* SENTRY].   You may go.

                                                                    [*Exit* SENTRY.]

[*To* ANTIGONÊ.] Tell me, tell me briefly:
Had you heard my proclamation touching this matter?
ANTIGONÊ.   It was public. Could I help hearing it?
CREON.   And yet you dared defy the law.
ANTIGONÊ.   I dared.
It was not God's proclamation. That final Justice
That rules the world below makes no such laws.

360   Your edict, King, was strong.
But all your strength is weakness itself against
The immortal unrecorded laws of God.
They are not merely now: they were, and shall be,
Operative for ever, beyond man utterly.

I knew I must die, even without your decree:
I am only mortal. And if I must die
Now, before it is my time to die,
Surely this is no hardship: can anyone
Living, as I live, with evil all about me,
370   Think Death less than a friend? This death of mine

Is of no importance; but if I had left my brother
Lying in death unburied, I should have suffered.
Now I do not.
                          You smile at me. Ah Creon,
Think me a fool, if you like; but it may well be
That a fool convicts me of folly.
CHORAGOS.   Like father, like daughter: both headstrong, deaf to reason!
     She has never learned to yield:
CREON.   She has much to learn.
     The inflexible heart breaks first, the toughest iron
     Cracks first, and the wildest horses bend their necks
     At the pull of the smallest curb.
380   Pride? In a slave?
     This girl is guilty of a double insolence,
     Breaking the given laws and boasting of it.
     Who is the man here,
     She or I, if this crime goes unpunished?
     Sister's child, or more than sister's child,
     Or closer yet in blood—she and her sister
     Win bitter death for this!
     [*To* SERVANTS.]   Go, some of you,
     Arrest Ismenê. I accuse her equally.
390 Bring her: you will find her sniffling in the house there.

     Her mind's a traitor: crimes kept in the dark
     Cry for light, and the guardian brain shudders;
     But how much worse than this
     Is brazen boasting of barefaced anarchy!
ANTIGONÊ.   Creon, what more do you want than my death?
CREON.   Nothing.
     That gives me everything.
ANTIGONÊ.   Then I beg you: kill me.
     This talking is a great weariness: your words
400 Are distasteful to me, and I am sure that mine
     Seem so to you. And yet they should not seem so:
     I should have praise and honor for what I have done.
     All these men here would praise me
     Were their lips not frozen shut with fear of you.
     [*Bitterly.*] Ah the good fortune of kings,
     Licensed to say and do whatever they please!
CREON.   You are alone here in that opinion.
ANTIGONÊ.   No, they are with me. But they keep their tongues in leash.
CREON.   Maybe. But you are guilty, and they are not.
410 ANTIGONÊ.   There is no guilt in reverence for the dead.
CREON.   But Eteoclês—was he not your brother too?
ANTIGONÊ.   My brother too.
CREON.   And you insult his memory?
ANTIGONÊ [*softly*].   The dead man would not say that I insult it.
CREON.   He would: for you honor a traitor as much as him.
ANTIGONÊ.   His own brother, traitor or not, and equal in blood.

CREON.   He made war on his country. Eteoclês defended it.

ANTIGONÊ.   Nevertheless, there are honors due all the dead.

CREON.   But not the same for the wicked as for the just.

420   ANTIGONÊ.   Ah Creon, Creon,
Which of us can say what the gods hold wicked?

CREON.   An enemy is an enemy, even dead.

ANTIGONÊ.   It is my nature to join in love, not hate.

CREON [*finally losing patience*].   Go join them then; if you must have your
love,
Find it in hell!

CHORAGOS.   But see, Ismenê comes:

[*Enter* ISMENÊ, *guarded.*]

Those tears are sisterly, the cloud
That shadows her eyes rains down gentle sorrow.

CREON.   You too, Ismenê,

430   Snake in my ordered house, sucking my blood
Stealthily—and all the time I never knew
That these two sisters were aiming at my throne!

Ismenê,
Do you confess your share in this crime, or deny it?
Answer me.

ISMENÊ.   Yes, if she will let me say so. I am guilty.

ANTIGONÊ [*coldly*].   No, Ismenê. You have no right to say so.
You would not help me, and I will not have you help me.

ISMENÊ.   But now I know what you meant; and I am here
To join you, to take my share of punishment.

440   ANTIGONÊ.   The dead man and the gods who rule the dead
Know whose act this was. Words are not friends.

ISMENÊ.   Do you refuse me, Antigonê? I want to die with you:
I too have a duty that I must discharge to the dead.

ANTIGONÊ.   You shall not lessen my death by sharing it.

ISMENÊ.   What do I care for life when you are dead?

ANTIGONÊ.   Ask Creon. You're always hanging on his opinions.

ISMENÊ.   You are laughing at me. Why, Antigonê?

ANTIGONÊ.   It's a joyless laughter, Ismenê.

ISMENÊ.   But can I do nothing?

450   ANTIGONÊ.   Yes. Save yourself. I shall not envy you.
There are those who will praise you; I shall have honor, too.

ISMENÊ.   But we are equally guilty!

ANTIGONÊ.   No more, Ismenê.
You are alive, but I belong to Death.

CREON [*to the* CHORUS.].   Gentlemen, I beg you to observe these girls:
One has just now lost her mind; the other,
It seems, has never had a mind at all.

ISMENÊ.   Grief teaches the steadiest minds to waver, king.

CREON.   Yours certainly did, when you assumed guilt with the guilty!

460   ISMENÊ.   But how could I go on living without her?

CREON.   You are.
She is already dead.

ISMENÊ.   But your own son's bride!

CREON.   There are places enough for him to push his plow.
  I want no wicked women for my sons!
ISMENÊ.   O dearest Haimon, how your father wrongs you!
CREON.   I've had enough of your childish talk of marriage!
CHORAGOS.   Do you really intend to steal this girl from your son?
CREON.   No; Death will do that for me.
CHORAGOS.   Then she must die?
CREON [*ironically*].   You dazzle me.
470   —But enough of this talk!
  [*To* GUARDS.] You, there, take them away and guard them well:
  For they are but women, and even brave men run
  When they see Death coming.

                              [*Exeunt* ISMENÊ, ANTIGONÊ, *and* GUARDS.]

ODE II

[STROPHE 1]

CHORUS.   Fortunate is the man who has never tasted God's vengeance!
  Where once the anger of heaven has struck, that house is shaken
  For ever: damnation rises behind each child
  Like a wave cresting out of the black northeast,
  When the long darkness under sea roars up
  And bursts drumming death upon the windwhipped sand.

[ANTISTROPHE 1]

480   I have seen this gathering sorrow from time long past
  Loom upon Oedipus' children: generation from generation
  Takes the compulsive rage of the enemy god.
  So lately this last flower of Oedipus' line
  Drank the sunlight! but now a passionate word
  And a handful of dust have closed up all its beauty.

[STROPHE 2]

    What mortal arrogance
    Transcends the wrath of Zeus?
  Sleep cannot lull him nor the effortless long months
  Of the timeless gods: but he is young for ever,
490 And his house is the shining day of high Olympos.
    All that is and shall be,
    And all the past, is his.
  No pride on earth is free of the curse of heaven.

[ANTISTROPHE 2]

  The straying dreams of men
    May bring them ghosts of joy:
  But as they drowse, the waking embers burn them;
  Or they walk with fixed eyes, as blind men walk.
  But the ancient wisdom speaks for our own time:
    Fate works most for woe
500   *With Folly's fairest show.*
  Man's little pleasure is the spring of sorrow.

SCENE III

CHORAGOS.   But here is Haimon, King, the last of all your sons.
 Is it grief for Antigonê that brings him here,
 And bitterness at being robbed of his bride?

[Enter HAIMON.]

CREON.   We shall soon see, and no need of diviners.
             —Son,
 You have heard my final judgment on that girl:
 Have you come here hating me, or have you come
 With deference and with love, whatever I do?
HAIMON.   I am your son, father. You are my guide.
510 You make things clear for me, and I obey you.
 No marriage means more to me than your continuing wisdom.
CREON.   Good. That is the way to behave: subordinate
 Everything else, my son, to your father's will.
 This is what a man prays for, that he may get
 Sons attentive and dutiful in his house,
 Each one hating his father's enemies,
 Honoring his father's friends. But if his sons
 Fail him, if they turn out unprofitably,
 What has he fathered but trouble for himself
 And amusement for the malicious?
520   So you are right
 Not to lose your head over this woman.
 Your pleasure with her would soon grow cold, Haimon,
 And then you'd have a hellcat in bed and elsewhere.
 Let her find her husband in Hell!
 Of all the people in this city, only she
 Has had contempt for my law and broken it.

 Do you want me to show myself weak before the people?
 Or to break my sworn word? No, and I will not.
 The woman dies.
530 I suppose she'll plead "family ties." Well, let her.
 If I permit my own family to rebel,
 How shall I earn the world's obedience?
 Show me the man who keeps his house in hand,
 He's fit for public authority.
          I'll have no dealings
 With lawbreakers, critics of the government:
 Whoever is chosen to govern should be obeyed—
 Must be obeyed, in all things, great and small,
 Just and unjust! O Haimon,
 The man who knows how to obey, and that man only,
540 Knows how to give commands when the time comes.
 You can depend on him, no matter how fast
 The spears come: he's a good soldier, he'll stick it out.

Anarchy, anarchy! Show me a greater evil!
This is why cities tumble and the great houses rain down,
This is what scatters armies!
No, no: good lives are made so by discipline.
We keep the laws then, and the lawmakers,
And no woman shall seduce us. If we must lose,
Let's lose to a man, at least! Is a woman stronger than we?

550 CHORAGOS.   Unless time has rusted my wits,
What you say, King, is said with point and dignity.

HAIMON [*boyishly earnest*].   Father:
Reason is God's crowning gift to man, and you are right
To warn me against losing mine. I cannot say—
I hope that I shall never want to say!—that you
Have reasoned badly. Yet there are other men
Who can reason, too; and their opinions might be helpful.
You are not in a position to know everything
That people say or do, or what they feel:

560 Your temper terrifies—everyone
Will tell you only what you like to hear.
But I, at any rate, can listen; and I have heard them
Muttering and whispering in the dark about this girl.
They say no woman has ever, so unreasonably,
Died so shameful a death for a generous act:
"She covered her brother's body. Is this indecent?
She kept him from dogs and vultures. Is this a crime?
Death? She should have all the honor that we can give her!"

This is the way they talk out there in the city.

570 You must believe me:
Nothing is closer to me than your happiness.
What could be closer? Must not any son
Value his father's fortune as his father does his?
I beg you, do not be unchangeable:
Do not believe that you alone can be right.
The man who thinks that,
The man who maintains that only he has the power
To reason correctly, the gift to speak, the soul—
A man like that, when you know him, turns out empty.

580 It is not reason never to yield to reason!

In flood time you can see how some trees bend,
And because they bend, even their twigs are safe,
While stubborn trees are torn up, roots and all.
And the same thing happens in sailing:
Make your sheet fast, never slacken,—and over you go,
Head over heels and under: and there's your voyage.
Forget you are angry! Let yourself be moved!
I know I am young; but please let me say this:
The ideal condition

590   Would be, I admit, that men should be right by instinct;
        But since we are all too likely to go astray,
        The reasonable thing is to learn from those who can teach.
     CHORAGOS.   You will do well to listen to him, King,
        If what he says is sensible. And you, Haimon,
        Must listen to your father.—Both speak well.
     CREON.   You consider it right for a man of my years and experience
        To go to school to a boy?
     HAIMON.   It is not right
        If I am wrong. But if I am young, and right,
600   What does my age matter?
     CREON.   You think it right to stand up for an anarchist?
     HAIMON.   Not at all. I pay no respect to criminals.
     CREON.   Then she is not a criminal?
     HAIMON.   The City would deny it, to a man.
     CREON.   And the City proposes to teach me how to rule?
     HAIMON.   Ah. Who is it that's talking like a boy now?
     CREON.   My voice is the one voice giving orders in this City!
     HAIMON.   It is no City if it takes orders from one voice.
     CREON.   The State is the King!
610 HAIMON.   Yes, if the State is a desert.

                                                          [Pause.]

     CREON.   This boy, it seems, has sold out to a woman.
     HAIMON.   If you are a woman: my concern is only for you.
     CREON.   So? Your "concern"! In a public brawl with your father!
     HAIMON.   How about you, in a public brawl with justice?
     CREON.   With justice, when all that I do is within my rights?
     HAIMON.   You have no right to trample on God's right.
     CREON [completely out of control].   Fool, adolescent fool! Taken in by a
        woman!
     HAIMON.   You'll never see me taken in by anything vile.
     CREON.   Every word you say is for her!
620 HAIMON [quietly, darkly].   And for you.
        And for me. And for the gods under the earth.
     CREON.   You'll never marry her while she lives.
     HAIMON.   Then she must die.—But her death will cause another.
     CREON.   Another?
        Have you lost your senses? Is this an open threat?
     HAIMON.   There is no threat in speaking to emptiness.
     CREON.   I swear you'll regret this superior tone of yours!
        You are the empty one!
     HAIMON.   If you were not my father,
630   I'd say you were perverse.
     CREON.   You girl-struck fool, don't play at words with me!
     HAIMON.   I am sorry. You prefer silence.
     CREON.   Now, by God—
        I swear, by all the gods in heaven above us,
        You'll watch it, I swear you shall!
     [To the SERVANTS.]   Bring her out!

Bring the woman out! Let her die before his eyes!
Here, this instant, with her bridegroom beside her!
HAIMON.   Not here, no; she will not die here, king.
And you will never see my face again.
640   Go on raving as long as you've a friend to endure you.

[*Exit* HAIMON.]

CHORAGOS.   Gone, gone.
Creon, a young man in a rage is dangerous!
CREON.   Let him do, or dream to do, more than a man can.
He shall not save these girls from death.
CHORAGOS.   These girls?
You have sentenced them both?
CREON.   No, you are right.
I will not kill the one whose hands are clean.
CHORAGOS.   But Antigonê?
CREON [*somberly*].   I will carry her far away
Out there in the wilderness, and lock her
Living in a vault of stone. She shall have food,
650   As the custom is, to absolve the State of her death.
And there let her pray to the gods of hell:
They are her only gods:
Perhaps they will show her an escape from death,
Or she may learn,
                        though late,
That piety shown the dead is pity in vain.

[*Exit* CREON.]

ODE III

[STROPHE]

CHORUS.   Love, unconquerable
Waster of rich men, keeper
Of warm lights and all-night vigil
660   In the soft face of a girl:
Sea-wanderer, forest-visitor!
Even the pure Immortals cannot escape you,
And mortal man, in his one day's dusk,
Trembles before your glory.

[ANTISTROPHE]

Surely you swerve upon ruin
The just man's consenting heart,
As here you have made bright anger
Strike between father and son—
And none has conquered but Love!
670   A girl's glance working the will of heaven:
Pleasure to her alone who mocks us,
Merciless Aphroditê.[7]

---

[7] The goddess of love.

SCENE IV

CHORAGOS [*as* ANTIGONÊ *enters guarded*].   But I can no longer stand in awe
    of this,
  Nor, seeing what I see, keep back my tears.
  Here is Antigonê, passing to that chamber
  Where all find sleep at last.

[STROPHE 1]

ANTIGONÊ.   Look upon me, friends, and pity me
  Turning back at the night's edge to say
  Good-by to the sun that shines for me no longer;
680 Now sleepy Death
  Summons me down to Acheron,[8] that cold shore:
  There is no bridesong there, nor any music.
CHORUS.   Yet not unpraised, not without a kind of honor,
  You walk at last into the underworld;
  Untouched by sickness, broken by no sword.
  What woman has ever found your way to death?

[ANTISTROPHE 1]

ANTIGONÊ.   How often I have heard the story of Niobê,[9]
  Tantalos' wretched daughter, how the stone
  Clung fast about her, ivy-close: and they say
690 The rain falls endlessly
  And sifting soft snow; her tears are never done.
  I feel the loneliness of her death in mine.
CHORUS.   But she was born of heaven, and you
  Are woman, woman-born. If her death is yours,
  A mortal woman's, is this not for you
  Glory in our world and in the world beyond?

[STROPHE 2]

ANTIGONÊ.   You laugh at me. Ah, friends, friends,
  Can you not wait until I am dead? O Thebes,
  O men many-charioted, in love with Fortune,
700 Dear springs of Dircê, sacred Theban grove,
  Be witnesses for me, denied all pity,
  Unjustly judged! and think a word of love
  For her whose path turns
  Under dark earth, where there are no more tears.
CHORUS.   You have passed beyond human daring and come at last
  Into a place of stone where Justice sits.
  I cannot tell
  What shape of your father's guilt appears in this.

---

  [8] The river separating this world from the Underworld.
  [9] To punish Niobê's impiety in claiming god-like qualities in herself and her children,
Apollo and Artemis slew all fourteen of her offspring. In her grief, Niobê turned to stone, yet
her tears continued to feed the mountain streams.

[ANTISTROPHE 2]

ANTIGONÊ.   You have touched it at last: that bridal bed
710   Unspeakable, horror of son and mother mingling:
      Their crime, infection of all our family!
      O Oedipus, father and brother!
      Your marriage strikes from the grave to murder mine.
      I have been a stranger here in my own land:
      All my life
      The blasphemy of my birth has followed me.
CHORUS.   Reverence is a virtue, but strength
      Lives in established law: that must prevail.
      You have made your choice,
720   Your death is the doing of your conscious hand.

[EPODE]

ANTIGONÊ.   Then let me go, since all your words are bitter,
      And the very light of the sun is cold to me.
      Lead me to my vigil, where I must have
      Neither love nor lamentation; no song, but silence.

[CREON *interrupts impatiently.*]

CREON.   If dirges and planned lamentations could put off death,
      Men would be singing for ever.
      [*To the* SERVANTS.]   Take her, go!
      You know your orders: take her to the vault
      And leave her alone there. And if she lives or dies,
730   That's her affair, not ours: our hands are clean.
ANTIGONÊ.   O tomb, vaulted bride-bed in eternal rock,
      Soon I shall be with my own again
      Where Persephonê[10] welcomes the thin ghosts underground:
      And I shall see my father again, and you, mother,
      And dearest Polyneicês—
                              dearest indeed
      To me, since it was my hand
      That washed him clean and poured the ritual wine:
      And my reward is death before my time!

      And yet, as men's hearts know, I have done no wrong,
740   I have not sinned before God. Or if I have,
      I shall know the truth in death. But if the guilt
      Lies upon Creon who judged me, then, I pray,
      May his punishment equal my own.
CHORAGOS.   O passionate heart,
      Unyielding, tormented still by the same winds!
CREON.   Her guards shall have good cause to regret their delaying.
ANTIGONÊ.   Ah! That voice is like the voice of death!
CREON.   I can give you no reason to think you are mistaken.
ANTIGONÊ.   Thebes, and you my father's gods,

---

[10] The queen of the Underworld.

750   And rulers of Thebes, you see me now, the last
      Unhappy daughter of a line of kings,
      Your kings, led away to death. You will remember
      What things I suffer, and at what men's hands,
      Because I would not transgress the laws of heaven.
      [*To the* Guards, *simply.*] Come: let us wait no longer.

                              [*Exit* Antigonê, *left, guarded.*]

                        ODE IV
                                                [STROPHE 1]

Chorus.   All Danaê's beauty was locked away
      In a brazen cell where the sunlight could not come:
      A small room still as any grave, enclosed her.
      Yet she was a princess too,
760   And Zeus in a rain of gold poured love upon her.[11]
      O child, child,
      No power in wealth or war
      Or tough sea-blackened ships
      Can prevail against untiring Destiny!

                                                [ANTISTROPHE 1]

      And Dryas' son[12] also, that furious king,
      Bore the god's prisoning anger for his pride:
      Sealed up by Dionysos in deaf stone,
      His madness died among echoes.
      So at the last he learned what dreadful power
770   His tongue had mocked:
      For he had profaned the revels,
      And fired the wrath of the nine
      Implacable Sisters[13] that love the sound of the flute.

                                                [STROPHE 2]

      And old men tell a half-remembered tale
      Of horror where a dark ledge splits the sea
      And a double surf beats on the gray shores:
      How a king's new woman, sick
      With hatred for the queen he had imprisoned,[14]
      Ripped out his two sons' eyes with her bloody hands
780   While grinning Arês[15] watched the shuttle plunge
      Four times: four blind wounds crying for revenge,

---

[11] A prophet told Acrisius, king of Argos, that his daughter Danaê would give birth to a son who would kill the king. Acrisius tried to prevent Danaê from ever becoming pregnant by confining her within a bronze tower, but Zeus descended upon her in a shower of gold and their offspring, Perseus, did indeed kill Acrisius.

[12] Dryas's son Lycurgus opposed the worship of Dionysos, the god of wine and revelry. For vengeance, Dionysos drove him insane and Lycurgus died within a stonewalled prison.

[13] The nine Muses, who give inspiration for the creative arts and sciences.

[14] This stanza and the one that follows tell the story of Cleopatra (not the Egyptian queen, but an earlier, legendary figure), who was cast off by her husband Phineus and imprisoned in a cave. The "king's new woman" Eidothea, wishing to assure her own children's claim to the throne, used a weaving shuttle to blind the sons of Cleopatra.

[15] The god of war.

Crying tears and blood mingled.—Piteously born,
Those sons whose mother was of heavenly birth!
Her father was the god of the North Wind
And she was cradled by gales,
She raced with young colts on the glittering hills
And walked untrammeled in the open light:
But in her marriage deathless Fate found means
To build a tomb like yours for all her joy.

SCENE V

[*Enter blind* TEIRESIAS, *led by a boy. The opening speeches of* TEIRESIAS *should be in singsong contrast to the realistic lines of* CREON.]

790 TEIRESIAS.   This is the way the blind man comes. Princes, princes,
    Lockstep, two heads lit by the eyes of one.
CREON.   What new thing have you to tell us, old Teiresias?
TEIRESIAS.   I have much to tell you: listen to the prophet, Creon.
CREON.   I am not aware that I have ever failed to listen.
TEIRESIAS.   Then you have done wisely, King, and ruled well.
CREON.   I admit my debt to you. But what have you to say?
TEIRESIAS.   This, Creon: you stand once more on the edge of fate.
CREON.   What do you mean? Your words are a kind of dread.
TEIRESIAS.   Listen, Creon:
800 I was sitting in my chair of augury, at the place
Where the birds gather about me. They were all a-chatter,
As is their habit, when suddenly I heard
A strange note in their jangling, a scream, a
Whirring fury; I knew that they were fighting,
Tearing each other, dying
In a whirlwind of wings clashing. And I was afraid.
I began the rites of burnt-offering at the altar,
But Hephaistos[16] failed me: instead of bright flame,
There was only the sputtering slime of the fat thigh-flesh
810 Melting: the entrails dissolved in gray smoke,
The bare bone burst from the welter. And no blaze!

This was a sign from heaven. My boy described it,
Seeing for me as I see for others.

I tell you, Creon, you yourself have brought
This new calamity upon us. Our hearths and altars
Are stained with the corruption of dogs and carrion birds
That glut themselves on the corpse of Oedipus' son.
The gods are deaf when we pray to them, their fire
Recoils from our offering, their birds of omen
820 Have no cry of comfort, for they are gorged

---

[16] The god of fire.

With the thick blood of the dead.
                                        O my son,
These are no trifles! Think: all men make mistakes,
But a good man yields when he knows his course is wrong,
And repairs the evil. The only crime is pride.

Give in to the dead man, then: do not fight with a corpse—
What glory is it to kill a man who is dead?
Think, I beg you:
It is for your own good that I speak as I do.
You should be able to yield for your own good.

830 CREON.   It seems that prophets have made me their special province.
All my life long
I have been a kind of butt for the dull arrows
Of doddering fortune-tellers!
                                        No, Teiresias:
If your birds—if the great eagles of God himself
Should carry him stinking bit by bit to heaven,
I would not yield. I am not afraid of pollution:
No man can defile the gods.
                                        Do what you will,
Go into business, make money, speculate
In India gold or that synthetic gold from Sardis,[17]
840   Get rich otherwise than by my consent to bury him.
Teiresias, it is a sorry thing when a wise man
Sells his wisdom, lets out his words for hire!

TEIRESIAS.   Ah, Creon! Is there no man left in the world—
CREON.   To do what?—Come, let's have the aphorism!
TEIRESIAS.   No man who knows that wisdom outweighs any wealth?
CREON.   As surely as bribes are baser than any baseness.
TEIRESIAS.   You are sick, Creon! You are deathly sick!
CREON.   As you say: it is not my place to challenge a prophet.
TEIRESIAS.   Yet you have said my prophecy is for sale.
850 CREON.   The generation of prophets has always loved gold.
TEIRESIAS.   The generation of kings has always loved brass.
CREON.   You forget yourself! You are speaking to your King.
TEIRESIAS.   I know it. You are a king because of me.
CREON.   You have a certain skill; but you have sold out.
TEIRESIAS.   King, you will drive me to words that—
CREON.   Say them, say them!
     Only remember: I will not pay you for them.
TEIRESIAS.   No, you will find them too costly.
CREON.   No doubt. Speak:
     Whatever you say, you will not change my will.
TEIRESIAS.   Then take this, and take it to heart!
860   The time is not far off when you shall pay back
Corpse for corpse, flesh of your own flesh.
You have thrust the child of this world into living night,

---

[17] An ancient city in Asia Minor where coins were first minted during the sixth century B.C.

You have kept from the gods below the child that is theirs:
The one in a grave before her death, the other,
Dead, denied the grave. This is your crime:
And the Furies[18] and the dark gods of Hell
Are swift with terrible punishment for you.

Do you want to buy me now, Creon?

                Not many days,
And your house will be full of men and women weeping,
870   And curses will be hurled at you from far
Cities grieving for sons unburied, left to rot
Before the walls of Thebes.

These are my arrows, Creon: they are all for you.

[*To Boy.*] But come, child: lead me home.
Let him waste his fine anger upon younger men.
Maybe he will learn at last
To control a wiser tongue in a better head.

                         [*Exit* TEIRESIAS.]

CHORAGOS.   The old man has gone, King, but his words
   Remain to plague us. I am old, too.
880   But I cannot remember that he was ever false.
CREON.   That is true. . . . It troubles me.
   Oh it is hard to give in! but it is worse
   To risk everything for stubborn pride.
CHORAGOS.   Creon: take my advice.
CREON.   What shall I do?
CHORAGOS.   Go quickly: free Antigonê from her vault
   And build a tomb for the body of Polyneicês.
CREON.   You would have me do this!
CHORAGOS.   Creon, yes!
   And it must be done at once: God moves
890   Swiftly to cancel the folly of stubborn men.
CREON.   It is hard to deny the heart! But I
   Will do it: I will not fight with destiny.
CHORAGOS.   You must go yourself, you cannot leave it to others.
CREON.   I will go.
           —Bring axes, servants:
   Come with me to the tomb. I buried her, I
   Will set her free.
             Oh quickly!
   My mind misgives—
   The laws of the gods are mighty, and a man must serve them
   To the last day of his life!

                         [*Exit* CREON.]

---

[18] Three avenging spirits who pursue those who have offended the gods.

PAEAN[19]

[STROPHE 1]

900 CHORAGOS.   God of many names
CHORUS.   O Iacchos[20]
                                              son
of Kadmeian Sémelê
                    O born of the Thunder!
Guardian of the West
                         Regent
of Eleusis' plain[21]
                    O Prince of maenad[22] Thebes
and the Dragon Field by rippling Ismenós:[23]

[ANTISTROPHE 1]

CHORAGOS.   God of many names
CHORUS.   the flame of torches
    flares on our hills
                    the nymphs of Iacchos
dance at the spring of Castalia:[24]
from the vine-close mountain
                         come ah come in ivy:
910 *Evohé evohé!*[25] sings through the streets of Thebes.

[STROPHE 2]

CHORAGOS.   God of many names
CHORUS.   Iacchos of Thebes
    heavenly Child
                    of Sémelê bride of the Thunderer!
The shadow of plague is upon us:
                                      come
with clement feet
                    oh come from Parnasos
down the long slopes
                    across the lamenting water

[ANTISTROPHE 2]

CHORAGOS.   *Iô*[26] Fire! Chorister of the throbbing stars!
    O purest among the voices of the night!

---

[19] A song of praise, tribute, or prayer to the gods.
[20] Iacchos (more commonly spelled Bacchus) is another name for Dionysos, the god of wine and revelry. Zeus, the god of thunder, was his father while Sémelê, the daughter of Kadmos, was his mother.
[21] The site of the annual "mysteries" during which young Greek men were initiated into the rites of Dionysos.
[22] Maenads are female worshipers of Dionysos.
[23] According to legend, Kadmos sowed dragon's teeth in a field beside the Ismenos River. The crop was a band of fierce warriors who founded Thebes.
[24] The waters of the Castalian spring on Mount Parnassus were used by the Maenads in rites of purification.
[25] This cry of the Maenads means "come forth" or "appear."
[26] *Iô* means "Hail."

Thou son of God, blaze for us!

CHORUS.   Come with choric rapture of circling Maenads
Who cry *Iô Iacche!*

920   *God of many names!*

EXODUS

[*Enter* MESSENGER *from left.*]

MESSENGER.   Men of the line of Kadmos, you who live
Near Amphion's citadel,[27]

I cannot say
Of any condition of human life "This is fixed,
This is clearly good, or bad." Fate raises up,
And Fate casts down the happy and unhappy alike:
No man can foretell his Fate.

Take the case of Creon:
Creon was happy once, as I count happiness:
Victorious in battle, sole governor of the land,
Fortunate father of children nobly born.

930   And now it has all gone from him! Who can say
That a man is still alive when his life's joy fails?
He is a walking dead man. Grant him rich,
Let him live like a king in his great house:
If his pleasure is gone, I would not give
So much as the shadow of smoke for all he owns.

CHORAGOS.   Your words hint at sorrow: what is your news for us?

MESSENGER.   They are dead. The living are guilty of their death.

CHORAGOS.   Who is guilty? Who is dead? Speak!

MESSENGER.   Haimon.
Haimon is dead; and the hand that killed him

940   Is his own hand.

CHORAGOS.   His father's? or his own?

MESSENGER.   His own, driven mad by the murder his father had done.

CHORAGOS.   Teiresias, Teiresias, how clearly you saw it all!

MESSENGER.   This is my news: you must draw what conclusions you can
from it.

CHORAGOS.   But look: Eurydicê, our Queen:
Has she overheard us?

[*Enter* EURYDICÊ *from the palace, center.*]

---

[27] Amphion, the son of Zeus and Antiope, is said to have built the walls of Thebes by playing
music so beautiful that the stones leaped of themselves into place.

EURYDICÊ.   I have heard something, friends:
As I was unlocking the gate of Pallas'[28] shrine
For I needed her help today, I heard a voice
950   Telling of some new sorrow. And I fainted
There at the temple with all my maidens about me.
But speak again: whatever it is, I can bear it:
Grief and I are no strangers.
MESSENGER.   Dearest Lady,
I will tell you plainly all that I have seen.
I shall not try to comfort you: what is the use,
Since comfort could lie only in what is not true?
The truth is always best.
                                        I went with Creon
To the outer plain where Polyneicês was lying,
No friend to pity him, his body shredded by dogs.
960   We made our prayers in that place to Hecatê
And Pluto,[29] that they would be merciful. And we bathed
The corpse with holy water, and we brought
Fresh-broken branches to burn what was left of it,
And upon the urn we heaped up a towering barrow
Of the earth of his own land.
                                        When we were done, we ran
To the vault where Antigonê lay on her couch of stone.
One of the servants had gone ahead,
And while he was yet far off heard a voice
Grieving within the chamber, and he came back
970   And told Creon. And as the King went closer,
The air was full of wailing, the words lost,
And he begged us to make all haste. "Am I a prophet?"
He said, weeping, "And must I walk this road,
The saddest of all that I have gone before?
My son's voice calls me on. Oh quickly, quickly!
Look through the crevice there, and tell me
If it is Haimon, or some deception of the gods!"

We obeyed; and in the cavern's farthest corner
We saw her lying:
980   She had made a noose of her fine linen veil
And hanged herself. Haimon lay beside her,
His arms about her waist, lamenting her,
His love lost under ground, crying out
That his father had stolen her away from him.

When Creon saw him the tears rushed to his eyes
And he called to him: "What have you done, child? Speak to me.
What are you thinking that makes your eyes so strange?

---

[28] Pallas Athene is the goddess of wisdom.
[29] Pluto is the king of the Underworld. Hecatê is the goddess of witchcraft.

O my son, my son, I come to you on my knees!"
But Haimon spat in his face. He said not a word,
Staring—
990   And suddenly drew his sword
And lunged. Creon shrank back, the blade missed; and the boy,
Desperate against himself, drove it half its length
Into his own side, and fell. And as he died
He gathered Antigonê close in his arms again,
Choking, his blood bright red on her white cheek.
And now he lies dead with the dead, and she is his
At last, his bride in the house of the dead.

                            [*Exit* EURYDICÊ *into the palace.*]

CHORAGOS.   She has left us without a word. What can this mean?
MESSENGER.   It troubles me, too; yet she knows what is best,
1000   Her grief is too great for public lamentation,
And doubtless she has gone to her chamber to weep
For her dead son, leading her maidens in his dirge.

                                [*Pause.*]

CHORAGOS.   It may be so: but I fear this deep silence.
MESSENGER.   I will see what she is doing. I will go in.

                        [*Exit* MESSENGER *into the palace.*]

        [*Enter* CREON *with attendants, bearing* HAIMON's *body.*]

CHORAGOS.   But here is the king himself: oh look at him,
Bearing his own damnation in his arms.
CREON.   Nothing you say can touch me any more.
My own blind heart was brought me
From darkness to final darkness. Here you see
1010   The father murdering, the murdered son—
And all my civic wisdom!

Haimon my son, so young, so young to die,
I was the fool, not you; and you died for me.
CHORAGOS.   That is the truth; but you were late in learning it.
CREON.   This truth is hard to bear. Surely a god
Has crushed me beneath the hugest weight of heaven,
And driven me headlong a barbaric way
To trample out the thing I held most dear.

The pains that men will take to come to pain!

                        [*Enter* MESSENGER *from the palace.*]

1020 MESSENGER.   The burden you carry in your hands is heavy,
But it is not all: you will find more in your house.
CREON.   What burden worse than this shall I find there?
MESSENGER.   The Queen is dead.

CREON.   O port of death, deaf world,
  Is there no pity for me? And you, Angel of evil,
  I was dead, and your words are death again.
  Is it true, boy? Can it be true?
  Is my wife dead? Has death bred death?
MESSENGER.   You can see for yourself.

[*The doors are opened and the body of* EURYDICÊ *is disclosed within.*]

1030 CREON.   Oh pity!
  All true, all true, and more than I can bear!
  O my wife, my son!
MESSENGER.   She stood before the altar, and her heart
  Welcomed the knife her own hand guided,
  And a great cry burst from her lips for Megareus[30] dead,
  And for Haimon dead, her sons; and her last breath
  Was a curse for their father, the murderer of her sons.
  And she fell, and the dark flowed in through her closing eyes.
CREON.   O God, I am sick with fear.
1040   Are there no swords here? Has no one a blow for me?
MESSENGER.   Her curse is upon you for the deaths of both.
CREON.   It is right that it should be. I alone am guilty.
  I know it, and I say it. Lead me in,
  Quickly, friends.
  I have neither life nor substance. Lead me in.
CHORAGOS.   You are right, if there can be right in so much wrong.
  The briefest way is best in a world of sorrow.
CREON.   Let it come,
  Let death come quickly, and be kind to me.
1050   I would not ever see the sun again.
CHORAGOS.   All that will come when it will; but we, meanwhile,
  Have much to do. Leave the future to itself.
CREON.   All my heart was in that prayer!
CHORAGOS.   Then do not pray any more: the sky is deaf.
CREON.   Lead me away. I have been rash and foolish.
  I have killed my son and my wife.
  I look for comfort; my comfort lies here dead.
  Whatever my hands have touched has come to nothing.
  Fate has brought all my pride to a thought of dust.

[*As* CREON *is being led into the house, the* CHORAGOS *advances and speaks directly to the audience.*]

1060 CHORAGOS.   There is no happiness where there is no wisdom;
  No wisdom but in submission to the gods.
  Big words are always punished,
  And proud men in old age learn to be wise.

[441 B.C.]

---

30 The son of Eurydicê, killed along with Polyneicês and Eteoclês in the recent battle.

Critical Commentary on *Antigonê*

Antigonê is surely one of the most fascinating of the great Greek tragedies. In part audiences are attracted to the play because of Antigonê's rebellion against the combined forces of tyranny and the subordination of women, but the play is also stimulating because it is packed with conflicts and contrasts. We see youth against age (Antigonê's naïve impetuousness in conflict with Creon's cautious political conservatism); woman against man (Antigonê's physical weakness set against the sheer coercive power of Creon and the guards); religious law against political law (the burial of the dead as commanded by the gods as opposed to the need of the state to withhold honor from traitors); the claims of the dead against the claims of the living (in choosing to bury Polyneicês out of sororal love, Antigonê knowingly neglects her love for her fiancé Haimon); son against father (Haimon versus Creon); sister against sister (Antigonê versus Ismenê); brother against brother (in the battle of Eteoclês and Polyneicês); and citizen against citizen (in the civil war caused by the conflict between the brothers). As this summary indicates, the tragic conflict of wills between Antigonê and Creon grows out of and augments the breakdown in custom and law that is both the precursor and the consequence of civil war.

Many critics view Antigonê as a far more attractive and sympathetic character than Creon. That may be true, but she is also a more formidable and possibly more frightening personality. If in Scene I, we initially sympathize with Antigonê's piety and affection for her dead brothers, we may also be somewhat chilled by her sternness, self-righteousness, and love of death. In summarizing Creon's decree against the burial of Polyneicês, she fails to draw any distinction between the brother who died in defense of the city and the one who died while attacking its walls. The reasons for Creon's decree hold no interest for her, and she immediately goes on to present Ismenê with a stark set of options:

> There it is,
> And now you can prove what you are:
> A true sister, or a traitor to your family.

This is, of course, a classic example of the either/or fallacy in logic, for Ismenê (and Antigonê) have many other options apart from servile acquiescence in, or direct violation of, Creon's decree. Antigonê's unreasoning recognition of only two antithetical courses of conduct should immediately lead us to question the soundness of her judgment. Antigonê's final, frightening words in this first scene are permeated by her increasing hate for Ismenê and her fascination with death:

> ANTIGONÊ. Go away, Ismenê:
> I shall be hating you soon, and the dead will too,
> For your words are hateful. Leave me my foolish plan:
> I am not afraid of the danger; if it means death,
> It will not be the worst of deaths—death without honor.

Despite her chilling preoccupation with death, Antigonê is a fascinating and complex woman. In contrast, Creon first seems pompous and simplistic, an all-too-ordinary human being who is wholly inadequate to the problems about to confront him. To his infinite sorrow, he is about to find out the answer to the fateful question raised by the Choragos immediately before Creon first appears on stage:

In this auspicious dawn of his reign
What are the new complexities
That shifting Fate has woven for him?

Creon speaks pedantically in cliché-ridden prose of the "Ship of State," the "recent storms," and the "merciful wisdom of Heaven." Like many a bureaucrat, he binds himself to inflexible rules and principles, failing to recognize that "new complexities" often require new solutions. And throughout the play he is incapable of imagining any motives for those who defy his decrees except that oldest of motives: that "money talks, and the wisest / Have sometimes been known to count a few coins too many."

These unpleasant initial impressions of Creon intensify as the audience sees his reactions to the sentry's report that the corpse of Polyneicês has been sprinkled with "New dust on the slimy flesh." Instead of calmly contemplating the "new complexities" of the sentry's news, Creon flies into a rage. When the Choragos suggests that perhaps the gods had a hand in this burial, Creon calls the old men of the chorus "doddering wrecks" and scorns their "senile opinion." Instead of thanking the sentry for bringing this report, Creon browbeats him and threatens to put him to torture and a shameful death.

The contrasts between Antigonê and Creon prepare the way for their confrontation in Scene II. Whatever qualms the audience may have about Antigonê's motives and reasoning, viewers cannot help but admire her dignity as she proudly admits that she has violated Creon's law in full knowledge of the consequences. This is the first instance in Western literature of civil disobedience and passive resistance, and Sophocles is quick to develop the puzzling consequences of such action. The only true justification for civil disobedience is the commitment to some higher law, and Antigonê grounds her defense firmly on that principle. The laws of the gods, she says, "were, and shall be, / Operative for ever, beyond man utterly."

Concomitant with a growing pity for Antigonê, the audience may, however, also feel awed by her strength and distanced by her lack of true concern for life and the living. By the end of Scene IV she is addressing her tomb as a "vaulted bride-bed in eternal rock" where she will soon "be with [her] own again." In her farewell to the living, she fails to think of Ismenê, and not once in the play does she mention her fiancé Haimon. In the end she turns to the guards, saying "Come: let us wait no longer" and presumably leads them toward her place of entombment. Although clearly a heroic figure, she also makes the blood run cold.

The last two scenes of the play unfold the terrifying consequences of Creon's perversion of natural law in burying the living and leaving the dead unburied. Creon's confrontation with Teiresias in Scene V provides him with a full and fairly specific warning about the consequences of his willfulness and pride. The surprising thing about this play, however, is that almost as soon as Teiresias has left after delivering his warning, Creon repents and attempts to redress his errors. Unlike the typical tragic hero who grandly remains unbending until the will of the gods crushes down upon him, Creon seems to be a little man, out of his depth in ruling a city, muddling through with bluster and bravado, and finally changing his mind at this first real chance for meditation. Part of his tragedy is that fate gives him no opportunity for repentance. Teiresias has reassured Creon that

> all men make mistakes,
> But a good man yields when he knows his course is wrong,
> And repairs the evil. The only crime is pride.

Yet even after swallowing his pride and doing his best to repair the evil, Creon is destroyed by the unforgiving gods.

What, finally, should the audience make of this play? Whose tragedy is it? Possibly it is the tragedy of Antigonê, whose moral absolutism is sustained at a frightful price. But Antigonê dies midway through the play. Isn't her senseless death just a factor in the gods' punishment of Creon? Just as the altars of Teiresias are polluted by the corrupt flesh of Polyneicês, so too the virginal mind of Antigonê is warped by the thought of that same corrupt flesh. Yet it is Creon's crime that has caused these perversions of nature, for without that crime Antigonê would still be Haimon's loving bride, the future mother of Creon's grandchildren. And so we see that Creon's crimes against the dead cause their own punishment, and Antigonê is but an agent in unfolding will of the gods; *her* corpse is left offstage and largely forgotten while the bodies of Eurydicê and Haimon are tragically displayed, and Creon's agony confronts us.

Is Creon, then, the proper focus of this tragic movement? Perhaps. His household is destroyed and he is left, in the words of the messenger, "a walking dead man." He has lost one son in the war, and his other son and his wife have committed suicide. Indeed, as G. H. Gellie observes, Haimon's death pointedly demonstrates the complete destruction of Creon's family. When Haimon, that most respectful of sons, spits in his own father's face, we see how thoroughly the family has been rent by Creon's folly. And when Haimon turns his sword against himself—perhaps as much in disgust at what he has just done to his father as in grief over the death of Antigonê—we see how much Creon has lost. And yet Creon, too, is unsatisfactory as a tragic hero. He is too coarse and too common to meet the Aristotelian standard of a tragic hero who is more noble than ordinary men.

The play is also, however, part of the great tragedy of Oedipus. Oedipus's crimes of incest and parricide are still corrosively at work in Thebes. Two of the children of the incest, Polyneicês and Eteoclês, have caused the civil war.

Antigonê, the third of these polluted offspring, is the direct agent of the tragedy before us, and both the Chorus and Antigonê recognize the hand of Oedipus in her fate:

> CHORUS.   . . . I cannot tell
> What shape of your father's guilt appears in this.
>
> ANTIGONÊ.   You have touched it at last: that bridal bed
> Unspeakable, horror of son and mother mingling:
> Their crime, infection of all our family!
> O Oedipus, father and brother!

> Your marriage strikes from the grave to murder mine.
> I have been a stranger here in my own land:
> All my life
> The blasphemy of my birth has followed me.

Antigonê and Creon are fascinating dramatic characters, but it is at least plausible that the true tragic hero of the play never even appears on stage.

A Selective Bibliography on *Antigonê*

Benardete, Seth. "A Reading of Sophocles' *Antigonê*." *Interpretation: A Journal of Political Philosophy* 4.3 (1975): 148–96; 5.1 (1975): 1–55; 5.2 (1975): 148–84.

Bowra, C. M. *Sophoclean Tragedy*. Oxford: Clarendon P, 1944.

Ehrenberg, V. *Sophocles and Pericles*. Oxford: Blackwell, 1954.

Field, S. B. "Classic Festival at Siracusa: *Antigonê*." *Drama* 16 (1925): 47–50.

Gellie, G. H. *Sophocles: A Reading*. Carlton, Aus.: Melbourne UP, 1972. 29–52.

Goheen, Robert F. *The Imagery of Sophocles' Antigonê: A Study of Poetic Language and Structure*. Princeton: Princeton UP, 1951.

Hathorn, Richmond Y. "Sophocles' *Antigonê*: Eros in Politics." *Classical Journal* 54 (1958): 109–15.

———. *Tragedy, Myth and Mystery*. Bloomington: U of Indiana P, 1962. 62–78.

Jones, John. *On Aristotle and Greek Tragedy*. London: Chatto & Windus, 1962. 192–214.

Kanzer, M. "The *Oedipus* Trilogy." *Psychoanalytic Quarterly* 21 (1950): 565–69.

Kells, J. H. "Problems of Interpretation in the *Antigonê*." *Bulletin of the Institute for Classical Studies* 10 (1963): 47–64.

Kitto, H. D. F. *Form and Meaning in Drama*. London: Methuen, 1956. 138–78.

———. *Greek Tragedy: A Literary Study* London: Methuen, 1939. 125–30.

Knox, Bernard. *The Heroic Temper*. Berkeley: U of California P, 1964. 62–116.

Lane, Warren J. and Ann M. "The Politics of Antigonê." *Greek Tragedy and Political Theory*. Ed. J. Peter Euben. Berkeley: U of California P, 1986. 162–82.

Levy, C. "Antigonê's Motives: A Suggested Interpretation." *Transactions and Proceedings of the American Philological Association* 94 (1963): 137–44.

Linforth, I. M. "Antigonê and Creon." *University of California Publications in Classical Philology* 15.5 (1961): 183–260.

Margon, J. S. "The Second Burial of Polyneicês." *Classical Journal* 68 (1972): 39–49.

McCall, M. "Divine and Human Action in Sophocles: the Double Burial." *Yale Classical Studies* 22 (1972): 103–17.

Messemer, E. "The Double Burial of Polyneicês." *Classical Journal* 27 (1942): 515–26.

Musurillo, H. "Fire-Walking in Sophocles' *Antigonê* 618–619." *Transactions and Proceedings of the American Philological Association* 94 (1963): 167–75.

Norwood, Gilbert. *Greek Tragedy*. New York: Hill and Wang, 1960. 136–141.

O'Connell, M. "*Antigonê* and the *Oedipus* Plays as Unified." *Classical Bulletin* 44 (Dec. 1967): 22–25.

O'Brien, Joan. *Guide to Sophocles' Antigonê*. Carbondale: Southern Illinois UP, 1978.

Reinhardt, Karl. *Sophocles*. Oxford: Blackwell, 1979. 64–93.

Rockwell, K. "*Antigonê*: The 'Double Burial' Again." *Mnemosyne* 17 (1964): 156–57.

Rose, J. "The Problem of the Second Burial in Sophocles' *Antigonê*." *Classical Journal* 47 (1952): 219–22.

Scodel, Ruth. *Sophocles*. Boston: Twayne, 1984. 43–57.

Seale, David. *Vision and Stagecraft in Sophocles.* London: Croom Helm, 1982. 84–112.

Segal, C. P. *Tragedy and Civilization: An Interpretation of Sophocles.* Cambridge: Harvard UP, 1981.

Steiner, George. *Antigonês.* Oxford: Clarendon P, 1984.

Waldock, A. J. A. *Sophocles the Dramatist.* Cambridge, Eng.: Cambridge UP, 1951.

Winnington-Ingram, R. P. *Sophocles: An Interpretation.* Cambridge, Eng.: Cambridge UP, 1980.

Woodward, Thomas, ed. *Sophocles: A Collection of Critical Essays.* Englewood Cliffs, N.J.: Prentice-Hall, 1966. 60–100.

Sophocles (ca. 496–406 B.C.)
KING OEDIPUS

Translated by William Butler Yeats

PERSONS IN THE PLAY

OEDIPUS, *King of Thebes* TIRESIAS, *a seer*
JOCASTA, *wife of Oedipus* A PRIEST
ANTIGONE, *daughter of Oedipus* MESSENGER
ISMENE, *daughter of Oedipus* A HERDSMAN
CREON, *brother-in-law of Oedipus* CHORUS

SCENE: *The Palace of King* OEDIPUS *at Thebes.*

OEDIPUS. Children, descendants of old Cadmus,[1] why do you come before
me, why do you carry the branches of supplicants, while the city smokes
with incense and murmurs with prayer and lamentation? I would not learn
from any mouth but yours, old man, therefore I question you myself. Do
you know of anything that I can do and have not done? How can I, being
the man I am, being King Oedipus, do other than all I know? I were
indeed hard of heart did I not pity such suppliants.

PRIEST. Oedipus, King of my country, we who stand before your door are of
all ages, some too young to have walked so many miles, some—priests of
10 Zeus such as I—too old. Among us stand the pick of the young men, and
behind in the market-places the people throng, carrying suppliant branches.[2] We all stand here because the city stumbles towards death, hardly
able to raise up its head. A blight has fallen upon the fruitful blossoms of
the land, a blight upon flock and field and upon the bed of marriage—
plague ravages the city. Oedipus, King, not God but foremost of living
men, seeing that when you first came to this town of Thebes you freed us
from that harsh singer, the riddling Sphinx,[3] we beseech you, all we
suppliants, to find some help; whether you find it by your power as a man,
or because, being near the Gods, a God has whispered you. Uplift our
20 State; think upon your fame; your coming brought us luck, be lucky to us
still; remember that it is better to rule over men than over a waste place,
since neither walled town nor ship is anything if it be empty and no man
within it.

---

[1] Cadmus was the legendary founder of ancient Thebes, a city located about 30 miles
northwest of Athens, Greece.
[2] Before praying for help, the Greeks often laid laurel boughs at the temples of the gods.
[3] The Sphinx, a monster half female and half lion, terrorized Thebes by slaying every
traveller who failed to solve her riddle: "What goes on four feet in the morning, two at noon, and
three in the evening?" When Oedipus answered "Man" (who crawls in infancy, walks erect in
maturity, and leans on a cane in senility), the Sphinx leaped in despair from the side of a cliff.

OEDIPUS.   My unhappy children! I know well what need has brought you, what suffering you endure; yet, sufferers though you be, there is not a single one whose suffering is as mine—each mourns himself, but my soul mourns the city, myself, and you. It is not therefore as if you came to arouse a sleeping man. No! Be certain that I have wept many tears and searched hither and thither for some remedy. I have already done the
30   only thing that came into my head for all my search. I have sent the son of Menoeceus, Creon, my own wife's brother, to the Pythian House of Phoebus,[4] to hear if deed or word of mine may yet deliver this town. I am troubled, for he is a long time away—a longer time than should be—but when he comes I shall not be an honest man unless I do whatever the God commands.

PRIEST.   You have spoken at the right time. They have just signalled to us that Creon has arrived.

OEDIPUS.   O King Apollo, may he bring brighter fortune, for his face is shining!

40 PRIEST.   He brings good news, for he is crowned with bay.

OEDIPUS.   We shall know soon. Brother-in-law, Menoeceus' son, what news from the God?

CREON.   Good news; for pain turns to pleasure when we have set the crooked straight.

OEDIPUS.   But what is the oracle?—so far the news is neither good nor bad.

CREON.   If you would hear it with all these about you, I am ready to speak. Or do we go within?

OEDIPUS.   Speak before all. The sorrow I endure is less for my own life than these.

50 CREON.   Then, with your leave, I speak. Our lord Phoebus bids us drive out a defiling thing that has been cherished in this land.

OEDIPUS.   By what purification?[5]

CREON.   King Laius was our King before you came to pilot us.

OEDIPUS.   I know—but not of my own knowledge, for I never saw him.

CREON.   He was killed; and the God now bids us revenge it on his murderers, whoever they be.

OEDIPUS.   Where shall we come upon their track after all these years? Did he meet his death in house or field, at home or in some foreign land?

CREON.   In a foreign land: he was journeying to Delphi.

60 OEDIPUS.   Did no fellow-traveller see the deed? Was there none there who could be questioned?

---

[4] The priests of Phoebus Apollo (the god of the Sun, prophecy, truth, poetry, and music) were reputed to see into the future, though often expressing their knowledge in ambiguous quotations or riddles. Their golden house was called "Pythian" in honor of Apollo's victory over the serpent Python.

[5] In drafting this modernized version of the play, Yeats, who was himself a playwright of considerable reputation, frequently omitted portions of the original text that he found either redundant or dramatically inadvisable. Here, and in subsequent footnotes we have supplied the most significant of the omitted passages using the translation by Richard C. Jebb consulted by Yeats himself. Thus, Jebb's translation continues:

> CREON.   By banishing a man, or by bloodshed in quittance of bloodshed, since it is that blood which brings the tempest on our city.
> OEDIPUS.   And who is the man whose fate he thus reveals?

CREON.   All perished but one man who fled in terror and could tell for certain but one thing of all he had seen.

OEDIPUS.   One thing might be a clue to many things.

CREON.   He said that they were fallen upon by a great troop of robbers.

OEDIPUS.   What robbers would be so daring unless bribed from here?

CREON.   Such things were indeed guessed at, but Laius once dead no avenger arose. We were amid our troubles.

OEDIPUS.   But when royalty has fallen what troubles could have hindered
70   search?

CREON.   The riddling Sphinx put those dark things out of our thoughts—we thought of what had come to our own doors.

OEDIPUS.   But I will start afresh and make the dark things plain. In doing right by Laius I protect myself, for whoever slew Laius might turn a hand against me. Come, my children, rise up from the altar steps; lift up these suppliant boughs and let all the children of Cadmus be called thither that I may search out everything and find for all happiness or misery as God wills.

PRIEST.   May Phoebus, sender of the oracle, come with it and be our saviour
80   and deliverer!

[*The* CHORUS *enter.*]

CHORUS.   What message comes to famous Thebes from the Golden
        House?
What message of disaster from that sweet-throated Zeus?
What monstrous thing our fathers saw do the seasons bring?
Or what that no man ever saw, what new monstrous thing?
Trembling in every limb I raise my loud importunate cry,
And in a sacred terror wait the Delian God's[6] reply.

Apollo chase the God of Death that leads no shouting men,
Bears no rattling shield and yet consumes this form with pain.
90   Famine takes what the plague spares, and all the crops are lost;
No new life fills the empty place—ghost flits after ghost
To that God-trodden western shore, as flit benighted birds.
Sorrow speaks to sorrow, but no comfort finds in words.

Hurry him from the land of Thebes with a fair wind behind
Out on to that formless deep where not a man can find
Hold for an anchor-fluke, for all is world-ending sea;
Master of the thunder-cloud, set the lightning free,
And add the thunder-stone to that and fling them on his head,
For death is all the fashion now, till even Death be dead.

100   We call against the pallid face of this God-hated God
The springing heel of Artemis[7] in the hunting sandal shod,

---

[6] Apollo was supposedly born on Delos, an island about 90 miles east-southeast of Athens.
[7] Artemis (or Diana) was a goddess associated with chastity, hunting, and the moon.

The tousle-headed Maenads,[8] blown torch and drunken sound,
The stately Lysian king[9] himself with golden fillet crowned,
And in his hands the golden bow and the stretched golden string,
And Bacchus' wine-ensanguined face that all the Maenads sing.

OEDIPUS.   You are praying, and it may be that your prayer will be answered;
that if you hear my words and do my bidding you may find help out of all
your trouble. This is my proclamation, children of Cadmus. Whoever
among you knows by what man Laius, son of Labdacus, was killed, must
110   tell all he knows. If he fear for himself and being guilty denounce himself,
he shall be in the less danger, suffering no worse thing than banishment.
If on the other hand there be one that knows that a foreigner did the
deed, let him speak, and I shall give him a reward and my thanks: but if
any man keep silent from fear or to screen a friend, hear all what I will do
to that man. No one in this land shall speak to him, nor offer sacrifice
beside him; but he shall be driven from their homes as if he himself had
done the deed. And in this I am the ally of the Pythian God and of the
murdered man, and I pray that the murderer's life may, should he be so
hidden and screened, drop from him and perish away, whoever he may
120   be, whether he did the deed with others or by himself alone:[10] and on you
I lay it to make—so far as man may—these words good, for my sake, and
for the God's sake, and for the sake of this land. And even if the God had
not spurred us to it, it were a wrong to leave the guilt unpurged, when one
so noble, and he your King, had perished; and all have sinned that could
have searched it out and did not: and now since it is I who hold the power
which he held once, and have his wife for wife—she who would have borne
him heirs had he but lived—I take up this cause even as I would were it
that of my own father. And if there be any who do not obey me in it, I pray
that the Gods send them neither harvest of the earth nor fruit of the
130   womb; but let them be wasted by his plague, or by one more dreadful still.
But may all be blessed for ever who hear my words and do my will!
CHORUS.   We do not know the murderer, and it were indeed more fitting
that Phoebus, who laid the task upon us, should name the man.
OEDIPUS.   No man can make the Gods speak against their will.
CHORUS.   Then I will say what seems the next best thing.
OEDIPUS.   If there is a third course, show it.
CHORUS.   I know that our lord Teiresias is the seer most like to our lord
Phoebus, and through him we may unravel all.
OEDIPUS.   So I was advised by Creon, and twice already have I sent to bring
140   him.
CHORUS.   If we lack his help we have nothing but vague and ancient ru-
mours.
OEDIPUS.   What rumours are they? I would examine every story.
CHORUS.   Certain wayfarers were said to have killed the King.

---

[8] The Maenads were female followers of Bacchus (or Dionysus), the god of wine and revelry.
[9] Apollo.
[10] Jebb's translation continues: "And for myself I pray that if, with my privity, he should
become an inmate of my house, I may suffer the same things which even now I called down upon
others."

OEDIPUS.   I know, I know. But who was there that saw it?

CHORUS.   If there is such a man, and terror can move him, he will not keep silence when they have told him of your curses.

OEDIPUS.   He that such a deed did not terrify will not be terrified because of a word.

150 CHORUS.   But there is one who shall convict him. For the blind prophet comes at last—in whom alone of all men the truth lives.

[Enter TIRESIAS, *led by a boy.]*

OEDIPUS.   Tiresias, mast of all knowledge, whatever may be spoken, whatever is unspeakable, whatever omens of earth and sky reveal, the plague is among us, and from that plague, Great Prophet, protect us and save us. Phoebus in answer to our question says that it will not leave us till we have found the murderers of Laius, and driven them into exile or put them to death. Do you therefore neglect neither the voice of birds, nor any other sort of wisdom, but rescue yourself, rescue the State, rescue me, rescue all that are defiled by the deed. For we are in your hands, and what greater
160   task falls to a man than to help other men with all he knows and has?

TIRESIAS.   Aye, and what worse task than to be wise and suffer for it? I know this well; it slipped out of mind, or I would never have come.

OEDIPUS.   What now?

TIRESIAS.   Let me go home. You will bear your burden to the end more easily, and I bear mine—if you but give me leave for that.

OEDIPUS.   Your words are strange and unkind to the State that bred you.

TIRESIAS.   I see that you, on your part, keep your lips tight shut, and therefore I have shut mine that I may come to no misfortune.

OEDIPUS.   For God's love do not turn away—if you have knowledge. We
170   suppliants implore you on our knees.

TIRESIAS.   You are fools—I will bring misfortune neither upon you nor upon myself.

OEDIPUS.   What is this? You know all and will say nothing? You are minded to betray me and Thebes?

TIRESIAS.   Why do you ask these things? You will not learn them from me.

OEDIPUS.   What! Basest of the base! You would enrage the very stones. Will you never speak out? Cannot anything touch you?

TIRESIAS.   The future will come of itself though I keep silent.

OEDIPUS.   Then seeing that come it must, you had best speak out.

180 TIRESIAS.   I will speak no further. Rage if you have a mind to; bring out all the fierceness that is in your heart.

OEDIPUS.   That will I. I will not spare to speak my thoughts. Listen to what I have to say. It seems to me that you have helped to plot the deed; and, short of doing it with your own hands, have done the deed yourself. Had you eyesight I would declare that you alone had done it.

TIRESIAS.   So that is what you say? I charge you to obey the decree that you yourself have made, and from this day out to speak neither to these nor to me. You are the defiler of this land.

OEDIPUS.   So brazen in your impudence? How do you hope to escape pun-
190   ishment?

TIRESIAS.   I have escaped; my strength is in my truth.

OEDIPUS.   Who taught you this? You never got it by your art.

TIRESIAS.   You, because you have spurred me to speech against my will.

OEDIPUS.   What speech? Speak it again that I may learn it better.

TIRESIAS.   You are but tempting me—you understood me well enough.

OEDIPUS.   No; not so that I can say I know it; speak it again.

TIRESIAS.   I say that you are yourself the murderer that you seek.

OEDIPUS.   You shall rue it for having spoken twice such outrageous words.

TIRESIAS.   Would you that I say more that you may be still angrier?

200 OEDIPUS.   Say what you will. I will not let it move me.

TIRESIAS.   I say that you are living with your next of kin in unimagined shame.

OEDIPUS.   Do you think you can say such things and never smart for it?

TIRESIAS.   Yes, if there be strength in truth.

OEDIPUS.   There is; yes—for everyone but you. But not for you that are maimed in ear and in eye and in wit.

TIRESIAS.   You are but a poor wretch flinging taunts that in a little while everyone shall fling at you.

OEDIPUS.   Night, endless night has covered you up so that you can neither
210 hurt me nor any man that looks upon the sun.

TIRESIAS.   Your doom is not to fall by me. Apollo is enough: it is his business to work out your doom.

OEDIPUS.   Was it Creon that planned this or you yourself?

TIRESIAS.   Creon is not your enemy; you are your own enemy.

OEDIPUS.   Power, ability, position, you bear all burdens, and yet what envy you create! Great must that envy be if envy of my power in this town—a power put into my hands unsought—has made trusty Creon, my old friend Creon, secretly long to take that power from me; if he has suborned this scheming juggler, this quack and trickster, this man with eyes for his gains
220 and blindness in his art. Come, come, where did you prove yourself a seer? Why did you say nothing to set the townsmen free when the riddling Sphinx was here? Yet that riddle was not for the first-comer to read; it needed the skill of a seer. And none such had you! Neither found by help of birds, nor straight from any God. No, I came; I silenced her, I the ignorant Oedipus, it was I that found the answer in my mother-wit, untaught by any birds. And it is I that you would pluck out of my place, thinking to stand close to Creon's throne. But you and the plotter of all this shall mourn despite your zeal to purge the land. Were you not an old man, you had already learnt how bold you are and learnt it to your cost.

230 CHORUS.   Both this man's words and yours, Oedipus, have been said in anger. Such words cannot help us here, nor any but those that teach us to obey the oracle.

TIRESIAS.   King though you are, the right to answer when attacked belongs to both alike. I am not subject to you, but to Loxias;[11] and therefore I shall never be Creon's subject. And I tell you, since you have taunted me with blindness, that though you have your sight, you cannot see in what misery you stand, nor where you are living, nor with whom, unknowing what you do—for you do not know the stock you come of—you have been your own kin's enemy be they living or be they dead. And one day a mother's curse

---

[11] Another name for Apollo.

240   and father's curse alike shall drive you from this land in dreadful haste and darkness upon those eyes.[12] Therefore, heap your scorn on Creon and on my message if you have a mind to; for no one of living men shall be crushed as you shall be crushed.

OEDIPUS.   Begone this instant! Away, away! Get you from these doors!

TIRESIAS.   I had never come but that you sent for me.

OEDIPUS.   I did not know you were mad.

TIRESIAS.   I may seem mad to you, but your parents thought me sane.

OEDIPUS.   My parents! Stop! Who was my father?

TIRESIAS.   This day shall you know your birth; and it will ruin you.

250 OEDIPUS.   What dark words you always speak!

TIRESIAS.   But are you not most skilful in the unravelling of dark words?

OEDIPUS.   You mock me for that which made me great?

TIRESIAS.   It was that fortune that undid you.

OEDIPUS.   What do I care? For I delivered all this town.

TIRESIAS.   Then I will go: boy, lead me out of this.

OEDIPUS.   Yes, let him lead you. You take vexation with you.

TIRESIAS.   I will go: but first I will do my errand. For frown though you may you cannot destroy me. The man for whom you look, the man you have been threatening in all the proclamations about the death of Laius, the

260   man is here. He seems, so far as looks go, an alien; yet he shall be found a native Theban and shall nowise be glad of that fortune. A blind man, though now he has his sight; a beggar, though now he is most rich; he shall go forth feeling the ground before him with his stick;[13] so you go in and think on that, and if you find I am in fault say that I have no skill in prophecy.

*[*TIRESIAS *is led out by the boy.* OEDIPUS *enters the palace.]*

CHORUS.   The Delphian rock has spoken out, now must a wicked mind,
Planner of things I dare not speak and of this bloody wrack,
Pray for feet that are as fast as the four hoofs of the wind:
Cloudy Parnassus[14] and the Fates thunder at his back.

270   That sacred crossing-place of lines upon Parnassus' head,
Lines that have run through North and South, and run through West and East,
That navel of the world[15] bids all men search the mountain wood,
The solitary cavern, till they have found that infamous beast.

*[*CREON *enters from the house.]*

---

[12] Jebb's translation continues: "And what place shall not be harbour to thy shriek, what of all Cithaeron shall not ring with it soon when thou hast learnt the meaning of the nuptials in which, within that house, thou didst find a fatal haven, after a voyage so fair? And a throng of other ills thou guessest not, which shall make thee level with thy true self and with thine own brood."

[13] Jebb's translation continues: "And he shall be found at once brother and father of the children with whom he consorts; son and husband of the woman who bore him; heir to his father's bed, shedder of his father's blood."

[14] A mountain near Delphi, sacred to Apollo; hence, through metonymy, another name for Apollo himself.

[15] The "navel of the world" and the "sacred crossing place of lines" is Delphi.

CREON.   Fellow-citizens, having heard that King Oedipus accuses me of
dreadful things, I come in my indignation. Does he think that he has
suffered wrong from me in these present troubles, or anything that could
lead to wrong, whether in word or deed? How can I live under blame like
that? What life would be worth having if by you here, and by my nearest
280   friends, called a traitor through the town?
CHORUS.   He said it in anger, and not from his heart out.
CREON.   He said it was I put up the seer to speak those falsehoods.
CHORUS.   Such things were said.
CREON.   And had he his right mind saying it?
CHORUS.   I do not know—I do not know what my masters do.

[OEDIPUS *enters.*]

OEDIPUS.   What brought you here? Have you a face so brazen that you come
to my house—you, the proved assassin of its master—the certain robber of
my crown? Come, tell me in the face of the Gods what cowardice, or folly,
did you discover in me that you plotted this? Did you think that I would
290   not see what you were at till you had crept upon me, or seeing it would not
ward it off? What madness to seek a throne, having neither friends nor
followers!
CREON.   Now, listen, hear my answer, and then you may with knowledge
judge between us.
OEDIPUS.   You are plausible, but waste words now that I know you.
CREON.   Hear what I have to say. I can explain it all.
OEDIPUS.   One thing you will not explain away—that you are my enemy.
CREON.   You are a fool to imagine that senseless stubbornness sits well upon
you.
300 OEDIPUS.   And you to imagine that you can wrong a kinsman and escape the
penalty.
CREON.   That is justly said, I grant you; but what is this wrong that you
complain of?
OEDIPUS.   Did you advise, or not, that I should send for that notorious
prophet?
CREON.   And I am of the same mind still.
OEDIPUS.   How long is it, then, since Laius—
CREON.   What, what about him?
OEDIPUS.   Since Laius was killed by an unknown hand?
310 CREON.   That was many years ago.
OEDIPUS.   Was this prophet at his trade in those days?
CREON.   Yes; skilled as now and in equal honour.
OEDIPUS.   Did he ever speak of me?
CREON.   Never certainly when I was within earshot.
OEDIPUS.   And did you enquire into the murder?
CREON.   We did enquire but learnt nothing.
OEDIPUS.   And why did he not tell out his story then?
CREON.   I do not know. When I know nothing I say nothing.
OEDIPUS.   This much at least you know and can say out.
320 CREON.   What is that? If I know it I will say it.
OEDIPUS.   That if he had not consulted you he would never have said that it
was I who killed Laius.

CREON. You know best what he said; but now, question for question.

OEDIPUS. Question your fill—I cannot be proved guilty of that blood.

CREON. Answer me then. Are you not married to my sister?

OEDIPUS. That cannot be denied.

CREON. And do you not rule as she does? And with a like power?

OEDIPUS. I give her all she asks for.

CREON. And am not I the equal of you both?

330 OEDIPUS. Yes: and that is why you are so false a friend.

CREON. Not so; reason this out as I reason it, and first weigh this: who would prefer to lie awake amid terrors rather than to sleep in peace, granting that his power is equal in both cases? Neither I nor any sober-minded man. You give me what I ask and let me do what I want, but were I King I would have to do things I did not want to do. Is not influence and no trouble with it better than any throne, am I such a fool as to hunger after unprofitable honours? Now all are glad to see me, every one wishes me well, all that want a favour from you ask speech of me—finding in that their hope. Why should I give up these things and take those? No wise
340 mind is treacherous. I am no contriver of plots, and if another took to them he would not come to me for help. And in proof of this go to the Pythian Oracle, and ask if I have truly told what the Gods said: and after that, if you have found that I have plotted with the Soothsayer, take me and kill me; not by the sentence of one mouth only—but of two mouths, yours and my own. But do not condemn me in a corner, upon some fancy and without proof. What right have you to declare a good man bad or a bad good? It is as bad a thing to cast off a true friend as it is for a man to cast away his own life—but you will learn these things with certainty when the time comes; for time alone shows a just man; though a day can show
350 a knave.

CHORUS. King! He has spoken well, he gives himself time to think; a headlong talker does not know what he is saying.

OEDIPUS. The plotter is at his work, and I must counterplot headlong, or he will get his ends and I miss mine.

CREON. What will you do then? Drive me from the land?

OEDIPUS. Not so; I do not desire your banishment—but your death.

CREON. You are not sane.

OEDIPUS. I am sane at least in my own interest.

CREON. You should be in mine also.

360 OEDIPUS. No, for you are false.

CREON. But if you understand nothing?

OEDIPUS. Yet I must rule.

CREON. Not if you rule badly.

OEDIPUS. Hear him, O Thebes!

CREON. Thebes is for me also, not for you alone.

CHORUS. Cease, princes: I see Jocasta coming out of the house; she comes just in time to quench the quarrel.

[JOCASTA *enters.*]

JOCASTA. Unhappy men! Why have you made this crazy uproar? Are you not ashamed to quarrel about your own affairs when the whole country is in

370 trouble? Go back into the palace, Oedipus, and you, Creon, to your own house. Stop making all this noise about some petty thing.

CREON. Your husband is about to kill me—or to drive me from the land of my fathers.

OEDIPUS. Yes: for I have convicted him of treachery against me.

CREON. Now may I perish accursed if I have done such a thing!

JOCASTA. For God's love believe it, Oedipus. First, for the sake of his oath, and then for my sake, and for the sake of these people here.

CHORUS [*all*]. King, do what she asks.

OEDIPUS. What would you have me do?

380 CHORUS. Not to make a dishonourable charge, with no more evidence than rumour, against a friend who has bound himself with an oath.

OEDIPUS. Do you desire my exile or my death?

CHORUS. No, by Helios,[16] by the first of all the Gods, may I die abandoned by Heaven and earth if I have that thought! What breaks my heart is that our public griefs should be increased by your quarrels.

OEDIPUS. Then let him go, though I am doomed thereby to death or to be thrust dishonoured from the land; it is your lips, not his, that move me to compassion; wherever he goes my hatred follows him.

CREON. You are as sullen in yielding as you were vehement in anger, but

390 such natures are their own heaviest burden.

OEDIPUS. Why will you not leave me in peace and begone?

CREON. I will go away; what is your hatred to me? In the eyes of all here I am a just man.

[*He goes.*]

CHORUS. Lady, why do you not take your man in to the house?

JOCASTA. I will do so when I have learned what has happened.

CHORUS. The half of it was blind suspicion bred of talk; the rest the wounds left by injustice.

JOCASTA. It was on both sides?

CHORUS. Yes.

400 JOCASTA. What was it?

CHORUS. Our land is vexed enough. Let the thing alone now that it is over.

[*Exit leader of Chorus.*]

JOCASTA. In the name of the Gods, King, what put you in this anger?

OEDIPUS. I will tell you; for I honour you more than these men do. The cause is Creon and his plots against me.

JOCASTA. Speak on, if you can tell clearly how this quarrel arose.

OEDIPUS. He says that I am guilty of the blood of Laius.

JOCASTA. On his own knowledge, or on hearsay?

OEDIPUS. He has made a rascal of a seer his mouthpiece.

JOCASTA. Do not fear that there is truth in what he says. Listen to me, and

410 learn to your comfort that nothing born of woman can know what is to come. I will give you proof of that. An oracle came to Laius once, I will not say from Phoebus, but from his ministers, that he was doomed to die by

---

[16] Apollo.

the hand of his own child sprung from him and me. When his child was but three days old, Laius bound its feet together and had it thrown by sure hands upon a trackless mountain; and when Laius was murdered at the place where three highways meet, it was, or so at least the rumour says, by foreign robbers. So Apollo did not bring it about that the child should kill its father, nor did Laius die in the dreadful way he feared by his child's hand. Yet that was how the message of the seers mapped out the future.

420 Pay no attention to such things. What the God would show he will need no help to show it, but bring it to light himself.

OEDIPUS.   What restlessness of soul, lady, has come upon me since I heard you speak, what a tumult of the mind!

JOCASTA.   What is this new anxiety? What has startled you?

OEDIPUS.   You said that Laius was killed where three highways meet.

JOCASTA.   Yes: that was the story.

OEDIPUS.   And where is the place?

JOCASTA.   In Phocis where the road divides branching off to Delphi and to Daulia.

430 OEDIPUS.   And when did it happen? How many years ago?

JOCASTA.   News was published in this town just before you came into power.

OEDIPUS.   O Zeus! What have you planned to do unto me?

JOCASTA.   He was tall; the silver had just come into his hair; and in shape not greatly unlike to you.

OEDIPUS.   Unhappy that I am! It seems that I have laid a dreadful curse upon myself, and did not know it.

JOCASTA.   What do you say? I tremble when I look on you, my King.

OEDIPUS.   And I have a misgiving that the seer can see indeed. But I will know it all more clearly, if you tell me one thing more.

440 JOCASTA.   Indeed, though I tremble I will answer whatever you ask.

OEDIPUS.   Had he but a small troop with him; or did he travel like a great man with many followers?

JOCASTA.   There were but five in all—one of them a herald; and there was one carriage with Laius in it.

OEDIPUS.   Alas! It is now clear indeed. Who was it brought the news, lady?

JOCASTA.   A servant—the one survivor.

OEDIPUS.   Is he by chance in the house now?

JOCASTA.   No; for when he found you reigning instead of Laius he besought me, his hand clasped in mine, to send him to the fields among the cattle

450 that he might be far from the sight of this town; and I sent him. He was a worthy man for a slave and might have asked a bigger thing.

OEDIPUS.   I would have him return to us without delay.

JOCASTA.   Oedipus, it is easy. But why do you ask this?

OEDIPUS.   I fear that I have said too much, and therefore I would question him.

JOCASTA.   He shall come, but I too have a right to know what lies so heavy upon your heart, my King.

OEDIPUS.   Yes: and it shall not be kept from you now that my fear has grown so heavy. Nobody is more to me than you, nobody has the same right to

460 learn my good or evil luck. My father was Polybus of Corinth, my mother the Dorian Merope, and I was held the foremost man in all that town until a thing happened—a thing to startle a man, though not to make him

angry as it made me. We were sitting at the table, and a man who had drunk too much cried out that I was not my father's son—and I, though angry, restrained my anger for that day; but the next day went to my father and my mother and questioned them. They were indignant at the taunt and that comforted me—and yet the man's words rankled, for they had spread a rumour through the town. Without consulting my father or my mother I went to Delphi, but Phoebus told me nothing of the thing for

470 which I came, but much of other things—things of sorrow and of terror: that I should live in incest with my mother, and beget a brood that men would shudder to look upon; that I should be my father's murderer. Hearing those words I fled out of Corinth, and from that day have but known where it lies when I have found its direction by the stars. I sought where I might escape those infamous things—the doom that was laid upon me. I came in my flight to that very spot where you tell me this king perished. Now, lady, I will tell you the truth. When I had come close up to those three roads, I came upon a herald, and a man like him you have described seated in a carriage. The man who held the reins and the old

480 man himself would not give me room, but thought to force me from the path, and I struck the driver in my anger. The old man, seeing what I had done, waited till I was passing him and then struck me upon the head. I paid him back in full, for I knocked him out of the carriage with a blow of my stick. He rolled on his back, and after that I killed them all. If this stranger were indeed Laius, is there a more miserable man in the world than the man before you? Is there a man more hated of Heaven? No stranger, no citizen, may receive him into his house, not a soul may speak to him, and no mouth but my own mouth has laid this curse upon me. Am I not wretched? May I be swept from this world before I have endured this

490 doom!

CHORUS. These things, O King, fill us with terror; yet hope till you speak with him that saw the deed, and have learnt all.

OEDIPUS. Till I have learnt all, I may hope. I await the man that is coming from the pastures.

JOCASTA. What is it that you hope to learn?

OEDIPUS. I will tell you. If his tale agrees with yours, then I am clear.

JOCASTA. What tale of mine?

OEDIPUS. He told you that Laius met his death from robbers; if he keeps to that tale now and speaks of several slayers, I am not the slayer. But if he

500 says one lonely wayfarer, then beyond a doubt the scale dips to me.

JOCASTA. Be certain of this much at least, his first tale was of robbers. He cannot revoke that tale—the city heard it and not I alone. Yet, if he should somewhat change his story, King, at least he cannot make the murder of Laius square with prophecy; for Loxias plainly said of Laius that he would die by the hand of my child. That poor innocent did not kill him, for it died before him. Therefore from this out I would not, for all divination can do, so much as look to my right hand or to my left hand, or fear at all.

OEDIPUS. You have judged well; and yet for all that, send and bring this peasant to me.

510 JOCASTA. I will send without delay. I will do all that you would have of me—but let us come in to the house.

[They go in to the house.]

CHORUS. For this one thing above all I would be praised as a man,
That in my words and my deeds I have kept those laws in mind
Olympian Zeus, and that high clear Empyrean,[17]
Fashioned, and not some man or people of mankind,
Even those sacred laws nor age nor sleep can bind.

A man becomes a tyrant out of insolence,
He climbs and climbs, until all people call him great,
He seems upon the summit, and God flings him thence;
520 Yet an ambitious man may lift up a whole State,
And in his death be blessed, in his life fortunate.

And all men honour such; but should a man forget
The holy images, the Delphian Sibyl's trance,[18]
And the world's navel-stone, and not be punished for it
And seem most fortunate, or even blessed perchance,
Why should we honour the Gods, or join the sacred dance?

[JOCASTA enters from the palace.]

JOCASTA. It has come into my head, citizens of Thebes, to visit every altar of
the Gods, a wreath in my hand and a dish of incense. For all manner of
alarms trouble the soul of Oedipus, who instead of weighing new oracles
530 by old, like a man of sense, is at the mercy of every mouth that speaks
terror. Seeing that my words are nothing to him, I cry to you, Lysian
Apollo, whose altar is the first I meet: I come, a suppliant, bearing symbols
of prayer; O, make us clean, for now we are all afraid, seeing him afraid,
even as they who see the helmsman afraid.

[Enter MESSENGER.]

MESSENGER. May I learn from you, strangers, where is the home of King
Oedipus? Or better still, tell me where he himself is, if you know.
CHORUS. This is his house, and he himself, stranger, is within it, and this
lady is the mother of his children.
MESSENGER. Then I call a blessing upon her, seeing what man she has mar-
540 ried.
JOCASTA. May God reward those words with a like blessing, stranger! But
what have you come to seek or to tell?
MESSENGER. Good news for your house, lady, and for your husband.
JOCASTA. What news? From whence have you come?
MESSENGER. From Corinth, and you will rejoice at the message I am about to
give you; yet, maybe, it will grieve you.
JOCASTA. What is it? How can it have this double power?

---

[17] Zeus, the most powerful of the Greek gods, was said to live on Mt. Olympus, the highest
mountain in Greece. The Empyrean is the highest heaven.
[18] The Sibyl, a female soothsayer, fell into a trance while telling fortunes.

MESSENGER. The people of Corinth, they say, will take him for king.

JOCASTA. How then? Is old Polybus no longer on the throne?

550 MESSENGER. No. He is in his tomb.

JOCASTA. What do you say? Is Polybus dead, old man?

MESSENGER. May I drop dead if it is not the truth.

JOCASTA. Away! Hurry to your master with this news. O oracle of the Gods, where are you now? This is the man whom Oedipus feared and shunned lest he should murder him, and now this man has died a natural death, and not by the hand of Oedipus.

[*Enter* OEDIPUS.]

OEDIPUS. Jocasta, dearest wife, why have you called me from the house?

JOCASTA. Listen to this man, and judge to what the oracles of the Gods have come.

560 OEDIPUS. And he—who may he be? And what news has he?

JOCASTA. He has come from Corinth to tell you that your father, Polybus, is dead.

OEDIPUS. How, stranger? Let me have it from your own mouth.

MESSENGER. If I am to tell the story, the first thing is that he is dead and gone.

OEDIPUS. By some sickness or by treachery?

MESSENGER. A little thing can bring the aged to their rest.

OEDIPUS. Ah! He died, it seems, from sickness?

MESSENGER. Yes; and of old age.

570 OEDIPUS. Alas! Alas! Why, indeed, my wife, should one look to that Pythian seer, or to the birds that scream above our heads? For they would have it that I was doomed to kill my father. And now he is dead—hid already beneath the earth. And here am I—who had no part in it, unless indeed he died from longing for me. If that were so, I may have caused his death; but Polybus has carried the oracles with him into Hades—the oracles as men have understood them—and they are worth nothing.

JOCASTA. Did I not tell you so, long since?

OEDIPUS. You did, but fear misled me.

JOCASTA. Put this trouble from you.[19]

580 OEDIPUS. Those bold words would sound better, were not my mother living. But as it is—I have some grounds for fear; yet you have said well.

JOCASTA. Yet your father's death is a sign that all is well.

OEDIPUS. I know that: but I fear because of her who lives.

MESSENGER. Who is this woman who makes you afraid?

OEDIPUS. Merope, old man, the wife of Polybus.

MESSENGER. What is there in her to make you afraid?

OEDIPUS. A dreadful oracle sent from Heaven, stranger.

MESSENGER. Is it a secret, or can you speak it out?

---

[19] Jebb's translation continues:

OEDIPUS. But surely I must needs fear my mother's bed?

JOCASTA. Nay, what should mortal fear, for whom the decrees of fortune are supreme, and who hath clear foresight of nothing? 'Tis best to live at random, as one may. But fear not thou touching wedlock with thy mother. Many men ere now have so fared in dreams also: but he to whom these things are as nought bears his life most easily.

OEDIPUS. Loxias said that I was doomed to marry my own mother, and to
590   shed my father's blood. For that reason I fled from my house in Corinth;
   and I did right, though there is great comfort in familiar faces.

MESSENGER. Was it indeed for that reason that you went into exile?

OEDIPUS. I did not wish, old man, to shed my father's blood.

MESSENGER. King, have I not freed you from that fear?

OEDIPUS. You shall be fittingly rewarded.

MESSENGER. Indeed, to tell the truth, it was for that I came; to bring you
   home and be the better for it——

OEDIPUS. No! I will never go to my parents' home.

MESSENGER. Oh, my son, it is plain enough, you do not know what you do.

600 OEDIPUS. How, old man? For God's love, tell me.

MESSENGER. If for these reasons you shrink from going home.

OEDIPUS. I am afraid lest Phoebus has spoken true.

MESSENGER. You are afraid of being made guilty through Merope?

OEDIPUS. That is my constant fear.

MESSENGER. A vain fear.

OEDIPUS. How so, if I was born of that father and mother?

MESSENGER. Because they were nothing to you in blood.

OEDIPUS. What do you say? Was Polybus not my father?

MESSENGER. No more nor less than myself.

610 OEDIPUS. How can my father be no more to me than you who are nothing
   to me?

MESSENGER. He did not beget you any more than I.

OEDIPUS. No? Then why did he call me his son?

MESSENGER. He took you as a gift from these hands of mine.

OEDIPUS. How could he love so dearly what came from another's hands?

MESSENGER. He had been childless.

OEDIPUS. If I am not your son, where did you get me?

MESSENGER. In a wooded valley of Cithaeron.

OEDIPUS. What brought you wandering there?

620 MESSENGER. I was in charge of mountain sheep.

OEDIPUS. A shepherd—a wandering, hired man.

MESSENGER. A hired man who came just in time.

OEDIPUS. Just in time—had it come to that?

MESSENGER. Have not the cords left their marks upon your ankles?

OEDIPUS. Yes, that is an old trouble.

MESSENGER. I took your feet out of the spancel.[20]

OEDIPUS. I have had those marks from the cradle.

MESSENGER. They have given you the name you bear.[21]

OEDIPUS. Tell me, for God's sake, was that deed my mother's or my father's?

630 MESSENGER. I do not know—he who gave you to me knows more of that than
   I.

OEDIPUS. What? You had me from another? You did not chance on me
   yourself?

MESSENGER. No. Another shepherd gave you to me.

---

[20] A noose for tethering animals.
[21] Oedipus means "swollen-feet."

OEDIPUS.   Who was he? Can you tell me who he was?

MESSENGER.   I think that he was said to be of Laius' household.

OEDIPUS.   The king who ruled this country long ago?

MESSENGER.   The same—the man was herdsman in his service.

OEDIPUS.   Is he alive, that I might speak with him?

640 MESSENGER.   You people of this country should know that.

OEDIPUS.   Is there any one here present who knows the herd he speaks of?
Any one who has seen him in the town pastures? The hour has come when
all must be made clear.

CHORUS.   I think he is the very herd you sent for but now; Jocasta can tell you
better than I.

JOCASTA.   Why ask about that man? Why think about him? Why waste a
thought on what this man has said? What he has said is of no account.

OEDIPUS.   What, with a clue like that in my hands and fail to find out my
birth?

650 JOCASTA.   For God's sake, if you set any value upon your life, give up this
search—my misery is enough.

OEDIPUS.   Though I be proved the son of a slave, yes, even of three generations of slaves, you cannot be made base-born.

JOCASTA.   Yet, hear me, I implore you. Give up this search.

OEDIPUS.   I will not hear of anything but searching the whole thing out.

JOCASTA.   I am only thinking of your good—I have advised you for the best.

OEDIPUS.   Your advice makes me impatient.

JOCASTA.   May you never come to know who you are, unhappy man!

OEDIPUS.   Go, some one, bring the herdsman here—and let that woman
660   glory in her noble blood.

JOCASTA.   Alas, alas, miserable man! Miserable! That is all that I can call you
now or for ever.

[She goes out.]

CHORUS.   Why has the lady gone, Oedipus, in such a transport of despair?
Out of this silence will burst a storm of sorrows.

OEDIPUS.   Let come what will. However lowly my origin I will discover it.
That women, with all a woman's pride, grows red with shame at my base
birth. I think myself the child of Good Luck, and that the years are my
foster-brothers. Sometimes they have set me up, and sometimes thrown
me down, but he that has Good Luck for mother can suffer no dishonour.

670   That is my origin, nothing can change it, so why should I renounce this
search into my birth?

CHORUS.   Oedipus' nurse, mountain of many a hidden glen,
Be honoured among men;
A famous man, deep-thoughted, and his body strong;
Be honoured in dance and song.
Who met in the hidden glen? Who let his fancy run
Upon nymph of Helicon?[22]

---

[22] The Chorus speculates that perhaps Oedipus's mother was a Greek nymph seduced by
Pan (a playful god of the fields and forests), or Apollo, or Dionysus (the god of wine and revelry,
worshipped by his female followers, the Bacchantes).

Lord Pan or Lord Apollo or the mountain Lord
By the Bacchantes adored?

680 OEDIPUS.   If I, who have never met the man, may venture to say so, I think that
the herdsman we await approaches; his venerable age matches with this
stranger's, and I recognize as servants of mine those who bring him. But
you, if you have seen the man before, will know the man better than I.

CHORUS.   Yes, I know the man who is coming; he was indeed in Laius'
service, and is still the most trusted of the herdsmen.

OEDIPUS.   I ask you first, Corinthian stranger, is this the man you mean?

MESSENGER.   He is the very man.

OEDIPUS.   Look at me, old man! Answer my questions. Were you once in
Laius' service?

690 HERDSMAN.   I was: not a bought slave, but reared up in the house.

OEDIPUS.   What was your work—your manner of life?

HERDSMAN.   For the best part of my life I have tended flocks.

OEDIPUS.   Where, mainly?

HERDSMAN.   Cithaeron or its neighbourhood.

OEDIPUS.   Do you remember meeting with this man there?

HERDSMAN.   What man do you mean?

OEDIPUS.   This man. Did you ever meet him?

HERDSMAN.   I cannot recall him to mind.

MESSENGER.   No wonder in that, master; but I will bring back his memory. He
700 and I lived side by side upon Cithaeron. I had but one flock and he had
two. Three full half-years we lived there, from spring to autumn, and every
winter I drove my flock to my own fold, while he drove his to the fold of
Laius. Is that right? Was it not so?

HERDSMAN.   True enough; though it was long ago.

MESSENGER.   Come, tell me now—do you remember giving me a boy to rear
as my own foster-son?

HERDSMAN.   What are you saying? Why do you ask me that?

MESSENGER.   Look at that man, my friend, he is the child you gave me.

HERDSMAN.   A plague upon you! Cannot you hold your tongue?

710 OEDIPUS.   Do not blame him, old man; your own words are more blameable.

HERDSMAN.   And how have I offended, master?

OEDIPUS.   In not telling of that boy he asks of.

HERDSMAN.   He speaks from ignorance, and does not know what he is saying.

OEDIPUS.   If you will not speak with a good grace you shall be made to speak.

HERDSMAN.   Do not hurt me for the love of God, I am an old man.

OEDIPUS.   Some one there, tie his hands behind his back.

HERDSMAN.   Alas! Wherefore! What more would you learn?

OEDIPUS.   Did you give this man the child he speaks of?

HERDSMAN.   I did: would I had died that day!

720 OEDIPUS.   Well, you may come to that unless you speak the truth.

HERDSMAN.   Much more am I lost if I speak it.

OEDIPUS.   What! Would the fellow make more delay?

HERDSMAN.   No, no. I said before that I gave it to him.

OEDIPUS.   Where did you come by it? Your own child, or another?

HERDSMAN.   It was not my own child—I had it from another.

OEDIPUS.   From any of those here? From what house?

HERDSMAN.   Do not ask any more, master; for the love of God do not ask.

OEDIPUS.   You are lost if I have to question you again.

HERDSMAN.   It was a child from the house of Laius.

730 OEDIPUS.   A slave? Or one of his own race?

HERDSMAN.   Alas! I am on the edge of dreadful words.

OEDIPUS.   And I of hearing: yet hear I must.

HERDSMAN.   It was said to have been his own child. But your lady within can tell you of these things best.

OEDIPUS.   How? It was she who gave it to you?

HERDSMAN.   Yes, King.

OEDIPUS.   To what end?

HERDSMAN.   That I should make away with it.

OEDIPUS.   Her own child?

740 HERDSMAN.   Yes: from fear of evil prophecies.

OEDIPUS.   What prophecies?

HERDSMAN.   That he should kill his father.

OEDIPUS.   Why, then did you give him up to this old man?

HERDSMAN.   Through pity, master, believing that he would carry him to whatever land he had himself come from—but he saved him for dreadful mystery; for if you are what this man says, you are the most miserable of all men.

OEDIPUS.   O! O! All brought to pass! All truth! Now, O light, may I look my last upon you, having been found accursed in bloodshed, accursed in
750   marriage, and in my coming into the world accursed!

> [*He rushes into the palace.*]

CHORUS.   What can the shadow-like generations of man attain
But build up a dazzling mockery of delight that under their touch dissolves again?
Oedipus seemed blessed, but there is no man blessed amongst men.

Oedipus overcame the woman-breasted Fate;[23]
He seemed like a strong tower against Death and first among the fortunate;
He sat upon the ancient throne of Thebes, and all men called him great.

760   But, looking for a marriage-bed, he found the bed of his birth,
Tilled the field his father had tilled, cast seed into the same abounding earth;
Entered through the door that had sent him wailing forth.

Begetter and begot as one! How could that be hid?
What darkness cover up that marriage-bed? Time watches, he is eagle-eyed,
And all the works of man are known and every soul is tried.

Would you had never come to Thebes, nor to this house,

---

[23] I.e., the Sphinx, whose riddle Oedipus solved.

Nor riddled with the woman-breasted Fate, beaten off Death and
770   succoured us,
That I had never raised this song, heartbroken Oedipus!

SECOND MESSENGER [*coming from the house*].   Friends and kinsmen of this
house! What deeds must you look upon, what burden of sorrow bear, if
true to race you still love the House of Labdacus. For not Ister nor Phasis[24]
could wash this house clean, so many misfortunes have been brought upon
it, so many has it brought upon itself, and those misfortunes are always the
worst that a man brings upon himself.

CHORUS.   Great already are the misfortunes of this house, and you bring us
a new tale.

780 SECOND MESSENGER.   A short tale in the telling: Jocasta, our Queen, is dead.

CHORUS.   Alas, miserable woman, how did she die?

SECOND MESSENGER.   By her own hand. It cannot be as terrible to you as to
one that saw it with his eyes, yet so far as words can serve, you shall see it.
When she had come into the vestibule, she ran half crazed towards her
marriage-bed, clutching at her hair with the fingers of both hands, and
once within the chamber dashed the doors together behind her. Then
called upon the name of Laius, long since dead, remembering that son
who killed the father and upon the mother begot an accursed race. And
wailed because of that marriage wherein she had borne a two-fold race—
790   husband by husband, children by her child. Then Oedipus with a shriek
burst in and running here and there asked for a sword, asked where he
would find the wife that was no wife but a mother who had borne his
children and himself. Nobody answered him, we all stood dumb; but
supernatural power helped him, for, with a dreadful shriek, as though
beckoned, he sprang at the double doors, drove them in, burst the bolts
out of their sockets, and ran into the room. There we saw the woman
hanging in a swinging halter, and with a terrible cry he loosened the halter
from her neck. When that unhappiest woman lay stretched upon the
ground, we saw another dreadful sight. He dragged the golden brooches
800   from her dress and lifting them struck them upon his eyeballs, crying out,
"You have looked enough upon those you ought never to have looked
upon, failed long enough to know those that you should have known;
henceforth you shall be dark." He struck his eyes, not once, but many
times, lifting his hands and speaking such or like words. The blood poured
down and not with a few slow drops, but all at once over his beard in a dark
shower as it were hail.

[*The* CHORUS *wails and he steps further on to the stage.*]

Such evils have come forth from the deeds of those two and fallen not on
one alone but upon husband and wife. They inherited much happiness,
much good fortune; but to-day, ruin, shame, death, and loud crying, all
810   evils that can be counted up, all, all are theirs.

CHORUS.   Is he any quieter?

SECOND MESSENGER.   He cries for someone to unbar the gates and to show to
all the men of Thebes his father's murderer, his mother's—the unholy

---

[24] Two large rivers.

word must not be spoken. It is his purpose to cast himself out of the land that he may not bring all this house under his curse. But he has not the strength to do it. He must be supported and led away. The curtain is parting; you are going to look upon a sight which even those who shudder must pity.

[*Enter* OEDIPUS.]

OEDIPUS.   Woe, woe is me! Miserable, miserable that I am! Where am I?
820   Where am I going? Where am I cast away? Who hears my words?

CHORUS.   Cast away indeed, dreadful to the sight of the eye, dreadful to the ear.

OEDIPUS.   Ah, friend, the only friend left to me, friend still faithful to the blind man! I know that you are there; blind though I am, I recognise your voice.

CHORUS.   Where did you get the courage to put out your eyes? What unearthly power drove you to that?

OEDIPUS.   Apollo, friends, Apollo, but it was my own hand alone, wretched that I am, that quenched these eyes.

830 CHORUS.   You were better dead than blind.

OEDIPUS.   No, it is better to be blind. What sight is there that could give me joy? How could I have looked into the face of my father when I came among the dead, aye, or on my miserable mother, since against them both I sinned such things that no halter can punish? And what to me this spectacle, town, statue, wall, and what to me this people, since I, thrice wretched, I, noblest of Theban men, have doomed myself to banishment, doomed myself when I commanded all to thrust out the unclean thing?

CHORUS.   It had indeed been better if that herdsman had never taken your feet out of the spancel or brought you back to life.

840 OEDIPUS.   O three roads, O secret glen; O coppice[25] and narrow way where three roads met; you that drank up the blood I spilt, the blood that was my own, my father's blood: remember what deeds I wrought for you to look upon, and then, when I had come hither, the new deeds that I wrought. O marriage-bed that gave me birth and after that gave children to your child, creating an incestuous kindred of fathers, brothers, sons, wives, and mothers. Yes, all the shame and the uncleanness that I have wrought among men.

CHORUS.   For all my pity I shudder and turn away.

OEDIPUS.   Come near, condescend to lay your hands upon a wretched man;
850   listen, do not fear. My plague can touch no man but me. Hide me somewhere out of this land for God's sake, or kill me, or throw me into the sea where you shall never look upon me more.

[*Enter* CREON *and attendants.*]

CHORUS.   Here Creon comes at a fit moment; you can ask of him what you will, help or counsel, for he is now in your place. He is King.

OEDIPUS.   What can I say to him? What can I claim, having been altogether unjust to him.

CREON.   I have not come in mockery, Oedipus, nor to reproach you. Lead

---

[25] A thicket of small trees.

him in to the house as quickly as you can. Do not let him display his misery before strangers.

860 OEDIPUS. I must obey, but first, since you have come in so noble a spirit, you will hear me.

CREON. Say what you will.

OEDIPUS. I know that you will give her that lies within such a tomb as befits your own blood, but there is something more, Creon. My sons are men and can take care of themselves, but my daughters, my two unhappy daughters, that have ever eaten at my own table and shared my food, watch over my daughters, Creon. If it is lawful, let me touch them with my hands. Grant it, Prince, grant it, noble heart. I would believe, could I touch them, that I still saw them.

[ISMENE *and* ANTIGONE *are led in by attendants.*]

870 But do I hear them sobbing? Has Creon pitied me and sent my children, my darlings? Has he done this?

CREON. Yes, I ordered it, for I know how greatly you have always loved them.

OEDIPUS. Then may you be blessed, and may Heaven be kinder to you than it has been to me! My children, where are you? Come hither—hither— come to the hands of him whose mother was your mother; the hands that put out your father's eyes, eyes once as bright as your own; his who, understanding nothing, seeing nothing, became your father by her that bore him. I weep when I think of the bitter life that men will make you live, 880 and the days that are to come. Into what company dare you go, to what festival, but that you shall return home from it not sharing in the joys, but bathed in tears? When you are old enough to be married, what man dare face the reproach that must cling to you and your children? What misery is there lacking? Your father killed his father, he begat you at the spring of his own being, offspring of her that bore him. That is the taunt that would be cast upon you and on the man that you should marry. That man is not alive; my children, you must wither away in barrenness. Ah, son of Menoeceus,[26] listen. Seeing that you are the only father now left to them, for we their parents are lost, both of us lost, do not let them wander in 890 beggary—are they not your own kindred?—do not let them sink down into my misery. No, pity them, seeing them utterly wretched in helpless childhood if you do not protect them. Show me that you promise, generous man, by touching me with your hand. [CREON *touches him.*] My children, there is much advice that I would give you were you but old enough to understand, but all I can do now is bid you pray that you may live wherever you are let live, and that your life be happier than your father's.

CREON. Enough of tears. Pass into the house.

OEDIPUS. I will obey, though upon conditions.

CREON. Conditions?

900 OEDIPUS. Banish me from this country. I know that nothing can destroy me, for I wait some incredible fate; yet cast me upon Cithaeron, chosen by my father and my mother for my tomb.

CREON. Only the Gods can say yes or no to that.

---

[26] Creon.

OEDIPUS.   No, for I am hateful to the Gods.

CREON.   If that be so you will get your wish the quicker. They will banish that which they hate.

OEDIPUS.   Are you certain of that?

CREON.   I would not say it if I did not mean it.

OEDIPUS.   Then it is time to lead me within.

910   CREON.   Come, but let your children go.

OEDIPUS.   No, do not take them from me.

CREON.   Do not seek to be master; you won the mastery but could not keep it to the end.

[*He leads* OEDIPUS *into the palace, followed by* ISMENE, ANTIGONE, *and attendants.*]

CHORUS.   Make way for Oedipus. All people said,
   "That is a fortunate man";
   And now what storms are beating on his head!
   "That is a fortunate man,"
   Call no man fortunate that is not dead.
   The dead are free from pain.

[ca. 429 B.C.]

Critical Commentary on *King Oedipus*

Surely, there can be few plays so universally admired and so variously interpreted as *King Oedipus*. In the case of this play, however, the most influential interpretation is the least literary and probably also the least concerned with the values and attitudes of the play's characters. We are referring, of course, to Sigmund Freud's well-known treatment of the play in *The Interpretation of Dreams*.

Freud argues that although many other "tragedies of destiny" leave an audience unmoved, *Oedipus* indisputably succeeds in evoking pity and fear. What peculiarities make this play so powerful? Could it be, Freud asks, that *Oedipus* succeeds because there is something in it "which makes a voice within us ready to recognize the compelling force of destiny?" Oedipus does what many altogether normal men have only dreamed of doing—he murders his father and marries his mother. "His destiny moves us," Freud insists, "because it might have been ours—because the oracle laid the same curse upon us before birth as upon him." Oedipus's fate is every man's nightmare. He *does* what we dread—but also what we desire.

If Freud is correct, it is ironic that our subconscious desires are so different from our conscious revulsion at incest. However, that is but one of many ironies in the play. At the beginning of the play, Oedipus vows to bring the dark secret of Laius's killer to light. Even as he does so, this man, who had seen through the riddle of the Sphinx, is blind to his own moral faults. At the end of the play, Oedipus sees clearly who he is and what he has done, but he is physically blind. In contrast, blind Tiresias, the prophet, is capable of seeing more truly than sighted men, and his vision is the result of his service to Apollo, the sun god, who is also the god of foresight and insight. The religious and moral implications of this imagery seem clear: man errs in priding himself on clear-sightedness of eye or mind; instead he must recognize his weakness, his blindness, and his subservience to the all-seeing gods.

The chasm between the recognition of these ironies and the explanation of Sophocles' intention in creating them has proven difficult indeed to bridge. One set of critics would have us view the play only as an ingenious murder mystery in which the sleuth ironically is also the murderer. Thus, according to Frances Fergusson, "Oedipus takes the role of District Attorney; and when he at last convicts himself, we have a twist, a *coup de theatre*, of unparalleled excitement." And this twist transforms the play from an ingenious murder mystery into an archetypal quest for identity. Oedipus has achieved fame by telling the Sphinx what man in the abstract is, but he has failed to understand who he himself is. In seeking to know the murderer of Laius, Oedipus will eventually be forced to recognize the supremacy of Apollo and to live by the words inscribed on the walls at Delphi, "Know thyself!"

Other critics argue that the play's pervasive ironies are intended to humble humanity. Such critics believe that the gods destroy Oedipus to show their awful power and to teach him—and us all—a lesson. "This humbling," C. M. Bowra observes, "is not deserved. . . . The gods display their power because they will. But since they display it, man may draw a salutary lesson." But if this is true, then the play is almost too horrifying to read. What could be more repellent than the spectacle of an inherently good man who is destined at birth to commit unpardonable crimes and who does so through no fault of his own and despite his best efforts to remain innocent? If Oedipus, and all humans, are mere pawns of fate or of the gods, then what meaning can there be in life? If our efforts at foresight are inevitably clouded and if nothing we do can alter our fate, then maybe the only sensible thing to do is to follow Jocasta's advice and "live at random, as one may."

Still other critics claim that the gods in Sophocles see the future, but do not cause it to occur. No god forces Oedipus to flee Corinth or kill Laius or marry Jocasta. If Oedipus was fated to do such things, it was only because these actions unfold naturally from his basic character. Indeed, nearly all critics agree that Oedipus is destroyed by the very qualities of personality that originally brought him greatness. His intelligence and self-confidence produce in him an insolent and excessive self-esteem. It is true that these qualities make him capable of confronting and defeating the Sphinx, but a less proud man would have ignored the drunken Corinthian's insinuations about his legitimacy. A less proud and self-confident man, having heard the Delphic prophecy, would have returned to Corinth—despairing perhaps, but also giving in to the will of the gods (and thereby evading their prophecy). A less self-confident and less ambitious man would have avoided battle with older men and marriage to an older woman. A less proud man would not say, as Oedipus says to the Chorus, "You are praying, and it may be that your prayer will be answered; that if you hear my words and do my bidding you may find help out of all your trouble." Thus, as Victor Ehrenberg has pointed out, "Pride and self-confidence induce Oedipus to despise prophesy, and to feel almost superior to the gods." His faults in character are the cause of his undoing, and the trap that the gods have prepared for him would never have caught and crushed a lesser man.

Perhaps the play retains its vitality in part because it opens up such fascinating questions about human psychology, human motivation, and the relationship between mortal failings and divine will. In studying *King Oedipus*, you too have an active part to play. Ultimately, each of us must grapple with the questions about free will and predestination that this play so effectively raises.

A Collection of Critical Interpretations

ARISTOTLE, *THE POETICS**

VI

Of the poetry which imitates in hexameter verse, and of Comedy, we will speak hereafter. Let us now discuss Tragedy, resuming its formal definition, as resulting from what has been already said.

Tragedy, then, is an imitation of an action that is serious, complete, and of a certain magnitude; in language embellished with each kind of artistic ornament, the several kinds being found in separate parts of the play; in the form of action, not of narrative; through pity and fear affecting the proper purgation of these emotions. By "language embellished," I mean language into which rhythm, "harmony," and song enter. By "the several kinds in separate parts," I mean, that some parts are rendered through the medium of verse alone, others again with the aid of song.

Now as tragic imitation implies persons acting, it necessarily follows, in the first place, that Spectacular equipment will be a part of Tragedy. Next, Song and Diction, for these are the medium of imitation. By "Diction" I mean the mere metrical arrangement of the words: as for "Song," it is a term whose sense every one understands.

Again, Tragedy is the imitation of an action; and an action implies personal agents, who necessarily possess certain distinctive qualities both of character and thought; for it is by these that we qualify actions themselves, and these—thought and character—are the two natural causes from which actions spring, and on actions again all success or failure depends. Hence, the Plot is the imitation of the action—for by plot I here mean the arrangement of the incidents. By Character I mean that in virtue of which we ascribe certain qualities to the agents. Thought is required wherever a statement is proved, or, it may be, a general truth enunciated. Every Tragedy, therefore, must have six parts, which parts determine its quality—namely, Plot, Character, Diction, Thought, Spectacle, Song. Two of the parts constitute the medium of imitation, one the manner, and three the objects of imitation. And these complete the list. These elements have been employed, we may say, by the poets to a man; in fact, every play contains Spectacular elements as well as Character, Plot, Diction, Song, and Thought.

But most important of all is the structure of the incidents. For Tragedy is an imitation, not of men, but of an action and of life, and life consists in action, and its end is a mode of action, not a quality. Now character deter-

* Translated by S. H. Butcher. From S. H. Butcher, *Aristotle's Theory of Poetry and Fine Art*, 3rd. ed. (London: Macmillan, 1902) 37–46.

mines men's qualities, but it is by their actions that they are happy or the reverse. Dramatic action, therefore, is not with a view to the representation of character: character comes in as subsidiary to the actions. Hence the incidents and the plot are the end of a tragedy; and the end is the chief thing of all. Again, without action there cannot be a tragedy; there may be without character. The tragedies of most of our modern poets fail in the rendering of character; and of poets in general this is often true. It is the same in painting; and here lies the difference between Zeuxis and Polygnotus. Polygnotus delineates character well: the style of Zeuxis is devoid of ethical quality. Again, if you string together a set of speeches expressive of character, and well finished in point of diction and thought, you will not produce the essential tragic effect nearly so well as with a play which, however deficient in these respects, yet has a plot and artistically constructed incidents. Besides which, the most powerful elements of emotional interest in Tragedy—Reversal of the situation and Recognition scenes—are parts of the plot. A further proof is, that novices in the art attain to finish of diction and precision of portraiture before they can construct the plot. It is the same with almost all the early poets.

The Plot, then, is the first principle, and, as it were, the soul of a tragedy: Character holds the second place. A similar fact is seen in painting. The most beautiful colors, laid on confusedly, will not give as much pleasure as the chalk outline of a portrait. Thus Tragedy is the imitation of an action, and of the agents, mainly with a view to the action.

Third in order is Thought—that is, the faculty of saying what is possible and pertinent in given circumstances. In the case of oratory, this is the function of the political art and of the art of rhetoric: and so indeed the older poets make their characters speak the language of civic life; the poets of our time, the language of the rhetoricians. Character is that which reveals moral purpose, showing what kind of things a man chooses or avoids. Speeches, therefore, which do not make this manifest, or in which the speaker does not choose or avoid anything whatever, are not expressive of character. Thought, on the other hand, is found where something is proved to be or not to be, or a general maxim is enunciated.

Fourth among the elements enumerated comes Diction; by which I mean, as has been already said, the expression of the meaning in words; and its essence is the same both in verse and prose.

Of the remaining elements Song holds the chief place among the embellishments.

The Spectacle has, indeed, an emotional attraction of its own, but, of all the parts, it is the least artistic, and connected least with the art of poetry. For the power of Tragedy, we may be sure, is felt even apart from representation and actors. Besides, the production of spectacular effects depends more on the art of the stage machinist than on that of the poet.

x

Plots are either Simple or Complex, for the actions in real life, of which the plots are an imitation, obviously show a similar distinction. An action which is one and continuous in the sense above defined, I call Simple, when the change of fortune takes place without Reversal of the Situation and without Recognition.

A Complex action is one in which the change is accompanied by such Reversal or by Recognition, or by both. These last should arise from the internal structure of the plot, so that what follows should be the necessary or probable result of the preceding action. It makes all the difference whether any given event is a case of *propter hoc* or *post hoc.*

XI

Reversal of the Situation is a change by which the action veers round to its opposite, subject always to our rule of probability or necessity. Thus in the *Oedipus,* the messenger comes to cheer Oedipus and free him from his alarms about his mother, but by revealing who he is, he produces the opposite effect. Again in the *Lynceus,* Lynceus is being led away to his death, and Danaus goes with him, meaning to slay him; but the outcome of the action is, that Danaus is killed and Lynceus saved.

Recognition, as the name indicates, is a change from ignorance to knowledge, producing love or hate between the persons destined by the poet for good or bad fortune. The best form of recognition is coincident with a Reversal of the Situation, as in the *Oedipus.* There are indeed other forms. Even inanimate things of the most trivial kind may sometimes be objects of recognition. Again, we may recognize or discover whether a person has done a thing or not. But the recognition which is most intimately connected with the plot and action is, as we have said, the recognition of persons. This recognition, combined with Reversal will produce either pity or fear; and actions producing these effects are those which, by our definition, Tragedy represents. Moreover, it is upon such situations that the issues of good or bad fortune will depend. Recognition, then, being between persons, it may happen that one person only is recognized by the other—when the latter is already known—or it may be necessary that the recognition should be on both sides. Thus Iphigenia is revealed to Orestes by the sending of the letter; but another act of recognition is required to make Orestes known to Iphigenia.

Two parts, then, of the Plot—Reversal of the Situation and Recognition—turn upon surprises. A third part is the Scene of Suffering. The Scene of Suffering is a destructive or painful action, such as death on the stage, bodily agony, wounds, and the like. . . .

XIII

As the sequel to what has already been said, we must proceed to consider what the poet should aim at, and what he should avoid, in constructing his plots; and by what means the specific effect of Tragedy will be produced.

A perfect tragedy should, as we have seen, be arranged not on the simple but on the complex plan. It should, moreover, imitate actions which excite pity and fear, this being the distinctive mark of tragic imitation. It follows plainly, in the first place, that the change of fortune presented must not be the spectacle of a virtuous man brought from prosperity to adversity: for this moves neither pity nor fear; it merely shocks us. Nor, again, that of a bad man passing from adversity to prosperity: for nothing can be more alien to the spirit of Tragedy; it possesses no single tragic quality; it neither satisfies the moral sense, nor calls forth pity or fear. Nor, again, should the downfall of the utter villain be exhibited. A plot of this kind would, doubtless, satisfy the moral sense, but it would inspire neither pity nor fear; for pity is aroused by unmerited misfortune, fear by the misfortune of a man like ourselves. Such an event, therefore, will be neither pitiful nor terrible. There remains, then, the character between these two extremes, that of a man who is not eminently good and just, yet whose misfortune is brought about not by vice or depravity, but by some error or fraility. He must be one who is highly renowned and prosperous—a personage like Oedipus, Thyestes, or other illustrious men of such families.

A well-constructed plot should, therefore, be single in its issue, rather than double as some maintain. The change of fortune should be not from bad to good, but, reversely, from good to bad. It should come about as the result not of vice, but of some great error or fraility, in a character either such as we have described, or better rather than worse. The practice of the stage bears out our view. At first the poets recounted any legend that came in their way. Now, the best tragedies are founded on the story of a few houses—on the fortunes of Alcmaeon, Oedipus, Orestes, Meleager, Thyestes, Telephus, and those others who have done or suffered something terrible. A tragedy, then, to be perfect according to the rules of art should be of this construction. Hence they are in error who censure Euripides just because he follows this principle in his plays, many of which end unhappily. It is, as we have said, the right ending. The best proof is that on the stage and in dramatic competition, such plays, if well worked out, are the most tragic in effect; and Euripides, faulty though he may be in the general management of his subject, yet is felt to be the most tragic of all poets.

In the second rank comes the kind of tragedy which some place first. Like the *Odyssey*, it has a double thread of plot, and also an opposite catastrophe for the good and for the bad. It is accounted the best because of the weakness of the spectators; for the poet is guided in what he writes by the wishes of his audience. The pleasure, however, thence derived is not the true tragic pleasure. It is proper rather to Comedy, where those who, in the piece, are the deadliest enemies—like Orestes and Aegisthus—quit the stage as friends at the close, and no one slays or is slain.

XIV

Fear and pity may be aroused by spectacular means; but they may also result from the inner structure of the piece, which is the better way, and indicates a superior poet. For the plot ought to be so constructed that, even without the aid of the eye, he who hears the tale told will thrill with horror and melt to pity at what takes place. This is the impression we should receive from hearing the story of the *Oedipus*. But to produce this effect by the mere spectacle is a less artistic method, and dependent on extraneous aids. Those who employ spectacular means to create a sense not of the terrible but only of the monstrous, are strangers to the purpose of Tragedy; for we must not demand of Tragedy any and every kind of pleasure, but only that which is proper to it. And since the pleasure which the poet should afford is that which comes from pity and fear through imitation, it is evident that this quality must be impressed upon the incidents.

Let us then determine what are the circumstances which strike us as terrible or pitiful.

Actions capable of this effect must happen between persons who are either friends or enemies or indifferent to one another. If an enemy kills an enemy, there is nothing to excite pity either in the act or the intention—except so far as the suffering in itself is pitiful. So again with indifferent persons. But when the tragic incident occurs between those who are near or dear to one another—if, for example, a brother kills, or intends to kill, a brother, a son his father, a mother her son, a son his mother, or any other deed of the kind is done—these are the situations to be looked for by the poet. He may not indeed destroy the framework of the received legends—the fact, for instance, that Clytemnestra was slain by Orestes and Eriphyle by Alcmaeon—but he ought to show invention of his own, and skilfully handle the traditional material. Let us explain more clearly what is meant by skilful handling.

The action may be done consciously and with knowledge of the persons, in the manner of the older poets. It is thus too that Euripides makes Medea slay her children. Or, again, the deed of horror may be done, but done in ignorance, and the tie of kinship or friendship be discovered afterwards. The *Oedipus* of Sophocles is an example. Here, indeed, the incident is outside the drama proper; but cases occur where it falls within the action of the play: one may cite the *Alcmaeon* of Astydamas, or Telegonus in the *Wounded Odysseus*. Again, there is a third case, to be about to act with knowledge of the persons and then not to act. The fourth case is when someone is about to do an irreparable deed through ignorance, and makes the discovery before it is done. These are the only possible ways. For the deed must either be done or not done, and that wittingly or unwittingly. But of all these ways, to be about to act knowing the persons, and then not to act, is the worst. It is shocking without being tragic, for no disaster follows. It is, therefore, never, or very rarely, found in poetry. One instance, however, is in the *Antigone*, where Haimon threatens to kill Creon. The next and better way is that the deed should be perpetrated. Still better, that it should be perpetrated in ignorance, and the discovery made afterwards. There is then nothing to shock us, while the discovery produces a startling effect. The last case is the best, as when in the *Cresphontes* Merope is about to slay her son, but, recognizing who he is, spares his life. So in the *Iphigenia*, the sister recognizes the brother just in time. Again in the *Helle*, the son recognizes the mother when on the point of giving her up. This, then, is why a few families only, as has been already observed, furnish the subjects of tragedy. It was not art, but happy chance, that led poets to look for such situations and so impress the tragic quality upon their plots. They are compelled, therefore, to have recourse to those houses whose history contains moving incidents like these.

Enough has now been said concerning the structure of the incidents, and the proper constitution of the plot.

XV

In respect of Character there are four things to be aimed at. First, and most important, it must be good. Now any speech or action that manifests moral purpose of any kind will be expressive of character: the character will be good if the purpose is good. This rule is relative to each class. Even a woman may be good, and also a slave; though the woman may be said to be an inferior being, and the slave quite worthless. The second thing to aim at is propriety. There is a type of manly valor; but valor in a woman, or unscrupulous cleverness, is inappropriate. Thirdly, character must be true to life: for this is a distinct thing from goodness and propriety, as here described. The fourth point is consistency: for though the subject of the imitation, who suggested the type, be inconsistent, still he must be consistently inconsistent. As an example of motiveless degradation of character, we have Menelaus in the *Orestes:* of character indecorous and inappropriate, the lament of Odysseus in the *Scylla,* and the speech of Melanippe: of inconsistency, the *Iphigenia at Aulis,* for Iphigenia the suppliant in no way resembles her later self.

As in the structure of the plot, so too in the portraiture of character, the poet should always aim either at the necessary or the probable. Thus a person of a given character should speak or act in a given way, by the rule either of necessity or of probability; just as this event should follow that by necessary or probable sequence. It is therefore evident that the unraveling of the plot, no less than the complication, must arise out of the plot itself; it must not be brought about by the *Deus ex Machina*—as in the *Medea,* or in the Return of the Greeks in the *Iliad.* The *Deus ex Machina* should be employed only for events external to the drama—for antecedent or subsequent events, which lie beyond the range of human knowledge, and which require to be reported or foretold; for to the gods we ascribe the power of seeing all things. Within the action there must be nothing irrational. If the irrational cannot be excluded, it should be outside the scope of the tragedy. Such is the irrational element in the *Oedipus* of Sophocles.

Again, since Tragedy is an imitation of persons who are above the common level, the example of good portrait-painters should be followed. They, while reproducing the distinctive form of the original, make a likeness which is true to life and yet more beautiful. So too the poet, in representing men who are irascible or indolent, or have other defects of character, should preserve the type and yet ennoble it. In this way Achilles is portrayed by Agathon and Homer.

These then are rules the poet should observe. Nor should he neglect those appeals to the senses, which, though not among the essentials, are the concomitants of poetry; for here too there is much room for error. But of this enough has been said in the published treatises.

SIGMUND FREUD, "THE OEDIPUS COMPLEX"*

In my experience, which is already extensive, the chief part in the mental lives of all children who later become psychoneurotics is played by their parents. Being in love with the one parent and hating the other are among the essential constituents of the stock of psychical impulses which is formed at that time and which is of such importance in determining the symptoms of the later neurosis. It is not my belief, however, that psychoneurotics differ sharply in this respect from other human beings who remain normal—that they are able, that is, to create something absolutely new and peculiar to themselves. It is far more probable—and this is confirmed by occasional

* From Sigmund Freud, *The Interpretation of Dreams.* Translated and edited by James Strachey (New York: Basic Books, Inc., 1955) 260–64.

observations on normal children—that they are only distinguished by exhib-
iting on a magnified scale feelings of love and hatred to their parents which
occur less obviously and less intensely in the minds of most children.

This discovery is confirmed by a legend that has come down to us from
classical antiquity: a legend whose profound and universal power to move
can only be understood if the hypothesis I have put forward in regard to the
psychology of children has an equally universal validity. What I have in mind
is the legend of King Oedipus and Sophocles' drama which bears his name.

Oedipus, son of Laïus, King of Thebes, and of Jocasta, was exposed as an
infant because an oracle had warned Laïus that the still unborn child would
be his father's murderer. The child was rescued, and grew up as a prince in
an alien court, until, in doubts as to his origin, he too questioned the oracle
and was warned to avoid his home since he was destined to murder his father
and take his mother in marriage. On the road leading away from what he
believed was his home, he met King Laïus and slew him in a sudden quarrel.
He came next to Thebes and solved the riddle set him by the Sphinx who
barred his way. Out of gratitude the Thebans made him their king and gave
him Jocasta's hand in marriage. He reigned long in peace and honour, and
she who, unknown to him, was his mother bore him two sons and two daughters. Then at last a plague broke out and the Thebans made enquiry once
more of the oracle. It is at this point that Sophocles' tragedy opens. The
messengers bring back the reply that the plague will cease when the murderer of Laïus has been driven from the land.

> But he, where is he? Where shall now be read
> The fading record of this ancient guilt?

The action of the play consists in nothing other than the process of revealing,
with cunning delays and ever-mounting excitement—a process that can be
likened to the work of a psychoanalysis—that Oedipus himself is the murderer of Laïus, but further that he is the son of the murdered man and of
Jocasta. Appalled at the abomination which he has unwittingly perpetrated,
Oedipus blinds himself and forsakes his home. The oracle has been fulfilled.

Oedipus Rex is what is known as a tragedy of destiny. Its tragic effect is said
to lie in the contrast between the supreme will of the gods and the vain
attempts of mankind to escape the evil that threatens them. The lesson
which, it is said, the deeply moved spectator should learn from the tragedy
is submission to the divine will and realization of his own impotence. Modern
dramatists have accordingly tried to achieve a similar tragic effect by weaving
the same contrast into a plot invented by themselves. But the spectators have
looked on unmoved while a curse or an oracle was fulfilled in spite of all the
efforts of some innocent man: later tragedies of destiny have failed in their
effect.

If *Oedipus Rex* moves a modern audience no less than it did the contemporary Greek one, the explanation can only be that its effect does not lie in
the contrast between destiny and human will, but is to be looked for in the
particular nature of the material on which that contrast is exemplified. There
must be something which makes a voice within us ready to recognize the
compelling force of destiny in the *Oedipus,* while we can dismiss as merely

arbitrary such dispositions as are laid down in [Grillparzer's] *Die Ahnfrau* or other modern tragedies of destiny. And a factor of this kind is in fact involved in the story of King Oedipus. His destiny moves us only because it might have been ours—because the oracle laid the same curse upon us before our birth as upon him. It is the fate of all of us, perhaps, to direct our first sexual impulse towards our mother and our first hatred and our first murderous wish against our father. Our dreams convince us that that is so. King Oedipus, who slew his father Laïus, and married his mother Jocasta, merely shows us the fulfilment of our own childhood wishes. But, more fortunate than he, we have meanwhile succeeded, in so far as we have not become psychoneurotics, in detaching our sexual impulses from our mothers and in forgetting our jealousy of our fathers. Here is one in whom these primaeval wishes of our childhood have been fulfilled, and we shrink back from him with the whole force of the repression by which those wishes have since that time been held down within us. While the poet, as he unravels the past, brings to light the guilt of Oedipus, he is at the same time compelling us to recognize our own inner minds, in which those same impulses, though suppressed, are still to be found. The contrast with which the closing Chorus leaves us confronted—

> . . . Fix on Oedipus your eyes,
> Who resolved the dark enigma, noblest champion and most wise.
> Like a star his envied fortune mounted beaming far and wide:
> Now he sinks in seas of anguish, whelmed beneath a raging tide . . .

—strikes as a warning at ourselves and our pride, at us who since our childhood have grown so wise and so mighty in our own eyes. Like Oedipus, we live in ignorance of these wishes, repugnant to morality, which have been forced upon us by Nature, and after their revelation we may all of us well seek to close our eyes to the scenes of our childhood.

There is an unmistakable indication in the text of Sophocles' tragedy itself that the legend of Oedipus sprang from some primaeval dream-material which had as its content the distressing disturbance of a child's relation to his parents owing to the first stirrings of sexuality. At a point when Oedipus, though he is not yet enlightened, has begun to feel troubled by his recollection of the oracle, Jocasta consoles him by referring to a dream which many people dream, though, as she thinks, it has no meaning:

> Many a man ere now in dreams hath lain
> With her who bare him. He hath least annoy
> Who with such omens troubleth not his mind.

Today, just as then, many men dream of having sexual relations with their mothers, and speak of the fact with indignation and astonishment. It is clearly the key to the tragedy and the complement to the dream of the dreamer's father being dead. The story of Oedipus is the reaction of the imagination to these two typical dreams. And just as these dreams, when dreamt by adults, are accompanied by feelings of repulsion, so too the legend must include horror and self-punishment. Its further modification originates once again in a misconceived secondary revision of the material, which has sought to exploit it for theological purposes. The attempt to harmonize divine omnipotence with human responsibility must naturally fail in connection with this subject-matter just as with any other.

A Selective Bibliography on *King Oedipus*

Adams, S. M. *Sophocles the Playwright.* Toronto: U of Toronto P, 1957. 81–107.

Berkowitz, Luci and Theodore F. Brunner, eds. *Oedipus Tyrannus.* New York: Norton, 1970. This *Norton Critical Edition* includes classic essays by Aristotle, Nietzsche, and Freud along with a selection of more recent critical views.

Bowra, C. M. *Sophoclean Tragedy.* Oxford: Clarendon P, 1947.

Bushnell, Rebecca Weld. "Oracular Silence in *Oedipus the King* and *Macbeth.*" *Classical and Modern Literature: A Quarterly* 2.4 (1982): 195–204.

Cameron, Alister. *The Identity of Oedipus the King: Five Essays on the Oedipus Tyrannus.* New York: New York UP, 1968.

Cook, Albert. *Enactment: Greek Tragedy.* Chicago: Swallow, 1971. 136–48.

Culler, Jonathan. "Semiotic Consequences." *Studies in Twentieth Century Literature* 6.1–2 (1981–82): 5–15.

Damen, Mark. "Actor and Character in Greek Tragedy." *Theater Journal* (1989): 316–40.

Ehrenberg, Victor. *Sophocles and Pericles.* Oxford: Blackwell, 1954.

Fergusson, Frances. *The Idea of a Theater.* Princeton: Princeton UP, 1949.

Freud, Sigmund. "The Oedipus Complex." *The Interpretation of Dreams.* Trans. and ed. James Strachey. New York: Basic Books, 1955. 260–64.

Gardiner, Cynthia P. *The Sophoclean Chorus: A Study of Character and Function.* Iowa City: U of Iowa P, 1987.

Gellie, G. H. *Sophocles: A Reading.* Melbourne, Aus.: Melbourne UP, 1972.

Golden, Leon. "*Othello, Hamlet,* and Aristotelian Tragedy." *Shakespeare Quarterly* 2 (1984): 142–56.

Goodhart, Sandor. "Oedipus and Laius's Many Murderers." *Diacritics* 8 (1978): 55–71.

Green, Andre. "Oedipus, Freud, and Us." Trans. C. Coman. *Psychoanalytic Approaches to Literature and Film.* Ed. Maurice Charney and Joseph Reppen. Rutherford, NJ: Fairleigh Dickinson UP, 1987. 215–37.

Holland, Peter. "Space: The Final Frontier." *The Play Out of Context: Transferring Plays from Culture to Culture.* Ed. Hanna Scolnicov and Peter Holland. Cambridge: Cambridge UP, 1989. 45–62.

Kane, Thomas S. "Human Suffering and Divine Justice in the *Oedipus Rex.*" *College English* 37 (1975): 16–20.

Kitto, H. D. F. *Greek Tragedy: A Literary Study,* 3rd ed. London: Methuen, 1961.

Knox, Bernard. "Sophocles' Oedipus." *Tragic Themes in Western Literature.* Ed. Cleanth Brooks. New Haven: Yale UP, 1955.

Norwood, Gilbert. *Greek Tragedy.* New York: Hill and Wang, 1960. 145–54.

Musurillo, Herbert. "Sunken Imagery in Sophocles' *Oedipus.*" *American Journal of Philology* 77 (1957): 36–51.

Poole, Adrian. *Tragedy: Shakespeare and the Greek Example.* Oxford: Blackwell, 1987. 88–113.

Reid, Stephen A. "Teaching *Oedipus Rex.*" *College English* 29 (1968), 615–19.

Reinhardt, Karl. *Sophocles.* New York: Barnes & Noble, 1979. 94–134.

Schwartz, Joel D. "Human Action and Political Action in *Oedipus Tyrannos.*" *Greek Tragedy and Political Theory.* Ed. J. Peter Euben. Berkeley: U of California P, 1986. 183–209.

Scodel, Ruth. *Sophocles.* Boston: Twayne, 1984.

Seale, David. *Vision and Stagecraft in Sophocles.* London: Croom Helm, 1982. 215–60.

Vellacott, Philip. *Sophocles and Oedipus: A Study of* Oedipus Tyrannus *with a New Translation.* Ann Arbor: U of Michigan P, 1971.

Verhoeff, Han and Harly Sonne. "Does Oedipus Have His Complex?" *Style* 18.3 (1984): 261–83.

Vernant, Jean-Pierre and Pierre Vidal-Naquet. *Tragedy and Myth in Ancient Greece.* Sussex, Eng.: Harvester P, 1981. 62–119.

Waldock, A. J. A. *Sophocles the Dramatist.* Oxford: Cambridge UP, 1951.

Wilson, Barrie A., et al. *Interpretation, Meta-Interpretation, and Oedipus Tyrranus.* Berkeley: U of California P, 1980.

Woodard, Thomas, ed. *Sophocles: A Collection of Critical Essays.* Englewood Cliffs, NJ: Prentice Hall, 1966.

Euripides (ca. 480–406 B.C.)

HIPPOLYTUS

Translated by David Greene

CHARACTERS

APHRODITE, *goddess of love*
HIPPOLYTUS, *son of* THESEUS *and his former mistress Antiope*
CHORUS OF WOMEN, *servants in* PHAEDRA'S *house*
NURSE *to* PHAEDRA
PHAEDRA, *wife of* THESEUS

CHORUS LEADER
THESEUS, *ruler of Troezen*
ARTEMIS, *daughter of Zeus and goddess of the hunt*
A SERVANT
A MESSENGER

SCENE: TROEZEN, *in front of the house of* THESEUS.[1]

PROLOGUE

APHRODITE. I am called the Goddess Cypris[2]
I am mighty among men and they honor me by many names.
All those that live and see the light of sun
from Atlas' Pillars to the tide of Pontus[3]
are mine to rule,
Such as worship my power in all humility,
I exalt in honor.
But those whose pride is stiff-necked against me
I lay by the heels.
There is joy in the heart of a God also
when honored by men.

Now I will quickly tell you the truth of this story.

10   Hippolytus, son of Theseus by the Amazon,
pupil of holy Pittheus,
alone among the folk of this land of Troezen has blasphemed me
counting me vilest of the Gods in Heaven.
He will none of the bed of love nor marriage,
but honors Artemis, Zeus's daughter,

---

[1] Troezen is an ancient city southeast of Athens of which it was a dependency. Theseus is its ruler.

[2] An epithet for Aphrodite; born in the foam of the sea, she supposedly came ashore on the island of Cyprus.

[3] I.e., from the Atlantic Ocean to the Black Sea.

counting her greatest of the Gods in Heaven
he is with her continually, this Maiden Goddess, in the greenwood.
They hunt with hounds and clear the land of wild things,
mortal with immortal in companionship.

20   I do not grudge him such privileges: why should I?
But for his sins against me
I shall punish Hippolytus this day.
I have no need to toil to win my end:
much of the task has been already done.
Once he came from Pittheus' house[4] to the country of Pandion
that he might see and be initiate in the holy mysteries.
Phaedra saw him
and her heart was filled with the longings of love.
This was my work.
So before ever she came to Troezen

30   close to the rock of Pallas[5] in view of this land,
she dedicated a temple to Cypris.
For her love, too, dwelt in a foreign land.
Ages to come will call this temple after him,
the temple of the Goddess established here.
When Theseus left the land of Cecrops,
flying from the guilty stain of the murder of the Pallantids,[6]
condemning himself to a year's exile
he sailed with his wife to this land.
Phaedra groans in bitterness of heart
and the goads of love prick her cruelly,
and she is like to die.

40   But she breathes not a word of her secret and none of the servants
know of the sickness that afflicts her.
But her love shall not remain thus aimless and unknown.
I will reveal the matter to Theseus and all shall come out.
Father shall slay son with curses—
this son that is hateful to me.
For once the Lord Poseidon, Ruler of the Sea,
granted this favor to Theseus
that three of his prayers to the God should find answer.
Renowned shall Phaedra be in her death, but none the less

---

[4] "Pittheus' house": The historian Pausanias, relating the legend of Hippolytus, says: "King Theseus, when he married Phaedra, daughter of the king of Crete, was in a quandary what to do with Hippolytus, his son by his former mistress, Antiope the Amazon. He did not wish that after his own death Hippolytus should rule the children of his legitimate marriage, nor yet that Hippolytus should be ruled by them, for he loved him. So he sent the boy to be brought up by his grandfather Pittheus, who lived in Troezen and ruled there. Theseus hoped that when Pittheus died, Hippolytus might inherit the kingdom, and thus peace within the family be preserved, Hippolytus governing Troezen, and Phaedra's children holding sway in Athens." "Pandion's country" and "land of Cecrops" both signify Attica. Pandion and Cecrops were early legendary heroes of Attica. [Translator's note]

[5] The temple of Aphrodite which stood near the Acropolis in Athens, near a monument of Hippolytus.

[6] The Pallantids were the cousins of Theseus with whom he quarreled and then murdered.

die she must.
Her suffering does not weigh in the scale so much
that I should let my enemies go untouched
escaping payment of the retribution
50   that honor demands that I have.
Look, here is the son of Theseus, Hippolytus!
He has just left his hunting.
I must go away.
See the great crowd that throngs upon his heels
and shouts the praise of Artemis in hymns!
He does not know
that the doors of death are open for him,
that he is looking on his last sun.

SCENE I

[*Enter* Hippolytus, *attended by friends and servants carrying nets, hunting spears, etc.*]

Hippolytus.   Follow me singing
the praises of Artemis,
Heavenly One, Child of Zeus,
Artemis!
60   We are the wards of your care.

[*The Chorus of huntsmen chant.*]

Hail, Holy and Gracious!
Hail, Daughter of Zeus!
Hail, Maiden Daughter of Zeus and Leto![7]
Dweller in the spacious sky!
Maid of the Mighty Father!
Maid of the Golden Glistening House!
Hail!
Maiden Goddess most beautiful of all the Heavenly Host that lives in
70   Olympus!

[Hippolytus *advances to the altar of Artemis and lays a garland on it, praying.*]

My Goddess Mistress, I bring you ready woven
this garland. It was I that plucked and wove it,
plucked it for you in your inviolate Meadow.
No shepherd dares to feed his flock within it:
no reaper plies a busy scythe within it:
only the bees in springtime haunt the inviolate Meadow.
Its gardener is the spirit Reverence who
refreshes it with water from the river.
Not those who by instruction have profited

---

[7] Leto was the daughter of the Titans and the mother of Apollo and Artemis by Zeus.

80   to learn, but in whose very soul the seed
     of Chastity toward all things alike
     nature has deeply rooted, they alone
     may gather flowers there! the wicked may not.

     Loved mistress, here I offer you this coronal;
     it is a true worshipper's hand that gives it you
     to crown the golden glory of your hair.
     With no man else I share this privilege
     that I am with you and to your words
     can answer words. True, I may only hear:
     I may not see God face to face.
     So may I turn the post set at life's end
     even as I began the race.
SERVANT.   King—for I will not call you "Master," that belongs
     to the Gods only—will you take good advice?
90 HIPPOLYTUS.   Certainly I will take good advice, I am not a fool.
SERVANT.   In men's communities one rule holds good,
     do you know it, King?
HIPPOLYTUS.   Not I. What is this rule?
SERVANT.   Men hate the haughty of heart who will not be
     the friend of every man.
HIPPOLYTUS.   And rightly too:
     For haughty heart breeds arrogant demeanor.
SERVANT.   And affability wins favor, then?
HIPPOLYTUS.   Abundant favor. Aye, and profit, too,
     at little cost of trouble.
SERVANT.   Do you think
     that it's the same among the Gods in Heaven?
HIPPOLYTUS.   If we in our world and the Gods in theirs
     know the same usages—Yes.
SERVANT.   Then, King, how comes it
     that for a holy Goddess you have not even
     a word of salutation?
HIPPOLYTUS.   Which Goddess?
100 Be careful, or you will find that tongue of yours
     may make a serious mistake.
SERVANT.   This Goddess here
     who stands before your gates, the Goddess Cypris.
HIPPOLYTUS.   I worship her—but from a long way off,
     for I am chaste.
SERVANT.   Yet she's a holy Goddess,
     and fair is her renown throughout the world.
HIPPOLYTUS.   Men make their choice: one man honors one God,
     and one another.
SERVANT.   Well, good fortune guard you!
     if you have the mind you should have.
HIPPOLYTUS.   God of nocturnal prowess is not my God.
SERVANT.   The honors of the Gods you must not scant, my son.
HIPPOLYTUS.   Go, men, into the house and look to supper.

A plentiful table is an excellent thing
110   after the hunt. And you [*singling out two*] rub down my horses.
When I have eaten I shall exercise them.
For your Cypris here—a long goodbye to her!

[*The old man is left standing alone on the stage. He prays before the statue of Aphrodite.*]

O Cypris Mistress, we must not imitate
the young men when they have such thoughts as these.
As fits a slave to speak, here at your image
I bow and worship. You should grant forgiveness
when one that has a young tempestuous heart
speaks foolish words. Seem not to hear them.
120   You should be wiser than mortals, being Gods.

[*Enter* CHORUS *of women, servants in Phaedra's house.*]

[STROPHE]

CHORUS.   There is a rock streaming with water,
whose source, men say, is Ocean,
and it pours from the heart of its stone a spring
where pitchers may dip and be filled.
My friend was there and in the river water
she dipped and washed the royal purple robes,
and spread them on the rock's warm back
where the sunbeams played.
It was from her I heard at first
130   of the news of my mistress' sorrow.

[ANTISTROPHE]

She lies on her bed within the house,
within the house and fever wracks her
and she hides her golden head in fine-spun robes.
This is the third day
she has eaten no bread
and her body is pure and fasting.
For she would willingly bring her life to anchor
at the end of its voyage
140   the gloomy harbor of death.

[STROPHE]

Is it Pan's[8] frenzy that possesses you
or is Hecate's[9] madness upon you, maid?
Can it be the holy Corybantes,[10]
or the mighty Mother[11] who rules the mountains?
Are you wasted in suffering thus,

---

[8] The Arcadian shepherd god, the patron of hunters and shepherds, forests and wildlife.
[9] The goddess of the underworld.
[10] Divine beings who, like Pan and Hecate, were capable of possessing mortals.
[11] Cybele or Rhea, the Greek mother-goddess; her attendants were the Corybantes.

for a sin against Dictynna, Queen of hunters?[12]
Are you perhaps unhallowed, having offered
no sacrifice to her from taken victims?
For she goes through the waters of the Lake[13]
can travel on dry land beyond the sea,
150   the eddying salt sea.

[ANTISTROPHE]

Can it be that some other woman's love,
a secret love that hides itself from you,
has beguiled your husband
the son of Erechtheus[14]
our sovran lord, that prince of noble birth?
Or has some sailor from the shores of Crete
put in at this harbor hospitable to sailors,
bearing a message for our queen,
and so because he told her some calamity
her spirit is bound in chains of grief
160   and she lies on her bed in sorrow?

[EPODE]

Unhappy is the compound of woman's nature;
the torturing misery of helplessness,
the helplessness of childbirth and its madness
are linked to it for ever.
My body, too, has felt this thrill of pain,
and I called on Artemis, Queen of the Bow;
she has my reverence always
as she goes in the company of the Gods.

170   But here is the old woman, the queen's nurse
here at the door. She is bringing her mistress out.
There is a gathering cloud upon her face.
What is the matter? my soul is eager to know.
What can have made the queen so pale?
What can have wasted her body so?

SCENE II

[*Enter the* NURSE, *supporting* PHAEDRA.]

NURSE. A weary thing is sickness and its pains!
    What must I do now?
    Here is light and air, the brightness of the sky.
    I have brought out the couch on which you tossed
180   in fever—here clear of the house.

---

   [12] Dictynna, a Cretan goddess, identified with Artemis.
   [13] Limnae, the Lake, a district in Laconia, was the center of the worship of Artemis in the Peloponnese. From it she is sometimes called Limnasios, or Lady of the Lake. [Translator's note]
   [14] An Athenian king.

Your every word has been to bring you out,
but when you're here, you hurry in again.
You find no constant pleasure anywhere
for when your joy is upon you, suddenly
you're foiled and cheated.
There's no content for you in what you have
for you're forever finding something dearer,
some other thing—because you have it not.
It's better to be sick than nurse the sick.
Sickness is single trouble for the sufferer:
but nursing means vexation of the mind,
and hard work for the hands besides.
The life of man entire is misery:
190   he finds no resting place, no haven from calamity.
But something other dearer still than life
the darkness hides and mist encompasses;
we are proved luckless lovers of this thing
that glitters in the underworld: no man
can tell us of the stuff of it, expounding
what is, and what is not: we know nothing of it.
Idly we drift, on idle stories carried.

PHAEDRA [*to the servants*].   Lift me up! Lift my head up! All the muscles
are slack and useless. Here, you, take my hands.
200   They're beautiful, my hands and arms!
Take away this hat! It is too heavy to wear.
Take it away! Let my hair fall free on my shoulders.

NURSE.   Quiet, child! Do not so restlessly
keep tossing to and fro! It's easier
to bear an illness if you have some patience
and the spirit of good breeding.
We all must suffer sometimes: we are mortal.

PHAEDRA.   O,
if I could only draw from the dewy spring
a draught of fresh spring water!
210   If I could only lie beneath the poplars,
in the tufted meadow and find my rest there!

NURSE.   Child, why do you rave so? There are others here.
Cease tossing out these wild demented words
whose driver is madness.

PHAEDRA.   Bring me to the mountains! I *will* go to the mountains!
Among the pine trees where the huntsmen's pack
trails spotted stags and hangs upon their heels.
God, how I long to set the hounds on, shouting!
And poise the Thessalian javelin drawing it back—
220   here where my fair hair hangs above the ear—
I would hold in my hand a spear with a steel point.

NURSE.   What ails you, child? What is this love of hunting,
and you a lady! Draught of fresh spring water!
Here, beside the tower there is a sloping ridge
with springs enough to satisfy your thirst.

PHAEDRA.   Artemis, mistress of the Salty Lake,
   mistress of the ring echoing to the racers' hoofs,
230   if only I could gallop your level stretches,
   and break Venetian colts![15]
NURSE.   This is sheer madness,
   that prompts such whirling, frenzied, senseless words.
   Here at one moment you're afire with longing
   to hunt wild beasts and you'd go to the hills,
   and then again all your desire is horses,
   horses on the sands beyond the reach of the breakers.
   Indeed, it would need to be a mighty prophet
   to tell which of the Gods mischievously
   jerks you from your true course and thwarts your wits!
PHAEDRA.   O, I am miserable! What is this I've done?
240   Where have I strayed from the highway of good sense?
   I was mad. It was the madness sent from some God
   that caused my fall.
   I am unhappy, so unhappy! Nurse,
   cover my face again. I am ashamed
   of what I said. Cover me up. The tears
   are flowing, and my face is turned to shame.
   Rightness of judgment is bitterness to the heart.
   Madness is terrible. It is better then
   that I should die and know no more of anything.
250 NURSE.   There, now, you are covered up. But my own body
   when will death cover that? I have learned much
   from my long life. The mixing bowl of friendship,
   the love of one for the other, must be tempered.
   Love must not touch the marrow of the soul.
   Our affections must be breakable chains that we
   can cast them off or tighten them.
   That one soul so for two should be in travail
260   as I for her, that is a heavy burden.
   The ways of life that are most fanatical
   trip us up more, they say, than bring us joy.
   They're enemies to health. So I praise less
   the extreme than temperance in everything.
   The wise will bear me out.
CHORUS LEADER.   Old woman, you are Phaedra's faithful nurse.
   We can see that she is in trouble but the cause
   that ails her is black mystery to us.
270   We would like to hear you tell us what is the matter.
NURSE.   I have asked and know no more. She will not tell me.
CHORUS LEADER.   Not even what began it?
NURSE.   And my answer
   is still the same: of all this she will not speak.

---

[15] Veneto, a region of Italy famous for its horses.

CHORUS LEADER.   But see how ill she is, and how her body
   is wracked and wasted!
NURSE.   Yes, she has eaten nothing
   for two days now.
CHORUS LEADER.   Is this the scourge of madness?
   Or can it be . . . that death is what she seeks?
NURSE.   Aye, death. She is starving herself to death.
CHORUS LEADER.   I wonder that her husband suffers this.
NURSE.   She hides her troubles, swears that she isn't sick.
280 CHORUS LEADER.   But does he not look into her face and see
   a witness that disproves her?
NURSE.   No, he is gone.
   He is away from home, in foreign lands.
CHORUS LEADER.   Why, you must force her then to find the cause
   of this mind-wandering sickness!
NURSE.   Every means
   I have tried and still have won no foot of ground.
   But I'll not give up trying, even now.
   You are here and can in person bear me witness
   that I am loyal to my masters always,
   even in misfortune's hour.
   Dear child, let us both forget our former words.
   Be kinder, you: unknit that ugly frown.
290   For my part I will leave this track of thought:
   I cannot understand you there. I'll take
   another and a better argument.

   If you are sick and it is some secret sickness,
   here are women standing at your side to help.
   But if your troubles may be told to men,
   speak, that a doctor may pronounce upon it.
   So, not a word! Oh, why will you not speak?
   There is no remedy in silence, child.
   Either I am wrong and then you should correct me:
   or right, and you should yield to what I say.
300   Say something! Look at me!

   Women, I have tried and tried and all for nothing.
   We are as far as ever from our goal.
   It was the same before. She was not melted
   by anything I said. She would not obey me.

   But this you shall know, though to my reasoning
   you are more dumbly obstinate than the sea:
   If you die, you will be a traitor to your children.
   They will never know their share in a father's palace.
   No, by the Amazon Queen, the mighty rider
   who bore a master for your children, one
   bastard in birth but true-born son in mind,

you know him well—Hippolytus. . . .

310   So that has touched you?

PHAEDRA.   You have killed me, nurse. For God's sake, I entreat you,
never again speak that man's name to me.

NURSE.   You see? You have come to your senses, yet despite that,
you will not make your children happy nor
save your own life besides.

PHAEDRA.   I love my children.
It is another storm of fate that batters me.

NURSE.   There is no stain of blood upon your hands?

PHAEDRA.   My hands are clean: the stain is in my heart.

NURSE.   The hurt comes from outside? Some enemy?

PHAEDRA.   One I love destroys me. Neither of us wills it.

320 NURSE.   Has Theseus sinned a sin against you then?

PHAEDRA.   God keep me equally guiltless in his sight!

NURSE.   What is this terror urging you to death?

PHAEDRA.   Leave me to my sins. My sins are not against you.

NURSE.   Not of my will, but yours, you cast me off.

PHAEDRA.   Would you force confession, my hand-clasping suppliant?

NURSE.   Your knees too—and my hands will never free you.

PHAEDRA.   Sorrow, nurse, sorrow, you will find my secret.

NURSE.   Can I know greater sorrow than losing you?

PHAEDRA.   You will kill me. My honor lies in silence.

330 NURSE.   And then you will hide this honor, though I beseech you?

PHAEDRA.   Yes, for I seek to win good out of shame.

NURSE.   Where honor is, speech will make you more honorable.

PHAEDRA.   O God, let go my hand and go away!

NURSE.   No, for you have not given me what you should.

PHAEDRA.   I yield. Your suppliant hand compels my reverence.

NURSE.   I will say no more. Yours is the word from now.

PHAEDRA.   Unhappy mother, what a love was yours!

NURSE.   It is her love for the bull[16] you mean, dear child?

PHAEDRA.   Unhappy sister, bride of Dionysus![17]

340 NURSE.   Why these ill-boding words about your kin?

PHAEDRA.   And I the unlucky third, see how I end!

NURSE.   Your words are wounds. Where will your tale conclude?

PHAEDRA.   Mine is an inherited curse.[18] It is not new.

NURSE.   I have not yet heard what I most want to know.

PHAEDRA.   If you could say for me what I must say for myself.

NURSE.   I am no prophet to know your hidden secrets.

PHAEDRA.   What is this thing, this love, of which they speak?

NURSE.   Sweetest and bitterest, both in one, at once.

PHAEDRA.   One of the two, the bitterness, I've known.

350 NURSE.   Are you in love, my child? And who is he?

---

[16] The allusion is to the story of Phaedra's ancestor Pasiphae, wife of King Minos of Crete, who lusted after and mated with a bull, producing the Minotaur.

[17] Phaedra's sister Ariadne, the daughter of Minos and Pasiphae, deserted Dionysus for Theseus, creating a situation which now parallels her own.

[18] A reference to the stain of lust which has infected the female members of her family.

PHAEDRA.   There is a man, . . . his mother was an Amazon. . . .
NURSE.   You mean Hippolytus?
PHAEDRA.   You
  have spoken it, not I.
NURSE.   What do you mean? This is my death.
  Women, this is past bearing. I'll not bear
  life after this. A curse upon the daylight!
  A curse upon this shining sun above us!
  I'll throw myself from a cliff, throw myself headlong!
  I'll be rid of life somehow, I'll die somehow!
  Farewell to all of you! This is the end for me.

  The chaste, they love not vice of their own will,
  but yet they love it. Cypris, you are no God.
360 You are something stronger than God if that can be.
  You have ruined her and me and all this house.

[The NURSE *goes off. The* CHORUS *forms into two half-choruses.]*

FIRST HALF-CHORUS.   Did you hear, did you hear
  the queen crying aloud,
  telling of a calamity
  which no ear should hear?
SECOND HALF-CHORUS.   I would rather die
  than think such thoughts as hers.
FIRST HALF-CHORUS.   I am sorry for her trouble.
SECOND HALF-CHORUS.   Alas for troubles, man-besetting.
FIRST HALF-CHORUS [*turning to* PHAEDRA].   You are dead, you yourself
  have dragged your ruin to the light.
  What can happen now in the long
  dragging stretch of the rest of your days?
370 Some new thing will befall the house.
CHORUS [*united*].   We know now, we know now
  how your love will end,
  poor unhappy Cretan girl!
PHAEDRA.   Hear me, you women of Troezen who live
  in this extremity of land, this anteroom to Argos.
  Many a time in night's long empty spaces
  I have pondered on the causes of a life's shipwreck.
  I think that our lives are worse than the mind's quality
  would warrant. There are many who know virtue.
380 We know the good, we apprehend it clearly.
  But we can't bring it to achievement. Some
  are betrayed by their own laziness, and others
  value some other pleasure above virtue.
  There are many pleasures in a woman's life—
  long gossiping talks and leisure, that sweet curse.
  Then there is shame that thwarts us. Shame is of two kinds.
  The one is harmless, but the other a plague.
  For clarity's sake, we should not talk of "shame,"
  a single word for two quite different things.

390   These then are my thoughts. Nothing can now seduce me
to the opposite opinion. I will tell you
in my own case the track which my mind followed.
At first when love had struck me, I reflected
how best to bear it. Silence was my first plan.
Silence and concealment. For the tongue
is not to be trusted: it can criticize
another's faults, but on its own possessor
it brings a thousand troubles.
Then I believed that I could conquer love,
conquer it with discretion and good sense.

400   And when that too failed me, I resolved to die.
And death is the best plan of them all. Let none of you
dispute that.
It would always be my choice
to have my virtues known and honored. So
when I do wrong I could not endure to see
a circle of condemning witnesses.
I know what I have done: I know the scandal:
and all too well I know that I am a woman,
object of hate to all. Destruction light
upon the wife who herself plays the tempter
and strains her loyalty to her husband's bed

410   by dalliance with strangers. In the wives
of noble houses first this taint begins:
when wickedness approves itself to those
of noble birth, it will surely be approved
by their inferiors. Truly, too, I hate
lip-worshippers of chastity who own
a lecherous daring when they have privacy.
O Cypris, Sea-Born Goddess, how can they
look frankly in the faces of their husbands
and never shiver with fear lest their accomplice,
the darkness, and the rafters of the house
take voice and cry aloud?
This then, my friends, is my destruction:

420   I cannot bear that I should be discovered
a traitor to my husband and my children.
God grant them rich and glorious life in Athens—
famous Athens—freedom in word and deed,
and from their mother an honorable name.
It makes the stoutest-hearted man a slave
if in his soul he knows his parents' shame.

The proverb runs: "There is one thing alone
that stands the brunt of life throughout its course,
a quiet conscience,". . . a just and quiet conscience
whoever can attain it.
Time holds a mirror, as for a young girl,
and sometimes as occasion falls, he shows us

the ugly rogues of the world. I would not wish
430   that I should be seen among them.
   CHORUS LEADER.   How virtue is held lovely everywhere,
      and harvests a good name among mankind!

[*The* NURSE *returns.*]

NURSE.   Mistress, the trouble you have lately told me,
      coming on me so suddenly, frightened me;
      but now I realize that I was foolish.
      In this world second thoughts, it seems, are best.
      Your case is not so extraordinary,
      beyond thought or reason. The Goddess in her anger
      has smitten you, and you are in love. What wonder
      is this? There are many thousands suffer with you.
440   So, you will die for love! And all the others,
      who love, and who will love, must they die, too?
      How will that profit them? The tide of love,
      at its full surge, is not withstandable.
      Upon the yielding spirit she comes gently,
      but to the proud and the fanatic heart
      she is a torturer with the brand of shame.
      She wings her way through the air; she is in the sea,
      in its foaming billows; from her everything,
      that is, is born. For she engenders us
450   and sows the seed of desire whereof we're born,
      all we her children, living on the earth.
      He who has read the writings of the ancients
      and has lived much in books, he knows
      that Zeus once loved the lovely Semele;[19]
      he knows that Dawn, the bright light of the world,
      once ravished Cephalus[20] hence to the God's company
      for love's sake. Yet all these dwell in heaven.
      They are content, I am sure, to be subdued
      by the stroke of love.
      But you, you won't submit! Why, you should certainly
460   have had your father beget you on fixed terms
      or with other Gods for masters, if you don't like
      the laws that rule this world. Tell me, how many
      of the wise ones of the earth do you suppose
      see with averted eyes their wives turned faithless;
      how many erring sons have fathers helped
      with secret loves? It is the wise man's part
      to leave in darkness everything that is ugly.

---

[19] Semele, the daughter of Cadmus, died when Zeus appeared before her in full glory and scorched her with his lightning. At the time she was pregnant by Zeus with Dionysus, the Greek god of wine or revelry.
[20] Cephalus, the son of Deion and Diomede, was ravished by Eos, the goddess of dawn.

We should not in the conduct of our lives
be too exacting. Look, see this roof here—
these overarching beams that span your house—
could builders with all their skill lay them dead straight?
You've fallen into the great sea of love
470   and with your puny swimming would escape!
If in the sum you have more good luck than ill,
count yourself fortunate—for you are mortal.

Come, dear, give up your discontented mood.
Give up your railing. It's only insolent pride
to wish to be superior to the Gods.
Endure your love. The Gods have willed it so.
You are sick. Then try to find some subtle means
to turn your sickness into health again.
There are magic love charms, spells of enchantment;
we'll find some remedy for your love-sickness.
480   Men would take long to hunt devices out,
if we the women did not find them first.

CHORUS LEADER.   Phaedra, indeed she speaks more usefully
for today's troubles. But it is you I praise.
And yet my praise brings with it more discomfort
than her words: it is bitterer to the ear.

PHAEDRA.   This is the deadly thing which devastates
well-ordered cities and the homes of men—
that's it, this art of oversubtle words.
It's not the words ringing delight in the ear
that one should speak, but those that have the power
to save their hearer's honorable name.

490   NURSE.   This is high moralizing! What you want
is not fine words, but the man! Come, let's be done.
And tell your story frankly and directly.
For if there were no danger to your life,
as now there is—or if you could be prudent,
I never would have led you on so far,
merely to please your fancy or your lust.
But now a great prize hangs on our endeavors,
and that's the saving of a life—yours, Phaedra,
there's none can blame us for our actions now.

PHAEDRA.   What you say is wicked, wicked! Hold your tongue!
I will not hear such shameful words again.

500   NURSE.   O, they are shameful! But they are better than
your noble-sounding moral sentiments.
"The deed" is better if it saves your life:
than your "good name" in which you die exulting.

PHAEDRA.   For God's sake, do not press me any further!
What you say is true, but terrible!
My very soul is subdued by my love
and if you plead the cause of wrong so well
I shall fall into the abyss
from which I now am flying.

Nurse.　If that is what you think, you should be virtuous.
　　　But if you are not, obey me: that is next best.
510　　It has just come to my mind, I have at home
　　　some magic love charms. They will end your trouble;
　　　they'll neither harm your honor nor your mind.
　　　They'll end your trouble, ... only you must be brave.
Phaedra.　Is this a poison ointment or a drink?
Nurse.　I don't know. Don't be overanxious, child,
　　　to find out what it is. Accept its benefits.
Phaedra.　I am afraid of you: I am afraid
　　　that you will be too clever for my good.
Nurse.　You are afraid of everything. What is it?
520　Phaedra.　You surely will not tell this to Hippolytus?
Nurse.　Come, let that be: I will arrange all well.
　　　Only, my lady Cypris of the Sea,
　　　be my helper you. The other plans I have
　　　I'll tell to those we love within the house;
　　　that will suffice.

　　　　　　　　　　　　　　　　　　　　[*The* Nurse *goes off.*]

　　　　　　　　　　　　　　　　　　　　　　　[STROPHE]

Chorus.　Love distills desire upon the eyes,
　　　love brings bewitching grace into the heart
　　　of those he would destroy.
　　　I pray that love may never come to me
　　　with murderous intent,
　　　in rhythms measureless and wild.
530　　Not fire nor stars have stronger bolts
　　　than those of Aphrodite sent
　　　by the hand of Eros, Zeus's child.[21]

　　　　　　　　　　　　　　　　　　　　　　[ANTISTROPHE]

　　　In vain by Alpheus' stream,[22]
　　　in vain in the halls of Phoebus' Pythian shrine[23]
　　　the land of Greece increases sacrifice.
540　　But Love the King of Men they honor not,
　　　although he keeps the keys
　　　of the temple desire,
　　　although he goes destroying through the world,
　　　author of dread calamities
　　　and ruin when he enters human hearts.

　　　　　　　　　　　　　　　　　　　　　　　[STROPHE]

　　　The Oechalian maiden who had never known
　　　the bed of love, known neither man nor marriage,
　　　the Goddess Cypris gave to Heracles.

---

[21] The god of love.
[22] Alpheus, the river god.
[23] The shrine of Phoebus, the sun god, at Delphi.

She took her from the home of Eurytus,[24]
maiden unhappy in her marriage song,
550   wild as a Naiad or a Bacchanal,[25]
with blood and fire, a murderous hymenaeal!

O Holy walls of Thebes and Dirce's fountain[26]
bear witness you, to Love's grim journeying:
once you saw Love bring Semele to bed,
lull her to sleep, clasped in the arms of Death,
560   pregnant with Dionysus by the thunder king.
Love is like a flitting bee in the world's garden
and for its flowers, destruction is in his breath.

SCENE III

[PHAEDRA *is standing listening near the central door of the palace.*]

PHAEDRA.   Women, be silent!

[*She listens and then recoils.*]

Oh, I am destroyed forever.
CHORUS LEADER.   What is there terrible within the house?
PHAEDRA.   Hush, let me hear the voices within!
CHORUS LEADER.   And I obey. But this is sorrow's prelude.
570   PHAEDRA. [*cries out*].   Oh, I am the most miserable of women!

[*The* CHORUS LEADER *and the* CHORUS *babble excitedly among themselves.*]

What does she mean by her cries?
Why does she scream?
Tell us the fear-winged word, Mistress, the fear-winged word,
rushing upon the heart.
PHAEDRA.   I am lost. Go, women, stand and listen there yourselves
and hear the tumult that falls on the house.
CHORUS LEADER.   Mistress, you stand at the door.
It is you who can tell us best
580   what happens within the house.
PHAEDRA.   Only the son of the horse-loving Amazon,
Hippolytus, cursing a servant maid.
CHORUS LEADER.   My ears can catch a sound,
but I can hear nothing clear.
I can only hear a voice
scolding in anger.
PHAEDRA.   It is plain enough. He cries aloud against

---

[24] Eurytus was the King of Oechalia. He was killed by Hercules, the son of Zeus, when, after teaching Hercules to use a bow, he refused to surrender to him his wife, Antiope.

[25] The Naiads were female deities of fountains and lakes; a bacchanal refers to a drunken revelry after Bacchus, the Greek god of wine.

[26] Dirce, after being gored to death by a wild bull, became a fountain.

590   the mischievous bawd who betrays her mistress' love.

Chorus Leader.   Lady, you are betrayed!
   How can I help you?
   What is hidden is revealed.
   You are destroyed.
   Those you love have betrayed you.

Phaedra.   She loved me and she told him of my troubles,
   and so has ruined me. She was my doctor,
   but her cure has made my illness mortal now.

Chorus Leader.   What will you do? There is no cure.

Phaedra.   I know of one, and only one—quick death.
600   That is the only cure for my disease.

[*She retires into the palace through one of the side doors just as* Hippolytus *issues through the central door, dogged by the* Nurse. Phaedra *is conceived of as listening from behind her door during the entire conversation between the* Nurse *and* Hippolytus.]

Hippolytus.   O Mother Earth! O Sun and open sky!
   What words I have heard from this accursed tongue!

Nurse.   Hush, son! Someone may hear you.

Hippolytus.   You cannot
   expect that I hear horror and stay silent.

Nurse.   I beg of you, entreat you by your right hand,
   your strong right hand, . . . don't speak of this!

Hippolytus.   Don't lay your hand on me! Let go my cloak!

Nurse.   By your knees then, . . . don't destroy me!

Hippolytus.   What is this?
   Don't you declare that you have done nothing wrong?

Nurse.   Yes, but the story, son, is not for everyone.

Hippolytus.   Why not? A pleasant tale makes pleasanter telling,
610   when there are many listeners.

Nurse.   You will not break your oath to me, surely you will not?

Hippolytus.   My tongue swore, but my mind was still unpledged.

Nurse.   Son, what would you do?
   You'll not destroy your friends?

Hippolytus.   "Friends" you say!
   I spit the word away. None of the wicked
   are friends of mine.

Nurse.   Then pardon, son. It's natural
   that we should sin, being human.

Hippolytus.   Women! This coin which men find counterfeit!
   Why, why, Lord Zeus, did you put them in the world,
   in the light of the sun? If you were so determined
   to breed the race of man, the source of it
   should not have been women. Men might have dedicated
620   in your own temples images of gold,
   silver, or weight of bronze, and thus have bought
   the seed of progeny, . . . to each been given
   his worth in sons according to the assessment

of his gift's value. So we might have lived
in houses free of the taint of women's presence.
But now, to bring this plague into our homes
we drain the fortunes of our homes. In this
we have a proof how great a curse is woman.
For the father who begets her, rears her up,
must add a dowry gift to pack her off
to another's house and thus be rid of the load.

630   And he again that takes the cursed creature
rejoices and enriches his heart's jewel
with dear adornment, beauty heaped on vileness.
With lovely clothes the poor wretch tricks her out
spending the wealth that underprops his house.
That husband has the easiest life whose wife
is a mere nothingness, a simple fool,
uselessly sitting by the fireside.

640   I hate a clever woman—God forbid
that I should ever have a wife at home
with more than woman's wits! Lust breeds mischief
in the clever ones. The limits of their minds
deny the stupid lecherous delights.
We should not suffer servants to approach them,
but give them as companions voiceless beasts,
dumb, . . . but with teeth, that they might not converse,
and hear another voice in answer.
But now at home the mistress plots the mischief,

650   and the maid carries it abroad. So you, vile woman,
came here to me to bargain and to traffic
in the sanctity of my father's marriage bed.
I'll go to a running stream and pour its waters
into my ear to purge away the filth.
Shall I who cannot even hear such impurity,
and feel myself untouched, . . . shall I turn sinner?
Woman, know this. It is my piety saves you.
Had you not caught me off my guard and bound
my lips with an oath, by heaven I would not refrain
from telling this to my father.
Now I will go and leave this house until
Theseus returns from his foreign wanderings,

660   and I'll be silent. But I'll watch you close.
I'll walk with my father step by step and see
how you look at him, . . . you and your mistress both.
I have tasted of the daring of your infamy.
I'll know it for the future. Curses on you!
I'll hate you women, hate and hate and hate you,
and never have enough of hating. . . .
                                Some
say that I talk of this eternally,
yes, but eternal, too, is woman's wickedness.
Either let someone teach them to be chaste,
or suffer me to trample on them forever.

[PHAEDRA *comes out from behind the door. Exit* HIPPOLYTUS.]

PHAEDRA.   Bitter indeed is woman's destiny!
670   I have failed. What trick is there now, what cunning plea
       to loose the knot around my neck?
       I have had justice. O earth and the sunlight!
       Where shall I escape from my fate?
       How shall I hide my trouble?
       What God or man would appear
       to bear hand or part in my crime?
       There is a limit to all suffering and I have reached it.
       I am the unhappiest of women.
680 CHORUS.   Alas, mistress, all is over now
       your servant's schemes have failed and you are ruined.

                                              [*Enter the* NURSE.]

PHAEDRA.   This is fine service you have rendered me,
       corrupted, damned seducer of your friends!
       May Zeus, the father of my fathers' line,
       blot you out utterly, raze you from the world
       with thunderbolts! Did I not see your purpose,
       did I not say to you, "Breathe not a word of this"
       which now overwhelms me with shame? But you,
       you did not hold back. And therefore I must die
       and die dishonored.
       Enough of this. We have a new theme now.
       The anger of Hippolytus is whetted.
690   He will tell his father all the story of your sin
       to my disparagement. He will tell old Pittheus, too.
       He will fill all the land with my dishonor.
       May my curse
       light upon you, on you and all the others
       who eagerly help unwilling friends to ruin.
NURSE.   Mistress, you may well blame my ill-success,
       for sorrow's bite is master of your judgment.
       But I have an answer to make if you will listen.
       I reared you up, I am your loyal servant.
       I sought a remedy for your love's sickness,
       and found, . . . not what I sought.
700   Had I succeeded, I had been a wise one.
       Our wisdom varies in proportion to
       our failure or achievement.
PHAEDRA.   So, that's enough
       for me? Do I have justice if you deal me
       my death blow and then say "I was wrong: I grant it."
NURSE.   We talk too long. True I was not wise then.
       But even from this desperate plight, my child,
       you can escape.
PHAEDRA.   You, speak no more to me.
       You have given me dishonorable advice.

What you have tried has brought dishonor too.
Away with you!
Think of yourself. For me and my concerns
I will arrange all well.

[*Exit* NURSE.]

710   You noble ladies of Troezen, grant me this,
       this one request, that what you have heard here
       you wrap in silence.
CHORUS LEADER.   I swear by holy Artemis, child of Zeus,
       never to bring your troubles to the daylight.
PHAEDRA.   I thank you. I have found one single blessing
       in this unhappy business, one alone,
       that I can pass on to my children after me
       life with an uncontaminated name,
       and myself profit by the present throw
       of Fortune's dice. For I will never shame you,
720   my Cretan home, nor will I go to face
       Theseus, defendant on an ugly charge,
       never—for one life's sake.
CHORUS LEADER.   What is the desperate deed you mean to do,
       the deed past cure?
PHAEDRA.   Death. But the way of it, that
       is what I now must plan.
CHORUS LEADER.   Oh, do not speak of it!
PHAEDRA.   No, I'll not speak of it. But on this day
       when I shake off the burden of this life
       I shall delight the Goddess who destroys me,
       the Goddess Cypris.
       Bitter will have been the love that conquers me,
       but in my death I shall at least bring sorrow,
       upon another, too, that his high heart
       may know no arrogant joy at my life's shipwreck;
730   he will have his share in this my mortal sickness
       and learn of chastity in moderation.

[STROPHE]

CHORUS.   Would that I were under the cliffs, in the secret
       hiding-places of the rocks,
       that Zeus might change me to a winged bird
       and set me among the feathered flocks.
       I would rise and fly to where the sea
       washes the Adriatic coast,
       and to the waters of Eridanus.[27]
       Into that deep-blue tide,
       where their father, the Sun, goes down,
       the unhappy maidens weep
740   tears from their amber-gleaming eyes

---

[27] A mythical river named after the river god Eridanus.

in pity for Phaethon.[28]

I would win my way to the coast,
apple-bearing Hesperian coast,[29]
of which the minstrels sing.
Where the Lord of the Ocean
denies the voyager further sailing,
and fixes the solemn limit of Heaven
which Giant Atlas[30] upholds.
There the streams flow with ambrosia
by Zeus's bed of love,
750   and holy earth, the giver of life,
yields to the Gods rich blessedness.

O Cretan ship with the white sails,
from a happy home you brought her,
my mistress over the tossing foam, over the salty sea,
to bless her with a marriage unblest.
Black was the omen that sped her here,
black was the omen for both her lands,
for glorious Athens and her Cretan home,
760   as they bound to Munychia's pier[31]
the cables' ends with their twisted strands
and stepped ashore on the continent.

The presage of the omen was true;
Aphrodite has broken her spirit
with the terrible sickness of impious love.
The waves of destruction are over her head,
from the roof of her room with its marriage bed,
770   she is tying the twisted noose.
And now it is around her fair white neck!
The shame of her cruel fate has conquered.
She has chosen good name rather than life:
she is easing her heart of its bitter load of love.
NURSE [*within*].   Ho, there, help!
You who are near the palace, help!
My mistress, Theseus' wife, has hanged herself.
CHORUS LEADER.   It is done, she is hanged in the dangling rope.
Our Queen is dead.

---

[28] Phaethon, the son of Apollo, rode his father's chariot across the sky only to be struck by a thunderbolt from Zeus. He fell into the Eridanus and became a swan. As he fell, his sisters, the Helides, wept amber tears for him.

[29] Hesperia, the West. The Hesperides, the daughters of the evening, guarded the golden apple tree in the West, a symbol of immortality.

[30] Atlas was punished for supporting the Titans against Zeus by being forced to carry the weight of the world on his shoulders.

[31] A hero who gave his name to a small harbor, one of Athens' ancient ports.

780 NURSE [*within*].   Quick! Someone bring a knife!
  Help me cut the knot around her neck.

[The CHORUS talks among itself.]

FIRST WOMAN.   What shall we do, friends? Shall we cross the threshold,
  and take the Queen from the grip of the tight-drawn cords?
SECOND WOMAN.   Why should we? There are servants enough within
  for that. Where hands are overbusy,
  there is no safety.
NURSE [*within*].   Lay her out straight, poor lady.
  Bitter shall my lord find her housekeeping.
THIRD WOMAN.   From what I hear, the queen is dead.
  They are already laying out the corpse.

SCENE IV

[THESUS enters.]

790 THESEUS.   Women, what is this crying in the house?
  I heard heavy wailing on the wind,
  as it were servants, mourning. And my house
  deigns me no kindly welcome, though I come
  crowned with good luck from Delphi.[32]
  The doors are shut against me. Can it be
  something has happened to my father. He is old.
  His life has traveled a great journey,
  but bitter would be his passing from our house.
CHORUS LEADER.   King, it is not the old who claim your sorrow.
  Young is the dead and bitterly you'll grieve.
THESEUS.   My children . . . has death snatched a life away?
800 CHORUS LEADER.   Your children live—but sorrowfully, King.
  Their mother is dead.
THESEUS.   It cannot be true, it cannot.
  My wife! How could she be dead?
CHORUS LEADER.   She herself tied the rope around her neck.
THESEUS.   Was it grief and numbing loneliness drove her to it,
  or has there been some violence at work?
CHORUS LEADER.   I know no more than this. I, too, came lately
  to mourn for you and yours, King Theseus.
THESEUS.   Oh,
  Why did I plait this coronal of leaves,
  and crown my head with garlands, I the envoy
  who find my journey end in misery.

[To the servants within.]

---

[32] Delphi, on the slopes of Mount Parnassus, was the home of a famous oracle of Apollo.
Theseus had gone to Delphi to expiate the guilt caused by his murder of the sons of Pallas.

Open the doors! Unbar the fastenings,
  that I may see this bitter sight, my wife
810 who killed me in her own death.

[*The doors are opened, and* Theseus *goes inside. The* Chorus *in the Orchestra divide again into half-choruses and chant.*]

First Half-chorus. Woman unhappy, tortured,
  your suffering, your death,
  has shaken this house to its foundations.
Second Half-chorus. You were daring, you who died
  in violence and guilt.
  Here was a wrestling: your own hand against your life.
Chorus [*united*]. Who can have cast a shadow on your life?

SCENE V

[*Enter* Theseus.]

Theseus. O city, city! Bitterness of sorrow!
  Extremest sorrow that a man can suffer!
  Fate, you have ground me and my house to dust,
  fate in the form of some ineffable
820 pollution, some grim spirit of revenge.
  The file has whittled away my life until
  it is a life no more.
  I am like a swimmer that falls into a great sea:
  I cannot cross this towering wave I see before me.

  My wife! I cannot think
  of anything said or done to drive you to this horrible death.
  You are like a bird that has vanished out of my hand.
  You have made a quick leap out of my arms
  into the land of Death.
830 It must be the sin of some of my ancestors in the dim past
  God in his vengeance makes me pay now.
Chorus Leader. You are not the only one, King.
  Many another as well as you
  has lost a noble wife.
Theseus. Darkness beneath the earth, darkness beneath the earth!
  How good to lie there and be dead,
  now that I have lost you, my dearest comrade.
840 Your death is no less mine.
  Will any of you
  tell me what happened?
  Or does the palace keep a flock of you for nothing?

  God, the pain I saw in the house!
  I cannot speak of it, I cannot bear it.
  I cannot speak of it, I cannot bear it. I am a dead man.

My house is empty and my children orphaned.
You have left them, you
my loving wife—
850   the best of wives
of all the sun looks down on or the blazing stars of the night.
CHORUS.   Woe for the house! Such storms of ill assail it.
My eyes are wells of tears and overrun,
and still I fear the evil that shall come.
THESEUS.   Let her be, let her be:
What is this tablet fastened to her dear hand?[33]
What can she wish to tell me of news?
Have you written begging me to care
for our children or, in entreaty,
860   about another woman? Sad one, rest confident.
There is no woman in the world who shall come to this house
and sleep by my side.
Look, the familiar signet ring,
hers who was once my wife!
Come, I will break the seals,
and see what this letter has to tell me.

[*The* CHORUS *of women speak singly.*]

FIRST WOMAN.   Surely some God
brings sorrow upon sorrow in succession.
870 SECOND WOMAN.   The house of our lords is destroyed: it is no more.
THIRD WOMAN.   God, if it so may be, hear my prayer.
Do not destroy this house utterly. I am a prophet:
I can see the omen of coming trouble.
THESEUS.   Alas, here is endless sorrow upon sorrow.
It passes speech, passes endurance.
CHORUS LEADER.   What is it? Tell us if we may share the story.
THESEUS.   It cries aloud, this tablet, cries aloud,
880   and Death is its song!
CHORUS LEADER.   Prelude of ruin!
THESEUS.   I shall no longer hold this secret prisoner
in the gates of my mouth. It is horrible,
yet I will speak.
Citizens,
Hippolytus has dared to rape my wife.
He has dishonored God's holy sunlight.

[*He turns in the direction of the sea.*]

Father Poseidon, once you gave to me
three curses.[34] . . . Now with one of these, I pray,

---

[33] Scholars surmise that this tablet was probably two wax-coated boards containing a letter and bound with ribbons which she had tied to her hand.

[34] According to legend, Poseidon, the god of the sea, had given Theseus three prayers or promises which he had pledged himself to fulfill.

kill my son. Suffer him not to escape,
890   this very day, if you have promised truly.
Chorus Leader.   Call back your curses, King, call back your curses.
Else you will realize that you were wrong
another day, too late. I pray you, trust me.
Theseus.   I will not. And I now make this addition:
I banish him from this land's boundaries.
So fate shall strike him, one way or the other,
either Poseidon will respect my curse,
and send him dead into the House of Hades,
or exiled from this land, a beggar wandering,
on foreign soil, his life shall suck the dregs
of sorrow's cup.
Chorus Leader.   Here comes your son, and seasonably, King Theseus.
900   Give over your deadly anger. You will best
determine for the welfare of your house.

                                        [*Enter* Hippolytus *with companions.*]

Hippolytus.   I heard you crying, father, and came quickly.
I know no cause why you should mourn.
Tell me.

                                        [*Suddenly he sees the body of* Phaedra.]

O father, father—Phaedra! Dead! She's dead!
I cannot believe it. But a few moments since
I left her. . . . And she is still so young.
But what could it be? How did she die, father?
910   I *must* hear the truth from you. You say nothing to me?

When you are in trouble is no time for silence
The heart that would hear everything
is proved most greedy in misfortune's hour.
You should not hide your troubles from your friends,
and, father, those who are closer than your friends.
Theseus.   What fools men are! You work and work for nothing,
you teach ten thousand tasks to one another,
invent, discover everything. One thing only
you do not know: one thing you never hunt for—
920   a way to teach fools wisdom.
Hippolytus.   Clever indeed
would be the teacher able to compel
the stupid to be wise! This is no time
for such fine logic chopping.
                                        I am afraid
your tongue runs wild through sorrow.
Theseus.   If there were
some token now, some mark to make the division
clear between friend and friend, the true and the false!
All men should have two voices, one the just voice,

and one as chance would have it. In this way
930   the treacherous scheming voice would be confuted
by the just, and we should never be deceived.
HIPPOLYTUS.   Some friend has poisoned your ear with slanderous tales.
Am I suspected, then, for all my innocence?
I am amazed. I am amazed to hear
your words. They are distraught. They go indeed
far wide of the mark!
THESEUS.   The mind of man—how far will it advance?
Where will its daring impudence find limits?
If human villainy and human life
shall wax in due proportion, if the son
shall always grow in wickedness past his father,
940   the Gods must add another world to this
that all the sinners may have space enough.

Look at this man! He was my son and he
dishonors my wife's bed! By the dead's testimony
he's clearly proved the vilest, falsest wretch.
Come—you could stain your conscience with the impurity—
show me your face; show it to me, your father.

You are the veritable holy man!
You walked with Gods in chastity immaculate!
950   I'll not believe your boasts of God's companionship:
the Gods are not so simple nor so ignorant.
Go, boast that you eat no meat, that you have Orpheus
for your king.[35] Read until you are demented
your great thick books whose substance is as smoke.
For I have found you out. I tell you all,
avoid such men as he. They hunt their prey
with holy-seeming words, but their designs
are black and ugly. "She is dead," you thought,
"and that will save me." Fool, it is chiefly that
960   which proves your guilt. What oath that you can swear,
what speech that you can make for your acquittal
outweighs this letter of hers? You'll say, to be sure,
she was your enemy and that the bastard son
is always hateful to the legitimate line.
Your words would argue her a foolish merchant
whose stock of merchandise was her own life
if she should throw away what she held dearest
to gratify her enmity for you.

Or you will tell me that this frantic folly
is inborn in a woman's nature; man
is different: I know that young men

---

[35] The son of Apollo, noted for his skill with the lyre. Orpheus's disciples believed that a
vegetable diet led to purification.

are no more to be trusted than a woman
when love disturbs the youthful blood in them.
970 The very male in them will make them false.
But why should I debate against you in words?
Here is the dead, surest of witnesses.
Get from this land with all the speed you can
to exile—may you rot there! Never again
come to our city, God-built Athens, nor
to countries over which my spear is king.

If I should take this injury at your hands
and pardon you, then Sinis of the Isthmus,
whom once I killed,[36] would vow I never killed him,
but only bragged of the deed. And Sciron's rocks[37]
washed by the sea would call me liar when
980 I swore I was a terror to ill-doers.

CHORUS LEADER.   I cannot say of any man: he is happy.
See here how former happiness lies uprooted!

HIPPOLYTUS.   Your mind and intellect are subtle, father:
here you have a subject dressed in eloquent words;
but if you lay the matter bare of words,
the matter is not eloquent. I am
no man to speak with vapid, precious skill
before a mob, although among my equals
and in a narrow circle I am held
not unaccomplished in the eloquent art.
That is as it should be. The demagogue
who charms a crowd is scorned by cultured experts.
990 But here in this necessity I must speak.
First I shall take the argument you first
urged as so irrefutable and deadly.
You see the earth and air about you, father?
In all of that there lives no man more chaste
than I, though you deny it.
It is my rule to honor the Gods first
and then to have as friends only such men
as do no sin, nor offer wicked service,
nor will consent to sin to serve a friend
as a return for kindness. I am no railer
1000 at my companions. Those who are my friends
find me as much their friends when they are absent
as when we are together.

There is one thing that I have never done, the thing
of which you think that you convict me, father,
I am a virgin to this very day.

---

[36] Sinis was an outlaw whom Theseus killed at the Isthmus of Corinth by tying him to two pine trees and tearing him asunder.

[37] Sciron was another robber killed by Theseus at the so-called Cliffs of Sciron on the island of Salamis.

Save what I have heard or what I have seen in pictures,
I'm ignorant of the deed. Nor do I wish
to see such things, for I've a maiden soul.
But say you disbelieve my chastity.
Then tell me how it was *your* wife seduced me:
was it because she was more beautiful
1010 than all the other women in the world?
Or did I think, when I had taken her,
to win your place and kingdom for a dowry
and live in your own house? I would have been
a fool, a senseless fool, if I had dreamed it.
Was rule so sweet? Never, I tell you, Theseus,
for the wise. A man whom power has so enchanted
must be demented. I would wish to be
first in the contests of the Greeks,
but in the city I'd take second place
and an enduring happy life among
the best society who are my friends.
So one has time to work, and danger's absence
1020 has charms above the royal diadem.
But a word more and my defense is finished.
If I had one more witness to my character,
if I were tried when *she* still saw the light,
deeds would have helped you as you scanned your friends
to know the true from the false. But now I swear,
I swear to you by Zeus, the God of oaths,
by this deep-rooted fundament of earth,
I never sinned against you with your wife
nor would have wished or thought of it.
If I have been a villain, may I die
unfamed, unknown, a homeless stateless beggar,
1030 an exile! May the earth and sea refuse
to give my body rest when I am dead!
Whether your wife took her own life because
she was afraid, I do not know. I may not speak
further than this.
Virtuous she was in deed, although not virtuous:
I that have virtue used it to my ruin.
CHORUS LEADER.   You have rebutted the charge enough by your oath:
it is a great pledge you took in the God's name.
THESEUS.   Why, here's a spell-binding magician for you!
He wrongs his father and then trusts his craft,
1040 his smooth beguiling craft to lull my anger.
HIPPOLYTUS.   Father, I must wonder at this in you.
If I were father now, and you were son,
I would not have banished you to exile! I
would have killed you if I thought you touched my wife.
THESEUS.   This speech is worthy of you: but you'll not die so.
A quick death is the easiest of ends
for miserable men. No, you'll go wandering

far from your fatherland and beg your way.
1050   This is the payment of the impious man.
    HIPPOLYTUS.   What will you do? You will not wait until
    time's pointing finger proves me innocent.
    Must I go at once to banishment?
    THESEUS.   Yes, and had I the power,
    your place of banishment would be beyond
    the limits of the world, the encircling sea
    and the Atlantic Pillars.[38]
    That is the measure of my hate, my son.
    HIPPOLYTUS.   Pledges, oaths, and oracles—you will not test them?
    You will banish me from the kingdom without trial?
    THESEUS.   This letter here is proof without lot-casting.
    The ominous birds may fly above my head:
    they do not trouble me.
    HIPPOLYTUS.   Eternal Gods!
1060   Dare I speak out, since I am ruined now
    through loyalty to the oath I took by you?
    No, he would not believe who should believe
    and I should be false to my oath for nothing.
    THESEUS.   This is more of your holy juggling!
    I cannot stomach it. Away with you!
    Get from this country—and go quickly!
    HIPPOLYTUS.   Where shall I turn? What friend will take me in,
    when I am banished on a charge like this?
    THESEUS.   Doubtless some man who loves to entertain
    his wife's seducers welcoming them at the hearth.
1070 HIPPOLYTUS.   That blow went home.
    I am near crying when I think that I
    am judged to be guilty and that it is you who are judge.
    THESEUS.   You might have sobbed and snivelled long ago,
    and thought of that before when you resolved
    to rape your father's wife.
    HIPPOLYTUS.   House, speak for me!
    Take voice and bear me witness if I have sinned.
    THESEUS.   You have a clever trick of citing witnesses,
    whose testimony is dumb. Here is your handiwork.

                            [Points to the body.]

    It, too, can't speak—but it convicts you.
    HIPPOLYTUS.   If I could only find
    another *me* to look me in the face
    and see my tears and all that I am suffering!
1080 THESEUS.   Yes, in self-worship you are certainly practiced.
    You are more at home there than in the other virtues,
    justice, for instance, and duty toward a father.

---

[38] The Pillars of Hercules, the twin promontories guarding the entrance to the Atlantic at the straits of Gibraltar, consisted of the Rock of Gibraltar to the north and the Jebel Musa in Morroco to the south.

HIPPOLYTUS.   Unhappy mother mine, and bitter birth-pangs,
　　when you gave me to the world! I would not wish
　　on any of my friends a bastard's birth.
THESEUS [*to the servants*].   Drag him away!
　　Did you not hear me, men, a long time since
　　proclaiming his decree of banishment?
HIPPOLYTUS.   Let one of them touch me at his peril! But you,
　　you drive me out yourself—if you have the heart!
THESEUS.   I'll do it, too, unless you go at once.
　　No, there is no chance that pity for your exile
　　will steal on my hard heart and make me change.

[THESEUS *goes out.*]

1090 HIPPOLYTUS.   So, I'm condemned and there is no release.
　　I know the truth and dare not tell the truth.

[*He turns to the statue of Artemis.*)

Daughter of Leto, dearest of the Gods to me,
comrade and partner in the hunt, behold me,
banished from famous Athens.
Farewell, city! Farewell Erechtheus' land!
Troezen, farewell! So many happy times
you knew to give a young man, growing up.
This is the last time I shall look upon you,
the last time I shall greet you.

[*To his companions.*]

Come friends, you are of my age and of this country,
say your farewells and set me on my way.
1100 You will not see a man more innocent—
innocent despite my judge!—condemned to banishment.

[HIPPOLYTUS *goes out.*]
[STROPHE]

CHORUS.   The care of God for us is a great thing,
　　if a man believe it at heart:
　　it plucks the burden of sorrow from him.
　　So I have a secret hope
　　of someone, a God, who is wise and plans;
　　but my hopes grow dim when I see
　　the deeds of men and their destinies.

For fortune is ever veering, and the currents of life are shifting
1110 shifting, wandering forever.

[ANTISTROPHE]

This is the lot in life I seek
and I pray that God may grant it me,
luck and prosperity

and a heart untroubled by anguish.
And a mind that is neither false clipped coin,
nor too clear-eyed in sincerity,
that I may lightly change my ways,
my ways of today when tomorrow comes,
and so be happy all my life long.

[STROPHE]

1120 My heart is no longer clear:
I have seen what I never dreamed,
I have seen the brightest star of Athens,
stricken by a father's wrath,
banished to an alien land.

Sands of the seashore!
Thicket of the mountain!
Where with his pacing hounds
he hunted wild beasts and killed
1130 to the honor of holy Dictynna.

[ANTISTROPHE]

He will never again mount his car
with its span of Venetian mares,
nor fill the ring of Limnae with the sound of horses' hoofs.
The music which never slept
on the strings of his lyre, shall be dumb,
shall be dumb in his father's house.
The haunts of the Goddess Maid
in the deep rich meadow shall want their crowns.
1140 You are banished: there's an end
of the rivalry of maids for your love.

[EPODE]

But my sorrow shall not die,
still my eyes shall be wet with tears
for your heartless doom.
Sad mother, you bore him in vain:
I am angry against the Gods.
Sister Graces, why did you let him go
guiltless, out of his native land,
1150 out of his father's house?

But here I see Hippolytus' servant
in haste making for the house, his face sorrowful.

SCENE VI

[*Enter a* MESSENGER.]

MESSENGER. Where shall I go to find King Theseus, women?
If you know, tell me. Is he within doors?
CHORUS. Here he is coming out.

MESSENGER.   King Theseus,
   I bring you news worthy of much thought
   for you and all the citizens who live
   in Athens' walls and boundaries of Troezen.
1160 THESEUS.   What is it? Has some still newer disaster
   seized my two neighboring cities?
MESSENGER.   Hippolytus is dead: I may almost say dead:
   he sees the light of day still, though the balance
   that holds him in this world is slight indeed.
THESEUS.   Who killed him? I can guess that someone hated him,
   whose wife he raped, as he did mine, his father's.
MESSENGER.   It was the horses of his own car that killed him,
   they, and the curses of your lips,
   the curses you invoked against your son,
   and prayed the Lord of Ocean to fulfil them.
THESEUS.   O God—Poseidon, you are then truly
1170   my father! You have heard my prayers.
   How did he die? Tell me. How did the beam
   of Justice's dead-fall strike him, my dishonorer?
MESSENGER.   We were combing our horses' coats beside the sea,
   where the waves came crashing to the shore. And we were crying
   for one had come and told us that our master,
   Hippolytus, should walk this land no more,
   since you had laid hard banishment upon him.
   Then he came himself down to the shore to us,
   with the same refrain of tears,
   and with him walked a countless company
1180   of friends and young men his own age.

   But at last he gave over crying and said:
   Why do I rave like this? It is my father
   who has commanded and I must obey him.
   Prepare my horses, men, and harness them.
   There is no longer a city of mine.
   Then every man made haste. Before you could say the words,
   there was the chariot ready before our master.
   He put his feet into the driver's rings,
   and took the reins from the rail into his hands.
1190   But first he folded his hands like this and prayed:
   Zeus, let me die now, if I have been guilty!
   Let my father know that he has done me wrong,
   whether I live to see the day or not.

   With that, he took the goad and touched the horses.
   And we his servants followed our master's car,
   close by the horses' heads, on the straight road
   that leads to Argos and to Epidaurus.[39]
   When we were entering the lonely country

---

[39] Two towns on the Peloponnesus, a peninsula in southern Greece.

1200 the other side of the border, where the shore
      goes down to the Saronic Gulf,[40] a rumbling
      deep in the earth, terrible to hear,
      growled like the thunder of Father Zeus.
      The horses raised their heads, pricked up their ears,
      and gusty fear was on us all to know,
      whence came the sound. As we looked toward the shore,
      where the waves were beating, we saw a wave appear,
      a miracle wave, lifting its crest to the sky,
      so high that Sciron's coast was blotted out
      from my eye's vision. And it hid the Isthmus
1210 and the Asclepius Rock.[41] To the shore it came,
      swelling, boiling, crashing, casting its surf around,
      to where the chariot stood.
      But at the very moment when it broke,
      the wave threw up a monstrous savage bull.
      Its bellowing filled the land, and the land echoed it,
      with shuddering emphasis. And sudden panic
      fell on the horses in the car. But the master—
      he was used to horses' ways—all his life long
1220 he had been with horses—took a firm grip of the reins
      and lashed the ends behind his back and pulled
      like a sailor at the oar. The horses bolted:
      their teeth were clenched upon the fire-forged bit.
      They heeded neither the driver's hand nor harness
      nor the jointed car. As often as he would turn them
      with guiding hand to the soft sand of the shore,
      the bull appeared in front to head them off,
      maddening the team with terror.
1230 But when in frenzy they charged toward the cliffs,
      the bull came galloping beside the rail,
      silently following until he brought disaster,
      capsizing the car, striking the wheel on a rock.
      Then all was in confusion. Axles of wheels,
      and lynch-pins flew up into the air,
      and he the unlucky driver, tangled in the reins,
      was dragged along in an inextricable
      knot, and his dear head pounded on the rocks,
      his body bruised. He cried aloud and terrible
1240 his voice rang in our ears: Stand, horses, stand!
      You were fed in my stables. Do not kill me!
      My father's curse! His curse! Will none of you
      save me? I am innocent. Save me!

      Many of us had will enough, but all
      were left behind in the race. Getting free of the reins,
      somehow he fell. There was still life in him.

---

[40] A gulf near Troezen, named after one of its kings.
[41] The Acropolis of Epidaurus, a town in Peloponnesus, north of Argos.

But the horses vanished and that ill-omened monster,
somewhere, I know not where, in the rough cliffs.

I am only a slave in your household, King Theseus,
1250   but I shall never be able to believe
that your son was guilty, not though the tribe of women
were hanged for it, not though the weight of tablets
of a high pine of Ida,[42] filled with writing,
accused him—for I know that he was good.
CHORUS LEADER.   It has been fulfilled, this bitter, new disaster,
for what is doomed and fated there is no quittance.
THESEUS.   For hatred of the sufferer I was glad
at what you told me. Still, he was my son.
As such I have reverence for him and the Gods:
1260   I neither rejoice nor sorrow at this thing.
MESSENGER.   What is your pleasure that we do with him?
Would you have him brought to you? If I might counsel,
you would not be harsh with your son—now he is unfortunate.
THESEUS.   Bring him to me that I may see his face.
He swore that he had never wronged my wife.
I will refute him with God's punishing stroke.
CHORUS.   Cypris, you guide men's hearts
and the inflexible
hearts of the Gods and with you
1270   comes Love with the flashing wings,
comes Love with the swiftest of wings.
Over the earth he flies
and the loud-echoing salt-sea.
He bewitches and maddens the heart
of the victim he swoops upon.
He bewitches the race of the mountain-hunting
lions and beasts of the sea,
and all the creatures that earth feeds,
and the blazing sun sees—
and man, too—
1280   over all you hold kingly power,
Love, you are only ruler
over all these.

EPILOGUE

ARTEMIS.   I call on the noble king, the son of Aegeus,[43]
to hear me! It is I, Artemis, child of Leto.

Miserable man, what joy have you in this?
You have murdered a son, you have broken nature's laws.

---

[42] Mount Ida, near Troy.
[43] The father of Theseus.

Dark indeed was the conclusion
you drew from your wife's lying accusations,
but plain for all to see is the destruction
to which they led you.
1290   There is a hell beneath the earth: haste to it,
and hide your head there! Or will you take wings,
and choosing the life of a bird instead of man
keep your feet from destruction's path in which they tread?
Among good men, at least, you have no share in life.
Hear me tell you, Theseus, how these things came to pass.
I shall not better them, but I will give you pain.
I have come here for this—to show you that your son's heart
was always just, so just that for his good name
he endured to die. I will show you, too,
1300   the frenzied love that seized your wife, or I may call it,
a noble innocence. For that most hated Goddess,
hated by all of us whose joy is virginity,
drove her with love's sharp prickings to desire
your son. She tried to overcome her love
with the mind's power, but at last against her will,
she fell by the nurse's strategems,
the nurse, who told your son under oath her mistress loved him.
But he, just man, did not fall in with her
counsels, and even when reviled by you
refused to break the oath he had pledged.
Such was his piety. But your wife fearing
1310   lest she be proved the sinner wrote a letter,
a letter full of lies; and so she killed
your son by treachery; but she convinced you.
THESEUS.   Alas!
ARTEMIS.   This is a bitter story, Theseus. Stay,
hear more that you may groan the more.
You know you had three curses from your father,
three, clear for you to use? One you have launched,
vile wretch, at your own son, when you might have
spent it upon an enemy. Your father,
King of the Sea, in loving kindness to you
gave you, by his bequest, all that he ought.
1320   But you've been proved at fault both in his eyes
and mine in that you did not stay for oaths
nor voice or oracles, nor gave a thought
to what time might have shown; only too quickly
you hurled the curses at your son and killed him.
THESEUS.   Mistress, I am destroyed.
ARTEMIS.   You have sinned indeed, but yet you may win pardon.
For it was Cypris managed the thing this way
to gratify her anger against Hippolytus.
This is the settled custom of the Gods:
No one may fly in the face of another's wish:
1330   we remain aloof and neutral. Else, I assure you,

had I not feared Zeus, I never would have endured
such shame as this—my best friend among men
killed, and I could do nothing.
As for you, in the first place ignorance acquits you,
and then your wife, by her death, destroyed the proofs,
the verbal proofs which might have still convinced you.
You and I are the chief sufferers, Theseus.
Misfortune for you, grief for me.

1340 The Gods do not rejoice when pious worshippers die:
the wicked we destroy, children, house and all.
 CHORUS. Here comes the suffering Hippolytus,
his fair young body and his golden head,
a battered wreck. O trouble of the house,
what double sorrow from the hand of God
has been fulfilled for this our royal palace!
 HIPPOLYTUS. A battered wreck of body! Unjust father,
and oracle unjust—this is your work.

1350 Woe for my fate!
My head is filled with shooting agony,
and in my brain there is a leaping fire.
Let me be!
For I would rest my weary frame awhile.
Curse on my team! How often have I fed you
from my own hand, you who have murdered me!
O, O!
In God's name touch my wounded body gently.

1360 Who is this standing on the right of me?
Come lift me carefully, bear me easily,
a man unlucky, cursed by my own father
in bitter error. Zeus, do you see this,
see me that worshipped God in piety,
me that excelled all men in chastity,
see me now go to death which gapes before me;
all my life lost, and all for nothing now
labors of piety in the face of men?

1370 O the pain, that comes upon me!
Let me be, let me be, you wretches!
May death the healer come for me at last!
You kill me ten times over with this pain.
O for a spear with a keen cutting edge
to shear me apart—and give me my last sleep!
Father, your deadly curse!

1380 This evil comes from some manslaying of old,
some ancient tale of murder among my kin.
But why should it strike me, who am clear of guilt?
What is there to say? How can I shake from me
this pitiless pain? O death, black night of death,
resistless death, come to me now the miserable,
and give me sleep!

ARTEMIS.   Unhappy boy! You are yoked to a cruel fate.
1390   The nobility of your soul has proved your ruin.
HIPPOLYTUS.   O divine fragrance! Even in my pain
   I sense it, and the suffering is lightened.
   The Goddess Artemis is near this place.
ARTEMIS.   She is, the dearest of the Gods to you.
HIPPOLYTUS.   You see my suffering, mistress?
ARTEMIS.   I see it. Heavenly law forbids my tears.
HIPPOLYTUS.   Gone is your huntsman, gone your servant now.
ARTEMIS.   Yes, truly: but you die beloved by me.
HIPPOLYTUS.   Gone is your groom, gone your shrine's guardian.
1400 ARTEMIS.   Cypris, the worker of mischief, so contrived.
HIPPOLYTUS.   Alas, I know the Goddess who destroyed me!
ARTEMIS.   She blamed your disrespect, hated your chastity.
HIPPOLYTUS.   She claimed us three as victims then, did Cypris?
ARTEMIS.   Your father, you, and me to make a third.
HIPPOLYTUS.   Yes, I am sorry for my father's suffering.
ARTEMIS.   Cypris deceived him by her cunning snares.
HIPPOLYTUS.   O father, this is sorrow for you indeed!
THESEUS.   I, too, am dead now. I have no more joy in life.
HIPPOLYTUS.   I sorrow for you in this more than myself.
1410 THESEUS.   Would that it was I who was dying instead of you!
HIPPOLYTUS.   Bitter were Poseidon's gifts, my father, bitter.
THESEUS.   Would that they had never come into my mouth.
HIPPOLYTUS.   Even without them, you would have killed me—
   you were so angry.
THESEUS.   A God tripped up my judgment.
HIPPOLYTUS.   O, if only men might be a curse to Gods!
ARTEMIS.   Hush, that is enough! You shall not be unavenged,
   Cypris shall find the angry shafts she hurled
   against you for your piety and innocence
   shall cost her dear.
1420   I'll wait until she loves a mortal next time,
   and with this hand—with these unerring arrows
   I'll punish him.

   To you, unfortunate Hippolytus,
   by way of compensation for these ills,
   I will give the greatest honors of Troezen.
   Unwedded maids before the day of marriage
   will cut their hair in your honor. You will reap
   through the long cycle of time, a rich reward in tears.
   And when young girls sing songs, they will not forget you,
   your name will not be left unmentioned,
1430   nor Phaedra's love for you remain unsung.

[*To* THESEUS.]

   Son of old Aegeus, take your son
   to your embrace. Draw him to you. Unknowing

you killed him. It is natural for men
to err when they are blinded by the Gods.

[*To* HIPPOLYTUS.]

Do not bear a grudge against your father.
It was fate that you should die so.
Farewell, I must not look upon the dead.
My eye must not be polluted by the last
gaspings for breath. I see you are near this.
1440 HIPPOLYTUS.   Farewell to you, too holy maiden! Go in peace.
You can lightly leave a long companionship.
You bid me end my quarrel with my father,
and I obey. In the past, too, I obeyed you.

The darkness is upon my eyes already.

Father, lay hold on me and lift me up.
THESEUS.   Alas, what are you doing to me, my son?
HIPPOLYTUS.   I am dying. I can see the gates of death.
THESEUS.   And so you leave me, my hands stained with murder.
HIPPOLYTUS.   No, for I free you from all guilt in this.
1450 THESEUS.   You will acquit me of blood guiltiness?
HIPPOLYTUS.   So help me Artemis of the conquering bow!
THESEUS.   Dear son, how noble you have proved to me!
HIPPOLYTUS.   Yes, pray to heaven for such legitimate sons.
THESEUS.   Woe for your goodness, piety, and virtue.
HIPPOLYTUS.   Farewell to you, too, father, a long farewell!
THESEUS.   Dear son, bear up. Do not forsake me.
HIPPOLYTUS.   This is the end of what I have to bear.
I'm gone. Cover my face up quickly.
THESEUS.   Pallas Athene's famous city,
1460   what a man you have lost! Alas for me!
Cypris, how many of your injuries
I shall remember.
CHORUS.   This is a common grief for all the city;
it came unlooked for. There shall be
a storm of multitudinous tears for this;
the lamentable stories of great men
prevail more than of humble folk.

[428 B.C.]

Critical Commentary on *Hippolytus*

The legendary story of the chaste youth Hippolytus and his stepmother
Phaedra, who falls in love with him, accuses him of rape when rebuffed, and
subsequently commits suicide, is one that plainly fascinated Euripides and
his Athenian contemporaries. That it has continued to fascinate writers and

audiences is indicated by the many other versions of the story, including those by Seneca in first-century A.D. Rome, by Racine in seventeenth-century France, and by O'Neill (in a somewhat different form) in twentieth-century America. Euripides had already treated the story in an earlier play, now lost, *Hippolytus Veiled,* which apparently shocked its Athenian audience by focusing on Phaedra's passion in such a way as to reduce her to a harlot. Despite its failure, Euripides remained intrigued by the theme and, perhaps stimulated by the knowledge that Sophocles had dramatized the story with considerable success, decided to produce a new and very different version. When the second *Hippolytus* was performed as a part of a trilogy during the festival of Dionysus in 428 B.C., Euripides was awarded first place.

Hippolytus is one of the best of Euripides' surviving plays. It is praised for its unity, for the depth and realism of its psychological portraits, for its satire of both traditional mythology and contemporary philosophy, and for the way in which Euripides recasts the traditional role of the chorus by removing it from the dramatic action of the play. Yet *Hippolytus* is also a play that raises a series of critical issues and questions about which there is substantial disagreement.

One of the most basic of these critical disagreements concerns the identity of the protagonist. Despite its title, and Aphrodite's clear statement in her opening speech that she intends to "punish Hippolytus this day" using Phaedra as her agent, it is often suggested that Phaedra, rather than Hippolytus, is the character of central interest. Such a view is easy enough to understand. It originates no doubt in the elaborate dramatic treatment given Phaedra's anguish and suffering as she attempts to come to grips with the implications of her own sexuality and the multitude of human emotions it in turn releases: vanity, pride, fear, jealousy, anger, hatred, and the desire for revenge. In developing the character of Phaedra, Euripides has taken on a formidable task. He must make credible as a "good" woman someone who kills herself and in essence murders an innocent man. That he succeeds is clear. Phaedra, in whom honor and intellect battle with instinct and passion, is one of the most fully realized and interesting characters in all of dramatic literature. Such an achievement does not, however, necessarily qualify Phaedra as the play's protagonist.

Part of the temptation to regard her as such clearly has to do with Hippolytus himself. When as astute a classical scholar as H. D. F. Kitto argues that the play's "rhythm goes the wrong way, from the very dramatic Phaedra to the less dramatic Hippolytus," he is simply stating the obvious. Hippolytus is an unworldly, asexual, and overbearingly self-righteous young man who is not nearly as attractive (or as convincing and believable) as the intense and passionate Phaedra. Many readers will surely agree with Kitto's verdict that Hippolytus is a "chilly," "disappointing" and much "too negative" character.

Hippolytus is indeed a difficult figure for modern readers and theatergoers to come to admire. By turns an odd and unpredictable mixture of unwordliness and arrogance, Hippolytus prides himself on his goodness and purity, even as he goes out of his way to insult Aphrodite. Although we cannot fail to be repelled by the cruel and tactless attitude he exhibits before Phaedra's obvious suffering, we nonetheless must also grant Hippolytus the sincerity of his pursuit of virtue, the clear love of beauty he displays in his prayer to Artemis, and the fact that his actions and conduct are generally praiseworthy, particularly his refusal to break his oath to Phaedra even though doing so might save his life. His weakness is, of course, tied to his refusal to acknowledge the legitimacy of sexual passion as a constituent part of the human condition. As a result, as G. M. A. Grube points out, "Hippolytus has the essentially limited outlook of a youth whose adoration is reserved for a negative purity, with the result that admiration of his own perfection makes him incapable of understanding or sympathizing with others, or of admitting any greatness in what he fails to understand." If Grube is correct about Hippolytus's lack of self-knowledge, then his observation helps to explain why Hippolytus does such a poor job of defending himself against the charges that his father, Theseus, levels against him.

Many critics subject the character of Hippolytus to a variety of psychoanalytic interpretations, for they see his self-conscious abstinence as a classic case of arrested adolescent development with clear Freudian overtones. "The difference between *Hippolytus* and a modern psychiatric history—and a fortunate difference—," John Gassner observes, "is only the fact that the psychological conflict in Euripides' tragedy is presented poetically rather than clinically. The play is suggestive rather than matter-of-fact, and the atmosphere exudes the wonder and magic of ancient legend."

Phaedra's character is an equally complex and conflicted one. Surely Hazel Barnes is correct when she sees Phaedra as torn between two opposing desires: the desire to maintain her reputation by concealing her love and the desire to find release through a confession of love. As a result, as Barnes contends,

> Phaedra's conflict is waged in bad faith. First of all, she will not admit to herself that fear of betrayal is balanced by a hope of what betrayal might win. Secondly, she plays the game in such a way that she can persuade herself that she has never willingly confessed her love but was compelled by extreme forces. From the beginning her conduct and words are calculated to make further inquiry inevitable. Her resolve to die by fasting (in itself an overreaction) is certain to attract attention. It enables Phaedra to think that she has chosen death in preference to wrongdoing; yet it keeps her alive in case the situation should change. In other words she is not so much ill as the result of repressed love as she is making herself ill as a way of expressing her love and in order to be forced to speak it openly.

Phaedra's motives and behavior (including whether or not she knows that the nurse intends to betray her to Hippolytus) are, in short, anything but simple and straightforward. In her case, as in the case of Hippolytus, the motives are partially subconscious and thus Phaedra herself may only be partially responsible for her own actions and fate.

But if the characters are not fully responsible, is ultimate responsibility to be borne by the gods—particularly by Artemis and Aphrodite in their proud battle for power and devotees? And what do these gods represent anyway? We know that Euripides viewed the Olympians far differently than his predecessors. He came to intellectual maturity at a time when skepticism was in the air and the old legends and gods had lost much of their former potency. At a certain level Euripides is surely satirizing the moral authority of the gods, but their presence in the play cannot be ignored.

Even knowing what we do of Euripides' frequently iconoclastic and satiric treatment of the gods, what are we to make of the callous vindictiveness of Aphrodite, who vows to punish Hippolytus for spurning her in favor of Artemis? What are we to think of Poseidon for his willingness to grant any three wishes that Theseus (a mere mortal) may ask— though one of them results in the undeserving death of Hippolytus? And how are we to regard Artemis's inability (or unwillingness) to intervene on behalf of Hippolytus, who has devoted his life to her service?

It may help our understanding if we view these deities, as some scholars invite us to do, not as anthropomorphic gods but rather as symbols of chastity (Artemis) and sexual love (Aphrodite). Sensible human beings should recognize that both are virtues, but how can one strike a balance between these seemingly incompatible values? Is there a golden mean between Hippolytus's cold chastity and Phaedra's boiling passion? Would the "second thoughts" that the nurse so frequently recommends have allowed Hippolytus and Phaedra to find some golden mean?

Whatever we decide about the role and meaning of Euripides's gods, there can be no question that they are dramatically effective. "What we feel as the play ends," Grube concludes, "is an intense pity for those poor mortals in the power of terrifying forces of these gods who have them at their mercy; but we feel pride too that men can at least find reconciliation which the gods cannot or will not know."

A Selective Bibliography on *Hippolytus*

Barnes, Hazel E. "The Hippolytus of Drama and Myth." *Hippolytus in Drama and Myth: The Hippolytus of Euripides*. Trans. Donald Sutherland. Lincoln: U of Nebraska P, 1960. 69–123.

Buxton, R. G. A. *Persuasion in Greek Tragedy: A Study of Peitho*. Cambridge, Eng.: Cambridge UP, 1982.

Des Bouvrie, Synnove. *Women in Greek Tragedy: An Anthropological Approach*. Oslo: Norwegian UP, 1990.

Dimock, G. E. "Euripides' Hippolytus, or Virtue Rewarded." *Yale Classical Studies* 25 (1977): 239–58.

Ferguson, John. *A Companion to Greek Tragedy*. Austin: U of Texas P, 1972. 276–93.

Fitzgerald, G. J. "Misconception, Hypocrisy, and the Structure of Euripides' Hippolytus." *Ramus* 2 (1973): 20–40.

Glenn, J. "The Phantasies of Phaedra: A Psychoanalytic Reading." *Classical World* 69 (1976): 435–42.

Goff, Barbara E. *The Noose of Words: Readings of Desire, Violence, and Language in Euripides' Hippolytus*. Cambridge, Eng.: Cambridge UP, 1990.

Goodkin, Richard E. *The Tragic Middle: Racine, Aristotle, Euripides*. Madison: U of Wisconsin P, 1991.

Goldhill, Simon. *Reading Greek Tragedy*. Cambridge: Cambridge UP, 1986.

Greenwood, L. H. G. *Aspects of Euripidean Tragedy*. Oxford: Cambridge UP, 1972. 42–48.

Gregory, Justina. *Euripides and the Instruction of the Athenians*. Ann Arbor: U of Michigan P, 1991.

Grube, G. M. A. *The Drama of Euripides*. New York: Barnes & Noble, 1961. 177–97.

Herington, C. J. *Poetry into Drama: Early Tragedy and the Greek Poetic Tradition.* Berkeley: U of California P, 1985.

Kitto, H. D. F. *Greek Tragedy: A Literary Study.* London: Methuen, 1968. 186–287.

Knox, Bernard. "The *Hippolytus* of Euripides." *Yale Classical Studies* 13 (1952): 3–31.

———. *Word and Action: Essays on the Ancient Theater.* Baltimore: Johns Hopkins UP, 1979. 205–30.

Kovacs, David. *The Heroic Muse: Studies in the Hippolytus and Hecuba of Euripides.* Baltimore: Johns Hopkins UP, 1987.

Larmour, David H. J. "Phaedra and the Chariot-ride." *Eranos* 86 (1988): 25–30.

Lattimore, R. "Phaedra and Hippolytus." *Arion* 13 (1962): 5–18.

Loraux, Nicole. *Tragic Ways of Killing a Woman.* Trans. Anthony Forster. Cambridge: Harvard UP, 1987.

Luschnig, C. A. E. *Time Holds the Mirror: A Study of Knowledge in Euripides' Hippolytus.* New York: Brill, 1988.

Norwood, Gilbert. *Essays on Euripidean Drama.* Berkeley: U of California P, 1954. 74–111.

Padel, Ruth. *In and Out of Mind: Greek Images of the Tragic Self.* Princeton: Princeton UP, 1992.

Rankin, A. V. "Euripides' Hippolytus: A Psychopathological Hero." *Areth* 7 (1974): 71–94.

Segal, Charles. *Interpreting Greek Tragedy: Myth, Poetry, Text.* Ithaca: Cornell UP, 1986. 165–221.

Snell, Bruno. *Scenes from Greek Tragedy.* Berkeley: U of California P, 1964. 23–69.

Willink, C. W. "Some Problems of Text and Interpretation in the Hippolytus." *Classical Quarterly* 62 (1968): 11–43.

Zimmerman, Bernhardt. *Greek Tragedy: An Introduction.* Trans. Thomas Marier. Baltimore: Johns Hopkins UP, 1991.

Aristophanes (ca. 450—385 B.C.)

LYSISTRATA

Translated by Douglass Parker

CHARACTERS

LYSISTRATA⎱
KLEONIKE ⎰*Athenian women*
MYRRHINE ⎰
LAMPITO, *a Spartan woman*
ISMENIA, *a Boiotian girl*
KORINTHIAN GIRL
POLICEWOMAN
KORYPHAIOS OF THE MEN
CHORUS OF OLD MEN *of Athens*
KORYPHAIOS OF THE WOMEN
CHORUS OF OLD WOMEN *of Athens*
COMMISSIONER OF PUBLIC SAFETY

FOUR POLICEMEN
KINESIAS, *Myrrhine's husband*
CHILD *of Kinesias and Myrrhine*
SLAVE
SPARTAN HERALD
SPARTAN AMBASSADOR
FLUTE-PLAYER
ATHENIAN WOMEN
PELOPONNESIAN WOMEN
PELOPONNESIAN MEN
ATHENIAN MEN

SCENE

A street in Athens. In the background, the Akropolis; center, its gateway, the Propylaia. The time is early morning. LYSISTRATA *is discovered alone, pacing back and forth in furious impatience.*

LYSISTRATA. *Women!*
 Announce a debauch in honor of Bacchos,
 a spree for Pan,[1] some footling fertility fieldday,
 and traffic stops—the streets are absolutely clogged
 with frantic females banging on tambourines. No urging
 for an orgy!
    But *today*—there's not one woman here.

            [*Enter* KLEONIKE.]

 Correction: one. Here comes my next door neighbor.
 —Hello, Kleonike.
KLEONIKE.   Hello to *you*, Lysistrata.
 —But what's the fuss? Don't look so barbarous, baby;
10 knitted brows just aren't your style.
LYSISTRATA.   It doesn't

---

[1] Bacchos (or Bacchus) is the Greek god of wine and revelry. Pan, the god of the fields and forests, is usually depicted as a lecherous satyr with the head and torso of a man but the horns and shaggy hindquarters of a goat.

matter, Kleonike—I'm on fire right down to the bone.
I'm positively ashamed to be a woman—a member
of a sex which can't even live up to male slanders!
To hear our husbands talk, we're *sly*: deceitful,
always plotting, monsters of intrigue. . . .
KLEONIKE [*Proudly*].   That's us!
LYSISTRATA.   And so we agreed to meet today and plot
an intrigue that really deserves the name of monstrous . . .
and WHERE are the women?
                                        Slyly asleep at home—
they won't get up for anything!
20 KLEONIKE.   Relax, honey.
They'll be here. You know a woman's way is hard—
mainly the way out of the house: fuss over hubby,
wake the maid up, put the baby down, bathe him,
feed him . . .
LYSISTRATA.   Trivia. They have more fundamental business to
     engage in.
KLEONIKE.   Incidentally, Lysistrata, just why are
you calling this meeting? Nothing teeny, I trust?
LYSISTRATA.   Immense.
KLEONIKE.   Hmmm. And pressing?
LYSISTRATA   Unthinkably tense.
KLEONIKE.   Then where IS everybody?
LYSISTRATA.   Nothing like that. If it were,
we'd already be in session. Seconding motions.
30   —No, *this* came to hand some time ago. I've spent
my nights kneading it, mulling it, filing it down. . . .
KLEONIKE.   Too bad. There can't be very much left.
LYSISTRATA.   Only this:
the hope and salvation of Hellas lies with the WOMEN!
KLEONIKE.   Lies with the women? Now *there's* a last resort.
LYSISTRATA.   It lies with us to decide affairs of state
and foreign policy.
                              The Spartan Question:[2] Peace
or Extirpation?
KLEONIKE.   How *fun!*
                                        I cast an Aye for Extirpation
LYSISTRATA.   The Utter Annihilation of every last Boiotian?
40 KLEONIKE.   AYE!—I mean Nay. Clemency, please, for those
     scrumptious eels.[3]
LYSISTRATA.   And as for Athens . . . I'd rather not put
the thought into words. Just fill in the blanks, if you will.

---

   [2] "The Spartan Question" is a reference to the Peloponnesian War (431–404 B.C.) which was
dominating Athenian life at the time this play was written (411 B.C.). The war was fought between
Sparta and Athens, the most powerful of the city-states in Greece (also called Hellas). The
various women in the play gather from all parts of Greece and represent the contending factions
and their allies.
   [3] Eels from Lake Kopais in Boiotia were considered a delicacy.

—To the point: if we can meet and reach agreement
here and now with the girls from Thebes and the Peloponnese,
we'll form an alliance and save the States of Greece!

KLEONIKE.   Us? Be practical. Wisdom from women? There's nothing
cosmic about cosmetics—and Glamor is our only talent.
All we can do is *sit*, primped and painted,
made up and dressed up,

> [*Getting carried away in spite of her argument.*]

> ravishing in saffron wrappers,
50   peekaboo peignoirs, exquisite negligees, those chic,
expensive little slippers that come from the East . . .

LYSISTRATA.   Exactly. You've hit it. I see our way to salvation
in just such ornamentation—in slippers and slips, rouge
and perfumes, negligees and decolletage. . . .

KLEONIKE.   How so?

LYSISTRATA.   So effectively that not one husband will take up his spear
against another . . .

KLEONIKE.   Peachy!
> I'll have that kimono
dyed . . .

LYSISTRATA.   . . . or shoulder his shield . . .

KLEONIKE.   . . . squeeze into that
daring negligee . . .

LYSISTRATA.   . . . or unsheathe his sword!

KLEONIKE.   . . . and buy those
slippers!

60 LYSISTRATA.   Well, now. Don't you think the girls should be here?

KLEONIKE.   *Be* here? Ages ago—they should have flown!

> [*She stops.*]

But no. You'll find out. These are authentic Athenians:
no matter what they do, they do it late.

LYSISTRATA.   But what about the out-of-town delegations? There isn't
a woman here from the Shore; none from Salamis . . .

KLEONIKE.   *That's* quite a trip. They usually get on board
at sunup. Probably riding at anchor now.

LYSISTRATA.   I thought the girls from Acharnai would be here first.
I'm especially counting on them. And they're not here.

70 KLEONIKE.   I think Theogenes' wife is under way.
When I went by, she was hoisting her sandals . . .

> [*Looking off right.*]

> But look!

Some of the girls are coming!

[*Women enter from the right.* LYSISTRATA *looks off to the left where more—a ragged lot—are straggling in.*]

LYSISTRATA.   And more over here!

KLEONIKE.   Where did you find *that* group?
LYSISTRATA.   They're from the outskirts.
KLEONIKE.   Well, that's something. If you haven't done anything
   else, you've really ruffled up the outskirts.

[MYRRHINE *enters guiltily from the right.*]

MYRRHINE.   Oh, Lysistrata,
   we aren't late, are we?
                    Well, *are* we?
                              Speak to me!
LYSISTRATA.   What is it, Myrrhine? Do you want a medal for tardiness?
   Honestly, such behavior, with so much at stake . . .
MYRRHINE.   I'm sorry. I couldn't find my girdle in the dark.
80   And anyway, we're here now. So tell us all about it,
   whatever it is.
KLEONIKE.   No, wait a minute. Don't
   begin just yet. Let's wait for those girls from Thebes
   and the Peloponnese.
LYSISTRATA.   Now *there* speaks the proper attitude.

[LAMPITO, *a strapping Spartan woman, enters left, leading a pretty Boiotian girl*
(ISMENIA) *and a huge, steatopygous*[4] *Korinthian.*]

   And here's our lovely Spartan.
                    Hel*lo,* Lampito
   dear. Why darling, you're simply ravishing! Such
   a blemishless complexion—so clean, so out-of-doors!
   And will you look at that figure—the pink of perfection!
KLEONIKE.   I'll bet you could strangle a bull.
LAMPITO.   I calklate so.
   Hit's fitness whut done it, fitness and dancin'. You know
   the step?

[*Demonstrating.*]

90   Foot it out back'ards an' toe yore twitchet.

[*The women crowd around* LAMPITO.]

KLEONIKE.   What unbelievably beautiful bosoms!
LAMPITO.   Shuckins,
   whut fer you tweedlin' me up so? I feel like a heifer
   come fair-time.
LYSISTRATA [*Turning to* ISMENIA].   And who is this young lady here?
LAMPITO.   Her kin's purt-near the bluebloodiest folk in Thebes—
   the First Fam'lies of Boiotia.
LYSISTRATA [*As they inspect* ISMENIA].   Ah, picturesque Boiotia:
   her verdant meadows, her fruited plain . . .
KLEONIKE [*Peering more closely*].   Her sunken
   garden where no grass grows. A cultivated country.

---

[4] Big-buttocked.

LYSISTRATA [*Gaping at the gawking* KORINTHIAN].
And who is *this*—er—little thing?
LAMPITO.   She hails
from over by Korinth, but her kinfolk's quality—mighty
big back there.
100 KLEONIKE [*On her tour of inspection*].   She's mighty big back *here.*
LAMPITO.   The womenfolk's all assemblied. Who-all's notion
was this-hyer confabulation?
LYSISTRATA.   Mine.
LAMPITO.   Git on with the give-out.
I'm hankerin' to hear.
MYRRHINE.   Me, too! I can't imagine
what could be so important. Tell us about it!
LYSISTRATA.   Right away.
                    —But first, a question. It's not
an involved one. Answer yes or no.

[*A pause.*]

MYRRHINE.   Well, ASK it!
LYSISTRATA.   It concerns the fathers of your children—your husbands,
absent on active service. I know you all have men
abroad.
                    —Wouldn't you like to have them home?
110 KLEONIKE.   My husband's been gone for the last five months! Way up
to Thrace, watchdogging military waste. It's horrible!
MYRRHINE.   Mine's been posted to Pylos for seven whole months!
LAMPITO.   My man's no sooner rotated out of the line
than he's plugged back in. Hain't no discharge in this war!
KLEONIKE.   And lovers can't be had for love or money,
not even synthetics. Why, since those beastly Milesians
revolted and cut off the leather trade, that handy
do-it-yourself kit's *vanished* from the open market!
LYSISTRATA.   If I can devise a scheme for ending the war,
I gather I have your support?
120 KLEONIKE.   You can count on me!
If you need money, I'll pawn the shift off my back—[*Aside.*] and drink
up
the cash before the sun goes down.
MYRRHINE.   Me, too! I'm ready to split myself right up
the middle like a mackerel, and give you half!
LAMPITO.   Me, too! I'd climb Taygetos Mountain plumb
to the top to git the leastes' peek at Peace!
LYSISTRATA.   Very well, I'll tell you. No reason to keep a secret.

[*Importantly, as the women cluster around her.*]

We can force our husbands to negotiate Peace,
Ladies, by exercising steadfast Self-Control—
By Total Abstinence . . . [*A pause.*]
KLEONIKE.   From WHAT?
MYRRHINE.   Yes, what?
130 LYSISTRATA.   You'll do it?

KLEONIKE.   Of course we'll do it! We'd even *die!*
LYSISTRATA.   Very well,
   then here's the program:
                        Total Abstinence
                             from SEX!

                             [*The cluster of women dissolves.*]

—Why are you turning away? Where are you going?

                             [*Moving among the women.*]

—What's this? Such stricken expressions! Such gloomy gestures!
—Why so pale?
             —Whence these tears?
                             —What IS this?
   Will you do it or won't you?
                        Cat got your tongue?

KLEONIKE.   Afraid I can't make it. Sorry.
                             On with the War!
MYRRHINE.   Me neither. Sorry.
                        On with the War!
LYSISTRATA.   *This* from
   my little mackerel? The girl who was ready, a minute
140   ago, to split herself right up the middle?
KLEONIKE [*Breaking in between* LYSISTRATA *and* MYRRHINE].   Try something
      else. Try anything. If you say so,
   I'm willing to walk through fire barefoot.
                                    But not
   to give up SEX—there's nothing like it, Lysistrata!
LYSISTRATA [*To* MYRRHINE].   And you?
MYRRHINE.   Me, too! I'll walk through fire.
LYSISTRATA.   *Women!*
   Utter sluts, the entire sex! Will-power,
   nil. We're perfect raw material for Tragedy,
   the stuff of heroic lays. "Go to bed with a god
   and then get rid of the baby"—that sums us up!

                             [*Turning to* LAMPITO.]

—Oh, Spartan, be a dear. If *you* stick by me,
150   just you, we still may have a chance to win.
   Give me your vote.

LAMPITO.   Hit's right onsettlin' fer gals
   to sleep all lonely-like, withouten no humpin'.
   But I'm on yore side. We shore need Peace, too.
LYSISTRATA.   You're a darling—the only woman here
   worthy of the name!
KLEONIKE.   Well, just suppose we *did,*
   as much as possible, abstain from . . . what you said,
   you know—not that we *would*—could something like

that bring Peace any sooner?

LYSISTRATA.   Certainly. Here's how it works:
We'll paint, powder, and pluck ourselves to the last
160   detail, and stay inside, wearing those filmy
tunics that set off everything we *have*—

                         and then
slink up to the men. They'll snap to attention, go
absolutely *mad* to love us—

                  but we won't let them. We'll Abstain.
—I imagine they'll conclude a treaty rather quickly.

LAMPITO [*Nodding*]. Menelaos he tuck one squint at Helen's bubbies
all nekkid, and plumb throwed up.

                             [*Pause for thought.*]

                   Throwed up his sword.

KLEONIKE. Suppose the men just leave us flat?

LYSISTRATA.   In that case,
we'll have to take things into our own hands.

KLEONIKE. There simply isn't any reasonable facsimile!
170   —Suppose they take us by force and drag us off
to the bedroom against our wills?

LYSISTRATA.   Hang on to the door.

KLEONIKE. Suppose they beat us?

LYSISTRATA.   Give in——but be bad sports.
Be nasty about it—they don't enjoy these forced
affairs. So make them suffer.

                  Don't worry; they'll stop
soon enough. A married man wants harmony—
cooperation, not rape.

KLEONIKE.   Well, I suppose so. . . .

              [*Looking from* LYSISTRATA *to* LAMPITO.]

If *both* of you approve this, then so do we.

LAMPITO. Hain't worried over our menfolk none. We'll bring 'em
round to makin' a fair, straightfor'ard Peace
180   withouten no nonsense about it. But take this rackety
passel in Athens: I misdoubt no one could make 'em
give over thet blabber of theirn.

LYSISTRATA.   They're our concern.
Don't worry. We'll bring them around.

LAMPITO.   Not likely.
Not long as they got ships kin still sail straight,
an' thet fountain of money up thar in Athene's temple.[5]

LYSISTRATA. That point is quite well covered:

                    We're taking over
The Akropolis, including Athene's temple, today.

---

[5] The Athenians kept a reserve fund of one thousand silver coins in the back of Athene's temple, located on a hill called the Akropolis.

It's set: Our oldest women have their orders.
They're up there now, pretending to sacrifice, waiting
190   for us to reach an agreement. As soon as we do,
they seize the Akropolis.

LAMPITO.   The way you put them thengs,
I swear I can't see how we kin possibly lose!

LYSISTRATA.   Well, now that it's settled, Lampito, let's not lose
any time. Let's take the Oath to make this binding.

LAMPITO.   Just trot out thet-thar Oath. We'll swear it.

LYSISTRATA.   Excellent.
—Where's a policewoman?

[*A huge girl, dressed as a Skythian archer (the Athenian police) with bow and circular
shield, lumbers up and gawks.*]

                    —What are *you* looking for?

                              [*Pointing to a spot in front of the women.*]

Put your shield down here.

                                        [*The girl obeys.*]

No, hollow *up!*

                    [*The girl reverses the shield.* LYSISTRATA *looks about brightly.*]
—Someone give me the entrails.

                                        [*A dubious silence.*]

KLEONIKE.   Lysistrata, what kind
of an Oath are we supposed to swear?

LYSISTRATA.   The Standard.
Aischylos[6] used it in a play, they say—the one where
you slaughter a sheep and swear on a shield.

200 KLEONIKE.   Lysistrata,
you *do not* swear an Oath for *Peace* on a *shield!*

LYSISTRATA.   What Oath do you want?

                                                  [*Exasperated.*]

                    Something bizarre and expensive?
A fancier victim—"Take one white horse and
disembowel"?

KLEONIKE.   *White horse:* The symbolism's too obscure.

LYSISTRATA.   *Then how
do we swear this oath?*

KLEONIKE.   Oh, *I* can tell you
that, if you'll let me.
                    First, we put an enormous
black cup right here—hollow up, of course.

---

⁶ Aeschylus (525–456 B.C.) was the earliest of the great Greek playwrights.

Next, into the cup we slaughter a jar of Thasian
210   wine, and swear a mighty Oath that we won't . . .
dilute it with water.
LAMPITO [*To* KLEONIKE]. Let me corngratulate you—
that were the beatenes' Oath I ever heerd on!
LYSISTRATA [*Calling inside*]. Bring out a cup and a jug of wine!

[*Two women emerge, the first staggering under the weight of a huge black cup, the
second even more burdened with a tremendous wine jar.* KLEONIKE *addresses them.*]

KLEONIKE.   You darlings!
What a tremendous display of pottery!

[*Fingering the cup.*]

A girl
could get a glow just *holding* a cup like this!

[*She grabs it away from the first woman, who exits.*]

LYSISTRATA [*Taking the wine jar from the second serving woman (who exits), she
barks at* KLEONIKE]. Put that down and help me butcher this boar!

[KLEONIKE *puts down the cup, over which she and* LYSISTRATA *together hold the jar of
wine (the "boar").* LYSISTRATA *prays.*]

O Mistress Persuasion,
O Cup of Devotion,
Attend our invocation:
220   Accept this oblation,
Grant our petition,
Favor our mission.

[LYSISTRATA *and* KLEONIKE *tip up the jar and pour the gurgling wine into the cup.*
MYRRHINE, LAMPITO, *and the others watch closely.*]

MYRRHINE.   Such an attractive shade of blood. And the spurt—
pure Art!
LAMPITO.   Hit shore do smell mighty purty!

[LYSISTRATA *and* KLEONIKE *put down the empty wine jar.*]

KLEONIKE.   Girls, let me be the first [*Launching herself at the cup.*] to take
the Oath!
LYSISTRATA [*Hauling* KLEONIKE *back*]. You'll have to wait your turn like
everyone else.
—Lampito, how do we manage with this mob?

Cumbersome.
—Everyone place her right hand on the cup.

[*The women surround the cup and obey.*]

I need a spokeswoman. One of you to take
the Oath in behalf of the rest.

[The women edge away from KLEONIKE, *who reluctantly finds herself elected.]*

The rite will conclude

230   with a General Pledge of Assent by all of you, thus
        confirming the Oath. Understood?

[Nods from the women. LYSISTRATA *addresses* KLEONIKE.]*

Repeat after me:

LYSISTRATA.   **I will withhold all rights of access or entrance**
KLEONIKE.   I will withhold all rights of access or entrance
LYSISTRATA.   **From every husband, lover, or casual acquaintance**
KLEONIKE.   from every husband, lover, or casual acquaintance
LYSISTRATA.   **Who moves in my direction in erection.**

—Go on

KLEONIKE.   who m-moves in my direction in erection.

Ohhhhh!

—Lysistrata, my knees are shaky. Maybe I'd better . . .
240 LYSISTRATA. **I will create, imperforate in cloistered chastity,**
KLEONIKE.   I will create, imperforate in cloistered chastity,
LYSISTRATA.   **A newer, more glamorous, supremely seductive me**
KLEONIKE.   a newer, more glamorous, supremely seductive me
LYSISTRATA.   **And fire my husband's desire with my molten allure—**
KLEONIKE.   and fire my husband's desire with my molten allure—
LYSISTRATA.   **But remain, to his panting advances, icily pure.**
KLEONIKE.   but remain, to his panting advances, icily pure.
LYSISTRATA.   **If he should force me to share the connubial couch,**
KLEONIKE.   If he should force me to share the connubial couch,
250 LYSISTRATA. **I refuse to return his stroke with the teeniest twitch.**
KLEONIKE.   I refuse to return his stroke with the teeniest twitch.
LYSISTRATA.   **I will not lift my slippers to touch the thatch**
KLEONIKE.   I will not lift my slippers to touch the thatch
LYSISTRATA.   **Or submit sloping prone in a hangdog crouch.**
KLEONIKE.   or submit sloping prone in a hangdog crouch.
LYSISTRATA.   **If I this oath maintain,**
                                   may I drink this glorious wine.
KLEONIKE.   If I this oath maintain,
                                   may I drink this glorious wine.
260 LYSISTRATA.   **But if I slip or falter,**
                                   let me drink water.
KLEONIKE.   But if I slip or falter,
                                   let me drink water.
LYSISTRATA.   —And now the General Pledge of Assent:
WOMEN.   **A-MEN!**
LYSISTRATA.   Good. I'll dedicate the oblation.

[She drinks deeply.]

KLEONIKE.   Not too much,
        darling. You know how anxious we are to become

allies and friends.
                    Not to mention *staying* friends.

[*She pushes* LYSISTRATA *away and drinks. As the women take their turns at the cup, loud cries and alarums are heard offstage.*]

LAMPITO.   What-all's that bodacious ruckus?
LYSISTRATA.   Just what I told you:
  It means the women have taken the Akropolis. Athene's
  Citadel is ours!
                    It's time for you to go,
270 Lampito, and set your affairs in order in Sparta.

                    [*Indicating the other women in* LAMPITO'*s group.*]

Leave these girls here as hostages.

                    [LAMPITO *exits left.* LYSISTRATA *turns to the others.*]
                                        Let's hurry inside
  the Akropolis and help the others shoot the bolts.
KLEONIKE.   Don't you think the men will send reinforcements
  against us as soon as they can?
LYSISTRATA.   So where's the worry?
  The men can't burn their way in or frighten us out.
  The Gates are ours—they're proof against fire and fear—
  and they open only on our conditions.
KLEONIKE.   Yes!
  That's the spirit—let's deserve our reputations:

                    [*As the women hurry off into the Akropolis.*]

280 UP THE SLUTS!
                    WAY FOR THE OLD IMPREGNABLES!

[*The door shuts behind the women, and the stage is empty. A pause, and the* CHORUS OF MEN *shuffles on from the left in two groups, led by their* KORYPHAIOS.[7] *They are incredibly aged Athenians; though they may acquire spryness later in the play, at this point they are sheer decrepitude. Their normally shaky progress is impeded by their burdens: each man not only staggers under a load of wood across his shoulders, but has his hands full as well—in one, an earthen pot containing fire (which is in constant danger of going out); in the other, a dried vinewood torch, not yet lit. Their progress toward the Akropolis is very slow.*]

KORYPHAIOS OF MEN.   [*To the right guide of the* FIRST SEMICHORUS, *who is stumbling along in mild agony.*]
  Forward, Swiftly, keep 'em in step! Forget your shoulder.
  I know these logs are green and heavy—but duty, boy, duty!
SWIFTY.   [*Somewhat inspired, he quavers into slow song to set a pace for his group.*]

---

[7] A term for the leader of the chorus.

I'm never surprised. At my age, life
is just one damned thing after another.
And yet, I never thought my wife
was anything more than a home-grown bother.
    But now, dadblast her,
    she's a National Disaster!

FIRST SEMICHORUS OF MEN.   What a catastrophe—

290   MATRIARCHY!
They've brought Athene's statue[8] to heel,
they've put the Akropolis under a seal,
they've copped the whole damned commonweal . . .
What is there left for them to steal?

KORYPHAIOS OF MEN.   [*To the right guide of the* SECOND SEMICHORUS—*a slower
soul, if possible, than* SWIFTY.]
Now, Chipper, speed's the word. The Akropolis, on the double!
Once we're there, we'll pile these logs around them, and convene
a circuit court for a truncated trial. Strictly impartial:
With a show of hands, we'll light a spark of justice under
every woman who brewed this scheme. We'll burn them all
on the first ballot—and the first to go is Ly . . .

                                          [*Pause for thought.*]

300   is Ly . . .

            [*Remembering and pointing at a spot in the audience.*]

is *Lykon's* wife—and there she is, right over there![9]

CHIPPER   [*Taking up the song again*].
            I won't be twitted, I won't be guyed,
            I'll teach these women not to trouble us!
            Kleomenes the Spartan tried
            expropriating our Akropolis[10]
                some time ago—
                ninety-five years or so—

SECOND SEMICHORUS OF MEN.   but he suffered damaging losses
                when he ran across US!

310   He breathed defiance—and more as well:
            No bath for six years—you could tell.
            We fished him out of the Citadel
            and quelled his spirit—but not his smell.

KORYPHAIOS OF MEN.   That's how I took him. A savage siege:
                                            Seventeen ranks

---

[8] A wooden statue thought of as the guardian of the city.

[9] "Rhodia, wife of the demagogue Lykon, was a real person, frequently lampooned for her morality. In a not unusual breaking of the dramatic illusion, her name occurs here as a surprise for the expected 'Lysistrata.' " [Translator's note.]

[10] "Kleomenes' occupation of the Akropolis in 508, high point of his unsuccessful bid to help establish the Athenian aristocrats, lasted rather less than the six years which the Chorus seems to remember. The actual time was two days." [Translator's note.]

of shields were massed at that gate, with blanket infantry cover.
I slept like a baby.
　　　　　　　　So when mere women (who gall the gods
and make Euripides[11] sick) try the same trick, should I
sit idly by?
Then demolish the monument I won at Marathon![12]

FIRST SEMICHORUS OF MEN　[*Singly*].
　　　　　　　—The last lap of our journey!

320　　　　　　—I greet it with some dismay.
　　　　　　　—The danger doesn't deter me,
　　　　　　　　　　　　　　　—but
it's uphill
　　　—all the way.
—Please, somebody,
　　　　　—find a jackass
　　　　　to drag these logs
　　　　　　　　　　to the top.
　　　　　—I ache to join the fracas,
330　　　　　　　　　　　　—but
　　　　　my shoulder's aching
　　　　　　　　　　　—to stop.
SWIFTY.　　　　Backward there's no turning.
　　　　　Upward and onward, men!
　　　　　And keep those firepots burning, or
　　　　　we make this trip again.
CHORUS OF MEN　[*Blowing into their firepots, which promptly send forth clouds of smoke*].
　　　　　　With a puff (pfffff)....
　　　　　　and a cough (hhhhhh)....
　　　　　The smoke! I'll choke! Turn it off!
SECOND SEMICHORUS OF MEN　[*Singly*].
　　　　　—Damned embers.
　　　　　　　　—Should be muzzled.
　　—There oughta be a law.
　　—They jumped me
　　　　　　—when I whistled
　　　　　　　　　　—and then
they gnawed my eyeballs
　　　　　　　—raw.
—There's lava in my lashes.
—My lids are oxidized.
—My brows are braised.
340　　　　　　　—These ashes are
　　volcanoes
　　　　　—in disguise.
CHIPPER.　　This way, men. And remember,

---

[11] A Greek playwright (ca. 480–407 B.C.).
[12] The site of a famous Greek victory over the Persians in 490 B.C.

The Goddess needs our aid.
So don't be stopped by cinders. Let's
press on to the stockade!

CHORUS OF MEN [*Blowing again into their firepots, which erupt as before*].
With a huff (hfffff). . . .
and a chuff (chffff). . . .
Drat that smoke. Enough is enough!

KORYPHAIOS OF MEN [*Signalling the* CHORUS, *which has now tottered into
position before the Akropolis gate, to stop, and peering into his firepot*].
Praise be to the gods, it's awake. There's fire in the old fire yet.
—Now the directions. See how they strike you:

First, we deposit
350   these logs at the entrance and light our torches. Next, we crash
the gate. When that doesn't work, we request admission. Politely.
When *that* doesn't work, we burn the damned door down, and smoke
these women into submission.

That seem acceptable? Good.
Down with the load . . . ouch, that smoke! Sonofabitch!

[*A horrible tangle results as the* CHORUS *attempts to deposit the logs. The* KORYPHAIOS
turns to the audience.]

Is there a general in the house? We have a logistical
problem. . . .

[*No answer. He shrugs.*]

Same old story. Still at loggerheads over in Samos.[13]

[*With great confusion, the logs are placed somehow.*]

That's better. The pressure's off. I've got my backbone back.

[*To his firepot.*]

What, pot? You forgot your part in the plot?
360   Urge that smudge.
to be hot on the dot and scorch my torch.
Got it, pot?

[*Praying.*]

Queen Athene, let these strumpets
crumple before our attack.
Grant us victory, male supremacy . . .
and a testimonial plaque.

[*The men plunge their torches into firepots and arrange themselves purposefully before
the gate. Engaged in their preparations, they do not see the sudden entrance, from the*

---

[13] After the annihilation of the Athenian forces sent to the island of Sicily in 415 B.C., most
of the remaining generals were sent to Samos (a Greek island off Asia Minor) in an effort to
shore up the allegiance and prepare an attack against those city states that had defected to
Sparta.

right, of the Chorus of Women, *led by their* Koryphaios. *These wear long cloaks and carry pitchers of water. They are very old—though not so old as the men—but quite spry. In their turn, they do not perceive the* Chorus of Men.]

Koryphaios of Women   [*Stopping suddenly*].
   What's this—soot? And smoke as well? I may be all wet,
   but this might mean fire. Things look dark, girls; we'll
   have to dash.

[*They move ahead, at a considerably faster pace than the men.*]

First Semichorus of Women.

[*Singly.*]

Speed! Celerity!	Save our sorority
370 from arson. Combustion.	And heat exhaustion.
Don't let our sisterhood	shrivel to blisterhood.

    Fanned into slag by hoary typhoons.
    By flatulent, nasty, gusty baboons.
      We're late! Run!
      The girls might be done

[*Tutte.*[14]]

Filling my pitcher	was absolute torture:
The fountains in town	are so *crowded* at dawn,
glutted with masses	of the lower classes
blatting and battering,	shoving, and shattering
380 jugs. But I juggled	my burden, and wriggled
away to extinguish	the igneous anguish

    of neighbor, and sister, and daughter—
      Here's Water!

Second Semichorus of Women.

[*Singly.*]

Get wind of the news?	The gaffers are loose.
The blowhards are off	with fuel enough
to furnish a bathhouse.	But the finish is pathos:

    They're scaling the heights with a horrid proposal.
    They're threatening women with rubbish disposal!
      How ghastly—how gauche![15]
390   burned up with the trash!

[*Tutte.*]

Preserve me, Athene,	from gazing on any
matron or maid	auto-da-fé'd.[16]
Cover with grace	these redeemers of Greece
from battles, insanity,	Man's inhumanity.

---

[14] All together.
[15] Awkward, graceless.
[16] Burned at the stake.

Gold-browed goddess,   hither to aid us!
Fight as our ally,   join in our sally
     against pyromaniac slaughter—
     Haul Water!

KORYPHAIOS OF WOMEN [*Noticing for the first time the* CHORUS OF MEN, *still busy
     at their firepots, she cuts off a member of her* CHORUS *who seems about to
     continue the song.*]   Hold it. What have we here? You don't catch
400   true-blue patriots red-handed. These are authentic degenerates, male,
     taken *in flagrante.*[17]

KORYPHAIOS OF MEN.   Oops. Female troops. This could be upsetting.
     I didn't expect such a flood of reserves.

KORYPHAIOS OF WOMEN.   Merely a spearhead.
     If our numbers stun you, watch that yellow streak
     spread. We represent just one percent of one percent of
     This Woman's Army.

KORYPHAIOS OF MEN.   Never been confronted with such backtalk. Can't
     allow it. Somebody pick up a log and pulverize that brass.

                                             Any volunteers?

                    [*There are none among the male chorus.*]

KORYPHAIOS OF WOMEN.   Put down the pitchers, girls. If they start waving
     that lumber, we don't want to be encumbered.

KORYPHAIOS OF MEN.   Look, men, a few sharp jabs
     will stop that jawing. It never fails.
410   The poet Hipponax
     swears by it.[18]

               [*Still no volunteers. The* KORYPHAIOS OF WOMEN *advances.*]

KORYPHAIOS OF WOMEN.   Then step right up. Have a jab at me.
     Free shot.

KORYPHAIOS OF MEN [*Advancing reluctantly to meet her*].   Shut up!
     I'll peel your pelt. I'll pit your pod.

KORYPHAIOS OF WOMEN.   The name is Stratyllis. I dare you to lay one finger
     on me.

KORYPHAIOS OF MEN.   I'll lay on you with a fistful. Er—any specific threats?

KORYPHAIOS OF WOMEN [*Earnestly*].   I'll crop your lungs and reap your
     bowels, bite by bite, and leave no balls on the body for other bitches
     to gnaw.

KORYPHAIOS OF MEN [*Retreating hurriedly*].   Can't beat Euripides for insight.
     And I quote:
               *No creature's found
     so lost to shame as Woman.*
                         Talk about realist playwrights!
420 KORYPHAIOS OF WOMEN.   Up with the water, ladies. Pitchers at the ready,
          place!

KORYPHAIOS OF MEN.   Why the water, you sink of iniquity? More sedition?

---

[17] In the act.
[18] The Greek refers to Boupalos, a sculptor, who was frequently mocked by Hipponax: e.g.,
"Hold my clothes; I'll sock Boupalos in the jaw."

KORYPHAIOS OF WOMEN.   Why the fire, you walking boneyard?
   Self-cremation?
KORYPHAIOS OF MEN.   I brought this fire to ignite a pyre and fricassee your
   friends.
KORYPHAIOS OF WOMEN.   I brought this water to douse your pyre. Tit for tat.
KORYPHAIOS OF MEN.   *You'll* douse my fire? Nonsense!
KORYPHAIOS OF WOMEN.   You'll see, when the facts soak in.
KORYPHAIOS OF MEN.   I have the torch right here. Perhaps I should
   barbecue *you*.
KORYPHAIOS OF WOMEN.   If you have any soap, I could give you a bath.
KORYPHAIOS OF MEN.   A bath from those
430 polluted hands?
KORYPHAIOS OF WOMEN.   Pure enough for a blushing young bridegroom.
KORYPHAIOS OF MEN.   Enough of that insolent lip.
KORYPHAIOS OF WOMEN.   It's merely freedom of speech.
KORYPHAIOS OF MEN.   I'll stop that screeching!
KORYPHAIOS OF WOMEN.   You're helpless outside the jury-box.
KORYPHAIOS OF MEN   [*Urging his men, torches at the ready, into a charge*].
   Burn, fire, burn!
KORYPHAIOS OF WOMEN   [*As the women empty their pitchers over the men*].
   And cauldron bubble.
KORYPHAIOS OF MEN   [*Like his troops, soaked and routed*].
                                             Arrgh!
KORYPHAIOS OF WOMEN.   Goodness.
   What seems to be the trouble? Too hot?
KORYPHAIOS OF MEN.   Hot, hell! Stop it!
   What do you think you're doing?
KORYPHAIOS OF WOMEN.   If you must know, I'm gardening.
   Perhaps you'll bloom.
KORYPHAIOS OF MEN.   Perhaps I'll fall right off the vine!
   I'm withered, frozen, shaking . . .
KORYPHAIOS OF WOMEN.   Of course. But, providentially,
   you brought along your smudgepot.
440   The sap should rise eventually.

[*Shivering, the* CHORUS OF MEN *retreats in utter defeat.*]

[*A* COMMISSIONER *of Public Safety enters from the left, followed quite reluctantly by a squad of police—four Skythian archers. He surveys the situation with disapproval.*]

COMMISSIONER.   Fire, eh? Females again—spontaneous combustion
   of lust. Suspected as much.
                                 Rubadubdubbing, incessant
incontinent keening for wine, damnable funeral
foofaraw for Adonis resounding from roof to roof—
heard it all before . . .[19]

---

[19] In mythology Adonis was adored by Aphrodite, the goddess of love, but he was killed
while hunting a boar after disregarding a warning from Aphrodite. His death was mourned by
the Greek women in annual religious festivals. During one of the festivals of Adonis the ill-fated
Sicilian expedition was debated in the Athenian assembly. In the following lines the Commissioner recalls the arguments in favor of sending out a naval task force and manning it with
troops drafted on the island of Zakynthos.

[Savagely, as the KORYPHAIOS OF MEN *tries to interpose a remark.]*

and WHERE?
                                   The ASSEMBLY!
Recall, if you can, the debate on the Sicilian Question:
That bullbrained demagogue Demostratos (who will rot, I trust)
rose to propose a naval task force.
                                        His wife,
writing with religion on a handy roof, bleated
a dirge:
450   "BEREFT! OH WOE OH WOE FOR ADONIS!"
And so of course Demostratos, taking his cue,
outblatted her:
                    "A DRAFT! ENROLL THE WHOLE OF ZAKYNTHOS!"
His wife, a smidgin stewed, renewed her yowling:
"OH GNASH YOUR TEETH AND BEAT YOUR
BREASTS FOR ADONIS!"
And so of course Demostratos (that god-detested blot,
that foul-lunged son of an ulcer) gnashed tooth and nail
and voice, and bashed and rammed his program through.
And THERE is the Gift of Women:
460   MORAL CHAOS!

KORYPHAIOS OF MEN.   Save your breath for actual felonies, Commissioner;
    see what's happened to us! Insolence, insults,
    these we pass over, but not lèse-majesté.[20]
                                        We're flooded
    with indignity from those bitches' pitchers—like a bunch
    of weak-bladdered brats. Our cloaks are sopped. We'll sue!
COMMISSIONER.   Useless. Your suit won't hold water. Right's on their side.
    For female depravity, gentlemen, WE stand guilty—
    we, their teachers, preceptors of prurience, accomplices
    before the fact of fornication. We sowed them in sexual
    license, and now we reap rebellion.
470   The proof?
    Consider. Off we trip to the goldsmith's to leave
    an order:
        "That bangle you fashioned last spring for my wife
        is sprung. She was thrashing around last night, and the prong
        popped out the bracket. I'll be tied up all day—I'm
        boarding the ferry right now—but my wife'll be home.
        If you get the time, please stop by the house in a bit
        and see if you can't do something—anything—to fit
        a new prong into the bracket of her bangle."
480   And bang.
    Another one ups to a cobbler—young, but no apprentice,
    full kit of tools, ready to give his awl—

----

[20] Treason.

and delivers this gem:
>"My wife's new sandals are tight.
>The cinch pinches her pinkie right where she's sensitive.
>Drop in at noon with something to stretch her cinch
>and give it a little play."
>   And a cinch it is.
Such hanky-panky we have to thank for today's
Utter Anarchy: I, a Commissioner of Public
Safety, duly invested with extraordinary powers
to protect the State in the Present Emergency, have secured
a source of timber to outfit our fleet and solve

490   the shortage of oarage. I need the money immediately . . .
and WOMEN, no less, have locked me out of the Treasury!

[Pulling himself together.]

—Well, no profit in standing around.

[To one of the archers.]

>   Bring
the crowbars. I'll jack these women back on their
pedestals!
>   —WELL, you slack-jawed jackass? What's the
attraction? Wipe that thirst off your face. I said *crow*bar,
not saloon!—all right, men, all together. Shove those
bars underneath the gate and HEAVE!

[Grabbing up a crowbar.]

>   I'll take this side.
And now let's root them out, men, ROOT them out.

500   One, Two . . .

[The gates to the Akropolis burst open suddenly, disclosing Lysistrata. *She is perfectly composed and bears a large spindle. The* Commissioner *and the* Police *fall back in consternation.]*

Lysistrata.   Why the moving equipment?
I'm quite well motivated, thank you, and here I am.
Frankly, you don't need crowbars nearly so much as
brains.
Commissioner.   Brains? O name of infamy! Where's a policeman?

[He grabs wildly for the First Archer *and shoves him toward* Lysistrata.]

Arrest that woman!
>   Better tie her hands behind her.

Lysistrata.   By Artemis, goddess of the hunt, if he lays a finger
on me, he'll rue the day he joined the force!

[She jabs the spindle viciously at the First Archer, *who leaps, terrified, back to his comrades.]*

COMMISSIONER.   What's this—retreat? never! Take her on the flank.

[*The* FIRST ARCHER *hangs back. The* COMMISSIONER *grabs the* SECOND ARCHER.]

510   —Help him.
              —Will the two of you kindly TIE HER UP?

[*He shoves them toward* LYSISTRATA. KLEONIKE, *carrying a large chamber pot, springs out of the entrance and advances on the* SECOND ARCHER.]

KLEONIKE.   By Artemis, goddess of the dew, if you so much
        as touch her, I'll stomp the shit right out of you!

                              [*The two* ARCHERS *run back to their group.*]

COMMISSIONER.   *Shit?* Shameless! Where's another policeman?

                    [*He grabs the* THIRD ARCHER *and propels him toward* KLEONIKE.]

        Handcuff *her* first. Can't stand a foul-mouthed female.

[MYRRHINE, *carrying a large, blazing lamp, appears at the entrance and advances on the* THIRD ARCHER.]

MYRRHINE.   By Artemis, bringer of light, if you lay a finger
        on her, you won't be able to stop the swelling!

                    [*The* THIRD ARCHER *dodges her swing and runs back to the group.*]

COMMISSIONER.   *Now* what? Where's an officer?

                              [*Pushing the* FOURTH ARCHER *toward* MYRRHINE.]

                                        Apprehend that woman!
        I'll see that *somebody* stays to take the blame!

[ISMENIA *the Boiotian, carrying a huge pair of pincers, appears at the entrance and advances on the* FOURTH ARCHER.]

ISMENIA.   By Artemis, goddess of Tauris, if you go near
520   that girl, I'll rip the hair right out of your head!

                              [*The* FOURTH ARCHER *retreats hurriedly.*]

COMMISSIONER.   What a colossal mess: Athens' Finest—
        finished!

                              [*Arranging the* ARCHERS.]

        —Now, men, a little *esprit de corps.*[21] Worsted
        by women? Drubbed by drabs?
                        Never!
                              Regroup,

---

[21] Group spirit.

reform that thin red line.

Ready?
CHARGE!

[*He pushes them ahead of him.*]

LYSISTRATA.   I warn you. We have four battalions behind us—
full-armed combat infantrywomen, trained
from the cradle . . .
COMMISSIONER.   Disarm them, Officers! Go for the hands!
LYSISTRATA.

[*Calling inside the Akropolis.*]

MOBILIZE THE RESERVES!

[*A horde of women, armed with household articles, begins to pour from the Akropolis.*]

Onward, you ladies from hell!

530   Forward, you market militia, you battle-hardened
bargain hunters, old sales compaigners, grocery
grenadiers, veterans never bested by an overcharge!
You troops of the breadline, doughgirls—
INTO THE FRAY!

Show them no mercy!
Push!
Jostle!
Shove!
Call them nasty names!
Don't be ladylike.

[*The women charge and rout the* ARCHERS *in short order.*]

Fall back—don't strip the enemy! The day is ours!

[*The women obey, and the* ARCHERS *run off left. The* COMMISSIONER, *dazed, is left muttering to himself.*]

COMMISSIONER.   Gross ineptitude. A sorry day for the Force.
LYSISTRATA.   Of course. What did you expect? We're not slaves;
we're freeborn Women, and when we're scorned, we're
540   full of fury. Never Underestimate the Power of a Woman.
COMMISSIONER.   Power? You mean Capacity. I should have remembered
the proverb: *The lower the tavern, the higher the dudgeon.*
KORYPHAIOS OF MEN.   Why cast your pearls before swine, Commissioner? I
know you're a civil
servant, but don't overdo it. Have you forgotten the bath
they gave us—in public,
fully dressed,
totally soapless?
Keep rational discourse for *people!*

[*He aims a blow at the* KORYPHAIOS OF WOMEN, *who dodges and raises her pitcher.*]

KORYPHAIOS OF WOMEN.   I might point out that lifting
one's hand against a neighbor is scarcely civilized
behavior—and entails, for the lifter, a black eye.
                        I'm really peaceful by nature,
compulsively inoffensive—a perfect doll. My ideal is a
well-bred repose that doesn't even stir up dust . . .

                   [*Swinging at the* KORYPHAIOS OF MEN *with the pitcher.*]

550   unless some no-good lowlife
tries to rifle my hive and gets my dander up!

[*The* KORYPHAIOS OF MEN *backs hurriedly away, and the* CHORUS OF MEN *goes into
a worried dance.*]

CHORUS OF MEN.

                                                                  [*Singly.*]

        O Zeus, what's the use of this constant abuse?
        How do we deal with this female zoo?
        Is there no solution to Total Immersion?
            What can a poor man DO?

                                                                  [*Tutti.*]

            Query the Adversary!
            Ferret out their story!
            What end did they have in view,
            to seize the city's sanctuary,
560   snatch its legendary eyrie,[22]
            snare an area so very
                terribly taboo?

KORYPHAIOS OF MEN [*To the* COMMISSIONER].   Scrutinize those women! Scour
        their depositions—assess their rebuttals!
    Masculine honor demands this affair be probed to the bottom!
COMMISSIONER [*Turning to the women from the Akropolis*].   All right, you.
    Kindly inform me, dammit, in your own words:
    What possible object could you have had in blockading the Treasury?
LYSISTRATA.   We thought we'd deposit the money in escrow and withdraw
    you men from the war.
COMMISSIONER.   The money's the cause of the war?
LYSISTRATA.   And all our internal
570   disorders—the Body Politic's chronic bellyaches: What
    causes Peisandros' frantic rantings, or the raucous cau-
    cuses of the Friends of Oligarchy?[23] The chance for graft.
                    But now, with the money up there,

---

[22] Eagle's nest—hence, the Acropolis, a stronghold on a hill overlooking the rest of Athens.
[23] One of the political clubs in Athens that sought public offices for their members.

they can't upset the City's equilibrium—or lower its
   balance.
COMMISSIONER.   And what's your next step?
LYSISTRATA.   Stupid question. We'll budget
   the money.
COMMISSIONER.   *You'll budget the money?*
LYSISTRATA.   Why should you find that so shocking?
   We budget the household accounts, and you don't object
580   at all.
COMMISSIONER.   That's different.
LYSISTRATA.   Different? How?
COMMISSIONER.   The War Effort needs this money!
LYSISTRATA.   Who needs the War Effort?
COMMISSIONER.   Every patriot who pulses to save
   all that Athens holds near and dear . . .
LYSISTRATA.   Oh, *that*. Don't worry.
   We'll save you.
COMMISSIONER.   *You* will save us?
LYSISTRATA.   Who else?
COMMISSIONER.   But this is unscrupulous!
LYSISTRATA.   We'll save you. You can't deter us.
COMMISSIONER.   Scurrilous!
LYSISTRATA.   You seem disturbed.
   This makes it difficult. But, still—we'll save you.
COMMISSIONER.   Doubtless illegal!
LYSISTRATA.   We deem it a duty. For friendship's sake.
COMMISSIONER.   Well, forsake this friend:
   I DO NOT WANT TO BE SAVED, DAMMIT!
LYSISTRATA.   All the more reason.
590   It's not only Sparta; now we'll have to save you from you.
COMMISSIONER.   Might I ask where you women conceived this concern
   about War and Peace?
LYSISTRATA [*Loftily*].   We shall explain.
COMMISSIONER [*Making a fist*].   Hurry up, and you won't
   get hurt.
LYSISTRATA.   Then *listen*. And do try to keep your hands to
   yourself.
COMMISSIONER [*Moving threateningly toward her*].   I can't. Righteous anger
   forbids restraint, and decrees . . .
KLEONIKE [*Brandishing her chamber pot*].   Multiple fractures?
   COMMISSIONER [*Retreating*].   Keep those croaks for yourself, you old crow!

                                                      [*To* LYSISTRATA.]
   All right, lady, I'm ready. Speak.

LYSISTRATA.   I shall proceed:
   When the War began, like the prudent, dutiful wives that
   we are, we tolerated you men, and endured your actions
600   in silence. (Small wonder—
      you wouldn't let us say boo.)
                           You were not precisely the answer

to a matron's prayer—we knew you too well, and found out more.
Too many times, as we sat in the house, we'd hear that
you'd done it again—manhandled another affair of
state with your usual staggering incompetence. Then,
masking our worry with a nervous laugh,
we'd ask you, brightly, "How was the Assembly today, dear? Anything
in the minutes about Peace?" And my husband would give his stock
    reply.
"What's that to you? Shut up!" And I did.

KLEONIKE [*Proudly*].   *I* never shut up!

COMMISSIONER.   I trust you were shut up. Soundly.

610 LYSISTRATA.   Regardless, *I* shut up.
And then we'd learn that you'd passed another decree,
fouler than the first, and we'd ask again: "Darling, how
did you manage anything so idiotic?" And my
husband, with his customary glare, would tell me to spin
my thread, or else get a clout on the head.
And of course he'd quote from Homer:
                        Yᵉ menne must husband yᵉ warre.[24]

COMMISSIONER.   Apt and irrefutably right.

LYSISTRATA.   *Right*, you miserable misfit?
To keep us from giving advice while you fumbled the
City away in the Senate? Right, indeed!
                    But this time was really too much:

620 Wherever we went, we'd hear you engaged in the same conversation:
"What Athens needs is a Man."
                 "But there isn't a Man in the country."
"You can say that again."
            There was obviously no time to lose.
We women met in immediate convention and passed a
unanimous resolution: To work in concert for safety and
Peace in Greece. We have valuable advice to impart,
and if you can possibly deign to emulate our silence,
and take your turn as audience, we'll rectify you—
we'll straighten you out and set you right.

COMMISSIONER. *You'll* set *us* right? You go too far. I cannot permit
such a statement to . . .

LYSISTRATA.   Shush.

COMMISSIONER.   I categorically decline to shush

630 for some confounded woman, who wears—as a constant
reminder of congenital inferiority, an injunction to
public silence—a veil!
Death before such dishonor!

LYSISTRATA [*Removing her veil*].
              If that's the only obstacle . . .

---

[24] From the *Iliad*, Book 6, line 492.

I feel you need a new panache,
  so take the veil, my dear Commissioner, and drape it thus—
                                          and SHUSH!

[*As she winds the veil around the startled* COMMISSIONER'*s head,* KLEONIKE *and* MYRRHINE, *with carding-comb and wool-basket, rush forward and assist in transforming him into a woman.*]

KLEONIKE.   Accept, I pray, this humble comb.
MYRRHINE.   Receive this basket of fleece as well.
640 LYSISTRATA.   Hike up your skirts, and card your wool,
                  and gnaw your beans—and stay at home!
                  While we rewrite Homer:
                  Y^e WOMEN must WIVE ye warre!

[*To the* CHORUS *of* WOMEN, *as the* COMMISSIONER *struggles to remove his new outfit.*]

Women, weaker vessels, arise!
                                 Put down your pitchers.
It's our turn, now. Let's supply our friends with some
moral support.

[*The* CHORUS OF WOMEN *dances to the same tune as the* MEN, *but with much more confidence.*]

CHORUS OF WOMEN.

                                                         [*Singly.*]

      Oh, yes! I'll dance to bless their success.
      Fatigue won't weaken my will. Or my knees.
650   I'm ready to join in any jeopardy.
          with girls as good as *these!*

                                                         [*Tutte.*]

          A tally of their talents
          convinces me they're giants
          of excellence. To commence:
          there's Beauty, Duty, Prudence, Science,
          Self-Reliance, Compliance, Defiance,
          and Love of Athens in balanced alliance
              with Common Sense!

KORYPHAIOS OF WOMEN   [*To the women from the Akropolis*].
   Autochthonous[25] daughters of Attika, sprung from the
   soil that bore your mothers, the spiniest, spikiest
660   nettles known to man, prove your mettle and attack!
   Now is no time to dilute your anger. You're

---

[25] Native.

running ahead of the wind!

LYSISTRATA.   We'll wait for the wind
from heaven. The gentle breath of Love and his Kyprian
mother[26] will imbue our bodies with desire, and raise a
storm to tense and tauten these blasted men until they
crack. And soon we'll be on every tongue in
Greece—the *Pacifiers*.

COMMISSIONER.   That's quite
a mouthful. How will you win it?

LYSISTRATA.   First, we intend to withdraw
that crazy Army of Occupation from the downtown
670   shopping section.

KLEONIKE.   Aphrodite be praised!

LYSISTRATA.   The pottery shop and the grocery stall
are overstocked with soldiers, clanking around like
those maniac Korybants,[27]
armed to the teeth for a battle.

COMMISSIONER.   A Hero is Always Prepared!

LYSISTRATA.   I suppose he is. But it does look silly to shop for sardines
from behind a shield.

KLEONIKE.   I'll second that. I saw
a cavalry captain buy vegetable soup on horseback. He
carried the whole mess home in his helmet.

                                   And then that fellow from Thrace,
shaking his buckler and spear—a menace straight from the stage.
680   The saleslady was stiff with fright. He was hogging her ripe figs—free.

COMMISSIONER.   I admit, for the moment, that Hellas' affairs are in one
hell of a snarl. But how can you set them straight?

LYSISTRATA.   Simplicity itself.

COMMISSIONER.   Pray demonstrate.

LYSISTRATA.   It's rather like yarn. When a hank's in a tangle,
we lift it—*so*— and work out the snarls by winding it up
on spindles, now this way, now that way.

                                   That's how we'll wind up the War,
if allowed: We'll work out the snarls by sending Special Commissions—
back and forth, now this way, now that way—to ravel
these tense international kinks.

COMMISSIONER.   I lost your thread, but I know there's a hitch.
Spruce up the world's disasters with spindles—typically
woolly female logic.

690 LYSISTRATA.   If *you* had a scrap of logic, you'd adopt
our wool as a master plan for Athens.

COMMISSIONER.   What course of action
does the wool advise?

LYSISTRATA.   Consider the City as fleece, recently
shorn. The first step is Cleansing: Scrub it in a public

---

[26] Aphrodite; Kyprian because she was said to have been born from the sea near Cyprus.
[27] Armed priests of Cybele, the goddess of Nature.

bath, and remove all corruption, offal, and sheepdip.
                              Next, to the couch
for Scutching and Plucking: Cudgel the leeches and
similar vermin loose with a club, then pick the prickles
and cockleburs out. As for the clots—those lumps
that clump and cluster in knots and snarls to snag
important posts—you comb these out,
twist off their heads, and discard.

700   Next, to raise the City's
nap, you card the citizens together in a single basket
of common weal and general welfare. Fold in our loyal
Resident Aliens, all Foreigners of proven and tested
friendship, and any Disenfranchised Debtors. Combine
    these closely with the rest.
Lastly, cull the colonies settled by our own people:
these are nothing but flocks of wool from the City's
fleece, scattered throughout the world. So gather home
these far-flung flocks, amalgamate them with the others.

710   Then, drawing this blend
of stable fibers into one fine staple, you spin a mighty
bobbin of yarn—and weave, without bias or seam, a
cloak to clothe the City of Athens!

COMMISSIONER.   This is too much! The City's
died in the wool, worsted by the distaff side—by women
who bore no share in the War. . . .

LYSISTRATA.   None, you hopeless hypocrite?
The quota we bear is double. First, we delivered our
sons to fill out the front lines in Sicily . . .

COMMISSIONER.   Don't tax me with that memory.

LYSISTRATA.   Next, the best years of our lives were levied. Top-level
strategy attached our joy, and we sleep alone.

                              But it's not the matrons
720   like us who matter. I mourn for the virgins, bedded in
single blessedness, with nothing to do but grow old.

COMMISSIONER.   Men *have* been known
to age, as well as women.

LYSISTRATA.   No, not as well as—better.
A man, an absolute antique, comes back from the war, and he's barely
doddered into town before he's married the veriest nymphet.
But a woman's season is brief; it slips, and she'll have
no husband, but sit out her life groping at omens—and finding no men.

COMMISSIONER.   Lamentable state of affairs. Perhaps we can rectify matters:

                                        [*To the audience.*]

TO EVERY MAN JACK, A CHALLENGE:
                              ARISE!
Provided you can . . .

LYSISTRATA.   Instead, Commissioner, why not simply curl up and *die?*
730   Just buy a coffin; here's the place.

[*Banging him on the head with her spindle.*]

I'll knead you a cake for the wake—and *these*

[*Winding the threads from the spindle around him.*]

make excellent wreaths. So Rest In Peace.

KLEONIKE. [*emptying the chamber pot over him*].   Accept these tokens of
deepest grief.

MYRRHINE [*breaking her lamp over his head*].   A final garland for the dear
deceased.

LYSISTRATA.   May I supply any last request?
                    Then run along. You're due at the wharf:
                        Charon's[28] anxious to sail—
                        you're holding up the boat for Hell!

COMMISSIONER.   This is monstrous—maltreatment of a public official—
maltreatment of ME!

740   I must repair directly
to the Board of Commissioners, and present my
colleagues concrete evidence of the sorry specifics of
this shocking attack!

[*He staggers off left.* LYSISTRATA *calls after him.*]

LYSISTRATA.   You won't haul us into court on a charge of neglecting
the dead, will you? (How like a man to insist
on his rights—even his last ones.) Two days between
death and funeral, that's the rule.
                                Come back here early
day after tomorrow, Commissioner:
                                We'll lay you out.

[LYSISTRATA *and her women re-enter the Akropolis. The* KORYPHAIOS OF MEN *advances to address the audience.*]

KORYPHAIOS OF MEN.   Wake up, Athenians! Preserve your freedom—the
750   time is Now!

[*To the* CHORUS OF MEN.]

Strip for action, men. Let's cope with the current mess.

[*The men put off their long mantles, disclosing short tunics underneath, and advance toward the audience.*]

CHORUS OF MEN.   This trouble may be terminal; it has a loaded odor,
an ominous aroma of constitutional rot.
My nose gives a prognosis of radical disorder—
it's just the first installment of an absolutist plot!
The Spartans are behind it:
they must have masterminded

---

[28] The boatman who ferries dead souls across the river Styx.

some morbid local contacts (engineered by Kleisthenes).[29]
    Predictably infected,
760   the women straightway acted
to commandeer the City's cash. They're feverish to freeze
    my be-all,
    my end-all . . .
    my *payroll!*

KORYPHAIOS OF MEN. The symptoms are clear. Our birthright's already
    nibbled. And oh, so
daintily: WOMEN ticking off troops for improper etiquette.
WOMEN propounding their featherweight views on the fashionable use
and abuse of the shield. And (if any more proof were needed) WOMEN
nagging us to trust the Nice Spartan, and put our heads
770 in his toothy maw—to make a dessert and call it Peace.
They've woven the City a seamless shroud, bedecked with the legend
DICTATORSHIP.
               But I won't be hemmed in. I'll use
their weapon against them, and uphold the right by sneakiness
            With knyf under cloke,
gauntlet in glove, sword in olivebranch,

           [*Slipping slowly toward the* KORYPHAIOS *of* WOMEN.]

                  I'll take up my post
in Statuary Row, beside our honored National Heroes,
in the natural foes of tyranny: Harmodios,
                    Aristogeiton,
                        and Me.[30]

                        [*Next to her.*]

Striking an epic pose, so, with the full approval
of the immortal gods,
          I'll bash this loathesome hag in the jaw!

    [*He does, and runs cackling back to the Men. She shakes a fist after him.*]

KORYPHAIOS OF WOMEN. Mama won't know her little boy when he gets home!

    [*To the Women, who are eager to launch a full-scale attack.*]

780   Let's not be hasty, fellow . . . hags. Cloaks off first.

[*The Women remove their mantles, disclosing tunics very like those of the Men, and advance toward the audience.*]

CHORUS OF WOMEN. We'll address you, citizens, in beneficial, candid,
    patriotic accents, as our breeding says we must,
since, from the age of seven, Athens graced me with a

---

[29] Kleisthenes was a notoriously effeminate contemporary of Aristophanes'—hence, suspected of being in league with the women.

[30] Statues of the heroes Harmodios and Aristogeiton were carved by the sculptor Kritios.

splendid string of civic triumphs to signalize her trust:
>I was Relic-Girl quite early,
>then advanced to Maid of Barley;
in Artemis' "Pageant of the Bear" I played the lead.
>To cap this proud progression,
790   I led the whole procession
at Athene's Celebration, certified and pedigreed
>—that cachet[31]
>so distingué[32]—
>Lady!

KORYPHAIOS OF WOMEN.

>[To the audience.]

I trust this establishes my qualifications. I may, I take it,
address the City to its profit? Thank you.
>I admit to being a woman—
but don't sell my contribution short on that account.
It's better than the present panic. And my word is as
good as my bond, because I hold stock in Athens—
800   stock I paid for in sons.

>[To the CHORUS OF MEN.]

—But you, you doddering bankrupts, where are your
shares in the State?

>[Slipping slowly toward the KORYPHAIOS OF MEN.]

Your grandfathers willed you the Mutual Funds from the Persian
>   War—
and where are they?[33]

>[Nearer.]

>You dipped into capital, then lost interest . . .
and now a pool of your assets won't fill a hole in the ground.
All that remains is one last potential killing—Athens.
Is there any rebuttal?

[The KORYPHAIOS OF MEN gestures menacingly. She ducks down, as if to ward off a
blow, and removes a slipper.]

>Force is a footling resort. I'll take
my very sensible shoe, and paste you in the jaw!

---

[31] Official seal.
[32] Distinguished.
[33] "This money originally made up the treasury of the Delian League, an alliance of Greek
states against Persia formed by the Athenian Aristeides in 477; following its transfer, for safety's
sake, from the island of Delos to Athens in 454, it became for all practical purposes Athenian
property, supported by tribute from the Allies. Athens' heavy expenses in Sicily, followed by the
Allies' nonpayment and defection, made this question all too pointed in early 411." [Translator's
note.]

[She does so, and runs back to the women.]

810 CHORUS OF MEN.   Their native respect for our manhood is small,
           and keeps getting smaller. Let's bottle their gall.
           The man who won't battle has no balls at all!
KORYPHAIOS OF MEN.   All right, men, skin out of the skivvies. Let's give them
  a whiff of Man, full strength. No point in muffling the essential Us.

[The men remove their tunics.]

CHORUS OF MEN.   A century back, we soared to the Heights[34]
         and beat down Tyranny there.
      Now's the time to shed our moults
        and fledge our wings once more,
820   to rise to the skies in our reborn force,
        and beat back Tyranny here!
KORYPHAIOS OF MEN.   No fancy grappling with these grannies;
  straightforward strength. The tiniest
toehold, and those nimble, fiddling fingers will have their
foot in the door, and we're done for.
                 *No amount of know-how can lick
a woman's knack.*
       They'll want to build ships . . . next thing we know,
we're all at sea, fending off female boarding parties.
(Artemisia fought us at Salamis. Tell me, has anyone
caught her yet?)
830   But we're *really* sunk if they take up horses. Scratch
the Cavalry:
        A woman is an easy rider with a natural seat.
Take her over the jumps bareback, and she'll never slip
her mount. (That's how the Amazons nearly took Athens. On
  horseback.
Check on Mikon's mural down in the Stoa.)
                     Anyway,
the solution is obvious. Put every woman in her place—
stick her in the stocks.
    To do this, first snare your woman around the neck.

[He attempts to demonstrate on the KORYPHAIOS OF WOMEN. *After a brief tussle, she works loose and chases him back to the Men.]*

CHORUS OF WOMEN.   The beast in me's eager and fit for a brawl.
         Just rile me a bit and she'll kick down the wall.
840   You'll bawl to your friends that you've no balls at all.
KORYPHAIOS OF WOMEN.   All right, ladies, strip for action. Let's give them a whiff
  of *Femme Enragée*—piercing and pungent, but not at all tart.

---

[34] The men of the family of Pericles held out in the mountains north of Athens during their first attempt to overthrow the tyrant Hippias in 513 B.C.

[*The women remove their tunics.*]

CHORUS OF WOMEN.   We're angry. The brainless bird who tangles
                                 with *us* has gummed his last mush.
                         In fact, the coot who even heckles
                                 is being daringly rash.
                         So look to your nests, you reclaimed eagles—
                                 whatever you lay, we'll squash!

850 KORYPHAIOS OF WOMEN.   Frankly, you don't faze me. *With* me, I have my
           friends—
     Lampito from Sparta; that genteel girl from Thebes, Ismenia—
     committed to me forever. *Against* me, *you*—permanently
     out of commission. So do your damnedest.
                                                   Pass a law.
     Pass seven. Continue the winning ways that have made
     your name a short and ugly household word.
                                         Like yesterday:
     I was giving a little party, nothing fussy, to honor
     the goddess Hekate. Simply to please my daughters,
     I'd invited a sweet little thing from the neighborhood—flawless
           pedigree, perfect
860 taste, a credit to any gathering—a Boiotian eel.
     But she had to decline. Couldn't pass the border. You'd passed a law.
     Not that you care for my party. You'll overwork your right of passage
     till your august body is overturned,
                                 and you break your silly neck!

[*She deftly grabs the* KORYPHAIOS OF MEN *by the ankle and upsets him. He scuttles
back to the Men, who retire in confusion.*]

[LYSISTRATA *emerges from the citadel, obviously distraught.*]

KORYPHAIOS OF WOMEN [*Mock-tragic*].   *Mistress, queen of this our subtle scheme
                                         why burst you from the hall with
                                                 brangled brow?*
LYSISTRATA.   *Oh, wickedness of woman! The female mind
                         does sap my soul and set my wits a-totter.*
KORYPHAIOS OF WOMEN.   *What drear accents are these?*
LYSISTRATA.   *The merest truth.*
KORYPHAIOS OF WOMEN.   *Be nothing loath to tell the tale to friends.*
870 LYSISTRATA.   *'Twere shame to utter, pain to hold unsaid.*
KORYPHAIOS OF WOMEN.   *Hide not from the affliction which we share.*
LYSISTRATA.   *In briefest compass,*

                                                   [*Dropping the paratragedy.*]

                         we want to get laid.
KORYPHAIOS OF WOMEN.   By Zeus!
LYSISTRATA.   No, no, not HIM!
                         Well, that's the way things are.
     I've lost my grip on the girls—they're mad for men!

But sly—they slip out in droves.
                                    A minute ago,
I caught one scooping out the little hole
that breaks through just below Pan's grotto.[35]
                                    One
had jerry-rigged some block-and-tackle business
and was wriggling away on a rope.
                                    Another just flat
deserted.
880   Last night I spied one mounting a sparrow,
all set to take off for the nearest bawdyhouse. I hauled
her back by the hair.
                    And excuses, pretexts for overnight
passes? I've heard them all.
                    Here comes one. Watch.

[*To the* FIRST WOMAN, *as she runs out of the Akropolis.*]

—You, there! What's your hurry?

FIRST WOMAN.   I have to get home.
I've got all this lovely Milesian wool in the house,
and the moths will simply batter it to bits!
LYSISTRATA.   I'll bet.
Get back inside.
FIRST WOMAN.   I swear I'll hurry right back!
—Just time enough to spread it out on the couch?
LYSISTRATA.   Your wool will stay unspread. And you'll stay here.
FIRST WOMAN.   Do I have to let my piecework *rot*?
890 LYSISTRATA.   Possibly.

[*The* SECOND WOMAN *runs on.*]

SECOND WOMAN.   Oh dear, oh goodness, what shall I do—my flax!
I left and forgot to peel it!
LYSISTRATA.   Another one.
She suffers from unpeeled flax.
                    —Get back inside!
SECOND WOMAN.   I'll be right back. I just have to pluck the fibers.
LYSISTRATA.   No. No plucking. You start it, and everyone else
will want to go and do their plucking, too.

[*The* THIRD WOMAN, *swelling conspicuously, hurries on, praying loudly.*]

THIRD WOMAN.   *O Goddess of Childbirth, grant that I not deliver*
    until I get me from out this sacred precinct!
LYSISTRATA.   What sort of nonsense is *this*?
THIRD WOMAN.   I'm due—any second!
LYSISTRATA.   You weren't pregnant yesterday.
900 THIRD WOMAN.   Today I am—

---

[35] A cave on the Acropolis.

a miracle!
           Let me go home for a midwife, *please!*
I may not make it!
LYSISTRATA [*Restraining her*].   You can do better than that.

        [*Tapping the woman's stomach and receiving a metallic clang.*]

What's this? It's hard.
THIRD WOMAN.   I'm going to have a boy.
LYSISTRATA.   Not unless he's made of bronze. Let's see.

    [*She throws open the* THIRD WOMAN's *cloak, exposing a huge bronze helmet.*]

Of all the brazen . . . You've stolen the helmet from
Athene's statue! Pregnant, indeed!
THIRD WOMAN.   I am *so* pregnant!
LYSISTRATA.   Then why the helmet?
THIRD WOMAN.   I thought my time might come
while I was still on forbidden ground. If it did,
I could climb inside Athene's helmet and have
my baby there.
910   The pigeons do it all the time.
LYSISTRATA.   Nothing but excuses!

               [*Taking the helmet.*]

           This is your baby. I'm afraid
you'll have to stay until we give it a name.
THIRD WOMAN.   But the Akropolis is *awful*. I can't even sleep! I saw
the snake that guards the temple.
LYSISTRATA.   That snake's a fabrication.
THIRD WOMAN.   I don't care *what* kind it is—I'm *scared!*

    [*The other women, who have emerged from the citadel, crowd around.*]

KLEONIKE.   And those goddamned holy owls; All night long,
tu-wit; tu-wu—they're hooting me into my grave!
LYSISTRATA.   Darlings, let's call a halt to this hocus-pocus.
You miss your men—now isn't that the trouble?

           [*Shamefaced nods from the group.*]

920   Don't you think they miss you just as much?
I can assure you, their nights are every bit
as hard as yours. So be good girls; endure!
Persist a few days more, and Victory is ours.
It's fated: a current prophecy declares that the men
will go down to defeat before us, provided that *we*
maintain a United Front.

           [*Producing a scroll.*]

         I happen to have
a copy of the prophecy.

KLEONIKE.   Read it!

LYSISTRATA.   Silence, *please:*

[Reading from the scroll.]

> **But when the swallows, in flight from the**
>   **hoopoes, have flocked to a hole**
> *930*   **on high, and stoutly eschew their**
>   **accustomed perch on the pole,**
> **yea, then shall Thunderer Zeus to**
>   **their suff'ring establish a stop,**
> **by making the lower the upper . . .**

KLEONIKE.   Then *we'll* be lying on top?

LYSISTRATA.   **But should these swallows, indulging their**
>   **lust for the perch, lose heart,**
> **dissolve their flocks in winged dissension,**
>   **and singly depart**
> *940*   **the sacred stronghold, breaking the**
>   **bands that bind them together—**
> **then know them as lewd, the pervertedest**
>   **birds that ever wore feather.**

KLEONIKE.   There's nothing obscure about *that* oracle. Ye gods!

LYSISTRATA.   Sorely beset as we are, we must not flag
or falter. So back to the citadel!

[As the women troop inside.]

And if we fail
that oracle, darlings, our image is absolutely *mud!*

[She follows them in. A pause, and the CHORUSES *assemble.]*

CHORUS OF MEN.   I have a simple
tale to relate you,
950   a sterling example
of masculine virtue:

The huntsman bold Melanion
was once a harried quarry.
The women in town tracked him down
and badgered him to marry.

Melanion knew the cornered male
eventually cohabits.
Assessing the odds, he took to the woods
and lived by trapping rabbits.

960   He stuck to the virgin stand, sustained
by rabbit meat and hate,
and never returned, but ever remained
an alfresco[36] celibate.

---

[36] Outdoor.

> Melanion is our ideal;
>   his loathing makes us free.
> Our dearest aim is the gemlike flame
>   of his misogyny.[37]

OLD MAN.   Let me kiss that wizened cheek ...
OLD WOMAN.

[Threatening with a fist.]

> A wish too rash for that withered flesh.

970 OLD MAN.   and lay you low with a highflying kick.

[He tries one and misses.]

OLD WOMAN.   Exposing an overgrown underbrush.
OLD MAN.   A hairy behind, historically, means
     masculine force: Myronides
  harassed the foe with his mighty mane,
     and furry Phormion swept the seas
        of enemy ships, never meeting his match—
        such was the nature of his thatch.[38]

CHORUS OF WOMEN.   I offer an anecdote
                   for your opinion,
980   an adequate antidote
                   for your Melanion:
                   Timon, the noted local grouch,
                      put rusticating hermits
                   out of style by building his wilds
                      inside the city limits

> He shooed away society
>   with natural battlements:
> his tongue was edged; his shoulder, frigid;
>   his beard, a picket fence

990   When random contacts overtaxed him,
                   he didn't stop to pack,
                but loaded curses on the male of the species,
                   left town, and never came back.

> Timon, you see, was a misanthrope
>   in a properly narrow sense:
> his spleen was vented only on men ...
>   *we* were his dearest friends.

OLD WOMAN [*Making a fist*].   Enjoy a chop to that juiceless chin?
OLD MAN [*Backing away*].   I'm jolted already. Thank you, no.
1000 OLD WOMAN.   Perhaps a trip from a well-turned shin?

---

[37] Hatred of women.
[38] Myronides, an Athenian general, and Phormion, an Athenian admiral, won important military battles many years before the action in the play.

[She tries a kick and misses.]

OLD MAN.   Brazenly baring the mantrap below.
OLD WOMAN.   At least it's *neat*. I'm not too sorry
   to have you see my daintiness.
  My habits are still depilatory;
    age hasn't made me a bristly mess.
     Secure in my smoothness, I'm never in doubt—
      though even down is out.

[LYSISTRATA mounts the platform and scans the horizon. When her gaze reaches the left, she stops suddenly.]

LYSISTRATA.   Ladies, attention! Battle stations, please!
  And quickly!

[A general rush of women to the battlements.]

KLEONIKE.   What is it?
1010 MYRRHINE.   What's all the shouting for?
LYSISTRATA.   A MAN!

[Consternation.]

        Yes, it's a man. And he's coming this way!
Hmm. Seems to have suffered a seizure. Broken out
with a nasty attack of love.

[Prayer, aside.]

         O Aphrodite,
   Mistress all-victorious,
   mysterious, voluptuous,
   you who make the crooked straight . . .
   don't let this happen to US!
KLEONIKE.   I don't care who he is—*where is he?*
LYSISTRATA *[Pointing]*.   Down there—
  just flanking that temple—Demeter the Fruitful.
KLEONIKE.   My.
  Definitely a man.
1020 MYRRHINE *[Craning for a look]*.   I wonder who it can be?
LYSISTRATA.   See for yourselves.—Can anyone identify him?
MYRRHINE.   Oh lord, I can.
          That is my husband—Kinesias.
LYSISTRATA *[To MYRRHINE]*.   Your duty is clear.
                Pop him on the griddle, twist
  the spit, braize him, baste him, stew him in his own
  juice, do him to a turn. Sear him with kisses,
  coyness, caresses, *everything*—
             but stop where Our Oath
  begins.
MYRRHINE.   Relax. I can take care of this.
LYSISTRATA.   Of course

you can, dear. Still, a little help can't hurt, now
can it? I'll just stay around for a bit
and—er—poke up the fire.
1030   —Everyone else inside!

[*Exit all the women but* LYSISTRATA, *on the platform, and* MYRRHINE, *who stands near
the Akropolis entrance, hidden from her husband's view.* KINESIAS *staggers on, in
erection and considerable pain, followed by a male slave who carries a baby boy.*]

KINESIAS.   OUCH!
                    Omigod.
Hypertension, twinges. . . . I can't hold out much more.
I'd rather be dismembered.
                    How long, ye gods, how long?
LYSISTRATA.

                                                      [*Officially.*]

WHO GOES THERE?
               WHO PENETRATES OUR POSITIONS?
KINESIAS.   Me.
LYSISTRATA.   —A Man?
KINESIAS.   Every inch.
LYSISTRATA.   Then inch yourself out
   of here. Off Limits to Men.
KINESIAS.   This *is* the limit.
   Just who are *you* to throw me out?
LYSISTRATA.   The Lookout.
1040 KINESIAS.   Well, look here, Lookout. I'd like to see Myrrhine.
   How's the outlook?
LYSISTRATA.   Unlikely. Bring Myrrhine
   to you? The idea!
                    Just by the by, who are you?
KINESIAS.   A private citizen. Her husband, Kinesias.
LYSISTRATA.   No!
   Meeting you—I'm overcome!
                    Your name, you know,
   is not without its fame among us girls.

                                                      [*Aside.*]

—Matter of fact, we have a name for *it.*—
I swear, you're never out of Myrrhine's mouth.
She won't even nibble a quince, or swallow an egg,
without reciting, "Here's to Kinesias!"

KINESIAS.   For god's sake,
   will you . . .
1050 LYSISTRATA [*Sweeping on over his agony*].
                    Word of honor, it's true. Why, when
   we discuss our husbands (you know how women are),
   Myrrhine refuses to argue. She simply insists:

"Compared with Kinesias, the rest have *nothing!*"
Imagine!

KINESIAS. *Bring her out here!*

LYSISTRATA. Really? And what would I
get out of this?

KINESIAS. You see my situation. I'll raise
whatever I can. This can all be yours.

LYSISTRATA. Goodness.
It's really her place. I'll go and get her.

[*She descends from the platform and moves to* MYRRHINE, *out of* KINESIAS' *sight.*]

KINESIAS. Speed!
—Life is a husk. She left our home, and happiness
1060 went with her. Now pain is the tenant. Oh, to enter
that wifeless house, to sense that awful emptiness,
to eat that tasteless, joyless food—it makes
it hard, I tell you. Harder all the time.

MYRRHINE [*Still out of his sight, in a voice to be overheard*].
Oh, I *do* love him! I'm mad about him! But he
doesn't want my love. Please don't make me see him.

KINESIAS. Myrrhine darling, why do you *act* this way?
Come down here!

MYRRHINE [*Appearing at the wall*].
Down there? Certainly not!

KINESIAS. It's me, Myrrhine. I'm begging you. Please come down.

MYRRHINE. I don't see why you're begging me. You don't need me.

1070 KINESIAS. I don't need you? I'm at the end of my rope!

MYRRHINE. I'm leaving.

[*She turns.* KINESIAS *grabs the boy from the slave.*]

KINESIAS. No! Wait! At least you'll have to listen
to the voice of your child.

[*To the boy, in a fierce undertone.*]

—(Call your mother!)

[*Silence.*]

. . . to the voice
of your very own child . . .
—(Call your mother, brat!)

CHILD. MOMMYMOMMYMOMMY!

KINESIAS. Where's your maternal instinct? He hasn't been washed
or fed for a week. How can you be so pitiless?

MYRRHINE. *Him* I pity. Of all the pitiful excuses
for a father. . . .

KINESIAS. Come down here, dear. For the baby's sake.

MYRRHINE. Motherhood! I'll have to come. I've got no choice.

KINESIAS [*Soliloquizing as she descends*].

1080   It may be me, but I'll swear she looks years younger—
and gentler—her eyes caress me. And then they flash:
that anger, that verve, that high-and-mighty air!
She's fire, she's ice—and I'm stuck right in the middle.

MYRRHINE [*Taking the baby*].   Sweet babykins with such a nasty daddy!
Here, let Mummy kissums. Mummy's little darling.

KINESIAS [*The injured husband*].   You should be ashamed of yourself, letting
those women
lead you around. Why do you DO these things?
You only make me suffer and hurt your poor,
sweet self.

MYRRHINE.   Keep your hands away from me!

1090 KINESIAS.   But the house, the furniture, everything we own—you're
letting it go to hell!

MYRRHINE.   Frankly, I couldn't care less.

KINESIAS.   But your weaving's unraveled—the loom is full of
chickens! You couldn't care less about *that*?

MYRRHINE.   I certainly couldn't.

KINESIAS.   And the holy rites of Aphrodite? Think how long
that's been.
           Come on, darling, let's go home.

MYRRHINE.   I absolutely refuse!
                    Unless you agree to a truce
to stop the war.

KINESIAS.   Well, then, if that's your decision,
we'll STOP the war!

MYRRHINE.   Well, then, if that's your decision,
I'll come back—*after* it's done.
                 But, for the present,
I've sworn off.

1100 KINESIAS.   At least lie down for a minute.
We'll talk.

MYRRHINE.   I know what you're up to—NO!
  —And yet. . . . I really can't say I don't love you . . .

KINESIAS.   You love me?
So what's the trouble? *Lie down.*

MYRRHINE.   Don't be disgusting.
In front of the baby?

KINESIAS.   Er . . . no. Heaven Forfend.

[*Taking the baby and pushing it at the slave.*]

—Take this home.

[*The slave obeys.*]

—Well, darling, we're rid of the kid . . .
let's go to bed?

MYRRHINE.   Poor dear.

But where does one do

this sort of thing?

KINESIAS.   Where? All we need is a little

nook. . . . We'll try Pan's grotto. Excellent spot.

MYRRHINE.

[*With a nod at the Akropolis.*]

I'll have to be pure to get back in *there*. How can I

expunge my pollution?

1110 KINESIAS.   Sponge off in the pool next door.

MYRRHINE.   I did swear an Oath. I'm supposed to perjure myself?

KINESIAS.   Bother the Oath. Forget it—I'll take the blame. [*A pause.*]

MYRRHINE.   Now I'll go get us a cot.

KINESIAS.   No! Not a cot!

The ground's enough for us.

MYRRHINE.   *I'll get the cot.*

For all your faults, I refuse to put you to bed

in the dirt.

[*She exits into the Akropolis.*]

KINESIAS.   She certainly loves me. That's nice to know.

MYRRHINE [*returning with a rope-tied cot*].   Here. You hurry to bed while I

undress.

[KINESIAS *lies down.*]

Gracious me—I forgot. We need a mattress.

KINESIAS.   Who wants a mattress? Not me!

MYRRHINE.   Oh, yes, you do.

It's perfectly squalid on the ropes.

1120 KINESIAS.   Well, give me a kiss

to tide me over.

MYRRHINE.   *Voilà.*

[*She pecks at him and leaves.*]

KINESIAS.   OolaLAlala!

—Make it a quick trip, dear.

MYRRHINE.

[*Entering with the mattress, she waves* KINESIAS *off the cot and lays the mattress on it.*]

Here we are.

Our mattress. Now hurry to bed while I undress.

[KINESIAS *lies down again.*]

Gracious me—I forgot. You don't have a pillow.

KINESIAS.   I do *not* need a pillow.

MYRRHINE.   I know, but *I* do.

[*She leaves.*]

KINESIAS.   What a lovefeast! Only the table gets laid.
MYRRHINE [*Returning with a pillow*].
   Rise and shine!

[KINESIAS *jumps up. She places the pillow.*]

   And now I have everything I need.

KINESIAS   [*Lying down again*].
   You certainly do.
                        Come here, my little jewelbox!
MYRRHINE.   Just taking off my bra.
                        Don't break your promise:
   no cheating about the Peace.
1130 KINESIAS.   I swear to god,
   I'll die first!
MYRRHINE.

[*Coming to him.*]

   Just look. You don't have a blanket.
KINESIAS.   I didn't plan to go camping—I want to make love!
MYRRHINE.   Relax. You'll get your love. I'll be right back.

[*She leaves.*]

KINESIAS.   Relax? I'm dying a slow death by dry goods!
MYRRHINE [*Returning with the blanket*].   Get up!
KINESIAS. [*Getting out of bed*].
   I've been up for hours. I was up before I was up.

[MYRRHINE *spreads the blanket on the mattress, and he lies down again.*]

MYRRHINE.   I presume you want perfume?
KINESIAS.   Positively NO!
MYRRHINE.   Absolutely *yes*—whether you want it or not.
                                          [*She leaves.*]

KINESIAS.   Dear Zeus, I don't ask for much—but please let her spill it.
MYRRHINE [*Returning with a bottle*].   Hold out your hand like a good boy.
1140   Now rub it in.
KINESIAS [*Obeying and sniffing*].   *This* is to quicken desire? Too strong. It
   grabs
   your nose and bawls out: *Try again tomorrow.*
MYRRHINE.   I'm *awful!* I brought you that rancid Rhodian brand.

[*She starts off with the bottle.*]

KINESIAS.   This is just *lovely.* Leave it, woman!
MYRRHINE.   Silly!

[*She leaves.*]

KINESIAS.   God damn the clod who first concocted perfume!
MYRRHINE [*Returning with another bottle*].   Here, try this flask.

KINESIAS.   Thanks—but you try mine.
   Come to bed, you witch—
                        and please stop bringing
   things!
MYRRHINE.   *That* is exactly what I'll do.
   There go my shoes.
1150   Incidentally, darling, you *will*
   remember to vote for the truce?
KINESIAS.   **I'LL THINK IT OVER!**

                           [*Myrrhine runs off for good.*]

That woman's laid me waste—destroyed me, root
and branch!
       I'm scuttled,
           gutted,
              up the spout!
     And Myrrhine's gone!

                [*In a parody of a tragic kommos.*[39]]

       Out upon't! But how? But where?
       Now I have lost the fairest fair,
       how screw my courage to yet another
       sticking-place? Aye, there's the rub—
       And yet, this wagging, wanton babe
1160   must soon be laid to rest, or else . . .
       Ho, Pandar!
                Pandar!
                       I'd hire a nurse.
KORYPHAIOS OF MEN.

       Grievous your bereavement, cruel
       the slow tabescence[40] of your soul.
       I bid my liquid pity mingle.

       Oh, where the soul, and where, alack!
       the cod to stand the taut attack
       of swollen prides, the scorching tensions
       that ravine up the lumbar regions?
           His morning lay
1170   has gone astray.
KINESIAS [*In agony*].   O Zeus, reduce the throbs, the throes!
KORYPHAIOS OF MEN.   I turn my tongue to curse the cause
       of your affliction—that jade, that slut,
       that hag, that ogress . . .

KINESIAS.   No! Slight not
   my light-o'-love, my dove, my sweet!
KORYPHAIOS OF MEN.   Sweet!

---

[39] A lyric performed by the actor and chorus together.
[40] Wasting away.

> O Zeus who rul'st the sky,
> snatch that slattern up on high,
> crack thy winds, unleash thy thunder,
> tumble her over, trundle her under,
> *1180*   juggle her from hand to hand;
> twirl her ever near the ground—
> drop her in a well-aimed fall
> on our comrade's tool! That's all.

[KINESIAS *exits left.*]

[A SPARTAN HERALD *enters from the right, holding his cloak together in a futile attempt to conceal his condition.*]

HERALD.   This Athens? Where-all kin I find the Council of Elders
or else the Executive Board? I brung some news.

[*The* COMMISSIONER, *swathed in his cloak, enters from the left.*]

COMMISSIONER.   And what are you—a man? a signpost? a joint-stock
company?
HERALD.   A herald, sonny, a honest-to-Kastor[41]
herald. I come to chat 'bout thet-there truce.
COMMISSIONER.   . . . carrying a concealed weapon? Pretty underhanded.
HERALD.

[*Twisting to avoid the* COMMISSIONER'S *direct gaze.*]

Hain't done no sech a thang!

1190 COMMISSIONER.   Very well, stand still.
Your cloak's out of crease—hernia? Are the roads that bad?
HERALD.   I swear this feller's plumb tetched in the haid!
COMMISSIONER [*throwing open the* SPARTAN'S *cloak, exposing the phallus.*].

You clown,
you've got an erection!
HERALD [*Wildly embarrassed*].
Hain't got no sech a thang!
You stop this-hyer foolishment!
COMMISSIONER.   What *have* you got there, then?
HERALD.   Thet-thur's a Spartan *epistle.*[42] In code.
COMMISSIONER.   I have the key.

[*Throwing open his cloak.*]

Behold another Spartan *epistle.* In code.

[*Tiring of teasing.*]

---

[41] The twin gods, Castor and Pollux, were especially revered by the Spartans.

[42] A rod used in sending coded messages. The original message was written on a strip of paper spiralled around the rod. Once unwrapped it could only be deciphered if wrapped around an identical rod.

Let's get down to cases. I know the score,
so tell me the truth.
　　　　　　　　　　How are things with you in Sparta?

1200　HERALD.　Thangs is up in the air. The whole Alliance
　　　is purt-near 'bout to explode. We-uns'll need barrels,
　　　'stead of women.
COMMISSIONER.　What was the cause of this outburst?
　　　The great god Pan?
HERALD.　　　　　　　　　Nope. I'll lay 'twere Lampito,
　　　most likely. She begun, and then they was off
　　　and runnin' at the post in a bunch, every last little gal
　　　in Sparta, drivin' their menfolk away from the winner's
　　　circle.
COMMISSIONER.　How are you taking this?
HERALD.　　　　　　　　　　　　　　Painful-like.
　　　Everyone's doubled up worse as a midget nursin'
　　　a wick in a midnight wind come moon-dark time.
1210　Cain't even tetch them little old gals on the moosey
　　　without we all agree to a Greece-wide Peace.
COMMISSIONER.　Of course!
　　　　　　　　　　A universal female plot—all Hellas
　　　risen in rebellion—I should have known!
　　　　　　　　　　　　　　　Return
　　　to Sparta with this request:
　　　　　　　　　　　　Have them despatch us
　　　A Plenipotentiary Commission, fully empowered
　　　to conclude an armistice. I have full confidence
　　　that I can persuade our Senate to do the same,
　　　without extending myself. The evidence is at hand.
HERALD.　I'm a-flyin', Sir! I hev never heered your equal!

　　　[*Exeunt hurriedly, the* COMMISSIONER *to the left, the* HERALD *to the right.*]

1220　KORYPHAIOS OF MEN.　The most unnerving work of nature,
　　　the pride of applied immorality,
　　　is the common female human.
　　　No fire can match, no beast can best her.
　　　O Unsurmountability,
　　　thy name—worse luck—is Woman.
KORYPHAIOS OF WOMEN.　After such knowledge, why persist
　　　in wearing out this feckless
　　　war between the sexes?
　　　When can I apply for the post
1230　of ally, partner, and general friend?
KORYPHAIOS OF MEN.　I won't be ployed to revise, re-do,
　　　amend, extend, or bring to an end
　　　my irreversible credo:
　　　Misogyny Forever!
　　　—The answer's never.
KORYPHAIOS OF WOMEN.　All right. Whenever you choose.

But, for the present, I refuse
to let you look your absolute worst,
parading around like an unfrocked freak:
1240   I'm coming over and get you dressed.

[*She dresses him in his tunic, an action* (*like others in this scene*) *imitated by the members of the* CHORUS OF WOMEN *toward their opposite numbers in the* CHORUS OF MEN.]

KORYPHAIOS OF MEN.   This seems sincere. It's not a trick.
   Recalling the rancor with which I stripped,
   I'm overlaid with chagrin.
KORYPHAIOS OF WOMEN.   Now you resemble a man,
   not some ghastly practical joke.
   And if you show me a little respect
   (and promise not to kick), I'll extract
   the beast in you.
KORYPHAIOS OF MEN [*Searching himself*].
                     What beast in me?
1250 KORYPHAIOS OF WOMEN.   That insect. There. The bug that's stuck
       in your eye.
KORYPHAIOS OF MEN [*playing along dubiously*].
               This gnat?
KORYPHAIOS OF WOMEN.   Yes, nitwit!
KORYPHAIOS OF MEN.   Of course.
   That steady, festering agony. . . .
   You've put your finger on the source
   of all my lousy troubles. Please
   roll back the lid and scoop it out.
   I'd like to see it.
KORYPHAIOS OF WOMEN.   All right, I'll do it.

                              [*Removing the imaginary insect.*]

1260   Although, of all the impossible cranks. . . .
       Do you sleep in a swamp? Just look at this.
       I've never seen a bigger chigger.

KORYPHAIOS OF MEN.   Thanks.
   Your kindness touches me deeply. For years,
   that thing's been sinking wells in my eye.
   Now you've unplugged me. Here come the tears.
KORYPHAIOS OF WOMEN.   I'll dry your tears, though I can't say why.

                              [*Wiping away the tears.*]

   Of all the irresponsible boys. . . .
   And I'll kiss you.

1270 KORYPHAIOS OF MEN.   Don't you kiss me!
     KORYPHAIOS OF WOMEN.   What made you think you had a choice?

                              [*She kisses him.*]

KORYPHAIOS OF MEN.   All right, damn you, that's enough of that ingrained
    palaver.
I can't dispute the truth or logic of the pithy old proverb:
       Life with women is hell.
       Life without women is hell, too.
And so we conclude a truce with you, on the following terms:
in future, a mutual moratorium on mischief in all its forms.
Agreed?—Let's make a single chorus and start our song.

                     [The two CHORUSES *unite and face the audience.]*

CHORUS OF MEN.

1280
          We're not about to introduce
          the standard personal abuse—
             the Choral Smear
          Of Present Persons (usually,
          in every well-made comedy,
             inserted here).
          Instead, in deed and utterance, we
          shall now indulge in philanthropy
             because we feel
          that members of the audience
          endure, in the course of current events,
1290
             sufficient hell.
          Therefore, friends, be rich! Be flush!
          Apply to us, and borrow cash
             in large amounts.
          The Treasury stands behind us—there—
          and we can personally take care
             of small accounts.
          Drop up today. Your credit's good.
          Your loan won't have to be repaid
             in full until
1300
          the war is over. And then, your debt
          is only the money you actually get—
             nothing at all.

CHORUS OF WOMEN.

          Just when we meant to entertain
          some madcap gourmets from out of town
             —such flawless taste!—
          the present unpleasantness intervened,
          and now we fear the feast we planned
             will go to waste.
          The soup is waiting, rich and thick;
1310
          I've sacrificed a suckling pig
             —the *pièce de résistance*[43]—
          whose toothsome cracklings should amaze
          the most fastidious gourmets—
             you, for instance.

---

[43] Main dish.

To everybody here, I say
take potluck at my house today
    with me and mine.
    Bathe and change as fast as you can.
    bring the children, hurry down,
1320   and walk right in.
Don't bother to knock. No need at all.
My house is yours. Liberty Hall.
    What are friends for?
Act self-possessed when you come over;
it may help out when you discover
    I've locked the door.

[*A delegation of Spartans enters from the right, with difficulty. They have removed their cloaks, but hold them before themselves in an effort to conceal their condition.*]

KORYPHAIOS OF MEN.   What's this? Behold the Spartan ambassadors,
        dragging their beards,
    pussy-footing along. It appears they've developed
1330   a hitch in the crotch.

[*Advancing to greet them.*]

    Men of Sparta, I bid you welcome!
                        And now
    to the point: What predicament brings you among us?
SPARTAN.   We-uns is up a stump. Hain't fit fer chatter.

[*Flipping aside his cloak.*]

    Here's our predicament. Take a look for yourselfs.
KORYPHAIOS OF MEN.   Well, I'll be damned—a regular disaster area.
    Inflamed. I imagine the temperature's rather intense?
SPARTAN.   Hit ain't the heat, hit's the tumidity.
                        But words
    won't help what ails us. We-uns come after Peace.
    Peace from any person, at any price.

[*Enter the Athenian delegation from the left, led by* KINESIAS. *They are wearing cloaks, but are obviously in as much travail as the Spartans.*]

1340 KORYPHAIOS OF MEN.   Behold our local Sons of the Soil, stretching
    their garments away from their groins, like wrestlers.
    Grappling with their plight. Some sort of athlete's disease, no doubt.
    An outbreak of epic proportions.
                        Athlete's foot?
    No. Could it be athlete's . . . ?
KINESIAS [*breaking in*].   Who can tell us
    how to get hold of Lysistrata? We've come as delegates
    to the Sexual Congress.

[*Opening his cloak.*]

    Here are our credentials.

KORYPHAIOS OF MEN.

[*Ever the scientist, looking from the Athenians to the Spartans and back again.*]

The words are different, but the malady seems the same.

[*To Kinesias.*]

Dreadful disease. When the crisis reaches its height,
what do you take for it?

KINESIAS.   Whatever comes to hand.
1350   But now we've reached the bitter end. It's Peace
or we fall back on Kleisthenes.

                              And he's got a waiting list.

KORYPHAIOS OF MEN [*To the* SPARTANS].   Take my advice and put your
        clothes on. If someone
from that self-appointed Purity League comes by, you
may be docked. They do it to the statues of Hermes,
they'll do it to you.[44]

KINESIAS. [*Since he has not yet noticed the Spartans, he interprets the warning as
meant for him, and hurriedly pulls his cloak together, as do the other
Athenians.*]

            Excellent advice.

SPARTAN.   Hit shorely is.
Hain't nothing to argue after. Let's git dressed.

        [*As they put on their cloaks, the Spartans are finally noticed by* KINESIAS.]

KINESIAS.   Welcome, men of Sparta! This is a shameful
        disgrace to masculine honor.

SPARTAN.   Hit could be worser.
1360   Ef them Herm-choppers seed us all fired up,
        they'd *really* take us down a peg or two.

KINESIAS.   Gentlemen, let's descend to details. Specifically,
        why are you here?

SPARTAN.   Ambassadors. We come to dicker
        'bout thet-thur Peace.

KINESIAS.   Perfect! Precise our purpose.
        Let's send for Lysistrata. Only she can reconcile
        our differences. There'll be no Peace for us without her.

SPARTAN.   We-uns ain't fussy. Call Lysistratos, too, if you want.

[*The gates to the Akropolis open, and* LYSISTRATA *emerges, accompanied by her hand-
maid,* PEACE—*a beautiful girl without a stitch on.* PEACE *remains out of sight by the
gates until summoned.*]

KORYPHAIOS OF MEN.   Hail, most virile of women! Summon up all your
        experience:

---

[44] In 415 B.C. the Athenian statues of Hermes, the god of messengers and thieves, were
mutilated by vandals.

Be terrible and tender,
                    lofty and lowbrow,
                                        severe and demure.
1370   Here stand the Leaders of Greece, enthralled by your charm.
        They yield the floor to you and submit their claims for your arbitration.
LYSISTRATA.   Really, it shouldn't be difficult, if I can catch them
        all bothered, before they start to solicit each other.
        I'll find out soon enough. Where's Peace?
                                        —Come here.

[PEACE *moves from her place by the gates to* LYSISTRATA. *The delegations goggle at her.*]

        Now, dear, first get those Spartans and bring them to me.
        Take them by the hand, but don't be pushy about it,
        not like our husbands (no savoir-faire[45] at all!).
        Be a lady, be proper, do just what you'd do at home:
        if hands are refused, conduct them by the handle.

                    [PEACE *leads the Spartans to a position near* LYSISTRATA.]

1380   And now a hand to the Athenians—it doesn't matter
        where; accept any offer—and bring *them* over.

[PEACE *conducts the Athenians to a position near* LYSISTRATA, *opposite the Spartans.*]

        You Spartans move up closer —right *here*—

                                        [*To the Athenians.*]

                                        and *you*
        stand over *here*.
                    —And now attend my speech.

[*This the delegations do with some difficulty, because of the conflicting attractions of* PEACE, *who is standing beside her mistress.*]

        I am a woman—but not without some wisdom:
        my native wit is not completely negligible,
        and I've listened long and hard to the discourse of my
        elders—my education is not entirely despicable.
                                        Well,
        now that I've got you, I intend to give you hell,
        and I'm perfectly right. Consider your actions:
                                        At festivals,
1390   in Pan-Hellenic harmony, like true blood-brothers, you share
        the selfsame basin of holy water, and sprinkle
        altars all over Greece—Olympia, Delphoi,
        Thermopylai . . . (I could go on and on, if length
        were my only object.)
                    But now, when the Persians sit by
        and wait, in the very presence of your enemies, you fight

─────────────
[45] Knowledge of the gracious way to do things.

each other, destroy *Greek* men, destroy *Greek* cities!
—Point One of my address is now concluded.

KINESIAS [*Gazing at* PEACE].   *I'm* destroyed, if this is drawn out much
longer!

LYSISTRATA [*Serenely unconscious of the interruption*].
—Men of Sparta, I direct these remarks to you.

1400   Have you forgotten that a Spartan suppliant once came
to beg assistance from Athens? Recall Perikleidas:
Fifty years ago, he clung to our altar,
his face dead-white above his crimson robe, and pleaded
for an army. Messene was pressing you hard in revolt,
and to this upheaval, Poseidon, the Earthshaker, added
another.
            But Kimon took four thousand troops
from Athens—an army which saved the state of Sparta.
Such treatment have you received at the hands of Athens,

1410   you who devastate the country that came to your aid!

KINESIAS [*Stoutly; the condemnation of his enemy has made him forget the girl
momentarily*].   You're right, Lysistrata. The Spartans are clearly in the
wrong!

SPARTAN. [*Guiltily backing away from* PEACE, *whom he has attempted to pat*].
Hit's wrong, I reckon, but that's the purtiest behind . . .

LYSISTRATA [*Turning to the Athenians*].   —Men of Athens, do you think I'll
let *you* off?
Have you forgotten the Tyrant's days,[46] when you wore
the smock of slavery, when the Spartans turned to the
spear, cut down the pride of Thessaly, despatched the
friends of tyranny, and dispossessed your oppressors?
                                    Recall:
On that great day, your only allies were Spartans;
your liberty came at their hands, which stripped away
your servile garb and clothed you again in Freedom!

1420 SPARTAN [*Indicating* LYSISTRATA].   Hain't never seed no higher type of
woman.

KINESIAS [*Indicating* PEACE].   Never saw one I wanted so much to top.

LYSISTRATA [*Oblivious to the byplay, addressing both groups*].
With such a history of mutual benefits conferred
and received, why are you fighting? Stop this wickedness!
Come to terms with each other! What prevents you?

SPARTAN.   We'd a heap sight druther make Peace, if we was
indemnified with a plumb strategic location.

[*Pointing at* PEACE's *rear.*]

We'll take thet butte.[47]

---

[46] "The reign of Hippias, expelled by Athenians in 510 with the aid of Kleomenes and his
Spartans, who defeated the tyrant's Thessalian allies." [Translator's note.]

[47] In the lines that follow, the discussion of the terms for peace is packed with *double entendre.*
"That butte" is both a prominent part of the female anatomy and a reference to the promontory
of Pylos, a region in Greece that the Spartans longed to control.

LYSISTRATA. Butte?
SPARTAN. The Promontory of Pylos—Sparta's Back Door.
  We've missed it fer a turrible spell.

[*Reaching.*]

                              Hev to keep our
  hand in.
KINESIAS [*Pushing him away*]. The price is too high—you'll never take that!
LYSISTRATA. Oh, let them have it.
KINESIAS.   What room will we have left
1430 for maneuvers?
LYSISTRATA.   Demand another spot in exchange.
KINESIAS. [*surveying* PEACE *like a map as he addresses the Spartan*].
  Then you hand over to us—uh, let me see—
  let's try Thessaly[48]

                    [*Indicating the relevant portions of* PEACE.]

                    First of all, Easy Mountain . . .
  then the Maniac Gulf behind it . . .
                              and down to Megara
  for the legs . . .
SPARTAN.   You cain't take all of thet! Yore plumb
  out of yore mind!
LYSISTRATA [*to* KINESIAS.]
                    Don't argue. Let the legs go.

              [KINESIAS *nods. A pause. General smiles of agreement.*]

KINESIAS [*doffing his cloak*]. I feel an urgent desire to plow a few furrows.
SPARTAN [*doffing his cloak*]. Hit's time to work a few loads of fertilizer in.
LYSISTRATA. Conclude the treaty and the simple life is yours.
1440 If such is your decision convene your councils,
  and then deliberate the matter with your allies.
KINESIAS. *Deliberate? Allies?*
                    We're over-extended already!
  Wouldn't every ally approve our position—
  Union Now?
SPARTAN.   I know I kin speak for ourn.
KINESIAS. And I for ours.
                    They're just a bunch of gigolos.
LYSISTRATA. I heartily approve.
                    Now first attend to your purification,
  then we, the women, will welcome you to the Citadel

---

  [48] "Puns on proper names, particularly geographical ones, rarely transfer well, as the following bits of sexual cartography will show. "Easy Mountain": an impossible pun on Mt. Oita,
replacing the Greek's *Echinous*, a town in Thessaly whose name recalls *echinos* "hedgehog"—
slang for the female genitalia. "Maniac Gulf": for Maliac Gulf, with less dimension than the
Greek's *Mêlia kolpon*, which puns both on bosom and pudendum. The "legs of Megara" are the
walls that connected that city with her seaport, Nisaia." [Translator's note.]

and treat you to all the delights of a home-cooked
banquet. Then you'll exchange your oaths and pledge
1450   your faith, and every man of you will take his wife and
depart for home.

> [LYSISTRATA *and* PEACE *enter the Akropolis.*]

KINESIAS.   Let's hurry!
SPARTAN.   Lead on, everwhich
   way's yore pleasure.
KINESIAS.   This way, then—and HURRY!

> [*The delegations exeunt at a run.*]

CHORUS OF WOMEN.

      I'd never stint on anybody.
      And now I include, in my boundless bounty,
        the younger set.
      Attention, you parents of teengage girls
      about to debut in the social whirl.
        Here's what you get:
      Embroidered linens, lush brocades,
1460   a huge assortment of ready-mades,
        from mantles to shifts;
      plus bracelets and bangles of solid gold—
      every item my wardrobe holds—
        absolute gifts!
      Don't miss this offer. Come to my place,
      barge right in, and make your choice.
        You can't refuse.
      Everything there must go today.
      Finders keepers—cart it away!
1470   How can you lose?
      Don't spare me. Open all the locks.
      Break every seal. Empty every box.
        Keep ferreting—
      And your sight's considerably better than mine
      if you should possibly chance to find
        a single thing.

CHORUS OF MEN.

      Troubles, friend? Too many mouths
      to feed, and not a scrap in the house
        to see you through?
1480   Faced with starvation? Don't give it a thought.
      Pay attention; I'll tell you what
        I'm gonna do.
      I overbought. I'm overstocked.
      Every room in my house is clogged
        with flour (best ever),
      glutted with luscious loaves whose size
      you wouldn't believe. I need the space;
        do me a favor:

Bring gripsacks, knapsacks, duffle bags,
1490 pitchers, cisterns, buckets, and kegs
          around to me.
A courteous servant will see to your needs;
he'll fill them up with A-1 wheat—
          and all for free!
—Oh. Just one final word before
you turn your steps to my front door:
          I happen to own
a dog. Tremendous animal.
Can't stand a leash. And bites like hell—
1500   better stay home.

[*The united* CHORUS *flocks to the door of the Akropolis.*]

KORYPHAIOS OF MEN [*Banging at the door*].   Hey, open up in there!

[*The door opens, and the* COMMISSIONER *appears. He wears a wreath, carries a torch, and is slightly drunk. He addresses the* KORYPHAIOS.]

COMMISSIONER.   You know the Regulations.
   Move along!

[*He sees the entire* CHORUS.]

     —And why are YOU lounging around?
I'll wield my trusty torch and scorch the lot!

[*The* CHORUS *backs away in mock horror. He stops and looks at his torch.*]

—*This* is the bottom of the barrel. A cheap burlesque bit.
I refuse to do it. I have my pride.

[*With a start, he looks at the audience, as though hearing a protest. He shrugs and addresses the audience.*]

          —No choice, eh?
Well, if that's the way it is, we'll take the trouble.
Anything to keep you happy.

[*The* CHORUS *advances eagerly.*]

KORYPHAIOS OF MEN.   Don't forget us!
   We're in this too. Your trouble is ours!
COMMISSIONER. [*Resuming his character and jabbing with his torch
      at the* CHORUS].   Keep moving!
   Last man out of the way goes home without hair!
1510   Don't block the exit. Give the Spartans some room.
   They've dined in comfort; let them go home in peace.

[*The* CHORUS *shrinks back from the door.* KINESIAS, *wreathed and quite drunk, appears at the door. He speaks his first speech in Spartan.*]

KINESIAS.   Hain't never seed sech a spread! Hit were splendiferous!
COMMISSIONER.   I gather the Spartans won friends and influenced people?

KINESIAS. And *we've* never been so brilliant. It was the wine.
COMMISSIONER. Precisely.

> The reason? A sober Athenian is just
> *non compos.*[49] If I can carry a little proposal
> I have in mind, our Foreign Service will flourish,
> guided by this rational rule:

No Ambassador

Without a Skinful.

> Reflect on our past performance:

1520
> Down to a Spartan parley we troop, in a state
> of disgusting sobriety, looking for trouble. It muddles
> our senses: we read between the lines; we hear,
> not what the Spartans say, but what we suspect
> they might have been about to be going to say.
> We bring back paranoid reports—cheap fiction, the fruit
> of temperance. Cold-water diplomacy, pah!

> Contrast
> this evening's total pleasure, the free-and-easy
> give-and-take of friendship: If we were singing,

> *Just Kleitagora and me,*
> *Alone in Thessaly,*

1530
> and someone missed his cue and cut in loudly,

> *Ajax, son of Telamon,*
> *He was one hell of a man—*

> no one took it amiss, or started a war;
> we clapped him on the back and gave three cheers.

[*During this recital, the* CHORUS *has sidled up to the door.*]

—Dammit, are you back here again?

[*Waving his torch.*]

> Scatter!
> Get out of the road! Gangway, you gallowsbait!

KINESIAS. Yes, everyone out of the way. They're coming out.

[*Through the door emerge the Spartan delegation, a flutist, the Athenian delegation,* LYSISTRATA, KLEONIKE, MYRRHINE, *and the rest of the women from the citadel, both Athenian and Peloponnesian. The* CHORUS *splits into its male and female components and draws to the sides to give the procession room.*]

SPARTAN [*To the flutist*]. Friend and kinsman, take up them pipes a yourn.
1540 I'd like fer to shuffle a bit and sing a right sweet
> song in honor of Athens and us'uns, too.
COMMISSIONER [*To the flutist*]. Marvelous, marvelous—come, take up your
> pipes!

[*To the Spartan.*]

---

[49] *Non compos mentis,* not of sound mind.

I certainly love to see you Spartans dance.

[*The flutist plays, and the Spartan begins a slow dance.*]

SPARTAN.

Memory,
send me
your Muse,
who knows
our glory,
knows Athens'—
Tell the story:
At Artemision
like gods, they stampeded
the hulks of the Medes, and
beat them.[50]
And Leonidas
leading us—
the wild boars
whetting their tusks.
And the foam flowered,
flowered and flowed,
down our cheeks
to our knees below.
The Persians there
like the sands of the sea—
Hither, huntress,
virgin, goddess,
tracker, slayer,
to our truce!
Holds us ever
fast together;
bring our pledges
love and increase;
wean us from the
fox's wiles—
Hither, huntress!
Virgin, hither!

1550

1560

1570

LYSISTRATA. [*Surveying the assemblage with a proprietary air.*]
Well, the preliminaries are over—very nicely, too.
So, Spartans,

[*Indicating the Peloponnesian women who have been hostages.*]

take these girls back home. And *you*

[*To the Athenian delegation, indicating the women from the Akropolis.*]

---

[50] Near Artemision in 480 B.C. the Athenian navy defeated the navy of the Persians (or Medes). Meanwhile Leonidas with 300 Spartans held the pass at Thermopylae against the entire Persian army.

take *these* girls. Each man stand by his wife, each wife
1580   by her husband. Dance to the gods' glory, and thank
them for the happy ending. And, from now on, please be
careful. Let's not make the same mistakes again.

[*The delegations obey; the men and women of the chorus join again for a rapid ode.*]

CHORUS.[51]   Start the chorus dancing,
                      Summon all the Graces,
        Send a shout to Artemis in invocation.
               Call upon her brother,
                  healer, chorus master,
    Call the blazing Bacchus, with his maddened muster.

           Call the flashing, fiery Zeus, and
1590   call his mighty, blessed spouse, and
            call the gods, call all the gods,
             to witness now and not forget
      our gentle, blissful Peace—the gift,
               the deed of Aphrodite.
                    Ai!
                Alalai! Paion!
              Leap you! Paion!
              Victory! Alalai!
        Hail!   Hail!   Hail!
1600 LYSISTRATA.   Spartan, let's have another song from you, a new one.
     SPARTAN.[52]   Leave darlin' Taygetos,
               Spartan Muse! Come to us
             once more, flyin'
             and glorifyin'
            Spartan themes:
           the god at Amyklai,
           bronze-house Athene,
            Tyndaros' twins,
            the valiant ones,
1610   playin' still by Eurotas' streams.

                  Up! Advance!
               Leap to the dance!

---

[51] The Athenian chorus concludes with a song invoking many of the Greek gods: Artemis, the goddess of chastity; her brother Apollo, the god of medicine and music; Bacchus, the god of wine and revelry; Zeus, the leader of the gods; and Hera, the wife of Zeus. Fittingly, the song concludes with an appeal to Aphrodite, the goddess of love—for love, as stimulated by the sex-strike and the nude figure of Peace, has brought an end to the war.

[52] The Spartan's song celebrates Apollo, worshipped in the Spartan town of Amyklai; Athene, whose temple in Sparta was bronze-plated; Kastor and Pollux, the twin sons of Tyndaros, who were supposedly born by the Eurotas River in Sparta; and Helen, wife of the Spartan king Menelaos and the indirect cause of the Trojan War. Fittingly, the Spartan's song concludes with the praises of Athene, the patroness of Athens—thus reaffirming the peace between Sparta and Athens.

> Help us hymn Sparta,
> lover of dancin',
> lover of foot-pats,
> where girls go prancin'
> like fillies along Eurotas' banks,
> whirlin' the dust, twinklin' their shanks,
> shakin' their hair
1620
> like Maenads playin'
> and jugglin' the thyrsis,
> in frenzy obeyin'
> Leda's daughter, the fair, the pure
> Helen, the mistress of the choir.

> Here, Muse, here!
> Bind up your hair!

> Stamp like a deer! Pound your feet!
> Clap your hands! Give us a beat!

1630
> *Sing* the greatest,
> *sing* the mightiest,
> *sing* the conqueror,
> *sing* to honor her—

> Athene of the Bronze House!
> Sing Athene!

[*Exeunt omnes, dancing and singing.*]

[411 B.C.]

Critical Commentary on *Lysistrata*

Lysistrata is a ribald and shocking play—but it is also a serious feminist attack against masculine militarism. In our current era of giggle and jiggle comedy, we may snicker at all the right moments, while still failing to recognize that Aristophanes was dramatizing important moral and ethical points through his carnal humor. That such a play could be performed as part of a religious observation and that leather phalluses could be part of the expected costuming are ideas completely alien to modern readers. Indeed, the play merits study in part because it reminds us that the traditions and values of modern America are far from permanent or universal.

As the action begins, Athens is in grave danger. The Peloponnesian War has already dragged on for nearly twenty years. The unity among the city states that had helped to make Greece great has degenerated into fractious regional warfare. Just as there is a lack of love between Athens and Sparta, there is also a lack of love between husband and wife. The men on both sides have been posted to the frontiers; the women languish at home. The men insist on running—and ruining—the affairs of state without feminine meddling; the women are restricted to housework and repressed by being seen mainly as brainless sexual toys.

Thus, the problems of the nation are fused with, and in a sense created by, the problems in the family—a fact that Aristophanes cleverly carries over into the imagery of the play. Not only are the men's weapons (their swords and spears) conventional phallic symbols, but the sex-starved men explicitly compare the bodies of the women to the fertile ground for which they have battled. In the resolution of the play, Peace, in the form of a beautiful nude maiden, is brought on stage to reunify both the divided states and the divided families. During the negotiations for Peace, the Spartans and Athenians cast lustful eyes on parts of her anatomy that can also stand for parts of Greece: a butte here, the easy mountains up there, the legs of Megara beneath, and so on. Once both sides have given up something they desire in order to retain something else, they retire from their overextended positions in order to "plow a few furrows" and "work a few loads of fertilizer in."

The analogy between sexual and physical geography is carried even farther, however. In the central action of the play, the women bar the gates of love just as they bar the gates of the Acropolis. They then control both the fertile womb from which all soldiers must emerge and the womb (the Treasury) from which all armaments flow. In a series of parallel scenes, we see the Commissioner, the chorus of men, and Kinesias attempt to open the gates through force—the typical masculine solution to both domestic and diplomatic problems. When the old men of the chorus struggle to light their fires and to lift their logs in an attack upon the women's gates, we are witness to *double entendre* on a truly massive scale. Peace and reunification are unattainable, however, until the men agree to listen to a woman. Lysistrata then guides the representatives of Sparta and Athens toward an equitable agreement. Thereafter, the divided chorus is reunified, the men return to their wives, and the play ends with odes to love and wisdom.

The problems raised by the play are nearly as pervasive in modern society as they were in 411 B.C. In particular, *Lysistrata* explores sex stereotypes and male attitudes still rampant today. At first even the women (except for Lysistrata) see themselves as inferior, flighty sex objects. When Lysistrata suggests that the women form an alliance and save the states of Greece, Kleonike replies:

> Us? Be practical. Wisdom from women? There's nothing cosmic about cosmetics—and Glamor is our only talent. All we can do is *sit*, primped and painted, made up and dressed up [*Getting carried away in spite of her argument*], ravishing in saffron wrappers, peekaboo peignoirs, exquisite negligees, those chic, expensive little slippers that come from the East . . .

The women have in fact endorsed the stereotype. But as the play develops, it becomes evident that the kind of self-control exhibited by the women in abstaining from sexual relations is also what is needed in the state. Unlike the passionate and impulsive men, women demonstrate that they have the financial and emotional self-restraint needed to shut the doors to the Treasury, to throw waters on the fires of sexual rivalry and state rivalry, and to use reason instead of passion and violence. This self-control is dramatically illustrated in the tantalizing scene between Kinesias and Myrrhine, but the philosophical core of the play grows out of Lysistrata's extended similes on diplomacy and political corruption: Ending the war is like unsnarling a hank of yarn: you need to send shuttles flying back and forth to work out the tense international kinks. And ending political corruption is like cleansing a fleece: first you "scrub it in a public bath" to remove the filth and corruption; then after clubbing any remaining vermin, you can "card the citizens together in a single basket of common weal, . . . spin a mighty bobbin of yarn—and weave, without bias or seam, a cloak to clothe the City of Athens."

Ironically, as the household similes of these speeches indicate, the women have been prepared to assume political power precisely because they have been denied it so long. The management of household accounts has taught them frugality, weaving and sewing have taught them to exercise patience and meticulous care, and physical weakness has taught them to reprehend violence. Aristophanes' play is comic, but his recipe for peace is serious and practical.

A Selective Bibliography on *Lysistrata*

Dover, K. J. *Aristophanic Comedy*. Berkeley: U of California P, 1972.

Ehrenberg, Victor. *The People of Aristophanes*, 2nd ed. Oxford: Blackwell, 1951.

Harriott, Rosemary M. *Aristophanes: Poet and Dramatist*. Baltimore: Johns Hopkins UP, 1986.

Henderson, Jeffrey. *The Maculate Muse: Obscene Language in Attic Comedy*, 2nd ed. New York: Oxford UP, 1991.

Hubbard, Thomas K. *The Mask of Comedy: Aristophanes and the Intertextual Parabasis*. Ithaca: Cornell UP, 1991.

Lloyd-Jones, Hugh. *Greek Comedy, Hellenistic Literature, Greek Religion, and Miscellanea*. Oxford, Eng.: Clarendon, 1990.

McLeish, Kenneth. *The Theatre of Aristophanes*. London: Thames and Hudson, 1980.

Murray, Gilbert. *Aristophanes*. Oxford: Clarendon, 1933.

Norwood, Gilbert. *Greek Comedy*. Boston: Luce, 1932.

Parker, Douglass. "Introduction." *Lysistrata*. Ann Arbor: U of Michigan P, 1964.

Polesso, P. "Searching for a Satyr Play: The Significance of the 'Parados'." *New Theatre Quarterly* 4 (1988): 321–25.

Smith, N. D. "Diviners and Divination in Aristophanic Comedy." *Classical Antiquity* 8 (1989): 140–58.

Solomos, Alexes. *The Living Aristophanes*. Ann Arbor: U of Michigan P, 1974.

Spatz, Lois. *Aristophanes*. Boston: Twayne, 1978. 91–102.

Whitman, Cedric H. *Aristophanes and the Comic Hero*. Cambridge: Harvard UP, 1964. 200–16.

Worthington, I. "Aristophanes' *Lysistrata* 526: An Unnoticed Military Pun?" *Mnemosyne* 39 (1986): 388–89.

Anonymous

THE SECOND SHEPHERD'S PLAY [1]

CHARACTERS

PRIMUS PASTOR,[2] COLL   JILL, *Mak's wife*
SECUNDUS PASTOR, GIB   ANGEL
TERCIUS PASTOR, DAW   JESUS
MAK   MARY

[*The setting is an open field on the cold, windy eve of the birth of Christ.* COLL, *the first shepherd, enters alone.*]

COLL.   Lord, how these weathers are cold! and I am ill wrapped;
    I am nearhand dold° so long have I napped.   *nearly numb*
    My legs they fold, my fingers are chapped;
    It is not as I wold°, for I am all lapped   *would*
      In sorrow.
    In storms and tempest,
    Now in the east, now in the west,
    Woe is him has never rest
      Mid-day nor morrow!

10   But we silly shepherds that walk on the moor,
    In faith we are near hands out° of the door;   *shoved out*
    No wonder as it stands if we be poor,
    For the tilling of our lands lies fallow as the floor,
      As you ken.°   *know*
    We are so hemmed,
    Overtaxed and rammed,
    We are made hand-tamed
      By these gentlery° men.   *gentle*

    Thus they rob us of our rest—our Lady them harry
20   These men that are lord-fast,[3] they cause the plow tarry.
    What men say is for the best, we find it contrary;

---

[1] Modernized spellings, translation of archaisms, and addition of stage directions by Jeffrey D. Hoeper.

[2] *Pastor* is Latin for *shepherd*, but the author may also have been playing satirically with the religious connotations of the word *pastor*. *Primus, secundus,* and *tercius* are Latin for first, second, and third.

[3] *Lord-fast* men are presumably those stewarts or overseers who are devoted to serving the nobility.

Thus are husbands oppressed, almost to miscarry
    In life.
Thus hold they us under;
Thus they bring us in blunder;
It were great wonder,
    If ever should we thrive

For may he get a painted sleeve° or a brooch nowadays,   *a costly shirt*
Woe is him that him grieve or once gainsays!
30   Dare no man him reprieve° whatever he craves,   *reprove*
And yet may no man believe one word that he says,
    No letter.
He can make purveyance°   *a claim on produce*
With boast and bragance,°   *braggery*
And all is through maintenance
    Of men that are greater.

There shall come a swain° as proud as a po,°   *shepherd/peacock*
He must borrow my wain,° my plough also.   *wagon*
Then I am full fain° to grant ere° he go.   *forced/before*
40   Thus live we in pain, anger, and woe,
    By night and day;
He must have if he long it;
If I should forgo it,
I were better be hanged
    Than once say him nay.

It does me good as I walk thus by mine own,
Of this world for to talk in manner of moan.
To my sheep will I stalk and hearken anon,°   *listen awhile*
There abide on a balk° or sit on a stone   *ridge*
50   Full soon.
For I trust, perde,°   *by God*
True men if they be,
We get more company
    Ere it be noon.

[GIB, *the second shepherd, staggers in, bent over against the force of the wind.*]

GIB.   Benste and dominus![4] What may this mean?
    Why fares this world thus? Oft have we not seen,
    Lord, these weathers are spiteous° and the winds full keen,   *spiteful*
    And the frosts so hideous they water mine eeyne?°   *eyes*
        No lie.
    Now in dry, now in wet,
60   Now in snow, now in sleet,
    When my shoes freeze to my feet,
        It is not all easy.

---

[4] *Benedicite* and *Dominus*: Latin meaning *bless us* and *lord*.

But as far as I ken° or yet as I go,   *know*
We silly wedmen° suffer much woe.   *married men*
We have sorrow then and then; it falls oft so.
Silly Capyle, our hen, both to and fro
   She cackles;
But begin she to croak,
To groan or to cluck,
70   Woe is him is our cock,
     For he is in the shackles.

These men that are wed have not all their will,
When they are full hard sted° they sigh full still.°   *beset/constantly*
God knows they are led full hard and full ill.
In bower° nor in bed they say nought theretill   *bedroom*
   This tide.°   *time*
My part have I found;
I know my lesson:
Woe is him that is bound,
80   For he must abide.

But now late in our lives, a marvel to me
That I think my heart rives° such wonders to see!   *breaks*
What that destiny drives, it should so be:
Some men will have two wives and some men three
   In store;
Some are woe that has any,
But so far as know I,
Woe is him that has many,
     For he feels it sore.

90   But young men of wooing, for God that you bought,
Beware well of wedding and think in your thought,
"Had I wist"° is a thing it serves of nought;   *known*
Much endless mourning has wedding home brought,
   And griefs,
With many a sharp shower,
For thou may catch in an hour
That shall savor° full sour   *taste*
     As long as thou lives.

For, as ever read I Epistle, I have one to my fair°   *mate*
100 As sharp as a thistle, as rough as a briar;
She is browed like a bristle with a sour looking cheer;
Had she once wet her whistle she could sing full clear
   Her "Pater Noster."°   *"Our Father"*
She is great as a whale;
She has a gallon of gall;
By him that died for us all,
     I would I had run till I had lost her.

COLL [*amiably to* GIB, *who has not yet noticed him*].   God watch over the
   raw!° [*pause*] Full deafly ye stand.   *land*

110 GIB [*resentfully*].   Yea, the devil in thy maw.° [*pause*] So tarrying,   *mouth*
    Saw thou ought of Daw?
COLL.   Yea, on a lea° land   *meadow*
    Heard I him blow; he comes here at hand,
      Not far;
    Stand still.
GIB.   Why?
COLL.   For he comes, hope I.
GIB.   He will tell us both a lie
      But if we beware.

[DAW, *a lad employed to watch* GIB'*s sheep, enters without at first noticing the other two.*]

120 DAW.   Christ's cross me speed and Saint Nicholas!
    Thereof had I need: it is worse than it was.
    Whoso could, take heed and let the world pass,
    It is ever in dreed° and brittle as glass,   *danger*
      And slithers.
    This world fared never so
    With marvels mo° and mo,   *more*
    Now in weal, now in woe
      And everything withers.

    Was never since Noah's flood such floods seen;
130   Winds and rains so rude and storms so keen;
    Some stammered, some stood in doubt, as I ween;°   *believe*
    Now God turn all to good. I say as I mean,
      For ponder:
    These foods so they drown
    Both in fields and in town
    And bears all down,
      And that is a wonder.

[Daw *now sees* COLL *and* GIB *peering at him but does not yet recognize them.*]

    We that walk on the nights our cattle to keep,
    We see sudden sights when other men sleep,
    Yet methink my heart lights: I see shrews° peep.   *rascals*
140   Ye are two all-wights;° I will give my sheep   *big men*
      A turn.
    [*Suddenly changing his mind.*] But full ill have I meant.
    As I walk on this bent,°   *field*
    I may lightly repent
      My toes if I spurn.[5]

                     [*going up to* COLL *and* GIB]

---

[5] Upon seeing Coll and Gib, Daw's first thought is to protect his sheep from these potential thieves. After reflection, however, he decides not to spurn the possibility of sharing their food and drink.

Ah, sir, God you save and master mine!
A drink fain° would I have and somewhat to dine.   *eagerly*
COLL.   Christ's curse, my knave, thou art a ledyr hyne!°   *wicked rascal*
GIB.   What! the boy likes to rave; abide unto sign
150   We have made it.
Ill thrift° on thy pate!°   *bad luck/head*
Though the shrew came late,
Yet is he in state
To dine if he had it.

DAW.   Such servants as I that sweats and swinks°   *works*
Eats our bread full dry and that me forthinks;°   *displeases*
We are oft wet and weary when master-men winks,
Yet comes full lately both dinners and drinks.
160   But nately°   *neatly*
Both our dame and our sire,
When we have run in the mire,
They can nip at° our hire,°   *cut back/wages*
And pay us full lately.

But hear my troth,° master: for the fare that ye make,   *vow*
I shall do thereafter work as I take;°   *am paid*
I shall do a little, sir, and then ever slake,°   *slack off*
For yet lay my supper never on my stomach
In fields.
Why then should I reap?
170 With my staff I can leap,
And men say "light cheap
Letherly for-yields."[6]

COLL.   Thou were an ill lad to ride a-wooing
With a man that had but little of spending.
GIB.   Peace, boy, I bid no more jangling,
Or I shall make thee full sad, by the heaven's king,
With thy frauds!
Where are our sheep, boy? We scorn—
180 DAW.   Sir, this same day at morn
I left them in the corn
When they rang lauds.[7]

They have pasture good; they can not go wrong.
COLL.   That is right, by the rood!° These nights are long,   *cross*
Yet I would, ere we yode,° once give us a song.   *left*
GIB.   So I thought as I stood, to mirth us among.
DAW.   I grant.
COLL.   Let me sing the tenor.

---

[6] "A penny-pinching bargain yields little."   [7] Bells rung for religious services at dawn.

GIB.   And I the treble so high.

190 DAW.   Then the mean° falls to me.   *middle part*
       Let's see how you chant.

                   [Mak *now enters wearing a cloak over his tunic.*]

MAK [*pretending not to see the shepherds*].   Now Lord, for thy names seven,
       that made both moon and starryness
     More than all numbers even,—thy will, Lord, make my harness.
     I am all uneven; my mind reels at thy largess.°   *generosity*
     Now would God I were in heaven, for there weap no barnes°   *children*
       So still.°   *constantly*
COLL.   Who is't that pipes° so poor?   *sings*
MAK.   Would God you wist° how I foor!°   *knew/fare*
     Lo, a man that walks on the moor,
200   And has not all his will!

GIB.   Mak, where has thou gone? Tell us tiding.
DAW [*whispering to his companions*].   Is *he* coming?
     Then ylkon° take heed to his thing.   *everyone*

[*And he takes the cloak from* MAK, *shaking it to see if* MAK *has concealed any stolen
goods within.*]

MAK.   What! I be a yeoman, I tell you, of the king,
     The self and the same, sond° from a great lordling   *sent*
       And such.
     Fie on you! Go hence—
     Out of my presence!
210   Why, who be I?

COLL.   Why make you it so quaint? Mak, you do wrong.
GIB.   But, Mak, play you the saint? For that do you long?
DAW [*whispering*].   I trust the shrew can paint! The devil might him hang!
MAK.   I shall make complaint and on you the whip shall twang
       At a word,
     If I tell what you dooth.
COLL.   But, Mak, is that truth?
     Now take out that southern tooth,
       And set it in a turd!⁸

220 GIB.   Mak, the devil in your eye. A stroke would I lay on you.
DAW.   Mak, know you not me? [*aside*] By God I could pain you.
MAK.   God look to you all three! Methought I had seen you;
     You are a fair company.
COLL.   Know us now, do you?
GIB.   Shrew, peep°   *Rascal, sneak about*
     Thus late as thou goes,

---

⁸ Mak has been using the southern accent of a royal official. Coll crudely tells him to quit
pretending.

What will men suppose?
For thou has an ill nose°   *reputation*
   Of stealing of sheep.

230 MAK. That I am true as steel, all men waytt,°   *acknowledge*
But a sickness I feel that holds me full haytt;°   *hot*
My belly fairs not weal;° it is out of estate.—   *healthily*
DAW [*skeptically aside*]. Seldom lies the devil dead by the gate.
MAK. Therefore
   Full sorry am I and so ill
   That I stand stone-still.
   I ate not a needle
     This month and more.

COLL. How fares thy wife? By my hood, how well does she go?
240 MAK. Lies wallowing by the rood° by the fire, low!   *cross*
With a houseful of brood.° She drinks well too;   *children*
There is no good that she will do!
   But she
   Eats as fast as she can,
   And each year that comes to man
   She brings forth a laken°   *baby*
     And some years two.

Even if I were more gracious and richer by far,
I were eaten out of house and of harbor;
250 Yet is she a foul louse if you came near
There is none that trows° nor knows a worse   *believes in*
   Than know I.
Now will you see what I proffer?
   To give all in my coffer
   Tomorrow morn to offer
     Her deadmass° penny!   *funeral mass*

GIB. I know so long-waked is none in this shire:
I would sleep though I taked less for my hire.
DAW. I am cold and naked and would have a fire.
260 COLL. I am weary for-rakyd° and run in the mire.   *from walking*

                [*Turning to* GIB *who is beginning to doze*]

   Wake thou!
GIB. Nay, I will lie down by,
   For I must sleep truly.
DAW. As good a man's son was I
     As any of you.

But, Mak, com hither! Between shall thou lie down.
MAK [*snidely with reference to* DAW]. Then might I hinder that whispering
   clown,
   Take heed!
   From my top to my toe,

270   Manus tuas commendo,
        Poncio Pilato,[9]
            Christ's cross me speed!

> [*Once the three shepherds fall asleep,* MAK *cautiously rises and says:*]

Now were time for a man that lacks what he would
To stalk secretly then unto a fold,°   sheep fold
And nimbly to work then and be not too bold,
For he might damn the deal if it were told
    At the ending.

> [MAK *stares for a moment at the sleeping shepherds and then continues reflectively:*]

Now were time to act pellmell,
But he needs good counsel
280   That fain would fare well,
        And has but little spending.

Put about you a circle as round as a moon,
Till I have done what I will, till that it be noon
That you lie stone still until I am done,
And I shall sing theretill of good words this tune:
    "On height
Over your heads my hand I lift.
Out go your eyes; forego your sight!"
But yet I must make better shift
290   Ere it be right.

> [MAK *completes his incantation with a flourish of arm movements, then carefully checks each of the sleeping shepherds while speaking the following words:*]

Lord! How they sleep hard! That may you all hear.
Was I never a shepherd, but now will I lear.°   learn
If the flock be scared, yet shall I nip° near.   slip
How? Draws it hitherward? Now mends this our cheer
    From sorrow.
A fat sheep, I dare say!
A good fleece dare I lay—
Requite° when I may—   Pay back
    But this I will borrow!

> [*After snatching up the closest sheep,* MAK *sneaks back to his hut.*]

300   How, Jill, art thou in? Give us some light.
JILL.   Who makes such a din at this time of night?
        I am set for to spin—I hope not I might
        Rise a penny to win—I beshrew° them on height!   curse
            So fares

---

[9] "I commend your hands to the care of Pontius Pilate"—a garbled version of Luke 23:46.

A housewife that has been
To be raised thus between.
Here may no work be seen
   For such small cares.

MAK.   Good wife, open the hatch! Seest thou not what I bring?
310 JILL.   I'll draw the bolt. You pull the latch. Ah, come in, my sweeting!
MAK.   Yea, you wouldn't budge an inch despite my long standing
JILL [*catching sight of the stolen sheep*].   By the naked neck are you likely to
   hang!
MAK.   Do way!°   *cut it out!*
   I am worthy my meat,
   For in a strait can I get
   More than they that swink° and sweat   *toil*
      All the long day.

   Thus it fell to my lot, Jill. I had such grace—
JILL.   It were a foul blot to be hanged for the case!
320 MAK.   I have escaped, Jilly, many as hard a maze.
JILL.   "Only so long goes the pot to the water," men says,
      "At last
   Comes it home broken."
MAK.   Well know I the token,
   But let it never be spoken!
      But come and help fast.

   I would he were flain.° I long to eat.   *skinned*
   This twelvemonth was I not so eager for one sheep's meat!
JILL.   Come they ere he be slain and hear the sheep bleat?
330 MAK.   Then might I be ta'en,° that were a cold sweat!   *taken*
      Hurry,
      Bar the gate.
JILL.   Yes, Mak,
   For if they come at thy back—
MAK.   Then might I get from all that pack
      The devil of a worry.

JILL.   A good trick have I spied since you know none:
   Here shall we hide him, till they be gone,
   In my cradle abide. Let me alone,
   And I shall lie beside in childbed and groan.
340 MAK.   Well said!
   And I shall say you came light°   *gave birth*
   Of a knave child this night.
JILL.   Joyful was the day so bright
      When I was bred.

   This is a good guise and a far cast.°   *fine trick*
   Yet a woman's advise helps at the last!

I know never who spies. Again go thou fast!
MAK.   Hope I come ere they rise! Else blows a cold blast!
    I will go sleep.

[MAK *hurries back to the sleeping shepherds and lies down.*]

350   Yet sleeps all this band,
    And I shall be slyly on hand
    As if I never had planned
        To carry off their sheep.
COLL.   Resurrex a mortruus![10] Have hold of my hand!
    Judas carnas dominus![11] I may not well stand.
    My foot sleeps, by Jesus, and I totter fasting.
    I thought that we laid us full near England!
GIB.   I see.
    Lord! How I have slept well!
360   As fresh as an eel,
    As light I me feel
        As a leaf on a tree.

DAW.   Benste be herein! So my heart quakes,
    My heart jumps from my skin? What is it that shakes
    Me? Who makes all this din so that my head aches?
    To the door will I win. Hark fellows! Wake us!
    We were four.
    See you ought of Mak now?
COLL.   We were up ere thou.
370 GIB.   Man, I give God a vow
    That he went nowhere.

DAW.   Methought he was lapped° in a wolfskin.   *wrapped*
COLL.   So are many happed now, namely within.
GIB.   When he had long napped methought with a gin°   *trick*
    A fat sheep he trapped, but he made no din.
DAW.   Be still!
    Thy dream makes thee wood;°   *insane*
    It is but phantom, by the rood.
COLL.   Now God turn all to good,
380   If it be his will.

GIB.   Rise, Mak, for shame! Thou liest right long.

[MAK *stirs making a great show of grogginess and stiffness in the bones.*]

MAK.   Now Christ's holy name be us among!
    What is this? For Saint James I may not well go on!
    I think I am the same. Ah! My neck has lain along
        Some bump. [GIB *helps him up.*]

---

[10] Corrupt Latin for "resurrected from the dead."
[11] Corrupt Latin for "Judas, lord incarnate."

Much thanks. Since yestereven
Now, by Saint Stephen,
I was flayed with a swevyn°— *dream*
   My heart gave a jump.

390   I thought Jill began to croak and travail° full sad. *labor*
Wellnigh at the first cock, she birthed a young lad
For to mend our flock; then be I never glad.
I have wool on my rock° more than ever I had. *distaff or rod*
   A, my head!
A houseful of young pains!
The devil knock out their brains!
Woe is him with brats to maintain
   And thereto little bread!

I must go home, by your leave, to Jill as I thought.
400   I pray you look in my sleeve that I steal nought.
I am loath you to grieve or from you take aught.
DAW.   Go forth, ill might thou chafe! [MAK *goes*] Now would I we sought,
   This morn,
That we had all our store.
COLL.   But I will go before;
   Let us meet.
GIB.   Where?
DAW.   At the crooked thorn.

[MAK *returns to his hut and begins pounding on the door.* JILL, *who has been sleeping soundly, is at first quite crotchety. Once she realizes that it is* MAK *at the door, she tries to pretend that she has been hard at work.*]

MAK.   Undo this door! Who is here? How long shall I stand?
410 JILL.   Who makes the deaf hear? Now walk in a dark land!
MAK.   Ah, Jill, what cheer? It is I, Mak, your husband.
JILL.   Then may we see here the devil in a band.° *noose*
   [*Opening the door.*] Sir Guile!
Lo, he comes with a croak
As he were held by the throat.
I may not sit at my note° *housework*
   A hand-long while.

MAK.   Will you hear what fare she makes to get her a glose,° *excuse*
And does nought but fakes and scratches her toes.
420 JILL.   Why, who wanders? Who wakes? Who comes? Who goes? Who
   brews?
Who bakes? What makes me thus hose?° *hoarse*
   And then
It is rueful to behold,
Now in hot, now in cold,
Full woeful is the household
   That wants a woman.

But what end has thou made with the herders, Mak?
Mak.   The last word that they said when I turned my back,
   They would look that they had their sheep—all the pack.
430 I hope they will not be well paid when they their sheep lack,
   Perde.°   *By God*
   But howso the game goes,
   To me they will suppose,
   And make a foul noise,
     And cry out upon me.

   But thou must do as thou hyght.°   *promised*
Jill.   I accord me theretill.
   I shall swadle him right in my cradle.
   If it were a greater sleight, yet could I help still.
   I will lie down straight; come wrap me;
440 Mak.   I will.

        [Mak *tries to embrace her. She pushes him away and says dryly:*]

Jill.   Behind
   Come Coll and his marrow,°   *comrade*
   They will nip us full narrow.
Mak.   But I may cry "out, harrow!"
   The sheep if they find.

Jill.   Hearken aye when they call. They will come anon.
   Come and make ready all and sing by thine own.°   *by yourself*
   Sing lullaby thou shall, for I must groan
   And cry out by the wall on Mary and John,
     So sore.
450 Sing lullaby now fast
   When you hear them at last.
   If I don't play a false cast,°   *trick*
     Trust me no more.

        [Coll, Gib, *and* Daw *meet near the crooked thorn.*]

Daw.   Ah, Coll, good morning. Why sleepest thou not?
Coll.   Alas, that ever I was born! We have a foul blot.
   A fat wether must we mourn.
Daw.   Mary, God forbot!°   *forbid*
Gib.   Who should do us that scorn? That were a foul spot.
Coll.   Some shrew.
460 I have sought with my dogs
   All Horbury Shrogs
   And of fifteen hogs°   *young sheep*
     Found I but one ewe.

Daw.   Now trust me, if ye will, by Saint Thomas of Kent,
   Either Mak or Jill was at° that event.   *behind*

Coll.   Peace, man, be still! I saw when we went;
    Thou slanders him ill. Thou ought to repent
       God speed.
470 Gib.   Now as ever might I thrive,
    If I should even here die,
    I would say it were he
       That did that same deed.

Daw.   Go we thither in dread and run on our feet.
    May I never eat bread, the truth till I greet.
Coll.   Nor drink in my head with him till I meet.
Gib.   I will rest in no stead till that I him greet.
    My brother,
    I swear by my might
480   Till I see him in sight
    Shall I never sleep one night
       Where I do another.

[The three shepherds sneak up to Mak's *door. Within,* Mak *is singing a lullaby and* Jill *is loudly groaning.]*

Daw.   Will you hear how they hack? Our sire likes to croon.
Coll.   Heard I never none crack so clear out of tune.
    Call on him.
Gib.   Mak! Undo your door soon.
Mak.   Who is it that spak,° as it were noon   *spoke*
    Aloft?
    Who is that, I say?
490 Daw [*looking nervously about him*].   Good fellows, were it day!
Mak.   As far as you may,
    Good friends, speak soft

    Over a sick woman's head that suffers malaise;
    I had rather be dead ere she had any disease.
Jill.   Go to another stead;° I may not well wheeze.   *place*
    Each foot that you tred my head seems to squeeze
       In two.
Coll.   Tell us, Mak, if you may,
    How fare you, I say?
500 Mak [*with false solicitude*].   But are you in this town today?
       How do you do?

    You have run in the mire and are wet yet!
    I shall make you a fire if you will sit.
    A nurse would I hire! Think of it.
    Well quit is my hire; my dream, this is it
       In season.
    I have barnes,° if you knew,   *children*
    Well more than a few,

But we must drink as we brew,
510   And that is but reason.

I would you dined ere you goed. Methink that you sweat.
GIB.   Nay, neither mends our mode drink nor meat.
MAK.   Why sir, ails you ought but good?
DAW.   Yea, our sheep that we get
  Are stolen as they strode; our loss is great!
MAK [*jovially*].   Sirs, drink?
  Had I been there,
  Some should have bought it full sore.
520 COLL [*dryly*].   Mary, some men believe you were,
    And that makes us think.

GIB.   Mak, some men think that it should be ye.
DAW.   Either you or your spouse, so say we.
MAK.   Now if you have supposed this of Jill or me,
  Come and rip our house and then may you see
    Who had her,
  If I any sheep got,
  Either cow or stot;°   *young bull*
  And Jill, my wife, rose not
530   Here since she laid her.

                     [MAK *points to the "infant" in the cradle.*]

As I am true and appeal to God, here I pray
That this be the first meal that I shall eat this day.
COLL.   Mak, by heaven's seal, advise thee, I say:
  He learned timely to steal that could not say nay.
JILL.   I wilt!
  Out, thieves, from my home!
  You've come to rob us this time.
MAK.   Hear you not how she groans?
    Your hearts should melt.

540 JILL.   Out, thieves, from my barne!° Nigh° him not there.   *child/come near*
MAK.   If you knew what she's borne, your hearts would be sore.
  You do wrong, I you warn, that thus come before
  A woman that this morn has been in labor. No more!
JILL.   Ah, my middle!
  I pray to God so mild,
  If ever I you beguiled,
  That I eat this child
    That lies in this cradle.

MAK.   Peace, woman, for God's pain and cry not so.
550   Thou spillest thy brain and make me full woe.
GIB.   I know our sheep is slain. What find you two?

DAW.   We work all in vain. We may as well go.
　　No matter.
　　I can find no flesh,
　　Hard nor mashed,
　　Salt nor fresh,
　　　But two bare platters.

　　　　　　　　　　[Pointing to the "infant," DAW continues.]

　　No livestock but this, tame nor wild!
　　None, as have I bliss, as foul as *he* smelled!
560 JILL *[feigning outrage]*.   No, so God me bless and give me joy of my child!
COLL.   We have worked amiss. I hold us beguiled!
GIB.   'Tis done.
　　Sir, our Lady him save,
　　Is your child a knave?
MAK.   Any lord might him have
　　　This child to his son.

　　When he wakens he kicks, that joy is to see.
DAW.   Good fortune to his hips and glee.
570 　But who was his gossips° so soon ready?　　　　　　　*god parents*
MAK.   So fair fall their lips—
COLL *[aside]*.   Hark now, a lie!
MAK.   —So God them thanks,
　　Perkin and Gibbon Waller, I say,
　　And gentle John Horn, in good faith,
　　He made all the display,
　　　With the great shanks.

GIB.   Mak, friends will we be, for we are all one.
MAK.   We? It's all right with me, for amends get I none.
580 　Farewell all three. *[aside]* And glad when you're gone.

　　　　　　　　　　　　　　[The shepherds leave.]

DAW.   Fair words may there be, but love is there none
　　　This year.
COLL.   Gave you the child anything?
GIB.   I think not one farthing.
DAW.   Fast again will I fling.
　　　Wait for me there.

　　　　　　　　　　　　　　[DAW returns to the hut.]

　　Mak, take it as no grief if I come to your child.
MAK.   Nay, you called me a thief. You have me defiled.
DAW.   The child will it not grieve, that daystar mild.
590 　Mak, with your leave let me give your child
　　　But sixpence.
MAK.   Nay, go away. He sleeps.

Daw. Methink he peeps.
Mak. When he wakens he weeps.
    I pray you go hence.

[The other shepherds return.]

Daw.   Give me leave to kiss him and lift up the clout.°   *blanket*

                      [Seeing the sheep, but not yet fully recognizing it].

    What the devil is this? He has a long snout!
Coll.   He is made amiss. *[gesturing toward* Jill*]* We shouldn't wait about.
Gib.   An ill-spun web like this always comes out.
    Ah, so!
600   He is like to our sheep!
Daw.   How, Gib? May I peep?
Coll.   I know kind° will creep   *nature*
    Where it may not go.°   *walk*

Gib.   This was a quaint gaud° and a far cast,   *sly trick*
    It was a high fraud.
Daw.   Yea, sirs, was't.
    Let's burn this bawd and bind her fast.
    A false scold hangs at the last;
      So shall thou.
610   Will you see how they swaddle
    His four feet in the middle?
    Saw I never in a cradle
    A horned lad ere now.

Mak *[desperately].*   Peace bid I. What! Let be your blare;
    I am he that him begot, and yon woman him bare.
Coll.   What devilish name's his lot, Mak? Lord God, Mak's heir!
Gib.   Let be all that. Now God give him care.
    Enough.
Jill.   A pretty child is he
620   As sits on a woman's knee!
    A dillydown,° perde,   *dear child*
    To make a man laugh.

Daw.   I know him by the earmark. That is a good token!
Mak.   I tell you, sirs, hark! His nose it was broken.
    Then, too, told me a clerk that he was forspoken.°   *enchanted*
Coll.   This is a false work. I would fain be wroken.°   *avenged*
    Get weapons!
Jill.   He was taken by an elf,
    I saw it myself.
630   When the clock struck twelve
    He turned misshapen.

Gib.   You two are quite deft—paired in one sty!
Daw.   Since they maintain their theft, let's make them die.

MAK.   If I trespass eft, then cut off my
    Head. To your judgement I'm left.

COLL.   Here say I:
    For this trespass
  We will neither ban nor deride,
  Fight nor chide,
  But now end his pride

640   And cast him in canvas.

                              [*They toss* MAK *in a blanket.*]

  Lord, how I am sore, almost ready to burst.
  In faith I may no more. Therefore will I rest.

GIB.   As a sheep of seven score he weighed in my fist.
  For to sleep anywhere methink that I'd be blessed.

DAW.   Now I pray you,
  Lie down on this bank.

COLL.   On these thieves yet I think.

DAW.   They're not worth a blink.

650   Do as I say you.

      [*The* ANGEL *comes on singing "Gloria in Excelsis." Then he speaks:*]

ANGEL.   Rise, herdsmen kind! For now is he born
  That shall take from the field what from Adam was shorn.
  That warlock to forfend, this night he is born.
  God is made your friend now at this morn.
    His behest:
  At Bethlehem go see—
  There lies the baby
  In a crib full poorly
    Between two beasts.

660 COLL [*after the* ANGEL *has gone*].   This was as quaint a dream as ever yet I
    heard.
  It is a marvel to name, thus to be scared.

GIB.   Of God's son of heaven he spoke strange words.
  All the woods he made seem as if lightning occurred
    So clear.

DAW.   He spoke of one born
  In Bethlehem, I you warn.

COLL.   That betokens yon starne.°   *star*
  Let us seek him there.

GIB.   Say, what was his song? Heard you not how he cracked it?
  Three briefs to a long.

670 DAW.   Yea, merrily he hacked it.
  Was no crochet° wrong nor no thing that lacked it.   *quarter note*

COLL.   For to sing us among, right as he knacked it,
    I can.

GIB.   Let's see how you croon.
  Can you bark at the moon?

DAW.   Hold your tongues, have done!
COLL.   Hark after, then.

GIB.   To Bethlehem he bade that we should go on.
 I am afraid that we tarry too long.
680 DAW.   Be merry and not sad; of mirth is our song.
 Everlasting gladness the meed we may find
   Without nose.
COLL.   Let's go in a hurry—
 Though we be wet and weary—
 To that child and that lady.
   We've no time to lose.

GIB.   We find by the prophecy—let be your din—
 Of David and Isiah and more than I myn,°   *have in mind*
 That prophesied by clergy that in a virgin
690 Should he light and lie to slacken our sin
   And slake it,
 Our kind from woe;
 For Isiah said so:
 "Ecce virgo
   Concipiet[12] a child that is naked."

DAW.   Full glad may we be and await that day
 That lovely one to see, that has all things in sway.
 Lord, well were me for once and for aye,
 Might I kneel on my knees some word for to say
700   To that child.
 But the angel said
 In a crib was he laid.
 He was poorly arrayed,
   Both meek and mild.

COLL.   Patriarchs that have been and prophets before
 That desired to have seen this child that is born—
 They are gone full clean. How they might mourn!
 We shall see him, I ween,° ere it be morn,   *believe*
   As a token.
710 When I see him and feel,
 Then know I full well
 It is true as steel
   What prophets have spoken:

 To so poor as we are that he would appear
 First found, and declare by his messenger.
GIB.   Go we now, let us fare. The place is us near.
DAW.   I am ready right here; go we in cheer
   To that bright.

---

[12] "Behold, a virgin shall conceive."

Lord, if thy will be—
We are lewd all three—
720   Thou grant us some kinds of glee
    To comfort thy wight.°   *off-spring*

                          [They arrive at the stable.]

COLL.   Hail, comely and clean! Hail, young child!
   Hail, Maker, as I mean, born of a maiden so mild!
   Thou has worried, I ween,° the warlock so wild;   *believe*
   The false beguiler often, now goes he beguiled.
    Lo, he's merry!
   Lo, he laughs, my sweeting!
   A well fair meeting.
730   I have held to my meeting!
    Have a bob of cherries.

GIB.   Hail, suffering Savior! For thou has us sought.
   Hail, first fruit and flower, that all things has wrought!
   Hail, full of favor, that made all of nought!
   Hail! I kneel and I cower. A bird have I brought
    From afar.
   Hail, little tiny mop!
   Of our creed thou art crop.
   I would drink of thy cup,
740   Little day-star.

DAW.   Hail, darling dear, full of godhead!
   I pray thee be near when that I have need.
   Hail! Sweet is thy cheer! My heart would bleed
   To see thee set here in so poor weed,°   *clothing*
    With no pennies.
   Hail! Put thy hand out full.
   I bring thee but a ball:
   Have and play thee withal,
    And go to the tennis.

750 MARY.   The Father of heaven, God omnipotent,
   That set all in seven days, his Son has he sent.
   His name he had chosen to alight ere he went.
   I conceived him full even through might, as he meant,
    And now is he born.
   He'll keep you from woe.
   I shall pray him so.
   Tell forth as you go,
    And remember this morn.

COLL.   Farewell, lady so fair to behold,
760   With thy child on thy knee!
GIB.   But he lies full cold.

Lord, well is me! Now we go, thou behold.
DAW.   Forsooth already it seems to be told
    Full oft.
COLL.   What grace we have found!
GIB.   Come forth! Now are we won!
DAW.   To sing are we bound.
    Let's sing aloft.

[*Here ends the shepherds' pageant.*]

[ca. 1400]

Critical Commentary on *The Second Shepherd's Play*

To some, the events in *The Second Shepherd's Play* represent an offensive parody of the birth of Christ. To an extent, of course, such readers are correct. The play is indeed a parody in which the attempt of Mak and Jill to conceal a stolen lamb by wrapping it in swaddling clothes, laying it in a cradle, and pretending that it is their newborn child is the cause for much horseplay and hilarity. Partially concealed behind this horseplay, there is, in the view of these readers, the sacrilegious notion that those who believe in the divinity of Christ are just as credulous and simple as a person who could believe in the humanity of a goat wrapped in swaddling clothes. Counteracting this interpretation, of course, is the surprising fact that this play was part of the Towneley cycle, and therefore both countenanced by the religious authorities and even partially sponsored by them.

During the fourteenth and fifteenth centuries in England, sequences of plays on biblical subjects were performed in several of the emerging English cities in honor of Corpus Christi Day. *The Second Shepherd's Play* is one of at least thirty-two plays that comprised the Towneley cycle performed in Wakefield in the fifteenth century. The plays were sponsored by the various guilds of professional craftsmen (the smiths, the tanners, the bakers, etc.), and were performed on temporary stages or even moveable wagons or floats. The playwrights were usually members of the Catholic clergy.

The question that most baffles contemporary audiences is how a religious writer could ever have written this work and why the bourgeois guildsmen of Wakefield would devote their time and money to producing a play that appears to be so sacrilegious. An answer to these questions begins to emerge when we consider the play's setting. Note that the seemingly irreligious events in the play take place prior to the birth of Christ. That is, they take place while humanity is still in its *fallen* state.

Before Christ has redeemed the world, it is not only possible, but even appropriate for there to be this diabolical reversal of sacred events. The horned young goat (with its satanic overtones) is in a position similar to that soon to be taken by the baby Jesus, the Lamb of God. And yet this birth is not a birth at all. The joy that should—and indeed shall—attend the birth of Christ is replaced here by deception, crime, and sorrow. The birth of Christ at the end of the play brings with it a change of tone and of seriousness. After being buffoons or even thugs throughout most of the play, the shepherds suddenly become pious, caring, and kind: they merely toss Mak in a blanket when by law he might have been hung, and they forget their profanity in pious prayer and gift-giving at the cradle of the baby Jesus.

The coarse and comic realism in the portrayal of the shepherds plays an important role both thematically and liturgically. As Thomas P. Campbell has argued, "The medieval audience was simultaneously aware of the shepherds as both historical participants in the Nativity drama and as contemporary people, caught up in the trials and complaints of the late Middle Ages." Campbell goes on to explain that this seeming anachronism actually served a purpose in early Christian ritual by showing "the similarity between the Christian community established around the manger, and their own community of Christian worshipers in the medieval church." In much the same way, of course, Catholic liturgy used (and continues to use) the bread and wine of the Eucharist as a means of recreating the Christian community of the Last Supper.

Thus, the apparent parody of Christ's birth actually serves a religious purpose in establishing links between the present and the past and in demonstrating contrasts between the fallen world before Christ and the more tolerant "Christian" world that commences with his birth.

A Selective Bibliography on *The Second Shepherd's Play*

Campbell, Thomas P. "Why Do the Shepherd's Prophesy?" *The Drama in the Middle Ages: Comparative and Critical Essays.* Ed. Clifford Davidson, C. J. Gianakaris, and John H. Stroupe. New York: AMS, 1982. 169–82.

Cantelupe, E. B. and R. Griffith. "The Gifts of the Shepherds in the Wakefield *Secunda Pastorum:* An Iconographical Interpretation." *Mediaeval Studies* 28 (1966): 328–35.

Cargill, Oscar. "The Authorship of the *Secunda Pastorum.*" *PMLA* 41 (1926): 810–31.

Carpenter, Nan Cooke. "Music in the *Secunda Pastorum.*" *Medieval Drama: Essays Critical and Contextual.* Ed. Jerome Taylor and Allan H. Nelson. Chicago: U of Chicago P, 1972. 212–17.

Cosbey, R. C. "The Mak Story and Its Folklore Analogues." *Speculum* 20 (1945): 310–17.

Gardner, John. *The Construction of the Wakefield Cycle.* Carbondale: Southern Illinois UP, 1974. 85–95.

Helterman, Jeffrey. *Symbolic Action in the Plays of the Wakefield Master.* Athens: U of Georgia P, 1981. 95–114.

Johnson, Wallace. "The Origin of the *Second Shepherds Play.*" *Quarterly Journal of Speech* 52 (1966): 47–57.

Lampe, David. "The Magi and Modes of Meaning: The *Second Shepherd's Play* as an Index of the Criticism of Medieval Drama." *Early Drama to 1600.* Ed. Albert H. Tricomi. Binghamton: Center for Medieval and Early Renaissance Studies, SUNY, 1987. 107–20.

Manly, William M. "Shepherds and Prophets: Religious Unity in the Townley *Secunda Pastorum.*" *PMLA* 78 (1963): 151–55.

Marshall, Linda E. " 'Sacral Parody' in the *Secunda Pastorum.*" *Speculum* 47 (1972): 720–36.

Morgan, Margery M. "'High Fraud': Paradox and Double-Plot in the Towneley *Secunda Pastorum.*" *PMLA* 78 (1963): 676.

Robinson, J. W. "Form in the *Second Shepherd's Play.*" *Proceedings of the PMR Conference: Annual Publication of the International Patristic, Mediaeval and Renaissance Conference* 8 (1983): 71–78.

Roney, Lois. "The Wakefield *First* and *Second Shepherd's Plays* as Complements in Psychology and Parody." *Speculum* 58 (1983): 696–723.

Ross, Lawrence J. "Symbol and Structure in the *Secunda Pastorum.*" *Comparative Drama* 1 (1967): 122–49.

Stevens, Martin. *Four Middle English Mystery Cycles: Textual, Contextual, and Critical Interpretations.* Princeton: Princeton UP, 1987. 174–79.

Thompson, Francis J. "Unity in *The Second Shepherd's Play.*" *MLN* 64 (1949): 302–6.

Vaughan, M. F. "Mak and the Proportions of *The Second Shepherd's Play.*" *Papers on Language and Literature* 18.4 (1982): 355–67.

Watt, Homer A. "The Dramatic Unity of the *Secunda Pastorum.*" *Essays and Studies in Honor of Carleton Brown.* New York: New York UP, 1940. 158–66.

Anonymous

EVERYMAN

CHARACTERS

MESSENGER	KNOWLEDGE
GOD	CONFESSION
DEATH	BEAUTY
EVERYMAN	STRENGTH
FELLOWSHIP	DISCRETION
COUSIN	FIVE WITS
KINDRED	ANGEL
GOODS	DOCTOR
GOOD DEEDS	

Here beginneth a treatise how the High Father of Heaven sendeth DEATH *to summon every creature to come and give account of their lives in this world, and is in manner of a moral play.*

[*Enter* MESSENGER *as Prologue.*]

MESSENGER. I pray you all give your audience,
And hear this manner with reverence,
By figure° a moral play—   kind or type
The *Summoning of Everyman* called it is,
That of our lives and ending shows
How transitory we be all day.
This matter is wondrous precious,
But the intent of it is more gracious,
And sweet to bear away.
10   The story saith: Man, in the beginning,
Look well, and take good heed to the ending,
Be you never so gay!
Ye think sin in the beginning full sweet,
Which in the end causeth the soul to weep,
When the body lieth in clay.
Here shall you see how Fellowship and Jollity,
Both Strength, Pleasure, and Beauty,
Will fade from thee as flower in May.
For ye shall hear how our Heaven King
20   Calleth Everyman to a general reckoning.
Give audience, and hear what he doth say. [*Exit.*]

[GOD *speaks from above.*]

GOD. I perceive, here in my majesty,
   How that all creatures be to me unkind,
   Living without dread in worldly prosperity.
   Of ghostly° sight the people be so blind,   *spiritual*
   Drowned in sin, they know me not for their God.
   In worldly riches is all their mind,
   They fear not my rightwiseness,° the sharp rod;   *righteousness*
   My love that I showed when I for them died
30   They forget clean, and shedding of my blood red;
   I hanged between two, it cannot be denied;
   To get them life I suffered to be dead;
   I healed their feet, with thorns hurt was my head.
   I could do no more than I did, truly;
   And now I see the people do clean forsake me.
   They use the seven deadly sins damnable,
   As pride, covetise,° wrath, and lechery,   *covetousness*
   Now in the world be made commendable;
   And thus they leave of angels the heavenly company.
40   Every man liveth so after his own pleasure,
   And yet of their life they be nothing sure.
   I see the more that I them forbear
   The worse they be from year to year;
   All that liveth appaireth° fast.   *degenerates*
   Therefore I will, in all the haste,
   Have a reckoning of every man's person;
   For, and° I leave the people thus alone   *if*
   In their life and wicked tempests,
   Verily they will become much worse than beasts;
50   For now one would by envy another up eat;
   Charity they all do clean forget.
   I hoped well that every man
   In my glory should make his mansion,
   And thereto I had them all elect,°   *saved*
   But now I see, like traitors deject,°   *downcast*
   They thank me not for the pleasure that I to them meant,
   Nor yet for their being that I them have lent.
   I proffered the people great multitude of mercy,
   And few there be that asketh it heartily;
60   They be so cumbered with worldly riches,
   That needs° on them I must do justice,   *necessarily*
   On every man living without fear.
   Where art thou, Death, thou mighty messenger?

                                 [Enter DEATH.]

DEATH. Almighty God, I am here at your will,
   Your commandment to fulfil.
GOD. Go thou to Everyman,
   And show him, in my name,
   A pilgrimage he must on him take,

Which he in no wise may escape;
70 And that he bring with him a sure reckoning
Without delay or any tarrying.

[*Exit* GOD.]

DEATH.   Lord, I will in the world go run over all,
And cruelly out search both great and small.
Every man will I beset that liveth beastly
Out of God's laws, and dreadeth not folly.
He that loveth riches I will strike with my dart,
His sight to blind, and from heaven to depart,
Except that alms be his good friend,
In hell for to dwell, world without end.

[EVERYMAN *enters, at a distance.*]

80 Lo, yonder I see Everyman walking;
Full little he thinketh on my coming.
His mind is on fleshly lusts and his treasure,
And great pain it shall cause him to endure
Before the Lord, Heaven King.
Everyman, stand still! Whither art thou going
Thus gaily? Hast thou thy Maker forgot?
EVERYMAN.   Why askest thou?
Wouldst thou wete?°   *know*
DEATH.   Yea, sir, I will show you:
90 In great haste I am sent to thee
From God out of his Majesty.
EVERYMAN.   What, sent to me?
DEATH.   Yea, certainly.
Though thou have forgot him here,
He thinketh on thee in the heavenly sphere,
As, ere we depart, thou shalt know.
EVERYMAN.   What desireth God of me?
DEATH.   That shall I show thee:
A reckoning he will needs have
100 Without any longer respite.
EVERYMAN.   To give a reckoning, longer leisure I crave.
This blind matter troubleth my wit.
DEATH.   On thee thou must take a long journey;
Therefore thy book of count° with thee thou bring;   *accounting*
For turn again thou can not by no way.
And look thou be sure of thy reckoning,
For before God thou shalt answer and show
Thy many bad deeds, and good but a few,
How thou hast spent thy life, and in what wise,
110 Before the Chief Lord of paradise.
Have ado° that we were in that way,°   *Have at it/on our way*
For, wete thou well, thou shalt make none° attourney.   *shall have no*
EVERYMAN.   Full unready I am such reckoning to give.
I know thee not. What messenger art thou?

DEATH.   I am Death, that no man dreadeth.°   *dreads no man*
   For every man I 'rest,° and no man spareth;   *arrest*
   For it is God's commandment
   That all to me should be obedient.
EVERYMAN.   O Death! thou comest when I had thee least in mind!
120   In thy power it lieth me to save.
   Yet of my goods will I give thee, if thou will be kind;
   Yea, a thousand pound shalt thou have,
   If thou defer this matter till another day.
DEATH.   Everyman, it may not be, by no way!
   I set not by° gold, silver, nor riches,   *set no value in*
   Nor by pope, emperor, king, duke, nor princes.
   For, and I would receive gifts great,
   All the world I might get;
   But my custom is clean contrary.
130   I give thee no respite. Come hence, and not tarry.
EVERYMAN.   Alas! shall I have no longer respite?
   I may say Death giveth no warning.
   To think on thee, it maketh my heart sick,
   For all unready is my book of reckoning.
   But twelve year and I might have abiding,
   My counting-book I would make so clear,
   That my reckoning I should not need to fear.
   Wherefore, Death, I pray thee, for God's mercy,
   Spare me till I be provided of remedy.
140 DEATH.   Thee availeth not to cry, weep, and pray;
   But haste thee lightly that thou were gone that journey,
   And prove thy friends if thou can.
   For wete thou well the tide abideth no man;
   And in the world each living creature
   For Adam's sin must die of nature.
EVERYMAN.   Death, if I should this pilgrimage take,
   And my reckoning surely make,
   Show me, for saint charity,
   Should I not come again shortly?
150 DEATH.   No, Everyman; and° thou be once there,   *if*
   Thou mayest never more come here,
   Trust me verily.
EVERYMAN.   O gracious God, in the high seat celestial,
   Have mercy on me in this most need!
   Shall I have no company from this vale terrestrial
   Of mine acquaintance that way me to lead?
DEATH.   Yea, if any be so hardy,
   That would go with thee and bear thee company.
   Hie° thee that thou were gone to God's magnificence,   *Haste*
160   Thy reckoning to give before his presence.
   What! weenest° thou thy life is given thee,   *think*
   And thy worldly goods also?
EVERYMAN.   I had weened so, verily.
DEATH.   Nay, nay; it was but lent thee;

For, as soon as thou art gone,
Another a while shall have it, and then go therefrom
Even as thou hast done.
Everyman, thou art mad! Thou hast thy wits five,
And here on earth will not amend thy life;
170   For suddenly I do come.
EVERYMAN.   O wretched caitiff!° whither shall I flee,   *prisoner*
   That I might 'scape endless sorrow?
   Now, gentle Death, spare me till tomorrow,
   That I may amend me
   With good advisement.°   *forewarning*
DEATH.   Nay, thereto I will not consent,
   Nor no man will I respite,
   But to the heart suddenly I shall smite
   Without any advisement.
180   And now out of thy sight I will me hie;
   See thou make thee ready shortly,
   For thou mayst say this is the day
   That no man may 'scape away.

                                              [Exit DEATH.*]*

EVERYMAN.   Alas! I may well weep with sighs deep.
   Now have I no manner of company
   To help me in my journey and me to keep;
   And also my writing is full unready.
   How shall I do now for to excuse me?
   I would to God I had never been get!°   *born*
190   To my soul a full great profit it had be,
   For now I fear pains huge and great.
   The time passeth; Lord, help, that all wrought.°   *created*
   For though I mourn it availeth naught.
   The day passeth, and is almost a-go;°   *gone*
   I wot° not well what for to do.   *know*
   To whom were I best my complaint to make?
   What if I to Fellowship thereof spake,
   And showed him of this sudden chance?
   For in him is all mine affiance,°   *trust*
200   We have in the world so many a day
   Been good friends in sport and play.
   I see him yonder, certainly;
   I trust that he will bear me company;
   Therefore to him will I speak to ease my sorrow.

                                        [Enter FELLOWSHIP.*]*

   Well met, good Fellowship, and good morrow!
FELLOWSHIP.   Everyman, good morrow, by this day!
   Sir, why lookest thou so piteously?
   If any thing be amiss, I pray thee me say,
   That I may help to remedy.
210 EVERYMAN.   Yea, good Fellowship, yea,
   I am in great jeopardy.

FELLOWSHIP.   My true friend, show to me your mind.
   I will not forsake thee to my life's end
   In the way of good company.
EVERYMAN.   That was well spoken, and lovingly.
FELLOWSHIP.   Sir, I must needs know your heaviness;
   I have pity to see you in any distress;
   If any have you wronged, ye shall revenged be,
   Though I on the ground be slain for thee,
220   Though that I know before that I should die.
EVERYMAN.   Verily, Fellowship, gramercy.°   *thank you*
FELLOWSHIP.   Tush! by thy thanks I set not a straw!
   Show me your grief, and say no more.
EVERYMAN.   If I my heart should to you break,
   And then you to turn your mind from me,
   And would not me comfort when you hear me speak,
   Then should I ten times sorrier be.
FELLOWSHIP.   Sir, I say as I will do, indeed.
EVERYMAN.   Then be you a good friend at need;
230   I have found you true here before.
FELLOWSHIP.   And so ye shall evermore;
   For, in faith, and thou go to hell,
   I will not forsake thee by the way!
EVERYMAN.   Ye speak like a good friend. I believe you well;
   I shall deserve it, and° I may.   *if*
FELLOWSHIP.   I speak of no deserving, by this day!
   For he that will say and nothing do
   Is not worthy with good company to go;
   Therefore show me the grief of your mind,
240   As to your friend most loving and kind.
EVERYMAN.   I shall show you how it is:
   Commanded I am to go a journey,
   A long way, hard and dangerous,
   And give a strait° count without delay   *strict*
   Before the high judge, Adonai.°   *God*
   Wherefore, I pray you, bear me company,
   As ye have promised, in this journey.
FELLOWSHIP.   That is matter indeed! Promise is duty;
   But, and° I should take such a voyage on me,   *if*
250   I know it well, it should be to my pain.
   Also it maketh me afeared,° certain.   *afraid*
   But let us take counsel here as well as we can,
   For your words would fear° a strong man.   *frighten*
EVERYMAN.   Why, ye said if I had need,
   Ye would me never forsake, quick° nor dead,   *living*
   Though it were to hell, truly.
FELLOWSHIP.   So I said, certainly,
   But such pleasures be set aside, the sooth° to say.   *truth*
   And also, if we took such a journey,
260   When should we come again?
EVERYMAN.   Nay, never again till the day of doom.

FELLOWSHIP.   In faith, then will not I come there!
   Who hath you these tidings brought?
EVERYMAN.   Indeed, Death was with me here.
FELLOWSHIP.   Now, by God that all hath bought,
   If Death were the messenger,
   For no man that is living today
   I will not go that loath° journey—   *loathsome*
   Not for the father that begat me!
270 EVERYMAN.   Ye promised otherwise, pardie.°   *by the Lord*
FELLOWSHIP.   I wot° well I said so, truly;   *know*
   And yet if thou wilt eat, and drink, and make good cheer,
   Or haunt to women the lusty company,
   I would not forsake you while the day is clear,
   Trust me verily!
EVERYMAN.   Yea, thereto you would be ready.
   To go to mirth, solace, and play,
   Your mind will sooner apply
   Than to bear me company in my long journey.
280 FELLOWSHIP.   Now, in good faith, I will not that way.
   But and° thou wilt murder, or any man kill,   *if*
   In that I will help thee with a good will!
EVERYMAN.   O, that is a simple advice indeed!
   Gentle fellow, help me in my necessity;
   We have loved long, and now I need,
   And now, gentle Fellowship, remember me!
FELLOWSHIP.   Whether ye have loved me or no,
   By Saint John, I will not with thee go.
EVERYMAN.   Yet, I pray thee, take the labor, and do so much for me
290   To bring me forward, for saint charity,
   And comfort me till I come without° the town.   *outside*
FELLOWSHIP.   Nay, and° thou would give me a new gown,   *if*
   I will not a foot with thee go;
   But, and° thou had tarried, I would not have left thee so.   *if*
   And as now God speed thee in thy journey,
   For from thee I will depart as fast as I may.
EVERYMAN.   Whither away, Fellowship? Will you forsake me?
FELLOWSHIP.   Yea, by my fay,° to God I betake° thee.   *faith / commend*
EVERYMAN.   Farewell, good Fellowship! For thee my heart is sore;
300 Adieu for ever! I shall see thee no more.
FELLOWSHIP.   In faith, Everyman, farewell now at the end!
   For you I will remember that parting is mourning.

                                                 [Exit FELLOWSHIP.*]*

EVERYMAN.   Alack! shall we thus depart indeed
   (Ah, Lady, help), without any more comfort?
   Lo, Fellowship foresaketh me in my most need.
   For help in this world whither shall I resort?
   Fellowship here before with me would merry make,
   And now little sorrow for me doth he take.
   It is said, "In prosperity men friends may find,

310   Which in adversity be full unkind."
     Now whither for succor shall I flee,
     Sith° that Fellowship hath forsaken me?   *since*
     To my kinsmen I will, truly,
     Praying them to help me in my necessity;
     I believe that they will do so,
     For "kind° will creep where it may not go.°"   *kindred/walk*
     I will go say,° for yonder I see them go.   *test it*
     Where be ye now, my friends and kinsmen?

                                    [*Enter* KINDRED *and* COUSIN.]

KINDRED.   Here be we now, at your commandment.
320   Cousin, I pray you show us your intent
     In any wise, and do not spare.
COUSIN.   Yea, Everyman, and to us declare
     If ye be disposed to go any whither,
     For, wete° you well, we will live and die together.   *know*
KINDRED.   In wealth and woe we will with you hold,
     For over his kin a man may be bold.
EVERYMAN.   Gramercy, my friends and kinsmen kind.
     Now shall I show you the grief of my mind.
     I was commanded by a messenger
330   That is a high king's chief officer;
     He bade me go a pilgrimage, to my pain,
     And I know well I shall never come again;
     Also I must give a reckoning straight,
     For I have a great enemy that hath me in wait,
     Which intended me for to hinder.
KINDRED.   What account is that which ye must render?
     That would I know.
EVERYMAN.   Of all my works I must show
     How I have lived, and my days spent;
340   Also of ill deeds that I have used
     In my time, sith life was me lent;
     And of all virtues that I have refused.
     Therefore I pray you go thither with me,
     To help to make mine account, for saint charity.
COUSIN.   What, to go thither? Is that the matter?
     Nay, Everyman, I had liefer° fast bread and water   *rather*
     All this five year and more.
EVERYMAN.   Alas, that ever I was bore!
     For now shall I never be merry
350   If that you forsake me.
KINDRED.   Ah, sir, what! Ye be a merry man!
     Take good heart to you, and make no moan.
     But one thing I warn you, by Saint Anne,
     As for me, ye shall go alone.
EVERYMAN.   My Cousin, will you not with me go?
COUSIN.   No, by our Lady! I have the cramp in my toe.

Trust not to me, for, so God me speed,
I will deceive you in your most need.
KINDRED.   It availeth not us to tice.°   *entice*
360   Ye shall have my maid with all my heart;
She loveth to go to feasts, there to be nice,°   *wanton*
And to dance, and abroad to start;
I will give her leave to help you in that journey,
If that you and she may agree.
EVERYMAN.   Now show me the very effect of your mind.
Will you go with me, or abide behind?
KINDRED.   Abide behind? Yea, that will I, and° I may!   *if*
Therefore, farewell till another day.

[*Exit* KINDRED.]

EVERYMAN.   How should I be merry or glad?
370   For fair promises men to me make,
But when I have most need, they me forsake.
I am deceived; that maketh me sad.
COUSIN.   Cousin Everyman, farewell now,
For verily I will not go with you;
Also of mine own life an unready reckoning
I have to account; therefore I make tarrying.
Now, God keep thee, for now I go.

[*Exit* COUSIN.]

EVERYMAN.   Ah, Jesus! is all come hereto?
Lo, fair words maketh fools fain;°   *happy*
380   They promise and nothing will do, certain.
My kinsmen promised me faithfully
For to abide with me steadfastly,
And now fast away do they flee.
Even so Fellowship promised me.
What friend were best me of to provide?
I lose my time here longer to abide.
Yet in my mind a thing there is:
All my life I have loved riches;
If that my good° now help me might,   *goods*
390   He would make my heart full light.
I will speak to him in this distress.
Where art thou, my Goods and riches?

[GOODS *speaks from within.*]

GOODS.   Who calleth me? Everyman? What, hast thou haste?
I lie here in corners, trussed and piled so high,
And in chests I am locked so fast,
Also sacked in bags—thou mayest see with thine eye—
I cannot stir; in packs low I lie.
What would ye have? Lightly me say.°   *tell me*
EVERYMAN.   Come hither, Goods, in all the haste thou may.
400   For of counsel I must desire thee.

[*Enter* GOODS.]

GOODS.   Sir, and° ye in the world have sorrow or adversity,   *if*
 That can I help you to remedy shortly.
EVERYMAN.   It is another disease that grieveth me;
 In this world it is not, I tell thee so.
 I am sent for another way to go,
 To give a strict count general
 Before the highest Jupiter of all;
 And all my life I have had joy and pleasure in thee,
 Therefore I pray thee go with me,
410 For, peradventure, thou mayst before God Almighty
 My reckoning help to clean and purify;
 For it is said ever among,
 That "money maketh all right that is wrong."
GOODS.   Nay, Everyman; I sing another song,
 I follow no man in such voyages;
 For, and° I went with thee,   *if*
 Thou shouldst fare much the worse for me;
 For because on me thou did set thy mind,
 Thy reckoning I have made blotted and blind,
420 That thine account thou cannot make truly;
 And that hast thou for the love of me.
EVERYMAN.   That would grieve me full sore,
 When I should come to that fearful answer.
 Up, let us go thither together.
GOODS.   Nay, not so! I am too brittle, I may not endure;
 I will follow no man one foot, be ye sure.
EVERYMAN.   Alas! I have thee loved, and had great pleasure
 All my life-days on goods and treasure.
GOODS.   That is to thy damnation, without lesing!°   *lying*
430 For my love is contrary to the love everlasting.
 But if thou had me loved moderately during,
 As to the poor to give part of me,
 Then shouldst thou not in this dolor be,
 Nor in this great sorrow and care.
EVERYMAN.   Lo, now was I deceived ere I was ware,°   *aware*
 And all I may wyte° my spending of time.   *attribute to*
GOODS.   What, weenest thou that I am thine?
EVERYMAN.   I had weened so.
GOODS.   Nay, Everyman, I say no;
440 As for a while I was lent thee,
 A season thou hast had me in prosperity.
 My condition is man's soul to kill;
 If I save one, a thousand I do spill;°   *stay*
 Weenest thou that I will follow thee
 From this world? Nay, verily.
EVERYMAN.   I had weened otherwise.
GOODS.   Therefore to thy soul Goods is a thief;
 For when thou art dead, this is my guise,°   *scheme*
 Another to deceive in the same wise
450 As I have done thee, and all to his soul's reprief.°   *reproof*

EVERYMAN.   O false Goods, curséd may thou be!
　Thou traitor to God, that hast deceived me
　And caught me in thy snare.
GOODS.   Marry! thou brought thyself in care,°　　　　　*trouble*
　Whereof I am right glad.
　I must needs laugh, I cannot be sad.
EVERYMAN.   Ah, Goods, thou hast had long my heartly love;
　I gave thee that which should be the Lord's above.
　But wilt thou not go with me indeed?
460　I pray thee truth to say.
GOODS.   No, so God me speed!
　Therefore farewell, and have good day.

　　　　　　　　　　　　　　　　　　[Exit GOODS.]

EVERYMAN.   O, to whom shall I make my moan
　For to go with me in that heavy journey?
　First Fellowship said he would with me gone;
　His words were very pleasant and gay,
　But afterward he left me alone.
　Then spake I to my kinsmen, all in despair,
　And also they gave me words fair,
470　They lacked no fair speaking,
　But all forsook me in the ending.
　Then went I to my Goods, that I loved best,
　In hope to have comfort, but there had I least;
　For my Goods sharply did me tell
　That he bringeth many into hell.
　Then of myself I was ashamed,
　And so I am worthy to be blamed;
　Thus may I well myself hate.
　Of whom shall I now counsel take?
480　I think that I shall never speed
　Till that I go to my Good Deeds.
　But alas! she is so weak
　That she can neither go nor speak.
　Yet will I venture on her now.
　My Good Deeds, where be you?

　　　　　　　　　　　[GOOD DEEDS *speaks from the ground.*]

GOOD DEEDS.   Here I lie, cold in the ground.
　Thy sins hath me sore bound,
　That I cannot stir.
EVERYMAN.   O Good Deeds, I stand in fear!
490　I must you pray of counsel,
　For help now should come right well.
GOOD DEEDS.   Everyman, I have understanding
　That ye be summoned account to make
　Before Messias, of Jerusalem King;
　And° you do by me,° that journey with you will I take.　　*If/as I say*
EVERYMAN.   Therefore I come to you my moan to make;
　I pray you that ye will go with me.

GOOD DEEDS.   I would full fain, but I cannot stand, verily.
EVERYMAN.   Why, is there anything on you fall?
500 GOOD DEEDS.   Yea, sir, I may thank you of all;
      If ye had perfectly cheered° me,   *cherished*
      Your book of count full ready had be.
      Look, the books of your works and deeds eke,°   *also*
      Behold how they lie under the feet,
      To your soul's heaviness.
EVERYMAN.   Our Lord Jesus help me!
      For one letter here I can not see.
GOOD DEEDS.   There is a blind reckoning in time of distress!
EVERYMAN.   Good Deeds, I pray you, help me in this need,
510   Or else I am for ever damned indeed.
      Therefore help me to make my reckoning
      Before the Redeemer of all thing,
      That King is, and was, and ever shall.
GOOD DEEDS.   Everyman, I am sorry of your fall,
      and fain would I help you, and I were able.
EVERYMAN.   Good Deeds, your counsel I pray you give me.
GOOD DEEDS.   That shall I do verily;
      Though that on my feet I may not go,
      I have a sister that shall with you also,
520   Called Knowledge, which shall with you abide,
      To help you to make that dreadful reckoning.

                                                              [*Enter* KNOWLEDGE.]

KNOWLEDGE.   Everyman, I will go with thee, and be thy guide,
      In thy most need to go by thy side.
EVERYMAN.   In good condition I am now in every thing,
      And am wholly content with this good thing;
      Thanked be God my Creator.
GOOD DEEDS.   And when he hath brought thee there,
      Where thou shalt heal thee of thy smart,
      Then go you with your reckoning and your Good Deeds together
530   For to make you joyful at heart
      Before the blessed Trinity.
EVERYMAN.   My Good Deeds, gramercy!
      I am well content, certainly,
      With your words sweet.
KNOWLEDGE.   Now go we together lovingly
      To Confession, that cleansing river.
EVERYMAN.   For Joy I weep; I would we were there!
      But, I pray you, give me cognition°   *knowledge*
      Where dwelleth that holy man, Confession.
540 KNOWLEDGE.   In the house of salvation,
      We shall find him in that place,
      That shall us comfort, by God's grace.

                                                              [*Enter* CONFESSION.]

Lo, this is Confession. Kneel down and ask mercy,
For he is in good conceit° with God almighty. *favor*

EVERYMAN. O glorious fountain, that all uncleanness doth clarify,
Wash from me the spots of vice unclean,
That on me no sin may be seen.
I come with Knowledge, for my redemption,
Redempt with hearty and full contrition;
550 For I am commanded a pilgrimage to take,
And great accounts before God to make.
Now, I pray you, Shrift,° mother of salvation, *forgiveness*
Help my Good Deeds for my piteous exclamation.
CONFESSION. I know your sorrow well, Everyman.
Because with Knowledge ye come to me,
I will you comfort as well as I can,
And a precious jewel I will give thee,
Called penance, voider of adversity.
Therewith shall your body chastised be
560 With abstinence and perseverance in God's service.
Here shall you receive that scourge of me

[*Gives* EVERYMAN *a scourge.*]

Which is penance strong that ye must endure
To remember thy Savior was scourged for thee
With sharp scourges and suffered it patiently.
So must thou ere thou 'scape° that painful pilgrimage. *escape*
Knowledge, keep him in this voyage,
And by that time Good Deeds will be with thee.
But in any wise be sure of mercy,
For your time draweth fast, and ye will saved be;
570 Ask God mercy, and He will grant truly;
When with the scourge of penance man doth him bind,
The oil of forgiveness then shall he find.

[*Exit* CONFESSION.]

EVERYMAN. Thanked be God for his gracious work!
For now I will my penance begin;
This hath rejoiced and lighted my heart,
Though the knots be painful and hard within.
KNOWLEDGE. Everyman, look your penance that ye fulfil,
What pain that ever it to you be,
And Knowledge shall give you counsel at will
580 How your account ye shall make clearly.

[EVERYMAN *kneels.*]

EVERYMAN. O eternal God! O heavenly figure!
O way of rightwiseness! O goodly vision!
Which descended down in a virgin pure
Because he would Everyman redeem,

Which Adam forfeited by his disobedience.
O blessèd Godhead! elect and high divine,
Forgive me my grievous offence;
Here I cry thee mercy in this presence.
O ghostly treasure! O ransomer and redeemer!
590   Of all the world hope and conductor,
Mirror of joy, and founder of mercy,
Which illumineth heaven and earth thereby,
Hear my clamorous complaint, though it late be.
Receive my prayers; unworthy in this heavy life.
Though I be a sinner most abominable,
Yet let my name be written in Moses' table.
O Mary! pray to the Maker of all thing,
Me for to help at my ending,
And save me from the power of my enemy,
600   For Death assaileth me strongly.
And, Lady, that I may be means of thy prayer
Of your Son's glory to be partner,
By the means of his passion I it crave.
I beseech you, help my soul to save.

[He rises.]

Knowledge, give me the scourge of penance.
My flesh therewith shall give you a quittance.°   *complete payment*
I will now begin, if God give me grace.
KNOWLEDGE. Everyman, God give you time and space.
Thus I bequeath you in the hands of our Savior,
610   Now may you make your reckoning sure.
EVERYMAN. In the name of the Holy Trinity,
My body sore punished shall be.

[Scourges himself.]

Take this, body, for the sin of the flesh.
Also thou delightest to go gay and fresh,
And in the way of damnation thou did me bring;
Therefore suffer now strokes of punishing.
Now of penance I will wade the water clear,
To save me from purgatory, that sharp fire.

[GOOD DEEDS rises.]

GOOD DEEDS. I thank God, now I can walk and go,
620   And am delivered of my sickness and woe.
Therefore with Everyman I will go, and not spare;
His good works I will help him to declare.
KNOWLEDGE. Now, Everyman, be merry and glad!
Your Good Deeds cometh now, ye may not be sad.
Now is your Good Deeds whole and sound,
Going upright upon the ground.
EVERYMAN. My heart is light, and shall be evermore.
Now will I smite faster than I did before.
GOOD DEEDS. Everyman, pilgrim, my special friend,

630   Blesséd be thou without end.
      For thee is prepared the eternal glory.
      Ye have me made whole and sound,
      Therefore, I will bide by thee in every stound.°   *circumstance*
    EVERYMAN.   Welcome, my Good Deeds; now I hear thy voice,
      I weep for very sweetness of love.
    KNOWLEDGE.   Be no more sad, but ever rejoice;
      God seeth thy living in his throne above.
      Put on this garment to thy behoof,°   *benefit*
      Which is wet with your tears,
640   Or else before God you may it miss,
      When you to your journey's end come shall.
    EVERYMAN.   Gentle Knowledge, what do ye it call?
    KNOWLEDGE.   It is the garment of sorrow;
      From pain it will you borrow,
      Contrition it is
      That getteth forgiveness;
      It pleaseth God passing well.
    GOOD DEEDS.   Everyman, will you wear it for your heal?

                     [EVERYMAN *puts on garment of contrition.*]

    EVERYMAN.   Now blesséd be Jesu, Mary's Son,
650   For now have I on true contrition.
      And let us go now without tarrying;
      Good Deeds, have we clear our reckoning?
    GOOD DEEDS.   Yea, indeed I have it here.
    EVERYMAN.   Then I trust we need not fear.
      Now, friends, let us not part in twain.
    KNOWLEDGE.   Nay, Everyman, that will we not, certain.
    GOOD DEEDS.   Yet must thou lead with thee
      Three persons of great might.
    EVERYMAN.   Who should they be?
660 GOOD DEEDS.   Discretion and Strength they hight,°   *are called*
      And thy Beauty may not abide behind.
    KNOWLEDGE.   Also ye must call to mind
      Your Five Wits as for your counselors.
    GOOD DEEDS.   You must have them ready at all hours.
    EVERYMAN.   How shall I get them hither?
    KNOWLEDGE.   You must call them all together,
      And they will hear you incontinent.°   *immediately*
    EVERYMAN.   My friends, come hither and be present,
      Discretion, Strength, my Five Wits, and Beauty.

            [*Enter* DISCRETION, STRENGTH, FIVE WITS, *and* BEAUTY.]

670 BEAUTY.   Here at your will we be all ready.
      What will ye that we should do?
    GOOD DEEDS.   That ye would with Everyman go,
      And help him in his pilgrimage.
      Advise you, will ye with him or not in that voyage?

STRENGTH.   We will bring him all thither,
   To his help and comfort, ye may believe me.
DISCRETION.   So will we go with him all together.
EVERYMAN.   Almighty God, lovéd may thou be!
   I give thee laud° that I have hither brought   *praise*
680 Strength, Discretion, Beauty, and Five Wits. Lack I naught.
   And my Good Deeds, with Knowledge clear,
   All be in company at my will here.
   I desire no more to my business.
STRENGTH.   And I, Strength, will by you stand in distress,
   Though thou would in battle fight on the ground.
FIVE WITS.   And though it were through the world round,
   We will not depart for sweet nor sour.
BEAUTY.   No more will I, unto death's hour,
   Whatsoever thereof befall.
690 DISCRETION.   Everyman, advise you first of all,
   Go with a good advisement and deliberation.
   We all give you virtuous monition°   *warning*
   That all shall be well.
EVERYMAN.   My friends, hearken what I will tell:
   I pray God reward you in his heavenly sphere.
   Now hearken, all that be here,
   For I will make my testament
   Here before you all present:
   In alms half my goods I will give my hands twain
700 In the way of charity, with good intent,
   And the other half still shall remain,
   I it bequeath to be returned there it ought to be.
   This I do in despite of the fiend of hell,
   To go quite out of his peril
   Ever after and this day.
KNOWLEDGE.   Everyman, hearken what I say;
   Go to Priesthood, I you advise,
   And receive of him in any wise
   The holy sacrament and ointment together,
710 Then shortly see ye turn again hither;
   We will all abide you here.
FIVE WITS.   Yea, Everyman, hie you that ye ready were.
   There is no emperor, king, duke, nor baron,
   That of God hath commission
   As hath the least priest in the world being;
   For of the blesséd sacraments pure and benign
   He beareth the keys, and thereof hath the cure
   For man's redemption—it is ever sure—
   Which God for our soul's medicine
720 Gave us out of his heart with great pain,
   Here in this transitory life, for thee and me.
   The blesséd sacraments seven there be:
   Baptism, confirmation, with priesthood good,
   And the sacrament of God's precious flesh and blood,

    Marriage, the holy extreme unction, and penance.
    These seven be good to have in remembrance,
    Gracious sacraments of high divinity.
EVERYMAN.   Fain would I receive that holy body
    And meekly to my ghostly father I will go.
730 FIVE WITS.   Everyman, that is the best that ye can do.
    God will you to salvation bring,
    For priesthood exceedeth all other thing;
    To us Holy Scripture they do teach,
    And converteth man from sin, heaven to reach;
    God hath to them more power given,
    Than to any angel that is in heaven.
    With five words he may consecrate
    God's body in flesh and blood to make,
    And handleth his Maker between his hands.
740   The priest bindeth and unbindeth all bands,
    Both in earth and in heaven.
    Though we kissed thy feet, thou wert worthy;
    Thou art the surgeon that cureth sin deadly:
    No remedy we find under God
    But all only priesthood.
    Everyman, God gave priests that dignity,
    And setteth them in his stead among us to be;
    Thus be they above angels, in degree.

         [EVERYMAN *goes out to receive the last rites of the church.*]

750 KNOWLEDGE.   If priests be good, it is so, surely.
    But when Jesus hanged on the cross with great smart,
    There he gave out of his blesséd heart
    The same sacrament in great torment.
    He sold them not to us, that Lord omnipotent.
    Therefore Saint Peter the Apostle doth say
    That Jesus' curse hath all they
    Which God their Savior do buy or sell,
    Or they for any money do take or tell.°   *count*
    Sinful priests giveth the sinners example bad;
760   Their children sitteth by other men's fires, I have heard;
    And some haunteth women's company
    With unclean life, as lusts of lechery.
    These be with sin made blind.
  FIVE WITS.   I trust to God no such way we find.
    Therefore let us priesthood honor,
    And follow their doctrine for our souls' succor.
    We be their sheep, and they shepherds be
    By whom we all be kept in surety.
    Peace! for yonder I see Everyman come,
770   Which hath made true satisfaction.
  GOOD DEEDS.   Methinketh it is he indeed.

                                 [*Re-enter* EVERYMAN.]

EVERYMAN.   Now Jesu be your alder speed.°   *final help*
  I have received the sacrament for my redemption,
  And then mine extreme unction.
  Bléssed be all they that counseled me to take it!
  And now, friends, let us go without longer respite.
  I thank God that ye have tarried so long.
  Now set each of you on this rood° your hand,   *cross*
  And shortly follow me.
780 I go before, there I would be. God be our guide.
  STRENGTH.   Everyman, we will not from you go,
    Till ye have done this voyage long.
  DISCRETION.   I, Discretion, will bide by you also.
  KNOWLEDGE.   And though this pilgrimage be never so strong,°   *difficult*
    I will never part you fro.°   *from*
    Everyman, I will be as sure by thee
    As ever I did by Judas Maccabee.

                                                        [*They go to a grave.*]

  EVERYMAN.   Alas! I am so faint I may not stand,
    My limbs under me do fold.
790 Friends, let us not turn again to this land,
    Not for all the world's gold;
    For into this cave must I creep
    And turn to earth, and there to sleep.
  BEAUTY.   What, into this grave? Alas!
  EVERYMAN.   Yea, there shall you consume, more and less.
  BEAUTY.   And what, should I smother here?
  EVERYMAN.   Yea, by my faith, and never more appear.
    In this world live no more we shall,
    But in heaven before the highest Lord of all.
800 BEAUTY.   I cross out all this; adieu; by Saint John!
    I take my cap in my lap and am gone.
  EVERYMAN.   What, Beauty, whither will ye?
  BEAUTY.   Peace! I am deaf. I look not behind me,
    Not and° thou would give me all the gold in thy chest.   *if*

                                                            [*Exit* BEAUTY.]

  EVERYMAN.   Alas, whereto may I trust?
    Beauty goeth fast away from me;
    She promised with me to live and die.
  STRENGTH.   Everyman, I will thee also forsake and deny.
    Thy game liketh me not at all.
810 EVERYMAN.   Why, then ye will forsake me all?
    Sweet Strength, tarry a little space.
  STRENGTH.   Nay, sir, by the rood of grace,
    I will hie me from thee fast,
    Though thou weep till thy heart to-brast.°   *break*
  EVERYMAN.   Ye would ever bide by me, ye said.
  STRENGTH.   Yea, I have you far enough conveyed.

Ye be old enough, I understand,
Your pilgrimage to take on hand.
I repent me that I hither came.

820 EVERYMAN.   Strength, you to displease I am to blame;
Yet promise is debt, this ye well wot.

STRENGTH.   In faith, I care not!
Thou art but a fool to complain.
You spend your speech and waste your brain.
Go, thrust thee into the ground.

[Exit STRENGTH.*]*

EVERYMAN.   I had weened surer I should you have found.
He that trusteth in his Strength
She him deceiveth at the length.
Both Strength and Beauty forsaketh me,
830 Yet they promised me fair and lovingly.

DISCRETION.   Everyman, I will after Strength be gone;
As for me I will leave you alone.

EVERYMAN.   Why, Discretion, will ye forsake me?

DISCRETION.   Yea, in faith I will go from thee;
For when Strength goeth before
I follow after evermore.

EVERYMAN.   Yet, I pray thee, for the love of the Trinity,
Look in my grave once piteously.

DISCRETION.   Nay, so nigh will I not come.
840 Farewell, every one!

[Exit DISCRETION.*]*

EVERYMAN.   O all thing faileth, save God alone,
Beauty, Strength, and Discretion;
For when Death bloweth his blast,
They all run from me full fast.

FIVE WITS.   Everyman, my leave now of thee I take;
I will follow the other, for her I thee forsake.

EVERYMAN.   Alas! then may I wail and weep,
For I took you for my best friend.

FIVE WITS.   I will no longer thee keep;
850 Now farewell, and there an end.

[Exit FIVE WITS.*]*

EVERYMAN.   O Jesu, help! All hath forsaken me!

GOOD DEEDS.   Nay, Everyman; I will bide with thee,
I will not forsake thee indeed;
Thou shalt find me a good friend at need.

EVERYMAN.   Gramercy, Good Deeds! Now may I true friends see.
They have forsaken me, every one;
I loved them better than my Good Deeds alone.
Knowledge, will ye forsake me also?

KNOWLEDGE.   Yea, Everyman, when ye to death shall go;
860 But not yet, for no manner of danger.

EVERYMAN. Gramercy, Knowledge, with all my heart.
KNOWLEDGE. Nay, yet I will not from hence depart
  Till I see where ye shall be come.
EVERYMAN. Methink, alas, that I must be gone
  To make my reckoning and my debts pay,
  For I see my time is nigh spent away.
  Take example, all ye that this do hear or see,
  How they that I loved best do forsake me,
  Except my Good Deeds that bideth truly.
870 GOOD DEEDS. All earthly things is but vanity.
  Beauty, Strength, and Discretion do man forsake,
  Foolish friends and kinsmen, that fair spake,
  All fleeth save Good Deeds, and that am I.
EVERYMAN. Have mercy on me, God most mighty;
  And stand by me, thou Mother and Maid, holy Mary!
GOOD DEEDS. Fear not, I will speak for thee.
EVERYMAN. Here I cry God mercy!
GOOD DEEDS. Short° our end, and 'minish° our pain.   *shorten/diminish*
  Let us go and never come again.
880 EVERYMAN. Into thy hands, Lord, my soul I commend.
  Receive it, Lord, that it be not lost.
  As thou me boughtest, so me defend.
  And save me from the fiend's boast,
  That I may appear with that blesséd host.
  That shall be saved at the day of doom.
  In manus tuas—of might's most
  For ever—*commendo spiritum meum.*[1]

                    [EVERYMAN *and* GOOD DEEDS *go into the grave.*]

KNOWLEDGE. Now hath he suffered that we all shall endure;
  The Good Deeds shall make sure.
890   Now hath he made ending.
  Methinketh that I hear angels sing
  And make great joy and melody
  Where Everyman's soul received shall be.
ANGEL. Come, excellent elect spouse to Jesu!
  Here above thou shalt go
  Because of thy singular virtue.
  Now the soul is taken the body fro,
  Thy reckoning is crystal clear.
  Now shalt thou into the heavenly sphere,
900   Unto the which all ye shall come
  That liveth well before the day of doom.

                              [*Exit* KNOWLEDGE.]

                    [*Enter* DOCTOR° *as Epilogue.*]   *Teacher*

---

[1] "Into your hands . . . I commend my spirit."

DOCTOR.   This moral men may have in mind;
    Ye hearers, take it of worth, old and young,
    And forsake Pride, for he deceiveth you in the end,
    And remember Beauty, Five Wits, Strength, and Discretion,
    They all at the last do Everyman forsake,
    Save his Good Deeds there doth he take.
    But beware, and they be small
    Before God he hath no help at all.
910   None excuse may be there for Everyman.
    Alas, how shall he do then?
    For, after death, amends may no man make,
    For then mercy and pity doth him forsake.
    If his reckoning be not clear when he doth come,
    God will say, "*Ite, maledicti, in ignem aeternum.*"[2]
    And he that hath his account whole and sound,
    High in heaven he shall be crowned.
    Unto which place God bring us all thither,
    That we may live body and soul together.
920   Thereto help the Trinity!
    Amen, say ye, for saint charity.

Thus endeth this moral play of EVERYMAN.

[ca. 1490]

Critical Commentary on *Everyman*

Everyman is the best surviving example of a medieval morality play, a form of didactic drama in which the characters represent such abstractions as Faith, Hope, and Charity in contention with Worldliness, Passion, and Sin for the welfare of the human soul. Among the other extant morality plays are *The Pride of Life* (before 1400), *The Castle of Perseverance* (ca. 1410), *Mankind* (ca. 1470), *Wisdom* (ca. 1470), and *Youth* (1520). The aims of morality plays are openly devotional, suggesting that they are written, or at least approved, by members of the Catholic clergy; in *Everyman,* for example, there is a lengthy, and largely irrelevant, digression on the powers and importance of the priesthood.

Almost nothing is known about the original staging of morality plays, although there is some evidence that on occasion they were performed individually by touring troupes of players. Both the staging and the characterization were probably designed to contribute to the allegorical effect. It is easy to imagine *Everyman* being performed on the village green using a platform stage with three levels. With this staging, God would appear at the highest level of the scaffolding; Death would climb up from the depths of the curtained ground-level; and the main events in Everyman's process of dying would occur on the "earth" of the middle platform.

This crude symbolism could easily be extended to include the characterization as well. As the play begins, for example, Everyman might be seen

---

[2]   "Go, accursed ones, into eternal fire."

enjoying a raucous and dissipated banquet with his friends at a table in one corner of the stage. As he stumbles drunkenly to center stage, he is suddenly confronted by the grim visage of Death. His boon companions at table prove unreliable one by one, starting with the superficially smiling Fellowship and the clattering, junk-laden Goods and continuing through the devious Cousin and the cheerfully irresponsible Kindred (who offers to lend Everyman his maid, a girl never known to refuse a man's companionship). Meanwhile, of course, Good Deeds is lying limply in a corner, too weak to come to Everyman's assistance.

As in other great allegories (such as Edmund Spenser's *The Faerie Queene*), the power of *Everyman* derives from the multiple perspectives from which it can be understood. Most directly, we see the very human failings of Everyman as he confronts his inevitable mortality. Everyman is, of course, a representative of us all, but he is also a unique human being. We watch with sympathy and occasional amusement as his friends, his relations, his possessions, and ultimately the characteristics of his own body desert him in his hour of need. We see, for example, his initial horror at the approach of death and the panicky naiveté with which he blurts out his condition to Fellowship and demands sympathy and companionship. After that first rejection, he grows clever and uses roundabout language in explaining his circumstances to Kindred and Cousin. He no longer mentions Death at all, describing instead how a "high king's chief officer" has commanded him to go on a "pilgrimage" from which he will never return. The plaintively human touches in Everyman's conduct and the amusing dodges of his unreliable companions give a great deal of surface appeal to the action.

At the moral level *Everyman* creates its most forceful message. Like so many other literary works of the Middle Ages, this one carries the implicit religious admonition: *Respice finem!*—"Look to the end!" Life was a chancey matter in the Middle Ages, apt to be cut short by plague, warfare, footpads, falls from horses, starvation, gluttony, childbirth, and every paltry breed of bacteria. Even today, of course, the vicissitudes of life are great, and few thoughtful readers remain unmoved by this representation of our own moral plight at death. We too recognize that in a moral and spiritual sense we shall be judged by the pitiful quantity of our good deeds.

From yet another perspective *Everyman* accurately portrays the physical processes of death. A dying man first takes leave of his friends and relatives as he gradually loses both his strength and beauty. In Roman Catholicism he confesses his sins, takes Holy Communion, and receives the last rites of Extreme Unction. Just before death he begins to lose control of his senses, his discretion, and finally his consciousness and knowledge.

For the modern reader, however, the most interesting reading of the play is apt to be psychological. Through the work of Elizabeth Kubler-Ross, we have become familiar with the common psychological stages in the process of dying: denial and isolation, anger, bargaining, depression, and finally acceptance. In *Everyman* we see a remarkably full exposition of several of these psychological stages, first in his bargaining with Death for more time "to give a reckoning" and culminating in the reverent acceptance of his final words:

Into thy hands, Lord, my soul I commend:
Receive it, Lord, that it be not lost.

As thou me boughtest, so me defend
And save me from the fiend's boast,
That I may appear with that blesséd host
That shall be saved at the day of doom.
In manus tuas,° of might's most,   *Into your hand*
Forever—*commendo spiritum meum.°*   *I commend my spirit*

Perhaps we are most moved by this work written half a millennium ago
because it reminds us of the ageless frailty of all flesh.

A Selective Bibliography on *Everyman*

Chessell, Del. "A Constant Shaping Pressure: Mortality in Poetry." *The Critical Review*
25 (1984): 3–17.

Conley, John. "*Everyman* 504: Ase, Behold, or 'Ah, See'?" *Notes and Queries* 29 (1982):
399–400.

———."The Identity of Discretion in *Everyman*." *Notes and Queries* 30 (1983): 394–96.

———." 'Cruelly' in *Everyman* 75." *Notes and Queries* 34 (1987): 10–11.

Cowling, Douglas. "The Angel's Song in *Everyman*." *Notes and Queries* 35 (1988):
301–3.

Dietrich, Julia. "*Everyman*, Lines 364–47." *The Explicator* 40 (1982): 5.

Duclow, Donald F. "*Everyman* and the *Ars Moriendi*: Fifteenth Century Ceremonies of
Dying." *Fifteenth–Century Studies* 6 (1983): 93–113.

Fletcher, Alan J. "*Everyman*: An Unrecorded Sermon Analogue." *English Studies* 66
(1985): 296–99.

Garner, Stanton B., Jr. "Theatricality in *Mankind* and *Everyman*." *Studies in Philology*
84 (1987): 272–85.

Hillman, Richard. "*Everyman* and the Energies of Stasis." *Florilegium* 7 (1985): 206–
26.

McRae, Murdo William. "Everyman's Last Rites and the Digression on Priesthood."
College Literature 13 (1986): 305–9.

Munson, William. "Knowing and Doing in *Everyman*." *The Chaucer Review* 19 (1985):
252–71.

Peek, George S. "Sermon Themes and Sermon Structure in *Everyman*." *South Central
Bulletin* 40 (1980): 159–60.

Ryan, Lawrence V. "Doctrine and Dramatic Structure in *Everyman*." *Speculum* 32
(1957): 722–35.

Spinrad, Phoebe S. "The Last Temptation of Everyman." *Philological Quarterly* 64
(1985): 185–94.

Strietman, Elsa. "The Middle Dutch *Elckerlijc* and the English *Everyman*." *Medium
Aevum* 52 (1983): 111–14.

Van Dyke, Carolyn. "The Intangible and Its Image: Allegorical Discourse and the
Cast of *Everyman*." Eds. Mary J. Carruthers and Elizabeth D. Kirk. *Acts of Interpretation: The Text in Its Contexts*, 700–1600. Norman: U of Oklahoma P, 1982. 311–
24.

Van Laan, Thomas F. "*Everyman*: A Structural Analysis." *PMLA* 78 (1963): 465–75.

White, D. Jerry. *Early English Drama: Everyman to 1580: A Reference Guide*. Boston:
G. K. Hall, 1986.

White, Patricia S. "Everybody: On Stage in New York." *Research Opportunities in
Renaissance Drama* 29 (1986–1987): 105–7.

Christopher Marlowe (1564–1593)
THE TRAGEDY OF DOCTOR FAUSTUS

Text Edited by Fredson Bowers

CHARACTERS

DOCTOR FAUSTUS	HORSE-COURSER
WAGNER, *his servant*	CARTER
VALDES ⎫ *Students of*	HOSTESS
CORNELIUS ⎭ *magic*	GOOD ANGEL
THREE SCHOLARS	BAD ANGEL
MEPHOSTOPHILIS	LUCIFER
An OLD MAN	BEELZEBUB
POPE ADRIAN	PRIDE ⎫
RAYMOND, *King of Hungary*	COVETOUSNESS ⎪
BRUNO, *the rival Pope*	ENVY ⎪ *the Seven*
CARDINALS OF FRANCE AND PADUA	WRATH ⎬ *Deadly*
ARCHBISHOP OF RHEIMS	GLUTTONY ⎪ *Sins*
CHARLES V, *Emperor of Germany*	SLOTH ⎪
MARTINO ⎫	LECHERY ⎭
FREDERICKE ⎬*Knights at his court*	ALEXANDER THE GREAT ⎫
BENVOLIO ⎭	HIS PARAMOUR ⎪
DUKE OF SAXONY	DARIUS, *King of Persia* ⎬ *Spirits*
DUKE OF VANHOLT	HELEN ⎪
DUCHESS OF VANHOLT	TWO CUPIDS ⎭
ROBIN, *the Clown*	BISHOPS, MONKS, FRIARS,
DICK	SOLDIERS, ATTENDANTS, DEVILS,
VINTNER	A PIPER

[*Enter* CHORUS.]
[CHORUS I]

CHORUS. Not marching in the fields of *Thrasimen,*
    Where *Mars* did mate° the warlicke *Carthagens,*[1]   *become an ally of*
    Nor sporting in the dalliance of love
    In Courts of Kings, where state is over-turn'd,
    Nor in the pompe of proud audacious deeds,
    Intends our Muse° to vaunt° his heavenly verse;   *our poet / display, show off*
    Onely this, Gentles: we must now performe
    The forme of *Faustus* fortunes, good or bad,

---

[1] Though we have no record of a play concerning the victory of Hannibal and the Carthaginians at Lake Thrasymenus in 217 B.C., the chorus is apparently referring to another play in the company's repertoire. Mars, of course, is the Roman god of war.

And now to patient judgements we appeale,
10   And speake for *Faustus* in his infancie.
Now is he borne, of parents base of stocke,
In *Germany*, within a Towne cal'd *Rhode:*[2]
At riper yeares to *Wittenberg*,[3] he went,
Whereas° his kinsmen chiefly brought him up;   *where*
So much he profits in Divinitie,
The fruitfull plot of Scholerisme grac'd,
That shortly he was grac'd with Doctors name,
Excelling all, whose sweete delight's dispute
In th' heavenly matters of Theologie,
20   Till swolne with cunning of a selfe conceit,
His waxen wings did mount above his reach,[4]
And melting, heavens conspir'd his over-throw:
For falling to a divellish exercise,
And glutted now with learnings golden gifts,
He surfets upon cursed Necromancie:
Nothing so sweet as Magicke is to him,
Which he preferres before his chiefest bliss;°   *his hope of salvation after death*
And this the man that in his study sits.

[*Exit.*]

SCENE I

[*Enter* FAUSTUS *in his study.*]

FAUSTUS.   Settle thy studies *Faustus*, and begin
30   To sound the depth of that thou wilt professe,
Having commenc'd, be a Divine in shew,°   *appearance*
Yet levell at the end of every Art,
And live and die in *Aristotles* workes.
Sweet *Analitikes*,[5] tis thou hast ravisht me,
Bene disserere est finis logices.[6]
Is to dispute well Logickes chiefest end?
Affoords this Art no greater miracle?
Then read no more, thou hast attain'd that end;
A greater subject fitteth *Faustus* wit:°   *intelligence*
40   Bid *on kai me on*[7] farewell, *Galen*[8] come:
Seeing *ubi desinit philosophus, ibi incipit medicus.*[9]

---

[2] Roda, a town in central Germany (now known as Stadtroda).
[3] A university town in eastern Germany, identified with Martin Luther.
[4] The allusion is to the death of Icarus, whose "waxen wings" melted when he flew too near the sun, causing him to fall into the sea.
[5] Works on logic and proof in argument by Aristotle.
[6] Petrus Ramus's (1515–1572) definition: "To argue well is the end of logic."
[7] "Being and not being."
[8] Galen (ca. A.D. 130–200), the Greek physician and author, was a recognized authority on medicine throughout the Middle Ages.
[9] "Where the philosopher stops, the doctor begins."

Be a Phisitian *Faustus,* heape up gold,
And be eterniz'd for some wondrous cure:
Summum bonum medicinæ sanitas,[10]
The end of Physicke is our bodies health:
Why *Faustus,* hast thou not attain'd that end?
Is not thy common talke sound Aphorismes?[11]
Are not thy bils° hung up as monuments,   *prescriptions*
Wherby whole Cities have escap't the plague,
50   And thousand desperate maladies beene cur'd?
Yet art thou still but *Faustus,* and a man.
Couldst thou make men to live eternally,
Or being dead, raise them to life againe,
Then this profession were to be esteem'd.
Physicke farewell: where is *Justinian?*[12]
Si una eademque res legatur duobus, alter rem, alter valorem rei, &c.
A petty case of paltry Legacies:
Exhereditare filium non potest pater, nisi—[13]
Such is the subject of the *Institute,*
60   And universall body of the law.
This study fits a Mercenarie drudge,
Who aimes at nothing but externall trash,
Too servile and illiberall for mee.
When all is done, *Divinitie* is best:
Jeromes Bible[14] *Faustus,* view it well:
Stipendium peccati mors est: ha, *Stipendium, &c.*
The reward of sin is death? that's hard:
Si peccasse negamus, fallimur, et nulla est in nobis veritas:
If we say that we have no sinne we deceive our selves, and there
70   is no truth in us.
Why then belike
We must sinne, and so consequently die,
I, we must die, an everlasting death.
What doctrine call you this? *Che sera, sera:*[15]
What will be, shall be; *Divinitie* adeiw.
These Metaphisicks of Magitians,
And Negromantick bookes are heavenly.
Lines, Circles, Signes, Letters, and Characters,
I these are those that *Faustus* most desires.
80   O what a world of profite and delight,
Of power, of honour, and omnipotence,
Is promised to the Studious Artizan?°   *artist*

---

[10] Faustus translates the Latin himself in the next line.
[11] A well-known medical textbook by Hippocrates (ca. 460–377 B.C.), the so-called "Fatherof Medicine."
[12] Emperor Justinian (483–561) reorganized and codified the whole of Roman law in his *Institutes*. The following line, from the *Institutes,* reads: "If one and the same thing is bequeathed to two persons, one should have the thing, the other its value."
[13] Again from the *Institutes:* "A father cannot disinherit his son unless. . . ."
[14] The edition of the Latin, of Vulgate, Bible by St. Jerome (ca. 340–420); the passages that Faustus cites below are from Romans, vi.23 and I John, i.8.
[15] "Whatever will be, will be."

All things that move betweene the quiet Poles[16]
Shall be at my command: Emperors and Kings,
Are but obey'd in their severall Provinces:
Nor can they raise the winde, or rend the cloudes:
But his dominion that exceeds in this,
Stretcheth as farre as doth the mind of man:
A sound Magitian is a Demi-god,
90   Here tire my braines to get a Deity.

                                                   [*Enter* WAGNER.]

Wagner, commend me to my deerest friends,
The Germane *Valdes* and *Cornelius,*
Request them earnestly to visit me.
WAGNER.   I will sir.

                                                          [*Exit.*]

FAUSTUS.   Their conference will be a greater helpe to me,
Then all my labours, plod I ne're so fast.

                             [*Enter the* ANGELL *and* SPIRIT (BAD ANGEL).]

GOOD ANGEL.   O *Faustus,* lay that damned booke aside,
And gaze not on it least it tempt thy soule,
And heape Gods heavy wrath upon thy head.
100   Reade, reade the Scriptures: that is blasphemy.
BAD ANGEL.   Go forward *Faustus* in that famous Art
Wherein all natures treasury is contain'd:
Be thou on earth as *Jove*[17] is in the skye,
Lord and Commander of these elements.

                                             [*Exeunt* ANGELS.]

FAUSTUS.   How am I glutted with conceipt of° this?   *drunk with the thought of*
Shall I make spirits fetch me what I please?
Resolve me of all ambiguities?
Performe what desperate enterprise I will?
I'le have them flie to *India* for gold;
110   Ransacke the Ocean for Orient Pearle,
And search all corners of the new-found-world
For pleasant fruites, and Princely delicates.°   *delicacies*
I'le have them read° me strange Philosophy,   *teach*
And tell the secrets of all forraine Kings:
I'le have them wall all *Germany* with Brasse,
And make swift *Rhine,* circle faire *Wittenberge:*
I'lle have them fill the publique Schooles with silke,
Wherewith the Students shall be bravely° clad.   *smartly*

---

[16] The quiet poles of the universe, "quiet" because they do not move.
[17] It was not unusual in the Renaissance, scholars tell us, to find the name of a pagan deity applied to the Christian God.

I'le leavy souldiers with the coyne they bring,
120 And chase the Prince of *Parma*[18] from our Land,
And raigne sole King of all our Provinces.
Yea stranger engines for the brunt of warre,
Then was the fiery keele at *Antwerpe* bridge,
I'le make my servile spirits to invent.
Come *Germane Valdes* and *Cornelius*,
And make me blest with your sage conference.

[*Enter* VALDES *and* CORNELIUS.]

Valdes, sweete *Valdes*, and *Cornelius*,
Know that your words have won me at the last,
To practise Magicke and concealed Arts.
130 Yet not your words onely, but mine owne fantasie,
That will receive no object,[19] for my head
But ruminates on Negromantique skill.
Philosophy is odious and obscure,
Both Law and Physicke are for petty wits:
Divinitie is basest of the three,
Unpleasant, harsh, contemptible and vilde:
'Tis magick, magick, that hath ravisht me.
Then gentle friends aid me in this attempt,
And I, that have with concise Sillogismes
140 Gravel'd° the Pastors of the Germane Church,   *confused*
And made the flowring pride of *Wittenberg*
Swarme to my Problemes, as th'infernall spirits
On sweet *Musæus*[20] when he came to hell,
Will be as cunning as *Agrippa*[21] was,
Whose shadows made all *Europe* honour him.
VALDES. *Faustus*, these bookes, thy wit, and our experience,
Shall make all Nations to Canonize us:
As Indian *Moores*,[22] obey their Spanish Lords,
So shall the spirits of every element,
150 Be alwaies serviceable to us three:
Like Lyons shall they guard us when we please,
Like *Almaine* Rutters with their horsemens staves,[23]
Or Lapland Giants trotting by our sides:
Sometimes like women or unwedded Maides,
Shadowing° more beauty in their Airie° browes,   *concealing/heavenly*

---

[18] The Prince of Parma was the governor-general of the Netherlands from 1579 to 1592, and perhaps the foremost soldier of his time. He built a bridge over the river Scheldt during the siege of Antwerp which was subsequently destroyed by a fire-ship in April of 1585.

[19] The precise meaning of this line is unclear, and scholars have given it so many interpretations that one may well conclude that it is corrupt. "That appearance will think of nothing else" will serve as well as any.

[20] In Greek mythology Musaeus was a poet-musician and a pupil of Orpheus.

[21] Henry Cornelius Agrippa von Nettesheim (1486–1535) was a reported magician who wrote an occult subjects. He was said to be able to call up the "shadows" of the dead.

[22] American Indians, in the the sense of dark-skinned people.

[23] Like German cavalry with lances.

Then has the white breasts of the Queene of love.[24]
From *Venice* shall they drag huge *Argosies*,°   *treasure ships*
And from *America* the Golden Fleece,[25]
That yearely stuffes old *Phillips*[26] treasury,
160   If learned *Faustus* will be resolute.
FAUSTUS.   *Valdes*, as resolute am I in this,
As thou to live, therefore object it not.°   *do not object to it*
CORNELIUS.   The miracles that magick will performe,
Will make thee vow to study nothing else.
He that is grounded in Astrology,
Inricht with tongues,[27] well seene in Minerals,[28]
Hath all the Principles Magick doth require:
Then doubt not *Faustus* but to be renowm'd,
And more frequented for this mysterie,
170   Then heeretofore the *Delphian* Oracle.[29]
The spirits tell me they can dry the sea,
And fetch the treasure of all forraine wrackes:
Yea all the wealth that our fore-fathers hid,
Within the massy° entrailes of the earth: *massive*
Then tell me *Faustus* what shall we three want?
FAUSTUS.   Nothing *Cornelius;* O this cheeres my soule:
Come, shew me some demonstrations Magicall,
That I may conjure in some bushy Grove,
And have these joies in full possession.
180 VALDES.   Then hast thee to some solitary Grove,
And beare wise *Bacons*, and *Abanus* workes,[30]
The *Hebrew* Psalter, and new Testament;
And whatsoever else is requisite,
We will informe thee e're our conference cease.
CORNELIUS.   *Valdes*, first let him know the words of Art,
And then all our ceremonies learn'd,
Faustus may try his cunning° by himselfe.   *skill*
VALDES.   First I'le instruct thee in the rudiments,
And then wilt thou be perfecter then I.
190 FAUSTUS.   Then come and dine with me, and after meate
We'le canvase every quidditie° thereof: *discuss every detail*
For e're I sleep, I'le try what I can do:
This night I'le conjure tho I die therefore.

[*Exeunt omnes.*]

---

[24] Venus.

[25] The allusion, of course, is to the golden fleece sought by Jason and his fellow Argonauts.

[26] King Philip II (1165–1223) of Spain.

[27] It was commonly believed that the spirits had to be addressed in Latin, Greek, and Hebrew.

[28] Well informed in the properties of minerals.

[29] The oracle of Apollo at Delphi.

[30] Roger Bacon (ca. 1214–1294) was an Oxford professor who, rumor had it, also dealt in black magic. Abanus, scholars surmise, refers to Pietro d'Abano (ca. 1215–1316), an Italian physician and philosopher, who also dabbled in the occult.

SCENE II

[*Enter two* SCHOLLERS.]

1. SCHOLLER.   I wonder what's become of *Faustus* that
Was wont to make our schooles ring, with *sic probo*.[31]

[*Enter* WAGNER.]

2. SCHOLLER.   That shall we presently know, here comes his boy.
1. SCHOLLER.   How now sirra, where's thy Maister?
WAGNER.   God in heaven knowes.
2. SCHOLLER.   Why, dost not thou know then.
200 WAGNER.   Yes, I know, but that followes not.
1. SCHOLLER.   Go to sirra, leave your jesting, and tell us where
he is.
WAGNER.   That followes not by force of argument, which you,
being *Licentiats*,° should stand upon; therefore acknowledge   *graduates*
your errour, and be attentive.
2. SCHOLLER.   Then you will not tell us?
WAGNER.   You are deceiv'd, for I will tell you: yet if you were
not dunces, you would never aske me such a question: For is
he not *Corpus naturale*? and is not that *Mobile*?[32] Then
210 wherefore should you aske me such a question? But that I
am by nature flegmatique, slow to wrath, and prone to
letcherie (to love I would say) it were not for you to come
within fortie foot of the place of execution,[33] although I do
not doubt but to see you both hang'd the next Sessions.°   *court sessions*
Thus having triumpht over you, I will set my counteance
like a Precisian,° and begin to speake thus: Truely my   *Puritan*
deere brethren, my Maister is within at dinner, with *Valdes*
and *Cornelius,* as this wine, if it could speake, would informe
your Worships: and so the Lord blesse you, preserve you,
and keepe you, my deere brethren.

[*Exit.*]

1. SCHOLLER.   O *Faustus,*
220 Then I feare that which I have long suspected:
That thou art falne into that damned Art
For which they two are infamous through the world.
2. SCHOLLER.   Were he a stranger, not allyed to me,
The danger of his soule would make me mourne:
But come, let us go, and informe the *Rector:*[34]
It may be his grave counsell may reclaime him.

---

[31] "I prove it thus;" a term from scholastic debate.
[32] *Corpus naturale . . . Mobile:* a natural body that is movable—the current scholastic definition for the subject matter of physics.
[33] I.e., the dining room.
[34] The head or president of a university.

1. SCHOLLER.   I feare me, nothing will reclaime him now.
2. SCHOLLER.   Yet let us see what we can do.

[*Exeunt.*]

SCENE III

[*Thunder. Enter* LUCIFER *and foure devils (above),* FAUSTUS *to them with this speech.*]

FAUSTUS.   Now that the gloomy shadow of the night,
230   Longing to view *Orions* drisling looke,[35]
        Leapes from th'Antarticke world unto the skie,[36]
        And dyms the *Welkin,*° with her pitchy breathe: *heavens*
        Faustus, begin thine Incantations,
        And try if devils will obey thy Hest,
        Seeing thou hast pray'd and sacrific'd to them.
        Within this circle is *Jehova's* Name,
        Forward, and backward, *Anagramatis'd:*
        Th'abreviated names of holy Saints,
        Figures of every adjunct to the heavens,
240   And Characters of Signes, and erring Starres,[37]
        By which the spirits are inforc'd to rise:[38]
        Then feare not *Faustus* to be resolute
        And try the utmost Magicke can performe.

Thunder.

Sint mihi Dei Acherontis propitii, valeat numen triplex Jehovæ,
    Ignei, Aerii, Aquatici, Terreni, spiritus salvete: Orientis Princeps
    Lucifer, Belzebub inferni ardentis monarcha, et Demogorgon,
    propitiamus vos, ut appareat, et surgat Mephostophilis.

Dragon.

Quid tu moraris; per Jehovam, Gehennam, et consecratam aquam
    quam nunc spargo; signumque crucis quod nunc facio; et per
250   *vota nostra ipse nunc surgat nobis dicatus Mephostophilis.*[39]

[*Enter a* DEVILL.]

        I charge thee to returne, and change thy shape,
        Thou art too ugly to attend on me:

---

[35] The constellation of Orion was associated with wet weather.

[36] Marlowe was apparently under the impression that the evening advanced from the southern hemisphere.

[37] Signs of the Zodiac and planets.

[38] Faustus, before he begins to conjure, engages in the ritual of drawing a circle inscribed with certain signs around himself.

[39] "May the gods of Acheron [one of the rivers in the Greek underworld] grant me favor. Away with the threefold spirit of Jehova! Welcome spirits of fire, air, water, and earth! Lucifer, prince of the East, Belzebub, monarch of burning hell, and Demogorgon [a god of creation, antedating classical mythology], we ask that Mephostophilis may rise up and appear. Why do you delay? By Jehova, by hell, and by the holy water which I now sprinkle, and by the sign of the cross which I now make, and by our prayer, may Mephostophilis now rise, compelled to obey us."

Go and returne an old *Franciscan* Frier,
That holy shape becomes a devill best.

[*Exit* Devill.]

I see there's vertue in my heavenly words.
Who would not be proficient in this Art?
How pliant is this *Mephostophilis?*
Full of obedience and humility,
Such is the force of Magicke, and my spels.
260 Now *Faustus,* thou art Conjurer laureate[40]
That canst commaund great *Mephostophilis,*
Quin redis Mephostophilis fratris imagine.[41]

[*Enter* Mephostophilis.]

MEPHOSTOPHILIS.   Now *Faustus* what wouldst thou have me do?
FAUSTUS.   I charge thee waite upon me whilst I live
    To do what ever *Faustus* shall command:
    Be it to make the Moone drop from her Sphere,
    Or the Ocean to overwhelme the world.
MEPHOSTOPHILIS.   I am a servant to great *Lucifer,*
    And may not follow thee without his leave;
270 No more then he commands, must we performe.
FAUSTUS.   Did not he charge thee to appeare to me?
MEPHOSTOPHILIS.   No, I came now hether of mine owne accord.
FAUSTUS.   Did not my conjuring speeches raise thee? speake.
MEPHOSTOPHILIS.   That was the cause, but yet *per accidens:*[42]
    For when we heare one racke° the name of God,   *distort*
    Abjure the Scriptures, and his Saviour Christ;
    We flye in hope to get his glorious soule:
    Nor will we come unlesse he use such meanes,
    Whereby he is in danger to be damn'd:
280 Therefore the shortest cut for conjuring
    Is stoutly to abjure the Trinity,
    And pray devoutely to the Prince of hell.
FAUSTUS.   So *Faustus* hath already done, and holds this principle,
    There is no chiefe but onely *Beelzebub:*
    To whom *Faustus* doth dedicate himselfe.
    This word Damnation, terrifies not me,
    For I confound hell in *Elizium:*[43]
    My Ghost be with the old Phylosophers.[44]
    But leaving these vaine trifles of mens soules,
290 Tell me, what is that *Lucifer,* thy Lord?

---

[40] Poets in ancient Greece were crowned with a laurel wreath. In this sense, a conjuror of special distinction.
[41] "Mephostophilis, why don't you return in the likeness of a friar."
[42] Incidentally, not because of Faustus's powers as a conjuror.
[43] Doesn't distinguish between hell and Elysium, the Greek afterlife.
[44] With those who share his disbelief in eternity with its rewards and punishments.

MEPHOSTOPHILIS.   Arch-regent and Commander of all Spirits.
FAUSTUS.   Was not that *Lucifer* an Angell once?
MEPHOSTOPHILIS.   Yes *Faustus*, and most deerely lov'd of God.
FAUSTUS.   How comes it then that he is Prince of Devils?
MEPHOSTOPHILIS.   O: by aspiring pride and insolence,
   For which God threw him from the face of heaven.
FAUSTUS.   And what are you that live with *Lucifer?*
MEPHOSTOPHILIS.   Unhappy spirits that feel with *Lucifer*,
   Conspir'd against our God with *Lucifer*,
300   And are for ever damn'd with *Lucifer*.
FAUSTUS.   Where are you damn'd?
MEPHOSTOPHILIS.   In hell.
FAUSTUS.   How comes it then that thou art out of hell?
MEPHOSTOPHILIS.   Why this is hell: nor am I out of it.
   Think'st thou that I who saw the face of God,
   And tasted the eternall Joyes of heaven,
   Am not tormented with ten thousand hels,
   In being depriv'd of everlasting blisse?
   O *Faustus* leave these frivolous demandes,
310   Which strike a terror to my fainting soule.
FAUSTUS.   What, is great *Mephostophilis* so passionate
   For being deprived of the Joyes of heaven?
   Learne thou of *Faustus* manly fortitude,
   And scorne those Joyes thou never shalt possesse.
   Go beare these tydings to great *Lucifer*,
   Seeing *Faustus* hath incur'd eternall death,
   By desperate thoughts against *Joves* Deity:
   Say he surrenders up to him his soule,
   So he will spare him foure and twenty yeares,
320   Letting him live in all voluptuousnesse,
   Having thee ever to attend on me,
   To give me whatsoever I shall aske;
   To tell me whatsoever I demand:
   To slay mine enemies, and aid my friends,
   And alwaies be obedient to my will.
   Go, and return to mighty *Lucifer*,
   And meet me in my Study, at Midnight,
   And then resolve me° of thy Maisters mind.   *report to me*
MEPHOSTOPHILIS.   I will *Faustus*.

                                                      [*Exit.*]

330 FAUSTUS.   Had I as many soules, as there be Starres,
   I'de give them all for *Mephostophilis*.
   By him, I'le be great Emperour of the world,
   And make a bridge, thorough the moving Aire,
   To passe the Ocean with a band of men,
   I'le joyne the Hils that bind the *Affrick* shore,[45]

---

[45] The hills that line the Straits of Gibraltar, thus creating a single continent out of Europe and Africa.

And make that Country, continent to° *Spaine,*   *touching*
And both contributary to my Crowne.
The Emperour shall not live, but by my leave,
Nor any Potentate of *Germany.*
340   Now that I have obtain'd what I desir'd
I'le live in speculation° of this Art   *study*
Till *Mephostophilis* returne againe.

[*Exeunt* Faustus; Lucifer *and devils above.*]

SCENE IV

[*Enter* Wagner *and* (Robin) *the Clowne.*]

Wagner.   Come hither sirra boy.
Robin.   Boy? O disgrace to my person: Zounds, boy in your
    face, you have seene many boyes with such pickadevaunts[46] I
    am sure.
Wagner.   Sirra, hast thou no commings in?°   *income*
Robin.   Yes, and goings out too, you may see sir.
Wagner.   Alas poore slave, see how poverty jests in his
    nakednesse, I know the Villaines out of service, and so
350   hungry, that he would give his soule to the devill, for a
    shoulder of Mutton, tho it were bloud raw.
Robin.   Not so neither; I had need to have it well rosted, and
    good sauce to it, if I pay so deere, I can tell you.
Wagner.   Sirra, wilt thou be my man and waite on me? and I
    will make thee go, like *Qui mihi discipulus.*[47]
Robin.   What, in Verse?
Wagner.   No slave, in beaten° silke, and staves-aker.[48]   *embroidered*
Robin.   Staves-aker? that's good to kill Vermine: then belike if
    I serve you, I shall be lousy.
360 Wagner.   Why so thou shalt be, whether thou dost it or no: for
    sirra, if thou dost not presently bind thy selfe to me for
    seven yeares, I'le turne all the lice about thee into Familiars,°   *demons*
    and make them tare thee in peeces.
Robin.   Nay sir, you may save your selfe a labour, for they are
    as familiar with me, as if they payd for their meate and
    drinke, I can tell you.
Wagner.   Well sirra, leave your jesting, and take these
        Guilders.°   *Dutch florins*
Robin.   Yes marry sir, and I thanke you to.
Wagner.   So, now thou art to bee at an howres warning,
370   whensoever, and wheresoever the devill shall fetch thee.
Robin.   Here, take your Guilders againe, I'le none of 'em.

---

[46] Fashionable beards trimmed to a sharp point.
[47] "You who are my student."
[48] A potion used to kill vermin.

WAGNER.   Not I, thou art Prest,° prepare thy selfe, for I will   *hired*
  presently raise up two devils to carry thee away: *Banio, Belcher.*

                                                              [*Calls.*]

ROBIN.   *Belcher?* and° *Belcher* come here, I'le belch him: I am not   *if*
  afraid of a devill.

                                                    [*Enter two devils.*]

WAGNER.   How now sir, will you serve me now?
ROBIN.   I good *Wagner,* take away the devill then.

                                                            [*Exeunt.*]

WAGNER.   Spirits away.
  Now sirra follow me.
380 ROBIN.   I will sir; but hearke you Maister, will you teach me this
  conjuring Occupation?
WAGNER.   I sirra, I'le teach thee to turne thy selfe to a Dog, or
  a Cat, or a Mouse, or a Rat, or any thing.
ROBIN.   A Dog, or a Cat, or a Mouse, or a Rat? O brave *Wagner.*
WAGNER.   Villaine, call me Maister *Wagner,* and see that you
  walke attentively, and let your right eye be alwaies
  Diametrally° fixt upon my left heele, that thou maist,   *in a straight line*
  *Quasi vestigiis nostris insistere.*⁴⁹

ROBIN.   Well sir, I warrant you.

                                                            [*Exeunt.*]

                           SCENE V

                                       [*Enter* FAUSTUS *in his Study.*]

FAUSTUS.   Now *Faustus,* must thou needs be damn'd,
390   And canst not now be sav'd.
    What bootes° it then to thinke on God or Heaven?   *avails*
    Away with such vaine fancies, and despaire,
    Despair in *GOD,* and trust in *Belzebub:*
    Now go not backward: no, *Faustus,* be resolute.
    Why waverst thou? O something soundeth in mine eares,
    Abjure this Magicke, turne to God againe.
    I and *Faustus* will turne to God againe.
    To God? he loves thee not:
    The god thou serv'st is thine owne appetite,
400   Wherein is fixt the love of *Belzebub,*

---

⁴⁹ "As if to walk in my footsteps."

To him, I'le build an Altar and a Church,
And offer luke-warme bloud, of new borne babes.

[Enter the two ANGELS.]

BAD ANGEL.   Go forward *Faustus* in that famous Art.
GOOD ANGEL.   Sweete *Faustus* leave that execrable Art.
FAUSTUS.   Contrition, Prayer, Repentance? what of these?
GOOD ANGEL.   O they are meanes to bring thee unto heaven.
BAD ANGEL.   Rather illusions, fruits of lunacy,
That makes men foolish that do use them most.
GOOD ANGEL.   Sweet *Faustus* think of heaven, and heavenly things.
410 BAD ANGEL.   No *Faustus*, thinke of honour, and of wealth.

[Exeunt ANGELS.]

FAUSTUS.   Wealth?
Why, the Signory of *Embden*,[50] shall be mine:
When *Mephostophilis* shall stand by me,
What god can hurt me? *Faustus* thou art safe.
Cast no more doubts; *Mephostophilis* come
And bring glad tydings from great *Lucifer*.
Ist not midnight? come *Mephostophilis*.
Veni veni Mephostophile.[51]

[Enter MEPHOSTOPHILIS.]

Now tell me what saith *Lucifer* thy Lord.
420 MEPHOSTOPHILIS.   That I shall waite on *Faustus* whilst he lives,
So he will buy my service with his soule.
FAUSTUS.   Already *Faustus* hath hazarded° that for thee.   *jeopardized*
MEPHOSTOPHILIS.   But now thou must bequeath it solemnly,°   *formally*
And wright a Deed of Gift with thine owne bloud;
For that security craves *Lucifer*.
If thou deny it I must backe to hell.
FAUSTUS.   Stay *Mephostophilis*
And tell me, what good will my soule do thy Lord?
MEPHOSTOPHILIS.   Enlarge his Kingdome.
430 FAUSTUS.   Is that the reason why he tempts us thus?
MEPHOSTOPHILIS.   *Solamen miseris socios habuisse doloris.*[52]
FAUSTUS.   Why, have you any paine that torture other?°   *others*
MEPHOSTOPHILIS.   As great as have the humane soules of men.
But tell me *Faustus*, shall I have thy soule?
And I will be thy slave and waite on thee,
And give thee more then thou hast wit to aske.
FAUSTUS.   I *Mephostophilis*, I'le give it him.°   *to Lucifer*
MEPHOSTOPHILIS.   Then *Faustus* stab thy Arme couragiously,

---

[50] The governorship of Emden, a wealthy port city in northwest Germany at the mouth of the Ems River.
[51] "Come, O Come Mephostophilis."
[52] "Misery loves company."

And bind thy soule, that at some certaine day
440   Great *Lucifer* may claime it as his owne,
And then be thou as great as *Lucifer*.
FAUSTUS.   Loe *Mephostophilis*, for love of thee
Faustus hath cut his arme, and with his proper° bloud   *own*
Assures° his soule to be great *Lucifers*,   *binds, conveys*
Chiefe Lord and Regent of perpetuall night.
Veiw here this bloud that trickles from mine arme,
And let it be propitious° for my wish.   *acceptable*
MEPHOSTOPHILIS.   But *Faustus*
Write it in manner of a Deed of Gift.
450 FAUSTUS.   I so I do; but *Mephostophilis*,
My bloud congeales, and I can write no more.
MEPHOSTOPHILIS.   I'le fetch thee fire to dissolve it streight.

[*Exit.*]

FAUSTUS.   What might the staying of my bloud portend?
Is it unwilling I should write this byll?
Why streames it not, that I may write a fresh?
Faustus gives to thee his soule: ah there it staid.
Why shouldst thou not? is not thy soule thine owne?
Then write againe: *Faustus* gives to thee his soule.

[*Enter* MEPHOSTOPHILIS *with the Chafer° of Fire.*]   *brazier*

MEPHOSTOPHILIS.   See *Faustus* here is fire, set it on.[53]
460 FAUSTUS.   So, now the bloud begins to cleere againe:
Now will I make an end immediately.
MEPHOSTOPHILIS [*aside*].   What will not I do to obtaine his soule?
FAUSTUS.   *Consummatum est:*[54] this byll is ended,
And *Faustus* hath bequeath'd his soule to *Lucifer*.
But what is this Inscription on mine Arme?
Homo fuge:[55] whether should I flye?
If unto God, hee'le throw me downe to hell.
My sences are deceiv'd, here's nothing writ:
O yes, I see it plaine, even heere is writ
470   *Homo fuge:* yet shall not *Faustus* flye.
MEPHOSTOPHILIS.   I'le fetch him somewhat to delight his minde.

[*Exit.*]

[*Enter Devils, giving Crownes and rich apparell to* FAUSTUS: *they dance, and then depart.*]

[*Enter* MEPHOSTOPHILIS.]

FAUSTUS.   What meanes this shew? speake *Mephostophilis*.
MEPHOSTOPHILIS.   Nothing *Faustus* but to delight thy mind,
And let thee see what Magicke can performe.

---

[53] That is, set the dish on the fire.
[54] "It is finished."
[55] "Fly, O Man."

Faustus.   But may I raise such spirits when I please?
Mephostophilis.   I *Faustus,* and do greater things then these.
Faustus.   Then *Mephostophilis* receive this scrole,
A Deed of Gift, of body and of soule:
But yet conditionally, that thou performe
480   All Covenants, and Articles, betweene us both.
Mephostophilis.   *Faustus,* I sweare by *Hell* and *Lucifer,*
To effect all promises betweene us made.
Faustus.   Then heare me read it *Mephostophilis.*
On these conditions following:

First, that Faustus *may be a spirit in forme and substance.*
Secondly, that Mephostophilis *shall be his servant, and be by him commanded.*
Thirdly, that Mephostophilis *shall doe for him, and bring him whatsoever.*
490   *Fourthly, that he shall be in his chamber or house invisible.*
Lastly, that hee shall appeare to the said John Faustus, *at all times, in what shape or forme soever he please.*
I John Faustus *of* Wittenberg, *Doctor, by these presents,*° *doe*   articles
give both body and soule to Lucifer, *Prince of the East, and his*
Minister Mephostophilis, *and furthermore grant unto them that*
foure and twentie yeares being expired, and these Articles above
written being inviolate, full power to fetch or carry the said
John Faustus, *body and soule, flesh and bloud, into their*
habitation wheresoever.
500   *By me* John Faustus.

Mephostophilis.   Speake *Faustus,* do you deliver this as your Deed?
Faustus.   I, take it, and the devill give thee good of it.
Mephostophilis.   So, now *Faustus* aske me what thou wilt.
Faustus.   First, I will question with thee about hell:
Tell me, where is the place that men call Hell?
Mephostophilis.   Under the heavens.
Faustus.   I, so are all things else; but whereabouts?
Mephostophilis.   Within the bowels of these Elements,[56]
510   Where we are tortur'd, and remaine for ever.
Hell hath no limits, nor is circumscrib'd,°   limited
In one selfe° place: but where we are is hell,   particular
And where hell is there must we ever be.
And to be short, when all the world dissolves,
And every creature shall be purif'd,
All places shall be hell that is not heaven.
Faustus.   I thinke Hel's a fable.
Mephostophilis.   I, thinke so still, till experience change thy mind.
Faustus.   Why, dost thou think that *Faustus* shall be damn'd?

---

[56] The four elements of contemporary cosmology: earth, air, fire, and water.

MEPHOSTOPHILIS.   I, of necessity, for here's the scrowle
520   In which thou hast given thy soule to *Lucifer*.
FAUSTUS.   I, and body too, but what of that:
        Think'st thou that *Faustus*, is so fond° to imagine,   *foolish*
        That after this life there is any paine?
        Tush, these are trifles, and meere old wives Tales.
MEPHOSTOPHILIS.   But I am an instance to prove the contrary:
        For I tell thee I am damn'd, and now in hell.
FAUSTUS.   Nay, and this be hell, I'le willingly be damn'd.
        What, sleeping, eating, walking and disputing?
        But leaving this, let me have a wife, the fairest Maid in *Germany*,
530   for I am wanton and lascivious, and cannot live without a wife.
MEPHOSTOPHILIS.   Well *Faustus*, thou shalt have a wife.

                                        [*He fetches in a woman devill.*]

FAUSTUS.   What sight is this?
MEPHOSTOPHILIS.   Now *Faustus* wilt thou have a wife?
FAUSTUS   Here's a hot whore indeed; no, I'le no wife.
MEPHOSTOPHILIS.   Marriage is but a ceremoniall toy,
        And if thou lovest me thinke no more of it.
        I'le cull thee out the fairest Curtezans,
        And bring them every morning to thy bed:
        She whom thine eye shall like, thy heart shall have,
540   Were she as chaste as was *Penelope*,
        As wise as *Saba*,[57] or as beautifull
        As was bright *Lucifer* before his fall.
        Hold, take this booke, peruse it thoroughly:
        The iterating° of these lines brings gold;   *repetition*
        The framing of this circle on the ground
        Brings Thunder, Whirle-winds, Storme and Lightning:
        Pronouce this thrice devoutly to thy selfe,
        And men in harnesse° shall appeare to thee,   *armor*
        Ready to execute what thou commandst.
550 FAUSTUS.   Thankes *Mephostophilis* for this sweete booke.
        This will I keepe, as chary° as my life.   *dear*
        Yet faine would I have a booke wherein I might beholde al
        spels and incantations, that I might raise up spirits when
        I please.

MEPHOSTOPHILIS.   Here they are in this booke.

                                        [*There turne to them.*]

FAUSTUS.   Now would I have a booke where I might see al
        characters of planets of the heavens, that I might knowe
        their motions and dispositions.°   *locations*

---

[57] Penelope was the faithful wife of Ulysses, who outlasted the suitors until he returned
from the Trojan war. Saba, the Queen of Sheba, posed difficult questions to King Solomon (I
Kings, x).

560 MEPHOSTOPHILIS.   Heere they are too.

[*Turne to them.*]

FAUSTUS.   Nay let me have one booke more, and then I have
   done, wherein I might see al plants, hearbes and trees that
   grow upon the earth.
MEPHOSTOPHILIS.   Here they be.
FAUSTUS.   O thou art deceived.
MEPHOSTOPHILIS.   Tut I warrant° thee.   *assure*

[*Turne to them.*]

[*Exeunt.*]

SCENE VI

[*Enter* FAUSTUS *in his Study, and* MEPHOSTOPHILIS.]

FAUSTUS.   When I behold the heavens then I repent
   And curse thee wicked *Mephostophilis*,
   Because thou hast depriv'd me of those Joyes.
MEPHOSTOPHILIS.   'Twas thine own seeking *Faustus*, thanke thy
   selfe.
   But think'st thou heaven is such a glorious thing?
   I tell thee *Faustus* it is not halfe so faire
   As thou, or any man that breathes on earth.
FAUSTUS.   How prov'st thou that?
560 MEPHOSTOPHILIS.   'Twas made for man; then he's more excellent.
FAUSTUS.   If Heaven was made for man, 'twas made for me:
   I will renounce this Magicke and repent.

[*Enter the two* ANGELS.]

GOOD ANGEL.   *Faustus* repent, yet God will pitty thee.
BAD ANGEL.   Thou art a spirit, God cannot pitty thee.
FAUSTUS.   Who buzzeth in mine eares I am a spirit?
   Be I a devill yet God may pitty me,
   Yea, God will pitty me if I repent.
BAD ANGEL.   I, but *Faustus* never shall repent.

[*Exeunt* ANGELS.]

FAUSTUS.   My heart is hardned, I cannot repent:
570   Scarce can I name salvation, faith, or heaven,
   But feareful ecchoes thunder in mine eares,
   Faustus, thou art damn'd, then swords and knives,
   Gunnes, poyson, halters,° and invenomb'd steele,   *hangman's ropes*
   Are laid before me to dispatch my selfe:
   And long e're this, I should have done the deed,
   Had not sweete pleasure conquer'd deepe despaire.
   Have not I made blind *Homer* sing to me

Of *Alexanders* love, and *Oenons* death?[58]
And hath not he that built the walles of *Thebes*
580   With ravishing sound of his melodious Harpe,[59]
Made musicke with my *Mephostophilis?*
Why should I die then, or basely despaire?
I am resolv'd, *Faustus* shall not repent.
Come *Mephostophilis* let us dispute againe,
And reason of divine Astrology.
Speake, are there many Spheares above the Moone?
Are all Celestiall bodies but one Globe,
As in the substance of this centricke° earth?   *central*
MEPHOSTOPHILIS.   As are the elements, such are the heavens,
590   Even from the Moone unto the Emperiall Orbe,
Mutually folded in each others Spheares,
And jointly move upon one Axle-tree,
Whose termine, is tearmed the worlds wide Pole.
Nor are the names of *Saturne, Mars,* or *Jupiter,*
Fain'd, but are erring Starres.[60]
FAUSTUS.   But have they all
One motion, both *situ et tempore?*°   *in place and time*
MEPHOSTOPHILIS.   All move from East to West, in foure and
twenty houres, upon the poles of the world, but differ
in their motions upon the poles of the Zodiacke.[61]
600 FAUSTUS.   These slender questions *Wagner* can decide:
Hath *Mephostophilis* no greater skill?
Who knowes not the double motion of the Planets?
That the first is finisht in a naturall day?
The second thus: *Saturne* in thirty yeares, *Jupiter* in twelve,
Mars in four, the *Sun, Venus,* and *Mercury* in a yeare;
the Moone in twenty eight daies. Tush, these are fresh
mens suppositions:[62] But tell me, hath every
Spheare a Dominion, or *Intelligentia?*[63]
MEPHOSTOPHILIS.   I.
FAUSTUS.   How many Heavens, or Spheares, are there?
610 MEPHOSTOPHILIS.   Nine, the seven Planets, the Firmament,
and the Emperiall heaven.
FAUSTUS.   But is there not *Cœlum igneum,* and *Christalinum?*[64]
MEPHOSTOPHILIS.   No *Faustus* they be but Fables.

---

[58] Alexander (or Paris, as Homer called him) fell in love with the nymph Oenone before becoming enamored of Helen of Troy. She subsequently committed suicide.
[59] According to mythology, when Amphion, a son of Zeus, played the harp, the stones rose up to form the walls of the city of Thebes.
[60] Faustus wants to know if the entire universe is a single ball like the earth. Mephostophilis responds that, just like the four elements, the heavenly spheres rotate on a single axis, each circling around the one above it.
[61] The common axis on which the spheres revolve.
[62] The elementary facts that every first year college student learns as the basis of argument.
[63] A ruling spirit or intelligence.
[64] A burning heaven and a crystalline heaven—two concepts from the Ptolemaic theory of the universe.

FAUSTUS.   Resolve° me then in this one question: *answer*
    Why are not Conjunctions, Oppositions, Aspects, Eclipses,[65]
    all at one time, but in some years we have more, in some lesse?
MEPHOSTOPHILIS.   *Per inæqualem motum respectu totius.*[66]
FAUSTUS.   Well, I am answer'd: now tell me who made the
    world?
MEPHOSTOPHILIS.   I will not.
620 FAUSTUS.   Sweet *Mephostophilis* tell me.
MEPHOSTOPHILIS.   Move° me not *Faustus*.   *anger*
FAUSTUS.   Villaine, have I not bound thee to tell me any thing?
MEPHOSTOPHILIS.   I, that is not against our Kingdome: this is.
    Thou art damn'd, think thou of hell.
FAUSTUS.   Thinke *Faustus* upon God, that made the world.
MEPHOSTOPHILIS.   Remember this.——

[Exit.]

FAUSTUS.   I, go accursed spirit to ugly hell:
    'Tis thou hast damn'd distressed *Faustus* soule.
    Ist not too late?

[Enter the two ANGELS.]

630 BAD ANGEL.   Too late.
GOOD ANGEL.   Never too late, if *Faustus* will repent.
BAD ANGEL.   If thou repent, devils will teare thee in peeces.
GOOD ANGEL.   Repent and they shall never raise° thy skin.   *graze*

[Exeunt ANGELS.]

FAUSTUS.   Ah Christ my Saviour, my Saviour,
    Helpe to save distressed *Faustus* soule.

[Enter LUCIFER, BELZEBUB, and MEPHOSTOPHILIS.]

LUCIFER.   Christ cannot save thy soule, for he is just,
    There's none but I have interest in° the same.   *a legal claim on*
FAUSTUS.   O what art thou that look'st so terrible.
LUCIFER.   I am *Lucifer,*
640 And this is my companion Prince in hell.
FAUSTUS.   O *Faustus* they are come to fetch thy soule.
BELZEBUB.   We are come to tell thee thou dost injure us.
LUCIFER.   Thou calst on Christ contrary to thy promise.
BELZEBUB.   Thou should'st not thinke on God.
LUCIFER.   Thinke of the devill.
BELZEBUB.   And his dam° to.   *mother*
FAUSTUS.   Nor will I henceforth: pardon me for this,
    And *Faustus* vowes never to looke to heaven,

---

[65] These are astrological terms for the position of the heavenly planets.
[66] "On account of the unequal motion with regard to the whole"—the different speeds at
which the various planets of the universe move.

Never to name God, or to pray to him,
650   To burne his Scriptures, slay his Ministers,
And make my spirites pull his churches downe.
LUCIFER.   So shalt thou shew thy selfe an obedient servant,
And we will highly gratify° thee for it.   *reward*
BELZEBUB.   *Faustus* we are come from hell in person to shew
thee some pastime: sit downe and thou shalt behold the
seven deadly sinnes appeare to thee in their owne proper
shapes and likenesse.
FAUSTUS.   That sight will be as pleasant to me, as Paradise was
to *Adam* the first day of his creation.
LUCIFER.   Talke not of Paradice or Creation, but marke the
660   shew. Go *Mephostophilis*, fetch them in.

[*Enter the* SEVEN DEADLY SINNES (*led by a* PIPER).]

BELZEBUB.   Now *Faustus*, question them of their names and
dispositions.
FAUSTUS.   That shall I soone: What art thou the first?
PRIDE.   I am *Pride;* I disdaine to have any parents: I am like to
Ovids Flea,[67] I can creepe into every corner of a Wench:
Sometimes, like a Perriwig, I sit upon her Brow: next, like a
Neckelace I hang about her Necke: Then, like a Fan of
Feathers, I kisse her lippes; And then turning my selfe to a
wrought° Smocke do what I list. But fye, what a smell is   *embroidered*
670   heere? I'le not speake a word more for a Kings ransome,
unlesse the ground be perfum'd, and cover'd with cloth of
Arras.[68]
FAUSTUS.   Thou art a proud knave indeed: What art thou the
second?
COVETOUSNESSE.   I am *Covetousnesse:* begotten of an old Churle°   *miser*
in a leather bag;° and might I now obtaine my wish, this   *money bag*
house, you and all, should turne to Gold, that I might locke
you safe into my Chest: O my sweete Gold!
FAUSTUS.   And what art thou the third?
ENVY.   I am *Envy,* begotten of a Chimney-sweeper, and an
680   Oyster-wife: I cannot read, and therefore wish all books
burn'd. I am leane with seeing others eate: O that there
would come a famine over all the world, that all might die,
and I live alone, then thou should'st see how fat I'de be. But
must thou sit, and I stand? come downe with a vengeance.
FAUSTUS.   Out envious wretch: But what art thou the fourth?
WRATH.   I am *Wrath:* I had neither father nor mother, I leapt
out of a Lyons mouth when I was scarce an houre old, and
ever since have run up and downe the world with these case°   *pair*
of Rapiers, wounding my selfe when I could get none to

---

[67] A medieval poem, attributed to Ovid.
[68] A rich Flemish tapestry.

690   fight withall: I was borne in hell, and look to it, for some of
         you shall be my father.
     FAUSTUS.   And what are thou the fift?
     GLUTTONY.   I am *Gluttony;* my parents are all dead, and the
         devill a peny they have left me, but a bare pention, and that
         buyes me thirty meales a day, and ten Beavers°: a small trifle   *light snacks*
         to suffice nature. I come of a Royall Pedigree, my father was
         a Gammon of Bacon, and my mother was a Hogshead of
         Claret Wine. My godfathers were these: Peter
         Pickeld-herring, and Martin Martlemasse-beefe:[69] But my
700   godmother, O she was an ancient Gentlewoman, her name
         was Margery March-beere:[70] Now *Faustus* thou hast heard all
         my progeny,° wilt thou bid me to supper?   *lineage*
     FAUSTUS.   Not I.
     GLUTTONY.   Then the devill chooke thee.
     FAUSTUS.   Choke thy selfe Glutton: What are thou the sixt?
     SLOTH.   Hey ho; I am *Sloth:* I was begotten on a sunny bank:
         where I have laine ever since, and you have done me great
         injury to bring me from thence, let me be carried thither
         againe by Gluttony and Letchery,
                             hey ho: I'le not speake an
     other word.
     FAUSTUS.   And what are you Mistris Minkes, the seventh and
         last?
     LETCHERY.   Who I sir? I am one that loves an inch of raw Mut-
         ton,[71] better then an ell of fryde Stockfish: and the first let-
710   ter of my name begins with *Letchery.*
     LUCIFER.   Away to hell, away: on piper.

                                               [*Exeunt the* SEVEN SINNES.]

     FAUSTUS.   O how this sight doth delight my soule.
     LUCIFER.   Tut *Faustus,* in hell is all manner of delight.
     FAUSTUS.   O might I see hell, and returne againe safe, how
         happy were I then.
     LUCIFER.   *Faustus,* thou shalt, at midnight I will send for thee;
         Meane while peruse this booke, and view it throughly,
         And thou shalt turne thy selfe into what shape thou wilt.
     FAUSTUS.   Thankes mighty *Lucifer:*
     This will I keepe as chary° as my life.   *carefully*
720 LUCIFER.   Now *Faustus* farewell.
     FAUSTUS.   Farewell great *Lucifer:* come *Mephostophilis.*

                                      [*Exeunt omnes, severall waies.*]

---

[69] Salted beef hung for the winter on Martinmas day, November 11th.
[70] A fine ale brewed in the spring and aged for two years.
[71] Mutton is a slang for whore.

SCENE VII

[Enter (Robin) *the* Clowne.]

Robin. What *Dick,* looke to the horses there till I come againe.
   I have gotten one of Doctor *Faustus* conjuring bookes, and
   now we'le have such knavery, as't passes.

[Enter Dick.]

Dick. What *Robin,* you must come away and walk the horses.
Robin. I walke the horses, I scorn't 'faith, I have other matters
   in hand, let the horses walk themselves and they will. *A*
   per se, a, t. h. e. the: o per se, o, demy orgon, gorgon:[72] keepe
   further from me O thou illiterate, and unlearned Hostler.
730 Dick. 'Snayles,[73] what hast thou got there, a book? why thou
   canst not tell ne're a word on't.
Robin. That thou shalt see presently: keep out of the circle, I
   say, least I send you into the Ostry° with a vengeance.   inn
Dick. That's like, 'faith: you had best leave your foolery, for an
   my Maister come, he'le conjur you 'faith.
Robin. My Maister conjure me? I'le tell thee what, an° my   if
   Maister come here, I'le clap as faire a paire of hornes on's
   head[74] as e're thou sawest in thy life.
Dick. Thou needst not do that, for my Mistresse hath done it.
740 Robin. I, there be of us here, that have waded as deepe into
   matters, as other men, if they were disposed to talke.
Dick. A plague take you, I thought you did not sneake up and
   downe after her for nothing. But I prethee tell me, in good
   sadnesse° *Robin,* is that a conjuring booke?   seriousness
Robin. Do but speake what thou't have me to do, and I'le do't:
   If thou't dance naked, put off thy cloathes, and I'le conjure
   thee about presently: Or if thou't go but to the Taverne with
   me, I'le give thee white wine, red wine, claret wine, Sacke,
   Muskadine, Malmesey and Whippincrust,[75] hold belly hold,°   a belly-full
750   and wee'le not pay one peny for it.
Dick. O brave, prethee let's to it presently, for I am as dry as
   a dog.
Robin. Come then let's away.

[Exeunt.]

[Enter the Chorus.]

---

[72] Robin, of course, reads only with great difficulty.
[73] "By God's snails," an oath.
[74] The mark of the cuckhold, a man whose wife is unfaithful.
[75] The names of various wines.

[CHORUS 2]

CHORUS.   Learned *Faustus*
    To find the secrets of Astronomy,
    Graven in the booke of *Joves* high firmament,
    Did mount him up to scale *Olimpus* top.
    Where sitting in a Chariot burning bright,
    Drawne by the strength of yoked Dragons neckes;
760   He viewes the cloudes, the Planets, and the Starres,
    The Tropicks, Zones, and quarters of the skye,
    From the bright circle of the horned Moone,
    Even to the height of *Primum Mobile:*[76]
    And whirling round with this circumference,
    Within the concave compasse of the Pole,
    From East to West his Dragons swiftly glide,
    And in eight daies did bring him home againe.
    Not long he stayed within his quiet house,
    To rest his bones after his weary toyle,
770   But new exploits do hale him out agen,
    And mounted then upon a Dragons backe,
    That with his wings did part the subtle aire,
    He now is gone to prove° *Cosmography,*   *test the accuracy of*
    That measures costs, and kingdomes of the earth:
    And as I guesse will first arrive at *Rome,*
    To see the Pope and manner of his Court,
    And take some part of holy *Peters* feast,[77]
    The which this day is highly solemnized.

[*Exit.*]

SCENE VIII

[*Enter* FAUSTUS *and* MEPHOSTOPHILIS.]

FAUSTUS.   Having now my good *Mephostophilis,*
780   Past with delight the stately Towne of *Trier:*[78]
    Invironed round with airy mountaine tops,
    With wals of Flint, and deepe intrenched Lakes,°   *castle moats*
    Not to be wonne by any conquering Prince:
    From *Paris* next, costing the Realme of *France,*
    We saw the River *Maine,* fall into *Rhine,*
    Whose bankes are set with Groves of fruitfull Vines.
    Then up to *Naples* rich *Campania,*
    The buildings faire, and gorgeous to the eye,
    Whose streetes straight forth,° and paved with finest   *in straight lines*
790   bricke,

---

[76] The highest or outermost sphere of Ptolemaic astronomy that moves the other nine.
[77] St. Peter's Feast day, June 29th.
[78] Treves, a German city on the Moselle River.

790   Quarter the towne in foure equivolence.

    There saw we learned *Maroes*° golden tombe: *Virgil's*

    The way he cut, an English mile in length,

    Thorough a rocke of stone in one nights space:

    From thence to *Venice, Padua,* and the rest,

    In midst of which a sumptuous Temple stands,

    That threates the starres with her aspiring top,

    Whose frame is paved with sundry coloured stones,

    And roof't aloft with curious worke in gold.[79]

    Thus hitherto hath *Faustus* spent his time.

800   But tell me now, what resting place is this?

    Hast thou, as earst° I did command,   *formerly*

    Conducted me within the walles of *Rome?*

MEPHOSTOPHILIS.   I have my *Faustus,* and for proofe thereof,

    This is the goodly Palace of the Pope:

    And cause we are no common guests,

    I chuse his privy° chamber for our use.   *private*

FAUSTUS.   I hope his Holinesse will bid us welcome.

MEPHOSTOPHILIS.   All's one, for wee'l be bold with his Venison.

    But now my *Faustus,* that thou maist perceive,

810   What *Rome* containes for to delight thine eyes,

    Know that this City stands upon seven hils,

    That underprop the ground-worke of the same:

    Just through the midst runnes flowing *Tybers* streame,

    With winding bankes that cut it in two parts;

    Over the which foure stately Bridges leane,

    That make safe passage, to each part of *Rome.*

    Upon the Bridge, call'd *Ponte Angelo,*

    Erected is a Castle passing strong,

    Where thou shalt see such store of Ordinance,

820   As that the double Cannons[80] forg'd of brasse,

    Do match the number of the daies contain'd,

    Within the compasse of one compleat yeare:

    Beside the gates, and high Pyramydes,°   *obelisks*

    That *Julius Cæsar* brought from *Affrica.*

FAUSTUS.   Now by the Kingdomes of Infernall Rule,

    Of *Stix,* of *Acheron,* and the fiery Lake,

    Of ever-burning *Phlegeton,*[81] I sweare,

    That I do long to see the Monuments

    And situation° of bright splendent *Rome,*   *lay-out*

830   Come therefore, let's away.

MEPHOSTOPHILIS.   Nay stay my *Faustus:* I know you'd see the Pope

    And take some part of holy *Peters* feast,

    The which this day with high solemnity,

---

[79] St. Mark's Cathedral in Venice.

[80] Apparently canons of a very high calibre.

[81] The Styx, Acheron, and Phlegethon are three of the five rivers in Hades, the Greek underworld.

This day is held through *Rome* and *Italy,*
In honour of the Popes triumphant victory.

Faustus. Sweete *Mephostophilis,* thou pleasest me:
Whilst I am here on earth let me be cloyd°   *satiated*
With all things that delight the heart of man.
My foure and twenty yeares of liberty
840 I'le spend in pleasure and in daliance,
That *Faustus* name, whilst this bright frame doth stand,
May be admired through the furthest Land.

Mephostophilis. 'Tis well said *Faustus,* come then stand by me
And thou shalt see them come immediately.

Faustus. Nay stay my gentle *Mephostophilis,*
And grant me my request, and then I go.
Thou know'st within the compasse° of eight daies,   *take part in*
We veiw'd the face of heaven, of earth and hell.
So high our Dragons soar'd into the aire,
850 That looking downe the earth appear'd to me,
No bigger than my hand in quantity.
There did we view the Kingdomes of the world,
And what might please mine eye, I there beheld.
Then in this shew let me an Actor be,
That this proud Pope may *Faustus* cunning see.

Mephostophilis. Let it be so my *Faustus,* but first stay,
And view their triumphs,° as they passe this way.   *spectacular displays*
And then devise what best contents thy minde,
By cunning in thine Art to crosse the Pope,
860 Or dash the pride of this solemnity;
To make his Monkes and Abbots stand like Apes,
And point like Antiques° at his triple Crowne: *clowns*
To beate the beades about the Friers Pates,
Or clap huge hornes, upon the Cardinals heads:
Or any villany thou canst devise,
And I'le performe it *Faustus:* heark they come:
This day shall make thee be admir'd° in *Rome.*   *marvelled over*

[*Enter the* Cardinals *and* Bishops, *some bearing Crosiers, some the Pillars,*[82] Monkes
and Friers, *singing their Procession: Then the* Pope, *and* Raymond *King of* Hungary, *with* Bruno *led in chaines.*][83]

Pope. Cast downe our Foot-stoole.

Raymond.   Saxon *Bruno* stoope,
Whilst on thy backe his hollinesse ascends
870 Saint *Peters* Chaire and State° Pontificall.   *throne*

Bruno. Proud *Lucifer,* that State belongs to me:

---

[82] Portable pillars carried by cardinals as a symbol of their office; crosiers are staffs resembling shepherd's crooks carried by bishops and abbots for the same purpose.
[83] Pope Adrian (1154–1159) ultimately captured and deposed his rival Bruno, who had
been made Pope by Holy Roman Emperor Frederick Barbarossa. Frederick, who reigned from
1152 to 1190, was subsequently forced to yield to Pope Alexander (1159–1181) and acknowledge his supremacy.

But thus I fall to *Peter,* not to thee.
POPE.   To me and *Peter,* shalt thou groveling lie,
And crouch before the Papall dignity:
Sound Trumpets then, for thus Saint *Peters* Heire,
From *Bruno's* backe, ascends Saint *Peters* Chaire.

[*A Flourish while he ascends.*]

Thus, as the Gods creepe on with feete of wool,
Long ere with Iron hands they punish men,[84]
So shall our sleeping vengeance now arise,
880   And smite with death thy hated enterprise.
Lord Cardinals of *France* and *Padua,*
Go forth-with to our holy Consistory,[85]
And read amongst the Statues Decretall°,   *papal decrees*
What by the holy Councell held at *Trent,*[86]
The sacred Sinod° hath decreed for him,   *general council*
That doth assume the Papall government,
Without election, and a true consent:
Away and bring us word with speed.

1. CARDINAL.   We go my Lord.

[*Exeunt* CARDINALS.]

890 POPE.   Lord *Raymond*——

[*They talk apart.*]

FAUSTUS.   Go hast thee gentle *Mephostophilis,*
Follow the Cardinals to the Consistory;
And as they turne their superstitious Bookes,
Strike them with sloth, and drowsy idlenesse;
And make them sleepe so sound, that in their shapes,
Thy selfe and I, may parly with this Pope:
This proud confronter of the Emperour,
And in despite of all his Holinesse
Restore this *Bruno* to his liberty,
900   And beare him to the States of *Germany.*
MEPHOSTOPHILIS.   *Faustus,* I goe.
FAUSTUS.   Dispatch it soone,
The Pope shall curse that *Faustus* came to *Rome.*

[*Exeunt* FAUSTUS *and* MEPHOSTOPHILIS.]

BRUNO.   Pope *Adrian* let us have some right of Law,
I was elected by the Emperour.
POPE.   We will depose the Emperour for that deed,

---

[84] The Pope's reference is to a proverb: "God comes with leaden (woolen) feet, but strikes with iron hands."
[85] The meeting place of the papal senate.
[86] The Council of Trent sat from 1545 to 1563.

And curse the people that submit to him;
Both he and thou shalt stand excommunicate,
And interdict° from Churches priviledge,   *debar*
910 And all society of holy men:
He growes to prowd in his authority,
Lifting his loftie head above the clouds,
And like a Steeple over-peeres the Church.
But wee'le pul downe his haughty insolence:
And as Pope *Alexander* our Progenitour,°   *predecessor*
Trode on the neck of Germane *Fredericke*,
Adding this golden sentence to our praise;
That *Peters* heires should tread on Emperours,
And walke upon the dreadfull Adders backe,
920 Treading the Lyon, and the Dragon downe,
And fearelesse spurne the killing Basiliske:[87]
So will we quell that haughty Schismatique;
And by authority Apostolicall
Depose him from his Regall Government.
BRUNO.   Pope *Julius* swore to Princely *Sigismond*,[88]
For him, and the succeeding Popes of *Rome*,
To hold the Emperours their lawfull Lords.
POPE.   Pope *Julius* did abuse the Churches Rites,
And therefore none of his Decrees can stand.
930 Is not all power on earth bestowed on us?
And therefore tho we would we cannot erre.
Behold this Silver Belt whereto is fixt
Seven golden keys[89] fast sealed with seven seales,
In token of our seven-fold power from heaven,
To binde or loose, lock fast, condemne, or judge,
Resigne,° or seale, or what so pleaseth us.   *unseal*
Then he and thou, and all the world shall stoope,
Or be assured of our dreadfull curse,
To light as heavy as the paines of hell.

[*Enter* FAUSTUS *and* MEPHOSTOPHILIS *like the* CARDINALS.]

940 MEPHOSTOPHILIS.   Now tell me *Faustus,* are we not fitted well?
FAUSTUS.   Yes *Mephostophilis,* and two such Cardinals
Ne're serv'd a holy Pope, as we shall do.
But whilst they sleepe within the Consistory,
Let us salute his reverend Father-hood.
RAYMOND.   Behold my Lord, the Cardinals are return'd.
POPE.   Welcome grave Fathers, answere presently,
What have our holy Councell there decreed,
Concerning *Bruno* and the Emperour,

---

[87] A mythical monster that killed by its look.
[88] Sigismund (1368–1437) was Holy Roman Emperor from 1411 to 1437. There were three popes named Julian, but none was a contemporary of Sigismund's.
[89] The symbolic keys of St. Peter.

In quittance of their late conspiracie
950　　Against our State, and Papall dignitie?
FAUSTUS.　Most sacred Patron of the Church of *Rome*,
By full consent of all the reverend Synod
Of Priests and Prelates, it is thus decreed:
That *Bruno*, and the Germane Emperour
Be held as Lollords,[90] and bold Schismatiques,
And proud disturbers of the Churches peace.
And if that *Bruno* by his owne assent,
Without inforcement° of the German Peeres,　　　　　　*compulsion from*
Did seeke to weare the triple Dyadem,
960　　And by your death to clime Saint *Peters* Chaire,
The Statutes Decretall have thus decreed,
He shall be streight condemn'd of heresie,
And on a pile of Fagots burnt to death.
POPE.　It is enough: here, take him to your charge,
And beare him streight to *Ponte Angelo*,[91]
And in the strongest Tower inclose him fast.
To morrow, sitting in our Consistory,
With all our Colledge of grave Cardinals,[92]
We will determine of his life or death.
970　　Here, take his triple Crowne along with you,
And leave it in the Churches treasury.
Make haste againe, my good Lord Cardinalls,
And take our blessing Apostolicall.
MEPHOSTOPHILIS.　So, so, was never Divell thus blest before.
FAUSTUS.　Away sweet *Mephostophilis* be gone,
The Cardinals will be plagu'd for this anon.

[*Exeunt* FAUSTUS *and* MEPHOSTOPHILIS (*with* BRUNO).]

POPE.　Go presently, and bring a banket° forth,　　　　　　*banquet*
That we may solemnize Saint *Peters* feast,
And with Lord *Raymond*, King of *Hungary*,
980　　Drinke to our late and happy victory.

[*Exeunt.*]

SCENE IX

[*A Senit*[93] *while the Banquet is brought in; and then Enter* FAUSTUS *and*
MEPHOSTOPHILIS *in their owne shapes.*]

MEPHOSTOPHILIS.　Now *Faustus*, come prepare thy selfe for mirth,
The sleepy Cardinals are hard at hand,

90　Lollards was the name given to the followers of John Wyclif (ca. 1320–1384), the English
religious reformer and Bible translator who was declared a heretic by the Church.
91　To a castle standing by the bridge.
92　The College of Cardinals, the official name for the Pope's council.

To censure *Bruno*, that is posted hence,
And on a proud pac'd Steed, as swift as thought,
Flies ore the Alpes to fruitfull *Germany*,
There to salute the wofull Emperour.

FAUSTUS. The Pope will curse them for their sloth to day,
That slept both *Bruno* and his crowne away.
But now, that *Faustus* may delight his minde,
990 And by their folly make some merriment,
Sweet *Mephostophilis* so charme me here,
That I may walke invisible to all,
And doe what ere I please, unseene of any.

MEPHOSTOPHILIS. *Faustus* thou shalt, then kneele downe presently,
Whilst on thy head I lay my hand,
And charme thee with this Magicke wand,
First weare this girdle, then appeare
Invisible to all are here:
The Planets seven, the gloomy aire,
1000 *Hell and the Furies forked haire,*[94]
Pluto's blew fire,[95] *and Hecat's tree,*[96]
With Magicke spels so compasse thee,
That no eye may thy body see.
So *Faustus*, now for all their holinesse,
Do what thou wilt, thou shalt not be discern'd.

FAUSTUS. Thankes *Mephostophilis:* now Friers take heed,
Lest *Faustus* make your shaven crownes to bleed.

MEPHOSTOPHILIS. *Faustus* no more: see where the Cardinals come.

[*Enter* POPE *and all the* LORDS. *Enter the* CARDINALS *with a Booke.*]

POPE. Welcome Lord Cardinals: come sit downe.
1010 Lord *Raymond*, take your seate, Friers attend,
And see that all things be in readinesse,
As best beseemes this solemne festivall.

1. CARDINAL. First, may it please your sacred Holinesse,
To view the sentence of the reverend Synod,
Concerning *Bruno* and the Emperour.

POPE. What needs this question? Did I not tell you,
To morrow we would sit i'th Consistory,
And there determine of his punishment?
You brought us word even now, it was decreed,
1020 That *Bruno* and the cursed Emperour
Were by the holy Councell both condemn'd
For lothed Lollords, and base Schismatiques:
Then wherefore would you have me view that booke?

1. CARDINAL. Your Grace mistakes, you gave us no such charge.

---

[94] It has been suggested that the allusion is to the forked tongues of snakes which formed the hair of the Furies, the Roman goddesses of vengeance.

[95] Pluto was the Greek god of the Underworld or Hades.

[96] Hecate was the name sometimes given to Trivia, a goddess of the crossroads where the gallows tree was often erected.

RAYMOND.   Deny it not, we all are witnesses
    That *Bruno* here was late delivered you,
    With his rich triple crowne to be reserv'd,°   *preserved*
    And put into the Churches treasury.
BOTH CARDINALS.   By holy *Paul* we saw him not.
1030 POPE.   By *Peter* you shall dye,
    Unlesse you bring them forth immediatly:
    Hale them to prison, lade their limbes with gyves:°   *shackles*
    False Prelates, for this hatefull treachery,
    Curst be your soules to hellish misery.

                                      [Exeunt CARDINALS *attended.]*

FAUSTUS.   So, they are safe: now *Faustus* to the feast,
    The Pope had never such a frolicke guest.
POPE.   Lord Archbishop of *Reames,* sit downe with us.
ARCHBISHOP.   I thank your Holinesse.
FAUSTUS.   Fall to, the Divell choke you an you spare.
1040 POPE.   Who's that spoke? Friers looke about.
    Lord *Raymond* pray fall too, I am beholding
    To the Bishop of *Millaine,* for this so rare a present.
FAUSTUS.   I thanke you sir.

                                              [Snatch it.]

POPE.   How now? who snatch't the meat from me!
    Villaines why speake you not?
    My good Lord Archbishop, heres a most daintie dish,
    Was sent me from a Cardinall in *France.*
FAUSTUS.   I'le have that too.

                                              [Snatch it.]

POPE.   What Lollards do attend our Hollinesse,
1050   That we receive such great indignity?
    Fetch me some wine.
FAUSTUS.   I, pray do, for *Faustus* is a dry.
POPE.   Lord *Raymond,* I drink unto your grace.
FAUSTUS.   I pledge your grace.

                                            [Snatch it.]

POPE.   My wine gone too? yee Lubbers° look about   *clumsy fellows*
    And find the man that doth this villany,
    Or by our sanctitude you all shall die.
    I pray my Lords have patience at this troublesome banquet.
ARCHBISHOP.   Please it your holinesse, I thinke it be some Ghost
1060   crept out of Purgatory, and now is come unto your holinesse
    for his pardon.
POPE.   It may be so:
    Go then command our Priests to sing a Dirge,°   *a requiem mass*
    To lay the fury of this same troublesome ghost.

> [*The* Pope *crosseth himselfe.*]

Faustus.   How now?
　Must every bit be spiced with a Crosse?
　Nay then take that.

> [Faustus *hits him a boxe of the eare.*]

Pope.   O I am slaine, help me my Lords:
　O come and help to beare my body hence:
1070　Damb'd be this soule for ever, for this deed.

> [*Exeunt the* Pope *and his traine.*]

Mephostophilis.   Now *Faustus*, what will you do now? for I can
　tell you, you'le be curst with Bell, Booke, and Candle.
Faustus.   Bell, Booke, and Candle; Candle, Booke, and Bell,
　Forward and backward, to curse *Faustus* to hell.[97]

> [*Enter the* Friers *with Bell, Booke, and Candle, for the Dirge.*]

1. Frier.   Come brethren, let's about our businesse with good devotion.
　Cursed be he that stole away his holinesse meate from the Table.
　　Maledicat Dominus.[98]
　Cursed be he that stroke his holinesse a blow on the face.
1080　　*Maledicat Dominus.*

> [Faustus *strikes a friar.*]

　Cursed be he that strucke fryer Sandelo a blow on the pate.
　　Maledicat Dominus.
　Cursed be he that disturbeth our holy Dirge.
　　Maledicat Dominus.
　Cursed be he that tooke away his holinesse wine.
　　Maledicat Dominus.
　　Et omnes sancti.[99] *Amen.*

> Beate the Friers, *fling fire workes among them,*
> 　*and Exeunt.*

> [*Exeunt.*]

SCENE X

> [*Enter (*Robin *the)* Clowne *and* Dick, *with a Cup.*]

Dick.   Sirra *Robin*, we were best looke that your devill can　an-
　swere the stealing of this same cup, for the Vintners boy　fol-
1090　lowes us at the hard heeles.°　　　　　　　　　*right on our heels*

---

[97] At the conclusion of an excommunication ceremony, the bell is tolled, the book is closed,
and the candle is extinguished.
[98] "May the Lord curse him."
[99] "And all the saints."

ROBIN: 'Tis no matter, let him come; an he follow us, I'le so
conjure him, as he was never conjur'd in his life, I warrant
him: let me see the cup.

[*Enter* VINTNER.]

DICK.   Here 'tis: Yonder he comes: Now *Robin*, now or never
shew thy cunning.

VINTNER.   O, are you here? I am glad I have found you, you are
a couple of fine companions: pray where's the cup you stole
from the Taverne?

ROBIN.   How, how? we steale a cup? take heed what you say, we
1100   looke not like cup-stealers I can tell you.

VINTNER.   Never deny't, for I know you have it, and I'le search
you.

ROBIN.   Search me? I and spare not: hold the cup *Dick*, come,
come, search me, search me.

VINTNER.   Come on sirra, let me search you now.

DICK.   I, I, do, do, hold the cup *Robin*, I feare not your searching; we scorne to steale your cups I can tell you.

VINTNER.   Never out face me for the matter,[100] for sure the cup
is betweene you two.

ROBIN.   Nay there you lie, 'tis beyond us both.

1110 VINTNER.   A plague take you, I thought 'twas your knavery to
take it away: Come, give it me againe.

ROBIN.   I much: when, can you tell? *Dick*, make me a circle,
and stand close at my backe, and stir not for thy life, *Vintner*
you shall have your cup anon, say nothing *Dick: O per se o,
demogorgon,*[101] *Belcher* and *Mephostophilis.*

[*Enter* MEPHOSTOPHILIS. *Exit* VINTNER *running.*]

MEPHOSTOPHILIS.   You Princely Legions of infernall Rule,
How am I vexed by these villaines Charmes?
From *Constantinople* have they brought me now,
Onely for pleasure of these damned slaves.

1120 ROBIN.   By Lady sir, you have had a shroud° journey of it, will   *tiresome*
it please you to take a shoulder of Mutton to supper, and a
Tester° in your purse, and go backe againe.   *sixpence*

DICK.   I, I pray you heartily sir; for wee cal'd you but in jeast I
promise you.

MEPHOSTOPHILIS.   To purge the rashnesse of this cursed deed,
First, be thou turned to this ugly shape,
For Apish° deeds transformed to an Ape.   *foolish*

ROBIN.   O brave, an Ape? I pray sir, let me have the carrying of
him about to shew some trickes.

1130 MEPHOSTOPHILIS.   And so thou shalt: be thou transformed to
A dog, and carry him upon thy backe;
Away be gone.

---

[100] "Never brazen the matter out with me."
[101] This echoes Robin's earlier attempt.

ROBIN.   A dog? that's excellent: let the Maids looke well to
their porridge-pots, for I'le into the Kitchin presently: come
Dick, come.

[*Exeunt the two* CLOWNES.]

MEPHOSTOPHILIS.   Now with the flames of ever-burning fire,
I'le wing my selfe and forth-with flie amaine
Unto my *Faustus* to the great Turkes Court.

[*Exit.*]

[*Enter* CHORUS.]
[CHORUS 3]

CHORUS.   When *Faustus* had with pleasure tane° the view   *taken*
Of rarest things, and royal courts of kings,
1140   Hee stayde his course,° and so returned home,   *stopped his travelling*
Where such as beare his absence but with griefe,
I meane his friends and nearest companions,
Did gratulate his safetie with kinde words,
And in their conference of what befell,
Touching his journey through the world and ayre,
They put forth questions of Astrologie,
Which *Faustus* answered with such learned skill,
As they admirde and wondred at his wit.
Now is his fame spread forth in every land,
1150   Amongst the rest the Emperour is one,
Carolus the fift,[102] at whose pallace now
Faustus is feasted mongst his noblemen.
What there he did in triall of his art,
I leave untold, your eyes shall see performd.

[*Exit.*]

SCENE XI

[*Enter* MARTINO, *and* FREDERICK *at severall dores.*]

MARTINO.   What ho, Officers, Gentlemen,
Hye to the presence° to attend the Emperour.   *audience chamber*
Good *Fredericke* see the roomes be voyded straight,°   *immediately cleared*
His Majesty is comming to the Hall;
Go backe, and see the State° in readinesse.   *throne*
1160 FREDERICKE.   But where is *Bruno* our elected Pope,
That on a furies back came post from *Rome*,
Will not his grace consort° the Emperour?   *accompany*
MARTINO.   O yes,
And with him comes the Germane Conjurer,

---

[102] Charles V (1500–1558), who reigned as Holy Roman Emperor from 1519 to 1556.

The learned *Faustus,* fame of *Wittenberge,*
The wonder of the world for Magick Art;
And he intends to shew great *Carolus,*
The race of all his stout progenitors;
And bring in presence of his Majesty,
1170   The royall shapes and warlike° semblances   *heroic*
  Of *Alexander* and his beauteous Paramour.[103]

FREDERICKE.   Where is *Benvolio?*
MARTINO.   Fast a sleepe I warrant you,
  He took his rouse° with stopes° of Rhennish wine,   *bout of drinking/measures*
  So kindly yesternight to *Bruno's* health,
  That all this day the sluggard keepes his bed.
FREDERICKE.   See, see his window's ope, we'l call to him.
MARTINO.   What hoe, *Benvolio.*

    [*Enter* BENVOLIO *above at a window, in his nightcap: buttoning.*]

BENVOLIO.   What a devill ayle you two?
1180 MARTINO.   Speak softly sir, least the devil heare you:
  For *Faustus* at the Court is late arriv'd,
  And at his heeles a thousand furies waite,
  To accomplish what soever the Doctor please.
BENVOLIO.   What of this?
MARTINO.   Come leave thy chamber first, and thou shalt see
  This Conjurer performe such rare exploits,
  Before the Pope and royall Emperour,
  As never yet was seene in *Germany.*
BENVOLIO.   Has not the Pope enough of conjuring yet? He was
1190   upon the devils backe late enough; and if he be so farre in
  love with him, I would he would post with him to *Rome*
  againe.
FREDERICKE.   Speake, wilt thou come and see this sport?
BENVOLIO.   Not I.
MARTINO.   Wilt thou stand in thy Window, and see it then?
BENVOLIO.   I, and I fall not asleepe i'th meane time.
MARTINO.   The Emperour is at hand, who comes to see
  What wonders by blacke spels may compast be.
BENVOLIO.   Well, go you attend the Emperour: I am content for
1200   this once to thrust my head out at a window: for they say, if
  a man be drunke over night, the Divell cannot hurt him in
  the morning: if that bee true, I have a charme in my head,
  shall controule him as well as the Conjurer, I warrant you.

          [*Exeunt* MARTINO *and* FREDERICKE.]

    [*A Senit. Enter* CHARLES *the Germane Emperour,* BRUNO, (*Duke of*) SAXONY,
FAUSTUS, MEPHOSTOPHILIS, FREDERICKE, MARTINO, *and Attendants.*]

EMPEROUR.   Wonder of men, renown'd Magitian,

---

[103] Alexander the Great, King of Macedon (356–323 B.C.); the paramour is presumably
Alexander's wife, Roxana.

Thrice learned *Faustus*, welcome to our Court.
This deed of thine, in setting *Bruno* free
From his and our professed enemy,
Shall adde more excellence unto thine Art,
Then if by powerfull Necromantick spels,
1210 Thou couldst command the worlds obedience:
For ever be belov'd of *Carolus*.
And if this *Bruno* thou hast late redeem'd,
In peace possesse the triple Diadem,
And sit in *Peters* Chaire, despite of chance,
Thou shalt be famous through all *Italy*,
And honour'd of the Germane Emperour.
FAUSTUS.   These gracious words, most royall *Carolus*,
Shall make poore *Faustus* to his utmost power,
Both love and serve the Germane Emperour,
1220 And lay his life at holy *Bruno's* feet.
For proofe whereof, if so your Grace be pleas'd,
The Doctor stands prepar'd, by power of Art,
To cast his Magicke charmes, that shall pierce through
The Ebon gates of ever-burning hell,
And hale the stubborne Furies from their caves,
To compasse° whatsoere your grace commands.   *embrace*
BENVOLIO.   Bloud, he speakes terribly: but for all that, I doe not
greatly beleeve him, he lookes as like a Conjurer as the Pope
to a Coster-monger.°   *fruit seller*
1230 EMPEROUR.   Then *Faustus* as thou late didst promise us,
We would behold that famous Conquerour,
Great *Alexander*, and his Paramour,
In their true shapes, and state Majesticall,
That we may wonder at their excellence.
FAUSTUS.   Your Majesty shall see them presently.
Mephostophilis away,
And with a solemne noyse of trumpets sound,
Present before this royall Emperour,
Great *Alexander* and his beauteous Paramour.
1240 MEPHOSTOPHILIS.   *Faustus* I will.

[*Exit.*]

BENVOLIO.   Well Master Doctor, an your Divels come not away
quickly, you shall have me asleepe presently: zounds I could
eate my selfe for anger, to thinke I have beene such an Asse
all this while, to stand gaping after the divels Governor,° and   *teacher*
can see nothing.
FAUSTUS.   Il'e make you feele something anon, if my Art faile me
not.
My Lord, I must forewarne your Majesty,
That when my Spirits present the royall shapes
1250 Of *Alexander* and his Paramour,
Your grace demand no questions of the King,
But in dumbe silence let them come and goe.

EMPEROUR.   Be it as *Faustus* please, we are content.

BENVOLIO.   I, I, and I am content too: and thou bring *Alexander*
and his Paramour before the Emperour, Il'e be *Acteon,* and
turne my selfe to a Stagge.[104]

FAUSTUS.   And Il'e play *Diana,* and send you the hornes presently.

[*Enter* MEPHOSTOPHILIS.]

[*Senit. Enter at one dore the Emperour* ALEXANDER, *at the other* DARIUS;[105] *they
meete,* DARIUS *is throwne downe,* ALEXANDER *kils him; takes off his Crowne, and
offering to goe out, his Paramour meetes him, he embraceth her, and sets* DARIUS
*Crowne upon his head; and comming backe, both salute the Emperour, who leaving
his State, offers to embrace them, which* FAUSTUS *seeing, suddenly staies him. Then
trumpets cease, and Musicke sounds.*]

My gracious Lord, you doe forget your selfe,
These are but shadowes, not substantiall.

1260 EMPEROUR.   O pardon me, my thoughts are ravished so
With sight of this renowned Emperour,
That in mine armes I would have compast° him.   *embraced*
But *Faustus,* since I may not speake to them,
To satisfie my longing thoughts at full,
Let me this tell thee: I have heard it said,
That this faire Lady, whilest she liv'd on earth,
Had on her necke a little wart, or mole;
How may I prove that saying to be true?

FAUSTUS.   Your Majesty may boldly goe and see.

1270 EMPEROUR.   *Faustus* I see it plaine,
And in this sight thou best pleasest me,
Then if I gain'd another Monarchie.

FAUSTUS.   Away, be gone.

[*Exit Show.*]

See, see, my gracious Lord, what strange beast is yon, that
thrusts his head out at the window.

EMPEROUR.   O wondrous sight: see Duke of *Saxony,*
Two spreading hornes most strangely fastened
Upon the head of yong *Benvolio.*

SAXONY.   What, is he asleepe, or dead?

1280 FAUSTUS.   He sleeps my Lord, but dreames not of his hornes.

EMPEROUR.   This sport is excellent: wee'l call and wake him.
What ho, *Benvolio.*

BENVOLIO.   A plague upon you, let me sleepe a while.

EMPEROUR.   I blame thee not to sleepe much, having such a
head of thine owne.

SAXONY.   Looke up *Benvolio,* tis the Emperour calls.

BENVOLIO.   The Emperour? where? O zounds my head.

---

[104] Actaeon, a young hunter, spied on Diana who was bathing naked and, in retaliation, she
turned him into a stag. His own dogs tore him to pieces.

[105] King Darius of Persia was defeated by Alexander the Great at Granicus in 334 B.C.

EMPEROUR.   Nay, and thy hornes hold, tis no matter for thy
      head, for that's arm'd sufficiently.
1290 FAUSTUS.   Why how now sir Knight, what, hang'd by the
      hornes? this is most horrible: fie, fie, pull in your head for
      shame, let not all the world wonder at you.
      BENVOLIO.   Zounds Doctor, is this your villany?
      FAUSTUS.   O say not so sir: the Doctor has no skill,
      No Art, no cunning, to present these Lords,
      Or bring before this royall Emperour
      The mightie Monarch, warlicke *Alexander.*
      If *Faustus* do it, you are streight resolv'd,
      In bold *Acteons* shape to turne a Stagge.
1300 And therefore my Lord, so please your Majesty,
      Il'e raise a kennell of Hounds shall hunt him so,
      As all his footmanship° shall scarce prevaile,   *running skill*
      To keepe his Carkasse from their bloudy phangs.
      Ho, *Belimoth, Argiron, Asteroth.*[106]
      BENVOLIO.   Hold, hold: zounds hee'l raise up a kennell of
      Divels I thinke anon: good my Lord intreate for me: 'sbloud
      I am never able to endure these torments.
      EMPEROUR.   Then good Master Doctor,
      Let me intreate you to remove his hornes,
1310 He has done penance now sufficiently.
      FAUSTUS.   My gracious Lord, not so much for injury done to
      me, as to delight your Majesty with some mirth, hath *Faustus*
      justly requited this injurious° knight, which being all I desire,   *insulting*
      I am content to remove his hornes. *Mephostophilis,* transforme
      him; and hereafter sir, looke you speake well of Schollers.
      BENVOLIO.   Speake well of yee? 'sbould and Schollers be such
      Cuckold-makers to clap hornes of honest mens heades o'this
      order, Il'e nere trust smooth faces, and small ruffes[107] more.
      But an I be not reveng'd for this, would I might be turn'd to
1320 a gaping Oyster, and drinke nothing but salt water.

                                                          [*Exit.*]

      EMPEROUR.   Come *Faustus* while the Emperour lives.
      In recompence of this thy high desert,
      Thou shalt command the state of *Germany,*
      And live belov'd of mightie *Carolus.*

                                                    [*Exeunt omnes.*]

                          SCENE XII

            [*Enter* BENVOLIO, MARTINO, FREDERICKE, *and Souldiers.*]

      MARTINO.   Nay sweet *Benvolio,* let us sway thy thoughts
      From this attempt against the Conjurer.

---

[106] These references are unclear.
[107] Beardless scholars in academic regalia.

BENVOLIO.   Away, you love me not, to urge me thus,
    Shall I let slip so great an injury,
    When every servile groome° jeasts at my wrongs,   *lowly fellow*
1330   And in their rusticke gambals proudly° say,   *insolently*
    Benvolio's head was grac't with hornes to day?
    O may these eye-lids never close againe,
    Till with my sword I have that Conjurer slaine.
    If you will aid me in this enterprise,
    Then draw your weapons, and be resolute:
    If not, depart: here will *Benvolio* die,
    But° *Faustus* death shall quit° my infamie.   *unless/avenge*
FREDERICKE.   Nay, we will stay with thee, betide what may,
    And kill that Doctor if he come this way.
1340 BENVOLIO.   Then gentle *Fredericke* hie thee to the grove,
    And place our servants, and our followers
    Close° in an ambush there behinde the trees,   *hidden*
    By this° (I know) the Conjurer is neere,   *by this time*
    I saw him kneele, and kisse the Emperours hand,
    And take his leave, laden with rich rewards.
    Then Souldiers boldly fight; if *Faustus* die,
    Take you the wealth, leave us the victorie.
FREDERICKE.   Come souldiers, follow me unto the grove,
    Who kils him shall have gold, and endlesse love.

                       [*Exit* FREDERICKE *with the Souldiers.*]

1350 BENVOLIO.   My head is lighter then it was by th'hornes,
    But yet my heart's more ponderous then my head,
    And pants untill I see that Conjurer dead.
MARTINO.   Where shall we place our selves *Benvolio?*
BENVOLIO.   Here will we stay to bide the first assault,
    O were that damned Hell-hound but in place,°   *on the spot*
    Thou soone shouldst see me quit my foule disgrace.

                           [*Enter* FREDERICKE.]

FREDERICKE.   Close, close, the Conjurer is at hand,
    And all alone, comes walking in his gowne;
    Be ready then, and strike the Peasant° downe.   *rascal*
1360 BENVOLIO.   Mine be that honour then: now sword strike home,
    For hornes he gave, Il'e have his head anone.

                    [*Enter* FAUSTUS *with the false head.*]

MARTINO.   See, see he comes.
BENVOLIO.   No words: this blow ends all,
    Hell take his soule, his body thus must fall.
FAUSTUS.   Oh.
FREDERICKE.   Grone you Master Doctor?
BENVOLIO.   Breake may his heart with grones: deere *Frederik* see,
    Thus will I end his griefes° immediatly.   *mischiefs*
MARTINO.   Strike with a willing hand, his head is off.

BENVOLIO.   The Divel's dead, the Furies now may laugh.
1370 FREDERICKE.   Was this that sterne aspect, that awfull frowne,
        Made the grim monarch of infernall spirits,
        Tremble and quake at his commanding charmes?
MARTINO.   Was this that damned head, whoses heart conspir'd
        Benvolio's shame before the Emperour?
BENVOLIO.   I, that's the head, and here the body lies,
        Justly rewarded for his villanies.
FREDERICKE.   Come, let's devise how we may adde more shame
        To the blacke scandall of his hated name.
BENVOLIO.   First, on his head, in quittance of my wrongs,
1380   Il'e naile huge forked hornes, and let them hang
        Within the window where he yoak'd me first,
        That all the world may see my just revenge.
MARTINO.   What use shall we put his beard to?
BENVOLIO.   Wee'l sell it to a Chimny-sweeper: it will weare out
        ten birchin broomes I warrant you.
FREDERICKE.   What shall his eyes doe?
BENVOLIO.   Wee'l put out his eyes, and they shall serve for but-
        tons to his lips, to keepe his tongue from catching cold.
MARTINO.   An excellent policie:° and now sirs, having divided   *scheme*
1390   him, what shall the body doe?

                                                [FAUSTUS *rises.*]

BENVOLIO.   Zounds the Divel's alive agen.
FREDERICKE.   Give him his head for Gods sake.
FAUSTUS.   Nay keepe it: *Faustus* will have heads and hands,
        I, all your hearts to recompence this deed.
        Knew you not Traytors, I was limitted°   *allowed*
        For foure and twenty yeares, to breathe on earth?
        And had you cut my body with your swords,
        Or hew'd this flesh and bones as small as sand,
        Yet in a minute had my spirit return'd,
1400   And I had breath'd a man made free from harme.
        But wherefore doe I dally° my revenge?   *trifle with*
        Asteroth, Belimoth, Mephostophilis,

                        [*Enter* MEPHOSTOPHILIS *and other Divels.*]

        Go horse these traytors on your fiery backes,
        And mount aloft with them as high as heaven,
        Thence pitch them headlong to the lowest hell:
        Yet stay, the world shall see their miserie,
        And hell shall after plague their treacherie.
        Go *Belimothe,* and take this caitife hence,
        And hurle him in some lake of mud and durt:
1410   Take thou this other, dragge him through the woods,
        Amongst the pricking thornes, and sharpest briers,
        Whils, with my gentle *Mephostophilis,*
        This Traytor flies unto some steepie rocke,

That rowling downe, may breake the villaines bones,
As he intended to dismember me.
Fly hence, dispatch my charge immediatly.
FREDERICKE.   Pitie us gentle *Faustus,* save our lives.
FAUSTUS.   Away.
FREDERICKE.   He must needs goe that the Divell drives.[108]

[Exeunt Spirits with the knights.]

[Enter the ambusht Souldiers.]

1420 1. SOLDIER.   Come sirs, prepare your selves in readinesse,
Make hast to help these noble Gentlemen,
I heard them parly with the Conjurer.
2. SOLDIER.   See where he comes, dispatch, and kill the slave.
FAUSTUS.   What's here? an ambush to betray my life:
Then *Faustus* try thy skill: base pesants stand,
For loe these Trees remove at my command,
And stand as Bulwarkes twixt your selves and me,
To sheild me from your hated treachery:
Yet to encounter this your weake attempt,
1430 Behold an Army comes incontinent.°   *immediately*

[FAUSTUS *strikes the dore, and enter a devill playing on a Drum, after him another bearing an Ensigne: and divers with weapons,* MEPHOSTOPHILIS *with fire-workes; they set upon the Souldiers and drive them out.*]

[Exeunt omnes.]

SCENE XIII

[*Enter at severall dores,* BENVOLIO, FREDERICKE, *and* MARTINO, *their heads and faces bloudy, and besmear'd with mud and durt; all having hornes on their heads.*]

MARTINO.   What ho, *Benvolio.*
BENVOLIO.   Here, what *Frederick,* ho.
FREDERICKE.   O help me gentle friend; where is *Martino?*
MARTINO.   Deere *Frederick* here,
Halfe smother'd in a Lake of mud and durt,
Through which the Furies drag'd me by the heeles.
FREDERICKE.   *Martino* see,
Benvolio's hornes againe.
MARTINO.   O misery.
How now *Benvolio?*
BENVOLIO.   Defend me heaven, shall I be haunted still?
1440 MARTINO.   Nay feare not man, we have no power to kill.
BENVOLIO.   My friends transformed thus: O hellish spite,
Your heads are all set with hornes.
FREDERICKE.   You hit it right,
It is your owne you meane, feele on your head.

---

[108] A well-known proverb.

BENVOLIO.   'Zons, hornes againe.
MARTINO.   Nay chafe not man,
  we all are sped.°   *provided for*
BENVOLIO.   What devill attends this damn'd Magician,
  That spite of spite,° our wrongs are doubled?   *in spite of everything*
FREDERICKE.   What may we do, that we may hide our shames?
BENVOLIO.   If we should follow him to worke revenge,
  He'd joyne long Asses eares to these huge hornes,
1450   And make us laughing stockes to all the world.
MARTINO.   What shall we then do deere *Benvolio?*
BENVOLIO.   I have a Castle joyning neere these woods,
  And thither wee'le repaire and live obscure,
  Till time shall alter this our brutish shapes:
  Sith° blacke disgrace hath thus eclipst our fame,   *seeing that*
  We'le rather die with griefe, then live with shame.

                                                          [*Exeunt omnes.*]

SCENE XIV

                    [*Enter* FAUSTUS, *and the* HORSE-COURSER.[109]]

HORSE-COURSER.   I beseech your Worship accept of these forty
  Dollors.
FAUSTUS.   Friend, thou canst not buy so good a horse, for so
1460   small a price: I have no great need to sell him, but if thou
  likest him for ten Dollors more, take him, because I see thou
  hast a good minde to him.
HORSE-COURSER.   I beseech you sir accept of this; I am a very
  poore man, and have lost very much of late by horse flesh,
  and this bargaine will set me up againe.
FAUSTUS.   Well, I will not stand° with thee, give me the money: *haggle*
  now sirra I must tell you, that you may ride him o're hedge
  and ditch, and spare him not; but do you heare? in any case,
  ride him not into the water.[110]
1470 HORSE-COURSER.   How sir, not into the water? why will he not
  drink of all waters?
FAUSTUS.   Yes, he will drinke of all waters,° but ride him not   *go anywhere*
  into the water; o're hedge and ditch, or where thou wilt, but
  not into the water: Go bid the Hostler deliver him unto you,
  and remember what I say.
HORSE-COURSER.   I warrant you sir; O joyfull day: Now am I a
  made man for ever.

                                                                    [*Exit.*]

FAUSTUS.   What art thou *Faustus* but a man condemn'd to die?
  Thy fatall time° drawes to a finall end;   *time granted by fate*

---

[109] Horse dealer, and as such an individual whose honesty is at once suspect.
[110] The horse is magical and water will destroy the spell that created it.

1480   Despaire doth drive distrust into my thoughts.
        Confound these passions with a quiet sleepe:
        Tush, Christ did call the Theefe upon the Crosse,
        Then rest thee *Faustus* quiet in conceit.°   *in mind*

                                                    [*He sits to sleepe.*]

                                        [*Enter the* HORSE-COURSER *wet.*]

HORSE-COURSER.   O what a cosening° Doctor was this? I riding   *cheating*
    my horse into the water, thinking some hidden mystery had
    beene in the horse, I had nothing under me but a little
    straw, and had much ado to escape drowning: Well I'le go
    rouse him, and make him give me my forty Dollors
    againe. Ho sirra Doctor, you cosening scab;° Maister   *rascal*
1490 Doctor awake, and rise, and give me my mony againe, for
    your horse is turned to a bottle° of Hay,—Maister Doctor.   *bundle*

                                                [*He puls off his leg.*]

    Alas I am undone, what shall I do? I have puld off his leg.
FAUSTUS.   O help, help, the villaine hath murder'd me.
HORSE-COURSER.   Murder or not murder, now he has but one
    leg, I'le out-run him, and cast this leg into some ditch or
    other.

                                                            [*Exit.*]

FAUSTUS.   Stop him, stop him, stop him—ha, ha, ha, *Faustus*
    hath his leg againe, and the Horse-courser a bundle of hay
    for his forty Dollors.

                                                    [*Enter* WAGNER.]

    How now *Wagner* what newes with thee?
1500 WAGNER.   If it please you, the Duke of *Vanholt* doth earnestly
    entreate your company, and hath sent some of his men to
    attend you with provision fit for your journey.
FAUSTUS.   The Duke of *Vanholt's* an honourable Gentleman, and
    one to whom I must be no niggard of my cunning; Come,
    away.

                                                        [*Exeunt.*]

                        SCENE XV

        [*Enter* (ROBIN) *the* CLOWNE, DICK, HORSE-COURSER, *and a* CARTER.]

CARTER.   Come my Maisters, I'le bring you to the best beere in
    Europe, what ho, Hostis; where be these Whores?

                                                    [*Enter* HOSTIS.]

HOSTESSE.   How now, what lacke you? What my old Guesse?
   welcome.
ROBIN.   Sirra *Dick*, dost thou know why I stand so mute?
1510 DICK.   No *Robin*, why is't?
ROBIN.   I am eighteene pence on the score,° but say nothing,   *in debt*
   see if she have forgotten me.
HOSTESSE.   Who's this, that stands so solemnly by himselfe: what
   my old Guest?
ROBIN.   O Hostesse how do you? I hope my score stands still.
HOSTESSE.   I there's no doubt of that, for me thinkes you make
   no hast to wipe it out.
DICK.   Why Hostesse, I say, fetch us some Beere.
HOSTESSE.   You shall presently: look up into th' hall there ho.

                                                                                    [*Exit.*]

1520 DICK.   Come sirs, what shall we do now till mine Hostesse
   comes?
CARTER.   Marry sir, I'le tell you the bravest tale how a Conjurer
   serv'd me; you know Doctor *Fauster?*
HORSE-COURSER.   I, a plague take him, heere's some on's have
   cause to know him; did he conjure thee too?
CARTER.   I'le tell you how he serv'd me: As I was going to
   Wittenberge t'other day, with a loade of Hay, he met me,
   and asked me what he should give me for as much Hay as he
   could eate; now sir, I thinking that a little would serve his
   turne, bad him take as much as he would for three-farthings;
1530 so he presently gave me my mony, and fell to eating; and as
   I am a cursen° man, he never left eating, till he had eate up   *Christian*
   all my loade of hay.
ALL.   O monstrous, eate a whole load of Hay!
ROBIN.   Yes, yes, that may be; for I have heard of one, that ha's
   eate a load of logges.
HORSE-COURSER.   Now sirs, you shall heare how villanously he
   serv'd mee: I went to him yesterday to buy a horse of him,
   and he would by no meanes sell him under forty Dollors; so
   sir, because I knew him to be such a horse, as would run
   over hedge and ditch, and never tyre, I gave him his money;
1540 so when I had my horse, Doctor *Fauster* bad me ride him
   night and day, and spare him no time; but, quoth he, in any
   case ride him not into the water. Now sir, I thinking the
   horse had had some rare quality that he would not have me
   know of, what did I but rid him into a great river, and when
   I came just to the midst my horse vanisht away, and I sate
   straddling upon a bottle of Hay.
ALL.   O brave Doctor.
HORSE-COURSER.   But you shall heare how bravely I serv'd him
   for it; I went me home to his house, and there I found him
   asleepe; I kept a hallowing and whooping in his eares, but
1550 all could not wake him: I seeing that, tooke him by the leg,

and never rested pulling, till I had pul'd me his leg quite off,
and now 'tis at home in mine Hostry.

DICK.   And has the Doctor but one leg then? that's excellent,
for one of his devils turn'd me into the likenesse of an Apes
face.

CARTER.   Some more drinke Hostesse.

ROBIN.   Hearke you, we'le into another roome and drinke a
while, and then we'le go seeke out the Doctor.

[*Exeunt omnes.*]

SCENE XVI

[*Enter the* DUKE OF VANHOLT; *his* DUTCHES, FAUSTUS, *and* MEPHOSTOPHILIS.]

DUKE.   Thankes Maister Doctor, for these pleasant sights, nor
1560   know I how sufficiently to recompence your great deserts in
erecting this inchanted Castle in the Aire: the sight whereof
so delighted me, as nothing in the world could please me more.

FAUSTUS.   I do thinke my selfe my good Lord, highly recom-
penced, in that it pleaseth your grace to thinke but well of
that which *Faustus* hath performed. But gratious Lady, it may
be, that you have taken no pleasure in those sights; therefor
I pray you tell me, what is the thing you most desire to have?
be it in the world, it shall be yours: I have heard that great
bellyed women, do long for things, are rare and dainty.

1570   LADY.   True Maister Doctor, and since I finde you so kind I will
make knowne unto you what my heart desires to have, and
were it now Summer, as it is January, a dead time of the Winter, I would request no better meate, then a dish of ripe grapes.

FAUSTUS.   This is but a small matter: Go *Mephostophilis*, away.

[*Exit* MEPHOSTOPHILIS.]

Madam, I will do more then this for your content.

[*Enter* MEPHOSTOPHILIS *agen with the grapes.*]

Here, now taste yee these, they should be good, for they come
from a farre Country I can tell you.

DUKE.   This makes me wonder more then all the rest, that at
this time of the yeare, when every Tree is barren of his
1580   fruite, from whence you had these ripe grapes.

FAUSTUS.   Please it your grace, the yeare is divided into two circles over the whole world, so that when it is Winter with us,
in the contrary circle it is likewise Summer with them, as in
India, Saba, [111] and such Countries that lye farre East, where
they have fruit twice a yeare. From whence, by meanes of a

---

[111] Sheba, an ancient country in southern Arabia (now Yemen).

swift spirit that I have, I had these grapes brought as you
see.

LADY.   And trust me, they are the sweetest grapes that e're I tasted.

[*The* CLOWNES *bounce° at the gate, within.*]   bang

DUKE.   What rude disturbers have we at the gate?
Go pacifie their fury, set it ope,
1590   And then demand of them, what they would have.

[*They knocke againe, and call out to talke with* FAUSTUS.]

A SERVANT.   Why how now Maisters, what a coyle° is there?   disturbance
What is the reason you disturbe the Duke?
DICK.   We have no reason for it, therefore a fig for him.
SERVANT.   Why saucy varlets, dare you be so bold.
HORSE-COURSER.   I hope sir, we have wit enough to be more
bold then welcome.
SERVANT.   It appeares so, pray be bold else-where,
And trouble not the Duke.
DUKE.   What would they have?
1600 SERVANT.   They all cry out to speake with Doctor *Faustus.*
CARTER.   I, and we will speake with him.
DUKE.   Will you sir? Commit the Rascals.
DICK.   Commit with us, he were as good commit with his father,
as commit with us.
FAUSTUS.   I do beseech your grace let them come in,
They are good subject for a merrriment.
DUKE.   Do as thou wilt *Faustus,* I give thee leave.
FAUSTUS.   I thanke your grace.

[*Enter (*ROBIN*) the* CLOWNE, DICK, CARTER, *and* HORSE-COURSER.]

Why, how now my good friends?
'Faith you are too outragious,° but come neere,   violent
1610   I have procur'd your pardons: welcome all.
ROBIN.   Nay sir, we will be wellcome for our mony, and we will
pay for what we take: What ho, give's halfe a dosen of Beere
here, and be hang'd.
FAUSTUS.   Nay, hearke you, can you tell me where you are?
CARTER.   I marry can I, we are under heaven.
SERVANT.   I but sir sauce box,[112] know you in what place?
HORSE-COURSER.   I, I, the house is good enough to drink in:
Zons fill us some Beere, or we'll breake all the barrels in the
house, and dash out all your braines with your Bottles.
1620 FAUSTUS.   Be not so furious: come you shall have Beere.
My Lord, beseech you give me leave a while,
I'le gage° my credit, 'twill content your grace.   stake
DUKE.   With all my heart kind Doctor, please thy selfe,

---

[112] Someone who is impertinent, saucy.

Our servants, and our Courts at thy command.

FAUSTUS.   I humbly thanke your grace: then fetch some Beere.

HORSE-COURSER.   I mary, there spake a Doctor indeed, and
    'faith Ile drinke a health to thy woodden leg for that word.

FAUSTUS.   My woodden leg? what dost thou meane by that?

CARTER.   Ha, ha, ha, dost heare him *Dick,* he has forgot his
    legge.

1630 HORSE-COURSER.   I, I, he does not stand much upon° that.   *make much of*

FAUSTUS.   No faith, not much upon a woodden leg.

CARTER.   Good Lord, that flesh and bloud should be so fraile
    with your Worship: Do not you remember a Horse-courser
    you sold a horse to?

FAUSTUS.   Yes, I remember I sold one a horse.

CARTER.   And do you remember you bid he should not ride him
    into the water?

FAUSTUS.   Yes, I do verie well remember that.

CARTER.   And do you remember nothing of your leg?

1640 FAUSTUS.   No in good sooth.

CARTER.   And do you remember your curtesie.°   *courteous bow*

FAUSTUS.   I thank you sir.

CARTER.   'Tis not so much worth; I pray you tel me one thing.

FAUSTUS.   What's that?

CARTER.   Be both your legs bedfellowes every night together?

FAUSTUS.   Wouldst thou make a *Colossus*[113] of me, that thou ask-
    est me such questions?

CARTER.   No truelie sir, I would make nothing of you, but I
    would faine know that.

                    [*Enter* HOSTESSE (*brought hither by magic*) *with drinke.*]

1650 FAUSTUS.   Then I assure thee certainelie they are.

CARTER.   I thanke you, I am fully satisfied.

FAUSTUS.   But wherefore dost thou aske?

CARTER.   For nothing sir: but me thinkes you should have a
    wooden bedfellow of one of 'em.

HORSE-COURSER.   Why, do you heare sir, did not I pull off one
    of your legs when you were asleepe?

FAUSTUS.   But I have it againe now I am awake: looke you
    heere sir.

ALL.   O horrible, had the Doctor three legs?

CARTER.   Do you remember sir, how you cosened me and eat
1660 up my load of———

                                              [FAUSTUS *charmes him dumb.*]

DICK.   Do you remember how you made me weare an Apes———

                                              [FAUSTUS *charmes him dumb.*]

---

[113] The Colossus of Rhodes, a giant statute, whose legs were said to straddle the harbor
entrance.

HORSE-COURSER.   You whoreson conjuring scab, do you remember
how you cosened me with a ho——

> [FAUSTUS *charmes him dumb.*]

ROBIN.   Ha' you forgotten me? you thinke to carry it away with
your *Hey-passe,* and *Re-passe:*[114] do you remember the dogs
fa——

> [FAUSTUS *charmes him dumb. Exeunt* CLOWNES.]

HOSTESSE.   Who payes for the Ale? heare you Maister Doctor,
now you have sent away my guesse, I pray who shall pay me
for my A——?

> [FAUSTUS *charmes her dumb. Exit* HOSTESSE.]

LADY.   My Lord,
1670   We are much beholding to this learned man.
DUKE.   So are we Madam, which we will recompence
With all the love and kindnesse that we may.
His Artfull sport, drives all sad thoughts away.

> [*Exeunt.*]

SCENE XVII

[*Thunder and lightning: Enter devils with cover'd dishes;* MEPHOSTOPHILIS *leades
them into* FAUSTUS *Study: Then enter* WAGNER.]

WAGNER.   I think my Maister means to die shortly, he has made
his will, and given me his wealth, his house, his goods, and
store of golden plate; besides two thousands duckets° ready   *ducats*
coin'd: I wonder what he meanes, if death were nie, he
would not frolick thus: hee's now at supper with the schollers, where ther's such belly-cheere, as *Wagner* in his life nere
1680   saw the like: and see where they come, belike° the feast is   *no doubt*
done.

> [*Exit.*]

[*Enter* FAUSTUS, MEPHOSTOPHILIS, *and two or three* SCHOLLERS.]

1. SCHOLLER.   Master Doctor *Faustus,* since our conference
about faire Ladies, which was the beautifullest in all the
world, we have determin'd with our selves, that *Hellen of
Greece* was the admirablest Lady that ever liv'd: therefore
Master Doctor, if you will doe us so much favour, as to let us
see that peerelesse dame of *Greece,* whom all the world admires for Majesty, we should thinke our selves much beholding unto you.

---

[114] Terms used by a conjuror and juggler during their acts (like abracadabra).

FAUSTUS. Gentlemen,
  For that I know your friendship is unfain'd,
1690 And *Faustus* custome is not to deny
  The just requests of those that wish him well,
  You shall behold that peerelesse dame of *Greece,*
  No otherwaies for pompe or Majesty,
  Then when sir *Paris* crost the seas with her,
  And brought the spoyles to rich *Dardania:*[115]
  Be silent then, for danger is in words.

[*Musicke sound,* MEPHOSTOPHILIS *brings in* HELLEN, *she passeth over the stage.*]

2. SCHOLLER. Too simple is my wit to tell her worth,
  Whom all the world admires for majesty.
3. SCHOLLER. No marvel tho the angry Greekes pursu'd
1700 With tenne yeares warre the rape of such a queene,
  Whose heavenly beauty passeth all compare.
1. SCHOLLER. Now we have seene the pride of Natures worke,
  And only Paragon of excellence,
  Let us depart, and for this blessed sight
  Happy and blest be *Faustus* evermore.

[*Exeunt* SCHOLLERS.]

FAUSTUS. Gentlemen farewell: the same wish I to you.

[*Enter an* OLD MAN.]

OLD MAN. O gentle *Faustus* leave this damned Art,
  This Magicke, that will charme thy soule to hell,
  And quite bereave thee of salvation.
1710 Though thou hast now offended like a man,
  Doe not persever in it like a Divell;
  Yet, yet, thou hast an amiable soule,
  If sin by custome grow not into nature:
  Then *Faustus,* will repentance come too late,
  Then thou art banisht from the sight of heaven;
  No mortall can expresse the paines of hell.
  It may be this my exhortation
  Seemes harsh, and all unpleasant; let it not,
  For gentle sonne, I speake it not in wrath,
1720 Or envy of° thee, but in tender love,   *ill will toward*
  And pitty of thy future miserie.
  And so have hope, that this my kinde rebuke,
  Checking° thy body, may amend thy soule.   *warning*
FAUSTUS. Where art thou *Faustus?* wretch, what hast thou done?
  Damned art thou *Faustus,* damned, despaire and die,

---

[115] The city called Troy; it was built by Dardanus on the Hellespont (Dardanelles). The abduction of Helen, Queen of Sparta, by Paris, who carried her off to Troy, initiated the great epic event of the classical world.

[Mephostophilis *gives him a dagger.*]

Hell claimes his right, and with a roaring voyce,
Saies *Faustus* come, thine houre is almost come,
And *Faustus* now will come to do thee right.°							*pay you your rightful due*

[*Offers to stab himself.*]

Old Man.   Ah stay good *Faustus*, stay thy desperate steps.
1730	I see an Angell hover ore thy head,
	And with a vyoll full of pretious grace,
	Offers to poure the same into thy soule,
	Then call for mercy, and avoyd despaire.
Faustus.   Ah my sweete friend,
	I feele thy words to comfort my distressed soule,
	Leave me a while, to ponder on my sinnes.
Old Man.   *Faustus* I leave thee, but with griefe of heart,
	Fearing the enemy of thy haplesse soule.

[*Exit.*]

Faustus.   Accursed *Faustus*, where is mercy now?
1740	I do repent, and yet I doe despaire,
	Hell strives with grace for conquest in my breast:
	What shall I doe to shun the snares of death?
Mephostophilis.   Thou traytor *Faustus*, I arrest thy soule,
	For disobedience to my soveraigne Lord,
	Revolt,° or I'le in peece-meale tear thy flesh.						*restore your allegiance*
Faustus.   I do repent I ere offended him,
	Sweet *Mephostophilis*, intreat thy Lord
	To pardon my unjust presumption,
	And with my bloud againe I will confirme
1750	The former vow I made to *Lucifer*.
Mephostophilis. Do it then *Faustus*, with unfained° heart,						*honest*
	Lest greater dangers do attend thy drift.°							*drifting*
Faustus.   Torment sweet friend, that base and crooked age,
	That durst disswade me from thy *Lucifer*,
	With greatest torments that our hell affoords.
Mephostophilis.   His faith is great, I cannot touch his soule;
	But what I may afflict his body with,
	I will attempt, which is but little worth.
Faustus.   One thing good servant let me crave of thee,
1760	To glut the longing of my hearts desire,
	That I may have unto my paramour,
	That heavenly *Hellen*, which I saw of late,
	Whose sweet embraces may extinguish cleare,
	Those thoughts that do disswade me from my vow,
	And keepe mine oath I made to *Lucifer*.
Mephostophilis.   This, or what else my *Faustus* shall desire,
	Shall be perform'd in twinkling of an eye.

[*Enter* Hellen *againe, passing over betweene two* Cupids.]

FAUSTUS. Was this the face that Launcht a thousand ships,
And burnt the toplesse Towers of *Ilium?*°   *Troy*
1770 Sweet *Hellen,* make me immortall with a kisse:
Her lips sucke forth my soule, see where it flies.
Come *Hellen,* come, give me my soule againe,
Here will I dwell, for heaven is in these lippes,
And all is drosse that is not *Helena.*

[*Enter* OLD MAN (*aloof*).]

I will be *Paris,* and for love of thee,
In stead of *Troy* shall *Wittenberg* be sack't,
And I will combat with weake *Menelaus,*[116]
And weare thy colours on my plumed crest.
Yea, I will wound *Achilles* in the heele,[117]
1780 And then returne to *Hellen* for a kisse.
O thou art fairer then the evenings aire,
Clad in the beauty of a thousand starres:
Brighter art thou then flaming *Jupiter,*
When he appear'd to haplesse *Semele:*[118]
More lovely then the Monarch of the sky,
In wanton *Arethusa's* azur'd armes,[119]
And none but thou shalt be my Paramour.

[*Exeunt.*]

OLD MAN. Accursed *Faustus,* miserable man,
That from thy soule exclud'st the grace of heaven,
1790 And fliest the throne of his tribunall seate.

[*Enter the* DIVELLES.]

Sathan begins to sift me with his pride:
As in this furnace God shal try my faith,
My faith, vile hel, shall triumph over thee,
Ambitious fiends, see how the heavens smiles
At your repulse, and laughs your state to scorne,
Hence hel, for hence I flie unto my God.

[*Exeunt.*]

---

[116] Helen's husband.
[117] Achilles was the greatest warrior at Troy. He was killed when Paris shot him in the heel with a poison arrow. The heel was Achilles's single vulnerable part; it had been left unprotected when his mother dipped him in the river Styx to render him invulnerable to attack.
[118] Semele was killed by lightning when her lover Jupiter (Zeus) appeared before her in all his divine glory.
[119] The particular episode referred to here is unclear. Arethusa was a wood nymph who became transformed into a spring.

SCENE XVIII

[*Thunder. Enter (above)* Lucifer, Belzebub, *and* Mephostophilis.]

LUCIFER.   Thus from infernall *Dis°* do we ascend   *Hades*
 To view the subjects of our Monarchy,
 Those soules which sinne seales the blacke sonnes of hell,
1800 'Mong which as chiefe, *Faustus* we come to thee,
 Bringing with us lasting damnation,
 To wait upon thy soule; the time is come
 Which makes it forfeit.
MEPHOSTOPHILIS.   And this gloomy night,
 Here in this roome will wretched *Faustus* be.
BELZEBUB.   And here wee'l stay,
 To marke him now he doth demeane himselfe.
MEPHOSTOPHILIS.   How should he, but in desperate lunacie.
 Fond worldling, now his heart bloud dries with griefe;
 His conscience kils it, and his labouring braine,
1810 Begets a world of idle fantasies,
 To over-reach the Divell, but all in vaine;
 His store of pleasures must be sauc'd with paine.
 He and his servant *Wagner* are at hand,
 Both come from drawing *Faustus* latest will.
 See where they come.

            [*Enter* Faustus *and* Wagner.]

FAUSTUS.   Say *Wagner*, thou hast perus'd my will,
 How dost thou like it?
WAGNER.   Sir, so wondrous well,
 As in all humble dutie, I do yeeld
 My life and lasting service for your love.

            [*Enter the* Schollers.]

1820 FAUSTUS.   Gramercies° *Wagner*. Welcome gentlemen.   *thank you*

            [*Exit* Wagner.]

1. SCHOLLER.   Now worthy *Faustus:* me thinks your looks are
 chang'd.
FAUSTUS.   Ah gentlemen.
2. SCHOLLER.   What ailes *Faustus?*
FAUSTUS.   Ah my sweet chamber-fellow, had I liv'd with thee, then
 had I lived still, but now must dye eternally.
 Looke sirs, comes he not, comes he not?
1. SCHOLLER.   O my deere *Faustus* what imports this feare?
2. SCHOLLER.   Is all our pleasure turn'd to melancholy?
3. SCHOLLER.   He is not well with being over solitarie.
1830 2. SCHOLLER.   If it be so, wee'l have Physitians,
 And *Faustus* shall bee cur'd.
3. SCHOLLER.   Tis but a surfet sir, feare nothing.

FAUSTUS.   A surfet of deadly sin, that hath damn'd both body
and soule.

2. SCHOLLER.   Yet *Faustus* looke up to heaven, and remember
Gods mercy is infinite.

FAUSTUS.   But *Faustus* offence can nere be pardoned, the serpent that tempted *Eve* may be saved, but not *Faustus*. Ah
gentlemen, heare me with patience, and tremble not at my
1840   speeches. Though my heart pant and quiver to remember
that I have beene a student here these thirty yeares, O would
I had never seene *Wittenberg*, never read book: and what
wonders I have done, all *Germany* can witnesse, yea all the
world: for which *Faustus* hath lost both *Germany* and the
world, yea heaven it selfe: heaven the seate of God, the
Throne of the Blessed, the Kingdome of Joy, and must remaine in hell for ever. Hell, ah hell for ever. Sweet friends,
what shall become of *Faustus* being in hell for ever?

2. SCHOLLER.   Yet *Faustus* call on God.

FAUSTUS.   On God, whom *Faustus* hath abjur'd? on God, whom
1850   *Faustus* hath blasphem'd? Ah my God, I would weepe, but
the Divell drawes in my teares. Gush forth bloud in stead of
teares, yea life and soule: oh hee stayes my tongue: I would
lift up my hands, but see they hold 'em, they hold 'em.

ALL.   Who, *Faustus?*

FAUSTUS.   Why, *Lucifer* and *Mephostophilis:*
Ah gentlemen, I gave them my soule for my cunning.

ALL.   O God forbid.

FAUSTUS.   God forbade it indeed, but *Faustus* hath done it: for
the vaine pleasure of foure and twenty yeares hath *Faustus*
1860   lost eternall joy and felicitie. I writ them a bill° with mine   deed
owne bloud, the date is expired: this is the time, and he will
fetch mee.

1. SCHOLLER.   Why did not *Faustus* tell us of this before, that
Divines might have prayd for thee?

FAUSTUS.   Oft have I thought to have done so: but the Divel
threatned to teare me in peeces if I nam'd God: to fetch me
body and soule, if I once gave eare to Divinitie: and now 'tis
too late. Gentlemen away, least you perish with me.

2. SCHOLLER.   O what may we do to save *Faustus?*

FAUSTUS.   Talke not of me, but save your selves and depart.

1870 3. SCHOLLER.   God will strengthen me, I will stay with *Faustus.*

1. SCHOLLER.   Tempt not God sweet friend, but let us into the
next roome, and there pray for him.

FAUSTUS.   I, pray for me, pray for me: and what noyse soever
you heare, come not unto me, for nothing can rescue me.

2. SCHOLLER.   Pray thou, and we will pray, that God may have
mercie upon thee.

FAUSTUS.   Gentlemen farewell: if I live till morning, Il'e visit
you: if not, *Faustus* is gone to hell.

ALL.   *Faustus*, farewell.

[Exeunt SCHOLLERS.]

[Enter MEPHOSTOPHILIS *below.]*

1880 MEPHOSTOPHILIS.   I, *Faustus,* now thou hast no hope of heaven,
  Therefore despaire, thinke onely upon hell;
  For that must be thy mansion, there to dwell.
FAUSTUS.   O thou bewitching fiend, 'twas thy temptation,
  Hath rob'd me of eternall happinesse.
MEPHOSTOPHILIS.   I doe confesse it *Faustus,* and rejoyce;
  'Twas I, that when thou wer't i'the way to heaven,
  Damb'd up thy passage; when thou took'st the booke,
  To view the Scriptures, then I turn'd the leaves
  And led thine eye.
1890   What, weep'st thou? 'tis too late, despaire, farewell,
  Fooles that will laugh on earth, must weepe in hell.

[Exit.]

[Enter the GOOD ANGEL, *and the* BAD ANGELL *at severall doores.]*

GOOD ANGEL.   Oh *Faustus,* if thou hadst given eare to me,
  Innumerable joyes had followed thee.
  But thou didst love the world.
BAD ANGEL.   Gave eare to me,
  And now must taste hels paines perpetually.
GOOD ANGEL.   O what will all thy riches, pleasures, pompes,
  Availe thee now?
BAD ANGEL.   Nothing but vexe thee more,
  To want in hell, that had on earth such store.

[Musicke while the Throne descends.]

GOOD ANGEL.   O thou hast lost celestiall happinesse,
1900   Pleasures unspeakeable, blisse without end.
  Hadst thou affected° sweet divinitie,   *devoted yourself to*
  Hell, or the Divell, had had no power on thee.
  Hadst thou kept on that way, *Faustus* behold,
  In what resplendant glory thou hadst set
  In yonder throne, like those bright shining Saints,
  And triumpht over hell: that hast thou lost,
  And now poore soule must thy good Angell leave thee,
  The jawes of hell are open to receive thee.

[Exit. Throne ascends. Hell is discovered.]

BAD ANGEL.   Now *Faustus* let thine eyes with horror stare
1910   Into that vaste perpetuall torture-house,
  There are the Furies tossing damned soules,
  On burning forkes: their bodies boyle in lead.
  There are live quarters broyling on the coles,
  That ner'e can die: this ever-burning chaire,

Is for ore-tortur'd soules to rest them in.
These, that are fed with soppes of flaming fire,
Were gluttons, and lov'd only delicates,
And laught to see the poore starve at their gates:
But yet all these are nothing, thou shalt see
1920   Ten thousand tortures that more horrid be.
FAUSTUS. O, I have seene enough to torture me.
BAD ANGEL. Nay, thou must feele them, taste the smart of all:
He that loves pleasure, must for pleasure fall.
And so I leave thee *Faustus* till anon,
Then wilt thou tumble in confusion.

                            [*Exit. Hell closes. The Clock strikes eleven.*]

FAUSTUS. Ah *Faustus*,
Now hast thou but one bare houre to live,
And then thou must be damn'd perpetually.
Stand still you ever moving Spheares of heaven,
1930   That time may cease, and midnight never come.
Faire natures eye, rise, rise againe and make
Perpetuall day: or let this houre be but
A yeare, a month, a weeke, a naturall day,
That *Faustus* may repent, and save his soule.
O lente lente currite noctis equi:[120]
The Stars move still, Time runs, the Clocke will strike,
The devill will come, and *Faustus* must be damn'd.
O I'le leape up to my God: who puls me downe?
See see where Christs bloud streames in the firmament,
1940   One drop would save my soule, halfe a drop, ah my Christ.
Rend not my heart, for naming of my Christ,
Yet will I call on him: O spare me *Lucifer*.
Where is it now? 'tis gone. And see where God
Stretcheth out his Arme, and bends his irefull Browes:
Mountaines and Hils, come, come, and fall on me,
And hide me from the heavy wrath of God.
No, no?
Then will I headlong run into the earth:
Gape earth; O no, it will not harbour me.
1950   You Starres that raign'd at my nativity,
Whose influence hath allotted death and hell;
Now draw up *Faustus* like a foggy mist,
Into the entrals of yon labouring cloud,
That when you vomite forth into the aire,
My limbes may issue from your smoky mouthes,
So that my soule may but ascend to heaven.

                            [*The Watch° strikes.*] *clock*

---

[120] The quotation is adapted from Ovid's *Amores:* "Go slowly, slowly, you horses of the night."

Ah halfe the houre is past: 'twill all be past anone:
O God, if thou wilt not have mercy on my soule,
Yet for Christs sake, whose bloud hath ransom'd me,
1960   Impose some end to my incessant paine:
Let *Faustus* live in hell a thousand yeares,
A hundred thousand, and at last be sav'd.
No end is limited° to damned soules.   *fixed*
Why wert thou not a creature wanting soule?
Or why is this immortall that thou hast?
Ah *Pythagoras Metemsycosis;*[121] were that true,
This soule should flie with me, and I be chang'd
Unto some brutish beast.
All beasts are happy, for when they die,
1970   Their soules are soone dissolv'd in elements,
But mine must live still to be plagu'd in hell.
Curst be the parents that ingendred me;
No *Faustus,* curse thy selfe, curse *Lucifer,*
That hath depriv'd thee of the joies of heaven.

                 [*The clocke striketh twelve.*]

It strikes, it strikes; now body turne to aire,
Or *Lucifer* will beare thee quicke° to hell.   *living*
O soule be chang'd into little water drops,
And fall into the Ocean, ne're be found.

               [*Thunder, and enter the devils.*]

My God, my God, looke not so fierce on me;
1980   Adders and serpents, let me breathe a while:
Ugly hell gape not; come not *Lucifer,*
I'le burne my bookes; ah *Mephostophilis.*

                     [*Exeunt with him.*]

           [*Exeunt* LUCIFER *and devils above.*]

SCENE XIX

                    [*Enter the* SCHOLLERS.]

1. SCHOLLER.   Come Gentlemen, let us go visit *Faustus,*
For such a dreadful night, was never seene,
Since first the worlds creation did begin.
Such fearefull shrikes, and cries, were never heard,
Pray heaven the Doctor have escapt the danger.
2. SCHOLLER.   O help us heaven, see, here are *Faustus* limbs,
All torne asunder by the hand of death.

---

[121] The Greek philosopher Pythagoras (d. ca. 497 B.C.) was associated with the belief in metempsychosis, the transmigration of souls.

1990 3. SCHOLLER.   The devils whom *Faustus* serv'd have torne him thus:
       For twixt the houres of twelve and one, me thought
       I heard him shreeke and call aloud for helpe:
       At which selfe time the house seem'd all on fire,
       With dreadfull horror of these damned fiends.
    2. SCHOLLER.   Well Gentlemen, tho *Faustus* end be such
       As every Christian heart laments to thinke on:
       Yet for he was a Scholler, once admired
       For wondrous knowledge in our Germane schooles,°   *universities*
       We'll give his mangled limbs due buryall:
2000   And all the Students clothed in mourning blacke,
       Shall waite upon° his heavy° funerall.   *attend/sad*

                                                                          [*Exeunt.*]

                                                                    [*Enter* CHORUS.]
                                                                         [CHORUS 4.]

CHORUS.   Cut is the branch that might have growne full straight,
       And burned is *Apollo's* Lawrell bough,
       That sometime° grew within this learned man: *at one time*
       Faustus is gone, regard his hellish fall,
       Whose fiendfull fortune may exhort the wise
       Onely to wonder at unlawfull things,
       Whose deepnesse doth intice such forward wits,
       To practise more then heavenly power permits.

                                                                             [*Exit.*]

              Terminat hora diem, Terminat Author opus.[122]
                              FINIS
                                                                          [ca. 1589]

Critical Commentary on *Doctor Faustus*

Christopher Marlowe's *Doctor Faustus* (ca. 1588–1589), a play now generally
regarded as the first great Elizabethan tragedy, is indebted for its plot as well
as for many of its most distinctive details (including the comic material of the
middle scenes) to the English translation of a slender book titled *The History
of the Damnable Life and Deserved Death of Doctor John Faustus,* originally published in Frankfurt, Germany, in 1587. The "Faust Book," as it came to be
known, purported to tell the "history" of an itinerant scholar and conjuror of
the early sixteenth century named Georg or Johannes Faustus, whose shadowy existence had been associated with many of the legendary stories about
witchcraft and the black arts that have been circulating in Europe for centuries. Not surprisingly, the story of Faustus's blasphemy and punishment

---

[122] "The hour ends the day, the author ends his work."

enjoyed enormous popularity among the clergy of the Protestant Reformation, who saw it as a convenient and powerful weapon with which to instill a healthy fear of evil and combat religious skepticism.

Doctor Faustus also draws heavily on the tradition of the medieval morality play, a tradition that Marlowe's Elizabethan audiences both immediately recognized and understood. The story of a man who sells his soul in return for twenty-four years of pleasure and then is banished to eternal damnation (together with such stock characters as the Good Angel, the Bad Angel, the parade of the Seven Deadly Sins, and the Old Man who pleads with Faustus to repent) clearly belongs to the tradition that produced plays like *Mankind* and *Everyman*.

Had Marlowe been content simply to repeat the story of the "Faust Book," or to dramatize that story in the manner of his medieval predecessors, it is doubtful that his play would be remembered for anything but its color and theatricality. The world of the medieval morality play is thoroughly predictable. The universe it presents is a divinely ordered and moral one, in which a benevolent God offers to all men the promise of salvation through the redemptive love of Christ. Moral issues and moral choices are immediately recognizable and clear cut.

The world of Christopher Marlowe's *Doctor Faustus,* by contrast, is anything but secure and settled. It is, rather, a place of genuine terror and tragedy. Although from the point of view of Christian orthodoxy Marlowe's play may have a satisfactory ending (Faustus, having completed his twenty-four allotted years is indeed carried off to hell), Marlowe's play does not simply repeat the moral patterns and reach the comfortable moral conclusions of *Mankind* and *Everyman*. What gives *Doctor Faustus* its power, and its final meaning, is Marlowe's ability to use his main character to explore the tensions and contradictions that lie at the heart of the Hebraic-Christian view of the universe as that view collided with the emerging aspirations unleashed by the English Renaissance. By focusing the central attention of the play not upon external events but inwardly upon on the deeply divided soul of Faustus himself, Marlowe produced not only the first great blank verse tragedy of the Elizabethan England, but a play which Richard B. Sewall has called the first great Christian tragedy.

Marlowe's Faustus is a Promethean character, who embodies the Renaissance spirit of restless curiosity and risk-taking. He longs to explore the geographical and intellectual boundaries of the age to the point of being willing to defy (and attempt to transcend) the limitations of the human condition. Marlowe was clearly fascinated by the heroic aspects of Faustus's search: by the soaring sweep of his imagination, by his belief in the infinite capacity of the human mind, and by his genuine willingness to risk everything—including human damnation—to reach beyond the known.

The tragedy of *Doctor Faustus* does not, however, lie in the search itself, or even in the defeated pride and arrogance of its hero. Rather, the essential tragedy of Marlowe's *Doctor Faustus* lies within Faustus himself. What finally renders Faustus a tragic hero is the fact that by the end of the play he has come to learn, as Richard B. Sewall notes,

the truth of his own nature—a truth which it was his peculiar Renaissance compulsion to forget or deny: that he is creature as well as creator; a man and not a god; a dependent, responsible part of a greater whole. He learns that his soul is not a mere trifle of his own, to use as a commodity, and that "contrition, prayer, repentance," hell and damnation, are not (as the Evil Angel told him) . . . "illusions, fruits of lunacy, / That make men foolish that do trust them most."

It is in his final awareness—the knowledge that, consumed by the sense of his own omnipotence, he has isolated himself from both his fellow men and from his God—that Faustus becomes most humanized and thereby achieves the status of a tragic hero. The central dramatic tension of the play can perhaps best be summarized as the tension between the spirit of the Renaissance which would propel men boldly forward to some unknown destiny and the older Christian orthodoxy with its emphasis on human limitations and imperfections that hold man back.

Students of *Doctor Faustus* are also called upon to deal with the problem of the play's "middle." Although it is almost universally agreed that the play's beginning and ending are strong and illustrate Marlowe at his dramatic best, the middle sections of the play, by contrast, are often characterized as being weak, haphazard, and disconnected—a clear violation of the Aristotelian premise that a play's middle must serve to further the development of the plot. The middle of *Doctor Faustus*, with its intrusion of low comedy, burlesque, and slapstick, it is often said, serves no such structural function. Though these scenes may succeed as theatrical spectacle (accomplished in the Elizabethan theater with the aid of trap doors and smokepots), the basic triviality of their content, so the argument goes, serves only to weaken the play's sense of dignity and tragedy. One convenient way out of this dilemma (and a way that many commentators have chosen) is simply to dismiss these scenes as the work of Marlowe's successors, for it has long been known that the text of the play, not published until after Marlowe's death, exists only in mutilated form. In a very real sense, however, to dismiss these scenes entirely is to dismiss the play.

These middle scenes do, to be sure, have their defenders. They argue that far from being superfluous these scenes serve effectively to develop Faustus's character, intensify his inner conflict, and dramatize effectively the stages of his decline and progressive disintegration. The middle scenes not only throw the play's beginning and end into sharp relief but thoroughly expose the essential tawdriness and final emptiness of the way of life that Faustus has chosen. Without them, Doctor Faustus's development and the meaning of his experience would remain unclear and incomplete. The middle scenes, in short, as Cleanth Brooks and Robert Heilman argue, "present the conduct by which Faustus comes to deserve his fate, and they become what we may call a 'moral middle.' "

Flaws and all, Marlowe's *Doctor Faustus* remains a powerful play—and its final climactic scene surely ranks as one of the greatest in all of Elizabethan drama. In fact, Marlowe's gifts were so great and his life so short that we are inevitably left to ponder what might have been—particularly if Marlowe had been like Shakespeare a playwright who reached his maturity relatively late and then maintained those gifts in full creative flower for two decades.

The text for the play is taken from Fredson Bowers's authoritative edition of *The Complete Works of Christopher Marlowe,* Volume II (Cambridge University Press, 1973). Bowers based his edition on the so-called B-text version of 1616, with some emendations from the earlier 1604 "bad Quarto" or A-text version of the play.

A Selective Bibliography on *Doctor Faustus*

Bloom, Harold, ed. *Christopher Marlowe's Doctor Faustus.* New York: Chelsea House, 1988.

Bowers, Fredson. "The Text of Marlowe's Faustus," *Modern Philology* 69 (1952): 195–204.

Cox, Gerald H., III. "Marlowe's *Doctor Faustus* and 'Sin against the Holy Ghost.' " *Huntington Library Quarterly* 36 (1973): 119–37.

Cutts, John P. *The Left Hand of God: A Critical Interpretation of the Plays of Christopher Marlowe.* Haddonfield, N.J.: Haddonfield House, 1973. 108–48.

Farnham, Willard, ed. *Twentieth Century Interpretations of Doctor Faustus.* Englewood Cliffs, N.J.: Prentice-Hall, 1969.

French, A. L. "Philosophy of Doctor Faustus." *Essays in Criticism* 20 (1970): 123–42 and 21 (1971): 101–6.

Giamatti, Bartlett. "Marlowe: The Arts of Illusion." *Yale Review* 61 (1972); 530–43.

Honderich, Pauline. "John Calvin and Doctor Faustus." *Modern Language Review* 68 (1973): 1–13.

Kirschbaum, Leo. "Marlowe's *Faustus:* A Reconsideration." *Review of English Studies* 19 (1943): 225–41.

Kocher, Paul H. "Witchcraft Basis in Marlowe's *Faustus.*" *Modern Philology* 38 (1940): 9–36.

Kuriyama, Constance Brown. *Hammer or Anvil: Psychological Patterns in Christopher Marlowe's Plays.* New Brunswick, N.J.: Rutgers UP, 1980. 95–136.

Longo, Joseph A. "Marlowe's *Doctor Faustus:* Allegorical Parody in Act Five." *Greyfriar* 15 (1974): 38–49.

Manley, Frank. "The Nature of Faustus." *Modern Philology* 66 (1969): 218–31.

Matalene, H. W. "Marlowe's Faustus and the Comforts of Academicism." *Journal of English Literary History* 39 (1972): 495–520.

O'Brien, Margaret A. "Christian Belief in *Doctor Faustus.*" *Journal of English Literary History* 37 (1970): 1–11.

Pettitt, Thomas. "Formulaic Dramaturgy in *Doctor Faustus.*" *A Poet and a Filthy Playmaker: New Essays on Christopher Marlowe.* Eds. Kenneth Friedenreich, Roma Gill, and Constance B. Kuriyama. New York: AMS, 1988. 167–91.

Pinciss, Gerald. *Christopher Marlowe.* New York: Ungar, 1975. 69–91.

Ricks, Christopher. "*Doctor Faustus* and Hell on Earth." *Essays in Criticism* 35 (1985): 101–20.

Sanders, Wilbur. *The Dramatist and the Received Idea: Studies in the Plays of Marlowe and Shakespeare.* Cambridge, Eng.: Cambridge UP, 1968. 205–52.

Sewall, Richard B. *The Vision of Tragedy.* 2nd ed. New Haven: Yale UP, 1980. 57–67.

Shepherd, Simon. *Marlowe and the Politics of Elizabethan Theatre.* Brighton, Eng.: Harvester, 1986. 91–98, 134–41.

Snow, Edward A. "Marlowe's *Doctor Faustus* and the Ends of Desire." *Two Renaissance*

Mythmakers: Christopher Marlowe and Ben Jonson. Ed. Alvin Kernan. Baltimore: Johns Hopkins UP, 1977. 70–110.

Snyder, Susan. "Marlowe's Doctor Faustus as an Inverted Saint's Life." *Studies in Philology* 63 (1966): 565–77.

Steane, J. B. *Marlowe: A Critical Study.* Cambridge, Eng.: Cambridge UP, 1964. 154–65.

Stockholder, Kay. " 'Within the massy entrailes of the earth': Faustus's Relation to Women," *"A Poet and a Filthy Play-maker": New Essays on Christopher Marlowe.* Eds. Kenneth Friedenreich, Roma Gill, and Constance B. Kuriyama. New York: AMS, 1988. 203–19.

Stroup, Thomas B. "Doctor Faustus and Hamlet: Contrasting Kinds of Christian Tragedy." *Comparative Drama* 5 (1971–1972): 243–53.

West, Robert H. "The Impatient Magic of *Doctor Faustus.*" *English Literary Renaissance* 4 (1974): 218–40.

Westlund, Joseph. "The Orthodox Christian Framework of Marlowe's *Faustus.*" *Studies in English Literature* 3 (1963): 191–205.

Wyman, Linda. "How Plot and Sub-Plot Unite in Marlowe's *Faust.*" *CEA Critic,* 37 (1974): 14–16.

William Shakespeare (1564–1616)
A MIDSUMMER NIGHT'S DREAM

CHARACTERS

THESEUS, *Duke of Athens*

EGEUS, *Father to* HERMIA

LYSANDER ⎫
DEMETRIUS ⎭ *in love with* HERMIA

PHILOSTRATE, *Master of the Revels to*
    THESEUS

QUINCE, *a Carpenter*

SNUG, *a Joiner*

BOTTOM, *a Weaver*

FLUTE, *a Bellows-mender*

SNOUT, *a Tinker*

STARVELING, *a Tailor*

HIPPOLYTA, *Queen of the Amazons,*
    betrothed to THESEUS

HERMIA, *in love with* LYSANDER

HELENA, *in love with* DEMETRIUS

OBERON, *King of the Fairies*

TITANIA, *Queen of the Fairies*

PUCK *or* ROBIN-GOODFELLOW

PEAS-BLOSSOM ⎫
COBWEB   ⎪
MOTH   ⎬ *Fairies*
MUSTARD-SEED ⎭

PYRAMUS ⎫
THISBE   ⎪ *Characters in the*
WALL   ⎬ *Interlude performed*
MOONSHINE ⎪ *by the "rude*
LION   ⎭ *mechanicals"*

Other Fairies attending their Queen
    and King

Attendants *on* THESEUS *and*
    HIPPOLYTA

SCENE: *Athens; and a Wood near it.*

ACT I

SCENE I

ATHENS.   *A Room in the Palace of* THESEUS.

[*Enter* THESEUS, HIPPOLYTA, PHILOSTRATE, *and* Attendants.]

THESEUS.   Now, fair Hippolyta, our nuptial hour
  Draws on apace; four happy days bring in
  Another moon: but, oh, methinks, how slow
  This old moon wanes! she lingers° my desires,   *delays*
  Like to a step-dame, or a dowager,
  Long withering out a young man's revenue.[1]
HIPPOLYTA.   Four days will quickly steep themselves in°   *be swallowed up in*
    nights;

---

[1] The allusion is to a stepmother or a widow who draws upon her deceased husband's estate thus depleting the son's inheritance.

Four nights will quickly dream away the time;
And then the moon, like to a silver bow

10 New bent in heaven, shall behold the night
Of our solemnities.

THESEUS.   Go, Philostrate,
Stir up the Athenian youth to merriments;
Awake the pert° and nimble spirit of mirth: *lively*
Turn melancholy forth to funerals,—
The pale companion is not for our pomp.°   *celebration*

[*Exit* PHILOSTRATE.]

Hippolyta, I woo'd thee with my sword,
And won thy love, doing thee injuries;
But I will wed thee in another key,

20 With pomp, with triumph,° and with revelling.   *festive entertainment*

[*Enter* EGEUS, HERMIA, LYSANDER, *and* DEMETRIUS.]

EGEUS.   Happy be Theseus, our renownèd duke!
THESEUS.   Thanks, good Egeus: what's the news with thee!
EGEUS.   Full of vexation come I, with complaint
Against my child, my daughter Hermia.—
Stand forth, Demetrius.—My noble lord,
This man hath my consent to marry her.—
Stand forth, Lysander:—and, my gracious duke,
This man hath bewitch'd the bosom of my child:—
Thou, thou, Lysander, thou hast given her rhymes,

30 And interchang'd love-tokens with my child:
Thou hast by moon-light at her window sung,
With feigning voice, verses of feigning love;
And stol'n th' impression of her fantasy
With bracelets of thy hair, rings, gawds,° conceits,°   *bits of finery/fancy articles*
Knacks,° trifles, nosegays, sweet-meats (messengers   *knick knacks*
Of strong prevailment° in unharden'd youth):   *influence*
With cunning hast thou filch'd my daughter's heart;
Turn'd her obedience, which is due to me,
To stubborn harshness:—and, my gracious duke,

40 Be it so she will not here before your grace
Consent to marry with Demetrius,
I beg the ancient privilege of Athens,—
As she is mine, I may dispose of her:
Which shall be either to this gentleman,
Or to her death, according to our law
Immediately provided° in that case.   *expressly stipulated*

THESEUS.   What say you, Hermia? be advis'd, fair maid:
To you your father should be as a god;
One that compos'd your beauties; yea, and one

50 To whom you are but as a form in wax,
By him imprinted, and within his power
To leave the figure, or disfigure° it.   *destroy*
Demetrius is a worthy gentleman.

HERMIA. So is Lysander.

THESEUS.   In himself he is;

    But, in this kind, wanting your father's voice,

    The other must be held the worthier.

HERMIA.   I would my father look'd but with my eyes.

THESEUS.   Rather, your eyes must with his judgment look.

60 HERMIA.   I do entreat your grace to pardon me.

    I know not by what power I am made bold,

    Nor how it may concern° my modesty,   *befit*

    In such a presence here, to plead my thoughts;

    But I beseech your grace, that I may know

    The worst that may befall me in this case,

    If I refuse to wed Demetrius.

THESEUS.   Either to die the death,° or to abjure   *be put to death*

    For ever the society of men.

    Therefore, fair Hermia, question your desires;

70   Know of your youth, examine well your blood,°   *feelings*

    Whether, if you yield not to your father's choice,

    You can endure the livery° of a nun;   *habit*

    For aye to be in shady cloister mew'd,°   *shut up, confined*

    To live a barren sister all your life,

    Chanting faint hymns to the cold fruitless moon.

    Thrice blessèd they, that master so their blood,

    To undergo such maiden pilgrimage;

    But earthlier happy is the rose distill'd,°   *reduced to its essence*

    Than that which, withering on the virgin thorn

80   Grows, lives, and dies, in single blessedness.

HERMIA. So will I grow, so live, so die, my lord,

    Ere I will yield my virgin patent° up   *right to my virginity*

    Unto his lordship, whose unwishèd yoke

    My soul consents not to give sovereignty.

THESEUS. Take time to pause; and, by the next new moon,—

    The sealing-day betwixt my love and me

    For everlasting bond of fellowship,—

    Upon that day either prepare to die

    For disobedience to your father's will,

90   Or else to wed Demetrius, as he would;

    Or on Diana's altar to protest,°   *vow*

    For aye, austerity° and single life.   *abstinence*

DEMETRIUS. Relent, sweet Hermia:—and, Lysander, yield

    Thy crazèd° title to my certain right.   *unsound*

LYSANDER. You have her father's love, Demetrius;

    Let me have Hermia's: do you marry him.

EGEUS. Scornful Lysander! true, he hath my love,—

    And what is mine my love shall render him;

    And she is mine, and all my right of her

100   I do estate unto° Demetrius.   *bestow upon*

LYSANDER. I am, my lord, as well deriv'd° as he,   *as of good an ancestry*

    As well possess'd;° my love is more than his;   *endowed*

    My fortunes every way as fairly rank'd

(If not with vantage,°) as Demetrius';   *indeed better*
And, which is more than all these boasts can be,
I am belov'd of beauteous Hermia:
Why should not I, then, prosecute my right?
Demetrius, I'll avouch it to his head,°   *to his face*
Made love to Nedar's daughter, Helena,
110 And won her soul; and she, sweet lady, dotes,
Devoutly dotes, dotes in idolatry,
Upon this spotted° and inconstant man.   *blemished*
THESEUS.   I must confess that I have heard so much,
And with Demetrius thought to have spoke thereof;
But, being over-full of self-affairs,°   *my own concerns*
My mind did lose it.—But, Demetrius, come;
And come, Egeus: you shall go with me,
I have some private schooling for you both.—
For you, fair Hermia, look you arm° yourself   *ready*
120 To fit your fancies to your father's will;
Or else the law of Athens yields you up
(Which by no means we may extenuate)°   *mitigate*
To death, or to a vow of single life.—
Come, my Hippolyta: what cheer, my love?—
Demetrius, and Egeus, go along:
I must employ you in some business
Against° our nuptial; and confer with you   *in preparation for*
Of something nearly° that concerns yourselves.   *closely*
EGEUS.   With duty and desire we follow you.

[*Exeunt* THESEUS, HIPPOLYTA, DEMETRIUS, *and train.*]

130 LYSANDER.   How now, my love! Why is your cheek so pale?
How chance the roses there do fade so fast?
HERMIA.   Belike,° for want of rain, which I could well   *probably*
Beteem° them from the tempest of mine eyes.   *grant*
LYSANDER.   Ah me! for aught that ever I could read,
Could ever hear by tale or history,
The course of true love never did run smooth:
But, either it was different in blood,°—   *parentage*
HERMIA.   O cross! too high to be enthrall'd to low!
LYSANDER.   Or else misgraffèd° in respect of years,—   *badly matched*
140 HERMIA.   O spite! too old to be engag'd to young!
LYSANDER.   Or else it stood upon the choice of friends,—
HERMIA.   O hell! to choose love by another's eye!
LYSANDER.   Or, if there were a sympathy° in choice,   *agreement*
War, death, or sickness, did lay siege to it,
Making it momentany° as a sound,   *momentary*
Swift as a shadow, short as any dream;
Brief as the lightning in the collied° night,   *black*
That, in a spleen,° unfolds both heaven and earth,   *fit of passion*
And ere a man hath power to say,—Behold!

150   The jaws of darkness do devour it up:
        So quick bright things come to confusion.
    HERMIA.   If, then true lovers have been ever cross'd,°   *thwarted*
        It stands as an edict in destiny:
        Then let us teach our trial patience,
        Because it is a customary cross,
        As due to love as thoughts, and dreams, and sighs,
        Wishes, and tears, poor fancy's° followers.   *love's*
    LYSANDER.   A good persuasion:° therefore, hear me, Hermia.   *doctrine*
        I have a widow aunt, a dowager
160   Of great revènue, and she hath no child:
        From Athens is her house remote seven leagues;
        And she respects° me as her only son.   *looks upon*
        There, gentle Hermia, may I marry thee:
        And to that place the sharp Athenian law
        Cannot pursue us. If thou lov'st me, then,
        Steal forth thy father's house to-morrow night;
        And in the wood, a league without° the town,   *outside*
        Where I did meet thee once with Helena,
        To do observance to a morn of May,
170   There will I stay for thee.
    HERMIA.   My good Lysander!
        I swear to thee, by Cupid's strongest bow;
        By his best arrow with the golden head;
        By the simplicity of Venus' doves;
        By that which knitteth souls and prospers loves,
        And by that fire which burn'd the Carthage queen,
        When the false Trojan under sail was seen;[2]
        By all the vows that ever men have broke,
        In number more than ever women spoke;—
180   In that same place thou hast appointed me,
        To-morrow truly will I meet with thee.
    LYSANDER.   Keep promise, love. Look, here comes Helena.

                                          [*Enter* HELENA.]

    HERMIA.   God speed fair Helena! Whither away?
    HELENA.   Call you me fair? that fair again unsay.
        Demetrius loves your fair°: O happy fair!   *beauty*
        Your eyes are lode-stars°; and your tongue's sweet air   *guiding stars*
        More tuneable° than lark to shepherd's ear,   *tuneful*
        When wheat is green, when hawthorn buds appear.
        Sickness is catching: O, were favour° so,   *beauty*
190   Yours would I catch, fair Hermia! ere I go,
        My ear should catch your voice, my eye your eye,

---

    [2] The allusion is to Dido, Queen and founder of Carthage, who, according to Virgil's *Aeneid*, watched her Trojan lover, Aeneas, sail away and then committed suicide by throwing herself upon her own funeral pyre.

My tongue should catch your tongue's sweet melody.
Were the world mine, Demetrius being bated,°   *excepted*
The rest I'll give to be to you translated.°   *transformed*
O, teach me how you look; and with what art
You sway the motion of Demetrius' heart!

HERMIA.   I frown upon him, yet he loves me still.

HELENA.   O that your frowns would teach my smiles such skill.

HERMIA.   I give him curses, yet he gives me love.

200 HELENA.   O that my prayers could such affection move!

HERMIA.   The more I hate, the more he follows me.

HELENA.   The more I love, the more he hateth me.

HERMIA.   His folly, Helena, is no fault of mine.

HELENA.   None, but your beauty: would that fault were mine!

HERMIA.   Take comfort: he no more shall see my face;
Lysander and myself will fly this place.—
Before the time I did Lysander see,
Seem'd Athens as a paradise to me:
O, then, what graces in my love do dwell,
210 That he hath turn'd a heaven unto a hell!

LYSANDER.   Helen, to you our minds we will unfold:
To-morrow night, when Phoebe³ doth behold
Her silver visage in the wat'ry glass,
Decking with liquid pearl the bladed grass,
(A time that lovers' flights doth still° conceal,)   *always*
Through Athens' gates have we devis'd to steal.

HERMIA.   And in the wood, where often you and I
Upon faint° primrose-beds were wont to lie,   *pale*
Emptying our bosoms of their counsel sweet,
220 There my Lysander and myself shall meet;
And thence from Athens turn away our eyes,
To seek new friends and stranger companies.⁴
Farewell, sweet playfellow; pray thou for us;
And good luck grant thee thy Demetrius!—
Keep word, Lysander: we must starve our sight
From lovers' food till morrow deep midnight.

LYSANDER.   I will, my Hermia—

                                                            [*Exit* HERMIA.]

                    Helena, adieu:
As you on him, Demetrius dote on you!

                                                            [*Exit.*]

HELENA.   How happy some, o'er other some° can be!   *some others*
230 Through Athens I am thought as fair as she:
But what of that? Demetrius thinks not so;
He will not know, what all but he do know;

---

³ Another name for Diana, the goddess of the moon.
⁴ That is, the company or fellowship of strangers.

And as he errs, doting on Hermia's eyes,
So I, admiring of his qualities.
Things base and vile, holding no quantity,
Love can transpose to form and dignity:
Love looks not with the eyes, but with the mind;
And therefore is wing'd Cupid painted blind:

240   Nor hath Love's mind of any judgment taste;
240   Wings, and no eyes, figure° unheedy haste: *symbolize*
And therefore is Love said to be a child,
Because in choice he is so oft beguil'd.
As waggish° boys in game° themselves forswear,   *mischievous/jest, sport*
So the boy Love is perjur'd every where:
For ere Demetrius look'd on Hermia's eyne,°   *eyes*
He hail'd down oaths that he was only mine;
And when this hail some heat from Hermia felt,
So he dissolv'd, and showers of oaths did melt.
I will go tell him of fair Hermia's flight:

250   Then to the wood will he, to-morrow night,
Pursue her; and for this intelligence°   *information*
If I have thanks it is a dear expense:°   *a great sacrifice*
But herein mean I to enrich my pain,
To have his sight thither and back again.

[*Exit.*]

SCENE II

ATHENS.   *A room in* QUINCE's *House.*

[*Enter* QUINCE, SNUG, BOTTOM, FLUTE, SNOUT, *and* STARVELING.]

QUINCE.   Is all our company here?
BOTTOM.   You were best to call them generally, man by man,
according to the scrip.°   *written paper*
QUINCE.   Here is the scroll of every man's name, which is
thought fit, through all Athens, to play in our interlude°   *play*
260   before the duke and the duchess on his wedding-day at
night.
BOTTOM.   First, good Peter Quince, say what the play treats on;
then read the names of the actors; and so grow to a
point.°   *conclusion*
QUINCE.   Marry,[5] our play is—The most lamentable comedy,
and most cruel death of Pyramus and Thisby.
BOTTOM.   A very good piece of work, I assure you, and a
merry.—Now, good Peter Quince, call forth your actors by
the scroll.—Masters, spread yourselves.
270   QUINCE.   Answer, as I call you.—Nick Bottom, the weaver.
BOTTOM.   Ready. Name what part I am for, and proceed.

---

[5] A mild oath, from the Virgin Mary.

QUINCE. You, Nick Bottom, are set down for Pyramus.
BOTTOM. What is Pyramus? a lover, or a tyrant?
QUINCE. A lover, that kills himself most gallantly for love.
BOTTOM. That will ask some tears in the true performing of it:
  if I do it, let the audience look to their eyes; I will move
  storms, I will condole° in some measure. To the rest:—   *lament*
  yet my chief humour is for a tyrant: I could play Ercles°   *Hercules*
  rarely, or a part to tear a cat° in, to make all split.   *rant and rave*

280
                    "The raging rocks
                    And shivering shocks
                    Shall break the locks
                       Of prison-gates;

                    And Phibbus' car[6]
                    Shall shine from far,
                    And make and mar
                       The foolish fates."

  This was lofty!—Now name the rest of the players.—This is
  Ercles' vein, a tyrant's vein;—a lover is more condoling.
290 QUINCE. Francis Flute, the bellows-mender.
  FLUTE. Here, Peter Quince.
  QUINCE. You must take Thisby on you.
  FLUTE. What is Thisby? a wandering knight?
  QUINCE. It is the lady that Pyramus must love.
  FLUTE. Nay, faith, let not me play a woman; I have a beard
    coming.
  QUINCE. That's all one: you shall play it in a mask, and you
    may speak as small as you will.
  BOTTOM. An° I may hide my face, let me play this Thisby too: *if*
300   I'll speak in a monstrous little voice;—"Thisne, Thisne"—
    "Ah, Pyramus, my lover dear! thy Thisby dear, and lady
    dear!"
  QUINCE. No, no; you must play Pyramus:—and, Flute, you
    Thisby.
  BOTTOM. Well, proceed.
  QUINCE. Robin Starveling, the tailor.
  STARVELING. Here, Peter Quince.
  QUINCE. Robin Starveling, you must play Thisby's mother.—
    Tom Snout, the tinker.
310 SNOUT. Here, Peter Quince.
  QUINCE. You, Pyramus's father;—myself, Thisby's father;—
    Snug, the joiner, you, the lion's part:—and, I hope, here is a
    play fitted.
  SNUG. Have you the lion's part written? pray you, if it be, give
    it me, for I am slow of study.
  QUINCE. You may do it extempore, for it is nothing but
    roaring.

---

[6] The chariot of Phoebus, the sun god.

BOTTOM.   Let me play the lion too: I will roar, that I will do
any man's heart good to hear me; I will roar, that I will
320   make the duke say, "Let him roar again, let him roar again."
QUINCE.   An° you should do it too terribly, you would fright the   *if*
duchess and the ladies, that they would shriek; and that were
enough to hang us all.
ALL.   That would hang us, every mother's son.
BOTTOM.   I grant you, friends, if that you should fright the ladies out of their wits, they would have no more discretion°   *choice*
but to hang us: but I will aggravate° my voice so, that I will   *moderate*
roar you as gently as any sucking dove; I will roar you an
'twere° any nightingale.   *as if it were*
330 QUINCE.   You can play no part but Pyramus; for Pyramus is a
sweet-faced man; a proper° man, as one shall see in a sum-   *handsome*
mer's day; a most lovely, gentlemanlike man: therefore, you
must needs play Pyramus.
BOTTOM.   Well, I will undertake it. What beard were I best to
play it in?
QUINCE.   Why, what you will.
BOTTOM.   I will discharge° it in either your straw-colour beard,   *perform*
your orange-tawny beard, your purple-in-grain° beard, or   *purple*
your French-crown-colour beard, your perfect yellow.
340 QUINCE.   Some of your French crowns have no hair at all, and
then you will play bare-faced.—But masters, here are your
parts: and I am to entreat you, request you, and desire you,
to con° them by to-morrow night; and meet me in the palace   *learn*
wood, a mile without the town, by moon-light; there will we
rehearse,—for if we meet in the city, we shall be dogged with
company, and our devices known. In the meantime, I will
draw a bill° of properties, such as our play wants. I pray you,   *list*
fail me not.
BOTTOM.   We will meet; and there we may rehearse more ob-
350   scenely, and courageously. Take pains; be perfect; adieu.
QUINCE.   At the duke's oak we meet.
BOTTOM.   Enough; hold, or cut bow-strings.[7]

[*Exeunt.*]

ACT II

SCENE I

A Wood near Athens.

[*Enter a* FAIRY *and* PUCK, *from opposite sides.*]

PUCK.   How now, spirit! whither wander you?
FAIRY.   Over hill, over dale,
          Thorough bush, thorough° brier,   *through*

---

[7] Apparently a proverbial expression derived from archery.

	Over park, over pale,°	*fence*

Over park, over pale,°   *fence*
   Thorough flood, thorough fire,
I do wander every where,
Swifter than the moon's sphere;[8]
360   And I serve the fairy queen,
To dew her orbs upon the green;[9]
The cowslips tall her pensioners° be;   *retinue, guards*
In their gold coats spots you see;
Those be rubies, fairy favours,
In those freckles live their savours°   *fragrances*
I must go seek some dew-drops here,
And hang a pearl in every cowslip's ear.
Farewell, thou lob° of spirits; I'll be gone: *bumpkin*
Our queen and all her elves come here anon.°   *presently*
370 PUCK. The king doth keep his revels here to-night:
Take heed the queen come not within his sight;
For Oberon is passing fell and wrath,°   *exceedingly angry*
Because that she, as her attendant, hath
A lovely boy, stol'n from an Indian king;
She never had so sweet a changeling:[10]
And jealous Oberon would have the child
Knight of his train, to trace° the forests wild;   *traverse, range over*
But she, perforce, withholds the loved boy,
Crowns him with flowers, and makes him all her joy:
380 And now they never meet in grove or green,
By fountain clear, or spangled star-light sheen,°   *bright*
But they do square°; that° all their elves, for fear,   *quarrel/so that*
Creep into acorn cups, and hide them there.
FAIRY. Either I mistake your shape and making quite,
Or else you are that shrewd° and knavish sprite,   *mischievous*
Call'd Robin Good-fellow: are you not he
That frights the maidens of the villagery;
Skims milk,[11] and sometimes labours in the quern,[12]
And bootless° makes the breathless housewife churn;   *fruitlessly*
390 And sometime makes the drink to bear no barm°;   *froth or head*
Misleads night-wanderers, laughing at their harm?
Those that Hobgoblin call you, and sweet Puck,
You do their work, and they shall have good luck:
Are not you he?
PUCK.   Thou speak'st aright
I am that merry wanderer of the night.
I jest to Oberon, and make him smile,

---

[8] According to the Ptolemaic astronomy of Shakespeare's day, the sun, moon, and stars revolved around the earth in spheres.

[9] Dark, circular rings of grass thought in Shakespeare's time to be the work of fairies.

[10] Changelings were the children (often ugly or stupid) that the fairies substituted for those they stole. Here, however, the reference is to the child stolen.

[11] Steals the cream.

[12] A hand-mill used for grinding grain.

When I a fat and bean-fed° horse beguile,	*well-fed*

Neighing in likeness of a filly foal:
400 And sometime lurk I in a gossip's bowl,[13]
        In very likeness of a roasted crab;°   *crabapple*
        And, when she drinks, against her lips I bob,
        And on her wither'd dew-lap[14] pour the ale.
        The wisest aunt, telling the saddest° tale,   *most serious*
        Sometime for three-foot stool mistaketh me;
        Then slip I from her bum, down topples she,
        And "tailor"[15] cries, and falls into a cough;
        And then the whole quire° hold their hips, and loffe;   *company*
        And waxen° in their mirth, and neeze,° and swear   *increase/sneeze*
410 A merrier hour was never wasted there.—
        But, room,° Fairy! here comes Oberon.   *give room, stand aside*
FAIRY.   And here my mistress—Would that he were gone!

SCENE II

The same.

[*Enter* OBERON *from one side, with his train; and* TITANIA *from the other, with hers.*]

OBERON.   Ill met by moon-light, proud Titania.
TITANIA.   What, jealous Oberon! Fairies, skip hence:
        I have forsworn his bed and company.
OBERON.   Tarry, rash wanton:° am not I thy lord?   *rebel*
TITANIA.   Then, I must be thy lady: but I know
        When thou hast stol'n away from fairy land,
        And in the shape of Corin[16] sat all day,
420 Playing on pipes of corn, and versing love°   *composing love poetry*
        To amorous Phillida. Why art thou here,
        Come from the farthest steep° of India,   *mountain range*
        But that, forsooth, the bouncing Amazon,
        Your buskin'd° mistress and your warrior love,   *wearing hunter's boots*
        To Theseus must be wedded? and you come
        To give their bed joy and prosperity.
OBERON.   How canst thou thus, for shame, Titania,
        Glance° at my credit with Hippolyta,   *hint critically*
        Knowing I know thy love to Theseus?
430 Didst thou not lead him through the glimmering night

---

[13] A popular drink made of ale, nutmeg, sugar, and roasted crabapples.
[14] The pendulous folds of flesh hanging from the throat.
[15] The reference is unclear.
[16] Corin, like Phillida (l. 411), were common names in pastoral poetry for a shepherd and a shepherdess.

From Perigenia,[17] whom he ravishèd?
And make him with fair Æglé break his faith,
With Ariadne, and Antiopa?

TITANIA.   These are the forgeries° of jealousy: *inventions*
And never, since the middle summer's spring,°   *beginning*
Met we on hill, in dale, forest, or mead,
By pavèd° fountain, or by rushy brook,   *pebbled*
Or on the beachèd margent° of the sea,   *margin*
To dance our ringlets° to the whistling wind,   *circular dances*
440   But with thy brawls° thou hast disturb'd our sport.   *noisiness*
Therefore the winds, piping to us in vain,
As in revenge, have suck'd up from the sea
Contagious° fogs; which, falling in the land,   *noxious*
Have every pelting° river made so proud,   *insignificant*
That they have overborne their continents:°   *banks*
The ox hath therefore stretch'd his yoke in vain,
The ploughman lost his sweat; and the green corn
Hath rotted ere his youth attain'd a beard:
The fold stands empty in the drownèd field,
450   And crows are fatted with the murrain° flock   *diseased*
The nine-men's morris[18] is fill'd up with mud;
And the quaint mazes in the wanton green,°   *lush grass*
For lack of tread are undistinguishable:
The human mortals want their winter here;
No night is now with hymn or carol blest:—
Therefore the moon, the governess of floods,
Pale in her anger, washes all the air,
That rheumatic° diseases do abound: *cold-like*
And thorough this distemperature° we see   *disorder*
460   The seasons alter: hoary-headed frosts
Fall in the fresh lap of the crimson rose;
And on old Hyem's° chin, and icy crown,   *winter's*
An odorous chaplet of sweet summer buds
Is, as in mockery, set. The spring, the summer,
The childing° autumn, angry winter, change   *fruitful*
Their wonted° liveries; and the 'mazèd° world,   *usual/bewildered*
By their increase,° now knows not which is which: *produce*
And this same progeny of evils comes
From our debate,° from our dissension;   *quarrel*
470   We are their parents and original.

OBERON.   Do you amend it, then; it lies in you:
Why should Titania cross her Oberon?
I do but beg a little changeling boy,
To be my henchman.°   *page boy*

TITANIA.   Set your heart at rest:

---

[17] Scholars believe that Shakespeare found this name, like those of Aegle, Ariadne, and Antiopa, in a contemporary translation of Plutarch's *Life of Theseus*.
[18] A game played outdoors on a kind of chess board laid out in the grass.

The fairy land buys not the child of me.
His mother was a votaress° of my order: *woman who has taken vows*
And, in the spicèd Indian air, by night,
Full often hath she gossip'd by my side;
480 And sat with me on Neptune's[19] yellow sands,
Marking th' embarkèd traders° on the flood;   *trading ship*
When we have laugh'd to see the sails conceive,
And grow big-bellied, with the wanton wind;
Which she, with pretty and with swimming gait°   *regular motion*
Following,° (her womb then rich with my young squire)   *resembling*
Would imitate, and sail upon the land,
To fetch me trifles, and return again,
As from a voyage, rich with merchandize.
But she, being mortal, of that boy did die;
490 And for her sake I do rear up her boy;
And for her sake I will not part with him.
OBERON.   How long within this wood intend you stay?
TITANIA.   Perchance till after Theseus' wedding-day.
If you will patiently dance in our round,
And see our moonlight revels, go with us;
If not, shun me, and I will spare° your haunts.   *avoid*
OBERON.   Give me that boy, and I will go with thee.
TITANIA.   Not for thy fairy kingdom.—Fairies, away!
We shall chide° downright, if I longer stay.   *quarrel*

[*Exit* TITANIA, *with her train.*]

500 OBERON.   Well, go thy way: thou shalt not from this grove,
Till I torment thee for this injury.—
My gentle Puck, come hither. Thou remember'st
Since° once I sat upon a promontory,   *when*
And heard a mermaid, on a dolphin's back,
Uttering such dulcet and harmonious breath,
That the rude° sea grew civil at her song,   *rough*
And certain stars shot madly from their spheres,
To hear the sea-maid's music.
PUCK.   I remember.
510 OBERON.   That very time I saw (but thou couldst not),
Flying between the cold moon and the earth,
Cupid all arm'd: a certain aim he took
At a fair vestal thronèd by° the west,   *in the region of*
And loos'd his love-shaft smartly from his bow,
As it should pierce a hundred thousand hearts:
But I might see young Cupid's fiery shaft
Quench'd in the chaste beams of the wat'ry moon,
And the imperial vot'ress passèd on,
In maiden meditation, fancy-free.
520 Yet mark'd I where the bolt of Cupid fell

---

[19] The Roman god of the sea.

It fell upon a little western flower,
Before milk-white, now purple with love's wound,
And maidens call it, love-in-idleness.°   *the pansy*
Fetch me that flower; the herb I show'd thee once:
The juice of it on sleeping eyelids laid,
Will make or man or woman madly dote
Upon the next live creature that it sees.
Fetch me this herb; and be thou here again,
Ere the leviathan° can swim a league.   *sea monster, whale*
530 PUCK.   I'll put a girdle round about the earth
In forty minutes.

                                                                    [Exit.]

OBERON.   Having once this juice,
I'll watch Titania when she is asleep,
And drop the liquor of it in her eyes.
The next thing then she waking looks upon,
(Be it on lion, bear, or wolf, or bull,
On meddling monkey, or on busy ape,)
She shall pursue it with the soul° of love: *single-minded devotion*
And ere I take this charm off from her sight,
540 (As I can take it with another herb)
I'll make her render up her page to me.
But who comes here? I am invisible;
And I will over-hear their conference.

                             [Enter DEMETRIUS, HELENA *following him.]*

DEMETRIUS.   I love thee not, therefore pursue me not.
Where is Lysander, and fair Hermia?
The one I'll slay, the other slayeth me.
Thou told'st me they were stol'n into this wood;
And here am I, and wood° within this wood,   *frantic, mad*
Because I cannot meet my Hermia.
Hence! I get thee gone, and follow me no more.
550 HELENA.   You draw me, you hard-hearted adamant;[20]
But yet you draw not iron, for my heart
Is true as steel: leave you° your power to draw,   *give up*
And I shall have no power to follow you.
DEMETRIUS.   Do I entice you? Do I speak you fair?
Or, rather, do I not in plainest truth
Tell you, I do not nor I cannot love you?
HELENA.   And even for that do I love you the more.
I am your spaniel; and, Demetrius,
560 The more you beat me, I will fawn on you:
Use me but as your spaniel, spurn me, strike me,
Neglect me, lose me; only give me leave,
Unworthy as I am, to follow you.

---

[20] A stone of impenetrable hardness and magnetic properties.

What worser place can I beg in your love,
(And yet a place of high respect with me,)
Than to be usèd as you use your dog?
DEMETRIUS.   Tempt not too much the hatred of my spirit;
For I am sick when I do look on thee.
HELENA.   And I am sick when I look not on you.
570 DEMETRIUS.   You do impeach° your modesty too much,   *call in question*
To leave the city, and commit yourself
Into the hands of one that loves you not;
To trust the opportunity of night,
And the ill counsel of a desert place,
With the rich worth of your virginity.
HELENA.   Your virtue is my privilege. For that°   *because*
It is not night when I do see your face,
Therefore I think I am not in the night;
Nor doth this wood lack worlds of company,
580 For you, in my respect,° are all the world: *estimation*
Then how can it be said I am alone,
When all the world is here to look on me?
DEMETRIUS.   I'll run from thee and hide me in the brakes,°   *thickets*
And leave thee to the mercy of wild beasts.
HELENA.   The wildest hath not such a heart as you.
Run when you will, the story shall be chang'd,—
Apollo flies, and Daphne holds the chase;[21]
The dove pursues the griffin[22]; the mild hind°   *doe*
Makes speed to catch the tiger,—bootless° speed,   *useless*
590 When cowardice pursues, and valour flies!
DEMETRIUS.   I will not stay thy° questions; let me go: *stay for*
Or, if thou follow me, do not believe
But I shall do thee mischief in the wood.
HELENA.   Ay, in the temple, in the town, the field,
You do me mischief. Fie, Demetrius!
Your wrongs do set a scandal on my sex:
We cannot fight for love, as men may do;
We should be woo'd, and were not made to woo.
I'll follow thee, and make a heaven of hell,
600 To die upon° the hand I love so well.   *by means of*

[*Exeunt* DEMETRIUS *and* HELENA.]

OBERON.   Fare thee well, nymph: ere he do leave this grove,
Thou shalt fly him, and he shall seek thy love.—

[*Re-enter* PUCK.]

Hast thou the flower there? Welcome, wanderer.
PUCK.   Ay, there it is.

---

[21] The allusion is to the nymph Daphne, who, fleeing the embraces of Apollo, became changed into a laurel tree.
[22] A mythological creature, half lion and half eagle.

OBERON.   I pray thee, give it me.
I know a bank where the wild thyme blows,
Where ox-lips, and the nodding violet grows;
Quite over-canopied with luscious woodbine,
With sweet musk-roses, and with eglantine:
610 Where sleeps Titania some time° of the night,   *at some time*
Lull'd in these flowers with dances and delight,
And there the snake throws her enamel'd skin,
Weed° wide enough to wrap a fairy in.   *garment*
And with the juice of this I'll streak° her eyes,   *mark*
And make her full of hateful fantasies.
Take thou some of it, and seek through this grove:
A sweet Athenian lady is in love
With a disdainful youth: anoint his eyes;
But do it, when the next thing he espies
620 May be the lady. Thou shalt know the man
By the Athenian garments he hath on.
Effect it with some care, that he may prove
More fond on her, than she upon her love:
And look thou meet me ere the first cock crow.
PUCK.   Fear not, my lord, your servant shall do so.

                                                              [*Exit.*]

SCENE III

Another part of the Wood.

                                                    [*Enter* TITANIA, *with her train.*]

TITANIA.   Come, now a roundel,° and a fairy song;   *a dance in a ring*
Then, for the third part of a minute, hence;—
Some, to kill cankers° in the musk-rose buds;   *caterpillars*
Some, war with rear-mice° for their leathern wings,   *bats*
630 To make my small elves coats; and some, keep back
The clamorous owl, that nightly hoots, and wonders
At our quaint° spirits. Sing me now asleep;   *dainty*
Then to your offices,° and let me rest.   *duties*

                          SONG

           1 FAIRY.   Ye spotted snakes, with double° tongue,   *forked*
                 Thorny hedge-hogs, be not seen;
                 Newts, and blind-worms,[23] do no wrong;
                 Come not near our fairy queen:
           CHORUS.   Philomel,° with melody,   *the nightingale*
                 Sing in our sweet lullaby;
640   Lulla, lulla, lullaby; lulla, lulla, lullaby:
                 Never harm,

---

[23] Both were thought to be venomous at one time.

                  Nor spell nor charm,
                  Come our lovely lady nigh;
                  So, good night, with lullaby.
        2 FAIRY.   Weaving spiders, come not here;
                  Hence, you long legg'd spinners, hence!
                  Beetles black, approach not near;
                  Worm, nor snail, do no offence.°   *harm*
        CHORUS.   Philomel, with melody, &c.
650   1 FAIRY.   Hence, away! now all is well.
                  One, aloof, stand sentinel.

                                  [*Exeunt Fairies.* TITANIA *sleeps.*]

                                      [*Enter* OBERON.]

OBERON [*squeezes the flower on* TITANIA's *eye-lids*].   What thou
    seest when thou dost wake,
    Do it for thy true love take;
    Love, and languish for his sake:
    Be it ounce,° or cat,° or bear,   *lynx/wildcat*
    Pard,° or boar with bristled hair,   *leopard*
    In thy eye that shall appear
    When thou wak'st, it is thy dear.
    Wake when some vile thing is near.

                                          [*Exit.*]

                            [*Enter* LYSANDER *and* HERMIA.]

660 LYSANDER.   Fair love, you faint with wandering in the wood;
        And to speak troth,° I have forgot our way: *truth*
        We'll rest us, Hermia, if you think it good,
        And tarry for the comfort of the day.
    HERMIA.   Be it so, Lysander: find you out a bed;
        For I upon this bank will rest my head.
    LYSANDER.   One turf shall serve as pillow for us both;
        One heart, one bed, two bosoms, and one troth.
    HERMIA.   Nay, good Lysander; for my sake, my dear,
        Lie farther off yet; do not lie so near.
670 LYSANDER.   O, take the sense, sweet, of my innocence!
        Love takes the meaning in love's conference.
        I mean, that my heart unto yours is knit,
        So that but one heart we can make of it:
        Two bosoms interchainèd with an oath;
        So then, two bosoms, and a single troth.
        Then, by your side no bed-room me deny;
        For, lying so, Hermia, I do not lie.
    HERMIA.   Lysander riddles very prettily:—
        Now much beshrew° my manners and my pride,   *curse upon*
680   If Hermia meant to say, Lysander lied.
        But, gentle friend, for love and courtesy
        Lie farther off; in human modesty,

Such separation as may well be said
Becomes a virtuous bachelor and a maid,—
So far be distant; and, good night, sweet friend.
Thy love ne'er alter till thy sweet life end!

LYSANDER.   Amen, amen, to that fair prayer, say I;
And then end life, when I end loyalty!
Here is my bed: sleep give thee all his rest!

690 HERMIA.   With half that wish the wisher's eyes be press'd!

[They sleep.]

[Enter PUCK.*]*

PUCK.   Through the forest have I gone,
But Athenian found I none,
On whose eyes I might approve°   put to the test
This flower's force in stirring love.
Night and silence! who is here?
Weeds of Athens he doth wear:
This is he, my master said,
Despisèd the Athenian maid;
And here the maiden, sleeping sound,
700   On the dank and dirty ground:—
Pretty soul! she durst not lie
Near this lack-love, this kill-courtesy,

[Squeezes the flower on LYSANDER'S *eyelids.]*

Churl, upon thy eyes I throw
All the power this charm doth owe.°   possess
When thou wak'st, let love forbid
Sleep his seat on thy eyelid:
So awake when I am gone,
For I must now to Oberon.

[Exit.]

[Enter DEMETRIUS *and* HELENA, *running.]*

HELENA.   Stay, though thou kill me, sweet Demetrius.
710 DEMETRIUS.   I charge thee, hence; and do not haunt me thus.
HELENA.   O, wilt thou darkling° leave me? do not so.   in the dark
DEMETRIUS.   Stay, on thy peril: I alone will go.

[Exit DEMETRIUS.*]*

HELENA.   O, I am out of breath in this fond° chase!   foolish
The more my prayer, the lesser is my grace.°   luck, fortune
Happy is Hermia, wheresoe'er she lies;
For she hath blessèd and attractive eyes.
How came her eyes so bright? Not with salt tears:
If so, my eyes are oftener wash'd than hers.
No, no, I am as ugly as a bear;

720   For beasts that meet me, run away for fear:
     Therefore no marvel though Demetrius
     Do, as a monster, fly my presence thus.
     What wicked and dissembling glass of mine
     Made me compare with Hermia's sphery eyne?°—   *starry eyes*
     But who is here?—Lysander!—on the ground!
     Dead? or asleep?—I see no blood, no wound.—
     Lysander, if you live, good Sir, awake.
LYSANDER [*awaking*].   And run through fire I will, for thy sweet
     sake.
     Transparent Helena! Nature here shows art,
730   That through thy bosom makes me see thy heart.
     Where is Demetrius? O, how fit a word
     Is that vile name to perish on my sword!
HELENA.   Do not say so, Lysander; say not so.
     What though he love your Hermia? Lord, what though?
     Yet Hermia still loves you: then be content.
LYSANDER.   Content with Hermia! No; I do repent
     The tedious minutes I with her spent.
     Not Hermia, but Helena I love:
     Who will not change a raven for a dove?
740   The will of man is by his reason sway'd;
     And reason says you are the worthier maid.
     Things growing are not ripe until their season:
     So I, being young, till now ripe not to reason;
     And touching now the point° of human skill,   *highest point*
     Reason becomes the marshal to my will,
     And leads me to your eyes; where I o'erlook°   *read*
     Love's stories, written in love's richest book.
HELENA.   Wherefore was I to this keen mockery born?
     When, at your hands, did I deserve this scorn?
750   Is't not enough, is't not enough, young man,
     That I did never, no, nor never can,
     Deserve a sweet look from Demetrius' eye,
     But you must flout my insufficiency?
     Good troth, you do me wrong,—good sooth,° you do,—   *truly*
     In such disdainful manner me to woo.
     But fare you well: perforce I must confess,
     I thought you lord of more true gentleness.°   *gentility*
     O, that a lady, of one man refus'd,
     Should of another therefore be abus'd!

                                      [*Exit.*]

760 LYSANDER.   She sees not Hermia.—Hermia, sleep thou there:
     And never may'st thou come Lysander near!
     For, as a surfeit of the sweetest things
     The deepest loathing to the stomach brings;
     Or, as the heresies, that men do leave,
     Are hated most of those they did deceive;

So thou, my surfeit and my heresy,
Of all be hated, but the most of me!
And, all my powers, address° your love and might   *apply*
To honour Helen, and to be her knight.

[*Exit.*]

770 HERMIA [*awaking*].   Help me, Lysander, help me! do thy best
To pluck this crawling serpent from my breast!
Ah me, for pity!—what a dream was here!
Lysander, look how I do quake with fear:
Methought a serpent eat my heart away,
And you sat smiling at his cruel prey.°—   *preying*
Lysander!—What, remov'd?—Lysander! lord!—
What, out of hearing? gone? no sound, no word?
Alack! where are you? speak, an if you hear;
780   Speak, of all loves! I swoon almost with fear.
No?—then I well perceive you are not nigh:
Either death, or you, I'll find immediately.

[*Exit.*]

ACT III

SCENE I

The Wood. TITANIA *lying asleep.*

[*Enter* QUINCE, SNUG, BOTTOM, FLUTE, SNOUT, *and* STARVELING.]

BOTTOM.   Are we all met?
QUINCE.   Pat, pat°; and here's a marvellous convenient place   *on the dot*
for our rehearsal. This green plot shall be our stage, this
hawthorn brake our 'tiring-house° and we will do it in   *dressing room*
action, as we will do it before the duke.
BOTTOM.   Peter Quince,—
QUINCE.   What say'st thou, bully° Bottom?   *worthy*
BOTTOM.   There are things in this comedy of "Pyramus and
790   Thisby," that will never please. First, Pyramus must draw a
sword to kill himself; which the ladies cannot abide. How
answer you that?
SNOUT.   By'rklakin²⁴ a parlous° fear.   *perilous*
STARVELING.   I believe we must leave the killing out, when all is
done.
BOTTOM.   Not a whit: I have a device to make all well. Write me
a prologue; and let the prologue seem to say, we will do no
harm with our swords, and that Pyramus is not killed indeed; and, for the more better assurance, that I, Pyramus,
am not Pyramus, but Bottom the weaver. This will put them
out of fear.

---

²⁴ An oath, "By Our Lady."

QUINCE.   Well, we will have such a prologue; and it shall be
800   written in eight and six.[25]

BOTTOM.   No, make it two more; let it be written in eight and
eight.

SNOUT.   Will not the ladies be afeard of the lion?

STARVELING.   I fear it, I promise you.

BOTTOM.   Masters, you ought to consider with yourselves to
bring in, —God shield us!—a lion among ladies, is a most
dreadful thing; for there is not a more fearful wild-fowl than
your lion, living; and we ought to look to it.

SNOUT.   Therefore, another prologue must tell he is not a lion.

BOTTOM.   Nay, you must name his name, and half his face must
810   be seen through the lion's neck, and he himself must speak
through, saying thus, or to the same defect,—"Ladies,—or,
fair ladies,—I would wish you,—or, I would request you,—or,
I would entreat you, —not to fear, not to tremble: my life for
yours. If you think I come hither as a lion, it were pity of my
life: no, I am no such thing; I am a man as other men
are:"—and there, indeed, let him name his name, and tell
them plainly, he is Snug, the joiner.

QUINCE.   Well, it shall be so. But there is two hard things,—that
is, to bring the moonlight into a chamber, for, you know,
820   Pyramus and Thisby meet by moonlight.

SNUG.   Doth the moon shine that night we play our play?

BOTTOM.   A calendar, a calendar! look in the almanack; find
out moonshine, find out moonshine.

QUINCE.   Yes, it doth shine that night.

BOTTOM.   Why, then may you leave a casement of the great
chamber window, where we play, open; and the moon may
shine in at the casement.

QUINCE.   Ay; or else one must come in with a bush of thorns[26]
and a lanthorn,° and say he comes to disfigure, or to   *lantern*
830   present, the person of moonshine. Then, there is another
thing: we must have a wall in the great chamber; for Pyramus and Thisby, says the story, did talk through the chink of
a wall.

SNUG.   You can never bring in a wall.—What say you, Bottom?

BOTTOM.   Some man or other must present wall: and let him
have some plaster, or some loam, or some rough-cast[27] about
him, to signify wall; and let him hold his fingers thus, and
through that cranny shall Pyramus and Thisby whisper.

QUINCE.   If that may be, then all is well. Come, sit down, every
840   mother's son, and rehearse your parts. Pyramus, you begin.
When you have spoken your speech, enter into that brake;—
and so every one according to his cue.

---

[25] In alternating lines of eight and six syllables, the meter of traditional ballads.

[26] According to a popular legend then current, the moon was often characterized as a man
with a bundle of sticks (or thorns) on his back.

[27] A mixture of lime and gravel used for plastering the outside of walls.

[Enter PUCK *behind.]*

PUCK.   What hempen home-spuns° have we swaggering here,   *rustics*
    So near the cradle of the fairy queen?
    What, a play toward!° I'll be an auditor;   *in preparation*
    An actor too, perhaps if I see cause.
QUINCE.   Speak, Pyramus.—Thisby, stand forth.
PYRAMUS.   "Thisby, the flowers of odious savours sweet,"—
QUINCE.   "Odours," "odours."
PYRAMUS.   —"odours savours sweet:
    So hath thy breath, my dearest Thisby, dear.—
850   But hark, a voice! stay thou but here a while,
    And by and by I will to thee appear."

[Exit.]

PUCK *[aside].*   A stranger Pyramus than e'er play'd here!

[Exit.]

THISBE.   Must I speak now?
QUINCE.   Ay, marry, must you; for you must understand he goes
    but to see a noise that he heard, and is to come again.
THISBE.   "Most radiant Pyramus, most lily-white of hue,
    Of colour like the red rose on triumphant° brier,   *magnified*
    Most brisky juvenal,° and eke° most lovely Jew,[28]   *lively youth/also*
    As true as truest horse, that yet would never tire,
860   I'll meet thee, Pyramus, at Ninny's tomb."
QUINCE.   "Ninus' tomb," man. Why, you must not speak that
    yet; that you answer to Pyramus: you speak all your part at
    once, cues and all.—Pyramus, enter: your cue is past; it is,
    "never tire."
THISBE.   O,—"As true as truest horse, that yet would never tire."

[Re-enter PUCK *and* BOTTOM *with an ass's head.]*

PYRAMUS.   "If I were, fair Thisby, I were only thine:"—
QUINCE.   O monstrous! O strange! we are haunted.—
    Pray, masters! fly, masters!—Help!

[Exit, with SNUG, FLUTE, SNOUT, *and* STARVELING.]

PUCK.   I'll follow you, I'll lead you about a round,°   *roundabout*
    Through bog, through bush, through brake, through brier;
870   Sometime a horse I'll be, sometime a hound,
    A hog, a headless bear, sometime a fire;
    And neigh, and bark, and grunt, and roar, and burn,
    Like horse, hound, hog, bear, fire, at every turn.

[Exit.]

---

[28] Jewel? The exact meaning of the word is unclear.

BOTTOM. Why do they run away? this is a knavery of them, to
make me afeard.

[*Re-enter* SNOUT.]

SNOUT. O Bottom! thou art changed! what do I see on thee?
BOTTOM. What do you see? you see an ass's head of your own,
do you?

[*Exit* SNOUT.]

[*Re-enter* QUINCE.]

QUINCE. Bless thee, Bottom! bless thee! thou art translated.°   *transformed*

[*Exit.*]

BOTTOM. I see their knavery: this is to make an ass of me, to
fright me, if they could. But I will not stir from this place, do
880   what they can: I will walk up and down here, and I will sing,
that they shall hear I am not afraid.

[*Sings.*]

The ousel-cock°, so black of hue,   *blackbird*
With orange-tawny bill,
The throstle° with his note so true,   *thrush*
The wren with little quill:°— *song*

TITANIA [*awaking*]. What angel wakes me from my flowery bed?
BOTTOM [*sings*].

The finch, the sparrow, and the lark,
The plain-song cuckoo gray,
Whose note full many a man doth mark,
890   And dares not answer, nay;—

for, indeed, who would set his wit to so foolish a bird? who
would give a bird the lie, though he cry "cuckoo" never so?
TITANIA. I pray thee, gentle mortal, sing again:
Mine ear is much enamour'd of thy note
So is mine eye enthrallèd to thy shape;
And thy fair virtue's force, perforce doth move me,
On the first view, to say, to swear, I love thee.
BOTTOM. Methinks, mistress, you should have little reason for
900   that: and yet, to say the truth, reason and love keep little
company now-a-days;—the more the pity, that some
honest neighbours will not make them friends. Nay, I can
gleek° upon occasion.   *joke*
TITANIA. Thou art as wise as thou art beautiful.
BOTTOM. Not so, neither: but if I had wit enough to get out of
this wood, I have enough to serve mine own turn.
TITANIA. Out of this wood do not desire to go:
Thou shalt remain here, whether thou wilt or no.
I am a spirit of no common rate,°—   *estimation*

The summer still doth tend upon my state;
910   And I do love thee: therefore go with me;
I'll give thee fairies to attend on thee;
And they shall fetch thee jewels from the deep,
And sing, while thou on pressèd flowers dost sleep:
And I will purge thy mortal grossness so,
That thou shalt like an airy spirit go.°—
Peas-blossom! Cobweb! Moth! and Mustard-seed!

[*Enter* PEAS-BLOSSOM, COBWEB, MOTH, *and* MUSTARD-SEED.]

PEAS-BLOSSOM.   Ready.
COBWEB.   And I.
MOTH.   And I.
MUSTARD-SEED.   And I.
ALL FOUR.   Where shall we go?
TITANIA.   Be kind and courteous to this gentleman:
Hop in his walks, and gambol in his eyes;
920   Feed him with apricocks,° and dewberries,°   *apricots/blackberries*
With purple grapes, green figs, and mulberries;
The honey-bags steal from the humble-bees,
And for night tapers crop their waxen thighs,
And light them at the fiery glow-worm's eyes,
To have my love to bed, and to arise;
And pluck the wings from painted butterflies,
To fan the moon-beams from his sleeping eyes:
Nod to him, elves, and do him courtesies.
PEAS-BLOSSOM.   Hail, mortal!
930 COBWEB.   Hail!
MOTH.   Hail!
MUSTARD-SEED.   Hail!
BOTTOM.   I cry° your worships' mercy,° heartily.—I beseech   *beg/pardon*
your worship's name.
COBWEB.   Cobweb.
BOTTOM.   I shall desire you of more acquaintance, good master
Cobweb: if I cut my finger, I shall make bold with you.[29]—
Your name, honest gentleman?
PEAS-BLOSSOM.   Peas-blossom.
940 BOTTOM.   I pray you, commend me to mistress Squash,[30] your
mother, and to master Peascod, your father. Good master
Peas-blossom, I shall desire you of more acquaintance
too.—Your name, I beseech you, Sir?
MUSTARD-SEED.   Mustard-seed.
BOTTOM.   Good master Mustard-seed, I know your patience
well: that same cowardly, giant-like ox-beef, hath devoured
many a gentleman of your house: I promise you, your kindred hath made my eyes water ere now. I desire you of more
acquaintance, good master Mustard-seed.

---

[29] In Shakespeare's time cobwebs were applied to stop bleeding.
[30] The name of the unripe pod of a pea (or peascod).

TITANIA.   Come, wait upon him; lead him to my bower.
950   The moon, methinks, looks with a wat'ry eye,
And when she weeps, weeps every little flower,
Lamenting some enforcèd° chastity.   *violated*
Tie up my love's tongue, bring him silently.

[*Exeunt.*]

SCENE II

Another part of the Wood.

[*Enter* OBERON.]

OBERON.   I wonder if Titania be awak'd;
Then, what it was that next came in her eye,
Which she must dote on in extremity.—
Here comes my messenger.—

[*Enter* PUCK.]

How now, mad spirit!
What night-rule° now about this haunted grove?   *diversions or disorders*
                                                                      of the night
PUCK.   My mistress with a monster is in love.
960   Near to her close° and consecrated bower,   *secret*
While she was in her dull and sleeping hour,
A crew of patches,° rude mechanicals,°   *clowns/working men*
That work for bread upon Athenian stalls,
Were met together to rehearse a play,
Intended for great Theseus' nuptial day.
The shallowest thick-skin of that barren sort,°   *dull company*
Who Pyramus presented, in their sport
Forsook his scene, and enter'd in a brake.
When I did him at this advantage take.
970   An ass's nowl° I fixèd on his head: *head*
Anon his Thisbe must be answerèd,
And forth my mimic° comes. When they him spy,   *comic actor*
As wild geese that the creeping fowler eye,
Or russet-pated choughs,° many in sort,   *grey-headed jackdaws*
Rising and cawing at the gun's report,
Sever themselves,° and madly sweep the sky;   *scatter*
So, at his sight, away his fellows fly;
And, at our stamp, here o'er and o'er one falls;
He murder cries, and help from Athens calls.
980   Their sense thus weak, lost with their fears thus strong,
Made senseless things begin to do them wrong,
For briers and thorns at their apparel snatch;
Some, sleeves,—some, hats,—from yielders all things catch.
I led them on in this distracted fear,
And left sweet Pyramus translated° there.   *transformed*
When in that moment (so it came to pass,)
Titania wak'd, and straightway lov'd an ass.

OBERON. This falls out better than I could devise.
  But hast thou yet latch'd° the Athenian's eyes   *captured*
990   With the love-juice, as I did bid thee do?
PUCK.   I took him sleeping, (that is finish'd too,)
  And the Athenian woman by his side;
  That, when he wak'd, of force° she must be ey'd.   *necessity*

[*Enter* DEMETRIUS *and* HERMIA.]

OBERON.   Stand close: this is the same Athenian.
PUCK.   This is the woman; but not this the man.
DEMETRIUS.   O, why rebuke you him that loves you so
  Lay breath so bitter on your bitter foe.
HERMIA.   Now I but chide; but I should use thee worse,
  For thou, I fear, hast given me cause to curse.
1000   If thou hast slain Lysander in his sleep,
  Being o'er shoes in° blood, plunge in the deep,   *waded in*
  And kill me too.
  The sun was not so true unto the day,
  As he to me: would he have stol'n away
  From sleeping Hermia? I'll believe as soon,
  This whole earth may be bor'd; and that the moon
  May through the centre creep, and so displease
  Her brother's noon-tide with th' Antipodes.
  It cannot be but thou hast murder'd him;
1010   So should a murderer look,—so dead°, so grim.   *deadly*
DEMETRIUS.   So should the murder'd look; and so should I,
  Pierc'd through the heart with your stern cruelty:
  Yet you, the murderer, look as bright, as clear,
  As yonder Venus³¹ in her glimmering sphere.
HERMIA.   What's this to my Lysander? where is he?
  Ah, good Demetrius, wilt thou give him me?
DEMETRIUS.   I had rather give his carcase to my hounds.
HERMIA.   Out, dog! out, cur! thou driv'st me past the bounds
  Of maiden's patience. Hast thou slain him, then?
1020   Henceforth be never number'd among men!
  O, once° tell true, tell true, e'en for my sake!   *once for all*
  Durst thou have look'd upon him being awake,
  And hast thou kill'd him sleeping? O brave touch°!   *deed*
  Could not a worm,° an adder, do so much?   *snake*
  An adder did it; for with doubler° tongue   *more deceitful*
  Than thine, thou serpent, never adder stung.
DEMETRIUS.   You spend your passion on a mispris'd mood°:   *mistaken anger*
  I am not guilty of Lysander's blood;
  Nor is he dead, for aught that I can tell.
1030 HERMIA.   I pray thee, tell me, then, that he is well.
DEMETRIUS.   An if I could, what should I get therefore?
HERMIA.   A privilege, never to see me more:—

---

³¹ Venus, the evening star, is also the goddess of love.

And from thy hated presence part I so:
See me no more, whether he be dead or no.

                                        [Exit.]

DEMETRIUS.   There is no following her in this fierce vein:
    Here therefore, for a while I will remain.
    So sorrow's heaviness doth heavier grow
    For debt that bankrupt sleep doth sorrow owe;
    Which now in some slight measure it will pay,
1040   If for his tender° here I make some stay.   *offer*

                       [Lies down and sleeps.]

OBERON.   What hast thou done? thou hast mistaken quite,
    And laid the love-juice on some true-love's sight:
    Of thy misprison° must perforce ensue   *mistake*
    Some true-love turn'd, and not a false turn'd true.
PUCK.   Then fate o'er-rules; that, one man holding troth,
    A million fail, confounding oath on oath.
OBERON.   About the wood go swifter than the wind,
    And Helena of Athens look thou find:
    All fancy-sick° she is, and pale of cheer°   *love-sick/face*
1050   With sighs of love, that cost the fresh blood dear:[32]
    By some illusion see thou bring her here:
    I'll charm his eyes against° she do appear,   *in expectation of when*
PUCK.   I go, I go; look how I go,—
    Swifter than arrow from the Tartar's[33] bow.

                          [Exit.]

OBERON.   Flower of this purple die,
    Hit with Cupid's archery,

        [Squeezes the flower on DEMETRIUS's *eyelids.]*

    Sink in apple° of his eye!   *pupil*
    When his love he doth espy,
    Let her shine as gloriously
1060   As the Venus of the sky.—
    When thou wak'st, if she be by,
    Beg of her for remedy.

                     [Re-enter PUCK.]

PUCK.   Captain of our fairy band,
    Helena is here at hand;
    And the youth, mistook by me,
    Pleading for a lover's fee.°   *reward*
    Shall we their fond pageant° see?   *foolish spectacle*

---

[32] An allusion to the popular belief that a sigh causes the loss of a drop of blood.
[33] The Tartars were savage tribesmen from central Asia.

Lord, what fools these mortals be!

OBERON.   Stand aside: the noise they make
1070   Will cause Demetrius to awake.

PUCK.   Then will two at once woo one,—
    That must needs be sport alone°;   *unique*
    And those things do best please me,
    That befall preposterously.

[*Enter* LYSANDER *and* HELENA.]

LYSANDER.   Why should you think that I should woo in scorn?
    Scorn and derision never come in tears:
    Look, when I vow, I weep, and vows so born,
      In their nativity all truth appears.[34]
    How can these things in me seem scorn to you,
1080   Bearing the badge of faith,° to prove them true?   *i.e., his tears*

HELENA.   You do advance your cunning more and more.
    When truth kills truth, O devilish-holy fray!
    These vows are Hermia's: will you give her o'er?
      Weigh oath with oath, and you will nothing weigh:
    Your vows to her and me, put in two scales,
    Will even weigh; and both as light as tales.

LYSANDER.   I had no judgment when to her I swore.

HELENA.   Nor none, in my mind, now you give her o'er.

LYSANDER.   Demetrius loves her, and he loves not you.

1090 DEMETRIUS [*awaking*].   O Helen, goddess, nymph, perfect, divine!
    To what, my love, shall I compare thine eyne?
    Crystal is muddy. O, how ripe in show
    Thy lips, those kissing cherries, tempting grow!
    That pure congealèd white, high Taurus[35] snow,
    Fann'd with the eastern wind, turns to a crow
    When thou hold'st up thy hand: O, let me kiss
    This princess of pure white, this seal of bliss!

HELENA.   O spite! O hell! I see you all are bent
    To set against me, for your merriment:
1100   If you were civil, and knew courtesy,
    You would not do me thus much injury.
    Can you not hate me, as I know you do,
    But you must join in souls[36] to mock me too?
    If you were men, as men you are in show,
    You would not use a gentle lady so;
    To vow, and swear, and superpraise my parts,°   *qualities*
    When I am sure you hate me with your hearts.
    You both are rivals, and love Hermia;
    And now both rivals, to mock Helena:
1110   A trim° exploit, a manly enterprise,   *fine*

---

[34] That is, vows born in weeping are truthful ones.
[35] A high mountain range in Turkey.
[36] Heart and soul, with your whole being.

To conjure tears up in a poor maid's eyes
With your derision! none of noble sort
Would so offend a virgin, and extort
A poor soul's patience, all to make you sport.
LYSANDER.   You are unkind, Demetrius; be not so;
For you love Hermia;—this you know I know:
And here, with all good-will, with all my heart,
In Hermia's love I yield you up my part;
And yours of Helena to me bequeath,
1120   Whom I do love, and will do to my death.
HELENA.   Never did mockers waste more idle breath.
DEMETRIUS.   Lysander, keep thy Hermia; I will none:[37]
If e'er I lov'd her, all that love is gone.
My heart to her but as guest-wise sojourn'd,
And now to Helen is it home return'd,
There to remain.
LYSANDER.   Helen, it is not so.
DEMETRIUS.   Disparage not the faith thou dost not know,
Lest, to thy peril, thou aby it dear.°—   *pay dearly for it*
Look, where thy love comes; yonder is thy dear.

                                           [*Re-enter* HERMIA.]

1130 HERMIA.   Dark night, that from the eye his function takes,
The ear more quick of apprehension makes;
Wherein it doth impair the seeing sense,
It pays the hearing double recompense.—
Thou art not by mine eye, Lysander, found;
Mine ear, I thank it, brought me to thy sound.
But why unkindly didst thou leave me so?
LYSANDER.   Why should he stay, whom love doth press to go?
HERMIA.   What love could press Lysander from my side?
LYSANDER.   Lysander's love, that would not let him bide,—
1140   Fair Helena; who more engilds the night
Than all you fiery oes and eyes° of light.   *stars*
Why seek'st thou me? could not this make thee know,
The hate I bear thee made me leave thee so?
HERMIA.   You speak not as you think: it cannot be.
HELENA.   Lo, she is one of this confederacy!
Now I perceive they have conjoin'd, all three,
To fashion this false sport in spite° of me.   *contempt*
Injurious° Hermia! most ungrateful maid!   *insulting*
Have you conspir'd, have you with these contriv'd
1150   To bait me with this foul derision?
Is all the counsel that we two have shar'd,
The sisters' vows, the hours that we have spent,
When we have chid the hasty-footed time
For parting us,—O! is all forgot?

---

[37] I want no part of her.

All school-days' friendship, childhood innocence?
We, Hermia, like two artificial° gods,   *highly skilled in art*
Have with our needls° created both one flower,   *needles*
Both on one sampler, sitting on one cushion,
Both warbling of one song, both in one key;
1160   As if our hands, our sides, voices, and minds,
Had been incorporate. So we grew together,
Like to a double cherry, seeming parted;
But yet a union in partition,
Two lovely berries moulded on one stem;
So, with two seeming bodies, but one heart;
Two of the first, like coats in heraldry,
Due to one, and crownèd with one crest.
And will you rent° our ancient love asunder,   *rend*
To join with men in scorning your poor friend?
1170   It is not friendly, 'tis not maidenly:
Our sex, as well as I, may chide you for it,
Though I alone do feel the injury.
HERMIA.   I am amazèd at your passionate words.
I scorn you not: it seems that you scorn me.
HELENA.   Have you not set Lysander, as in scorn,
To follow me, and praise my eyes and face?
And made your other love, Demetrius,
(Who even but now did spurn me with his foot,)
To call me goddess, nymph, divine, and rare,
1180   Precious, celestial? Wherefore speaks he this
To her he hates? and wherefore doth Lysander
Deny your love, so rich within his soul,
And tender me, forsooth, affection,
But by your setting on, by your consent?
What though I be not so in grace as you,
So hung upon with love, so fortunate;
But miserable most to love unlov'd?
This you should pity, rather than despise.
HERMIA.   I understand not what you mean by this.
1190 HELENA.   Ay, do, persèver, counterfeit sad° looks,   *serious*
Make mouths upon me when I turn my back;
Wink each at other; hold° the sweet jest up: *keep*
This sport, well carried, shall be chronicled.
If you have any pity, grace, or manners,
You would not make me such an argument.°   *subject of merriment*
But, fare ye well: 'tis partly mine own fault;
Which death, or absence, soon shall remedy.
LYSANDER.   Stay, gentle Helena; hear my excuse:
My love, my life, my soul, fair Helena!
1200 HELENA.   O excellent!
HERMIA.   Sweet, do not scorn her so.
DEMETRIUS.   If she cannot entreat, I can compel.
LYSANDER.   Thou canst compel no more than she entreat:
Thy threats have no more strength than her weak prayers.—

Helen, I love thee; by my life, I do:
I swear by that which I will lose for thee,
To prove him false that says I love thee not.
DEMETRIUS.   I say I love thee more than he can do.
LYSANDER.   If thou say so, withdraw, and prove it too.
1210 DEMETRIUS.   Quick, come!
HERMIA.   Lysander, whereto tends all this?
LYSANDER.   Away, you Ethiop!°   *Ethiopian*
DEMETRIUS.   No, no, Sir:—
Seem to break loose, take on, as³⁸ you would follow;
But yet come not: you are a tame man, go!
LYSANDER [*to* HERMIA].   Hang off, thou cat, thou burr! vile thing,
    let loose,
Or I will shake thee from me like a serpent!
HERMIA.   Why are you grown so rude? what change is this,
1220   Sweet love?
LYSANDER.   Thy love? out, tawny Tartar, out!
Out, loathèd medìcine! O hated potion, hence!
HERMIA.   Do you not jest?
HELENA.   Yes, 'sooth; and so do you.
LYSANDER.   Demetrius, I will keep my word with thee.
DEMETRIUS.   I would I had your bond, for I perceive
A weak bond holds you: I'll not trust your word.
LYSANDER.   What, should I hurt her, strike her, kill her dead?
Although I hate her, I'll not harm her so.
1230 HERMIA.   What, can you do me greater harm than hate?
Hate me! wherefore? O me! what news, my love?
Am not I Hermia? Are not you Lysander?
I am as fair now, as I was erewhile.
Since night, you lov'd me; yet, since night you left me:
Why, then you left me (O, the gods forbid!)
In earnest, shall I say?
LYSANDER.   Ay, by my life;
And never did desire to see thee more.
Therefore be out of hope, of question, of doubt:
1240   Be certain, nothing truer; 'tis no jest,
That I do hate thee, and love Helena.
HERMIA.   O me!—you juggler!° you canker-blossom!°   *trickster / blighted blossom*
You thief of love! what, have you come by night,
And stol'n my love's heart from him?
HELENA.   Fine, i' faith!
Have you no modesty, no maiden shame,
No touch of bashfulness? What, will you tear
Impatient answers from my gentle tongue?
Fie, fie! you counterfeit,° you puppet you!   *cheat*
1250 HERMIA.   Puppet! why, so: ay, that way goes the game.
Now I perceive that she hath made compare

---

³⁸ Make a commotion as if.

Between our statures; she hath urg'd her height;
And with her personage,° her tall personage,   *figure*
Her height, forsooth, she hath prevail'd with him.—
And are you grown so high in his esteem,
Because I am so dwarfish and so low?
How low am I, thou painted maypole? speak;
How low am I? I am not yet so low,
But that my nails can reach unto thine eyes.

1260 HELENA.   I pray you, though you mock me, gentlemen,
Let her not hurt me. I was never curst;°   *fierce*
I have no gift at all in shrewishness;
I am a right° maid for my cowardice: *real*
Let her not strike me. You perhaps may think,
Because she is something° lower than myself,   *somewhat*
That I can match her.

HERMIA.   Lower! hark, again.

HELENA.   Good Hermia, do not be so bitter with me.
I evermore did love you, Hermia,
1270 Did ever keep your counsels, never wrong'd you;
Save that, in love unto Demetrius,
I told him of your stealth° unto this wood.   *stealing away*
He follow'd you, for love, I follow'd him;
But he hath chid me hence, and threaten'd me
To strike me, spurn me, nay, to kill me too:
And now, so you will let me quiet go,
To Athens will I bear my folly back,
And follow you no farther: let me go:
You see how simple and how fond° I am.   *tender*

1280 HERMIA.   Why, get you gone: who is't that hinders you?

HELENA.   A foolish heart, that I leave here behind.

HERMIA.   What, with Lysander?

HELENA.   With Demetrius.

LYSANDER.   Be not afraid; she shall not harm thee, Helena.

DEMETRIUS.   No, Sir, she shall not, though you take her part.

HELENA.   O, when she is angry, she is keen and shrewd!
She was a vixen when she went to school;
And though she be but little, she is fierce.

HERMIA.   Little again! nothing but low and little!—
1290 Why will you suffer her to flout me thus?
Let me come to her.

LYSANDER.   Get you gone, you dwarf!
You minimus,° of hindering knot-grass[39] made;   *insignificant creature*
You bead, you acorn!

DEMETRIUS.   You are too officious
In her behalf that scorns your services.
Let her alone: speak not of Helena;
Take not her part; for, if thou dost intend

---

[39] A tough weed.

　　　　　　Never so little show of love to her,
1300　　　Thou shalt aby° it,　　　　　　　　　　　　　　　　　　　*pay for*
　　　LYSANDER.　　　　　　　Now she holds me not;
　　　　　　Now follow, if thou dar'st, to try whose right,—
　　　　　　Or thine or mine,—is most in Helena.
　　　DEMETRIUS.　Follow? nay, I'll go with thee, cheek by jole.°　　　*jowl*

　　　　　　　　　　　　　　　　[*Exeunt* LYSANDER *and* DEMETRIUS.]

　　　HERMIA.　You, mistress, all this coil° is 'long of° you:　　*turmoil/because*
　　　　　　Nay, go not back.
　　　HELENA.　　　　　　　I will not trust you, I,
　　　　　　Nor longer stay in your curst company.
　　　　　　Your hands, than mine, are quicker for a fray;
1310　　　My legs are longer though, to run away.

　　　　　　　　　　　　　　　　　　　　　　　　[*Exit.*]

　　　HERMIA.　I am amaz'd, and know not what to say.

　　　　　　　　　　　　　　　　　　　　　　　　[*Exit.*]

　　　OBERON.　This is thy negligence: still thou mistak'st,
　　　　　　Or else commit'st thy knaveries wilfully.
　　　PUCK.　Believe me, king of shadows, I mistook.
　　　　　　Did not you tell me I should know the man
　　　　　　By the Athenian garments he had on?
　　　　　　And so far blameless proves my enterprise,
　　　　　　That I have 'nointed an Athenian's eyes;
　　　　　　And so far am I glad it so did sort,°　　　　　　　　　*turn out*
1320　　　As this their jangling I esteem a sport.
　　　OBERON.　Thou seest, these lovers seek a place to fight:
　　　　　　Hie° therefore, Robin, overcast the night;　　　　　　*hasten*
　　　　　　The starry welkin° cover thou anon　　　　　　　　　　*sky*
　　　　　　With drooping fog, as black as Acheron;[40]
　　　　　　And lead these testy rivals so astray,
　　　　　　As° one come not within another's way.　　　　　　　　*that*
　　　　　　Like to Lysander sometime frame thy tongue,
　　　　　　Then stir Demetrius up with bitter wrong;°　　　　　　*insult*
　　　　　　And sometimes rail thou like Demetrius;
1330　　　And from each other look thou lead them thus,
　　　　　　Till o'er their brows death-counterfeiting sleep
　　　　　　With leaden legs and batty° wings doth creep:　　　　*bat-like*
　　　　　　Then crush this herb into Lysander's eye;
　　　　　　Whose liquor hath this virtuous° property,　　　　　　*powerful*
　　　　　　To take from thence all error with his might,
　　　　　　And make his eye-balls roll with wonted sight.
　　　　　　When they next wake, all this derision
　　　　　　Shall seem a dream, and fruitless vision;

---

[40] Acheron is one of the four rivers of Hades, the underworld.

And back to Athens shall the lovers wend,
1340 With league, whose date° till death shall never end.   *duration*
Whiles I in this affair do thee employ,
I'll to my queen, and beg her Indian boy;
And then I will her charmèd eye release
From monster's view, and all things shall be peace.
PUCK.   My fairy lord, this must be done with haste,
For night's swift dragons[41] cut the clouds full fast,
And yonder shines Aurora's harbinger;[42]
At whose approach, ghosts, wandering here and there,
Troop home to church-yards: damnèd spirits all,
That in cross-ways and floods have burial,
1350 Already to their wormy beds are gone;
For fear lest day should look their shames upon,
They wilfully themselves exile from light,
And must for aye consort with black-brow'd night.
OBERON.   But we are spirits of another sort:
I with the morning's love have oft made sport;
And, like a forester, the groves may tread,
Even till the eastern gate, all fiery-red,
Opening on Neptune[43] with fair blessèd beams,
1360 Turns into yellow gold his salt green streams.
But, notwithstanding, haste; make no delay:
We may effect this business yet ere day.

                                                                 [*Exit* OBERON.]

PUCK.   Up and down, up and down,
I will lead them up and down:
I am fear'd in field and town:
Goblin, lead them up and down.
Here comes one.

                                                                 [*Re-enter* LYSANDER.]

LYSANDER.   Where art thou, proud Demetrius? speak thou now.
PUCK.   Here, villain! drawn° and ready. Where art thou?   *with sword drawn*
1370 LYSANDER.   I will be with thee straight.
PUCK.   Follow me, then,
To plainer° ground.   *more level or open*

                                                                 [*Exit* LYSANDER *as following the voice.*]

                                                                 [*Re-enter* DEMETRIUS.]

DEMETRIUS.   Lysander! speak again.
Thou runaway, thou coward, art thou fled?
Speak! In some bush? Where dost thou hide thy head?

---

[41] The chariot of Cynthia, the Roman goddess of moon, was said to be pulled across the sky by dragons.
[42] Aurora is the Roman goddess of the dawn; her harbinger is Venus, the morning star.
[43] The Roman god of waters.

PUCK. Thou coward! art thou bragging to the stars,
  Telling the bushes that thou look'st for wars,
  And wilt not come? Come, recreant; come, thou child;
  I'll whip thee with a rod: he is defil'd
  That draws a sword on thee.
1380 DEMETRIUS.   Yea, art thou there?
PUCK.   Follow my voice: we'll try no manhood here.

                                     [Exeunt.]

                           [Re-enter LYSANDER.]

LYSANDER. He goes before me, and still dares me on:
  When I come where he calls, then he is gone.
  The villain is much lighter-heel'd than I:
  I follow'd fast, but faster he did fly;
  That fallen am I in dark uneven way,
  And here will rest me. *[Lies down.]* Come, thou gentle day!
  For if but once thou show me thy grey light,
  I'll find Demetrius, and revenge this spite.

                                     [Sleeps.]

                     [Re-enter PUCK and DEMETRIUS.]

1390 PUCK. Ho! ho! ho! Coward, why com'st thou not?
DEMETRIUS. Abide° me, if thou dar'st; for well I wot°   *face/know*
  Thou runn'st before me, shifting every place,
  And dar'st not stand, nor look me in the face.
  Where art thou now?
PUCK.   Come hither: I am here.
DEMETRIUS. Nay, then, thou mock'st me. Thou shalt 'by this dear,
  If ever I thy face by day-light see
  Now, go thy way. Faintness constraineth me
  To measure out my length on this cold bed.
1400   By day's approach look to be visited.

                               [Lies down and sleeps.]

                               [Re-enter HELENA.]

HELENA. O weary night! O long and tedious night!
  Abate° thy hours: shine, comforts, from the east,   *shorten*
  That I may back to Athens, by day-light,
  From these that my poor company detest:
  And sleep, that sometimes shuts up sorrow's eye,
  Steal me a while from mine own company.

                               [Lies down and sleeps.]

PUCK. Yet but three? Come one more;
  Two of both kinds make up four.
  Here she comes, curst° and sad:—   *short tempered*
1410   Cupid is a knavish lad,
  Thus to make poor females mad.

[*Re-enter* HERMIA.]

HERMIA.   Never so weary, never so in woe;
 Bedabbled with the dew, and torn with briers;
I can no farther crawl, no farther go;
 My legs can keep no pace with my desires.
Here will I rest me till the break of day.
Heavens shield Lysander, if they mean a fray!

[*Lies down and sleeps.*]

PUCK.   On the ground sleep sound:
 I'll apply to your eye,
1420 Gentle lover, remedy.

[*Squeezing the herb on* LYSANDER'*s eyelids.*]

When thou wak'st, thou tak'st
True delight in the sight
Of thy former lady's eye:
And the country proverb known,
That every man should take his own,
In your waking shall be shown:
 Jack shall have Jill;
 Naught shall go ill;
The man shall have his mare again,
1430 And all shall be well.

[*Exit.*]

ACT IV

SCENE I

The Wood.

[*Enter* TITANIA *and* BOTTOM; LYSANDER, DEMETRIUS, HERMIA, *and* HELENA, *still lying asleep.*
PEAS-BLOSSOM, COBWEB, MOTH, MUSTARD-SEED, *and other Fairies attending;* OBERON *behind
unseen.*]

TITANIA.   Come, sit thee down upon this flowery bed,
 While I thy amiable° cheeks do coy,°   *lovely/caress*
And stick musk-roses in thy sleek smooth head,
And kiss thy fair large ears, my gentle joy.
BOTTOM.   Where's Peas-blossom?
PEAS-BLOSSOM.   Ready.
BOTTOM.   Scratch my head, Peas-blossom.—Where's monsieur
Cobweb?
COBWEB.   Ready.
BOTTOM.   Monsieur Cobweb, good monsieur, get your weapons
1440 in your hand, and kill me a red-hipped humble-bee on the
top of a thistle; and, good monsieur, bring me the honey-
bag. Do not fret yourself too much in the action, monsieur;

and, good monsieur, have a care the honey-bag break not; I
would be loath to have you overflown with a honey-bag, signior.—Where's monsieur Mustard-seed?

MUSTARD-SEED.   Ready.

BOTTOM.   Give me your neif,° monsieur Mustard-seed. Pray   *fist*
you, leave your courtesy,° good monsieur.   *omit formality*

MUSTARD-SEED.   What's your will?

BOTTOM.   Nothing, good monsieur, but to help cavalery°   *cavalier*
1450   Cobweb to scratch. I must to the barber's, monsieur; for methinks I am marvellous hairy about the face; and I am such a
tender ass, if my hair do but tickle me, I must scratch.

TITANIA.   What, wilt thou hear some music, my sweet love?

BOTTOM.   I have a reasonable good ear in music: let
us have the tongs and the bones.°   *crude musical instruments*

TITANIA.   Or say, sweet love, what thou desir'st to eat:

BOTTOM.   Truly, a peck of provender: I could munch your
good dry oats. Methinks I have a great desire to a bottle° of   *bundle*
hay: good hay, sweet hay, hath no fellow.

1460 TITANIA.   I have a venturous fairy that shall seek
The squirrel's hoard, and fetch thee new nuts.

BOTTOM.   I had rather have a handful or two of dried peas.
But, I pray you, let none of your people stir me: I have an
exposition of sleep come upon me.

TITANIA.   Sleep thou, and I will wind thee in my arms.—
Fairies, be gone, and be all ways° away.—   *in every direction*

[*Exeunt Fairies.*]

So doth the woodbine the sweet honeysuckle
Gently entwist: the female ivy so
Enrings the barky fingers of the elm.
1470   O, how I love thee, how I dote on thee!

[*They sleep.*]

[*Enter* PUCK.]

OBERON [*advancing*].   Welcome, good Robin. Seest thou this sweet sight?
Her dotage now I do begin to pity:
For, meeting her of late behind the wood,
Seeking sweet favours° for this hateful fool,   *gifts of flowers*
I did upbraid her, and fall out with her;
For she his hairy temples then had rounded
With coronet of fresh and fragrant flowers;
And that same dew, which sometime on the buds
1480   Was wont to swell, like round and orient° pearls,   *lustrous*
Stood now within the pretty flow'rets' eyes,
Like tears, that did their own disgrace bewail.
When I had at my pleasure taunted her,
And she in mild terms begg'd my patience,
I then did ask of her her changeling child;
Which straight she gave me; and her fairies sent

To bear him to my bower in fairy land.
And now I have the boy, I will undo
This hateful imperfection of her eyes:
1490 And, gentle Puck, take this transformèd scalp
From off the head of this Athenian swain;
That he, awaking when the other° do,   *others*
May all to Athens back again repair,°   *return*
And think no more of this night's accidents,
But as the fierce vexation of a dream.
But first I will release the fairy queen.

[*Touching her eyes with a herb.*]

Be, as thou wast wont to be;
See, as thou wast wont to see:
Dian's bud o'er Cupid's flower°   *the pansy*
1500 Hath such force and blessèd power.
Now, my Titania; wake you, my sweet queen.

TITANIA. My Oberon! what visions have I seen!
Methought I was enamour'd of an ass.
OBERON. There lies your love.
TITANIA.   How came these things to pass?
O, how mine eyes do loathe this visage now!
OBERON. Silence, awhile.—Robin, take off this head.—
Titania, music call; and strike more dead
Than common sleep, of all these five the sense.
1510 TITANIA. Music, ho! music! such as charmeth sleep.

[*Still music.*]

PUCK. Now, when thou wak'st, with thine own fool's eyes peep.
OBERON. Sound, music! Come, my queen, take hands with me,
And rock the ground whereon these sleepers be.
Now thou and I are new in amity,
And will to-morrow midnight solemnly
Dance in Duke Theseus' house triumphantly,
And bless it to all fair prosperity.
There shall the pairs of faithful lovers be
1520 Wedded, with Theseus, all in jollity.
PUCK. Fairy king, attend, and mark:
I do hear the morning lark.
OBERON. Then, my queen, in silence sad,
Trip we after the night's shade:
We the globe can compass soon,
Swifter than the wandering moon.
TITANIA. Come, my lord; and in our flight,
Tell me how it came this night,
That I sleeping here was found
With these mortals on the ground.

[*Exeunt. Horns sound within.*]

[*Enter* THESEUS, HIPPOLYTA, EGEUS, *and train.*]

THESEUS.   Go, one of you, find out the forester;
      For now our observation° is perform'd;   *the observance of May Day rites*
      And since we have the vaward° of the day,   *early part*
      My love shall hear the music of my hounds;
      Uncouple° in the western valley; let them go: *unleash*
      Despatch, I say, and find the forester.—

                                                      [*Exit an* Attendant.]

      We will, fair queen, up to mountain's top,
      And mark the musical confusion
      Of hounds and echo in conjunction.

HIPPOLYTA.   I was with Hercules and Cadmus once,
1540 When in a wood of Crete they bay'd° the bear   *brought to bay*
      With hounds of Sparta:[44] never did I hear
      Such gallant chiding°; for, besides the groves,   *noise*
      The skies, the fountains, every region near
      Seem'd all one mutual cry: I never heard
      So musical a discord, such sweet thunder.
THESEUS.   My hounds are bred out of the Spartan kind,
      So flew'd,° so sanded°; and their heads are hung   *with large chaps/sandy-colored*
      With ears that sweep away the morning dew;
      Crook-knee'd, and dew-lapp'd like Thessalian bulls;
1550 Slow in pursuit, but match'd in mouth like bells,
      Each under each. A cry more tuneable°   *melodious*
      Was never holla'd to, nor cheer'd with horn,
      In Crete, in Sparta, nor in Thessaly:
      Judge, when you hear.—But, soft!° what nymphs are these?   *stop*
EGEUS.   My lord, this is my daughter here asleep;
      And this, Lysander; this Demetrius is;
      This Helena, old Nedar's Helena:
      I wonder of their being here together.
THESEUS.   No doubt they rose up early to observe
1560 The rite of May; and, hearing our intent,
      Came here in grace of° our solemnity.—   *to grace*
      But speak, Egeus; is not this the day
      That Hermia should give answer of her choice?
EGEUS.   It is, my lord.
THESEUS.   Go, bid the huntsmen wake them with their horns.

[*Exit an* Attendant. *Horns, and shout within.* LYSANDER, DEMETRIUS, HERMIA, *and*
HELENA, *awake and start up.*]

      Good-morrow, friends. Saint Valentine° is past: *Saint Valentine's Day*
      Begin these wood-birds but to couple now?

LYSANDER.   Pardon, my lord.

                                                      [*He and the rest kneel.*]

_____

[44] Hercules and Cadmus (though unrelated) were figures of classical antiquity; Crete and
Sparta were both famous for their hounds.

THESEUS.   I pray you all, stand up.
1570   I know you two are rival enemies:
     How comes this gentle concord in the world,
     That hatred is so far from jealousy,°   *suspicion, mistrust*
     To sleep by hate, and fear no enmity?
LYSANDER. My lord, I shall reply amazedly,
     Half sleep, half waking: but as yet, I swear,
     I cannot truly say how I came here;
     But, as I think, (for truly would I speak,—
     And now I do bethink me, so it is)
     I came with Hermia hither: our intent
1580   Was to be gone from Athens, where we might,
     Without° the peril of the Athenian law—   *beyond*
EGEUS.   Enough, enough, my lord; you have enough
     I beg the law, the law, upon his head.—
     They would have stol'n away; they would, Demetrius,
     Thereby to have defeated° you and me,   *cheated*
     You of your wife, and me of my consent,—
     Of my consent that she should be your wife.
DEMETRIUS. My lord, fair Helen told me of their stealth,
     Of this their purpose hither to this wood;
1590   And I in fury hither follow'd them,
     Fair Helena in fancy following me.
     But, my good lord, I wot° not by what power,   *know*
     (But by some power it is,) my love to Hermia,
     Melted as the snow, seems to me now
     As the remembrance of an idle gawd,°   *worthless toy*
     Which in my childhood I did dote upon;
     And all the faith, the virtue of my heart,
     The object, and the pleasure of mine eye,
     Is only Helena. To her, my lord,
1600   Was I betroth'd ere I saw Hermia:
     But, like in sickness, did I loathe this food;
     But, as in health, come to my natural taste,
     Now do I wish it, love it, long for it.
     And will for evermore be true to it.
THESEUS.   Fair lovers, you are fortunately met:
     Of this discourse we more will hear anon.—
     Egeus, I will overbear your will;
     For in the temple, by and by, with us,
     These couples shall eternally be knit.
1610   And, for the morning now is something worn,
     Our purpos'd hunting shall be set aside.
     Away, with us, to Athens: three and three,
     We'll hold a feast in great solemnity.°—   *celebration*
     Come, Hippolyta.

             [*Exeunt* THESEUS, HIPPOLYTA, EGEUS, *and train.*]

DEMETRIUS. These things seem small and undistinguishable,
     Like far-off mountains turnèd into clouds.

HERMIA.   Methinks I see these things with parted eye,°   *eyes out of focus*
    When every thing seems double.
HELENA.   So methinks:
1620   And I have found Demetrius, like a jewel,
    Mine own, and not mine own.
DEMETRIUS.   Are you sure
    That we are awake? It seems to me
    That yet we sleep, we dream.—Do not you think
    The duke was here, and bid us follow him?
HERMIA.   Yea; and my father.
HELENA.   And Hippolyta.
LYSANDER.   And he did bid us follow to the temple.
DEMETRIUS.   Why then, we are awake: let's follow him;
1630   And by the way let us recount our dreams.

              [*Exeunt* LYSANDER, DEMETRIUS, HERMIA, *and* HELENA.]

BOTTOM [*awaking*].   When my cue comes, call me, and I will
    answer: —my next is, "Most fair Pyramus."—Hey, no!—
    Peter Quince! Flute, the bellows-mender! Snout, the tinker!
    Starveling!—God's my life! stolen hence, and left me asleep!
    I have had a most rare vision. I have had a dream,—past the
    wit of man to say what dream it was: man is but an ass, if he
    go about to expound this dream. Methought I was—there is
    no man can tell what. Methought I was, and methought I
    had,—but man is but a patched° fool, if he will offer to say   *motley*
1640   what methought I had. The eye of man hath not heard, the
    ear of man hath not seen, man's hand is not able to taste, his
    tongue to conceive, nor his heart to report, what my dream
    was. I will get Peter Quince to write a ballad of this dream: it
    shall be called Bottom's Dream, because it hath no bottom;
    and I will sing it in the latter end of a play, before the duke:
    peradventure, to make it the more gracious,° I shall sing it at   *appealing*
    her death.

                                                [*Exit.*]

SCENE II

ATHENS.   *A Room in* QUINCE's *House.*

              [*Enter* QUINCE, FLUTE, SNOUT, *and* STARVELING.]

QUINCE.   Have you sent to Bottom's house? is he come home
    yet?
STARVELING.   He cannot be heard of. Out of doubt, he is
    transported.°   *carried away*
FLUTE.   If he come not, then the play is marred: it goes not
    forward, doth it?
1650 QUINCE.   It is not possible: you have not a man in all Athens
    able to discharge° Pyramus but he.   *act*

FLUTE. No, he hath simply the best wit° of any handycraft man   *mind*
in Athens.

QUINCE. Yea, and the best person° too; and he is very   *appearance*
paramour for a sweet voice.

FLUTE. You must say, paragon: a paramour is, God bless us! a
thing of naught.°   *something wicked*

[*Enter* SNUG.]

SNUG. Masters, the duke is coming from the temple, and there
is two or three lords and ladies more married: if our sport
1660   had gone forward, we had all been made men.[45]

FLUTE. O sweet bully Bottom! Thus hath he lost sixpence a-day
during his life; he could not have 'scaped sixpence a-day:
an° the duke had not given him sixpence a-day for playing   *if*
Pyramus, I'll be hanged; he would have deserved it: sixpence
a-day in Pyramus, or nothing.

[*Enter* BOTTOM.]

BOTTOM. Where are these lads? where are these hearts?°   *good fellows*

QUINCE. Bottom!—O most courageous day! O most happy
hour!

BOTTOM. Masters, I am to discourse wonders: but ask me not
what; for if I tell you, I am no true Athenian. I will tell you
every thing, right as it fell out.

1670   QUINCE. Let us hear, sweet Bottom.

BOTTOM. Not a word of me. All that I will tell you is, that the
duke hath dined. Get your apparel together, good strings to
your beards, new ribbons to your pumps°; meet presently at   *shoes*
the palace; every man look o'er his part; for the short and
the long is, our play is preferred.° In any case, let Thisby   *recommended*
have clean linen; and let not him that plays the lion pare his
nails, for they shall hang out for the lion's claws. And, most
dear actors, eat no onions nor garlick, for we are to utter
sweet breath; and I do not doubt but to hear them say, it is a
sweet comedy. No more words: away! go; away!

[*Exeunt.*]

ACT V

SCENE I

ATHENS. *An Apartment in the Palace of* THESEUS.

[*Enter* THESEUS, HIPPOLYTA, PHILOSTRATE, Lords, *and* Attendants.]

1680   HIPPOLYTA. 'Tis strange, my Theseus, that these lovers speak of.

THESEUS. More strange than true: I never may believe
These antique° fables, nor these fairy toys.°   *fantastic/idle tales*

---

[45] Our fortunes would have been made.

Lovers and madmen have such seething brains,
Such shaping fantasies, that apprehend
More than cool reason ever comprehends.
The lunatic, the lover, and the poet,
Are of imagination all compact:°—   *composed*
One sees more devils than vast hell can hold,—
That is, the madman, the lover, all as frantic,
1690 Sees Helen's beauty[46] in a brow of Egypt.°   *gypsy's face*
The poet's eye, in a fine frenzy rolling,
Doth glance from heaven to earth, from earth to heaven;
And, as imagination bodies forth
The forms of things unknown, the poet's pen
Turns them to shapes, and gives to airy nothing
A local habitation and a name.
Such tricks hath strong imagination,
That, if it would but apprehend some joy,
1700 It comprehends some bringer of that joy,
Or in the night, imagining some fear,
How easy is a bush suppos'd a bear!
HIPPOLYTA.   But all the story of the night told over,
And all their minds transfigur'd so together,
More witnesseth than fancy's images,
And grows to something of great constancy;°   *consistency*
But, howsoever, strange and admirable.°   *to be wondered at*
THESEUS.   Here come the lovers, full of joy and mirth.

[*Enter* LYSANDER, DEMETRIUS, HERMIA, *and* HELENA.]

Joy, gentle friends! joy, and fresh days of love,
1710 Accompany your hearts!

LYSANDER.   More than to us
Wait in your royal walks, your board, your bed!
THESEUS.   Come now; what masks,[47] what dances shall we have,
To wear away this long age of three hours,
Between our after-supper,° and bed-time?   *dessert*
Where is our usual manager of mirth?
What revels are in hand? Is there no play,
To ease the anguish of a torturing hour?
Call Philostrate.
PHILOSTRATE.   Here, mighty Theseus.
1720 THESEUS.   Say, what abridgment° have you for this evening?   *pastime*
What mask? what music? How shall we beguile
The lazy time, if not with some delight?
PHILOSTRATE.   There is a brief° how many sports are ripe: *summary*
Make choice of which your highness will see first.

[*Giving a paper.*]

---

[46] The allusion is to Helen of Troy, famous for her beauty.
[47] Entertainments, or masques, featuring masked dancers.

THESEUS [*reads*].   "The battle with the Centaurs,[48] to be sung
   By an Athenian eunuch to the harp."—
We'll none of that: that have I told my love,
In glory of my kinsman Hercules.—
[*Reads.*] "The riot of the tipsy Bacchanals,
1730   Tearing the Thracian singer[49] in their rage."—
That is an old device;° and it was play'd   *entertainment*
When I from Thebes came last a conqueror.—
[*Reads.*] "The thrice three Muses mourning for the death
   Of learning, late deceas'd in beggary."—
That is some satire, keen and critical,
Not sorting° with a nuptial ceremony.—   *appropriate to*
[*Reads.*] "A tedious brief scene of young Pyramus,
   And his love Thisbe; very tragical mirth."—
Merry and tragical! Tedious and brief!
1740 That is, hot ice and wondrous strange snow.
How shall we find the concord of this discord?
PHILOSTRATE.   A play there is, my lord, some ten words long,
Which is as brief as I have known a play;
But by ten words, my lord, it is too long,
Which makes it tedious; for in all the play
There is not one word apt, one player fitted:
And tragical, my noble lord, it is;
For Pyramus therein doth kill himself.
Which, when I saw rehears'd, I must confess,
1750 Made mine eyes water; but more merry tears
The passion of loud laughter never shed.
THESEUS.   What are they that do play it?
PHILOSTRATE.   Hard-handed men, that work in Athens here,
Which never labour'd in their minds till now;
And now have toil'd their unbreath'd° memories   *unpracticed*
With this same play, against your nuptial.
THESEUS.   And we will hear it.
PHILOSTRATE.   No, my noble lord;
It is not for you: I have heard it over,
1760 And it is nothing, nothing in the world;
Unless you can find sport in their intents,
Extremely stretch'd and conn'd° with cruel pain,   *strained and pored over*
To do you service.
THESEUS.   I will hear that play;
For never any thing can be amiss,
When simpleness and duty tender it.
Go, bring them in:—and take your places, ladies.

                                           [*Exit* PHILOSTRATE.]

---

[48] A race of men, half-human and half-horse.
[49] The allusion is to Orpheus, the son of Apollo, who played the lyre with great sweetness.
According to the legend referred to here, Apollo was torn apart by followers of the god Bacchus.

HIPPOLYTA. 　I love not to see wretchedness o'ercharg'd,° 　　　　　*overburdened*
　　　And duty in his service perishing.
1770 THESEUS. 　Why, gentle sweet, you shall see no such thing.
HIPPOLYTA. 　He says they can do nothing in this kind.
THESEUS. 　The kinder we, to give them thanks for nothing.
　　　Our sport shall be to take what they mistake:
　　　And what poor duty cannot do,
　　　Noble respect takes it in might, not merit.
　　　Where I have come, great clerks° have purposèd 　　　　*scholars*
　　　To greet me with premeditated welcomes;
　　　Where I have seen them shiver and look pale,
　　　Make periods in the midst of sentences,
1780 　　Throttle their practis'd accent in their fears,
　　　And, in conclusion, dumbly have broke off,
　　　Not paying me a welcome. Trust me, sweet,
　　　Out of this silence, yet, I pick'd a welcome;
　　　And in the modesty° of fearful° duty 　　　　　*deference/timid*
　　　I read as much, as from the rattling tongue
　　　Of saucy and audacious eloquence.
　　　Love, therefore, and tongue-tied simplicity,
　　　In least speak most, to my capacity.° 　　　　　*understanding*

[*Enter* PHILOSTRATE.]

PHILOSTRATE. 　So please your grace, the prologue is addrest.° 　　*ready*
1790 THESEUS. 　Let him approach.

[*Flourish of trumpets.*]

[*Enter* PROLOGUE.]

PROLOGUE. 　"If we offend, it is with our good will.
　　　　That you should think, we come not to offend,
　　　But with good-will. To show our simple skill,
　　　　That is the true beginning of our end.
　　　Consider, then, we come but in despite.° 　　*in ill-will to spite you*
　　　　We do not come as minding to content you,
　　　Our true intent is. All for your delight,
　　　　We are not here. That you should here repent you,
　　　The actors are at hand; and, by their show,
1800 　　　You shall know all, that you are like to know."
THESEUS. 　This fellow doth not stand upon points.
LYSANDER. 　He hath rid his prologue like a rough colt; he
　　knows not the stop. A good moral, my lord: it is not enough
　　to speak, but to speak true.
HIPPOLYTA. 　Indeed, he hath played on his prologue,
　　like a child on a recorder°; a sound, but not in 　　*flute-like instrument*
　　government.° 　　　　　　　　　　　　　　　*under control*
THESEUS. 　His speech was like a tangled chain; nothing im-
　　paired, but all disordered. Who is next?

[*Enter* PYRAMUS *and* THISBE, WALL, MOONSHINE, *and* LION, *as in dumb show.*]

PROLOGUE. "Gentles, perchance you wonder at this show;
1810   But wonder on, till truth make all things plain.
          This man is Pyramus, if you would know;
             This beauteous lady Thisby is, certain.
          This man, with lime and rough-cast, doth present
             Wall, that vile Wall which did these lovers sunder;
          And through Wall's chink, poor souls, they are content
             To whisper; at the which let no man wonder.
          This man, with lantern, dog, and bush of thorn,
             Presenteth Moonshine; for, if you will know,
          By moonshine did these lovers think no scorn
1820   To meet at Ninus' tomb, there, there to woo.
          This grisly beast, which Lion hight° by name,   *is called*
          The trusty Thisby, coming first by night,
          Did scare away, or rather did affright;
          And, as she fled, her mantle she did fall,°   *let fall*
             Which Lion vile with bloody mouth did stain.
          Anon comes Pyramus, sweet youth and tall,°   *valiant*
             And finds his trusty Thisby's mantle slain:
          Whereat, with blade, with bloody blameful blade,
             He bravely broach'd° his boiling bloody breast: *stabbed*
1830   And Thisby, tarrying in mulberry shade,
             His dagger drew, and died. For all the rest,
          Let Lion, Moonshine, Wall, and lovers twain,
          At large discourse, while here they do remain."

                 [*Exeunt* PROLOGUE, THISBE, LION, *and* MOONSHINE.]

THESEUS. I wonder, if the lion be to speak.
DEMETRIUS. No wonder, my lord:
   One lion may, when many asses do.
WALL. "In this same interlude it doth befall,
   That I, one Snout by name, present a wall;
   And such a wall, as I would have you think,
1840   That had in it a cranny'd hole or chink,
   Through which the lovers, Pyramus and Thisby,
   Did whisper often very secretly.
   This lime, this rough-cast, and this stone, doth show
   That I am that same wall; the truth is so:
   And this the cranny is, right and sinister,°   *left*
   Through which the fearful lovers are to whisper."
THESEUS. Would you desire lime and hair to speak better?
DEMETRIUS. It is the wittiest° partition that ever I heard discourse,   *cleverest*
   my lord.
THESEUS. Pyramus draws near the wall: silence!

                                         [*Enter* PYRAMUS.]

1850 PYRAMUS. "O grim-look'd night! O night with hue so black!
          O night, which ever art when day is not!
        O night, O night! alack, alack, alack!
        I fear my Thisby's promise is forgot!—

And thou, O wall, O sweet, O lovely wall,
 That stand'st between her father's ground and mine;
Thou wall, O wall, O sweet, and lovely wall,
 Show me thy chink to blink through with mine eyne!

              [Wall *holds up his fingers.*]

Thanks, courteous wall: Jove shield thee well for this!
 But what see I? No Thisby do I see.
1860 O wicked wall, through whom I see no bliss!
 Curst be thy stones for thus deceiving me!"

THESEUS. The wall, methinks, being sensible,° should   *capable of feeling*
 curse again.
PYRAMUS. No, in truth, Sir, he should not. "Deceiving me," is
 Thisby's cue: she is to enter now, and I am to spy her
 through the wall. You shall see, it will fall° pat as I told *occur*
 you.—Yonder she comes.

                [*Enter* THISBE.]

THISBE. "O wall, full often hast thou heard my moans,
 For parting my fair Pyramus and me!
My cherry lips have often kiss'd thy stones,
 Thy stones with lime and hair knit up in thee."
1870 PYRAMUS. "I see a voice: now will I to the chink,
  To spy an I can hear my Thisby's face.—
 Thisby!"
THISBE. "My love! thou art my love, I think."
PYRAMUS. "Think what thou wilt, I am thy lover's grace°; *i.e., your grace*
 And, like Limander, am I trusty still."
THISBE. "And I like Helen,⁵⁰ till the fates me kill."
PYRAMUS. "Not Shafalus to Procrus was so true."
THISBE. "As Shafalus to Procrus,⁵¹ I to you."
PYRAMUS. "O! kiss me through the hole of this vile wall!"
1880 THISBE. "I kiss the wall's hole, not your lips at all."
PYRAMUS. "Wilt thou at Ninny's tomb meet me straightway?"
THISBE. "Tide° life, 'tide death, I come without delay." *come*

            [*Exeunt* PYRAMUS *and* THISBE.]

WALL. "Thus have I, wall, my part dischargèd so;
 And, being done, thus wall away doth go."

                  [*Exit.*]

THESEUS. Now is the mural° down between the two neighbours. *wall*

---

 ⁵⁰ Limander and Helen are errors for what should be Leander and Hero, two famous classical lovers. Leander nightly swam across the Hellespont to be with his beloved. One night he drowned. Hero, overcome by grief, then drowned herself by leaping into the sea.
 ⁵¹ Again errors, for Cephalus and his faithful wife, Procris, whom he accidently killed with a javelin.

DEMETRIUS.   No remedy, my lord, when walls are so wilful to
   hear without warning.
HIPPOLYTA.   This is the silliest stuff that ever I heard.
THESEUS.   The best in this kind are but shadows; and the worst
1890   are no worse, if imagination amend them.
HIPPOLYTA.   It must be your imagination then, and not theirs.
THESEUS.   If we imagine no worse of them than they of themselves, they may pass for excellent men.—Here come two
   noble beasts in, a moon and a lion.

> [*Enter* LION *and* MOONSHINE.]

LION.   "You, ladies, you, whose gentle hearts do fear
      The smallest monstrous mouse that creeps on floor,
   May now perchance both quake and tremble here,
      When lion rough in wildest rage doth roar.
   Then know that I, one Snug the joiner, am
1900   No lion fell,° nor else no lion's dam;   *lion's skin*
   For, if I should as lion come in strife
   Into this place, 'twere pity of my life."
THESEUS.   A very gentle beast, and of a good conscience.
DEMETRIUS.   The very best at a beast, my lord, that e'er I saw.
LYSANDER.   This lion is a very fox for his valour.
THESEUS.   True; and a goose for his discretion.
DEMETRIUS.   Not so, my lord; for his valour cannot carry his
   discretion; and the fox carries the goose.
THESEUS.   His discretion, I am sure, cannot carry his valour; for
1910   the goose carries not the fox. It is well: leave it to his discre-
   tion, and let us listen to the moon.
MOONSHINE.   "This lantern doth the horned moon present;"—
DEMETRIUS.   He should have worn the horns on his head.[52]
THESEUS.   He is no crescent,° and his horns are invisible   *new or waxing moon*
   within the circumference.
MOONSHINE.   "This lantern doth the horned moon present;
   Myself the man i' the moon do seem to be."
THESEUS.   This is the greatest error of all the rest: the man
   should be put into the lantern. How is it else the man i' the
   moon?
DEMETRIUS.   He dares not come there for° the candle; for, you   *because of*
1920   see, it is already in snuff.°   *anger*
HIPPOLYTA.   I am aweary of this moon: would he would change!
THESEUS.   It appears, by his small light of discretion, that he is
   in the wane; but yet, in courtesy, in all reason, we must stay°   *await*
   the time.
LYSANDER.   Proceed, moon.
MOONSHINE.   All that I have to say, is, to tell you that the lantern is the moon; I, the man in the moon; this thorn-bush,
   my thorn-bush; and this dog, my dog.

---

[52] The allusion is to the horns of a cuckold.

DEMETRIUS.   Why, all these should be in the lantern; for all
these are in the moon. But, silence! here comes Thisbe.

[*Enter* THISBE.]

1930   THISBE.   "This is old Ninny's tomb. Where is my love?"
LION [*roaring*].   "Oh—."

[THISBE *runs off.*]

DEMETRIUS.   Well roared, lion.
THESEUS.   Well run, Thisbe.
HIPPOLYTA.   Well shone, moon.—Truly, the moon shines with a
good grace.

[*The* Lion *tears* THISBE's *mantle, and exit.*]

THESEUS.   Well moused,° lion.   *torn*
DEMETRIUS.   And then came Pyramus.
LYSANDER.   And so the lion vanished.

[*Enter* PYRAMUS.]

PYRAMUS.   "Sweet moon, I thank thee for thy sunny beams
1940   I thank thee, moon, for shining now so bright;
      For, by thy gracious, golden, glittering streams,
        I trust to taste of truest Thisbe's sight.
            But stay,—O spite!—
            But mark, poor knight,
   What dreadful dole° is here!   *cause for grief*
        Eyes, do you see?
        How can it be?
   O dainty duck! O dear!
          Thy mantle good,
1950   What, stain'd with blood?
   Approach, ye furies fell!
         O fates,[53] come, come,
         Cut thread and thrum[54];
      Quail,° crush, conclude, and quell°!"   *overpower/kill*
THESEUS.   This passion,° and the death of a dear friend, would   *suffering*
go near to make a man look sad.
HIPPOLYTA.   Beshrew my heart, but I pity the man.
PYRAMUS.   "O wherefore, nature, didst thou lions frame?
      Since lion vile hath here deflower'd my dear:
1960   Which is—no, no—which was the fairest dame
      That liv'd, that lov'd, that lik'd, that look'd with cheer.
          Come, tears, confound;
          Out, sword, and wound

---

[53] The Roman goddesses of vengeance. The Fates were the three goddesses who spun, drew
out, and then cut the thread of human life.
[54] The warp and weft of the loom; here used as a synonym for everything together.

The pap of Pyramus,—
    Ay, that left pap,
    Where heart doth hop:—

                                      [*Stabs himself.*]

Thus die I, thus, thus, thus!
    Now am I dead,
    Now am I fled;
My soul is in the sky:
1980   Tongue, lose thy light!
        Moon, take thy flight!

                              [*Exit* MOONSHINE.]

Now die, die, die, die, die."

                                      [*Dies.*]

DEMETRIUS. No die, but an ace, for him; for he is but one.
LYSANDER. Less than an ace, man; for he is dead; he is nothing.
THESEUS. With the help of a surgeon, he might yet recover,
    and prove an ass.
HIPPOLYTA. How chance moonshine is gone, before Thisbe
    comes back and finds her lover?
1990 THESEUS. She will find him by starlight.—Here she comes; and
    her passion ends the play.

                             [*Re-enter* THISBE.]

HIPPOLYTA. Methinks she should not use a long one for such a
    Pyramus: I hope she will be brief.
DEMETRIUS. A mote° will turn the balance, which°   *small particle/whether*
    Pyramus, which° Thisbe, is the better; he for a man, God   *or*
    warrant° us,—she for a woman, God bless us.   *defend*
LYSANDER. She hath spied him already with those sweet eyes.
DEMETRIUS. And thus she moans, *videlicet*:—
THISBE.   "Asleep, my love?
2000   What, dead, my dove?
            O Pyramus, arise!
             Speak, speak. Quite dumb?
             Dead, dead? A tomb
        Must cover thy sweet eyes.
             These lily lips,
             This cherry nose,
        These yellow cowslip cheeks,
             Are gone, are gone:
             Lovers, make moan:
2020   His eyes were green as leeks.
             O, sisters three,[55]
             Come, come to me,

---

[55] The Fates, see Note 53.

With hands as pale as milk;
   Lay them in gore,
   Since you have shore°   *shorn*
With shears his thread of silk.
   Tongue, not a word:
   Come, trusty sword;
Come, blade, my breast imbrue:°   *stain with blood*

2020   [*Stabs herself.*]

   And farewell, friends,—
   Thus Thisby ends,—
Adieu, adieu, adieu."

                                               [*Dies.*]

THESEUS.   Moonshine and Lion are left to bury the dead.
DEMETRIUS.   Ay, and Wall too.
BOTTOM.   No, I assure you; the wall is down that parted their
   fathers. Will it please you to see the epilogue, or to hear a
   Bergomask[56] dance between two of our company?
THESEUS.   No epilogue, I pray you; for your play needs no excuse. Never excuse; for when the players are all dead, there
2030   need none to be blamed. Marry, if he that writ it, had play'd
   Pyramus, and hanged himself in Thisbe's garter, it would
   have been a fine tragedy: and so it is, truly; and very notably
   discharged. But come, your Bergomask: let your epilogue
   alone.

                                               [*A dance.*]

The iron tongue° of midnight hath told twelve:—   *of a bell*
Lovers, to bed; 'tis almost fairy time.
I fear we shall out-sleep the coming morn,
As much as we this night have overwatch'd.°   *kept watch over*
This palpable gross° play hath well beguil'd   *stupid*
The heavy gait of night.—Sweet friends, to bed.—
2040 A fortnight hold we this solemnity,
In nightly revels, and new jollity.

                                            [*Exeunt.*]

SCENE II

                                         [*Enter* PUCK.]

PUCK.   Now the hungry lion roars,
   And the wolf behowls the moon;
   Whilst the heavy ploughman snores,
   All with weary task fordone.°   *exhausted*

---

[56] A rustic dance that originated in northern Italy among the people of Bergamo.

Now the wasted° brands do glow,   *burned out*
　　Whilst the screech-owl, screeching loud,
Puts the wretch that lies in woe,
　　In remembrance of a shroud.
Now it is the time of night,
2050　　That the graves, all gaping wide,
Every one lets forth his sprite,
　　In the church-way paths to glide:
And we fairies, that do run
　　By the triple Hecate's team,[57]
From the presence of the sun,
　　Following darkness like a dream,
Now are frolic°: not a mouse   *merry*
Shall disturb this hallow'd house:
2060　I am sent, with broom, before,
To sweep the dust behind the door.

　　　　　　　　　　　　　　　　 [*Enter* OBERON *and* TITANIA, *with their train.*]

OBERON.　Through the house give glimmering light,
　　By the dead and drowsy fire:
Every elf, and fairy sprite,
　　Hop as light as bird from brier;
And this ditty, after me,
　　Sing, and dance it trippingly.
TITANIA.　First, rehearse your song by rote,
　　To each word a warbling note:
2070　Hand in hand, with fairy grace,
Will we sing, and bless this place.

　　　　　　　　　　　　　　　　　　　　　　　　　 [*Song and dance.*]

OBERON.　Now, until the break of day,
　　Through this house each fairy stray.
To the best bride-bed will we,
　　Which by us shall blessed be;
And the issue there create°   *created*
　　Ever shall be fortunate.
So shall all the couples three
　　Ever true in loving be;
2080　And the blots of nature's hand
　　Shall not in their issue stand;
Never mole, hare-lip, nor scar,
　　Nor mark prodigious,° such as are   *birthmark*
Despisèd in nativity,
　　Shall upon their children be.
With this field-dew consecrate,°   *consecrated*
　　Every fairy take his gait;°   *way*
And each several° chamber bless,   *separate*

---

[57] Hecate is the goddess of the moon; her team is her chariot.

Through this palace, with sweet peace:
2090 Ever shall in safety rest,
And the owner of it blest.
Trip away; make no stay;
Meet me all by break of day.

[*Exeunt* OBERON, TITANIA, *and train.*]

PUCK. If we shadows have offended,
Think but this, (and all is mended,)
That you have but slumber'd here,
While these visions did appear.
And this weak and idle theme,
No more yielding but a dream,
2100 Gentles,° do not reprehend: *gentlefolk*
If you pardon, we will mend.°   *improve*
And, as I'm an honest Puck,
If we have unearnèd luck
Now to 'scape the serpent's tongue,°   *hisses*
We will make amends ere long;
Else the Puck a liar call:
So, good night unto you all.
Give me your hands,° if we be friends,   *applause*
And Robin shall restore amends.°   *return satisfaction*

[*Exit.*]

[ca. 1594–1596]

Critical Commentary on *A Midsummer Night's Dream*

England's cowslips were golden cups, spotted with rich rubies, and a pearl of dew hung in each. The woodlands were carpeted with thick primrose beds, and its springtime outrivalled that of Theocritus in greenery: the song of the lark in the season when wheat is green and hawthorn buds appear, roused English villages betimes to do observances to the month of May. The fields are asparkle with the dew-drop's liquid pearl: the woods are lighted with the fiery glow-worm's eyes. Morning has mountain top and western valley filled with music of the hounds. . . . And evening ushers in the midnight revels on hill, in dale, forest or mead, by paved fountain or by rushy brook, or in the beached margent of the sea, where ringlets are danced in quaint mazes to the whistling of the wind. This is the land of *A Midsummer Night's Dream*.

—H. B. Charlton (1966)

As Charlton suggests, the world of Shakespeare's comedies is a bucolic, pastoral world which skillfully blends and reconciles the competing claims of realism and romance. Nowhere is this truer than in *A Midsummer Night's Dream*, which in the rich variety of its meter and verse forms, its highly pictorial imagery, and its clever use of parody and irony demonstrates the range of talents that William Shakespeare brought to the business of writing plays. Many scholars and critics insist that comedy rather than tragedy was

William Shakespeare's natural calling. Drawing upon both classical models, the traditions of English medieval drama, and the works of his immediate English predecessors and contemporaries, Shakespeare developed very early in his career a kind of tightly-knit, controlled comedy that was uniquely and truly his own.

A Midsummer Night's Dream, which explores and celebrates the foolishness and irrationality of love, is one of Shakespeare's most popular, most admired, and most remarkable plays. In fact, it is often regarded as the best of the early comedies; it is certainly his happiest. It belongs to the remarkable period of Shakespeare's first flowering in the late 1580s and into the 1590s that saw him bring to the stage a full thirteen of the thirty-eight plays that are now part of the Shakespeare canon. Though we have little definite information to go on, the play is usually dated between 1594 and 1596.

The origins of *A Midsummer Night's Dream*, like the date of its composition, are not entirely clear. Because the plot deliberately culminates in the wedding celebration of Theseus and Hippolyta, it has been speculated that the play was written on commission to be privately performed at the wedding celebration of an aristocrat in his great country house or at court. But it is also a play which, when performed on the public stage (initially by Shakespeare's own company, the Lord Chamberlain's Men) broadly appealed to a wide cross-section of Elizabethan society.

The play's remarkable synthesis of comic materials is clear. It consists of three groups of characters and three distinct but intersecting subplots (or "layers" of action as they have been called) tightly woven together into a balanced and satisfying whole. The worlds of Theseus and Hippolyta and the four young lovers, of King Oberon, Queen Titania, Puck, and the other fairies, and of Peter Quince, Nick Bottom and their fellow "crew of patches, rude mechanicals" are very different and disparate ones. Shakespeare draws these characters together in an enchanted wood near Athens, temporarily suspends the laws of everyday reality, allows them to play themselves off against one another, and then looks on "in amazement," in the words of David Zesmer, "as the madness called love scrambles the three worlds almost beyond recognition." He resolves the mistakes, quarrels, and confusion by bringing the parties to a triple wedding, an event which promptly gives way to one of the great final scenes in all of dramatic literature, uniting the once-disentangled threads in an hilarious, happy, and poetic conclusion.

As the introductory quotation from H. B. Charlton suggests, both time and place in their blending of folklore and myth are critically important in creating the play's lyrical atmosphere and theatrical effect. The time is Midsummer Eve, the summer solstice, a traditional holiday rooted in antiquity and associated both with merrymaking and magic. On Midsummer's Eve, according to English folk tradition, spirits and other strange beings were abroad in the land, and inexplicable and unworldly events took place. Woods were the domain of such spirits and it was there that such mid-summer rioting most frequently took place. In the woods, it was widely believed, these spirits were most free to work their enchantment on those unfortunate mortals who mistakenly wandered into their domain.

The moon-drenched woods of Shakespeare's play are precisely such a place. Here confusion and unreason reign supreme, and love becomes blind, as represented most clearly by Titania, who awakes in wonder to become enamored with Bottom the weaver, whose head has been transformed into that of an ass. The farcical behavior that overtakes all who enter into this haunted and topsy-turvy world serves to illustrate all too well the truth of Bottom's assertion of Act III that "reason and love keep little company together now-a-days." The magical other-worldliness of Shakespeare's setting is, in short, the perfect place to stage a play bent on demonstrating the reality-distorting power of love—a theme that finds its most definitive statement in Theseus's speech opening Act V:

> Lovers and madmen have such seething brains,
> Such shaping fantasies, that apprehend
> More than cool reason ever comprehends.
> The lunatic, the lover, and the poet,
> Are of imagination all compact.

Though Theseus may well serve as an authorial spokesman, the final truth of the matter, of course, is that, as Alexander Leggatt observes, "love imposes its own peculiar kind of vision, which renders any other opinion—including that of common sense—irrelevant."

Shakespeare uses the residents of these woods—Oberon, Titania, Puck, and the other forest sprites—not only to parallel and reinforce the larger thematic concerns of the play but as a means of suggesting those external mysterious forces in the universe which can, and often do, interrupt and influence the affairs of men and render them something akin to helpless pawns. It is important to note that for all their general benevolence toward humans, Puck and Oberon have their darker, demonic and malevolent sides; they are potentially dangerous and capable of considerable mischief. As such they may be said to hint at the darker realities of life—realities from which comedy of the sort that Shakespeare himself writes may temporarily allow us to escape. Productions of the play which reduce Titania, Puck, Oberon, and their train to utterly harmless and fun-loving characters, dismissing this darker vision of things, are thus guilty of portraying these wonderful characters in a way never intended by Shakespeare and in a way that would have seemed quite foreign to the audiences of Shakespeare's day. Indeed, the name Puck seems to have been a generic Old English name for mischievous spirits and by the sixteenth century had come to be identified with "a shrewd and knavish sprite" otherwise known as Robin Goodfellow and Hobgoblin. In *A Midsummer Night's Dream*, of course, Shakespeare gave Puck immortality.

A Selective Bibliography on *A Midsummer Night's Dream*

Alexander, Marguerite. *An Introduction to Shakespeare and His Contemporaries.* London: Pan Books, 1979. 50–57.

Anderson, Linda. *A Kind of Wild Justice: Revenge in Shakespeare's Comedies.* Newark: U of Delaware P, 1987. 47–56.

Arthos, John. *Shakespeare's Use of Dream and Vision.* Totowa, N.J.: Roman and Littlefield, 1977. 15–84.

Bellringer, Alan W. "The Act of Change in *A Midsummer Night's Dream.*" *English Studies* 64 (1983): 201–17.

Berry, Ralph. *Shakespeare's Comedies: Explorations in Form.* Princeton: Princeton UP, 1972. 89–110.

Bevington, David. " 'But We Are Spirits of Another Sort': The Dark Side of Love and Magic in *A Midsummer Night's Dream.*" *Medieval and Renaissance Studies.* Ed. Siegfried Wenzel. Chapel Hill: U of North Carolina P, 1978. 80–92.

Bonazza, Blaze Odell. *Shakespeare's Early Comedies: A Structural Analysis.* The Hague: Mouton, 1966. 105–24.

Bryant, J. A., Jr. *Shakespeare and the Uses of Comedy.* Lexington: U of Kentucky P, 1986. 57–80.

Calderwood, James L. *Shakespearean Metadrama.* Minneapolis: U of Minnesota P, 1971. 120–48.

Champion, Larry S. *The Evolution of Shakespeare's Comedy.* Cambridge: Harvard UP, 1970. 47–59, 197–202.

Charlton, H. B. *Shakespearian Comedy.* New York: Macmillan, 1938. 100–22.

Clayton, Thomas. " 'Fie What a Question That If Thou Wert Near a Lewd Interpreter,' The Wall Scene in *A Midsummer Night's Dream.*" *Shakespeare Studies* 7 (1974): 101–23.

Cody, Richard. *The Landscape of the Mind: Pastoralism and Platonic Theory in Tasso's 'Aminta' and Shakespeare's Early Comedies.* Oxford: Clarendon, 1969. 127–50.

Cope, Jackson I. *The Theater and the Dream: From Metaphor to Form in Renaissance Drama.* Baltimore: Johns Hopkins UP, 1973. 211–44.

Cutts, John P. *The Shattered Glass: A Dramatic Pattern in Shakespeare's Early Plays.* Detroit: Wayne State UP, 1968. 49–55.

Faber, M. D. "Hermia's Dream: Royal Road to *A Midsummer Night's Dream.*" *Literature and Psychology* 22.4 (1972): 179–90.

Falk, Florence. "Dream and Ritual in *A Midsummer Night's Dream.*" *Comparative Drama* 14 (1980); 263–79.

Farrell, Kirby. *Shakespeare's Creation: The Language of Magic & Play.* Amherst: U of Massachusetts P, 1975. 97–116.

Fergusson, Francis. *Shakespeare: The Pattern in His Carpet.* New York: Delacorte, 1970. 120–27.

Foakes, R. A. "Introduction." *A Midsummer Night's Dream.* Cambridge, Eng.: Cambridge UP, 1984. 1–41.

Garber, Marjorie. *Coming of Age in Shakespeare.* London: Methuen, 1981. 116–43.

———. *Dream in Shakespeare: From Metaphor to Metamorphosis.* New Haven: Yale UP, 1974. 59–87.

Garner, Shirley Nelson. "*A Midsummer Night's Dream*: 'Jack shall have Jill; / Nought shall go ill.' " *Women's Studies* 9 (1981): 47–63.

Gilman, Ernest B. *The Curious Perspective: Literary and Pictorial Wit in the Seventeenth Century.* New Haven: Yale UP, 1978. 129–66.

Girard, Rene. "Myth and Ritual in Shakespeare's *A Midsummer Night's Dream.*" *Textual Strategies: Perspectives in Post-Structuralist Criticism.* Ed. Josue V. Harari. Ithaca: Cornell UP, 1979. 189–212.

Goldstein, Melvin. "Identity Crises in a Midsummer Nightmare: Comedy as Terror in Disguise." *Psychoanalytic Review* 60 (1973): 169–204.

Guilhamet, Leon. "*A Midsummer Night's Dream* as the Imitation of an Action." *Studies in English Literature* 15 (1975): 257–71.

Hamilton, A. C. *The Early Shakespeare.* San Marino, CA: Huntington Library, 1967. 216–33.

Hartman, Vicki Shahly. "*A Midsummer Night's Dream*: A Gentle Concord to the Oedipal Problem." *American Imago* 40 (1983): 355–69.

Hassel, R. Chris, Jr. *Faith and Folly in Shakespeare's Romantic Comedies*. Athens: U of Georgia P, 1980. 52–76.

Hawkins, Harriett. *Likenesses of Truth in Elizabethan and Restoration Drama*. Oxford: Clarendon, 1972. 27–50.

Henze, Richard. "*A Midsummer Night's Dream*: Analogues Image." *Shakespeare Studies* 7 (1974): 115–23.

Herbert, T. Walter. *Oberon's Mazed World: A Judicious Young Elizabethan Contemplates A Midsummer Night's Dream*. Baton Rouge: Louisiana State UP, 1977.

Holland, Norman N. "Freud on Shakespeare." *PMLA* 75 (1960): 163–73.

———. "Hermia's Dream." *Representing Shakespeare: New Psychoanalytic Essays*. Eds. Murray M. Schwartz and Coppelia Kahn. Baltimore: Johns Hopkins UP, 1980. 1–20.

Huston, J. Denis. "Bottom's Waking: Shakespeare's 'Most Rare Vision.'" *Studies in English Literature* 13 (1973): 208–22.

———. *Shakespeare's Comedies of Play*. New York: Columbia UP, 1981. 94–121.

Isaacs, Neil D. and Jack E. Reese. "Dithyramb and Paean in *A Midsummer Night's Dream*." *English Studies* 55 (1974): 351–57.

Kernan, Alvin B. *The Playwright as Magician: Shakespeare's Image of the Poet in the English Public Theater*. New Haven: Yale UP, 1979. 74–79.

Kott, Jan. *The Bottom Translation: Marlowe and Shakespeare and the Carnival Tradition*. Trans. Daniela Miedzyrzecka and Lillian Vallee. Evanston: Northwestern UP, 1987.

Knight, G. W. *The Shakespearian Tempest*. London: Methuen, 1953. 141–68.

Krieger, Elliot. *A Marxist Study of Shakespeare's Comedies*. New York: Macmillan, 1979. 37–69.

Lamb, M. E. "*A Midsummer Night's Dream*: The Myth of Theseus and the Minotaur." *Texas Studies in Literature and Language* 21 (1979): 478–91.

Leggatt, Alexander. *Shakespeare's Comedy of Love*. London: Methuen, 1974. 89–115.

MacCary, W. Thomas. *Friends and Lovers: The Phenomenology of Desire in Shakespeare's Comedy*. New York: Columbia UP, 1985. 134–49.

McFarland, Thomas. *Shakespeare's Pastoral Comedy*. Chapel Hill: U of North Carolina P. 1972. 78–97.

Marcus, Mordecai. "*A Midsummer Night's Dream*: The Dialect of Eros-Thanatos." *American Imago* 35 (1981): 269–78.

Marshall, David. "Exchanging Visions: Reading *A Midsummer Night's Dream*." *English Literary History* 49 (1982): 543–75.

Martz, William J. *Shakespeare's Universe of Comedy*. New York: D. Lewis, 1971. 61–79.

Mebane, John S. "Structure, Source, and Meaning in *A Midsummer Night's Dream*." *Texas Studies in Literature and Language* 24 (1982): 255–70.

Miller, Ronald F. "*A Midsummer Night's Dream*: The Fairies, Bottom, and the Mystery of Things." *Shakespeare Quarterly* 26 (1975): 254–68.

Muir, Kenneth, ed. *Shakespeare: The Comedies, A Collection of Critical Essays*. Englewood Cliffs, N.J.: Prentice-Hall, 1965.

———. *Shakespeare's Comic Sequence*. Liverpool, Eng.: Liverpool UP, 1979. 42–50.

Nevo, Ruth. *Comic Transformations in Shakespeare*. London: Methuen, 1980. 96–114.

Ormerod, David. "*A Midsummer Night's Dream*: The Monster in the Labyrinth." *Shakespeare Studies* 11 (1978): 39–52.

Paolucci, Anne. "The Lost Days in *A Midsummer Night's Dream.*" *Shakespeare Quarterly* 28 (1977): 317–26.

Parker, Douglas H. " 'Limander' and 'Helen' in *A Midsummer Night's Dream.*" *Shakespeare Quarterly* 33 (1982): 99–101.

Patterson, Annabel. *Shakespeare and the Popular Voice*. Oxford, Eng.,: Blackwell, 1989. 52–70.

Pearson, D'Orsay W. " 'Unkinde' Theseus: A Study in Renaissance Mythography." *English Literary Renaissance* 4 (1974): 276–98.

Richmond, Hugh M. *Shakespeare's Sexual Comedy: A Mirror for Lovers*. Indianapolis: Bobbs-Merrill, 1971. 102–22.

Riemer, A. P. *Antic Fables: Patterns on Evasion in Shakespeare's Comedies*. New York: St. Martin's, 1980. 68–75, 195–207.

Rose, Mark. *Shakespearean Design*. Cambridge, MA: Belknap, 1972. 1–26.

Selbourne, David. *The Making of A Midsummer Night's Dream*. London: Methuen, 1982.

Smidt, Kristian. *Unconformities in Shakespeare's Early Comedies*. Basinstoke, Eng.: Macmillan, 1986. 120–40.

Smith, Hallett. *Shakespeare's Romances: A Study of Some Ways of the Imagination*. San Marino, CA: Huntington Library, 1972. 121–39.

Smith, Jonathan C. "*A Midsummer Night's Dream* and the Allegory of Theologians." *Christianity and Literature* 28 (1979): 15–23.

Smith, Stephen L. "*A Midsummer Night's Dream*: Shakespeare, Play and Metaplay." *Centennial Review* 21 (1977): 194–209.

Snodgrass, W. D. *In Radical Pursuit: Critical Essays and Lectures*. New York: Harper, 1975. 203–40.

Stansbury, Joan. "Characterization of the Four Young Lovers in *A Midsummer Night's Dream.*" *Shakespeare Survey* 35 (1982): 57–83.

Swinden, Patrick. *An Introduction to Shakespeare's Comedies*. London: Macmillan, 1973. 51–64.

Taylor, Michael. "The Darker Purpose of *A Midsummer Night's Dream.*" *Studies in English Literature* 9 (1969): 259–73.

Toliver, Harold E. *Pastoral Forms and Attitudes*. Berkeley: U of California P, 1971. 82–115.

Vaughn, Jack A. *Shakespeare's Comedies*. New York: Ungar, 1980. 61–76.

Warren, Roger. *A Midsummer Night's Dream*. London: Macmillan, 1983.

Weiner, Andrew D. " 'Multforme Uniforme': *A Midsummer Night's Dream.*" *English Literary History* 38 (1971): 329–49.

Weiss, Theodore. *The Breadth of Clowns and Kings: Shakespeare's Early Comedies and Histories*. New York: Atheneum, 1971. 75–110.

Weld, John. *Meaning in Comedy: Studies in Elizabethan Romantic Comedy*. Albany: State U of New York P, 1975. 91–206.

Williams, Gary J. " 'The Concord of this Discord': Music in the Stage History of *A Midsummer Night's Dream.*" *Yale/Theatre* 4 (1973): 40–68.

Willson, Robert F., Jr. *"Their Form Confounded": Studies in the Burlesque Play from Udall to Sheridan*. The Hague: Mouton, 1975. 27–56.

Wyrick, Baker. "The Ass Motif in The Comedy of Errors and *A Midsummer Night's Dream.*" *Shakespeare Quarterly* 33 (1982): 432–48.

Young, David P. *Something of Great Constancy: The Art of A Midsummer Night's Dream*. New Haven: Yale University Press, 1966.

Zimbardo, R. A. "Regeneration and Reconciliation in *A Midsummer Night's Dream.*" *Shakespeare Studies* 6 (1972): 35–50.

William Shakespeare (1564–1616)
OTHELLO, THE MOOR OF VENICE

DRAMATIS PERSONAE

DUKE OF VENICE
BRABANTIO, *a senator, Desdemona's*
  father
OTHER SENATORS
GRATIANO, *brother to Brabantio*
LODOVICO, *kinsman to Brabantio*
OTHELLO, *a noble Moor in the service*
  of the Venetian state
CASSIO, *his lieutenant*
IAGO, *his ancient*
RODERIGO, *a Venetian gentleman*

MONTANO, *Othello's predecessor in the*
  government of Cyprus
CLOWN, *servant to Othello*
DESDEMONA, *daughter to Brabantio*
  and wife to Othello
EMILIA, *wife to Iago*
BIANCA, *mistress to Cassio*
SAILOR, MESSENGER, HERALD,
  OFFICERS, GENTLEMEN, MUSICIANS,
  and ATTENDANTS

SCENE: *Venice: a seaport in Cyprus.*

ACT I

SCENE I

Venice. A street.

[*Enter* RODERIGO *and* IAGO.]

RODERIGO. Tush, never tell me; I take it much unkindly
  That thou, Iago, who hast had my purse
  As if the strings were thine, shouldst know of this.
IAGO. 'Sblood, but you will not hear me.
  If ever I did dream of such a matter,
  Abhor me.
RODERIGO. Thou told'st me thou didst hold him in thy hate.
IAGO. Despise me, if I do not. Three great ones of the city,
  In personal suit to make me his lieutenant,
10 Off-caped° to him: and, by the faith of man,   *doffed caps*
  I know my price, I am worth no worse a place:
  But he, as loving his own pride and purposes,
  Evades them, with a bombast circumstance°   *pompous speech*
  Horribly stuffed with epithets of war;
  And, in conclusion,
  Nonsuits° my mediators; for, "Certes,"° says he,   *rejects / to be sure*
  "I have already chose my officer."
  And what was he?

Forsooth, a great arithmetician,°   *theorist*
20 One Michael Cassio, a Florentine,
A fellow almost damned in a fair wife;[1]
That never set a squadron in the field,
Nor the division of a battle knows
More than a spinster; unless the bookish theoric,
Wherein the togèd° consuls can propose,   *toga-wearing*
As masterly as he: mere prattle without practice
Is all his soldiership. But he, sir, had the election:
And I, of whom his eyes had seen the proof
At Rhodes, at Cyprus and on other grounds
30 Christian and heathen, must be be-lee'd and calmed°   *becalmed*
By debitor and creditor: this counter-caster,°   *bookkeeper*
He, in good time, must his lieutenant be,
And I—God bless the mark!—his Moorship's ancient.°   *standard-bearer*
RODERIGO.   By heaven, I rather would have been his hangman.
IAGO.   Why, there's no remedy; 'tis the curse of service,
Preferment goes by letter° and affection,   *references*
And not by old gradation,° where each second   *seniority*
Stood heir to the first. Now, sir, be judge yourself
Whether I in any just term am affined°   *bound*
To love the Moor.
40 RODERIGO.   I would not follow him then.
IAGO.   O, sir, content you;
I follow him to serve my turn upon him:
We cannot all be masters, nor all masters
Cannot be truly followed. You shall mark
Many a duteous and knee-crooking knave,
That doting on his own obsequious bondage
Wears out his time, much like his master's ass,
For nought but provender,° and when he's old, cashiered:°   *food / fired*
Whip me such honest knaves. Others there are
50 Who, trimmed° in forms and visages of duty,   *dressed*
Keep yet their hearts attending on themselves,
And throwing but shows of service on their lords
Do well thrive by them, and when they have lined their coats
Do themselves homage:° these fellows have some soul,   *serve*
And such a one do I profess myself.
For, sir,
It is as sure as you are Roderigo,
Were I the Moor, I would not be Iago:
In following him, I follow but myself;
60 Heaven is my judge, not I for love and duty,
But seeming so, for my peculiar° end: *personal*
For when my outward action doth demonstrate
The native act and figure of my heart

---

[1] Iago's meaning is unclear since Cassio is unmarried. However, in the source used by Shakespeare, Cassio was married and this reference to his fair wife is probably just a careless carryover.

In compliment extern,° 'tis not long after   *external appearance*
But I will wear my heart upon my sleeve
For daws° to peck at: I am not what I am.   *crows*
RODERIGO.   What a full fortune does the thick-lips° owe,°   *Othello / own*
  If he can carry't° thus!   *handle it*
IAGO.   Call up her father,
  Rouse him: make after him, poison his delight,
  Proclaim him in the streets; incense her kinsmen,
70 And, though he in a fertile climate dwell,
  Plague him with flies: though that his joy be joy,
  Yet throw such changes of vexation on't
  As it may lose some color.
RODERIGO.   Here is her father's house; I'll call aloud.
IAGO.   Do; with like timorous° accent and dire yell   *terrifying*
  As when, by night and negligence, the fire
  Is spied in populous cities.
RODERIGO.   What, ho, Brabantio! Signior Brabantio, ho!
IAGO.   Awake! what, ho, Brabantio! thieves! thieves! thieves!
80 Look to your house, your daughter and your bags!
  Thieves! thieves!

                    [BRABANTIO *appears above, at a window.*]

BRABANTIO.   What is the reason of this terrible summons?
  What is the matter there?
RODERIGO.   Signior, is all your family within?
IAGO.   Are your doors locked?
BRABANTIO.   Why, wherefore ask you this?
IAGO.   'Zounds,° sir, you're robbed; for shame, put on   *by God's wounds*
  your gown;
  Your heart is burst, you have lost half your soul;
  Even now, now, very now, an old black ram
  Is tupping° your white ewe. Arise, arise;   *coupling with*
90 Awake the snorting° citizens with the bell,   *snoring*
  Or else the devil will make a grandsire of you:
  Arise, I say.
BRABANTIO.   What, have you lost your wits?
RODERIGO.   Most reverend signior, do you know my voice?
BRABANTIO.   Not I: what are you?
RODERIGO.   My name is Roderigo.
BRABANTIO.   The worser welcome:
  I have charged thee not to haunt about my doors:
  In honest plainness thou hast heard me say
  My daughter is not for thee; and now, in madness,
  Being full of supper and distempering draughts,°   *befuddling drinks*
100 Upon malicious bravery,° dost thou come   *bravado*
  To start° my quiet.   *disturb*
RODERIGO.   Sir, sir, sir,—
BRABANTIO.   But thou must needs be sure
  My spirit and my place have in them power
  To make this bitter to thee.

RODERIGO.   Patience, good sir.

BRABANTIO.   What tell'st thou me of robbing? This is Venice;
   My house is not a grange.°   *farm*

RODERIGO.   Most grave Brabantio,
   In simple and pure soul I come to you.

IAGO.   'Zounds, sir, you are one of those that will not
   serve God, if the devil bid you. Because we come to do
110   you service and you think we are ruffians, you'll have your
   daughter covered with a Barbary° horse; you'll have your   *North African*
   nephews° neigh to you; you'll have coursers° for cousins,   *grandsons / horses*
   and gennets° for germans.°   *Spanish horses / kinfolk*

BRABANTIO.   What profane wretch art thou?

IAGO.   I am one, sir, that comes to tell you your daughter
   and the Moor are now making the beast with two backs.

BRABANTIO.   Thou art a villain.

IAGO.   You are—a senator.

BRABANTIO.   This thou shalt answer; I know thee, Roderigo.

RODERIGO.   Sir, I will answer any thing. But, I beseech you,
120   If't be your pleasure and most wise consent,
   As partly I find it is, that your fair daughter,
   At this odd-even° and dull watch o' the night,   *wee hour*
   Transported with no worse nor better guard
   But with a knave of common hire, a gondolier,
   To the gross clasps of a lascivious Moor,—
   If this be known to you, and your allowance,°   *permission*
   We then have done you bold and saucy° wrongs;   *impudent*
   But if you know not this, my manners tell me
   We have your wrong rebuke. Do not believe
130   That, from° the sense of all civility,   *contrary to*
   I thus would play and trifle with your reverence:
   Your daughter, if you have not given her leave,
   I say again, hath made a gross revolt,
   Tying her duty, beauty, wit and fortunes,
   In an extravagent and wheeling° stranger   *roving*
   Of here and everywhere. Straight satisfy yourself:
   If she be in her chamber or your house,
   Let loose on me the justice of the state
   For thus deluding you.

BRABANTIO.   Strike on the tinder, ho!
140   Give me a taper!° call up all my people!   *candle*
   This accident° is not unlike my dream: *event*
   Belief of it oppresses me already.
   Light, I say! light!

                                                    [Exit above.]

IAGO.   Farewell; for I must leave you:
   It seems not meet, nor wholesome to my place,
   To be produced—as, if I stay, I shall—
   Against the Moor: for I do know, the state,
   However this may gall him with some check,°   *reprimand*

Cannot with safety cast° him; for he's embarked   *dismiss*
150   With such loud reason to the Cyprus wars,
Which even now stand in act,° that, for their souls,   *have begun*
Another of his fathom° they have none   *capability*
To lead their business: in which regard,
Though I do hate him as I do hell-pains,
Yet for necessity of present life,
I must show out a flag and sign of love,
Which is indeed but sign. That you shall surely find him,
Lead to the Sagittary° the raised search;   *an inn*
And there will I be with him. So farewell.

                                        [*Exit.*]

[*Enter, below,* Brabantio, *in his night-gown, and* Servants *with torches.*]

Brabantio.   It is too true an evil: gone she is;
160   And what's to come of my despisèd time
Is nought but bitterness. Now, Roderigo,
Where didst thou see her? O unhappy girl!
With the Moor, say'st thou? Who would be a father!
How didst thou know 'twas she? O, she deceives me
Past thought! What said she to you? Get more tapers.
Raise all my kindred. Are they married, think you?
Roderigo.   Truly, I think they are.
Brabantio.   O heaven! How got she out? O treason of the blood!
Fathers, from hence trust not your daughters' minds
170   By what you see them act. Is there not charms
By which the property° of youth and maidhood   *true nature*
May be abused? Have you not read, Roderigo,
Of some such thing?
Roderigo.   Yes, sir, I have indeed.
Brabantio.   Call up my brother. O, would you had had her!
Some one way, some another. Do you know
Where we may apprehend her and the Moor?
Roderigo.   I think I can discover him, if you please
To get good guard and go along with me.
180 Brabantio.   Pray you, lead on. At every house I'll call;
I may command at most. Get weapons, ho!
And raise some special officers of night.
On, good Roderigo; I'll deserve° your pains.   *reward*

                                        [*Exeunt.*]

                    SCENE II
Another street.

                    [*Enter* Othello, Iago, *and* Attendants *with torches.*]

Iago.   Though in the trade of war I have slain men,
Yet do I hold it very stuff o' the conscience
To do no contrived murder: I lack iniquity
Sometimes to do me service: nine or ten times
I had thought to have yerked° him here under the ribs.   *stabbed*

OTHELLO.   'Tis better as it is.
IAGO.   Nay, but he prated
190   And spoke such scurvy and provoking terms
      Against your honor,
      That, with the little godliness I have,
      I did full hard forbear° him. But I pray you, sir,   with difficulty spare
      Are you fast married? Be assured of this,
      That the magnifico° is much beloved,   nobleman
      And hath in his effect a voice potential
      As double° as the duke's: he will divorce you,   strong
      Or put upon you what restraint and grievance
      The law, with all his might to enforce it on,
200   Will give him cable.°   scope
OTHELLO.   Let him do his spite:
      My services, which I have done the signiory,°   government
      Shall out-tongue° his complaints. 'Tis yet to know—   speak louder than
      Which, when I know that boasting is an honor,
      I shall promulgate—I fetch my life and being
      From men of royal siege,° and my demerits°   rank / merits
      May speak unbonneted° to as proud a fortune   proudly
      As this that I have reached: for know, Iago,
      But that I love the gentle Desdemona,
210   I would not my unhoused free condition
      Put into circumscription and confine°   i.e., marriage
      For the sea's worth. But, look! what lights come yond?
IAGO.   Those are the raisèd father and his friends:
      You were best go in.
OTHELLO.   Not I; I must be found:
      My parts,° my title and my perfect soul,   qualities
      Shall manifest me rightly. Is it they?
IAGO.   By Janus, I think no.

              [*Enter* CASSIO, *and certain* OFFICERS *with torches.*]

OTHELLO.   The servants of the duke, and my lieutenant.
      The goodness of the night upon you, friends!
220   What is the news?
CASSIO.   The duke does greet you, general,
      And he requires your haste-post-haste appearance,
      Even on the instant.
OTHELLO.   What is the matter, think you?
CASSIO.   Something from Cyprus, as I may divine:°   speculate
      It is a business of some heat:° the galleys   urgency
      Have sent a dozen sequent° messengers   successive
      This very night at one another's heels;
      And many of the consuls, raised and met,
      Are at the duke's already: you have been hotly called for;
      When, being not at your lodging to be found,
      The senate hath sent about three several° quests   separate
      To search you out.

230 OTHELLO.   'Tis well I am found by you.
      I will but spend a word here in the house,
      And go with you.

                                                              [*Exit.*]

CASSIO.   Ancient,° what makes he here?   *Ensign*
IAGO.   Faith, he tonight hath boarded a land carack:[2]
      If it prove lawful prize, he's made for ever.
CASSIO.   I do not understand.
IAGO.   He's married.
CASSIO.   To who?

                                                [*Re-enter* OTHELLO.]

IAGO.   Marry, to—Come, captain, will you go?
OTHELLO.   Have with you.
CASSIO.   Here comes another troop to seek for you.
IAGO.   It is Brabantio: general, be advised;
      He comes to bad intent.

           [*Enter* BRABANTIO, RODERIGO, *and* OFFICERS *with torches and weapons.*]

240 OTHELLO.   Holla! stand there!
      RODERIGO.   Signior, it is the Moor.
      BRABANTIO.   Down with him, thief!

                                              [*They draw on both sides.*]

IAGO.   You, Roderigo! come, sir, I am for you.
OTHELLO.   Keep up your bright swords, for the dew will rust them.
      Good signior, you shall more command with years
      Than with your weapons.
BRABANTIO.   O thou foul thief, where hast thou stowed my daughter?
      Damned as thou art, thou hast enchanted her;
250   For I'll refer me to all things of sense,°   *common sense*
      If she in chains of magic were not bound,
      Whether a maid so tender, fair and happy,
      So opposite to marriage that she shunned
      The wealthy curled° darlings of our nation,   *i.e., coiffured*
      Would ever have, to incur a general mock,
      Run from her guardage° to the sooty bosom   *legal home*
      Of such a thing as thou, to fear, not to delight.
      Judge me the world, if 'tis not gross° in sense   *obvious*
      That thou hast practised on her with foul charms,
260   Abused her delicate youth with drugs or minerals
      That weaken motion: I'll have't disputed on;
      'Tis probable, and palpable to thinking.
      I therefore apprehend and do attach° thee   *arrest*
      For an abuser of the world, a practiser

---

[2] A trading ship with a high stern; a treasure ship.

Of arts inhibited° and out of warrant.°   *prohibited / unlawful*
Lay hold upon him: if he do resist,
Subdue him at his peril.
OTHELLO.   Hold your hands,
Both you of my inclining and the rest:
Were it my cue to fight, I should have known it
270   Without a prompter. Where will you that I go
To answer this your charge?
BRABANTIO.   To prison, till fit time
Of law and course of direct session
Call thee to answer.
OTHELLO.   What if I do obey?
How may the duke be therewith satisfied,
Whose messengers are here about my side,
Upon some present business of the state
To bring me to him?
FIRST OFFICER.   'Tis true, most worthy signior;
The duke's in council, and your noble self,
I am sure, is sent for,
BRABANTIO.   How! the duke in council!
280   In this time of the night! Bring him away:
Mine's not an idle cause: the duke himself,
Or any of my brothers of the state,
Cannot but feel this wrong as 'twere their own;
For if such actions may have passage free,
Bond-slaves and pagans shall our statesmen be.

                                                          [*Exeunt.*]

                        SCENE III

A council-chamber.

        [*The* DUKE *and* SENATORS *sitting at a table;* OFFICERS *attending.*]

DUKE.   There is no composition° in these news   *consistency*
That gives them credit.
FIRST SENATOR.   Indeed they are disproportioned;
My letters say a hundred and seven galleys.
DUKE.   And mine, a hundred and forty.
SECOND SENATOR.   And mine, two hundred:
290   But though they jump° not on a just° account,—   *settle / precise*
As in these cases, where the aim° reports,   *trend*
'Tis oft with difference,—yet do they all confirm
A Turkish fleet, and bearing up to Cyprus.
DUKE.   Nay, it is possible enough to judgement:
I do not so secure me in° the error,   *take such assurance from*
But° the main article I do approve°   *But that / believe*
In fearful sense.
SAILOR [*within*]. What, ho! what, ho! what, ho!
FIRST OFFICER.   A messenger from the galleys.

[*Enter* SAILOR.]

DUKE.   Now, what's the business?

300 SAILOR.   The Turkish preparation makes for Rhodes;
So was I bid report here to the state
By Signior Angelo.

DUKE.   How say you by this change!

FIRST SENATOR.   This cannot be,
By no assay° of reason: 'tis a pageant°   *test / ploy*
To keep us in false gaze. When we consider
The importancy of Cyprus to the Turk,
And let ourselves again but understand
That as it more concerns the Turk than Rhodes,
So may he with more facile question° bear° it,   *battle / capture*
310 For that it stands not in such warlike brace,°   *condition*
But altogether lacks the abilities°   *strengths*
That Rhodes is dressed in: if we make thought of this,
We must not think the Turk is so unskilful
To leave that latest which concerns him first,
Neglecting an attempt of ease and gain,
To wake and wage° a danger profitless.   *risk*

DUKE.   Nay, in all confidence, he's not for Rhodes.

FIRST OFFICER.   Here is more news.

[*Enter a* MESSENGER.]

320 MESSENGER.   The Ottomites,° reverend and gracious,   *Turks*
Steering with due course toward the isle of Rhodes,
Have there injointed° them with an after° fleet.   *combined / following*

FIRST SENATOR.   Ay, so I thought. How many, as you guess?

MESSENGER.   Of thirty sail: and now they do re-stem°   *turn about to*
Their backward course, bearing with frank appearance
Their purposes toward Cyprus. Signior Montano,
Your trusty and most valiant servitor,
With his free duty recommends° you thus,   *informs*
And prays you to believe him.

DUKE.   'Tis certain then for Cyprus.
330 Marcus Luccicos, is not he in town?

FIRST SENATOR.   He's now in Florence.

DUKE.   Write from us to him; post-post-haste dispatch.

FIRST SENATOR.   Here comes Brabantio and the valiant Moor.

[*Enter* BRABANTIO, OTHELLO, IAGO, RODERIGO, *and* OFFICERS.]

DUKE.   Valiant Othello, we must straight employ you
Against the general enemy Ottoman.
[*To Brabantio.*] I did not see you; welcome, gentle signior;
We lacked your counsel and your help tonight.

BRABANTIO.   So did I yours. Good your grace, pardon me;
Neither my place nor aught I heard of business
340 Hath raised me from my bed, nor doth the general care
Take hold on me; for my particular grief

Is of so flood-gate° and o'erbearing nature   *overflowing*
That it engluts° and swallows other sorrows,   *engulfs*
And it is still itself.
DUKE.   Why, what's the matter?
BRABANTIO.   My daughter! O, my daughter!
ALL.   Dead?
BRABANTIO.   Ay, to me;
She is abused, stol'n from me and corrupted
By spells and medicines bought of mountebanks;°   *quacks*
For nature so preposterously to err,
Being not deficient, blind, or lame of sense,
350   Sans° witchcraft could not.   *without*
DUKE.   Who'er he be that in this foul proceeding
Hath thus beguiled your daughter of herself
And you of her, the bloody book of law
You shall yourself read in the bitter letter
After your own sense, yea, though our proper° son   *own*
Stood in your action.°   *court action*
BRABANTIO.   Humbly I thank your grace.
Here is the man, this Moor; whom now, it seems,
Your special mandate for the state-affairs
Hath hither brought.
ALL.   We are very sorry for't.
360 DUKE [*to Othello*]. What in your own part can you say to this?
BRABANTIO.   Nothing, but this is so.
OTHELLO.   Most potent, grave, and reverend signiors,
My very noble and approved good masters,
That I have ta'en away this old man's daughter,
It is most true; true, I have married her:
The very head and front of my offending
Hath this extent, no more. Rude am I in my speech,
And little blest with the soft phrase of peace;
370   For since these arms of mine had seven years' pith°,   *strength*
Till now some nine moons wasted, they have used
Their dearest° action in the tented field;   *most important*
And little of this great world can I speak,
More than pertains to feats of broil and battle;
And therefore little shall I grace my cause
In speaking for myself. Yet, by your gracious patience,
I will a round unvarnished tale deliver
Of my whole course of love; what drugs, what charms,
What conjuration and what mighty magic—
380   For such proceeding I am charged withal—
I won his daughter.
BRABANTIO.   A maiden never bold;
Of spirit so still and quiet that her motion°   *soul*
Blushed at herself; and she—in spite of nature,
Of years, of country, credit, everything—
To fall in love with what she feared to look on!
It is a judgement maimed and most imperfect

That will confess perfection so could err
Against all rules of nature; and must be driven
To find out practices of cunning hell,
390   Why this should be. I therefore vouch again,
That with some mixtures powerful o'er the blood,
Or with some dram conjured to this effect,
He wrought upon her.
DUKE.   To vouch° this, is no proof,   *assert*
Without more certain and more overt test
Than these thin habits° and poor likelihoods   *dressings*
Of modern° seeming do prefer against him.   *ordinary*
FIRST SENATOR.   But, Othello, speak:
Did you by indirect and forced courses
Subdue and poison this young maid's affections?
400   Or came it by request, and such fair question
As soul to soul affordeth?
OTHELLO.   I do beseech you,
Send for the lady to the Sagittary,
And let her speak of me before her father:
If you do find me foul in her report,
The trust, the office I do hold of you,
Not only take away, but let your sentence
Even fall upon my life.
DUKE.   Fetch Desdemona hither.
OTHELLO.   Ancient, conduct them; you best know the place.

                                        [*Exeunt* IAGO *and* ATTENDANTS.]

And till she come, as truly as to heaven
410   I do confess that vices of my blood,
So justly to your grave ears I'll present
How I did thrive in this fair lady's love
And she in mine.
DUKE.   Say it, Othello.
OTHELLO.   Her father loved me, oft invited me,
Still questioned me the story of my life
From year to year, the battles, sieges, fortunes,
That I have passed.
I ran it through, even from my boyish days
420   To the very moment that he bade me tell it:
Wherein I spake of most disastrous chances,
Of moving accidents by flood and field,
Of hair-breadth 'scapes i' the imminent deadly breach,
Of being taken by the insolent foe,
And sold to slavery, of my redemption thence,
And portance° in my travels' history: *deportment*
Wherein of antres° vast and deserts idle,   *caves*
Rough quarries, rocks, and hills whose heads touch heaven,
It was my hint to speak,—such was the process;
430   And of the Cannibals that each other eat,
The Anthropophagi,° and men whose heads   *man-eaters*

Do grow beneath their shoulders. This to hear
Would Desdemona seriously incline:
But still the house-affairs would draw her thence;
Which ever as she could with haste dispatch,
She'ld come again, and with a greedy ear
Devour up my discourse: which I observing,
Took once a pliant° hour, and found good means   convenient
To draw from her a prayer of earnest heart
440   That I would all my pilgrimage dilate.°   relate
Whereof by parcels she had something heard,
But not intentively:° I did consent,   attentively
And often did beguile her of her tears
When I did speak of some distressful stroke
That my youth suffered. My story being done,
She gave me for my pains a world of sighs:
She swore, in faith, 'twas strange, 'twas passing strange;
'Twas pitiful, 'twas wondrous pitiful:
She wished she had not heard it, yet she wished
450   That heaven had made her such a man: she thanked me,
And bade me, if I had a friend that loved her,
I should but teach him how to tell my story,
And that would woo her. Upon this hint I spake:
She loved me for the dangers I had passed,
And I loved her that she did pity them.
This only is the witchcraft I have used.
Here comes the lady; let her witness it.

                          [*Enter* DESDEMONA, IAGO, *and* ATTENDANTS.]

DUKE.   I think this tale would win my daughter too.
        Good Brabantio,
460   Take up this mangled matter at the best:
        Men do their broken weapons rather use
        Than their bare hands.
BRABANTIO.   I pray you, hear her speak:
        If she confess that she was half the wooer,
        Destruction on my head, if my bad blame
        Light on the man! Come hither, gentle mistress:
        Do you perceive in all this noble company
        Where most you owe obedience?
DESDEMONA.   My noble father,
        I do perceive here a divided duty:
        To you I am bound for life and education;
470   My life and education both do learn me
        How to respect you; you are the lord of duty,
        I am hitherto your daughter: but here's my husband,
        And so much duty as my mother showed
        To you, preferring you before her father,
        So much I challenge° that I may profess   assert

Due to the Moor my lord.

BRABANTIO.   God be with you! I have done.
Please it your grace, on to the state-affairs:
I had rather to adopt a child than get° it.   *beget*
Come hither, Moor:
480   I here do give thee that with all my heart,
Which, but thou hast already, with all my heart
I would keep from thee. For your sake, jewel,
I am glad at soul I have no other child;
For thy escape would teach me tyranny,
To hang clogs° on them. I have done, my lord.   *weights*

DUKE.   Let me speak like yourself, and lay a sentence
Which, as a grise° or step, may help these lovers   *degree*
Into your favor.
When remedies are past, the griefs are ended
490   By seeing the worst, which late° on hopes depended.   *until lately*
To mourn a mischief that is past and gone
Is the next way to draw new mischief on.
What cannot be preserved when fortune takes,
Patience her injury a mockery makes.
The robbed that smiles steals something from the thief;
He robs himself that spends a bootless° grief.   *useless*

BRABANTIO.   So let the Turk of Cyprus us beguile;
We lose it not so long as we can smile.
He bears the sentence well, that nothing bears
500   But the free comfort which from thence he hears;
But he bears both the sentence and the sorrow,
That, to pay grief, must of poor patience borrow.
These sentences, to sugar or to gall,
Being strong on both sides, are equivocal:
But words are words; I never yet did hear
That the bruised heart was piercèd° through the ear.   *relieved (lanced)*
I humbly beseech you, proceed to the affairs of state.

DUKE.   The Turk with a most mighty preparation makes for
Cyprus. Othello, the fortitude of the place is best known
510   to you; and though we have there a substitute of most
allowed° sufficiency, yet opinion, a sovereign mistress of   *acknowledged*
effects, throws a more safer voice on you: you must
therefore be content to slubber° the gloss of your new   *sully*
fortunes with this more stubborn and boisterous expedition.

OTHELLO.   The tyrant custom, most grave senators,
Hath made the flinty and steel couch of war
My thrice-driven° bed of down: I do agnize°   *thrice-sifted / recognize*
A natural and prompt alacrity
I find in hardness; and do undertake
520   These present wars against the Ottomites.
Most humbly therefore bending to your state,
I crave fit disposition° for my wife,   *provision*
Due reference° of place and exhibition,°   *assignment / funds*

With such accommodation and besort°   *company*
   As levels with her breeding.
DUKE.   If you please,
   Be 't at her father's.
BRABANTIO.   I'll not have it so.
OTHELLO.   Nor I.
DESDEMONA.   Nor I, I would not there reside,
   To put my father in impatient thoughts
   By being in his eye. Most gracious duke,
530   To my unfolding lend your prosperous ear,
   And let me find a charter° in your voice   *permission*
   To assist my simpleness.
DUKE.   What would you, Desdemona?
DESDEMONA.   That I did love the Moor to live with him,
   My downright violence and storm of fortunes
   May trumpet to the world: my heart's subdued
   Even to the very quality° of my lord: *appearance*
   I saw Othello's visage in his mind,
   And to his honor and his valiant parts
540   Did I my soul and fortunes consecrate.
   So that, dear lords, if I be left behind,
   A moth of peace, and he go to the war,
   The rites for which I love him are bereft me,
   And I a heavy interim shall support
   By his dear absence. Let me go with him.
OTHELLO.   Let her have your voices.
   Vouch with me, heaven, I therefore beg it not,
   To please the palate of my appetite;
   Nor to comply with heat°—the young affects°   *lust / youthful passions*
550   In me defunct—and proper° satisfaction;   *personal*
   But to be free and bounteous to her mind:
   And heaven defend° your good souls, that you think   *forbid*
   I will your serious and great business scant
   For° she is with me. No, when light-winged toys   *Because*
   Of feathered Cupid seel° with wanton dullness   *blind*
   My speculative and officed instruments,[3]
   That my disports° corrupt and taint my business,   *diversions*
   Let housewives make a skillet of my helm,°   *helmet*
   And all indign° and base adversities   *unworthy*
560   Make head against my estimation!°   *reputation*
DUKE.   Be it as you shall privately determine,
   Either for her stay or going: the affair cries haste,
   And speed must answer 't; you must hence tonight.
DESDEMONA.   Tonight, my lord?
DUKE.   This night.
OTHELLO.   With all my heart.
DUKE.   At nine i' the morning here we'll meet again.

---

[3] My clear-sighted and properly functioning faculties.

Othello, leave some officer behind,
And he shall our commission bring to you;
With such things else of quality and respect
As doth import° you.   *matter to*
OTHELLO.   So please your grace, my ancient;
570 A man he is of honesty and trust:
To his conveyance I assign my wife,
With what else needful your good grace shall think
To be sent after me.
DUKE.   Let it be so.
Good night to every one. [*To* BRABANTIO] And, noble signior,
If virtue no delighted° beauty lack,   *delightful*
Your son-in-law is far more fair than black.
FIRST SENATOR.   Adieu, brave Moor; use Desdemona well.
BRABANTIO.   Look to her, Moor, if thou has eyes to see:
She has deceived her father, and may thee.

[*Exeunt* DUKE, SENATORS, OFFICERS, &c.]

580 OTHELLO.   My life upon her faith! Honest Iago,
My Desdemona must I leave to thee:
I prithee, let thy wife attend on her;
And bring them after in the best advantage.°   *opportunity*
Come, Desdemona; I have but an hour
Of love, of worldly matters and direction,
To spend with thee: we must obey the time.

[*Exeunt* OTHELLO *and* DESDEMONA.]

RODERIGO.   Iago!
IAGO.   What say'st thou, noble heart?
RODERIGO.   What will I do, thinkest thou?
590 IAGO.   Why, go to bed and sleep.
RODERIGO.   I will incontinently° drown myself.   *immediately*
IAGO.   If thou dost, I shall never love thee after. Why, thou silly
     gentleman!
RODERIGO.   It is silliness to live when to live is torment; and
     then have we a prescription to die when death is our physi-
     cian.
IAGO.   O villainous! I have looked upon the world for four times
     seven years; and since I could distinguish betwixt a benefit
     and an injury, I never found man that knew how to love
600 himself. Ere I would say I would drown myself for the love of
     a guinea-hen,° I would change my humanity with a baboon.   *whore*
RODERIGO.   What should I do? I confess it is my shame to be so
     fond; but it is not in my virtue to amend it.
IAGO.   Virtue! a fig! 'tis in ourselves that we are thus or
     thus. Our bodies are gardens; to the which our wills are
     gardeners: so that if we will plant nettles° or sow lettuce,   *weeds*
     set hyssop° and weed up thyme, supply it with one gender   *a mint*
     of herbs or distract it with many, either to have it sterile

with idleness or manured with industry, why, the power
610   and corrigible° authority of this lies in our wills. If the   *corrective*
balance of our lives had not one scale of reason to poise°   *counterweight*
another of sensuality, the blood and baseness of our natures
would conduct us to most preposterous conclusions: but
we have reason to cool our raging motions, our carnal stings,
our unbitted° lusts; whereof I take this, that you call love,   *unbridled*
to be a sect° or scion.°   *cutting / graft*
RODERIGO.   It cannot be.
IAGO.   It is merely a lust of the blood and a permission of the
will. Come, be a man: drown thyself! drown cats and blind
620   puppies. I have professed me thy friend, and I confess me
knit to thy deserving with cables of perdurable° toughness: *everlasting*
I could never better stead° thee than now. Put money in thy   *assist*
purse; follow thou the wars; defeat° thy favor° within an   *disguise / face*
usurped° beard; I say, put money in thy purse. It cannot   *false*
be that Desdemona should long continue her love to the
Moor—put money in thy purse—nor he his to her: it was a
violent commencement, and thou shalt see an answerable
sequestration;° put but money in thy purse. These Moors   *similar separation*
630   are changeable in their wills:—fill thy purse with money.
The food that to him now is as luscious as locusts, shall be to
him shortly as bitter as coloquintida.° She must change for   *bitter apple*
youth: when she is sated with his body, she will find the er-
ror of her choice: she must have change, she must: therefore
put money in thy purse. If thou wilt needs damn thyself, do
it a more delicate way than drowning. Make all the money
thou canst: if sanctimony and a frail vow betwixt an erring
barbarian and a supersubtle Venetian be not too hard for my
wits and all the tribe of hell, thou shalt enjoy her; therefore
640   make money. A pox of drowning thyself! it is clean out of
the way: seek thou rather to be hanged in compassing°   *attaining*
thy joy than to be drowned and go without her.
RODERIGO.   Wilt thou be fast° to my hopes, if I depend on the   *true*
issue?
IAGO.   Thou art sure of me: go, make money: I have told thee
often, and I retell thee again and again, I hate the Moor: my
cause is hearted;° thine hath no less reason. Let us be   *heart-felt*
conjunctive° in our revenge against him: if thou canst cuckold   *joined*
650   him, thou dost thyself a pleasure, me a sport. There are
many events in the womb of time, which will be delivered.
Traverse; go; provide thy money. We will have more of this
tomorrow. Adieu.
RODERIGO.   Where shall we meet 'i the morning?
IAGO.   At my lodging.
RODERIGO.   I'll be with thee betimes.°   *early*
IAGO.   Go to; farewell. Do you hear, Roderigo?
RODERIGO.   What say you?
IAGO.   No more of drowning, do you hear?

RODERIGO.   I am changed: I'll go sell all my land. [*Exit.*]
660 IAGO.   Thus do I ever make my fool my purse;
      For I mine own gained knowledge should profane,
      If I would time expend with such a snipe°   *fool*
      But for my sport and profit. I hate the Moor;
      And it is thought abroad that 'twixt my sheets
      He has done my office: I know not if't be true;
      But I for mere suspicion in that kind
      Will do as if for surety.° He holds me well;   *certainty*
      The better shall my purpose work on him.
      Cassio's a proper° man: let me see now;   *handsome*
670   To get his place, and to plume up° my will   *satisfy*
      In double knavery—How, how?—Let's see:—
      After some time, to abuse Othello's ear
      That he is too familiar with his wife.
      He hath a person and a smooth dispose°   *disposition*
      To be suspected; framed to make women false.
      The Moor is of a free and open nature,
      That thinks men honest that but seem to be so;
      And will as tenderly be led by the nose
      As asses are.
680   I have 't. It is engendered. Hell and night
      Must bring this monstrous birth to the world's light. [*Exit.*]

ACT II

SCENE I

A seaport in Cyprus. An open place near the quay.

[*Enter* MONTANO *and two* GENTLEMEN.]

MONTANO.   What from the cape can you discern at sea?
FIRST GENTLEMAN.   Nothing at all: it is a high-wrought flood;
      I cannot, 'twixt the heaven and the main,
      Descry° a sail.   *See*
MONTANO.   Methinks the wind hath spoke aloud at land;
      A fuller blast ne'er shook our battlements:
      If it hath ruffianed° so upon the sea,   *raged*
690   What ribs of oak, when mountains melt on them,
      Can hold the mortise?[4] What shall we hear of this?
SECOND GENTLEMAN.   A segregation° of the Turkish fleet: *dispersal*
      For do but stand upon the foaming shore,
      The chidden° billow seems to pelt the clouds;   *driven*
      The wind-shaked surge, with high and monstrous mane,
      Seems to cast water on the burning bear,°   *a constellation*

---

[4] The slot into which the ribs of the ship are fitted.

And quench the guards[5] of the ever-fixèd pole:
I never did like molestation° view   *disruption*
On the enchafèd flood.°   *raging sea*
MONTANO.   If that the Turkish fleet
Be not ensheltered and embayed, they are drowned;
700   It is impossible to bear it out.

                                       [*Enter a third* GENTLEMAN.]

THIRD GENTLEMAN.   News, lads! Our wars are done.
The desperate tempest hath so banged the Turks,
That their designment° halts: a noble ship of Venice   *plan*
Hath seen a grievous wreck and sufferance°   *suffering*
On most part of their fleet.
MONTANO.   How! Is this true?
THIRD GENTLEMAN.   The ship is here put in,
A Veronesa; Michael Cassio,
Lieutenant to the warlike Moor Othello,
Is come on shore: the Moor himself at sea,
710   And is in full commission here for Cyprus.
MONTANO.   I am glad on't; 'tis a worthy governor.
THIRD GENTLEMAN.   But this same Cassio, though he speak of comfort
Touching the Turkish loss, yet he looks sadly
And prays the Moor be safe; for they were parted
With foul and violent tempest.
MONTANO.   Pray heavens he be;
For I have served him, and the man commands
Like a full soldier. Let's to the seaside, ho!
As well to see the vessel that's come in
As to throw out our eyes for brave Othello,
720   Even till we make the main and the aerial blue
An indistinct regard.°   *view (horizon)*
THIRD GENTLEMAN.   Come, let's do so;
For every minute is expectancy
Of more arrivance.

                                               [*Enter* CASSIO.]

CASSIO.   Thanks, you the valiant of this warlike isle,
That so approve the Moor! O, let the heavens
Give him defence against the elements,
For I have lost him on a dangerous sea.
MONTANO.   Is he well shipped?
CASSIO.   His bark is stoutly timbered, and his pilot
730   Of very expert and approved allowance;°   *acclaim*
Therefore my hopes, not surfeited to death,°   *not excessive*
Stand in bold cure.°   *in good stead*

                         [*A cry within:* "A sail, a sail, a sail!"]

---

[5] The stars near (or guarding) the North Star.

[*Enter a fourth* Gentleman.]

Cassio.   What noise?

Fourth Gentleman.   The town is empty; on the brow o' the sea
   Stand ranks of people, and then cry "A sail!"

Cassio.   My hopes do shape him for the governor.

[*Guns heard.*]

Second Gentlemen.   They do discharge their shot of courtesy:
   Our friends at least.

740 Cassio.   I pray you, sir, go forth,
   And give us truth who 'tis that is arrived.

Second Gentleman.   I shall.

[*Exit.*]

Montano.   But, good lieutenant, is your general wived?

Cassio.   Most fortunately: he hath achieved a maid
   That paragons° description and wild fame;   *tops*
   One that excels the quirks of blazoning° pens,   *praising*
   And in the essential vesture° of creation   *clothing*
   Does tire the ingener.°   *creator of the praise*

[*Re-enter second* Gentleman.]

   How now! who has put in?

Second Gentleman.   'Tis one Iago, ancient to the general.

750 Cassio.   He has had most favorable and happy speed:
   Tempests themselves, high seas, and howling winds,
   The guttered° rocks, and congregated sands,   *jagged*
   Traitors ensteeped° to clog° the guiltless keel,   *submerged / obstruct*
   As having sense of beauty, do omit°   *neglect*
   Their mortal° natures, letting go safely by   *deadly*
   The divine Desdemona.

Montano.   What is she?

Cassio.   She that I spake of, our great captain's captain,
   Left in the conduct of the bold Iago;
   Whose footing° here anticipates our thoughts   *setting foot*
760 A se'nnight's° speed. Great Jove, Othello guard,   *week's*
   And swell his sail with thine own powerful breath,
   That he may bless this bay with his tall ship,
   Make love's quick pants in Desdemona's arms,
   Give renewed fire to our extinct spirits,
   And bring all Cyprus comfort.

[*Enter* Desdemona, Emilia, Iago, Roderigo, *and* Attendants.]

                    O, behold,
   The riches of the ship is come on shore!
   Ye men of Cyprus, let her have your knees.

Hail to thee, lady! and the grace of heaven,
Before, behind thee, and on every hand,
Enwheel° thee round!   *Encircle*

770 DESDEMONA.   I thank you, valiant Cassio.
What tidings can you tell me of my lord?
CASSIO.   He is not yet arrived: nor know I aught
But that he's well and will be shortly here.
DESDEMONA.   O, but I fear—How lost you company?
CASSIO.   The great contention of the sea and skies
Parted our fellowship—But, hark! a sail.

[*A cry within:* "A sail, a sail!" *Guns heard.*]

SECOND GENTLEMAN.   They give their greeting to the citadel:
This likewise is a friend.
CASSIO.   See for the news.

[*Exit* GENTLEMAN.]

780   Good ancient, you are welcome. [*To* EMILIA.] Welcome, mistress:
Let it not gall your patience, good Iago,
That I extend° my manners; 'tis my breeding   *show*
That gives me this bold show of courtesy.

[*Kissing her.*]

IAGO.   Sir, would she give you so much of her lips
As of her tongue she oft bestows on me,
You'd have enough.
DESDEMONA.   Alas, she has no speech.
IAGO.   In faith, too much;
I find it still when I have list° to sleep: *desire*
Marry, before your ladyship, I grant,
790   She puts her tongue a little in her heart
And chides with thinking.
EMILIA.   You have little cause to say so.
IAGO.   Come on, come on; you are pictures out of doors,
Bells in your parlors, wild-cats in your kitchens,
Saints in your injuries, devils being offended,
Players in your housewifery, and housewives° in your   *i.e., hard working*
beds,
DESDEMONA.   O, fie upon thee, slanderer!
IAGO.   Nay, it is true, or else I am a Turk:
You rise to play, and go to bed to work.
EMILIA.   You shall not write my praise.
800 IAGO.   No, let me not.
DESDEMONA.   What wouldst thou write of me, if thou shouldst
praise me?
IAGO.   O gentle lady, do not put me to't;
For I am nothing if not critical.

DESDEMONA.   Come on, assay°—There's one gone to the harbor?   *try*
IAGO.   Ay, madam.
DESDEMONA.   I am not merry; but I do beguile°   *divert attention from*
    The thing I am by seeming otherwise.
    Come, how wouldst thou praise me?
810 IAGO.   I am about it; but indeed my invention
    Comes from my pate as birdlime does from frize;[6]
    It plucks out brains and all: but my Muse labors,
    And thus she is delivered.
    If she be fair° and wise, fairness and wit,   *blonde, pretty*
    The one's for use, the other useth it.
DESDEMONA.   Well praised! How if she be black° and witty?   *brunette, ugly*
IAGO.   If she be black, and thereto have a wit,
    She'll find a white° that shall her blackness fit.   *fair person*
DESDEMONA.   Worse and worse.
EMILIA.   How if fair and foolish?
820 IAGO.   She never yet was foolish that was fair;
    For even her folly helped her to an heir.
DESDEMONA.   These are old fond° paradoxes to make fools laugh   *foolish*
    i' the alehouse. What miserable praise hast thou for her
    that's foul and foolish?
IAGO.   There's none so foul, and foolish thereunto,
    But does foul pranks which fair and wise ones do.
DESDEMONA.   O heavy ignorance! thou praisest the worst best.
    But what praise couldst thou bestow on a deserving woman
    indeed, one that in the authority of her merit did justly
830   put on° the vouch° of very malice itself?   *claim / praise*
IAGO.   She that was ever fair and never proud,
    Had tongue at will and yet was never loud,
    Never lacked gold and yet went never gay,°   *gaily dressed*
    Fled from her wish and yet said "Now I may;"
    She that, being angered, her revenge being nigh,
    Bade her wrong stay and her displeasure fly;
    She that in wisdom never was so frail
    To change the cod's head for the salmon's tail;[7]
840   She that could think and ne'er disclose her mind,
    See suitors following and not look behind;
    She was a wight,° if ever such wight were,—   *person*
DESDEMONA.   To do what?
IAGO.   To suckle fools and chronicle small beer.°   *keep trivial accounts*
DESDEMONA.   O most lame and impotent conclusion! Do not
    learn of him, Emilia, though he be thy husband. How say
    you, Cassio? Is he not a most profane and liberal°   *lewd*
    counsellor?

---

[6] I.e., but indeed my ideas come from my brain as unwillingly as tar comes unstuck from coarse cloth.
[7] The cod, a common edible fish, is often said to be all head. The salmon is a delicacy, but its tail would be inedible.

CASSIO.   He speaks home,° madam: you may relish him more   *pointedly*
   in the soldier than in the scholar.
850 IAGO [*aside*]. He takes her by the palm: ay, well said, whisper:
   with as little a web as this will I ensnare as great a fly as
   Cassio. Ay, smile upon her, do; I will gyve° thee in thine   *fetter*
   own courtship. You say true; 'tis so, indeed: if such tricks
   as these strip you out of your lieutenantry, it had been
   better you had not kissed your three fingers so oft, which
   now again you are most apt to play the sir° in.   *gentleman*
   Very good; well kissed! an excellent courtesy! 'tis so, indeed.
   Yet again your fingers to your lips? Would they were clyster-
   pipes° for your sake! [*Trumpet within.*] The Moor! I   *enema tubes*
   know his trumpet.
860 CASSIO.   'Tis truly so.
DESDEMONA.   Let's meet him and receive him.
CASSIO.   Lo, where he comes!

                    [*Enter* OTHELLO *and* ATTENDANTS.]

OTHELLO.   O my fair warrior!
DESDEMONA.   My dear Othello!
OTHELLO.   It gives me wonder great as my content
   To see you here before me. O my soul's joy!
   If after every tempest come such calms,
   May the winds blow till they have wakened death!
   And let the laboring bark climb hills of seas
870   Olympus-high and duck again as low
   As hell's from heaven! If it were now to die,
   'Twere now to be most happy; for I fear,
   My soul hath her content so absolute
   That not another comfort like to this
   Succeeds in unknown fate.
DESDEMONA.   The heavens forbid
   But that our loves and comforts should increase,
   Even as our days do grow!
OTHELLO.   Amen to that, sweet powers!
   I cannot speak enough of this content;
   It stops me here; it is too much of joy:
880   And this, and this, the greatest discords be

                      [*Kissing her.*]

   That e'er our hearts shall make!
IAGO.   [*Aside*] O, you are well tuned now!
   But I'll set down the pegs that make this music
   As honest as I am.[8]
OTHELLO.   Come, let us to the castle.
   News, friends; our wars are done, the Turks are drowned.

---

   [8] I.e., Iago will untune the heartstrings of Othello and Desdemona until their loving music
is no more honest (harmonious) than he is.

How does my old acquaintance of this isle?
Honey, you shall be well desired in Cyprus;
I have found great love amongst them. O my sweet,
I prattle out of fashion, and I dote
In mine own comforts. I prithee, good Iago,
890   Go to the bay, and disembark my coffers:°   *chests*
Bring thou the master to the citadel;
He is a good one, and his worthiness
Does challenge° much respect. Come, Desdemona,   *lay claim to*
Once more well met at Cyprus.

                          [*Exeunt all but* IAGO *and* RODERIGO.]

IAGO.   Do thou meet me presently at the harbor. Come hither.
If thou be'st valiant—as, they say, base men being in love
have then a nobility in their natures more than is native to
them—list° me. The lieutenant tonight watches on the court   *hear*
900   of guard. First, I must tell thee this: Desdemona is directly in
love with him.
RODERIGO.   With him! why, 'tis not possible.
IAGO.   Lay thy finger thus,° and let thy soul be instructed. Mark   *on your lips*
me with what violence she first loved the Moor, but for brag-
ging and telling her fantastical lies: and will she love him still
for prating? Let not thy discreet heart think it. Her eye must
be fed; and what delight shall she have to look on the devil?
When the blood is made dull with the act of sport, there
should be, again to inflame it and to give satiety a fresh appe-
910   tite, loveliness in favor,° sympathy in years, manners and   *face*
beauties; all which the Moor is defective in: now, for want of
these required conveniences, her delicate tenderness will find
itself abused, begin to heave the gorge,° disrelish and abhor   *vomit*
the Moor; very nature will instruct her in it and compel her
to some second choice. Now, sir, this granted—as it is a most
pregnant° and unforced position—who stands so eminently   *well conceived*
in the degree of this fortune as Cassio does? A knave very
voluble; no further conscionable than in putting on the mere
form of civil and humane seeming, for the better compassing
920   of his salt° and most hidden loose affection? Why, none; why,   *salty, lustful*
none: a slipper° and subtle knave; a finder out of occasions;   *slippery*
that has an eye can stamp and counterfeit advantages, though
true advantage never present itself: a devilish knave! Besides,
the knave is handsome, young, and hath all those requisites
in him that folly and green minds look after: a pestilent complete knave; and the woman hath found him already.
RODERIGO.   I cannot believe that in her; she's full of most blest
condition.
IAGO.   Blest fig's-end! The wine she drinks is made of grapes: if
930   she had been blest, she would never have loved the Moor:
blest pudding! Didst thou not see her paddle° with the palm   *toy*
of his hand? Didst not mark that?
RODERIGO.   Yes, that I did; but that was but courtesy.

IAGO.   Lechery, by this hand; an index and obscure prologue to
the history of lust and foul thoughts. They met so near with
their lips that their breaths embraced together. Villanous
thoughts, Roderigo! When these mutualities so marshal the
way, hard at hand comes the master and main exercise, the
incorporate° conclusion: pish! But, sir, be you ruled by me: I   *carnal*
940   have brought you from Venice. Watch you tonight; for the
command, I'll lay't upon you: Cassio knows you not: I'll not
be far from you: do you find some occasion to anger Cassio,
either by speaking too loud or tainting° his discipline, or   *discrediting*
from what other course you please, which the time shall
more favorably minister.

RODERIGO.   Well.

IAGO.   Sir, he is rash and very sudden in choler,° and haply may   *anger*
950   strike at you: provoke him, that he may; for even out of that
will I cause these of Cyprus to mutiny; whose qualification°   *equanimity*
shall come into no true taste again but by the displanting of
Cassio. So shall you have a shorter journey to your desires by
the means I shall then have to prefer° them, and the impedi-   *advance*
ment most profitably removed, without the which there were
no expectation of our prosperity.

RODERIGO.   I will do this, if I can bring it to any opportunity.

IAGO.   I warrant° thee. Meet me by and by at the citadel: I must   *promise*
fetch his necessaries ashore. Farewell.

960 RODERIGO.   Adieu. [*Exit.*]

IAGO.   That Cassio loves her, I do well believe it;
That she loves him, 'tis apt° and of great credit:°   *possible / credibility*
The Moor, howbeit that I endure him not,
Is of a constant, loving, noble nature;
And I dare think he'll prove to Desdemona
A most dear husband. Now, I do love her too,
Not out of absolute lust, though peradventure°   *perhaps*
I stand accountant for as great a sin,
But partly led to diet° my revenge,   *feed*
970   For that I do suspect the lusty Moor
Hath leaped into my seat;° the thought whereof   *i.e., cuckolded me*
Doth like a poisonous mineral gnaw my inwards;
And nothing can or shall content my soul
Till I am evened with him, wife for wife;
Or failing so, yet that I put the Moor
At least into a jealousy so strong
That judgement cannot cure. Which thing to do,
If this poor trash of Venice, whom I trash°   *restrain*
For his quick hunting, stand the putting on,°   *on (the scent)*
980   I'll have our Michael Cassio on the hip,°   *i.e., the ground*
Abuse him to the Moor in the rank garb;°   *insinuating style*
For I fear Cassio with my night-cap° too;   *wife*
Make the Moor thank me, love me and reward me,
For making him egregiously an ass
And practising upon his peace and quiet

Even to madness. 'Tis here, but yet confused:
Knavery's plain face is never seen till used. [*Exit.*]

SCENE II

A street.

[*Enter a* HERALD *with a proclamation;* PEOPLE *following.*]

HERALD.   It is Othello's pleasure, our noble and valiant general,
    that upon certain tidings now arrived, importing the mere
990   perdition°of the Turkish fleet, every man put himself into   *total loss*
    triumph; some to dance, some to make bonfires, each man
    to what sport and revels his addiction° leads him: for, besides   *inclination*
    these beneficial news, it is the celebration of his nuptial.
    So much was his pleasure should be proclaimed. All offices°   *mess-halls*
    are open, and there is full liberty of feasting from this present
    hour of five till the bell have told eleven. Heaven bless the
    isle of Cyprus and our noble general Othello! [*Exeunt.*]

SCENE III

A hall in the castle.

[*Enter* OTHELLO, DESDEMONA, CASSIO *and* ATTENDANTS.]

OTHELLO.   Good Michael, look you to the guard tonight:
    Let's teach ourselves that honorable stop,°   *self-restraint*
1000 Not to outsport discretion.
CASSIO.   Iago hath direction what to do;
    But notwithstanding with my personal eye
    Will I look to't.
OTHELLO.   Iago is most honest.
    Michael, good night: tomorrow with your earliest
    Let me have speech with you. Come, my dear love,
    The purchase made, the fruits are to ensue;
    That profit's yet to come 'tween me and you.
    Good night. [*Exeunt* OTHELLO, DESDEMONA, *and* ATTENDANTS.]

[*Enter* IAGO.]

1010 CASSIO.   Welcome, Iago; we must to the watch.
IAGO.   Not this hour, lieutenant; 'tis not yet ten 'o
    the clock. Our general cast° us thus early for the love of his   *dismissed*
    Desdemona; who let us not therefore blame: he hath not
    yet made wanton the night with her, and she is sport for
    Jove.
CASSIO.   She's a most exquisite lady.
IAGO.   And, I'll warrant her, full of game.
CASSIO.   Indeed she's a most fresh and delicate creature.

IAGO.   What an eye she has! Methinks it sounds° a parley°   *signals / conference*
    to provocation.°   *sexual excitement*
1020 CASSIO.   An inviting eye; and yet methinks right modest.
IAGO.   And when she speaks, is it not an alarum° to love?   *call*
CASSIO.   She is indeed perfection.
IAGO.   Well, happiness to their sheets! Come, lieutenant, I have
    a stoup° of wine; and here without are a brace° of   *half-gallon / pair*
    Cyprus gallants that would fain have a measure to the health
    of black Othello.
CASSIO.   Not tonight, good Iago: I have very poor and unhappy
    brains for drinking: I could well wish courtesy would invent
    some other custom of entertainment.
1030 IAGO.   O, they are our friends; but one cup: I'll drink for you.
CASSIO.   I have drunk but one cup tonight, and that was
    craftily qualified° too, and behold what innovation° it   *diluted / change*
    makes here: I am unfortunate in the infirmity and dare not
    task my weakness with any more.
IAGO.   What, man! 'Tis a night of revels: the gallants desire it.
CASSIO.   Where are they?
IAGO.   Here at the door; I pray you, call them in.
CASSIO.   I'll do 't; but it dislikes me. [*Exit.*]
1040 IAGO.   If I can fasten but one cup upon him,
    With that which he hath drunk tonight already,
    He'll be as full of quarrel and offence
    As my young mistress' dog. Now my sick fool Roderigo,
    Whom love hath turned almost the wrong side out,
    To Desdemona hath tonight caroused
    Potations pottle-deep;° and he's to watch: *by the potful*
    Three lads of Cyprus, noble swelling spirits,
    That hold their honors in a wary distance,°   *touchily*
    The very elements of this warlike isle,
1050   Have I tonight flustered with flowing cups,
    And they watch too. Now, 'mongst this flock of drunkards,
    Am I to put our Cassio in some action
    That may offend the isle. But here they come:
    If consequence° do but approve° my dream,   *events / confirm*
    My boat sails freely, both with wind and stream.

[*Re-enter* CASSIO; *with him* MONTANO *and* GENTLEMEN; SERVANTS *following with*
wine.]

CASSIO.   'Fore God, they have given me a rouse° already.   *drink*
MONTANO.   Good faith, a little one; not past a pint, as I am a
    soldier.
IAGO.   Some wine, ho!
    [*Sings.*] And let me the canakin° clink, clink;   *little pot*
1060   And let me the canakin clink:
            A soldier's a man;
            A life's but a span;
          Why then let a soldier drink.
    Some wine, boys!
CASSIO.   'Fore God, an excellent song.

IAGO.   I learned it in England, where indeed they are most
    potent in potting:° your Dane, your German, and your swag-   *draining pots*
    bellied Hollander,—Drink, ho!—are nothing to your English.
1070 CASSIO.   Is your Englishman so expert in his drinking?
IAGO.   Why, he drinks you with facility your Dane dead drunk;
    he sweats not to overthrow your Almain;° he gives your   *German*
    Hollander a vomit ere the next pottle° can be filled.   *pot*
CASSIO.   To the health of our general!
MONTANO.   I am for it, lieutenant, and I'll do you justice.°   *equal you*
IAGO.   O sweet England!

    [*Sings.*] King Stephen was a worthy peer,
          His breeches cost him but a crown;
1080   He held them sixpence all too dear,
          With that he called the tailor lown.°   *rascal*

    He was a wight of high renown,
          And thou are but of low degree:
    'Tis pride that pulls the country down;
          Then take thine auld° cloak about thee.   *old*

    Some wine, ho!
CASSIO.   Why, this is a more exquisite song than the other.
IAGO.   Will you hear't again?
CASSIO.   No; for I hold him to be unworthy of his place that
1090   does those things. Well: God's above all; and there be souls
    must be saved, and there be souls must not be saved.
IAGO.   It's true, good lieutenant.
CASSIO.   For mine own part—no offence to the general, nor any
    man of quality—I hope to be saved.
IAGO.   And so do I too, lieutenant.
CASSIO.   Ay, but, by your leave, not before me; the lieutenant
    is to be saved before the ancient. Let's have no more of
    this; let's to our affairs. God forgive us our sins! Gentlemen,
    let's look to our business. Do not think, gentlemen, I am
1100   drunk: this is my ancient: this is my right hand, and this
    is my left. I am not drunk now; I can stand well enough,
    and speak well enough.
ALL.   Excellent well.
CASSIO.   Why, very well then; you must not think then that I am
    drunk. [*Exit.*]
MONTANO.   To the platform, masters; come, let's set the watch.
IAGO.   You see this fellow that is gone before;
    He is a soldier fit to stand by Caesar
    And give direction: and do but see his vice;
1110   'Tis to his virtue a just equinox,°   *an exact equal*
    The one as long as the other: 'tis pity of him.
    I fear the trust Othello puts him in
    On some odd time of his infirmity
    Will shake this island.
MONTANO.   But is he often thus?

IAGO.   'Tis evermore the prologue to his sleep:
He'll watch the horologe° a double set,°   *clock / twice around*
If drink rock not his cradle.
MONTANO.   It were well
1120   The general were put in mind of it.
Perhaps he sees it not, or his good nature
Prizes the virtue that appears in Cassio
And looks not on his evils: is not this true?

[*Enter* RODERIGO.]

IAGO [*aside to him*].   How now, Roderigo!
I pray you, after the lieutenant; go. [*Exit* RODERIGO.]
MONTANO.   And 'tis great pity that the noble Moor
Should hazard such a place as his own second
With one of an ingraft° infirmity: *ingrained*
It were an honest action to say
1130   So to the Moor.
IAGO.   Not I, for this fair island:
I do love Cassio well, and would do much
To cure him of this evil:—But, hark! what noise?
[*A cry within:* "Help! help!"]

[*Re-enter* CASSIO, *driving in* RODERIGO.]

CASSIO.   'Zounds! you rogue! you rascal!
MONTANO.   What's the matter, lieutenant?
CASSIO.   A knave teach me my duty! But I'll beat the knave into
a wicker bottle.
RODERIGO.   Beat me!
CASSIO.   Dost thou prate, rogue?

[*Striking* RODERIGO.]

1140 MONTANO.   Nay, good lieutenant; I pray, you, sir, hold your hand.
CASSIO.   Let me go, sir, or I'll knock you o'er the mazzard.°   *head*
MONTANO.   Come, come, you're drunk.
CASSIO.   Drunk!

[*They fight.*]

IAGO [*Aside to* RODERIGO].   Away, I say; go out, and cry a mutiny.

[*Exit* RODERIGO.]

Nay, good lieutenant! God's will, gentlemen!
Help, ho!—Lieutenant,—sir,—Montano—sir;—
Help, masters!—Here's a goodly watch indeed!

[*A bell rings.*]

Who's that that rings the bell?—Diablo,° ho!   *The devil*
The town will rise: God's will, lieutenant, hold;
You will be shamed forever.

[*Re-enter* OTHELLO *and* ATTENDANTS.]

1150 OTHELLO.   What is the matter here?

MONTANO.   'Zounds, I bleed still; I am hurt to the death.

                                                                    [*Faints.*]

OTHELLO.   Hold, for your lives!
IAGO.   Hold, ho! Lieutenant,—sir,—Montano,—Gentlemen,—
    Have you forgot all sense of place and duty?
    Hold! the general speaks to you; hold, hold, for shame!
OTHELLO.   Why, how now, ho! from whence ariseth this?
    Are we turned Turks, and to ourselves do that
    Which heaven hath forbid the Ottomites?
1160 For Christian shame, put by this barbarous brawl;
    He that stirs next to carve for his own rage
    Holds his soul light; he dies upon his motion.
    Silence that dreadful bell! It frights the isle
    From her propriety. What is the matter, masters?
    Honest Iago, that look'st dead with grieving,
    Speak, who began this? On thy love, I charge thee.
IAGO.   I do not know: friends all but now, even now,
    In quarter,° and in terms like bride and groom   *on watch*
    Devesting° them for bed; and then, but now,   *disrobing*
1170 As if some planet had unwitted men,
    Swords out, and tilting one at other's breast,
    In opposition bloody. I cannot speak
    Any beginning to this peevish odds;°   *fight*
    And would in action glorious I had lost
    Those legs that brought me to a part of it!
OTHELLO.   How comes it, Michael, you are thus forgot?
CASSIO.   I pray you, pardon me; I cannot speak.
OTHELLO.   Worthy Montano, you were wont be civil;
    The gravity and stillness of your youth
1180 The world hath noted, and your name is great
    In mouths of wisest censure:° what's the matter,   *opinion*
    That you unlace your reputation thus,
    And spend your rich opinion for the name
    Of a night-brawler? Give me answer to it.
MONTANO.   Worthy Othello, I am hurt to danger:
    Your officer, Iago, can inform you—
    While I spare speech, which something now offends° me—   *pains*
    Of all that I do know: nor know I aught
    By me that's said or done amiss this night;
1190 Unless self-charity be sometimes a vice,
    And to defend ourselves it be a sin
    When violence assails us.
OTHELLO.   Now, by heaven,
    My blood begins my safer guides to rule,
    And passion, having my best judgement collied,°   *blackened*
    Assays° to lead the way: if I once stir,   *attempts*
    Or do but lift this arm, the best of you
    Shall sink in my rebuke. Give me to know
    How this foul rout began, who set it on,

1200   And he that is approved° in this offence,   *convicted*
        Though he had twinned with me, both at a birth,
        Shall lose me. What! in a town of war,
        Yet wild, the people's hearts brimful of fear,
        To manage private and domestic quarrel,
        In night, and on the court and guard of safety!
        'Tis monstrous. Iago, who began 't?
MONTANO.   If partially affined,° or leagued in office,   *obligated*
        Thou dost deliver more or less than truth,
        Thou art no soldier.
1210 IAGO.   Touch me not so near:
        I had rather have this tongue cut from my mouth
        Than it should do offence to Michael Cassio;
        Yet, I persuade myself, to speak the truth
        Shall nothing wrong him. Thus it is, general.
        Montano and myself being in speech,
        There comes a fellow crying out for help,
        And Cassio following him with determined sword,
        To execute upon him. Sir, this gentleman
        Steps in to Cassio and entreats his pause:
1220   Myself the crying fellow did pursue,
        Lest by his clamor—as it so fell out—
        The town might fall in fright: he, swift of foot,
        Outran my purpose; and I returned the rather
        For that I heard the clink and fall of swords,
        And Cassio high in oath; which till tonight
        I ne'er might say before. When I came back—
        For this was brief—I found them close together,
        At blow and thrust; even as again they were
        When you yourself did part them.
1230   More of this matter cannot I report:
        But men are men; the best sometimes forget:
        Though Cassio did some little wrong to him,
        As men in rage strike those that wish them best,
        Yet surely Cassio, I believe, received
        From him that fled some strange indignity,
        Which patience could not pass.
OTHELLO.   I know, Iago,
        Thy honesty and love doth mince this matter,
        Making it light to Cassio. Cassio, I love thee;
1240   But never more be officer of mine.

                          [*Re-enter* DESDEMONA, *attended.*]

        Look, if my gentle love be not raised up!
        I'll make thee an example.

DESDEMONA.   What's the matter?
OTHELLO.   All's well now, sweeting; come away to bed.
        Sir, for your hurts, myself will be your surgeon:
        Lead him off.

                        [*To* MONTANO, *who is led off.*]

        Iago, look with care about the town,

And silence those whom this vile brawl distracted.
Come, Desdemona: 'tis the soldiers' life
1250 To have their balmy slumbers waked with strife.

[*Exeunt all but* Iago *and* Cassio.]

Iago. What, are you hurt, lieutenant?

Cassio. Ay, past all surgery.

Iago. Marry, heaven forbid!

Cassio. Reputation, reputation, reputation! O, I have lost my
reputation! I have lost the immortal part of myself, and what
remains is bestial. My reputation, Iago, my reputation!

Iago. As I am an honest man, I thought you had received
some bodily wound; there is more sense in that than in repu-
1260 tation. Reputation is an idle and most false imposition;°   *covering*
oft got without merit and lost without deserving: you have
lost no reputation at all, unless you repute yourself such a
loser. What, man! there are ways to recover the general
again: you are but now cast° in his mood,° a punishment   *dismissed / anger*
more in policy than in malice; even so as one would beat his
offenceless dog to affright an imperious lion: sue to him
again, and he's yours.

Cassio. I will rather sue to be despised than to deceive so
good a commander with so slight, so drunken, and so
1270 indiscreet an officer. Drunk? and speak parrot?°   *i.e., like a parrot*
and squabble? swagger? swear? and discourse fustian° with   *poppycock*
one's own shadow? O thou invisible spirit of wine, if thou hast
no name to be known by, let us call thee devil!

Iago. What was he that you followed with your sword?
What had he done to you?

Cassio. I know not.

Iago. Is't possible?

Cassio. I remember a mass of things, but nothing distinctly, a
quarrel, but nothing wherefore. O God, that men should put
an enemy in their mouths to steal sway their brains! that we
should, with joy, pleasance, revel and applause, transform
ourselves into beasts!

Iago. Why, but you are now well enough: how came you thus
recovered?

1280 Cassio. It hath pleased the devil drunkenness to give place to
the devil wrath: one unperfectness shows me another, to
make me frankly despise myself.

Iago. Come, you are too severe a moraler: as the time, the
place, and the condition of this country stands, I could heartily wish this had not befallen; but since it is as it is, mend it
for your own good.

Cassio. I will ask him for my place again; he shall tell me I am
1290 a drunkard! Had I as many mouths as Hydra,[9] such an answer would stop them all. To be now a sensible man, by and
by a fool, and presently a beast! O strange! Every inordinate
cup is unblest, and the ingredient is a devil.

---

[9] A mythical monster with nine heads.

IAGO.   Come, come, good wine is a good familiar creature, if it
be well used: exclaim no more against it. And, good lieutenant, I think you think I love you.

CASSIO.   I have well approved° it, sir. I drunk!   *demonstrated*

IAGO.   You or any man living may be drunk at some time, man.
I'll tell you what you shall do. Our general's wife is now the
1300   general. I may say so in this respect, for that he hath devoted and given up himself to the contemplation, mark and
denotement° of her parts and graces: confess yourself freely   *notation*
to her; importune her help to put you in your place again:
she is of so free,° so kind, so apt, so blessed a disposition,   *generous*
she holds it a vice in her goodness not to do more than she
is requested: this broken joint between you and her husband
entreat her to splinter;° and, my fortunes against   *splint, repair*
any lay° worth naming, this crack of your love shall   *wager*
grow stronger than it was before.

CASSIO.   You advise me well.

IAGO.   I protest, in the sincerity of love and honest kindness.

1310 CASSIO.   I think it freely; and betimes° in the morning I will   *early*
beseech the virtuous Desdemona to undertake for me: I am
desperate of my fortunes if they check me here.

IAGO.   You are in the right. Good night, lieutenant; I must to
the watch.

CASSIO.   Good night, honest Iago.

                                                                      [*Exit.*]

IAGO.   And what's he then that says I play the villain?
When this advice is free I give and honest,
Probal° to thinking, and indeed the course   *probable*
1320   To win the Moor again? For 'tis most easy
The inclining Desdemona to subdue°   *win over*
In any honest suit. She's framed as fruitful
As the free elements. And then for her
To win the Moor—were't to renounce his baptism,
All seals and symbols of redeemèd sin—
His soul is so enfettered to her love,
That she may make, unmake, do what she list,°   *likes*
Even as her appetite shall play the god
With his weak function.° How am I then a villain   *(as commander)*
1330   To counsel Cassio to this parallel course,
Directly to his good? Divinity of hell!
When devils will the blackest sins put on,
They do suggest at first with heavenly shows,
As I do now: for whiles this honest fool
Plies Desdemona to repair his fortunes,
And she for him pleads strongly to the Moor,
I'll pour this pestilence into his ear,
That she repeals° him for her body's lust: *appeals for*
And by how much she strives to do him good,
1340   She shall undo her credit with the Moor.
So will I turn her virtue into pitch;

And out of her own goodness make the net
That shall enmesh them all.

[*Enter* RODERIGO.]

How now, Roderigo!

RODERIGO.   I do follow here in the chase, not like a hound that
hunts, but one that fills up the cry.° My money is almost   *pack*
spent; I have been tonight exceedingly well cudgelled;° and I   *beaten*
think the issue will be, I shall have so much experience for
my pains; and so, with no money at all and a little more wit,
return again to Venice.

1350 IAGO.   How poor are they that have not patience!
What wound did ever heal but by degrees?
Thou know'st we work by wit and not by witchcraft,
And wit depends on dilatory time.
Does't not go well? Cassio hath beaten thee,
And thou by that small hurt hast cashiered Cassio:
Though other things grow fair against the sun,
Yet fruits that blossom first will first be ripe:
Content thyself awhile. By the mass, 'tis morning;
Pleasure and action make the hours seem short.
1360 Retire thee; go where thou art billeted:
Away, I say; thou shalt know more hereafter:
Nay, get thee gone. [*Exit* RODERIGO.] Two things are to be done:
My wife must move° for Cassio to her mistress: *plead*
I'll set her on;
Myself the while to draw the Moor apart,
And bring him jump° when he may Cassio find   *just*
Soliciting his wife: ay, that's the way;
Dull not device by coldness and delay.

[*Exit.*]

ACT III

SCENE I

Before the castle.

[*Enter* CASSIO *and some* MUSICIANS.]

CASSIO.   Masters, play here; I will content° your pains;   *reward*
1370 Something that's brief; and bid "Good morrow, general."
[*Music.*]

[*Enter* CLOWN.]

CLOWN.   Why, masters, have your instruments been in Naples,
that they speak i' the nose thus?[10]

---

[10] A reference to the nasal Neapolitan accent but also to the free-wheeling reputation and
endemic syphilis (damaging the nose in advanced stages) of this sailors' town.

FIRST MUSICIAN. How, sir, how!

CLOWN. Are these, I pray you, wind-instruments?

FIRST MUSICIAN. Ay, marry, are they, sir.

CLOWN. O, thereby hangs a tail.

FIRST MUSICIAN. Whereby hangs a tale, sir?

CLOWN. Marry, sir, by many a wind-instrument that I know.

1380 But, masters, here's money for you: and the general so likes
your music, that he desires you, for love's sake, to make no
more noise with it.

FIRST MUSICIAN. Well, sir, we will not.

CLOWN. If you have any music that may not be heard, to 't
again: but, as they say, to hear music the general does not
greatly care.

FIRST MUSICIAN. We have none such, sir.

CLOWN. Then put up your pipes in your bag, for I'll away: go;
vanish into air; away!

[*Exeunt* MUSICIANS.]

CASSIO. Dost thou hear, my honest friend?

1390 CLOWN. No, I hear not your honest friend; I hear you.

CASSIO. Prithee, keep up thy quillets.° There's a poor piece of   *quibbles*
gold for thee: if the gentlewoman that attends the general's
wife be stirring, tell her there's one Cassio entreats her a
little favor of speech: wilt thou do this?

CLOWN. She is stirring, sir; if she will stir hither, I shall seem
to notify unto her.

CASSIO. Do, good my friend.

[*Exit* CLOWN.]

[*Enter* IAGO.]

In happy time, Iago.

IAGO. You have not been a-bed, then?

CASSIO. Why, no; the day had broke

1400 Before we parted. I have made bold, Iago.
To send in to your wife: my suit to her
Is, that she will to virtuous Desdemona
Procure me some access.

IAGO.   I'll send her to you presently;
And I'll devise a mean to draw the Moor
Out of the way, that your converse and business
May be more free.

CASSIO. I humbly thank you for't. [*Exit* IAGO.] I never knew
A Florentine more kind and honest.

[*Enter* EMILIA.]

EMILIA. Good morrow, good lieutenant: I am sorry

1410 For your displeasure; but all will sure be well.
The general and his wife are talking of it,

And speaks for you stoutly: the Moor replies,
That he you hurt is of great fame in Cyprus
And great affinity,° and that in wholesome wisdom   *family*
He might not but refuse you; but he protests he loves you,
And needs no other suitor but his likings
To take the safest occasion by the front°   *forelock*
To bring you in again.

Cassio.   Yet, I beseech you,
If you think fit, or that it may be done,
1420   Give me advantage of some brief discourse
With Desdemona alone.

Emilia.   Pray you, come in:
I will bestow you where you shall have time
To speak your bosom freely.

Cassio.   I am much bound to you.

[Exeunt.]

SCENE II

A room in the castle.

[Enter Othello, Iago, *and* Gentlemen.*]*

Othello.   These letters give, Iago, to the pilot;
And by him do my duties to the senate:
That done, I will be walking on the works;°   *fortifications*
Repair there to me.

Iago.   Well, my good lord, I'll do't.

Othello.   This fortification, gentlemen, shall we see't?

Gentleman.   We'll wait upon your lordship.

[Exeunt.]

SCENE III

The garden of the castle.

[Enter Desdemona, Cassio, *and* Emilia.*]*

1430 Desdemona.   Be thou assured, good Cassio, I will do
All my abilities in thy behalf.

Emilia.   Good madam, do: I warrant it grieves my husband
As if the case were his.

Desdemona.   O, that's an honest fellow. Do not doubt, Cassio,
But I will have my lord and you again
As friendly as you were.

Cassio.   Bounteous madam,
Whatever shall become of Michael Cassio,
He's never any thing but your true servant.

Desdemona.   I know 't: I thank you. You do love my lord:

1440　You have known him long; and be you well assured
　　　He shall in strangeness° stand no farther off　　　　　*estrangement*
　　　Than in a politic° distance.　　　　　　　　　　　　　*diplomatic*
CASSIO.　　　　　　　　　　　　Ay, but, lady,
　　　That policy may either last so long,
　　　Or feed upon such nice and waterish diet,
　　　Or breed itself so out of circumstance,
　　　That, I being absent and my place supplied,
　　　My general will forget my love and service.
DESDEMONA.　Do not doubt° that; before Emilia here　　　*fear*
　　　I give thee warrant of thy place: assure thee,
1450　If I do vow a friendship, I'll perform it
　　　To the last article: my lord shall never rest;
　　　I'll watch him tame[11] and talk him out of patience;
　　　His bed shall seem a school, his board a shrift;°　　　*confessional*
　　　I'll intermingle every thing he does
　　　With Cassio's suit: therefore be merry, Cassio;
　　　For thy solicitor shall rather die
　　　Than give thy cause away.

　　　　　　　　　　　　[*Enter* OTHELLO *and* IAGO, *at a distance.*]

EMILIA.　Madam, here comes my lord.
CASSIO.　Madam, I'll take my leave.
1460　DESDEMONA.　Nay, stay and hear me speak.
CASSIO.　Madam, not now: I am very ill at ease,
　　　Unfit for mine own purposes.
DESDEMONA.　Well, do your discretion.

　　　　　　　　　　　　　　　　　　　　　　[*Exit* CASSIO.]

IAGO.　Ha! I like not that.
OTHELLO.　What dost thou say?
IAGO.　Nothing, my lord: or if—I know not what.
OTHELLO.　Was not that Cassio parted from my wife?
IAGO.　Cassio, my lord! No, sure, I cannot think it,
　　　That he would steal away so guilty-like,
　　　Seeing you coming.
1470　OTHELLO.　　　　　　　　I do believe 'twas he.
DESDEMONA.　How now, my lord!
　　　I have been talking with a suitor here,
　　　A man that languishes in your displeasure.
OTHELLO.　Who is't you mean?
DESDEMONA.　Why, your lieutenant, Cassio. Good my lord,
　　　If I have any grace or power to move you,
　　　His present reconciliation take;
　　　For if he be not one that truly loves you,
　　　That errs in ignorance and not in cunning,
1480　I have no judgement in an honest face:
　　　I prithee, call him back.

　　　　　───────────────
　　　[11] Hawks are sometimes kept awake until tamed.

OTHELLO. Went he hence now?

DESDEMONA. Ay, sooth;° so humbled, *true*
  That he hath left part of his grief with me,
  To suffer with him. Good love, call him back.

OTHELLO. Not now, sweet Desdemona; some other time.

DESDEMONA. But shall't be shortly?

OTHELLO. The sooner, sweet, for you.

DESDEMONA. Shall't be tonight at supper?

OTHELLO. No, not tonight.

DESDEMONA. Tomorrow dinner then?

OTHELLO. I shall not dine at home;
  I meet the captains at the citadel.

1490 DESDEMONA. Why then tomorrow night; or Tuesday morn;
  On Tuesday noon, or night; on Wednesday morn:
  I prithee, name the time; but let it not
  Exceed three days: in faith, he's penitent;
  And yet his trespass, in our common reason—
  Save that, they say, the wars must make examples
  Out of their best—is not almost a fault
  To incur a private check.° When shall he come? *rebuke*
  Tell me, Othello: I wonder in my soul,
  What you would ask me, that I should deny,

1500   Or stand so mammering° on. What! Michael Cassio, *hesitant*
  That came a-wooing with you, and so many a time
  When I have spoke of you dispraisingly
  Hath ta'en your part; to have so much to do
  To bring him in! Trust me, I could do much—

OTHELLO. Prithee, no more: let him come when he will;
  I will deny thee nothing.

DESDEMONA. Why, this is not a boon;° *gift*
  'Tis as I should entreat you wear your gloves,
  Or feed on nourishing dishes, or keep you warm,
  Or sue to you to do a peculiar profit

1510   To your own person: nay, when I have a suit
  Wherein I mean to touch your love indeed,
  It shall be full of poise° and difficult weight, *matter*
  And fearful to be granted.

OTHELLO. I will deny thee nothing:
  Whereon, I do beseech thee, grant me this,
  To leave me but a little to myself.

DESDEMONA. Shall I deny you? No: farewell, my lord.

OTHELLO. Farewell, my Desdemona: I'll come to thee straight.

DESDEMONA. Emilia, come. Be as your fancies teach you;
  Whate'er you be, I am obedient.

                          [Exeunt DESDEMONA *and* EMILIA.]

1520 OTHELLO. Excellent wretch! Perdition catch my soul,
  But I do love thee! And when I love thee not,
  Chaos is come again.

IAGO. My noble lord,—

OTHELLO. What dost thou say, Iago?

IAGO.   Did Michael Cassio, when you wooed my lady,
 Know of your love?
OTHELLO.   He did, from first to last: why dost thou ask?
IAGO.   But for a satisfaction of my thought;
 No further harm.
OTHELLO.   Why of thy thought, Iago?
IAGO.   I did not think he had been acquainted with her.
OTHELLO.   O, yes, and went between us very oft.
1530 IAGO.   Indeed!
OTHELLO.   Indeed! ay, indeed: discern'st thou aught in that?
 Is he not honest?
IAGO.   Honest, my lord!
OTHELLO.   Honest! ay, honest.
IAGO.   My lord, for aught I know.
OTHELLO.   What dost thou think?
IAGO.   Think, my lord!
OTHELLO.   Think, my lord! By heaven, he echoes me,
1540 As if there were some monster in his thought
 Too hideous to be shown. Thou dost mean something:
 I heard thee say even now, thou likedst not that,
 When Cassio left my wife: what didst not like?
 And when I told thee he was of my counsel
 In my whole course of wooing, thou criedst 'Indeed!'
 And didst contract and purse thy brow together,
 As if thou then hadst shut up in thy brain
 Some horrible conceit:° if thou dost love me,   *idea*
 Show me thy thought.
IAGO.   My lord, you know I love you.
1550 OTHELLO.   I think thou dost;
 And for I know thou'rt full of love and honesty
 And weigh'st thy words before thou givest them breath,
 Therefore these stops of thine fright me the more:
 For such things in a false disloyal knave
 Are tricks of custom; but in a man that's just
 They're close delations,° working from the heart,   *secret charges*
 That passion cannot rule.
IAGO.   For Michael Cassio,
 I dare be sworn I think that he is honest.
OTHELLO.   I think so too.
IAGO.   Men should be what they seem;
1560 Or those that be not, would they might seem none!
OTHELLO.   Certain, men should be what they seem.
IAGO.   Why then I think Cassio's an honest man.
OTHELLO.   Nay, yet there's more in this:
 I prithee, speak to me as to thy thinkings,
 As thou dost ruminate, and give thy worst of thoughts
 The worst of words.
IAGO.   Good my lord, pardon me:
 Though I am bound to every act of duty,
 I am not bound to that all slaves are free to.

Utter my thoughts? Why, say they are vile and false;
1570   As where's that palace whereinto foul things
        Sometimes intrude not? Who has a breast so pure,
        But some uncleanly apprehensions
        Keep leets° and law-days, and in session sit   *courts*
        With meditations lawful?
OTHELLO.   Thou dost conspire against thy friend, Iago,
        If thou but think'st him wronged and makest his ear
        A stranger to thy thoughts.
IAGO.   I do beseech you—
        Though I perchance am vicious in my guess,
        As, I confess, it is my nature's plague
        To spy into abuses, and oft my jealousy
1580   Shapes faults that are not—that your wisdom yet,
        From one that so imperfectly conceits,°   *speculates*
        Would take no notice, nor build yourself a trouble
        Out of his scattering and unsure observance.
        It were not for your quiet nor your good,
        Nor for my manhood, honesty, or wisdom,
        To let you know my thoughts.
OTHELLO.   What dost thou mean?
IAGO.   Good name in man and woman, dear my lord,
        Is the immediate jewel of their souls:
1590   Who steals my purse steals trash; 'tis something, nothing;
        'Twas mine, 'tis his, and has been slave to thousands;
        But he that filches from me my good name
        Robs me of that which not enriches him
        And makes me poor indeed.
OTHELLO.   By heaven, I'll know thy thoughts.
IAGO.   You cannot, if my heart were in your hand;
        Nor shall not, whilst 'tis in my custody.
OTHELLO.   Ha!
IAGO.   O, beware, my lord, of jealousy;
        It is the green-eyed monster, which doth mock°   *torment*
1600   The meat it feeds on: that cuckold lives in bliss
        Who, certain of his fate, loves not his wronger;
        But, O, what damnèd minutes tells he o'er
        Who dotes, yet doubts, suspects, yet strongly loves!
OTHELLO.   O misery!
IAGO.   Poor and content is rich, and rich enough;
        But riches fineless° is as poor as winter   *without end*
        To him that ever fears he shall be poor:
        Good heaven, the souls of all my tribe defend
        From jealousy!
OTHELLO.   Why, why is this?
1610   Think'st thou I'ld make a life of jealousy,
        To follow still the changes of the moon
        With fresh suspicions? No; to be once in doubt
        Is once to be resolved: exchange me for a goat,
        When I shall turn the business of my soul

To such exsufflicate° and blown° surmises,   *puffed up / swollen*
Matching thy inference. 'Tis not to make me jealous
To say my wife is fair, feeds well, loves company,
Is free of speech, sings, plays and dances well;
Where virtue is, these are more virtuous:

1620   Nor from mine own weak merits will I draw
The smallest fear or doubt of her revolt;
For she had eyes, and chose me. No, Iago;
I'll see before I doubt; when I doubt, prove;
And on the proof, there is no more but this,
Away at once with love or jealousy!

IAGO.   I am glad of it; for now I shall have reason
To show the love and duty that I bear you
With franker spirit: therefore, as I am bound,
Receive it from me. I speak not yet of proof.

1630   Look to your wife; observe her well with Cassio;
Wear your eye thus, not jealous nor secure:
I would not have your free and noble nature
Out of self-bounty° be abused; look to 't: *your own kindness*
I know our country disposition well;
In Venice they do let heaven see the pranks
They dare not show their husbands; their best conscience
Is not to leave 't undone, but keep 't unknown.

OTHELLO.   Dost thou say so?

IAGO.   She did deceive her father, marrying you;

1640   And when she seemed to shake and fear your looks,
She loved them most.

OTHELLO.   And so she did.

IAGO.   Why, go to° then;   *go on*
She that so young could give out such a seeming,
To seel° her father's eyes up close as oak—   *sew*
He thought 'twas witchcraft—but I am much to blame;
I humbly do beseech you of your pardon
For too much loving you.

OTHELLO.   I am bound to thee for ever.

IAGO.   I see this hath a little dashed your spirits.

OTHELLO.   Not a jot,° not a jot.   *bit*

IAGO.   I' faith, I fear it has.
I hope you will consider what is spoke

1650   Comes from my love; but I do see you're moved:
I am to pray you not to strain my speech
To grosser issues nor to larger reach
Than to suspicion.

OTHELLO.   I will not.

IAGO.   Should you do so, my lord,
My speech should fall into such vile success
As my thoughts aim not at. Cassio's my worthy friend—
My lord, I see you're moved.

OTHELLO.   No, not much moved:
I do not think but Desdemona's honest.°   *chaste*

Iago.   Long live she so! and long live you to think so!
1660 Othello.   And yet, how nature erring from itself—
Iago.   Ay, there's the point: as—to be bold with you—
    Not to affect° many proposèd matches   *like*
    Of her own clime, complexion and degree,
    Whereto we see in all things nature tends—
    Foh! one may smell in such a will° most rank,   *lust*
    Foul disproportion, thoughts unnatural.
    But pardon me: I do not in position°   *hypothesis*
    Distinctly speak of her; though I may fear
    Her will, recoiling to her better judgement,
1670   May fall° to match you with her country forms,°   *happen / countrymen*
    And happily° repent.   *perhaps*
Othello.   Farewell, farewell:
    If more thou dost perceive, let me know more;
    Set on thy wife to observe: leave me, Iago.
Iago [*going*].   My lord, I take my leave.
Othello.   Why did I marry? This honest creature doubtless
    Sees and knows more, much more, than he unfolds.
Iago [*returning*].   My lord, I would I might entreat your honor
    To scan° this thing no further; leave it to time: *analyze*
1680   Though it be fit that Cassio have his place,
    For sure he fills it up with great ability,
    Yet, if you please to hold him off awhile,
    You shall by that perceive him and his means:
    Note if your lady strain° his entertainment°   *urge / employment*
    With any strong or vehement importunity;
    Much will be seen in that. In the mean time,
    Let me be thought too busy in my fears—
    As worthy cause I have to fear I am—
    And hold her free,° I do beseech your honor.   *guiltless*
1690 Othello.   Fear not my government.°   *self-control*
Iago.   I once more take my leave.

                                                                                           [*Exit.*]

Othello.   This fellow's of exceeding honesty,
    And knows all qualities,° with a learnèd spirit,   *natures*
    Of human dealings. If I do prove her haggard,°   *a strayed hawk*
    Though that her jesses° were my dear heart-strings,   *restraining straps*
    I'ld whistle her off and let her down° the wind   *fly down*
    To prey° at fortune.° Haply, for I am black   *hunt / random*
    And have not those soft parts of conversation
    That chamberers° have, or for I am declined   *womanizers*
1700   Into the vale of years,—yet that's not much—
    She's gone; I am abused, and my relief
    Must be to loathe her. O curse of marriage,
    That we can call these delicate creatures ours,
    And not their appetites! I had rather be a toad,
    And live upon the vapor of a dungeon,
    Than keep a corner in the thing I love

For others' uses. Yet, 'tis the plague of great ones;
Prerogatived are they less than the base;
'Tis destiny unshunnable, like death:
1710   Even then this forkèd plague° is fated to us   *cuckoldry*
When we do quicken.° Desdemona comes: *are conceived*

[*Re-enter* DESDEMONA *and* EMILIA.]

If she be false, O, then heaven mocks itself!
I'll not believe 't.

DESDEMONA.   How now, my dear Othello!
Your dinner, and the generous islanders
By you invited, do attend your presence.
OTHELLO.   I am to blame.
DESDEMONA.   Why do you speak so faintly?
Are you not well?
OTHELLO.   I have a pain upon my forehead here.
DESDEMONA.   Faith, that's with watching; 'twill away again:
1720   Let me but bind it hard, within this hour
It will be well.
OTHELLO.   Your napkin is too little;

[*He puts the handkerchief from him; and she drops it.*]

Let it alone. Come, I'll go in with you.
DESDEMONA.   I am very sorry that you are not well.

[*Exeunt* OTHELLO *and* DESDEMONA.]

EMILIA.   I am glad I have found this napkin:
This was her first remembrance from the Moor:
My wayward husband hath a hundred times
Woo'd me to steal it; but she so loves the token,
For he conjured her she should ever keep it,
That she reserves it evermore about her
1730   To kiss and talk to. I'll have the work ta'en out,°   *copied*
And give 't Iago: what he will do with it
Heaven knows, not I;
I nothing but to please his fantasy.°   *whim*

[*Re-enter* IAGO.]

IAGO.   How now! What do you here alone?
EMILIA.   Do not you chide; I have a thing for you.
IAGO.   A thing for me? It is a common thing—
EMILIA.   Ha!
IAGO.   To have a foolish wife.
EMILIA.   O, is that all? What will you give me now
For that same handkerchief?
1740 IAGO.   What handkerchief?
EMILIA.   What handkerchief!
Why, that the Moor first gave to Desdemona;
That which so often you did bid me steal.

IAGO.   Hast stol'n it from her?

EMILIA.   No, faith; she let it drop by negligence,
And, to the advantage, I being here took 't up.
Look, here it is.

IAGO.   A good wench; give it me.

EMILIA.   What will you do with 't, that you have been so earnest

1750   To have me filch it?

IAGO [*snatching it*].   Why, what's that to you?

EMILIA.   If 't be not for some purpose of import,°   *importance*
Give 't me again: poor lady, she'll run mad
When she shall lack it.

IAGO.   Be not acknown on 't;° I have use for it.   *knowledgeable about it*
Go, leave me.

                                                          [*Exit* EMILIA.]

I? will in Cassio's lodging lose this napkin,
And let him find it. Trifles light as air
Are to the jealous confirmations strong

1760   As proofs of holy writ: this may do something.
The Moor already changes with my poison:
Dangerous conceits are in their natures poisons,
Which at the first are scarce found to distaste,
But with a little act upon the blood
Burn like the mines of sulphur. I did say so:
Look, where he comes!

                                                       [*Re-enter* OTHELLO.]

                    Not poppy, nor mandragora,°   *a narcotic*
Nor all the drowsy syrups of the world,
Shall ever medicine thee to that sweet sleep
Which thou owedst° yesterday.   *owned*

OTHELLO.   Ha! ha! false to me?

1770 IAGO.   Why, how now, general! no more of that.

OTHELLO.   Avaunt! Be gone! thou hast set me on the rack:
I swear 'tis better to be much abused
Than but to know't a little.

IAGO.   How now, my lord!

OTHELLO.   What sense had I of her stol'n hours of lust?
I saw't not, thought it not, it harmed not me:
I slept the next night well, was free and merry;
I found not Cassio's kisses on her lips:
He that is robbed, not wanting what is stol'n,
Let him not know't and he's not robbed at all.

1780 IAGO.   I am sorry to hear this.

OTHELLO.   I had been happy, if the general camp,
Pioners° and all, had tasted her sweet body,   *Privates*
So I had nothing known. O, now forever
Farewell the tranquil mind! farewell content!
Farewell the plumèd troop and the big wars
That make ambition virtue! O, farewell,
Farewell the neighing steed and the shrill trump,

The spirit-stirring drum, the ear-piercing fife,
The royal banner and all quality,
1790   Pride, pomp and circumstances° of glorious war!   *pageantry*
And, O you mortal engines,° whose rude throats   *cannons*
The immortal Jove's dread clamors counterfeit,
Farewell! Othello's occupation's gone!
IAGO.   Is't possible, my lord?
OTHELLO.   Villain, be sure thou prove my love a whore;
Be sure of it; give me the ocular proof;
Or, by the worth of man's eternal soul,
Thou hadst been better have been born a dog
Than answer my waked wrath!
IAGO.   Is't come to this?
1800 OTHELLO.   Make me to see't; or at the least so prove it,
That the probation° bear no hinge nor loop   *proof*
To hang a doubt on; or woe upon thy life!
IAGO.   My noble lord,—
OTHELLO.   If thou dost slander her and torture me,
Never pray more; abandon all remorse;
On horror's head horrors accumulate;
Do deeds to make heaven weep, all earth amazed;
For nothing canst thou to damnation add
Greater than that.
IAGO.   O grace! O heaven defend me!
1810   Are you a man? Have you a soul or sense?
God be wi' you; take mine office. O wretched fool,
That livest to make thine honesty a vice!
O monstrous world! Take note, take note, O world,
To be direct and honest is not safe.
I thank you for this profit,° and from hence   *gain (in wisdom)*
I'll love no friend sith° love breeds such offence.   *since*
OTHELLO.   Nay, stay: thou shouldst be honest.
IAGO.   I should be wise; for honesty's a fool,
And loses that it works for.
OTHELLO.   By the world,
1820   I think my wife be honest, and think she is not;
I think that thou are just, and think thou are not:
I'll have some proof. Her name, that was as fresh
As Dian's° visage, is now begrimed and black   *goddess of chastity*
As mine own face. If there be cords, or knives,
Poison, or fire, or suffocating streams,
I'll not endure it. Would I were satisfied!
IAGO.   I see, sir, you are eaten up with passion:
I do repent me that I put it to you.
You would be satisfied?
OTHELLO.   Would! nay, I will.
1830 IAGO.   And may: but, how? How satisfied, my lord?
Would you, the supervisor, grossly gape on?
Behold her topped?
OTHELLO.   Death and damnation! O!
IAGO.   It were a tedious difficulty, I think,

To bring them to that prospect: damn them then,
If ever mortal eyes do see them bolster°   *sleep together*
More than their own! What then? How then?
What shall I say? Where's satisfaction?
It is impossible you should see this,
Were they as prime° as goats, as hot as monkeys,   *lustful*
1840 As salt° as wolves in pride,° and fools as gross   *desirous / heat*
As ignorance made drunk. But yet, I say,
If imputation and strong circumstances,
Which lead directly to the door of truth,
Will give you satisfaction, you may have't.
OTHELLO.   Give me a living reason she's disloyal.
IAGO.   I do not like the office:
But sith I am entered in this cause so far,
Pricked° to 't by foolish honesty and love,   *Driven*
I will go on. I lay with Cassio lately,
1850 And being troubled with a raging tooth,
I could not sleep.
There are a kind of men so loose of soul,
That in their sleeps will mutter their affairs:
One of this kind is Cassio:
In sleep I heard him say "Sweet Desdemona,
Let us be wary, let us hide our loves";
And then, sir, would he gripe° and wring my hand,   *grip*
Cry "O sweet creature!" and then kiss me hard,
As if he plucked up kisses by the roots,
1860 That grew upon my lips: then laid his leg
Over my thigh, and sighed and kissed, and then
Cried "Cursed fate that gave thee to the Moor!"
OTHELLO.   O monstrous! monstrous!
IAGO.   Nay, this was but his dream.
OTHELLO.   But this denoted a foregone conclusion:
'Tis a shrewd doubt,° though it be but a dream.   *astute suspicion*
IAGO.   And this may help to thicken other proofs
That do demonstrate thinly.
OTHELLO.   I'll tear her all to pieces.
IAGO.   Nay, but be wise: yet we see nothing done;
She may be honest yet. Tell me but this;
1870 Have you not sometimes seen a handkerchief
Spotted with strawberries in your wife's hand?
OTHELLO.   I gave her such a one; 'twas my first gift.
IAGO.   I know not that: but such a handkerchief—
I am sure it was your wife's—did I today
See Cassio wipe his beard with.
OTHELLO.   If it be that,—
IAGO.   If it be that, or any that was hers,
It speaks against her with the other proofs.
OTHELLO.   O, that the slave had forty thousand lives!
One is too poor, too weak for my revenge.
1880 Now do I see 'tis true. Look here, Iago;
All my fond love thus do I blow to heaven:

'Tis gone.
Arise, black vengeance, from thy hollow cell!
Yield up, O love, thy crown and hearted throne
To tyrannous hate! Swell, bosom, with thy fraught,°   *freight*
For 'tis of aspics' tongues!
IAGO.   Yet be content.
OTHELLO.   O, blood, blood, blood!
IAGO.   Patience, I say; your mind perhaps may change.
OTHELLO.   Never, Iago. Like to the Pontic sea,°   *Black Sea*
1890   Whose icy current and compulsive course
Ne'er feels retiring ebb, but keeps due on
To the Propontic and the Hellespont;[12]
Even so my bloody thoughts, with violent pace,
Shall ne'er look back, ne'er ebb to humble love,
Till that a capable° and wide revenge   *capacious*
Swallow them up. Now, by yond marble heaven,
In the due reverence of a sacred vow [*Kneels.*]
I here engage my words.
IAGO.   Do not rise yet [*Kneels.*]
Witness, you ever-burning lights above,
1900   You elements that clip° us round about,   *encircle*
Witness that here Iago doth give up
The execution° of his wit, hands, heart,   *action*
To wronged Othello's service! Let him command,
And to obey shall be in me remorse,°   *an act of pity*
What bloody business ever.
OTHELLO.   I greet thy love,
Not with vain thanks, but with acceptance bounteous,
And will upon the instant put thee to 't:
Within these three days let me hear thee say
That Cassio's not alive.
1910 IAGO.   My friend is dead; 'tis done at your request:
But let her live.
OTHELLO.   Damn her, lewd minx! O, damn her!
Come, go with me apart: I will withdraw,
To furnish me with some swift means of death
For the fair devil. Now art thou my lieutenant.
IAGO.   I am your own for ever.

                                                                                [*Exeunt.*]

SCENE IV

Before the castle.

                                          [*Enter* DESDEMONA, EMILIA, *and* CLOWN.]

DESDEMONA.   Do you know, sirrah, where Lieutenant Cassio lies?
CLOWN.   I dare not say he lies any where.

---

[12] The "Propontic" is another name for the Sea of Marmara; the "Hellespont" is an ancient
name for the Dardanelles through which Sea of Marmara drains into the Mediterranean Sea.

Desdemona.   Why, man?
Clown.   He's a soldier; and for one to say a soldier lies,
1920   is° stabbing.   *i.e., is cause for*
Desdemona.   Go to: where lodges he?
Clown.   To tell you where he lodges, is to tell you where I lie.
Desdemona.   Can any thing be made of this?
Clown.   I know not where he lodges; and for me to devise
    a lodging, and say he lies here or he lies there, were to lie
    in mine own throat.
Desdemona.   Can you inquire him out and be edified by report?
Clown.   I will catechize the world for him; that is, make ques-
    tions and by them answer.
1930 Desdemona.   Seek him, bid him come hither: tell him I have
    moved my lord on his behalf and hope all will be well.
Clown.   To do this is within the compass of man's wit, and
    therefore I will attempt the doing it.

                                                                    [*Exit.*]

Desdemona.   Where should I lose that handkerchief, Emilia?
Emilia.   I know not, madam.
Desdemona.   Believe me, I had rather have lost my purse
    Full of crusadoes:° and, but my noble Moor   *gold coins*
    Is true of mind and made of no such baseness
    As jealous creatures are, it were enough
    To put him to ill thinking.
Emilia.   Is he not jealous?
1940 Desdemona.   Who, he? I think the sun where he was born
    Drew all such humors° from him.   *feelings*
Emilia.   Look, where he comes.
Desdemona.   I will not leave him now till Cassio
    Be called to him.

                                                        [*Enter* Othello.]

                How is 't with you, my lord?
Othello.   Well, my good lady. [*Aside*] O, hardness to dissemble!
    How do you, Desdemona?
Desdemona.   Well, my good lord.
Othello.   Give me your hand: this hand is moist, my lady.
1950 Desdemona.   It yet has felt no age nor known no sorrow.
Othello.   This argues fruitfulness and liberal heart:
    Hot, hot, and moist: this hand of yours requires
    A sequester° from liberty, fasting and prayer,   *separation*
    Much castigation, exercise devout;
    For here's a young and sweating devil here,
    That commonly rebels. 'Tis a good hand,
    A frank one.
Desdemona.   You may, indeed, say so;
    For 'twas that hand that gave away my heart.
Othello.   A liberal hand: the hearts of old gave hands;
    But our new heraldry is hands, not hearts.

1960 DESDEMONA.   I cannot speak of this. Come now, your promise.
OTHELLO.   What promise, chuck?°   *dear*
DESDEMONA.   I have sent to bid Cassio come speak with you.
OTHELLO.   I have a salt and sorry rheum° offends me;   *cold*
   Lend me thy handkerchief.
DESDEMONA.   Here, my lord.
OTHELLO.   That which I gave you.
DESDEMONA.   I have it not about me.
OTHELLO.   Not?
1970 DESDEMONA.   No, indeed, my lord.
OTHELLO.   That's a fault. That handkerchief
   Did an Egyptian to my mother give;
   She was a charmer,° and could almost read   *magician*
   The thoughts of people: she told her, while she kept it
   'Twould make her amiable and subdue my father
   Entirely to her love, but if she lost it
   Or made a gift of it, my father's eye
   Should hold her loathed and his spirits should hunt
   After new fancies: she dying gave it me,
1980   And bid me, when my fate would have me wive,
   To give it her. I did so: and take heed on 't;
   Make it a darling like your precious eye;
   To lose 't or give 't away were such perdition
   As nothing else could match.
DESDEMONA.   Is't possible?
OTHELLO.   'Tis true: there's magic in the web of it:
   A sibyl,° that had numbered in the world   *prophetess*
   The sun to course two hundred compasses,
   In her prophetic fury sewed the work;
   The worms were hallowed that did breed the silk;
1990   And it was dyed in mummy° which the skillful   *fluid from mummies*
   Conserved of maidens' hearts.
DESDEMONA.   Indeed! is't true?
OTHELLO.   Most veritable; therefore look to 't well.
DESDEMONA.   Then would to God that I had never seen 't!
OTHELLO.   Ha! wherefore?
DESDEMONA.   Why do you speak so startingly and rash?
OTHELLO.   Is 't lost? Is 't gone? Speak, is it out 'o the way?
DESDEMONA.   Heaven bless us!
OTHELLO.   Say you?
DESDEMONA.   It is not lost; but what an if it were?
2000 OTHELLO.   How!
DESDEMONA.   I say, it is not lost.
OTHELLO.   Fetch 't, let me see it.
DESDEMONA.   Why, so I can, sir, but I will not now.
   This is a trick to put me from my suit:
   Pray you, let Cassio be received again.
OTHELLO.   Fetch me the handkerchief: my mind misgives.
DESDEMONA.   Come, come;
   You'll never meet a more sufficient° man.   *able*
OTHELLO.   The handkerchief!

DESDEMONA.   I pray, talk me of Cassio.
OTHELLO.   The handkerchief!
2010 DESDEMONA.   A man that all his time
 Hath founded his good fortunes on your love,
 Shared dangers with you,—
OTHELLO.   The handkerchief!
DESDEMONA.   In sooth, you are to blame.
OTHELLO.   Away!

                   [Exit.]

EMILIA.   Is not this man jealous?
DESDEMONA.   I ne'er saw this before.
 Sure there's some wonder in this handkerchief:
 I am most unhappy in the loss of it.
2020 EMILIA.   'Tis not a year or two shows us a man:
 They are all but stomachs and we all but food;
 They eat us hungerly, and when they are full
 They belch us. Look you, Cassio and my husband.

           [Enter CASSIO and IAGO.]

IAGO.   There is no other way; 'tis she must do 't:
 And, lo, the happiness!° Go and importune her.   *luck*
DESDEMONA.   How now, good Cassio! What's the news with you?
CASSIO.   Madam, my former suit: I do beseech you
 That by your virtuous means I may again
 Exist, and be a member of his love
 Whom I with all the office° of my heart   *service*
2030 Entirely honor: I would not be delayed.
 If my offence be of such moral kind
 That nor my service past nor present sorrows
 Nor purposed merit in futurity
 Can ransom me into his love again,
 But to know so must be my benefit;
 So shall I clothe me in a forced content
 And shut myself up in some other course
 To fortune's alms.
DESDEMONA.   Alas, thrice-gentle Cassio!
2040 My advocation° is not now in tune;   *advocacy*
 My lord is not my lord, nor should I know him
 Were he in favor° as in humor altered.   *appearance*
 So help me every spirit sanctified,
 As I have spoken for you all my best
 And stood within the blank° of his displeasure   *center*
 For my free speech! You must awhile be patient:
 What I can do I will; and more I will
 Than for myself I dare: let that suffice you.
IAGO.   Is my lord angry?
2050 EMILIA.   He went hence but now,
 And certainly in strange unquietness.
IAGO.   Can he be angry? I have seen the cannon,

When it hath blown his ranks into the air,
And, like the devil, from his very arm
Puffed his own brother; and can he be angry?
Something of moment then: I will go meet him:
That's matter in't indeed if he be angry.
DESDEMONA.   I prithee, do so.

[*Exit* IAGO.]

                       Something sure of state,
Either from Venice or some unhatched practice°   *uncovered plot*
2060   Made demonstrable here in Cyprus to him,
Hath puddled° his clear spirit; and in such cases   *muddied*
Men's natures wrangle with inferior things,
Though great ones are their object. 'Tis even so;
For let our finger ache, and it indues°   *brings*
Our other healthful members even to that sense
Of pain: nay, we must think men are not gods,
Nor of them look for such observancy°   *observances*
As fits the bridal. Beshrew° me much, Emilia,   *Curse*
I was, unhandsome° warrior as I am,   *unfitting*
2070   Arraigning his unkindness with my soul;
But now I find I had suborned° the witness,   *induced to perjury*
And he's indicted falsely.

EMILIA.   Pray heaven it be state-matters, as you think,
And no conception nor no jealous toy
Concerning you.
DESDEMONA.   Alas the day, I never gave him cause!
EMILIA.   But jealous souls will not be answered so;
They are not ever jealous for the cause,
But jealous for they are jealous: 'tis a monster
2080   Begot upon itself, born on itself.
DESDEMONA.   Heaven keep that monster from Othello's mind!
EMILIA.   Lady, amen.
DESDEMONA.   I will go seek him. Cassio, walk hereabout:
If I do find him fit, I'll move your suit,
And seek to effect it to my uttermost.
CASSIO.   I humbly thank your ladyship.

[*Exeunt* DESDEMONA *and* EMILIA. *Enter* BIANCA.]

BIANCA.   Save you, friend Cassio!
CASSIO.   What make you from home?
How is it with you, my most fair Bianca?
I' faith, sweet love, I was coming to your house
2090 BIANCA.   And I was going to your lodging, Cassio.
What, keep a week away? Seven days and nights?
Eight score eight hours? And lovers' absent hours,
More tedious than the dial° eight score times?   *whole day*
O weary reckoning!
CASSIO.   Pardon me, Bianca:
I have this while with leaden thoughts been pressed;

But I shall in a more continuate° time   *uninterrupted*
Strike off this score° of absence. Sweet Bianca,   *account*

[*Giving her Desdemona's handkerchief.*]

Take me this work out.
BIANCA.   O Cassio, whence came this?
2100   This is some token from a newer friend:
To the felt absence now I feel a cause:
Is 't come to this? Well, well.
CASSIO.   Go to, woman!
Throw your vile guesses in the devil's teeth,
From whence you have them. You are jealous now
That this is from some mistress, some remembrance:
No, by my faith, Bianca.
BIANCA.   Why, whose is it?
CASSIO.   I know not, sweet: I found it in my chamber.
I like the work well: ere it be demanded—
As like enough it will—I'd have it copied:
2110   Take it, and do 't; and leave me for this time.
BIANCA.   Leave you! Wherefore?
CASSIO.   I do attend here on the general;
And think it no addition, nor my wish,
To have him see me womaned.°   *with a woman*
BIANCA.   Why, I pray you?
CASSIO.   Not that I love you not.
BIANCA.   But that you do not love me.
I pray you, bring me on the way a little;
And say if I shall see you soon at night.
CASSIO.   'Tis but a little way that I can bring you;
For I attend here: but I'll see you soon.
2120 BIANCA.   'Tis very good; I must be circumstanced.°   *ruled by circumstances*

[*Exeunt.*]

ACT IV

SCENE I

Cyprus. Before the castle.

[*Enter* OTHELLO *and* IAGO.]

IAGO.   Will you think so?
OTHELLO.   Think so, Iago!
IAGO.   What,
To kiss in private?
OTHELLO.   An unauthorized kiss.
IAGO.   Or to be naked with her friend in bed
An hour or more, not meaning any harm?
OTHELLO.   Naked in bed, Iago, and not mean harm!
It is hypocrisy against the devil:

They that mean virtuously and yet do so,
The devil their virtue tempts and they tempt heaven.

IAGO.   So they do nothing, 'tis a venial slip:
2130   But if I give my wife a handkerchief—

OTHELLO.   What then?

IAGO.   Why, then, 'tis hers, my lord; and being hers,
She may, I think, bestow 't on any man.

OTHELLO.   She is protectress of her honor too:
May she give that?

IAGO.   Her honor is an essence that's not seen;
They have it very oft that have it not:
But for the handkerchief—

OTHELLO.   By heaven, I would most gladly have forgot it:
2140   Thou said'st—O, it comes o'er my memory,
As doth the raven° o'er the infected house,   *(emblem of death)*
Boding to all—he had my handkerchief.

IAGO.   Ay, what of that?

OTHELLO.   That's not so good now.

IAGO.   What
If I had said I had seen him do you wrong?
Or heard him say—as knaves be such abroad,
Who having, by their own importunate suit
Or voluntary dotage of° some mistress,   *doting on*
Convincèd° or supplied° them, cannot choose   *seduced / met the desires of*
But they must blab—

OTHELLO.   Hath he said anything?
2150 IAGO.   He hath, my lord; but be you well assured,
No more than he'll unswear.

OTHELLO.   What hath he said?

IAGO.   Faith, that he did—I know not what he did.

OTHELLO.   What? What?

IAGO.   Lie—

OTHELLO.   With her?

IAGO.   With her, on her; what you will.

OTHELLO.   Lie with her! lie on her!—We say lie on her, when
they belie her.—Lie with her! 'Zounds, that's fulsome!°   *disgusting*
Handkerchief—confessions—handkerchief!—To confess,
and be hanged for his labor; first, to be hanged, and then
to confess. I tremble at it. Nature would not invest herself
in such shadowing passion without some instruction.[13]
2160   It is not words that shakes me thus. Pish! Noses, ears and
lips. Is 't possible?—Confess?—Handkerchief?—O devil!

[*Falls in a trance.*]

IAGO.   Work on,
My medicine, work! thus credulous fools are caught;
And many worthy and chaste dames even thus,

---

[13] I.e., my nature would not be so darkened with passion unless there were some cause.

And guiltless, meet reproach. What, ho! my lord!
My lord, I say! Othello!

[Enter CASSIO.]

How now, Cassio!

CASSIO.   What's the matter?
IAGO.   My lord is fall'n into an epilepsy:
   This is his second fit; he had one yesterday.
2170 CASSIO.   Rub him about the temples.
IAGO.   No, forbear;
   The lethargy° must have his quiet course: *stupor*
   If not, he foams at mouth, and by and by
   Breaks out to savage madness. Look, he stirs:
   Do you withdraw yourself a little while,
   He will recover straight: when he is gone,
   I would on great occasion° speak with you.   *important matters*

[Exit CASSIO.]

   How is it, general? Have you not hurt your head?
OTHELLO.   Dost thou mock me?
IAGO.   I mock you! No, by heaven.
2180   Would you would bear your fortune like a man!
OTHELLO.   A hornèd° man's a monster and a beast.   *cuckolded*
IAGO.   There's many a beast then in a populous city,
   And many a civil monster.
OTHELLO.   Did he confess it?
IAGO.   Good sir, be a man;
   Think every bearded fellow that's but yoked°   *married*
   May draw with you: there's millions now alive
   That nightly lie in those unproper° beds   *unchaste*
   Which they dare swear peculiar:° your case is better.   *theirs alone*
   O, 'tis the spite of hell, the fiend's arch-mock,
2190   To lip° a wanton in a secure couch.   *kiss*
   And to suppose her chaste! No, let me know;
   And knowing what I am, I know what she shall be.
OTHELLO.   O, thou art wise; 'tis certain.
IAGO.   Stand you awhile apart;
   Confine yourself but in a patient list.°   *mood*
   Whilst you were here o'erwhelmed with your grief—
   A passion most unsuiting such a man—
   Cassio came hither: I shifted him away,
   And laid good 'scuse upon your ecstasy;°   *trance*
   Bade him anon return and here speak with me;
2200   The which he promised. Do but encave° yourself,   *conceal*
   And mark the fleers,° the gibes and notable scorns,   *sneers*
   That dwell in every region of his face;
   For I will make him tell the tale anew,
   Where, how, how oft, how long ago and when

He hath and is again to cope° your wife: *cover*
I say, but mark his gesture. Marry,° patience;   *Indeed*
Or I shall say you are all in all in spleen,°   *passion*
And nothing of a man.

OTHELLO.   Dost thou hear, Iago?
2210 I will be found most cunning in my patience;
But—dost thou hear?—most bloody.

IAGO.   That's not amiss;
But yet keep time in all. Will you withdraw?

[OTHELLO *retires.*]

Now will I question Cassio of Bianca,
A housewife that by selling her desires
Buys herself bread and clothes: it is a creature
That dotes on Cassio; as 'tis the strumpet's plague
To beguile many and be beguiled by one.
He, when he hears of her, cannot refrain
From the excess of laughter. Here he comes.

[*Re-enter* CASSIO.]

As he shall smile, Othello shall go mad;
2220 And his unbookish° jealousy must construe   *ignorant*
Poor Cassio's smiles, gestures and light behavior,
Quite in the wrong. How do you now, lieutenant?

CASSIO.   The worser that you give me the addition°   *additional title*
Whose want even kills me.

IAGO.   Ply Desdemona well, and you are sure on 't.
Now, if this suit lay in Bianca's power,
How quickly should you speed!

CASSIO.   Alas, poor caitiff!°   *wretch*

OTHELLO.   Look, how he laughs already!

IAGO.   I never knew a woman love man so.

2230 CASSIO.   Alas, poor rogue! I think, i' faith, she loves me.

OTHELLO.   Now he denies it faintly and laughs it out.

IAGO.   Do you hear, Cassio?

OTHELLO.   Now he importunes him
To tell it o'er: go to; well said, well said.

IAGO.   She gives it out that you shall marry her.
Do you intend it?

CASSIO.   Ha, ha, ha!

OTHELLO.   Do you triumph, Roman? Do you triumph?

CASSIO.   I marry her! what, a customer!° I prithee, bear some   *prostitute*
charity to my wit; do not think it so unwholesome.
2240   Ha, ha, ha!

OTHELLO.   So, so, so, so: they laugh that win.

IAGO.   Faith, the cry goes that you shall marry her.

CASSIO.   Prithee, say true.

IAGO.   I am a very villain else.

OTHELLO.   Have you scored me?° Well.   *paid me back*

CASSIO.   This is the monkey's own giving out: she is persuaded
   I will marry her, out of her own love and flattery, not out of
   my promise.
OTHELLO.   Iago beckons me; now he begins the story.
2250 CASSIO.   She was here even now; she haunts me in every place.
   I was the other day talking on the sea-bank with certain
   Venetians; and thither comes the bauble,° and, by this   *plaything*
   hand, she falls me thus about my neck—
OTHELLO.   Crying "O dear Cassio!" as it were: his gesture im-
   ports it.
CASSIO.   So hangs and lolls and weeps upon me; so hales°   *drags*
   and pulls me: ha, ha, ha!
OTHELLO.   Now he tells how she plucked him to my chamber.
2260   O, I see that nose of yours, but not that dog I shall throw it
   to.
CASSIO.   Well, I must leave her company.
IAGO.   Before me! Look, where she comes.
CASSIO.   'Tis such another fitchew!° Marry, a perfumed one.   *polecat, harlot*

                                                            [*Enter* BIANCA.]

   What do you mean by this haunting of me?
BIANCA.   Let the devil and his dam haunt you! What did you
   mean by that same handkerchief you gave me even now? I
   was a fine fool to take it. I must take out the work? A
   likely piece of work, that you should find it in your chamber, and not know who left it there! This is some minx's
2270   token, and I must take out the work? There; give it your
   hobby-horse:° wheresoever you had it, I'll take out no   *rocking horse, whore*
   work on 't.
CASSIO.   How now, my sweet Bianca! How now! How now!
OTHELLO.   By heaven, that should be my handkerchief!
BIANCA.   An you'll come to supper tonight, you may; an
   you will not, come when you are next prepared for.

                                                                  [*Exit.*]

IAGO.   After her, after her.
CASSIO.   Faith, I must; she'll rail i' the street else.
IAGO.   Will you sup there?
2280 CASSIO.   Faith, I intend so.
IAGO.   Well, I may chance to see you; for I would very
   fain speak with you.
CASSIO.   Prithee, come; will you?
IAGO.   Go to; say no more.

                                                              [*Exit* CASSIO.]

OTHELLO [*advancing*].   How shall I murder him, Iago?
IAGO.   Did you perceive how he laughed at his vice?
OTHELLO.   O Iago!
IAGO.   And did you see the handkerchief?

OTHELLO. Was that mine?

2290 IAGO. Yours, by this hand: and to see how he prizes the foolish
     woman your wife! She gave it him, and he hath given it his
     whore.

OTHELLO. I would have him nine years a-killing. A fine woman!
     a fair woman! a sweet woman!

IAGO. Nay, you must forget that.

OTHELLO. Ay, let her rot, and perish, and be damned tonight;
     for she shall not live: no, my heart is turned to stone; I strike
     it, and it hurts my hand. O, the world hath not a sweeter
2300   creature: she might lie by an emperor's side, and command
     him tasks.

IAGO. Nay, that's not your way.

OTHELLO. Hang her! I do but say what she is: so delicate with
     her needle: an admirable musician: O, she will sing the sav-
     ageness out of a bear: of so high and plenteous wit and in-
     vention:—

IAGO. She's the worse for all this.

OTHELLO. O, a thousand thousand times: and then, of so gen-
     tle a condition!°   *nature*

IAGO. Aye, too gentle.°   *generous*

2310 OTHELLO. Nay, that's certain: but yet the pity of it, Iago! O
     Iago, the pity of it, Iago!

IAGO. If you are so fond over her iniquity, give her patent° to   *permission*
     offend; for, if it touch not you, it comes near nobody.

OTHELLO. I will chop her into messes.° Cuckold me!   *porridge*

IAGO. O, 'tis foul in her.

OTHELLO. With mine officer!

IAGO. That 's fouler.

OTHELLO. Get me some poison, Iago; this night. I'll not expos-
     tulate with her, lest her body and beauty unprovide° my mind   *unsettle*
     again: this night, Iago.

2320 IAGO. Do it not with poison, strangle her in her bed,
     even the bed she hath contaminated.

OTHELLO. Good, good: the justice of it pleases: very good.

IAGO. And for Cassio, let me be his undertaker: you shall
     hear more by midnight.

OTHELLO. Excellent good. [*A trumpet within.*] What trumpet
     is that same?

IAGO. Something from Venice, sure. 'Tis Lodovico come
     from the duke: and, see, your wife is with him.

[*Enter* LODOVICO, DESDEMONA, *and* ATTENDANTS.]

LODOVICO. God save the worthy general!

2330 OTHELLO.   With all my heart, sir.

LODOVICO. The duke and senators of Venice greet you.

[*Gives him a letter.*]

OTHELLO. I kiss the instrument of their pleasures.

[*Opens the letter, and reads.*]

DESDEMONA.   And what's the news, good cousin Lodovico?

IAGO.   I am very glad to see you, signior;
   Welcome to Cyprus.

LODOVICO.   I thank you. How does Lieutenant Cassio?

IAGO.   Lives, sir.

DESDEMONA.   Cousin, there's fall'n between him and my lord
   An unkind breach: but you shall make all well.

2340 OTHELLO.   Are you sure of that?

DESDEMONA.   My lord?

OTHELLO [*reads*].   "This fail you not to do, as you will—"

LODOVICO.   He did not call; he's busy in the paper.
   Is there division 'twixt my lord and Cassio?

DESDEMONA.   A most unhappy one: I would do much
   To atone° them, for the love I bear to Cassio   *reunite*

OTHELLO.   Fire and brimstone!

DESDEMONA.   My lord?

OTHELLO.   Are you wise?

DESDEMONA.   What, is he angry?

2350 LODOVICO.   May be the letter moved him;
   For, as I think, they do command him home,
   Deputing° Cassio in his government.°   *substituting* / *office*

DESDEMONA.   By my troth, I am glad on 't.

OTHELLO.   Indeed!

DESDEMONA.   My lord?

OTHELLO.   I am glad to see you mad.

DESDEMONA.   Why, sweet Othello?

OTHELLO.   Devil! [*Striking her.*]

DESDEMONA.   I have not deserved this.

LODOVICO.   My lord, this would not be believed in Venice,
   Though I should swear I saw 't: 'tis very much:
   Make her amends; she weeps.

OTHELLO.   O devil, devil!

2360 If that the earth could teem° with woman's tears,   *bear offspring*
   Each drop she falls would prove a crocodile.[14]
   Out of my sight!

DESDEMONA.   I will not stay to offend you. [*Going.*]

LODOVICO.   Truly, an obedient lady:
   I do beseech your lordship, call her back.

OTHELLO.   Mistress!

DESDEMONA.   My lord?

OTHELLO.   What would you with her, sir?

LODOVICO.   Who, I, my lord?

OTHELLO.   Ay; you did wish that I would make her turn:
   Sir, she can turn and turn, and yet go on,

2370 And turn again; and she can weep, sir, weep;

---

[14] The crocodile was thought to shed false tears over its victims.

And she's obedient, as you say, obedient,
Very obedient. Proceed you in your tears.
Concerning this, sir,—O well-painted passion!—
I am commanded home. Get you away;
I'll send for you anon. Sir, I obey the mandate,
And will return to Venice. Hence, avaunt!°   *be gone*

[*Exit* DESDEMONA.]

Cassio shall have my place. And, sir, tonight,
I do entreat that we may sup together:
You are welcome, sir, to Cyprus. Goats and monkeys!

[*Exit.*]

2380 LODOVICO.   Is this the noble Moor whom our full senate
Call all in all sufficient? This the nature
Whom passion could not shake? whose solid virtue
The shot of accident nor dart of chance
Could neither graze nor pierce?
IAGO.   He is much changed.
LODOVICO.   Are his wits safe? Is he not light of brain?
IAGO.   He's that he is: I may not breathe my censure°   *adverse opinion*
What he might be: if what he might he is not,
I would to heaven he were!
LODOVICO.   What, strike his wife!
IAGO.   Faith, that was not so well; yet would I knew
That stroke would prove the worst!
2390 LODOVICO.   Is it his use?°   *habit*
Or did the letters work upon his blood,
And new create this fault?
IAGO.   Alas, alas!
It is not honesty in me to speak
What I have seen and known. You shall observe him,
And his own courses will denote him so
That I may save my speech: do but go after,
And mark how he continues.
LODOVICO.   I am sorry that I am deceived in him.

[*Exeunt.*]

SCENE II

A room in the castle.

[*Enter* OTHELLO *and* EMILIA.]

OTHELLO.   You have seen nothing, then?
2400 EMILIA.   Nor ever heard, nor ever did suspect.
OTHELLO.   Yes, you have seen Cassio and she together.
EMILIA.   But then I saw no harm, and then I heard
Each syllable that breath made up between them.

OTHELLO.   What, did they never whisper?
EMILIA.   Never, my lord.
OTHELLO.   Nor send you out o' the way?
EMILIA.   Never.
OTHELLO.   To fetch her fan, her gloves, her mask, nor nothing?
EMILIA.   Never, my lord.
OTHELLO.   That's strange.

2410 EMILIA.   I durst, my lord, to wager she is honest,°   *chaste*
     Lay down my soul at stake:° if you think other,   *as wager*
     Remove your thought; it doth abuse your bosom.
     If any wretch have put this in your head,
     Let heaven requite it with the serpent's curse!
     For if she be not honest, chaste and true,
     There's no man happy; the purest of their wives
     Is foul as slander.
OTHELLO.   Bid her come hither: go.

                                                            [*Exit* EMILIA.]

     She says enough: yet she's a simple bawd
     That cannot say as much. This is a subtle whore,
2420 A closet lock and key of villanous secrets:
     And yet she'll kneel and pray; I have seen her do 't.

                                      [*Enter* DESDEMONA *with* EMILIA.]

DESDEMONA.   My lord, what is your will?
OTHELLO.   Pray, chuck, come hither.
DESDEMONA.   What is your pleasure?
OTHELLO.   Let me see your eyes;
     Look in my face.
DESDEMONA.   What horrible fancy's this?
OTHELLO [*to* EMILIA].   Some of your function,[15] mistress;
     Leave procreants° alone and shut the door;   *fornicators*
     Cough, or cry hem, if anybody come:
     Your mystery,° your mystery: nay, dispatch.   *trade*

                                                            [*Exit* EMILIA.]

DESDEMONA.   Upon my knees, what doth your speech import?
2430 I understand a fury in your words,
     But not the words.
OTHELLO.   Why, what are thou?
DESDEMONA.   Your wife, my lord; your true and loyal wife.
OTHELLO.   Come, swear it, damn thyself;
     Lest, being like one of heaven, the devils themselves
     Should fear to seize thee: therefore be double-damned;
     Swear thou art honest.
DESDEMONA.   Heaven doth truly know it.

---

[15] I.e., perform your function as madam of the brothel.

OTHELLO.   Heaven truly knows that thou art false as hell.

DESDEMONA.   To whom, my lord? With whom? How am I false?

2440 OTHELLO.   O Desdemona! Away! away! away!

DESDEMONA.   Alas the heavy day! Why do you weep?
    Am I the motive of these tears, my lord?
    If haply° you my father do suspect   *perhaps*
    An instrument of this your calling back,
    Lay not your blame on me: if you have lost him,
    Why, I have lost him too.

OTHELLO.   Had it pleased heaven
    To try me with affliction; had they rained
    All kinds of sores and shames on my bare head,
    Steeped me in poverty to the very lips,
2450   Given to captivity me and my utmost hopes,
    I should have found in some place of my soul
    A drop of patience: but, alas, to make me
    A fixèd figure for the time of scorn
    To point his slow unmoving finger at!
    Yet could I bear that too; well, very well:
    But there, where I have garnered° up my heart,   *stored*
    Where either I must live or bear no life,
    The fountain from the which my current runs,
    Or else dries up; to be discarded thence!
2460   Or keep it as a cistern for foul toads
    To knot and gender° in! Turn thy complexion° there,   *mate / Turn pale*
    Patience, thou young and rose-lipped cherubin,—
    Ay, there, look grim as hell!

DESDEMONA.   I hope my noble lord esteems me honest.

OTHELLO.   O, ay; as summer flies are in the shambles,°   *butcher shop*
    That quicken even with blowing.[16] O thou weed,
    Who art so lovely fair and smell'st so sweet
    That the sense aches at thee, would thou hadst ne'er been born!

2470 DESDEMONA.   Alas, what ignorant° sin have I committed?   *unwitting*

OTHELLO.   Was this fair paper, this most goodly book,
    Made to write "whore" upon? What committed!
    Committed! O thou public commoner!°   *whore*
    I should make very forges of my cheeks,
    That would to cinders burn up modesty,
    Did I but speak thy deeds. What committed!
    Heaven stops the nose at it, and the moon winks;
    The bawdy wind, that kisses all it meets,
    Is hushed within the hollow mine of earth,
2480   And will not hear it. What committed!
    Impudent strumpet!

DESDEMONA.   By heaven, you do me wrong.

OTHELLO.   Are not you a strumpet!

DESDEMONA.   No, as I am a Christian:

---

[16] That are impregnated even the moment after giving birth.

If to preserve this vessel for my lord
From any other foul unlawful touch
Be not to be a strumpet, I am none.
OTHELLO.   What, not a whore?
DESDEMONA.   No, as I shall be saved.
OTHELLO.   Is 't possible?
DESDEMONA.   O, heaven forgive us!
OTHELLO.   I cry you mercy then:
   I took you for that cunning whore of Venice
2490   That married with Othello. [*Raising his voice*] You, mistress,
   That have the office opposite to Saint Peter,
   And keep the gate of hell!

                                                                        [*Re-enter* EMILIA.]

                                    You, you, ay, you!
   We have done our course;° there's money for your pains: *sexual encounter*
   I pray you, turn the key, and keep our counsel.

                                                                                 [*Exit.*]

EMILIA.   Alas, what does this gentleman conceive?
   How do you, madam? How do you, my good lady?
DESDEMONA.   Faith, half asleep.
EMILIA.   Good madam, what's the matter with my lord?
DESDEMONA.   With who?
2500 EMILIA.   Why, with my lord, madam.
DESDEMONA.   Who is thy lord?
EMILIA.   He that is yours, sweet lady.
DESDEMONA.   I have none: do not talk to me, Emilia;
   I cannot weep, nor answer have I none
   But what should go by water.° Prithee, tonight   *tears*
   Lay on my bed my wedding sheets: remember;
   And call thy husband hither.
EMILIA.   Here's a change indeed!

                                                                                 [*Exit.*]

DESDEMONA.   'Tis meet I should be used so, very meet.
   How have I been behaved, that he might stick°   *put*
   The small'st opinion° on my least misuse?°   *suspicion / error*

                                                                 [*Re-enter* EMILIA *with* IAGO.]

2510 IAGO.   What is your pleasure, madam? How is't with you?
DESDEMONA.   I cannot tell. Those that do teach young babes
   Do it with gentle means and easy tasks:
   He might have chid me so; for, in good faith,
   I am a child to chiding.
IAGO.   What's the matter, lady?
EMILIA.   Alas, Iago, my lord hath so bewhored her,
   Thrown such despite° and heavy terms upon her,   *scorn*
   As true hearts cannot bear.

DESDEMONA.   Am I that name, Iago?

IAGO.   What name, fair lady?

DESDEMONA.   Such as she says my lord did say I was.

2520 EMILIA.   He called her whore: a beggar in his drink
      Could not have laid such terms upon his callat.°   *slut*

IAGO.   Why did he so?

DESDEMONA.   I do not know; I am sure I am none such.

IAGO.   Do not weep, do not weep. Alas the day!

EMILIA.   Hath she forsook so many noble matches,
      Her father and her country and her friends,
      To be called whore? Would it not make one weep?

DESDEMONA.   It is my wretched fortune.

IAGO.   Beshrew° him for't!   *Evil befall*
      How comes this trick° upon him?   *foolishness*

DESDEMONA.   Nay, heaven doth know.

2530 EMILIA.   I will be hanged, if some eternal villain,
      Some busy and insinuating rogue,
      Some cogging,° cozening° slave, to get some office.   *cheating / deceiving*
      Have not devised this slander; I'll be hanged else.

IAGO.   Fie, there is no such man; it is impossible.

DESDEMONA.   If any such there be, heaven pardon him!

EMILIA.   A halter pardon him! And hell gnaw his bones!
      Why should he call her whore? Who keeps her company?
      What place? What time? What form? What likelihood?
      The Moor's abused by some most villanous knave,
2540 Some base notorious knave, some scurvy fellow,
      O heaven, that such companions thou'ldst unfold,°   *expose*
      And put in every honest hand a whip
      To lash the rascals naked through the world
      Even from the east to the west!

IAGO.   Speak within door.°   *quietly*

EMILIA.   O, fie upon them! Some such squire he was
      That turned your wit the seamy side without,
      And made you to suspect me with the Moor.

IAGO.   You are a fool; go to.

DESDEMONA.   O good Iago,
      What shall I do to win my lord again?
2550 Good friend, go to him; for, by this light of heaven,
      I know not how I lost him. Here I kneel:
      If e'er my will did trespass 'gainst his love
      Either in discourse of thought or actual deed,
      Or that mine eyes, mine ears, or any sense,
      Delighted them in any other form,
      Or that I do not yet, and ever did,
      And ever will, though he do shake me off
      To beggarly divorcement, love him dearly,
      Comfort forswear° me! Unkindness may do much;   *forsake*
2560 And his unkindness may defeat my life,
      But never taint my love. I cannot say "whore":
      It doth abhor me now I speak the word;

     To do the act that might the addition° earn   *name*
     Not the world's mass of vanity could make me.
Iago.   I pray you, be content; 'tis but his humor;
     The business of the state does him offense.
     And he does chide with you.
Desdemona.   If 'twere no other,—
Iago.   'Tis but so, I warrant. [*Trumpet within.*]
2570   Hark, how these instruments summon to supper!
     The messengers of Venice stay° the meat: *await*
     Go in, and weep not; all things shall be well.

                    [*Exeunt* Desdemona *and* Emilia.]

                          [*Enter* Roderigo.]

     How now, Roderigo!
Roderigo.   I do not find that thou dealest justly with me.
Iago.   What in the contrary.
Roderigo.   Every day thou daffest me° with some device,   *turn me aside*
     Iago; and rather, as it seems to me now, keepest from me all
     conveniency° than suppliest me with the least advantage of   *opportunity*
2580   hope. I will indeed no longer endure it; nor am I yet per-
     suaded to put up in peace what already I have foolishly suf-
     fered.
Iago.   Will you hear me, Roderigo?
Roderigo.   Faith, I have heard too much; for your words and
     performances are no kin together.
Iago.   You charge me most unjustly.
Roderigo.   With nought but truth. I have wasted myself out
     of my means. The jewels you have had from me to deliver
     to Desdemona would half have corrupted a votarist:°   *nun*
     you have told me she hath received them and returned me
2590   expectations and comforts of sudden° respect and   *immediate*
     acquaintance; but I find none.
Iago.   Well; go to; very well.
Roderigo.   Very well! Go to! I cannot go to, man; nor 'tis
     not very well: by this hand, I say 'tis very scurvy, and begin to
     find myself fopped° in it.   *made foolish*
Iago.   Very well.
Roderigo.   I tell you 'tis not very well. I will make myself known
     to Desdemona: if she will return me my jewels, I will give
     over my suit and repent my unlawful solicitation; if not,
2600   assure yourself I will seek satisfaction of you.
Iago.   You have said now?
Roderigo.   Ay, and said nothing but what I protest intendment°   *intention*
     of doing.
Iago.   Why, now I see there's mettle° in thee; and even from   *spirit*
     this instant do build on thee a better opinion than ever
     before. Give me thy hand, Roderigo: thou hast taken against
     me a most just exception; but yet, I protest, I have dealt
     most directly in thy affair.

RODERIGO.   It hath not appeared.

2610 IAGO.   I grant indeed it hath not appeared, and your suspicion
is not without wit and judgement. But, Roderigo, if thou hast
that in thee indeed, which I have greater reason to believe
now than ever, I mean purpose, courage and valor, this
night show it; if thou the next night following enjoy not
Desdemona, take me from this world with treachery and
devise engines° for my life.   *instruments of torture*

RODERIGO.   Well, what is it? Is it within reason and compass?°   *reach*

IAGO.   Sir, there is especial commission come from Venice
to depute Cassio in Othello's place.

2620 RODERIGO.   Is that true? Why then Othello and Desdemona
return again to Venice.

IAGO.   O, no; he goes into Mauritania, and takes away
with him the fair Desdemona, unless his abode be lingered
here by some accident: wherein none can be so determinate°   *convincing*
as the removing of Cassio.

RODERIGO.   How do you mean, removing of him?

IAGO.   Why, by making him uncapable of Othello's place;
knocking out his brains.

RODERIGO.   And that you would have me to do?

2630 IAGO.   Ay, if you dare do yourself a profit and a right. He sups
tonight with a harlotry, and thither will I go to him: he
knows not yet of his honorable fortune. If you will watch his
going thence, which I will fashion to fall out between twelve
and one, you may take him at your pleasure: I will be near
to second your attempt, and he shall fall between us. Come,
stand not amazed at it, but go along with me; I will show you
such a necessity in his death that you shall think yourself
bound to put it on him. It is now high supper-time, and the
night grows to waste: about it.

2640 RODERIGO.   I will hear further reason for this.

IAGO.   And you shall be satisfied.

[*Exeunt.*]

SCENE III

Another room in the castle.

[*Enter* OTHELLO, LODOVICO, DESDEMONA, EMILIA, *and* ATTENDANTS.]

LODOVICO.   I do beseech you, sir, trouble yourself no further.

OTHELLO.   O, pardon me; 'twill do me good to walk.

LODOVICO.   Madam, good night; I humbly thank your ladyship.

DESDEMONA.   Your honor is most welcome.

OTHELLO.   Will you walk sir?
O,—Desdemona,—

DESDEMONA.   My lord?

OTHELLO.   Get you to bed on the instant; I will be returned
2650   forthwith: dismiss your attendant there: look it be done.

DESDEMONA.   I will, my lord.

[*Exeunt* Othello, Lodovico, *and* Attendants.]

EMILIA.   How goes it now? He looks gentler than he did.

DESDEMONA.   He says he will return incontinent:°   *immediately*
He hath commanded me to go to bed,
And bade me to dismiss you.

EMILIA.   Dismiss me!

DESDEMONA.   It was his bidding; therefore, good Emilia,
Give me my nightly wearing, and adieu:
We must not now displease him.

EMILIA.   I would you had never seen him!

2660 DESDEMONA.   So would not I: my love doth so approve him,
That even his stubbornness, his checks,° his frowns,—   *rebukes*
Prithee, unpin me,—have grace and favor in them.

EMILIA.   I have laid those sheets you bade me on the bed.

DESDEMONA.   All's one. Good faith, how foolish are our minds!
If I do die before thee, prithee, shroud me
In one of those same sheets.

EMILIA.   Come, come, you talk.

DESDEMONA.   My mother had a maid called Barbara:
She was in love; and he she loved proved mad
And did forsake her: she had a song of "willow";
2670 An old thing 'twas, but it expressed her fortune,
And she died singing it: that song tonight
Will not go from my mind; I have much to do
But to go hang my head all at one side
And sing it like poor Barbara. Prithee, dispatch.

EMILIA.   Shall I go fetch your nightgown.

DESDEMONA.   No, unpin me here.
This Lodovico is a proper man.

EMILIA.   A very handsome man.

DESDEMONA.   He speaks well.

EMILIA.   I know a lady in Venice would have walked
2680 barefoot to Palestine for a touch of his nether° lip.   *lower*

DESDEMONA [*singing*].   "The poor soul sat sighing by a
    sycamore tree,
    Sing all a green willow;
Her hand on her bosom, her head on her knee,
    Sing willow, willow, willow:
The fresh streams ran by her, and murmured her moans;
    Sing willow, willow, willow;
Her salt tears fell from her, and softened the stones"—
Lay by these:—
2690 [*Singing*.] "Sing willow, willow, willow."
Prithee, hie° thee; he'll come anon:°—   *hasten / soon*
[*Singing*.] "Sing all a green willow must be my garland.
    Let nobody blame him; his scorn I approve"—
Nay, that's not next. Hark! who is't that knocks?

EMILIA.   It's the wind.

DESDEMONA [*singing*].   "I called my love false love; but what said
    he then?

Sing willow, willow, willow:
If I court moe° women, you'll couch with moe men."   *more*
2700   So get thee gone; good night. Mine eyes do itch;
Doth that bode weeping?
EMILIA.   'Tis neither here nor there.
DESDEMONA.   I have heard it said so. O, these men, these men!
Dost thou in conscience think,—tell me, Emilia,—
That there be women do abuse their husbands
In such gross kind?
EMILIA.   There be some such, no question.
DESDEMONA.   Wouldst thou do such a deed for all the world?
EMILIA.   Why, would not you?
DESDEMONA.   No, by this heavenly light!
EMILIA.   Nor I neither by this heavenly light; I might do't
as well i' the dark.
2710 DESDEMONA.   Wouldst thou do such a deed for all the world?
EMILIA.   The world's a huge thing: it is a great price
For a small vice.
DESDEMONA.   In troth, I think thou wouldst not.
EMILIA.   In troth, I think I should; and undo 't when I had
done. Marry, I would not do such a thing for a joint-ring,°   *cheap ring*
nor for measures of lawn,° nor for gowns, petticoats, nor   *fine linen*
caps, nor any petty exhibition; but, for the whole
world,—why, who would not make her husband a cuckold to
make him a monarch? I should venture purgatory for 't.
DESDEMONA.   Beshrew me, if I would do such a wrong
2720   For the whole world.
EMILIA.   Why, the wrong is but a wrong i' the world; and having
the world for your labor, 'tis a wrong in your own world,
and you might quickly make it right.
DESDEMONA.   I do not think there is any such woman.
EMILIA.   Yes, a dozen; and as many to the
Vantage° as would store° the world they played for.   *to boot / people*
But I do think it is their husbands' faults
If wives do fall: say that they slack their duties
2730   And pour our treasures into foreign laps,
Or else break out in peevish jealousies,
Throwing restraint upon us, or say they strike us,
Or scant° our former having° in despite,   *reduce / allowance*
Why, we have galls,° and though we have some grace,   *tempers*
Yet have we some revenge. Let husbands know
Their wives have sense like them: they see and smell
And have their palates both for sweet and sour,
As husbands have. What is it that they do
When they change us for others? Is it sport?
2740   I think it is: and doth affection breed it?
I think it doth: is 't frailty that thus errs?
It is so too: and have not we affections,
Desires for sport, and frailty, as men have?
Then let them use us well: else let them know,
The ills we do, their ills instruct us so.

DESDEMONA.   Good night, good night: heaven me such uses° send,   *habits*
    Not to pick bad from bad, but by bad mend!

[*Exeunt.*]

ACT V

SCENE I

Cyprus. A street.

[*Enter* IAGO *and* RODERIGO.]

IAGO.   Here, stand behind this bulk;° straight will he come: *framework*
    Wear thy good rapier bare, and put it home:
2750   Quick, quick; fear nothing; I'll be at thy elbow:
    It makes us, or it mars us; think on that,
    And fix most firm thy resolution.
RODERIGO.   Be near at hand; I may miscarry in 't.
IAGO.   Here, at thy hand: be bold, and take thy stand.

[*Retires.*]

RODERIGO.   I have no great devotion to the deed;
    And yet he hath given me satisfying reasons:
    'Tis but a man gone. Forth, my sword: he dies.
2760 IAGO.   I have rubbed this young quat° almost to the sense,°   *pimple / quick*
    And he grows angry. Now, whether he kill Cassio,
    Or Cassio him, or each do kill the other,
    Every way makes my gain: live Roderigo,
    He calls me to a restitution large
    Of gold and jewels that I bobbed° from him,   *filched*
    As gifts to Desdemona:
    It must not be: if Cassio do remain,
    He hath a daily beauty in his life
    That makes me ugly; and besides, the Moor
2770   May unfold° me to him; there stand I in much peril: *expose*
    No, he must die. Be 't so. I hear him coming.

[*Enter* CASSIO.]

RODERIGO.   I know his gait; 'tis he. Villain, thou diest!
    [*Makes a pass at* CASSIO.]
CASSIO.   That thrust had been mine enemy indeed,
    But that my coat is better than thou know'st:
    I will make proof of thine. [*Draws, and wounds* RODERIGO.]
RODERIGO.   O, I am slain!
    [IAGO *from behind wounds* CASSIO *in the leg, and exit.*]
CASSIO.   I am maimed forever. Help, ho! murder! murder!
    [*Falls.*]

[*Enter* OTHELLO.]

OTHELLO.   The voice of Cassio: Iago keeps his word.

RODERIGO.   O, villain that I am!
OTHELLO.   It is even so.
2780 CASSIO.   O, help, ho! light! a surgeon!
OTHELLO.   'Tis he. O brave Iago, honest and just,
    That hast such noble sense of thy friend's wrong!
    Thou teachest me. Minion,° your dear lies dead,   *Mistress*
    And your unblest fate hies:° strumpet, I come!   *hastens*
    Forth of my heart these charms, thine eyes, are blotted;
    Thy bed lust-stained shall with lust's blood be spotted.

                                                          [Exit.]

                             [Enter LODOVICO *and* GRATIANO.]

CASSIO.   What, ho! No watch?° No passage?° Murder!   *sentries / passersby*
    Murder!
GRATIANO.   'Tis some mischance;° the cry is very direful.   *mishap*
2790 CASSIO.   O, help!
LODOVICO.   Hark!
RODERIGO.   O wretched villain!
LODOVICO.   Two or three groan: it is a heavy night:
    These may be counterfeits: let's think 't unsafe
    To come in to the cry without more help.
RODERIGO.   Nobody come? Then shall I bleed to death.
LODOVICO.   Hark!

                              [Re-enter IAGO, *with a light.]*

GRATIANO.   Here's one comes in his shirt, with light and weapons.
IAGO.   Who's there? Whose noise is this that cries on murder?
LODOVICO.   We do not know.
2800 IAGO.   Did not you hear a cry?
CASSIO.   Here, here! For heaven's sake, help me!
IAGO.   What's the matter?
GRATIANO.   This is Othello's ancient, as I take it.
LODOVICO.   The same indeed; a very valiant fellow.
IAGO.   What are you here that cry so grievously?
CASSIO.   Iago? O, I am spoiled, undone by villains!
    Give me some help.
IAGO.   O me, lieutenant! What villains have done this?
CASSIO.   I think that one of them is hereabout,
    And cannot make away.
IAGO.   O treacherous villains!
2810   What are you there? Come in and give some help.

                          [To LODOVICO *and* GRATIANO.]

RODERIGO.   O, help me here!
CASSIO.   That's one of them.
IAGO.   O murderous slave! O villain!

                                [Stabs RODERIGO.]

RODERIGO.   O damned Iago! O inhuman dog!
IAGO.   Kill men i' the dark! Where be these bloody thieves?
   How silent is this town! Ho! murder! murder!
   What may you be? Are you of good or evil!
LODOVICO.   As you shall prove us, praise us.
IAGO.   Signior Lodovico?
2820 LODOVICO.   He, sir.
IAGO.   I cry you mercy. Here's Cassio hurt by villains.
GRATIANO.   Cassio!
IAGO.   How is 't, brother?
CASSIO.   My leg is cut in two.
IAGO.   Marry, heaven forbid!
   Light, gentlemen: I'll bind it with my shirt.

                                        [Enter BIANCA.*]*

BIANCA.   What is the matter, ho? Who is't that cried?
IAGO.   Who is't that cried!
BIANCA.   O my dear Cassio! My sweet Cassio! O Cassio, Cassio, Cassio!
2830 IAGO.   O notable strumpet! Cassio, may you suspect
   Who they should be that have thus mangled you?
CASSIO.   No.
GRATIANO.   I am sorry to find you thus: I have been to seek you.
IAGO.   Lend me a garter. So. O, for a chair.
   To bear him easily hence!
BIANCA.   Alas, he faints! O Cassio, Cassio, Cassio!
IAGO.   Gentlemen all, I do suspect this trash
   To be a party in this injury,
   Patience awhile, good Cassio. Come, come;
2840   Lend me a light. Know we this face or no?
   Alas, my friend and my dear countryman
   Roderigo? No:—yes, sure: O heaven! Roderigo.
GRATIANO.   What, of Venice?
IAGO.   Even he sir. Did you know him?
GRATIANO.   Know him! Ay.
IAGO.   Signior Gratiano? I cry you gentle pardon;
   These bloody accidents must excuse my manners,
   That so neglected you.
GRATIANO.   I am glad to see you.
IAGO.   How do you, Cassio? O, a chair, a chair!
GRATIANO.   Roderigo!
IAGO.   He, he, 'tis he. *[A chair brought in.]* O, that's well
2850   said; the chair:
   Some good man bear him carefully from hence;
   I'll fetch the general's surgeon. *[To* BIANCA.*]* For you, mistress,
   Save you your labor. He that lies slain here, Cassio,
   Was my dear friend. What malice was between you?
CASSIO.   None in the world; nor do I know the man.
IAGO *[to* BIANCA*]*.   What, look you pale? O, bear him out o' the air.

                        [CASSIO and RODERIGO *are borne off.]*

Stay you, good gentlemen. Look you pale, mistress?
2860 Do you perceive the gastness° of her eye?   *ghastliness*
Nay, if you stare, we shall hear more anon.
Behold her well; I pray you, look upon her.
Do you see, gentlemen? Nay, guiltiness will speak,
Though tongues were out of use.

[*Enter* EMILIA.]

EMILIA. 'Las, what's the matter? What's the matter, husband?
IAGO. Cassio hath here been set on in the dark
By Roderigo, and fellows that are 'scaped:
He's almost slain, and Roderigo dead.
EMILIA. Alas, good gentleman! Alas, good Cassio!
2870 IAGO. This is the fruit of whoring. Prithee, Emilia,
Go know of Cassio where he supped tonight.
What, do you shake at that?
BIANCA. He supped at my house: but I therefore shake not.
IAGO. O, did he so? I charge you, go with me.
EMILIA. Fie, fie upon thee, strumpet!
BIANCA. I am no strumpet; but of life as honest
As you that thus abuse me.
EMILIA.   As I! Foh! Fie upon thee!
IAGO. Kind gentlemen, let's go see poor Cassio dressed.°   *bandaged*
2880 Come, mistress, you must tell's another tale.
Emilia, run you to the citadel,
And tell my lord and lady what hath happed!
Will you go on? I pray. [*Aside*] This is the night
That either makes me or fordoes° me quite.   *undoes*

[*Exeunt.*]

SCENE II

A bedchamber in the castle: DESDEMONA *in bed asleep; a light burning.*

[*Enter* OTHELLO.]

OTHELLO. It is the cause, it is the cause, my soul:
Let me not name it to you, you chaste stars!
It is the cause. Yet I'll not shed her blood,
Nor scar that whiter skin of hers than snow
2890 And smooth as monumental alabaster.
Yet she must die, else she'll betray more men.
Put out the light, and then put out the light:
If I quench thee, thou flaming minister,
I can again thy former light restore,
Should I repent me: but once put out thy light,
Thou cunning'st pattern of excelling nature,
I know not where is that Promethean[17] heat

---

[17] In Greek mythology Prometheus stole fire from the gods and gave it to man.

That can thy light relume.° When I have plucked the rose,   *restore*
I cannot give it vital growth again,
2900   It must needs wither. I'll smell it on the tree.

                                                                    [*Kissing her.*]

Ah, balmy breath, that dost almost persuade
Justice to break her sword! One more, one more:
Be thus when thou art dead, and I will kill thee,
And love thee after. One more, and this the last.
So sweet was ne'er so fatal. I must weep,
But they are cruel tears. This sorrow's heavenly;
It strikes where it doth love. She wakes.
DESDEMONA.   Who's there? Othello?
OTHELLO.   Ay, Desdemona.
DESDEMONA.   Will you come to bed, my lord?
OTHELLO.   Have you prayed tonight, Desdemona?
2910 DESDEMONA.   Ay, my lord.
OTHELLO.   If you bethink yourself of any crime
Unreconciled as yet to heaven and grace,
Solicit for it straight.
DESDEMONA.   Alas, my lord, what may you mean by that?
OTHELLO.   Well, do it, and be brief: I will walk by.
I would not kill thy unprepared spirit.
No, heaven forfend!° I would not kill thy soul.   *forbid*
DESDEMONA.   Talk you of killing?
OTHELLO.   Ay, I do.
2920 DESDEMONA.   Then heaven have mercy on me!
OTHELLO.   Amen, with all my heart!
DESDEMONA.   If you say so, I hope you will not kill me.
OTHELLO.   Hum!
DESDEMONA.   And yet I fear you; for you are fatal then
When your eyes roll so. Why I should fear I know not.
Since guiltiness I know not; but yet I feel I fear.
OTHELLO.   Think on thy sins.
DESDEMONA.   They are loves I bear to you.
OTHELLO.   Ay, and for that thou diest.
DESDEMONA.   That death's unnatural that kills for loving.
2930   Alas, why gnaw you so your nether° lip?   *lower*
Some bloody passion shakes your very frame:
These are portents;° but yet I hope, I hope,   *omens*
They do not point on me.
OTHELLO.   Peace, and be still!
DESDEMONA.   I will so. What's the matter?
OTHELLO.   That handkerchief which I so loved and gave thee
Thou gavest to Cassio.
DESDEMONA.   No, by my life and soul!
Send for the man, and ask him.
OTHELLO.   Sweet soul, take heed,
Take heed of perjury; thou art on thy deathbed.
DESDEMONA.   Ay, but not yet to die.

OTHELLO.   Yes, presently:
2940   Therefore confess thee freely of thy sin;
         For to deny each article with oath
         Cannot remove nor choke° the strong conception°   *stifle / belief*
         That I do groan withal. Thou art to die.
DESDEMONA.   Then Lord have mercy on me!
OTHELLO.   I say, amen.
DESDEMONA.   And have you mercy too! I never did
         Offend you in my life; never loved Cassio
         But with such general warranty of heaven
         As I might love. I never gave him token.
OTHELLO.   By heaven, I saw my handkerchief in 's hand.
2950   O perjured woman! Thou dost stone° my heart,   *harden*
         And makest me call what I intend to do
         A murder, which I thought a sacrifice.
         I saw the handkerchief.
DESDEMONA.   He found it then;
         I never gave it him. Send for him hither;
         Let him confess a truth.
OTHELLO.   He hath confessed.
DESDEMONA.   What, my lord?
OTHELLO.   That he hath used thee.
DESDEMONA.   How? Unlawfully?
OTHELLO.   Ay.
DESDEMONA.   He will not say so.
2960 OTHELLO.   No, his mouth is stopped;
         Honest Iago hath ta'en order for't.
DESDEMONA.   O, my fear interprets!° What, is he dead?   *explains (itself)*
OTHELLO.   Had all his hairs been lives, my great revenge
         Had stomach° for them all.   *appetite*
DESDEMONA.   Alas, he is betrayed, and I undone!
OTHELLO.   Out, strumpet! Weep'st thou for him to my face?
DESDEMONA.   O, banish me, my lord, but kill me not!
OTHELLO.   Down, strumpet!
DESDEMONA.   Kill me tomorrow; let me live tonight!
2970 OTHELLO.   Nay, if you strive,—
DESDEMONA.   But half an hour!
OTHELLO.   Being done, there is no pause.
DESDEMONA.   But while I say one prayer!
OTHELLO.   It is too late. [*He stifles her.*]
EMILIA [*within*].   My lord, my lord! What, ho! My lord, my lord!
OTHELLO.   What noise is this? Not dead? Not yet quite dead?
         I that am cruel am yet merciful;
         I would not have thee linger in thy pain.
         So, so.
EMILIA [*within*].   What, ho! My lord, my lord!
2980 OTHELLO.   Who's there?
EMILIA [*within*].   O, good my lord, I would speak a word with you!
OTHELLO.   Yes: 'tis Emilia. By and by. She's dead.
         'Tis like she comes to speak of Cassio's death.

The noise was here. Ha! No more moving?
Still as the grave. Shall she come in? Were 't good?
I think she stirs again. No. What's best to do?
If she comes in, she'll sure speak to my wife.
2990 My wife! My wife! What wife? I have no wife.
O, insupportable! O heavy hour!
Methinks it should be now a huge eclipse
Of sun and moon, and that the affrighted globe
Should yawn° at alteration.   *i.e., in earthquake*
EMILIA [*within*].   I do beseech you
That I may speak with you, O, good my lord!
OTHELLO.   I had forgot thee. O, come in, Emilia.
Soft;° by and by. Let me the curtains draw.   *Quietly*
Where art thou? [*Unlocks the door.*]

[*Enter* EMILIA.]

What's the matter with thee now?
EMILIA.   O, my good lord, yonder's foul murders done!
OTHELLO.   What, now?
EMILIA.   But now, my lord.
3000 OTHELLO.   It is the very error of the moon;
She comes more nearer earth than she was wont
And makes men mad.
EMILIA.   Cassio, my lord, hath killed a young Venetian
Called Roderigo.
OTHELLO.   Roderigo killed!
And Cassio killed!
EMILIA.   No, Cassio is not killed.
OTHELLO.   Not Cassio killed! Then murder's out of tune,
And sweet revenge grows harsh.
DESDEMONA.   O, falsely, falsely murdered!
EMILIA.   Alas, what cry is that?
OTHELLO.   That! What?
3010 EMILIA.   Out; and alas! That was my lady's voice.
Help! Help, ho! Help! O lady, speak again!
Sweet Desdemona! O sweet mistress, speak!
DESDEMONA.   A guiltless death I die.
EMILIA.   O, who hath done this deed?
DESDEMONA.   Nobody; I myself. Farewell.
Commend me to my kind lord. O, farewell! [*Dies.*]
OTHELLO.   Why, how should she be murdered?
EMILIA.   Alas, who knows?
OTHELLO.   You heard her say herself, it was not I.
3020 EMILIA.   She said so. I must needs report the truth.
OTHELLO.   She's like a liar gone to burning hell.
'Twas I that killed her.
EMILIA.   O, the more angel she,
And you the blacker devil!
OTHELLO.   She turned to folly and she was a whore.

EMILIA.   Thou dost belie her and thou art a devil.
OTHELLO.   She was false as water.
EMILIA.   Thou art rash as fire, to say
   That she was false. O, she was heavenly true!
OTHELLO.   Cassio did top her; ask thy husband else.
   O, I were damned beneath all depth in hell,
3030   But that I did proceed upon just grounds
   To this extremity. Thy husband knew it all.
EMILIA.   My husband!
OTHELLO.   Thy husband.
EMILIA.   That she was false to wedlock?
OTHELLO.   Ay, with Cassio. Nay, had she been true,
   If heaven would make me such another world
   Of one entire and perfect chrysolite,°   *topaz*
   I'd not have sold her for it.
EMILIA.   My husband!
OTHELLO.   Ay, 'twas he that told me first.
3040   An honest man he is, and hates the slime
   That sticks on filthy deeds.
EMILIA.   My husband!
OTHELLO.   What needs this iteration, woman? I say thy husband.
EMILIA.   O mistress, villainy hath made mocks with° love!   *a mockery of*
   My husband say that she was false!
OTHELLO.   He, woman;
   I say thy husband. Dost understand the word?
   My friend, thy husband, honest, honest Iago.
EMILIA.   If he say so, may his pernicious soul
   Rot half a grain a day! He lies to the heart.
   She was too fond of her most filthy bargain.
3050 OTHELLO.   Ha!
EMILIA.   Do thy worst:
   This deed of thine is no more worthy heaven
   Than thou wast worthy her.
OTHELLO.   Peace, you were best.
EMILIA.   Thou hast not half that power to do me harm
   As I have to be hurt. O gull!° O dolt!   *simpleton*
   As ignorant as dirt! Thou hast done a deed—
   I care not for thy sword; I'll make thee known,
   Though I lost twenty lives. Help! Help! ho! Help!
   The Moor hath killed my mistress! Murder! Murder!

        [*Enter* MONTANO, GRATIANO, IAGO, *and others.*]

3060 MONTANO.   What is the matter? How now, general!
EMILIA.   O, are you come, Iago? You have done well,
   That men must lay their murders on your neck.
GRATIANO.   What is the matter?
EMILIA.   Disprove this villain, if thou be'st a man.
   He says thou told'st him that his wife was false.
   I know thou didst not, thou'rt not such a villain.

Speak, for my heart is full.

IAGO.   I told him what I thought, and told no more
Than what he found himself was apt and true.

3070 EMILIA.   But did you ever tell him she was false?

IAGO.   I did.

EMILIA.   You told a lie, an odious, damnèd lie;
Upon my soul, a lie, a wicked lie!
She false with Cassio! Did you say with Cassio?

IAGO.   With Cassio, mistress. Go to, charm° your tongue.   control

EMILIA.   I will not charm my tongue; I am bound to speak:
My mistress here lies murdered in her bed,—

ALL.   O heavens forfend!

EMILIA.   And your reports have set the murder on.

3080 OTHELLO.   Nay, stare not, masters. It is true indeed.

GRATIANO.   'Tis a strange truth.

MONTANO.   O monstrous act!

EMILIA.   Villainy, villainy, villainy!
I think upon't. I think. I smell't. O villainy!
I thought so then. I'll kill myself for grief,
O villainy, villainy!

IAGO.   What, are you mad? I charge you, get you home.

EMILIA.   Good gentlemen, let me have leave to speak.
'Tis proper I obey him, but not now.
Perchance, Iago, I will ne'er go home.

OTHELLO.   O! O! O! [*Falling on the bed.*]

3090 EMILIA.   Nay, lay thee down and roar;
For thou hast killed the sweetest innocent
That e'er did lift up eye.

OTHELLO [*rising*].   O, she was foul!
I scarce did know you, uncle. There lies your niece,
Whose breath indeed these hands have newly stopped.
I know this act shows° horrible and grim.   looks

GRATIANO.   Poor Desdemona! I am glad thy father's dead.
Thy match was mortal to him, and pure grief
Shore his old thread in twain. Did he live now,

3100 This sight would make him do a desperate turn;°   deed
Yea, curse his better angel from his side,
And fall to reprobation.°   damnation

OTHELLO.   'Tis pitiful; but yet Iago knows
That she with Cassio hath the act of shame
A thousand times committed; Cassio confessed it.
And she did gratify his amorous works
With that recognizance and pledge of love
Which I first gave her; I saw it in his hand.
It was a handkerchief, an antique token

3110 My father gave my mother.

EMILIA.   O heaven! O heavenly powers!

IAGO.   'Zounds! Hold your peace.

EMILIA.   'Twill out, 'twill out. I peace!
No, I will speak as liberal° as the north.°   freely / north wind

Let heaven and men and devils let them all,
All, all, cry shame against me, yet I'll speak.
IAGO.   Be wise, and get you home.
EMILIA.   I will not.

[IAGO *offers to stab* EMILIA.]

GRATIANO.   Fie!
Your sword upon a woman!
EMILIA.   O thou dull Moor! That handkerchief thou speak'st of
3120   I found by fortune and did give my husband;
For often with a solemn earnestness,
More than indeed belonged to such a trifle,
He begged of me to steal it.
IAGO.   Villainous whore!
EMILIA.   She give it Cassio! No, alas, I found it,
And I did give't my husband.
IAGO.   Filth, thou liest!
EMILIA.   By heaven, I do not, I do not, gentlemen.
O murderous coxcomb!° What should such a fool   *dunce*
Do with so good a wife!
OTHELLO.   Are there no stones in heaven
3130   But what serve for the thunder?[18] Precious villain!

[*He runs at* IAGO. IAGO, *from behind, stabs* EMILIA, *and exit*.]

GRATIANO.   The woman falls; sure, he hath killed his wife.
EMILIA.   Ay, ay. O, lay me by my mistress' side.
GRATIANO.   He's gone, but his wife's killed.
MONTANO.   'Tis a notorious villain. Take you this weapon,
Which I have here recovered from the Moor.
Come, guard the door without; let him not pass,
But kill him rather. I'll after that same villain,
For 'tis a damned slave.

[*Exeunt all but* OTHELLO *and* EMILIA.]

OTHELLO.   I am not valiant neither,
But every puny whipster° gets my sword.   *whipping boy*
3140   But why should honor outlive honesty?
Let it go all.
EMILIA.   What did thy song bode, lady?
Hark, canst thou hear me? I will play the swan,
And die in music. [*Singing*.] Willow, willow, willow.
Moor, she was chaste; she loved thee, cruel Moor;
So come my soul to bliss, as I speak true;
So speaking as I think, I die, I die. [*Dies*.]
OTHELLO.   I have another weapon in this chamber;
It is a sword of Spain, the ice-brook's temper.°—   *i.e., tempered in ice-water*
O, here it is. Uncle, I must come forth.

---

[18] Thunder was thought by some Elizabethans to be caused by huge boulders falling from
the sky and bouncing along the ground.

3150 GRATIANO [*within*].   If thou attempt it, it will cost thee dear.
    Thou hast no weapon, and perforce must suffer.
OTHELLO.   Look in upon me then, and speak with me,
    Or, naked as I am, I will assault thee.

                                         [*Re-enter* GRATIANO.]

GRATIANO.   What is the matter?
OTHELLO.   Behold, I have a weapon;
    A better never did itself sustain
    Upon a soldier's thigh. I have seen the day
    That with this little arm and this good sword
    I have made my way through more impediments
    Than twenty times your stop.° But, O vain boast!   *opposition*
3160 Who can control his fate? 'Tis not so now.
    Be not afraid, though you do see me weaponed;
    Here is my journey's end, here is my butt°   *target*
    And very sea-mark° of my utmost° sail.   *marker / farthest*
    Do you go back dismayed? 'Tis a lost fear:
    Man but a rush° against Othello's breast,   *reed*
    And he retires. Where should Othello go?
    Now, how dost thou look now? O ill-starred wench!
    Pale as thy smock! When we shall meet at compt,°   *Judgment*
    This look of thine will hurl my soul from heaven,
3170 And fiends will snatch at it. Cold, cold, my girl!
    Even like thy chastity. O cursed slave!
    Whip me, ye devils,
    From the possession of this heavenly sight!
    Blow me about in winds! Roast me in sulphur!
    Wash me in steep-down gulfs of liquid fire!
    O Desdemona! Desdemona! Dead!
    Oh! Oh! Oh!

[*Enter* LODOVICO, MONTANO, CASSIO *carried in a chair, and* OFFICERS *with* IAGO, *prisoner.*]

LODOVICO.   Where is this rash and most unfortunate man?
OTHELLO.   That's he that was Othello. Here I am.
3180 LODOVICO.   Where is that viper? Bring the villain forth.
OTHELLO.   I look down towards his feet; but that's a fable.
    If that thou be'st a devil,° I cannot kill thee.   *i.e., with cloven feet*

                                         [*Wounds* IAGO.]

LODOVICO.   Wrench his sword from him.
IAGO.   I bleed, sir, but not killed.
OTHELLO.   I am not sorry neither. I'ld have thee live;
    For, in my case, 'tis happiness to die.
LODOVICO.   O thou Othello, that wert once so good,
    Fall'n in the practice° of a damnèd slave,   *scheming*
    What shall be said to thee?
OTHELLO.   Why, any thing.
    An honorable murderer, if you will;
3190 For nought did I in hate, but all in honor.

LODOVICO.   This wretch hath part confessed his villainy.
  Did you and he consent in Cassio's death?
OTHELLO.   Ay.
CASSIO.   Dear general, I never gave you cause.
OTHELLO.   I do believe it, and I ask your pardon.
  Will you, I pray, demand that demi-devil
  Why he hath thus ensnared my soul and body?
IAGO.   Demand me nothing; what you know, you know.
  From this time forth I never will speak word.
LODOVICO.   What, not to pray?
3200 GRATIANO.   Torments will ope your lips.
OTHELLO.   Well, thou dost best.
LODOVICO.   Sir, you shall understand what hath befall'n,
  Which, as I think, you know not. Here is a letter
  Found in the pocket of the slain Roderigo,
  And here another. The one of them imports
  The death of Cassio to be undertook
  By Roderigo.
OTHELLO.   O villain!
CASSIO.   Most heathenish and most gross!
LODOVICO.   Now here's another discontented paper,
3210   Found in his pocket too; and this, it seems,
  Roderigo meant to have sent this damned villain;
  But that, belike, Iago in the interim
  Came in and satisfied him.
OTHELLO.   O the pernicious caitiff!°   *villain*
  How came you, Cassio, by that handkerchief
  That was my wife's?
CASSIO.   I found it in my chamber.
  And he himself confessed but even now
  That there he dropped it for a special purpose
  Which wrought to his desire.
OTHELLO.   O fool! fool! fool!
CASSIO.   There is besides in Roderigo's letter,
3220   How he upbraids Iago, that he made him
  Brave° me upon the watch; whereon it came   *Defy*
  That I was cast,° and even but now he spake   *dismissed*
  After long seeming dead, Iago hurt him,
  Iago set him on.
LODOVICO.   You must forsake this room, and go with us.
  Your power and your command is taken off,
  And Cassio rules in Cyprus. For this slave,
  If there be any cunning cruelty
  That can torment him much and hold him long,
3230   It shall be his. You shall close prisoner rest,
  Till that the nature of your fault be known
  To the Venetian state. Come, bring away.
OTHELLO.   Soft you; a word or two before you go.
  I have done the state some service, and they know't.
  No more of that. I pray you, in your letters,

When you shall these unlucky deeds relate,
Speak of me as I am; nothing extenuate,
Nor set down aught in malice. Then must you speak
Of one that loved not wisely but too well;
3240 Of one not easily jealous but, being wrought,
Perplexed in the extreme; of one whose hand,
Like the base Indian, threw a pearl away
Richer than all his tribe; of one whose subdued eyes,
Albeit unused to the melting mood,
Drop tears as fast as the Arabian trees
Their medicinal gum. Set you down this;
And say besides, that in Aleppo once,
Where a malignant and a turbaned Turk
Beat a Venetian and traduced° the state,   *slandered*
3250 I took by the throat the circumcisèd dog
And smote him, thus. [*Stabs himself.*]
LODOVICO.   O bloody period!
GRATIANO.   All that's spoke is marred.
OTHELLO.   I kissed thee ere I killed thee. No way but this,
Killing myself, to die upon a kiss.

[*Falls on the bed, and dies.*]

CASSIO.   This did I fear, but thought he had no weapon;
For he was great of heart.
LODOVICO [*to* IAGO].   O Spartan[19] dog,
More fell° than anguish, hunger, or the sea!   *cruel*
Look on the tragic loading of this bed;
This is thy work.The object poisons sight;
3260 Let it be hid. Gratiano, keep the house,
And seize upon the fortunes of the Moor,
For they succeed on you. To you, lord governor,
Remains the censure of this hellish villain,
The time, the place, the torture: O, enforce it!
Myself will straight aboard, and to the state
This heavy act with heavy heart relate.

[*Exeunt.*]

[1604]

Critical Commentary on *Othello*

Act III, Scene III, of *Othello* is perhaps the most stunning *tour de force* in all
of Shakespearean drama. During this scene alone, Othello, under Iago's diabolical tutelage, changes from loving and trusting his wife Desdemona, to
believing himself cuckolded by her and planning to murder her. At the same
time, and as a result of his growing sexual jealousy, Othello changes from a

---

[19] The Spartans were famous for ferocity.

just and wise ruler to a tyrant. These dramatically convincing psychological changes take place in full view of the audience, which looks on with growing horror as Othello relies more and more on the guidance of his devilish "ancient" and distances himself more and more from his angelic wife.

What's more, Iago even warns Othello to resist his growing jealousy:

> O, beware, my lord, of jealousy;
> It is the green-eyed monster, which doth mock
> The meat it feeds on:

What is it in Othello that makes him the easy victim of Iago's predations?

First of all, Othello is perhaps too well aware of his own virtues and importance. His first significant speech is given over to a summary of his services to the state and a proud statement about his lineage; he speaks self-confidently of his "parts," his "title," and his "perfect soul." There is nothing factually wrong about his proud self-evaluation, but his consciousness of his own value and the importance he gives to his dignity will be important causes of his insane jealousy later in the play. The thought that his wife could value Cassio more than she values him is intolerable.

Othello's decisiveness is another important element in his personality. He knows instinctively that he must let himself be found by Brabantio; he decides immediately to prevent a sword-fight between his men and Brabantio's; he immediately accepts the Duke's command to leave for Cyprus (even though it interrupts his wedding night); and he immediately acquiesces in Desdemona's request for permission to follow him to Cyprus. For a general, decisiveness is an essential trait, but it can be a fatal flaw in a spouse. Note the decisiveness in Othello's marriage to Desdemona: They have known each other for fewer than nine months before their marriage. No sooner did Othello recognize Desdemona's interest in him, than he decided to court her. No sooner did their courtship begin, than they decided to elope. They have not yet had time to build up mutual experiences or deep knowledge of each other. Such early demonstrations of impulsive passion make it all the more credible that Othello should be an easy victim of impulsive jealousy later.

Nonetheless, Othello would never have distrusted Desdemona were it not for the malicious suggestions of Iago. Indeed, by the play's end Othello turns and asks the pathetic rhetorical question: "Will you, I pray, demand that demi-devil [Iago] why he hath thus ensnared my soul and body?"

However evil Iago's actions may be, his manipulation of Othello is soundly based on an understanding of human psychology. In the presence of Othello, he always conceals his cunning and acts the part of the blunt and brave old soldier. He spurs Othello's jealousy with subtle innuendo, making Othello begin to suspect Desdemona before any charge is made. On seeing Cassio leave Desdemona in Act III, Scene III, Iago says, "Ha! I like not that." And he goes on to deny that Cassio would "steal away so guilty-like."

By feigning reluctance to speak against his friend Cassio, Iago forces Othello to draw him out, making the point that Cassio "seems" honest and "Certain, men should be what they seem." As he begins to explain his suspicions, Iago is careful to protect himself by confessing his own jealous nature and warning Othello against jealousy. Indeed, by casting doubt on his "suspicions," he persuades Othello that he expresses himself too cautiously and knows more than he is willing to say. Once Iago sees that Othello has begun to believe that his wife is untrue, he plays upon Othello's limited knowledge of Venetian women in general and Desdemona in particular to suggest that it is in character for such women as Desdemona to "let heaven see the pranks / They dare not show their husbands." Desdemona's duplicity is demonstrated, Iago asserts, by the fact that

> She did deceive her father, marrying you;
> And when she seemed to shake and fear your looks,
> She loved them most.

When opportunity offers, Iago is also quick to point out the "unnatural" racial difference between Othello and Desdemona: "Foh! one may smell in such a will most rank, / Foul disproportion, thoughts unnatural." And finally, he slyly uses his knowledge that Cassio has sought Desdemona's help in regaining Othello's favor:

> Note if your lady strain his entertainment
> With any strong or vehement importunity;
> Much will be seen in that.

After all this, the fortunate accident of obtaining the handkerchief becomes only a helpful aid in confirming Desdemona's infidelity—an aid which the clever Iago could have fabricated in a dozen different ways.

Yet for all Iago's effectiveness as an agent of deviltry, he could not have succeeded if Othello had not had faults of character that made him susceptible to Iago's arguments. Certainly, Othello is quick to sense the innuendo in Iago's words, and he starts to test Desdemona before Iago has even begun to develop his suspicions. At the very beginning of Act III, Scene III, for example, Othello sees Cassio parting from his wife. He and Iago have commented upon that fact. And yet when Desdemona says that she has been speaking to "a suitor" who "languishes in your displeasure," Othello seems to test his wife's honesty by his reply, "Who is't you mean?" And since he knows very well that Cassio has just been with Desdemona, he tests her again in asking, "Went he hence now?" Then when Desdemona leaves after browbeating poor Othello into agreeing to see Cassio, Othello comments,

> Excellent wretch! Perdition catch my soul,
> But I do love thee! And when I love thee not,
> Chaos is come again.

Some critics see these lines as merely an instance of dramatic irony, but isn't it also possible to see in them Othello's first speculations on the consequences of the infidelity that he is already beginning to suspect in Desdemona?

Not only does Othello in some ways anticipate Iago's accusations, but he also draws those accusations out of Iago with an unseemly relish. He wants to hear (and is inclined to believe) the worst about Desdemona. He says to Iago, "give thy worst of thoughts / The worst of words." When Iago notes Desdemona's past duplicity ("She did deceive her father, marrying you"), Othello is quick to agree, "And so she did." Instead of hoping to prove Desdemona's innocence, Othello commands Iago to prove her guilt: "Villain, be sure thou prove my love a whore."

Indeed, Iago need not even be present for Othello's jealousy to develop. When Othello reenters after having gone in with Desdemona, it is clear that he has spent his offstage moments imagining her infidelity, "her stol'n hours of lust." He even goes so far as to imagine his situation if "the general camp, / Pioneers and all, had tasted her sweet body." What troubles him most is the blow to his pride:

> I had rather be a toad,
> And live upon the vapor of a dungeon,
> Than keep a corner in the thing I love
> For others' uses.

Thus, the development of Othello's jealousy is the result of an alliance between Iago and Othello. Together they are driven to worse actions—more harmful to themselves as well as others—than would have been possible had they acted separately. The moment in which they kneel together and swear fidelity is an appropriate substitution of a new marriage for the one that they are allied in destroying—and within a matter of hours this evil union, pregnant with malice, yields its grim and bloody burden.

A Collection of Critical Interpretations

MADELON GOHLKE SPRENGNETHER, " 'I WOOED THEE WITH MY SWORD': SHAKESPEARE'S TRAGIC PARADIGMS."*

. . . I am particularly interested in Shakespeare's tragedies, in what seem to me to be shared fictions on the part of the heroes about femininity and about their own vulnerability in relation to women, fictions interweaving women with violence, generating a particular kind of heterosexual dilemma.

The primacy of metaphor in the structures of individual consciousness, as in the collective fiction of the plot, appears in an early tragedy, *Romeo and Juliet*, where the failure of the play to achieve the generic status of comedy may be read as the result of the way in which heterosexual relations are imagined. In the conversation between the servants Sampson and Gregory, sexual intercourse, through a punning reference to the word "maidenhead," comes to be described as a kind of murder.

> SAMPSON. 'Tis all one. I will show myself a tyrant. When I have fought with the men, I will be civil with the maids—I will cut off their heads.
> GREGORY. The heads of the maids?
> SAMPSON. Ay, the heads of the maids or their maidenheads. Take it in what sense thou wilt. (I.i.)

To participate in the masculine ethic of this play is to participate in the feud, which defines relations among men as intensely competitive, and re-

---

* From *The Woman's Part: Feminist Criticism of Shakespeare.* Ed. Carolyn Ruth Swift Lenz, Gayle Greene, and Carol Thomas Neely (Urbana: U of Illinois P, 1980) 150–70.

lations with women as controlling and violent, so that women in Sampson's language "being the weaker vessels, are ever thrust to the wall" (I.i.). That Romeo initially rejects this ethic would seem to redefine the nature and structure of male/female relationships. What is striking about the relationship between Romeo and Juliet, however, is the extent to which it anticipates and ultimately incorporates violence.

Both lovers have a lively imagination of disaster. While Romeo ponders "some vile forfeit of untimely death" (I.iv.), Juliet speculates "If he is married, / My grave is like to be my wedding bed" (I.v.). Premonition, for both, has the force of self-fulfilling prophecy. While Romeo seeks danger by courting Juliet, and death by threatening suicide in the wake of Tybalt's death, Juliet, under pressure, exclaims: "I'll to my wedding bed; / And death, not Romeo, take my maidenhead!" (III.ii.). Read metaphorically, the plot validates the perception expressed variously in the play that love kills.

The paradigm offered by *Romeo and Juliet*, with some modifications, may be read in the major tragedies as well. Here, the structures of male dominance, involving various strategies of control, expressed in the language of prostitution, rape, and murder, conceal deeper structures of fear, in which women are perceived as powerful, and the heterosexual relation one which is either mutually violent or at least deeply threatening to the man. . . .

The paradox of prostitution in the tragedies is based on the masculine perception of the prostitute as not so much the victim as the agent of exploitation. If women are classed as prostitutes and treated as sexual objects, it is because they are deeply feared as sexually untrustworthy, as creatures whose intentions and desires are fundamentally unreadable. Thus, while Helen in *Troilus and Cressida* is verbally degraded, as the Trojans discuss her in terms of soiled goods and contaminated meat, she is, through her infidelity to Menelaus, the source of the sexual pride and humiliation that animate the entire conflict between the two warring nations. Honor among men in this play, though it takes the form of combat, is ultimately a sexual matter, depending largely on the fidelity or infidelity of women. For a man to be betrayed by a woman is to be humiliated or dishonored. To recover his honor he must destroy the man or woman who is responsible for his humiliation, for placing him in a position of vulnerability. . . .

If I seem to be arguing that the tragedies are largely about the degeneration of heterosexual relationships, or marriages that fail, it is because I am reading the development from the comedies through the problem plays and the major tragedies in terms of an explosion of the sexual tensions that threaten without rupturing the surface of the earlier plays. Throughout, a woman's power is less social or political (though it may have social and political ramifications) than emotional, expressed in her capacity to give or to withhold love. In a figure like Isabella the capacity to withhold arouses lust and a will to power in someone like Angelo, whose enforcing tactics amount to rape. In Portia, the threat of infidelity, however jokingly presented, is a weapon in her struggle with Antonio for Bassanio's allegiance. Male resistance, comic and exaggerated in Benedick, sullen and resentful in Bertram, stems from fears of occupying a position of weakness, taking in essence a "feminine" posture in relation to a powerful woman.

The feminine posture for a male character is that of the betrayed, and it is the man in this position who portrays women as whores. Since Iago occupies this position in relation to Othello, it makes sense that he seeks to destroy him, in the same way that Othello seeks to destroy the agent of his imagined betrayal, Desdemona. There is no reason to suppose, moreover, that Iago's consistently degraded view of women conceals any less hostile attitude in his actual relations with women. He, after all, like Othello, kills his wife. The difference between the two men lies not in their fear and mistrust of women but in the degree to which they are able to accept an emotional involvement. It is Othello, not Iago, who wears his heart on his sleeve, "for daws to peck at" (I.i.). Were it not for Othello's initial vulnerability to Desdemona he would not be susceptible to Iago's machinations. Having made himself vulnerable, moreover, he attaches an extraordinary significance to the relation. "And when I love thee not, / Chaos is come again" (III.iii.) "But there where I have garnered up my heart, / Where either I must live or bear no life, / The fountain from the which my current runs / Or else dries up" (IV.ii.).

Once Othello is convinced of Desdemona's infidelity (much like Claudio, on the flimsiest of evidence), he regards her, not as a woman who has committed a single transgression, but as a whore, one whose entire behavior may be explained in terms of lust. As such, he may humiliate her in public, offer her services to the Venetian ambassadors, pass judgment on her, and condemn her to death. Murder, in this light, is a desperate attempt to control. It is Desdemona's power to hurt which Othello seeks to eliminate by ending her life. While legal and social sanctions may be invoked against the prostitute, the seemingly virtuous woman suspected of adultery may be punished by death. In either case it is the fear or pain of victimization on the part of the man that leads to his victimization of women. It is those who perceive themselves to be powerless who may be incited to the acts of greatest violence.

The paradox of violence in *Othello*, not unlike in *Macbeth*, is that the exercise of power turns against the hero. In this case the murder of a woman leads to self-murder, and the hero dies attesting to the erotic destructiveness at the heart of his relation with Desdemona. "I kissed thee ere I killed thee. No way but this, / Killing myself, to die upon a kiss" (V.ii.). If murder may be a loving act, love may be a murdering act, and consummation of such a love possible only through the death of both parties.

Marianne Novy, "Marriage and Mutuality in *Othello*."*

In an article entitled "Marriage and the Construction of Reality," the sociologists Peter Berger and Hansfried Kellner say, "Unlike an earlier situation in which the establishment of the new marriage simply added to the differentiation and complexity of an already existing social world, the marriage partners are now embarked on the often difficult task of constructing for themselves the little world in which they will live." By this definition, Othello and Desdemona seem to begin their marriage in a situation more modern than traditional. Othello is cut off from his ancestry; Desdemona is disowned

---

* From *Love's Argument: Gender Relations in Shakespeare* (Chapel Hill: U of North Carolina P, 1984) 125–33.

by her father. They spend most of the play in Cyprus, a setting native to neither of them. Thus they have some of both the opportunities and the difficulties of constructing their own world that Berger and Kellner discuss. "The re-construction of the world in marriage," they continue, "occurs principally in the course of conversation. . . . The implicit problem of this conversation is how to match two individual definitions of reality."

Marriage for Berger and Kellner, as, I have argued, for Shakespeare's comedies, involves a combination of ideals of mutuality and assumptions of patriarchy, though of course patriarchy takes a different form in twentieth-century America than in seventeenth-century England. Though the balance may tip in one direction or the other, the predominance of playfulness and of festive disguise helps to remove threatening elements. In Shakespeare's tragedies, however, the combination of patriarchy and mutuality breaks down. We never see Othello and Desdemona creating together a private game-like world of conversation onstage. All the early scenes where they both speak are public, and events in the outside world remain important to their relationship. Othello's public role as warrior is part of what Desdemona loves in him. Furthermore, Berger and Kellner assume a situation in which "the husband typically talks with his wife about his friend, but not with his friend about his wife"; in *Othello* the opposite is true. One principal representative of the already existing social world stays with Othello and Desdemona—Iago. And accompanying his presence is the persistence of conventional attitudes from the outside world in Othello's mind. Othello cannot completely free himself from the conventional assumption that Desdemona's marriage to him is unnatural. He cannot keep distrust of women out of his marriage. Brabantio may not be physically present, but his message, "She has deceived her father, and may thee" (1.3), rings in Othello's memory. And after Othello has stopped believing anything Desdemona says, Iago's presence makes it impossible for Othello to keep out of his marriage a code of proving manhood by violent revenge. Between patriarchy and racism, the initial mutuality between Desdemona and Othello is destroyed. To restore it is the aim of Othello's suicide.

In Shakespeare's comedies we usually see mutuality being established; in *Othello* we hear the process described. Othello calls it, "How I did thrive in this fair lady's love / And she in mine" (1.3). While he told his life story to her father,

> This to hear
> Would Desdemona seriously incline;
> But still the house affairs would draw her thence;
> Which ever as she could with haste dispatch,
> She'd come again, and with a greedy ear
> Devour up my discourse. Which I observing,
> Took once a pliant hour, and found good means
> To draw from her a prayer of earnest heart
> That I would all my pilgrimage dilate,
> Whereof by parcels she had something heard,
> But not intentively. I did consent,
> And often did beguile her of her tears

> When I did speak of some distressful stroke
> That my youth suffered. (1.3)

Here Othello gives a description of a process of initiative and response leading to further response—Othello talks, Desdemona listens, Othello sees her listening and encourages it, hopes she will ask to hear more; she does, he agrees, and she responds with tears of sympathy. Othello is gratified by her initial interest in his performance and draws her out for more active participation.

While this scene fits some conventions of patriarchy—male activity and female response—the imagery by which Othello's words become food that Desdemona devours should signal that roles here are not altogether limited to conventional ones. As Brabantio says, Othello's story portrays Desdemona as "half the wooer" (1.3). She goes beyond the audience's responsiveness to initiate courtship by her hint. The content of their conversation in this story is Othello's experience, not Desdemona's, but we should notice how closely he has observed her, how carefully he has elicited her request. While Desdemona has been an audience to Othello's performance, he has also behaved like an audience in closely observing her. In the narrative Othello tells, he has judged Desdemona's feelings from her gestures, guessed at meaning beneath her words, and he has been right about her interest in him—beyond his dreams. Othello describes a powerful experience of emotional sharing—he has gone back to his youth and relived his sufferings and she has felt them along with him: "She loved me for the dangers I had passed, / And I loved her that she did pity them" (1.3).

Yet in spite of her active participation, Desdemona describes her loyalty to Othello as a matter of duty. Furthermore, Desdemona makes as many concessions as she can to her father in explaining her "divided duty" (1.3); she speaks first of her bonds as a daughter, and she compares her choice of Othello with her mother's choice of her father. One of few Shakespearean women who claim to imitate their mothers, she is trying to reassure Brabantio by putting her marriage into an orderly continuity of marriages, trying to remind him that his marriage too was won at the cost of separation from a father.

In these introductory statements by Othello and Desdemona, their marriage appears as a combination of patriarchy and mutuality. Othello makes the marriage proposal and keeps the title of lord, yet there is a genuine emotional sharing and companionship. Desdemona further emphasizes both these elements later on in this scene. "That I did love the Moor to live with him," she says,

> My downright violence, and storm of fortunes,
> May trumpet to the world. (1.3)

She joins him in *his* imagery as in his career. "My heart's subdued / Even to the very quality of my lord" (1.3). She identifies with him in a way that subordinates her. He does not, for example, ask that she accompany him to Cyprus until after she does, and he makes a point of saying that he asks it only as a magnanimous gesture, "to be free and bounteous to her mind"

(1.3). Although his description of their courtship revealed the importance to him of her emotional response—the mutual dependence that they have created—he wants to deny his need of her and, most emphatically, to deny any sexual appetite that would clamor for satisfaction—"Not to comply with heat—the young affects / In me defunct" (1.3). . . .

Why is Iago so successful in his attempts to destroy the relationship between Othello and Desdemona? Many different approaches can work toward answers to this question; here I am interested in looking at what the play shows about the vulnerability of the combination of patriarchy and mutuality that we see in that relationship, and about how Iago manipulates Othello's persisting need for mutuality.

If mutuality and patriarchy are to be combined, as we have already suggested, the woman must make the gesture of subordinating herself to the man; in addition, in *Othello*, much more than in the comedies, the man believes he must subdue qualities in himself that he considers would make him woman-like or too dependent on a woman. Othello's need for control to assert his manliness often coalesces with the need for control to assert that he is civilized and not a barbarian slave to passion. It is important to note here the overlap between the stereotypes of the woman and of the Moor: conventional Renaissance European views would see both as excessively passionate. Othello's first appearance, contrary to this stereotype, is an amazing show of self-possession under Brabantio's attacks. Even in his description of his life history, he recounts his adventures in a controlled tone. He is, however, moved when Desdemona cries over them; if he beguiles her of her tears, she can express his emotions for him. It further suggests his control, based on his sense of social distinctions, that *Desdemona* first speaks of love, and Othello can see himself as loving only in response, and therefore rationally. Indeed, he is, as we have seen, curiously emphatic about his lack of sexual passion.

Othello's stress on control of passion may add to the implications of his dismissal of Cassio. Just after the announcement that Othello has proclaimed a general festivity because of the coincidence of the victory over the Turks and the celebration of his nuptial, Othello says to Cassio:

> Good Michael, look you to the guard to-night.
> Let's teach ourselves that honorable stop,
> Not to outsport discretion. (2.3)

Here Othello seems to be identifying himself with Cassio, the potential drunkard, in a common need for control. A few lines later, Othello leaves with Desdemona, saying

> Come, my dear love.
> The purchase made, the fruits are to ensue;
> That profit's yet to come 'tween me and you. (2.3)

After the first line, this is a rather business-like description for the sexual initiation of a wedding night. Again it suggests a concern for sharing, but it is odd that he should turn pleasure into financial imagery. Iago's words a few lines later suggest one kind of language Othello has avoided using: "He hath not yet made wanton the night with her, and she is sport for Jove" (2.3).

Thus, while Cassio drinks too much and gets into a fight with Roderigo and then with Montano, the characters and the audience are frequently reminded that Othello and Desdemona are meeting in bed for the first time. Iago, in fact, brings this juxtaposition shockingly into focus when he describes the fight to Othello, who has been called back by its clamor:

> Friends all, but now, even now,
> In quarter, and in terms like bride and groom
> Devesting them for bed; and then but now—
> As if some planet had unwitted men—
> Swords out, and tilting one at other's breast
> In opposition bloody. (2.3)

What Iago has described is perilously close to the reality of the wedding night, when at least briefly rational control must be abandoned and blood must be shed.

I suggest that, partly under Iago's influence, partly because of his own emphasis on self-control, Othello feels guilty about the passion involved in his intercourse with Desdemona; he identifies with the offender who has also let passion run away with him, and in effect he makes Cassio a scapegoat for himself. When he dismisses Cassio, as later when he kills Desdemona, he insists that he is acting justly when he is really moved by his emotions. Here he returns to Desdemona saying "All's well now, sweeting" (2.3), because Cassio is dismissed, and so too, Othello thinks, is the disturbing image of sexuality becoming violent with which Iago has associated him. Like Stanley Cavell, I think that Othello's guilt about sexuality is an important subtext of the play; but in addition to the guilt about hurting Desdemona, which Cavell stresses, I see him as feeling guilty for loss of control of his passions, such loss of control as many medieval theologians whose views were still reflected in some Elizabethan sermons thought made sex inevitably suspect even within marriage.

Of course, *Othello* is a play about passionate love; but part of its impact comes from the tension between that passion and the restraints that Othello is constantly trying to place on it, as suggested by his words. Furthermore, Othello's very idealization of Desdemona has a passionate component. He is passionate in wishing her to be totally fused in identification with him, in a symbiosis possible only for the mother and infant before the infant's discovery of sex. In one of his final confrontations with Desdemona, he describes her, in language that brings to mind the dependence of the infant at the mother's breast, as the place

> Where either I must love or bear no life,
> The fountain from the which my current runs
> Or else dries up. (4.2)

C. L. Barber has suggested that many of Shakespeare's female characters have the resonance for the hero, and for the audience, of the Virgin Mary; Shakespeare's audience still had the fantasy of a total and pure relationship such as one could have only with a mother who was perpetually a virgin, and this fantasy could no longer be dealt with through religious symbolism and ritual because of the Reformation. Thus Othello projects the kind of religious need onto Desdemona that no merely human being could fulfill.

Diane Elizabeth Dreher, "Desdemona: Love's Sweet Victim."*

Alternately canonized and criticized for loving Othello, Desdemona has been praised for her devotion and censured for her sexuality, described as deceptive, proud, and manipulative or as helplessly passive. She is herself a tragic paradox. A spirited, courageous young woman, Desdemona is moved by the depth of her love to conform to a static and fatal ideal of feminine behavior. Among those critics for whom she shines as a saintly ideal, Irving Ribner said that "in the perfection of her love Desdemona reflects the love of Christ for man," and G. Wilson Knight found her a "divinity comparable with Dante's Beatrice." Yet W. H. Auden observed "One cannot but share Iago's doubts as to the durability of the marriage," predicting that "given a few more years of Othello and of Emilia's influence and she might well, one feels, have taken a lover." Jan Kott, too, found her strong sexuality disturbing: "Of all Shakespeare's female characters she is the most sensuous. . . . Desdemona is faithful but must have something of a slut in her."

Beyond a doubt, Desdemona is affectionate and sensual, but this does not make her a slut any more than the absence of sexuality would sanctify her. Too often her critics themselves have fallen victim to the virgin-whore complex, the false dilemma that dominates the perception of women in traditional society. A few critics have recognized the simple fact that Desdemona is both a virtuous and a passionate woman.

The elopement has been cited as proof of her courage or evidence of her deceptive nature: "a measure of her determination to have a life that seems to offer the promise of excitement denied her as a sheltered Venetian senator's daughter"; "her deception of her own father makes an unpleasant impression." We may laugh at Thomas Rymer's oversimplified reading of the play as "a caution to all Maidens of Quality how, without their Parents consent, they run away with Blackamoors" and "a warning to all good Wives, that they look well to their Linnen." Desdemona's critics range from the sublime to the ridiculous. Predominantly male, they have seen her as either willful and manipulative or helplessly passive: "a determined young woman . . . eager to get her own way; her advocacy for Cassio demonstrating her desire to dominate Othello, revealing a strong case of penis envy.". . .

Bradley, by contrast, found her "helplessly passive," an innocent, loving martyr:

> Desdemona is helplessly passive. She can do nothing whatever. She cannot retaliate even in speech: no, not even in silent feeling. And the chief reason of her helplessness only makes the sight of her suffering more exquisitely painful. She is helpless because her nature is infinitely sweet and her love absolute. . . . Desdemona's suffering is like that of the most loving of dumb creatures tortured without cause by the being he adores. . . .

The history of Desdemona on the stage parallels these changing critical estimations. Until Fanny Kemble, Helena Faucit, and Ellen Terry endowed her with a new dynamism, Desdemona was portrayed as a pathetic girl, not

* From *Domination and Defiance: Fathers and Daughters in Shakespeare* (Lexington: U P Kentucky, 1986) 87–95.

a tragic heroine. In the nineteenth century her part was diminished by extensive cuts, and William Charles Macready tried to dissuade Fanny Kemble from playing it, arguing that this was no part for a great actress. Kemble persevered, creating a Desdemona who was softly feminine but also forthright and courageous. Her Desdemona, like Helena Faucit's, fought for her life in the final scene. According to Ellen Terry, most people believed that Desdemona was "a ninny, a pathetic figure," that "an actress of the dolly type, a pretty young thing with a vapid, innocent expression, is well suited to the part," but she felt that Desdemona was "a woman of strong character," requiring the talents of a great tragic actress. . . .

She is by nature unconventional, a sensuous and virtuous woman in a culture that prized a cold, chaste ideal. Dynamic and courageous when the traditional feminine norm was passivity, she transcends patriarchal order and degree, reaching out in loving kindness to all. Desdemona behaved with daughterly decorum in her father's house but revealed her assertiveness and magnanimity in her love for Othello. Her enthusiastic and affectionate nature are evident in Othello's description of their courtship, especially in the Folio version. This apparently docile maiden would rush from her household chores to "devour" his stories "with a greedy ear." She was fascinated by this man of men and the adventurous life he led. So far was she from Brabantio's conventional "maiden never bold" that she gave Othello for his pains "a world of kisses," in the Folio reading far more assertive than the Quarto's "sighs.". . .

In her elopement, Desdemona "successfully defies the Father," Brabantio himself and "the symbol of Authority and Force" he represents. Harold Goddard contrasts her to the submissive Ophelia and Hamlet, who fail to break free from paternal authority. True, her love liberates her long enough to elope with Othello, but in her concept of marriage she again succumbs to the yoke of convention, adopting the traditional role inherited from her mother, a relationship in which the wife becomes her husband's submissive, obedient subject. . . .

Critics have found an echo of the traditional father-daughter relationship, pointing to Othello's age, which makes him a father surrogate, and noting that he was her father's friend before the elopement. Some psychological critics have seen her choice of him as motivated by an Oedipus complex, in which she sought either to marry someone like her father or to punish her father for being faithless to her in childhood. . . .

But one need not resort to incest and Oedipus complexes to explain Desdemona's behavior. We have seen in her love for Othello a highly idealistic strain as well as a passionate attachment, an almost religious fervor and dedication. All her young life she had longed for a heroic mission, a cause. Because she is a woman, unable to pursue her heroic ideals, she finds her cause in loving Othello, subordinating herself in her role as his wife, even as he subordinates his ego to the demands of war. It is not only Othello who "agnize[s] / A natural and prompt alacrity . . . in hardness" (I.iii.). Desdemona, as well, longs for heroic commitment and sacrifice. Given the limits of her culture, she can find this only indirectly, some would say masochistically, by devoting herself to Othello.

Thus we have the paradox that explains Desdemona's contradictory image. She is courageous, heroic, passive, and vulnerable. She is both extremes because of her love, which makes of her an oxymoronic "excellent wretch"

(III.iii). On the altar of holy love she sacrifices her dynamic self to the image of her dreams, becoming not a "moth of peace" (I.ii.) but an equally diminished shadow of herself. As she rejects the "wealthy curled darlings" (I.ii.) of Venice, leaving her father and embracing the man of her dreams, it would seem that she has resolved for herself the crisis of identity. But in her marriage she does not commit herself with the dynamic energy that flourished in her courtship and elopement. She chooses a new identity, a controlled, ever modest and obedient self, not Desdemona but the model wife, because this is what she feels Othello deserves. She becomes a victim of the convention she embraces, a neurotic self-effacement amounting to slow suicide. She, too, loves "not wisely, but too well" (V.ii.), affirming a static ideal, a polished surface of behavior that will not withstand the tempests her marriage faces on Cyprus. . . .

Othello is the bleakest of tragedies, for although these two people love each other dearly, their love is not enough. They fail because they do not know who they are. Othello knows only what it means to be a soldier, a heroic leader who makes decisions on the battlefield, in an instant discerning friend from foe and taking violent action. Like Coriolanus, he is one of Shakespeare's warrior heroes who calls the heroic ideal into question. The same behavior that makes him a hero on the battlefield only destroys him in peacetime. Desdemona knows how to be a dutiful daughter, the traditional role she rejects in courageously following Othello and her heroic dreams. Her short-lived self-affirmation in love, however, turns to bondage in marriage. In I.iii. she acknowledges the ritual transfer that makes her not her father's but her husband's chattel, surrendering her dynamic self for the passive feminine ideal. Both Othello and Desdemona err in conforming to traditional male and female stereotypes, adopting persona behavior which prevents real intimacy and trust. Desdemona's chastity becomes more important to both of them than Desdemona herself. Othello kills her and she sacrifices herself to affirm the traditional ideal. As we have seen in considering Hero, nothing the traditional woman can do will alter men's misperceptions of her. In the world of traditional male-female roles, males act and females react. Desdemona cannot change Othello's perceptions. Her loving unselfishness becomes compulsive compliance which actually prevents her from defending herself.

Iago's assessment of Desdemona is correct. She attempts to please everyone, fulfilling the role of the good woman. She: "is of so free, so kind, so apt, so blessed a disposition, she holds it a vice in her goodness not to do more than she is requested" (II.iii.). Desdemona's error is that of the traditional woman who lives for others, choosing goodness over selfishness. In attempting to nurture everyone around her, she fails herself. She pleads eloquently to the duke about her love for Othello. In her boundless empathy, she pleads for Cassio, but, characteristically woman, she cannot plead for herself. . . .

Enslaved by the traditional ideal that not only dominates her behavior but distorts her perceptions, Desdemona sinks into passivity until in IV.ii. she tells Emilia she is "half asleep" in shock. Attempting to conform to "what should be," she fails to see "what is," refusing to recognize Othello's jealousy and the danger it represents. The traditional norms have given her no means of defending herself. She is told only to bear chiding with all patience and obedience, and so she does. The idealism and all-consuming nature of her love lead her into a closed-image syndrome not uncommon among battered wives: she refuses to believe all this is happening. Othello cannot really be jealous; she never gave him cause. Every shock to her system is met with a new denial, a new affirmation of her innocence and obedience in the role of perfect wife. Her inability to accept Othello's jealousy is compounded by her previously sheltered life, which did not prepare her for anything like this. In loving Othello, she has risked everything, given up home, father, and country. Her identity as Othello's wife has become her *only* identity; her belief system at this point will not tolerate his rejection, which would make her a nonentity and turn her world to chaos.

A significant line early in the play is Othello's response to the street brawl: "Are we turn'd Turks, and to ourselves do that / Which heaven hath forbid the Ottomites?" (II.iii.). Are we, he asks, our own worst enemies? His accusation holds true for all the principal characters in the play. Iago betrays his humanity in his murderous revenge. Cassio betrays himself by drinking to excess. Othello loses his faith in Desdemona's love, betrayed by his own insecurities. In his *anagnorisis* he acknowledges this, executing justice upon himself as he had done to the "turban'd Turk," arch enemy of the Venetian state (V.ii.). Desdemona, too, has been an enemy to herself in slavishly following the traditional ideal of female behavior, which undermines her self-esteem. Her unselfish devotion to Othello makes her a martyr to love. Desdemona's last words have been read many ways: a final act of loving kindness, a benevolent lie to protect Othello. As Emilia asks her who has done this deed and Desdemona answers, "Nobody; I myself" (V.ii.), there is surely some truth in her admission. She dies upholding the impossible standard of the good woman, impossible because even though she was innocent and chaste, the man she loved failed to perceive her so.

Like Ophelia and Hero, Desdemona is in her own way a dominated daughter, a dominated woman in a patriarchal society that will not allow women to grow up, to assert themselvs in their adult lives, or even to act in their own defense. In her attempt to be a good wife, she loses her vitality and self-confidence, drawing her identity from her husband's perceptions. Despite her forebodings, she lies in bed waiting for him in V.ii. And as he murders her, she becomes the ultimate embodiment of the feminine ideal: silent, cold, and chaste, as beautiful as a marble statue: "Cold, cold, my girl! / Even like thy chastity" (V.ii.). The element of necrophilia in Othello's adoration of her sleeping form is no accident ("Be thus when thou art dead, and I will kill thee / And love thee after"). Carried to its logical extreme, the traditional ideal repesents a woman's denial of her thoughts and desires, her very essence, an ultimate obliteration of the self. In her death, Desdemona finally becomes the "perfect" Renaissance woman.

KAREN NEWMAN," 'AND WASH THE ETHIOP WHITE': FEMININITY AND THE MONSTROUS IN *OTHELLO*."*

> Shakespeare, who is accountable both to the *Eyes* and to the *Ears*, And to convince the very heart of an Audience, shews that *Desdemona* was won by hearing *Othello* talk. . . . This was the Charm, this was the philtre, the love-

---

* From *Shakespeare Reproduced: The Text in History and Ideology.* Ed. Jean E. Howard and Marion F. O'Connor (New York: Methuen, 1987) 143–62.

powder, that took the Daughter of this Noble Venetian. This was sufficient to make the Black-amoor White, and reconcile all, tho' there had been a Cloven-foot into the bargain.

(Rymer, 1693, 221–2)

It would be something monstrous to conceive this beautiful Venetian girl falling in love with a veritable negro.

(Coleridge I, 42)

To a great many people the word "negro" suggests at once the picture of what they would call a "nigger", the woolly hair, thick lips, round skull, blunt features, and burnt-cork blackness of the traditional nigger minstrel. Their sub-conscious generalization is as silly as that implied in Miss Preston's "the African race" or Coleridge's "veritable negro". There are more races than one in Africa, and that a man is black in colour is no reason why he should, even to European eyes, look subhuman. One of the finest heads I have ever seen on any human being was that of a negro conductor on an American Pullman car. He had lips slightly thicker than an ordinary European's, and he had somewhat curly hair; for the rest he had a long head, a magnificent forehead, a keenly chiselled nose, rather sunken cheeks, and his expression was grave, dignified, and a trifle melancholy. He was coal-black, but he might have sat to a sculptor for a statue of Caesar.

(Ridley, 1958, li)

M. R. Ridley's "they" is troublesome. As scholars and teachers, we use his Arden edition of *Othello* and find ourselves implicated in his comfortable assumptions about "a great many people." In answer to the long critical history which sought to refute Othello's blackness, Ridley affirms that Othello was black, but he hastens to add the adversative "but." Othello was not a "veritable negro," he assures us, a type from vaudeville and the minstrel show, a figure of ridicule unworthy of tragedy who would evidently appear "sub-human" to European eyes, but a black who looks white and might have represented the most renowned general of the western tradition, Caesar. What are we to make of a widely used scholarly edition of Shakespeare which, in the very act of debunking, canonizes the prejudices of Rymer and Coleridge? Can we shrug our shoulders, certain that Ridley's viewpoint represents a long ago past of American Pullman cars and dignified black conductors? Are such prejudices dismantled by the most recent reprint which represents on its cover a "veritable negro" of exactly the physiognomy Ridley assures us "a great many people" are wrong in imagining?

Much of the disgust Rymer, Coleridge, and other critics betray comes not from the fact of Othello's individual blackness, but from the *relation* of that blackness to Desdemona's fair purity. Coleridge calls it "monstrous." Embedded in commentaries on the play which seek to ward off Othello's blackness is the fear of miscegenation, and particularly the white man's fear of the union of black man with white woman. Such commentators occupy the rhetorical position of Roderigo, Brabantio, and Iago who view the marriage of Othello and Desdemona as against all sense and nature: "I'll refer me to all things of sense, / . . . Whether a maid, so tender, fair, and happy, / . . . Would ever have (to incur a general mock) / Run from her guardage to the sooty bosom / Of such a thing as thou?" (I.ii.)

In *Othello,* the black Moor and the fair Desdemona are united in a marriage which all the other characters view as unthinkable. Shakespeare uses their assumption to generate the plot itself—Iago's ploy to string Roderigo along is his assurance that Desdemona could not, contrary to nature, long love a black man. Even his manipulation of Othello depends on the Moor's own prejudices against his blackness and belief that the fair Desdemona would prefer the white Cassio.

Miscegenation is an issue not only on the level of plot, but also of language, for linked oppositions, especially of black and white and their cultural associations, characterize the play's discourse. "Black ram" tups "white ewe;" "fair" Desdemona runs to Othello's "sooty bosom." The Duke mollifies Brabantio with "Your son-in-law is far more fair than black." Desdemona is described, in what for the Renaissance would have been an oxymoron, as a "fair devil," and as "fair paper" and a "goodly book" across the white pages of which Othello fears is written "whore." In the final scene Emilia exclaims in response to Othello's confession that he has killed Desdemona, "O, the more angel she, / And you the blacker devil!" Like the proverb "to wash an Ethiop white," Emilia's lines exemplify what I will term rhetorical miscegenation, for despite the semantics of antithesis, the chiasmus allies the opposing terms rhetorically.

In the Renaissance no other colors so clearly implied opposition or were so frequently used to denote polarization. As Winthrop Jordan points out in his monumental study, *White over Black*, the meaning of *black* even before the sixteenth century, according to the *OED*, included "deeply stained with dirt, soiled, dirty, foul. . . . Having dark or deadly purposes, malignant; pertaining to or involving death, deadly, baneful, disastrous . . . iniquitous, atrocious, horrible, wicked . . . indicating disgrace, censure, liability to punishment, etc."[2] . . . *White* represented the opposite. The emphasis in *Othello* on Desdemona's fairness and purity, "that whiter skin of hers than snow / And smooth as monumental alabaster" (V. ii), and the idealization of fair female beauty it implies—the entire apparatus of Petrarchanism—is usually said to point up the contrast between Desdemona and Othello. But I want to argue to the contrary that femininity is not opposed to blackness and monstrosity, as white is to black, but identified with the monstrous, an identification that makes miscegenation doubly fearful. The play is structured around a cultural aporia, miscegenation.

Femininity interrupts not only the characterological, but also the critical discourse of the play. In his commentary, Ridley continues after the passage quoted above:

> to give an insult any point and barb it must have some relation to the facts. A woman may call a pale-complexioned rival "pasty" or "whey-faced", but it would be silly to call her swarthy . . . in the same way, "thick lips" would lose all its venom if it could not be recognizably applicable to Othello's mouth.
>
> (I.ii.)

Ridley's justification of Othello's blackness and his reading of "thick lips" betray a woefully inadequate sense of irony: literary discourse often works by means of negative example, as in Shakespeare's vaunt "My mistress' eyes are

---

[2] Winthrop Jordan, *White Over Black* (Chapel Hill: U of North Carolina P, 1968) 7.

nothing like the sun." But more important than Ridley's limitations as a reader of texts is how he illustrates his point about Othello's blackness: he evokes a cultural prejudice against women, their supposed cattiness in response to a rival. Femininity interrupts Ridley's commentary on Othello's blackness; pitting women against women, the critic displaces the struggle of white against black man onto a cultural femininity.

Miscegenation: Blacks and the Monstrous

Until the late sixteenth century, speculation about the cause of blackness depended on classical sources rather than experience or observation. In the myth of Phaëton, for example, and Ptolemy's *Tetrabiblos*, Africans' blackness was explained by their proximity to the sun. With the publication in 1589 of the many travel accounts and geographies in Hakluyt's *Principal Navigations*, however, the rehearsal of this ancient topos though often quoted, was usually countered by the observation that many peoples living equally close to the sun in the Indies and other parts of the New World were of olive complexion and thus disproved the ancients' latitudinal etiology. Myth and empirical observation collided.

In his *Discourse* (1578, repr. in Hakluyt, 1600), George Best, an English traveler, gives an early account of miscegenation and the causes of blackness:

> I my selfe have seene an Ethiopian as blacke as a cole brought into England, who taking a faire English woman to wife, begat a sonne in all respects as blacke as the father was, although England were his native countrey, and an English woman his mother: whereby it seemeth this blacknes proceedeth rather of some natural infection of that man, which was so strong, that neither the nature of the Clime, neither the good complexion of the mother concurring, coulde any thing alter.
>
> (Hakluyt, 262)

Best's account of miscegenation is designed to refute the conventional latitudinal explanation, but it does much more. Not only does it emphasize the contrariety of black and white, "blacke as a cole" and "faire English woman;" his repetitions also betray the Englishman's ethnocentric preoccupation with his native isle.

Best also proffers an alternative explanation of blackness which he substitutes for the ancients' geographical theory: "this blacknes proceedeth rather of some natural infection of that man." Best's claim is more radical than his metaphor of disease implies because to assert that black and white were "naturally" different also posed a theological problem. If the union of black and white always results in black offspring, "in all respects as blacke as the father," then how can we account for the origin of blacks from our first parents? And so Best goes on to explain his claim by referring to Scripture and the story in Genesis of Noah and his three sons,

> who all three being white, and their wives also, by course of nature should have begotten and brought foorth white children. But the envie of our great and continuall enemie the wicked Spirite is such, that as hee coulde not suffer our olde father Adam to live in the felicitie and Angelike state wherein hee was first created, but tempting him, sought and procured his ruine and fall: so againe, finding at this flood none but a father and three sonnes living, hee so caused

one of them to transgresse and disobey his father's commaundement, that after
him all his posteritie shoulde bee accursed. The fact of disobedience was this:
When Noe at the commandement of God had made the Arke and entered
therein . . . hee straitely commaunded his sonnes and their wives, that they . . .
should use continencie, and abstaine from carnall copulation with their
wives. . . . Which good instructions and exhortations notwithstanding his wicked
sonne Cham disobeyed, and being perswaded that the first childe borne after
the flood (by right and Lawe of nature) should inherite and possesse all the
dominions of the earth, hee contrary to his fathers commandement while they
were yet in the Arke, used company with his wife, and craftily went about
thereby to dis-inherite the off-spring of his other two brethren: for the which
wicked and detestable fact, as an example for contempt of Almightie God, and
disobedience of parents, God would a sonne should bee borne whose name was
Chus, who not onely it selfe, but all his posteritie after him should bee so blacke
and lothsome, that it might remaine a spectacle of disobedience to all the
worlde. And of this blacke and cursed Chus came all these blacke Moores which
are in Africa.

(Best, 1578 [repr. in Hakluyt, 1600, 263–4])

Best's myth of a second fall is an extraordinarily rich rehearsal of early
English social attitudes. In it are revealed the stock prejudices against blacks
in Elizabethan and Jacobean culture: the link between blackness and the
devil, the myth of black sexuality, the problem of black subjection to authority, here displaced onto obedience owed to the father and to God. Best's story
passes "segregation off as natural—and as the very law of the origin." Derrida's words about apartheid are suggestive for understanding not only Best's
Discourse, but travel writing more generally:

there's no racism without a language. The point is not that acts of racial violence are only words but rather that they have to have a word. Even though it
offers the excuse of blood, color, birth—or, rather, because it uses this natu-
ralist and sometimes creationist discourse—racism always betrays the perversion of man, the "talking animal."[3]

. . . Best's nationalism and fear of difference demarcate attitudes characteristic of the period. Even by 1578 the English had a considerable material
investment in Africa: English explorers had begun to compete with Portu-
guese traders; John Hawkins had organized the first successful slave-trading
venture between Africa and the West Indies in 1563. Best's is not just a
fantasy about Africa and blackness, but an enabling discourse which sustains
a series of material and economic practices and interests. In England itself,
by 1596, blacks were numerous enough to generate alarm. Elizabeth wrote to
the Lord Mayor of London and to other towns and observed "there are of
late divers blackmoores brought into this realme, of which kinde of people
there are allready to manie, consideringe howe God hath blessed this land
with great increase of people of our own nation;" a week later she observed

---

[3] Jacques Derrida, "Racism's Last Word." Trans. Peggy Kamuf. *Critical Inquiry* 12 (1985):
292.

that "those kinde of people may be well spared in this realme, being so populous," and licensed a certain Casper van Senden, a merchant of Lübeck who had freed eighty-nine Englishmen imprisoned in Spain and Portugal, "to take up so much blackamoores here in this realme and to transport them into Spain and Portugal" for his expenses. . . .

Other travel accounts of the period display the intersection of ancient legends and myths about black Africa with contemporary experience, observation, and prejudice. Interspersed with descriptions of African tribal customs, language, and landscape were the legendary stories from Pliny and other classical sources, probably via Mandeville (whose popular *Travels* were included in the first [1589] edition of Hakluyt's *Principal Navigations*), of the Anthropophagi who wore skins and ate human flesh, of people without heads or speech, of satyrs and Troglodytes who lived in caves and dens. The African landscape was presented descriptively in terms of safe harbors, intense heat, and gigantic waterfalls, but also mythically, as traversed by flames and fire which reached as high as the moon, and as ringing with the sound of pipes, trumpets, and drums. Always we find the link between blackness and the monstrous, and particularly a monstrous sexuality. Early travelers describe women held in common and men "furnisht with such members as are after a sort burthensome unto them." These accounts often bore no relation to African sexual habits, but they did confirm earlier discourses and representations of African sexuality found in Herodotus, Diodorus, and other classical authors. . . .

Such attitudes, both inherited from the past and reconstructed by contemporary historiographers, humanists, and travelers, were quickly assimilated into the drama and culture of early modern England. In *Titus Andronicus*, for example, the lustful union of Aaron and Tamor resulted in a black baby called "a devil" in the play. In *Tamar Cam* (1592) there is an entry of "Tartars, Geates, Amozins, Negars, olive cullord moores, Canniballs, Hermaphrodites, Pigmes . . ." company which testifies to the contemporary link between blackness and the monstrous. Similarly, Volpone's copulations resulting in his monstrous offspring, the fool, dwarf, and hermaphrodite, are accomplished with "beggars, gipseys and Jewes, and black moores." In Bacon's *New Atlantis* (1624), a holy hermit "desired to see the Spirit of Fornication; and there appeared to him a foul little Aethiop." Treatises on witchcraft and trials of the period often reported that the devil appeared to the possessed as a black man. Finally, contemporary ballads and broadsides, the Renaissance equivalent of the news story, popularized monstrous births such as one recorded by the Stationers' Register (1580): a child, born at Fenstanton in Huntingdonshire, was described as "a monster with a black face, the Mouth and Eyes like a Lyon which was both Male and Female."

Monstrous Desire in *Othello*

In *Renaissance Self-Fashioning*, Stephen Greenblatt has argued persuasively that Othello submits to narrative self-fashioning, his own and Iago's. He demonstrates the congruence between their narratives and the ideological narratives of Renaissance culture, most powerfully the orthodox Christian attitude toward sexuality, and he shows how Iago and Othello are linked by shared, if dialectically opposed, cultural values about women and sexuality. Greenblatt quotes Kenneth Burke's claim that they are "consubstantial":

> Iago, to arouse Othello, must talk a language that Othello knows as well as he, a language implicit in the nature of Othello's love as the idealization of his private property in Desdemona. This language is the dialectical opposite of Othello's; but it so thoroughly shares a common ground with Othello's language that its insinuations are never for one moment irrelevant to Othello's thinking. Iago must be cautious in leading Othello to believe them as true: but Othello never for a moment doubts them as *values*.

For Greenblatt, Othello's "identity depends upon a constant performance, as we have seen, of his story, a loss of his own origins, an embrace and perpetual reiteration of the norms of another culture" (245).

What are Othello's lost origins? Greenblatt implies as somehow anterior to identity-as-performance an essential self, an ontological subjectivity, an Edenic moment of black identity prior to discourse, outside, in Derrida's phrase quoted earlier, "the perversion of man, the 'talking animal.'" Derrida's words about racism are also pertinent to a discussion of origins and permit the substitution of ontology for race: "there are no origins without a language." "Othello" doesn't lose "his own origins;" his only access to those origins are the exotic ascriptions of European colonial discourse. Othello's stories of slavery and adventure are *precisely* a rehearsal of his origins, from his exotic tales of monstrous races to the story of the handkerchief's genealogy in witchcraft and Sibylline prophecy. Othello charms by reiterating his origins even as he submits and embraces the dominant values of Venetian culture. His successful courtship of Desdemona suggests that those origins are not simply repressive, but also enabling. Greenblatt is moving in his representation of Othello's submission to such cultural plots, but by focusing on Othello's ideological complicity, he effectively erases the other which is constituted discursively in the play as both woman and black. Othello is both a speaking subject, a kind of George Best recounting his tales of conquest, and at the same time the object of his "Travellours historie" by virtue of his blackness which originates with the very monstrous races he describes.

Similarly he is both the representative and upholder of a rigorous sexual code which prohibits desire and defines it even within marriage as adulterous, as Greenblatt claims, and yet also the sign of a different, unbridled sexuality. Greenblatt effaces the profound paradox of the black Othello's embrace of Christian sexual mores: Othello is both monster and hero, and his own sexuality is appropriately indecipherable. As the champion of Christian cultural codes he assures the senators his wish to take his bride with him to Cyprus is not "to please the palate of my appetite, / Nor to comply with heat, the young affects / In my defunct, and proper satisfaction" (I. iii.). He loves Desdemona "but to be free and bounteous of her mind." Like Brabantio, Iago, and Roderigo, Othello perceives of his love and indeed his human, as opposed to bestial, identity as depending on property rights, on absolute ownership:

> O curse of marriage,
> That we can call these delicate creatures ours,
> And not their appetites! I had rather be a toad,

And live upon the vapour in a dungeon,
Than keep a corner in a thing I love,
For others' uses:

(III. iii.)

But opposed to the representation of Othello's participation in the play's dominant sex/gender system is a conventional representation of black sexuality evoked by other characters and by Othello himself in his traveler's tales and through his passionate action. The textual allusions to bestiality, lubriciousness, and the demonic have been often noted. Iago rouses Brabantio with "an old black ram / Is tupping your white ewe . . . / . . . the devil will make a grandsire of you" (I. i.), and "you'll have your daughter cover'd with a Barbary horse; you'll have your nephews neigh to you; you'll have coursers for cousins, and gennets for germans." "Your daughter and the Moor, are now making the beast with two backs" (115–16) and Desdemona is transported, according to Roderigo, "to the gross clasps of a lascivious Moor." Not until the third scene is the Moor named, and the delay undoubtedly dramatizes Othello's blackness and the audience's shared prejudices which are vividly conjured up by Iago's pictorial visions of carnal knowledge. To read Othello as congruent with the attitudes toward sexuality and femininity expressed in the play by the Venetians—Iago, Brabantio, Roderigo and Cassio—and opposed to Desdemona's desire is to ignore the threatening sexuality of the other which divides the representation of Othello's character. Othello internalizes alien cultural values, but the otherness which divides him from that culture and links him to the play's other marginality, femininity, remains in visual and verbal allusion.

For the white male characters of the play, the black man's power resides in his sexual difference from a white male norm. Their preoccupation with black sexuality is not an eruption of a normally repressed animal sexuality in the "civilized" white male, but of the feared power and potency of a different and monstrous sexuality which threatens the white male sexual norm represented in the play most emphatically by Iago. For however evil Iago reveals himself to be, like the Vice in the medieval morality, or, we could add, the trickster/slave of Latin comedy, Iago enjoys a privileged relation with the audience. He possesses what can be termed the discourse of knowledge in *Othello* and annexes not only the other characters, but the resisting spectator as well, into his world and its perspective. By virtue of his manipulative power and his superior knowledge and control over the action, which we share, we are implicated in his machinations and the cultural values they imply. Iago is a cultural hyperbole; he does not oppose cultural norms so much as hyperbolize them.

Before the English had wide experience of miscegenation, they seem to have believed, as George Best recounts, that the black man had the power to subjugate his partner's whiteness, to make both his "victim" and her offspring resemble him, to make them both black, a literal blackness in the case of a child, a metaphorical blackness in the case of a sexual partner. So in *Othello*, Desdemona becomes "thou black weed" (IV. iii.) and the white pages of her "goodly book" are blackened by writing when Othello imagines "whore" inscribed across them. At IV. iii, she explicitly identifies herself with her mother's maid Barbary whose name connotes blackness. The union of

Desdemona and Othello represents a sympathetic identification between femininity and the monstrous which offers a potentially subversive recognition of sexual and racial difference. . . .

Colonialism and Sexual Difference

Was Shakespeare a racist who condoned the negative image of blacks in his culture? Is Desdemona somehow guilty in her stubborn defense of Cassio and her admiring remark "Ludovico is a proper man?" Or in a new critical vocabulary, in her "erotic submission, [which] conjoined with Iago's murderous cunning, far more effectively, if unintentionally, subverts her husband's carefully fashioned identity" (Greenblatt, 244)? Readers preoccupied with formal dramatic features claim such questions are moot, that the questions themselves expose the limits of moral or political readings of texts because they raise the specters of intention or ignore the touted transcendence of history by art. But as much recent poststructuralist and/or political criticism has demonstrated, even highly formalist readings are political, inscribed in the discourses both of the period in which the work was produced and of those in which it is consumed.

The task of a political criticism is not merely to expose or demystify the ideological discourses which organize literary texts, but to *reconstitute* those texts, to reread canonical texts in noncanonical ways which reveal the contingency of so-called canonical readings, which disturb conventional interpretations and discover them as partisan, constructed, made rather than given, natural, and inevitable. Such strategies of reading are particularly necessary in drama because the dramatic immediacy of theatrical representation obscures the fact that the audience is watching a highly artificial enactment of what, in the case of *Othello*, a non-African and a man has made into a vision of blackness and femininity, of passion and desire in the other, those marginal groups which stand outside culture and simultaneously within it.

Shakespeare was certainly subject to the racist, sexist, and colonialist discourses of his time, but by making the black Othello a hero, and by making Desdemona's love for Othello, and her transgression of her society's norms for women in choosing him, sympathetic, Shakespeare's play stands in a contestatory relation to the hegemonic ideologies of race and gender in early modern England. Othello is, of course, the play's hero only within the terms of a white, elitist male ethos, and he suffers the generic "punishment" of tragedy, but he is nevertheless represented as heroic and tragic at a historical moment when the only role blacks played on stage was that of a villain of low status. The case of Desdemona is more complex because the fate she suffers is the conventional fate assigned to the desiring woman. Nevertheless, Shakespeare's representation of her as at once virtuous and desiring, and of her choice in love as heroic rather than demonic, dislocates the conventional ideology of gender the play also enacts.

We need to read Shakespeare in ways which produce resistant readings, ways which contest the hegemonic forces the plays at the same time affirm. Our critical task is not merely to describe the formal parameters of a play, nor is it to make claims about Shakespeare's politics, conservative or subversive, but to reveal the discursive and dramatic evidence for such representations, and their counterparts in criticism, as representations.

MICHAEL NEILL, "UNPROPER BEDS: RACE, ADULTERY, AND THE HIDEOUS IN *OTHELLO*.*

The ending of *Othello* is perhaps the most shocking in Shakespearean tragedy. "I am glad that I have ended my revisal of this dreadful scene," wrote Dr. Johnson; "it is not to be endured." His disturbed response is one that the play conspicuously courts: indeed Johnson does no more than paraphrase the reaction of the scandalized Venetians, whose sense of the unendurable nature of what is before them produces the most violently abrupted of all Shakespearean endings. Though its catastrophe is marked by a conventional welter of stabbing and slaughter, *Othello* is conspicuously shorn of the funeral dignities that usually serve to put a form of order upon such spectacles of ruin: in the absence of any witness sympathetic enough to tell the hero's story, the disgraced Othello has to speak what amounts to his own funeral oration—and it is one whose lofty rhetoric is arrested in mid-line by the "bloody period" of his own suicide (5.2). "All that's spoke is marred," observed Gratiano, but no memorializing tributes ensue. Even Cassio's "he was great of heart" may amount to nothing more than a faint plea in mitigation for one whose heart was swollen to bursting with intolerable emotion; and in place of the reassuring processional exeunt announced by the usual command to take up the tragic bodies, we get only Lodovico's curt order to close up the scene of butchery: "The object poisons sight: / Let it be hid." The tableau on the bed announces a kind of plague, one that taints the sight as the deadly effluvia of pestilence poison the nostrils.

The congruence between Dr. Johnson's desperately averted gaze and Lodovico's fear of contamination is striking; but it is only Johnson's agitated frankness that makes it seem exceptional. It makes articulate the anxiety evident almost everywhere in the play's history—a sense of scandal that informs the textual strategies of editors and theatrical producers as much as it does the disturbed reactions of audiences and critics. Contemplating the "unutterable agony" of the conclusion, the Variorum editor, Furness, came to wish that the tragedy had never been written; and his choice of the word "unutterable" is a telling one, for this ending, as its stern gestures of erasure demonstrate, has everything to do with what cannot be uttered and must not be seen.

The sensational effect of the scene upon its earliest audiences is apparent from the imitations it spawned and from the mesmerized gaze of Henry Jackson, who left the first surviving account of *Othello* in performance. He saw *Othello* acted by the King's Men at Oxford in 1610 and wrote how

> the celebrated Desdemona, *slayn in our presence by her husband*, although she pleaded her case very effectively throughout, yet moved us more after she was dead, when *lying in her bed*, she entreated the pity of the spectators by her very countenance. (Hankey, 18).

More than any other scene, it was this show of a wife murdered by her husband that gripped Jackson's imagination; but even more disturbing than the killing itself seems to have been the sight of the dead woman "lying in her

* From *Shakespeare Quarterly* 40 (Winter 1989): 383–412.

bed"—a phrase that echoes Emilia's outrage: "My mistress here lies murdered in her bed" (5.2). For Jackson, the *place* seems to matter almost as much as the fact of wife-murder—just as it did to the nineteenth-century Desdemona, Fanny Kemble, when she confessed to "feel[ing] horribly at the idea of being murdered *in my bed*" (Hankey, 315).

The same anxious fascination is reflected in the first attempts to represent the play pictorially: it was the spectacle of the violated marriage bed that Nicholas Rowe selected to epitomize the tragedy in the engraving for his 1709 edition; and his choice was followed by the actors David Garrick and Sarah Siddons, wanting memorials of their own performances. In the great period of Shakespeare illustration from the 1780s to the 1920s, the bedchamber scene was overwhelmingly preferred by publishers and artists, whose images combined to grant it the same representative significance as the graveyard in *Hamlet* or the monument in *Antony and Cleopatra*—as if announcing in this display of death-in-marriage a gestic account of the play's key meanings. Both graveyard and monument, however, in their different ways help to clothe the tragic ending in traditional forms of rhetoric and ceremony that mitigate its terrors, shackling death within a frame of decorum. What makes the ending of *Othello* so unaccountably disturbing and so threatening to its spectators is precisely the brutal violation of decorum that is registered in the quasi-pornographic explicitness of the graphic tradition. The illustrators' voyeuristic manipulation of the parted curtains and their invariable focus upon the unconscious invitation of Desdemona's gracefuly exposed body serve to foreground not merely the perverse eroticism of the scene but its aspect of forbidden disclosure.

Even more striking is the fact that these images were often designed to draw readers into texts whose bowdlerizing maneuvers aimed, as far as possible, to conceal everything that their frontispieces offer to reveal. While they could scarcely contrive to remove the scandalous property itself, late eighteenth- and nineteenth-century editors sought to restrict the curiosity that the final scene gratifies and to obscure its most threatening meanings by progressively excising from the text every explicit reference to the bed.

Predictably enough, an even more anxious censorship operated in the theatre itself, where, however, its consequences were much more difficult to predict. In the most striking of many effacements, it became the practice for nineteenth-century Othellos to screen the murder from the audience by closing the curtains upon the bed. This move was ostensibly consistent with a general attempt at de-sensationalizing the tragedy, an attempt whose most obvious manifestation was the restrained "Oriental" Moor developed by Macready and others. But the actual effect of the practice was apparently quite opposite, raising to a sometimes unbearable intensity the audience's scandalized fascination with the now-invisible scene. Years later Westland Marston could still recall the "thrilling" sensation as Macready thrust "his dark despairing face, through the curtains," its "contrast with the drapery" producing "a marvelous piece of colour" (Hankey, 64, 317); and so shocking was this moment, according to John Forster, that in his presence a woman "hysterically fainted" at it (Hankey, 64).

The reasons for so extreme a reaction can be glimpsed in the offended tone of the Melbourne *Argus* critic, attacking an 1855 production that had flouted this well-established convention: "[The] consummation," he indignantly insisted, "should take place behind the curtain and out of sight"

(Hankey, 317). The revealing word "consummation," when set beside the "hysterical" reaction to Macready's "marvelous piece of colour," suggests that the bed was so intensely identified with the anxieties about race and sex stirred up by the play that it needed, as far as possible, to be removed from the public gaze. Yet the effect of such erasure was only to give freer play to the fantasy it was designed to check, so that the violent chiaroscuro of Macready's blackened face thrust between the virgin-white curtains was experienced as a shocking sado-erotic climax. It was, of course, a stage picture that significantly repeated an off-stage action twice imagined in the first half of the play, when Othello, first in Venice (1.2) and then in Cyprus (2.3), is unceremoniously roused from his nuptial bed. The unconscious repetition must have had the effect of underlining the perverse eroticism of the murder just at the point where the parting of the bed-curtains and the display of Desdemona's corpse was about to grant final satisfaction to the audience's terrible curiosity about the absent scene that dominates so much of the play's action.

For all their ostentatious pudency, then, the Victorian attempts at containing the danger of the play's ending reveal a reading unsettlingly consistent with the most sensational recent productions, like Bernard Miles's 1971 Mermaid *Othello* or Ronald Eyre's at the National in 1979, with their extraordinary emphasis on the significance and visibility of a bed. It is a reading in which the stage direction opening 5.2, *"Enter . . . Desdemona in her bed,"* announces ocular proof of all that the audience have most desired and feared to look upon, exposing to cruel light the obscure erotic fantasies that the play both explores and disturbingly excites in its audience. Forster's story of the woman who fainted at the sight of Macready's "dark despairing face" records a moment when (despite more than half a century of bleaching, "civilizing," and bowdlerizing) a subterranean image erupted to confirm the deep fears of the racial/sexual otherness on which the play trades—fears that are made quite embarrassingly explicit in the feverish self-betrayals of a nineteenth-century Russian literary lady reacting to Ira Aldridge's performance of the part. In her account the play exhibits nothing less than the symbolic rape of the European "spirit" by the "savage, wild flesh" of black otherness:

> A full-blooded Negro, incarnating the profoundest creations of Shakespearean art, giving *flesh and blood* for the aesthetic judgment of educated European society. . . . How much nearer can one get to truth, to the very source of the highest aesthetic satisfaction? But *what is truth. . .* ? As the spirit is not the body, so the truth of art is not this profoundly raw flesh which we can take hold of, and call by name and, if you please, feel, pinch with our unbelieving, all-feeling hand. . . . Not the Moscow Maly Theatre, but the African jungle should have been filled and resounded with . . . the cries of this black, powerful, howling flesh. But by the very fact that that flesh is so powerful—that it is genuinely black, so naturally *un-white* does it howl—that savage flesh did its fleshly work. It murdered and crushed the spirit. . . . one's spirit cannot accept it—and in place of the highest enjoyment, this blatant flesh introduced into art, this *natural* black Othello, pardon me, causes only . . . revulsion.*

---

* N. S. Sokhanskaya ("N. Kokhanovskaya") in a letter to the Slavophile newspaper *Dyen* (1863), quoted in Herbert Marshall and Mildred Stock, *Ira Aldridge: The Negro Tragedian* (London: Rockliff, 1958) 265–66.

It is as if in Macready's coup the strange mixture of thrilled agitation, horror, and shame voiced here became focused with an unbearable intensity upon the occupation of the bed, where the transgression of racial boundaries was displayed as an offence punishable by death. . . .

One of the terrifying things about *Othello* is that its racial poisons seem so casually concocted, as if racism were just something that Iago, drawing in his improvisational way on a gallimaufry of quite unsystematic prejudices and superstitions, made up as he went along. The characteristic pleasure he takes in his own felicitous invention only makes the effect more shocking. Iago lets horrible things loose and delights in watching them run; and the play seems to share that narcissistic fascination—or perhaps, better, Iago is the voice of its own fascinated self-regard. The play thinks abomination into being and then taunts the audience with the knowledge that it can never be *un*thought: "What you know, you know." It is a technique that works close to the unstable ground of consciousness itself; for it would be almost as difficult to say whether its racial anxieties are ones that the play discovers or implants in an audience as to say whether jealousy is something that Iago discovers or implants in Othello. Yet discovery, in the most literal theatrical sense, is what the last scene cruelly insists on. Like no other drama, *Othello* establishes an equivalency between psychological event (what happens "inside") and off-stage action (what happens "within"); thus it can flourish its disclosure of the horror on the bed like a psychoanalytic revelation.

The power of the offstage scene over the audience's prying imagination is immediately suggested by the irritable speculation of Thomas Rymer, the play's first systematic critic. Rymer spends several pages of his critique exposing what he regards as ludicrous inconsistencies between what the play tells the audience and what verisimilitude requires them to believe about the occupation of "the Matrimonial Bed." The time scheme, he insists, permits Othello and his bride to sleep together only once, on the first night in Cyprus, but "*once* will not do the Poets business: the *Audience* must suppose a great many bouts, to make the plot operate. They must deny their senses, to reconcile it to common sense."

Rymer's method is taken to extraordinary extremes in a recent article by T. G. A. Nelson and Charles Haines, who set out to demonstrate, with a mass of circumstantial detail, that the marriage of Othello and Desdemona was never consummated at all. In this previously unsuspected embarrassment is to be found an explanation for the extreme suggestibility of the hero, and thus the hidden spring of the entire tragic action. Their essay is remarkable not for the ingenuity of its finally unsustainable argument about the sequential "facts" of a plot whose time-scheme is so notoriously undependable, but for what it unconsciously reveals about the effect of *Othello* upon its audiences. Their entire procedure mirrors with disturbing fidelity the habit of obsessive speculation about concealed offstage action, into which the play entraps the viewer as it entraps its characters. Nelson and Haines become victims, like the hero himself, of the scopophile economy of this tragedy and prey to its voyeuristic excitements.

Recently, Norman Nathan has attempted a point-by-point rebuttal of Nelson and Haines, the ironic effect of which is to entrap him in the very speculation he wishes to cut short. "If a lack of consummation is so important to this play, why isn't the audience informed?" he somewhat testily enquires (Nathan, 81). An answer might be—to make them ask the question. *Othello* persistently goads its audience into speculation about what is happening behind the scenes. This preoccupation with offstage action is unique in Shakespeare. Elsewhere, whenever offstage action is of any importance, it is almost always carefully described, usually by an eyewitness whose account is not open to question, so that nothing of critical importance is left to the audience's imagination. But in *Othello* the real imaginative focus of the action is always the hidden marriage-bed, an inalienably private location, shielded, until the very last scene, from every gaze. This disquietingly absent presence creates the margin within which Iago can operate as a uniquely deceitful version of the *nuntius*, whose vivid imaginary descriptions taint the vision of the audience even as they colonize the minds of Brabantio and Othello:

> Iago: Even now, now, very now, an old black ram
>   Is tupping your white ewe. . . .
>   you'll have your daughter covered with a Barbary horse. . . . your daughter
>   and the moor are now making the beast with two backs.
>
>   (1.i.)

. . . In early modern culture the marriage bed had a peculiar topographic and symbolic significance. It was a space at once more private and more public than for us. More private because (with the exception of the study or cabinet) it was virtually the *only* place of privacy available to the denizens of sixteenth- and early seventeenth-century households; more public because as the domain of the most crucial of domestic offices—perpetuation of the lineage—it was the site of important public rituals of birth, wedding, and death. In the great houses of France, this double public/private function was even symbolized by the existence of two beds: an "official bed, majestic but unoccupied," located in the *chambre de parement,* and a private bed, screened from view in the more intimate domain of the bedchamber proper. Everywhere the same double role was acknowledged in the division of the bridal ritual between the public bringing to bed of bride and groom by a crowd of relatives and friends, and the private rite of consummation which ensued after the formal drawing of the bed curtains. Part of the scandal of *Othello* arises from its structural reversal of this solemn division: the offstage elopement in Act I turning the public section of the bridal into a furtive and private thing; the parted curtains of Act 5 exposing the private scene of the bed to a shockingly public gaze. . . .

The principal cause of these anxieties, and hence of the fiercely defended privacy of the marriage bed, lay in the fact that it was a place of licensed sexual and social metamorphosis, where the boundaries of self and other, of family allegiance and of gender, were miraculously abolished as man and wife became "one flesh." Because it was a space that permitted a highly specialized naturalization of what would otherwise constitute a wholly "unnatural" collapsing of differences, it must itself be protected by taboos of the most intense character. In the cruel system of paradoxy created by this play's ideas of race and adultery, Othello as both stranger and husband can be *both* the violator of these taboos and the seeming victim of their violation—

adulterer and cuckold—as he is both black and "fair," Christian general and erring barbarian, insider and outsider, the author of a "monstrous act" and Desdemona's "kind lord." As the most intimate site of these contradictions, it was inevitable that the bed should become the imaginative center of the play—the focus of Iago's corrupt fantasy, of Othello's tormented speculation, and always of the audience's intensely voyeuristic compulsions.

At the beginning of the play, the monstrousness of Desdemona's passion is marked for Brabantio by its being fixed upon an object "naturally" unbearable to sight: "To fall in love with what she feared to look on! / . . . Against all rules of nature" (1.3). At the end she has become, for Lodovico, part of the "object [that] poisons sight." The bed now is the visible sign of *what has been improperly revealed* and must now be hidden from view again—the unnamed horror that Othello fatally glimpsed in the dark cave of Iago's imagination: "some monster in his thought / Too hideous to be shown" (3.3.); it is the token of everything that must not be seen and cannot be spoken ("Let me not name it to you, you chaste stars" [5.2]), everything that the second nature of culture seeks to efface or disguise as "unnatural"—all that should be banished to outer (or consigned to inner) darkness; a figure for unlicensed desire itself. That banishment of what must not be contemplated is what is embodied in Lodovico's gesture of stern erasure. But, as Othello's quibble upon the Latin root of the word suggests, a *monster* is also what, by virtue of its very hideousness, demands to be *shown*. What makes the tragedy of *Othello* so shocking and painful is that it engages its audience in a conspiracy to lay naked the scene of forbidden desire, only to confirm that the penalty for such exposure is death and oblivion; in so doing, the play takes us into territory we recognize but would rather not see. It doesn't "oppose racism," but (much more disturbingly) illuminates the process by which such visceral superstitions were implanted in the very body of the culture that formed us. The object that "poisons sight" is nothing less than a mirror for the obscene desires and fears that *Othello* arouses in its audiences—monsters that the play at once invents and naturalizes, declaring them unproper, even as it implies that they were always "naturally" there.

If the ending of this tragedy is unendurable, it is because it first tempts us with the redemptive vision of Desdemona's sacrificial self-abnegation and then insists, with all the power of its swelling rhetorical music, upon the hero's magnificence as he dismantles himself for death—only to capitulate to Iago's poisoned vision at the very moment when it has seemed poised to reaffirm the transcendent claims of their love—the claims of kind and kindness figured in the union between a black man and a white woman and the bed on which it was made.

A Selective Bibliography on *Othello*

Adamson, Jane. Othello *as Tragedy: Some Problems of Judgment and Feeling.* Cambridge, Eng.: Cambridge UP, 1980.
Africanus, Leo. *Historie of Africa.* Antwerp, 1526, rpt. 1556.
Bayley, John. *Shakespeare and Tragedy.* London: Routledge, 1981. 200–20.

Bennett, William E. "Shakespeare's Iago: The Kierkegardian Aesthete." *The Upstart Crow* 5 (1984): 156–59.

Berry, Ralph. "Pattern in *Othello*." *Shakespeare Quarterly* 23 (1972): 3–19.

Bloom, Allan D. "Cosmopolitan Man and the Political Community: An Interpretation of *Othello*." *American Political Science Review* 54 (1960): 130–57.

Bodkin, Maud. "The Hero and the Devil." *Archetypal Patterns in Poetry*. London: Oxford UP, 1963.

Boose, Lynda E. "Othello's 'Chrysolite' and the Song of Songs Tradition." *Philological Quarterly* 60 (1981): 427–37.

———. "Othello's Handkerchief: The Recognition of Pledge and Love." *English Literary Renaissance* 5 (1975): 208–13.

Bradley, A. C. *Shakespearean Tragedy*. 2nd ed. New York: St. Martin's, 1967.

Buchman, Lorne M. "Orson Welles's *Othello*: A Study of Time in Shakespearean Tragedy." *Shakespeare Survey* 39 (1987): 53–65.

Burgess, C. F. "Othello's Occupation." *Shakespeare Quarterly* 26 (1975): 208–13.

Butcher, Philip. "Othello's Racial Identity." *Shakespeare Quarterly* 2 (1951): 233–39.

Calaghan, Dympna. *Women and Gender in Renaissance Tragedy: A Study of King Lear, Othello, The Dutchess of Malfi, and The White Devil*. New York: Harvester Wheatsheaf, 1989.

Calderwood, James L. "Speech and Self in *Othello*." *Shakespeare Quarterly* 38 (1987): 293–303.

Camden, Carroll. "Iago on Women." *Journal of English and Germanic Philology* 48 (1949): 47–71.

Campbell, Lily B. *Shakespeare's Tragic Heroes: Slaves of Passion*. Cambridge, Eng.: Cambridge UP, 1930.

Cartwright, Kent. *Shakespearean Tragedy and Its Double: The Rhythms of Audience Response*. University Park: Pennsylvania State UP, 1991.

Clemen, Wolfgang. *The Development of Shakespeare's Imagery*. Cambridge, MA: Harvard UP, 1951.

Cohen, Derek. "Patriarchy and Jealousy in *Othello* and *The Winter's Tale*." *Modern Language Quarterly* 48 (1987): 207–23.

Coleridge, S. T. *Shakespearean Criticism*. Ed. Thomas M. Raysor. New York: Dutton, 1960.

Creeth, Edmund. *Mankynde in Shakespeare*. Athens: U of Georgia P, 1972. 73–110.

Draper, J. W. *The Othello of Shakespeare's Audience*. Paris: Didier, 1952. Rpt. New York: Octagon, 1966.

Elliott, George R. *Flaming Minister: A Study of Othello as Tragedy of Love and Hate*. Durham, NC: Duke UP, 1953.

Elliott, Martin. *Shakespeare's Invention of Othello*. New York: St. Martin's, 1988.

Emery, John P. "Othello's Epilepsy." *Psychoanalysis and the Psychoanalytic Review* 46 (1959): 30–32.

Engles, Balz. "Othello's Great Heart." *English Studies* 68 (1987): 129–36.

Evans, Bertrand. *Shakespeare's Tragic Muse*. Oxford, Eng.: Oxford UP, 1979. 115–46.

Evans, K. W. "The Racial Factor in *Othello*." *Shakespeare Survey* 5 (1970): 124–40.

Everett, Barbara. " 'Spanish' Othello: The Making of Shakespeare's Moor." *Shakespeare Survey* 35 (1982): 101–12.

Faber, M. D. "Suicidal Patterns in *Othello*." *Literature and Psychology* 14 (1964): 85–96.

Fleissner, R. F. "The Case of the 'Base Judean' Revisited." *The Upstart Crow* 6 (1986): 44–53.

Foreman, Walter C., Jr. *The Muse of Close: The Final Scene of Shakespeare's Tragedies.* Lexington: UP of Kentucky, 1978. 159–75.

Furness, H. H., ed. *The Variorum Othello.* Philadelphia, 1886.

Gajowski, Evelyn. *The Art of Loving: Female Subjectivity and Male Discursive Traditions in Shakespeare's Tragedies.* Newark: U of Delaware P, 1992.

Gardner, Helen. "*Othello*: A Retrospect, 1900–67." *Shakespeare Survey* 21 (1968): 1–11.

———. *The Noble Moor.* New York: Oxford UP, 1956.

Gardner, S. N. "Shakespeare's Desdemona." *Shakespeare Studies* 9 (1976): 233–52.

Gohlke, Madelon. " 'All that is Spoke is Marred': Language and Consciousness in *Othello.*" *Women's Studies* 9 (1982): 157–76.

Golden, Leon. "*Othello, Hamlet,* and Aristotelian Tragedy." *Shakespeare Quarterly* 35 (1984): 142–56.

Gonzalez, Alexander G. "The Infection and Spread of Evil: Some Major Patterns of Imagery and Language in Othello." *South Atlantic Review* 50 (1985): 35–49.

Granville-Barker, Harley. *Prefaces to Shakespeare.* Princeton, NJ: Princeton UP, 1947. Vol. 1.

Gray, Garry. "Iago's Metamorphosis." *College Language Association Journal* 28 (1985): 393–403.

Greenblatt, Stephen. *Renaissance Self-Fashioning from More to Shakespeare.* Chicago: U of Chicago P, 1980.

———. *Shakespearean Negotiations: The Circulation of Social Energy.* Berkeley: U of California P, 1988.

Grennan, Eamon. "The Women's Voices in *Othello*: Speech, Song, Silence." *Shakespeare Quarterly* 38 (1987): 275–92.

Guilfoyle, Cherrell. "Mactacio Desdemonae: Medieval Scenic Form in the Last Scene of *Othello.*" *Comparative Drama* 19 (1985): 305–20.

———. *Shakespeare's Play Within Play: Medieval Imagery and Scenic Form in Hamlet, Othello, and King Lear.* Kalamazoo: Medieval Institute, 1990.

Gutierrez, Nancy A. "An Allusion to 'India' and Pearls." *Shakespeare Quarterly* 36 (1985): 220.

Hall, Michael. *The Structure of Love: Representational Patterns and Shakespeare's Love Tragedies.* Charlottesville: UP of Virginia, 1989.

Hankey, Julie, ed. *Othello.* Plays in Performance Series. Bristol, Eng., 1987.

Harrison, G. B. *Shakespeare's Tragedies.* London: Routledge, 1951.

Heilman, Robert. *Magic in the Web: Action and Language in* Othello. Lexington, KY, 1956. Rpt. Westport, Conn.: Greenwood, 1976.

Holderness, Graham. "Are Shakespeare's Tragic Heroes 'Fatally Flawed'?" *Critical Survey* 1 (1989): 53–62.

Hollindale, Peter. "Othello and Desdemona." *Critical Survey* 1 (1989): 43–52.

Honigmann, E. A. J. *Shakespeare: Seven Tragedies.* London: Macmillan, 1976. 77–100.

Hyman, Stanley E. *Iago: Some Approaches to the Illusion of His Motivation.* New York: Atheneum, 1970.

Jones, Elred D. *Othello's Countrymen: The African in English Renaissance Drama.* New York: Oxford UP, 1965.

Kaplan, Paul H. "The Earliest Images of Othello." *Shakespeare Quarterly* 39 (1988): 171–86.

Kay, Caril McGinnis. "Othello's Need for Mirrors." *Shakespeare Quarterly* 34 (1983): 261–70.

King, Rosalind. " 'The murder's out of tune': The Music and Structure of *Othello*." *Shakespeare Survey* 39 (1987): 149–58.

Kirsch, Arthur. *The Passions of Shakespeare's Tragic Heroes*. Charlottesville: UP of Virginia, 1990.

Knight, G. Wilson. "The Othello Music." *The Wheel of Fire*. 4th ed. London: Methuen, 1965.

Kott, Jan. "Othello's Marriage Is Consummated." *Cahiers Élisabéthains* 34 (1988): 79–82.

Lake, James H. "Othello and the Comforts of Love." *American Imago* 45 (1988): 327–35.

Leavis, F. R. "Diabolic Intellect and the Noble Hero: A Note on *Othello*." *The Common Pursuit*. London: Chatto & Windus, 1952.

Lerner, Laurence. "The Machiavel and the Moor." *Essays in Criticism* 9 (1959): 339–60.

Levin, Richard. "The Indian/Iudean Crux in *Othello*: An Addendum." *Shakespeare Quarterly* 34 (1983): 72.

Mehl, Dieter. *Shakespeare's Tragedies: An Introduction*. Cambridge, Eng.: Cambridge UP, 1983. 56–77.

Melchiori, Giogio. "The Rhetoric of Character Construction: *Othello*." *Shakespeare Survey* 34 (1981): 61–72.

Mendonça, Barbara H. C. de. "*Othello*: A Tragedy Built on a Comic Structure." *Shakespeare Survey* 21 (1968): 31–38.

Mercer, Peter. "Othello and the Form of Heroic Tragedy." *Critical Quarterly* 11 (1969): 45–61.

Milward, Peter. *Biblical Influences in Shakespeare's Great Tragedies*. Bloomington: Indiana UP, 1987.

Miola, Robert S. *Shakespeare and Classical Tragedy: The Influence of Seneca*. New York: Oxford UP, 1992.

Mooney, Michael E. *Shakespeare's Dramatic Transactions*. Durham: Duke UP, 1990.

Nathan, Norman. "Othello's Marriage Is Consummated." *Cahiers Élisabéthains* 34 (1988): 79–82.

Neill, Michael. "Changing Places in *Othello*." *Shakespeare Survey* 37 (1984): 115–31.

Nelson, Bonnie. "Much Ado About Something: The Law of Lombardy and the 'Othello Play' Phenomenon." *Studia Neophilologica* 58 (1986): 71–83.

Nelson, T. G. A. and C. Haines. "Othello's Unconsummated Marriage." *Essays in Criticism* 33 (1983): 1–18.

Orkin, Martin. "Othello and the 'Plain Face' of Racism." *Shakespeare Quarterly* 38 (1987): 166–88.

Paris, Bernard J. " 'His Scorn I Approve': The Self-Effacing Desdemona." *American Journal of Psychoanalysis* 44 (1984): 413–24.

Parten, Anne. "Masculine Adultery and Feminine Rejoinders in Shakespeare, Dekker, and Sharpham." *Mosaic* 17 (1984): 9–18.

Poole, Adrian. *Tragedy: Shakespeare and the Greek Example*. Oxford: Blackwell, 1987.

Ridley, M. R., ed. *Othello by William Shakespeare*. London, 1959, rpt. 1977.

Roddier, Henri. "A Freudian Detective's Shakespeare." *Modern Philology* 48 (1950): 122–29.

Rogers, Robert. "Endopsychic Drama in *Othello*." *Shakespeare Quarterly* 20 (1969): 205–15.

Rose, Mark. "Othello's Occupation: Shakespeare and the Romance of Chivalry." *English Literary Renaissance* 15 (1985): 293–311.

Rosenberg, Marvin. *The Masks of Othello.* Berkeley: U of California P, 1961.

Rozett, Martha Tuck. "Othello, Otello, and the Comic Tradition." *Bulletin of Research in the Humanities* 85 (1982): 386–411.

Rudnytsky, Peter L. "A Woman Killed with Kindness as Subtext of *Othello.*" *Renaissance Drama* 14 (1983): 103–24.

Rymer, Thomas. "A Short View of Tragedy." *Critical Essays of the Seventeenth Century.* Ed. J. E. Spingarn. Bloomington: Indiana UP, 1957.

Sanders, Norman. *Othello.* Cambridge, Eng.: Cambridge UP, 1984.

Shaheen, Naseeb. *Biblical References in Shakespeare's Tragedies.* Newark: U of Delaware P, 1987.

Siegel, Paul N. "The Damnation of Othello: An Addendum." *PMLA* 68 (1953): 1068–78.

———. *Shakespearean Tragedy and the Elizabethan Compromise.* New York: New York UP, 1957.

Siemon, James R. " 'Nay, That's Not Next': *Othello,* V, ii, in Performance, 1760–1900." *Shakespeare Quarterly* 37 (1986): 38–51.

Smith, Gordon Ross. "Iago the Paranoiac." *American Imago* 16 (1959): 155–67.

Smith, John Hazel. *Shakespeare's Othello: A Bibliography.* Ann Arbor: AMS, 1988.

Snyder, Susan, ed. *Othello: Critical Essays.* New York: Garland, 1988.

Sorelius, Gunnar. "*Othello* and the Language of Cosmos." *Studia Neophilologica* 55 (1983): 11–17.

Splitter, Rudolf. "Language, Sexual Conflict and 'Symbiosis Anxiety' in *Othello.*" *Mosaic* 15 (1982): 17–26.

Sproat, Kezia Vanmeter. "Rereading *Othello,* II, i." *The Kenyon Review* 7 (1985): 44–51.

Spurgeon, Caroline. *Shakespeare's Imagery and What It Tells Us.* Cambridge, Eng.: Cambridge UP, 1965.

Stockholder, Kay. "Form as Metaphor: *Othello* and Love–Death Romance." *Dalhousie Review* 64 (1984–1985): 736–47.

Stoll, E. E. *Othello: An Historical and Comparative Study.* Minneapolis: U of Minnesota P, 1915. Rpt. New York: Octagon, 1964.

Sturrock, June. "*Othello:* Women and 'Woman.' " *Atlantis: A Women's Studies Journal* 9 (1984): 1–8.

Taylor, Gary. "The Folio Copy for *Hamlet, King Lear,* and *Othello.*" *Shakespeare Quarterly* 34 (1983): 44–61.

Teague, Frances. "*Othello* and New Comedy." *Comparative Drama* 20 (1986): 54–64.

Thompson, Ann and John Thompson. " 'To Look so Low as Where They Are': Hand and Heart Synecdoches in *Othello.*" *Southern Review* 19 (1986): 53–66.

Turnbull, William Robertson. *Othello: A Critical Study.* New York: AMS, 1973.

Wangh, Martin. "*Othello:* The Tragedy of Iago." *Psychoanalytic Quarterly* 19 (1950): 202–12.

Watermeier, Daniel J. "Edwin Booth's Iago." *Theatre History Studies* 6 (1986): 32–55.

West, Robert H. "The Christianness of *Othello.*" *Shakespeare Quarterly* 15 (1964): 333–44.

Williams, George Walton. "Yet Another Early Use of Iudean." *Shakespeare Quarterly* 34 (1983): 44–61.

Wilson, Rob. "Othello: Jealousy as Mimetic Contagion." *American Imago* 44 (1987): 213–33.

Young, David. *Action to the Word: Structure and Style in Shakespearean Tragedy.* New Haven: Yale UP, 1990.

Ben Jonson (1572–1637)
VOLPONE; OR, THE FOX

Edited by Brinsley Nicholson and C. H. Hereford

CHARACTERS

VOLPONE, *a Magnifico°*	gentleman	ANDROGYNO, *an Hermaphrodite*
MOSCA, *his Parasite*		GREGE *(or Mob)*
VOLTORE, *an Advocate°*	lawyer	COMMANDADORI, *Officers of Justice*
CORBACCIO, *an old Gentleman*		MERCATORI, *three Merchants*
CORVINO, *a Merchant*		AVOCATORI, *four Magistrates*
BONARIO, *son to Corbaccio*		NOTARIO, *the Register°* clerk of the court
SIR POLITICK WOULD-BE, *a Knight*		LADY-WOULD-BE, *Sir Politick's Wife*
PEREGRINE, *a Gentleman Traveller*		CELIA, *Corvino's Wife*
NANO, *a Dwarf*		Servitori, *Servants, two*
CASTRONE, *an Eunuch*		*waiting-women*

SCENE: *Venice*

THE ARGUMENT

V olpone, childless, rich, feigns sick, despairs,
O ffers his state° to hopes of several heirs,   *estate*
L ies languishing: his parasite receives
P resents of all, assures, deludes; then weaves
O ther cross plots, which ope° themselves, are told.   *develop*
N ew tricks for safety are sought; they thrive: when bold,
E ach tempts the other again, and all are sold.°   *betrayed*

PROLOGUE

Now, luck yet send us, and a little wit
   Will serve to make our play hit:
10   (According to the palates° of the season)   *taste*
   Here is rhyme, not empty of reason.
This we were bid to credit° from our poet.[1]   *believe*
   Whose true scope,° if you would know it,   *aim*
In all his poems still° hath been this measure,   *always*
   To mix profit with your pleasure;
And not as some, whose throats their envy failing,
   Cry hoarsely, All he writes is railing:°   *abuse*

---

[1] Asked by our poet to believe.

And when his plays come forth, think they can flout them,
  With saying, He was a year about them.
20 To this there needs no lie,° but this his creature,°   *challenge/his play*
  Which was two months since no feature:[2]
And though he dares give them five lives to mend it,
  'Tis known, five weeks fully penned it.
From his own hand, without a coadjutor,°   *co-author*
  Novice, journeyman,° or tutor.°   *assistant/corrector*
Yet thus much I can give you as a token
  Of his play's worth, no eggs are broken,
Nor quaking custards with fierce teeth affrighted,
  Wherewith your rout° are so delighted;[3]   *mob*
30 Nor hales° he in a gull° old ends reciting,   *hauls/fool*
  To stop gaps in his loose writing;
With such a deal of monstrous and forced action,
  As might make Bethlem a faction:[4]
Nor made he his play for jests stolen from each table,
  But makes jests to fit his fable;
And so presents quick° comedy refined,   *lively*
  As best critics have designed;[5]
The laws of time, place, persons he observeth,
  From no needful rule he swerveth.
40 All gall and copperas[6] from his ink he draineth,
  Only a little salt remaineth,
Wherewith he'll rub your cheeks, till red with laughter,
  They shall look fresh a week after.

ACT THE FIRST

SCENE I

A Room in Volpone's House

[*Enter* VOLPONE *and* MOSCA.]

VOLPONE.   Good morning to the day; and next, my gold!
  Open the shrine, that I may see my saint.

[MOSCA *withdraws the curtain, and discovers piles of gold, plate, jewels, etc.*]

Hail the world's soul, and mine! more glad than is
The teeming earth to see the longed-for sun

---

   [2] Which two months ago did not exist.
   [3] Scholars agree that the allusion is to a custard pie featured at the Lord Mayor of London's inaugural banquet into which an attendant fool was made to jump. It may also refer, in a more general sense, to custard pies thrown about the stage as slapstick comedy.
   [4] St. Mary of Bethlehem, or Bedlam, was a London asylum for lunatics. The line thus reads "As might turn lunatics into supporters."
   [5] The three Aristotelian unities, said to govern drama.
   [6] Gall and coppers are ingredients of ink.

      Peep through the horns of the celestial Ram,[7]

      Am I, to view thy splendour darkening his:

50   That lying here, amongst my other hoards,

      Show'st like a flame by night, or like the day

      Struck out of chaos, when all darkness fled

      Unto the centre. O thou son of Sol,°   *the sun*

      But brighter than thy father, let me kiss,

      With adoration, thee, and every relic

      Of sacred treasure in this blessed room.

      Well did wise poets, by thy glorious name.

      Title that age° which they would have the best;   *the golden age*

      Thou being the best of things, and far transcending

60   All style of joy, in children, parents, friends.

      Or any other waking dream on earth:

      Thy looks when they° to Venus did ascribe,   *classical poets*

      They should have given her twenty thousand Cupids;[8]

      Such are thy beauties and our loves! Dear saint,

      Riches, the dumb god, that giv'st all men tongues,

      That canst do nought, and yet mak'st men do all things;

      The price of souls; even hell, with thee to boot,°   *as part of the bargain*

      Is made worth heaven. Thou art virtue, fame

      Honour, and all things else. Who can get thee,

70   He shall be noble, valiant, honest, wise——

Mosca.   And what he will, sir. Riches are in fortune

      A greater good than wisdom is in nature.

Volpone.   True, my beloved Mosca. Yet I glory

      More in the cunning purchase° of my wealth,   *acquisition*

      Than in the glad possession, since I gain

      No common way; I use no trade, no venture;°   *speculation*

      I wound no earth with ploughshares, fat no beasts

      To feed the shambles;° have no mills for iron,   *slaughterhouses*

      Oil, corn, or men, to grind them into powder:

80   I blow no subtle° glass, expose no ships   *intricate*

      To threat'ning of the furrow-faced sea;

      I turn° no monies in the public bank,[9]   *exchange*

      No usurer private.°[10]   *private moneylending*

Mosca.   No sir, nor devour

      Soft prodigals. You shall have some will swallow

      A melting heir[11] as glibly as your Dutch

      Will pills of butter,[12] and ne'er purge for it;

      Tear forth the fathers of poor families

---

    [7] The Zodiacal sign of Aries; the sun enters the sign at the vernal equinox, March 21, initiating spring.

    [8] The classical poets described Venus as "golden;" as such she should not, Volpone says, have produced one offspring but twenty.

    [9] In Jonson's time the allusion is to money changing and money lending.

    [10] Volpone is making fun here of the traditional ways of making money.

    [11] Cheat an heir out of recently inherited wealth.

    [12] Mosca is making fun of the well-known proclivity of the Dutch for butter.

Out of their beds, and coffin them alive
90   In some kind clasping prison, where their bones
May be forthcoming, when the flesh is rotten:
But your sweet nature doth abhor these courses;
You loathe the widow's or the orphan's tears
Should wash your pavements, or their piteous cries
Ring in your roofs, and beat the air for vengeance.
VOLPONE.   Right, Mosca; I do loathe it.
MOSCA.   And besides, sir,
You are not like the thresher that doth stand
With a huge flail, watching a heap of corn,
100   And, hungry, dares not taste the smallest grain,
But feeds on mallows, and such bitter herbs;
Nor like the merchant, who hath filled his vaults
With Romagnia, and rich Candian wines,
Yet drinks the lees of Lombard's vinegar:[13]
You will not lie in straw, whilst moths and worms
Feed on your sumptuous hangings and soft beds;
You know the use of riches, and dare give now
From that bright heap, to me, your poor observer,°   *follower*
Or to your dwarf, or your hermaphrodite,
110   Your eunuch, or what other household trifle°   *pet*
Your pleasure allows maintenance——
VOLPONE.   Hold thee, Mosca, [*Gives him money.*]
Take of my hand; thou strik'st on truth in all,
And they are envious term thee parasite.
Call forth my dwarf, my eunuch, and my fool,
And let them make me sport [*Exit* MOSCA.] What should I do,
But cocker up° my genius, and live free   *indulge*
To all delights my fortune calls me to?
I have no wife, no parent, child, ally,
120   To give my substance° to; but whom I make   *possessions*
Must be my heir; and this makes men observe me:
This draws new clients daily to my house,
Women and men of every sex and age,
That bring me presents, send me plate, coin, jewels
With hope that when I die (which they expect
Each greedy minute) it shall then return
Tenfold upon them; whilst some, covetous
Above the rest, seek to engross° me whole,   *monopolize*
And counter-work the one unto the other,°   *undermine each other*
130   Contend in gifts, as they would seem in love:
All which I suffer,° playing with their hopes,   *allow*
And am content to coin them into profit,
And look upon their kindness, and take more,

---

[13] Romagnia was a sweet wine; Candia, or Candy as it became known, in Crete produced another type of sweet wine. Lombard refers to Lombardy, a region in northern Italy; vinegar to a poor grade of wine.

And look on that; still bearing them in hand,°   *deluding them*
Letting the cherry[14] knock against their lips,
And draw it by their mouths, and back again.—
How now!

[*Re-enter* MOSCA *with* NANO, ANDROGYNO, *and* CASTRONE.]

NANO. "Now, room for fresh gamesters, who do will you
      to know,
140   They do bring you neither play nor university show;
And therefore do intreat you that whatsoever they rehearse,°   *recite*
May not fare a whit the worse, for the false pace of the verse.
If you wonder at this, you will wonder more ere we pass,
For know, here[15] is enclosed the soul of Pythagoras,
That juggler divine, as hereafter shall follow;
Which soul, fast and loose,° sir, came first from Apollo,[16]   *slippery*
And was breathed into Æthalides,[17] Mercurius his son,
Where it had the gift to remember all that ever was done.
From whence it fled forth, and made quick transmigration
150   To goldy-locked Euphorbus, who was killed in good fashion,
At the siege of old Troy, by the cuckold of Sparta,[18]
Hermotimus[19] was next (I find it in my charta),°   *text*
To whom it did pass, where no sooner it was missing,
But with one Pyrrhus of Delos[20] it learned to go a-fishing;
And thence did it enter the sophist of Greece.[21]
From Pythagore, she went into a beautiful piece,
Hight° Aspasio, the meretrix;° and the next toss of her   *named / prostitute*
Was again of a whore, she became a philosopher,
Crates the cynick[22] as itself doth relate it:
160   Since kings, knights, and beggars, knaves, lords, and fools
      gat it,
Besides ox and ass, camel, mule, goat, and brock,°   *badger*
In all which it hath spoke, as in the cobbler's cock.[23]
But I come not here to discourse of that matter,
Or his one, two, or three, or his great oath, BY QUATER!

---

[14] The allusion is to the game of bob-cherry in which the players try to bite a cherry dangling before them on a string.
[15] Nano points to Androgyno.
[16] The god of prophecy, healing, and music.
[17] The herald of the Argonauts. Aethalides is the first of series of individuals to be introduced to whose bodies the soul of Pythagoras (d. c. 497 B.C.), the Greek philosopher and mathematician, is said to have been transmitted. The story that Nano tells here is taken from *The Dream*, a dialogue by the poet Lucian.
[18] Menelaus, the husband of Helen.
[19] Another early Greek philosopher.
[20] A Greek philosopher who, according to tradition, had once been a fisherman at Delos, an island of Greece.
[21] Pythagoras.
[22] Crates of Thebes, a pupil of the famous cynic philosopher Diogenes (412?–323 B.C.).
[23] In Lucian's dialogue the cock, in whose body Pythagoras's soul had come to rest, tells his story to his master, the cobbler.

His musics, his trigon,° his golden thigh,   *triangle*
Or his telling how elements shift;[24] but I
Would ask, how of late thou hast suffered translation,
And shifted thy coat in these days of reformation.
170 ANDROGYNO.   Like one of the reformed, a fool, as you see,
       Counting all old doctrine heresy.
NANO.   But not on thine own forbid meats hast thou vent-
       ured?
ANDROGYNO.   On fish, when first a Carthusian[25] I entered.
NANO.   Why, then thy dogmatical silence[26] hath left thee?
ANDROGYNO.   Of that an obstreperous lawyer bereft me.
NANO.   O wonderful change, when sir lawyer forsook thee!
       For Pythagore's sake, what body then took thee?
ANDROGYNO.   A good dull mule.
180 NANO.   And how! by that means
       Thou wert brought to allow of the eating of beans?
ANDROGYNO.   Yes.
NANO.   But from the mule into whom didst thou pass?
ANDROGYNO.   Into a very strange beast, by some writers
       called an ass;
       By others a precise, pure, illuminate brother°   *Puritan*
       Of those devour flesh, and sometimes one another:
       And will drop you forth a libel, or a sanctified lie,
       Betwixt every spoonful of a nativity-pie.[27]
190 NANO.   Now quit thee, for heaven, of that profane nation,
       And gently report thy next transmigration.
ANDROGYNO.   To the same that I am.
NANO.   A creature of delight,
       And, what is more than a fool, an hermaphrodite!
       Now, prithee, sweet soul, in all thy variation,
       Which body wouldst thou choose to keep up thy station?
ANDROGYNO.   Troth, this I am in: even here would I tarry.
NANO.   'Cause here the delight of each sex thou canst
       vary!
200 ANDROGYNO.   Alas, those pleasures be stale and forsaken;
       No, 'tis your fool wherewith I am so taken,
       The only one creature that I can call blessed;
       For all other forms I have proved most distressed.
NANO.   Spoke true, as thou wert in Pythagoras still,
       This learned opinion we celebrate will,
       Fellow eunuch, as behoves us, with all our wit and art,
       To dignify that whereof ourselves are so great and special a part."
VOLPONE.   Now, very, very pretty; Mosca, this
       Was thy invention?

------

[24] Allusions to Pythagoras's theories of numbers, music, and geometry and to the fact that he is said to have had a golden thigh.
[25] The Carthusians were a strict monastic order. They did, however, eat fish which Pythagoras forbid. He also forbid the eating of beans (see line 181).
[26] Pythagoras imposed five years of silence upon his followers.
[27] I.e., of a Christmas-pie. [Editors' note]

210 MOSCA.   If it please my patron,
       Not else.
     VOLPONE.   It doth, good Mosca.
     MOSCA.   Then it was, sir.

                                          [NANO *and* CASTRONE *sing*.]²⁸

                 "Fools, they are the only nation
                 Worth men's envy or admiration;
                 Free from care or sorrow-taking,
                 Selves and others merry making:
                 All they speak or do is sterling.
                 Your fool he is your great man's darling,
220   And your ladies' sport and pleasure;
                 Tongue and bauble are his treasure.
                 E'en his face begetteth laughter,
                 And he speaks truth free from slaughter;°   *with impunity*
                 He's the grace of every feast,
                 And sometimes the chiefest guest;
                 Hath his trencher° and his stool,   *wooden plate*
                 When wit waits upon the fool.
                    O, who would not be
                    He, he, he?"
                                                   [*Knocking without.*]

230 VOLPONE.   Who's that? Away! [*Exeunt* NANO *and* CASTRONE.] Look, Mosca.
       Fool, begone!

                                                   [*Exit* ANDROGYNO.]

     MOSCA.   'Tis Signior Voltore, the advocate; I know him by his knock.
     VOLPONE.   Fetch me my gown,
       My furs, and night-caps; say my couch is changing.°   *is being changed*
       And let him entertain himself awhile
       Without i' the gallery. [*Exit* MOSCA.] Now, now my clients
       Begin their visitation! Vulture, kite,
       Raven, and gorcrow,²⁹ all my birds of prey,
       That think me turning carcase, now they come:
240   I am not for them yet.

                                          [*Re-enter* MOSCA, *with the gown, etc.*]

                          How now! the news?
     MOSCA.   A piece of plate,° sir.   *gold or silver plate*
     VOLPONE.   Of what bigness?
     MOSCA.   Huge,
       Massy, and antique, with your name inscribed,
       And arms engraven.
     VOLPONE.   Good! and not a fox

---

²⁸ Their song is made up of passages from the works of the Dutch scholar Erasmus
(c. 1466–1536).
²⁹ A crow that eats carrion.

Stretched on the earth, with fine delusive sleights,
Mocking a gaping crow? ha, Mosca!
250 MOSCA.   Sharp, sir.
VOLPONE.   Give me my furs.

                                 [Puts on his sick dress.]

Why dost thou laugh so, man?
MOSCA.   I cannot choose, sir, when I apprehend
  What thoughts he was without now, as he walks:
  That this might be the last gift he should give;
  That this would fetch you; if you died to-day,
  And gave him all, what he should be to-morrow;
  What large return would come of all his ventures
  How he should worshipped be, and reverenced;
260   Ride with his furs, and foot-cloths;[30] waited on
  By herds of fools and clients; have clear way
  Made for his mule, as lettered° as himself   *learned*
  Be called the great and learned advocate:
  And then concludes, there's nought impossible.
VOLPONE: Yes, to be learned, Mosca.
MOSCA.   O, no: rich
  Implies it. Hood an ass with reverend purple,
  So you can hide his two ambitious° ears,°   *prominent*
  And he shall pass for a cathedral doctor.°   *doctor of theology*
270 VOLPONE.   My caps, my caps, good Mosca. Fetch him in.
MOSCA.   Stay, sir; your ointment for your eyes.
VOLPONE: That's true;
  Dispatch, dispatch:° I long to have possession   *hurry, hurry*
  Of my new present.
MOSCA.   That, and thousands more,
  I hope to see you lord of.
VOLPONE.   Thanks, kind Mosca.
MOSCA.   And that, when I am lost in blended dust,
  And hundreds such as I am, in succession—
280 VOLPONE: Nay, that were too much, Mosca.
MOSCA.   You shall live
  Still to delude these harpies.
VOLPONE: Loving Mosca!
  'Tis well: my pillow now, and let him enter. *[Exit* MOSCA.*]*
  Now, my feigned cough, my phtisic,[31] and my gout,
  My apoplexy, palsy, and catarrhs,
  Help, with your forced functions, this my posture,
  Wherein, this three year, I have milked their hopes.
  He comes; I hear him—Uh *[coughing.]* uh! uh! uh! O—

        [Re-enter MOSCA, *introducing* VOLTORE *with a piece of Plate.]*

---

[30] Ornamental cloths or tapestries laid over the back of a horse or mule.
[31] Consumptive condition.

290   Mosca.   You still are what you were, sir. Only you,
        Of all the rest, are he commands his love,
        And you do wisely to preserve it thus,
        With early visitation, and kind notes°   *tokens*
        Of your good meaning to him, which, I know,
        Cannot but come most grateful. Patron! sir!
        Here's Signior Voltore is come—
    Volpone [*faintly*].   What say you?
    Mosca.   Sir, Signior Voltore is come this morning
        To visit you.
300   Volpone.   I thank him.
    Mosca.   And hath brought
        A piece of antique plate, bought of St. Mark,[32]
        With which he here presents you.
    Volpone.   He is welcome.
        Pray him to come more often.
    Mosca.   Yes.
    Voltore.   What says he?
    Mosca.   He thanks you, and desires you to see him often.
    Volpone.   Mosca.
310   Mosca.   My patron!
    Volpone.   Bring him near, where is he?
        I long to feel his hand.
    Mosca.   The plate is here, sir.
    Voltore.   How fare you, sir?
    Volpone.   I thank you, Signior Voltore;
        Where is the plate? mine eyes are bad.
    Voltore [*putting it into his hands*].   I'm sorry
        To see you still thus weak.
    Mosca.   That he's not weaker.   [*Aside.*]
320   Volpone.   You are too munificent.
    Voltore.   No, sir; would to heaven,
        I could as well give health to you, as that plate!
    Volpone.   You give, sir, what you can; I thank you. Your
        love
        Hath taste° in this, and shall not be unanswered: *proves itself*
        I pray you see me often.
    Voltore.   Yes, I shall, sir.
    Volpone.   Be not far from me.
    Mosca.   Do you observe that, sir?
330   Volpone.   Hearken unto me still; it will concern you.
    Mosca.   You are a happy man, sir; know your good.
    Volpone.   I cannot now last long—
    Mosca.   You are his heir, sir.

---

[32] In one of the shops in St. Mark's square.

VOLTORE.   Am I?

VOLPONE.   I feel me going: Uh! uh! uh! uh!
   I'm sailing to my port, Uh! uh! uh! uh!
   And I am glad I am so near my haven.

MOSCA.   Alas, kind gentleman! Well, we must all go—

VOLTORE.   But, Mosca—

340 MOSCA.   Age will conquer.

VOLTORE.   Pray thee, hear me;
   Am I inscribed his heir for certain?

MOSCA.   Are you!
   I do beseech you, sir, you will vouchsafe
   To write me in your family.[33] All my hopes
   Depend upon your worship: I am lost
   Except the rising sun do shine on me.

VOLTORE.   It shall both shine, and warm thee, Mosca.

MOSCA.   Sir,
350 I am a man that hath not done your love
   All the worst offices: here I wear your keys,
   See all your coffers and your caskets locked,
   Keep the poor inventory of your jewels,
   Your plate, and monies; am your steward, sir,
   Husband° your goods here.   *protect*

VOLTORE.   But am I sole heir?

MOSCA.   Without a partner, sir: confirmed this morning:
   The wax is warm yet, and the ink scarce dry
   Upon the parchment.

360 VOLTORE.   Happy, happy me!
   By what good chance, sweet Mosca?

MOSCA.   Your desert, sir;
   I know no second cause.

VOLTORE.   Thy modesty
   Is not to know it; well, we shall requite it.

MOSCA.   He ever liked your course, sir; that first took him.
   I oft have heard him say how he admired
   Men of your large profession, that could speak
   To every cause, and things mere contraries,
370 Till they were hoarse again, yet all be law;
   That, with most quick agility, could turn,
   And return; make knots, and undo them;
   Give forked° counsel; take provoking gold   *equivocal*
   On either hand, and put it up; these men,
   He knew, would thrive with their humility.
   And, for his part, he thought he should be blest
   To have his heir of such a suffering spirit,
   So wise, so grave, of so perplexed a tongue,
   And loud withal, that would not wag, nor scarce

---

[33] Include me in the list of your household servants and retainers.

380 Lie still, without a fee; when every word
     Your worship but lets fall, is a chequin!—[34]

                                                    [*Knocking without.*]

     Who's that? one knocks; I would not have you seen sir.
     And yet—pretend you came, and went in haste;
     I'll fashion an excuse—and, gentle sir,
     When you do come to swim in golden lard,
     Up to the arms in honey, that your chin
     Is borne up stiff with fatness of the flood,
     Think on your vassal; but remember me:
     I have not been your worst of clients.
390 VOLTORE.   Mosca!—
     MOSCA.   When will you have your inventory brought, sir?
     Or see a copy of the Will?—Anon!°   *Coming!*
     I'll bring them to you, sir. Away, begone,
     Put business in your face.

                                                    [*Exit* VOLTORE.]

     VOLPONE [*springing up*]. Excellent Mosca!
     Come hither, let me kiss thee.
     MOSCA.   Keep you still, sir.
     Here is Corbaccio.
     VOLPONE.   Set the plate away:
400 The vulture's gone, and the old raven's come.
     MOSCA.   Betake you of your silence, and your sleep.
     Stand there and multiply. [*Putting the plate to the rest.*]
        Now we shall see
     A wretch who is indeed more impotent
     Than this can feign to be; yet hopes to hop
     Over his grave.

                                                    [*Enter* CORBACCIO.]

              Signior Corbaccio!
        You're very welcome, sir.
     CORBACCIO   How does your patron?
410 MOSCA.   Troth, as he did, sir; no amends.
     CORBACCIO.   What! mends he?
     MOSCA.   No, sir: he's rather worse.
     CORBACCIO.   That's well. Where is he?
     MOSCA.   Upon his couch, sir, newly fall'n asleep.
     CORBACCIO.   Does he sleep well?
     MOSCA.   No wink, sir, all this night,
        Nor yesterday; but slumbers.°   *dozes*
     CORBACCIO.   Good! he should take

---

[34] A Venetian gold coin.

Some counsel of physicians: I have brought him
420   An opiate here, from mine own doctor.
    MOSCA.   He will not hear of drugs.
    CORBACCIO.   Why? I myself
       Stood by while it was made, saw all the ingredients;
       And know it cannot but most gently work:
       My life for his, 'tis but to make him sleep.
    VOLPONE.   Ay, his last sleep, if he would take it.   *[Aside]*
    MOSCA.   Sir,
       He has no faith in physic.°   *medicine*
    CORBACCIO.   Say you, say you?
430 MOSCA.   He has no faith in physic: he does think
       Most of your doctors are the greater danger,
       And worse disease, to escape. I often have
       Heard him protest that your physician
       Should never be his heir.
    CORBACCIO.   Not I his heir?
    MOSCA.   Not your physician, sir.
    CORBACCIO.   O, no, no, no.
       I do not mean it.
    MOSCA.   No, sir, nor their fees
440   He cannot brook: he says they flay a man
       Before they kill him.
    CORBACCIO.   Right, I do conceive° you.   *understand*
    MOSCA.   And then they do it by experiment;³⁵
       For which the law not only doth absolve them,
       But gives them great reward: and he is loth
       To hire his death so.
    CORBACCIO.   It is true, they kill
       With as much license as a judge.
    MOSCA.   Nay, more;
450   For he but kills, sir, where the law condemns,
       And these can kill him too.
    CORBACCIO.   Ay, or me;
       Or any man. How does his apoplex?°   *apoplexy*
       Is that strong on him still?
    MOSCA.   Most violent.
       His speech is broken, and his eyes are set.
       His face drawn longer than 'twas wont—
    CORBACCIO.   How! how!
       Stronger than he was wont?
460 MOSCA.   No, sir; his face
       Drawn longer than 'twas wont.
    CORBACCIO.   Oh, good!

---

³⁵ Try it out as an experiment.

Mosca.   His mouth
  Is ever gaping, and his eyelids hang.
Corbaccio.   Good.
Mosca.   A freezing numbness stiffens all his joints,
  And makes the colour of his flesh like lead.
Corbaccio.   'Tis good.
Mosca.   His pulse beats slow, and dull.
470 Corbaccio.   Good symptoms still.
Mosca.   And from his brain—
Corbaccio.   I conceive you; good.
Mosca.   Flows a cold sweat, with a continual rheum,°   *discharge*
  Forth the resolved° corners of his eyes.   *drooping*
Corbaccio.   Is't possible? Yet° I am better, ha!   *again*
  How does he with the swimming of his head?
Mosca.   O, sir, 'tis past the scotomy;[36] he now
  Hath lost his feeling, and hath left to snort:°   *stopped snorting*
  You hardly can perceive him, that he breathes.
480 Corbaccio.   Excellent, excellent! sure I shall outlast him:
  This makes me young again, a score of years.
Mosca.   I was a-coming for you, sir.
Corbaccio.   Has he made his Will?
  What has he given me?
Mosca.   No, sir.
Corbaccio.   Nothing! ha?
Mosca.   He has not made his Will, sir.
Corbaccio.   Oh, oh, oh!
  What then did Voltore, the lawyer, here?
490 Mosca.   He smelt a carcase, sir, when he but heard
  My master was about his testament;°   *making his will*
  As I did urge him to it for your good—
Corbaccio.   He came unto him, did he? I thought so.
Mosca.   Yes, and presented him this piece of plate.
Corbaccio.   To be his heir?
Mosca.   I do not know, sir.
Corbaccio.   True:
  I know it too.
Mosca.   By your own scale, sir.   *[Aside.]*
500 Corbaccio.   Well,
  I shall prevent° him yet. See, Mosca, look   *anticipate*
  Here I have brought a bag of bright chequines,
  Will quite weigh down his plate.
Mosca *[taking the bag]*.   Yea, marry, sir.
  This is true physic, this your sacred medicine;
  No talk of opiates[37] to this great elixir!

---

[36] Scotomia is a dizziness or swimming in the head. [Editors' note]
[37] No opiates can compare to . . . !

CORBACCIO. 'Tis aurum palpabile, if not potabile.[38]

MOSCA. It shall be ministered to him in his bowl.

CORBACCIO. Ay, do, do, do.

510 MOSCA. Most blessed cordial!°   *restorative medicine*
    This will recover him.

CORBACCIO. Yes, do, do, do.

MOSCA. I think it were not best, sir.

CORBACCIO. What?

MOSCA. To recover him.

CORBACCIO. O, no, no, no; by no means.

MOSCA. Why, sir, this
    Will work some strange effect, if he but feel it.

CORBACCIO. 'Tis true, therefore forbear; I'll take my venture:°   *investment*

520   Give me it again.

MOSCA. At no hand: pardon me:
    You shall not do yourself that wrong, sir. I
    Will so advise you, you shall have it all.

CORBACCIO. How?

MOSCA. All, sir; 'tis your right, your own; no man
    Can claim a part: 'tis yours without a rival,
    Decreed by destiny.

CORBACCIO. How, how, good Mosca?

MOSCA. I'll tell you, sir. This fit he shall recover.

530 CORBACCIO. I do conceive you.

MOSCA. And on first advantage°   *opportunity*
    Of his gained sense, will I re-importune him
    Unto the making of his testament:
    And show him this.   *[Pointing to the money.]*

CORBACCIO. Good, good.

MOSCA. 'Tis better yet,
    If you will hear, sir.

CORBACCIO. Yes, with all my heart.

MOSCA. Now would I counsel you, make home with speed;

540   There, frame a Will; whereto you shall inscribe
    My master your sole heir.

CORBACCIO. And disinherit
    My son!

MOSCA. O, sir, the better: for that colour
    Shall make it much more taking.[39]

CORBACCIO. O, but colour?

MOSCA. This Will, sir, you shall send it unto me.
    Now, when I come to inforce, as I will do,
    Your cares, your watchings, and your many prayers,

550   Your more than many gifts, your this day's present,

---

[38] It is gold that can be felt if not drunk. Aurum potabile, "drinkable gold"—particles of gold in oil, thought to act as a stimulant.

[39] The pretext will make it much more attractive or successful.

And last, produce your Will; where, without thought,
Or least regard, unto your proper° issue,   *own*
A son so brave, and highly meriting,
The stream of your diverted love hath thrown you
Upon my master, and made him your heir:
He cannot be so stupid, or stone dead,
But out of conscience and mere gratitude—

CORBACCIO.   He must pronounce me his?
MOSCA.   'Tis true.
560 CORBACCIO.   This plot
    Did I think on before.
MOSCA.   I do believe it.
CORBACCIO.   Do you not believe it?
MOSCA.   Yes, sir.
CORBACCIO.   Mine own project.
MOSCA.   Which, when he hath done, sir—
CORBACCIO.   Published me his heir?
MOSCA.   And you so certain to survive him—
CORBACCIO.   Ay.
570 MOSCA.   Being so lusty a man—
CORBACCIO.   'Tis true.
MOSCA.   Yes, sir—
CORBACCIO.   I thought on that, too. See, how he should be
    The very organ to express my thoughts!
MOSCA.   You have not only done yourself a good—
CORBACCIO.   But multiplied it on my son.
MOSCA.   'Tis right, sir.
CORBACCIO.   Still, my invention.
MOSCA.   'Las, sir! heaven knows,
580   It hath been all my study, all my care,
    (I e'en grow gray withal,) how to work things—
CORBACCIO.   I do conceive, sweet Mosca.
MOSCA.   You are he
    For whom I labour here.
CORBACCIO.   Ay, do, do, do:
    I'll straight about it.

                                                          [Going.]

MOSCA.   Rook go with you,° raven! *[Aside.]*   *may you be fooled*
CORBACCIO.   I know thee honest.
MOSCA.   You do lie, sir!
590 CORBACCIO.   And—
MOSCA.   Your knowledge is no better than your ears, sir.
CORBACCIO.   I do not doubt to be a father to thee.
MOSCA.   Nor I to gull° my brother of his blessing.[40]   *cheat*
CORBACCIO.   I may have my youth restored to me, why not?
MOSCA.   Your worship is a precious ass!

---

[40] The allusion is to Jacob and Esau (Genesis 27).

CORBACCIO.   What sayest thou?

MOSCA.   I do desire your worship to make haste, sir.

CORBACCIO.   'Tis done, 'tis done; I go.

                                                    [Exit.]

VOLPONE [*leaping from his couch*].   O, I shall burst!

600   Let out my sides, let out my sides—

MOSCA.   Contain

    Your flux° of laughter, sir: you know this hope   *burst*

    Is such a bait, it covers any hook.

VOLPONE.   O, but thy working, and thy placing it!

    I cannot hold;° good rascal, let me kiss thee: *contain myself*

    I never knew thee in so rare a humour.°   *mood*

MOSCA.   Alas, sir, I but do as I am taught;

    Follow your grave instructions; give them words;°   *fool them*

    Pour oil into their ears, and send them hence.

610 VOLPONE.   'Tis true, 'tis true. What a rare punishment.

    Is avarice to itself![41]

MOSCA.   Ay, with our help, sir.

VOLPONE.   So many cares, so many maladies,

    So many fears attending on old age.

    Yea, death so often called on, as no wish

    Can be more frequent with them, their limbs faint,

    Their senses dull, their seeing, hearing, going,°   *ability to work*

    All dead before them; yea, their very teeth,

    Their instruments of eating, failing them:

620   Yet this is reckoned life! nay, here was one,

    Is now gone home, that wishes to live longer!

    Feels not his gout, nor palsy; feigns himself

    Younger by scores of years, flatters his age

    With confident belying it, hopes he may

    With charms like Æson,[42] have his youth restored;

    And with these thoughts so battens,° as if fate   *grows fat*

    Would be as easily cheated on as he,

    And all turns air! [*knocking within.*] Who's that there,

        now? a third!

630 MOSCA.   Close,° to your couch again; I hear his voice.   *hide yourself*

    It is Corvino, our spruce merchant.

VOLPONE [*lies down as before*].   Dead.[43]

MOSCA.   Another bout, sir, with your eyes [*annointing*

    them.][44] Who's there?

                                             [Enter CORVINO.]

    Signior Corvino! come most wished for! O,

    How happy were you, if you knew it, now!

---

[41] Volpone is paraphrasing a line from Seneca's (c. 4 B.C.–65 A.D.) *Epistle* CXV.

[42] Aeson, King of Thessaly and father of Jason, was restored to youth by the magic of his daughter-in-law, Medea.

[43] Volpone is lying down pretending to be dead.

[44] So as to renew his disguise.

CORVINO.   Why? what? wherein?

MOSCA.   The tardy hour is come, sir.

CORVINO.   He is not dead?

640 MOSCA.   Not dead, sir, but as good;
    He knows no man.

CORVINO.   How shall I do then?

MOSCA.   Why, sir?

CORVINO.   I have brought him here a pearl.

MOSCA.   Perhaps he has
    So much remembrance left as to know you, sir:
    He still° calls on you; nothing but your name   *constantly*
    Is in his mouth. Is your pearl orient,[45] sir?

CORVINO.   Venice was never owner of the like.

650 VOLPONE [*faintly*].   Signior Corvino!

MOSCA.   Hark.

VOLPONE.   Signior Corvino.

MOSCA.   He calls you: step and give it him—He's here, sir.
    And he has brought you a rich pearl.

CORVINO.   How do you, sir?
    Tell him it doubles the twelve caract.[46]

MOSCA.   Sir,
    He cannot understand, his hearing's gone;
    And yet it comforts him to see you—

660 CORVINO.   Say
    I have a diamond for him, too.

MOSCA.   Best show it, sir;
    Put it into his hand: 'tis only there
    He apprehends: he has his feeling yet.
    See how he grasps it!

CORVINO.   'Las, good gentleman!
    How pitiful the sight is!

MOSCA.   Tut, forget, sir.
    The weeping of an heir should still be laughter
670   Under a visor.°   *deceiving countenance, mask*

CORVINO.   Why, am I his heir?

MOSCA.   Sir, I am sworn, I may not show the Will
    Till he be dead; but here has been Corbaccio,
    Here has been Voltore, here were others too,
    I cannot number 'em, they were so many;
    All gaping here for legacies: but I,
    Taking the vantage of his naming you,
    Signior Corvino, Signior Corvino, took
    Paper, and pen, and ink, and there I asked him
680   Whom he would have his heir! *Corvino.* Who
    Should be executor? *Corvino.* And

---

[45] That is, is your pearl of the purest luster? Originally such pearls came from the East or Orient.

[46] I.e., carat. That is, it weighs 24 carats. [Editors' note]

To any question he was silent to,
I still interpreted the nods he made,
Through weakness, for consent: and sent home th' others,
Nothing bequeathed them, but to cry and curse.
CORVINO.   O, my dear Mosca. [*They embrace.*] Does he not
    perceive us?
MOSCA.   No more than a blind harper.[47] He knows no man,
No face of friend, nor name of any servant,
690   Who 'twas that fed him last, or gave him drink:
Not those he had begotten, or brought up.
Can he remember.
CORVINO.   Has he children?
MOSCA.   Bastards,
Some dozen, or more, that he begot on beggars,
Gypsies, and Jews, and black-moors when he was drunk.
Knew you not that, sir? 'tis the common fable.
The dwarf, the fool, the eunuch, are all his;
He's the true father of his family,
700   In all save me:—but he has given them nothing.
CORVINO.   That's well, that's well! Art sure he does not
    hear us?
MOSCA.   Sure, sir! why, look you, credit your own sense.

                                   [*Shouts in* VOLPONE'S *ear.*]

The pox° approach, and add to your diseases,   *syphilis*
If it would send you hence the sooner, sir,
For your incontinence, it hath deserved it
Throughly and throughly, and the plague to boot!—
You may come near, sir.—Would you once° close   *once and for all*
Those filthy eyes of yours, that flow with slime,
710   Like two frog-pits; and those same hanging cheeks,
Covered with hide instead of skin—Nay, help, sir—
That look like frozen dish-clouts° set on end!   *cloths*
CORVINO [*aloud*].   Or like an old smoked wall, on which
    the rain
Ran down in streaks!
MOSCA.   Excellent, sir! speak out:
You may be louder yet; a culverin°   *pistol*
Discharged in his ear would hardly bore° it.   *penetrate*
CORVINO.   His nose is like a common sewer, still running.
720 MOSCA.   'Tis good! And what his mouth!
CORVINO.   A very draught.°   *cesspool*
MOSCA.   O, stop it up—
CORVINO.   By no means.
MOSCA.   Pray you, let me:
Faith I could stifle him rarely° with a pillow   *excellently*
As well as any woman that should keep° him.   *look after*
CORVINO.   Do as you will; but I'll begone.

---

[47] A proverbial saying.

MOSCA.   Be so;
   It is your presence makes him last so long.
730 CORVINO.   I pray you use no violence.
MOSCA.   No, sir! why?
   Why should you be thus scrupulous, pray you, sir?
CORVINO.   Nay, at your discretion.
MOSCA.   Well, good sir, be gone.
CORVINO.   I will not trouble you now to take my pearl.
MOSCA.   Puh! nor your diamond. What a needless care.
   Is this afflicts you? Is not all here yours?
   Am not I here, whom you have made your creature?
   That owe my being to you?
740 CORVINO.   Grateful Mosca!
   Thou art my friend, my fellow, my companion,
   My partner, and shalt share in all my fortunes.
MOSCA.   Excepting one.
CORVINO.   What's that?
MOSCA.   Your gallant° wife, sir.   *fine, beautiful*

                                                            [*Exit* CORVINO.]

   Now he is gone: we had no other means
   To shoot him hence but this.
VOLPONE.   My divine Mosca!
   Thou hast to-day outgone thyself. [*Knocking within.*] Who's
750   there?
   I will be troubled with no more. Prepare
   Me music, dances, banquets, all delights;
   The Turk is not more sensual in his pleasures
   Than will Volpone. [*Exit* MOSCA.] Let me see; a pearl!
   A diamond! plate! chequines! Good morning's purchase.°   *haul, loot*
   Why, this is better than rob churches, yet;
   Or fat,° by eating, once a month, a man—   *grow fat*

                                                            [*Re-enter* MOSCA.]

   Who is 't?
MOSCA.   The beauteous Lady Would-be, sir,
760   Wife to the English knight, Sir Politick Would-be,
   (This is the style, sir, is directed me,)[48]
   Hath sent to know how you have slept to-night,°   *last night*
   And if you would be visited?
VOLPONE.   Not now:
   Some three hours hence.
MOSCA.   I told the squire° so much.   *attendant*
VOLPONE.   When I am high with mirth and wine; then, then:
   'Fore heaven, I wonder at the desperate valour
   Of the bold English, that they dare let loose
770   Their wives to all encounters!

---

[48] This is the manner in which I have been directed to announce her.

MOSCA.   Sir, this knight
   Had not his name for nothing, he is *politick,*
   And knows, howe'er his wife affect strange airs,
   She hath not yet the face° to be dishonest:°   *looks/unfaithful*
   But had she Signior Corvino's wife's face—
VOLPONE.   Hath she so rare a face?
MOSCA.   O, sir, the wonder,
   The blazing star of Italy! a wench
   Of the first year,[49] a beauty ripe as harvest!
780   Whose skin is whiter than a swan all over,
   Than silver, snow, or lilies; a soft lip,
   Would tempt you to eternity of kissing!
   And flesh that melteth in the touch to blood!
   Bright as your gold, and lovely as your gold!
VOLPONE.   Why had not I known this before?
MOSCA.   Alas, sir,
   Myself but yesterday discovered it.
VOLPONE.   How might I see her?
MOSCA.   O, not possible;
790   She's kept as warily as is your gold;
   Never does come abroad, never takes air
   But at a window. All her looks are sweet,
   As the first grapes or cherries, and are watched
   As near° as they are.   *closely*
VOLPONE.   I must see her.
MOSCA.   Sir,
   There is a guard of spies ten thick upon her,
   All his whole household; each of which is set
   Upon his fellow,° and have their charge,°   *fellow-servant/instruction*
800   When he goes out, when he comes in, examined.
VOLPONE.   I will go see her, though but at her window.
MOSCA.   In some disguise then.
VOLPONE.   That is true; I must
   Maintain mine own shape still the same: we'll think.

                                                            [*Exeunt.*]

ACT THE SECOND

SCENE I

St. Mark's Place; a retired corner before CORVINO's *House.*

                  [*Enter* SIR POLITICK WOULD-BE, *and* PEREGRINE.]

SIR POLITICK.   Sir, to a wise man, all the world's his soil:°   *country*
   It is not Italy, nor France, nor Europe,
   That must bound me, if my fates call me forth,

---

[49] A woman in the prime of life.

Yet I protest, it is no salt° desire   *excessive*
   Of seeing countries, shifting a religion,
810   Nor any disaffection to the state
   Where I was bred, and unto which I owe
   My dearest plots, hath brought me out; much less
   That idle, antique, stale, grey-headed project
   Of knowing men's minds and manners, with Ulysses!
   But a peculiar humour° of my wife's   *particular whim*
   Laid for this height of Venice,[50] to observe,
   To quote,° to learn the language, and so forth—   *take notes on*
   I hope you travel, sir, with licence?
PEREGRINE.   Yes.
820 SIR POLITICK.   I dare the safelier converse[51]—How long, sir,
   Since you left England?
PEREGRINE.   Seven weeks.
SIR POLITICK.   So lately!
   You have not been with my lord ambassador?[52]
PEREGRINE.   Not yet, sir.
SIR POLITICK.   Pray you, what news, sir, vents° our climate?   *circulates about*
   I heard last night a most strange thing reported
   By some of my lord's followers, and I long
   To hear how 'twill be seconded.°   *confirmed*
830 PEREGRINE.   What was 't, sir?
SIR POLITICK.   Marry, sir, of a raven[53] that should build°   *is said to have built*
   In a ship royal of the king's.
PEREGRINE.   This fellow,
   Does he gull° me, trow?° or is gulled? [*Aside.*] Your   *trick / do you think?*
   name, sir?
SIR POLITICK.   My name is Politick Would-be.
PEREGRINE.   O, that speaks him. [*Aside.*]
   A knight, sir?
SIR POLITICK.   A poor knight, sir.
840 PEREGRINE.   Your lady
   Lies° here in Venice, for intelligence°   *stays / information*
   Of tires° and fashions, and behavior,   *attires*
   Among the courtezans? the fine Lady Would-be?
SIR POLITICK.   Yes, sir; the spider and the bee ofttimes
   Suck from one flower.
PEREGRINE.   Good Sir Politick,
   I cry you mercy;° I have heard much of you: *beg your pardon*
   'Tis true, sir, of your raven.
SIR POLITICK.   On your knowledge?
850 PEREGRINE.   Yes, and your lion's whelping in the Tower.[54]
SIR POLITICK.   Another whelp?
PEREGRINE.   Another, sir.

---

[50] That is, directed toward the latitude of Venice.
[51] I feel more safe in being seen talking with you.
[52] Sir Henry Wotton was then the English ambassador to Venice.
[53] The raven was traditionally regarded as an omen of bad luck.
[54] The Tower of London where lions were in fact kept.

SIR POLITICK.   Now heaven!
   What prodigies be these? The fires at Berwick![55]
   And the new star![56] these things concurring, strange,
   And full of omen! Saw you those meteors?
PEREGRINE.   I did, sir.
SIR POLITICK.   Fearful! Pray you, sir, confirm me,
   Were there three porpoises seen above the bridge,
860   As they give out?
PEREGRINE.   Six, and a sturgeon, sir.
SIR POLITICK.   I am astonished.
PEREGRINE.   Nay, sir, be not so;
   I'll tell you a greater prodigy than these.
SIR POLITICK.   What should these things portend?
PEREGRINE.   The very day
   (Let me be sure) that I put forth from London,
   There was a whale discovered in the river,
   As high as Woolwich, that had waited there,
870   Few know how many months, for the subversion
   Of the Stode fleet.[57]
SIR POLITICK.   Is't possible? believe it,
   'Twas either sent from Spain, or the archduke's:[58]
   Spinola's whale,[59] upon my life, my credit!
   Will they not leave these projects? Worthy sir,
   Some other news.
PEREGRINE.   Faith, Stone[60] the fool is dead.
   And they do lack a tavern fool extremely.
SIR POLITICK.   Is Mass° Stone dead?   *Master*
880 PEREGRINE.   He's dead, sir; why, I hope
   You thought him not immortal?—O, this knight,
   Were he well known, would be a precious thing
   To fit our English stage: he that should write
   But such a fellow,[61] should be thought to feign
   Extremely, if not maliciously.   *[Aside.]*
SIR POLITICK.   Stone dead!
PEREGRINE.   Dead.—Lord! how deeply, sir, you apprehend it!
   He was no kinsman to you?
SIR POLITICK.   That I know of.
890   Well! that same fellow was an unknown fool.

---

[55] In January of 1605, a strange apparition of men fighting appeared among the hills near Berwick.

[56] A new and brilliant star had been reported in September, 1604.

[57] Stode (Stade) was a German port used by the ships of the English Merchant Adventurers, an export–import company.

[58] The Archdukes was a joint title given to Isabella, the daughter of Philip II of Spain, and her husband Albert when the Netherlands was ceded to them in 1602.

[59] General Ambrogio Spinola (1569–1630) took command of the Spanish army in Netherlands in 1604. His whale was his reputed secret weapon, which was to be used in attacking London.

[60] A popular contemporary figure about whom little is known.

[61] That is, should insert a character like Sir Politick into a play.

PEREGRINE.   And yet you knew him, it seems?
SIR POLITICK.   I did so. Sir,
   I knew him one of the most dangerous heads
   Living within the state, and so I held him.
PEREGRINE.   Indeed, sir?
SIR POLITICK.   While he lived, in action.
   He has received weekly intelligence,
   Upon my knowledge, out of the Low Countries,
   For all parts of the world, in cabbages;
900   And those dispensed again to ambassadors,
   In oranges, musk-melons, apricots,
   Lemons, pome-citrons,° and such-like; sometimes   *lemon-like fruits*
   In Colchester oysters, and your Selsey cockles.
PEREGRINE.   You make me wonder.
SIR POLITICK.   Sir, upon my knowledge.
   Nay, I've observed him, at your public ordinary,°   *tavern*
   Take his advertisement° from a traveller,   *instructions*
   A concealed statesman, in a trencher° of meat;   *plate*
   And instantly, before the meal was done,
910   Convey an answer in a tooth-pick.
PEREGRINE.   Strange!
   How could this be, sir?
SIR POLITICK.   Why, the meat was cut
   So like his character,[62] and so laid as he
   Must easily read the cypher.
PEREGRINE.   I have heard,
   He could not read, sir.
SIR POLITICK.   So 'twas given out,
   In policy, by those that did employ him:
920   But he could read, and had your languages.
   And to 't, as sound a noddle[63]—
PEREGRINE.   I have heard, sir,
   That your baboons were spies, and that they were
   A kind of subtle nation near to China.
SIR POLITICK.   Ay, ay, your Mamaluchi.[64] Faith, they had
   Their hand in a French plot or two; but they
   Were so extremely given to women, as
   They made discovery of all: yet I
   Had my advices here, on Wednesday last,
930   From one of their own coat,° they were returned,   *party*
   Made their relations,° as the fashion is,   *reports*
   And now stand fair° for fresh employment.   *ready*
PEREGRINE.   Heart![65]
   This Sir Pol will be ignorant of nothing.   [*Aside.*]
   It seems, sir, you know all.

---

[62] It was fashionable at the time to cut one's meat in the shape of letters.
[63] And in addition, as level a head.
[64] An Arabic slave.
[65] An oath: "By God's heart!"

SIR POLITICK.   Not all, sir; but
    I have some general notions. I do love
    To note and to observe: though I live out,
    Free from the active torrent, yet I'd mark
940   The currents and the passages of things.
    For mine own private use; and know the ebbs
    And flows of state.
PEREGRINE.   Believe it, sir, I hold
    Myself in no small tie unto my fortunes,[66]
    For casting me thus luckily upon you,
    Whose knowledge, if your bounty equal it,
    May do me great assistance, in instruction
    For my behavior, and my bearing, which
    Is yet so rude and raw.
950 SIR POLITICK.   Why? came you forth
    Empty of rules for travel?
PEREGRINE.   Faith, I had
    Some common ones, from out that vulgar grammar,
    Which he that cried Italian to me, taught me.
SIR POLITICK.   Why, this it is that spoils all our brave bloods,°   *young gallants*
    Trusting our hopeful gentry unto pedants,
    Fellows of outside, and mere bark.° You seem   *surface*
    To be a gentleman of ingenuous race:°—   *teachers of noble birth*
    I not profess it, but my fate hath been
960   To be, where I have been consulted with,
    In this high kind, touching some great men's sons,
    Persons of blood° and honour.—   *noble birth*

[*Enter* MOSCA *and* NANO *disguised, followed by persons with materials for erecting a Stage.*]

PEREGRINE.   Who be these, sir?
MOSCA.   Under that window, there 't must be. The same.
SIR POLITICK.   Fellows, to mount a bank. Did your instructor
    In the dear tongues,° never discourse to you   *valued languages*
    Of the Italian mountebanks?
PEREGRINE.   Yes, sir.
SIR POLITICK.   Why,
970   Here you shall see one.
PEREGRINE.   They are quacksalvers,° [67]   *quacks*
    Fellows that live by venting° oils and drugs.   *selling*
SIR POLITICK.   Was that the character he gave you of them?
PEREGRINE.   As I remember.
SIR POLITICK.   Pity his ignorance.
    They are the only knowing men of Europe!
    Great general scholars, excellent physicians,

---

[66] That is, I thank my lucky stars.
[67] An Italian term: a person who sells quack medicines from a platform.

Most admired statesmen, profest favourites,

And cabinet° counsellors to the greatest princes;   *private*

980   The only languaged° men of all the world!   *best spoken*

PEREGRINE.   And, I have heard, they are the most lewd°   *ignorant*
    imposters;

Made all of terms° and shreds; no less beliers   *jargon/bits and pieces*

Of great men's favours, than their own vile med'cines;   *of knowledge*

Which they will utter° upon monstrous oaths;   *sell*

Selling that drug for twopence, ere they part,

Which they have valued at twelve crowns° before.   *silver coins*

SIR POLITICK.   Sir, calumnies are answered best with silence.

Yourself shall judge.—Who is it mounts, my friends?

990 MOSCA.   Scoto of Mantua,[68] sir.

SIR POLITICK.   Is't he? Nay, then

I'll proudly promise, sir, you shall behold

Another man that has been phant'sied° to you.   *imaginatively described*

I wonder yet, that he should mount his bank,

Here in this nook, that has been wont t' appear

In face of the Piazza!—Here he comes.

[*Enter* VOLPONE, *disguised as a mountebank Doctor, and followed by a crowd of people.*]

VOLPONE.   Mount, zany.[69] [*To* NANO.]

MOB.   Follow, follow, follow, follow!

SIR POLITICK.   See how the people follow him! he's a man

1000   May write ten thousand crowns in bank here. Note,

[VOLPONE *mounts the stage.*]

Mark but his gesture:—I do use to observe

The state he keeps in getting up.

PEREGRINE.   'Tis worth it, sir.

VOLPONE.   "Most noble gentlemen, and my worthy patrons! It
may seem strange that I, your Scoto Mantuano, who was ever
wont to fix my bank in the face of the public Piazza, near
the shelter of the Portico to the Procuratia,[70] should now,
after eight months' absence from this illustrious city of Venice, humbly retire myself into an obscure nook of the Pi-

1010   azza."

SIR POLITICK.   Did not I now object the same?

PEREGRINE.   Peace, sir.

VOLPONE.   "Let me tell you: I am not, as your Lombard proverb saith, cold on my feet;[71] or content to part with my com-
modities at a cheaper rate than I am accustomed: look not

---

[68] A late-sixteenth-century Italian entertainer.

[69] A mountebank's comic assistant.

[70] The colonnade or portico along the Piazza San Marco where the Procuratia, the city's
leading administrators, resided.

[71] That is, to be so poor as to have to sell one's goods at a loss.

for it. Nor that the calumnious reports of that impudent de-
tractor, and shame to our profession (Alessandro Buttone,[72]
I mean), who gave out, in public, I was condemned a
sforzato° to the galleys, for poisoning the Cardinal Bem-　　　*galley slave*

1020　　bo's[73]—cook, hath at all attached, much less dejected me.
No, no, worthy gentlemen; to tell you true, I cannot endure
to see the rabble of these ground ciarlitani,[74] that spread
their cloaks on the pavement, as if they meant to do feats of
activity, and then come in lamely, with their mouldy tales out
of Boccacio, like stale Tabarine, the fabulist:[75] some of them
discoursing their travels, and of their tedious captivity in the
Turk's galleys, when, indeed, were the truth known, they
were the Christian's galleys, where very temperately they eat
bread, and drunk water, as a wholesome penance enjoined

1030　　them by their confessors, for base pilferies."
　　SIR POLITICK.　Note but his bearing, and contempt of these.
　　VOLPONE.　"These turdy-facy-nasty-paty-lousy-fartical rogues,
with one poor groat's-worth of unprepared antimony,[76]
finely wrapt up in several scartoccios,[77] are able, very well, to
kill their twenty a week, and play; yet these meagre, starved
spirits, who have half stopt the organs of their minds with
earthly oppilations,° want not their favourers among your　　*obstructions*
shrivelled salad-eating artisans, who are overjoyed that they
may have their half-per'th° of physic; though it purge　　*half-penny's worth*

1040　　them into another world, it makes no matter."
　　SIR POLITICK.　Excellent! have you heard better language, sir?
　　VOLPONE.　"Well, let them go. And, gentlemen, honourable
gentlemen, know, that for this time, our bank, being thus
removed from the clamours of the canaglia,° shall be the　　*mob*
scene of pleasure and delight; for I have nothing to sell, lit-
tle or nothing to sell."
　　SIR POLITICK.　I told you, sir, his end.
　　PEREGRINE.　You did so, sir.
　　VOLPONE.　"I protest, I, and my six servants, are not able to

1050　　make of this precious liquor, so fast as it is fetched away
from my lodging by gentlemen of your city; strangers of the
Terra-firma;[78] worshipful merchants; ay, and senators too:
who, ever since my arrival, have detained me to their uses,
by their splendidous liberalities. And worthily; for, what
avails your rich man to have his magazines° stuft with mos-　　*storehouses*

---

[72] The allusion is unclear.
[73] Pietro Bembo (1470–1547), a noted humanist of the Italian Renaissance, spent the last
six years of his life as a cardinal.
[74] Petty charlatans, imposters. [Editors' note]
[75] Boccaccio (1313–1375) was the author of *The Decameron* (1353), the great collection of
Renaissance stories. Tambarin was another well-known contemporary Venetian entertainer.
[76] A metallic ingredient used in contemporary medicine.
[77] I.e., covers, folds of paper. [Editors' note]
[78] Terra Firma is the part of Venice located on the mainland.

cadelli,[79] or of the purest grape, when his physicians prescribe him, on pain of death, to drink nothing but water
cocted° with aniseeds? O, health! health! the blessing of the   *boiled*
rich! the riches of the poor! who can buy thee at too dear a
1060   rate, since there is no enjoying this world without thee? Be
not then so sparing of your purses, honourable gentlemen,
as to abridge the natural course of life—"
PEREGRINE.   You see his end.
SIR POLITICK.   Ay, is't not good?
VOLPONE.   "For when a humid flux,° or catarrh, by the mutabil-   *runny nose*
ity of air, falls from your head into an arm or shoulder, or
any other part; take you a ducket, or your chequin of gold,
and apply to the place affected: see what good effect it can
work. No, no, 'tis this blessed unguento,° this rare extraction,   *ointment*
1070   that hath only power to disperse all malignant humours,[80]
that proceed either of hot, cold, moist, or windy causes—"
PEREGRINE.   I would he had put in dry too.
SIR POLITICK.   Pray you observe.
VOLPONE.   "To fortify the most indigest and crude° stomach,   *upset*
ay, were it of one that, through extreme weakness, vomited
blood, applying only a warm napkin to the place, after the
unction and fricace;°— for the vertigine° in the head, put-   *massage / vertigo*
ting but a drop into your nostrils, likewise behind the ears; a
most sovereign and approved remedy; the mal caduco,°   *epilepsy*
1080   cramps, convulsions, paralysies, epilepsies, tremorcordia,°   *heart palpatations*
retired nerves, ill vapours of the spleen, stopping
of the liver, the stone,° the strangury,°   *kidney stones / painful urinations*
hernia ventosa,° iliaca passio;° stops a dysenteria immedi-   *rupture / gas*
ately; easeth the torsion of the small guts; and cures melan-
cholia hypondriaca,° being taken and applied, according to   *depression*
my printed receipt. [*Pointing to his bill and his vial.*] For this is
the physician, this the medicine; this counsels, this cures; this
gives the direction, this works the effect; and, in sum, both
together may be termed an abstract of the theorick and
1090   practick in the Æsculapian[81] art. 'Twill cost you eight crowns.
And,—Zan Fritada,[82] prithee sing a verse extempore in honour of it."
SIR POLITICK.   How do you like him, sir?
PEREGRINE.   Most strangely, I!
SIR POLITICK.   Is not his language rare?
PEREGRINE.   But° alchemy, I never heard the like; or Brought-   *except for*
on's books.[83]

---

[79] An Italian wine.
[80] The medieval psychological theory of the four humors (hotness, coldness, wetness, and
dryness) whose combination was said to determine the human temperament.
[81] The Greek god of healing.
[82] Literally, Jack Pancake.
[83] Hugh Broughton (1549–1612) was a Puritan minister and a rabbinical scholar who wrote
abstruse treatises.

[NANO *sings*.]

Had old Hippocrates, or Galen,[84]
That to their books put med'cines all in,
But known this secret, they had never
(Of which they will be guilty ever)
Been murderers of so much paper,
Or wasted many a hurtless taper;
No Indian drug had e'er been famed,
Tobacco, sassafras not named;
Ne yet of guacum[85] one small stick, sir,
Nor Raymund Lully's great elixir.[86]
Ne had been known the Danish Gonswart,[87]
Or Paracelsus, with his long sword.[88]

1110 PEREGRINE.   All this, yet, will not do; eight crowns his high.
VOLPONE.   "No more.—Gentlemen, if I had but time to discourse to you the miraculous effects of this my oil, surnamed
Oglio del Scoto;° with the countless catalogue of those I have   *Scoto's oil*
cured of the aforesaid, and many more diseases; the patents
and privileges of all the princes and commonwealths of
Christendom; or but the depositions of those that appeared
on my part, before the signiori of the Sanita[89] and most
learned College of Physicians; where I was authorised, upon
notice taken of the admirable virtues of my medicaments,
1120 and mine own excellency in matter of rare and unknown secrets, not only to disperse them publicly in this famous city,
but in all the territories, that happily joy under the government of the most pious and magnificent states of Italy. But
may some other gallant fellow say, O, there be divers that
make profession to have as good, and as experimented
receipts° as yours: indeed, very many have assayed, like   *tested formulas*
apes, in imitation of that, which is really and essentially in
me, to make of this oil; bestowed great cost in furnaces, stills,
alembecks,° continual fires, and preparation of the   *distilling equipment*
1130 ingredients (as indeed there goes to it six hundred several
simples,° besides some quantity of human fat, for the   *herbs*
conglutination,° which we buy of the anatomists),   *gluing together*
but when these practitioners come to the last decoction,°   *boiling down*
blow, blow, puff, puff, and all flies in fumo:° ha, ha, ha! Poor   *smoke*

---

[84] Two famous Greek physicians.
[85] The wood of the guacum tree from the West Indies, like both tobacco and sassafras, was
then used medicinally.
[86] The medieval Spaniard Raymond Lull (1235–1315) was an alchemist who was thought to
have discovered the philosopher's stone, which transmuted base metal into gold.
[87] The allusion is unclear.
[88] Theophrastus Bombastus von Hohenheim (1493–1541), or Paracelsus as he was known,
was a German chemist and physician who is supposed to have kept secret remedies hidden in
the hilt of his sword.
[89] The Venetian board of examiners which licensed physicians and mountebanks.

wretches! I rather pity their folly and indiscretion, than their loss of time and money; for these may be recovered by industry: but to be a fool born, is a disease incurable.

"For myself, I always from my youth have endeavored to get the rarest secrets, and book them, either in exchange, or for money: I spared nor cost nor labour, where anything was worthy to be learned. And, gentlemen, honourable gentlemen, I will undertake, by virtue of chemical art, out of the honourable hat that covers your head, to extract the four elements; that is to say, the fire, air, water, and earth, and return you your felt without burn or stain. For, whilst others have been at the Balloo,[90] have been at my book; and am now past the craggy paths of study, and come to the flowery plains of honour and reputation."

SIR POLITICK.   I do assure you, sir, that is his aim.

VOLPONE.   "But to our price—"

PEREGRINE.   And that withal, Sir Pol.

VOLPONE.   "You all know, honourable gentlemen, I never valued this ampulla, or vial, at less than eight crowns; but for this time, I am content to be deprived of it for six; six crowns is the price, and less in courtesy I know you cannot offer me; take it or leave it, howsoever, both it and I am at your service. I ask you not as the value of the thing, for then I should demand of you a thousand crowns, so the Cardinals Montalto, Fernese, the great Duke of Tuscany,[91] my gossip,°   *godfather* with divers other princes, have given me; but I despise money. Only to show my affection to you, honourable gentlemen, and your illustrious State here, I have neglected the messages of these princes, mine own offices, framed my journey hither, only to present you with the fruits of my travels.— Tune your voices once more to the touch of your instruments, and give the honourable assembly some delightful recreation."

PEREGRINE.   What monstrous and most painful circumstance
Is here, to get some three or four gazettes,°   *small change*
Some threepence in the whole! for that 'twill come to.

[NANO *sings.*]

You that would last long, list to my song,
Make no more coil,° but buy of this oil.   *ado*
Would you be ever fair and young?
Stout of teeth, and strong of tongue?
Tart of palate? quick of ear?
Sharp of sight? of nostril clear?
Moist of hand? and light of foot?

---

[90] A game in which a huge ball is driven forward by a flat piece of wood fastened to the arm. [Editors' note]

[91] Three historical figures of sixteenth-century Italy.

> Or, I will come nearer to't,
> Would you live free from all diseases?
> 1180   Do the act your mistress pleases,
> Yet fright all aches from your bones?
> Here's a med'cine for the nones."

VOLPONE.   "Well, I am in a humour at this time to make a
present of the small quantity my coffer contains; to the rich
in courtesy, and to the poor for God's sake. Wherefore now
mark: I asked you six crowns; and six crowns, at other times,
you have paid me; you shall not give me six crowns, nor five,
nor four, nor three, nor two, nor one; nor half a ducat; no,
nor a moccinigo.[92] Sixpence it will cost you, or six hundred
1190   pound—expect no lower price, for, by the banner of my   *a small coin*
front, I will not bate a bagatine,° —that I will have, only,
a pledge of your loves, to carry something from amongst
you, to show I am not contemned by you. Therefore, now,
toss your handkerchiefs, cheerfully, cheerfully; and be
advertised,° that the first heroic spirit that deigns to grace   *aware*
me with a handkerchief, I will give it a little remembrance of
something, beside, shall please it better than if I had pre-
sented it with a double pistolet."°   *Spanish gold piece*
PEREGRINE.   Will you be that *herioc spark,*° Sir Pol?   *young gentleman*

[CELIA, *at a window above, throws down her handkerchief.*]

1200   O, see! the window has prevented° you.   *anticipated*
VOLPONE.   "Lady, I kiss your bounty; and for this timely grace
you have done your poor Scoto of Mantua, I will return you,
over and above my oil, a secret of that high and inestimable
nature, shall make you for ever enamoured on that minute,
wherein your eye first descended on so mean, yet not altogether to be despised, an object. Here is a powder concealed
in this paper, of which, if I should speak to the worth, nine
thousand volumes were but as one page, that page as a line,
that line as a word; so short is this pilgrimmage of man
1210   (which some call life) to the expressing of it. Would I reflect
on the price? why, the whole world is but as an empire, that
empire as a province, that province as a bank, that bank as a
private purse to the purchase of it. I will only tell you; it is
the powder that made Venus a goddess (given her by
Apollo), that kept her perpetually young, cleared her wrin-
kles, firmed her gums, filled her skin, coloured her hair;
from her derived° to Helen, and at the sack of Troy unfortu-   *conveyed*
nately lost: til now, in this our age, it was as happily recovered, by a studious antiquary, out of some ruins of Asia, who
1220   sent a moiety° of it to the court of France (but much sophis-   *part*
ticated), wherewith the ladies there now colour their hair.

---

[92] A small coin used in Venice worth about ninepence. [Editors' note]

The rest, at this present, remains with me; extracted to a
quintessence: so that, wherever it but touches, in youth it
perpetually preserves, in age restores the complexion; seats
your teeth, did they dance like virginal jacks,[93] firm as a
wall: makes them white as ivory, that were black as——"

                                                                    [*Enter* Corvino.]

CORVINO.   Spite o' the devil, and my shame! come down here;
   Come down;—No house but mine to make your scene?
   Signior Flaminio,[94] will you down, sir? down?
1230   What, is my wife your Fransciscina, sir?
   No windows on the whole Piazza, here,
   To make your properties, but mine? but mine?

                                                      [*Beats away* Volpone, Nano, &c.]

   Heart! ere to-morrow I shall be new christened,
   And called the Pantalone di Besogniosi,[95]
   About the town.
PEREGRINE.   What should this mean, Sir Pol?
SIR POLITICK.   Some trick of state, believe it; I will home.
PEREGRINE.   It may be some design on you.
SIR POLITICK.   I know not.
1240 I'll stand upon my guard.
PEREGRINE.   It is your best, sir.
SIR POLITICK.   This three weeks, all my advices, all my letters,
   They have been intercepted.
PEREGRINE.   Indeed sir!
   Best have a care.
SIR POLITICK.   Nay, so I will.
PEREGRINE.   This knight,
   I may not lose him, for my mirth, till night.   [*Exeunt.*]

SCENE II

A room in Volpone's *House*

                                                      [*Enter* Volpone *and* Mosca.]

VOLPONE.   O, I am wounded!
1250 MOSCA.   Where, sir?
VOLPONE.   Not without;
   Those blows were nothing: I could bear them ever.
   But angry Cupid, bolting° from her eyes,   *shooting bolts*
   Hath shot himself into me like a flame;

---

[93] The keys of a small spinet.
[94] Some scholars believe that this is a reference to a contemporary Venetian actor.
[95] The Pantaloon of Beggars, a comic figure of contemporary Italian theater, the *commedia dell'arte.*

Where now he flings about his burning heat,
As in a furnace an ambitious° fire,   *growing*
Whose vent is stopt. The fight is all within me.
I cannot live, except thou help me, Mosca;
My liver melts,[96] and I, without the hope
1260   Of some soft air, from her refreshing breath,
Am but a heap of cinders.
MOSCA.   'Las, good sir,
Would you had never seen her!
VOLPONE.   Nay, would thou
Hadst never told me of her!
MOSCA.   Sir, 'tis true;
I do confess I was unfortunate,
And you unhappy; but I'm bound in conscience,
No less than duty, to effect my best
1270   To your release of torment, and I will, sir.
VOLPONE.   Dear Mosca, shall I hope?
MOSCA.   Sir, more than dear,
I will not bid you to despair of aught
Within a human compass.
VOLPONE.   O, there spoke
My better angel. Mosca, take my keys,
Gold, plate, and jewels, all's at thy devotion;°   *service*
Employ them how thou wilt: nay, coin me too:
So thou in this but crown my longings, Mosca.
1280 MOSCA.   Use but your patience.
VOLPONE.   So I have.
MOSCA.   I doubt not
To bring success to your desires.
VOLPONE.   Nay, then,
I not repent me of my late disguise.
MOSCA.   If you can horn° him, sir, you need not.   *cuckold*
VOLPONE.   True:
Besides, I never meant him for my heir.
Is not the colour of my beard and eyebrows
1290   To make me known?
MOSCA.   No jot.
VOLPONE.   I did it well.
MOSCA.   So well, would I could follow you in mine,
With half the happiness! and yet I would
Escape your epilogue.[97]   *[Aside.]*
VOLPONE.   But were they gulled
With a belief that I was Scoto?
MOSCA.   Sir,
Scoto himself could hardly have distinguished!

---

[96] The liver was thought to be the source of such passions as love and jealousy.
[97] That is, the beating you received.

1300   I have not time to flatter you now, we'll part:
        And as I prosper, so applaud my art.   [*Exeunt.*]

SCENE III

A room in CORVINO'S *House*

     [*Enter* CORVINO, *with his sword in his hand, dragging in* CELIA.]

CORVINO.   Death to mine honour, with the city's fool!
     A juggling, tooth-drawing, prating mountebank!
     And at a public window! where, whilst he,
     With his strained action, and his dole° of faces,   *mask*
     To his drug-lecture draws your itching ears,
     A crew of old, unmarried, noted letchers,
     Stood leering up like satyrs: and you smile
     Most graciously, and fan your favours° forth,   *shower your approval*
1310   To give your hot spectators satisfaction!
     What, was your montebank their call? their whistle?
     Or were you enamoured on his copper rings,
     His saffron jewel, with the toad-stone[98] in't,
     Or his embroidered suit, with the cope-stitch,°   *used in embroidering*
     Made of a herse cloth? or his old tilt-feather?°   *plume feather*
     Or his starched beard! Well you shall have him, yes!
     He shall come home, and minister unto you
     The fricare for the mother.[99] Or, let me see,
     I think you'd rather mount; would you not mount?
1320   Why, if you'll mount, you may; yes, truly, you may!
     And so you may be seen, down to the foot.
     Get you a cittern,° Lady Vanity,[100]   *a kind of guitar*
     And be a dealer with the virtuous man;
     Make one: I'll but protest myself a cuckold,
     And save your dowry. I'm a Dutchman, I!
     For if you thought me an Italian,
     You would be damned ere you did this, you whore!
     Thou'dst tremble, to imagine, that the murder
     Of father, mother, brother, all thy race,
1330   Should follow, as the subject of my justice.
CELIA.   Good sir, have patience.
CORVINO.   What couldst thou propose
     Less to thyself, than in this heat of wrath,
     And stung with my dishonour, I should strike
     This steel into thee, with as many stabs
     As thou wert gazed upon with goatish eyes?

---

[98] An agate-like stone worn as a charm.
[99] Literally, a massage for hysteria, which was then thought to be connected with the womb.
There is sexual innuendo here as in the dialogue that follows.
[100] An allegorical stock character out of an English morality play.

CELIA.   Alas, sir, be appeased! I could not think
    My being at the window should more now
    Move your impatience than at other times.
1340 CORVINO.   No! not to seek and entertain a parley
    With a known knave, before a multitude!
    You were an actor with your handkerchief,
    Which he most sweetly kist in the receipt,
    And might, no doubt, return it with a letter,
    And point the place where you might meet; your sister's,
    Your mother's or your aunt's might serve the turn.
CELIA.   Why, dear sir, when do I make these excuses
    Or ever stir abroad, but to the church?
    And that so seldom—
1350 CORVINO.   Well, it shall be less;
    And thy restraint before was liberty,
    To what I now decree: and therefore mark me.
    First, I will have this bawdy light dammed up;
    And till't be done, some two or three yards off,
    I'll chalk a line; o'er which if thou but chance
    To set thy desperate foot, more hell, more horror,
    More wild remorseless rage shall seize on thee,
    Than on a conjuror that had heedless left
    His circle's[101] safety ere his devil was laid.°   *exorcised*
1360   Then here's a lock° which I will hang upon thee,   *chastity belt*
    And, now I think on't, I will keep thee backwards;
    Thy lodging shall be backwards; thy walks backwards;
    Thy prospect, all be backwards; and no pleasure,
    That thou shalt know but backwards: nay, since you force
    My honest nature, know, it is your own,
    Being too open, makes me use you thus:
    Since you will not contain your subtle nostrils
    In a sweet room, but they must snuff the air
    Of rank and sweaty passengers.°   *passers by*

                                                            [*Knocking within.*]

1370   One knocks.
    Away, and be not seen, pain of thy life;
    Nor look toward the window; if thou dost—
    Nay, stay, hear this—let me not prosper, whore,
    But I will make thee an anatomy.°   *use you as a cadaver*
    Dissect thee mine own self, and read a lecture
    Upon thee to the city, and in public.
    Away!—

                                                            [*Exit* CELIA]

                                                            [*Enter* SERVANT.]

    Who's there?
SERVANT.   'Tis Signior Mosca, sir.

---

[101] The conjuror's circle in which he was safe from any devil he called up.

1380   Corvino.   Let him come in. [*Exit Servant.*] His master's
      dead; there's yet
      Some good to help the bad.

                                                [*Enter* Mosca.]

                         My Mosca, welcome!
      I guess your news.
      Mosca.   I fear you cannot, sir.
      Corvino.   Is't not his death?
      Mosca.   Rather the contrary.
      Corvino.   Not his recovery.
      Mosca.   Yes, sir.
1390   Corvino.   I am cursed,
      I am bewitched, my crosses meet to vex me.
      How? how? how? how?
      Mosca.   Why, sir, with Scoto's oil;
      Corbaccio and Voltore brought of it,
      Whilst I was busy in an inner room—
      Corvino.   Death! that damned mountebank! but for the law
      Now, I could kill the rascal: it cannot be
      His oil should have that virtue. Have not I
      Known him a common rogue, come fiddling in
1400   To the osteria,[102] with a tumbling whore,
      And, when he has done all his forced tricks, been glad
      Of a poor spoonful of dead wine, with flies in't?
      It cannot be. All his ingredients
      Are a sheep's gall, a roasted bitch's marrow,
      Some few sod° earwigs, pounded caterpillars,   *boiled*
      A little capon's grease, and fasting spittle:[103]
      I know them to a dram.
      Mosca.   I know not, sir;
      But some on't, there, they poured into his ears,
1410   Some in his nostrils, and recovered him;
      Applying but the fricace.
      Corvino.   Pox o' that fricace!°   *massage*
      Mosca.   And since, to seem the more officious°   *helpful*
      And flatt'ring of his health, there, they have had,
      At extreme fees, the college of physicians
      Consulting on him, how they might restore him;
      Where one would have a cataplasm° of spices,   *poultice*
      Another a flayed ape clapped to his breast,
      A third would have it a dog, a fourth an oil,
1420   With wild cats' skins: at last, they all resolved
      That to preserve him, was no other means
      But some young woman must be straight sought out,

---

[102] The inn or hotel. [Editors' note]
[103] That is, from someone who has been fasting and is thus hungry.

Lusty, and full of juice, to sleep by him;
And to this service most unhappily,
And most unwillingly, am I now employed,
Which here I thought to pre-acquaint you with,
For your advice, since it concerns you most;
Because I would not do that thing might cross
Your ends, on whom I have my sole dependence, sir;
1430   Yet, if I do it not, they may delate°   *complain of*
My slackness to my patron, work me out
Of his opinion; and there all your hopes,
Ventures, or whatsoever, are all frustrate!
I do but tell you, sir. Besides, they are all
Now striving who shall first present him; therefore—
I could entreat you, briefly conclude somewhat;°   *decide on something*
Prevent them if you can.
    CORVINO.   Death to my hopes,
This is my villainous fortune! Best to hire
1440   Some common courtezan.
    MOSCA.   Ay. I thought on that, sir;
But they are all so subtle, full of art—
And age again doting and flexible,
So as—I cannot tell—we may, perchance,
Light on a quean° may cheat us all.   *whore*
    CORVINO.   'Tis true.
    MOSCA.   No, no: it must be one that has no tricks, sir,
Some simple thing, a creature made unto it;
Some wench you may command. Have you no kinswoman?
1450   Odso[104]—Think, think, think, think, think, think, think, sir.
One o' the doctors offered there his daughter.
    CORVINO.   How!
    MOSCA.   Yes, Signior Lupo,[105] the physician.
    CORVINO.   His daughter!
    MOSCA.   And a virgin, sir. Why, alas,
He knows the state of's body, what it is;
That nought can warm his blood, sir, but a fever;
Nor any incantation raise his spirit:
A long forgetfulness hath seized that part.
1460   Besides, sir, who shall know it? some one or two—
    CORVINO.   I pray thee give me leave. [*Walks aside.*] If any man
But I had had this luck—The thing in't self,
I know, is nothing—Wherefore should not I
As well command my blood° and my affections   *passions*
As this dull doctor? In the point of honour,
The cases are all one of wife and daughter.   [*Aside.*]
    MOSCA.   I hear him coming.°   *coming around*
    CORVINO.   She shall do't: 'tis done.

---

[104] An oath: "By God's soul."
[105] Lupo is Italian for wolf.

Slight!¹⁰⁶ if this doctor, who is not engaged,°   *not deeply involved*
1470   Unless 't be for his counsel, which is nothing,
        Offer his daughter, what should I, that am
        So deeply in? I will prevent him: Wretch!
        Covetous wretch!—Mosca, I have determined.
MOSCA. How, sir?
CORVINO. We'll make sure. The party you wot° of   *know*
        Shall be mine own wife, Mosca.
MOSCA. Sir, the thing,
        But that I would not seem to counsel you,
        I should have motioned° to you, at the first: *proposed*
1480   And make your count, you have cut all their throats.
        Why, 'tis directly taking a possession!
        And in his next fit, we may let him go.
        'Tis but to pull the pillow from his head,
        And he is throttled: it had been done before
        But for your scrupulous doubts.
CORVINO. Ay, a plague on't,
        My conscience fools my wit!° Well, I'll be brief,   *reason*
        And so be thou, lest they should be before us:
        Go home, prepare him, tell him with what zeal
1490   And willingness I do it: swear it was
        On the first hearing, as thou mayst do, truly,
        Mine own free motion.°   *will*
MOSCA. Sir, I warrant you,
        I'll so possess° him with it, that the rest   *impress*
        Of his starved clients shall be banished all;
        And only you received. But come not, sir.
        Until I send, for I have something else
        To ripen for your good, you must not know't.
CORVINO. But do not you forget to send now.
1500 MOSCA. Fear not.   [*Exit.*]
CORVINO. Where are you, wife? my Celia! wife!

                                                          [*Re-enter* CELIA.]

            —What, blubbering?
        Come, dry those tears. I think thou thought'st me in earnest;
        Ha! by this light I talked so but to try thee:
        Methinks, the lightness of the occasion
        Should have confirmed° thee. Come, I am not jealous.   *assured*
CELIA. No!
CORVINO. Faith I am not, I, nor never was;
        It is a poor unprofitable humour.°   *disposition*
1510   Do not I know, if women have a will,°   *sexual appetite*
        They'll do° 'gainst all the watches° of the world,   *betray their husbands / guards*
        And that the fiercest spies are tamed with gold?
        Tut, I am confident in thee, thou shalt see't;

_____
¹⁰⁶ An oath: "By God's light!"

And see I'll give thee cause too, to believe it.
Come kiss me. Go, and make thee ready straight,
In all thy best attire, thy choicest jewels,
Put them all on, and, with them, thy best looks:
We are invited to a solemn feast,
At old Volpone's, where it shall appear
1520 How far I am free from jealousy or fear.   [*Exeunt.*]

ACT THE THIRD

SCENE I

A Street

[*Enter* MOSCA.]

MOSCA.   I fear I shall begin to grow in love
With my dear self, and my most prosperous parts,°   *talents*
They do so spring and burgeon; I can feel
A whimsy° in my blood: I know not how,   *giddiness*
Success hath made me wanton. I could skip
Out of my skin now, like a subtle° snake,   *cunning*
I am so limber. O! your parasite
Is a most precious thing, dropt from above,
Not bred 'mongst clods and clodpoles,° here on earth.   *numbskulls*
1530 I muse, the mystery° was not made a science,   *craft*
It is so liberally profest!° Almost   *widely practiced*
All the wise world is little else, in nature,
But parasites or sub-parasites. And yet
I mean not those that have your bare town-art,[107]
To know who's fit to feed them; have no house,
No family, no care, and therefore mould°   *invent*
Tales for men's ears, to bait that sense; or get
Kitchen-invention,[108] and some stale° receipts   *old*
To please the belly, and the groin; nor those,
1540 With their court dog-tricks, that can fawn and fleer,°   *bow and smirk*
Make their revenue out of legs and faces,
Echo my lord, and lick away a moth:
But your fine elegant rascal, that can rise
And stoop, almost together, like an arrow;
Shoot through the air as nimbly as a star;°   *meteor*
Turn short as doth a swallow; and be here,
And there, and here, and yonder, all at once;
Present to any humour, all occasion;
And change a visor° swifter than a thought!   *mask*
1550 This is the creature had the art born with him;
Toils not to learn it, but doth practice it

---

[107] Wise in the ways of town life.
[108] Presumably new recipes.

Out of most excellent nature:° and such sparks°   *natural talent / dandies*
Are the true parasites, others but their zanis.°   *mimics*

[*Enter* BONARIO.]

Who's this? Bonario, old Corbaccio's son?
The person I was bound to seek. Fair sir,
You are happily met.
BONARIO.   That cannot be by thee.
MOSCA.   Why, sir?
BONARIO.   Nay, pray thee know thy way, and leave me:
1560   I would be loth to interchange discourse
With such a mate° as thou art.   *rogue*
MOSCA.   Courteous sir,
Scorn not my poverty.
BONARIO.   Not I, by heaven;
But thou shalt give me leave to hate thy baseness.
MOSCA.   Baseness!
BONARIO.   Ay; answer me, is not thy sloth
Sufficient argument? thy flattery?
Thy means of feeding?
1570 MOSCA.   Heaven be good to me!
These imputations are too common, sir,
And easily stuck on virtue when she's poor.
You are unequal° to me, and however   *unjust*
Your sentence may be righteous, yet you are not,
That, ere you know me, thus proceed in censure:
St. Mark[109] bear witness 'gainst you, 'tis inhuman.   [*Weeps.*]
BONARIO.   What! does he weep? the sign is soft and good:
I do repent me that I was so harsh.   [*Aside.*]
MOSCA.   'Tis true, that, swayed by strong necessity,
1580   I am enforced to eat my careful° bread   *hard earned*
With too much obsequy;° 'tis true, beside,   *obsequiousness*
That I am fain° to spin mine own poor raiment   *compelled*
Out of my mere observance,° being not born   *service*
To a free fortune: but that I have done
Base offices, in rending friends asunder,
Dividing families, betraying counsels,
Whispering false lies, or mining° men with praises,   *undermining*
Trained° their credulity with perjuries,   *encouraged*
Corrupted chastity, or am in love
1590   With mine own tender ease, but would not rather
Prove° the most rugged and laborious course,   *endure*
That might redeem my present estimation,°   *restore my good name*
Let me here perish, in all hope of goodness,
BONARIO.   This cannot be a personated° passion. [*Aside.*]   *pretended*
I was to blame, so to mistake thy nature;
Prithee forgive me: and speak out thy business.
MOSCA.   Sir, it concerns you; and though I may seem

---

[109] St. Mark is the patron saint of Venice.

At first to make a main° offence in manners,	*major*
And in my gratitude unto my master;	

1600   Yet for the pure love which I bear all right,
And hatred of the wrong, I must reveal it.
This very hour your father is in purpose
To disinherit you—

BONARIO.   How!

MOSCA.   And thrust you forth,
As a mere stranger to his blood: 'tis true, sir.
The work no way engageth me, but, as
I claim an interest in the general state
Of goodness and true virtue, which I hear

1610   To abound in you; and for which mere respect,°   *for which reason alone*
Without a second aim, sir, I have done it.

BONARIO.   This tale hath lost thee much of the late trust
Thou hadst with me; it is impossible:
I know not how to lend it any thought,
My father should be so unnatural.

MOSCA.   It is a confidence that well becomes
Your piety:° and formed, no doubt, it is   *filial love*
From your own simple innocence: which makes
Your wrong more monstrous and abhorred. But, sir,

1620   I now will tell you more. This very minute,
It is, or will be doing; and if you
Shall be but pleased to go with me, I'll bring you,
I dare not say where you shall see, but where
Your ear shall be a witness of the deed;
Hear yourself written bastard, and profest
The common issue of the earth.[110]

BONARIO.   I am mazed!°   *dazed*

MOSCA.   Sir, if I do it not, draw your just sword,
And score your vengeance on my front° and face;   *forehead*

1630   Mark me your villain: you have too much wrong,
And I do suffer for you, sir. My heart
Weeps blood in anguish—

BONARIO.   Lead: I follow thee.   [*Exeunt.*]

SCENE II

A Room in VOLPONE'S *House*

[*Enter* VOLPONE.]

VOLPONE.   Mosca stays long, methinks.—Bring forth your
      sports,
And help to make the wretched time more sweet.

[*Enter* NANO, ANDROGYNO, *and* CASTRONE.]

---

[110] A son of the earth.

NANO.   "Dwarf, fool, and eunuch, well met here we be.
 A question it were now, whether° of us three,   *which*
 Being all the known delicates° of a rich man,   *acknowledged favorites*
1640 In pleasing him, claim the precedency can?"
CASTRONE.   "I claim for myself."
ANDROGYNO.   "And so doth the fool."
NANO.   " 'Tis foolish indeed: let me set you both to school.[111]
 First for your dwarf, he's little and witty,
 And everything, as it is little, is pretty;
 Else why do men say to a creature of my shape,
 So soon as they see him, It's a pretty little ape?
 And why a pretty ape, but for pleasing imitation
 Of greater men's actions, in a ridiculous fashion?
1650 Beside, this feat° body of mine doth not crave   *graceful, trim*
 Half the meat, drink, and cloth, one of your bulks will
  have.
 Admit° your fool's face be the mother of laughter,   *granted*
 Yet, for his brain, it must always come after;
 And though that do feed him, it's a pitiful case,
 His body is beholding° to such a bad face."   *beholden*

          [*Knocking within.*]

VOLPONE.   Who's there? my couch; away! look! Nano, see:

       [*Exeunt* ANDROGYNO *and* CASTRONE.]

 Give me my caps first—go, inquire. [*Exit* NANO.] Now,
  Cupid
1660 Send it be Mosca, and with fair return!
NANO [*within*].   It is the beauteous madam—
VOLPONE.   Would-be—is it?
NANO.   The same.
VOLPONE.   Now torment on me! Squire her in;
 For she will enter, or dwell here for ever:
 Nay, quickly. [*Retires to his couch.*] That my fit were past!
  I fear
 A second hell too, that my loathing this°   *Lady Would-be*
 Will quite expel my appetite to the other:°   *Celia*
1670 Would she were taking now her tedious leave.
 Lord, how it threats me what I am to suffer!

     [*Re-enter* NANO *with* LADY POLITICK WOULD-BE.]

LADY POLITICK.   I thank you, good sir. Pray you signify
 Unto your patron I am here.—This band°   *ruff*
 Shows not my neck enough.—I trouble you, sir;
 Let me request you bid one of my women
 Come hither to me. In good faith, I am drest

---

[111] Teach you both a lesson.

Most favourably to-day! It is no matter:
'Tis well enough.

[*Enter* 1st WAITING-WOMAN.]

Look, see these petulant° things,   troublesome
1680   How they have done this!
    VOLPONE. I do feel the fever
    Entering in at mine ears; O, for a charm,
    To fright it hence!   [*Aside.*]
    LADY POLITICK. Come nearer: is this curl
    In his right place, or this? Why is this higher
    Than all the rest? You have not washed your eyes yet!
    Or do they not stand even in your head?
    Where is your fellow? call her.

[*Exit* 1st WOMAN.]

    NANO. Now, St. Mark
1690   Deliver us! anon she'll beat her women,
    Because her nose is red.

[*Re-enter* 1st *with* 2nd WOMAN]

    LADY POLITICK. I pray you view.
    This tire,° forsooth: are all things apt, or no?   hair arrangement
    1ST WOMAN. One hair a little here sticks out, forsooth.
    LADY POLITICK. Does't so, forsooth, and where was your
        dear sight.
    When it did so, forsooth! What now! bird-eyed?
    And you, too? Pray you, both approach and mend it.
    Now, by that light I muse° you are not ashamed!   wonder
1700   I, that have preached these things so oft unto you.
    Read you the principles, argued all the grounds,
    Disputed every fitness, every grace,
    Called you to counsel of so frequent dressings.
    NANO. More carefully than of your fame or honour.   [*Aside.*]
    LADY POLLITICK. Made you acquainted what an ample dowry
    The knowledge of these things would be unto you,
    Able alone to get you noble husbands
    At your return: and you thus to neglect it!
    Besides, you seeing what a curious° nation   fastidious
1710   The Italians are, what will they say of me?
    The English lady cannot dress herself.
    Here's a fine imputation to our country!
    Well, go your ways, and stay in the next room.
    This focus° was too coarse too; it's no matter—   cosmetic
    Good sir, you'll give them entertainment?°   provide for them

[*Exeunt* NANO *and* WAITING-WOMEN.]

    VOLPONE. The storm comes toward me.
    LADY POLITICK [*goes to the couch*]. How does my Volpone?

VOLPONE.   Troubled with noise, I cannot sleep; I dreamt
   That a strange fury[112] entered now my house,
1720 And, with the dreadful tempest of her breath,
   Did cleave my roof asunder.
LADY POLITICK.   Believe me, and I
   Had the most fearful dream, could I remember't—
VOLPONE.   Out on my fate!° I had given her the occasion   *curse my luck!*
   How to torment me: she will tell me hers.   *[Aside.]*
LADY POLITICK.   Methought the golden mediocrity,°   *golden mean*
   Polite, and delicate—
VOLPONE.   O, if you do love me,
   No more: I sweat, and suffer, at the mention
1730 Of any dream; feel how I tremble yet.
LADY POLITICK.   Alas, good soul! the passion of the heart.°   *heartburn*
   Seed-pearl[113] were good now, boiled with syrup of apples,
   Tincture of gold, and coral, citron-pills,
   Your elicampane root, myrobalanes—
VOLPONE.   Ah me, I have ta'en a grasshopper by the wing!   *[Aside.]*
LADY POLITICK.   Burnt silk and amber. You have muscadel°   *wine*
   Good in the house—
VOLPONE.   You will not drink, and part?
LADY POLITICK.   No, fear not that. I doubt we shall not get
1740 Some English saffron, half a dram would serve;
   Your sixteen cloves, a little musk, dried mints;
   Bugloss, and barley-meal—
VOLPONE.   She's in again!
   Before I feigned diseases, now I have one.   *[Aside.]*
LADY POLITICK.   And these applied with a right scarlet cloth.
VOLPONE.   Another flood of words! a very torrent!   *[Aside.]*
LADY POLITICK.   Shall I, sir, make you a poultice?
VOLPONE.   No, no, no.
   I'm very well, you need prescribe no more.
1750 LADY POLITICK.   I have a little studied physic; but now
   I'm all for music, save, in the forenoons,
   An hour or two for painting, I would have
   A lady, indeed, to have° all letters and arts,   *know*
   Be able to discourse, to write, to paint,
   But principal, as Plato holds, your music,
   And so does wise Pythagoras, I take it,
   Is your true rapture: when there is concent[114]
   In face, in voice, and clothes: and is, indeed,
   Our sex's chiefest ornament.
1760 VOLPONE.   The poet
   As old in time as Plato, and as knowing,
   Say that your highest female grace is silence.

---

[112] The Furies were the Greek goddesses of vengeance.
[113] A popular remedy. It is followed by a catalog of such recipes.
[114] I.e., agreement or harmony. [Editors' note]

LADY POLITICK.　Which of your poets? Petrarch,[115] or Tasso,
　　or Dante?
　　Guarini, Ariosto? Aretine?
　　Cieco di Hadria? I have read them all.
VOLPONE.　Is everything a cause to my destruction?　　　　　*[Aside.]*
LADY POLITICK.　I think I have two or three of them about
　　me.
1770　VOLPONE.　The sun, the sea, will sooner both stand still
　　Than her eternal tongue! nothing can scape it.　　　　　*[Aside.]*
LADY POLITICK.　Here's Pastor Fido—[116]
VOLPONE.　Profess obstinate silence;
　　That now my safest.° *[Aside.]*　　　　　　　　　　　　　*my safest course*
LADY POLITICK.　All our English writers,
　　I mean such as are happy° in the Italian,　　　　　　　　　　*fluent*
　　Will deign to steal out of this author, mainly;
　　Almost as much as from Montagnié:[117]
　　He has so modern and facile° a vein,　　　　　　　　　　　*up to date*
1780　Fitting the time, and catching the court-ear!
　　Your Petrarch is more passionate,[118] yet he,
　　In days of sonnetting, trusted them with much;
　　Dante is hard, and few can understand him.
　　But for a desperate° wit, there's Aretine;[119]　　　　　　　*outrageous*
　　Only his pictures are a little obscene—
　　You mark me not.
VOLPONE.　Alas, my mind's perturbed.
LADY POLITICK.　Why, in such cases, we must cure ourselves.
　　Make use of our philosophy—
1790　VOLPONE.　Oh me!
LADY POLITICK.　And as we find our passions do rebel,
　　Encounter them with treason, or divert them,
　　By giving scope unto some other humour
　　Of lesser danger: as, in politic° bodies,　　　　　　　　　*governing*
　　There's nothing more doth overwhelm the judgment,
　　And cloud the understanding, than too much
　　Settling and fixing, and, as 'twere, subsiding
　　Upon one object. For the incorporating
　　Of these same outward things, into that part,

---

　[115] Petrarch (1304–1374), Tasso (1554–1595), Dante (1265–1321), Guarini (1538–1612), Ariosto (1474–1533), Aretino (1492–1556), Cieco di Hadria (1541–1585). These and the other poets and writers named below were Italians who became well-known in England during the Renaissance.
　[116] *The Faithful Shepherd* (1590), a popular pastoral comedy by Giovanni Battista Guarini (1538–1612).
　[117] Michel de Montaigne (1533–1592) was the famous French essayist and sceptic.
　[118] The allusion is to Petrarch's well-known sequence of over 300 love sonnets.
　[119] The notorious Italian writer Pietro Aretino (1492–1556), authored satirical and often scurrilous sonnets and produced equally obscene engravings.

1800   Which we call mental, leaves some certain fæces°   *sediment*
       That stop the organs, and, as Plato says,
       Assassinate our knowledge.
    Volpone.   Now, the spirit
       Of patience help me!   *[Aside.]*
    Lady Politick.   Come, in faith, I must
       Visit you more a days;° and make you well: *on more or other days*
       Laugh and be lusty.°   *merry, lustful*
    Volpone.   My good angel save me!   *[Aside.]*
    Lady Politick.   There was but one sole man in all the world
1810   With whom I e'er could sympathise; and he
       Would lie you, often, three, four hours together
       To hear me speak; and be sometime so rapt,
       As he would answer me quite from the purpose,°   *off the point*
       Like you, and you are like him, just. I'll discourse,
       An't be but only sir, to bring you asleep,
       How we did spend our time and loves together,
       For some six years.
    Volpone.   Oh, oh, oh, oh, oh, oh!
    Lady Politick.   For we were coætanei,° and brought up—   *of the same age*
1820 Volpone.   Some power, some fate, some fortune rescue me!

                                                  [Enter Mosca.*]*

    Mosca.   God save you, madam!
    Lady Politick.   Good sir.
    Volpone.   Mosca! welcome,
       Welcome to my redemption.
    Mosca.   Why, sir?
    Volpone.   Oh,
       Rid me of this my torture, quickly, there;
       My madam with the everlasting voice:
       The bells, in time of pestilence,[120] ne'er made
1830   Like noise, or were in that perpetual motion!
       The Cock-pit[121] comes not near it. All my house,
       But now, steamed like a bath with her thick breath,
       A lawyer could not have been heard; nor scarce
       Another woman, such a hail of words
       She has let fall. For hell's sake, rid her hence.
    Mosca.   Has she presented?°   *handed over a present*
    Volpone.   Oh, I do not care!
       I'll take her absence upon any price,
       With any loss.
1840 Mosca.   Madam—
    Lady Politick.   I have brought your patron
       A toy,° a cap here, of mine own work.   *trifle*
    Mosca.   'Tis well.

---

[120] In time of plague the bells of London were rung continuously.
[121] The enclosed arena where cock fights were held, noted for its noise.

I had forgot to tell you I saw your knight,
Where you would little think it.—
LADY POLITICK.   Where?
MOSCA.   Marry,°   *Virgin Mary*
Where yet, if you make haste, you may apprehend him,
Rowing upon the water in a gondole,°   *gondola*
1850   With the most cunning courtezan of Venice.
LADY POLITICK.   Is't true?
MOSCA.   Pursue them, and believe your eyes:
Leave me to make your gift.   [*Exit* LADY POLITICK *hastily.*]
I knew 'twould take:
For, lightly,° they that use themselves most licence,   *commonly*
Are still most jealous.
VOLPONE.   Mosca, hearty thanks,
For thy quick fiction, and delivery of me.
Now to my hopes, what sayst thou?

[*Re-enter* LADY POLITICK WOULD-BE.]

1860   LADY POLITICK.   But do you hear, sir?—
VOLPONE.   Again! I fear a paroxysm.
LADY POLITICK.   Which way
Rowed they together?
MOSCA.   Toward the Rialto.[122]
LADY POLITICK.   I pray you lend me your dwarf.
MOSCA.   I pray you take him.   [*Exit* LADY POLITICK.]
Your hopes, sir, are like happy blossoms, fair,
And promise timely fruit, if you will stay
But the maturing; keep you at your couch,
1870   Corbaccio will arrive straight, with the Will;   [*Exit*]
When he is gone, I'll tell you more.
VOLPONE.   My blood,
My spirits are returned; I am alive;
And, like your wanton° gamester° at primero,[123]   *reckless, lecherous / gambler*
Whose thought had whispered to him, not go less,
Methinks I lie, and draw—for an encounter.

[*The scene closes upon* VOLPONE.]

SCENE III

The Passage leading to VOLPONE'S *Chamber*

[*Enter* MOSCA *and* BONARIO.]

MOSCA.   Sir, here concealed [*shows him a closet.*] you may hear all. But
pray you,
Have patience, sir [*knocking within.*]—the same's your father knocks:

---

122 The bridge over Venice's Grand Canal.
123 Primero was a card game of the period.

1880　　I am compelled to leave you. 　　　　　　　　　　　　　　*[Exit.]*
　　BONARIO.　Do so.—Yet.
　　　　Cannot my thought imagine this a truth.

　　　　　　　　　　　　　　　　　　　　　[Goes into the closet.]

SCENE IV

　　Another part of the Same

　　　　　　　　　　[Enter MOSCA *and* CORVINO, CELIA *following.]*

　　MOSCA.　Death on me! you are come too soon, what meant you?
　　　　Did not I say I would send?
　　CORVINO.　Yes, but I feared
　　　　You might forget it, and then they prevent us.
　　MOSCA.　Prevent! Did e'er man haste so for his horns?° 　　*the horns of a cuckold*
　　　　A courtier would not ply it so for a place.° 　　*[Aside.]* 　　*sinecure, position at court*
　　　　Well, now there is no helping it, stay here;
1890　　I'll presently return.
　　CORVINO.　Where are you, Celia?
　　　　You know not wherefore I have brought you hither?
　　CELIA.　Not well, except you told me.° 　　　　　*only what you told me before*
　　CORVINO.　Now I will:
　　　　Hark hither. 　　　　　　　　　　　　　　　　　*[Exeunt.]*

SCENE V

　　A Closet opening into a Gallery

　　　　　　　　　　　　[Enter MOSCA *and* BONARIO.]

　　MOSCA.　Sir, your father hath sent word,
　　　　It will be half an hour ere he come;
　　　　And therefore, if you please to walk the while
　　　　Into that gallery—at the upper end,
1900　　There are some books to entertain the time:
　　　　And I'll take care no man shall come unto you, sir.
　　BONARIO.　Yes, I will stay there—I do doubt this fellow.

　　　　　　　　　　　　　　　　　　　　[Aside, and exit.]

　　MOSCA *[looking after him]*.　There; he is far enough; he
　　　　can hear nothing:
　　　　And for his father, I can keep him off. 　　　　　*[Exit.]*

SCENE VI

　　VOLPONE's *Chamber,* VOLPONE *on his couch.* MOSCA *sitting by him.*

　　　　　　　　　　　　[Enter CORVINO, *forcing in* CELIA.]

　　CORVINO.　Nay, now, there is no starting back, and therefore,
　　　　Resolve upon it: I have so decreed.
　　　　It must be done. Nor would I move't° afore, 　　　*urge, propose*

Because I would avoid all shifts° and tricks,   *evasions*
1910   That might deny me.
    CELIA.   Sir, let me beseech you,
      Affect not these strange trials; if you doubt
      My chastity, why, lock me up for ever;
      Make me the heir of darkness. Let me live
      Where I may please your fears,° if not your trust.   *set your fears at rest*
    CORVINO.   Believe it, I have no such humour,° I.   *pretence*
      All that I speak I mean; yet I'm not mad;
      Not horn-mad, you see? Go to, show yourself
      Obedient, and a wife.
1920 CELIA.   O heaven!
    CORVINO.   I say it,
      Do so.
    CELIA.   Was this the train?°   *trap, trick*
    CORVINO.   I've told you reasons;
      What the physicians have set down; how much
      It may concern me;° what my engagements are;   *I stand to gain*
      My means, and the necessity of those means
      For my recovery: wherefore, if you be
      Loyal, and mine, be won, respect° my venture.   *support*
1930 CELIA.   Before your honour?
    CORVINO.   Honour? tut, a breath:
      There's no such thing in nature; a mere term
      Invented to awe fools. What is my gold
      The worse for touching, clothes for being looked on?
      Why, this 's no more. An old decrepit wretch,
      That has no sense, no sinew; takes his meat
      With others' fingers:° only knows to gape   *must be fed*
      When you do scald his gums; a voice, a shadow;
      And what can this man hurt you?
1940 CELIA.   Lord! what spirit
      Is this hath entered him?   *[Aside.]*
    CORVINO.   And for your fame,
      That's such a jig;° as if I would go tell it,   *farce, joke*
      Cry it on the Piazza! who shall know it
      But he that cannot speak it, and this fellow,
      Whose lips are in my pocket? Save yourself,
      (If you'll proclaim't, you may,) I know no other
      Should come to know it.
    CELIA.   Are heaven and saints then nothing?
1950   Will they be blind or stupid?
    CORVINO.   How!
    CELIA.   good sir,
      Be jealous still, emulate them;° and think   *i.e., the saints*
      What hate they burn with toward every sin.
    CORVINO.   I grant you: if I thought it were a sin
      I would not urge you. Should I offer this
      To some young Frenchman, or hot Tuscan blood
      That had read Aretine, conned all his prints,
      Knew every quirk within lust's labyrinth,

1960   And were profest critic° in lechery,   *expert*
        And° I would look upon him, and applaud him,   *if*
        This were a sin: but here, 'tis contrary,
        A pious work, mere charity for physic,
        And honest polity, to assure mine own.
    CELIA.   O heaven! canst thou suffer such a change?
    VOLPONE.   Thou art mine honour, Mosca, and my pride
        My joy, my tickling, my delight! Go bring them.
    MOSCA [*advancing*].   Please you draw near, sir.
    CORVINO.   Come on, what—
1970   You will not be rebellious? by that light—
    MOSCA.   Sir,
        Signior Corvino, here, is come to see you.
    VOLPONE.   Oh!
    MOSCA.   And hearing of the consultation had,
        So lately, for your health, is come to offer,
        Or rather, sir to prostitute—
    CORVINO.   Thanks, sweet Mosca.
    MOSCA.   Freely, unasked, or unintreated—
    CORVINO.   Well.
1980 MOSCA.   As the true fervent instance of his love,
        His own most fair and proper wife; the beauty
        Only of price° in Venice—   *the only precious beauty*
    CORVINO.   'Tis well urged.
    MOSCA.   To be your comfortress, and to preserve you.
    VOLPONE.   Alas, I am past, already! Pray you, thank him
        For his good care and promptness; but for that,
        'Tis a vain labour e'en to fight 'gainst heaven;
        Applying fire to stone—uh, uh, uh, uh!   [*Coughing.*]
        Making a dead leaf grow again. I take
1990   His wishes gently, though; and you may tell him
        What I have done for him: marry, my state is hopeless.
        Will him to pray for me; and to use his fortune
        With reverence when he comes to 't.
    MOSCA.   Do you hear, sir?
        Go to him with your wife.
    CORVINO.   Heart of my father!
        Wilt thou persist thus? Come, I pray thee, come.
        Thou see'st 'tis nothing, Celia. By this hand
        I shall grow violent. Come, do't, I say.
2000 CELIA.   Sir, kill me, rather: I will take down poison,
        Eat burning coals, do anything—
    CORVINO.   Be damned!
        Heart, I will drag thee hence home by the hair;
        Cry thee a strumpet through the streets; rip up
        Thy mouth unto thine ears, and slit thy nose,
        Like a raw rochet![124]—Do not tempt me: come,
        Yield, I am loth—Death! I will buy some slave

---

[124] A *rochet* or *rouget*, so named for its red colour, is a fish of the gurnet kind. [Editors' note]

Whom I will kill, and bind thee to him alive!
And at my window hang you forth, devising
2010   Some monstrous crime, which I, in capital letters,
Will eat into thy flesh with aquafortis,°   *nitric acid*
And burning corsives,° on this stubborn breast.   *corrosives*
Now, by the blood thou hast incensed, I'll do it!
CELIA.   Sir, what you please, you may, I am your martyr.
CORVINO.   Be not thus obstinate, I have not deserved it:
Think who it is intreats you. Prithee, sweet;—
Good faith, thou shalt have jewels, gowns, attires,
What thou wilt think, and ask. Do but go kiss him.
Or touch him but. For my sake. At my suit—
2020   This once. No! not! I shall remember this.
Will you disgrace me thus? do you thirst my undoing?
MOSCA.   Nay, gentle lady, be advised.
CORVINO.   No, no.
She has watched her time. Ods precious,[125] this is scurvy,
'Tis very scurvy; and you are—
MOSCA.   Nay, good sir.
CORVINO.   An arrant locust—by heaven, a locust!°—   *a destructive pestilence*
Whore, crocodile, that hast thy tears prepared,   *or blight*
Expecting how thou'lt bid them flow—
2030 MOSCA.   Nay, pray you, sir!
She will consider.
CELIA.   Would my life would serve
To satisfy—
CORVINO.   'Sdeath![126] if she would but speak to him,
And save my reputation, it were somewhat;
But spitefully to affect my utter ruin!
MOSCA.   Ay, now you have put your fortune in her hands.
Why i'faith, it is her modesty, I must quit° her.   *acquit*
If you were absent, she would be more coming;°   *subservient*
2040   I know it: and dare undertake for her.
What woman can before her husband? pray you,
Let us depart, and leave her here.
CORVINO.   Sweet Celia,
Thou mayst redeem all yet; I'll say no more:
If not, esteem yourself as lost. Nay, stay there.

                                        [*Shuts the door and exit with* MOSCA.]

CELIA.   O God, and his good angels! whither, whither,
Is shame fled human breasts? that with such ease,
Men dare put off your honours, and their own?
Is that, which ever was a cause of life,
2050   Now placed beneath the basest circumstance,
And modesty an exile made, for money?

---

[125] An oath: "By God's precious blood."
[126] An oath: "By God's death!"

VOLPONE.   Ay, in Corvino, and such earth-fed minds,

[*Leaping from his couch.*]

That never tasted the true heaven of love.
Assure thee, Celia, he that would sell thee,
Only for hope of gain, and that uncertain,
He would have sold his part of Paradise
For ready money, had he met a cope-man.[127]
Why art thou mazed° to see me thus revived?   amazed
Rather applaud thy beauty's miracle;
2060   'Tis thy great work: that hath, not now alone,
But sundry times raised me, in several shapes,
And, but this morning, like a mountebank,
To see thee at thy window: ay, before
I would have left my practice,° for thy love,   scheming
In varying figures, I would have contented
With the blue Proteus,[128] or the horned flood.[129]
Now art thou welcome.
CELIA.   Sir!
VOLPONE.   Nay, fly me not.
2070   Nor let thy false imagination
That I was bed-rid, make thee think I am so:
Thou shalt not find it. I am now as fresh,
As hot, as high, and in as jovial plight
As, when, in that so celebrated scene,
At recitation of our comedy,
For entertainment of the great Valois,[130]
I acted young Antinous;[131] and attracted
The eyes and ears of all the ladies present,
To admire each graceful gesture, note, and footing.°   dance step

[*Sings.*]

2080   Come, my Celia, let us prove°   engage in, test
                  While we can, the sports of love,
                  Time will not be ours for ever,
                  He, at length, our good will sever;°   end
                  Spend not then his gifts in vain:
                  Suns that set may rise again;
                  But if once we lost this light,
                  'Tis with us perpetual night.
                  Why should we defer our joys?

---

[127] I.e., chapman, peddler, trader. [Editors' note]

[128] The Old Man of the Sea of Greek mythology, a sea god who had the ability to transform himself into various shapes.

[129] An allusion to the river god Achelous. One of his protean incarnations was as a bull.

[130] Henry III (1551–1589), King of France from 1574 to 1589. On his visit to Venice in 1574 he was regally entertained.

[131] Antinous, a young man noted for his beauty, was a favorite of the Emperor Hadrian (76–138 A.D.).

	Fame and rumour are but toys.°	*toys*
2090	Cannot we delude the eyes	
	Of a few poor household spies?	
	Or his easier ears beguile,	
	Thus removed by our wile?	

'Tis no sin love's fruits to steal;
But the sweet thefts to reveal:
To be taken, to be seen,
These have crimes accounted been.

CELIA.   Some serene° blast me, or dire lightning strike   *noxious vapors*
This my offending face!

2100 VOLPONE.   Why droops my Celia?
Thou hast, in the place of a base husband found
A worthy lover: use thy fortune well,
With secrecy and pleasure. See, behold,
What thou art queen of; not in expectation,
As I feed others: but possessed and crowned.
See, here, a rope of pearl; and each more orient
Than the brave Ægyptian queen caroused:[132]
Dissolve and drink them. See, a carbuncle,°   *a red gem*
May put out both the eyes of our St. Mark;

2110 A diamond would have bought Lollia Paulina,
When she came in like star-light, hid with jewels,
That were the spoils of provinces,[133] take these
And wear, and lose them; yet remains an earring
To purchase them again, and this whole state.
A gem but worth a private partrimony,
Is nothing; we will eat such a meal.
The heads of parrots, tongues of nightingales,
The brains of peacocks, and of estriches,
Shall be our food, and, could we get the phoenix,[134]

2120 Though nature lost her kind, she were our dish.
CELIA.   Good sir, these things might move a mind affected
With such delights; but I, whose innocence
Is all I can think wealthy, or worth th' enjoying,
And which, once lost, I have nought to lose beyond it.
Cannot be taken with these sensual baits:
If you have conscience—
VOLPONE.   'Tis the beggar's virtue;
If thou hast wisdom, hear me, Celia,
Thy baths shall be the juice of July-flowers,

2130 Spirit of roses, and of violets,

---

[132] The allusion is to Cleopatra of Egypt, who during a banquet drank pearls dissolved in vinegar on a wager from Antony.

[133] The historian Pliny reported that Lollia Paulina, the wife of a Roman governor, appeared in public resplendent in jewels looted by her husband from several provinces.

[134] Only one of these mythical birds was said to live at any one time.

The milk of unicorns, and panthers' breath[135]
Gathered in bags, and mixed with Cretan wines.[136]
Our drink shall be prepared gold and amber;
Which we will take until my roof whirl round
With the vertigo: and my dwarf shall dance,
My eunuch sing, my fool make up the antic,°   *grotesque dance*
Whilst we, in changed shapes, act Ovid's tales,[137]
Thou, like Europa now, and I like Jove,[138]
Then I like Mars, and thou like Erycine:[139]
So of the rest, till we have quite run through,
And wearied all the fables of the gods,
Then will I have thee in more modern forms,
Attired like some sprightly dame of France,
Brave Tuscan lady, or proud Spanish beauty;
Sometimes unto the Persian sophy's[140] wife;
Or the grand signior's[141] mistress; and for change,
To one of our most artful courtezans,
Or some quick° Negro, or cold Russian: *vigorous*
And I will meet thee in as many shapes:
Where we may so transfuse our wandering souls
Out at our lips, and score up sums of pleasures,   [*Sings.*]

That the curious shall not know
How to tell° them as they flow;   *count*
And the envious, when they find
What their number is, be pined.°   *pine with envy*

CELIA.   If you have ears that will be pierced—or eyes
That can be opened—a heart that may be touched—
Or any part that yet sounds man above you—
If you have touch of holy saints—or heaven
Do me the grace to let 'scape—if not,
Be bountiful and kill me. You do know,
I am a creature, hither ill betrayed,
By one whose shame I would forget it were:
If you will deign me neither of these graces,
Yet feed your wrath, sir, rather than your lust,
(It is a vice comes nearer manliness,)
And punish that unhappy crime of nature,
Which you miscall my beauty: flay my face,
Or poison it with ointments for seducing
Your blood to this rebellion. Rub these hands

2140 *(line 2140)*
2150 *(line 2150)*
2160 *(line 2160)*
2170 *(line 2170)*

---

[135] The panther was said to use its breath to lure its victims.
[136] Crete was noted for its sweet wines.
[137] The *Metamorphoses*.
[138] Jove (Zeus) carried off the goddess Europa to Crete while disguised as a bull.
[139] Mars is the Roman god of war; Erycine is the Greek epithet for Aphrodite, the goddess of love.
[140] The Shah of Persia.
[141] The grand signor refers to the Sultan of Turkey.

With what may cause an eating leprosy,
E'en to my bones and marrow: anything
That may disfavour° me, save in my honour—   *disfigure*
And I will kneel to you, pray for you, pay down
A thousand hourly vows, sir, for your health;
Report, and think you virtuous—

VOLPONE.   Think me cold,
    Frozen, and impotent, and so report me?
    That I had Nestor's hernia,[142] thou wouldst think.
2180   I do degenerate,° and abuse my nation   *violate my own nature*
    To play with opportunity thus long;
    I should have done the act, and then have parleyed.
    Yield, or I'll force thee.   [*Seizes her.*]
CELIA.   O! just God!
VOLPONE.   In vain—
BONARIO [*rushing in*].   Forbear, foul ravisher! libidinous
    swine!
    Free the forced lady, or thou diest, impostor.
    But that I'm loth to snatch thy punishment
2190   Out of the hand of justice, thou shouldst yet
    Be made the timely sacrifice of vengeance,
    Before this altar and this dross, thy idol.—
    Lady, let's quit the place, it is the den
    Of villainy; fear nought, you have a guard:
    And he ere long shall meet his just reward.

                  [*Exeunt* BONARIO *and* CELIA..]

VOLPONE.   Fall on me, roof, and bury me in ruin!
    Become my grave, that wert my shelter! O!
    I am unmasked, unspirited, undone,
    Betrayed to beggary, to infamy—

              [*Enter* MOSCA *wounded and bleeding.*]

2200 MOSCA.   Where shall I run, most wretched shame of men,
    To beat out my unlucky brains?
VOLPONE.   Here, here.
    What dost thou bleed?
MOSCA.   O, that his well-driven sword
    Had been so courteous to have cleft me down
    Unto the navel, ere I lived to see
    My life, my hopes, my spirits, my patron, all
    Thus desperately engaged by my error!
VOLPONE.   Woe on thy fortune!
2210 MOSCA.   And my follies, sir.
VOLPONE.   Thou hast made me miserable.
MOSCA.   And myself, sir,

---

[142] The allusion is to impotence. The aged Nestor, King of Pylos, was one of the Greek
commanders at Troy.

Who would have thought he would have hearkened so?
VOLPONE.   What shall we do?
MOSCA.   I know not; if my heart
    Could expiate the mischance, I'd pluck it out.
    Will you be pleased to hang me, or cut my throat?
    And I'll requite you,° sir. Let's die like Romans   *reciprocate*
    Since we have lived like Grecians.[143]   [*Knocking within.*]
2220 VOLPONE.   Hark! who's there?
    I hear some footing; officers, the saffi,°   *Venetian police*
    Come to apprehend us! I do feel the brand
    Hissing already at my forehead; now
    Mine ears are boring.[144]
MOSCA.   To your couch, sir, you.
    Make that place good, however. [VOLPONE *lies down as before.*]
    Guilty men
    Suspect what they deserve still.

                                 [*Enter* CORBACCIO.]

    Signior Corbaccio!
CORBACCIO.   Why, how now, Mosca?
2230 MOSCA.   O, undone, amazed, sir.
    Your son, I know not by what accident,
    Acquainted with your purpose to my patron,
    Touching your Will, and making him your heir,
    Entered our house with violence, his sword drawn,
    Sought for you, called you wretch, unnatural,
    Vowed he would kill you.
CORBACCIO.   Me!
MOSCA.   Yes, and my patron.
CORBACCIO.   This act shall disinherit him indeed:
2240   Here is the Will.
MOSCA.   'Tis well, sir.
CORBACCIO.   Right and well:
    Be you as careful° now for me.   *full of concern*

                                 [*Enter* VOLTORE *behind.*]

MOSCA.   My life, sir.
    Is not more tendered;° I am only yours.   *taken care of*
CORBACCIO.   How does he? will he die shortly, think'st thou?
MOSCA.   I fear
    He'll outlast May.
CORBACCIO.   To-day?
2250 MOSCA.   No, last out May, sir.
CORBACCIO.   Couldst thou not give him a dram?
MOSCA.   O, by no means, sir.

---

[143] The Romans were known for dying stoically by falling on their swords to avoid dishonor, the Greeks for living an indulgent life of luxury.

[144] Criminals were then often punished by being branded or marked by having holes bored in their ears.

CORBACCIO. Nay, I'll not bid you.
VOLTORE [*coming forward.*] This is a knave, I see.
MOSCA [*seeing* VOLTORE]. How! Signior Voltore! did he
    hear me?   [*Aside.*]
VOLTORE. Parasite!
MOSCA. Who's that?—O, sir, most timely welcome—
VOLTORE. Scarce,
2260   To the discovery of your tricks, I fear.
    You are his, *only?* and mine also, are you not?
MOSCA. Who? I, sir!
VOLTORE. You, sir. What device is this
    About a Will?
MOSCA. A plot for you, sir.
VOLTORE. Come,
    Put not your foists° upon me; I shall scent them.   *tricks*
MOSCA. Did you not hear it?
VOLTORE. Yes, I hear Corbaccio
2270   Hath made your patron there his heir.
MOSCA. 'Tis true,
    By my device, drawn to it by my plot,
    With hope—
VOLTORE. Your patron should reciprocate?
    And you have promised?
MOSCA. For your good I did, sir.
    Nay, more, I told his son, brought, hid him here,
    Where he might hear his father pass the deed;
    Being persuaded to it by this thought, sir,
2280   That the unnaturalness first, of the act,
    And then his father's oft disclaiming in° him,   *repudiating*
    (Which I did mean t' help on), would sure enrage him
    To do some violence upon his parent,
    On which the law should take sufficient hold,
    And you be stated° in a double hope: *installed*
    Truth be my comfort, and my conscience,
    My only aim was to dig you a fortune
    Out of these two old rotten sepulchres—
VOLTORE. I cry thee mercy, Mosca.
2290 MOSCA. Worth your patience,
    And your great merit, sir. And see the change!
VOLTORE. Why, what success?
MOSCA. Most hapless! you must help, sir.
    Whilst we expected the old raven, in comes
    Corvino's wife, sent hither by her husband—
VOLTORE. What, with a present?
MOSCA. No, sir, on visitation;
    (I'll tell you how anon;) and staying long,
    The youth he grows impatient, rushes forth,
2300   Seizeth the lady, wounds me, makes her swear
    (Or he would murder her, that was his vow)
    To affirm my patron to have done her rape:

Which how unlike it is, you see! and hence,
With that pretext he's gone, to accuse his father,
Defame my patron, defeat you—
VOLTORE.   Where is her husband?
   Let him be sent for straight.
MOSCA.   Sir, I'll go fetch him.
VOLTORE.   Bring him to the Scrutineo.°   *court of law*
2310 MOSCA.   Sir, I will.
VOLTORE.   This must be stopt.
MOSCA.   O you do nobly, sir.
   Alas, 'twas laboured all, sir, for your good;
   Nor was there want of counsel in the plot:
   But fortune can, at any time, o'erthrow
   The projects of a hundred learned clerks,° sir.   *scholars*
CORBACCIO [*listening*].   What's that?
VOLTORE.   Wilt please you, sir, to go along?

                        [*Exit* CORBACCIO, *followed by* VOLTORE.]

MOSCA.   Patron, go in, and pray for our success.
2320 VOLPONE [*rising from his couch*].   Need makes devotion:[145]
   heaven your labour bless!   [*Exeunt.*]

ACT THE FOURTH

SCENE I

A Street

                [*Enter* SIR POLITICK WOULD-BE *and* PEREGRINE.]

SIR POLITICK.   I told you, sir, it was a plot you see
   What observation is! You mentioned me
   For some instructions: I will tell you, sir,
   (Since we are met here in this height° of Venice.)   *climate*
   Some few particulars I have set down,
   Only for this meridian, fit to be known
   Of your crude traveller; and they are these.
   I will not touch, sir, at your phrase, or clothes,
2330   For they are old.
PEREGRINE.   Sir, I have better.
SIR POLITICK.   Pardon,
   I meant, as they are themes.
PEREGRINE.   O, sir, proceed:
   I'll slander you no more of wit, good sir.
SIR POLITICK.   First, for your garb, it must be grave and
     serious,

---

[145] Desperation fosters pity.

Very reserved and locked; not tell a secret
On any terms, not to your father: scarce

2340   A fable, but with caution: make sure choice
Both of your company and discourse; beware
You never speak a truth—

PEREGRINE.   How!

SIR POLITICK.   Not to strangers,
For those be they you must converse with most;
Others I would not know, sir, but at distance.
So as I still might be a saver[146] in them:
You shall have tricks else past upon you hourly.
And then, for your religion, profess none,

2350   But wonder at the diversity of all;
And, for your part, protest, were there no other
But simply the laws o' th' land, you could content you.
Nic. Machiavel[147] and Monsieur Bodin,[148] both
Were of this mind. Then must you learn the use
And handling of your silver fork[149] at meals,
The metal° of your glass; (these are main matters   *material*
With your Italian;) and to know the hour
When you must eat your melons and your figs.

PEREGRINE.   Is that a point of state too?

2360 SIR POLITICK.   Here it is:
For your Venetian, if he see a man
Preposterous in the least, he has him straight;
He has, he strips him. I'll acquaint you, sir,
I now have lived here 'tis some fourteen months:
Within the first week of my landing here,
And took me for a citizen of Venice,
I knew the forms so well—

PEREGRINE.   And nothing else.   [*Aside.*]

SIR POLITICK.   I had read Contarene,[150] took me a house,

2370   Dealt with my Jews[151] to furnish it with movables—
Well, if I could but find one man, one man
To mine own heart, whom I durst trust, I would—

PEREGRINE.   What, what, sir?

SIR POLITICK.   Make him rich; make him a fortune:
He should not think again. I would command it.

PEREGRINE.   As how?

SIR POLITICK.   With certain projects that I have;
Which I may not discover.

---

[146] "Saver" is a gambling term for someone who escapes without winning or losing.

[147] Niccolo Machiavelli (1469–1527), author of *The Prince,* the great Italian political theorist and expert on the realities of statecraft.

[148] Monsieur Bodin was a French lawyer of eminence, and a very voluminous writer. [Editors' note]

[149] At the time of the play, forks were as yet uncommon in England.

[150] Cardinal Gasparo Contarini had written a well-known book on the Venetian Republic in 1589.

[151] The sizable Jewish community in Venice.

PEREGINE.   If I had
2380   But one to wager with, I would lay odds now,
He tells me instantly.   *[Aside.]*
SIR POLITICK.   One is, and that
I care not greatly who knows, to serve the state
Of Venice with red herrings for three years,
And at a certain rate, from Rotterdam,
Where I have correspondence. There's a letter,
Sent me from one o' the states,[152] and to that purpose:
He cannot write his name, but that's his mark.
PEREGINE.   He is a chandler?
2390 SIR POLITICK.   No, a cheesemonger.[153]
There are some others too with whom I treat
About the same negotiation;
And I will undertake it: for 'tis thus,
I'll do't with ease, I have cast it all.° Your hoy°   *figured it all out / small sloop*
Carries but three men in her, and a boy;
And she shall make me three returns a year:
So if there come but one of three, I save;
If two, I can defalk°:—but this is now,   *reduce expenses*
If my main project fail.
2400 PEREGINE.   Then you have others?
SIR POLITICK.   I should be loth to draw the subtle air
Of such a place, without my thousand aims.
I'll not dissemble, sir: where'er I come,
I love to be considerative; and 'tis true,
I have at my free hours thought upon
Some certain goods unto the state of Venice,
Which I do call *my Cautions;*° and, sir, which   *precautions*
I mean, in hope of pension, to propound
To the Great Council, then unto the Forty,
2410   So to the Ten.[154] My means are made already—
PEREGINE.   By whom?
SIR POLITICK.   Sir, one that though his place be obscure,
Yet he can sway, and they will hear him. He's
A commandador.°   *arresting or summoning officer*
PEREGINE.   What! a common serjeant?
SIR POLITICK.   Sir, such as they are, put it in their mouths,
What they should say, sometimes; as well as greater:
I think I have my notes to show you—

                                                            [Searching his pockets.]

PEREGINE.   Good sir.

---

[152] Of the States General of Holland, the Dutch legislative assembly.
[153] A candle and cheese seller.
[154] The allusion is to the complex, multilevel system of Venetian government which included the Great Council (open to all males over twenty-five), three Councils of Forty, and the Council of Ten (the Doge and his senior advisers).

2420 SIR POLITICK.   But you shall swear unto me, on your gentry,°   *as you are*
Not to anticipate—   *gentlemen*
PEREGRINE.   I, sir!
SIR POLITICK.   Nor reveal
A circumstance—My paper is not with me.
PEREGRINE.   O, but you remember, sir.
SIR POLITICK.   My first is
Concerning tinder-boxes. You must know,
No family is here without its box.
Now, sir, it being so portable a thing,
2430 Put case, that you or I were ill affected
Unto the state, sir; with it in our pockets,
Might not I go into the Arsenal,[155]
Or you come out again, and none the wiser?
PEREGRINE.   Except yourself, sir.
SIR POLITICK.   Go to, then. I therefore
Advertise to the state, how fit it were
That none but such as were known patriots,
Sound lovers of their country, should be suffered
To enjoy them in their houses; and even those
2440 Sealed° at some office, and at such a bigness   *licensed*
As might not lurk in pockets.
PEREGRINE.   Admirable!
SIR POLITICK.   My next is, how to inquire, and be resolved,
By present demonstration, whether a ship,
Newly arrived from Soria,[156] or from
Any suspected part of all the Levant,°   *the East*
Be guilty of the plague: and where they use
To lie out forty, fifty days, sometimes,
About the Lazaretto,[157] for their trial;
2450 I'll save that charge and loss unto the merchant,
And in an hour clear the doubt.
PEREGRINE.   Indeed, sir!
SIR POLITICK.   Or—I will lose my labour.
PEREGRINE.   My faith, that's much.
SIR POLITICK.   Nay, sir, conceive me. It will cost me in onions,
Some thirty livres—[158]
PEREGRINE.   Which is one pound sterling.
SIR POLITICK.   Beside my waterworks: for this I do, sir.
First, I bring in your ship 'twixt two brick walls;
2460 But those the state shall venture.° On the one   *invest in*
I strain° me a fair tarpauling, and in that   *stretch*
I stick my onions, cut in halves; the other
Is full of loopholes, out of which I thrust
The noses of my bellows; and those bellows

---

[155] Where Venetian ships were built, repaired, and fitted with ornaments and gunpowder.
[156] I.e., Syria. [Editors' note]
[157] Venice's two Lazarettos, or quarantine hospitals, were located on the city's outer islands to prevent contagion, particularly bubonic plague.
[158] French coins of small value.

I keep, with waterworks, in perpetual motion,
Which is the easiest matter of a hundred.
Now, sir, your onion, which doth naturally
Attract the infection, and your bellows blowing
The air upon him, will show instantly,
2470　By his changed colour, if there be contagion;
Or else remain as fair as at the first.
Now it is known, 'tis nothing.
PEREGRINE.　You are right, sir.
SIR POLITICK.　I would I had my note.
PEREGRINE.　Faith, so would I:
　But you have done well for once, sir.
SIR POLITICK.　Were I false,
　Or would be made so, I could show you reasons
　How I could sell this state now to the Turk,
2480　Spite of their galleys, or their—

　　　　　　　　　　　　　　　　　　　[Examining his papers.]

PEREGRINE.　Pray you, Sir Pol.
SIR POLITICK.　I have them not about me.
PEREGRINE.　That I feared:
　They are there, sir.
SIR POLITICK.　No, this is my diary,
　Wherein I note my actions of the day.
PEREGRINE.　Pray you let's see, sir. What is here?
　　Notandum°,　　　　　　　　　　　　　　　　*Take note*

　　　　　　　　　　　　　　　　　　　　　　[Reads.]

　"A rat had gnawed my spur-leathers; notwithstanding,
2490　I put on new, and did go forth; but first
　I threw three beans over the threshold. Item,
　I went and bought two toothpicks, whereof one
　I burst immediately, in a discourse
　With a Dutch merchant, 'bout ragion del stato.°　　*reasons of state*
　From him I went and paid a moccinigo°　　　　　　*small coin*
　For piecing° my silk stockings; by the way　　　　*mending*
　I cheapened sprats;° and at St. Mark's I urined."　*bargained for fish*

　Faith these are politic notes!
SIR POLITICK.　Sir, I do slip°　　　　　　　　　　*pass over*
2500　No action of my life, but thus I quote it.
PEREGRINE.　Believe me, it is wise!
SIR POLITICK.　Nay, sir, read forth.

[Enter, at a distance, LADY POLITICK WOULD-BE, NANO, *and two* WAITING-WOMEN.]

LADY POLITICK.　Where should this loose knight be, trow?
　sure he's housed.°　　　　　　　　　　　　　　*indoors*
NANO.　Why, then he's fast.°　　　　　　　　　　*safe*

LADY POLITICK.   Ay, he plays both with me.
　I pray you stay. This heat will do more harm
　To my complexion than his heart is worth.
　(I do not care to hinder, but to take him.)
2510　How it comes off!　　　　　　　　　　　　[*Rubbing her cheeks.*]
1ST WOMAN.   My master's yonder.
LADY POLITICK.   Where?
2ND WOMAN.   With a young gentleman.
LADY POLITICK.   That same's the party;
　In man's apparel!¹⁵⁹ Pray you, sir, jog my knight:
　I will be tender to his reputation,
　However he demerit.°　　　　　　　　　　　*he is at fault*
SIR POLITICK [*seeing her*].   My lady!
PEREGRINE.   Where?
2520 SIR POLITICK.   'Tis she indeed, sir; you shall know her. She is,
　Were she not mine, a lady of that merit,
　For fashion and behaviour; and for beauty
　I durst compare—
PEREGRINE.   It seems you are not jealous,
　That dare commend her.
SIR POLITICK.   Nay, and for discourse—
PEREGRINE.   Being your wife, she cannot miss that.
SIR POLITICK [*introducing* PEREGRINE].   Madam,
　Here is a gentleman, pray you, use him fairly;
2530　He seems a youth, but he is—
LADY POLITICK.   None.
SIR POLITICK.   Yes one
　Has put his face as soon into the world—
LADY POLITICK.   You mean, as early? but to-day?
SIR POLITICK.   How's this?
LADY POLITICK.   Why, in this habit, sir; you apprehend me:
　Well, Master Would-be, this doth not become you;
　I had thought the odour, sir, of your good name
　Had been more precious to you; that you would not
2540　Have done this dire massacre on your honour;
　One of your gravity, and rank besides!
　But knights, I see, care little for the oath
　They make to ladies; chiefly their own ladies.
SIR POLITICK.   Now, by my spurs, the symbol of my
　　knighthood—
PEREGRINE.   Lord, how this brain is humbled for an oath!　　[*Aside.*]
SIR POLITICK.   I reach° you not.　　　　　　　　　*understand*
LADY POLITICK.   Right, sir, your policy°　　　　　　*cunning*
　May bear it through thus. Sir, a word with you.

　　　　　　　　　　　　　　　　　　　　　　[*To* PEREGRINE.]

2550　I would be loth to contest publicly

---

¹⁵⁹ That is, a transvestite.

With any gentlewoman, or to seem
Froward,° or violent, as the courtier[160] says;   *unreasonable*
It comes too near rusticity in a lady,
Which I would shun by all means: and however
I may deserve from Master Would-be, yet
T' have one fair gentlewoman thus be made
The unkind instrument to wrong another,
And one she knows not, ay, and to perséver:
In my poor judgment, is not warranted°   *guaranteed*
2560   From being a solecism in our sex,
If not in manners.
PEREGRINE.   How is this!
SIR POLITICK.   Sweet madam,
Come nearer to your aim.
LADY POLITICK.   Marry, and will, sir.
Since you provoke me with your impudence,
And laughter of your light° land-syren here,   *immoral*
Your Sporus,[161] your hermaphrodite—
PEREGRINE.   What's here?
2570   Poetic fury and historic storms!
SIR POLITICK.   The gentleman, believe it, is of worth
And of our nation.
LADY POLITICK.   Ay, your Whitefriars nation.[162]
Come, I blush for you, Master Would-be, I;
And am ashamed you should have no more forehead,°   *modesty*
Than thus to be the patron, or St. George,[163]
To a lewd harlot, a base fricatrice,°   *whore*
A female devil, in a male outside.
SIR POLITICK.   Nay,
2580   An you be such a one, I must bid adieu
To your delights. The case appears too liquid.°   *clear*

                                             [*Exit.*]

LADY POLITICK.   Ay, you may carry't clear, with your state
          face!°   *solemn face*
But for your carnival concupiscence,
Who here is fled for liberty of conscience,
From furious persecution of the marshal,
Her will I dis'ple.°   *discipline*
PEREGRINE.   This is fine, i' faith!

---

[160] *The Courtier* (1528), by Castiglione (1478–1529), was a well-known Italian manual of courtly behavior and etiquette.
[161] Sporus was a favorite eunuch of the Emperor Nero (A.D. 54–68).
[162] Whitefriars was at this time a privileged spot, in which fraudulent debtors, gamblers, prostitutes, and other outcasts of society usually resided. [Editors' note]
[163] St. George was noted for rescuing women.

And do you use this° often? Is this part   *act in this way*
2590   Of your wit's exercise, 'gainst you have occasion?
    Madam—
LADY POLITICK. Go to, sir.
PEREGRINE. Do you hear me, lady?
    Why, if your knight have set you to beg shirts,
    Or to invite me home, you might have done it
    A nearer° way by far.   *more direct*
LADY POLITICK. This cannot work you
    Out of my snare.
PEREGRINE. Why, am I in it, then?
2600   Indeed your husband told me you were fair,
    And so you are; only now your nose inclines,
    That side that's next to the sun, to the queen-apple.[164]
LADY POLITICK. This cannot be endured by any patience.

                                        [*Enter* MOSCA.]

MOSCA. What is the matter, madam?
LADY POLITICK. If the senate
    Right not my quest in this, I will protest° them   *publish*
    To all the world no aristocracy.
MOSCA. What is the injury, lady?
LADY POLITICK. Why, the callet[165]
2610   You told me of, here I have ta'en disguised.
MOSCA. Who? this! what means your ladyship? the crea-
    ture
    I mentioned to you is apprehended now,
    Before the senate; you shall see her—
LADY POLITICK. Where?
MOSCA. I'll bring you to her. This young gentleman,
    I saw him land this morning at the port.
LADY POLITICK. Is't possible! how has my judgment wan-
    dered?
2620   Sir, I must, blushing, say to you, I have erred;
    And plead your pardon.
PEREGRINE. What, more changes yet!
LADY POLITICK. I hope you have not the malice to re-
    member
    A gentlewoman's passion. If you stay
    In Venice here, please you to use me, sir—
MOSCA. Will you go, madam?
LADY POLITICK. Pray you, sir use me; in faith,
    The more you see me the more I shall conceive
2630   You have forgot our quarrel.

                  [*Exeunt* LADY WOULD-BE, MOSCA, NANO, *and* WAITING-WOMEN.]

---

[164] A large red apple, apparently in reference to Lady Politick's nose.
[165] *Callet, callat,* or *calot,* is used by all our old writers for a strumpet of the basest kind. [Editors' note]

PEREGRINE.   This is rare!
　　Sir Politick Would-be? no, Sir Politick Bawd,
　　To bring me thus acquainted with his wife!
　　Well, wise Sir Pol, since you have practiced° thus   *plotted*
　　Upon my freshman-ship, I'll try your salt-head,
　　What proof it is against a counter-plot.   [*Exit.*]

SCENE II

The Scrutineo, or Senate House

　　　　　　　　　　　[*Enter* VOLTORE, CORBACCIO, CORVINO, *and* MOSCA.]

VOLTORE.   Well, now you know the carriage° of the business,   *procedure*
　　Your constancy is all that is required
　　Unto the safety of it.
2640 MOSCA.   Is the lie
　　Safely conveyed amongst us? is that sure?
　　Knows every man his burden?
CORVINO.   Yes.
MOSCA.   Then shrink not.
CORVINO.   But knows the advocate the truth?
MOSCA.   O, sir,
　　By no means; I devised a formal tale,
　　That salved° your reputation. But be valiant, sir.   *saved*
CORVINO.   I fear no one but him that this his pleading
2650 Should make him stand for a co-heir—
MOSCA.   Co-halter!
　　Hang him: we will but use his tongue, his noise,
　　As we do croaker's here.
CORVINO.   Ay, what shall he do?
MOSCA.   When we have done, you mean?
CORVINO.   Yes.
MOSCA.   Why, we'll think:
　　Sell him for mummia:[166] he's half dust already.
　　Do you not smile, [*to* VOLTORE.] to see this buffalo,
2660 How he doth sport it with his head?[167] I should,
　　If all were well and past. [*Aside.*] Sir, [*to* CORBACCIO.]
　　　only you
　　Are he that shall enjoy the crop of all,
　　And these not know for whom they toil.
CORBACCIO.   Ay, peace.
MOSCA [*turning to* CORVINO].   But you shall eat it.
　　　Much! [*Aside.*] Worshipful sir, [*to* VOLTORE]
　　Mercury sit upon your thundering tongue,

---

[166] The powdered remains of mummies were in fact sold as medicine.
[167] An allusion to a cuckold's horns.

Or the French Hercules,[168] and make your language
2670   As conquering as his club, to beat along,
    As with a tempest, flat, our adversaries;
    But much more yours, sir.
VOLTORE.   Here they come, have done.
MOSCA.   I have another witness, if you need, sir, I can produce.
VOLTORE.   Who is it?
MOSCA.   Sir, I have her.

[*Enter* AVOCATORI, *and take their seats*, BONARIO, CELIA, NOTARIO, COMMANDADORI,
SAFFI, *and other Officers of Justice.*]

1ST AVOCATORI.   The like of this the senate never heard of.
2ND AVOCATORI.   'Twill come most strange to them when
    we report it.
2680 4TH AVOCATORI.   The gentlewoman has been ever held
    Of unreproved name.
3RD AVOCATORI.   So has the youth.
4TH AVOCATORI.   The more unnatural part that of his father.
2ND AVOCATORI.   More of the husband.
1ST AVOCATORI.   I not know° to give   *I do not know how*
    His act a name, it is so monstrous!
4TH AVOCATORI.   But the impostor, he's a thing created
    To exceed example!°   *precedent*
1ST AVOCATORI.   And all after-times!°   *future possibilities*
2690 2ND AVOCATORI.   I never heard a true voluptuary
    Described but him.
3RD AVOCATORI.   Appear yet those were cited?°   *summoned to court*
NOTARIO.   All but the old magnifico,° Volpone.   *gentleman*
1ST AVOCATORI.   Why is not he here?
MOSCA.   Please your fatherhoods,
    Here is his advocate: himself so weak,
    So feeble—
4TH AVOCATORI.   Who are you?
BONARIO.   His parasite,
2700   His knave, his pander. I beseech the court
    He may be forced to come, that your grave eyes
    May bear strong witness of his strange impostures.
VOLTORE.   Upon my faith and credit with your virtues,
    He is not able to endure the air.
2ND AVOCATORI.   Bring him, however.
3RD AVOCATORI.   We will see him.
4TH AVOCATORI.   Fetch him.
VOLTORE.   Your fatherhoods' fit pleasures be obeyed;

[*Exeunt* OFFICERS.]

But sure, the sight will rather move your pities

---

[168] The gods Mercury and Hercules, among other things, were noted for their eloquence.

2710 Than indignation. May it please the court,
In the mean time, he may be heard in me:
I know this place most void of prejudice,
And therefore crave it, since we have no reason
To fear our truth should hurt our cause.
3RD AVOCATORI.   Speak free.
VOLTORE.   Then know, most honoured fathers, I must now
Discover to your strangely abused° ears,   *deceived*
The most prodigious and most frontless° piece   *shameless*
Of solid impudence, and treachery,
2720 That ever vicious nature yet brought forth
To shame the state of Venice. This lewd woman,
That wants no artificial looks or tears
To help the vizor° she has now put on,   *mask*
Hath long been known a close° adulteress   *secret*
To that lascivious youth there; not suspected,
I say, but known, and taken in the act
With him; and by this man, the easy husband,
Pardoned; whose timeless° bounty makes him now   *untimely*
Stand here, the most unhappy, innocent person,
2730 That ever man's own goodness made accused.
For these not knowing how to owe° a gift   *own*
Of that dear grace,° but with their shame; being placed   *preciousness*
So above all powers of their gratitude,
Began to hate the benefit; and in place
Of thanks, devise to extirpe° the memory   *extirpate*
Of such an act: wherein I pray your fatherhoods
To observe the malice, yea, the rage of creatures
Discovered in their evils: and what heart°   *boldness*
Such take, even from their crimes:—but that anon
2740 Will more appear.—This gentleman, the father,
Hearing of this foul fact,° with many others,   *crime*
Which daily struck at his too tender ears,
And grieved in nothing more than that he could not
Preserve himself a parent (his son's ills
Growing to that strange flood), at last decreed
To disinherit him.
1ST AVOCATORI.   These be strange turns!
2ND AVOCATORI.   The young man's fame was ever fair and
honest.
2750 VOLTORE.   So much more full of danger is his vice,
That can beguile to under shade of virtue.
But, as I said, my honoured sires, his father
Having this settled purpose, by what means
To him betrayed, we know not, and this day
Appointed for the deed; that parricide,
I cannot style him better, by confederacy°   *conspiracy*
Preparing this and his paramour to be there,
Entered Volpone's house (who was the man,
Your fatherhoods must understand, designed°   *designated*

2760 For the inheritance), there sought his father:—
But with what purpose sought he him, my lords?
I tremble to pronounce it, that a son
Unto a father, and to such a father,
Should have so foul, felonious intent!
It was to murder him: when being prevented
By his more happy absence, what then did he?
Not check his wicked thoughts; no, now new deeds;
(Mischief doth never end where it begins)
An act of horror, fathers! he dragged forth
2770 The aged gentleman that had there lain bed-rid
Three years and more, out of his innocent couch,
Naked upon the floor, there left him; wounded
His servant in the face; and with this strumpet,
The stale° to his forged practice, who was glad   *decoy, pretext*
To be so active,—(I shall here desire
Your fatherhoods to note but my collections,°   *conclusions*
As most remarkable,—) thought at once to stop
His father's ends, discredit his free choice
In° the old gentleman, redeem themselves,   *of*
2780 By laying infamy upon this man,
To whom, with blushing, they should owe their lives.
1st Avocatori. What proofs have you of this?
Bonario. Most honoured fathers,
 I humbly crave there be no credit given
 To this man's mercenary tongue.
2nd Avocatori. Forbear.
Bonario. His soul moves in his fee.
3rd Avocatori. O, sir.
Bonario. This fellow,
2790 For six sols° more would plead against his Maker.   *French coins*
1st Avocatori. You do forget yourself.
Voltore. Nay, nay, grave fathers,
 Let him have scope; can any man imagine
 That he will spare his accuser, that would not
 Have spared his parent?
1st Avocatori. Well, produce your proofs.
Celia. I would I could forget I were a creature.
Voltore. Signior Corbaccio!

[Corbaccio *comes forward.*]

4th Avocatori. What is he?
2800 Voltore. The father.
2nd Avocatori. Has he had an oath?
Notario. Yes.
Corbaccio. What must I do now?
Notario. Your testimony's craved.
Corbaccio. Speak to the knave?

I'll have my mouth first stopt with earth; my heart
Abhors his knowledge:° I disclaim in him.   *to recognize him*
1ST AVOCATORI.   But for what cause?
CORBACCIO.   The mere portent of nature!
2810   He is an utter stranger to my loins.
BONARIO.   Have they made you to this?
CORBACCIO.   I will not hear thee,
     Monster of men, swine, goat, wolf, parricide!
     Speak not, thou viper.
BONARIO.   Sir, I will sit down,
     And rather wish my innocence should suffer
     Than I resist the authority of a father.
VOLTORE.   Signior Corvino!

                                                    [CORVINO *comes forward.*]

2ND AVOCATORI.   This is strange.
2820   1ST AVOCATORI.   Who's this?
NOTORIO.   The husband.
4TH AVOCATORI.   Is he sworn?
NOTARIO.   He is.
3RD AVOCATORI.   Speak then.
CORVINO.   This woman, please your fatherhoods, is a
          whore,
     Of most hot exercise, more than a partrich,[169]
     Upon record—
1ST AVOCATORI.   No more.
2830   CORVINO.   Neighs like a jennet.[170]
NOTARIO.   Preserve the honour of the court.
CORVINO.   I shall,
     And modesty of your most reverend ears.
     And I hope that I may say these eyes
     Have seen her glued unto that piece of cedar,
     That fine well timbered gallant: and that here
     The letters may be read, thorough° the horn,   *through*
     That makes the story perfect.
MOSCA.   Excellent sir.
2840   CORVINO.   There is no shame in this now, is there?   [*Aside to* MOSCA.]
MOSCA.   None.
CORVINO.   Or if I said, I hoped that she were onward
     To her damnation, if there be a hell
     Greater than whore and woman; a good Catholic
     May make the doubt.
3RD AVOCATORI.   His grief hath made him frantic.
1ST AVOCATORI.   Remove him hence.
2ND AVOCATORI.   Look to the woman.   [CELIA *swoons.*]

---

[169] A partridge, by reputation, was the most lecherous of birds.
[170] A Spanish breed of horses.

CORVINO.   Rare!°   *marvellous*
2850   Prettily feigned again!
       4TH AVOCATORI.   Stand from about her.
       1ST AVOCATORI.   Give her the air.
       3RD AVOCATORI.   What can you say?   [*To* MOSCA.]
       MOSCA.   My wound,
           May it please your wisdoms, speaks for me, received
           In aid of my good patron, when he mist
           His sought-for father, when that well-taught dame
           Had her cue given her to cry out, A rape!
       BONARIO.   O most laid° impudence! Fathers—   *well planned*
2860   3RD AVOCATORI.   Sir, be silent;
           You had your hearing free, so must they theirs.
       2ND AVOCATORI.   I do begin to doubt the imposture here.
       4TH AVOCATORI.   This woman has too many moods.
       VOLTORE.   Grave fathers,
           She is a creature of a most profest
           And prostituted lewdness.
       CORVINO.   Most impetuous,
           Unsatisfied, grave fathers!
       VOLTORE.   May her feignings
2870   Not take° your wisdoms: but this day she baited   *take in*
           A stranger, a grave knight, with her loose eyes,
           And more lascivious kisses. This man saw them
           Together on the water, in a gondola.
       MOSCA.   Here is the lady herself, that saw them too,
           Without; who then had in the open streets
           Pursued them, but for saving her knight's honour.
       1ST AVOCATORI.   Produce that lady.
       2ND AVOCATORI.   Let her come.

                                                                    [*Exit* MOSCA.]

       4TH AVOCATORI.   These things,
2880   They strike with wonder.
       3RD AVOCATORI.   I am turned a stone.

                                          [*Re-enter* MOSCA *with* LADY WOULD-BE.]

       MOSCA.   Be resolute, madam.
       LADY POLITICK.   Ay, this same is she.   [*Pointing to* CELIA.]
           Out, thou camelion harlot! now thine eyes
           Vie tears with the hyæna. Dar'st thou look
           Upon my wronged face? I cry your pardons,
           I fear I have forgettingly transgrest
           Against the dignity of the court—
       2ND AVOCATORI.   No, madam.
2890   LADY POLITICK.   And been exorbitant—
       2ND AVOCATORI.   You have not, lady.
       4TH AVOCATORI.   These proofs are strong.

LADY POLITICK.   Surely, I had no purpose
  To scandalize your honours, or my sex's.
3RD AVOCATORI.   We do believe it.
LADY POLITICK.   Surely you may believe it.
2ND AVOCATORI.   Madam, we do.
LADY POLITICK.   Indeed you may; my breeding
  Is not so coarse—
2900 4TH AVOCATORI.   We know it.
LADY POLITICK.   To offend
  With pertinancy—°   *pertinacity*
3RD AVOCATORI.   Lady—
LADY POLITICK.   Such a presence!°   *presence room, court room*
  No surely.
1ST AVOCATORI.   We well think it.
LADY POLITICK.   You may think it.
1ST AVOCATORI.   Let her o'ercome. What witnesses have you,
  To make good your report?
2910 BONARIO.   Our consciences.
CELIA.   And heaven, that never fails the innocent.
4TH AVOCATORI.   These are no testimonies.
BONARIO.   Not in your courts,
  Where multitude and clamour overcomes.
1ST AVOCATORI.   Nay, then you do wax insolent.

                   [*Re-enter* OFFICERS, *bearing* VOLPONE *on a couch.*]

VOLTORE.   Here, here.
  The testimony comes that will convince,
  And put to utter dumbness their bold tongues!
  See here, grave fathers, here's the ravisher,
2920   The rider on men's wives, the great impostor,
  The grand voluptuary! Do you not think
  These limbs should affect venery?° or these eyes   *lust*
  Covet a concubine? pray you mark these hands;
  Are they not fit to stroke a lady's breasts?
  Perhaps he doth dissemble!
BONARIO.   So he does.
VOLTORE.   Would you have him tortured?
BONARIO.   I would have him proved.
VOLTORE.   Best try him then with goads, or burning irons;
2930   Put him to the strappado;[171] I have heard
  The rack hath cured the gout; faith, give it him,
  And help him of a malady; be courteous.
  I'll undertake, before these honoured fathers,
  He shall have yet as many left diseases,
  As she has known adulterers, or thou strumpets.

---

[171] A common torture of the day, in which the victim was hung by his wrists which were
strapped together behind his back.

O, my most equal hearers, if these deeds,
Acts of this bold and most exorbitant strain,
May pass with sufferance, what one citizen
But owes the forfeit of his life, yea, fame,
2940   To him that dares traduce him? which of you
Are safe, my honoured fathers? I would ask,
With leave of your grave fatherhoods, if their plot
Have any face or colour° like to truth?   *appearance or semblance*
Or if, unto the dullest nostril here,
It smell not rank, and most abhorred slander?
I crave your care of this good gentleman,
Whose life is much endangered by their fable;
And as for them, I will conclude with this,
That vicious persons, when they're hot, and fleshed°   *violent and hardened*
2950   In impious acts, their constancy abounds:
Damned deeds are done with greatest confidence.
1st Avocatori.   Take them to custody, and sever them.
2nd Avocatori.   'Tis pity two such prodigies° should live.   *monsters*
1st Avocatori.   Let the old gentleman be returned with care.

                              [*Exeunt* Officers *with* Volpone.]

I'm sorry our credulity hath wronged him.
4th Avocatori.   These are two creatures!
3rd Avocatori.   I've an earthquake in me.°   *I'm overwhelmed*
2nd Avocatori.   Their shame, even in their cradles, fled
    their faces.
2960 4th Avocatori.   You have done a worthy service to the
    state, sir,
In their discovery.

                                     [*To* Voltore.]

1st Avocatori.   You shall hear, ere night,
What punishment the court decrees upon them.

       [*Exeunt* Avocatori, Notario, *and* Officers *with* Bonario *and* Celia.]

Voltore.   We thank your fatherhoods. How like you it?
Mosca.   Rare.
I'd have your tongue, sir, tipt with gold for this;
I'd have you be the heir to the whole city;
The earth I'd have want men ere you want living:°   *employment*
2970   They're bound to erect your statue in St. Mark's.[172]
Signior Corvino, I would have you go
And show yourself that you have conquered.
Corvino.   Yes.
Mosca.   It was much better that you should profess
Yourself a cuckold thus, than that the other
Should have been proved.

---

[172] Venice's central square.

CORVINO.   Nay, I considered that:
   Now it is her fault.
MOSCA.   Then it had been yours.
2980 CORVINO.   True; I do doubt this advocate still.
MOSCA.   I' faith,
   You need not, I dare ease you of that care.
CORVINO.   I trust thee, Mosca.

                                              [Exit.]

MOSCA.   As your own soul, sir.
CORBACCIO.   Mosca!
MOSCA.   Now for your business, sir.
CORBACCIO.   How! have you business?
MOSCA.   Yes, yours, sir.
CORBACCIO.   O, none else.
2990 MOSCA.   None else, not I.
CORBACCIO.   Be careful then.
MOSCA.   Rest you with both your eyes, sir.
CORBACCIO.   Dispatch it.
MOSCA.   Instantly.
CORBACCIO.   And look that all,
   Whatever, be put in, jewels, plate, moneys,
   Household stuff, bedding, curtains.
MOSCA.   Curtain-rings, sir:
   Only the advocate's fee must be deducted.
3000 CORBACCIO.   I'll pay him now; you'll be too prodigal.
MOSCA.   Sir, I must tender it.
CORBACCIO.   Two chequines is well.
MOSCA.   No, six, sir.
CORBACCIO.   'Tis too much.
MOSCA.   He talked a great while;
   You must consider that, sir.
CORBACCIO.   Well, there's three—
MOSCA.   I'll give it him.
CORBACCIO.   Do so, and there's for thee.

                                              [Exit.]

3010 MOSCA.   Bountiful bones! What horrid strange offence
   Did he commit 'gainst nature, in his youth,
   Worthy this age? *[Aside.]* You see, sir, *[to* VOLTORE.*]* how I
     work
   Unto your ends: take you no notice.
VOLTORE.   No,
   I'll leave you.

                                              [Exit.]

MOSCA.   All is yours, the devil and all:
   Good advocate!—Madam, I'll bring you home.

LADY POLITICK.   No, I'll go see your patron.

3020 MOSCA.   That you shall not:
  I'll tell you why. My purpose is to urge
  My patron to reform° his will, and for   *rewrite*
  The zeal you have shown to-day, whereas before
  You were but third or fourth, you shall be now
  Put in the first; which would appear as begged
  If you were present. Therefore—

LADY POLITICK.   You shall sway me.

                                                      [Exeunt.]

ACT THE FIFTH

SCENE I

A Room in VOLPONE'S *House*

                                           [Enter VOLPONE.*]*

VOLPONE.   Well, I am here, and all this brunt° is past.   *crisis, trouble*
  I ne'er was in dislike with my disguise
3030 Till this fled° moment: here 'twas good, in private;   *past*
  But in your public—*cave*° whilst I breathe.   *beware*
  'Fore God, my left leg 'gan° to have the cramp,   *began*
  And I apprehended straight some power had struck me
  With a dead palsy. Well! I must be merry,
  And shake it off. A many of these fears
  Would put me into some villainous disease,
  Should they come thick upon me: I'll prevent 'em.
  Give me a bowl of lusty wine, to fright
  This humour from my heart. *[Drinks.]* Hum, hum, hum!
3040 'Tis almost gone already; I shall conquer.
  Any device now of rare ingenious knavery,
  That would possess me with a violent laughter,
  Would make me up° again. *[Drinks again.]* So, so, so, so!   *restore me*
  This heat is life; 'tis blood by this time:—Mosca!

                                           [Enter MOSCA.*]*

MOSCA.   How now, sir? does the day look clear again?
  Are we recovered, and wrought out of error,
  Into our way, to see our path before us?
  Is our trade free once more?

VOLPONE.   Exquisite Mosca!

3050 MOSCA.   Was it not carried learnedly?

VOLPONE.   And stoutly:
  Good wits are greatest in extremities.

MOSCA.   It were folly beyond thought to trust
  Any grand act unto a cowardly spirit:
  You are not taken with it enough, methinks.

VOLPONE.   O, more than if I had enjoyed the wench:
　The pleasure of all woman-kind's not like it.
MOSCA.   Why, now you speak, sir. We must here be fixed;
　Here we must rest; this is our masterpiece;
3060　We cannot think to go beyond this.
VOLPONE.   True,
　Thou hast played thy prize, my precious Mosca.
MOSCA.   Nay, sir,
　To gull the court—
VOLPONE.   And quite divert the torrent
　Upon the innocent.
MOSCA.   Yes, and to make
　So rare a music out of discords—
VOLPONE.   Right.
3070　That yet to me's the strangest, how thou hast borne it!
　That these, being so divided amongst themselves,
　Should not scent somewhat, or in me or thee,
　Or doubt their own side.
MOSCA.   True, they will not see't,
　Too much light blinds them, I think. Each of them
　Is so possest and stuft with his own hopes
　That anything unto the contrary,
　Never so true, or never so apparent,
　Never so palpable, they will resist it—
3080 VOLPONE.   Like a temptation of the devil.
MOSCA.   Right, sir.
　Merchants may talk of trade, and your great signiors
　Of land that yields well; but if Italy
　Have any glebe° more fruitful than these fellows,   *soil*
　I am deceived. Did not your advocate rare?°   *rarely*
VOLPONE.   O—"My most honoured fathers, my grave fathers,
　Under correction of your fatherhoods,
　What face of truth is here? If these strange deeds
　May pass, most honoured fathers"—I had much ado
3090　To forbear laughing.
MOSCA.   It seemed to me, you sweat, sir.
VOLPONE.   In troth, I did a little.
MOSCA.   But confess, sir,
　Were you not daunted?
VOLPONE.   In good faith, I was
　A little in a mist, but not dejected;
　Never but still myself.
MOSCA.   I think it, sir.
　Now, so truth help me, I must needs say this, sir,
3100　And out of conscience for your advocate,
　He has taken pains, in faith, sir, and deserved
　In my poor judgment, I speak it under favour,°   *with permission*
　Not to contrary you, sir, very richly—
　Well—to be cozened.°   *cheated*
VOLPONE.   Troth and I think so too,
　By that I heard him in the latter end.

MOSCA.   O, but before, sir: had you heard him first
   Draw it to certain heads,[173] then aggravate,°   *emphasize*
   Then use his vehement figures[174]—I looked still
3110   When he would shift° a shirt; and doing this   *change*
   Out of pure love, no hope of gain—
VOLPONE.   'Tis right.
   I cannot answer° him Mosca, as I would,   *repay*
   Not yet; but for thy sake, at thy entreaty,
   I will begin, even now—to vex them all,
   This very instant.
MOSCA.   Good sir.
VOLPONE.   Call the dwarf
   And eunuch forth.
3120 MOSCA.   Castrone, Nano!

                          [Enter CASTRONE and NANO.]

NANO.   Here.
VOLPONE.   Shall we have a jig now?
MOSCA.   What you please, sir.
VOLPONE.   Go,
   Straight give out about the streets, you two,
   That I am dead; do it with constancy,°   *conviction*
   Sadly,° do you hear? impute it to the grief   *seriously*
   Of this late slander.

                          [Exeunt CASTRONE and NANO.]

MOSCA.   What do you mean, sir?
3130 VOLPONE.   O,
   I shall have instantly my Vulture, Crow,
   Raven, come flying hither, on the news,
   To peck for carrion, my she-wolf, and all,
   Greedy, and full of expectation—
MOSCA.   And then to have it ravished from their mouths!
VOLPONE   'Tis true. I will have thee put on a gown,
   And take upon thee,° as thou wert mine heir;   *act as though*
   Show them a Will. Open that chest, and reach
   Forth one of those that has the blanks; I'll straight
3140   Put in thy name.
MOSCA.   It will be rare, sir.   *[Gives him a paper.]*
VOLPONE.   Ay,
   When they ev'n gape, and find themselves deluded—
MOSCA.   Yes.
VOLPONE.   And thou use them scurvily!
   Dispatch, get on thy gown.
MOSCA *[putting on a gown]*.   But what, sir, if they ask
   After the body?

---

[173] That is, collect together his argument under certain topics.
[174] Rhetorical figures.

VOLPONE.   Say, it was corrupted.
3150 MOSCA.   I'll say it stunk, sir; and was fain° to have it   *obliged*
    Coffined up instantly, and sent away.
VOLPONE.   Anything; what thou wilt. Hold, here's my Will.
    Get thee a cap, a count-book,° pen and ink,   *account book*
    Papers afore thee; sit as thou wert taking
    An inventory of parcels: I'll get up
    Behind the curtain, on a stool, and hearken:
    Sometime peep over, see how they do look,
    With what degrees their blood doth leave their faces.
    O, 'twill afford me a rare meal of laughter!
3160 MOSCA [*putting on a cap, and setting out the table, etc.*]
    Your advocate will turn stark dull upon it.
VOLPONE.   It will take off his oratory's edge.
MOSCA.   But your clarissimo°, old roundback, he   *Venetian nobleman*
    Will crump you° like a hog-louse, with the touch.   *curl up*
VOLPONE.   And what Corvino?
MOSCA.   O, sir, look for him.
    To-morrow morning, with a rope and dagger,°   *suicidal*
    To visit all the streets; he must run mad,
    My lady too, that came into the court,
3170   To bear false witness for your worship—
VOLPONE.   Yes,
    And kissed me 'fore the fathers, when my face
    Flowed all with oils—
MOSCA.   And sweat, sir. Why, your gold
    Is such another med'cine, it dries up
    All those offensive savours: it transforms
    The most deformed, and restores them lovely,
    As 'twere the strange poetical girdle.[175] Jove
    Could not invent t' himself a shroud° more subtle   *disguise*
3180 To pass Acrisius' guards.[176] It is the thing
    Makes all the world her grace, her youth, her beauty.
VOLPONE.   I think she loves me.
MOSCA.   Who? the lady, sir?
    She's jealous of you.
VOLPONE.   Dost thou say so?   [*Knocking within.*]
MOSCA.   Hark,
    There's some already.
VOLPONE.   Look.
MOSCA.   It is the Vulture;
3190 He has the quickest scent.
VOLPONE.   I'll to my place,
    Thou to thy posture.°   *pretense*

---

[175] The allusion is to the girdle of Venus which bestowed on its wearers both grace and beauty.
[176] The allusion is to the story of Jove (Jupiter), who entered the locked chamber of the daughter of Acrisius by transforming himself into a shower of gold.

[Goes behind the curtain.]

MOSCA.   I am set.
VOLPONE.   But, Mosca,
   Play the artificer° now, torture them rarely.   trickster

[Enter VOLTORE.*]*

VOLTORE.   How now, my Mosca?
MOSCA *[writing]*.   "Turkey carpets, nine—"
VOLTORE.   Taking an inventory! that is well.
MOSCA.   "Two suits° of bedding, tissue°—"   sets / rich cloth
3200 VOLTORE.   Where's the Will?
   Let me read the while.

[Enter SERVANTS *with* CORBACCIO *in a chair.]*

CORBACCIO.   So, set me down,
   And get you home.

[Exeunt SERVANTS.*]*

VOLTORE.   Is he come now, to trouble us!
MOSCA.   "Of cloth of gold, two more—"
CORBACCIO.   Is it done, Mosca?
MOSCA.   "Of several velvets, eight—"
VOLTORE.   I like his care.
CORBACCIO.   Dost thou not hear?

[Enter CORVINO.*]*

3210 CORVINO.   Ha! is the hour come, Mosca?
VOLPONE *[peeping over the curtain]*.   Ay, now they muster.
CORVINO.   What does the advocate here,
   Or this Corbaccio?
CORBACCIO.   What do these here?

[Enter LADY POLITICK WOULD-BE.*]*

LADY POLITICK.   Mosca!
   Is his thread spun?
MOSCA.   "Eight chests of linen—"
VOLPONE.   O,
   My fine Dame Would-be too!
3220 CORVINO.   Mosca, the Will,
   That I may show it these, and rid them hence.
MOSCA.   "Six chests of diaper,° four of damask"—There   linen

[Gives them the Will carelessly, over his shoulder.]

CORBACCIO.   Is that the Will?
MOSCA.   "Down-beds, and bolsters—
VOLPONE.   Rare!
   Be busy still. Now they begin to flutter:

They never think of me. Look, see, see, see!
How their swift eyes run over the long deed,
Unto the name, and to the legacies,
3230   What is bequeathed them there—
Mosca.   "Ten suits of hangings—"
Volpone.   Ay, in their garters,[177] Mosca. Now their hopes
    Are at the gasp.°   *last gasp*
Voltore.   Mosca the heir.
Corbaccio.   What's that?
Volpone.   My advocate is dumb; look to my merchant,
    He has heard of some strange storm, a ship is lost,
    He faints; my lady will swoon. Old glazen-eyes,°   *wearing glasses*
    He hath not reached his despair yet.
3240 Corbaccio.   All these
    Are out of hope; I am, sure, the man.   *[Takes the Will.]*
Corvino.   But, Mosca—
Mosca.   "Two cabinets—"
Corvino.   Is this in earnest?
Mosca.   "One
    Of ebony—"
Corvino.   Or do you but delude me?
Mosca.   "The other, mother of pearl"—
    I am very busy.
3250   Good faith, it is a fortune thrown upon me—
    "Item one salt° of agate"—not my seeking.   *saltcellar*
Lady Politick.   Do you hear, sir?
Mosca.   "A perfumed box"—Pray you forbear,
    You see I'm troubled—"made of an onyx—"
Lady Politick.   How!
Mosca.   To-morrow or next day, I shall be at leisure
    To talk with you all.
Corvino.   Is this my large hope's issue?
Lady Politick.   Sir, I must have a fairer answer.
3260 Mosca.   Madam!
    Marry, and shall: pray you, fairly° quit my house.   *once and for all*
    Nay, raise no tempest with your looks; but hark you,
    Remember what your ladyship offered me
    To put you in an heir; go to, think on it:
    And what you said e'en your best madams did
    For maintenance; and why not you? Enough.
    Go home, and use the poor Sir Pol, your knight, well,
    For fear I tell some riddles;° go, be melancholy.   *secrets*

                                            [Exit Lady Would-be.*]*

Volpone.   O, my fine devil!
3270 Corvino.   Mosca, pray you a word.
Mosca.   Lord! will not you take your dispatch hence yet?

---

[177] That is, they hang themselves in their own garters.

Methinks, of all, you should have been the example.
Why should you stay here? with what thought, what
    promise?
Hear you; do you not know, I know you an ass,
And that you would most fain have been a wittol°   *willing cuckold*
If fortune would have let you? that you are
A declared cuckold, on good terms?° This pearl,   *fair and square*
You'll say, was yours? right: this diamond?
3280   I'll not deny't, but thank you. Much here else?
It may be so. Why, think that these good works
May help to hide your bad. I'll not betray you;
Although you be but extraordinary,
And have it only in title,[178] it sufficeth:
Go home, be melancholy too, or mad.

                              [*Exit* CORVINO.]

VOLPONE.   Rare Mosca! how his villainy becomes him!
VOLTORE.   Certain he doth delude all these for me.
CORBACCIO.   Mosca the heir!
VOLPONE.   O, his four eyes[179] have found it.
3290 CORBACCIO.   I am cozened, cheated, by a parasite slave;
    Harlot,° thou hast gulled me.   *scoundrel*
MOSCA.   Yes, sir. Stop your mouth,
    Or I shall draw the only tooth is left.
    Are not you he, that filthy covetous wretch,
    With the three legs,[180] that here, in hope of prey,
    Have, any time this three years, snuffed about,
    With your most grovelling nose, and would have hired
    Me to the poisoning of my patron, sir:
    Are not you he that have to-day in court
3300   Professed the disinheriting of your son?
    Perjured yourself? Go home, and die, and stink;
    If you but croak a syllable, all comes out:
    Away, and call your porters! [*Exit* CORBACCIO.] Go, go,
    stink.
VOLPONE.   Excellent varlet!
VOLTORE.   Now, my faithful Mosca,
    I find thy constancy—
MOSCA.   Sir!
VOLTORE.   Sincere.
3310 MOSCA [*writing*].   "A table
    Of porphyry"—I marle° you'll be thus troublesome.   *marvel*
VOLTORE.   Nay, leave off now, they are gone.
MOSCA.   Why, who are you?
    What! who did send for you? O, cry you mercy,

---

[178] Although you are not a real cuckold but simply doing your best to be one.
[179] Carbaccio wears spectacles.
[180] Including his cane.

Reverend sir! Good faith, I am grieved for you,
That any chance° of mine should thus defeat　　　　　　　*luck*
Your (I must needs say) most deserving travails:
But I protest, sir, it was cast upon me,
And I could almost wish to be without it,
3320　But that the will o' the dead must be observed,
Marry, my joy is that you need it not;
You have a gift, sir (thank your education),
Will never let you want, while there are men,
And malice, to breed causes.° Would I had　　　　　　　*legal suits*
But half the like, for all my fortune, sir!
If I have any suits, as I do hope,
Things being so easy and direct, I shall not,
I will make bold with your obstreperous aid,
Conceive me—for your fee, sir.[181] In mean time,
3330　You that have so much law, I know have the conscience
Not to be covetous of what is mine.
Good sir, I thank you for my plate; 'twill help
To set up a young man. Good faith, you look
As you were costive;° best go home and purge, sir.　　　*constipated*

　　　　　　　　　　　　　　　　　　　　　　　　[*Exit* VOLTORE.]

VOLPONE [*comes from behind the curtain.*]　Bid him eat
　　lettuce well.[182] My witty mischief,
　Let me embrace thee. O that I could now
　Transform thee to a Venus!—Mosca, go,
　Straight take my habit° of clarissimo,　　　　　　　　*costume*
3340　And walk the streets; be seen, torment them more:
　We must pursue, as well as plot. Who would
　Have lost his feast?
MOSCA.　I doubt it will lose them.
VOLPONE.　O, my recovery shall recover all.
　That I could now but think on some disguise
　To meet them in, and ask them questions:
　How I would vex them still at every turn!
MOSCA.　Sir, I can fit you.
VOLPONE.　Canst thou?
3350 MOSCA.　Yes, I know
　One o' the commandadori, sir, so like you;
　Him will I straight make drunk, and bring you his habit.
VOLPONE.　A rare disguise, and answering thy brain!
　O, I will be a sharp disease unto them.
MOSCA.　Sir, you must look for curses—
VOLPONE.　Till they burst;
　The Fox fares ever best when he is curst.

　　　　　　　　　　　　　　　　　　　　　　　　　[*Exeunt.*]

---

[181] It is understood that I will pay your fee.
[182] Lettuce taken as a laxative.

SCENE II

A Hall in SIR POLITICK'S *House*

[*Enter* PEREGRINE *disguised, and three* MERCHANTS.]

PEREGRINE.   Am I enough disguised?

1ST MERCHANT.   I warrant° you.   assure

3360   PEREGRINE.   All my ambition is to fright him only.

2ND MERCHANT.   If you could ship him away, 'twere excellent.

3RD MERCHANT.   To Zant, or to Aleppo![183]

PEREGRINE.   Yes, and have his
    Adventures put i' the Book of Voyages,[184]
    And his gulled story° registered for truth.   story of being gulled
    Well, gentlemen, when I am in a while,
    And that you think us warm in our discourse,
    Know your approaches.

1ST MERCHANT.   Trust it to our care.   [*Exeunt* MERCHANTS.]

[*Enter* WAITING-WOMAN.]

3370   PEREGRINE.   Save you, fair lady! Is Sir Pol within?

WOMAN.   I do not know, sir.

PEREGRINE.   Pray you say unto him
    Here is a merchant, upon urgent business,
    Desires to speak with him.

WOMAN.   I will see, sir.

[*Exit.*]

PEREGRINE.   Pray you.
    I see the family is all female here.

[*Re-enter* WAITING-WOMAN.]

WOMAN.   He says, sir, he has weighty affairs of state,
    That now require him whole;° some other time   his whole attention
3380   You may possess him.

PEREGRINE.   Pray you say again,
    If those require him whole, these will exact him,
    Whereof I bring him tidings. [*Exit* WOMAN.] What might be
    His grave affair of state now! how to make
    Bolognian sausages here in Venice, sparing
    One o' the ingredients?

[*Re-enter* WAITING-WOMAN.]

WOMAN.   Sir, he says, he knows
    By your word *tidings*, that you are no statesman,[185]
    And therefore wills you stay.

---

[183] To Byzantium, or to Aleppo in Syria.

[184] One of any number of popular contemporary books of travel adventures.

[185] A real statesman would probably use a word like "intelligence."

3390 PEREGRINE.   Sweet, pray you return° him;   *reply to*
    I have not read so many proclamations,
    And studied them for words, as he has done——
    But—here he deigns to come.   [*Exit* WOMAN.]

                         [*Enter* SIR POLITICK.]

SIR POLITICK.   Sir, I must crave
    Your courteous pardon. There hath chanced to-day
    Unkind disaster 'twixt my lady and me;
    And I was penning my apology,
    To give her satisfaction, as you came now.
PEREGRINE.   Sir, I am grieved I bring you worse disaster:
3400 The gentleman you met at the port to-day,
    That told you he was newly arrived—
SIR POLITICK.   Ay, was
    A fugitive punk?°   *prostitute*
PEREGRINE.   No, sir, a spy set on you:
    And he has made relation to the senate,
    That you profest to him to have a plot
    To sell the State of Venice to the Turk.
SIR POLITICK.   O me!
PEREGRINE.   For which warrants are signed by this time,
3410 To apprehend you, and to search your study
    For papers—
SIR POLITICK.   Alas, sir, I have none, but notes
    Drawn out of play-books——
PEREGRINE.   All the better, sir.
SIR POLITICK.   And some essays. What shall I do?
PEREGRINE.   Sir, best
    Convey yourself into a sugar-chest:
    Or, if you could lie round,° a frail[186] were rare.   *curl up*
    And I could send you aboard.
3420 SIR POLITICK.   Sir, I but talked so,
    For discourse sake merely.   [*Knocking within.*]
PEREGRINE.   Hark! they are there.
SIR POLITICK.   I am a wretch, a wretch!
PEREGRINE.   What will you do, sir?
    Have you ne'er a currant-butt° to leap into?   *cask for currants*
    They'll put you to the rack; you must be sudden.
SIR POLITICK.   Sir, I have an ingine°—   *contrivance, invention*
3RD MERCHANT [*within*].   Sir Politick Would-be!
2ND MERCHANT [*within*].   Where is he?
3430 SIR POLITICK.   That I have thought upon before time.
PEREGRINE.   What is it?
SIR POLITICK.   I shall ne'er endure the torture,
    Marry, it is, sir, of a tortoise-shell,
    Fitted for these extremities: pray you, sir, help me.

---

[186] A rush basket for packing figs or raisins.

Here I've a place, sir, to put back my legs.
Please you to lay it on, sir, [*Lies down while* PEREGRINE
places the shell upon him.]—with this cap,
And my black gloves. I'll lie, sir, like a tortoise,
Till they are gone.
3440 PEREGRINE.   And call you this an ingine?
SIR POLITICK.   Mine own device—Good sir, bid my wife's
      women
   To burn my papers.   [*Exit* PEREGRINE.]

[*The three* MERCHANTS *rush in.*]

1ST MERCHANT.   Where is he hid?
3RD MERCHANT.   We must,
   And will sure find him.
2ND MERCHANT.   Which is his study?

[*Re-enter* PEREGRINE.]

1ST MERCHANT.   What
   Are you, sir?
3450 SIR POLITICK.   I am a merchant, that came here
   To look upon this tortoise.
3RD MERCHANT.   How!
1ST MERCHANT.   St. Mark!
   What beast is this?
PEREGRINE.   It is a fish.
2ND MERCHANT.   Come out here!
PEREGRINE.   Nay, you may strike him, sir, and tread upon
   him:
   He'll bear a cart.
3460 1ST MERCHANT.   What, to run over him?
PEREGRINE.   Yes, sir.
3RD MERCHANT.   Let's jump upon him.
2ND MERCHANT.   Can he not go?°   *move*
PEREGRINE.   He creeps, sir.
1ST MERCHANT.   Let's see him creep.
PEREGRINE.   No, good sir, you will hurt him.
2ND MERCHANT.   Heart, I will see him creep, or prick his
   guts.
3RD MERCHANT.   Come out here!
3470 PEREGRINE.   Pray you, sir—Creep a little.   [*Aside to* SIR POLITICK.]
1ST MERCHANT.   Forth.
2ND MERCHANT.   Yet farther.
PEREGRINE.   Good sir!—Creep.
2ND MERCHANT.   We'll see his legs.

[*They pull off the shell and discover him.*]

3RD MERCHANT.   Ods so, he has garters!

1st Merchant.   Ay, and gloves!
2nd Merchant.   Is this
   Your fearful tortoise?
Peregrine [*discovering himself*].   Now, Sir Pol, we are even;
3480   For your next project I shall be prepared:
   I am sorry for the funeral of your notes, sir.
1st Merchant.   'Twere a rare motion to be seen in Fleet Street.[187]
2nd Merchant.   Ay, in the Term.[188]
1st Merchant.   Or Smithfield, in the fair.[189]
3rd Merchant.   Methinks 'tis but a melancholy sight.
Peregrine.   Farewell, most politic tortoise!

                  [*Exeunt* Peregrine *and* Merchants.]

                  [*Re-enter* Waiting-woman.]

Sir Politick.   Where's my lady?
   Knows she of this?
Woman.   I know not, sir.
3490 Sir Politick.   Enquire.—
   O, I shall be the fable of all feasts,
   The freight of the gazetti,[190] ship-boys' tale;
   And, which is worst, even talk for ordinaries.°   *tavern gossip*
Woman.   My lady's come most melancholy home,
   And says, sir, she will straight to sea, for physic.°   *for her health*
Sir Politick.   And I, to shun this place and clime for ever,
   Creeping with house on back, and think it well
   To shrink° my poor head in my politic shell.   *draw in*

                           [*Exeunt.*]

SCENE III

A Room in Volpone's *House*

[*Enter* Mosca *in the habit of a clarissimo, and* Volpone *in that of a commanda-dore.*]

Volpone.   Am I then like him?
3500 Mosca.   O, sir, you are he:
   No man can sever you.
Volpone.   Good.
Mosca.   But what am I?

---

[187] A puppet show in London's Fleet Street where such performances often took place.
[188] London's Inns of Court are located near Fleet Street and "in Term," when the Inns of
Court were in session, these street fairs provided a popular diversion.
[189] The famous Bartholomew Fair was held annually in Smithfield, north of London.
[190] I.e., newspapers. [Editors' note]

VOLPONE.   'Fore heaven, a brave clarissimo; thou becom'st it!
     Pity thou wert not born one.

MOSCA.   If I hold°   *retain*
     My made one,° 'twill be well. [*Aside.*]   *assumed guise*

VOLPONE.   I'll go and see
     What news first at the court.

3510   MOSCA.   Do so. My Fox
     Is out of his hole, and ere he shall re-enter,
     I'll make him languish in his borrowed case,°   *disguise*
     Except he come to composition with me.—[191]
     Androgyno, Castrone, Nano!

                        [*Enter* ANDROGYNO, CASTRONE, *and* NANO.]

ALL.   Here.

MOSCA.   Go, recreate yourselves abroad; go, sport,—

                                     [*Exeunt.*]

     So, now I have the keys, and am possest.
     Since he will needs be dead afore his time,
     I'll bury him, or gain by him: I am his heir,

3520   And so will keep me,° till he share at least.   *remain*
     To cozen him of all, were but a cheat
     Well placed: no man would construe it a sin:
     Let his sport pay for 't. This is called the Fox-trap.

                                     [*Exit.*]

SCENE IV

     A Street

                            [*Enter* CORBACCIO *and* CORVINO.]

CORBACCIO.   They say the court is set.

CORVINO.   We must maintain

3530   Our first tale good, for both our reputations.

CORBACCIO.   Why, mine's no tale: my son would there have
     killed me.

CORVINO.   That's true, I had forgot:—mine is, I'm sure.   [*Aside.*]

3530   But for your Will, sir.

CORBACCIO.   Ay, I'll come up on him
     For that hereafter, now his patron's dead.

                                 [*Enter* VOLPONE.]

VOLPONE.   Signior Corvino! and Corbaccio! sir,
     Much joy unto you.

---

[191] Unless he makes a deal with me.

CORVINO.   Of what?

VOLPONE.   The sudden good
   Dropt down upon you—

CORBACCIO.   Where?

VOLPONE.   And none knows how,
3540   From old Volpone, sir.

CORBACCIO.   Out, arrant knave!

VOLPONE.   Let not your too much wealth, sir, make you
   furious.

CORBACCIO.   Away, thou varlet.¹⁹²

VOLPONE.   Why, sir?

CORBACCIO.   Dost thou mock me?

VOLPONE.   You mock the world, sir; did you not change
   Wills?

CORBACCIO.   Out, harlot!

3550 VOLPONE.   O! belike° you are the man,   *perhaps*
   Signior Corvino? faith, you carry it well;
   You grow not mad withal; I love your spirit;
   You are not over-leavened with your fortune.
   You should have some would swell now, like a wine-fat,
   With such an autumn—Did he give you all, sir?

CORVINO.   Avoid,° you rascal!   *be gone*

VOLPONE.   Troth, your wife has shown
   Herself a very° woman; but you are well,   *true*
   You need not care, you have a good estate,
3560   To bear it out, sir, better by this chance:
   Except Corbaccio have a share.

CORBACCIO.   Hence, varlet.

VOLPONE.   You will not be acknown,° sir; why, 'tis wise.   *acknowledged*
   Thus do all gamesters, at all games, dissemble:
   No man will seem to win.

                            [*Exeunt* CORVINO *and* CORBACCIO.]

   Here comes my vulture,
   Heaving his beak up in the air, and snuffing.

                                   [*Enter* VOLTORE.]

VOLTORE.   Outstript thus, by a parasite! a slave
   Would run on errands, and make legs° for crumbs.   *bow and scrape*
3570   Well, what I'll do—

VOLPONE.   The court stays for your worship.
   I e'en rejoice, sir, at your worship's happiness,
   And that it fell into so learned hands,
   That understand the fingering—

VOLTORE.   What do you mean?

---

¹⁹² Rascal, but also the title of a court officer or sergeant.

VOLPONE.   I mean to be a suitor to your worship.
  For the small tenement, out of reparations,°   *repair*
  That, at the end of your long row of houses,
  By the Piscaria:[193] it was, in Volpone's time,
3580 Your predecessor, ere he grew diseased,
  A handsome, pretty, customed° bawdy-house   *much frequented*
  As any was in Venice, none dispraised;°   *slighted*
  But fell with him: his body and that house
  Decayed together.
VOLTORE.   Come, sir, leave your prating.
VOLPONE.   Why, if your worship give me but your hand,°   *handshake or signature*
  That I may have the refusal, I have done
  'Tis a mere toy to you, sir; candle-rents;[194]
  As your learned worship knows—
3590 VOLTORE.   What do I know?
VOLPONE.   Marry, no end of your wealth, sir; God decrease it!
VOLTORE.   Mistaking knave! what, mock'st thou my misfortune?   [*Exit.*]
VOLPONE.   His blessing on your heart, sir; would t'were more!——
  Now to my first again, at the next corner.   [*Exit.*]

SCENE V

Another part of the Street

[*Enter* CORBACCIO *and* CORVINO;—MOSCA *passes over the Stage, before them.*]

CORBACCIO.   See, in our habit! see the impudent varlet!
CORVINO.   That I could shoot mine eyes at him, like gun-
    stones!°   *stone cannonballs*

[*Enter* VOLPONE.]

VOLPONE.   But is this true, sir, of the parasite?
CORBACCIO.   Again, to afflict us! monster!
3600 VOLPONE.   In good faith, sir,
  I'm heartily grieved, a beard of your grave length
  Should be so over-reached.° I never brooked°   *out-witted / could stand*
  That parasite's hair; methought his nose should cozen:
  There still was somewhat° in his look, did promise   *something*
  The bane of a clarissimo.
CORBACCIO.   Knave—
VOLPONE.   Methinks
  Yet you, that are so traded in the world,
  A witty merchant, the fine bird, Corvino,
3610 That have such moral emblems[195] on your name,

---

[193] A fish street or market.
[194] Income derived from deteriorating property.
[195] The allusion is to emblem books, collections of engravings accompanied by explicit moral lessons, often in verse.

Should not have sung your shame, and dropt your cheese,
To let the Fox laugh at your emptiness.
CORVINO.　Sirrah, you think the privilege of the place,
And your red saucy cap, that seems to me
Nailed to your jolt-head° with those two chequines,[196]　　　　　*blockhead*
Can warrant your abuses; come you hither:
You shall perceive, sir, I dare beat you; approach.
VOLPONE.　No haste, sir, I do know your valour well,
Since you durst publish what you are, sir.
3620 CORVINO.　Tarry,
I'd speak with you.
VOLPONE.　Sir, sir, another time—
CORVINO.　Nay, now.
VOLPONE.　O lord, sir! I were a wise man,
Would stand the fury of a distracted cuckold.

> [*As he is running off, re-enter* MOSCA.]

CORBACCIO.　What, come again!
VOLPONE.　Upon 'em, Mosca; save me.
CORBACCIO.　The air's infected where he breathes.
CORVINO.　Let's fly him.

> [*Exeunt* CORVINO *and* CORBACCIO.]

3630 VOLPONE.　Excellent basilisk![197] turn upon the vulture.

> [*Enter* VOLTORE.]

VOLTORE.　Well, flesh-fly, it is summer with you now;
Your winter will come on.
MOSCA.　Good advocate,
Prithee not rail, nor threaten out of place thus;
Thou'lt make a solecism, as madam says.
Get you a biggin[198] more; your brain breaks loose.

> [*Exit.*]

VOLTORE.　Well, sir.
VOLPONE.　Would you have me beat the insolent slave,
Throw dirt upon his first good clothes?
3640 VOLTORE.　This same
Is doubtless some familiar.
VOLPONE.　Sir, the court,
In troth, stays for you. I am mad, a mule
That never read Justinian,[199] should get up,
And ride an advocate. Had you not quirk°　　　　　　　*trick*
To avoid gullage,° sir, by such a creature?　　　　　　*deceit*

---

[196] The two gilt buttons on the commandadori's red cap.
[197] A mythical creature whose look was fatal.
[198] A kind of *coif*, or night-cap. [Editors' note]
[199] The Emperor Justinian (483–565) codified Roman law.

I hope you do but jest; he has not done it:
'Tis but confederacy° to blind the rest.   *conspiracy*
You are the heir.
3650 VOLTORE. A strange, officious,
Troublesome knave! thou dost torment me.
VOLPONE. I know—
It cannot be, sir, that you should be cozened;
'Tis not within the wit of man to do it;
You are so wise, so prudent; and 'tis fit
That wealth and wisdom still should go together.

[*Exeunt*]

SCENE VI

The Scrutineo or Senate House

[*Enter* AVOCATORI, NOTARIO, BONARIO, CELIA, CORBACCIO, CORVINO, COMMAN-
DADORI, SAFFI, *etc.*]

3660 1ST AVOCATORI. Are all the parties here?
NOTARIO. All but the advocate.
2ND AVOCATORI. And here he comes.

[*Enter* VOLTORE *and* VOLPONE.]

1ST AVOCATORI. Then bring them forth to sentence.
VOLTORE. O, my most honoured fathers, let your mercy
Once win upon your justice, to forgive—
I am distracted—
VOLPONE. What will he do now?   [*Aside.*]
VOLTORE. O,
3670 I know not which to address myself to first;
Whether your fatherhoods, or these innocents—
CORVINO. Will he betray himself?   [*Aside.*]
VOLTORE. Whom equally
I have abused, out of most covetous ends—
CORVINO. The man is mad!
CORBACCIO. What's that?
CORVINO. He is possest.
VOLTORE. For which, now struck in conscience, here I prostrate
Myself at your offended feet, for pardon.
1ST, 2ND AVOCATORI. Arise.
CELIA. O heaven, how just thou art!
VOLTORE. I am caught
In mine own noose—   [*Aside.*]
3680 CORVINO [*to* CORBACCIO]. Be constant, sir; nought now
Can help but impudence.
1ST AVOCATORI. Speak forward.
COMMANDADORI. Silence!

VOLTORE.   It is not passion in me, reverend fathers,
    But only conscience, conscience, my good sires,
    That makes me now tell truth. That parasite,
    That knave, hath been the instrument of all.
1ST AVOCATORI.   Where is that knave? fetch him.
VOLPONE.   I go.   [*Exit.*]
3690 CORVINO.   Grave fathers,
    This man's distracted; he confest it now:
    For, hoping to be old Volpone's heir,
    Who now is dead—
3RD AVOCATORI.   How!
2ND AVOCATORI.   Is Volpone dead?
CORVINO.   Dead since, grave fathers.
BONARIO.   O sure vengeance!
1ST AVOCATORI.   Stay,
    Then he was no deceiver.
3700 VOLTORE.   O no, none:
    This parasite, grave fathers.
CORVINO.   He does speak
    Out of mere envy 'cause the servant's made
    The thing he gaped for: please your fatherhoods,
    This is the truth, though I'll not justify
    The other, but he may be some-deal faulty.
VOLTORE.   Ay, to your hopes, as well as mine, Corvino:
    But I'll use modesty. Pleaseth your wisdoms,
    To view these certain notes, and but confer° them;   *compare*
3710 And as I hope favour, they shall speak clear truth.
CORVINO.   The devil has entered him!
BONARIO.   Or bides in you.
4TH AVOCATORI.   We have done ill, by a public officer
    To send for him, if he be heir.
2ND AVOCATORI.   For whom?
4TH AVOCATORI.   Him that they call the parasite.
3RD AVOCATORI.   'Tis true,
    He is a man of great estate, now left.
4TH AVOCATORI.   Go you, and learn his name, and say the court
3720 Entreats his presence here, but to the clearing
    Of some few doubts.   [*Exit* NOTARY.]
2ND AVOCATORI.   This same's a labyrinth!
1ST AVOCATORI.   Stand you unto your first report?
CORVINO.   My state,
    My life, my fame—
BONARIO.   Where is it?
CORVINO.   Are at the stake.
1ST AVOCATORI.   Is yours so too?
CORBACCIO.   The advocate's a knave,
3730 And has a forked tongue—
2ND AVOCATORI.   Speak to the point.
CORBACCIO.   So is the parasite too.
1ST AVOCATORI.   This is confusion.

VOLTORE. I do beseech your fatherhoods, read but those—

[Giving them papers.]

CORVINO. And credit nothing the false spirit hath writ:
It cannot be but he's possest, grave fathers.

[The scene closes.]

SCENE VII

A Street

[Enter VOLPONE.]

VOLPONE. To make a snare for mine own neck! and run
My head into it, wilfully! with laughter!
When I had newly scaped, was free and clear,
Out of mere wantonness! O, the dull devil
3740   Was in this brain of mine when I devised it,
And Mosca gave it second; he must now
Help to sear up° this vein, or we bleed dead.   *cauterize*

[Enter NANO, ANDROGYNO, and CASTRONE.]

How now! who let you loose? whither go you now?
What, to buy gingerbread, or to drown kitlings?°   *kittens*
NANO. Sir, Master Mosca called us out of doors,
And bid us all go play, and took the keys.
ANDROGYNO. Yes.
VOLPONE. Did Master Mosca take the keys? why, so!
I'm farther in. These are my fine conceits!°   *notions*
3750   I must be merry, with a mischief to me!
What a vile wretch was I, that could not bear
My fortune soberly? I must have my crochets,°   *fancies*
And my conundrums!° Well, go you, and seek him: *whims*
His meaning may be truer than my fear.
Bid him, he straight come to me to the court;
Thither will I, and, if't be possible,
Unscrew my advocate, upon° new hopes: *by means of*
When I provoked him, then I lost myself.

[Exeunt.]

SCENE VIII

The Scrutineo, or Senate House

*[AVOCATORI, BONARIO, CELIA, CORBACCIO, CORVINO, COMMANDADORI, SAFFI, etc.,
as before.]*

3760 1ST AVOCATORI. These things can ne'er be reconciled. He
    here

[Showing the papers.]

Professeth that the gentleman was wronged,
And that the gentlewoman was brought thither,
Forced by her husband, and there left.

VOLTORE.   Most true.

CELIA.   How ready is heaven to those that pray!

1ST AVOCATORI.   But that
Volpone would have ravished her, he holds
Utterly false, knowing his impotence.

3770 CORVINO.   Grave fathers, he's possest; again, I say,
Possest: nay, if there be possession, and
Obsession, he has both.

3RD AVOCATORI.   Here comes our officer.

[*Enter* VOLPONE.]

VOLPONE.   The parasite will straight be here, grave fathers.

4TH AVOCATORI.   You might invent some other name, sir
varlet.

3RD AVOCATORI.   Did not the notary meet him?

VOLPONE.   Not that I know.

4TH AVOCATORI.   His coming will clear all.

3780 2ND AVOCATORI.   Yet it is misty.°   *obscure*

VOLTORE.   May't please your fatherhoods—

VOLPONE [*whispers* VOLTORE].   Sir, the parasite
Willed me to tell you that his master lives;
That you are still the man; your hopes the same;
And this was only a jest—

VOLTORE.   How?

VOLPONE.   Sir, to try
If you were firm, and how you stood affected.

VOLTORE.   Art sure he lives?

3790 VOLPONE.   Do I live sir?

VOLTORE.   O me!
I was too violent.

VOLPONE.   Sir, you may redeem it.
They said you were possest: fall down, and seem so:
I'll help to make it good. [VOLTORE *falls.*] God bless the
man!—
Stop your wind hard, and swell—See, see, see, see!
He vomits crooked pins! his eyes are set,
Like a dead hare's hung in a poulterer's° shop!   *poultry*

3800 His mouth's running away! Do you see, signior?
Now it is in his belly.

CORVINO.   Ay, the devil!

VOLPONE.   Now in his throat.

CORVINO.   Ay, I perceive it plain.

VOLTORE.   'Twill out, 'twill out! stand clear. See where it flies,
In shape of a blue toad, with a bat's wings!
Do you not see it, sir?

CORBACCIO.   What? I think I do.

CORVINO.   'Tis too manifest.

3810 VOLPONE.   Look! he comes to himself!

VOLTORE.   Where am I?

VOLPONE.   Take good heart, the worst is past, sir.
   You are dispossest.

1ST AVOCATORI.   What accident is this!

2ND AVOCATORI.   Sudden, and full of wonder!

3RD AVOCATORI.   If he were
   Possest, as it appears, all this is nothing.

CORVINO.   He has been often subject to these fits.

1ST AVOCATORI.   Show him that writing:—do you know it, sir?

3820 VOLPONE [*whispers* VOLTORE].   Deny it, sir, forswear it; know it not.

VOLTORE.   Yes, I do know it well, it is my hand;
   But all that it contains is false.

BONARIO.   O practice!°   *deceit*

2ND AVOCATORI.   What maze is this!

1ST AVOCATORI.   Is he not guilty then,
   Whom you there name the parasite?

VOLTORE.   Grave fathers,
   No more than his good patron, old Volpone.

4TH AVOCATORI.   Why, he is dead.

3830 VOLTORE.   O no, my honoured fathers,
   He lives—

1ST AVOCATORI.   How! lives?

VOLTORE.   Lives.

2ND AVOCATORI.   This is subtler yet!

3RD AVOCATORI.   You said he was dead.

VOLTORE.   Never.

3RD AVOCATORI.   You said so.

CORVINO.   I heard so.

4TH AVOCATORI.   Here comes the gentleman; make him way.

[*Enter* MOSCA.]

3840 3RD AVOCATORI.   A stool.

4TH AVOCATORI.   A proper° man; and were Volpone dead,   *handsome*
   A fit match for my daughter.   [*Aside.*]

3RD AVOCATORI.   Give him way.

VOLPONE.   Mosca, I was almost lost; the advocate
   Had betrayed all; but now it is recovered;
   All's on the hinge again—Say I am living.

[*Aside to* MOSCA.]

MOSCA.   What busy° knave is this!—Most reverend fathers   *meddlesome*
   I sooner had attended your grave pleasures,
   But that my order for the funeral

3850   Of my dear patron did require me—

VOLPONE.   Mosca!   [*Aside.*]

MOSCA.   Whom I intend to bury like a gentleman.

VOLPONE.   Ay, quick,° and cozen me of all. [*Aside.*]   *alive*

2ND AVOCATORI.   Still stranger!

More intricate!

1st Avocatori.   And come about again!

4th Avocatori.   It is a match, my daughter is bestowed.   [*Aside.*]

Mosca.   Will you give me half?

[*Aside to* Volpone.]

Volpone.   First I'll be hanged.

3860 Mosca.   I know
Your voice is good, cry not so loud.

1st Avocatori.   Demand.°   *question*
The advocate.—Sir, did you not affirm
Volpone was alive?

Volpone.   Yes, and he is;
This gentleman told me so.—Thou shalt have half.

[*Aside to* Mosca.]

Mosca.   Whose drunkard is this same? speak, some that
know him:
I never saw his face.—I cannot now
3870 Afford it you so cheap.

[*Aside to* Volpone.]

Volpone.   No!

1st Avocatori.   What say you?

Voltore.   The officer told me.

Volpone.   I did, grave fathers,
And will maintain he lives, with mine own life,
And that this creature [*points to* Mosca.] told me.—I was
born
With all good stars my enemies.   [*Aside.*]

Mosca.   Most grave fathers,
3880 If such an insolence as this must pass
Upon me, I am silent; 'twas not this
For which you sent, I hope.

2nd Avocatori.   Take him away.

Volpone.   Mosca!

3rd Avocatori.   Let him be whipt.

Volpone.   Wilt thou betray me?
Cozen me?

3rd Avocatori.   And taught to bear himself
Toward a person of his rank.

3890 4th Avocatori.   Away

[*The* Officers *seize* Volpone.]

Mosca.   I humbly thank your fatherhoods.

Volpone.   Soft, soft:° Whipt!   *easy, easy*
And lose all that I have! If I confess,
It cannot be much more.   [*Aside.*]

4th Avocatori.   Sir, are you married?

VOLPONE.   They'll be allied anon; I must be resolute;
    The Fox shall here uncase.   *[Throws off his disguise.]*
MOSCA.   Patron!
VOLPONE   Nay, now
3900   My ruin shall not come alone; your match
    I'll hinder sure: my substance shall not glue you,
    Nor screw you into a family.
MOSCA.   Why, patron!
VOLPONE.   I am Volpone, and this is my knave;

                                    [Pointing to MOSCA.*]*

    This [*to* VOLTORE], his own knave; this [*to* CORBACCIO],
        avarice's fool;
    This [*to* CORVINO], a chimera[200] of wittol, fool, and knave:
    And, reverend fathers, since we all can hope
    Nought but a sentence, let's not now despair it.
3910   You hear me brief.
CORVINO.   May it please your fatherhoods—
COMMANDADORI.   Silence.
1ST AVOCATORI.   The knot is now undone by miracle.
2ND AVOCATORI.   Nothing can be more clear.
3RD AVOCATORI.   Or can more prove
    These innocent.
1ST AVOCATORI.   Give them their liberty.
BONARIO.   Heaven could not long let such gross crimes be
    hid.
3920 2ND AVOCATORI.   If this be held the highway to get riches,
    May I be poor!
3RD AVOCATORI.   This is not the gain, but torment.
1ST AVOCATORI.   These possess wealth, as sick men possess fevers,
    Which trulier may be said to posses them.
2ND AVOCATORI.   Disrobe that parasite.
CORVINO and MOSCA.   Most honoured fathers—
1ST AVOCATORI.   Can you plead aught to stay the course of justice?
    If you can, speak.
CORVINO and VOLTORE.   We beg favour.
3930 CELIA.   And mercy.
1ST AVOCATORI.   You hurt your innocence, suing for the guilty.
    Stand forth; and first the parasite. You appear
    T'have been the chiefest minister, if not plotter,
    In all these lewd impostures, and now, lastly,
    Have with your impudence abused° the court,   *deceived*
    And habit of a gentleman of Venice,
    Being a fellow of no birth or blood:
    For which our sentence is, first, thou be whipt;
    Then live a perpetual prisoner in our galleys.
3940 VOLPONE.   I thank you for him.

---

[200] A mythical creature resembling in composite a lion, goat, and serpent.

MOSCA.   Bane° to thy wolfish nature!   *poison*
1ST AVOCATORI.   Deliver him to the saffi. [MOSCA *is carried*
     out.] Thou, Volpone,
   By blood and rank a gentleman, canst not fall
   Under like censure; but our judgment on thee
   Is, that thy substance° all be straight confiscate   *property*
   To the hospital of the Incurabili:°   *incurables*
   And since the most was gotten by imposture,
   By feigning lame, gout, palsy, and such diseases,
3950   Thou art to lie in prison, cramp'd with irons,
   Till thou be'st sick and lame indeed. Remove him.

                                  [*He is taken from the Bar.*]

VOLPONE.   This is called mortifying° of a Fox.   *chastening*
1ST AVOCATORI.   Thou, Voltore, to take away the scandal,
   Thou hast given all worthy men of my profession,
   Art banished from their fellowship, and our state.
   Corbaccio!—bring him near. We here possess
   Thy son of all thy state,° and confine thee   *estate*
   To the monastery of San Spirito;[201]
   Where, since thou knewest not how to live well here,
3960   Thou shalt be learned to die well.
CORBACCIO.   Ha! what said he?
COMMANDADORI.   You shall know anon, sir.
1ST AVOCATORI.   Thou, Corvino, shalt
   Be straight embarked from thine own house, and rowed
   Round about Venice, through the grand canale,
   Wearing a cap, with fair long ass's ears,
   Instead of horns! and so to mount, a paper
   Pinned on thy breast, to the Berlina.[202]
CORVINO.   Yes,
3970   And have mine eyes beat out with stinking fish,
   Bruised fruit, and rotten eggs—'tis well. I am glad
   I shall not see my shame yet.°   *still*
1ST AVOCATORI.   And to expiate
   Thy wrongs done to thy wife, thou are to send her
   Home to her father, with her dowry trebled:
   And these are all your judgments.
ALL.   Honoured fathers—
1ST AVOCATORI.   Which may not be revoked. Now you begin,
   When crimes are done, and past, and to be punished,
3980   To think what your crimes are: away with them.
   Let all that see these vices thus rewarded
   Take heart and love to study 'em. Mischiefs feed
   Like beasts, till they be fat, and then they bleed.   [*Exeunt.*]

---

[201] The monastery of the Holy Spirit.
[202] A *pillory*, or ducking-stool [for publicly dunking offenders in water]. [Editors' note]

[VOLPONE *comes forward.*]

"The seasoning of a play is the applause.
Now, though the Fox be punished by the laws,
He yet doth hope, there is no suffering due,
For any fact° which he hath done 'gainst you;   *crime*
If there be, censure him; here he doubtful stands:
If not, fare jovially, and clap your hands."

[*Exit.*]

[ca. 1606]

Critical Commentary on *Volpone*

According to tradition, Jonson wrote *Volpone* in only five weeks. Then, early
in 1606 the play was performed before enthusiastic audiences, first at London's famous Globe Theater and later that same year at both Oxford and
Cambridge. Published in quarto in 1607 and then in the famous folio edition
of *The Works of Benjamin Jonson* in 1616, *Volpone* continued to enjoy popular
success on the English stage. Surviving records indicate that it was revived by
the King's Men in 1624, 1630, and 1638, and that it was frequently performed after the theaters were reopened in 1660 with the restoration of
Charles II. In our own time *Volpone* is generally regarded not just as one of
Jonson's major plays, but also as one of the great comedies of the English
language.

Volpone, the "magnifico," most assuredly ranks as one of the great characters in all of literature. Jonson uses his voluptuous title character and his
schemes as a vehicle for unleashing a satiric and heavily sardonic attack upon
human acquisitiveness and cupidity and the social pretentiousness that so
often accompanies the mad pursuit of opulence and wealth. The play's subtitle, *The Fox*, is an allusion to an old beast fable ("The Fox Who Feigned
Death") which tells the story of a sly fox who pretends to be dead in order to
turn the tables on birds of prey who come to devour him.

There can be little doubt that Jonson's choice of setting—luxurious and
exotic Venice—is perfect. In Jonson's day Venice enjoyed a well-established
reputation throughout Europe for its culture and refinement as well as for its
corruption, commercial materialism, licentiousness, and intrigue. English
travelers of Jonson's day, and for many years to come, were advised to be
wary of Italy and Venice and the temptations they offered to vice and depravity. Jonson's play clearly appeals to just such prejudices. To be sure,
Venice also enjoyed a reputation for the swift rendering of justice, which
gives the two trial scenes of Act IV and Act V a ring of credibility that Jonson's
contemporary audiences would recognize at once.

Like the fabled fox, Volpone is the consummate deceiver and con man, a
Protean figure able to assume a multitude of guises and masks and to use
them free from any moral restraint. The roguish, conscienceless Volpone is
in fact so attractive and vital in his rascality, audacity, bravado, and sheer
mental agility as to arouse our genuine admiration to the point that few
readers (or members of the audience) wish to see his stratagems fail. Even in

his wooing of Celia, with the famous *carpe diem* lyric "Come my Celia, let us prove," Volpone is, as Harold Bloom has observed, "positively endearing as he gets carried away in transports of voluptuousness." Given the surrounding cast of characters, such feelings are hardly surprising. With the exception of the passively innocent Celia and Bonario, whose virtues are real enough, most of Volpone's victims surely deserve to be victimized. Jonson's achievement, in short, is to create a character so vital and alive as to manage, in John W. Creaser's words, "to walk a knife-edge between moral condemnation and existential admiration."

Volpone makes his basic motive, the desire for wealth and power, together with his modus operandi immediately clear. Not only do we see him as the play opens kneeling in worship to offer a morning hymn to his hoard of gold ("Good morning to the day; and next, my gold"), but he soon announces,

> What should I do,
> But cocker up my genius and live free
> To all delights my fortune calls me to?
> I have no wife, no parent, child, ally,
> To give my substance to; but whom I make
> Must be my heir; and this makes men observe me.

The motives of money and power are not, of course, particularly unusual. What makes their pursuit particularly interesting in the case of Volpone is the kind of double consciousness that he adopts toward them. "What we have in Volpone," as C. N. Manlove observes, "is a man whose scale of values is entirely perverted by money, but who, at the same time, without applying the condition to himself, is able to see how wealth overthrows all values in other people. He is a man who has taken on an Olympian position, but who himself is one of those he mocks—a man who is in a fundamentally ironic position throughout the play."

To test Volpone's basic proposition about the corrupting power of wealth, Jonson introduces an almost perfect cast of fellow rogues. There is Mosca, the apparently faithful parasite and social climber, who aids Volpone's machinations with an almost effortless efficiency until he overplays his hand, succumbs to his own greed and betrays Volpone in Act 5. There are the three principal dupes, the birds of prey of the fable: the merchant Corvino (the crow); the miser Corbaccio (the raven) and the advocate Voltore (the vulture). Though all three conceal their private greed and spiritual poverty behind a veneer of respectability, each is so obsessed with becoming Volpone's heir that he becomes a willing and eager participant in his own gulling. Voltore is willing to sacrifice the truth which as a lawyer he has pledged to serve. The doddering and deaf Corbaccio is willing to disinherit and then betray his own son. Corvino is willing to offer up his own wife and her honor to satisfy Volpone's lust.

As is the case with most of Jonson's plays, *Volpone* consists of a tightly constructed five act plot, in which the first two acts serve to introduce the characters and initiate the conflict, the third to increase the complication, the fourth to offer a resolution that turns out to be false, and the fifth to provide the real conclusion. By the end of Act IV, Volpone, as crafty as the fox of the fable, seems to be triumphant in his manipulations. The helpless Celia and

Bonario have been declared guilty of adultery and slander, Volpone has convinced all concerned that he is dying, and the Venetian court, the arbiter of justice, seems to have been fooled. Stephen Greenblatt praises Jonson's use of what he calls a "false ending" as a means of testing the moral sensitivities and sensibilities of his audience. What in effect would the world be like, Jonson seems to be asking, if it mirrored the state of affairs—the kind of "justice"—displayed in Act IV? Having implicitly raised this question, having challenged the reader and playgoer to ponder these possibilities, Greenblatt contends that Jonson is then content to correct himself and to let the play reach a different, and apparently more satisfying, if grim, ending—at least in terms of our sense of justice.

Such a view as Greenblatt's is not, however, universally shared and any number of critics from John Dryden (1688) to the present have faulted the play's ending as forced, unduly contrived, and unsatisfactory. The somber and subdued nature of the ending results in happiness for no one, and is very unlike what one expects to find in a comedy of the conventional sort. To be sure, the Avocatori of Venice punish the wrong-doers with a severity that underscores the play's moral point, but as for happy survivors and a sense of resulting pleasure, there is little here for audience or reader to celebrate. Indeed, as John Gordon Sweeney observes, "The climax of the play is a remarkably protracted affair, extending through one and one-half acts and featuring several false resolutions. It demonstrates nothing about the inevitability of comic justice. Until the very last moment of the play, the entire plot might have been saved had Mosca and Volpone been able to reach a settlement."

What is absent here, in other words, is anything resembling a final optimistic statement about the possibilities of the human spirit to transcend the corruption and perversity that so strongly marks Jonson's play. In fact it is Volpone himself who comes forward to speak the play's Epilogue, appealing for our empathy, "joviality" and applause, and reminding us, as R. B. Parker suggests, that "theatrically and imaginatively the Fox survives because he represents something permanent in all of us, a corruption that is closely linked to our vitality."

A Selective Bibliography on *Volpone*

Anderson, Mark A. "Structure and Response in *Volpone.*" *Renaissance and Modern Studies* 19 (1975): 47–71.

Barish, Jonas A. "The Double Plot in *Volpone.*" *Modern Philology* 51 (1953): 83–92.

———, ed. *Volpone: A Case Book.* London: Macmillan, 1972.

Barton, Anne. *Ben Jonson, Dramatist.* Cambridge, Eng.: Cambridge UP, 1984. 105–19.

Beaurline, L. A. *Jonson and Elizabeth Comedy: Essays in Dramatic Rhetoric.* San Marino, Ca.: Huntington Library, 1978. 160–94.

Bloom, Harold, ed. *Ben Jonson.* New York: Chelsea, 1987.

Brock, D. Heyward. *A Ben Jonson Companion.* Bloomington: Indiana UP, 1983.

Broude, Ronald. "Volpone and the Triumph of Truth: Some Antecedents and Analogues of the Main Plot of *Volpone.*" *Studies in Philology* 77 (1980): 227–46.

Bryant, J. A., Jr. *The Compassionate Satirist: Ben Jonson and His Imperfect World.* Athens: U of Georgia P, 1972. 56–91.

Clary, Frank N., Jr. "The Vol and the Pone: A Reconsideration." *English Language Notes* 10 (1972): 102–07.

Creaser, John. "Volpone: The Mortifying of the Fox." *Essays in Criticism* 25 (1975): 329–56.

Davison, P. H. "Volpone and the Old Comedy." *Modern Language Quarterly* 24 (1963): 151–57.

Dessen, Alan C. *Jonson's Moral Comedy.* Evanston: Northwestern UP, 1971: 74–106.

Donaldson, Ian. "Volpone: Quick and Dead." *Essays in Criticism* 21 (1971): 121–34.

Duncan, Douglas. *Ben Jonson and the Lucianic Tradition.* Cambridge, Eng.: Cambridge UP, 1979.

Empson, William. "Volpone." *Hudson Review* 21 (1968–1969): 651–66.

Gertmenian, Donald. "Volpone's Mortification." *Essays in Criticism* 26 (1976): 274–77.

Gossett, S. "Best Men are Molded out of Faults': Marrying the Rapist in Jacobean Drama." *English Literary Renaissance* 14 (1984): 305–27.

Greenblatt, Stephen J. "The False Ending in *Volpone.*" *Journal of English and Germanic Philology* 75 (1976): 90–104.

Grene, Nicholas. *Shakespeare, Jonson, Moliere: The Comic Contract.* London: Macmillan, 1980.

Hallett, Charles A. "Jonson's Celia: A Reinterpretation of *Volpone.*" *Studies in Philology* 68 (1971): 50–69.

———. "The Satanic Nature of Volpone." *Philological Quarterly* 49 (1970): 41–55.

Hill, W. Speed. "Biography, Autobiography, and *Volpone.*" *Studies in English Literature* 12 (1972): 309–28.

Hurd, Myles. "Between Crime and Punishment in Jonson's *Volpone.*" *College Literature* 10 (1983): 172–83.

Hyland, Peter. *Disguise and Role-Playing in Ben Jonson's Drama.* Salzburg: U of Salzburg, 1977.

Jones, Robert C. *Engagement with Knavery: Point of View in Richard III, The Jew of Malta, Volpone, and The Revenger's Tragedy.* Durham: Duke UP, 1986.

Knoll, Robert E. *Ben Jonson's Plays: An Introduction.* Lincoln: U of Nebraska P, 1964. 79–104.

Leggatt, Alexander. *Ben Jonson: His Vision and His Art.* London: Methuen, 1981.

Manlove, C. N. "The Double View in *Volpone,*" *Studies in English Literature* 19 (1979): 239–52.

McPherson, David C. *Shakespeare, Jonson, and the Myth of Venice.* Newark: U of Delaware P, 1990. i.

Miles, Rosalind. *Ben Jonson: His Life and Work.* London: Routledge, 1986. 108–111.

———. *Ben Jonson: His Art and Craft.* London: Routledge, 1990.

Murray, Timothy. "From Foul Sheets to Legitimate Model: Antitheater, Text, Ben Jonson." *New Literary History* 14 (1983): 641–64.

Nardo, A.K. "The Transmigrations of Folly: Volpone's Innocent Grotesques." *English Studies* 58 (1977): 105–09.

Parker, R. B. "Introduction." *Volpone or, The Fox.* Manchester, Eng.: Manchester UP, 1983. 1–65.

Paster, Gail Kern. "Ben Jonson's Comedy of Limitation." *Studies in Philology* 72 (1975): 51–71.

Salingar, Leo. "Comic Form in Ben Jonson: Volpone and the Philosopher's Stone." *English Drama: Forms of Development.* Eds. Marie Axton and Raymond Williams. Cambridge, Eng: Cambridge UP, 1977. 48–69.

Shapiro, James S. *Rival Playwrights: Marlowe, Jonson, Shakespeare*. New York: Columbia UP, 1991.

Simmons, Joseph L. "Volpone as Antinous: Jonson and 'Th' Overthrow of Stage-Playes.' " *Modern Language Review* 70 (1975): 13–19.

Summers, Claude J. and Ted-Larry Pebworth. *Ben Jonson*. Boston: Twayne, 1979. 61–70.

Sweeney, John Gordon, III. *Jonson and the Psychology of Public Theater*. Princeton: Princeton UP, 1985. 70–104.

Watson, Robert N. *Ben Jonson's Parodic Strategy: Literary Imperialism in the Comedies*. Cambridge: Harvard UP, 1987. 82–97.

Womack, Peter. *Ben Jonson*. New York: Blackwell, 1986.

Molière (Jean-Baptiste Poquelin) (1622–1673)

TARTUFFE OR THE HYPOCRITE
(L'IMPOSTEUR)
A COMEDY

Translated by A. R. Waller

CHARACTERS

MADAME PERNELLE, *Orgon's mother*
ORGON, *Elmire's husband*
ELMIRE, *Orgon's wife*
DAMIS, *Orgon's son, Elmire's stepson*
MARIANE, *Orgon's daughter, Elmire's stepdaughter, and Valère's lover*
VALÈRE, *Mariane's lover*

CLÉANTE, *Orgon's brother-in-law*
TARTUFFE, *a hypocrite*
DORINE, *Mariane's maid*
M. LOYAL, *A bailiff*
POLICE OFFICER
FLIPOTE, *Mme. Pernelle's servant*
LAURENT, *Tartuffe's servant*

SCENE: *Paris*

ACT I

SCENE I

MADAME PERNELLE *and* FLIPOTE, *her servant,* ELMIRE, MARIANE, DORINE, DAMIS, CLÉANTE

MME. PERNELLE. Come along, Flipote, come along; let me get away from them.

ELMIRE. You walk so fast that I can scarcely keep up with you.

MME. PERNELLE. You need not come any further, child. I can dispense with such ceremony.

ELMIRE. We only give what is due to you. But, mother, why are you in such a hurry to leave us?

MME. PERNELLE. Because I cannot bear to see such goings on and no one takes any pains to meet my wishes. Yes, I leave your house not very well pleased: you ignore all my advice, you do not show any respect for anything, everyone says what he likes, and it is just like the Court of King Pétaud.[1]

DORINE. If . . .

MME. PERNELLE. You are far too free with your tongue for your position, my lass, and too saucy. You offer your advice about everything.

DAMIS. But . . .

MME. PERNELLE. You are a fool thrice over, my boy, though it is your own

---

[1] A court without order where every man is his own master.

grandmother who says it. I have told your father a hundred times that you will become a ne'er-do-well, and will cause him nothing but trouble.

20 MARIANE.   I think . . .

MME. PERNELLE.   As for you, his sister, you put on such a demure air that it is difficult to catch you tripping. But, as the saying is, still waters are the most dangerous, and I hate your underhand ways.

ELMIRE.   But, mother . . .

MME. PERNELLE.   Let me tell you, daughter, that your whole conduct is entirely wrong. You ought to set them a good example: their late mother did much better. You are extravagant: I am shocked to see you decked out like a princess. If a woman wishes to please her husband only, she has no need for so much finery, my child.

30 CLÉANTE.   But, madam, after all . . .

MME. PERNELLE.   As for you, sir, who are her brother, I think very highly of you, and I both love and respect you, but, at the same time, if I were my son, her husband, I should request you not to enter our house. You are always laying down rules of conduct which respectable people should not follow. I speak rather frankly to you, but that is my nature: I do not mince matters when I have anything on my mind.

DAMIS.   Your Mr. Tartuffe is, no doubt, an excellent person . . .

MME. PERNELLE.   He is a very worthy man, one who should be listened to; and it makes me very angry to hear him sneered at by a fool like you.

40 DAMIS.   What! Am I to permit a censorious bigot to exercise a tyrannical influence in the family; and are we not to be allowed any pleasures unless this good gentleman condescends to give his consent?

DORINE.   Were we to listen to him and to put faith in his maxims, we should look upon all our acts as criminal, for the zealous critic finds fault with everything.

MME. PERNELLE.   And whatever he finds fault with deserves censure. He wants to lead you to Heaven, and it is my son's duty to teach you to value him.

DAMIS.   No; look here, grandmother, neither my father nor anyone else shall ever induce me to think well of him: I should be false to myself were 50   I to speak otherwise. His ways irritate me constantly. I can see what the consequence will be: that underbred fellow and I will soon quarrel.

DORINE.   Surely it is a scandalous thing to see a stranger exercise such authority in this house: to see a beggar, who, when he came, had not shoes on his feet, and whose whole clothing may have been worth twopence, so far forget himself as to interfere with everything, and play the master.

MME. PERNELLE.   Ah! mercy on me! it would be much better if everything were done in accordance with his good rules.

DORINE.   He is a saint in your opinion, but, in mine, he is a hypocrite.

MME. PERNELLE.   What language!

60 DORINE.   I should not like to trust myself either with him or with his man Laurent, without good security.

MME. PERNELLE.   I do not know what the servant may be at heart, but I will swear the master is a worthy man. You all hate and flout him because he tells you unpleasant truths. His anger is directed against sin, and his only desire is to further the cause of Heaven.

DORINE.   Yes; but why, especially for some time past, can he not bear any one to come to the house? Why is a polite call so offensive to Heaven that he

needs make noise enough about it to split our heads? Between ourselves
I will tell you what I think. Upon my word, I believe that he is jealous of
70   Madame.

MME. PERNELLE.   Hold your tongue, and take care what you say. He is not the
only person who blames these visits. The whole neighborhood is annoyed
by the bustle of the people you receive, their carriages always waiting
before the door, and the noisy crowd of servants. I am willing to believe
that there is no actual harm done, but people will talk, and it is better not
to give them cause.

CLÉANTE.   Ah! madam, how can you stop people talking? It would be a sorry
thing if in this world we had to give up our best friends, because of idle
chatter aimed at us. And even if we could bring ourselves to do so, do you
80   think it would stop people's tongues? There is not any protection against
slander. Do not let us pay any attention to foolish gossip, but endeavour
to live honestly and leave the scandal-mongers to say what they will.

DORINE.   Probably our neighbor Daphné, and her little husband, are at the
bottom of all this slander. Those who are the most ridiculous in their own
conduct are always the first to libel others. They are quick to get hold of
the slightest rumor of a love-affair, to spread it abroad with high glee,
giving the story just what twist they like. They paint the actions of others
in their own colors, thinking thereby to justify their own conduct to the
world; and in the vain hope of a resemblance they try to give their in-
90   trigues some show of innocence, or else to shift to other shoulders a part
of that blame with which they themselves are overburdened.

MME. PERNELLE.   All these arguments have nothing to do with the matter.
Everybody knows that Orante leads an exemplary life, and that all her
thoughts are towards heaven. Well, I have been told that she strongly
disapproves of the company who visit here.

DORINE.   The example is admirable, and the lady is beyond reproach! It is
true that she lives an austere life, but age is responsible for her fervent
zeal, and people know that she is a prude because she cannot help it. She
made the most of all her advantages while she had the power of attracting
100   attention. But now that her eyes have lost their luster she renounces the
world which renounces her, and hides under the pompous cloak of prudence the decay of her worn-out charms. Such is the last shift of a modern
coquette. Mortified to see their lovers fall away from them, their gloomy
despair sees nothing for it, when thus forsaken, but the rôle of prudery;
and in their strictness these good women censure everything and pardon
nothing. They loudly condemn the actions of others, not from principles
of charity, but out of envy, since they cannot bear to see another taste
those pleasures for which age has taken away their appetite.

MME. PERNELLE.   These are idle tales told to please you. I have to be silent in
110   your house, my child, for madam, by gossiping, holds the dice the whole
day.[2] Still, I mean to have my say in my turn. I tell you that my son never
did a wiser act than when he received this good man into his family;
Heaven mercifully sent him into your house to convert your erring
thoughts. You ought to hear him for your soul's sake, since he censures

---

[2] I.e., she dominates the conversation.

nothing but that which deserves censure. All these visits, these balls, these tales, are inventions of the evil one. Not one good word is heard at them, nothing but idle gossip, songs and chatter. Often enough the neighbor comes in for his share, and there is scandal right and left. Indeed the heads of sensible people are quite turned by the distraction of these gath-
120   erings. A thousand ill-natured stories are spread abroad in no time; and, as a certain doctor very truly said the other day, it is a perfect tower of Babylon, for every one babbles as long as he likes. And to tell the story which brought this up . . . Here is this gentleman giggling already! Go and find the fools who make you laugh, and unless . . . Good-bye, my child. I'll say no more. My regard for your house has fallen by one-half, and it will be a very long time before I set foot in it again. [*Slapping* FLIPOTE's *face.*] Come along, you, don't stand there dreaming and gaping. Good Lord! I'll warm your ears for you, come on, hussy, come on.

SCENE II

CLÉANTE, DORINE

CLÉANTE.   I will not follow her lest she should begin scolding me again. How
130   that old woman . . .
DORINE.   Ah! truly it is a pity that she does not hear you use such language. She would soon tell you *your* age, and that *she* is not yet old enough to deserve that title.
CLÉANTE.   What a passion she got into with us about nothing, and how infatuated she seems with her Tartuffe!
DORINE.   Oh! indeed, her infatuation is nothing in comparison with her son's, and if you could see him you would say he was far worse! During our civil troubles he gained a reputation for sense, and showed some courage in serving his prince, but he has become an idiot since his head has been
140   full of Tartuffe. He calls him brother, and in his heart loves him a hundred times more than he loves mother, son, daughter, and wife. He makes him the sole confidant of all his secrets, and the sage adviser of all his actions. He caresses him, kisses him, and I do not think he could show more affection to a mistress. He will have him seated at the head of the table, and is delighted to see him eat as much as half-a-dozen other people. All the choice morsels are given to him, and if he chance to hiccup he says to him, "God bless you!" In short, he is crazy about him; he is his all, his hero; he admires him at all points, quotes him on all occasions; he considers that his most trifling actions are miracles, and every word he utters
150   an oracle. Tartuffe, who understands his dupe, and wishes to make the most profit out of him, is clever enough to impose upon him in a hundred different shams. He constantly extorts money from him by his cant, and takes upon himself the right to find fault with us all. Even that puppy of a footboy of his has the cheek to lecture us; he preaches at us with indignant looks, and throws away our ribbons, rouge, and patches.[3] Only the

---

[3] It was the fashion at the time for women to wear small black patches to cover up blemishes (or scars from smallpox) on their faces.

other day the wretch tore a handkerchief to pieces which he found in a 'Flower of the Saints,' saying that it was an abominable sin to put the devil's trappings side by side with holy things.

SCENE III

ELMIRE, MARIANE, DAMIS, CLÉANTE, DORINE

160 ELMIRE. You are very lucky to have missed the sermon she gave us at the door. But I have just seen my husband, and as he did not see me I shall go and wait upstairs for him.

CLÉANTE. I will wait for him here for a little longer, only to bid him "Good-morning."

DAMIS. Sound him a little about my sister's marriage. I suspect that Tartuffe opposes it, because he puts my father up to so many evasions; and you know what a great interest I take in it. If the same passion influences my sister and Valère, his sister is, as you know, dear to me, and if it were necessary . . .

DORINE. Here he is.

SCENE IV

ORGON, CLÉANTE, DORINE

170 ORGON. Ah! good-morning, brother.

CLÉANTE. I am glad to see you back. I was just going away. The country is not very attractive just now.

ORGON. Dorine . . . Just one moment, brother, I beg. You will, I know, let me relieve my mind by asking how things have gone here. Has all been well during the last two days? What has happened? How are they all?

DORINE. The day before yesterday Madam was feverish from morning to night, with a splitting headache.

ORGON. And Tartuffe?

DORINE. Tartuffe? He is in excellent health, stout and fat, with a fresh
180 complexion and ruddy lips.

ORGON. Poor man!

DORINE. In the evening she felt very sick, and her head ached so violently she could not touch anything at supper.

ORGON. And Tartuffe?

DORINE. He took his supper, in her presence, and very devoutly ate a brace of partridges and half a leg of mutton hashed.

ORGON. Poor man!

DORINE. She passed the whole night without closing her eyes for a moment, kept from sleeping by her feverishness, and we were obliged to sit up with
190 her until morning.

ORGON. And Tartuffe?

DORINE. Comfortably drowsy when he got up from the table, he went to his bedroom and quickly tumbled into his warmed bed, where he slept undisturbed till the morning.

ORGON.   Poor man!

DORINE.   At length we prevailed upon her to be bled,[4] and immediately she felt relieved.

ORGON.   And Tartuffe?

DORINE.   He took heart again, as was only right, and to fortify himself against
200   all ills, and to make up for the blood which Madam had lost, he drank four large bumpers of wine at breakfast.

ORGON.   Poor man!

DORINE.   Both are now well again, and I will go and tell Madam how pleased you are at her recovery.

SCENE V

ORGON, CLÉANTE

CLÉANTE.   She is making game of you, brother, to your face, and, without wishing to vex you, I tell you frankly there is good reason for it. Who ever heard of such a whim? How can you be so infatuated with a man at this time of day as to forget everything else for him? And, after having saved him from want by taking him into your own house you should go so far
210   as . . .

ORGON.   Stop there, brother, you do not know the man of whom you speak.

CLÉANTE.   I do not know him then, if you like; but, after all, to know what sort of a man he is . . .

ORGON.   Brother, you would be only too glad to know him, and your astonishment would be boundless. He is a man . . . who . . . ha! . . . a man . . . in fact, a man. He who follows attentively his precepts enjoys a profound peace, and looks upon the rest of the world as so much dross. Yes, I am quite another man since I conversed with him. He teaches me that I must not set my affections upon anything; he detaches my heart from all ties;
220   and I could see my brother, children, mother and wife die without caring as much as a snap of the fingers.

CLÉANTE.   Humane feelings these, brother!

ORGON.   Oh! had you but seen him as I first saw him, you would have for him the same affection that I have. Every day he would come to church, and with mild looks kneel down in front of me. He drew upon himself the attention of the whole congregation by the fervor of his prayers to Heaven; he sighed deeply in his saintly raptures and kissed the ground humbly every moment, and when I came out he would steal quickly before me to the door to offer me holy water. Having learnt who he was, and that he was
230   poor—through his footboy—who copies everything he does—I gave him presents, but he always modestly wished to return me some part of them. "It is too much, too much by half," he would say, "I do not deserve your pity." And when I refused to take it back he distributed it to the poor before my eyes. At last Heaven moved me to take him into my house, and

---

[4] Doctors in Molière's day frequently opened a vein in a patient's arm in an effort to drain off the tainted blood thought to cause illness.

since then everything has seemed to prosper here. He reproves every-thing, and, with a view to my honor, he shows an extreme solicitude even towards my wife. He tells me of those who cast sweet looks her way, and he is six times more jealous of her than I am. You would never guess how far he carries his zeal: he accuses himself of sin over the slightest trifle; a mere nothing is enough to shock him; he even accused himself the other day for having killed a flea too angrily which he caught whilst saying his prayers.

240

CLÉANTE.   Really, brother, I think you must be crazy. Are you joking at my expense with this nonsense? How can you pretend that all this foolery . . .?

ORGON.   Brother, your talk savors of free thought: you are somewhat tainted with it; and, as I have repeatedly told you, you will draw down some heavy judgment upon your head.

CLÉANTE.   That is the usual style of talking among your set; they want ev-eryone to be as blind as themselves. To be clear-sighted is to be a free-thinker, and he who does not bow down to idle affectations has neither respect for nor faith in sacred things. I tell you none of your sermons frighten me: I know what I say, and Heaven sees my heart. We are not ruled by your formalists. There are pretenders to devotion as to courage; and even as those who are truly brave when honor calls are not those who make the most noise, so the good and truly pious, in whose footsteps we ought to follow, are not those who make so many grimaces. What? will you not make any distinction between hypocrisy and sincerity? Will you speak of them in the same words, and render the same homage to the mask as to the face, put artifice on a level with sincerity, confound the appearance with the reality, value the shadow as much as the substance and false coin as good? Men, truly, are strange beings! They are never seen in their proper nature; reason's boundaries are too limited for them; in every character they overact the part; and they often mar that which is most noble by too much exaggeration and by wilful extremes. But this, brother, is by the way.

250

260

ORGON.   Yes, you are doubtless a doctor, revered by all; all the learning of the ages is concentrated in you; you alone are wise, enlightened, an oracle, a Cato[5] for the present age; and compared with you, all men are fools.

CLÉANTE.   No, brother, I am not a revered teacher, nor do I possess all wisdom; my learning is simply the knowledge of how to tell the false from the true. And since I do not know any character more admirable than the truly devout, nor anything in the world more noble and more beautiful than the righteous fervor of a sincere piety, neither do I know anything more odious than the whited sepulchre of a specious zeal; than these barefaced hypocrites, these hireling bigots, whose sacrilegious and deceit-ful mouthings impose on people with impunity, who jest as they please with all that men hold most holy and sacred; these slaves of self-interest who barter religion and make a trade of it, and who would purchase honor and reputation with a false uplifting of the eyes and affected groans. These men, I say, whom we see possessed of such uncommon ardor, make their

270

---

[5] Marcus Porcius Cato (234–149 B.C.), a Roman consul renowned for devotion to virtue; or his great-grandson, Marcus Porcius Cato, the Younger (95–46 B.C.), a philosopher.

280 fortunes in this world by way of the next; themselves asking each day some new favor, they preach solitude in the midst of the Court, burning with zeal and great in prayer. They know how to reconcile their profession with their vices, are passionate, revengeful, faithless, full of deceit, and, in order to ruin a man, insolently cover their fierce resentment with the cloak of Heaven's interests. They are doubly dangerous in their bitter wrath for they use against us the weapons we revere; and their anger, for which they are commended, prompts them to kill us with a consecrated blade. There are too many of these false characters; the truly devout are easily recognised. Our age, brother, has shown us some who should serve us as glo-
290 rious examples: look at Ariston, look at Périandre, Oronte, Alcidamas, Polydore, Clitandre[6]—no one denies their title. These are not boasters of virtue; unbearable ostentation is not seen in them; their piety is human, is reasonable; they do not condemn all our actions: they think there is too much arrogance in these censures; and, leaving haughty words to others, they reprove our actions by their own. They do not build upon the appearances of evil, and their minds are inclined to think well of others. No spirit of cabal is found in them; they have no intrigues to scent out; their sole care is to live rightly. They do not persecute a sinner; it is only the sin itself they hate. Neither do they desire to vindicate the interests of Heaven
300 with a keener zeal than Heaven itself shows. These are the people I admire; that is the right way to live; there is, in short, the example to be followed. Your man, to speak truly, is not of this mold: you applaud his piety in good faith, but I believe you are dazzled by a false glitter.

ORGON. Have you said your say, my dear brother?

CLÉANTE. Yes.

ORGON. I am your humble servant [*going*].

CLÉANTE. One word, brother, I pray. Let us drop this discussion. You know you promised Valère he should become your son-in-law?

ORGON. Yes.

310 CLÉANTE. And that you had fixed the happy day.

ORGON. True.

CLÉANTE. Why, then, defer the ceremony?

ORGON. I do not know.

CLÉANTE. Have you another design in view?

ORGON. Perhaps.

CLÉANTE. You will break your word?

ORGON. I do not say that.

CLÉANTE. No obstacle, I believe, can prevent you fulfilling your promises.

ORGON. That depends.

320 CLÉANTE. Why so much circumspection about a word? Valère sent me to see you on this matter.

ORGON. Heaven be praised!

CLÉANTE. But what shall I tell him?

ORGON. What you please.

CLÉANTE. But it is necessary to know your intentions. What, then, are they?

---

[6] Fictitious, not historical, persons.

Orgon.　To perform the will of Heaven.

Cléante.　Come, speak to the point. Valère has your word. Will you keep it or not?

Orgon.　Good-bye.

330 Cléante.　I am afraid his love will not run smooth, and I ought to tell him what is going on.

ACT II

SCENE I

Orgon, Mariane

Orgon.　Mariane

Mariane.　Yes, father.

Orgon.　Come here, I have something to say to you privately.

Mariane.　What are you looking for?

Orgon [*looking into a small side-room*].　I am looking to see whether anyone is there who might overhear us; this is a most likely little place for such a purpose. Now, we are all right. Mariane, I have always found you very good-natured, and you have always been dear to me.

340 Mariane.　I am very grateful for your fatherly love.

Orgon.　That is well said, my child, and in order to deserve it your chief care ought to be to please me.

Mariane.　It is my dearest wish.

Orgon.　Very well. What do you think of our guest Tartuffe?

Mariane.　Who, I?

Orgon.　You. Think well before you answer.

Mariane.　Oh, dear! I will say anything you like.

Orgon.　That is sensibly spoken. Tell me, then, my child, that he is a man whose virtues shine forth, that you love him, and that it would make you

350 very happy were I to choose him for your husband. Eh?

Mariane [*draws back, surprised*].　Eh?

Orgon.　What is the matter?

Mariane.　What did you say?

Orgon.　What?

Mariane.　Am I mistaken?

Orgon.　Why?

Mariane.　Whom do you wish me to say I love, father? Whom do I wish you to choose as my husband?

Orgon.　Tartuffe

360 Mariane.　I don't wish anything of the kind, father, I assure you. Why would you make me tell such a lie?

Orgon.　But I wish it to be the truth, and it is enough for you that I have made up my mind on the subject.

Mariane.　What, father, would you . . .?

Orgon.　Yes, my child, I intend to unite Tartuffe to my family by your marriage. I have decided that he shall be your husband, and since you have promised, I . . .

SCENE II

DORINE, ORGON, MARIANE

ORGON.   What are you doing here? Your curiosity must be very great, my girl, to urge you to come and listen to us in this way.

370 DORINE.   Indeed, I don't know whether the report is conjecture or simply chance words, but I have just heard some news about this marriage and I treated it as a mere jest.

ORGON.   Why? Is the thing incredible?

DORINE.   So much so that I could not believe it from your lips, Monsieur.

ORGON.   I know how to make you believe it, though.

DORINE.   Yes, yes, you tell us a pretty story.

ORGON.   I tell you what you will see happen very shortly.

DORINE.   Nonsense!

ORGON.   I am not jesting, my child.

380 DORINE.   Come, do not believe your father, he is joking.

ORGON.   I tell you . . .

DORINE.   No, you may say what you like, and no one will believe you.

ORGON.   My anger will very soon . . .

DORINE.   Very well, we will believe you, but so much the worse for you. What, is it possible, Monsieur, with that air of wisdom and your well-bearded face, that you would be silly enough to want . . .

ORGON.   Now listen: you have taken certain liberties in this house, my girl, which I do not like.

DORINE.   Let us talk without becoming angry, Monsieur, I beg. Are you

390 making game of everybody by means of this scheme? Your daughter will never do for a bigot: he has other things to think about. Besides, what good will such an alliance be to you? Why, with all your wealth, do you choose a beggar for a son-in-law?

ORGON.   Be quiet. If he has nothing he ought to be the more esteemed. His poverty is, without doubt, a noble poverty; it should raise him above all worldly greatness since he has allowed himself to be deprived of his wealth by caring too little for earthly affairs, and by his ardent attachment to things eternal. My help may be the means of getting him out of his troubles and of restoring his property to him: his estates are well known

400 in his native place, but even as he is he is a gentleman.

DORINE.   Well, he says he is, but this vanity, Monsieur, does not agree well with his piety. He who embraces the simplicity of a holy life should not boast of his name and lineage: the humble ways of goodness have nothing in common with the glare of ambition. Why such pride? But what I say vexes you: let us speak of himself and leave his quality. Can you have the heart to bestow such a daughter as yours upon a man of his stamp? Ought you not to have some regard for propriety and foresee the consequences of this union? You must know the girl's virtue is not safe when she is married against her inclinations, that her living virtuously depends upon

410 the qualities of the husband who is given to her, and that those who have the finger of scorn pointed at them make their wives what we see they are. It is truly no easy task to be faithful to certain husbands; and he who gives

his daughter to a man she hates is responsible to heaven for the sins she commits. Consider, then, to what perils your design exposes you.

ORGON.   I see I shall have to learn from her how to live.

DORINE.   You could not do better than follow my advice.

ORGON.   Do not let us waste time, my child, with this silly talk. I am your father, and I know what is good for you. I had betrothed you to Valère, but I hear he is inclined to gambling, and I also suspect he is a free-thinker,

420   for I never see him at church.

DORINE.   Would you like him to go there at stated times like those who go to be seen?

ORGON.   I don't ask your advice upon the matter. Tartuffe is on the best possible terms with heaven, and that is a treasure second to none. This union will crown your wishes with every blessing. It will be full of pleasure and joy. You will live together in faithful love like two young children, like turtledoves, there will not be any miserable disputes between you, and you will make anything you like of him.

DORINE.   She? Why, I am sure she will never make anything of him but a fool.

430 ORGON.   Good gracious! what language!

DORINE.   I tell you he looks it all over, and his destiny, Monsieur, will be stronger than your daughter's virtue.

ORGON.   Don't interrupt me. Try to hold your tongue without poking your nose into what does not concern you.

DORINE.   I only speak for your good, Monsieur. [*She interrupts him every time he turns to speak to his daughter.*]

ORGON.   You are too good! Be quiet, will you?

DORINE.   If I did not like you . . .

ORGON.   I do not need affection.

440 DORINE.   But I will care for you, Monsieur, in spite of yourself.

ORGON.   Ah!

DORINE.   Your honor is dear to me, and I cannot bear that you should be jeered at by every one.

ORGON.   Will you be silent?

DORINE.   It is a shame to let you make such an alliance.

ORGON.   Will you hold your peace, you viper, whose brazen face . . .

DORINE.   What! you a religious man and you give way to anger?

ORGON.   Yes, my choler is roused to fury by your nonsense. I insist upon your holding your tongue.

450 DORINE.   Very well. But if I cannot speak I shall think all the more.

ORGON.   Think, if you like, but take care not to tell your thoughts to me, or . . . beware. [*Turning towards his daughter.*] I have deliberately weighed everything as a prudent man should.

DORINE.   It makes me furious not to be allowed to speak. [*She is silent when he looks towards her.*]

ORGON.   Without being a fop Tartuffe's looks are such . . .

DORINE.   Yes, he has a fine mug.

ORGON.   That even if you do not appreciate his other qualities . . . [*He turns towards her, and looks at her, his arms folded.*]

460 DORINE.   There's a fine bargain! If I were in her place, depend upon it no man should marry me against my will with impunity. I would soon let him

see, after the wedding-day, that a woman has always her vengeance in her own hands.

ORGON.   Then you do not mean to take any notice of what I say?

DORINE.   What are you complaining about? I was not speaking to you.

ORGON.   What were you doing then?

DORINE.   I was speaking to myself.

ORGON.   All right. I must give her the back of my hand for her unbearable insolence. [*He prepares to slap* DORINE's *face; and* DORINE *stands silent and erect*
470   *each time he looks at her.*] You ought to approve of my plan, my child . . . and have faith in the husband . . . I have chosen for you . . . Why do you not speak to yourself?

DORINE.   Because I have no more to say to myself.

ORGON.   Only a little word.

DORINE.   It does not suit me.

ORGON.   I was waiting for you.

DORINE.   I am not such a fool.

ORGON.   In short, my girl, you must obey, and show all deference to my choice.

480 DORINE   [*running away*]. I would take care I would not marry such a husband.

ORGON.   [*He tries to slap* DORINE's *face and misses her.*] You have a pestilent hussy there, my child, with whom I cannot live without forgetting myself. I feel I am not fit now to continue the conversation. Such insolent speeches have put me in so great a passion that I must have a breath of air to compose myself.

SCENE III

DORINE, MARIANE

DORINE.   Tell me, have you lost your tongue; must I play your part in this matter? To think you allow such an absurd proposal to be made to you without your saying a word against it!

490 MARIANE.   What would you have me do against a tyrannical father?

DORINE.   Anything to ward off such a fate.

MARIANE.   But what?

DORINE.   Tell him a heart cannot love at the bidding of another, that you marry to please yourself not him, that, as the matter concerns you alone it is you, not him, whom the husband must please, and that, since he is so charmed with his Tartuffe, he can marry him himself without any hindrance.

MARIANE.   A father has such authority over us that I admit I have not had the courage to say anything.

500 DORINE.   Let us talk it all over. Valère has proposed to you: do you love him, pray, or do you not?

MARIANE.   Oh! Dorine, you are very unjust to me. How can you ask me such a question? Have I not opened my heart to you a hundred times on this subject? Do you not know how much I love him?

DORINE.   How do I know your lips have spoken what your heart felt and that you really care for this lover?

MARIANE.   You wrong me greatly, Dorine, to doubt it. Surely my real feelings
    have shown themselves only too plainly.

DORINE.   Then you love him?

MARIANE.   Yes, passionately.

510 DORINE.   And apparently he loves you just as ardently.

MARIANE.   I believe so.

DORINE.   And you both are eager to be married.

MARIANE.   Most certainly.

DORINE.   What do you mean to do, then, about this other match?

MARIANE.   To kill myself if I am forced into it.

DORINE.   Good! I had not thought of that way out of the difficulty; you have
    but to die to be rid of troubles; what an excellent remedy! It puts me out
    of all patience to hear such talk.

MARIANE.   Good heavens! what a temper you are in, Dorine. You have no
520   sympathy for people in their troubles.

DORINE.   I have no pity for those who talk nonsense and give way at the
    critical moment as you do.

MARIANE.   But what can I do? I am afraid.

DORINE.   Love asks for courage.

MARIANE.   Have I wavered in my love of Valère? Is it not his place to win me
    from my father?

DORINE.   What if your father is a downright lunatic, who has gone clean crazy
    over his Tartuffe, and who does not keep his promise about this marriage:
    is your lover to be blamed for that?

530 MARIANE.   But am I, by haughty refusal and contemptuous disdain, to let
    everyone see my own heart is too deeply smitten? However much I desire
    Valère, am I to cast aside for him my womanly modesty and my filial duty?
    And would you have me show my heart to the whole world . . .?

DORINE.   No, no! I won't ask you to do anything. I see you wish to belong to
    Monsieur Tartuffe; and I should do wrong, now I come to think of it, were
    I to dissuade you from such a marriage. What excuse have I for opposing
    your wishes? The match in itself is very advantageous. Monsieur Tartuffe!
    oh! oh! is it nothing that is proposed? Indeed, Monsieur Tartuffe, to look
    at the thing in the right light, is not a man to be trifled with by any means,
540   and it is not a piece of bad luck to be his better half. The world has already
    crowned him with glory; he passes for an aristocrat in his own parish, well
    set up in person, with his red ears and his florid complexion. How very
    happy you will be with such a husband!

MARIANE.   Oh! dear . . .

DORINE.   What delight you will experience when you become the wife of such
    a bridegroom!

MARIANE.   Oh! stop such talk, I beg you, and show me the way to avoid this
    marriage. Let us make an end of it. I give in, and am ready to do anything.

DORINE.   A daughter should obey her father even if he wished her to marry
550   an ape. Yours is an enviable fate; of what do you complain? You will go in
    the coach to his native town and find yourself rich in uncles and cousins
    whom it will delight you exceedingly to entertain. You will soon be intro-
    duced into the best society; you will begin by visits to the magistrate's wife
    and the tax-surveyor's lady, who will honor you with a folding-stool. At
    carnival time you may hope for a ball there, the grand local band, con-

sisting of two bagpipes, in attendance, and possibly the learned ape will be present and marionettes, only, if your husband . . .

MARIANE.   Oh! you are enough to kill me. Help me rather with your advice.

DORINE.   I am your servant.

560 MARIANE.   Ah! Dorine, for pity's sake . . .

DORINE.   This matter ought to go through in order to punish you.

MARIANE.   My dear girl!

DORINE.   No.

MARIANE.   If my declared vows . . .

DORINE.   No. Tartuffe is your man, and you must have him.

MARIANE.   You know I have always trusted in you. Help me . . .

DORINE.   No, upon my word you shall be tartuffed.

MARIANE.   Very well, since my fate fails to move you, leave me alone henceforth with my despair: my heart shall borrow help from that, and I know

570 there is one unfailing remedy for my misery. [*She turns to go.*]

DORINE.   Here! stop, stop, come back. I won't be angry any longer. It seems I must take pity on you, in spite of everything.

MARIANE.   Dorine, you may be sure if they force me to endure this cruel martyrdom I shall surely die.

DORINE.   Do not worry yourself. We will be too clever for them, and prevent . . . But here comes your lover Valère.

SCENE IV

VALÈRE, MARIANE, DORINE

VALÈRE.   I have just been told a very pretty piece of news which I did not know.

MARIANE.   What is it?

580 VALÈRE.   That you are to marry Tartuffe.

MARIANE.   It is true my father has this design in his head.

VALÈRE.   Your father, Madam . . .

MARIANE.   Has changed his mind: he has just proposed this thing to me.

VALÈRE.   What, seriously?

MARIANE.   Yes, seriously. He has declared himself openly for this match.

VALÈRE.   And what is your own decision in the matter, Madam?

MARIANE.   I do not know.

VALÈRE.   A candid answer. You do not know?

MARIANE.   No.

590 VALÈRE.   No?

MARIANE.   What do you advise me?

VALÈRE.   I? I advise you to accept this husband.

MARIANE.   You advise me that?

VALÈRE.   Yes.

MARIANE.   In earnest?

VALÈRE.   Without doubt: the choice is excellent and well worth considering.

MARIANE.   Very well, then, sir, I will act on the advice.

VALÈRE.   That will not be very disagreeable, I imagine.

MARIANE.   Not more painful than for you to give it.

600 VALÈRE.   I? I gave it to please you, Madam.

MARIANE.   And I? I shall follow it to please you.

DORINE.   Let us see what will come of this.

VALÈRE.   This, then, is your affection? And it was deception when you . . .

MARIANE.   Pray do not let us talk any more of that. You told me plainly I ought to accept the husband selected for me: and I declare I intend to do so, since you have given me that salutary advice.

VALÈRE.   Do not make my advice your excuse. You had already made up your mind, and you seized a frivolous pretext to justify the breaking of your word.

610 MARIANE.   Very true, and well put.

VALÈRE.   No doubt; and you never really loved me.

MARIANE.   Alas! think so if you please.

VALÈRE.   Yes, yes, if I please; but my slighted love may perchance forestall you in a similar design; and I know where to offer both my heart and my hand.

MARIANE.   Ah! I do not doubt it. The love which merit can command . . .

VALÈRE.   For Heaven's sake, let us leave merit out of the question: there is but little of it in me, no doubt, and you have given proof of it. But I have great hopes of the kindness another woman will have for me, and I know
620 whose heart will not be ashamed to consent to make up for my loss when I am free.

MARIANE.   The loss is not great; and you will be consoled easily enough by this exchange.

VALÈRE.   I shall do my best, you may depend. To be forgotten wounds self-love; every endeavor must be used to forget also; and if one does not succeed, one must at least pretend to do so; for it is an unpardonable weakness to appear loving when forsaken.

MARIANE.   Truly, what noble and praiseworthy sentiments.

VALÈRE.   Most certainly; and they should be approved by everyone. What?
630 Would you have me for ever cherish in my heart the warmth of my passion for you? Am I to see you throw yourself into the arms of another before my face, and not elsewhere bestow the heart you no longer want?

MARIANE.   On the contrary: I confess that is exactly what I desire. I wish the thing were done already.

VALÈRE.   You wish it?

MARIANE.   Yes.

VALÈRE.   You insult me, Madam. I will go at once to satisfy you. [*He turns to go but keeps on coming back.*]

MARIANE.   Very well.

640 VALÈRE.   Recollect at least that it is you yourself who drive me to this extremity.

MARIANE.   Yes.

VALÈRE.   And that the design I have in my mind is but to follow your example.

MARIANE.   My example let it be.

VALÈRE.   Be it so: you will be served just as you wish.

MARIANE.   I am very glad.

VALÈRE.   You see me for the last time in your life.

MARIANE.   That is all right.

650 VALÈRE.   Eh? [*He goes; and when he is near the door he returns.*]
    MARIANE.   What?
    VALÈRE.   Did you call me?
    MARIANE.   I? You are dreaming.
    VALÈRE.   Ah! well, I will go my way then. Farewell, Madam.
    MARIANE.   Farewell, Monsieur.
    DORINE.   I think you are mad to talk such nonsense; I have left you to quarrel
    all this time to see how far you would go. Stop there, seigneur Valère! [*She*
    takes hold of his arm to stop him, and he makes a great show of resistance.]
    VALÈRE.   Well, what do you want, Dorine?
660 DORINE.   Come here.
    VALÈRE.   No, no, I am too indignant. Do not turn me away from doing her
    will.
    DORINE.   Stop.
    VALÈRE.   No, do you not see my mind is made up?
    DORINE.   Ah!
    MARIANE.   He cannot bear to see me, my presence drives him away. I had
    much better give up the place to him.
    DORINE.   [*She leaves* VALÈRE *and runs to* MARIANE.] Here goes another. Where
    are you running off to?
670 MARIANE.   Let me go.
    DORINE.   You must come back.
    MARIANE.   No, no, Dorine, it is in vain for you to try to keep me.
    VALÈRE.   I see plainly the sight of me annoys her, and doubtless I had better
    rid her of my presence.
    DORINE.   [*She leaves* MARIANE *and runs to* VALÈRE.] Again? Deuce take you if I
    wish it! Stop this fooling and come here, both of you. [*She seizes hold of them*
    both.]
    VALÈRE.   What do you want?
    MARIANE.   What are you going to do?
680 DORINE.   To bring you together again, and set things straight. Are you mad
    to wrangle like this?
    VALÈRE.   Did you not hear how she spoke to me?
    DORINE.   Are you an idiot to have got into such a passion?
    MARIANE.   Did you not see how it all happened, and how he treated me?
    DORINE.   Folly on both sides. She has no other wish than to remain yours; I
    can vouch for it. He loves you only, and desires nothing else than to be
    your husband; I will answer for it with my life.
    MARIANE.   Why, then, did you give me such advice?
    VALÈRE.   Why did you ask for it on such a subject?
690 DORINE.   What a couple of fools you are. Come, now, give me your hands
    here.
    VALÈRE   [*giving his hand to* DORINE]. What is the good of my hand?
    DORINE.   Ah! now, then, yours.
    MARIANE   [*also giving her hand*]. What is the good of my hand?
    DORINE.   Goodness! be quick, come on. You both are fonder of each other
    than you think.
    VALÈRE.   Don't do things with such a bad grace, then, but give a man a civil
    look. [MARIANE *turns her eyes on* VALÈRE *and smiles a little.*]
    DORINE.   What silly creatures lovers are, to be sure!

700 VALÈRE. But still, have I not cause to complain of you? And, to say the least, were you not unkind to utter such cruel things to me?

MARIANE. But you, are you not also the most ungrateful man . . .?

DORINE. Let us leave all this talk for another time, and consider how we can avert this wretched marriage.

MARIANE. Tell us, then, what plans we must prepare.

DORINE. We will try every means. Your father is only jesting, and it is mere talk; but as for you, you had better pretend to humor his whim dutifully, so that in case of alarm it would be easier for you to put the wedding off indefinitely. In gaining time, we remedy everything. Sometimes you will
710 give sudden illness as an excuse, and so cause delays; at other times you will bring forward some ill-omen: you had the ill-luck to meet a corpse, broke a mirror, or dreamt of muddy water. But the best of all is that they cannot marry you either to others or to him unless you say "yes." However, the best way to succeed, I think, is for you two not to be seen talking together. [*To* VALÈRE.] Go away at once, and without delay employ your friends to make her father keep his promise to you. We will enlist the efforts of his brother and the interest of the step-mother on our side. Good-bye.

VALÈRE [*to* MARIANE]. Whatever efforts we all make my greatest hope is really
720 in you.

MARIANE [*to* VALÈRE]. I cannot answer for the will of a father, but I will not belong to any one but Valère.

VALÈRE. Oh! how happy you make me. And whatever they may attempt . . .

DORINE. Ah! lovers never weary of chattering. Be off, I tell you.

VALÈRE. [*He goes a step and returns.*] In short . . .

DORINE. What a cackle you make! You take yourself off that way; and you, the other. [*Pushing each by the shoulder.*]

ACT III

SCENE I

DAMIS, DORINE

DAMIS. May I be struck down by lightning this very moment, may everybody look upon me as the greatest of scamps, if there is any respect or power to
730 stop me from doing something rash!

DORINE. For heaven's sake control your temper: your father merely mentioned the matter. People do not carry out all they propose: there is many a slip 'twixt the cup and the lip.

DAMIS. I must put a stop to this fellow's intrigues and whisper a few words in his ear.

DORINE. Gently, gently, let your stepmother manage him, and your father as well. She has some influence over Tartuffe; he agrees with all she says, and very likely he has a tender feeling for her. Would to heaven it were true! That would be a fine thing! Indeed, she has thought it best to send for him
740 in your interest: she wants to sound him about the marriage which makes you so furious, to find out his feelings, and to let him know what unhappy contentions it would cause were he to entertain the least hope of realising

this scheme. His man told me he was at his prayers so I could not see him; but he said he was just coming down; therefore, pray be gone and leave me to wait for him.

DAMIS.   I want to be present throughout this interview.

DORINE.   Certainly not: they must be alone.

DAMIS.   I will not say anything to him.

750 DORINE.   You deceive yourself: we know what rages you get into, and that would be the surest way to spoil everything. Go away.

DAMIS.   No; I will look on, without losing my temper.

DORINE.   How tiresome you are! Here he comes. Do go away.

SCENE II

TARTUFFE, LAURENT, DORINE

TARTUFFE   [*perceiving* DORINE]. Laurent, lock up my hairshirt and my scourge, and pray heaven ever to enlighten you. If any one comes to see me, say I have gone to the prisoners to distribute the alms I have received.

DORINE.   What affectation and boasting!

TARTUFFE.   What do you want?

DORINE.   To tell you . . .

TARTUFFE.   [*He takes a handkerchief out of his pocket.*] Ah! for the sake of heaven,
760   pray take this handkerchief before you speak to me.

DORINE.   What for?

TARTUFFE.   To cover that bosom which I cannot bear to see. Such a sight is injurious to the soul and gives birth to sinful thoughts.

DORINE.   You are mightily susceptible, then, to temptation, and the flesh seems to make a great impression on your senses. Truly, I do not know why you should take fire so quickly: as for me, my passions are not so easily roused, were I to see you unclothed from top to toe your hide would not tempt me.

TARTUFFE.   Be a little more modest in your conversation, or I shall leave you
770   at once.

DORINE.   No, no, I am going to leave you in peace, and I have only two words to say to you. Madame is coming down into this room, and wishes the favor of a few moments' talk with you.

TARTUFFE.   Alas! most willingly.

DORINE   [*to herself*]. How sweet we are! Upon my word, I still stick to what I said about it.

TARTUFFE.   Will she soon be here?

DORINE.   I think I hear her. Yes, here she is. I will leave you together.

SCENE III

ELMIRE, TARTUFFE

TARTUFFE.   May a supremely bountiful heaven ever bestow upon you health
780   of body and of soul, and bless your days as abundantly as the humblest of its servants can desire.

ELMIRE.   I am much obliged for this pious wish. But let us sit down, to be a little more at ease.

TARTUFFE.   Have you quite recovered from your indisposition?

ELMIRE.   Quite: the fever soon left me.

TARTUFFE.   My prayers are not worthy to have drawn down such favor from heaven; but I have not offered up a single pious aspiration which has not had your recovery for its object.

ELMIRE.   You are too solicitous in my behalf.

790 TARTUFFE.   It is impossible to be too anxious concerning your precious health; I would have sacrificed my own to re-establish yours.

ELMIRE.   You carry Christian charity to an extreme; I am much indebted to you for all this kindness.

TARTUFFE.   I do much less for you than you deserve.

ELMIRE.   I wished to speak privately to you on a certain matter. I am very glad no one is watching us.

TARTUFFE.   I am equally delighted, and it is indeed very pleasant, Madame, to find myself quite alone with you. I have often implored heaven to grant me this favor, but until now it has been denied me.

800 ELMIRE.   I too wish a few words with you; I hope you will speak openly to me and not hide anything from me.

TARTUFFE.   I have but the wish, in return for this singular favor, to lay bare my whole soul to you, and to swear to you that the reports which I have spread abroad concerning the visits paid here to your charms do not spring from any hatred towards you, but rather from a passionate zeal which carries me away, and from a pure motive . . .

ELMIRE.   I quite understand, I feel sure the pains you take are for my welfare.

TARTUFFE.   [*He presses the end of her fingers.*] Yes, Madame, you are right, and such is my devotion . . .

810 ELMIRE.   Oh! you squeeze me too hard.

TARTUFFE.   It is from excess of zeal. I never had any intention of doing you any other ill; I would much sooner . . . [*He places his hand on her knee.*]

ELMIRE.   Why do you put your hand there?

TARTUFFE.   I am feeling your dress: the stuff is very soft.

ELMIRE.   Oh! please, leave off, I am very ticklish. [*She pushes back her chair, and* TARTUFFE *draws his nearer.*]

TARTUFFE.   Heavens! how marvellous is the workmanship of this lace! Work nowadays is wonderfully skilful; one could not imagine anything more beautifully made.

820 ELMIRE.   It is true. But let us talk a little about our business. They say my husband wishes to break his word and give you his daughter. Tell me, is it true?

TARTUFFE.   He did just mention it; but, Madame, to tell you the truth, that is not the happiness for which I sigh; I see elsewhere the perfect attractions of that bliss which is the end of all my desires.

ELMIRE.   That is because you have no love for the things of the earth.

TARTUFFE.   My breast does not contain a heart of flint.

ELMIRE.   I quite believe all your sighs tend heavenwards, and that nothing here below satisfies your desires.

830 TARTUFFE.   Our love for the beauty which is eternal does not stifle in us the love for things fleeting; our senses can easily be charmed with the perfect

works which heaven has created. Its reflected loveliness shines forth in such as are like you; but in you yourself it displays its choicest wonders. It has lavished on your face a beauty which dazzles the eyes and transports the heart, and I am unable to gaze on you, you perfect creature, without adoring in you the author of nature, and without feeling my heart seized with a passionate love for the most beautiful of the portraits in which he has delineated himself. At first I feared lest this secret tenderness might be but an artful assault of the evil one; and my heart even resolved to flee

840 from your eyes, fearing you might be a stumbling-block in the way of my salvation. But at last I learnt, ah! most entrancing beauty, that this passion need not be a guilty one, that I could reconcile it with modesty, and so I have let my heart give way to it. It is, I own, a very great presumption in me to dare to offer you this heart; but my love expects everything from your kindness, and nothing from the vain efforts of my weakness. In you is my hope, my happiness, my peace, on you depends my torment or my bliss; in truth, I shall be happy if you will it, or unhappy if such be your pleasure: you are the sole arbitress.

ELMIRE.   The declaration is most gallant, but it is certainly a little surprising.

850 I think you ought to have guarded your heart more carefully, and have reflected a little upon such a design. A pious man like you, whose name is in every one's mouth . . .

TARTUFFE.   Ah! I may be pious, but I am none the less a man; and when your heavenly charms are seen the heart surrenders without reasoning. I know such language from me must seem strange; but, after all, Madame, I am not an angel, and, if you condemn my avowal, you must lay the blame on your captivating attractions. You became the queen of my heart the moment your ethereal beauty first shone upon me; the ineffable sweetness of your divine looks broke down the resistance of my obstinate heart; it

860 overcame everything—fasting, prayers, tears, and diverted all my thoughts to the consideration of your charms. My looks and my sighs have declared this to you a thousand times, and to make it still clearer I now add my voice. If it should happen that you would look upon the sufferings of your unworthy slave a little kindly, if you would only of your bounty take compassion upon me and deign to stoop even to my insignificance, I should ever have for you, ah! miracle of grace, a devotion beyond comparison. With me your reputation is not in danger, and you need not fear any disgrace from me. All those court gallants upon whom women dote are noisy in their doings and boastful in their talk, ceaselessly bragging of

870 their successes; they do not receive any favors which they do not divulge, and their indiscreet tongues, in which people believe, dishonor the altar where their hearts worship. But people like ourselves love more discreetly, and our secrets are always safely kept. The care which we take of our reputation is a sufficient safeguard to the woman loved, who finds, in accepting our devotion, love without scandal and pleasure without fear.

ELMIRE.   I have listened to what you say, and your eloquence expresses itself to me in sufficiently strong terms. Are you not afraid I may be disposed to tell my husband of this ardent devotion, and that the sudden knowledge of such a feeling may well cause him to change his friendship for you?

880 TARTUFFE.   I know you are too gracious, and that you will forgive my boldness; you will excuse, in consideration of human frailty, the passionate

raptures of a love which offends you, and you will consider, when you look in your mirror, that people are not blind, and that a man is of the flesh.

ELMIRE.   Others may perhaps take all this in a different way, but I will exercise discretion. I will not speak to my husband about the matter, but I want one thing from you in return: and that is, to forward honestly and openly the union of Valère and Mariane, and to renounce the unjust power which would enrich you with what belongs to another, and . . .

SCENE IV

DAMIS, ELMIRE, TARTUFFE

DAMIS   [*coming out of the little room in which he had been hiding*]. No, Madame,
890   no; this ought to be made public. I have been in here, where I have overheard everything; and heaven in its goodness seems to have directed me here to confound the pride of a traitor who wrongs me, to point out a way to take vengeance on his hypocrisy and his insolence, to undeceive my father and to show him plainly the heart of the scoundrel who speaks to you of love.

ELMIRE.   No, Damis: it is sufficient that he promises to amend and tries to deserve the forgiveness to which I have committed myself. Since I have promised it, do not make me break my word. I have no mind to cause a scandal: a woman laughs at such follies, and never troubles her husband's
900   ears with them.

DAMIS.   You have your reasons for acting thus and I have mine also for dealing otherwise. It is a mockery to wish to spare him; the insolent pride of his bigotry has lorded it over my just anger but too often, and he has caused too many troubles in our house. The knave has governed my father too long, and he has thwarted my love as well as Valère's. It is necessary my father should have his eyes opened to this treachery, and Providence has offered me for that an easy opportunity for which I am thankful. It is too favorable to be neglected: and were I not to use it whilst I have it in my hands, I should deserve to have it snatched away from me.

910 ELMIRE.   Damis . . .

DAMIS.   No, by your leave, I must take my own counsel. My heart is now overjoyed: it is in vain for you to try to persuade me to give up the pleasure of revenging myself. I shall disclose the affair without delay, and here is just the very opportunity I want.

SCENE V

ORGON, DAMIS, TARTUFFE, ELMIRE

DAMIS.   Come, father, we will enliven your arrival with an altogether novel and very surprising piece of news. You are well rewarded for all your caresses; this gentleman amply recompenses your kindness. His great zeal for you has just revealed itself: it aims at nothing less than to dishonor you. I have here overheard him make shameful avowal of a guilty passion. She,
920   being too prudent and good-natured, insisted at all hazards upon keeping

the matter secret; but I cannot countenance such impudence, and I should wrong you were I to keep silence.

ELMIRE.   Yes, I hold that it is better never to disturb the peace of mind of one's husband by such silly nonsense. Honor does not depend on the confession of attacks upon it, and it is enough for us that we know how to protect ourselves. These are my own sentiments. You would not have said anything, Damis, if I had had more influence over you.

SCENE VI

ORGON, DAMIS, TARTUFFE

ORGON.   What do I hear? Good heavens, is it possible?

TARTUFFE.   Yes, brother, I am a wicked, miserable and guilty sinner, full of
930   iniquity, the greatest wretch who ever lived. Every moment of my life is weighed down with pollution; it is nothing but a mass of crime and corruption, and I see that heaven, for my punishment, intends to mortify me on this occasion. I throw away the pride of self-defence no matter what great crime I may be accused of. Believe what they tell you, let your wrath take up arms and drive me, like a criminal, from your house. I deserve even greater shame than I shall have in being turned away.

ORGON   [to his son]. Ah! you villain, how dare you try to sully the purity of his virtue by such falsehoods?

DAMIS.   What? Does the feigned meekness of this hypocrite make you give
940   the lie to . . .?

ORGON.   Be quiet, you accursed plague.

TARTUFFE.   Oh! let him speak: you chide him wrongfully and you had much better believe his story. Why be favorable to me in the face of such an assertion? Are you aware, after all, of what I am capable? Why trust in my bearing, brother? Why believe me good because of my outward professions? No, no; you suffer yourself to be deceived by appearances, and I am, alas! just what these people think. The world takes me for a worthy man; but the simple truth is that I am worthless. [Addressing DAMIS.] Yes, my dear boy, speak: accuse me of treachery, infamy, theft, murder; over-
950   whelm me with still more despicable names. I do not deny them, I have deserved them; on my knees I will bear the shameful ignominy due to the sins of my life.

ORGON   [to TARTUFFE]. This is too much, my brother. [To his son.] Wretch, does not your heart relent?

DAMIS.   What? can his words so far deceive you . . .?

ORGON.   Hold your tongue, rascal. [To TARTUFFE.] Oh! rise, my brother, I beseech you. [To his son.] Infamous scoundrel!

DAMIS.   He can . . .

ORGON.   Be quiet.

960 DAMIS.   Intolerable! What! I am taken for . . .

ORGON.   If you say another word I will break every bone.

TARTUFFE.   Control yourself, my brother, in heaven's name. I would rather suffer the greatest injury than that he should receive the slightest hurt on my account.

ORGON   [to his son]. Ungrateful wretch!

TARTUFFE.   Leave him alone. If I must on my knees ask you to forgive him . . .

ORGON   [*to* TARTUFFE]. Oh! you jest? [*To his son.*] Rascal! See how good he is.

DAMIS.   Then . . .

ORGON.   Cease.

970 DAMIS.   What? I . . .

ORGON.   Cease, I say. I know well the motive which makes you accuse him. You all hate him; and I now see my wife, children and servants all incensed against him. You try every impudent trick to drive this saintly person away from me. But the more you strive to send him away, the greater efforts I shall make to keep him here longer, and I will haste my daughter's marriage to him to crush the pride of the whole family.

DAMIS.   You mean to force her to take him?

ORGON.   Yes, scoundrel, this very night, to confound you all. Ah! I defy the whole household. I will let you know I am the master and must be obeyed.

980   You wretch, come and retract what you have said, and throw yourself instantly at his feet to beg his pardon.

DAMIS.   Who, I? Of this villain who, by his impostures . . .

ORGON.   Ah! you refuse, you scamp, and abuse him besides? A stick! A stick! [*To* TARTUFFE.] Do not prevent me. [*To his son.*] Begone this instant out of my sight, and never have the face to set foot in my house again.

DAMIS.   Yes, I will go; but . . .

ORGON.   Quick, leave the place. I disinherit you, you hangdog, and curse you, as well.

SCENE VII

ORGON, TARTUFFE

ORGON.   To affront a holy person in such a manner!

990 TARTUFFE.   Oh Heaven! forgive him the pain he causes me. [*To* ORGON.] If you only knew with what anguish I see them endeavor to blacken my character in the eyes of my brother . . .

ORGON.   Alas!

TARTUFFE.   The very thought of such ingratitude is so great a torture to me that . . . The horror I feel . . . My heart is too full to speak, and I believe I shall die.

ORGON.   [*He runs in tears to the door through which he had driven his son.*] Villain! How I regret I held my hand and that I did not instantly make an end of you on the spot. Compose yourself, brother, and do not grieve.

1000 TARTUFFE.   Let us put an end to these miserable disputes. I see what great friction I cause in this house, and I feel sure it is needful, my brother, that I should go away.

ORGON.   What? You are not in earnest?

TARTUFFE.   They hate me, and I see they will seek to rouse suspicion in you as to my integrity.

ORGON.   What does it matter? Do you think I pay any attention to what they say?

TARTUFFE.   They will not fail to continue, never fear, and the same stories which now you reject you may at another time credit.

1010 ORGON.   No, brother, never.

TARTUFFE.   Oh! my brother, a wife can very easily influence the mind of her husband.

ORGON.   No, no.

TARTUFFE.   Let me leave here at once and thus remove all occasion for their attacks.

ORGON.   No, you shall stay: my life is at stake.

TARTUFFE.   Ah! well, then I must mortify myself. Nevertheless, if you would . . .

ORGON.   Ah!

TARTUFFE.   Be it so: let us not say anything more about it. But I know how I
1020   must act in the future. Honor is a delicate matter, and friendship enjoins
me to prevent reports and not to give cause for suspicion. I will shun your
wife, and you shall not see me . . .

ORGON.   No, you shall see her frequently in spite of everyone. I desire nothing more than to jolt society, and I wish her to be seen in your company
at all hours. Nor is this all: the better to defy them all you shall be my sole
heir, and I will go forthwith to arrange in due form that the whole of my
property shall be made yours. A good and faithful friend, whom I take for
son-in-law, is far dearer to me than son, wife, or kindred. Will you not
accept my offer?

1030 TARTUFFE.   The will of heaven be done in all things!

ORGON.   Poor man! Let us go quickly to draw up the deed: then may envy
itself burst with spite.

ACT IV

SCENE I

CLÉANTE, TARTUFFE

CLÉANTE.   Indeed, you may believe me, everybody is talking about it. The
scandal which this rumor makes is not to your credit. I have met you,
Monsieur, very seasonably, and I can tell you plainly my view of the
matter, in two words. I do not sift these reports to the bottom; I pass them
by and admit the worst view of the case. Let us grant that Damis has not
acted wisely, and it may be you have been accused in error: does it not
become a Christian to forgive the offence and to extinguish in him every
1040   desire for vengeance? And, because of your quarrel, ought you to suffer a
father to drive a son out of his house? I repeat it, and I tell you candidly,
high and low are scandalised by it. If you take my advice, you will make
peace and not push matters to extremes. Make an offering to God of all
your resentment, and restore the son to the father's favor.

TARTUFFE.   Alas! So far as I am concerned I would do so with all my heart. I
do not bear him any ill-will, Monsieur, I forgive him everything. I do not
blame him for anything. I would serve him to the best of my power. But
the interests of heaven cannot consent to it; and if he returns home I must
go away. After his unparalleled behavior intercourse between us would
1050   give rise to scandal. Heaven knows what every one would think of it at
once! They would impute it to sheer policy on my part, and it would be
said everywhere that, knowing myself to be guilty, I affect a charitable zeal

for my accuser; that I am afraid of him; and that I wish to conciliate him
in order to bribe him in an underhand manner to silence.

CLÉANTE.　You are putting us off, Monsieur, with sham excuses. All your
arguments are too far-fetched. Why do you take upon yourself the interests of heaven? Cannot it punish sinners without our help? Leave vengeance to it, leave vengeance to it, and remember only the forgiveness
which it directs towards offences. Do not trouble yourself about men's
1060　　judgments when you follow the sovereign edicts of heaven. What? Shall
the paltry fear of men's opinion prevent the accomplishment of a good
deed? No, no; let us always do what heaven commands, and not trouble
our minds with any other care.

TARTUFFE.　I have already told you, Monsieur, that I forgive him as heaven
enjoins. But, after the scandal and insult of today, heaven does not ordain
that I should live with him.

CLÉANTE.　And does it require you, Monsieur, to lend your ears to what a
mere whim dictates to his father, and to accept the gift which is made
you of a property to which in justice you cannot pretend to have any
1070　　claim?

TARTUFFE.　Those who know me will not think I act from interested motives.
All the riches of this world have few attractions for me. I am not dazzled
by their false glitter. If I bring myself to take this gift which the father
wishes to make to me, it is merely because I fear all this wealth will fall into
wicked hands, and that it will be shared only by those who will put it here
to bad uses, and not employ it, as I propose to do, for the glory of heaven
and the well-being of my fellow-men.

CLÉANTE.　Ah! Monsieur, do not entertain these delicate scruples, which may
give ground of complaint to a rightful heir. Allow him, without giving
1080　　yourself any anxiety, to enjoy his rights at his own peril; and consider that
it is far better for him to make a bad use of it than that people should
accuse you of defrauding him of it. I only wonder you could have suffered
unblushingly such a proposal to be made you. For, in truth, do we find
among the maxims of true piety one which teaches how to plunder a
lawful heir? And, if it is a fact that heaven has put in your heart an
invincible obstacle against your living with Damis, would it not be better
for you, as a discreet person, honorably to retire from this house, rather
than to allow the son of the house to be turned out of it, against all reason,
on your account? Believe me, Monsieur, it would give a proof of your
1090　　probity . . .

TARTUFFE.　Monsieur, it is half-past three: a certain religious exercise calls
me upstairs; pray excuse me for leaving you so soon.

CLÉANTE.　Ah!

SCENE II

ELMIRE, MARIANE, DORINE, CLÉANTE

DORINE.　For pity's sake join us in all we do for her, Monsieur. She is suffering great misery, and the agreement which her father has concluded
for tonight drives her every moment to despair. Here he comes. Let us

unite our efforts, I beseech you, to try, either by force or by skill to frustrate this unhappy design which causes us all this trouble.

SCENE III

ORGON, ELMIRE, MARIANE, CLÉANTE, DORINE

ORGON.   Ah! I am delighted to find you all here. [*To* MARIANE] I have some-
2000   thing in this document which will please you: you know already what I mean.

MARIANE   [*on her knees*]. Father, in the name of that heaven which knows my grief, in the name of everything that can move your heart, forego a little of a father's rights and do not exact this obedience from me. Do not compel me, by this harsh command, to reproach heaven with my duty to you; do not, oh my father, render most miserable the life which, alas! you gave me. If, contrary to the sweet hopes I had cherished, you forbid me to belong to the one whom I have dared to love, I implore you on my knees at least, of your goodness, to spare me the horror of belonging to one
2010   whom I abhor. Do not drive me to despair by exerting all your authority over me.

ORGON   [*feeling himself soften*]. Be firm, my heart; none of this human weakness.

MARIANE.   I do not feel aggrieved at your tenderness for him; indulge in it, give him your wealth, and, if that is not enough, add all mine to it: I consent with all my heart and give it to you. But, at least, do not go so far as to include my person, let me wear out in the hardships of a convent the rest of the sad days that heaven has allotted to me.

ORGON.   Ah! girls always wish to become nuns when a father crosses their
2020   love-sick inclinations. Get up: the more your heart recoils from accepting the offer, the greater will be your merit. Mortify your senses by this marriage, and do not trouble me any further.

DORINE.   But what . . .?

ORGON.   You hold your tongue: mind your own business. I absolutely forbid you to dare to say a single word.

CLÉANTE.   If you will allow me to speak and advise . . .

ORGON.   Brother, your advice is the best in the world, and I value it highly: you will permit me, however, not to take it.

ELMIRE   [*to* ORGON]. In the face of all this I do not know I can say more than
2030   that I am astonished at your blindness. You must be quite bewitched with the man and altogether prejudiced in his favor, to deny the truth of what we tell you took place today.

ORGON.   I am your humble servant, but I judge by appearances. I know how lenient you are towards my rascal of a son, and you were afraid to disown the trick which he wished to play on the poor fellow. In fact, you took it too calmly to be believed. You should have been a little more disturbed.

ELMIRE.   Is it necessary one's honor should take up arms so furiously at a simple declaration of tender feelings? Is it not possible to give a fitting answer without anger in the eyes and invective on the lips? For myself, I
2040   simply laugh at such talk; it does not please me to make a noise about it.

I prefer to show that prudence can be accompanied by gentleness. I am not at all like the savage prudes who defend their honor with tooth and nail, and who are ready, at the slightest word, to tear a man's eyes out. Heaven preserve me from such discretion! I prefer a virtue that has nothing of the tigress about it, and I believe a quiet and cold rebuff is not less efficient in repelling an advance.

ORGON. Nevertheless, I understand the whole affair and I will not be imposed upon.

ELMIRE. Once more, I wonder at this strange weakness: but what answer
2050 would your incredulity give me, if I made you see we have told you the truth?

ORGON. See?

ELMIRE. Yes.

ORGON. Nonsense.

ELMIRE. Never mind! Suppose I found a way of convincing you irresistibly?

ORGON. Moonshine.

ELMIRE. What a man you are! At least, answer me. I do not ask you to believe us, but, look here, suppose we found a place where you could plainly see and hear everything, what would you say then of your good man?

2060 ORGON. In that case I should say . . . I should not say anything, for such a thing could not be.

ELMIRE. Your delusion has lasted too long, and you have taxed us too much with imposture. You must, to satisfy me, and without going any further, be a witness of all that has been told you.

ORGON. Be it so. I take you at your word. We will see your cleverness and how you can carry out this undertaking.

ELMIRE. Make him come here.

DORINE. He is very crafty and perhaps it will be difficult to catch him.

ELMIRE. No; people are easily duped by those whom they love. Self-love
2070 leads the way to self-deceit. [*Speaking to* CLÉANTE *and to* MARIANE.] Tell him to come down to me. And you, withdraw.

SCENE IV

ELMIRE, ORGON

ELMIRE. Let us bring this table nearer and you go under it.

ORGON. Why?

ELMIRE. It is necessary you should be well concealed.

ORGON. Why under this table?

ELMIRE. Oh! good heavens, never mind; I have thought out my plan, and you shall judge of it. Go under there, I tell you; and, when you are there, take care you are neither seen nor heard.

ORGON. I must say my complaisance in this matter is great, but I will see you
2080 through with your scheme.

ELMIRE. You will not have anything with which to reproach me, that I swear. [*To her husband, under the table.*] Now mind! I am going to speak on a strange subject and you must not be shocked in any way. As I have undertaken to convince you, I must be allowed to say whatever I choose.

Since I am compelled to it, I shall flatter this hypocrite until he lets fall his mask: I shall encourage the impudent desires of his love, and give free scope to his audacity. As I am going to pretend to yield to his wishes for your sake alone, and the better to confound him, things need not go any further than you like, and I will cease as soon as you are convinced. I leave
2090   it to you to stop his mad passion when you think matters have gone far enough, to spare your wife, and not to expose me longer than is necessary to disabuse you. This is your concern, you must decide, and . . . Here he comes. Keep still, and do not show yourself.

SCENE V

TARTUFFE, ELMIRE, ORGON

TARTUFFE.   They tell me you wish to speak to me here.
ELMIRE.   Yes. I have some secrets to reveal to you. But shut the door before I begin to tell them to you. Look everywhere, lest we should be surprised. We must certainly not have such an affair here as we had a little while ago. I was never so surprised. Damis put me in a terrible fright on your account. You saw I tried all I could to baffle his design and to calm his anger.
2100   In fact I was so confused that the thought of denying what he said never occurred to me; but, nevertheless, thank heaven, it was all for the best and things are on a surer footing. The esteem in which you are held has dispelled the storm, and my husband cannot be offended with you. He wishes us to be together constantly, the better to set at defiance the spiteful remarks which people spread abroad, and that is the reason why I may be shut up here alone with you, without fear of being blamed. This justifies me in opening my heart to you, a little too readily, perhaps, in response to your love.
TARTUFFE.   This language, Madam, is a little difficult to comprehend. You
2110   spoke but lately in a different strain.
ELMIRE.   Ah! if such a refusal has offended you, how very little you know a woman's heart, how little you understand what we mean when we defend ourselves so feebly. At such times our modesty always struggles with any tender sentiments we may feel. Whatever reasons we may find for the love which conquers us, there is always a little shame in the avowal of it. We resist at first, but from our manner it can easily be seen our heart surrenders, that our words oppose our wishes for the sake of honor, and that we refuse in such a way as to promise everything. I am making a very free confession to you, to be sure, and I am not sparing woman's modesty; but,
2120   since these words have at last escaped me, should I have been anxious to restrain Damis, should I, I ask you, have listened to you so long and with so much patience, when you offered me your heart, should I have taken the thing as I did, if the offer of your heart had not given me pleasure? What could you infer from such an action when I myself tried to make you renounce the proposed marriage, if it were not that I took an interest in you, and that I should have been grieved if such a marriage had taken place and you had in the least divided that affection which I wanted to be wholly mine?

TARTUFFE.   It is certainly, Madam, extremely pleasant to hear such words
2130   from the lips one loves. Their honey generously diffuses through all my
senses a sweetness which I never before knew. The happiness of pleasing
you is my supreme study, and it is the delight of my heart to carry out your
wishes, but, with your leave, my heart presumes still to doubt a little of its
felicity. It may be that these words are a plausible stratagem to compel me
to break off the approaching marriage; and, if I must speak candidly to
you, I shall not trust in these tender words until I am assured they mean
what they say by a few of those favors for which I sigh, which will establish
in my heart a firm belief in the kindly sentiments you bear towards me.
ELMIRE.   [*She coughs to warn her husband.*] What? would you proceed so fast
2140   and exhaust the kindness of my heart all at once? I commit myself in
making such a tender admission; yet that is not enough for you. Will
nothing satisfy you but to push things to their furthest extremity?
TARTUFFE.   The less a blessing is merited the less one ventures to hope for it.
Our love can hardly be satisfied with words. A condition full-fraught with
happiness is difficult to realise and we wish to enjoy it before we believe in
it. I so little deserve your favors that I doubt the success of my boldness;
and I shall not believe anything, Madam, until you have satisfied my
passion by real proofs.
ELMIRE.   Good Heavens! How very tyrannical is your love, and into what
2150   strange agitation it throws me! What an irresistible power it exercises over
the heart, and how violently it clamors for what it desires! What? Is there
no avoiding your pursuit? Will you not give me time to breathe? Is it
decent to be so very exacting, to insist without quarter upon those things
which you demand, and, by your pressing ardor, thus to take advantage of
the weakness which you see is felt for you?
TARTUFFE.   But if you look upon my address with a favorable eye, why refuse
me convincing proofs?
ELMIRE.   How can I comply with your desires without offending that heaven
of which you constantly speak?
2160 TARTUFFE.   If heaven is the only thing which opposes my wishes I can easily
remove such an obstacle; that need not be any restraint upon your love.
ELMIRE.   But the judgments of heaven are terrifying.
TARTUFFE.   I can dispel these absurd fears from you, Madam; I know the art
of removing scruples. Heaven, it is true, forbids certain gratifications; but
there are ways of compounding with it. It is a science to stretch the strings
of our conscience according to divers needs and to rectify the immorality
of the act with the purity of our intention. I can initiate you into these
secrets, Madam; you have only to allow yourself to be led. Satisfy my
desire, and do not be afraid: I will be answerable for you in everything,
2170   and I will take the sin upon myself. You cough a good deal, Madam.
ELMIRE.   Yes, it racks me.
TARTUFFE.   Would you please to take a piece of this liquorice?
ELMIRE.   It is a troublesome cold, to be sure; and I very much fear all the
liquorice in the world will not do it any good now.
TARTUFFE.   It is certainly very tiresome.
ELMIRE.   Yes, more than I can say.
TARTUFFE.   In short your scruple is easily overcome. You may be sure the
secret will be well kept here, and no harm is done unless the thing is

noised abroad. The scandal of the world is what makes the offence, and to
2180 sin in secret is not to sin at all.

ELMIRE [*after having coughed again*].   Well, I see I must make up my mind to
yield: that I must consent to grant you everything: and that with less than
this I ought not to expect you should be satisfied, or convinced. It is
indeed very hard to come to this, and it is greatly against my will that I
venture so far, but, since people persist in driving me to this; since they
will not believe anything that is said to them, and since they wish for more
convincing testimony, one must even resolve upon it and satisfy them. If
this gratification carries any offense in it, so much the worse for those who
force me to this violence; the fault, assuredly, is not mine.

2190 TARTUFFE.   Yes, Madam, I take it upon myself, and the thing itself . . .

ELMIRE.   Open the door a little, and pray, look if my husband is not in that
passage.

TARTUFFE.   Why need you trouble yourself so much about him? Between
ourselves, he is a man to be led by the nose. He is inclined to be proud of
our intercourse, and I have brought him so far as to see everything without
believing anything.

ELMIRE.   Nevertheless, pray, go out for a moment and look carefully everywhere outside.

SCENE VI

ORGON, ELMIRE

ORGON [*coming from under the table*].   Well! he is an abominable man, I admit.
2200 I cannot get over it, it has stunned me.

ELMIRE.   What? you come out so soon? You make fools of people. Go back
under the table-cloth, it is not time yet; stay to the end to make sure of
things, and do not trust to mere conjectures.

ORGON.   No: no one more wicked ever came out of hell.

ELMIRE.   Good Heavens! You ought not to believe things too easily: let yourself be fully convinced before you give in, and do not hurry, lest you
should be mistaken. [*She pushes her husband behind her.*]

SCENE VII

TARTUFFE, ELMIRE, ORGON

TARTUFFE.   Everything conspires, Madam, to my satisfaction. I have looked
everywhere, there is no one here; and my ravished soul . . .

2100 ORGON [*stopping him*]. Gently, you are too eager in your amorous wishes; you
ought not to be so impetuous. Ah! ah! my good man, you want to rob me
of my wife. How your soul is led away by temptations! You would marry my
daughter and covet my wife. I have very much doubted for a long time
whether you were in earnest, and I always thought you would change your
tone. But the proof has gone quite far enough: I am satisfied, and for my
part I do not want any more.

ELMIRE [*to* TARTUFFE]. The part I have played is contrary to my inclinations, but I was obliged to the necessity of treating you thus.

TARTUFFE. What? Do you believe . . .?

2110 ORGON. Come, pray, no more talk, leave this place, and without ceremony.

TARTUFFE. I intended . . .

ORGON. Your speeches are no longer in season. You must quit this house immediately.

TARTUFFE. It is for you to leave, you who speak as though you were the master of it. The house belongs to me, and I will make you know it. I will show you plainly it is useless to resort to these cowardly tricks in order to pick a quarrel with me. You have made a great mistake in insulting me. I have it in my power to confound and to punish imposture, to avenge an offended heaven, and to make those repent who talk of turning me away.

SCENE VIII

ELMIRE, ORGON

2120 ELMIRE. What talk is this? What does he mean?

ORGON. Alas! I am ashamed; it is no laughing matter.

ELMIRE. Why?

ORGON. I see my fault by what he says, and the deed of gift troubles my mind.

ELMIRE. The deed of gift . . .

ORGON. Yes, the thing is done, but there is still something else which makes me anxious.

ELMIRE. What is that?

ORGON. You shall know all, but let us see first if a particular box is still
2130 upstairs.

ACT V

SCENE I

ORGON, CLÉANTE

CLÉANTE. Where are you going so fast?

ORGON. Indeed, I do not know.

CLÉANTE. It seems to me the first thing to be done is to consult together concerning what steps we can take in this matter.

ORGON. This box troubles me greatly; it distresses me more than anything else.

CLÉANTE. Then it contains an important secret?

ORGON. It is a trust that Argas himself, my unfortunate friend, put secretly into my hands: he selected me for this, when he fled. And, from what he
2140 told me, on these papers depend his life and his fortune.

CLÉANTE. Then why did you trust them to any other hands?

ORGON. It was from a conscientious motive. I went straight away to that wretch in utter confidence, and his arguments persuaded me it was better

to give him the box to keep, so that, in case of enquiry, I could deny
having it. I might have the help of a subterfuge in readiness, by which my
conscience might be quite safe in swearing against the truth.

CLÉANTE.   If one may judge by appearances, you are in a bad case. The deed
of gift and this trust are, to speak frankly, steps taken with little consideration. You may be carried great lengths by such pledges. Since this man
2150   has these advantages over you, it is still greater imprudence in you to
irritate him: you ought to seek some gentler method.

ORGON.   What? To conceal such a false heart and such a wicked soul under
so fair an appearance of ardent zeal! And I, who received him as a beggar
and penniless . . . It is all over, I renounce all pious people: I shall hold
them henceforth in utter abhorrence, and shall become worse to them
than the devil.

CLÉANTE.   Is not that just like your hasty ways? You never judge anything
calmly. You never keep in due reason. You always rush from one extreme
to the other. You see your error, and you realise you have been imposed
2160   upon by a false piety. But is it reasonable that, in order to correct one
mistake, you should commit a greater, and not make any difference between the heart of a perfidious rascal and that of a good man? What?
because a villain has shamelessly imposed upon you, under the pompous
mask of austerity, would you have it that all men are like him, and that
there is not a sincere worshipper to be found now-a-days? Leave these
foolish deductions to unbelievers; distinguish between virtue and the appearance of it; do not bestow your esteem so rashly; and keep in this the
rightful middle course. Do not honor imposture, if you can avoid doing so,
but at the same time, do not attack true virtue. If you must fall into an
2170   extremity, err, rather, on the other side.

SCENE II

DAMIS, ORGON, CLÉANTE

DAMIS.   Is it true, father, that this scoundrel threatens you, that he has forgotten every benefit he has received, and that his cowardly and shameless
arrogance turns your goodness to him into arms against you?

ORGON.   Yes, my son, and it causes me inexpressible grief.

DAMIS.   Leave him to me, I will crop his two ears for him: you must not flinch
before his insolence. I will rid you of him at a stroke, and, to put an end
to the matter, I will put an end to him.

CLÉANTE.   That is exactly how a mere boy talks. Try to moderate these violent outbursts. We live under a government, and in an age in which vio-
2180   lence only makes matters worse.

SCENE III

MADAME PERNELLE, MARIANE, ELMIRE, DORINE, DAMIS, ORGON, CLÉANTE

MME. PERNELLE.   What is the matter? What are these dreadful, mysterious
reports I hear?

ORGON. They are of things which I have seen with my own eyes, and you see how I am paid for my kindness. I eagerly take in a man out of charity, I shelter him, and treat him as my own brother. I heap benefits upon him every day, I give him my daughter and everything I possess, and, all the while, the villain, the traitor, harbors the black design of seducing my wife. Not content even with this vile attempt, he dares to threaten me with my own gifts; and, in order to ruin me, he intends to use the advantage he has 2190 obtained through my unwise good nature to drive me out of my estate which I made over to him, and to reduce me to the same condition from which I rescued him.

DORINE. Poor man!

MME. PERNELLE. I can never believe, my son, that he would commit so black a deed.

ORGON. Why?

MME. PERNELLE. Good people are always envied.

ORGON. What do you mean by that, mother?

MME. PERNELLE. Why, there are strange goings-on in your house. It is very 2200 plain to see the ill-will they bear him.

ORGON. What has this hatred to do with what I have just told you?

MME. PERNELLE. When you were a child I told you a hundred times that in this world virtue is ever persecuted, and that the envious may die, but envy never.

ORGON. But what has this speech to do with what has happened today?

MME. PERNELLE. They have most likely fabricated a hundred idle stories against him for your benefit.

ORGON. I have already told you I have seen everything myself.

MME. PERNELLE. The spite of slanderers is great.

2210 ORGON. You would drive me mad, mother. I tell you I saw with my own eyes this monstrous crime.

MME. PERNELLE. Tongues are always ready to spit venom: nothing here below is proof against them.

ORGON. That remark seems to lack common sense. I have seen it, I tell you, seen it, with my own eyes, seen it, what people call seen it. Must I drum it in your ears a hundred times and shout at the top of my voice?

MME. PERNELLE. Well, appearances deceive more often than not: you must not always judge by what you see.

ORGON. I'm furious.

2220 MME. PERNELLE. We are naturally subject to false suspicions, and a bad construction is often put on a good deed.

ORGON. Must I regard his desire to kiss my wife as charitable?

MME. PERNELLE. You should have just cause before you accuse people. You ought to have waited until you were sure you saw these things.

ORGON. How the devil could I better satisfy myself? Ought I then to have waited, mother, until before my eyes he had . . . You will make me say something obscene.

MME. PERNELLE. Indeed I am sure his soul burns with too pure a zeal; I cannot possibly believe he would attempt the things of which people ac-
2230 cuse him.

ORGON. Enough! If you were not my mother I do not know what I might say to you, you make me so angry.

DORINE.   Such is the just reward of acts in this world, Monsieur. You would
not believe and now you are not believed.

CLÉANTE.   We waste time in mere trifles which we ought to use in taking
measures. We ought not to sleep when a knave threatens.

DAMIS.   What? would his effrontery go to such lengths?

ELMIRE.   For my part, I do not believe he can possibly make out a case: his
ingratitude would be too glaring.

2240 CLÉANTE.   You must not trust to that. He will find means to justify his actions
against you: for less than this a powerful party has involved people in sad
troubles. I tell you again, armed as he is, you ought never to have driven
him thus far.

ORGON.   That is true, but what could I do? I was not the master of my
feelings when I saw the insolence of this traitor.

CLÉANTE.   I wish, with all my heart, we could arrange for even the shadow of
peace between you two.

ELMIRE.   If I had known he had such weapons in his hands I would not have
made so much noise about the matter, and my . . .

2250 ORGON.   What does that man want? Go quickly, and see. A nice condition I
am in for seeing anybody.

SCENE IV

M. LOYAL, MADAME PERNELLE, ORGON, DAMIS, MARIANE, DORINE, ELMIRE,
CLÉANTE

M. LOYAL.   Good-morning, my dear sister, pray let me speak to your master.

DORINE.   He is engaged with friends, and I doubt whether he can see anyone
at present.

M. LOYAL.   I do not want to be intrusive in his own house. I do not think my
presence concerns anything that will distress him. I have come upon a
matter which will please him.

DORINE.   What is your name?

M. LOYAL.   Simply tell him I come, on behalf of Monsieur Tartuffe, for his
2260   good.

DORINE.   He is a man who comes with a civil message from Monsieur
Tartuffe, concerning a matter which he says will please you.

CLÉANTE.   You must see who this man is, and what he can want.

ORGON.   Perhaps he comes here to reconcile us. In what way shall I behave
to him?

CLÉANTE.   You ought not to show your resentment; and if he speaks of an
agreement you ought to listen to him?

M. LOYAL.   Your servant, Monsieur. May heaven destroy those who wish you
harm, and may it be as favorable to you as I wish.

2270 ORGON.   This civil beginning bears out my opinion, and augurs already
some reconciliation.

M. LOYAL.   I was your father's servant, and your whole household has ever
been dear to me.

ORGON.   I am greatly ashamed, Monsieur, and I beg your pardon in that I do
not know you or your name.

M. LOYAL.   My name is Loyal, I am a native of Normandy, and, in spite of envious people, a bailiff. Thanks to heaven, I have had, for the last forty years, the happiness of holding this office with much credit. I have come to you, Monsieur, by your leave, to serve a writ of a certain kind . . .

2280 ORGON. What? are you here . . .?

M. LOYAL. Calm yourself, Sir. It is nothing but a summons, an order to remove you and yours hence, to take your furniture away, and to make way for others, without delay or remission, as hereby decreed.

ORGON. I to leave this house?

M. LOYAL. Yes, Monsieur, if it pleases you. The house, at present, as you well know, belongs unquestionably to good Monsieur Tartuffe. Henceforth, of all your goods he is lord and master, by virtue of a contract which I have with me. It is in due form and nothing can be said against it.

DAMIS. Truly I admire this impudence: it is colossal.

2290 M. LOYAL. Monsieur, I have not any business with you. It is with this gentleman. He is both reasonable and civil, and he knows the duty of a sensible man too well to wish to resist what is in any way just.

ORGON. But . . .

M. LOYAL. Yes, Monsieur, I know you would not rebel for a million, and that you will, like a gentleman, allow me to execute here the orders which have been given me.

DAMIS. Monsieur Bailiff, it may happen that you will here get the stick laid across your black gown.

M. LOYAL. Order your son to be silent or withdraw, Monsieur. I should be
2300 sorry to have to put your name down in my official report.

DORINE. This Monsieur Loyal has a very disloyal air.

M. LOYAL. I have much sympathy with all worthy people, and I would not have burdened myself, Monsieur, with these documents save to oblige you and to do you service, to take away in this manner the chance of someone else being chosen who, not having for you the esteem I have, would have proceeded in a less gentle manner.

ORGON. What can be worse than to order people out of their own house?

M. LOYAL. Monsieur, you are given time, and I will suspend proceedings under the writ until tomorrow, I will simply come to pass the night here,
2310 with ten of my men, without scandal and without noise. For the sake of form, you will be so good as to bring me the keys of your door before you go to bed. I will take care not to disturb your repose, and not to allow anything unseemly. But tomorrow, early in the morning, you must be ready to clear the house even to the smallest utensil. My men will help you. I have chosen strong fellows, so that they can assist you to take everything away. It is not possible to act better than I am acting, I feel sure, and, since I treat you with great consideration, Monsieur, I beg that on your part you will treat me properly and that you will not annoy me in any way in the execution of the duties of my office.

2320 ORGON. With the best heart in the world would I give just now a hundred of the brightest louis d'or[7] that are left me could I have the pleasure of giving one of the soundest clouts possible on his beak.

CLÉANTE. Be quiet, do not make matters worse.

---

[7] Gold coins issued during the reigns of Louis XIII through Louis XVI—that is, from 1610 through 1792.

DAMIS.   I can hardly contain myself. My hand itches at this monstrous impertinence.

DORINE.   Upon my word, Monsieur Loyal, a drubbing with a stick would not sit ill on your broad back.

M. LOYAL.   We could easily punish those shameful words, my girl; women, also, are answerable to the law.

2330 CLÉANTE.   Let us end all this, Monsieur, there has been enough of it. Give up this paper, for goodness' sake, quickly, and leave us.

M. LOYAL.   Good-bye for the present. May Heaven keep you all in happiness!

ORGON.   May it confound you and him who sent you!

SCENE V

ORGON, CLÉANTE, MARIANE, ELMIRE, MADAME PERNELLE, DORINE, DAMIS

ORGON.   Ah! well. You see now, mother, I was right, and you can judge of the rest by the warrant. Do you acknowledge his treachery at last?

MME. PERNELLE.   I am quite thunderstruck: I feel as though I had dropped from the clouds!

DORINE.   You have not any reason to complain, or to blame him. His pious
2340   designs are confirmed by this. His virtue reaches its consummation in the love of his neighbor. He knows that riches very often corrupt a man, and, out of pure charity, he would take away from you everything which could become an obstacle in the way of your salvation.

ORGON.   Hold your tongue. I am continually telling you to be quiet.

CLÉANTE.   Let us see what course we ought to follow.

ELMIRE.   Go and expose the ungrateful wretch's audacity. His proceeding destroys the validity of the contract. His disloyalty will appear too black to allow him to gain the success he expects.

SCENE VI

VALÈRE, ORGON, CLÉANTE, ELMIRE, MARIANE, etc.

2350 VALÈRE.   I am very sorry, Monsieur, that I come to trouble you, but I am forced to it by the urgency of the danger. A friend who is united to me by the closest ties, and who knows the interest I take in you, has, by a hazardous step, violated for my sake the secrecy due to affairs of state and has just sent me some intelligence in consequence of which you will be compelled to make a sudden flight. About an hour ago, the knave, who has imposed upon you for so long, thought proper to accuse you to the king, and, amongst the charges which he brings against you, he has put into his hands the important documents of a state criminal whose guilty secret he says you have kept in contempt of the duty of a subject. I do not know the
2360   details of the crime with which you are charged, but a warrant is out against your person, and the better to execute it, he himself is appointed to accompany the person who is to arrest you.

CLÉANTE.   His pretensions are now armed, and it is by this means that the traitor seeks to render himself master of your property.

ORGON.   I tell you the fellow is a vile brute.

VALÈRE.   The least delay may be fatal to you. My coach is at the door to take you away, and I have brought you a thousand louis d'or. Do not let us lose any time; the bolt is shot, and this is one of those blows which must be parried by flight. I myself offer to conduct you to a safe retreat, and I will
2370   accompany you even to the end of your flight.

ORGON.   Alas! what do I not owe to your thoughtful care? I must thank you another time. I beg that heaven will be propitious enough to enable me to acknowledge some day this generous service. Farewell. The rest of you be careful . . .

CLÉANTE.   Go quickly, brother, we will see to everything necessary.

LAST SCENE

A POLICE OFFICER, TARTUFFE, VALÈRE, ORGON, ELMIRE, MARIANE, *etc.*

TARTUFFE.   Gently, Monsieur, gently, do not run so fast. You will not have to go very far in order to find your lodging; we take you prisoner in the King's name.

ORGON.   Wretch! You have kept this shaft for the last. This is the blow,
2380   villain, by which you dispatch me, and it crowns all your evil deeds.

TARTUFFE.   Your abuse has no power to disturb me; I am accustomed to endure all things for the sake of heaven.

CLÉANTE.   Your moderation is great, to be sure.

DAMIS.   How impudently the villain plays with heaven!

TARTUFFE.   All your abuse cannot move me. I do not think of anything but of doing my duty.

MARIANE.   You may aspire to great glory from *this* duty. And this task is a very proper one for *you* to undertake.

TARTUFFE.   A task cannot but be glorious when it proceeds from the power
2390   which sends me to this place.

ORGON.   Ungrateful wretch, do you remember that it was my charitable hand which raised you from a miserable condition?

TARTUFFE.   Yes, I know what assistance I had from you, but the interest of the King is my first duty. The imperative obligation of that sacred duty stifles all gratitude in my heart, and I would sacrifice friend, wife, parents and myself with them to so powerful a bond.

ELMIRE.   The hypocrite!

DORINE.   How well and artfully he knows how to make himself a fine cloak out of all that men hold sacred.

2400 CLÉANTE.   But if this zeal which fills you, and upon which you plume yourself, is as perfect as you say it is, why did it not appear before he happened to surprise you soliciting his wife? Why did you not think to denounce him until his honor obliged him to turn you away? I do not say the gift of all his property he recently made you should have prevented you from doing your duty, but why did you agree to take anything of his when you intended to treat him as a criminal today?

TARTUFFE [*to the* POLICE OFFICER]. Pray, Monsieur, deliver me from this
clamor, and be so good as to execute your warrant.

POLICE OFFICER.   Certainly. We have delayed the execution too long, without
2410   doubt. Your words aptly remind me to fulfil it. My warrant will be exe-
cuted if you follow me directly to the prison which is assigned you for your
dwelling.

TARTUFFE.   Who? I, Monsieur.

POLICE OFFICER.   Yes, you.

TARTUFFE.   Why, then, to prison?

POLICE OFFICER.   I have no account to render to you. Compose yourself,
Monsieur, after so great an alarm. We live under a king who is an enemy
to fraud, a king whose eyes look into the depths of all hearts, and who
cannot be deceived by the most artful imposter. Gifted with a fine dis-
2420   cernment, his lofty soul at all times sees things in the right light. He is
never betrayed into exaggeration, and his sound judgment never falls into
any excess. He confers an everlasting glory upon men of worth; but this
zeal does not radiate blindly: his esteem for the sincere does not close his
heart to the horror aroused by those who are treacherous. Even this person was not the man to overreach him: he has guarded himself against
more subtle snares. From the first his quick perception pierced through
all the vileness coiled round that man's heart, who, coming to accuse you,
betrayed himself, and by a righteous act of divine justice revealed himself
to the King as a notorious rogue, of whose deeds, under another name,
2430   the King was aware. His life is one long series of utterly black actions, of
which volumes might be written. In short, the monarch detested his vile
ingratitude and his disloyalty towards you; to his other misdeeds he has
added this crime; and I am placed in this matter under his orders, so that
the lengths to which his impudence would carry him might be seen, and
in order to make him give you entire satisfaction. Yes, I am instructed to
take away from the wretch all your documents of which he declares he is
the owner, and to place them in your hands. By his sovereign power he
annuls the terms of the contract which made over to that man all your
wealth, and, finally, he pardons you the secret offense into which the flight
2440   of a friend caused you to fall. This is the reward he bestows for the zeal
which he formerly saw you display in the support of his rights, to show that
his heart knows, when least suspected, how to recompense a good action,
that merit is never ignored by him, and that he remembers good much
better than evil.

DORINE.   Heaven be praised!

MADAME PERNELLE.   Now I breathe again.

ELMIRE.   What a happy end to our troubles!

MARIANE.   Who would have dared to foretell this?

ORGON [*to* TARTUFFE]. Ah! well, there you go, traitor!

2450 CLÉANTE.   Ah! my brother, stay, do not descend to abuse. Leave the wretch
to his evil fate, and do not add to the remorse which overwhelms him.
Much rather hope his heart may today make a happy return to the bosom
of virtue; that he may reform his life in detesting his crime, and thus cause
our glorious King to temper justice; whilst you throw yourself on your
knees in return for his lenity and render the thanks such mild treatment
demands.

ORGON. Yes, it is well said. Let us joyfully throw ourselves at his feet and praise the goodness which his heart has shown to us. Then, having acquitted ourselves a little of this first duty, let us apply ourselves to the pressing claims of another, and by a happy wedding let us crown in Valère the ardor of a generous and sincere lover.

END

[1667]

Critical Commentary on *Tartuffe*

Molière's *Tartuffe,* like Aristophanes' *Lysistrata* and Shaw's *Mrs Warren's Profession,* was long banished from the stage because of its content. But while the other two plays were censored for transgressions against narrow codes of sexual morality, *Tartuffe* calls into question the ethics and the sexual mores of those religious fanatics and hypocrites who are most likely to impose censorship. The radical religious groups of Molière's own day successfully prevented public performances of the play for the five years between 1664 and 1669. During this period, Molière continued to work on the play and he struggled to convince the king and court that *Tartuffe* satirized only religious impostors and not religion itself. Indeed, the fawning praise of the king in the fifth act is an insertion obviously designed to win the support Molière needed in order to bring his work before the public. When professional performances were finally authorized in 1669, the play quickly established itself as a classic of popular drama.

The element of religious satire in the play is most prominent in the treatment of the title character, Tartuffe. He is, as Dorine says in the last scene, one who can artfully "make himself a fine cloak out of all that men hold sacred." He knows how to give his every action a coat of pious whitewash. Thus, when Damis reports having heard Tartuffe make indecent proposals to Elmire, the hypocrite merely humbles himself and piously begs for even greater humiliation: "accuse me of treachery, infamy, theft, murder; overwhelm me with still more despicable names. I do not deny them, I have deserved them" (III, vi). He justifies taking Damis' rightful inheritance by claiming that such wealth were better bestowed on one indifferent to it, like himself, than on one who might put it to evil use, like Damis. He even manages to praise heaven, purity, and God's creation all the while he is suggesting an adulterous affair to his benefactor's wife.

Tartuffe's hypocrisy, however, is so obvious that it fools only Orgon and Mme. Pernelle. More subtle, and perhaps more disturbing to some religious authorities, is the depiction of Tartuffe's enthusiastic supporter, Orgon. In many respects Orgon becomes the embodiment of the puritanical zealot, but his excesses make ridiculous many views that are often accepted and praised. He condemns the free-thinking of Deists like Cléante. He takes a poor man into his house and bestows his own wealth upon him. He disassociates himself from worldly personal interests and devotes all of his attention to the hereafter and to following the advice of his religious counselor. He even paraphrases the Scripture when he remarks that Tartuffe "teaches me that I must not set my affections upon anything; he detaches my heart from all ties; and I could see my brother, children, mother and wife die without caring as much as a snap of the fingers" (I, v). In the end, Orgon's ridiculous credulity jeopardizes his own future and that of his family.

Most critics conclude, however, that the play is less a satire on religion than on extremism in general. Like many other neoclassical comedies, *Tartuffe* obtains much of its humor by ridiculing immoderate or unreasonable conduct. Its major characters are conceived as comic "types" that are made recognizable as such through the exaggeration of some attitude or characteristic. Thus, Tartuffe, "the impostor," becomes a figure of fun when we learn that "he even accused himself the other day for having killed a flea too angrily which he caught whilst saying his prayers" (I, v). And his first words in the play, "Laurent, lock up my hairshirt and my scourge" (III, ii), suggest, in an understated manner, his ridiculous posturing. Saints may have once worn hairshirts and mortified their flesh, but unlike Tartuffe they made no public show of their sufferings.

Similarly, Orgon, "the dupe," is made ludicrous because of his excessive fondness for Tartuffe. In Act 1, Scene IV, for example, Orgon returns from a trip and is told by the maid, Dorine, that his wife has been ill during his absence. His only response is to ask, "And Tartuffe?"—a question that he repeats three more times as he is told that Elmire could not touch her supper, that she spent a sleepless night, and that she was finally bled by the physician. The startled Dorine tells Orgon that Tartuffe has been "in excellent health, stout and fat;" that he dined very devoutly on "a brace of partridges and half a leg of mutton hashed;" that he slept soundly all night; and that, "to make up for the blood which Madame had lost, he drank four large bumpers of wine for breakfast." Each tidbit of information about his dear Tartuffe prompts Orgon to exclaim, "Poor man!" And the bewildered Dorine exits after observing wryly, "Both are now well again, and I will go and tell Madame how pleased you are at her recovery."

A number of the minor figures in the play are also characterized by their comic excesses. Madame Pernelle is a comic exaggeration of "the mother-in-law," Damis is "the hot-headed youth," Mariane and Valère are "the young lovers," and Dorine is "the impertinent maid." The comic excesses of these characters are all the more obvious because Molière gives us models of moderate and reasonable behavior in Elmire and Cléante.

According to neoclassical thinking, all immoderation is capable of disrupting society. Jacques Guicharnaud and Hallam Walker argue, however, that the various excesses in *Tartuffe* specifically threaten the family structure and, by extension, the state itself. In the very first scene the curtain rises on a family dispute and the household is explicitly compared with the flawed court of King Pétaud. When Orgon returns home shortly thereafter, Elmire and the young people quickly scatter, indicating what Walker calls "the fragmenting of the family." The fragmentation is, as Dorine observes, the direct result of Tartuffe's intrusion into the family: "Surely it is a scandalous thing to see a stranger exercise such authority in this house . . . and play the master" (I, i). Tartuffe's place in the family is, in turn, the result of Orgon's tyrannical desire for power. The greater the opposition to Tartuffe, the more Orgon becomes determined to have his way. Thus, Orgon tells Mariane, "I am your father, and I know what is good for you" (II, ii). And he decides that she *shall* love Tartuffe: "I wish it to be the truth, and it is enough for you that I have made up my mind on the subject" (II, i). In the attempt to subdue his rebellious family, Orgon makes Tartuffe his heir, gives him the title to his home, and even entrusts him with a compromising box of papers.

Such actions are clearly an abuse of Orgon's paternal authority. He is led astray by his own warped love for Tartuffe. Affection that should naturally be given to his wife and children is lavished on Tartuffe: "He caresses him, kisses him, and I do not think he could show more affection to a mistress" (I, ii). At least twice Orgon and Tartuffe embrace on stage—though Molière avoids overt impropriety by making these embraces inadvertent and by staging them after Orgon has recognized Tartuffe's hypocrisy. Nonetheless, this perversion of love is paralleled by disruptions in other love relationships. Elmire is estranged from her husband; Damis is disinherited by his father; the betrothal of Mariane and Valère is broken. Furthermore, Tartuffe, who should be devoted only to the love of God, is forever leering at Dorine's bosom or Elmire's knee.

In the end the king must intervene to reestablish the proper relationships within the family, and it is appropriate that he should. The patriarchal family contains in miniature the same power structure as the absolute monarchy of Louis XIV—a fact that helps to explain the scattered and obscure references to the recent rebellion against the king. If Louis were to tolerate the usurpations of a Tartuffe within the family, he would be setting a precedent that eventually could shake his own throne, for the proper functioning of the family is necessary in a secure and prosperous state. Fortunately, the king is "gifted with a fine discernment, his lofty soul at all times sees things in the right light. He is never betrayed into exaggeration, and his sound judgment never falls into any excess" (V, vii). Only the intervention of this nearly omnipotent embodiment of reason prevents Tartuffe's total victory and allows the play to conclude, as so many other comedies do, with an anticipated marriage between young lovers and happiness all around.

A Selective Bibliography on *Tartuffe*

Auerbach, Erich. *Mimesis*. Trans. Willard Trask. Princeton: Princeton UP, 1953. 359–94.

Cairncross, John. *New Light on Molière*. Geneva: Droz, 1956.

Gossman, Lionel. *Men and Masks: A Study of Molière*. Baltimore: Johns Hopkins UP, 1963. 101–44.

Fernandez, Ramon. *Molière: The Man Seen Through His Plays*. New York, 1980. 122–26, 129–41.

Guicharnaud, Jacques. *Molière, une aventure theatrale*. Paris: Gallimard, 1963. 170–73.

———. *Molière: A Collection of Critical Essays*. Englewood Cliffs, N.J.: Prentice-Hall, 1964.

Hall, H. G. *Molière: Tartuffe*. London: Arnold, 1960.

Howarth, W. D. *Molière: A Playwright and His Audience*. Cambridge, Eng.: Cambridge UP, 1982. 195–204.

Hubert, J. D. *Molière & and the Comedy of Intellect*. Berkeley: U of California P., 1962. 91–112.

Jagendorf, Zvi. *The Happy End of Comedy: Jonson, Molière, and Shakespeare*. Newark: U of Delaware P. 1984. 93–100.

Knutson, Harold C. *Molière: An Archetypal Approach*. Toronto: U of Toronto P, 1976. 76–83.

————. *The Triumph of Wit: Molière and Restoration Comedy.* Columbus: Ohio State UP, 1988.

Phillips, Henry. "Molière and Tartuffe: Recrimination and Reconciliation." *The French Review: Journal of the American Association of Teachers of French* 62.5 (1989): 749–63.

McBride, Robert. *The Sceptical Vision of Molière.* New York: Barnes & Noble, 1977. 31–78.

Moore, W. G. *Molière: A New Criticism.* Rev. Ed. Garden City: Doubleday, 1962. 44–50.

Nurse, Peter H. "*Tartuffe*: Comedy or Drama?" *Modern Languages* 70.2 (1989): 118–22.

Walker, Hallam. *Molière.* Rev. Ed. New York: Twayne, 1990. 81–98.

Henrik Ibsen (1828–1906)
A DOLL'S HOUSE

Translated by William Archer

CHARACTERS

TORVALD HELMER
NORA, *his wife*
DOCTOR RANK
MRS. LINDEN
NILS KROGSTAD

THE HELMERS' *three children*
ANNA, *their nurse*
ELLEN, *a maidservant*
A Porter

The action passes in Helmer's house (a flat) in Christiania.

ACT I

A room, comfortably and tastefully, but not expensively, furnished. In the back, on the right, a door leads to the hall; on the left another door leads to HELMER'S *study. Between the two doors a pianoforte. In the middle of the left wall a door, and nearer the front a window. Near the window a round table with armchairs and a small sofa. In the right wall, somewhat to the back, a door, and against the same wall, further forward, a porcelain stove; in front of it a couple of armchairs and a rocking-chair. Between the stove and the side-door a small table. Engravings on the walls. A what-not with china and bric-à-brac.[1] A small bookcase filled with handsomely bound books. Carpet. A fire in the stove. It is a winter day. A bell rings in the hall outside. Presently the outer door of the flat is heard to open.*

[NORA *enters, humming gayly. She is in outdoor dress, and carries several parcels, which she lays on the right-hand table. She leaves the door into the hall open, and a Porter is seen outside, carrying a Christmas tree and a basket, which he gives to the Maidservant who has opened the door.*]

NORA. Hide the Christmas tree carefully, Ellen; the children must on no account see it before this evening, when it's lighted up. [*To the Porter, taking out her purse.*] How much?
PORTER. Fifty öre.[2]
NORA. There is a crown. No, keep the change. [*The Porter thanks her and goes.* NORA *shuts the door. She continues smiling in quiet glee as she takes off her outdoor things. Taking from her pocket a bag of macaroons, she eats one or two. Then she goes on tiptoe to her husband's door and listens.*] Yes; he is at home. [*She begins humming again, crossing to the table on the right.*]

---

[1] A what-not is a stand with shelves for holding bric-a-brac, small decorative objects.
[2] The basic unit of Swedish currency is the krona, or crown, worth one hundred öre.

HELMER [*in his room*].   Is that my lark twittering there?

NORA [*busy opening some of her parcels*].   Yes, it is.

HELMER.   Is it the squirrel frisking around?

10 NORA.   Yes!

HELMER.   When did the squirrel get home?

NORA.   Just this minute. [*Hides the bag of macaroons in her pocket and wipes her mouth.*] Come here, Torvald, and see what I've been buying.

HELMER.   Don't interrupt me. [*A little later he opens the door and looks in, pen in hand.*] Buying, did you say? What! All that? Has my little spendthrift been making the money fly again?

NORA.   Why, Torvald, surely we can afford to launch out a little now. It's the first Christmas we haven't had to pinch.

HELMER.   Come, come; we can't afford to squander money.

20 NORA.   Oh, yes, Torvald, do let us squander a little, now—just the least little bit! You know you'll soon be earning heaps of money.

HELMER.   Yes, from New Year's Day. But there's a whole quarter before my first salary is due.

NORA.   Never mind; we can borrow in the mean time.

HELMER.   Nora! [*He goes up to her and takes her playfully by the ear.*] Still my little featherbrain! Supposing I borrowed a thousand crowns to-day, and you made ducks and drakes of them during Christmas week, and then on New Year's Eve a tile blew off the roof and knocked my brains out.

NORA [*laying her hand on his mouth*].   Hush! How can you talk so horridly?

30 HELMER.   But supposing it were to happen—what then?

NORA.   If anything so dreadful happened, it would be all the same to me whether I was in debt or not.

HELMER.   But what about the creditors?

NORA.   They! Who cares for them? They're only strangers.

HELMER.   Nora, Nora! What a *woman* you are! But seriously, Nora, you know my principles on these points. No debts! No borrowing! Home life ceases to be free and beautiful as soon as it is founded on borrowing and debt. We two have held out bravely till now, and we are not going to give in at the last.

40 NORA [*going to the fireplace*].   Very well—as you please. Torvald.

HELMER [*following her*].   Come, come; my little lark mustn't droop her wings like that. What? Is my squirrel in the sulks? [*Takes out his purse.*] Nora, what do you think I have here?

NORA [*turning around quickly*].   Money!

HELMER.   There! [*Gives her some notes.*] Of course, I know all sorts of things are wanted at Christmas.

NORA [*counting*].   Ten, twenty, thirty, forty. Oh, thank you, thank you, Torvald! This will go a long way.

HELMER.   I should hope so.

50 NORA.   Yes, indeed; a long way! But come here, and let me show you all I've been buying. And so cheap!. Look, here's a new suit for Ivar, and a little sword. Here are a horse and a trumpet for Bob. And here are a doll and a cradle for Emmy. They're only common; but they're good enough for her to pull to pieces. And dress-stuffs and kerchiefs for the servants. I ought to have got something better for old Anna.

HELMER.   And what's in that other parcel?

NORA [*crying out*].   No, Torvald, you're not to see that until this evening!

HELMER.   Oh! Ah! But now, tell me, you little spendthrift, have you thought of anything for yourself?

60 NORA.   For myself! Oh, I don't want anything.

HELMER.   Nonsense! Just tell me something sensible you would like to have.

NORA.   No, really I don't know of anything—Well, listen, Torvald—

HELMER.   Well?

NORA [*playing with his coat-buttons, without looking him in the face*].   If you really want to give me something, you might, you know—you might—

HELMER.   Well? Out with it!

NORA [*quickly*].   You might give me money, Torvald. Only just what you think you can spare; then I can buy something with it later on.

HELMER.   But, Nora—

70 NORA.   Oh, please do, dear Torvald, please do! I should hang the money in lovely gilt paper on the Christmas tree. Wouldn't that be fun?

HELMER.   What do they call the birds that are always making the money fly?

NORA.   Yes, I know—spendthrifts, of course. But please do as I ask you, Torvald. Then I shall have time to think what I want most. Isn't that very sensible, now?

HELMER [*smiling*].   Certainly; that is to say, if you really kept the money I gave you, and really spent it on something for yourself. But it all goes in housekeeping, and for all manner of useless things, and then I have to pay up again.

80 NORA.   But, Torvald—

HELMER.   Can you deny it, Nora dear? [*He puts his arm round her.*] It's a sweet little lark, but it gets through a lot of money. No one would believe how much it costs a man to keep such a little bird as you.

NORA.   For shame! How can you say so? Why, I save as much as ever I can.

HELMER [*laughing*].   Very true—as much as you can—but that's precisely nothing.

NORA [*hums and smiles with covert glee*].   H'm! If you only knew, Torvald, what expenses we larks and squirrels have.

HELMER.   You're a strange little being! Just like your father—always on the
90   lookout for all the money you can lay your hands on; but the moment you have it, it seems to slip through your fingers; you never know what becomes of it. Well, one must take you as you are. It's in the blood. Yes, Nora, that sort of thing is hereditary.

NORA.   I wish I had inherited many of papa's qualities.

HELMER.   And I don't wish you anything but just what you are—my own, sweet little song-bird. But I say—it strikes me you look so—so—what shall I call it?—so suspicious today—

NORA.   Do I?

HELMER.   You do, indeed. Look me full in the face.

100 NORA [*looking at him*].   Well?

HELMER [*threatening with his finger*].   Hasn't the little sweet-tooth been playing pranks today?

NORA.   No; how can you think such a thing!

HELMER.   Didn't she just look in at the confectioner's?

NORA.   No, Torvald; really—

HELMER.   Not to sip a little jelly?

NORA.   No; certainly not.

HELMER.   Hasn't she even nibbled a macaroon or two?

NORA.   No, Torvald, indeed, indeed!

110 HELMER.   Well, well, well; of course I'm only joking.

NORA [*goes to the table on the right*].   I shouldn't think of doing what you disapprove of.

HELMER.   No, I'm sure of that; and, besides, you've given me your word— [*Going toward her.*] Well, keep your little Christmas secrets to yourself, Nora darling. The Christmas tree will bring them all to light, I dare say.

NORA.   Have you remembered to invite Doctor Rank?

HELMER.   No. But it's not necessary; he'll come as a matter of course. Besides, I shall ask him when he looks in today. I've ordered some capital wine. Nora, you can't think how I look forward to this evening.

120 NORA.   And I, too. How the children will enjoy themselves, Torvald!

HELMER.   Ah, it's glorious to feel that one has an assured position and ample means. Isn't it delightful to think of?

NORA.   Oh, it's wonderful!

HELMER.   Do you remember last Christmas? For three whole weeks beforehand you shut yourself up every evening till long past midnight to make flowers for the Christmas tree, and all sorts of other marvels that were to have astonished us. I was never so bored in my life.

NORA.   I didn't bore myself at all.

HELMER [*smiling*].   But it came to little enough in the end, Nora.

130 NORA.   Oh, are you going to tease me about that again? How could I help the cat getting in and pulling it all to pieces?

HELMER.   To be sure you couldn't, my poor little Nora. You did your best to give us all pleasure, and that's the main point. But, all the same, it's a good thing the hard times are over.

NORA.   Oh, isn't it wonderful?

HELMER.   Now I needn't sit here boring myself all alone; and you needn't tire your blessed eyes and your delicate little fingers—

NORA [*clapping her hands*].   No, I needn't, need I, Torvald? Oh, how wonderful it is to think of? [*Takes his arm.*] And now I'll tell you how I think we

140 ought to manage, Torvald. As soon as Christmas is over—[*The hall doorbell rings.*] Oh, there's a ring! [*Arranging the room.*] That's somebody come to call. How tiresome!

HELMER.   I'm "not at home" to callers; remember that.

ELLEN [*in the doorway*].   A lady to see you, ma'am.

NORA.   Show her in.

ELLEN [*to* HELMER].   And the doctor has just come, sir.

HELMER.   Has he gone into my study?

ELLEN.   Yes, sir.

[HELMER *goes into his study.*]

[ELLEN *ushers in* MRS. LINDEN, *in traveling costume, and goes out, closing the door.*]

MRS. LINDEN [*embarrassed and hesitating*].   How do you do, Nora?

150 NORA [*doubtfully*].   How do you do?

MRS. LINDEN.   I see you don't recognize me.

NORA. No, I don't think—oh, yes!—I believe—[*Suddenly brightening.*] What, Christina! Is it really you?

MRS. LINDEN. Yes; really I!

NORA. Christina! And to think I didn't know you! But how could I—[*More softly.*] How changed you are, Christina!

MRS. LINDEN. Yes, no doubt. In nine or ten years—

NORA. Is it really so long since we met? Yes, so it is. Oh, the last eight years have been a happy time, I can tell you. And now you have come to town?
160   All that long journey in mid-winter! How brave of you!

MRS. LINDEN. I arrived by this morning's steamer.

NORA. To have a merry Christmas, of course. Oh, how delightful! Yes, we *will* have a merry Christmas. Do take your things off. Aren't you frozen? [*Helping her.*] There; now we'll sit cozily by the fire. No, you take the armchair; I shall sit in this rocking chair. [*Seizes her hands.*] Yes, now I can see the dear old face again. It was only at the first glance—But you're a little paler, Christina,—and perhaps a little thinner.

MRS. LINDEN. And much, much older, Nora.

NORA. Yes, perhaps a little older—not much—ever so little. [*She suddenly
170   checks herself; seriously.*] Oh, what a thoughtless wretch I am! Here I sit chattering on, and—Dear, dear Christina, can you forgive me!

MRS. LINDEN. What do you mean, Nora?

NORA [*softly*]. Poor Christina! I forgot: you are a widow.

MRS. LINDEN. Yes; my husband died three years ago.

NORA. I know, I know; I saw it in the papers. Oh, believe me, Christina, I did mean to write to you; but I kept putting it off, and something always came in the way.

MRS. LINDEN. I can quite understand that, Nora, dear.

NORA. No, Christina; it was horrid of me. Oh, you poor darling! how much
180   you must have gone through!—And he left you nothing?

MRS. LINDEN. Nothing.

NORA. And no children?

MRS. LINDEN. None.

NORA. Nothing, nothing at all?

MRS. LINDEN. Not even a sorrow or a longing to dwell upon.

NORA [*looking at her incredulously*]. My dear Christina, how is that possible?

MRS. LINDEN [*smiling sadly and stroking her hair*]. Oh, it happens so sometimes, Nora.

NORA. So utterly alone! How dreadful that must be! I have three of the
190   loveliest children. I can't show them to you just now; they're out with their nurse. But now you must tell me everything.

MRS. LINDEN. No, no; I want you to tell me—

NORA. No, you must begin; I won't be egotistical today. Today I'll think only of you. Oh! but I must tell you one thing—perhaps you've heard of our great stroke of fortune?

MRS. LINDEN. No. What is it?

NORA. Only think! my husband has been made manager of the Joint Stock Bank.

MRS. LINDEN. Your husband! Oh, how fortunate!

200 NORA. Yes; isn't it? A lawyer's position is so uncertain, you see, especially

when he won't touch any business that's the least bit—shady, as of course
Torvald never would; and there I quite agree with him. Oh! You can
imagine how glad we are. He is to enter on his new position at the New
Year, and then he'll have a large salary, and percentages. In future we
shall be able to live quite differently—just as we please, in fact. Oh, Christina, I feel so light-hearted and happy! It's delightful to have lots of
money, and no need to worry about things, isn't it?

MRS. LINDEN.   Yes; at any rate, it must be delightful to have what you need.

NORA.   No, not only what you need, but heaps of money—*heaps!*

210   MRS. LINDEN [*smiling*].   Nora, Nora, haven't you learned reason yet? In our
schooldays you were a shocking little spendthrift.

NORA [*quietly smiling*].   Yes; that's what Torvald says I am still. [*Holding up her
forefinger.*] But "Nora, Nora," is not so silly as you all think. Oh! I haven't
had the chance to be much of a spendthrift. We have both had to work.

MRS. LINDEN.   You, too?

NORA.   Yes, light fancy work: crochet, and embroidery, and things of that
sort; [*carelessly*] and other work too. You know, of course, that Torvald left
the Government service when we were married. He had little chance of
promotion, and of course he required to make more money. But in the

220   first year after our marriage he overworked himself terribly. He had to
undertake all sorts of extra work, you know, and to slave early and late. He
couldn't stand it, and fell dangerously ill. Then the doctors declared he
must go to the South.

MRS. LINDEN.   You spent a whole year in Italy, didn't you?

NORA.   Yes, we did. It wasn't easy to manage, I can tell you. It was just after
Ivar's birth. But of course we had to go. Oh, it was a wonderful, delicious
journey! And it saved Torvald's life. But it cost a frightful lot of money,
Christina.

MRS. LINDEN.   So I should think.

230   NORA.   Twelve hundred dollars! Four thousand eight hundred crowns! Isn't
that a lot of money?

MRS. LINDEN.   How lucky you had the money to spend.

NORA.   We got it from father, you must know.

MRS. LINDEN.   Ah, I see. He died just about that time, didn't he?

NORA.   Yes, Christina, just then. And only think! I couldn't go and nurse
him! I was expecting little Ivar's birth daily; and then I had my poor sick
Torvald to attend to. Dear, kind old father! I never saw him again, Christina. Oh! That's the hardest thing I have had to bear since my marriage.

MRS. LINDEN.   I know how fond you were of him. But then you went to Italy?

240   NORA.   Yes; you see, we had the money, and the doctors said we must lose no
time. We started a month later.

MRS. LINDEN.   And your husband came back completely cured.

NORA.   Sound as a bell.

MRS. LINDEN.   But—the doctor?

NORA.   What do you mean?

MRS. LINDEN.   I thought as I came in your servant announced the doctor—

NORA.   Oh, yes; Doctor Rank. But he doesn't come professionally. He is our
best friend, and never lets a day pass without looking in. No, Torvald
hasn't had an hour's illness since that time. And the children are so healthy

250   and well, and so am I. [*Jumps up and claps her hands.*] Oh, Christina,

Christina, what a wonderful thing it is to live and to be happy!—Oh but it's really too horrid of me! Here am I talking about nothing but my own concerns. [*Seats herself upon a footstool close to* CHRISTINA, *and lays her arms on her friend's lap.*] Oh, don't be angry with me! Now, tell me, is it really true that you didn't love your husband? What made you marry him, then?

MRS. LINDEN.   My mother was still alive, you see, bedridden and helpless; and then I had my two younger brothers to think of. I didn't think it would be right for me to refuse him.

NORA.   Perhaps it wouldn't have been. I suppose he was rich then?

260 MRS. LINDEN.   Very well off, I believe. But his business was uncertain. It fell to pieces at his death, and there was nothing left.

NORA.   And then—?

MRS. LINDEN.   Then I had to fight my way by keeping a shop, a little school, anything I could turn my hand to. The last three years have been one long struggle for me. But now it is over, Nora. My poor mother no longer needs me; she is at rest. And the boys are in business, and can look after themselves.

NORA.   How free your life must feel!

MRS. LINDEN.   No, Nora; only inexpressibly empty. No one to live for! [*Stands*
270 *up restlessly.*] That's why I could not bear to stay any longer in that out-of-the-way corner. Here it must be easier to find something to take one up—to occupy one's thoughts. If I could only get some settled employment—some office work.

NORA.   But, Christina, that's such drudgery, and you look worn out already. It would be ever so much better for you to go to some watering-place and rest.

MRS. LINDEN [*going to the window*].   I have no father to give me the money, Nora.

NORA [*rising*].   Oh, don't be vexed with me.

280 MRS. LINDEN [*going to her*].   My dear Nora, don't you be vexed with me. The worst of a position like mine is that it makes one so bitter. You have no one to work for, yet you have to be always on the strain.[3] You must live; and so you become selfish. When I heard of the happy change in your fortunes—can you believe it?—I was glad for my own sake more than for yours.

NORA.   How do you mean? Ah, I see! You think Torvald can perhaps do something for you.

MRS. LINDEN.   Yes; I thought so.

NORA.   And so he shall, Christina. Just you leave it all to me. I shall lead up to it beautifully!—I shall think of some delightful plan to put him in a
290 good humor! Oh, I should so love to help you.

MRS. LINDEN.   How good of you, Nora, to stand by me so warmly! Doubly good in you, who know so little of the troubles and burdens of life.

NORA.   I? I know so little of—?

MRS. LINDEN [*smiling*].   Oh, well—a little fancy-work, and so forth.—You're a child, Nora.

NORA [*tosses her head and paces the room*].   Oh, come, you mustn't be so patronizing!

---

3 I.e., always struggling to make ends meet.

Mrs. Linden.   No?

Nora.   You're like the rest. You all think I'm fit for nothing really serious—

300 Mrs. Linden.   Well, well—

Nora.   You think I've had no troubles in this weary world.

Mrs. Linden.   My dear Nora, you've just told me all your troubles.

Nora.   Pooh—those trifles! [*Softly.*] I haven't told you the great thing.

Mrs. Linden.   The great thing? What do you mean?

Nora.   I know you look down upon me, Christina; but you have no right to. You are proud of having worked so hard and so long for your mother.

Mrs. Linden.   I am sure I don't look down upon any one; but it's true I am both proud and glad when I remember that I was able to keep my mother's last days free from care.

310 Nora.   And you're proud to think of what you have done for your brothers, too.

Mrs. Linden.   Have I not the right to be?

Nora.   Yes, indeed. But now let me tell you, Christina,—I, too, have something to be proud and glad of.

Mrs. Linden.   I don't doubt it. But what do you mean?

Nora.   Hush! Not so loud. Only think, if Torvald were to hear! He mustn't—not for worlds! No one must know about it, Christina,—no one but you.

Mrs. Linden.   Why, what can it be?

Nora.   Come over here. [*Draws her down beside her on the sofa.*] Yes, Chris-

320 tina,—I, too, have something to be proud and glad of. I saved Torvald's life.

Mrs. Linden.   Saved his life? How?

Nora.   I told you about our going to Italy. Torvald would have died but for that.

Mrs. Linden.   Well—and your father gave you the money.

Nora [*smiling*].   Yes, so Torvald and every one believes; but—

Mrs. Linden.   But—?

Nora.   Papa didn't give us one penny. It was *I* that found the money.

Mrs. Linden.   You? All that money?

330 Nora.   Twelve hundred dollars. Four thousand eight hundred crowns. What do you say to that?

Mrs. Linden.   My dear Nora, how did you manage it? Did you win it in the lottery?

Nora [*contemptuously*].   In the lottery? Pooh! Any one could have done *that!*

Mrs. Linden.   Then, wherever did you get it from?

Nora [*hums and smiles mysteriously*].   H'm; tra-la-la-la.

Mrs. Linden.   Of course you couldn't borrow it.

Nora.   No? Why not?

Mrs. Linden.   Why, a wife can't borrow without her husband's consent.

340 Nora [*tossing her head*].   Oh! When the wife has some idea of business, and knows how to set about things—

Mrs. Linden.   But, Nora, I don't understand—

Nora.   Well, you needn't. I never said I borrowed the money. There are many ways I may have got it. [*Throws herself back on the sofa.*] I may have got it from some admirer. When one is so—attractive as I am—

Mrs. Linden.   You're too silly, Nora.

Nora.   Now, I'm sure you're dying of curiosity, Christina,—

MRS. LINDEN.   Listen to me, Nora, dear: haven't you been a little rash?

NORA [*sitting upright again*].   Is it rash to save one's husband's life?

350 MRS. LINDEN.   I think it was rash of you, without his knowledge—

NORA.   But it would have been fatal for him to know! Can't you understand that? He wasn't even to suspect how ill he was. The doctors came to me privately and told me his life was in danger—that nothing could save him but a winter in the South. Do you think I didn't try diplomacy first? I told him how I longed to have a trip abroad, like other young wives; I wept and prayed; I said he ought to think of my condition, and not to thwart me; and then I hinted that he could borrow the money. But then, Christina, he got almost angry. He said I was frivolous, and that it was his duty as a husband not to yield to my whims and fancies—so he called them. Very

360 well, thought I, but saved you must be; and then I found the way to do it.

MRS. LINDEN.   And did your husband never learn from your father that the money was not from him?

NORA.   No; never. Papa died at that very time. I meant to have told him all about it, and begged him to say nothing. But he was so ill—unhappily, it wasn't necessary.

MRS. LINDEN.   And you have never confessed to your husband?

NORA.   Good Heavens! What can you be thinking of? *Tell him,* when he has such a loathing of debt! And, besides,—how painful and humiliating it would be for Torvald, and his manly self-respect, to know that he owed

370 anything to me! It would utterly upset the relation between us; our beautiful, happy home would never again be what it is.

MRS. LINDEN.   Will you never tell him?

NORA [*thoughtfully, half-smiling*].   Yes, some time, perhaps,—many, many years hence, when I'm—not so pretty. You mustn't laugh at me! Of course, I mean when Torvald is not so much in love with me as he is now; when it doesn't amuse him any longer to see me dancing about, and dressing up and acting. Then it might be well to have something in reserve. [*Breaking off.*] Nonsense! Nonsense! That time will never come. Now, what do you say to my grand secret, Christina? Am I fit for nothing now? You may

380 believe it has cost me a lot of anxiety. It has been no joke to meet my engagements punctually. You must know, Christina, that in business there are things called installments, and quarterly interest, that are terribly hard to provide for. So I've had to pinch a little here and there, wherever I could. I couldn't save much out of the housekeeping, for, of course, Torvald had to live well. And I couldn't let the children go about badly dressed; all I got for them, I spent on them, the blessed darlings!

MRS. LINDEN.   Poor Nora! So it had to come out of your own pocket-money.

NORA.   Yes, of course. After all, the whole thing was my doing. When Torvald gave me money for clothes, and so on, I never spent more than half

390 of it; I always bought the simplest and cheapest things. It's a mercy that everything suits me so well—Torvald never had any suspicions. But it was often very hard, Christina, dear. For it's nice to be beautifully dressed—now, isn't it?

MRS. LINDEN.   Indeed it is.

NORA.   Well, and besides that, I made money in other ways. Last winter I was so lucky—I got a heap of copying to do. I shut myself up every evening and wrote far into the night. Oh, sometimes I was so tired, so tired. And

yet it was splendid to work in that way and earn money. I almost felt as if
I was a man.

400 Mrs. Linden.   Then how much have you been able to pay off?

Nora.   Well, I can't precisely say. It's difficult to keep that sort of business
clear. I only know that I've paid everything I could scrape together. Sometimes I really didn't know where to turn. [*Smiles.*] Then I used to sit here
and pretend that a rich old gentleman was in love with me—

Mrs. Linden.   What! What gentleman?

Nora.   Oh, nobody!—that he was dead, now, and that when his will was
opened, there stood in large letters: "Pay over at once everything of which
I die possessed to that charming person, Mrs. Nora Helmer."

Mrs. Linden.   But, my dear Nora,—what gentleman do you mean?

410 Nora.   Oh, dear, can't you understand? There wasn't any old gentleman: it
was only what I used to dream and dream when I was at my wits' end for
money. But it doesn't matter now—the tiresome old creature may stay
where he is for me. I care nothing for him or his will; for now my troubles
are over. [*Springing up.*] Oh, Christina, how glorious it is to think of! Free
from all anxiety! Free, quite free. To be able to play and romp about with
the children; to have things tasteful and pretty in the house, exactly as
Torvald likes it! And then the spring will soon be here, with the great blue
sky. Perhaps then we shall have a little holiday. Perhaps I shall see the sea
again. Oh, what a wonderful thing it is to live and to be happy!

[*The hall doorbell rings.*]

420 Mrs. Linden [*rising*].   There's a ring. Perhaps I had better go.

Nora.   No; do stay. No one will come here. It's sure to be some one for
Torvald.

Ellen [*in the doorway*].   If you please, ma'am, there's a gentleman to speak to
Mr. Helmer.

Nora.   Who is the gentleman?

Krogstad [*in the doorway*].   It is I, Mrs. Helmer.

[Mrs. Linden *starts and turns away to the window.*]

Nora [*goes a step toward him, anxiously, speaking low*].   You? What is it? What
do you want with my husband?

Krogstad.   Bank business—in a way. I hold a small post in the Joint Stock
430   Bank, and your husband is to be our new chief, I hear.

Nora.   Then it is—?

Krogstad.   Only tiresome business, Mrs. Helmer; nothing more.

Nora.   Then will you please go to his study.

[Krogstad *goes. She bows indifferently while she closes the door into the hall. Then she
goes to the stove and looks to the fire.*]

Mrs. Linden.   Nora—who was that man?

Nora.   A Mr. Krogstad—a lawyer.

Mrs. Linden.   Then it was really he?

Nora.   Do you know him?

Mrs. Linden.   I used to know him—many years ago. He was in a lawyer's
office in our town.

440 Nora. Yes, so he was.

Mrs. Linden. How he has changed!

Nora. I believe his marriage was unhappy.

Mrs. Linden. And he is a widower now?

Nora. With a lot of children. There! Now it will burn up. [*She closes the stove, and pushes the rocking-chair a little aside.*]

Mrs. Linden. His business is not of the most creditable, they say?

Nora. Isn't it? I dare say not. I don't know. But don't let us think of business—it's so tiresome.

[Doctor Rank *comes out of* Helmer's *room.*]

Rank [*still in the doorway*]. No, no; I'm in your way. I shall go and have a chat
450 with your wife. [*Shuts the door and sees* Mrs. Linden.] Oh, I beg your pardon. I'm in the way here too.

Nora. No, not in the least. [*Introduces them.*] Doctor Rank—Mrs. Linden.

Rank. Oh, indeed; I've often heard Mrs. Linden's name; I think I passed you on the stairs as I came up.

Mrs. Linden. Yes; I go so very slowly. Stairs try me so much.

Rank. Ah—you are not very strong?

Mrs. Linden. Only overworked.

Rank. Nothing more? Then no doubt you've come to town to find rest in a round of dissipation?

460 Mrs. Linden. I have come to look for employment.

Rank. Is that an approved remedy for overwork?

Mrs. Linden. One must live, Doctor Rank.

Rank. Yes, that seems to be the general opinion.

Nora. Come, Doctor Rank,—you want to live yourself.

Rank. To be sure I do. However wretched I may be, I want to drag on as long as possible. All my patients, too, have the same mania. And it's the same with people whose complaint is moral. At this very moment Helmer is talking to just such a moral incurable—

Mrs. Linden [*softly*]. Ah!

470 Nora. Whom do you mean?

Rank. Oh, a fellow named Krogstad, a man you know nothing about,—corrupt to the very core of his character. But even he began by announcing as a matter of vast importance, that he must live.

Nora. Indeed? And what did he want with Torvald?

Rank. I haven't an idea; I only gathered that it was some bank business.

Nora. I didn't know that Krog—that this Mr. Krogstad had anything to do with the Bank?

Rank. Yes. He has got some sort of place there. [*To* Mrs. Linden.] I don't know whether, in your part of the country, you have people who go grub-
480 bing and sniffing around in search of moral rottenness—and then, when they have found a "case," don't rest till they have got their man into some good position, where they can keep a watch upon him. Men with a clean bill of health they leave out in the cold.

Mrs. Linden. Well, I suppose the—delicate characters require most care.

Rank [*shrugs his shoulders*]. There we have it! It's that notion that makes society a hospital. [Nora, *deep in her own thoughts, breaks into half-stifled*

laughter and claps her hands.] Why do you laugh at that? Have you any idea
what "society" is?

NORA.   What do I care for your tiresome society? I was laughing at some-
490   thing else—something excessively amusing. Tell me, Doctor Rank, are all
the employees at the Bank dependent on Torvald now?

RANK.   Is that what strikes you as excessively amusing?

NORA [*smiles and hums*].   Never mind, never mind! [*Walks about the room.*] Yes,
it is funny to think that we—that Torvald has such power over so many
people. [*Takes the bag from her pocket.*] Doctor Rank, will you have a macaroon?

RANK.   What!—macaroons! I thought they were contraband here.

NORA.   Yes; but Christina brought me these.

MRS. LINDEN.   What! I—?

500 NORA.   Oh, well! Don't be frightened. You couldn't possibly know that Torvald had forbidden them. The fact is, he's afraid of me spoiling my teeth.
But, oh, bother, just for once!—That's for you, Doctor Rank! [*Puts a macaroon into his mouth.*] And you too, Christina. And I'll have one while we're
about it—only a tiny one, or at most two. [*Walks about again.*] Oh, dear, I
am happy! There's only one thing in the world I really want.

RANK.   Well; what's that?

NORA.   There's something I should so like to say—in Torvald's hearing.

RANK.   Then why don't you say it?

NORA.   Because I daren't, it's so ugly.

510 MRS. LINDEN.   Ugly!

RANK.   In that case you'd better not. But to us you might—What is it you
would so like to say in Helmer's hearing?

NORA.   I should so love to say, "Damn it all!"

RANK.   Are you out of your mind?

MRS. LINDEN.   Good gracious, Nora—!

RANK.   Say it—there he is!

NORA [*hides the macaroons*].   Hush—sh—

[HELMER *comes out of his room, hat in hand, with his overcoat on his arm.*]

[*Going to him*]. Well, Torvald, dear, have you got rid of him?

HELMER.   Yes; he has just gone.

520 NORA.   Let me introduce you—this is Christina, who has come to town—

HELMER.   Christina? Pardon me, I don't know—

NORA.   Mrs. Linden, Torvald, dear,—Christina Linden.

HELMER [*to* MRS. LINDEN].   Indeed! A school-friend of my wife's, no doubt?

MRS. LINDEN.   Yes; we knew each other as girls.

NORA.   And only think! She has taken this long journey on purpose to speak
to you.

HELMER.   To speak to me!

MRS. LINDEN.   Well, not quite—

NORA.   You see, Christina is tremendously clever at office work, and she's so
530   anxious to work under a first-rate man of business in order to learn still
more—

HELMER [*to* MRS. LINDEN].   Very sensible, indeed.

NORA.   And when she heard you were appointed manager—it was telegraphed, you know—she started off at once, and—Torvald, dear, for my sake, you must do something for Christina. Now, can't you?

HELMER.   It's not impossible. I presume Mrs. Linden is a widow?

MRS. LINDEN.   Yes.

HELMER.   And you have already had some experience of business?

MRS. LINDEN.   A good deal.

540 HELMER.   Well, then, it's very likely I may be able to find a place for you.

NORA [*clapping her hands*].   There now! There now!

HELMER.   You have come at a fortunate moment, Mrs. Linden.

MRS. LINDEN.   Oh, how can I thank you—?

HELMER [*smiling*].   There is no occasion. [*Puts on his overcoat.*] But for the present you must excuse me—

RANK.   Wait; I am going with you.

[*Fetches his fur coat from the hall and warms it at the fire.*]

NORA.   Don't be long, Torvald, dear.

HELMER.   Only an hour; not more.

NORA.   Are you going too, Christina?

550 MRS. LINDEN [*putting on her walking things*].   Yes; I must set about looking for lodgings.

HELMER.   Then perhaps we can go together?

NORA [*helping her*].   What a pity we haven't a spare room for you; but it's impossible—

MRS. LINDEN.   I shouldn't think of troubling you. Good-bye, dear Nora, and thank you for all your kindness.

NORA.   Good-bye for the present. Of course, you'll come back this evening. And you, too, Doctor Rank. What! If you're well enough? Of course you'll be well enough. Only wrap up warmly. [*They go out, talking, into the hall.*
560 *Outside on the stairs are heard children's voices.*] There they are! There they are! [*She runs to the outer door and opens it. The Nurse,* ANNA, *enters the hall with the children.*] Come in! Come in! [*Stoops down and kisses the children.*] Oh, my sweet darlings! Do you see them, Christina? Aren't they lovely?

RANK.   Don't let us stand here chattering in the draught.

HELMER.   Come, Mrs. Linden; only mothers can stand such a temperature.

[DOCTOR RANK, HELMER, *and* MRS. LINDEN *go down the stairs.*]

[ANNA *enters the room with the children;* NORA *also, shutting the door.*]

NORA.   How fresh and bright you look! And what red cheeks you've got! Like apples and roses. [*The children chatter to her during what follows.*] Have you had great fun? That's splendid! Oh, really! You've been giving Emmy and Bob a ride on your sledge!—both at once, only think! Why, you're quite a
570 man, Ivar. Oh, give her to me a little, Anna. My sweet little dolly! [*Takes the smallest from the nurse and dances with her.*] Yes, yes; mother will dance with Bob, too. What! Did you have a game of snowballs? Oh, I wish I'd been there. No; leave them, Anna; I'll take their things off. Oh, yes, let me do it; it's such fun. Go to the nursery; you look frozen. You'll find some hot coffee on the stove. [*The Nurse goes into the room on the left.* NORA *takes off the children's things and throws them down anywhere, while the children talk all*

together.] Really! A big dog ran after you? But he didn't bite you? No; dogs
don't bite dear little dolly children. Don't peep into those parcels, Ivar.
What is it? Wouldn't you like to know? Take care—it'll bite! What? Shall we
580   have a game? What shall we play at? Hide-and-seek? Yes, let's play hide-
and-seek. Bob shall hide first. Am I to? Yes, let me hide first.

[*She and the children play, with laughter and shouting, in the room and the adjacent
one to the right. At last* NORA *hides under the table; the children come rushing in, look
for her, but cannot find her, hear her half-choked laughter, rush to the table, lift up
the cover and see her. Loud shouts. She creeps out, as though to frighten them. Fresh
shouts.*
    *Meanwhile there has been a knock at the door leading into the hall. No one has
heard it. Now the door is half opened and* KROGSTAD *appears. He waits a little; the
game is renewed.*]

KROGSTAD.   I beg your pardon, Mrs. Helmer—
NORA [*with a suppressed cry, turns round and half jumps up*].   Ah! What do you
    want?
KROGSTAD.   Excuse me; the outer door was ajar—somebody must have for-
    gotten to shut it—
NORA [*standing up*].   My husband is not at home, Mr. Krogstad.
KROGSTAD.   I know it.
NORA.   Then what do you want here?
590 KROGSTAD.   To say a few words to you.
NORA.   To me? [*To the children, softly.*] Go in to Anna. What? No, the strange
    man won't hurt mamma. When he's gone we'll go on playing. [*She leads the
    children into the left-hand room, and shuts the door behind them. Uneasy, in
    suspense.*] It is to me you wish to speak?
KROGSTAD.   Yes, to you.
NORA.   Today! But it's not the first yet—
KROGSTAD.   No, today is Christmas Eve. It will depend upon yourself whether
    you have a merry Christmas.
NORA.   What do you want? I'm not ready today—
600 KROGSTAD.   Never mind that just now. I have come about another matter.
    You have a minute to spare?
NORA.   Oh, yes, I suppose so; although—
KROGSTAD.   Good. I was sitting in the restaurant opposite, and I saw your
    husband go down the street—
NORA.   Well?
KROGSTAD.   With a lady.
NORA.   What then?
KROGSTAD.   May I ask if the lady was a Mrs. Linden?
NORA.   Yes.
610 KROGSTAD.   Who has just come to town?
NORA.   Yes. Today.
KROGSTAD.   I believe she is an intimate friend of yours.
NORA.   Certainly. But I don't understand—
KROGSTAD.   I used to know *her* too.
NORA.   I know you did.
KROGSTAD.   Ah! You know all about it. I thought as much. Now, frankly, is
    Mrs. Linden to have a place in the Bank?

NORA.   How dare you catechize me in this way, Mr. Krogstad—you, a subordinate of my husband's? But since you ask, you shall know. Yes, Mrs.
620   Linden is to be employed. And it is I who recommended her, Mr. Krogs-
tad. Now you know.
KROGSTAD.   Then my guess was right.
NORA [*walking up and down*].   You see one has a wee bit of influence, after all.
It doesn't follow because one's only a woman—When people are in a
subordinate position, Mr. Krogstad, they ought really to be careful how
they offend anybody who—h'm—
KROGSTAD.   Who has influence?
NORA.   Exactly.
KROGSTAD [*taking another tone*].   Mrs. Helmer, will you have the kindness to
630   employ your influence on my behalf?
NORA.   What? How do you mean?
KROGSTAD.   Will you be so good as to see that I retain my subordinate posi-
tion in the Bank?
NORA.   What do you mean? Who wants to take it from you?
KROGSTAD.   Oh, you needn't pretend ignorance. I can very well understand
that it cannot be pleasant for your friend to meet me; and I can also
understand now for whose sake I am to be hounded out.
NORA.   But I assure you—
KROGSTAD.   Come, come, now, once for all: there is time yet, and I advise you
640   to use your influence to prevent it.
NORA.   But, Mr. Krogstad, I have no influence—absolutely none.
KROGSTAD.   None? I thought you said a moment ago—
NORA.   Of course, not in that sense. I! How can you imagine that I should
have any such influence over my husband?
KROGSTAD.   Oh, I know your husband from our college days. I don't think he
is any more inflexible than other husbands.
NORA.   If you talk disrespectfully of my husband, I must request you to leave
the house.
KROGSTAD.   You are bold, madam.
650 NORA.   I am afraid of you no longer. When New Year's Day is over, I shall
soon be out of the whole business.
KROGSTAD [*controlling himself*].   Listen to me, Mrs. Helmer. If need be, I shall
fight as though for my life to keep my little place in the Bank.
NORA.   Yes, so it seems.
KROGSTAD.   It's not only for the salary: that is what I care least about. It's
something else—Well, I had better make a clean breast of it. Of course,
you know, like every one else, that some years ago I—got into trouble.
NORA.   I think I've heard something of the sort.
KROGSTAD.   The matter never came into court; but from that moment all
660   paths were barred to me. Then I took up the business you know about. I
had to turn my hand to something; and I don't think I've been one of the
worst. But now I must get clear of it all. My sons are growing up; for their
sake I must try to recover my character as well as I can. This place in the
Bank was the first step; and now your husband wants to kick me off the
ladder, back into the mire.
NORA.   But I assure you, Mr. Krogstad, I haven't the least power to help you.
KROGSTAD.   That is because you have not the will; but I can compel you.
NORA.   You won't tell my husband that I owe you money?

KROGSTAD.   H'm; suppose I were to?

670 NORA.   It would be shameful of you. [*With tears in her voice.*] The secret that
is my joy and my pride—that he should learn it in such an ugly, coarse
way—and from you. It would involve me in all sorts of unpleasantness—

KROGSTAD.   Only unpleasantness?

NORA [*hotly*].   But just do it. It's you that will come off worst, for then my
husband will see what a bad man you are, and then you certainly won't
keep your place.

KROGSTAD.   I asked whether it was only domestic unpleasantness you feared?

NORA.   If my husband gets to know about it, he will, of course, pay you off at
once, and then we shall have nothing more to do with you.

680 KROGSTAD [*coming a pace nearer*].   Listen, Mrs. Helmer: either your memory
is defective, or you don't know much about business. I must make the
position a little clearer to you.

NORA.   How so?

KROGSTAD.   When your husband was ill, you came to me to borrow twelve
hundred dollars.

NORA.   I knew of nobody else.

KROGSTAD.   I promised to find you the money—

NORA.   And you did find it.

KROGSTAD.   I promised to find you the money, on certain conditions. You
690 were so much taken up at the time about your husband's illness, and so
eager to have the wherewithal for your journey, that you probably did not
give much thought to the details. Allow me to remind you of them. I
promised to find you the amount in exchange for a note of hand, which
I drew up.

NORA.   Yes, and I signed it.

KROGSTAD.   Quite right. But then I added a few lines, making your father
security for the debt. Your father was to sign this.

NORA.   Was to—? He did sign it!

KROGSTAD.   I had left the date blank. That is to say, your father was himself
700 to date his signature. Do you recollect that?

NORA.   Yes, I believe—

KROGSTAD.   Then I gave you the paper to send to your father, by post. Is not
that so?

NORA.   Yes.

KROGSTAD.   And of course you did so at once; for within five or six days you
brought back the document with your father's signature; and I handed
you the money.

NORA.   Well? Have I not made my payments punctually?

KROGSTAD.   Fairly—yes. But to return to the point: You were in great trouble
710 at the time, Mrs. Helmer.

NORA.   I was, indeed!

KROGSTAD.   Your father was very ill, I believe?

NORA.   He was on his death-bed.

KROGSTAD.   And died soon after?

NORA.   Yes.

KROGSTAD.   Tell me, Mrs. Helmer; do you happen to recollect the day of his
death? The day of the month, I mean?

NORA.   Father died on the 29th of September.

KROGSTAD. Quite correct. I have made inquiries. And here comes in the
720   remarkable point—[*produces a paper*] which I cannot explain.

NORA. What remarkable point? I don't know—

KROGSTAD. The remarkable point, madam, that your father signed this paper three days after his death!

NORA. What! I don't understand—

KROGSTAD. Your father died on the 29th of September. But look here: he
has dated his signature October 2nd! Is not that remarkable, Mrs. Helmer?
[NORA *is silent.*] Can you explain it? [NORA *continues silent.*] It is noteworthy,
too, that the words "October 2nd" and the year are not in your father's
handwriting, but in one that I believe I know. Well, this may be explained;
730   your father may have forgotten to date his signature, and somebody may
have added the date at random, before the fact of your father's death was
known. There is nothing wrong in that. Everything depends on the signature. Of course, it is genuine, Mrs. Helmer? It was really your father
himself who wrote his name here?

NORA [*after a short silence, throws her head back and looks defiantly at him*]. No,
it was not. *I* wrote father's name.

KROGSTAD. Ah!—Are you aware, madam, that that is a dangerous admission?

NORA. How so? You will soon get your money.

740 KROGSTAD. May I ask you one more question? Why did you not send the
paper to your father?

NORA. It was impossible. Father was ill. If I had asked him for his signature,
I should have had to tell him why I wanted the money; but he was so ill I
really could not tell him that my husband's life was in danger. It was
impossible.

KROGSTAD. Then it would have been better to have given up your tour.

NORA. No, I couldn't do that; my husband's life depended on that journey.
I couldn't give it up.

KROGSTAD. And did it never occur to you that you were playing me false?

750 NORA. That was nothing to me. I didn't care in the least about you. I
couldn't endure you for all the cruel difficulties you made, although you
knew how ill my husband was.

KROGSTAD. Mrs. Helmer, you evidently do not realize what you have been
guilty of. But I can assure you it was nothing more and nothing worse that
made me an outcast from society.

NORA. You! You want me to believe that you did a brave thing to save your
wife's life?

KROGSTAD. The law takes no account of motives.

NORA. Then it must be a very bad law.

760 KROGSTAD. Bad or not, if I produce this document in court, you will be
condemned according to law.

NORA. I don't believe that. Do you mean to tell me that a daughter has no
right to spare her dying father trouble and anxiety?—that a wife has no
right to save her husband's life? I don't know much about the law, but I'm
sure you'll find, somewhere or another, that that is allowed. And you don't
know that—you, a lawyer! You must be a bad one, Mr. Krogstad.

KROGSTAD. Possibly. But business—such business as ours—I do understand.
You believe that? Very well; now, do as you please. But this I may tell you,

that if I am flung into the gutter a second time, you shall keep me com-
770   pany.

[*Bows and goes out through hall.*]

NORA [*stands a while thinking, then tosses her head*].   Oh, nonsense! He wants to
frighten me. I'm not so foolish as that. [*Begins folding the children's clothes.
Pauses.*] But—? No, it's impossible! Why, I did it for love!

CHILDREN [*at the door, left*].   Mamma, the strange man has gone now.

NORA.   Yes, yes, I know. But don't tell any one about the strange man. Do
you hear? Not even papa!

CHILDREN.   No, mamma; and now will you play with us again?

NORA.   No, no; not now.

CHILDREN.   Oh, do, mamma; you know you promised.

780   NORA.   Yes, but I can't just now. Run to the nursery; I have so much to do.
Run along, run along, and be good, my darlings! [*She pushes them gently into
the inner room, and closes the door behind them. Sits on the sofa, embroiders a few
stitches, but soon pauses.*] No! [*Throws down the work, rises, goes to the hall door
and calls out.*] Ellen, bring in the Christmas tree! [*Goes to table, left, and opens
the drawer; again pauses.*] No, it's quite impossible!

ELLEN [*with Christmas tree*].   Where shall I stand it, ma'am?

NORA.   There, in the middle of the room.

ELLEN.   Shall I bring in anything else?

NORA.   No, thank you, I have all I want.

[ELLEN, *having put down the tree, goes out.*]

790   NORA [*busy dressing the tree*].   There must be a candle here—and flowers
there.—That horrible man! Nonsense, nonsense! there's nothing to be
afraid of. The Christmas tree shall be beautiful. I'll do everything to please
you, Torvald; I'll sing and dance, and—

[*Enter* HELMER *by the hall door, with a bundle of documents.*]

NORA.   Oh! You're back already?

HELMER.   Yes. Has anybody been here?

NORA.   Here? No.

HELMER.   That's odd. I saw Krogstad come out of the house.

NORA.   Did you? Oh, yes, by the bye, he was here for a minute.

HELMER.   Nora, I can see by your manner that he has been begging you to
800   put in a good word for him.

NORA.   Yes.

HELMER.   And you were to do it as if of your own accord? You were to say
nothing to me of his having been here. Didn't he suggest that, too?

NORA.   Yes, Torvald; but—

HELMER.   Nora, Nora! And you could condescend to that! To speak to such
a man, to make him a promise! And then to tell me an untruth about it!

NORA.   An untruth!

HELMER.   Didn't you say that nobody had been here? [*Threatens with his
finger.*] My little bird must never do that again! A song-bird must sing clear
810   and true; no false notes. [*Puts his arm round her.*] That's so, isn't it? Yes, I
was sure of it. [*Lets her go.*] And now we'll say no more about it. [*Sits down

before the fire.] Oh, how cozy and quiet it is here! [*Glances into his documents.*]

NORA [*busy with the tree, after a short silence*]. Torvald!

HELMER. Yes.

NORA. I'm looking forward so much to the Stenborgs' fancy ball the day after tomorrow.

HELMER. And I'm on tenterhooks to see what surprise you have in store for me.

NORA. Oh, it's too tiresome!

820 HELMER. What is?

NORA. I can't think of anything good. Everything seems so foolish and meaningless.

HELMER. Has little Nora made that discovery?

NORA [*behind his chair, with her arms on the back*]. Are you very busy, Torvald?

HELMER. Well—

NORA. What papers are those?

HELMER. Bank business.

NORA. Already!

HELMER. I have got the retiring manager to let me make some necessary
830 changes in the staff and the organization. I can do this during Christmas week. I want to have everything straight by the New Year.

NORA. Then that's why that poor Krogstad—

HELMER. H'm.

NORA [*still leaning on the chair-back and slowly stroking his hair*]. If you hadn't been so very busy, I should have asked you a great, great favor, Torvald.

HELMER. What can it be? Out with it.

NORA. Nobody has such perfect taste as you; and I should so love to look well at the fancy ball. Torvald, dear, couldn't you take me in hand, and settle what I'm to be, and arrange my costume for me?

840 HELMER. Aha! So my willful little woman is at a loss, and making signals of distress.

NORA. Yes, please, Torvald. I can't get on without your help.

HELMER. Well, well, I'll think it over, and we'll soon hit upon something.

NORA. Oh, how good that is of you! [*Goes to the tree again; pause.*] How well the red flowers show.—Tell me, was it anything so very dreadful this Krogstad got into trouble about?

HELMER. Forgery, that's all. Don't you know what that means?

NORA. Mayn't he have been driven to it by need?

HELMER. Yes; or, like so many others, he may have done it in pure heed-
850 lessness. I am not so hard-hearted as to condemn a man absolutely for a single fault.

NORA. No, surely not, Torvald!

HELMER. Many a man can retrieve his character, if he owns his crime and takes the punishment.

NORA. Punishment—?

HELMER. But Krogstad didn't do that. He evaded the law by means of tricks and subterfuges; and that is what has morally ruined him.

NORA. Do you think that—?

HELMER. Just think how a man with a thing of that sort on his conscience
860 must be always lying and canting and shamming. Think of the mask he must wear even toward those who stand nearest him—toward his own wife

and children. The effect on the children—that's the most terrible part of it, Nora.

NORA.   Why?

HELMER.   Because in such an atmosphere of lies home life is poisoned and contaminated in every fiber. Every breath the children draw contains some germ of evil.

NORA [*closer behind him*].   Are you sure of that?

HELMER.   As a lawyer, my dear, I have seen it often enough. Nearly all cases
870   of early corruption may be traced to lying mothers.

NORA.   Why—mothers?

HELMER.   It generally comes from the mother's side; but of course the father's influence may act in the same way. Every lawyer knows it too well. And here has this Krogstad been poisoning his own children for years past by a life of lies and hypocrisy—that is why I call him morally ruined. [*Holds out both hands to her.*] So my sweet little Nora must promise not to plead his cause. Shake hands upon it. Come, come, what's this? Give me your hand. That's right. Then it's a bargain. I assure you it would have been impossible for me to work with him. It gives me a positive sense of physical
880   discomfort to come in contact with such people.

[NORA *draws her hand away, and moves to the other side of the Christmas tree.*]

NORA.   How warm it is in here. And I have so much to do.

HELMER [*rises and gathers up his papers*].   Yes, and I must try to get some of these papers looked through before dinner. And I shall think over your costume too. Perhaps I may even find something to hang in gilt paper on the Christmas tree. [*Lays his hand on her head.*] My precious little song-bird!

[*He goes into his room and shuts the door.*]

NORA [*softly, after a pause*].   It can't be. It's impossible. It must be impossible!

ANNA [*at the door, left*].   The little ones are begging so prettily to come to
890   mamma.

NORA.   No, no, no; don't let them come to me! Keep them with you, Anna.

ANNA.   Very well, ma'am. [*Shuts the door.*]

NORA [*pale with terror*].   Corrupt my children!—Poison my home! [*Short pause. She throws back her head.*] It's not true! It can never, never be true!

ACT II

The same room. In the corner, beside the piano, stands the Christmas tree, stripped, and with the candles burned out. NORA's *outdoor things lie on the sofa.*

[NORA, *alone, is walking about restlessly. At last she stops by the sofa, and takes up her cloak.*]

NORA [*dropping the cloak*].   There's somebody coming! [*Goes to the hall door*
900   *and listens.*] Nobody; of course nobody will come today, Christmas Day; nor tomorrow either. But perhaps—[*Opens the door and looks out.*]—No, nothing in the letter box; quite empty. [*Comes forward.*] Stuff and nonsense! Of course he won't really do anything. Such a thing couldn't happen. It's impossible! Why, I have three little children.

[ANNA *enters from the left, with a large cardboard box.*]

900 ANNA.   I've found the box with the fancy dress at last.

NORA.   Thanks; put it down on the table.

ANNA [*doing so*].   But I'm afraid it's very much out of order.

NORA.   Oh, I wish I could tear it into a hundred thousand pieces!

ANNA.   Oh, no. It can easily be put to rights—just a little patience.

NORA.   I shall go and get Mrs. Linden to help me.

ANNA.   Going out again? In such weather as this! You'll catch cold, ma'am, and be ill.

NORA.   Worse things might happen.—What are the children doing?

ANNA.   They're playing with their Christmas presents, poor little dears;
910   but—

NORA.   Do they often ask for me?

ANNA.   You see they've been so used to having their mamma with them.

NORA.   Yes; but, Anna, I can't have them so much with me in future.

ANNA.   Well, little children get used to anything.

NORA.   Do you think they do? Do you believe they would forget their mother if she went quite away?

ANNA.   Gracious me! Quite away?

NORA.   Tell me, Anna,—I've so often wondered about it,—how could you bring yourself to give your child up to strangers?

920 ANNA.   I had to when I came to nurse my little Miss Nora.

NORA.   But how could you make up your mind to it?

ANNA.   When I had the chance of such a good place? A poor girl who's been in trouble must take what comes. That wicked man did nothing for me.

NORA.   But your daughter must have forgotten you.

ANNA.   Oh, no, ma'am, that she hasn't. She wrote to me both when she was confirmed and when she was married.

NORA [*embracing her*].   Dear old Anna—you were a good mother to me when I was little.

ANNA.   My poor little Nora had no mother but me.

930 NORA.   And if my little ones had nobody else, I'm sure you would—Nonsense, nonsense! [*Opens the box.*] Go in to the children. Now I must—You'll see how lovely I shall be tomorrow.

ANNA.   I'm sure there will be no one at the ball so lovely as my Miss Nora.

[*She goes into the room on the left.*]

NORA [*takes the costume out of the box, but soon throws it down again*].   Oh, if I dared go out. If only nobody would come. If only nothing would happen here in the mean time. Rubbish; nobody is coming. Only not to think. What a delicious muff! Beautiful gloves, beautiful gloves! To forget—to forget! One, two, three, four, five, six—[*With a scream.*] Ah, there they come. [*Goes toward the door, then stands irresolute.*]

[MRS. LINDEN *enters from the hall, where she has taken off her things.*]

940 NORA.   Oh, it's you, Christina. There's nobody else there? I'm so glad you have come.

MRS. LINDEN.   I hear you called at my lodgings.

NORA.   Yes, I was just passing. There's something you *must* help me with. Let us sit here on the sofa—so. Tomorrow evening there's to be a fancy ball at Consul Stenborg's overhead, and Torvald wants me to appear as a Neapolitan fisher-girl,[4] and dance the *tarantella;*[5] I learned it at Capri.[6]

MRS. LINDEN.   I see—quite a performance.

NORA.   Yes, Torvald wishes it. Look, this is the costume; Torvald had it made for me in Italy. But now it's all so torn, and I don't know—

950 MRS. LINDEN.   Oh, we shall soon set that to rights. It's only the trimming that has come loose here and there. Have you a needle and thread? Ah, here's the very thing.

NORA.   Oh, how kind of you.

MRS. LINDEN [*sewing*].   So you're to be in costume tomorrow, Nora? I'll tell you what—I shall come in for a moment to see you in all your glory. But I've quite forgotten to thank you for the pleasant evening yesterday.

NORA [*rises and walks across the room*].   Oh, yesterday, it didn't seem so pleasant as usual.—You should have come to town a little sooner, Christina.— Torvald has certainly the art of making home bright and beautiful.

960 MRS. LINDEN.   You, too, I should think, or you wouldn't be your father's daughter. But tell me—is Doctor Rank always so depressed as he was last evening?

NORA.   No, yesterday it was particularly noticeable. You see, he suffers from a dreadful illness. He has spinal consumption, poor fellow. They say his father was a horrible man, who kept mistresses and all sorts of things—so the son has been sickly from his childhood, you understand.

MRS. LINDEN [*lets her sewing fall into her lap*].   Why, my darling Nora, how do you come to know such things?

NORA [*moving about the room*].   Oh, when one has three children, one some-
970 times has visits from women who are half—half doctors—and they talk of one thing and another.

MRS. LINDEN [*goes on sewing; a short pause*].   Does Doctor Rank come here every day?

NORA.   Every day of his life. He has been Torvald's most intimate friend from boyhood, and he's a good friend of mine, too. Doctor Rank is quite one of the family.

MRS. LINDEN.   But tell me—is he quite sincere? I mean, isn't he rather given to flattering people?

NORA.   No, quite the contrary. Why should you think so?

980 MRS. LINDEN.   When you introduced us yesterday he said he had often heard my name; but I noticed afterwards that your husband had no notion who I was. How could Doctor Rank—?

NORA.   He was quite right, Christina. You see, Torvald loves me so indescribably, he wants to have me all to himself, as he says. When we were first married, he was almost jealous if I even mentioned any of my old friends at home; so naturally I gave up doing it. But I often talk of the old times to Doctor Rank, for he likes to hear about them.

---

    [4] I.e., dress like a peasant girl from Naples, Italy.
    [5] An Italian folk dance in a teasing, flirtatious style. The dance is associated with tarantism, a form of hysteria arising from frenetic dance. According to folklore, the poison of the tarantula spider could be counteracted by such behavior.
    [6] An island near Naples.

MRS. LINDEN.   Listen to me, Nora! You are still a child in many ways. I am older than you, and have had more experience. I'll tell you something? You ought to get clear of all this with Doctor Rank.

NORA.   Get clear of what?

MRS. LINDEN.   The whole affair, I should say. You were talking yesterday of a rich admirer who was to find you money—

NORA.   Yes, one who never existed, worse luck. What then?

MRS. LINDEN.   Has Doctor Rank money?

NORA.   Yes, he has.

MRS. LINDEN.   And nobody to provide for?

NORA.   Nobody. But—?

MRS. LINDEN.   And he comes here every day?

NORA.   Yes, I told you so.

MRS. LINDEN.   I should have thought he would have had better taste.

NORA.   I don't understand you a bit.

MRS. LINDEN.   Don't pretend, Nora. Do you suppose I can't guess who lent you the twelve hundred dollars?

NORA.   Are you out of your senses? How can you think such a thing? A friend who comes here every day! Why, the position would be unbearable!

MRS. LINDEN.   Then it really is not he?

NORA.   No, I assure you. It never for a moment occurred to me—Besides, at that time he had nothing to lend; he came into his property afterwards.

MRS. LINDEN.   Well, I believe that was lucky for you, Nora, dear.

NORA.   No, really, it would never have struck me to ask Doctor Rank—And yet, I'm certain that if I did—

MRS. LINDEN.   But of course you never would.

NORA.   Of course not. It's inconceivable that it should ever be necessary. But I'm quite sure that if I spoke to Doctor Rank—

MRS. LINDEN.   Behind your husband's back?

NORA.   I must get clear of the other thing; that's behind his back too. I *must* get clear of that.

MRS. LINDEN.   Yes, yes, I told you so yesterday; but—

NORA [*walking up and down*].   A man can manage these things much better than a woman.

MRS. LINDEN.   One's own husband, yes.

NORA.   Nonsense. [*Stands still.*] When everything is paid, one gets back the paper.

MRS. LINDEN.   Of course.

NORA.   And can tear it into a hundred thousand pieces, and burn it up, the nasty, filthy thing!

MRS. LINDEN [*looks at her fixedly, lays down her work, and rises slowly*].   Nora, you are hiding something from me.

NORA.   Can you see it in my face?

MRS. LINDEN.   Something has happened since yesterday morning. Nora, what is it?

NORA [*going toward her*].   Christina—! [*Listens.*] Hush! There's Torvald coming home. Do you mind going into the nursery for the present? Torvald can't bear to see dressmaking going on. Get Anna to help you.

MRS. LINDEN [*gathers some of the things together*].   Very well; but I shan't go away until you have told me all about it.

[*She goes out to the left.* HELMER *enters from the hall.*]

NORA [*runs to meet him*].   Oh, how I've been longing for you to come, Torvald, dear!

1040 HELMER.   Was that the dressmaker—?

NORA.   No, Christina. She's helping me with my costume. You'll see how nice I shall look.

HELMER.   Yes, wasn't that a happy thought of mine?

NORA.   Splendid! But isn't it good of me, too, to have given in to you about the *tarantella*?

HELMER [*takes her under the chin*].   Good of you! To give in to your own husband? Well, well, you little madcap, I know you don't mean it. But I won't disturb you. I dare say you want to be "trying on."

NORA.   And you are going to work, I suppose?

1050 HELMER.   Yes. [*Shows her a bundle of papers.*] Look here. I've just come from the Bank—

[*Goes toward his room.*]

NORA.   Torvald.

HELMER [*stopping*].   Yes?

NORA.   If your little squirrel were to beg you for something so prettily—

HELMER.   Well?

NORA.   Would you do it?

HELMER.   I must know first what it is.

NORA.   The squirrel would skip about and play all sorts of tricks if you would only be nice and kind.

1060 HELMER.   Come, then, out with it.

NORA.   Your lark would twitter from morning till night—

HELMER.   Oh, that she does in any case.

NORA.   I'll be an elf and dance in the moonlight for you, Torvald.

HELMER.   Nora—you can't mean what you were hinting at this morning?

NORA [*coming nearer*].   Yes, Torvald, I beg and implore you!

HELMER.   Have you really the courage to begin that again?

NORA.   Yes, yes; for my sake, you *must* let Krogstad keep his place in the Bank.

HELMER.   My dear Nora, it's his place I intend for Mrs. Linden.

1070 NORA.   Yes, that's so good of you. But instead of Krogstad, you could dismiss some other clerk.

HELMER.   Why, this is incredible obstinacy! Because you have thoughtlessly promised to put in a word for him, I am to—!

NORA.   It's not that, Torvald. It's for your own sake. This man writes for the most scurrilous newspapers; you said so yourself. He can do you no end of harm. I'm so terribly afraid of him—

HELMER.   Ah, I understand; it's old recollections that are frightening you.

NORA.   What do you mean?

HELMER.   Of course, you're thinking of your father.

1080 NORA.   Yes—yes, of course. Only think of the shameful slanders wicked people used to write about father. I believe they would have got him dismissed if you hadn't been sent to look into the thing, and been kind to him, and helped him.

HELMER.   My little Nora, between your father and me there is all the difference in the world. Your father was not altogether unimpeachable. I am;
and I hope to remain so.

NORA.   Oh, no one knows what wicked men may hit upon. We could live so
quietly and happily now, in our cozy, peaceful home, you and I and the
children, Torvald! That's why I beg and implore you—

1090 HELMER.   And it is just by pleading his cause that you make it impossible for
me to keep him. It's already known at the Bank that I intend to dismiss
Krogstad. If it were now reported that the new manager let himself be
turned round by his wife's little finger—

NORA.   What then?

HELMER.   Oh, nothing, so long as a willful woman can have her way—! I am
to make myself a laughing-stock to the whole staff, and set people saying
that I am open to all sorts of outside influence? Take my word for it, I
should soon feel the consequences. And besides—there is one thing that
makes Krogstad impossible for me to work with—

1100 NORA.   What thing?

HELMER.   I could perhaps have over-looked his moral failings at a pinch—

NORA.   Yes, couldn't you, Torvald?

HELMER.   And I hear he is good at his work. But the fact is, he was a college
chum of mine—there was one of those rash friendships between us that
one so often repents of later. I may as well confess it at once—he calls me
by my Christian name; and he is tactless enough to do it even when others
are present. He delights in putting on airs of familiarity—Torvald here,
Torvald there! I assure you it's most painful to me. He would make my
position at the Bank perfectly unendurable.

1110 NORA.   Torvald, surely you're not serious?

HELMER.   No? Why not?

NORA.   That's such a petty reason.

HELMER.   What! Petty! Do you consider me petty!

NORA.   No, on the contrary, Torvald, dear; and that's just why—

HELMER.   Never mind; you call my motives petty; then I must be petty too.
Petty! Very well!—Now we'll put an end to this, once for all. [*Goes to the
door into the hall and calls.*] Ellen!

NORA.   What do you want?

HELMER [*searching among his papers*].   To settle the thing. [ELLEN *enters.*] Here;
1120 take this letter; give it to a messenger. See that he takes it at once. The
address is on it. Here's the money.

ELLEN.   Very well, sir.

[*Goes with the letter.*]

HELMER [*putting his papers together*].   There, Madam Obstinacy.

NORA [*breathless*].   Torvald—what was in the letter?

HELMER.   Krogstad's dismissal.

NORA.   Call it back again, Torvald! There's still time. Oh, Torvald, call it
back again! For my sake, for your own, for the children's sake! Do you
hear, Torvald? Do it! You don't know what that letter may bring upon
us all.

1130 HELMER.   Too late.

NORA. Yes, too late.

HELMER. My dear Nora, I forgive your anxiety, though it's anything but flattering to me. Why should you suppose that *I* would be afraid of a wretched scribbler's spite? But I forgive you all the same, for it's a proof of your great love for me. [*Takes her in his arms.*] That's as it should be, my own dear Nora. Let what will happen—when it comes to the pinch, I shall have strength and courage enough. You shall see: my shoulders are broad enough to bear the whole burden.

NORA [*terror-struck*]. What do you mean by that?

1140 HELMER. The whole burden, I say—

NORA [*with decision*]. That you shall never, never do!

HELMER. Very well; then we'll share it, Nora, as man and wife. That is how it should be. [*Petting her.*] Are you satisfied now? Come, come, come, don't look like a scared dove. It's all nothing—foolish fancies.—Now you ought to play the *tarantella* through and practice with the tambourine. I shall sit in my inner room and shut both doors, so that I shall hear nothing. You can make as much noise as you please. [*Turns round in doorway.*] And when Rank comes, just tell him where I'm to be found.

[*He nods to her, and goes with his papers into his room, closing the door.*]

NORA [*bewildered with terror, stands as though rooted to the ground, and whispers*].

1150 He would do it. Yes, he would do it. He would do it, in spite of all the world.—No, never that, never, never! Anything rather than that! Oh, for some way of escape! What shall I do—! [*Hall bell rings.*] Doctor Rank—! Anything, anything, rather than —! [NORA *draws her hands over her face, pulls herself together, goes to the door and opens it.* RANK *stands outside hanging up his fur coat. During what follows it begins to grow dark.*] Good-afternoon, Doctor Rank. I knew you by your ring. But you mustn't go to Torvald now. I believe he's busy.

RANK. And you?

[*Enters and closes the door.*]

NORA. Oh, you know very well, I have always time for *you.*

1160 RANK. Thank you. I shall avail myself of your kindness as long as I can.

NORA. What do you mean? As long as you can?

RANK. Yes. Does *that* frighten you?

NORA. I think it's an odd expression. Do you expect anything to happen?

RANK. Something I have long been prepared for; but I didn't think it would come so soon.

NORA [*catching at his arm.*] What have you discovered? Doctor Rank, you must tell me!

RANK [*sitting down by the stove*]. I am running down hill. There's no help for it.

1170 NORA [*drawing a long breath of relief*]. It's *you*—?

RANK. Who else should it be?—Why lie to one's self? I am the most wretched of all my patients, Mrs. Helmer. In these last days I have been auditing my life-account—bankrupt! Perhaps before a month is over, I shall lie rotting in the churchyard.

NORA. Oh! What an ugly way to talk.

RANK. The thing itself is so confoundedly ugly, you see. But the worst of it is, so many other ugly things have to be gone through first. There is only one last investigation to be made, and when that is over I shall know pretty certainly when the break-up will begin. There's one thing I want to say to you: Helmer's delicate nature shrinks so from all that is horrible: I will not have him in my sick-room—

NORA. But, Doctor Rank—

RANK. I won't have him, I say—not on any account. I shall lock my door against him.—As soon as I am quite certain of the worst, I shall send you my visiting-card with a black cross on it; and then you will know that the final horror has begun.

NORA. Why, you're perfectly unreasonable today; and I did so want you to be in a really good humor.

RANK. With death staring me in the face?—And to suffer thus for another's sin! Where's the justice of it? And in one way or another you can trace in every family some such inexorable retribution—

NORA [*stopping her ears*]. Nonsense, nonsense! Now, cheer up!

RANK. Well, after all, the whole thing's only worth laughing at. My poor innocent spine must do penance for my father's wild oats.

NORA [*at table, left*]. I suppose he was too fond of asparagus and Strasbourg pâté,[7] wasn't he?

RANK. Yes; and truffles.[8]

NORA. Yes, truffles, to be sure. And oysters, I believe?

RANK. Yes, oysters; oysters, of course.

NORA. And then all the port and champagne! It's sad that all these good things should attack the spine.

RANK. Especially when the luckless spine attacked never had any good of them.

NORA. Ah, yes, that's the worst of it.

RANK [*looks at her searchingly*]. H'm—

NORA [*a moment later*]. Why did you smile?

RANK. No; it was you that laughed.

NORA. No; it was you that smiled, Doctor Rank.

RANK [*standing up*]. I see you're deeper than I thought.

NORA. I'm in such a crazy mood today.

RANK. So it seems.

NORA [*with her hands on his shoulders*]. Dear, dear Doctor Rank, death shall not take you away from Torvald and me.

RANK. Oh, you'll easily get over the loss. The absent are soon forgotten.

NORA [*looks at him anxiously*]. Do you think so?

RANK. People make fresh ties, and then—

NORA. Who make fresh ties?

RANK. You and Helmer will, when I am gone. You yourself are taking time by the forelock, it seems to me. What was that Mrs. Linden doing here yesterday?

NORA. Oh!—you're surely not jealous of poor Christina?

---

[7] A liver paste thought to be a delicacy.

[8] Fungi that grow underground and are considered edible delicacies.

RANK. Yes, I am. She will be my successor in this house. When I am out of the way, this woman will, perhaps—

NORA. Hush! Not so loud! She's in there.

RANK. Today as well? You see!

NORA. Only to put my costume in order—dear me, how unreasonable you are! [*Sits on sofa.*] Now, do be good, Doctor Rank! Tomorrow you shall see how beautifully I shall dance; and then you may fancy that I'm doing it all to please you—and of course Torvald as well. [*Takes various things out of*
1230 *box.*] Doctor Rank, sit down here, and I'll show you something.

RANK [*sitting*]. What is it?

NORA. Look here. Look!

RANK. Silk stockings.

NORA. Flesh-colored. Aren't they lovely? It's so dark here now; but tomorrow—No, no, no; you must only look at the feet. Oh, well, I suppose you may look at the rest too.

RANK. H'm—

NORA. What are you looking so critical about? Do you think they won't fit me?

1240 RANK. I can't possibly give any competent opinion on that point.

NORA [*looking at him a moment*]. For shame! [*Hits him lightly on the ear with the stockings.*] Take that. [*Rolls them up again.*]

RANK. And what other wonders am I to see?

NORA. You shan't see anything more; for you don't behave nicely. [*She hums a little and searches among the things.*]

RANK [*after a short silence*]. When I sit here gossiping with you, I can't imagine—I simply cannot conceive—what would have become of me if I had never entered this house.

NORA [*smiling*]. Yes, I think you do feel at home with us.

1250 RANK [*more softly—looking straight before him*]. And now to have to leave it all—

NORA. Nonsense. You shan't leave us.

RANK [*in the same tone*]. And not to be able to leave behind the slightest token of gratitude; scarcely even a passing regret—nothing but an empty place, that can be filled by the first comer.

NORA. And if I were to ask you for—? No—

RANK. For what?

NORA. For a great proof of your friendship.

RANK. Yes—yes?

1260 NORA. I mean—for a very, very great service—

RANK. Would you really, for once, make me so happy?

NORA. Oh, you don't know what it is.

RANK. Then tell me.

NORA. No, I really can't, Doctor Rank. It's far, far too much—not only a service, but help and advice, besides—

RANK. So much the better. I can't think what you can mean. But go on. Don't you trust me?

NORA. As I trust no one else. I know you are my best and truest friend. So I will tell you. Well, then, Doctor Rank, there is something you must help
1270 me to prevent. You know how deeply, how wonderfully Torvald loves me; he wouldn't hesitate a moment to give his very life for my sake.

RANK [*bending toward her*]. Nora—do you think he is the only one who—

Nora [*with a slight start*].   Who—?

Rank.   Who would gladly give his life for you?

Nora [*sadly*].   Oh!

Rank.   I have sworn that you shall know it before I—go. I shall never find a
  better opportunity.—Yes, Nora, now I have told you; and now you know
  that you can trust me as you can no one else.

Nora [*standing up; simply and calmly*].   Let me pass, please.

1280 Rank [*makes way for her, but remains sitting*].   Nora—

Nora [*in the doorway*].   Ellen, bring the lamp. [*Crosses to the stove.*] Oh, dear,
  Doctor Rank, that was too bad of you.

Rank [*rising*].   That I have loved you as deeply as—any one else? Was that
  too bad of me?

Nora.   No, but that you should have told me so. It was so unnecessary—

Rank.   What do you mean? Did you know—? [Ellen *enters with the lamp; sets
  it on the table and goes out again.*] Nora—Mrs. Helmer—I ask you, did you
  know?

Nora.   Oh, how can I tell what I knew or didn't know? I really can't say—

1290 How could you be so clumsy, Doctor Rank? It was all so nice!

Rank.   Well, at any rate, you know now that I am at your service, body and
  soul. And now, go on.

Nora [*looking at him*].   Go on—now?

Rank.   I beg you to tell me what you want.

Nora.   I can tell you nothing now.

Rank.   Yes, yes! You mustn't punish me in that way. Let me do for you
  whatever a man can.

Nora.   You can do nothing for me now—Besides, I really want no help. You
  shall see it was only my fancy. Yes, it must be so. Of course! [*Sits in the*

1300 *rocking-chair, looks at him and smiles.*] You are a nice person, Doctor Rank!
  Aren't you ashamed of yourself, now that the lamp is on the table?

Rank.   No; not exactly. But perhaps I ought to go—forever.

Nora.   No, indeed you mustn't. Of course, you must come and go as you've
  always done. You know very well that Torvald can't do without you.

Rank.   Yes, but you?

Nora.   Oh, you know I always like to have you here.

Rank.   That is just what led me astray. You are a riddle to me. It has often
  seemed to me as if you liked being with me almost as much as being with
  Helmer.

1310 Nora.   Yes; don't you see? There are people one loves, and others one likes
  to talk to.

Rank.   Yes—there's something in that.

Nora.   When I was a girl, of course, I loved papa best. But it always delighted me to steal into the servants' room. In the first place they never
  lectured me, and in the second it was such fun to hear them talk.

Rank.   Ah, I see; then it's *their* place I have taken?

Nora [*jumps up and hurries toward him*].   Oh, my dear Doctor Rank, I don't
  mean that. But you understand, with Torvald it's the same as with papa—

[Ellen *enters from the hall.*]

Ellen.   Please, ma'am— [*Whispers to* Nora, *and gives her a card.*]

1320 Nora [*glancing at card*].   Ah! [*Puts it in her pocket.*]

RANK.   Anything wrong?

NORA.   No, no, not in the least. It's only—it's my new costume—

RANK.   Your costume! Why, it's there.

NORA.   Oh, that one, yes. But this is another that—I have ordered it—
          Torvald mustn't know—

RANK.   Aha! So that's the great secret.

NORA.   Yes, of course. Please go to him; he's in the inner room. Do keep him
          while I—

RANK.   Don't be alarmed; he shan't escape.

[Goes into HELMER'S *room.]*

1330   NORA [*to* ELLEN].   Is he waiting in the kitchen?

       ELLEN.   Yes, he came up the back stair—

       NORA.   Didn't you tell him I was engaged.

       ELLEN.   Yes, but it was no use.

       NORA.   He won't go away?

       ELLEN.   No, ma'am, not until he has spoken to you.

       NORA.   Then let him come in; but quietly. And, Ellen—say nothing about it;
                 it's a surprise for my husband.

       ELLEN.   Oh, yes, ma'am, I understand.

[She goes out.]

       NORA.   It is coming! The dreadful thing is coming, after all. No, no, no, it
1340   can never be; it shall not!

[She goes to HELMER'S *door and slips the bolt.* ELLEN *opens the hall door for* KROGS-
TAD, *and shuts it after him. He wears a traveling-coat, high boots, and a fur cap.]*

NORA [*goes toward him*].   Speak softly; my husband is at home.

KROGSTAD.   All right. That's nothing to me.

NORA.   What do you want?

KROGSTAD.   A little information.

NORA.   Be quick, then. What is it?

KROGSTAD.   You know I have got my dismissal.

NORA.   I couldn't prevent it, Mr. Krogstad. I fought for you to the last, but
          it was of no use.

KROGSTAD.   Does your husband care for you so little? He knows what I can
1350   bring upon you, and yet he dares—

NORA.   How could you think I should tell him?

KROGSTAD.   Well, as a matter of fact, I didn't think it. It wasn't like my friend
          Torvald Helmer to show so much courage—

NORA.   Mr. Krogstad, be good enough to speak respectfully of my husband.

KROGSTAD.   Certainly, with all due respect. But since you are so anxious to
          keep the matter secret, I suppose you are a little clearer than yesterday as
          to what you have done.

NORA.   Clearer than you could ever make me.

KROGSTAD.   Yes, such a bad lawyer as I—

1360   NORA.   What is it you want?

KROGSTAD.   Only to see how you are getting on, Mrs. Helmer. I've been
          thinking about you all day. Even a mere money-lender, a gutter-journalist,
          a—in short, a creature like me—has a little bit of what people call feeling.

NORA.　Then show it; think of my little children.

KROGSTAD.　Did you and your husband think of mine? But enough of that. I only wanted to tell you that you needn't take this matter too seriously. I shall not lodge any information, for the present.

NORA.　No, surely not. I knew you wouldn't.

KROGSTAD.　The whole thing can be settled quite amicably. Nobody need
1370　know. It can remain among us three.

NORA.　My husband must never know.

KROGSTAD.　How can you prevent it? Can you pay off the balance?

NORA.　No, not at once.

KROGSTAD.　Or have you any means of raising the money in the next few days?

NORA.　None—that I will make use of.

KROGSTAD.　And if you had, it would not help you now. If you offered me ever so much money down, you should not get back your I O U.

NORA.　Tell me what you want to do with it.

1380　KROGSTAD.　I only want to keep it—to have it in my possession. No outsider shall hear anything of it. So, if you have any desperate scheme in your head—

NORA.　What if I have?

KROGSTAD.　If you should think of leaving your husband and children—

NORA.　What if I do?

KROGSTAD.　Or if you should think of—something worse—

NORA.　How do you know that?

KROGSTAD.　Put all that out of your head.

NORA.　How did you know what I had in my mind?

1390　KROGSTAD.　Most of us think of *that* at first. I thought of it, too; but I hadn't the courage—

NORA [*tonelessly*].　Nor I.

KROGSTAD [*relieved*].　No, one hasn't. You haven't the courage either, have you?

NORA.　I haven't, I haven't.

KROGSTAD.　Besides, it would be very foolish.—Just one domestic storm, and it's all over. I have a letter in my pocket for your husband—

NORA.　Telling him everything?

KROGSTAD.　Sparing you as much as possible.

1400　NORA [*quickly*].　He must never read the letter. Tear it up. I will manage to get the money somehow—

KROGSTAD.　Pardon me, Mrs. Helmer, but I believe I told you—

NORA.　Oh, I'm not talking about the money I owe you. Tell me how much you demand from my husband—I will get it.

KROGSTAD.　I demand no money from your husband.

NORA.　What *do* you demand, then?

KROGSTAD.　I will tell you. I want to regain my footing in the world. I want to rise; and your husband shall help me to do it. For the last eighteen months my record has been spotless; I have been in bitter need all the time; but
1410　I was content to fight my way up, step by step. Now, I've been thrust down again, and I will not be satisfied with merely being reinstated as a matter of grace. I want to rise, I tell you. I must get into the Bank again, in a higher position than before. Your husband shall create a place on purpose for me—

NORA.   He will never do that!

KROGSTAD.   He will do it; I know him—he won't dare to show fight! And
when he and I are together there, you shall soon see! Before a year is out
I shall be the manager's right hand. It won't be Torvald Helmer, but Nils
Krogstad, that manages the Joint Stock Bank.

1420 NORA.   That shall never be.

KROGSTAD.   Perhaps you will—?

NORA.   *Now* I have the courage for it.

KROGSTAD.   Oh, you don't frighten me! A sensitive, petted creature like you—

NORA.   You shall see, you shall see!

KROGSTAD.   Under the ice, perhaps? Down into the cold, black water? And
next spring to come up again, ugly, hairless, unrecognizable—

NORA.   You can't terrify me.

KROGSTAD.   Nor you me. People don't do that sort of thing, Mrs. Helmer.
And, after all, what would be the use of it? I have your husband in my
1430   pocket, all the same.

NORA.   Afterwards? When I am no longer—?

KROGSTAD.   You forget, your reputation remains in my hands! [NORA *stands
speechless and looks at him.*] Well, now you are prepared. Do nothing foolish.
As soon as Helmer has received my letter, I shall expect to hear from him.
And remember that it is your husband himself who has forced me back
into such paths. That I will never forgive him. Good-bye, Mrs. Helmer.

[*Goes out through the hall.* NORA *hurries to the door, opens it a little, and listens.*]

NORA.   He's going. He's not putting the letter into the box. No, no, it would
be impossible! [*Opens the door further and further.*] What's that. He's standing still; not going downstairs. Has he changed his mind? Is he—? [*A letter
1440   falls into the box.* KROGSTAD'S *footsteps are heard gradually receding down the
stair.* NORA *utters a suppressed shriek, and rushes forward towards the sofa-table;
pause.*] In the letter-box! [*Slips shrinkingly up to the hall door.*] There it
lies.—Torvald, Torvald—now we are lost!

[MRS. LINDEN *enters from the left with the costume.*]

MRS. LINDEN.   There, I think it's all right now. Shall we just try it on?

NORA [*hoarsely and softly*].   Christina, come here.

MRS. LINDEN [*throws down the dress on the sofa*].   What's the matter? You look
quite distracted.

NORA.   Come here. Do you see that letter? *There*, see,—through the glass of
the letter-box.

1450 MRS. LINDEN.   Yes, yes, I see it.

NORA.   That letter is from Krogstad—

MRS. LINDEN.   Nora—it was Krogstad who lent you the money?

NORA.   Yes; and now Torvald will know everything.

MRS. LINDEN.   Believe me, Nora, it's the best thing for both of you.

NORA.   You don't know all yet. I have forged a name—

MRS. LINDEN.   Good Heavens!

NORA.   Now, listen to me, Christina; you shall bear me witness—

MRS. LINDEN.   How "witness"? What am I to—

NORA.   If I should go out of my mind—it might easily happen—

1460 Mrs. Linden.   Nora!

Nora.   Or if anything else should happen to me—so that I couldn't be here—!

Mrs. Linden.   Nora, Nora, you're quite beside yourself!

Nora.   In case any one wanted to take it all upon himself—the whole blame—you understand—

Mrs. Linden.   Yes, yes; but how can you think—?

Nora.   You shall bear witness that it's not true, Christina. I'm not out of my mind at all; I know quite well what I'm saying; and I tell you nobody else knew anything about it; I did the whole thing, I myself. Remember that.

1470 Mrs. Linden.   I shall remember. But I don't understand what you mean—

Nora.   Oh, how should you? It's the miracle come to pass.

Mrs. Linden.   The miracle?

Nora.   Yes, the miracle. But it's so terrible, Christina; it mustn't happen for all the world.

Mrs. Linden.   I shall go straight to Krogstad and talk to him.

Nora.   Don't; he'll do you some harm.

Mrs. Linden.   Once he would have done anything for me.

Nora.   He?

Mrs. Linden.   Where does he live?

1480 Nora.   Oh, how can I tell?—Yes—[*Feels in her pocket.*] Here's his card. But the letter, the letter—!

Helmer [*knocking outside*].   Nora!

Nora [*shrieks in terror*].   Oh, what is it? What do you want?

Helmer.   Well, well, don't be frightened. We're not coming in; you've bolted the door. Are you trying on your dress?

Nora.   Yes, yes, I'm trying it on. It suits me so well, Torvald.

Mrs. Linden [*who has read the card*].   Why, he lives close by here.

Nora.   Yes, but it's no use now. We are lost. The letter is there in the box.

Mrs. Linden.   And your husband has the key?

1490 Nora.   Always.

Mrs. Linden.   Krogstad must demand his letter back, unread. He must find some pretext—

Nora.   But this is the very time when Torvald generally—

Mrs. Linden.   Prevent him. Keep him occupied. I shall come back as quickly as I can. [*She goes out hastily by the hall door.*]

Nora [*opens* Helmer's *door and peeps in*].   Torvald!

Helmer.   Well, may one come into one's own room again at last? Come, Rank, we'll have a look—[*In the doorway.*] But how's this?

Nora.   What, Torvald, dear?

1500 Helmer.   Rank led me to expect a grand transformation.

Rank [*in the doorway*].   So I understood. I suppose I was mistaken.

Nora.   No, no one shall see me in my glory till tomorrow evening.

Helmer.   Why, Nora, dear, you look so tired. Have you been practicing too hard?

Nora.   No, I haven't practiced at all yet.

Helmer.   But you'll have to—

Nora.   Oh, yes, I must, I must! But, Torvald, I can't get on at all without your help. I've forgotten everything.

Helmer.   Oh, we shall soon freshen it up again.

1510 NORA. Yes, do help me. Torvald. You must promise me—Oh, I'm so nervous about it. Before so many people—This evening you must give yourself up entirely to me. You mustn't do a stroke of work; you mustn't even touch a pen. Do promise, Torvald, dear!

HELMER. I promise. All this evening I shall be your slave. Little helpless thing—! But, by the bye, I must just— [*Going to hall door.*]

NORA. What do you want there?

HELMER. Only to see if there are any letters.

NORA. No, no, don't do that, Torvald.

HELMER. Why not?

1520 NORA. Torvald, I beg you not to. There are none there.

HELMER. Let me just see. [*Is going.* NORA, *at the piano, plays the first bars of the tarantella. At the door, stops*]. Aha!

NORA. I can't dance tomorrow if I don't rehearse with you first.

HELMER [*going to her*]. Are you really so nervous, dear Nora?

NORA. Yes, dreadfully! Let me rehearse at once. We have time before dinner. Oh, do sit down and play for me, Torvald, dear; direct me and put me right, as you used to do.

HELMER. With all the pleasure in life, since you wish it.

[*Sits at piano.* NORA *snatches the tambourine out of the box, and hurriedly drapes herself in a long parti-colored shawl; then, with a bound, stands in the middle of the floor.*]

NORA. Now, play for me! Now I'll dance!

[HELMER *plays and* NORA *dances.* RANK *stands at the piano behind* HELMER *and looks on.*]

1530 HELMER [*playing*]. Slower! Slower!

NORA. Can't do it slower!

HELMER. Not so violently, Nora.

NORA. I must! I must!

HELMER [*stops*]. No, no, Nora,—that will never do.

NORA [*laughs and swings her tambourine*]. Didn't I tell you so!

RANK. Let me play for her.

HELMER [*rising*]. Yes, do,—then I can direct her better.

[RANK *sits down to the piano and plays;* NORA *dances more and more wildly.* HELMER *stands by the stove and addresses frequent corrections to her; she seems not to hear. Her hair breaks loose, and falls over her shoulders. She does not notice it, but goes on dancing.*]

[MRS. LINDEN *enters and stands spellbound in the doorway.*]

MRS. LINDEN. Ah—!

NORA [*dancing*]. We're having such fun here, Christina!

1540 HELMER. Why, Nora, dear, you're dancing as if it were a matter of life and death.

NORA. So it is.

HELMER.   Rank, stop! This is the merest madness. Stop, I say! [RANK *stops playing, and* NORA *comes to a sudden standstill. Going toward her*]. I couldn't have believed it. You've positively forgotten all I taught you.

NORA [*throws the tambourine away*].   You see for yourself.

HELMER.   You really do want teaching.

NORA.   Yes, you see how much I need it. You must practice with me up to the last moment. Will you promise me, Torvald?

1550   HELMER.   Certainly, certainly.

NORA.   Neither today nor tomorrow must you think of anything but me. You mustn't open a single letter—mustn't look at the letter-box.

HELMER.   Ah, you're still afraid of that man—

NORA.   Oh, yes, yes, I am.

HELMER.   Nora, I can see it in your face—there's a letter from him in the box.

NORA.   I don't know, I believe so. But you're not to read anything now; nothing ugly must come between us until all is over.

RANK [*softly, to* HELMER].   You mustn't contradict her.

1560   HELMER [*putting his arm around her*].   The child shall have her own way. But tomorrow night, when the dance is over—

NORA.   Then you shall be free.

[ELLEN *appears in the doorway, right.*]

ELLEN.   Dinner is on the table, ma'am.

NORA.   We'll have some champagne, Ellen.

ELLEN.   Yes. ma'am.

[*Goes out.*]

HELMER.   Dear me! Quite a banquet.

NORA.   Yes, and we'll keep it up till morning. [*Calling out.*] And macaroons, Ellen,—plenty,—just this once.

HELMER [*seizing her hand*].   Come, come, don't let us have this wild excite-
1570   ment! Be my own little lark again.

NORA.   Oh, yes, I will. But now go into the dining-room; and you, too, Doctor Rank. Christina, you must help me to do up my hair.

RANK [*softly, as they go*].   There's nothing in the wind? Nothing—I mean—?

HELMER.   Oh, no, nothing of the kind. It's merely this babyish anxiety I was telling you about.

[*They go out to the right.*]

NORA.   Well?

MRS. LINDEN.   He's gone out of town.

NORA.   I saw it in your face.

MRS. LINDEN.   He comes back tomorrow evening. I left a note for him.

1580   NORA.   You shouldn't have done that. Things must take their course. After all, there's something glorious in waiting for the miracle.

MRS. LINDEN.   What is it you're waiting for?

NORA.   Oh, you can't understand. Go to them in the dining-room; I shall come in a moment. [MRS. LINDEN *goes into the dining-room.* NORA *stands for a moment as though collecting her thoughts; then looks at her watch.*] Five. Seven hours till midnight. Then twenty-four hours till the next midnight. Then the *tarantella* will be over. Twenty-four and seven? Thirty-one hours to live.

[HELMER *appears at the door, right.*]

HELMER.   What has become of my little lark?
1590 NORA [*runs to him with open arms*].   Here she is!

ACT III

The same room. The table, with the chairs around it, in the middle. A lighted lamp on the table. The door to the hall stands open. Dance music is heard from the floor above.

[MRS. LINDEN *sits by the table and absently turns the pages of a book. She tries to read, but seems unable to fix her attention; she frequently listens and looks anxiously toward the hall door.*]

MRS. LINDEN [*looks at her watch*].   Not here yet; and the time is nearly up. If only he hasn't—[*Listens again.*] Ah, there he is. [*She goes into the hall and cautiously opens the outer door; soft footsteps are heard on the stairs; she whispers.*] Come in; there is no one here.
KROGSTAD [*in the doorway*].   I found a note from you at my house. What does it mean?
MRS. LINDEN.   I *must* speak to you.
KROGSTAD.   Indeed? And in this house?
MRS. LINDEN.   I could not see you at my rooms. They have no separate
1600   entrance. Come in; we are quite alone. The servants are asleep, and the Helmers are at the ball upstairs.
KROGSTAD [*coming into the room*].   Ah! So the Helmers are dancing this evening? Really?
MRS. LINDEN.   Yes. Why not?
KROGSTAD.   Quite right. Why not?
MRS. LINDEN.   And now, let us talk a little.
KROGSTAD.   Have we two anything to say to each other?
MRS. LINDEN.   A great deal.
KROGSTAD.   I should not have thought so.
1610 MRS. LINDEN.   Because you have never really understood me.
KROGSTAD.   What was there to understand? The most natural thing in the world—a heartless woman throws a man over when a better match offers.
MRS. LINDEN.   Do you really think me so heartless? Do you think I broke with you lightly?
KROGSTAD.   Did you not?
MRS. LINDEN.   Do you really think so?
KROGSTAD.   If not, why did you write me that letter?
MRS. LINDEN.   Was it not best? Since I had to break with you, was it not right that I should try to put an end to all that you felt for me?
1620 KROGSTAD [*clenching his hands together*].   So that was it? And all this—for the sake of money!
MRS. LINDEN.   You ought not to forget that I had a helpless mother and two

little brothers. We could not wait for you, Nils, as your prospects then stood.

KROGSTAD. Perhaps not; but you had no right to cast me off for the sake of others, whoever the others might be.

MRS. LINDEN. I don't know. I have often asked myself whether I had the right.

KROGSTAD [*more softly*]. When I had lost you, I seemed to have no firm
1630   ground left under my feet. Look at me now. I am a shipwrecked man clinging to a spar.

MRS. LINDEN. Rescue may be at hand.

KROGSTAD. It *was* at hand; but then you came and stood in the way.

MRS. LINDEN. Without my knowledge, Nils. I did not know till today that it was you I was to replace in the Bank.

KROGSTAD. Well, I take your word for it. But now that you do know, do you mean to give way?

MRS. LINDEN. No; for that would not help you in the least.

KROGSTAD. Oh, help, help—! I should do it whether or no.

1640 MRS. LINDEN. I have learned prudence. Life and bitter necessity have schooled me.

KROGSTAD. And life has taught me not to trust fine speeches.

MRS. LINDEN. Then life has taught you a very sensible thing. But deeds you *will* trust?

KROGSTAD. What do you mean?

MRS. LINDEN. You said you were a shipwrecked man, clinging to a spar.

KROGSTAD. I have good reason to say so.

MRS. LINDEN. I, too, am shipwrecked, and clinging to a spar. I have no one to mourn for, no one to care for.

1650 KROGSTAD. You made your own choice.

MRS. LINDEN. No choice was left me.

KROGSTAD. Well, what then?

MRS. LINDEN. Nils, how if we two shipwrecked people could join hands?

KROGSTAD. What!

MRS. LINDEN. Two on a raft have a better chance than if each clings to a separate spar.

KROGSTAD. Christina!

MRS. LINDEN. What do you think brought me to town?

KROGSTAD. Had you any thought of me?

1660 MRS. LINDEN. I must have work or I can't bear to live. All my life, as long as I can remember, I have worked; work has been my one great joy. Now I stand quite alone in the world, aimless and forlorn. There is no happiness in working for one's self. Nils, give me somebody and something to work for.

KROGSTAD. I cannot believe in all this. It is simply a woman's romantic craving for self-sacrifice.

MRS. LINDEN. Have you ever found me romantic?

KROGSTAD. Would you really—? Tell me: do you know all my past?

MRS. LINDEN. Yes.

1670 KROGSTAD. And do you know what people say of me?

MRS. LINDEN. Did you not say just now that with me you could have been another man?

KROGSTAD. I am sure of it.

MRS. LINDEN.   Is it too late?

KROGSTAD.   Christina, do you know what you are doing? Yes, you do; I see it
in your face. Have you the courage, then—?

MRS. LINDEN.   I need some one to be a mother to, and your children need a
mother. You need me, and I—I need you. Nils, I believe in your better
self. With you I fear nothing.

1680 KROGSTAD [*seizing her hands*].   Thank you—thank you, Christina. Now I shall
make others see me as you do.—Ah, I forgot—

MRS. LINDEN [*listening*].   Hush! The *tarantella!* Go! Go!

KROGSTAD.   Why? What is it?

MRS. LINDEN.   Don't you hear the dancing overhead? As soon as that is over
they will be here.

KROGSTAD.   Oh, yes, I shall go. Nothing will come of this, after all. Of course,
you don't know the step I have taken against the Helmers.

MRS. LINDEN.   Yes, Nils, I do know.

KROGSTAD.   And yet you have the courage to—?

1690 MRS. LINDEN.   I know to what lengths despair can drive a man.

KROGSTAD.   Oh, if I could only undo it!

MRS. LINDEN.   You could. Your letter is still in the box.

KROGSTAD.   Are you sure?

MRS. LINDEN.   Yes; but—

KROGSTAD [*looking to her searchingly*].   Is that what it all means? You want to
save your friend at any price. Say it out—is that your idea?

MRS. LINDEN.   Nils, a woman who has once sold herself for the sake of others,
does not do so again.

KROGSTAD.   I shall demand my letter back again.

1700 MRS. LINDEN.   No, no.

KROGSTAD.   Yes, of course. I shall wait till Helmer comes; I shall tell him to
give it back to me—that it's only about my dismissal—that I don't want it
read—

MRS. LINDEN.   No, Nils, you must not recall the letter.

KROGSTAD.   But tell me, wasn't that just why you got me to come here?

MRS. LINDEN.   Yes, in my first alarm. But a day has passed since then, and in
that day I have seen incredible things in this house. Helmer must know
everything; there must be an end to this unhappy secret. These two must
come to a full understanding. They must have done with all these shifts

1710 and subterfuges.

KROGSTAD.   Very well, if you like to risk it. But *one* thing I can do, and at
once—

MRS. LINDEN [*listening*].   Make haste! Go, go! The dance is over; we're not
safe another moment.

KROGSTAD.   I shall wait for you in the street.

MRS. LINDEN.   Yes, do; you must see me home.

KROGSTAD.   I never was so happy in all my life!

[KROGSTAD *goes out by the outer door. The door between the room and the hall remains
open.*]

MRS. LINDEN [*arranging the room and getting her outdoor things together*].   What

a change! What a change! To have some one to work for, to live for; a
1720 home to make happy! Well, it shall not be my fault if I fail.—I wish they
would come.—[*Listens.*] Ah, there they are! I must get my things on. [*Takes
bonnet and cloak.*]

[HELMER'S *and* NORA'S *voices are heard outside, a key is turned in the lock, and*
HELMER *drags* NORA *almost by force into the hall. She wears the Italian costume with
a large black shawl over it. He is in evening dress and wears a black domino,*[9] *open.*]

NORA [*struggling with him in the doorway*].   No, no, no! I won't go in! I want to
go upstairs again; I don't want to leave so early!
HELMER.   But, my dearest girl—!
NORA.   Oh, please, please, Torvald, I beseech you—only one hour more!
HELMER.   Not one minute more, Nora, dear; you know what we agreed.
Come, come in; you're catching cold here.

[*He leads her gently into the room in spite of her resistance.*]

MRS. LINDEN.   Good-evening.
1730 NORA.   Christina!
HELMER.   What, Mrs. Linden! You here so late?
MRS. LINDEN.   Yes, I ought to apologize. I did so want to see Nora in her
costume.
NORA.   Have you been sitting here waiting for me?
MRS. LINDEN.   Yes; unfortunately, I came too late. You had gone upstairs
already, and I felt I couldn't go away without seeing you.
HELMER [*taking* NORA'S *shawl off*].   Well, then, just look at her! I assure you
she's worth it. Isn't she lovely, Mrs. Linden?
MRS. LINDEN.   Yes, I must say—
1740 HELMER.   Isn't she exquisite? Every one said so. But she's dreadfully obstinate dear little creature. What's to be done with her? Just think, I had
almost to force her away.
NORA.   Oh, Torvald, you'll be sorry some day that you didn't let me stay, if
only for one half-hour more.
HELMER.   There! You hear her, Mrs. Linden? She dances her *tarantella* with
wild applause, and well she deserved it, I must say,—though there was,
perhaps, a little too much nature in her rendering of the idea,—more than
was, strictly speaking, artistic. But never mind—the point is, she made a
great success, a tremendous success. Was I to let her remain after that—to
1750 weaken the impression? Not if I know it. I took my sweet little Capri
girl—my capricious little Capri girl, I might say—under my arm; a rapid
turn round the room, a curtsy to all sides, and—as they say in novels—the
lovely apparition vanished! An exit should always be effective, Mrs. Linden; but I can't get Nora to see it. By Jove! it's warm here. [*Throws his
domino on a chair and opens the door to his room.*] What! No light there? Oh,
of course. Excuse me—

[*Goes in and lights candles.*]

---

[9] A hooded cloak, worn with a mask at a masquerade.

NORA [*whispers breathlessly*]. Well?

MRS. LINDEN [*softly*]. I've spoken to him.

NORA. And—?

1760 MRS. LINDEN. Nora—you must tell your husband everything—

NORA [*tonelessly*]. I knew it!

MRS. LINDEN. You have nothing to fear from Krogstad; but you must speak out.

NORA. I shall not speak!

MRS. LINDEN. Then the letter will.

NORA. Thank you, Christina. Now I know what I have to do. Hush—!

HELMER [*coming back*]. Well, Mrs. Linden, have you admired her?

MRS. LINDEN. Yes; and now I must say good-night.

HELMER. What, already? Does this knitting belong to you?

1770 MRS. LINDEN [*takes it*]. Yes, thanks; I was nearly forgetting it.

HELMER. Then you do knit?

MRS. LINDEN. Yes.

HELMER. Do you know, you ought to embroider instead?

MRS. LINDEN. Indeed! Why?

HELMER. Because it's so much prettier. Look, now! You hold the embroidery in the left hand, so, and then work the needle with the right hand, in a long, graceful curve—don't you?

MRS. LINDEN. Yes, I suppose so.

HELMER. But knitting is always ugly. Just look—your arms close to your

1780 sides, and the needles going up and down—there's something Chinese about it.—They really gave us splendid champagne tonight.

MRS. LINDEN. Well, good-night, Nora, and don't be obstinate any more.

HELMER. Well said, Mrs. Linden!

MRS. LINDEN. Good-night, Mr. Helmer.

HELMER [*accompanying her to the door*]. Good-night, good-night; I hope you'll get safely home. I should be glad to—but you have such a short way to go. Good-night, good-night. [*She goes;* HELMER *shuts the door after her and comes forward again.*] At last we've got rid of her; she's a terrible bore.

NORA. Aren't you very tired, Torvald?

1790 HELMER. No, not in the least.

NORA. Nor sleepy?

HELMER. Not a bit. I feel particularly lively. But you? You do look tired and sleepy.

NORA. Yes, very tired. I shall soon sleep now.

HELMER. There, you see. I was right, after all, not to let you stay longer.

NORA. Oh, everything you do is right.

HELMER [*kissing her forehead*]. Now my lark is speaking like a reasonable being. Did you notice how jolly Rank was this evening?

NORA. Indeed? Was he? I had no chance of speaking to him.

1800 HELMER. Nor I, much; but I haven't seen him in such good spirits for a long time. [*Looks at* NORA *a little, then comes nearer her.*] It's splendid to be back in our own home, to be quite alone together!—Oh, you enchanting creature!

NORA. Don't look at me in that way, Torvald.

HELMER. I am not to look at my dearest treasure?—at all the loveliness that is mine, mine only, wholly and entirely mine?

NORA [*going to the other side of the table*].   You mustn't say these things to me
this evening.

HELMER [*following*].   I see you have the *tarantella* still in your blood—and that
1810   makes you all the more enticing. Listen! the other people are going now.
[*More softly.*] Nora—soon the whole house will be still.

NORA.   Yes, I hope so.

HELMER.   Yes, don't you, Nora, darling? When we are among strangers, do
you know why I speak so little to you, and keep so far away, and only steal
a glance at you now and then—do you know why I do it? Because I am
fancying that we love each other in secret, that I am secretly betrothed to
you, and that no one dreams that there is anything between us.

NORA.   Yes, yes, yes. I know all your thoughts are with me.

HELMER.   And then, when the time comes to go, and I put the shawl about
1820   your smooth, soft shoulders, and this glorious neck of yours, I imagine you
are my bride, that our marriage is just over, that I am bringing you for the
first time to my home—that I am alone with you for the first time—quite
alone with you, in your trembling loveliness! All this evening I have been
longing for you, and you only. When I watched you swaying and whirling
in the *tarantella*—my blood boiled—I could endure it no longer; and that's
why I made you come home with me so early—

NORA.   Go, now, Torvald! Go away from me. I won't have all this.

HELMER.   What do you mean? Ah, I see you're teasing me, little Nora!
Won't—won't! Am I not your husband—?

[*A knock at the outer door.*]

1830 NORA [*starts*].   Did you hear—?

HELMER [*going toward the hall*].   Who's there?

RANK [*outside*].   It is I; may I come in for a moment?

HELMER [*in a low tone, annoyed*].   Oh! What can he want just now? [*Aloud.*]
Wait a moment. [*Opens door.*] Come, it's nice of you to look in.

RANK.   I thought I heard your voice, and that put it into my head. [*Looks
round.*] Ah, this dear old place! How cozy you two are here!

HELMER.   You seemed to find it pleasant enough upstairs, too.

RANK.   Exceedingly. Why not? Why shouldn't one take one's share of everything in this world? All one can, at least, and as long as one can. The wine
1840   was splendid—

HELMER.   Especially the champagne.

RANK.   Did you notice it? It's incredible the quantity I contrived to get down.

NORA.   Torvald drank plenty of champagne, too.

RANK.   Did he?

NORA.   Yes, and it always puts him in such spirits.

RANK.   Well, why shouldn't one have a jolly evening after a well-spent day?

HELMER.   Well-spent! Well, I haven't much to boast of in that respect.

RANK [*slapping him on the shoulder*].   But I *have*, don't you see?

NORA.   I suppose you have been engaged in a scientific investigation, Doctor
1850   Rank?

RANK.   Quite right.

HELMER.   Bless me! Little Nora talking about scientific investigations!

NORA.   Am I to congratulate you on the result?

RANK.   By all means.

NORA.   It was good, then?

RANK.   The best possible, both for doctor and patient—certainty.

NORA [*quickly and searchingly*].   Certainty?

RANK.   Absolute certainty. Wasn't I right to enjoy myself after that?

NORA.   Yes, quite right, Doctor Rank.

1860 HELMER.   And so say I, provided you don't have to pay for it tomorrow.

RANK.   Well, in this life nothing is to be had for nothing.

NORA.   Doctor Rank—I'm sure you are very fond of masquerades?

RANK.   Yes, when there are plenty of amusing disguises—

NORA.   Tell me, what shall we two be at our next masquerade?

HELMER.   Little featherbrain! Thinking of your next already!

RANK.   We two? I'll tell you. You must go as a good fairy.

HELMER.   Ah, but what costume would indicate *that*?

RANK.   She has simply to wear her everyday dress.

HELMER.   Capital! But don't you know what you will be yourself?

1870 RANK.   Yes, my dear friend, I am perfectly clear upon that point.

HELMER.   Well?

RANK.   At the next masquerade I shall be invisible.

HELMER.   What a comical idea!

RANK.   There's a big black hat—haven't you heard of the invisible hat? It
    comes down all over you, and then no one can see you.

HELMER [*with a suppressed smile*].   No, you're right there.

RANK.   But I'm quite forgetting what I came for. Helmer, give me a cigar—
    one of the dark Havanas.[10]

HELMER.   With the greatest pleasure. [*Hands cigar-case.*]

1880 RANK [*takes one and cuts the end off*].   Thank you.

NORA [*striking a wax match*].   Let me give you a light.

RANK.   A thousand thanks. [*She holds the match. He lights his cigar at it.*] And
    now, good-bye!

HELMER.   Good-bye, good-bye, my dear fellow.

NORA.   Sleep well, Doctor Rank.

RANK.   Thanks for the wish.

NORA.   Wish me the same.

RANK.   You? Very well, since you ask me—sleep well. And thanks for the
    light.

[*He nods to them both and goes out.*]

1890 HELMER [*in an undertone*].   He's been drinking a good deal.

NORA [*absently*].   I dare say. [HELMER *takes his bunch of keys from his pocket and
    goes into the hall.*] Torvald, what are you doing there?

HELMER.   I must empty the letter-box; it's quite full; there will be no room
    for the newspapers tomorrow morning.

NORA.   Are you going to work tonight?

HELMER.   You know very well I am not.—Why, how is this? Some one has
    been at the lock.

NORA.   The lock—?

---

[10] Cigars from Havana, Cuba, are especially prized for their aroma and taste.

HELMER. I'm sure of it. What does it mean? I can't think that the servants—?
1900   Here's a broken hairpin. Nora, it's one of yours.

NORA [*quickly*]. It must have been the children—

HELMER. Then you must break them of such tricks.—There! At last I've got it open. [*Takes contents out and calls into the kitchen.*] Ellen!—Ellen, just put the hall door lamp out. [*He returns with letters in his hand, and shuts the inner door.*] Just see how they've accumulated. [*Turning them over.*] Why, what's this?

NORA [*at the window*]. The letter! Oh, no, no, Torvald!

HELMER. Two visiting-cards—from Rank.

NORA. From Doctor Rank?

1910   HELMER [*looking at them*]. Doctor Rank. They were on the top. He must just have put them in.

NORA. Is there anything on them?

HELMER. There's a black cross over the name. Look at it. What an unpleasant idea! It looks just as if he were announcing his own death.

NORA. So he is.

HELMER. What! Do you know anything? Has he told you anything?

NORA. Yes. These cards mean that he has taken his last leave of us. He is going to shut himself up and die.

HELMER. Poor fellow! Of course, I knew we couldn't hope to keep him long.
1920   But so soon—! And to go and creep into his lair like a wounded animal—

NORA. When we *must* go, it is best to go silently. Don't you think so, Torvald?

HELMER [*walking up and down*]. He had so grown into our lives, I can't realize that he is gone. He and his sufferings and his loneliness formed a sort of cloudy background to the sunshine of our happiness.—Well, perhaps it's best as it is—at any rate, for him. [*Stands still.*] And perhaps for us, too, Nora. Now we two are thrown entirely upon each other. [*Takes her in his arms.*] My darling wife! I feel as if I could never hold you close enough. Do you know, Nora, I often wish some danger might threaten you, that I might risk body and soul, and everything, everything, for your dear sake.

1930   NORA [*tears herself from him and says firmly*]. Now you shall read your letters, Torvald.

HELMER. No, no; not tonight. I want to be with you, my sweet wife.

NORA. With the thought of your dying friend—?

HELMER. You are right. This has shaken us both. Unloveliness has come between us—thoughts of death and decay. We must seek to cast them off. Till then—we will remain apart.

NORA [*her arms round his neck*]. Torvald! Good-night! good-night!

HELMER [*kissing her forehead*]. Good-night, my little song-bird. Sleep well, Nora. Now I shall go and read my letters.

[*He goes with the letters in his hand into his room and shuts the door.*]

1940   NORA [*with wild eyes, gropes about her, seizes* HELMER's *domino, throws it around her, and whispers quickly, hoarsely, and brokenly*]. Never to see him again. Never, never, never. [*Throws her shawl over her head.*] Never to see the children again. Never, never.—Oh, that black, icy water! Oh that bottomless—! If it were only over! Now he has it; he's reading it. Oh, no, no, no, not yet. Torvald, good-bye—! Good-bye, my little ones—!

[*She is rushing out by the hall; at the same moment* HELMER *flings his door open and stands there with an open letter in his hand.*]

HELMER. Nora!

NORA [*shrieks*]. Ah—!

HELMER. What is this? Do you know what is in this letter?

NORA. Yes, I know. Let me go! Let me pass!

1950 HELMER [*holds her back*]. Where do you want to go?

NORA [*tries to break away from him*]. You shall not save me, Torvald.

HELMER [*falling back*]. True! Is what he writes true? No, no, it is impossible that this can be true.

NORA. It *is* true. I have loved you beyond all else in the world.

HELMER. Pshaw—no silly evasions!

NORA [*a step nearer him*]. Torvald—!

HELMER. Wretched woman—what have you done!

NORA. Let me go—you shall not save me! You shall not take my guilt upon yourself!

1960 HELMER. I don't want any melodramatic airs. [*Locks the outer door.*] Here you shall stay and give an account of yourself. Do you understand what you have done? Answer! Do you understand it?

NORA [*looks at him fixedly, and says with a stiffening expression*]. Yes; now I begin fully to understand it.

HELMER [*walking up and down*]. Oh, what an awful awakening! During all these eight years—she who was my pride and my joy—a hypocrite, a liar—worse, worse—a criminal. Oh, the unfathomable hideousness of it all! Ugh! Ugh! [NORA *says nothing, and continues to look fixedly at him.*] I ought to have known how it would be. I ought to have foreseen it. All your

1970 father's want of principle—be silent!—all your father's want of principle you have inherited—no religion, no morality, no sense of duty. How I am punished for screening him! I did it for your sake; and you reward me like this.

NORA. Yes—like this.

HELMER. You have destroyed my whole happiness. You have ruined my future. Oh, it's frightful to think of! I am in the power of a scoundrel; he can do whatever he pleases with me, demand whatever he chooses; he can domineer over me as much as he likes, and I must submit. And all this disaster and ruin is brought upon me by an unprincipled woman!

1980 NORA. When I am out of the world, you will be free.

HELMER. Oh, no fine phrases. Your father, too, was always ready with them. What good would it do me, if you were "out of the world," as you say? No good whatever! He can publish the story all the same; I might even be suspected of collusion. People will think I was at the bottom of it all and egged you on. And for all this I have you to thank—you whom I have done nothing but pet and spoil during our whole married life. Do you understand now what you have done to me?

NORA [*with cold calmness*]. Yes.

HELMER. The thing is so incredible, I can't grasp it. But we must come to an

1990 understanding. Take that shawl off. Take it off, I say! I must try to pacify him in one way or another—the matter must be hushed up, cost what it may.—As for you and me, we must make no outward change in our way of life—no *outward* change, you understand. Of course, you will continue to live here. But the children cannot be left in your care. I dare not trust them to you.—Oh, to have to say this to one I have loved so tenderly—whom I still—! But that must be a thing of the past. Henceforward there can be no question of happiness, but merely of saving the ruins, the shreds, the show—[*A ring;* HELMER *starts.*] What's that? So late! Can it be the worst? Can he—? Hide yourself, Nora; say you are ill.

[NORA *stands motionless.* HELMER *goes to the door and opens it.*]

2000 ELLEN [*half dressed, in the hall.*]   Here is a letter for you, ma'am.
   HELMER.   Give it to me. [*Seizes the letter and shuts the door.*] Yes, from him. You shall not have it. I shall read it.
   NORA.   Read it!
   HELMER [*by the lamp*].   I have hardly the courage to. We may both be lost, both you and I. Ah! I *must* know. [*Hastily tears the letter open; reads a few lines, looks at an enclosure; with a cry of joy.*] Nora! [NORA *looks inquiringly at him.*] Nora!—Oh! I must read it again.—Yes, yes, it is so. I am saved! Nora, I am saved!
   NORA.   And I?
2010 HELMER.   You, too, of course; we are both saved, both of us. Look here—he sends you back your promissory note. He writes that he regrets and apologizes that a happy turn in his life—Oh, what matter what he writes. We are saved, Nora! No one can harm you. Oh, Nora, Nora; but first to get rid of this hateful thing. I'll just see—[*Glances at the I O U.*] No, I will not look at it; the whole thing shall be nothing but a dream to me. [*Tears the I O U and both letters in pieces. Throws them into the fire and watches them burn.*] There! it's gone!—He said that ever since Christmas Eve—Oh, Nora, they must have been three terrible days for you!
   NORA.   I have fought a hard fight for the last three days.
2020 HELMER.   And in your agony you saw no other outlet but—No; we won't think of that horror. We will only rejoice and repeat—it's over, all over! Don't you hear, Nora? You don't seem able to grasp it. Yes, it's over. What is this set look on your face? Oh, my poor Nora, I understand; you cannot believe that I have forgiven you. But I have, Nora; I swear it. I have forgiven everything. I know that what you did was all for love of me.
   NORA.   That is true.
   HELMER.   You loved me as a wife should love her husband. It was only the means that, in your inexperience, you misjudged. But do you think I love you the less because you cannot do without guidance? No, no. Only lean
2030 on me; I will counsel you, and guide you. I should be no true man if this very womanly helplessness did not make you doubly dear in my eyes. You mustn't dwell upon the hard things I said in my first moment of terror, when the world seemed to be tumbling about my ears. I have forgiven you, Nora,—I swear I have forgiven you.
   NORA.   I thank you for your forgiveness.

[*Goes out, to the right.*]

HELMER.   No stay—! [*Looking through the doorway.*] What are you going to do?
NORA [*inside*].   To take off my masquerade dress.

HELMER [*in the doorway*]. Yes, do, dear. Try to calm down, and recover your balance, my scared little song-bird. You may rest secure. I have broad
2040 wings to shield you. [*Walking up and down near the door.*] Oh, how lovely— how cozy our home is, Nora! Here you are safe; here I can shelter you like a hunted dove whom I have saved from the claws of the hawk. I shall soon bring your poor beating heart to rest; believe me, Nora, very soon. To-morrow all this will seem quite different—everything will be as before. I shall not need to tell you again that I forgive you; you will feel for yourself that it is true. How could you think I could find it in my heart to drive you away, or even so much as to reproach you? Oh, you don't know a true man's heart, Nora. There is something indescribably sweet and soothing to a man in having forgiven his wife—honestly forgiven her, from the
2050 bottom of his heart. She becomes his property in a double sense. She is as though born again; she has become, so to speak, at once his wife and his child. That is what you shall henceforth be to me, my bewildered, helpless darling. Don't be troubled about anything, Nora; only open your heart to me, and I will be both will and conscience to you. [NORA *enters in everyday dress.*] Why, what's this? Not gone to bed? You have changed your dress?

NORA. Yes. Torvald; now I have changed my dress.

HELMER. But why now, so late—?

NORA. I shall not sleep tonight.

HELMER. But, Nora, dear—

2060 NORA [*looking at her watch*]. It's not so late yet. Sit down, Torvald; you and I have much to say to each other. [*She sits at one side of the table.*]

HELMER. Nora—what does this mean? Your cold, set face—

NORA. Sit down. It will take some time. I have much to talk over with you. [HELMER *sits at the other side of the table.*]

HELMER. You alarm me, Nora. I don't understand you.

NORA. No, that is just it. You don't understand me; and I have never understood you—till tonight. No, don't interrupt. Only listen to what I say.—We must come to a final settlement, Torvald.

HELMER. How do you mean?

2070 NORA [*after a short silence*]. Does not one thing strike you as we sit here?

HELMER. What should strike me?

NORA. We have been married eight years. Does it not strike you that this is the first time we two, you and I, man and wife, have talked together seriously?

HELMER. Seriously! What do you call seriously?

NORA. During eight whole years, and more—ever since the day we first met—we have never exchanged one serious word about serious things.

HELMER. Was I always to trouble you with the cares you could not help me to bear?

2080 NORA. I am not talking of cares. I say that we have never yet set ourselves seriously to get to the bottom of anything.

HELMER. Why, my dearest Nora, what have you to do with serious things?

NORA. There we have it! You have never understood me.—I have had great injustice done me, Torvald; first by father, and then by you.

HELMER. What! By your father and me?—By us, who have loved you more than all the world?

NORA [*shaking her head*]. You have never loved me. You only thought it amusing to be in love with me.

HELMER.   Why, Nora, what a thing to say!
2090 NORA.   Yes, it is so, Torvald. While I was at home with father, he used to tell me all his opinions, and I held the same opinions. If I had others, I said nothing about them, because he wouldn't have liked it. He used to call me his doll-child, and played with me as I played with my dolls. Then I came to live in your house—
HELMER.   What an expression to use about our marriage!
NORA [*undisturbed*].   I mean I passed from father's hands into yours. You arranged everything according to your taste; and I got the same tastes as you; or I pretended to—I don't know which—both ways, perhaps; some-times one and sometimes the other. When I look back on it now, I seem
2100 to have been living here like a beggar, from hand to mouth. I lived by performing tricks for you, Torvald. But you would have it so. You and father have done me a great wrong. It is your fault that my life has come to nothing.
HELMER.   Why, Nora, how unreasonable and ungrateful you are! Have you not been happy here?
NORA.   No, never. I thought I was; but I never was.
HELMER.   Not—not happy!
NORA.   No; only merry. And you have always been so kind to me. But our house has been nothing but a play-room. Here I have been your doll-wife,
2110 just as at home I used to be papa's doll-child. And the children, in their turn, have been my dolls. I thought it fun when you played with me, just as the children did when I played with them. That has been our marriage, Torvald.
HELMER.   There is some truth in what you say, exaggerated and overstrained though it be. But henceforth it shall be different. Play-time is over; now comes the time for education.
NORA.   Whose education? Mine, or the children's?
HELMER.   Both, my dear Nora.
NORA.   Oh, Torvald, you are not the man to teach me to be a fit wife for you.
2120 HELMER.   And you can say that?
NORA.   And I—how have I prepared myself to educate the children?
HELMER.   Nora!
NORA.   Did you not say yourself, a few minutes ago, you dared not trust them to me?
HELMER.   In the excitement of the moment! Why should you dwell upon that?
NORA.   No—you were perfectly right. That problem is beyond me. There is another to be solved first—I must try to educate myself. You are not the man to help me in that. I must set about it alone. And that is why I am
2130 leaving you.
HELMER [*jumping up*].   What—do you mean to say—?
NORA.   I must stand quite alone if I am ever to know myself and my sur-roundings; so I cannot stay with you.
HELMER.   Nora! Nora!
NORA.   I am going at once. I dare say Christina will take me in for tonight—
HELMER.   You are mad! I shall not allow it! I forbid it!
NORA.   It is of no use your forbidding me anything now. I shall take with me what belongs to me. From you I will accept nothing, either now or after-wards.

2140 HELMER.   What madness this is!

NORA.   Tomorrow I shall go home—I mean to what was my home. It will be easier for me to find some opening there.

HELMER.   Oh, in your blind inexperience—

NORA.   I must try to *gain* experience, Torvald.

HELMER.   To forsake your home, your husband, and your children! And you don't consider what the world will say.

NORA.   I can pay no heed to that. I only know that I must do it.

HELMER.   This is monstrous! Can you forsake your holiest duties in this way?

NORA.   What do you consider my holiest duties?

2150 HELMER.   Do I need to tell you that? Your duties to your husband and your children.

NORA.   I have other duties equally sacred.

HELMER.   Impossible! What duties do you mean?

NORA.   My duties toward myself.

HELMER.   Before all else you are a wife and a mother.

NORA.   That I no longer believe. I believe that before all else I am a human being, just as much as you are—or at least that I should try to become one. I know that most people agree with you, Torvald, and that they say so in books. But henceforth I can't be satisfied with what most people say, and
2160   what is in books. I must think things out for myself, and try to get clear about them.

HELMER.   Are you not clear about your place in your own home? Have you not an infallible guide in questions like these? Have you not religion?

NORA.   Oh, Torvald, I don't really know what religion is.

HELMER.   What do you mean?

NORA.   I know nothing but what Pastor Hansen told me when I was confirmed. He explained that religion was this and that. When I get away from all this and stand alone, I will look into that matter too. I will see whether what he taught me is right, or, at any rate, whether it is right
2170   for me.

HELMER.   Oh, this is unheard of! And from so young a woman! But if religion cannot keep you right, let me appeal to your conscience—for I suppose you have some moral feeling? Or, answer me: perhaps you have none?

NORA.   Well, Torvald, it's not easy to say. I really don't know—I am all at sea about these things. I only know that I think quite differently from you about them. I hear, too, that the laws are different from what I thought; but I can't believe that they can be right. It appears that a woman has no right to spare her dying father, or to save her husband's life! I don't believe that.

2180 HELMER.   You talk like a child. You don't understand the society in which you live.

NORA.   No, I do not. But now I shall try to learn. I must make up my mind which is right—society or I.

HELMER.   Nora, you are ill; you are feverish; I almost think you are out of your senses.

NORA.   I have never felt so much clearness and certainty as tonight.

HELMER.   You are clear and certain enough to forsake husband and children?

NORA.   Yes, I am.

2190 HELMER.   Then there is only one explanation possible.

NORA.   What is that?

HELMER.   You no longer love me.

NORA.   No; that is just it.

HELMER.   Nora!—Can you say so!

NORA.   Oh, I'm so sorry, Torvald; for you've always been so kind to me. But I can't help it. I do not love you any longer.

HELMER [*mastering himself with difficulty*].   Are you clear and certain on this point too?

NORA.   Yes, quite. That is why I will not stay here any longer.

2200 HELMER.   And can you also make clear to me how I have forfeited your love?

NORA.   Yes, I can. It was this evening, when the miracle did not happen; for then I saw you were not the man I had imagined.

HELMER.   Explain yourself more clearly; I don't understand.

NORA.   I have waited so patiently all these eight years; for, of course, I saw clearly enough that miracles don't happen everyday. When this crushing blow threatened me, I said to myself so confidently, "Now comes the miracle!" When Krogstad's letter lay in the box, it never for a moment occurred to me that you would think of submitting to that man's condi-tions. I was convinced that you would say to him, "Make it known to all the
2210 world"; and that then—

HELMER.   Well? When I had given my own wife's name up to disgrace and shame—?

NORA.   Then I firmly believed that you would come forward, take everything upon yourself, and say, "I am the guilty one."

HELMER.   Nora—!

NORA.   You mean I would never have accepted such sacrifice? No, certainly not. But what would my assertions have been worth in opposition to yours?—*That* was the miracle that I hoped for and dreaded. And it was to hinder *that* that I wanted to die.

2220 HELMER.   I would gladly work for you day and night, Nora,—bear sorrow and want for your sake. But no man sacrifices his honor, even for one he loves.

NORA.   Millions of women have done so.

HELMER.   Oh, you think and talk like a silly child.

NORA.   Very likely. But you neither think nor talk like the man I can share my life with. When your terror was over—not for what threatened me, but for yourself—when there was nothing more to fear—then it seemed to you as though nothing had happened. I was your lark again, your doll, just as before—whom you would take twice as much care of in future, because she
2230 was so weak and fragile. [*Stands up.*] Torvald—in that moment it burst upon me that I had been living here these eight years with a strange man, and had borne him three children.—Oh, I can't bear to think of it! I could tear myself to pieces!

HELMER [*sadly*].   I see it, I see it; an abyss has opened between us.—But, Nora, can it never be filled up?

NORA.   As I now am, I am no wife for you.

HELMER.   I have strength to become another man.

NORA.   Perhaps—when your doll is taken away from you.

HELMER.   To part—to part from you! No, Nora, no; I can't grasp the thought.

2240 NORA [*going into room on the right*].   The more reason for the thing to happen.

[*She comes back with outdoor things and a small traveling-bag, which she places on a chair.*]

HELMER.   Nora, Nora, not now! Wait till tomorrow.

NORA [*putting on cloak*].   I can't spend the night in a strange man's house.

HELMER.   But can we not live here, as brother and sister—?

NORA [*fastening her hat*].   You know very well that wouldn't last long. [*Puts on the shawl.*] Good-bye Torvald. No, I won't go to the children. I know they are in better hands than mine. As I now am, I can be nothing to them.

HELMER.   But some time, Nora—some time—?

NORA.   How can I tell? I have no idea what will become of me.

2250 HELMER.   But you are my wife, now and always!

NORA.   Listen, Torvald,—when a wife leaves her husband's house, as I am doing, I have heard that in the eyes of the law he is free from all duties toward her. At any rate, I release you from all duties. You must not feel yourself bound, any more than I shall. There must be perfect freedom on both sides. There, I give you back your ring. Give me mine.

HELMER.   That, too?

NORA.   That, too.

HELMER.   Here it is.

NORA.   Very well. Now it is all over. I lay the keys here. The servants know
2260 about everything in the house—better than I do. Tomorrow, when I have started, Christina will come to pack up the things I brought with me from home. I will have them sent after me.

HELMER.   All over! All over! Nora, will you never think of me again?

NORA.   Oh, I shall often think of you, and the children, and this house.

HELMER.   May I write to you, Nora?

NORA.   No—never. You must not.

HELMER.   But I must send you—

NORA.   Nothing, nothing.

HELMER.   I must help you if you need it.

2270 NORA.   No, I say. I take nothing from strangers.

HELMER.   Nora—can I never be more than a stranger to you?

NORA [*taking her traveling-bag*].   Oh, Torvald, then the miracle of miracles would have to happen—

HELMER.   What is the miracle of miracles?

NORA.   Both of us would have to change so that—Oh, Torvald, I no longer believe in miracles.

HELMER.   But *I* will believe. Tell me! We must so change that—?

NORA.   That communion between us shall be a marriage. Good-bye.

[*She goes out by the hall door.*]

HELMER [*sinking into a chair by the door with his face in his hands*].   Nora! Nora!
2280 [*He looks round and rises.*] Empty. She is gone. [*A hope springs up in him.*] Ah! The miracle of miracles—?

[*From below is heard the reverberation of a heavy door closing.*]

[1879]

Critical Commentary on *A Doll's House*

At the beginning Henrik Ibsen's *A Doll's House,* a doorbell rings and a key turns in a lock; at the end, a door slams shut. Between these two events, Ibsen's first audience in 1879 witnessed the birth of modern drama.

For the first time that audience saw ordinary life become the subject of serious art. Nora's situation as wife, mother, and homemaker is transformed into great drama, and the reverberations of the door she slams on the conventional roles of women continue to be felt throughout the western world.

As the title of the play suggests, Nora is initially a doll in a doll's house. Torvald's little terms of endearment (squirrel, lark, spendthrift, featherbrain) all serve to create a relationship in which he is wise, important, and dignified, while she is supportive, childish, and scatterbrained. Yet there is little that is pernicious here. At the play's beginning Torvald and Nora are a very ordinary couple, working jointly to sustain the illusion of contentment. They both play-act in their doll's house. Nora goes out of her way to seem coyly feminine; Torvald complements her performance with his solemn masculinity. While Torvald remains detached and dignified in his study, Nora romps with the children, whom she calls her dollies. That she and the children decide to play hide-and-seek, with Nora being the first to hide, is nicely symbolic of her broader concealment and deception. And yet, for all that, Nora and Torvald are happy in their pretenses, or so it seems.

Soon, however, we begin to realize how little truthfulness and sharing exists between them. Nora is forever concealing things from Torvald (her borrowing, her reasons for wanting a Christmas gift of money, her taste for macaroons, her work as a copyist). Torvald is supercilious, scornful of women, and far too concerned about his dignity. Moreover, their ethical beliefs are completely at odds. Nora would be perfectly happy living on borrowed money; Torvald would be ashamed to spend what he did not earn. Nora cares little for the fate of the strangers who might lend her money; Torvald, a banker, believes strongly in protecting the interests of creditors. Having experienced suffering herself, Nora is able to empathize with the misfortunes of Christina and even Krogstad; believing that we are all wholly responsible for our own fates, Torvald is often selfish and callous.

The arrival in Act I of Nora's childhood friend Christina eventually disrupts the illusion of harmony between Torvald and Nora, in part because Nora indulges in that very human folly of confiding in a friend. Nora tells her troubles to Christina and explains just how much she has worked and sacrificed to secure the illegal loan that saved her husband's life. In doing so, she reveals that she doesn't wish everyone to think of her as a carefree little child, yet there is much childishness in her. She doesn't know how much of her loan she has paid off or care about legal niceties. What she really enjoys is the prospect that her husband's new job will finally allow her to spend money freely.

Christina is, of course, Nora's foil, just as Krogstad is Torvald's foil. Christina has aged; Nora has not. Christina has remained childless; Nora is a child among her children. Christina has realized that her first marriage was empty; Nora has yet to do so. But they are very similar too. Nora has committed perjury and forgery in order to save her family, and Christina too has committed a form of perjury by marrying a man she knew she didn't love.

Similarly, Torvald and Krogstad are carefully contrasted. Where Torvald is a rising manager, Krogstad is a lowly clerk. Where Torvald makes his living through "honest" banking; Krogstad earns extra cash through usury. Ironically, Torvald himself prompts us to compare the two by insisting that "Krogstad [has] been poisoning his own children for years past by a life of lies and hypocrisy." Little does he know that his own life is even more deeply rooted in hypocrisy than that of his unfortunate clerk.

In contrast to the sham marriage of Nora and Torvald, Ibsen shows us the development of a stronger and more truthful union between Krogstad and Christina. By the middle of Act III, Ibsen's purposes grow clear. Christina and Krogstad have lived lives of dishonesty and deception in the past, but in their new relationship they are committed to unflinching honesty, to each other and to others. They are, as they describe themselves, "two shipwrecked people" clinging to one another in an effort to survive. In their own commitment to clear-sightedness, they demand it of others. When Krogstad contemplates asking Torvald to return unopened the letter exposing Nora's illegal borrowing, Christina stops him, saying "These two must come to a full understanding. They must have done with all these shifts and subterfuges."

Juxtaposed to this scene of honesty between Christina and Krogstad, we have a scene that shows the deceptive dishonesty of Nora and Torvald on the evening of the dance. Torvald tries to exude charm in his conversation with Christina when he really thinks her a dreadful bore; he is effusive in greeting Dr. Rank when he really wonders why the man is intruding upon his romantic evening. In watching Nora dance the Tarantella and pretend to passions that she doesn't feel, Torvald is filled with secret sexual fantasies that heighten his lust for her. And then Torvald opens the mail and finally learns from Krogstad what his wife has done and who she is. In dreading these revelations, Nora at first fantasizes about a tragically romantic suicide in the "black, icy water." Then, even more unrealistically she begins to anticipate the "miracle" in which her husband saves her by shouldering the blame for her misdeed.

When the truth finally does emerge, there is no romance. Torvald angrily demands an end to her "melodramatic airs," but he doesn't know how painful the end of their play-acting will be. His first reactions are selfish, but because of that, they are also human—and understandable. He immediately justifies himself and blames everything on Nora, quite the reverse of the miracle she had desired. His most disgraceful moment comes when he opens Krogstad's second letter (containing the forged loan papers) and, thinking nothing of her feelings, announces, "I am saved. Nora, I am saved!"

Even in attempting to explain his selfishness and make light of Nora's errors, he unwittingly points out what is false and even humiliating to Nora in their relationship. He thinks there is something "indescribably sweet and soothing to a man in forgiving his wife. . . . She becomes his property again in a double sense"—both a wife and an erring child. And when she agrees that she has been no more than a child, he exclaims that "playtime is over" and schooltime has just begun. This is perhaps true, but he is not to be the teacher. Nora at last gets out of her costume and insists on having a truthful, mature conversation. She sees the distinction between lightheartedness and happiness and demands a chance to grow into the latter. Such growth requires seriousness, independence, competence, and self-knowledge. She realizes that only absolute freedom for both husband and wife can give rise to a true marriage—and she slams the door on the false one behind her.

A Selective Bibliography on *A Doll's House*

Archer, William. "Character and Psychology." *Play-making: A Manual of Craftsmanship.* New York: Dodd, 1937. 245–61.

Baruch, Elaine H. "Ibsen's *Doll House:* A Myth for Our Time." *Yale Review* 69 (1980): 374–87.

Bradbrook, Muriel C. *Ibsen, the Norwegian: A Revaluation.* 1948. Hamden, Conn.: Archon, 1966. 116–21.

Clurman, Harold. *Ibsen.* New York: Collier, 1977.

Dukore, Bernard F. "Doors in the Doll House." *Theatre History Studies 9* (1989): 37–40.

———. "Karl Marx's Youngest Daughter and 'A Doll's House.' " *Theatre Journal* 42.3 (1990): 308–22.

———. *Money and Politics in Ibsen, Shaw, and Brecht.* Columbia: Missouri UP, 1980.

Durbach, Errol. *A Doll's House: Ibsen's Myth of Transformation.* Boston: Twayne, 1991.

Ganz, Arthur F. "Miracle and Vine Leaves: An Ibsen Play Rewrought." *PMLA* 94 (1979): 9–21.

Gilman, Richard. *The Making of Modern Drama.* New York: Farrar, 1972.

Gray, Ronald D. *Ibsen, A Dissenting View: A Study of the Last Twelve Plays.* Cambridge, Eng.: Cambridge UP, 1977.

Hardwick, Elizabeth. "Ibsen's Women." *Seduction and Betrayal: Women and Literature.* New York: Random House, 1974. 31–83.

Hornby, Richard. "Ibsen's *A Doll House.*" *Script into Performance: A Structuralist View of Play Production.* Austin: U of Texas P, 1977. 153–72.

———. *Patterns in Ibsen's Middle Plays.* Lewistown, PA: Bucknell UP, 1981.

Ibsen, Henrik. "*A Doll's House:* Notes for the Modern Tragedy." *Playwrights on Play-writing.* Ed. Toby Cole. New York: Hill & Wang, 1960. 151–54.

Johnston, Brian. *The Ibsen Cycle: The Design of the Plays from Pillars of Society to When We Dead Awaken.* Boston: Twayne, 1975.

———. *Text and Supertext in Ibsen's Drama.* University Park: Pennsylvania State UP, 1989. 137–64.

Kiberd, Declan. *Men and Feminism in Modern Literature.* New York: St. Martin's, 1985. 61–84.

Northam, John R. *Ibsen: A Critical Study.* Cambridge, Eng.: Cambridge UP, 1973.

———. *Ibsen's Dramatic Method.* 2nd ed. Oslo: Norwegian UP, 1971. 15–38.

Rogers, Katharine M. "A Woman Appreciates Ibsen." *Centennial Review* 18 (1974): 91–108.

Rosenberg, Marvin. "Ibsen vs. Ibsen, or: Two Versions of *A Doll's House.*" *Modern Drama* 12 (1969): 187–96.

Shafer, Yvonne. *Approaches to Teaching Ibsen's* A Doll House. *Approaches to Teaching Masterpieces of World Lit.* 7. New York: MLA, 1985.

Shaw, George Bernard. *The Quintessence of Ibsenism.* New York: Hill & Wang, 1958. 77–81.

Spacks, Patricia M. "Confrontation and Escape in Two Social Dramas." *Modern Drama* 11 (1968): 61–72.

Styan, J. L. "Ibsen's Contribution to Realism." *Modern Drama in Theory and Practice.* Cambridge, Eng: Cambridge UP, 1980. Vol. 1. 17–30.

Templeton, Joan. "The *Doll House* Backlash: Criticism, Feminism, and Ibsen." *PMLA* 104 (1989): 28–40.

Tufts, Carol Strongin. "Recasting *A Doll House:* Narcissism as Character Motivation in Ibsen's Play." *Comparative Drama* 20.2 (1986): 140–59.

Valency, Maurice. *The Flower and the Castle: An Introduction to Modern Drama.* New York: Macmillan, 1963. 149–59.

Weigand, H. J. *The Modern Ibsen: A Reconsideration.* 1925. New York: Dutton, 1960. 26–75.

Zucker, A. A. "The Forgery in Ibsen's *Doll House.*" *Scandinavian Studies* 17 (1943): 309–13.

August Strindberg (1849–1912)

MISS JULIA

A NATURALISTIC TRAGEDY

Translated by Edwin Björkman

CHARACTERS

MISS JULIA, *twenty-five*
JEAN, *a valet, aged thirty*
CHRISTINE, *a cook, aged thirty-five*

The action takes place on Midsummer Eve, in the kitchen of the count's country house.

A large kitchen: the ceiling and the side walls are hidden by draperies and hangings. The rear wall runs diagonally across the stage, from the left side and away from the spectators. On this wall, to the left, there are two shelves full of utensils made of copper, iron, and tin. The shelves are trimmed with scalloped paper.

A little to the right may be seen three-fourths of the big arched doorway leading to the outside. It has double glass doors, through which are seen a fountain with a cupid, lilac shrubs in bloom, and the tops of some Lombardy poplars.

On the left side of the stage is seen the corner of a big cookstove built of glazed bricks; also a part of the smoke-hood above it.

From the right protrudes one end of the servants' dining-table of white pine, with a few chairs about it.

The stove is dressed with bundled branches of birch. Twigs of juniper are scattered on the floor.

On the table end stands a big Japanese spice pot full of lilac blossoms.

An icebox, a kitchen-table, and a wash-stand.

Above the door hangs a big old-fashioned bell on a steel spring, and the mouthpiece of a speaking-tube appears at the left of the door.

CHRISTINE is standing by the stove, frying something in a pan. She has on a dress of light-colored cotton, which she has covered up with a big kitchen apron.

JEAN enters, dressed in livery and carrying a pair of big, spurred riding-boots, which he places on the floor in such manner that they remain visible to the spectators.

JEAN. Tonight Miss Julia is crazy again; absolutely crazy.
CHRISTINE. So you're back again?
JEAN. I took the count to the station, and when I came back by the barn, I went in and had a dance, and there I saw the young lady leading the dance with the gamekeeper. But when she caught sight of me, she rushed right up to me and asked me to dance the ladies' waltz with her. And ever since she's been waltzing like—well, I never saw the like of it. She's crazy!
CHRISTINE. And has always been, but never the way it's been this last fortnight, since her engagement was broken.

10 JEAN.   Well, what kind of a story was that anyhow? He's a fine fellow, isn't he, although he isn't rich? Ugh, but they're so full of notions. [*Sits down at the end of the table.*] It's peculiar anyhow, that a young lady—hm!—would rather stay at home with the servants—don't you think?—than go with her father to their relatives!

CHRISTINE.   Oh, I guess she feels sort of embarrassed by that rumpus with her fellow.

JEAN.   Quite likely. But there was some backbone to that man just the same. Do you know how it happened, Christine? I saw it, although I didn't care to let on.

20 CHRISTINE.   No, did you?

JEAN.   Sure, I did. They were in the stable-yard one evening, and the young lady was training him, as she called it. Do you know what that meant? She made him leap over her horse-whip the way you teach a dog to jump. Twice he jumped and got a cut each time. The third time he took the whip out of her hand and broke it into a thousand bits. And then he got out.

CHRISTINE.   So that's the way it happened! You don't say!

JEAN.   Yes, that's how that thing happened. Well, Christine, what have you got that's tasty?

CHRISTINE [*serves from the pan and puts the plate before* JEAN].   Oh, just some
30   kidney which I cut out of the veal roast.

JEAN [*smelling the food*].   Fine! That's my great *délice.*[1] [*Feeling the plate.*] But you might have warmed the plate.

CHRISTINE.   Well, if you ain't harder to please than the count himself! [*Pulls his hair playfully.*]

JEAN [*irritated*].   Don't pull my hair! You know how sensitive I am.

CHRISTINE.   Well, well, it was nothing but a love pull, you know.

[*JEAN eats.* CHRISTINE *opens a bottle of beer.*]

JEAN.   Beer—on Midsummer Eve? No, thank you! Then I have something better myself. [*Opens a table-drawer and takes out a bottle of claret with yellow cap.*] Yellow seal, mind you! Give me a glass—and you use those with stems
40   when you drink it *pure.*

CHRISTINE [*returns to the stove and puts a small pan on the fire*].   Heaven preserve her that gets you for a husband, Mr. Finicky!

JEAN.   Oh, rot! You'd be glad enough to get a smart fellow like me. And I guess it hasn't hurt you that they call me your beau. [*Tasting the wine.*] Good! Pretty good! Just a tiny bit too cold. [*He warms the glass with his hands.*] We got this at Dijon. It cost us four francs per litre, not counting the bottle. And there was the duty besides. What is it you're cooking—with that infernal smell?

CHRISTINE.   Oh, it's some deviltry the young lady is going to give Diana.

50 JEAN.   You should choose your words with more care, Christine. But why should you be cooking for a bitch on a holiday eve like this? Is she sick?

CHRISTINE.   Ye-es, she is sick. She's been running around with the gatekeeper's pug—and now's there's trouble—and the young lady just won't hear of it.

---

[1] "Delight."

JEAN.   The young lady is too stuck up in some ways and not proud enough in others—just as was the countess while she lived. She was most at home in the kitchen and among the cows, but she would never drive with only one horse. She wore her cuffs till they were dirty, but she had to have cuff buttons with a coronet on them. And speaking of the young lady, she

60   doesn't take proper care of herself and her person. I might say even that she's lacking in refinement. Just now, when she was dancing in the barn, she pulled the gamekeeper away from Anna and asked him herself to come and dance with her. We wouldn't act in that way. But that's just how it is: when upper-class people want to demean themselves, then they grow—mean! But she's splendid! Magnificent! Oh, such shoulders! And— and so on!

CHRISTINE.   Oh, well, don't brag too much! I've heard Clara talking, who tends to her dressing.

JEAN.   Pooh, Clara! You're always jealous of each other. I, who have been out

70   riding with her—And then the way she dances!

CHRISTINE.   Say, Jean, won't you dance with me when I'm done?

JEAN.   Of course I will.

CHRISTINE.   Do you promise?

JEAN.   Promise? When I say so, I'll do it. Well, here's thanks for the good food. It tasted fine! [*Puts the cork back into the bottle.*]

JULIA [*appears in the doorway, speaking to somebody on the outside*].   I'll be back in a minute. You go right on in the meantime.

[JEAN *slips the bottle into the table-drawer and rises respectfully.*]

JULIA [*enters and goes over to* CHRISTINE *by the wash-stand*].   Well, is it done yet?

[CHRISTINE *signs to her that* JEAN *is present.*]

JEAN [*gallantly*].   The ladies are having secrets, I believe.

80 JULIA [*strikes him in the face with her handkerchief*].   That's for you, Mr. Pry!

JEAN.   Oh, what a delicious odor that violet has!

JULIA [*with coquetry*].   Impudent! So you know something about perfumes also? And know pretty well how to dance—Now don't peep! Go away!

JEAN [*with polite impudence*].   Is it some kind of witches' broth the ladies are cooking on Midsummer Eve— something to tell fortunes by and bring out the lucky star in which one's future love is seen?

JULIA [*sharply*].   If you can see that, you'll have good eyes, indeed! [*To* CHRIS-TINE.] Put it in a pint bottle and cork it well. Come and dance a *schottische*[2] with me now, Jean.

90 JEAN [*hesitatingly*].   I don't want to be impolite, but I had promised to dance with Christine this time—

JULIA.   Well, she can get somebody else—can't you, Christine? Won't you let me borrow Jean from you?

CHRISTINE.   That isn't for me to say. When Miss Julia is so gracious, it isn't for him to say no. You just go along, and be thankful for the honor, too!

JEAN.   Frankly speaking, but not wishing to offend in any way, I cannot help wondering if it's wise for Miss Julia to dance twice in succession with the

---

[2] A Scottish dance resembling a polka.

same partner, especially as the people here are not slow in throwing out hints—

100 JULIA [*flaring up*].   What is that? What kind of hints? What do you mean?

JEAN [*submissively*].   As you don't want to understand, I have to speak more plainly. It don't look well to prefer one servant to all the rest who are expecting to be honored in the same unusual way—

JULIA.   Prefer! What ideas! I'm surprised! I, the mistress of the house, deign to honor this dance with my presence, and when it so happens that I actually want to dance, I want to dance with one who knows how to lead, so that I am not made ridiculous.

JEAN.   As you command, Miss Julia! I am at your service!

JULIA [*softened*].   Don't take it as a command. Tonight we should enjoy our-
110   selves as a lot of happy people, and all rank should be forgotten. Now give me your arm. Don't be afraid, Christine! I'll return your beau to you!

[JEAN *offers his arm to* MISS JULIA *and leads her out*.]

PANTOMIME

Must be acted as if the actress were really alone in the place. When necessary she turns her back to the public. She should not look in the direction of the spectators, and she should not hurry as if fearful that they might become impatient.

CHRISTINE *is alone. A* schottische *tune played on a violin is heard faintly in the distance.*

While humming the tune, CHRISTINE *clears off the table after* JEAN, *washes the plate at the kitchen-table, wipes it, and puts it away in a cupboard.*

Then she takes off her apron, pulls out a small mirror from one of the table-drawers and leans it against the flower jar on the table; lights a tallow candle and heats a hairpin, which she uses to curl her front hair.

Then she goes to the door and stands there listening. Returns to the table. Discovers the handkerchief which MISS JULIA *has left behind, picks it up, and smells it, spreads it out absent-mindedly and begins to stretch it, smooth it, fold it up, and so forth.*

JEAN [*enters alone*].   Crazy, that's what she is! The way she dances! And the people stand behind the doors and grin at her. What do you think of it, Christine?

CHRISTINE.   Oh, she has her time now, and then she is always a little queer like that. But are you going to dance with me now?

JEAN.   You are not mad at me because I disappointed you?

CHRISTINE.   No!—Not for a little thing like that, you know! And also, I know my place—

120 JEAN [*putting his arm around her waist*].   You are a sensible girl, Christine, and I think you'll make a good wife—

JULIA [*enters and is unpleasantly surprised; speaks with forced gayety*].   Yes, you are a fine partner—running away from your lady!

JEAN.   On the contrary, Miss Julia. I have, as you see, looked up the one I deserted.

JULIA [*changing tone*].   Do you know, there is nobody that dances like you!— But why do you wear your livery on an evening like this? Take it off at once.

JEAN. Then I must ask you to step outside for a moment, as my black coat
130 is hanging right here.

[*Points toward the right and goes in that direction.*]

JULIA. Are you bashful on my account? Just to change a coat? Why don't you
go into your own room and come back again? Or, you can stay right here,
and I'll turn my back on you.
JEAN. With your permission, Miss Julia.

[*Goes further over to the right; one of his arms can be seen as he changes his coat.*]

JULIA [*to* CHRISTINE]. Are you and Jean engaged, that he's so familiar with
you?
CHRISTINE. Engaged? Well, in a way. We call it that.
JULIA. Call it?
CHRISTINE. Well, Miss Julia, you have had a fellow of your own, and—
140 JULIA. We were really engaged—
CHRISTINE. But it didn't come to anything just the same—

[JEAN *enters, dressed in black frock coat and black derby.*]

JULIA. *Très gentil, Monsieur Jean! Très gentil!*[3]
JEAN. *Vous voulez plaisanter, Madame!*[4]
JULIA. *Et vous voulez parler français!*[5] Where did you learn it?
JEAN. In Switzerland, while I worked as *sommelier*[6] in one of the big hotels at
Lucerne.
JULIA. But you look like a real gentleman in your frock coat! Charming! [*Sits
down at the table.*]
JEAN. Oh, you flatter me.
150 JULIA [*offended*]. Flatter—you!
JEAN. My natural modesty does not allow me to believe that you could be
paying genuine compliments to one like me, and so I dare to assume that
you are exaggerating, or, as we call it, flattering.
JULIA. Where did you learn to use your words like that? You must have been
to the theatre a great deal?
JEAN. That, too. I have been to a lot of places.
JULIA. But you were born in this neighbourhood?
JEAN. My father was a cotter[7] on the county attorney's property right by
here, and I can recall seeing you as a child, although you, of course, didn't
160 notice me.
JULIA. No, really!
JEAN. Yes, and I remember one time in particular—but of that I can't speak.
JULIA. Oh, yes, do! Why—just for once.
JEAN. No, really, I cannot do it now. Another time, perhaps.
JULIA. Another time is no time. It is as bad as that?

---

3 "Very fashionable, Monsieur Jean! Very fashionable!"
4 "You wish to jest, Madam!"
5 "And you wish to speak French!"
6 Wine steward.
7 One who lives in a cottage, a peasant.

JEAN.   It isn't bad, but it comes a little hard. Look at that one! [*Points to* CHRISTINE, *who has fallen asleep on a chair by the stove.*]

JULIA.   She'll make a pleasant wife. And perhaps she snores, too.

JEAN.   No, she doesn't, but she talks in her sleep.

170 JULIA [*cynically*].   How do you know?

JEAN [*insolently*].   I have heard it.

[*Pause during which they study each other.*]

JULIA.   Why don't you sit down?

JEAN.   It wouldn't be proper in your presence.

JULIA.   But if I order you to do it?

JEAN.   Then I obey.

JULIA.   Sit down, then!—But wait a moment! Can you give me something to drink first?

JEAN.   I don't know what we have got in the icebox. I fear it is nothing but beer.

180 JULIA.   And you call that nothing? My taste is so simple that I prefer it to wine.

JEAN [*takes a bottle of beer from the icebox and opens it; gets a glass and a plate from the cupboard, and serves the beer*].   Allow me!

JULIA.   Thank you. Don't you want some yourself?

JEAN.   I don't care very much for beer, but if it is a command, of course—

JULIA.   Command?—I should think a polite gentleman might keep his lady company.

JEAN.   Yes, that's the way it should be.

[*Opens another bottle and takes out a glass.*]

JULIA.   Drink my health now!

[JEAN *hesitates.*]

190 JULIA.   Are you bashful—a big, grown-up man?

JEAN [*kneels with mock solemnity and raises his glass*].   To the health of my liege lady!

JULIA.   Bravo!—And now you must also kiss my shoe in order to get it just right.

[JEAN *hesitates a moment; then he takes hold of her foot and touches it lightly with his lips.*]

JULIA.   Excellent! You should have been on the stage.

JEAN [*rising to his feet*].   This won't do any longer, Miss Julia. Somebody might see us.

JULIA.   What would that matter?

JEAN.   Oh, it would set the people talking—that's all! And if you only knew

200 how their tongues were wagging up there a while ago—

JULIA.   What did they have to say? Tell me—Sit down now!

JEAN [*sits down*].   I don't want to hurt you, but they were using expressions—which cast reflections of a kind that—oh, you know it yourself! You are not a child, and when a lady is seen alone with a man, drinking—no matter if he's only a servant—and at night—then—

JULIA.   Then what? And besides, we are not alone. Isn't Christine with us?

JEAN.   Yes—asleep!

JULIA.   Then I'll wake her. [*Rising.*] Christine, are you asleep?

CHRISTINE [*in her sleep*].   Blub-blub-blub-blub!

210 JULIA.   Christine!—Did you ever see such a sleeper.

CHRISTINE [*in her sleep*].   The count's boots are polished—put on the coffee— yes, yes, yes—my—my—pooh!

JULIA [*pinches her nose*].   Can't you wake up?

JEAN [*sternly*].   You shouldn't bother those that sleep.

JULIA [*sharply*].   What's that?

JEAN.   One who has stood by the stove all day has a right to be tired at night. And sleep should be respected.

JULIA [*changing tone*].   It is fine to think like that, and it does you honor—I thank you for it. [*Gives* JEAN *her hand.*] Come now and pick some lilacs for
220 me.

[*During the following scene* CHRISTINE *wakes up. She moves as if still asleep and goes out to the right in order to go to bed.*]

JEAN.   With you, Miss Julia?

JULIA.   With me!

JEAN.   But it won't do! Absolutely not!

JULIA.   I can't understand what you are thinking of. You couldn't possibly imagine—

JEAN.   No, not I, but the people.

JULIA.   What? That I am fond of the valet?

JEAN.   I am not at all conceited, but such things have happened—and to the people nothing is sacred.

230 JULIA.   You are an aristocrat, I think.

JEAN.   Yes, I am.

JULIA.   And I am stepping down—

JEAN.   Take my advice, Miss Julia, don't step down. Nobody will believe you did it on purpose. The people will always say that you fell down.

JULIA.   I think better of the people than you do. Come and see if I am not right. Come along! [*She ogles him.*]

JEAN   You're mighty queer, do you know!

JULIA.   Perhaps. But so are you. And for that matter, everything is queer. Life, men, everything—just a mush that floats on top of the water until it
240 sinks, sinks down! I have a dream that comes back to me ever so often. And just now I am reminded of it. I have climbed to the top of a column and sit there without being able to tell how to get down again. I get dizzy when I look down, and I must get down, but I haven't the courage to jump off. I cannot hold on, and I am longing to fall, and yet I don't fall. But there will be no rest for me until I get down, down on the ground. And if I did reach the ground, I should want to get still further down, into the ground itself—Have you ever felt like that?

JEAN.   No, my dream is that I am lying under a tall tree in a dark wood. I want to get up, up to the top, so that I can look out over the smiling landscape, where the sun is shining, and so that I can rob the nest in which
250 lie the golden eggs. And I climb and climb, but the trunk is so thick and smooth, and it is so far to the first branch. But I know that if I could only

reach that first branch, then I should go right on to the top as on a ladder. I have not reached it yet, but I am going to, if it only be in my dreams.

JULIA.   Here I am chattering to you about dreams! Come along! Only into the park!

[*She offers her arm to him, and they go toward the door.*]

JEAN.   We must sleep on nine midsummer flowers tonight, Miss Julia—then our dreams will come true.

[*They turn around in the doorway, and* JEAN *puts one hand up to his eyes.*]

JULIA.   Let me see what you have got in your eye.
260 JEAN.   Oh, nothing—just some dirt—it will soon be gone.
JULIA.   It was my sleeve that rubbed against it. Sit down and let me help you. [*Takes him by the arm and makes him sit down; takes hold of his head and bends it backwards; tries to get out the dirt with a corner of her handkerchief.*] Sit still now, absolutely still! [*Slaps him on the hand.*] Well, can't you do as I say? I think you are shaking—a big, strong fellow like you! [*Feels his biceps.*] And with such arms!
JEAN [*ominously*].   Miss Julia!
JULIA.   Yes, Monsieur Jean.
JEAN.   *Attention! Je ne suis qu' un homme.*[8]
270 JULIA.   Can't you sit still!—There now! Now it's gone. Kiss my hand now, and thank me.
JEAN [*rising*].   Miss Julia, listen to me. Christine has gone to bed now—Won't you listen to me?
JULIA.   Kiss my hand first.
JEAN.   Listen to me!
JULIA.   Kiss my hand first!
JEAN.   All right, but blame nobody but yourself!
JULIA.   For what?
JEAN.   For what? Are you still a mere child at twenty-five? Don't you know
280 that it is dangerous to play with fire?
JULIA.   Not for me. I am insured.
JEAN [*boldly*].   No, you are not. And even if you were, there are inflammable surroundings to be counted with.
JULIA.   That's you, I suppose?
JEAN.   Yes. Not because I am I, but because I am a young man—
JULIA.   Of handsome appearance—what an incredible conceit! A Don Juan, perhaps. Or a Joseph? Oh my soul, I think you are a Joseph!
JEAN.   Do you?
JULIA.   I fear it almost.

[JEAN *goes boldly up to her and takes her around the waist in order to kiss her.*]

290 JULIA [*gives him a cuff on the ear*].   Shame!
JEAN.   Was that in play or in earnest?
JULIA.   In earnest.

---

[8] "Watch out! I am only a man."

JEAN.   Then you were in earnest a moment ago also. Your playing is too serious, and that's the dangerous thing about it. Now I am tired of playing, and I ask to be excused in order to resume my work. The count wants his boots to be ready for him, and it is after midnight already.

JULIA.   Put away the boots.

JEAN.   No, it's my work, which I am bound to do. But I have not undertaken to be your playmate. It's something I can never become—I hold myself too good for it.

JULIA.   You're proud!

JEAN.   In some ways, and not in others.

JULIA.   Have you ever been in love?

JEAN.   We don't use that word. But I have been fond of a lot of girls, and once I was taken sick because I couldn't have the one I wanted: sick, you know, like those princes in the Arabian Nights who cannot eat or drink for sheer love.

JULIA.   Who was it?

[JEAN *remains silent.*]

JULIA.   Who was it?

JEAN.   You cannot make me tell you.

JULIA.   If I ask you as an equal, ask you as—a friend: who was it?

JEAN.   It was you.

JULIA [*sits down*].   How funny!

JEAN.   Yes, as you say—it was ludicrous. That was the story, you see, which I didn't want to tell you a while ago. But now I am going to tell it. Do you know how the world looks from below—no, you don't. No more than do hawks and falcons, of whom we never see the back because they are always floating about high up in the sky. I lived in the cotter's hovel, together with seven other children, and a pig—out there on the grey plain, where there isn't a single tree. But from our windows I could see the wall around the count's park, and apple-trees above it. That was the Garden of Eden, and many fierce angels were guarding it with flaming swords. Nevertheless I and some other boys found our way to the Tree of Life—now you despise me?

JULIA.   Oh, stealing apples is something all boys do.

JEAN.   You may say so now, but you despise me nevertheless. However— once I got into the Garden of Eden with my mother to weed the onion beds. Near by stood a Turkish pavillion, shaded by trees and covered with honeysuckle. I didn't know what it was used for, but I had never seen a more beautiful building. People went in and came out again, and one day the door was left wide open. I stole up and saw the walls covered with pictures of kings and emperors, and the windows were hung with red, fringed curtains—now you know what I mean. I—[*Breaks off a lilac sprig and holds it under* MISS JULIA's *nose.*]—I had never been inside the manor, and I had never seen anything but the church—and this was much finer. No matter where my thoughts ran, they returned always—to that place. And gradually a longing arose within me to taste the full pleasure of—*enfin!*[9] I sneaked in, looked and admired. Then I heard somebody coming. There

9 "Finally!"

340   was only one way out for fine people, but for me there was another, and
       I could do nothing else but choose it.

                     [JULIA *who has taken the lilac sprig, lets it drop on the table.*]

       JEAN.   Then I started to run, plunged through a hedge of raspberry bushes,
            chased right across a strawberry plantation, and came out on the terrace
            where the roses grow. There I caught sight of a pink dress and pair of
            white stockings—that was you! I crawled under a pile of weeds—right into
            it, you know—into stinging thistles and wet, ill-smelling dirt. And I saw
            you walking among the roses, and I thought: if it be possible for a robber
            to get into heaven and dwell with the angels, then it is strange that a
            cotter's child, here on God's own earth, cannot get into the park and play
            with the count's daughter.
350   JULIA [*sentimentally*].   Do you think all poor children have the same thoughts
            as you had in this case?
       JEAN [*hesitatingly at first; then with conviction*].   If *all* poor—yes—of course. Of
            course!
       JULIA.   It must be a dreadful misfortune to be poor.
       JEAN [*in a tone of deep distress and with rather exaggerated emphasis*].   Oh, Miss
            Julia! Oh!—A dog may lie on her ladyship's sofa; a horse may have his
            nose patted by the young lady's hand, but a servant—[*Changing his tone.*]—
            oh well, here and there you meet one made of different stuff, and he
            makes a way for himself in the world, but how often does it happen?—
360   However, do you know what I did? I jumped into the mill brook with my
            clothes on, and was pulled out, and got a licking. But the next Sunday,
            when my father and the rest of the people were going over to my grand-
            mother's, I fixed it so that I could stay at home. And then I washed myself
            with soap and hot water, and put on my best clothes, and went to church,
            where I could see you. I did see you, and went home determined to die.
            But I wanted to die beautifully and pleasantly, without any pain. And then
            I recalled that it was dangerous to sleep under an elder bush. We had a big
            one that was in full bloom. I robbed it of all its flowers, and then I put them
            in the big box where the oats were kept and lay down in them. Did you
370   ever notice the smoothness of oats? Soft to the touch as the skin of the
            human body! However, I pulled down the lid and closed my eyes—fell
            asleep and was waked up a very sick boy. But I didn't die, as you can see.
            What I wanted—that's more than I can tell. Of course, there was not the
            least hope of winning you—but you symbolized the hopelessness of trying
            to get out of the class into which I was born.
       JULIA.   You narrate splendidly, do you know! Did you ever go to school?
       JEAN.   A little. But I have read a lot of novels and gone to the theater a good
            deal. And besides, I have listened to the talk of better-class people, and
            from that I have learned most of all.
380   JULIA.   Do you stand around and listen to what we are saying?
       JEAN.   Of course! And I have heard a lot, too, when I was on the box of the
            carriage, or rowing the boat. Once I heard you, Miss Julia, and one of your
            girl friends—
       JULIA.   Oh!—What was it you heard then?
       JEAN.   Well, it wouldn't be easy to repeat. But I was rather surprised, and I

couldn't understand where you had learned all those words. Perhaps, at bottom, there isn't quite so much difference as they think between one kind of people and another.

JULIA.   You ought to be ashamed of yourself! We don't live as you do when
390   we are engaged.

JEAN [*looking hard at her*].   Is it so certain?—Well, Miss Julia, it won't pay to make yourself out so very innocent to me—

JULIA.   The man on whom I bestowed my love was a scoundrel.

JEAN.   That's what you always say—afterwards.

JULIA.   Always?

JEAN.   Always, I believe, for I have heard the same words used several times before, on similar occasions.

JULIA.   What occasions?

JEAN.   Like the one of which we were speaking. The last time—

400   JULIA [*rising*].   Stop! I don't want to hear any more!

JEAN.   Nor did *she*—curiously enough! Well, then I ask permission to go to bed.

JULIA [*gently*].   Go to bed on Midsummer Eve?

JEAN.   Yes, for dancing with that mob out there has really no attraction for me.

JULIA.   Get the key to the boat and take me out on the lake—I want to watch the sunrise.

JEAN.   Would that be wise?

JULIA.   It sounds as if you were afraid of your reputation.

410   JEAN.   Why not? I don't care to be made ridiculous, and I don't care to be discharged without a recommendation, for I am trying to get on in the world. And then I feel myself under a certain obligation to Christine.

JULIA.   So it's Christine now—

JEAN.   Yes, but it's you also—Take my advice and go to bed!

JULIA.   Am I to obey you?

JEAN.   For once—and for your own sake! The night is far gone. Sleepiness makes us drunk, and the head grows hot. Go to bed! And besides—if I am not mistaken—I can hear the crowd coming this way to look for me. And if we are found together here, you are lost!

420   CHORUS [*is heard approaching*].
Through the fields come two ladies a-walking,
Treederee-derallah, treederee-derah.
And one has her shoes full of water,
Treederee-derallah-lah.

They're talking of hundreds of dollars,
Treederee-derallah, treederee-derah.
But have not between them a dollar
Treederee-derallah-lah.

This wreath I give you gladly,
430   Treederee-derallah, treederee-derah.
But love another madly,
Treederee-derallah-lah.

JULIA. I know the people, and I love them, just as they love me. Let them come, and you'll see.

JEAN. No, Miss Julia, they don't love you. They take your food and spit at your back. Believe me. Listen to me—can't you hear what they are singing?—No, don't pay any attention to it!

JULIA [*listening*]. What is it they are singing?

JEAN. Oh, something scurrilous. About you and me.

440 JULIA. How infamous! They ought to be ashamed! And the treachery of it!

JEAN. The mob is always cowardly. And in such a fight as this there is nothing to do but to run away.

JULIA. Run away? Where to? We cannot get out. And we cannot go into Christine's room.

JEAN. Oh, we cannot? Well, into my room, then! Necessity knows no law. And you can trust me, for I am your true and frank and respectful friend.

JULIA. But think only—think if they should look for you in there!

JEAN. I shall bolt the door. And if they try to break it open, I'll shoot!—Come! [*Kneeling before her.*] Come!

450 JULIA [*meaningly*]. And you promise me—?

JEAN. I swear!

[MISS JULIA *goes quickly out to the right.* JEAN *follows her eagerly.*]

BALLET

The peasants enter. They are decked out in their best and carry flowers in their hats. A fiddler leads them. On the table they place a barrel of small-beer and a keg of "bränn-vin," or white Swedish whiskey, both of them decorated with wreathes woven out of leaves. First they drink. Then they form in ring and sing and dance to the melody heard before:
"Through the fields come two ladies a-walking."
The dance finished, they leave singing.

JULIA [*Enters alone. On seeing the disorder in the kitchen, she claps her hands together. Then she takes out a powder-puff and begins to powder her face.*]

JEAN [*enters in a state of exaltation*]. There you see! And you heard, didn't you? Do you think it possible to stay here?

JULIA. No, I don't think so. But what are we to do?

JEAN. Run away, travel, far away from here.

JULIA. Travel? Yes—but where?

JEAN. To Switzerland, the Italian lakes—you have never been there?

JULIA. No. Is the country beautiful?

JEAN. Oh! Eternal summer! Orange trees! Laurels! Oh!

460 JULIA. But then—what are we to do down there?

JEAN. I'll start a hotel, everything first class, including the customers.

JULIA. Hotel?

JEAN. That's the life, I tell you! Constantly new faces and new languages. Never a minute free for nerves or brooding. No trouble about what to do—for the work is calling to be done: night and day, bells that ring, trains that whistle, buses that come and go; and gold pieces raining on the counter all the time. That's the life for you!

JULIA.   Yes, that is life. And I?

JEAN.   The mistress of everything, the chief ornament of the house. With
470   your looks—and your manners—oh, success will be assured! Enormous!
You'll sit like a queen in the office and keep the slaves going by the touch
of an electric button. The guests will pass in review before your throne and
timidly deposit their treasures on your table. You cannot imagine how
people tremble when a bill is presented to them—I'll salt the items, and
you'll sugar them with your sweetest smiles. Oh, let us get away from
here—[*Pulling a time-table from his pocket.*]—at once, with the next train!
We'll be in Malmö at 6:30; in Hamburg at 8:40 to-morrow morning; in
Frankfort and Basel a day later. And to reach Como by way of the St.
Gotthard it will take us—let me see—three days. Three days!

480 JULIA.   All that is all right. But you must give me some courage—Jean. Tell
me that you love me. Come and take me in your arms.

JEAN [*reluctantly*].   I should like to—but I don't dare. Not in this house again.
I love you—beyond doubt—or, can you doubt it, Miss Julia?

JULIA [*with modesty and true womanly feeling*].   Miss?—Call me Julia. Between
us there can be no barriers hereafter. Call me Julia!

JEAN [*disturbed*].   I cannot! There will be barriers between us as long as we
stay in this house—there is the past, and there is the count—and I have
never met another person for whom I felt such respect. If I only catch sight
of his gloves on a chair I feel small. If I only hear that bell up there, I jump
490   like a shy horse. And even now, when I see his boots standing there so stiff
and perky, it is as if something made my back bend. [*Kicking at the boots.*]
It's nothing but superstition and tradition hammered into us from childhood—but it can be as easily forgotten again. Let us only get to another
country, where they have a republic, and you'll see them bend their backs
double before my liveried porter. You see, backs have to be bent, but not
mine. I wasn't born to that kind of thing. There's better stuff in me—
character—and if I only get hold of the first branch, you'll see me do some
climbing. Today I am a valet, but next year I'll be a hotel owner. In ten
years I can live on the money I have made, and then I'll go to Romania
500   and get myself an order. And I may—note that I say *may*—end my days as
a count.

JULIA.   Splendid, splendid!

JEAN.   Yes, in Romania the title of count can be had for cash, and so you'll
be a countess after all. My countess!

JULIA.   What do I care about all I now cast behind me! Tell me that you love
me: otherwise—yes, what am I otherwise?

JEAN.   I will tell you so a thousand times—later. But not here. And above all,
no sentimentality, or everything will be lost. We must look at the matter in
cold blood, like sensible people. [*Takes out a cigar, cuts off the point, and
510   lights it.*] Sit down there now, and I'll sit here, and then we'll talk as if
nothing had happened.

JULIA [*in despair*].   Good Lord! Have you then no feelings at all?

JEAN.   I? No one is more full of feeling than I am. But I know how to control
myself.

JULIA.   A while ago you kissed my shoe—and now!

JEAN [*severely*].   Yes, that was then. Now we have other things to think of.

JULIA.   Don't speak harshly to me!

JEAN.   No, but sensibly. One folly has been committed—don't let us commit
any more! The count may be here at any moment, and before he comes
520   our fate must be settled. What do you think of my plans for the future? Do
you approve of them?

JULIA.   They seem acceptable, on the whole. But there is one question: a big
undertaking of that kind will require a big capital—have you got it?

JEAN [chewing his cigar].   I? Of course! I have my expert knowledge, my vast
experience, my familiarity with several languages. That's the very best
kind of capital, I should say.

JULIA.   But it won't buy you a railroad ticket even.

JEAN.   That's true enough. And that is just why I am looking for a backer to
advance the needful cash.

530   JULIA.   Where could you get one all of a sudden?

JEAN.   It's for you to find him if you want to become my partner.

JULIA.   I cannot do it, and I have nothing myself. [Pause.]

JEAN.   Well, then that's off—

JULIA.   And—

JEAN.   Everything remains as before.

JULIA.   Do you think I am going to stay under this roof as your concubine?
Do you think I'll let the people point their fingers at me? Do you think I
can look my father in the face after this? No, take me away from here,
from all this humiliation and disgrace!—Oh, what have I done? My God,
540   my God! [Breaks into tears.]

JEAN.   So we have got around to that tune now!—What you have done?
Nothing but what many others have done before you.

JULIA [crying hysterically].   And now you're despising me!—I'm falling, I'm
falling!

JEAN.   Fall down to me, and I'll lift you up again afterwards.

JULIA.   What horrible power drew me to you? Was it the attraction which the
strong exercises on the weak—the one who is rising on one who is falling?
Or was it love? This—love! Do you know what love is?

JEAN.   I? Well, I should say so! Don't you think I have been there before?

550   JULIA.   Oh, the language you use, and the thoughts you think!

JEAN.   Well, that's the way I was brought up, and that's the way I am. Don't
get nerves now and play the exquisite, for now one of us is just as good as
the other. Look here, my girl, let me treat you to a glass of something
superfine.

[He opens the table-drawer, takes out the wine bottle and fills up two glasses that have
already been used.]

JULIA.   Where did you get that wine?

JEAN.   In the cellar.

JULIA.   My father's Burgundy!

JEAN.   Well, isn't it good enough for a son-in-law?

JULIA.   And I am drinking beer—I!

560   JEAN.   It shows merely that I have better taste than you.

JULIA.   Thief!

JEAN.   Do you mean to tell on me?

JULIA.   Oh, oh! The accomplice of a house thief! Have I been drunk, or have

I been dreaming all this night? Midsummer Eve! The feast of innocent
games—

JEAN.   Innocent—hm!

JULIA [*walking back and forth*].   Can there be another human being on earth
so unhappy as I am at this moment?

JEAN.   But why should you be? After such a conquest? Think of Christine in
570   there. Don't you think she has feelings also?

JULIA.   I thought so a while ago, but I don't think so any longer. No, a menial
is a menial—

JEAN.   And a whore a whore!

JULIA [*on her knees, with folded hands*].   O God in heaven, make an end of this
wretched life! Take me out of the filth into which I am sinking! Save me!
Save me!

JEAN.   I cannot deny that I feel sorry for you. When I was lying among the
onions and saw you up there among the roses—I'll tell you now—I had the
same nasty thoughts that all boys have.

580   JULIA.   And you who wanted to die for my sake!

JEAN.   Among the oats. That was nothing but talk.

JULIA.   Lies in other words!

JEAN [*beginning to feel sleepy*].   Just about. I think I read the story in a paper,
and it was about a chimney-sweep who crawled into a wood-box full of
lilacs because a girl had brought suit against him for not supporting her
kid—

JULIA.   So that's the sort you are!

JEAN.   Well, I had to think of something—for it's the high-faluting stuff that
the women bite on.

590   JULIA.   Scoundrel!

JEAN.   Rot!

JULIA.   And now you have seen the back of the hawk—

JEAN.   Well, I don't know—

JULIA.   And I was to be the first branch—

JEAN.   But the branch was rotten—

JULIA.   I was to be the sign in front of the hotel—

JEAN.   And I the hotel.—

JULIA.   Sit at your counter, and lure your customers, and doctor your bills—

JEAN.   No, that I should have done myself—

600   JULIA.   That a human soul can be so steeped in dirt!

JEAN.   Well, wash it off!

JULIA.   You lackey, you menial, stand up when I talk to you!

JEAN.   You lackey-love, you mistress of a menial—shut up and get out of
here! You're the right one to come and tell me that I am vulgar. People
of my kind would never in their lives act as vulgarly as you have acted
tonight. Do you think any servant girl would go for a man as you did? Did
you ever see a girl of my class throw herself at anybody in that way? I have
never seen the like of it except among beasts and prostitutes.

JULIA [*crushed*].   That's right: strike me, step on me—I haven't deserved any
610   better! I am a wretched creature. But help me! Help me out of this, if there
be any way to do so!

JEAN [*in a milder tone*].   I don't want to lower myself by a denial of my share
in the honor of seducing. But do you think a person in my place would

have dared to raise his eyes to you, if the invitation to do so had not come
from yourself? I am still sitting here in a state of utter surprise—

JULIA. And pride—

JEAN. Yes, why not? Although I must confess that the victory was too easy to
bring with it any real intoxication.

JULIA. Strike me some more!

620 JEAN [*rising*]. No! Forgive me instead what I have been saying. I don't want
to strike one who is disarmed, and least of all a lady. On one hand I cannot
deny that it has given me pleasure to discover that what has dazzled us
below is nothing but catgold;[10] that the hawk is simply grey on the back
also; that there is powder on the tender cheek; that there may be black
borders on the polished nails; and that the handkerchief may be dirty,
although it smells of perfume. But on the other hand it hurts me to have
discovered that what I was striving to reach is neither better nor more
genuine. It hurts me to see you sinking so low that you are far beneath
your own cook—it hurts me as it hurts to see the Fall flowers beaten down
630 by the rain and turned into mud.

JULIA. You speak as if you were already above me?

JEAN. Well, so I am. Don't you see: I could have made a countess of you, but
you could never make me a count.

JULIA. But I am born of a count, and that's more than you can ever achieve.

JEAN. That's true. But I might be the father of counts—if—

JULIA. But you are a thief—and I am not.

JEAN. Thief is not the worst. There are other things still farther down. And
then, when I serve in a house, I regard myself in a sense as a member of
the family, as a child of the house, and you don't call it theft when children
640 pick a few of the berries that load down the vines. [*His passion is aroused
once more.*] Miss Julia, you are a magnificent woman, and far too good for
one like me. You were swept along by a spell of intoxication, and now you
want to cover up your mistake by making yourself believe that you are in
love with me. Well, you are not, unless possibly my looks might tempt
you—in which case your love is no better than mine. I could never rest
satisfied with having you care for nothing in me but the mere animal, and
your love I can never win.

JULIA. Are you so sure of that?

JEAN. You mean to say that it might be possible? That I might love you: yes,
650 without doubt—for you are beautiful, refined [*Goes up to her and takes hold
of her hand.*], educated, charming when you want to be so, and it is not
likely that the flame will ever burn out in a man who has once been set on
fire by you. [*Puts his arm around her waist.*] You are like burnt wine with
strong spices in it, and one of your kisses——

[*He tries to lead her away, but she frees herself gently from his hold.*]

JULIA. Leave me alone! In that way you cannot win me.

JEAN. How then?—Not in that way! Not by caresses and sweet words! Not by
thought for the future, by escape from disgrace! How then?

JULIA. How? How? I don't know—Not at all! I hate you as I hate rats, but I
cannot escape from you!

---

[10] False glitter.

660 JEAN.   Escape *with* me!

JULIA [*straightening up*].   Escape? Yes, we must escape!—But I am so tired. Give me a glass of wine.

[JEAN *pours out wine.*]

JULIA [*looks at her watch*].   But we must have a talk first. We have still some time left. [*Empties her glass and holds it out for more.*]

JEAN.   Don't drink so much. It will go to your head.

JULIA.   What difference would that make?

JEAN.   What difference would it make? It's vulgar to get drunk—What was it you wanted to tell me?

JULIA.   We must get away. But first we must have a talk—that is, I must talk, 670 for so far you have done all the talking. You have told me about your life. Now I must tell you about mine, so that we know each other right to the bottom before we begin the journey together.

JEAN.   One moment, pardon me! Think first, so that you don't regret it afterwards, when you have already given up the secrets of your life.

JULIA.   Are you not my friend?

JEAN.   Yes, at times—but don't rely on me.

JULIA.   You only talk like that—and besides, my secrets are known to everybody. You see, my mother was not of noble birth, but came of quite plain people. She was brought up in the ideas of her time about equality, and 680 woman's independence, and that kind of thing. And she had a decided aversion to marriage. Therefore, when my father proposed to her, she said she wouldn't marry him—and then she did it just the same. I came into the world—against my mother's wish, I have come to think. Then my mother wanted to bring me up in a perfectly natural state, and at the same time I was to learn everything that a boy is taught, so that I might prove that a woman is just as good as a man. I was dressed as a boy, and was taught how to handle a horse, but could have nothing to do with the cows. I had to groom and harness and go hunting on horseback. I was even forced to learn something about agriculture. And all over the estate men 690 were set to do women's work, and women to do men's—with the result that everything went to pieces and we became the laughingstock of the whole neighborhood. At last my father must have recovered from the spell cast over him, for he rebelled, and everything was changed to suit his own ideas. My mother was taken sick—what kind of sickness it was I don't know, but she fell often into convulsions, and she used to hide herself in the garret or in the garden, and sometimes she stayed out all night. Then came the big fire, of which you have heard. The house, the stable, and the barn were burned down, and this under circumstances which made it look as if the fire had been set on purpose. For the disaster occurred the day 700 after our insurance expired, and the money sent for renewal of the policy had been delayed by the messenger's carelessness, so that it came too late. [*She fills her glass again and drinks.*]

JEAN.   Don't drink any more.

JULIA.   Oh, what does it matter!—We were without a roof over our heads and had to sleep in the carriages. My father didn't know where to get money for the rebuilding of the house. Then my mother suggested that he try to borrow from a childhood friend of hers, a brick manufacturer living not

far from here. My father got the loan, but was not permitted to pay any
interest, which astonished him. And so the house was built up again.
710   [*Drinks again.*] Do you know who set fire to the house?
    JEAN.   Her ladyship, your mother!
    JULIA.   Do you know who the brick manufacturer was?
    JEAN.   Your mother's lover?
    JULIA.   Do you know to whom the money belonged?
    JEAN.   Wait a minute—no, that I don't know.
    JULIA.   To my mother.
    JEAN.   In other words, to the count, if there was no settlement.
    JULIA.   There was no settlement. My mother possessed a small fortune of her
        own which she did not want to leave in my father's control, so she invested
720   it with—her friend.
    JEAN.   Who copped it.
    JULIA.   Exactly! He kept it. All this came to my father's knowledge. He
        couldn't bring suit; he couldn't pay his wife's lover; he couldn't prove that
        it was his wife's money. That was my mother's revenge because he had
        made himself master in his own house. At that time he came near shooting
        himself—it was even rumored that he had tried and failed. But he took a
        new lease of life, and my mother had to pay for what she had done. I can
        tell you that those were five years I'll never forget! My sympathies were
        with my father, but I took my mother's side because I was not aware of the
730   true circumstances. From her I learned to suspect and hate men—for she
        hated the whole sex, as you have probably heard—and I promised her on
        my oath that I would never become a man's slave.
    JEAN.   And so you became engaged to the County Attorney.
    JULIA.   Yes, in order that he should be my slave.
    JEAN.   And he didn't want to?
    JULIA.   Oh, he wanted, but I wouldn't let him. I got tired of him.
    JEAN.   Yes, I saw it—in the stable-yard.
    JULIA.   What did you see?
    JEAN.   Just that—how he broke the engagement.
740 JULIA.   That's a lie! It was I who broke it. Did he say he did it, the scoundrel?
    JEAN.   Oh, he was no scoundrel, I guess. So you hate men, Miss Julia?
    JULIA.   Yes! Most of the time. But now and then—when the weakness comes
        over me—oh, what shame!
    JEAN.   And you hate me too?
    JULIA.   Beyond measure! I should like to kill you like a wild beast—
    JEAN.   As you make haste to shoot a mad dog. Is that right?
    JULIA.   That's right!
    JEAN.   But now there is nothing to shoot with—and there is no dog. What are
        we to do then?
750 JULIA.   Go abroad.
    JEAN.   In order to plague each other to death?
    JULIA.   No—in order to enjoy ourselves: a couple of days, a week, as long as
        enjoyment is possible. And then—die!
    JEAN.   Die? How silly! Then I think it's much better to start a hotel.
    JULIA [*without listening to* JEAN].   —At Lake Como, where the sun is always
        shining, and the laurels stand green at Christmas, and the oranges are
        glowing.

JEAN. Lake Como is a rainy hole, and I could see no oranges except in the groceries. But it is a good place for tourists, as it has a lot of villas that can
760   be rented to loving couples, and that's a profitable business—do you know why? Because they take a lease for six months—and then they leave after three weeks.

JEAN [*naïvely*]. Why after three weeks?

JEAN. Because they quarrel, of course. But the rent has to be paid just the same. And then you can rent the house again. And that way it goes on all the time, for there is plenty of love—even if it doesn't last long.

JULIA. You don't want to die with me?

JEAN. I don't want to die at all. Both because I am fond of living, and because I regard suicide as a crime against the Providence which has
770   bestowed life on us.

JULIA. Do you mean to say that *you* believe in God?

JEAN. Of course, I do. And I go to church every other Sunday. Frankly speaking, now I am tired of all this, and now I am going to bed.

JULIA. So! And you think that will be enough for me? Do you know what you owe a woman that you have spoiled?

JEAN [*takes out his purse and throws a silver coin on the table*]. You're welcome! I don't want to be in anybody's debt.

JULIA [*pretending not to notice the insult*]. Do you know what the law provides—

780 JEAN. Unfortunately the law provides no punishment for a woman who seduces a man.

JULIA [*as before*]. Can you think of any escape except by our going abroad and getting married, and then getting a divorce?

JEAN. Suppose I refuse to enter into this *mésaillance*?[11]

JULIA. *Mésaillance*—

JEAN. Yes, for me. You see, I have better ancestry than you, for nobody in my family was ever guilty of arson.

JULIA. How do you know?

JEAN. Well, nothing is known to the contrary, for we keep no pedigrees—
790   except in the police bureau. But I have read about your pedigree in a book that was lying on the drawing-room table. Do you know who was your first ancestor? A miller who let his wife sleep with the king one night during the war with Denmark. I have no such ancestry. I have none at all, but I can become an ancestor myself.

JULIA. That's what I get for unburdening my heart to one not worthy of it; for sacrificing my family's honor—

JEAN. Dishonor! Well, what was it I told you? You shouldn't drink, for then you talk. And you *must* not talk!

JULIA. Oh, how I regret what I have done! How I regret it! If at least you
800   loved me!

JEAN. For the last time: what do you mean? Am I to weep? Am I to jump over your whip? Am I to kiss you, and lure you down to Lake Como for three weeks, and so on? What am I to do? What do you expect? This is getting to be rather painful! But that's what comes from getting mixed up

---

[11] "Mismatch."

with women. Miss Julia! I see that you are unhappy; I know that you are suffering; but I cannot understand you. We never carry on like that. There is never any hatred between us. Love is to us a play, and we play at it when our work leaves us time to do so. But we have not the time to do so all day and all night, as you have. I believe you are sick—I am sure you are sick.

810 JULIA.   You should be good to me—and now you speak like a human being.

JEAN.   All right, but be human yourself. You spit on me, and then you won't let me wipe myself—on you!

JULIA.   Help me, help me! Tell me only what I am to do—where I am to turn?

JEAN.   O Lord, if I only knew that myself!

JULIA.   I have been exasperated, I have been mad, but there ought to be some way of saving myself.

JEAN.   Stay right here and keep quiet. Nobody knows anything.

JULIA.   Impossible! The people know, and Christine knows.

820 JEAN.   They don't know, and they would never believe it possible.

JULIA [*hesitating*].   But—it might happen again.

JEAN.   That's true.

JULIA.   And the results?

JEAN [*frightened*].   The results! Where was my head when I didn't think of that! Well, then there is only one thing to do—you must leave. At once! I can't go with you, for then everything would be lost, so you must go alone—abroad—anywhere!

JULIA.   Alone? Where?—I can't do it.

JEAN.   You must! And before the count gets back. If you stay, then you know

830   what will happen. Once on the wrong path, one wants to keep on, as the harm is done anyhow. Then one grows more and more reckless—and at last it all comes out. So you must get away! Then you can write to the count and tell him everything, except that it was me. And he would never guess it. Nor do I think he would be very anxious to find out.

JULIA.   I'll go if you come with me.

JEAN.   Are you stark mad, woman? Miss Julia to run away with her valet! It would be in the papers in another day, and the count could never survive it.

JULIA.   I can't leave! I can't stay! Help me! I am so tired, so fearfully tired.

840   Give me orders! Set me going, for I can no longer think, no longer act—

JEAN.   Do you see now what good-for-nothings you are! Why do you strut and turn up your noses as if you were the lords of creation? Well, I am going to give you orders. Go up and dress. Get some traveling money, and then come back again.

JULIA [*in an undertone*].   Come up with me!

JEAN.   To your room? Now you're crazy again! [*Hesitates a moment.*] No, you must go at once! [*Takes her by the hand and leads her out.*]

JULIA [*on her way out*].   Can't you speak kindly to me, Jean?

JEAN.   An order must always sound unkind. Now you can find out how it

850   feels!

[JULIA *goes out.* JEAN, *alone, draws a sigh of relief; sits down at the table; takes out note-book and a pencil; figures aloud from time to time; dumb play until* CHRISTINE *enters dressed for church; she has a false shirt front and a white tie in one of her hands.*]

CHRISTINE. Goodness gracious, how the place looks! What have you been up to anyhow?

JEAN. Oh, it was Miss Julia who dragged in the people. Have you been sleeping so hard that you didn't hear anything at all?

CHRISTINE. I have been sleeping like a log.

JEAN. And dressed for church already?

CHRISTINE. Yes, didn't you promise to come with me to communion today?

JEAN. Oh, yes, I remember now. And there you've got the finery. Well, come on with it. [*Sits down;* CHRISTINE *helps him to put on the shirt front and the white*
860   *tie. Pause.*]

JEAN [*sleepily*]. What's the text today?

CHRISTINE. Oh, about John the Baptist beheaded, I guess.

JEAN. That's going to be a long story, I'm sure. My, but you choke me! Oh, I'm so sleepy, so sleepy!

CHRISTINE. Well, what has been keeping you up all night? Why, man, you're just green in the face!

JEAN. I have been sitting here talking with Miss Julia.

CHRISTINE. She hasn't an idea of what's proper, that creature! [*Pause.*]

JEAN. Say, Christine.
870 CHRISTINE. Well?

JEAN. Isn't it funny anyhow, when you come to think of it? Her!

CHRISTINE. What is it that's funny?

JEAN. Everything! [*Pause.*]

CHRISTINE [*seeing the glasses on the table that are only half emptied*]. So you've been drinking together also?

JEAN. Yes.

CHRISTINE. Shame on you! Look me in the eye!

JEAN. Yes.

CHRISTINE. Is it possible? Is it possible?
880 JEAN [*after a moment's thought*]. Yes, it is!

CHRISTINE. Ugh! That's worse than I could ever have believed. It's awful!

JEAN. You are not jealous of her, are you?

CHRISTINE. No, not of her. Had it been Clara or Sophie, then I'd have scratched your eyes out. Yes, that's the way I feel about it, and I can't tell why. Oh my, but that was nasty!

JEAN. Are you mad at her then?

CHRISTINE. No, but at you! It was wrong of you, very wrong! Poor girl! No, I tell you, I don't want to stay in this house any longer, with people for whom it is impossible to have any respect.

890 JEAN. Why should you have any respect for them?

CHRISTINE. And you who are such a smarty can't tell that! You wouldn't serve people who don't act decently, would you? It's to lower oneself, I think.

JEAN. Yes, but it ought to be a consolation to us that they are not a bit better than we.

CHRISTINE. No, I don't think so. For if they're no better, then it's no use trying to get up to them. And just think of the count! Think of him who has had so much sorrow in his day! No, I don't want to stay any longer in this house—And with a fellow like you, too. If it had been the County Attorney—if it had only been some one of her own sort—

900 JEAN. Now look here!

CHRISTINE. Yes, yes! You're all right in your way, but there's after all some difference between one kind of people and another—No, but this is something I'll never get over!—And the young lady who was so proud, and so tart to the men, that you couldn't believe she would ever let one come near her—and such one at that! And she who wanted to have poor Diana shot because she had been running around with the gamekeeper's pug!—Well, I declare!—But I won't stay here any longer, and next October I get out of here.

JEAN. And then?

910 CHRISTINE. Well, as we've come to talk of that now, perhaps it would be just as well if you looked for something, seeing that we're going to get married after all.

JEAN. Well, what could I look for? As a married man I couldn't get a place like this.

CHRISTINE. No, I understand that. But you could get a job as a janitor, or maybe as a messenger in some government bureau. Of course, the public loaf is always short in weight, but it comes steady, and then there is a pension for the widow and the children—

JEAN [*making a face*]. That's good and well, but it isn't my style to think of

920 dying all at once for the sake of wife and children. I must say that my plans have been looking toward something better than that kind of thing.

CHRISTINE. Your plans, yes—but you've got obligations also, and those you had better keep in mind!

JEAN. Now don't you get my dander up by talking of obligations! I know what I've got to do anyhow. [*Listening for some sound on the outside.*] However, we've plenty of time to think of all this. Go in now and get ready, and then we'll go to church.

CHRISTINE. Who is walking around up there?

JEAN. I don't know, unless it be Clara.

930 CHRISTINE [*going out*]. It can't be the count, do you think, who's come home without anybody hearing him?

JEAN [*scared*]. The count? No, that isn't possible, for then he would have rung for me.

CHRISTINE [*as she goes out*]. Well, God help us all! Never have I seen the like of it!

[*The sun has risen and is shining on the tree tops in the park. The light changes gradually until it comes slantingly in through the windows. JEAN goes to the door and gives a signal.*]

JULIA [*enters in traveling dress and carrying a small bird-cage covered up with a towel; this she places on a chair*]. Now I am ready.

JEAN. Hush! Christine is awake.

JULIA [*showing extreme nervousness during the following scene*]. Did she suspect

940 anything?

JEAN. She knows nothing at all. But, my heavens, how you look!

JULIA. How do I look?

JEAN. You're as pale as a corpse, and—pardon me, but your face is dirty.

JULIA. Let me wash it then—Now! [*She goes over to the washstand and washes her face and hands.*] Give me a towel—Oh!—That's the sun rising!

JEAN. And then the ogre bursts.

JULIA. Yes, ogres and trolls were abroad last night!—But listen, Jean. Come with me, for now I have the money.

JEAN [*doubtfully*]. Enough?

950 JULIA. Enough to start with. Come with me, for I cannot travel alone today. Think of it—Midsummer Day, on a stuffy train, jammed with people who stare at you—and standing still at stations when you want to fly. No, I cannot! I cannot! And then the memories will come: childhood memories of Midsummer Days, when the inside of the church was turned into a green forest—birches and lilacs; the dinner at the festive table with relatives and friends; the afternoon in the park, with dancing and music, flowers and games! Oh, you may run and run, but your memories are in the baggage-car, and with them remorse and repentance!

JEAN. I'll go with you—but at once, before it's too late. This very moment!

960 JULIA. Well, get dressed then. [*Picks up the cage.*]

JEAN. But no baggage! That would only give us away.

JULIA. No, nothing at all! Only what we can take with us in the car.

JEAN [*has taken down his hat*]. What have you got there? What is it?

JULIA. It's only my finch. I can't leave it behind.

JEAN. Did you ever! Dragging a bird-cage along with us! You must be raving mad! Drop the cage!

JULIA. The only thing I take with me from my home! The only living creature that loves me since Diana deserted me! Don't be cruel! Let me take it along!

970 JEAN. Drop the cage, I tell you! And don't talk so loud—Christine can hear us.

JULIA. No, I won't let it fall into strange hands. I'd rather have you kill it!

JEAN. Well, give it to me, and I'll wring its neck.

JULIA. Yes, but don't hurt it. Don't—no, I cannot!

JEAN. Let me—I can!

JULIA [*takes the bird out of the cage and kisses it*]. Oh, my little birdie, must it die and go away from its mistress!

JEAN. Don't make a scene, please. Don't you know it's a question of your life, of your future? Come, quick! [*Snatches the bird away from her, carries it to the*
980 *chopping-block and picks up an axe.* MISS JULIA *turns away.*]

JEAN. You should have learned how to kill chickens instead of shooting with a revolver—[*Brings down the axe.*]—then you wouldn't have fainted for a drop of blood.

JULIA [*screaming*]. Kill me too! Kill me! You who can take the life of an innocent creature without turning a hair! Oh, I hate and despise you! There is blood between us! Cursed be the hour when I first met you! Cursed be the hour when I came to life in my mother's womb!

JEAN. Well, what's the use of all that cursing? Come on!

JULIA [*approaching the chopping-block as if drawn to it against her will*]. No, I
990 don't want to go yet. I cannot—I must see—Hush! There's a carriage coming up the road. [*Listening without taking her eyes off the block and the axe.*] You think I cannot stand the sight of blood. You think I am as weak as that—oh, I should like to see your blood, your brains, on that block there. I should like to see your whole sex swimming in blood like that thing there. I think I could drink out of your skull, and bathe my feet in your open breast, and eat your heart from the spit!—You think I am weak; you

think I love you because the fruit of my womb was yearning for your seed;
you think I want to carry your offspring under my heart and nourish it
with my blood—bear your children and take your name! Tell me, you,
what are you called anyhow? I have never heard your family name—and
maybe you haven't any. I should become Mrs. "Hovel," or Mrs. "Backyard"—you dog there, that's wearing my collar; you lackey with my coat of
arms on your buttons—and I should share with my cook, and be the rival
of my own servant. Oh! Oh! Oh!—You think I am a coward and want to
run away! No, now I'll stay—and let the lightning strike! My father will
come home—will find his chiffonier[12] opened—the money gone! Then
he'll ring—twice for the valet—and then he'll send for the sheriff—and
then I shall tell everything! Everything! Oh, but it will be good to get an
end to it—if it only be the end! And then his heart will break, and he
dies!—So there will be an end to all of us—and all will be quiet—peace—
eternal rest!—And then the coat of arms will be shattered on the coffin—and the count's line will be wiped out—but the lackey's line goes on
in the orphan asylum—wins laurels in the gutter, and ends in jail.

JEAN.   There spoke the royal blood! Bravo, Miss Julia! Now you put the
miller back in his sack!

[CHRISTINE *enters dressed for church and carrying a hymn-book in her hand.*]

JULIA [*hurries up to her and throws herself into her arms as if seeking protection*].
Help me, Christine! Help me against this man!

CHRISTINE [*unmoved and cold*].   What kind of performance is this on the Sabbath morning? [*Catches sight of the chopping-block.*] My, what a mess you
have made!—What's the meaning of all this? And the way you shout and
carry on!

JULIA.   You are a woman, Christine, and you are my friend. Beware of that
scoundrel!

JEAN [*a little shy and embarrassed*].   While the ladies are discussing I'll get
myself a shave. [*Slinks out to the right.*]

JULIA.   You must understand me, and you must listen to me.

CHRISTINE.   No, really, I don't understand this kind of trolloping. Where are
you going in your traveling dress—and he with his hat on—what?—What?

JULIA.   Listen, Christine, listen, and I'll tell you everything—

CHRISTINE.   I don't want to know anything—

JULIA.   You must listen to me—

CHRISTINE.   What is it about? Is it about this nonsense with Jean? Well, I don't
care about it at all, for it's none of my business. But if you're planning to
get him away with you, we'll put a stop to that!

JULIA [*extremely nervous*].   Please try to be quiet, Christine, and listen to me.
I cannot stay here, and Jean cannot stay here—and so we must leave—

CHRISTINE.   Hm, hm!

JULIA [*brightening up*].   But now I have got an idea, you know. Suppose all
three of us should leave—go abroad—go to Switzerland and start a hotel
together—I have money, you know—and Jean and I could run the whole

---

[12] Dresser.

thing—and you, I thought, could take charge of the kitchen—Wouldn't that be fine!—Say yes, now! And come along with us! Then everything is fixed!—Oh, say yes! [*She puts her arms around* CHRISTINE *and pats her.*]

CHRISTINE [*coldly and thoughtfully*]. Hm, hm!

JULIA [*presto tempo*].[13]   You have never traveled, Christine—you must get out and have a look at the world. You cannot imagine what fun it is to travel on a train—constantly new people—new countries—and then we get to Hamburg and take in the Zoological Gardens in passing—that's what you like—and then we go to the theaters and to the opera—and when we get

1050   to Munich, there, you know, we have a lot of museums, where they keep Rubens and Raphael and all those big painters, you know—Haven't you heard of Munich, where King Louis[14] used to live—the king, you know, that went mad—And then we'll have a look at his castle—he has still some castles that are furnished just as in a fairy tale—and from there it isn't very far to Switzerland—and the Alps, you know—just think of the Alps, with snow on top of them in the middle of the summer—and there you have orange trees and laurels that are green all the year around—

[JEAN *is seen in the right wing, sharpening his razor on a strop which he holds between his teeth and his left hand; he listens to the talk with a pleased mien and nods approval now and then.*]

JULIA [*tempo prestissimo*].[15]   And then we get a hotel—and I sit in the office, while Jean is outside receiving tourists—and goes out marketing—and

1060   writes letters—That's a life for you—Then the train whistles, and the bus drives up, and it rings upstairs, and it rings in the restaurant—and then I make out the bills—and I am going to salt them, too—You can never imagine how timid tourists are when they come to pay their bills! And you—you will sit like a queen in the kitchen. Of course, you are not going to stand at the stove yourself. And you'll have to dress neatly and nicely in order to show yourself to people—and with your looks—yes, I am not flattering you—you'll catch a husband some fine day—some rich English-man, you know—for those fellows are so easy [*Slowing down.*] to catch—and then we grow rich—and we build us a villa at Lake Como—of course,

1070   it is raining a little in that place now and then—but [*Limply.*] the sun must be shining sometimes—although it looks dark—and—then—or else we can go home again—and come back—here—or some other place—

CHRISTINE. Tell me, Miss Julia, do you believe in all that yourself?

JULIA [*crushed*]. Do I believe in it myself?

CHRISTINE. Yes.

JULIA [*exhausted*]. I don't know: I believe no longer in anything. [*She sinks down on the bench and drops her head between her arms on the table.*] Nothing! Nothing at all!

---

[13] "Rapidly."

[14] Louis II (1845–1886), King of Bavaria from 1864 to 1886, drowned himself after being declared insane.

[15] "Very rapidly."

CHRISTINE [*turns to the right, where* JEAN *is standing*].   So you were going to run
1080   away!

JEAN [*abashed, puts the razor on the table*].   Run away? Well, that's putting it
rather strong. You have heard what the young lady proposes, and though
she is tired out now by being up all night, it's a proposition that can be put
through all right.

CHRISTINE.   Now you tell me: did you mean me to act as cook for that one
there—?

JEAN [*sharply*].   Will you please use decent language in speaking to your
mistress! Do you understand?

CHRISTINE.   Mistress!

1090 JEAN   Yes!

CHRISTINE.   Well, well! Listen to him!

JEAN.   Yes, it would be better for you to listen a little more and talk a little
less. Miss Julia is your mistress, and what makes you disrespectful to her
now should make you feel the same way about yourself.

CHRISTINE.   Oh, I have always had enough respect for myself—

JEAN.   To have none for others!

CHRISTINE.   —not to go below my own station. You can't say that the count's
cook has had anything to do with the groom or the swineherd. You can't
say anything of the kind!

1100 JEAN.   Yes, it's your luck that you have had to do with a gentleman.

CHRISTINE.   Yes, a gentleman who sells the oats out of the count's stable!

JEAN.   What's that to you who get a commission on the groceries and bribes
from the butcher?

CHRISTINE.   What's that?

JEAN.   And so you can't respect your master and mistress any longer! You—
you!

CHRISTINE.   Are you coming with me to church? I think you need a good
sermon on top of such a deed.

JEAN.   No, I am not going to church today. You can go by yourself and
1110   confess your own deeds.

CHRISTINE.   Yes, I'll do that, and I'll bring back enough forgiveness to cover
you also. The Savior suffered and died on the cross for all our sins, and if
we go to him with a believing heart and a repentant mind, he'll take all our
guilt on himself.

JULIA.   Do you believe that, Christine?

CHRISTINE.   It is my living belief, as sure as I stand here, and the faith of my
childhood which I have kept since I was young, Miss Julia. And where sin
abounds, grace abounds too.

JULIA.   Oh, if I had your faith! Oh, if—

1120 CHRISTINE.   Yes, but you don't get it without the special grace of God, and
that is not bestowed on everybody—

JULIA.   On whom is it bestowed then?

CHRISTINE.   That's just the great secret of the work of grace, Miss Julia, and
the Lord has no regard for persons, but there those that are last shall be
the foremost—

JULIA.   Yes, but that means he has regard for those that are last.

CHRISTINE [*going right on*].   —and it is easier for a camel to go through a

needle's eye than for a rich man to get into heaven. That's the way it is, Miss Julia. Now I am going, however—alone—and as I pass by, I'll tell the
1130 stableman not to let out the horses if anybody should like to get away before the count comes home. Good-bye!

[*Goes out.*]

JEAN.   Well, ain't she a devil!—And all for the sake of a finch!

JULIA [*apathetically*].   Never mind the finch!—Can you see any way out of this, any way to end it?

JEAN [*ponders*].   No!

JULIA.   What would you do in my place?

JEAN.   In your place? Let me see. As one of gentle birth, as a woman, as one who has—fallen. I don't know—yes, I do know!

JULIA [*picking up the razor with a significant gesture*].   Like this?

1140 JEAN.   Yes!—But please observe that I myself wouldn't do it, for there is a difference between us.

JULIA.   Because you are a man and I a woman? What is the difference?

JEAN.   It is the same—as—that between man and woman.

JULIA [*with the razor in her hand*].   I want to, but I cannot!—My father couldn't either, that time he should have done it.

JEAN.   No, he should not have done it, for he had to get his revenge first.

JULIA.   And now it is my mother's turn to revenge herself again, through me.

JEAN.   Have you not loved your father, Miss Julia?

JULIA.   Yes, immensely, but I must have hated him, too. I think I must have
1150 been doing so without being aware of it. But he was the one who reared me in contempt for my own sex—half woman and half man! Whose fault is it, this that has happened? My father's—my mother's—my own? My own? Why, I have nothing that is my own. I haven't a thought that didn't come from my father; not a passion that didn't come from my mother; and now this last—this about all human creatures being equal—I got that from him, my fiancé—whom I call a scoundrel for that reason! How can it be my own fault? To put the blame on Jesus, as Christine does—no, I am too proud for that, and know too much—thanks to my father's teachings— And that about a rich person not getting into heaven, it's just a lie, and
1160 Christine, who has money in the savings-bank, wouldn't get in anyhow. Whose is the fault?—What does it matter whose it is? For just the same I am the one who must bear the guilt and the results—

JEAN.   Yes, but—

[*Two sharp strokes are rung on the bell.* MISS JULIA *leaps to her feet.* JEAN *changes his coat.*]

JEAN.   The count is back. Think if Christine— [*Goes to the speaking-tube, knocks on it, and listens.*]

JULIA.   Now he has been to the chiffonier!

JEAN.   It is Jean, your lordship! [*Listening again, the spectators being unable to hear what the count says.*] Yes, your lordship! [*Listening.*] Yes, your lordship! At once! [*Listening.*] In a minute, your lordship! [*Listening.*] Yes, yes! In half
1170 an hour!

JULIA [*with intense concern*].   What did he say? Lord Jesus, what did he say?
JEAN.   He called for his boots and wanted his coffee in half an hour.
JULIA.   In half an hour then! Oh, I am so tired. I can't do anything; can't
repent, can't run away, can't stay, can't live—can't die! Help me now!
Command me, and I'll obey you like a dog! Do me this last favor—save my
honor, and save his name! You know what my will ought to do, and what
it cannot do—now give me your will, and make me do it!
JEAN.   I don't know why—but now I can't either—I don't understand—It is
just as if this coat here made a—I cannot command you—and now, since
1180   I've heard the count's voice—now—I can't quite explain it—but—Oh, that
damned menial is back in my spine again. I believe if the count should
come down here, and if he should tell me to cut my own throat—I'd do it
on the spot!
JULIA.   Make believe that you are he, and that I am you!—You did some fine
acting when you were on your knees before me—then you were the nobleman—or—have you ever been to a show and seen one who could
hypnotize people?

[JEAN *makes a sign of assent.*]

JULIA.   He says to his subject: get the broom. And the man gets it. He says:
sweep. And the man sweeps.
1190 JEAN.   But then the other person must be asleep.
JULIA [*ecstatically*].   I am asleep already—there is nothing in the whole room
but a lot of smoke—and you look like a stove—that looks like a man in
black clothes and a high hat—and your eyes glow like coals when the fire
is going out—and your face is a lump of white ashes. [*The sunlight has
reached the floor and is now falling on* JEAN.] How warm and nice it is! [*She rubs
her hands as if warming them before a fire.*] And so light—and so peaceful!
JEAN [*takes the razor and puts it in her hand*].   There's the broom! Go now, while
it is light—to the barn—and— [*Whispers something in her ear.*]
JULIA [*awake*].   Thank you! Now I shall have rest! But tell me first—that the
1200   foremost also receive the gift of grace. Say it, even if you don't believe it.
JEAN.   The foremost? No, I can't do that!—But wait—Miss Julia—I know!
You are no longer among the foremost—now when you are among the—
last!
JULIA.   That's right. I am among the last of all: I am the very last. Oh!—But
now I cannot go—Tell me once more that I must go!
JEAN.   No, now I can't do it either. I cannot!
JULIA.   And those that are foremost shall be the last.
JEAN.   Don't think, don't think! Why, you are taking away my strength, too,
so that I become a coward—What? I thought I saw the bell moving!—To
1210   be that scared of a bell! Yes, but it isn't only the bell—there is somebody
behind it—a hand that makes it move—and something else that makes the
hand move—but if you cover up your ears—just cover up your ears! Then
it rings worse than ever! Rings and rings, until you answer it—and then it's
too late—then comes the sheriff—and then—

[*Two quick rings from the bell.*]

JEAN [*shrinks together; then he straightens himself up*].   It's horrid! But there's no other end to it!—Go!

[JULIA *goes firmly out through the door.*]

CURTAIN

[1888]

Critical Commentary on *Miss Julia*

At the time Strindberg composed *Miss Julia,* he was a fervent admirer of literary naturalism, especially as expressed in the novels of Emile Zola (1840–1902). Zola believed that the novelist was an experimenter akin to a chemist or a biologist. On the basis of accurate observation, the writer was to illustrate how the forces of nature (particularly heredity, psychology, social pressure, and the environment) determine all human conduct. In his famous preface to *Miss Julia,* Strindberg embraced these ideas and explained their application to the play.

The premise of the play illustrates Darwinian survival of the fittest. In the clash between the aristocratic Miss Julia and the ambitious servant Jean, we see not only the triumph of the dominant individual, but also the extinction of a family and the symbolic conquest of the entire class of conniving peasants over the exhausted gentry. Strindberg commented with equanimity upon the bloodshed that often flows from such clashes, observing that

> When we have grown as hardened as the first French revolutionaries were, then
> it will without question produce only a happy and wholesome impression to see
> the crown parks weeded out and ridded of rotting, super-annuated trees that
> too long have stood in the way of others, equally entitled to their day of veg-
> etation—the kind of impression one experiences when one sees somebody with
> an incurable disease taken by death.

Of course, the action of the play can only be convincingly naturalistic if we believe that the characters act realistically, with plausible motivations. Here, Strindberg's contribution to modern drama is unique and still debatable. He argued that most playwrights err by oversimplifying the complexity of human motives and by making their characters too consistent. Instead, Strindberg intentionally created characters that "use their brains only intermittently as people do in real life where, during a conversation, one cog in a person's brain may find itself, more or less by chance, geared into another cog; and where no topic is completely exhausted." As a result, the characters in *Miss Julia* tend to be "vacillating, disjointed: a blending of the old and the new."

Consider, for example, Miss Julia herself. Strindberg envisioned her as typical of the modern (and in his opinion degenerate) "half-woman . . . who pushes herself forward." But she is also "a remnant of the old war nobility, which is now giving way to the new aristocracy of the mind with its nervous driving force." According to Strindberg, her sexual attraction to the socially inferior footman springs from a combination of forces:

the mother's fundamental instincts, the father's wrong upbringing of the girl, her own strange nature, and the suggestive influence of her fiancé upon an insipid, vapid, and degenerated mind. In addition, and more directly, the festal mood of Midsummer Eve, the absence of her father, her monthly period, her preoccupancy with animals, the excitement of the dance, the long twilight of the night, the strongly aphrodisiac influence of the flowers, and lastly, the chance bringing together of the two alone in a secluded room—not to mention the aroused passion of a bold and aggressive man.

In much the same way that a city dump asserts its presence through the foulness of its intermingled odors, Julia's very humanity is defined by a complex collection of past experiences, primitive urges, natural phenomena, and chance encounters. Prior to Strindberg, no playwright had so consciously taken this naturalistic view of human behavior.

Strindberg's plays are also innovative, however, in their elements of symbolism and expressionism. Expressionism was a literary movement that emerged early in the twentieth century (most directly in Strindberg's *A Dream Play* [1902]) as a reaction against excessive realism. It strove to create a particular atmosphere, often eerie and unsettling, through the use of symbols, irrationality, and rebellion against theatrical convention. We see this expressionism in Julia's sadistic pleasure while striking her fiancé with a riding crop; in the curious use of mime and ballet; in the Freudian symbolism and uncanny parallelism of the dreams related by Julia and Jean; in the bizarre and ornate anecdote Jean tells about creeping into the "Garden of Eden," being trapped in the Turkish pavilion (an outdoor privy), and spying upon Julia while hiding beneath a reeking pile of refuse; in the grotesque on-stage beheading of Julia's pet bird; and in the curiously hypnotic way in which Jean reacts to his lackey's uniform and the Count's boots and in which Julia marches offstage.

Thus, Strindberg has combined naturalism (an outgrowth of realism) with expressionism (a rebellion against realism). This fascination with contrarieties is typical of his art and personality. He was a divided soul, torn by the cross-currents of contemporary existence. Perhaps his plays retain their pathos because his characters are pummeled by the same winds that swirl about us.

A Selective Bibliography on *Miss Julia*

Bellquist, John Eric. "Rereading *Fröken Julie:* Undercurrents in Strindberg's Naturalistic Intent." *Scandinavian Studies* 60 (1988): 1–11.

Bergholz, Harry. "*Miss Julia:* Strindberg's Response to J. P. Jacobsen's *Fru Marie Grubbe.*" *Scandinavica* 11 (1972): 13–19.

Brustein, Robert. "Male and Female in August Strindberg." *Tulane Drama Review* 7.2 (Winter 1962): 154–60.

———. *Theatre of Revolt.* Boston: Little Brown, 1964. 112–19.

Dahlstrom, Carl. "Strindberg and Naturalistic Tragedy." *Scandinavian Studies* 30 (1958): 1–18.

Dodd, Philip. "Fairy Tales, the Unconscious and Strindberg's *Miss Julie.*" *Literature and Psychology* 28 (1978): 145–50.

Greenway, John L. "Strindberg and Suggestion in *Miss Julie.*" *South Atlantic Review* 51.2 (1986): 21–34.

Hauptman, Ira. "Strindberg's Realistic Plays." *Yale/Theatre* 5.3 (1974): 87–94.

Hayes, Stephen G. and Jules Zentner. "Strindberg's *Miss Julie:* Lilacs and Beer." *Scandinavian Studies* 45 (1973): 59–64.

Johnson, Walter. *August Strindberg.* Boston: Twayne, 1976.

Lally, M. L. K. "Strindberg's *Miss Julie.*" *Explicator* 48 (1990): 196–98.

Lamm, Martin. *August Strindberg.* New Ed. Trans. Harry G. Carlson. New York: Blom, 1971.

Lucas, F. L. *The Drama of Ibsen and Strindberg.* London: Cassell, 1962. 363–81.

Marker, Frederick J. and Lise-Lone Marker. "Love without Lovers: Ingmar Bergman's Julie." In *Strindberg's Dramaturgy.* Ed. Goran Stockenstrom. Minneapolis: U of Minnesota P, 1988. 152–63.

Mattson, Margareta. "Strindberg's *Miss Julie* in English: The Value of Literalness in Translation." *Scandinavica* 13 (1974): 131–36.

Napieralski, Edmund A. "*Miss Julie:* Strindberg's Tragic Fairy Tale." *Modern Drama* 26 (1983): 282–89.

Offenbacher, Emil. "A Contribution to the Origin of Strindberg's *Miss Julie.*" *Psychoanalytic Review* 31 (1944); 81–87.

Ollen, Gunner. *August Strindberg.* New York: Ungar, 1972.

Parker, Brian. "Strindberg's *Miss Julie* and the Legend of Salome." *Modern Drama* 32 (1989): 469–84.

Powell, Jocelyn. "Demons That Live in Sunlight: Problems in Staging Strindberg." *Yearbook of English Studies* 9 (1979): 116–34.

Roberts, Patrick. "Strindberg: The Strong and Cruel Struggle." *The Psychology of Tragic Drama.* London: Routledge, 1975. 56–68.

Rokem, Freddie. "The Camera and the Aesthetics of Repetition: Strindberg's Use of Space and Scenography in *Miss Julie, A Dream Play,* and *The Ghost Sonata.*" In *Strindberg's Dramaturgy.* Ed. Goran Stockenstrom. Minneapolis: U of Minnesota P, 1988. 107–28.

Smith, Molly. "Strindberg's Dramatic Art as Search for Self: *The Father, Miss Julie,* and *A Dream Play.*" *Journal of Evolutionary Psychology* 9 (1988): 43–51.

Sprinchorn, Evert. "Julie's End." In *Essays on Strindberg.* Ed. Carl R. Smedmark. Stockholm: Beckmans, 1966. 55–66.

Steene, Birgitta. *The Greatest Fire: A Study of August Strindberg.* Carbondale, IL: SIU Press, 1973.

Strindberg, August. "Miss Julie." In *Playwrights on Playwrighting.* Ed. Toby Cole. New York: Hill and Wang, 1960. 171–82.

Templeton, Alice. " 'Miss Julie' as a 'Naturalistic Tragedy.' " *Theatre Journal* 40.4 (1990); 468–80.

Valency, Maurice. *The Flower and the Castle: An Introduction to Modern Drama.* New York: Macmillan, 1963. 274–78.

Young, Vernon. "The History of *Miss Julie.*" *Hudson Review* 8 (1955): 123–30.

Henrik Ibsen (1828–1906)

HEDDA GABLER

Translated by William Archer and Sir Edmund Gosse

CHARACTERS

GEORGE TESMAN
HEDDA TESMAN *his wife*
MISS JULIANA TESMAN *his aunt*
MRS. ELVSTED

JUDGE BRACK
EILERT LÖVBORG
BERTA *servant at the Tesmans'*

SCENE: TESMAN'S *villa, in the west end of Christiania.*

ACT I

A spacious, handsome and tastefully furnished drawing-room, decorated in dark colors. In the back, a wide doorway with curtains drawn back, leading into a smaller room decorated in the same style as the drawing-room. In the right-hand wall of the front room, a folding door leading out to the hall. In the opposite wall, on the left, a glass door, also with curtains drawn back. Through the panes can be seen part of a verandah outside, and trees covered with autumn foliage. An oval table, with a cover on it, and surrounded by chairs, stands well forward. In front, by the wall on the right, a wide stove of dark porcelain, a high-backed arm-chair, a cushioned foot-rest, and two foot-stools. A settee, with a small round table in front of it, fills the upper right-hand corner. In front, on the left, a little way from the wall, a sofa. Farther back than the glass door, a piano. On either side of the doorway at the back a whatnot with terra-cotta and majolica ornaments.[1]—Against the back wall of the inner room a sofa, with a table, and one or two chairs. Over the sofa hangs the portrait of a handsome elderly man in a General's uniform. Over the table a hanging lamp, with an opal glass shade.—A number of bouquets are arranged about the drawing-room, in vases and glasses. Others lie upon the tables. The floors in both rooms are covered with thick carpets.—Morning light. The sun shines in through the glass door.

MISS JULIANA TESMAN, with her bonnet on and carrying a parasol, comes in from the hall, followed by BERTA, who carries a bouquet wrapped in paper. MISS TESMAN is a comely and pleasant-looking lady of about sixty-five. She is nicely but simply dressed in a gray walking-costume. BERTA is a middle-aged woman of plain and rather countrified appearance.

MISS TESMAN [*stops close to the door, listens, and says softly*]. Upon my word, I don't believe they are stirring yet!

---

[1] A *whatnot* is a stand with shelves for small decorative articles. *Terra-cotta* is a brownish-red clay used in pottery, and *majolica* is a kind of glazed and richly decorated pottery from Italy.

BERTA [*also softly*].   I told you so, Miss. Remember how late the steamboat got in last night. And then, when they got home!—good Lord, what a lot the young mistress had to unpack before she could get to bed.

MISS TESMAN.   Well, well—let them have their sleep out. But let us see that they get a good breath of the fresh morning air when they do appear. [*She goes to the glass door and throws it open.*]

BERTA [*beside the table, at a loss what to do with the bouquet in her hand*].   I declare
10   there isn't a bit of room left. I think I'll put it down here, Miss. [*She places it on the piano.*]

MISS TESMAN.   So you've got a new mistress now, my dear Berta. Heaven knows it was a wrench to me to part with you.

BERTA [*on the point of weeping*].   And do you think it wasn't hard for me too, Miss? After all the blessed years I've been with you and Miss Rina.

MISS TESMAN.   We must make the best of it, Berta. There was nothing else to be done. George can't do without you, you see—he absolutely can't. He has had you to look after him ever since he was a little boy.

BERTA.   Ah, but, Miss Julia, I can't help thinking of Miss Rina lying helpless
20   at home there, poor thing. And with only that new girl, too! She'll never learn to take proper care of an invalid.

MISS TESMAN.   Oh, I shall manage to train her. And of course, you know, I shall take most of it upon myself. You needn't be uneasy about my poor sister, my dear Berta.

BERTA.   Well, but there's another thing, Miss. I'm so mortally afraid I shan't be able to suit the young mistress.

MISS TESMAN.   Oh, well—just at first there may be one or two things—

BERTA.   Most like she'll be terrible grand in her ways.

MISS TESMAN.   Well, you can't wonder at that—General Gabler's daughter!
30   Think of the sort of life she was accustomed to in her father's time. Don't you remember how we used to see her riding down the road along with the General? In that long black habit—and with feathers in her hat?

BERTA.   Yes, indeed—I remember well enough—! But good Lord, I should never have dreamt in those days that she and Master George would make a match of it.

MISS TESMAN.   Nor I.—But, by-the-bye, Berta—while I think of it: in future you mustn't say Master George. You must say Dr. Tesman.

BERTA.   Yes, the young mistress spoke of that too—last night—the moment they set foot in the house. Is it true, then, Miss?

40 MISS TESMAN.   Yes, indeed it is. Only think, Berta—some foreign university has made him a doctor—while he has been abroad, you understand. I hadn't heard a word about it, until he told me himself upon the pier.

BERTA.   Well, well, he's clever enough for anything, he is. But I didn't think he'd have gone in for doctoring people too.

MISS TESMAN.   No, no, it's not that sort of doctor he is. [*Nods significantly.*] But let me tell you, we may have to call him something still grander before long.

BERTA.   You don't say so! What can that be, Miss?

MISS TESMAN [*smiling*].   H'm—wouldn't you like to know! [*With emotion.*] Ah,
50   dear, dear—if my poor brother could only look up from his grave now, and see what his little boy has grown into! [*Looks around.*] But bless me,

Berta—why have you done this? Taken the chintz[2] covers off all the furniture?

BERTA.   The mistress told me to. She can't abide covers on the chairs, she says.

MISS TESMAN.   Are they going to make this their everyday sitting-room then?

BERTA.   Yes, that's what I understood—from the mistress. Master George—the doctor—he said nothing.

[GEORGE TESMAN *comes from the right into the inner room, humming to himself, and carrying an unstrapped empty portmanteau.*[3] *He is a middle-sized, young-looking man of thirty-three, rather stout, with a round, open, cheerful face, fair hair and beard. He wears spectacles, and is somewhat carelessly dressed in comfortable indoor clothes.*]

MISS TESMAN.   Good morning, good morning, George.

60 TESMAN [*in the doorway between the rooms*].   Aunt Julia! Dear Aunt Julia! [*Goes up to her and shakes hands warmly.*] Come all this way—so early! Eh?

MISS TESMAN.   Why of course I had to come and see how you were getting on.

TESMAN.   In spite of your having had no proper night's rest?

MISS TESMAN.   Oh, that makes no difference to me.

TESMAN.   Well, I suppose you got home all right from the pier? Eh?

MISS TESMAN.   Yes, quite safely, thank goodness. Judge Brack was good enough to see me right to my door.

TESMAN.   We were so sorry we couldn't give you a seat in the carriage. But you saw what a pile of boxes Hedda had to bring with her.

70 MISS TESMAN.   Yes, she had certainly plenty of boxes.

BERTA [*to* TESMAN].   Shall I go in and see if there's anything I can do for the mistress?

TESMAN.   No thank you, Berta—you needn't. She said she would ring if she wanted anything.

BERTA [*going towards the right*].   Very well.

TESMAN.   But look here—take this portmanteau with you.

BERTA [*taking it*].   I'll put it in the attic.

[*She goes out by the hall door.*]

TESMAN.   Fancy, Auntie—I had the whole of that portmanteau chock full of copies of documents. You wouldn't believe how much I have picked up 80 from all the archives I have been examining—curious old details that no one has had any idea of—

MISS TESMAN.   Yes, you don't seem to have wasted your time on your wedding trip, George.

TESMAN.   No, that I haven't. But do take off your bonnet, Auntie. Look here! Let me untie the strings—eh?

MISS TESMAN [*while he does so*].   Well, well—this is just as if you were still at home with us.

---

[2] A printed cotton fabric.
[3] A leather trunk.

TESMAN [*with the bonnet in his hand, looks at it from all sides*]. Why, what a gorgeous bonnet you've been investing in!

90   MISS TESMAN.   I bought it on Hedda's account.

TESMAN.   On Hedda's account? Eh?

MISS TESMAN.   Yes, so that Hedda needn't be ashamed of me if we happened to go out together.

TESMAN [*patting her cheek*].   You always think of everything, Aunt Julia. [*Lays the bonnet on a chair beside the table.*] And now, look here—suppose we sit comfortably on the sofa and have a little chat, till Hedda comes. [*They seat themselves. She places her parasol*[4] *in the corner of the sofa.*]

MISS TESMAN [*takes both his hands and looks at him*].   What a delight it is to have you again, as large as life, before my very eyes, George! My George—my poor brother's own boy!

100   TESMAN.   And it's a delight for me, too, to see you again, Aunt Julia. You, who have been father and mother in one to me.

MISS TESMAN.   Oh, yes, I know you will always keep a place in your heart for your old aunts.

TESMAN.   And what about Aunt Rina? No improvement—eh?

MISS TESMAN.   Oh, no—we can scarcely look for any improvement in her case, poor thing. There she lies, helpless, as she has lain for all these years. But heaven grant I may not lose her yet awhile! For if I did, I don't know what I should make of my life, George—especially now that I haven't you to look after any more.

110   TESMAN [*patting her back*].   There, there, there—!

MISS TESMAN [*suddenly changing her tone*].   And to think that here you are a married man, George!—And that you should be the one to carry off Hedda Gabler, the beautiful Hedda Gabler! Only think of it—she, that was so beset with admirers!

TESMAN [*hums a little and smiles complacently*].   Yes, I fancy I have several good friends about town who would like to stand in my shoes—eh?

MISS TESMAN.   And then this fine long wedding-tour you have had! More than five—nearly six months—

TESMAN.   Well, for me it has been a sort of tour of research as well. I have had

120   to do so much grubbing among old records—and to read no end of books too, Auntie.

MISS TESMAN.   Oh, yes, I suppose so. [*More confidentially, and lowering her voice a little.*] But listen now, George—have you nothing—nothing special to tell me?

TESMAN.   As to our journey?

MISS TESMAN.   Yes.

TESMAN.   No, I don't know of anything except what I have told you in my letters. I had a doctor's degree conferred on me—but that I told you yesterday.

130   MISS TESMAN.   Yes, yes, you did. But what I mean is—haven't you any—any—expectations—?

TESMAN.   Expectations?

---

[4] A flimsy sun umbrella.

Miss Tesman.   Why, you know, George—I'm your old auntie!

Tesman.   Why, of course I have expectations.

Miss Tesman.   Ah!

Tesman.   I have every expectation of being a professor one of these days.

Miss Tesman.   Oh, yes, a professor—

Tesman.   Indeed, I may say I am certain of it. But my dear Auntie—you know all about that already!

140 Miss Tesman [*laughing at herself*].   Yes, of course I do. You are quite right there. [*Changing the subject.*] But we were talking about your journey! It must have cost a great deal of money, George?

Tesman.   Well, you see—my handsome traveling-scholarship went a good way.

Miss Tesman.   But I can't understand how you can have made it go far enough for two.

Tesman.   No, that's not so easy to understand—eh?

Miss Tesman.   And especially traveling with a lady—they tell me that makes it ever so much more expensive.

150 Tesman.   Yes, of course—it makes it a little more expensive. But Hedda had to have this trip, Auntie! She really had to. Nothing else would have done.

Miss Tesman.   No, no, I suppose not. A wedding-tour seems to be quite indispensable nowadays.—But tell me now—have you gone thoroughly over the house yet?

Tesman.   Yes, you may be sure I have. I have been afoot ever since daylight.

Miss Tesman.   And what do you think of it all?

Tesman.   I'm delighted! Quite delighted! Only I can't think what we are to do with the two empty rooms between the parlor and Hedda's bedroom.

Miss Tesman [*laughing*].   Oh, my dear George, I dare say you may find some
160 use for them—in the course of time.

Tesman.   Why of course you are right, Aunt Julia! You mean as my library increases—eh?

Miss Tesman.   Yes, quite so, my dear boy. It was your library I was thinking of.

Tesman.   I am specially pleased on Hedda's account. Often and often, before we were engaged, she said that she would never care to live anywhere but in Secretary Falk's villa.

Miss Tesman.   Yes, it was lucky that this very house should come into the market, just after you had started.

170 Tesman.   Yes, Aunt Julia, the luck was on our side, wasn't it—eh?

Miss Tesman.   But the expense, my dear George! You will find it very expensive, all this.

Tesman [*looks at her, a little cast down*].   Yes, I suppose I shall, Aunt!

Miss Tesman.   Oh, frightfully!

Tesman.   How much do you think? In round numbers—eh?

Miss Tesman.   Oh, I can't even guess until all the accounts come in.

Tesman.   Well, fortunately, Judge Brack has secured the most favorable terms for me,—so he said in a letter to Hedda.

Miss Tesman.   Yes, don't be uneasy, my dear boy.—Besides, I have given
180 security for the furniture and all the carpets.

Tesman.   Security? You? My dear Aunt Julia—what sort of security could you give?

MISS TESMAN.   I have given a mortgage on our annuity.

TESMAN [*jumps up*].   What! On your—and Aunt Rina's annuity!

MISS TESMAN.   Yes, I knew of no other plan, you see.

TESMAN [*placing himself before her*].   Have you gone out of your senses, Auntie!
Your annuity—it's all that you and Aunt Rina have to live upon.

MISS TESMAN.   Well, well, don't get so excited about it. It's only a matter of
form you know—Judge Brack assured me of that. It was he that was kind

190   enough to arrange the whole affair for me. A mere matter of form, he said.

TESMAN.   Yes, that may be all very well. But nevertheless—

MISS TESMAN.   You will have your own salary to depend upon now. And, good
heavens, even if we did have to pay up a little—! To eke things out a bit
at the start—! Why, it would be nothing but a pleasure to us.

TESMAN.   Oh, Auntie—will you never be tired of making sacrifices for me!

MISS TESMAN [*rises and lays her hands on his shoulders*].   Have I had any other
happiness in this world except to smooth your way for you, my dear boy?
You, who have had neither father nor mother to depend on. And now we
have reached the goal, George! Things have looked black enough for us,

200   sometimes; but, thank heaven, now you have nothing to fear.

TESMAN.   Yes, it is really marvelous how everything has turned out for the
best.

MISS TESMAN.   And the people who opposed you—who wanted to bar the way
for you—now you have them at your feet. They have fallen, George. Your
most dangerous rival—his fall was the worst.—And now he has to lie on
the bed he has made for himself—poor misguided creature.

TESMAN.   Have you heard anything of Eilert? Since I went away, I mean.

MISS TESMAN.   Only that he is said to have published a new book.

TESMAN.   What! Eilert Lövborg! Recently—eh?

210   MISS TESMAN.   Yes, so they say. Heaven knows whether it can be worth anything! Ah, when your new book appears—that will be another story,
George! What is it to be about?

TESMAN.   It will deal with the domestic industries of Brabant during the
Middle Ages.

MISS TESMAN.   Fancy—to be able to write on such a subject as that!

TESMAN.   However, it may be some time before the book is ready. I have all
these collections to arrange first, you see.

MISS TESMAN.   Yes, collecting and arranging—no one can beat you at that.
There you are my poor brother's own son.

220   TESMAN.   I am looking forward eagerly to setting to work at it; especially now
that I have my own delightful home to work in.

MISS TESMAN.   And, most of all, now that you have got the wife of your heart,
my dear George.

TESMAN [*embracing her*].   Oh, yes, yes, Aunt Julia. Hedda—she is the best part
of all! [*Looks toward the doorway.*] I believe I hear her coming—eh?

[HEDDA *enters from the left through the inner room. She is a woman of nine-and-
twenty. Her face and figure show refinement and distinction. Her complexion is pale
and opaque. Her steel-grey eyes express a cold, unruffled repose. Her hair is of an
agreeable medium brown, but not particularly abundant. She is dressed in a tasteful,
somewhat loose-fitting morning-gown.*]

Miss Tesman [*going to meet* Hedda]. Good morning, my dear Hedda! Good morning, and a hearty welcome.

Hedda [*holds out her hand*]. Good morning, dear Miss Tesman! So early a call! This is kind of you.

230 Miss Tesman [*with some embarrassment*]. Well—has the bride slept well in her new home?

Hedda. Oh yes, thanks. Passably.

Tesman [*laughing*]. Passably! Come, that's good, Hedda! You were sleeping like a stone when I got up.

Hedda. Fortunately. Of course one has always to accustom one's self to new surroundings, Miss Tesman—little by little. [*Looking towards the left.*] Oh—there the servant has gone and opened the verandah door, and let in a whole flood of sunshine.

Miss Tesman [*going towards the door*]. Well, then, we will shut it.

240 Hedda. No, no, not that! Tesman, please draw the curtains. That will give a softer light.

Tesman [*at the door*]. All right—all right. There now, Hedda, now you have both shade and fresh air.

Hedda. Yes, fresh air we certainly must have, with all these stacks of flowers—But—won't you sit down, Miss Tesman?

Miss Tesman. No, thank you. Now that I have seen that everything is all right here—thank heaven!—I must be getting home again. My sister is lying longing for me, poor thing.

Tesman. Give her my very best love, Auntie; and say I shall look in and see
250   her later in the day.

Miss Tesman. Yes, yes, I'll be sure to tell her. But by-the-bye, George— [*feeling in her dress pocket*]—I have almost forgotten—I have something for you here.

Tesman. What is it, Auntie? Eh?

Miss Tesman [*produces a flat parcel wrapped in newspaper and hands it to him*]. Look here, my dear boy.

Tesman [*opening the parcel*]. Well, I declare! Have you really saved them for me, Aunt Julia! Hedda, isn't this touching—eh?

Hedda [*beside the whatnot on the right*]. Well, what is it?

260 Tesman. My old morning-shoes! My slippers.

Hedda. Indeed. I remember you often spoke of them while we were abroad.

Tesman. Yes, I missed them terribly. [*Goes up to her.*] Now you shall see them, Hedda!

Hedda [*going towards the stove*]. Thanks, I really don't care about it.

Tesman [*following her*]. Only think—ill as she was, Aunt Rina embroidered these for me. Oh you can't think how many associations cling to them.

Hedda [*at the table*]. Scarcely for me.

Miss Tesman. Of course not for Hedda, George.

Tesman. Well, but now that she belongs to the family, I thought—

270 Hedda [*interrupting*]. We shall never get on with this servant, Tesman.

Miss Tesman. Not get on with Berta?

Tesman. Why, dear, what puts that in your head? Eh?

Hedda [*pointing*]. Look there! She has left her old bonnet lying about on a chair.

TESMAN [*in consternation, drops the slippers on the floor*].   Why, Hedda—
HEDDA.   Just fancy, if any one should come in and see it.
TESMAN.   But Hedda—that's Aunt Julia's bonnet.
HEDDA.   Is it!
MISS TESMAN [*taking up the bonnet*].   Yes, indeed it's mine. And what's more,
280   it's not old, Madame Hedda.
HEDDA.   I really did not look closely at it, Miss Tesman.
MISS TESMAN [*trying on the bonnet*].   Let me tell you it's the first time I have
      worn it—the very first time.
TESMAN.   And a very nice bonnet it is too—quite a beauty!
MISS TESMAN.   Oh, it's no such great thing, George. [*Looks around her.*] My
      parasol—? Ah, here. [*Takes it.*] For this is mine too—[*mutters*]—not Berta's.
TESMAN.   A new bonnet and a new parasol! Only think, Hedda!
HEDDA.   Very handsome indeed.
TESMAN.   Yes, isn't it? But Auntie, take a good look at Hedda before you go!
290   See how handsome she is!
MISS TESMAN.   Oh, my dear boy, there's nothing new in that. Hedda was
      always lovely. [*She nods and goes towards the right.*]
TESMAN [*following*].   Yes, but have you noticed what splendid condition she is
      in? How she has filled out on the journey?
HEDDA [*crossing the room*].   Oh, do be quiet—?
MISS TESMAN [*who has stopped and turned*].   Filled out?
TESMAN.   Of course you don't notice it so much now that she has that dress
      on. But I, who can see—
HEDDA [*at the glass door, impatiently*].   Oh, you can't see anything.
300 TESMAN.   It must be the mountain air in the Tyrol—
HEDDA [*curtly, interrupting*].   I am exactly as I was when I started.
TESMAN.   So you insist; but I'm quite certain you are not. Don't you agree
      with me, Auntie?
MISS TESMAN [*who has been gazing at her with folded hands*].   Hedda is lovely—
      lovely—lovely. [*Goes up to her, takes her head between both hands, draws it
      downwards, and kisses her hair*]. God bless and preserve Hedda Tesman—for
      George's sake.
HEDDA [*gently freeing herself*].   Oh—! Let me go.
MISS TESMAN [*in quiet emotion*].   I shall not let a day pass without coming to
310   see you.
TESMAN.   No you won't, will you, Auntie? Eh?
MISS TESMAN.   Good-bye—good-bye!

[*She goes out by the hall door.* TESMAN *accompanies her. The door remains half open.*
TESMAN *can be heard repeating his message to Aunt Rina and his thanks for the
slippers.*
      In the meantime, HEDDA *walks about the room raising her arms and clenching her
hands as if in desperation. Then she flings back the curtains from the glass door, and
stands there looking out.*
      Presently TESMAN *returns and closes the door behind him.*]

TESMAN [*picks up the slippers from the floor*].   What are you looking at, Hedda?
HEDDA [*once more calm and mistress of herself*].   I am only looking at the leaves.
      They are so yellow—so withered.

Tesman [*wraps up the slippers and lays them on the table*].   Well, you see, we are
well into September now.

Hedda [*again restless*].   Yes, to think of it!—Already in—in September.

Tesman.   Don't you think Aunt Julia's manner was strange, dear? Almost
320   solemn? Can you imagine what was the matter with her? Eh?

Hedda.   I scarcely know her, you see. Is she often like that?

Tesman.   No, not as she was today.

Hedda [*leaving the glass door*].   Do you think she was annoyed about the
bonnet?

Tesman.   Oh, scarcely at all. Perhaps a little, just at the moment—

Hedda.   But what an idea, to pitch her bonnet about in the drawing-room!
No one does that sort of thing.

Tesman.   Well you may be sure Aunt Julia won't do it again.

Hedda.   In any case, I shall manage to make my peace with her.

330   Tesman.   Yes, my dear, good Hedda, if you only would.

Hedda.   When you call this afternoon, you might invite her to spend the
evening here.

Tesman.   Yes, that I will. And there's one thing more you could do that
would delight her heart.

Hedda.   What is it?

Tesman.   If you could only prevail on yourself to say *du*[5] to her. For my sake,
Hedda? Eh?

Hedda.   No, no, Tesman—you really mustn't ask that of me. I have told you
so already. I shall try to call her "Aunt"; and you must be satisfied with
340   that.

Tesman.   Well, well. Only I think now that you belong to the family, you—

Hedda.   H'm—I can't in the least see why—[*She goes up towards the middle
doorway.*]

Tesman [*after a pause*].   Is there anything the matter with you, Hedda? Eh?

Hedda.   I'm only looking at my old piano. It doesn't go at all well with all the
other things.

Tesman.   The first time I draw my salary, we'll see about exchanging it.

Hedda.   No, no—no exchanging. I don't want to part with it. Suppose we
put it there in the inner room, and then get another here in its place.
When it's convenient, I mean.

350   Tesman [*a little taken aback*].   Yes—of course we could do that.

Hedda [*takes up the bouquet from the piano*].   These flowers were not here last
night when we arrived.

Tesman.   Aunt Julia must have brought them for you.

Hedda [*examining the bouquet*].   A visiting-card. [*Takes it out and reads.*] "Shall
return later in the day." Can you guess whose card it is?

Tesman.   No. Whose? Eh?

Hedda.   The name is "Mrs. Elvsted."

Tesman.   Is it really? Sheriff Elvsted's wife? Miss Rysing that was.

Hedda.   Exactly. The girl with the irritating hair, that she was always show-
360   ing off. An old flame of yours, I've been told.

---

[5] Like the French and Germans, Norwegians reserve the familiar form of the pronoun "you"
(*du*) for conversations between lovers and intimate friends; the more formal *de* is used between
strangers and casual acquaintances.

TESMAN [*laughing*].   Oh, that didn't last long; and it was before I knew you,
   Hedda. But fancy her being in town!
HEDDA.   It's odd that she should call upon us. I have scarcely seen her since
   we left school.
TESMAN.   I haven't seen her either for—heaven knows how long. I wonder
   how she can endure to live in such an out-of-the-way hole—eh?
HEDDA [*after a moment's thought says suddenly*].   Tell me, Tesman—isn't it
   somewhere near there that he—that—Eilert Lövborg is living?
TESMAN.   Yes, he is somewhere in that part of the country.

                                            [BERTA *enters by the hall door.*]

370 BERTA.   That lady, ma'am, that brought some flowers a little while ago, is
   here again. [*Pointing.*] The flowers you have in your hand, ma'am.
HEDDA.   Ah, is she? Well, please show her in.

[BERTA *opens the door for* MRS. ELVSTED, *and goes out herself.—*MRS. ELVSTED *is a
woman of fragile figure, with pretty, soft features. Her eyes are light blue, large,
round, and somewhat prominent, with a startled, inquiring expression. Her hair is
remarkably light, almost flaxen, and unusually abundant and wavy. She is a couple
of years younger than* HEDDA. *She wears a dark visiting dress, tasteful, but not quite
in the latest fashion.*]

HEDDA [*receives her warmly*].   How do you do, my dear Mrs. Elvsted? It's
   delightful to see you again.
MRS. ELVSTED [*nervously, struggling for self-control*].   Yes, it's a very long time
   since we met.
TESMAN [*gives her his hand*].   And we too—eh?
HEDDA.   Thanks for your lovely flowers—
MRS. ELVSTED.   Oh, not at all—I would have come straight here yesterday
380   afternoon; but I heard that you were away—
TESMAN.   Have you just come to town? Eh?
MRS. ELVSTED.   I arrived yesterday, about midday. Oh, I was quite in despair
   when I heard that you were not at home.
HEDDA.   In despair! How so?
TESMAN.   Why, my dear Mrs. Rysing—I mean Mrs. Elvsted—
HEDDA.   I hope that you are not in any trouble?
MRS. ELVSTED.   Yes, I am. And I don't know another living creature here that
   I can turn to.
HEDDA [*laying the bouquet on the table*].   Come—let us sit here on the sofa—
390 MRS. ELVSTED.   Oh, I am too restless to sit down.
HEDDA.   Oh no, you're not. Come here. [*She draws* MRS. ELVSTED *down upon
   the sofa and sits at her side.*]
TESMAN.   Well? What is it, Mrs. Elvsted?
HEDDA.   Has anything in particular happened to you at home?
MRS. ELVSTED.   Yes—and no. Oh—I am so anxious you should not misun-
   derstand me—
HEDDA.   Then your best plan is to tell us the whole story, Mrs. Elvsted.
TESMAN.   I suppose that's what you have come for—eh?
MRS. ELVSTED.   Yes, yes—of course it is. Well then, I must tell you—if you
400   don't already know—that Eilert Lövborg is in town, too.

Hedda. Lövborg—!

Tesman. What! Has Eilert Lövborg come back? Fancy that, Hedda!

Hedda. Well, well—I hear it.

Mrs. Elvsted. He has been here a week already. Just fancy—a whole week! In this terrible town, alone! With so many temptations on all sides.

Hedda. But my dear Mrs. Elvsted—how does he concern you so much?

Mrs. Elvsted [*looks at her with a startled air, and says rapidly*]. He was the children's tutor.

Hedda. Your children's?

410 Mrs. Elvsted. My husband's. I have none.

Hedda. Your step-children's, then?

Mrs. Elvsted. Yes.

Tesman [*somewhat hesitantly*]. Then was he—I don't know how to express it—was he—regular enough in his habits to be fit for the post? Eh?

Mrs. Elvsted. For the last two years his conduct has been irreproachable.

Tesman. Has it indeed? Fancy that, Hedda!

Hedda. I hear it.

Mrs. Elvsted. Perfectly irreproachable, I assure you! In every respect. But all the same—now that I know he is here—in this great town—and with a
420 large sum of money in his hands—I can't help being in mortal fear for him.

Tesman. Why did he not remain where he was? With you and your husband? Eh?

Mrs. Elvsted. After his book was published he was too restless and unsettled to remain with us.

Tesman. Yes, by-the-bye, Aunt Julia told me he had published a new book.

Mrs. Elvsted. Yes, a big book, dealing with the march of civilization—in broad outline, as it were. It came out about a fortnight ago. And since it has sold so well, and been so much read—and made such a sensation—

430 Tesman. Has it indeed? It must be something he has had lying by since his better days.

Mrs. Elvsted. Long ago, you mean?

Tesman. Yes.

Mrs. Elvsted. No, he has written it all since he has been with us—within the last year.

Tesman. Isn't that good news, Hedda? Think of that.

Mrs. Elvsted. Ah, yes, if only it would last!

Hedda. Have you seen him here in town?

Mrs. Elvsted. No, not yet. I have had the greatest difficulty in finding out
440 his address. But this morning I discovered it at last.

Hedda [*looks searchingly at her*]. Do you know, it seems to me a little odd of your husband—h'm—

Mrs. Elvsted [*starting nervously*]. Of my husband! What?

Hedda. That he should send you to town on such an errand—that he does not come himself and look after his friend.

Mrs. Elvsted. Oh, no, no—my husband has no time. And besides, I—I had some shopping to do.

Hedda [*with a slight smile*]. Ah, that is a different matter.

Mrs. Elvsted [*rising quickly and uneasily*]. And now I beg and implore you,
450 Mr. Tesman—receive Eilert Lövborg kindly if he comes to you! And that

he is sure to do. You see you were such great friends in the old days. And then you are interested in the same studies—the same branch of science—so far as I can understand.

TESMAN.   We used to be, at any rate.

MRS. ELVSTED.   That is why I beg so earnestly that you—you too—will keep a sharp eye upon him. Oh, you will promise me that, Mr. Tesman—won't you?

TESMAN.   With the greatest of pleasure, Mrs. Rysing—

HEDDA.   Elvsted.

460 TESMAN.   I assure you I shall do all I possibly can for Eilert. You may rely upon me.

MRS. ELVSTED.   Oh, how very, very kind of you! [Presses his hands.] Thanks, thanks, thanks! [Frightened.] You see, my husband is very fond of him!

HEDDA [rising].   You ought to write to him, Tesman. Perhaps he may not care to come to you of his own accord.

TESMAN.   Well, perhaps it would be the right thing to do, Hedda? Eh?

HEDDA.   And the sooner the better. Why not at once?

MRS. ELVSTED [imploringly].   Oh, if you only would!

TESMAN.   I'll write this moment. Have you his address, Mrs.—Mrs. Elvsted?

470 MRS. ELVSTED.   Yes. [Takes a slip of paper from her pocket, and hands it to him.] Here it is.

TESMAN.   Good, good. Then I'll go in—[Looks about him.] By-the-bye,—my slippers? Oh, here. [Takes the packet, and is about to go.]

HEDDA.   Be sure you write him a cordial, friendly letter. And a good long one too.

TESMAN.   Yes, I will.

MRS. ELVSTED.   But please, please don't say a word to show that I have suggested it.

TESMAN.   No, how could you think I would? Eh?

[He goes out to the right, through the inner room.]

480 HEDDA [goes up to MRS. ELVSTED, smiles, and says in a low voice].   There. We have killed two birds with one stone.

MRS. ELVSTED.   What do you mean?

HEDDA.   Could you not see that I wanted him to go?

MRS. ELVSTED.   Yes, to write the letter—

HEDDA.   And that I might speak to you alone.

MRS. ELVSTED [confused].   About the same thing?

HEDDA.   Precisely.

MRS. ELVSTED [apprehensively].   But there is nothing more, Mrs. Tesman! Absolutely nothing!

490 HEDDA.   Oh, yes, but there is. There is a great deal more—I can see that. Sit here—and we'll have a cosy confidential chat. [She forces MRS. ELVSTED to sit in the easy-chair beside the stove, and seats herself on one of the foot-stools.]

MRS. ELVSTED [anxiously, looking at her watch].   But, my dear Mrs. Tesman—I was really on the point of going.

HEDDA.   Oh, you can't be in such a hurry.—Well? Now tell me something about your life at home.

MRS. ELVSTED.   Oh, that is just what I care least to speak about.

HEDDA. But to me, dear—? Why, weren't we school-fellows?

MRS. ELVSTED. Yes, but you were in the class above me. Oh, how dreadfully
500   afraid of you I was then!

HEDDA. Afraid of me?

MRS. ELVSTED. *Yes,* dreadfully. For when we met on the stairs you used always
to pull my hair.

HEDDA. Did I, really?

MRS. ELVSTED. Yes, and once you said you would burn it off my head.

HEDDA. Oh, that was all nonsense, of course.

MRS. ELVSTED. Yes, but I was so silly in those days.—And since then, too—we
have drifted so far—far apart from each other. Our circles have been so
entirely different.

510 HEDDA. Well, then, we must try to drift together again. Now listen! At school
we said *du* to each other; and we called each other by our Christian
names—

MRS. ELVSTED. No, I am sure you must be mistaken.

HEDDA. No, not at all! I can remember quite distinctly. So now we are going
to renew our old friendship. [*Draws the foot-stool closer to* MRS. ELVSTED.]
There now! [*Kisses her cheek.*] You must say *du* to me and call me Hedda.

MRS. ELVSTED [*presses and pats her hands*]. Oh, how good and kind you are! I
am not used to such kindness.

HEDDA. There, there, there! And I shall say *du* to you, as in the old days, and
520   call you my dear Thora.

MRS. ELVSTED. My name is Thea.

HEDDA. Why, of course! I meant Thea. [*Looks at her compassionately.*] So you
are not accustomed to goodness and kindness, Thea? Not in your own
home?

MRS. ELVSTED. Oh, if I only had a home! But I haven't any; I have never had
a home.

HEDDA [*looks at her for a moment*]. I almost suspected as much.

MRS. ELVSTED [*gazing helplessly before her*]. Yes—yes—yes.

HEDDA. I don't quite remember—was it not as housekeeper that you first
530   went to Mr. Elvsted's?

MRS. ELVSTED. I really went as governess. But his wife—his late wife—was an
invalid,—and rarely left her room. So I had to look after the housekeeping
as well.

HEDDA. And then—at last—you became mistress of the house.

MRS. ELVSTED [*sadly*]. Yes, I did.

HEDDA. Let me see—about how long ago was that?

MRS. ELVSTED. My marriage?

HEDDA. Yes.

MRS. ELVSTED. Five years ago.

540 HEDDA. To be sure; it must be that.

MRS. ELVSTED. Oh, those five years—! Or at all events the last two or three
of them! Oh, if you could only imagine—

HEDDA [*giving her a little slap on the hand*]. De?[6] Fie, Thea!

---

[6] *De* is the formal second-person pronoun. Hedda wishes Thea to use the more intimate
pronoun *du.*

MRS. ELVSTED.   Yes, yes, I will try—Well if—you could only imagine and understand—

HEDDA [*lightly*].   Eilert Lövborg has been in your neighborhood about three years, hasn't he?

MRS. ELVSTED [*looks at her doubtfully*].   Eilert Lövborg? Yes—he has.

HEDDA.   Had you known him before, in town here?

550 MRS. ELVSTED.   Scarcely at all. I mean—I knew him by name of course.

HEDDA.   But you saw a good deal of him in the country?

MRS. ELVSTED.   Yes, he came to us every day. You see, he gave the children lessons; for in the long run I couldn't manage it all myself.

HEDDA.   No, that's clear.—And your husband—? I suppose he is often away from home?

MRS. ELVSTED.   Yes. Being Sheriff, you know, he has to travel about a good deal in his district.

HEDDA [*leaning against the arm of the chair*].   Thea—my poor, sweet Thea—now you must tell me everything—exactly as it stands.

560 MRS. ELVSTED.   Well then, you must question me.

HEDDA.   What sort of a man is your husband, Thea? I mean—you know—in everyday life. Is he kind to you?

MRS. ELVSTED [*evasively*].   I am sure he means well in everything.

HEDDA.   I should think he must be altogether too old for you. There is at least twenty years' difference between you, is there not?

MRS. ELVSTED [*irritably*].   Yes, that is true, too. Everything about him is repellent to me! We have not a thought in common. We have no single point of sympathy—he and I.

HEDDA.   But is he not fond of you all the same? In his own way?

570 MRS. ELVSTED.   Oh, I really don't know. I think he regards me simply as a useful property. And then it doesn't cost much to keep me. I am not expensive.

HEDDA.   That is stupid of you.

MRS. ELVSTED [*shakes her head*].   It cannot be otherwise—not with him. I don't think he really cares for any one but himself—and perhaps a little for the children.

HEDDA.   And for Eilert Lövborg, Thea.

MRS. ELVSTED [*looking at her*].   For Eilert Lövborg? What puts that into your head?

580 HEDDA.   Well, my dear—I should say, when he sends you after him all the way to town—[*smiling almost imperceptibly*]. And besides, you said so yourself, to Tesman.

MRS. ELVSTED [*with a little nervous twitch*].   Did I? Yes, I suppose I did. [*Vehemently, but not loudly.*] No—I may just as well make a clean breast of it at once! For it must all come out in any case.

HEDDA.   Why, my dear Thea—

MRS. ELVSTED.   Well, to make a long story short: My husband did not know that I was coming.

HEDDA.   What! Your husband didn't know it!

590 MRS. ELVSTED.   No, of course not. For that matter, he was away from home himself—he was traveling. Oh, I could bear it no longer, Hedda! I couldn't indeed—so utterly alone as I should have been in future.

HEDDA.   Well? And then?

Mrs. Elvsted.   So I put together some of my things—what I needed most—as quietly as possible. And then I left the house.

Hedda.   Without a word?

Mrs. Elvsted.   Yes—and took the train straight to town.

Hedda.   Why, my dear, good Thea—to think of you daring to do it!

Mrs. Elvsted [*rises and moves about the room*].   What else could I possibly do?

600 Hedda.   But what do you think your husband will say when you go home again?

Mrs. Elvsted [*at the table, looks at her*].   Back to him?

Hedda.   Of course.

Mrs. Elvsted.   I shall never go back to him again.

Hedda [*rising and going towards her*].   Then you have left your home—for good and all?

Mrs. Elvsted.   Yes. There was nothing else to be done.

Hedda.   But then—to take flight so openly.

Mrs. Elvsted.   Oh, it's impossible to keep things of that sort secret.

610 Hedda.   But what do you think people will say of you, Thea?

Mrs. Elvsted.   They may say what they like for aught *I* care. [*Seats herself wearily and sadly on the sofa.*] I have done nothing but what I had to do.

Hedda [*after a short silence*].   And what are your plans now? What do you think of doing?

Mrs. Elvsted.   I don't know yet. I only know this, that I must live here, where Eilert Lövborg is—if I am to live at all.

Hedda [*takes a chair from the table, seats herself beside her, and strokes her hands*]. My dear Thea—how did this—this friendship—between you and Eilert Lövborg come about?

620 Mrs. Elvsted.   Oh, it grew up gradually. I gained a sort of influence over him.

Hedda.   Indeed?

Mrs. Elvsted.   He gave up his old habits. Not because I asked him to, for I never dared do that. But of course he saw how repulsive they were to me; and so he dropped them.

Hedda [*concealing an involuntary smile of scorn*].   Then you have reclaimed him—as the saying goes—my little Thea.

Mrs. Elvsted.   So he says himself, at any rate. And he, on his side, has made a real human being of me—taught me to think, and to understand so
630 many things.

Hedda.   Did he give you lessons too, then?

Mrs. Elvsted.   No, not exactly lessons. But he talked to me—talked about such an infinity of things. And then came the lovely, happy time when I began to share in his work—when he allowed me to help him!

Hedda.   Oh, he did, did he?

Mrs. Elvsted.   Yes! He never wrote anything without my assistance.

Hedda.   You were two good comrades, in fact?

Mrs. Elvsted [*eagerly*].   Comrades! Yes, fancy Hedda—that is the very word he used!—Oh, I ought to feel perfectly happy; and yet I cannot; for I don't
640 know how long it will last.

Hedda.   Are you no surer of him than that?

Mrs. Elvsted [*gloomily*].   A woman's shadow stands between Eilert Lövborg and me.

HEDDA [*looks at her anxiously*].   Who can that be?

MRS. ELVSTED.   I don't know. Some one he knew in his—in his past. Some one he has never been able wholly to forget.

HEDDA.   What has he told you—about this?

MRS. ELVSTED.   He has only once—quite vaguely—alluded to it.

HEDDA.   Well! And what did he say?

650 MRS. ELVSTED.   He said that when they parted, she threatened to shoot him with a pistol.

HEDDA [*with cold composure*].   Oh, nonsense! No one does that sort of thing here.

MRS. ELVSTED.   No. And that is why I think it must have been that red-haired singing woman whom he once—

HEDDA.   Yes, very likely.

MRS. ELVSTED.   For I remember they used to say of her that she carried loaded firearms.

HEDDA.   Oh—then of course it must have been she.

660 MRS. ELVSTED [*wringing her hands*].   And now just fancy, Hedda—I hear that this singing-woman—that she is in town again! Oh, I don't know what to do—

HEDDA [*glancing towards the inner room*].   Hush! Here comes Tesman. [*Rises and whispers.*] Thea—all this must remain between you and me.

MRS. ELVSTED [*springing up*].   Oh, yes, yes! for heaven's sake—!

[GEORGE TESMAN, *with a letter in his hand, comes from the right through the inner room.*]

TESMAN.   There now—the epistle is finished.

HEDDA.   That's right. And now Mrs. Elvsted is just going. Wait a moment—I'll go with you to the garden gate.

TESMAN.   Do you think Berta could post the letter, Hedda dear?

670 HEDDA [*takes it*].   I will tell her so.

[BERTA *enters from the hall.*]

BERTA.   Judge Brack wishes to know if Mrs. Tesman will receive him.

HEDDA.   Yes, ask Judge Brack to come in. And look here—put this letter in the post.

BERTA [*taking the letter*].   Yes, ma'am.

[*She opens the door for* JUDGE BRACK *and goes out herself.* BRACK *is a man of forty-five; thick-set, but well-built and elastic in his movements. His face is roundish with an aristocratic profile. His hair is short, still almost black, and carefully dressed. His eyes are lively and sparkling. His eyebrows thick. His moustaches are also thick, with short-cut ends. He wears a well-cut walking-suit, a little too youthful for his age. He uses an eye-glass, which he now and then lets drop.*]

JUDGE BRACK [*with his hat in his hand, bowing*].   May one venture to call so early in the day?

HEDDA.   Of course one may.

TESMAN [*presses his hand*].   You are welcome at any time. [*Introducing him.*] Judge Brack—Miss Rysing—

680 HEDDA.   Oh—!

BRACK [*bowing*]. Ah—delighted—

HEDDA [*looks at him and laughs*].   It's nice to have a look at you by daylight, Judge!

BRACK.   Do you find me—altered?

HEDDA.   A little younger, I think.

BRACK.   Thank you so much.

TESMAN.   But what do you think of Hedda—eh? Doesn't she look flourishing? She has actually—

HEDDA.   Oh, do leave me alone. You haven't thanked Judge Brack for all the
690   trouble he has taken—

BRACK.   Oh, nonsense—it was a pleasure to me—

HEDDA.   Yes, you are a friend indeed. But here stands Thea, all impatience to be off—so *au revoir,* Judge. I shall be back again presently.

[*Mutual salutations.* MRS. ELVSTED *and* HEDDA *go out by the hall door.*]

BRACK.   Well,—is your wife tolerably satisfied—

TESMAN.   Yes, we can't thank you sufficiently. Of course she talks of a little re-arrangement here and there; and one or two things still wanting. We shall have to buy some additional trifles.

BRACK.   Indeed!

700 TESMAN.   But we won't trouble you about these things. Hedda says she herself will look after what is wanting.—Shan't we sit down? Eh?

BRACK.   Thanks, for a moment. [*Seats himself beside the table.*] There is something I wanted to speak to you about, my dear Tesman.

TESMAN.   Indeed? Ah, I understand! [*Seating himself.*] I suppose it's the serious part of the frolic that is coming now. Eh?

BRACK.   Oh, the money question is not so very pressing; though, for that matter, I wish we had gone a little more economically to work.

TESMAN.   But that would never have done, you know! Think of Hedda, my dear fellow! You, who know her so well—. I couldn't possibly ask her to put
710   up with a shabby style of living!

BRACK.   No, no—that is just the difficulty.

TESMAN.   And then—fortunately—it can't be long before I receive my appointment.

BRACK.   Well, you see—such things are often apt to hang fire for a time.

TESMAN.   Have you heard anything definite? Eh?

BRACK.   Nothing exactly definite—[*interrupting himself*]. But by-the-bye—I have one piece of news for you.

TESMAN.   Well?

BRACK.   Your old friend, Eilert Lövborg, has returned to town.

720 TESMAN.   I know that already.

BRACK.   Indeed! How did you learn it?

TESMAN.   From that lady who went out with Hedda.

BRACK.   Really? What was her name? I didn't quite catch it.

TESMAN.   Mrs. Elvsted.

BRACK.   Aha—Sheriff Elvsted's wife? Of course—he has been living up in their regions.

TESMAN.   And fancy—I'm delighted to hear that he is quite a reformed character!

BRACK.   So they say.

730 TESMAN.   And then he has published a new book—eh?

BRACK.   Yes, indeed he has.

TESMAN.   And I hear it has made some sensation!

BRACK.   Quite an unusual sensation.

TESMAN.   Fancy—isn't that good news! A man of such extraordinary talents—I felt so grieved to think he had gone irretrievably to ruin.

BRACK.   That was what everybody thought.

TESMAN.   But I cannot imagine what he will take to now! How in the world will he be able to make his living? Eh?

[*During the last words,* HEDDA *has entered by the hall door.*]

HEDDA [*to* BRACK, *laughing with a touch of scorn*].   Tesman is forever worrying
740   about how people are to make their living.

TESMAN.   Well, you see, dear—we were talking about poor Eilert Lövborg.

HEDDA [*glancing at him rapidly*].   Oh, indeed? [*Seats herself in the arm-chair beside the stove and asks indifferently.*] What is the matter with him?

TESMAN.   Well—no doubt he has run through all his property long ago; and he can scarcely write a new book every year—eh? So I really can't see what is to become of him.

BRACK.   Perhaps I can give you some information on that point.

TESMAN.   Indeed!

BRACK.   You must remember that his relations have a good deal of influence.

750 TESMAN.   Oh, his relations, unfortunately have entirely washed their hands of him.

BRACK.   At one time they called him the hope of the family.

TESMAN.   At one time, yes! But he has put an end to all that.

HEDDA.   Who knows? [*With a slight smile.*] I hear they have reclaimed him up at Sheriff Elvsted's—

BRACK.   And then this book he has published—

TESMAN.   Well, well, I hope to goodness they may find something for him to do. I have just written to him. I asked him to come and see us this evening, Hedda dear.

760 BRACK.   But, my dear fellow, you are booked for my bachelors' party this evening. You promised on the pier last night.

HEDDA.   Had you forgotten, Tesman?

TESMAN.   Yes, I had utterly forgotten.

BRACK.   But it doesn't matter, for you may be sure he won't come.

TESMAN.   What makes you think that? Eh?

BRACK [*with a little hesitation, rising and resting his hands on the back of his chair*].   My dear Tesman—and you too, Mrs. Tesman—I think I ought not to keep you in the dark about something that—that—

TESMAN.   That concerns Eilert—?

770 BRACK.   Both you and him.

TESMAN.   Well, my dear Judge, out with it.

BRACK.   You must be prepared to find your appointment deferred longer than you desired or expected.

TESMAN [*jumping up uneasily*].   Is there some hitch about it? Eh?

BRACK.   The nomination may perhaps be made conditional on the result of a competition—

TESMAN.   Competition! Think of that, Hedda!

HEDDA [*leans farther back in the chair*].   Aha—aha!

TESMAN.   But who can my competitor be? Surely not—?

780 BRACK.   Yes, precisely—Eilert Lövborg.

TESMAN [*clasping his hands*].   No, no—it's quite inconceivable! Quite impossible! Eh?

BRACK.   H'm—that is what it may come to, all the same.

TESMAN.   Well but, Judge Brack—it would show the most incredible lack of consideration for me. [*Gesticulates with his arms.*] For—just think—I'm a married man. We have been married on the strength of these prospects, Hedda and I; and run deep into debt; and borrowed money from Aunt Julia too. Good heavens, they had as good as promised me the appointment. Eh?

790 BRACK.   Well, well, well—no doubt you will get it in the end; only after a contest.

HEDDA [*immovable in her arm-chair*].   Fancy, Tesman, there will be a sort of sporting interest in that.

TESMAN.   Why, my dearest Hedda, how can you be so indifferent about it?

HEDDA [*as before*].   I am not at all indifferent. I am most eager to see who wins.

BRACK.   In any case, Mrs. Tesman, it is best that you should know how matters stand. I mean—before you set about the little purchases I hear you are threatening.

800 HEDDA.   This can make no difference.

BRACK.   Indeed! Then I have no more to say. Good-bye! [*To* TESMAN.] I shall look in on my way back from my afternoon walk, and take you home with me.

TESMAN.   Oh yes, yes—your news has quite upset me.

HEDDA [*reclining, holds out her hand*].   Good-bye, Judge; and be sure to call in the afternoon.

BRACK.   Many thanks. Good-bye, good-bye!

TESMAN [*accompanying him to the door*].   Good-bye, my dear Judge! You must really excuse me—

[JUDGE BRACK *goes out by the hall door.*]

810 TESMAN [*crosses the room*].   Oh, Hedda—one should never rush into adventures. Eh?

HEDDA [*looks at him, smiling*].   Do you do that?

TESMAN.   Yes, dear—there is no denying—it was adventurous to go and marry and set up house upon mere expectations.

HEDDA.   Perhaps you are right there.

TESMAN.   Well—at all events, we have our delightful home, Hedda! Fancy, the home we both dreamed of—the home we were in love with, I may almost say. Eh?

HEDDA [*rising slowly and wearily*].   It was part of our compact that we were to
820   go into society—to keep open house.

TESMAN.   Yes, if you only knew how I had been looking forward to it! Fancy—to see you as hostess—in a select circle? Eh? Well, well, well—for the present we shall have to get on without society, Hedda—only invite Aunt Julia now and then.—Oh, I intended you to lead such an utterly different life, dear—!

HEDDA.   Of course I cannot have my man in livery just yet.

TESMAN.   Oh no, unfortunately. It would be out of the question for us to keep
a footman, you know.

HEDDA.   And the saddle-horse I was to have had—

830 TESMAN [*aghast*].   The saddle-horse!

HEDDA.   —I suppose I must not think of that now.

TESMAN.   Good heavens, no!—that's as clear as daylight.

HEDDA [*goes up the room*].   Well, I shall have one thing at least to kill time with
in the meanwhile.

TESMAN [*beaming*].   Oh, thank heaven for that! What is it, Hedda? Eh?

HEDDA [*in the middle doorway, looks at him with covert scorn*].   My pistols, George.

TESMAN [*in alarm*].   Your pistols!

HEDDA [*with cold eyes*].   General Gabler's pistols.

[*She goes out through the inner room, to the left.*]

TESMAN [*rushes up to the middle doorway and calls after her.*]   No, for heaven's
840   sake, Hedda darling—don't touch those dangerous things! For my sake,
Hedda! Eh?

ACT II

The room at the TESMANS' *as in the first act, except that the piano has been removed,
and an elegant little writing-table with bookshelves put in its place. A smaller table
stands near the sofa at the left. Most of the bouquets have been taken away.* MRS.
ELVSTED's *bouquet is upon the large table in front.—It is afternoon.*

HEDDA, *dressed to receive callers, is alone in the room. She stands by the open glass
door, loading a revolver. The fellow to it lies in an open pistol-case on the writing-
table.*

HEDDA [*looks down the garden, and calls*].   So you are here again, Judge!

BRACK [*is heard calling from a distance*].   As you see, Mrs. Tesman!

HEDDA [*raises the pistol and points*].   Now I'll shoot you, Judge Brack!

BRACK [*calling unseen*].   No, no, no! Don't stand aiming at me!

HEDDA.   This is what comes of sneaking in by the back way. [*She fires.*]

BRACK [*nearer*].   Are you out of your senses—!

HEDDA.   Dear me—did I happen to hit you?

850 BRACK [*still outside*].   I wish you would let these pranks alone!

HEDDA.   Come in then, Judge.

[JUDGE BRACK, *dressed as though for a men's party, enters by the glass door. He carries
a light overcoat over his arm.*]

BRACK.   What the deuce—haven't you tired of that sport, yet? What are you
shooting at?

HEDDA.   Oh, I am only firing in the air.

BRACK [*gently takes the pistol out of her hand*].   Allow me, madam! [*Looks at it.*]
Ah— I know this pistol well! [*Looks around.*] Where is the case? Ah, here it
is. [*Lays the pistol in it, and shuts it.*] Now we won't play at that game any
more today.

HEDDA.   Then what in heaven's name would you have me do with myself?

860 BRACK. Have you had no visitors?

HEDDA [*closing the glass door*]. Not one. I suppose all our set are still out of town.

BRACK. And is Tesman not at home either?

HEDDA [*at the writing-table putting the pistol-case in a drawer which she shuts*]. No. He rushed off to his aunt's directly after lunch; he didn't expect you so early.

BRACK. H'm—how stupid of me not to have thought of that!

HEDDA [*turning her head to look at him*]. Why stupid?

BRACK. Because if I had thought of it I should have come a little—earlier.

870 HEDDA [*crossing the room*]. Then you would have found no one to receive you; for I have been in my room changing my dress ever since lunch.

BRACK. And is there no sort of little chink that we could hold a parley through?

HEDDA. You have forgotten to arrange one.

BRACK. That was another piece of stupidity.

HEDDA. Well, we must just settle down here—and wait. Tesman is not likely to be back for some time yet.

BRACK. Never mind; I shall not be impatient.

[HEDDA *seats herself in the corner of the sofa.* BRACK *lays his overcoat over the back of the nearest chair, and sits down, but keeps his hat in his hand. A short silence. They look at each other.*]

HEDDA. Well?

880 BRACK [*in the same tone*]. Well?

HEDDA. I spoke first.

BRACK [*bending a little forward*]. Come, let us have a cosy little chat, Mrs. Hedda.

HEDDA [*leaning further back in the sofa*]. Does it not seem like a whole eternity since our last talk? Of course I don't count those few words yesterday evening and this morning.

BRACK. You mean since our last confidential talk? Our last *tête-à-tête*?[7]

HEDDA. Well, yes—since you put it so.

BRACK. Not a day has passed but I have wished that you were home again.

890 HEDDA. And I have done nothing but wish the same thing.

BRACK. You? Really, Mrs. Hedda. And I thought you had been enjoying your tour so much!

HEDDA. Oh, yes, you may be sure of that!

BRACK. But Tesman's letters spoke of nothing but happiness.

HEDDA. Oh, Tesman! You see, he thinks nothing so delightful as grubbing in libraries and making copies of old parchments, or whatever you call them.

BRACK [*with a spice of malice*]. Well, that is his vocation in life—or part of it at any rate.

900 HEDDA. Yes, of course; and no doubt when it's your vocation—But *I*! Oh, my dear Mr. Brack, how mortally bored I have been.

BRACK [*sympathetically*]. Do you really say so? In downright earnest?

---

[7] A private conversation.

HEDDA.   Yes, you can surely understand it—! To go for six whole months
without meeting a soul that knew anything of our circle, or could talk
about the things we are interested in.
BRACK.   Yes, yes—I too should feel that a deprivation.
HEDDA.   And then, what I found most intolerable of all—
BRACK.   Well?
HEDDA.   —was being everlastingly in the company of—one and the same
910   person—
BRACK [*with a nod of assent*].   Morning, noon, and night, yes—at all possible
times and seasons.
HEDDA.   I said "everlastingly."
BRACK.   Just so. But I should have thought, with our excellent Tesman, one
could—
HEDDA.   Tesman is—a specialist, my dear Judge.
BRACK.   Undeniably.
HEDDA.   And specialists are not at all amusing to travel with. Not in the long
run at any rate.
920   BRACK.   Not even—the specialist one happens to love?
HEDDA.   Faugh—don't use that sickening word!
BRACK [*taken aback*].   What do you say, Mrs. Hedda?
HEDDA [*half laughing, half irritated*].   You should just try it! To hear of nothing
but the history of civilization, morning, noon, and night—
BRACK.   Everlastingly.
HEDDA.   Yes, yes, yes! And then all this about the domestic industry of the
middle ages—! That's the most disgusting part of it!
BRACK [*looks searchingly at her*].   But tell me—in that case, how am I to un-
derstand your—? H'm—
930   HEDDA.   My accepting George Tesman, you mean?
BRACK.   Well, let us put it so.
HEDDA.   Good heavens, do you see anything so wonderful in that?
BRACK.   Yes and no—Mrs. Hedda.
HEDDA.   I had positively danced myself tired, my dear Judge. My day was
done— [*With a slight shudder.*] Oh no—I won't say that; nor think it either!
BRACK.   You have assuredly no reason to.
HEDDA.   Oh, reasons— [*Watching him closely.*] And George Tesman—after all,
you must admit that he is correctness itself.
BRACK.   His correctness and respectability are beyond all question.
940   HEDDA.   And I don't see anything absolutely ridiculous about him.—Do you?
BRACK.   Ridiculous? N—no—I shouldn't exactly say so—
HEDDA.   Well—and his powers of research, at all events are untiring.—I see
no reason why he should not one day come to the front, after all.
BRACK [*looks at her hesitatingly*].   I thought that you, like every one else, expected him to attain the highest distinction.
HEDDA [*with an expression of fatigue*].   Yes, so I did.—And then, since he was
bent, at all hazards, on being allowed to provide for me—and I really
don't know why I should not have accepted his offer?
BRACK.   No—if you look at it in that light—
950   HEDDA.   It was more than my other adorers were prepared to do for me, my
dear Judge.
BRACK [*laughing*].   Well, I can't answer for all the rest; but as for myself, you

know quite well that I have always entertained a—a certain respect for the marriage tie—for marriage as an institution, Mrs. Hedda.

HEDDA [*jestingly*].   Oh, I assure you I have never cherished any hopes with respect to you.

BRACK.   All I require is a pleasant and intimate interior, where I can make myself useful in every way, and am free to come and go as—a trusted friend—

960 HEDDA.   Of the master of the house, do you mean?

BRACK [*bowing*].   Frankly—of the mistress first of all; but of course of the master, too, in the second place. Such a triangular friendship—if I may call it so—is really a great convenience for all parties, let me tell you.

HEDDA.   Yes, I have many a time longed for some one to make a third on our travels. Oh—those railway-carriage *tête-à-têtes*—!

BRACK.   Fortunately your wedding journey is over now.

HEDDA [*shaking her head*].   Not by a long—long way. I have only arrived at a station on the line.

BRACK.   Well, then the passengers jump out and move about a little, Mrs.
970 Hedda.

HEDDA.   I never jump out.

BRACK.   Really?

HEDDA.   No—because there is always some one standing by to—

BRACK [*laughing*].   To look at your ankles, do you mean?

HEDDA.   Precisely.

BRACK.   Well but, dear me—

HEDDA [*with a gesture of repulsion*].   I won't have it. I would rather keep my seat where I happen to be—and continue the *tête-à-tête*.

BRACK.   But suppose a third person were to jump in and join the couple.

980 HEDDA.   Ah—that is quite another matter!

BRACK.   A trusted, sympathetic friend—

HEDDA.   —with a fund of conversation on all sorts of lively topics—

BRACK.   —and not the least bit of a specialist!

HEDDA [*with an audible sigh*].   Yes, that would be a relief indeed.

BRACK [*hears the front door open, and glances in that direction*].   The triangle is completed.

HEDDA [*half aloud*].   And on goes the train.

[GEORGE TESMAN, *in a gray walking-suit, with a soft felt hat, enters from the hall. He has a number of unbound books under his arm and in his pockets.*]

TESMAN [*goes up to the table beside the corner settee*].   Ouf—what a load for a warm day—all these books. [*Lays them on the table.*] I'm positively perspir-
990 ing, Hedda. Hallo—are you there already, my dear Judge? Eh? Berta didn't tell me.

BRACK [*rising*].   I came in through the garden.

HEDDA.   What books have you got here?

TESMAN [*stands looking them through*].   Some new books on my special subjects—quite indispensable to me.

HEDDA.   Your special subjects?

BRACK.   Yes, books on his special subjects, Mrs. Tesman. [BRACK *and* HEDDA *exchange a confidential smile.*]

HEDDA.   Do you need still more books on your special subjects?

1000 TESMAN.   Yes, my dear Hedda, one can never have too many of them. Of course one must keep up with all that is written and published.

HEDDA.   Yes, I suppose one must.

TESMAN [*searching among his books*].   And look here—I have got hold of Eilert Lövborg's new book too. [*Offering it to her.*] Perhaps you would like to glance through it, Hedda? Eh?

HEDDA.   No, thank you. Or rather—afterwards perhaps.

TESMAN.   I looked into it a little on the way home.

BRACK.   Well, what do you think of it—as a specialist?

TESMAN.   I think it shows quite remarkable soundness of judgment. He never 1010 wrote like that before. [*Putting the books together.*] Now I shall take all these into my study. I'm longing to cut the leaves—! And then I must change my clothes. [*To* BRACK.] I suppose we needn't start just yet? Eh?

BRACK.   Oh, dear no—there is not the slightest hurry.

TESMAN.   Well then, I will take my time. [*Is going with his books, but stops in the doorway and turns.*] By-the-bye, Hedda—Aunt Julia is not coming this evening.

HEDDA.   Not coming? Is it that affair of the bonnet that keeps her away?

TESMAN.   Oh, not at all. How could you think such a thing of Aunt Julia? Just fancy—! The fact is, Aunt Rina is very ill.

1020 HEDDA.   She always is.

TESMAN.   Yes, but today she is much worse than usual, poor dear.

HEDDA.   Oh, then it's only natural that her sister should remain with her. I must bear my disappointment.

TESMAN.   And you can't imagine, dear, how delighted Aunt Julia seemed to be—because you had come home looking so flourishing!

HEDDA [*half aloud, rising*].   Oh, those everlasting aunts!

TESMAN.   What?

HEDDA [*going to the glass door*].   Nothing.

TESMAN.   Oh, all right.

[*He goes through the inner room, out to the right.*]

1030 BRACK.   What bonnet were you talking about?

HEDDA.   Oh, it was a little episode with Miss Tesman this morning. She had laid down her bonnet on the chair there—[*looks at him and smiles*].—And I pretended to think it was the servant's.

BRACK [*shaking his head*].   Now my dear Mrs. Hedda, how could you do such a thing? To that excellent old lady, too!

HEDDA [*nervously crossing the room*].   Well, you see—these impulses come over me all of a sudden; and I cannot resist them. [*Throws herself down in the easy-chair by the stove.*] Oh, I don't know how to explain it.

BRACK [*behind the easy-chair*].   You are not really happy—that is the bottom of 1040 it.

HEDDA [*looking straight before her*].   I know of no reason why I should be—happy. Perhaps you can give me one?

BRACK.   Well—amongst other things, because you have got exactly the home you had set your heart on.

HEDDA [*looks up at him and laughs*].   Do you too believe in that legend?

BRACK. Is there nothing in it, then?

HEDDA. Oh, yes, there is something in it.

BRACK. Well?

HEDDA. There is this in it, that I made use of Tesman to see me home from
1050   evening parties last summer—

BRACK. I, unfortunately, had to go quite a different way.

HEDDA. That's true. I know you were going a different way last summer.

BRACK [*laughing*]. Oh fie, Mrs. Hedda! Well, then—you and Tesman—?

HEDDA. Well, we happened to pass here one evening; Tesman, poor fellow,
    was writhing in the agony of having to find conversation; so I took pity on
    the learned man—

BRACK [*smiles doubtfully*]. You took pity? H'm—

HEDDA. Yes, I really did. And so—to help him out of his torment—I hap-
    pened to say, in pure thoughtlessness, that I should like to live in this villa.

1060 BRACK. No more than that?

HEDDA. Not that evening.

BRACK. But afterwards?

HEDDA. Yes, my thoughtlessness had consequences, my dear Judge.

BRACK. Unfortunately that too often happens, Mrs. Hedda.

HEDDA. Thanks! So you see it was this enthusiasm for Secretary Falk's villa
    that first constituted a bond of sympathy between George Tesman and me.
    From that came our engagement and our marriage, and our wedding
    journey, and all the rest of it. Well, well, my dear Judge—as you make your
    bed so you must lie, I could almost say.

1070 BRACK. This is exquisite! And you really cared not a rap about it all the time?

HEDDA. No, heaven knows I didn't.

BRACK. But now? Now that we have made it so homelike for you?

HEDDA. Uh—the rooms all seem to smell of lavender and dried rose-
    leaves.—But perhaps it's Aunt Julia that has brought that scent with her.

BRACK [*laughing*]. No, I think it must be a legacy from the late Mrs. Secre-
    tary Falk.

HEDDA. Yes, there is an odor of mortality about it. It reminds me of a
    bouquet—the day after the ball. [*Clasps her hands behind her head, leans back
    in her chair and looks at him.*] Oh, my dear Judge—you cannot imagine how
1080   horribly I shall bore myself here.

BRACK. Why should not you, too, find some sort of vocation in life, Mrs.
    Hedda?

HEDDA. A vocation—that should attract me?

BRACK. If possible, of course.

HEDDA. Heaven knows what sort of a vocation that could be. I often wonder
    whether—[*breaking off*]. But that would never do either.

BRACK. Who can tell? Let me hear what it is.

HEDDA. Whether I might not get Tesman to go into politics, I mean.

BRACK [*laughing*]. Tesman? No, really now, political life is not the thing for
1090   him—not at all in his line.

HEDDA. No, I daresay not.—But if I could get him into it all the same?

BRACK. Why—what satisfaction could you find in that? If he is not fitted for
    that sort of thing, why should you want to drive him into it?

HEDDA. Because I am bored, I tell you! [*After a pause.*] So you think it quite
    out of the question that Tesman should ever get into the ministry?

BRACK. H'm—you see, my dear Mrs. Hedda—to get into the ministry, he would have to be a tolerably rich man.

HEDDA [*rising impatiently*]. Yes, there we have it! It is this genteel poverty I have managed to drop into—! [*Crosses the room.*] That is what makes life so
1100   pitiable! So utterly ludicrous!—For that's what it is.

BRACK. Now *I* should say the fault lay elsewhere.

HEDDA. Where, then?

BRACK. You have never gone through any really stimulating experience.

HEDDA. Anything serious, you mean?

BRACK. Yes, you may call it so. But now you may perhaps have one in store.

HEDDA [*tossing her head*]. Oh, you're thinking of the annoyances about this wretched professorship! But that must be Tesman's own affair. I assure you I shall not waste a thought upon it.

BRACK. No, no. I daresay not. But suppose now that what people call—in
1110   elegant language—a solemn responsibility were to come upon you? [*Smiling.*] A new responsibility, Mrs. Hedda?

HEDDA [*angrily*]. Be quiet! Nothing of that sort will ever happen!

BRACK [*warily*]. We will speak of this again a year hence—at the very outside.

HEDDA [*curtly*]. I have no turn for anything of the sort, Judge Brack. No responsibilities for me!

BRACK. Are you so unlike the generality of women as to have no turn for the duties which—?

HEDDA [*beside the glass door*]. Oh, be quiet, I tell you! I often think there is only one thing in the world I have any turn for.

1120 BRACK [*drawing near to her*]. And what is that, if I may ask?

HEDDA [*stands looking out*]. Boring myself to death. Now you know it. [*Turns, looks towards the inner room, and laughs*]. Yes, as I thought! Here comes the Professor.

BRACK [*softly, in a tone of warning*]. Come, come, come, Mrs. Hedda!

[GEORGE TESMAN, *dressed for the party, with his gloves and hat in his hand, enters from the right through the inner room.*]

TESMAN. Hedda, has no message come from Eilert Lövborg? Eh?

HEDDA. No.

TESMAN. Then you'll see he'll be here presently.

BRACK. Do you really think he will come?

TESMAN. Yes, I am almost sure of it. For what you were telling us this morn-
1130   ing must have been a mere floating rumor.

BRACK. You think so?

TESMAN. At any rate, Aunt Julia said she did not believe for a moment that he would ever stand in my way again. Fancy that!

BRACK. Well then, that's all right.

TESMAN [*placing his hat and gloves on a chair on the right*]. Yes, but you must really let me wait for him as long as possible.

BRACK. We have plenty of time yet. None of my guests will arrive before seven or half-past.

TESMAN. Then meanwhile we can keep Hedda company, and see what hap-
1140   pens. Eh?

HEDDA [*placing* BRACK'S *hat and overcoat upon the corner settee*]. And at the worst Mr. Lövborg can remain here with me.

BRACK [*offering to take his things*].   Oh, allow me, Mrs. Tesman!—What do you mean by "At the worst"?

HEDDA.   If he won't go with you and Tesman.

TESMAN [*looks dubiously at her*].   But, Hedda dear—do you think it would quite do for him to remain with you? Eh? Remember, Aunt Julia can't come.

HEDDA.   No, but Mrs. Elvsted is coming. We three can have a cup of tea together.

1150 TESMAN.   Oh, yes, that will be all right.

BRACK [*smiling*].   And that would perhaps be the safest plan for him.

HEDDA.   Why so?

BRACK.   Well, you know, Mrs. Tesman, how you used to gird at my little bachelor parties. You declared they were adapted only for men of the strictest principles.

HEDDA.   But no doubt Mr. Lövborg's principles are strict enough now. A converted sinner—

[BERTA *appears at the hall door.*]

BERTA.   There's a gentleman asking if you are at home, ma'am—

HEDDA.   Well, show him in.

1160 TESMAN [*softly*].   I'm sure it is he! Fancy that!

[EILERT Lövborg *enters from the hall. He is slim and lean; of the same age as* TESMAN, *but looks older and somewhat worn-out. His hair and beard are of a blackish brown, his face long and pale, but with patches of color on the cheek-bones. He is dressed in a well-cut black visiting suit, quite new. He has dark gloves and a silk hat. He stops near the door, and makes a rapid bow, seeming somewhat embarrassed.*]

TESMAN [*goes up to him and shakes him warmly by the hand*].   Well, my dear Eilert—so at last we meet again!

EILERT Lövborg [*speaks in a subdued voice*].   Thanks for your letter, Tesman. [*Approaching* HEDDA.] Will you too shake hands with me, Mrs. Tesman?

HEDDA [*taking his hand*].   I am glad to see you, Mr. Lövborg. [*With a motion of her hand.*] I don't know whether you two gentlemen—?

Lövborg [*bowing slightly*].   Judge Brack, I think.

BRACK [*doing likewise*].   Oh, yes—in the old days—

TESMAN [*to* Lövborg, *with his hands on his shoulders*].   And now you must make
1170   yourself entirely at home, Eilert! Mustn't he, Hedda?—For I hear you are going to settle in town again? Eh?

Lövborg.   Yes, I am.

TESMAN.   Quite right, quite right. Let me tell you, I have got hold of your new book; but I haven't had time to read it yet.

Lövborg.   You may spare yourself the trouble.

TESMAN.   Why so?

Lövborg.   Because there is very little in it.

TESMAN.   Just fancy—how can you say so?

BRACK.   But it has been very much praised, I hear.

1180 Lövborg.   That was what I wanted; so I put nothing into the book but what every one would agree with.

BRACK.   Very wise of you.

TESMAN.   Well but, my dear Eilert—

Lövborg.   For now I mean to win myself a position again—to make a fresh start.

TESMAN [*a little embarrassed*].   Ah, that is what you wish to do? Eh?

Lövborg [*smiling, lay down his hat, and draws a packet, wrapped in paper, from his coat pocket*].   But when this one appears, George Tesman, you will have to read it. For this is the real book—the book I have put my true self into.

1190 TESMAN.   Indeed? And what is it?

Lövborg.   It is the continuation.

TESMAN.   The continuation? Of what?

Lövborg.   Of the book.

TESMAN.   Of the new book?

Lövborg.   Of course.

TESMAN.   Why, my dear Eilert—does it not come down to our own days?

Lövborg.   Yes, it does; and this one deals with the future.

TESMAN.   With the future! But, good heavens, we know nothing of the future!

Lövborg.   No; but there is a thing or two to be said about it all the same.

1200 [*Opens the packet.*] Look here—

TESMAN.   Why, that's not your handwriting.

Lövborg.   I dictated it. [*Turning over the pages.*] It falls into two sections. The first deals with the civilizing forces of the future. And here is the second— [*running through the pages towards the end*]—forecasting the probable line of development.

TESMAN.   How odd now! I should never have thought of writing anything of that sort.

HEDDA [*at the glass door, drumming on the pane*].   H'm—I daresay not.

Lövborg [*replacing the manuscript in its paper and laying the packet on the table*]. I brought it, thinking I might read you a little of it this evening.

1210 TESMAN.   That was very good of you, Eilert. But this evening—? [*Looking at BRACK.*] I don't quite see how we can manage it—

Lövborg.   Well then, some other time. There is no hurry.

BRACK.   I must tell you, Mr. Lövborg—there is a little gathering at my house this evening—mainly in honor of Tesman, you know—

Lövborg [*looking for his hat*].   Oh—then I won't detain you—

BRACK.   No, but listen—will you not do me the favor of joining us?

Lövborg [*curtly and decidedly*].   No, I can't—thank you very much.

BRACK.   Oh, nonsense—do! We shall be quite a select little circle. And I assure you we shall have a "lively time," as Mrs. Hed—as Mrs. Tesman

1220 says.

Lövborg.   I have no doubt of it. But nevertheless—

BRACK.   And then you might bring your manuscript with you, and read it to Tesman at my house. I could give you a room to yourselves.

TESMAN.   Yes, think of that, Eilert,—why shouldn't you? Eh?

HEDDA [*interposing*].   But, Tesman, if Mr. Lövborg would really rather not! I am sure Mr. Lövborg is much more inclined to remain here and have supper with me.

Lövborg [*looking at her*].   With you, Mrs. Tesman?

HEDDA.   And with Mrs. Elvsted?

1230 Lövborg.   Ah— [*Lightly.*] I saw her for a moment this morning.

HEDDA.   Did you? Well, she is coming this evening. So you see you are almost bound to remain, Mr. Lövborg, or she will have no one to see her home.

Lövborg.   That's true. Many thanks, Mrs. Tesman—in that case I will remain.

HEDDA.   Then I have one or two orders to give the servant—

[*She goes to the hall door and rings.* Berta *enters.* Hedda *talks to her in a whisper, and points towards the inner room.* Berta *nods and goes out again.*]

Tesman [*at the same time, to* Lövborg]. Tell me, Eilert—is it this new subject—the future—that you are going to lecture about?

Lövborg. Yes.

Tesman. They told me at the bookseller's, that you are going to deliver a
1240 course of lectures this autumn.

Lövborg. That is my intention. I hope you won't take it ill, Tesman.

Tesman. Oh no, not in the least! But—?

Lövborg. I can quite understand that it must be disagreeable to you.

Tesman [*cast down*]. Oh, I can't expect you, out of consideration for me, to—

Lövborg. But I shall wait till you have received your appointment.

Tesman. Will you wait? Yes, but—yes, but—are you not going to compete with me? Eh?

Lövborg. No; it is only the moral victory I care for.

Tesman. Why, bless me—then Aunt Julia was right after all! Oh yes—I knew
1250 it! Hedda! Just fancy—Eilert Lövborg is not going to stand in our way!

Hedda [*curtly*]. Our way? Pray leave me out of the question.

[*She goes up towards the inner room, where* Berta *is placing a tray with decanters and glasses on the table.* Hedda *nods approval, and comes forward again.* Berta *goes out.*]

Tesman [*at the same time*]. And you, Judge Brack—what do you say to this? Eh?

Brack. Well, I say that a moral victory—h'm—may be all very fine—

Tesman. Yes, certainly. But all the same—

Hedda [*looking at* Tesman *with a cold smile*]. You stand there looking as if you were thunderstruck—

Tesman. Yes—so I am—I almost think—

Brack. Don't you see, Mrs. Tesman, a thunderstorm has just passed over?

1260 Hedda [*pointing towards the inner room*]. Will you not take a glass of cold punch, gentlemen?

Brack [*looking at his watch*]. A stirrup-cup? Yes, it wouldn't come amiss.

Tesman. A capital idea, Hedda! just the thing! Now that the weight has been taken off my mind—

Hedda. Will you not join them, Mr. Lövborg?

Lövborg [*with a gesture of refusal*]. No, thank you. Nothing for me.

Brack. Why, bless me—cold punch is surely not poison.

Lövborg. Perhaps not for every one.

Hedda. I will keep Mr. Lövborg company in the meantime.

1270 Tesman. Yes, yes, Hedda dear, do.

[*He and* Brack *go into the inner room, seat themselves, drink punch, smoke cigarettes, and carry on a lively conversation during what follows.* Eilert Lövborg *remains beside the stove.* Hedda *goes to the writing-table.*]

Hedda [*raising her voice a little*]. Do you care to look at some photographs, Mr. Lövborg? You know Tesman and I made a tour in the Tyrol[8] on our way home?

---

[8] The Tyrolese mountains discussed in the subsequent exchanges are all in Northern Italy near the Austrian border.

[*She takes up an album, and places it on the table beside the sofa, in the further corner of which she seats herself.* EILERT Lövborg *approaches, stops, and looks at her. Then he takes a chair and seats himself at her left, with his back towards the inner room.*]

HEDDA [*opening the album*]. Do you see this range of mountains, Mr. Lövborg? It's the Ortler group. Tesman has written the name underneath. Here it is: "The Ortler group near Meran."

Lövborg [*who has never taken his eyes off her, says softly and slowly*]. Hedda— Gabler!

HEDDA [*glancing hastily at him*]. Ah! Hush!

1280 Lövborg [*repeats softly*]. Hedda Gabler!

HEDDA [*looking at the album*]. That was my name in the old days—when we two knew each other.

Lövborg. And I must teach myself never to say Hedda Gabler again—never, as long as I live.

HEDDA [*still turning over the pages*]. Yes, you must. And I think you ought to practice in time. The sooner the better, I should say.

Lövborg [*in a tone of indignation*]. Hedda Gabler married? And married to—George Tesman!

HEDDA. Yes—so the world goes.

1290 Lövborg. Oh, Hedda, Hedda—how could you[9] throw yourself away!

HEDDA [*looks sharply at him*]. What? I can't allow this!

Lövborg. What do you mean? [TESMAN *comes into the room and goes towards the sofa.*]

HEDDA [*hears him coming and says in an indifferent tone*]. And this is a view from the Val d'Ampezzo, Mr. Lövborg. Just look at these peaks! [*Looks affectionately up at* TESMAN.] What's the name of these curious peaks, dear?

TESMAN. Let me see? Oh, those are the Dolomites.

HEDDA. Yes, that's it—Those are the Dolomites, Mr. Lövborg.

TESMAN. Hedda, dear,—I only wanted to ask whether I shouldn't bring you a little punch after all? For yourself at any rate—eh?

1300 HEDDA. Yes, do, please; and perhaps a few biscuits.

TESMAN. No cigarettes?

HEDDA. No.

TESMAN. Very well.

[*He goes into the inner room and out to the right.* BRACK *sits in the inner room, and keeps an eye from time to time on* HEDDA *and* Lövborg.]

Lövborg [*softly, as before*]. Answer me, Hedda—how could you go and do this?

HEDDA [*apparently absorbed in the album*]. If you continue to say *du* to me I won't talk to you.

Lövborg. May I not say *du* when we are alone?

HEDDA. No. You may think it: but you mustn't say it.

1310 Lövborg. Ah, I understand. It is an offense against George Tesman, whom you[10]—love.

---

[9] Lövborg uses the intimate pronoun *du.*
[10] Here Lövborg begins using the formal pronoun *de.*

HEDDA [*glances at him and smiles*].   Love? What an idea!

Lövborg.   You don't love him then!

HEDDA.   But I won't hear of any sort of unfaithfulness! Remember that.

Lövborg.   Hedda—answer me one thing—

HEDDA.   Hush!

[TESMAN *enters with a small tray from the inner room.*]

TESMAN.   Here you are! Isn't this tempting? [*He puts the tray on the table.*]

HEDDA.   Why do you bring it yourself?

TESMAN [*filling the glasses*].   Because I think it's such fun to wait upon you,
1320   Hedda.

HEDDA.   But you have poured out two glasses. Mr. Lövborg said he wouldn't
have any—

TESMAN.   No, but Mrs. Elvsted will soon be here, won't she?

HEDDA.   Yes, by-the-bye—Mrs. Elvsted—

TESMAN.   Had you forgotten her? Eh?

HEDDA.   We were so absorbed in these photographs. [*Shows him a picture.*] Do
you remember this little village?

TESMAN.   Oh, it's that one just below the Brenner Pass. It was there we
passed the night—

1330 HEDDA.   —and met that lively party of tourists.

TESMAN.   Yes, that was the place. Fancy—if we could only have had you with
us, Eilert! Eh?

[*He returns to the inner room and sits beside* BRACK.]

Lövborg.   Answer me this one thing, Hedda—

HEDDA.   Well?

Lövborg.   Was there no love in your friendship for me either? Not a spark—
not a tinge of love in it?

HEDDA.   I wonder if there was? To me it seems as though we were two good
comrades—two thoroughly intimate friends. [*Smilingly.*] You especially
were frankness itself.

1340 Lövborg.   It was you that made me so.

HEDDA.   As I look back upon it all, I think there was really something beautiful, something fascinating—something daring—in—in that secret intimacy—that comradeship which no living creature so much as dreamed of.

Lövborg.   Yes, yes, Hedda! Was there not?—When I used to come to your
father's in the afternoon—and the General sat over at the window reading
his papers—with his back towards us—

HEDDA.   And we two sat on the corner sofa—

Lövborg.   Always the same illustrated paper before us—

HEDDA.   For want of an album, yes.

1350 Lövborg.   Yes, Hedda, and when I made my confessions to you—told you
about myself, things that at that time no one else knew! There I would sit
and tell you of my escapades—my days and nights of devilment. Oh,
Hedda—what was the power in you that forced me to confess these things?

HEDDA.   Do you think it was any power in me?

Lövborg.   How else can I explain it? And all those—those roundabout questions you used to put to me—

HEDDA.   Which you understood so particularly well—

Lövborg.   How could you sit and question me like that? Question me quite
frankly—

1360 HEDDA.   In roundabout terms, please observe.

Lövborg.   Yes, but frankly nevertheless. Cross-question me about—all that
sort of thing?

HEDDA.   And how could you answer, Mr. Lövborg?

Lövborg.   Yes, that is just what I can't understand—in looking back upon it.
But tell me now, Hedda—was there not love at the bottom of our friendship? On your side, did you not feel as though you might purge my stains
away if I made you my confessor? Was it not so?

HEDDA.   No, not quite.

Lövborg.   What was your motive, then?

1370 HEDDA.   Do you think it quite incomprehensible that a young girl—when it
can be done—without any one knowing—

Lövborg.   Well?

HEDDA.   —should be glad to have a peep, now and then, into a world which—

Lövborg.   Which—?

HEDDA.   —which she is forbidden to know anything about?

Lövborg.   So that was it?

HEDDA.   Partly. Partly—I almost think.

Lövborg.   Comradeship in the thirst for life. But why should not that, at any
rate, have continued?

1380 HEDDA.   The fault was yours.

Lövborg.   It was you that broke with me.

HEDDA.   Yes, when our friendship threatened to develop into something
more serious. Shame upon you, Eilert Lövborg! How could you think of
wronging your—your frank comrade?

Lövborg [clenching his hands].   Oh, why did you not carry out your threat?
Why did you not shoot me down?

HEDDA.   Because I have such a dread of scandal.

Lövborg.   Yes, Hedda, you are a coward at heart.

HEDDA.   A terrible coward. [Changing her tone.] But it was a lucky thing for
1390 you. And now you have found ample consolation at the Elvsteds'.

Lövborg.   I know what Thea has confided to you.

HEDDA.   And perhaps you have confided to her something about us?

Lövborg.   Not a word. She is too stupid to understand anything of that sort.

HEDDA.   Stupid?

Lövborg.   She is stupid about matters of that sort.

HEDDA.   And I am cowardly. [Bends over towards him, without looking him in the
face, and says more softly—] But now I will confide something to you.

Lövborg [eagerly].   Well?

HEDDA.   The fact that I dared not shoot you down—

1400 Lövborg.   Yes!

HEDDA.   —that was not my most arrant cowardice—that evening.

Lövborg [looks at her a moment, understands, and whispers passionately].   Oh,
Hedda! Hedda Gabler! Now I begin to see a hidden reason beneath our
comradeship! You and I—! After all, then, it was your craving for life—

HEDDA [softly, with a sharp glance].   Take care! Believe nothing of the sort!

[Twilight has begun to fall. The hall door is opened from without by BERTA.]

Hedda [*closes the album with a bang and calls smilingly*].   Ah, at last! My darling
   Thea,—come along!

[Mrs. Elvsted *enters from the hall. She is in evening dress. The door is closed behind
her.*]

Hedda [*on the sofa, stretches out her arms towards her*].   My sweet Thea—you
   can't think how I have been longing for you!

[Mrs. Elvsted, *in passing, exchanges slight salutations with the gentlemen in the
inner room, then goes up to the table and gives* Hedda *her hands.* Eilert Lövborg
has risen. He and Mrs. Elvsted *greet each other with a silent nod.*]

1410 Mrs. Elvsted.   Ought I to go in and talk to your husband for a moment?
Hedda.   Oh, not at all. Leave those two alone. They will soon be going.
Mrs. Elvsted.   Are they going out?
Hedda.   Yes, to a supper party?
Mrs. Elvsted [*quickly, to* Lövborg].   Not you?
Lövborg.   No.
Hedda.   Mr. Lövborg remains with us.
Mrs. Elvsted [*takes a chair and is about to seat herself at his side*].   Oh, how nice
   it is here!
Hedda.   No, thank you, my little Thea! Not there! You'll be good enough to
1420   come over here to me. I will sit between you.
Mrs. Elvsted.   Yes, just as you please.

[*She goes round the table and seats herself on the sofa on* Hedda's *right.* Lövborg
re-seats himself on his chair.]

Lövborg [*after a short pause, to* Hedda].   Is not she lovely to look at?
Hedda [*lightly stroking her hair*].   Only to look at?
Lövborg.   Yes. For we two—she and I—are two real comrades. We have
   absolute faith in each other; so we can sit and talk with perfect frankness—
Hedda.   Not round about, Mr. Lövborg?
Lövborg.   Well—
Mrs. Elvsted [*softly, clinging close to* Hedda].   Oh, how happy I am, Hedda;
   for, only think, he says I have inspired him too.
1430 Hedda [*looks at her with a smile*].   Ah! Does he say that, dear?
Lövborg.   And then she is so brave, Mrs. Tesman!
Mrs. Elvsted.   Good heavens—am I brave?
Lövborg.   Exceedingly—where your comrade is concerned.
Hedda.   Ah, yes—courage! If one only had that!
Lövborg.   What then? What do you mean?
Hedda.   Then life would perhaps be liveable, after all. [*With a sudden change
   of tone.*] But now, my dearest Thea, you really must take a glass of cold
   punch.
Mrs. Elvsted.   No, thanks—I never take anything of that kind.
1440 Hedda.   Well then, you, Mr. Lövborg.
Lövborg.   Nor I, thank you.
Mrs. Elvsted.   No, he doesn't either.
Hedda [*looks fixedly at him*].   But if I say you shall?
Lövborg.   It would be no use.
Hedda [*laughing*].   Then I, poor creature, have no sort of power over you?

LÖVBORG.   Not in that respect.

HEDDA.   But seriously, I think you ought to—for your own sake.

MRS. ELVSTED.   Why, Hedda—

LÖVBORG.   How so?

1450 HEDDA.   Or rather on account of other people.

LÖVBORG.   Indeed?

HEDDA.   Otherwise people might be apt to suspect that—in your heart of hearts—you did not feel quite secure—quite confident of yourself.

MRS. ELVSTED [*softly*].   Oh please, Hedda—

LÖVBORG.   People may suspect what they like—for the present.

MRS. ELVSTED [*joyfully*].   Yes, let them!

HEDDA.   I saw it plainly in Judge Brack's face a moment ago.

LÖVBORG.   What did you see?

HEDDA.   His contemptuous smile, when you dared not go with them into the
1460 inner room.

LÖVBORG.   Dared not? Of course I preferred to stop here and talk to you.

MRS. ELVSTED.   What could be more natural, Hedda?

HEDDA.   But the Judge could not guess that. And I saw, too, the way he smiled and glanced at Tesman when you dared not accept his invitation to this wretched little supper-party of his.

LÖVBORG.   Dared not! Do you say I dared not?

HEDDA.   *I* don't say so. But that was how Judge Brack understood it.

LÖVBORG.   Well, let him.

HEDDA.   Then you are not going with them?

1470 LÖVBORG.   I will stay here with you and Thea.

MRS. ELVSTED.   Yes, Hedda—how can you doubt that?

HEDDA [*smiles and nods approvingly to* LÖVBORG].   Firm as a rock! Faithful to your principles, now and forever! Ah, that is how a man should be! [*Turns to* MRS. ELVSTED *and caresses her.*] Well now, what did I tell you, when you came to us this morning in such a state of distraction—

LÖVBORG [*surprised*].   Distraction!

MRS. ELVSTED [*terrified*].   Hedda—oh Hedda—!

HEDDA.   You can see for yourself; you haven't the slightest reason to be in such mortal terror—[*interrupting herself*]. There! Now we can all three
1480 enjoy ourselves!

LÖVBORG [*who has given a start*].   Ah—what is all this, Mrs. Tesman?

MRS. ELVSTED.   Oh my God, Hedda! What are you saying? What are you doing?

HEDDA.   Don't get excited! That horrid Judge Brack is sitting watching you.

LÖVBORG.   So she was in mortal terror! On my account!

MRS. ELVSTED [*softly and piteously*].   Oh, Hedda—now you have ruined everything!

LÖVBORG [*looks fixedly at her for a moment. His face is distorted*].   So that was my comrade's frank confidence in me?

1490 MRS. ELVSTED [*imploringly*].   Oh, my dearest friend—only let me tell you—

LÖVBORG [*takes one of the glasses of punch, raises it to his lips, and says in a low, husky voice*].   Your health, Thea! [*He empties the glass, puts it down, and takes the second.*]

MRS. ELVSTED [*softly*].   Oh, Hedda, Hedda—how could you do this?

HEDDA.   *I* do it? *I*? Are you crazy?

Lövborg.   Here's your health, too, Mrs. Tesman. Thanks for the truth. Hurrah for the truth! [*He empties the glass and is about to re-fill it.*]

Hedda [*lays her hand on his arm*].   Come, come—no more for the present. Remember you are going out to supper.

Mrs. Elvsted.   No, no, no!

Hedda.   Hush! They are sitting watching you.

1500 Lövborg [*putting down the glass*].   Now. Thea—tell me the truth—

Mrs. Elvsted.   Yes.

Lövborg.   Did your husband know that you had come after me?

Mrs. Elvsted [*wringing her hands*].   Oh, Hedda—do you hear what he is asking?

Lövborg.   Was it arranged between you and him that you were to come to town and look after me? Perhaps it was the Sheriff himself that urged you to come? Aha, my dear—no doubt he wanted my help in his office! Or was it at the card-table that he missed me?

Mrs. Elvsted [*softly, in agony*].   Oh, Lövborg, Lövborg—!

1510 Lövborg [*seizes a glass and is on the point of filling it*].   Here's a glass for the old Sheriff too!

Hedda [*preventing him*].   No more just now. Remember, you have to read your manuscript to Tesman.

Lövborg [*calmly, putting down the glass*].   It was stupid of me all this, Thea—to take it in this way, I mean. Don't be angry with me, my dear, dear comrade. You shall see—both of you and the others—that if I was fallen once—now I have risen again! Thanks to you, Thea.

Mrs. Elvsted [*radiant with joy*].   Oh, heaven be praised—!

[Brack *has in the meantime looked at his watch. He and* Tesman *rise and come into the drawing-room.*]

Brack [*takes his hat and overcoat*].   Well, Mrs. Tesman, our time has come.

1520 Hedda.   I suppose it has.

Lövborg [*rising*].   Mine too, Judge Brack.

Mrs. Elvsted [*softly and imploringly*].   Oh, Lövborg, don't do it!

Hedda [*pinching her arm*].   They can hear you!

Mrs. Elvsted [*with a suppressed shriek*].   Ow!

Lövborg [*to* Brack].   You were good enough to invite me.

Brack.   Well, are you coming after all?

Lövborg.   Yes, many thanks.

Brack.   I'm delighted—

Lövborg [*to* Tesman, *putting the parcel of MS. in his pocket*].   I should like to

1530 show you one or two things before I send it to the printer's.

Tesman.   Fancy—that will be delightful. But, Hedda dear, how is Mrs. Elvsted to get home? Eh?

Hedda.   Oh, that can be managed somehow.

Lövborg [*looking towards the ladies*].   Mrs. Elvsted? Of course, I'll come again and fetch her. [*Approaching.*] At ten or thereabouts, Mrs. Tesman? Will that do?

Hedda.   Certainly. That will do capitally.

Tesman.   Well, then, that's all right. But you must not expect me so early, Hedda.

1540 HEDDA.   Oh, you may stop as long—as long as ever you please.

MRS. ELVSTED [*trying to conceal her anxiety*].   Well then, Mr. Lövborg—I shall remain here until you come.

LÖVBORG [*with his hat in his hand*].   Pray do, Mrs. Elvsted.

BRACK.   And now off goes the excursion train, gentlemen! I hope we shall have a lively time, as a certain fair lady puts it.

HEDDA.   Ah, if only the fair lady could be present unseen—!

BRACK.   Why unseen?

HEDDA.   In order to hear a little of your liveliness at first hand, Judge Brack.

BRACK [*laughing*].   I should not advise the fair lady to try it.

1550 TESMAN [*also laughing*].   Come, you're a nice one, Hedda! Fancy that!

BRACK.   Well, good-bye, good-bye, ladies.

LÖVBORG [*bowing*].   About ten o'clock, then.

[BRACK, LÖVBORG, and TESMAN *go out by the hall door. At the same time* BERTA *enters from the inner room with a lighted lamp, which she places on the dining-room table; she goes out by the way she came.*]

MRS. ELVSTED [*who has risen and is wandering restlessly about the room*].   Hedda—Hedda—what will come of all this?

HEDDA.   At ten o'clock—he will be here. I can see him already—with vine-leaves in his hair[11]—flushed and fearless—

MRS. ELVSTED.   Oh, I hope he may.

HEDDA.   And then, you see—then he will have regained control over himself. Then he will be a free man for all his days.

1560 MRS. ELVSTED.   Oh God!—if he would only come as you see him now!

HEDDA.   He will come as I see him—so, and not otherwise! [*Rises and approaches* THEA.] You may doubt him as long as you please; I believe in him. And now we will try—

MRS. ELVSTED.   You have some hidden motive in this, Hedda!

HEDDA.   Yes, I have. I want for once in my life to have power to mold a human destiny.

MRS. ELVSTED.   Have you not the power?

HEDDA.   I have not—and have never had it.

MRS. ELVSTED.   Not your husband's?

1570 HEDDA.   Do you think that is worth the trouble? Oh, if you could only understand how poor I am. And fate has made you so rich! [*Clasps her passionately in her arms.*] I think I must burn your hair off, after all.

MRS. ELVSTED.   Let me go! Let me go! I am afraid of you, Hedda!

BERTA [*in the middle doorway*].   Tea is laid in the dining-room, ma'am.

HEDDA.   Very well. We are coming.

MRS. ELVSTED.   No, no, no! I would rather go home alone! At once.

HEDDA.   Nonsense! First you shall have a cup of tea, you little stupid. And then—at ten o'clock—Eilert Lövborg will be here—with vine-leaves in his hair. [*She drags* MRS. ELVSTED *almost by force towards the middle doorway.*]

---

[11] Bacchus, the Greek and Roman god of wine and revelry, was often portrayed with vine leaves in his hair.

ACT III

The room at the TESMANS'. *The curtains are drawn over the middle doorway, and also over the glass door. The lamp, half turned down and with a shade over it, is burning on the table. In the stove, the door of which stands open, there has been a fire, which is now nearly burnt out.*

MRS. ELVSTED, *wrapped in a large shawl, and with her feet upon a foot-rest, sits close to the stove, sunk back in the arm-chair.* HEDDA, *fully dressed, lies sleeping upon the sofa, with a sofa-blanket over her.*

1580   MRS. ELVSTED [*after a pause, suddenly sits up in her chair and listens eagerly. Then she sinks back again wearily, moaning to herself*]. Not yet!—Oh God—oh God—not yet!

[BERTA *slips in by the hall door. She has a letter in her hand.*]

MRS. ELVSTED [*turns and whispers eagerly*]. Well—has any one come?

BERTA [*softly*]. Yes, a girl has brought this letter.

MRS. ELVSTED [*quickly, holding out her hand*]. A letter! Give it to me!

BERTA. No, it's for Dr. Tesman, ma'am.

MRS. ELVSTED. Oh, indeed.

BERTA. It was Miss Tesman's servant that brought it. I'll lay it here on the table.

MRS. ELVSTED. Yes, do.

1590   BERTA [*laying down the letter*]. I think I had better put out the lamp. It's smoking.

MRS. ELVSTED. Yes, put it out. It must soon be daylight now.

BERTA [*putting out the lamp*]. It is daylight already, ma'am.

MRS. ELVSTED. Yes, broad day! And no one come back yet—!

BERTA. Lord bless you, ma'am! I guessed how it would be.

MRS. ELVSTED. You guessed?

BERTA. Yes, when I saw that a certain person had come back to town—and that he went off with them. For we've heard enough about that gentleman before now.

1600   MRS. ELVSTED. Don't speak so loud! You will awaken Mrs. Tesman.

BERTA [*looks towards the sofa and sighs*]. No, no—let her sleep, poor thing. Shan't I put some wood on the fire?

MRS. ELVSTED. Thanks, not for me.

BERTA. Oh, very well.

[*She goes softly out by the hall door.*]

HEDDA [*is awakened by the shutting of the door, and looks up*]. What's that—?

MRS. ELVSTED. It was only the servant—

HEDDA [*looking about her*]. Oh, we're here—! Yes, now I remember. [*Sits erect upon the sofa, stretches herself, and rubs her eyes.*] What o'clock is it, Thea?

MRS. ELVSTED [*looks at her watch*]. It's past seven.

1610   HEDDA. When did Tesman come home?

MRS. ELVSTED. He has not come.

HEDDA. Not come home yet?

MRS. ELVSTED [*rising*]. No one has come.

HEDDA. Think of our watching and waiting here till four in the morning—

MRS. ELVSTED [*wringing her hands*].   And how I watched and waited for him!

HEDDA [*yawns, and says with her hand before her mouth*].   Well, well—we might have spared ourselves the trouble.

MRS. ELVSTED.   Did you get a little sleep?

HEDDA.   Oh yes; I believe I slept pretty well. Have you not?

1620   MRS. ELVSTED.   Not for a moment. I couldn't, Hedda!—not to save my life.

HEDDA [*rising and goes towards her*].   There, there, there! There's nothing to be so alarmed about. I understand quite well what has happened.

MRS. ELVSTED.   Well, what do you think? Won't you tell me?

HEDDA.   Why, of course it has been a very late affair at Judge Brack's—

MRS. ELVSTED.   Yes, yes, that is clear enough. But all the same—

HEDDA.   And then, you see, Tesman hasn't cared to come home and ring us up in the middle of the night. [*Laughing.*] Perhaps he wasn't inclined to show himself either—immediately after a jollification.

MRS. ELVSTED.   But in that case—where can he have gone?

1630   HEDDA.   Of course he has gone to his aunts' and slept there. They have his old room ready for him.

MRS. ELVSTED.   No, he can't be with them; for a letter has just come for him from Miss Tesman. There it lies.

HEDDA.   Indeed? [*Looks at the address.*] Why yes, it's addressed in Aunt Julia's own hand. Well then, he has remained at Judge Brack's. And as for Eilert Lövborg—he is sitting, with vine-leaves in his hair, reading his manuscript.

MRS. ELVSTED.   Oh Hedda, you are just saying things you don't believe a bit.

HEDDA.   You really are a little blockhead, Thea.

1640   MRS. ELVSTED.   Oh yes, I suppose I am.

HEDDA.   And how mortally tired you look.

MRS. ELVSTED.   Yes, I am mortally tired.

HEDDA.   Well then, you must do as I tell you. You must go into my room and lie down for a little while.

MRS. ELVSTED.   Oh no, no—I shouldn't be able to sleep.

HEDDA.   I am sure you would.

MRS. ELVSTED.   Well, but your husband is certain to come soon now; and then I want to know at once—

HEDDA.   I shall take care to let you know when he comes.

1650   MRS. ELVSTED.   Do you promise me, Hedda?

HEDDA.   Yes, rely upon me. Just you go in and have a sleep in the meantime.

MRS. ELVSTED.   Thanks; then I'll try to. [*She goes off through the inner room.*]

[HEDDA *goes up to the glass door and draws back the curtains. The broad daylight streams into the room. Then she takes a little hand-glass from the writing-table, looks at herself in it, and arranges her hair. Next she goes to the hall door and presses the bell-button.* BERTA *presently appears at the hall door.*]

BERTA.   Did you want anything, ma'am?

HEDDA.   Yes; you must put some more wood in the stove. I am shivering.

BERTA.   Bless me—I'll make up the fire at once. [*She rakes the embers together and lays a piece of wood upon them; then stops and listens.*] That was a ring at the front door, ma'am.

HEDDA.   Then go to the door. I will look after the fire.

BERTA.   It'll soon burn up. [*She goes out by the hall door.*]

[HEDDA *kneels on the foot-rest and lays some more pieces of wood in the stove. After a short pause,* GEORGE TESMAN *enters from the hall. He looks tired and rather serious. He steals on tiptoe towards the middle doorway and is about to slip through the curtains.*]

1660 HEDDA [*at the stove, without looking up*].   Good morning.

TESMAN [*turns*].   Hedda! [*Approaching her.*] Good heavens—are you up so early? Eh?

HEDDA.   Yes, I am up very early this morning.

TESMAN.   And I never doubted you were still sound asleep! Fancy that, Hedda!

HEDDA.   Don't speak so loud. Mrs. Elvsted is resting in my room.

TESMAN.   Has Mrs. Elvsted been here all night?

HEDDA.   Yes, since no one came to fetch her.

TESMAN.   Ah, to be sure.

1670 HEDDA [*closes the door of the stove and rises*].   Well, did you enjoy yourself at Judge Brack's?

TESMAN.   Have you been anxious about me? Eh?

HEDDA.   No, I should never think of being anxious. But I asked if you had enjoyed yourself.

TESMAN.   Oh, yes,—for once in a way. Especially the beginning of the evening; for then Eilert read me part of his book. We arrived more than an hour too early—fancy that! And Brack had all sorts of arrangements to make—so Eilert read to me.

HEDDA [*seating herself by the table on the right*].   Well? Tell me, then—

1680 TESMAN [*sitting on a foot-stool near the stove*].   Oh Hedda, you can't conceive what a book that is going to be! I believe it is one of the most remarkable things that have ever been written. Fancy that!

HEDDA.   Yes, yes; I don't care about that—

TESMAN.   I must make a confession to you, Hedda. When he had finished reading—a horrid feeling came over me.

HEDDA.   A horrid feeling?

TESMAN.   I felt jealous of Eilert for having had it in him to write such a book. Only think, Hedda!

HEDDA.   Yes, yes, I am thinking!

1690 TESMAN.   And then how pitiful to think that he—with all his gifts—should be irreclaimable after all.

HEDDA.   I suppose you mean that he has more courage than the rest?

TESMAN.   No, not at all—I mean that he is incapable of taking his pleasures in moderation.

HEDDA.   And what came of it all—in the end?

TESMAN.   Well, to tell the truth, I think it might best be described as an orgy, Hedda.

HEDDA.   Had he vine-leaves in his hair?

TESMAN.   Vine-leaves? No, I saw nothing of the sort. But he made a long,
1700   rambling speech in honor of the woman who had inspired him in his work—that was the phrase he used.

HEDDA.   Did he name her?

TESMAN.   No, he didn't; but I can't help thinking he meant Mrs. Elvsted. You
    may be sure he did.
HEDDA.   Well—where did you part from him?
TESMAN.   On the way to town. We broke up—the last of us at any rate—all
    together; and Brack came with us to get a breath of fresh air. And then,
    you see, we agreed to take Eilert home; for he had had far more than was
    good for him.
1710 HEDDA.   I daresay.
TESMAN.   But now comes the strange part of it, Hedda; or, I should rather
    say, the melancholy part of it. I declare I am almost ashamed—on Eilert's
    account—to tell you—
HEDDA.   Oh, go on—!
TESMAN.   Well, as we were getting near town, you see, I happened to drop a
    little behind the others. Only for a minute or two—fancy that!
HEDDA.   Yes, yes, yes, but—?
TESMAN.   And then, as I hurried after them—what do you think I found by
    the wayside? Eh?
1720 HEDDA.   Oh, how should I know!
TESMAN.   You mustn't speak of it to a soul, Hedda! Do you hear! Promise
    me, for Eilert's sake. [*Draws a parcel, wrapped in paper, from his coat pocket.*]
    Fancy, dear—I found this.
HEDDA.   Is not that the parcel he had with him yesterday?
TESMAN.   Yes, it is the whole of his precious, irreplaceable manuscript! And
    he had gone and lost it, and knew nothing about it. Only fancy, Hedda! So
    deplorably—
HEDDA.   But why did you not give him back the parcel at once?
TESMAN.   I didn't care to—in the state he was then in—
1730 HEDDA.   Did you not tell any of the others that you had found it?
TESMAN.   Oh, far from it! You can surely understand that, for Eilert's sake, I
    wouldn't do that.
HEDDA.   So no one knows that Eilert Lövborg's manuscript is in your pos-
    session?
TESMAN.   No. And no one must know it.
HEDDA.   Then what did you say to him afterwards?
TESMAN.   I didn't talk to him again at all; for when we got among the streets,
    he and two or three of the others gave us the slip and disappeared. Fancy
    that!
1740 HEDDA.   Indeed! They must have taken him home then.
TESMAN.   Yes, so it would appear. And Brack, too, left us.
HEDDA.   And what have you been doing with yourself since?
TESMAN.   Well, I and some of the others went home with one of the party, a
    jolly fellow, and took our morning coffee with him; or perhaps I should
    rather call it our night coffee—eh? But now, when I have rested a little,
    and given Eilert, poor fellow, time to have his sleep out, I must take this
    back to him.
HEDDA [*holds out her hand for the packet*].   No—don't give it to him! Not in
    such a hurry, I mean. Let me read it first.
1750 TESMAN.   No, my dearest Hedda, I mustn't, I really mustn't.
HEDDA.   You must not?

TESMAN. No—for you can imagine what a state of despair he will be in when he awakens and misses the manuscript. He has no copy of it, you must know! He told me so.

HEDDA [*looking searchingly at him*]. Can such a thing not be reproduced? Written over again?

TESMAN. No, I don't think that would be possible. For the inspiration, you see—

HEDDA. Yes, yes—I suppose it depends on that. [*Lightly.*] But, by-the-bye—
1760   here is a letter for you.

TESMAN. Fancy—!

HEDDA [*handing it to him*]. It came early this morning.

TESMAN. It's from Aunt Julia! What can it be? [*He lays the packet on the other foot-stool, opens the letter, runs his eyes through it, and jumps up*]. Oh, Hedda— she says that poor Aunt Rina is dying!

HEDDA. Well, we were prepared for that.

TESMAN. And that if I want to see her again, I must make haste. I'll run in to them at once.

HEDDA [*suppressing a smile*]. Will you run?

1770 TESMAN. Oh, dearest Hedda—if you could only make up your mind to come with me! Just think!

HEDDA [*rises and says wearily, repelling the idea*]. No, no, don't ask me. I will not look upon sickness and death. I loathe all sorts of ugliness.

TESMAN. Well, well, then—! [*Bustling around.*] My hat—my overcoat—? Oh, in the hall—I do hope I mayn't come too late, Hedda! Eh?

HEDDA. Oh, if you run—

[BERTA *appears at the hall door.*]

BERTA. Judge Brack is at the door, and wishes to know if he may come in.

TESMAN. At this time! No, I can't possibly see him.

HEDDA. But I can. [*To* BERTA.] Ask Judge Brack to come in.

[BERTA *goes out.*]

1780 HEDDA [*quickly whispering*]. The parcel, Tesman! [*She snatches it up from the stool.*]

TESMAN. Yes, give it to me!

HEDDA. No, no, I will keep it till you come back.

[*She goes to the writing-table and places it in the book-case.* TESMAN *stands in a flurry of haste, and cannot get his gloves on.* JUDGE BRACK *enters from the hall.*]

HEDDA [*nodding to him*]. You are an early bird, I must say.

BRACK. Yes, don't you think so? [*To* TESMAN.] Are you on the move, too?

TESMAN. Yes, I must rush off to my aunts'. Fancy—the invalid one is lying at death's door, poor creature.

BRACK. Dear me, is she indeed? Then on no account let me detain you. At such a critical moment—

TESMAN. Yes, I must really rush—Good-bye! Good-bye!

[*He hastens out by the hall door.*]

1790 HEDDA [*approaching*].   You seem to have made a particularly lively night of it
at your rooms, Judge Brack.

BRACK.   I assure you I have not had my clothes off, Mrs. Hedda.

HEDDA.   Not you, either?

BRACK.   No, as you may see. But what has Tesman been telling you of the
night's adventures?

HEDDA.   Oh, some tiresome story. Only that they went and had coffee somewhere or other.

BRACK.   I have heard about that coffee-party already. Eilert Lövborg was not
with them, I fancy?

1800 HEDDA.   No, they had taken him home before that.

BRACK.   Tesman, too?

BRACK.   No, but some of the others, he said.

BRACK. [*smiling*].   George Tesman is really an ingenuous creature, Mrs.
Hedda.

HEDDA.   Yes, heaven knows he is. Then is there something behind all this?

BRACK.   Yes, perhaps there may be.

HEDDA.   Well then, sit down, my dear Judge, and tell your story in comfort.

[*She seats herself to the left of the table.* BRACK *sits near her, at the long side of the
table.*]

HEDDA.   Now then?

BRACK.   I had special reasons for keeping track of my guests—or rather of
1810 some of my guests—last night.

HEDDA.   Of Eilert Lövborg among the rest, perhaps?

BRACK.   Frankly, yes.

HEDDA.   Now you make me really curious—

BRACK.   Do you know where he and one or two of the others finished the
night, Mrs. Hedda?

HEDDA.   If it is not quite unmentionable, tell me.

BRACK.   Oh no, it's not at all unmentionable. Well, they put in an appearance
at a particularly animated soirée.[12]

HEDDA.   Of the lively kind?

1820 BRACK.   Of the very liveliest—

HEDDA.   Tell me more of this, Judge Brack—

BRACK.   Lövborg, as well as the others, had been invited in advance. I knew
all about it. But he had declined the invitation; for now, as you know, he
has become a new man.

HEDDA.   Up at the Elvsteds', yes. But he went after all, then?

BRACK.   Well, you see, Mrs. Hedda—unhappily the spirit moved him at my
rooms last evening—

HEDDA.   Yes, I hear he found inspiration.

BRACK.   Pretty violent inspiration. Well, I fancy, that altered his purpose; for
1830 we men folk are unfortunately not always so firm in our principles as we
ought to be.

HEDDA.   Oh, I am sure you are an exception, Judge Brack. But as to
Lövborg—?

---

[12] An evening party.

BRACK. To make a long story short—he landed at last in Mademoiselle
    Diana's rooms.

HEDDA. Mademoiselle Diana's?

BRACK. It was Mademoiselle Diana that was giving the soirée to a select
    circle of her admirers and her lady friends.

HEDDA. Is she a red-haired woman?

1840 BRACK. Precisely.

HEDDA. A sort of a—singer?

BRACK. Oh yes—in her leisure moments. And moreover a mighty hunt-
    ress—of men—Mrs. Hedda. You have no doubt heard of her. Eilert
    Lövborg was one of her most enthusiastic protectors—in the days of his
    glory.

HEDDA. And how did all this end?

BRACK. Far from amicably, it appears. After a most tender meeting, they
    seem to have come to blows—

HEDDA. Lövborg and she?

1850 BRACK. Yes. He accused her or her friends of having robbed him. He de-
    clared that his pocket-book had disappeared—and other things as well. In
    short, he seems to have a made a furious disturbance.

HEDDA. And what came of it all?

BRACK. It came to a general scrimmage, in which the ladies as well as the
    gentlemen took part. Fortunately the police at last appeared on the scene.

HEDDA. The police too?

BRACK. Yes. I fancy it will prove a costly frolic for Eilert Lövborg, crazy being
    that he is.

HEDDA. How so?

1860 BRACK. He seems to have made a violent resistance—to have hit one of the
    constables on the head and torn the coat off his back. So they had to
    march him off to the police-station with the rest.

HEDDA. How have you learnt all this?

BRACK. From the police themselves.

HEDDA [*gazing straight before her*]. So that is what happened. Then he had no
    vine-leaves in his hair.

BRACK. Vine-leaves, Mrs. Hedda?

HEDDA [*changing her tone*]. But tell me now, Judge—what is your real reason
    for tracking out Eilert Lövborg's movements so carefully?

1870 BRACK. In the first place, it could not be entirely indifferent to me if it
    should appear in the police-court that he came straight from my house.

HEDDA. Will the matter come into court, then?

BRACK. Of course. However, I should scarcely have troubled so much about
    that. But I thought that, as a friend of the family, it was my duty to supply
    you and Tesman with a full account of his nocturnal exploits.

HEDDA. Why so, Judge Brack?

BRACK. Why, because I have a shrewd suspicion that he intends to use you
    as a sort of blind.

HEDDA. Oh, how can you think such a thing!

1880 BRACK. Good heavens, Mrs. Hedda—we have eyes in our head. Mark my
    words! This Mrs. Elvsted will be in no hurry to leave town again.

HEDDA. Well, even if there should be anything between them, I suppose
    there are plenty of other places where they could meet.

BRACK. Not a single home. Henceforth, as before, every respectable house will be closed against Eilert Lövborg.

HEDDA. And so ought mine to be, you mean?

BRACK. Yes. I confess it would be more than painful to me if this personage were to be made free of your house. How superfluous, how intrusive, he would be, if he were to force his way into—

1890 HEDDA. —into the triangle?

BRACK. Precisely. It would simply mean that I should find myself homeless.

HEDDA [looks at him with a smile]. So you want to be the one cock in the basket—that is your aim.

BRACK [nods slowly and lowers his voice]. Yes, that is my aim. And for that I will fight—with every weapon I can command.

HEDDA [her smile vanishing]. I see you are a dangerous person—when it comes to the point.

BRACK. Do you think so?

HEDDA. I am beginning to think so. And I am exceedingly glad to think—

1900 that you have no sort of hold over me.

BRACK [laughing equivocally]. Well, well, Mrs. Hedda—perhaps you are right there. If I had, who knows what I might be capable of?

HEDDA. Come, come now, Judge Brack. That sounds almost like a threat.

BRACK [rising]. Oh, not at all! The triangle, you know, ought, if possible, to be spontaneously constructed.

HEDDA. There I agree with you.

BRACK. Well, now I have said all I had to say; and I had better be getting back to town. Good-bye, Mrs. Hedda. [He goes toward the glass door.]

HEDDA [rising]. Are you going out through the garden?

1910 BRACK. Yes, it's a short cut for me.

HEDDA. And then it is the back way, too.

BRACK. Quite so. I have no objection to back ways. They may be piquant enough at times.

HEDDA. When there is ball practice going on, you mean?

BRACK [in the doorway, laughing to her]. Oh, people don't shoot their tame poultry, I fancy.

HEDDA [also laughing]. Oh no, when there is only one cock in the basket—

[They exchange laughing nods of farewell. He goes. She closes the door behind him. HEDDA, who has become quite serious, stands for a moment looking out. Presently she goes and peeps through the curtain over the middle doorway. Then she goes to the writing-table, takes Lövborg's packet out of the book-case, and is on the point of looking through its contents. BERTA is heard speaking loudly in the hall. HEDDA turns and listens. Then she hastily locks up the packet in the drawer, and lays the key on the inkstand. EILERT Lövborg, with his great coat on and his hat in his hand, tears open the hall door. He looks somewhat confused and irritated.]

Lövborg [looking toward the hall]. And I tell you I must and will come in! There!

[He closes the door, turns and sees HEDDA, at once regains his self-control, and bows.]

1920 HEDDA [at the writing-table]. Well, Mr. Lövborg, this is rather a late hour to call for Thea.

Lövborg.   You mean rather an early hour to call on you. Pray pardon me.

Hedda.   How do you know that she is still here?

Lövborg.   They told me at her lodgings that she had been out all night.

Hedda [*going to the oval table*].   Did you notice anything about the people of the house when they said that?

Lövborg [*looks inquiringly at her*].   Notice anything about them?

Hedda.   I mean, did they seem to think it odd?

Lövborg [*suddenly understanding*].   Oh yes, of course! I am dragging her
1930   down with me! However, I didn't notice anything—I suppose Tesman is not up yet?

Hedda.   No—I think not—

Lövborg.   When did he come home?

Hedda.   Very late.

Lövborg.   Did he tell you anything?

Hedda.   Yes, I gathered that you had had an exceedingly jolly evening at Judge Brack's.

Lövborg.   Nothing more?

Hedda.   I don't think so. However, I was so dreadfully sleepy—

[Mrs. Elvsted *enters through the curtains of the middle doorway.*]

1940   Mrs. Elvsted [*going towards him*].   Ah, Lövborg! At last—!

Lövborg.   Yes, at last. And too late!

Mrs. Elvsted [*looks anxiously at him*].   What is too late?

Lövborg.   Everything is too late now. It is all over with me.

Mrs. Elvsted.   Oh no no—don't say that!

Lövborg.   You will say the same when you hear—

Mrs. Elvsted.   I won't hear anything!

Hedda.   Perhaps you would prefer to talk to her alone! If so, I will leave you.

Lövborg.   No, stay—you too. I beg of you to stay.

Mrs. Elvsted.   Yes, but I won't hear anything, I tell you.

1950   Lövborg.   It is not last night's adventures that I want to talk about.

Mrs. Elvsted.   What is it then—?

Lövborg.   I want to say that now our ways must part.

Mrs. Elvsted.   Part!

Hedda [*involuntarily*].   I knew it!

Lövborg.   You can be of no more service to me, Thea.

Mrs. Elvsted.   How can you stand there and say that! No more service to you! Am I not to help you now, as before? Are we not to go on working together?

Lövborg.   Henceforward I shall do no work.

1960   Mrs. Elvsted [*despairingly*].   Then what am I to do with my life?

Lövborg.   You must try to live your life as if you had never known me.

Mrs. Elvsted.   But you know I cannot do that!

Lövborg.   Try if you cannot, Thea. You must go home again—

Mrs. Elvsted [*in vehement protest*].   Never in this world! Where you are, there will I be also! I will not let myself be driven away like this! I will remain here! I will be with you when the book appears.

Hedda [*half aloud, in suspense*].   Ah yes—the book!

Lövborg [*looks at her*].   My book and Thea's; for that is what it is.

MRS. ELVSTED.   Yes, I feel that it is. And that is why I have a right to be with
1970   you when it appears! I will see with my own eyes how respect and honor
pour in upon you afresh. And the happiness—the happiness—oh, I must
share it with you!

LÖVBORG.   Thea—our book will never appear.

HEDDA.   Ah!

MRS. ELVSTED.   Never appear!

LÖVBORG.   Can never appear.

MRS. ELVSTED [*in agonized foreboding*].   Lövborg—what have you done with the
manuscript?

HEDDA [*looks anxiously at him*].   Yes, the manuscript—?

1980 MRS. ELVSTED.   Where is it?

LÖVBORG.   Oh Thea—don't ask me about it!

MRS. ELVSTED.   Yes, yes I will know. I demand to be told at once.

LÖVBORG.   The manuscript—Well then—I have torn the manuscript into a
thousand pieces.

MRS. ELVSTED [*shrieks*].   Oh no, no—!

HEDDA [*involuntarily*].   But that's not—

LÖVBORG [*looks at her*].   Not true, you think?

HEDDA [*collecting herself*].   Oh well, of course—since you say so. But it sounded
so improbable—

1990 LÖVBORG.   It is true, all the same.

MRS. ELVSTED [*wringing her hands*].   Oh God—oh God, Hedda—torn his own
work to pieces!

LÖVBORG.   I have torn my own life to pieces. So why should I not tear my
life-work too—?

MRS. ELVSTED.   And you did this last night?

LÖVBORG.   Yes, I tell you! Tore it into a thousand pieces and scattered them
on the fiord—far out. There there is cool sea-water at any rate—let them
drift upon it—drift with the current and the wind. And then presently they
will sink—deeper and deeper—as I shall, Thea.

2000 MRS. ELVSTED.   Do you know, Lövborg, that what you have done with the
book—I shall think of it to my dying day as though you had killed a little
child.

LÖVBORG.   Yes, you are right. It is a sort of child-murder.

MRS. ELVSTED.   How could you, then—! Did not the child belong to me too?

HEDDA [*almost inaudibly*].   Ah, the child—

MRS. ELVSTED [*breathing heavily*].   It is all over then. Well, well, now I will go,
Hedda.

HEDDA.   But you are not going away from town?

MRS. ELVSTED.   Oh, I don't know what I shall do. I see nothing but darkness
2010   before me.

[*She goes out by the hall door.*]

HEDDA [*stands waiting for a moment*].   So you are not going to see her home,
Mr. Lövborg?

LÖVBORG.   I? Through the streets? Would you have people see her walking
with me?

HEDDA.   Of course I don't know what else may have happened last night. But
is it so utterly irretrievable?

Lövborg.   It will not end with last night—I know that perfectly well. And the
thing is that now I have no taste for that sort of life either. I won't begin
it anew. She has broken my courage and my power of braving life out.

2020 HEDDA [*looking straight before her*].   So that pretty little fool has had her fingers in a man's destiny. [*Looks at him.*] But all the same, how could you
treat her so heartlessly?

Lövborg.   Oh, don't say that it was heartless!

HEDDA.   To go and destroy what has filled her whole soul for months and
years. You do not call that heartless!

Lövborg.   To you I can tell the truth, Hedda.

HEDDA.   The truth?

Lövborg.   First promise me—give me your word—that what I now confide
to you Thea shall never know.

2030 HEDDA.   I give you my word.

Lövborg.   Good. Then let me tell you what I said just now was untrue.

HEDDA.   About the manuscript?

Lövborg.   Yes. I have not torn it to pieces—nor thrown it into the fiord.

HEDDA.   No, no—But—where is it then?

Lövborg.   I have destroyed it none the less—utterly destroyed it, Hedda!

HEDDA.   I don't understand.

Lövborg.   Thea said that what I had done seemed to her like a child-murder.

HEDDA.   Yes, so she said.

Lövborg.   But to kill his child—that is not the worst thing a father can do to
2040   it.

HEDDA.   Not the worst?

Lövborg.   No. I wanted to spare Thea from hearing the worst.

HEDDA.   Then what is the worst?

Lövborg.   Suppose now, Hedda, that a man—in the small hours of the
morning—came home to his child's mother after a night of riot and
debauchery, and said: "Listen—I have been here and there—in this place
and in that. And I have taken our child with me—to this place and to that.
And I have lost the child—utterly lost it. The devil knows into what hands
it may have fallen—who may have had their clutches on it."

2050 HEDDA.   Well—but when all is said and done, you know—that was only a
book—

Lövborg.   Thea's pure soul was in that book.

HEDDA.   Yes, so I understand.

Lövborg.   And you can understand, too, that for her and me together no
future is possible.

HEDDA.   What path do you mean to take then?

Lövborg.   None. I will only try to make an end of it all—the sooner the
better.

HEDDA [*a step nearer to him*].   Eilert Lövborg—listen to me. Will you not try
2060   to—to do it beautifully?

Lövborg.   Beautifully? [*Smiling.*] With vine-leaves in my hair, as you used to
dream in the old days—?

HEDDA.   No, no. I have lost my faith in the vine-leaves. But beautifully,
nevertheless! For once in a way!—Good-bye! You must go now—and do
not come here any more.

Lövborg.   Good-bye, Mrs. Tesman. And give George Tesman my love. [*He
is on the point of going.*]

HEDDA.   No, wait! I must give you a memento to take with you.

[*She goes to the writing-table and opens the drawer and the pistol-case; then returns to* Lövborg *with one of the pistols.*]

Lövborg [*looks at her*].   This? Is this the memento?
2070   HEDDA [*nodding slowly*].   Do you recognize it? It was aimed at you once.
Lövborg.   You should have used it then.
HEDDA.   Take it—and do you use it now.
Lövborg [*puts the pistol in his breast pocket*].   Thanks!
HEDDA.   And beautifully, Eilert Lövborg. Promise me that!
Lövborg.   Good-bye, Hedda Gabler. [*He goes out by the hall door.*]

[HEDDA *listens for a moment at the door. Then she goes up to the writing-table, takes out the packet of manuscript, peeps under the cover, draws a few of the sheets half out, and looks at them. Next she goes over and seats herself in the arm-chair beside the stove, with the packet in her lap. Presently she opens the stove door, and then the packet.*]

HEDDA [*throws one of the quires into the fire and whispers to herself*].   Now I am burning your child, Thea!—Burning it, curly-locks! [*Throwing one or two more quires into the stove.*] Your child and Eilert Lövborg's. [*Throws the rest in.*] I am burning—I am burning your child.

ACT IV

The same rooms at the TESMANS'. *It is evening. The drawing-room is in darkness. The back room is lighted by the hanging lamp over the table. The curtains over the glass door are drawn close.*

HEDDA, dressed in black, walks to and fro in the dark room. Then she goes into the back room and disappears for a moment to the left. She is heard to strike a few chords on the piano. Presently she comes in sight again, and returns to the drawing-room. BERTA *enters from the right, through the inner room, with a lighted lamp, which she places on the table in front of the corner settee in the drawing-room. Her eyes are red with weeping, and she has black ribbons in her cap. She goes quietly and circumspectly out to the right.* HEDDA *goes up to the glass door, lifts the curtain a little aside, and looks out into the darkness. Shortly afterwards,* MISS TESMAN, *in mourning, with a bonnet and veil on, comes in from the hall.* HEDDA *goes towards her and holds out her hand.*

MISS TESMAN.   Yes, Hedda, here I am, in mourning and forlorn; for now my
2080   poor sister has at last found peace.
HEDDA.   I have heard the news already, as you see. Tesman sent me a card.
MISS TESMAN.   Yes, he promised me he would. But nevertheless I thought that to Hedda—here in the house of life—I ought myself to bring the tidings of death.
HEDDA.   That was very kind of you.
MISS TESMAN.   Ah, Rina ought not to have left us just now. This is not the time for Hedda's house to be a house of mourning.
HEDDA [*changing the subject*].   She died quite peacefully, did she not, Miss Tesman?

2090 MISS TESMAN.   Oh, her end was so calm, so beautiful. And then she had the unspeakable happiness of seeing George once more—and bidding him good-bye.—Has he come home yet?

HEDDA.   No. He wrote that he might be detained. But won't you sit down?

MISS TESMAN.   No thank you, my dear, dear Hedda. I should like to, but I have so much to do. I must prepare my dear one for her rest as well as I can. She shall go to her grave looking her best.

HEDDA.   Can I not help you in any way?

MISS TESMAN.   Oh, you must not think of it! Hedda Tesman must have no hand in such mournful work. Nor let her thoughts dwell on it either—not
2100   at this time.

HEDDA.   One is not always mistress of one's thoughts—

MISS TESMAN [*continuing*].   Ah yes, it is the way of the world. At home we shall be sewing a shroud; and here there will soon be sewing too, I suppose—but of another sort, thank God!

[GEORGE TESMAN *enters by the hall door.*]

HEDDA.   Ah, you have come at last!

TESMAN.   You here, Aunt Julia? With Hedda? Fancy that!

MISS TESMAN.   I was just going, my dear boy. Well, have you done all you promised?

TESMAN.   No; I'm really afraid I have forgotten half of it. I must come to you
2110   again tomorrow. Today my brain is all in a whirl. I can't keep my thoughts together.

MISS TESMAN.   Why, my dear George, you mustn't take it in this way.

TESMAN.   Mustn't—? How do you mean?

MISS TESMAN.   Even in your sorrow you must rejoice, as I do—rejoice that she is at rest.

TESMAN.   Oh yes, yes—you are thinking of Aunt Rina.

HEDDA.   You will feel lonely now, Miss Tesman.

MISS TESMAN.   Just at first, yes. But that will not last very long, I hope. I daresay I shall soon find an occupant for poor Rina's little room.

2120 TESMAN.   Indeed? Who do you think will take it? Eh?

MISS TESMAN.   Oh, there's always some poor invalid or other in want of nursing, unfortunately.

HEDDA.   Would you really take such a burden upon you again?

MISS TESMAN.   A burden! Heaven forgive you, child—it has been no burden to me.

HEDDA.   But suppose you had a total stranger on your hands—

MISS TESMAN.   Oh, one soon makes friends with sick folks; and it's such an absolute necessity for me to have some one to live for. Well, heaven be praised, there may soon be something in this house, too, to keep an old
2130   aunt busy.

HEDDA.   Oh, don't trouble about anything here.

TESMAN.   Yes, just fancy what a nice time we three might have together, if—?

HEDDA.   If—?

TESMAN [*uneasily*].   Oh, nothing. It will all come right. Let us hope so—eh?

MISS TESMAN.   Well, well, I daresay you two want to talk to each other. [*Smiling.*] And perhaps Hedda may have something to tell you too, George.

Good-bye! I must go home to Rina. [*Turning at the door.*] How strange it is to think that now Rina is with me and with my poor brother as well!

TESMAN.   Yes, fancy that, Aunt Julia! Eh?

[MISS TESMAN *goes out by the hall door.*]

2140 HEDDA [*follows* TESMAN *coldly and searchingly with her eyes*].   I almost believe your Aunt Rina's death affects you more than it does your Aunt Julia.

TESMAN.   Oh, it's not that alone. It's Eilert I am so terribly uneasy about.

HEDDA [*quickly*].   Is there anything new about him?

TESMAN.   I looked in at his rooms this afternoon, intending to tell him the manuscript was in safe-keeping.

HEDDA.   Well, did you not find him?

TESMAN.   No. He wasn't at home. But afterwards I met Mrs. Elvsted, and she told me he had been here early this morning.

HEDDA.   Yes, directly after you had gone.

2150 TESMAN.   And he said he had torn his manuscript to pieces—eh?

HEDDA.   Yes, so he declared.

TESMAN.   Why, good heavens, he must have been completely out of his mind! And I suppose you thought it best not to give it back to him, Hedda?

HEDDA.   No, he did not get it.

TESMAN.   But of course you told him that we had it?

HEDDA.   No. [*Quickly.*] Did you tell Mrs. Elvsted?

TESMAN.   No; I thought I had better not. But you ought to have told him. Fancy, if, in desperation, he should go and do himself some injury! Let me have the manuscript, Hedda! I will take it to him at once. Where is it?

2160 HEDDA [*cold and immovable, leaning on the arm-chair*].   I have not got it.

TESMAN.   Have not got it? What in the world do you mean?

HEDDA.   I have burnt it—every line of it.

TESMAN [*with a violent movement of terror*].   Burnt! Burnt Eilert's manuscript!

HEDDA.   Don't scream so. The servant might hear you.

TESMAN.   Burnt! Why, good God—! No, no, no! It's impossible!

HEDDA.   It is so, nevertheless.

TESMAN.   Do you know what you have done, Hedda? It's unlawful appropriation of lost property. Fancy that! Just ask Judge Brack, and he'll tell you what it is.

2170 HEDDA.   I advise you not to speak of it—either to Judge Brack, or to any one else.

TESMAN.   But how could you do anything so unheard-of? What put it into your head? What possessed you? Answer me that—eh?

HEDDA [*suppressing an almost imperceptible smile*].   I did it for your sake, George.

TESMAN.   For my sake!

HEDDA.   This morning, when you told me about what he had read to you—

TESMAN.   Yes, yes—what then?

HEDDA.   You acknowledged that you envied his work.

2180 TESMAN.   Oh, of course I didn't mean that literally.

HEDDA.   No matter—I could not bear the idea that any one should throw you into the shade.

TESMAN [*in an outburst of mingled doubt and joy*].   Hedda! Oh, is this true? But—but—I never knew you to show your love like that before. Fancy that!

HEDDA.   Well, I may as well tell you that—just at this time—[*impatiently, breaking off*]. No, no; you can ask Aunt Julia. She will tell you, fast enough.

TESMAN.   Oh, I almost think I understand you, Hedda! [*Clasps his hands together.*] Great heavens! do you really mean it! Eh?

HEDDA.   Don't shout so. The servant might hear.

2190 TESMAN [*laughing in irrepressible glee*].   The servant! Why, how absurd you are, Hedda. It's only my old Berta! Why, I'll tell Berta myself.

HEDDA [*clenching her hands together in desperation*].   Oh, it is killing me—it is killing me, all this!

TESMAN.   What is, Hedda? Eh?

HEDDA [*coldly, controlling herself*].   All this—absurdity—George.

TESMAN.   Absurdity! Do you see anything absurd in my being overjoyed at the news! But after all perhaps I had better not say anything to Berta.

HEDDA.   Oh—why not that too?

TESMAN.   No, no, not yet! But I must certainly tell Aunt Julia. And then that
2200 you have begun to call me George too! Fancy that! Oh, Aunt Julia will be so happy—so happy.

HEDDA.   When she hears that I have burnt Eilert Lövborg's manuscript—for your sake?

TESMAN.   No, by-the-bye—that affair with the manuscript—of course nobody must know about that. But that you love me so much, Hedda—Aunt Julia must really share my joy in that! I wonder, now, whether this sort of thing is usual in young wives? Eh?

HEDDA.   I think you had better ask Aunt Julia that question too.

TESMAN.   I will indeed, some time or other. [*Looks uneasy and downcast again.*]
2210 And yet the manuscript—the manuscript! Good God! it is terrible to think what will become of poor Eilert now.

[MRS. ELVSTED, *dressed as in the first act, with hat and cloak, enters by the hall door.*]

MRS. ELVSTED [*greets them hurriedly, and says in evident agitation*].   Oh, dear Hedda, forgive me coming again.

HEDDA.   What is the matter with you, Thea?

TESMAN.   Something about Eilert Lövborg again—eh?

MRS. ELVSTED.   Yes! I am dreadfully afraid some misfortune has happened to him.

HEDDA [*seizes her arm*].   Ah,—do you think so?

TESMAN.   Why, good Lord—what makes you think that, Mrs. Elvsted?

2220 MRS. ELVSTED.   I heard them talking of him at my boarding-house—just as I came in. Oh, the most incredible rumors are afloat about him today.

TESMAN.   Yes, fancy, so I heard too! And I can bear witness that he went straight home to bed last night. Fancy that!

HEDDA.   Well, what did they say at the boarding-house?

MRS. ELVSTED.   Oh, I couldn't make out anything clearly. Either they knew nothing definite, or else— They stopped talking when they saw me; and I did not dare to ask.

TESMAN [*moving about uneasily*].   We must hope—we must hope that you misunderstood them, Mrs. Elvsted.

2230 MRS. ELVSTED.   No, no; I am sure it was of him they were talking. And I heard something about the hospital or—

TESMAN.   The hospital?

HEDDA.   No—surely that cannot be!

MRS. ELVSTED.   Oh, I was in such mortal terror! I went to his lodgings and asked for him there.

HEDDA.   You could make up your mind to that, Thea!

MRS. ELVSTED.   What else could I do? I really could bear the suspense no longer.

TESMAN.   But you didn't find him either—eh?

2240 MRS. ELVSTED.   No. And the people knew nothing about him. He hadn't been home since yesterday afternoon, they said.

TESMAN.   Yesterday! Fancy, how could they say that?

MRS. ELVSTED.   Oh, I am sure something terrible must have happened to him.

TESMAN.   Hedda dear—how would it be if I were to go and make inquiries—?

HEDDA.   No, no—don't mix yourself up in this affair.

[JUDGE BRACK, *with his hat in his hand, enters by the hall door, which* BERTA *opens, and closes behind him. He looks grave and bows in silence.*]

TESMAN.   Oh, is that you, my dear Judge? Eh?

BRACK.   Yes. It was imperative I should see you this evening.

TESMAN.   I can see you have heard the news about Aunt Rina.

2250 BRACK.   Yes, that among other things.

TESMAN.   Isn't it sad—eh?

BRACK.   Well, my dear Tesman, that depends on how you look at it.

TESMAN [*looks doubtfully at him*].   Has anything else happened?

BRACK.   Yes.

HEDDA [*in suspense*].   Anything sad, Judge Brack?

BRACK.   That, too, depends on how you look at it, Mrs. Tesman.

MRS. ELVSTED [*unable to restrain her anxiety*].   Oh! it is something about Eilert Lövborg!

BRACK [*with a glance at her*].   What makes you think that, Madam? Perhaps

2260 you have already heard something—?

MRS. ELVSTED [*in confusion*].   No, nothing at all, but—

TESMAN.   Oh, for heaven's sake, tell us!

BRACK [*shrugging his shoulders*].   Well, I regret to say Eilert Lövborg has been taken to the hospital. He is lying at the point of death.

MRS. ELVSTED [*shrieks*].   Oh God! Oh God—

TESMAN.   To the hospital! And at the point of death.

HEDDA [*involuntarily*].   So soon then—

MRS. ELVSTED [*wailing*].   And we parted in anger, Hedda!

HEDDA [*whispers*].   Thea—Thea—be careful!

2270 MRS. ELVSTED [*not heeding her*].   I must go to him! I must see him alive!

BRACK.   It is useless, Madam. No one will be admitted.

MRS. ELVSTED.   Oh, at least tell me what has happened to him? What is it?

TESMAN.   You don't mean to say that he has himself—Eh?

HEDDA.   Yes, I am sure he has.

TESMAN.   Hedda, how can you—?

BRACK [*keeping his eyes fixed upon her*].   Unfortunately you have guessed quite correctly, Mrs. Tesman.

MRS. ELVSTED.   Oh, how horrible!

TESMAN.   Himself, then! Fancy that!

2280 HEDDA.   Shot himself!

BRACK.   Rightly guessed again, Mrs. Tesman.

MRS. ELVSTED [*with an effort at self-control*].   When did it happen, Mr. Brack?

BRACK.   This afternoon—between three and four.

TESMAN.   But, good Lord, where did he do it? Eh?

BRACK [*with some hesitation*].   Where? Well—I suppose at his lodgings.

MRS. ELVSTED.   No, that cannot be; for I was there between six and seven.

BRACK.   Well, then, somewhere else. I don't know exactly. I only know that
    he was found—. He had shot himself—in the breast.

MRS. ELVSTED.   Oh, how terrible! That he should die like that!

2290 HEDDA [*to* BRACK].   Was it in the breast?

BRACK.   Yes—as I told you.

HEDDA.   Not in the temple?

BRACK.   In the breast, Mrs. Tesman.

HEDDA.   Well, well—the breast is a good place, too.

BRACK.   How do you mean, Mrs. Tesman?

HEDDA [*evasively*].   Oh, nothing—nothing.

TESMAN.   And the wound is dangerous, you say—eh?

BRACK.   Absolutely mortal. The end has probably come by this time.

MRS. ELVSTED.   Yes, yes, I feel it. The end! The end! Oh, Hedda—!

2300 TESMAN.   But tell me, how have you learnt all this?

BRACK [*curtly*].   Through one of the police. A man I had some business with.

HEDDA [*in a clear voice*].   At last a deed worth doing!

TESMAN [*terrified*].   Good heavens, Hedda! what are you saying?

HEDDA.   I say there is beauty in this.

BRACK.   H'm, Mrs. Tesman—

TESMAN.   Beauty! Fancy that!

MRS. ELVSTED.   Oh, Hedda, how can you talk of beauty in such an act!

HEDDA.   Eilert Lövborg has himself made up his account with life. He has
    had the courage to do—the one right thing.

2310 MRS. ELVSTED.   No, you must never think that was how it happened! It must
    have been in delirium that he did it.

TESMAN.   In despair!

HEDDA.   That he did not, I am certain of that.

MRS. ELVSTED.   Yes, yes! In delirium! Just as when he tore up our manuscript.

BRACK [*starting*].   The manuscript? Has he torn that up?

MRS. ELVSTED.   Yes, last night.

TESMAN [*whispers softly*].   Oh, Hedda, we shall never get over this.

BRACK.   H'm, very extraordinary.

TESMAN [*moving about the room*].   To think of Eilert going out of the world in
2320   this way! And not leaving behind him the book that would have immor-
    talized his name—

MRS. ELVSTED.   Oh, if only it could be put together again!

TESMAN.   Yes, if it only could! I don't know what I would not give—

MRS. ELVSTED.   Perhaps it can, Mr. Tesman.

TESMAN.   What do you mean?

MRS. ELVSTED [*searches in the pocket of her dress*].   Look here. I have kept all the
    loose notes he used to dictate from.

HEDDA [*a step forward*].   Ah—!

TESMAN.   You have kept them, Mrs. Elvsted! Eh?

2330 MRS. ELVSTED.   Yes, I have them here. I put them in my pocket when I left home. Here they still are—

TESMAN.   Oh, do let me see them!

MRS. ELVSTED [*hands him a bundle of papers*].   But they are in such disorder—all mixed up.

TESMAN.   Fancy, if we could make something out of them, after all! Perhaps if we two put our heads together—

MRS. ELVSTED.   Oh, yes, at least let us try—

TESMAN.   We will manage it! We must! I will dedicate my life to this task.

HEDDA.   You, George? Your life?

2340 TESMAN.   Yes, or rather all the time I can spare. My own collections must wait in the meantime. Hedda—you understand, eh? I owe it to Eilert's memory.

HEDDA.   Perhaps.

TESMAN.   And so, my dear Mrs. Elvsted, we will give our whole minds to it. There is no use in brooding over what can't be undone—eh? We must try to control our grief as much as possible, and—

MRS. ELVSTED.   Yes, yes, Mr. Tesman, I will do the best I can.

TESMAN.   Well then, come here. I can't rest until we have looked through the notes. Where shall we sit? Here? No, in there, in the back room. Excuse
2350   me, my dear Judge. Come with me, Mrs. Elvsted.

MRS. ELVSTED.   Oh, if only it were possible!

[TESMAN *and* MRS. ELVSTED *go into the back room. She takes off her hat and cloak. They both sit at the table under the hanging lamp, and are soon deep in an eager examination of the papers.* HEDDA *crosses to the stove and sits in the arm-chair. Presently* BRACK *goes up to her.*]

HEDDA [*in a low voice*].   Oh, what a sense of freedom it gives one, this act of Eilert Lövborg's.

BRACK.   Freedom. Mrs. Hedda? Well, of course, it is a release for him—

HEDDA.   I mean for me. It gives me a sense of freedom to know that a deed of deliberate courage is still possible in this world,—a deed of spontaneous beauty.

BRACK [*smiling*].   H'm—my dear Mrs. Hedda—

HEDDA.   Oh, I know what you are going to say. For you are a kind of spe-
2360   cialist too, like—you know!

BRACK [*looking hard at her*].   Eilert Lövborg was more to you than perhaps you are willing to admit to yourself. Am I wrong?

HEDDA.   I don't answer such questions. I only know Eilert Lövborg has had the courage to live his life after his own fashion. And then—the last great act, with its beauty! Ah! that he should have the will and the strength to turn away from the banquet of life—so early.

BRACK.   I am sorry, Mrs. Hedda,—but I fear I must dispel an amiable illusion.

HEDDA.   Illusion?

2370 BRACK.   Which could not have lasted long in any case.

HEDDA.   What do you mean?

BRACK.   Eilert Lövborg did not shoot himself voluntarily.

HEDDA.   Not voluntarily?

BRACK.   No. The thing did not happen exactly as I told it.

HEDDA [*in suspense*].   Have you concealed something? What is it?

BRACK.   For poor Mrs. Elvsted's sake I idealized the facts a little.

HEDDA.   What are the facts?

BRACK.   First, that he is already dead.

HEDDA.   At the hospital?

2380 BRACK.   Yes—without regaining consciousness.

HEDDA.   What more have you concealed?

BRACK.   This—the event did not happen at his lodgings.

HEDDA.   Oh, that can make no difference.

BRACK.   Perhaps it may. For I must tell you—Eilert Lövborg was found shot in—in Mademoiselle Diana's boudoir.

HEDDA [*makes a motion as if to rise, but sinks back again*].   That is impossible, Judge Brack! He cannot have been there again today.

BRACK.   He was there this afternoon. He went there, he said, to demand the return of something which they had taken from him. Talked wildly about

2390 a lost child—

HEDDA.   Ah—so that was why—

BRACK.   I thought probably he meant his manuscript; but now I hear he destroyed that himself. So I suppose it must have been his pocket-book.

HEDDA.   Yes, no doubt. And there—there he was found?

BRACK.   Yes, there. With a pistol in his breastpocket, discharged. The ball had lodged in a vital part.

HEDDA.   In the breast—yes.

BRACK.   No—in the bowels.

HEDDA [*looks up at him with an expression of loathing*].   That too! Oh, what curse

2400 is it that makes everything I touch turn ludicrous and mean?

BRACK.   There is one point more, Mrs. Hedda—another disagreeable feature in the affair.

HEDDA.   And what is that?

BRACK.   The pistol he carried—

HEDDA [*breathless*].   Well? What of it?

BRACK.   He must have stolen it?

HEDDA [*leaps up*].   Stolen it! That is not true! He did not steal it!

BRACK.   No other explanation is possible. He must have stolen it—Hush!

[TESMAN *and* MRS. ELVSTED *have risen from the table in the back room, and come into the drawing-room.*]

TESMAN [*with the papers in both his hands*].   Hedda dear, it is almost impossible

2410 to see under that lamp. Think of that!

HEDDA.   Yes, I am thinking.

TESMAN.   Would you mind our sitting at your writing-table—eh?

HEDDA.   If you like. [*Quickly.*] No, wait! Let me clear it first!

TESMAN.   Oh, you needn't trouble, Hedda. There is plenty of room.

HEDDA.   No, no; let me clear it, I say! I will take these things in and put them on the piano. There!

[*She has drawn out an object, covered with sheet music, from under the book-case, places several other pieces of music upon it, and carries the whole into the inner room, to the left.* TESMAN *lays the scraps of paper on the writing-table, and moves the lamp there from the corner table,* HEDDA *returns.*]

HEDDA [*behind* MRS. ELVSTED's *chair, gently ruffling her hair*].   Well, my sweet Thea,—how goes it with Eilert Lövborg's monument?

MRS. ELVSTED [*looks dispiritedly up at her*].   Oh, it will be terribly hard to put in
2420   order.

TESMAN.   We must manage it. I am determined. And arranging other people's papers is just the work for me.

[HEDDA *goes over to the stove, and seats herself on one of the foot-stools.* BRACK *stands over her, leaning on the arm-chair.*]

HEDDA [*whispers*].   What did you say about the pistol?

BRACK [*softly*].   That he must have stolen it.

HEDDA.   Why stolen it?

BRACK.   Because every other explanation ought to be impossible, Mrs. Hedda.

HEDDA.   Indeed?

BRACK [*glances at her*].   Of course Eilert Lövborg was here this morning. Was
2430   he not?

HEDDA.   Yes.

BRACK.   Were you alone with him?

HEDDA.   Part of the time.

BRACK.   Did you not leave the room whilst he was here?

HEDDA.   No.

BRACK.   Try to recollect. Were you not out of the room a moment?

HEDDA.   Yes, perhaps just a moment—out in the hall.

BRACK.   And where was your pistol-case during that time?

HEDDA.   I had it locked up in—

2440 BRACK.   Well, Mrs. Hedda?

HEDDA.   The case stood there on the writing-table.

BRACK.   Have you looked since, to see whether both the pistols are there?

HEDDA.   No.

BRACK.   Well, you need not. I saw the pistol found in Lövborg's pocket, and I knew it at once as the one I had seen yesterday—and before, too.

HEDDA.   Have you it with you?

BRACK.   No; the police have it.

HEDDA.   What will the police do with it?

BRACK.   Search till they find the owner.

2450 HEDDA.   Do you think they will succeed?

BRACK [*bends over her and whispers*].   No, Hedda Gabler—not so long as I say nothing.

HEDDA [*looks frightened at him*].   And if you do not say nothing,—what then?

BRACK [*shrugs his shoulders*].   There is always the possibility that the pistol was stolen.

HEDDA [*firmly*].   Death rather than that.

BRACK [*smiling*].   People say such things—but they don't do them.

HEDDA [*without replying*].   And supposing the pistol was stolen, and the owner is discovered? What then?

2460 BRACK.   Well, Hedda—then comes the scandal.

HEDDA.   The scandal.

BRACK. Yes, the scandal—of which you are mortally afraid. You will, of course, be brought before the court—both you and Mademoiselle Diana. She will have to explain how the thing happened—whether it was an accidental shot or murder. Did the pistol go off as he was trying to take it out of his pocket, to threaten her with? Or did she tear the pistol out of his hand, shoot him, and push it back into his pocket? That would be quite like her; for she is an able-bodied young person, this same Mademoiselle Diana.

2470 HEDDA. But *I* have nothing to do with all this repulsive business.

BRACK. No. But you will have to answer the question: Why did you give Eilert Lövborg the pistol? And what conclusions will people draw from the fact that you did give it to him?

HEDDA [*lets her head sink*]. That is true. I did not think of that.

BRACK. Well, fortunately, there is no danger, so long as I say nothing.

HEDDA [*looks up at him*]. So I am in your power, Judge Brack. You have me at your beck and call, from this time forward.

BRACK [*whispers softly*]. Dearest Hedda—believe me—I shall not abuse my advantage.

2480 HEDDA. I am in your power none the less. Subject to your will and demands. A slave, a slave then! [*Rises impetuously.*] No, I cannot endure the thought of that! Never!

BRACK [*looks half-mockingly at her*]. People generally get used to the inevitable.

HEDDA [*returns his look*]. Yes, perhaps. [*She crosses to the writing-table. Suppressing an involuntary smile, she imitates* TESMAN's *intonations.*] Well? Are you getting on, George? Eh?

TESMAN. Heaven knows, dear. In any case it will be the work of months.

HEDDA [*as before*]. Fancy that? [*Passes her hands softly through* MRS. ELVSTED's
2490 *hair.*] Doesn't it seem strange to you, Thea? Here are you sitting with Tesman—just as you used to sit with Eilert Lövborg?

MRS. ELVSTED. Ah, if I could only inspire your husband in the same way.

HEDDA. Oh, that will come too—in time.

TESMAN. Yes, do you know, Hedda—I really think I begin to feel something of the sort. But won't you go and sit with Brack again?

HEDDA. Is there nothing I can do to help you two?

TESMAN. No, nothing in the world. [*Turning his head.*] I trust to you to keep Hedda company, my dear Brack.

BRACK [*with a glance at* HEDDA]. With the very greatest of pleasure.

2500 HEDDA. Thanks. But I am tired this evening. I will go in and lie down a little on the sofa.

TESMAN. Yes, do dear—eh?

[HEDDA *goes into the back room and draws the curtains. A short pause. Suddenly she is heard playing a wild dance on the piano.*]

MRS. ELVSTED [*starts from her chair*]. Oh—what is that?

TESMAN [*runs to the doorway*]. Why, my dearest Hedda—don't play dance music tonight! Just think of Aunt Rina! And of Eilert too!

HEDDA [*puts her head out between the curtains*]. And of Aunt Julia. And of all the rest of them.—After this, I will be quiet. [*Closes the curtains again.*]

TESMAN [*at the writing-table*]. It's not good for her to see us at this distressing

2510 work. I'll tell you what, Mrs. Elvsted,—you shall take the empty room at
Aunt Julia's, and then I will come over in the evenings, and we can sit and
work there—eh?

HEDDA [*in the inner room*].   I hear what you are saying, Tesman. But how am
I to get through the evenings out here?

TESMAN [*turning over the papers*].   Oh, I daresay Judge Brack will be so kind
as to look in now and then, even though I am out.

BRACK [*in the arm-chair, calls out gaily*].   Every blessed evening, with all the
pleasure in life, Mrs. Tesman! We shall get on capitally together, we two!

HEDDA [*speaking loud and clear*].   Yes, don't you flatter yourself we will, Judge
Brack? Now that you are the one cock in the basket—

[*A shot is heard from within.* TESMAN, MRS. ELVSTED, *and* BRACK *leap to their feet.*]

2520 TESMAN.   Oh, now she is playing with those pistols again.

[*He throws back the curtains and runs in, followed by* MRS. ELVSTED. HEDDA *lies
stretched out on the sofa, lifeless. Confusion and cries.* BERTA *enters in alarm from the
right.*]

TESMAN [*shrieks to* BRACK].   Shot herself! Shot herself in the temple! Fancy
that!

BRACK [*half-fainting in the arm-chair*].   Good God!—people don't do such
things.

[1890]

Critical Commentary on *Hedda Gabler*

Hedda Gabler is a study of a pathological personality—incapable of love, yet
possessed by jealousy; repulsed by any reference to pregnancy, yet consumed
by a longing for spiritual fertility; fearful of the task of molding a child's life,
yet eager to control a man's life. Each audience must determine for itself—in
part as a result of the actors' interpretation—the extent to which Hedda's
sickness is innate or is societally induced. The sickness itself, however, is
hardly a matter of dispute. It is stunningly displayed through Hedda's heartless actions—first in burning Eilert's manuscript, next in encouraging Eilert
to commit suicide "beautifully," and then in destroying her unborn child
along with herself. Hedda's actions are nearly as horrifying as Abbie Cabot's
infanticide in *Desire Under the Elms*, but Abbie was guided to some extent by
love while Hedda is guided by a petty fear of scandal, a scorn for the genteel
poverty into which she has fallen, and a loathing of her own carnality that
verges upon a denial of life itself.

The play is particularly worthy of study because it is approachable from so
many different critical perspectives. First and foremost it is a marvel of
dramatic craftsmanship. Indeed, Harold Clurman has written of *Hedda
Gabler*, "To novices in dramatic craftsmanship in the realm of modern realism I would recommend the play as a model." The play begins with a brilliant
exposition of characters and situation through the conversation between
Berta and Miss Tesman. The disruption of the status quo is nicely foreshadowed by the bouquet of flowers and visiting card from Mrs. Elvsted. From this

very natural and unstrained beginning, the events of the play unfold, inexorably bearing Hedda toward death. Furthermore, each act of the play builds toward its own crisis, which is spotlighted in curtain lines of incandescent brilliance. And these four crises build in dramatic intensity to their culmination in the final pistol shot. In realistic drama, as Chekhov once contended, if you introduce a pistol in the first act of a play, it must go off before the final curtain falls.

Surely, for most members of the audience the focus of the play is upon the peculiar psychological make-up of its central character, Hedda Gabler. That she is always referred to by her maiden name, Gabler, instead of her married name, Tesman, is one indication of her difficulty in accepting the traditional role of femininity. Note, too, that she refrains from using the intimate pronoun *du* in speaking with her husband, she shudders at the thought of becoming part of a tight family circle with George and Aunt Julia, she refuses to acknowledge her pregnancy, and she secretly despises the expensive home that George bought just to please her. To what extent is this play a feminist critique of the limited roles of women in a patriarchal society? To what extent is Hedda's desire to have her "fingers in a man's destiny" actually indicative of a desire to *be* a man? We know from biographical evidence that ever since writing an early draft for *Rosmersholm,* Ibsen had been concerned about what happens to a young woman who finds herself "highly gifted, without any application for her talents." To what extent is this play a further exploration of a particularly female dilemma of the past?

Whatever one thinks of the psychology of Hedda or of the feminist basis for that psychology, these elements of the play must in the end be somehow related to the life and human development of their creator, Henrik Ibsen. In his definitive book *Ibsen: A Biography,* Michael Meyer draws our attention to the historical models for Hedda in Emelie Bardach, Sophie Magelssen, Sally Svendsen, and others, but the most intriguing biographical speculation involves the relationship between the play and Ibsen himself. Meyer summarizes the contention of Arne Duve that "Lövborg and Tesman both represent aspects of Ibsen's own self: Lövborg an idealized portrait of himself as he had been in the wild days of his youth, Tesman a *reductio ad absurdam* of what he had chosen to become."

Among the great plenitude of critical interpretations of the play, one of the more interesting involves its many references to myths and archetypes. According to Elinor Fuchs, Lövborg, with "vine leaves in his hair," is obviously Dionysian; Mademoiselle Diana, "a mighty huntress of men," is reminiscent of the goddess Diana; Thea with her golden hair owes something to the Norse goddess Sis; Aunt Julia, who "stitches away at shrouds and buntings, hoping for the worst," is one of the Fates; the lustful Brack is both satyr and chorus; and Hedda herself is "Hecate, goddess of the underworld, the white bitch." Fuchs argues that this witches' brew of pagan deities is "representative of Ibsen's own view of civilization's diminished spirit." In the modern world, such deities are but pale shadows of themselves. A character such as Hedda, who wishes to worship a living Dionysus and secretly observe those modern mysteries of Eleusis forbidden to women, has no place in the world of bank balances and treatises on the domestic industries of Brabant in the middle ages. She kills herself, Fuchs argues, because modern life offers her (and us) "No glory, no terror left anywhere."

A Selective Bibliography on *Hedda Gabler*

Behrendt, Patricia Flanagan. "The Narcissus Paradigm in *Hedda Gabler*." *Journal of Evolutionary Psychology* 6 (1985): 202–10.

Belkin, Roslyn. "Prisoners of Convention: Ibsens's 'Other' Women." *Journal of Women's Studies in Literature* 1 (1979): 142–58.

Blau, Herbert. "*Hedda Gabler*: The Irony of Decadence." *Educational Theatre Journal* 5 (1953): 112–16.

Bradbrook, M. C. *Ibsen the Norwegian: A Revaluation*. New York, 1948; rpt. Hamden, Conn.: Archon Books, 1966. 116–21.

————. "Ibsen and the Past Imperfect." *Contemporary Approaches to Ibsen*. Oslo: Universitetsforlaget, 1971.

Braunmuller, A. R. "*Hedda Gabler* and the Sources of Symbolism." *Drama and Symbolism*. Ed. James Redmond. Cambridge, Eng.: Cambridge UP, 1982. 57–70.

Breitbart, Sara. "*Hedda Gabler*: A Critical Analysis." *American Journal of Psychoanalysis* 8 (1948): 55–58.

Cardullo, Bert. "Ibsen's *Hedda Gabler* and *Ghosts*." *Explicator* 46.1 (1987): 23–5.

Cima, Gay Gibson. "Discovering Signs: The Emergence of the Critical Actor in Ibsen." *Theater Journal* 35 (March 1983): 5–22.

Clurman, Harold. *Ibsen*. New York: Macmillan, 1977. 155–66.

Dacre, Kathleen. "Charles Marowitz's *Hedda* (and *An Enemy of the People*)." *Drama Review* 25 (1981): 5.

Dorcy, Michael M. "Ibsen's *Hedda Gabler*: Tragedy as Denouement." *College English* 29 (1967): 223–27.

Dukore, Bernard F. "Half a Kingdom for a Horse: Ibsenite Tragicomedy." *Modern Drama* 22 (1979): 217–51.

Durbach, Errol. "The Apotheosis of Hedda Gabler," *Scandinavian Studies* 43 (1971): 143–59.

————. *"Ibsen the Romantic": Analogues of Paradise in the Later Plays*. Athens, Ga.: U of Georgia P, 1982. 22–24, 34–52, and 71–74.

Finney, Gail. "Maternity and Hysteria: Ibsen's *Hedda Gabler*." *Women in Modern Drama: Freud, Feminism, and European Theater at the Turn of the Century*. Ithaca: Cornell UP, 1989. 149–65.

Fleischmann, Wolfgang B. "*Hedda Gabler*: A Cascade of Triangles." *Scandinavia* 8 (1969): 49–53.

Fuchs, Elinor. "Mythic Structure in *Hedda Gabler*: The Mask Behind the Face." *Comparative Drama* 19 (Fall 1985): 209–21.

Ganz, Arthur. "Miracle and Vine Leaves: An Ibsen Play Rewrought." *PMLA* 94 (1979): 9–21.

Gray, Ronald. *Ibsen—A Dissenting View: A Study of the Last Twelve Plays*. Cambridge, Eng.: Cambridge UP, 1977. 131–48.

Hardwick, Elizabeth. *Seduction and Betrayal: Women and Literature*. New York: Random House, 1974. 31–83.

Jacobs, Elizabeth. "Henrik Ibsen and the Doctrine of Self-Realization." *Journal of English and Germanic Philology* 38 (1939): 416–30.

Jacobsen, Per Schelde and Barbara Fass Leavy. *Ibsen's Forsaken Merman: Folklore in the Late Plays*. New York: New York UP, 1988. 136–41 and 211–14.

James, Henry. "On the Occasion of *Hedda Gabler*." *Discussions of Henrik Ibsen*. Ed. James W. McFarlane. Boston: Heath, 1962.

Jones, David R. "The Virtues of *Hedda Gabler*." *Educational Theatre Journal* 29 (1977): 447–62.

Kildahl, Erling E. "The 'Social Conditions and Principles' of *Hedda Gabler*." *Educational Theatre Journal* 13 (1961): 207–13.

Knight, G. Wilson. *Henrik Ibsen*. New York: Grove, 1964.

Krook, Dorothea. *Elements of Tragedy*. New Haven: Yale UP, 1969. 81–118.

Lester, Elenore. "Ibsen's Unliberated Heroines." *Scandinavian Review* 65 (1978): 58–66.

Lucas, F. L. *The Drama of Ibsen and Strindberg*. London: Cassell, 1962. 220–42.

Matherne, Beverly M. "A Kierkegaardian Study of *Hedda Gabler*." *Western Journal of Speech Communication* 42 (1978): 258–69.

Mayerson, Caroline W. "Thematic Symbols in *Hedda Gabler*." *Ibsen: A Collection of Critical Essays*. Ed. Rolf Fjelde. Englewood Cliffs, N.J.: Prentice-Hall, 1965. 131–39.

Meyer, Michael. *Ibsen: A Biography*. Garden City, N.Y.: Doubleday, 1971. 642–49.

Northam, John. *Ibsen: A Critical Study*. Cambridge, Eng.: Cambridge UP, 1973.

———— *Ibsen's Dramatic Method: A Study of the Prose Dramas*. Oslo: Universitetsforlaget, 1971. 147–71.

Olsen, Stein Haugom. "Why Does Hedda Gabler Marry Jorgen Tesman?" *Modern Drama* 28 (1985): 591–610.

Popovich, Helen. "Shelf of Dolls: A Modern View of Ibsen's Emancipated Women." *College English Association Critic* 39 (1977): 4–8.

Reed, Walter. "*The Cherry Orchard* and *Hedda Gabler*." *Homer to Brecht: The European Epic and Dramatic Traditions*. Eds. Michael Seidel and Edward Mendelson. New Haven: Yale UP, 1977. 317–35.

Saari, Sandra E. "Hedda Gabler: The Past Recaptured." *Modern Drama* 20 (September 1977): 299–316.

Sandstroem, Yvonne L. "Problems of Identity in *Hedda Gabler*." *Scandinavian Studies* 51 (1979): 368–74.

Schatia, Viva. "Hedda Gabler's Doll's House." *Psychoanalytic Review* 26 (1939): 33–38.

Spacks, Patricia Meyer. "The World of *Hedda Gabler*." *Tulane Drama Review* 7 (1962): 155–64.

Suzman, Janet. "*Hedda Gabler*: The Play in Performance." *Ibsen and the Theater*. Ed. Errol Durbach. London: Macmillan, 1980. 83–104.

Theopharis, Theopharis C. "*Hedda Gabler* and the 'The Dead.' " *English Literary History* 50 (1983): 791–809.

Valency, Maurice. *The Flower and the Castle*. New York: Macmillan, 1963. 192–201.

Walkington, J. W. "Women and Power in Henrik Ibsen and Adrienne Rich." *English Journal* 80.3 (1991): 64–9.

Webb, Eugene. *The Dark Dove: The Sacred and the Secular in Modern Literature*. Seattle: U of Washington P, 1979. 47–63.

Weigand, Hermann J. *The Modern Ibsen: A Reconsideration*. New York: Holt, 1925; rpt, New York, 1960. 242–73.

Wiedner, Elsie M. "Emma Bovary and Hedda Gabler: A Comparative Study." *Modern Language Studies* 8 (1978): 56–64.

Wisdom, John O. "The Lust for Power in *Hedda Gabler*." *Psychoanalytic Review* 31 (1944): 419–39.

Zucker, A. E. "Ibsen's Bardach Episode and *Hedda Gabler*." *Philological Quarterly* 8 (1929): 288–95.

George Bernard Shaw (1856–1950)
MRS WARREN'S PROFESSION

CHARACTERS

PRAED *an architect*

VIVIE WARREN

KITTY WARREN, *Vivie's mother*

SIR GEORGE CROFTS

FRANK GARDNER

REV. SAMUEL GARDNER, *Frank's father*

ACT I

Summer afternoon in a cottage garden on the eastern slope of a hill a little south of Haslemere[1] *in Surrey. Looking up the hill, the cottage is seen in the left hand corner of the garden, with its thatched roof and porch, and a large latticed window to the left of the porch. A paling completely shuts in the garden, except for a gate on the right. The common*[2] *rises uphill beyond the paling to the sky line. Some folded canvas garden chairs are leaning against the side bench in the porch. A lady's bicycle is propped against the wall, under the window. A little to the right of the porch a hammock is slung from two posts. A big canvas umbrella, stuck in the ground, keeps the sun off the hammock, in which a young lady lies reading and making notes, her head towards the cottage and her feet towards the gate. In front of the hammock, and within reach of her hand, is a common kitchen chair, with a pile of serious-looking books and a supply of writing paper on it.*

A gentleman walking on the common comes into sight from behind the cottage. He is hardly past middle age, with something of the artist about him, unconventionally but carefully dressed, and clean-shaven except for a moustache, with an eager susceptible face and very amiable and considerate manners. He has silky black hair, with waves of grey and white in it. His eyebrows are white, his moustache black. He seems not certain of his way. He looks over the palings; takes stock of the place; and sees the young lady.

THE GENTLEMAN [*taking off his hat*].   I beg your pardon. Can you direct me to Hindhead View—Mrs Alison's?

THE YOUNG LADY [*glancing up from her book*].   This is Mrs Alison's. [*She resumes her work*].

THE GENTLEMAN.   Indeed! Perhaps—may I ask are you Miss Vivie Warren?

THE YOUNG LADY [*sharply, as she turns on her elbow to get a good look at him*].   Yes.

---

[1] Haslemere is an English town about 40 miles southwest of London. The action in the play takes place near the end of the nineteenth century.

[2] A public field.

THE GENTLEMAN [*daunted and conciliatory*].   I'm afraid I appear intrusive. My
name is Praed. [VIVIE *at once throws her books upon the chair, and gets out of the
hammock*]. Oh, pray dont[3] let me disturb you.
10   VIVIE [*striding to the gate and opening it for him*].   Come in, Mr Praed. [*He comes
in*]. Glad to see you. [*She proffers her hand and takes his with a resolute and
hearty grip. She is an attractive specimen of the sensible, able, highly-educated
young middle-class Englishwoman. Age 22. Prompt, strong, confident, self-
possessed. Plain business-like dress, but not dowdy. She wears a chatelaine[4] at her
belt, with a fountain pen and a paper knife among its pendants*].
PRAED.   Very kind of you indeed. Miss Warren. [*She shuts the gate with a
vigorous slam. He passes in to the middle of the garden, exercising his fingers,
which are slightly numbed by her greeting*]. Has your mother arrived?
VIVIE [*quickly, evidently scenting aggression*].   Is she coming?
20   PRAED [*surprised*].   Didnt you expect us?
VIVIE.   No.
PRAED.   Now, goodness me, I hope Ive not mistaken the day. That would be
just like me, you know. Your mother arranged that she was to come down
from London and that I was to come over from Horsham to be introduced
to you.
VIVIE [*not at all pleased*].   Did she? Hm! My mother has rather a trick of taking
me by surprise—to see how I behave myself when she's away, I suppose. I
fancy I shall take my mother very much by surprise one of these days, if
she makes arrangements that concern me without consulting me before-
30   hand. She hasnt come.
PRAED [*embarrassed*].   I'm really very sorry.
VIVIE [*throwing off her displeasure*].   It's not your fault, Mr Praed, is it? And I'm
very glad youve come. You are the only one of my mother's friends I have
ever asked her to bring to see me.
PRAED [*relieved and delighted*].   Oh, now this is really very good of you, Miss
Warren!
VIVIE.   Will you come indoors; or would you rather sit out here and talk!
PRAED.   It will be nicer out here, dont you think?
VIVIE.   Then I'll go and get you a chair. [*She goes to the porch for a garden
40   chair*].
PRAED [*following her*].   Oh, pray, pray! Allow me. [*He lays hands on the chair*].
VIVIE [*letting him take it*].   Take care of your fingers: theyre rather dodgy
things, those chairs. [*She goes across to the chair with the books on it; pitches
them into the hammock; and brings the chair forward with one swing*].
PRAED [*who has just unfolded his chair*].   Oh, now d o let me take that hard
chair. I like hard chairs.
VIVIE.   So do I. Sit down, Mr Praed. [*This invitation she gives with genial
peremptoriness, his anxiety to please her clearly striking her as a sign of weakness
of character on his part. But he does not immediately obey*].
50   PRAED.   By the way, though, hadnt we better go to the station to meet your
mother?

---

[3] Shaw advocated a number of reforms in spelling and typography. Thus, in this play
apostrophes are omitted from many contractions ("dont" instead of "don't") and spacing replaces italics for emphasis ("N e v e r!" instead of *"Never!"*).
[4] A decorative clasp or chain.

Vivie [*coolly*].   Why? She knows the way.

Praed [*disconcerted*].   Er—I suppose she does [*he sits down*].

Vivie.   Do you know, you are just like what I expected. I hope you are disposed to be friends with me.

Praed [*again beaming*].   Thank you, my d e a r Miss Warren: thank you. Dear me! I'm so glad your mother hasnt spoilt you!

Vivie.   How?

Praed.   Well, in making you too conventional. You know, my dear Miss
60   Warren, I am a born anarchist. I hate authority. It spoils the relations between parent and child: even between mother and daughter. Now I was always afraid that your mother would strain her authority to make you very conventional. It's such a relief to find that she hasnt.

Vivie.   Oh! have I been behaving unconventionally?

Praed.   Oh no: oh dear no. At least not conventionally unconventionally, you understand. [*She nods and sits down. He goes on, with a cordial outburst*]. But it was so charming of you to say that you were disposed to be friends with me! You modern young ladies are splendid: perfectly splendid!

Vivie [*dubiously*].   Eh? [*watching him with dawning disappointment as to the quality
70   of his brains and character*].

Praed.   When I was your age, young men and women were afraid of each other: there was no good fellowship. Nothing real. Only gallantry copied out of novels, and as vulgar and affected as it could be. Maidenly reserve! gentlemanly chivalry! always saying no when you meant yes! simple purgatory for shy and sincere souls.

Vivie.   Yes, I imagine there must have been a frightful waste of time. Especially women's time.

Praed.   Oh, waste of life, waste of everything. But things are improving. Do you know, I have been in a positive state of excitement about meeting you
80   ever since your magnificent achievements at Cambridge: a thing unheard of in my day. It was perfectly splendid, your tieing with the third wrangler.[5] Just the right place, you know. The first wrangler is always a dreamy, morbid fellow, in whom the thing is pushed to the length of a disease.

Vivie.   It doesnt pay. I wouldnt do it again for the same money.

Praed [*aghast*].   The same money!

Vivie.   I did it for £ 50.

Praed.   Fifty pounds!

Vivie.   Yes. Fifty pounds. Perhaps you dont know how it was. Mrs Latham, my tutor at Newnham,[6] told my mother that I could distinguish myself in
90   the mathematical tripos[7] if I went in for it in earnest. The papers were full just then of Phillipa Summers beating the senior wrangler. You remember about it, of course.

Praed [*shakes his head energetically*]!!!

Vivie.   Well anyhow she did; and nothing would please my mother but that I should do the same thing. I said flatly it was not worth my while to face the grind since I was not going in for teaching; but I offered to try for

---

[5] The third wrangler was the Cambridge University student graduating with the third highest mark in mathematics.

[6] A women's college, now part of Cambridge University in England.

[7] An examination for the B.A. with honors in mathematics.

fourth wrangler or thereabouts for £ 50. She closed with me at that, after a little grumbling; and I was better than my bargain. But I wouldnt do it again for that. £ 200 would have been nearer the mark.

100 PRAED [*much damped*].   Lord bless me! Thats a very practical way of looking at it.

VIVIE.   Did you expect to find me an unpractical person?

PRAED.   But surely it's practical to consider not only the work these honors cost, but also the culture they bring.

VIVIE.   Culture! My dear Mr Praed: do you know what the mathematical tripos means? It means grind, grind, grind for six to eight hours a day at mathematics, and nothing but mathematics. I'm supposed to know something about science; but I know nothing except the mathematics it involves. I can make calculations for engineers, electricians, insurance

110   companies, and so on; but I know next to nothing about engineering or insurance. I dont even know arithmetic well. Outside mathematics, lawn-tennis, eating, sleeping, cycling, and walking, I'm a more ignorant barbarian than any woman could possibly be who hadnt gone in for the tripos.

PRAED [*revolted*].   What a monstrous, wicked, rascally system! I knew it! I felt at once that it meant destroying all that makes womanhood beautiful.

VIVIE.   I dont object to it on that score in the least. I shall turn it to very good account, I assure you.

PRAED.   Pooh! In what way?

120 VIVIE.   I shall set up in chambers[8] in the City, and work at actuarial calculations and conveyancing. Under cover of that I shall do some law, with one eye on the Stock Exchange all the time. Ive come down here by myself to read law: not for a holiday, as my mother imagines. I hate holidays.

PRAED.   You make my blood run cold. Are you to have no romance, no beauty in your life?

VIVIE.   I dont care for either, I assure you.

PRAED.   You cant mean that.

VIVIE.   Oh yes I do. I like working and getting paid for it. When I'm tired of working, I like a comfortable chair, a cigar, a little whisky, and a novel with

130   a good detective story in it.

PRAED [*rising in a frenzy of repudiation*].   I dont believe it. I am an artist; and I cant believe it: I refuse to believe it. It's only that you havnt discovered yet what a wonderful world art can open up to you.

VIVIE.   Yes I have. Last May I spent six weeks in London with Honoria Fraser. Mamma thought we were doing a round of sightseeing together; but I was really at Honoria's chambers in Chancery Lane[9] every day, working away at actuarial calculations for her, and helping her as well as a greenhorn could. In the evenings we smoked and talked, and never dreamt of going out except for exercise. And I never enjoyed myself more

140   in my life. I cleared all my expenses, and got initiated into the business without a fee into the bargain.

PRAED.   But bless my heart and soul, Miss Warren, do you call that discovering art?

---

[8] A law office.
[9] A section of London containing law and judicial offices.

VIVIE.   Wait a bit. That wasnt the beginning. I went up to town on an invitation from some artistic people in Fitzjohn's Avenue: one of the girls was a Newnham chum. They took me to the National Gallery—

PRAED [*approving*].   Ah!! [*He sits down, much relieved*].

VIVIE [*continuing*].   —to the Opera—

PRAED [*still more pleased*].   Good!

150 VIVIE.   —and to a concert where the band played all the evening: Beethoven and Wagner and so on. I wouldnt go through that experience again for anything you could offer me. I held out for civility's sake until the third day; and then I said, plump out, that I couldnt stand any more of it, and went off to Chancery Lane. N o w you know the sort of perfectly splendid modern young lady I am. How do you think I shall get on with my mother?

PRAED [*startled*].   Well, I hope—er—

VIVIE.   It's not so much what you hope as what you believe, that I want to know.

PRAED.   Well, frankly, I am afraid your mother will be a little disappointed.
160   Not from any shortcoming on your part, you know: I dont mean that. But you are so different from her ideal.

VIVIE.   Her what?!

PRAED.   Her ideal.

VIVIE.   Do you mean her ideal of ME?

PRAED.   Yes.

VIVIE.   What on earth is it like?

PRAED.   Well, you must have observed, Miss Warren, that people who are dissatisfied with their own bringing-up generally think that the world would be all right if everybody were to be brought up quite differently.
170   Now your mother's life has been—er—I suppose you know—

VIVIE.   Dont suppose anything, Mr Praed. I hardly know my mother. Since I was a child I have lived in England, at school or college, or with people paid to take charge of me. I have been boarded out all my life. My mother has lived in Brussels or Vienna and never let me go to her. I only see her when she visits England for a few days. I dont complain: it's been very pleasant; for people have been very good to me; and there has always been plenty of money to make things smooth. But dont imagine I know anything about my mother. I know far less than you do.

PRAED [*very ill at ease*].   In that case—[*He stops, quite at a loss. Then, with a forced*
180   *attempt at gaiety*] But what nonsense we are talking! Of course you and your mother will get on capitally. [*He rises, and looks abroad at the view*]. What a charming little place you have here!

VIVIE [*unmoved*].   Rather a violent change of subject, Mr Praed. Why wont my mother's life bear being talked about?

PRAED.   Oh, you really mustnt say that. Isnt it natural that I should have a certain delicacy in talking to my old friend's daughter about her behind her back? You and she will have plenty of opportunity of talking about it when she comes.

VIVIE.   No: s h e wont talk about it either. [*Rising*] However, I daresay you
190   have good reasons for telling me nothing. Only, mind this, Mr Praed. I expect there will be a battle royal when my mother hears of my Chancery Lane project.

PRAED [*ruefully*].   I'm afraid there will.

VIVIE.   Well, I shall win, because I want nothing but my fare to London to start there to-morrow earning my own living by devilling[10] for Honoria. Besides, I have no mysteries to keep up; and it seems she has. I shall use that advantage over her if necessary.

PRAED [*greatly shocked*].   Oh no! No, pray. Youd not do such a thing.

VIVIE.   Then tell me why not.

PRAED.   I really cannot. I appeal to your good feeling. [*She smiles at his
200   sentimentality*]. Besides, you may be too bold. Your mother is not to be trifled with when she's angry.

VIVIE.   You cant frighten me, Mr Praed. In that month at Chancery Lane I had opportunities of taking the measure of one or two women v e r y like my mother. You may back me to win. But if I hit harder in my ignorance than I need, remember that it is you who refuse to enlighten me. Now, let us drop the subject. [*She takes her chair and replaces it near the hammock with the same vigorous swing as before*].

PRAED [*taking a desperate resolution*].   One word, Miss Warren. I had better tell you. It's very difficult; but—

[MRS WARREN *and* SIR GEORGE CROFTS *arrive at the gate.* MRS WARREN *is between 40 and 50, formerly pretty, showily dressed in a brilliant hat and a gay blouse fitting tightly over her bust and flanked by fashionable sleeves. Rather spoilt and domineering, and decidedly vulgar, but, on the whole, a genial and fairly presentable old blackguard of a woman.*

CROFTS *is a tall powerfully-built man of about 50, fashionably dressed in the style of a young man. Nasal voice, reedier than might be expected from his strong frame. Clean-shaven bulldog jaws, large flat ears, and thick neck: gentlemanly combination of the most brutal types of city man, sporting man, and man about town.*]

210 VIVIE.   Here they are. [*Coming to them as they enter the garden*] How do, mater? Mr Praed's been here this half hour, waiting for you.

MRS WARREN.   Well, if youve been waiting, Praddy, it's your own fault: I thought youd have had the gumption to know I was coming by the 3.10 train. Vivie: put your hat on, dear: you'll get sunburnt. Oh, I forgot to introduce you. Sir George Croft: my little Vivie.

[CROFTS *advances to* VIVIE *with his most courtly manner. She nods, but makes no motion to shake hands.*]

CROFTS.   May I shake hands with a young lady whom I have known by reputation very long as the daughter of one of my oldest friends?

VIVIE [*who has been looking him up and down sharply*].   If you like. [*She takes his tenderly proffered hand and gives it a squeeze that makes him open his eyes; then
220   turns away, and says to her mother*] Will you come in, or shall I get a couple more chairs? [*She goes into the porch for the chairs*].

MRS WARREN.   Well, George, what do you think of her?

CROFTS [*ruefully*].   She has a powerful fist. Did you shake hands with her, Praed?

PRAED.   Yes: it will pass off presently.

CROFTS.   I hope so. [VIVIE *reappears with two more chairs. He hurries to her assistance*]. Allow me.

MRS WARREN [*patronizingly*].   Let Sir George help you with the chairs, dear.

---

[10] Acting as a legal assistant.

Vivie [*pitching them into his arms*].   Here you are. [*She dusts her hands and turns*
230   *to* Mrs Warren]. Youd like some tea, wouldnt you?

Mrs Warren [*sitting in* Praed's *chair and fanning herself*].   I'm dying for a drop
to drink.

Vivie.   I'll see about it. [*She goes into the cottage*].

[Sir George *has by this time managed to unfold a chair and plant it beside* Mrs
Warren, *on her left. He throws the other on the grass and sits down, looking dejected
and rather foolish, with the handle of his stick in his mouth.* Praed, *still very uneasy,
fidgets about the garden on their right.*]

Mrs Warren [*to* Praed, *looking at* Crofts].   Just look at him, Praddy: he looks
cheerful, dont he? He's been worrying my life out these three years to have
that little girl of mine shewn to him; and now that Ive done it, he's quite
out of countenance. [*Briskly*] Come! sit up, George; and take your stick out
of your mouth. [Crofts *sulkily obeys*].

Praed.   I think, you know—if you dont mind my saying so—that we had
240   better get out of the habit of thinking of her as a little girl. You see she has
really distinguished herself; and I'm not sure, from what I have seen of
her, that she is not older than any of us.

Mrs Warren [*greatly amused*].   Only listen to him, George! Older than any of
us! Well, she h a s been stuffing you nicely with her importance.

Praed.   But young people are particularly sensitive about being treated in
that way.

Mrs Warren.   Yes; and young people have to get all that nonsense taken out
of them, and a good deal more besides. Dont you interfere, Praddy: I
know how to treat my own child as well as you do. [Praed, *with a grave shake*
250   *of his head, walks up the garden with his hands behind his back.* Mrs. Warren
*pretends to laugh, but looks after him with perceptible concern. Then she whispers
to* Crofts]. Whats the matter with him? What does he take it like that for?

Crofts [*morosely*].   Youre afraid of Praed.

Mrs Warren.   What! Me! Afraid of dear old Praddy! Why, a fly wouldnt be
afraid of him.

Crofts.   Y o u r e afraid of him.

Mrs Warren [*angry*].   I'll trouble you to mind your own business, and not try
any of your sulks on me. I'm not afraid of y o u, anyhow. If you cant make
yourself agreeable, youd better go home. [*She gets up, and, turning her back*
260   *on him, finds herself face to face with* Praed]. Come, Praddy, I know it was only
your tender-heartedness. Youre afraid I'll bully her.

Praed.   My dear Kitty: you think I'm offended. Dont imagine that: pray
dont. But you know I often notice things that escape you; and though you
never take my advice, you sometimes admit afterwards that you ought to
have taken it.

Mrs Warren.   Well, what do you notice now?

Praed.   Only that Vivie is a grown woman. Pray, Kitty, treat her with every
respect.

Mrs Warren [*with genuine amazement*].   Respect! Treat my own daughter with
270   respect! What next, pray!

Vivie [*appearing at the cottage door and calling to* Mrs Warren].   Mother: will
you come to my room before tea?

Mrs Warren.   Yes, dearie. [*She laughs indulgently at* Praed's *gravity, and pats him on the cheek as she passes him on her way to the porch*]. Dont be cross, Praddy. [*She follows* VIVIE *into the cottage*].

CROFTS [*furtively*]. I say, Praed.

PRAED. Yes.

CROFTS. I want to ask you a rather particular question.

PRAED. Certainly. [*He takes* MRS WARREN's *chair and sits close to* CROFTS].

280 CROFTS. Thats right: they might hear us from the window. Look here: did Kitty ever tell you who that girl's father is?

PRAED. Never.

CROFTS. Have you any suspicion of who it might be?

PRAED. None.

CROFTS [*not believing him*]. I know, of course, that you perhaps might feel bound not to tell if she had said anything to you. But it's very awkward to be uncertain about it now that we shall be meeting the girl every day. We dont exactly know how we ought to feel towards her.

PRAED. What difference can that make? We take her on her own merits.

290 What does it matter who her father was?

CROFTS [*suspiciously*]. Then you know who he was?

PRAED [*with a touch of temper*]. I said no just now. Did you not hear me?

CROFTS. Look here, Praed. I ask you as a particular favor. If you d o know [*movement of protest from* PRAED]—I only say, if you know, you might at least set my mind at rest about her. The fact is, I feel attracted.

PRAED [*sternly*]. What do you mean?

CROFTS. Oh, dont be alarmed: it's quite an innocent feeling. Thats what puzzles me about it. Why, for all I know, *I* might be her father.

PRAED. You! Impossible!

300 CROFTS [*catching him up cunningly*]. You know for certain that I'm not?

PRAED. I know nothing about it, I tell you, any more than you. But really, Crofts—oh, no, it's out of the question. Theres not the least resemblance.

CROFTS. As to that, theres no resemblance between her and her mother that I can see. I suppose she's not y o u r daughter, is she?

PRAED [*rising indignantly*]. Really, Crofts—!

CROFTS. No offence, Praed. Quite allowable as between two men of the world.

PRAED [*recovering himself with an effort and speaking gently and gravely*]. Now listen to me, my dear Crofts. [*He sits down again*]. I have nothing to do with

310 that side of Mrs Warren's life, and never had. She has never spoken to me about it; and of course I have never spoken to her about it. Your delicacy will tell you that a handsome woman needs s o m e friends who are not—well, not on that footing with her. The effect of her own beauty would become a torment to her if she could not escape from it occasionally. You are probably on much more confidential terms with Kitty than I am. Surely you can ask her the question yourself.

CROFTS. I have asked her, often enough. But she's so determined to keep the child all to herself that she would deny that it ever had a father if she could. [*Rising*] I'm thoroughly uncomfortable about it, Praed.

320 PRAED [*rising also*]. Well, as you are, at all events, old enough to be her father, I dont mind agreeing that we both regard Miss Vivie in a parental way, as a young girl whom we are bound to protect and help. What do you say?

CROFTS [*aggressively*].   I'm no older than you, if you come to that.

PRAED.   Yes you are, my dear fellow: you were born old. I was born a boy: Ive never been able to feel the assurance of a grown-up man in my life. [*He folds his chair and carries it to the porch*].

MRS WARREN [*calling from within the cottage*].   Prad-dee! George! Tea-ea-ea-ea!

CROFTS [*hastily*].   She's calling us. [*He hurries in*].

[PRAED *shakes his head bodingly, and is following* CROFTS *when he is hailed by a young gentleman who has just appeared on the common, and is making for the gate. He is pleasant, pretty, smartly dressed, cleverly good-for-nothing, not long turned 20, with a charming voice and agreeably disrespectful manners. He carries a light sporting magazine rifle.*]

330   THE YOUNG GENTLEMAN.   Hallo! Praed!

PRAED.   Why, Frank Gardner! [FRANK *comes in and shakes hands cordially*]. What on earth are you doing here?

FRANK.   Staying with my father.

PRAED.   The Roman[11] father?

FRANK.   He's rector here. I'm living with my people this autumn for the sake of economy. Things came to a crisis in July: the Roman father had to pay my debts. He's stony broke in consequence; and so am I. What are you up to in these parts? Do you know the people here?

PRAED.   Yes: I'm spending the day with a Miss Warren.

340   FRANK [*enthusiastically*].   What! Do you know Vivie? Isn't she a jolly girl? I'm teaching her to shoot with this [*putting down the rifle*]. I'm so glad she knows you: youre just the sort of fellow she ought to know. [*He smiles, and raises the charming voice almost to a singing tone as he exclaims*] It's e v e r so jolly to find you here, Praed.

PRAED.   I'm an old friend of her mother. Mrs Warren brought me over to make her daughter's acquaintance.

FRANK.   The mother! Is s h e here?

PRAED.   Yes: inside at tea.

MRS WARREN [*calling from within*].   Prad-dee-ee-ee-eee! The tea-cake'll be

350   cold.

PRAED [*calling*].   Yes, Mrs Warren. In a moment. Ive just met a friend here.

MRS WARREN.   A what?

PRAED [*louder*].   A friend.

MRS WARREN.   Bring him in.

PRAED.   All right. [*To* FRANK] Will you accept the invitation?

FRANK [*incredulous, but immensely amused*].   Is that Vivie's mother?

PRAED.   Yes.

FRANK.   By Jove! What a lark! Do you think she'll like me?

PRAED.   Ive no doubt youll make yourself popular, as usual. Come in and try

360   [*moving towards the house*].

FRANK.   Stop a bit. [*Seriously*] I want to take you into my confidence.

---

[11]   I.e., noble and dutiful—*not* Roman Catholic. Gardner's father is an Anglican clergyman— *rector* (see next line) means "parish priest" or "pastor." Anglican clergymen are often referred to as "priests" and addressed as "Father," but unlike Roman Catholic clergy they are allowed to marry.

PRAED.   Pray dont. It's only some fresh folly, like the barmaid at Redhill.

FRANK.   It's ever so much more serious than that. You say youve only just met Vivie for the first time?

PRAED.   Yes.

FRANK [rhapsodically].   Then you can have no idea what a girl she is. Such character! Such sense! And her cleverness! Oh, my eye, Praed, but I can tell you she i s clever! And—need I add?—she loves me.

CROFTS [putting his head out of the window].   I say, Praed: what are you about? Do come along. [He disappears].

FRANK.   Hallo! Sort of chap that would take a prize at a dog show, ain't he? Who's he?

PRAED.   Sir George Crofts, an old friend of Mrs Warren's. I think we had better come in.

[On their way to the porch they are interrupted by a call from the gate. Turning, they see an elderly clergyman looking over it.]

THE CLERGYMAN [calling].   Frank!

FRANK.   Hallo! [To PRAED] The Roman father. [To the clergyman] Yes, gov'nor: all right: presently. [To PRAED] Look here, Praed: youd better go in to tea. I'll join you directly.

PRAED.   Very good. [He goes into the cottage].

[THE CLERGYMAN remains outside the gate, with his hands on the top of it. THE REV. SAMUEL GARDNER, a beneficed clergyman of the Established Church,[12] is over 50. Externally he is pretentious, booming, noisy, important. Really he is that obsolescent social phenomenon the fool of the family dumped on the Church by his father the patron, clamorously asserting himself as father and clergyman without being able to command respect in either capacity.]

REV. SAMUEL.   Well, sir. Who are your friends here, if I may ask?

FRANK.   Oh, it's all right, gov'nor! Come in.

REV. SAMUEL.   No, sir; not until I know whose garden I am entering.

FRANK.   It's all right. It's Miss Warren's.

REV. SAMUEL.   I have not seen her at church since she came.

FRANK.   Of course not: she's a third wrangler. Ever so intellectual. Took a higher degree than you did; so why should she go to hear you preach?

REV. SAMUEL.   Dont be disrespectful, sir.

FRANK.   Oh, it dont matter: nobody hears us. Come in. [He opens the gate, unceremoniously pulling his father with it into the garden]. I want to introduce you to her. Do you remember the advice you gave me last July, gov'nor?

REV. SAMUEL [severely].   Yes. I advised you to conquer your idleness and flippancy, and to work your way into an honorable profession and live on it and not upon me.

FRANK.   No: thats what you thought of afterwards. What you actually said was that since I had neither brains nor money, I'd better turn my good looks to account by marrying somebody with both. Well, look here. Miss Warren has brains: you cant deny that.

---

[12] The Church of England or Anglican Church, called the Episcopal Church in the U.S. It is called "Established" because it was founded by King Henry VIII and has been the State religion of England ever since.

REV. SAMUEL.   Brains are not everything.

FRANK.   No, of course not: theres the money—

400 REV. SAMUEL [*interrupting him austerely*].   I was not thinking of money, sir. I was speaking of higher things. Social position, for instance.

FRANK.   I dont care a rap about that.

REV. SAMUEL.   But I do, sir.

FRANK.   Well, nobody wants you to marry her. Anyhow, she has what amounts to a high Cambridge degree; and she seems to have as much money as she wants.

REV. SAMUEL [*sinking into a feeble vein of humor*].   I greatly doubt whether she has as much money as y o u will want.

FRANK.   Oh, come: I havnt been so very extravagant. I live ever so quietly; I
410   dont drink; I dont bet much; and I never go regularly on the razzle-dazzle as you did when you were my age.

REV. SAMUEL [*booming hollowly*].   Silence, sir.

FRANK.   Well, you told me yourself, when I was making ever such an ass of myself about the barmaid at Redhill, that you once offered a woman £ 50 for the letters you wrote to her when—

REV. SAMUEL [*terrified*].   Sh-sh-sh, Frank, for Heaven's sake! [*He looks round apprehensively. Seeing no one within earshot he plucks up courage to boom again, but more subduedly*]. You are taking an ungentlemanly advantage of what I confided to you for your own good, to save you from an error you would
420   have repented all your life long. Take warning by your father's follies, sir; and dont make them an excuse for your own.

FRANK.   Did you ever hear the story of the Duke of Wellington[13] and his letters?

REV. SAMUEL.   No, sir; and I dont want to hear it.

FRANK.   The old Iron Duke didnt throw away £ 50: not he. He just wrote: "Dear Jenny: publish and be damned! Yours affectionately, Wellington." Thats what you should have done.

REV. SAMUEL [*piteously*].   Frank, my boy: when I wrote those letters I put
430   myself into that woman's power. When I told you about them I put myself, to some extent, I am sorry to say, in your power. She refused my money with these words, which I shall never forget. "Knowledge is power" she said; "and I never sell power." Thats more than twenty years ago; and she has never made use of her power or caused me a moment's uneasiness. You are behaving worse to me than she did, Frank.

FRANK.   Oh yes I dare say! Did you ever preach at her the way you preach at me every day?

REV. SAMUEL [*wounded almost to tears*].   I leave you, sir. You are incorrigible. [*He turns toward the gate*].

440 FRANK [*utterly unmoved*].   Tell them I shant be home to tea, will you, gov'nor, like a good fellow? [*He moves towards the cottage door and is met by* PRAED *and* VIVIE *coming out*].

VIVIE [*to* FRANK].   Is that your father, Frank? I do so want to meet him.

FRANK.   Certainly. [*Calling after his father*] Gov'nor. Youre wanted. [*The parson*

---

[13] The reference is to Arthur Wellesley (1769–1852), the first Duke of Wellington, who defeated Napoleon at Waterloo in 1815 and later became prime minister of England (1828–1830).

turns at the gate, fumbling nervously at his hat. PRAED *crosses the garden to the opposite side, beaming in anticipation of civilities*]. My father: Miss Warren.
VIVIE [*going to the clergyman and shaking his hand*].   Very glad to see you here, Mr Gardner. [*Calling to the cottage*] Mother: come along: youre wanted.

[MRS WARREN *appears on the threshold, and is immediately transfixed, recognizing the clergyman.*]

VIVIE [*continuing*].   Let me introduce—
450 MRS WARREN [*swooping on the* REVEREND SAMUEL].   Why, it's Sam Gardner, gone into the Church! Well, I never! Dont you know us, Sam? This is George Crofts, as large as life and twice as natural. Dont you remember me?
REV. SAMUEL [*very red*].   I really—er—
MRS WARREN.   Of course you do. Why, I have a whole album of your letters still: I came across them only the other day.
REV. SAMUEL [*miserably confused*].   Miss Vavasour, I believe.
MRS WARREN [*correcting him quickly in a loud whisper*].   Tch! Nonsense! Mrs Warren: dont you see my daughter there?

ACT II

Inside the cottage after nightfall. Looking eastward from within instead of westward from without, the latticed window, with its curtains drawn, is now seen in the middle of the front wall of the cottage, with the porch door to the left of it. In the left-hand side wall is the door leading to the kitchen. Farther back against the same wall is a dresser with a candle and matches on it, and FRANK's *rifle standing beside them, with the barrel resting in the plate-rack. In the centre a table stands with a lighted lamp on it.* VIVIE's *books and writing materials are on a table to the right of the window, against the wall. The fireplace is on the right, with a settle: there is no fire. Two of the chairs are set right and left of the table.*

The cottage door opens, shewing a fine starlit night without; and MRS. WARREN, *her shoulders wrapped in a shawl borrowed from* VIVIE, *enters, followed by* FRANK, *who throws his cap on the window seat. She has had enough of walking, and gives a gasp of relief as she unpins her hat; takes it off; sticks the pin through the crown; and puts it on the table.*

MRS WARREN.   O Lord! I dont know which is the worst of the country, the
460 walking or the sitting at home with nothing to do. I could do with a whisky and soda now very well, if only they had such a thing in this place.
FRANK.   Perhaps Vivie's got some.
MRS WARREN.   Nonsense! What would a young girl like her be doing with such things! Never mind: it dont matter. I wonder how she passes her time here! I'd a good deal rather be in Vienna.
FRANK.   Let me take you there. [*He helps her to take off her shawl, gallantly giving her shoulders a very perceptible squeeze as he does so*].
MRS WARREN.   Ah! would you? I'm beginning to think youre a chip of the old block.
470 FRANK.   Like the gov'nor, eh? [*He hangs the shawl on the nearest chair, and sits down*].
MRS WARREN.   Never you mind. What do you know about such things? Youre only a boy. [*She goes to the hearth, to be farther from temptation*].

FRANK.   Do come to Vienna with me? It'd be ever such larks.

MRS WARREN.   No, thank you. Vienna is no place for you—at least not until youre a little older. [*She nods at him to emphasize this piece of advice. He makes a mock-piteous face, belied by his laughing eyes. She looks at him; then comes back to him*]. Now, look here, little boy [*taking his face in her hands and turning it up to her*]: I know you through and through and by your likeness to your father,
480   better than you know yourself. Dont you go taking any silly ideas into your head about me. Do you hear?

FRANK [*gallantly wooing her with his voice*].   Cant help it, my dear Mrs Warren: it runs in the family.

[*She pretends to box his ears; then looks at the pretty laughing upturned face for a moment, tempted. At last she kisses him, and immediately turns away, out of patience with herself.*]

MRS WARREN.   There! I shouldnt have done that. I a m wicked. Never you mind, my dear: it's only a motherly kiss. Go and make love to Vivie.

FRANK.   So I have.

MRS WARREN [*turning on him with a sharp note of alarm in her voice*].   What!

FRANK.   Vivie and I are ever such chums.

MRS WARREN.   What do you mean? Now see here: I wont have any young
490   scamp tampering with my little girl. Do you hear? I wont have it.

FRANK [*quite unabashed*].   My dear Mrs Warren: dont you be alarmed. My intentions are honorable: ever so honorable; and your little girl is jolly well able to take care of herself. She dont need looking after half so much as her mother. She aint so handsome, you know.

MRS WARREN [*taken aback by his assurance*].   Well, you have got a nice healthy two inches thick of cheek all over you. I dont know where you got it. Not from your father, anyhow.

CROFTS [*in the garden*].   The gipsies, I suppose?

REV. SAMUEL [*replying*].   The broomsquires[14] are far worse.

500   MRS WARREN [*to* FRANK].   S-sh! Remember! youve had your warning.

[CROFTS *and the* REVEREND SAMUEL *come in from the garden, the clergyman continuing his conversation as he enters.*]

REV. SAMUEL.   The perjury at the Winchester assizes[15] is deplorable.

MRS WARREN.   Well? what became of you two? And wheres Praddy and Vivie?

CROFTS [*putting his hat on the settle and his stick in the chimney corner*].   They went up the hill. We went to the village. I wanted a drink. [*He sits down on the settle, putting his legs up along the seat*].

MRS WARREN.   Well, she oughtnt to go off like that without telling me. [*To* FRANK] Get your father a chair, Frank: where are your manners? [FRANK *springs up and gracefully offers his father his chair; then takes another from the wall and sits down at the table, in the middle, with his father on his right and* MRS
510   WARREN *on his left*]. George: where are you going to stay to-night? You cant stay here. And whats Praddy going to do?

CROFTS.   Gardner'll put me up.

---

[14] Squatters on the English wasteland who live by tying heath into brooms.
[15] Court sessions.

MRS WARREN.   Oh, no doubt youve taken care of yourself! But what about Praddy?

CROFTS.   Dont know. I suppose he can sleep at the inn.

MRS WARREN.   Havnt you room for him, Sam?

REV. SAMUEL.   Well—er—you see, as rector here, I am not free to do as I like. Er—what is Mr Praed's social position?

MRS WARREN.   Oh, he's all right: he's an architect. What an old stick-in-the-
520   mud you are, Sam!

FRANK.   Yes, it's all right, gov'nor. He built that place down in Wales for the Duke. Caernarvon Castle[16] they call it. You must have heard of it [*He winks with lightning smartness at* MRS WARREN, *and regards his father blandly*].

REV. SAMUEL.   Oh, in that case, of course we shall only be too happy. I suppose he knows the Duke personally.

FRANK.   Oh, ever so intimately! We can stick him in Georgina's old room.

MRS WARREN.   Well, thats settled. Now if those two would only come in and let us have supper. Theyve no right to stay out after dark like this.

CROFTS [*aggressively*].   What harm are they doing you?

530   MRS WARREN.   Well, harm or not, I dont like it.

FRANK.   Better not wait for them, Mrs Warren. Praed will stay out as long as possible. He has never known before what it is to stray over the heath on a summer night with my Vivie.

CROFTS [*sitting up in some consternation*].   I say, you know! Come!

REV. SAMUEL [*rising, startled out of his professional manner into real force and sincerity*].   Frank, once for all, it's out of the question. Mrs Warren will tell you that it's not to be thought of.

CROFTS.   Of course not.

FRANK [*with enchanting placidity*].   Is that so, Mrs Warren?

540   MRS WARREN [*reflectively*].   Well, Sam, I dont know. If the girl wants to get married, no good cause can come of keeping her unmarried.

REV. SAMUEL [*astounded*].   But married to him!—your daughter to my son! Only think: it's impossible.

CROFTS.   Of course it's impossible. Dont be a fool, Kitty.

MRS WARREN [*nettled*].   Why not? Isnt my daughter good enough for your son?

REV. SAMUEL.   But surely, my dear Mrs Warren, you know the reasons—

MRS WARREN [*defiantly*].   I know no reasons. If you know any, you can tell them to the lad, or to the girl, or to your congregation, if you like.

550   REV. SAMUEL [*collapsing helplessly into his chair*].   You know very well that I couldn't tell anyone the reasons. But my boy will believe me when I tell him there a r e reasons.

FRANK.   Quite right, Dad: he will. But has your boy's conduct ever been influenced by your reasons?

CROFTS.   You cant marry her; and thats all about it. [*He gets up and stands on the hearth, with his back to the fireplace, frowning determinedly*].

MRS WARREN [*turning on him sharply*].   What have you got to do with it, pray?

---

[16] Caernarvon Castle is one of the most famous tourist attractions in the United Kingdom, but it was built in 1283. Frank is brazenly making fun of his father's ignorance by pretending that Praed designed the castle for the Duke of Wales. There is, however, no *Duke* of Wales; Wales is a *principality* and its lord is the *Prince* of Wales.

FRANK [*with his prettiest lyrical cadence*].   Precisely what I was going to ask, myself, in my own graceful fashion.

560 CROFTS [*to* MRS WARREN].   I suppose you dont want to marry the girl to a man younger than herself and without either a profession or twopence to keep her on. Ask Sam, if you dont believe me. [*To the parson*] How much more money are you going to give him?

REV. SAMUEL.   Not another penny. He has had his patrimony; and he spent the last of it in July. [MRS WARREN's *face falls*].

CROFTS [*watching her*].   There! I told you. [*He resumes his place on the settle and puts up his legs on the seat again, as if the matter were finally disposed of*].

FRANK [*plaintively*].   This is ever so mercenary. Do you suppose Miss Warren's going to marry for money? If we love one another—

570 MRS WARREN.   Thank you. Your love's a pretty cheap commodity, my lad. If you have no means of keeping a wife, that settles it: you cant have Vivie.

FRANK [*much amused*].   What do y o u say, gov'nor, eh?

REV. SAMUEL.   I agree with Mrs Warren.

FRANK.   And good old Crofts has already expressed his opinion.

CROFTS [*turning angrily on his elbow*].   Look here: I want none of y o u r cheek.

FRANK [*pointedly*].   I'm ever so sorry to surprise you, Crofts; but you allowed yourself the liberty of speaking to me like a father a moment ago. One father is enough, thank you.

CROFTS [*contemptuously*].   Yah! [*He turns away again*].

580 FRANK [*rising*].   Mrs Warren: I cannot give my Vivie up, even for your sake.

MRS WARREN [*muttering*].   Young scamp!

FRANK [*continuing*].   And as you no doubt intend to hold out other prospects to her, I shall lose no time in placing my case before her. [*They stare at him; and he begins to declaim gracefully*].

> He either fears his fate too much,
> Or his deserts are small,
> That dares not put it to the touch
> To gain or lose it all.[17]

[*The cottage door opens whilst he is reciting; and* VIVIE *and* PRAED *come in. He breaks off.* PRAED *puts his hat on the dresser. There is an immediate improvement in the company's behavior.* CROFTS *takes down his legs from the settle and pulls himself together as* PRAED *joins him at the fireplace.* MRS WARREN *loses her ease of manner and takes refuge in querulousness.*]

MRS WARREN.   Wherever have you been, Vivie?

590 VIVIE [*taking off her hat and throwing it carelessly on the table*].   On the hill.

MRS WARREN.   Well, you shouldnt go off like that without letting me know. How could I tell what had become of you? And night coming on too!

VIVIE [*going to the door of the kitchen and opening it, ignoring her mother*].   Now, about supper? [*All rise except* MRS WARREN]. We shall be rather crowded in here, I'm afraid.

MRS WARREN.   Did you hear what I said, Vivie?

VIVIE [*quietly*].   Yes, mother. [*Reverting to the supper difficulty*] How many are

---

[17] From "My Dear and Only Love" by the Marquis of Montrose (1612–1650).

we? [*Counting*] One, two, three, four, five, six. Well, two will have to wait until the rest are done: Mrs Alison has only plates and knives for four.

600 PRAED.   Oh, it doesnt matter about me. I—

VIVIE.   You have had a long walk and are hungry, Mr Praed: you shall have your supper at once. I can wait myself. I want one person to wait with me. Frank: are you hungry?

FRANK.   Not the least in the world. Completely off my peck, in fact.

MRS WARREN [*to* CROFTS].   Neither are you, George. You can wait.

CROFTS.   Oh, hang it, Ive eaten nothing since tea-time. Cant Sam do it?

FRANK.   Would you starve my poor father?

REV. SAMUEL [*testily*].   Allow me to speak for myself, sir. I am perfectly willing to wait.

610 VIVIE [*decisively*].   Theres no need. Only two are wanted. [*She opens the door of the kitchen*]. Will you take my mother in, Mr Gardner. [*The parson takes* MRS WARREN; *and they pass into the kitchen.* PRAED *and* CROFTS *follow. All except* PRAED *clearly disapprove of the arrangement, but do not know how to resist it.* VIVIE *stands at the door looking in at them*]. Can you squeeze past to that corner, Mr Praed: it's rather a tight fit. Take care of your coat against the white-wash: thats right. Now, are you all comfortable?

PRAED [*within*].   Quite, thank you.

MRS WARREN [*within*].   Leave the door open, dearie. [VIVIE *frowns; but* FRANK *checks her with a gesture, and steals to the cottage door, which he softly sets wide* 620 *open*]. Oh Lor, what a draught! You'd better shut it, dear.

[VIVIE *shuts it with a slam, and then, noting with disgust that her mother's hat and shawl are lying about, takes them tidily to the window seat, whilst* FRANK *noiselessly shuts the cottage door.*]

FRANK [*exulting*].   Aha! Got rid of em. Well, Vivvums: what do you think of my governor?

VIVIE [*preoccupied and serious*].   Ive hardly spoken to him. He doesnt strike me as being a particularly able person.

FRANK.   Well, you know, the old man is not altogether such a fool as he looks. You see, he was shoved into the Church rather; and in trying to live up to it he makes a much bigger ass of himself than he really is. I dont dislike him as much as you might expect. He means well. How do you think you'll get on with him?

630 VIVIE [*rather grimly*].   I dont think my future life will be much concerned with him, or with any of that old circle of my mother's, except perhaps Praed. [*She sits down on the settle*]. What do you think of my mother?

FRANK.   Really and truly?

VIVIE.   Yes, really and truly.

FRANK.   Well, she's ever so jolly. But she's rather a caution, isnt she? And Crofts! Oh, my eye, Crofts! [*He sits beside her*].

VIVIE.   What a lot, Frank!

FRANK.   What a crew!

VIVIE [*with intense contempt for them*].   If I thought that *I* was like that—that I 640 was going to be a waster, shifting along from one meal to another with no purpose, and no character, and no grit in me, I'd open an artery and bleed to death without one moment's hesitation.

FRANK.   Oh no, you wouldnt. Why should they take any grind when they can
   afford not to? I wish I had their luck. No: what I object to is their form. It
   isnt the thing: it's slovenly, ever so slovenly.

VIVIE.   Do you think your form will be any better when youre as old as Crofts,
   if you dont work?

FRANK.   Of course I do. Ever so much better. Vivvums mustnt lecture: her
   little boy's incorrigible. [*He attempts to take her face caressingly in his hands*].

650 VIVIE [*striking his hands down sharply*].   Off with you: Vivvums is not in a
   humor for petting her little boy this evening. [*She rises and comes forward to
   the other side of the room*].

FRANK [*following her*].   How unkind!

VIVIE [*stamping at him*].   Be serious. I'm serious.

FRANK.   Good. Let us talk learnedly. Miss Warren: do you know that all the
   most advanced thinkers are agreed that half the disease of modern civilization are due to starvation of the affections of the young. Now, *I*—

VIVIE [*cutting him short*].   You are very tiresome. [*She opens the inner door*].
   Have you room for Frank there? He's complaining of starvation.

660 MRS WARREN [*within*].   Of course there is [*clatter of knives and glasses as she
   moves the things on the table*]. Here! theres room now beside me. Come
   along, Mr. Frank.

FRANK.   Her little boy will be ever so even with his Vivvums for this. [*He passes
   into the kitchen*].

MRS WARREN [*within*].   Here, Vivie: come on you too, child. You must be
   famished. [*She enters, followed by* CROFTS, *who holds the door open for* VIVIE *with
   marked deference. She goes out without looking at him; and he shuts the door after
   her*]. Why, George, you cant be done: youve eaten nothing. Is there anything wrong with you?

670 CROFTS.   Oh, all I wanted was a drink. [*He thrusts his hands in his pockets, and
   begins prowling about the room, restless and sulky*].

MRS WARREN.   Well, I like enough to eat. But a little of that cold beef and
   cheese and lettuce goes a long way. [*With a sigh of only half repletion she sits
   down lazily on the settle*].

CROFTS.   What do you go encouraging that young pup for?

MRS WARREN [*on the alert at once*].   Now see here, George: what are you up to
   about that girl? Ive been watching your way of looking at her. Remember:
   I know you and what your looks mean.

CROFTS.   Theres no harm in looking at her, is there?

680 MRS WARREN.   I'd put you out and pack you back to London pretty soon if I
   saw any of your nonsense. My girl's little finger is more to me than your
   whole body and soul. [CROFTS *receives this with a sneering grin.* MRS WARREN,
   *flushing a little at her failure to impose on him in the character of a theatrically
   devoted mother, adds in a lower key*] Make your mind easy: the young pup has
   no more chance than you have.

CROFTS.   Maynt a man take an interest in a girl?

MRS WARREN.   Not a man like you.

CROFTS.   How old is she?

MRS WARREN.   Never you mind how old she is.

690 CROFTS.   Why do you make such a secret of it?

MRS WARREN.   Because I choose.

CROFTS.   Well, I'm not fifty yet; and my property is as good as ever it was—

Mrs Warren [*interrupting him*].   Yes; because youre as stingy as youre vicious.

Crofts [*continuing*].   And a baronet isnt to be picked up every day. No other man in my position would put up with you for a mother-in-law. Why shouldnt she marry me?

Mrs Warren.   You!

Crofts.   We three could live together quite comfortably. I'd die before her and leave her a bouncing widow with plenty of money. Why not? It's been
700   growing in my mind all the time Ive been walking with that fool inside there.

Mrs Warren [*revolted*].   Yes: it's the sort of thing that w o u l d grow in your mind.

[*He halts in his prowling; and the two look at one another, she steadfastly, with a sort of awe behind her contemptuous disgust: he stealthily, with a carnal gleam in his eye and a loose grin.*]

Crofts [*suddenly becoming anxious and urgent as he sees no sign of sympathy in her*].   Look here, Kitty: youre a sensible woman: you neednt put on any moral airs. I'll ask no more questions; and you need answer none. I'll settle the whole property on her; and if you want a cheque for yourself on the wedding day, you can name any figure you like—in reason.

Mrs Warren.   So it's come to that with you, George, like all the other worn-
710   out old creatures!

Crofts [*savagely*].   Damn you!

[*Before she can retort the door of the kitchen is opened; and the voices of the others are heard returning.* Crofts, *unable to recover his presence of mind, hurries out of the cottage. The clergyman appears at the kitchen door.*]

Rev. Samuel [*looking around*].   Where is Sir George?

Mrs Warren.   Gone out to have a pipe. [*The clergyman takes his hat from the table, and joins* Mrs Warren *at the fireside. Meanwhile* Vivie *comes in, followed by* Frank, *who collapses into the nearest chair with an air of extreme exhaustion.* Mrs Warren *looks round at* Vivie *and says, with her affectation of maternal patronage even more forced than usual*] Well, dearie: have you had a good supper?

Vivie.   You know what Mrs Alison's suppers are. [*She turns to* Frank *and pets*
720   *him*]. Poor Frank! was all the beef gone? did it get nothing but bread and cheese and ginger beer? [*Seriously, as if she had done quite enough trifling for one evening*] Her butter is really awful. I must get some down from the stores.

Frank.   Do, in Heaven's name!

[Vivie *goes to the writing-table and makes a memorandum to order the butter.* Praed *comes in from the kitchen, putting up his handkerchief, which he has been using as a napkin.*]

Rev. Samuel.   Frank, my boy: it is time for us to be thinking of home. Your mother does not know yet that we have visitors.

Praed.   I'm afraid we're giving trouble.

Frank [*rising*].   Not the least in the world: my mother will be delighted to see you. She's a genuinely intellectual artistic woman; and she sees nobody

730 here from one year's end to another except the gov'nor; so you can imagine how jolly dull it pans out for her. [*To his father*] Y o u r e not intellectual or artistic: are you, pater? So take Praed home at once; and I'll stay here and entertain Mrs Warren. Youll pick up Crofts in the garden. He'll be excellent company for the bull-pup.

PRAED [*taking his hat from the dresser, and coming close to* FRANK]. Come with us, Frank. Mrs Warren has not seen Miss Vivie for a long time; and we have prevented them from having a moment together yet.

FRANK [*quite softened, and looking at* PRAED *with romantic admiration*]. Of course, I forgot. Ever so thanks for reminding me. Perfect gentleman, Praddy.
740 Always were. My ideal through life. [*He rises to go, but pauses a moment between the two older men, and puts his hand on* PRAED'S *shoulder*]. Ah, if you had only been my father instead of this unworthy old man! [*He puts his other hand on his father's shoulder*].

REV. SAMUEL. [*blustering*]. Silence, sir, silence: you are profane.

MRS WARREN [*laughing heartily*]. You should keep him in better order, Sam. Good-night. Here: take George his hat and stick with my compliments.

REV. SAMUEL [*taking them*]. Good-night. [*They shake hands. As he passes* VIVIE *he shakes hands with her also and bids her good-night. Then, in booming command, to* FRANK.] Come along, sir, at once. [*He goes out*].
750 MRS WARREN. Byebye, Praddy.

PRAED. Byebye, Kitty.

[*They shake hands affectionately and go out together, she accompanying him to the garden gate.*]

FRANK [*to* VIVIE]. Kissums?

VIVIE [*fiercely*]. No. I hate you. [*She takes a couple of books and some paper from the writing-table, and sits down with them at the middle table, at the end next the fireplace*].

FRANK [*grimacing*]. Sorry. [*He goes for his cap and rifle.* MRS WARREN *returns. He takes her hand*] Good-night, dear Mrs Warren. [*He kisses her hand. She snatches it away, her lips tightening, and looks more than half disposed to box his ears. He laughs mischievously and runs off, clapping-to the door behind him*].
760 MRS WARREN [*resigning herself to an evening of boredom now that the men are gone*]. Did you ever in your life hear anyone rattle on so? Isnt he a tease? [*She sits at the table*]. Now that I think of it, dearie, dont you go encouraging him. I'm sure he's a regular good-for-nothing.

VIVIE [*rising to fetch more books*]. I'm afraid so. Poor Frank! I shall have to get rid of him; but I shall feel sorry for him, though he's not worth it. That man Crofts does not seem to me to be good for much either: is he? [*She throws the books on the table rather roughly*].

MRS WARREN [*galled by* VIVIE'S *indifference*]. What do you know of men, child, to talk that way about them? Youll have to make up your mind to see a
770 good deal of Sir George Crofts, as he's a friend of mine.

VIVIE [*quite unmoved*]. Why? [*She sits down and opens a book*]. Do you expect that we shall be much together? You and I, I mean?

MRS WARREN [*staring at her*]. Of course: until youre married. Youre not going back to college again.

VIVIE. Do you think my way of life would suit you? I doubt it.

MRS WARREN.   Y o u r way of life! What do you mean?

VIVIE [*cutting a page of her book with the paper knife on her chatelaine*].   Has it really never occurred to you, mother, that I have a way of life like other people?

780 MRS WARREN.   What nonsense is this youre trying to talk? Do you want to shew your independence, now that youre a great little person at school? Dont be a fool, child.

VIVIE [*indulgently*].   Thats all you have to say on the subject, is it, mother?

MRS WARREN [*puzzled, then angry*].   Dont you keep on asking me questions like that. [*Violently*] Hold your tongue. [VIVIE *works on, losing no time, and saying nothing*]. You and your way of life, indeed! What next? [*She looks at* VIVIE *again. No reply*]. Your way of life will be what I please, so it will. [*Another pause*]. Ive been noticing these airs in you ever since you got that tripos or whatever you call it. If you think I'm going to put up with them

790 youre mistaken; and the sooner you find it out, the better. [*Muttering*] All I have to say on the subject, indeed! [*Again raising her voice angrily*] Do you know who youre speaking to, Miss?

VIVIE [*looking across at her without raising her head from her book*].   No. Who are you? What are you?

MRS WARREN [*rising breathless*].   You young imp!

VIVIE.   Everybody knows my reputation, my social standing, and the profession I intend to pursue. I know nothing about you. What is that way of life which you invite me to share with you and Sir George Crofts, pray?

MRS WARREN.   Take care. I shall do something I'll be sorry for after, and you

800 too.

VIVIE [*putting aside her books with cool decision*].   Well, let us drop the subject until you are better able to face it. [*Looking critically at her mother*] You want some good walks and a little lawn tennis to set you up. You are shockingly out of condition: you were not able to manage twenty yards uphill today without stopping to pant; and your wrists are mere rolls of fat. Look at mine. [*She holds out her wrists*].

MRS WARREN [*after looking at her helplessly, begins to whimper*].   Vivie—

VIVIE [*springing up sharply*].   Now pray dont begin to cry. Anything but that. I really cannot stand whimpering. I will go out of the room if you do.

810 MRS WARREN [*piteously*].   Oh, my darling, how can you be so hard on me? Have I no rights over you as your mother?

VIVIE.   A r e you my mother?

MRS WARREN [*appalled*].   A m I your mother! Oh, Vivie!

VIVIE.   Then where are our relatives? my father? our family friends? You claim the rights of a mother: the right to call me fool and child; to speak to me as no woman in authority over me in college dare speak to me; to dictate my way of life; and to force on me the acquaintance of a brute whom anyone can see to be the most vicious sort of London man about town. Before I give myself the trouble to resist such claims, I may as well

820 find out whether they have any real existence.

MRS WARREN [*distracted, throwing herself on her knees*].   Oh no, no. Stop, stop. I a m your mother: I swear it. Oh, you cant mean to turn on me—my own child! it's not natural. You believe me, dont you? Say you believe me.

VIVIE.   Who was my father?

MRS WARREN.   You dont know what youre asking. I cant tell you.

VIVIE [*determinedly*].   Oh yes you can, if you like. I have a right to know; and you know very well that I have that right. You can refuse to tell me, if you please; but if you do, you will see the last of me tomorrow morning.

MRS WARREN.   Oh, it's too horrible to hear you talk like that. You wouldnt—
830   you c o u l d n t leave me.

VIVIE [*ruthlessly*].   Yes, without a moment's hesitation, if you trifle with me about this. [*Shivering with disgust*] How can I feel sure that I may not have the contaminated blood of that brutal waster in my veins?

MRS WARREN.   No, no. On my oath it's not he, nor any of the rest that you have ever met. I'm certain of that, at least.

[VIVIE'S *eyes fasten sternly on her mother as the significance of this flashes on her.*]

VIVIE [*slowly*].   You are certain of that, at l e a s t. Ah! You mean that that is all you are certain of. [*Thoughtfully*] I see. [MRS WARREN *buries her face in her hands*]. Dont do that, mother: you know you dont feel it a bit. [MRS WARREN *takes down her hands and looks up deplorably at* VIVIE, *who takes out her watch*
840   *and says*] Well, that is enough for tonight. At what hour would you like breakfast? Is half-past eight too early for you?

MRS WARREN [*wildly*].   My God, what sort of woman are you?

VIVIE [*coolly*].   The sort the world is mostly made of, I should hope. Other- wise I dont understand how it gets its business done. Come [*taking her mother by the wrist, and pulling her up pretty resolutely*]: pull yourself together. Thats right.

MRS WARREN [*querulously*].   Youre very rough with me, Vivie.

VIVIE.   Nonsense. What about bed? It's past ten.

MRS WARREN [*passionately*].   Whats the use of my going to bed? Do you think
850   I could sleep?

VIVIE.   Why not? I shall.

MRS WARREN.   You! youve no heart. [*She suddenly breaks out vehemently in her natural tongue—the dialect of a woman of the people—with all her affectations of maternal authority and conventional manners gone, and an overwhelming inspi- ration of true conviction and scorn in her*] Oh, I wont bear it: I wont put up with the injustice of it. What right have you to set yourself up above me like this? You boast of what you are to me—to m e, who gave you the chance of being what you are. What chance had I? Shame on you for a bad daughter and a stuck-up prude!

860 VIVIE [*sitting down with a shrug, no longer confident; for her replies, which have sounded sensible and strong to her so far, now begin to ring rather woodenly and even priggishly against the new tone of her mother*].   Dont think for a moment I set myself above you in any way. You attacked me with the conventional authority of a mother: I defended myself with the conventional superiority of a respectable woman. Frankly, I am not going to stand any of your nonsense; and when you drop it I shall not expect you to stand any of mine. I shall always respect your right to your own opinions and your own way of life.

MRS WARREN.   My own opinions and my own way of life! Listen to her talk-
870   ing! Do you think I was brought up like you? able to pick and choose my own way of life? Do you think I did what I did because I liked it, or thought it right, or wouldnt rather have gone to college and been a lady if I'd had the chance?

VIVIE.   Everybody has some choice, mother. The poorest girl alive may not

be able to choose between being Queen of England or Principal of Newnham; but she can choose between ragpicking and flowerselling, according
to her taste. People are always blaming their circumstances for what they
are. I dont believe in circumstances. The people who get on in this world
are the people who get up and look for the circumstances they want, and,
880   if they cant find them, make them.

MRS WARREN.   Oh, it's easy to talk, very easy, isnt it? Here! would you like to
know what m y circumstances were?

VIVIE.   Yes: you had better tell me. Wont you sit down?

MRS WARREN.   Oh, I'll sit down: dont you be afraid. [*She plants her chair farther
forward with brazen energy, and sits down.* VIVIE *is impressed in spite of herself*].
D'you know what your gran'mother was?

VIVIE.   No.

MRS WARREN.   No you dont. I do. She called herself a widow and had a
fried-fish shop down by the Mint, and kept herself and four daughters out
890   of it. Two of us were sisters: that was me and Liz; and we were both
good-looking and well made. I suppose our father was a well-fed man:
mother pretended he was a gentleman; but I dont know. The other two
were only half sisters: undersized, ugly, starved looking, hard working,
honest poor creatures: Liz and I would have half-murdered them if mother
hadnt half-murdered u s to keep our hands off them. They were the
respectable ones. Well, what did they get by their respectability? I'll tell
you. One of them worked in a whitelead factory twelve hours a day for nine
shillings a week until she died of lead poisoning. She only expected to get
her hands a little paralyzed; but she died. The other was always held up to
900   us as a model because she married a Government laborer in the Deptford
victualling yard, and kept his room and the three children neat and tidy
on eighteen shillings a week—until he took to drink. That was worth being
respectable for, wasn't it?

VIVIE [*now thoughtfully attentive*].   Did you and your sister think so?

MRS WARREN.   Liz didnt, I can tell you: she had more spirit. We both went to
a church school—that was part of the ladylike airs we gave ourselves to be
superior to the children that knew nothing and went nowhere—and we
stayed there until Liz went out one night and never came back. I know the
schoolmistress thought I'd soon follow her example; for the clergyman
910   was always warning me that Lizzie'd end by jumping off Waterloo Bridge.
Poor fool: that was all he knew about it! But I was more afraid of the
whitelead factory than I was of the river; and so would you have been in
my place. That clergyman got me a situation as scullery maid in a temperance restaurant where they sent out for anything you liked. Then I was
waitress; and then I went to the bar at Waterloo station: fourteen hours a
day serving drinks and washing glasses for four shillings a week and my
board. That was considered a great promotion for me. Well, one cold,
wretched night, when I was so tired I could hardly keep myself awake, who
should come up for a half of Scotch but Lizzie, in a long fur cloak, elegant
920   and comfortable, with a lot of sovereigns in her purse.

VIVIE [*grimly*].   My aunt Lizzie!

MRS WARREN.   Yes; and a very good aunt to have, too. She's living down at
Winchester now, close to the cathedral, one of the most respectable ladies
there. Chaperones girls at the county ball, if you please. No river for Liz,

thank you! You remind me of Liz a little: she was a first-rate business woman—saved money from the beginning—never let herself look too like what she was—never lost her head or threw away a chance. When she saw I'd grown up good-looking she said to me across the bar "What are you doing there, you little fool? wearing out your health and your appearance
930 for other people's profit!" Liz was saving money then to take a house for herself in Brussels; and she thought we two could save faster than one. So she lent me some money and gave me a start; and I saved steadily and first paid her back, and then went into business with her as her partner. Why shouldnt I have done it? The house in Brussels was real high class: a much better place for a woman to be in than the factory where Anne Jane got poisoned. None of our girls were ever treated as I was treated in the scullery of that temperance place, or at the Waterloo bar, or at home. Would you have had me stay in them and become a worn out old drudge before I was forty?
940 VIVIE [*intensely interested by this time*]. No; but why did you choose that business? Saving money and good management will succeed in any business.
MRS WARREN. Yes, saving money. But where can a woman get the money to save in any other business? Could y o u save out of four shillings a week and keep yourself dressed as well? Not you. Of course, if youre a plain woman and cant earn anything more; or if you have a turn for music, or the stage, or newspaper-writing: thats different. But neither Liz nor I had any turn for such things: all we had was our appearance and our turn for pleasing men. Do you think we were such fools as to let other people trade in our good looks by employing us as shopgirls, or barmaids, or waitresses,
950 when we could trade in them ourselves and get all the profits instead of starvation wages? Not likely.
VIVIE. You were certainly quite justified—from the business point of view.
MRS WARREN. Yes; or any other point of view. What is any respectable girl brought up to do but to catch some rich man's fancy and get the benefit of his money by marrying him?—as if a marriage ceremony could make any difference in the right or wrong of the thing! Oh, the hypocrisy of the world makes me sick! Liz and I had to work and save and calculate just like other people; elseways we should be as poor as any good-for-nothing drunken waster of a woman that thinks her luck will last for ever. [*With
960 great energy*] I despise such people: theyve no character; and if theres a thing I hate in a woman, it's want of character.
VIVIE. Come now, mother: frankly! Isnt it part of what you call character in a woman that she should greatly dislike such a way of making money?
MRS WARREN. Why, of course. Everybody dislikes having to work and make money; but they have to do it all the same. I'm sure Ive often pitied a poor girl, tired out and in low spirits, having to try to please some man that she doesnt care two straws for—some half-drunken fool that thinks he's making himself agreeable when he's teasing and worrying and disgusting a woman so that hardly any money could pay her for putting up with it. But
970 she has to bear with disagreeables and take the rough with the smooth, just like a nurse in a hospital or anyone else. It's not work that any woman would do for pleasure, goodness knows; though to hear the pious people talk you would suppose it was a bed of roses.
VIVIE. Still, you consider it worth while. It pays.

MRS WARREN. Of course it's worth while to a poor girl, if she can resist temptation and is good-looking and well conducted and sensible. It's far better than any other employment open to her. I always thought that oughtnt to be. It c a n t be right, Vivie, that there shouldn't be better opportunities for women. I stick to that: it's wrong. But it's so, right or
980   wrong; and a girl must make the best of it. But of course it's not worth while for a lady. If you took to it youd be a fool; but I should have been a fool if I'd taken to anything else.

VIVIE [*more and more deeply moved*].   Mother: suppose we were both as poor as you were in those wretched old days, are you quite sure that you wouldnt advise me to try the Waterloo bar, or marry a laborer, or even go into the factory?

MRS WARREN [*indignantly*].   Of course not. What sort of mother do you take me for! How could you keep your self-respect in such starvation and slavery? And whats a woman worth? whats life worth? without self-respect!
990   Why am I independent and able to give my daughter a first-rate educa- tion, when other women that had just as good opportunities are in the gutter? Because I always knew how to respect myself and control myself. Why is Liz looked up to in a cathedral town? The same reason. Where would we be now if we'd minded the clergyman's foolishness? Scrubbing floors for one and six-pence a day and nothing to look forward to but the workhouse infirmary. Dont you be led astray by people who dont know the world, my girl. The only way for a woman to provide for herself decently is for her to be good to some man that can afford to be good to her. If she's in his own station of life, let her make him marry her; but if she's far
1000   beneath him she cant expect it: why should she? it wouldnt be for her own happiness. Ask any lady in London society that has daughters; and she'll tell you the same, except that I tell you straight and she'll tell you crooked. Thats all the difference.

VIVIE [*fascinated, gazing at her*].   My dear mother: you are a wonderful woman: you are stronger than all England. And are you really and truly not one wee bit doubtful—or—or—ashamed?

MRS WARREN.   Well, of course, dearie, it's only good manners to be ashamed of it: it's expected from a woman. Women have to pretend to feel a great deal that they dont feel. Liz used to be angry with me for plumping out the
1010   truth about it. She used to say that when every woman could learn enough from what was going on in the world before her eyes, there was no need to talk about it to her. But then Liz was such a perfect lady! She had the true instinct of it; while I was always a bit of a vulgarian. I used to be so pleased when you sent me your photos to see that you were growing up like Liz: youve just her ladylike, determined way. But I cant stand saying one thing when everyone knows I mean another. Whats the use in such hypocrisy? If people arrange the world that way for women, theres no good pretending it's arranged the other way. No: I never was a bit ashamed really. I consider I had a right to be proud of how we managed
1020   everything so respectably, and never had a word against us, and how the girls were so well taken care of. Some of them did very well: one of them married an ambassador. But of course now I darent talk about such things: whatever would they think of us! [*She yawns*]. Oh dear! I do believe I'm

getting sleepy after all. [*She stretches herself lazily, thoroughly relieved by her explosion, and placidly ready for her night's rest*].

VIVIE.   I believe it is I who will not be able to sleep now. [*She goes to the dresser and lights the candle. Then she extinguishes the lamp, darkening the room a good deal*]. Better let in some fresh air before locking up. [*She opens the cottage door, and finds that it is broad moonlight*]. What a beautiful night! Look! [*She*
1030   *draws aside the curtains of the window. The landscape is seen bathed in the radiance of the harvest moon rising over Blackdown*].

MRS WARREN [*with a perfunctory glance at the scene*].   Yes, dear; but take care you dont catch your death of cold from the night air.

VIVIE [*contemptuously*].   Nonsense.

MRS WARREN [*querulously*].   Oh yes: everything I say is nonsense, according to you.

VIVIE [*turning to her quickly*].   No: really that is not so, mother. You have got completely the better of me tonight, though I intended it to be the other way. Let us be good friends now.

1040 MRS WARREN [*shaking her head a little ruefully*].   So it h a s been the other way. But I suppose I must give in to it. I always got the worst of it from Liz; and now I suppose it'll be the same with you.

VIVIE.   Well, never mind. Come: good-night, dear old mother. [*She takes her mother in her arms*].

MRS WARREN [*fondly*].   I brought you up well, didnt I, dearie?

VIVIE.   You did.

MRS WARREN.   And youll be good to your poor old mother for it, wont you?

VIVIE.   I will, dear. [*Kissing her*] Good-night.

MRS WARREN [*with unction*].   Blessings on my own dearie darling! a mother's
1050   blessing!

[*She embraces her daughter protectingly, instinctively looking upward for divine sanction.*]

ACT III

In the Rectory garden next morning, with the sun shining from a cloudless sky. The garden wall has a five-barred wooden gate, wide enough to admit a carriage, in the middle. Beside the gate hangs a bell on a coiled spring, communicating with a pull outside. The carriage drive comes down the middle of the garden and then swerves to its left, where it ends in a little gravelled circus[18] opposite the Rectory porch. Beyond the gate is seen the dusty high road, parallel with the wall, bounded on the farther side by a strip of turf and an unfenced pine wood. On the lawn, between the house and the drive, is a clipped yew tree, with a garden bench in its shade. On the opposite side, the garden is shut in by a box hedge; and there is a sundial on the turf, with an iron chair near it. A little path leads off through the box hedge, behind the sundial.

FRANK, seated on the chair near the sundial, on which he has placed the morning papers, is reading The Standard. His father comes from the house, red-eyed and shivery, and meets FRANK's eye with misgiving.

---

[18] Circle.

FRANK [*looking at his watch*].   Half-past eleven. Nice hour for a rector to come
down to breakfast!

REV. SAMUEL.   Dont mock, Frank: dont mock. I am a little—er—[*Shivering*]—

FRANK.   Off color?

REV. SAMUEL [*repudiating the expression*].   No, sir: u n w e l l this morning.
Wheres your mother?

FRANK.   Dont be alarmed: she's not here. Gone to town by the 11.13 with
Bessie. She left several messages for you. Do you feel equal to receiving
them now, or shall I wait til youve breakfasted?

1060 REV. SAMUEL.   I h a v e breakfasted, sir. I am surprised at your mother going
to town when we have people staying with us. Theyll think it very strange.

FRANK.   Possibly she has considered that. At all events, if Crofts is going to
stay here, and you are going to sit up every night with him until four,
recalling the incidents of your fiery youth, it is clearly my mother's duty,
as a prudent housekeeper, to go up to the stores and order a barrel of
whisky and a few hundred siphons.

REV. SAMUEL.   I did not observe that Sir George drank excessively.

FRANK.   You were not in a condition to, gov'nor.

REV. SAMUEL.   Do you mean to say that I—?

1070 FRANK [*calmly*].   I never saw a beneficed clergyman less sober. The anecdotes
you told about your past career were so awful that I really dont think
Praed would have passed the night under your roof if it hadnt been for the
way my mother and he took to one another.

REV. SAMUEL.   Nonsense, sir. I am Sir George Crofts' host. I must talk to him
about something; and he has only one subject. Where is Mr Praed now?

FRANK.   He is driving my mother and Bessie to the station.

REV. SAMUEL.   Is Crofts up yet?

FRANK.   Oh, long ago. He hasnt turned a hair: he's in much better practice
than you. Has kept it up ever since, probably. He's taken himself off

1080 somewhere to smoke.

[FRANK *resumes his paper. The parson turns disconsolately towards the gate; then
comes back irresolutely.*]

REV. SAMUEL.   Er—Frank.

FRANK.   Yes.

REV. SAMUEL.   Do you think the Warrens will expect to be asked here after
yesterday afternoon?

FRANK.   Theyve been asked already.

REV. SAMUEL [*appalled*].   What!!!

FRANK.   Crofts informed us at breakfast that you told him to bring Mrs
Warren and Vivie over here to-day, and to invite them to make this house
their home. My mother then found she must go to town by the 11.13 train.

1090 REV. SAMUEL [*with despairing vehemence*].   I never gave any such invitation. I
never thought of such a thing.

FRANK [*compassionately*].   How do you know, gov'nor, what you said and
thought last night?

PRAED [*coming in through the hedge*].   Good morning.

REV. SAMUEL.   Good morning. I must apologize for not having met you at
breakfast, I have a touch of—of—

FRANK. Clergyman's sore throat, Praed. Fortunately not chronic.

PRAED [*changing the subject*]. Well, I must say your house is in a charming
spot here. Really most charming.

1100 REV. SAMUEL. Yes: it is indeed. Frank will take you for a walk, Mr Praed, if
you like. I'll ask you to excuse me: I must take the opportunity to write my
sermon while Mrs Gardner is away and you are all amusing yourselves.
You wont mind, will you?

PRAED. Certainly not. Dont stand on the slightest ceremony with me.

REV. SAMUEL. Thank you. I'll—er—er—[*He stammers his way to the porch and
vanishes into the house*].

PRAED. Curious thing it must be writing a sermon every week.

FRANK. Ever so curious, if h e did it. He buys em. He's gone for some soda
water.

1110 PRAED. My dear boy: I wish you would be more respectful to your father.
You know you can be so nice when you like.

FRANK. My dear Praddy: you forget that I have to live with the governor.
When two people live together—it dont matter whether theyre father and
son or husband and wife or brother and sister—they cant keep up the
polite humbug thats so easy for ten minutes on an afternoon call. Now the
governor, who unites to many admirable domestic qualities the irresolute-
ness of a sheep and the pompousness and aggressiveness of a jackass—

PRAED. No, pray, pray, my dear Frank, remember! He is your father.

FRANK. I give him due credit for that. [*Rising and flinging down his paper*] But
1120 just imagine his telling Crofts to bring the Warrens over here! He must
have been ever so drunk. You know, my dear Praddy, my mother wouldnt
stand Mrs Warren for a moment. Vivie mustnt come here until she's gone
back to town.

PRAED. But your mother doesnt know anything about Mrs Warren, does
she? [*He picks up the paper and sits down to read it*].

FRANK. I dont know. Her journey to town looks as if she did. Not that my
mother would mind in the ordinary way: she has stuck like a brick to lots
of women who had got into trouble. But they were all nice women. Thats
what makes the real difference. Mrs Warren, no doubt, has her merits; but
1130 she's ever so rowdy; and my mother simply wouldnt put up with her.
So—hallo! [*This exclamation is provoked by the reappearance of the clergyman,
who comes out of the house in haste and dismay*].

REV. SAMUEL. Frank: Mrs Warren and her daughter are coming across the
heath with Crofts: I saw them from the study windows. What a m I to say
about your mother?

FRANK. Stick on your hat and go out and say how delighted you are to see
them; and that Frank's in the garden; and that mother and Bessie have
been called to the bedside of a sick relative, and were ever so sorry they
couldnt stop; and that you hope Mrs Warren slept well; and—and—say
1140 any blessed thing except the truth, and leave the rest to Providence.

REV. SAMUEL. But how are we to get rid of them afterwards?

FRANK. Theres no time to think of that now. Here! [*He bounds into the house*].

REV. SAMUEL. He's so impetuous. I dont know what to do with him, Mr
Praed.

FRANK [*returning with a clerical felt hat, which he claps on his father's head*]. Now:
off with you. [*Rushing him through the gate*]. Praed and I'll wait here, to give

the thing an unpremeditated air. [*The clergyman, dazed but obedient, hurries off*].

FRANK.   We must get the old girl back to town somehow, Praed. Come!
1150   Honestly, dear Praddy, do you like seeing them together?

PRAED.   Oh, why not?

FRANK [*his teeth on edge*].   Dont it make your flesh creep ever so little? that wicked old devil, up to every villainy under the sun, I'll swear, and Vivie—ugh!

PRAED.   Hush, pray. Theyre coming.

[*The clergyman and* CROFTS *are seen coming along the road, followed by* MRS WARREN *and* VIVIE *walking affectionately together.*]

FRANK.   Look: she actually has her arm round the old woman's waist. It's her right arm: she began it. She's gone sentimental, by God! Ugh! ugh! Now do you feel the creeps? [*The clergyman opens the gate; and* MRS WARREN *and* VIVIE *pass him and stand in the middle of the garden looking at the house.* FRANK,
1160   *in an ecstasy of dissimulation, turns gaily to* MRS WARREN, *exclaiming.*] Ever so delighted to see you, Mrs Warren. This quiet old rectory garden becomes you perfectly.

MRS WARREN.   Well, I never! Did you hear that, George? He says I look well in a quiet old rectory garden.

REV. SAMUEL [*still holding the gate for* CROFTS, *who loafs through it, heavily bored*].   You look well everywhere, Mrs Warren.

FRANK.   Bravo, gov'nor! Now look here: lets have a treat before lunch. First lets see the church. Everyone has to do that. It's a regular old thirteenth century church, you know: the gov'nor's ever so fond of it, because he got
1170   up a restoration fund and had it completely rebuilt six years ago. Praed will be able to shew its points.

PRAED [*rising*].   Certainly, if the restoration has left any to shew.

REV. SAMUEL [*mooning hospitably at them*].   I shall be pleased, I'm sure, if Sir George and Mrs Warren really care about it.

MRS WARREN.   Oh, come along and get it over.

CROFTS [*turning back towards the gate*].   Ive no objection.

REV. SAMUEL.   Not that way. We go through the fields, if you dont mind. Round here. [*He leads the way by the little path through the box hedge*].

CROFTS.   Oh, all right. [*He goes with the parson.* PRAED *follows with* MRS WARREN.
1180   VIVIE *does not stir: she watches them until they have gone, with all the lines of purpose in her face marking it strongly.*]

FRANK.   Aint you coming?

VIVIE.   No. I want to give you a warning, Frank. You were making fun of my mother just now when you said that about the rectory garden. That is barred in future. Please treat my mother with as much respect as you treat your own.

FRANK.   My dear Viv: she wouldnt appreciate it: the two cases require different treatment. But what on earth has happened to you? Last night we were perfectly agreed as to your mother and her set. This morning I find
1190   you attitudinizing sentimentally with your arm round your parent's waist.

VIVIE [*flushing*].   Attitudinizing!

FRANK.   That was how it struck me. First time I ever saw you do a second-rate
thing.

VIVIE [*controlling herself*].   Yes, Frank: there has been a change; but I dont
think it a change for the worse. Yesterday I was a little prig.

FRANK.   And today?

VIVIE [*wincing; then looking at him steadily*].   Today I know my mother better
than you do.

FRANK.   Heaven forbid!

1200 VIVIE.   What do you mean?

FRANK.   Viv: theres a freemasonry among thoroughly immoral people that
you know nothing of. Youve too much character. T h a t s the bond
between your mother and me: thats why I know her better than youll ever
know her.

VIVIE.   You are wrong: you know nothing about her. If you knew the circumstances against which my mother had to struggle—

FRANK [*adroitly finishing the sentence for her*].   I should know why she is what
she is, shouldnt I? What difference would that make? Circumstances or no
circumstances, Viv, you wont be able to stand your mother.

1210 VIVIE [*very angry*].   Why not?

FRANK.   Because she's an old wretch, Viv. If you ever put your arm round her
waist in my presence again, I'll shoot myself there and then as a protest
against an exhibition with revolts me.

VIVIE.   Must I choose between dropping your acquaintance and dropping
my mother's?

FRANK [*gracefully*].   That would put the old lady at ever such a disadvantage.
No, Viv: your infatuated little boy will have to stick to you in any case. But
he's all the more anxious that you shouldnt make mistakes. It's no use,
Viv: your mother's impossible. She may be a good sort; but she's a bad lot,

1220 a very bad lot.

VIVIE [*hotly*].   Frank—! [*He stands his ground. She turns away and sits down on the
bench under the yew tree, struggling to recover her self-command. Then she says*]
Is she to be deserted by all the world because she's what you call a bad lot?
Has she no right to live?

FRANK.   No fear of that, Viv: s h e wont ever be deserted. [*He sits on the bench
beside her*].

VIVIE.   But I am to desert her, I suppose.

FRANK [*babyishly, lulling her and making love to her with his voice*].   Mustnt go
live with her. Little family group of mother and daughter wouldnt be a

1230 success. Spoil o u r little group.

VIVIE [*falling under the spell*].   What little group?

FRANK.   The babes in the wood: Vivie and little Frank. [*He nestles against her
like a weary child*]. Lets go and get covered up with leaves.

VIVIE [*rhythmically, rocking him like a nurse*].   Fast asleep, hand in hand, under
the trees.

FRANK.   The wise little girl with her silly little boy.

VIVIE.   The dear little boy with his dowdy little girl.

FRANK.   Ever so peaceful, and relieved from the imbecility of the little boy's
father and the questionableness of the little girl's—

1240 VIVIE [*smothering the word against her breast*].   Sh-sh-sh-sh! little girl wants to forget all about her mother. [*They are silent for some moments, rocking one another. Then* VIVIE *wakes up with a shock, exclaiming*] What a pair of fools we are! Come: sit up. Gracious! your hair. [*She smooths it*]. I wonder do all grown up people play in that childish way when nobody is looking. I never did it when I was a child.

FRANK.   Neither did I. You are my first playmate. [*He catches her hand to kiss it, but checks himself to look round first. Very unexpectedly, he sees* CROFTS *emerging from the box hedge*]. Oh damn!

VIVIE.   Why damn, dear?

1250 FRANK [*whispering*].   Sh! Here's this brute Crofts. [*He sits farther away from her with an unconcerned air*].

CROFTS.   Could I have a few words with you, Miss Vivie?

VIVIE.   Certainly.

CROFTS [*to* FRANK].   Youll excuse me, Gardner. Theyre waiting for you in the church, if you dont mind.

FRANK [*rising*].   Anything to oblige you, Crofts—except church. If you should happen to want me, Vivvums, ring the gate bell. [*He goes into the house with unruffled suavity*].

CROFTS [*watching him with a crafty air as he disappears, and speaking to* VIVIE *with
1260   an assumption of being on privileged terms with her*].   Pleasant young fellow that, Miss Vivie. Pity he has no money, isnt it?

VIVIE.   Do you think so?

CROFTS.   Well, whats he to do? No profession. No property. Whats he good for?

VIVIE.   I realize his disadvantages, Sir George.

CROFTS [*a little taken aback at being so precisely interpreted*].   Oh, it's not that. But while we're in this world we're in it; and money's money. [*Vivie does not answer*]. Nice day, isnt it?

VIVIE [*with scarcely veiled contempt for this effort at conversation*].   Very.

1270 CROFTS [*with brutal good humor, as if he liked her pluck*].   Well, thats not what I came to say. [*Sitting down beside her.*] Now listen, Miss Vivie. I'm quite aware that I'm not a young lady's man.

VIVIE.   Indeed, Sir George?

CROFTS.   No; and to tell you the honest truth I dont want to be either. But when I say a thing I mean it; when I feel a sentiment I feel it in earnest; and what I value I pay hard money for. Thats the sort of man I am.

VIVIE.   It does you great credit, I'm sure.

CROFTS.   Oh, I dont mean to praise myself. I have my faults. Heaven knows: no man is more sensible of that than I am. I know I'm not perfect: thats
1280   one of the advantages of being a middle-aged man; for I'm not a young man, and I know it. But my code is a simple one, and, I think, a good one. Honor between man and man; fidelity between man and woman; and no cant about this religion or that religion, but an honest belief that things are making for good on the whole.

VIVIE [*with biting irony*].   "A power, not ourselves, that makes for righteousness,"[19] eh?

---

[19] The quotation is from the first chapter of Matthew Arnold's *Literature and Dogma: An Essay toward a Better Apprehension of the Bible* (1873) in which God is defined as "the enduring power,

CROFTS [*taking her seriously*]. Oh certainly. Not ourselves, of course. You
understand what I mean. Well, now as to practical matters. You may have
an idea that Ive flung my money about; but I havnt: I'm richer today than
1290   when I first came into the property. Ive used my knowledge of the world
to invest my money in ways that other men have overlooked; and whatever
else I may be, I'm a safe man from the money point of view.

VIVIE. It's very kind of you to tell me all this.

CROFTS. Oh well, come, Miss Vivie: you neednt pretend you dont see what
I'm driving at. I want to settle down with a Lady Crofts. I suppose you
think me very blunt, eh?

VIVIE. Not at all: I am much obliged to you for being so definite and businesslike. I quite appreciate the offer: the money, the position, Lady Crofts,
and so on. But I think I will say no, if you dont mind. I'd rather not. [*She
1300   rises, and strolls across to the sundial to get out of his immediate neighborhood*].

CROFTS [*not at all discouraged, and taking advantage of the additional room left him
on the seat to spread himself comfortably, as if a few preliminary refusals were part
of the inevitable routine of courtship*]. I'm in no hurry. It was only just to let
you know in case young Gardner should try to trap you. Leave the question open.

VIVIE [*sharply*]. My no is final. I wont go back from it.

[CROFTS *is not impressed. He grins; leans forward with his elbows on his knees to prod
with his stick at some unfortunate insect in the grass; and looks cunningly at her. She
turns away impatiently.*]

CROFTS. I'm a good deal older than you. Twenty-five years: quarter of a
century. I shant live for ever; and I'll take care that you shall be well off
1310   when I'm gone.

VIVIE. I am proof against even that inducement, Sir George. Dont you think
youd better take your answer? There is not the slightest chance of my
altering it.

CROFTS [*rising, after a final slash at a daisy, and coming nearer to her*]. Well, no
matter. I could tell you some things that would change your mind fast
enough; but I wont, because I'd rather win you by honest affection. I was
a good friend to your mother: ask her whether I wasnt. She'd never have
made the money that paid for your education if it hadnt been for my
advice and help, not to mention the money I advanced her. There are not
1320   many men would have stood by her as I have. I put not less than £ 40,000
into it, from first to last.

VIVIE [*staring at him*]. Do you mean to say you were my mother's business
partner?

CROFTS. Yes. Now just think of all the trouble and the explanations it would
save if we were to keep the whole thing in the family, so to speak. Ask your
mother whether she'd like to have to explain all her affairs to a perfect
stranger.

VIVIE. I see no difficulty, since I understand that the business is wound up,
and the money invested.

---

not ourselves, which makes for righteousness."

CROFTS [*stopping short, amazed*].   Wound up! Wind up a business thats paying
1330   35 per cent in the worst years! Not likely. Who told you that?
VIVIE [*her color quite gone*].   Do you mean that it is still—? [*She stops abruptly,
and puts her hand on the sundial to support herself. Then she gets quickly to the
iron chair and sits down*]. What business are you talking about?
CROFTS.   Well, the fact is it's not what would be considered exactly a high-
class business in my set—the county set, you know—o u r set it will be if
you think better of my offer. Not that theres any mystery about it: dont
think that. O f course you know by your mother's being in it that it's
perfectly straight and honest. Ive known her for many years; and I can say
of her that she'd cut off her hands sooner than touch anything that was not
1340   what it ought to be. I'll tell you all about it if you like. I dont know whether
youve found in travelling how hard it is to find a really comfortable private
hotel.
VIVIE [*sickened, averting her face*].   Yes: go on.
CROFTS.   Well, thats all it is. Your mother has a genius for managing such
things. We've got two in Brussels, one in Ostend, one in Vienna, and two
in Budapest. Of course there are others besides ourselves in it; but we hold
most of the capital; and your mother's indispensable as managing director. Youve noticed, I daresay, that she travels a good deal. But you see you
cant mention such things in society. Once let out the word hotel and
1350   everybody says you keep a public-house.[20] You wouldnt like people to say
that of your mother, would you? Thats why we're so reserved about it. By
the way, youll keep it to yourself, wont you? Since it's been a secret so long,
it had better remain so.
VIVIE.   And this is the business you invite me to join you in?
CROFTS.   Oh no. My wife shant be troubled with business. Youll not be in it
more than youve always been.
VIVIE.   *I* always been! What do you mean?
CROFTS.   Only that youve always lived on it. It paid for your education and
the dress you have on your back. Dont turn up your nose at business, Miss
1360   Vivie: where would your Newnhams and Girtons[21] be without it.
VIVIE [*rising, almost beside herself*].   Take care. I know what this business is.
CROFTS [*starting, with a suppressed oath*].   Who told you?
VIVIE.   Your partner. My mother.
CROFTS [*black with rage*].   The old—
VIVIE.   Just so.

[*He swallows the epithet and stands for a moment swearing and raging foully to
himself. But he knows that his cue is to be sympathetic. He takes refuge in generous
indignation.*]

CROFTS.   She ought to have had more consideration for you. *I*'d never have
told you.
VIVIE.   I think you would probably have told me when we were married: it
would have been a convenient weapon to break me in with.

---

[20] I.e., a house of ill-repute, a brothel.
[21] Newnham and Girton are now women's colleges within Cambridge University.

1370 CROFTS [*quite sincerely*].   I never intended that. On my word as a gentleman I didnt.

[VIVIE *wonders at him. Her sense of the irony of his protest cools and braces her. She replies with contemptuous self-possession.*]

VIVIE.   It does not matter. I suppose you understand that when we leave here today our acquaintance ceases.

CROFTS.   Why? Is it for helping your mother?

VIVIE.   My mother was a very poor woman who had no reasonable choice but to do as she did. You were a rich gentleman; and you did the same for the sake of 35 per cent. You are a pretty common sort of scoundrel, I think. That is my opinion of you.

CROFTS [*after a stare: not at all displeased, and much more at his ease on these frank*
1380   *terms than on their former ceremonious ones*].   Ha! ha! ha! ha! Go it, little missie, go it: it doesnt hurt me and it amuses you. Why the devil shouldnt I invest my money that way? I take the interest on my capital like other people: I hope you dont think I dirty my own hands with the work. Come! you wouldnt refuse the acquaintance of my mother's cousin the Duke of Belgravia because some of the rents he gets are earned in queer ways. You wouldnt cut the Archbishop of Canterbury, I suppose, because the Ecclesiastical Commissioners have a few publicans[22] and sinners among their tenants. Do you remember your Crofts scholarship at Newnham? Well, that was founded by my brother the M.P.[23] He gets his 22 per cent out of
1390   a factory with 600 girls in it, and not one of them getting wages enough to live on. How d'ye suppose they manage when they have no family to fall back on? Ask your mother. And do you expect me to turn my back on 35 per cent when all the rest are pocketing what they can, like sensible men? No such fool! If youre going to pick and choose your acquaintances on moral principles, youd better clear out of this country, unless you want to cut yourself out of all decent society.

VIVIE [*conscience stricken*].   You might go on to point out that I myself never asked where the money I spent came from. I believe I am just as bad as you.

1400 CROFTS [*greatly reassured*].   Of course you are; and a very good thing too! What harm does it do after all? [*Rallying her jocularly.*] So you dont think me such a scoundrel now you come to think it over. Eh?

VIVIE.   I have shared profits with you; and I admitted you just now to the familiarity of knowing what I think of you.

CROFTS [*with serious friendliness*].   To be sure you did. You wont find me a bad sort: I dont go in for being superfine intellectually; but Ive plenty of honest human feeling; and the old Crofts breed comes out in a sort of instinctive hatred of anything low, in which I'm sure youll sympathize with me. Believe me, Miss Vivie, the world isn't such a bad place as the croak-
1410   ers[24] make out. As long as you dont fly openly in the face of society, society doesnt ask any inconvenient questions; and it makes precious short work

---

22 Innkeepers.
23 Member of Parliament.
24 Chronic complainers.

of the cads who do. There are no secrets better than the secrets everybody guesses. In the class of people I can introduce you to, no lady or gentleman would so far forget themselves as to discuss my business affairs or your mother's. No man can offer you a safer position.

VIVIE [*studying him curiously*].   I suppose you really think youre getting on famously with me.

CROFTS.   Well, I hope I may flatter myself that you think better of me than you did at first.

1420 VIVIE [*quietly*].   I hardly find you worth thinking about at all now. When I think of the society that tolerates you, and the laws that protect you! when I think of how helpless nine out of ten young girls would be in the hands of you and my mother! the unmentionable woman and her capitalist bully—

CROFTS [*livid*].   Damn you!

VIVIE.   You need not. I feel among the damned already.

[*She raises the latch of the gate to open it and go out. He follows her and puts his hand heavily on the top bar to prevent its opening.*]

CROFTS [*panting with fury*].   Do you think I'll put up with this from you, you young devil?

VIVIE [*unmoved*].   Be quiet. Some one will answer the bell. [*Without flinching*
1430   *a step she strikes the bell with the back of her hand. It clangs harshly; and he starts back involuntarily. Almost immediately* FRANK *appears at the porch with his rifle.*]

FRANK [*with cheerful politeness*].   Will you have the rifle, Viv; or shall I operate?

VIVIE.   Frank: have you been listening?

FRANK [*coming down into the garden*].   Only for the bell, I assure you; so that you shouldnt have to wait. I think I shewed great insight into your character, Crofts.

CROFTS.   For two pins I'd take that gun from you and break it across your head.

FRANK [*stalking him cautiously*].   Pray dont. I'm ever so careless in handling
1440   firearms. Sure to be a fatal accident, with a reprimand from the coroner's jury for my negligence.

VIVIE.   Put the rifle away, Frank: it's quite unnecessary.

FRANK.   Quite right, Viv. Much more sportsmanlike to catch him in a trap. [CROFTS, *understanding the insult, makes a threatening movement*]. Crofts: there are fifteen cartridges in the magazine here; and I am a dead shot at the present distance and at an object of your size.

CROFTS.   Oh, you neednt be afraid. I'm not going to touch you.

FRANK.   Ever so magnanimous of you under the circumstances! Thank you.

CROFTS.   I'll just tell you this before I go. It may interest you, since youre so
1450   fond of one another. Allow me, Mister Frank, to introduce you to your half-sister, the eldest daughter of the Reverend Samuel Gardner. Miss Vivie, your half-brother. Good morning. [*He goes out through the gate and along the road*].

FRANK [*after a pause of stupefaction, raising the rifle*].   Youll testify before the coroner that it's an accident, Viv. [*He takes aim at the retreating figure of* CROFTS. VIVIE *seizes the muzzle and pulls it round against her breast*].

VIVIE.   Fire now. You may.

FRANK [*dropping his end of the rifle hastily*].   Stop! take care. [*She lets it go. It falls on the turf*]. Oh, youve given your little boy such a turn. Suppose it had
1460   gone off! ugh! [*He sinks on the garden seat, overcome*].

VIVIE.   Suppose it had: do you think it would not have been a relief to have some sharp physical pain tearing through me?

FRANK [*coaxingly*].   Take it ever so easy, dear Viv. Remember: even if the rifle scared that fellow into telling the truth for the first time in his life, that only makes us the babes in the wood in earnest. [*He holds out his arms to her*]. Come and be covered up with leaves again.

VIVIE [*with a cry of disgust*].   Ah, not that, not that. You make all my flesh creep.

FRANK.   Why, whats the matter?

1470 VIVIE.   Goodbye. [*She makes for the gate*].

FRANK [*jumping up*].   Hallo! Stop! Viv! Viv! [*She turns in the gateway*] Where are you going to? Where shall we find you?

VIVIE.   At Honoria Fraser's chambers, 67 Chancery Lane, for the rest of my life. [*She goes off quickly in the opposite direction to that taken by* CROFTS].

FRANK.   But I say—wait—dash it! [*He runs after her*].

ACT IV

Honoria Fraser's chambers in Chancery Lane. An office at the top of New Stone Buildings, with a plate-glass window, distempered[25] *walls, electric light, and a patent stove. Saturday afternoon. The chimneys of Lincoln's Inn and the western sky beyond are seen through the window. There is a double writing table in the middle of the room, with a cigar box, ash pans, and a portable electric reading lamp almost snowed up in heaps of papers and books. This table has knee holes and chairs right and left and is very untidy. The clerk's desk, closed and tidy, with its high stool, is against the wall, near a door communicating with the inner rooms. In the opposite wall is the door leading to the public corridor. Its upper panel is of opaque glass, lettered in black on the outside,* FRASER AND WARREN. *A baize screen hides the corner between this window and the window.*

FRANK, *in a fashionable light-colored coaching suit, with his stick, gloves, and white hat in his hands, is pacing up and down the office. Somebody tries the door with a key.*

FRANK [*calling*].   Come in. It's not locked.

[VIVIE *comes in, in her hat and jacket. She stops and stares at him.*].

VIVIE [*sternly*].   What are you doing here?

FRANK.   Waiting to see you. Ive been here for hours. Is this the way you attend to your business? [*He puts his hat and stick on the table, and perches
1480   himself with a vault on the clerk's stool, looking at her with every appearance of being in a specially restless, teasing, flippant mood*].

VIVIE.   Ive been away exactly twenty minutes for a cup of tea. [*She takes off her hat and jacket and hangs them up behind the screen*]. How did you get in?

FRANK.   The staff had not left when I arrived. He's gone to play cricket on Primrose Hill. Why dont you employ a woman, and give your sex a chance?

---

[25] I.e., colored.

VIVIE. What have you come for?

FRANK [*springing off the stool and coming close to her*]. Viv: lets go and enjoy the Saturday half-holiday somewhere, like the staff. What do you say to Richmond,[26] and then a music hall, and a jolly supper?

1490 VIVIE. Cant afford it. I shall put in another six hours work before I go to bed.

FRANK. Cant afford it, cant we? Aha! Look here. [*He takes out a handful of sovereigns and makes them chink.*] Gold, Viv: gold!

VIVIE. Where did you get it?

FRANK. Gambling, Viv: gambling. Poker.

VIVIE. Pah! It's meaner than stealing it. No: I'm not coming. [*She sits down to work at the table, with her back to the glass door, and begins turning over the papers*].

FRANK [*remonstrating piteously*]. But, my dear Viv, I want to talk to you ever so seriously.

1500 VIVIE. Very well: sit down in Honoria's chair and talk here. I like ten minutes chat after tea. [*He murmurs*]. No use groaning: I'm inexorable. [*He takes the opposite seat disconsolately*]. Pass that cigar box, will you?

FRANK [*pushing the cigar box across*]. Nasty womanly habit. Nice men dont do it any longer.

VIVIE. Yes: they object to the smell in the office: and weve had to take to cigarets. See! [*She opens the box and takes out a cigaret, which she lights. She offers him one; but he shakes his head with a wry face. She settles herself comfortably in her chair, smoking*]. Go ahead.

FRANK. Well, I want to know what youve done—what arrangements youve
1510 made.

VIVIE. Everything was settled twenty minutes after I arrived here. Honoria has found the business too much for her this year; and she was on the point of sending for me and proposing a partnership when I walked in and told her I hadnt a farthing in the world. So I installed myself and packed her off for a fortnight's holiday. What happened at Haslemere when I left?

FRANK. Nothing at all. I said youd gone to town on particular business.

VIVIE. Well?

FRANK. Well, either they were too flabbergasted to say anything, or else
1520 Crofts had prepared your mother. Anyhow, she didnt say anything; and Crofts didnt say anything; and Praddy only stared. After tea they got up and went; and Ive not seen them since.

VIVIE [*nodding placidly with one eye on a wreath of smoke*]. Thats all right.

FRANK [*looking round disparagingly*]. Do you intend to stick in this confounded place?

VIVIE [*blowing the wreath decisively away, and sitting straight up*]. Yes. These two days have given me back all my strength and self-possession. I will never take a holiday again as long as I live.

FRANK [*with a very wry face*]. Mps! You look quite happy. And as hard as nails.

1530 VIVIE [*grimly*]. Well for me that I am!

FRANK [*rising*]. Look here, Viv: we must have an explanation. We parted the

---

[26] A riverside resort on the Thames about ten miles southwest of London.

other day under a complete misunderstanding. [*He sits on the table, close to her*].

VIVIE [*putting away the cigaret*].   Well: clear it up.

FRANK.   You remember what Crofts said?

VIVIE.   Yes.

FRANK.   That revelation was supposed to bring about a complete change in the nature of our feeling for one another. It placed us on the footing of brother and sister.

1540 VIVIE.   Yes.

FRANK.   Have you ever had a brother?

VIVIE.   No.

FRANK.   Then you dont know what being brother and sister feels like? Now I have lots of sisters; and the fraternal feeling is quite familiar to me. I assure you my feeling for you is not the least in the world like it. The girls will go their way; I will go mine; and we shant care if we never see one another again. Thats brother and sister. But as to you, I cant be easy if I have to pass a week without seeing you. Thats not brother and sister. It's exactly what I felt an hour before Crofts made his revelation. In short,

1550   dear Viv, it's love's young dream.

VIVIE [*bitingly*].   The same feeling, Frank, that brought your father to my mother's feet. Is that it?

FRANK [*so revolted that he slips off the table for a moment*].   I very strongly object, Viv, to have my feelings compared to any which the Reverend Samuel is capable of harboring; and I object still more to a comparison of you to your mother. [*Resuming his perch*]. Besides, I dont believe the story. I have taxed my father with it, and obtained from him what I consider tantamount to a denial.

VIVIE.   What did he say?

1560 FRANK.   He said he was sure there must be some mistake.

VIVIE.   Do you believe him?

FRANK.   I am prepared to take his word as against Crofts'.

VIVIE.   Does it make any difference? I mean in your imagination or conscience; for of course it makes no real difference.

FRANK [*shaking his head*].   None whatever to me.

VIVIE.   Nor to me.

FRANK [*staring*].   But this is ever so surprising! [*He goes back to his chair*]. I thought our whole relations were altered in your imagination and conscience, as you put it, the moment those words were out of that brute's

1570   muzzle.

VIVIE.   No: it was not that. I didnt believe him. I only wish I could.

FRANK.   Eh?

VIVIE.   I think brother and sister would be a very suitable relation for us.

FRANK.   You really mean that?

VIVIE.   Yes. It's the only relation I care for, even if we could afford any other. I mean that.

FRANK [*raising his eyebrows like one on whom a new light has dawned, and rising with quite an effusion of chivalrous sentiment*].   My dear Viv: why didnt you say so before? I am ever so sorry for persecuting you. I understand, of course.

1580 VIVIE [*puzzled*].   Understand what?

FRANK.   Oh, I'm not a fool in the ordinary sense: only in the Scriptural sense of doing all the things the wise man declared to be folly, after trying them himself on the most extensive scale. I see I am no longer Vivvum's little boy. Dont be alarmed: I shall never call you Vivvums again—at least unless you get tired of your new little boy, whoever he may be.

VIVIE.   My new little boy!

FRANK [*with conviction*].   Must be a new little boy. Always happens this way. No other way, in fact.

VIVIE.   None that you know of, fortunately, for you.

[*Someone knocks at the door*].

1590   FRANK.   My curse upon yon caller, whoe'er he be!

VIVIE.   It's Praed. He's going to Italy and wants to say goodbye. I asked him to call this afternoon. Go and let him in.

FRANK.   We can continue our conversation after his departure for Italy. I'll stay him out. [*He goes to the door and opens it*]. How are you, Praddy? Delighted to see you. Come in.

[PRAED, *dressed for travelling, comes in, in high spirit*].

PRAED.   How do you do, Miss Warren? [*She presses his hand cordially, though a certain sentimentality in his high spirits jars on her*]. I start in an hour from Holborn Viaduct. I wish I could persuade you to try Italy.

VIVIE.   What for?

1600   PRAED.   Why, to saturate yourself with beauty and romance, of course.

[VIVIE, *with a shudder, turns her chair to the table, as if the work waiting for her there were a support to her*. PRAED *sits opposite to her*. FRANK *places a chair near* VIVIE, *and drops lazily and carelessly into it, talking at her over his shoulder*].

FRANK.   No use, Praddy. Viv is a little Philistine. She is indifferent to my romance, and insensible to my beauty.

VIVIE.   Mr Praed: once for all, there is no beauty and no romance in life for me. Life is what it is; and I am prepared to take it as it is.

PRAED [*enthusiastically*].   You will not say that if you come with me to Verona and on to Venice. You will cry with delight at living in such a beautiful world.

FRANK.   This is most eloquent, Praddy. Keep it up.

PRAED.   Oh, I assure you *I* have cried—I shall cry again, I hope—at fifty! At

1610   your age, Miss Warren, you would not need to go so far as Verona. Your spirits would absolutely fly up at the mere sight of Ostend. You would be charmed with the gaiety, the vivacity, the happy air of Brussels.

VIVIE [*springing up with an exclamation of loathing*].   Agh!

PRAED [*rising*].   Whats the matter?

FRANK [*rising*].   Hallo, Viv!

VIVIE [*to* PRAED, *with deep reproach*].   Can you find no better example of your beauty and romance than Brussels to talk to me about?

PRAED [*puzzled*].   Of course it's very different from Verona. I dont suggest for a moment that—

1620   VIVIE [*bitterly*].   Probably the beauty and romance come to much the same in both places.

PRAED [*completely sobered and much concerned*].   My dear Miss Warren: I—[*looking enquiringly of* FRANK] Is anything the matter?

FRANK.   She thinks your enthusiasm frivolous, Praddy. She's had ever such a serious call.

VIVIE [*sharply*].   Hold your tongue, Frank. Dont be silly.

FRANK [*sitting down*].   Do you call this good manners, Praed?

PRAED [*anxious and considerate*].   Shall I take him away, Miss Warren? I feel sure we have disturbed you at your work.

1630 VIVIE.   Sit down: I'm not ready to go back to work yet. [PRAED *sits*]. You both think I have an attack of nerves. Not a bit of it. But there are two subjects I want dropped, if you dont mind. One of them [*to* FRANK] is love's young dream in any shape or form: the other [*to* PRAED] is the romance and beauty of life, especially Ostend and the gaiety of Brussels. You are welcome to any illusions you may have left on these subjects: I have none. If we three are to remain friends, I must be treated as a woman of business, permanently single [*to* FRANK] and permanently unromantic [*to* PRAED].

FRANK.   I also shall remain permanently single until you change your mind. Praddy: change the subject. Be eloquent about something else.

1640 PRAED [*diffidently*].   I'm afraid theres nothing else in the world that I c a n talk about. The Gospel of Art is the only one I can preach. I know Miss Warren is a great devotee of the Gospel of Getting On; but we cant discuss that without hurting your feelings, Frank, since you are determined not to get on.

FRANK.   Oh, dont mind my feelings. Give me some improving advice by all means: it does me ever so much good. Have another try to make a successful man of me, Viv. Come: lets have it all: energy, thrift, foresight, self-respect, character. Dont you hate people who have no character, Viv?

VIVIE [*wincing*].   Oh, stop, stop: let us have no more of that horrible cant. Mr
1650 Praed: if there are really only those two gospels in the world, we had better all kill ourselves; for the same taint is in both, through and through.

FRANK [*looking critically at her*].   There is a touch of poetry about you today, Viv, which has hitherto been lacking.

PRAED [*remonstrating*].   My dear Frank: arent you a little unsympathetic?

VIVIE [*merciless to herself*].   No: it's good for me. It keeps me from being sentimental.

FRANK [*bantering her*].   Checks your strong natural propensity that way, dont it?

VIVIE [*almost hysterically*].   Oh yes: go on: dont spare me. I was sentimental for
1660 one moment in my life—beautifully sentimental—by moonlight; and now—

FRANK [*quickly*].   I say, Viv: take care. Dont give yourself away.

VIVIE.   Oh, do you think Mr Praed does not know all about my mother? [*Turning on* PRAED] You had better have told me that morning, Mr Praed. You are very old fashioned in your delicacies, after all.

PRAED.   Surely it is you who are a little old fashioned in your prejudices, Miss Warren. I feel bound to tell you, speaking as an artist, and believing that the most intimate human relationships are far beyond and above the scope of the law, that though I know that your mother is an unmarried
1670 woman, I do not respect her the less on that account. I respect her more.

FRANK [*airily*].   Hear! hear!

VIVIE [*staring at him*].   Is that a l l you know?

PRAED.   Certainly that is all.

VIVIE.   Then you neither of you know anything. Your guesses are innocence itself compared to the truth.

PRAED [*rising, startled and indignant, and preserving his politeness with an effort*]. I hope not. [*More emphatically*] I hope not, Miss Warren.

FRANK [*whistles*].   Whew!

VIVIE.   You are not making it easy for me to tell you, Mr Praed.

1680 PRAED [*his chivalry drooping before their conviction*].   If there i s anything worse—that is, anything else—are you sure you are right to tell us, Miss Warren?

VIVIE.   I am sure that if I had the courage I should spend the rest of my life in telling everybody—stamping and branding it into them until they all felt their part in its abomination as I feel mine. There is nothing I despise more than the wicked convention that protects these things by forbidding a woman to mention them. And yet I cant tell you. The two infamous words that describe what my mother is are ringing in my ears and struggling on my tongue; but I cant utter them: the shame of them is too

1690 horrible for me. [*She buries her face in her hands. The two men, astonished, stare at one another and then at her. She raises her head again desperately and snatches a sheet of paper and a pen*]. Here; let me draft you a prospectus.

FRANK.   Oh, she's mad. Do you hear, Viv? mad. Come! pull yourself together.

VIVIE.   You shall see. [*She writes*]. "Paid up capital: not less than £ 40,000 standing in the name of Sir George Crofts, Baronet, the chief shareholder. Premises at Brussels, Ostend, Vienna, and Budapest. Managing director: Mrs Warren"; and now dont let us forget h e r qualifications: the two words. [*She writes the words and pushes the paper to them*]. There! Oh no: dont

1700 read it: dont!

[*She snatches it back and tears it to pieces; then seizes her head in her hands and hides her face on the table.*

FRANK, *who has watched the writing over her shoulder, and opened his eyes very widely at it, takes a card from his pocket; scribbles the two words on it; and silently hands it to* PRAED, *who reads it with amazement, and hides it hastily in his pocket*].

FRANK [*whispering tenderly*].   Viv, dear: thats all right. I read what you wrote: so did Praddy. We understand. And we remain, as this leaves us at present, yours ever so devotedly.

PRAED.   We do indeed, Miss Warren. I declare you are the most splendidly courageous woman I ever met.

[*This sentimental compliment braces* VIVIE. *She throws it away from her with an impatient shake, and forces herself to stand up, though not without some support from the table*].

FRANK.   Dont stir, Viv, if you dont want to. Take it easy.

VIVIE.   Thank you. You can always depend on me for two things: not to cry and not to faint. [*She moves a few steps toward the door of the inner room, and stops close to* PRAED *to say*] I shall need much more courage than that when

1710 I tell my mother that we have come to the parting of the ways. Now I must go into the next room for a moment to make myself neat again, if you dont mind.

PRAED.   Shall we go away?

VIVIE.   No: I'll be back presently. Only for a moment. [*She goes into the other room,* PRAED *opening the door for her*].

PRAED.   What an amazing revelation! I'm extremely disappointed in Crofts: I am indeed.

FRANK.   I'm not in the least. I feel he's perfectly accounted for at last. But what a facer for me, Praddy! I cant marry her now.

1720 PRAED [*sternly*].   Frank! [*The two look at one another,* FRANK *unruffled,* PRAED *deeply indignant*]. Let me tell you, Gardner, that if you desert her now you will behave very despicably.

FRANK.   Good old Praddy! Ever chivalrous! But you mistake: it's not the moral aspect of the case: it's the money aspect. I really cant bring myself to touch the old woman's money now!

PRAED.   And was that what you were gong to marry on?

FRANK.   What else? *I* havnt any money, nor the smallest turn for making it. If I married Viv now she would have to support me; and I should cost her more than I am worth.

1730 PRAED.   But surely a clever bright fellow like you can make something by your own brains.

FRANK.   Oh yes, a little. [*He takes out his money again*]. I made all that yesterday in an hour and a half. But I made it in a highly speculative business. No, dear Praddy: even if Bessie and Georgina marry millionaires and the governor dies after cutting them off with a shilling, I shall have only four hundred a year. And he wont die until he's three score and ten: he hasnt originality enough. I shall be on short allowance for the next twenty years. No short allowance for Viv, if I can help it. I withdraw gracefully and leave the field to the gilded youth of England. So thats settled. I shant worry her

1740   about it: I'll just send her a little note after we're gone. She'll understand.

PRAED [*grasping his hand*].   Good fellow, Frank! I heartily beg your pardon. But must you never see her again?

FRANK.   Never see her again! Hang it all, be reasonable. I shall come along as often as possible, and be her brother. I can n o t understand the absurd consequences you romantic people expect from the most ordinary transactions. [*A knock at the door*]. I wonder who this is. Would you mind opening the door? If it's a client it will look more respectable than if I appeared.

PRAED.   Certainly. [*He goes to the door and opens it.* FRANK *sits down in* VIVIE'S *chair to scribble a note*]. My dear Kitty: come in: come in.

[MRS WARREN *comes in, looking apprehensively round for* VIVIE. *She has done her best to make herself matronly and dignified. The brilliant hat is replaced by a sober bonnet, and the gay blouse covered by a costly black silk mantle. She is pitiably anxious and ill at ease: evidently panic-stricken*].

1750 MRS WARREN [*to* FRANK].   What! Y o u r e here, are you?

FRANK [*turning in his chair from his writing, but not rising*].   Here, and charmed to see you. You come like a breath of spring.

MRS WARREN.   Oh, get out with your nonsense. [*In a low voice*] Wheres Vivie?

[FRANK *points expressively to the door of the inner room, but says nothing*].

MRS WARREN [*sitting down suddenly and almost beginning to cry*].   Praddy: wont
she see me, dont you think?

PRAED.   My dear Kitty: dont distress yourself. Why should she not?

MRS WARREN.   Oh, you never can see why not: youre too innocent. Mr Frank:
did she say anything to you?

FRANK [*folding his note*].   She m u s t see you, if [*very expressively*] you wait til
1760   she comes in.

MRS WARREN [*frightened*].   Why shouldnt I wait?

[FRANK *looks quizzically at her; puts his note carefully on the ink-bottle, so that* VIVIE
*cannot fail to find it when next she dips her pen; then rises and devotes his attention
entirely to her.*]

FRANK.   My dear Mrs Warren: suppose you were a sparrow—ever so tiny and
pretty a sparrow hopping in the roadway—and you saw a steam roller
coming in your direction, would you wait for it?

MRS WARREN.   Oh, dont bother me with your sparrows. What did she run
away from Haslemere like that for?

FRANK.   I'm afraid she'll tell you if you rashly await her return.

MRS WARREN.   Do you want me to go away?

FRANK.   No: I always want you to stay. But I a d v i s e you to go away.

1770   MRS WARREN.   What! And never see her again!

FRANK.   Precisely.

MRS WARREN [*crying again*].   Praddy: dont let him be cruel to me. [*She hastily
checks her tears and wipes her eyes*]. She'll be so angry if she sees Ive been
crying.

FRANK [*with a touch of real compassion in his airy tenderness*].   You know that
Praddy is the soul of kindness, Mrs Warren. Praddy: what do y o u say? Go
or stay?

PRAED [*to* MRS WARREN].   I really should be very sorry to cause you unnecessary pain; but I think perhaps you had better not wait. The fact is—[VIVIE
1780   *is heard at the inner door*].

FRANK.   Sh! Too late. She's coming.

MRS WARREN.   Dont tell her I was crying. [VIVIE *comes in. She stops gravely on
seeing* MRS WARREN, *who greets her with hysterical cheerfulness*]. Well, dearie, So
here you are at last.

VIVIE.   I am glad you have come: I want to speak to you. You said you were
going, Frank, I think.

FRANK.   Yes. Will you come with me, Mrs Warren? What do you say to a trip
to Richmond, and the theatre in the evening? There is safety in Richmond. No steam roller there.

1790   VIVIE.   Nonsense, Frank. My mother will stay here.

MRS WARREN [*scared*].   I dont know: perhaps I'd better go. We're disturbing
you at your work.

VIVIE [*with quiet decision*].   Mr Praed: please take Frank away. Sit down,
mother.

[MRS WARREN *obeys helplessly*].

PRAED.   Come, Frank. Goodbye, Miss Vivie.

VIVIE [*shaking hands*].   Goodbye. A pleasant trip.

PRAED.   Thank you: thank you. I hope so.

FRANK [*to* MRS WARREN].   Goodbye: youd ever so much better have taken my
  advice. [*He shakes hands with her. Then airily to* VIVIE] Byebye, Viv.

1800 VIVIE.   Goodbye. [*He goes out gaily without shaking hands with her*].

PRAED [*sadly*].   Goodbye, Kitty.

MRS WARREN [*snivelling*].   —oobye!

[PRAED *goes.* VIVIE, *composed and extremely grave, sits down in Honoria's chair, and
waits for her mother to speak.* MRS WARREN, *dreading a pause, loses no time in
beginning*].

MRS WARREN.   Well, Vivie, what did you go away like that for without saying
  a word to me? How could you do such a thing! And what have you done
  to poor George? I wanted him to come with me; but he shuffled out of it.
  I could see that he was quite afraid of you. Only fancy: he wanted me not
  to come. As if [*trembling*] I should be afraid of you, dearie. [VIVIE's *gravity
  deepens*]. But of course I told him it was all settled and comfortable between
  us, and that we were on the best of terms. [*She breaks down*]. Vivie: whats
1810   the meaning of this? [*She produces a commercial envelope, and fumbles at the
  enclosure with trembling fingers*]. I got it from the bank this morning.

VIVIE.   It is my month's allowance. They sent it to me as usual the other
  day. I simply sent it back to be placed to your credit, and asked them
  to send you the lodgment receipt.[27] In future I shall support myself.

MRS WARREN [*not daring to understand*].   Wasnt it enough? Why didn't you tell
  me? [*With a cunning gleam in her eye?*] I'll double it: I was intending to
  double it. Only let me know how much you want.

VIVIE.   You know very well that that has nothing to do with it. From this time
  I go my own way in my own business and among my own friends. And you
1820   will go yours. [*She rises*]. Goodbye.

MRS WARREN [*rising, appalled*].   Goodbye?

VIVIE.   Yes: goodbye. Come: dont let us make a useless scene: you understand perfectly well. Sir George Crofts has told me the whole business.

MRS WARREN [*angrily*].   Silly old—[*She swallows an epithet, and turns white at the
  narrowness of her escape from uttering it*].

VIVIE.   Just so.

MRS WARREN.   He ought to have his tongue cut out. But I thought it was
  ended: you said you didnt mind.

VIVIE [*steadfastly*].   Excuse me: I d o mind.

1830 MRS WARREN.   But I explained—

VIVIE.   You explained how it came about. You did not tell me that it is still
  going on. [*She sits*].

[MRS WARREN, *silenced for a moment, looks forlornly at* VIVIE, *who waits, secretly
hoping that the combat is over. But the cunning expression comes back into* MRS
WARREN's *face; and she bends across the table, sly and urgent, half whispering*].

MRS WARREN.   Vivie: do you know how rich I am?

VIVIE.   I have no doubt you are very rich.

MRS WARREN.   But you dont know all that that means: youre too young. It

_____
[27] Deposit slip.

means a new dress every day; it means theatres and balls every night; it means having the pick of all the gentlemen in Europe at your feet; it means a lovely house and plenty of servants; it means the choicest of eating and drinking; it means everything you like, everything you want,
1840 everything you can think of. And what are you here? A mere drudge, toiling and moiling early and late for your bare living and two cheap dresses a year. Think over it. [*Soothingly*] Youre shocked, I know. I can enter into your feelings; and I think they do you credit; but trust me, nobody will blame you: you may take my word for that. I know what young girls are; and I know youll think better of it when youve turned it over in your mind.

Vivie.   So that's how it's done, is it? You must have said all that to many a woman, mother, to have it so pat.

Mrs Warren [*passionately*].   What harm am I asking you to do? [Vivie *turns*
1850 *away contemptuously.* Mrs Warren *continues desperately*] Vivie: listen to me: you dont understand: youve been taught wrong on purpose: you dont know what the world is really like.

Vivie [*arrested*].   Taught wrong on purpose! What do you mean?

Mrs Warren.   I mean that youre throwing away all your chances for nothing. You think that people are what they pretend to be: that the way you were taught at school and college to think right and proper is the way things really are. But it's not: it's all only a pretence, to keep the cowardly slavish common run of people quiet. Do you want to find that out, like other women, at forty, when youve thrown yourself away and lost your chances;
1860 or wont you take it in good time now from your own mother, that loves you and swears to you that it's truth: gospel truth? [*Urgently*] Vivie: the big people, the clever people, the managing people, all know it. They do as I do, and think what I think. I know plenty of them. I know them to speak to, to introduce you to, to make friends of for you. I dont mean anything wrong: thats what you dont understand: your head is full of ignorant ideas about me. What do the people that taught you know about life or about people like me? When did they ever meet me, or speak to me, or let anyone tell them about me? the fools! Would they ever have done anything for you if I hadn't paid them? Havnt I told you that I want you to be
1870 respectable? Havnt I brought you up to be respectable? And how can you keep it up without my money and my influence and Lizzie's friends? Cant you see that youre cutting your own throat as well as breaking my heart in turning your back on me?

Vivie.   I recognize the Crofts philosophy of life, mother. I heard it all from him that day at the Gardners'.

Mrs Warren.   You think I want to force that played-out old sot on you! I dont, Vivie: on my oath I dont.

Vivie.   It would not matter if you did: you would not succeed. [Mrs Warren *winces, deeply hurt by the implied indifference towards her affectionate intention.*
1880 Vivie, *neither understanding this nor concerning herself about it, goes on calmly*] Mother: you dont at all know the sort of person I am. I dont object to Crofts more than to any other coarsely built man of his class. To tell you the truth, I rather admire him for being strongminded enough to enjoy himself in his own way and make plenty of money instead of living the usual shooting, hunting, dining-out, tailoring, loafing life of his set merely because all the rest do it. And I'm perfectly aware that if I'd been in the

same circumstances as my aunt Liz, I'd have done exactly what she did. I
dont think I'm more prejudiced or straitlaced than you: I think I'm less.
I'm certain I'm less sentimental. I know very well that fashionable morality
1890   is all a pretence, and that if I took your money and devoted the rest of my
life to spending it fashionably, I might be as worthless and vicious as the
silliest woman could possibly want to be without having a word said to me
about it. But I dont want to be worthless. I shouldnt enjoy trotting about
the park to advertize my dressmaker and carriage builder, or being bored
at the opera to shew off a shopwindowfull of diamonds.
MRS WARREN [*bewildered*].   But—
VIVIE.   Wait a moment: Ive not done. Tell me why you continue your business now that you are independent of it. Your sister, you told me, has left
all that behind her. Why dont you do the same?
1900   MRS WARREN.   Oh, it's all very easy for Liz: she likes good society, and has the
air of being a lady. Imagine m e in a cathedral town! Why, the very rooks
in the trees would find me out even if I could stand the dulness of it. I must
have work and excitement, or I should go melancholy mad. And what else
is there for me to do? The life suits me: I'm fit for it and not for anything
else. If I didnt do it somebody else would; so I dont do any real harm by
it. And then it brings in money; and I like making money. No: it's no use:
I cant give it up—not for anybody. But what need you know about it? I'll
never mention it. I'll keep Crofts away. I'll not trouble you much: you see
I have to be constantly running about from one place to another. Youll be
1910   quit of me altogether when I die.
VIVIE.   No: I am my mother's daughter. I am like you: I must have work, and
must make more money than I spend. But my work is not your work, and
my way not your way. We must part. It will not make much difference to
us: instead of meeting one another for perhaps a few moments in twenty
years, we shall never meet: thats all.
MRS WARREN [*her voice stifled in tears*].   Vivie: I meant to have been more with
you: I did indeed.
VIVIE.   It's no use, mother: I am not to be changed by a few cheap tears and
entreaties any more than you are, I daresay.
1920   MRS WARREN [*wildly*].   Oh, you call a mother's tears cheap.
VIVIE.   They cost you nothing; and you ask me to give you the peace and
quietness of my whole life in exchange for them. What use would my
company be to you if you could get it? What have we two in common that
could make either of us happy together?
MRS WARREN [*lapsing recklessly into her dialect*].   We're mother and daughter. I
want my daughter. Ive a right to you. Who is to care for me when I'm old?
Plenty of girls have taken to me like daughters and cried at leaving me;
but I let them all go because I had you to look forward to. I kept myself
lonely for you. Youve no right to turn on me now and refuse to do your
1930   duty as a daughter.
VIVIE [*jarred and antagonized by the echo of the slums in her mother's voice*].   My
duty as a daughter! I thought we should come to that presently. Now once
for all, mother, you want a daughter and Frank wants a wife. I dont want
a mother; and I dont want a husband. I have spared neither Frank nor
myself in sending him about his business. Do you think I will spare y o u?
MRS WARREN [*violently*].   Oh, I know the sort you are: no mercy for yourself
or anyone else. *I* know. My experience has done that for me anyhow: I can

tell the pious, canting, hard, selfish woman when I meet her. Well, keep
yourself to yourself: *I* dont want you. But listen to this. Do you know what
1940   I would do with you if you were a baby again? aye, as sure as there's a
Heaven above us.

VIVIE.   Strangle me, perhaps.

MRS WARREN.   No: I'd bring you up to be a real daughter to me, and not what
you are now, with your pride and your prejudices and the college education you stole from me: yes, stole: deny it if you can: what was it but
stealing? I'd bring you up in my own house, I would.

VIVIE [*quietly*].   In one of your own houses.

MRS WARREN [*screaming*].   Listen to her! listen to how she spits on her mother's grey hairs! Oh, may you live to have your own daughter tear and
1950   trample on you as you have trampled on me. And you will: you will. No
woman ever had luck with a mother's curse on her.

VIVIE.   I wish you wouldn't rant, mother. It only hardens me. Come: I suppose I am the only young woman you ever had in your power that you did
good to. Dont spoil it all now.

MRS WARREN.   Yes, Heaven forgive me, it's true; and you are the only one
that ever turned on me. Oh, the injustice of it! the injustice! the injustice!
I always wanted to be a good woman. I tried honest work; and I was
slave-driven until I cursed the day I ever heard of honest work. I was a
good mother; and because I made my daughter a good woman she turns
1960   me out as if I was a leper. Oh, if I only had my life to live over again! I'd
talk to that lying clergyman in the school. From this time forth, so help me
Heaven in my last hour, I'll do wrong and nothing but wrong. And I'll
prosper on it.

VIVIE.   Yes: it's better to choose your line and go through with it. If I had
been you, mother, I might have done as you did; but I should not have
lived one life and believed in another. You are a conventional woman at
heart. That is why I am bidding you goodbye now. I am right, am I not?

MRS WARREN [*taken aback*].   Right to throw away all my money!

VIVIE.   No: right to get rid of you? I should be a fool not to? Isnt that so?

1970 MRS WARREN [*sulkily*].   Oh well, yes if you come to that, I suppose you are. But
Lord help the world if everybody took to doing the right thing! And now
I'd better go than stay where I'm not wanted. [*She turns to the door*].

VIVIE [*kindly*].   Wont you shake hands?

MRS WARREN [*after looking at her fiercely for a moment with a savage impulse to strike
her*].   No, thank you. Goodbye.

VIVIE [*matter-of-factly*].   Goodbye. [MRS WARREN *goes out, slamming the door behind her. The strain on* VIVIE's *face relaxes; her grave expression breaks up into one
of joyous content; her breath goes out in a half sob, half laugh of intense relief. She
goes buoyantly to her place at the writing-table; pushes the electric lamp out of the*
1980   *way; pulls over a great sheaf of papers; and is in the act of dipping her pen in the
ink when she finds* FRANK's *note. She opens it unconcernedly and reads it quickly,
giving a little laugh at some quaint turn of expression in it*]. And goodbye Frank.
[*She tears the note up and tosses the pieces into the waste-paper basket without a
second thought. Then she goes at her work with a plunge, and soon becomes
absorbed in its figures*].

                                                                                                                    [1902]

Critical Commentary on *Mrs Warren's Profession*

Mrs Warren's Profession, Shaw's third full-length play, was written in 1893–1894, but not published until 1898, not performed at all until 1902, and not performed commercially until 1905. The lengthy lapse between composition and production was not the result of any deficiency in the play; but, in writing about prostitution and touching on incest, Shaw had prodded sensitive areas in Victorian life, and the Lord Chamberlain, who was empowered to censor offensive productions, succeeded in keeping the play off the English stage. Private performances by the Stage Society in 1902 naturally reached only a small audience and failed to satisfy Shaw's desire for publicity. Thus, the first public performance of the play in New York in 1905 was an event of major importance in Shaw's dramatic career. Unfortunately, the police, having heard that the play was banned in England, swooped down on the theater and arrested both the producer and the entire company. When the judge read the play, however, he could find nothing immoral or profane in it. The charges were dismissed, the show opened, and the people packed the theater, having been attracted in part by the scandal. This sudden popularity encouraged Shaw to bring out an American edition of *Plays, Pleasant and Unpleasant,* containing six of his "Problem Plays," and thereafter his fame in America was assured.

While the actual content of Shaw's play is unobjectionable, the problems posed by prostitution in Victorian London were serious and appalling. It is estimated that every sixtieth house in London was a brothel and that the average man (married or single) made 2.4 visits to a brothel each week. In writing about prostitution, Shaw became the first English-speaking playwright to focus on the kinds of social problems that had provided Ibsen with subject matter during the preceding twenty years. And *Mrs Warren's Profession* is a particularly effective indictment of a society that puts its poorest women in the position of having to choose between prostitution and ill-paid, exhausting, and often unhealthful labor as factory workers, shop girls, or barmaids. As Shaw himself argued in his lengthy preface to the play, Mrs. Warren's defense of her profession is unanswerable.

> But it is no defence at all of the vice which she organizes. It is no defence of an immoral life to say that the alternative offered by society collectively to poor women is a miserable life, starved, overworked, fetid, ailing, ugly. Though it is quite natural and right for Mrs. Warren to choose what is, according to her lights, the least immoral alternative, it is none the less infamous of society to offer such alternatives. For the alternatives offered are not morality and immorality, but two sorts of immorality.

Near the end of act II, Mrs. Warren bitterly tells Vivie of the factory where one of her sisters died of lead poisoning, of the single room where another sister fed and clothed a husband and three children on eighteen shillings a week, and of the bar where she herself worked fourteen hours a day for four shillings a week. These are accurate and chilling representations of *laissez faire* capitalism in operation. At the same time, Shaw goes to considerable effort to contradict the unrealistic literary version of prostitution (as, for example, in Dumas' *La Dame aux Camelias*) in which the beautiful, elegant, and sophisticated courtesan is eventually turned out by her aristocratic "protector" but rescued at the last moment by her childhood lover, in whose arms she dies most touchingly. In contrast, Mrs. Warren is a vulgar businesswoman who unsentimentally sees each prostitute she employs as a worker—"just like a nurse in a hospital or anyone else"—who must sometimes overcome fatigue or low-spirits to "try to please some man that she doesn't care two straws for—some half-drunken fool that thinks he's making himself agreeable when he's teasing and worrying and disgusting a woman so that hardly any money could pay her for putting up with it."

At heart, Shaw's technique is to overturn our expectations of what prostitutes are like, of who is responsible for prostitution, and of what sort of society necessitates it. But the ironic reversals of expectations are not confined just to Shaw's discussions of his major themes. Instead, they are an integral part of his whole approach to drama. The surprises begin in the very first pages of the play and continue without abatement until the end. Vivie, for example, should be the naive, feminine product of her sheltered upbringing. Yet when Vivie first shakes hands with Praed, she "takes his with a resolute and hearty grip" that leaves his fingers tingling afterwards. She slams the gate vigorously behind him. She likes hard chairs. She pursues academic distinction for money, not honor. She hates holidays and prefers actuarial calculations to music, opera, and art. When she is tired of working, she likes "a comfortable chair, a cigar, a little whiskey, and a novel with a good detective story in it."

In a play by Shaw, nothing wholly conforms to convention. Frank, the son of the clergyman, is neither respectful nor particularly moral. The clergyman himself does not merit respect, for he obtained his social status through family influence, he purchases his sermons, and he cautiously refrains from any contact with poor or disreputable people (i.e., those most plainly in need of moral counsel) because he is afraid of compromising his position in society. Mrs. Warren, the supposedly corrupt harlot, turns out to be a woman of vitality, thrift, and honesty who has brought up her daughter to be pure, reserved, and intelligent. These four characters together create a delightfully ironic contrast that Shaw took pains to point out in his preface: "The dramatic reason for making the clergyman what Mrs. Warren calls 'an old stick-in-the-mud,' whose son, in spite of much capacity and charm, is a cynically worthless member of society, is to set up a mordant contrast between him and the woman of infamous profession, with her well-brought-up, straightforward, hardworking daughter."

These ironies are even further heightened when it turns out that this clergyman, so conspicuously concerned with his position in the upper class, had once been the passionate lover of that women in the lowest of classes—and may well have been the father of her child. Similarly, Sir George Crofts, a member of the English nobility, turns out to be a silent partner in Mrs. Warren's bordellos and a suitor for Vivie Warren's hand—if indeed he can convince himself that he is not her father.

Mrs. Warren and Vivie are particularly round and complex characters. As mother and daughter, they are inevitably quite similar. Both like money. Both like whiskey. Both want to get ahead in the world. Both reject conventional notions. Both believe "life is what it is" and are prepared to take it as it is. Even their attitudes toward sex are not all that different: Mrs. Warren views it with professional detachment, Vivie with virginal distaste.

Ultimately, however, the two women are incompatible, and their incompatibility is at least as much the result of Vivie's youthful ignorance as of Mrs. Warren's moral imperfections. Vivie tends to seek absolute purity. In Act II she prides herself on her own respectability and in Act IV she unnecessarily severs all acquaintance with her mother when it is hard to see how the continuation of their occasional meetings could do her any harm. She even rejects the beauty of Vienna and Brussels because she cannot bear the thought that these cities, like all others, harbor brothels. In becoming "a woman of business, permanently single [*to Frank*], and permanently unromantic [*to Praed*]," she cuts herself off from much that makes life worthwhile. Indeed, there is a hint of tragedy in her outburst against the Gospel of Art and the Gospel of Getting On: "Oh, stop, stop," she pleads. "Let us have no more of that horrible cant. Mr. Praed: if there are really only those two gospels in the world, we had better all kill ourselves; for the same taint is in both, through and through."

In the end, Shaw refuses to take sides in the dispute between Vivie and her mother, observing only that "Mrs. Warren is not a whit a worse woman than the reputable daughter who cannot endure her." If there is a solution to the rift between these women and if there is an alternative to the two Gospels of life that seem to confront them, Shaw does not say, and the play is all the stronger for the absence of didacticism.

A Selective Bibliography on *Mrs Warren's Profession*

Berdan, Marshall S. "Watson and Shaw: Subtle Echoes in the Canon." *The Baker Street Journal: An Irregular Quarterly of Sherlockiana.* 39.4 (1989): 206–8.

Berst, Charles A. *Bernard Shaw and the Art of Drama.* Urbana: U of Illinois P, 1973. 3–19.

Carpenter, Charles A. *Bernard Shaw and the Art of Destroying Ideals.* Madison: U of Wisconsin P, 1969. 49–69.

Crane, Gladys M. "Directing Early Shaw: Acting and Meaning in *Mrs Warren's Profession,*" *Shaw: The Annual of Bernard Shaw Studies* 3 (1983): 29–39.

Dolid, William A. "Vivie Warren and the Tripos" *Shaw Review* 23 (1980): 52–56.

Dukore, Bernard F. *Bernard Shaw, Playwright.* Columbia: U of Missouri P, 1973. 70–79, 262–264.

Gibbs, A. M. *The Art and Mind of Shaw.* London: Macmillan, 1983. 49–56.

Grene, Nicholas. *Bernard Shaw: A Critical View.* New York: St. Martin's, 1984. 20–25.

Morgan, Margery M. *The Shavian Playground.* London: Methuen, 1972. 36–45.

Potter, Rosanne G. "Changes in Shaw's Dramatic Rhetoric: *Mrs. Warren's Profession, Major Barbara,* and *Heartbreak House.*" *Literary Computing and Literary Criticism: Theoretical and Practical Essays on Theme and Rhetoric.* Ed. Rosanne G. Potter. Philadelphia: U of Pennsylvania P, 1989. 225–58.

Rao, Valli. "Vivie Warren in the Blakean World of Experience." *Shaw Review* 22 (1979): 123–34.

Salih, Sabah A. "*The New York Times* and Arnold Daly's Production of *Mrs. Warren's Profession.*" *The Independent Shavian* 26.3 (1988): 57–60.

Stafford, T. "*Mrs Warren's Profession:* In the Garden of Respectability." *Shaw Review* 2 (1982): 3–11.

Turco, Alfred. *Shaw's Moral Vision.* Ithaca, NY: Cornell UP, 1976. 68–76.

Valency, Maurice. *The Cart and the Trumpet.* New York: Oxford UP, 1973. 93–9.

West, Alick. *George Bernard Shaw: "A Good Man Fallen Among Fabians."* New York: International, 1950. 55–66.

Yae, Young-Soo. "Individual Will and Social Environment in G. B. Shaw's *Mrs. Warren's Profession.*" *The Journal of English Language and Literature* 37 (1991): 213–32.

Wiley, Catherine. "The Matter with Manners: The New Woman and the Problem Play." *Women in Theatre.* Ed. James Redmond. Cambridge, Eng.: Cambridge UP, 1989. 109–27.

Anton Pavlovich Chekhov (1860–1904)
THE CHERRY ORCHARD

Translated by David Magarshack

CHARACTERS

LYUBOV (LYUBA) ANDREYEVNA
  RANEVSKY, *a landowner*
ANYA, *her daughter, aged
  seventeen*
VARYA, *her adopted daughter, aged
  twenty-four*
LEONID ANDREYEVICH GAYEV, *Mrs.
  Ranevsky's brother*
YERMOLAY ALEXEYEVICH LOPAKHIN, *a
  businessman*
PETER (PYOTR) SERGEYEVICH
  TROFIMOV, *a student*

BORIS BORISOVICH
  SIMEONOV-PISHCHIK, *a landowner*
CHARLOTTE IVANOVNA, *a governess*
SIMON PANTELEYEVICH YEPIKHODOV, *a
  clerk*
DUNYASHA, *a maid*
FIRS, *a manservant, aged eighty-seven*
YASHA, *a young manservant*
A HIKER
A STATIONMASTER
A POST OFFICE CLERK
GUESTS *and* SERVANTS

SCENE: *The action takes place on* MRS. RANEVSKY'S *estate.*

ACT I

A room which is still known as the nursery. One of the doors leads to ANYA'S *room. Daybreak; the sun will be rising soon. It is May. The cherry trees are in blossom, but it is cold in the orchard. Morning frost. The windows of the room are shut. Enter* DUNYASHA, *carrying a candle, and* LOPAKHIN *with a book in his hand.*

LOPAKHIN.   The train's arrived, thank goodness. What's the time?
DUNYASHA.   Nearly two o'clock, sir. [*Blows out the candle.*] It's light already.
LOPAKHIN.   How late was the train? Two hours at least. [*Yawns and stretches.*] What a damn fool I am! Came here specially to meet them at the station and fell asleep. . . . Sat down in a chair and dropped off. What a nuisance! Why didn't you wake me?
DUNYASHA.   I thought you'd gone, sir. [*Listens.*] I think they're coming.
LOPAKHIN [*listening*].   No. . . . I should have been there to help them with the luggage and so on. [*Pause.*] Mrs. Ranevsky's been abroad for five years. I
10   wonder what she's like now. . . . She's such a nice person. Simple, easy-going. I remember when I was a lad of fifteen, my late father—he used to keep a shop in the village—punched me in the face and made my nose bleed. We'd gone into the yard to fetch something, and he was drunk. Mrs. Ranevsky—I remember it as if it happened yesterday, she was such a young girl then and so slim—took me to the washstand in this very room, the nursery. "Don't cry, little peasant," she said, "it won't matter by the

time you're wed." [*Pause.*] Little peasant. . . . It's quite true my father was a peasant, but here I am wearing a white waistcoat and brown shoes. A dirty peasant in a fashionable shop. . . . Except, of course, that I'm a rich man now, rolling in money. But, come to think of it, I'm a plain peasant still. . . . [*Turns the pages of his book.*] Been reading this book and haven't understood a word. Fell asleep reading it.

[*Pause.*]

DUNYASHA.   The dogs have been awake all night; they know their masters are coming.
LOPAKHIN.   What's the matter, Dunyasha? Why are you in such a state?
DUNYASHA.   My hands are shaking. I think I'm going to faint.
LOPAKHIN.   A little too refined, aren't you, Dunyasha? Quite the young lady. Dress, hair. It won't do, you know. Remember your place!

[*Enter* YEPIKHODOV *with a bunch of flowers; he wears a jacket and brightly polished high-boots which squeak loudly; on coming in, he drops the flowers.*]

YEPIKHODOV [*picking up the flowers*].   The gardener sent these. Said to put them in the dining room. [*Hands the flowers to* DUNYASHA.]
LOPAKHIN.   Bring me some kvass[1] while you're about it.
DUNYASHA.   Yes, sir. [*Goes out.*]
YEPIKHODOV.   Thirty degrees, morning frost, and the cherry trees in full bloom. Can't say I think much of our climate, sir. [*Sighs.*] Our climate isn't particularly accommodating, is it, sir? Not when you want it to be, anyway. And another thing. The other day I bought myself this pair of boots, and believe me, sir, they squeak so terribly that it's more than a man can endure. Do you happen to know of something I could grease them with?
LOPAKHIN.   Go away. You make me tired.
YEPIKHODOV.   Every day, sir, I'm overtaken by some calamity. Not that I mind. I'm used to it. I just smile. [DUNYASHA *comes in and hands* LOPAKHIN *the kvass.*] I'll be off. [*Bumps into a chair and knocks it over.*] There you are, sir. [*Triumphantly.*] You see, sir, pardon the expression, this sort of circumstance . . . I mean to say . . . Remarkable! Quite remarkable. [*Goes out.*]
DUNYASHA.   I simply must tell you, sir: Yepikhodov has proposed to me.
LOPAKHIN.   Oh?
DUNYASHA.   I really don't know what to do, sir. He's ever such a quiet fellow, except that sometimes he starts talking and you can't understand a word he says. It sounds all right and it's ever so moving, only you can't make head or tail of it. I like him a little, I think. I'm not sure though. He's madly in love with me. He's such an unlucky fellow, sir. Every day something happens to him. Everyone teases him about it. They've nicknamed him Twenty-Two Calamities.
LOPAKHIN [*listens*].   I think I can hear them coming.
DUNYASHA.   They're coming! Goodness, I don't know what's the matter with me. I've gone cold all over.
LOPAKHIN.   Yes, they are coming all right. Let's go and meet them. Will she recognize me? We haven't seen each other for five years.
DUNYASHA [*agitated*].   I'm going to faint. Oh dear, I'm going to faint!

---

[1] An alcoholic beverage somewhat like beer.

[*Two carriages can be heard driving up to the house.* LOPAKHIN *and* DUNYASHA *go out quickly. The stage is empty. People can be heard making a noise in the adjoining rooms.* FIRS, *who has been to meet* MRS. RANEVSKY *at the station, walks across the stage hurriedly, leaning on a stick. He wears an old-fashioned livery coat and a top hat; he keeps muttering to himself, but it is impossible to make out a single word. The noise offstage becomes louder. A voice is heard: "Let's go through here."* MRS. RANEVSKY, ANYA, *and* CHARLOTTE, *with a lap dog on a little chain, all wearing traveling clothes,* VARYA, *wearing an overcoat and a head scarf,* GAYEV, SIMEONOV-PISHCHIK, LOPAKHIN, DUNYASHA, *carrying a bundle and an umbrella, and other* SERVANTS *with luggage walk across the stage.*]

60 ANYA.   Let's go through here. Remember this room, Mother?
MRS. RANEVSKY [*joyfully, through tears*].   The nursery!
VARYA.   It's so cold. My hands are quite numb. [*To* MRS. RANEVSKY.] Your rooms, the white one and the mauve one, are just as you left them, Mother dear.
MRS. RANEVSKY.   The nursery! My dear, my beautiful room! I used to sleep here when I was a little girl. [*Cries.*] I feel like a little girl again now. [*Kisses her brother and* VARYA, *and then her brother again.*] Varya is the same as ever. Looks like a nun. And I also recognize Dunyasha. [*Kisses* DUNYASHA.]
GAYEV.   The train was two hours late. How do you like that? What a way to
70   run a railway!
CHARLOTTE [*to* PISHCHIK].   My dog also eats nuts.
PISHCHIK [*surprised*].   Good Lord!

[*All, except* ANYA *and* DUNYASHA, *go out.*]

DUNYASHA.   We thought you'd never come. [*Helps* ANYA *off with her coat and hat.*]
ANYA.   I haven't slept for four nights on our journey. Now I'm chilled right through.
DUNYASHA.   You left before Easter. It was snowing and freezing then. It's different now, isn't it? Darling Anya! [*Laughs and kisses her.*] I've missed you so much, my darling, my precious! Oh, I must tell you at once! I can't keep
80   it to myself a minute longer. . . .
ANYA [*apathetically*].   What is it this time?
DUNYASHA.   Our clerk, Yepikhodov, proposed to me after Easter.
ANYA.   Always the same. [*Tidying her hair.*] I've lost all my hairpins. [*She is so tired, she can hardly stand.*]
DUNYASHA.   I don't know what to think. He loves me so much, so much!
ANYA [*tenderly, looking through the door into her room*].   My own room, my own windows, just as if I'd never been away! I'm home again! As soon as I get up in the morning, I'll run out into the orchard. . . . Oh, if only I could sleep. I didn't sleep all the way back, I was so worried.
90 DUNYASHA.   Mr. Trofimov arrived the day before yesterday.
ANYA [*joyfully*].   Peter!
DUNYASHA.   He's asleep in the bathhouse. He's been living there. Afraid of being a nuisance, he says. [*Glancing at her watch.*] I really ought to wake him, except that Miss Varya told me not to. "Don't you dare wake him!" she said.

[VARYA *comes in with a bunch of keys at her waist.*]

VARYA.   Dunyasha, coffee quick! Mother's asking for some.

DUNYASHA.   I won't be a minute! [*Goes out.*]

VARYA.   Well, thank goodness you're all back. You're home again, my darling. [*Caressing her.*] My darling is home again! My sweet child is home 100 again.

ANYA.   I've had such an awful time!

VARYA.   I can imagine it.

ANYA.   I left before Easter. It was terribly cold then. All the way Charlotte kept talking and doing her conjuring tricks. Why did you force Charlotte on me?

VARYA.   But you couldn't have gone alone, darling, could you? You're only seventeen!

ANYA.   In Paris it was also cold and snowing. My French is awful. I found Mother living on the fourth floor. When I got there, she had some French 110 visitors, a few ladies and an old Catholic priest with a book. The place was full of tobacco smoke and terribly uncomfortable. Suddenly I felt sorry for Mother, so sorry that I took her head in my arms, held it tightly, and couldn't let go. Afterwards Mother was very sweet to me. She was crying all the time.

VARYA [*through tears*].   Don't go on, Anya. Please don't.

ANYA.   She'd already sold her villa near Mentone. She had nothing left. Nothing! I hadn't any money, either. There was hardly enough for the journey. Mother just won't understand! We had dinner at the station and she would order the most expensive things and tip the waiters a ruble 120 each. Charlotte was just the same. Yasha, too, demanded to be given the same kind of food. It was simply awful! You see, Yasha is Mother's manservant. We've brought him back with us.

VARYA.   Yes, I've seen the scoundrel.

ANYA.   Well, what's been happening? Have you paid the interest on the mortgage?

VARYA.   Heavens, no!

ANYA.   Dear, oh dear . . .

VARYA.   The estate will be up for sale in August.

ANYA.   Oh dear!

130 LOPAKHIN [*puts his head through the door and bleats*].   Bah-h-h! [*Goes out.*]

VARYA [*through tears*].   Oh, I'd like to hit him! [*Shakes her fist.*]

ANYA [*gently embracing* VARYA].   Varya, has he proposed to you? [VARYA *shakes her head.*] But he loves you. Why don't you two come to an understanding? What are you waiting for?

VARYA.   I don't think anything will come of it. He's so busy. He can't be bothered with me. Why, he doesn't even notice me. I wish I'd never known him. I can't stand the sight of him. Everyone's talking about our wedding, everyone's congratulating me, while there's really nothing in it. It's all so unreal. Like a dream. [*In a different tone of voice.*] You've got a new brooch. 140 Like a bee, isn't it?

ANYA [*sadly*].   Yes, Mother bought it. [*Goes to her room, talking quite happily, like a child.*] You know, I went up in a balloon in Paris!

VARYA.   My darling's home again! My dearest one's home again! [DUNYASHA *has come back with a coffeepot and is making coffee;* VARYA *is standing at the door of* ANYA's *room.*] All day long, darling, I'm busy about the house, and all the time I'm dreaming, dreaming. If only we could find a rich husband for you! My mind would be at rest then. I'd go into a convent and later on a pilgrimage to Kiev . . . to Moscow. Just keep going from one holy place to another. On and on. . . . Wonderful!

150 ANYA.   The birds are singing in the orchard. What's the time?

VARYA.   It's past two. It's time you were asleep, darling. [*Goes into* ANYA's *room.*] Wonderful!

[*Enter* YASHA *with a traveling rug and a small bag.*]

YASHA [*crossing the stage, in an affected genteel voice*].   May I be permitted to go through here?

DUNYASHA.   I can hardly recognize you, Yasha. You've changed so much abroad.

YASHA.   Hmmm . . . And who are you, may I ask?

DUNYASHA.   When you left, I was no bigger than this. [*Shows her height from the floor with her hand.*] I'm Dunyasha, Fyodor Kozoedov's daughter. Don't you

160   remember me?

YASHA.   Mmmm . . . Juicy little cucumber! [*Looks round, then puts his arms around her; she utters a little scream and drops a saucer.* YASHA *goes out hurriedly.*]

VARYA [*in the doorway, crossly*].   What's going on there?

DUNYASHA [*in tears*].   I've broken a saucer.

VARYA.   That's lucky.

ANYA [*coming out of her room*].   Mother must be told Peter's here.

VARYA.   I gave orders not to wake him.

ANYA [*pensively*].   Father died six years ago. A month after our brother,

170   Grisha, was drowned in the river. Such a pretty little boy. He was only seven. Mother took it badly. She went away, went away never to come back. [*Shudders.*] Peter Trofimov was Grisha's tutor. He might remind her . . .

[FIRS *comes in, wearing a jacket and a white waistcoat.*]

FIRS [*walks up to the coffeepot anxiously*].   Madam will have her coffee here. [*Puts on white gloves.*] Is the coffee ready? [*Sternly, to* DUNYASHA.] You there! Where's the cream?

DUNYASHA.   Oh dear! [*Goes out quickly.*]

FIRS [*fussing round the coffeepot*].   The nincompoop! [*Muttering to himself.*] She's come from Paris. . . . Master used to go to Paris. . . . Aye, by coach. . . . [*Laughs.*]

180 VARYA.   What are you talking about, Firs?

FIRS.   Sorry, what did you say? [*Joyfully.*] Madam is home again! Home at last! I can die happy now. [*Weeps with joy.*]

[*Enter* MRS. RANEVSKY, GAYEV, *and* SIMEONOV-PISHCHIK, *the last one wearing a Russian long-waisted coat of expensive cloth and wide trousers. As he enters,* GAYEV *moves his arms and body as if he were playing billiards.*]

MRS. RANEVSKY.   How does it go now? Let me think. Pot the red in the corner. Double into the middle pocket.

GAYEV.   And straight into the corner! A long time ago, Lyuba, you and I slept in this room. Now I'm fifty-one. . . . Funny, isn't it!

LOPAKHIN.   Aye, time flies.

GAYEV.   I beg your pardon?

LOPAKHIN.   "Time flies," I said.

190 GAYEV.   The place reeks of patchouli.[2]

ANYA.   I'm off to bed. Good night, Mother. [*Kisses her mother.*]

MRS. RANEVSKY.   My sweet little darling! [*Kisses her hands.*] You're glad to be home, aren't you? I still can't believe it.

ANYA.   Good night, Uncle.

GAYEV [*kissing her face and hands*].   God bless you. You're so like your mother! [*To his sister.*] You were just like her at that age, Lyuba.

[ANYA *shakes hands with* LOPAKHIN *and* PISHCHIK. *Goes out and shuts the door behind her.*]

MRS. RANEVSKY.   She's terribly tired.

PISHCHIK.   It was a long journey.

VARYA [*to* LOPAKHIN *and* PISHCHIK.].   Well, gentlemen, it's past two o'clock.

200   You mustn't outstay your welcome, must you?

MRS. RANEVSKY [*laughs*].   You're just the same, Varya. [*Draws* VARYA *to her and kisses her.*] Let me have my coffee first and then we'll all go. [FIRS *puts a little cushion under her feet.*] Thank you, Firs dear. I've got used to having coffee. I drink it day and night. Thank you, Firs, thank you, my dear old man. [*Kisses* FIRS.]

VARYA.   I'd better make sure they've brought all the things in. [*Goes out.*]

MRS. RANEVSKY.   Is it really me sitting here? [*Laughs.*] I feel like jumping about, waving my arms. [*Covers her face with her hands.*] And what if it's all a dream? God knows, I love my country. I love it dearly. I couldn't look out

210   of the train for crying. [*Through tears.*] But, I suppose I'd better have my coffee. Thank you, Firs, thank you, dear old man. I'm so glad you're still alive.

FIRS.   The day before yesterday . . .

GAYEV.   He's a little deaf.

LOPAKHIN.   At five o'clock I've got to leave for Kharkov. What a nuisance! I wish I could have had a good look at you, a good talk with you. You're still as magnificent as ever. . . .

PISHCHIK [*breathing heavily*].   Lovelier, I'd say. Dressed in the latest Paris fashion. If only I were twenty years younger—ho-ho-ho!

220 LOPAKHIN.   This brother of yours says that I'm an ignorant oaf, a tightfisted peasant, but I don't mind. Let him talk. All I want is that you should believe in me as you used to, that you should look at me as you used to with those wonderful eyes of yours. Merciful heavens! My father was a serf of your father and your grandfather, but you, you alone, did so much for me in the past that I forgot everything, and I love you just as if you were my own flesh and blood, more than my own flesh and blood.

MRS. RANEVSKY.   I can't sit still, I can't. . . . [*Jumps up and walks about the room in great agitation.*] This happiness is more than I can bear. Laugh at me if you like. I'm making such a fool of myself. Oh, my darling little bookcase

230   . . . [*Kisses the bookcase.*] My sweet little table . . .

---

[2] A plant from the mint family, at that time a popular fragrance.

GAYEV. You know, of course, that Nanny died here while you were away.

MRS. RANEVSKY [*sits down and drinks her coffee*]. Yes, God rest her soul. They wrote to tell me about it.

GAYEV. Anastasy, too, is dead. Boss-eyed Peter left me for another job. He's with the Police Superintendent in town now. [*Takes a box of fruit drops out of his pocket and sucks one.*]

PISHCHIK. My daughter Dashenka—er—wishes to be remembered to you.

LOPAKHIN. I'd like to say something very nice and cheerful to you. [*Glances at his watch.*] I shall have to be going in a moment and there isn't much
240   time to talk. As you know, your cherry orchard's being sold to pay your debts. The auction is on the twenty-second of August. But there's no need to worry, my dear. You can sleep soundly. There's a way out. Here's my plan. Listen carefully, please. Your estate is only about twelve miles from town, and the railway is not very far away. Now, all you have to do is break up your cherry orchard and the land along the river into building plots and lease them out for country cottages. You'll then have an income of at least twenty-five thousand a year.

GAYEV. I'm sorry, but what utter nonsense!

MRS. RANEVSKY. I don't quite follow you, Lopakhin.

250 LOPAKHIN. You'll be able to charge your tenants at least twenty-five rubles a year for a plot of about three acres. I bet you anything that if you advertise now, there won't be a single plot left by the autumn. They will all be snapped up. In fact, I congratulate you. You are saved. The site is magnificent and the river is deep enough for bathing. Of course, the place will have to be cleared, tidied up. . . . I mean, all the old buildings will have to be pulled down, including, I'm sorry to say, this house, but it isn't any use to anybody any more, is it? The old cherry orchard will have to be cut down.

MRS. RANEVSKY. Cut down? My dear man, I'm very sorry but I don't think
260   you know what you're talking about. If there's anything of interest, anything quite remarkable, in fact, in the whole county, it's our cherry orchard.

LOPAKHIN. The only remarkable thing about this orchard is that it's very large. It only produces a crop every other year, and even then you don't know what to do with the cherries. Nobody wants to buy them.

GAYEV. Why, you'll find our orchard mentioned in the encyclopedia.

LOPAKHIN [*glancing at his watch*]. If we can't think of anything and if we can't come to any decision, it won't be only your cherry orchard but your whole estate that will be sold at auction on the twenty-second of August. Make up
270   your mind. I tell you, there is no other way. Take my word for it. There isn't.

FIRS. In the old days, forty or fifty years ago, the cherries used to be dried, preserved, made into jam, and sometimes—

GAYEV. Do shut up, Firs.

FIRS. —and sometimes cartloads of dried cherries were sent to Moscow and Kharkov. Fetched a lot of money, they did. Soft and juicy, those cherries were. Sweet and such a lovely smell . . . They knew the recipe then. . . .

MRS. RANEVSKY. And where's the recipe now?

FIRS. Forgotten. No one remembers it.

280 PISHCHIK [*to* MRS. RANEVSKY]. What was it like in Paris? Eh? Eat any frogs?

MRS. RANEVSKY.   I ate crocodiles.

PISHCHIK.   Good Lord!

LOPAKHIN.   Till recently there were only the gentry and the peasants in the
country. Now we have holiday-makers. All our towns, even the smallest,
are surrounded by country cottages. I shouldn't be surprised if in twenty
years the holiday-maker multiplies enormously. All your holiday-maker
does now is drink tea on the veranda, but it's quite in the cards that if he
becomes the owner of three acres of land, he'll do a bit of farming on the
side, and then your cherry orchard will become a happy, prosperous,
290   thriving place.

GAYEV [*indignantly*].   What nonsense!

[*Enter* VARYA *and* YASHA.]

VARYA.   I've got two telegrams in here for you, Mother dear. [*Picks out a key
and unlocks the old-fashioned bookcase with a jingling noise.*] Here they are.

MRS. RANEVSKY.   They're from Paris. [*Tears the telegrams up without reading
them.*] I've finished with Paris.

GAYEV.   Do you know how old this bookcase is, Lyuba? Last week I pulled out
the bottom drawer and saw some figures burned into it. This bookcase was
made exactly a hundred years ago. What do you think of that? Eh? We
ought really to celebrate its centenary. An inanimate object, but say what
300   you like, it's a bookcase after all.

PISHCHIK [*amazed*].   A hundred years! Good Lord!

GAYEV.   Yes, indeed. It's quite something. [*Feeling round the bookcase with his
hands.*] Dear, highly esteemed bookcase, I salute you. For over a hundred
years you have devoted yourself to the glorious ideals of goodness and
justice. Throughout the hundred years your silent appeal to fruitful work
has never faltered. It sustained [*through tears*] in several generations of our
family, their courage and faith in a better future and fostered in us the
ideals of goodness and social consciousness.

[*Pause.*]

LOPAKHIN.   Aye. . . .

310   MRS. RANEVSKY.   You haven't changed a bit, have you, darling Leonid?

GAYEV [*slightly embarrassed*].   Off the right into a corner! Pot into the middle
pocket!

LOPAKHIN [*glancing at his watch*].   Well, afraid it's time I was off.

YASHA [*handing* MRS. RANEVSKY *her medicine*].   Your pills, ma'am.

PISHCHIK.   Never take any medicines, dear lady. I don't suppose they'll do
you much harm, but they won't do you any good either. Here, let me have
'em, my dear lady. [*Takes the box of pills from her, pours the pills into the palm
of his hand, blows on them, puts them all into his mouth, and washes them down
with kvass.*] There!

320   MRS. RANEVSKY [*alarmed*].   You're mad!

PISHCHIK.   Swallowed the lot.

LOPAKHIN.   The glutton!

[*All laugh.*]

FIRS. He was here at Easter, the gentleman was. Ate half a bucketful of pickled cucumbers, he did. . . . [*Mutters.*]

MRS. RANEVSKY. What is he saying?

VARYA. He's been muttering like that for the last three years. We've got used to it.

YASHA. Old age!

[CHARLOTTE, *in a white dress, very thin and tightly laced, a lorgnette*[3] *dangling from her belt, crosses the stage.*]

LOPAKHIN. I'm sorry, Miss Charlotte, I haven't had the chance of saying
330 how-do-you-do to you. [*Tries to kiss her hand.*]

CHARLOTTE [*snatching her hand away*]. If I let you kiss my hand, you'll want to kiss my elbow, then my shoulder . . .

LOPAKHIN. It's not my lucky day. [*They all laugh.*] My dear Charlotte, show us a trick, please.

MRS. RANEVSKY. Yes, do show us a trick, Charlotte.

CHARLOTTE. I won't. I'm off to bed. [*Goes out.*]

LOPAKHIN. We'll meet again in three weeks. [*Kisses* MRS. RANEVSKY's *hand.*] Good-bye for now. I must go. [*To* GAYEV.] So long. [*Embraces* PISHCHIK.] So long. [*Shakes hands with* VARYA *and then with* FIRS *and* YASHA.] I wish I didn't
340 have to go. [*To* MRS. RANEVSKY.] Let me know if you make up your mind about the country cottages. If you decide to go ahead, I'll get you a loan of fifty thousand or more. Think it over seriously.

VARYA [*angrily*]. For goodness' sake, go!

LOPAKHIN. I'm going, I'm going. . . . [*Goes out.*]

GAYEV. The oaf! However, I'm sorry. Varya's going to marry him, isn't she? He's Varya's intended.

VARYA. Don't say things you'll be sorry for, Uncle.

MRS. RANEVSKY. But why not, Varya? I should be only too glad. He's a good man.

PISHCHIK. A most admirable fellow, to tell the truth. My Dashenka—er—
350 also says that—er—says all sorts of things. [*Drops off and snores, but wakes up immediately.*] By the way, my dear lady, you will lend me two hundred and forty rubles, won't you? Must pay the interest on the mortgage tomorrow.

VARYA [*terrified*]. We have no money; we haven't!

MRS. RANEVSKY. We really haven't any, you know.

PISHCHIK. Have a good look around—you're sure to find it. [*Laughs.*] I never lose hope. Sometimes I think it's all over with me, I'm done for, then—hey presto—they build a railway over my land and pay me for it. Something's bound to turn up, if not today, then tomorrow. I'm certain of it. Dashenka
360 might win two hundred thousand. She's got a ticket in the lottery, you know.

MRS. RANEVSKY. Well, I've finished my coffee. Now to bed.

FIRS [*brushing* GAYEV's *clothes admonishingly*]. Put the wrong trousers on again, sir. What am I to do with you?

---

[3] A pair of eyeglasses with a handle instead of earpieces.

VARYA [*in a low voice*].   Anya's asleep. [*Opens a window quietly.*] The sun has
risen. It's no longer cold. Look, Mother dear. What lovely trees! Heavens,
what wonderful air! The starlings are singing.

GAYEV [*opens another window*].   The orchard's all white. Lyuba, you haven't
forgotten, have you? The long avenue there—it runs on and on, straight
370   as an arrow. It gleams on moonlit nights. Remember? You haven't forgotten, have you?

MRS. RANEVSKY [*looking through the window at the orchard*].   Oh, my childhood,
oh, my innocence! I slept in this nursery. I used to look out at the orchard
from here. Every morning happiness used to wake with me. The orchard
was just the same in those days. Nothing has changed. [*Laughs happily.*]
White, all white! Oh, my orchard! After the dark, rainy autumn and the
cold winter, you're young again, full of happiness; the heavenly angels
haven't forsaken you. If only this heavy load could be lifted from my heart;
if only I could forget my past!

380 GAYEV.   Well, and now they're going to sell the orchard to pay our debts.
Funny, isn't it?

MRS. RANEVSKY.   Look! Mother's walking in the orchard in . . . a white dress!
[*Laughs happily.*] It *is* Mother!

GAYEV.   Where?

VARYA.   Really, Mother dear, what are you saying?

MRS. RANEVSKY.   There's no one there. I just imagined it. Over there, on the
right, near the turning to the summer house, a little white tree's leaning
over. It looks like a woman. [*Enter* TROFIMOV. *He is dressed in a shabby
student's uniform and wears glasses.*] What an amazing orchard! Masses of
390   white blossom. A blue sky . . .

TROFIMOV.   I say, Mrs. Ranevsky . . . [*She looks round at him.*] I've just come to
say hello. I'll go at once. [*Kisses her hand warmly.*] I was told to wait till
morning, but I—I couldn't. I couldn't.

[MRS. RANEVSKY *gazes at him in bewilderment.*]

VARYA [*through tears*].   This is Peter Trofimov.

TROFIMOV.   Peter Trofimov. Your son Grisha's old tutor. I haven't changed
so much, have I?

[MRS. RANEVSKY *embraces him and weeps quietly.*]

GAYEV [*embarrassed*].   There, there, Lyuba.

VARYA [*cries*].   I did tell you to wait till tomorrow, didn't I, Peter?

MRS. RANEVSKY.   Grisha, my . . . little boy, Grisha . . . my son.

400 VARYA.   It can't be helped, Mother. It was God's will.

TROFIMOV [*gently, through tears*].   Now, now . . .

MRS. RANEVSKY [*weeping quietly*].   My little boy died, drowned. Why? Why, my
friend? [*More quietly.*] Anya's asleep in there and here I am shouting,
making a noise. . . . Well, Peter? You're not as good-looking as you were,
are you? Why not? Why have you aged so much?

TROFIMOV.   A peasant woman in a railway carriage called me "a moth-eaten
gentleman."

MRS. RANEVSKY.   You were only a boy then. A charming young student. Now

you're growing thin on top, you wear glasses. . . . You're not still a student,
410 are you? [*Walks toward the door.*]

TROFIMOV.   I expect I shall be an eternal student.

MRS. RANEVSKY [*kisses her brother and then* VARYA].   Well, go to bed now. You,
Leonid, have aged too.

PISHCHIK [*following her*].   So, we're off to bed now, are we? Oh dear, my gout!
I think I'd better stay the night here. Now, what about letting me have
the—er—two hundred and forty rubles tomorrow morning, dear lady?
Early tomorrow morning. . . .

GAYEV.   He does keep on, doesn't he?

PISHCHIK.   Two hundred and forty rubles—to pay the interest on the mort-
420 gage.

MRS. RANEVSKY.   But I haven't any money, my dear man.

PISHCHIK.   I'll pay you back, dear lady. Such a trifling sum.

MRS. RANEVSKY.   Oh, all right. Leonid will let you have it. Let him have it,
Leonid.

GAYEV.   Let him have it? The hell I will.

MRS. RANEVSKY.   What else can we do? Let him have it, please. He needs it.
He'll pay it back.

[MRS. RANEVSKY, TROFIMOV, PISHCHIK, *and* FIRS *go out.* GAYEV, VARYA, *and* YASHA
remain.]

GAYEV.   My sister hasn't got out of the habit of throwing money about. [*To*
YASHA.] Out of my way, fellow. You reek of the hen house.

430 YASHA [*grins*].   And you, sir, are the same as ever.

GAYEV.   I beg your pardon? [*To* VARYA.] What did he say?

VARYA [*to* YASHA].   Your mother's come from the village. She's been sitting in
the servant's quarters since yesterday. She wants to see you.

YASHA.   Oh, bother her!

VARYA.   You shameless bounder!

YASHA.   I don't care. She could have come tomorrow, couldn't she? [*Goes
out.*]

VARYA.   Dear Mother is just the same as ever. Hasn't changed a bit. If you let
her, she'd give away everything.

440 GAYEV.   I suppose so. [*Pause.*] When a lot of remedies are suggested for an
illness, it means that the illness is incurable. I've been thinking, racking
my brains; I've got all sorts of remedies, lots of them, which, of course,
means that I haven't got one. It would be marvelous if somebody left us
some money. It would be marvelous if we found a very rich husband for
Anya. It would be marvelous if one of us went to Yaroslavl to try out luck
with our great-aunt, the Countess. She's very rich, you know. Very rich.

VARYA [*crying*].   If only God would help us.

GAYEV.   Don't howl! Our aunt is very rich, but she doesn't like us. First,
because my sister married a lawyer and not a nobleman. . . . [ANYA *appears*
450 *in the doorway.*] She did not marry a nobleman, and she has not been
leading an exactly blameless life, has she? She's a good, kind, nice person.
I love her very much. But, however much you try to make allowances for
her, you have to admit that she is an immoral woman. You can sense it in
every movement she makes.

VARYA [*in a whisper*].   Anya's standing in the doorway.

GAYEV.   I beg your pardon? [*Pause.*] Funny thing, there's something in my right eye. Can't see properly. On Thursday, too, in the district court . . .

[ANYA *comes in.*]

VARYA.   Why aren't you asleep, Anya?

ANYA.   I can't sleep, I can't.

460 GAYEV.   My little darling. [*Kisses* ANYA'S *face and hands.*] My dear child! [*Through tears.*] You're not my niece, you're my angel. You're everything to me. Believe me. Do believe me.

ANYA.   I believe you, Uncle. Everyone loves you, everyone respects you, but, dear Uncle, you shouldn't talk so much. What were you saying just now about Mother, about your own sister? What did you say it for?

GAYEV.   Well, yes, yes. [*He takes her hand and covers his face with it.*] You're quite right. It was dreadful. Dear God, dear God, help me! That speech I made to the bookcase today—it was so silly. The moment I finished it, I realized how silly it was.

470 VARYA.   It's quite true, Uncle dear. You oughtn't to talk so much. Just don't talk, that's all.

ANYA.   If you stopped talking, you'd feel much happier yourself.

GAYEV.   Not another word. [*Kisses* ANYA'S *and* VARYA'S *hands.*] Not another word. Now to business. Last Thursday I was at the county court, and, well—er—I met a lot of people there, and we started talking about this and that, and—er—it would seem that we might manage to raise some money on a promissory note and pay the interest to the bank.

VARYA.   Oh, if only God would help us!

GAYEV.   I shall be there again on Tuesday, and I'll have another talk. [*To*
480 VARYA.] For goodness' sake, don't howl! [*To* ANYA.] Your mother will have a talk with Lopakhin. I'm sure he won't refuse her. After you've had your rest, you'll go to Yaroslavl to see your great-aunt, the Countess. That's how we shall tackle the problem from three different sides, and I'm sure we'll get it settled. The interest we shall pay. Of that I'm quite sure. [*Puts a fruit drop in his mouth.*] I give you my word of honor, I swear by anything you like, the estate will not be sold! [*Excitedly.*] Why, I'll stake my life on it! Here's my hand; call me a rotten scoundrel if I allow the auction to take place. I stake my life on it!

ANYA [*has regained her composure; she looks happy*].   You're so good, Uncle
490 dear! So clever! [*Embraces him.*] I'm no longer worried now. Not a bit worried. I'm happy.

[*Enter* FIRS.]

FIRS [*reproachfully*].   Have you no fear of God, sir? When are you going to bed?

GAYEV.   Presently, presently. Go away, Firs. Never mind, I'll undress this time. Well, children, bye-bye now. More about it tomorrow. Now you must go to bed. [*Kisses* ANYA *and* VARYA.] I'm a man of the eighties. People don't think much of that time, but let me tell you, I've suffered a great deal for my convictions during my life. It's not for nothing that the peasants love me. You have to know your peasant, you have to know how to—

500 ANYA. There you go again, Uncle.

VARYA. Please, Uncle dear, don't talk so much.

FIRS [*angrily*]. Sir!

GAYEV. I'm coming, I'm coming. You two go to bed. Off two cushions into the middle. Pot the white!

[GAYEV *goes out,* FIRS *shuffling off after him.*]

ANYA. I'm not worried any longer now. I don't feel like going to Yaroslavl. I don't like my great-aunt, but I'm no longer worried. I ought to thank Uncle for that. [*Sits down.*]

VARYA. I ought to go to bed, and I shall be going in a moment, I must tell you first that something unpleasant happened here while you were away.
510   You know, of course, that only a few old servants live in the old servants' quarters: Yefimushka, Polia, Evstigney, and, well, also Karp. They had been letting some tramps sleep there, but I didn't say anything about it. Then I heard that they were telling everybody that I'd given orders for them to be fed on nothing but dried peas. I'm supposed to be a miser, you see. It was all that Evstigney's doing. Well, I said to myself, if that's how it is, you just wait! So I sent for Evstigney. [*Yawns.*] He comes. "What do you mean," I said, "Evstigney, you silly old fool?" [*Looks at* ANYA.] Darling! [*Pause.*] Asleep . . . [*Takes* ANYA *by the arm.*] Come to bed, dear. . . . Come on! [*Leads her by the arm.*] My darling's fallen asleep. Come along. [*They go
520   out. A shepherd's pipe is heard playing from far away on the other side of the orchard.* TROFIMOV *walks across the stage and, catching sight of* VARYA *and* ANYA, *stops.*] Shh! She's asleep, asleep. Come along, my sweet.

ANYA [*softly, half asleep*]. I'm so tired. . . . I keep hearing harness bells. Uncle . . . dear . . . Mother and Uncle . . .

VARYA. Come on, my sweet, come on. . . .

[*They go into* ANYA's *room.*]

TROFIMOV [*deeply moved*]. My sun! My spring!

ACT II

Open country. A small tumbledown wayside chapel. Near it, a well, some large stones, which look like old gravestones, and an old bench. A road can be seen leading to GAYEV's *estate. On one side, a row of tall dark poplars; it is there that the cherry orchard begins. In the distance, some telegraph poles, and far, far away on the horizon, the outlines of a large town that is visible only in very fine, clear weather. The sun is about to set.* CHARLOTTE, YASHA, *and* DUNYASHA *are sitting on the bench;* YEPIKHODOV *is standing nearby and is playing a guitar; they all sit sunk in thought.* CHARLOTTE *wears a man's old peaked hat; she has taken a shotgun from her shoulder and is adjusting the buckle on the strap.*

CHARLOTTE [*pensively*]. I haven't a proper passport, I don't know how old I am, and I can't help thinking that I'm still a young girl. When I was a little girl, my father and mother used to travel the fairs and give perform-
530   ances—very good ones. I used to do the *salto mortale*[4] and all sorts of other

---

[4] Death-leap.

tricks. When Father and Mother died, a German lady adopted me and began educating me. Very well. I grew up and became a governess, but where I came from and who I am, I do not know. Who my parents were, I do not know either. They may not even have been married. I don't know. [*Takes a cucumber out of her pocket and starts eating it.*] I don't know anything. [*Pause.*] I'm longing to talk to someone, but there is no one to talk to. I haven't anyone. . . .

YEPIKHODOV [*plays his guitar and sings*].   "What care I for the world and its bustle? What care I for my friends and my foes?" . . . Nice to play a
540   mandolin.

DUNYASHA.   It's a guitar, not a mandolin. [*She looks at herself in a hand mirror and powders her face.*]

YEPIKHODOV.   To a madman in love, it's a mandolin. [*Sings softly.*] "If only my heart was warmed by the fire of love requited."

[YASHA *joins in.*]

CHARLOTTE.   How terribly these people sing! Ugh! Like hyenas.

DUNYASHA [*to* YASHA].   All the same, you're ever so lucky to have been abroad.

YASHA.   Why, of course. Can't help agreeing with you there. [*Yawns, then lights a cigar.*]

YEPIKHODOV.   Stands to reason. Abroad, everything's in excellent complex-
550   ion. Been like that for ages.

YASHA.   Naturally.

YEPIKHODOV.   I'm a man of some education, I read all sorts of remarkable books, but what I simply can't understand is where it's all leading to. I mean, what do I really want—to live or to shoot myself? In any case, I always carry a revolver. Here it is. [*Shows them his revolver.*]

CHARLOTTE.   That's done. Now I can go. [*Puts the shotgun over her shoulder.*] You're a very clever man, Yepikhodov. You frighten me to death. Women must be madly in love with you. Brrr! [*Walking away.*] These clever people are all so stupid. I've no one to talk to. Always alone, alone, I've no one,
560   and who I am and what I am for is a mystery. [*Walks off slowly.*]

YEPIKHODOV.   Strictly speaking, and apart from all other considerations, what I ought to say about myself, among other things, is that Fate treats me without mercy, like a storm a small boat. Even supposing I'm mistaken, why in that case should I wake up this morning and suddenly find a spider of quite enormous dimensions on my chest? As big as that. [*Uses both hands to show the spider's size.*] Or again, I pick up a jug of kvass and there's something quite outrageously indecent in it, like a cockroach. [*Pause.*] Have you ever read Buckle's *History of Civilization?*[5] [*Pause.*] May I have a word or two with you, Dunyasha?

570 DUNYASHA.   Oh, all right. What is it?

YEPIKHODOV.   I'd be very much obliged if you'd let me speak to you in private. [*Sighs.*]

DUNYASHA [*embarrassed*].   All right, only first bring me my cape, please. It's hanging near the wardrobe. It's so damp here.

---

[5] Henry Thomas Buckle (1821–1862) is best known for his *History of Civilization in England* (1857–1861).

YEPIKHODOV. Very well, I'll fetch it. . . . Now I know what to do with my revolver. [*Picks up his guitar and goes out strumming it.*]

YASHA. Twenty-two Calamities! A stupid fellow, between you and me. [*Yawns.*]

DUNYASHA. I hope to goodness he won't shoot himself. [*Pause.*] I'm ever so
580   nervous. I can't help being worried all the time. I was taken into service when I was a little girl, and now I can't live like a peasant any more. See my hands? They're ever so white, as white as a young lady's. I've become so nervous, so sensitive, so like a lady. I'm afraid of everything. I'm simply terrified. So if you deceived me, Yasha, I don't know what would happen to my nerves.

YASHA [*kisses her*]. Little cucumber! Mind you, I expect every girl to be respectable. What I dislike most is for a girl to misbehave herself.

DUNYASHA. I've fallen passionately in love with you, Yasha. You're so educated. You can talk about anything

                                         [*Pause.*]

590 YASHA [*yawning*]. You see, in my opinion, if a girl is in love with somebody, it means she's immoral. [*Pause.*] It is so pleasant to smoke a cigar in the open air. [*Listens.*] Someone's coming. It's them. . . . [DUNYASHA *embraces him impulsively.*] Please go home and look as if you've been down to the river for a swim. Take that path or they'll think I had arranged to meet you here. Can't stand that sort of thing.

DUNYASHA [*coughing quietly*]. Your cigar has given me an awful headache. [*Goes out.*]

[YASHA *remains sitting near the chapel. Enter* MRS. RANEVSKY, GAYEV, *and* LOPA-KHIN.]

LOPAKHIN. You must make up your minds once and for all. There's not much time left. After all, it's quite a simple matter. Do you agree to lease
600   your land for country cottages or don't you? Answer me in one word: yes or no. Just one word.

MRS. RANEVSKY. Who's been smoking such horrible cigars here? [*Sits down.*]

GAYEV. Now that they've built the railway, things are much more convenient. [*Sits down.*] We've been to town for lunch—pot the red in the middle! I really should have gone in to have a game first.

MRS. RANEVSKY. There's plenty of time.

LOPAKHIN. Just one word. [*Imploringly.*] Please give me your answer!

GAYEV [*yawns*]. I beg your pardon?

MRS. RANEVSKY [*looking in her purse*]. Yesterday I had a lot of money, but I've
610   hardly any left today. My poor Varya! Tries to economize by feeding everybody on milk soup and the old servants in the kitchen on peas, and I'm just throwing money about stupidly. [*Drops her purse, scattering some gold coins.*] Goodness gracious, all over the place! [*She looks annoyed.*]

YASHA. Allow me to pick 'em up, madam. It won't take a minute. [*Starts picking up the coins.*]

MRS. RANEVSKY. Thank you, Yasha. Why on earth did I go out to lunch? That disgusting restaurant of yours with its stupid band, and those tablecloths smelling of soap. Why did you have to drink so much, Leonid? Or eat so

much? Or talk so much? You did talk a lot again in the restaurant today
620   and all to no purpose. About the seventies and the decadents[6] . . . And
who to? Talking about the decadents to waiters!

LOPAKHIN.   Aye. . . .

GAYEV [*waving his arm*].   I'm incorrigible, that's clear. [*Irritably to* YASHA.]
What are you hanging around here for?

YASHA [*laughs*].   I can't hear your voice without laughing, sir.

GAYEV [*to his sister*].   Either he or I.

MRS. RANEVSKY.   Go away, Yasha. Run along.

YASHA [*returning the purse to* MRS. RANEVSKY].   At once, madam. [*Is hardly able
to suppress his laughter.*] This very minute. [*Goes out.*]

630 LOPAKHIN.   The rich merchant Deriganov is thinking of buying your estate.
I'm told he's coming to the auction himself.

MRS. RANEVSKY.   Where did you hear that?

LOPAKHIN.   That's what they're saying in town.

GAYEV.   Our Yaroslavl great-aunt has promised to send us money, but when
and how much we do not know.

LOPAKHIN.   How much will she send? A hundred thousand? Two hundred?

MRS. RANEVSKY.   Well, I hardly think so. Ten or fifteen thousand at most. We
must be thankful for that.

LOPAKHIN.   I'm sorry, but such improvident people as you, such peculiar,
640   unbusinesslike people, I've never met in my life! You're told in plain
language that your estate's going to be sold, and you don't seem to understand.

MRS. RANEVSKY.   But what are we to do? Tell us, please.

LOPAKHIN.   I tell you every day. Every day I go on repeating the same thing
over and over again. You must let out the cherry orchard and the land for
country cottages, and you must do it now, as quickly as possible. The auction
is on top of you! Try to understand! The moment you decide to let your
land, you'll be able to raise as much money as you like, and you'll be saved.

MRS. RANEVSKY.   Country cottages, holiday-makers—I'm sorry, but it's so vul-
650   gar.

GAYEV.   I'm of your opinion entirely.

LOPAKHIN.   I shall burst into tears or scream or have a fit. I can't stand it.
You've worn me out! [*To* GAYEV.] You're a silly old woman!

GAYEV.   I beg your pardon?

LOPAKHIN.   A silly old woman! [*He gets up to go.*]

MRS. RANEVSKY [*in dismay*].   No, don't go. Please stay. I beg you. Perhaps we'll
think of something.

LOPAKHIN.   What is there to think of?

MRS. RANEVSKY.   Please don't go. I beg you. Somehow I feel so much more
660   cheerful with you here. [*Pause.*] I keep expecting something to happen, as
though the house was going to collapse on top of us.

GAYEV [*deep in thought*].   Cannon off the cushion. Pot into the middle
pocket. . . .

MRS. RANEVSKY.   I'm afraid we've sinned too much—

LOPAKHIN.   You sinned!

---

[6] A name adopted by a group of French and English writers of the late nineteenth century
because of their admiration for the decadent period in Roman civilization.

GAYEV [*putting a fruit drop into his mouth*].   They say I squandered my entire fortune on fruit drops. [*Laughs.*]

MRS. RANEVSKY.   Oh, my sins! . . . I've always thrown money about aimlessly, like a madwoman. Why, I even married a man who did nothing but pile up
670   debts. My husband died of champagne. He drank like a fish. Then, worse luck, I fell in love with someone, had an affair with him, and it was just at that time—it was my first punishment, a blow that nearly killed me—that my boy was drowned in the river here. I went abroad, never to come back, never to see that river again. I shut my eyes and ran, beside myself, and *he* followed me—pitilessly, brutally. I bought a villa near Mentone because *he* had fallen ill. For the next three years I knew no rest, nursing him day and night. He wore me out. Everything inside me went dead. Then, last year, I had to sell the villa to pay my debts. I left for Paris, where he robbed me, deserted me, and went to live with another woman. I tried to poison
680   myself. Oh, it was all so stupid, so shaming. . . . It was then that I suddenly felt an urge to go back to Russia, to my homeland, to my daughter. [*Dries her eyes.*] Lord, O Lord, be merciful! Forgive me my sins! Don't punish me any more! [*Takes a telegram from her pocket.*] I received this telegram from Paris today. He asks me to forgive him. He implores me to go back. [*Tears up the telegram.*] What's that? Music? [*Listens intently.*]

GAYEV.   That's our famous Jewish band. Remember? Four fiddles, a flute, and a double bass.

MRS. RANEVSKY.   Does it still exist? We ought to arrange a party and have them over to the house.

690   LOPAKHIN [*listening*].   I don't hear anything. [*Sings quietly.*] "And the Germans, if you pay 'em, will turn a Russian into a Frenchman." [*Laughs.*] I saw an excellent play at the theatre last night. It was very amusing.

MRS. RANEVSKY.   I don't suppose it was amusing at all. You shouldn't be watching plays, but should be watching yourselves more often. What dull lives you live. What nonsense you talk.

LOPAKHIN.   Perfectly true. Let's admit quite frankly that the life we lead is utterly stupid. [*Pause.*] My father was a peasant, an idiot. He understood nothing. He taught me nothing. He just beat me when he was drunk and always with a stick. As a matter of fact, I'm just as big a blockhead and an
700   idiot myself. I never learnt anything, and my handwriting is so abominable that I'm ashamed to let people see it.

MRS. RANEVSKY.   You ought to get married, my friend.

LOPAKHIN.   Yes. That's true.

MRS. RANEVSKY.   Married to our Varya. She's a nice girl.

LOPAKHIN.   Aye. . . .

MRS. RANEVSKY.   Her father was a peasant too. She's a hard-working girl, and she loves you. That's the important thing. Why, you've been fond of her for a long time yourself.

LOPAKHIN.   Very well. I've no objection. She's a good girl.

[*Pause.*]

710   GAYEV.   I've been offered a job in a bank. Six thousand a year. Have you heard, Lyuba?

MRS. RANEVSKY.   You in a bank! You'd better stay where you are.

[FIRS *comes in carrying an overcoat.*]

FIRS [*to* GAYEV]. Please put it on, sir. It's damp out here.

GAYEV [*putting on the overcoat*]. You're a damned nuisance, my dear fellow.

FIRS. Come along, sir. Don't be difficult. . . . This morning, too, you went off without saying a word. [*Looks him over.*]

MRS. RANEVSKY. How you've aged, Firs!

FIRS. What's that, ma'am?

LOPAKHIN. Your mistress says you've aged a lot.

720 FIRS. I've been alive a long time. They were trying to marry me off before your dad was born. . . . [*Laughs.*] When freedom[7] came, I was already chief valet. I refused to accept freedom and stayed on with my master. [*Pause.*] I well remember how glad everyone was, but what they were glad about, they did not know themselves.

LOPAKHIN. It wasn't such a bad life before, was it? At least, they flogged you.

FIRS [*not hearing him*]. I should say so. The peasants stuck to their masters and the masters to their peasants. Now everybody does what he likes. You can't understand nothing.

GAYEV. Shut up, Firs. I have to go to town tomorrow. I've been promised an

730   introduction to a general who might lend us some money on a promissory note.

LOPAKHIN. Nothing will come of it. You won't pay the interest, either. You may be sure of that.

MRS. RANEVSKY. Oh, he's just imagining things. There aren't any generals.

[*Enter* TROFIMOV, ANYA, *and* VARYA.]

GAYEV. Here they are at last.

ANYA. There's Mother.

MRS. RANEVSKY [*affectionately*]. Come here, come here, my dears. [*Embracing* ANYA *and* VARYA.] If you only knew how much I love you both. Sit down beside me. That's right.

[*All sit down.*].

740 LOPAKHIN. Our eternal student is always walking about with the young ladies.

TROFIMOV. Mind your own business.

LOPAKHIN. He's nearly fifty and he's still a student.

TROFIMOV. Do drop your idiotic jokes.

LOPAKHIN. Why are you so angry, you funny fellow?

TROFIMOV. Well, stop pestering me.

LOPAKHIN [*laughs*]. Tell me, what do you think of me?

TROFIMOV. Simply this: You're a rich man and you'll soon be a millionaire. Now, just as a beast of prey devours everything in its path and so helps to

750   preserve the balance of nature, so you, too, perform a similar function.

[*They all laugh.*]

VARYA. You'd better tell us about the planets, Peter.

MRS. RANEVSKY. No, let's carry on with what we were talking about yesterday.

---

[7] The emancipation of the Russian serfs took place in 1861.

TROFIMOV. What was that?

GAYEV. Pride.

TROFIMOV. We talked a lot yesterday, but we didn't arrive at any conclusion. As you see it, there's something mystical about the proud man. You may be right for all I know. But try to look at it simply, without being too clever. What sort of pride is it, is there any sense in it, if, physiologically, man is far from perfect? If, in fact, he is, in the vast majority of cases, coarse, 760 stupid, and profoundly unhappy? It's time we stopped admiring ourselves. All we must do is—work!

GAYEV. We're going to die all the same.

TROFIMOV. Who knows? And what do you mean by "we're going to die"? A man may possess a hundred senses. When he dies, he loses only the five we know. The other ninety-five live on.

MRS. RANEVSKY. How clever you are, Peter!

LOPAKHIN [*ironically*]. Oh, frightfully!

TROFIMOV. Mankind marches on, perfecting its powers. Everything that is incomprehensible to us now, will one day become familiar and compre- 770 hensible. All we have to do is to work and do our best to assist those who are looking for truth. Here in Russia only a few people are working so far. The vast majority of the educated people I know, do nothing. They aren't looking for anything. They are quite incapable of doing any work. They call themselves intellectuals, but speak to their servants as inferiors and treat the peasants like animals. They're not particularly keen on their studies, they don't do any serious reading, they are bone idle, they merely talk about science, and they understand very little about art. They are all so solemn, they look so very grave, they talk only of important matters, they philosophize. Yet anyone can see that our workers are abominably 780 fed, sleep on bare boards, thirty and forty to a room—bedbugs everywhere, stench, damp, moral turpitude. It's therefore obvious that all our fine phrases are merely a way of deluding ourselves and others. Tell me, where are all those children's crèches people are talking so much about? Where are the reading rooms? You find them only in novels. Actually, we haven't any. All we have is dirt, vulgarity, brutality. I dislike and I'm frightened of all these solemn countenances, just as I'm frightened of all serious conversations. Why not shut up for once?

LOPAKHIN. Well, I get up at five o'clock in the morning. I work from morning till night, and I've always lots of money on me—mine and other 790 people's—and I can see what the people around me are like. One has only to start doing something to realize how few honest, decent people there are about. Sometimes when I lie awake, I keep thinking; Lord, you've given us vast forests, boundless plains, immense horizons, and living here, we ourselves ought really to be giants—

MRS. RANEVSKY. You want giants, do you? They're all right only in fairy tales. Elsewhere they frighten me. [YEPIKHODOV *crosses the stage in the background, playing his guitar. Pensively.*] There goes Yepikhodov.

ANYA [*pensively*]. There goes Yepikhodov.

GAYEV. The sun's set, ladies and gentlemen.

800 TROFIMOV. Yes.

GAYEV [*softly, as though declaiming*]. Oh, nature, glorious nature! Glowing with eternal radiance, beautiful and indifferent, you, whom we call Mother,

uniting in yourself both life and death, you—life-giver and destroyer . . .
VARYA [*imploringly*].   Darling uncle!
ANYA.   Uncle, again!
TROFIMOV.   You'd far better pot the red in the middle.
GAYEV.   Not another word! Not another word!

[*They all sit deep in thought. Everything is still. The silence is broken only by the subdued muttering of* FIRS. *Suddenly a distant sound is heard. It seems to come from the sky, the sound of a breaking string, slowly dying away, melancholy.*]

MRS. RANEVSKY.   What's that?
LOPAKHIN.   I don't know. I expect a bucket must have broken somewhere far
810   away in a coal mine, but somewhere a very long distance away.
GAYEV.   Perhaps it was a bird, a heron or something.
TROFIMOV.   Or an eagle-owl.
MRS. RANEVSKY [*shudders*].   It makes me feel dreadful for some reason.

[*Pause.*]

FIRS.   Same thing happened before the misfortune: the owl hooted and the
samovar[8] kept hissing.
GAYEV.   Before what misfortune?
FIRS.   Before they gave us our freedom.

[*Pause.*]

MRS. RANEVSKY.   Come, let's go in, my friends. It's getting dark. [*To* ANYA.]
There are tears in your eyes. What's the matter, darling. [*Embraces her.*]
820 ANYA.   It's nothing, Mother. Nothing.
TROFIMOV.   Someone's coming.

[*A* HIKER *appears. He wears a shabby white peaked cap and an overcoat; he is slightly drunk.*]

HIKER.   Excuse me, is this the way to the station?
GAYEV.   Yes, follow that road.
HIKER.   I'm greatly obliged to you sir. [*Coughs.*] Glorious weather . . .
[*Declaiming.*] Brother, my suffering brother, come to the Volga, you whose
groans[9] . . . [*To* VARYA.] Mademoiselle, won't you give thirty kopecks to a
starving Russian citizen?

[VARYA, *frightened, utters a little scream.*]

LOPAKHIN [*angrily*].   There's a limit to the most disgraceful behavior.
MRS. RANEVSKY [*at a loss*].   Here, take this. [*Looks for some money in her purse.*]
830   No silver. Never mind, have this gold one.
HIKER.   Profoundly grateful to you, ma'am. [*Goes out.*]

[*Laughter.*]

---

[8] A metal urn used in Russia for making tea.
[9] The hiker is quoting from poems by Syomon Nadson (1862–1887) and Nikolay Nekrasov (1821–1878).

VARYA [*frightened*]. I'm going away. I'm going away. Good heavens, Mother dear, there's no food for the servants in the house, and you gave him a gold sovereign!

MRS. RANEVSKY. What's to be done with a fool like me? I'll give you all I have when we get home. You'll lend me some more money, Lopakhin, won't you?

LOPAKHIN. With pleasure.

MRS. RANEVSKY. Let's go in. It's time. By the way, Varya, we've found you a
840   husband here. Congratulations.

VARYA [*through tears*]. This isn't a joking matter, Mother.

LOPAKHIN. Okhmelia, go to a nunnery!¹⁰

GAYEV. Look at my hands. They're shaking. It's a long time since I had a game of billiards.

LOPAKHIN. Okhmelia, O nymph, remember me in your prayers!

MRS. RANEVSKY. Come along, come along, it's almost supper time.

VARYA. That man frightened me. My heart's still pounding.

LOPAKHIN. Let me remind you, ladies and gentlemen: The cherry orchard is up for sale on the twenty-second of August. Think about it! Think!

[*They all go out except* TROFIMOV *and* ANYA.]

850 ANYA [*laughing*]. I'm so glad the hiker frightened Varya. Now we are alone.

TROFIMOV. Varya's afraid we might fall in love. That's why she follows us around for days on end. With her narrow mind she cannot grasp that we are above love. The whole aim and meaning of our life is to bypass everything that is petty and illusory, that prevents us from being free and happy. Forward! Let us march on irresistibly toward the bright star shining there in the distance! Forward! Don't lag behind, friends!

ANYA [*clapping her hands excitedly*]. You talk so splendidly! [*Pause.*] It's so heavenly here today!

TROFIMOV. Yes, the weather is wonderful.

860 ANYA. What have you done to me, Peter? Why am I no longer as fond of the cherry orchard as before? I loved it so dearly. I used to think there was no lovelier place on earth than our orchard.

TROFIMOV. The whole of Russia is our orchard. The earth is great and beautiful. There are lots of lovely places on it. [*Pause.*] Think, Anya: your grandfather, your greatgrandfather, and all your ancestors owned serfs. They owned living souls. Can't you see human beings looking at you from every cherry tree in your orchard, from every leaf and every tree trunk? Don't you hear their voices? To own living souls—that's what has changed you all so much, you who are living now and those who lived before you.
870   That's why your mother, you yourself, and your uncle no longer realize that you are living on borrowed capital, at other people's expense, at the expense of those whom you don't admit farther than your entrance hall. We are at least two hundred years behind the times. We haven't got anything at all. We have no definite attitude toward our past. We just philosophize, complain of depression, or drink vodka. Isn't it abundantly

---

¹⁰ Here, and below, Lopakhin alludes imprecisely to Hamlet's address to Ophelia in Act 3, Scene 1, lines 89–90 and 121.

clear that before we start living in the present, we must atone for our past,
make an end of it? And atone for it we can only by suffering, by extraordinary, unceasing labor. Understand that, Anya.

ANYA.   The house we live in hasn't really been ours for a long time. I'm going
880   to leave it. I give you my word.

TROFIMOV.   If you have the keys of the house, throw them into the well and
go away. Be free as the wind.

ANYA [*rapturously*].   How well you said it!

TROFIMOV.   Believe me, Anya, believe me! I'm not yet thirty, I'm young, I'm
still a student, but I've been through hell more than once. I'm driven from
pillar to post. In winter I'm half-starved, I'm ill, worried, poor as a beggar.
You can't imagine the terrible places I've been to! And yet, always, every
moment of the day and night, my heart was full of ineffable visions of the
future. I feel, I'm quite sure, that happiness is coming, Anya. I can see it
890   coming already.

ANYA [*pensively*].   The moon is rising.

[YEPIKHODOV *can be heard playing the same sad tune as before on his guitar. The
moon rises. Somewhere near the poplars* VARYA *is looking for* ANYA *and calling,
"Anya, where are you?"*]

TROFIMOV.   Yes, the moon is rising. [*Pause.*] There it is—happiness! It's coming nearer and nearer. Already I can hear its footsteps, and if we never see
it, if we never know it, what does it matter? Others will see it.

VARYA [*offstage*].   Anya, where are you?

TROFIMOV.   That Varya again! [*Angrily.*] Disgusting!

ANYA.   Never mind, let's go to the river. It's lovely there.

TROFIMOV.   Yes, let's.

[*They go out.*]

VARYA [*offstage*].   Anya! Anya!

ACT III

*The drawing room, separated by an archway from the ballroom. A candelabra is
alight. The Jewish band can be heard playing in the entrance hall. It is the same band
that is mentioned in Act Two. Evening. In the ballroom people are dancing the
Grande Ronde.* SIMEONOV-PISHCHIK'S *voice van be heard crying out, "Promenade à
une paire!"*[11] *They all come out into the drawing room;* PISHCHIK *and* CHARLOTTE *the
first couple,* TROFIMOV *and* MRS. RANEVSKY *the second,* ANYA *and a* POST OFFICE
CLERK *the third,* VARYA *and the* STATIONMASTER *the fourth, and so on.* VARYA *is quietly
crying and dries her eyes as she dances. The last couple consists of* DUNYASHA *and a
partner. They walk across the drawing room.* PISHCHIK *shouts, "Grande Ronde
balancez!"*[12] *and "Les cavaliers à genoux et remerciez vos dames!"*[13]

FIRS, *wearing a tailcoat, brings in soda water on a tray.* PISHCHIK *and* TROFIMOV
come into the drawing room.

---

[11] "March in a pair!"
[12] "Grand circle, pause!"
[13] "Gentlemen on your knees and thank your ladies!"

900 PISHCHIK.   I've got high blood-pressure. I've had two strokes already, and I
find dancing hard work. But, as the saying goes, if you're one of a pack,
wag your tail, whether you bark or not. As a matter of fact, I'm as strong
as a horse. My father, may he rest in peace, liked his little joke, and
speaking about our family pedigree, he used to say that the ancient
Simeonov-Pishchiks came from the horse that Caligula had made a senator.[14] [*Sits down.*] But you see, the trouble is that I have no money. A
hungry dog believes only in meat. [*Snores, but wakes up again at once.*] I'm
just the same. All I can think of is money.

TROFIMOV.   There really is something horsy about you.

910 PISHCHIK.   Well, a horse is a good beast. You can sell a horse.

[*From an adjoining room comes the sound of people playing billiards.* VARYA *appears
in the ballroom under the archway.*]

TROFIMOV [*teasing her*].   Mrs. Lopakhin! Mrs. Lopakhin!

VARYA [*angrily*].   Moth-eaten gentleman!

TROFIMOV.   Well, I am a moth-eaten gentleman and proud of it.

VARYA [*brooding bitterly*].   We've hired a band, but how we are going to pay for
it, I don't know. [*Goes out.*]

TROFIMOV [*to* PISHCHIK].   If the energy you have wasted throughout your life
looking for money to pay the interest on your debts had been spent on
something else, you'd most probably have succeeded in turning the world
upside down.

920 PISHCHIK.   Nietzsche[15] the famous philosopher—a great man, a man of great
intellect—says in his works that there's nothing wrong about forging bank
notes.

TROFIMOV.   Have you read Nietzsche?

PISHCHIK.   Well, actually, Dashenka told me about it. I don't mind telling
you, though, that in my present position I might even forge bank notes.
The day after tomorrow I've got to pay three hundred and ten rubles. I've
already got one hundred and thirty. [*Feels his pockets in alarm.*] My money's
gone, I've lost my money! [*Through tears.*] Where is it? [*Happily.*] Ah, here
it is, in the lining. Lord the shock brought me out in a cold sweat!

[*Enter* MRS. RANEVSKY *and* CHARLOTTE.]

930 MRS. RANEVSKY [*hums a popular Georgian dance tune*].   Why is Leonid so late?
What's he doing in town? [*To* DUNYASHA.] Offer the band tea, please.

TROFIMOV.   I don't suppose the auction has taken place.

MRS. RANEVSKY.   What a time to have a band! What a time to have a party!
Oh, well, never mind. [*Sits down and hums quietly.*]

CHARLOTTE [*hands* PISHCHIK *a pack of cards*].   Here's a pack of cards. Think of
a card.

PISHCHIK.   All right.

CHARLOTTE.   Now shuffle the pack. That's right. Now give it to me. Now,
then, my dear Mr. Pishchik, *eins, zwei, drei!*[16] Look in your breast pocket.
940   Is it there?

---

[14] The mad emperor Caligula (A.D. 12–41) appointed a horse to serve in the Roman Senate.
[15] Friedrich Wilhelm Nietzsche (1844–1900), a German philosopher.
[16] "One, two, three!"

PISHCHIK [*takes the card out of his breast pocket*].   The eight of spades! Absolutely right! [*Surprised.*] Good Lord!

CHARLOTTE [*holding a pack of cards on the palm of her hand, to* TROFIMOV].   Tell me, quick, what's the top card?

TROFIMOV.   Well, let's say the queen of spades.

CHARLOTTE.   Here it is. [*To* PISHCHIK.] What's the top card now?

PISHCHIK.   The ace of hearts.

CHARLOTTE.   Here you are! [*Claps her hands and the pack of cards disappears.*] What lovely weather we've having today. [*A mysterious female voice, which*
950   *seems to come from under the floor, answers. "Oh yes, glorious weather, madam!"*] You're my ideal, you're so nice! [*The voice: "I like you very much too, madam."*]

STATIONMASTER [*clapping his hands*].   Bravo, Madam Ventriloquist!

PISHCHIK [*looking surprised*].   Good Lord! Enchanting, Miss Charlotte, I'm simply in love with you.

CHARLOTTE.   In love! Are you sure you can love? *Guter Mensch, aber schlechter Musikant.*[17]

TROFIMOV [*claps* PISHCHIK *on the shoulder*].   Good old horse!

CHARLOTTE.   Attention, please. One more trick. [*She takes a rug from a chair.*] Here's a very good rug. I'd like to sell it. [*Shaking it.*] Who wants to buy it?
960 PISHCHIK [*surprised*].   Good Lord!

CHARLOTTE.   *Eins, zwei, drei!*

[*Quickly snatching up the rug, which she had let fall, she reveals* ANYA *standing behind it.* ANYA *curtseys, runs to her mother, embraces her, and runs back to the ballroom, amid general enthusiasm.*]

MRS. RANEVSKY [*applauding*].   Bravo, bravo!

CHARLOTTE.   Now, once more. *Eins, zwei, drei!* [*Lifts the rug; behind it stands* VARYA, *who bows.*]

PISHCHIK [*surprised*].   Good Lord!

CHARLOTTE.   The end! [*Throws the rug over* PISHCHIK, *curtseys, and runs off to the ballroom.*]

PISHCHIK [*running after her*].   The hussy! What a woman, eh? What a woman! [*Goes out.*]

970 MRS. RANEVSKY.   Still no Leonid. I can't understand what he can be doing in town all this time. It must be over now. Either the estate has been sold or the auction didn't take place. Why keep us in suspense so long?

VARYA [*trying to comfort her*].   I'm certain Uncle must have bought it.

TROFIMOV [*sarcastically*].   Oh, to be sure!

VARYA.   Our great-aunt sent him power of attorney to buy the estate in her name and transfer the mortgage to her. She's done it for Anya's sake. God will help us and Uncle will buy it. I'm sure of it.

MRS. RANEVSKY.   Your great-aunt sent fifteen thousand to buy the estate in her name. She doesn't trust us—but the money wouldn't even pay the
980   interest. [*She covers her face with her hands.*] My whole future is being decided today, my future. . . .

TROFIMOV [*teasing* VARYA].   Mrs. Lopakhin!

------

[17] "A good man, but a bad musician." A line by Heinrich Heine (1799–1856), a German poet.

VARYA [*crossly*].   Eternal student! Expelled twice from the university, weren't you?

MRS. RANEVSKY.   Why are you so cross, Varya? He's teasing you about Lopakhin. Well, what of it? Marry Lopakhin if you want to. He is a nice, interesting man. If you don't want to, don't marry him. Nobody's forcing you, darling.

990 VARYA.   I regard such a step seriously, Mother dear. I don't mind being frank about it: He is a nice man, and I like him.

MRS. RANEVSKY.   Well, marry him. What are you waiting for? That's what I can't understand.

VARYA.   But, Mother dear, I can't very well propose to him myself, can I? Everybody's been talking to me about him for the last two years. Everyone! But he either says nothing or makes jokes. I quite understand. He's making money. He has his business to think of, and he hasn't time for me. If I had any money, just a little, a hundred rubles, I'd give up everything and go right away as far as possible. I'd have gone into a convent.

TROFIMOV.   Wonderful!

1000 VARYA [*to* TROFIMOV].   A student ought to be intelligent! [*In a gentle voice, through tears.*] How plain you've grown, Peter! How you've aged! [*To* MRS. RANEVSKY, *no longer crying.*] I can't live without having something to do, Mother! I must be doing something all the time.

[*Enter* YASHA.]

YASHA [*hardly able to restrain his laughter*].   Yepikhodov's broken a billiard cue! [*Goes out.*]

VARYA.   What's Yepikhodov doing here? Who gave him permission to play billiards? Can't understand these people! [*Goes out.*]

MRS. RANEVSKY.   Don't tease her, Peter. Don't you see she is unhappy enough already?

1010 TROFIMOV.   She's a bit too conscientious. Pokes her nose into other people's affairs. Wouldn't leave me and Anya alone all summer. Afraid we might have an affair. What business is it of hers? Besides, the idea never entered my head. Such vulgarity is beneath me. We are above love.

MRS. RANEVSKY.   So, I suppose I must be beneath love. [*In great agitation.*] Why isn't Leonid back? All I want to know is: Has the estate been sold or not? Such a calamity seems so incredible to me that I don't know what to think. I'm completely at a loss. I feel like screaming, like doing something silly. Help me, Peter. Say something. For God's sake, say something!

1020 TROFIMOV.   What does it matter whether the estate's been sold today or not? The estate's been finished and done with long ago. There's no turning back. The road to it is closed. Stop worrying, my dear. You mustn't deceive yourself. Look the truth straight in the face for once in your life.

MRS. RANEVSKY.   What truth? You can see where truth is and where it isn't, but I seem to have gone blind. I see nothing. You boldly solve all important problems, but tell me, dear boy, isn't it because you're young, isn't it because you haven't had the time to live through the consequences of any of your problems? You look ahead boldly, but isn't it because you neither see nor expect anything terrible to happen to you, because life is still hidden from your young eyes? You're bolder, more honest, you see much

1030   deeper than any of us, but think carefully, try to understand our position,
be generous even a little, spare me. I was born here, you know. My father
and mother lived here, and my grandfather also. I love this house. Life has
no meaning for me without the cherry orchard, and if it has to be sold,
then let me be sold with it. [*Embraces* TROFIMOV *and kisses him on the forehead.*] Don't you see, my son was drowned here. [*Weeps.*] Have pity on me,
my good, kind friend.

TROFIMOV.   You know I sympathize with you with all my heart.

MRS. RANEVSKY.   You should have put it differently. [*Takes out her handkerchief. A telegram falls on the floor.*] My heart is so heavy today. You can't
1040   imagine how heavy. I can't bear this noise. The slightest sound makes me
shudder. I'm trembling all over. I'm afraid to go to my room. I'm terrified
to be alone. . . . Don't condemn me, Peter. I love you as my own son. I'd
gladly let Anya marry you, I swear I would. Only, my dear, boy, you must
study, you must finish your course at the university. You never do anything. You just drift from one place to another. That's what's so strange.
Isn't that so? Isn't it? And you should do something about your beard.
Make it grow, somehow. [*Laughs.*] You are funny!

TROFIMOV [*picking up the telegram*].   I have no wish to be handsome.

MRS. RANEVSKY.   That telegram's from Paris. I get one every day. Yesterday
1050   and today. That wild man is ill again, in trouble again. He asks me to
forgive him. He begs me to come back to him, and I really think I ought
to be going back to Paris to be near him for a bit. You're looking very
stern, Peter. But what's to be done, my dear boy? What am I to do? He's
ill. He's lonely. He's unhappy. Who'll look after him there? Who'll stop
him from doing something silly? Who'll give him his medicine at the right
time? And, why hide it? Why be silent about it? I love him. That's obvious.
I love him. I love him. He's a millstone round my neck and he's dragging
me down to the bottom with him, but I love the millstone, and I can't live
without it. [*Presses* TROFIMOV'*s hand.*] Don't think badly of me, Peter. Don't
1060   say anything. Don't speak.

TROFIMOV [*through tears*].   For God's sake—forgive my being so frank, but he
left you penniless!

MRS. RANEVSKY.   No, no, no! You mustn't say that. [*Puts her hands over her
ears.*]

TROFIMOV.   Why, he's a scoundrel, and you're the only one who doesn't seem
to know it. He's a petty scoundrel, a nonentity.

MRS. RANEVSKY [*angry but restraining herself*].   You're twenty-six or twenty-
seven, but you're still a schoolboy—a sixth-grade schoolboy!

TROFIMOV.   What does that matter?

1070 MRS. RANEVSKY.   You ought to be a man. A person of your age ought to
understand people who are in love. You ought to be in love yourself. You
ought to fall in love. [*Angrily.*] Yes! Yes! And you're not so pure either.
You're just a prude, a ridiculous crank, a freak!

TROFIMOV [*horrified*].   What is she saying?

MRS. RANEVSKY.   "I'm above love!" You're not above love, you're simply what
Firs calls a nincompoop. Not have a mistress at your age!

TROFIMOV [*horrified*].   This is terrible! What is she saying? [*Walks quickly into
the ballroom, clutching his head.*] It's dreadful! I can't! I'll go away! [*Goes out*

1080 *but immediately comes back.*] All is at an end between us! [*Goes out into the hall.*]

MRS. RANEVSKY [*shouting after him*].   Peter, wait! You funny boy, I was only joking. Peter!

[*Someone can be heard running rapidly up the stairs and then suddenly falling downstairs with a crash.* ANYA *and* VARYA *scream, followed immediately by laughter.*]

MRS. RANEVSKY.   What's happened?

ANYA [*laughing, runs in*].   Peter's fallen down the stairs! [*Runs out.*]

MRS. RANEVSKY.   What an eccentric! [*The* STATIONMASTER *stands in the middle of the ballroom and recites "The Fallen Woman" by Alexey Tolstoy.*[18] *The others listen. But he has hardly time to recite a few lines when the sound of a waltz comes from the entrance hall, and the recitation breaks off. Everybody dances.* TROFIMOV, ANYA, VARYA, *and* MRS. RANEVSKY *enter from the hall.*] Well, Peter dear, you

1090 pure soul, I'm sorry. . . . Come, let's dance. [*Dances with* TROFIMOV.]

[ANYA *and* VARYA *dance together.* FIRS *comes in and stands his walking stick near the side door.* YASHA *has also come in from the drawing room and is watching the dancing.*]

YASHA.   Well, Grandpa!

FIRS.   I'm not feeling too well. We used to have generals, barons, and admirals at our dances before, but now we send for the post office clerk and the stationmaster. Even they are not too keen to come. Afraid I'm getting weak. The old master, the mistress's grandfather that is, used to give us powdered sealing wax for medicine. It was his prescription for all illnesses. I've been taking sealing wax every day for the last twenty years or more. That's perhaps why I'm still alive.

YASHA.   You make me sick, Grandpa. [*Yawns.*] I wish you was dead.

1100 FIRS.   Ugh, you nincompoop! [*Mutters.*]

[TROFIMOV *and* MRS. RANEVSKY *dance in the ballroom and then in the drawing room.*]

MRS. RANEVSKY.   *Merci.*[19] I think I'll sit down a bit. [*Sits down.*] I'm tired.

[*Enter* ANYA.]

ANYA [*agitated*].   A man in the kitchen said just now that the cherry orchard has been sold today.

MRS. RANEVSKY.   Sold? Who to?

ANYA.   He didn't say. He's gone away now.

[ANYA *dances with* TROFIMOV; *both go off to the ballroom.*]

YASHA.   Some old man gossiping, madam. A stranger.

FIRS.   Master Leonid isn't here yet. Hasn't returned. Wearing his light autumn overcoat. He might catch cold. Oh, these youngsters!

---

[18] Alexey Tolstoy (1817–1875) was a popular Russian poet and playwright. He is not Leo Tolstoy (1828–1910), Russian novelist, author of *War and Peace*.

[19] "Thank you."

MRS. RANEVSKY.   I shall die! Yasha, go and find out who bought it.

1110 YASHA.   But he's gone, the old man has. [*Laughs.*]

MRS. RANEVSKY [*a little annoyed*].   Well, what are you laughing at? What are you so pleased about?

YASHA.   Yepikhodov's a real scream. Such a fool. Twenty-two Calamities!

MRS. RANEVSKY.   Firs, where will you go if the estate's sold?

FIRS.   I'll go wherever you tell me, ma'am.

MRS. RANEVSKY.   You look awful! Are you ill? You'd better go to bed.

FIRS.   Me to bed, ma'am? [*Ironically.*] If I goes to bed, who's going to do the waiting? Who's going to look after everything? I'm the only one in the whole house.

1120 YASHA [*to* MRS. RANEVSKY.].   I'd like to ask you a favor, madam. If you go back to Paris, will you take me with you? It's quite impossible for me to stay here. [*Looking round, in an undertone.*] You know perfectly well yourself what an uncivilized country this is—the common people are so immoral—and besides, it's so boring here, the food in the kitchen is disgusting, and on top of it, there's that old Firs wandering about, muttering all sorts of inappropriate words. Take me with you, madam, please!

[*Enter* PISHCHIK.]

PISHCHIK.   May I have the pleasure of a little dance, fair lady? [MRS. RANEVSKY *goes with him.*] I'll have one hundred and eighty rubles off you all the same, my dear, charming lady. . . . I will, indeed. [*They dance.*] One hundred and

1130 eighty rubles. . . .

[*They go into the ballroom.*]

YASHA [*singing softly*].   "Could you but feel the agitated beating of my heart."

[*In the ballroom a woman in a gray top hat and check trousers can be seen jumping about and waving her arms. Shouts of "Bravo, Charlotte! Bravo!"*]

DUNYASHA [*stops to powder her face*].   Miss Anya told me to join the dancers because there are lots of gentlemen and very few ladies. But dancing makes me dizzy and my heart begins beating so fast. I say, Firs, the post office clerk said something to me just now that quite took my breath away.

[*The music becomes quieter.*]

FIRS.   What did he say to you?

DUNYASHA.   "You're like a flower," he said.

YASHA [*yawning*].   What ignorance! [*Goes out.*]

DUNYASHA.   Like a flower! I'm ever so delicate, and I love people saying nice

1140 things to me!

FIRS.   You'll come to a bad end, my girl. Mark my words.

[*Enter* YEPIKHODOV.]

YEPIKHODOV.   You seem to avoid me, Dunyasha. Just as if I was some insect. [*Sighs.*] Oh, life!

DUNYASHA.   What do you want?

YEPIKHODOV.   No doubt you may be right. [*Sighs.*] But, of course, if one looks at things from a certain point of view, then, if I may say so and if you'll forgive my frankness, you have reduced me absolutely to a state of mind. I know what Fate has in store for me. Every day some calamity overtakes me, but I got used to it so long ago that I just look at my Fate and smile.

1150   You gave me your word, and though I—

DUNYASHA.   Let's talk about it some other time. Leave me alone now. Now, I am dreaming. [*Plays with her fan.*]

YEPIKHODOV.   Every day some calamity overtakes me and I—let me say it quite frankly—why, I just smile, laugh even.

[*Enter* VARYA *from the ballroom.*]

VARYA.   Are you still here, Simon! What an ill-mannered fellow you are, to be sure! [*To* DUNYASHA.] Be off with you, Dunyasha. [*To* YEPIKHODOV.] First you go and play billiards and break a cue, and now you wander about the drawing room as if you were a guest.

YEPIKHODOV.   It's not your place to reprimand me, if you don't mind my

1160   saying so.

VARYA.   I'm not reprimanding you. I'm telling you. All you do is drift about from one place to another without ever doing a stroke of work. We're employing an office clerk, but goodness knows why.

YEPIKHODOV [*offended*].   Whether I work or drift about, whether I eat or play billiards, is something which only people older than you, people who know what they're talking about, should decide.

VARYA.   How dare you talk to me like that? [*Flaring up.*] How dare you? I don't know what I'm talking about, don't I? Get out of here! This instant!

YEPIKHODOV [*cowed*].   Express yourself with more delicacy, please.

1170 VARYA [*beside herself*].   Get out of here this minute! Out! [*He goes toward the door, and she follows him.*] Twenty-two Calamities! Don't let me see you here again! Never set foot here again! [YEPIKHODOV *goes out. He can be heard saying behind the door. "I'll lodge a complaint."*] Oh, so you're coming back, are you? [*Picks up the stick which* FIRS *has left near the door.*] Come on, come on, I'll show you! Coming are you? Well, take that! [*Swings the stick as* LOPAKHIN *comes in.*]

LOPAKHIN.   Thank you very much!

VARYA [*angrily and derisively*].   I'm so sorry!

LOPAKHIN.   It's quite all right. Greatly obliged to you for the kind reception.

1180 VARYA.   Don't mention it. [*Walks away, then looks around and inquires gently.*] I didn't hurt you, did I?

LOPAKHIN.   Oh no, not at all. There's going to be an enormous bump on my head for all that.

[*Voices in the ballroom:* "LOPAKHIN's *arrived.* LOPAKHIN!"]

PISHCHIK.   Haven't heard from you or seen you for ages, my dear fellow! [*Embraces* LOPAKHIN.] Do I detect a smell of brandy, dear boy? We're doing very well here, too.

[*Enter* MRS. RANEVSKY.]

MRS. RANEVSKY.   Is it you, Lopakhin? Why have you been so long? Where's Leonid?

LOPAKHIN.   He came back with me. He'll be here in a moment.

1190 MRS. RANEVSKY [*agitated*].   Well, what happened? Did the auction take place? Speak, for heaven's sake!

LOPAKHIN [*embarrassed, fearing to betray his joy*].   The auction was over by four o'clock. We missed our train and had to wait till half past nine. [*With a deep sigh.*] Oh dear, I'm afraid I feel a little dizzy.

[*Enter* GAYEV. *He carries some parcels in his right hand and wipes away his tears with his left.*]

MRS. RANEVSKY.   What's the matter, Leonid? Well! [*Impatiently, with tears.*] Quick, tell me for heaven's sake!

GAYEV [*doesn't answer, only waves his hands resignedly; to* FIRS, *weeping*].   Here, take these—anchovies, Kerch herrings. . . I've had nothing to eat all day. I've had a terrible time. [*The door of the billiard room is open; the click of*
1200 *billiard balls can be heard and* YASHA's *voice: "Seven and eighteen!"* GAYEV's *expression changes. He is no longer crying.*] I'm awfully tired. Come and help me change, Firs.

[GAYEV *goes off through the ballroom to his own room, followed by* FIRS.]

PISHCHIK.   Well, what happened at the auction? Come, tell us!

MRS. RANEVSKY.   Has the cherry orchard been sold?

LOPAKHIN.   It has.

MRS. RANEVSKY.   Who bought it?

LOPAKHIN.   I bought it. [*Pause.* MRS. RANEVSKY *is crushed; she would have collapsed on the floor if she had not been standing near an armchair.* VARYA *takes the keys from her belt, throws them on the floor in the center of the drawing room, and*
1210 *goes out.*] I bought it! One moment, please, ladies and gentlemen. I feel dazed. I can't talk. . . . [*Laughs.*] Deriganov was already there when we got to the auction. Gayev had only fifteen thousand, and Deriganov began his bidding at once with thirty thousand over and above the mortgage. I realized the position at once and took up his challenge. I bid forty. He bid forty-five. He kept raising his bid by five thousand and I by adding another ten thousand. Well, it was soon over. I bid ninety thousand on top of the arrears, and the cherry orchard was knocked down to me. Now the cherry orchard is mine! Mine! [*Laughs loudly.*] Merciful heavens, the cherry orchard's mine! Come on, tell me, tell me I'm drunk. Tell me I'm out of
1220 my mind. Tell me I'm imagining it all. [*Stamps his feet.*] Don't laugh at me! If my father and my grandfather were to rise from their graves and see what's happened, see how their Yermolay, their beaten and half-literate Yermolay, Yermolay who used to run around barefoot in winter, see how that same Yermolay bought this estate, the most beautiful estate in the world! I've bought the estate where my father and grandfather were slaves, where they weren't even allowed inside the kitchen. I must be dreaming. I must be imagining it all. It can't be true. It's all a figment of your imagination, shrouded in mystery. [*Picks up the keys, smiling affectionately.*] She's thrown down the keys. Wants to show she's no longer the mistress
1230 here. [*Jingles the keys.*] Oh well, never mind. [*The band is heard tuning up.*] Hey you, musicians, play something! I want to hear you. Come, all of you!

Come and watch Yermolay Lopakhin take an axe to the cherry orchard. Watch the trees come crashing down. We'll cover the place with country cottages, and our grandchildren and great-grandchildren will see a new life springing up here. Strike up the music! [*The band plays.* MRS. RANEVSKY *has sunk into a chair and is weeping bitterly. Reproachfully.*] Why did you not listen to me? You poor dear, you will never get it back now. [*With tears.*] Oh, if only all this could be over soon, if only our unhappy, disjointed life could somehow be changed son.

1240 PISHCHIK [*takes his arm, in an undertone*].   She's crying. Let's go into the ball-room. Let's leave her alone. Come on. [*Takes his arm and leads him away to the ballroom.*]

LOPAKHIN.   What's the matter? You there in the band, play up, play up! Let's hear you properly. Let's have everything as I want it now. [*Ironically.*] Here comes the new landowner, the owner of the cherry orchard! [*Knocks against a small table accidentally and nearly knocks over the candelabra.*] I can pay for everything!

[LOPAKHIN *goes out with* PISHCHIK. *There is no one left in the ballroom except* MRS. RANEVSKY, *who remains sitting in a chair, hunched up and crying bitterly. The band plays quietly.* ANYA *and* TROFIMOV *come in quickly.* ANYA *goes up to her mother and kneels in front of her.* TROFIMOV *remains standing by the entrance to the ballroom.*]

ANYA.   Mother, Mother, why are you crying? My dear, good, kind Mother, my darling Mother, I love you; God bless you, Mother. The cherry or-
1250   chard is sold. It's gone. That's true, quite true, but don't cry, Mother. You still have your life ahead of you, and you've still got your kind and pure heart. . . . Come with me, darling. Come. Let's go away from here. We shall plant a new orchard, an orchard more splendid than this one. You will see it, you will understand, and joy, deep, serene joy, will steal into your heart, sink into it like the sun in the evening, and you will smile, Mother! Come, darling! Come!

ACT IV

The scene is the same as in the first act. There are no curtains at the windows or pictures on the walls. Only a few pieces of furniture are left. They have been stacked in one corner as if for sale. There is a feeling of emptiness. Near the front door and at the back of the stage, suitcases, traveling bags, etc., are piled up. The door on the left is open and the voices of VARYA *and* ANYA *can be heard.* LOPAKHIN *stands waiting.* YASHA *is holding a tray with glasses of champagne. In the entrance hall* YEPIKHODOV *is tying up a box. There is a constant murmur of voices offstage, the voices of peasants who have come to say good-bye.* GAYEV's *voice is heard: "Thank you, my dear people, thank you."*

YASHA.   The peasants have come to say good-bye. In my opinion, sir, the peasants are decent enough fellows, but they don't understand a lot.

[*The murmur of voices dies away.* MRS. RANEVSKY *and* GAYEV *come in through the entrance hall; she is not crying, but she is pale. Her face is quivering. She cannot speak.*]

GAYEV. You gave them your purse, Lyuba. You shouldn't. You really
1260   shouldn't.
MRS. RANEVSKY. I—I couldn't help it. I just couldn't help it.

[*Both go out.*]

LOPAKHIN [*calling through the door after them*]. Please take a glass of champagne. I beg you. One glass each before we leave. I forgot to bring any
from town, and I could find only one bottle at the station. Please! [*Pause.*]
Why, don't you want any? [*Walks away from the door.*] If I'd known, I
wouldn't have bought it. Oh well, I don't think I'll have any, either. [YASHA
puts the tray down carefully on a chair.] You'd better have some, Yasha.
YASHA. Thank you, sir. To those who're going away! And here's to you, sir,
who're staying behind! [*Drinks.*] This isn't real champagne. Take it from
1270   me, sir.
LOPAKHIN. Paid eight rubles a bottle. [*Pause.*] Damn cold here.
YASHA. The stoves haven't been lit today. We're leaving, anyway. [*Laughs.*]
LOPAKHIN. What's so funny?
YASHA. Oh, nothing. Just feeling happy.
LOPAKHIN. It's October, but it might just as well be summer: it's so sunny and
calm. Good building weather. [*Glances at his watch and calls through the
door.*] I say, don't forget the train leaves in forty-seven minutes. In twenty
minutes we must start for the station. Hurry up!

[TROFIMOV *comes in from outside, wearing an overcoat.*]

TROFIMOV. I think it's about time we were leaving. The carriages are at the
1280   door. Where the blazes could my galoshes have got to? Disappeared without a trace. [*Through the door.*] Anya, I can't find my galoshes! Can't find
them!
LOPAKHIN. I've got to go to Kharkov. I'll leave with you on the same train.
I'm spending the winter in Kharkov. I've been hanging about here too
long. I'm worn out with having nothing to do. I can't live without work.
Don't know what to do with my hands. They just flop about as if they
belonged to someone else.
TROFIMOV. Well, we'll soon be gone and then you can resume your useful
labors.
1290 LOPAKHIN. Come on, have a glass of champagne.
TROFIMOV. No, thank you.
LOPAKHIN. So you're off to Moscow, are you?
TROFIMOV. Yes. I'll see them off to town, and I'm off to Moscow tomorrow.
LOPAKHIN. I see. I suppose the professors have stopped lecturing while
you've been away. They're all waiting for you to come back.
TROFIMOV. Mind your own business.
LOPAKHIN. How many years have you been studying at the university?
TROFIMOV. Why don't you think of something new for a change? This is
rather old, don't you think?—and stale. [*Looking for his galoshes.*] I don't
1300   suppose we shall ever meet again, so let me give you a word of advice as
a farewell gift: Don't wave your arms about. Get rid of the habit of throwing your arms about. And another thing: To build country cottages in the
hope that in the fullness of time vacationers will become landowners is the

same as waving your arms about. Still, I like you in spite of everything. You've got fine sensitive fingers, like an artist's, and you have a fine sensitive soul.

LOPAKHIN [*embraces him*].   My dear fellow, thanks for everything. Won't you let me lend you some money for your journey? You may need it.

TROFIMOV.   Need it? Whatever for?

1310   LOPAKHIN.   But you haven't any, have you?

TROFIMOV.   Oh, but I have. I've just got some money for a translation. Got it here in my pocket. [*Anxiously.*] Where could those galoshes of mine have got to?

VARYA [*from another room*].   Oh, take your filthy things! [*Throws a pair of galoshes onto the stage.*]

TROFIMOV.   Why are you so cross, Varya? Good heavens, these are not my galoshes!

LOPAKHIN.   I had about three thousand acres of poppy sown last spring. Made a clear profit of forty thousand. When my poppies were in bloom,

1320   what a beautiful sight they were! Well, so you see, I made forty thousand and I'd be glad to lend you some of it because I can afford to. So why be so high and mighty? I'm a peasant. . . . I'm offering it to you without ceremony.

TROFIMOV.   Your father was a peasant, my father was a pharmacist, all of which proves exactly nothing. [LOPAKHIN *takes out his wallet.*] Put it back! Put it back! If you offered me two hundred thousand, I wouldn't accept it. I'm a free man. Everything you prize so highly, everything that means so much to all of you, rich or poor, has no more power over me than a bit of fluff blown about in the air. I can manage without you. I can pass you by.

1330   I'm strong and proud. Mankind is marching toward a higher truth, toward the greatest happiness possible on earth, and I'm in the front ranks!

LOPAKHIN.   Will you get there?

TROFIMOV.   I will. [*Pause.*] I will get there or show others the way to get there.

[*The sound of an axe striking a tree can be heard in the distance.*]

LOPAKHIN.   Well, good-bye, my dear fellow. Time to go. You and I are trying to impress one another, but life goes on regardless. When I work hard for hours on end, I can think more clearly, and then I can't help feeling that I, too, know what I live for. Have you any idea how many people in Russia exist goodness only knows why? However, no matter. It isn't they who make the world go round. I'm told Gayev has taken a job at the bank at six

1340   thousand a year. He'll never stick to it. Too damn lazy.

ANYA [*in the doorway*].   Mother asks you not to begin cutting down the orchard till she's gone.

TROFIMOV.   Really, haven't you any tact at all? [*Goes out through the hall.*]

LOPAKHIN.   Sorry, I'll see to it at once, at once! The damned idiots! [*Goes out after* TROFIMOV.]

ANYA.   Has Firs been taken to the hospital?

YASHA.   I told them to this morning. They must have taken him, I should think.

ANYA [*to* YEPIKHODOV, *who is crossing the ballroom*].   Please find out if Firs has

1350   been taken to the hospital.

YASHA [*offended*].   I told Yegor this morning. I haven't got to tell him a dozen times, have I?

YEPIKHODOV.   Old man Firs, if you want my final opinion, is beyond repair, and it's high time he was gathered to his fathers. So far as I'm concerned, I can only envy him. [*Puts a suitcase on a hatbox and squashes it.*] There, you see! I knew it. [*Goes out.*]

YASHA [*sneeringly*].   Twenty-two Calamities!

VARYA [*from behind the door*].   Has Firs been taken to the hospital?

ANYA.   He has.

1360   VARYA.   Why didn't they take the letter for the doctor?

ANYA.   We'd better send it on after him. [*Goes out.*]

VARYA [*from the next room*].   Where's Yasha? Tell him his mother's here. She wants to say good-bye to him.

YASHA [*waves his hand impatiently*].   Oh, that's too much!

[*All this time* DUNYASHA *has been busy with the luggage. Now that* YASHA *is alone, she goes up to him.*]

DUNYASHA.   You haven't even looked at me once, Yasha. You're going away, leaving me behind. [*Bursts out crying and throws her arms around his neck.*]

YASHA.   Must you cry? [*Drinks champagne.*] I'll be back in Paris in a week. Tomorrow we catch the express and off we go! That's the last you'll see of us. I can hardly believe it, somehow. *Vive la France!*[20] I hate it here. It

1370   doesn't suit me at all. It's not the kind of life I like. I'm afraid it can't be helped. I've had enough of all this ignorance. More than enough. [*Drinks champagne.*] So what's the use of crying? Behave yourself and you won't end up crying.

DUNYASHA [*powdering her face, looking in a hand mirror*].   Write to me from Paris, please. I did love you, Yasha, after all. I loved you so much. I'm such an affectionate creature, Yasha.

YASHA.   They're coming here. [*Busies himself around the suitcases, humming quietly.*]

[*Enter* MRS. RANEVSKY, GAYEV, ANYA, *and* CHARLOTTE.]

GAYEV.   We ought to be going. There isn't much time left. [*Looking at* YASHA.]

1380   Who's smelling of pickled herrings here?

MRS. RANEVSKY.   In another ten minutes we ought to be getting into the carriages. [*Looks round the room.*] Good-bye, dear house, good-bye, old grandfather house! Winter will pass, spring will come, and you won't be here any more. They'll have pulled you down. The things these walls have seen! [*Kisses her daughter affectionately.*] My precious one, you look radiant. Your eyes are sparkling like diamonds. Happy? Very happy?

ANYA.   Oh yes, very! A new life is beginning, Mother!

GAYEV [*gaily*].   It is, indeed. Everything's all right now. We were all so worried and upset before the cherry orchard was sold, but now, when every-

1390   thing has been finally and irrevocably settled, we have all calmed down and even cheered up. I'm a bank official now, a financier. Pot the red in

---

[20] "Long live France!"

the middle. As for you, Lyuba, say what you like, but you too are looking a lot better. There's no doubt about it.

Mrs. Ranevsky.   Yes, my nerves are better, that's true. [*Someone helps her on with her hat and coat.*] I sleep well. Take my things out, Yasha. It's time. [*To* Anya.] We'll soon be seeing each other again, darling. I'm going to Paris. I'll live there on the money your great-aunt sent from Yaroslayl to buy the estate—three cheers for Auntie!—but the money won't last long, I'm afraid.

1400 Anya.   You'll come home soon, Mother, very soon. I'm going to study, pass my school exams, and then I'll work and help you. We shall read all sorts of books together, won't we, Mother? [*Kisses her mother's hands.*] We shall read during the autumn evenings. We'll read lots and lots of books, and a new, wonderful world will open up to us. [*Dreamily.*] Oh, do come back, Mother!

Mrs. Ranevsky.   I'll come back, my precious. [*Embraces her daughter.*]

[*Enter* Lopakhin. Charlotte *quietly hums a tune.*]

Gayev.   Happy Charlotte! She's singing!

Charlotte [*picks up a bundle that looks like a baby in swaddling clothes*].   My darling baby, go to sleep, my baby. [*A sound of a baby crying is heard.*] Hush,
1410   my sweet, my darling boy. [*The cry is heard again.*] Poor little darling, I'm so sorry for you! [*Throws the bundle down.*] So you will find me another job, won't you? I can't go on like this.

Lopakhin.   We'll find you one, don't you worry.

Gayev.   Everybody's leaving us. Varya's going away. All of a sudden, we're no longer wanted.

Charlotte.   I haven't anywhere to live in town. I must go away. [*Sings quietly.*] It's all the same to me. . . .

[*Enter* Pishchik.]

Lopakhin.   The nine days' wonder!

Pishchik [*out of breath*].   Oh dear, let me get my breath back! I'm all in. Dear
1420   friends . . . a drink of water, please.

Gayev.   Came to borrow some money, I'll be bound. Not from me this time. Better make myself scarce. [*Goes out.*]

Pishchik.   Haven't seen you for ages, dearest lady. [*To* Lopakhin.] You here too? Glad to see you . . . man of immense intellect. . . . Here, that's for you, take it. [*Gives* Lopakhin *money.*] Four hundred rubles. That leaves eight hundred and forty I still owe you.

Lopakhin [*puzzled, shrugging his shoulders*].   I must be dreaming. Where did you get it?

Pishchik.   One moment . . . Terribly hot . . . Most extraordinary thing hap-
1430   pened. Some Englishmen came to see me. They found some kind of white clay on my land. [*To* Mrs. Ranevsky.] Here's four hundred for you too, beautiful ravishing lady. [*Gives her the money.*] The rest later. [*Drinks some water.*] Young fellow in the train just now was telling me that some—er— great philosopher advises people to jump off roofs. "Jump!" he says, and that'll solve all your problems. [*With surprise.*] Good Lord! More water, please.

LOPAKHIN. Who were these Englishmen?

PISHCHIK. I let them a plot of land with the clay on a twenty-four years' lease. And now you must excuse me, my friends. I'm in a hurry. Must be rushing off somewhere else. To Znoykov's, to Kardamonov's . . . Owe them all money. [*Drinks.*] Good-bye. I'll look in on Thursday.

MRS. RANEVSKY. We're just leaving for town. I'm going abroad tomorrow.

PISHCHIK. What? [*In a worried voice.*] Why are you going to town? Oh! I see! The furniture, the suitcases . . . Well, no matter. [*Through tears.*] No matter. Men of immense intellect, these Englishmen. . . . No matter. . . . No matter. I wish you all the best. May God help you. . . . No matter. Everything in this world comes to an end. [*Kisses* MRS. RANEVSKY'S *hand.*] When you hear that my end has come, remember the—er—old horse and say: Once there lived a man called Simeonov-Pishchik; may he rest in peace. Remarkable weather we've been having. . . . Yes. [*Goes out in great embarrassment, but immediately comes back and says, standing in the doorway.*] My Dashenka sends her regards. [*Goes out.*]

MRS. RANEVSKY. Well, we can go now. I'm leaving with two worries on my mind. One concerns Firs. He's ill. [*With a glance at her watch.*] We still have about five minutes.

ANYA. Firs has been taken to the hospital, Mother. Yasha sent him off this morning.

MRS. RANEVSKY. My other worry concerns Varya. She's used to getting up early and working. Now that she has nothing to do, she's like a fish out of water. She's grown thin and pale, and she's always crying, poor thing. [*Pause.*] You must have noticed it, Lopakhin. As you very well know, I'd always hoped to see her married to you. Indeed, everything seemed to indicate that you two would get married. [*She whispers to* ANYA, *who nods to* CHARLOTTE, *and they both go out.*] She loves you, you like her, and I simply don't know why you two always seem to avoid each other. I don't understand it.

LOPAKHIN. To tell you the truth, neither do I. The whole thing's odd somehow. If there's still time, I'm ready even now. . . . Let's settle it at once and get it over. I don't feel I'll ever propose to her without you here.

MRS. RANEVSKY. Excellent! Why, it shouldn't take more than a minute. I'll call her at once.

LOPAKHIN. And there's champagne here too. Appropriate to the occasion. [*Looks at the glass.*] They're empty. Someone must have drunk it. [YASHA *coughs.*] Lapped it up, I call it.

MRS. RANEVSKY [*excitedly*]. Fine! We'll go out, Yasha, *allez!*[21] I'll call her. [*Through the door.*] Varya, leave what you're doing and come here for a moment. Come on.

[MRS. RANEVSKY *goes out with* YASHA.]

LOPAKHIN [*glancing at his watch*]. Aye. . . .

[*Pause. Behind the door suppressed laughter and whispering can be heard. Enter* VARYA.]

---

[21] "Let's go!"

VARYA [*spends a long time examining the luggage*]. Funny, can't find it.
1480 LOPAKHIN. What are you looking for?
VARYA. Packed it myself, and can't remember.

[*Pause.*]

LOPAKHIN. Where are you going now, Varya?
VARYA. Me? To the Ragulins'. I've agreed to look after their house—to be their housekeeper, I suppose.
LOPAKHIN. In Yashnevo, isn't it? About fifty miles from here. [*Pause.*] Aye. . . . So life's come to an end in this house.
VARYA [*examining the luggage*]. Where can it be? Must have put it in the trunk. Yes, life's come to an end in this house. It will never come back.
LOPAKHIN. I'm off to Kharkov by the same train. Lots to see to there. I'm
1490 leaving Yepikhodov here to keep an eye on things. I've given him the job.
VARYA. Have you?
LOPAKHIN. This time last year it was already snowing, you remember. Now it's calm and sunny. A bit cold, though. Three degrees of frost.
VARYA. I haven't looked. [*Pause.*] Anyway, our thermometer's broken.

[*Pause. A voice from outside, through the door: "Mr.* LOPAKHIN!*"*]

LOPAKHIN [*as though he had long been expecting this call*]. Coming! [*Goes out quickly.*]

[VARYA *sits down on the floor, lays her head on a bundle of clothes, and sobs quietly. The door opens and* MRS. RANEVSKY *comes in cautiously.*]

MRS. RANEVSKY. Well? [*Pause.*] We must go.
VARYA [*no longer crying, dries her eyes*]. Yes, it's time, Mother dear. I'd like to get to the Ragulins' today, I only hope we don't miss the train.
1500 MRS. RANEVSKY [*calling through the door*]. Anya, put your things on.

[*Enter* ANYA, *followed by* GAYEV *and* CHARLOTTE. GAYEV *wears a warm overcoat with a hood.* SERVANTS *and* COACHMEN *come in.* YEPIKHODOV *is busy with the luggage.*]

MRS. RANEVSKY. Now we can be on our way.
ANYA [*joyfully*]. On our way. Oh, yes!
GAYEV. My friends, my dear, dear friends, leaving this house for good, how can I remain silent, how can I, before parting from you, refrain from expressing the feelings which now pervade my whole being—
ANYA [*imploringly*]. Uncle!
VARYA. Uncle dear, please don't.
GAYEV [*dejectedly*]. Double the red into the middle. . . . Not another word!

[*Enter* TROFIMOV, *followed by* LOPAKHIN.]

TROFIMOV. Well, ladies and gentlemen, it's time to go.
1510 LOPAKHIN. Yepikhodov, my coat!
MRS. RANEVSKY. Let me sit down a minute. I feel as though I've never seen the walls and ceilings of this house before. I look at them now with such eagerness, with such tender emotion. . . .
GAYEV. I remember when I was six years old sitting on this window sill on Trinity Sunday and watching Father going to church.

MRS. RANEVSKY. Have all the things been taken out?

LOPAKHIN. I think so. [*To* YEPIKHODOV *as he puts on his coat.*] Mind, everything's all right here, Yepikhodov.

YEPIKHODOV [*in a hoarse voice*]. Don't you worry, sir.

1520 LOPAKHIN. What's the matter with your voice?

YEPIKHODOV. I've just had a drink of water and I must have swallowed something.

YASHA [*contemptuously*]. What ignorance!

MRS. RANEVSKY. There won't be a soul left in this place when we've gone.

LOPAKHIN. Not till next spring.

[VARYA *pulls an umbrella out of a bundle of clothes with such force that it looks as if she were going to hit someone with it;* LOPAKHIN *pretends to be frightened.*]

VARYA. Good heavens, you didn't really think that—

TROFIMOV. Come on, let's get into the carriages! It's time. The train will be in soon.

VARYA. There are your galoshes, Peter. By that suitcase. [*Tearfully.*] Oh, how
1530   dirty they are, how old. . . .

TROFIMOV [*putting on his galoshes*]. Come along, ladies and gentlemen.

[*Pause.*]

GAYEV [*greatly put out, afraid of bursting into tears*]. Train . . . station . . . in off into the middle pocket . . . double the white into the corner.

MRS. RANEVSKY. Come along!

LOPAKHIN. Is everyone here? No one left behind? [*Locks the side door on the left.*] There are some things in there. I'd better keep it locked. Come on!

ANYA. Good-bye, old house! Good-bye, old life!

TROFIMOV. Welcome new life!

[TROFIMOV *goes out with* ANYA. VARYA *casts a last look round the room and goes out unhurriedly.* YASHA *and* CHARLOTTE, *carrying her lap dog, go out.*]

LOPAKHIN. So, it's till next spring. Come along, ladies and gentlemen. Till
1540   we meet again. [*Goes out.*]

[MRS. RANEVSKY *and* GAYEV *are left alone. They seem to have been waiting for this moment. They fling their arms around each other, sobbing quietly, restraining themselves, as though afraid of being overheard.*]

GAYEV [*in despair*]. My sister! My sister!

MRS. RANEVSKY. Oh, my dear, my sweet, my beautiful orchard! My life, my youth, my happiness, good-bye! . . .

ANYA [*offstage, happily, appealingly*]. Mo-ther!

TROFIMOV [*offstage, happily, excited*]. Where are you?

MRS. RANEVSKY. One last look at the walls and the windows. Mother loved to walk in this room.

GAYEV. My sister, my sister!

ANYA [*offstage*]. Mo-ther!

1550 TROFIMOV [*offstage*]. Where are you?

MRS. RANEVSKY. We're coming.

[*They go out. The stage is empty. The sound of all the doors being locked is heard, then of carriages driving off. It grows quiet. The silence is broken by the muffled noise of an axe striking a tree, sounding forlorn and sad. Footsteps can be heard.* FIRS *appears from the door on the right. He is dressed, as always, in a jacket and white waistcoat. He is wearing slippers. He looks ill.*]

FIRS [*walks up to the door and tries the handle*]. Locked! They've gone. [*Sits down on the sofa.*] Forgot all about me. Never mind. Let me sit down here for a bit. Forgotten to put on his fur coat, the young master has. Sure of it. Gone off in his light overcoat. [*Sighs anxiously.*] I should have seen to it. . . . Oh, these youngsters! [*Mutters something which cannot be understood.*] My life's gone just as if I'd never lived. . . . [*Lies down.*] I'll lie down a bit. No strength left. Nothing's left. Nothing. Ugh, you—nincompoop! [*Lies motionless.*]

[*A distant sound is heard, which seems to come from the sky, the sound of a breaking string, slowly dying away, melancholy. It is followed by silence, broken only by the sound of an axe striking a tree far away in the orchard.*]

CURTAIN

[1904]

Critical Commentary on *The Cherry Orchard*

Toward the end of Act 2 of *The Cherry Orchard,* the characters hear a strange sound in the distance: "It seems to come from the sky, the sound of a breaking string, slowly dying away, melancholy." In the exchanges that follow, each character reflects briefly on the meaning of this sound. For Lopakhin, a merchant preoccupied with commerce, it is an indication that "a bucket must have broken somewhere far away in a coal mine." For the romantic aristocratic Gayev, it is more apt to be the cry of a heron, a notion that his scholarly antagonist Trofimov naturally rejects, describing the cry as that of an owl (the traditional symbol of wisdom). Somewhat surprisingly, however, the antiquated servant Firs puts forth the most thought-provoking suggestion. He says, "Same thing happened before the misfortune: the owl hooted and the samovar kept hissing." When asked "what misfortune," Firs replies, "Before they gave us [the serfs] our freedom."

Of course, we should not make the naïve mistake of taking Firs' view as Chekhov's. Chekhov came from peasant stock himself, but had risen from an impoverished childhood to become a successful doctor, a famous author, and a wealthy landowner. He shared none of Firs' nostalgic fondness for a past in which both man and master knew his proper place. Yet just *because* of these roots, Chekhov was capable of understanding the enormous changes that had been wrought in Russia by the emancipation of the serfs. Old manservants like Firs had lost their purpose in life; younger servants like Yasha and Dunyasha aspired to a level of aristocratic sophistication that was itself effete and doomed; and masses of displaced former serfs like the Hiker, who appears immediately after this exchange, wander the countryside hungry and ready for revolution.

The theme of the entire play is thus symbolized by this snapping string, for there had been since the time of "the misfortune" a rupture in Russian life, and the various citizens of the land must either adapt to the great changes taking place around them or be crushed by the weight of events. Indeed, the changes brewing in Czarist Russia motivate all of the action and percolate through the conversations of the characters. These conversations contain repeated allusions to the advent of the railroad, the suburbanization of the countryside, and the revolution that broods in the faces of the hungry and jobless peasants. Until 1861 serfs had made the great estates profitable, but once they were freed there was no one to do the manual labor—no one to harvest the fruit of the cherry orchard, no one to process it, and no one to carry it to market. The emancipation of the serfs fundamentally changed Russian society and doomed its effete aristocracy.

Thus, change is the subject of the play, and we see the importance of change not only in the allusions to grand historical events, but also in the mundane lives of the characters. Mme. Lyubov Andreyevna Ranevsky has been away from home for five years, and in the first moments of the play Lopakhin wonders "what she's like now." During her absence, the maid Dunyasha has gone through adolescence and changed so greatly that the footman Yasha fails to recognize her. During Lyubov's absence, the family nurse has died, Lopakhin has grown rich, and the mortgages on the family estate have grown so burdensome that the sale of the cherry orchard is imminent.

The play's title appropriately emphasizes its subject, for the cherry orchard, which has been so resistant to change that it was even mentioned in the Encyclopedia, is a symbol of stability, aristocracy, elegance, and beauty. But it also symbolizes an archaic and unproductive way of life—no one even remembers how to process its occasional harvest. Thus, the cherry orchard must give way before a new age dedicated to productivity, pragmatism, and profit.

While events in Russia are undergoing rapid change, the characters in the play are, for the most part, unable or unwilling to adapt to the times. They are always saying things such as, "you're just the same, Varya"; "You haven't changed a bit, have you, darling Leonid"; "and you, sir, are the same as ever;" and "Dear Mother is just the same as ever. Hasn't changed a bit. If you let her, she'd give away everything."

Apart from Lopakhin, all of Chekhov's characters are comic, ineffectual, and yet lovable people who are doomed to sorrow and declining fortunes because of their inability to adjust to the world around them. Thus, Lyubov Andreyevna remains a passionate and supremely generous woman even though her excesses of heart and hand are ruining her family. Gayev remains a liberal aristocrat of the 1880s twenty years after such notions have passed into oblivion. Pishchik remains a compulsively idle borrower despite the fact that such scrambling merely delays—but does not prevent—disaster. And Firs remains a devoted serf forty years after his liberation.

Even the younger characters, whom one might expect to be flexible, are frequently committed to potentially ruinous lifestyles. Anya seems as ready as her mother to embark upon an irresponsible series of love affairs. Varya is just as addicted to work as Lopakhin and just as unable as he to express her emotions and obtain love. Charlotte performs her futile slights of hand without knowing who she is or where she is going. Yepikhodov contemplates his "twenty-two Calamities," laments that he can't understand his own state of mind, and carries a revolver just in case he should want to shoot himself. Trofimov remains "the eternal student" twenty years after entering school. And Dunyasha repeatedly falls in love as if eager to be ruined by some cad like Yasha.

None of these characters is capable of productive work; none seems capable of growth and change; and none takes an active part in the transformation of Russia. Things change, situations change, but people—Chekhov seems to be saying—never change. Even so simple a task as taking the ailing Firs to a hospital is beyond the competencies of these people. At the end of the play, Firs is left behind—a solitary relic of the past imprisoned in an empty shell.

A Selective Bibliography on *The Cherry Orchard*

Anderson, Greta. "The Music of *The Cherry Orchard:* Repetitions in the Russian Text." *Modern Drama* 34 (1991): 340–50.

Barricelli, Jean-Pierre, ed. *Chekhov's Great Plays: A Critical Anthology.* New York: New York UP, 1981.

Beckerman, Bernard. "Dramatic Analysis and Literary Interpretation: *The Cherry Orchard* as Exemplum." *New Literary History* 2 (1971): 391–406.

Durkin, Andrew R. "*The Cherry Orchard* in English: An Overview." *Yearbook of Comparative and General Literature* 33 (1984): 74–82.

Fergusson, Francis. *The Idea of a Theater.* Princeton: Princeton UP, 1953, 174–90.

Foster, Verna A. "The Dramaturgy of Mood in *Twelfth Night* and *The Cherry Orchard.*" *Modern Language Quarterly* 48 (1987): 162–85.

Grawe, Paul H. *Comedy in Space, Time, and the Imagination.* Chicago: Nelson-Hall, 1983, 205–20.

Hahn, Beverly. *Chekhov: A Study of the Major Stories and Plays.* London: Cambridge UP, 1977.

———. "Chekhov: *The Cherry Orchard.*" *Critical Review* 16 (1973): 56–72.

Hubbs, Clayton A. and Joanna T. Hubbs. "The Goddess of Love and the Tree of Knowledge: Some Elements of Myth and Folklore in Chekhov's *The Cherry Orchard.*" *South Carolina Review* 14 (1982): 66–77.

Jackson, Robert Louis, ed. *Chekhov: A Collection of Critical Essays.* Englewood Cliffs, N.J.: Prentice-Hall, 1967.

Kelson, John. "Allegory and Myth in *The Cherry Orchard.*" *Western Humanities Review* 13 (Summer 1959): 321–24.

Kirk, Irina. *Anton Chekhov.* Boston: Twayne, 1981.

Kramer, Karl D. "Love and Comic Instability in *The Cherry Orchard.*" *Russian Literature and American Critics.* Ed. Kenneth N. Borstrom. Ann Arbor: U of Michigan, 1984, 295–307.

Laffitte, Sophie. *Chekhov: 1860–1904.* Trans. Moura Budberg and Gordon Latta. New York: Scribner's, 1973.

Latham, Jacqueline. "*The Cherry Orchard* as Comedy." *Educational Theatre Journal* 10 (March 1958): 21–29.

Magarshack, David. *Chekhov the Dramatist.* New York: Lehmann, 1952. 264–86.

Melchinger, Siegfried. *Anton Chekhov.* Trans. Edith Tarcov. New York: Ungar, 1972.

Peace, Richard. *Chekhov: A Study of Four Major Plays*. New Haven: Yale UP, 1983.

Pitcher, Harvey. *The Chekhov Play: A New Interpretation*. London: Chatto and Windus, 1973. 158–213.

Quintus, John Allen. "The Loss of Dear Things: Chekhov and Williams in Perspective." *English Language Notes* 18 (1981): 201–6.

Rayfield, Donald. *Chekhov: The Evolutions of His Art*. London: Elek, 1975. 219–29.

Reed, Walter. "*The Cherry Orchard* and *Hedda Gabler*." *Homer to Brecht: The European Epic and Dramatic Traditions*. Eds. Michael Seidel and Edward Mendelson. New Haven: Yale UP, 1977. 317–35.

Silverstein, Norman. "Chekhov's Comic Spirit and *The Cherry Orchard*." *Modern Drama* 1 (1958): 91–100.

Styan, John L. "The Cherry Orchard." *Critical Essays on Anton Chekhov*. Ed. Thomas Eekman. Boston: G. K. Hall, 1989. 192–200.

Tulloch, John. *Chekhov: A Structuralist Study*. London: Macmillan, 1980. 185–204.

Valency, Maurice. *The Breaking String: The Plays of Anton Chekhov*. New York: Oxford UP, 1966. 251–88.

Susan Glaspell (1882–1948)

TRIFLES

CHARACTERS

COUNTY ATTORNEY
MRS. PETERS, *the sheriff's wife*
SHERIFF HENRY PETERS

MR. HALE, *a neighbor*
MRS. HALE

The kitchen in the now abandoned farmhouse of JOHN WRIGHT, *a gloomy kitchen, and left without having been put in order—unwashed pans under the sink, a loaf of bread outside the breadbox, a dish towel on the table—other signs of incompleted work. At the rear the outer door opens, and the* SHERIFF *comes in, followed by the* COUNTY ATTORNEY *and* HALE. *The* SHERIFF *and* HALE *are men in middle life, the* COUNTY ATTORNEY *is a young man; all are much bundled up and go at once to the stove. They are followed by the two women—the* SHERIFF'S WIFE *first; she is a slight wiry woman, a thin nervous face.* MRS. HALE *is larger and would ordinarily be called more comfortable looking, but she is disturbed now and looks fearfully about as she enters. The women have come in slowly and stand close together near the door.*

COUNTY ATTORNEY [*rubbing his hands*].   This feels good. Come up to the fire, ladies.

MRS. PETERS [*after taking a step forward*].   I'm not—cold.

SHERIFF [*unbuttoning his overcoat and stepping away from the stove as if to mark the beginning of official business*].   Now, Mr. Hale, before we move things about, you explain to Mr. Henderson just what you saw when you came here yesterday morning.

COUNTY ATTORNEY.   By the way, has anything been moved? Are things just as you left them yesterday?

10 SHERIFF [*looking about*].   It's just the same. When it dropped below zero last night, I thought I'd better send Frank out this morning to make a fire for us—no use getting pneumonia with a big case on; but I told him not to touch anything except the stove—and you know Frank.

COUNTY ATTORNEY.   Somebody should have been left here yesterday.

SHERIFF.   Oh—yesterday. When I had to send Frank to Morris Center for that man who went crazy—I want you to know I had my hands full yesterday. I knew you could get back from Omaha by today, and as long as I went over everything here myself—

COUNTY ATTORNEY.   Well, Mr. Hale, tell just what happened when you came

20 here yesterday morning.

HALE.   Harry and I had started to town with a load of potatoes. We came along the road from my place; and as I got here, I said, "I'm going to see if I can't get John Wright to go in with me on a party telephone." I spoke to Wright about it once before, and he put me off, saying folks talked too much anyway, and all he asked was peace and quiet—I guess you know about how much he talked himself; but I thought maybe if I went to the house and talked about it before his wife, though I said to Harry that I didn't know as what his wife wanted made much difference to John—

COUNTY ATTORNEY. Let's talk about that later, Mr. Hale. I do want to talk
30 about that, but tell now just what happened when you got to the house.

HALE. I didn't hear or see anything; I knocked at the door, and still it was all quiet inside. I knew they must be up, it was past eight o'clock. So I knocked again, and I thought I heard somebody say, "Come in." I wasn't sure, I'm not sure yet, but I opened the door—this door [*indicating the door by which the two women are still standing*], and there in that rocker—[*pointing to it*] sat Mrs. Wright.

[*They all look at the rocker.*]

COUNTY ATTORNEY. What—was she doing?

HALE. She was rockin' back and forth. She had her apron in her hand and was kind of—pleating it.

40 COUNTY ATTORNEY. And how did she—look?

HALE. Well, she looked queer.

COUNTY ATTORNEY. How do you mean—queer?

HALE. Well, as if she didn't know what she was going to do next. And kind of done up.

COUNTY ATTORNEY. How did she seem to feel about your coming?

HALE. Why, I don't think she minded—one way or other. She didn't pay much attention. I said, "How do, Mrs. Wright, it's cold, ain't it?" And she said, "Is it?"—and went on kind of pleating at her apron. Well, I was surprised; she didn't ask me to come up to the stove, or to set down, but
50 just sat there, not even looking at me, so I said, "I want to see John." And then she—laughed. I guess you would call it a laugh. I thought of Harry and the team outside, so I said a little sharp: "Can't I see John?" "No," she says, kind o' dull like. "Ain't he home?" says I. "Yes," says she, "he's home." "Then why can't I see him?" I asked her, out of patience. " 'Cause he's dead," says she. *"Dead?"* says I. She just nodded her head, not getting a bit excited, but rockin' back and forth. "Why—where is he?" says I, not knowing what to say. She just pointed upstairs—like that [*himself pointing to the room above*]. I got up, with the idea of going up there. I walked from there to here—then I says, "Why, what did he die of?" "He died of a rope
60 around his neck," says she, and just went on pleatin' at her apron. Well, I went out and called Harry. I thought I might—need help. We went upstairs, and there he was lyin'—

COUNTY ATTORNEY. I think I'd rather have you go into that upstairs, where you can point it all out. Just go on now with the rest of the story.

HALE. Well, my first thought was to get that rope off. I looked . . . [*Stops, his face twitches.*] . . . but Harry, he went up to him, and he said, "No, he's dead all right, and we'd better not touch anything." So we went back downstairs. She was still sitting that same way. "Has anybody been notified?" I asked. "No," says she, unconcerned. "Who did this, Mrs. Wright?" said Harry.
70 He said it businesslike—and she stopped pleatin' of her apron. "I don't

know," she says. "You don't *know*?" says Harry. "No," says she. "Weren't you sleepin' in the bed with him?" says Harry. "Yes," says she, "but I was on the inside." Somebody slipped a rope round his neck and strangled him, and you didn't wake up?" says Harry. "I didn't wake up," she said after him. We must 'a looked as if we didn't see how that could be, for after a minute she said, "I sleep sound." Harry was going to ask her more questions, but I said maybe we ought to let her tell her story first to the coroner, or the sheriff, so Harry went fast as he could to Rivers' place, where there's a telephone.

80 COUNTY ATTORNEY.   And what did Mrs. Wright do when she knew that you had gone for the coroner?

HALE.   She moved from that chair to this over here . . . [*Pointing to a small chair in the corner.*] . . . and just sat there with her hands held together and looking down. I got a feeling that I ought to make some conversation, so I said I had come in to see if John wanted to put in a telephone, and at that she started to laugh, and then she stopped and looked at me—scared. [*The* COUNTY ATTORNEY, *who has had his notebook out, makes a note.*] I dunno, maybe it wasn't scared. I wouldn't like to say it was. Soon Harry got back, and then Dr. Lloyd came, and you, Mr. Peters, and so I guess that's all I

90   know that you don't.

COUNTY ATTORNEY   [*looking around*].   I guess we'll go upstairs first—and then out to the barn and around there. [*To the* SHERIFF.] You're convinced that there was nothing important here—nothing that would point to any motive?

SHERIFF.   Nothing here but kitchen things.

[*The* COUNTY ATTORNEY, *after again looking around the kitchen, opens the door of a cupboard closet. He gets up on a chair and looks on a shelf. Pulls his hand away, sticky.*]

COUNTY ATTORNEY.   Here's a nice mess.

[*The women draw nearer.*]

MRS. PETERS [*to the other woman*].   Oh, her fruit; it did freeze. [*To the* LAWYER.] She worried about that when it turned so cold. She said the fir'd go out and her jars would break.

100 SHERIFF.   Well, can you beat the women! Held for murder and worryin' about her preserves.

COUNTY ATTORNEY.   I guess before we're through she may have something more serious than preserves to worry about.

HALE.   Well, women are used to worrying over trifles.

[*The two women move a little closer together.*]

COUNTY ATTORNEY [*with the gallantry of a young politician*].   And yet, for all their worries, what would we do without the ladies? [*The women do not unbend. He goes to the sink, takes a dipperful of water from the pail and, pouring it into a basin, washes his hands. Starts to wipe them on the roller towel, turns it for a cleaner place.*] Dirty towels! [*Kicks his foot against the pans under the sink.*] Not

110   much of a housekeeper, would you say, ladies?

MRS. HALE [*stiffly*].   There's a great deal of work to be done on a farm.

COUNTY ATTORNEY.   To be sure. And yet . . . [*With a little bow to her.*] . . . I know there are some Dickson county farmhouses which do not have such roller towels. [*He gives it a pull to expose its full length again.*]

MRS. HALE   Those towels get dirty awful quick. Men's hands aren't always as clean as they might be.

COUNTY ATTORNEY.   Ah, loyal to your sex, I see. But you and Mrs. Wright were neighbors. I suppose you were friends, too.

MRS. HALE [*shaking her head*].   I've not seen much of her of late years. I've not
120   been in this house—it's more than a year.

COUNTY ATTORNEY.   And why was that? You didn't like her?

MRS. HALE.   I liked her all well enough. Farmers' wives have their hands full, Mr. Henderson. And then—

COUNTY ATTORNEY.   Yes—?

MRS. HALE [*looking about*].   It never seemed a very cheerful place.

COUNTY ATTORNEY.   No—it's not cheerful. I shouldn't say she had the home-making instinct.

MRS. HALE.   Well, I don't know as Wright had, either.

COUNTY ATTORNEY.   You mean that they didn't get on very well?

130   MRS. HALE.   No, I don't mean anything. But I don't think a place'd be any cheerfuler for John Wright's being in it.

COUNTY ATTORNEY.   I'd like to talk more of that a little later. I want to get the lay of things upstairs now. [*He goes to the left, where three steps lead to a stair door.*]

SHERIFF.   I suppose anything Mrs. Peters does'll be all right. She was to take in some clothes for her, you know, and a few little things. We left in such a hurry yesterday.

COUNTY ATTORNEY.   Yes, but I would like to see what you take, Mrs. Peters, and keep an eye out for anything that might be of use to us.

140   MRS. PETERS.   Yes, Mr. Henderson.

[*The women listen to the men's steps on the stairs, then look about the kitchen.*]

MRS. HALE.   I'd hate to have men coming into my kitchen, snooping around and criticizing. [*She arranges the pans under sink which the* LAWYER *had shoved out of place.*]

MRS. PETERS.   Of course it's no more than their duty.

MRS. HALE.   Duty's all right, but I guess that deputy sheriff that came out to make the fire might have got a little of this on. [*Gives the roller towel a pull.*] Wish I'd thought of that sooner. Seems mean to talk about her for not having things slicked up when she had to come away in such a hurry.

MRS. PETERS [*who has gone to a small table in the left rear corner of the room, and
150   lifted one end of a towel that covers a pan*]. She had bread set. [*Stands still.*]

MRS. HALE [*eyes fixed on a loaf of bread beside the breadbox, which is on a low shelf at the other side of the room. Moves slowly toward it*].   She was going to put this in there. [*Picks up loaf, then abruptly drops it. In a manner of returning to familiar things.*] It's a shame about her fruit. I wonder if it's all gone. [*Gets up on the chair and looks.*] I think there's some here that's all right, Mrs. Peters. Yes—here; [*Holding it toward the window.*] this is cherries, too. [*Looking again.*] I declare I believe that's the only one. [*Gets down, bottle in her hand. Goes to the sink and wipes it off on the outside.*] She'll feel awful bad

after all her hard work in the hot weather. I remember the afternoon I put
160   up my cherries last summer. [*She puts the bottle on the big kitchen table, center
of the room, front table. With a sigh, is about to sit down in the rocking chair.
Before she is seated realizes what chair it is; with a slow look at it, steps back. The
chair, which she has touched, rocks back and forth.*]

MRS. PETERS.   Well, I must get those things from the front-room closet. [*She
goes to the door at the right, but after looking into the other room steps back.*] You
coming with me, Mrs. Hale? You could help me carry them.

[*They go into the other room; reappear,* MRS. PETERS *carrying a dress and skirt,* MRS.
HALE *following with a pair of shoes.*]

MRS. PETERS.   My, it's cold in there. [*She puts the cloth on the big table, and
hurries to the stove.*]

MRS. HALE [*examining the skirt*].   Wright was close. I think maybe that's why
170   she kept so much to herself. She didn't even belong to the Ladies' Aid. I
suppose she felt she couldn't do her part, and then you don't enjoy things
when you feel shabby. She used to wear pretty clothes and be lively, when
she was Minnie Foster, one of the town girls singing in the choir. But
that—oh, that was thirty years ago. This all you was to take in?

MRS. PETERS.   She said she wanted an apron. Funny thing to want, for there
isn't much to get you dirty in jail, goodness knows. But I suppose just to
make her feel more natural. She said they was in the top drawer in this
cupboard. Yes, here. And then her little shawl that always hung behind the
door. [*Opens stair door and looks.*] Yes, here it is. [*Quickly shuts door leading
180   upstairs.*]

MRS. HALE [*abruptly moving towards her*].   Mrs. Peters?

MRS. PETERS.   Yes, Mrs. Hale?

MRS. HALE.   Do you think she did it?

MRS. PETERS [*in a frightened voice*].   Oh, I don't know.

MRS. HALE.   Well, I don't think she did. Asking for an apron and her little
shawl. Worrying about her fruit.

MRS. PETERS [*starts to speak, glances up, where footsteps are heard in the room above.
In a low voice*].   Mr. Peters says it looks bad for her. Mr. Henderson is
awful sarcastic in a speech, and he'll make fun of her sayin' she didn't wake
190   up.

MRS. HALE.   Well, I guess John Wright didn't wake when they was slipping
that rope under his neck.

MRS. PETERS.   No, it's strange. It must have been done awful crafty and still.
They say it was such a—funny way to kill a man, rigging it all up like that.

MRS. HALE.   That's just what Mr. Hale said. There was a gun in the house.
He says that's what he can't understand.

MRS. PETERS.   Mr. Henderson said coming out that what was needed for the
case was a motive; something to show anger, or—sudden feeling.

MRS. HALE [*who is standing by the table*].   Well, I don't see any signs of anger
200   around here. [*She puts her hand on the dish towel which lies on the table, stands
looking down at the table, one half of which is clean, the other half messy.*] It's
wiped here. [*Makes a move as if to finish work, then turns and looks at loaf of
bread outside the breadbox. Drops towel. In that voice of coming back to familiar
things.*] Wonder how they are finding things upstairs? I hope she had it a

little more red-up there. You know, it seems kind of *sneaking.* Locking her up in town and then coming out here and trying to get her own house to turn against her!

MRS. PETERS.   But, Mrs. Hale, the law is the law.

MRS. HALE.   I s'pose 'tis. [*Unbuttoning her coat.*] Better loosen up your things,
210   Mrs. Peters. You won't feel them when you go out.

[MRS. PETERS *takes off her fur tippet,*[1] *goes to hang it on hook at back of room, stands looking at the under part of the small corner table.*]

MRS. PETERS.   She was piecing a quilt. [*She brings the large sewing basket, and they look at the bright pieces.*]

MRS. HALE.   It's log cabin pattern. Pretty, isn't it? I wonder if she was goin' to quilt or just knot it?

[*Footsteps have been heard coming down the stairs. The* SHERIFF *enters, followed by* HALE *and the* COUNTY ATTORNEY.]

SHERIFF.   They wonder if she was going to quilt it or just knot it. [*The men laugh, the women look abashed.*]

COUNTY ATTORNEY [*rubbing his hands over the stove*]. Frank's fire didn't do much up there, did it? Well, let's go out to the barn and get that cleared up.

[*The men go outside.*]

MRS. HALE [*resentfully*].   I don't know as there's anything so strange, our
220   takin' up our time with little things while we're waiting for them to get the evidence. [*She sits down at the big table, smoothing out a block with decision.*] I don't see as it's anything to laugh about.

MRS. PETERS [*apologetically*].   Of course they've got awful important things on their minds. [*Pulls up a chair and joins* MRS. HALE *at the table.*]

MRS. HALE [*examining another block.*].   Mrs. Peters, look at this one. Here, this is the one she was working on, and look at the sewing! All the rest of it has been so nice and even. And look at this! It's all over the place! Why, it looks as if she didn't know what she was about! [*After she has said this, they look at each other, then start to glance back at the door. After an instant* MRS. HALE
230   *has pulled at a knot and ripped the sewing.*]

MRS. PETERS.   Oh, what are you doing, Mrs. Hale?

MRS. HALE [*mildly*].   Just pulling out a stitch or two that's not sewed very good. [*Threading a needle.*] Bad sewing always made me fidgety.

MRS. PETERS [*nervously*].   I don't think we ought to touch things.

MRS. HALE.   I'll just finish up this end. [*Suddenly stopping and leaning forward.*] Mrs. Peters?

MRS. PETERS.   Yes, Mrs. Hale?

MRS. HALE.   What do you suppose she was so nervous about?

MRS. PETERS.   Oh—I don't know. I don't know as she was nervous. I some-
240   times sew awful queer when I'm just tired. [MRS. HALE *starts to say something,*

---

[1] A small scarf.

looks at Mrs. Peters, *then goes on sewing.*] Well, I must get these things wrapped up. They may be through sooner than we think. [*Putting apron and other things together.*] I wonder where I can find a piece of paper, and string.

Mrs. Hale.   In that cupboard, maybe.

Mrs. Peters [*looking in cupboard*].   Why, here's a birdcage. [*Holds it up.*] Did she have a bird, Mrs. Hale?

Mrs. Hale.   Why, I don't know whether she did or not—I've not been here for so long. There was a man around last year selling canaries cheap, but
250   I don't know as she took one; maybe she did. She used to sing real pretty herself.

Mrs. Peters [*glancing around*].   Seems funny to think of a bird here. But she must have had one, or why should she have a cage? I wonder what happened to it?

Mrs. Hale.   I s'pose maybe the cat got it.

Mrs. Peters.   No, she didn't have a cat. She's got that feeling some people have about cats—being afraid of them. My cat got in her room, and she was real upset and asked me to take it out.

Mrs. Hale.   My sister Bessie was like that. Queer, ain't it?

260 Mrs. Peters [*examining the cage*].   Why, look at this door. It's broke. One hinge is pulled apart.

Mrs. Hale [*looking, too*].   Looks as if someone must have been rough with it.

Mrs. Peters.   Why, yes. [*She brings the cage forward and puts it on the table.*]

Mrs. Hale.   I wish if they're going to find any evidence they'd be about it. I don't like this place.

Mrs. Peters.   But I'm awful glad you came with me, Mrs. Hale. It would be lonesome for me sitting here alone.

Mrs. Hale.   It would, wouldn't it? [*Dropping her sewing.*] But I tell you what I do wish, Mrs. Peters. I wish I had come over sometimes when *she* was
270   here. I—[*Looking around the room.*]—wish I had.

Mrs. Peters.   But of course you were awful busy, Mrs. Hale—your house and your children.

Mrs. Hale.   I could've come. I stayed away because it weren't cheerful—and that's why I ought to have come. I—I've never liked this place. Maybe because it's down in a hollow, and you don't see the road. I dunno what it is, but it's a lonesome place and always was. I wish I had come over to see Minnie Foster sometimes. I can see now—[*shakes her head*].

Mrs. Peters.   Well, you mustn't reproach yourself, Mrs. Hale. Somehow we just don't see how it is with other folks until—something comes up.

280 Mrs. Hale.   Not having children makes less work—but it makes a quiet house, and Wright out to work all day, and no company when he did come in. Did you know John Wright, Mrs. Peters?

Mrs. Peters.   Not to know him; I've seen him in town. They say he was a good man.

Mrs. Hale.   Yes—good; he didn't drink, and kept his word as well as most, I guess, and paid his debts. But he was a hard man, Mrs. Peters. Just to pass the time of day with him. [*Shivers.*] Like a raw wind that gets to the bone. [*Pauses, her eye falling on the cage.*] I should think she would 'a wanted a bird. But what do you suppose went with it?

290 MRS. PETERS.   I don't know, unless it got sick and died. [*She reaches over and swings the broken door, swings it again; both women watch it.*]

MRS. HALE.   You weren't raised round here, were you? [MRS. PETERS *shakes her head.*] You didn't know—her?

MRS. PETERS.   Not till they brought her yesterday.

MRS. HALE.   She—come to think of it, she was kind of like a bird herself—real sweet and pretty, but kind of timid and—fluttery. How—she—did—change. [*Silence; then as if struck by a happy thought and relieved to get back to everyday things.*] Tell you what, Mrs. Peters, why don't you take the quilt in with you? It might take up her mind.

300 MRS. PETERS.   Why, I think that's a real nice idea, Mrs. Hale. There couldn't possibly be any objection to it, could there? Now, just what would I take? I wonder if her patches are in here—and her things. [*They look in the sewing basket.*]

MRS. HALE.   Here's some red. I expect this has got sewing things in it. [*Brings out a fancy box.*] What a pretty box. Looks like something somebody would give you. Maybe her scissors are in here. [*Opens box. Suddenly puts her hand to her nose.*] Why—[MRS. PETERS *bends nearer, then turns her face away.*] There's something wrapped up in this piece of silk.

MRS. PETERS.   Why, this isn't her scissors.

310 MRS. HALE [*lifting the silk*].   Oh, Mrs. Peters—it's—[MRS. PETERS *bends closer.*]

MRS. PETERS.   It's the bird.

MRS. HALE [*jumping up*].   But, Mrs Peters—look at it. Its neck! Look at its neck! It's all—other side *to.*

MRS. PETERS.   Somebody—wrung—its neck.

[*Their eyes meet. A look of growing comprehension of horror. Steps are heard outside.* MRS. HALE *slips box under quilt pieces, and sinks into her chair. Enter* SHERIFF *and* COUNTY ATTORNEY. MRS. PETERS *rises.*]

COUNTY ATTORNEY [*as one turning from serious things to little pleasantries*].   Well, ladies, have you decided whether she was going to quilt it or knot it?

MRS. PETERS.   We think she was going to—knot it.

COUNTY ATTORNEY.   Well, that's interesting, I'm sure. [*Seeing the birdcage.*] Has the bird flown?

320 MRS. HALE [*putting more quilt pieces over the box*].   We think the—cat got it.

COUNTY ATTORNEY [*preoccupied*].   Is there a cat?

[MRS. HALE *glances in a quick covert way at* MRS. PETERS.]

MRS. PETERS.   Well, not now. They're superstitious, you know. They leave.

COUNTY ATTORNEY [*to* SHERIFF PETERS, *continuing an interrupted conversation*].   No sign at all of anyone having come from the outside. Their own rope. Now let's go up again and go over it piece by piece. [*They start upstairs.*] It would have to have been someone who knew just the—

[MRS. PETERS *sits down. The two women sit there not looking at one another, but as if peering into something and at the same time holding back. When they talk now, it is in the manner of feeling their way over strange ground, as if afraid of what they are saying, but as if they cannot help saying it.*]

MRS. HALE.   She liked the bird. She was going to bury it in that pretty box.

MRS. PETERS [*in a whisper*].   When I was a girl—my kitten—there was a boy
took a hatchet, and before my eyes—and before I could get there—[*covers*
330   *her face an instant*]. If they hadn't held me back, I would have—[*catches*
herself, looks upstairs where steps are heard, falters weakly]—hurt him.

MRS. HALE [*with a slow look around her*].   I wonder how it would seem never to
have had any children around. [*Pause.*] No, Wright wouldn't like the
bird—a thing that sang. She used to sing. He killed that, too.

MRS. PETERS [*moving uneasily*].   We don't know who killed the bird.

MRS. HALE.   I knew John Wright.

MRS. PETERS.   It was an awful thing was done in this house that night, Mrs.
Hale. Killing a man while he slept, slipping a rope around his neck that
choked the life out of him.

340 MRS. HALE.   His neck. Choked the life out of him.

[*Her hand goes out and rests on the birdcage.*]

MRS. PETERS [*with rising voice*].   We don't know who killed him. We don't
know.

MRS. HALE [*her own feeling not interrupted*].   If there'd been years and years of
nothing, then a bird to sing to you, it would be awful—still, after the bird
was still.

MRS. PETERS [*something within her speaking*].   I know what stillness is. When we
homesteaded in Dakota, and my first baby died—after he was two years
old, and me with no other then—

MRS. HALE [*moving*].   How soon do you suppose they'll be through, looking
350   for evidence?

MRS. PETERS.   I know what stillness is. [*Pulling herself back.*] The law has got
to punish crime, Mrs. Hale.

MRS. HALE [*not as if answering that*].   I wish you'd seen Minnie Foster when
she wore a white dress with blue ribbons and stood up there in the choir
and sang. [*A look around the room.*] Oh, I *wish* I'd come over here once in
a while! That was a crime! That was a crime! Who's going to punish that?

MRS. PETERS [*looking upstairs*].   We mustn't—take on.

MRS. HALE.   I might have known she needed help! I know how things can
be—for women. I tell you, it's queer, Mrs. Peters. We live close together,
360   and we live far apart. We all go through the same things—it's all just a
different kind of the same thing. [*Brushes her eyes, noticing the bottle of fruit,
reaches out for it.*] If I was you, I wouldn't tell her her fruit was gone. Tell
her it *ain't.* Tell her it's all right. Take this in to prove it to her. She—she
may never know whether it was broke or not.

MRS. PETERS [*takes the bottle, looks about for something to wrap it in; takes petticoat
from the clothes brought from the other room, very nervously begins winding this
around the bottle. In a false voice*].   My, it's a good thing the men couldn't
hear us. Wouldn't they just laugh! Getting all stirred up over a little thing
like a—dead canary. As if that could have anything to do with—with—
370   wouldn't they *laugh!*

[*The men are heard coming downstairs.*]

MRS. HALE [*under her breath*].   Maybe they would—maybe they wouldn't.
COUNTY ATTORNEY.   No, Peters, it's all perfectly clear except a reason for doing it. But you know juries when it comes to women. If there was some definite thing. Something to show—something to make a story about—a thing that would connect up with this strange way of doing it.

[*The women's eyes meet for an instant. Enter* HALE *from outer door.*]

MRS. HALE.   Well, I've got the team around. Pretty cold out there.
COUNTY ATTORNEY.   I'm going to stay here awhile by myself. [*To the* SHERIFF.] You can send Frank out for me, can't you? I want to go over everything. I'm not satisfied that we can't do better.
380 SHERIFF.   Do you want to see what Mrs. Peters is going to take in?

[*The* LAWYER *goes to the table, picks up the apron, laughs.*]

COUNTY ATTORNEY.   Oh, I guess they're not very dangerous things the ladies have picked up. [*Moves a few things about, disturbing the quilt pieces which cover the box. Steps back.*] No, Mrs. Peters doesn't need supervising. For that matter, a sheriff's wife is married to the law. Ever think of it that way, Mrs. Peters?
MRS. PETERS.   Not—just that way.
SHERIFF [*chuckling*].   Married to the law. [*Moves toward the other room.*] I just want you to come in here a minute, George. We ought to take a look at these windows.
390 COUNTY ATTORNEY [*scoffingly*].   Oh, windows!
SHERIFF.   We'll be right out, Mr. Hale.

[HALE *goes outside. The* SHERIFF *follows the* COUNTY ATTORNEY *into the other room. Then* MRS. HALE *rises, hands tight together, looking intensely at* MRS. PETERS, *whose eyes take a slow turn, finally meeting* MRS. HALE's. *A moment* MRS. HALE *holds her, then her own eyes point the way to where the box is concealed. Suddenly* MRS. PETERS *throws back quilt pieces and tries to put the box in the bag she is wearing. It is too big. She opens box, starts to take bird out, cannot touch it, goes to pieces, stands there helpless. Sound of a knob turning in the other room.* MRS. HALE *snatches the box and puts it in the pocket of her big coat. Enter* COUNTY ATTORNEY *and* SHERIFF.]

COUNTY ATTORNEY [*facetiously*].   Well, Henry, at least we found out that she was not going to quilt it. She was going to—what is it you call it, ladies?
MRS. HALE [*her hand against her pocket*].   We call it—knot it, Mr. Henderson.

[1916]

Critical Commentary on *Trifles*

Susan Glaspell's *Trifles* (1916) has established itself as a classic for good reason. In the first place, the play is an exciting murder mystery in which the audience is challenged to join with Mrs. Hale and Mrs. Peters in identifying the killer and piecing together the evidence on motive. While the elements of mystery keep the attention of the audience, the play also develops interesting psychological insights concerning the causes of the murder. As Mrs.

Hale and Mrs. Peters begin to reconstruct Minnie Foster Wright's bleak existence, they and the audience increasingly become aware of the shared plight of *all* women in a society dominated by men. The play's crisis and resolution turn not so much on the discovery of "whodunit" or even why she did it as on the dilemma of Mrs. Hale and Mrs. Peters. By concealing what they know and even destroying evidence that could be used against Mrs. Wright, they decide to take justice into their own hands, feeling that only women who have experienced what Mrs. Wright herself experienced can serve as a "jury of her peers."

In 1916 when this play was first produced, women lacked many of the legal and political rights of men. In only eleven states were women granted the right to vote in state elections; the nineteenth amendment to the Constitution, granting women the right to vote in national elections, was still unratified; women had few property rights independent of their husbands and often could not even serve as the legal guardians of their own children; in general, women were not admitted to law school and hence a woman like Minnie Foster Wright could not be represented by a member of her own sex, nor would her judge be a woman. Indeed, in most places women were not even allowed to serve as members of a jury.

Although the political and economic oppression of women was beginning to change at the time *Trifles* was written, the play continues even today to pack a feminist punch. In many parts of the country, the changes in the law have had little effect upon the traditional upbringing and roles of women. In Appalachia and Arkansas, in Texas and Michigan, indeed throughout the land in cities as on farms, many women continue to experience the hard labor, the slights, and the repression which in *Trifles* lead Mrs. Hale and Mrs. Peters to band together in a minor rebellion against the domination of men. Glaspell effectively underscores the subservient positions of these two protagonists by naming them only through their relationship to their husbands: they are referred to only as "Mrs. Hale" and "Mrs. Peters." We know neither their given names nor their maiden names—as if they had no existence prior to or apart from their marriages. In the case of Mrs. Wright, the murder of her husband is a direct rebellion against male domination and evidently earns her the right to be remembered as Minnie Foster. But even here Glaspell's references to her maiden identity are designed to emphasize the sad transformation that took place in Minnie Foster after her subjection to John Wright's callousness and indifference.

As the play's title indicates, much of the plot develops from the contrast between the "trifles" that occupy the attention of the women and the "awful important things" that concern the men. As it happens, the women's concern with trifles allows them to discover circumstantial evidence of Minnie's guilt and her motive. It is, for example, a trifle that Minnie is worried about her preserves and asks for an apron to wear while in jail. But these trifles indicate that she is indeed a good and industrious housekeeper. She was able to tell Mrs. Peters that her apron would be "in the top drawer in this cupboard" and that her shawl "always hung behind the door." Thus, the agitated state of mind of this good housekeeper is convincingly demonstrated by the general disarray of her household—the dirty towels, the unwashed pans, the half-wiped table, the unbaked bread, and the sloppy quilting. Clearly, something troubled Minnie so gravely on the day before Wright's death that she was unable to keep her mind on her routine chores. The women, in their concern for trifles, recognize this evidence for what it is, while the men, with their minds on important things, merely conclude that Minnie was "not much of a housekeeper."

In belittling the women for their concern over trifles, the men eventually cause them to band together with Minnie Foster and against male domination. This process takes place slowly over the course of the play, but it reaches a turning point in the discussion of the quilting. The three men come down from the upstairs bedroom just as Mrs. Hale is admiring Minnie's log cabin pattern and wondering "if she was goin' to quilt or just knot it." The sheriff mockingly repeats her words and the men all laugh before going out to the barn. Hitherto, the men had only made fun of *Minnie's* household concerns; now they are belittling Mrs. Hale as well, and she doesn't like it, commenting resentfully, "I don't know as there's anything so strange, our takin' up our time with little things while we're waiting for them to get the evidence. . . . I don't see as it's anything to laugh about." She then examines the quilt carefully and notices that the sewing on the last block is sloppy and unlike the rest. Perhaps realizing that this is evidence of Minnie's agitation and now siding with her fellow woman, Mrs. Hale pulls out the erratic stitching and begins to redo it.

Mrs. Peters, the wife of the sheriff, does not reach the same state of covert rebellion until she and Mrs. Hale have pieced together Minnie's motive like a quilt composed of fragments and scraps. They realize how lonely Minnie must have been in a depressing home without children and with a cold, hard man for a husband. They see the parallels between Minnie herself and the bird she had bought for comfort and companionship. And they discover the empty birdcage with the violently broken hinge and the bird itself with its neck wrung. All of this is particularly meaningful for Mrs. Peters. She is "a slight wiry woman, a thin nervous face," and her life has at times been as empty as Minnie's. She remembers how lonesome she felt in Dakota when her first child died and she remembers how murderously she felt as a child when a boy killed her kitten with a hatchet. Even before she has consciously expressed these emotions, she feels them. And hence, she too begins to side with and protect Minnie when the county attorney asks, "(. . . *as one turning from serious things to little pleasantries*). Well, ladies, have you decided whether she was going to quilt it or knot it?" Her response, "We think she was going to—knot it," is psychologically revealing. In knotting a quilt, the squares of fabric are joined by yarn knots only at the corners; in true quilting, the squares are sewn all the way around. Clearly, Minnie was going to quilt it rather than knot it. Why does Mrs. Peters not say so? Two possibilities present themselves. First, the men already believe that Minnie was a poor homemaker; by telling them that Minnie was taking the easy, sloppy way in piecing her quilt, Mrs. Peters may be trying to keep them from recognizing how "trifles" like the dirty towels and unbaked bread might be used "to get her own house to turn against her." Perhaps, too, Mrs. Peters is tired of being laughed at for being a woman and is returning the men's mockery with a subtle twist of her own. She evidently feels that these self-important men will never bother to check the quilting, or that if they did, they would not recognize the significance of such trifling distinctions as quilting it or knotting it.

The matter of the quilting comes up for a third time in the very last lines of the play, and there it is again used to emphasize the subtle rebellion of these women against all men. They have just conspired in hiding the quilting box with the dead canary in it. Without this evidence of motive, they know that Minnie Foster has a much better chance of being acquitted of the murder of her husband. The county attorney, having found no evidence of motive, turns facetiously and says, "Well, Henry, at least we found out that she was not going to quilt it. She was going to—what is it you call it, ladies?" Mrs. Hale responds, with her hand against the pocket concealing the canary, "We call it—knot it, Mr. Henderson." Her response, confirming that of Mrs. Peters, reiterates her role in conspiring to help Minnie and dryly mocks male ignorance. But it may also do more. Is there not also an element of truth in her words? While Minnie may not have been going to knot the quilt, she did in fact knot the cord around her husband's neck. Yet in giving a response that, on so many levels, the county attorney cannot understand, Mrs. Hale is also rendering a verdict of innocent ("not it") to the charge of murder against Minnie Foster. Thus, in this play only women are capable of collecting the evidence concerning the death of John Wright and only women, a jury of Minnie's peers, are capable of evaluating it fairly. When they do so, they find that Minnie Foster was a victim of her husband and her society. If she did indeed choke the life out of John Wright one evening, it was only because he had choked the life out of her for many years.

A Selective Bibliography on *Trifles*

Alkalay-Gut, Karen. "A Jury of Her Peers: The Importance of Trifles." *Studies in Short Fiction* 21 (1984): 1–10.

Ben-Zvi, Linda. " 'Murder, She Wrote': The Genesis of Susan Glaspell's *Trifles*." *Theatre Journal* 44.2 (1992): 141–52.

———. "Susan Glaspell and Eugene O'Neill." *Eugene O'Neill Newsletter* 6.2 (1982): 21–29.

Bigsby, C.W.E. "Introduction." *Plays by Susan Glaspell*. Cambridge, Eng.: Cambridge UP, 1987. 1–12

Brater, Enoch, ed. *Feminine Focus: The New Women Playwrights*. New York: Oxford UP, 1989.

Brown, Janet. *Feminist Drama: Definition and Critical Analysis*. Metuchen, NJ: Scarecrow, 1979.

Dickinson, Thomas H. *Playwrights of the New American Theatre*. New York: Macmillan, 1925. 208–18.

Dymkowski, Christine. "On the Edge: The Plays of Susan Glaspell." *Modern Drama* 31 (March 1988): 91–105.

Kolodny, Annette. "A Map for Rereading: Or, Gender and the Interpretation of Literary Texts." *New Literary History* 11 (1980): 451–67.

Kriegel, Harriet. *Women in Drama*. New York: NAL, 1975. 341–55.

Mael, Phyllis. " 'Trifles': The Path to Sisterhood." *Literature–Film Quarterly* 17.4 (1989): 281–4.

Mustazza, Leonard. "Generic Translation and Thematic Shift in Susan Glaspell's *Trifles* and *A Jury of Her Peers*." *Studies in Short Fiction* 26.4 (1989): 489–96.

Natalle, Elizabeth J. *Feminist Theatre: A Study in Persuasion*. Metuchen, NJ: Scarecrow, 1985.

Noe, Marcia. "Region as Metaphor in the Plays of Susan Glaspell," *Western Illinois Regional Studies* 4.1 (1981): 77–85.

———. *Susan Glaspell: A Voice from the Heartland*. Macomb: Western Illinois U, 1983.

Schlueter, June, ed. *Modern American Drama: The Female Canon*. Rutherford: Fairleigh Dickinson UP, 1990.

Smith, Beverly A. "Women's Work—Trifles? The Skill and Insight of Playwright Susan Glaspell." *International Journal of Women's Studies* 5 (1982): 172–84.

Stein, Karen. "The Women's World of Glaspell's *Trifles*." *Women in American Theatre*. Ed. Helen K. Chinoy and Linda W. Jenkins. New York: Theater Communications Group, 1981. 251–54.

Stowell, Sheila. *A Stage of Their Own: Feminist Playwrights of the Suffrage Era*. Ann Arbor: U of Michigan P, 1992.

Sutherland, Cynthia. "American Women Playwrights as Mediators of the 'Woman Problem.' " *Modern Drama* 21 (1976): 319–36.

Waterman, Arthur. *Susan Glaspell*. New York: Twayne, 1966.

———. "Susan Glaspell and the Provincetown." *Modern Drama* 7 (1964): 174–84.

———. "Susan Glaspell (1882?–1948)." *American Literary Realism* 4 (Spring 1971): 183–91.

Luigi Pirandello 1867–1936

SIX CHARACTERS IN SEARCH OF AN AUTHOR:

A PLAY IN THE MAKING

Translated by Frederick May[1]

THE CHARACTERS OF THE PLAY IN THE MAKING

THE FATHER
THE MOTHER
THE STEPDAUGHTER
THE SON

THE BOY *(non-speaking)*
THE LITTLE GIRL *(non-speaking)*
MADAM PACE *(who is called into being)*

THE ACTORS IN THE COMPANY

THE PRODUCER
THE LEADING LADY
THE LEADING MAN
THE SECOND FEMALE LEAD*
THE INGENUE
THE JUVENILE LEAD
OTHER ACTORS AND ACTRESSES

THE STAGE-MANAGER
THE PROMPTER
THE PROPERTY MAN
THE FOREMAN OF THE STAGE CREW
THE PRODUCER'S SECRETARY
THE COMMISSIONAIRE
STAGE HANDS AND OTHER THEATRE PERSONNEL

(*She is referred to as THE SECOND ACTRESS in the text.)

ACT I

DAYTIME: THE STAGE OF A THEATRE

N.B.—*The play has neither acts nor scenes. Its performance will be interrupted twice: once—though the curtain will not be lowered—when the PRODUCER and the principal CHARACTERS go away to write the script and the ACTORS leave the stage, and a second time when the Man on the Curtain lets it fall by mistake.*

When the audience enters the auditorium the curtain is up and the stage is just as it would be during the daytime. There is no set and there are no wings; it is empty and in almost total darkness. This is in order that right from the very beginning the audience shall receive the impression of being present, not at a performance of a carefully rehearsed play, but at a performance of a play that suddenly happens.

Two small flights of steps, one right and one left, give access to the stage from the auditorium.

---

[1] Frederick May's translation is based on Pirandello's final, definitive version of *Sei personaggi in cerca d'autore*. Although Pirandello envisioned this as a play without separate acts, we have followed the traditional division of the play into acts, in part as a convenience for critical discussion.

On the stage itself, the prompter's dome[2] has been removed, and is standing just to one side of the prompt box.

Downstage, on the other side, a small table and an armchair with its back turned to the audience have been set for the PRODUCER.

Two more small tables, one rather larger than the other, together with several chairs, have been set downstage so that they are ready if needed for the rehearsal. There are other chairs scattered about to the left and to the right for the actors, and, in the background, to one side and almost hidden, there is a piano.

When the house lights go down the FOREMAN *comes on to the stage through the door back. He is dressed in blue dungarees and carries his tools in a bag slung at his belt. From a corner at the back of the stage he takes one or two slats of wood, brings them down front, kneels down and starts nailing them together. At the sound of his hammer the* STAGE-MANAGER *rushes in from the direction of the dressing-rooms.*

STAGE-MANAGER.   Hey. What are you doing?

FOREMAN.   What am I doing? Hammering . . . nails.

STAGE-MANAGER.   At this time of day? [*He looks at his watch.*] It's gone half-past ten! The Producer'll be here any minute now and he'll want to get on with his rehearsal.

FOREMAN.   And let me tell *you* something . . . I've got to have time to do *my* work, too.

STAGE-MANAGER.   You'll get it, you'll get it. . . . But you can't do that *now*.

FOREMAN.   When can I do it then?

10 STAGE-MANAGER.   After the rehearsal. Now, come on. . . . Clear up all this mess, and let me get on with setting the second set of *The Game As He Played It*.

[*The* FOREMAN *gathers his pieces of wood together, muttering and grumbling all the while, and goes off. Meanwhile, the* ACTORS OF THE COMPANY *have begun to come on to the stage through the door back. First one comes in, then another, then two together . . . just as they please. There are nine or ten of them in all—as many as you would suppose you would need for the rehearsal of Pirandello's play,* The Game As He Played It, *which has been called for today. As they come in they greet one another and the* STAGE-MANAGER *with a cheery 'Good morning'. Some of them go off to their dressing-rooms; others, and among them the* PROMPTER, *who is carrying the prompt copy rolled up under his arm, remain on the stage, waiting for the* PRODUCER *to come and start the rehearsal. While they are waiting—some of them standing, some seated about in small groups—they exchange a few words among themselves. One lights a cigarette, another complains about the part that he's been given and a third reads out an item of news from a theatrical journal for the benefit of the other actors. It would be best if all the* ACTORS AND ACTRESSES *could be dressed in rather bright and gay clothes. This first improvised scene should be played very naturally and with great vivacity. After a while, one of the comedy men can sit down at the piano and start playing a dance-tune. The younger* ACTORS AND ACTRESSES *start dancing.*]

STAGE-MANAGER [*clapping his hands to restore order*].   Come on, now, come on! That's enough of that! Here's the producer!

---

[2] A dome-shaped cover that conceals the prompter from the audience's sight.

[*The music and dancing come to a sudden stop. The* Actors *turn and look out into the auditorium and see the* Producer, *who is coming in through the door. He comes up the gangway between the stalls, bowler hat on head, stick under arm, and a large cigar in his mouth, to the accompaniment of a chorus of 'Good-mornings' from the* Actors *and climbs up one of the flights of steps on to the stage. His* Secretary *offers him his post—a newspaper or so, a script.*]

Producer.　Any letters?
Secretary.　None at all. This is all the post there is.
Producer [*handing him back the script*].　Put it in my office. [*Then, looking around and turning to the* Stage-Manager.] Oh, you can't see a thing here! Ask them to give us a spot of light, please.
20 Stage-Manager.　Right you are!

[*He goes off to give the order and a short while after the whole of the right side of the stage, where the* Actors *are standing, is lit up by a bright white light. In the meantime the* Prompter *has taken his place in his box, switched on his light and spread his script out in front of him.*]

Producer [*clapping his hands*].　Come on, let's get started! [*To the* Stage-Manager.] Anyone missing?
Stage-Manager.　The Leading Lady.
Producer.　As usual! [*Looks at his watch.*] We're ten minutes late already. Make a note, will you, please, to remind me to give her a good talking-to about being so late? It might teach her to get to rehearsals on time in the future.

[*He has scarcely finished his rebuke when the voice of the* Leading Lady *is heard at the back of the auditorium.*]

Leading Lady.　No, please don't! Here I am! Here I am!

[*She is dressed completely in white, with a large and rather dashing and provocative hat, and is carrying a dainty little lap-dog. She runs down the aisle and hastily climbs up the steps on to the stage.*]

Producer.　You've set your heart on always keeping us waiting, haven't you?
30 Leading Lady.　Forgive me! I hunted everywhere for a taxi so that I should get here on time! But you haven't started yet, anyway. And I don't come on immediately. [*Then, calling the* Stage-Manager *by name, she gives him the lap-dog.*] Please put him in my dressing-room . . . and mind you shut the door!
Producer [*grumblingly*].　And she has to bring a dog along too! As if there weren't enough dogs around here! [*He claps his hands again and turns to the* Prompter.] Come on now, let's get on with Act II of *The Game As He Played It.* [*He sits down in the armchair.*] Now, ladies and gentlemen, who's on?

[*The* Actors and Actresses *clear away from the front of the stage and go and sit to one side, except for the three who start the scene, and the* Leading Lady. *She has paid no attention to the* Producer's *question and has seated herself at one of the little tables.*]

PRODUCER [*to the* LEADING LADY].   Ah! So you're in this scene, are you?

40 LEADING LADY.   Me? Oh, no!

PRODUCER [*annoyed*].   Then for God's sake get off!

[*And the* LEADING LADY *gets up and goes and sits with the others.*]

PRODUCER [*to the* PROMPTER].   Now, let's get started!

PROMPTER [*reading from his script*].   "The house of Leone Gala. A strange room, half dining-room, half study."

PRODUCER [*turning to the* STAGE-MANAGER].   We'll use the red set.

STAGE-MANAGER [*making a note on a sheet of paper*].   The red set. Right!

PROMPTER [*continuing to read from his script*].   "A table laid for a meal and a desk with books and papers. Bookshelves with books on them. Glass-fronted cupboards containing valuable china. A door back leading into

50   Leone's bedroom. A side door left, leading into the kitchen. The main entrance is right."

PRODUCER [*getting up and pointing*].   Right! Now listen carefully—over there, the main entrance. And over here, the kitchen. [*Turning to the actor who is to play the part of Socrates.*] You'll make your entrances and exits this side. [*To the* STAGE-MANAGER.] We'll have that green-baize door at the back there . . . and some curtains. [*He goes and sits down again.*]

STAGE-MANAGER [*making a note*].   Right you are!

PROMPTER [*reading*].   "Scene I. Leone Gala, Guido Venanzi, Filippo, who is called Socrates." [*To the* PRODUCER.] Do I have to read the stage directions

60   as well?

PRODUCER.   Yes, yes, of course! I've told you that a hundred times!

PROMPTER [*reading*].   "When the curtain rises, Leone Gala, wearing a cook's hat and apron, is busy beating an egg in a basin with a wooden spoon. Filippo, also dressed as a cook, is beating another egg. Guido Venanzi is sitting listening to them."

LEADING MAN [*to the* PRODUCER].   Excuse me, but do I really have to wear a cook's hat?

PRODUCER [*irritated by this observation*].   So it seems! That's certainly what's written there! [*He points to the script.*]

70 LEADING MAN.   Forgive me for saying so, but it's ridiculous.

PRODUCER [*bounding to his feet in fury*].   Ridiculous! Ridiculous! What do you expect me to do if the French haven't got any more good comedies to send us, and we're reduced to putting on plays by Pirandello? And if you can understand *his* plays . . . you're a better man than I am! He deliberately goes out of his way to annoy people, so that by the time the play's through everybody's fed up . . . actors, critics, audience, everybody!

[*The* ACTORS *laugh. Then getting up and going over to the* LEADING MAN, *the* PRODUCER *cries*].

Yes, my dear fellow, a cook's hat! And you beat eggs! And do you think that, having these eggs to beat, you then have nothing more on your

80   hands? Oh, no, not a bit of it. . . . You have to represent the shell of the eggs that you're beating!

[*The* ACTORS *start laughing again and begin to make ironical comments among themselves.*]

Shut up! And listen when I'm explaining things! [*Turning again to the* LEADING MAN.] Yes, my dear fellow, the shell . . . or, as you might say, the empty form of reason, without that content of instinct which is blind! You are reason and your wife is instinct, in a game where you play the parts which have been given you. And all the time you're playing your part, you are the self-willed puppet of yourself. Understand?

LEADING MAN [*spreading out his hands*].   Me? No!

PRODUCER [*returning to his seat*].   Neither do I! However, let's get on with it! It's going to be a wonderful flop, anyway! [*In a confidential tone.*] I suggest you turn to the audience a bit more . . . about three-quarters face. Otherwise, what with the abstruseness of the dialogue, and the audience's not being able to hear you, the whole thing'll go to hell. [*Clapping his hands again.*] Now, come along! *Come along!* Let's get started!

PROMPTER.   Excuse me, sir, do you mind if I put the top back on my box? There's a bit of a draught.

PRODUCER.   Of course! Go ahead! Go ahead!

[*Meanwhile the* COMMISSIONAIRE[3] *has entered the auditorium. He is wearing a braided cap and having covered the length of the aisle, he comes up to the edge of the stage to announce the arrival of the* SIX CHARACTERS *to the* PRODUCER. *They have followed the* COMMISSIONAIRE *into the auditorium and have walked behind him as he has come up to the stage. They look about them, a little perplexed and a little dismayed.*

In any production of this play it is imperative that the producer should use every means possible to avoid any confusion between the SIX CHARACTERS *and the* ACTORS. *The placings of the two groups, as they will be indicated in the stage-directions once the* CHARACTERS *are on the stage, will no doubt help. So, too, will their being lit in different colours. But the most effective and most suitable method of distinguishing them that suggests itself, is the use of special masks for the* CHARACTERS, *masks specially made from some material which will not grow limp with perspiration and will at the same time be light enough to be worn by the actors playing these parts. They should be cut so as to leave the eyes, the nose and the mouth free. In this way the deep significance of the play can be brought out. The* CHARACTERS *should not, in fact, appear as phantasms, but as created realities, unchangeable creations of the imagination and, therefore, more real and more consistent than the ever-changing naturalness of the* ACTORS. *The masks will assist in giving the impression of figures constructed by art, each one fixed immutably in the expression of that sentiment which is fundamental to it. That is to say in* REMORSE *for the* FATHER, REVENGE *for the* STEPDAUGHTER, CONTEMPT *for the* SON *and* SORROW *for the* MOTHER. *Her mask should have wax tears fixed in the corners of the eyes and coursing down the cheeks, just like those which are carved and painted in the representations of the Mater Dolorosa[4] that are to be seen in churches. Her dress, too, should be of a special material and cut. It should be severely plain,*

---

[3] A doorman or porter.
[4] Statues or paintings of the grieving Virgin Mary.

its folds stiff, giving in fact the appearance of having been carved, and not of being made of any material that you can just go out and buy or have cut-out and made up into a dress by any ordinary dressmaker.

The FATHER *is a man of about fifty. He is not bald but his reddish hair is thin at the temples. His moustache is thick and coils over his still rather youthful-looking mouth, which all too often falls open in a purposeless, uncertain smile. His complexion is pale and this is especially noticeable when one has occasion to look at his forehead which is particularly broad. His blue, oval-shaped eyes are very clear and piercing. He is wearing a dark jacket and light-coloured trousers. At times his manner is all sweetness and light, at others it is hard and harsh.*

The MOTHER *appears as a woman crushed and terrified by an intolerable weight of shame and abasement. She is dressed in a modest black and wears a thick crêpe widow's veil. When she lifts her veil she reveals a wax-like face; it is not, however, at all sickly looking. She keeps her eyes downcast all the time. The* STEPDAUGHTER, *who is eighteen, is defiant, bold, arrogant—almost shamelessly so. She is very beautiful. She, too, is dressed in mourning but carries it with a decided air of showy elegance. She shows contempt for the very timid, dejected, half-frightened manner of her younger brother, a rather grubby and unprepossessing* BOY *of fourteen, who is also dressed in black. On the other hand she displays a very lively tenderness for her small sister, a* LITTLE GIRL *of about four, who is wearing a white frock with a black silk sash round the waist.*

The SON *is a tall young man of twenty-two. He is wearing a mauve coloured overcoat and has a long green scarf twisted round his neck. He appears as if he has stiffened into an attitude of contempt for the* FATHER *and of supercilious indifference towards the* MOTHER.]

COMMISSIONAIRE [*cap in hand*]. Excuse me, sir.

PRODUCER [*snapping at him rudely*]. Now what's the matter?

100 COMMISSIONAIRE. There are some people here, sir, asking for you.

[*The* PRODUCER *and the* ACTORS *turn in astonishment and look out into the auditorium.*]

PRODUCER [*furiously*]. But I've got a rehearsal on at the moment! And you know quite well that no one's allowed in here while a rehearsal's going on. [*Then addressing the* CHARACTERS.] Who are you? What do you want?

FATHER [*he steps forward, followed by the others, and comes to the foot of one of the flights of steps*]. We are here in search of an author.

PRODUCER [*caught between anger and utter astonishment*]. In search of an author? Which author?

FATHER. Any author, sir.

PRODUCER. But there's no author here. . . . We're not rehearsing a new play.

110 STEPDAUGHTER [*vivaciously, as she rushes up the steps*]. So much the better! Then so much the better, sir! *We* can be your new play.

ONE OF THE ACTORS [*amidst the lively comments and laughter of the others*]. Oh, just listen to her! *Listen* to her!

FATHER [*following the* STEPDAUGHTER *on to the stage*]. Yes, but if there isn't any author. . . . [*To the* PRODUCER.] Unless *you'd* like to be the author. . . .

[*Holding the* LITTLE GIRL *by the hand, the* MOTHER, *followed by the* BOY, *climbs up the first few steps leading to the stage and stands there expectantly. The* SON *remains morosely below.*]

PRODUCER.   Are you people trying to be funny?

FATHER.   No. . . . How can you suggest such a thing? On the contrary, we are bringing you a terrible and grievous drama.

STEPDAUGHTER.   And we might make your fortune for you.

120   PRODUCER.   Perhaps you'll do me the kindness of getting out of this theatre! We've got no time to waste on lunatics!

FATHER [*he is wounded by this, but replies in a gentle tone*].   Oh. . . . But you know very well, don't you, that life is full of things that are infinitely absurd, things that, for all their impudent absurdity, have no need to masquerade as truth, because they are true.

PRODUCER.   What the devil are you talking about?

FATHER.   What I'm saying is that reversing the usual order of things, forcing oneself to a contrary way of action, may well be construed as madness. As, for instance, when we create things which have all the appearance of
130   reality in order that they shall look like the realities themselves. But allow me to observe that if this indeed be madness, it is, nonetheless, the sole *raison d'être*[5] of your profession.

[*The* ACTORS *stir indignantly at this.*]

PRODUCER [*getting up and looking him up and down*].   Oh, yes? So you think ours is a profession of lunatics, do you?

FATHER.   Yes, making what isn't true *seem* true . . . without having to . . . for fun. . . . Isn't it your function to give life on the stage to imaginary characters?

PRODUCER [*immediately, making himself spokesman for the growing anger of his actors*].   I should like you to know, my dear sir, that the actor's profession
140   is a most noble one. And although nowadays, with things in the state they are, our playwrights give us stupid comedies to act, and puppets to represent instead of men, I'd have you know that it is our boast that we have given life, here on these very boards, to immortal works!

[*The* ACTORS *satisfiedly murmur their approval and applaud the* PRODUCER.]

FATHER [*breaking in and following hard on his argument*].   There you are! Oh, that's it exactly! To living beings . . . to beings who are more alive than those who breathe and wear clothes! Less real, perhaps but truer! We're in complete agreement!

[*The* ACTORS *look at each other in utter astonishment.*]

PRODUCER.   But . . . What on earth! . . . But you said just now . . .

FATHER.   No, I said that because of your . . . because you shouted at us that
150   you had no time to waste on lunatics . . . while nobody can know better than you that nature makes use of the instrument of human fantasy to pursue her work of creation on a higher level.

PRODUCER.   True enough! True enough! But where does all this get us?

FATHER.   Nowhere. I only wish to show you that one is born into life in so many ways, in so many forms. . . . As a tree, or as a stone; as water or as

---

[5] *raison d'être*: rationale.

a butterfly.... Or as a woman. And that one can be born a character.

PRODUCER [*ironically, feigning amazement*].   And you, together with these other
people, were born a character?

FATHER.   Exactly. And alive, as you see. [*The* PRODUCER *and the* ACTORS *burst out*
160   *laughing as if at some huge joke.*] [*Hurt.*] I'm sorry that you laugh like that
because, I repeat, we carry within ourselves a terrible and grievous drama,
as you can deduce for yourselves from this woman veiled in black.

[*And so saying, he holds out his hand to the* MOTHER *and helps her up the last few steps
and, continuing to hold her hand, leads her with a certain tragic solemnity to the other
side of the stage, which immediately lights up with a fantastic kind of light. The* LITTLE
GIRL *and the* BOY *follow their* MOTHER. *Next, the* SON *comes up and goes and stands
to one side, in the background. Then the* STEPDAUGHTER *follows him on to the stage;
she stands downstage, leaning against the proscenium arch. The* ACTORS *are at first
completely taken aback and then, caught in admiration at this development, they burst
into applause—just as if they had had a show put on for their benefit.*]

PRODUCER [*at first utterly astonished and then indignant*].   Shut up! What the ...!
[*Then turning to the* CHARACTERS.] And you get out of here! Clear out of here!
[*To the* STAGE-MANAGER.] For God's sake, clear them out!

STAGE-MANAGER [*coming forward, but then stopping as if held back by some strange
dismay*].   Go away! Go away!

FATHER [*to the* PRODUCER].   No, no! Listen.... We....

PRODUCER [*shouting*].   I tell you, we've got work to do!

170 LEADING MAN.   You can't go about playing practical jokes like this....

FATHER [*resolutely coming forward*].   I wonder at your incredulity. Is it perhaps
that you're not accustomed to seeing the characters created by an author
leaping to life up here on the stage, when they come face to face with each
other? Or is it, perhaps, that there's no script there [*he points to the prompt
box*] that contains us?

STEPDAUGHTER [*smiling, she steps towards the* PRODUCER; *then, in a wheedling voice*].
Believe me, sir, we really are six characters ... and very, very interesting!
But we've been cut adrift.

FATHER [*brushing her aside*].   Yes, that's it, we've been cut adrift. [*And then
180   immediately to the* PRODUCER.] In the sense, you understand, that the author
who created us as living beings, either couldn't or wouldn't put us mate-
rially into the world of art. And it was truly a crime ... because he who has
the good fortune to be born a living character may snap his fingers at
Death even. He will never die! Man ... The writer ... The instrument of
creation ... Will die.... But what is created by him will never die. And in
order to live eternally he has not the slightest need of extraordinary gifts
or of accomplishing prodigies. Who was Sancho Panza?[6] Who was Don
Abbondio?[7] And yet they live eternally because—living seeds—they had
the good fortune to find a fruitful womb—a fantasy which knew how to
190   raise and nourish them, and to make them live through all eternity.

---

[6] Sancho Panza is the commonsensical squire in Miguel de Cervantes Saavedra's famous
novel *Don Quixote* (1605).

[7] Don Abbondio is the parish priest in Alessandro Manzoni's novel *The Betrothed*
(1825–1827).

PRODUCER.   All this is very, very fine indeed. . . . But what do you want here?
FATHER.   We wish to live, sir!
PRODUCER [*ironically*].   Through all eternity?
FATHER.   No, sir; just for a moment . . . in you.
AN ACTOR.   Listen to him! . . . listen to him!
LEADING LADY.   They want to live in us!
JUVENILE LEAD [*pointing to the* STEPDAUGHTER].   I've no objection . . . so long as
    I get her.
FATHER.   Listen! Listen! The play is in the making. [*To the* PRODUCER.] But if
200 you and your actors are willing, we can settle it all between us without
    further delay.
PRODUCER [*annoyed*].   But what do you want to settle? We don't go in for that
    sort of concoction here! We put on comedies and dramas here.
FATHER.   Exactly! That's the very reason why we came to you.
PRODUCER.   And where's the script?
FATHER.   It is in us, sir. [*The* ACTORS *laugh.*] the drama is in us. *We* are the
    drama and we are impatient to act it—so fiercely does our inner passion
    urge us on.
STEPDAUGHTER [*scornful, treacherous, alluring, with deliberate shamelessness*].   My
210 passion. . . . If you only knew! My passion . . . for him!

[*She points to the* FATHER *and makes as if to embrace him, but then bursts into strident
laughter.*]

FATHER [*at once, angrily*].   You keep out of this for the moment! And please
    don't laugh like that!
STEPDAUGHTER.   Oh . . . mayn't I? Then perhaps *you'll* allow me, ladies and
    gentlemen. . . . Although it's scarcely two months since my father died . . .
    just you watch how I can dance and sing!

[*Mischievously she starts to sing Dave Stamper's "Prends garde à Tchou-Thin-
Tchou"*[8] *in the fox-trot or slow one-step version by François Salabert. She sings the
first verse, accompanying it with a dance.*]

Les chinois sont un peuple malin,
De Shangaï à Pékin,
Ils ont mis des écriteaux partout:
Prenez garde à Tchou-Thin-Tchou!

[*While she is singing and dancing, the* ACTORS, *and especially the younger ones, as if
attracted by some strange fascination, move towards her and half raise their hands as
though to catch hold of her. She runs away, and when the* ACTORS *burst into applause,
and the* PRODUCER *rebukes her, she stands where she is, quietly, abstractedly, and as
if her thoughts were far away.*]

220 ACTORS AND ACTRESSES [*laughing and clapping*].   Well done! Jolly good!
PRODUCER [*irately*].   Shut up! What do you think this is . . . a cabaret? [*Then*

---

    [8] *Prends garde à Tchou-Thin-Tchou:* "Beware of Tchou-Thin-Tchou," a song from the *Ziegfeld
Follies of 1917*, a popular song-and-dance revue. The rest of the lyrics continue: "The Chinese
are a cunning people,/From Shanghai to Beijing,/They have posted warnings everywhere:/
Beware of Tchou-Thin-Tchou."

taking the FATHER *a little to one side, he says with a certain amount of consternation.*] Tell me something. . . . Is she mad?

FATHER.   What do you mean, mad? It's worse than that!

STEPDAUGHTER [*immediately rushing up to the* PRODUCER].   Worse! Worse! Oh it's something very much worse than that! Listen! Let's put this drama on at once. . . . Please! Then you'll see that at a certain moment I . . . when this little darling here. . . . [*Takes the* LITTLE GIRL *by the hand and brings her over to the* PRODUCER.] . . . Isn't she a dear? [*Takes her in her arms and kisses her.*]

230   You little darling! . . . You dear little darling! [*Puts her down again, adding in a moved tone, almost without wishing to.*] Well, when God suddenly takes this child away from her poor mother, and that little imbecile there [*roughly grabbing hold of the* BOY *by the sleeve and thrusting him forward*] does the stupidest of all stupid things, like the idiot he is [*pushing him back towards the* MOTHER] . . . Then you will see me run away. Yes, I shall run away! And, oh, how I'm longing for that moment to come! Because after all the very intimate things that have happened between him and me [*with a horrible wink in the direction of the* FATHER] I can't remain any longer with these people . . . having to witness my mother's anguish because of that

240   queer fish there [*pointing to the* SON]. Look at him! Look at him! See how indifferent, how frigid he is . . . because he's the legitimate son . . . *he* is! He despises me, he despises him [*pointing to the* BOY], he despises that dear little creature. . . . Because we're bastards! Do you understand? . . . Because we're *bastards!* [*She goes up to the* MOTHER *and embraces her.*] And he doesn't want to recognise this poor woman as his mother. . . . This poor woman . . . who is the mother of us all! He looks down on her as if she were only the mother of us three bastards! The wretch! [*She says all this very quickly and very excitedly. She raises her voice at the word 'bastards' and the final 'wretch' is delivered in a low voice and almost spat out.*]

250   MOTHER [*to the* PRODUCER, *an infinity of anguish in her voice*].   Please, in the name of these two little children . . . I beg you. . . . [*She grows faint and sways on her feet.*] Oh, my God! [*Consternation and bewilderment among the* ACTORS.]

FATHER [*rushing over to support her, accompanied by most of the* ACTORS].   Quick . . . a chair. . . . A chair for this poor widow!

ACTORS [*rushing over*].   Has she fainted? Has she fainted?

PRODUCER.   Quick, get a chair . . . get a chair!

[*One of the* ACTORS *brings a chair, the others stand around, anxious to help in any way they can. The* MOTHER *sits on the chair; she attempts to prevent the* FATHER *from lifting the veil which hides her face.*]

FATHER.   Look at her. . . . Look at her. . . .

MOTHER.   No, No! My God! Stop it, please!

260   FATHER.   Let them see you. [*He lifts her veil.*]

MOTHER [*rising and covering her face with her hands in desperation*].   I beg you, sir, . . . Don't let this man carry out his plan! You must prevent him. . . . It's horrible!

PRODUCER [*utterly dumbfounded*].   I don't get this at all. . . . I haven't got the slightest idea what you're talking about. [*To the* FATHER.] Is this lady your wife?

FATHER [*immediately*].   Yes, sir, my wife.

PRODUCER.   Then how does it come about that she's a widow if you're still alive?

[*The* ACTORS *find relief for their bewilderment and astonishment in a noisy burst of laughter.*]

270 FATHER [*wounded, speaking with sharp resentment*].   Don't laugh! Don't laugh like that, for pity's sake! It is in this fact that her drama lies. She had another man. Another man who ought to be here.

MOTHER [*with a cry*].   No! No!

STEPDAUGHTER.   He's got the good luck to be dead. . . . He died two months ago, as I just told you. We're still wearing mourning for him, as you can see.

FATHER.   But it's not because he's dead that he's not here. No, he's not here because . . . Look at her! Look at her, please, and you'll understand immediately! Her drama does not lie in the love of two men for whom she,
280 being incapable of love, could feel nothing. . . . Unless, perhaps, it be a little gratitude . . . to him, not to me. She is not a woman. . . . She is a mother. And her drama. . . . And how powerful it is! How powerful it is! . . . Her drama lies entirely, in fact, in these four children. . . . The children of the two men that she had.

MOTHER.   Did you say that I had them? Do you dare to say that I *had* these two men . . . to suggest that I wanted them? [*To the* PRODUCER.] It was his doing. He gave him to me! He forced him on me! He forced me. . . . He forced me to go away with that other man!

STEPDAUGHTER [*at once, indignantly*].   It's not true!
290 MOTHER [*startled*].   Not true?

STEPDAUGHTER.   It's not true! It's not true, I say.

MOTHER.   And what can you possibly know about it?

STEPDAUGHTER.   It's not true! [*To the* PRODUCER.] Don't believe her! Do you know why she said that? Because of him. [*Pointing to the* SON.] That's why she said it! Because she tortures herself, wears herself out with anguish, because of the indifference of that son of hers. She wants him to believe that if she abandoned him when he was two years old it was because he [*pointing to the* FATHER] forced her to do it.

MOTHER [*forcefully*].   He forced me to do it! He forced me, as God is my
300 witness! [*To the* PRODUCER.] Ask him [*pointing to her* HUSBAND] if it's not true! Make him tell my son! She [*pointing to her* DAUGHTER] knows nothing at all about the matter.

STEPDAUGHTER.   I know that while my father lived you were always happy. . . . You had a peaceful and contented life together. Deny it if you can!

MOTHER.   I don't deny it! No. . . .

STEPDAUGHTER.   He was always most loving, always kindness itself towards you. [*To the* BOY, *angrily.*] Isn't it true? Go on. . . . Say it's true! Why don't you speak, you stupid little idiot?

MOTHER.   Leave the poor boy alone! Why do you want to make me appear
310 an ungrateful woman? I don't want to say anything against your father. . . . I only said that it wasn't my fault, and that it wasn't just to satisfy my own desires that I left his house and abandoned my son.

FATHER.   What she says is true. It was my doing.

[*There is a pause.*]

LEADING MAN [*to the other* ACTORS].   My God! What a show!
LEADING LADY.   And we're the audience this time!
JUVENILE LEAD.   For once in a while.
PRODUCER [*who is beginning to show a lively interest*].   Let's listen to this! Let's
   hear what they've got to say!

[*And saying this he goes down the steps into the auditorium and stands in front of the
stage, as if to get an impression of the scene from the audience's point of view.*]

SON [*without moving from where he is, speaking coldly, softly, ironically*].   Yes!
320   Listen to the chunk of philosophy you're going to get now! He will tell you
   all about the Dæmon of Experiment.
FATHER.   You're a cynical idiot, as I've told you a hundred times. [*Down to the*
   PRODUCER.] He mocks me because of this expression that I've discovered in
   my own defence.
SON [*contemptuously*].   Words! Words!
FATHER.   Yes! Words! Words! They can always bring consolation to us. . . . To
   everyone of us. . . . When we're confronted by something for which there's
   no explanation. . . . When we're face to face with an evil that consumes
   us. . . . The consolation of finding a word that tells us nothing, but that
330   brings us peace.
STEPDAUGHTER.   And dulls our sense of remorse, too. Yes! That above all!
FATHER.   Dulls our sense of remorse? No, that's not true. It wasn't with words
   alone that I quietened remorse within me.
STEPDAUGHTER.   No, you did it with a little money as well. Yes! Oh, yes! with
   a little money as well! With the hundred lire[9] that he was going to offer me
   . . . as payment, ladies and gentlemen!

[*A movement of horror on the part of the* ACTORS.]

SON [*contemptuously to his* STEPSISTER].   That was vile!
STEPDAUGHTER.   Vile? There they were, in a pale blue envelope, on the little
   mahogany table in the room behind Madame Pace's shop. Madame
340   Pace. . . . One of those *Madames* who pretend to sell *Robes et Manteaux*[10] so
   that they can attract us poor girls from decent families into their work-
   rooms.
SON.   And she's bought the right to tyrannise over the whole lot of us with
   those hundred lire that he was going to pay her. . . . But by good fortune. . . . And let me emphasize this. . . . He had no reason to pay her
   anything.
STEPDAUGHTER.   Yes, but it was a very near thing! Oh, yes, it was, you know!
   [*She bursts out laughing.*]
MOTHER [*rising to protest*].   For shame! For shame!
350 STEPDAUGHTER [*immediately*].   Shame? No! This is my revenge! I'm trembling

---

[9] A lira is a unit of Italian currency, roughly comparable to the U.S. dollar.
[10] *Robes et Manteaux:* dresses and coats.

with desire. . . . Simply trembling with desire to live that scene! That room. . . . Over here is the shop-window with all the coats in it. . . . And over there the divan, the long mirror and a screen. . . . And in front of the window that little mahogany table. . . . And the pale blue envelope with the hundred lire inside. Yes, I can see it quite clearly! I'd only have to stretch out my hand and I could pick it up! But you gentlemen really ought to turn your backs now, because I'm almost naked. I no longer blush, because he's the one who does the blushing now [*pointing to the* FATHER]. But, let me tell you, he was very pale then. . . . Very pale indeed! 360 [*To the* PRODUCER.] You can believe *me*!

PRODUCER.   I haven't the vaguest idea what you're talking about!

FATHER.   I can well believe it! When you get things hurled at you like that. Put your foot down. . . . And let me speak before you believe all these horrible slanders she's so viciously heaping upon me. . . . Without letting me get a word of explanation in.

STEPDAUGHTER.   Ah, but this isn't the place for your long-winded fairy-stories, you know!

FATHER.   But I'm not going to. . . . I want to explain things to him!

STEPDAUGHTER.   Oh yes . . . I bet you do! You'll explain everything so that it 370 suits you, won't you?

[At this point the PRODUCER *comes back on stage to restore order.]*

FATHER.   But can't you see that here we have the cause of all the trouble! In the use of words! Each one of us has a whole world of things inside him. . . . And each one of us has his own particular world. How can we understand each other if into the words which I speak I put the sense and the value of things as I understand them within myself. . . . While at the same time whoever is listening to them inevitably assumes them to have the sense and value that they have for him. . . . The sense and value that they have in the world that he has within him? We think we understand one another. . . . But we never really do understand! Look at this situation, 380 for example! All my pity, all the pity that I feel for this woman [*pointing to the* MOTHER] *she* sees as the most ferocious cruelty.

MOTHER.   But you turned me out of the house!

FATHER.   There! Do you hear? I turned her out! She really believed that I was turning her out!

MOTHER.   You know how to talk . . . I don't. . . . But believe me [*turning to the* PRODUCER] after he had married me. . . . Goodness knows why! For I was a poor, humble woman. . . .

FATHER.   But it was just because of that. . . . It was your humility that I loved in you. I married you for your humility, believing . . . [*He breaks off, for she* 390 *is making gestures of contradiction. Then, seeing how utterly impossible it is to make her understand him he opens his arms wide in a gesture of despair and turns to the* PRODUCER.] No! . . . You see? She says no! It's terrifying, believe me! It's really terrifying, this deafness [*he taps his forehead*]. . . . This mental deafness of hers! Affection. . . . Yes! . . . For her children! But deaf. . . . Mentally deaf. . . . Deaf to the point of desperation.

STEPDAUGHTER.   True enough! But now you make him tell us what good all his cleverness has ever done us.

FATHER. If we could only foresee all the ill that can result from the good that we believe we are doing.

[*Meanwhile the* LEADING LADY, *with ever-increasing fury, has been watching the* LEADING MAN, *who is busy carrying on a flirtation with the* STEPDAUGHTER. *Unable to stand it any longer she now steps forward and says to the* PRODUCER.]

400 LEADING LADY. Excuse me, but are you going on with the rehearsal?
PRODUCER. Why, of course! Of course! But just at the moment I want to hear what these people have to say!
JUVENILE LEAD. This is really something quite new!
INGENUE. It's most interesting!
LEADING LADY. For those that are interested! [*And she looks meaningly in the direction of the* LEADING MAN.]
PRODUCER [*to the* FATHER]. But you'll have to explain everything clearly. [*He goes and sits down.*]
FATHER. Yes. . . . Well. . . . You see . . . I had a poor man working under
410 me. . . . He was my secretary, and devoted to me. . . . Who understood *her* in every way. . . . In everything [*pointing to the* MOTHER]. Oh, there wasn't the slightest suspicion of anything wrong. He was a good man. A humble man. . . . Just like her. . . . They were incapable . . . both of them . . . not only of doing evil . . . but even of thinking it!
STEPDAUGHTER. So, instead, he thought about it for them! And then got on with it.
FATHER. It's not true! I thought that what I should be doing would be for their good. . . . And for mine, too. . . . I confess it! Yes, things had come to such a pass that I couldn't say a single word to either of them without their
420 immediately exchanging an understanding look. . . . Without the one's immediately trying to catch the other's eye. . . . For advice as to how to take what I had said. . . . So that I shouldn't get into a bad temper. As you'll readily appreciate it was enough to keep me in a state of continual fury. . . . Of intolerable exasperation!
PRODUCER. But. . . . Forgive my asking. . . . Why didn't you give the secretary of yours the sack?
FATHER. That's exactly what I did do, as a matter of fact. But then I had to watch that poor woman wandering forlornly about the house like some poor lost creature. . . . Like one of those stray animals you take in out of
430 charity.
MOTHER. But . . .
FATHER [*immediately turning on her, as if to forestall what she is about to say*]. Your son! You were going to tell him about your son, weren't you?
MOTHER. But first of all he tore my son away from me!
FATHER. Not out of any desire to be cruel though! I took him away so that, by living in the country, in contact with Nature, he might grow up strong and healthy.
STEPDAUGHTER [*pointing to him, ironically*]. And just look at him!
FATHER [*immediately*]. And is it my fault, too, that he's grown up the way he
440 has? I sent him to a wet-nurse in the country . . . a peasant's wife . . . because my wife didn't seem strong enough to me. . . . Although she came of a humble family, and it was for that reason that I'd married her! Just a

whim maybe. . . . But then . . . what was I to do? I've always had this cursed longing for a certain solid moral healthiness.

[*At this the* STEPDAUGHTER *breaks out afresh into noisy laughter.*]

Make her stop that noise! I can't stand it!

PRODUCER.   Be quiet! Let me hear what he has to say, for God's sake!

[*At the* PRODUCER'S *rebuke she immediately returns to her former attitude. . . . Absorbed and distant, a half-smile on her lips. The* PRODUCER *comes down off the stage again to see how it looks from the auditorium.*]

FATHER.   I could no longer stand the sight of that woman near me [*pointing to the* MOTHER]. Not so much because of the irritation she caused me . . . the nausea . . . the very real nausea with which she inspired me. . . . But rather
450   because of the pain . . . the pain and the anguish that I was suffering on her account.

MOTHER.   And he sent me away!

FATHER.   Well provided with everything. . . . To that other man. . . . So that she might be free of me.

MOTHER.   And so that he might be free as well!

FATHER.   Yes, I admit it. And a great deal of harm came as a result of it. . . . But I meant well. . . . And I did it more for her sake than for my own. I swear it! [*He folds his arms. Then immediately turning to the* MOTHER.] Did I ever lose sight of you? Tell me, did I ever lose sight of you until that fellow
460   took you away suddenly to some other town . . . all unknown to me. . . . Just because he'd got some queer notion into his head about the interest I was showing in you. . . . An interest which was pure, I assure you, sir. . . . Without the slightest suspicion of any ulterior motive about it! I watched the new little family that grew up around her with incredible tenderness. She can testify to that [*he points to the* STEPDAUGHTER].

STEPDAUGHTER.   Oh, I most certainly can! I was such a sweet little girl. . . . Such a sweet little girl, you see. . . . With plaits down to my shoulders . . . and my knickers a little bit longer than my frock. I used to see him standing there by the door of the school as I came out. He came to see how
470   I was growing up. . . .

FATHER.   Oh, this is vile! Treacherous! Infamous!

STEPDAUGHTER.   Oh, no! What makes you say it's infamous?

FATHER.   It's infamous! Infamous! [*Then turning excitedly to the* PRODUCER *he goes on in an explanatory tone.*] After she'd gone away [*pointing to the* MOTHER], my house suddenly seemed empty. She had been a burden on my spirit, but she had filled my house with her presence! Left alone I wandered through the rooms like some lost soul. This boy here [*pointing to the* SON], having been brought up away from home . . . I don't know . . . But . . . But when he returned home he no longer seemed to be my son. With no
480   mother to link him to me, he grew up entirely on his own. . . . A creature apart . . . absorbed in himself . . . with no tie of intellect or affection to bind him to me. And then. . . . And, strange as it may seem, it's the simple truth . . . I became curious about her little family. . . . Gradually I was attracted to this family which had come into being as a result of what I had done. And the thought of it began to fill the emptiness that I felt all

around me. I felt a real need . . . a very real need . . . to believe that she was happy, at peace, absorbed in the simple everyday duties of life. I wanted to look on her as being fortunate because she was far removed from the complicated torments of my spirit. And so, to have some proof

490   of this, I used to go and watch that little girl come out of school.

STEPDAUGHTER.   I should just say he did! He used to follow me along the street. He would smile at me and when I reached home he'd wave to me . . . like this. I would look at him rather provocatively, opening my eyes wide. I didn't know who he might be. I told my mother about him and she knew at once who it must be. [*The* MOTHER *nods agreement.*] At first she didn't want to let me go to school again. . . . And she kept me away for several days. And when I did go back, I saw him waiting for me at the door again . . . looking so ridiculous . . . with a brown paper bag in his hand. He came up to me and patted me. . . . And then he took a lovely large straw

500   hat out of the bag . . . with lots of lovely little roses on it. . . . And all for me.

PRODUCER.   This is a bit off the point, you know.

SON [*contemptuously*].   Yes. . . . Literature! Literature!

FATHER.   Literature indeed! This is life! Passion!

PRODUCER.   It may be. But you certainly can't act this sort of stuff!

FATHER.   I agree with you. Because all this is only leading up to the main action. I'm not suggesting that this part should be acted. And as a matter of fact, as you can quite well see, she [*pointing to the* STEPDAUGHTER] is no longer that little girl with plaits down to her shoulders. . . .

510   STEPDAUGHTER.   . . . and her knickers a little bit longer than her frock!

FATHER.   It is now that the drama comes! Something new, something complex. . . .

STEPDAUGHTER [*coming forward, her voice gloomy, fierce*].   As soon as my father died. . . .

FATHER [*at once, not giving her a chance to continue*].   . . . they fell into the most wretched poverty! They came back here. . . . And because of her stupidity [*pointing to the* MOTHER] I didn't know a thing about it. It's true enough that she can hardly write her own name. . . . But she might have got her daughter or that boy to write and tell me that they were in need!

520   MOTHER.   Now tell me, sir, how was I to know that this was how he'd feel?

FATHER.   That's exactly where you went wrong, in never having got to know how I felt about anything.

MOTHER.   After so many years away from him. . . . And after all that had happened. . . .

FATHER.   And is it my fault that that fellow took you away from here as he did? [*Turning to the* PRODUCER.] I tell you, they disappeared overnight. . . . He'd found some sort of a job away from here . . . I couldn't trace them at all. . . . So, of necessity, my interest in them dwindled. And this was how it was for quite a number of years. The drama broke out, unforeseen and

530   violent in its intensity, when they returned. . . . When I was impelled by the demands of my miserable flesh, which is still alive with desire. . . . Oh, the wretchedness, the unutterable wretchedness of the man who's alone and who detests the vileness of casual affairs! When he's not old enough to do without a woman, and not really young enough to be able to go and look for one without feeling a sense of shame. Wretchedness, did I say? It's

horrible! It's horrible! Because no woman is any longer capable of giving him love. And when he realises this, he ought to do without. . . . Yes, yes, I know! . . . Each one of us, when he appears before his fellow men, is clothed with a certain dignity. But deep down inside himself he knows
540   what unconfessable things go on in the secrecy of his own heart. We give way . . . we give way to temptation. . . . Only to rise up again immediately, filled with a great eagerness to re-establish our dignity in all its solid entirety. . . . Just as if it were a tombstone on some grave in which we had buried, in which we had hidden from our eyes, every sign, and the very memory itself of our shame. And everyone is just like that! Only there are some of us who lack the courage to talk about certain things.

STEPDAUGHTER.   They've got the courage to do them, though. . . . All of them!

FATHER.   Yes, all of them! But only in secret! And that's why it needs so much more courage to talk about them! A man's only got to mention these
550   things, and the words have hardly left his lips before he's been labelled a cynic. And all the time it's not true. He's just like everybody else. . . . In fact he's better than they are, because he's not afraid to reveal with the light of his intelligence that red blush of shame which is inherent in human bestiality. . . . That shame to which bestial man closes his eyes, in order not to see it. And woman. . . . Yes, woman. . . . What kind of a being is she? She looks at you, tantalisingly, invitingly. You take her in your arms! And no sooner is she clasped firmly in your arms than she shuts her eyes. It is the sign of her mission, the sign by which she says to man, "Blind yourself, for I am blind."

560 STEPDAUGHTER.   And what about when she no longer shuts her eyes? When she no longer feels the need to hide her blushing shame from herself by closing her eyes? When she sees instead . . . dry-eyed and dispassionate . . . the blushing shame of man, who has blinded himself without love? Oh, what disgust, what unutterable disgust, does she feel then for all these intellectual complications, for all this philosophy which reveals the beast in man and then tries to save him, tries to excuse him . . . I just can't stand here and listen to him! Because when a man is obliged to 'simplify' life bestially like that—when he throws overboard every vestige of 'humanity', every chaste desire, every pure feeling. . . . All sense of idealism, of duty,
570   of modesty and of shame. . . . Then nothing is more contemptible, infuriating and revoltingly nauseating than their maudlin remorse. . . . Those crocodile tears!

PRODUCER.   Now let's get back to the point! Let's get to the point! This is just a lot of beating about the bush!

FATHER.   Very well. But a fact is like a sack. . . . When it's empty it won't stand up. And in order to make it stand up you must first of all pour into it all the reasons and all the feelings which have caused it to exist. I couldn't possibly be expected to know that when that man died and they returned here in such utter poverty, she [*pointing to the* MOTHER] would go out to
580   work as a dress-maker in order to support the children. . . . Nor that, of all people, she'd gone to work for that . . . for Madame Pace.

STEPDAUGHTER.   Who's a high-class dress-maker, if you ladies and gentlemen would really like to know. On the surface she does work for only the best sort of people. But she arranges things so that these fine ladies act as a screen . . . without prejudice to the others . . . who are only so-so.

MOTHER. Believe me, it never entered my head for one moment that that old hag gave me work because she had her eye on my daughter. . . .

STEPDAUGHTER. Poor Mummy! Do you know what that woman used to do when I took her back the work that my mother had done? She would point
590 out to me how the material had been ruined by giving it to my mother to sew. . . . Oh, she'd grumble about this! And she'd grumble about that! And so, you understand, I had to pay for it. . . . And all the time this poor creature thought she was sacrificing herself for me and for those two children, as she sat up all night sewing away at work for Madame Pace. [*Gestures and exclamations of indignation from the* ACTORS.]

PRODUCER [*immediately*]. And it was there, one day, that you met . . .

STEPDAUGHTER [*pointing to the* FATHER]. . . . him! Yes, him! An old client! Now there's a scene for you to put on! Absolutely superb!

FATHER. With her . . . the Mother . . . arriving. . . .

600 STEPDAUGHTER [*immediately, treacherously*]. . . . almost in time!

FATHER [*a cry*]. No! In time! In time! Fortunately I recognised her in time! And I took them all back home with me! Now you can imagine what the situation is like for both of us. She, just as you see her. . . . And I, no longer able to look her in the face.

STEPDAUGHTER. It's utterly ridiculous! How can I possibly be expected, after all that, to be a modest young miss . . . well-bred and virtuous . . . in accordance with his confounded aspirations for a "solid moral healthiness"?

FATHER. My drama lies entirely in this one thing. . . . In my being conscious
610 that each one of us believes himself to be a single person. But it's not true. . . . Each one of us is many persons. . . . Many persons . . . according to all the possibilities of being that there are within us. . . . With some people we are one person. . . . With others we are somebody quite different. . . . And all the time we are under the illusion of always being one and the same person for everybody. . . . We believe that we are always this one person in whatever it is we may be doing. But it's not true! It's not true! And we see this very clearly when by some tragic chance we are, as it were, caught up whilst in the middle of doing something and find ourselves suspended in mid-air. And then we perceive that all of us was not in what
620 we were doing, and that it would, therefore, be an atrocious injustice to us to judge us by that action alone. . . . To keep us suspended like that. . . . To keep us in a pillory . . . throughout all existence . . . as if our whole life were completely summed up in that one deed. Now do you understand the treachery of this girl? She surprised me somewhere where I shouldn't have been . . . and doing something that I shouldn't have been doing with her. . . . She surprised an aspect of me that should never have existed for her. And now she is trying to attach to me a reality such as I could never have expected I should have to assume for her. . . . The reality that lies in one fleeting, shameful moment of my life. And this, this above all, is what
630 I feel most strongly about. And as you can see, the drama acquires a tremendous value from this concept. Then there's the position of the others. . . . His . . . [*pointing to the* SON].

SON [*shrugging his shoulders scornfully*]. Leave me alone! I've got nothing to do with all this!

FATHER. What do you mean . . . you've got nothing to do with all this?

SON. I've got nothing to do with it. . . . And I don't want to have anything to do with it, because, as you quite well know, I wasn't meant to be mixed up in all this with the rest of you!

STEPDAUGHTER. Common, that's what we are! And he's a fine gentleman!
640 But, as you may have noticed, every now and again I fix him with a contemptuous look, and he lowers his eyes. . . . Because he knows the harm he's done me!

SON [*scarcely looking at her*]. I?

STEPDAUGHTER. Yes, you! You! It's all your fault that I became a prostitute! [*A movement of horror from the* ACTORS.] Did you or did you not deny us, by the attitude you adopted—I won't say the intimacy of your home—but even that mere hospitality which makes guests feel at their ease? We were invaders who had come to disturb the kingdom of your legitimacy. I should just like you [*this to the* PRODUCER] to be present at certain little
650 scenes that took place between him and me. He says that I tyrannised over everybody. . . . But it was just because of the way that he behaved that I took advantage of the thing that he calls 'vile'. . . . Why I exploited the reason for my coming into his house with my mother. . . . Who is his mother as well! And I went into that house as mistress of it!

SON [*slowly coming forward*]. It's all very easy for them. . . . It's fine sport. . . . All of them ganging-up against me. But just imagine the position of a son whose fate it is one fine day, while he's sitting quietly at home, to see arriving an impudent and brazen young woman who asks for his father— and heaven knows what her business is with him! Later he sees her come
660 back, as brazen as ever, bringing that little girl with her. And finally he sees her treating his father—without knowing in the least why—in a very equivocal and very much to-the-point manner . . . asking him for money, in a tone of voice which leads you to suppose that he must give it to her. . . . Must give it to her, because he has every obligation to do so. . . .

FATHER. As indeed I have! It's an obligation I owe your mother!

SON. How should I know that? When had I ever seen or even heard of her? Then one day I see her arrive with *her* [*pointing to the* STEPDAUGHTER] together with that boy and the little girl. And they say to me, "This is *your* mother, too, you know." Little by little I begin to understand. . . . Largely
670 as a result of the way she goes on [*pointing to the* STEPDAUGHTER *again*]. . . . Why it is that they've come to live with us. . . . So suddenly. . . . So unexpectedly. . . . What I feel, what I experience, I neither wish, nor am able, to express. I wouldn't even wish to confess it to myself. No action, therefore, can be hoped for from me in this affair. Believe me, I am a dramatically unrealised character . . . and I do not feel the least bit at ease in their company. So please leave me out of it!

FATHER. What! But it's just because you're like that. . . .

SON [*in violent exasperation*]. And what do you know about it? How do you know what I'm like? When have you ever bothered yourself about me?
680 FATHER. I admit it! I admit it! But isn't that a dramatic situation in itself? This aloofness of yours, which is so cruel to me and to your mother. . . . Your mother who returns home and sees you almost for the first time. . . . You're so grown up that she doesn't recognise you, but she knows that you're her son. [*Pointing to the* MOTHER *and addressing the* PRODUCER.] There, look! She's crying!

STEPDAUGHTER [*angrily, stamping her foot*]. Like the fool she is!

FATHER [*pointing to the* STEPDAUGHTER]. She can't stand him! [*Then returning to*

the subject of the SON.] He says he's got nothing to do with all this, when, as
a matter of fact, almost the whole action hinges on him. Look at that little
690   boy. . . . See how he clings to his mother all the time, frightened and
humiliated. . . . And it's *his* fault that he's like that! Perhaps his position is
the most painful of all. . . . More than any of them he feels himself to be
an outsider. And so the poor little chap feels mortified, humiliated at
being taken into my home . . . out of charity, as it were. [*Confidentially.*]
He's just like his father. Humble. . . . Doesn't say a word. . . .

PRODUCER.   I don't think it's a good idea to have him in. You've no idea what
a nuisance boys are on the stage.

FATHER.   Oh, . . . but he won't be a nuisance for long. . . . He disappears
almost immediately. And the little girl, too. . . . In fact, she's the first to go.

700 PRODUCER.   This is excellent! I assure you I find this all very interesting. . . .
Very interesting indeed! I can see we've got the makings of a pretty good
play here.

STEPDAUGHTER [*trying to butt in*].   When you've got a character like me!

FATHER [*pushing her to one side in his anxiety to hear what decision the* PRODUCER *has
come to*].   You be quiet!

PRODUCER [*continuing, heedless of the interruption*].   And it's certainly something new. . . . Yes! . . .

FATHER.   Absolutely brand new!

PRODUCER.   You had a nerve, though, I must say. . . . Coming here and
710   chucking the idea at me like that. . . .

FATHER.   Well, you understand, born as we are for the stage. . . .

PRODUCER.   Are you amateur actors?

FATHER.   No . . . I say that we're born for the stage because . . .

PRODUCER.   Oh, don't try and come that one with me! You're an old hand at
this game.

FATHER.   No. I only act as much as anyone acts the part that he sets himself
to perform, or the part that he is given in life. And in me it is passion itself,
as you can see, that always becomes a little theatrical of its own accord . . .
as it does in everyone . . . once it becomes exalted.

720 PRODUCER.   Oh well, that as may be! That as may be! . . . But you do understand, without an author . . . I could give you the address of somebody
who'd . . .

FATHER.   No! . . . Look here. . . . You be the author!

PRODUCER.   Me? What the devil are you talking about?

FATHER.   Yes, you! You! why not?

PRODUCER.   Because I've never written anything in my life! That's why not!

FATHER.   Then why not try your hand at it now? There's nothing to it. Everybody's doing it! And your job's made all the easier for you because we
are here, all of us, alive before you. . . .

730 PRODUCER.   That's not enough!

FATHER.   Not enough? When you see us live our drama. . . .

PRODUCER.   Yes! Yes! But we'll still need somebody to write the play.

FATHER.   No. . . . Someone to take it down possibly, while we act it out, scene
by scene. It'll be quite sufficient if we make a rough sketch of it first and
then have a run through.

PRODUCER [*climbing back on to the stage, tempted by this*].   H'm! . . . You almost
succeed in tempting me. . . . H'm! It would be rather fun! We could certainly have a shot at it.

FATHER. Of course! Oh, you'll see what wonderful scenes'll emerge! I can tell
740   you what they are here and now.

PRODUCER. You tempt me. . . . You tempt me. . . . Let's have a go at it! . . .
Come with me into my office. [*Turning to the* ACTORS.] You can have a few
minutes' break. . . . But don't go too far away. I want you all back again in
about a quarter of an hour or twenty minutes. [*To the* FATHER.] Well, let's
see what we can make of it! We might get something really extraordinary
out of it. . . .

FATHER. There's no *might* about it! They'd better come along too, don't you
think? [*Pointing to the other* CHARACTERS.]

PRODUCER. Yes, bring 'em along! Bring 'em along! [*Starts going off and then
750   turns back to the* ACTORS.] Now remember, don't be late back! You've got a
quarter of an hour!

[*The* PRODUCER *and the* SIX CHARACTERS *cross the stage and disappear. The* ACTORS
remain looking at one another in astonishment.]

LEADING MAN. Is he serious? What's he going to do?

JUVENILE LEAD. This is utter madness!

A THIRD ACTOR. Does he expect us to knock up a play in five minutes?

JUVENILE LEAD. Yes . . . like the actors in the old Commedia dell' Arte.[11]

LEADING LADY. Well, if he thinks that I'm going to have anything to do with
fun and games of that sort. . . .

INGENUE. And you certainly don't catch me joining in!

A FOURTH ACTOR. I should like to know who those people are. [*He is alluding
760   to the* CHARACTERS.]

THIRD ACTOR. Who do you think they're likely to be? They're probably
escaped lunatics. . . . Or crooks!

JUVENILE LEAD. And does he really take what they say seriously?

INGENUE. Vanity! That's what it is. . . . The vanity of appearing as an author!

LEADING MAN. It's absolutely unheard of! If the stage has come to this. . . .

A FIFTH ACTOR. I'm rather enjoying it!

THIRD ACTOR. Oh, well! After all, we shall have the pleasure of seeing what
comes of it all!

[*And talking among themselves in this way the* ACTORS *leave the stage. Some go out
through the door back, some go in the direction of the dressing-rooms. The curtain
remains up.*

The performance is suspended for twenty minutes.]

ACT II

The call-bells ring, warning the audience that the performance is about to be resumed.

The ACTORS, *the* STAGE-MANAGER, *the* FOREMAN *of the stage crew, the* PROMPTER
and the PROPERTY MAN *reassemble on stage. Some come from the dressing-rooms, some
through the door back, some even from the auditorium. The* PRODUCER *enters from his
office accompanied by the* SIX CHARACTERS.

The houselights are extinguished and the stage lighting is as before.

---

[11] An early Italian form of improvised comedy using such stock characters as the Harlequin
or the Pantaloon.

PRODUCER. Now come on, ladies and gentlemen! Are we all here? Let me
770   have your attention please! Now let's make a start! [*Then calls the* FORE-
MAN.]
FOREMAN. Yes, sir?
PRODUCER. Set the stage for the parlour scene. A couple of flats and a door
    will do. As quickly as you can!

[*The* FOREMAN *runs off at once to carry out this order and is setting the stage as
directed whilst the* PRODUCER *is making his arrangements with the* STAGE-MANAGER,
the PROPERTY MAN, *the* PROMPTER *and the* ACTORS. *The flats he has set up are painted
in pink and gold stripes.*]

PRODUCER [*to* PROPERTY MAN]. Just have a look, please, and see if we've got
    some sort of sofa or divan in the props room.
PROPERTY MAN. There's the green one, sir.
STEPDAUGHTER. No, no, green won't do! It was yellow . . . yellow flowered
    plush. . . . A huge thing . . . and most comfortable.
780 PROPERTY MAN. Well, we haven't got anything like that.
PRODUCER. It doesn't matter! Give me what there is!
STEPDAUGHTER. What do you mean, it doesn't matter? Madame Pace's fa-
    mous sofa!
PRODUCER. We only want it for this run-through. Please don't interfere. [*To
    the* STAGE-MANAGER.] Oh, and see if we've got a shop-window . . . something
    rather long and narrowish is what we want.
STEPDAUGHTER. And a little table . . . the little mahogany table for the pale
    blue envelope!
STAGE-MANAGER [*to* PRODUCER]. There's that little one. . . . You know, the
790   gold-painted one.
PRODUCER. That'll do fine! Shove it on!
FATHER. You need a long mirror.
STEPDAUGHTER. And the screen! I must have a screen, please. . . . Else how
    can I manage?
STAGE-MANAGER. Don't you worry, Miss! We've got masses of them!
PRODUCER [*to the* STEPDAUGHTER]. And some clothes-hangers and so on, h'm?
STEPDAUGHTER. Oh, yes, lots!
PRODUCER [*to the* STAGE-MANAGER]. See how many we've got and get some-
    body to bring them up.
800 STAGE-MANAGER. Right you are sir, I'll see to it!

[*The* STAGE-MANAGER *goes off about his business and while the* PRODUCER *is talking
to the* PROMPTER *and later to the* CHARACTERS *and* ACTORS, *he gets the stage hands to
bring up the furniture and properties and proceeds to arrange them in what he thinks
is the best sort of order.*]

PRODUCER [*to the* PROMPTER]. Now if you'll get into position while they're
    setting the stage. . . . Look, here's an outline of the thing. . . . Act I . . . Act
    II . . . [*he holds out some sheets of paper to him*]. But you'll really have to excel
    yourself this time.
PROMPTER. You mean, take it down in shorthand?
PRODUCER [*pleasantly surprised*]. Oh, good man! Can you do shorthand?
PROMPTER. I mayn't know much about prompting, but shorthand. . . .

PRODUCER. Better and better. [*Turning to a* STAGE-HAND.] Go and get some paper out of my room. . . . A large wadge.[12] . . . As much as you can find!

[*The* STAGE-HAND *hurries off and returns shortly with a thick wadge of paper which he gives to the* PROMPTER.]

810 PRODUCER [*to the* PROMPTER]. Follow the scenes closely as we play them and try and fix the lines . . . or at least the most important ones. [*Then, turning to the* ACTORS.] Right, ladies and gentlemen, clear the stage, please! No, come over this side [*he waves them over to his left*] . . . and pay careful attention to what goes on.

LEADING LADY. Excuse me, but we . . .

PRODUCER [*forestalling what she is going to say*]. There won't be any improvising to do, don't you worry!

LEADING MAN. What *do* we have to do, then?

PRODUCER. Nothing. For the moment all you've got to do is to stay over
820 there and watch what happens. You'll get your parts later. Just now we're going to have a rehearsal . . . or as much of one as we can in the circumstances! And *they'll* be doing the rehearsing [*he points to the* CHARACTERS].

FATHER [*in consternation, as if he had tumbled from the clouds into the midst of all the confusion on stage*]. We are? But, excuse me, in what way will it be a rehearsal?

PRODUCER. Well . . . a rehearsal . . . a rehearsal for *their* benefit.

[*He points to the* ACTORS.]

FATHER. But if we're the characters . . .

PRODUCER. Just so, "the characters." But it's not characters that act here. It's actors who do the acting here. The characters remain there, in the script
830 [*he points to the prompt box*]. . . . When there is a script!

FATHER. Precisely! And since there is no script and you have the good fortune to have the characters here alive before your very eyes. . . .

PRODUCER. Oh, this is wonderful. Do you want to do everything on your own? Act . . . present yourselves to the public?

FATHER. Yes, just as we are.

PRODUCER. And let me tell you you'd make a wonderful sight!

LEADING MAN. And what use should we be then?

PRODUCER. You're not going to pretend that you can act, are you? Why, it's enough to make a cat laugh. . . . [*And as a matter of fact, the* ACTORS *burst out*
840 *laughing.*] There you are, you see, they're laughing at the idea! [*Then, remembering.*] But, to the point! I must tell you what your parts are. That's not so very difficult. They pretty well cast themselves. [*To the* SECOND ACTRESS.] You, the Mother. [*To the* FATHER.] We'll have to find a name for her.

FATHER. Amalia.

PRODUCER. But that's your wife's name. We can hardly call her by her real name.

FATHER. And why not, when that's her name? But, perhaps, if it has to be that lady . . . [*a slight gesture to indicate the* SECOND ACTRESS] I see *her* [*pointing to the* MOTHER] as Amalia. But do as you like. . . . [*His confusion grows.*] I

---

[12] Loose stack.

850   don't know what to say to you. . . . I'm already beginning. . . . I don't know
        how to express it . . . to hear my own words ringing false . . . as if they had
        another sound from the one I had meant to give them. . . .

PRODUCER.   Now don't you worry about that! Don't you worry about it at all!
        We'll think about how to get the right tone of voice. And as for the
        name. . . . If you want it to be Amalia, Amalia it shall be. Or we'll find some
        other name. Just for the present we'll refer to the characters in this way.
        [*To the* JUVENILE LEAD.] You, the Son. . . . [*To the* LEADING LADY.] And you'll
        play the Stepdaughter, of course. . . .

STEPDAUGHTER [*excitedly*].   What! What did you say? That woman there. . . .
860   Me! [*She bursts out laughing.*]

PRODUCER [*angrily*].   And what's making you laugh?

LEADING LADY [*indignantly*].   Nobody has ever dared to laugh at me before!
        Either you treat me with respect or I'm walking out!

STEPDAUGHTER.   Oh, no, forgive me! I wasn't laughing at you.

PRODUCER [*to* STEPDAUGHTER].   You should feel yourself honoured to be played
        by . . .

LEADING LADY [*immediately, disdainfully*].   . . . "that woman there."

STEPDAUGHTER.   But my remark wasn't meant as a criticism of you . . . I was
        thinking about myself. . . . Because I can't see myself in you at all. I don't
870   know how to . . . you're not a bit like me!

FATHER.   Yes, that's the point I wanted to make! Look . . . all that we ex-
        press. . . .

PRODUCER.   What do you mean . . . *all that you express?* Do you think that this
        whatever-it-is that you express is something you've got inside you? Not a
        bit of it.

FATHER.   Why . . . aren't even the things we express our own?

PRODUCER.   Of course they aren't! The things that you express become ma-
        terial here for the actors, who give it body and form, voice and gesture.
        And, let me tell you, my actors have given expression to much loftier
880   material than this. This stuff of yours is so trivial that, believe me, if it
        comes off on the stage, the credit will all be due to my actors.

FATHER.   I don't dare to contradict you! But please believe me when I tell you
        that we . . . who have these bodies . . . these features. . . . Who are as you
        see us now. . . . We are suffering horribly. . . .

PRODUCER [*cutting in impatiently*].   . . . But the make-up will remedy all
        that. . . . At least as far as your faces are concerned!

FATHER.   Perhaps. . . . But what about our voices? . . . What about our ges-
        tures? . . .

PRODUCER.   Now, look here! You, as yourself, just cannot exist here! Here
890   there's an actor who'll play you. And let that be an end to all this argu-
        ment!

FATHER.   I understand. . . . And now I think I see why our author didn't wish
        to put us on the stage after all. . . . He saw us as we are. . . . Alive. . . . He
        saw us as living beings. . . . I don't want to offend your actors. . . . Heaven
        forbid that I should! . . . But I think that seeing myself acted now . . . by I
        don't know whom . . .

LEADING MAN [*rising with some dignity and coming over, followed by a laughing
        group of young actresses*].   By me, if you have no objection.

FATHER [*humbly, mellifluously*].   I am deeply honoured, sir. [*He bows.*] But. . . .
900   Well. . . . I think that however much of his art this gentleman puts into
absorbing me into himself. . . . However much he wills it. . . . [*He becomes
confused.*]

LEADING MAN.   Go on! Go on! [*The actresses laugh.*]

FATHER.   Well, I should say that the performance he'll give. . . . Even if he
makes himself up to look as much like me as he can. . . . I should say that
with his figure . . . [*All the* ACTORS *laugh.*] . . . it will be difficult for it to be
a performance of me . . . of me as I really am. It will rather be . . . leaving
aside the question of his appearance. . . . It will be how he interprets what
I am . . . how he sees me. . . . If he sees me as anything at all. . . . And not
910   as I, deep down within myself, feel myself to be. And it certainly seems to
me that whoever is called upon to criticise us will have to take this into
account.

PRODUCER.   So you're already thinking about what the critics will say, are
you? And here am I, still trying to get the play straight! The critics can say
what they like. We'd be much better occupied in thinking about getting
the play on. . . . If we can. [*Stepping out of the group and looking around him.*]
Now, come on, let's make a start! Is everything ready? [*To the* ACTORS *and*
CHARACTERS.] Come on, don't clutter up the place! Let me see how it looks!
[*He comes down from the stage.*] And now, don't let's lose any more time! [*To*
920   *the* STEPDAUGHTER.] Do you think the set looks all right?

STEPDAUGHTER.   To be perfectly honest, I just don't recognise it at all!

PRODUCER.   Good Lord, you surely didn't hope that we were going to reconstruct that room behind Madame Pace's shop here on the stage, did
you? [*To the* FATHER.] You did tell me it had flowered wallpaper, didn't
you?

FATHER.   Yes, white.

PRODUCER.   Well, it's not white—and it's got stripes on it—but it'll have to
do! As for the furniture, I think we've more or less got everything we need.
Bring that little table down here a bit! [*The* STAGE HANDS *do so. Then he says*
930   *to the* PROPERTY MAN.] Now, will you go and get an envelope. . . . A pale
blue one if you can. . . . And give it to that gentleman. [*He points to the*
FATHER.]

PROPERTY MAN.   The kind you put letters in?

PRODUCER AND FATHER.   Yes, the kind you put letters in!

PROPERTY MAN.   Yes, sir! At once, sir! [*Exit.*]

PRODUCER.   Now, come on! First scene—the young lady. [*The* LEADING LADY
comes forward.] No! No! Wait a moment! I said the young lady! [*Pointing to*
the STEPDAUGHTER.] You stay there and watch. . . .

STEPDAUGHTER [*immediately adding*]. . . . how I make it live!

940 LEADING LADY [*resentfully*].   I'll know how to make it live, don't you worry,
once I get started!

PRODUCER [*with his hands to his head*].   Ladies and gentlemen, don't let's have
any arguing! Please! Right! Now . . . The first scene is between the young
lady and Madame Pace. Oh! [*He looks around rather helplessly and then comes*
back on stage.] What about this Madame Pace?

FATHER.   She's not with us, sir.

PRODUCER.   And what do we do about her?

FATHER.   But she's alive! She's alive too!

PRODUCER.   Yes, yes! But where is she?

950 FATHER.   If you'll just allow me to have a word with your people. . . . [*Turning to the* ACTRESSES.] I wonder if you ladies would do me the kindness of lending me your hats for a moment.

THE ACTRESSES [*a chorus . . . half-laughing, half-surprised.*].   What?
   Our hats?
   What did he say?
   Why?
   Listen to the man!

PRODUCER.   What are you going to do with the women's hats? [*The* ACTORS *laugh.*]

960 FATHER.   Oh, nothing . . . I just want to put them on these pegs for a moment. And perhaps one of you ladies would be so kind as to take off your coat, too.

THE ACTORS [*laughter and surprise in their voices*].   Their coats as well?
   And after that?
   The man must be mad!

ONE OR TWO OF THE ACTRESSES [*surprise and laughter in their voices*].   But why?
   Only our coats?

FATHER.   So that I can hang them here. . . . Just for a moment or so. . . . Please do me this favour. Will you?

970 THE ACTRESSES [*they take off their hats. One or two take off their coats as well, all laughing the while. They go over and hang the coats here and there on the pegs and hangers*].
   And why not?
   Here you are!
   This really is funny!
   Do we have to put them on show?

FATHER.   Precisely. . . . You have to put them on show. . . . Like this!

PRODUCER.   Is one allowed to know what you're up to?

FATHER.   Why, yes. If we set the stage better, who knows whether she may not
980   be attracted by the objects of her trade and perhaps appear among us. . . .
   [*He invites them to look towards the door at the back of the stage.*] Look! Look!

[*The door opens and* MADAME PACE *comes in and takes a few steps forward. She is an enormously fat old harridan of a woman, wearing a pompous carrot-coloured tow wig with a red rose stuck into one side of it, in the Spanish manner. She is heavily made up and dressed with clumsy elegance in a stylish red silk dress. In one hand she carries an ostrich feather fan; the other hand is raised and a lighted cigarette is poised between two fingers. Immediately they see this apparition, the* ACTORS *and the* PRODUCER *bound off the stage with howls of fear, hurling themselves down the steps into the auditorium and making as if to dash up the aisle. The* STEPDAUGHTER, *however, rushes humbly up to* MADAME PACE, *as if greeting her mistress.*]

STEPDAUGHTER [*rushing up to her*].   Here she is! Here she is!

FATHER [*beaming*].   It's Madame Pace! What did I tell you? Here she is!

PRODUCER [*his first surprise overcome, he is now indignant*].   What sort of a game do you call this?

Leading Man. ⎫

Juvenile Lead. ⎪   *[Almost at the*

Ingenue. ⎪   *same moment*

990   ⎬   *and all*

Leading Lady. ⎪   *speaking at*

           ⎭   *once.]*

⎧ Hang it all, what's going on?

Where did *she* spring from?

They were keeping her in reserve!

So it's back to the music hall and conjuring tricks, is it?

Father [*dominating the protesting voices*]. One moment, please! Why should you wish to destroy this prodigy of reality, which was born, which was evoked, attracted and formed by this scene itself? . . . A reality which has more right to live here than you have. . . . Because it is so very much more alive than you are. . . . Why do you want to spoil it all, just because of some niggling, vulgar convention of truth? . . . Which of you actresses will be playing the part of Madame Pace? Well, *that* woman *is* Madame Pace! Grant me at least that the actress who plays her will be less true than she is. . . . For *she* is Madame Pace in person! Look! My daughter recognised her and went up to her at once. Now, watch this scene! Just watch it! [*Hesitantly the* Producer *and the* Actors *climb back on to the stage. But while the* Actors *have been protesting and the* Father *has been replying to them, the scene between the* Stepdaughter *and* Madame Pace *has begun. It is carried on in an undertone, very quietly—naturally in fact—in a manner that would be quite impossible on the stage. When the* Actors *obey the* Father's *demand that they shall watch what is happening, they see that* Madame Pace *has already put her hand under the* Stepdaughter's *chin to raise her head and is talking to her. Hearing her speak in a completely unintelligible manner they are held for a moment. But almost immediately their attention flags.*]

Producer. Well?

Leading Man. But what's she saying?

Leading Lady. We can't hear a thing!

Juvenile Lead. Speak up! Louder!

Stepdaughter [*she leaves* Madame Pace *and comes down to the group of* Actors. Madame Pace *smiles—a priceless smile*]. Did you say, 'Louder?' What do you mean, 'Louder?' What we're talking about is scarcely the sort of thing to be shouted from the roof-tops. I was able to yell it out just now so that I could shame *him* [*pointing to the* Father]. . . . So that I could have my revenge! But it's quite another matter for Madame Pace. . . . It would mean prison for her.

Producer. Indeed? So that's how it is, is it? But let me tell you something, my dear young lady. . . . Here in the theatre you've got to make yourself heard! The way you're doing this bit at the moment even those of us who're on stage can't hear you! Just imagine what it'll be like with an audience out front. This scene's got to be got over. And anyway there's nothing to prevent you from speaking up when you're on together. . . . We shan't be here to listen to you. . . . We're only here now because it's a rehearsal. Pretend you're alone in the room behind the shop, where nobody can hear you.

[*The* Stepdaughter *elegantly, charmingly—and with a mischievous smile—wags her finger two or three times in disagreement.*]

PRODUCER.   What do you mean, 'No?'

STEPDAUGHTER [*in a mysterious whisper*].   There's someone who'll hear us if *she* [*pointing to* MADAME PACE] speaks up.

PRODUCER [*in utter consternation*].   Do you mean to say that there's somebody else who's going to burst in on us? [*The* ACTORS *make as if to dive off the stage again.*]

FATHER.   No! No! They're alluding to me. I have to be there, waiting behind the door. . . . And Madame Pace knows it. So, if you'll excuse me, I'll go. . . . So that I'm all ready to make my entrance. [*He starts off towards the back of the stage.*]

1040

PRODUCER [*stopping him*].   No! No! Wait a moment! When you're here you have to respect the conventions of the theatre! Before you get ready to go on to that bit. . . .

STEPDAUGHTER.   No! Let's get on with it at once! At once! I'm dying with desire, I tell you . . . to live this scene. . . . To live it! If he wants to get on with it right away, I'm more than ready!

PRODUCER [*shouting*].   But first of all, the scene between you and her [*pointing to* MADAME PACE] has got to be got over! Do you understand?

1050 STEPDAUGHTER.   Oh, my God! She's just been telling me what *you* already know. . . . That once again my mother's work has been badly done. . . . That the dress is spoilt. . . . And that I must be patient if she is to go on helping us in our misfortune.

MADAME PACE [*stepping forward, a grand air of importance about her*].   But, yes, señor, porque[13] I not want to make profit . . . to take advantàge. . . .

PRODUCER [*more than a touch of terror in his voice*].   What? Does she speak like that?

[*The* ACTORS *burst into noisy laughter.*]

STEPDAUGHTER [*laughing too*].   Yes, she speaks like that, half in English, half in Spanish. . . . It's most comical.

1060 MADAME PACE.   Ah, no, it does not to me seem good manners that you laugh of me when I . . . force myself to . . . hablar,[14] as I can, English, señor!

PRODUCER.   Indeed, no! It's very wrong of us! You speak like that! Yes, speak like that, Madame! It'll bring the house down! We couldn't ask for anything better. It'll bring a little comic relief into the crudity of the situation. Yes, you talk like that! It's absolutely wonderful!

STEPDAUGHTER.   Wonderful! And why not? When you hear a certain sort of suggestion made to you in a lingo like that. . . . There's not much doubt about what your answer's going to be. . . . Because it almost seems like a joke. You feel inclined to laugh when you hear there's an 'old señor' who wants to 'amuse himself with me'. An 'old señor', eh, Madame?

1070 MADAME PACE.   Not so very old. . . . Not quite so young, yes? And if he does not please to you. . . . Well, he has . . . *prudencia*.[15]

MOTHER [*absorbed as they are in the scene the* ACTORS *have been paying no attention to her. Now, to their amazement and consternation, she leaps up and*

---

13 Because.
14 Speak.
15 Discretion.

attacks MADAME PACE. *At her cry they jump, then hasten smilingly to restrain her, for she, meanwhile, has snatched off* MADAME PACE's *wig and has thrown it to the ground*]. You old devil! You old witch! You murderess! Oh, my daughter!

STEPDAUGHTER [*rushing over to restrain her* MOTHER]. No, Mummy, no! Please!

FATHER [*rushing over at the same time*]. Calm yourself, my dear! Just be calm! Now . . . come and sit down again!

MOTHER. Take that woman out of my sight, then!

[*In the general excitement the* PRODUCER, *too, has rushed over and the* STEPDAUGHTER *now turns to him.*]

STEPDAUGHTER. It's impossible for my mother to remain here!

FATHER [*to the* PRODUCER]. They can't be here together. That's why, when we first came, that woman wasn't with us. If they're on at the same time the whole thing is inevitably given away in advance.

PRODUCER. It doesn't matter! It doesn't matter a bit! This is only a first run-through. . . . Just to give us a rough idea how it goes. Everything'll come in useful . . . I can sort out the bits and pieces later. . . . I'll make something out of it, even if it is all jumbled up. [*Turning to the* MOTHER *and leading her back to her chair.*] Now, please be calm, and sit down here, nice and quietly.

[*Meanwhile the* STEPDAUGHTER *has gone down centre stage again. She turns to* MADAME PACE.]

STEPDAUGHTER. Go on, Madame, go on!

MADAME PACE [*offended*]. Ah, no thank you! Here I do not do nothing more with your mother present!

STEPDAUGHTER. Now, come on! Show in the 'old señor' who wants to 'amuse himself with me.' [*Turning imperiously on the rest.*] Yes, this scene has got to be played. So let's get on with it! [*To* MADAME PACE.] You can go!

MADAME PACE. Ah, I am going . . . I am going. . . . Most assuredly I am going! [*Exit furiously, ramming her wig back on and glowering at the* ACTORS, *who mockingly applaud her.*]

STEPDAUGHTER [*to the* FATHER]. And now you make your entrance! There's no need for you to go out and come in again! Come over here! Pretend that you've already entered! Now, I'm standing here modestly, my eyes on the ground. Come on! Speak up! Say, 'Good afternoon, Miss,' in that special tone of voice . . . you know. . . . Like somebody who's just come in from the street.

PRODUCER [*by this time he is down off the stage*]. Listen to her! Are you running this rehearsal, or am I? [*To the* FATHER *who is looking perplexed and undecided.*] Go on, do as she tells you! Go to the back of the stage. . . . Don't exit! . . . And then come forward again.

[*The* FATHER *does as he is told. He is troubled and very pale. But as he approaches from the back of the stage he smiles, already absorbed in the reality of his created life. He smiles as if the drama which is about to break upon him is as yet unknown to him. The* ACTORS *become intent on the scene which is beginning.*]

PRODUCER [*whispering quickly to the* PROMPTER, *who has taken up his position*]. Get ready to write now!

THE SCENE

FATHER. [*coming forward, a new note in his voice*].   Good afternoon, Miss.

STEPDAUGHTER [*her head bowed, speaking with restrained disgust*].   Good afternoon!

FATHER [*studying her a little, looking up into her face from under the brim of her hat (which almost hides it), and perceiving that she is very young, exclaims, almost to himself, a little out of complacency, a little, too, from the fear of compromising himself in a risky adventure*].   H'm! But. . . . M'm. . . . This won't be the first
1120   time, will it? The first time that you've been here?

STEPDAUGHTER [*as before*].   No, sir.

FATHER.   You've been here before? [*And since the STEPDAUGHTER nods in affirmation.*] More than once? [*He waits a little while for her reply, resumes his study of her, again looking up into her face from under the brim of her hat, smiles and then says.*] Then . . . well . . . it shouldn't any longer be so. . . . May I take off your hat?

STEPDAUGHTER [*immediately forestalling him, unable to restrain her disgust*].   No, sir, I'll take it off myself! [*Convulsed, she hurriedly takes it off.*]

[*The MOTHER is on tenterhooks throughout. The TWO CHILDREN cling to their MOTHER and they, she and the SON form a group on the side opposite the ACTORS, watching the scene. The MOTHER follows the words and the actions of the STEPDAUGHTER and the FATHER with varying expressions of sorrow, of indignation, of anxiety and of horror; from time to time she hides her face in her hands and sobs.*]

MOTHER.   Oh, my God! My God!
1130 FATHER [*he remains for a moment as if turned to stone by this sob. Then he resumes in the same tone of voice as before*].   Here, let me take it. I'll hang it up for you. [*He takes the hat from her hands.*] But such a charming, such a dear little head really ought to have a much smarter hat than this! Would you like to come and help me choose one from among these hats of Madame's? Will you?

INGENUE [*breathing in*].   Oh, I say! Those are *our* hats!

PRODUCER [*at once, furiously*].   For God's sake, shut up! Don't try to be funny! We're doing our best to rehearse this scene, in case you weren't aware of the fact! [*Turning to STEPDAUGHTER.*] Go on from where you left off, please.
1140 STEPDAUGHTER [*continuing*].   No thank you, sir.

FATHER.   Come now, don't say no. Do say you'll accept it. . . . Just to please me. I shall be most upset if you won't. . . . Look, here are some rather nice ones. And then it would please Madame. She puts them out on show on purpose, you know.

STEPDAUGHTER.   No . . . listen! I couldn't wear it.

FATHER.   You're thinking perhaps about what they'll say when you come home wearing a new hat? Well now, shall I tell you what to do? Shall I tell you what to say when you get home?

STEPDAUGHTER [*quickly—she is at the end of her tether*].   No, it's not that! I
1150   couldn't wear it because I'm . . . As you see. . . . You should have noticed already . . . [*indicating her black dress*].

FATHER.   That you're in mourning! Of course. . . . Oh, forgive me! Of course! Oh, I beg your pardon! Believe me. . . . I'm most profoundly sorry. . . .

STEPDAUGHTER [*summoning all her strength and forcing herself to conquer her contempt, her indignation and her nausea*].   Stop! Please don't say any more! I really ought to be thanking you. There's no need for you to feel so very sorry or upset! Please don't give another thought to what I said! I, too, you understand. . . . [*Tries hard to smile and adds.*] I really must forget that I'm dressed like this!

1160 PRODUCER [*interrupting them; he climbs back on to the stage and turns to the* PROMPTER].   Hold it! Stop a minute! Don't write that down. Leave out that last bit. [*Turning to the* FATHER *and the* STEPDAUGHTER.] It's going very well! Very well indeed! [*Then to the* FATHER.] And then you go on as we arranged. [*To the* ACTORS.] Rather delightful, that bit where he offers her the hat, don't you think?

STEPDAUGHTER.   Ah, but the best bit's coming now! Why aren't we going on?

PRODUCER.   Now be patient, please! Just for a little while! [*Turning to the* ACTORS.] Of course it'll have to be treated rather lightly. . . .

LEADING MAN. . . . M'm . . . and put over slickly. . . .

1170 LEADING LADY.   Of course! There's nothing difficult about it at all. [*To the* LEADING MAN.] Shall we try it now?

LEADING MAN.   As far as I'm . . . I'll go and get ready for my entrance. [*Exit to take up his position outside the door back.*]

PRODUCER [*to the* LEADING LADY].   Now, look. . . . The scene between you and Madame Pace is finished. I'll get down to writing it up properly afterwards. You're standing. . . . Where are you going?

LEADING LADY.   Just a moment! I want to put my hat back on. . . . [*Goes over, takes her hat down and puts it on.*]

PRODUCER.   Good! Now you stand here. With your head bowed down a bit.

1180 STEPDAUGHTER [*amused*].   But she's not dressed in black!

LEADING LADY.   I *shall* be dressed in black. . . . And much more becomingly than you are.

PRODUCER [*to the* STEPDAUGHTER].   Shut up . . . please! And watch! You'll learn something. [*Claps his hands.*] Now come on! Let's get going! Entrance! [*He goes down from the stage again to see how it looks from out front. The door back opens and the* LEADING MAN *steps forward. He has the lively, raffish, self-possessed air of an elderly gallant. The playing of this scene by the* ACTORS *will appear from the very first words as something completely different from what was played before, without its having, even in the slightest degree, the air of a parody. It should appear*

1190 *rather as if the scene has been touched up. Quite naturally the* FATHER *and the* STEPDAUGHTER, *not being able to recognise themselves at all in the* LEADING LADY *and* LEADING MAN, *yet hearing them deliver the very words they used, react in a variety of ways, now with a gesture, now with a smile, with open protest even, to the impression they receive. They are surprised, lost in wonder, in suffering . . . as we shall see. The* PROMPTER's *voice is clearly heard throughout the scene.*]

LEADING MAN.   Good afternoon, Miss!

FATHER [*immediately, unable to restrain himself*].   No! No! [*And the* STEPDAUGHTER, *seeing the* LEADING MAN *enter in this way, bursts out laughing.*]

PRODUCER [*infuriated*].   Shut up! And once and for all . . . Stop that laughing!

1200 We shan't get anywhere if we go on like this!

STEPDAUGHTER [*moving away from the proscenium*].   Forgive me . . . but I couldn't help laughing! This lady [*pointing to the* LEADING LADY] stands just where you put her, without budging an inch . . . But if she's meant to be me. . . . I can assure you that if I heard anybody saying 'Good afternoon' to me in that way and in that tone of voice I'd burst out laughing. . . . So I had to, you see.

FATHER [*coming forward a little, too*].   Yes, that's it exactly. . . . His manner. . . . The tone of voice. . . .

PRODUCER.   To hell with your manner and your tone of voice! Just stand to
1210   one side, if you don't mind, and let me get a look at this rehearsal.

LEADING MAN [*coming forward*].   Now if I've got to play an old fellow who's coming into a house of rather doubtful character. . . .

PRODUCER.   Oh, don't take any notice of him! Now, *please!* Start again, please! It was going very nicely. [*There is a pause—he is clearly waiting for the* LEADING MAN *to begin again.*] Well?

LEADING MAN.   Good afternoon, Miss.

LEADING LADY.   Good afternoon!

LEADING MAN [*repeating the* FATHER's *move—that is, looking up into the* LEADING LADY's *face from under the brim of her hat; but then expressing very clearly first his*
1220   *satisfaction and then his fear*].   M'm . . . this won't be the first time, I hope. . . .

FATHER [*unable to resist the temptation to correct him*].   Not 'hope'—'will it', 'will it?'

PRODUCER.   You say 'will it?' . . . It's a question.

LEADING MAN [*pointing to the* PROMPTER].   I'm sure he said, 'hope.'

PRODUCER.   Well, it's all one! 'Hope' or whatever it was! Go on, please! Go on. . . . Oh, there was one thing . . . I think perhaps it ought not to be quite so heavy. . . . Hold on, I'll show you what I mean. Watch me. . . . [*Comes back on to the stage. Then, making his entrance, he proceeds to play the part.*] Good afternoon, Miss.

1230   LEADING LADY.   Good afternoon. . . .

PRODUCER.   M'm . . . [*Turning to the* LEADING MAN *to impress on him the way he has looked up at the* LEADING LADY *from under the brim of her hat.*] Surprise, fear and satisfaction. [*Then turning back to the* LEADING LADY.] It won't be the first time, will it, that you've been here? [*Turning again to the* LEADING MAN *enquiringly.*] Is that clear? [*To the* LEADING LADY.] And then you say, 'No, sir.' [*To the* LEADING MAN.] There you are. . . . It wants to be a little more . . . what shall I say? . . . A little more *flexible.* A little more *souple!* [*He goes down from the stage again.*]

LEADING LADY.   No, sir. . . .

1240   LEADING MAN.   You've been here before? More than once?

PRODUCER.   Wait a minute! You must let her [*pointing to the* LEADING LADY] get her nod in first. You've been here before? [*The* LEADING LADY *lifts her head a little, closing her eyes painfully as if in disgust and then when the* PRODUCER *says* Down, *nods twice.*]

STEPDAUGHTER [*unable to restrain herself*].   Oh, my God! [*And immediately she puts her hand over her mouth to stifle her laughter.*]

PRODUCER [*turning*].   What's the matter?

STEPDAUGHTER [*immediately*].   Nothing! Nothing!

PRODUCER [*to the* LEADING MAN].   It's your cue. . . . Carry straight on.

1250   LEADING MAN.   More than once? Well then . . . Come along. . . . May I take off your hat?

[*The* LEADING MAN *says this last line in such a tone of voice and accompanies it with such a gesture that the* STEPDAUGHTER, *who has remained with her hands over her mouth, can no longer restrain herself. She tries desperately to prevent herself from laughing but a noisy burst of laughter comes irresistibly through her fingers.*]

LEADING LADY [*turning indignantly*].   I'm not going to stand here and be made a fool of by that woman!

LEADING MAN.   And neither am I. Let's pack the whole thing in.

PRODUCER [*shouting at the* STEPDAUGHTER].   Once and for all, will you shut up!

STEPDAUGHTER.   Yes. . . . Forgive me, please! . . . Forgive me!

PRODUCER.   The trouble with you is that you've got no manners! You go too far!

FATHER [*trying to intervene*].   Yes, sir, you're quite right! Quite right! But you
1260   must forgive her. . . .

PRODUCER [*climbing back on to the stage*].   What do you want me to forgive? It's absolutely disgusting the way she's behaving!

FATHER.   Yes. . . . But . . . Oh, believe me . . . Believe me, it has such a strange effect. . . .

PRODUCER.   Strange! How do you mean, 'Strange'? What's so strange about it?

FATHER.   You see, sir, I admire . . . I admire your actors. . . . That gentleman there [*pointing to the* LEADING MAN] and that lady [*pointing to the* LEADING LADY] . . . But . . . Well . . . The truth is . . . They're certainly not us!

1270 PRODUCER.   I should hope not! How do you expect them to be *you* if they're actors?

FATHER.   Just so, actors. And they play our parts well, both of them. But when they act . . . To us they seem to be doing something quite different. They want to be the same . . . And all the time they just aren't.

PRODUCER.   But how aren't they the same? What are they then?

FATHER.   Something that becomes theirs . . . And no longer ours.

PRODUCER.   But that's inevitable! I've told you that already.

FATHER.   Yes, I understand . . . I understand that. . . .

PRODUCER.   Well then, let's hear no more on the subject! [*Turning to the*
1280   ACTORS.] We'll run through it later by ourselves in the usual way. I've always had a strong aversion to holding rehearsals with the author present. He's never satisfied! [*Turning to the* FATHER *and the* STEPDAUGHTER.] Now, come on, let's get on with it! And let's see if we can have no more laughing! [*To the* STEPDAUGHTER.]

STEPDAUGHTER.   Oh, I shan't laugh any more! I promise you! My big bit's coming now. . . . Just you wait and see!

PRODUCER.   Well, then. . . . When you say, 'Please don't give another thought to what I said! I, too, you understand. . . .' [*Turning to the* FATHER.] You come in at once with, 'I understand! I understand!' and immediately ask . . .

1290 STEPDAUGHTER [*interrupting him*].   What? What does he ask?

PRODUCER.   . . . why you're in mourning.

STEPDAUGHTER.   Oh, no! That's not it at all! Listen! When I told him that I mustn't think about my being in mourning, do you know what his answer was? 'Well, then, let's take this little frock off at once, shall we?'

PRODUCER.   That would be wonderful! Wonderful! That *would* bring the house down!

STEPDAUGHTER.   But it's the truth!

PRODUCER.   But what's the truth got to do with it? Acting's what *we're* here for! Truth's all very fine . . . But only up to a point.

1300 STEPDAUGHTER.   And what do you want then?

PRODUCER.   You'll see! You'll see. Leave everything to me.

STEPDAUGHTER.   No, I won't! What you'd like to do, no doubt, is to concoct a romantic, sentimental little affair out of my disgust, out of all the reasons, each more cruel, each viler than the other, why I am this sort of woman, why I am what I am! An affair with him! He asks me why I'm in mourning and I reply with tears in my eyes that my father died only two months ago. No! No! He must say what he said then, 'Well, then, let's take this little frock off at once, shall we?' And I . . . my heart still grieving for my father's death. . . . I went behind there . . . Do you understand? . . . There, behind

1310 that screen! And then, my fingers trembling with shame and disgust, I took off my frock, undid my brassière. . . .

PRODUCER [*running his hands through his hair*].   For God's sake! What on earth are you saying, girl?

STEPDAUGHTER [*crying out excitedly*].   The truth! The truth!

PRODUCER.   Yes, it probably is the truth! I'm not denying it! And I understand . . . I fully appreciate all your horror. But you must realise that we simply can't put this kind of thing on the stage.

STEPDAUGHTER.   Oh, you can't, can't you? If that's how things are, thanks very much! I'm going!

1320 PRODUCER.   No! No! Look here! . . .

STEPDAUGHTER.   I'm going! I'm not stopping here! You worked it all out together, didn't you? . . . The pair of you. . . . You and him. . . . When you were in there. . . . You worked out what was going to be possible on the stage. Oh, thanks very much! I understand! He wants to jump to the bit where he presents his spiritual torments! [*This is said harshly.*] But I want to present my own drama! *Mine! Mine!*

PRODUCER [*his shoulders shaking with annoyance*].   Ah! There we have it! *Your* drama! Look here . . . you'll have to forgive me for telling you this . . . but there isn't only your part to be considered! Each of the others has

1330 his drama, too. [*He points to the* FATHER.] He has his and your Mother has hers. You can't have one character coming along like this, becoming too prominent, invading the stage in and out of season and overshadowing all the rest. All the characters must be contained within one harmonious picture, and presenting only what it is proper to present. I'm very well aware that everyone carries a complete life within himself and that he wants to put it before the whole world. But it's here that we run into difficulties: how are we to bring out only just so much as is absolutely necessary? . . . And at the same time, of course, to take into account all the other characters. . . . And yet in that small fragment we have to be

1340 able to hint at all the rest of the secret life of that character. Ah, it would be all very pleasant if each character could have a nice little monologue. . . . Or without making any bones about it, give a lecture, in which he could tell his audience what's bubbling and boiling away inside him. [*His tone is good-humoured, conciliatory.*] You must restrain yourself. And believe me, it's in your own interest, too. Because all this fury . . . this exasperation and this disgust . . . They make a bad impression. Especially when . . . And pardon me for mentioning this. . . . You yourself have confessed that you'd had other men there at Madame Pace's before him. . . . And more than once!

1350 STEPDAUGHTER [*bowing her head. She pauses a moment in recollection and then, a deeper note in her voice*]. That is true! But you must remember that those other men mean *him* for me, just as much as he himself does!

PRODUCER [*uncomprehending*]. What? The other men mean *him?* What do you mean?

STEPDAUGHTER. Isn't it true that in the case of someone who's gone wrong, the person who was responsible for the first fault is responsible for all the faults which follow? And in my case, he is responsible. . . . Has been ever since before I was born. Look at him, and see if it isn't true!

PRODUCER. Very well, then! And does this terrible weight of remorse that is
1360 resting on his spirit seem so slight a thing to you? Give him the chance of acting it!

STEPDAUGHTER. How? How can he act all his 'noble' remorse, all his 'moral' torments, if you want to spare him all the horror of one day finding in his arms. . . . After he had asked her to take off her frock . . . her grief still undulled by time. . . . The horror of finding in his arms that child. . . . A woman now, and a fallen woman already. . . . That child whom he used to go and watch as she came out of school? [*She says these last words in a voice trembling with emotion. The* MOTHER, *hearing her talk like this, is overcome by distress which expresses itself at first in stifled sobs. Finally*
1370 *she breaks out into a fit of bitter crying. Everyone is deeply moved. There is a long pause.*]

STEPDAUGHTER [*gravely and resolutely, as soon as the* MOTHER *shows signs of becoming a little quieter*]. At the moment we are here, unknown as yet by the public. Tomorrow you will present us as you wish. . . . Making up your play in your own way. But would you really like to see our drama? To see it flash into life as it did in reality?

PRODUCER. Why, of course! I couldn't ask for anything better, so that from now on I can use as much as possible of it.

STEPDAUGHTER. Well, then, ask my Mother to leave us.

1380 MOTHER [*rising, her quiet weeping changed to a sharp cry*]. No! No! Don't you allow them to do it! Don't allow them to do it!

PRODUCER. But it's only so that I can see how it goes.

MOTHER. I can't bear it! I can't bear it!

PRODUCER. But since it's already happened, I don't understand!

MOTHER. No, it's happening now! It happens all the time! My torment is no pretence, sir. I am alive and I am present always. . . . At every moment of my torment. . . . A torment which is for ever renewing itself. Always alive and always present. But those two children there. . . . Have you heard them say a single word? They can no longer speak! They cling to me
1390 still. . . . In order to keep my torment living and present! But for themselves they no longer exist! They no longer exist! And she [*pointing to the* STEPDAUGHTER] . . . She has run away. . . . Run away from me and is lost. . . . Lost! . . . And if I see her here before me it is for this reason and for this reason alone. . . . To renew at all times. . . . Forever. . . . To bring before me again, present and living, the anguish that I have suffered on her account too.

FATHER [*solemnly*]. The eternal moment, as I told you, sir. She [*he points to the* STEPDAUGHTER] . . . She is here in order to fix me. . . . To hold me suspended throughout all eternity. . . . In the pillory of that one fleeting

1400   shameful moment in my life. She cannot renounce her rôle. . . . And you, sir, cannot really spare me my agony.

PRODUCER.   Quite so, but I didn't say that I wouldn't present it. As a matter of fact it'll form the basis of the first act. . . . Up to the point where she surprises you [*pointing to the* MOTHER].

FATHER.   That is right. Because it is my sentence. All our passion. . . . All our suffering. . . . Which must culminate in *her* cry [*pointing to the* MOTHER].

STEPDAUGHTER.   I can still hear it ringing in my ears! That cry sent me mad! You can play me just as you like. . . . It doesn't matter. Dressed, if you like, provided that I can have my arms bare at least. . . . Just my arms bare. . . .

1410   Because, you see, standing there . . . [*She goes up to the* FATHER *and rests her head on his chest.*] with my head resting on his chest like this . . . and with my arms round his neck . . . I could see a vein throbbing away in my arm. And then . . . Just as if that pulsing vein alone gave me a sense of horror . . . I shut my eyes tight and buried my head in his chest. [*Turning towards the* MOTHER.] Scream, Mummy! Scream! [*She buries her head in the* FATHER's *chest and, raising her shoulders as if in order not to hear the cry, adds in a voice stifled with torment.*] Scream, as you screamed then!

MOTHER [*rushing upon them to separate them*].   No! No! She's my daughter! [*And having torn her daughter away.*] You brute! You brute! She's my daugh-

1420   ter! Can't you see that she's my daughter?

PRODUCER [*retreating at the cry right up to the footlights, amid the general dismay of the* ACTORS].   Excellent! Excellent! And then . . . Curtain! Curtain!

FATHER [*rushing over to him convulsively*].   Yes, because that's how it really happened!

PRODUCER [*quite convinced, admiration in his voice*].   Oh, yes, we must have the curtain there. . . . That cry and then . . . Curtain! Curtain!

[*At the repeated shouts of the* PRODUCER *the* STAGE HAND *on the curtain lets it down, leaving the* PRODUCER *and the* FATHER *between it and the footlights.*]

PRODUCER [*looking up, his arms raised*].   Oh, the damned fool! I say, 'Curtain' . . . Meaning that I want the act to end there. . . . And he really does go and bring the curtain down. [*To the* FATHER, *lifting up a corner of the curtain.*]

1430   Oh, yes! That's absolutely wonderful! Very good indeed! That'll get them! There's no *if or but* about it. . . . That line and then . . . *Curtain!* We've got something in that first act . . . or I'm a Dutchman! [*Disappears through the curtain with the* FATHER.]

ACT III

When the curtain goes up again the audience sees that the STAGE HANDS *have dismantled the previous set and put on in its place a small garden fountain. On one side of the stage the* ACTORS *are sitting in a row, and on the other side, the* CHARACTERS. *The* PRODUCER *is standing in a meditative attitude in the middle of the stage with his hand clenched over his mouth. There is a brief pause; then:*

PRODUCER [*with a shrug of his shoulders*].   Oh, well! . . . Let's get on with Act II! Now if you'll only leave it all to me, as we agreed, everything'll sort itself out.

STEPDAUGHTER. This is where we make our entry into his house. . . . [*Pointing to the* FATHER.] In spite of him! [*Pointing to the* SON.]

1440 PRODUCER [*out of patience*]. Yes, yes! But leave it to me, I tell you!

STEPDAUGHTER. Well. . . . So long as it's made quite clear that it was against his wishes.

MOTHER [*from the corner, shaking her head*]. For all the good that's come of it. . . .

STEPDAUGHTER [*turning to her quickly*]. That doesn't matter! The more harm that it's done us, the more remorse for him!

PRODUCER [*impatiently*]. I understand all that! I'll take it all into account! Don't you worry about it!

MOTHER [*a supplicant note in her voice*]. But I do beg you, sir . . . To set my
1450 conscience at rest. . . . To make it quite plain that I tried in every way I could to . . .

STEPDAUGHTER [*interrupting contemptuously and continuing her* MOTHER's *speech*].
. . . to pacify me, to persuade me not to get my own back. . . . [*To the* PRODUCER.] Go on . . . do what she asks you! Give her that satisfaction. . . . Because she's quite right, you know! I'm enjoying myself no end, because . . . Well, just look. . . . The meeker she is, the more she tries to wriggle her way into his heart, the more he holds himself aloof, the more distant he becomes. I can't think why she bothers!

PRODUCER. Are we going to get started on the second act or are we not?

1460 STEPDAUGHTER. I won't say another word! But, you know, it won't be possible to play it all in the garden, as you suggested.

PRODUCER. Why not?

STEPDAUGHTER. Because he [*pointing to the* SON *again*] shuts himself up in his room all the time. . . . Holding himself aloof. . . . And, what's more, there's all the boy's part. . . . Poor bewildered little devil. . . . As I told you, all that takes place indoors.

PRODUCER. I know all about that! On the other hand you do understand that we can hardly stick up notices telling the audience what the scene is. . . . *Or* change the set three or four times in one act.

1470 LEADING MAN. They used to in the good old days.

PRODUCER. Oh, yes. . . . When the intelligence of the audience was about up to the level of that little girl's there. . . .

LEADING LADY. And it does make it easier to get the sense of illusion.

FATHER [*immediately, rising*]. Illusion, did you say? For Heaven's sake, please don't use the word illusion! Please don't use that word. . . . It's a particularly cruel one for us!

PRODUCER [*astounded*]. And why's that?

FATHER. It's cruel! Cruel! You should have known that!

PRODUCER. What ought we to say then? We were referring to the illusion that
1480 we have to create on this stage . . . for the audience. . . .

LEADING MAN. . . . with our acting. . . .

PRODUCER. . . . the illusion of a reality!

FATHER. I understand, sir. But you . . . Perhaps you can't understand us. Forgive me! Because . . . you see . . . for you and for your actors, all this is only . . . and quite rightly so. . . . All this is only a game.

LEADING LADY [*indignantly interrupting him*]. What do you mean, a game? We're not children! We're serious actors!

FATHER.   I don't deny it! And in fact, in using the term, I was referring to
your art which must, as this gentleman has said, create a perfect illusion of
1490   reality.
PRODUCER.   Precisely!
FATHER.   Now just consider the fact that we [*pointing quickly to himself and to the
other* FIVE CHARACTERS] as ourselves, have no other reality outside this illusion!
PRODUCER [*in utter astonishment, looking round at his actors who show the same
bewildered amazement*].   And what does all that mean?
FATHER [*the ghost of a smile on his face. There is a brief pause while he looks at them
all*].   As I said. . . . What other reality should we have? What for you is an
illusion that you have to create, for us, on the other hand, is our sole
1500   reality. The only reality we know. [*There is a short pause. Then he takes a step
or two towards the* PRODUCER *and adds.*] But it's not only true in our case, you
know. Just think it over. [*He looks into his eyes.*] Can you tell me who you
are? [*And he stands there pointing his index finger at him.*]
PRODUCER [*disturbed, a half-smile on his lips*].   What? Who am I? I'm myself!
FATHER.   And suppose I were to tell you that that wasn't true? Suppose I told
you that you were me? . . .
PRODUCER.   I should say that you were mad! [*The* ACTORS *laugh.*]
FATHER.   You're quite right to laugh, because here everything's a game. [*To
the* PRODUCER.] And you can object, therefore, that it's only in fun that that
1510   gentleman [*pointing to the* LEADING MAN] who is *himself* must be *me* who, on
the contrary, am myself. . . . That is, *the person you see here*. There, you see.
I've caught you in a trap! [*The* ACTORS *laugh again.*]
PRODUCER [*annoyed*].   But you said all this not ten minutes ago! Do we have
to go over all that again?
FATHER.   No. As a matter of fact that wasn't what I intended. I should like to
invite you to abandon this game. . . . [*Looking at the* LEADING LADY *as if to
forestall what she will say.*] Your art! Your art! . . . The game that is customary for you and your actors to play here in this theatre. And once again I
ask you in all seriousness. . . . Who are you?
1520   PRODUCER [*turning to the* ACTORS *in utter amazement, an amazement not unmixed
with irritation*].   What a cheek the fellow has! A man who calls himself a
character comes here and asks me who I am!
FATHER [*with dignity, but in no way haughtily*].   A character, sir, may always ask
a man who he is. Because a character has a life which is truly his, marked
with his own special characteristics. . . . And as a result he is always somebody! Whilst a man. . . . And I'm not speaking of you personally at the
moment. . . . Man in general . . . Can quite well be nobody.
PRODUCER.   That as may be! But you're asking *me* these questions. Me, do
you understand? The Producer! The boss!
1530   FATHER [*softly, with gentle humility*].   But only in order to know if you, you as
you really are now, are seeing yourself as, for instance, after all the time
that has gone by, you see yourself as you were at some point in the
past. . . . With all the illusions that you had then . . . with everything . . . all
the things you had deep down inside you . . . everything that made up
your external world . . . everything as it appeared to you then . . . and as
it *was*, as it was in reality for you then! Well . . . thinking back on those
illusions which you no longer have . . . on all those things that no longer

seem to be what they *were* once upon a time . . . don't you feel that . . . I won't say these boards. . . . No! . . . That the very earth itself is slipping
1540 away from under your feet, when you reflect that in the same way this *you* that you now feel yourself to be . . . all your reality as it is today . . . is destined to seem an illusion tomorrow?

PRODUCER [*not having understood much of all this, and somewhat taken aback by this specious argument*]. Well? And where does all this get us, anyway?

FATHER. Nowhere. I only wanted to make you see that if we [*again pointing to himself and to the other* CHARACTERS] have no reality outside the world of illusion, it would be as well if you mistrusted your own reality. . . . The reality that you breathe and touch today. . . . Because like the reality of yesterday, it is fated to reveal itself as a mere illusion tomorrow.

1550 PRODUCER [*deciding to make fun of him*]. Oh, excellent! And so you'd say that you and this play of yours that you've been putting on for my benefit are more real than I am?

FATHER [*with the utmost seriousness*]. Oh, without a doubt.

PRODUCER. Really?

FATHER. I thought that you'd understood that right from the very beginning.

PRODUCER. More real than I am.

FATHER. If your reality can change from one day to the next. . . .

PRODUCER. But everybody knows that it can change like that! It's always
1560 changing. . . . Just like everybody else's!

FATHER [*with a cry*]. No, ours doesn't change! You see. . . . That's the difference between us! Our reality doesn't change. . . . It can't change. . . . It can never be in any way different from what it is. . . . Because it is already fixed. . . . Just as it is. . . . For ever! For ever it is *this* reality. . . . It's terrible! . . . This immutable reality. . . . It should make you shudder to come near us!

PRODUCER [*quickly, suddenly struck by an idea. He moves over and stands squarely in front of him*]. I should like to know, however, when anyone ever saw a character step out of his part and begin a long dissertation on it like the
1570 one you've just been making. . . . Expounding it. . . . Explaining it. . . . Can you tell me? . . . I've never seen it happen before!

FATHER. You have never seen it happen before because authors usually hide the details of their work of creation. Once the characters are alive. . . . Once they are standing truly alive before their author. . . . He does nothing but follow the words and gestures that they suggest to him. . . . And he must want them to be what they themselves want to be. For woe betide him if he doesn't do what they wish him to do! When a character is born he immediately acquires such an independence. . . . Even of his own author. . . . That everyone can imagine him in a whole host of situations in
1580 which his author never thought of placing him. . . . They can even imagine his acquiring, sometimes, a significance that the author never dreamt of giving him.

PRODUCER. Yes. . . . I know all that!

FATHER. Well, then, why are you so astonished at seeing us? Just imagine what a misfortune it is for a character to be born alive. . . . Created by the imagination of an author who afterwards sought to deny him life. . . . Now tell me whether a character who has been left unrealised in this way. . . .

Living, yet without a life. . . . Whether this character hasn't the right to do
what we are doing now. . . . Here and now. . . . For your benefit? . . . After
1590   we had spent . . . Oh, such ages, believe me! . . . Doing it for his benefit . . .
Trying to persuade him, trying to urge him to realise us. . . . First of all I
would present myself to him. . . . Then she would . . . [*pointing to the* STEP-
DAUGHTER]. . . . And then her poor Mother. . . .

STEPDAUGHTER [*coming forward as if in a trance*].   Yes, what he says is true. . . .
I would go and tempt him. . . . There, in his gloomy study. . . . Just at
twilight. . . . He would be sitting there, sunk in an armchair. . . . Not bothering to stir himself and switch on the light. . . . Content to let the room
get darker and darker. . . . Until the whole room was filled with a darkness
that was alive with our presence. . . . We were there to tempt him. . . . [*And
1600   then, as if she saw herself as still in that study and irritated by the presence of all
those actors.*] Oh, go away. . . . All of you! Leave us alone! Mummy . . . and
her son. . . . I and the little girl. . . . The boy by himself. . . . Always by
himself. . . . Then he and I together [*a faint gesture in the direction of the*
FATHER]. And then. . . . By myself. . . . By myself . . . alone in that darkness
[*a sudden turn round as if she wished to seize and fix the vision that she has of
herself, the living vision that she sees shining in the darkness*]. Yes, my life! Ah,
what scenes, what wonderful scenes we suggested to him! And I . . . I
tempted him more than any of them. . . .

FATHER.   Indeed you did! And it may well be that it's all your fault that he
1610   wouldn't give us the life we asked for. . . . You were too persistent. . . . Too
impudent. . . . You exaggerated too much. . . .

STEPDAUGHTER.   What? When it was he who wanted me to be what I am? [*She
goes up to the* PRODUCER *and says confidentially.*] I think it's much more likely
that he refused because he felt depressed . . . or because of his contempt
for the theatre. . . . Or at least, for the present-day theatre with all its
pandering to the box-office. . . .

PRODUCER.   Let's get on! Let's get on, for God's sake! Let's have some action!

STEPDAUGHTER.   It looks to me as if we've got too much action for you already. . . . Just staging our entry into his house [*pointing to the* FATHER]. You
1620   yourself said that you couldn't stick up notices or be changing the set every
five minutes.

PRODUCER.   And neither can we! Of course we can't! What we've got to do is
to combine and group all the action into one continuous well-knit
scene. . . . Not the sort of thing that you want. . . . With, first of all, your
younger brother coming home from school and wandering about the
house like some lost soul. . . . Hiding behind doors and brooding on a
plan that . . . What did you say it does to him?

STEPDAUGHTER.   Dries him up. . . . Shrivels him up completely.

PRODUCER.   M'm! Well, as you said. . . . And all the time you can see it more
1630   and more clearly in his eyes. . . . Wasn't that what you said?

STEPDAUGHTER.   Yes. . . . Just look at him! [*Pointing to where he is standing by his*
MOTHER.]

PRODUCER.   And then, at the same time, you want the child to be playing in
the garden, blissfully unaware of everything. The boy in the house, the
little girl in the garden. . . . I ask you!

STEPDAUGHTER.   Yes . . . happily playing in the sun! That is the only pleasure
that I have. . . . Her happiness. . . . All the joy that she gets from playing

in the garden. . . . After the wretchedness and the squalor of that horrible room where we all four slept together. . . . And she had to sleep with
1640   me. . . . Just think of it. . . . My vile contaminated body next to hers! . . . With her holding me tight in her loving, innocent, little arms! She only had to get a glimpse of me in the garden and she'd run up to me and take me by the hand. She wasn't interested in the big flowers . . . she'd run about looking for the . . . 'weeny' ones. . . . So that she could point them out to me. . . . And she'd be so happy. . . . So excited. . . .

[*As she says this she is torn by the memory of it all and gives a long, despairing cry, dropping her head on to her hands which are lying loosely on the little table in front of her. At the sight of her emotion everyone is deeply moved. The* PRODUCER *goes up to her almost paternally and says comfortingly.*]

PRODUCER.   We'll have the garden in . . . Don't you worry . . . We'll have the garden scene in. . . . Just you wait and see. . . . You'll be quite satisfied with how I arrange it. . . . We'll play everything in the garden. [*Calling a* STAGE-HAND.] Hey [*his name*]! Let me have something in the shape of a tree or
1650   two. . . . A couple of not-too-large cypresses in front of this fountain! [*Two small cypress trees descend from the flies. The* FOREMAN *dashes up and fixes them with struts and nails.*]
PRODUCER [*to the* STEPDAUGHTER].   That'll do. . . . For the moment anyway. . . . It'll give us a rough idea. [*Calls to the* STAGE-HAND *again.*] Oh [*his name*], let me have something for a sky, will you?
STAGE-HAND [*up aloft*].   Eh?
PRODUCER.   Something for a sky! A backcloth to go behind the fountain! [*And a white backcloth descends from the flies.*]
PRODUCER.   Not white! I said I wanted a sky! Oh, well, it doesn't matter. . . .
1660   Leave it! Leave it! . . . I'll fix it myself. . . . [*Calls.*] Hey! . . . You there on the lights! . . . Everything off. . . . And let me have the moonlight blues on! . . . Blues in the batten! . . . A couple of blue spots on the backcloth! . . . Yes, that's it! That's just right!

[*There is now a mysterious moonlit effect about the scene, and the* ACTORS *are prompted to move about and to speak as they would if they were indeed walking in a moonlit garden.*]

PRODUCER [*to the* STEPDAUGHTER].   There, do you see? Now the Boy, instead of hiding behind doors inside the house, can move about the garden and hide behind these trees. But, you know, it'll be rather difficult to find a little girl to play that scene with you. . . . The one where she shows you the flowers. [*Turning to the* BOY.] Now come down here a bit! Let's see how it works out! [*Then, since the* BOY *doesn't move.*] Come on! Come on! [*He drags*
1670   *him forward and tries to make him hold his head up. But after every attempt down it falls again.*] Good God, here's a fine how d'ye do. . . . There's something queer about this boy. . . . What's the matter with him? . . . My God, he'll have to say *something*. . . . [*He goes up to him, puts a hand on his shoulder and places him behind one of the trees.*] Now. . . . Forward a little! . . . Let me see you! . . . Mm! . . . Now hide yourself. . . . That's it! . . . Now try popping your head out a bit . . . Take a look round. . . . [*He goes to one side to study the effect and the* BOY *does what he has been told to do. The* ACTORS *look on, deeply*

affected and quite dismayed.] That's excellent! . . . Yes, excellent! [*Turning
again to the* STEPDAUGHTER.] Suppose the little girl were to catch sight of him
1680   there as he was looking out, and run over to him. . . . Wouldn't that drag
a word or two out of him?

STEPDAUGHTER [*rising*].   It's no use your hoping that he'll speak. . . . At least
not so long as *he's* here [*pointing to the* SON]. If you want him to speak, you'll
have to send *him* away first.

SON [*going resolutely towards the steps down into the auditorium*].   Willingly! I'm
only too happy to oblige! Nothing could possibly suit me better!

PRODUCER [*immediately catching hold of him*].   Hey! Oh no you don't! Where are
you going? You hang on a minute!

[*The* MOTHER *rises in dismay, filled with anguish at the thought that he really is going
away. She instinctively raises her arms to prevent him from going, without, however,
moving from where she is standing.*]

SON [*he has reached the footlights*].   I tell you . . . There's absolutely nothing for
1690   me to do here! Let me go, please! Let me go! [*This to the* PRODUCER.]

PRODUCER.   What do you mean . . . There's nothing for you to do?

STEPDAUGHTER [*placidly, ironically*].   Don't bother to hold him back! He won't
go away!

FATHER.   He has to play that terrible scene with his Mother in the garden.

SON [*immediately, fiercely, resolutely*].   I'm not playing anything! I've said that
all along! [*To the* PRODUCER.] Let me go!

STEPDAUGHTER [*running over, then addressing the* PRODUCER].   Do you mind?
[*She gets him to lower the hand with which he has been restraining the* SON.] Let
him go! [*Then turning to the* SON, *as soon as the* PRODUCER *has dropped his arm.*]
1700   Well, go on. . . . Leave us!

[*The* SON *stands where he is, still straining in the direction of the steps, but, as if held
back by some mysterious force, he cannot go down them. Then, amidst the utter dismay
and anxious bewilderment of the* ACTORS, *he wanders slowly along the length of the
footlights in the direction of the other flight of steps. Once there, he again finds himself
unable to descend, much as he would wish to. The* STEPDAUGHTER *has watched his
progress intently, her eyes challenging, defiant. Now she bursts out laughing.*]

STEPDAUGHTER.   He can't, you see! He can't leave us! He must remain
here. . . . He has no choice but to remain with us! He's chained to us. . . .
Irrevocably! But if I . . . Who really do run away when what is inevitable
happens. . . . And I run away because of my hatred for him. . . . I run away
just because I can no longer bear the sight of him. . . . Well, if I can still
stay here. . . . If I can still put up with his company and with having to have
him here before my eyes. . . . Do you think it's likely that he can run away?
Why, he has to stay here with that precious father of his. . . . With his
mother. . . . Because now she has no other children but him. . . . [*Turning
1710   to her* MOTHER.] Come on, Mummy! Come on. . . . [*Turning to the* PRODUCER
and pointing to the MOTHER.] There. . . . You see. . . . She'd got up to prevent him from going. . . . [*To her* MOTHER, *as if willing her actions by some
magic power.*] Come on! Come on! [*Then to the* PRODUCER.] You can imagine
just how reluctant she is to give this proof of her affection in front of your
actors. But so great is her desire to be with him that . . . There! . . . You

see? . . . She's willing to live out again her scene with him! [*And as a matter of fact the* MOTHER *has gone up to her* SON, *and scarcely has the* STEPDAUGHTER *finished speaking before she makes a gesture to indicate her agreement.*]

SON [*immediately*]. No! No! You're not going to drag me into this! If I can't
1720 get away, I shall stay here! But I repeat that I'm not going to do any acting at all!

FATHER [*trembling with excitement, to the* PRODUCER]. You can force him to act!

SON. Nobody can force me!

FATHER. I can and I will!

STEPDAUGHTER. Wait! Wait! First of all the little girl has to go to the fountain. . . . [*Goes over to the* LITTLE GIRL. *She drops on to her knees in front of her and takes her face in her hands.*] Poor little darling. . . . You're looking so bewildered. . . . With those beautiful big eyes. . . . You must be wondering just where you are. We're on a stage, dear! What's a stage? Well . . . It's a
1730 place where you play at being serious. They put on plays here. And now *we're* putting a play on. Really and truly! Even you. . . . [*Embracing her, clasping her to her breast and rocking her for a moment or so.*] Oh, you little darling. . . . My dear little darling, what a terrible play for you. . . . What a horrible end they've thought out for you! The garden, the fountain. . . . Yes, it's a make-believe fountain. . . . The pity is, darling, that everything's make-believe here. . . . But perhaps you like a make-believe fountain better than a real one. . . . So that you can play in it. . . . M'm? No. . . . It'll be a game for the others. . . . Not for you unfortunately . . . Because you're real. . . . And you really play by a real fountain. . . . A lovely big green one,
1740 with masses of bamboo palms casting shadows. . . . Looking at your reflection in the water. . . . And lots and lots of little baby ducklings swimming about in it, breaking the shadow into a thousand little ripples. You try to take hold of one of the ducklings . . . [*With a shriek which fills everybody with dismay.*] No, Rosetta, no! Your Mummy's not looking after you. . . . And all because of that swine there. . . . Her son! I feel as if all the devils in hell were loose inside me. . . . And he . . . [*Leaves the* LITTLE GIRL *and turns with her usual scorn to the* BOY.] What are you doing . . . drooping there like that? . . . Always the little beggarboy! It'll be your fault too if that baby drowns. . . . Because of the way you go on. . . . As if I didn't pay for every-
1750 body when I got you into his house. [*Seizing his arm to make him take his hand out of his pocket.*] What have you got there? What are you trying to hide? Out with it! Take that hand out of your pocket! [*She snatches his hand out of his pocket and to everybody's horror reveals that it is clenched round a revolver. She looks at him for a little while, as if satisfied. Then she says sombrely.*] M'm! Where did you get that gun from? . . . And how did you manage to lay your hands on it? [*And since the* BOY, *in his utter dismay—his eyes are staring and vacant— does not reply.*] You idiot! If I'd been you I shouldn't have killed myself. . . . I'd have killed one of *them.* . . . Or the pair of them! Father and son together!

[*She hides him behind the cypress tree where he was lurking before. Then she takes the* LITTLE GIRL *by the hand and leads her towards the fountain. She puts her into the basin of the fountain, and makes her lie down so that she is completely hidden. Finally she goes down on her knees and buries her head in her hands on the rim of the basin of the fountain.*]

1760 PRODUCER. That's it! Good! [*Turning to the* SON.] And at the same time. . . .
 SON [*angrily*]. What do you mean . . . 'And at the same time'? Oh, no! . . .
   Nothing of the sort! There never was any scene between her and me!
   [*Pointing to the* MOTHER.] You make her tell you what really happened!
   [*Meanwhile the* SECOND ACTRESS *and the* JUVENILE LEAD *have detached themselves*
   from the group of ACTORS *and are standing gazing intently at the* MOTHER *and the*
   SON *so that later they can act these parts.*]
 MOTHER. Yes, it's true, sir! I'd gone to his room at the time.
 SON. There! Did you hear? To my room! Not into the garden!
 PRODUCER. That doesn't matter at all! As I said we'll have to run all the
1770   action together into one composite scene!
 SON [*becoming aware that the* JUVENILE LEAD *is studying him*]. What do *you* want?
 JUVENILE LEAD. Nothing! I was just looking at you.
 SON [*turning to the* SECOND ACTRESS]. Oh! . . . And *you're* here too, are you? All
   ready to play *her* part, I suppose? [*Pointing to the* MOTHER.]
 PRODUCER. That's the idea! And if you want my opinion you ought to be
   damned grateful for all the attention they're paying you.
 SON. Indeed? Thank you! But hasn't it dawned on you yet that you aren't
   going to be able to stage this play? Not even the tiniest vestige of us is to
   be found in you. . . . And all the time your actors are studying us from the
1780   outside. Do you think it's possible for us to live confronted by a mirror
   which, not merely content with freezing us in that particular picture which
   is the fixing of our expression, has to throw an image back at us which we
   can no longer recognise? . . . Our own features, yes. . . . But twisted into a
   horrible grimace.
 FATHER. He's quite right! He's quite right, you know!
 PRODUCER [*to the* JUVENILE LEAD *and* SECOND ACTRESS]. Right you are! Get back
   with the others!
 SON. It's no use your bothering! I'm not having anything to do with this!
 PRODUCER. You be quiet for the moment, and let me listen to what your
1790   mother has to say! [*To the* MOTHER.] You were saying? . . . You'd gone to his
   room? . . .
 MOTHER. Yes, I'd gone to his room. . . . I couldn't bear the strain any longer!
   I wanted to pour out my heart to him. . . . I wanted to tell him of all the
   anguish that was tormenting me. . . . But as soon as he saw me come in . . .
 SON. There was no scene between us! I rushed out of the room. . . . I didn't
   want to get involved in any scenes! Because I never have been involved in
   any! Do you understand?
 MOTHER. Yes! That *is* what happened! That is what happened.
 PRODUCER. But for the purposes of this play we've simply *got* to have a scene
1800   between you and him! Why . . . it's absolutely *essential*!
 MOTHER. I'm quite ready to take part in one! Oh, if you could only find
   some way to give me an opportunity of speaking to him . . . if only for a
   moment. . . . So that I can pour out my heart to him!
 FATHER [*going up to the* SON, *in a great rage*]. You'll do what she asks, do you
   understand? You'll do what your Mother asks!
 SON [*more stubbornly than ever*]. I'm doing nothing!
 FATHER [*taking hold of him by the lapels of his coat and shaking him*]. My God,
   you'll do what I tell you! Or else . . . Can't you hear how she's pleading
   with you? Haven't you a spark of feeling in you for your Mother?

1810 SON [*grappling with the* FATHER].   No, I haven't! For God's sake let's have done
with all this. . . . Once and for all, let's have done with it!

[*General agitation. The* MOTHER *is terrified and tries to get between them in order to
separate them.*]

MOTHER.   Please! *Please!*
FATHER [*without relinquishing his hold*].   You must obey me! You *must!*
SON [*struggling with him and finally hurling him to the ground. He falls near the
steps amidst general horror*].   What's come over you? Why are you in this
terrible state of frenzy? Haven't you any sense of decency? . . . Going
about parading your shame. . . . And ours, too. I'm having nothing to do
with this affair! Nothing, do you hear? And by making this stand I am
interpreting the wishes of our author, who didn't wish to put us on the
1820   stage!
PRODUCER.   Oh, God! You come along here and . . .
SON [*pointing to the* FATHER].   He did! I didn't!
PRODUCER.   Aren't you here now?
SON.   It was he who wanted to come. . . . And he dragged us all along with
him. Then the pair of them went in there with you and agreed on what was
to go into the play. But he didn't only stick to what really did occur. . . .
No, as if that wasn't enough for any man, he had to put in things that
never even happened.
PRODUCER.   Well, then, you tell me what really happened! You can at least do
1830   that! You rushed out of your room without saying a word?
SON [*he hesitates for a moment*].   Without saying a word! I didn't want to get
involved in a scene!
PRODUCER [*pressing him*].   And then? What did you do then?
SON [*everybody's attention is on him; amidst the anguished silence he takes a step or
two across the front of the stage*].   Nothing. . . . As I was crossing the garden
. . . [*he breaks off and becomes gloomy and absorbed*].
PRODUCER [*urging him to speak, very much moved by this extraordinary reserve*].
Well? As you were crossing the garden?
SON [*in exasperation, shielding his face with his arm*].   Why do you want to force
1840   me to tell you? It's horrible!

[*The* MOTHER *is trembling all over and stifled sobs come from her as she looks towards
the fountain.*]

PRODUCER [*slowly, quietly . . . he has seen where the* MOTHER *is looking and he now
turns to the* SON *with growing apprehension*].   The little girl?
SON [*staring straight in front of him, out into the auditorium*].   There . . . In the
fountain. . . .
FATHER [*from where he is on the floor, pointing with tender pity to the* MOTHER].
She was following him. . . .
PRODUCER [*anxiously to the* SON].   And what did you do?
SON [*slowly, continuing to stare in front of him*].   I rushed up to the fountain. . . .
I was about to dive in and fish her out. . . . Then all of a sudden I pulled
1850   up short. . . . Behind that tree I saw something that made my blood run
cold. . . . The boy. . . . The boy was standing there. . . . Stock still. . . . With
madness in his eyes. . . . Staring like some insane creature at his little

sister, who was lying drowned in the fountain! [*The* STEPDAUGHTER, *who has all this while been bent over the fountain in order to hide the* LITTLE GIRL, *is sobbing desperately—her sobs coming like an echo from the background. There is a pause.*] I moved towards him. . . . And then . . . [*And from behind the trees where the* BOY *is hidden a revolver shot rings out.*]

MOTHER [*with a heartrending cry she rushes behind the trees accompanied by the* SON *and all the* ACTORS. *There is general confusion*]. Oh, my son! My son! [*And*
1860   *then amidst the general hubbub and shouting.*] Help! Oh, help!

PRODUCER [*amidst all the shouting, he tries to clear a space while the* BOY *is carried off behind the skycloth*]. Is he wounded? Is he badly hurt?

[*By now everybody, except for the* PRODUCER *and the* FATHER, *who is still on the ground by the steps, has disappeared behind the skycloth. They can be heard muttering and exclaiming in great consternation. Then first from one side, then from the other, the* ACTORS *re-enter.*]

LEADING LADY [*re-entering right, very much moved*]. He's dead, poor boy! He's dead! Oh what a terrible thing to happen!

LEADING MAN [*re-entering left, laughing*]. What do you mean, dead? It's all make-believe! It's all just a pretence! Don't get taken in by it!

OTHER ACTORS [*entering from the right*]. Make-believe? Pretence? Reality! Reality! He's dead!

OTHERS [*from the left*]. No! Make-believe! It's all a pretence!

1870 FATHER [*rising and crying out to them*]. What do you mean, pretence? Reality, ladies and gentlemen, reality! Reality! [*And desperation in his face, he too disappears behind the backcloth*].

PRODUCER [*at the end of his tether*]. Pretence! Reality! Go to hell, the whole lot of you! Lights! Lights! Lights!

[*The stage and the auditorium are suddenly flooded with very bright light. The* PRODUCER *breathes again as if freed from a tremendous burden. They all stand there looking into one another's eyes, in an agony of suspense and dismay.*]

PRODUCER. My God! Nothing like this has ever happened to me before! I've lost a whole day on their account! [*He looks at his watch.*] You can go home now. . . . All of you! There's nothing we can do now! It's too late to start rehearsing again! I'll see you all this evening. [*And as soon as the* ACTORS *have said 'Goodbye!' and gone he calls out to the* ELECTRICIAN.] Hey [*his name*]!
1880   Everything off! [*He has hardly got the words out before the theatre is plunged for a moment into utter darkness.*] Hell! You might at least leave me one light on, so that I can see where I'm going!

[*And immediately behind the backcloth, a green flood lights up. It projects the silhouettes of the* CHARACTERS [*minus the* BOY *and the* LITTLE GIRL], *clear-cut and huge, on to the backcloth. The* PRODUCER *is terrified and leaps off the stage. As he does so the green flood is switched off—rather as if its having come on in the first instance had been due to the* ELECTRICIAN's *having pulled the wrong switch—and the stage is again lit in blue. Slowly the* CHARACTERS *come in and advance to the front of the stage. The* SON *comes in first, from the right, followed by the* MOTHER, *who has her arms outstretched towards him. Then the* FATHER *comes in from the left. They stop half-way down the stage and stand there like people in a trance. Last of all the* STEPDAUGHTER *comes in from the left and runs towards the steps which lead down into the auditorium.*]

With her foot on the top step she stops for a moment to look at the other three and bursts into strident laughter. Then she hurls herself down the steps and runs up the aisle. She stops at the back of the auditorium and turns to look at the three figures standing on the stage. She bursts out laughing again. And when she has disappeared from the auditorium you can still hear her terrible laughter coming from the foyer beyond. A short pause and then,

CURTAIN

[1921]

Critical Commentary on *Six Characters in Search of an Author*

Six Characters in Search of an Author is, as its subtitle suggests, a play about the creation of a play; it presents a dramatic account of how the story embodied in the six characters is explored by an author and ultimately rejected as unstageable. Their story includes marital infidelity, prostitution, attempted incest, and the death of two children—one of them by suicide and the other by drowning. Yet Pirandello calls this story a *commedia*, a word that means "drama" but also has connotations of comedy. The humor in the play, such as it is, has nothing to do with the story that the six characters wish to tell. Instead it arises from the story of their efforts to tell the story. Within *this* story there is a great deal of humor: there is, for example, the humorous incongruity in the efforts of the Leading Man and Leading Lady to perform the seduction scene that the Father and the Stepdaughter have just *lived* before them:

> LEADING MAN.   You've been here before? . . . More than once? Well then . . .
>   Come along. . . . May I take off your hat?

> [*The* LEADING MAN *says this last line in such a tone of voice and accompanies it with such a gesture that the* STEPDAUGHTER, *who has remained with her hands over her mouth, can no longer restrain herself. She tries desperately to prevent herself from laughing but a noisy burst of laughter comes irresistibly through her fingers.*]

Similarly, there is the moment of farce when the wicked procuress Madame Pace is found to have a ludicrous accent. There is even slapstick when, for example, the curtain drops at the end of Act II even though the Producer only wished to indicate that it *would* drop then during an actual performance of the play that he is attempting to write. Ultimately, the play turns into a satire about the conventional notions of what "will play." It is for that reason, and for that reason alone, that Pirandello feels comfortable including the vexed reaction of the Producer to the "deaths" of the two children at the end of the play:

> Pretense! Reality! Go to hell, the whole lot of you! Lights! Lights! Lights! . . .
> My God! Nothing like this has ever happened to me before! I've lost a whole
> day on their account!

To understand this play about the failure to make a play, we may wish to consider how Pirandello has used the standard elements of a dramatic plot: *exposition, complication, crisis, falling action,* and *resolution.*

Consider the plight of the Producer at the beginning of the play. We learn from the initial expository pages that the Producer is unhappily attempting to stage a play by Pirandello entitled *The Game As He Played It:*

> Ridiculous! Ridiculous! What do you expect me to do if the French haven't got any more good comedies to send us, and we're reduced to putting on plays by Pirandello? And if you can understand *his* plays . . . you're a better man than I am! He deliberately goes out of his way to annoy people, so that by the time the play's through everybody's fed up . . . actors, critics, audience, everybody!

Is the Producer not ripe for inspiration? Ready to imagine a play that is more worthy of performance than the one he actually has on hand?

The complication follows almost immediately when the Prompter feels "a bit of a draught." A door has opened to allow the entrance of the six characters. Our first question is "What are they?" Are they—can they truly be—characters whose author refused to put them into a book and who wander in search of an author? (Pirandello was in fact noted for conversing aloud with his characters as he composed his stories and plays!) Or should we think of this as a metaphor of the creative process and realize that characters could enter the mind of an author (the Producer) in very much this fashion, as a result of his dissatisfaction with the foolishly pretentious play he is staging? (Does it clear things up or only muddy the waters even more if we recognize that they are actually actors pretending to be characters?)

Only by seeing this as a play about the making of plays can we understand the relevance of many of the Father's comments. He is critical of the realistic theater which seeks to create "things which have all the appearance of reality in order that they shall look like the realities themselves." He points out that in fact, "life is full of things that are infinitely absurd, things that, for all their impudent absurdity, have no need to masquerade as truth, because they are true." Thus conventional drama, with its insistence upon realism, falsifies life. Although the characters in a play achieve a fixed and static form in "the book," living human beings are *always* changing so that what occurs today will probably not be remembered at all five years hence.

Being a practical man, the Producer listens with little comprehension and even less sympathy to the Father's theorizing about drama, but he does begin to be interested in the six characters when he first perceives the pathos in their story. Their story of adultery leading toward incest is exactly the kind of sordid soap opera that would strike the bourgeois Producer as being highly dramatic. It includes a mother who is driven by her own husband into the arms of another man—and abandons her firstborn son in order to do so. It includes the torment of a man for whom it is easier to lose his wife than to be prey to her reproachful looks and to observe her shared sympathies with a rival. It includes scandalous hints of prostitution and incestuous seduction. Because there is no "book," however, we see only tantalizing and disorganized glimpses of the action that would be part of the book.

As the complications in the play develop in Acts I and II, we see that the Father and the Stepdaughter disagree less about what happened than about the meaning of what happened. For example, the Stepdaughter thinks that the Father's secretive observations of her as a young child are but one more illustration of his salacious character. For the Father, those same events grow out of his remorse over the wrong that he had done by marrying the Mother and the well-intentioned harm he caused by driving her away. The Father believes that, in watching over the Stepdaughter, he is not lustful, but protective. All that he asks of the Producer is an opportunity to explain his motives. In contrast, all that the Stepdaughter asks is the opportunity to act her part. The Producer recognizes, however, that the Father's explanations would be too windy for the stage and the daughter's actions too pornographic. When he hesitates to let her play a scene naked, she explodes:

> THE STEPDAUGHTER.   I'm going! I'm not stopping here! You worked it all out together, didn't you? . . . The pair of you. . . . You and him. . . . When you were in there. . . . You worked out what was going to be possible on the stage. Oh, thanks very much! I understand! He wants to jump to the bit where he presents his spiritual torments! [*This is said harshly.*] But I want to present my own drama! *Mine! Mine!*

Recognizing the problems caused by these dilemmas more rapidly than the Producer, the Father reflects by the middle of Act II, "I think I see why our author didn't wish to put us on the stage after all. . . . He saw us as we are. . . . Alive." The Father realizes that the author didn't want them changed to suit the stage. Indeed, in the process of adapting the story for the stage, it would doubtless have lost all that made it interesting and unusual (the inner torment of the characters, the nudity, etc.) and would instead have become another cheap melodrama.

Paradoxically, of course, in this play about the reasons why the story of the six characters cannot be performed on the contemporary stage, Pirandello has actually found the perfect form for bringing it to the stage. We *do* hear the Father's lengthy rationales, and even if we *don't* see the Stepdaughter play her climactic scene in the nude, we at least imagine her doing so. The most obvious implication of this is also the most difficult of Pirandello's paradoxes for an audience to understand. If the characters of a play have no reality apart from the reality given to them in "the book," then *these* characters have no existence apart from the existence we see. They are not restaging events that happened in the past; the events themselves are happening *now*. They are caught in the "eternal moment." When Madame Pace appears as if by magic, that is the way in which she always appears, the only way she has ever appeared! As the scene between the Father and the Stepdaughter begins to unfold, the Mother expresses this clearly. She denies that the scene took place in the past: "No, it's happening now! It happens all the time." In another moment the Mother screams and steps forward to separate the Father and the Stepdaughter. The Producer then exclaims gleefully "Excellent! Excellent! And then . . . Curtain! Curtain!" And the Father adds, "Yes, because that's how it really happened!" And then the curtain *does* come down—because that's the way it really happened, the only way.

In the third act of the play Pirandello clarifies and develops the implications about the nature of the theater that he has introduced in the first two acts. There, for example, the Stepdaughter speculates that the author abandoned the play "because of his contempt for the theatre. . . . Or at least, for the present-day theatre with all its pandering to the box-office." There the Father continues to reflect that "if we (the characters) have no reality outside the world of illusion, it would be as well if you (the Producer) mistrusted your own reality. . . . Because like the reality of yesterday, it is fated to reveal itself as a mere illusion tomorrow." And there the Producer ruefully wonders "when anyone ever saw a character step out of his part and begin a long dissertation on it like the one you've just been making?" And yet in this startlingly original play about six characters in search of an author, Pirandello has found an ideal form for expressing his complex philosophy about our shifting, unstable realities.

A Selective Bibliography on *Six Characters in Search of an Author*

Bently, Eric. "Father's Day." *The Drama Review* 13.1 (1968): 57–72.

Bermel, Albert. *Contradictory Characters: An Interpretation of the Modern Theatre*. New York: Dutton, 1973. 122–43.

Bishop, Thomas. *Pirandello and the French Theater*. New York: New York UP, 1960. 19–23.

Brustein, Robert. *The Theatre of Revolt*. Boston: Little Brown, 1964. 279–318.

Budel, Oscar. *Pirandello*. 2nd ed. New York: Hillary House, 1969.

Cambon, Glauco, ed. *Pirandello: A Collection of Critical Essays*. Englewood Cliffs, NJ: Prentice-Hall, 1967.

Cannon, Jo Ann. "The Question of Frame in Pirandello's Metatheatrical Trilogy." *Modern Language Studies* 16.3 (1986): 44–56.

Charney, Maurice. "Shakespearean and Pirandellian: *Hamlet* and *Six Characters in Search of an Author*." *Modern Drama* 24 (1981): 323–29.

Clark, Hoover W. "Existentialism and Pirandello's *Sei Personaggi*." *Italica* 43 (1966): 276–84.

Gordon, Jan B. "*Sei Personnaggi in Cerca D'autore:* Myth, Ritual, and Pirandello's Anti-Symbolist Theatre." *Forum Italicum* 6 (1972): 333–55.

Fergusson, Francis. *The Idea of a Theater*. Princeton, NJ: U of Princeton P, 1949. 198–206.

Groff, Edward. "Point of View in Modern Drama." *Modern Drama* 2 (1960): 268–82.

Herman, William. "Pirandello and Possibility." *Tulane Drama Review* 10.3 (1966): 91–111.

Hodess, Kenneth Mark. *In Search of the Divided Self: A Psychoanalytic Inquiry into Selected Plays of Luigi Pirandello*. Ann Arbor: University Microfilms, 1979. 131–66.

Illiano, Antonio. "Pirandello's *Six Characters In Search of an Author: A Comedy in the Making*." *Italica* 44 (1967): 1–12.

———. " 'Six Characters': An American Opera." *Review of National Literatures* 14 (1987): 136–59.

Kennedy, Andrew K. "*Six Characters:* Pirandello's Last Tape." *Modern Drama* 12 (1969): 1–9.

Kernan, Alvin B. "Truth and Dramatic Mode in the Modern Theater: Chekhov, Pirandello, and Williams." *Modern Drama* 1 (1958): 101–14.

Kligerman, Charles. "A Psychoanalytic Study of Pirandello's *Six Characters in Search of an Author*." *Journal of the American Psychoanalytic Association* 10 (1962): 731–44.

Liebler, Naomi Conn. " 'Give o'er the play': Closure in Shakespeare's *Hamlet* and Pirandello's *Six Characters in Search of an Author*." *Modern Drama* 24 (1981): 314–22.

Lorch, Jennifer. "The 1925 Text of *Sei personnaggi in cerca d'autore* and Pitoeff's Production of 1923." *Yearbook of the British Pirandello Society* 2 (1982): 32–47.

McDonald, David. "Derrida and Pirandello: A Post-Structuralist Analysis of *Six Characters in Search of an Author*." *Modern Drama* 20 (1977): 421–36.

Needler, Howard I. "On the Art of Pirandello: Theory and Praxis." *Texas Studies in Literature and Language* 15 (1974): 735–58.

Nolan, David. "Theory in Action: Pirandello's *Sei Personnaggi*." *Forum for Modern Language Studies* 4 (1968): 269–76.

Oliver, Robert W. *Dreams of Passion: the Theater of Luigi Pirandello*. New York: New York UP, 1979.

Paolucci, Anne. "Pirandello and the Waiting Stage of the Absurd (with Some Observations on a New 'Critical Language')." *Modern Drama* 23 (1980): 102–11.

———. *Pirandello's Theater*. Carbondale: Southern Illinois UP, 1974.

Pirandello, Luigi. "Preface to *Six Characters in Search of an Author*." *Naked Masks*. Ed. Eric Bentley. New York: Dutton, 1952. 363–75.

Ragusa, Olga. *Luigi Pirandello: An Approach to His Theatre*. Edinburgh: University Press, 1980.

———. "Teaching *Six Characters*." *Teaching Language through Literature* 24.2 (1985): 3–14.

Sogliuzzo, Richard. *Luigi Pirandello: the Playwright in the Theatre*. Metuchen, NJ: Scarecrow, 1982.

———. "The Uses of Masks in *The Great God Brown* and *Six Characters in Search of an Author*." *Educational Theatre Journal* 18 (1966): 224–9.

Starkie, Walter. *Luigi Pirandello*. 3rd ed. Berkeley: U of California P, 1965. 205–20.

Styan, J. L. "Pirandellian Theatre Games: Spectator as Victim." *Modern Drama* 23 (1980): 95–101.

Thompson, Doug. "Pirandello's 'Inferno': Time and Punishment in *Sei personaggi in cerca d'autore*." *Perspectives on Contemporary Literature* 12 (1986): 65–72.

Witt, Mary Ann Frese. "Six Characters in Search of an Author and the Battle of the Lexis." *Modern Drama* 30 (1987): 396–404.

Zaiser, Rainer and Gretchen Wieshan. "*En Attendant Godot:* Reflections on Some Parallels between Beckett and Pirandello." *Journal of European Studies* 72 (1988): 253–66.

Eugene O'Neill (1888–1953)
DESIRE UNDER THE ELMS

CHARACTERS

EPHRAIM CABOT

SIMEON ⎤
PETER ⎬ *His sons*
EBEN ⎦

ABBIE PUTNAM

YOUNG GIRL, TWO FARMERS, THE FIDDLER, A SHERIFF, AND OTHER FOLK FROM THE NEIGHBORING FARMS.

The action of the entire play takes place in, and immediately outside of, the Cabot farmhouse in New England, in the year 1850. The south end of the house faces front to a stone wall with a wooden gate at center opening on a country road. The house is in good condition but in need of paint. Its walls are a sickly grayish, the green of the shutters faded. Two enormous elms are on each side of the house. They bend their trailing branches down over the roof. They appear to protect and at the same time subdue. There is a sinister maternity in their aspect, a crushing, jealous absorption. They have developed from their intimate contact with the life of man in the house an appalling humaneness. They brood oppressively over the house. They are like exhausted women resting their sagging breasts and hands and hair on its roof, and when it rains their tears trickle down monotonously and rot on the shingles.

There is a path running from the gate around the right corner of the house to the front door. A narrow porch is on this side. The end wall facing us has two windows in its upper story, two larger ones on the floor below. The two upper are those of the father's bedroom and that of the brothers. On the left, ground floor, is the kitchen—on the right, the parlor, the shades of which are always drawn down.

PART I

SCENE 1

Exterior of the farmhouse. It is sunset of a day at the beginning of summer in the year 1850. There is no wind and everything is still. The sky above the roof is suffused with deep colors, the green of the elms glows, but the house is in shadow, seeming pale and washed out by contrast.

A door opens and EBEN CABOT *comes to the end of the porch and stands looking down the road to the right. He has a large bell in his hand and this he swings mechanically, awakening a deafening clangor. Then he puts his hands on his hips and stares up at the sky. He sighs with a puzzled awe and blurts out with halting appreciation.*

EBEN.   God! Purty! [*His eyes fall and he stares about him frowningly. He is twenty-five, tall and sinewy. His face is well-formed, good-looking, but its expression is resentful and defensive. His defiant, dark eyes remind one of a wild animal's in captivity. Each day is a cage in which he finds himself trapped but inwardly unsubdued. There is a fierce repressed vitality about him. He has black hair, mustache, a thin curly trace of beard. He is dressed in rough farm clothes.*]

He spits on the ground with intense disgust, turns and goes back into the house. SIMEON *and* PETER *come in from their work in the fields. They are tall men, much older than their half-brother (*SIMEON *is thirty-nine and* PETER *thirty-seven), built on a squarer, simpler model, fleshier in body, more bovine and homelier in face, shrewder and more practical. Their shoulders stoop a bit from years of farm work. They clump heavily along in their clumsy thick-soled boots caked with earth. Their clothes, their faces, hands, bare arms and throats are earth-stained. They smell of earth. They stand together for a moment in front of the house and, as if with the one impulse, stare dumbly up at the sky, leaning on their hoes. Their faces have a compressed, unresigned expression. As they look upward, this softens.*]

SIMEON [*grudgingly*].   Purty.
PETER.   Ay-eh.
SIMEON [*suddenly*].   Eighteen year ago.
10 PETER.   What?
SIMEON.   Jenn. My woman. She died.
PETER.   I'd fergot.
SIMEON.   I rec'lect—now an' agin. Makes it lonesome. She'd hair long's a hoss' tail—an' yaller like gold!
PETER.   Waal—she's gone. [*This with indifferent finality—then after a pause.*] They's gold in the West, Sim.
SIMEON [*still under the influence of sunset—vaguely*].   In the sky?
PETER.   Waal—in the manner o' speakin'—thar's the promise. [*Growing excited.*] Gold in the sky—in the West—Golden Gate—Californi-a!—Goldest
20 West!—fields o' gold!
SIMEON [*excited in his turn*].   Fortunes layin' just atop o' the ground waitin' t' be picked! Solomon's mines,[1] they says! [*For a moment they continue looking up at the sky—then their eyes drop.*]
PETER [*with sardonic bitterness*].   Here—it's stones atop o' the ground—stones atop o' stones—makin' stone walls—year atop o' year—him 'n' yew 'n' me 'n' then Eben—makin' stone walls fur him to fence us in!
SIMEON.   We've wuked. Give our strength. Give our years. Plowed 'em under in the ground—[*he stamps rebelliously.*]—rottin'—makin' soil for his crops! [*A pause.*] Waal—the farm pays good for hereabouts.
30 PETER.   If we plowed in Californi-a, they'd be lumps o' gold in the furrow!
SIMEON.   Californi-a's t'other side o' earth, a'most. We got t' calc'late—
PETER [*after a pause*].   'Twould be hard fur me, too, to give up what we've 'arned here by our sweat. [*A pause.* EBEN *sticks his head out of the dining-room window, listening.*]

---

[1] According to legend, the fabulous wealth of Solomon (king of Israel in the tenth century B.C.) was extracted from rich gold and silver mines.

SIMEON. Ay-eh. [*A pause*] Mebbe—he'll die soon.

PETER [*doubtfully*]. Mebbe.

SIMEON. Mebbe—fur all we knows—he's dead now.

PETER. Ye'd need proof.

SIMEON. He's been gone two months—with no word.

40 PETER. Left us in the fields an evenin' like this. Hitched up an' druv off into the West. That's plum onnateral. He hain't never been off this farm 'ceptin' t' the village in thirty year or more, not since he married Eben's maw. [*A pause. Shrewdly*] I calc'late we might git him declared crazy by the court.

SIMEON. He skinned 'em too slick. He got the best o' all on 'em. They'd never b'lieve him crazy. [*A pause.*] We got t' wait—til he's under ground.

EBEN [*with a sardonic chuckle*]. Honor thy father! [*They turn, startled, and stare at him. He grins, then scowls.*] I pray he's died. [*They stare at him. He continues matter-of-factly.*] Supper's ready.

SIMEON and PETER [*together*]. Ayeh.

50 EBEN [*gazing up at the sky*]. Sun's downin' purty.

SIMEON and PETER [*together*]. Ay-eh. They's gold in the West.

EBEN. Ay-eh. [*Pointing*] Yonder atop o' the hill pasture, ye mean?

SIMEON and PETER [*together*]. In Californi-a!

EBEN. Hunh? [*Stares at them indifferently for a second, then drawls.*] Waal—supper's gittin' cold. [*He turns back into kitchen.*]

SIMEON [*startled—smacks his lips*]. I air hungry!

PETER [*sniffing*]. I smells bacon!

SIMEON [*with hungry appreciation*]. Bacon's good!

PETER [*in same tone*]. Bacon's bacon! [*They turn, shouldering each other, their*
60 *bodies bumping and rubbing together as they hurry clumsily to their food, like two friendly oxen toward their evening meal. They disappear around the right corner of house and can be heard entering the door.*]

CURTAIN

SCENE II

The color fades from the sky. Twilight begins. The interior of the kitchen is now visible. A pine table is at center, a cookstove in the right rear corner, four rough wooden chairs, a tallow candle on the table. In the middle of the rear wall is fastened a big advertising poster with a ship in full sail and the word "California" in big letters. Kitchen utensils hang from nails. Everything is neat and in order but the atmosphere is of a men's camp kitchen rather than that of a home.

Places for three are laid. EBEN takes boiled potatoes and bacon from the stove and puts them on the table, also a loaf of bread and a crock of water. SIMEON and PETER shoulder in, slump down in their chairs without a word. EBEN joins them. The three eat in silence for a moment, the two elder as naturally unrestrained as beasts of the field, EBEN picking at his food without appetite, glancing at them with a tolerant dislike.

SIMEON [*suddenly turns to* EBEN]. Looky here! Ye'd oughtn't t' said that, Eben.

PETER. 'Twa'n't righteous.

EBEN. What?

SIMEON. Ye prayed he'd died.

EBEN. Waal—don't yew pray it? [*A pause.*]

PETER. He's our Paw.

EBEN [*violently*]. Not mine!

70 SIMEON [*dryly*]. Ye'd not let no one else say that about yer Maw! Ha! [*He gives one abrupt sardonic guffaw.* PETER *grins.*]

EBEN [*very pale*]. I meant—I hain't his'n—I hain't like him—he hain't me!

PETER [*dryly*]. Wait til ye've growed his age!

EBEN [*intensely*]. I'm Maw—every drop o' blood! [*A pause. They stare at him with indifferent curiosity.*]

PETER [*reminiscently*]. She was good t' Sim 'n' me. A good Stepmaw's scurse.

SIMEON. She was good t' everyone.

EBEN [*greatly moved, gets to his feet and makes an awkward bow to each of them— stammering*]. I be thankful t' ye. I'm her—her heir. [*He sits down in con-*
80 *fusion.*]

PETER [*after a pause—judicially*]. She was good even t' him.

EBEN [*fiercely*]. An' fur thanks he killed her!

SIMEON [*after a pause*]. No one never kills nobody. It's allus somethin'. That's the murderer.

EBEN. Didn't he slave Maw t' death?

PETER. He's slaved himself t' death. He's slaved Sim 'n' me 'n' yew t' death— on'y none o' us hain't died—yit.

SIMEON. It's somethin'—drivin' him—t' drive us!

EBEN [*vengefully*]. Waal—I hold him t' jedgment! [*Then scornfully*] Some-
90 thin'! What's somethin'?

SIMEON. Dunno.

EBEN [*sardonically*]. What's drivin' yew to Californi-a, mebbe? [*They look at him in surprise.*] Oh, I've heerd ye! [*Then, after a pause.*] But ye'll never go t' the gold fields!

PETER [*assertively*]. Mebbe!

EBEN. Whar'll ye git the money?

PETER. We kin walk. It's an a'mighty ways—Californi-a—but if yew was t' put all the steps we've walked on this farm end t' end we'd be in the moon!

EBEN. The Injuns'll skulp ye on the plains.

100 SIMEON [*with grim humor*]. We'll mebbe make 'em pay a hair fur a hair!

EBEN [*decisively*]. But t'aint that. Ye won't never go because ye'll wait here fur yer share o' the farm, thinkin' allus he'll die soon.

SIMEON [*after a pause*]. We've a right.

PETER. Two-thirds belongs t'us.

EBEN [*jumping to his feet*]. Ye've no right! She wa'n't yewr Maw! It was her farm! Didn't he steal it from her? She's dead. It's my farm.

SIMEON [*sardonically*]. Tell that t' Paw—when he comes! I'll bet ye a dollar he'll laugh—fur once in his life. Ha! [*He laughs himself in one single mirthless bark.*]

110 PETER [*amused in turn, echoes his brother*]. Ha!

SIMEON [*after a pause*]. What've ye got held agin us, Eben? Year arter year it's skulked in yer eye—somethin'.

PETER. Ay-eh.

EBEN. Ay-eh. They's somethin'. [*Suddenly exploding.*] Why didn't ye never stand between him 'n' my Maw when he was slavin' her to her grave—t' pay her back fur the kindness she done t' yew? [*There is a long pause. They stare at him in surprise.*]

SIMEON. Waal—the stock'd got t' be watered.

PETER. 'R they was woodin' t' do.

120 SIMEON. 'R plowin'.

PETER. 'R hayin'.

SIMEON. 'R spreadin' manure.

PETER. 'R weedin'.

SIMEON. 'R prunin'.

PETER. 'R milkin'.

EBEN [*breaking in harshly*]. An' makin' walls—stone atop o' stone—makin' walls till yer heart's a stone ye heft up out o' the way o' growth onto a stone wall t' wall in yer heart!

SIMEON [*matter-of-factly*]. We never had no time t' meddle.

130 PETER [*To* EBEN]. Yew was fifteen afore yer Maw died—an' big fur yer age. Why didn't ye never do nothin'?

EBEN [*harshly*]. They was chores t' do, wa'n't they? [*A pause—then slowly*] It was on'y arter she died I come to think o' it. Me cookin'—doin' her work—that made me know her, suffer her sufferin'—she'd come back t' help—come back t' bile potatoes—come back t' fry bacon—come back t' bake biscuits—come back all cramped up t' shake the fire, an' carry ashes, her eyes weepin' an' bloody with smoke an' cinders same's they used t' be. She still comes back—stands by the stove thar in the evenin'—she can't find it nateral sleepin' an' restin' in peace. She can't git used t' bein'

140 free—even in her grave.

SIMEON. She never complained none.

EBEN. She'd got too tired. She'd got too used t' bein' too tired. That was what he done. [*With vengeful passion.*] An' sooner'r later, I'll meddle. I'll say the thin's I didn't say then t' him! I'll yell 'em at the top o' my lungs. I'll see t' it my Maw gits some rest an' sleep in her grave! [*He sits down again, relapsing into a brooding silence. They look at him with a queer indifferent curiosity.*]

PETER [*after a pause*]. Whar in tarnation d'ye s'pose he went, Sim?

SIMEON. Dunno. He druv off in the buggy, all spick an' span, with the mare

150 all breshed an' shiny, druv off clackin' his tongue an' wavin' his whip. I remember it right well. I was finishin' plowin', it was spring an' May an' sunset, an' gold in the West, an' he druv off into it. I yells "Whar ye goin', Paw?" an' he hauls up by the stone wall a jiffy. His old snake's eyes was glitterin' in the sun like he'd been drinkin' a jugful an' he says with a mule's grin: "Don't ye run away till I come back!"

PETER. Wonder if he knowed we was wantin' fur Californi-a?

SIMEON. Mebbe. I didn't say nothin' and he says, lookin' kinder queer an' sick: "I been hearin' the hens cluckin' an' the roosters crowin' all the durn day. I been listenin' t' the cows lowin' an everythin' else kickin' up till I

160 can't stand it no more. It's spring an' I'm feelin' damned," he says. "Damned like an old bare hickory tree fit on'y fur burnin'," he says. An' then I calc'late I must've looked a mite hopeful, fur he adds real spry and vicious: "But don't git no fool idee I'm dead. I've sworn t' live a hundred an' I'll do it, if on'y t' spite yer sinful greed! An' now I'm ridin' out t' learn God's message t' me in the spring, like the prophets done. An' yew git

back t' yer plowin'," he says. An' he druv off singin' a hymn. I thought he was drunk—'r I'd stopped him goin'.

EBEN [*scornfully*].   No, ye wouldn't! Ye're scared o' him. He's stronger—inside—than both o' ye put together!

170 PETER [*sardonically*].   An' yew—be yew Samson?[2]

EBEN.   I'm gittin' stronger. I kin feel it growin' in me—growin' an' growin'—till it'll bust out—! [*He gets up and puts on his coat and a hat. They watch him, gradually breaking into grins. EBEN avoids their eyes sheepishly.*] I'm goin' out fur a spell—up the road.

PETER.   T' the village?

SIMEON.   T' see Minnie?

EBEN [*defiantly*].   Ay-eh!

PETER [*jeeringly*].   The Scarlet Woman!

SIMEON.   Lust—that's what's growin' in ye!

180 EBEN.   Waal—she's purty!

PETER.   She's been purty fur twenty year!

SIMEON.   A new coat o' paint'll make a heifer out of forty.

EBEN.   She hain't forty.

PETER.   If she hain't, she's teeterin' on the edge.

EBEN [*desperately*].   What d'yew know—

PETER.   All they is . . . Sim knew her—an' then me arter—

SIMEON.   An' Paw kin tell yew somethin' too! He was fust!

EBEN.   D'ye mean t' say he . . .

SIMEON [*with a grin*].   Ay-eh! We air his heirs in everythin'!

190 EBEN [*intensely*].   That's more to it! That grows on it! It'll bust soon! [*Then violently.*] I'll go smash my fist in her face! [*He pulls open the door in rear violently.*]

SIMEON [*with a wink at PETER—drawlingly*].   Mebbe—but the night's wa'm—purty—by the time ye git thar mebbe ye'll kiss her instead.

PETER.   Sart'n he will! [*They both roar with coarse laughter. EBEN rushes out and slams the door—then the outside front door—comes around the corner of the house and stands still by the gate, staring up at the sky.*]

SIMEON [*looking after him*].   Like his Paw.

PETER.   Dead spit an' image!

200 SIMEON.   Dog'll eat dog!

PETER.   Ay-eh. [*Pause. With yearning.*] Mebbe a year from now we'll be in Californi-a.

SIMEON.   Ay-eh. [*A pause. Both yawn.*] Let's git t'bed. [*He blows out the candle. They go out door in rear. EBEN stretches his arms up to the sky—rebelliously.*]

EBEN.   Waal— thar's a star, an' somewhar's they's him, an' here's me, an' thar's Min up the road—in the same night. What if I does kiss her? She's like t'night, she's soft 'n' wa'm, her eyes kin wink like a star, her mouth's wa'm, her arms're wa'm, she smells like a wa'm plowed field, she's purty . . . Ay-eh! By God A'mighty she's purty, an' I don't give a damn how many

210 sins she's sinned afore mine or who she's sinned 'em with, my sin's as purty as any one on 'em! [*He strides off down the road to the left.*]

---

[2] An Israelite noted for his great strength. He was ultimately betrayed by his mistress Delilah. See the Bible, Judges, Chapters 13–16.

SCENE III

It is the pitch darkness just before dawn. EBEN *comes in from the left and goes around to the porch, feeling his way, chuckling bitterly and cursing half-aloud to himself.*

EBEN. The cussed old miser! [*He can be heard going in the front door. There is a pause as he goes upstairs, then a loud knock on the bedroom door of the brothers*] Wake up!

SIMEON [*startledly*]. Who's thar?

EBEN [*pushing open the door and coming in, a lighted candle in his hand. The bedroom of the brothers is revealed. Its ceiling is the sloping roof. They can stand upright only close to the center dividing wall of the upstairs.* SIMEON *and* PETER *are in a double bed, front.* EBEN's *cot is to the rear.* EBEN *has a mixture of silly grin and*
220   *vicious scowl on his face*]. I be!

PETER [*angrily*]. What in hell's-fire . . . ?

EBEN. I got news fur ye! Ha! [*He gives one abrupt sardonic guffaw.*]

SIMEON [*angrily*]. Couldn't ye hold it 'til we'd got our sleep?

EBEN. It's nigh sunup. [*Then explosively.*] He's gone an' married agen!

SIMEON *and* PETER [*explosively*]. Paw!

EBEN. Got himself hitched to a female 'bout thirty-five—an' purty, they says . . .

SIMEON [*aghast*]. It's a durn lie!

PETER. Who says?

230 SIMEON. They been stringin' ye!

EBEN. Think I'm a dunce, do ye? The hull village says. The preacher from New Dover, he brung the news—told it t' our preacher—New Dover, that's whar the old loon got himself hitched—that's whar the woman lived—

PETER [*no longer doubting—stunned*]. Waal . . . !

SIMEON [*the same*]. Waal . . . !

EBEN [*sitting down on a bed—with vicious hatred*]. Ain't he a devil out o' hell? It's jest t' spite us—the damned old mule!

PETER [*after a pause*]. Everythin'll go t' her now.

SIMEON. Ay-eh. [*A pause—dully*] Waal—if it's done—

240 PETER. It's done us. [*Pause—then persuasively*] They's gold in the fields o' Californi-a, Sim. No good a-stayin' here now.

SIMEON. Jest what I was a-thinkin'. [*Then with decision.*] S'well fust's last! Let's light out and git this mornin'.

PETER. Suits me.

EBEN. Ye must like walkin'.

SIMEON [*sardonically*]. If ye'd grow wings on us we'd fly thar!

EBEN. Ye'd like ridin' better—on a boat, wouldn't ye? [*Fumbles in his pocket and takes out a crumpled sheet of foolscap.*] Waal, if ye sign this ye kin ride on a boat. I've had it writ out an' ready in case ye'd ever go. It says fur three
250   hundred dollars t' each ye agree yewr shares o' the farm is sold t' me. [*They look suspiciously at the paper. A pause.*]

SIMEON [*wonderingly*]. But if he's hitched agen—

PETER. An' whar'd yew git that sum o' money, anyways?

EBEN [*cunningly*]. I know whar it's hid. I been waitin'—Maw told me. She knew whar it lay fur years, but she was waitin' . . . It's her'n—the money he hoarded from her farm an' hid from Maw. It's my money by rights now.

PETER.   Whar's it hid?

EBEN [*cunningly*].   Whar yew won't never find it without me. Maw spied on
him—'r she'd never knowed. [*A pause. They look at him suspiciously, and he at*
260   *them.*] Waal, is it fa'r trade?

SIMEON.   Dunno.

PETER.   Dunno.

SIMEON [*looking at window*].   Sky's grayin'.

PETER.   Ye better start the fire, Eben.

SIMEON.   An' fix some vittles.

EBEN.   Ay-eh. [*Then with a forced jocular heartiness.*] I'll git ye a good one. If
ye're startin' t' hoof it t' Californi-a ye'll need somethin' that'll stick t' yer
ribs. [*He turns to the door, adding meaningly.*] But ye kin ride on a boat if ye'll
swap. [*He stops at the door and pauses. They stare at him.*]

270   SIMEON [*suspiciously*].   Whar was ye all night?

EBEN [*defiantly*].   Up t' Min's. [*Then slowly.*] Walkin' thar, fust I felt 's if I'd kiss
her; then I got a-thinkin' o' what ye'd said o' him an' her an' I says, I'll bust
her nose fur that! Then I got t' the village an heerd the news an' I got
madder'n hell an' run all the way t' Min's not knowin' what I'd do— [*He*
pauses— then sheepishly but more defiantly.] Waal—when I seen her, I didn't
hit her—nor I didn't kiss her nuther—I begun t' beller like a calf an' cuss
at the same time. I was durn mad—an' she got scared—an' I jest grabbed
holt an' tuk her— [*Proudly.*] Yes, sirree! I tuk her. She may've been his'n—
an' your'n, too—but she's mine now!

280   SIMEON [*dryly*].   In love, air yew?

EBEN [*with lofty scorn*].   Love! I don't take no stock in sech slop!

PETER [*winking at* SIMEON].   Mebbe Eben's aimin' t' marry, too.

SIMEON.   Min'd make a true faithful he'pmeet! [*They snicker.*]

EBEN.   What do I care fur her—'ceptin' she's round an' wa'm? The p'int is
she was his'n—an' now she b'longs t' me! [*He goes to the door—then turns—*
rebelliously.] An' Min hain't sech a bad un. They's worse'n Min in the world,
I'll bet ye! Wait'll we see this cow the Old Man's hitched t'! She'll beat Min,
I got a notion! [*He starts to go out.*]

SIMEON [*suddenly*].   Mebbe ye'll try t' make her your'n, too?

290   PETER.   Ha! [*He gives a sardonic laugh of relish at this idea.*]

EBEN [*spitting with disgust*].   Her—here—sleepin' with him—stealin' my
Maw's farm! I'd as soon pet a skunk 'r kiss a snake! [*He goes out. The two*
stare after him suspiciously. A pause. They listen to his steps receding.]

PETER.   He's startin' the fire.

SIMEON.   I'd like t' ride t' Californi-a—but—

PETER.   Min might o' put some scheme in his head.

SIMEON.   Mebbe it's all a lie 'bout Paw marryin'. We'd best wait an' see the
bride.

PETER.   An' don't sign nothin' til we does!

300   SIMEON.   Nor til we've tested it's good money. [*Then with a grin.*] But if Paw's
hitched we'd be sellin' Eben somethin we'd never git nohow!

PETER.   We'll wait an' see. [*Then with sudden vindictive anger.*] An' til he comes,
let's yew 'n' me not wuk a lick, let Eben tend to thin's if he's a mind t', let's
us jest sleep an' eat an' drink likker, an' let the hull damned farm go t'
blazes!

SIMEON [*excitedly*].   By God, we've 'arned a rest! We'll play rich fur a change.
I hain't a-going to stir outa bed till breakfast's ready.
PETER.   An' on the table!
SIMEON [*after a pause—thoughtfully*].   What d'ye calc'late she'll be like—our
310   new Maw? Like Eben thinks?
PETER.   More'n likely.
SIMEON [*vindictively*].   Waal—I hope she's a she-devil that'll make him wish
he was dead an' living in the pit o' hell fur comfort!
PETER [*fervently*].   Amen!
SIMEON [*imitating his father's voice*].   "I'm ridin' out t' learn God's message t'
me in the spring like the prophets done," he says. I'll bet right then an'
thar he knew plumb well he was goin' whorin', the stinkin' old hypocrite!

SCENE IV

*Same as Scene II—Shows the interior of the kitchen with a lighted candle on table.
It is gray dawn outside.* SIMEON *and* PETER *are just finishing their breakfast.* EBEN *sits
before his plate of untouched food, brooding frowningly.*

PETER [*glancing at him rather irritably*].   Lookin' glum don't help none.
SIMEON [*sarcastically*].   Sorrowin' over his lust o' the flesh!
320   PETER [*with a grin*].   Was she yer fust?
EBEN [*angrily*].   None o' yer business. [*A pause*] I was thinkin' o' him. I got a
notion he's gittin' near—I kin feel him comin' on like yew kin feel malaria
chill afore it takes ye.
PETER.   It's too early yet.
SIMEON.   Dunno. He'd like t' catch us nappin'—jest t' have somethin' t' hoss
us 'round over.
PETER [*mechanically gets to his feet.* SIMEON *does the same*].   Waal—let's git t'wuk.
[*They both plod mechanically toward the door before they realize. Then they stop
short.*]
330   SIMEON [*grinning*].   Ye're a cussed fool, Peter—and I be wuss! Let him see we
hain't wukin'! We don't give a durn!
PETER [*as they go back to the table*].   Not a damned durn! It'll serve t' show him
we're done with him. [*They sit down again.* EBEN *stares from one to the other
with surprise.*]
SIMEON [*grins at him*].   We're aimin' t' start bein' lilies o' the field.[3]
PETER.   Nary a toil 'r spin 'r lick o' wuk do we put in!
SIMEON.   Ye're sole owner—till he comes—that's what ye wanted. Waal, ye
got t' be sole hand, too.
PETER.   The cows air bellerin'. Ye better hustle at the milkin'.
340   EBEN [*with excited joy*].   Ye mean ye'll sign the paper?
SIMEON [*dryly*].   Mebbe.
PETER.   Mebbe.
SIMEON.   We're considerin'. [*Peremptorily.*] Ye better git t' wuk.
EBEN [*with queer excitement*].   It's Maw's farm agen! It's my farm! Them's my

---

[3]   See Matthew 6:34: "Consider the lilies of the field, how they grow; they toil not, neither do
they spin."

cows! I'll milk my durn fingers off fur cows o' mine! [*He goes out door in rear, they stare after him indifferently.*]

SIMEON.   Like his Paw.

PETER.   Dead spit 'n' image!

SIMEON.   Waal— let dog eat dog! [EBEN *comes out of front door and around the* 350 *corner of the house. The sky is beginning to grow flushed with sunrise.* EBEN *stops by the gate and stares around him with glowing, possessive eyes. He takes in the whole farm with his embracing glance of desire.*]

EBEN.   It's purty! It's damned purty! It's mine! [*He suddenly throws his head back boldly and glares with hard, defiant eyes at the sky.*] Mine, d'ye hear? Mine! [*He turns and walks quickly off left, rear, toward the barn. The two brothers light their pipes.*]

SIMEON [*putting his muddy boots up on the table, tilting back his chair, and puffing defiantly*]. Waal—this air solid comfort—fur once.

PETER.   Ay-eh. [*He follows suit. A pause. Unconsciously they both sigh.*]

360 SIMEON [*suddenly*].   He never was much o' a hand at milkin', Eben wa'n't.

PETER [*with a snort*].   His hands air like hoofs! [*A pause.*]

SIMEON.   Reach down the jug thar! Let's take a swaller. I'm feelin' kind o' low.

PETER.   Good idee! [*He does so—gets two glasses—they pour out drinks of whiskey.*] Here's t' the gold in Californi-a!

SIMEON.   An' luck t' find it! [*They drink—puff resolutely—sigh—take their feet down from the table.*]

PETER.   Likker don't pear t' sot right.

SIMEON.   We hain't used t' it this early. [*A pause. They become very restless.*]

370 PETER.   Gittin' close in this kitchen.

SIMEON [*with immense relief*].   Let's git a breath o' air. [*They arise briskly and go out rear—appear around house and stop by the gate. They stare up at the sky with a numbed appreciation.*]

PETER.   Purty!

SIMEON.   Ay-eh. Gold's t' the East now.

PETER.   Sun's startin' with us fur the Golden West.

SIMEON [*staring around the farm, his compressed face tightened, unable to conceal emotion*].   Waal—it's our last mornin'—mebbe.

PETER [*the same*].   Ay-eh.

380 SIMEON [*stamps his foot on the earth and addresses it desperately*].   Waal—ye've thirty year o' me buried in ye—spread out over ye—blood an' bone an' sweat—rotted away—fertilizin' ye—richin' yer soul—prime manure, by God, that's what I been t' ye!

PETER.   Ay-eh! An' me!

SIMEON.   An' yew, Peter. [*He sighs—then spits.*] Waal—no use'n cryin' over spilt milk.

PETER.   They's gold in the West—an' freedom, mebbe. We been slaves t' stone walls here.

SIMEON [*defiantly*].   We hain't nobody's slaves from this out—nor nothin's 390 slave nuther. [*A pause—restlessly.*] Speaking o' milk, wonder how Eben's managin'?

PETER.   I s'pose he's managin'.

SIMEON.   Mebbe we'd ought t' help—this once.

PETER.   Mebbe. The cows knows us.

SIMEON. An' likes us. They don't know him much.

PETER. An' the hosses, an' pigs, an' chickens. They don't know him much.

SIMEON. They knows us like brothers—an' likes us! [*Proudly.*] Hain't we raised 'em to' be fust-rate, number one prize stock?

PETER. We hain't not no more.

400 SIMEON [*dully*]. I was fergittin'. [*Then resignedly*] Waal, let's go help Eben a spell an' git waked up.

PETER. Suits me. [*They are starting off down left, rear, for the barn when* EBEN *appears from there hurrying toward them, his face excited.*]

EBEN [*breathlessly*]. Waal—har they be! The old mule an' the bride! I seen 'em from the barn down below at the turnin'.

PETER. How could ye tell that far?

EBEN. Hain't I as far-sight as he's near-sight? Don't I know the mare 'n' buggy, an' two people settin' in it? Who else . . . ? An' I tell ye I kin feel 'em a-coming', too! [*He squirms as if he had the itch.*]

410 PETER [*beginning to be angry*]. Waal—let him do his own unhitchin'!

SIMEON [*angry in his turn*]. Let's hustle in an' git our bundles an' be a-goin' as he's a-comin'. I don't want never t' step inside the door agen arter he's back. [*They both start back around the corner of the house.* EBEN *follows them.*]

EBEN [*anxiously*]. Will ye sign it afore ye go?

PETER. Let's see the color o' the old skinflint's money an' we'll sign. [*They disappear left. The two brothers clump upstairs to get their bundles.* EBEN *appears in the kitchen, runs to window, peers out, comes back and pulls up a strip of flooring in under stove, takes out a canvas bag and puts it on table, then sets the floorboard back in place. The two brothers appear a moment after. They carry old*

420   *carpet bags.*]

EBEN [*puts his hand on bag guardingly*]. Have ye signed?

SIMEON [*shows paper in his hand*]. Ay-eh. [*Greedily.*] Be that the money?

EBEN [*opens bag and pours out pile of twenty-dollar gold pieces*]. Twenty-dollar pieces—thirty on 'em. Count 'em. [*Peter does so, arranging them in stacks of five, biting one or two to test them.*]

PETER. Six hundred. [*He puts them in bag and puts it inside his shirt carefully.*]

SIMEON [*handing paper to* EBEN]. Har ye be.

EBEN [*after glance, folds it carefully and hides it under his shirt—gratefully*]. Thank yew.

430 PETER. Thank yew fur the ride.

SIMEON. We'll send ye a lump o' gold fur Christmas. [*A pause.* EBEN *stares at them and they at him.*]

PETER [*awkwardly*]. Waal—we're a-goin'.

SIMEON. Comin' out t' the yard?

EBEN. No. I'm waitin' in here a spell. [*Another silence. The brothers edge awkwardly to door in rear—then turn and stand.*]

SIMEON. Waal—good-by.

PETER. Good-by.

EBEN. Good-by. [*They go out. He sits down at the table, faces the stove and pulls*

440   *out the paper. He looks from it to the stove. His face, lighted up by the shaft of sunlight from the window, has an expression of trance. His lips move. The two brothers come out to the gate.*]

PETER [*looking off toward barn*]. Thar he be—unhitchin'.

SIMEON [*with a chuckle*]. I'll bet ye he's riled.

PETER. An' thar she be.

SIMEON. Let's wait 'n' see what our new Maw looks like.

PETER [*with a grin*]. An' give him our partin' cuss!

SIMEON [*grinning*]. I feel like raisin' fun. I feel light in my head an' feet.

PETER. Me, too. I feel like laffin' till I'd split up the middle.

450 SIMEON. Reckon it's the likker?

PETER. No. My feet feel itchin' t' walk an' walk—an' jump high over thin's— an' . . .

SIMEON. Dance? [*A pause.*]

PETER [*puzzled*]. It's plumb onnateral.

SIMEON [*a light coming over his face*]. I calc'late it's 'cause school's out. It's holiday. Fur once we're free!

PETER [*dazedly*]. Free?

SIMEON. The halter's broke—the harness is busted—the fence bars is down—the stone walls air crumblin' an' tumblin'! We'll be kickin' up an'

460 tearin' away down the road!

PETER [*drawing a deep breath—oratorically*]. Anybody that wants this stinkin' old rock-pile of a farm kin hev it. T'ain't our'n, no sirree!

SIMEON [*takes the gate off its hinges and puts it under his arm*]. We harby 'bolishes shet gates, an' open gates, an' all gates, by thunder!

PETER. We'll take it with us fur luck an' let 'er sail free down some river.

SIMEON [*as a sound of voices comes from left, rear*]. Har they comes! [*The two brothers congeal into two stiff, grim-visaged statues. EPHRAIM CABOT and ABBIE PUTNAM come in. CABOT is seventy-five, tall and gaunt, with great, wiry, concentrated power, but stoop-shouldered from toil. His face is as hard as if it were hewn*

470 *out of a boulder, yet there is a weakness in it, a petty pride in its own narrow strength. His eyes are small, close together, and extremely near-sighted, blinking continually in the effort to focus on objects, their stare having a straining, ingrowing quality. He is dressed in his dismal black Sunday suit. ABBIE is thirty-five, buxom, full of vitality. Her round face is pretty but marred by its rather gross sensuality. There is strength and obstinacy in her jaw, a hard determination in her eyes, and about her whole personality the same unsettled, untamed, desperate quality which is so apparent in EBEN.*]

CABOT [*as they enter—a queer strangled emotion in his dry cracking voice*]. Har we be t' hum, Abbie.

480 ABBIE [*with lust for the word*]. Hum! [*Her eyes gloating on the house without seeming to see the two stiff figures at the gate.*] It's purty—purty! I can't b'lieve it's r'ally mine.

CABOT [*sharply*]. Yewr'n? Mine! [*He stares at her penetratingly. She stares back. He adds relentingly.*] Our'n—mebbe! It was lonesome too long. I was growin' old in the spring. A hum's got t' hev a woman.

ABBIE [*her voice taking possession*]. A woman's got t' hev a hum.

CABOT [*nodding uncertainly*]. Ay-eh. [*then irritably*] Whar be they? Ain't thar nobody about—'r wukin'—r' nothin'?

ABBIE [*sees the brothers. She returns their stare of cold appraising contempt with*

490 *interest—slowly*]. Thar's two men loafin' at the gate an' starin' at me like a couple o' strayed hogs.

CABOT [*straining his eyes*]. I kin see 'em—but I can't make out. . . .

SIMEON. It's Simeon.

PETER. It's Peter.

CABOT [*exploding*]. Why hain't ye wukin'?

SIMEON [*dryly*]. We're waitin' t' welcome ye hum—yew an' the bride!

CABOT [*confusedly*]. Huh? Waal—this be yer new Maw, boys. [*She stares at them and they at her.*]

SIMEON [*turns away and spits contemptuously*]. I see her!

500 PETER [*spits also*]. An' I see her!

ABBIE [*with the conqueror's conscious superiority*]. I'll go in an' look at *my* house. [*She goes slowly around to porch.*]

SIMEON [*with a snort*]. *Her* house!

PETER [*calls after her*]. Ye'll find Eben inside. Ye better not tell him it's *your* house.

ABBIE [*mouthing the name*]. Eben. [*Then quietly.*] I'll tell Eben.

CABOT [*with a contemptuous sneer*]. Ye needn't heed Eben. Eben's a dumb fool—like his Maw—soft an' simple!

SIMEON [*with his sardonic burst of laughter*]. Ha! Eben's a chip o' yew—spit 'n'
510   image—hard 'n' bitter's a hickory tree! Dog'll eat dog. He'll eat ye yet, old man!

CABOT [*commandingly*]. Ye git t' wuk!

SIMEON [*as* ABBIE *disappears in house—winks at* PETER *and says tauntingly*]. So thar's our new Maw, be it? Whar in hell did ye dig her up? [*He and* PETER *laugh.*]

PETER. Ha! Ye'd better turn her in the pen with the other sows. [*They laugh uproariously, slapping their thighs.*]

CABOT [*so amazed at their effrontery that he stutters in confusion*]. Simeon! Peter! What's come over ye? Air ye drunk?

520 SIMEON. We're free, old man—free o' yew an' the hull damned farm! [*They grow more and more hilarious and excited.*]

PETER. An' we're startin' out fur the gold fields o' Californi-a!

SIMEON. Ye kin take this place an' burn it!

PETER. An' bury it—fur all we cares!

SIMEON. We're free, old man! [*He cuts a caper.*]

PETER. Free! [*He gives a kick in the air.*]

SIMEON [*in a frenzy*]. Whoop!

PETER. Whoop! [*They do an absurd Indian war dance about the old man who is petrified between rage and the fear that they are insane.*]

530 SIMEON. We're free as Injuns! Lucky we don't skulp ye!

PETER. An' burn yer barn an' kill the stock!

SIMEON. An' rape yer new woman! Whoop! [*He and* PETER *stop their dance, holding their sides, rocking with wild laughter.*]

CABOT [*edging away*]. Lust fur gold—fur the sinful, easy gold o' Californi-a! It's made ye mad!

SIMEON [*tauntingly*]. Wouldn't ye like us to send ye back some sinful gold, ye old sinner?

PETER. They's gold besides what's in Californi-a! [*He retreats back beyond the vision of the old man and takes the bag of money and flaunts it in the air above his
540   head, laughing.*]

SIMEON. And sinfuller, too!

PETER. We'll be voyagin' on the sea! Whoop! [*He leaps up and down.*]

SIMEON. Livin' free! Whoop! [*He leaps in turn.*]

CABOT [*suddenly roaring with rage*]. My cuss on ye!

SIMEON. Take our'n in trade fur it! Whoop!

CABOT. I'll hev ye both chained up in the asylum.

PETER. Ye old skinflint! Good-by!

SIMEON. Ye old blood sucker! Good-by!

CABOT. Go afore I . . . !

550 PETER. Whoop! [*He picks a stone from the road.* SIMEON *does the same.*]

SIMEON. Maw'll be in the parlor.

PETER. Ay-eh! One! Two!

CABOT [*frightened*]. What air ye . . . ?

PETER. Three! [*They both throw, the stones hitting the parlor window with a crash of glass, tearing the shade.*]

SIMEON. Whoop!

PETER. Whoop!

CABOT [*in a fury now, rushing toward them*]. If I kin lay hands on ye—I'll break yer bones fur ye! [*But they beat a capering retreat before him,* SIMEON *with the*

560   *gate still under his arm.* CABOT *comes back, panting with impotent rage. Their voices as they go off take up the song of the gold-seekers to the old tune of "'Oh, Susannah!"*]

> "I jumped aboard the Liza ship,
> And traveled on the sea,
> And every time I thought of home
> I wished it wasn't me!
> Oh! Californi-a,
> That's the land fur me!
> I'm off to Californi-a!

570 > With my wash bowl on my knee."

[*In the meantime, the window of the bedroom on right is raised and* ABBIE *sticks her head out. She looks down at* CABOT *with a sigh of relief.*]

ABBIE. Waal—that's the last o' them two, hain't it? [*He doesn't answer. Then in possessive tones*] This here's a nice bedroom, Ephraim. It's a r'al nice bed. Is it my room, Ephraim?

CABOT [*grimly—without looking up*]. Our'n! [*She cannot control a grimace of aversion and pulls back her head slowly and shuts the window. A sudden horrible thought seems to enter* CABOT'S *head.*] They been up to somethin'! Mebbe— mebbe they've pizened the stock—'r somethin'! [*He almost runs off down toward the barn. A moment later the kitchen door is slowly pushed open and* ABBIE *enters. For a moment she stands looking at* EBEN. *He does not notice her at first.*

580   *Her eyes take him in penetratingly with a calculating appraisal of his strength as against hers. But under this her desire is dimly awakened by his youth and good looks. Suddenly he becomes conscious of her presence and looks up. Their eyes meet. He leaps to his feet, glowering at her speechlessly.*]

ABBIE [*in her most seductive tones which she uses all through this scene*]. Be you— Eben? I'm Abbie— [*She laughs*] I mean, I'm yer new Maw.

EBEN [*viciously*]. No, damn ye!

ABBIE [*as if she hadn't heard—with a queer smile*]. Yer Paw's spoke a lot o' yew. . . .

EBEN. Ha!

590 ABBIE. Ye mustn't mind him. He's an old man. [*A long pause. They stare at*

each other] I don't want t' pretend playin' Maw t' ye, Eben. [*Admiringly*] Ye're too big an' too strong fur that. I want t' be frens with ye. Mebbe with me fur a fren ye'd find ye'd like livin' here better. I kin make it easy fur ye with him, mebbe. [*With a scornful sense of power.*] I calc'late I kin git him t' do most anythin' fur me.

EBEN [*with bitter scorn*].   Ha! [*They stare again,* EBEN *obscurely moved, physically attracted to her—in forced stilted tones.*] Yew kin go t' the devil!

ABBIE [*calmly*].   If cussin' me does ye good, cuss all ye've a mind t'. I'm all prepared t' have ye agin me—at fust. I don't blame ye nuther. I'd feel the

600 same at any stranger comin' t' take my Maw's place. [*He shudders. She is watching him carefully.*] Yew must've cared a lot fur yewr Maw, didn't ye? My Maw died afore I'd growed. I don't remember her none. [*A pause*] But yew won't hate me long, Eben. I'm not the wust in the world—an' yew an' me've got a lot in common. I kin tell that by lookin' at ye. Waal—I've had a hard life, too—oceans o' trouble an' nuthin' but wuk fur reward. I was a orphan early an' had t' wuk fur others in other folks' hums. Then I married an' he turned out a drunken spreer an' so he had to wuk fur others an' me too agen in other folks' hums, an' the baby died, an' my husband got sick an' died too, an' I was glad sayin' now I'm free fur once, on'y I

610 diskivered right away all I was free fur was t' wuk agen in other folks' hums, doin' other folks' wuk til I'd most give up hope o' ever doin' my own wuk in my own hum, an' then your Paw come. . . . [CABOT *appears returning from the barn. He comes to the gate and looks down the road the brothers have gone. A faint strain of their retreating voices is heard: "Oh, Californi-a! That's the place for me." He stands glowering, his fist clenched, his face grim with rage.*]

EBEN [*fighting against his growing attraction and sympathy—harshly*].   An' bought yew—like a harlot! [*She is stung and flushes angrily. She has been sincerely moved by the recital of her troubles. He adds furiously.*] An' the price he's payin' ye—this farm—was my Maw's, damn ye!—an' mine now!

620 ABBIE [*with a cool laugh of confidence*].   Yewr'n? We'll see 'bout that! [*Then strongly*] Waal—what if I did need a hum? What else'd I marry an old man like him fur?

EBEN [*maliciously*].   I'll tell him ye said that!

ABBIE [*smiling*].   I'll say ye're lyin' a-purpose—an' he'll drive ye off the place!

EBEN.   Ye devil!

ABBIE [*defying him*].   This be my farm—this be my hum—this be my kitchen—!

EBEN [*furiously, as if he were going to attack her*].   Shut up, damn ye!

ABBIE [*walks up to him—a queer coarse expression of desire in her face and body—*

630 *slowly*].   An' upstairs—that be my bedroom—an' my bed! [*He stares into her eyes, terribly confused and torn. She adds softly.*] I hain't bad nor mean—'ceptin' fur an enemy—but I got t' fight fur what's due me out o' life, if I ever 'spect t' git it. [*Then putting her hand on his arm—seductively.*] Let's yew 'n' me be frens, Eben.

EBEN [*stupidly—as if hypnotized*].   Ay-eh. [*Then furiously flinging off her arm.*] No, ye durned old witch! I hate ye! [*He rushes out the door.*]

ABBIE [*looks after him smiling satisfiedly—then half to herself, mouthing the word*].   Eben's nice. [*She looks at the table, proudly.*] I'll wash up *my* dishes now. [EBEN *appears outside, slamming the door behind him. He comes around corner, stops on*

640 *seeing his father, and stands staring at him with hate.*]

CABOT [*raising his arms to heaven in the fury he can no longer control*].   Lord God
    o' Hosts, smite the undutiful sons with Thy wust cuss!
EBEN [*breaking in violently*].   Yew 'n' yewr God! Allus cussin' folks—allus nag-
    gin' 'em!
CABOT [*oblivious to him—summoningly*].   God o' the old! God o' the lonesome!
EBEN [*mockingly*].   Naggin' His sheep t' sin! T' hell with yewr God! [CABOT
    turns. He and EBEN *glower at each other.*]
CABOT [*harshly*].   So it's yew. I might've knowed it. [*Shaking his finger threat-
    eningly at him.*] Blasphemin' fool! [*Then quickly*] Why hain't ye t' wuk?
650 EBEN.   Why hain't yew? They've went. I can't wuk it all alone.
CABOT [*contemptuously*].   Nor noways! I'm wuth ten o' ye yit, old's I be! Ye'll
    never be more'n half a man! [*Then, matter-of-factly.*] Waal—let's get t' the
    barn. [*They go. A last faint note of the "Californi-a" song is heard from the
    distance.* ABBIE *is washing her dishes.*]

CURTAIN

PART II

SCENE I

The exterior of the farmhouse, as in Part I—a hot Sunday afternoon two months
later. ABBIE, dressed in her best, is discovered sitting in a rocker at the end of the porch.
She rocks listlessly, enervated by the heat, staring in front of her with bored, half-closed
eyes.

EBEN sticks his head out of his bedroom window. He looks around furtively and tries
to see—or hear—if anyone is on the porch, but although he has been careful to make
no noise, ABBIE has sensed his movement. She stops rocking, her face grows animated
and eager, she waits attentively. EBEN seems to feel her presence, he scowls back his
thoughts of her and spits with exaggerated disdain—then withdraws back into the
room.

ABBIE waits, holding her breath as she listens with passionate eagerness for every
sound within the house.

EBEN comes out. Their eyes meet; his falter. He is confused, he turns away and
slams the door resentfully. At this gesture, ABBIE laughs tantalizingly, amused but at
the same time piqued and irritated. He scowls, strides off the porch to the path and
starts to walk past her to the road with a grand swagger of ignoring her existence. He
is dressed in his store suit, spruced up, his face shines from soap and water. ABBIE leans
forward on her chair, her eyes hard and angry now, and, as he passes her, gives a
sneering, taunting chuckle.

EBEN [*stung—turns on her furiously*].   What air yew cacklin' 'bout?
ABBIE [*triumphant*].   Yew!
EBEN.   What about me?
ABBIE.   Ye look all slicked up like a prize bull.
EBEN [*with a sneer*].   Waal—ye hain't so durned purty yerself, be ye? [*They
660   stare into each other's eyes, his held by hers in spite of himself, hers glowingly
    possessive. Their physical attraction becomes a palpable force quivering in the hot
    air.*]

Abbie [*softly*]. Ye don't mean that, Eben. Ye may think ye mean it, mebbe, but ye don't. Ye can't. It's agin nature, Eben. Ye been fightin' yer nature ever since the day I come—tryin' t' tell yerself I hain't purty t'ye. [*She laughs a low humid laugh without taking her eyes from his. A pause—her body squirms desirously—she murmurs languorously.*] Hain't the sun strong an' hot? Ye kin feel it burnin' into the earth—Nature—makin' thin's grow—bigger 'n' bigger—burnin' inside ye—makin' ye want t' grow—into somethin'
670   else—till ye're jined with it—an' it's your'n—but it owns ye, too—an' makes ye grow bigger—like a tree—like elums— [*She laughs again softly, holding his eyes. He takes a step toward her, compelled against his will.*] Nature'll beat ye, Eben. Ye might's well own up t' it fust 's last.
Eben [*trying to break from her spell—confusedly*]. If Paw'd hear ye goin' on. . . . [*Resentfully*] But ye've made such a damned idjit out o' the old devil. . . . [Abbie *laughs.*]
Abbie. Waal—hain't it easier fur yew with him changed softer?
Eben [*defiantly*]. No. I'm fightin' him—fightin' yew—fightin' fur Maw's rights t' her hum! [*This breaks her spell for him. He glowers at her.*] An' I'm
680   onto ye. Ye hain't foolin' me a mite. Ye're aimin' t' swaller up everythin' an' make it your'n. Waal, you'll find I'm a heap sight bigger hunk nor yew kin chew! [*He turns from her with a sneer.*]
Abbie [*trying to regain her ascendancy—seductively*]. Eben!
Eben. Leave me be! [*He starts to walk away.*]
Abbie [*more commandingly*]. Eben!
Eben [*stops—resentfully*]. What d'ye want?
Abbie [*trying to conceal a growing excitement*]. Whar air ye goin'?
Eben [*with malicious nonchalance*]. Oh—up the road a spell.
Abbie. T' the village?
690 Eben [*airily*]. Mebbe.
Abbie [*excitedly*]. T' see that Min, I s'pose?
Eben. Mebbe.
Abbie [*weakly*]. What d'ye want t' waste time on her fur?
Eben [*revenging himself now—grinning at her*]. Ye can't beat Nature, didn't ye say? [*He laughs and again starts to walk away.*]
Abbie [*bursting out*]. An ugly old hake!
Eben [*with a tantalizing sneer*]. She's purtier'n yew be!
Abbie. That every wuthless drunk in the country has. . . .
Eben [*tauntingly*]. Mebbe—but she's better'n yew. She owns up fa'r 'n' squar'
700   t' her doin's.
Abbie [*furiously*]. Don't ye dare compare. . . .
Eben. She don't go sneakin' an' stealin'—what's mine.
Abbie [*savagely seizing on his weak point*]. Your'n? Yew mean—my farm?
Eben. I mean the farm yew sold yerself fur like any other old whore—my farm!
Abbie [*stung—fiercely*]. Ye'll never live t' see the day when even a stinkin' weed on it'll belong t' ye! [*Then in a scream.*] Git out o' my sight! Go on t' yer slut—disgracin' yer Paw 'n' me! I'll git yer Paw t' horsewhip ye off the place if I want t'! Ye're only livin' here 'cause I tolerate ye! Git along! I hate
710   the sight o' ye! [*She stops, panting and glaring at him.*]
Eben [*returning her glance in kind*]. An' I hate the sight o' yew! [*He turns and strides off up the road. She follows his retreating figure with concentrated hate. Old*

CABOT *appears coming up from the barn. The hard, grim expression of his face has changed. He seems in some queer way softened, mellowed. His eyes have taken on a strange, incongruous dreamy quality. Yet there is no hint of physical weakness about him—rather he looks more robust and younger.* ABBIE *sees him and turns away quickly with unconcealed aversion. He comes slowly up to her.*]

CABOT [*mildly*].   War yew an' Eben quarrelin' agen?

ABBIE [*shortly*].   No.

720 CABOT.   Ye was talkin' a'mighty loud. [*He sits down on the edge of porch.*]

ABBIE [*snappishly*].   If ye heerd us they hain't no need askin' questions.

CABOT.   I didn't hear what ye said.

ABBIE [*relieved*].   Waal—it wa'n't nothin' t' speak on.

CABOT [*after a pause*].   Eben's queer.

ABBIE [*bitterly*].   He's the dead spit 'n' image o' yew!

CABOT [*queerly interested*].   D'ye think so, Abbie? [*After a pause, ruminatingly.*] Me 'n' Eben's allus fit 'n' fit. I never could b'ar him noways. He's so thunderin' soft—like his Maw.

ABBIE [*scornfully*].   Ay-eh! 'Bout as soft as yew be!

730 CABOT [*as if he hadn't heard*].   Mebbe I been too hard on him.

ABBIE [*jeeringly*].   Waal—ye're gittin' soft now—soft as slop! That's what Eben was sayin'.

CABOT [*his face instantly grim and ominous*].   Eben was sayin'? Waal, he'd best not do nothin' t' try me 'r he'll soon diskiver. . . . [*A pause. She keeps her face turned away. His gradually softens. He stares up at the sky.*] Purty, hain't it?

ABBIE [*crossly*].   I don't see nothin' purty.

CABOT.   The sky. Feels like a wa'm field up thar.

ABBIE [*sarcastically*].   Air yew aimin' t' buy up over the farm too? [*She snickers contemptuously.*]

740 CABOT [*strangely*].   I'd like t' own my place up thar. [*A pause.*] I'm gittin' old, Abbie. I'm gittin' ripe on the bough. [*A pause. She stares at him mystified. He goes on.*] It's allus lonesome cold in the house—even when it's bilin' hot outside. Hain't yew noticed?

ABBIE.   No.

CABOT.   It's wa'm down t' the barn—nice smellin' an' warm—with the cows. [*A pause.*] Cows is queer.

ABBIE.   Like yew?

CABOT.   Like Eben. [*A pause.*] I'm gittin t' feel resigned t' Eben—jest as I got t' feel 'bout his Maw. I'm gittin' t' learn to b'ar his softness—jest like her'n

750 I calc'late I c'd a'most take t' him—if he wa'n't sech a dumb fool! [*A pause.*] I s'pose it's old age a-creepin' in my bones.

ABBIE [*indifferently*].   Waal—ye hain't dead yet.

CABOT [*roused*].   No, I hain't, yew bet—not by a hell of a sight—I'm sound 'n' tough as hickory! [*then moodily.*] But arter three score and ten the Lord warns ye t' prepare. [*A pause.*] That's why Eben's come in my head. Now that his cussed sinful brothers is gone their path t' hell, they's no one left but Eben.

ABBIE [*resentfully*].   They's me, hain't they? [*Agitatedly.*] What's all this sudden likin' ye've tuk to Eben? Why don't ye say nothin' 'bout me? Hain't I yer

760 lawful wife?

CABOT [*simply*].   Ay-eh. Ye be. [*A pause—he stares at her desirously—his eyes grow avid—then with a sudden movement he seizes her hands and squeezes them, de-*

claiming in a queer camp meeting preacher's tempo.] Yew air my Rose o' Sharon.[4] Behold, yew air fair; yer eyes air doves; yer lips air like scarlet; yer two breasts air like two fawns; yer navel be like a round goblet; yer belly be like a heap o' wheat. . . . [*He covers her hand with kisses. She does not seem to notice. She stares before her with hard angry eyes.*]

ABBIE [*jerking her hands away—harshly*].   So ye're plannin' t' leave the farm t' Eben, air ye?

770 CABOT [*dazedly*].   Leave . . . ? [*Then with resentful obstinacy.*] I hain't a-givin' it t' no one!

ABBIE [*remorselessly*].   Ye can't take it with ye.

CABOT [*thinks a moment—then reluctantly*].   No, I calc'late not. [*After a pause—with a strange passion*] But if I could, I would, by the Eternal! 'R if I could, in my dyin' hour, I'd set it afire an' watch it burn—this house an' every ear o' corn an' every tree down t' the last blade o' hay! I'd sit an' know it was all a'dying with me an' no one else'd ever own what was mine, what I'd made out o' nothin' with my own sweat 'n' blood! [*A pause—then he adds with a queer affection.*] 'Ceptin' the cows. Them I'd turn free.

780 ABBIE [*harshly*].   An' me?

CABOT [*with a queer smile*].   Ye'd be turned free, too.

ABBIE [*furiously*].   So that's the thanks I git fur marryin' ye—t' have ye change kind to Eben who hates ye, an' talk o' turnin' me out in the road.

CABOT [*hastily*].   Abbie! Ye know I wa'n't. . . .

ABBIE [*vengefully*].   Just let me tell ye a thing or two 'bout Eben! Whar's he gone? T' see that harlot, Min! I tried fur t' stop him. Disgracin' yew an' me—on the Sabbath, too!

CABOT [*rather guiltily*].   He's a sinner—nateral-born. It's lust eatin' his heart.

ABBIE [*enraged beyond endurance—wildly vindictive*].   An' his lust fur me! Kin ye
790 find excuses fur that?

CABOT [*stares at her—after a dead pause*].   Lust—fur yew?

ABBIE. [*defiantly*].   He was tryin' t' make love t' me—when ye heerd us quarrlin'.

CABOT [*stares at her—then a terrible expression of rage comes over his face—he springs to his feet shaking all over*].   By the A'mighty God—I'll end him!

ABBIE [*frightened now for* EBEN].   No! Don't ye!

CABOT [*violently*].   I'll git the shotgun an' blow his soft brains t' the top o' them elums!

ABBIE [*throwing her arms around him*].   No, Ephraim!

800 CABOT [*pushing her away violently*].   I will, by God!

ABBIE [*in a quieting tone*].   Listen, Ephraim. 'Twa'n't nothin' bad—on'y a boy's foolin'—'twa'n't meant serious—jest jokin' an' teasin' . . .

CABOT.   Then why did ye say—lust?

ABBIE.   It must hev sounded wusser'n I meant. An' I was mad at thinkin'—ye'd leave him the farm.

CABOT [*quieter but still grim and cruel*].   Waal then, I'll horsewhip him off the place if that much'll content ye.

ABBIE [*reaching out and taking his hand*].   No. Don't think o' me! Ye mustn't

---

[4] Here, and in the following lines, Cabot is echoing the Song of Solomon in the Bible, one of the most impassioned love poems in all of literature.

drive him off. 'Tain't sensible. Who'll ye get to help ye on the farm? They's
810   no one hereabouts.
CABOT [*considers this—then nodding his appreciation*].   Ye got a head on ye.
[*Then irritably.*] Waal, let him stay. [*He sits down on the edge of the porch. She
sits beside him. He murmurs contemptuously.*] I oughtn't t' git riled so—at that
'ere fool calf. [*A pause.*] But har's the p'int. What son o' mine'll keep on
here t' the farm—when the Lord does call me? Simeon an' Peter air gone
t' hell—an' Eben's follerin' 'em.
ABBIE.   They's me.
CABOT.   Ye're on'y a woman.
ABBIE.   I'm yewr wife.
820   CABOT.   That hain't me. A son is me—my blood—mine. Mine ought t' git
mine. An' then it's still mine—even though I be six foot under. D'ye see?
ABBIE [*giving him a look of hatred*].   Ay-eh. I see. [*She becomes very thoughtful, her
face growing shrewd, her eyes studying* CABOT *craftily.*]
CABOT.   I'm gittin' old—ripe on the bough. [*Then with a sudden forced reassurance.*] Not but what I hain't a hard nut t' crack even yet—an' fur many
a year t' come! By the Etarnal, I kin break most o' the young fellers' backs
at any kind o' work any day o' the year!
ABBIE [*suddenly*].   Mebbe the Lord'll give *us* a son.
CABOT [*turns and stares at her eagerly*].   Ye mean—a son—t' me 'n' yew?
830   ABBIE [*with a cajoling smile*].   Ye're a strong man yet, hain't ye? 'Tain't noways
impossible, be it? We know that. Why d'ye stare so? Hain't ye never thought
o' that afore? I been thinkin' o' it all along. Ay-eh—an' I been prayin' it'd
happen, too.
CABOT [*his face growing full of joyous pride and a sort of religious ecstasy*].   Ye been
prayin', Abbie?—fur a son?—t' us?
ABBIE.   Ay-eh. [*With a grim resolution*] I want a son now.
CABOT [*excitedly clutching both of her hands in his*].   It'd be the blessin' o' God
Abbie—the blessin' o' God A'mighty on me—in my old age—in my lonesomeness! They hain't nothin' I wouldn't do fur ye then, Abbie. Ye'd hev
840   on'y t' ask it—anythin' ye'd a mind t'!
ABBIE [*interrupting*].   Would ye will the farm t' me then—t' me an' it . . . ?
CABOT [*vehemently*].   I'd do anythin' ye axed, I tell ye! I swar it! May I be
everlastin' damned t' hell if I wouldn't! [*He sinks to his knees pulling her down
with him. He trembles all over with the fervor of his hopes.*] Pray t' the Lord
agen, Abbie. It's the Sabbath! I'll jine ye! Two prayers air better nor one.
"An' God hearkened unto Rachel"![5] An' God hearkened unto Abbie! Pray,
Abbie! Pray fur him to hearken! [*He bows his head, mumbling. She pretends to
do likewise but gives him a side glance of scorn and triumph.*]

SCENE II

*About eight in the evening. The interior of the two bedrooms on the top floor is
shown.* EBEN *is sitting on the side of his bed in the room on the left. On account of the
heat he has taken off everything but his undershirt and pants. His feet are bare. He*

---

[5] The allusion is to Genesis 30:22. Rachel, the wife of Jacob, remained barren for many years
until "God hearkened to her" and she bore Jacob a son in his old age.

faces front, brooding moodily, his chin propped on his hands, a desperate expression on his face.

In the other room CABOT *and* ABBIE *are sitting side by side on the edge of their bed, an old four-poster with feather mattress. He is in his night shirt, she in her nightdress. He is still in the queer, excited mood into which the notion of a son has thrown him. Both rooms are lighted dimly and flickeringly by tallow candles.*

CABOT.   The farm needs a son.

850   ABBIE.   I need a son.

CABOT.   Ay-eh. Sometimes ye air the farm an' sometimes the farm be yew. That's why I clove t' ye in my lonesomeness. [*A pause. He pounds his knee with his fist*] Me an' the farm has got t' beget a son!

ABBIE.   Ye'd best go to' sleep. Ye're gittin' thin's all mixed.

CABOT [*with an impatient gesture*].   No, I hain't. My mind's clear's a well. Ye don't know me, that's it. [*He stares hopelessly at the floor.*]

ABBIE [*indifferently*].   Mebbe. [*In the next room* EBEN *gets up and paces up and down distractedly.* ABBIE *hears him. Her eyes fasten on the intervening wall with concentrated attention.* EBEN *stops and stares. Their hot glances seem to meet*
860   *through the wall. Unconsciously he stretches out his arms for her and she half rises. Then aware, he mutters a curse at himself and flings himself face downward on the bed, his clenched fists above his head, his face buried in the pillow.* ABBIE *relaxes with a faint sigh but her eyes remain fixed on the wall; she listens with all her attention for some movement from* EBEN.]

CABOT [*suddenly raises his head and looks at her—scornfully*].   Will ye ever know me—'r will any man 'r woman? [*Shaking his head.*] No. I calc'late 't wa'n't t' be. [*He turns away.* ABBIE *looks at the wall. Then, evidently unable to keep silent about his thoughts, without looking at his wife, he puts out his hand and clutches her knee. She starts violently, looks at him, sees he is not watching her, concentrates*
870   *again on the wall and pays no attention to what he says.*] Listen, Abbie. When I come here fifty odd year ago—I was jest twenty an' the strongest an' hardest ye ever seen—ten times as strong an' fifty times as hard as Eben. Waal—this place was nothin' but fields o' stones. Folks laughed when I tuk it. They couldn't know what I knowed. When ye kin make corn sprout out o' stones, God's livin' in yew! They wa'n't strong enuf fur that! They reckoned God was easy. They laughed. They don't laugh no more. Some died hereabouts. Some went West an' died. They're all under ground—fur follerin' arter an easy God. God hain't easy. [*He shakes his head slowly.*] An' I growed hard. Folks kept allus sayin' he's a hard man like 'twas sinful t'
880   be hard, so's at last I said back at 'em: Waal then, by thunder, ye'll git me hard an' see how ye like it! [*Then suddenly—.*] But I give in t' weakness once. 'Twas arter I'd been here two year. I got weak—despairful—they was so many stones. They was a party leavin', givin' up, goin' West. I jined 'em. We tracked on 'n on. We come t' broad medders, plains, whar the soil was black an' rich as gold. Nary a stone. Easy. Ye'd on'y to plow an' sow an' then set an' smoke yer pipe an' watch thin's grow. I could o' been a rich man—but somethin' in me fit me an' fit me—the voice o' God sayin': "This hain't wuth nothin' t' Me. Git ye back t' hum!" I got afeered o' that voice an' I lit out back t' hum here, leavin' my claim an' crops t' whoever'd a
890   mind t' take 'em. Ay-eh. I actoolly give up what was rightful mine! God's hard, not easy! God's in the stones! Build my church on a rock—out o'

stones an' I'll be in them! That's what He meant t' Peter![6] [*He sighs
heavily—a pause.*] Stones. I picked 'em up an' piled 'em into walls. Ye kin
read the years of my life in them walls, every day a hefted stone, climbin'
over the hills up and down, fencin' in the fields that was mine, whar I'd
make thin's grow out o' nothin'—like the will o' God, like the servant o'
His hand. It wa'n't easy. It was hard an' He made me hard fur it. [*He
pauses.*] All the time I kept gittin' lonesomer. I tuk a wife. She bore Simeon
an' Peter. She was a good woman. She wuked hard. We was married
900   twenty year. She never knowed me. She helped but she never knowed what
she was helpin'. I was allus lonesome. She died. After that it wa'n't so
lonesome fur a spell. [*A pause*] I lost count o' the years. I had no time t' fool
away countin' 'em. Sim an' Peter helped. The farm growed. It was all
mine! When I thought o' that I didn't feel lonesome. [*A pause.*] But ye can't
hitch yer mind t' one thin' day an' night. I tuk another wife—Eben's Maw.
Her folks was contestin' me at law over my deeds t' the farm—my farm!
That's why Eben keeps a-talkin', his fool talk o' this bein' his Maw's farm.
She bore Eben. She was purty—but soft. She tried t' be hard. She couldn't.
She never knowed me nor nothin'. It was lonesomer 'n hell with her. After
910   a matter o' sixteen odd years, she died. [*A pause*] I lived with the boys.
They hated me 'cause I was hard. I hated them 'cause they was soft. They
coveted the farm without knowin' what it meant. It made me bitter 'n
wormwood. It aged me—them coveting what I'd made fur mine. Then this
spring the call come—the voice o' God cryin' in my wilderness, in my
lonesomeness—t' go out an seek an' find! [*Turning to her with strange
passion—.*] I sought ye an I found ye! Yew air my Rose o' Sharon! Yer eyes
air like. . . . [*She has turned a blank face, resentful eyes to his. He stares at her for
a moment—then harshly.*] Air ye any the wiser fur all I've told ye?

ABBIE [*confusedly*].   Mebbe.

920 CABOT [*pushing her away from him—angrily*].   Ye don't know nothin'—nor
never will. If ye don't hev a son t' redeem ye. . . . [*This in a tone of cold
threat.*]

ABBIE [*resentfully*].   I've prayed, hain't I?

CABOT [*bitterly*].   Pray agen—fur understandin'!

ABBIE [*a veiled threat in her tone*].   Ye'll have a son out o' me. I promise ye.

CABOT.   How kin ye promise?

ABBIE.   I got second-sight mebbe. I kin foretell. [*She gives a queer smile.*]

CABOT.   I believe ye have. Ye give me the chills sometimes. [*He shivers.*] It's
cold in this house. It's oneasy. They's thin's pokin' about in the dark—in
930   the corners. [*He pulls on his trousers, tucking in his night shirt, and pulls on his
boots.*]

ABBIE [*surprised*].   Whar air ye goin'?

CABOT [*queerly*].   Down whar it's restful—whar it's warm—down t' the barn.
[*Bitterly.*] I kin talk t' the cows. They know. They know the farm an' me.
They'll give me peace. [*He turns to go out the door.*]

ABBIE [*a bit frightenedly*].   Air ye ailin' tonight, Ephraim?

CABOT.   Growin'. Growin' ripe on the bough. [*He turns and goes, his boots

---

[6] "Upon this rock I will build my church"—Matthew 16:18.

clumping down the stairs. EBEN *sits up with a start, listening.* ABBIE *is conscious of his movement and stares at the wall.* CABOT *comes out of the house around the*
940   *corner and stands by the gate, blinking at the sky. He stretches up his hands in a tortured gesture*] God A'mighty, call from the dark! [*He listens as if expecting an answer. Then his arms drop, he shakes his head and plods off toward the barn.* EBEN *and* ABBIE *stare at each other through the wall.* EBEN *sighs heavily and* ABBIE *echoes it. Both become terribly nervous, uneasy. Finally* ABBIE *gets up and listens, her ear to the wall. He acts as if he saw every move she was making, he becomes resolutely still. She seems driven into a decision—goes out the door in rear determinedly. His eyes follow her. Then as the door of his room is opened softly, he turns away, waits in an attitude of strained fixity.* ABBIE *stands for a second staring at him, her eyes burning with desire. Then with a little cry she runs over and throws*
950   *her arms about his neck, she pulls his head back and covers his mouth with kisses. At first, he submits dumbly; then he puts his arms about her neck and returns her kisses, but finally, suddenly aware of his hatred, he hurls her away from him, springing to his feet. They stand speechless and breathless, panting like two animals.*]

ABBIE [*at last—painfully*].   Ye shouldn't, Eben—ye shouldn't—I'd make ye happy!

EBEN [*harshly*].   I don't want t' be happy—from yew!

ABBIE [*helplessly*].   Ye do, Eben! Ye do! Why d'ye lie?

EBEN [*viciously*].   I don't take t'ye, I tell ye! I hate the sight o' ye!

960   ABBIE [*with an uncertain troubled laugh*].   Waal, I kissed ye anyways—an' ye kissed back—yer lips was burnin'—we can't lie 'bout that! [*Intensely.*] If ye don't care, why did ye kiss me back—why was yer lips burnin'?

EBEN [*wiping his mouth*].   It was like pizen on 'em. [*Then tauntingly.*] When I kissed ye back, mebbe I thought 'twas someone else.

ABBIE [*wildly*].   Min?

EBEN.   Mebbe.

ABBIE [*torturedly*].   Did ye go t' see her? Did ye r'ally go? I thought ye mightn't. Is that why ye throwed me off jest now?

EBEN [*sneeringly*].   What if it be?

970   ABBIE [*raging*].   Then ye're a dog, Eben Cabot!

EBEN [*threateningly*].   Ye can't talk that way t' me!

ABBIE [*with a shrill laugh*].   Can't I? Did ye think I was in love with ye—a weak thin' like yew? Not much! I on'y wanted ye fur a purpose o' my own—an' I'll hev ye fur it yet 'cause I'm stronger'n yew be!

EBEN [*resentfully*].   I knowed well it was on'y part o' yer plan t' swaller everythin'!

ABBIE [*tauntingly*].   Mebbe!

EBEN [*furious*].   Git out o' my room!

ABBIE.   This air my room an' ye're on'y hired help!

980   EBEN [*threateningly*].   Git out afore I murder ye!

ABBIE [*quite confident now*].   I hain't a mite afeerd. Ye want me, don't ye? Yes, ye do! An' yer Paw's son'll never kill what he wants! Look at yer eyes! They's lust fur me in 'em, burnin' 'em up! Look at yer lips now! They're tremblin' an' longin' t' kiss me, an' yer teeth t' bite! [*He is watching her now with a horrible fascination. She laughs a crazy triumphant laugh.*] I'm a-goin' to' make all o' this hum my hum! They's one room hain't mine yet, but it's a-goin' t' be tonight. I'm a-goin' down now an' light up! [*She makes him a mocking bow.*] Won't ye come courtin' me in the best parlor, Mister Cabot?

EBEN [*staring at her—horribly confused—dully*].   Don't ye dare! It hain't been
990   opened since Maw died an' was laid out thar! Don't ye . . . ! [*But her eyes are fixed on his so burningly that his will seems to wither before hers. He stands swaying toward her helplessly.*]

ABBIE [*holding his eyes and putting all her will into her words as she backs out the door*].   I'll expect ye afore long, Eben.

EBEN [*stares after her for a while, walking toward the door. A light appears in the parlor window. He murmurs*].   In the parlor? [*This seems to arouse connotations, for he comes back and puts on his white shirt, collar, half ties the tie mechanically, puts on coat, takes his hat, stands barefooted looking about him in bewilderment, mutters wonderingly.*] Maw! Whar air yew? [*Then goes slowly
1000   toward the door in rear.*]

SCENE III

A few minutes later. The interior of the parlor is shown. A grim, repressed room like a tomb in which the family has been interred alive. ABBIE *sits on the edge of the horsehair sofa. She has lighted all the candles and the room is revealed in all its preserved ugliness. A change has come over the woman. She looks awed and frightened now, ready to run away.*

The door is opened and EBEN *appears. His face wears an expression of obsessed confusion. He stands staring at her, his arms hanging disjointedly from his shoulders, his feet bare, his hat in his hand.*

ABBIE [*after a pause—with a nervous, formal politeness*].   Won't ye set?

EBEN [*dully*].   Ay-eh. [*Mechanically he places his hat carefully on the floor near the door and sits stiffly beside her on the edge of the sofa. A pause. They both remain rigid, looking straight ahead with eyes full of fear.*]

ABBIE.   When I fust come in—in the dark—they seemed somethin' here.

EBEN [*simply*].   Maw.

ABBIE.   I kin still feel—somethin'. . . .

EBEN.   It's Maw.

ABBIE.   At fust I was feered o' it. I wanted t' yell an' run. Now—since yew
1010   come—seems like it's growin' soft an' kind t' me. [*Addressing the air—queerly.*] Thank yew.

EBEN.   Maw allus loved me.

ABBIE.   Mebbe it knows I love yew, too. Mebbe that makes it kind t' me.

EBEN [*dully*].   I dunno. I should think she'd hate ye.

ABBIE [*with certainty*].   No. I kin feel it don't—not no more.

EBEN.   Hate ye fur stealin' her place—here in her hum—settin' in her parlor whar she was laid—[*He suddenly stops, staring stupidly before him.*]

ABBIE.   What is it, Eben?

EBEN [*in a whisper*].   Seems like Maw didn't want me t' remind ye.

1020 ABBIE [*excitedly*]   I knowed, Eben! It's kind t' me! It don't b'ar me no grudges fur what I never knowed an' couldn't help!

EBEN.   Maw b'ars him a grudge.

ABBIE.   Waal, so does all o' us.

EBEN.   Ay-eh. [*With passion*] I does, by God!

ABBIE [*taking one of his hands in hers and patting it*].   Thar! Don't git riled thinkin' o' him. Think o' yer Maw who's kind t' us. Tell me about yer Maw, Eben.

EBEN.   They hain't nothin' much. She was kind. She was good.

ABBIE [*putting one arm over his shoulder. He does not seem to notice—passionately*].
1030   I'll be kind an' good t' ye!

EBEN.   Sometimes she used t' sing fur me.

ABBIE.   I'll sing fur ye!

EBEN.   This was her hum. This was her farm.

ABBIE.   This is my hum! This is my farm!

EBEN.   He married her t' steal 'em. She was soft an' easy. He couldn't 'preciate her.

ABBIE.   He can't 'preciate me!

EBEN.   He murdered her with his hardness.

ABBIE.   He's murderin' me!

1040 EBEN.   She died. [*A pause.*] Sometimes she used to sing fur me. [*He bursts into a fit of sobbing.*]

ABBIE [*both her arms around him—with wild passion*].   I'll sing fur ye! I'll die fur ye! [*In spite of her overwhelming desire for him, there is a sincere maternal love in her manner and voice—a horribly frank mixture of lust and mother love.*] Don't cry, Eben! I'll take yer Maw's place! I'll be everythin' she was t' ye! Let me kiss ye, Eben! [*She pulls his head around. He makes a bewildered pretense of resistance. She is tender.*] Don't be afeered! I'll kiss ye pure. Eben—same's if I was a Maw t' ye—an' ye kin kiss me back 's if yew was my son—my boy—sayin' good-night t' me! Kiss me, Eben. [*They kiss in
1050   restrained fashion. Then suddenly wild passion overcomes her. She kisses him lustfully again and again and he flings his arms about her and returns her kisses. Suddenly, as in the bedroom, he frees himself from her violently and springs to his feet. He is trembling all over, in a strange state of terror. ABBIE strains her arms toward him with fierce pleading.*] Don't ye leave me, Eben! Can't ye see it hain't enuf—lovin' ye like a Maw— can't ye see it's got t' be that an' more—much more—a hundred times more—fur me t' be happy—fur yew t' be happy?

EBEN [*to the presence he feels in the room*].   Maw! Maw! What d'ye want? What air ye tellin' me?

1060 ABBIE.   She's tellin' ye t' love me. She knows I love ye an' I'll be good t' ye. Can't ye feel it? Don't ye know? She's tellin' ye t' love me, Eben!

EBEN.   Ay-eh. I feel—mebbe she—but—I can't figger out—why—when ye've stole her place—here in her hum—in the parlor whar she was—

ABBIE [*fiercely*].   She knows I love ye!

EBEN [*his face suddenly lighting up with a fierce, triumphant grin*].   I see it! I sees why. It's her vengeance on him—so's she kin rest quiet in her grave!

ABBIE [*wildly*].   Vengeance o' God on the hull o' us! What d'we give a durn? I love ye, Eben! God knows I love ye! [*She stretches out her arms for him.*]

EBEN [*throws himself on his knees beside the sofa and grabs her in his arms—releasing
1070   all his pent-up passion*].   An' I love ye, Abbie!—now I kin say it! I been dyin' fur want o' ye—every hour since ye come! I love ye! [*Their lips meet in a fierce, bruising kiss.*]

SCENE IV

Exterior of the farmhouse. It is just dawn. The front door at right is opened and
Eben *comes out and walks around to the gate. He is dressed in his working clothes. He*
seems changed. His face wears a bold and confident expression, he is grinning to
himself with evident satisfaction. As he gets near the gate, the window of the parlor is
heard opening and the shutters are flung back and Abbie *sticks her head out. Her hair*
tumbles over her shoulders in disarray, her face is flushed, she looks at Eben *with*
tender, languorous eyes and calls softly.

Abbie.   Eben. [*As he turns— playfully.*] Jest one more kiss afore ye go. I'm
  goin' to miss ye fearful all day.

Eben.   An' me yew, ye kin bet! [*He goes to her. They kiss several times. He draws*
  away, laughingly.] Thar. That's enuf, hain't it? Ye won't hev none left fur
  next time.

Abbie.   I got a million o' 'em left fur yew! [*Then a bit anxiously.*] D'ye r'ally love
  me, Eben?

1080 Eben [*emphatically*].   I like ye better'n any gal I ever knowed! That's gospel!

Abbie.   Likin' hain't lovin'.

Eben.   Waal then—I love ye. Now air yew satisfied?

Abbie.   Ay-eh. I be. [*She smiles at him adoringly.*]

Eben.   I better git t' the barn. The old critter's liable t' suspicion an' come
  sneakin' up.

Abbie [*with a confident laugh*].   Let him! I kin allus pull the wool over his eyes.
  I'm goin' t' leave the shutters open and let in the sun 'n' air. This room's
  been dead long enuf. Now it's goin' t' be my room!

Eben [*frowning*].   Ay-eh.

1090 Abbie [*hastily*].   I meant—our room.

Eben.   Ay-eh.

Abbie.   We made it our'n last night, didn't we? We give it life—our lovin' did.
  [*A pause.*]

Eben [*with a strange look*].   Maw's gone back t' her grave. She kin sleep now.

Abbie.   May she rest in peace! [*Then tenderly rebuking.*] Ye oughtn't t' talk o'
  sad thin's—this mornin'.

Eben.   It jest come up in my mind o' itself.

Abbie.   Don't let it. [*He doesn't answer. She yawns.*] Waal, I'm a-goin' t' steal a
  wink o' sleep. I'll tell the Old Man I hain't feelin' pert. Let him git his own
1100 vittles.

Eben.   I see him comin' from the barn. Ye better look smart an' git upstairs.

Abbie.   Ay-eh. Good-by. Don't ferget me. [*She throws him a kiss. He grins—then*
  squares his shoulders and awaits his father confidently. Cabot *walks slowly up from*
  the left, staring up at the sky with a vague face.]

Eben [*jovially*].   Mornin', Paw. Star-gazin' in daylight?

Cabot.   Purty, hain't it?

Eben [*looking around him possessively*].   It's a durned purty farm.

Cabot.   I mean the sky.

Eben [*grinning*].   How d'ye know? Them eyes o' your'n can't see that fur.
1110 [*This tickles his humor and he slaps his thigh and laughs.*] Ho-ho! That's a
  good un!

CABOT [*grimly sarcastic*].   Ye're feeling right chipper, hain't ye? Whar'd ye steal the likker?

EBEN [*good-naturedly*].   'Tain't likker. Jest life. [*Suddenly holding out his hand—soberly.*] Yew 'n' me is quits. Let's shake hands.

CABOT [*suspiciously*].   What's come over ye?

EBEN.   Then don't. Mebbe it's jest as well. [*A moment's pause.*] What's come over me? [*Queerly.*] Didn't ye feel her passin' goin' back t' her grave?

CABOT [*dully*].   Who?

1120 EBEN.   Maw. She kin rest now an' sleep content. She's quits with ye.

CABOT [*confusedly*].   I rested. I slept good—down with the cows. They know how t' sleep. They're teachin' me.

EBEN [*suddenly jovial again*].   Good fur the cows! Waal—ye better git t' work.

CABOT [*grimly amused*].   Air yew bossin' me, ye calf?

EBEN [*beginning to laugh*].   Ay-eh! I'm bossin' yew! Ha-ha-ha-ha! See how ye like it. Ha-ha-ha! I'm the prize rooster o' this roost. Ha-ha-ha! [*He goes off toward the barn laughing.*]

CABOT [*looks after him with scornful pity*].   Soft-headed. Like his Maw. Dead spit 'n' image. No hope in him! [*He spits with contemptuous disgust.*] A born
1130 fool! [*Then matter-of-factly.*] Waal—I'm gittin' peckish. [*He goes toward the door.*]

CURTAIN

PART III

SCENE I

A night in late spring the following year. The kitchen and the two bedrooms upstairs are shown. The two bedrooms are dimly lighted by a tallow candle in each. EBEN *is sitting on the side of the bed in his room, his chin propped on his fists, his face a study of the struggle he is making to understand his conflicting emotions. The noisy laughter and music from below where a kitchen dance is in progress annoy and distract him. He scowls at the floor.*

In the next room a cradle stands beside the double bed.

In the kitchen all is festivity. The stove has been taken down to give more room to the dancers. The chairs, with wooden benches added, have been pushed back against the walls. On these are seated, squeezed in tight against one another, farmers and their wives and their young folks of both sexes from the neighboring farms. They are all chattering and laughing loudly. They evidently have some secret joke in common. There is no end of winking, of nudging, of meaning nods of the head toward CABOT *who, in a state of extreme hilarious excitement increased by the amount he has drunk, is standing near the rear door where there is a small keg of whisky and serving drinks to all the men. In the left corner, front, dividing the attention with her husband,* ABBIE *is sitting in a rocking chair, a shawl wrapped about her shoulders. She is very pale, her face is thin and drawn, her eyes are fixed anxiously on the open door in rear as if waiting for someone.*

The musician is tuning his fiddle, seated in the far right corner. He is a lanky young fellow with a long, weak face. His pale eyes blink incessantly and he grins about him slyly with a greedy malice.

ABBIE [*suddenly turning to a young girl on her right*]. Whar's Eben?

YOUNG GIRL [*eyeing her scornfully*]. I dunno, Mrs. Cabot. I hain't seen Eben in ages. [*Meaningly*] Seems like he's spent most o' his time t' hum since yew come.

ABBIE [*vaguely*]. I tuk his Maw's place.

YOUNG GIRL. Ay-eh. So I've heerd. [*She turns away to retail this bit of gossip to her mother sitting next to her.* ABBIE *turns to her left to a big stoutish middle-aged man whose flushed face and starting eyes show the amount of "likker" he has* 1140 *consumed.*]

ABBIE. Ye hain't seen Eben, hev ye?

MAN. No, I hain't. [*Then he adds with a wink.*] If yew hain't, who would?

ABBIE. He's the best dancer in the country. He'd ought t' come an' dance.

MAN [*with a wink*]. Mebbe he's doin' the dutiful an' walkin' the kid t' sleep. It's a boy, hain't it?

ABBIE [*nodding vaguely*]. Ay-eh—born two weeks back—purty's a picter.

MAN. They all is—t' their Maws. [*Then in a whisper, with a nudge and a leer.*] Listen, Abbie—if ye ever git tired o' Eben, remember me! Don't forgit now! [*He looks at her uncomprehending face for a second—then grunts disgust-* 1150 *edly.*] Waal—guess I'll likker agin. [*He goes over and joins* CABOT *who is arguing noisily with an old farmer over cows. They all drink.*]

YOUNG GIRL [*this time appealing to nobody in particular*]. Wonder what Eben's a-doin'? [*Her remark is repeated down the line with many a guffaw and titter until it reaches the fiddler. He fastens his blinking eyes on* ABBIE.]

FIDDLER [*raising his voice*]. Bet I kin tell ye. Abbie, what Eben's doin'! He's down t' the church offerin' up prayers o' thanksgivin'. [*They all titter expectantly.*]

A MAN. What fur? [*Another titter.*]

FIDDLER. 'Cause unto him a—[*He hesitates just long enough.*] brother is born! 1160 [*A roar of laughter. They all look from* ABBIE *to* CABOT. *She is oblivious, staring at the door.* CABOT, *although he hasn't heard the words, is irritated by the laughter and steps forward, glaring about him. There is an immediate silence.*]

CABOT. What're ye all bleatin' about—like a flock o' goats? Why don't ye dance, damn ye? I axed ye here t' dance—t' eat, drink an' be merry—an' thar ye set cacklin' like a lot o' wet hens with the pip! Ye've swilled my likker an' guzzled my vittles like hogs, hain't ye? Then dance fur me, can't ye? That's fa'r an' squar', hain't it? [*A grumble of resentment goes around but they are all evidently in too much awe of him to express it openly.*]

FIDDLER [*slyly*]. We're waitin' fur Eben. [*A suppressed laugh.*]

1170 CABOT [*with a fierce exultation*]. T'hell with Eben! Eben's done fur now! I got a new son! [*His mood switching with drunken suddenness.*] But ye needn't t' laugh at Eben, none o' ye! He's my blood, if he be a dumb fool. He's better nor any o' yew! He kin do a day's work a'most up r' what I kin—an' that'd put any o' yew pore critters t' shame!

FIDDLER An' he kin do a good night's work, too! [*A roar of laughter.*]

CABOT. Laugh, ye damn fools! Ye're right jist the same, Fiddler. He kin work day an' night too, like I kin, if need be!

OLD FARMER [*from behind the keg where he is weaving drunkenly back and forth—with great simplicity*]. They hain't many t' touch ye, Ephraim—a son at 1180 seventy-six. That's a hard man fur ye! I be on'y sixty-eight an' I couldn't do it. [*A roar of laughter in which* CABOT *joins uproariously.*]

CABOT [*slapping him on the back*].   I'm sorry fur ye, H. I'd never suspicion sech weakness from a boy like yew!

FARMER.   An' I never reckoned yew had it in ye nuther, Ephraim. [*There is another laugh.*]

CABOT [*suddenly grim*].   I got a lot in me—a hell of a lot—folks don't know on. [*Turing to the fiddler*] Fiddle 'er up, durn ye! Give 'em somethin' t' dance t'! What air ye, an ornament? Hain't this a celebration? Then grease yer elbow an' go it!

1190 FIDDLER [*seizes a drink which the* OLD FARMER *holds out to him and downs it*].   Here goes! [*He starts to fiddle "Lady of the Lake." Four young fellows and four girls form in two lines and dance a square dance. The* FIDDLER *shouts directions for the different movements, keeping his words in the rhythm of the music and interspersing them with jocular personal remarks to the dancers themselves. The people seated along the walls stamp their feet and clap their hands in unison.* CABOT *is especially active in this respect. Only* ABBIE *remains apathetic, staring at the door as if she were alone in a silent room.*]

FIDDLER.   Swing your partner t' the right! That's it, Jim! Give her a b'ar hug. Her Maw hain't lookin'. [*Laughter.*] Change partners! That suits ye, don't

1200 it, Essie, now ye got Reub afore ye? Look at her redden up, will ye? Waal, life is short an' so's love, as the feller says. [*Laughter.*]

CABOT [*excitedly, stamping his foot*].   Go it, boys! go it, gals!

FIDDLER [*with a wink at the others*].   Ye're the spryest seventy-six ever I sees, Ephraim! Now if ye'd on'y good eye-sight . . . ! [*Suppressed laughter. He gives* CABOT *no chance to retort but roars.*] Promenade! Ye're walkin' like a bride down the aisle, Sarah! Waal, while they's life they's allus hope, I've heerd tell. Swing your partner to the left! Gosh A'mighty, look at Johnny Cook high-steppin'! they hain't goin' t' be much strength left fur howin' in the corn lot t'morrow. [*Laughter.*]

1210 CABOT.   Go it! Go it! [*Then suddenly, unable to restrain himself any longer, he prances into the midst of the dancers, scattering them, waving his arms about wildly.*] Ye're all hoofs! Git out o' my road! Give me room! I'll show ye dancin'. Ye're all too soft! [*He pushes them roughly away. They crowd back toward the walls, muttering, looking at him resentfully.*]

FIDDLER [*jeeringly*].   Go it, Ephraim! Go it! [*He starts "Pop, Goes the Weasel," increasing the tempo with every verse until at the end he is fiddling crazily as fast as he can go.*]

CABOT [*starts to dance, which he does very well and with tremendous vigor. Then he begins to improvise, cuts incredibly grotesque capers, leaping up and cracking his*

1220 *heels together, prancing around in a circle with body bent in an Indian war dance, then suddenly straightening up and kicking as high as he can with both legs. He is like a monkey on a string. And all the while he intersperses his antics with shouts and derisive comments*].   Whoop! Here's dancin' fur ye! Whoop! See that! Seventy-six, if I'm a day! Hard as iron yet! Beatin' the young 'uns like I allus done! Look at me! I'd invite ye t' dance on my hundredth birthday on'y ye'll all be dead by then. Ye're a sickly generation! Yer hearts air pink, not red! Yer veins is ful o' mud an' water! I be the on'y man in the country! Whoop! See that! I'm a Injun! I've killed Injuns in the West afore ye was born—an' skulped 'em too! They's a arrer wound on my backside I c'd

1230 show ye! The hull tribe chased me. I outrun 'em all—with the arrer stuck in me! An' I tuk vengeance on e'm. Ten eyes fur an eye, that was my motter! Whoop! Look at me! I kin kick the ceiling' off the room! Whoop!

FIDDLER [*stops playing—exhaustedly*].   God A'mighty, I got enuf. Ye got the devil's strength in ye.

CABOT [*delightedly*].   Did I beat yew, too? Waal, ye played smart. Hev a swig. [*He pours whisky for himself and* FIDDLER. *They drink. The others watch* CABOT *silently with cold, hostile eyes. There is a dead pause. The* FIDDLER *rests.* CABOT *leans against the keg, panting, glaring around him confusedly. In the room above,* EBEN *gets to his feet and tiptoes out the door in rear, appearing a moment later in* 1240   *the other bedroom. He moves silently, even frightenedly, toward the cradle and stands there looking down at the baby. His face is as vague as his reactions are confused, but there is a trace of tenderness, of interested discovery. At the same moment that he reaches the cradle* ABBIE *seems to sense something. She gets up weakly and goes to* CABOT]

ABBIE.   I'm goin' up t' the baby.

CABOT [*with real solicitation*].   Air ye able fur the stairs? D'ye want me t' help ye, Abbie?

ABBIE.   No. I'm able. I'll be down agen soon.

CABOT.   Don't ye git wore out! He needs ye, remember—our son does! [*He* 1250   *grins affectionately, patting her on the back. She shrinks from his touch.*]

ABBIE [*dully*].   Don't—tech me. I'm goin'—up. [*She goes.* CABOT *looks after her. A whisper goes around the room.* CABOT *turns. It ceases. He wipes his forehead steaming with sweat. He is breathing pantingly.*]

CABOT.   I'm a-goin' out t' git fresh air. I'm feelin' a mite dizzy. Fiddle up thar! Dance, all o' ye! Here's likker fur them as wants it. Enjoy yerselves. I'll be back. [*He goes, closing the door behind him.*]

FIDDLER [*sarcastically*].   Don't hurry none on our account! [*A suppressed laugh. He imitates* ABBIE]. Whar's Eben? [*More laughter.*]

A WOMAN [*loudly*].   What's happened in this house is plain as the nose on yer 1260   face! [ABBIE *appears in the doorway upstairs and stands looking in surprise and adoration at* EBEN *who does not see her.*]

A MAN.   Ssshh! He's li'ble t' be listenin' at the door. That'd be like him. [*Their voices die to an intensive whispering. Their faces are concentrated on this gossip. A noise as of dead leaves in the wind comes from the room.* CABOT *has come out from the porch and stands by the gate, leaning on it, staring at the sky blinkingly.* ABBIE *comes across the room silently.* EBEN *does not notice her until quite near.*]

EBEN [*starting*].   Abbie!

ABBIE.   Ssshh! [*She throws her arms around him. They kiss—then bend over the* 1270   *cradle together.*] Ain't he purty?—dead spit 'n' image o' yew!

EBEN [*pleased*].   Air he? I can't tell none.

ABBIE.   Exactly like!

EBEN [*frowningly*].   I don't like this. I don't like lettin' on what's mine's his'n. I been doin' that all my life. I'm gittin' t' the end o' b'arin' it.

ABBIE [*putting her finger on his lips*].   We're doin' the best we kin. We got t' wait. Somethin's bound t' happen. [*She puts her arms around him.*] I got t' go back.

EBEN.   I'm goin' out. I can't b'ar it with the fiddle playin' an the laughin'.

ABBIE.   Don't git feelin' low. I love ye, Eben. Kiss me. [*He kisses her. They* 1280   *remain in each other's arms.*]

CABOT [*at the gate, confusedly*].   Even the music can't drive it out—somethin'.

Ye kin feel it droppin' off the elums, climbin' up the roof, sneakin' down the chimney, pokin' in the corners! They's no peace in houses, they's no rest livin' with folks. Somethin's always livin' with ye. [*With a deep sigh.*] I'll go t' the barn an' rest a spell. [*He goes wearily toward the barn.*]

FIDDLER [*tuning up*].   Let's celebrate the old skunk gittin' fooled! We kin have some fun now he's went. [*He starts to fiddle "Turkey in the Straw." There is real merriment now. The young folks get up to dance.*]

SCENE II

*A half hour later—Exterior—*EBEN *is standing by the gate looking up at the sky, an expression of dumb pain bewildered by itself on his face.* CABOT *appears, returning from the barn, walking wearily, his eyes on the ground. He sees* EBEN *and his whole mood immediately changes. He becomes excited, a cruel, triumphant grin comes to his lips, he strides up and slaps* EBEN *on the back. From within comes the whining of the fiddle and the noise of stamping feet and laughing voices.*

CABOT.   So har ye be.

1290 EBEN [*startled, stares at him with hatred for a moment—then dully*].   Ay-eh.

CABOT [*surveying him jeeringly*].   Why hain't ye been in t' dance? They was all axin' fur ye.

EBEN.   Let 'em ax!

CABOT.   They's a hull passel o' purty gals.

EBEN.   T' hell with 'em!

CABOT.   Ye'd ought t' be marryin' one o' 'em soon.

EBEN.   I hain't marryin' no one.

CABOT.   Ye might 'arn a share o' a farm that way.

EBEN [*with a sneer*].   Like yew did, ye mean? I hain't that kind.

1300 CABOT [*stung*].   Ye lie! 'Twas ye Maw's folks aimed t' steal my farm from me.

EBEN.   Other folks don't say so. [*After a pause—defiantly.*] An' I got a farm, anyways!

CABOT [*derivisely*].   Whar?

EBEN [*stamps a foot on the ground*].   Har!

CABOT [*throws his head back and laughs coarsely*].   Ho-ho! Ye hev, hev ye? Waal, that's a good un!

EBEN [*controlling himself—grimly*].   Ye'll see!

CABOT [*stares at him suspiciously, trying to make him out—a pause—then with scornful confidence*].   Ay-eh. I'll see. So'l ye. It's ye that's blind—blind as a
1310   mole underground. [EBEN *suddenly laughs, one short sardonic bark: "Ha." A pause.* CABOT *peers at him with renewed suspicion.*] What air ye hawin' 'bout? [EBEN *turns away without answering.* CABOT *grows angry.*] God A'mighty, yew air a dumb dunce! They's nothin' in that thick skull o' your'n but noise— like a empty keg it be! [EBEN *doesn't seem to hear.* CABOT'S *rage grows.*] Yewr farm! God A'mighty! If ye wa'n't a born donkey ye'd know ye'll never own stick nor stone on it, specially now arter him bein' born. It's his'n. I tell ye—his'n arter I die—but I'll live a hundred jest t' fool ye all—an' he'll be growed then—yewr age a'most! [EBEN *laughs again his sardonic "Ha." This drives* CABOT *into a fury.*] Ha? Ye think ye kin git 'round that someways, do
1320   ye? Waal, it'll be her'n, too—Abbie's—ye won't git 'round her—she knows yer tricks—she'll be too much fur ye—she wants the farm her'n—she was

afeerd o' ye—she told me ye was sneakin' 'round tryin' t' make love t' her t' git her on yer side . . . ye . . . ye mad fool, ye! [*He raises his clenched fists threateningly.*]

EBEN [*confronting him, choking with rage*]. Ye lie, ye old skunk! Abbie never said no sech thing!

CABOT [*suddenly triumphant when he sees how shaken* EBEN *is*]. She did. An' I says, I'll blow his brains t' the top o' them elums—an' she says no, that hain't sense, who'll ye git t' help ye on the farm in his place—an' then she says yew'n me ought t' have a son—I know we kin, she says—an' I says, if we do, ye kin have anythin' I've got ye've a mind t'. An' she says, I wants Eben cut off so' this farm'll be mine when ye die! [*With terrible gloating.*] An' that's what's happened, hain't it? An' the farm's her'n! An' the dust o' the road—that's you'rn! Ha! Now who's hawin'?

EBEN [*has been listening, petrified with grief and rage—suddenly laughs wildly and brokenly*]. Ha-ha-ha! So that's her sneakin' game—all along!—like I suspicioned at fust—t' swaller it all—an' me, too . . . ! [*Madly.*] I'll murder her! [*He springs toward the porch but* CABOT *is quicker and gets in between.*]

CABOT. No, ye don't!

EBEN. Git out o' my road! [*He tries to throw* CABOT *aside. They grapple in what becomes immediately a murderous struggle. The old man's concentrated strength is too much for* EBEN. CABOT *gets one hand on his throat and presses him back across the stone wall. At the same moment,* ABBIE *comes out on the porch. With a stifled cry she runs toward them.*]

ABBIE. Eben! Ephraim! [*She tugs at the hand on* EBEN'S *throat.*] Let go, Ephraim! Ye're chokin' him!

CABOT [*removes his hand and flings* EBEN *full length on the grass, gasping and choking. With a cry,* ABBIE *kneels beside him trying to take his head on her lap, but he pushes her away.* CABOT *stands looking down with fierce triumph*]. Ye needn't t've fret, Abbie. I wa'n't aimin' t' kill him. He hain't wuth hangin' fur—not by a hell of a sight! [*More and more triumphantly.*] Seventy-six an' him not thirty yit—an' look whar he be fur thinkin' his Paw was easy! No, by God, I hain't easy! An' him upstairs, I'll raise him t' be like me! [*He turns to leave them.*] I'm goin' in an' dance!—sing an' celebrate! [*He walks to the porch—then turns with a great grin*] I don't calc'late it's left in him, but if he gits pesky, Abbie, ye jest sing out. I'll come a-runnin' an by the Etarnal, I'll put him across my knee an' birch him! Ha-ha-ha! [*He goes into the house laughing. A moment later his loud "whoop" is heard.*]

ABBIE [*tenderly*]. Eben. Air ye hurt? [*She tries to kiss him but he pushes her violently away and struggles to a sitting position.*]

EBEN [*gaspingly*]. T'hell—with ye!

ABBIE [*not believing her ears*]. It's me, Eben—Abbie—don't ye know me?

EBEN [*glowering at her with hatred*]. Ay-eh—I know ye—now! [*He suddenly breaks down, sobbing weakly.*]

ABBIE [*fearfully*]. Eben—what's happened t'ye—why did ye look at me 's if ye hated me?

EBEN [*violently, between sobs and gasps*]. I do hate ye! Ye're a whore—a damn trickin' whore!

ABBIE [*shrinking back horrified*]. Eben! Ye don't know what ye're sayin'!

EBEN [*scrambling to his feet and following her—accusingly*]. Ye're nothin' but a stinkin' passel o' lies! Ye've been lyin' t' me every word ye spoke, day an' night, since we fust—done it. Ye've kept sayin' ye loved me. . . .

ABBIE [*frantically*]. I do love ye! [*She takes his hand but he flings her away.*]

EBEN [*unheeding*]. Ye've made a fool o' me—a sick, dumb fool—a-purpose! Ye've been on'y playin' yer sneakin', stealin' game all along—gittin' me t' lie with ye so's ye'd hev a son he'd think was his'n, an' makin' him promise he'd give ye the farm and let me eat dust, if ye did git him a son! [*Staring at her with anguished bewildered eyes.*] They must be a devil livin' in ye! T'ain't human t' be as bad as that be!

1380 ABBIE [*stunned—dully*]. He told yew . . . ?

EBEN. Hain't it true? It hain't no good in yew lyin'.

ABBIE [*pleading*]. Eben, listen—ye must listen—it was long ago—afore we done nothin'—yew was scornin' me—goin' t' see Min—when I was lovin' ye—an' I said it t' him t' git vengeance on ye!

EBEN [*unheedingly. With tortured passion*]. I wish ye was dead! I wish I was dead along with ye afore this come! [*Ragingly.*] But I'll git my vengeance too! I'll pray Maw t' come back t' help me—t' put her cuss on yew an' him!

ABBIE [*brokenly*]. Don't ye, Eben! Don't ye! [*She throws herself on her knees*
1390 *before him, weeping*] I didn't mean t' do bad t' ye! Fergive me, won't ye?

EBEN [*not seeming to hear her—fiercely*]. I'll git squar' with the old skunk—an' yew! I'll tell him the truth about the son he's so proud o'! Then I'll leave ye here t' pizen each other—with Maw comin' out o' her grave at nights— an' I'll go t' the gold fields o' Californi-a whar Sim an' Peter be!

ABBIE [*terrified*]. Ye won't leave me? Ye can't!

EBEN [*with fierce determination*]. I'm a-goin', I tell ye! I'll git rich thar an' come back an' fight him fur the farm he stole—an' I'll kick ye both out in the road—t' beg an' sleep in the woods—an' yer son along with ye—t' starve an' die! [*He is hysterical at the end.*]

1400 ABBIE [*with a shudder—humbly*]. He's yewr son, too, Eben.

EBEN [*torturedly*]. I wish he never was born! I wish he'd die this minit! I wish I'd never sot eyes on him! It's him—yew havin' him—a-purpose t' steal— that's changed everythin'!

ABBIE [*gently*]. Did ye believe I loved ye—afore he come?

EBEN. Ay-eh—like a dumb ox!

ABBIE. An' ye don't believe no more?

EBEN. B'lieve a lyin' thief! Ha!

ABBIE [*shudders—then humbly*]. An' did ye r'ally love me afore?

EBEN [*brokenly*]. Ay-eh—an' ye was trickin' me!

1410 ABBIE. An' ye don't love me now!

EBEN [*violently*]. I hate ye, I tell ye!

ABBIE. An' ye're truly goin' West—goin' t' leave me—all account o' him being born?

EBEN. I'm a-goin' in the mornin'—or may God strike me t' hell!

ABBIE [*after a pause—with a dreadful cold intensity—slowly*]. If that's what his comin's done t' me—killin' yewr love—takin' yew away—my on'y joy—the on'y joy I ever knowed—like heaven t' me—purtier'n heaven—then I hate him, too, even if I be his Maw!

EBEN [*bitterly*]. Lies! Ye love him! He'll steal the farm fur ye! [*Brokenly.*] But
1420 t'ain't the farm so much—not no more—it's yew foolin' me—gittin' me t' love ye—lyin' yew loved me—jest t' git a son t' steal!

ABBIE [*distractedly*]. He won't steal! I'd kill him fust! I do love ye! I'll prove t' ye . . .

EBEN [*harshly*].   T'ain't no use lyin' no more. I'm deaf t' ye! [*He turns away.*]
    I hain't seein' ye agen. Good-by!

ABBIE [*pale with anguish*].   Hain't ye even goin' t' kiss me—not once—arter all
    we loved?

EBEN [*in a hard voice*].   I hain't wantin' t' kiss ye never agen! I'm wantin' t'
    forget I ever sot eyes on ye!

1430 ABBIE.   Eben!—ye mustn't—wait a spell—I want t' tell ye. . . .

EBEN.   I'm a-goin' in t' git drunk. I'm a-goin' t' dance.

ABBIE [*clinging to his arm—with passionate earnestness*].   If I could make it—'s if
    he'd never come up between us—if I could prove t' ye I wa'n't schemin' t'
    steal from ye—so's everythin' could be jest the same with us, lovin' each
    other jest the same, kissin' an' happy the same's we've been happy afore
    he come—if I could do it—ye'd love me agen, wouldn't ye? Ye'd kiss me
    agen? Ye wouldn't never leave me, would ye?

EBEN [*moved*].   I calc'late not. [*Then shaking her hand off his arm—with a bitter
    smile.*] But ye hain't God, be ye?

1440 ABBIE [*exultantly*].   Remember ye've promised! [*Then with strange intensity.*]
    Mebbe I kin take back one thin' God does.

EBEN [*peering at her*].   Ye're gittin' cracked, hain't ye? [*Then going towards
    door.*] I'm a-goin' t' dance.

ABBIE [*calls after him intensely*].   I'll prove t' ye! I'll prove I love ye better'n. . . .
    [*He goes in the door, not seeming to hear. She remains standing where she is
    looking after him—then she finishes desperately.*] Better'n everythin' else in the
    world!

SCENE III

Just before dawn in the morning—shows the kitchen and CABOT's *bedroom. In the
kitchen, by the light of a tallow candle on the table,* EBEN *is sitting, his chin propped
on his hands, his drawn face blank and expressionless. His carpetbag is on the floor
beside him. In the bedroom, dimly lighted by a small whale-oil lamp,* CABOT *lies asleep.*
ABBIE *is bending over the cradle, listening, her face full of terror yet with an under-
current of desperate triumph. Suddenly, she breaks down and sobs, appears about to
throw herself on her knees beside the cradle; but the old man turns restlessly, groaning
in his sleep, and she controls herself, and, shrinking away from the cradle with a
gesture of horror, backs swiftly toward the door in rear and goes out. A moment later
she comes into the kitchen and, running to* EBEN, *flings her arms about his neck and
kisses him wildly. He hardens himself, he remains unmoved and cold, he keeps his eyes
straight ahead.*

ABBIE [*hysterically*].   I done it, Eben! I told ye I'd do it! I've proved I love
    ye—better'n everythin'—so's ye can't never doubt me no more!

1450 EBEN [*dully*].   Whatever ye done, it hain't no good now.

ABBIE [*wildly*].   Don't ye say that! Kiss me, Eben, won't ye? I need ye t' kiss me
    arter what I done! I need ye t' say ye love me!

EBEN [*kisses her without emotion—dully*].   That's fur good-by. I'm a-goin' soon.

ABBIE.   No! No! Ye won't go—not now!

EBEN [*going on with his own thoughts*].   I been a-thinkin'—an I hain't goin' t'
    tell Paw nothin'. I'll leave Maw t' take vengeance on ye. If I told him, the
    old skunk'd jest be stinkin' mean enuf to take it out on that baby. [*His voice*

showing emotion in spite of him.] An' I don't want nothin' bad t' happen t' him. He hain't t' blame fur yew. [*He adds with a certain queer pride.*] An' he
1460   looks like me! An' by God, he's mine! An' some day I'll be a-comin' back an' . . . !

ABBIE [*too absorbed in her own thoughts to listen to him—pleadingly*].   They's no cause fur ye t' go now—they's no sense—it's all the same's it was—they's nothin' come b'tween us now—arter what I done!

EBEN [*something in her voice arouses him. He stares at her a bit frightenedly*].   Ye look mad, Abbie. What did ye do?

ABBIE.   I—I killed him, Eben.

EBEN [*amazed*].   Ye killed him?

ABBIE [*dully*].   Ay-eh.

1470 EBEN [*recovering from his astonishment—savagely*].   An' serves him right! But we got t' do somethin' quick t' make it look 'sif the old skunk'd killed himself when he was drunk. We kin prove by 'em all how drunk he got.

ABBIE [*wildly*].   No! No! Not him! [*Laughing distractedly.*] But that's what I ought t' done, hain't it? I oughter killed him instead! Why didn't ye tell me?

EBEN [*appalled*],   Instead? What d'ye mean?

ABBIE.   Not him.

EBEN [*his face grown ghastly*].   Not—not that baby!

ABBIE [*dully*].   Ay-eh!

1480 EBEN [*falls to his knees as if he'd been struck—his voice trembling with horror*].   Oh, God A'mighty! A'mighty God! Maw, whar was ye, why didn't ye stop her?

ABBIE [*simply*].   She went back t' her grave that night we fust done it, remember? I hain't felt her about since. [*A pause.* EBEN *hides his head in his hands, trembling all over as if he had the ague. She goes on dully.*] I left the piller over his little face. Then he killed himself. He stopped breathin'. [*She begins to weep softly.*]

EBEN [*rage beginning to mingle with grief*].   He looked like me. He was mine, damn ye!

ABBIE [*slowly and brokenly*].   I didn't want t' do it. I hated myself fur doin' it.
1490   I loved him. He was so purty—dead spit 'n' image o' yew. But I loved yew more—an' yew was goin' away—far off whar I'd never see ye agen, never kiss ye, never feel ye pressed agin me agen—an' ye said ye hated me fur havin' him—ye said ye hated him an' wished he was dead—ye said if it hadn't been fur him comin' it'd be the same's afore between us.

EBEN [*unable to endure this, springs to his feet in a fury, threatening her, his twitching fingers seeming to reach out for her throat*].   Ye lie! I never said—I never dreamed ye'd—I'd cut off my head afore I'd hurt his finger!

ABBIE [*piteously, sinking on her knees*].   Eben, don't ye look at me like that— hatin' me—not after what I done fur ye—fur us—so's we could be happy
1500   agen—

EBEN [*furiously now*].   Shut up, or I'll kill ye! I see yer game now—the same old sneakin' trick—ye're aimin' t' blame me fur the murder ye done!

ABBIE [*moaning—putting her hands over her ears*].   Don't ye, Eben! Don't ye! [*She grasps his legs.*]

EBEN [*his mood suddenly changing to horror, shrinks away from her*].   Don't ye tech me! Ye're pizen! How could ye—t' murder a pore little critter—Ye must've swapped yer soul t' hell! [*Suddenly raging.*] Ha! I kin see why ye

1510 done it! Not the lies ye jest told—but 'cause ye wanted t' steal agen—steal the last thin' ye'd left me—my part o' him—no, the hull o' him—ye saw he looked like me—ye knowed he was all mine—an' ye couldn't b'ar it—I know ye! Ye killed him fur bein' mine! [*All this has driven him almost insane. He makes a rush past her for the door—then turns—shaking both fists at her, violently.*] But I'll take vengeance now! I'll git the Sheriff! I'll tell him everythin'! Then I'll sing "I'm off to Californi-a!" an' go—gold—Golden Gate—gold sun—fields o' gold in the West! [*This last he half shouts, half croons incoherently, suddenly breaking off passionately.*] I'm a-goin' fur the Sheriff t' come an' git ye! I want ye tuk away, locked up from me! I can't stand t' luk at ye! Murderer an' thief 'r not, ye still tempt me! I'll give ye up t' the Sheriff! [*He turns and runs out, around the corner of house, panting*
1520 *and sobbing, and breaks into a swerving sprint down the road.*]

ABBIE [*struggling to her feet, runs to the door, calling after him*].   I love ye, Eben! I love ye! [*She stops at the door weakly, swaying, about to fall.*] I don't care what ye do—if ye'll on'y love me agen—[*She falls limply to the floor in a faint.*]

SCENE IV

About an hour later. Same as Scene III. Shows the kitchen and CABOT's *bedroom. It is after dawn. The sky is brilliant with the sunrise. In the kitchen,* ABBIE *sits at the table, her body limp and exhausted, her head bowed down over her arms, her face hidden. Upstairs,* CABOT *is still asleep but awakens with a start. He looks toward the window and gives a snort of surprise and irritation—throws back the covers and begins hurriedly pulling on his clothes. Without looking behind him, he begins talking to* ABBIE *whom he supposes is beside him.*

CABOT.   Thunder 'n' lightin', Abbie! I hain't slept this late in fifty year! Looks 's if the sun was ful riz a'most. Must've been the dancin' an' likker. Must be gittin' old. I hope Eben's t' wuk. Ye might've tuk the trouble t' rouse me, Abbie. [*He turns—sees no one here—surprised.*] Waal—whar air she? Gittin' vittles, I calc'late. [*He tiptoes to the cradle and peers down—proudly.*] Mornin', sonny. Purty's a picter! Sleepin' sound. He don't beller all night
1530 like most o' 'em. [*He goes quietly out the door in rear—a few moments later enters kitchen—sees* ABBIE—*with satisfaction.*] So thar ye be. Ye got any vittles cooked?

ABBIE [*without moving*].   No.

CABOT [*coming to her, almost sympathetically*].   Ye feelin' sick?

ABBIE.   No.

CABOT [*pats her on shoulder. She shudders*].   Ye'd best lie down a spell. [*Half jocularly.*] Yer son'll be needin' ye soon. He'd ought t' wake up with a gnashin' appetite, the sound way he's sleepin'.

ABBIE [*shudders—then in a dead voice*].   He hain't never goin' t' wake up.

1540 CABOT [*jokingly*].   Takes after me this mornin'. I hain't slept so late in . . .

ABBIE.   He's dead.

CABOT [*stares at her—bewilderedly*].   What. . . .

ABBIE.   I killed him.

CABOT [*stepping back from her—aghast*].   Air ye drunk—'r crazy—'r . . . !

ABBIE [*suddenly lifts her head and turns on him—wildly*].   I killed him. I tell ye!

I smothered him. Go up an' see if ye don't b'lieve me! [CABOT *stares at her a second, then bolts out the rear door, can be heard bounding up the stairs, and rushes into the bedroom and over to the cradle.* ABBIE *has sunk back lifelessly into her former position.* CABOT *puts his hand down on the body in the crib. An* 1550 *expression of fear and horror comes over his face.*]

CABOT [*shrinking away—tremblingly*].   God A'mighty! God A'mighty. [*He stumbles out the door—in a short while returns to the kitchen—comes to* ABBIE, *the stunned expression still on his face—hoarsely.*] Why did ye do it? Why? [*As she doesn't answer, he grabs her violently by the shoulder and shakes her.*] I ax ye why ye done it! Ye'd better tell me 'r . . . !

ABBIE [*gives him a furious push which sends him staggering back and springs to her feet—with rage and hatred*].   Don't ye dare tech me! What right hev ye t' question me 'bout him? He wa'n't yewr son! Think I'd have a son by yew? I'd die fust! I hate the sight o' ye an' allus did! It's yew I should've mur1560 dered, if I'd had good sense! I hate ye! I love Eben. I did from the fust. An' he was Eben's son—mine an' Eben's —not your'n!

CABOT [*stands looking at her dazedly—a pause—finding his words with an effort—dully*].   That was it—what I felt—pokin' round the corners—while ye lied—holdin' yerself from me—sayin' ye'd a'ready conceived—[*He lapses into crushed silence—then with a strange emotion.*] He's dead, sart'n. I felt his heart. Pore little critter! [*He blinks back one tear, wiping his sleeve across his nose.*]

ABBIE [*hysterically*].   Don't ye! Don't ye! [*She sobs unrestrainedly.*]

CABOT [*with a concentrated effort that stiffens his body into a rigid line and hardens 1570 his face into a stony mask—through his teeth to himself*].   I got t' be—like a stone—a rock o' jedgment! [*A pause. He gets complete control over himself—harshly.*] If he was Eben's, I be glad he air gone! An' mebbe I suspicioned it all along. I felt they was somethin' onnateral—somewhars—the house got so lonesome—an' cold—drivin' me down t' the barn—t' the beasts o' the field. . . . Ay-eh. I must've suspicioned—somethin'. Ye didn't fool me— not altogether, leastways—I'm too old a bird—growin' ripe on the bough. . . . [*He becomes aware he is wandering, straightens again, looks at* ABBIE *with a cruel grin.*] So ye'd liked t' hev murdered me 'stead o' him, would ye? Waal, I'll live to be a hundred! I'll live t' see ye hung! I'll deliver ye up t' 1580 the jedgment o' God an' the law! I'll git the Sheriff now. [*Starts for the door.*]

ABBIE [*dully*].   Ye needn't. Eben's gone fur him.

CABOT [*amazed*].   Eben—gone fur the Sheriff?

ABBIE.   Ay-eh.

CABOT.   T' inform agen ye?

ABBIE.   Ay-eh.

CABOT [*considers this—a pause—then in a hard voice*].   Waal, I'm thankful fur him savin' me the trouble. I'll git t' wuk. [*He goes to the door—then turns—in a voice full of strange emotion.*] He'd ought t' been my son, Abbie. Ye'd ought t' loved me. I'm a man. If ye'd loved me, I'd never told no Sheriff on ye 1590 no matter what ye did, if they was t' brile me alive!

ABBIE [*defensively*].   They's more to it nor yew know, makes him tell.

CABOT [*dryly*].   Fur yewr sake, I hope they be. [*He goes out—comes around to the gate—stares up at the sky. His control relaxes. For a moment he is old and weary. He murmurs despairingly.*] God A'mighty, I be lonesomer'n ever! [*He hears running footsteps from the left, immediately is himself again.* EBEN *runs in, panting exhaustedly, wild-eyed and mad looking. He lurches through the gate.* CABOT *grabs him by the shoulder.* EBEN *stares at him dumbly.*] Did ye tell the Sheriff?

EBEN [*nodding stupidly*].   Ay-eh.

CABOT [*gives him a push away that sends him sprawling—laughing with withering contempt*].   Good fur ye! A prime chip o' yer Maw ye be! [*He goes toward the barn, laughing harshly.* EBEN *scrambles to his feet. Suddenly* CABOT *turns—grimly threatening.*] Git off this farm when the Sheriff takes her—or, by God, he'll have t' come back an' git me fur murder, too! [*He stalks off.* EBEN *does not appear to have heard him. He runs to the door and comes into the kitchen.* ABBIE *looks up with a cry of anguished joy.* EBEN *stumbles over and throws himself on his knees beside her sobbing brokenly.*]

EBEN.   Fergive me!

ABBIE [*happily*].   Eben! [*She kisses him and pulls his head over against her breast.*]

EBEN.   I love ye! Fergive me!

ABBIE [*ecstatically*].   I'd fergive ye all the sins in hell fur sayin' that! [*She kisses his head, pressing it to her with a fierce passion of possession.*]

EBEN [*brokenly*].   But I told the Sheriff. He's comin' fur ye!

ABBIE.   I kin b'ar what happens t' me—now!

EBEN.   I woke him up. I told him. He says, wait 'til I git dressed. I was waiting. I got to thinkin' o' yew. I got to thinkin' how I'd loved ye. It hurt like somethin' was bustin' in my chest an' head. I got t' cryin'. I knowed sudden I loved ye yet, an' allus would love ye!

ABBIE [*caressing his hair—tenderly*].   My boy, hain't ye!

EBEN.   I begun t' run back. I cut across the fields an' through the woods. I thought ye might have time t' run away—with me—an' . . .

ABBIE [*shaking her head*].   I got t' take my punishment—t' pay fur my sin.

EBEN.   Then I want t' share it with ye.

ABBIE.   Ye didn't do nothin'.

EBEN.   I put it in yer head. I wisht he was dead! I as much as urged ye t' do it!

ABBIE.   No. It was me alone!

EBEN.   I'm as guilty as yew be! He was the child o' our sin.

ABBIE [*lifting her head as if defying God*].   I don't repent that sin! I hain't askin' God t' fergive that!

EBEN.   Nor me—but it led up t' the other—an' the murder ye did, ye did 'count o' me—an' it's my murder, too, I'll tell the Sheriff—an' if ye deny it, I'll say we planned it t'gether—an' they'll all b'lieve me, fur they suspicion everythin' we've done, an' it'll seem likely an' true to 'em. An' it is true—way down. I did help ye—somehow.

ABBIE [*laying her head on his—sobbing*].   No! I don't want yew t' suffer!

EBEN.   I got t' pay fur my part o' the sin! An' I'd suffer wuss leavin' ye, goin' West, thinkin' o' ye day an' night, bein' out when yew was in—[*Lowering his voice.*] 'r bein' alive, when yew was dead. [*A pause.*] I want t' share with ye, Abbie—prison 'r death 'r hell 'r anythin'! [*He looks into her eyes and forces a trembling smile.*] If I'm sharin' with ye, I won't feel lonesome, leastways.

ABBIE [*weakly*].   Eben! I won't let ye! I can't let ye!

EBEN [*kissing her—tenderly*].   Ye can't he'p yerself. I got ye beat fur once!

ABBIE [*forcing a smile—adoringly*].   I hain't beat—s'long's I got ye!

EBEN [*hears the sound of feet outside*].   Ssshh! Listen! They've come t' take us!

ABBIE. No, it's him. Don't give him no chance to fight ye, Eben. Don't say nothin'—no matter what he says. An' I won't neither. [*It is* CABOT. *He comes up from the barn in a great state of excitement and strides into the house and then into the kitchen.* EBEN *is kneeling beside* ABBIE, *his arm around her, hers around him. They stare straight ahead.*]

1650 CABOT [*stares at them, his face hard. A long pause—vindictively*]. Ye make a slick pair o' murderin' turtle doves! Ye'd ought t' be both hung on the same limb an' left thar t' swing in the breeze an' rot—a warnin' t' old fools like me t' b'ar their lonesomeness alone—an' fur young fools like ye t' hobble their lust. [*A pause. The excitement returns to his face, his eyes snap, he looks a bit crazy.*] I couldn't work today. I couldn't take no interest. T' hell with the farm! I'm leavin' it! I've turned the cows an' other stock loose! I've druv 'em into the woods whar they kin be free! By freein' 'em, I'm freein' myself! I'm quittin' here today! I'll set fire t' house an' barn an' watch 'em burn, an' I'll leave yer Maw t' haunt the ashes, an' I'll will the fields back

1660 t' God, so that nothin' human kin never touch 'em! I'll be a-goin' to Californi-a—t' jine Simeon an' Peter—true sons o' mine if they be dumb fools—an' the Cabots'll find Solomon's Mines t'gether! [*He suddenly cuts a mad caper.*] Whoop! What was the song they sung? "Oh, Californi-a! That's the land fur me." [*He sings this—then gets on his knees by the floor-board under which the money was hid.*] An' I'll sail thar on one o' the finest clippers I kin find! I've got the money! Pity ye didn't know whar this was hidden so's ye could steal. . . . [*He has pulled up the board. He stares—feels—stares again. A pause of dead silence. He slowly turns, slumping into a sitting position on the floor, his eyes like those of a dead fish, his face the sickly green of an attack of nausea. He

1670 swallows painfully several times—forces a weak smile at last.*] So—ye did steal it!

EBEN [*emotionlessly*]. I swapped it t' Sim an' Peter fur their share o' the farm— t' pay their passage t' Californi-a.

CABOT [*with one sardonic*]. Ha! [*He begins to recover. Gets slowly to his feet—strangely.*] I calc'late God give it to 'em—not yew! God's hard, not easy! Mebbe they's easy gold in the West but it hain't God's gold. It hain't fur me. I kin hear His voice warnin' me agen t' be hard an' stay on my farm. I kin see his hand usin' Eben t' steal t' keep me from weakness. I kin feel I be in the palm o' His hand, His fingers guidin' me. [*A pause—then he mutters sadly.*] It's a-goin' t' be lonesomer now than ever it war afore—an'

1680 I'm gittin' old, Lord—ripe on the bough. . . . [*Then stiffening.*] Waal—what d'ye want? God's lonesome, hain't He? God's hard an' lonesome! [*A pause. The* SHERIFF *with two men comes up the road from the left. They move cautiously to the door. The* SHERIFF *knocks on it with the butt of his pistol.*]

SHERIFF. Open in the name o' the law. [*They start.*]

CABOT. They've come fur ye. [*He goes to the rear door.*] Come in, Jim! [*The three men enter.* CABOT *meets them in doorway.*] Jest a minit, Jim. I got 'em safe here. [*The* SHERIFF *nods. He and his companions remain in the doorway.*]

EBEN [*suddenly calls*]. I lied this mornin', Jim. I helped her to do it. Ye kin take me, too.

1690 ABBIE [*brokenly*]. No!

CABOT. Take 'em both. [*He comes forward—stares at* EBEN *with a trace of grudging admiration.*] Purty good—fur yew! Waal, I got t' round up the stock. Good-by.

EBEN. Good-by.

CABOT. Good-by. [CABOT *turns and strides past the men—comes out and around the corner of the house, his shoulders squared, his face stony, and stalks grimly toward the barn. In the meantime the* SHERIFF *and men have come into the room.*]

SHERIFF [*embarrassedly*]. Waal—we'd best start.

ABBIE. Wait. [*Turns to* EBEN]. I love ye, Eben.

1700 EBEN. I love ye, Abbie. [*They kiss. The three men grin and shuffle embarrassedly.* EBEN *takes* ABBIE's *hand. They go out the door in rear, the men following, and come from the house, walking hand in hand to the gate.* EBEN *stops there and points to the sunrise sky*] Sun's a-rizin'. Purty, hain't it?

ABBIE. Ay-eh. [*They both stand for a moment looking up raptly in attitudes strangely aloof and devout.*]

SHERIFF [*looking around at the farm enviously—to his companions*]. It's a jim-dandy farm, no denyin'. Wished I owned it!

CURTAIN

[1924]

Critical Commentary on *Desire Under the Elms*

Generations of novelists have fantasized about writing the great American novel. Playwrights seem to have no such fantasy. Perhaps they recognize that so gaudy a dream, while achievable in the sprawling verbal continent of fiction, is inappropriate to the narrow confines of the stage. Nevertheless, a handful of major plays by such authors as Susan Glaspell, Tennessee Williams, and Arthur Miller have succeeded in capturing key aspects of the American experience. No single play, however, comes closer to defining the sweep of our national history and ambitions than Eugene O'Neill's *Desire Under the Elms*. Set in New England in the year 1850, the play presents a tidy synopsis of the forces that have guided American development ever since the arrival of the first Puritan settlers in 1607.

As the biblical overtones of the characters' names suggest, this play is set firmly upon the bedrock of Protestant theology—albeit a theology that has been distorted by the environment of the New World. Despite obvious flaws in his conduct and values, Ephraim Cabot is very much the Puritan patriarch. He believes that "God's hard, not easy"; that work is a form of worship; and that success itself is a sign of God's favor and approval. He claims that "When ye kin make corn sprout out o' stones, God's livin' in yew!"

In keeping with these beliefs, he gives his sons Old Testament names, and two of his three sons are named after the most prominent features of his farm, the stones: *Peter* means "stone" and *Eben* means "little stone." In a moment of insight, Eben recognizes the symbolic significance of the stone wall that is so visible on the stage. Among the many chores about the farm, one is the making of walls: "stone atop o' stone—makin' walls till yer heart's a stone ye heft up out o' the way o' growth onto a stone wall t' wall in yer heart."

The stone God of the Puritan work ethic is only one of the elements of Americana in the play. Note, as well, the influence of the West and the westering impulse. Ephraim Cabot himself had once been part of the great westward migration, having carved out a farm in the rich soil of the Great Plains, only to discover that *he* (or his God) could find no value in a life of ease. Ephraim's sons, like perhaps all American sons, fail fully to share their father's values. Simeon and Peter work the farm, but they do not love it with Ephraim's passion. For them, the sunset in the west holds the golden promise of California. By the end of Part I, they join the great American migration known as the California gold rush. Like many Americans of every generation, they reject the hard life of heaving stones from furrows and dream instead of an easy life where gold stones lie "just atop o' the ground waitin' t' be picked!"

Their brother Eben, however, is a truer son of Ephraim. For him, the sun doesn't set way off in California, but rather "yonder atop the hill pasture." But while Eben may seem superficially different from his brothers, his basic weakness of character is the same. All of the characters in the play are dominated by desire: desire for easy wealth, desire for the farm, desire for power, desire for sexual gratification. In different ways each of these desires drives these characters toward their destruction. They want possessions. They want, as Eben says of Abbie, to "swaller up everythin' an' make it your'n." Thus, the language of the play is packed with personal pronouns: *my* farm, *my* room, *my* bed, and, most tragically, *my* son.

O'Neill felt that American capitalism led inevitably to materialism, selfishness, and possessiveness. What these characters lack—and what Americans in general *may* lack—is the willingness and ability to share. Old Ephraim, for all his faults, begins dimly to develop toward sharing as the action unfolds. Even at the very beginning, when Abbie stares lustfully at the farmhouse and exclaims, "I can't b'lieve it's r'ally mine," Cabot quickly backs away from claiming it as his alone, to add relentingly, "Our'n—mebbe!" Later, he senses a coldness and loneliness in the house and starts spending more of his time in the barn with the cows, where at least an animal warmth can be shared and where, he says, the cows are "teaching" him. Instead of gazing possessively at his farmland, he gazes myopically at the sky, longing to make a place for himself up there. After the birth of Abbie's child, Cabot attends to his young wife "*with real solicitation,*" offering to help her climb the stairs. And even when he knows that the murdered infant was not his own son, he is still moved to tears by the tragedy of its death. Sadly, though, Ephraim pulls back into himself in the closing moments of the play, seeing the hand of God in his misfortunes and hearing the voice of God telling him to resist weakness, stay on the farm, and learn to bear his lonesomeness stoically.

Paradoxically, Abbie and Eben, the two characters most driven by desire, are also the two who come closest to true sharing. At the beginning of the play, Abbie marries Ephraim solely to gain a home, but she soon discovers that he will not leave the farm to her unless she bears him a son. She initiates the affair with Eben as much because she needs his seed to become pregnant as because she desires sexual pleasure. Similarly, Eben enters into the affair with Abbie for the same reasons that he had earlier forced himself upon the local trollop Min; he tells Simeon and Peter: "I jest grabbed holt an' tuk her—[*Proudly*] Yes, siree! She may've been his'n—an' your'n, too—but she's mine now!" Both enter into the affair as a result of a desire that is materialistic, but it is soon transformed into primitive carnal passion. Their first kisses leave them "speechless and breathless, panting like two animals."

Ironically, their physical desire offers them an escape from the more despicable and harmful force of materialism. As Abbie astutely observes, human sexuality is a natural force like that of the sun:

> Ye kin feel it burnin' into the earth—Nature—makin' thin's grow—bigger 'n' bigger—burnin' inside ye—makin' ye want t' grow—into somethin' else—till ye're jined with it—an' it's your'n—but it owns ye, too—an' makes ye grow bigger. . . .

Although they are first joined by lust, Abbie and Eben do grow together until at the end of the play they realize that they truly love each other. Eben speaks for them both when he says, "I want t' share with ye, Abbie—prison 'r death 'r hell 'r anythin'!" They discover that sharing banishes the lonesomeness that is the reward of worshipping Cabot's hard god of materialism. And through sharing they begin to experience moral growth, realizing that they must suffer for their selfish sins of the past.

Whatever optimism about America we may feel in observing this rudimentary morality is, however, undermined by our knowledge that it has come too late. Abbie and Eben will be hung or imprisoned. The land is controlled by Cabot, now childless and stonier than ever. And after he dies, to whom will it pass? The closing lines of the play give us a clue. As Abbie and Eben join hands to share, as we all can share, in the natural beauty of the sunrise, the sheriff has eyes only for the farm. He looks around it "enviously" and comments to his companions, "It's a jim-dandy farm, no denyin'. Wished I owned it!" Possessiveness will prevail.

A Selective Bibliography on *Desire Under the Elms*

Berlin, Normand. *Eugene O'Neill.* New York: Grove, 1982.

Bloom, Harold, ed. *Eugene O'Neill.* New York: Chelsea, 1987.

Bogard, Travis. *Contour in Time: The Plays of Eugene O'Neill.* New York: Oxford UP, 1972.

Cargill, Oscar, N. B. Fagin, and W. J. Fisher, eds. *O'Neill and His Plays: Four Decades of Criticism.* New York: New York UP, 1961.

Carpenter, Frederic I. *Eugene O'Neill.* Boston: Twayne, 1979.

Chabrowe, Leonard. *Ritual and Pathos: The Theater of O'Neill.* Lewisburg, Pa.: Bucknell UP, 1976.

Conlin, Matthew T. "The Tragic Effect in *Autumn Fire* and *Desire Under the Elms.*" *Modern Drama* 1 (1959): 228–35.

Eaton, Walter Pritchard. "O'Neill: New Risen Attic Stream?" *American Scholar* 6 (1937): 304–12.

Engel, Edwin. *The Haunted Heroes of Eugene O'Neill.* Cambridge: Harvard UP, 1953.

Fambrough, Preston. "The Tragic Cosmology of O'Neill's *Desire Under the Elms.*" *The Eugene O'Neill Newsletter* 10.2 (1986): 25–29.

Falk, Doris V. *Eugene O'Neill and the Tragic Tension.* 2nd ed. New York: Gordian Press, 1982.

Floyd, Virginia. *The Plays of Eugene O'Neill: A New Assessment.* New York: Ungar, 1985. 270–87.

Gassner, John. *O'Neill: A Collection of Critical Essays.* Englewood Cliffs, N.J.: Prentice-Hall, 1964.

Griffin, Ernest G., ed. *Eugene O'Neill: A Collection of Criticism.* New York: McGraw-Hill, 1976.

Hays, Peter L. "Biblical Perversions in *Desire Under the Elms.*" *Modern Drama* 9 (1969): 423–28.

Hinden, Michael. "Desire and Forgiveness: O'Neill's Diptych." *Comparative Drama* 14 (1980): 240–50.

Hoover, Marjorie L. "Three O'Neill Plays in 1920s Productions by Tairov's Kamerny." *Theatre History Studies* 11 (1991): 123–27.

Kalson, Albert E. "Up-Staged and Off-Staged by the Director and Designer: *The Hairy Ape* and *Desire Under the Elms* in London." *The Eugene O'Neill Newsletter* 11.2 (1987): 36–40.

Kolin, Philip C. "Parallels between *Desire Under the Elms* and *Sweet Bird of Youth.*" *The Eugene O'Neill Review* 13.2 (1989): 23–35.

Lemanis, Mara. "*Desire Under the Elms* and Tragic Form: A Study of Misalliance." *South Dakota Review* 16.3 (1978): 46–55.

Mandl, Bette. "Family Ties: Landscape and Gender in *Desire under the Elms.*" *The Eugene O'Neill Newsletter* 11.2 (1987): 19–23.

Meyers, Jay Ronald. "O'Neill's Use of the Phedre Legend in *Desire Under the Elms.*" *Révue de Litterature Comparée* 41 (1967): 120–25.

Mikos, Michael and David Mulroy. "Reymont's *The Peasants:* A Probable Influence on *Desire Under the Elms.*" *The Eugene O'Neill Newsletter* 10.1 (1986): 4–15.

Miller, Jordan Y. *Playwright's Progress: O'Neill and the Critics.* Chicago: Scott, Foresman, 1965.

McVeigh, Terrence A. "A Tragic Senex Amans: O'Neill's Ephraim Cabot." *Classical and Modern Literature* 11.1 (1990): 67–75.

Moorton, Richard F., ed. *Eugene O'Neill's Century.* New York: Greenwood, 1991.

Nolan, Patrick J. "*Desire Under the Elms:* Characters by Jung." *The Eugene O'Neill Newsletter* 5.2 (1981): 5–10.

Ranald, Margaret Loftus. *The Eugene O'Neill Companion.* Westport, Conn.: Greenwood, 1985.

Reardon, William R. "The Path of a Classic: *Desire Under the Elms.*" *Southern Speech Journal* 31 (1966): 295–300.

Robinson, James A. "Buried Children: Fathers and Sons in O'Neill and Shepard." *Eugene O'Neill and the Emergence of American Drama.* Ed. Mart Maufort. Amsterdam: Rodopi, 1989. 151–57.

———, "O'Neill's Indian Elms." *The Eugene O'Neill Review* 13.1 (1989): 40–46.

Schlueter, June and Arthur Lewis. "Cabot's Conflict: The Stones and Cows in O'Neill's *Desire Under the Elms.*" *Critical Essays on Eugene O'Neill.* Ed. James J. Martine. Boston: G. K. Hall, 1984. 111–14.

Skinner, Richard Dana. *Eugene O'Neill: A Poet's Quest.* New York: Russell, 1964.

Stroupe, John H. *Critical Approaches to O'Neill.* New York: AMS, 1988.

Tiusanen, Timo. *O'Neill's Scenic Images.* Princeton: Princeton UP, 1968.

Wainscott, Ronald H. *Staging O'Neill: The Experimental Years, 1920–1934.* New Haven: Yale UP, 1988. 157–69.

Waterstradt, Jean A. "Another View of Ephraim Cabot: A Footnote to *Desire Under the Elms.*" *The Eugene O'Neill Newsletter* 9.2 (1985): 27–31.

Weiss, Samuel A. "O'Neill, Nietzsche, and Cows." *Modern Drama* 34 (1991): 494–98.

Winther, Sophus Keith. "*Desire Under the Elms:* A Modern Tragedy," *Modern Drama* 3 (1960): 326–32.

Tennessee Williams (1911–1983)

THE GLASS MENAGERIE

SCENE: *An Alley in St. Louis*

>Part I. Preparation for a Gentleman Caller.
>Part II. The Gentleman calls.

TIME: *Now and the Past*

THE CHARACTERS

AMANDA WINGFIELD (*the mother*). A little woman of great but confused vitality clinging frantically to another time and place. Her characterization must be carefully created, not copied from type. She is not paranoiac, but her life is paranoia. There is much to admire in Amanda, and as much to love and pity as there is to laugh at. Certainly she has endurance and a kind of heroism, and though her foolishness makes her unwittingly cruel at times, there is tenderness in her slight person.

LAURA WINGFIELD (*her daughter*). Amanda, having failed to establish contact with reality, continues to live vitally in her illusions, but Laura's situation is even graver. A childhood illness has left her crippled, one leg slightly shorter than the other, and held in a brace. This defect need not be more than suggested on the stage. Stemming from this, Laura's separation increases till she is like a piece of her own glass collection, too exquisitely fragile to move from the shelf.

TOM WINGFIELD (*her son and the narrator of the play*). A poet with a job in a warehouse. His nature is not remorseless, but to escape from a trap he has to act without pity.

JIM O'CONNOR (*the gentleman caller*). A nice, ordinary, young man.

PRODUCTION NOTES

Being a "memory play," *The Glass Menagerie* can be presented with unusual freedom of convention. Because of its considerably delicate or tenuous material, atmospheric touches and subtleties of direction play a particularly important part. Expressionism and all other unconventional techniques in drama have only one valid aim, and that is a closer approach to truth. When a play employs unconventional techniques, it is not, or certainly shouldn't be, trying to escape its responsibility of dealing with reality, or interpreting experience, but is actually or should be attempting to find a closer approach, a more penetrating and vivid expression of things as they are. The straight realistic play with its genuine Frigidaire and authentic ice-cubes, its characters who speak exactly as its audience speaks, corresponds to the academic landscape and has the same virtue of a photographic likeness. Everyone should know nowadays the unimportance of the photographic in art: that truth, life, or reality is an organic thing which the poetic imagination can represent or suggest, in essence, only through transformation, through changing into other forms than those which were merely present in appearance.

These remarks are not meant as a preface only to this particular play. They have to do with a conception of a new, plastic theatre which must take the place of the exhausted theatre of realistic conventions if the theatre is to resume vitality as a part of our culture.

THE SCREEN DEVICE: There is *only one important difference between the original and the acting version of the play* and that is the *omission* in the latter of the device that I tentatively included in my *original* script. This device was the use of a screen on which were projected magic-lantern slides bearing images or titles. I do not regret the omission of this device from the original Broadway production. The extraordinary power of Miss Taylor's[1] performance made it suitable to have the utmost simplicity in the physical production. But I think it may be interesting to some readers to see how this device was conceived. So I am putting it into the published manuscript. These images and legends, projected from behind, were cast on a section of wall between the front-room and dining-room areas, which should be indistinguishable from the rest when not in use.

The purpose of this will probably be apparent. It is to give accent to certain values in each scene. Each scene contains a particular point (or several) which is structurally the most important. In an episodic play, such as this, the basic structure or narrative line may be obscured from the audience; the effect may seem fragmentary rather than architectural. This may not be the fault of the play so much as the lack of attention in the audience. The legend or image upon the screen will strengthen the effect of what is merely allusion in the writing and allow the primary point to be made more simply and lightly than if the entire responsibility were on the spoken lines. Aside from this structural value, I think the screen will have a definite emotional appeal, less definable but just as important. An imaginative producer or director may invent many other uses for this device than those indicated in the present script. In fact the possibilities of the device seem much larger to me than the instance of this play can possibly utilize.

THE MUSIC: Another extra-literary accent in this play is provided by the use of music.[2] A single recurring tune, "The Glass Menagerie," is used to give emotional emphasis to suitable passages. This tune is like circus music, not when you are on the grounds or in the immediate vicinity of the parade, but when you are at some distance and very likely thinking of something else. It seems under those circumstances to continue almost interminably and it weaves in and out of your preoccupied consciousness; then it is the lightest, most delicate music in the world and perhaps the saddest. It expresses the surface vivacity of life with the underlying strain of immutable and inexpressible sorrow. When you look at a piece of delicately spun glass you think

---

[1] Laurette Taylor (1884–1946) played the part of Amanda in the original production of the play.
[2] Paul Bowles (1910–) composed the music for the first production.

of two things: how beautiful it is and how easily it can be broken. Both of those ideas should be woven into the recurring tune, which dips in and out of the play as if it were carried on a wind that changes. It serves as a thread of connection and allusion between the narrator with his separate point in time and space and the subject of his story. Between each episode it returns as reference to the emotion, nostalgia, which is the first condition of the play. It is primarily Laura's music and therefore comes out most clearly when the play focuses upon her and the lovely fragility of glass which is her image.

THE LIGHTING: The lighting in the play is not realistic. In keeping with the atmosphere of memory, the stage is dim. Shafts of light are focused on selected areas or actors, sometimes in contradistinction to what is the apparent center. For instance, in the quarrel scene between Tom and Amanda, in which Laura has no active part, the clearest pool of light is on her figure. This is also true of the supper scene, when her silent figure on the sofa should remain the visual center. The light upon Laura should be distinct from the others, having a peculiar pristine clarity such as light used in early religious portraits of female saints or madonnas. A certain correspondence to light in religious paintings, such as El Greco's,[3] where the figures are radiant in atmosphere that is relatively dusky, could be effectively used throughout the play. (It will also permit a more effective use of the screen.) A free, imaginative use of light can be of enormous value in giving a mobile, plastic quality to plays of a more or less static nature.

Tennessee Williams

SCENE I

The Wingfield apartment is in the rear of the building, one of those vast hive-like conglomerations of cellular living-units that flower as warty growths in overcrowded urban centers of lower middle-class population and are symptomatic of the impulse of this largest and fundamentally enslaved section of American society to avoid fluidity and differentiation and to exist and function as one interfused mass of automatism.

The apartment faces an alley and is entered by a fire escape, a structure whose name is a touch of accidental poetic truth, for all of these huge buildings are always burning with the slow and implacable fires of human desperation. The fire escape is part of what we see—that is, the landing of it and steps descending from it.

The scene is memory and is therefore nonrealistic. Memory takes a lot of poetic license. It omits some details; others are exaggerated, according to the emotional value of the articles it touches, for memory is seated predominantly in the heart. The interior is therefore rather dim and poetic.

At the rise of the curtain, the audience is faced with the dark, grim rear wall of the Wingfield tenement. This building is flanked on both sides by dark, narrow alleys which run into murky canyons of tangled clotheslines, garbage cans, and the sinister

---

[3] El Greco (1541–1614 was born in Crete but painted primarily in Spain. His paintings are noted for their elongated human shapes, their odd color schemes, and their eerie lighting.

latticework of neighboring fire escapes. It is up and down these side alleys that exterior entrances and exits are made during the play. At the end of Tom's opening commentary, the dark tenement wall slowly becomes transparent and reveals the interior of the ground-floor Wingfield apartment.

Nearest the audience is the living room which also serves as a sleeping room for Laura, the sofa unfolding to make her bed. Just beyond, separated from the living room by a wide arch or second proscenium with transparent faded portieres (or second curtain), is the dining room. In an old-fashioned whatnot[4] in the living room are seen scores of transparent glass animals. A blown-up photograph of the father hangs on the wall of the living room, to the left of the archway. It is the face of a very handsome young man in a doughboy's[5] First World War cap. He is gallantly smiling, ineluctably smiling, as if to say "I will be smiling forever."

Also hanging on the wall, near the photograph, are a typewriter keyboard chart and a Gregg shorthand diagram. An upright typewriter on a small table stands beneath the charts.

The audience hears and sees the opening scene in the dining room through both the transparent fourth wall of the building and the transparent gauze portieres of the dining-room arch. It is during this revealing scene that the fourth wall slowly ascends, out of sight. This transparent exterior wall is not brought down again until the very end of the play, during Tom's final speech.

The narrator is an undisguised convention of the play. He takes whatever license with dramatic convention is convenient to his purposes.

Tom enters, dressed as a merchant sailor, and strolls across to the fire escape. There he stops and lights a cigarette. He addresses the audience.

TOM.   Yes I have tricks in my pocket, I have things up my sleeve. But I am the opposite of a stage magician. He gives you illusion that has the appearance of truth. I give you truth in the pleasant disguise of illusion.

To begin with, I turn back time. I reverse it to that quaint period, the thirties, when the huge middle class of America was matriculating in a school for the blind. Their eyes had failed them, or they had failed their eyes, and so they were having their fingers pressed forcibly down on the fiery Braille alphabet of a dissolving economy.

10   In Spain there was revolution.[6] Here there was only shouting and confusion. In Spain there was Guernica. Here there were disturbances of labor, sometimes pretty violent, in otherwise peaceful cities such as Chicago, Cleveland, Saint Louis . . . This is the social background of the play.

[*Music begins to play.*]

---

[4] A stand with shelves for decorative articles.

[5] An American infantryman.

[6] The Spanish Civil War (1936–39) pitted the Nationalist forces of Francisco Franco against a coalition of socialists, anarchists, and communists. Guernica in northern Spain was heavily damaged in 1937 by German bombers supporting Franco.

The play is memory. Being a memory play, it is dimly lighted, it is sentimental, it is not realistic. In memory everything seems to happen to music. That explains the fiddle in the wings.

I am the narrator of the play, and also a character in it. The other characters are my mother, Amanda, my sister, Laura, and a gentleman caller who appears in the final scenes. He is the most realistic character in the play, being an emissary from a world of reality that we were somehow
20   set apart from. But since I have a poet's weakness for symbols, I am using this character also as a symbol; he is the long-delayed but always expected something that we live for.

There is a fifth character in the play who doesn't appear except in this larger-than-life-size photograph over the mantel. This is our father who left us a long time ago. He was a telephone man who fell in love with long distances; he gave up his job with the telephone company and skipped the light fantastic out of town . . .

The last we heard of him was a picture postcard from Mazatlan, on the Pacific coast of Mexico, containing a message of two words: "Hello—
30   Goodbye!" and no address.

I think the rest of the play will explain itself. . . .

[AMANDA's *voice becomes audible through the portieres.*]

[*Legend on screen:* "Ou sont les neiges."[7]]

[TOM *divides the portieres and enters the dining room.* AMANDA *and* LAURA *are seated at a drop-leaf table. Eating is indicated by gestures without food or utensils.* AMANDA *faces the audience.* TOM *and* LAURA *are seated in profile. The interior has lit up softly and through the scrim*[8] *we see* AMANDA *and* LAURA *seated at the table.*]

AMANDA [*calling*].   Tom?
TOM.   Yes, Mother.
AMANDA.   We can't say grace until you come to the table!
TOM.   Coming, Mother. [*He bows slightly and withdraws, reappearing a few moments later in his place at the table.*]
AMANDA [*to her son*].   Honey, don't *push* with your *fingers*. If you have to push with something, the thing to push with is a crust of bread. And chew—chew! Animals have secretions in their stomachs which enable them to
40   digest food without mastication, but human beings are supposed to chew their food before they swallow it down. Eat food leisurely, son, and really enjoy it. A well-cooked meal has lots of delicate flavors that have to be held in the mouth for appreciation. So chew your food and give your salivary glands a chance to function!

[TOM *deliberately lays his imaginary fork down and pushes his chair back from the table.*]

TOM.   I haven't enjoyed one bite of this dinner because of your constant directions on how to eat it. It's you that make me rush through meals with

---

[7] "Where are the snows [of yesteryear]," a line from a poem by François Villon (1431–1461?).
[8] A thin fabric curtain or screen which can be transparent or opaque, depending on the lighting.

your hawklike attention to every bite I take. Sickening—spoils my appetite—all this discussion of—animals' secretion—salivary glands—mastication!

50 AMANDA [*lightly*].   Temperament like a Metropolitan star![9] [TOM *rises and walks toward the living room.*] You're not excused from the table.

TOM.   I'm getting a cigarette.

AMANDA.   You smoke too much.

[LAURA *rises.*]

LAURA.   I'll bring in the blanc mange.[10]

[TOM *remains standing with his cigarette by the portieres.*]

AMANDA [*rising*].   No, sister, no sister—you be the lady this time and I'll be the darky.

LAURA.   I'm already up.

AMANDA.   Resume your seat, little sister—I want you to stay fresh and pretty—for gentlemen callers!

60 LAURA [*sitting down*].   I'm not expecting any gentlemen callers.

AMANDA [*crossing out to the kitchenette, airily*].   Sometimes they come when they are least expected! Why, I remember one Sunday afternoon in Blue Mountain—

[*She enters the kitchenette.*]

TOM.   I know what's coming!

LAURA.   Yes. But let her tell it.

TOM.   Again?

LAURA.   She loves to tell it.

[AMANDA *returns with a bowl of dessert.*]

AMANDA.   One Sunday afternoon in Blue Mountain—your mother received—*seventeen!*—gentlemen callers! Why, sometimes there weren't chairs
70 enough to accommodate them all. We had to send the nigger over to bring in folding chairs from the parish house.

TOM [*remaining at the portieres*].   How did you entertain those gentlemen callers?

AMANDA.   I understood the art of conversation!

TOM.   I bet you could talk.

AMANDA.   Girls in those days *knew* how to talk, I can tell you.

TOM.   Yes?

[*Image on screen:* AMANDA *as a girl on a porch, greeting callers.*]

AMANDA.   They knew how to entertain their gentlemen callers. It wasn't enough for a girl to be possessed of a pretty face and a graceful figure—
80 although I wasn't slighted in either respect. She also needed to have a nimble wit and a tongue to meet all occasions.

TOM.   What did you talk about?

---

[9] I.e., an opera star.

[10] A sweet pudding made with milk and cornstarch.

AMANDA. Things of importance going on in the world! Never anything coarse or common or vulgar.

[*She addresses* TOM *as though he were seated in the vacant chair at the table though he remains by the portieres.*[11] *He plays this scene as though reading from a script.*]

My callers were gentlemen—all! Among my callers were some of the most prominent young planters of the Mississippi Delta—planters and sons of planters!

[TOM *motions for music and a spot light on* AMANDA. *Her eyes lift, her face glows, her voice becomes rich and elegiac.*]

[*Screen legend:* "Ou sont les neiges d'antan?"]

There was young Champ Laughlin who later became vice-president of the Delta Planters Bank. Hadley Stevenson who was drowned in Moon Lake
90   and left his widow one hundred and fifty thousand in Government bonds. There were the Cutrere brothers, Wesley and Bates. Bates was one of my bright particular beaux! He got in a quarrel with that wild Wainwright boy. They shot it out on the floor of Moon Lake Casino. Bates was shot through the stomach. Died in the ambulance on his way to Memphis. His widow was also well provided-for, came into eight or ten thousand acres, that's all. She married him on the rebound—never loved her—carried my picture on him the night he died! And there was that boy that every girl in the Delta had set her cap for! That beautiful, brilliant young Fitzhugh boy from Greene County!
100 TOM. What did he leave his widow?
AMANDA. He never married! Gracious, you talk as though all of my old admirers had turned up their toes to the daisies!
TOM. Isn't this the first you've mentioned that still survives?
AMANDA. That Fitzhugh boy went North and made a fortune—came to be known as the Wolf of Wall Street! He had the Midas touch, whatever he touched turned to gold! And I could have been Mrs. Duncan J. Fitzhugh, mind you! But—I picked your *father!*
LAURA [*rising*]. Mother, let me clear the table.
AMANDA. No, dear, you go in front and study your typewriter chart. Or
110   practice your shorthand a little. Stay fresh and pretty!—It's almost time for our gentlemen callers to start arriving. [*She flounces girlishly toward the kitchenette.*] How many do you suppose we're going to entertain this afternoon?

[TOM *throws down the paper and jumps up with a groan.*]

LAURA [*alone in the dining room*]. I don't believe we're going to receive any, Mother.
AMANDA [*reappearing, airily*]. Why? No one—not one? You must be joking!

[LAURA *nervously echoes her laugh. She slips in a fugitive manner through the half-open portieres and draws them gently behind her. A shaft of very clear light is*

---

[11] Curtains in a doorway.

thrown on her face against the faded tapestry of the curtains. Faintly the music of "The Glass Menagerie" is heard as she continues, lightly.]

Not one gentleman caller? It can't be true! There must be a flood, there must have been a tornado!

LAURA.   It isn't a flood, it's not a tornado, Mother. I'm just not popular like
120   you were in Blue Mountain. . . . [Tom *utters another groan.* LAURA *glances at him with a faint, apologetic smile. Her voice catches a little:*] Mother's afraid I'm going to be an old maid.

[*The scene dims out with the "Glass Menagerie" music.*]

SCENE II

On the dark stage the screen is lighted with the image of blue roses. Gradually LAURA's *figure becomes apparent and the screen goes out. The music subsides.*

  LAURA *is seated in the delicate ivory chair at the small claw-foot table. She wears a dress of soft violet material for a kimono—her hair is tied back from her forehead with a ribbon. She is washing and polishing her collection of glass.* AMANDA *appears on the fire escape steps. At the sound of her ascent,* LAURA *catches her breath, thrusts the bowl of ornaments away, and seats herself stiffly before the diagram of the typewriter keyboard as though it held her spellbound. Something has happened to* AMANDA. *It is written in her face as she climbs to the landing: a look that is grim and hopeless and a little absurd. She has on one of those cheap or imitation velvety-looking cloth coats with imitation fur collar. Her hat is five or six years old, one of those dreadful cloche*[12] *hats that were worn in the late Twenties, and she is clutching an enormous black patent-leather pocketbook with nickel clasps and initials. This is her full-dress outfit, the one she usually wears to the D.A.R.*[13] *Before entering she looks through the door. She purses her lips, opens her eyes very wide, rolls them upward and shakes her head. Then she slowly lets herself in the door. Seeing her mother's expression* LAURA *touches her lips with a nervous gesture.*

LAURA.   Hello, Mother, I was— [*She makes a nervous gesture toward the chart on the wall.* AMANDA *leans against the shut door and stares at* LAURA *with a martyred look.*]
AMANDA.   Deception? Deception? [*She slowly removes her hat and gloves, continuing the sweet suffering stare. She lets the hat and gloves fall on the floor—a bit of acting.*]
LAURA [*shakily*].   How was the D.A.R. meeting?

[AMANDA *slowly opens her purse and removes a dainty white handkerchief which she shakes out delicately and delicately touches to her lips and nostrils.*]

130   Didn't you go to the D.A.R. meeting, Mother?
AMANDA [*faintly, almost inaudibly*].   —No.—No. [*then more forcibly:*] I did not have the strength—to go to the D.A.R. In fact, I did not have the courage! I wanted to find a hole in the ground and hide myself in it forever! [*She*

---

[12] A bell-shaped, close-fitting hat.
[13] Daughters of the American Revolution, an organization for women whose ancestors fought the British in the Revolutionary War.

crosses slowly to the wall and removes the diagram of the typewriter keyboard. She holds it in front of her for a second, staring at it sweetly and sorrowfully—then bites her lips and tears it in two pieces.]

LAURA [*faintly*]: Why did you do that, Mother? [AMANDA *repeats the same procedure with the chart of the Gregg Alphabet.*] Why are you—

AMANDA. Why? Why? How old are you, Laura?

140 LAURA: Mother, you know my age.

AMANDA. I thought that you were an adult; it seems that I was mistaken. [*She crosses slowly to the sofa and sinks down and stares at* LAURA.]

LAURA. Please don't stare at me, Mother.

[AMANDA *closes her eyes and lowers her head. There is a ten-second pause.*]

AMANDA. What are we going to do, what is going to become of us, what is the future?

[*There is another pause.*]

LAURA. Has something happened, Mother? [AMANDA *draws a long breath, takes out the handkerchief again, goes through the dabbing process.*] Mother, has—something happened?

AMANDA. I'll be all right in a minute, I'm just bewildered—[*She hesitates.*]—by

150 life. . . .

LAURA. Mother, I wish that you would tell me what's happened!

AMANDA. As you know, I was supposed to be inducted into my office at the D.A.R. this afternoon.

[*Screen image:* A swarm of typewriters.]

But I stopped off at Rubicam's Business College to speak to your teacher about your having a cold and ask them what progress they thought you were making down there.

LAURA. Oh. . . .

AMANDA. I went to the typing instructor and introduced myself as your mother. She didn't know who you were. "Wingfield," she said, "We don't

160 have any such student enrolled at the school!"

I assured her she did, that you had been going to classes since early in January.

"I wonder," she said, "If you could be talking about that terribly shy little girl who dropped out of school after only a few days' attendance?"

"No," I said, "Laura, my daughter, has been going to school every day for the past six weeks!"

"Excuse me," she said. She took the attendance book out and there was your name, unmistakably printed, and all the dates you were absent until they decided that you had dropped out of school.

170 I still said, "No, there must have been some mistake! There must have been some mix-up in the records!"

And she said, "No—I remember her perfectly now. Her hands shook so that she couldn't hit the right keys! The first time we gave a speed test, she broke down completely—was sick at the stomach and almost had to be carried to the wash room! After that morning she never showed up any more. We phoned the house but never got any answer"—While I was

working at Famous–Barr, I suppose, demonstrating those— [*She indicates a brassiere with her hands.*] Oh! I felt so weak I could barely keep on my feet! I had to sit down while they got me a glass of water! Fifty dollars' tuition,
180   all of our plans—my hopes and ambitions for you—just gone up the spout, just gone up the spout like that. [LAURA *draws a long breath and gets awkwardly to her feet. She crosses to the Victrola*[14] *and winds it up.*] What are you doing?

LAURA.   Oh! [*She releases the handle and returns to her seat.*]

AMANDA.   Laura, where have you been going when you've gone out pretending that you were going to business college?

LAURA.   I've just been going out walking.

AMANDA.   That's not true.

LAURA.   It is. I just went walking.

190 AMANDA.   Walking? Walking? In winter? Deliberately courting pneumonia in that light coat? Where did you walk to, Laura?

LAURA.   All sorts of places—mostly in the park.

AMANDA.   Even after you'd started catching that cold?

LAURA.   It was the lesser of two evils, Mother.

[*Screen image:* Winter scene in a park.]

I couldn't go back there. I—threw up—on the floor!

AMANDA.   From half past seven till after five every day you mean to tell me you walked around the park, because you wanted to make me think that you were still going to Rubicam's Business College?

LAURA.   It wasn't as bad as it sounds. I went inside places to get warmed up.

200 AMANDA.   Inside where?

LAURA.   I went in the art museum and the bird houses at the Zoo. I visited the penguins every day! Sometimes I did without lunch and went to the movies. Lately I've been spending most of my afternoons in the Jewel Box, that big glass house where they raise the tropical flowers.

AMANDA.   You did all this to deceive me, just for deception? [LAURA *looks down.*] Why?

LAURA.   Mother, when you're disappointed, you get that awful suffering look on your face, like the picture of Jesus' mother in the museum!

AMANDA.   Hush!

210 LAURA.   I couldn't face it.

[*There is a pause. A whisper of strings is heard. Legend on screen:* "The Crust of Humility."]

AMANDA [*hopelessly fingering the huge pocketbook*].   So what are we going to do the rest of our lives? Stay home and watch the parades go by? Amuse ourselves with the glass menagerie, darling? Eternally play those worn-out phonograph records your father left as a painful reminder of him? We won't have a business career—we've given that up because it gave us nervous indigestion! [*She laughs wearily.*] What is there left but dependency all our lives? I know so well what becomes of unmarried women who aren't prepared to occupy a position. I've seen such pitiful cases in

---

[14] A brand name that is often used generically for an early record player.

the South—barely tolerated spinsters living upon the grudging patron-
220 age of sister's husband or brother's wife!—stuck away in some little
mousetrap of a room—encouraged by one in-law to visit another—little
birdlike women without any nest—eating the crust of humility all their
life!

Is that the future that we've mapped out for ourselves? I swear it's the
only alternative I can think of! [*She pauses.*] It isn't a very pleasant alternative, is it? [*She pauses again.*] Of course—some girls *do marry.* [Laura
twists her hands nervously.] Haven't you ever liked some boy?

Laura. Yes. I liked one once. [*She rises.*] I came across his picture a while
ago.

230 Amanda [*with some interest*].   He gave you his picture?

Laura.   No, it's in the yearbook.

Amanda [*disappointed*].   Oh—a high school boy.

[*Screen image:* Jim as the high school hero bearing a silver cup.]

Laura.   Yes. His name was Jim. [*She lifts the heavy annual from the claw-foot
table.*] Here he is in *The Pirates of Penzance.*[15]

Amanda. [*absently*].   The what?

Laura.   The operetta the senior class put on. He had a wonderful voice and
we sat across the aisle from each other Mondays, Wednesdays and Fridays
in the Aud. Here he is with the silver cup for debating! See his grin?

Amanda [*absently*].   He must have had a jolly disposition.

240 Laura.   He used to call me—Blue Roses.

[*Screen image:* Blue roses.]

Amanda.   Why did he call you such a name as that?

Laura.   When I had that attack of pleurosis—he asked me what was the
matter when I came back. I said pleurosis—he thought that I said Blue
Roses! So that's what he always called me after that. Whenever he saw me,
he'd holler, "Hello, Blue Roses!" I didn't care for the girl that he went out
with. Emily Meisenbach. Emily was the best-dressed girl at Soldan. She
never struck me, though, as being sincere . . . It says in the Personal
Section—they're engaged. That's—six years ago! They must be married
by now.

250 Amanda.   Girls that aren't cut out for business careers usually wind up married to some nice man. [*She gets up with a spark of revival.*] Sister, that's what
you'll do!

[Laura *utters a startled, doubtful laugh. She reaches quickly for a piece of glass.*]

Laura.   But, Mother—

Amanda.   Yes? [*She goes over to the photograph.*]

Laura [*in a tone of frightened apology*].   I'm—crippled!

Amanda.   Nonsense! Laura, I've told you never, never to use that word. Why,
you're not crippled, you just have a little defect—hardly noticeable, even!

---

[15] A comic opera written in 1879 by Sir William Schwenck Gilbert (1836–1911) and Sir
Arthur Sullivan (1842–1900).

When people have some slight disadvantage like that, they cultivate other things to make up for it—develop charm—and vivacity—and—*charm!* That's all you have to do! [*She turns again to the photograph.*] One thing your 260 father had *plenty of*—was *charm!*

[*The scene fades out with music.*]

SCENE III

Legend on screen: "After the fiasco—"
TOM *speaks from the fire escape landing.*

TOM. After the fiasco at Rubicam's Business College, the idea of getting a gentleman caller for Laura began to play a more and more important part in Mother's calculations. It became an obsession. Like some archetype of the universal unconscious, the image of the gentleman caller haunted our small apartment. . . .

[*Screen image:* A young man at the door of a house with flowers.]

An evening at home rarely passed without some allusion to this image, this specter, this hope. . . . Even when he wasn't mentioned, his presence hung in Mother's preoccupied look and in my sister's frightened, apologetic manner—hung like a sentence passed upon the Wingfields!
270   Mother was a woman of action as well as words. She began to take logical steps in the planned direction. Late that winter and in the early spring—realizing that extra money would be needed to properly feather the nest and plume the bird—she conducted a vigorous campaign on the telephone, roping in subscribers to one of those magazines for matrons called *The Homemaker's Companion,* the type of journal that features the serialized sublimations of ladies of letters who think in terms of delicate cuplike breasts, slim, tapering waists, rich, creamy thighs, eyes like wood smoke in autumn, fingers that soothe and caress like strains of music, bodies as powerful as Etruscan sculpture.[16]

[*Screen image:* The cover of a glamor magazine.]

[AMANDA *enters with the telephone on a long extension cord. She is spotlighted in the dim stage.*]

280 AMANDA. Ida Scott? This is Amanda Wingfield! We *missed* you at the D.A.R. last Monday! I said to myself: She's probably suffering with that sinus condition! How is that sinus condition?
     Horrors! Heaven have mercy!—You're a Christian matryr, yes, that's what you are, a Christian martyr! Well, I just now happened to notice that your subscription to the *Companion*'s about to expire! Yes, it expires with the next issue, honey!—just when that wonderful new serial by Bessie Mae

---

[16] The Etruscans who dominated central Italy in the fifth century B.C. were noted for their naturalistic sculpture.

Hopper is getting off to such an exciting start. Oh, honey, it's something that you can't miss! You remember how *Gone with the Wind* took everybody by storm? You simply couldn't go out if you hadn't read it. All everybody
290   talked was Scarlett O'Hara. Well, this is a book that critics already compare to *Gone with the Wind*. It's the *Gone with the Wind* of the post-World-War generation!—What?—Burning?—Oh, honey, don't let them burn, go take a look in the oven and I'll hold the wire! Heavens—I think she's hung up!

[*The scene dims out.*]

[*Legend on screen:* "You think I'm in love with Continental Shoemakers?"]

[*Before the lights come up again, the violent voices of* Tom *and* Amanda *are heard. They are quarreling behind the portieres. In front of them stands* Laura *with clenched hands and panicky expression. A clear pool of light is on her figure throughout this scene.*]

Tom.   What in Christ's name am I—
Amanda [*shrilly*].   Don't you use that—
Tom.   —supposed to do!
Amanda.   —expression! Not in my—
Tom.   Ohhh!
Amanda.   —presence! Have you gone out of your senses?
300 Tom.   I have, that's true, *driven* out!
Amanda.   What is the matter with you, you—big—big—IDIOT!
Tom.   Look!—I've got *no thing*, no single thing—
Amanda.   Lower your voice!
Tom.   —in my life here that I can call my OWN! Everything is—
Amanda.   Stop that shouting!
Tom.   Yesterday you confiscated my books! You had the nerve to—
Amanda.   I took that horrible novel back to the library—yes! That hideous book by that insane Mr. Lawrence.[17] [Tom *laughs wildly.*] I cannot control the output of diseased minds or people who cater to them— [Tom *laughs*
310   *still more wildly.*] BUT I WON'T ALLOW SUCH FILTH BROUGHT INTO MY HOUSE! No, no, no, no, no!
Tom.   House, house! Who pays rent on it, who makes a slave of himself to—
Amanda [*fairly screeching*].   Don't you DARE to—
Tom.   No, no, *I* mustn't say things! *I've* got to just—
Amanda.   Let me tell you—
Tom.   I don't want to hear any more!

[*He tears the portieres open. The dining-room area is lit with a turgid smoky red glow. Now we see* Amanda; *her hair is in metal curlers and she is wearing a very old bathrobe, much too large for her slight figure, a relic of the faithless Mr. Wingfield. The upright typewriter now stands on the drop-leaf table, along with a wild disarray of manuscripts. The quarrel was probably precipitated by* Amanda's *interruption of* Tom's *creative labor. A chair lies overthrown on the floor. Their gesticulating shadows are cast on the ceiling by the fiery glow.*]

---

[17] D.H. Lawrence (1885–1930) was a poet and novelist who openly advocated eroticism and sexual freedom.

AMANDA. You *will* hear more, you—

TOM. No, I won't hear more, I'm going out!

AMANDA. You come right back in—

320 TOM. Out, out, out! Because I'm—

AMANDA. Come back here, Tom Wingfield! I'm not through talking to you!

TOM. Oh, go—

LAURA [*desperately*]. —Tom!

AMANDA. You're going to listen, and no more insolence from you! I'm at the
    end of my patience!

[*He comes back toward her.*]

TOM. What do you think I'm at? Aren't I supposed to have any patience to
    reach the end of, Mother? I know, I know. It seems unimportant to you,
    what I'm *doing*—what I *want* to do—having a little *difference* between them!
    You don't think that—

330 AMANDA. I think you've been doing things that you're ashamed of. That's
    why you act like this. I don't believe that you go every night to the movies.
    Nobody goes to the movies night after night. Nobody in their right minds
    goes to the movies as often as you pretend to. People don't go to the
    movies at nearly midnight, and movies don't let out at two A.M. Come in
    stumbling. Muttering to yourself like a maniac! You get three hours' sleep
    and then go to work. Oh, I can picture the way you're doing down there.
    Moping, doping, because you're in no condition.

TOM [*wildly*]. No, I'm in no condition!

AMANDA. What right have you got to jeopardize your job? Jeopardize the
340   security of us all? How do you think we'd manage if you were—

TOM. Listen! You think I'm crazy about the *warehouse*? [*He bends fiercely
    toward her slight figure.*] You think I'm in love with the Continental Shoe-
    makers? You think I want to spend fifty-five *years* down there in that—
    celotex interior! with—*fluorescent—tubes!* Look! I'd rather somebody picked
    up a crowbar and battered out my brains—than go back mornings! I *go!*
    Every time you come in yelling that Goddamn *"Rise and Shine!" "Rise and
    Shine!"* I say to myself, "How *lucky dead* people are!" But I get up. I *go!* For
    sixty-five dollars a month I give up all that I dream of doing and being
    ever! And you say self—*self's* all I ever think of. Why, listen, if self is what
350   I thought of, Mother, I'd be where he is—GONE! [*He points to his father's
    picture.*] As far as the system of transportation reaches! [*He starts past her.
    She grabs his arm.*] Don't grab at me, Mother!

AMANDA. Where are you going?

TOM. I'm going to the *movies!*

AMANDA. I don't believe that lie!

[TOM *crouches toward her, overtowering her tiny figure. She backs away, gasping.*]

TOM. I'm going to opium dens! Yes, opium dens, dens of vice and criminals'
    hangouts, Mother. I've joined the Hogan Gang, I'm a hired assassin, I
    carry a tommy gun in a violin case! I run a string of cat houses in the
    Valley! They call me Killer, Killer Wingfield, I'm leading a double-life, a
360   simple, honest warehouse worker by day, by night a dynamic *czar* of the
    underworld, Mother. I go to gambling casinos, I spin away fortunes on the

roulette table! I wear a patch over one eye and a false mustache, sometimes I put on green whiskers. On those occasions they call me—*El Diablo!*
Oh, I could tell you many things to make you sleepless! My enemies plan
to dynamite this place. They're going to blow us all sky-high some night!
I'll be glad, very happy, and so will you! You'll go up, up on a broomstick,
over Blue Mountain with seventeen gentlemen callers! You ugly—babbling old—*witch.* . . . [*He goes through a series of violent, clumsy movements,
seizing his overcoat, lunging to the door, pulling it fiercely open. The women watch
370   him, aghast. His arm catches in the sleeve of his coat as he struggles to pull it on.
For a moment he is pinioned by the bulky garment. With an outraged groan he tears
the coat off again, splitting the shoulder of it, and hurls it across the room. It strikes
against the shelf of* LAURA's *glass collection, and there is a tinkle of shattering glass.*
LAURA *cries out as if wounded.*]

[*Music.*]

[*Screen legend:* "The Glass Menagerie."]

LAURA [*shrilly*].   My *glass!*—menagerie. . . . [*She covers her face and turns away.*]

[*But* AMANDA *is still stunned and stupefied by the "ugly witch" so that she barely notices
this occurrence. Now she recovers her speech.*]

AMANDA [*in an awful voice*].   I won't speak to you—until you apologize!

[*She crosses through the portieres and draws them together behind her.* TOM *is left with*
LAURA. LAURA *clings weakly to the mantel with her face averted.* TOM *stares at her
stupidly for a moment. Then he crosses to the shelf. He drops awkwardly on his knees
to collect the fallen glass, glancing at* LAURA *as if he would speak but couldn't.*]

["*The Glass Menagerie*" *music steals in as the scene dims out.*]

SCENE IV

*The interior of the apartment is dark. There is a faint light in the alley. A deep-voiced
bell in a church is tolling the hour of five.*
    TOM *appears at the top of the alley. After each solemn boom of the bell in the tower,
he shakes a little noisemaker or rattle as if to express the tiny spasm of man in contrast
to the sustained power and dignity of the Almighty. This and the unsteadiness of his
advance make it evident that he has been drinking. As he climbs the few steps to the fire
escape landing light steals up inside.* LAURA *appears in the front room in a nightdress.
She notices that* TOM's *bed is empty.* TOM *fishes in his pockets for his door key,
removing a motley assortment of articles in the search, including a shower of movie
ticket stubs and an empty bottle. At last he finds the key, but just as he is about to insert
it, it slips from his finger. He strikes a match and crouches below the door.*]

TOM [*bitterly*].   One crack—and it falls through!

[LAURA *opens the door.*]

LAURA.   Tom! Tom, what are you doing?
TOM.   Looking for a door key.
380   LAURA.   Where have you been all this time?

Tom.   I have been to the movies.

Laura.   All this time at the movies?

Tom.   There was a very long program. There was a Garbo[18] picture and a
Mickey Mouse and a travelogue and a newsreel and a preview of coming
attractions. And there was an organ solo and a collection for the Milk
Fund—simultaneously—which ended up in a terrible fight between a fat
lady and an usher!

Laura [*innocently*].   Did you have to stay through everything?

Tom.   Of course! And, oh, I forgot! There was a big stage show! The head-
390   liner on this stage show was Malvolio the Magician. He performed wonderful tricks, many of them, such as pouring water back and forth between
pitchers. First it turned to wine and then it turned to beer and then it
turned to whisky. I know it was whisky it finally turned into because he
needed somebody to come up out of the audience to help him and I came
up—both shows! It was Kentucky Straight Bourbon. A very generous fellow, he gave souvenirs. [*He pulls from his back pocket a shimmering rainbow-
colored scarf.*] He gave me this. This is his magic scarf. You can have it,
Laura. You wave it over a canary cage and you get a bowl of goldfish. You
wave it over the goldfish bowl and they fly away canaries. . . . But the
400   wonderfullest trick of all was the coffin trick. We nailed him into a coffin
and he got out of the coffin without removing one nail. [*He has come inside.*]
There is a trick that would come in handy for me—get me out of this
two-by-four situation! [*He flops onto the bed and starts removing his shoes.*]

Laura.   Tom—shhh!

Tom.   What're you shushing me for?

Laura.   You'll wake up Mother.

Tom.   Goody, goody! Pay 'er back for all those "Rise an' Shines." [*He lies
down, groaning.*] You know it don't take much intelligence to get yourself
into a nailed-up coffin, Laura. But who in hell ever got himself out of one
410   without removing one nail?

[*As if in answer, the father's grinning photograph lights up. The scene dims out.*]

[*Immediately following, the church bell is heard striking six. At the sixth stroke the
alarm clock goes off in* Amanda's *room, and after a few moments we hear her calling:
"Rise and Shine! Rise and Shine!* Laura, *go tell your brother to rise and shine!"*]

Tom [*sitting up slowly*].   I'll rise—but I won't shine.

[*The light increases.*]

Amanda.   Laura, tell your brother his coffee is ready.

[Laura *slips into the front room.*]

Laura.   Tom!—It's nearly seven. Don't make Mother nervous. [*He stares at
her stupidly. Beseechingly:*] Tom, speak to Mother this morning. Make up
with her, apologize, speak to her!

Tom.   She won't to me. It's her that started not speaking.

Laura.   If you just say you're sorry she'll start speaking.

---

[18] Greta Garbo (1905–1990) a Swedish film actress renowned for her beauty and her aura
of detachment.

TOM.   Her not speaking—is that such a tragedy?

LAURA.   Please—please!

420 AMANDA [*calling from the kitchenette*].   Laura, are you going to do what I asked you to do, or do I have to get dressed and go out myself?

LAURA.   Going, going—soon as I get on my coat! [*She pulls on a shapeless felt hat with a nervous, jerky movement, pleadingly glancing at* TOM. *She rushes awkwardly for her coat. The coat is one of* AMANDA's, *inaccurately made-over, the sleeves too short for* LAURA.] Butter and what else?

AMANDA [*entering from the kitchenette*].   Just butter. Tell them to charge it.

LAURA.   Mother, they make such faces when I do that.

AMANDA.   Sticks and stones can break our bones, but the expression on Mr. Garfinkel's face won't harm us! Tell your brother his coffee is getting
430 cold.

LAURA [*at the door*].   Do what I asked you, will you, will you, Tom?

[*He looks sullenly away.*]

AMANDA.   Laura, go now or just don't go at all!

LAURA [*rushing out*].   Going—going!

[*A second later she cries out.* TOM *springs up and crosses to the door.* TOM *opens the door.*]

TOM.   Laura?

LAURA.   I'm all right. I slipped, but I'm all right.

AMANDA [*peering anxiously after her*].   If anyone breaks a leg on those fire-escape steps, the landlord ought to be sued for every cent he possesses!

[*She shuts the door. Now she remembers she isn't speaking to* TOM *and returns to the other room.*]

[*As* TOM *comes listlessly for his coffee, she turns her back to him and stands rigidly facing the window on the gloomy gray vault of the areaway. Its light on her face with its aged but childish features is cruelly sharp, satirical as a Daumier[19] print.*]

[*The music of "Ave Maria" is heard softly.*]

[TOM *glances sheepishly but sullenly at her averted figure and slumps at the table. The coffee is scalding hot; he sips it and gasps and spits it back in the cup. At his gasp,* AMANDA *catches her breath and half turns. Then she catches herself and turns back to the window.* TOM *blows on his coffee, glancing sidewise at his mother. She clears her throat.* TOM *clears his. He starts to rise, sinks back down again, scratches his head, clears his throat again.* AMANDA *coughs.* TOM *raises his cup in both hands to blow on it, his eyes staring over the rim of it at his mother for several moments. Then he slowly sets the cup down and awkwardly and hesitantly rises from the chair.*]

TOM [*hoarsely*].   Mother. I—I apologize, Mother. [AMANDA *draws a quick, shuddering breath. Her face works grotesquely. She breaks into childlike tears.*]

---

[19] Honoré Daumier (1808–1879), a French lithographer, painter, and sculptor whose satirical prints often lampooned politicians.

440 I'm sorry for what I said, for everything that I said, I didn't mean it.

AMANDA [*sobbingly*].   My devotion has made me a witch and so I make myself hateful to my children!

TOM.   *No, you* don't.

AMANDA.   I worry so much, don't sleep, it makes me nervous!

TOM [*gently*].   I understand that.

AMANDA.   I've had to put up a solitary battle all these years. But you're my right-hand bower![20] Don't fall down, don't fail!

TOM [*gently*].   I try, Mother.

AMANDA [*with great enthusiasm*].   Try and you will *succeed!* [*The notion makes her*
450 *breathless.*] Why, you—you're just *full* of natural endowments! Both my children—they're *unusual* children! Don't you think I know it? I'm so— *proud!* Happy and—feel I've—so much to be thankful for but—promise me one thing, son!

TOM.   What, Mother?

AMANDA.   Promise, son, you'll—never be a drunkard!

TOM [*turns to her grinning*].   I will never be a drunkard, Mother.

AMANDA.   That's what frightened me so, that you'd be drinking! Eat a bowl of Purina!

TOM.   Just coffee, Mother.

460 AMANDA.   Shredded wheat biscuit?

TOM.   No. No, Mother, just coffee.

AMANDA.   You can't put in a day's work on an empty stomach. You've got ten minutes—don't gulp! Drinking too-hot liquids makes cancer of the stomach. . . . Put cream in.

TOM.   No, thank you.

AMANDA.   To cool it.

TOM.   No! No, thank you, I want it black.

AMANDA.   I know, but it's not good for you. We have to do all that we can to build ourselves up. In these trying times we live in, all that we have to cling
470 to is—each other. . . . That's why it's so important to—Tom, I—I sent out your sister so I could discuss something with you. If you hadn't spoken I would have spoken to you. [*She sits down.*]

TOM [*gently*].   What is it, Mother, that you want to discuss?

AMANDA.   *Laura!*

[TOM *puts his cup down slowly.*]

[*Legend on screen:* "Laura." *Music:* "The Glass Menagerie."]

TOM.   —Oh.—Laura . . .

AMANDA [*touching his sleeve*].   You know how Laura is. So quiet but—still water runs deep! She notices things and I think she—broods about them. [TOM *looks up.*] A few days ago I came in and she was crying.

TOM.   What about?

480 AMANDA.   You.

TOM.   Me?

AMANDA.   She has an idea that you're not happy here.

---

[20] The Jack of trumps, the highest card in certain card games.

TOM. What gave her that idea?

AMANDA. What gives her any idea? However, you do act strangely. I—I'm not criticizing, understand *that!* I know your ambitions do not lie in the warehouse, that like everybody in the whole wide world—you've had to—make sacrifices, but—Tom—Tom—life's not easy, it calls for—Spartan endurance! There's so many things in my heart that I cannot describe to you! I've never told you but I—*loved*—your father....

490 TOM [*gently*]. I know that, Mother.

AMANDA. And you—when I see you taking after his ways! Staying out late—and—well, you *had* been drinking the night you were in that—terrifying condition! Laura says that you hate the apartment and that you go out nights to get away from it! Is that true, Tom?

TOM. No. You say there's so much in your heart that you can't describe to me. That's true of me, too. There's so much in my heart that I can't describe to *you!* So let's respect each other's—

AMANDA. But, why—*why*, Tom—are you always so *restless?* Where do you *go* to, nights?

500 TOM. I—go to the movies.

AMANDA. Why do you go to the movies so much, Tom?

TOM. I go to the movies because—I like adventure. Adventure is something I don't have much of at work, so I go to the movies.

AMANDA. But, Tom, you go to the movies *entirely* too *much!*

TOM. I like a lot of adventure.

[AMANDA *looks baffled, then hurt. As the familiar inquisition resumes,* TOM *becomes hard and impatient again.* AMANDA *slips back into her querulous attitude toward him.*]

[*Image on screen:* A sailing vessel with Jolly Roger.]

AMANDA. Most young men find adventure in their careers.

TOM. Then most young men are not employed in a warehouse.

AMANDA. The world is full of young men employed in warehouses and offices and factories.

510 TOM. Do all of them find adventure in their careers?

AMANDA. They do or they do without it! Not everybody has a craze for adventure.

TOM. Man is by instinct a lover, a hunter, a fighter, and none of those instincts are given much play at the warehouse!

AMANDA. Man is by instinct! Don't quote instinct to me! Instinct is something that people have got away from! It belongs to animals! Christian adults don't want it!

TOM. What do Christian adults want, then, Mother?

AMANDA. Superior things! Things of the mind and the spirit! Only animals 520 have to satisfy instincts! Surely your aims are somewhat higher than theirs! Than monkeys—pigs—

TOM. I reckon they're not.

AMANDA. You're joking. However, that isn't what I wanted to discuss.

TOM [*rising*]. I haven't much time.

AMANDA [*pushing his shoulders*]. Sit down.

TOM. You want me to punch in red at the warehouse, Mother?

AMANDA.   You have five minutes. I want to talk about Laura.

[*Screen legend:* "Plans and Provisions."]

Tom.   All right! What about Laura?

AMANDA.   We have to be making some plans and provisions for her. She's
530   older than you, two years, and nothing has happened. She just drifts along
        doing nothing. It frightens me terribly how she just drifts along.

Tom.   I guess she's the type that people call home girls.

AMANDA.   There's no such type, and if there is, it's a pity! That is unless the
        home is hers, with a husband!

Tom.   What?

AMANDA.   Oh, I can see the handwriting on the wall as plain as I see the nose
        in front of my face! It's terrifying! More and more you remind me of your
        father! He was out all hours without explanation!—Then *left! Goodbye!* And
        me with the bag to hold. I saw that letter you got from the Merchant
540   Marine. I know what you're dreaming of. I'm not standing here blind-
        folded. [*She pauses.*] Very well, then. Then *do* it! But not till there's some-
        body to take your place.

Tom.   What do you mean?

AMANDA.   I mean that as soon as Laura has got somebody to take care of her,
        married, a home of her own, independent—why, then you'll be free to go
        wherever you please, on land, on sea, whichever way the wind blows you!
        But until that time you've got to look out for your sister. I don't say me
        because I'm old and don't matter! I say for your sister because she's young
        and dependent.
550   I put her in business college—a dismal failure! Frightened her so it
        made her sick at the stomach. I took her over to the Young People's
        League at the church. Another fiasco. She spoke to nobody, nobody spoke
        to her. Now all she does is fool with those pieces of glass and play those
        worn-out records. What kind of life is that for a girl to lead?

Tom.   What can I do about it?

AMANDA.   Overcome selfishness! Self, self, self is all that you ever think of!

[*Tom springs up and crosses to get his coat. It is ugly and bulky. He pulls on a cap
with earmuffs.*]

Where is your muffler? Put your wool muffler on!

[*He snatches it angrily from the closet, tosses it around his neck and pulls both ends
tight.*]

Tom! I haven't said what I had in mind to ask you.

Tom.   I'm too late to—

560 AMANDA [*catching his arm—very importunately; then shyly*].   Down at the ware-
        house, aren't there some—nice young men?

Tom.   No!

AMANDA.   There *must* be—*some* . . .

Tom.   Mother—[*He gestures.*]

AMANDA.   Find out one that's clean-living—doesn't drink and ask him out for
        sister!

Tom. What?
Amanda. For *sister!* To *meet!* Get *acquainted!*
Tom [*stamping to the door*]. Oh, my *go-osh!*
570 Amanda. Will you? [*He opens the door. She says, imploringly:*] Will you? [*He starts down the fire escape.*] Will you? *Will* you, dear?
Tom [*calling back*]. *Yes!*

[*Amanda closes the door hesitantly and with a troubled but faintly hopeful expression.*]

[*Screen image:* The cover of a glamor magazine.]

[*The spotlight picks up* Amanda *at the phone.*]

Amanda. Ella Cartwright? This is Amanda Wingfield! How are you, honey? How is that kidney condition? [*There is a five-second pause.*] Horrors! [*There is another pause.*] You're a Christian martyr, yes, honey, that's what you are, a Christian matryr! Well, I just now happened to notice in my little red book that your subscription to the *Companion* has just run out! I knew that you wouldn't want to miss out on the wonderful serial starting in this new issue. It's by Bessie May Hopper, the first thing she's written since *Hon-*
580 *eymoon for Three*. Wasn't that a strange and interesting story? Well, this one is even lovelier, I believe. It has a sophisticated, society background. It's all about the horsey set on Long Island!

[*The light fades out.*]

SCENE V

Legend on the screen: "Annunciation."
Music is heard as the light slowly comes on.
It is early dusk of a spring evening. Supper has just been finished in the Wingfield apartment. Amanda *and* Laura, *in light-colored dresses, are removing dishes from the table in the dining room, which is shadowy, their movements formalized almost as a dance or ritual, their moving forms as pale and silent as moths.* Tom, *in white shirt and trousers, rises from the table and crosses toward the fire escape.*

Amanda [*as he passes her*]. Son, will you do me a favor?
Tom. What?
Amanda. Comb your hair! You look so pretty when your hair is combed!

[*Tom slouches on the sofa with the evening paper. Its enormous headline reads:* "Franco[21] Triumphs."]

There is only one respect in which I would like you to emulate your father.
Tom. What respect is that?
Amanda. The care he always took of his appearance. He never allowed himself to look untidy.

[*He throws down the paper and crosses to the fire escape.*]

---

[21] General Francisco Franco (1892–1975), the leader of the Nationalist forces during the Spanish Civil War. His forces triumphed in 1939.

590   Where are you going?

TOM.   I'm going out to smoke.

AMANDA.   You smoke too much. A pack a day at fifteen cents a pack. How much would that amount to in a month? Thirty times fifteen is how much, Tom? Figure it out and you will be astounded at what you could save. Enough to give you a night-school course in accounting at Washington U.! Just think what a wonderful thing that would be for you, son!

[*TOM is unmoved by the thought.*]

TOM.   I'd rather smoke. [*He steps out on the landing, letting the screen door slam.*]

AMANDA [*sharply*].   I know! That's the tragedy of it. . . . [*Alone, she turns to look at her husband's picture.*]

[*Dance music: "The World Is Waiting for the Sunrise!"*]

600 TOM [*to the audience*].   Across the alley from us was the Paradise Dance Hall. On evenings in spring the windows and doors were open and the music came outdoors. Sometimes the lights were turned out except for a large glass sphere that hung from the ceiling. It would turn slowly about and filter the dusk with delicate rainbow colors. Then the orchestra played a waltz or a tango, something that had a slow and sensuous rhythm. Couples would come outside, to the relative privacy of the alley. You could see them kissing behind ash pits and telephone poles. This was the compensation for lives that passed like mine, without any change or adventure. Adventure and change were imminent in this year. They were waiting
610   around the corner for all these kids. Suspended in the mist over Berchtesgaden,[22] caught in the folds of Chamberlain's[23] umbrella. In Spain there was Guernica! But here there was only hot swing music and liquor, dance halls, bars, and movies, and sex that hung in the gloom like a chandelier and flooded the world with brief, deceptive rainbows. . . . All the world was waiting for bombardments!

[AMANDA *turns from the picture and comes outside.*]

AMANDA. [*sighing*].   A fire escape landing's a poor excuse for a porch. [*She spreads a newspaper on a step and sits down, gracefully and demurely as if she were settling into a swing on a Mississippi veranda.*] What are you looking at?

TOM.   The moon.

620 AMANDA.   Is there a moon this evening?

TOM.   It's rising over Garfinkel's Delicatessen.

AMANDA.   So it is! A little silver slipper of a moon. Have you made a wish on it yet?

TOM.   Um-hum.

AMANDA.   What did you wish for?

TOM.   That's a secret.

AMANDA.   A secret, huh? Well, I won't tell mine either. I will be just as mysterious as you.

---

[22] A town in the German Alps, the site of Adolf Hitler's vacation villa.

[23] Neville Chamberlain (1869–1940) was the prime minister of Great Britain who sought to avoid war with Hitler through a policy of appeasement.

TOM. I bet I can guess what yours is.
630 AMANDA. Is my head so transparent?
TOM. You're not a sphinx.
AMANDA. No, I don't have secrets. I'll tell you what I wished for on the moon.
    Success and happiness for my precious children! I wish for that whenever
    there's a moon, and when there isn't a moon, I wish for it, too.
TOM. I thought perhaps you wished for a gentleman caller.
AMANDA. Why do you say that?
TOM. Don't you remember asking me to fetch one?
AMANDA. I remember suggesting that it would be nice for your sister if you
    brought home some nice young man from the warehouse. I think that I've
640   made that suggestion more than once.
TOM. Yes, you have made it repeatedly.
AMANDA. Well?
TOM. We are going to have one.
AMANDA. *What?*
TOM. A gentleman caller!

> [*The annunciation is celebrated with music.*]

> [AMANDA *rises.*]

> [*Image on screen:* A caller with a bouquet.]

AMANDA. You mean you have asked some nice young man to come over?
TOM. Yep. I've asked him to dinner.
AMANDA. You really did?
TOM. I did!
650 AMANDA. You did, and did he—*accept?*
TOM. He did!
AMANDA. Well, well—well, well! That's—lovely!
TOM. I thought that you would be pleased.
AMANDA. It's definite then.
TOM. Very definite.
AMANDA. Soon?
TOM. Very soon.
AMANDA. For heaven's sake, stop putting on and tell me some things, will
    you?
660 TOM. What things do you want me to tell you?
AMANDA. *Naturally* I would like to know when he's *coming!*
TOM. He's coming tomorrow.
AMANDA. *Tomorrow?*
TOM. Yep. Tomorrow.
AMANDA. But, Tom!
TOM. Yes, Mother?
AMANDA. Tomorrow gives me no time!
TOM. Time for what?
AMANDA. Preparations! Why didn't you phone me at once, as soon as you
670   asked him, the minute that he accepted? Then, don't you see, I could have
    been getting ready!
TOM. You don't have to make any fuss.

AMANDA.   Oh, Tom, Tom, Tom, of course I have to make a fuss! I want things nice, not sloppy! Not thrown together. I'll certainly have to do some fast thinking, won't I?

TOM.   I don't see why you have to think at all.

AMANDA.   You just don't know. We can't have a gentleman caller in a pigsty! All my wedding silver has to be polished, the monogrammed table linen ought to be laundered! The windows have to be washed and fresh curtains
680   put up. And how about clothes? We have to *wear* something, don't we?

TOM.   Mother, this boy is no one to make a fuss over!

AMANDA.   Do you realize he's the first young man we've introduced to your sister? It's terrible, dreadful, disgraceful that poor little sister has never received a single gentleman caller! Tom, come inside! [*She opens the screen door.*]

TOM.   What for?

AMANDA.   I want to ask you some things.

TOM.   If you're going to make such a fuss, I'll call it off, I'll tell him not to come!

690   AMANDA.   You certainly won't do anything of the kind. Nothing offends people worse than broken engagements. It simply means I'll have to work like a Turk! We won't be brilliant, but we will pass inspection. Come on inside. [TOM *follows her inside, groaning.*] Sit down.

TOM.   Any particular place you would like me to sit?

AMANDA.   Thank heavens I've got that new sofa! I'm also making payments on a floor lamp I'll have sent out! And put the chintz covers on, they'll brighten things up! Of course I'd hoped to have these walls re-papered. . . . What is the young man's name?

TOM.   His name is O'Connor.

700   AMANDA.   That, of course, means fish—tomorrow is Friday! I'll have that salmon loaf—with Durkee's dressing! What does he do? He works at the warehouse?

TOM.   Of course! How else would I—

AMANDA.   Tom, he—doesn't drink?

TOM.   Why do you ask me that?

AMANDA.   Your father *did!*

TOM.   Don't get started on that!

AMANDA.   He *does* drink, then?

TOM.   Not that I know of!

710   AMANDA.   Make sure, be certain! The last thing I want for my daughter's a boy who drinks!

TOM.   Aren't you being a little bit premature? Mr. O'Connor has not yet appeared on the scene!

AMANDA.   But will tomorrow. To meet your sister, and what do I know about his character? Nothing! Old maids are better off than wives of drunkards!

TOM.   Oh, my God!

AMANDA.   Be still!

TOM [*leaning forward to whisper*].   Lots of fellows meet girls whom they don't marry!

720   AMANDA.   Oh, talk sensibly, Tom—and don't be sarcastic! [*She has gotten a hairbrush.*]

TOM.   What are you doing?

AMANDA. I'm brushing that cowlick down! [*She attacks his hair with the brush.*] What is this young man's position at the warehouse?

TOM [*submitting grimly to the brush and the interrogation*]. This young man's position is that of a shipping clerk, Mother.

AMANDA. Sounds to me like a fairly responsible job, the sort of a job *you* would be in if you just had more *get-up*. What is his salary? Have you any idea?

730 TOM. I would judge it to be approximately eighty-five dollars a month.

AMANDA. Well—not princely, but—

TOM. Twenty more than I make.

AMANDA. Yes, how well I know! But for a family man, eighty-five dollars a month is not much more than you can just get by on. . . .

TOM. Yes, but Mr. O'Connor is not a family man.

AMANDA. He might be, mightn't he? Some time in the future?

TOM. I see. Plans and provisions.

AMANDA. You are the only young man that I know of who ignores the fact that the future becomes the present, the present the past, and the past

740 turns into everlasting regret if you don't plan for it!

TOM. I will think that over and see what I can make of it.

AMANDA. Don't be supercilious with your mother! Tell me some more about this—what do you call him?

TOM. James D. O'Connor. The D. is for Delaney.

AMANDA. Irish on *both* sides! *Gracious!* And doesn't drink?

TOM. Shall I call him up and ask him right this minute?

AMANDA. The only way to find out about those things is to make discreet inquiries at the proper moment. When I was a girl in Blue Mountain and it was suspected that a young man drank, the girl whose attentions he had

750 been receiving, if any girl *was*, would sometimes speak to the minister of his and sort of feel him out on the young man's character. That is the way such things are discreetly handled to keep a young woman from making a tragic mistake!

TOM. Then how did you happen to make a tragic mistake?

AMANDA. That innocent look of your father's had everyone fooled! He *smiled*—the world was *enchanted!* No girl can do worse than put herself at the mercy of a handsome appearance! I hope that Mr. O'Connor is not too good-looking.

TOM. No, he's not too good-looking. He's covered with freckles and hasn't

760 too much of a nose.

AMANDA. He's not right-down homely, though?

TOM. Not right-down homely. Just medium homely, I'd say.

AMANDA. Character's what to look for in a man.

TOM. That's what I've always said, Mother.

AMANDA. You've never said anything of the kind and I suspect you would never give it a thought.

TOM. Don't be suspicious of me.

AMANDA. At least I hope he's the type that's up and coming.

TOM. I think he really goes in for self-improvement.

770 AMANDA. What reason have you to think so?

TOM. He goes to night school.

AMANDA [*beaming*]. Splendid! What does he do, I mean study?

Toм.   Radio engineering and public speaking!

AMANDA.   Then he has visions of being advanced in the world! Any young man who studies public speaking is aiming to have an executive job some day! And radio engineering? A thing for the future! Both of these facts are very illuminating. Those are the sort of things that a mother should know concerning any young man who comes to call on her daughter. Seriously or—not.

780 Toм.   One little warning. He doesn't know about Laura. I didn't let on that we had dark ulterior motives. I just said, why don't you come and have dinner with us? He said okay and that was the whole conversation.

AMANDA.   I bet it was! You're eloquent as an oyster. However, he'll know about Laura when he gets here. When he sees how lovely and sweet and pretty she is, he'll thank his lucky stars he was asked to dinner.

Toм.   Mother, you mustn't expect too much of Laura.

AMANDA.   What do you mean?

Toм.   Laura seems all those things to you and me because she's ours and we love her. We don't even notice she's crippled any more.

790 AMANDA.   Don't say crippled! You know that I never allow that word to be used!

Toм.   But face facts, Mother. She is and—that's not all—

AMANDA.   What do you mean "not all?"

Toм.   Laura is very different from other girls.

AMANDA.   I think the difference is all to her advantage.

Toм.   Not quite all—in the eyes of others—strangers—she's terribly shy and lives in a world of her own and those things make her seem a little peculiar to people outside the house.

AMANDA.   Don't say peculiar.

800 Toм.   Face the facts. She is.

[*The dance hall music changes to a tango that has a minor and somewhat ominous tone.*]

AMANDA.   In what way is she peculiar—may I ask?

Toм [*gently*].   She lives in a world of her own—a world of little glass ornaments, Mother. . . .

[*He gets up.* AMANDA *remains holding the brush, looking at him, troubled.*]

She plays old phonograph records and—that's about all—[*He glances at himself in the mirror and crosses to the door.*]

AMANDA [*sharply*].   Where are you going?

Toм.   I'm going to the movies. [*He goes out the screen door.*]

AMANDA.   Not to the movies, every night to the movies! [*She follows quickly to the screen door.*] I don't believe you always go to the movies! [*He is gone.*

810 AMANDA *looks worriedly after him for a moment. Then vitality and optimism return and she turns from the door, crossing to the portieres.*] Laura, Laura!

[LAURA *answers from the kitchenette.*]

LAURA.   Yes, Mother.

AMANDA.   Let those dishes go and come in front! [LAURA *appears with a dish towel.* Amanda *speaks to her gaily.*] Laura, come here and make a wish on the moon!

[*Screen image:* The Moon.]

Laura [*entering*].   Moon—moon?

Amanda.   A little silver slipper of a moon. Look over your left shoulder, Laura, and make a wish! [Laura *looks faintly puzzled as if called out of sleep.* Amanda *seizes her shoulders and turns her at an angle by the door.*] Now! Now, 820   darling, *wish!*

Laura.   What shall I wish for, Mother?

Amanda [*her voice trembling and her eyes suddenly filling with tears*].   Happiness! Good fortune!

[*The sound of the violin rises and the stage dims out.*]

SCENE VI

The light comes up on the escape landing. Tom *is leaning against the grill, smoking.*
[*Screen image:* The high school hero.]

Tom.   And so the following evening I brought Jim home to dinner. I had known Jim slightly in high school. In high school Jim was a hero. He had tremendous Irish good nature and vitality with the scrubbed and polished look of white chinaware. He seemed to move in a continual spotlight. He was a star in basketball, captain of the debating club, president of the senior class and the glee club and he sang the male lead in the annual light 830   operas. He was always running or bounding, never just walking. He seemed always at the point of defeating the law of gravity. He was shooting with such velocity through his adolescence that you would logically expect him to arrive at nothing short of the White House by the time he was thirty. But Jim apparently ran into more interference after his graduation from Soldan. His speed had definitely slowed. Six years after he left high school he was holding a job that wasn't much better than mine.

[*Screen image:* The Clerk.]

He was the only one at the warehouse with whom I was on friendly terms. I was valuable to him as someone who could remember his former glory, who had seen him win basketball games and the silver cup in debating. He 840   knew of my secret practice of retiring to a cabinet of the washroom to work on poems when business was slack in the warehouse. He called me Shakespeare. And while the other boys in the warehouse regarded me with suspicious hostility, Jim took a humorous attitude toward me. Gradually his attitude affected the others, their hostility wore off and they also began to smile at me as people smile at an oddly fashioned dog who trots across their path at some distance.

I knew that Jim and Laura had known each other at Soldan, and I had heard Laura speak admiringly of his voice. I didn't know if Jim remembered her or not. In high school Laura had been as unobtrusive as Jim had 850   been astonishing. If he did remember Laura, it was not as my sister, for

when I asked him to dinner, he grinned and said, "You know, Shakespeare, I never thought of you as having folks!"
 He was about to discover that I did. . . .

[*Legend on screen:* "The accent of a coming foot."]

[*The light dims out on* TOM *and comes up in the Wingfield living room—a delicate
lemony light. It is about five on a Friday evening of late spring which comes "scattering poems in the sky."*]

[AMANDA *has worked like a Turk in preparation for the gentleman caller. The results are astonishing. The new floor lamp with its rose silk shade is in place, a
colored paper lantern conceals the broken light fixture in the ceiling, new billowing
white curtains are at the windows, chintz covers are on the chairs and sofa, a pair
of new sofa pillows make their initial appearance. Open boxes and tissue paper are
scattered on the floor.*]

[LAURA *stands in the middle of the room with lifted arms while* AMANDA *crouches before
her, adjusting the hem of a new dress, devout and ritualistic. The dress is colored and
designed by memory. The arrangement of* LAURA'S *hair is changed; it is softer and more
becoming. A fragile, unearthly prettiness has come out in* LAURA: *she is like a piece of
translucent glass touched by light, given a momentary radiance, not actual, not
lasting.*]

AMANDA [*impatiently*].   Why are you trembling?
LAURA.   Mother, you've made me so nervous!
AMANDA.   How have I made you nervous?
LAURA.   By all this fuss! You make it seem so important!
AMANDA.   I don't understand you, Laura. You couldn't be satisfied with just
     sitting home, and yet whenever I try to arrange something for you, you
860   seem to resist it. [*She gets up.*] Now take a look at yourself. No, wait! Wait
     just a moment—I have an idea!
LAURA.   What is it now?

[AMANDA *produces two powder puffs which she wraps in handkerchiefs and stuffs in*
LAURA'S *bosom.*]

LAURA.   Mother, what are you doing?
AMANDA.   They call them "Gay Deceivers"!
LAURA.   I won't wear them!
AMANDA.   You will!
LAURA.   Why should I?
AMANDA.   Because, to be painfully honest, your chest is flat.
LAURA.   You make it seem like we were setting a trap.
870 AMANDA.   All pretty girls are a trap, a pretty trap, and men expect them to
     be.

[*Legend on screen:* "A pretty trap."]

 Now look at yourself, young lady. This is the prettiest you will ever be! [*She
 stands back to admire* LAURA.] I've got to fix myself now! You're going to be
 surprised by your mother's appearance!

[AMANDA *crosses through the portieres, humming gaily.* LAURA *moves slowly to the long mirror and stares solemnly at herself. A wind blows the white curtains inward in a slow, graceful motion and with a faint, sorrowful sighing.*]

AMANDA [*from somewhere behind the portieres*].   It isn't dark enough yet.

[LAURA *turns slowly before the mirror with a troubled look.*]

[*Legend on screen:* "This is my sister: Celebrate her with strings!" *Music plays.*]

AMANDA [*laughing, still not visible*].   I'm going to show you something. I'm going to make a spectacular appearance!

LAURA.   What is it, Mother?

AMANDA.   Possess your soul in patience—you will see! Something I've resur-
880   rected from that old trunk! Styles haven't changed so terribly much after all. . . . [*She parts the portieres.*] Now just look at your mother! [*She wears a girlish frock of yellowed voile with a blue silk sash. She carries a bunch of jonquils—the legend of her youth is nearly revived. Now she speaks feverishly:*] This is the dress in which I led the cotillion. Won the cakewalk twice at Sunset Hill, wore one Spring to the Governor's Ball in Jackson! See how I sash-ayed around the ballroom, Laura? [*She raises her skirt and does a mincing step around the room.*] I wore it on Sundays for my gentleman callers! I had it on the day I met your father. . . . I had malaria fever all that Spring. The change of climate from East Tennessee to the Delta—weakened resis-
890   tance. I had a little temperature all the time—not enough to be serious—just enough to make me restless and giddy! Invitations poured in—parties all over the Delta! "Stay in bed," said Mother, "you have a fever!"—but I just wouldn't. I took quinine but kept on going, going! Evenings, dances! Afternoons, long, long rides! Picnics—lovely! So lovely, that country in May—all lacy with dogwood, literally flooded with jonquils! That was the spring I had the craze for jonquils. Jonquils became an absolute obsession. Mother said, "Honey, there's no more room for jonquils." And still I kept on bringing in more jonquils. Whenever, wherever I saw them, I'd say, "Stop! Stop! I see jonquils!" I made the young men help me gather the
900   jonquils! It was a joke, Amanda and her jonquils. Finally there were no more vases to hold them, every available space was filled with jonquils. No vases to hold them? All right, I'll hold them myself! And then I—[*She stops in front of the picture. Music plays.*] met your father! Malaria fever and jonquils and then—this—boy. . . . [*She switches on the rose-colored lamp.*] I hope they get here before it starts to rain. [*She crosses the room and places the jonquils in a bowl on the table.*] I gave your brother a little extra change so he and Mr. O'Connor could take the service car home.

LAURA [*with an altered look*].   What did you say his name was?

AMANDA.   O'Connor.

910   LAURA.   What is his first name?

AMANDA.   I don't remember. Oh, yes, I do. It was—Jim!

[LAURA *sways slightly and catches hold of a chair.*]

[*Legend on screen:* "Not Jim!"]

LAURA [*faintly*]:   Not—Jim!

AMANDA.   Yes, that was it, it was Jim! I've never known a Jim that wasn't nice!

[*The music becomes ominous.*]

LAURA.   Are you sure his name is Jim O'Connor?
AMANDA.   Yes. Why?
LAURA.   Is he the one that Tom used to know in high school?
AMANDA.   He didn't say so. I think he just got to know him at the warehouse.
LAURA.   There was a Jim O'Connor we both knew in high school—[*then, with effort*] If that is the one that Tom is bringing to dinner—you'll have to
920   excuse me, I won't come to the table.
AMANDA.   What sort of nonsense is this?
LAURA.   You asked me once if I'd ever liked a boy. Don't you remember I showed you this boy's picture?
AMANDA.   You mean the boy you showed me in the yearbook?
LAURA.   Yes, that boy.
AMANDA.   Laura, Laura, were you in love with that boy?
LAURA.   I don't know, Mother. All I know is I couldn't sit at the table if it was him!
AMANDA.   It won't be him! It isn't the least bit likely. But whether it is or not,
930   you will come to the table. You will not be excused.
LAURA.   I'll have to be, Mother.
AMANDA.   I don't intend to humor your silliness, Laura. I've had too much from you and your brother, both! So just sit down and compose yourself till they come. Tom has forgotten his key so you'll have to let them in, when they arrive.
LAURA [*panicky*].   Oh, Mother—*you* answer the door!
AMANDA [*lightly*].   I'll be in the kitchen—busy!
LAURA.   Oh, Mother, please answer the door, don't make me do it!
AMANDA [*crossing into the kitchenette*].   I've got to fix the dressing for the
940   salmon. Fuss, fuss—silliness!—over a gentleman caller!

[*The door swings shut.* LAURA *is left alone.*]

[*Legend on screen:* "Terror!"]

[*She utters a low moan and turns off the lamp—sits stiffly on the edge of the sofa, knotting her fingers together.*]

[*Legend on screen:* "The Opening of a Door!"]

[Tom *and* JIM *appear on the fire escape steps and climb to the landing. Hearing their approach,* LAURA *rises with a panicky gesture. She retreats to the portieres. The doorbell rings.* LAURA *catches her breath and touches her throat. Low drums sound.*]

AMANDA [*calling*].   Laura, sweetheart! The door!

[LAURA *stares at it without moving.*]

JIM.   I think we just beat the rain.
TOM.   Uh-huh. [*He rings again, nervously.* JIM *whistles and fishes for a cigarette.*]

AMANDA [*very, very gaily*]. Laura, that is your brother and Mr. O'Connor! Will you let them in, darling?

[LAURA *crosses toward the kitchenette door.*]

LAURA [*breathlessly*]. Mother—you go to the door! [AMANDA *steps out of the kitchenette and stares furiously at* LAURA. *She points imperiously at the door.*]
LAURA. Please, please!
AMANDA [*in a fierce whisper*]. What is the matter with you, you silly thing?
950 LAURA [*desperately*]. Please, you answer it, *please!*
AMANDA. I told you I wasn't going to humor you, Laura. Why have you chosen this moment to lose your mind?
LAURA. Please, please, please, you go!
AMANDA. You'll have to go to the door because I can't!
LAURA [*despairingly*]. I can't either!
AMANDA. *Why?*
LAURA. I'm *sick!*
AMANDA. I'm sick, too—of your nonsense! Why can't you and your brother be normal people? Fantastic whims and behavior! [TOM *gives a long ring.*]
960 Preposterous goings on! Can you give me one reason—[*She calls out lyrically.*] Coming! Just one second!—why you should be afraid to open a door? Now you answer it, Laura!
LAURA. Oh, oh, oh . . . [*She returns through the portieres, darts to the Victrola, winds it frantically and turns it on.*]
AMANDA. Laura Wingfield, you march right to that door!
LAURA. Yes—yes, Mother!

[*A faraway, scratchy rendition of "Dardanella" softens the air and gives her strength to move through it. She slips to the door and draws it cautiously open.* TOM *enters with the caller,* JIM O'CONNOR.]

TOM. Laura, this is Jim. Jim, this is my sister, Laura.
JIM [*stepping inside*]. I didn't know that Shakespeare had a sister!
LAURA [*retreating, stiff and trembling, from the door*]. How—how do you do?
970 JIM [*heartily, extending his hand*]. Okay!

[LAURA *touches it hesitantly with hers.*]

JIM. Your hand's *cold*, Laura!
LAURA. Yes, well—I've been playing the Victrola. . . .
JIM. Must have been playing classical music on it! You ought to play a little hot swing music to warm you up!
LAURA. Excuse me—I haven't finished playing the Victrola. . . . [*She turns awkwardly and hurries into the front room. She pauses a second by the Victrola. Then she catches her breath and darts through the portieres like a frightened deer.*]
JIM [*grinning*]. What was the matter?
TOM. Oh—with Laura? Laura is—terribly shy.
980 JIM. Shy, huh? It's unusual to meet a shy girl nowadays. I don't believe you ever mentioned you had a sister.
TOM. Well, now you know. I have one. Here is the *Post Dispatch.* You want a piece of it?

JIM.   Uh-huh.

TOM.   What piece? The comics?

JIM.   Sports! [*He glances at it.*] Ole Dizzy Dean is on his bad behavior.

TOM [*uninterested*].   Yeah? [*He lights a cigarette and goes over to the fire-escape door.*]

JIM.   Where are *you* going?

990   TOM.   I'm going out on the terrace.

JIM [*going after him*].   You know, Shakespeare—I'm going to sell you a bill of goods!

TOM.   What goods?

JIM.   A course I'm taking.

TOM.   Huh?

JIM.   In public speaking! You and me, we're not the warehouse type.

TOM.   Thanks—that's good news. But what has public speaking got to do with it?

JIM.   It fits you for—executive positions!

1000   TOM.   Awww.

JIM.   I tell you it's done a helluva lot for me.

[*Image on screen:* Executive at his desk.]

TOM.   In what respect?

JIM.   In every! Ask yourself what is the difference between you an' me and men in the office down front? Brains?—No!—Ability?—No! Then what? Just one little thing—

TOM.   What is that one little thing?

JIM.   Primarily it amounts to—social poise! Being able to square up to people and hold your own on any social level!

AMANDA [*from the kitchenette*].   Tom?

1010   TOM.   Yes, Mother?

AMANDA.   Is that you and Mr. O'Connor?

TOM.   Yes, Mother.

AMANDA.   Well, you just make yourselves comfortable in there.

TOM.   Yes, Mother.

AMANDA.   Ask Mr. O'Connor if he would like to wash his hands.

JIM.   Aw, no—no—thank you—I took care of that at the warehouse. Tom—

TOM.   Yes?

JIM.   Mr. Mendoza was speaking to me about you.

TOM.   Favorably?

1020   JIM.   What do you think?

TOM.   Well—

JIM.   You're going to be out of a job if you don't wake up.

TOM.   I am waking up—

JIM.   You show no signs.

TOM.   The signs are interior.

[*Image on screen:* The sailing vessel with the Jolly Roger again.]

TOM.   I'm planning to change. [*He leans over the fire-escape rail, speaking with quiet exhilaration. The incandescent marquees and signs of the first-run movie houses light his face from across the alley. He looks like a voyager.*] I'm

right at the point of committing myself to a future that doesn't include
the warehouse and Mr. Mendoza or even a night-school course in public
speaking.

JIM.   What are you gassing about?

TOM.   I'm tired of the movies.

JIM.   Movies!

TOM.   Yes, movies! Look at them—[*a wave toward the marvels of Grand Avenue*]
All of those glamorous people—having adventures—hogging it all, gob-
bling the whole thing up! You know what happens? People go to the
movies instead of *moving!* Hollywood characters are supposed to have all
the adventures for everybody in America, while everybody in America sits
in a dark room and watches them have them! Yes, until there's a war.
That's when adventure becomes available to the masses! *Everyone's* dish,
not only Gable's![24] Then the people in the dark room come out of the
dark room to have some adventures themselves—goody, goody! It's our
turn now, to go to the South Sea Island—to make a safari—to be exotic,
far-off! But I'm not patient. I don't want to wait till then. I'm tired of the
movies and I am *about* to *move!*

JIM [*incredulously*].   Move?

TOM.   Yes.

JIM.   When?

TOM.   Soon!

JIM.   Where? Where?

[*The music seems to answer the question, while* TOM *thinks it over. He searches in his
pockets.*]

TOM.   I'm starting to boil inside. I know I seem dreamy, but inside—well,
I'm boiling! Whenever I pick up a shoe, I shudder a little thinking how
short life is and what I am doing! Whatever that means, I know it
doesn't mean shoes—except as something to wear on a traveler's feet!
[*He finds what he has been searching for in his pockets and holds out a paper
to* JIM.] Look—

JIM.   What?

TOM.   I'm a member.

JIM [*reading*].   The Union of Merchant Seamen.

TOM.   I paid my dues this month, instead of the light bill.

JIM.   You will regret it when they turn the lights off.

TOM.   I won't be here.

JIM.   How about your mother?

TOM.   I'm like my father. The bastard son of a bastard! Did you notice how
he's grinning in his picture in there? And he's been absent going on
sixteen years!

JIM.   You're just talking, you drip. How does your mother feel about it?

TOM.   Shhh! Here comes Mother! Mother is not acquainted with my plans!

AMANDA [*coming through the portieres*].   Where are you all?

TOM.   On the terrace, Mother.

---

[24] Clark Gable (1901–1960), the famous leading man in such films as *Gone With the Wind*
(1940) and *The Misfits* (1960).

[*They start inside. She advances to them.* TOM *is distinctly shocked at her appearance. Even* JIM *blinks a little. He is making his first contact with girlish Southern vivacity and in spite of the night-school course in public speaking is somewhat thrown off the beam by the unexpected outlay of social charm. Certain responses are attempted by* JIM *but are swept aside by* AMANDA'S *gay laughter and chatter.* TOM *is embarrassed but after the first shock* JIM *reacts very warmly. He grins and chuckles, is altogether won over.*]

[*Image on screen:* Amanda as a girl.]

AMANDA [*coyly smiling, shaking her girlish ringlets*].   Well, well, well, so this is Mr. O'Connor. Introductions entirely unnecessary. I've heard so much about you from my boy. I finally said to him, Tom—good gracious!—why don't you bring this paragon to supper? I'd like to meet this nice young man at the warehouse!—instead of just hearing him sing your praises so much! I don't know why my son is so stand-offish—that's not Southern behavior!

 Let's sit down and—I think we could stand a little more air in here!
1080 Tom, leave the door open. I felt a nice fresh breeze a moment ago. Where has it gone to? Mmm, so warm already! And not quite summer, even. We're going to burn up when summer really gets started. However, we're having—we're having a very light supper. I think light things are better fo' this time of year. The same as light clothes are. Light clothes an' light food are what warm weather calls fo'. You know our blood gets so thick during th' winter—it takes a while fo' us to *adjust* ou'selves!—when the season changes . . . It's come so quick this year. I wasn't prepared. All of a sud-den—heavens! Already summer! I ran to the trunk an' pulled out this light dress—terribly old! Historical almost! But feels so good—so good an'
1090 co-ol, y' know. . . .
TOM.   Mother—
AMANDA.   Yes, honey?
TOM.   How about—supper?
AMANDA.   Honey, you go ask Sister if supper is ready! You know that Sister is in full charge of supper! Tell her you hungry boys are waiting for it. [*to* JIM] Have you met Laura?
JIM.   She—
AMANDA.   Let you in? Oh, good, you've met already! It's rare for a girl as sweet an' pretty as Laura to be domestic! But Laura is, thank heavens, not
1100 only pretty but also very domestic. I'm not at all. I never was a bit. I never could make anything but angel-food cake. Well, in the South we had so many servants. Gone, gone, gone. All vestige of gracious living! Gone completely! I wasn't prepared for what the future brought me. All of my gentleman callers were sons of planters and of course I assumed that I would be married to one and raise my family on a large piece of land with plenty of servants. But man proposes[25]—and woman accepts the pro-posal! To vary that old, old saying a little bit—I married no planter! I married a man who worked for the telephone company! That gallantly

---

[25] The old saying is, "Man proposes, but God disposes."

smiling gentleman over there! [*She points to the picture.*] A telephone man
1110   who—fell in love with long-distance! Now he travels and I don't even know
where! But what am I going on for about my—tribulations? Tell me
yours—I hope you don't have any! Tom?

Tom [*returning*]. Yes, Mother?

Amanda. Is supper nearly ready?

Tom. It looks to me like supper is on the table.

Amanda. Let me look—[*She rises prettily and looks through the portieres.*] Oh,
lovely! But where is Sister?

Tom. Laura is not feeling well and she says that she thinks she'd better not
come to the table.

1120 Amanda. What? Nonsense! Laura? Oh, Laura!

Laura [*from the kitchenette, faintly*]. Yes, Mother.

Amanda. You really must come to the table. We won't be seated until you
come to the table! Come in, Mr. O'Connor. You sit over there, and I'll . . .
Laura? Laura Wingfield! You're keeping us waiting, honey! We can't say
grace until you come to the table!

[*The kitchenette door is pushed weakly open and* Laura *comes in. She is obviously
quite faint, her lips trembling, her eyes wide and staring. She moves unsteadily toward
the table.*]

[*Screen legend:* "Terror!"]

[*Outside a summer storm is coming on abruptly. The white curtains billow inward at
the windows and there is a sorrowful murmur from the deep blue dusk.*]

[Laura *suddenly stumbles; she catches at a chair with a faint moan.*]

Tom. Laura!

Amanda. Laura! [*There is a clap of thunder.*]

[*Screen legend:* "Ah!"]

[*despairingly*] Why, Laura, you *are* ill, darling! Tom, help your sister into
the living room, dear! Sit in the living room, Laura—rest on the sofa. Well!
1130   [*to* Jim *as* Tom *helps his sister to the sofa in the living room*] Standing over the
hot stove made her ill! I told her that it was just too warm this evening,
but— [Tom *comes back to the table.*] Is Laura all right now?

Tom. Yes.

Amanda. What *is* that? Rain? A nice cool rain has come up! [*She gives* Jim *a
frightened look.*] I think we may—have grace—now . . . [Tom *looks at her
stupidly.*] Tom, honey—you say grace!

Tom. Oh . . . "For these and all thy mercies—"

[*They bow their heads,* Amanda *stealing a nervous glance at* Jim. *In the living room*
Laura, *stretched on the sofa, clenches her hand to her lips, to hold back a shuddering
sob.*]

God's Holy Name be praised—

[*The scene dims out.*]

SCENE VII

It is half an hour later. Dinner is just being finished in the dining room, LAURA *is still huddled upon the sofa, her feet drawn under her, her head resting on a pale blue pillow, her eyes wide and mysteriously watchful. The new floor lamp with its shade of rose-colored silk gives a soft, becoming light to her face, bringing out the fragile, unearthly prettiness which usually escapes attention. From outside there is a steady murmur of rain, but it is slackening and soon stops; the air outside becomes pale and luminous as the moon breaks through the clouds. A moment after the curtain rises, the lights in both rooms flicker and go out.*

JIM.   Hey, there, Mr. Light Bulb!

[AMANDA *laughs nervously.*]

[*Legend on screen:* "Suspension of a public service."]

1140   AMANDA.   Where was Moses when the lights went out? Ha-ha. Do you know the answer to that one, Mr. O'Connor?

JIM.   No, Ma'am, what's the answer?

AMANDA.   In the dark! [JIM *laughs appreciatively.*] Everybody sit still. I'll light the candles. Isn't it lucky we have them on the table? Where's a match? Which of you gentleman can provide a match?

JIM.   Here.

AMANDA.   Thank you, Sir.

JIM.   Not at all, Ma'am!

AMANDA [*as she lights the candles*].   I guess the fuse has burned out. Mr. O'Con-
1150   nor, can you tell a burnt-out fuse? I know I can't and Tom is a total loss when it comes to mechanics. [*They rise from the table and go into the kitchen-ette, from where their voices are heard.*] Oh, be careful you don't bump into something. We don't want our gentleman caller to break his neck. Now wouldn't that be a fine howdy-do?

JIM.   Ha-ha! Where is the fuse-box?

AMANDA.   Right here next to the stove. Can you see anything?

JIM.   Just a minute.

AMANDA.   Isn't electricity a mysterious thing? Wasn't it Benjamin Franklin who tied a key to a kite? We live in such a mysterious universe, don't we?
1160   Some people say that science clears up all the mysteries for us. In my opinion it only creates more! Have you found it yet?

JIM.   No, Ma'am. All these fuses look okay to me.

AMANDA.   Tom!

TOM.   Yes, Mother?

AMANDA.   That light bill I gave you several days ago. The one I told you we got the notices about?

[*Legend on screen:* "Ha!"]

TOM.   Oh—yeah.

AMANDA.   You didn't neglect to pay it by any chance?

TOM.   Why, I—
1170   AMANDA.   Didn't! I might have known it!

JIM.   Shakespeare probably wrote a poem on that light bill, Mrs. Wingfield.

Amanda. I might have known better than to trust him with it! There's such a high price for negligence in this world!

Jim. Maybe the poem will win a ten-dollar prize.

Amanda. We'll just have to spend the remainder of the evening in the nineteenth century, before Mr. Edison made the Mazda lamp!

Jim. Candlelight is my favorite kind of light.

Amanda. That shows you're romantic! But that's no excuse for Tom. Well, we got through dinner. Very considerate of them to let us get through dinner
1180   before they plunged us into everlasting darkness, wasn't it, Mr. O'Connor?

Jim. Ha-ha!

Amanda. Tom, as a penalty for your carelessness you can help me with the dishes.

Jim. Let me give you a hand.

Amanda. Indeed you will not!

Jim. I ought to be good for something.

Amanda. Good for something! [*Her tone is rhapsodic.*] You? Why, Mr. O'Connor, nobody, *nobody's* given me this much entertainment in years—as you have!

1190 Jim. Aw, now, Mrs. Wingfield!

Amanda. I'm not exaggerating, not one bit! But Sister is all by her lonesome. You go keep her company in the parlor! I'll give you this lovely old candelabrum that used to be on the altar at the Church of the Heavenly Rest. It was melted a little out of shape when the church burnt down. Lightning struck it one spring. Gypsy Jones was holding a revival at the time and he intimated that the church was destroyed because the Episcopalians gave card parties.

Jim. Ha-ha.

Amanda. And how about you coaxing Sister to drink a little wine? I think it
1200   would be good for her! Can you carry both at once?

Jim. Sure. I'm Superman!

Amanda. Now, Thomas, get into this apron!

[Jim *comes into the dining room, carrying the candelabrum, its candles lighted, in one hand and a glass of wine in the other. The door of the kitchenette swings closed on* Amanda's *gay laughter; the flickering light approaches the portieres.* Laura *sits up nervously as* Jim *enters. She can hardly speak from the almost intolerable strain of being alone with a stranger.*]

[*Screen legend:* "I don't suppose you remember me at all!"]

[*At first, before* Jim's *warmth overcomes her paralyzing shyness,* Laura's *voice is thin and breathless, as though she had just run up a steep flight of stairs.* Jim's *attitude is gently humorous. While the incident is apparently unimportant, it is to* Laura *the climax of her secret life.*]

Jim. Hello there, Laura.

Laura [*faintly*]. Hello.

[*She clears her throat.*]

Jim. How are you feeling now? Better?

Laura. Yes. Yes, thank you.

JIM. This is for you. A little dandelion wine. [*He extends the glass toward her with extravagant gallantry.*]

LAURA. Thank you.

1210 JIM. Drink it—but don't get drunk! [*He laughs heartily.* LAURA *takes the glass uncertainly; she laughs shyly.*] Where shall I set the candles?

LAURA. Oh—oh, anywhere . . .

JIM. How about here on the floor? Any objections?

LAURA. No.

JIM. I'll spread a newspaper under to catch the drippings. I like to sit on the floor. Mind if I do?

LAURA. Oh, no.

JIM. Give me a pillow?

LAURA. What?

1220 JIM. A pillow!

LAURA. Oh . . . [*She hands him one quickly.*]

JIM. How about you? Don't you like to sit on the floor?

LAURA. Oh—yes.

JIM. Why don't you, then?

LAURA. I—will.

JIM. Take a pillow! [LAURA *does. He sits on the floor on the other side of the candelabrum.* JIM *crosses his legs and smiles engagingly at her.*] I can't hardly see you sitting way over there.

LAURA. I can—see you.

1230 JIM. I know, but that's not fair, I'm in the limelight. [LAURA *moves her pillow closer.*] Good! Now I can see you! Comfortable?

LAURA. Yes.

JIM. So am I. Comfortable as a cow! Will you have some gum?

LAURA. No, thank you.

JIM. I think that I will indulge, with your permission. [*He musingly unwraps a stick of gum and holds it up.*] Think of the fortune made by the guy that invented the first piece of chewing gum. Amazing, huh? The Wrigley Building is one of the sights of Chicago—I saw it when I went up to the Century of Progress. Did you take in the Century of Progress?[26]

1240 LAURA. No, I didn't.

JIM. Well, it was quite a wonderful exposition. What impressed me most was the Hall of Science. Gives you an idea of what the future will be in America, even more wonderful than the present time is! [*There is a pause.* JIM *smiles at her.*] Your brother tells me you're shy. Is that right, Laura?

LAURA. I—don't know.

JIM. I judge you to be an old-fashioned type of girl. Well, I think that's a pretty good type to be. Hope you don't think I'm being too personal—do you?

LAURA [*hastily, out of embarrassment*]. I believe I *will* take a piece of gum, if

1250 you—don't mind. [*clearing her throat*] Mr. O'Connor, have you—kept up with your singing?

JIM. Singing? Me?

LAURA. Yes, I remember what a beautiful voice you had.

---

[26] The byname of the 1933–1934 World's Fair in Chicago.

JIM.   When did you hear me sing?

[LAURA *does not answer, and in the long pause which follows a man's voice is heard singing offstage.*]

VOICE:

O blow, ye winds,
heigh-ho,
A-roving, I will go!
I'm off to my love
With a boxing glove—
Ten thousand miles away!

1260

JIM.   You say you've heard me sing?

LAURA.   Oh, yes! Yes, very often ... I—don't suppose—you remember me—at all?

JIM [*smiling doubtfully*].   You know I have an idea I've seen you before. I had that idea soon as you opened the door. It seemed almost like I was about to remember your name. But the name that I started to call you—wasn't a name! And so I stopped myself before I said it.

LAURA.   Wasn't it—Blue Roses?

1270 JIM [*springing up, grinning*].   Blue Roses! By gosh, yes—Blue Roses! That's what I had on my tongue when you opened the door! Isn't it funny what tricks your memory plays? I didn't connect you with high school somehow or other. But that's where it was; it was high school. I didn't even know you were Shakespeare's sister! Gosh, I'm sorry.

LAURA.   I didn't expect you to. You—barely knew me!

JIM.   But we did have a speaking acquaintance, huh?

LAURA.   Yes, we—spoke to each other.

JIM.   When did you recognize me?

LAURA.   Oh, right away!

1280 JIM.   Soon as I came in the door?

LAURA.   When I heard your name I thought it was probably you. I knew that Tom used to know you a little in high school. So when you came in the door—well, then I was—sure.

JIM.   Why didn't you *say* something, then?

LAURA [*breathless*].   I didn't know what to say, I was—too surprised!

JIM.   For goodness' sakes! You know, this sure is funny!

LAURA.   Yes! Yes, isn't it, though ...

JIM.   Didn't we have a class in something together?

LAURA.   Yes, we did.

1290 JIM.   What class was that?

LAURA.   It was—singing—chorus!

JIM.   Aw!

LAURA.   I sat across the aisle from you in the Aud.

JIM.   Aw.

LAURA.   Mondays, Wednesdays, and Fridays.

JIM.   Now I remember—you always came in late.

LAURA.   Yes, it was so hard for me, getting upstairs. I had that brace on my leg—it clumped so loud!

JIM.   I never heard any clumping.

1300 LAURA [*wincing at the recollection*].   To me it sounded like—thunder!

JIM.   Well, well, well, I never even noticed.

LAURA.   And everybody was seated before I came in. I had to walk in front of all those people. My seat was in the back row. I had to go clumping all the way up the aisle with everyone watching!

JIM.   You shouldn't have been self-conscious.

LAURA.   I know, but I was. It was always such a relief when the singing started.

JIM.   Aw, yes, I've placed you now! I used to call you Blue Roses. How was it that I got started calling you that?

1310   LAURA.   I was out of school a little while with pleurosis. When I came back you asked what was the matter. I said I had pleurosis—you thought I said *Blue Roses*. That's what you always called me after that!

JIM.   I hope you didn't mind.

LAURA.   Oh, no—I liked it. You see, I wasn't acquainted with many—people. . . .

JIM.   As I remember you sort of stuck by yourself.

LAURA.   I—I—never have had much luck at—making friends.

JIM.   I don't see why you wouldn't.

LAURA.   Well, I—started out badly.

1320   JIM.   You mean being—

LAURA.   Yes, it sort of—stood between me—

JIM.   You shouldn't have let it!

LAURA.   I know, but it did, and—

JIM.   You were shy with people!

LAURA.   I tried not to be but never could—

JIM.   Overcome it?

LAURA.   No, I—I never could!

JIM.   I guess being shy is something you have to work out of kind of gradually.

1330   LAURA [*sorrowfully*].   Yes—I guess it—

JIM.   Takes time!

LAURA.   Yes—

JIM.   People are not so dreadful when you know them. That's what you have to remember! And everybody has problems, not just you, but practically everybody has got some problems. You think of yourself as having the only problems, as being the only one who is disappointed. But just look around you and you will see lots of people as disappointed as you are. For instance, I hoped when I was going to high school that I would be further along at this time, six years later, than I am now. You remember that

1340   wonderful write-up I had in *The Torch*?

LAURA.   Yes! [*She rises and crosses to the table.*]

JIM.   It said I was bound to succeed in anything I went into! [LAURA *returns with the high school yearbook.*] Holy Jeez! *The Torch!*

[*He accepts it reverently. They smile across the book with mutual wonder.* LAURA *crouches beside him and they begin to turn the pages.* LAURA's *shyness is dissolving in his warmth.*]

LAURA.   Here you are in *The Pirates of Penzance!*

JIM [*wistfully*].   I sang the baritone lead in that operetta.

Laura [*raptly*]. So—*beautifully!*

Jim [*protesting*]. Aw—

Laura. Yes, yes—beautifully—beautifully!

Jim. You heard me?

1350 Laura. All three times!

Jim. No!

Laura. Yes!

Jim. All three performances?

Laura [*looking down*]. Yes.

Jim. Why?

Laura. I—wanted to ask you to—autograph my program. [*She takes the program from the back of the yearbook and shows it to him.*]

Jim. Why didn't you ask me to?

Laura. You were always surrounded by your own friends so much that I

1360 never had a chance to.

Jim. You should have just—

Laura. Well, I—thought you might think I was—

Jim. Thought I might think you was—what?

Laura. Oh—

Jim [*with reflective relish*]. I was beleaguered by females in those days.

Laura. You were terribly popular!

Jim. Yeah—

Laura. You had such a—friendly way—

Jim. I was spoiled in high school.

1370 Laura. Everybody—liked you!

Jim. Including you?

Laura. I—yes, I—did, too—[*She gently closes the book in her lap.*]

Jim. Well, well, well! Give me that program, Laura. [*She hands it to him. He signs it with a flourish.*] There you are—better late than never!

Laura. Oh, I—what a—surprise!

Jim. My signature isn't worth very much right now. But some day—maybe—it will increase in value! Being disappointed is one thing and being discouraged is something else. I am disappointed but I am not discouraged. I'm twenty-three years old. How old are you?

1380 Laura. I'll be twenty-four in June.

Jim. That's not old age!

Laura. No, but—

Jim. You finished high school?

Laura [*with difficulty*]. I didn't go back.

Jim. You mean you dropped out?

Laura. I made bad grades in my final examinations. [*She rises and replaces the book and the program on the table. Her voice is strained.*] How is—Emily Meisenbach getting along?

Jim. Oh, that kraut-head!

1390 Laura. Why do you call her that?

Jim. That's what she was.

Laura. You're not still—going with her?

Jim. I never see her.

Laura. It said in the "Personal" section that you were—engaged!

Jim. I know, but I wasn't impressed by that—propaganda!

LAURA.   It wasn't—the truth?
JIM.   Only in Emily's optimistic opinion!
LAURA.   Oh—

[*Legend:* "What have you done since high school?"]

[JIM *lights a cigarette and leans indolently back on his elbows smiling at* LAURA *with a warmth and charm which lights her inwardly with altar candles. She remains by the table, picks up a piece from the glass menagerie collection, and turns it in her hands to cover her tumult.*]

JIM [*after several reflective puffs on his cigarette*].   What have you done since
1400   high school? [*She seems not to hear him.*] Huh? [LAURA *looks up.*] I said what
       have you done since high school, Laura?
LAURA.   Nothing much.
JIM.   You must have been doing something these six long years.
LAURA.   Yes.
JIM.   Well, then, such as what?
LAURA.   I took a business course at business college—
JIM.   How did that work out?
LAURA.   Well, not very—well—I had to drop out, it gave me—indigestion—

[JIM *laughs gently.*]

JIM.   What are you doing now?
1410 LAURA.   I don't do anything—much. Oh, please don't think I sit around
       doing nothing! My glass collection takes up a good deal of time. Glass is
       something you have to take good care of.
JIM.   What did you say—about glass?
LAURA.   Collection I said—I have one—[*She clears her throat and turns away
       again, acutely shy.*]
JIM [*abruptly*].   You know what I judge to be the trouble with you? Inferiority
       complex! Know what that is? That's what they call it when someone low-
       rates himself! I understand it because I had it, too. Although my case was
       not so aggravated as yours seems to be. I had it until I took up public
1420   speaking, developed my voice, and learned that I had an aptitude for
       science. Before that time I never thought of myself as being outstanding
       in any way whatsoever! Now I've never made a regular study of it, but I
       have a friend who says I can analyze people better than doctors that make
       a profession of it. I don't claim that to be necessarily true, but I can sure
       guess a person's psychology, Laura! [*He takes out his gum.*] Excuse me,
       Laura. I always take it out when the flavor is gone. I'll use this scrap of
       paper to wrap it in. I know how it is to get it stuck on a shoe. [*He wraps the
       gum in paper and puts it in his pocket.*] Yep—that's what I judge to be your
       principal trouble. A lack of confidence in yourself as a person. You don't
1430   have the proper amount of faith in yourself. I'm basing that fact on a
       number of your remarks and also on certain observations I've made. For
       instance that clumping you thought was so awful in high school. You say
       that you even dreaded to walk into class. You see what you did? You
       dropped out of school, you gave up an education because of a clump,
       which as far as I know was practically non-existent! A little physical defect

is what you have. Hardly noticeable even! Magnified thousands of times by imagination! You know what my strong advice to you is? Think of yourself as *superior* in some way!

LAURA. In what way would I think?

1440 JIM. Why, man alive, Laura! Just look about you a little. What do you see? A world full of common people! All of 'em born and all of 'em going to die! Which of them has one-tenth of your good points! Or mine! Or anyone else's, as far as that goes—gosh! Everybody excels in some one thing. Some in many! [*He unconsciously glances at himself in the mirror.*] All you've got to do is discover in *what!* Take me, for instance. [*He adjusts his tie at the mirror.*] My interest happens to lie in electro-dynamics. I'm taking a course in radio engineering at night school, Laura, on top of a fairly responsible job at the warehouse. I'm taking that course and studying public speaking.

LAURA. Ohhhh.

1450 JIM. Because I believe in the future of television! [*turning his back to her.*] I wish to be ready to go up right along with it. Therefore I'm planning to get in on the ground floor. In fact I've already made the right connections and all that remains is for the industry itself to get under way! Full steam—[*His eyes are starry.*] Knowledge—Zzzzzp! Money—Zzzzzzp!—Power! That's the cycle democracy is built on! [*His attitude is convincingly dynamic.* LAURA *stares at him, even her shyness eclipsed in her absolute wonder. He suddenly grins.*] I guess you think I think a lot of myself!

LAURA. No—o-o-o, I—

JIM. Now how about you? Isn't there something you take more interest in
1460 than anything else?

LAURA. Well, I do—as I said—have my—glass collection—

[*A peal of girlish laughter rings from the kitchenette.*]

JIM. I'm not right sure I know what you're talking about. What kind of glass is it?

LAURA. Little articles of it, they're ornaments mostly! Most of them are little animals made out of glass, the tiniest little animals in the world. Mother calls them a glass menagerie! Here's an example of one, if you'd like to see it! This one is one of the oldest. It's nearly thirteen.

[*Music: "The Glass Menagerie."*]

[*He stretches out his hand.*]

Oh, be careful—if you breathe, it breaks!

JIM. I'd better not take it. I'm pretty clumsy with things.

1470 LAURA. Go on, I trust you with him! [*She places the piece in his palm.*] There now—you're holding him gently! Hold him over the light, he loves the light! You see how the light shines through him?

JIM. It sure does shine!

LAURA. I shouldn't be partial, but he is my favorite one.

JIM. What kind of thing is this one supposed to be?

LAURA. Haven't you noticed the single horn on his forehead?

JIM. A unicorn, huh?

LAURA. Mmmm-hmmm!

Jim. Unicorns—aren't they extinct in the modern world?
1480 Laura. I know!
Jim. Poor little fellow, he must feel sort of lonesome.
Laura [*smiling*]. Well, if he does, he doesn't complain about it. He stays on
    a shelf with some horses that don't have horns and all of them seem to get
    along nicely together.
Jim. How do you know?
Laura [*lightly*]. I haven't heard any arguments among them!
Jim [*grinning*]. No arguments, huh? Well, that's a pretty good sign! Where
    shall I set him?
Laura. Put him on the table. They all like a change of scenery once in a
1490   while!
Jim. Well, well, well, well—[*He places the glass piece on the table, then raises his
    arms and stretches.*] Look how big my shadow is when I stretch!
Laura. Oh, oh, yes—it stretches across the ceiling!
Jim [*crossing to the door*]. I think it's stopped raining. [*He opens the fire-escape
    door and the background music changes to a dance tune.*] Where does the music
    come from?
Laura. From the Paradise Dance Hall across the alley.
Jim. How about cutting a rug a little, Miss Wingfield?
Laura. Oh, I—
1500 Jim. Or is your program filled up? Let me have a look at it. [*He grasps an
    imaginary card.*] Why, every dance is taken! I'll just have to scratch some
    out.

[*Waltz music:* "La Golondrina."]

    Ahhh, a waltz! [*He executes some sweeping turns by himself, then holds his arms
    toward Laura.*]
Laura [*breathlessly*]. I—can't dance!
Jim. There you go, that inferiority stuff!
Laura. I've never danced in my life!
Jim. Come on, try!
Laura. Oh, but I'd step on you!
1510 Jim. I'm not made out of glass.
Laura. How—how—how do we start?
Jim. Just leave it to me. You hold your arms out a little.
Laura. Like this?
Jim [*taking her in his arms*]. A little bit higher. Right. Now don't tighten up,
    that's the main thing about it—relax.
Laura [*laughing breathlessly*]. It's hard not to.
Jim. Okay.
Laura. I'm afraid you can't budge me.
Jim. What do you bet I can't? [*He swings her into motion.*]
1520 Laura. Goodness, yes, you can!
Jim. Let yourself go, now Laura, just let yourself go.
Laura. I'm—
Jim. Come on!
Laura. —trying!
Jim. Not so stiff—easy does it!
Laura. I know but I'm—

JIM.   Loosen th' backbone! There now, that's a lot better.

LAURA.   Am I?

JIM.   Lots, lots better! [*He moves her about the room in a clumsy waltz.*]

1530 LAURA.   Oh, my!

JIM.   Ha-ha!

LAURA.   Oh, my goodness!

JIM.   Ha-ha-ha! [*They suddenly bump into the table, and the glass piece on it falls to the floor. JIM stops the dance.*] What did we hit on?

LAURA.   Table.

JIM.   Did something fall off it? I think—

LAURA.   Yes.

JIM.   I hope that it wasn't the little glass horse with the horn!

LAURA.   Yes [*She stoops to pick it up.*]

1540 JIM.   Aw, aw, aw. Is it broken?

LAURA.   Now it is just like all the other horses.

JIM.   It's lost its—

LAURA.   Horn! It doesn't matter. Maybe it's a blessing in disguise.

JIM.   You'll never forgive me. I bet that that was your favorite piece of glass.

LAURA.   I don't have favorites much. It's no tragedy, Freckles. Glass breaks so easily. No matter how careful you are. The traffic jars the shelves and things fall off them.

JIM.   Still I'm awfully sorry that I was the cause.

LAURA [*smiling*].   I'll just imagine he had an operation. The horn was re-
1550 moved to make him feel less—freakish! [*They both laugh.*] Now he will feel more at home with the other horses, the ones that don't have horns. . . .

JIM.   Ha-ha, that's very funny! [*Suddenly he is serious.*] I'm glad to see that you have a sense of humor. You know—you're—well—very different! Surprisingly different from anyone else I know! [*His voice becomes soft and hesitant with a genuine feeling.*] Do you mind me telling you that? [LAURA *is abashed beyond speech.*] I mean it in a nice way— [LAURA *nods shyly, looking away.*] You make me feel sort of—I don't know how to put it! I'm usually pretty good at expressing things, but—this is something that I don't know how to say! [LAURA *touches her throat and clears it—turns the broken unicorn in her hands.*
1560 *His voice becomes softer.*] Has anyone ever told you that you were pretty? [*There is a pause, and the music rises slightly.* LAURA *looks up slowly, with wonder, and shakes her head.*] Well, you are! In a very different way from anyone else. And all the nicer because of the difference, too. [*His voice becomes low and husky.* LAURA *turns away, nearly faint with the novelty of her emotions.*] I wish that you were my sister. I'd teach you to have some confidence in yourself. The different people are not like other people, but being different is nothing to be ashamed of. Because other people are not such wonderful people. They're one hundred times one thousand. You're one times one! They walk all over the earth. You just stay here. They're common as—
1570 weeds, but—you—well, you're—*Blue Roses!*

[*Image on screen:* Blue Roses.]

[*The music changes.*]

LAURA.   But blue is wrong for—roses. . . .

JIM.   It's right for you! You're—pretty!

LAURA.   In what respect am I pretty?

JIM. In all respects—believe me! Your eyes—your hair—are pretty! Your hands are pretty! [*He catches hold of her hand.*] You think I'm making this up because I'm invited to dinner and have to be nice. Oh, I could do that! I could put on an act for you, Laura, and say lots of things without being very sincere. But this time I am. I'm talking to you sincerely. I happened to notice you had this inferiority complex that keeps you from feeling
1580 comfortable with people. Somebody needs to build your confidence up and make you proud instead of shy and turning away and—blushing. Somebody—ought to—*kiss* you, Laura! [*His hand slips slowly up her arm to her shoulder as the music swells tumultuously. He suddenly turns her about and kisses her on the lips. When he releases her,* LAURA *sinks on the sofa with a bright, dazed look.* JIM *backs away and fishes in his pocket for a cigarette.*]

[*Legend on screen:* "A souvenir."]

Stumblejohn! [*He lights the cigarette, avoiding her look. There is a peal of girlish laughter from* AMANDA *in the kitchenette.* LAURA *slowly raises and opens her hand. It still contains the little broken glass animal. She looks at it with a tender, bewildered expression.*] Stumblejohn! I shouldn't have done that—that was
1590 way off the beam. You don't smoke, do you? [*She looks up, smiling, not hearing the question. He sits beside her rather gingerly. She looks at him speechlessly—waiting. He coughs decorously and moves a little farther aside as he considers the situation and senses her feelings, dimly, with perturbation. He speaks gently.*] Would you—care for a—mint? [*She doesn't seem to hear him but her look grows brighter even.*] Peppermint? Life Saver? My pocket's a regular drugstore—wherever I go. . . . [*He pops a mint in his mouth. Then he gulps and decides to make a clean breast of it. He speaks slowly and gingerly.*] Laura, you know, if I had a sister like you, I'd do the same thing as Tom. I'd bring out fellows and—introduce her to them. The right type of boys—of a type
1600 to—appreciate her. Only—well—he made a mistake about me. Maybe I've got no call to be saying this. That may not have been the idea in having me over. But what if it was? There's nothing wrong with that. The only trouble is that in my case—I'm not in a situation to—do the right thing. I can't take down your number and say I'll phone. I can't call up next week and—ask for a date. I thought I had better explain the situation in case you—misunderstood it and—I hurt your feelings. . . .

[*There is a pause. Slowly, very slowly,* LAURA'S *look changes, her eyes returning slowly from his to the glass figure in her palm.* AMANDA *utters another gay laugh in the kitchenette.*]

LAURA [*faintly*]. You—won't—call again?
JIM. No, Laura, I can't. [*He rises from the sofa.*] As I was just explaining, I've—got strings on me. Laura, I've—been going steady! I go out all the
1610 time with a girl named Betty. She's a home-girl like you, and Catholic, and Irish, and in a great many ways we—get along fine. I met her last summer on a moonlight boat trip up the river to Alton, on the *Majestic*. Well—right away from the start it was—love!

[*Legend:* Love!]

[LAURA *sways slightly forward and grips the arm of the sofa. He fails to notice, now enrapt in his own comfortable being.*] Being in love has made a new man of me! [*Leaning stiffly forward, clutching the arm of the sofa,* LAURA *struggles visibly with her storm. But* JIM *is oblivious; she is a long way off.*] The power of love is really pretty tremendous! Love is something that—changes the whole world, Laura! [*The storm abates a little and* LAURA *leans back. He notices her again.*] It happened that Betty's aunt took sick, she got a wire and had to go to Centralia. So Tom—when he asked me to dinner—I naturally just accepted the invitation, not knowing that you—that he—that I—[*He stops awkwardly.*] Huh—I'm a stumblejohn! [*He flops back on the sofa. The holy candles on the altar of* LAURA'S *face have been snuffed out. There is a look of almost infinite desolation.* JIM *glances at her uneasily.*] I wish that you would—say something. [*She bites her lip which was trembling and then bravely smiles. She opens her hand again on the broken glass figure. Then she gently takes his hand and raises it level with her own. She carefully places the unicorn in the palm of his hand, then pushes his fingers closed upon it.*] What are you—doing that for? You want me to have him? Laura? [*She nods.*] What for?

LAURA.   A—souvenir. . . .

[*She rises unsteadily and crouches beside the Victrola to wind it up.*]

[*Legend on screen:* "Things have a way of turning out so badly!" *Or image:* "Gentleman caller waving goodbye—gaily."]

[*At this moment* AMANDA *rushes brightly back into the living room. She bears a pitcher of fruit punch in an old-fashioned cut-glass pitcher, and a plate of macaroons. The plate has a gold border and poppies painted on it.*]

AMANDA.   Well, well, well! Isn't the air delightful after the shower? I've made you children a little liquid refreshment. [*She turns gaily to* JIM.] Jim, do you know that song about lemonade?

> "Lemonade, lemonade
> Made in the shade and stirred with a spade—
> Good enough for any old maid!"

JIM [*uneasily*].   Ha-ha! No—I never heard it.

AMANDA.   Why, Laura! You look so serious!

JIM.   We were having a serious conversation.

AMANDA.   Good! Now you're better acquainted!

JIM [*uncertainly*].   Ha-ha! Yes.

AMANDA.   You modern young people are much more serious-minded than my generation. I was so gay as a girl!

JIM.   You haven't changed, Mrs. Wingfield.

AMANDA.   Tonight I'm rejuvenated! The gaiety of the occasion, Mr. O'Connor! [*She tosses her head with a peal of laughter, spilling some lemonade.*] Ooo! I'm baptizing myself!

JIM.   Here—let me—

AMANDA [*setting the pitcher down*].   There now. I discovered we had some maraschino cherries. I dumped them in, juice and all!

JIM.   You shouldn't have gone to that trouble, Mrs. Wingfield.

AMANDA.   Trouble, trouble? Why, it was loads of fun! Didn't you hear me cutting up in the kitchen? I bet your ears were burning! I told Tom how outdone with him I was for keeping you to himself so long a time! He should have brought you over much, much sooner! Well, now that you've

found your way, I want you to be a very frequent caller! Not just occasional but all the time. Oh, we're going to have a lot of gay times together! I see them coming! Mmm, just breath that air! So fresh, and the moon's so
1660   pretty! I'll skip back out—I know where my place is when young folks are having a—serious conversation!

JIM.   Oh, don't go out, Mrs. Wingfield. The fact of the matter is I've got to be going.

AMANDA.   Going, now? You're joking! Why, it's only the shank of the evening, Mr. O'Connor!

JIM.   Well, you know how it is.

AMANDA.   You mean you're a young workingman and have to keep working-man's hours. We'll let you off early tonight. But only on the condition that next time you stay later. What's the best night for you? Isn't Saturday night
1670   the best night for you workingmen?

JIM.   I have a couple of time-clocks to punch, Mrs. Wingfield. One at morn-ing, another one at night!

AMANDA.   My, but you *are* ambitious! You work at night, too?

JIM.   No, Ma'am, not work but—Betty!

[*He crosses deliberately to pick up his hat. The band at the Paradise Dance Hall goes into a tender waltz.*]

AMANDA.   Betty? Betty? Who's—Betty!

[*There is an ominous cracking sound in the sky.*]

JIM.   Oh, just a girl. The girl I go steady with!

[*He smiles charmingly. The sky falls.*]

[*Legend:* "The Sky Falls."]

AMANDA [*a long-drawn exhalation*].   Ohhh . . . Is it a serious romance, Mr. O'Connor?

JIM.   We're going to be married the second Sunday in June.

1680 AMANDA.   Ohhhh—how nice! Tom didn't mention that you were engaged to be married.

JIM.   The cat's not out of the bag at the warehouse yet. You know how they are. They call you Romeo and stuff like that. [*He stops at the oval mirror to put on his hat. He carefully shapes the brim and the crown to give a discreetly dashing effect.*] It's been a wonderful evening, Mrs. Wingfield. I guess this is what they mean by Southern hospitality.

AMANDA.   It really wasn't anything at all.

JIM.   I hope it don't seem like I'm rushing off. But I promised Betty I'd pick her up at the Wabash depot, an' by the time I get my jalopy down there
1690   her train'll be in. Some women are pretty upset if you keep 'em waiting.

AMANDA.   Yes, I know—the tyranny of women! [*She extends her hand.*] Good-bye, Mr. O'Connor. I wish you luck—and happiness—and success! All three of them, and so does Laura! Don't you, Laura?

LAURA.   Yes!

JIM [*taking* LAURA's *hand*].   Goodbye, Laura. I'm certainly going to treasure that souvenir. And don't you forget the good advice I gave you. [*He raises his voice to a cheery shout.*] So long, Shakespeare! Thanks again, ladies. Good night!

[*He grins and ducks jauntily out. Still bravely grimacing,* AMANDA *closes the door on the gentleman caller. Then she turns back to the room with a puzzled expression. She and* LAURA *don't dare to face each other.* LAURA *crouches beside the Victrola to wind it.*]

AMANDA [*faintly*].   Things have a way of turning out so badly. I don't believe
1700   that I would play the Victrola. Well, well—well! Our gentleman caller was
        engaged to be married! [*She raises her voice.*] Tom!
TOM [*from the kitchenette*].   Yes, Mother?
AMANDA.   Come in here a minute. I want to tell you something awfully funny.
TOM [*entering with a macaroon and a glass of lemonade*].   Has the gentleman
        caller gotten away already?
AMANDA.   The gentleman caller has made an early departure. What a won-
        derful joke you played on us!
TOM.   How do you mean?
AMANDA.   You didn't mention that he was engaged to be married.
1710 TOM.   Jim? Engaged?
AMANDA.   That's what he just informed us.
TOM.   I'll be jiggered! I didn't know about that.
AMANDA.   That seems very peculiar.
TOM.   What's peculiar about it?
AMANDA.   Didn't you call him your best friend down at the warehouse?
TOM.   He is, but how did I know?
AMANDA.   It seems extremely peculiar that you wouldn't know your best
        friend was going to be married!
TOM.   The warehouse is where I work, not where I know things about peo-
1720   ple!
AMANDA.   You don't know things anywhere! You live in a dream; you man-
        ufacture illusions!

                                                    [*He crosses to the door.*]

Where are you going?
TOM.   I'm going to the movies.
AMANDA.   That's right, now that you've had us make such fools of ourselves.
        The effort, the preparations, all the expense! The new floor lamp, the rug,
        the clothes for Laura! All for what? To entertain some other girl's fiancé!
        Go to the movies, go! Don't think about us, a mother deserted, an un-
        married sister who's crippled and has no job! Don't let anything interfere
1730   with your selfish pleasure! Just go, go, go—to the movies!
TOM.   All right, I will! The more you shout about my selfishness to me the
        quicker I'll go, and I won't go to the movies!
AMANDA.   Go, then! Go to the moon—you selfish dreamer!

[TOM *smashes his glass on the floor. He plunges out on the fire escape, slamming the door.* LAURA *screams in fright. The dance-hall music becomes louder.* TOM *stands on the fire escape, gripping the rail. The moon breaks through the storm clouds, illumi- nating his face.*]

[*Legend on screen:* "And so goodbye . . ."]

[TOM's *closing speech is timed with what is happening inside the house. We see, as though through soundproof glass, that* AMANDA *appears to be making a comforting speech to* LAURA, *who is huddled upon the sofa. Now that we cannot hear the mother's speech, her silliness is gone and she has dignity and tragic beauty.* LAURA's *hair hides her face until, at the end of the speech, she lifts her head to smile at her mother.* AMANDA's *gestures are slow and graceful, almost dancelike, as she comforts her daughter. At the end of her speech she glances a moment at the father's picture—then withdraws through the portieres. At the close of* TOM's *speech,* LAURA *blows out the candles, ending the play.*]

TOM.   I didn't go to the moon, I went much further—for time is the longest distance between two places. Not long after that I was fired for writing a poem on the lid of a shoe-box. I left Saint Louis. I descended the steps of this fire escape for a last time and followed, from then on, in my father's footsteps, attempting to find in motion what was lost in space. I traveled around a great deal. The cities swept about me like dead leaves, leaves that 1740 were brightly colored but torn away from the branches. I would have stopped, but I was pursued by something. It always came upon me unawares, taking me altogether by surprise. Perhaps it was a familiar bit of music. Perhaps it was only a piece of transparent glass. Perhaps I am walking along a street at night, in some strange city, before I have found companions. I pass the lighted window of a shop where perfume is sold. The window is filled with pieces of colored glass, tiny transparent bottles in delicate colors, like bits of a shattered rainbow. Then all at once my sister touches my shoulder. I turn around and look into her eyes. Oh, Laura, Laura, I tried to leave you behind me, but I am more faithful than 1750 I intended to be! I reach for a cigarette, I cross the street, I run into the movies or a bar, I buy a drink, I speak to the nearest stranger—anything that can blow your candles out!

[LAURA *bends over the candles.*]

For nowadays the world is lit by lightning! Blow out your candles, Laura— and so goodbye. . . .

[*She blows the candles out.*]

[1944]

Critical Commentary on *The Glass Menagerie*

Every morning of his life Tennessee Williams sat down before a portable typewriter and spent four hours writing. Often he would revise works drafted earlier, and *The Glass Menagerie* was one of the most thoroughly revised of all his compositions. In one of its earliest incarnations Williams envisioned it as a screenplay entitled *The Gentleman Caller*. At one point he turned it into a short story, "Portrait of a Girl in Glass." It also became a one-act play, *The Pretty Trap*, and provided scenes for countless spin-offs into other one-act plays, short stories, and poems. The play itself went through innumerable drafts and even now it remains in two very different printed versions, the "acting version" and the "reading edition" reproduced in this text.

Perhaps because of all this revision, the play is a particularly rich and rewarding piece of literature, but the causes of Williams' compulsive editing are clearly rooted in the relationship between the play and events in his own life. *The Glass Menagerie* is an imaginative and somewhat fictionalized autobiography in which the narrator even bears the same first name as the author. Although there are important differences between the events in the play and the events in Williams' life, there are also many parallels, including the absentee father, the talkative Southern-belle mother, the shy and fragile sister, the abortive enrollment at Rubicam's Business College, the squalid apartment, the preoccupation with gentleman callers, and the poet's unhappiness at the International Shoe Company. Like the narrator, Williams himself was haunted by the fate of his sister Rose, who apparently suffered from shyness, nervousness, sexual repression, and assorted phobias. He felt he had abandoned her by going away to college and he never forgave his mother for authorizing Rose's lobotomy; nor did he ever forgive himself for leaving Rose unprotected in her period of gravest vulnerability.

Perhaps because Williams was using *The Glass Menagerie* to work out his own feelings about an unhappy past, the play itself is dominated by time, as Sam Bluefarb argues in his essay, "*The Glass Menagerie*: Three Visions of Time." We are accustomed to thinking of time as a constant, flowing continuum to be coped with by reasonable people in reasonable ways. As Amanda explains it in Scene V: ". . . the future becomes the present, the present the past, and the past turns into everlasting regret if you don't plan for it!" In normal life we presume that the present will dominate both the memories of the past and the preparation for the future, but there are in fact others ways to view time—and these characters embrace them.

Specifically, *The Glass Menagerie* is a play in which the past is preeminent. It is a memory play—Tom's attempt to make his future possible by exorcising the past. Within that remembered past, Tom has little ability to cope with a present made unhappy by his detestation of his work and his rejection of his mother's obsessive desire to control his future. At first he escapes to the movies for adventurous fantasy, but ultimately he makes permanent his escape by joining the Merchant Marines. Amanda, too, is unhappy with the present. Whenever possible, she retreats into her pleasant memories of the past in Blue Mountain. Most of her attempts to control her children are really attempts to restore the happiness she once felt while surrounded by suitors in Blue Mountain. Laura, because of her limp and her fearful shyness, cannot escape to the movies as Tom does or to a romanticized past as Amanda does. Instead she tends to her glass menagerie, creating a brittle and pristine world of imagination apart from the jarring commotion of reality.

These three characters are very equal in importance. Ostensibly, the dominant role is that of Amanda Wingfield, an almost archetypal mother seeking successes for her children that she herself has been unable to attain. Within her very complex character, Williams combines almost equal portions of foolishness, pathos, and nobility. As Edmund Napieralski has observed, Amanda attempts to become the domineering director of her children's lives: "Amanda not only dramatizes her own behavior and image of herself but also attempts to create roles for, to direct, prompt, and even costume the other characters in a drama of which she is author, producer, director, and leading lady." Hence, she is always telling Tom how to comb his hair, what to say, and how to behave. When the gentleman caller finally appears, she redecorates the apartment, puts Laura in costume (complete with "gay deceivers"), and scripts the action right down to who should open the door. In the end, however, nothing works out the way she wanted it to. The gentleman caller turns out to be engaged to someone else, Tom deserts her in much the same way her husband had done years earlier, and now both Laura and Amanda will have to chew upon the crust of humility.

Tom, however, makes good his escape, much like the magician who gets out of a sealed coffin without removing one nail. Perhaps he is the dominant character. As narrator, Tom's outlook informs and controls everything. He would like us to see Amanda as a somewhat pushy and ludicrous stage director (though, in actuality, of course, he is that director). Ultimately, we recognize that the rather unflattering portrait of Amanda has very likely been created by Tom as a way of laying off on her some of the guilt he feels for having deserted his mother and sister. He would like to feel that he was forced to leave them in poverty in order to retain for himself some slim chance of achieving his dream of becoming a writer.

Not only is the entire play a somewhat suspect and self-serving amalgamation of Tom's memories, but through the use of captions, we see Tom obviously striving to manipulate our responses. Many of these captions are almost undisguised, mocking attempts to distance us from Amanda, as when the legend "The Crust of Humility" precedes Amanda's lecture to Laura about the fate of spinsters. Not until the very end of the play do we see (but not hear) Amanda removed from the filtering consciousness of Tom. And then she begins to take on an aura of nobility; in a stage direction Williams writes: "Now that we cannot hear the mother's speech, her silliness is gone and she has dignity and tragic beauty." What purpose can such a stage direction serve other than suggesting that Tom is not an entirely trustworthy narrator? Tom would have us believe that Amanda thwarted his dreams and that the shoe factory stifled his creativity, but in the years that have passed, he has not become a poet. He stands before us throughout the play dressed in the uniform of an ordinary sailor, not even having attained rank among those coarse manual laborers.

At heart, however, it seems to be Laura who really controls the play's emotional tone and much of its action. Williams signals the importance of Laura by naming the play *The Glass Menagerie,* with a very conscious awareness of the symbolism evoked therein. Although Amanda has been unable to revitalize the past and Tom has been unable to escape into the future, Laura has been all too successful in crystallizing the present. In her secluded corner of the living room, to the repetitious accompaniment of her father's antique collection of records, she lives in the translucent, otherworldly light of her glass menagerie. For Laura, as for her collection of glass ornaments, no change is possible. All her time is taken up in tending to her collection, arranging and polishing animals that are as fleshless, motionless, and lustless as she would like to be. Yet when change does force itself upon her world—

when the jar of traffic dislodges a piece or when a gentleman caller intrudes—Laura sheds a tear, heaves a sigh, and goes back to polishing and arranging the remainder. She will not even keep the unicorn once it has fallen and become an ordinary horse, for to do so would be an acceptance of change, a reminder of the transformation she once imagined for herself in the arms of the gentleman caller, Jim.

In the end the play achieves its power primarily because of the stubborn unworldliness emanating from Laura. And in the end it is Laura's rigid fragility that finally helps Tom to the fulfillment of his dreams. He cannot blow her candles out, and time cannot efface his memories of her. And so he becomes a playwright—the poet he once dreamed of being. Each night on stage he is caught with Amanda in Laura's glass menagerie, which we see "as though viewed through soundproof glass." And Laura's story never ends; it is merely suspended as she blows her candles out—to begin anew for another audience on the next night of its endless, unearthly run.

The Life of Tennessee Williams 1911–1983

Thomas Lanier (Tennessee) Williams was born on March 26, 1911, in Columbus, Mississippi. His father Cornelius was at first a traveling representative for the telephone company; later he became a salesman for a shoe company. Because Cornelius liked to gamble, drink with his friends, and flirt with other women, it is perhaps inevitable that the family home was unhappy. Indeed, Edwina (Tennessee's mother) returned to live with her parents soon after her marriage to Cornelius and continued to do so until young Tom was nearly eight years old.

Late in 1918 Cornelius was hired as a manager of the International Shoe Company and the family moved with him to St. Louis. Tom's best friend in St. Louis turned out to be a little girl named Hazel Kramer, whom he met when she was nine and he was eleven. They used to make up stories together: Tennessee would invent the plot and Hazel would draw illustrations. He later commented that she was "the great extrafamilial love" of his life, but Edwina disapproved of her. She frowned on all of Tom's friends. As Williams put it in his *Memoirs*, "The boys were too rough for her delicate son, Tom, and the girls were, of course, too 'common.' " Nonetheless, Tom and Hazel remained very close for the next eleven years.

As an adolescent he was very shy, blushing whenever anyone looked him in the eyes, as if hiding "some quite dreadful or abominable secret." He felt that "somewhere deep in my nerves there was imprisoned a young girl, a sort of blushing school maiden." Only in his writing was he able to express himself freely. By age sixteen he was already writing for publication; his short story, "The Vengeance of Nitocris," appeared in a magazine called *Weird Tales* in 1928.

At seventeen he was taken by his grandfather on a summer tour of Europe. There in the cathedral at Cologne he first truly felt himself in the presence of God: "It was as if an impalpable hand was placed upon my head, and at the instant of that touch, the phobia [that was tormenting me] was lifted away as lightly as a snowflake though it had weighted on my head like a skull-breaking block of iron." A little later his phobia returned, but this time he exorcised it himself through the composition of a poem in which he recognizes himself as just one more member in the great human masses:

> then all at once my hot woe
> cools like a cinder dropped on snow.

This insight later seemed to him "a most important recognition—perhaps the most important of all, at least in the quest for balance of mind."

In 1929 he enrolled at the University of Missouri. There he became a member of Alpha Tau Omega fraternity and commenced a university education that was unmarked by academic distinction but formative in other ways. For the first time he was out from under the hawklike gaze of his mother and, like many other undergraduates, he discovered wine, women, and song. He also discovered other men. By the end of his first day on campus he had written a letter proposing marriage to Hazel Kramer. (She demurred.) Despite his shyness, he dated several girls, but his most intense sexual experiences occurred with a fraternity brother who made veiled attempts at seduction.

More important than these sensual distractions were the formative intellectual experiences of the young writer. His academic performance was mediocre, in large part because he spent much of his time writing poetry and talking about it with his friends. He also discovered the works of Ibsen and Strindberg. These playwrights, along with Chekhov whom he read a little later, were formative influences upon his conception of drama. During this period, too, he won an honorable mention for a one-act play, *Beauty Is the Word,* that he submitted in a contest sponsored by the Dramatic Arts Club.

Cornelius Williams did not believe that his son's grades warranted a return to college for a second year, so in the summer of 1932 Tom, out of necessity, began three years of intermittent employment in International Shoe Company. His misery in that employment is recorded with some poetic license in *The Glass Menagerie.* After his daily stint at the factory, he would fix himself great pots of strong coffee and stay up all night smoking cigarettes and writing short stories and poems. Compounding his stress at the time was the unexpected revelation that Hazel had married a young man at the University of Wisconsin. Tom began noticing palpitations of his heart, and one evening during a tense taxi ride with his sister Rose (who was already beginning to show symptoms of mental illness), Tom felt his chest tightening; in a nervous panic he insisted that he be taken to the hospital. Tests failed to show anything more serious than undernourishment and exhaustion, but for the rest of his life, Williams was always concerned about his heart condition.

In the months following his nervous collapse, Williams recuperated at the home of his maternal grandparents in Memphis, and there in 1934 his play entitled *Cairo, Shanghai, Bombai!* was produced by an amateur theatre. Williams complained that the leading lady sounded more like a fishmonger than an actress, but even so the experience delighted him. In his *Memoirs,* Williams recounts that "the laughter, genuine and loud, at the comedy I had written enchanted me. Then and there the theatre and I found each other for better and for worse."

Williams subsequently enrolled in Washington University in St. Louis before completing his degree at the University of Iowa in 1938. At both schools he devoted himself more to his writing than to his studies. Williams' poems began appearing in college literary magazines, and a one-act play called *The Magic Tower* won first prize in a contest sponsored by the Webster Groves Theatre Guild. In March 1937, the St. Louis Mummers, another amateur group, presented his first full-length play, *Candles to the Sun.*

Throughout this period his sister Rose continued to grow more unstable, falling victim to uncontrollable rages and sexual fantasies. In the summer of 1937 she was first confined to a mental institution. Perhaps this unrest at home—intensified by difficulties in the marriage between Edwina and Cornelius—was a factor in Tom's decision to transfer that fall to the University of Iowa. In any event Williams was away at school when his parents authorized the doctors to perform a prefrontal lobotomy on Rose, emphatically stopping her sexual fantasies but also condemning her to a life of sharply limited mental acuity. Williams blamed his mother and never forgave her. He remained guilt-stricken and strongly protective of Rose for the rest of his life.

Between 1938 and 1944 Williams struggled to establish himself as a professional writer. A cataract in his left eye kept him out of the army but also limited his employment options. He wandered the country taking on brief jobs in Chicago, New Orleans, Los Angeles, New York, Provincetown, and Key West—working as a waiter, a feather picker on a chicken farm, an elevator attendant, a teletype operator. And always he wrote.

Oddly enough, his first big break came in 1939 in a literary contest that he failed to win. He had submitted a series of one-act plays entitled *American Blues* in a contest sponsored by the influential Group Theatre in New York. The plays failed to win the $500 first prize, but the chief reader, Molly Day Thacher, insisted on a special $100 prize as an encouragement for Williams to continue writing. "There's a wonderful young playwright riding around Southern California on a bicycle," she told her husband (Elia Kazan) and the group's leader (Harold Clurman). Kazan later directed many of Williams' most important plays, and Clurman became the most influential theatre critic in New York. Thacher also arranged for Williams to sign a contract with the influential literary agent Audrey Wood, who not only looked after the unworldly Williams' literary affairs but also took care of a great many practical details that he was too absent-minded to handle.

In 1943 Audrey Wood negotiated for Williams a six-month contract as a writer for MGM at the then-extravagant fee of $250 a week. His job was to write a suitable screenplay—he later called it a "celluloid brassiere"—for Lana Turner. He tried, but was told that "the dialogue was beyond the young lady's comprehension" even though he had scrupulously avoided polysyllabic words. After being pulled from that project, he spent the rest of his time working on a screenplay that he called *The Gentleman Caller.* MGM rejected the script.

During the next several months, Williams rewrote his screenplay for the stage. On December 26, 1944, *The Glass Menagerie* opened in Chicago with the legendary actress Laurette Taylor in the role of Amanda. The first audience was unenthusiastic, but two influential Chicago critics began championing the play as a masterpiece. By the spring of 1945, he was earning $1,000 a week in royalties and plans were afoot for an opening on Broadway.

In 1947 Williams moved back to New Orleans and commenced hard work on a script that he was then calling *The Poker Night* but which ultimately became his most successful play, *A Streetcar Named Desire*. In an essay written that year, he commented, "I live near the main street of the Quarter. Down this street, running on the same tracks, are two streetcars, one named 'Desire' and the other named 'Cemeteries.' Their indiscourageable progress up and down Royal Street struck me as having some symbolic bearing on the broad nature on the life in the Vieux Carré—and everywhere else, for that matter."

Streetcar opened in New York on December 3, 1947, with Marlon Brando and Jessica Tandy in the leading roles and directed by Elia Kazan. It was a stupendous success. The audience applauded for more than half an hour; the critics joined in the general praise. In 1951 the film version of *Streetcar* came out starring Brando and Vivien Leigh and was greeted with equal acclaim.

Unfortunately, this harvest of glory also brought with it the seed of decay. Williams had always used the stimulant of black coffee to help him write in the mornings, but in the 1950s he began using amphetamines and barbiturates, often in combination with alcohol. He later referred to this as his "stoned age," but he never entirely escaped it. He continued to write religiously—creating such important plays as *Summer and Smoke, Cat on a Hot Tin Roof, Camino Real,* and *The Night of the Iguana*—but his personal behavior became more and more erratic until in 1969 he was committed to a mental institution. His doctors cut him off from all his drugs "cold turkey," and the result was that he suffered from three *grand mal* seizures and two heart attacks in a period of three days.

Williams recuperated, but he was never quite the same. He wrote many more plays, and his autobiography *Memoirs*, with its blatant revelations about his homosexuality, was a huge commercial success in 1975, but he had lost something and could not regain it. Eventually, he relapsed into a pattern of drug abuse, and on the night of February 24, 1983, while apparently attempting to swallow a Seconal tablet, he aspirated the bottle cap and suffocated.

A Collection of Critical Interpretations

NANCY M. TISCHLER, *TENNESSEE WILLIAMS: REBELLIOUS PURITAN*[*]

The setting of *The Glass Menagerie* was interesting in its symbolism and technical experimentation. Moving from the deep South to St. Louis for his story, Williams retains the memory of the South, as a haunting presence under the superimposed Midwestern setting. The audience, never seeing the gracious mansion that was the scene of Amanda's girlhood, feels its remembered glory and its contrast to the mean present. Awareness of the past is always an element in Williams' plays. His characters live beyond the fleeting moments of the drama—back into a glowing past and shrinking from a terrifying

[*] From Tischler, *Tennessee Williams: Rebellious Puritan* (New York: Citadel Press, 1961) 101–105.

future. For both Amanda and the later Blanche of *Streetcar,* the South forms an image of youth, love, purity, all of the ideals that have crumbled along with the mansions and the family fortunes.

Since the setting in *Menagerie* is that of a memory play, Tennessee Williams could feel free in its staging. His theory of expressionism is propounded in the introductory production notes, which are, in fact, directly applied in the play. His concept of the "new, plastic theatre" was probably influenced by Erwin Piscator, a German director who had helped him at the New School Seminar. He suggests that in *The Glass Menagerie*'s "considerably delicate or tenuous material, atmospheric touches and subtleties of direction play a particularly important part." Williams justifies such unconventional techniques as expressionism or impressionism on the basis that their subjectivity provides a "closer approach to truth." No playwright should use such devices in an effort to avoid the "responsibility of dealing with reality, or interpreting experience." But he believes that the new drama has followed the other arts in recognizing that realism is not the key to reality.

"The straight realistic play with its genuine frigidaire and authentic ice-cubes, its characters that speak exactly as its audience speaks," he says, "corresponds to the academic landscape and has the same virtue of a photographic likeness." Then, with unique optimism regarding current artistic tastes, he continues, "Everyone should know nowadays the unimportance of the photographic in art: that truth, life, or reality is an organic thing which the poetic imagination can represent or suggest, in essence, only through transformation, through changing into other forms than those which were merely present in appearance." The philosophy expressed here is in accord with the nineteenth century romantics and their followers in this century. The expressionistic concepts propounded in this preface have proved so effective in Tennessee Williams' work that set-designers have usually chosen to use expressionistic even when realistic settings are called for in Williams' manuscripts. Williams has a poet's weakness for symbols, and this modern technique frees his hand for scattering them about the stage. Their use to reflect, emphasize, and contrast with the meanings of the actions and the words has become a trademark of the Williams play.

The Glass Menagerie projected symbolic elements in line with Williams' newly enunciated theory. To reinforce the spoken word the author recommends the use of a screen device. A legend or image projected on the screen for the duration of the scene emphasizes the most important phrase. For example, in the scene where Jim remembers that Laura is the girl who was stricken with pleurosis, whom he mistakenly nicknamed "Blue Roses,' the legend on the screen accents the peculiarity of the name, and the audience, along with Laura, is made more keenly aware that although blue is beautiful, it is wrong for roses. Eddie Dowling considered this device superfluous and omitted it from the stage production, and wisely so. Mr. Gassner also considered the screen device "redundant and rather precious." Williams is "straining for effect not knowing that his simple tale, so hauntingly self-sufficient, needs no adornments."

Williams' expressionist theory also leads him to another variation from strictly realistic drama. The lighting changes with the mood. The stage is as dim as the participants' lives. Shafts of light flicker onto selected areas or actors, "sometimes in contradiction to what is the apparent center." When Tom and Amanda are quarreling, the light on them is low red, while Laura stands in a pool of light of that "peculiar pristine clarity such as light used in early religious portraits of saints or madonnas." The tone, strength, and occurrence of the lights have the power of emotional emphasis. In a technique reminiscent of Chekhov's, Williams heightens the emotional truths of the scenes and the reality of the internal action through unusual external effects.

The musical accompaniment of *The Glass Menagerie* is another element of Tennessee Williams' expressionism that characterizes his dramas. The theme is a tune called "The Glass Menagerie," composed by Paul Bowles. It is "like circus music, not when you are on the grounds or in the immediate vicinity of the parade, but when you are at some distance and very likely thinking of something else. . . . It expresses the surface vivacity of life and the underlying strain of immutable and inexpressible sorrow." The music becomes Laura's symbol: of this world which is like a circus for her—heard from a safe distance; and of her retreat into a world of music as well as of glass.

The depiction of the Wingfields' apartments also follows the dicta of expressionism. The ugly uniformity of the tenements depresses Tom and makes him frantic to escape. The place is described as "one of those vast hive-like conglomerations of cellular living-units that flower as warty growths in overcrowded urban centers of lower middle-class populations." They are, says the temporarily socially conscious author, "symptomatic of the impulse of this largest and fundamentally enslaved section of American society to avoid fluidity and differentiation and to exist and function as one interfused mass of automatism." Of the characters in the play, only Tom seems aware of this grotesque uniformity; and since the whole story takes place in his memory, he would naturally exaggerate the dismal reality he sees.

On both sides of the building, dark, narrow alleys run into "murky canyons of tangled clotheslines, garbage cans and sinister lattice-work of neighboring fire escapes." The meaning of these alleys is clear if the reader recalls Tom's picture of "Death Valley," where cats were trapped and killed by a vicious dog. The predicament becomes a symbol of his factory work, murderous to his creative imagination. For Laura, the alley represents the ugly world from which she retreats to gaze into her tiny glass figures. For Amanda, too, the alley is the world of her present hopeless poverty and convulsion from which she retreats into her make-believe world of memory and pretense. Inside the apartment, where she tries to create an illusion of gentility, her husband's portrait grins at her futile efforts.

The apartment is entered by a fire escape, "a structure whose name is a touch of accidental poetic truth, for all those huge buildings are always burning with the slow and implacable fires of human desperation." On this fire escape, Tom Wingfield seeks liberation from his private hell. It is no mere coincidence that this play's solution (like those of *Battle of Angels* and *Stairs to the Roof*) centers around the stairway. Stairs are the tangible sign of man's change in levels of reality.

It would seem that every item of the setting is symbolic—even the Paradise Dance Hall, across the alley. There sexual gratification provides the cliff-dwellers of the neighborhood a temporary paradise. In their moments

of closeness, they achieve the escape that Tom finds in his movies and poetry.

SAM BLUEFARB, "*THE GLASS MENAGERIE*: THREE VISIONS OF TIME"*

The effort to escape both the restriction of time and its demands forms the
thematic and motivational basis of Tennessee Williams' play *The Glass Menagerie*. In attempting to effect such an escape, Amanda, Tom, and Laura
Wingfield (the latter with some qualification) eventually find that they can
never quite succeed in breaking the bonds of their world. . . .

However, in all three instances—whether in Amanda's yearning for the
past, Tom's eager thrust toward the future, or Laura's imprisonment in the
jailhouse of her thwarted present—the past dominates as the present or
future can never do. The past not only casts its shadow upon the present and
the future, but actually determines the course that each of these shall take.
Thus the present and, by implication, the future are prevented from *taking* a
course. For while the future has yet to be born, the present is a static, stillborn
entity. In this play, the characters do not *live* in the present but in a past and
a future that have never quite effected a coalescence in a livable present. Yet
if, as in the case of Tom Wingfield, they plan for the future, that plan can
only be put into operation to the extent that an attempt is made to abolish
both the past and the present . . .

Amanda Wingfield, the mother, lives in a world that is emotionally
bounded by the past. Although she quite literally inhabits the present, she is
incapable of inhabiting that present other than in terms of the past. Her life
as a vivacious Southern belle can be of significance only if the memory of that
life is nourished and kept alive in the fertile earth of her nostalgia. Periodically, she must recall every word, every gesture, every event that ever took
place within the context of her East Tennessee girlhood. Amanda Wingfield
can never quite extricate herself from the past in order to come to terms with
the flow of life in the present, or what that present bodes for the future. Since
the past for Amanda dominates the present, the future is untenable (or
un*tenant*-able), in spite of her moments of concern for Laura's future. . . .

Amanda's obsession, of course, translated into the practical everyday
world, is to superimpose her own past on daughter Laura's future. Essentially, she desires for Laura the supposed benefits which she herself enjoyed
in that earlier time of her vanished girlhood: the balls, the dresses, the
attentions, but, above all, the numerous (if we can believe her) gentleman
callers. If such a gentleman caller can be summoned up in this latter day, he
may well turn out to be a likely candidate for the hand of the hapless,
crippled Laura. . . . Amanda will even accept—as in fact she does—the sparse
comfort of one of Tom's fellow workers from the shoe warehouse, a person-
able, but not overly-dashing chap by the name of Jim O'Connor. . . .

This is the final touch of pathos that drives Tom Wingfield out of the St.
Louis tenement he shares so uncomfortably with mother and sister, out into

---

* From Bluefarb, "*The Glass Menagerie*: Three Visions of Time," *College English* 24 (1963)
513–18.

the world of vagabondage, toward the romance of the sea and the ships, to the presumably freer life of the seafarer. This time he can no longer satisfy himself with the synthetic escape he has, until now, found in the darkened movie houses. This time the romance and the escape must have greater substance. And at first glance it would seem that Tom's escape to sea is essentially a romantic escape, an escape whose vistas point away from Amanda's past and his own present toward a brighter future. So it would appear. Yet, even after he makes the break, he is still tied, through guilt, to his own immediate past which, through the reawakened image of the lost Laura, he has abandoned:

> I pass the lighted windows of a shop where perfume is sold. The window is filled with pieces of colored glass . . . like bits of shattered rainbow. Then all at once my sister touches my shoulder. I turn around and look into her eyes. . . . Oh, Laura, Laura, I tried to leave you behind me, but I am more faithful than I intended to be! I reach for a cigarette, I cross the street, I run into the movies or a bar, I buy a drink, I speak to the nearest stranger—anything that can blow your candles out!

Tom Wingfield, then, has never really succeeded in running away from the past. And perhaps he never really meant to. Ostensibly, he was fired from the shoe warehouse for writing poetry on the lid of a shoe box. But this in itself doesn't make of Tom Wingfield a poet. Neither does his running off to sea. For his poetry writing and his seafaring are not so much the gestures of a young man searching for the *ultima Thule* of romance, as they are the expression of a man's desperation to escape the drab present and a past that prevents that present from fulfilling itself in a future. Actually, the act of writing that poem on the lid of a shoe box (a shoe box!) may well have been Tom Wingfield's way, at perhaps the deepest level of the subconscious, of expressing an overwhelming need—the need, perhaps, to bring down on his head the wrath of the warehouse foreman, a gesture not so much of the poet as of the rebel. And of the rebel, let it be said, who somehow cannot make the best of both worlds, but must expiate his "sin" by preferring one world to the other, getting himself fired for it. The act is thus both an act of destruction and of expiation. It is also a rebellion against the deadening romanticism of his mother, of her past, and of all that her past represents—the clamping, limiting strictures on the present. The poetry is only the means, the excuse, the trigger mechanism, which will catapult Tom along the trajectory of his life into the future. . . .

Laura, unlike her brother and her mother, *can* face the present—but only to the extent that she recognizes the truth about herself in that present. This would appear to hold a paradox. Yet, in this paradox, as at the heart of all paradox, there lies a kernel of truth. For Laura sees her lameness as a true debility, even if her mother prefers not to:

AMANDA.   Girls that aren't cut out for business careers usually wind up married
    to some nice man. . . . Sister, that's what you'll do.
LAURA.   But, mother—
AMANDA.   Yes?
LAURA.   I'm crippled!

AMANDA. Nonsense! Laura, I've told you never, never to use that word. Why, you're not crippled, you just have a little defect—hardly noticeable, even!

As far back as high school days, Laura's infirmity has affected and thus determined her attitude toward the world. Her entire personality has been forced to turn in upon itself; driven into the mold of her desperation and, finally, resignation with each heavy-footed descent of her lame foot onto the floor of the high school auditorium. When Laura surrenders to the timeless world of her glass animals, it is not simply because she wishes to escape from the world of the present into a world of fantasy and delusion, but precisely because she can look the present fully in the face—if only with fragmented vision. For Amanda it is a past which sustains the shimmering image of her nostalgia, a past by which the present and possibly the future may be illuminated. For Tom it is a future which offers escape from the shadows of a darkened present, made dark by the dark light of Amanda's past. For Laura, however, it is neither past, present, nor future which holds the semblance of reality; nor does the past or future offer even the simulacrum of a make-believe reality. For time has ceased to have any meaning whatever for Laura; her whole existence turns on a fulcrum of no-time. . . .

Ostensibly, one should lavish pity on such hapless creatures as Tom and Laura, and perhaps even experience a certain smug satisfaction from Amanda's plight; it seems to be a kind of poetic justice wreaked upon her for having ruined her children's lives. We should perhaps pity the hapless victims of a selfish mother who wanted, above all else, to bury her children in the crypt of her own past. Yet, when all has been said on behalf of the three, it is Amanda that finally invites the truest and deepest pity. For while each of her children has somehow managed to handle his own dilemma in his own way, Amanda can never fully resolve hers. She is ever conscious of the disparity which lies between a present that is meaningless to her and a past that not only gave meaning to what her life once was, but to what it might have been. If these periodic excursions back into the past give her some sort of dubious solace in the present, it is at best a solace which points up the meaninglessness of that present.

Thus, none of the characters in *Glass Menagerie* can ever truly face the flow of time for any sustained span; they are forever condemned to search for something that is neither of the past, present, or future, but may perhaps be found, someday, within the unfinished meaning of their own fragmented lives.

EDMUND A NAPIERALSKI, "TENNESSEE WILLIAMS' *THE GLASS MENAGERIE:* THE DRAMATIC METAPHOR"*

A previously neglected feature of Williams' achievement in *The Glass Menagerie* lies in his use of dramatic metaphor, that is, a metaphor defined not only through the vehicle of language but through action, the mode that distinguishes drama from narrative. In *The Glass Menagerie* not language alone, but

* From Napieralski, "Tennessee Williams' *The Glass Menagerie:* The Dramatic Metaphor," *The Southern Quarterly* 16 (1977): 1–5.

stage positions, gesture, activity, and movement define Amanda as the center of a metaphor that is the drama itself. Amanda not only dramatizes her own behavior and image of herself but also attempts to create roles for, to direct, prompt, and even costume the other characters in a drama of which she is author, producer, director, and leading lady. This dramatic metaphor, fashioned out of Amanda's experience and with the reluctant cooperation of Laura and Tom, gives depth to the dramatic illusion of *The Glass Menagerie* and gives the play its special power. . . .

In Scene I Amanda's voice is heard even before the lights go up and the outer wall is raised out of sight. When the scene is illuminated, Amanda, seated at the table with Tom and Laura, faces the audience while the other characters are in profile. Her first words to Tom are a command, or better, directions given by a tyrannical director to a recalcitrant actor. First she instructs him on table manners: "Honey, don't *push* with your *fingers*. . . . And chew—chew!" When Tom refuses her direction, Amanda proceeds to accuse him, ironically, of having a "Temperament like a Metropolitan star!", and once more reprimands him, this time for smoking too much. Tom, then, for the first time in the play retreats to the portieres. Amanda, apparently used to Tom's rejection of her advice, proceeds to demonstrate her propensity for pretense, for impersonation; as Laura attempts to rise to get the dessert, Amanda directs, "No sister, no sister—you be the lady this time and I'll be the darky." Amanda's words and behavior here foreshadow the more elaborate impersonation she will devise for the play's climax in the last scene. Then, despite the sarcasm of Tom and with Laura's forbearance, Amanda tells once more the story of her gentleman callers in Blue Mountain, this time through reverie taking the role of her younger self with "a pretty face and a graceful figure" and a "nimble wit." After the story she transfers her pretense to Laura as she directs her to prepare for her own gentleman callers. Just as her brother did earlier in the scene, Laura attempts to take refuge from her mother's painful charade, slipping "*in a fugitive manner through the half-open portieres*," which she draws gently behind her. By the end of the first scene, then, Amanda has established the set as her stage, has assumed several roles, and has attempted to design a kind of scenario for two reluctant players whose gestures clearly evidence their own desire to escape Amanda's influence.

Scenes II and III continue to elaborate the dramatic metaphor as Amanda tries to shape the roles of Laura and Tom. In Scene II Amanda enters looking grim and hopeless after discovering that Laura has played truant from Rubicam's Business College. Williams' stage directions here make it clear that Amanda deliberately engages in "*a bit of acting.*" Before speaking to Laura, who watches her nervously, Amanda "*slowly opens her purse and removes a dainty white handkerchief which she shakes out delicately and delicately touches to her lips and nostrils.*" Amanda proceeds to re-enact for Laura's benefit the scene with the typing instructor, going so far even to quote the dialogue carefully. Laura, obviously shaken by her mother's accusations, explains how she spent the time her mother supposed her to be at school. When Amanda, continuing her dejected air, replies, "You did all this to deceive me, just for deception?" Laura calls attention to her mother's affected pose, a pose which is in effect another role for Amanda, the suffering Madonna: "Mother, when you're disappointed, you get that awful suffering look on your face, like the picture of Jesus' mother in the museum." Once Laura confesses, at her mother's prompting, to liking a high-school hero who called her "Blue Roses," Amanda becomes revived with the thought of a new plan—to get Laura married. Refusing to accept Laura's objection that she is crippled, Amanda effusively counsels her to "cultivate other things to make up for it," ironically recommending pretense or deception to one whom she had just berated for deception. It is clear throughout this scene that Amanda's pity and her fear of what the future may hold are directed more to herself than to Laura, that in effect she is here, as earlier and later in the play, priming Laura to assume the role of the young Amanda who reigned in the Delta.

In Scene III Amanda attempts to govern Tom as she governed Laura in the preceding scene. Her accusations of deception are now levelled at Tom, who bitterly resents Amanda's criticism of his reading D.H. Lawrence, his writing, his mediocre position at the warehouse, and his fondness for the movies. As in Scene II, Amanda's fear for herself obviously motivates her attack: "What right have you to jeopardize your job? Jeopardize the security of us all? How do you think we'd manage if you were—." But Tom cuts her off, pointing to his father's picture and threatening to leave as he did. One cannot avoid the suspicion here that just as Amanda tries to design Laura as a version of her younger self, she tries here and later in the play to design Tom as an idealized version of her deserting husband. Amanda's romantic conception of the past and her commitment to an idealized reincarnation of that past haunt the entire play. But Tom, unlike his delicate sister, struggles desperately to avoid his mother's despotic direction. Calling her an "ugly babbling old witch," he struggles to put on his coat to make an escape but tears the sleeve in the attempt and angrily hurls it across the room where it strikes Laura's glass collection, sending shattering glass to the floor. Laura, who has witnessed the bitter confrontation between mother and son cries, "My glass?—menagerie. . . ."

Although Laura does not explain until Scene VII that it is Amanda who has given the name "menagerie" to her glass collection, nowhere else in the play has the designation more appropriateness than it does here, coming as it does after Amanda's manipulation of Laura in Scene II and of Tom in this scene, to symbolize Amanda's relationship to her children. Amanda's choice of diction is significant because a menagerie is a place where animals are kept and trained, especially for exhibition.[1] The action of the play defines Amanda not only as a producer of a drama but also as a proprietress of a menagerie—like the drama a means of exhibition—in which Laura and Tom are caged, trained, and displayed. And like the animals in a menagerie, Laura and Tom have attempted escape, not only by resorting to their own fantasies and illusions but even physically by retreating as they do several times to and behind the portieres, as if straining against the confines of their cage.

---

[1] In "Portrait of a Girl in Glass," Williams' short story which served as a source for this play, the glass figures are referred to as "ornaments," "articles," and "pieces." His choice of "menagerie" signals the change in focus from story to play as Amanda assumes the central position formerly held by Laura. See *One Arm and Other Stories* (New York: New Directions, 1948), 97–112.

JUDITH J. THOMPSON, "SYMBOL, MYTH, AND RITUAL IN *THE GLASS MENAGERIE, THE ROSE TATTOO, AND ORPHEUS DESCENDING*"*

The Glass Menagerie is one of Williams' most symbolically informed plays. The symbols—concrete, allusive, and evocative—are so structured as to define a world which is at once existentially constrictive and metaphorically expansive. Even as the physical constructs of time and circumstance identify the characters by their human limitations, the metaphors through which their aspirations are expressed enlarge their individual dimensions to those of archetypal stature and elevate their personal plight to universal significance.

The principal symbol in the play is, as the title suggests, the glass menagerie. It is specifically Laura's symbol, the objective correlative of her fragile, other-worldly beauty. Its stylized animal forms image her own immobilized animal or sexual nature, her arrested emotional development, and her inability to cope with the demands of a flesh-and-blood world. Given broader implications, the separate pieces of the glass collection reflect the fixed attitudes of all the members of the Wingfield family as well as their isolation from one another. Presented as crystallized forms in Tom's memory, each character is shown to be psychologically encased in a world of his own. Seeking escape, refuge, or rebirth, each imagines different versions of a transcendent reality, themselves a collection of isolatos condemned to individual fragmentation and mutual misunderstanding. Finally, in its quintessential form, the glass menagerie is symbolic of status, that temporal mode central to the play's internal structure. The underlying structure of *The Glass Menagerie* is formed by a tension between the illusion of moving forward and the reality of moving backward, between dream and destiny, the two so perfectly balanced that the effect is the arrest of time. Within this frozen moment, however, resides the significant action of the play: a cyclical motion of repetition and recurrence, the acting out again and again of a single futile pattern.

The dynamic symbol of that recurrent pattern is Amanda's story of the courtship ritual, herein an ironic process of anticipation, momentary fulfillment, and subsequent loss, desolation, and disillusionment. As symbol, the story of Amanda and her seventeen gentleman callers forms a paradigm of experience which underlies the structure of the entire play. Life is envisioned as a series of losses, beginning with innocent expectations of its infinite possibilities and ending in confrontation with its inherent limitations. It is, indeed, this story told by Amanda at the beginning of the play which is re-enacted in its second half by Laura and Jim. Furthermore, every other event in the play repeats the process. A similar pattern of great expectations and subsequent despair informs the story of Tom, the aspiring poet whose dreams of life as a meaningful voyage end only in aimless drifting. Although Jim's ability to compromise with a diminished reality differentiates him from the other characters, the pattern also informs his story, for he is the high school hero—"The Pirate of Penzance"—who is reduced to a clerk in a warehouse, his romantic libretto exchanged for a paean to capitalistic enter-

---

* *Tennessee Williams: A Tribute.* Ed. Jack Tharpe (Jackson, Miss.: U P of Mississippi, 1977): 685–92.

prise. The pattern of anticipation, brief fulfillment, and subsequent loss is capsulized at the very beginning of the play in the message contained in the father's picture postcard: "Hello—Goodbye!," a microcosmic summary of the play's symbolic structure.

A symbolic embodiment of the last of the gentleman callers, the father is present throughout the play in the image of a larger-than-life-size photograph which lights up whenever Amanda recalls him, thereby reminding the audience of the entire pattern of her story, from its inflated beginnings to its prosaic end. The inevitability of the pattern is reinforced by implied analogies among the three male figures. As the suitor with the winning smile, the father is linked with Jim, the reincarnated gentleman caller, who shares his charm and grin. As the deserting husband, he is linked with Tom, the prodigal son, who shares his escapist impulse. All three embody the romantic concept of war as heroic adventure in their respective roles of World War I doughboy, make-believe pirate, and merchant seaman. Moreover, Jim's romantic stage role as the Pirate of Penzance in Gilbert and Sullivan's comic opera both foreshadows and mocks Tom's dream of playing a similarly romantic role by joining the Merchant Marines. Thus, Jim's stage symbol, the image of "a sailing vessel with Jolly Roger"—the black flag of the pirate ship—is flashed on the screen whenever Tom dreams of his maritime adventure, a subliminal undermining of Tom's transcendent aspirations. Even in their family name, juxtaposing *wing* with *field*, the symbols of transcendence are fused with the constructs of mundane reality, relentlessly suggesting the painful disparity between aspiration and actuality, or between what the characters would be and what they must be.

The tension between the ideal and the real is also exemplified in the religious imagery which ironically links both the members of this fragmented household and the romanticized Jim to the Christian Holy Family. The incongruity of superimposing the images of Christian archetypes of love and sacrifice onto pathetically inadequate representatives painfully emphasizes modern man's loss of that original mythic union between heaven and earth, the divine and the human, spirit and flesh. At the same time, it poignantly reveals a continued yearning for redemption from a world devoid of spiritually transcendent values. Thus, the intensity of Amanda's disappointment with Laura's failure to fulfill her expectations at Rubicam's Business College suggests her analogy to "the picture of Jesus' mother in the museum," the mater dolorosa of Christian art, image of martyred maternity. Laura herself evokes the image of saint, nun, or child of God whose relics, the profane collection of her father's phonograph records, assume the miraculous function of creating a harmonious sanctuary in which her crippled psyche is momentarily healed of the wounds incurred in a discordant reality. The All-American Jim is elevated to a Christ figure or savior, the news of his coming to dinner referred to as an "annunciation," the promise of birth. Tom suggests an ironic inversion of the archetypal Son, a "bastard son of a bastard," a dispossessed heir who "followed . . . in my father's footsteps" by his liberation from and repudiation of inherited responsibilities. The father himself, "a telephone man—who fell in love with long distance," is thus symbolic of the absent and incommunicado God of the modern world.

The play's symbols are not derived exclusively from Christian myth, however. Each character is invested with a matrix of multiple images, drawn from sources both sacred and secular, Christian and pagan. Amanda's character and monologues are infused with a nostalgia which taps an emotional memory far beyond her *"Gone With the Wind"* account of her southern girlhood. In her first monologue of the seventeen gentleman callers, the very exaggeration of the number of suitors recalls fairy tale and the legends of romance in which the princess is beleaguered by suitors until the perfect knight or prince appears. The pastoral implications of suitors who are "planters and sons of planters" recall both the Edenic garden and ancient myths of gods and goddesses of fertility. Amanda is an Aphrodite called on by multiple analogues of Adonis. Her story always begins the same, on a Sunday morning in Blue Mountain, combining the Christian religious day with overtones of Olympus, the archetypal point of epiphany. It always ends at Moon Lake, evoking the experience of a fall, from chastity or innocence. At Moon Lake, the pastoral scene disintegrates into a graveyard, the uprooted or unweeded garden, Amanda's admirers have "turned up their toes to the daisies" after meeting violent ends. Success or survival depends on transplantation, the exchange of those genteel values of the fertile Delta of Greene County for those of the cold North, where at least one of her former suitors is transformed from beauty and youth to a lone "Wolf of Wall Street," a modern Midas whose touch turns all sustenance to unregenerate gold. The significance of the allusive imagery and fatalistic pattern of Amanda's story extends beyond that of a paradigm for the historical collapse of the Plantation South in civil strife, beyond the corruption of the New World through mercenary exploitation. It evokes the myth of the Fall itself: humankind's expulsion from Eden, the subsequent violence of brother against brother, and the perversion by man's inherently defective nature of all attempts to cultivate "a paradise within."

In anticipation of a new gentleman caller, Amanda recounts a still earlier memory of spring and courtship, set in a kind of Dionysian meadow where the sexual and the spiritual were once reconciled: fever and flowers, the heat of passion and the sympathetic sensuousness of nature. Amanda's description of that momentous spring when she met her husband is perhaps one of the most lyrical passages in Williams' plays. At a breathless pace, Amanda more nearly sings than speaks her story, repeating the word *jonquils* until its sensuous and lyrical syllables assume incantatory power, invoking a flood of memories of rebirth and rejuvenation. Amanda is endowed with the archetypal attributes of May Queen, the spirit of vegetation and fertility crowned with flowers, who, amidst gaiety and dancing, enacts the ritual of spring, the mating rite. Because the boy she meets is also the husband who abandons her to the dark tenement in an impoverished reality, the story of Amanda also recalls the myth of Persephone, goddess of spring whom Pluto snatched from her flower-gathering to his dark underworld. Like Persephone, Amanda has lost her eternal spring and bitterly mourns the transitory nature of youth, love, and beauty. Her experience has taught her that beauty and charm may be enticements of seduction and love itself an instrument of exploitation. Thus, the youthful Amanda who triggers collective images of Aphrodite, May Queen, Persephone, and Princess also reveals the darker side of the feminine archetype, of woman as entrapment and danger. To Laura she speaks as femme fatale: "All pretty girls are a trap." To Tom, she is the Terrible Mother, the womb of the earth become the devouring maw of

the underworld, to which the fairy-tale analogue is the "ugly—babbling old—
witch," as Tom calls her. The anticipation of a gentleman caller, however, not
only permits Amanda to take on the attributes of May Queen again for a brief
time but also allows her to assume the benevolent role of fairy godmother,
attempting to transform the crippled Laura into a Cinderella, as she urges
her to wish on a "little silver slipper of a moon."

The symbolism associated with Laura is composed largely of religious and
ascetic images connoting the innocent other-worldiness of the saint, the
cloistered nun, and the chaste virgin. In "Production Notes," Williams says
that the light upon Laura should have "a peculiar pristine clarity such as
light used in early religious portraits of female saints or madonnas." Appropriately, candlelight, the halo of illumination set before shrines, is her mi-
lieu. Jim's attentions light "her inwardly with altar candles," the warmth of
religious devotion, while her final disappointment is revealed as if "the holy
candles on the altar of Laura's face have been snuffed out," the loss of faith.
In reinforcement of her saintly aspect, Amanda, Jim, and Tom call her
"Sister," the traditional address for a nun, and she calls herself "an old
maid," the eternal virgin. Her favorite animal in the glass menagerie is the
mythical unicorn, "emblem of chastity and the lover of virgins" (Frye, 152).
The recurrent music of *The Glass Menagerie*, which may be imagined as the
distant sound of a calliope on a merry-go-round, evokes all the other images
which characterize Laura's inner world: the tiny stationary glass animals, her
childlike nature, and her uniqueness—in circus terms called freakishness; in
religious terms, miraculous; in temporal terms, anachronistic. Her symbolic
name of "Blue Roses" emphasizes her unnatural or extraterrestrial nature, as
does her favorite retreat, "the Jewel Box, that big glass house where they
raise the tropical flowers," a metaphor for Laura's inner world, herself the
rara avis or exotic flower that cannot survive transplantation to the outside
world. Finally, Laura's name resembles *laurel*, the name of the flowering tree
into which the mythic Daphne was transformed after evading the sexual
pursuit of Appollo, thereby refusing the call to sexual maturity.

Images of modern existential man dominate Tom's symbolic characterization: the demonic images of fragmentation, suffocation, and alienation.
He identifies both the urban tenement and the warehouse as modern analogues of hell, himself sealed in a coffin, an ironic *"czar* of the *underworld*," his
deepest aspirations smoldering in frustration. Driven by the oppressive and
repressive circumstances of his life and seduced by the illusory images of the
movie screen to believe in a rainbow at the end of the journey, Tom attempts
the sea voyage which is not only his personal quest for self-realization, but
also represents the attempt of twentieth century man to restore to wholeness
the fragmented self, threatened by dehumanization and disintegration.
Tom's struggle to integrate the primal instincts of "a lover, a hunter, a
fighter" with the creative impulse of the poet suggests the attempt of modern
man to heal that deep split between body and soul, the senses and the spirit,
which characterizes the modern malaise. Liberated from Hades, however,
Tom finds himself an aimless drifter in its modern equivalent, the Wasteland,
self-exiled among the ruins of a nihilistic landscape. All the symbols of hope
through which the characters have expressed their private visions of transcendence—Amanda's colorful jonquils, Laura's iridescent glass figures,
Tom's flickering screen images, and the large glass sphere in the Paradise

Dance Hall—are ultimately revealed as fragments of broken dreams, as "bits of a shattered rainbow." Haunted by his abandonment of the others in his futile quest for self, Tom joins the ranks of other guilt-haunted wanderers—Cain, the Wandering Jew, the Flying Dutchman, the Ancient Mariner—representatives of archetypal alienation. Tom becomes the poète maudit, cursed with existential knowledge of the human condition and compelled to retell his story, a modern fable of the failure of love and of man's inability to transcend his solitude in a world devoid of transcendent goals.

Jim O'Connor is at once the most symbolic character in the play and the most realistic. Accordingly, the allusive imagery from which he is constructed is multiple and paradoxical, romantic and ironic. As a reincarnation of the gentleman caller, he evokes both the infinite possibilities suggested by all seventeen suitors and the limited reality defined by the last caller, the father who abandoned wife and family. Thus, Jim represents both that "long-delayed but always expected something that we live for" and, ironically, "a nice, ordinary, young man," both the ideal and the real. "Like some archetype of the universal unconscious," Jim is invested with multiple heroic images. As the reborn gentleman caller, he may be identified with a fertility god, the regenerative planter; his annunciation signals the rebirth or second coming of Christ as a savior; Amanda's wish upon "the little silver slipper of a moon" casts Jim in the role of Prince Charming to Laura's Cinderella and her Sleeping Beauty. He is the singing Pirate who will charm the Lady, and he is Superman who never fails to rescue Lois Lane. All of these symbols of expectation are invested in a character who is the epitome of the All-American boy—extroverted, dynamic, and optimistic—thoroughly acculturated to the popular version of happiness achieved through technological progress, status, and material success.

The enlargement of the characters through allusive imagery in the first part of the play is designed to heighten the emotional intensity of its climactic scene, the meeting between Laura and Jim. The mythicization of the characters combined with the symbolic value invested in the concrete props of the scene—Laura's physical transformation, the suggestion of rain, the circle of candlelight from the miraculously fire-salvaged candelabrum, and the glass of dandelion wine—all elevate the significance of their meeting beyond mere social ceremony to suggest the pagan ritual of fertility or initiation, the Christian rite of Holy Communion, and the romantic ideal of courtship. In this instance, however, symbol is divorced from substance, the mythical distinguished from the actual, and the bubbles of subjective reality in which the characters have insulated themselves are broken. At the same time, the infusion of symbolic meaning into ordinary human experience evokes an emotional response appropriate to an event of momentous import, thereby deepening the significance of the failure of union between Laura and Jim.

The process of demythicization begins with Jim's breaking of the unicorn, medieval emblem of chastity and innocence, which signals the beginning of Laura's healthy sexual and emotional development and the diminishment of her symbolic dimensions as virgin, saint, and child. As the unicorn divested of its horn is now "just like all the other horses," so Laura no longer feels freakish and estranged from vital human experience. Her emergence into Jim's world of dynamic optimism is dramatically expressed by her cavalier reaction to the broken unicorn, her private world of imaginary animals having become less important than the real one of human relationships. Thus, her use of popular slang parallels Jim's own idiomatic diction: "It's no tragedy, Freckles. Glass breaks so easily." While Laura's sexuality is awakened by Jim's natural exuberance, his deeper sensibilities are aroused by her vulnerability and virginal beauty. Thus, for the brief moment of their kiss, the symbolic fusion of experience and innocence, body and soul, sense and spirit, or reality and dream is achieved. Jim's subsequent revelation of his engagement to another girl and the finality of his departure not only abandon Laura to her shattered dreams but also deflate the entire matrix of mythical, romantic, and religious symbols. Mocked by their symbols of transcendence, the characters are identified starkly as "a mother deserted, an unmarried sister who's crippled" and a son who's a "selfish dreamer." The end of all the images and symbols developed in the play is to evoke an overwhelming sense of loss. The failure of Jim to save Laura is also the failure of the fertility god to complete the initiation rite, the failure of Christ's second coming, the failures of Prince Charming, the Pirate, and Superman to rescue the maiden in distress. Because Williams has so extended the symbolic meaning of Jim, the loss becomes one of "infinite desolation." It is the loss of all heroes, the death of all gods. Thus, through a profusion of symbolic references and a recurrent pattern of anticipation, momentary fulfillment, and ultimate despair, the meaning of the play is enlarged. It is not simply the story of one shy crippled girl, a neurotic mother, and a dreamer of a son, not the story of just one more broken family, but an analogue of modern man's alienation from God and isolation from his fellow man.

A Selective Bibliography on *The Glass Menagerie*

Adler, Thomas P. "The (Un)reliability of the Narrator in *The Glass Menagerie* and *Vieux Carré*." *The Tennessee Williams Review* 3.1 (1981): 6–9.

Balachandran, K. "Marriage and Family Life in Tennessee Williams." *Notes on Mississippi Writers* 21.2 (1989): 69–76.

Beaurline, Lester A. "*The Glass Menagerie:* From Story to Play." *Modern Drama* 8 (1965): 142–49.

Berkowitz, Gerald M. "Williams' 'Other places'—A Theatrical Metaphor in the Plays." Tharpe. 712–19.

Bloom, Harold. *Tennessee Williams's "The Glass Menagerie."* New York: Chelsea, 1988.

Bluefarb, Sam. "*The Glass Menagerie:* Three Visions of Time." *College English* 24 (1963): 513–18.

Boxhill, Roger. *Tennessee Williams.* New York: St. Martin's, 1986.

Cate, Hollis C. and Delma E. Presley. "Beyond Stereotype: Ambiguity in Amanda Wingfield." *Notes on Mississippi Writers* 3 (1971): 91–100.

Davis, Joseph K. "Landscapes of the Dislocated Mind in Williams' *The Glass Menagerie*." Tharpe 192–206.

Donahue, Francis. *The Dramatic World of Tennessee Williams.* New York: Ungar, 1964.

Frye, Northrop. *Fables of Identity: Studies in Poetic Mythology.* New York: Harcourt, 1963.

Ganz, Arthur. "The Desparate Morality of the Plays of Tennessee Williams." *American Scholar* 31 (1962): 278:94.

Griff, Louis K. "Fathers, Daughters, and Spiritual Sisters: Marsha Norman's *'night Mother* and Tennessee Williams's *The Glass Menagerie.*" *Text and Performance Quarterly* 9.3 (1989): 224–28.

Howell, Elmo. "The Function of Gentlemen Callers: A Note on Tennessee Williams' *The Glass Menagerie.*" *Notes on Mississippi Writers* 2 (1970): 83–90.

Jones, John H. "The Missing Link: The Father in *The Glass Menagerie.*" *Notes on Mississippi Writers* 20.1 (1988): 29–38.

Kahn, Sy. "Through a Glass Menagerie Darkly: The World of Tennessee Williams." *Modern American Drama: Essays in Criticism.* Ed. William E. Taylor. DeLand, FL: Everett/Edwards, 1968.

King, Thomas L. "Irony and Distance in *The Glass Menagerie.*" *Educational Theater Journal* 25 (1973): 207–14.

Londre, Felicia. *Tennessee Williams.* New York: Ungar, 1979.

Miller, Arthur. "Morality and Modern Drama." *Educational Theater Journal* 10 (1959): 190–202.

Napieralski, Edmund A. "Tennessee Williams' *The Glass Menagerie:* The Dramatic Metaphor." *Southern Quarterly* 16 (1977): 1–12.

Nelson, Benjamin. *Tennessee Williams: The Man and His Work.* New York: Obolensky, 1961.

Parker, Brian. "The Composition of *The Glass Menagerie:* An Argument for Complexity." *Modern Drama* 25.3 (1982): 409–22.

Parker, R. B. "The Circle Closed: A Psychological Reading of *The Glass Menagerie* and *The Two Character Play.*" *Modern Drama* 28.4 (1985): 517–34.

———. *The Glass Menagerie: A Collection of Critical Essays.* Englewood Cliffs: Prentice-Hall, 1983.

Scheye, Thomas E. "*The Glass Menagerie:* 'It's no tragedy, Freckles.' " Tharpe 207–13.

Smith, Harry W. "Tennessee Williams and Jo Mielziner: The Memory Plays." *Theatre Survey: The American Journal of Theatre History* 23.2 (1982): 223–35.

Stein, Roger B. "*The Glass Menagerie* Revisited: Catastrophe without Violence." *Western Humanities Review* 18 (1964): 141–53.

Tharpe, Jack, ed. *Tennessee Williams: A Tribute.* Jackson, Miss.: U P of Mississippi, 1977.

Thompson, Judith J. "Symbol, Myth, and Ritual in *The Glass Menagerie, The Rose Tattoo,* and *Orpheus Descending.*" Tharpe 679–711.

Tischler, Nancy M. *Tennessee Williams: Rebellious Puritan.* New York: Citadel Press, 1961.

Watson, Charles S. "The Revision of *The Glass Menagerie:* The Passing of Good Manners." *Southern Literary Journal* 8 (1976): 74–78.

Samuel Beckett (1906–1989)

ALL THAT FALL

A PLAY FOR RADIO

CHARACTERS

MRS. ROONEY (MADDY), *a lady in her seventies*

CHRISTY, *a carter*

MR. TYLER, *a retired bill-broker*

MR. SLOCUM, *Clerk of the Racecourse*

TOMMY, *a porter*

MR. BARRELL, *a station-master*

MISS FITT, *a lady in her thirties*

A FEMALE VOICE

DOLLY, *a small girl*

MR. ROONEY (DAN), *blind husband of Mrs. Rooney*

JERRY, *a small boy*

Rural sounds. Sheep, bird, cow, cock, severally, then together. Silence. MRS. ROONEY advances along country road towards railway station. Sound of her dragging feet. Music faint from house by way. "Death and the Maiden."[1] The steps slow down, stop.

MRS. ROONEY.   Poor woman. All alone in that ruinous old house.

[*Music louder. Silence but for music playing. The steps resume. Music dies. MRS. ROONEY murmurs, melody. Her murmur dies. Sound of approaching cartwheels. The cart stops. The steps slow down, stop.*]

MRS. ROONEY.   Is that you, Christy?
CHRISTY.   It is, Ma'am.
MRS. ROONEY.   I thought the hinny[2] was familiar. How is your poor wife?
CHRISTY.   No better, Ma'am.
MRS. ROONEY.   Your daughter then?
CHRISTY.   No worse, Ma'am.

[*Silence.*]

MRS. ROONEY.   Why do you halt? [*Pause.*] But why do I halt?

[*Silence*]

CHRISTY.   Nice day for the races, Ma'am.
10   MRS. ROONEY.   No doubt it is. [*Pause.*] But will it hold up? [*Pause. With emotion.*] Will it hold up?

[*Silence.*]

---

[1] "Death and the Maiden" ("Der Tod und das Mädchen") is a string quartet in D minor by the Austrian composer Franz Peter Schubert (1795–1828).
[2] The offspring of a stallion and a donkey.

CHRISTY.   I suppose you wouldn't—

MRS. ROONEY.   Surely to goodness that cannot be the up mail I hear already.

[*Silence. The hinny neighs. Silence.*]

CHRISTY.   Damn the mail.

MRS. ROONEY.   Oh thank God for that! I could have sworn I heard it, thundering up the track in the far distance. [*Pause.*] So hinnies whinny. Well, it is not surprising.

CHRISTY.   I suppose you wouldn't be in need of a small load of dung?

MRS. ROONEY.   Dung? What class of dung?

20 CHRISTY.   Stydung.

MRS. ROONEY.   Stydung . . . I like your frankness, Christy. [*Pause*] I'll ask the master. [*Pause*] Christy.

CHRISTY.   Yes, Ma'am.

MRS. ROONEY.   Do you find anything . . . bizarre about my way of speaking? [*Pause.*] I do not mean the voice. [*Pause.*] No, I mean the words. [*Pause. More to herself.*] I use none but the simplest words, I hope, and yet I sometimes find my way of speaking very . . . bizarre. [*Pause.*] Mercy! What was that?

CHRISTY.   Never mind her, Ma'am, she's very fresh in herself today.

[*Silence.*]

30 MRS. ROONEY.   Dung? What would we want with dung, at our time of life? [*Pause.*] Why are you on your feet down on the road? Why do you not climb up on the crest of your manure and let yourself be carried along? Is it that you have no head for heights?

[*Silence.*]

CHRISTY [*to the hinny*].   Yep! [*Pause. Louder.*] Yep wiyya to hell owwa that!

[*Silence.*]

MRS. ROONEY.   She does not move a muscle. [*Pause.*] I too should be getting along, if I do not wish to arrive late at the station. [*Pause.*] But a moment ago she neighed and pawed the ground. And now she refuses to advance. Give her a good welt on the rump. [*Sound of welt. Pause.*] Harder! [*Sound of welt. Pause.*] Well! If someone were to do that for me I should not dally.

40   [*Pause.*] How she gazes at me to be sure, with her great moist cleg-tormented[3] eyes! Perhaps if I were to move on, down the road, out of her field of vision. . . . [*Sound of welt.*] No, no, enough! Take her by the snaffle and pull her eyes away from me. Oh this is awful! [*She moves on. Sound of her dragging feet.*] What have I done to deserve all this, what, what? [*Dragging feet.*] So long ago. . . . No! No! [*Dragging feet. Quotes.*] "Sigh out a something something tale of things, Done long ago and ill done." [*She halts.*] How can I go on, I cannot. Oh let me just flop down flat on the road like a big fat jelly out of a bowl and never move again! A great big slop

---

[3] Fly-bitten.

thick with grit and dust and flies, they would have to scoop me up with a
50 shovel. [*Pause.*] Heavens, there is that up mail again, what will become of
me! [*The dragging steps resume.*] Oh I am just a hysterical old hag, I know,
destroyed with sorrow and pining and gentility and church-going and fat
and rheumatism and childlessness. [*Pause. Brokenly.*] Minnie! Little Minnie! [*Pause.*] Love, that is all I asked, a little love, daily, twice daily, fifty
years of twice daily love like a Paris horse-butcher's regular, what normal
woman wants affection? A peck on the jaw at morning near the ear, and
another at evening, peck, peck, till you grow whiskers on you. There is that
lovely laburnum[4] again.

[*Dragging feet. Sound of bicycle-bell. It is old* MR. TYLER *coming up behind her on his
bicycle, on his way to the station. Squeak of brakes. He slows down and rides abreast
of her.*]

MR. TYLER.   Mrs. Rooney! Pardon me if I do not doff my cap, I'd fall off.
60   Divine day for the meeting.
MRS. ROONEY.   Oh, Mr. Tyler, you startled the life out of me stealing up
behind me like that like a deer-stalker! Oh!
MR. TYLER [*playfully*].   I rang the bell, Mrs. Rooney, the moment I sighted
you I started tinkling my bell, now don't you deny it.
MRS. ROONEY.   Your bell is one thing, Mr. Tyler, and you are another. What
news of your poor daughter?
MR. TYLER.   Fair, fair. They removed everything, you know, the whole . . . er
. . . bag of tricks. Now I am grandchildless.

[*Dragging feet.*]

MRS. ROONEY.   Gracious how you wobble! Dismount, for mercy's sake, or ride
70   on.
MR. TYLER.   Perhaps if I were to lay my hand lightly on your shoulder, Mrs.
Rooney, how would that be? [*Pause.*] Would you permit that?
MRS. ROONEY.   No, Mr. Rooney, Mr. Tyler I mean, I am tired of light old
hands on my shoulders and other senseless places, sick and tired of them.
Heavens, here comes Connolly's van! [*She halts. Sound of motor-van. It
approaches, passes with thunderous rattle, recedes.*] Are you all right, Mr. Tyler?
[*Pause.*] Where is he? [*Pause.*] Ah there you are! [*The dragging steps resume.*]
That was a narrow squeak.
MR. TYLER.   I alit in the nick of time.
80 MRS. ROONEY.   It is suicide to be abroad. But what is it to be at home, Mr.
Tyler, what is it to be at home? A lingering dissolution. Now we are white
with dust from head to foot. I beg your pardon?
MR. TYLER.   Nothing, Mrs. Rooney, nothing, I was merely cursing, under my
breath. God and man, under my breath, and the wet Saturday afternoon
of my conception. My back tire has gone down again. I pumped it hard as
iron before I set out. And now I am on the rim.
MRS. ROONEY.   Oh what a shame!
MR. TYLER.   Now if it were the front I should not so much mind. But the

---

4 An ornamental shrub with bright yellow flowers.

back. The back! The chain! The oil! The grease! The hub! The brakes!
90   The gear! No! It is too much!

[*Dragging steps.*]

MRS. ROONEY.   Are we very late, Mr. Tyler? I have not the courage to look at
     my watch.
MR. TYLER [*bitterly*].   Late! I on my bicycle as I bowled along was already late.
     Now therefore we are doubly late, trebly, quadrupedly late. Would I had
     shot by you, without a word.

[*Dragging feet.*]

MRS. ROONEY.   Whom are you meeting, Mr. Tyler?
MR. TYLER.   Hardy. [*Pause.*] We used to climb together. [*Pause.*] I saved his
     life once. [*Pause.*] I have not forgotten it.

[*Dragging feet. They stop.*]

MRS. ROONEY.   Let us halt a moment and let this vile dust fall back upon the
100   viler worms.

[*Silence. Rural sounds.*]

MR. TYLER.   What sky! What light! Ah in spite of all it is a blessed thing to be
     alive in such weather, and out of hospital.
MRS. ROONEY.   Alive?
MR. TYLER.   Well half alive shall we say?
MRS. ROONEY.   Speak for yourself, Mr. Tyler. I am not half alive nor anything
     approaching it. [*Pause.*] What are we standing here for? The dust will not
     settle in our time. And when it does some great roaring machine will come
     and whirl it all skyhigh again.
MR. TYLER.   Well, shall we be getting along in that case?
110 MRS. ROONEY.   No.
MR. TYLER.   Come, Mrs. Rooney—
MRS. ROONEY.   Go, Mr. Tyler, go on and leave me, listening to the cooing of
     the ringdoves. [*Cooing.*] If you see my poor blind Dan tell him I was on my
     way to meet him when it all came over me again, like a flood. Say to him,
     Your poor wife, she told me to tell you it all came flooding over her again
     and . . . [*The voice breaks*] . . . she simply went back home . . . straight back
     home . . .
MR. TYLER.   Come, Mrs. Rooney, come, the mail has not yet gone up, just
     take my free arm and we'll be there with time and to spare.
120 MRS. ROONEY [*sobbing*].   What? What's all this now? [*Calmer.*] Can't you see
     I'm in trouble? [*With anger.*] Have you no respect for misery? [*Sobbing.*]
     Minnie! Little Minnie!
MR. TYLER.   Come, Mrs. Rooney, come, the mail has not yet gone up, just
     take my free arm and we'll be there with time to spare.
MRS. ROONEY [*brokenly*].   In her forties now she'd be, I don't know, fifty,
     girding up her lovely little loins, getting ready for the change . . .
MR. TYLER.   Come, Mrs. Rooney, come, the mail—
MRS. ROONEY [*exploding*].   Will you get along with you, Mr. Rooney, Mr.

Tyler I mean, will you get along with you now and cease molesting me?
130 What kind of a country is this where a woman can't weep her heart out
on the highways and byways without being tormented by retired bill-
brokers! [Mr. Tyler *prepares to mount his bicycle.*] Heavens you're not going to ride her flat! [Mr. Tyler *mounts.*] You'll tear your tube to ribbons!
[Mr. Tyler *rides off. Receding sound of bumping bicycle. Silence. Cooing.*] Venus birds! Billing in the woods all the long summer long. [*Pause.*] Oh
cursed corset! If I could let it out, without indecent exposure. Mr. Tyler!
Mr. Tyler! Come back and unlace me behind the hedge! [*She laughs
wildly, ceases.*] What's wrong with me, what's wrong with me, never tranquil, seething out of my dirty old pelt, out of my skull, oh to be in at-
140 oms, in atoms! [*Frenziedly.*] ATOMS! [*Silence. Cooing. Faintly.*] Jesus!
[*Pause.*] Jesus!

[*Sound of car coming up behind her. It slows down and draws up beside her, engine
running. It is* Mr. Slocum, *the Clerk of the Racecourse.*]

Mr. Slocum. Is anything wrong, Mrs. Rooney? You are bent all double.
Have you a pain in the stomach?

[*Silence.* Mrs. Rooney *laughs wildly. Finally.*]

Mrs. Rooney. Well if it isn't my old admirer the Clerk of the Course, in his
limousine.
Mr. Slocum. May I offer you a lift, Mrs. Rooney? Are you going in my
direction?
Mrs. Rooney. I am, Mr. Slocum, we all are. [*Pause.*] How is your poor
mother?
150 Mr. Slocum. Thank you, she is fairly comfortable. We manage to keep her
out of pain. That is the great thing, Mrs. Rooney, is it not?
Mrs. Rooney. Yes, indeed, Mr. Slocum, that is the great thing. I don't know
how you do it. [*Pause. She slaps her cheek violently.*] Ah these wasps!
Mr. Slocum [*coolly*]. May I then offer you a seat, Madam?
Mrs. Rooney [*with exaggerated enthusiasm*]. Oh that would be heavenly, Mr.
Slocum, just simply heavenly. [*Dubiously.*] But would I ever get in, you look
very high off the ground today, these new balloon tires I presume. [*Sound
of door opening and* Mrs. Rooney *trying to get in.*] Does this roof never come
off? No? [*Efforts of* Mrs. Rooney.] No . . . I'll never do it . . . you'll have to
160 get down, Mr. Slocum, and help me from the rear. [*Pause.*] What was that?
[*Pause. Aggrieved.*] This is all your suggestion, Mr. Slocum, not mine. Drive
on, Sir, drive on.
Mr. Slocum [*switching off the engine*]. I'm coming, Mrs. Rooney, I'm coming,
give me time, I'm as stiff as yourself.

[*Sound of* Mr. Slocum *extracting himself from driver's seat.*]

Mrs. Rooney. Stiff! Well I like that! And me heaving all over back and front.
[*To herself.*] The dry old reprobate!
Mr. Slocum [*in position behind her*]. Now, Mrs. Rooney, how shall we do this?
Mrs. Rooney. As if I were a bale, Mr. Slocum, don't be afraid. [*Pause. Sounds
of effort.*] That's the way! [*Effort.*] Lower! [*Effort.*] Wait! [*Pause.*] No, don't let
170 go! [*Pause.*] Suppose I do get up, will I ever get down?

MR. SLOCUM [*breathing hard*].   You'll get down, Mrs. Rooney, you'll get down. We may not get you up, but I warrant you we'll get you down.

[*He resumes his efforts. Sound of these.*]

MRS. ROONEY.   Oh! . . . Lower! . . . Don't be afraid! . . . We're past the age when . . . There! . . . Now! . . . Get your shoulder under it . . . Oh . . . [*Giggles.*] Oh glory! . . . Up! Up! . . . Ah! . . . I'm in! [*Panting of* MR. SLOCUM. *He slams the door. In a scream.*] My frock! You've nipped my frock! [MR. SLOCUM *opens the door.* MRS. ROONEY *frees her frock.* MR. SLOCUM *slams the door. His violent unintelligible muttering as he walks round to the other door. Tearfully.*] My nice frock! Look what you've done to my nice frock! [MR. SLOCUM *gets*
180   *into his seat, slams driver's door, presses starter. The engine does not start. He releases starter.*] What will Dan say when he sees me?
MR. SLOCUM.   Has he then recovered his sight?
MRS. ROONEY.   No, I mean when he knows, what will he say when he feels the hole? [MR. SLOCUM *presses starter. As before. Silence.*] What are you doing, Mr. Slocum?
MR. SLOCUM.   Gazing straight before me, Mrs. Rooney, through the windscreen, into the void.
MRS. ROONEY.   Start her up, I beseech you, and let us be off. This is awful!
MR. SLOCUM [*dreamily.*]   All morning she went like a dream and now she is
190   dead. That is what you get for a good deed. [*Pause. Hopefully.*] Perhaps if I were to choke her. [*He does so, presses the starter. The engine roars. Roaring to make himself heard.*] She was getting too much air!

[*He throttles down, grinds in his first gear, moves off, changes up in a grinding of gears.*]

MRS. ROONEY [*in anguish.*]   Mind the hen! [*Scream of brakes. Squawk of hen.*] Oh, mother, you have thrashed her, drive on, drive on! [*The car accelerates. Pause.*] What a death! One minute picking happy at the dung, on the road, in the sun, with now and then a dust bath, and then—bang!—all her troubles over. [*Pause.*] All the laying and the hatching. [*Pause.*] Just one great squawk and then . . . peace. [*Pause.*] They would have slit her weasand[5] in any case. [*Pause.*] Here we are, let me down. [*The car slows*
200   *down, stops, engine running.* MR. SLOCUM *blows his horn. Pause. Louder. Pause.*] What are you up to now, Mr. Slocum? We are at a standstill, all danger is past and you blow your horn. Now if instead of blowing it now you had blown it at that unfortunate—

[*Horn violently.* TOMMY *the porter appears at top of station steps.*]

MR. SLOCUM [*calling*].   Will you come down, Tommy, and help this lady out, she's stuck. [TOMMY *descends the steps.*] Open the door, Tommy, and ease her out.

[TOMMY *opens the door.*]

TOMMY.   Certainly, sir. Nice day for the races, sir. What would you fancy for—

---
[5] Throat.

MRS. ROONEY. Don't mind me. Don't take any notice of me. I do not exist.
210   That fact is well known.
MR. SLOCUM. Do as you're asked, Tommy, for the love of God.
TOMMY. Yessir. Now, Mrs. Rooney.

[He starts pulling her out.]

MRS. ROONEY. Wait, Tommy, wait now, don't bustle me, just let me wheel
round and get my feet to the ground. *[Her efforts to achieve this.]* Now.
TOMMY *[pulling her out.]* Mind your feather, Ma'am. *[Sounds of effort]*. Easy
now, easy.
MRS. ROONEY. Wait, for God's sake, you'll have me beheaded.
TOMMY. Crouch down, Mrs. Rooney, crouch down, and get your head in the
open.
220 MRS. ROONEY. Crouch down! At my time of life! This is lunacy!
TOMMY. Press her down, sir.

[Sounds of combined efforts.]

MRS. ROONEY. Pity!
TOMMY. Now! She's coming! Straighten up, Ma'am. There!

[MR. SLOCUM slams the door.]

MRS. ROONEY. Am I out?

[The voice of MR. BARRELL, the station-master, raised in anger.]

MR. BARRELL. Tommy! Tommy! Where the hell is he?

[MR. SLOCUM grinds in his gear.]

TOMMY *[hurriedly.]* You wouldn't have something for the Ladies Plate, sir. I
was given Flash Harry.
MR. SLOCUM *[scornfully]*. Flash Harry! That carthorse!
MR. BARRELL *[at the top of steps, roaring]*. Tommy! Blast your bleeding
230   bloody—*[He sees MRS. ROONEY]*. Oh, Mrs. Rooney . . . *[MR. SLOCUM drives
away in a grinding of gears.]* Who's that crucifying his gearbox, Tommy?
TOMMY. Old Cissy Slocum.
MRS. ROONEY. Cissy Slocum! That's a nice way to refer to your betters. Cissy
Slocum! And you an orphan!
MR. BARRELL *[angrily to TOMMY]*. What are you doing stravaging[6] down here
on the public road? This is no place for you at all! Nip up there on the
platform now and whip out the truck! Won't the twelve-thirty be on top of
us before we can turn around?
TOMMY *[bitterly]*. And that's the thanks you get for a Christian act.
240 MR. BARRELL *[violently]*. Get on with you now before I report you! *[Slow feet
of TOMMY climbing steps.]* Do you want me to come down to you with the
shovel? *[The feet quicken, recede, cease.]* Ah God forgive me, it's a hard life.
[Pause.] Well, Mrs. Rooney, it's nice to see you up and about again. You
were laid up there a long time.
MRS. ROONEY. Not long enough, Mr. Barrell. *[Pause.]* Would I were still in

---

[6] Roaming.

bed, Mr. Barrell. [*Pause.*] Would I were lying stretched out in my comfortable bed, Mr. Barrell, just wasting slowly, painlessly away, keeping up my strength with arrowroot and calves-foot jelly, till in the end you wouldn't see me under the blankets any more than a board. [*Pause.*] Oh no

250 coughing or spitting or bleeding or vomiting, just drifting gently down into the higher life, and remembering, remembering . . . [*The voice breaks*] . . . all the silly unhappiness . . . as though . . . it had never happened . . . What did I do with that handkerchief? [*Sound of handkerchief loudly applied.*] How long have you been master of this station now, Mr. Barrell?

Mr. Barrell. Don't ask me, Mrs. Rooney, don't ask me.

Mrs. Rooney. You stepped into your father's shoes, I believe, when he took them off.

Mr. Barrell. Poor Pappy! [*Reverent pause.*] He didn't live long to enjoy his ease.

260 Mrs. Rooney. I remember him clearly. A small ferrety purple-faced widower, deaf as a doornail, very testy and snappy. [*Pause.*] I suppose you'll be retiring soon yourself, Mr. Barrell, and growing your roses. [*Pause.*] Did I understand you to say the twelve-thirty would soon be upon us?

Mr. Barrell. Those were my words.

Mrs. Rooney. But according to my watch which is more or less right—or was—by the eight o'clock news the time is now coming up to twelve . . . [*pause as she consults her watch*] . . . thirty-six. [*Pause.*] And yet upon the other hand the up mail has not yet gone through. [*Pause.*] Or has it sped by unbeknown to me? [*Pause.*] For there was a moment there, I remember

270 now, I was so plunged in sorrow I wouldn't have heard a steam roller go over me. [*Pause.* Mr. Barrell *turns to go.*] Don't go, Mr. Barrell! [Mr. Barrell *goes. Loud.*] Mr. Barrell! [*Pause. Louder.*] Mr. Barrell!

[Mr. Barrell *comes back.*]

Mr. Barrell [*testily*]. What is it, Mrs. Rooney, I have my work to do.

[*Silence. Sound of wind.*]

Mrs. Rooney. The wind is getting up. [*Pause. Wind.*] The best of the day is over. [*Pause. Wind. Dreamily.*] Soon the rain will begin to fall and go on falling, all afternoon. [Mr. Barrell *goes.*] Then at evening the clouds will part, the setting sun will shine an instant, then sink, behind the hills. [*She realizes* Mr. Barrell *has gone.*] Mr. Barrell! Mr. Barrell! [*Silence.*] I estrange them all. They come towards me, uninvited, bygones bygones, full of

280 kindness, anxious to help . . . [*the voice breaks*] . . . genuinely pleased . . . to see me again . . . looking so well . . . [*Handkerchief.*] A few simple words . . . from my heart . . . and I am all alone . . . once more. . . . [*Handkerchief. Vehemently.*] I should not be out at all. I should never leave the grounds! [*Pause.*] Oh there is that Fitt woman, I wonder will she bow to me. [*Sound of* Miss Fitt *approaching, humming a hymn. She starts climbing the steps.*] Miss Fitt! [Miss Fitt *halts, stops humming.*] Am I then invisible, Miss Fitt? Is this cretonne[7] so becoming to me that I merge into the masonry? [Miss Fitt

---

[7] A strong cotton or linen cloth, generally used for upholstery or curtains.

descends a step.] That is right, Miss Fitt, look closely and you will finally distinguish a once female shape.

290 MISS FITT.   Mrs. Rooney! I saw you, but I did not know you.

MRS. ROONEY.   Last Sunday we worshipped together. We knelt side by side at the same altar. We drank from the same chalice. Have I so changed since then?

MISS FITT [*shocked*].   Oh but in church, Mrs. Rooney, in church I am alone with my Maker. Are not you? [*Pause.*] Why even the sexton himself, you know, when he takes up the collection, knows it is useless to pause before me. I simply do not see the plate, or bag, whatever it is they use, how could I? [*Pause.*] Why even when all is over and I go out into the sweet fresh air, why even then for the first furlong or so I stumble in a kind of daze as you
300 might say, oblivious to my co-religionists. And they are very kind I must admit—the vast majority—very kind and understanding. They know me now and take no umbrage. There she goes, they say, there goes the dark Miss Fitt, alone with her Maker, take no notice of her. And they step down off the path to avoid my running into them. [*Pause.*] Ah yes, I am distray,[8] very distray, even on week-days. Ask Mother, if you do not believe me. Hetty, she says, when I start eating my doily[9] instead of the thin bread and butter, Hetty, how can you be so distray? [*Sighs.*] I suppose the truth is I am not there, Mrs. Rooney, just not really there at all. I see, hear, smell, and so on, I go through the usual motions, but my heart is not in it, Mrs.
310 Rooney, but heart is in none of it. Left to myself, with no one to check me, I would soon be flown . . . home. [*Pause.*] So if you think I cut you just now, Mrs. Rooney, you do me an injustice. All I saw was a big pale blur, just another big pale blur. [*Pause.*] Is anything amiss, Mrs. Rooney, you do not look normal somehow. So bowed and bent.

MRS. ROONEY [*ruefully*].   Maddy Rooney, née Dunne, the big pale blur. [*Pause.*] You have piercing sight, Miss Fitt, if you only knew it, literally piercing.

[*Pause.*]

MISS FITT.   Well . . . is there anything I can do, now that I am here?

MRS. ROONEY.   If you would help me up the face of this cliff, Miss Fitt, I have
320 little doubt your Maker would requite you, if no one else.

MISS FITT.   Now, now, Mrs. Rooney, don't put your teeth in me. Requite! I make these sacrifices for nothing—or not at all. [*Pause. Sound of her descending steps.*] I take it you want to lean on me, Mrs. Rooney.

MRS. ROONEY.   I asked Mr. Barrell to give me his arm, just give me his arm. [*Pause.*] He turned on his heel and strode away.

MISS FITT.   Is it my arm you want then? [*Pause. Impatiently.*] Is it my arm you want, Mrs. Rooney, or what is it?

MRS. ROONEY [*exploding*].   Your arm! Any arm! A helping hand! For five seconds! Christ what a planet!

330 MISS FITT.   Really. . . . Do you know what it is, Mrs. Rooney, I do not think it is wise for you to be going about at all.

---

8 Distrait, absent-minded, troubled.
9 A small, decorative napkin.

Mrs. Rooney [*violently*].   Come down here, Miss Fitt, and give me your arm, before I scream down the parish!

[*Pause. Wind. Sound of* Miss Fitt *descending last steps.*]

Miss Fitt [*resignedly*].   Well, I suppose it is the Protestant thing to do.
Mrs. Rooney.   Pismires[10] do it for one another. [*Pause.*] I have seen slugs do it. [Miss Fitt *proffers her arm.*] No, the other side, my dear, if it's all the same to you, I'm left-handed on top of everything else. [*She takes* Miss Fitt's *right arm.*] Heavens, child, you're just a bag of bones, you need building up. [*Sound of her toiling up steps on* Miss Fitt's *arm.*] This is worse
340   than the Matterhorn, were you ever up the Matterhorn, Miss Fitt, great honeymoon resort. [*Sound of toiling.*] Why don't they have a handrail? [*Panting.*] Wait till I get some air. [*Pause.*] Don't let me go! [Miss Fitt *hums her hymn.*[11] *After a moment* Mrs. Rooney *joins in with the words.*] . . . the encircling gloo-oom . . . [Miss Fitt *stops humming*] . . . tum tum me on. [*Forte.*] The night is dark and I am far from ho-ome, tum tum—
Miss Fitt [*hysterically*].   Stop it, Mrs. Rooney, stop it, or I'll drop you!
Mrs. Rooney.   Wasn't it that they sung on the *Lusitania*?[12] Or Rock of Ages? Most touching it must have been. Or was it the *Titanic*?[13]

[*Attracted by the noise a group, including* Mr. Tyler, Mr. Barrell, *and* Tommy, *gathers at top of steps.*]

Mr. Barrell.   What the—

[*Silence.*]

350 Mr. Tyler.   Lovely day for the fixture.

[*Loud titter from* Tommy *cut short by* Mr. Barrell *with back-handed blow in the stomach. Appropriate noise from* Tommy.]

Female voice [*shrill*].   Oh look, Dolly, look!
Dolly.   What, Mamma?
Female voice.   They are stuck! [*Cackling laugh.*] They are stuck!
Mrs. Rooney.   Now we are the laughingstock of the twenty-six counties. Or is it thirty-six?
Mr. Tyler.   That is a nice way to treat your defenseless subordinates, Mr. Barrell, hitting them without warning in the pit of the stomach.
Miss Fitt.   Has anybody seen my mother?
Mr. Barrell.   Who is that?
360 Tommy.   The dark Miss Fitt.
Mr. Barrell.   Where is her face?
Mrs. Rooney.   Now, deary, I am ready if you are. [*They toil up remaining steps.*] Stand back, you cads!

[*Shuffle of feet.*]

---

10 Ants.
11 Her hymn: "Lead, Kindly Light" by John Henry Newman (1801–1890).
12 A British passenger ship sunk by German torpedoes on May 7, 1915.
13 A British passenger ship that sank after striking an iceberg on April 14, 1912.

FEMALE VOICE.   Mind yourself, Dolly!

MRS. ROONEY.   Thank you, Miss Fitt, thank you, that will do, just prop me up against the wall like a roll of tarpaulin and that will be all, for the moment. [*Pause.*] I am sorry for all this ramdam, Miss Fitt, had I known you were looking for your mother I should not have importuned you, I know what it is.

370 MR. TYLER [*in marvelling aside*].   Ramdam!

FEMALE VOICE.   Come, Dolly darling, let us take up our stand before the first class smokers. Give me your hand and hold me tight, one can be sucked under.

MR. TYLER.   You have lost your mother, Miss Fitt?

MISS FITT.   Good morning, Mr. Tyler.

MR. TYLER.   Good morning, Miss Fitt.

MR. BARRELL.   Good morning, Miss Fitt.

MISS FITT.   Good morning, Mr. Barrell.

MR. TYLER.   You have lost your mother, Miss Fitt?

380 MISS FITT.   She said she would be on the last train.

MRS. ROONEY.   Do not imagine, because I am silent, that I am not present, and alive, to all that is going on.

MR. TYLER [*to* MISS FITT].   When you say the last train—

MRS. ROONEY.   Do not flatter yourselves for one moment, because I hold aloof that my sufferings have ceased. No. The entire scene, the hills, the plain, the racecourse with its miles and miles of white rails and three red stands, the pretty little wayside station, even you yourselves, yes, I mean it, and over all the clouding blue, I see it all, I stand here and see it all with eyes . . . [*the voice breaks*] . . . through eyes . . . oh if you had my eyes

390 . . . you would understand . . . the things they have seen . . . and not looked away . . . this is nothing . . . nothing . . . what did I do with the handkerchief?

[*Pause.*]

MR. TYLER [*to* MISS FITT].   When you say the last train—[MRS. ROONEY *blows her nose violently and long*]—when you say the last train, Miss Fitt, I take it you mean the twelve-thirty.

MISS FITT.   What else could I mean, Mr. Tyler, what else could I *conceivably* mean?

MR. TYLER.   Then you have no cause for anxiety, Miss Fitt, for the twelve-thirty has not yet arrived. Look. [MISS FITT *looks.*] No, up the line. [MISS

400 FITT *looks. Patiently.*] No, Miss Fitt, follow the direction of my index. [Miss Fitt *looks.*] There. You see now. The signal. At the bawdy hour of nine. [*In rueful afterthought.*] Or three alas! [MR. BARRELL *stifles a guffaw.*] Thank you, Mr. Barrell.

MISS FITT.   But the time is now getting on for—

MR. TYLER [*patiently*].   We all know, Miss Fitt, we all know only too well what the time is now getting on for, and yet the cruel fact remains that the twelve-thirty has not yet arrived.

MISS FITT.   Not an accident, I trust! [*Pause.*] Do not tell me she has left the track! [*Pause.*] Oh darling mother! With the fresh sole for lunch!

[*Loud titter from* TOMMY, *checked as before by* MR. BARRELL.]

410 MR. BARRELL.   That's enough old guff out of you. Nip up to the box now and see has Mr. Case anything for me.

[TOMMY *goes.*]

MRS. ROONEY.   Poor Dan!

MISS FITT [*in anguish*].   What terrible thing has happened?

MR. TYLER.   Now now, Miss Fitt, do not—

MRS. ROONEY [*with vehement sadness*].   Poor Dan!

MR. TYLER.   Now now, Miss Fitt, do not give way . . . to despair, all will come right . . . in the end. [*Aside to* MR. BARRELL.] What *is* the situation, Mr. Barrell? Not a collision surely?

MRS. ROONEY [*enthusiastically*].   A collision! Oh that would be wonderful!

420 MISS FITT [*horrified*].   A collision! I knew it!

MR. TYLER.   Come, Miss Fitt, let us move a little up the platform.

MRS. ROONEY.   Yes, let us all do that. [*Pause.*] No? [*Pause.*] You have changed your mind? [*Pause.*] I quite agree, we are better here, in the shadow of the waiting-room.

MR. BARRELL.   Excuse me a moment.

MRS. ROONEY.   Before you slink away, Mr. Barrell, please, a statement of some kind, I insist. Even the slowest train on this brief line is not ten minutes and more behind its scheduled time without good cause, one imagines. [*Pause.*] We all know your station is the best kept of the entire network, but there are

430 times when that is not enough, just not enough. [*Pause.*] Now, Mr. Barrell, leave off chewing your whiskers, we are waiting to hear from you—we the unfortunate ticket-holders' nearest if not dearest.

[*Pause.*]

MR. TYLER [*reasonably*].   I do think we are owed some kind of explanation, Mr. Barrell, if only to set our minds at rest.

MR. BARRELL.   I know nothing. All I know is there has been a hitch. All traffic is retarded.

MRS. ROONEY [*derisively*].   Retarded! A hitch! Ah these celibates! Here we are eating our hearts out with anxiety for our loved ones and he calls that a hitch! Those of us like myself with heart and kidney trouble may collapse

440 at any moment and he calls that a hitch! In our ovens the Saturday roast is burning to a shrivel and he calls that—

MR. TYLER.   Here comes Tommy, running! I am glad I have been spared to see this.

TOMMY [*excitedly, in the distance*].   She's coming. [*Pause. Nearer.*] She's at the level-crossing!

[*Immediately exaggerated station sounds. Falling signals. Bells. Whistles. Crescendo of train whistle approaching. Sound of train rushing through station.*]

MRS. ROONEY [*above rush of train*].   The up mail! The up mail! [*The up mail recedes, the down train approaches, enters the station, pulls up with great hissing of steam and clashing of couplings. Noise of passengers descending, doors banging,* MR. BARRELL *shouting "Boghill! Boghill!", etc. Piercingly.*] Dan! . . . Are you all

450 right? . . . Where is he? . . . Dan! . . . Did you see my husband? . . . Dan! . . . [*Noise of station emptying. Guard's whistle. Train departing, receding. Silence*]. He isn't on it! The misery I have endured, to get here, and he isn't on it!

. . . Mr. Barrell! . . . Was he not on it? [*Pause.*] Is anything the matter, you look as if you had seen a ghost. [*Pause.*] Tommy! . . . Did you see the master?

TOMMY.   He'll be along, Ma'am, Jerry is minding him.

[MR. ROONEY *suddenly appears on platform, advancing on small boy* JERRY'S *arm. He is blind, thumps the ground with his stick and pants incessantly.*]

MRS. ROONEY.   Oh, Dan! There you are! [*Her dragging feet as she hastens towards him. She reaches him. They halt.*] Where in the world were you?

MR. ROONEY [*coolly*].   Maddy.

460 MRS. ROONEY.   Where were you all this time?

MR. ROONEY.   In the men's.

MRS. ROONEY.   Kiss me!

MR. ROONEY.   Kiss you? In public? On the platform? Before the boy? Have you taken leave of your senses?

MRS. ROONEY.   Jerry wouldn't mind. Would you, Jerry?

JERRY.   No, Ma'am.

MRS. ROONEY.   How is your poor father?

JERRY.   They took him away, Ma'am.

MRS. ROONEY.   Then you are all alone?

470 JERRY.   Yes, Ma'am.

MR. ROONEY.   Why are you here? You did not notify me.

MRS. ROONEY.   I wanted to give you a surprise. For your birthday.

MR. ROONEY.   My birthday?

MRS. ROONEY.   Don't you remember? I wished you your happy returns in the bathroom.

MR. ROONEY.   I did not hear you.

MRS. ROONEY.   But I gave you a tie! You have it on!

[*Pause.*]

MR. ROONEY.   How old am I now?

MRS. ROONEY.   Now never mind about that. Come.

480 MR. ROONEY.   Why did you not cancel the boy? Now we shall have to give him a penny.

MRS. ROONEY [*miserably*].   I forgot! I had such a time getting here! Such horrid nasty people! [*Pause. Pleading.*] Be nice to me, Dan, be nice to me today!

MR. ROONEY.   Give the boy a penny.

MRS. ROONEY.   Here are two halfpennies, Jerry. Run along now and buy yourself a nice gobstopper.

JERRY.   Yes, Ma'am.

MR. ROONEY.   Come for me on Monday, if I am still alive.

490 JERRY.   Yessir.

[*He runs off.*]

MR. ROONEY.   We could have saved sixpence. We have saved fivepence. [*Pause.*] But at what cost?

[*They move off along the platform arm in arm. Dragging feet, panting, thudding stick.*]

MRS. ROONEY.   Are you not well?

[*They halt, on* MR. ROONEY's *initiative.*]

MR. ROONEY.   Once and for all, do not ask me to speak and move at the same time. I shall not say this in this life again.

[*They move off. Dragging feet, etc. They halt at top of steps.*]

MRS. ROONEY.   Are you not—
MR. ROONEY.   Let us get this precipice over.
MRS. ROONEY.   Put your arm around me.
MR. ROONEY.   Have you been drinking again? [*Pause.*] You are quivering like
500   a blanc-mange. [*Pause.*] Are you in a condition to lead me? [*Pause.*] We shall fall into the ditch.
MRS. ROONEY.   Oh, Dan! It will be like old times!
MR. ROONEY.   Pull yourself together or I shall send Tommy for the cab. Then instead of having saved sixpence, no, fivepence, we shall have lost . . . [*calculating mumble*] . . . two and three less six one and no plus one one and no plus three one and nine and one ten and three two and one . . . [*normal voice*] two and one, we shall be the poorer to the tune of two and one. [*Pause.*] Curse that sun, it has gone in. What is the day doing?

[*Wind.*]

MRS. ROONEY.   Shrouding, shrouding, the best of it is past. [*Pause.*] Soon the
510   first great drops will fall splashing in the dust.
MR. ROONEY.   And yet the glass was firm. [*Pause.*] Let us hasten home and sit before the fire. We shall draw the blinds. You will read to me. I think Effie is going to commit adultery with the Major. [*Brief drag of feet.*] Wait! [*Feet cease. Stick tapping at steps.*] I have been up and down these steps five thousand times and still I do not know how many there are. When I think there are six there are four or five or seven or eight and when I remember there are five there are three or four or six or seven and when finally I realize there are seven there are five or six or eight or nine. Sometimes I wonder if they do not change them in the night. [*Pause. Irritably.*] Well?
520   How many do you make them today?
MRS. ROONEY.   Do not ask me to count, Dan, not now.
MR. ROONEY.   Not count! One of the few satisfactions in life!
MRS. ROONEY.   Not steps, Dan, please, I always get them wrong. Then you might fall on your wound and I would have that on my manure-heap on top of everything else. No, just cling to me and all will be well.

[*Confused noise of their descent. Panting, stumbling, ejaculations, curses. Silence.*]

MR. ROONEY.   Well! That is what you call well!
MRS. ROONEY.   We are down. And little the worse. [*Silence. A donkey brays. Silence.*] That was a true donkey. Its father and mother were donkeys.

[*Silence.*]

MR. ROONEY.   Do you know what it is, I think I shall retire.
530 MRS. ROONEY [*appalled*].   Retire! And live at home? On your grant!

MR. ROONEY.   Never tread these cursed steps again. Trudge this hellish road
for the last time. Sit at home on the remnants of my bottom counting the
hours—till the next meal. [*Pause.*] The very thought puts life in me! Forward, before it dies!

[*They move on. Dragging feet, panting, thudding stick.*]

MRS. ROONEY.   Now mind, here is the path . . . Up! . . . Well done! Now we
are in safety and a straight run home.
MR. ROONEY [*without halting, between gasps*].   A straight . . . run! . . . She calls
that . . . a straight . . . run! . . .
MRS. ROONEY.   Hush! Do not speak as you go along, you know it is not good
540   for your coronary. [*Dragging steps, etc.*] Just concentrate on putting one
foot before the next or whatever the expression is. [*Dragging feet, etc.*] That
is the way, now we are doing nicely. [*Dragging feet, etc. They suddenly halt, on*
MRS. ROONEY's *initiative.*] Heavens! I knew there was something! With all
the excitement I forgot!
MR. ROONEY [*quietly*].   Good God.
MRS. ROONEY.   But you must know, Dan, of course, you were on it. Whatever
happened? Tell me!
MR. ROONEY.   I have never known anything to happen.
MRS. ROONEY.   But you must—
550 MR. ROONEY [*violently*].   All this stopping and starting again is devilish, dev-
ilish! I get a little way on me and begin to be carried along when suddenly
you stop dead! Two hundred pounds of unhealthy fat! What possessed you
to come out at all! Let go of me!
MRS. ROONEY [*in great agitation*].   No, I must know, we won't stir from here till
you tell me. Fifteen minutes late! On a thirty-minute run! It's unheard of!
MR. ROONEY.   I know nothing. Let go of me before I shake you off.
MRS. ROONEY.   But you must know! You were on it! Was it at the terminus?
Did you leave on time? Or was it on the line? [*Pause.*] Did something
happen on the line? [*Pause.*] Dan! [*Brokenly.*] Why won't you tell me!

[*Silence. They move off. Dragging feet, etc. They halt. Pause.*]

560 MR. ROONEY.   Poor Maddy! [*Pause. Children's cries.*] What was that?

[*Pause for* MRS. ROONEY *to ascertain.*]

MRS. ROONEY.   The Lynch twins jeering at us.

[*Cries.*]

MR. ROONEY.   Will they pelt us with mud today, do you suppose?

[*Cries.*]

MRS. ROONEY.   Let us turn and face them. [*Cries. They turn. Silence.*] Threaten
them with your stick. [*Silence.*] They have run away!

[*Pause.*]

MR. ROONEY.   Did you ever wish to kill a child? [*Pause.*] Nip some young
doom in the bud. [*Pause.*] Many a time at night, in winter, and on the black

road home, I nearly attacked the boy. [*Pause.*] Poor Jerry! [*Pause.*] What
restrained me then? [*Pause.*] Not fear of man. [*Pause.*] Shall we go on
backwards now a little?

570 Mrs. Rooney.   Backwards?

Mr. Rooney.   Yes. Or you forwards and I backwards. The perfect pair. Like
Dante's damned, with their faces arsy-versy. Our tears will water our bottoms.

Mrs. Rooney.   What is the matter, Dan? Are you not well?

Mr. Rooney.   Well! Did you ever know me to be well? The day you met me
I should have been in bed. The day you proposed to me the doctors gave
me up. You knew that, did you not? The night you married me they came
for me with an ambulance. You have not forgotten that, I suppose? [*Pause.*]
No, I cannot be said to be well. But I am no worse. Indeed I am better than

580 I was. The loss of my sight was a great fillip. If I could go deaf and dumb
I think I might pant on to be a hundred. Or have I done so? [*Pause.*] Was
I a hundred today? [*Pause.*] Am I a hundred, Maddy?

[*Silence.*]

Mrs. Rooney.   All is still. No living soul in sight. There is no one to ask. The
world is feeding. The wind—[*brief wind*]—scarcely stirs the leaves and the
birds—[*brief chirp*]—are tired singing. The cows—[*brief moo*]—and sheep—
[*brief baa*]—ruminate in silence. The dogs—[*brief bark*]—are hushed and
the hens—[*brief cackle*]—sprawl torpid in the dust. We are alone. There is
no one to ask.

[*Silence.*]

Mr. Rooney [*clearing his throat, narrative tone*].   We drew out on the tick of
590 time, I can vouch for that. I was—

Mrs. Rooney.   How can you vouch for it?

Mr. Rooney [*normal tone, angrily*].   I can vouch for it, I tell you! Do you want
my relation or don't you? [*Pause. Narrative tone.*] On the tick of time. I had
the compartment to myself, as usual. At least I hope so, for I made no
attempt to restrain myself. My mind—[*Normal tone.*] But why do we not sit
down somewhere? Are we afraid we should never rise again?

Mrs. Rooney.   Sit down on what?

Mr. Rooney.   On a bench, for example.

Mrs. Rooney.   There is no bench.

600 Mr. Rooney.   Then on a bank, let us sink down upon a bank.

Mrs. Rooney.   There is no bank.

Mr. Rooney.   Then we cannot. [*Pause.*] I dream of other roads in other
lands. Of another home, another—[*he hesitates*]—another home. [*Pause.*]
What was I trying to say?

Mrs. Rooney.   Something about your mind.

Mr. Rooney [*startled*].   My mind? Are you sure? [*Pause. Incredulous.*] My
mind? . . . [*Pause.*] Ah yes. [*Narrative tone.*] Alone in the compartment my
mind began to work, as so often after office hours, on the way home, in the
tram, to the lilt of the bogeys. Your season-ticket, I said, costs you twelve

610 pounds a year and you earn, on an average, seven and six a day, that is to
say barely enough to keep you alive and twitching with the help of food,

drink, tobacco and periodicals until you finally reach home and fall into bed. Add to this—or subtract from it—rent, stationery, various subscriptions, tramfares to and fro, light and heat, permits and licenses, hairtrims and shaves, tips to escorts, upkeep of premises and appearances, and a thousand unspecifiable sundries, and it is clear that by lying at home in bed, day and night, winter and summer, with a change of pyjamas once a fortnight, you would add very considerably to your income. Business, I said—[*A cry. Pause. Again. Normal tone.*] Did I hear a cry?

620 Mrs. Rooney. Mrs. Tully I fancy. Her poor husband is in constant pain and beats her unmercifully.

[*Silence.*]

Mr. Rooney. That was a short knock. [*Pause.*] What was I trying to get at?
Mrs. Rooney. Business.
Mr. Rooney. Ah yes, business. [*Narrative tone.*] Business, old man, I said, retire from business, it has retired from you. [*Normal tone.*] One has these moments of lucidity.
Mrs. Rooney. I feel very cold and weak.
Mr. Rooney [*narrative tone*]. On the other hand, I said, there are the horrors of home life, the dusting, sweeping, airing, scrubbing, waxing, waning,
630 washing, mangling, drying, mowing, clipping, raking, rolling, scuffling, shovelling, grinding, tearing, pounding, banging, and slamming. And the brats, the happy little healthy little howling neighbour's brats. Of all this and much more the week-end, the Saturday intermission and then a day of rest, have given you some idea. But what must it be like on a working-day? A Wednesday? A Friday! What must it be like on a Friday! And I fell to thinking of my silent, backstreet, basement office, with its obliterated plate, rest-couch and velvet hangings, and what it means to be buried there alive, if only from ten to five, with convenient to the one hand a bottle of light pale ale and to the other a long ice-cold fillet of hake.[14]
640 Nothing, I said, not even fully certified death, can ever take the place of that. It was then I noticed we were at a standstill. [*Pause. Normal tone. Irritably.*] Why are you hanging out of me like that? Have you swooned away?
Mrs. Rooney. I feel very cold and faint. The wind—[*whistling wind*]—is whistling through my summer frock as if I had nothing on over my bloomers. I have had no solid food since my elevenses.[15]
Mr. Rooney. You have ceased to care. I speak—and you listen to the wind.
Mrs. Rooney. No no, I am agog, tell me all, we shall press on and never pause, never pause, till we come safe to haven.

[*Pause.*]

650 Mr. Rooney. Never pause . . . safe to haven . . . Do you know, Maddy, sometimes one would think you were struggling with a dead language.
Mrs. Rooney. Yes indeed, Dan, I know full well what you mean, I often have that feeling, it is unspeakably excruciating.

---

[14] A fish related to cod.
[15] A midmorning snack.

MR. ROONEY.   I confess I have it sometimes myself, when I happen to overhear what I am saying.

MRS. ROONEY.   Well, you know, it will be dead in time, just like our own poor
dear Gaelic, there is that to be said.

[*Urgent baa.*]

MR. ROONEY [*startled*].   Good God!

MRS. ROONEY.   Oh the pretty little woolly lamb, crying to suck its mother!
660   Theirs has not changed, since Arcady.[16]

[*Pause.*]

MR. ROONEY.   Where was I in my composition?

MRS. ROONEY.   At a standstill.

MR. ROONEY.   Ah yes. [*Clears his throat. Narrative tone.*] I concluded naturally
that we had entered a station and would soon be on our way again, and I
sat on, without misgiving. Not a sound. Things are very dull today, I said,
nobody getting down, nobody getting on. Then as time flew by and nothing happened I realized my error. We had not entered a station.

MRS. ROONEY.   Did you not spring up and poke your head out of the window?

670 MR. ROONEY.   What good would that have done me?

MRS. ROONEY.   Why to call out to be told what was amiss.

MR. ROONEY.   I did not care what was amiss. No, I just sat on, saying, if this
train were never to move again I should not greatly mind. Then gradually
a—how shall I say—a growing desire to—er—you know—welled up within
me. Nervous probably. In fact now I am sure. You know, the feeling of
being confined.

MRS. ROONEY.   Yes yes, I have been through that.

MR. ROONEY.   If we sit here much longer, I said, I really do not know what I
shall do. I got up and paced to and fro between the seats, like a caged
680   beast.

MRS. ROONEY.   That is a help sometimes.

MR. ROONEY.   After what seemed an eternity we simply moved off. And the
next thing was Barrell bawling the abhorred name. I got down and Jerry
let me to the men's, or Fir as they call it now, from Vir Viris I suppose, the
V becoming F, in accordance with Grimm's Law.[17] [*Pause.*] The rest you
know. [*Pause.*] You say nothing? [*Pause.*] Say something, Maddy. Say you
believe me.

MRS. ROONEY.   I remember once attending a lecture by one of these new
mind doctors, I forget what you call them. He spoke—

690 MR. ROONEY.   A lunatic specialist?

MRS. ROONEY.   No no, just the troubled mind. I was hoping he might shed a
little light on my lifelong preoccupation with horses' buttocks.

MR. ROONEY.   A neurologist.

MRS. ROONEY.   No no, just mental distress, the name will come back to me in
the night. I remember his telling us the story of a little girl, very strange

---

[16] A legendary region of pastoral beauty.
[17] The systematic change in consonants during the evolution of languages was first examined by Jacob Grimm in *Deutsche Grammatik* (1822).

and unhappy in her ways, and how he treated her unsuccessfully over a period of years and was finally obliged to give up the case. He could find nothing wrong with her, he said. The only thing wrong with her as far as he could see was that she was dying. And she did in fact die, shortly after

700 he washed his hands of her.

MR. ROONEY. Well? What is there so wonderful about that?

MRS. ROONEY. No, it was just something he said, and the way he said it, that have haunted me ever since.

MR. ROONEY. You lie awake at night, tossing to and fro brooding on it.

MRS. ROONEY. On it and other . . . wretchedness. [*Pause.*] When he had done with the little girl he stood there motionless for some time, quite two minutes I should say, looking down at his table. Then he suddenly raised his head and exclaimed, as if he had had a revelation, The trouble with her was she had never been really born! [*Pause.*] He spoke throughout

710 without notes. [*Pause.*] I left before the end.

MR. ROONEY. Nothing about your buttocks? [MRS. ROONEY *weeps. In affectionate remonstrance.*] Maddy!

MRS. ROONEY. There is nothing to be done for those people!

MR. ROONEY. For which is there? [*Pause.*] That does not sound right somehow. [*Pause.*] What way am I facing?

MRS. ROONEY. What?

MR. ROONEY. I have forgotten what way I am facing.

MRS. ROONEY. You have turned aside and are bowed down over the ditch.

MR. ROONEY. There is a dead dog down there.

720 MRS. ROONEY. No no, just the rotting leaves.

MR. ROONEY. In June? Rotting leaves in June?

MRS. ROONEY. Yes, dear, from last year, and from the year before last, and from the year before that again. [*Silence. Rainy wind. They move on. Dragging steps, etc.*] There is that lovely laburnum again. Poor thing, it is losing all its tassels. [*Dragging steps, etc.*] There are the first drops. [*Rain. Dragging feet, etc.*] Golden drizzle. [*Dragging steps, etc.*] Do not mind me, dear, I am just talking to myself. [*Rain heavier. Dragging steps, etc.*] Can hinnies procreate, I wonder?

[*They halt.*]

MR. ROONEY. Say that again.

730 MRS. ROONEY. Come on, dear, don't mind me, we are getting drenched.

MR. ROONEY [*forcibly*]. Can what what?

MRS. ROONEY. Hinnies procreate. [*Silence.*] You know, hinnies, or jinnies, aren't they barren, or sterile, or whatever it is? [*Pause.*] It wasn't an ass's colt[18] at all, you know, I asked the Regius Professor.[19]

[*Pause.*]

MR. ROONEY. He should know.

MRS. ROONEY. Yes, it was a hinny, he rode into Jerusalem or wherever it was on a hinny. [*Pause.*] That must mean something. [*Pause.*] It's like the

---

[18] *It* refers to the mule (or hinny) upon which Jesus rode into Jerusalem (see Matthew 21:2–8).

[19] A Regius professorship is one that has been endowed by the British royal family.

sparrows, than many of which we are of more value, they weren't sparrows at all.

740 MR. ROONEY.   Than many of which? . . . You exaggerate, Maddy.

MRS. ROONEY [*with emotion*].   They weren't sparrows at all!

MR. ROONEY.   Does that put our price up?

> [*Silence. They move on. Wind and rain. Dragging feet, etc. They halt.*]

MRS. ROONEY.   Do you want some dung? [*Silence. They move on. Wind and rain, etc. They halt.*] Why do you stop? Do you want to say something?

MR. ROONEY.   No.

MRS. ROONEY.   Then why do you stop?

MR. ROONEY.   It is easier.

MRS. ROONEY.   Are you very wet?

MR. ROONEY.   To the buff.

750 MRS. ROONEY.   The buff?

MR. ROONEY.   The buff. From buffalo.

MRS. ROONEY.   We shall hang up all our things in the hot-cupboard and get into our dressing-gowns. [*Pause.*] Put your arm round me. [*Pause.*] Be nice to me! [*Pause. Gratefully.*] Ah, Dan! [*They move on. Wind and rain. Dragging feet, etc. Faintly same music as before. They halt. Music clearer. Silence but for music playing. Music dies.*] All day the same old record! All alone in that great empty house. She must be a very old woman now.

MR. ROONEY [*indistinctly*].   Death and the Maiden.

> [*Silence.*]

MRS. ROONEY.   You are crying. [*Pause.*] Are you crying?

760 MR. ROONEY [*violently*].   Yes! [*They move on. Wind and rain. Dragging feet, etc. They halt. They move on. Wind and rain. Dragging feet, etc. They halt.*] Who is the preacher tomorrow? The incumbent?

MRS. ROONEY.   No.

MR. ROONEY.   Thank God for that. Who?

MRS. ROONEY.   Hardy.

MR. ROONEY.   "How to be Happy though Married?"

MRS. ROONEY.   No no, he died, you remember. No connexion.

MR. ROONEY.   Has he announced his text?

MRS. ROONEY.   "The Lord upholdeth all that fall and raiseth up all those that
770 be bowed down."[20] [*Silence. They join in wild laughter. They move on. Wind and rain. Dragging feet, etc.*] Hold me tighter, Dan! [*Pause.*] Oh yes!

> [*They halt.*]

MR. ROONEY.   I hear something behind us.

> [*Pause.*]

MRS. ROONEY.   It looks like Jerry. [*Pause.*] It is Jerry.

> [*Sound of* JERRY's *running steps approaching. He halts beside them, panting.*]

JERRY [*panting*].   You dropped—

---

[20] From Psalm 145, verse 14.

MRS. ROONEY. Take your time, my little man, you will burst a blood-vessel.

JERRY [*panting*]. You dropped something, sir. Mr. Barrell told me to run after you.

MRS. ROONEY. Show. [*She takes the object.*] What is it? [*She examines it.*] What is this thing, Dan?

780 MR. ROONEY. Perhaps it is not mine at all.

JERRY. Mr. Barrell said it was, sir.

MRS. ROONEY. It looks like a kind of ball. And yet it is not a ball.

MR. ROONEY. Give it to me.

MRS. ROONEY [*giving it*]. What *is* it, Dan?

MR. ROONEY. It is a thing I carry about with me.

MRS. ROONEY. Yes, but what—

MR. ROONEY [*violently*]. It is a thing I carry about with me!

[*Silence.* MRS. ROONEY *looks for a penny.*]

MRS. ROONEY. I have no small money. Have you?

MR. ROONEY. I have none of any kind.

790 MRS. ROONEY. We are out of change, Jerry. Remind Mr. Rooney on Monday and he will give you a penny for your pains.

JERRY. Yes, Ma'am.

MR. ROONEY. If I am alive.

JERRY. Yessir.

[JERRY *starts running back towards the station.*]

MRS. ROONEY. Jerry! [JERRY *halts.*] Did you hear what the hitch was? [*Pause.*] Did you hear what kept the train so late?

MR. ROONEY. How would he have heard? Come on.

MRS. ROONEY. What was it, Jerry?

JERRY. It was a—

800 MR. ROONEY. Leave the boy alone, he knows nothing! Come on!

MRS. ROONEY. What was it, Jerry?

JERRY. It was a little child, Ma'am.

[MR. ROONEY *groans.*]

MRS. ROONEY. What do you mean, it was a little child?

JERRY. It was a little child fell out of the carriage, Ma'am. [*Pause.*] On to the line, Ma'am. [*Pause.*] Under the wheels, Ma'am.

[*Silence.* JERRY *runs off. His steps die away. Tempest of wind and rain. It abates. They move on. Dragging steps, etc. They halt. Tempest of wind and rain.*]

END

[1957]

Critical Commentary on *All That Fall*

All That Fall is a characteristically Irish tragicomedy about the inevitability of decay and death. The characters in the play, who live in a town with the appropriately oxymoronic name of Boghill, experience a fall from health, a fall from beauty, a fall from happiness, a fall from dignity, and perhaps even a fall from grace. The melancholy mood of the play is well expressed in Maddy's frequent observations about the weather: "The best of the day is over. . . . Soon the rain will begin to fall and go on falling, all afternoon."

The general tone of melancholy depression is revealed in the title with its ironic allusion to the biblical verse, "The Lord upholdeth all that fall and raiseth all those that be bowed down." Within this play, of course, the Lord takes on no such role. In fact, the play is pervaded by death and forebodings of death ranging from the recurring melody from Schubert's "Death and the Maiden" to the final grim episode of the young child's death by falling from the train. As G. C. Barnard observes, "The references to death and severe illness are numerous; five of the characters to whom Mrs. Rooney talks, though healthy themselves, have a wife, daughter or father severely ill; a hen is killed on the road, and Mrs. Rooney mourns for her daughter Minnie who died while still a child."

The religious imagery introduced in the title permeates the entire play, so much so that Hersh Zeifman sees the road in the play as a symbol of the "road of life that leads to death and, possibly, salvation." In this sense we all travel through life in a single direction. Thus, when Mr. Slocum asks, "Are you going in my direction?" Maddy responds, "I am, Mr. Slocum, we all are." This eternal route through time is appropriately traveled, as Zeifman observes, by a "progressively more sophisticated series of vehicles: a dung cart, a bicycle, a car, and a van." Perhaps, then, Maddy's ascent into Mr. Slocum's car can be seen as an ascent to paradise; her grunts and struggles as she rises "Up! Up!" reach a culmination in her exclamation "Oh glory!" But if so, as Zeifman points out, this religious imagery only helps to create Beckett's characteristically ironic view of both religion and salvation. For although this scene and, to an almost equal extent, the entire play are pervaded by religious imagery, they are even more pervaded by sexual innuendo. During this scene, Maddy finds herself "heaving" and grunting in a close aural imitation of the sounds of sexual intercourse—a similarity made even more coarsely apparent by the fact that this is a radio play. Her exclamation "Oh glory!" occurs just as Mr. Slocum pushes most firmly against her ample posterior. And what are we to make of Mr. Slocum's own ejaculation, "I'm coming, Mrs. Rooney, I'm coming, give me time, I'm stiff as yourself"? For Zeifman, all this is an "outrageous burlesque" in which "the dream of paradise is . . . exploded."

Ultimately, of course, Mrs. Rooney does get up—and down again—in time to meet her husband at the station where the train has been mysteriously delayed. As one might expect, the play's ending has been the cause of considerable critical controversy. Some readers think that Dan has actually pushed the child onto the tracks and find numerous details to support this homicidal hypothesis, ranging from Dan's confessed desire to beat Jerry and his comment regarding the jeering Lynch twins ("Did you ever wish to kill a child? Nip some young doom in the bud?") to the oddity of Jerry returning to him a kind of ball that he had dropped on the platform. What would a blind man do with a ball? Could he have taken it from the child before pushing the child onto the tracks? Skeptics respond to these questions with others: How could a blind man as decrepit as Dan manage to murder even a small child? Where were the child's parents at the time? Would a blind man take the risk of such an open murder on a public train?

Many of these questions, of course, carry us beyond the text itself and all of them are unanswerable. The result is that Beckett's play ends in sadness and mystery. Life itself, we are perhaps to conclude, is just such a progress toward unhappiness, decay, and death, where the deity (if one exists) not only fails to uphold *all* that fall, but even refuses to intervene on the behalf of the most innocent of children. In the world Beckett gives us, it is even possible to die without having lived: Maddy at one point recalls a young girl who is said by a psychiatrist to have died because "The trouble with her was she had never been really born!" When the play ends, Maddy and Dan are reduced to silence, but we continue to hear their footsteps painfully dragging along as they are engulfed in the wind and rain of a hostile, apparently godless universe.

A Selective Bibliography on *All That Fall*

Alvarez, A. *Samuel Beckett*. London: Fontana, 1992.

Alpaugh, David J. "The Symbolic Structure of Samuel Beckett's *All That Fall*." *Modern Drama* 9 (December 1966): 324–32.

Barnard, Guy K. *Samuel Beckett: A New Approach*. New York: Dodd, Mead, 1970. 110–113.

Ben-Zvi, Linda. *Samuel Beckett*. Boston: Twayne, 1986. 185–86.

———. "Samuel Beckett's Media Plays." *Modern Drama* 28 (March 1985): 22–37.

Bloom, Harold, ed. *Samuel Beckett*. New York: Chelsea, 1985.

Cleveland, Louise O. "Trials in the Soundscape: The Radio Plays of Samuel Beckett." *Modern Drama* 11 (December 1968): 267–82.

Cohn, Ruby. *Back to Beckett*. Princeton: Princeton UP, 1973. 158–65.

Dolan, T. P. "Samuel Beckett's Dramatic Use of HibernoEnglish." *Irish University Review* 14 (Spring 1984): 46–56.

Esselin, Martin. "Samuel Beckett and the Art of Broadcasting." *Encounter* 45 (September 1975): 38–46.

Fletcher, Beryl and John. *A Student's Guide to the Plays of Samuel Beckett*. 2nd ed. London: Faber and Faber, 1985.

Fletcher, John and John Spurling. *Beckett: A Study of His Plays*. New York: Hill and Wang, 1972. 82–88.

Fletcher, John. "Literature and the Problem of Evil, II." *Theology* 79 (November 1976): 337–43.

———. "Beckett and the Medium: Rough for Radio?" *Caliban* 15.14 (1978): 2–18.

Hale, Jane A. *The Broken Window: Beckett's Dramatic Perspective*. West Lafayette, Ind.: Purdue UP, 1987.

Kenner, Hugh. *Samuel Beckett: A Critical Study*. New York: Grove Press, 1961. 167–74.

Levy, Shimon. *Beckett's Self-Referential Drama*. London: Macmillan, 1990.

Madelaine, R. E. R. "Happy-though-Married Hardy." *Notes and Queries* 29 (1982): 348–49.

Pilling, John. *Samuel Beckett*. London: Routledge, 1976. 94–98.

Pountney, Rosemary. *Theatre of Shadows: Samuel Beckett's Drama, 1956–1976*. Totowa, N.J.: Barnes & Noble, 1988. 103–07.

Robinson, Michael. *The Long Sonata of the Dead: A Study of Samuel Beckett*. London: Hart-Davis, 1969. 277–83.

Schirmer, Gregory A. "The Irish Connection: Ambiguity of Language in *All That Fall*." *College Literature* 8 (Fall 1981): 283–91.

Van Laan, Thomas F. *"All That Fall* as 'a Play for Radio.' " *Modern Drama* 28 (March 1985): 38–47.

Webb, Eugene. *The Plays of Samuel Beckett*. Seattle: U of Washington P, 1972. 42–53.

Wilcher, Robert. " 'Out of the Dark': Beckett's Texts for Radio." *Beckett's Later Fiction and Drama*. Eds. James Acheson et al. Basinstoke, Eng.: Macmillan, 1987. 1–17.

Worth, Katherine. "Beckett and the Radio Medium." *British Radio Drama*. Ed. J. Drakakis. Cambridge, Eng.: Cambridge UP, 1981. 191–217.

Zeifman, Hersh. "Religious Imagery in the Plays of Samuel Beckett." *Samuel Beckett*. Ed. Ruby Cohn. New York: McGraw-Hill, 1975. 85–94.

Lorraine Hansberry (1930–1965)

A RAISIN IN THE SUN

CHARACTERS

RUTH YOUNGER
TRAVIS YOUNGER
WALTER LEE YOUNGER (BROTHER)
BENEATHA YOUNGER
LENA YOUNGER (MAMA)

JOSEPH ASAGAI
GEORGE MURCHISON
KARL LINDNER
BOBO
MOVING MEN

The action of the play is set in Chicago's Southside, sometime between World War II and the present.

ACT I

SCENE I: *Friday morning.*
SCENE II: *The following morning.*

ACT II

SCENE I: *Later, the same day.*
SCENE II: *Friday night, a few weeks later.*
SCENE III: *Moving day, one week later.*

ACT III

An hour later.

ACT I

SCENE I

The YOUNGER *living room would be a comfortable and well-ordered room if it were not for a number of indestructible contradictions to this state of being. Its furnishings are typical and undistinguished and their primary feature now is that they have clearly had to accommodate the living of too many people for too many years—and they are tired. Still, we can see that at some time, a time probably no longer remembered by the family (except perhaps for* MAMA), *the furnishings of this room were actually selected with care and love and even hope—and brought to this apartment and arranged with taste and pride.*

That was a long time ago. Now the once loved pattern of the couch upholstery has to fight to show itself from under acres of crocheted doilies and couch covers which have themselves finally come to be more important than the upholstery. And here a table or a chair has been moved to disguise the worn places in the carpet; but the carpet has fought back by showing its weariness, with depressing uniformity, elsewhere on its surface.

Weariness has, in fact, won in this room. Everything has been polished, washed, sat on, used, scrubbed too often. All pretenses but living itself have long since vanished from the very atmosphere of this room.

Moreover, a section of this room, for it is not really a room unto itself, though the landlord's lease would make it seem so, slopes backward to provide a small kitchen area, where the family prepares the meals that are eaten in the living room proper, which must also serve as dining room. The single window that has been provided for these "two" rooms is located in this kitchen area. The sole natural light the family may enjoy in the course of a day is only that which fights its way through this little window.

At left, a door leads to a bedroom which is shared by MAMA *and her daughter,* BENEATHA. *At right, opposite, is a second room (which in the beginning of the life of this apartment was probably a breakfast room) which serves as a bedroom for* WALTER *and his wife,* RUTH.

TIME: *Sometime between World War II and the present.*

PLACE: *Chicago's Southside.*

At Rise: It is morning dark in the living room. TRAVIS *is asleep on the make-down bed at center. An alarm clock sounds from within the bedroom at right, and presently* RUTH *enters from that room and closes the door behind her. She crosses sleepily toward the window. As she passes her sleeping son she reaches down and shakes him a little. At the window she raises the shade and a dusky Southside morning light comes in feebly. She fills a pot with water and puts it on to boil. She calls to the boy, between yawns, in a slightly muffled voice.*

RUTH is about thirty. We can see that she was a pretty girl, even exceptionally so, but now it is apparent that life has been little that she expected, and disappointment has already begun to hang in her face. In a few years, before thirty-five even, she will be known among her people as a "settled woman."

She crosses to her son and gives him a good, final, rousing shake.

RUTH.   Come on now, boy, it's seven thirty! [*Her son sits up at last, in a stupor of sleepiness.*] I say hurry up, Travis! You ain't the only person in the world got to use a bathroom! [*The child, a sturdy, handsome little boy of ten or eleven, drags himself out of the bed and almost blindly takes his towels and "today's clothes" from drawers and a closet and goes out to the bathroom, which is in an outside hall and which is shared by another family or families on the same floor.* RUTH *crosses to the bedroom door at right and opens it and calls in to her husband.*] Walter Lee! . . . It's after seven thirty! Lemme see you do some waking up in there now! [*She waits.*] You better get up from there, man! It's after seven thirty I tell you. [*She waits again.*] All right, you just go ahead and lay there and next thing you know Travis be finished and Mr. Johnson'll be in there and you'll be fussing and cussing round here like a mad man! And be late too! [*She waits, at the end of patience.*] Walter Lee—it's time for you to get up!

[*She waits another second and then starts to go into the bedroom, but is apparently satisfied that her husband has begun to get up. She stops, pulls the door to, and returns to the kitchen area. She wipes her face with a moist cloth and runs her fingers through her sleep-disheveled hair in a vain effort and ties an apron around her housecoat. The bedroom door at right opens and her husband stands in the doorway in his pajamas, which are rumpled and mismated. He is a lean, intense young man in his middle thirties, inclined to quick nervous movements and erratic speech habits—and always in his voice there is a quality of indictment.*]

WALTER. Is he out yet?

RUTH. What you mean *out*? He ain't hardly got in there good yet.

WALTER [*wandering in, still more oriented to sleep than to a new day*]. Well, what was you doing all that yelling for if I can't even get in there yet? [*Stopping and thinking.*] Check coming today?

20 RUTH. They *said* Saturday and this is just Friday and I hopes to God you ain't going to get up here first thing this morning and start talking to me 'bout no money—'cause I 'bout don't want to hear it.

WALTER. Something the matter with you this morning?

RUTH. No—I'm just sleepy as the devil. What kind of eggs you want?

WALTER. Not scrambled. [RUTH *starts to scramble eggs.*] Paper come? [RUTH *points impatiently to the rolled up* Tribune *on the table, and he gets it and spreads it out and vaguely reads the front page.*] Set off another bomb yesterday.

RUTH [*maximum indifference*]. Did they?

WALTER [*looking up*]. What's the matter with you?

RUTH. Ain't nothing the matter with me. And don't keep asking me that this
30 morning.

WALTER. Ain't nobody bothering you. [*Reading the news of the day absently again.*] Say Colonel McCormick is sick.

RUTH [*affecting tea-party interest*]. Is he now? Poor thing.

WALTER [*sighing and looking at his watch*]. Oh, me. [*He waits.*] Now what is that boy doing in the bathroom all this time? He just going to have to start getting up earlier. I can't be being late to work on account of him fooling around in there.

RUTH [*turning on him*]. Oh, no he ain't going to be getting up no earlier no such thing! It ain't his fault that he can't get to bed no earlier nights 'cause
40 he got a bunch of crazy good-for-nothing clowns sitting up running their mouths in what is supposed to be his bedroom after ten o'clock at night . . .

WALTER. That's what you mad about, ain't it? The things I want to talk about with my friends just couldn't be important in your mind, could they?

[*He rises and finds a cigarette in her handbag on the table and crosses to the little window and looks out, smoking and deeply enjoying this first one.*]

RUTH [*almost matter of factly, a complaint too automatic to deserve emphasis*]. Why you always got to smoke before you eat in the morning?

WALTER [*at the window*]. Just look at 'em down there . . . Running and racing to work . . . [*He turns and faces his wife and watches her a moment at the stove, and then, suddenly.*] You look young this morning, baby.

50 RUTH [*indifferently*]. Yeah?

WALTER. Just for a second—stirring them eggs. It's gone now—just for a second it was—you looked real young again. [*Then, drily.*] It's gone now— you look like yourself again.

RUTH.   Man, if you don't shut up and leave me alone.

WALTER [*looking out to the street again*].   First thing a man ought to learn in life is not to make love to no colored woman first thing in the morning. You all some evil people at eight o'clock in the morning.

[TRAVIS *appears in the hall doorway, almost fully dressed and quite wide awake now, his towels and pajamas across his shoulders. He opens the door and signals for his father to make the bathroom in a hurry.*]

TRAVIS [*watching the bathroom*].   Daddy, come on!

[WALTER *gets his bathroom utensils and flies out to the bathroom.*]

RUTH.   Sit down and have your breakfast, Travis.

60 TRAVIS.   Mama, this is Friday. [*Gleefully.*] Check coming tomorrow, huh?

RUTH.   You get your mind off money and eat your breakfast.

TRAVIS [*eating*].   This is the morning we supposed to bring the fifty cents to school.

RUTH.   Well, I ain't got no fifty cents this morning.

TRAVIS.   Teacher say we have to.

RUTH.   I don't care what teacher say. I ain't got it. Eat your breakfast, Travis.

TRAVIS.   I *am* eating.

RUTH.   Hush up now and just eat!

[*The boy gives her an exasperated look for her lack of understanding, and eats grudgingly.*]

TRAVIS.   You think Grandmama would have it?

70 RUTH.   No! And I want you to stop asking your grandmother for money, you hear me?

TRAVIS [*outraged*].   Gaaaleee! I don't ask her, she just gimme it sometimes!

RUTH.   Travis Willard Younger—I got too much on me this morning to be—

TRAVIS.   Maybe Daddy—

RUTH.   *Travis!*

[*The boy hushes abruptly. They are both quiet and tense for several seconds.*]

TRAVIS [*presently*].   Could I maybe go carry some groceries in front of the supermarket for a little while after school then?

RUTH.   Just hush, I said. [*Travis jabs his spoon into his cereal bowl viciously, and rests his head in anger upon his fists.*] If you through eating, you can get over

80 there and make up your bed.

[*The boy obeys stiffly and crosses the room, almost mechanically, to the bed and more or less carefully folds the covering. He carries the bedding into his mother's room and returns with his books and cap.*]

TRAVIS [*sulking and standing apart from her unnaturally*].   I'm gone.

RUTH [*looking up from the stove to inspect him automatically.*]   Come here. [*He crosses to her and she studies his head.*] If you don't take this comb and fix this here head, you better! [*Travis puts down his books with a great sigh of oppression, and crosses to the mirror. His mother mutters under her breath about his "stubbornness."*] 'Bout to march out of here with that head looking just like

chickens slept in it! I just don't know where you get your stubborn ways . . .
And get your jacket, too. Looks chilly out this morning.

Travis [*with conspicuously brushed hair and jacket*].   I'm gone.

90 Ruth.   Get carfare and milk money—[*Waving one finger.*]— and not a single
penny for no caps, you hear me?

Travis [*with sullen politeness*].   Yes'm.

[*He turns in outrage to leave. His mother watches after him as in his frustration he
approaches the door almost comically. When she speaks to him, her voice has become
a very gentle tease.*]

Ruth [*mocking; as she thinks he would say it*].   Oh, Mama makes me so mad
sometimes, I don't know what to do! [*She waits and continues to his back as
he stands stock-still in front of the door.*] I wouldn't kiss that woman good-bye
for nothing in this world this morning! [*The boy finally turns around and rolls
his eyes at her, knowing the mood has changed and he is vindicated; he does not,
however, move toward her yet.*] Not for nothing in this world! [*She finally
laughs aloud at him and holds out her arms to him and we see that it is a way
100   between them, very old and practiced. He crosses to her and allows her to embrace
him warmly but keeps his face fixed with masculine rigidity. She holds him back
from her presently and looks at him and runs her fingers over the features of his
face. With utter gentleness—.*] Now—whose little old angry man are you?

Travis [*the masculinity and gruffness start to fade at last*].   Aw gaalee—Mama . . .

Ruth [*mimicking*].   Aw—gaaaaalleeeee, Mama! [*She pushes him, with rough
playfulness and finality, toward the door.*] Get out of here or you going to be
late.

Travis [*in the face of love, new aggressiveness*].   Mama, could I *please* go carry
groceries?

110 Ruth.   Honey, it's starting to get so cold evenings.

Walter [*coming in from the bathroom and drawing a make-believe gun from a
make-believe holster and shooting at his son*].   What is it he wants to do?

Ruth.   Go carry groceries after school at the supermarket.

Walter.   Well, let him go . . .

Travis [*quickly, to the ally*].   I *have* to—she won't gimme the fifty cents . . .

Walter [*to his wife only*].   Why not?

Ruth [*simply, and with flavor*].   'Cause we don't have it.

Walter [*to Ruth only*].   What you tell the boy things like that for? [*Reaching
down into his pants with a rather important gesture.*] Here, son—

[*He hands the boy the coin, but his eyes are directed to his wife's.* Travis *takes the
money happily.*]

120 Travis.   Thanks, Daddy.

[*He starts out,* Ruth *watches both of them with murder in her eyes.* Walter *stands and
stares back at her with defiance, and suddenly reaches into his pocket again on an
afterthought.*]

Walter [*without even looking at his son, still staring hard at his wife*].   In fact,
here's another fifty cents . . . Buy yourself some fruit today—or take a taxi
cab to school or something!

Travis.   Whoopee—

[*He leaps up and clasps his father around the middle with his legs, and they face each other in mutual appreciation; slowly* WALTER LEE *peeks around the boy to catch the violent rays from his wife's eyes and draws his head back as if shot.*]

WALTER.   You better get down now—and get to school, man.
TRAVIS [*at the door*].   O.K. Good-bye.

[*He exits.*]

WALTER [*after him, pointing with pride*].   That's *my* boy. [*She looks at him in disgust and turns back to her work.*] You know what I was thinking 'bout in the bathroom this morning?
130 RUTH.   No.
WALTER.   How come you always try to be so pleasant!
RUTH.   What is there to be pleasant 'bout!
WALTER.   You want to know what I was thinking 'bout in the bathroom or not!
RUTH.   I know what you was thinking 'bout.
WALTER [*ignoring her*].   'Bout what me and Willy Harris was talking about last night.
RUTH [*immediately—a refrain*].   Willy Harris is a good-for-nothing loud mouth.
140 WALTER.   Anybody who talks to me has got to be a good-for-nothing loud mouth, ain't he? And what you know about who is just a good-for-nothing loud mouth? Charlie Atkins was just a "good-for-nothing loud mouth" too, wasn't he! When he wanted me to go in the dry-cleaning business with him. And now—he's grossing a hundred thousand a year. A hundred thousand dollars a year! You still call *him* a loud mouth!
RUTH [*bitterly*].   Oh, Walter Lee . . .

[*She folds her head on her arms over on the table.*]

WALTER [*rising and coming to her and standing over her*].   You tired, ain't you? Tired of everything. Me, the boy, the way we live—this beat-up hole— everything. Ain't you? [*She doesn't look up, doesn't answer.*] So tired—moan-
150 ing and groaning all the time, but you wouldn't do nothing to help, would you? You couldn't be on my side that long for nothing, could you?
RUTH.   Walter, please leave me alone.
WALTER.   A man needs for a woman to back him up . . .
RUTH.   Walter—
WALTER.   Mama would listen to you. You know she listen to you more than she do me and Bennie. She think more of you. All you have to do is just sit down with her when you drinking your coffee one morning and talking 'bout things like you do and—[*He sits down beside her and demonstrates graphically what he thinks her methods and tone should be.*]—you just sip your
160 coffee, see, and say easy like that you been thinking 'bout that deal Walter Lee is so interested in, 'bout the store and all, and sip some more coffee, like what you saying ain't really that important to you— And the next thing you know, she be listening good and asking you questions and when I come home—I can tell her the details. This ain't no fly-by-night prop-osition, baby. I mean we figured it out, me and Willy and Bobo.

RUTH [*with a frown*]. Bobo?

WALTER. Yeah. You see, this little liquor store we got in mind cost seventy-five thousand and we figured the initial investment on the place be 'bout thirty thousand, see. That be ten thousand each. Course, there's a couple
170 of hundred you got to pay so's you don't spend your life just waiting for them clowns to let your license get approved—

RUTH. You mean graft?

WALTER [*frowning impatiently*]. Don't call it that. See there, that just goes to show you what women understand about the world. Baby, don't *nothing* happen for you in this world 'les you pay *somebody* off!

RUTH. Walter, leave me alone! [*She raises her head and stares at him vigorously—then says, more quietly.*] Eat your eggs, they gonna be cold.

WALTER [*straightening up from her and looking off*]. That's it. There you are. Man say to his woman: I got me a dream. His woman say: Eat your eggs.
180 [*Sadly, but gaining in power.*] Man say: I got to take hold of this here world, baby! And a woman will say: Eat your eggs and go to work. [*Passionately now.*] Man say: I got to change my life, I'm choking to death, baby! And his woman say—[*In utter anguish as he brings his fists down on his thighs.*]—Your eggs is getting cold!

RUTH [*softly*]. Walter, that ain't none of our money.

WALTER [*not listening at all or even looking at her*]. This morning, I was lookin' in the mirror and thinking about it ... I'm thirty-five years old; I been married eleven years and I got a boy who sleeps in the living room—[*very, very quietly*]—and all I got to give him is stories about how rich white
190 people live ...

RUTH. Eat your eggs, Walter.

WALTER. *Damn my eggs ... damn all the eggs that ever was!*

RUTH. Then go to work.

WALTER [*looking up at her*]. See—I'm trying to talk to you 'bout myself— [*Shaking his head with the repetition.*]—and all you can say is eat them eggs and go to work.

RUTH [*wearily*]. Honey, you never say nothing new. I listen to you every day, every night and every morning, and you never say nothing new. [*Shrugging.*] So you would rather *be* Mr. Arnold than be his chauffeur. So—I
200 would *rather* be living in Buckingham Palace.[1]

WALTER. That is just what is wrong with the colored woman in this world ... Don't understand about building their men up and making 'em feel like they somebody. Like they can do something.

RUTH [*drily, but to hurt*]. There *are* colored men who do things.

WALTER. No thanks to the colored woman.

RUTH. Well, being a colored woman, I guess I can't help myself none.

[*She rises and gets the ironing board and sets it up and attacks a huge pile of rough-dried clothes, sprinkling them in preparation for the ironing and then rolling them into tight fat balls.*]

WALTER [*mumbling*]. We one group of men tied to a race of women with small minds.

---

[1] The residence of the British royal family in London.

[*His sister* BENEATHA *enters. She is about twenty, as slim and intense as her brother. She is not as pretty as her sister-in-law, but her lean, almost intellectual face has a handsomeness of its own. She wears a bright-red flannel nightie, and her thick hair stands wildly about her head. Her speech is a mixture of many things; it is different from the rest of the family's insofar as education has permeated her sense of English—and perhaps the Midwestern rather than the South has finally—at last—won out in her inflection; but not altogether, because over all of it is a soft slurring and transformed use of vowels which is the decided influence of the Southside. She passes through the room without looking at either* RUTH *or* WALTER *and goes to the outside door and looks, a little blindly, out to the bathroom. She sees that it has been lost to the Johnsons. She closes the door with a sleepy vengeance and crosses to the table and sits down a little defeated*].

BENEATHA. I am going to start timing those people.

210 WALTER. You should get up earlier.

BENEATHA [*her face in her hands. She is still fighting the urge to go back to bed*]. Really—would you suggest dawn? Where's the paper?

WALTER [*pushing the paper across the table to her as he studies her almost clinically, as though he has never seen her before*]. You a horrible-looking chick at this hour.

BENEATHA [*drily*]. Good morning, everybody.

WALTER [*senselessly*]. How is school coming?

BENEATHA [*in the same spirit*]. Lovely. Lovely. And you know, biology is the greatest. [*Looking up at him.*] I dissected something that looked just like

220 you yesterday.

WALTER. I just wondered if you've made up your mind and everything.

BENEATHA [*gaining in sharpness and impatience*]. And what did I answer yesterday morning—and the day before that?

RUTH [*from the ironing board, like someone disinterested and old*]. Don't be so nasty, Bennie.

BENEATHA [*still to her brother*]. And the day before that and the day before that!

WALTER [*defensively*]. I'm interested in you. Something wrong with that? Ain't many girls who decide—

230 WALTER AND BENEATHA [*in unison*]. —"to be a doctor."

[*Silence.*]

WALTER. Have we figured out yet just exactly how much medical school is going to cost?

RUTH. Walter Lee, why don't you leave that girl alone and get out of here to work?

BENEATHA [*exits to the bathroom and bangs and bangs on the door*]. Come on out of there, please!

[*She comes back into the room.*]

WALTER [*looking at his sister intently*]. You know the check is coming tomorrow.

BENEATHA [*turning on him with a sharpness all her own*]. That money belongs to

240 Mama, Walter, and it's for her to decide how she wants to use it. I don't care if she wants to buy a house or a rocket ship or just nail it up somewhere and look at it. It's hers. Not ours—*hers*.

WALTER [*bitterly*].   Now ain't that fine! You just got your mother's interest at
   heart, ain't you, girl? You such a nice girl—but if Mama got that money she
   can always take a few thousand and help you through school too—can't she?
BENEATHA.   I have never asked anyone around here to do anything for me!
WALTER.   No! And the line between asking and just accepting when the time
   comes is big and wide—ain't it!
BENEATHA [*with fury*].   What do you want from me, Brother—that I quit school
250   or just drop dead, which!
WALTER.   I don't want nothing but for you to stop acting holy 'round here.
   Me and Ruth done made some sacrifices for you—why can't you do some-
   thing for the family?
RUTH.   Walter, don't be dragging me in it.
WALTER.   You are in it— Don't you get up and go work in somebody's kitchen
   for the last three years to help put clothes on her back?
RUTH.   Oh, Walter—that's not fair . . .
WALTER.   It ain't that nobody expects you to get on your knees and say thank
   you, Brother; thank you, Ruth; thank you, Mama—and thank you, Travis,
260   for wearing the same pair of shoes for two semesters—
BENEATHA [*dropping to her knees*].   Well—I *do*—all right?—thank everybody
   . . . and forgive me for ever wanting to be anything at all . . . forgive me,
   forgive me!
RUTH.   Please stop it! Your mama'll hear you.
WALTER.   Who the hell told you you had to be a doctor? If you so crazy 'bout
   messing 'round with sick people—then go be a nurse like other women
   —or just get married and be quiet . . .
BENEATHA.   Well—you finally got it said . . . It took you three years but you
   finally got it said. Walter, give up; leave me alone—it's Mama's money.
270 WALTER.   *He was my father, too!*
BENEATHA.   So what? He was mine, too—and Travis' grandfather—but the
   insurance money belongs to Mama. Picking on me is not going to make
   her give it to you to invest in any liquor stores—[*underbreath, dropping into
   a chair*]—and I for one say, God bless Mama for that!
WALTER [*to* RUTH].   See—did you hear? Did you hear!
RUTH.   Honey, please go to work.
WALTER.   Nobody in this house is ever going to understand me.
BENEATHA.   Because you're a nut.
WALTER.   Who's a nut?
280 BENEATHA.   You—you are a nut. Thee is mad, boy.
WALTER [*looking at his wife and his sister from the door, very sadly*].   The world's
   most backward race of people, and that's a fact.
BENEATHA [*turning slowly in her chair*].   And then there are all those prophets
   who would lead us out of the wilderness—[WALTER *slams out of the house*]—
   into the swamps!
RUTH.   Bennie, why you always gotta be pickin' on your brother? Can't you
   be a little sweeter sometimes?

[*Door opens.* WALTER *walks in.*]

WALTER [*to* RUTH].   I need some money for carfare.
RUTH [*looks at him, then warms; teasing, but tenderly*].   Fifty cents? [*She goes to her
290   bag and gets money.*] Here, take a taxi.

[WALTER *exits.* MAMA *enters. She is a woman in her early sixties, full-bodied and strong. She is one of those women of a certain grace and beauty who wear it so unobtrusively that it takes a while to notice. Her dark-brown face is surrounded by the total whiteness of her hair, and, being a woman who has adjusted to many things in life and overcome many more, her face is full of strength. She has, we can see, wit and faith of a kind that keep her eyes lit and full of interest and expectancy. She is, in a word, a beautiful woman. Her bearing is perhaps most like the noble bearing of the women of the Hereros of Southwest Africa—rather as if she imagines that as she walks she still bears a basket or a vessel upon her head. Her speech, on the other hand, is as careless as her carriage is precise—she is inclined to slur everything—but her voice is perhaps not so much quiet as simply soft.*]

MAMA.   Who that 'round here slamming doors at this hour?

[*She crosses through the room, goes to the window, opens it, and brings in a feeble little plant growing doggedly in a small pot on the window sill. She feels the dirt and puts it back out.*]

RUTH.   That was Walter Lee. He and Bennie was at it again.

MAMA.   My children and they tempers. Lord, if this little old plant don't get more sun than it's been getting it ain't never going to see spring again. [*She turns from the window.*] What's the matter with you this morning, Ruth? You looks right peaked. You aiming to iron all them things? Leave some for me. I'll get to 'em this afternoon. Bennie honey, it's too drafty for you to be sitting 'round half dressed. Where's your robe?

BENEATHA.   In the cleaners.

300 MAMA.   Well, go get mine and put it on.

BENEATHA   I'm not cold, Mama, honest.

MAMA.   I know—but you so thin . . .

BENEATHA [*irritably*].   Mama, I'm not cold.

MAMA [*seeing the make-down bed as* TRAVIS *has left it.*]   Lord have mercy, look at that poor bed. Bless his heart—he tries, don't he?

[*She moves to the bed* TRAVIS *has sloppily made up.*]

RUTH.   No—he don't half try at all 'cause he knows you going to come along behind him and fix everything. That's just how come he don't know how to do nothing right now—you done spoiled that boy so.

MAMA.   Well—he's a little boy. Ain't supposed to know 'bout housekeeping.

310   My baby, that's what he is. What you fix for his breakfast this morning?

RUTH [*angrily*].   I feed my son, Lena!

MAMA.   I ain't meddling—[*underbreath; busy-bodyish*] I just noticed all last week he had cold cereal, and when it starts getting chilly in the fall a child ought to have some hot grits or something when he goes out in the cold—

RUTH [*furious*].   I gave him hot oats—is that all right!

MAMA.   I ain't meddling. [*Pause.*] Put a lot of nice butter on it? [RUTH *shoots an angry look and does not reply.*] He likes lots of butter.

RUTH [*exasperated*].   Lena—

MAMA [*to* BENEATHA. MAMA *is inclined to wander conversationally sometimes*].   What
320   was you and your brother fussing 'bout this morning?

BENEATHA.   It's not important, Mama.

[*She gets up and goes to look out at the bathroom, which is apparently free, and she picks up her towels and rushes out.*]

MAMA. What was they fighting about?

RUTH. Now you know as well as I do.

MAMA [*shaking her head*]. Brother still worrying hisself sick about that money?

RUTH. You know he is.

MAMA. You had breakfast?

RUTH. Some coffee.

MAMA. Girl, you better start eating and looking after yourself better. You
330 almost as thin as Travis.

RUTH. Lena—

MAMA. Uh-hunh?

RUTH. What are you going to do with it?

MAMA. Now don't you start, child. It's too early in the morning to be talking about money. It ain't Christian.

RUTH. It's just that he got his heart set on that store—

MAMA. You mean that liquor store that Willy Harris want him to invest in?

RUTH. Yes—

MAMA. We ain't no business people, Ruth. We just plain working folks.

340 RUTH. Ain't nobody business people till they go into business. Walter Lee say colored people ain't never going to start getting ahead till they start gambling on some different kinds of things in the world—investments and things.

MAMA. What done got into you, girl? Walter Lee done finally sold you on investing.

RUTH. No. Mama, something is happening between Walter and me. I don't know what it is—but he needs something—something I can't give him any more. He needs this chance, Lena.

MAMA [*frowning deeply*]. But liquor, honey—

350 RUTH. Well—like Walter say—I spec people going to always be drinking themselves some liquor.

MAMA. Well—whether they drinks it or not ain't none of my business. But whether I go into business selling it to 'em *is*, and I don't want that on my ledger this late in life. [*Stopping suddenly and studying her daughter-in-law.*] Ruth Younger, what's the matter with you today? You look like you could fall right over.

RUTH. I'm tired.

MAMA. Then you better stay home from work today.

RUTH. I can't stay home. She'd be calling up the agency and screaming at
360 them, "My girl didn't come in today—send me somebody! My girl didn't come in!" Oh, she just have a fit . . .

MAMA. Well, let her have it. I'll just call her up and say you got the flu—

RUTH [*laughing.*] Why the flu?

MAMA. 'Cause it sounds respectable to 'em. Something white people get, too. They know 'bout the flu. Otherwise they think you been cut up or something when you tell 'em you sick.

RUTH. I got to go in. We need the money.

MAMA. Somebody would of thought my children done all but starved to

death the way they talk about money here late. Child, we got a great big
370   old check coming tomorrow.
   RUTH [*sincerely, but also self-righteously*].   Now that's your money. It ain't got
      nothing to do with me. We all feel like that—Walter and Bennie and
      me—even Travis.
   MAMA [*thoughtfully, and suddenly very far away*].   Ten thousand dollars—
   RUTH.   Sure is wonderful.
   MAMA.   Ten thousand dollars.
   RUTH.   You know what you should do, Miss Lena? You should take yourself
      a trip somewhere. To Europe or South America or someplace—
   MAMA [*throwing up her hands at the thought*].   Oh, child!
380 RUTH.   I'm serious. Just pack up and leave! Go on away and enjoy yourself
      some. Forget about the family and have yourself a ball for once in your
      life—
   MAMA [*drily*].   You sound like I'm just about ready to die. Who'd go with me?
      What I look like wandering 'round Europe by myself?
   RUTH.   Shoot—these here rich white women do it all the time. They don't
      think nothing of packing up they suitcases and piling on one of them big
      steamships and—swoosh!—they gone, child.
   MAMA.   Something always told me I wasn't no rich white woman.
   RUTH.   Well—what are you going to do with it then?
390 MAMA.   I ain't rightly decided. [*Thinking. She speaks now with emphasis.*] Some
      of it got to be put away for Beneatha and her schoolin'—and ain't nothing
      going to touch that part of it. Nothing. [*She waits several seconds, trying to
      make up her mind about something, and looks at* RUTH *a little tentatively before
      going on.*] Been thinking that we maybe could meet the notes on a little old
      two-story somewhere, with a yard where Travis could play in the summer-
      time, if we use part of the insurance for a down payment and everybody
      kind of pitch in. I could maybe take on a little day work again, a few days
      a week—
   RUTH [*studying her mother-in-law furtively and concentrating on her ironing, anx-*
400   *ious to encourage without seeming to.*]   Well, Lord knows, we've put enough
      rent into this here rat trap to pay for four houses by now . . .
   MAMA [*looking up at the words "rat trap" and then looking around and leaning back
      and sighing—in a suddenly reflective mood—*].   "Rat trap"—yes, that's all it
      is. [*Smiling.*] I remember just as well the day me and Big Walter moved in
      here. Hadn't been married but two weeks and wasn't planning on living
      here no more than a year. [*She shakes her head at the dissolved dream.*] We was
      going to get away, little by little, don't you know, and buy a little place out
      in Morgan Park. We had even picked out the house. [*Chuckling a little.*]
      Looks right dumpy today. But Lord, child, you should know all the dreams
410   I had 'bout buying that house and fixing it up and making me a little
      garden in the back—[*She waits and stops smiling.*] And didn't none of it
      happen.

                                 [*Dropping her hands in a futile gesture.*]

   RUTH [*keeps her head down, ironing*].   Yes, life can be a barrel of disappoint-
      ments, sometimes.

MAMA.   Honey, Big Walter would come in here some nights back then and slump down on that couch there and just look at the rug, and look at me and look at the rug and then back at me—and I'd know he was down then . . . really down. [*After a second very long and thoughtful pause; she is seeing back to times that only she can see.*] And then, Lord, when I lost that baby—little
420   Claude—I almost thought I was going to lose Big Walter too. Oh, that man grieved hisself! He was one man to love his children.

RUTH.   Ain't nothin' can tear at you like losin' your baby.

MAMA.   I guess that's how come that man finally worked hisself to death like he done. Like he was fighting his own war with this here world that took his baby from him.

RUTH.   He sure was a fine man, all right. I always liked Mr. Younger.

MAMA.   Crazy 'bout his children! God knows there was plenty wrong with Walter Younger—hard-headed, mean, kind of wild with women—plenty wrong with him. But he sure loved his children. Always wanted them to
430   have something—be something. That's where Brother gets all these notions, I reckon. Big Walter used to say, he'd get right wet in the eyes sometimes, lean his head back with the water standing in his eyes and say, "Seem like God didn't see fit to give the black man nothing but dreams—but He did give us children to make them dreams seem worth while." [*She smiles.*] He could talk like that, don't you know.

RUTH.   Yes, he sure could. He was a good man, Mr. Younger.

MAMA.   Yes, a fine man—just couldn't never catch up with his dreams, that's all.

[BENEATHA *comes in, brushing her hair and looking up to the ceiling, where the sound of a vacuum cleaner has started up.*]

BENEATHA.   What could be so dirty on that woman's rugs that she has to
440   vacuum them every single day?

RUTH.   I wish certain young women 'round here who I could name would take inspiration about certain rugs in a certain apartment I could also mention.

BENEATHA [*shrugging*].   How much cleaning can a house need, for Christ's sake.

MAMA [*not liking the Lord's name used thus*].   Bennie!

RUTH.   Just listen to her—just listen!

BENEATHA.   Oh, God!

MAMA.   If you use the Lord's name just one more time—
450 BENEATHA [*a bit of a whine.*]   Oh, Mama—

RUTH.   Fresh—just fresh as salt, this girl!

BENEATHA [*drily*].   Well—if the salt loses its savor—

MAMA.   Now that will do. I just ain't going to have you 'round here reciting the scriptures in vain—you hear me?

BENEATHA.   How did I manage to get on everybody's wrong side by just walking into a room?

RUTH.   If you weren't so fresh—

BENEATHA.   Ruth, I'm twenty years old.

MAMA.   What time you be home from school today?

460 BENEATHA.   Kind of late [*With enthusiasm.*] Madeline is going to start my
       guitar lessons today.

                        [MAMA *and* RUTH *look up with the same expression.*]

       MAMA.   Your *what* kind of lessons?
       BENEATHA.   Guitar.
       RUTH.   O, Father!
       MAMA.   How come you done taken it in your mind to learn to play the
       guitar?
       BENEATHA.   I just want to, that's all.
       MAMA [*smiling*].   Lord, child, don't you know what to do with yourself? How
       long it going to be before you get tired of this now—like you got tired of
470 that little play-acting group you joined last year? [*Looking at Ruth.*] And
       what was it the year before that?
       RUTH.   The horseback-riding club for which she bought that fifty-five-dollar
       riding habit that's been hanging in the closet ever since!
       MAMA [*to* BENEATHA].   Why you got to flit so from one thing to another, baby?
       BENEATHA [*sharply*].   I just want to learn to play the guitar. Is there anything
       wrong with that?
       MAMA.   Ain't nobody trying to stop you. I just wonders sometimes why you
       has to flit so from one thing to another all the time. You ain't never done
       nothing with all that camera equipment you brought home—
480 BENEATHA.   I don't flit! I—I experiment with different forms of expression—
       RUTH.   Like riding a horse?
       BENEATHA.   —People have to express themselves one way or another.
       MAMA.   What is it you want to express?
       BENEATHA [*angrily*].   Me! [MAMA *and* RUTH *look at each other and burst into
       raucous laughter.*] Don't worry—I don't expect you to understand.
       MAMA [*to change the subject*].   Who you going out with tomorrow night?
       BENEATHA [*with displeasure*].   George Murchison again.
       MAMA [*pleased*].   Oh—you getting a little sweet on him?
       RUTH.   You ask me, this child ain't sweet on nobody but herself—[*Under-
490 breath.*] Express herself!

                                                                [*They laugh.*]

       BENEATHA.   Oh—I like George all right, Mama. I mean I like him enough to
       go out with him and stuff, but—
       RUTH [*for devilment*].   What does *and stuff* mean?
       BENEATHA.   Mind your own business.
       MAMA.   Stop picking at her now, Ruth. [*A thoughtful pause, and then a suspi-
       cious sudden look at her daughter as she turns in her chair for emphasis.*] What
       does it mean?
       BENEATHA [*wearily*].   Oh, I just mean I couldn't ever really be serious about
       George. He's—he's so shallow.
500 RUTH.   Shallow—what do you mean he's shallow? He's *Rich!*
       MAMA.   Hush, Ruth.
       BENEATHA.   I know he's rich. He knows he's rich, too.
       RUTH.   Well—what other qualities a man got to have to satisfy you, little girl?

BENEATHA. You wouldn't even begin to understand. Anybody who married Walter could not possibly understand.

MAMA [*outraged*]. What kind of way is that to talk about your brother?

BENEATHA. Brother is a flip—let's face it.

MAMA [*to* RUTH, *helplessly*]. What's a flip?

RUTH [*glad to add kindling*]. She's saying he's crazy.

510 BENEATHA. Not crazy. Brother isn't really crazy yet—he—he's an elaborate neurotic.

MAMA. Hush your mouth!

BENEATHA. As for George. Well. George looks good—he's got a beautiful car and he takes me to nice places and, as my sister-in-law says, he is probably the richest boy I will ever get to know and I even like him sometimes—but if the Youngers are sitting around waiting to see if their little Bennie is going to tie up the family with the Murchisons, they are wasting their time.

RUTH. You mean you wouldn't marry George Murchison if he asked you someday? That pretty, rich thing? Honey, I knew you was odd—

520 BENEATHA. No I would not marry him if all I felt for him was what I feel now. Besides, George's family wouldn't really like it.

MAMA. Why not?

BENEATHA. Oh, Mama—the Murchisons are honest-to-God-real-*live*-rich colored people, and the only people in the world who are more snobbish than rich white people are rich colored people. I thought everybody knew that. I've met Mrs. Murchison. She's a scene!

MAMA. You must not dislike people 'cause they well off, honey.

BENEATHA. Why not? It makes just as much sense as disliking people 'cause they are poor, and lots of people do that.

530 RUTH [*in a wisdom-of-the-ages manner, to* MAMA]. Well, she'll get over some of this—

BENEATHA. Get over it? What are you talking about, Ruth? Listen, I'm going to be a doctor. I'm not worried about who I'm going to marry yet—if I ever get married.

MAMA *and* RUTH. *If!*

MAMA. Now, Bennie—

BENEATHA. Oh, I probably will . . . but first I'm going to be a doctor, and George, for one, still thinks that's pretty funny. I couldn't be bothered with that. I am going to be a doctor and everybody around here better

540 understand that!

MAMA [*kindly*]. 'Course you going to be a doctor, honey, God willing.

BENEATHA [*drily*]. God hasn't got a thing to do with it.

MAMA. Beneatha—that just wasn't necessary.

BENEATHA. Well—neither is God. I get sick of hearing about God.

MAMA. Beneatha!

BENEATHA. I mean it! I'm just tired of hearing about God all the time. What has He got to do with anything? Does he pay tuition?

MAMA. You 'bout to get your fresh little jaw slapped!

RUTH. That's just what she needs, all right!

550 BENEATHA. Why? Why can't I say what I want to around here, like everybody else?

MAMA. It don't sound nice for a young girl to say things like that—you wasn't brought up that way. Me and your father went to trouble to get you and Brother to church every Sunday.

BENEATHA.   Mama, you don't understand. It's all a matter of ideas, and God is just one idea I don't accept. It's not important. I am not going out and be immoral or commit crimes because I don't believe in God. I don't even think about it. It's just that I get tired of Him getting credit for all the things the human race achieves through its own stubborn effort. There simply is

560   no blasted God—there is only man and it is he who makes miracles!

[MAMA *absorbs this speech, studies her daughter and rises slowly and crosses to* BE-NEATHA *and slaps her powerfully across the face. After, there is only silence and the daughter drops her eyes from her mother's face, and* MAMA *is very tall before her.*]

MAMA.   Now—you say after me, in my mother's house there is still God. [*There is a long pause and* BENEATHA *stares at the floor wordlessly.* MAMA *repeats the phrase with precision and cool emotion.*] In my mother's house there is still God.

BENEATHA.   In my mother's house there is still God.

[*A long pause.*]

MAMA [*walking away from* BENEATHA, *too disturbed for triumphant posture. Stopping and turning back to her daughter*].   There are some ideas we ain't going to have in this house. Not long as I am at the head of this family.

BENEATHA.   Yes, ma'am.

[MAMA *walks out of the room.*]

570   RUTH [*almost gently, with profound understanding*].   You think you a woman, Bennie—but you still a little girl. What you did was childish—so you got treated like a child.

BENEATHA.   I see. [*Quietly.*] I also see that everybody thinks it's all right for Mama to be a tyrant. But all the tyranny in the world will never put a God in the heavens!

[*She picks up her books and goes out.*]

RUTH [*goes to* MAMA'S *door*].   She said she was sorry.

MAMA [*Coming out, going to her plant*].   They frightens me, Ruth. My children.

RUTH.   You got good children, Lena. They just a little off sometimes—but they're good.

580   MAMA.   No—there's something come down between me and them that don't let us understand each other and I don't know what it is. One done almost lost his mind thinking 'bout money all the time and the other done commence to talk about things I can't seem to understand in no form or fashion. What is it that's changing, Ruth?

RUTH [*soothingly, older than her years*].   Now . . . you taking it all too seriously. You just got strong-willed children and it takes a strong woman like you to keep 'em in hand.

MAMA [*looking at her plant and sprinkling a little water on it*].   They spirited all right, my children. Got to admit they got spirit—Bennie and Walter. Like

590   this little old plant that ain't never had enough sunshine or nothing—and look at it . . .

[*She has her back to* Ruth, *who has had to stop ironing and lean against something and put the back of her hand to her forehead.*]

Ruth [*trying to keep* Mama *from noticing*]. You . . . sure . . . loves that little old thing, don't you? . . .

Mama. Well, I always wanted me a garden like I used to see sometimes at the back of the houses down home. This plant is close as I ever got to having one. [*She looks out of the window as she replaces the plant.*] Lord, ain't nothing as dreary as the view from this window on a dreary day, is there? Why ain't you singing this morning, Ruth? Sing that "No Ways Tired." That song always lifts me up so—[*she turns at last to see that* Ruth *has slipped quietly into a chair, in a state of semiconsciousness.*] Ruth! Ruth honey—what's the matter with you . . . Ruth!

600

CURTAIN

SCENE II

It is the following morning; a Saturday morning, and house cleaning is in progress at the Youngers. *Furniture has been shoved hither and yon and* Mama *is giving the kitchen-area walls a washing down.* Beneatha, *in dungarees, with a handkerchief tied around her face, is spraying insecticide into the cracks in the walls. As they work, the radio is on and a Southside disk-jockey program is inappropriately filling the house with a rather exotic saxophone blues.* Travis, *the sole idle one, is leaning on his arms, looking out the window.*

Travis. Grandmama, that stuff Bennie is using smells awful. Can I go down-stairs, please?

Mama. Did you get all them chores done already? I ain't seen you doing much.

Travis. Yes'm—finished early. Where did Mama go this morning?

Mama [*looking at* Beneatha]. She had to go on a little errand.

Travis. Where?

Mama. To tend to her business.

610 Travis. Can I go outside then?

Mama. Oh, I guess so. You better stay right in front of the house, though . . . and keep a good lookout for the postman.

Travis. Yes'm. [*He starts out and decides to give his* Aunt Beneatha *a good swat on the legs as he passes her.*] Leave them poor little old cockroaches alone, they ain't bothering you none.

[*He runs as she swings the spray gun at him both viciously and playfully.* Walter *enters from the bedroom and goes to the phone.*]

Mama. Look out there, girl, before you be spilling some of that stuff on that child!

Travis [*teasing*]. That's right—look out now!

[*He exits.*]

Beneatha [*drily*]. I can't imagine that it would hurt him—it has never hurt

620 the roaches.

MAMA.   Well, little boys' hides ain't as tough as Southside roaches.

WALTER [*into phone*].   Hello—Let me talk to Willy Harris.

MAMA.   You better get over there behind the bureau. I seen one marching out of there like Napoleon yesterday.

WALTER.   Hello, Willy? It ain't come yet. It'll be here in a few minutes. Did the lawyer give you the papers?

BENEATHA.   There's really only one way to get rid of them, Mama—

MAMA.   How?

BENEATHA.   Set fire to this building.

630 WALTER.   Good. Good. I'll be right over.

BENEATHA.   Where did Ruth go, Walter?

WALTER.   I don't know.

[*He exits abruptly.*]

BENEATHA.   Mama, where did Ruth go?

MAMA [*looking at her with meaning*].   To the doctor, I think.

BENEATHA.   The doctor? What's the matter. [*They exchange glances.*] You don't think—

MAMA [*with her sense of drama*].   Now I ain't saying what I think. But I ain't never been wrong 'bout a woman neither.

[*The phone rings*].

BENEATHA [*at the phone*].   Hay-lo . . . [*Pause, and a moment of recognition.*] Well—

640   when did you get back! . . . And how was it? . . . Of course I've missed you—in my way . . . This morning? No . . . house cleaning and all that and Mama hates it if I let people come over when the house is like this . . . You *have?* Well, that's different . . . What is it—Oh, what the hell, come on over . . . Right, see you then.

[*She hangs up.*]

MAMA [*who has listened vigorously, as is her habit*].   Who is that you inviting over here with this house looking like this? You ain't got the pride you was born with!

BENEATHA.   Asagai doesn't care how houses look, Mama—he's an intellectual.

650 MAMA.   *Who?*

BENEATHA.   Asagai—Joseph Asagai. He's an African boy I met on campus. He's been studying in Canada all summer.

MAMA.   What's his name?

BENEATHA.   Asagai, Joseph. Ah-sah-guy . . . He's from Nigeria.

MAMA.   Oh, that's the little country that was founded by slaves way back . . .

BENEATHA.   No, Mama—that's Liberia.

MAMA.   I don't think I never met no African before.

BENEATHA.   Well, do me a favor and don't ask him a whole lot of ignorant questions about Africans. I mean, do they wear clothes and all that—

660 MAMA.   Well, now, I guess if you think we so ignorant 'round here maybe you shouldn't bring your friends here—

BENEATHA.   It's just that people ask such crazy things. All anyone seems to know about when it comes to Africa is Tarzan—

Mama [*indignantly*].   Why should I know anything about Africa?

Beneatha.   Why do you give money at church for the missionary work?

Mama.   Well, that's to help save people.

Beneatha.   You mean save them from *heathenism*—

Mama [*innocently*].   Yes.

Beneatha.   I'm afraid they need more salvation from the British and the
670   French.

[Ruth *comes in forlornly and pulls off her coat with dejection. They both turn to look at her.*]

Ruth [*dispiritedly*].   Well, I guess from all the happy faces—everybody knows.

Beneatha.   You pregnant?

Mama.   Lord have mercy, I sure hope it's a little old girl. Travis ought to
have a sister.

[Beneatha *and* Ruth *give her a hopeless look for this grandmotherly enthusiasm.*]

Beneatha.   How far along are you?

Ruth.   Two months.

Beneatha.   Did you mean to? I mean did you plan it or was it an accident?

Mama.   What do you know about planning or not planning?

Beneatha.   Oh, Mama.

680 Ruth [*wearily*].   She's twenty years old, Lena.

Beneatha.   Did you plan it, Ruth?

Ruth.   Mind your own business.

Beneatha.   It is my business—where is he going to live, on the *roof*? [*There is silence following the remark as the three women react to the sense of it.*] Gee—I didn't mean that, Ruth, honest. Gee, I don't feel like that at all. I—I think it is wonderful.

Ruth [*dully*].   Wonderful.

Beneatha.   Yes—really.

Mama [*looking at* Ruth, *worried*].   Doctor say everything going to be all right?

690 Ruth [*far away*].   Yes—she says everything is going to be fine . . .

Mama [*immediately suspicious*].   "She"—What doctor you went to?

[Ruth *folds over, near hysteria.*]

Mama [*worriedly hovering over* Ruth].   Ruth honey—what's the matter with you—you sick?

[Ruth *has her fists clenched on her thighs and is fighting hard to suppress a scream that seems to be rising in her.*]

Beneatha.   What's the matter with her, Mama?

Mama [*working her fingers in* Ruth's *shoulder to relax her*].   She be all right. Women gets right depressed sometimes when they get her way. [*Speaking softly, expertly, rapidly.*] Now you just relax. That's right . . . just lean back, don't think 'bout nothing at all . . . nothing at all—

Ruth.   I'm all right . . .

[*The glassy-eyed look melts and then she collapses into a fit of heavy sobbing. The bell rings.*]

700 BENEATHA.   Oh, my God—that must be Asagai.

MAMA [*to* RUTH].   Come on now, honey. You need to lie down and rest awhile
. . . then have some nice hot food.

[*They exit,* RUTH'S *weight on her mother-in-law.* BENEATHA *herself profoundly disturbed, opens the door to admit a rather dramatic-looking young man with a large
package.*]

ASAGAI.   Hello, Alaiyo—

BENEATHA [*holding the door open and regarding him with pleasure*].   Hello . . .
[*Long pause.*] Well—come in. And please excuse everything. My mother
was very upset about my letting anyone come here with the place like this.

ASAGAI [*coming into the room*].   You look disturbed too . . . Is something
wrong?

BENEATHA [*still at the door, absently*].   Yes . . . we've all got acute ghetto-itus.
710   [*She smiles and comes toward him, finding a cigarette and sitting.*] So—sit down!
How was Canada?

ASAGAI [*a sophisticate*].   Canadian.

BENEATHA [*looking at him*].   I'm very glad you are back.

ASAGAI [*looking back at her in turn*].   Are you really?

BENEATHA.   Yes—very.

ASAGAI.   Why—you were quite glad when I went away. What happened?

BENEATHA.   You went away.

ASAGAI.   Ahhhhhhhh.

BENEATHA.   Before—you wanted to be so serious before there was time.

720 ASAGAI.   How much time must there be before one knows what one feels?

BENEATHA [*stalling this particular conversation. Her hands pressed together, in a
deliberately childish gesture*].   What did you bring me?

ASAGAI [*handing her the package*].   Open it and see.

BENEATHA [*eagerly opening the package and drawing out some records and the colorful robes of a Nigerian woman*].   Oh, Asagai! . . . You got them for me! . . .
How beautiful . . . and the records too! [*She lifts out the robes and runs to the
mirror with them and holds the drapery up in front of herself.*]

ASAGAI [*coming to her at the mirror*].   I shall have to teach you how to drape
it properly. [*He flings the material about her for the moment and stands
730   back to look at her*]. Ah—Oh-pay-gay-day, oh-gbah-mu-shay. [*A Yoruba[2] exclamation for admiration.*] You wear it well . . . very well . . . mutilated hair
and all.

BENEATHA [*turning suddenly*].   My hair—what's wrong with my hair?

ASAGAI [*shrugging*].   Were you born with it like that?

BENEATHA [*reaching up to touch it*].   No . . . of course not.

[*She looks back to the mirror, disturbed*].

ASAGAI [*smiling*].   How then?

BENEATHA.   You know perfectly well how — as crinkly as yours . . . that's how.

ASAGAI.   And it is ugly to you that way?

BENEATHA [*quickly*].   Oh, no—not ugly . . . [*More slowly, apologetically.*] But it's
740   so hard to manage when it's, well—raw.

---

[2] The Yoruba tribe is prevalent in Southwest Nigeria. Yoruba culture is rich and varied,
particularly renowned for the sculpture of the Benin dynasty (ca. 1400–1897).

ASAGAI. And so to accommodate that—you mutilate it every week?

BENEATHA. It's not mutilation!

ASAGAI [*laughing aloud at her seriousness*]. Oh . . . please! I am only teasing you because you are so very serious about these things. [*He stands back from her and folds his arms across his chest as he watches her pulling at her hair and frowning in the mirror.*] Do you remember the first time you met me at school? . . . [*He laughs.*] You came up to me and you said—and I thought you were the most serious little thing I had ever seen—you said: [*He imitates her.*] "Mr. Agasai—I want very much to talk with you. About Africa.
750   You see, Mr. Asagai, I am looking for my *identity!*"

[*He laughs.*]

BENEATHA [*turning to him, not laughing*]. Yes—

[*Her face is quizzical, profoundly disturbed.*]

ASAGAI [*still teasing and reaching out and taking her face in his hands and turning her profile to him*]. Well . . . it is true that this is not so much a profile of a Hollywood queen as perhaps the queen of the Nile—[*A mock dismissal of the importance of the question.*] But what does it matter? Assimilationism is so popular in your country.

BENEATHA [*wheeling, passionately, sharply*]. I am not an assimilationist!

ASAGAI [*the protest hangs in the room for a moment and* ASAGAI *studies her, his laughter fading*]. Such a serious one. [*There is a pause.*] So—you like the
760   robes? You must take excellent care of them—they are from my sister's personal wardrobe.

BENEATHA [*with incredulity*]. You—you sent all the way home—for me?

ASAGAI [*with charm*]. For you—I would do much more . . . Well, that is what I came for. I must go.

BENEATHA. Will you call me Monday?

ASAGAI. Yes . . . We have a great deal to talk about. I mean about identity and time and all that.

BENEATHA. Time?

ASAGAI. Yes. About how much time one needs to know what one feels.

770 BENEATHA. You never understood that there is more than one kind of feeling which can exist between a man and a woman—or, at least, there should be.

ASAGAI [*shaking his head negatively but gently*]. No. Between a man and a woman there need be only one kind of feeling. I have that for you . . . Now even . . . right this moment . . .

BENEATHA. I know—and by itself—it won't do. I can find that anywhere.

ASAGAI. For a woman it should be enough.

BENEATHA. I know—because that's what it says in all the novels that men write. But it isn't. Go ahead and laugh—but I'm not interested in being
780   someone's little episode in America or—[*with feminine vengeance*]—one of them! [ASAGAI *has burst into laughter again.*] That's funny as hell, huh!

ASAGAI. It's just that every American girl I have known has said that to me. White—black—in this you are all the same. And the same speech, too!

BENEATHA [*angrily*]. Yuk, yuk, yuk!

ASAGAI. It's how you can be sure that the world's most liberated women are not liberated at all. You all talk about it too much!

[MAMA *enters and is immediately all social charm because of the presence of a guest.*]

BENEATHA. Oh—Mama—this is Mr. Asagai.

MAMA. How do you do?

ASAGAI [*total politeness to an elder*]. How do you do, Mrs. Younger. Please
790   forgive me for coming at such an outrageous hour on a Saturday.

MAMA. Well, you are quite welcome. I just hope you understand that our
house don't always look like this. [*Chatterish.*] You must come again. I
would love to hear all about—[*not sure of the name*]—your country. I think
it's so sad the way our American Negroes don't know nothing about Africa
'cept Tarzan and all that. And all that money they pour into these churches
when they ought to be helping you people over there drive out them
French and Englishmen done taken away your land.

[*The mother flashes a slightly superior look at her daughter upon completion of the recitation.*]

ASAGAI [*taken aback by this sudden and acutely unrelated expression of sympathy*].
Yes . . . yes . . .

800 MAMA [*smiling at him suddenly and relaxing and looking him over*]. How many
miles is it from here to where you come from?

ASAGAI. Many thousands.

MAMA [*looking at him as she would* WALTER]. I bet you don't half look after
yourself, being away from your mama either. I spec you better come
'round here from time to time and get yourself some decent home-cooked
meals . . .

ASAGAI [*moved*]. Thank you. Thank you very much. [*They are all quiet, then—.*]
Well . . . I must go. I will call you Monday, Alaiyo.

MAMA. What's that he call you?

810 ASAGAI. Oh—"Alaiyo." I hope you don't mind. It is what you would call a
nickname, I think. It is a Yoruba word. I am a Yoruba.

MAMA [*looking at* BENEATHA]. I—I thought he was from—

ASAGAI [*understanding*]. Nigeria is my country. Yoruba is my tribal origin—

BENEATHA. You didn't tell us what Alaiyo means . . . for all I know, you might
be calling me Little Idiot or something . . .

ASAGAI. Well . . . let me see . . . I do not know how just to explain it . . . The
sense of a thing can be so different when it changes languages.

BENEATHA. You're evading.

ASAGAI. No—really it is difficult . . . [*Thinking.*] It means . . . it means One
820   for Whom Bread—Food—Is Not Enough. [*He looks at her.*] Is that all right?

BENEATHA [*understanding, softly*]. Thank you.

MAMA [*looking from one to the other and not understanding any of it*]. Well . . .
that's nice . . . You must come see us again—Mr.—

ASAGAI. Ah-sah-guy . . .

MAMA. Yes . . . Do come again.

ASAGAI. Good-bye.

[*He exits.*]

MAMA [*after him*]. Lord, that's a pretty thing just went out here! [*In-
sinuatingly, to her daughter.*] Yes, I guess I see why we done com-

mence to get so interested in Africa 'round here. Missionaries my aunt
830   Jenny!

[*She exits.*]

BENEATHA.   Oh, Mama! . . .

[*She picks up the Nigerian dress and holds it up to her in front of the mirror again.
She sets the headdress on haphazardly and then notices her hair again and clutches at
it and then replaces the headdress and frowns at herself. Then she starts to wriggle in
front of the mirror as she thinks a Nigerian woman might.* TRAVIS *enters and regards
her.*]

TRAVIS.   You cracking up?
BENEATHA.   Shut up.

[*She pulls the headdress off and looks at herself in the mirror and clutches at her hair
again and squinches her eyes as if trying to imagine something. Then, suddenly, she
gets her raincoat and kerchief and hurriedly prepares for going out.*]

MAMA [*coming back into the room*].   She's resting now. Travis, baby, run next
door and ask Miss Johnson to please let me have a little kitchen cleanser.
This here can is empty as Jacob's kettle.
TRAVIS.   I just came in.
MAMA.   Do as you told. [*He exits and she looks at her daughter.*] Where you
going?
840   BENEATHA [*halting at the door*].   To become a queen of the Nile!

[*She exits in a breathless blaze of glory.* RUTH *appears in the bedroom doorway.*]

MAMA.   Who told you to get up?
RUTH.   Ain't nothing wrong with me to be lying in no bed for. Where did
Bennie go?
MAMA [*drumming her fingers*].   Far as I could make out—to Egypt. [RUTH *just
looks at her.*] What time is it getting to?
RUTH.   Ten twenty. And the mailman going to ring that bell this morning
just like he done every morning for the last umpteen years.

[TRAVIS *comes in with the cleanser can.*]

TRAVIS.   She say to tell you that she don't have much.
MAMA [*angrily*].   Lord, some people I could name sure is tight-fisted! [*Di-*
850   *recting her grandson.*] Mark two cans of cleanser down on the list there. If
she that hard up for kitchen cleanser, I sure don't want to forget to get her
none!
RUTH.   Lena—maybe the woman is just short on cleanser—
MAMA [*not listening*].   —Much baking powder as she done borrowed from me
all these years, she could of done gone into the baking business!

[*The bell sounds suddenly and sharply and all three are stunned—serious and silent—
mid-speech. In spite of all the other conversations and distractions of the morning, this
is what they have been waiting for, even* TRAVIS, *who looks helplessly from his mother
to his grandmother.* RUTH *is the first to come to life again.*]

RUTH [*to* TRAVIS].   *Get down them steps, boy!*

[TRAVIS *snaps to life and flies out to get the mail.*]

MAMA [*her eyes wide, her hand to her breast*].   You mean it done really come?
RUTH [*excited*].   Oh, Miss Lena!
MAMA [*collecting herself*].   Well . . . I don't know what we all so excited about
860   'round here for. We known it was coming for months.
RUTH.   That's a whole lot different from having it come and being able to
         hold it in your hands . . . a piece of paper worth ten thousand dollars . . .
         [TRAVIS *bursts back into the room. He holds the envelope high above his head, like
         a little dancer, his face is radiant and he is breathless. He moves to his grandmother
         with sudden slow ceremony and puts the envelope into her hands. She accepts it,
         and then merely holds it and looks at it.*] Come on! Open it . . . Lord have
         mercy, I wish Walter Lee was here!
TRAVIS.   Open it, Grandmama!
MAMA [*staring at it*].   Now you all be quiet. It's just a check.
870 RUTH.   Open it . . .
MAMA [*still staring at it*].   Now don't act silly . . . We ain't never been no
         people to act silly 'bout no money—
RUTH [*swiftly*].   We ain't never had none before—*open it!*

[MAMA *finally makes a good strong tear and pulls out the thin blue slice of paper and
inspects it closely. The boy and his mother study it raptly over* MAMA'S *shoulders.*]

MAMA.   *Travis!* [*She is counting off with doubt.*] Is that the right number of
         zeros?
TRAVIS.   Yes'm . . . ten thousand dollars. Gaalee, Grandmama, you rich.
MAMA [*she holds the check away from her, still looking at it. Slowly her face sobers into
         a mask of unhappiness*].   Ten thousand dollars. [*She hands it to* RUTH.] Put
         it away somewhere, Ruth. [*She does not look at* RUTH; *her eyes seem to be seeing
880   something somewhere very far off.*] Ten thousand dollars they give you. Ten
         thousand dollars.
TRAVIS [*to his mother, sincerely*].   What's the matter with Grandmama—don't
         she want to be rich?
RUTH [*distractedly*].   You go out and play now, baby. [TRAVIS *exits.* MAMA *starts
         wiping dishes absently, humming intently to herself.* RUTH *turns to her, with kind
         exasperation.*] You've gone and got yourself upset.
MAMA [*not looking at her*].   I spec if it wasn't for you all . . . I would just put
         that money away or give it to the church or something.
RUTH.   Now what kind of talk is that. Mr. Younger would just be plain mad
890   if he could hear you talking foolish like that.
MAMA [*stopping and staring off*].   Yes. . . . he sure would. [*Sighing.*] We got
         enough to do with that money, all right. [*She halts then, and turns and looks
         at her daughter-in-law hard;* RUTH *avoids her eyes and* MAMA *wipes her hands
         with finality and starts to speak firmly to* RUTH.] Where did you go today, girl?
RUTH.   To the doctor.
MAMA [*impatiently*].   Now, Ruth . . . you know better than that. Old Doctor
         Jones is strange enough in his way but there ain't nothing 'bout him make
         somebody slip and call him "she"—like you done this morning.
RUTH.   Well, that's what happened—my tongue slipped.

900 MAMA.   You went to see that woman, didn't you?
RUTH [*defensively, giving herself away*].   What woman you talking about?
MAMA [*angrily*].   That woman who—

[WALTER *enters in great excitement.*]

WALTER.   Did it come?
MAMA [*quietly*].   Can't you give people a Christian greeting before you start asking about money?
WALTER [*to* RUTH].   Did it come? [RUTH *unfolds the check and lays it quietly before him, watching him intently with thoughts of her own.* WALTER *sits down and grasps it close and counts off the zeros.*] Ten thousand dollars—[*He turns suddenly, frantically to his mother and draws some papers out of his breast pocket.*] Mama—
910   look. Old Willy Harris put everything on paper—
MAMA.   Son—I think you ought to talk to your wife . . . I'll go on out and leave you alone if you want—
WALTER.   I can talk to her later—Mama, look—
MAMA.   Son—
WALTER.   WILL SOMEBODY PLEASE LISTEN TO ME TODAY!
MAMA [*quietly*].   I don't 'low no yellin' in this house, Walter Lee, and you know it—[WALTER *stares at them in frustration and starts to speak several times.*] And there ain't going to be no investing in no liquor stores. I don't aim to have to speak on that again.

[*A long pause.*]

920 WALTER.   Oh—so you don't aim to have to speak on that again? So *you* have decided . . . [*Crumpling his papers.*] Well, *you* tell that to my boy tonight when you put him to sleep on the living-room couch . . . [*Turning to* MAMA *and speaking directly to her.*] Yeah—and tell it to my wife, Mama, tomorrow when she has to go out of here to look after somebody else's kids. And tell it to *me*, Mama, every time we need a new pair of curtains and I have to watch *you* go out and work in somebody's kitchen. Yeah, you tell me then!

[WALTER *starts out.*]

RUTH.   Where you going?
WALTER.   I'm going out!
RUTH.   Where?
930 WALTER.   Just out of this house somewhere—
RUTH [*getting her coat*].   I'll come too.
WALTER.   I don't want you to come!
RUTH.   I got something to talk to you about, Walter.
WALTER.   That's too bad.
MAMA [*still quietly*].   Walter Lee—[*she waits and he finally turns and looks at her.*] Sit down.
WALTER.   I'm a grown man, Mama.
MAMA.   Ain't nobody said you wasn't grown. But you still in my house and my presence. And as long as you are—you'll talk to your wife civil. Now sit
940   down.
RUTH [*suddenly*].   Oh, let him go on out and drink himself to death! He makes me sick to my stomach! [*She flings her coat against him.*]

WALTER [*violently*].   And you turn mine too, baby! [RUTH *goes into their bedroom and slams the door behind her.*] That was my greatest mistake—

MAMA [*still quietly*].   Walter, what is the matter with you?

WALTER.   Matter with me? Ain't nothing the matter with *me!*

MAMA.   Yes there is. Something eating you up like a crazy man. Something more than me not giving you this money. The past few years I been watching it happen to you. You get all nervous acting and kind of wild in
950   the eyes—[WALTER *jumps up impatiently at her words.*] I said sit there now, I'm talking to you!

WALTER.   Mama—I don't need no nagging at me today.

MAMA.   Seem like you getting to a place where you always tied up in some kind of knot about something. But if anybody ask you 'bout it you just yell at 'em and bust out the house and go out and drink somewheres. Walter Lee, people can't live with that. Ruth's a good, patient girl in her way—but you getting to be too much. Boy, don't make the mistake of driving that girl away from you.

WALTER.   Why—what she do for me?

960   MAMA.   She loves you.

WALTER.   Mama—I'm going out. I want to go off somewhere and be by myself for a while.

MAMA.   I'm sorry 'bout your liquor store, son. It just wasn't the thing for us to do. That's what I want to tell you about—

WALTER.   I got to go out, Mama—

[*He rises.*]

MAMA.   It's dangerous, son.

WALTER.   What's dangerous?

MAMA.   When a man goes outside his home to look for peace.

WALTER [*beseechingly*].   Then why can't there never be no peace in this house
970   then?

MAMA.   You done found it in some other house?

WALTER.   No—there ain't no woman! Why do women always think there's a woman somewhere when a man gets restless. [*Coming to her.*] Mama— Mama—I want so many things . . .

MAMA.   Yes, son—

WALTER.   I want so many things that they are driving me kind of crazy . . . Mama—look at me.

MAMA.   I'm looking at you. You a good-looking boy. You got a job, a nice wife, a fine boy and—

980   WALTER.   A job. [*Looks at her.*] Mama, a job? I open and close car doors all day long. I drive a man around in his limousine and I say, "Yes, sir; no, sir; very good, sir; shall I take the Drive, sir?" Mama, that ain't no kind of job . . . that ain't nothing at all. [*Very quietly.*] Mama, I don't know if I can make you understand.

MAMA.   Understand what, baby?

WALTER [*quietly*].   Sometimes it's like I can see the future stretched out in front of me—just plain as day. The future, Mama. Hanging over there at the edge of my days. Just waiting for me—a big, looming blank space—full of *nothing.* Just waiting for *me.* [*Pause.*] Mama—sometimes when I'm down-

990   town and I pass them cool, quiet-looking restaurants where them white boys are sitting back and talking 'bout things . . . sitting there turning deals worth millions of dollars . . . sometimes I see guys don't look much older than me—

MAMA.   Son—how come you talk so much 'bout money?

WALTER [*with immense passion*].   Because it is life, Mama!

MAMA [*quietly*].   Oh—[*Very quietly.*] So now it's life. Money is life. Once upon a time freedom used to be life—now it's money. I guess the world really do change . . .

WALTER.   No—it was always money, Mama. We just didn't know about it.

1000 MAMA.   No . . . something has changed. [*She looks at him.*] You something new, boy. In my time we was worried about not being lynched and getting to the North if we could and how to stay alive and still have a pinch of dignity too . . . Now here come you and Beneatha—talking 'bout things we ain't never even thought about hardly, me and your daddy. You ain't satisfied or proud of nothing we done. I mean that you had a home; that we kept you out of trouble till you was grown; that you don't have to ride to work on the back of nobody's streetcar— You my children—but how different we done become.

WALTER.   You just don't understand, Mama, you just don't understand.

1010 MAMA.   Son—do you know your wife is expecting another baby? [WALTER *stands, stunned, and absorbs what his mother has said.*] That's what she wanted to talk to you about. [WALTER *sinks down into a chair.*] This ain't for me to be telling—but you ought to know. [*She waits.*] I think Ruth is thinking 'bout getting rid of that child.

WALTER [*slowly understanding*].   No—no—Ruth wouldn't do that.

MAMA.   When the world gets ugly enough—a woman will do anything for her family. *The part that's already living.*

WALTER.   You don't know Ruth, Mama, if you think she would do that.

[RUTH *opens the bedroom door and stands there a little limp.*]

RUTH [*beaten*].   Yes I would too, Walter. [*Pause.*] I gave her a five-dollar down 1020   payment.

[*There is total silence as the man stares at his wife and the mother stares at her son.*]

MAMA [*presently*].   Well—[*Tightly.*] Well—son, I'm waiting to hear you say something . . . I'm waiting to hear how you be your father's son. Be the man he was . . . [*Pause.*] Your wife say she going to destroy your child. And I'm waiting to hear you talk like him and say we a people who give children life, not who destroys them—[*She rises.*] I'm waiting to see you stand up and look like your daddy and say we done give up one baby to poverty and that we ain't going to give up nary another one . . . I'm waiting.

WALTER.   Ruth—

1030 MAMA.   If you a son of mine, tell her! [WALTER *turns, looks at her and can say nothing. She continues, bitterly.*] You . . . you are a disgrace to your father's memory. Somebody get me my hat.

CURTAIN

ACT II

SCENE I

TIME: *Later the same day.*

At rise: RUTH *is ironing again. She has the radio going. Presently* BENEATHA'S *bedroom door opens and* RUTH'S *mouth falls and she puts down the iron in fascination.*

RUTH. What have we got on tonight!

BENEATHA [*emerging grandly room from the doorway so that we can see her thoroughly robed in the costume Asagai brought*]. You are looking at what a well-dressed Nigerian woman wears—[*She parades for* RUTH, *her hair completely hidden by the headdress; she is coquettishly fanning herself with an ornate oriental fan, mistakenly more like Butterfly than any Nigerian that ever was.*] Isn't it beauti-
1040   ful? [*She promenades to the radio and, with an arrogant flourish, turns off the good loud blues that is playing.*] Enough of this assimilationist junk! [RUTH *follows her with her eyes as she goes to the phonograph and puts on a record and turns and waits ceremoniously for the music to come up. Then, with a shout—*] OCOMOGOSIAY!

[RUTH *jumps. The music comes up, a lovely Nigerian melody.* BENEATHA *listens, enraptured, her eyes far away—"back to the past." She begins to dance.* RUTH *is dumfounded.*]

RUTH. What kind of dance is that?
BENEATHA. A folk dance.
RUTH [*Pearl Bailey*]. What kind of folks do that, honey?
BENEATHA. It's from Nigeria. It's a dance of welcome.
RUTH. Who you welcoming?
BENEATHA. The men back to the village.
1050 RUTH. Where they been?
BENEATHA. How should I know—out hunting or something. Anyway, they are coming back now . . .
RUTH. Well, that's good.
BENEATHA [*with the record*].
   Alundi, alundi
   Alundi alunya
   Jop pu a jeepua
   Ang gu sooooooooooo

1050   *Ai yai yae . . .*
   Ayehaye—alundi . . .

[WALTER *comes in during this performance; he has obviously been drinking. He leans against the door heavily and watches his sister, at first with distaste. Then his eyes look off—"back to the past"—as he lifts both his fists to the roof, screaming.*]

WALTER. YEAH . . . AND ETHIOPIA STRETCH FORTH HER HANDS AGAIN! . . .
RUTH [*drily, looking at him*]. Yes—and Africa sure is claiming her own to-night. [*She gives them both up and starts ironing again.*]

WALTER [*all in a drunken, dramatic shout*].   Shut up! . . . I'm digging them
drums . . . them drums move me! . . . [*He makes his weaving way to his wife's
face and leans in close to her.*] In my *heart of hearts*—[*he thumps his chest*]—I am
much warrior!

1060 RUTH [*without even looking up*].   In your heart of hearts you are much drunkard.

WALTER [*coming away from her and starting to wander around the room, shouting*].
Me and Jomo . . . [*Intently, in his sister's face. She has stopped dancing to watch
him in this unknown mood.*] That's my man, Kenyatta.³ [*Shouting and thump-
ing his chest.*] FLAMING SPEAR! HOT DAMN! [*He is suddenly in possession
of an imaginary spear and actively spearing enemies all over the room.*] OCO-
MOGOSIAY . . . THE LION IS WAKING . . . OWIMOWEH! [*He pulls his
shirt open and leaps up on a table and gestures with his spear. The bell rings. RUTH
goes to answer.*]

1070 BENEATHA [*to encourage WALTER, thoroughly caught up with this side of him*].
OCOMOGOSIAY, FLAMING SPEAR!

WALTER [*on the table, very far gone, his eyes pure glass sheets. He sees what he cannot,
that he is a leader of his people, a great chief, a descendant of Chaka, and that the
hour to march has come*].   Listen my black brothers—

BENEATHA.   OCOMOGOSIAY!

WALTER.   —Do you hear the waters rushing against the shores of the coast-
lands—

BENEATHA.   OCOMOGOSIAY!

WALTER.   —Do you hear the screeching of the cocks in yonder hills beyond
1080   where the chiefs meet in council for the coming of the mighty war—

BENEATHA.   OCOMOGOSIAY!

WALTER.   —Do you hear the beating of the wings of the birds flying low over
the mountains and the low places of our land—

[RUTH *opens the door.* GEORGE MURCHISON *enters.*]

BENEATHA.   OCOMOGOSIAY!

WALTER.   —Do you hear the singing of the women, singing the war songs of
our fathers to the babies in the great houses . . . singing the sweet war
songs? OH, DO YOU HEAR, MY BLACK BROTHERS!

BENEATHA [*completely gone*].   We hear you, Flaming Spear—

WALTER.   Telling us to prepare for the greatness of the time—[*To* GEORGE.]
1090   Black Brother!

[*He extends his hand for the fraternal clasp.*]

GEORGE.   Black Brother, hell!

RUTH [*having had enough, and embarrassed for the family*].   Beneatha, you got
company—what's the matter with you? Walter Lee Younger, get down off
that table and stop acting like a fool . . .

[WALTER *comes down off the table suddenly and makes a quick exit to the bathroom.*]

---

³ Jomo Kenyatta (1893?–1978) was a leader in the struggle of the Kenyans to gain independence from Great Britain. Imprisoned for terrorism in 1953 and then exiled, he became the
president of independent Kenya from 1964–1978, consolidating his power by suppressing and
banning all political opposition.

RUTH. He's had a little to drink . . . I don't know what her excuse is.

GEORGE [*to* BENEATHA]. Look honey, we're going *to* the theatre—we're not going to be *in* it . . . so go change, huh?

RUTH. You expect this boy to go out with you looking like that?

BENEATHA [*looking at* GEORGE]. That's up to George. If he's ashamed of his
1100   heritage—

GEORGE. Oh, don't be so proud of yourself, Bennie—just because you look eccentric.

BENEATHA. How can something that's natural be eccentric?

GEORGE. That's what being eccentric means—being natural. Get dressed.

BENEATHA. I don't like that, George.

RUTH. Why must you and your brother make an argument out of everything people say?

BENEATHA. Because I hate assimilationist Negroes!

RUTH. Will somebody please tell me what assimila-whoever means!

1110 GEORGE. Oh, it's just a college girl's way of calling people Uncle Toms—but that isn't what it means at all.

RUTH. Well, what does it mean?

BENEATHA [*cutting* GEORGE *off and staring at him as she replies to* RUTH]. It means someone who is willing to give up his own culture and submerge himself completely in the dominant, and in this case, *oppressive* culture!

GEORGE. Oh, dear, dear, dear! Here we go! A lecture on the African past! On our Great West African Heritage! In one second we will hear all about the great Ashanti empires;[4] the great Songhay civilizations; and the great sculpture of Bénin—and then some poetry in Bantu—and the whole
1120   monologue will end with the word *heritage!* [*Nastily.*] Let's face it, baby, your heritage is nothing but a bunch of raggedy-assed spirituals and some grass huts!

BENEATHA. *Grass huts!* [RUTH *crosses to her and forcibly pushes her toward the bedroom.*] See there . . . you are standing there in your splendid ignorance talking about people who were the first to smelt iron on the face of the earth! [RUTH *is pushing her through the door.*] The Ashanti were performing surgical operations when the English—[RUTH *pulls the door to, with* BE-NEATHA *on the other side, and smiles graciously at* GEORGE. BENEATHA *opens the door and shouts the end of the sentence defiantly at* GEORGE.]—were still tatooing
1130   themselves with blue dragons . . . [*She goes back inside.*]

RUTH. Have a seat, George. [*They both sit,* RUTH *folds her hands rather primly on her lap, determined to demonstrate the civilization of the family.*] Warm, ain't it? I mean for September. [*Pause.*] Just like they always say about Chicago weather: If it's too hot or cold for you, just wait a minute and it'll change. [*She smiles happily at this cliché of clichés.*] Everybody say it's got to do with them bombs and things they keep setting off. [*Pause.*] Would you like a nice cold beer?

GEORGE. No, thank you. I don't care for beer. [*He looks at his watch.*] I hope she hurries up.

---

[4] The Ashanti empire prospered during the 18th century in what is now Ghana; the Songhay empire dominated West Central Africa in the 15th century; the Benin dynasty ruled the coastal region near the mouth of the Niger River from about 1400 until the end of the 19th century; the Bantu language is spoken by most Africans living south of the equator.

1140 RUTH.   What time is the show?

GEORGE.   It's an eight-thirty curtain. That's just Chicago, though. In New York standard curtain time is eight-forty.

[*He is rather proud of this knowledge.*]

RUTH [*properly appreciating it*].   You get to New York a lot?

GEORGE [*offhand*].   Few times a year.

RUTH.   Oh—that's nice. I've never been to New York.

[WALTER *enters. We feel he has relieved himself, but the edge of unreality is still with him.*]

WALTER.   New York ain't got nothing Chicago ain't. Just a bunch of hustling people all squeezed up together—being "Eastern."

[*He turns his face into a screw of displeasure.*]

GEORGE.   Oh—you've been?

WALTER.   *Plenty* of times.

1150 RUTH [*shocked at the lie*].   Walter Lee Younger!

WALTER [*staring her down*].   Plenty! [*Pause.*] What we got to drink in this house? Why don't you offer this man some refreshment. [*To* GEORGE.] They don't know how to entertain people in this house, man.

GEORGE.   Thank you—I don't really care for anything.

WALTER [*feeling his head; sobriety coming*].   Where's Mama?

RUTH.   She ain't come back yet.

WALTER [*looking* MURCHISON *over from head to toe, scrutinizing his carefully casual tweed sports jacket over cashmere V-neck sweater over soft eyelet shirt and tie, and soft slacks, finished off with white buckskin shoes*].   Why all you college boys
1160   wear them fairyish-looking white shoes?

RUTH.   Walter Lee!

[GEORGE MURCHISON *ignores the remark.*]

WALTER [*to* RUTH].   Well, they look crazy as hell—white shoes, cold as it is.

RUTH [*crushed*].   You have to excuse him—

WALTER.   No he don't! Excuse me for what? What you always excusing me for! I'll excuse myself when I needs to be excused! [*A pause.*] They look as funny as them black knee socks Beneatha wears out of here all the time.

RUTH.   It's the college *style*, Walter.

WALTER.   Style, hell. She looks like she got burnt legs or something!

RUTH.   Oh, Walter—

1170 WALTER [*an irritable mimic*].   Oh, Walter! Oh, Walter! [*To* MURCHISON.] How's your old man making out? I understand you all going to buy that big hotel on the Drive?[5] [*He finds a beer in the refrigerator, wanders over to* MURCHISON, *sipping and wiping his lips with the back of his hand, and straddling a chair backwards to talk to the other man.*] Shrewd move. Your old man is all right, man. [*Tapping his head and half winking for emphasis.*] I mean he knows how

---

[5] Lake Shore Drive is a very prosperous strip of hotels and condominiums in Chicago along the shore of Lake Michigan.

to operate. I mean he thinks *big*, you know what I mean, I mean for a *home*, you know? But I think he's kind of running out of ideas now. I'd like to talk to him. Listen, man, I got some plans that could turn this city upside down. I mean I think like he does. *Big*. Invest big, gamble big, hell, lose
1180 *big* if you have to, you know what I mean. It's hard to find a man on this whole Southside who understands my kind of thinking—you dig? [*He scrutinizes* MURCHISON *again, drinks his beer, squints his eyes and leans in close, confidential, man to man.*] Me and you ought to sit down and talk sometimes, man. Man, I got me some ideas . . .

MURCHISON [*with boredom*]. Yeah—sometimes we'll have to do that, Walter.

WALTER [*understanding the indifference, and offended*]. Yeah—well, when you get the time, man. I know you a busy little boy.

RUTH. Walter, please—

WALTER [*bitterly, hurt*]. I know ain't nothing in this world as busy as you
1190 colored college boys with your fraternity pins and white shoes . . .

RUTH [*covering her face with humiliation*]. Oh, Walter Lee—

WALTER. I see you all all the time—with the books tucked under your arms— going to your [*British A—a mimic*] "clahsses." And for what! What the hell you learning over there? Filling up your heads—[*counting off on his fingers*]—with the sociology and the psychology—but they teaching you how to be a man? How to take over and run the world? They teaching you how to run a rubber plantation or a steel mill? Naw—just to talk proper and read books and wear white shoes . . .

GEORGE [*looking at him with distaste, a little above it all*]. You're all wacked up
1200 with bitterness, man.

WALTER [*intently, almost quietly, between the teeth, glaring at the boy*]. And you— ain't you bitter, man? Ain't you just about had it yet? Don't you see no stars gleaming that you can't reach out and grab? You happy?—you contented son-of-a-bitch—you happy? You got it made? Bitter? Man, I'm a volcano. Bitter? Here I am a giant—surrounded by ants! Ants who can't even understand what it is the giant is talking about.

RUTH [*passionately and suddenly*]. Oh, Walter—ain't you with nobody!

WALTER [*violently*]. No! 'Cause ain't nobody with me! Not even my own mother!

1210 RUTH. Walter, that's a terrible thing to say!

[BENEATHA *enters, dressed for the evening in a cocktail dress and earrings.*]

GEORGE. Well—hey, you look great.

BENEATHA. Let's go, George. See you all later.

RUTH. Have a nice time.

GEORGE. Thanks. Good night. [*To* WALTER, *sarcastically.*] Good night, Prometheus.[6]

[BENEATHA *and* GEORGE *exit.*]

WALTER [*to* RUTH]. Who is Prometheus?

RUTH. I don't know. Don't worry about it.

WALTER [*in fury, pointing after* GEORGE.] See there, they get to a point where

---

[6] In Greek mythology, Prometheus was one of the Titans. He is known as the supreme trickster and also as the god who gave fire to humanity.

they can't insult you man to man—they got to go talk about something
1220   ain't nobody never heard of!
RUTH.   How do you know it was an insult? [*To humor him.*] Maybe
Prometheus is a nice fellow.
WALTER.   Prometheus! I bet there ain't even no such thing! I bet that simple-
minded clown—
RUTH.   Walter—

[*She stops what she is doing and looks at him.*]

WALTER [*yelling*].   Don't start!
RUTH.   Start what?
WALTER.   Your nagging! Where was I? Who was I with? How much money
did I spend?
1230   RUTH [*plaintively*].   Walter Lee—why don't we just try to talk about it . . .
WALTER [*not listening*].   I been out talking with people who understand me.
People who care about the things I got on my mind.
RUTH [*wearily*].   I guess that means people like Willy Harris.
WALTER.   Yes, people like Willy Harris.
RUTH [*with a sudden flash of impatience*].   Why don't you all just hurry up and
go into the banking business and stop talking about it!
WALTER.   Why? You want to know why? 'Cause we all tied up in a race of peo-
ple that don't know how to do nothing but moan, pray and have babies!

[*The line is too bitter even for him and he looks at her and sits down.*]

RUTH.   Oh, Walter . . . [*Softly.*] Honey, why can't you stop fighting me?
1240   WALTER [*without thinking*].   Who's fighting you? Who even cares about you?

[*This line begins the retardation of his mood.*]

RUTH.   Well—[*she waits a long time, and then with resignation starts to put away
her things.*] I guess I might as well go on to bed . . . [*more or less to herself*] I
don't know where we lost it . . . but we have . . . [*then, to him*] I—I'm sorry
about this new baby, Walter. I guess maybe I better go on and do what I
started . . . I guess I just didn't realize how bad things was with us . . . I
guess I just didn't really realize—[*She starts out to the bathroom and stops.*]
You want some hot milk?
WALTER.   Hot milk?
RUTH.   Yes—hot milk.
1250   WALTER.   Why hot milk?
RUTH.   'Cause after all that liquor you come home with you ought to have
something hot in your stomach.
WALTER.   I don't want no milk.
RUTH.   You want some coffee then?
WALTER.   No, I don't want no coffee. I don't want nothing hot to drink.
[*Almost plaintively.*] Why you always trying to give me something to eat?
RUTH [*standing and looking at him helplessly*].   What else can I give you, Walter
Lee Younger?

[*She stands and looks at him and presently turns to go out again. He lifts his head and
watches her going away from him in a new mood which began to emerge when he asked
her "Who cares about you?".*]

WALTER.   It's been rough, ain't it, baby? [*She hears and stops but does not turn*
1260   *around and he continues to her back.*] I guess between two people there ain't
never as much understood as folks generally thinks there is. I mean like
between me and you—[*She turns to face him.*] How we gets to the place
where we scared to talk softness to each other. [*He waits, thinking hard to
himself.*] Why you think it got to be like that? [*He is thoughtful, almost as a
child would be.*] Ruth, what is it gets into people ought to be close?
RUTH.   I don't know, honey. I think about it a lot.
WALTER.   On account of you and me, you mean? The way things are with us.
The way something done come down between us.
RUTH.   There ain't so much between us, Walter . . . Not when you come to
1270   me and try to talk to me. Try to be with me . . . a little even.
WALTER [*total honesty*].   Sometimes . . . sometimes . . . I don't even know how
to try.
RUTH.   Walter—
WALTER.   Yes?
RUTH [*coming to him, gently and with misgiving, but coming to him*].   Honey . . .
life don't have to be like this. I mean sometimes people can do things so
that things are better . . . You remember how we used to talk when Travis
was born . . . about the way we were going to live . . . the kind of house . . .
[*She is stroking his head.*] Well, it's all starting to slip away from us . . .

[MAMA *enters, and* WALTER *jumps up and shouts at her.*]

1280 WALTER.   Mama, where have you been?
MAMA.   My—them steps is longer than they used to be. Whew! [*She sits down
and ignores him.*] How you feeling this evening, Ruth?

[RUTH *shrugs, disturbed some at having been prematurely interrupted and watching
her husband knowingly.*]

WALTER.   Mama, where have you been all day?
MAMA [*still ignoring him and leaning on the table and changing to more comfortable
shoes*].   Where's Travis?
RUTH.   I let him go out earlier and he ain't come back yet. Boy, is he going
to get it!
WALTER.   Mama!
MAMA [*as if she has heard him for the first time*].   Yes, son?
1290 WALTER.   Where did you go this afternoon?
MAMA.   I went down town to tend to some business that I had to tend to.
WALTER.   What kind of business?
MAMA.   You know better than to question me like a child, Brother.
WALTER [*rising and bending over the table*].   Where were you, Mama? [*Bringing
his fists down and shouting.*] Mama, you didn't go do something with that
insurance money, something crazy?

[*The front door opens slowly, interrupting him, and* TRAVIS *peeks his head in, less than
hopefully.*]

TRAVIS [*to his mother*].   Mama, I—
RUTH.   "Mama I" nothing! You're going to get it, boy! Get on in that bedroom and get yourself ready!
1300 TRAVIS.   But I—

Mama. Why don't you all never let the child explain hisself.

Ruth. Keep out of it now, Lena.

[Mama *clamps her lips together, and* Ruth *advances toward her son menacingly.*]

Ruth. A thousand times I have told you not to go off like that—

Mama [*holding out her arms to her grandson*]. Well—at least let me tell him something. I want him to be the first one to hear . . . Come here, Travis. [*The boy obeys, gladly.*] Travis—[*She takes him by the shoulders and looks into his face.*]—you know that money we got in the mail this morning?

Travis. Yes'm—

Mama. Well—what you think your grandmama gone and done with that
1310   money?

Travis. I don't know, Grandmama.

Mama [*putting her finger on his nose for emphasis*]. She went out and she bought you a house! [*The explosion comes from* Walter *at the end of the revelation and he jumps up and turns away from all of them in a fury.* Mama *continues, to* Travis.] You glad about the house? It's going to be yours when you get to be a man.

Travis. Yeah—I always wanted to live in a house.

Mama. All right, gimme some sugar then—[Travis *puts his arms around her neck as she watches her son over the boy's shoulder. Then, to* Travis, *after the embrace.*] Now when you say your prayers tonight, you thank God and your
1320   grandfather—'cause it was him who give you the house—in his way.

Ruth [*taking the boy from* Mama *and pushing him toward the bedroom*]. Now you get out of here and get ready for your beating.

Travis. Aw, Mama—

Ruth. Get on in there—[*Closing the door behind him and turning radiantly to her mother-in-law.*] So you went and did it!

Mama [*quietly, looking at her son with pain*]. Yes, I did.

Ruth [*raising both arms classically*]. Praise God! [*Looks at* Walter *a moment, who says nothing. She crosses rapidly to her husband.*] Please, honey—let me be glad . . . you be glad too. [*She has laid her hands on his shoulders, but he shakes
1330   himself free of her roughly, without turning to face her.*] Oh, Walter . . . a home . . . a home. [*She comes back to* Mama.] Well—where is it? How big is it? How much is it going to cost?

Mama. Well—

Ruth. When we moving?

Mama [*smiling at her*]. First of the month.

Ruth [*throwing back her head with jubilance*]. Praise God!

Mama [*tentatively, still looking at her son's back turned against her and* Ruth.] It's—it's a nice house too . . . [*She cannot help speaking directly to him. An imploring quality in her voice, her manner, makes her almost like a girl now.*]
1340   Three bedrooms—nice big one for you and Ruth. . . . Me and Beneatha still have to share our room, but Travis have one of his own—and—[*with difficulty*] I figures if the—new baby—is a boy, we could get one of them double-decker outfits . . . And there's a yard with a little patch of dirt where I could maybe get to grow me a few flowers . . . And a nice big basement . . .

Ruth. Walter honey, be glad—

Mama [*still to his back, fingering things on the table*]. 'Course I don't want to make it sound fancier than it is . . . It's just a plain little old house—but it's

made good and solid—and it will be *ours*. Walter Lee—it makes a differ-
1350 ence in a man when he can walk on floors that belong to *him* . . .

RUTH.   Where is it?

MAMA [*frightened at this telling*].   Well—well—it's out there in Clybourne
Park—

[RUTH's *radiance fades abruptly, and* WALTER *finally turns slowly to face his mother
with incredulity and hostility.*]

RUTH.   Where?

MAMA [*matter-of-factly*].   Four o six Clybourne Street, Clybourne Park.

RUTH.   Clybourne Park? Mama, there ain't no colored people living in Clybourne Park.

MAMA [*almost idiotically*].   Well, I guess there's going to be some now.

WALTER [*bitterly*].   So that's the peace and comfort you went out and bought
1360 for us today!

MAMA [*raising her eyes to meet his finally*].   Son—I just tried to find the nicest
place for the least amount of money for my family.

RUTH [*trying to recover from the shock*].   Well—well—'course I ain't one never
been 'fraid of no crackers,[7] mind you—but—well, wasn't there no other
houses nowhere?

MAMA.   Them houses they put up for colored in them areas way out all seem
to cost twice as much as other houses. I did the best I could.

RUTH [*struck senseless with the news, in its various degrees of goodness and trouble,
she sits a moment, her fists propping her chin in thought, and then she starts to rise,*
1370 *bringing her fists down with vigor, the radiance spreading from cheek to cheek
again*].   Well—well!—All I can say is—if this is my time in life—*my time*—to
say good-bye—[*and she builds with momentum as she starts to circle the room
with an exuberant, almost tearfully happy release*]—to these God-damned
cracking walls!—[*she pounds the walls*]—and these marching roaches!—[*she
wipes at an imaginary army of marching roaches*]—and this cramped little
closet which ain't now or never was no kitchen! . . . then I say it loud and
good, *Hallelujah! and good-bye misery . . . I don't never want to see your ugly face
again!* [*She laughs joyously, having practically destroyed the apartment, and flings
her arms up and lets them come down happily, slowly, reflectively, over her abdo-*
1380 *men, aware for the first time perhaps that the life therein pulses with happiness and
not despair.*] Lena?

MAMA [*moved, watching her happiness*].   Yes, honey?

RUTH [*looking off*].   Is there—is there a whole lot of sunlight?

MAMA [*understanding*].   Yes, child, there's a whole lot of sunlight.

[*Long pause.*]

RUTH [*collecting herself and going to the door of the room* TRAVIS *is in*].   Well—I
guess I better see 'bout Travis. [*To* MAMA.] Lord, I sure don't feel like
whipping nobody today!

[*She exits.*]

MAMA [*the mother and son are left alone now and the mother waits a long time,
considering deeply, before she speaks*].   Son—you—you understand what I
1390 done, don't you? [WALTER *is silent and sullen.*] I—I just seen my family

---

[7] A disparaging term generally applied to lower-class, white Southerners.

falling apart today . . . just falling to pieces in front of my eyes . . . We couldn't of gone on like we was today. We was going backwards 'stead of forwards—talking 'bout killing babies and wishing each other was dead . . . When it gets like that in life—you just got to do something different, push on out and do something bigger . . . [*She waits.*] I wish you say something, son . . . I wish you'd say how deep inside you you think I done the right thing—

WALTER [*crossing slowly to his bedroom door and finally turning there and speaking measuredly*].   What you need me to say you done right for? *You* the head

1400   of the family. You run our lives like you want to. It was your money and you did what you wanted with it. So what you need for me to say it was all right for? [*Bitterly, to hurt her as deeply as he knows is possible.*] So you butchered up a dream of mine—you—who always talking 'bout your children's dreams . . .

MAMA.   Walter Lee—

[*He just closes the door behind him.* MAMA *sits alone, thinking heavily.*]

CURTAIN

SCENE II

TIME: Friday night. A few weeks later.

At rise: Packing crates mark the intention of the family to move. BENEATHA *and* GEORGE *come in, presumably from an evening out again.*

GEORGE.   O.K. . . . O.K., whatever you say . . . [*They both sit on the couch. He tries to kiss her. She moves away.*] Look, we've had a nice evening; let's not spoil it, huh? . . .

[*He again turns her head and tries to nuzzle in and she turns away from him, not with distaste but with momentary lack of interest; in a mood to pursue what they were talking about.*]

BENEATHA.   I'm *trying* to talk to you.

1410 GEORGE.   We always talk.

BENEATHA.   Yes—and I love to talk.

GEORGE [*exasperated; rising*].   I know it and I don't mind it sometimes . . . I want you to cut it out, see— The moody stuff, I mean. I don't like it. You're a nice-looking girl . . . all over. That's all you need, honey, forget the atmosphere. Guys aren't going to go for the atmosphere—they're going to go for what they see. Be glad for that. Drop the Garbo[8] routine. It doesn't go with you. As for myself, I want a nice—[*Groping.*]—simple—[*Thoughtfully.*]—sophisticated girl . . . not a poet—O.K.?

[*She rebuffs him again and he starts to leave.*]

BENEATHA.   Why are you angry?

---

[8]   Greta Garbo (1905–1990), a Swedish actress who became famous for her air of remote sophistication in such films as *Grand Hotel* (1932) and *Anna Karenina* (1935).

1420 GEORGE.   Because this is stupid! I don't go out with you to discuss the nature
of "quiet desperation" or to hear all about your thoughts—because the
world will go on thinking what it thinks regardless—
BENEATHA.   Then why read books? Why go to school?
GEORGE [*with artificial patience, counting on his fingers*].   It's simple. You read
books—to learn facts—to get grades—to pass the course—to get a degree.
That's all—it has nothing to do with thoughts.

[*A long pause.*]

BENEATHA.   I see. [*A longer pause as she looks at him.*] Good night, George.

[GEORGE *looks at her a little oddly, and starts to exit. He meets* MAMA *coming in.*]

GEORGE.   Oh—hello, Mrs. Younger.
MAMA.   Hello, George, how you feeling?
1430 GEORGE.   Fine—fine, how are you?
MAMA.   Oh, a little tired. You know them steps can get you after a day's work.
You all have a nice time tonight?
GEORGE.   Yes—a fine time. Well, good night.
MAMA.   Good night. [*He exits.* MAMA *closes the door behind her.*] Hello, honey.
What you sitting like that for?
BENEATHA.   I'm just sitting.
MAMA.   Didn't you have a nice time?
BENEATHA.   No.
MAMA.   No? What's the matter?
1440 BENEATHA.   Mama, George is a fool—honest. [*She rises.*]
MAMA [*hustling around unloading the packages she has entered with. She stops*].   Is
he, baby?
BENEATHA.   Yes.

[BENEATHA *makes up* TRAVIS' *bed as she talks.*]

MAMA.   You sure?
BENEATHA.   Yes.
MAMA.   Well—I guess you better not waste your time with no fools.

[BENEATHA *looks up at her mother, watching her put groceries in the refrigerator.
Finally she gathers up her things and starts into the bedroom. At the door she stops and
looks back at her mother.*]

BENEATHA.   Mama—
MAMA.   Yes, baby—
BENEATHA.   Thank you.
1450 MAMA.   For what?
BENEATHA.   For understanding me this time.

[*She exits quickly and the mother stands, smiling a little, looking at the place where*
BENEATHA *just stood.* RUTH *enters.*]

RUTH.   Now don't you fool with any of this stuff, Lena—
MAMA.   Oh, I just thought I'd sort a few things out.

[*The phone rings.* RUTH *answers.*]

R<small>UTH</small> [*at the phone*]. Hello—Just a minute. [*Goes to door.*] Walter, it's Mrs. Arnold. [*Waits. Goes back to the phone. Tense.*] Hello. Yes, this is his wife speaking . . . He's lying down now. Yes . . . well, he'll be in tomorrow. He's been very sick. Yes—we know I should have called, but we were so sure he'd be able to come in today. Yes—yes, I'm very sorry. Yes . . . Thank you very much. [*She hangs up.* W<small>ALTER</small> *is standing in the doorway of the bedroom*
1460   *behind her.*] That was Mrs. Arnold.

W<small>ALTER</small> [*indifferently*]. Was it?

R<small>UTH</small>. She said if you don't come in tomorrow that they are getting a new man . . .

W<small>ALTER</small>. Ain't that sad—ain't that crying sad.

R<small>UTH</small>. She said Mr. Arnold has had to take a cab for three days . . . Walter, you ain't been to work for three days! [*This is a revelation to her.*] Where you been, Walter Lee Younger? [W<small>ALTER</small> *looks at her and starts to laugh.*] You're going to lose your job.

W<small>ALTER</small>. That's right . . .

1470 R<small>UTH</small>. Oh, Walter, and with your mother working like a dog every day—

W<small>ALTER</small>. That's sad too— Everything is sad.

M<small>AMA</small>. What you been doing for these three days, son?

W<small>ALTER</small>. Mama—you don't know all the things a man what got leisure can find to do in this city . . . What's this—Friday night? Well—Wednesday I borrowed Willy Harris' car and I went for a drive . . . just me and myself and I drove and drove . . . Way out . . . way past South Chicago, and I parked the car and I sat and looked at the steel mills all day long. I just sat in the car and looked at them big black chimneys for hours. Then I drove back and I went to the Green Hat. [*Pause.*] And Thursday—Thursday I
1480   borrowed the car again and I got in it and I pointed it the other way and I drove the other way—for hours—way, way up to Wisconsin, and I looked at the farms. I just drove and looked at the farms. Then I drove back and I went to the Green Hat. [*Pause.*] And today—today I didn't get the car. Today I just walked. All over the Southside. And I looked at the Negroes and they looked at me and finally I just sat down on the curb at Thirty-ninth and South Parkway and I just sat there and watched the Negroes go by. And then I went to the Green Hat. You all sad? You all depressed? And you know where I am going right now—

[R<small>UTH</small> *goes out quietly.*]

M<small>AMA</small>. Oh, Big Walter, is this the harvest of our days?

1490 W<small>ALTER</small>. You know what I like about the Green Hat? [*He turns the radio on and a steamy, deep blues pours into the room.*] I like this little cat they got there who blows a sax . . . He blows. He talks to me. He ain't but 'bout five feet tall and he's got a conked head and his eyes is always closed and he's all music—

M<small>AMA</small> [*rising and getting some papers out of her handbag*]. Walter—

W<small>ALTER</small>. And there's this other guy who plays the piano . . . and they got a sound. I mean they can work on some music . . . They got the best little combo in the world in the Green Hat . . . You can just sit there and drink and listen to them three men play and you realize that don't nothing
1500   matter worth a damn, but just being there—

MAMA.   I've helped do it to you, haven't I, son? Walter, I been wrong.

WALTER.   Naw—you ain't never been wrong about nothing, Mama.

MAMA.   Listen to me, now. I say I been wrong, son. That I been doing to you
what the rest of the world been doing to you. [*She stops and he looks up slowly
at her and she meets his eyes pleadingly.*] Walter—what you ain't never understood is that I ain't got nothing, don't own nothing, ain't never really
wanted nothing that wasn't for you. There ain't nothing as precious to me
. . . There ain't nothing worth holding on to, money, dreams, nothing
else—if it means—if it means it's going to destroy my boy. [*She puts her
papers in front of him and he watches her without speaking or moving.*] I paid the
man thirty-five hundred dollars down on the house. That leaves sixty-five
hundred dollars. Monday morning I want you to take this money and take
three thousand dollars and put it in a savings account for Beneatha's
medical schooling. The rest you put in a checking account—with your
name on it. And from now on any penny that comes out of it or that go in
it is for you to look after. For you to decide. [*She drops her hands a little
helplessly.*] It ain't much, but it's all I got in the world and I'm putting it in
your hands. I'm telling you to be the head of the family from now on like
you supposed to be.

WALTER [*stares at the money*].   You trust me like that, Mama?

MAMA.   I ain't never stop trusting you. Like I ain't never stop loving you.

[*She goes out, and WALTER sits looking at the money on the table as the music continues
in its idiom, pulsing in the room. Finally, in a decisive gesture, he gets up and, in a
furious action, flings the bedclothes wildly from his son's makeshift bed to all over the
floor—with a cry of desperation. Then he picks up the money and goes out in a hurry.*]

CURTAIN

SCENE III

TIME: *Saturday, moving day, one week later.*

*Before the curtain rises, RUTH's voice, a strident, dramatic church alto, cuts through
the silence.*

*It is, in the darkness, a triumphant surge, a penetrating statement of expectation:
"Oh, Lord, I don't feel no ways tired! Children, oh, glory hallelujah!"*

*As the curtain rises we see that RUTH is alone in the living room, finishing up the
family's packing. It is moving day. She is nailing crates and tying cartons. BENEATHA
enters, carrying a guitar case, and watches her exuberant sister-in-law.*

RUTH.   Hey!

BENEATHA [*putting away the case*].   Hi.

RUTH [*pointing at a package*].   Honey—look in that package there and see
what I found on sale this morning at South Center. [RUTH *gets up and moves
to the package and draws out some curtains.*] Lookahere—hand-turned hems!

BENEATHA.   How do you know the window size out there?

RUTH [*who hadn't thought of that*].   Oh—Well, they bound to fit something in
the whole house. Anyhow, they was too good a bargain to pass us. [RUTH

1530   *slaps her head, suddenly remembering something.*] Oh, Bennie—I meant to put a special note on that carton over there. That's your mama's good china and she wants 'em to be very careful with it.

BENEATHA.   I'll do it.

        [BENEATHA *finds a piece of paper and starts to draw large letters on it.*]

RUTH.   You know what I'm going to do as soon as I get in that new house?

BENEATHA.   What?

RUTH.   Honey—I'm going to run me a tub of water up to here . . . [*With her fingers practically up to her nostrils.*] And I'm going to get in it—and I am going to sit . . . and sit . . . and sit in that hot water and the first person who knocks to tell *me* to hurry up and come out—

1540 BENEATHA.   Gets shot at sunrise.

RUTH [*laughing happily*].   You said it, sister! [*Noticing how large* BENEATHA *is absent-mindedly making the note.*] Honey, they ain't going to read that from no airplane.

BENEATHA [*laughing herself*].   I guess I always think things have more emphasis if they are big, somehow.

RUTH [*looking up at her and smiling*].   You and your brother seem to have that as a philosophy of life. Lord, that man—done changed so 'round here. You know—you know what we did last night? Me and Walter Lee?

BENEATHA.   What?

1550 RUTH [*smiling to herself*].   We went to the movies. [*Looking at* BENEATHA *to see if she understands.*] We went to the movies. You know the last time me and Walter went to the movies together?

BENEATHA.   No.

RUTH.   Me neither. That's how long it been. [*Smiling again.*] But we went last night. The picture wasn't much good, but that didn't seem to matter. We went—and we held hands.

BENEATHA.   Oh, Lord!

RUTH.   We held hands—and you know what?

BENEATHA.   What?

1560 RUTH.   When we come out of the show it was late and dark and all the stores and things was closed up . . . and it was kind of chilly and there wasn't many people on the streets . . . and we was still holding hands, me and Walter.

BENEATHA.   You're killing me.

[WALTER *enters with a large package. His happiness is deep in him; he cannot keep still with his new-found exuberance. He is singing and wiggling and snapping his fingers. He puts his package in a corner and puts a phonograph record, which he has brought in with him, on the record player. As the music comes up he dances over to* RUTH *and tries to get her to dance with him. She gives in at last to his raunchiness and in a fit of giggling allows herself to be drawn into his mood and together they deliberately burlesque an old social dance of their youth.*]

BENEATHA [*regarding them a long time as they dance, then drawing in her breath for a deeply exaggerated comment which she does not particularly mean*].   Talk about—olddddddddddd-fashionedddddddd—Negroes!

WALTER [*stopping momentarily*].   What kind of Negroes?

[*He says this in fun. He is not angry with her today, nor with anyone. He starts to dance with his wife again.*]

BENEATHA.   Old-fashioned.
WALTER [*as he dances with* RUTH].   You know, when these *New Negroes* have
1570   their convention—[*pointing at his sister*]—that is going to be the chairman
of the Committee on Unending Agitation. [*He goes on dancing, then stops.*]
Race, race, race! . . . Girl, I do believe you are the first person in the
history of the entire human race to successfully brainwash yourself. [BE-
NEATHA *breaks up and he goes on dancing. He stops again, enjoying his tease.*]
Damn, even the N double A C P takes a holiday sometimes! [BENEATHA *and*
RUTH *laugh. He dances with* RUTH *some more and starts to laugh and stops and
pantomines someone over an operating table.*] I can just see that chick someday
looking down at some poor cat on an operating table before she starts to
slice him, saying . . . [*pulling his sleeves back maliciously*] "By the way, what
1580   are your views on civil rights down there? . . ."

[*He laughs at her again and starts to dance happily. The bell sounds.*]

BENEATHA.   Sticks and stones may break my bones but . . . words will never
hurt me!

[BENEATHA *goes to the door and opens it as* WALTER *and* RUTH *go on with the
clowning.* BENEATHA *is somewhat surprised to see a quiet-looking middle-aged white
man in a business suit holding his hat and a briefcase in his hand and consulting a
small piece of paper.*]

MAN.   Uh—how do you do, miss. I am looking for Mrs.—[*he looks at the slip
of paper*] Mrs. Lena Younger?
BENEATHA [*smoothing her hair with slight embarrassment*].   Oh—yes, that's my
mother. Excuse me. [*She closes the door and turns to quiet the other two.*] Ruth!
Brother! Somebody's here. [*Then she opens the door. The man casts a curious
quick glance at all of them.*] Uh—come in please.
MAN [*coming in*].   Thank you.
1590 BENEATHA.   My mother isn't here just now. Is it business?
MAN.   Yes . . . well, of a sort.
WALTER [*freely, the Man of the House*].   Have a seat. I'm Mrs. Younger's son. I
look after most of her business matters.

[RUTH *and* BENEATHA *exchange amused glances.*]

MAN [*regarding* WALTER, *and sitting*].   Well— My name is Karl Lindner . . .
WALTER [*stretching out his hand*].   Walter Younger. This is my wife—[RUTH
nods politely]—and my sister.
LINDNER.   How do you do.
WALTER [*amiably, as he sits himself easily on a chair, leaning with interest forward on
his knees and looking expectantly into the newcomer's face*].   What can we do for
1600   you, Mr. Lindner!
LINDNER [*some minor shuffling of the hat and briefcase on his knees*].   Well—I am
a representative of the Clybourne Park Improvement Association—
WALTER [*pointing*].   Why don't you sit your things on the floor?
LINDNER.   Oh—yes. Thank you. [*He slides the briefcase and hat under the chair.*]

And as I was saying—I am from the Clybourne Park Improvement Association and we have had it brought to our attention at the last meeting that you people—or at least your mother—has bought a piece of residential property at—[*he digs for the slip of paper again*]—four o six Clybourne Street . . .

1610 WALTER. That's right. Care for something to drink? Ruth, get Mr. Lindner a beer.

LINDNER [*upset for some reason*]. Oh—no, really. I mean thank you very much, but no thank you.

RUTH [*innocently*]. Some coffee?

LINDNER. Thank you, nothing at all.

[BENEATHA *is watching the man carefully.*]

LINDNER. Well, I don't know how much you folks know about our organization. [*He is a gentle man; thoughtful and somewhat labored in his manner.*] It is one of these community organizations set up to look after—oh, you know, things like block upkeep and special projects and we also have what we call
1620 our New Neighbors Orientation Committee . . .

BENEATHA [*drily*]. Yes—and what do they do?

LINDNER [*turning a little to her and then returning the main force to* WALTER]. Well—it's what you might call a sort of welcoming committee, I guess. I mean they, we, I'm the chairman of the committee—go around and see the new people who move into the neighborhood and sort of give them the lowdown on the way we do things out in Clybourne Park.

BENEATHA [*with appreciation of the two meanings, which escape* RUTH *and* WALTER]. Un-huh.

LINDNER. And we also have the category of what the association calls—[*he
1630 looks elsewhere*]—uh—special community problems . . .

BENEATHA. Yes—and what are some of those?

WALTER. Girl, let the man talk.

LINDNER [*with understated relief*]. Thank you. I would sort of like to explain this thing in my own way. I mean I want to explain to you in a certain way.

WALTER. Go ahead.

LINDNER. Yes. Well, I'm going to try to get right to the point. I'm sure we'll all appreciate that in the long run.

BENEATHA. Yes.

WALTER. Be still now!
1640 LINDNER. Well—

RUTH [*still innocently*]. Would you like another chair—you don't look comfortable.

LINDNER [*more frustrated than annoyed*]. No, thank you very much. Please. Well—to get right to the point I—[*a great breath, and he is off at last*] I am sure you people must be aware of some of the incidents which have happened in various parts of the city when colored people have moved into certain areas—[BENEATHA *exhales heavily and starts tossing a piece of fruit up and down in the air.*] Well—because we have what I think is going to be a unique type of organization in American community life—not only do we
1650 deplore that kind of thing—but we are trying to do something about it. [BENEATHA *stops tossing and turns with a new and quizzical interest to the man.*]

We feel—[*gaining confidence in his mission because of the interest in the faces of the people he is talking to*]—we feel that most of the trouble in this world, when you come right down to it—[*he hits his knee for emphasis*]— most of the trouble exists because people just don't sit down and talk to each other.

RUTH [*nodding as she might in church, pleased with the remark*].   You can say that again, mister.

LINDNER [*more encouraged by such affirmation*].   That we don't try hard enough
1660   in this world to understand the other fellow's problem. The other guy's point of view.

RUTH.   Now that's right.

[BENEATHA *and* WALTER *merely watch and listen with genuine interest.*]

LINDNER.   Yes—that's the way we feel out in Clybourne park. And that's why I was elected to come here this afternoon and talk to you people. Friendly like, you know, the way people should talk to each other and see if we couldn't find some way to work this thing out. As I say, the whole business is a matter of *caring* about the other fellow. Anybody can see that you are a nice family of folks, hard working and honest I'm sure. [BENEATHA *frowns slightly, quizzically, her head tilted regarding him.*] Today everybody knows
1670   what it means to be on the outside of *something*. And of course, there is always somebody who is out to take the advantage of people who don't always understand.

WALTER.   What do you mean?

LINDNER.   Well—you see our community is made up of people who've worked hard as the dickens for years to build up that little community. They're not rich and fancy people; just hard-working, honest people who don't really have much but those little homes and a dream of the kind of community they want to raise their children in. Now, I don't say we are perfect and there is a lot wrong in some of the things they want. But you've got to
1680   admit that a man, right or wrong, has the right to want to have the neighborhood he lives in a certain kind of way. And at the moment the overwhelming majority of our people out there feel that people get along better, take more of a common interest in the life of the community, when they share a common background. I want you to believe me when I tell you that race prejudice simply doesn't enter into it. It is a matter of the people of Clybourne Park believing, rightly or wrongly, as I say, that for the happiness of all concerned that our Negro families are happier when they live in their *own* communities.

BENEATHA [*with a grand and bitter gesture*].   This, friends, is the Welcoming
1690   Committee!

WALTER [*dumfounded, looking at* LINDNER].   Is this what you came marching all the way over here to tell us?

LINDNER.   Well, now we've been having a fine conversation. I hope you'll hear me all the way through.

WALTER [*tightly*].   Go ahead, man.

LINDNER.   You see—in the face of all things I have said, we are prepared to make your family a very generous offer . . .

BENEATHA.   Thirty pieces and not a coin less!

WALTER.   Yeah?

1700 LINDNER [*putting on his glasses and drawing a form out of the briefcase*].   Our
association is prepared, through the collective effort of our people, to buy
the house from you at a financial gain to your family.
RUTH.   Lord have mercy, ain't this the living gall!
WALTER.   All right, you through?
LINDNER.   Well, I want to give you the exact terms of the financial agreement—
WALTER.   We don't want to hear no exact terms of no arrangements. I want
to know if you got any more to tell us 'bout getting together?
LINDNER [*taking off his glasses*].   Well—I don't suppose that you feel . . .
1710 WALTER.   Never mind how I feel—you got any more to say 'bout how people
ought to sit down and talk to each other? . . . Get out of my house, man.

[*He turns his back and walks to the door.*]

LINDNER [*looking around at the hostile faces and reaching and assembling his hat and
briefcase*].   Well—I don't understand why you people are reacting this
way. What do you think you are going to gain by moving into a neighborhood where you just aren't wanted and where some elements—well—
people can get awful worked up when they feel that their whole way of life
and everything they've ever worked for is threatened.
WALTER.   Get out.
LINDNER [*at the door, holding a small card*].   Well—I'm sorry it went like this.
1720 WALTER.   Get out.
LINDNER [*almost sadly regarding* WALTER].   You just can't force people to
change their hearts, son.

[*He turns and puts his card on a table and exits.* WALTER *pushes the door to with
stinging hatred, and stands looking at it.* RUTH *just sits and* BENEATHA *just stands.
They say nothing.* MAMA *and* TRAVIS *enter.*]

MAMA.   Well—this all the packing got done since I left out of here this
morning. I testify before God that my children got all the energy of the
dead. What time the moving men due?
BENEATHA.   Four o'clock. You had a caller, Mama.

[*She is smiling, teasingly.*]

MAMA.   Sure enough—who?
BENEATHA [*her arms folded saucily*].   The Welcoming Committee.

[WALTER *and* RUTH *giggle.*]

MAMA [*innocently*].   Who?
1730 BENEATHA.   The Welcoming Committee. They said they're sure going to be
glad to see you when you get there.
WALTER [*devilishly*].   Yeah, they said they can't hardly wait to see your face.

[*Laughter.*]

MAMA [*sensing their facetiousness*].   What's the matter with you all?
WALTER.   Ain't nothing the matter with us. We just telling you 'bout the
gentleman who came to see you this afternoon. From the Clybourne Park
Improvement Association.

MAMA. What he want?

RUTH [*in the same mood as* BENEATHA *and* WALTER]. To welcome you, honey.

WALTER. He said they can't hardly wait. He said the one thing they don't
1740   have, that they just *dying* to have out there is a fine family of colored
people! [*To* RUTH *and* BENEATHA.] Ain't that right!

RUTH *and* BENEATHA [*mockingly*]. Yeah! He left his card in case—

[*They indicate the card, and* MAMA *picks it up and throws it on the floor—understanding and looking off as she draws her chair up to the table on which she has put
her plant and some sticks and some cord.*]

MAMA. Father, give us strength. [*Knowingly—and without fun.*] Did he
threaten us?

BENEATHA. Oh—Mama—they don't do it like that any more. He talked
Brotherhood. He said everybody ought learn how to sit down and hate
each other with good Christian fellowship.

[*She and* WALTER *shake hands to ridicule the remark.*]

MAMA [*sadly*]. Lord, protect us . . .

RUTH. You should hear the money those folks raised to buy the house from
1750   us. All we paid and then some.

BENEATHA. What they think we going to do—eat 'em?

RUTH. No, honey, marry 'em.

MAMA [*shaking her head*]. Lord, Lord, Lord . . .

RUTH. Well—that's the way the crackers crumble. Joke.

BENEATHA [*laughingly noticing what her mother is doing*]. Mama, what are you
doing?

MAMA. Fixing my plant so it won't get hurt none on the way . . .

BENEATHA. Mama, you going to take *that* to the new house?

MAMA. Un-huh.

1760 BENEATHA. That raggedy-looking old thing?

MAMA [*stopping and looking at her*]. It expresses *me*.

RUTH [*with delight, to* BENEATHA]. So there, Miss Thing!

[WALTER *comes to* MAMA *suddenly and bends down behind her and squeezes her in his
arms with all his strength. She is overwhelmed by the suddenness of it and, though
delighted, her manner is like that of* RUTH *with* TRAVIS.]

MAMA. Look out now, boy! You make me mess up my thing here!

WALTER [*his face lit, he slips down on his knees beside her, his arms still about her*].
Mama . . . you know what it means to climb up in the chariot?

MAMA [*gruffly, very happy*]. Get on away from me now . . .

RUTH [*near the gift-wrapped package, trying to catch* WALTER'S *eye*]. Psst—

WALTER. What the old song say, Mama . . .

RUTH. Walter—Now?

[*She is pointing to the package.*]

1770 WALTER [*speaking the lines, sweetly, playfully, in his mother's face*].

I got wings . . . you got wings. . .
All God's children got wings . . .

Mama. Boy—get out of my face and do some work . . .

Walter.

When I get to heaven gonna put on my wings,
Gonna fly all over God's heaven . . .

Beneatha [*teasingly, from across the room*]. Everybody talking 'bout heaven ain't going there!

Walter [*to* Ruth, *who is carrying the box across to them*]. I don't know, you think
1780　we ought to give her that . . . Seems to me she ain't been very appreciative around here.

Mama [*eying the box, which is obviously a gift*]. What is that?

Walter [*taking it from* Ruth *and putting it on the table in front of* Mama]. Well— what you all think. Should we give it to her?

Ruth. Oh—she was pretty good today.

Mama. I'll good you—

[*She turns her eyes to the box again.*]

Beneatha. Open it, Mama.

[*She stands up, looks at it, turns and looks at all of them, and then presses her hands together and does not open the package.*]

Walter [*sweetly*]. Open it, Mama. It's for you. [Mama *looks in his eyes. It is the first present in her life without its being Christmas. Slowly she opens her package*
1790　*and lifts out, one by one, a brand-new sparkling set of gardening tools.* Walter *continues, prodding.*] Ruth made up the note—read it . . .

Mama [*picking up the card and adjusting her glasses*]. "To our own Mrs. Miniver—Love from Brother, Ruth and Beneatha." Ain't that lovely . . .

Travis [*tugging at his father's sleeve*]. Daddy, can I give her mine now?

Walter. All right, son. [Travis *flies to get his gift.*] Travis didn't want to go in with the rest of us, Mama. He got his own. [*Somewhat amused.*] We don't know what it is . . .

Travis [*racing back in the room with a large hatbox and putting it in front of his grandmother*]. Here!

1800　Mama. Lord have mercy, baby. You done gone and bought your grand-mother a hat?

Travis [*very proud*]. Open it!

[*She does and lifts out an elaborate, but very elaborate, wide gardening hat, and all the adults break up at the sight of it.*]

Ruth. Travis, honey, what is that?

Travis [*who thinks it is beautiful and appropriate*]. It's a gardening hat! Like the ladies always have on in the magazines when they work in their gardens.

Beneatha [*giggling fiercely*]. Travis—we were trying to make Mama Mrs. Miniver—not Scarlett O'Hara!

Mama [*indignantly*]. What's the matter with you all! This here is a beautiful hat! [*Absurdly.*] I always wanted me one just like it!

[*She pops it on her head to prove it to her grandson, and the hat is ludicrous and considerably oversized.*]

1810 RUTH. Hot dog! Go, Mama!
WALTER [*doubled over with laughter*]. I'm sorry, Mama—but you look like you
ready to go out and chop you some cotton sure enough!

[*They all laugh except* MAMA, *out of deference to* TRAVIS' *feelings*]

MAMA [*gathering the boy up to her*]. Bless your heart—this is the prettiest hat
I ever owned—[WALTER, RUTH *and* BENEATHA *chime in—noisily, festively and
insincerely congratulating* TRAVIS *on his gift.*] What are we all standing around
here for? We ain't finished packin' yet. Bennie, you ain't packed one book.

[*The bell rings.*]

BENEATHA. That couldn't be the movers . . . it's not hardly two good yet—

[BENEATHA goes into her room. MAMA *starts for door.*]

WALTER [*turning, stiffening*]. Wait—wait—I'll get it.

[*He stands and looks at the door.*]

MAMA. You expecting company, son?
1820 WALTER [*just looking at the door*]. Yeah—yeah . . .

[MAMA *looks at* RUTH, *and they exchange innocent and unfrightened glances.*]

MAMA [*not understanding*]. Well, let them in, son.
BENEATHA [*from her room*]. We need some more string.
MAMA. Travis—you run to the hardware and get me some string cord.

[MAMA *goes out and* WALTER *turns and looks at* RUTH. TRAVIS *goes to a dish for
money.*]

RUTH. Why don't you answer the door, man?
WALTER [*suddenly bounding across the floor to her*]. 'Cause sometimes it hard
to let the future begin! [*Swooping down in her face.*]
I got wings! You got wings!
All God's children got wings!

[*He crosses to the door and throws it open. Standing there is a very slight little man
in a not too prosperous business suit and with haunted frightened eyes and a hat pulled
down tightly, brim up, around his forehead.* TRAVIS *passes between the men and exits.*
WALTER *leans deep in the man's face, still in his jubilance.*]

When I get to heaven gonna put on my wings,
1830 *Gonna fly all over God's heaven . . .*

[*The little man just stares at him.*]

Heaven—

[*Suddenly he stops and looks past the little man into the empty hallway.*]
Where's Willy, man?

BOBO. He ain't with me.
WALTER [*not disturbed*]. Oh—come on in. You know my wife.
BOBO [*dumbly, taking off his hat*]. Yes—h'you, Miss Ruth.
RUTH [*quietly, a mood apart from her husband already, seeing* BOBO]. Hello,
Bobo.

WALTER.   You right on time today . . . Right on time. That's the way! [*He slaps* BOBO *on his back.*] Sit down . . . lemme hear.

[RUTH *stands stiffly and quietly in back of them, as though somehow she senses death, her eyes fixed on her husband.*]

1840 BOBO [*his frightened eyes on the floor, his hat in his hands*].   Could I please get a drink of water, before I tell you about it, Walter Lee?

[WALTER *does not take his eyes off the man.* RUTH *goes blindly to the tap and gets a glass of water and brings it to* BOBO.]

WALTER.   There ain't nothing wrong, is there?
BOBO.   Lemme tell you—
WALTER.   Man—didn't nothing go wrong?
BOBO.   Lemme tell you—Walter Lee. [*Looking at* RUTH *and talking to her more than to* WALTER.] You know how it was. I got to tell you how it was. I mean first I got to tell you how it was all the way . . . I mean about the money I put in, Walter Lee . . .
WALTER [*with taut agitation now*].   What about the money you put in?
1850 BOBO.   Well—it wasn't much as we told you—me and Willy— [*He stops.*] I'm sorry, Walter. I got a bad feeling about it. I got a real bad feeling about it . . .
WALTER.   Man, what you telling me about all this for? . . . Tell me what happened in Springfield . . .
BOBO.   Springfield.
RUTH [*like a dead woman*].   What was supposed to happen in Springfield?
BOBO [*to her*].   This deal that me and Walter went into with Willy— Me and Willy was going to go down to Springfield and spread some money 'round so's we wouldn't have to wait so long for the liquor license . . . That's what
1860 we were going to do. Everybody said that was the way you had to do, you understand, Miss Ruth?
WALTER.   Man—what happened down there?
BOBO [*a pitiful man, near tears*].   I'm trying to tell you, Walter.
WALTER [*screaming at him suddenly*].   THEN TELL ME, GODDAMNIT . . . WHAT'S THE MATTER WITH YOU?
BOBO.   Man . . . I didn't go to no Springfield, yesterday.
WALTER [*halted, life hanging in the moment*].   Why not?
BOBO [*the long way, the hard way to tell*].   'Cause I didn't have no reason to . . .
WALTER.   Man, what are you talking about!
1870 BOBO.   I'm talking about the fact that when I got to the train station yester-day morning—eight o'clock like we planned . . . Man—*Willy didn't never show up.*
WALTER.   Why . . . where was he . . . where is he?
BOBO.   That's what I'm trying to tell you . . . I don't know . . . I waited six hours . . . I called his house . . . and I waited . . . six hours . . . I waited in that train station six hours . . . [*Breaking into tears.*] That was all the extra money I had in the world . . . [*Looking up at* WALTER *with the tears running down his face.*] Man, *Willy is gone.*
WALTER.   Gone, what you mean Willy is gone? Gone where? You mean he
1880 went by himself. You mean he went off to Springfield by himself—to take care of getting the license—[*Turns and looks anxiously at* RUTH.] You mean

maybe he didn't want too many people in on the business down there?
[*Looks to* RUTH *again, as before.*] You know Willy got his own ways. [*Looks back
to* BOBO.] Maybe you was late yesterday and he just went on down there
without you. Maybe—maybe—he's been callin' you at home tryin' to tell
you what happened or something. Maybe—maybe—he just got sick. He's
somewhere—he's got to be somewhere. We just got to find him—me and
you got to find him. [*Grabs* BOBO *senselessly by the collar and starts to shake
him.*] We got to!

1890 BOBO [*in sudden angry, frightened agony*].   What's the matter with you, Walter!
When a cat take off with your money he don't leave you no maps!

WALTER [*turning madly, as though he is looking for* WILLY *in the very room*].   Willy! . . . Willy . . . don't do it . . . Please don't do it . . . Man, not with that
money . . . Man, please, not with that money . . . Oh, God . . . Don't let it
be true . . . [*He is wandering around, crying out for Willy and looking for him or
perhaps for help from God.*] Man . . . I trusted you . . . Man, I put my life in
your hands . . . [*He starts to crumple down on the floor as* RUTH *just covers her
face in horror.* MAMA *opens the door and comes into the room, with* BENEATHA
behind her.] Man . . . [*He starts to pound the floor with his fists, sobbing wildly*]

1900 That money is made out of my father's flesh . . .

BOBO [*standing over him helplessly*].   I'm sorry, Walter . . . [*Only* WALTER'S *sobs
reply.* BOBO *puts on his hat*] I had my life staked on this deal, too . . .

[*He exits.*]

MAMA [*to* WALTER].   Son—[*She goes to him, bends down to him, talks to his bent
head.*] Son . . . Is it gone? Son, I gave you sixty-five hundred dollars. Is it
gone? All of it? Beneatha's money too?

WALTER [*lifting his head slowly*].   Mama . . . I never . . . went to the bank at
all . . .

MAMA [*not wanting to believe him*].   You mean . . . your sister's school money
. . . you used that too . . . Walter? . . .

1910 WALTER.   Yessss! . . . All of it . . . It's all gone . . .

[*There is total silence.* RUTH *stands with her face covered with her hands;* BENEATHA
leans forlornly against a wall, fingering a piece of red ribbon from the mother's gift.
MAMA *stops and looks at her son without recognition and then, quite without thinking
about it, starts to beat him senselessly in the face.* BENEATHA *goes to them and stops it.*]

BENEATHA.   Mama!

[MAMA *stops and looks at both of her children and rises slowly and wanders vaguely,
aimlessly away from them.*]

MAMA.   I seen . . . him . . . night after night . . . come in . . . and look at that
rug . . . and then look at me . . . the red showing in his eyes . . . the veins
moving in his head . . . I seen him grow thin and old before he was forty
. . . working and working and working like somebody's old horse . . .
killing himself . . . and you—you give it all away in a day . . .

BENEATHA.   Mama—

MAMA.   Oh, God . . . [*She looks up to Him.*] Look down here—and show me
the strength.

1920 BENEATHA.   Mama—

Mama [*folding over*]. Strength . . .
Beneatha [*plaintively*]. Mama . . .
Mama. Strength!

CURTAIN

ACT III

Time: *An hour later.*

> *At curtain, there is a sullen light of gloom in the living room, gray light not unlike that which began the first scene of Act I. At left we can see* Walter *within his room, alone with himself. He is stretched out on the bed, his shirt out and open, his arms* 1930 *under his head. He does not smoke, he does not cry out, he merely lies there, looking up at the ceiling, much as if he were alone in the world.*
>
> *In the living room* Beneatha *sits at the table, still surrounded by the now almost ominous packing crates. She sits looking off. We feel that this is a mood struck perhaps an hour before, and it lingers now, full of the empty sound of profound disappointment. We see on a line from her brother's bedroom the sameness of their attitudes. Presently the bell rings and* Beneatha *rises without ambition or interest in answering. It is* Asagai, *smiling broadly, striding into the room with energy and happy expectation and conversation.*

Asagai. I came over . . . I had some free time. I thought I might help with the packing. Ah, I like the look of packing crates! A household in preparation for a journey! It depresses some people . . . but for me . . . it is another feeling. Something full of the flow of life, do you understand? Movement, progress . . . It makes me think of Africa.

Beneatha. Africa!

Asagai. What kind of a mood is this? Have I told you how deeply you move me?

1920 Beneatha. He gave away the money, Asagai . . .

Asagai. Who gave away what money?

Beneatha. The insurance money. My brother gave it away.

Asagai. Gave it away?

Beneatha. He made an investment! With a man even Travis wouldn't have trusted.

Asagai. And it's gone?

Beneatha. Gone!

Asagai. I'm very sorry . . . And you, now?

Beneatha. Me? . . . Me? . . . Me I'm nothing . . . Me. When I was very small
1930 . . . we used to take our sleds out in the wintertime and the only hills we had were the ice-covered stone steps of some houses down the street. And we used to fill them in with snow and make them smooth and slide down them all day . . . and it was very dangerous you know . . . far too steep . . . and sure enough one day a kid named Rufus came down too fast and hit the sidewalk . . . and we saw his face just split open right there in front of us . . . And I remember standing there looking at his bloody open face thinking that was the end of Rufus. But the ambulance came and they took him to the hospital and they fixed the broken bones and they sewed it all

up . . . and the next time I saw Rufus he had just a little line down the
1940   middle of his face . . . I never got over that . . .

Asagai.   What?

Beneatha.   That that was what one person could do for another, fix him
up—sew up the problem, make him all right again. That was the most
marvelous thing in the world . . . I wanted to do that. I always thought it
was the one concrete thing in the world that a human being could do. Fix
up the sick, you know—and make them whole again. This was truly being
God . . .

Asagai.   You wanted to be God?

Beneatha.   No—I wanted to cure. It used to be so important to me. I wanted
1950   to cure. It used to matter. I used to care. I mean about people and how
their bodies hurt . . .

Asagai.   And you've stopped caring?

Beneatha.   Yes—I think so.

Asagai.   Why?

Beneatha.   Because it doesn't seem deep enough, close enough to the truth.

Asagai.   Truth? Why is it that you despairing ones always think that only you
have the truth? I never thought to see *you* like that. You! Your brother
made a stupid, childish mistake—and you are grateful to him. So that now
you can give up the ailing human race on account of it. You talk about
1960   what good is struggle; what good is anything? Where are we all going? And
why are we bothering?

Beneatha.   *And you cannot answer it!* All your talk and dreams about Africa
and Independence. Independence and then what? What about all the
crooks and petty thieves and just plain idiots who will come into power to
steal and plunder the same as before—only now they will be black and do
it in the name of the new Independence— You cannot answer that.

Asagai [*shouting over her*].   *I live the answer!* [*Pause.*] In my village at home it
is the exceptional man who can even read a newspaper . . . or who ever *sees*
a book at all. I will go home and much of what I will have to say will seem
1970   strange to the people of my village . . . But I will teach and work and
things will happen, slowly and swiftly. At times it will seem that nothing
changes at all . . . and then again . . . the sudden dramatic events which
make history leap into the future. And then quiet again. Retrogression
even. Guns, murder, revolution. And I even will have moments when I
wonder if the quiet was not better than all that death and hatred. But I will
look about my village at the illiteracy and disease and ignorance and I will
not wonder long. And perhaps . . . perhaps I will be a great man . . . I
mean perhaps I will hold on to the substance of truth and find my way
always with the right course . . . and perhaps for it I will be butchered in
1980   my bed some night by the servants of empire . . .

Beneatha.   *The martyr!*

Asagai.   . . . or perhaps I shall live to be a very old man respected and
esteemed in my new nation . . . And perhaps I shall hold office and this is
what I'm trying to tell you, Alaiyo; perhaps the things I believe now for my
country will be wrong and outmoded, and I will not understand and do
terrible things to have things my way or merely to keep my power. Don't
you see that there will be young men and women, not British soldiers then,
but my own black countrymen . . . to step out of the shadows some evening

and slit my then useless throat? Don't you see they have always been there
1990 ... that they always will be. And that such a thing as my own death will be
an advance? They who might kill me even ... actually replenish me!

BENEATHA. Oh, Asagai, I know all that.

ASAGAI. Good! Then stop moaning and groaning and tell me what you plan
to do.

BENEATHA. Do?

ASAGAI. I have a bit of a suggestion.

BENEATHA. What?

ASAGAI [*rather quietly for him*]. That when it is all over—that you come home
with me—

2000 BENEATHA [*slapping herself on the forehead with exasperation born of misunderstanding*]. Oh—Asagai—at this moment you decide to be romantic!

ASAGAI [*quickly understanding the misunderstanding*]. My dear, young creature
of the New World—I do not mean across the city—I mean across the
ocean; home—to Africa.

BENEATHA [*slowly understanding and turning to him with murmured amazement*].
To—to Nigeria?

ASAGAI. Yes! ... [*Smiling and lifting his arms playfully.*] Three hundred years
later the African Prince rose up out of the seas and swept the maiden back
across the middle passage over which her ancestors had come—

2010 BENEATHA [*unable to play*]. Nigeria?

ASAGAI. Nigeria. Home. [*Coming to her with genuine romantic flippancy.*] I will
show you our mountains and our stars; and give you cool drinks from
gourds and teach you the old songs and the ways of our people—and, in
time, we will pretend that—[*very softly*]—you have only been away for a
day—

[*She turns her back to him, thinking. He swings her around and takes her full in his
arms in a long embrace which proceeds to passion.*]

BENEATHA [*pulling away*]. You're getting me all mixed up—

ASAGAI. Why?

BENEATHA. Too many things—too many things have happened today. I must
sit down and think. I don't know what I feel about anything right this
2020 minute.

[*She promptly sits down and props her chin on her fist.*]

ASAGAI [*charmed*]. All right, I shall leave you. No—don't get up. [*Touching
her, gently, sweetly.*] Just sit awhile and think ... Never be afraid to sit
awhile and think. [*He goes to door and looks at her.*] How often I have looked
at you and said, "Ah—so this is what the New World hath finally
wrought ..."

[*He exits. BENEATHA sits on alone. Presently WALTER enters from his room and starts
to rummage through things, feverishly looking for something. She looks up and turns
in her seat.*]

BENEATHA [*hissing*]. Yes—just look at what the New World hath wrought! ...
Just look! [*She gestures with bitter disgust.*] There he is! *Monsieur le petit
bourgeois noir*—himself! There he is—Symbol of a Rising Class! Entrepre-

neur! Titan of the system! [WALTER *ignores her completely and continues fran-*
2030   *tically and destructively looking for something and hurling things to floor and*
tearing things out of their place in his search. BENEATHA *ignores the eccentricity of*
his actions and goes on with the monologue of insult.] Did you dream of yachts
on Lake Michigan, Brother? Did you see yourself on the Great Day sitting
down at the Conference Table, surrounded by all the mighty bald-headed
men in America? All halted, waiting, breathless, waiting for your pronouncements on industry? Waiting for you—Chairman of the Board?
[WALTER *finds what he is looking for—a small piece of white paper—and pushes*
it in his pocket and puts on his coat and rushes out without ever having looked at
her. She shouts after him.] I look at you and I see the final triumph of
2040   stupidity in the world!

[*The door slams and she returns to just sitting again.* RUTH *comes quickly out of*
MAMA'S *room.*]

RUTH.   Who was that?
BENEATHA.   Your husband.
RUTH.   Where did he go?
BENEATHA.   Who knows—maybe he has an appointment at U.S. Steel.
RUTH [*anxiously, with frightened eyes*].   You didn't say nothing bad to him, did
     you?
BENEATHA.   Bad? Say anything bad to him? No—I told him he was a sweet
     boy and full of dreams and everything is strictly peachy keen, as the ofay[9]
     kids say!

[MAMA *enters from her bedroom. She is lost, vague, trying to catch hold, to make some*
sense of her former command of the world, but it still eludes her. A sense of waste
overwhelms her gait; a measure of apology rides on her shoulders. She goes to her
plant, which has remained on the table, looks at it, picks it up and takes it to the
window sill and sits it outside, and she stands and looks at it a long moment. Then she
closes the window, straightens her body with effort and turns around to her children.]

2050 MAMA.   Well—ain't it a mess in here, though? [*A false cheerfulness, a beginning*
     of something.] I guess we all better stop moping around and get some work
     done. All this unpacking and everything we got to do. [RUTH *raises her head*
     slowly in response to the sense of the line; and BENEATHA *in similar manner turns*
     very slowly to look at her mother.] One of you all better call the moving people
     and tell 'em not to come.
RUTH.   Tell 'em not to come?
MAMA.   Of course, baby. Ain't no need in 'em coming all the way here and
     having to go back. They charges for that too. [*She sits down, fingers to her*
     brow, thinking.] Lord, ever since I was a little girl, I always remembers
2060   people saying, "Lena—Lena Eggleston, you aims too high all the time.
     You needs to slow down and see life a little more like it is. Just slow down
     some." That's what they always used to say down home—"Lord, that Lena
     Eggleston is a high-minded thing. She'll get her due one day!"
RUTH.   No, Lena . . .
MAMA.   Me and Big Walter just didn't never learn right.

---

[9] A slang word for *white.*

RUTH.   Lena, no! We gotta go. Bennie—tell her . . . [*She rises and crosses to* BENEATHA *with her arms outstretched.* BENEATHA *doesn't respond.*] Tell her we can still move . . . the notes ain't but a hundred and twenty five a month. We got four grown people in this house—we can work . . .

2070 MAMA [*to herself*].   Just aimed too high all the time—

RUTH [*turning and going to* MAMA *fast—the words pouring out with urgency and desperation*].   Lena—I'll work . . . I'll work twenty hours a day in all the kitchens in Chicago . . . I'll strap my baby on my back if I have to and scrub all the floors in America and wash all the sheets in America if I have to—but we got to move . . . We got to get out of here . . .

[MAMA *reaches out absently and pats* RUTH's *hand.*]

MAMA.   No—I sees things differently now. Been thinking 'bout some of the things we could do to fix this place up some. I seen a second-hand bureau over on Maxwell Street just the other day that could fit right there. [*She points to where the new furniture might go.* RUTH *wanders away from her.*] Would

2080 need some new handles on it and then a little varnish and then it look like something brand-new. And—we can put up them new curtains in the kitchen . . . Why this place be looking fine. Cheer us all up so that we forget trouble ever came . . . [*To* RUTH.] And you could get some nice screens to put up in your room round the baby's basinet . . . [*She looks at both of them, pleadingly.*] Sometimes you just got to know when to give up some things . . . and hold on to what you got.

[WALTER *enters from the outside, looking spent and leaning against the door, his coat hanging from him.*]

MAMA.   Where you been, son?

WALTER [*breathing hard*].   Made a call.

MAMA.   To who, son?

2090 WALTER.   To The Man.

MAMA.   What man, baby?

WALTER.   The Man, Mama. Don't you know who The Man is?

RUTH.   Walter Lee?

WALTER.   *The Man.* Like the guys in the streets say—The Man. Captain Boss—Mistuh Charley . . . Old Captain Please Mr. Bossman . . .

BENEATHA [*suddenly*].   Lindner!

WALTER.   That's right! That's good. I told him to come right over.

BENEATHA [*fiercely, understanding*].   For what? What do you want to see him for!

2100 WALTER [*looking at his sister*].   We going to do business with him.

MAMA.   What you talking 'bout, son?

WALTER.   Talking 'bout life, Mama. You all always telling me to see life like it is. Well—I laid in there on my back today . . . and I figured it out. Life just like it is. Who gets and who don't get. [*He sits down with his coat on and laughs.*] Mama, you know it's all divided up. Life is. Sure enough. Between the takers and the "tooken." [*He laughs.*] I've figured it out finally. [*He looks around at them.*] Yeah. Some of us always getting "tooken." [*He laughs.*] People like Willy Harris, they don't never get "tooken." And you know why the rest of us do? 'Cause we all mixed up. Mixed up bad. We get to

2110   looking 'round for the right and the wrong; and we worry about it and cry about it and stay up nights trying to figure out 'bout the wrong and the right of things all the time . . . And all the time, man, them takers is out there operating, just taking and taking. Willy Harris? Shoot—Willy Harris don't even count. He don't even count in the big scheme of things. But I'll say one thing for old Willy Harris . . . he's taught me something. He's taught me to keep my eye on what counts in the world. Yeah—[*Shouting out a little.*] Thanks, Willy!

RUTH.   What did you call that man for, Walter Lee?

WALTER.   Called him to tell him to come on over to the show. Gonna put on
2120   a show for the man. Just what he wants to see. You see, Mama, the man came here today and he told us that them people out there where you want us to move—well they so upset they willing to pay us not to move out there. [*He laughs again.*] And—and oh, Mama—you would of been proud of the way me and Ruth and Bennie acted. We told him to get out . . . Lord have mercy! We told the man to get out. Oh, we was some proud folks this afternoon, yeah. [*He lights a cigarette.*] We were still full of that old-time stuff . . .

RUTH [*coming toward him slowly*].   You talking 'bout taking them people's money to keep us from moving in that house?

2130 WALTER.   I ain't just talking 'bout it, baby—I'm telling you that's what's going to happen.

BENEATHA.   Oh, God! Where is the bottom! Where is the real honest-to-God bottom so he can't go any farther!

WALTER.   See—that's the old stuff. You and that boy that was here today. You all want everybody to carry a flag and a spear and sing some marching songs, huh? You wanna spend your life looking into things and trying to find the right and wrong part, huh? Yeah. You know what's going to happen to that boy someday—he'll find himself sitting in a dungeon, locked in forever—and the takers will have the key! Forget it, baby! There
2140   ain't no causes—there ain't nothing but taking in this world, and he who takes most is smartest—and it don't make a damn bit of difference *how.*

MAMA.   You making something inside me cry, son. Some awful pain inside me.

WALTER.   Don't cry, Mama. Understand. That white man is going to walk in that door able to write checks for more money than we ever had. It's important to him and I'm going to help him . . . I'm going to put on the show, Mama.

MAMA.   Son—I come from five generations of people who was slaves and sharecroppers—but ain't nobody in my family never let nobody pay 'em
2150   no money that was a way of telling us we wasn't fit to walk the earth. We ain't never been that poor. [*Raising her eyes and looking at him.*] We ain't never been that dead inside.

BENEATHA.   Well—we are dead now. All the talk about dreams and sunlight that goes on in this house. All dead.

WALTER.   What's the matter with you all! I didn't make this world! It was give to me this way! Hell, yes, I want me some yachts someday! Yes, I want to hang some real pearls 'round my wife's neck. Ain't she supposed to wear no pearls? Somebody tell me—tell me, who decides which women is sup-

pose to wear pearls in this world. I tell you I am a *man*—and I think my
2160 wife should wear some pearls in this world!

[*This last line hangs a good while and* Walter *begins to move about the room. The
word "Man" has penetrated his consciousness; he mumbles it to himself repeatedly
between strange agitated pauses as he moves about.*]

Mama. Baby, how you going to feel on the inside?
Walter. Fine! . . . Going to feel fine . . . a man . . .
Mama. You won't have nothing left then, Walter Lee.
Walter [*coming to her*]. I'm going to feel fine, Mama. I'm going to look that
son-of-a-bitch in the eyes and say—[*he falters*]—and say, "All right, Mr.
Lindner—[*he falters even more*]—that's your neighborhood out there. You
got the right to keep it like you want. You got the right to have it like you
want. Just write the check and—the house is yours." And, I am going to say
—[*His voice almost breaks.*] And you—you people just put the money in my
2170 hand and you won't have to live next to this bunch of stinking niggers! . . .
[*He straightens up and moves away from his mother, walking around the room.*]
Maybe—maybe I'll just get down on my black knees . . . [*He does so;* Ruth
and Bennie *and* Mama *watch him in frozen horror.*] Captain, Mistuh, Bossman.
[*He starts crying.*] A-hee-hee-hee! [*Wringing his hands in profoundly anguished
imitation.*] Yasssssuh! Great White Father, just gi' ussen de money, fo'
God's sake, and we's ain't gwine come out deh and dirty up yo' white folks
neighborhood . . .

[*He breaks down completely, then gets up and goes into the bedroom.*]

Beneatha. That is not a man. That is nothing but a toothless rat.
Mama. Yes—death done come in this here house. [*She is nodding, slowly,
2180 reflectively.*] Done come walking in my house. On the lips of my children.
You what supposed to be my harvest. [*To* Beneatha] You—you mourning
your brother?
Beneatha. He's no brother of mine.
Mama. What you say?
Beneatha. I said that that individual in that room is no brother of mine.
Mama. That's what I thought you said. You feeling like you better than he
is today? [Beneatha *does not answer.*] Yes? What you tell him a minute ago?
That he wasn't a man? Yes? You give him up for me? You done wrote his
epitaph too—like the rest of the world? Well, who give you the privilege?
2190 Beneatha. Be on my side for once! You saw what he just did, Mama! You saw
him—down on his knees. Wasn't it you who taught me—to despise any
man who would do that. Do what he's going to do.
Mama. Yes—I taught you that. Me and your daddy. But I thought I taught
you something else too . . . I thought I taught you to love him.
Beneatha. Love him? There is nothing left to love.
Mama. There is always something left to love. And if you ain't learned that,
you ain't learned nothing. [*Looking at her.*] Have you cried for that boy
today? I don't mean for yourself and for the family 'cause we lost the
money. I mean for him; what he been through and what it done to him.
2200 Child, when do you think is the time to love somebody the most; when

they done good and made things easy for everybody? Well then, you ain't through learning—because that ain't the time at all. It's when he's at his lowest and can't believe in hisself 'cause the world done whipped him so. When you starts measuring somebody, measure him right, child, measure him right. Make sure you done taken into account what hills and valleys he come through before he got to wherever he is.

[TRAVIS *bursts into the room at the end of the speech, leaving the door open.*]

TRAVIS.   Grandmama—the moving men are downstairs! The truck just pulled up.

MAMA [*turning and looking at him*].   Are they, baby? They downstairs?

[*She sighs and sits.* LINDNER *appears in the doorway. He peers in and knocks lightly, to gain attention, and comes in. All turn to look at him.*]

2210 LINDNER [*hat and briefcase in hand*].   Uh—hello . . .

[RUTH *crosses mechanically to the bedroom door and opens it and lets it swing open freely and slowly as the lights come up on* WALTER *within, still in his coat, sitting at the far corner of the room. He looks up and out through the room to* LINDNER]

RUTH.   He's here.

[*A long minute passes and* WALTER *slowly gets up.*]

LINDNER [*coming to the table with efficiency, putting his briefcase on the table and starting to unfold papers and unscrew fountain pens*].   Well, I certainly was glad to hear from you people. [WALTER *has begun the trek out of the room, slowly and awkwardly, rather like a small boy, passing the back of his sleeve across his mouth from time to time.*] Life can really be so much simpler than people let it be most of the time. Well—with whom do I negotiate? You, Mrs. Younger, or your son here? [MAMA *sits with her hands folded on her lap and her eyes closed as* WALTER *advances.* TRAVIS *goes close to* LINDNER *and looks at the*
2220   *papers curiously.*] Just some official papers, sonny.

RUTH.   Travis, you go downstairs.

MAMA [*opening her eyes and looking into* WALTER'S].   No. Travis, you stay right here. And you make him understand what you doing, Walter Lee. You teach him good. Like Willy Harris taught you. You show where our five generations done come to. Go ahead, son—

WALTER [*looks down into his boy's eyes.* TRAVIS *grins at him merrily and* WALTER *draws him beside him with his arm lightly around his shoulder*].   Well, Mr. Lindner. [BENEATHA *turns away.*] We called you—[*there is a profound, simple groping quality in his speech*]—because, well, me and my family [*He looks around and*
2230   *shifts from one foot to the other.*] Well—we are very plain people . . .

LINDNER.   Yes—

WALTER.   I mean—I have worked as a chauffeur most of my life—and my wife here, she does domestic work in people's kitchens. So does my mother. I mean—we are plain people . . .

LINDNER.   Yes, Mr. Younger—

WALTER [*really like a small boy, looking down at his shoes and then up at the man*].   And—uh—well, my father, well, he was a laborer most of his life.

LINDNER [*absolutely confused*].   Uh, yes—

WALTER [*looking down at his toes once again*].   My father almost beat a man to
2240   death once because this man called him a bad name or something, you
know what I mean?

LINDNER.   No, I'm afraid I don't.

WALTER [*finally straightening up*].   Well, what I mean is that we come from
people who had a lot of pride. I mean—we are very proud people. And
that's my sister over there and she's going to be a doctor—and we are very
proud—

LINDNER.   Well—I am sure that is very nice, but—

WALTER [*starting to cry and facing the man eye to eye*].   What I am telling you is
that we called you over here to tell you that we are very proud and that this
2250   is—this is my son, who makes the sixth generation of our family in this
country, and that we have all thought about your offer and we have decided
to move into our house because my father—my father—he earned it. [MAMA
*has her eyes closed and is rocking back and forth as though she were in church, with
her head nodding the amen yes.*] We don't want to make no trouble for nobody
or fight no causes—but we will try to be good neighbors. That's all we got
to say. [*He looks the man absolutely in the eye.*] We don't want your money.

[*He turns and walks away from the man.*]

LINDNER [*looking around at all of them*].   I take it then that you have decided
to occupy.

BENEATHA.   That's what the man said.

2260   LINDNER [*to* MAMA *in her reverie*].   Then I would like to appeal to you, Mrs.
Younger. You are older and wiser and understand things better I am
sure . . .

MAMA [*rising*].   I am afraid you don't understand. My son said we was going
to move and there ain't nothing left for me to say. [*Shaking her head with
double meaning.*] You know how these young folks is nowadays, mister.
Can't do a thing with 'em. Good-bye.

LINDNER [*folding up his materials*].   Well—if you are that final about it . . .
There is nothing left for me to say. [*He finishes. He is almost ignored by the
family, who are concentrating on* WALTER LEE. *At the door* LINDNER *halts and looks
2270   around.*] I sure hope you people know what you're doing.

[*He shakes his head and exits.*]

RUTH [*looking around and coming to life*].   Well, for God's sake—if the moving
men are here—LET'S GET THE HELL OUT OF HERE!

MAMA [*into action*].   Ain't it the truth! Look at all this here mess. Ruth put
Travis' good jacket on him . . . Walter Lee, fix your tie and tuck your shirt
in, you look just like somebody's hoodlum. Lord have mercy, where is my
plant? [*She flies to get it amid the general bustling of the family, who are deliberately trying to ignore the nobility of the past moment.*] You all start on down . . .
Travis child, don't go empty–handed . . . Ruth, were did I put that box with
my skillets in it? I want to be in charge of it myself . . . I'm going to make
2280   us the biggest dinner we ever ate tonight . . . Beneatha, what's the matter
with them stockings? Pull them things up, girl . . .

[*The family starts to file out as two moving men appear and begin to carry out the heavier pieces of furniture, bumping into the family as they move about.*]

BENEATHA.   Mama, Asagai—asked me to marry him today and go to Africa—
MAMA [*in the middle of her getting-ready activity*].   He did? You ain't old enough to marry nobody—[*Seeing the moving men lifting one of her chairs precariously.*] Darling, that ain't no bale of cotton, please handle it so we can sit in it again. I had that chair twenty-five years . . .

[*The movers sigh with exasperation and go on with their work.*]

BENEATHA [*girlishly and unreasonably trying to pursue the conversation*].   To go to Africa, Mama—be a doctor in Africa . . .
MAMA [*distractedly*].   Yes, baby—
2290 WALTER.   Africa! What he want you to go to Africa for?
BENEATHA.   To practice there . . .
WALTER.   Girl, if you don't get all them silly ideas out your head! You better marry yourself a man with some loot . . .
BENEATHA [*angrily, precisely as in the first scene of the play*].   What have you got to do with who I marry!
WALTER.   Plenty. Now I think George Murchison—

[*He and* BENEATHA *go out yelling at each other vigorously;* BENEATHA *is heard saying that she would not marry* GEORGE MURCHISON *if he were Adam and she were Eve, etc. The anger is loud and real till their voices diminish.* RUTH *stands at the door and turns to* MAMA *and smiles knowingly.*]

MAMA [*fixing her hat at last*].   Yeah—they something all right, my children . . .
RUTH.   Yeah—they're something. Let's go, Lena.
MAMA [*stalling, starting to look around at the house*].   Yes—I'm coming. Ruth—
2300 RUTH.   Yes?
MAMA [*quietly, woman to woman*].   He finally come into his manhood today, didn't he? Kind of like a rainbow after the rain . . .
RUTH [*biting her lip lest her own pride explode in front of* MAMA].   Yes, Lena.

[WALTER'S *voice calls for them raucously.*]

MAMA [*waving* RUTH *out vaguely*].   All right, honey—go on down. I be down directly.

[RUTH *hesitates, then exits.* MAMA *stands, at last alone in the living room, her plant on the table before her as the lights start to come down. She looks around at all the walls and ceilings and suddenly, despite herself, while the children call below, a great heaving thing rises in her and she puts her fist to her mouth, takes a final desperate look, pulls her coat about her, pats her hat and goes out. The lights dim down. The door opens and she comes back in, grabs her plant, and goes out for the last time.*]

CURTAIN

[1959]

Critical Commentary on *A Raisin in the Sun*

In 1959 *A Raisin in the Sun* won the New York Drama Critics' Circle Award as the best play of the year. A film version in 1961 won a special award at the Cannes Film Festival, and a musical adaptation in 1974 was awarded a Tony.

Through its remarkable success, Lorraine Hansberry's *A Raisin in the Sun* cleared and seeded new terrain for the creative cultivation of other African-American writers. It was the first play by a black woman to be produced on Broadway. It was the first play by an African-American author to win national awards and critical plaudits. It was the first major play to analyze the problems of the urban black family with sympathy and understanding. Its success prepared the way for other black playwrights such as Alice Childress, Imamu Amiri Baraka [LeRoi Jones], and most recently August Wilson.

To some extent, *A Raisin in the Sun* grew out of Hansberry's own experiences as a child growing up on the South Side of Chicago. When Lorraine was eight years old, her father Carl purchased a home in one of the city's white neighborhoods. The family was not welcomed. Mobs gathered; bricks were thrown; Lorraine was insulted and jostled on her way to school. Relying on ambiguities in the title and restrictive covenants in the local laws, community leaders sought to drive the Hansberrys from their new home. But Carl Hansberry fought back in the courts, initiating a civil rights suit that he eventually won in the United States Supreme Court.

Other aspects of the play are equally autobiographical. Walter Lee Younger, for example, aspires to become a member of the black middle class; in actuality Carl Hansberry did rise into the middle class and even the well-to-do, becoming a United States Deputy Marshall, a successful realtor, and the founder of a black-owned bank in Chicago. Similarly, Beneatha's interest in her African roots parallels Hansberry's own interest in African culture. Her uncle, William Leo Hansberry, was a well-known expert on African history at Howard University. Through him, Lorraine met many young African students who must to some extent have served as models for her dignified Nigerian student, Joseph Asagai.

The setting of the play, of course, draws heavily from Hansberry's childhood reminiscences, but it also serves a number of symbolic functions. Hansberry's first stage direction repeatedly emphasizes how the apartment and its furniture mirror the struggles and weariness of the characters. We are told that the living room furnishings "have clearly had to accommodate the living of too many people for too many years—and they are tired," and later that "weariness has, in fact, won in this room." If weariness has won, however, it has done so only by battle. Tables and chairs have been moved about to conceal worn places in the rug, "but the carpet has fought back by showing its weariness." Even the pattern on the upholstery of the couch "has to fight to show itself" under the couch covers and doilies. The weariness and struggle in the lives of the characters is therefore represented by the very chairs on which they sit and the carpets on which they walk.

The single window through which a dim natural light "fights its way" provides another powerful symbol of the restricted environment in which each of the Youngers strives for his or her own place in the sun. For Lena, the family matriarch, the struggle to make a home is particularly poignant. Her desire to raise a garden in her own backyard has, after many years, wilted to the tending of "a feeble little plant growing doggedly in a small pot." Indeed, Mama's own situation and the situation of each member of her family is like that of her drooping plant. These characters are all confined to small pots, growing root-bound in their narrow circumstances.

Much of this symbolism is implicit in the play's title, *A Raisin in the Sun*. That title contains an allusion to Langston Hughes's well-known poem "Harlem" in which he contemplates the results of the Negro's "dream deferred." Throughout *A Raisin in the Sun* we witness repeated references to the dreams of the characters, ranging from Walter's dream of opening a liquor store and Beneatha's dream of becoming a doctor to Lena's dream of owning her own home in the suburbs. All of these have been dreams deferred as the play opens, and the characters have been sagging under their weight for years. The action of the play thus tells us whether, in the words of Langston Hughes, these dreams "dry up / like a raisin in the sun"—or finally "explode."

A Selective Bibliography on *A Raisin in the Sun*

Abramson, Doris E. *Negro Playwrights in the American Theater, 1925–1959*. New York: Columbia UP, 1968. 230–54, 263–66.

Anderson, Mary Louise. "Black Matriarchy: Portrayal of Women in Three Plays." *Negro American Literature Forum* 10 (1976): 93–95.

Ashley, Leonard R. "Lorraine Hansberry and the Great Black Way." *Modern American Drama: The Female Canon*. Ed. June Schlueter. Rutherford: Fairleigh Dickinson UP, 1990. 151–60.

Baraka, Amiri. "*Raisin in the Sun's* Enduring Passion." *The Washington Post* 16 November 1989: F1–3.

Barthelemy, Anthony. "Mother, Sister, Wife: A Dramatic Perspective." *The Southern Review* 21.3 (1985): 770–89.

Berrian, Brenda. "The Afro-American-West African Marriage Question: Its Literary and Historical Contexts." *African Literature Today* 15 (1987): 152–59.

Bigsby, C. W. E. "Lorraine Hansberry." *Confrontation and Commitment: A Study of Contemporary American Drama, 1959–66*. Columbia, MO: U of Missouri P, 1968. 156–73.

Brown, Lloyd W. "Lorraine Hansberry as Ironist: A Reappraisal of *A Raisin in the Sun*." *Journal of Black Studies* 4.3 (1974): 237–47.

Brown-Guillory, Elizabeth. "Black Women Playwrights: Exorcising Myths." *Phylon* 48.3 (1987): 229–39.

Carter, Steven. *Hansberry's Drama: Commitment Amid Complexity*. Urbana: U of Illinois P, 1991.

Cheney, Anne. "Measure Him Right: *A Raisin in the Sun*." *Lorraine Hansberry*. Boston: Twayne, 1984. 55–71.

Cruse, Harold. "Lorraine Hansberry." *The Crisis of the Negro Intellectual*. New York: Morrow, 1967. 277–84.

Hooks, Bell. "*Raisin* in a New Light." *Christianity and Crisis*. 6 February 1989: 21–3.

Keyssar, Helene. "Rites and Responsibilities: The Drama of Black American Women." *Feminine Focus: The New Women Playwrights*. Ed. Enoch Brater. New York: Oxford UP, 1989. 226–40.

Nemiroff, Robert. "Introduction." *A Raisin in the Sun.* New York: Penguin, 1988. ix–xviii.

Olauson, Judith. "1950–1960." *The American Woman Playwright: A View of Criticism and Characterization.* Troy, NY: Whitson, 1981. 77–99.

Peerman, Dean. "*A Raisin in the Sun:* The Uncut Version." *The Christian Century* 25 January 1989: 71–3.

Washington, J. Charles. "*A Raisin in the Sun* Revisited." *Black American Literature Forum* 22 (1988): 109–24.

Wilkerson, Margaret B. "*A Raisin in the Sun:* Anniversary of an American Classic." *Theatre Journal* 38 (1986): 441–52.

Wole Soyinka (1934–   )

THE STRONG BREED

CHARACTERS

EMAN, *a stranger*
SUNMA, *Jaguna's daughter*
IFADA, *an idiot*
A GIRL
JAGUNA
OROGE
ATTENDANT STALWARTS, *The villagers*

From EMAN'S past:
OLD MAN, *his father*
OMAE, *his betrothed*
TUTOR
PRIEST
ATTENDANTS. *The villagers*

The scenes are described briefly, but very often a darkened stage with lit areas will not only suffice but is necessary. Except for the one indicated place, there can be no break in the action. A distracting scene-change would be ruinous.

A mud house, with space in front of it. EMAN, *in light buba[1] and trousers stands at the window, looking out. Inside,* SUNMA *is clearing the table of what looks like a modest clinic, putting the things away in a cupboard. Another rough table in the room is piled with exercise books, two or three worn text-books, etc.* SUMMA *appears agitated. Outside, just below the window crouches* IFADA. *He looks up with a shy smile from time to time, waiting for* EMAN *to notice him.*

SUNMA [*hesitant*].   You will have to make up your mind soon Eman. The lorry[2] leaves very shortly.

[*As* EMAN *does not answer,* SUNMA *continues her work, more nervously. Two villagers, obvious travellers, pass hurriedly in front of the house, the man has a small raffia[3] sack, the woman a cloth-covered basket, the man enters first, turns and urges the woman who is just emerging to hurry.*]

SUNMA [*seeing them, her tone is more intense*].   Eman, are we going or aren't we? You will leave it till too late.
EMAN [*quietly*].   There is still time—if you want to go.
SUNMA.   If I want to go . . . and you?

[EMAN *makes no reply.*]

---

[1] A traditional shirt worn by Africans of the Yoruba tribe.
[2] A passenger vehicle constructed on a large truck frame.
[3] A fiber made from palm leaves.

SUNMA [*bitterly*]. You don't really want to leave here. You never want to go
away—even for a minute.

[IFADA *continues his antics.* EMAN *eventually pats him on the head and the boy grins
happily. Leaps up suddenly and returns with a basket of oranges which he offers to*
EMAN.]

EMAN.   My gift for today's festival enh?

[IFADA *nods, grinning.*]

10 EMAN.   They look ripe—that's a change.
SUNMA [*she has gone inside the room. Looks round the door*].   Did you call me?
EMAN.   No. [*She goes back.*] And what will you do tonight Ifada? Will you take
part in the dancing? Or perhaps you will mount your own masquerade?[4]

[IFADA *shakes his head, regretfully.*]

EMAN.   You won't? So you haven't any? But you would like to own one.

[IFADA *nods eagerly.*]

EMAN.   Then why don't you make your own?

[IFADA *stares, puzzled by this idea.*]

EMAN.   Sunma will let you have some cloth you know. And bits of wool . . .
SUNMA [*coming out*].   Who are you talking to Eman?
EMAN.   Ifada. I am trying to persuade him to join the young maskers.
SUNMA [*losing control*].   What does he want here? Why is he hanging around
20   us?
EMAN [*amazed*].   What . . . ? I said Ifada, Ifada.
SUNMA.   Just tell him to go away. Let him go and play somewhere else!
EMAN.   What is this? Hasn't he always played here?
SUNMA.   I don't want him here. [*Rushes to the window.*] Get away idiot. Don't
bring your foolish face here any more, do you hear? Go on, go away from
here . . .
EMAN [*restraining her*].   Control yourself Sunma. What on earth has got into
you?

[IFADA, *hurt and bewildered, backs slowly away.*]

SUNMA.   He comes crawling round here like some horrible insect. I never
30   want to lay my eyes on him again.
EMAN.   I don't understand. It *is* Ifada you know. Ifada! The unfortunate one
who runs errands for you and doesn't hurt a soul.
SUNMA.   I cannot bear the sight of him.
EMAN.   You can't do what? It can't be two days since he last fetched water for
you.
SUNMA.   What else can he do except that? He is useless. Just because we have
been kind to him . . . Others would have put him in an asylum.
EMAN.   You are not making sense. He is not a madman, he is just a little

---

[4] A ritual festival in which masked dancers invoke supernatural spirits.

more unlucky than other children. [*Looks keenly at her.*] But what is the
40　matter?

SUNMA.　It's nothing. I only wish we had sent him off to one of those places
for creatures like him.

EMAN.　He is quite happy here. He doesn't bother anyone and he makes
himself useful.

SUNMA.　Useful! Is that one of any use to anybody? Boys of his age are already
earning a living but all he can do is hang around and drool at the mouth.

EMAN.　But he does work. You know he does a lot for you.

SUNMA.　Does he? And what about the farm you started for him! Does he ever
work on it? Or have you forgotten that it was really for Ifada you cleared
50　that bush. Now you have to go and work it yourself. You spend all your
time on it and you have no room for anything else.

EMAN.　That wasn't his fault. I should first have asked him if he was fond of
farming.

SUNMA.　Oh, so he can choose? As if he shouldn't be thankful for being
allowed to live.

EMAN.　Sunma!

SUNMA.　He does not like farming but he knows how to feast his dumb mouth
on the fruits.

EMAN.　But I want him to. I encourage him.

60　SUNMA.　Well keep him. I don't want to see him any more.

EMAN [*after some moments*].　But why? You cannot be telling all the truth. What
has he done?

SUNMA.　The sight of him fills me with revulsion.

EMAN [*goes to her and holds her*].　What really is it? [SUNMA *avoids his eyes.*] It is
almost as if you are forcing yourself to hate him. Why?

SUNMA.　That is not true. Why should I?

EMAN.　Then what is the secret? You've even played with him before.

SUNMA.　I have always merely tolerated him. But I cannot any more. Suddenly my disgust won't take him any more. Perhaps . . . perhaps it is the
70　new year. Yes, yes, it must be the new year.

EMAN.　I don't believe that.

SUNMA.　It must be. I am a woman, and these things matter. I don't want a
mis-shape near me. Surely for one day in the year, I may demand some
wholesomeness.

EMAN.　I do not understand you.

[SUNMA *is silent.*]

It was cruel of you. And to Ifada who is so helpless and alone. We are the
only friends he has.

SUNMA.　No, just you. I have told you, with me it has always been only an act
of kindness. And now I haven't any pity left for him.

80　EMAN.　No. He is not a wholesome being.

[*He turns back to looking through the window.*]

SUNMA [*half-pleading*].　Ifada can rouse your pity. And yet if anything, I need
more kindness from you. Every time my weakness betrays me, you close
your mind against me . . . Eman . . . Eman . . .

[*A* GIRL *comes in view, dragging an effigy by a rope attached to one of its legs. She stands for a while gazing at* EMAN. IFADA, *who has crept back shyly to his accustomed position, becomes somewhat excited when he sees the effigy. The girl is unsmiling. She possesses in fact, a kind of inscrutability which does not make her hard but is unsettling.*]

GIRL.   Is the teacher in?
EMAN. [*smiling*].   No.
GIRL.   Where is he gone?
EMAN.   I don't really know. Shall I ask?
GIRL.   Yes, do.
EMAN [*turning slightly*].   Sunma, a girl outside wants to know . . .

[SUNMA *turns away, goes into the inside room.*]

90 EMAN.   Oh. [*Returns to the girl, but his slight gaiety is lost.*] There is no one at
     home who can tell me.
GIRL.   Why are you not in?
EMAN.   I don't really know. Maybe I went somewhere.
GIRL.   All right. I will wait until you get back.

[*She pulls the effigy to her, sits down.*]

EMAN [*slowly regaining his amusement*].   So you are all ready for the new year.
GIRL [*without turning round*].   I am not going to the festival.
EMAN.   Then why have you got that?
GIRL.   Do you mean my carrier? I am unwell you know. My mother says it
     will take away my sickness with the old year.
100 EMAN.   Won't you share the carrier with your playmates?
GIRL.   Oh, no. Don't you know I play alone? The other children won't come
     near me. Their mothers would beat them.
EMAN.   But I have never seen you here. Why don't you come to the clinic?
GIRL.   My mother said No.

[*Gets up, begins to move off.*]

EMAN.   You are not going away?
GIRL.   I must not stay talking to you. If my mother caught me . . .
EMAN.   All right, tell me what you want before you go.
GIRL [*stops. For some moments she remains silent*].   I must have some clothes for
     my carrier.
110 EMAN.   Is that all? You wait a moment. [SUNMA *comes out as he takes down a buba
     from the wall. She goes to the window and glares almost with hatred at the girl. The
     girl retreats hastily, still impassive.*] By the way Sunma, do you know who that
     girl is?
SUNMA.   I hope you don't really mean to give her that.
EMAN.   Why not? I hardly ever use it.
SUNMA.   Just the same don't give it to her. She is not a child. She is as evil as
     the rest of them.
EMAN.   What has got into you today?
SUNMA.   All right, all right. Do what you wish.

[*She withdraws. Baffled,* EMAN *returns to the window.*]

120 EMAN.   Here . . . will this do? Come and look at it.

GIRL. Throw it.

EMAN. What is the matter? I am not going to eat you.

GIRL. No one lets me come near them.

EMAN. But I am not afraid of catching your disease.

GIRL. Throw it.

[EMAN *shrugs and tosses the buba. She takes it without a word and slips it on the effigy, completely absorbed in the task.* EMAN *watches for a while, then joins* SUNMA *in the inner room.*]

GIRL [*after a long, cool survey of* IFADA]. You have a head like a spider's egg, and your mouth dribbles like a roof. But there is no one else. Would you like to play?

[IFADA *nods eagerly, quite excited.*]

GIRL. You will have to get a stick.

[IFADA *rushes around, finds a big stick and whirls it aloft, bearing down on the carrier.*]

130 GIRL. Wait. I don't want you to spoil it. If it gets torn I shall drive you away. Now, let me see how you are going to beat it.

[IFADA *hits it gently.*]

GIRL. You may hit harder than that. As long as there is something left to hang at the end. [*She appraises him up and down.*] You are not very tall . . . will you be able to hang it from a tree?

[IFADA *nods, grinning happily.*]

GIRL. You will hang it up and I will set fire to it. [*Then, with surprising venom*] But just because you are helping me, don't think it is going to cure you. I am the one who will get well at midnight, do you understand? It is my carrier and it is for me alone. [*She pulls at the rope to make sure that it is well attached to the leg.*] Well don't stand there drooling. Let's go.

[*She begins to walk off, dragging the effigy in the dust.* IFADA *remains where he is for some moments, seemingly puzzled. Then his face breaks into a large grin and he leaps after the procession, belabouring the effigy with all his strength. The stage remains empty for some moments. Then the horn of a lorry is sounded and* SUNMA *rushes out. The hooting continues for some time with a rhythmic pattern.* EMAN *comes out.*]

140 EMAN. I am going to the village . . . I shan't be back before nightfall.

SUNMA [*blankly*]. Yes.

EMAN [*hesitates*]. Well what do you want me to do?

SUNMA. The lorry was hooting just now.

EMAN. I didn't hear it.

SUNMA. It will leave in a few minutes. And you did promise we could go away.

EMAN. I promised nothing. Will you go home by yourself or shall I come back for you?

SUNMA. You don't even want me here?

150 EMAN. But you have to go home haven't you?

SUNMA. I had hoped we would watch the new year together—in some other place.

EMAN. Why do you continue to distress yourself?

SUNMA. Because you will not listen to me. Why do you continue to stay where nobody wants you?

EMAN. That is not true.

SUNMA. It is. You are wasting your life on people who really want you out of their way.

EMAN. You don't know what you are saying.

160 SUNMA. You think they love you? Do you think they care at all for what you—or I—do for them?

EMAN. *Them?* These are your own people. Sometimes you talk as if you were a stranger too.

SUNMA. I wonder if I really sprang from here. I know they are evil and I am not. From the oldest to the smallest child, they are nourished in evil and unwholesomeness in which I have no part.

EMAN. You knew this when you returned?

SUNMA. You reproach me then for trying at all?

EMAN. I reproach you with nothing? But you must leave me out of your

170 plans. I can have no part in them.

SUNMA [*nearly pleading*]. Once I could have run away. I would have gone and never looked back.

EMAN. I cannot listen when you talk like that.

SUNMA. I swear to you, I do not mind what happens afterwards. But you must help me tear myself away from here. I can no longer do it by myself . . . It is only a little thing. And we have worked so hard this past year . . . surely we can go away for a week . . . even a few days would be enough.

EMAN. I have told you Sunma . . .

SUNMA [*desperately*]. Two days Eman. Only two days.

180 EMAN [*distressed*]. But I tell you I have no wish to go.

SUNMA [*suddenly angry*]. Are you so afraid then?

EMAN. Me? Afraid of what?

SUNMA. You think you will not want to come back.

EMAN [*pitying*]. You cannot dare me that way.

SUNMA. Then why won't you leave here, even for an hour? If you are so sure that your life is settled here, why are you afraid to do this thing for me? What is so wrong that you will not go into the next town for a day or two?

EMAN. I don't want to. I do not have to persuade you, or myself about anything. I simply have no desire to go away.

190 SUNMA [*his quiet confidence appears to incense her*]. You are afraid. You accuse me of losing my sense of mission, but you are afraid to put yours to the test.

EMAN. You are wrong Sunma. I have no sense of mission. But I have found peace here and I am content with that.

SUNMA. I haven't. For a while I thought that too, but I found there could be no peace in the midst of so much cruelty. Eman, tonight at least, the last night of the old year . . .

EMAN. No Sunma. I find this too distressing; you should go home now.

SUNMA. It is the time for making changes in one's life Eman. Let's breathe

200 in the new year away from here.

EMAN.   You are hurting yourself.

SUNMA.   Tonight. Only tonight. We will come back tomorrow, as early as you like. But let us go away for this one night. Don't let another year break on me in this place . . . you don't know how important it is to me, but I will tell you, I will tell you on the way . . . but we must not be here today, Eman, do this one thing for me.

EMAN [*sadly*].   I cannot.

SUNMA [*suddenly calm*].   I was a fool to think it would be otherwise. The whole village may use you as they will but for me there is nothing. Sometimes I
210   think you believe that doing anything for me makes you unfaithful to some part of your life. If it was a woman then I pity her for what she must have suffered. [EMAN *winces and hardens slowly.*. SUNMA *notices nothing.*] Keeping faith with so much is slowly making you inhuman. [*Seeing the change in* EMAN.] Eman. Eman. What is it?

[*As she goes towards him,* EMAN *goes into the house.*]

SUNMA [*apprehensive, follows him*].   What did I say? Eman, forgive me, forgive me please. [EMAN *remains facing into the slow darkness of the room.* SUNMA, *distressed, cannot decide what to do.*] I swear I didn't know . . . I would not have said it for all the world.

[*A lorry is heard taking off somewhere nearby. The sound comes up and slowly fades away into the distance.* SUNMA *starts visibly, goes slowly to the window.*]

SUNMA [*as the sound dies off, to herself*].   What happens now?
220   EMAN [*joining her at the window*].   What did you say?

SUNMA.   Nothing.

EMAN.   Was that not the lorry going off?

SUNMA.   It was.

EMAN.   I am sorry I couldn't help you.

[SUNMA, *about to speak, changes her mind.*]

EMAN.   I think you ought to go home now.

SUNMA.   No, don't send me away. It's the least you can do for me. Let me stay here until all the noise is over.

EMAN.   But are you not needed at home? You have a part in the festival.

SUNMA.   I have renounced it; I am Jaguna's eldest daughter only in name.
230   EMAN.   Renouncing one's self is not so easy—surely you know that.

SUNMA.   I don't want to talk about it. Will you at least let us be together tonight?

EMAN.   But . . .

SUNMA.   Unless you are afraid my father will accuse you of harbouring me.

EMAN.   All right, we will go out together.

SUNMA.   Go out? I want us to stay here.

EMAN.   When there is so much going on outside?

SUNMA.   Some day you will wish that you went away when I tried to make you.

EMAN.   Are we going back to that?
240   SUNMA.   No. I promise you I will not recall it again. But you must know that it was also for your sake that I tried to get us away.

EMAN.   For me? How?

SUNMA.   By yourself you can do nothing here. Have you not noticed how
   tightly we shut out strangers? Even if you lived here for a lifetime, you
   would remain a stranger.

EMAN.   Perhaps that is what I like. There is peace in being a stranger.

SUNMA.   For a while perhaps. But they would reject you in the end. I tell you
   it is only I who stand between you and contempt. And because of this you
   have earned their hatred. I don't know why I say this now, except that
250   somehow, I feel that it no longer matters. It is only I who have stood
   between you and much humiliation.

EMAN.   Think carefully before you say any more. I am incapable of feeling
   indebted to you. This will make no difference at all.

SUNMA.   I ask for nothing. But you must know it all the same. It is true I
   hadn't the strength to go by myself. And I must confess this now, if you
   had come with me, I would have done everything to keep you from returning.

EMAN.   I know that.

SUNMA.   You see, I bare myself to you. For days I had thought it over, this was
260   to be a new beginning for us. And I placed my fate wholly in your hands.
   Now the thought will not leave me, I have a feeling which will not be
   shaken off, that in some way, you have tonight totally destroyed my life.

EMAN.   You are depressed, you don't know what you are saying.

SUNMA.   Don't think I am accusing you. I say all this only because I cannot
   help it.

EMAN.   We must not remain shut up here. Let us go and be part of the living.

SUNMA.   No. Leave them alone.

EMAN.   Surely you don't want to stay indoors when the whole town is alive
   with rejoicing.

270 SUNMA.   Rejoicing! Is that what it seems to you? No, let us remain here.
   Whatever happens I must not go out until all this is over.

   [*There is silence. It has grown much darker.*]

EMAN.   I shall light the lamp.

SUNMA [*eager to do something*].   No, let me do it.

[*She goes into the inner room.*
   EMAN *paces the room, stops by a shelf and toys with the seeds in an 'ayo'[5] board,
   takes down the whole board and places it on a table, playing by himself.*
   The GIRL *is now seen coming back, still dragging her 'carrier'.* IFADA *brings up the
   rear as before. As he comes round the corner of the house two men emerge from the
   shadows. A sack is thrown over* IFADA's *head, the rope is pulled tight rendering him
   instantly helpless. The* GIRL *has reached the front of the house before she turns round
   at the sound of scuffle. She is in time to see* IFADA *thrown over the shoulders and borne
   away. Her face betraying no emotion at all, the* GIRL *backs slowly away, turns and
   flees, leaving the 'carrier' behind.* SUNMA *enters, carrying two kerosene lamps. She
   hangs one up from the wall.*]

   ⎯⎯⎯⎯⎯⎯⎯

   [5] Ayo is a game played on a wooden board with sixteen holes arranged in two parallel
   columns of eight holes apiece. Seeds are placed in these holes according to fixed rules. The
   object is to get four seeds in a hole.

EMAN.   One is enough.

SUNMA.   I want to leave one outside.

[*She goes out, hangs the lamp from a nail just above the door. As she turns she sees the effigy and gasps. EMAN rushes out.*]

EMAN.   What is it? Oh, is that what frightened you?

SUNMA.   I thought . . . I didn't really see it properly.

[EMAN *goes towards the object, stoops to pick it up.*]

EMAN.   It must belong to that sick girl.

SUNMA.   Don't touch it.

280   EMAN.   Let's keep it for her.

SUNMA.   Leave it alone. Don't touch it Eman.

EMAN [*shrugs and goes back*].   You are very nervous.

SUNMA.   Let's go in.

EMAN.   Wait. [*He detains her by the door, under the lamp.*] I know there is something more than you've told me. What are you afraid of tonight?

SUNMA.   I was only scared by that thing. There is nothing else.

EMAN.   I am not blind Sunma. It is true I would not run away when you wanted me to, but that doesn't mean I do not feel things. What does tonight really mean that it makes you so helpless?

290   SUNMA.   It is only a mood. And your indifference to me . . . let's go in.

[EMAN *moves aside and she enters; he remains there for a moment and then follows. She fiddles with the lamp, looks vaguely round the room, then goes and shuts the door, bolting it. When she turns, it is to meet EMAN's eyes, questioning.*]

SUNMA.   There is a cold wind coming in.

[EMAN *keeps his gaze on her.*]

SUNMA.   It *was* getting cold.

[*She moves guiltily to the table and stands by the 'ayo' board, rearranging the seeds. EMAN remains where he is a few moments, then brings a stool and sits opposite her. She sits down also and they begin to play in silence.*]

SUNMA.   What bought you here at all, Eman? And what makes you stay?

[*There is another silence.*]

SUNMA.   I am not trying to share your life. I know you too well by now. But at least we have worked together since you came. Is there nothing at all I deserve to know?

EMAN.   Let me continue a stranger—especially to you. Those who have much to give fulfil themselves only in total loneliness.

SUNMA.   Then there is no love in what you do.

300   EMAN.   There is. Love comes to me more easily with strangers.

SUNMA.   That is unnatural.

EMAN.   Not for me. I know I find consummation only when I have spent myself for a total stranger.

SUNMA.   It seems unnatural to me. But then I am a woman. I have a woman's longings and weaknesses. And the ties of blood are very strong in me.

EMAN [*smiling*].   You think I have cut loose from all these—ties of blood.
SUNMA.   Sometimes you are so inhuman.
EMAN.   I don't know what that means. But I am very much my father's son.

[*They play in silence. Suddenly* EMAN *pauses listening.*]

EMAN.   Did you hear that?
310 SUNMA [*quickly*].   I heard nothing . . . it's your turn.
EMAN.   Perhaps some of the mummers are coming this way.

[EMAN *about to play, leaps up suddenly.*]

SUNMA.   What is it? Don't you want to play any more?

[EMAN *moves to the door.*]

SUNMA.   No. Don't go out Eman.
EMAN.   If it's the dancers I want to ask them to stay. At least we won't have
   to miss everything.
SUNMA.   No, no. Don't open the door. Let us keep out everyone tonight.

[*A terrified and disordered figure bursts suddenly round the corner, past the window
and begins hammering at the door. It is* IFADA. *Desperate with terror, he pounds madly
at the door, dumb-moaning all the while.*]

EMAN.   Isn't that Ifada?
SUNMA.   They are only fooling about. Don't pay any attention.
EMAN [*looks round the window*].   That is Ifada. [*Begins to unbolt the door.*]
320 SUNMA [*pulling at his hands*].   It is only a trick they are playing on you. Don't
   take any notice Eman.
EMAN.   What are you saying? The boy is out of his senses with fear.
SUNMA.   No, no. Don't interfere Eman. For God's sake don't interfere.
EMAN.   Do you know something of this then?
SUNMA.   You are a stranger here Eman. Just leave us alone and go your own
   way. There is nothing you can do.
EMAN [*he tries to push her out of the way but she clings fiercely to him*].   Have you
   gone mad? I tell you the boy must come in.
SUNMA.   Why won't you listen to me Eman? I tell you it's none of your
330 business. For your own sake do as I say.

[EMAN *pushes her off, unbolts the door.* IFADA *rushes in, clasps* EMAN *round the knees,
dumb-moaning against his legs.*]

EMAN [*manages to re-bolt the door*].   What is it Ifada? What is the matter?

[*Shouts and voices are heard coming nearer the house.*]

SUNMA.   Before it's too late, let him go. For once Eman, believe what I tell
   you. Don't harbour him or you will regret it all your life.

[EMAN *tries to calm* IFADA *who becomes more and more abject as the outside voices get
nearer.*]

EMAN.   What have they done to him? At least tell me that. What is going on
   Sunma?

SUNMA [*with sudden venom*]. Monster! Could you not take yourself somewhere else?

EMAN. Stop talking like that.

SUNMA. He could have run into the bush couldn't he? Toad! Why must he
340 follow us with his own disasters!

VOICES OUTSIDE. It's here . . . Round the back . . . Spread, spread . . . this way
. . . no, head him off . . . use the bush path and head him off . . . get some
more lights . . .

[EMAN *listens. Lifts* IFADA *bodily and carries him into the inner room. Returns at once,
shutting the door behind him.*]

SUNMA [*slumps into a chair, resigned*]. You always follow your own way.

JAGUNA [*comes round the corner followed by* OROGE *and three men, one bearing a
torch*]. I knew he would come here.

OROGE. I hope our friend won't make trouble.

JAGUNA. He had better not. You, recall all the men and tell them to surround the house.

350 OROGE. But he may not be in the house after all.

JAGUNA. I know he is here . . . [*to the men*] . . . go on, do as I say. [*He bangs
on the door.*] Teacher, open your door . . . you two stay by the door. If I
need you I will call you.

[EMAN *opens the door.*]

JAGUNA [*speaks as he enters*]. We know he is here.

EMAN. Who?

JAGUNA. Don't let us waste time. We are grown men, teacher. You understand me and I understand you. But we must take back the boy.

EMAN. This is my house.

JAGUNA. Daughter, you'd better tell your friend. I don't think he quite knows
360 our ways. Tell him why he must give up the boy.

SUNMA. Father, I . . .

JAGUNA. Are you going to tell him or aren't you?

SUNMA. Father, I beg you, leave us alone tonight . . .

JAGUNA. I thought you might be a hindrance. Go home then if you will not
use your sense.

SUNMA. But there are other ways . . .

JAGUNA [*turning to the men*]. See that she gets home. I no longer trust her. If
she gives trouble carry her. And see that the women stay with her until all
this is over.

[SUNMA *departs, accompanied by one of the men.*]

370 JAGUNA. Now teacher . . .

OROGE [*restrains him*]. You see, Mister Eman, it is like this. Right now, nobody knows that Ifada has taken refuge here. No one except us and our
men—and they know how to keep their mouths shut. We don't want to
have to burn down the house you see, but if the word gets around, we
would have no choice.

JAGUNA. In fact, it may be too late already. A carrier should end up in the
bush, not in a house. Anyone who doesn't guard his door when the carrier

goes by has himself to blame. A contaminated house should be burnt down.

380 OROGE.   But we are willing to let it pass. Only, you must bring him out quickly.

EMAN.   All right. But at least you will let me ask you something.

JAGUNA.   What is there to ask? Don't you understand what we have told you?

EMAN.   Yes. But why did you pick on a helpless boy. Obviously he is not willing.

JAGUNA.   What is the man talking about? Ifada is a godsend. Does he have to be willing?

EMAN.   In my home, we believe that a man should be willing.

OROGE.   Mister Eman, I don't think you quite understand. This is not a
390   simple matter at all. I don't know what you do, but here, it is not a cheap task for anybody. No one in his senses would do such a job. Why do you think we give refuge to idiots like him? We don't know where he came from. One morning, he is simply there, just like that. From nowhere at all. You see, there is a purpose in that.

JAGUNA.   We only waste time.

OROGE.   Jaguna, be patient. After all, the man has been with us for some time now and deserves to know. The evil of the old year is no light thing to load on any man's head.

EMAN.   I know something about that.

400 OROGE.   You do? [*Turns to* JAGUNA *who snorts impatiently.*] You see I told you so didn't I? From the moment you came I saw you were one of the knowing ones.

JAGUNA.   Then let him behave like a man and give back the boy.

EMAN.   It is you who are not behaving like men.

JAGUNA [*advances aggressively*].   That is a quick mouth you have . . .

OROGE.   Patience Jaguna . . . if you want the new year to cushion the land there must be no deeds of anger. What did you mean my friend?

EMAN.   It is a simple thing. A village which cannot produce its own carrier contains no men.

410 JAGUNA.   Enough. Let there be no more talk or this business will be ruined by some rashness. You . . . come inside. Bring the boy out, he must be in the room there.

EMAN.   Wait.

[*The men hesitate.*]

JAGUNA [*hitting the nearer one and propelling him forward*].   Go on. Have you changed masters now that you listen to what he says?

OROGE [*sadly*].   I am sorry you would not understand Mister Eman. But you ought to know that no carrier may return to the village. If he does, the people will stone him to death. It has happened before. Surely it is too much to ask a man to give up his own soil.

420 EMAN.   I know others who have done more.

[IFADA *is brought out, abjectly dumb-moaning.*]

EMAN.   You can see him with your own eyes. Does it really have meaning to use one as unwilling as that?

OROGE [*smiling*].   He shall be willing. Not only willing but actually joyous. I
am the one who prepares them all, and I have seen worse. This one
escaped before I began to prepare him for the event. But you will see him
later tonight, the most joyous creature in the festival. Then perhaps you
will understand.

EMAN.   Then it is only a deceit. Do you believe the spirit of a new year is so
easily fooled?

430 JAGUNA.   Take him out. [*The men carry out* IFADA.] You see, it is so easy to talk. You say there are no men in this village because they cannot provide a willing carrier. And yet I heard Oroge tell you we only use strangers. There is only one other stranger in the village, but I have not heard him offer himself [*spits.*] It is so easy to talk is it not?

[*He turns his back on him. They go, off, taking* IFADA *with them, limp and silent. The only sign of life is that he strains his neck to keep his eyes on* EMAN *till the very moment that he disappears from sight.* EMAN *remains where they left him, staring after the group.*]

[*A black-out lasting no more than a minute. The lights come up slowly and* IFADA *is seen returning to the house. He stops at the window and looks in. Seeing no one, he bangs on the sill. Appears surprised that there is no response. He slithers down on his favourite spot, then sees the effigy still lying where the girl had dropped it in her flight. After some hesitation, he goes towards it, begins to strip it of the clothing. Just then the girl comes in.*]

GIRL.   Hey, leave that alone. You know it's mine.

[IFADA *pauses, then speeds up his action.*]

GIRL.   I said it is mine. Leave it where you found it.

[*She rushes at him and begins to struggle for possession of the carrier.*]

GIRL.   Thief! Thief! Let it go, it is mine. Let it go. You animal, just because I let you play with it. Idiot! Idiot!

[*The struggle becomes quite violent. The girl is hanging on to the effigy and* IFADA *lifts her with it, flinging her all about. The girl hangs on grimly.*]

GIRL.   You are spoiling it . . . why don't you get your own? Thief! Let it go
440   you thief!

[SUNMA *comes in walking very fast, throwing apprehensive glances over her shoulder. Seeing the two children, she becomes immediately angry. Advances on them.*]

SUNMA.   So you've made this place your playground. Get away you untrained pigs. Get out of here.

[IFADA *flees at once, the girl retreats also, retaining possession of the 'carrier'.*
SUNMA *goes to the door. She has her hand on the door when the significance of* IFADA's *presence strikes her for the first time. She stands rooted to the spot, then turns slowly round.*]

SUNMA.   Ifada! What are you doing here? [IFADA *is bewildered.* SUNMA *turns suddenly and rushes into the house, flying into the inner room and out again.*]

Eman! Eman! Eman! [*She rushes outside.*] Where did he go? Where did they take him? [IFADA *distressed, points.* SUNMA *seizes him by the arm, drags him off.*] Take me there at once. God help you if we are too late.
You loathsome thing, if you have let him suffer . . .

[*Her voice fades into other shouts, running footsteps, banged tins, bells, dogs, etc., rising in volume.*]

[*It is a narrow passage-way between two mud-houses. At the far end one man after another is seen running across the entry, the noise dying off gradually.*

About half-way down the passage, EMAN *is crouching against the wall, tense with apprehension. As the noise dies off, he seems to relax, but the alert hunted look is still in his eyes which are ringed in a reddish colour. The rest of his body has been whitened with a floury substance. He is naked down to the waist, wears a baggy pair of trousers, calf-length, and around both feet are bangles.*]

EMAN.   I will simply stay here till dawn. I have done enough.

[*A window is thrown open and a woman empties some slop from a pail. With a startled cry* EMAN *leaps aside to avoid it and the woman puts out her head.*]

450 WOMAN.   Oh, my head. What have I done! Forgive me neighbour. . . . Eh, it's the carrier! [*Very rapidly she clears her throat and spits on him, flings the pail at him and runs off, shouting.*] He's here. The carrier is hiding in the passage. Quickly, I have found the carrier!

[*The cry is taken up and* EMAN *flees down the passage. Shortly afterwards his pursuers come pouring down the passage in full cry. After the last of them come* JAGUNA *and* OROGE.]

OROGE.   Wait, wait. I cannot go so fast.
JAGUNA.   We will rest a little then. We can do nothing anyway.
OROGE.   If only he had let me prepare him.
JAGUNA.   They are the ones who break first, these fools who think they were born to carry suffering like a hat. What are we to do now?
OROGE.   When they catch him I must prepare him.
460 JAGUNA.   He? It will be impossible now. There can be no joy left in that one.
OROGE.   Still, it took him by surprise. He was not expecting what he met.
JAGUNA.   Why then did he refuse to listen? Did he think he was coming to sit down to a feast. He had not even gone through one compound before he bolted. Did he think he was taken round the people to be blessed? A woman, that is all he is.
OROGE.   No, no. He took the beating well enough. I think he is the kind who would let himself be beaten from night till dawn and not utter a sound. He would let himself be stoned until he dropped dead.
JAGUNA.   Then what made him run like a coward?
470 OROGE.   I don't know. I don't really know. It is a night of curses Jaguna. It is not many unprepared minds will remain unhinged under the load.
JAGUNA.   We must find him. It is a poor beginning for a year when our own curses remain hovering over our homes because the carrier refused to take them.

[*They go. The scene changes.* EMAN *is crouching beside some shrubs, torn and bleeding.*]

EMAN.   They are even guarding my house . . . as if I would go there, but I need water . . . they could at least grant me that . . . I can be thirsty too . . . [*he pricks his ears*] . . . there must be a stream nearby . . . [*As he looks round him, his eyes widen at a scene he encounters.*]

[*An old man, short and vigorous-looking, is seated on a stool. He also is wearing calf-length baggy trousers, white. On his head, a white cap. An attendant is engaged in rubbing his body with oil. Round his eyes two white rings have already been marked.*]

OLD MAN.   Have they prepared the boat?
480 ATTENDANT.   They are making the last sacrifice.
OLD MAN.   Good. Did you send for my son?
ATTENDANT.   He's on his way.
OLD MAN.   I have never met the carrying of the boat with such a heavy heart. I hope nothing comes of it.
ATTENDANT.   The gods will not desert us on that account.
OLD MAN.   A man should be at his strongest when he takes the boat my friend. To be weighed down inside and out is not a wise thing. I hope when the moment comes I shall have found my strength.

[*Enter* EMAN, *a wrapper round his waist and a 'danski'*[6] *over it.*]

OLD MAN.   I meant to wait until after my journey to the river, but my mind
490   is so burdened with my own grief and yours I could not delay it. You know I must have all my strength. But I sit here, feeling it all eaten slowly away by my unspoken grief. It helps to say it out. It even helps to cry sometimes. [*He signals to the attendant to leave them.*] Come nearer . . . we will never meet again son. Not on this side of the flesh. What I do not know is whether you will return to take my place.
EMAN.   I will never come back.
OLD MAN.   Do you know what you are saying? Ours is a strong breed my son. It is only a strong breed that can take this boat to the river year after year and wax stronger on it. I have taken down each year's evils for over twenty
500   years. I hoped you would follow me.
EMAN.   My life here died with Omae.
OLD MAN.   Omae died giving birth to your child and you think the world is ended. Eman, my pain did not begin when Omae died. Since you sent her to stay with me son, I lived with the burden of knowing that this child would die bearing your son.
EMAN.   Father . . .
OLD MAN.   Don't you know it was the same with you? And me? No woman survives the bearing of the strong ones. Son, it is not the mouth of the boaster that says he belongs to the strong breed. It is the tongue that is red
510   with pain and black with sorrow. Twelve years you were away my son, and

---

[6] A brief Yoruba attire.

for those twelve years I knew the love of an old man for his daughter and
the pain of a man helplessly awaiting his loss.

EMAN.   I wish I had stayed away. I wish I never came back to meet her.

OLD MAN.   It had to be. But you know now what slowly ate away my strength.
I awaited your return with love and fear. Forgive me then if I say that your
grief is light. It will pass. This grief may drive you now from home. But you
must return.

EMAN.   You do not understand. It is not grief alone.

OLD MAN.   What is it then? Tell me, I can still learn.

520 EMAN.   I was away twelve years. I changed much in that time.

OLD MAN.   I am listening.

EMAN.   I am unfitted for your work father. I wish to say no more. But I am
totally unfitted for your call.

OLD MAN.   It is only time you need son. Stay longer and you will answer the
urge of your blood.

EMAN.   That I stayed at all was because of Omae. I did not expect to find her
waiting. I would have taken her away, but hard as you claim to be, it would
have killed you. And I was a tired man. I needed peace. Because Omae was
peace, I stayed. Now nothing holds me here.

530 OLD MAN.   Other men would rot and die doing this task year after year. It is
strong medicine which only we can take. Our blood is strong like no other.
Anything you do in life must be less than this, son.

EMAN.   That is not true father.

OLD MAN.   I tell you it is true. Your own blood will betray you son, because
you cannot hold it back. If you make it do less than this, it will rush to your
head and burst it open. I say what I know my son.

EMAN.   There are other tasks in life father. This one is not for me. There are
even greater things you know nothing of.

OLD MAN.   I am very sad. You only go to give to others what rightly belongs
540   to us. You will use your strength among thieves. They are thieves because
they take what is ours, they have no claim of blood to it. They will even lack
the knowledge to use it wisely. Truth is my companion at this moment my
son. I know everything I say will surely bring the sadness of truth.

EMAN.   I am going father.

OLD MAN.   Call my attendant. And be with me in your strength for this last
journey. A-ah, did you hear that? It came out without my knowing it; this
is indeed my last journey. But I am not afraid.

[EMAN *goes out. A few moments later, the attendant enters.*]

ATTENDANT.   The boat is ready.

OLD MAN.   So am I.

[*He sits perfectly still for several moments. Drumming begins somewhere in the distance, and the old man sways his head almost imperceptibly. Two men come in bearing
a miniature boat, containing an indefinable mound. They rush it in and set it briskly
down near the old man, and stand well back. The old man gets up slowly, the
attendant watching him keenly. He signs to the men, who lift the boat quickly onto the
old man's head. As soon as it touches his head, he holds it down with both hands and
runs off, the men give him a start, then follow at a trot.*]

[*As the last man disappears* OROGE *limps in and comes face to face with* EMAN—*as carrier—who is now seen still standing beside the shrubs, staring into the scene he has just witnessed.* OROGE, *struck by the look on* EMAN's *face, looks anxiously behind him to see what has engaged* EMAN's *attention.* EMAN *notices him then, and the pair stare at each other. Jaguna enters, sees him and shouts, 'Here he is', rushes at* EMAN *who is whipped back to the immediate and flees,* JAGUNA *in pursuit. Three or four others enter and follow them.* OROGE *remains where he is, thoughtful.*]

550 JAGUNA [*re-enters*]. They have closed in on him now, we'll get him this time.
OROGE. It is nearly midnight.
JAGUNA. You were standing there looking at him as if he was some strange spirit. Why didn't you shout?
OROGE. You shouted didn't you? Did that catch him?
JAGUNA. Don't worry. We have him now. But things have taken a bad turn. It is no longer enough to drive him past every house. There is too much contamination about already.
OROGE [*not listening*]. He saw something. Why may I not know what it was?
JAGUNA. What are you talking about?
560 OROGE. Hm. What is it?
JAGUNA. I said there is too much harm done already. The year will demand more from this carrier than we thought.
OROGE. What do you mean?
JAGUNA. Do we have to talk with the full mouth?
OROGE. S-sh . . . look!

[Jaguna *turns just in time to see* SUNMA *fly at him, clawing at his face like a crazed tigress.*]

SUNMA. Murderer! What are you doing to him. Murderer! Murderer!

[JAGUNA *finds himself struggling really hard to keep off his daughter, he succeeds in pushing her off and striking her so hard on the face that she falls to her knees. He moves on her to hit her again.*]

OROGE [*comes between*]. Think what you are doing Jaguna, she is your daughter.
JAGUNA. My daughter! Does this one look like my daughter? Let me cripple
570 the harlot for life.
OROGE. That is a wicked thought Jaguna.
JAGUNA. Don't come between me and her.
OROGE. Nothing in anger—do you forget what tonight is?
JAGUNA. Can you blame me for forgetting?

[*Draws his hand across his cheek—it is covered with blood.*]

OROGE. This is an unhappy night for us all. I fear what is to come of it.
JAGUNA. Let's go. I cannot restrain myself in this creature's presence. My own daughter . . . and for a stranger . . .

[*They go off.* IFADA, *who came in with* SUNMA *and had stood apart, horror-stricken, comes shyly forward. He helps* SUNMA *up. They go off, he holding* SUNMA *bent and sobbing.*]

[*Enter* EMAN—*as carrier. He is physically present in the bounds of this next scene, a side of a round thatched hut. A young girl, about fourteen runs in, stops beside the hut. She looks carefully to see that she is not observed, puts her mouth to a little hole in the wall.*]

OMAE.   Eman . . . Eman . . .

[EMAN—*as carrier—responds, as he does throughout the scene, but they are unaware of him.*]

EMAN [*from inside*].   Who is it?
580 OMAE.   It is me, Omae.
    EMAN.   How dare you come here! [*Two hands appear at the hole and pushing outwards, create a much larger hole through which* EMAN *puts out his head. It is* EMAN *as a boy, the same age as the girl.*] Go away at once. Are you trying to get me into trouble!
    OMAE.   What is the matter?
    EMAN.   You. Go away.
    OMAE.   But I came to see you.
    EMAN.   Are you deaf? I say I don't want to see you. Now go before my tutor catches you.
590 OMAE.   All right. Come out.
    EMAN.   Do what!
    OMAE.   Come out.
    EMAN.   You must be mad.
    OMAE [*sits on the ground*].   All right, if you don't come out I shall simply stay here until your tutor arrives.
    EMAN [*about to explode, thinks better of it and the head disappears. A moment later he emerges from behind the hut.*]   What sort of a devil has got into you?
    OMAE.   None. I just wanted to see you.
    EMAN [*his mimicry is nearly hysterical*].   'None. I just wanted to see you.' Do you
600 think this place is the stream where you can go and molest innocent people?
    OMAE [*coyly*].   Aren't you glad to see me?
    EMAN.   I am not.
    OMAE.   Why?
    EMAN.   Why? Do you really ask me why? Because you are a woman and a most troublesome woman. Don't you know anything about this at all? We are not meant to see any woman. So go away before more harm is done.
    OMAE [*flirtatious*].   What is so secret about it anyway? What do they teach you?
    EMAN.   Nothing any woman can understand.
610 OMAE.   Ha ha. You think we don't know eh? You've all come to be circumcised.
    EMAN.   Shut up. You don't know anything.
    OMAE.   Just think, all this time you haven't been circumcised, and you dared make eyes at us women.
    EMAN.   Thank you—woman. Now go.
    OMAE.   Do they give you enough to eat?
    EMAN [*testily*].   No. We are so hungry that when silly girls like you turn up, we eat them.

Omae [*feigning tears*].   Oh, oh, oh, he's abusing me. He's abusing me.

620 Eman [*alarmed*].   Don't try that here. Go quickly if you are going to cry.

Omae.   All right, I won't cry.

Eman.   Cry or no cry, go away and leave me alone. What do you think will happen if my tutor turns up now.

Omae.   He won't.

Eman [*mimicking*].   'He won't.' I suppose you are his wife and he tells you where he goes. In fact this is just the time he comes round to our huts. He could be at the next hut this very moment.

Omae.   Ha-ha. You're lying. I left him by the stream, pinching the girls' bottoms. Is that the sort of thing he teaches you?

630 Eman.   Don't say anything against him or I shall beat you. Isn't it you loose girls who tease him, wiggling your bottoms under his nose?

Omae [*going tearful again*].   A-ah, so I am one of the loose girls eh?

Eman.   Now don't start accusing me of things I didn't say.

Omae.   But you said it. You said it.

Eman.   I didn't. Look Omae, someone will hear you and I'll be in disgrace. Why don't you go before anything happens.

Omae.   It's all right. My friends have promised to hold your old rascal tutor till I get back.

Eman.   Then you go back right now. I have work to do. [*Going in.*]

640 Omae [*runs after and tries to hold him.* Eman *leaps back, genuinely scared*].   What is the matter? I was not going to bite you.

Eman.   Do you know what you nearly did? You almost touched me!

Omae.   Well?

Eman.   Well! Isn't it enough that you let me set my eyes on you? Must you now totally pollute me with your touch? Don't you understand anything?

Omae.   Oh, that.

Eman [*nearly screaming*].   It is not 'oh that'. Do you think this is only a joke or a little visit like spending the night with your grandmother? This is an important period of my life. Look, these huts, we built them with our own

650 hands. Every boy builds his own. We learn things, do you understand? And we spend much time just thinking. At least, I do. It is the first time I have had nothing to do except think. Don't you see, I am becoming a man. For the first time, I understand that I have a life to fulfil. Has that thought ever worried you?

Omae.   You are frightening me.

Eman.   There. That is all you can say. And what use will that be when a man finds himself alone—like that? [*Points to the hut.*] A man must go on his own, go where no one can help him, and test his strength. Because he may find himself one day sitting alone in a wall as round as that. In there, my

660 mind could hold no other thought. I may never have such moments again to myself. Don't dare to come and steal any more of it.

Omae [*this time, genuinely tearful*].   Oh, I know you hate me. You only want to drive me away.

Eman [*impatiently*].   Yes, yes, I know I hate you—but go.

Omae [*going, all tears. Wipes her eyes, suddenly all mischief*].   Eman.

Eman.   What now?

Omae.   I only want to ask one thing . . . do you promise to tell me?

EMAN. Well, what is it?
OMAE [*gleefully*]. Does it hurt?

[*She turns instantly and flees, landing straight into the arms of the returning tutor.*]

670 TUTOR. Te-he-he . . . what have we here? What little mouse leaps straight
into the beak of the wise old owl eh?

[OMAE *struggles to free herself, flies to the opposite side, grimacing with distaste.*]

TUTOR. I suppose you merely came to pick some fruits eh? You did not
sneak here to see any of my children.
OMAE. Yes, I came to steal your fruits.
TUTOR. Te-he-he . . . I thought so. And that dutiful son of mine over there.
He saw you and came to chase you off my fruit trees didn't he? Te-he-he
. . . I'm sure he did, isn't that so my young Eman?
EMAN. I was talking to her.
TUTOR. Indeed you were. Now be good enough to go into your hut until I
680 decide your punishment. [EMAN *withdraws.*] Te-he-he . . . now now my little
daughter, you need not be afraid of me.
OMAE [*spiritedly*]. I am not.
TUTOR. Good. Very good. We ought to be friendly. [*His voice becomes leering.*]
Now this is nothing to worry you my daughter . . . a very small thing
indeed. Although of course if I were to let it slip that your young Eman
had broken a strong taboo, it might go hard on him you know. I am sure
you would not like that to happen, would you?
OMAE. No.
TUTOR. Good. You are sensible my girl. Can you wash clothes?
690 OMAE. Yes.
TUTOR. Good. If you will come with me now to my hut, I shall give you some
clothes to wash, and then we will forget all about this matter eh? Well,
come on.
OMAE. I shall wait here. You go and bring the clothes.
TUTOR. Eh? What is that? Now now, don't make me angry. You should know
better than to talk back at your elders. Come now.

[*He takes her by the arm, and tries to drag her off.*]

OMAE. No no, I won't come to your hut. Leave me. Leave me alone you
shameless old man.
TUTOR. If you don't come I shall disgrace the whole family of Eman, and
700 yours too.

[EMAN *re-enters with a small bundle.*]

EMAN. Leave her alone. Let us go Omae.
TUTOR. And where do you think you are going?
EMAN. Home.
TUTOR. Te-he-he . . . As easy as that eh? You think you can leave here any
time you please? Get right back inside that hut!

[EMAN *takes* OMAE *by the arm and begins to walk off.*]

TUTOR. Come back at once.

[*He goes after him and raises his stick.* EMAN *catches it, wrenches it from him and throws its away.*]

OMAE [*hopping delightedly*].   Kill him. Beat him to death.
TUTOR.   Help! Help! He is killing me! Help!

[*Alarmed,* EMAN *clamps his hand over his mouth.*]

EMAN.   Old tutor, I don't mean you any harm, but you mustn't try to harm
710   me either. [*He removes his hand.*]
TUTOR.   You think you can get away with your crime. My report shall reach
    the elders before you ever get into town.
EMAN.   You are afraid of what I will say about you? Don't worry. Only if you
    try to shame me, then I will speak. I am not going back to the village
    anyway. Just tell them I have gone, no more. If you say one word more
    than that I shall hear of it the same day and I shall come back.
TUTOR.   You are telling me what to do? But don't think to come back next
    year because I will drive you away. Don't think to come back here even ten
    years from now. And don't send your children.

[*Goes off with threatening gestures.*]

720   EMAN.   I won't come back.
OMAE.   Smoked vulture! But Eman, he says you cannot return next year.
    What will you do?
EMAN.   It is a small thing one can do in the big towns.
OMAE.   I thought you were going to beat him that time. Why didn't you crack
    his dirty hide?
EMAN.   Listen carefully Omae . . . I am going on a journey.
OMAE.   Come on. Tell me about it on the way.
EMAN.   No, I go that way. I cannot return to the village.
OMAE.   Because of that wretched man? Anyway you will first talk to your
730   father.
EMAN.   Go and see him for me. Tell him I have gone away for some time. I
    think he will know.
OMAE.   But Eman . . .
EMAN.   I haven't finished. You will go and live with him till I get back. I have
    spoken to him about you. Look after him!
OMAE.   But what is this journey? When will you come back?
EMAN.   I don't know. But this is a good moment to go. Nothing ties me
    down.
OMAE.   But Eman, you want to leave me.
740   EMAN.   Don't forget all I said. I don't know how long I will be. Stay in my
    father's house as long as you remember me. When you become tired of
    waiting, you must do as you please. You understand? You must do as you
    please.
OMAE.   I cannot understand anything Eman. I don't know where you are
    going or why. Suppose you never came back! Don't go Eman. Don't leave
    me by myself.
EMAN.   I must go. Now let me see you on your way.
OMAE.   I shall come with you.

EMAN.   Come with me! And who will look after you? Me? You will only be in
750   my way, you know that! You will hold me back and I shall desert you in a
strange place. Go home and do as I say. Take care of my father and let him
take care of you.

[*He starts going but* OMAE *clings to him.*]

OMAE.   But Eman, stay the night at least. You will only lose your way. Your
father Eman, what will he say? I won't remember what you said . . . come
back to the village . . . I cannot return alone Eman . . . come with me as far
as the crossroads.

[*His face set,* EMAN *strides off and* OMAE *loses balance as he increases his pace.
Falling, she quickly wraps her arms around his ankle, but* EMAN *continues unchecked,
dragging her along.*]

OMAE.   Don't go Eman . . . Eman, don't leave me, don't leave me . . . don't
leave your Omae . . . don't go Eman . . . don't leave your Omae . . .

[EMAN—*as carrier—makes a nervous move as if he intends to go after the vanished
pair. He stops but continues to stare at the point where he last saw them. There is
stillness for a while. Then the* GIRL *enters from the same place and remains looking at*
EMAN. *Startled,* EMAN *looks apprehensively round him. The* GIRL *goes nearer but
keeps beyond arm's length.*]

GIRL.   Are you the carrier?
760 EMAN.   Yes. I am Eman.
GIRL.   Why are you hiding?
EMAN.   I really came for a drink of water . . . er . . . is there anyone in front
of the house?
GIRL.   No.
EMAN.   But there might be people in the house. Did you hear voices?
GIRL.   There is no one here.
EMAN.   Good. Thank you. [*He is about to go, stops suddenly.*] Er . . . would you
. . . you will find a cup on the table. Could you bring me the water out
here? The water-pot is in a corner.

[*The* GIRL *goes. She enters the house, then, watching* EMAN *carefully, slips out and
runs off.*]

770 EMAN [*sitting*].   Perhaps they have all gone home. It will be good to rest. [*He
hears voices and listens hard.*] Too late. [*Moves cautiously nearer the house.*]
Quickly girl, I can hear people coming. Hurry up. [*Looks through the window.*] Where are you? Where is she? [*The truth dawns on him suddenly and he
moves off, sadly.*]

[*Enter* JAGUNA *and* OROGE, *led by the* GIRL.]

GIRL [*pointing*].   He was there.
JAGUNA.   Ay, he's gone now. He is a sly one is your friend. But it won't save
him for ever.
OROGE.   What was he doing when you saw him?
GIRL.   He asked me for a drink of water.
780 JAGUNA *and* OROGE.   Ah! [*They look at each other.*]

OROGE. We should have thought of that.

JAGUNA. He is surely finished now. If only we had thought of it earlier.

OROGE. It is not too late. There is still an hour before midnight.

JAGUNA. We must call back all the men. Now we need only wait for him—in the right place.

OROGE. Everyone must be told. We don't want anyone heading him off again.

JAGUNA. And it works so well. This is surely the help of the gods themselves Oroge. Don't you know at once what is on the path to the stream?

790 OROGE. The sacred trees.

JAGUNA. I tell you it is the very hand of the gods. Let us go.

[*An overgrown part of the village.* EMAN *wanders in, aimlessly, seemingly uncaring of discovery. Beyond him, an area lights up, revealing a group of people clustered round a spot, all the heads are bowed. One figure stands away and separate from them. Even as* EMAN *looks, the group breaks up and the people disperse, coming down and past him. Only three people are left, a man (*EMAN*) whose back is turned, the village priest and the isolated one. They stand on opposite sides of the grave, the man on the mound of earth. The priest walks round to the man's side and lays a hand on his shoulder.*]

PRIEST. Come.

EMAN. I will. Give me a few moments here alone.

PRIEST. Be comforted.

[*They fall silent.*]

EMAN. I was gone twelve years but she waited. She whom I thought had too much of the laughing child in her. Twelve years I was a pilgrim, seeking the vain shrine of secret strength. And all the time, strange knowledge, this silent strength of my child-woman.

PRIEST. We all saw it. It was a lesson to us; we did not know that such
800 goodness could be found among us.

EMAN. Then why? Why the wasted years if she had to perish giving birth to my child? [*They are both silent.*] I do not really know for what great meaning I searched. When I returned, I could not be certain I had found it. Until I reached my home and I found her a full-grown woman, still a child at heart. When I grew to believe it, I thought, this, after all, is what I sought. It was here all the time. And I threw away my new-gained knowledge. I buried the part of me that was formed in strange places. I made a home in my birthplace.

PRIEST. That was as it should be.

810 EMAN. Any truth of that was killed in the cruelty of her brief happiness.

PRIEST [*looks up and sees the figure standing away from them, the child in his arms. He is totally still*]. Your father—he is over there.

EMAN. I knew he would come. Has he my son with him?

PRIEST. Yes.

EMAN. He will let no one take the child. Go and comfort him priest. He loved Omae like a daughter, and you all know how well she looked after him. You see how strong we really are. In his heart of hearts the old man's love really awaited a daughter. Go and comfort him. His grief is more than mine.

[*The* PRIEST *goes. The* OLD MAN *has stood well away from the burial group. His face is hard and his gaze unswerving from the grave. The* PRIEST *goes to him, pauses, but sees that he can make no dent in the man's grief. Bowed, he goes on his way.*]

[EMAN, *as carrier, walking towards the graveside, the other* EMAN *having gone. His feet sink into the mound and he breaks slowly on to his knees, scooping up the sand in his hands and pouring it on his head. The scene blacks out slowly.*]

[*Enter* JAGUNA *and* OROGE.]

820 OROGE.   We have only a little time.

JAGUNA.   He will come. All the wells are guarded. There is only the stream left him. The animal must come to drink.

OROGE.   You are sure it will not fail—the trap I mean.

JAGUNA.   When Jaguna sets the trap, even elephants pay homage—their trunks downwards and one leg up in the sky. When the carrier steps on the fallen twigs, it is up in the sacred trees with him.

OROGE.   I shall breathe again when this long night is over.

[*They go out.*]

[*Enter* EMAN—*as carrier—from the same direction as the last two entered. In front of him is a still figure, the* OLD MAN *as he was, carrying the dwarf boat.*]

EMAN [*joyfully*].   Father.

[*The figure does not turn round.*]

EMAN.   It is your son. Eman. [*He moves nearer.*] Don't you want to look at me?

830   It is I, Eman. [*He moves nearer still.*]

OLD MAN.   You are coming too close. Don't you know what I carry on my head?

EMAN.   But Father, I am your son.

OLD MAN.   Then go back. We cannot give the two of us.

EMAN.   Tell me first where you are going.

OLD MAN.   Do *you* ask that? Where else but to the river?

EMAN [*visibly relieved*].   I only wanted to be sure. My throat is burning. I have been looking for the stream all night.

OLD MAN.   It is the other way.

840 EMAN.   But you said . . .

OLD MAN.   I take the longer way, you know how I must do this. It is quicker if you take the other way. Go now.

EMAN.   No, I will only get lost again. I shall go with you.

OLD MAN.   Go back my son. Go back.

EMAN.   Why? Won't you even look at me?

OLD MAN.   Listen to your father. Go back.

EMAN.   But father!

[*He makes to hold him. Instantly the* OLD MAN *breaks into a rapid trot.* EMAN *hesitates, then follows, his strength nearly gone.*]

EMAN.   Wait father. I am coming with you . . . wait . . . wait for me father . . .

[*There is a sound of twigs breaking, of a sudden trembling in the branches. Then silence.*]

[*The front of* EMAN's *house. The effigy is hanging from the sheaves.*[7] *Enter* SUNMA, *still supported by* IFADA, *she stands transfixed as she sees the hanging figure.* IFADA *appears to go mad, rushes at the object and tears it down.* SUNMA, *her last bit of will gone, crumbles against the wall. Some distance away from them, partly hidden, stands the* GIRL, *impassively watching.* IFADA *hugs the effigy to him, stands above* SUNMA. *The* GIRL *remains where she is, observing.*

Almost at once, the villagers begin to return, subdued and guilty.

They walk across the front, skirting the house as widely as they can. No word is exchanged. JAGUNA *and* OROGE *eventually appear.* JAGUNA *who is leading, sees* SUNMA *as soon as he comes in view. He stops at once, retreating slightly.*]

OROGE [*almost whispering*].   What is it?
850 JAGUNA.   The viper.

[OROGE *looks cautiously at the woman.*]

OROGE.   I don't think she will even see you.
JAGUNA.   Are you sure? I am in no frame of mind for another meeting with her.
OROGE.   Let's go home.
JAGUNA.   I am sick to the heart of the cowardice I have seen tonight.
OROGE.   That is the nature of men.
JAGUNA.   Then it is a sorry world to live in. We did it for them. It was all for their own common good. What did it benefit me whether the man lived or died. But did you see them? One and all they looked up at the man and
860   words died in their throats.
OROGE.   It was no common sight.
JAGUNA.   Women could not have behaved so shamefully. One by one they crept off like sick dogs. Not one could raise a curse.
OROGE.   It was not only him they fled. Do you see how unattended we are?
JAGUNA.   There are those who will pay for this night's work!
OROGE.   Ay, let us go home.

[*They go off.* SUNMA, IFADA *and* GIRL *remain as they are, the light fading slowly on them.*]

THE END

[1964]

Critical Commentary on *The Strong Breed*

I made a strange discovery this morning. I am pregnant.

For a long time I looked down on the evidence, wondering how it came to be. For there it was, firmly rounded and taut, an egg of a protuberance that had no business on my waist-line.

Considering my sex, it should not happen to me at all.

Those words begin the twenty-ninth chapter of *The Man Died: Prison Notes of Wole Soyinka.* Soyinka had been imprisoned almost eighteen months earlier

---

[7] The overhanging edge of the roof, or eaves.

as a result of his efforts to prevent the incipient civil war in his homeland of Nigeria. Despite his importance as a playwright of international repute, Soyinka had been kept in solitary confinement, often shackled. He was deprived of access to books and writing implements and subjected to lengthy interrogations. It turns out that his "pregnancy" had resulted from an extended hunger strike:

> The longer I fasted, the wider the gap of course [between trousers and abdomen] and the harder my lower belly strained to fill it. I seem to have built up over the months what must be in proportion to the body the largest abdominal set of muscles anywhere in the world. . . . a wad of rich, superabundant muscles, ready to step into any Mr. Universe contest of the abdomen.

Wole Soyinka, winner of the Nobel Prize for Literature in 1986, is far more than the author of two novels, four books of poetry, two volumes of autobiography, and a dozen major plays. He is a man who strongly believes that society advances only as a result of the insights of unique individuals. In addition, he believes that such individuals have a duty to communicate their insights even if by doing so they risk conflict with the authorities or the cultural traditions.

The history of civilization is, in large part, a history of those victims of persecution and often martyrdom who knew that their ideas were worthy of personal sacrifice. We remember such sacrifices by Plato, Jesus, Joan of Arc, Galileo, Mahatma Gandhi, and Martin Luther King, each of whom suffered imprisonment or death as a result of advancing a belief about truth or justice. Soyinka, too, has suffered for his beliefs and he continues to believe in the dignity and worth of suffering humanity.

The duty of the individual is at the heart of *The Strong Breed,* the story of Eman's attempt to change African cultural values through a chosen martyrdom. One of Soyinka's most abiding interests is in the many variations of religious myths of human sacrifice. This is the central element in *The Strong Breed*; it is part of *The Bacchae*; it is at the core of *Death and the King's Horseman*; and it has a significant role in *A Dance of the Forests* and *The Road*.

In *The Strong Breed* Soyinka signals the significance that he gives to the character of Eman by a series of carefully developed similarities between Eman and Jesus Christ. As Eldred Jones has noted in *The Writing of Wole Soyinka*, "like Christ, Eman is both teacher and healer." He devotes himself particularly to serving the sick and the poor. Like Christ, he takes the sins of the entire community upon himself. And as in Judas's betrayal of Christ, Eman is betrayed by one whom he has cared for and served. Jones continues,

> Other analogies with Christ are Eman's conscious sacrifice of himself for an ungrateful people, his supreme sacrifice taking the form of his being hanged on a sacred tree. Toward the climax of the physical sacrifice, his body flinches, and he needs water. Eman's pathetic appeal to the girl who betrays him parallels Christ's agonized cry 'I thirst'. Eman's death, like Christ's, stuns the people in whose name it had been demanded, and leaves a remarkable impression on some unlikely minds.

The Strong Breed begins with clear foreshadowing of the sacrifice to come. Sunma is "agitated" and her uneasiness in the presence of the harmless Ifada suggests her awareness that he is the likely candidate for the role of carrier. Her fervent desire that she and Eman go away from the village for at least that one night demonstrates her knowledge that Eman is the only other choice for carrier in this village which by tradition uses a stranger as its sacrificial victim.

What is less clear at the beginning is that Eman is far more knowledgeable than Sunma thinks he is. As a member of the strong breed of carriers for his native village, he must have suspicions about the nature of the New Year's festivities in this village. Is his presence in the village a sign of his willingness to assume the burden of self-sacrifice, or is he there because he rejects the burdens that his father bore?

Soyinka's attitude toward the rituals of human suffering is quite complex. He points out that the villagers tolerate the retarded child Ifada only because they expect to make him the next year's carrier. As the festival approaches, their attitude toward Ifada begins to change. Sunma had asked him to run errands and had even played with him in the past, but now she drives him away and says he is like "some horrible insect." This hardening of the heart and dehumanization of the victim is implicit in the ritual sacrifice. As Sunma says, "Suddenly my disgust won't take him any more. Perhaps . . . perhaps it is the new year. Yes, yes, it must be the new year."

Soyinka seems ambivalent about the value of the willing carriers like Jesus Christ, the Old Man (Eman's father), and ultimately Eman himself. On the one hand, the whole notion of having an innocent sacrificial victim carry the sins of an entire village or, in the case of Jesus, of all mankind may seem superstitious to a modern rationalist. Apparently, this is the opinion of Eman after he returns to his village following twelve years of travel and study. "I am unfitted for your work father," he says. "I wish to say no more. But I am totally unfitted for your call." He is too polite and too dutiful a son to tell his father that he no longer believes in the tribal carrier, but he does insist that there are "other tasks" and "greater things" in life. The tasks he chooses for himself are teaching and practicing medicine, two of the most respected modern ways of giving of oneself to others.

Soyinka, however, does not allow modern scientific rationalism to go unchallenged in this play. Eman's father sadly predicts that Eman will only "give to others what rightly belongs to us. . . . They will even lack the knowledge to use it wisely." He remains confident that Eman cannot reject the call of his own blood, the blood of the strong breed. If we reread the beginning of the play with this possibility in mind, we can see that Eman is half-consciously preparing himself to become the village carrier. He avoids true intimacy with Sunma, despite her love for him. He wilfully rejects her suggestion that they leave the village before the festival begins. On some level he must have recognized that in giving his cloak to the sick girl at the beginning of the play, he was offering himself up as a ritual carrier. At the very least her doll carrier should have served as a reminder of his past and a forewarning of the nature of the coming festival.

By the end of the play, however, Eman's self-sacrifice is quite different from his father's annual role in a ritual of expiation. Most directly, of course, he serves as carrier primarily to spare the boy Ifada from the beatings administered to the carrier and, more importantly, from the banishment that is the most painful part of the carrier's fate. Early in his ordeal, however, the significance of the event changes for Eman. He takes the first beating "well enough," and Oroge recognizes that "he is the kind who would let himself be beaten from night till dawn and not utter a sound."

Why, then, did he run? Was he trying to free the village from superstition by hiding out all night and breaking the tradition of annual expiation? His words and actions as he hides in the alley ("I will stay here until dawn. I have done enough.") are consistent with this hypothesis, but something changes in him after he is betrayed by the young girl and after he experiences his visions of his father and Omae.

The great strength of Omae was that as a full-grown woman, she was "still a child at heart." In contrast, the sick girl in this village is old and cunning and made evil by her superstitions. The childish innocence of Omae was physically destroyed by her union with the strong breed; perhaps the unnatural malice of the sick girl can be spiritually destroyed by Eman's tragic self-sacrifice.

When Eman follows the vision of his father on his last journey down to the river, Soyinka clearly suggests that Eman *chooses* his sacrificial death. Why? Could it be that he now recognizes that this village needs a stronger break with tradition than hiding out until morning would provide? As Jaguna and Oroge return from the grove where Eman was hung from the sacred tree, they are puzzled by the reactions of the villagers: "they all looked up at the man and words died in their throats." No man could raise a curse. Oroge and Jaguna, who had always been attended by subordinates earlier in the play, now slink back to the village unattended and afraid even of confronting Sunma. When Jaguna concludes that "There are those who will pay for this night's work," we may hope that he and Oroge are the ones who will pay and that Eman's self-sacrifice was the only way to end such sacrifices for all time. But it is characteristic of Soyinka's pessimism that the opposite is also possible. Eman's death may only diminish the number of decent human beings, leaving the world more easily controlled by men like Oroge and Jaguna, who make others pay for their crimes.

A Selective Bibliography on *The Strong Breed*

Adedeji, Joel 'Yinka. "Wole Soyinka and the Growth of Drama." *European-Language Writing in Sub-Saharan Africa.* Ed. Albert S. Gerard. Budapest: Akademiaj Kiado, 1986. 716–39.

Amosu, Tundonu. "Sociology and the Translator: Soyinka in Translation." *Babel: International Journal of Translation* 34.3 (1988): 141–51.

Avery, Greta M. *Index of Subjects, Proverbs, and Themes in the Writings of Wole Soyinka.* New York: Greenwood, 1988.

Bryan, Sylvia. "Images of Woman in Wole Soyinka's Work." *African Literature Today* 15 (1987): 119–30.

Carpenter, Charles A. "Studies of Wole Soyinka's Drama: An International Bibliography." *Modern Drama* 24 (1981): 96–101.

Galle, Etienne. "Wole Soyinka and Ritual Drama." *Commonwealth Essays and Studies* 7 (1984): 20–8.

Gibbs, James. "The Living Dramatist and Shakespeare: A Study of Shakespeare's Influence on Wole Soyinka." *Shakespeare Survey* 39 (1987): 169–78.

Gibbs, James, ed. *Critical Perspectives on Wole Soyinka*. Washington, D.C.: Three Continents, 1980.

————. *Wole Soyinka*. Basingstoke, Eng.: Macmillan, 1986.

Gopalakrishnan, Radhamani. "The Christ Figure in the Plays of Soyinka." *The Commonwealth Review* 1 (1989): 87–96.

Hepburn, Joan. "Mediators of Ritual Closure." *Black American Literature Forum* 22 (1988): 576–614.

Jones, Elred D. *The Writing of Wole Soyinka*. 3rd ed. Portsmouth, NH: Heinemann, 1988. 72–86.

Katrak, Ketu H. *Wole Soyinka and Modern Tragedy: A Study of Dramatic Theory and Practice*. Westport: Greenwood, 1986.

Maduakor, Obi. *Wole Soyinka: An Introduction to His Writings*. New York: Garland, 1987.

Moore, Gerald. *Wole Soyinka*. New York: Africana, 1971.

Ogunba, Oyin. *The Movement of Transition: A Study of the Plays of Wole Soyinka*. Ibadan, Nigeria: U of Ibadan P, 1975.

Peters, Jonathan. A. *A Dance of Masks: Senghor, Achebe, Soyinka*. Washington, D.C.: Three Continents, 1978.

Severac, Alain. "Soyinka's Tragedies: From Ritual to Drama." *Commonwealth Essays and Studies* 10 (1987): 26–40.

Sethuraman, R. "The Role of Women in the Plays of Wole Soyinka." *World Literature Written in English* 25.2 (1985): 222–7.

Soyinka, Wole. "Shakespeare and the Living Dramatist." *Shakespeare Survey* 36 (1983): 1–10.

Thompson, Paul. "An Introduction to the Works of Wole Soyinka." *Studies in English Language and Literature* 28 (1987): 39–63.

Wright, Derek. "The Ritual Context of Two Plays by Soyinka." *Theatre Research International* 12 (1987): 51–60.

————. "Soyinka's Carrier Complex." *Komparatistische Hefte* 13 (1986): 83–93.

Tom Stoppard (1937–   )
THE REAL INSPECTOR HOUND

CHARACTERS

MOON

BIRDBOOT

MRS. DRUDGE

SIMON

FELICITY

CYNTHIA

MAGNUS

INSPECTOR HOUND

The first thing is that the audience appear to be confronted by their own reflection in a huge mirror. Impossible. However, back there in the gloom—not at the foot-lights—a bank of plush seats and pale smudges of faces. (The total effect having been established, it can be progressively faded out as the play goes on, until the front row remains to remind us of the rest and then, finally, merely two seats in that row—one of which is now occupied by MOON. *Between* MOON *and the auditorium is an acting area which represents, in as realistic an idiom as possible, the drawing-room of Muldoon Manor. French windows at one side. A telephone fairly well upstage (i.e. towards* MOON). *The* BODY *of a man lies sprawled face down on the floor in front of a large settee. This settee must be of a size and design to allow it to be wheeled over the body, hiding it completely. Silence. The room. The* BODY. MOON.*

MOON stares blankly ahead. He turns his head to one side then the other, then up, then down—waiting. He picks up his program and reads the front cover. He turns over the page and reads.

He turns over the page and reads.

He turns over the page and reads.

He turns over the page and reads.

He looks at the back cover and reads.

He puts it down and crosses his legs and looks about. He stares front. Behind him and to one side, barely visible, a man enters and sits down: BIRDBOOT.

Pause. MOON *picks up his program, glances at the front cover and puts it down impatiently. Pause. . . . Behind him there is the crackle of a chocolate-box, absurdly loud.* MOON *looks round. He and* BIRDBOOT *see each other. They are clearly known to each other. They acknowledge each other with constrained waves.* MOON *looks straight ahead.* BIRDBOOT *comes down to join him.*

Note: Almost always, MOON *and* BIRDBOOT *converse in tones suitable for an auditorium, sometimes a whisper. However good the acoustics might be, they will have to have microphones where they are sitting. The effect must be not of sound picked up, amplified and flung out at the audience, but of sound picked up, carried and gently dispersed around the auditorium.*

Anyway, BIRDBOOT, *with a box of Black Magic,*[1] *makes his way down to join* MOON *and plumps himself down next to him, plumpish middle-aged* BIRDBOOT *and younger taller, less-relaxed* MOON.

BIRDBOOT [*sitting down; conspiratorially*].   Me and the lads have had a meeting in the bar and decided its first-class family entertainment but if it goes on beyond half-past ten it's self-indulgent—pass it on . . . [*and laughs jovially*] I'm on my own tonight, don't mind if I join you?

MOON.   Hello, Birdboot.

BIRDBOOT.   Where's Higgs?

MOON.   I'm standing in.

MOON AND BIRDBOOT.   Where's Higgs?

MOON.   Every time.

10 BIRDBOOT.   What?

MOON.   It is as if we only existed one at a time, combining to achieve continuity. I keep space warm for Higgs. My presence defines his absence, his absence confirms my presence, his presence precludes mine. . . . When Higgs and I walk down this aisle together to claim our common seat, the oceans will fall into the sky and the trees will hang with fishes.

BIRDBOOT [*he has not been paying attention, looking around vaguely, now catches up*].   Where's Higgs?

MOON.   The very sight of me with a complimentary ticket is enough. The streets are impassable tonight, the country is rising and the cry goes up

20   from hill to hill—Where—is—Higgs? [*Small pause.*] Perhaps he's dead at last, or trapped in a lift somewhere, or succumbed to amnesia, wandering the land with his turn-ups[2] stuffed with ticket-stubs.

[BIRDBOOT *regards him doubtfully for a moment.*]

BIRDBOOT.   Yes. . . . Yes, well I didn't bring Myrtle tonight—not exactly her cup of tea, I thought, tonight.

MOON.   Over her head, you mean?

BIRDBOOT.   Well, no—I mean it's a sort of *thriller*, isn't it?

MOON.   Is it?

BIRDBOOT.   That's what I heard. Who killed thing?—no one will leave the house.

30 MOON.   I suppose so. Underneath.

BIRDBOOT.   *Underneath*? ! ? It's a whodunnit, man!—Look at it! [*They look at it. The room. The* BODY. *Silence.*] Has it started yet?

MOON.   Yes. [*Pause. They look at it.*]

BIRDBOOT.   Are you sure?

MOON.   It's a pause.

BIRDBOOT.   You can't start with a *pause*! If you want my opinion there's total panic back there. [*Laughs and subsides.*] Where's Higgs tonight, then?

MOON.   It will follow me to the grave and become my epitaph—Here lies Moon the second string: where's Higgs? . . . Sometimes I dream of revo-

---

[1] A popular English brand of boxed chocolate candies.
[2] Trouser cuffs.

40 lution, a bloody *coup d'état*[3] by the second rank—troupes of actors slaughtered by their understudies, magicians sawn in half by indefatigably
smiling glamour girls, cricket[4] teams wiped out by marauding bands of
twelfth men—I dream of champions chopped down by rabbit-punching
sparring partners while eternal bridesmaids turn and rape the bride-
grooms over the sausage rolls and parliamentary private secretaries plant
bombs in the Minister's Humber[5]—comedians die on provincial stages,
robbed of their feeds[6] by mutely triumphant stooges—and—march—an
army of assistants and deputies, the seconds-in-command, the runners-up,
the right-hand men—storming the palace gates wherein the second son
50 has already mounted the throne having committed regicide with a
croquet-mallet—stand-ins of the world stand up!—[*Beat.*] Sometimes I
dream of Higgs.

[*Pause.* BIRDBOOT *regards him doubtfully. He is at a loss, and grasps reality in the
form of his box of chocolates.*]

BIRDBOOT [*Chewing into mike*]   Have a chocolate!
MOON.   What kind?
BIRDBOOT [*Chewing into mike*].   Black Magic.
MOON.   No thanks.

[*Chewing stops dead.*]

[*Of such tiny victories and defeats. . . .*]

BIRDBOOT.   I'll give you a tip, then. Watch the girl.
MOON.   You think she did it?
BIRDBOOT.   No, no—the *girl*, watch her.
60 MOON.   What girl?
BIRDBOOT.   You won't know her, I'll give you a nudge.
MOON.   *You* know her, do you?
BIRDBOOT [*suspiciously, bridling*].   What's *that* supposed to mean?
MOON.   I beg your pardon?
BIRDBOOT.   I'm trying to tip you a wink—give you a nudge as good as a
tip—for God's sake, Moon, what's the matter with you?—you could do
yourself some good, spotting her first time out—she's new, from the prov-
inces, going straight to the top. I don't want to put words into your mouth
but a word from us and we could make her.
70 MOON.   I suppose you've made dozens of them, like that.
BIRDBOOT [*instantly outraged*].   I'll have you know I'm a family man devoted to
my homely but good-natured wife, and if you're suggesting—
MOON.   No, no—
BIRDBOOT.   —A man of my scrupulous morality—
MOON.   I'm sorry—

---

  [3] Overthrow of the government by force.
  [4] A popular English game somewhat like baseball, played by teams of eleven men. Twelfth
men are, therefore, substitutes.
  [5] A British make of automobiles.
  [6] I.e., robbed of the feed-lines usually recited by the straight man.

BIRDBOOT.   —falsely besmirched.

MOON.   Is that her? [*For* MRS. DRUDGE *has entered.*]

BIRDBOOT.   —don't be absurd, wouldn't be seen dead with the old—ah.

[MRS. DRUDGE *is the char, middle-aged, turbanned. She heads straight for the radio, dusting on the trot.*]

MOON [*reading his program*].   Mrs. Drudge the Help.

80 RADIO [*without preamble, having been switched on by* MRS. DRUDGE].   We inter-
rupt our program for a special police message. [MRS. DRUDGE *stops to listen.*]
The search still goes on for the escaped madman who is on the run in
Essex.[7]

MRS. DRUDGE [*fear and dismay*].   Essex!

RADIO.   County police led by Inspector Hound have received a report that
the man has been seen in the desolate marshes around Muldoon Manor.
[*Fearful gasp from* MRS. DRUDGE.] The man is wearing a darkish suit with a
lightish shirt. He is of medium height and build and youngish. Anyone
seeing a man answering to this description and acting suspiciously, is
90   advised to phone the nearest police station. [*A man answering this description
has appeared behind* MRS. DRUDGE. *He is acting suspiciously. He creeps in. He
creeps out.* MRS. DRUDGE *does not see him. He does not see the body.*] That is the
end of the police message. [MRS. DRUDGE *turns off the radio and resumes her
cleaning. She does not see the body. Quite fortuitously, her view of the body is always
blocked, and when it isn't she has her back to it. However, she is dusting and
polishing her way towards it.*]

BIRDBOOT.   So that's what they say about me, is it?

MOON.   What?

BIRDBOOT.   Oh, I know what goes on behind my back—sniggers—slanders—
100   hole-in-corner innuendo—What have you heard?

MOON.   Nothing.

BIRDBOOT [*urbanely*].   Tittle tattle. Tittle, my dear fellow, tattle. I take no
notice of it—the sly envy of scandal mongers—I can afford to ignore them,
I'm a respectable married man—

MOON.   Incidentally—

BIRDBOOT.   Water off a duck's back, I assure you.

MOON.   Who was that lady I saw you with last night?

BIRDBOOT [*unexpectedly stung into fury*].   How dare you! Don't you come here
with your slimy insinuations! My wife Myrtle understands perfectly well
110   that a man of my critical standing is obliged occasionally to mingle with
the world of the footlights, simply by way of keeping *au fait*[8] with the
latest—

MOON.   I'm sorry—

BIRDBOOT.   That a critic of my scrupulous integrity should be vilified and
pilloried in the stocks of common gossip—

MOON.   Ssssh—

BIRDBOOT.   I have nothing to hide!—why, if this should reach the ears of my
beloved Myrtle—

---

[7] A county on the eastern coast of England.

[8] Up to date.

MOON.   Can I have a chocolate?

120 BIRDBOOT.   What? Oh—[*Mollified.*] Oh yes—my dear fellow—yes, let's have a
chocolate—No point in—yes, good show. [*Pops chocolate into his mouth and
chews.*] Which one do you fancy?—Cherry? Strawberry? Coffee cream?
Turkish delight?[9]

MOON.   I'll have a montelimar.

[Chewing stops.]

BIRDBOOT.   Ah. sorry. [*Just missed that one.*]

MOON.   Gooseberry fondue?

BIRDBOOT.   No.

MOON.   Pistachio fudge? Nectarine cluster? Hickory nut praline? Creme de
menthe cracknell?

130 BIRDBOOT.   I'm afraid not. . . . Caramel?

MOON.   Yes, all right.

BIRDBOOT.   Thanks very much. [*He gives* MOON *a chocolate. Pause.*] Incidentally, old chap, I'd be grateful if you didn't mention—I mean, you know
how these misunderstandings get about. . . .

MOON.   What?

BIRDBOOT.   The fact is, Myrtle simply doesn't *like* the theatre. . . . [*He tails off
hopelessly.* MRS. DRUDGE, *whose discovery of the body has been imminent, now—by
way of tidying the room—slides the couch over the corpse, hiding it completely. She
resumes dusting and humming.*]

140 MOON.   By the way, congratulations, Birdboot.

BIRDBOOT.   What?

MOON.   At the Hippodrome.[10] Your entire review reproduced in neon!

BIRDBOOT [*pleased*].   Oh . . . that old thing.

MOON.   You've seen it, of course.

BIRDBOOT [*vaguely*].   Well, I was passing. . . .

MOON.   I definitely intend to take a second look when it has settled down.

BIRDBOOT.   As a matter of fact I have a few color transparencies—I don't
know whether you'd care to?

MOON.   Please, please—love to, love to. . . . [BIRDBOOT *hands over a few color*
150 *slides and a battery-powered viewer which* MOON *holds up to his eyes as he speaks.*]
Yes . . . yes . . . lovely . . . awfully sound. It has scale, it has color, it is, in
the best sense of the word, electric. Large as it is, it is a small masterpiece—I would go so far as to say—kinetic without being pop, and having
said that, I think it must be said that here we have a review that adds a new
dimension to the critical scene. I urge you to make haste to the Hippodrome, for this is the stuff of life itself.

BIRDBOOT.   Most handsome of you, Moon.

MOON [*viewing*].   A critic who is not afraid to say so when he's had a frankly
appalling putrid lousy night in the theater.

160 BIRDBOOT.   'Appallingly frank but ridiculously right in the theater'—they
haven't quite got the hang of the thing—

---

[9] All these are flavors of fillings of chocolate candy. Birdboot is consulting the diagram
inside the lid of the candy-box that shows where each flavor is located.

[10] The name of a theater in London.

MOON [*handing back the slides, morosely*].   All I ever got was "Unforgettable" out-side. . . . What was it?

[*The phone rings.* MRS. DRUDGE *seems to have been waiting for it to do so and for the last few seconds has been dusting it with an intense concentration. She snatches it up.*]

MRS. DRUDGE [*into phone*].   Hello, the drawing-room of Lady Muldoon's country residence one morning in early spring? . . . He*llo!*—the draw—Who? Who did you wish to speak to? I'm afraid there is no one of that name here, this is all very mysterious and I'm sure it's leading up to something, I hope nothing is amiss for we, that is Lady Muldoon and her houseguests, are here cut off from the world, including Magnus, the wheelchair-ridden
170   half-brother of her ladyship's husband Lord Albert Muldoon who ten years ago went out for a walk on the cliffs and was never seen again—and all alone, for they had no children.
MOON.   Derivative, of course.
BIRDBOOT.   But quite sound.
MRS. DRUDGE.   Should a stranger enter our midst, which I very much doubt, I will tell him you called. Good-bye. [*She puts down the phone and catches sight of the previously seen suspicious character who has now entered again, more suspiciously than ever, through the french windows. He senses her stare, freezes, and straightens up.*]
180 SIMON.   Ah!—hello there! I'm Simon Gascoyne, I hope you don't mind, the door was open so I wandered in. I'm a friend of Lady Muldoon, the lady of the house, having made her acquaintance through a mutual friend, Felicity Cunningham, shortly after moving into this neighborhood just the other day.
MRS. DRUDGE.   I'm Mrs. Drudge. I don't live in but I pop in on my bicycle when the weather allows to help in the running of charming though somewhat isolated Muldoon Manor. Judging by the time [*she glances at the clock*] you did well to get here before high water cut us off for all practical purposes from the outside world.
190 SIMON.   I took the short cut over the cliffs and followed one of the old smugglers' paths through the treacherous swamps that surround this strangely inaccessible house.
MRS. DRUDGE.   Yes, many visitors have remarked on the topographical quirk in the local strata whereby there are no roads leading from the Manor, though there *are* ways of getting *to* it, weather allowing.
SIMON.   Yes, well I must say it's a lovely day so far.
MRS. DRUDGE.   Ah, but now that the cuckoo-beard is in bud there'll be fog before the sun hits Foster's Ridge.
SIMON.   I say, it's wonderful how you country people really know weather.
200 MRS. DRUDGE [*suspiciously*].   Know whether what?
SIMON [*glancing out of the window*].   Yes, it does seem to be coming on a bit foggy.
MRS. DRUDGE.   The fog is very treacherous around here—it rolls off the sea without warning, shrouding the cliffs in a deadly mantle of blind man's bluff.
SIMON.   Yes, I've heard it said.

MRS. DRUDGE.   I've known whole week-ends when Muldoon Manor, as this
lovely old Queen Anne House[11] is called, might as well have been floating
on the pack ice for all the good it would have done phoning the police. It
210   was on such a week-end as this that Lord Muldoon who had lately brought
his beautiful bride back to the home of his ancestors, walked out of this
house ten years ago, and his body was never found.
SIMON.   Yes, indeed, poor Cynthia.
MRS. DRUDGE.   His name was Albert.
SIMON.   Yes indeed, poor Albert. But tell me, is Lady Muldoon about?
MRS. DRUDGE.   I believe she is playing tennis on the lawn with Felicity Cun-
ningham.
SIMON [*startled*].   Felicity Cunningham?
MRS. DRUDGE.   A mutual friend, I believe you said. A happy chance. I will tell
220   them you are here.
SIMON.   Well, I can't really stay as a matter of fact—please don't disturb
them—I really should be off.
MRS. DRUDGE.   They would be very disappointed. It is some time since we have
had a four for pontoon bridge at the Manor, and I don't play cards myself.
SIMON.   There is another guest, then?
MRS. DRUDGE.   Major Magnus, the crippled half-brother of Lord Muldoon
who turned up out of the blue from Canada just the other day, completes
the house-party. [MRS. DRUDGE *leaves on this,* SIMON *is undecided.*]
MOON [*ruminating quietly*].   I think I must be waiting for Higgs to die.
230 BIRDBOOT.   What?
MOON.   Half afraid that I will vanish when he does.

[*The phone rings.* SIMON *picks it up.*]

SIMON.   Hello?
MOON.   I wonder if it's the same for Macafferty?
BIRDBOOT AND SIMON [*together*].   Who?
MOON.   Third string.
BIRDBOOT.   Your stand-in?
MOON.   Does he wait for Higgs and I to write each other's obituary—does he
dream—?
SIMON.   To whom did you wish to speak?
240 BIRDBOOT.   What's he like?
MOON.   Bitter.
SIMON.   There is no one of that name here.
BIRDBOOT.   No—as a critic, what's Macafferty like as a critic?
MOON [*laughs poisonously*].   Nobody knows—
SIMON.   You must have got the wrong number!
MOON.   —he's never been called upon to criticise.

[SIMON *replaces the phone and paces nervously. Pause.* BIRDBOOT *consults his program.*]

---

[11]   During the reign of Queen Anne (1702–1714), most houses were built of red brick to
meet practical needs with only simple and dignified ornamentation.

BIRDBOOT. Simon Gascoyne. It's not him, of course.

MOON. What?

BIRDBOOT. I said it's not him.

250 MOON. Who is it, then?

BIRDBOOT. My guess is Magnus.

MOON. In disguise, you mean?

BIRDBOOT. What?

MOON. You think he's Magnus in disguise?

BIRDBOOT. I don't think you're concentrating, Moon.

MOON. I thought you said—

BIRDBOOT. You keep chattering on about Higgs and Macafferty—what's the matter with you?

MOON [*thoughtfully*]. I wonder if they talk about me. . . ?

[*A strange impulse makes* SIMON *turn on the radio.*]

260 RADIO. Here is another police message. Essex county police are still searching in vain for the madman who is at large in the deadly marshes of the coastal region. Inspector Hound who is masterminding the operation, is not available for comment but it is widely believed that he has a secret plan. . . . Meanwhile police and volunteers are combing the swamps with loud-hailers, shouting, "Don't be a madman, give yourself up." That is the end of the police message.

[SIMON *turns off the radio. He is clearly nervous.* MOON *and* BIRDBOOT *are on separate tracks.*]

BIRDBOOT [*knowingly*]. Oh yes. . . .

MOON. Yes, I should think my name is seldom off Macafferty's lips . . . sad, really. I mean, it's no life at all, a stand-in's stand-in.

270 BIRDBOOT. Yes . . . yes . . .

MOON. Higgs never gives me a second thought. I can tell by the way he nods.

BIRDBOOT. Revenge, of course.

MOON. What?

BIRDBOOT. Jealousy.

MOON. Nonsense—there's nothing *personal* in it—

BIRDBOOT. The paranoid grudge—

MOON [*sharply first, then starting to career . . .*]. It is merely that it is not enough to wax at another's wane, to be held in reserve, to be on hand, on
280 call, to step in or not at all, the substitute—the near offer—the temporary-acting—for I am Moon, continuous Moon, in my own shoes, Moon in June, April, September, and no member of the human race keeps warm my bit of space—yes, I can tell by the way he nods.

BIRDBOOT. Quite mad, of course.

MOON. What?

BIRDBOOT. The answer lies out there in the swamps.

MOON. Oh.

BIRDBOOT. The skeleton in the cupboard is coming home to roost.

MOON. Oh yes. [*He clears his throat . . . for both he and* BIRDBOOT *have a "public"*
290 *voice, a critic voice which they turn on for sustained pronouncements of opinion.*]

Already in the opening stages we note the classic impact of the catalystic figure—the outsider—plunging through to the center of an ordered world and setting up the disruptions—the shock waves—which unless I am much mistaken, will strip these comfortable people—these crustaceans in the rock pool of society—strip them of their shells and leave them exposed as the trembling raw meat which, at heart, is all of us. But there is more to it than that—

BIRDBOOT. I agree—keep your eye on Magnus.

[*A tennis ball bounces through the french windows, closely followed by* FELICITY, *who is in her twenties. She wears a pretty tennis outfit, and carries a racket.*]

FELICITY [*calling behind her*]. Out! [*It takes her a moment to notice* SIMON *who is*
300   *standing shiftily to one side.* MOON *is stirred by a memory.*]

MOON. I say, Birdboot. . . .

BIRDBOOT. That's the one.

FELICITY [*Catching sight of* SIMON]. You! [FELICITY's *manner at the moment is one of great surprise but some pleasure.*]

SIMON [*nervously*]. Er, yes—hello again.

FELICITY. What are you doing here?

SIMON. Well, I. . . .

MOON. She's—

BIRDBOOT. Ssh. . . .

310 SIMON. No doubt you're surprised to see me.

FELICITY. Honestly, darling, you really are extraordinary.

SIMON. Yes, well, here I am.

FELICITY. You must have been desperate to see me—I mean, I'm *flattered,* but couldn't it wait till I got back?

SIMON [*bravely*]. There is something you don't know.

FELICITY. What is it?

SIMON. Look, about the things I said—it may be that I got carried away a little—we both did—

FELICITY [*stiffly*]. What are you trying to say?

320 SIMON. I love another!

FELICITY. I see.

SIMON. I didn't make any promises—I merely—

FELICITY. You don't have to say any more—

SIMON. Oh, I didn't want to hurt you—

FELICITY. Of all the nerve!—to march in here to tell me that!

SIMON. Well, I didn't exactly—

FELICITY. You philandering coward—

SIMON. Let me explain—

FELICITY. This is hardly the time and place—you think you can barge in
330   anywhere, whatever I happen to be doing—

SIMON. But I want you to know that my admiration for you is sincere—I don't want you to think that I didn't mean those things I said—

FELICITY. I'll kill you for this, Simon Gascoyne! [*She leaves in tears, passing* MRS. DRUDGE *who has entered in time to overhear her last remark.*]

MOON. It was her.

BIRDBOOT. I told you—straight to the top—

MOON. No, no—

BIRDBOOT. Ssssh. . . .

SIMON [*to* MRS. DRUDGE]. Yes what is it?

340 MRS. DRUDGE. I have come to set up the card table, sir.

SIMON. I don't think I can stay.

MRS. DRUDGE. Oh, Lady Muldoon *will* be disappointed.

SIMON. Does she know I'm here?

MRS. DRUDGE. Oh yes, sir, I just told her and it put her in quite a tizzy.

SIMON. Really? . . . Well, I suppose now that I've cleared the air. . . . Quite a
tizzy, you say . . . really . . . really . . . [*He and* MRS. DRUDGE *start setting up
for card game.* MRS. DRUDGE *leaves when this is done.*]

MOON. Felicity!—she's the one.

BIRDBOOT. Nonsense—red herring.

350 MOON. I mean, it was *her!*

BIRDBOOT [*exasperated*]. *What* was?

MOON. That lady I saw you with last night!

BIRDBOOT [*inhales with fury*]. Are you suggesting that a man of my scrupulous
integrity would trade his pen for a mess of potage?! Simply because in the
course of my profession I happen to have struck up an acquaintance—to
have, that is, a warm regard, if you like, for a fellow toiler in the vineyard
of greasepaint—I find it simply intolerable to be pillified and villoried—

MOON. I never implied—

BIRDBOOT. —to find myself the object of uninformed malice, the petty slan-
360 ders of little men—

MOON. I'm sorry—

BIRDBOOT. —to suggest that my good opinion in a journal of unimpeachable
integrity is at the disposal of the first actress who gives me what I want—

MOON. Sssssh—

BIRDBOOT. A ladies' man! . . . Why, Myrtle and I have been together now
for—

[*Enter* LADY CYNTHIA MULDOON *through french windows. A beautiful woman in her
thirties. She wears a cocktail dress, is formally coiffured, and carries a tennis racket.
Her effect on* BIRDBOOT *is also impressive. He half rises and sinks back agape.*]

CYNTHIA [*entering*]. Simon! [*A dramatic freeze between her and* SIMON.]

BIRDBOOT. I *say*—who's that?

MOON. Lady Muldoon.

370 BIRDBOOT. No, I mean—who *is* she?

SIMON [*coming forward*]. Cynthia!

CYNTHIA. Don't say anything for a moment—just hold me.

[*He seizes her and glues his lips to hers, as they say. While their lips are glued*—]

BIRDBOOT. She's *beautiful*—a vision of eternal grace, a poem. . . .

MOON. I think she's got her mouth open.

[CYNTHIA *breaks away dramatically.*]

CYNTHIA. We can't go on meeting like this!

SIMON. We have nothing to be ashamed of!

CYNTHIA. But darling, this is madness!

SIMON.   Yes!—I am mad with love for you!

CYNTHIA.   Please—remember where we are!

380 SIMON.   Cynthia, I love you!

CYNTHIA.   Don't—I love Albert!

SIMON.   He's dead! [*Shaking her.*] Do you understand me—Albert's dead!

CYNTHIA.   No—I'll never give up hope! Let me go! We are not free!

SIMON.   I don't care, we were meant for each other—had we but met in time.

CYNTHIA.   You're a cad, Simon! You will use me and cast me aside as you have cast aside so many others.

SIMON.   No, Cynthia!—you can make me a better person!

CYNTHIA.   You're ruthless—so strong, so cruel—

[*Ruthlessly he kisses her.*]

MOON.   The son she never had, now projected in this handsome stranger
390   and transformed into lover—youth, vigor, the animal, the athlete as aesthete—breaking down the barriers at the deepest level of desire.

BIRDBOOT.   By jove, I think you're right. Her mouth *is* open.

MOON.   But an archetypal victim if ever I saw one.

BIRDBOOT.   Lucky devil.

[CYNTHIA *breaks away.* MRS. DRUDGE *has entered.*]

CYNTHIA.   Stop—can't you see you're making a fool of yourself!

SIMON.   I'll kill anyone who comes between us!

CYNTHIA.   Yes, what is it, Mrs. Drudge?

MRS. DRUDGE.   Should I close the windows, my lady? The fog is beginning to roll off the sea like a deadly—

400 CYNTHIA.   Yes, you'd better. It looks as if we're in for one of those days. Are the cards ready?

MRS. DRUDGE.   Yes, my lady.

CYNTHIA.   Would you tell Miss Cunningham we are waiting.

MRS. DRUDGE.   Yes, my lady.

CYNTHIA.   And fetch the Major down.

MRS. DRUDGE.   I think I hear him coming downstairs now [*as she leaves.*]

[*She does: the sound of a wheelchair approaching down several flights of stairs with landings in between. It arrives bearing* MAGNUS *at about 15 m.p.h., knocking* SIMON *over violently.*]

CYNTHIA.   Simon!

MAGNUS [*roaring*].   Never had a chance! Ran under the wheels!

CYNTHIA.   Darling, are you all right?

410 MAGNUS.   I have witnesses!

CYNTHIA.   Oh, Simon—say something!

SIMON [*sitting up suddenly*].   I'm most frightfully sorry.

MAGNUS [*shouting yet*].   How long have you been a pedestrian?

SIMON.   Ever since I could walk.

CYNTHIA.   Can you walk now. . . ? [SIMON *rises and walks.*] Thank God! Magnus, this is Simon Gascoyne.

MAGNUS.   What's he doing here?

CYNTHIA.   He just turned up.

MAGNUS.   Really? How do you like it here?

420 FELICITY [*who has just entered*].   So—you're still here.

CYNTHIA.   Of course he's still here. We're going to play cards. Now you two
sit there . . . and there . . . Simon you help me with this sofa . . . there—
[*The sofa is shoved towards the card table, once more revealing the corpse, though
not to the players.*] Right—who starts?

MAGNUS.   I do.

[*A continuous mumble of card talk under the dialogue, dovetailed as follows:*]

CYNTHIA [*as* MAGNUS *rhubarbs*[12]].   Simon just happend to drop by for a game
of cards.

FELICITY [*plays, then as* CYNTHIA *plays*].   He's a bit of a cheat you know—aren't
you, Simon?

430 SIMON [*plays*].   Call me what you like, but I hold the cards.

CYNTHIA.   Well done, Simon!

[*Cards are thrown down and* MAGNUS *pays* SIMON. CYNTHIA *deals.*]

FELICITY.   I hear there's a dangerous madman on the loose. Personally I
think he's been hiding out in the deserted cottage on the cliffs.

CYNTHIA.   Your opening, Simon.

FELICITY [*as* SIMON *and* CYNTHIA *play*].   I couldn't sleep last night and happening to glance out of the window I saw a strange light shining from that
direction. What's the matter Simon, you seem nervous.

[MAGNUS *plays*—SIMON, CYNTHIA, FELICITY, MAGNUS *again and* SIMON *again, who
wins.*]

CYNTHIA.   No!—Simon your luck's in tonight?

[MAGNUS *pays him again.*]

FELICITY [*getting up and stalking out*].   We shall see—the night is not over yet,
440   Simon Gascoyne!

MAGNUS [*wheeling himself out*].   Well, I think I'll go and oil my gun.

[SIMON *and* CYNTHIA *have stood up.*]

CYNTHIA.   I think Felicity suspects something.

SIMON.   Let her think what she likes.

CYNTHIA.   But she's acting as if—Simon, was there something between you
and Felicity?

SIMON.   No, no—it's over between her and me, Cynthia—it was a mere
passing fleeting thing we had—but now that I have found you—

CYNTHIA.   If I find that you have been untrue to me—if I find that you have
falsely seduced me from my dear husband Albert—I will kill you, Simon
450   Gascoyne!

[MRS. DRUDGE *has entered silently to witness this. On this tableau, pregnant with
significance, the act ends, the body still undiscovered. Perfunctory applause.* MOON
and BIRDBOOT *seem to be completely preoccupied, becoming audible, as it were.*]

---

[12] Chatters unintelligibly in a low voice (a theatrical term).

MOON.   Camps it around the Old Vic[13] in his opera cloak and passes me the
  tat.
BIRDBOOT.   Do you believe in love at first sight?
MOON.   It's not that I think I'm a better critic—
BIRDBOOT.   I feel my whole life changing—
MOON.   I am but it's not that.
BIRDBOOT.   Oh, the world will laugh at me, I know. . . .
MOON.   It is not that they are much in the way of shoes to step into. . . .
BIRDBOOT.   . . . call me an infatuated old fool. . . .
460 MOON.   . . . They are not.
BIRDBOOT.   . . . condemn me. . . .
MOON.   He is standing in my light, that is all.
BIRDBOOT.   . . . betrayer of my class . . .
MOON.   . . . an almost continuous eclipse, interrupted by the phenomenon
  of moonlight.
BIRDBOOT.   I don't care, I'm a gonner.
MOON.   And I dream. . . .
BIRDBOOT.   The Blue Angel[14] all over again.
MOON.   . . . of the day his temperature climbs through the top of his
470 head. . . .
BIRDBOOT.   Ah, the sweet madness of love . . .
MOON.   . . . of the spasm on the stairs . . .
BIRDBOOT.   Myrtle, farewell . . .
MOON.   . . . dreaming of the stair he'll never reach—
BIRDBOOT.   —for I only live but once. . . .
MOON.   Sometimes I dream that I've killed him.
BIRDBOOT.   What?
MOON.   What? [*They pull themselves together.*]
BIRDBOOT.   Yes . . . yes. . . . A beautiful performance, a collector's piece. I
480 shall say so.
MOON.   A very promising debut. I'll put in a good word.
BIRDBOOT.   It would be as hypocritical of me to withhold praise on grounds
  of personal feelings, as to withhold censure.
MOON.   You're right. Courageous.
BIRDBOOT.   Oh, I know what people will say—There goes Birdboot buttering
  up his latest—
MOON.   Ignore them—
BIRDBOOT.   But I rise above that—The fact is I genuinely believe her per-
  formance to be one of the summits in the range of contemporary the-
490 atre.
MOON.   Trim-buttocked, that's the word for her.
BIRDBOOT.   —the radiance, the inner sadness—
MOON.   Does she actually come across with it?
BIRDBOOT.   The part as written is a mere cypher but she manages to make
  Cynthia a real person—
MOON.   *Cynthia?*

---

[13] A theater in London famous for excellent productions of Shakespeare's plays.
[14] A film made in 1930 [remade in 1959] about a slinky performer in a Berlin nightclub who
lures a middle-aged English teacher into degeneracy and corruption.

BIRDBOOT. And should she, as a result, care to meet me over a drink, simply by way of er—thanking me, as it were—

MOON. Well, you fickle old bastard!

[BIRDBOOT *shudders to a halt and clears his throat.*]

500 BIRDBOOT. Well now—shaping up quite nicely, wouldn't you say?

MOON. Oh yes, yes. A nice trichotomy of forces. One must reserve judgement of course, until the confrontation, but I think it's pretty clear where we're heading.

BIRDBOOT. I agree. It's Magnus a mile off. [*Small pause.*]

MOON. What's Magnus a mile off?

BIRDBOOT. If we knew that we wouldn't be here.

MOON [*clears throat*]. Let me at once say that it has *élan*[15] while at the same time avoiding *éclat*.[16] Having said that, and I think it must be said, I am bound to ask—does this play know where it is going?

510 BIRDBOOT. Well, it seems open and shut to me, Moon—Magnus is not what he pretends to be and he's got his next victim marked down—

MOON. Does it, I repeat, declare its affiliations? There are moments, and I would not begrudge it this, when the play, if we can call it that, and I think on balance we can, aligns itself uncompromisingly on the side of life. *Je suis*,[17] it seems to be saying, *ergo sum*.[18] But is that enough? I think we are entitled to ask. For what in fact is this play concerned with? It is my belief that here we are concerned with what I have referred to elsewhere as the nature of identity. I think we are entitled to ask—and here one is irresistibly reminded of Voltaire's cry, "*Voilà!*"[19]—I think we are entitled to ask—

520 *Where is God?*

BIRDBOOT [*stunned*]. Who?

MOON. Go-od.

BIRDBOOT [*peeping furtively into his program*]. God?

MOON. I think we are entitled to ask.

[*The phone rings. The set re-illumines to reveal* CYNTHIA, FELICITY *and* MAGNUS *about to take coffee, which is being taken round by* MRS. DRUDGE. SIMON *is missing. The body lies in position.*]

MRS. DRUDGE [*into phone*]. The same, half an hour later? . . . No, I'm sorry—there's no one of that name here. [*She replaces phone and goes round with coffee. To* CYNTHIA.] Black or white, my lady.

CYNTHIA. White please.

[MRS. DRUDGE *pours.*]

MRS. DRUDGE [*to* FELICITY]. Black or white, miss?

530 FELICITY. White please.

[MRS. DRUDGE *pours.*]

---

[15] Impetuous ardor.
[16] Showiness.
[17] I am.
[18] Therefore I am.
[19] There it is!

MRS. DRUDGE [*to* MAGNUS].   Black or white, Major?
MAGNUS.   White please.

[*Ditto.*]

MRS. DRUDGE [*to* CYNTHIA].   Sugar, my lady?
CYNTHIA.   Yes please.

[*Puts sugar in.*]

MRS. DRUDGE [*to* FELICITY].   Sugar, miss?
FELICITY.   Yes please.

[*Ditto.*]

MRS. DRUDGE [*to* MAGNUS].   Sugar, Major?
MAGNUS.   Yes please.

[*Ditto.*]

MRS. DRUDGE [*to* CYNTHIA].   Biscuit, my lady?
540 CYNTHIA.   No thank you.
BIRDBOOT [*writing elaborately in his notebook*].   The second act, however, fails to
    fulfil the promise. . . .
FELICITY.   If you ask me, there's something funny going on. [MRS. DRUDGE'S
    approach to FELICITY *makes* FELICITY *jump to her feet in impatience. She goes to the
    radio while* MAGNUS *declines his biscuit, and* MRS. DRUDGE *leaves.*]
RADIO.   We interrupt our program for a special police message. The search
    for the dangerous madman who is on the loose in Essex has now narrowed
    to the immediate vicinity of Muldoon Manor. Police are hampered by the
    deadly swamps and the fog, but believe that the madman spent last night
550   in a deserted cottage on the cliffs. The public is advised to stick together
    and make sure none of their number is missing.

[FELICITY *turns off the radio nervously. Pause.*]

CYNTHIA.   Where's Simon?
FELICITY.   Who?
CYNTHIA.   Simon. Have you seen him?
FELICITY.   No.
CYNTHIA.   Have you, Magnus?
MAGNUS.   No.
CYNTHIA.   Oh.
FELICITY.   Yes, there's something foreboding in the air, it is as if one of
560   us—
CYNTHIA.   Oh, Felicity, the house is locked up tight—no one can get in—and
    the police are practically on the doorstep.
FELICITY.   I don't know—it's just a feeling.
CYNTHIA.   It's only the fog.
MAGNUS.   Hound will never get through on a day like this.
CYNTHIA [*shouting at him*].   *Fog!*
FELICITY.   He means the Inspector.
CYNTHIA.   Is he bringing a dog?
FELICITY.   Not that I know of.

570 MAGNUS. —never get through the swamps. Yes, I'm afraid the madman can show his hand in safety now.

> [*A mournful baying hooting is heard in the distance, scary.*]

CYNTHIA. What's that?!
FELICITY [*tensely*]. It sounded like the cry of a gigantic hound!
MAGNUS. Poor devil!
CYNTHIA. Ssssh!

> [*They listen.*]

BIRDBOOT. . . . That poise, that profile. . . .
MOON. Has it ever struck you that there are probably hundreds of undiscovered murders every year?
BIRDBOOT. . . . the siren[20] on her sea-washed rock, beckoning, beckon-
580 ing. . . .
MOON. One tends to assume that the only murders which *happen* are the ones one reads about—
BIRDBOOT. . . . I must go to her . . .
MOON. But of course it's probably quite easy, provided that one's motive is sufficiently obtuse.
BIRDBOOT. . . . I can't stop myself. . . .
MOON. Because if the *motive* defies precedent and understanding, it would never occur to the simple minds of the police or the neighbors to speculate on the possibility, which is the natural thing to do when, for instance,
590 a large legacy or a lover turns up.
BIRDBOOT. —even if I wake and drown.
MOON. Yes, if one wanted to get rid of someone for a perfectly impenetrable reason, one could get away with murder.

[*The baying has been repeated during the above, with exclamations, getting nearer until—*]

FELICITY. There it is again!
CYNTHIA. It's coming this way—it's right outside the house!

> [MRS. DRUDGE *enters.*]

MRS. DRUDGE. Inspector Hound!
CYNTHIA. A *police* dog?

[*Enter* INSPECTOR HOUND. *On his head he wears a sort of miner's helmet with a flashing light. On his feet are his swamp boots. These are two inflatable—and inflated—pontoons with flat bottoms about two feet across. He carries a foghorn.*]

HOUND. Lady Muldoon?
CYNTHIA. Yes.
600 HOUND. I came as soon as I could. Where shall I put my foghorn and my swamp boots?

---

[20] One of two mythological females in Homer's *Odyssey* whose singing lures seamen to destruction.

CYNTHIA. Mrs. Drudge will take them out. How very resourceful.

HOUND [*divesting himself of hat, boots and foghorn*]. It takes more than a bit of weather to keep a policeman from his duty.

[MRS. DRUDGE *leaves with chattels. A pause.*]

CYNTHIA. Oh—er, Inspector Hound—Felicity Cunningham, Major Magnus Muldoon.

HOUND. Good evening. [*He and* CYNTHIA *continue to look expectantly at each other.*]

CYNTHIA AND HOUND [*together*]. Well?—Sorry—

610 CYNTHIA. No, do go on.

HOUND. Thank you. Well, tell me about it in your own words—take your time, begin at the beginning and don't leave anything out.

CYNTHIA. I beg your pardon?

HOUND. Fear nothing. You are in safe hands now. I hope you haven't touched anything.

CYNTHIA. I'm afraid I don't understand.

HOUND. I'm Inspector Hound.

CYNTHIA. Yes.

HOUND. Well, what's it all about?

620 CYNTHIA. I really have no idea.

HOUND. How did it begin?

CYNTHIA. What?

HOUND. The . . . thing.

CYNTHIA. What thing?

HOUND [*rapidly losing confidence but exasperated*]. The trouble!

CYNTHIA. There hasn't *been* any trouble!

HOUND. Didn't you phone the police?

CYNTHIA. No.

FELICITY. I didn't.

630 MAGNUS. What for?

HOUND. I see. [*Pause.*] This puts me in a very difficult position [*A steady pause.*] Well, I'll be getting along, then. [*He moves towards the door.*]

CYNTHIA. I'm terribly sorry.

HOUND [*stiffly*]. That's perfectly all right.

CYNTHIA. Thank you so much for coming.

HOUND. Not at all. You never know, there might have been a serious matter.

CYNTHIA. Drink?

HOUND. More serious than that, even.

CYNTHIA [*correcting*]. Drink before you go?

640 HOUND. No thank you. [*Leaves.*]

CYNTHIA [*through the door*]. I do hope you find him.

HOUND [*reappearing at once*]. Find who, Madam?—out with it!

CYNTHIA. I thought you were looking for the lunatic.

HOUND. And what do you know about that?

CYNTHIA. It was on the radio.

HOUND. Was it, indeed? Well, that's what I'm here about, really. I didn't want to mention it because I didn't know how much you knew. No point in causing unnecessary panic, even with a murderer in our midst.

FELICITY. Murderer, did you say?

650 HOUND. Ah—so that was not on the radio?

CYNTHIA. Whom has he murdered, Inspector?

HOUND. Perhaps no one—yet. Let us hope we are in time.

MAGNUS. You believe he is in our midst, Inspector?

HOUND. I do. If anyone of you have recently encountered a youngish good-looking fellow in a smart suit, white shirt, hatless, well-spoken—someone possibly claiming to have just moved into the neighborhood, someone who on the surface seems as sane as you or I, then now is the time to speak.

FELICITY. Inspector—

CYNTHIA. No, Felicity!

660 MAGNUS. Is one of us in danger, Inspector?

HOUND. Didn't it strike you as odd that on his escape the madman made a beeline for Muldoon Manor? It is my guess that he bears a deep-seated grudge against someone in this very house! Lady Muldoon—where is your husband?

FELICITY. My husband?—you don't mean—?

HOUND. I don't know—but I have a reason to believe that one of you is the real McCoy!

FELICITY. The real what?

HOUND. William Herbert McCoy who as a young man, meeting the mad-
670 man in the street and being solicited for sixpence for a cup of tea, replied, "Why don't you do a decent day's work, you shifty old bag of horse manure," in Canada all those many years ago and went on to make his fortune. [*He starts to pace intensely.*] The madman was a mere boy at the time but he never forgot that moment, and thenceforth carried in his heart the promise of revenge! [*At which point he finds himself standing on top of the corpse. He looks down carefully.*]

HOUND. Is there anything you have forgotten to tell me? [*They all see the corpse for the first time.*]

FELICITY. So the madman has struck!

680 CYNTHIA. Oh—it's horrible—horrible—

HOUND. Yes, just as I feared. Now you see the sort of man you are protecting.

CYNTHIA. I can't believe it!

FELICITY. I'll have to tell him, Cynthia—Inspector, a stranger of that description has indeed appeared in our midst—Simon Gascoyne. Oh, he had charm, I'll give you that, and he took me in completely. I'm afraid I made a fool of myself over him, and so did Cynthia.

HOUND. Where is he now?

MAGNUS. He must be around the house—he couldn't get away in these
690 conditions.

HOUND. You're right. Fear naught, Lady Muldoon—I shall apprehend the man who killed your husband.

CYNTHIA. My husband? I don't understand.

HOUND. Everything points to Gascoyne.

CYNTHIA. But who's that? [*The corpse.*]

HOUND. Your husband.

CYNTHIA. No, it's not.

HOUND. Yes, it is.
CYNTHIA. I tell you it's not.
700 HOUND. Are you sure?
CYNTHIA. For goodness sake!
HOUND. Then who is it?
CYNTHIA. I don't know.
HOUND. Anybody?
FELICITY. I've never seen him before.
MAGNUS. Quite unlike anybody I've ever met.
HOUND. I seem to have made a dreadful mistake. Lady Muldoon, I do
   apologize.
CYNTHIA. But what are we going to do?
710 HOUND [*snatching the phone*]. I'll phone the police!
CYNTHIA. But you are the police!
HOUND. Thank God I'm here—the lines have been cut!
CYNTHIA. You mean—?
HOUND. Yes!—we're on our own, cut off from the world and in grave dan-
   ger!
FELICITY. You mean—?
HOUND. Yes!—I think the killer will strike again!
MAGNUS. You mean—?
HOUND. Yes! One of us ordinary mortals thrown together by fate and cut off
720   by the elements, is the murderer! He must be found—search the house!

[*All depart speedily in different directions leaving a momentarily empty stage.* SIMON
strolls on.]

SIMON [*entering, calling*]. Anyone about?—funny. . . . [*He notices the corpse and
   is surprised. He approaches it and turns it over. He stands up and looks about in
   alarm. There is a shot.* SIMON *falls dead.* INSPECTOR HOUND *runs on and crouches
   down by* SIMON's *body.* CYNTHIA *appears at the french windows. She stops there and
   stares.*]
CYNTHIA. What happened, Inspector?!

[HOUND *turns to face her.*]

HOUND. He's dead. . . . [*He stands up thoughtfully.*] So we were all wrong,
   after all. We assumed that the body could not have been lying here before
   Simon Gascoyne entered the house . . . but . . . [*he slides the sofa over the
730 body*] . . . there's your answer. And now—who killed Simon Gascoyne? And
   why?

["CURTAIN": FREEZE, APPLAUSE, EXEUNT.]

BIRDBOOT. Obviously I wouldn't want to hurt Myrtle. . . .
MOON. I've just had a rather ghastly thought. . . .
BIRDBOOT. But I'm a creative sort of person—artistic you might say . . .
MOON. . . . even if I did, and got away with it, there'd still be Macafferty
   behind me. . . .
BIRDBOOT. . . . A free spirit, really—
MOON. . . . and if I could, so could he.

BIRDBOOT.   Yes, I know of this rather nice hotel, very discreet, run by a man
740   of the world—

MOON.   Does Macafferty dream of me?

BIRDBOOT.   Breakfast served in one's room and no questions asked—[*wakes
    up*]. Hello—what's happened?

MOON.   What? Oh yes—what do you make of it, so far?

BIRDBOOT [*clears throat*].   It is at this point that the play for me comes alive.
    The groundwork has been well and truly laid, and the author has taken
    the trouble to learn from the masters of the genre. He has created a real
    situation, and few will doubt his ability to resolve it with a startling de-
    nouement. Certainly that is what it so far lacks, but it has a beginning, a
750   middle and I have no doubt it will prove to have an end. For this let us give
    thanks, and double thanks for a good clean show without a trace of smut.
    But perhaps even all this would be for nothing were it not for a perfor-
    mance which I consider to be one of the summits in the range of contem-
    porary theatre. In what is possibly the finest Cynthia since the war—

MOON.   If we examine this more closely, and I think close examination is the
    least tribute that this play deserves, I think we will find that within the
    austere framework of what is seen to be on one level a country-house
    weekend, and what a useful symbol that is, the author has given us—yes,
    I will go so far—he has given us the human condition—

760 BIRDBOOT.   More talent in her little finger—

MOON.   An uncanny ear that might have belonged to a Van Gogh[21]—

BIRDBOOT.   —a public scandal that the Birthday Honors[22] to date have ne-
    glected—

MOON.   Faced as we are with such ubiquitous obliquity, it is hard, it is hard
    indeed, and therefore I will not attempt, to refrain from invoking the
    names of Kafka, Sartre, Shakespeare, St. Paul, Beckett, Birkett, Pinero,
    Pirandello, Dante and Dorothy L. Sayers.[23]

BIRDBOOT.   A rattling good evening out. I was held.

[*The phone starts to ring on the empty stage.* MOON *tries to ignore it.*]

MOON.   Harder still—Harder still if impossible—Harder still if it is possible
770   to be—Neither do I find it easy—Dante and Dorothy L. Sayers. Harder
    still—

BIRDBOOT.   Others taking part included—*Moon!*

[*For* MOON *has lost patience and is bearing down on the ringing phone. He is frankly
irritated.*]

MOON [*picking up phone, barks*].   Hel-lo! [*Pause, turns to* BIRDBOOT, *quietly.*] It's
    for you. [*Pause.*]

---

[21] A Dutch painter [1853–1890] who cut off his own ear in 1888.

[22] The Birthday Honors are titles or other signs of recognition bestowed by the British
Sovereign at the ruler's birthday celebration.

[23] This idiosyncratic list of world authors is notable primarily because of the omission of
Agatha Christie whose play, *The Mousetrap*, is imitated and parodied throughout *The Real Inspector Hound*.

[BIRDBOOT *gets up. He approaches cautiously.* MOON *gives him the phone and moves back to his seat.* BIRDBOOT *watches him go. He looks round and smiles weakly, expiating himself.*]

BIRDBOOT [*into phone*].   Hello. . . . [*Explosion.*] Oh, for God's sake, Myrtle!— I've told you never to phone me at work! [*He is naturally embarrassed, looking about with surreptitious fury.*] What? Last night? Good God, woman, this is hardly the time—I assure you, Myrtle, there is absolutely nothing going on between me and—that's a complete lie. I took her to dinner
780   simply by way of keeping *au fait* with the world of the paint and the motley[24]—That's nothing to do with her, I'm here simply doing my job— yes, I promise—Yes, I do—Yes, I *said* yes—I *do*—and you are mine too, Myrtle—darling—I can't—[*whispers*] *I'm not alone*—[*up.*]. No, she's not!— [*He looks around furtively, licks his lips and mumbles.*] All *right*! I love your little pink ears and you are my own fluffy bunny-boo—Now for God's sake— Good-bye, Myrtle—[*Puts down phone.* BIRDBOOT *mops his brow with his handkerchief. As he turns, a tennis ball bounces in through the french windows, followed by* FELICITY, *as before, in tennis outfit. The lighting is as it was. Everything is as it was. It is, let us say, the same moment of time. The only difference is that* FELICITY
790   *must be allowed changes of inflection and emphasis which now also "go with" the fact of a critic appearing in the middle of a play.*]
FELICITY [*calling*].   Out! [*She catches sight of* BIRDBOOT *and is amazed.*] You!
BIRDBOOT.   Er, yes—hello again.
FELICITY.   What are you doing here?!
BIRDBOOT.   Well, I . . .
FELICITY.   Honestly, darling, you really are extraordinary—
BIRDBOOT.   Yes, well, here I am. [*He looks round sheepishly.*]
FELICITY.   You must have been desperate to see me—I mean, I'm flattered, but couldn't it wait till I got back?
800   BIRDBOOT.   No, no, you've got it all wrong—
FELICITY.   What is it?
BIRDBOOT.   And about last night—perhaps I gave you the wrong impression—got carried away a bit, perhaps—
FELICITY [*stiffly*].   What are you trying to say?
BIRDBOOT.   I want to call it off.
FELICITY.   I see.
BIRDBOOT.   I didn't promise anything—and the fact is, I have my reputation—people do talk—
FELICITY.   You don't have to say any more—
810   BIRDBOOT.   And my wife, too—I don't know how she got to hear of it, but—
FELICITY.   Of all the nerve! To march in here and—
BIRDBOOT.   I'm sorry you had to find out like this—the fact is I didn't mean it this way—
FELICITY.   You philandering coward!
BIRDBOOT.   I'm sorry—but I want you to know that I meant those things I said—oh yes—shows brilliant promise—I shall say so—

---

[24] Grease paint and harlequin (clown-like) costume; i.e., the world of the theater.

FELICITY. I'll kill you for this, Simon Gascoyne! [*She leaves in tears, passing* MRS. DRUDGE *who has entered in time to overhear her last remark.*]

BIRDBOOT [*wide-eyed*]. Good God. . . .

820 MRS. DRUDGE. I have come to set up the card table, sir.

BIRDBOOT [*wildly*]. I can't stay for a game of *cards!*

MRS. DRUDGE. Oh, Lady Muldoon *will* be disappointed.

BIRDBOOT. You mean . . . you mean, she wants to meet me. . . ?

MRS. DRUDGE. Oh yes, sir, I just told her and it put her in quite a tizzy.

BIRDBOOT. Really? Yes, well, a man of my influence is not to be sneezed at— I think I have some small name for the making of reputations—mmm, yes, quite a tizzy, you say?

[MRS. DRUDGE *is busied with the card table.* BIRDBOOT *stands marooned and bemused for a moment.*]

MOON [*from his seat*]. Birdboot!—[*a tense whisper*]. Birdboot! [BIRDBOOT *looks round vaguely.*] What the hell are you doing?

830 BIRDBOOT. Nothing.

MOON. Stop making an ass of yourself. Come back.

BIRDBOOT. Oh, I know what you're thinking—but the fact is I genuinely consider her performance to be one of the summits—

[CYNTHIA *enters as before.* MRS. DRUDGE *has gone.*]

CYNTHIA. Darling!

BIRDBOOT. Ah, good evening—may I say that I genuinely consider—

CYNTHIA. Don't say anything for a moment—just hold me. [*She falls into his arms.*]

BIRDBOOT. All right!—let us throw off the hollow pretences of the gimcrack codes we live by! Dear lady, from the first moment I saw you, I felt my 840 whole life changing—

CYNTHIA [*breaking free*]. We can't go on meeting like this!

BIRDBOOT. I am not ashamed to proclaim nightly my love for you!—but fortunately that will not be necessary—I know of a very good hotel, discreet—run by a man of the world—

CYNTHIA. But darling, this is madness!

BIRDBOOT. Yes! I am mad with love.

CYNTHIA. Please!—remember where we are!

BIRDBOOT. I don't care! Let them think what they like, I love you!

CYNTHIA. Don't—I love Albert!

850 BIRDBOOT. He's dead. [*Shaking her.*] Do you understand me—Albert's dead!

CYNTHIA. No—I'll never give up hope! Let me go! We are not free!

BIRDBOOT. You mean Myrtle? She means nothing to me—nothing!—she's all cocoa and blue nylon fur slippers—not a spark of creative genius in her whole slumping knee-length-knickered[25] body—

CYNTHIA. You're a cad, Simon! You will use me and cast me aside as you have cast aside so many others!

BIRDBOOT. No, Cynthia—now that I have found you—

CYNTHIA. You're ruthless—so strong—so cruel—

---

[25] *Knickers* in England means women's underdrawers.

[BIRDBOOT *seizes her in an embrace, during which* MRS. DRUDGE *enters, and* MOON's *fevered voice is heard.*]

MOON.   Have you taken leave of your tiny mind?

[CYNTHIA *breaks free.*]

860 CYNTHIA.   Stop—can't you see you're making a fool of yourself!
MOON.   She's right.
BIRDBOOT [*to* MOON].   You keep out of this.
CYNTHIA.   Yes, what is it, Mrs. Drudge?
MRS. DRUDGE.   Should I close the windows, my lady? The fog—
CYNTHIA.   Yes, you'd better.
MOON.   Look, they've got your number—
BIRDBOOT.   I'll leave in my own time, thank you very much.
MOON.   It's the finish of you, I suppose you know that—
BIRDBOOT.   I don't need your twopenny Grubb Street prognostications—I
870   have found something bigger and finer—
MOON [*bemused, to himself*].   If only it were Higgs. . . .
CYNTHIA.   . . . And fetch the Major down.
MRS. DRUDGE.   I think I hear him coming down stairs now.

[*She leaves. The sound of a wheelchair's approach as before.* BIRDBOOT *prudently keeps out of the chair's former path but it enters from the next wing down and knocks him flying. A babble of anguish and protestation.*]

CYNTHIA.   Simon—say something!
BIRDBOOT.   That reckless bastard [*as he sits up*].
CYNTHIA.   Thank God!—
MAGNUS.   What's *he* doing here?
CYNTHIA.   He just turned up.
MAGNUS.   Really? How do you like it here?
880 BIRDBOOT.   I couldn't take it night after night.

[BIRDBOOT *limps across towards* MOON.]

BIRDBOOT.   Did you see that? I *told* you it was Magnus. Not that it *is* Magnus.
MOON.   What do you mean?
BIRDBOOT.   There's more in this than meets the eye, Moon.
MOON.   I don't know what you're talking about. For heaven's sake sit down—
    have a chocolate—relax—they've got no right—
BIRDBOOT [*looking over his shoulder*].   They need me to make up a four—

[*The card scene is set-up, the sofa moved, the body visible.* BIRDBOOT *takes his place. The card game of course dovetails into the game on page 1264, the dialogue of which is here reduced to stewed rhubarb, while the former rhubarb becomes as follows:*]

CYNTHIA.   Who starts?
MAGNUS.   I do. I'll dummy for a no-bid ruff and double my holding on
    south's queen. [*He does various things with cards.*]
890 FELICITY.   Pay twenty-ones or trump my contract.
CYNTHIA.   I'll trump your contract with five dummy's no-trump *there* [*dis-

cards] and I'll move West's rook for the re-bid with a banker ruff on his second trick *there. [Discards.]* Simon?

BIRDBOOT [*stupefied*]. Would you mind doing that again?

CYNTHIA [*takes back cards*]. —and I'll ruff your dummy with five no-bid trumps there [*discards*] and I support your rebid with a banker for the solo ruff in dummy trick there. [*Discards.*]

[BIRDBOOT *angrily gets to his feet and throws down his cards.*]

BIRDBOOT. And I'll call your bluff!

CYNTHIA. Well done, Simon! [*As they all inspect his cards.* MAGNUS *pays* SIMON
900   *about £50 in notes, while* CYNTHIA *deals.*] Right, Simon, it's your opening on the minor bid.

[BIRDBOOT *pockets the money warily. After looking carefully at the other players he gingerly extracts a card from his hand and puts it down.*]

CYNTHIA. Hm—hm—Let's see. I think I'll overbid the spade convention with two no-trumps and King's gambit offered there [*discards*] and West's dummy split double to QB4 there! Partner?

[MAGNUS *rolls dice.*]

MAGNUS [*disgusted*]. Snake eyes!

CYNTHIA. Simon?

BIRDBOOT [*triumphantly*]. I call your bluff!

CYNTHIA [*imperturbably*]. I meld.

FELICITY. I huff.
910   MAGNUS. I ruff.

BIRDBOOT. I bluff.

CYNTHIA. Twist.

FELICITY. I'll see you!

MAGNUS [*dice*]. Double top!

BIRDBOOT [*hysterically*]. Bingo!

CYNTHIA. No!—Simon, your luck's in tonight!

[MAGNUS *counts out another wad of money for* BIRDBOOT, *and finally jiggles around in his trouser pocket for a coin to add to the pile of notes. Meanwhile:*]

FELICITY [*leaving*]. We shall see, the night is not over yet, Simon Gascoyne!

[*But* BIRDBOOT *is staring at* MAGNUS.]

BIRDBOOT. Excuse me, but haven't I seen you somewhere before? There's something about you ... your voice. . . . [MAGNUS *keeps counting money.*]
920   Where was it?—I must have seen you in something—and yet, I don't think it was quite that—

MAGNUS [*departing*]. Well, I think I'm going to oil my gun.

CYNTHIA. I think Felicity suspects something.

BIRDBOOT [*watching* MAGNUS, *abstracted*]. What?

CYNTHIA. Simon—was there anything between you and Felicity?

BIRDBOOT [*coming round*]. No, no—that's all over now—I merely flattered her a little over a drink, told her she'd go far, that sort of thing—dear me, the fuss that's been made about a little flirtation—

CYNTHIA [*as* MRS. DRUDGE *enters behind*].   If I find you have falsely seduced me
930   from my dear husband Albert, I will kill you, Simon Gascoyne!

[*The* "CURTAIN" *as before.* MRS. DRUDGE *and* CYNTHIA *leave.* BIRDBOOT *starts to follow them.*]

MOON.   *Birdboot!*

[BIRDBOOT *stops.*]

MOON.   For God's sake pull yourself together.
BIRDBOOT.   I can't help it.
MOON.   What do you think you're doing? You're turning it into a complete
         farce!
BIRDBOOT.   I know, I know—but I can't live without her. [*He is making erratic
         neurotic journeys about the stage.*] I shall resign my position, of course. I don't
         care I'm a gonner, I tell you— [*He has arrived at the body. He looks at it in
         surprise, hesitates, bends and turns it over.*]
940   MOON.   Birdboot, think of your family, your friends—your high standing in
         the world of letters—I say, what are you doing? [BIRDBOOT *is staring at the
         body's face.*] Birdboot . . . leave it alone. Come and sit down—what's the
         matter with you?
BIRDBOOT [*dead-voiced*].   It's Higgs.
MOON.   What?
BIRDBOOT.   It's Higgs. [*Pause.*]
MOON.   Don't be silly.
BIRDBOOT.   I tell you it's Higgs! [MOON *half rises. Bewildered.*] I don't under-
         stand. . . . He's dead.
950   MOON.   Dead?
BIRDBOOT.   Who would want to. . . ?
MOON.   He must have been lying there all the time. . . .
BIRDBOOT.   . . . kill Higgs?
MOON.   But what's he doing here? I was standing in tonight. . . .
BIRDBOOT [*turning*].   Moon? . . .
MOON [*faltering*].   But I swear I. . . .
BIRDBOOT.   I've got it—
MOON.   But I didn't—
BIRDBOOT [*quietly*].   My God . . . so that was it. . . . [*Up.*] Moon—now I see—
960   MOON.   —I swear I didn't—
BIRDBOOT.   Now—finally—I see it all—

[*There is a shot and* BIRDBOOT *falls dead.*]

MOON.   Birdboot! [*He runs on, to* BIRDBOOT'*s body.*]

[CYNTHIA *appears at the french windows. She stops and stares. All as before.*]

CYNTHIA.   Oh my God—what happened, Inspector?

[MOON *turns to face her. He stands up and makes swiftly for his seat. Before he gets
there he is stopped by the sound of voices.* SIMON *and* HOUND *are occupying the critics'
seats.* MOON *freezes.*]

SIMON.   To say that it is without pace, point, focus, interest, drama, wit or
         originality is to say simply that it does not happen to be my cup of tea. One

has only to compare this ragbag with the masters of the genre to see that here we have a trifle that is not my cup of tea at all.

HOUND.   I'm sorry to be blunt but there is no getting away from it. It lacks pace. A complete ragbag.

970 SIMON.   I will go further. Those of you who were fortunate enough to be at the Comedie Francaise on Wednesday last, will not need to be reminded that hysterics are no substitute for *éclat*.

HOUND.   It lacks *élan*.

SIMON.   Some of the cast seem to have given up acting altogether, apparently aghast, with every reason, at finding themselves involved in an evening that would, and indeed will, make the angels weep.

HOUND.   I am not a prude but I fail to see any reason for the shower of filth and sexual allusion foisted on to an unsuspecting public in the guise of modernity at all costs. . . .

[*Behind* MOON, FELICITY, MAGNUS *and* MRS. DRUDGE *have made their entrances, so that he turns to face their semi-circle.*]

980 MAGNUS [*pointing to* BIRDBOOT'*s body*].   Well, Inspector, is this your man?

MOON [*warily*].   . . . Yes. . . . Yes. . . .

CYNTHIA.   It's Simon . . .

MOON.   Yes . . . yes . . . poor. . . . [*Up.*] Is this some kind of a joke?

MAGNUS.   If it is, Inspector, it's in very poor taste.

[MOON *pulls himself together and becomes galvanic, a little wild, in grief for* BIRD-BOOT.]

MOON.   All right! I'm going to find out who did this! I want everyone to go to the positions they occupied when the shot was fired—[*they move; hysterically*]: No one will leave the house! [*They move back.*]

MAGNUS.   I think we all had the opportunity to fire the shot, Inspector—but which of us would want to?

990 MOON.   Perhaps you, Major Magnus!

MAGNUS.   Why should I want to kill him!

MOON.   Because he discovered your secret!

MAGNUS.   What secret?

MOON.   *I* don't know—I think that lets me out of it pretty conclusively.

MRS. DRUDGE.   Excuse me, sir?

MOON.   Yes?

MRS. DRUDGE.   Happening to enter this room earlier in the day to set up the card table, I chanced to overhear a remark made by the deceased to her ladyship, viz., "I will kill anyone who comes between us."

1000 MOON.   Exactly!—an obvious reference to the first corpse.

CYNTHIA.   But he didn't come between us!

MAGNUS.   And who, then, killed Simon?

MRS. DRUDGE.   Subsequent to that reported remark, I also happened to be in earshot of a remark made by Lady Muldoon to the deceased, to the effect, "I will kill you, Simon Gascoyne!" I hope you don't mind my mentioning it.

MOON.   Not at all. I'm glad you did. It is from these chance remarks that we in the force build up our complete picture before moving in to make the

1010

arrest. It will not be long now, I fancy, and I must warn you, Lady Muldoon that anything you say—

CYNTHIA.   Yes!—I hated Simon Gascoyne, for he had me in his power!—But I didn't kill him!

MRS. DRUDGE.   Prior to that, Inspector, I also chanced to overhear a remark made by Miss Cunningham, no doubt in the heat of the moment, but it stuck in my mind as these things do, viz. "I will kill you for this, Simon Gascoyne!"

MOON.   Ah! The final piece of the jigsaw! I think I am now in a position to reveal the mystery. This man [*the corpse*] was, of course, McCoy, the Ca-

1020

nadian who, as we heard, meeting Gascoyne in the street and being so-licited for sixpence for a toffee apple, smacked him across the ear, with the cry, "How's that for a grudge to harbor, you sniffling little workshy!" all those many years ago. Gascoyne bided his time, but in due course tracked McCoy down to this house, having, on the way, met, in the neighborhood, a simple ambitious girl from the provinces. He was charming, persua-sive—told her, I have no doubt, that she would go straight to the top—and she, flattered by his sophistication, taken in by his promises to see her all right on the night, gave in to his simple desires. Perhaps she loved him. We shall never know. But in the very hour of her promised triumph, his eye fell on another—yes, I refer to Lady Cynthia Muldoon. From the

1030

moment he caught sight of her there was no other woman for him—he was in her spell, willing to sacrifice anything, even you, Felicity Cunningham. It was only today—unexpectedly finding him here—that you learned the truth. There was a bitter argument which ended with your promise to kill him—a promise that you carried out in this very room at your first op-portunity! And I must warn you that anything you say—

FELICITY.   But it doesn't make sense!

MOON.   Not at first glance, *perhaps*.

CYNTHIA.   So! So Simon was not the only murderer in our midst.

MAGNUS.   If indeed he was a murderer at all. Could not McCoy have been

1040

killed by the same person who killed Simon? Suppose Simon, as you surmised, Inspector, discovered the killer's secret.

FELICITY.   But why should any of us want to kill a perfect stranger?

MAGNUS.   Perhaps he was not a stranger to *one* of us.

MOON [*faltering*].   But Simon was the madman, wasn't he?

MAGNUS.   We only have your word for that, Inspector. We only have your word for a lot of things. For instance—McCoy. Who is he? Is his name McCoy? Is there any truth in that fantastic and implausible tale of the insult inflicted in the Canadian streets? Or is there something else, some-thing quite unknown to us, behind all this? Suppose for a moment that the

1050

madman, having killed this unknown stranger for private and inscrutable reasons of his own, was disturbed before he could dispose of the body, so having cut the telephone wires he decided to return to the scene of the crime, masquerading as—Police Inspector Hound!

MOON.   But . . . I'm not mad . . . I'm almost sure I'm not mad. . . .

MAGNUS.   . . . only to discover that in the house was a man, Simon Gascoyne, who happened to be a former inmate of the same asylum, and who, moreover, recognized the corpse as a man against whom you had held a deep-seated grudge—!

MOON.   But I didn't kill—I'm almost sure I—

1060   MAGNUS.   I put it to you!—are you the real Inspector Hound?!

MOON.   You know damn well I'm not! What's it all about?—I didn't kill
      anyone!

MAGNUS.   I'm afraid it all fits.

MOON.   I only dreamed . . . sometimes I dreamed—

CYNTHIA.   So it was you!

MRS. DRUDGE.   The madman!

FELICITY.   What made you realize that he was the lunatic, Major?

MAGNUS.   It was his funny hat which first put me on to it. But that wasn't
      all—you see, we had a shrewd suspicion he would turn up here—and he

1070   walked into the trap!

MOON.   What *trap*?

MAGNUS.   I am not the real Magnus Muldoon!—It was a mere subterfuge!—
      and [*standing up and removing his moustaches*] I now reveal myself as—

MOON [*recoils*].   Macafferty!

CYNTHIA.   You mean—?

MAGNUS.   Yes!—I am the real Inspector Hound!

MOON.   Macafferty. . . .

MAGNUS [*with pistol*].   Stand where you are, or I shoot!

MOON [*backing*].   You killed Higgs—and Birdboot tried to tell me—

1080   MAGNUS.   Stop in the name of the law! [MOON *turns to run.* MAGNUS *fires.* MOON
      drops to his knees.] He has paid his debt to society.

CYNTHIA.   So you are the real Inspector Hound.

MAGNUS.   Not only that!—I have been leading a double life—at *least!*

CYNTHIA.   You mean—?

MAGNUS.   Yes!—It's been ten long years, but don't you know me?

CYNTHIA.   You mean—?

MAGNUS.   Yes!—it is me, Albert!—who lost his memory and joined the force,
      rising by merit to the rank of Inspector, his past blotted out—until fate
      cast him back into the home he left behind, back to the beautiful woman

1090   he had brought here as his girlish bride—in short, my darling, my mem-
      ory has returned and your long wait is over!

CYNTHIA.   Oh, Albert!

[*They embrace.*]

MOON [*with a trace of admiration*].   Macafferty! . . . you cunning bastard.

[MOON *dies.*]

THE END

[1968]

Critical Commentary on *The Real Inspector Hound*

The Real Inspector Hound was the first stage play Stoppard completed after the
enormous success of *Rosencrantz and Guildenstern Are Dead*, and like its predecessor it profited from revision over a period of years. As in *Rosencrantz and
Guildenstern*, Stoppard attempts to entangle the audience in the play itself by

confusing the ordinarily sharp distinctions between reality, the action in the theater, and the action in a play-within-the-play. In this case two critics, who are ostensibly members of the audience, become involved in the action on stage and ultimately perish. They and the other major characters in the play all have multiple identities and multiple roles in the play's various fictional levels. The result is that Stoppard successfully demonstrates the relativity of reality: the meaning of any event depends very much on the perspective from which it is viewed and the assumptions made in explaining it.

Stoppard's delight in confusing appearance and reality is evident even in the basic description of the setting: "The first thing is that the audience appear to be confronted by their own reflection in a huge mirror." It is doubtful that Stoppard really wishes us to believe ourselves reflected in the personalities of Birdboot, Moon, and the other eccentric characters in the play, all of whom are too ridiculous to be wholly realistic. More likely, he is simply exploring (and undermining) the theatrical convention that a play takes place in a fictional world without direct ties to the real world.

Stoppard once again undermines conventions and questions the distinctions between theater and reality when Birdboot and Moon first begin to discuss the play they have come to see:

> BIRDBOOT. Yes. . . . Yes, well I didn't bring Myrtle tonight—not exactly her cup of tea, I thought, tonight.
> MOON. Over her head, you mean?
> BIRDBOOT. Well, no—I mean it's a sort of *thriller*, isn't it?
> MOON. Is it?
> BIRDBOOT. That's what I heard. Who killed thing?—no one will leave the house.
> MOON. I suppose so. Underneath.
> BIRDBOOT. *Underneath?!?* It's a whodunit, man!—Look at it! [*They look at it. The room. The body. Silence.*] Has it started yet?
> MOON. Yes. [*Pause. They look at it.*]
> BIRDBOOT. Are you sure?
> MOON. It's a pause.
> BIRDBOOT. You can't start with a *pause*! If you want my opinion there's total panic back there. [*Laughs and subsides.*] Where's Higgs tonight, then?

Evidently, Moon believes that the play-within-the-play has begun because the scene is exposed, an actor is present (the body), and an event of significance has already taken place (the murder). Birdboot demands action in drama, however; so for him the play cannot begin with a pause: it commences some moments later with the entrance of Mrs. Drudge. For real spectators, this whole discussion is a salient one, for Stoppard's play *does* begin with a pause. As the audience files into the theater, Moon is already in his seat, the curtain is up, the body in place. It is not hard to imagine conversations in the audience that almost exactly parallel the exchange between Moon and Birdboot. Does *The Real Inspector Hound*, as a theatrical event, begin when "MOON stares blankly ahead"? Or does it begin when we first suspect that Moon and Birdboot are actors and not members of the audience? Or does it, as Birdboot would have it, begin with the first verbal exchanges? In any event, the play almost certainly begins at a different moment for virtually every spectator.

We ourselves, as spectators, are in a situation exactly analogous to that of

Birdboot and Moon, and like them, we allow our expectations of drama to lead us into errors of interpretation. All of us assume, for example, that the body on the stage is that of an actor or dummy. It does not occur to Birdboot and Moon that "the body" could be that of a real corpse until very much later in the play. For viewers of the play this issue, too, is significant. Stoppard is obviously trying to make us wonder how long the complacent notion that "it's all an act" would last if a real body were discovered on opening night on the stage of the latest whodunit.

All of this is central to Stoppard's main goal in the play, which is to make us question the conventions of theater in general and of mysteries in particular. In doing so, the lines quoted above serve as an exposition of theme. They are also a very polished exposition of character, conflict, and plot. In them we find the first faint hint of Birdboot's marital infidelity. He is not accompanied by his wife, and moreover, he seems to think her such a dull person that she would be wholly out of place at a "thriller." Similarly, the question that concludes the extract—"Where's Higgs tonight, then?"—leads to a revelation of Moon's character and serves as an echoing refrain throughout the play. This is already the fourth time the question has been raised in less than three minutes, and here it provokes a tirade from Moon, who dreams "of revolution, a bloody *coup d'état* by the second rank." More to the point, however, the repetitious questions about Higgs do make us wonder what has happened to him, and Moon's uncontrolled anger in response to them eventually makes us question his sanity. Thus, when we discover that Higgs' body has been on stage all along, Moon is an obvious suspect—so much so that even his denial of guilt trails off into uncertainty: "But I didn't kill—I'm almost sure I—"

This subtle and thoroughly professional dramatic exposition is followed by the obvious and awkward exposition within the mystery play. Mrs. Drudge enters and turns on the radio just in time to hear a police warning about an escaped madman who is "wearing a darkish suit with a lightish shirt . . . [and] is of medium height and build and youngish." Every element of the play-within-the-play is a parody of the contrivance of mystery drama. In this case the undiscovered murder is the hilarious result of the cleaning woman's thoroughness in moving the sofa. The seclusion of the manor, the apparent vulnerability of its inhabitants, the treacherous fog, and the series of death threats are all standard in the genre, but Stoppard's tongue-in-cheek exaggeration exposes them as obvious contrivances.

The very ineptness of the inner play complements and develops the outer play. The madman mentioned in the radio dispatch is described so generally that he could be nearly anyone from Simon Gascoyne to Moon to Magnus. Inspector Hound is so incompetent that we are almost forced to consider him an imposter and to wonder who will turn out to be "the real Inspector Hound." The ridiculousness of a murder-mystery in which nobody recognizes the victim only becomes understandable when we learn that the murdered man is the critic Higgs and not an actor at all.

When Birdboot and Moon are finally drawn down onto the stage, the opportunities for exchanges with both "real" and "theatrical" meanings multiply. Thus, when Cynthia breaks free from Birdboot's embrace to exclaim, "We can't go on meeting like this!"—she may only be reciting a line meaning that they can't continue to have meetings at Muldoon Manor, but in "real" terms she may mean instead that they can't go on meeting on stage in the middle of a play. Birdboot chooses to interpret her words in the second sense and replies, "I am not ashamed to proclaim nightly my love for you!—but fortunately that will not be necessary—I know of a very good hotel, discreet— run by a man of the world." He has been drawn into a world of confusing theatrical deceptions and (perhaps like most of us) allows his desires to dictate how he will interpret reality. The same thing is true of Moon, who steps down onto the stage and assumes the role of Inspector because he grieves for his friend and longs to find his killer. There he finds that his own desires for the death of Higgs have made him the most likely suspect, and, unable to differentiate clearly between what he has done and what he only appears to have done, he flees and is shot as a fugitive murderer.

A Selective Bibliography on *The Real Inspector Hound*

Babula, William. "The Play-Life Metaphor in Shakespeare and Stoppard." *Modern Drama* 15 (1972): 281.

Bigsby, C. W. E. *Tom Stoppard.* Harlowe, Eng.: Longman, 1976.

Billington, Michael. *Stoppard: The Playwright.* London: Methuen, 1987. 62–68.

Bloom, Harold, ed. *Tom Stoppard.* New York: Chelsea, 1986.

Brassell, Tim. *Tom Stoppard: An Assessment.* New York: St. Martin's, 1985. 92–105.

Bratt, David. *Tom Stoppard: A Reference Guide.* Boston: G. K. Hall, 1982.

Cahn, Victor L. *Beyond Absurdity: The Plays of Tom Stoppard.* Rutherford, N.J.: Fairleigh Dickinson UP, 1979.

Corballis, Richard. *Stoppard: The Mystery and the Clockwork.* Oxford: Methuen, 1984. 49–54.

Crossley, Brian M. "An Investigation of Stoppard's 'Hound' and 'Foot.' " *Modern Drama* 20 (1977): 77–86.

Dean, Joan Fitzpatrick. *Tom Stoppard.* Columbia: U of Missouri P, 1981.

Durham, Weldon B. "Ritual and Riddance in Tom Stoppard's *The Real Inspector Hound.*" *Tom Stoppard: A Casebook.* Ed. John Harty. New York: Garland, 1988. 89–104.

Farish, Gillian. "Into the Looking-Glass Bowl: An Instant of Grateful Terror." *University of Windsor Review* 10 (1975): 14–29.

Gabbard, Lucina Pacquet. *The Stoppard Plays.* Troy, N.Y.: Whitston, 1982. 58–69.

Gitzen, Julian. "Tom Stoppard: Chaoes in Perspective." *Southern Humanities Review* 10 (1976): 143–52.

Hayman, Ronald. *Tom Stoppard.* 2nd ed. London: Heinemann, 1978.

Jenkins, Anthony. *Critical Essays on Tom Stoppard.* Boston: G. K. Hall, 1990.

———. *The Theatre of Tom Stoppard.* Cambridge, Eng.: Cambridge UP, 1987. 50–54.

Kelly, Katherine E. *Tom Stoppard and the Craft of Comedy.* Ann Arbor: U of Michigan P, 1991.

———. "Tom Stoppard Journalist: Through the Stage Door." *Modern Drama* 33 (1990): 380–93.

Kennedy, Andrew K. "Old and New In London Now." *Modern Drama* 11 (1969): 437–42.

Levenson, Jill. "Views from a Revolving Door: Tom Stoppard's Canon to Date." *Queen's Quarterly* 78 (1971): 431–42.

Londre, Felicia H. *Tom Stoppard.* New York: Ungar, 1981. p. 107–41.

Mason, Jeffrey D. "Foot-prints to the Moon: Detectives as Suspects in Hound and Magritte." *Tom Stoppard: A Casebook.* John Harty, ed. New York: Garland, 1988. 105–19.

Page, Malcolm. *File on Stoppard.* London: Methuen, 1986.

Roberts, Philip. "Tom Stoppard: Serious Artist or Siren?" *Critical Quarterly* 20 (1978): 84–92.

Rusinko, Susan. *Tom Stoppard.* Boston: Twayne, 1986. 69–71.

Sammells, Neil. *Tom Stoppard: The Artist as Critic.* Basingstoke, Eng.: Macmillan, 1988. 55–60.

Schlueter, June. "Stoppard's Moon and Birdboot, Rosencrantz and Guildenstern." *Metafictional Characters in Modern Drama.* New York: Columbia UP, 1979. 89–103.

Taylor, John Russell. "Tom Stoppard." *The Second Wave: British Drama for the Seventies.* New York: Hill & Wang, 1971. 94–107.

Whitaker, Thomas R. *Tom Stoppard.* New York: Grove, 1983. 69–75.

Alice Childress (1920–)
WINE IN THE WILDERNESS

CHARACTERS

BILL JAMESON, *an artist age*
  thirty-three

OLDTIMER, *an old roustabout*
  character in his sixties

SONNY-MAN, *a writer age twenty-seven*

TOMMY, *a woman factory worker age*
  thirty

CYNTHIA, *a social worker age*
  twenty-five, SONNY-MAN'S *wife.*

TIME: *The summer of 1964. Night of a riot.*

PLACE: *Harlem, New York City, New York, U.S.A.*

SCENE: *A one room apartment in a Harlem Tenement. It used to be a three room apartment but the tenant has broken out walls and is half finished with a redecorating job. The place is now only partly reminiscent of its past tawdry days, plaster broken away and lathing exposed right next to a new brick-faced portion of wall. The kitchen is now a part of the room. There is a three-quarter bed covered with an African throw, a screen is placed at the foot of the bed to insure privacy when needed. The room is obviously black dominated, pieces of sculpture, wall hangings, paintings. An artist's easel is standing with a drapery thrown across it so the empty canvas beneath it is hidden. Two other canvases the same size are next to it, they too are covered and conceal paintings. The place is in a beautiful, rather artistic state of disorder. The room also reflects an interest in other darker peoples of the world.... A Chinese incenseburner Buddha, an American Indian feathered war helmet, a Mexican serape, a Japanese fan, a West Indian travel poster. There is a kitchen table, chairs, floor cushions, a couple of box crates, books, bookcases, plenty of artist's materials. There is a small raised platform for model posing. On the platform is a backless chair. The tail end of a riot is going on out in the street. Noise and screaming can be heard in the distance . . . running feet, voices shouting over loudspeakers.*

OFFSTAGE VOICES.   Offa the street! Into your homes! Clear the street! [*The whine of a bullet is heard.*] Cover that roof! It's from the roof! [BILL *is seated on the floor with his back to the wall, drawing on a large sketch pad with charcoal pencil. He is very absorbed in his task but flinches as he hears the bullet sound, ducks and shields his head with upraised hand . . . then resumes sketching. The telephone rings, he reaches for phone with caution, pulls it toward him by the cord in order to avoid going near window or standing up.*]

BILL.   Hello? Yeah, my phone is on. How the hell I'm gonna be talkin' to you if it's not on? [*Sound of glass breaking in the distance.*] I could lose my damn life answerin' the phone. Sonny-man, what the hell you callin' me up for! I thought you and Cynthia might be downstairs dead. I banged on the

floor and hollered down the air-shaft, no answer. No stuff! Thought yall
was dead. I'm sittin' here drawin' a picture in your memory. In a bar! Yall
sittin' in a bar? See there, you done blew the picture that's in your memory
. . . No kiddin', they wouldn't let you in the block? Man, they can't keep
you outta your own house. Found? You found who? Model? What model?
Yeah, yeah, thanks, . . . but I like to find my own models. No! Don't bring
nobody up here in the middle of a riot . . . Hey, Sonny-man! Hey! [*Sound
of yelling and rushing footsteps in the hall.*]

20 WOMAN'S VOICE [*offstage*].   Damnit, Bernice! The riot is over! What you hidin'
in the hall for? I'm in the house, your father's in the house, . . . and you
out there hidin' in the hall!

GIRL'S VOICE [*offstage*].   The house might burn down!

BILL.   Sonny-man, I can't hear you!

WOMAN'S VOICE [*offstage*].   If it do burn down, what the hell you gon' do, run
off and leave us to burn up by ourself? The riot is over. The police say it's
over! Get back in the house! [*Sound of running feet and a knock on the door.*]

BILL.   They say it's over. Man, they oughta let you on your own block, in
your own house . . . Yeah, we still standin', this seventy-year-old house got
30 guts. Thank you, yeah, thanks but I like to pick my own models. You
drunk? Can't you hear when I say not to . . . Okay, all right, bring her. . . .
[*Frantic knocking at the door.*] I gotta go. Yeah, yeah, bring her. I gotta go
. . . [*Hangs up phone and opens the door for* OLDTIMER. *The old man is carrying
a haul of loot . . . two or three bottles of liquor, a ham, a salami and a suit with
price tags attached.*] What's this! Oh, no, no, no, Oldtimer, not here. . . .
[*Faint sound of a police whistle.*] The police after you? What you bring that
stuff in here for?

OLDTIMER [*runs past* BILL *to center as he looks for a place to hide the loot*].   No, no,
they not really after me but . . . I was in the basement so I could stash this
40 stuff, . . . but a fella told me they pokin' round down there . . . in the back
yard pokin' round . . . the police doin' a lotta pokin' round.

BILL.   If the cops are searchin' why you wanna dump your troubles on me?

OLDTIMER.   I don't wanna go to jail. I'm too old to go to jail. What we gonna
do?

BILL.   We can throw it the hell outta the window. Didn't you think of just
throwin' it away and not worry 'bout jail?

OLDTIMER.   I can't do it. It's like . . . I'm Oldtimer but my hands and arms is
somebody else that I don't know-a-tall. [BILL *pulls stuff out of* OLDTIMER'S
arms and places loot on the kitchen table. OLDTIMER'S *arms fall to his sides.*] Thank
50 you, son.

BILL.   Stealin' ain't worth a bullet through your brain, is it? You wanna get
shot down and drown in your own blood, . . . for what? A suit, a bottle of
whiskey? Gonna throw your life away for a damn ham?

OLDTIMER.   But I ain't really stole nothin', Bill, cause I ain' no thief. Them
others, . . . they smash the windows, they run in the stores and grab and
all. Me, I pick up what they left scatter in the street. Things they drop . . .
things they trample underfoot. What's in the street ain' like stealin'. This
is leavin's. What I'm gon' do if the police come?

BILL [*starts to gather the things in the tablecloth that is on the table*].   I'll throw it
60 out the air-shaft window.

OLDTIMER [*places himself squarely in front of the air-shaft window*].   I be damn.
Uh-uh, can't let you do it, Bill-Boy. [*Grabs the liquor and holds on.*]

BILL [*wraps the suit, the ham and the salami in the tablecloth and ties the ends together
in a knot*].   Just for now, then you can go down and get it later.

OLDTIMER [*getting belligerent*].   I say I ain' gon' let you do it.

BILL.   Sonny-man calls this "The people's revolution." A revolution should
not be looting and stealing. Revolutions are for liberation. [OLDTIMER *won't
budge from before the window.*] Okay, man, you win, it's all yours. [*Walks away
from* OLDTIMER *and prepares his easel for sketching.*]

70 OLDTIMER.   Don't be mad with me, Bill-Boy, I couldn't help myself.

BILL [*at peace with the old man*].   No hard feelin's.

OLDTIMER [*as he uncorks bottle*].   I don't blame you for bein' fed up with us, . . .
fella like you oughta be fed up with your people sometime. Hey, Billy, let's
you and me have a little taste together.

BILL.   Yeah, why not.

OLDTIMER [*at table pouring drinks*].   You mustn't be too hard on me. You see,
you talented, you got somethin' on the ball, you gonna make it on past
these white folk, . . . but not me, Billy-boy, it's too late in the day for that.
Time, time, time, . . . time done put me down. Father Time is a bad white

80 cat. Whatcha been paintin' and drawin' lately? You can paint me again if
you wanta, . . . no charge. Paint me 'cause that might be the only way I get
to stay in the world after I'm dead and gone. Somebody'll look up at your
paintin' and say, . . . "Who's that?" And you say, . . . "That's Oldtimer."
[BILL *joins* OLDTIMER *at table and takes one of the drinks.*] Well, here's lookin'
at you and goin' down me. [*Gulps drink down.*]

BILL [*raising his glass*].   Your health, Oldtimer.

OLDTIMER.   My day we didn't have all this grants and scholarship like now.
Whatcha been doin'?

BILL.   I'm working on the third part of a triptych.

90 OLDTIMER.   A what tick?

BILL.   A triptych.

OLDTIMER.   Hot-damn, that calls for another drink. Here's to the trip-tick.
Down the hatch. What is one-a-those?

BILL.   It's three paintings that make one work . . . three paintings that make
one subject.

OLDTIMER.   Goes together like a new outfit . . . hat, shoes and suit.

BILL.   Right. The title of my triptych is . . . "Wine in the Wilderness" . . .
Three canvases on black womanhood. . . .

OLDTIMER [*eyes light up*].   Are they naked pitchers?

100 BILL [*crosses to paintings*].   No, all fully clothed.

OLDTIMER [*wishing it was a naked picture*].   Man, ain' nothin' dirty 'bout naked
pitchers. That's art. What you call artistic.

BILL.   Right, right, right, but these are with clothes. That can be artistic too.
[*Uncovers one of the canvases and reveals painting of a charming little girl in
Sunday dress and hair ribbon.*] I call her . . . "Black girlhood."

OLDTIMER.   Awwwww, that's innocence! Don't know what it's all about. Ain't
that the little child that live right down the street? Yeah. That call for
another drink.

BILL.   Slow down, Oldtimer, wait till you see this. [*Covers the painting of the*

110   *little girl, then uncovers another canvas and reveals a beautiful woman, deep*
       mahogany complexion, she is cold but utter perfection, draped in startling colors of
       African material, very "Vogue" looking. She wears a golden head-dress sparkling
       with brilliants and sequins applied over the paint.] There she is . . . "Wine In
       The Wilderness" . . . Mother Africa, regal, black womanhood in her no-
       blest form.

OLDTIMER.   Hot damn. I'd die for her, no stuff, . . . oh, man. "Wine In The
       Wilderness."

BILL.   Once, a long time ago, a poet named Omar[1] told us what a paradise
       life could be if a man had a loaf of bread, a jug of wine and . . . a woman
120   singing to him in the wilderness. She is the woman, she is the bread, she
       is the wine, she is the singing. This Abyssinian maiden[2] is paradise, . . .
       perfect black womanhood.

OLDTIMER [*pours for* BILL *and himself*].   To our Abyssinian maiden.

BILL.   She's the Sudan, the Congo River, the Egyptian Pyramids. . . . Her
       thighs are African Mahogany . . . she speaks and her words pour forth
       sparkling clear as the waters . . . Victoria Falls.

OLDTIMER.   Ow! Victoria Falls! She got a pretty name.

BILL [*covers her up again*].   Victoria Falls is a waterfall not her name. Now,
       here's the one that calls for a drink. [*Snatches cover from the empty canvas.*]

130 OLDTIMER [*stunned by the empty canvas*].   Your . . . your pitcher is gone.

BILL.   Not gone . . . she's not painted yet. This will be the third part of the
       triptych. This is the unfinished third of "Wine In The Wilderness." She's
       gonna be the kinda chick that is grass roots, . . . no, not grass roots, . . . I
       mean she's underneath the grass roots. The lost woman, . . . what the
       society has made out of our women. She's as far from my African queen as
       a woman can get and still be female, she's as close to the bottom as you can
       get without crackin' up . . . she's ignorant, unfeminine, coarse, rude . . .
       vulgar . . . a poor, dumb chick that's had her behind kicked until it's numb
       . . . and the sad part is . . . she ain't together, you know . . . there's no hope
140   for her.

OLDTIMER.   Oh, man, you talkin 'bout my first wife.

BILL.   A chick that ain' fit for nothing' but to . . . to . . . just pass her by.

OLDTIMER.   Yeah, later for her. When you see her, cross over to the other side
       of the street.

BILL.   If you had to sum her up in one word it would be nothin'!

OLDTIMER [*roars with laughter*].   That call for a double!

BILL [*beginning to slightly feel the drinks. He covers the canvas again*].   Yeah,
       that's a double! The kinda woman that grates on your damn nerves. And
       Sonny-man just called to say he found her runnin' round in the middle-a
150   this riot. Sonny-man say she's the real thing from underneath them grass
       roots. A back-country chick right outa the wilds of Mississippi, . . . but she
       ain't never been near there. Born in Harlem, raised right here in
       Harlem, . . . but back country. Got the picture?

---

[1] Omar Khayyám (c. 1048–1122) was the author of *The Rubáiyát*, which was given its most
famous translation into English by Edward Fitzgerald in 1859.
[2] Abyssinia was a kingdom in Africa. Bill may be alluding to the Abyssinian maiden praised
in Samuel Taylor Coleridge's poem "Kubla Khan" (1816).

OLDTIMER [*full of laughter*]. When . . . when . . . when she get here let's us stomp her to death.

BILL. Not till after I paint her. Gonna put her right here on this canvas. [*Pats the canvas, walks in a strut around the table.*] When she gets put down on canvas, . . . then triptych will be finished.

OLDTIMER [*joins him in the strut*]. Trip-tick will be finish . . . trip-tick will be
160   finish . . .

BILL. Then "Wine In The Wilderness" will go up against the wall to improve the view of some post office . . . or some library . . . or maybe a bank . . . and I'll win a prize . . . and the queen, my black queen will look down from the wall so the messed up chicks in the neighborhood can see what a woman oughta be . . . and the innocent child on one side of her and the messed up chick on the other side of her . . . MY STATEMENT.

OLDTIMER [*turning the strut into a dance*]. Wine in the wilderness . . . up against the wall . . . wine in the wilderness . . . up against the wall . . .

WOMAN FROM UPSTAIRS APARTMENT [*offstage*]. What's the matter! The house on
170   fire?

BILL [*calls upstairs through the air-shaft window*]. No, baby! We down here paintin' pictures! [*Sound of police siren in distance.*]

WOMAN FROM UPSTAIRS APARTMENT [*offstage*]. So much-a damn noise! Cut out the noise! [*To her husband hysterically.*] Percy! Percy! You hear a police siren! Percy! That a fire engine?!

BILL. Another messed up chick. [*Gets a rope and ties it to* OLDTIMER's *bundle.*] Got an idea. We'll tie the rope to the bundle, . . . then . . . [*lowers bundle out of window*] lower the bundle outta the window . . . and tie it to this nail here behind the curtain. Now! Nobody can find it except you and me . . . Cops
180   come, there's no loot. [*Ties rope to nail under curtain.*]

OLDTIMER. Yeah, yeah, loot long gone 'til I want it. [*Makes sure window knot is secure.*] It'll be swingin' in the breeze free and easy. [*There is knocking on the door.*]

SONNY-MAN. Open up! Open up! Sonny-man and company.

BILL [*putting finishing touches on securing knot to nail*]. Wait, wait, hold on. . . .

SONNY-MAN. And-a here we come! [*Pushes the door open. Enters room with his wife* CYNTHIA *and* TOMMY. SONNY-MAN *is in high spirits. He is in his late twenties, his wife* CYNTHIA *is a bit younger. She wears her hair in a natural style, her clothing is tweedy and in good, quiet taste.* SONNY-MAN *is wearing slacks and a*
190   *dashiki over a shirt.* TOMMY *is dressed in a mis-matched skirt and sweater, wearing a wig that is not comical, but is wiggy looking. She has the habit of smoothing it every once in a while, patting to make sure it's in place. She wears sneakers and bobby sox, carries a brown paper sack.*]

CYNTHIA. You didn't think it was locked, did you?

BILL. Door not locked? [*Looking over* TOMMY.]

TOMMY. You oughta run him outta town, pushin' open people's door.

BILL. Come right on in.

SONNY-MAN [*standing behind* TOMMY *and pointing down at her to draw Bill's attention*]. Yes, sireeeeee.

200 CYNTHIA. Bill, meet a friend-a ours . . . This is Miss Tommy Fields. Tommy, meet a friend-a ours . . . this is Bill Jameson . . . Bill, Tommy.

BILL. Tommy, if I may call you that . . .

TOMMY [*likes him very much*].   Help yourself, Bill. It's a pleasure. Bill Jameson,
   well, all right.

BILL.   The pleasure is all mine. Another friend-a ours. Oldtimer.

TOMMY [*with respect and warmth*].   How are you, Mr. Timer?

BILL [*laughs along with others,* OLDTIMER *included*].   What you call him, baby?

TOMMY.   Mr. Timer, . . . ain't that what you say? [*They all laugh expansively.*]

BILL.   No, sugar pie, that's not his name, . . . we just say . . . "Oldtimer,"
210   that's what everybody call him. . . .

OLDTIMER.   Yeah, they all call me that . . . everybody say that . . . Oldtimer.

TOMMY.   That's cute, . . . but what's your name?

BILL.   His name is . . . er . . . er . . . What is your name?

SONNY-MAN.   Dog-bite, what's your name, man? [*There is a significant moment
   of self-consciousness as* CYNTHIA, SONNY *and* BILL *realize they don't know* OLD-
   TIMER'*s name.*]

OLDTIMER.   Well, it's . . . Edmond L. Matthews.

TOMMY.   Edmond *L.* Matthews. What's the L for?

OLDTIMER.   Lorenzo, . . . Edmond Lorenzo Matthews.

220 BILL AND SONNY-MAN.   Edmond Lorenzo Matthews.

TOMMY.   Pleased to meetcha, Mr. Matthews.

OLDTIMER.   Nobody call me that in a long, long time.

TOMMY.   I'll call you Oldtimer like the rest but I like to know who I'm
   meetin'. [OLDTIMER *gives her a chair.*] There you go. He's a gentleman too.
   Bet you can tell my feet hurt. I got one corn, . . . and that one is enough.
   Oh, it'll ask you for somethin'. [*General laughter.* BILL *indicates to* SONNY-MAN
   that TOMMY *seems right.* CYNTHIA *and* OLDTIMER *takes seats near* TOMMY.]

BILL.   You rest yourself, baby, er . . . er . . . Tommy. You did say Tommy.

TOMMY.   I cut it to Tommy . . . Tommy-Marie, I use both of 'em sometime.

230 BILL.   How 'bout some refreshment?

SONNY-MAN.   Yeah, how 'bout that. [*Pouring drinks.*]

TOMMY.   Don't yall carry me too fast, now.

BILL [*indicating liquor bottles*].   I got what you see and also some wine . . .
   couple-a cans-a beer.

TOMMY.   I'll take the wine.

BILL.   Yeah, I knew it.

TOMMY.   Don't wanta start nothin' I can't keep up. [OLDTIMER *slaps his thigh
   with pleasure.*]

BILL.   That's all right, baby, you just a wine-o.

240 TOMMY.   You the one that's got the wine, not me.

BILL.   I use it for cookin'.

TOMMY.   You like to get loaded while you cook? [OLDTIMER *is having a ball.*]

BILL [*as he pours wine for* TOMMY].   Oh, baby, you too much.

OLDTIMER [*admiring* TOMMY].   Oh, Lord, I wish, I wish, I wish I was young
   again.

TOMMY [*flirtatiously*].   Lively as you are, . . . I don't know what we'd do with
   you if you got any younger.

OLDTIMER.   Oh, hush now!

SONNY-MAN [*whispering to* BILL *and pouring drinks*].   Didn't I tell you! Know
250   what I'm talking about. You dig? All the elements man.

TOMMY [*worried about what the whispering means*].   Let's get somethin' straight.
   I didn't come bustin' in on the party . . . I was asked. If you married and

any wives or girl-friends round here . . . I'm innocent. Don't wanna get shot at, or jumped on. Cause I wasn't doin' a thing but mindin' my business! . . . [*Saying the last in loud tones to be heard in other rooms.*]

OLDTIMER. Jus' us here, that's all.

BILL. I'm single, baby. Nobody wants a poor artist.

CYNTHIA. Oh, honey, we wouldn't walk you into a jealous wife or girl friend.

260 TOMMY. You paint all-a these pitchers? [BILL *and* SONNY-MAN *hand out drinks.*]

BILL. Just about. Your health, baby, to you.

TOMMY [*lifts her wine glass*]. All right, and I got one for you. . . . Like my grampaw used-ta say, . . . Here's to the men's collars and the women's skirts, . . . may they never meet. [*General laughter.*]

OLDTIMER. But they ain't got far to go before they do.

TOMMY [*suddenly remembers her troubles*]. Niggers, niggers . . . niggers, . . . I'm sick-a niggers, ain't you? A nigger will mess up everytime. . . . Lemmie tell you what the niggers done . . .

BILL. Tommy, baby, we don't use that word around here. We can talk about
270 each other a little better than that.

CYNTHIA. Oh, she doesn't mean it.

TOMMY. What must I say?

BILL. Try Afro-Americans.

TOMMY. Well, . . . the Afro-Americans burnt down my house.

OLDTIMER. Oh, no they didn't!

TOMMY. Oh, yes they did . . . it's almost burn down. Then the firemen nailed up my door . . . the door to my room, nailed up shut tight with all I got in the world.

OLDTIMER. Shame, what a shame.

280 TOMMY. A *damn* shame. My clothes . . . Everything gone. This riot blew my life. All I got is gone like it never was.

OLDTIMER. I know it.

TOMMY. My transistor radio . . . that's gone.

CYNTHIA. Ah, gee.

TOMMY. The transistor . . . and a brand new pair-a shoes I never had on one time. . . . [*Raises her right hand.*] If I never move, that's the truth . . . new shoes gone.

OLDTIMER. Child, when hard luck fall it just keep fallin'.

TOMMY. And in my top dresser drawer I got a my-on-ase jar with forty-one
290 dollars in it. The fireman would not let me in to get it. . . . And it was a Afro-American fireman, don'tcha know.

OLDTIMER. And you ain't got no place to stay. [BILL *is studying her for portrait possibilities.*]

TOMMY [*rises and walks around room*]. That's a lie. I always got some place to go. I don't wanta boast but I ain't never been no place that I can't go back the second time. Woman I use to work for say . . . "Tommy, any time, any time you want a sleep-in place you come right here to me." . . . And that's Park Avenue, my own private bath and T.V. set. . . . But I don't want that . . . so I make it on out here to the dress factory. I got friends . . . not a lot
300 of 'em . . . but a few *good* ones. I call my friend—girl and her mother . . . they say . . . "Tommy, you come here, bring yourself over here." So Tommy got a roof with no sweat. [*Looks at torn walls.*] Looks like the

Afro-Americans got to you too. Breakin' up, breakin' down, . . . that's all they know.

BILL.   No, Tommy, . . . I'm redecorating the place . . .

TOMMY.   You mean you did this to yourself?

CYNTHIA.   It's gonna be wild . . . brick-face walls . . . wall to wall carpet.

SONNY-MAN.   She was breakin' up everybody in the bar . . . had us all laughin' . . . crackin' us up. In the middle of a riot . . . she's gassin' everybody!

310 TOMMY.   No need to cry. It's sad enough. They hollerin' whitey, whitey . . . but who they burn out? Me.

BILL.   The brothers and sisters are tired, weary of the endless get-no-where struggle.

TOMMY.   I'm standin' there in the bar . . . tellin' like it is . . . next thing I know they talkin' bout bringin' me to meet you. But you know what I say? Can't nobody pick nobody for nobody else. It don't work. And I'm standin' there in a mis-match skirt and top and these sneaker-shoes. I just went to put my dresses in the cleaner . . . Oh, Lord, wonder if they burn down the cleaner. Well, no matter, when I got back it was all over . . . They went in

320 the grocery store, rip out the shelves, pull out all the groceries . . . the hams . . . the . . . the can goods . . . everything . . . and then set fire . . . Now who you think live over the grocery? Me, that's who. I don't even go to the store lookin' this way . . . but this would be the time, when . . . folks got a fella they want me to meet.

BILL [*suddenly self-conscious*].   Tommy, they thought . . . they thought I'd like to paint you . . . that's why they asked you over.

TOMMY [*pleased by the thought but she can't understand it*].   Paint me? For what? If he was gonna paint somebody seems to me it'd be one of the pretty girls they show in the beer ads. They even got colored on television now, . . .

330 brushin' their teeth and smokin' cigarettes, . . . some of the prettiest girls in the world. He could get them, . . . couldn't you?

BILL.   Sonny-man and Cynthia were right. I want to paint you.

TOMMY [*suspiciously*].   Naked, with no clothes on?

BILL.   No, baby, dressed just as you are now.

OLDTIMER.   Wearin' clothes is also art.

TOMMY.   In the cleaner I got a white dress with a orlon sweater to match it, maybe I can get it out tomorrow and pose in that. [CYNTHIA, OLDTIMER *and* SONNY-MAN *are eager for her to agree.*]

BILL.   No, I will paint you today, Tommy, just as you are, holding your

340 brown paper bag.

TOMMY.   Mmmmmm, me holdin' the damn bag, I don't know 'bout that.

BILL.   Look at it this way, tonight has been a tragedy.

TOMMY.   Sure as hell has.

BILL.   And so I must paint you tonight, . . . Tommy in her moment of tragedy.

TOMMY.   I'm tired.

BILL.   Damn, baby, all you have to do is sit there and rest.

TOMMY.   I'm hungry.

SONNY-MAN.   While you're posin' Cynthia can run down to our house and fix

350 you some eggs.

CYNTHIA [*gives her husband a weary look*].   Oh, Sonny, that's such a lovely idea.

SONNY-MAN.   Thank you, darlin', I'm in there, . . . on the beam.

TOMMY [*ill at ease about posing*].   I don't want no eggs. I'm goin' to find me some Chinese food.

BILL.   I'll go. If you promise to stay here and let me paint you, . . . I'll get you anything you want.

TOMMY [*brightening up*].   Anything I want. Now, how he sound? All right, you comin' on mighty strong there. "Anything you want." When last you heard somebody say that? . . . I'm warnin' you, now, . . . I'm free, single and
360   disengage, . . . so you better watch yourself.

BILL [*keeping her away from ideas of romance*].   Now this is the way the program will go down. First I'll feed you, then I'll paint you.

TOMMY.   Okay, I'm game, I'm a good sport. First off, I want me some Chinese food.

CYNTHIA.   Order up, Tommy, the treat's on him.

TOMMY.   How come it is you never been married? All these girls runnin' round Harlem lookin' for husbands. [*To* CYNTHIA.] I don't blame 'em, 'cause I'm lookin' for somebody myself.

BILL.   I've been married, married and divorced, she divorced me, Tommy,
370   so maybe I'm not much of a catch.

TOMMY.   Look at it this-a-way. Some folks got bad taste. That woman had bad taste. [*All laugh except* BILL *who pours another drink.*] Watch it, Bill, you gonna rust the linin' of your stomach. Ain't this a shame? The riot done wipe me out and I'm sittin' here havin' me a ball. Sittin' here ballin'! [*As Bill refills her glass.*] Hold it, that's enough. Likker ain' my problem.

OLDTIMER.   I'm havin' me a good time.

TOMMY.   Know what I say 'bout divorce. [*Slaps her hands together in a final gesture.*] Anybody don' wantcha, . . . later, let 'em go. That's bad taste for you.

380 BILL.   Tommy, I don't wanta ever get married again. It's me and my work, I'm not gettin' serious about anybody. . . .

TOMMY.   He's spellin' at me, now. Nigger . . . I mean Afro-American . . . I ain' ask you nothin'. You hinkty, I'm hinkty too. I'm independent as a hog on ice, . . . and a hog on ice is dead, cold, well-preserved . . . and don't need a mother-grabbin' thing. [*All laugh heartily except* BILL *and* CYNTHIA.] I know models get paid. I ain' no square but this is a special night and so this one'll be on the house. Show you my heart's in the right place.

BILL.   I'll be glad to pay you, baby.

TOMMY.   You don't really like me, do you? That's all right, sometime it
390   happen that way. You can't pick for *nobody*. Friends get to matchin' up friends and they mess up everytime. Cynthia and Sonny-man done messed up.

BILL.   I like you just fine and I'm glad and grateful that you came.

TOMMY.   Good enough. [*Extends her hand. They slap hands together.*] You 'n me friends?

BILL.   Friends, baby, friends. [*Putting rock record on.*]

TOMMY [*trying out the model stand*].   Okay. Dad! Let's see 'bout this *anything I want* jive. Want me a bucket-a Egg Foo Yong, and you get you a shrimp-fry rice, we split that and each have some-a both. Make him give you the soy
400   sauce, the hot mustard and the duck sauce too.

BILL.　Anything else, baby?

TOMMY.　Since you ask, yes. If your money hold out, get me a double order egg roll. And a half order of the sweet and sour spare ribs.

BILL [*to* OLDTIMER *and* SONNY-MAN].　Come on, come on. I need some strong men to help me bring back your order, baby.

TOMMY [*going into her dance . . . simply standing and going through some boo-ga-loo motions*].　Better go get it 'fore I think up some more to go 'long with it. [*The men laugh and vanish out of the door. Steps heard descending stairs.*] Turn that off. [CYNTHIA *turns off record player.*] How could I forget your name,
410　good as you been to me this day. Thank you. Cynthia, thank you. I *like* him. Oh, I *like* him. But I don't wanta push him too fast. Oh, I got to play these cards right.

CYNTHIA [*a bit uncomfortable*].　Oh, Honey, . . . Tommy, you don't want a poor artist.

TOMMY.　Tommy's not lookin' for a meal ticket. I been doin' for myself all my life. It takes two to make it in this high-price world. A black man see a hard way to go. The both of you gotta pull together. That way you accomplish.

CYNTHIA.　I'm a social worker . . . and I see so many broken homes. Some of
420　these men! Tommy, don't be in a rush about the marriage thing.

TOMMY.　Keep it to yourself, . . . but I was thirty my last birthday and haven't ever been married. I coulda been. Oh, yes, indeed, coulda been. But I don't want any and everybody. What I want with a no-good piece-a nothin'? I'll never forget what the Reverend Martin Luther King said . . . "I have a dream." I liked him sayin' it 'cause truer words have never been spoke. [*Straightening the room.*] I have a dream, too. Mine is to find a man who'll treat me just half-way decent . . . just to meet me half-way is all I ask, to smile, be kind to me. Somebody in my corner. Not to wake up by myself in the mornin' and face this world all alone.

430　CYNTHIA.　About Bill, it's best not to ever count on anything, anything at all, Tommy.

TOMMY [*This remark bothers her for a split second but she shakes it off*].　Of course Cynthia, that's one of the foremost rules of life. Don't count on *nothin'!*

CYNTHIA.　Right, don't be too quick to put your trust in these men.

TOMMY.　You put your trust in one and got yourself a husband.

CYNTHIA.　Well, yes, but what I mean is. . . . Oh, you know. A man is a man and Bill is also an artist and his work comes before all else and there are other factors . . .

TOMMY [*sits facing* CYNTHIA].　What's wrong with me?

440　CYNTHIA.　I don't know what you mean.

TOMMY.　Yes you do. You tryin' to tell me I'm aimin' too high by lookin' at Bill.

CYNTHIA.　Oh, no, my dear.

TOMMY.　Out there in the street, in the bar, you and your husband were so sure that he'd *like* me and want to paint my picture.

CYNTHIA.　But he does want to paint you, he's very eager to . . .

TOMMY.　But why? Somethin' don't fit right.

CYNTHIA [*feeling sorry for* TOMMY].　If you don't want to do it, just leave and that'll be that.

450　TOMMY.　Walk out while he's buyin' me what I ask for, spendin' his money on

me? That'd be too dirty. [*Looks at books. Takes one from shelf.*] Books, books, books everywhere. "Afro-American History." I like that. What's wrong with me, Cynthia? Tell me, I won't get mad at you, I swear. If there's somethin' wrong that I can change, I'm ready to do it. Eighth grade, that's all I had of school. You a social worker, I know that means college. I come from poor people. [*Examining the book in her hand.*] Talkin' 'bout poverty this and poverty that and studyin' it. When you in it you don't be studyin' 'bout it. Cynthia, I remember my mother tyin' up her stockin's with strips-a rag 'cause she didn't have no garters. When I get home from school she'd
460 say, . . . "Nothin' much here to eat." Nothin' much might be grits, or bread and coffee. I got sick-a all that, got me a job. Later for school.

CYNTHIA. The Matriarchal Society.

TOMMY. What's that?

CYNTHIA. A Matriarchal Society is one in which the women rule . . . the women have the power . . . the women head the house.

TOMMY. We didn't have nothin' to rule over, not a pot nor a window. And my papa picked hisself up and run off with some finger-poppin' woman and we never hear another word 'til ten, twelve years later when a under-taker call up and ask if Mama wanta come claim his body. And don'cha
470 know, mama went over and claim it. A woman need a man to claim, even if it's a dead one. What's wrong with me? Be honest.

CYNTHIA. You're a fine person . . .

TOMMY. Go on, I can take it.

CYNTHIA. You're too brash. You're too used to looking out for yourself. It makes us lose our femininity. . . . It makes us hard . . . it makes us seem very hard. We do for ourselves too much.

TOMMY. If I don't, who's gonna do for me?

CYNTHIA. You have to let the black man have his manhood again. You have to give it back, Tommy.

480 TOMMY. I didn't take it from him, how I'm gonna give it back? What else is the matter with me? You had school, I didn't. I respect that.

CYNTHIA. Yes, I've had it, the degree and the whole bit. For a time I thought I was about to move into another world, the so-called "integrated" world, a place where knowledge and know-how could set you free and open all the doors, but that's a lie. I turned away from that idea. The first thing I did was give up dating white fellas.

TOMMY. I never had none to give up. I'm not soundin' on you. White folks nothin' happens when I look at 'em. I don't hate 'em, don't love 'em . . . just nothin' shakes a-tall. The dullest people in the world. The way they
490 talk . . . "Oh, hooty, hooty, hoo" . . . Break it down for me to A, B, C's. That Bill . . . I like him, with his black, uppity, high-handed ways. What do you do to get a man you want? A social worker oughta tell you things like that.

CYNTHIA. Don't chase him . . . at least don't let it look that way. Let him pursue you.

TOMMY. What if he won't? Men don't chase me much, not the kind I like.

CYNTHIA [*rattles off instructions glibly*]. Let him do the talking. Learn to listen. Stay in the background a little. Ask his opinion . . . "What do you think, Bill?"

500 TOMMY. Mmmmm. "Oh, hooty, hooty, hoo."

CYNTHIA. But why count on him? There are lots of other nice guys.

TOMMY. You don't think he'd go for me, do you?

CYNTHIA [*trying to be diplomatic*]. Perhaps you're not really his type.

TOMMY. Maybe not, but he's mine. I'm so lonesome . . . I'm *lonesome* . . . I want somebody to love. Somebody to say . . . "That's all right," when the World treats me mean.

CYNTHIA. Tommy, I think you're too good for Bill.

TOMMY. I don't wanta hear that. The last man that told me I was too good for him . . . was tryin' to get away. He's good enough for me. [*Straightening*
510 *room.*]

CYNTHIA. Leave the room alone. What we need is a little more sex appeal and a little less washing, cooking and ironing. [TOMMY *puts down the room straightening.*] One more thing . . . do you have to wear that wig?

TOMMY [*a little sensitive*]. I like how your hair looks. But some of the naturals I don't like. Can see all the lint caught up in the hair like it hasn't been combed since know not when. You a Muslim?[3]

CYNTHIA. No.

TOMMY. I'm just sick-a hair, hair, hair. Do it this way, don't do it, leave it natural, straighten it, process, no process. I get sick-a hair and talkin' 'bout
520 it and foolin' with it. That's why I wear the wig.

CYNTHIA. I'm sure your own must be just as nice or nicer than that.

TOMMY. It oughta be. I only paid nineteen ninety five for this.

CYNTHIA. You ought to go back to usin' your own.

TOMMY [*tensely*]. I'll be givin' that some thought.

CYNTHIA. You're pretty nice people just as you are. Soften up, Tommy. You might surprise yourself.

TOMMY. I'm listenin'.

CYNTHIA. Expect more. Learn to let men open doors for you . . .

TOMMY. What if I'm standin' there and they don't open it?

530 CYNTHIA [*trying to level with her*]. You're a fine person. He wants to paint you, that's all. He's doing a kind of mural thing and we thought he would enjoy painting you. I'd hate to see you expecting more out of the situation than what's there.

TOMMY. Forget it, sweetie-pie, don' nothin' happen that's not suppose to. [*Sound of laughter in the hall.* BILL, OLDTIMER *and* SONNY-MAN *enter.*]

BILL. No Chinese restaurant left, baby! It's wiped out. Gone with the revolution.

SONNY-MAN [*to* CYNTHIA]. Baby, let's move, split the scene, get on with it, time for home.

540 BILL. The revolution is here. Whatta you do with her? You paint her!

SONNY-MAN. You write her . . . you write the revolution. I'm gonna write the revolution into a novel nine hundred pages long.

BILL. Dance it! Sing it! "Down in the cornfield Hear dat mournful sound. . . . [SONNY-MAN *and* OLDTIMER *harmonize.*] Dear old Massa am-a

---

[3] The Muslims are believers in Islam, a monotheistic religion founded by the prophet Mohammed in the 7th century. The Black Muslims were established in the United States beginning in the 1930s under such leaders as Elijah Muhammed (1897–1975) and Malcolm X (1925–1965). They advocate racial separation and a very strict moral code involving, among other things, the subservience of women to men.

sleepin' A-sleepin' in the cold, cold ground." Now for "Wine In The Wilderness!" Triptych will be finished.

CYNTHIA [*in* BILL's *face*]. "Wine In The Wilderness," huh? Exploitation!

SONNY-MAN. Upstairs, all out, come on, Oldtimer. Folks can't create in a crowd. Cynthia, move it, baby.

550 OLD TIMER [*starting toward the window.*] My things! I got a package.

SONNY-MAN [*heads him off*]. Up and out. You don't have to go home, but you have to get outta here. Happy paintin', yall. [*One backward look and they are all gone.*]

BILL. Whatta night, whatta night, whatta night, baby. It will be painted, written, sung and discussed for generations.

TOMMY [*notices nothing that looks like Chinese food; he is carrying a small bag and a container*]. Where's the Foo-Yong?

BILL. They blew the restaurant, baby. All I could get was a couple-a franks and a orange drink from the stand.

560 TOMMY [*tersely*]. You brought me a frank-footer? That's what you think-a me, a frank-footer?

BILL. Nothin' to do with what I think. Place is closed.

TOMMY [*quietly surly*]. This is the damn City-a New York, any hour on the clock they sellin' the chicken in the basket, barbecue ribs, pizza pie, hot pastrami samitches; and you brought me a frank-footer?

BILL. Baby, don't break bad over somethin' to eat. The smart set, the jet, the beautiful people, kings and queens eat frankfurters.

TOMMY. If a queen sent you out to buy her a bucket-a Foo Yong, you wouldn't come back with no lonely-ass frank-footer.

570 BILL. Kill me 'bout it, baby! Go 'head and shoot me six times. That's the trouble with our women, yall always got your mind on food.

TOMMY Is that our trouble? [*Laughs.*] Maybe you right. Only two things to do. Either eat the frank-footer or walk on outta here. You got any mustard?

BILL [*gets mustard from the refrigerator*]. Let's face it, our folks are not together. The brothers and sisters have busted up Harlem . . . no plan, no nothin'. There's your black revolution, heads whipped, hospital full and we still in the same old bag.

TOMMY [*seated at the kitchen table*]. Maybe what everybody need is somebody

580 like you, who know how things oughta go, to get on out there and start some action.

BILL. You still mad about the frankfurter?

TOMMY. No. I keep seein' pitchers of what was in my room and how it all must be spoiled now. [*Sips the orange drink.*] A orange never been near this. Well, it's cold. [*Looking at an incense burner.*] What's that?

BILL. An incense burner, was given to me by the Chinese guy, Richard Lee. I'm sorry they blew his restaurant.

TOMMY. Does it help you to catch the number?

BILL. No, baby, I just burn incense sometime.

590 TOMMY. For what?

BILL. Just 'cause I feel like it. Baby, ain't you used to nothin'?

TOMMY. Ain't used to burnin' incent for nothin'.

BILL [*laughs*]. Burnin' what?

TOMMY. That stuff.

BILL.   What did you call it?

TOMMY.   Incent.

BILL.   It's not incent, baby. It's incense.

TOMMY.   Like the sense you got in your head. In-sense. Thank you. You're a
very correctable person, ain't you?

600 BILL.   Let's put you on canvas.

TOMMY [*stubbornly*].   I have to eat first.

BILL.   That's another thing 'bout black women, they wanta eat 'fore they do
anything else. Tommy, . . . Tommy, . . . I bet your name is Thomasina.
You look like a Thomasina.

TOMMY.   You could sit there and guess til your eyes pop out and you never
would guess my first name. You might could guess the middle name but
not the first one.

BILL.   Tell it to me.

TOMMY.   My name is Tomorrow.

610 BILL.   How's that?

TOMMY.   Tomorrow, . . . like yesterday and *tomorrow*, and the middle name is
just plain Marie. That's what my father name me. Tomorrow Marie. My
mother say he thought it had a pretty sound.

BILL.   Crazy! I never met a girl named Tomorrow.

TOMMY.   They got to callin' me Tommy for short, so I stick with that. Tomorrow Marie, . . . Sound like a promise that can never happen.

BILL [*straightens chair on stand; he is very eager to start painting.*]   That's what
Shakespeare said, . . . "Tomorrow and tomorrow and tomorrow." Tomorrow, you will be on this canvas.

620 TOMMY [*still uneasy about being painted*].   What's the hurry? Rome wasn't built
in a day, . . . that's another saying.

BILL.   If I finish in time, I'll enter you in the exhibition.

TOMMY [*loses interest in the food. Examines the room. Looks at portrait on the wall*].
He looks like somebody I know or maybe saw before.

BILL.   That's Frederick Douglass.[4] A man who used to be a slave. He escaped
and spent his life trying to make us all free. He was a great man.

TOMMY.   Thank you, Mr. Douglass. Who's the light colored man? [*Indicates a
frame next to the Douglass.*]

BILL.   He's white. That's John Brown.[5] They killed him for tryin' to shoot
630   the country outta the slavery bag. He dug us, you know. Old John said,
"Hell no, slavery must go."

TOMMY.   I heard all about him. Some folks say he was crazy.

BILL.   If he had been shootin' at *us* they wouldn't have called him a nut.

TOMMY.   School wasn't a great part-a my life.

BILL.   If it was you wouldn't-a found out too much 'bout black history cause
the books full-a nothin' but whitey, . . . all except the white ones who dug
us, . . . they not there either. Tell me, . . . who was Elijah Lovejoy?[6]

---

[4] Frederick Douglass (1817–1895) is best known for his autobiographical *Narrative of the Life
of Frederick Douglass, an American Slave* (1845).

[5] John Brown (1800–1859) was hung after leading an attack on a government arsenal at
Harpers Ferry, Virginia, in the hope of provoking a slave revolt.

[6] Elijah Parish Lovejoy (1802–1837), the founder and editor of an antislavery newspaper,
was tarred and feathered and later shot to death by pro-slavery extremists in Alton, Illinois.

TOMMY.   Elijah Lovejoy, . . . Mmmmmmm. I don't know. Have anything to
do with the Bible?

640 BILL.   No, that's another white fella, . . . Elijah had a printin' press and the
main thing he printed was "Slavery got to go." Well the man moved in on
him, smashed his press time after time . . . but he kept puttin' it back
together and doin' his thing. So, one final day, they came in a mob and
burned him to death.

TOMMY [*blows her nose with sympathy as she fights tears*].   That's dirty.

BILL [*as* TOMMY *glances at titles in book case*].   Who was Monroe Trotter?[7]

TOMMY.   Was he white?

BILL   No, soul brother. Spent his years tryin' to make it all right. Who was
Harriet Tubman?[8]

650 TOMMY.   I heard-a her. But don't put me through no test, Billy. [*Moving
around studying pictures and books.*] This room is full-a things I don' know
nothin' about. How'll I get to know?

BILL.   Read, go to the library, book stores, ask somebody.

TOMMY.   Okay, I'm askin'. Teach me things.

BILL.   Aw, baby, why torment yourself? Trouble with our women, . . . they all
wanta be great brains. Leave somethin' for a man to do.

TOMMY [*eager to impress him*].   What you think-a Martin Luther King?

BILL.   A great guy. But it's too late in the day for the singin' and prayin' now.

TOMMY.   What about Malcolm X?[9]

660 BILL.   Great cat . . . but there again . . . Where's the program?

TOMMY.   What about Adam Powell?[10] I voted for him. That's one thing bout
me. I vote. Maybe if everybody vote for the right people . . .

BILL.   The ballot box. It would take me all my life to straighten you on that
hype.

TOMMY.   I got the time.

BILL.   You gonna wind up with a king size headache. The Matriarchy gotta go.
Yall throw them suppers together, keep your husband happy, raise the kids.

TOMMY.   I don't have a husband. Course, that could be fixed. [*Leaving the
unspoken proposal hanging in the air.*]

670 BILL.   You know the greatest thing you could do for your people? Sit up
there and let me put you down on canvas.

TOMMY.   Bein' married and havin' a family might be good for your people as
a race, but I was thinkin' bout myself a little.

BILL.   Forget yourself sometime, sugar. On that canvas you'll be givin' and
givin' and givin'. . . . That's where you can do your thing best. What you
stallin' for?

TOMMY [*returns to table and sits in chair*].   I . . . I don't want to pose in this
outfit.

---

[7] [William] Monroe Trotter (1872–1934) was the founder and editor of the Boston *Guardian*
(1902–1934) and a militant civil rights activist in the first two decades of the twentieth century.

[8] Harriet Tubman (1820–1913) escaped from slavery herself and then helped 300 others to
escape through the Underground Railroad.

[9] Malcolm X, born Malcolm Little (1920–1965), was a militant Black Muslim leader before
his assassination in 1965.

[10] Adam Clayton Powell, Jr., (1908–1972) represented the residents of Harlem in the U.S.
Congress for over twenty years in the period from 1945–1969.

BILL [*patience is wearing thin*].   Why, baby, why?

680 TOMMY.   I don't feel proud-a myself in this.

BILL.   Art, baby, we are talkin' art. Whatcha want . . . Ribbons? Lace? False eyelashes?

TOMMY.   No, just my white dress with the orlon sweater, . . . or anything but this what I'm wearin'. You oughta see me in that dress with my pink linen shoes. Oh, hell, the shoes are gone. I forgot 'bout the fire . . .

BILL.   Oh, stop fightin' me! Another thing . . . our women don't know a damn thing bout bein' feminine. *Give in* sometime. It won't kill you. You tellin' me how to paint? Maybe you oughta hang out your shingle and give art lessons! You too damn opinionated. You gonna pose or you not gonna

690 pose? Say somethin'!

TOMMY.   You makin' me nervous! Hollerin' at me. My mama never holler at me. Hollerin'.

BILL.   But I'll soon be too tired to pick up the brush, baby.

TOMMY [*eye catches picture of white woman on the wall*].   That's a white woman! Bet you never hollered at her and I bet she's your girlfriend . . . too, and when she posed for her pitcher I bet yall was laughin' . . . and you didn't buy her no frank-footer!

BILL [*feels a bit smug about his male prowess*].   Awww, come on, cut that out, baby. That's a little blonde, blue-eyed chick who used to pose for me. That

700 ain't where it's at. This is a new day, the deal is goin' down different. This is the black moment, doll. Black, black, black is bee-yoo-tee-full. Got it? *Black is beautiful.*

TOMMY.   Then how come it is that I don't *feel* beautiful when you *talk* to me?!

BILL.   That's your hang-up, not mine. You supposed to stretch forth your wings like Ethiopia, shake off them chains that been holdin' you down. Langston Hughes[11] said let 'em see how beautiful you are. But you determined not to ever be beautiful. Okay, that's what makes you Tommy.

TOMMY.   Do you have a girl friend? And who is she?

BILL [*now enjoying himself to the utmost*].   Naw, naw, naw, doll. I *know* people,

710 but none-a this "tie-you-up-and-I-own-you" jive. I ain't mistreatin' nobody and there's enough-a me to go around. That's another thing with our women, . . . they wanta *latch* on. Learn to play it by ear, roll with the punches, cut down on some-a this "got-you-to-the-grave" kinda relationship. Was today all right? Good, be glad, . . . take what's at hand because tomorrow never comes, it's always today. [*She begins to cry.*] Awwww, I didn't mean it that way . . . I forgot your name. [*He brushes her tears away.*] You act like I belong to you. You're jealous of a picture?

TOMMY.   That's how women are, always studyin' each other and wonderin' how they look up 'gainst the next person.

720 BILL [*a bit smug*].   That's human nature. Whatcha call healthy competition.

TOMMY.   You think she's pretty?

BILL.   She was, perhaps still is. Long, silky hair. She could sit on her hair.

TOMMY [*with bitter arrogance*].   Doesn't *everybody*?

---

[11] Langston Hughes (1902–1967) was one of the most important poets of the twentieth century and a leading member of the Harlem Renaissance, a period of great creativity by black writers during the 1920s and 1930s.

BILL.   You got a head like a rock and gonna have the last word if it kills you, Baby. I bet you could knock out Mohammud Ali in the first round, then rare back and scream like Tarzan . . . "Now, I am the greatest!" [*He is very close to her and is amazed to feel a great sense of physical attraction.*] What we arguin' bout? [*Looks her over as she looks away. He suddenly wants to put the conversation on a more intimate level. His eye is on the bed.*] Maybe tomorrow
730   would be a better time for paintin'. Wanna freshen up, take a bath, baby? Water's nice n' hot.
TOMMY [*knows the sound and turns to check on the look; notices him watching the bed; starts weeping*].   No, I don't! Nigger!
BILL.   Was that nice? What the hell, let's paint the picture. Or are you gonna hold that back too?
TOMMY.   I'm posin'. Shall I take off the wig?
BILL.   No, it's a part of your image, ain't it? You must have a reason for wearin' it. [TOMMY *snatches up her orange drink and sits in the model's chair.*]
TOMMY [*with defiance*].   Yes, I wear it cause you and those like you go for long,
740   silky hair, and this is the only way I can have some without burnin' my mother-grabbin' brains out. Got it? [*She accidentally knocks over container of orange drink into her lap.*] Hell, I can't wear this. I'm soaked through. I'm not gonna catch no double pneumonia sittin' up here wringin' wet while you paint and holler at me.
BILL.   Bitch!
TOMMY.   You must be talkin' bout your mama!
BILL.   Shut up! Aw, shut-up! [*Phone rings. He finds an African throw-cloth and hands it to her.*] Put this on. Relax, don't go way mad, and all the rest-a that jazz. Change, will you? I apologize. I'm sorry. [*He picks up phone.*] Hello,
750   survivor of a riot speaking. Who's calling? [TOMMY *retires behind the screen with the throw. During the conversation she undresses and wraps the throw around her. We see* TOMMY *and* BILL *but they can't see each other.*] Sure, told you not to worry. I'll be ready for the exhibit. If you don't dig it, don't show it. Not time for you to see it yet. Yeah, yeah, next week. You just make sure your exhibition room is big enough to hold the crowds that's gonna congregate to see this fine chick I got here. [*This perks* TOMMY's *ears up.*] You oughta see her. The finest black woman in the world . . . No, . . . the finest *any* woman in the world . . . This gorgeous satin chick is . . . is . . . black velvet moon-light . . . an ebony queen of the universe . . . [TOMMY *can hardly believe her*
760   *ears.*] One look at her and you go back to Spice Islands . . . She's Mother Africa . . . You flip, double flip. She has come through everything that has been put on her . . . [*He unveils the gorgeous woman he has painted . . .* "Wine In The Wilderness." TOMMY *believes he is talking about her.*] Regal . . . grand . . . magnificent, fantastic . . . You would vote her the woman you'd most like to meet on a desert island, or around the corner from anywhere. She's here with me now . . . and I don't know if I want to show her to you or anybody else . . . I'm beginnin' to have this deep attachment . . . She sparkles, man, Harriet Tubman, Queen of the Nile . . . sweetheart, wife, mother, sister, friend . . . The night . . . a black diamond . . . A dark,
770   beautiful dream . . . A cloud with a silvery lining . . . Her wrath is a storm over the Bahamas. "Wine In The Wilderness" . . . The memory of Africa . . . The *now* of things . . . but best of all and most important . . . She's tomorrow . . . she's my tomorrow . . . [TOMMY *is dressed in the African wrap.*

She is suddenly awakened to the feeling of being loved and admired. She removes the wig and fluffs her hair. Her hair under the wig must not be an accurate, well-cut Afro . . . but should be rather attractive natural hair. She studies herself in a mirror. We see her taller, more relaxed and sure of herself. Perhaps braided hair will go well with Afro robe.] Aw, man, later. You don't believe in nothin'! *[He covers "Wine In The Wilderness." Is now in a glowing mood.]* Baby, when-
780   ever you ready. *[She emerges from behind the screen. Dressed in the wrap, sans wig. He is astounded.]* Baby, what . . . ? Where . . . where's the wig?

TOMMY.   I don't think I want to wear it, Bill.

BILL.   That is very becoming . . . the drape thing.

TOMMY.   Thank you.

BILL.   I don't know what to say.

TOMMY.   It's time to paint. *[Steps up on the model stand and sits in the chair. She is now a queen, relaxed and smiling her appreciation for his past speech to the art dealer. Her feet are bare.]*

BILL *[mystified by the change in her; tries to do a charcoal sketch]*.   It is quite late.

790 TOMMY.   Makes me no difference if it's all right with you.

BILL *[wants to create the other image]*.   Could you put the wig back on?

TOMMY.   You don't really like wigs, do you?

BILL.   Well, no.

TOMMY.   Then let's have things the way you like.

BILL *[has no answer for this. He makes a haphazard line or two as he tries to remember the other image]*.   Tell me something about yourself, . . . anything.

TOMMY *[now on sure ground]*.   I was born in Baltimore, Maryland and raised here in Harlem. My favorite flower is "Four O'clocks," that's a bush flower. My wearin' flower, corsage flower, is pink roses. My mama raised me,
800   mostly by herself, God rest the dead. Mama belonged to "The Eastern Star." Her father was a "Mason." If a man in the family is a "Mason" any woman related to him can be an "Eastern Star." My grandfather was a member of "The Prince Hall Lodge." I had a uncle who was an "Elk," . . . a member of "The Improved Benevolent Protective Order of Elks of the World": "The Henry Lincoln Johnson Lodge." You know, the white "Elks" are called "The Benevolent Protective Order of Elks" but the black "Elks" are called "The *Improved* Benevolent Protective Order of Elks of the World." That's because the black "Elks" got the copyright first but the white "Elks" took us to court about it to keep us from usin' the name. Over
810   fifteen hundred black folk went to jail for wearin' the "Elk" emblem on their coat lapel. Years ago, . . . that's what you call history.

BILL.   I didn't know about that.

TOMMY.   Oh, it's understandable. Only way I heard bout John Brown was because the black "Elks" bought his farmhouse where he trained his men to attack the government.

BILL.   The black "Elks" bought the John Brown Farm? What did they do with it?

TOMMY.   They built a outdoor theatre and put a perpetual light in his memory, . . . and they buildin' cottages there, one named for each state in the
820   union and . . .

BILL.   How do you know about it?

TOMMY.   Well, our "Elks" helped my cousin go through school with a scholarship. She won a speaking contest and wrote a composition titled "On-

ward and Upward, O, My Race." That's how she won the scholarship.
Coreen knows all that Elk history.

BILL [*seeing her with new eyes*]. Tell me some more about you, Tomorrow
Marie. I bet you go to church.

TOMMY. Not much as I used to. Early in life I pledged myself in the A.M.E.
Zion Church.

830 BILL [*studying her face, seeing her for the first time*]. A.M.E.

TOMMY. A.M.E. That's African Methodist Episcopal. We split off from the
white Methodist Episcopal and started our own in the year Seventeen
hundred and ninety six. We built our first buildin' in the year 1800. How
bout that?

BILL. That right?

TOMMY. Oh, I'm just showin' off. I taught Sunday School for two years and
you had to know the history of A.M.E. Zion . . . or else you couldn't teach.
My great, great grandparents was slaves.

BILL. Guess everybody's was.

840 TOMMY. Mine was slaves in a place called Sweetwater Springs, Virginia. We
tried to look it up one time but somebody at Church told us that Sweetwater Springs had become a part of Norfolk . . . so we didn't carry it any
further. . . . As it would be a expense to have a lawyer trace your people.

BILL [*throws charcoal pencil across room*]. No good! It won't work! I can't work
anymore.

TOMMY. Take a rest. Tell me about you.

BILL [*sits on bed*]. Everybody in my family worked for the Post Office. They
bought a home in Jamaica, Long Island. Everybody on that block bought
an aluminum screen door with a duck on it, . . . or was it a swan? I guess
850   that makes my favorite flower crab grass and hedges. I have a lot of bad
dreams. [TOMMY *massages his temples and the back of his neck.*] A dream like
suffocating, dying of suffocation. The worst kinda dream. People are
standing in a weird looking art gallery, they're looking and laughing at
everything I've ever done. My work begins to fade off the canvas, right
before my eyes. Everything I've ever done is laughed away.

TOMMY. Don't be so hard on yourself. If I was smart as you I'd wake up
singin' every mornin'. [*There is the sound of thunder. He kisses her.*] When it
thunders that's the angels in heaven playin' with their hoops, rollin' their
hoops and bicycle wheels in the rain. My Mama told me that.

860 BILL. I'm glad you're here. Black is beautiful, you're beautiful, A.M.E. Zion,
Elks, pink roses, bush flower, . . . blooming out of the slavery of Sweetwater Springs, Virginia.

TOMMY. I'm gonna take a bath and let the riot and the hell of living go down
the drain with the bath water.

BILL. Tommy, Tommy, Tomorrow Marie, let's save each other, let's be kind
and good to each other while it rains and the angels roll those hoops and
bicycle wheels. [*They embrace. The sound of rain.*]

[*Music in as lights come down. As lights fade down to darkness, music comes in louder.
There is a flash of lightning. We see* TOMMY *and* BILL *in each other's arms. It is very
dark. Music up louder, then softer and down to very soft. Music is mixed with the
sound of rain beating against the window. Music slowly fades as gray light of dawn
shows at window. Lights go up gradually. The bed is rumpled and empty.* BILL *is in*

the bathroom. TOMMY *is at the stove turning off the coffee pot. She sets table with cups and saucers, spoons.* TOMMY *is at the stove turning off the coffee pot. She sets table with cups and saucers, spoons.* TOMMY's *hair is natural, she wears another throw draped around her. She sings and hums a snatch of a joyous spiritual.*]

TOMMY. "Great day, Great day, the world's on fire, Great day . . ." [*Calling out to* BILL *who is in bath.*] Honey, I found the coffee, and it's ready. Nothin'
870   here to go with it but a cucumber and a Uneeda biscuit.
BILL [*offstage: joyous yell from offstage*].   Tomorrow and tomorrow and tomorrow! Good mornin', Tomorrow!
TOMMY [*more to himself than to* BILL].   "Tomorrow and tomorrow." That's Shakespeare. [*Calls to* BILL.] You say that was Shakespeare?
BILL [*offstage*].   Right, baby, right!
TOMMY. I bet Shakespeare was black! You know how we love poetry. That's what give him away. I bet he was passin'. [*Laughs.*]
BILL [*offstage*].   Just you wait, one hundred years from now all the honkys gonna claim our poets just like they stole our blues. They gonna try to
880   steal Paul Lawrence Dunbar and LeRoi and Margaret Walker.[12]
TOMMY [*to herself*].   God moves in a mysterious way, even in the middle of a riot. [*A knock on the door.*] Great day, great day the world's on fire . . . [*Opens the door,* OLDTIMER *enters. He is soaking wet. He does not recognize her right away.*]
OLDTIMER. 'Scuse me, I must be in the wrong place.
TOMMY [*patting her hair*].   This is me. Come on in, Edmond Lorenzo Matthews. I took off my hair-piece. This is me.
OLDTIMER [*very distracted and worried*].   Well, howdy-do and good mornin'. [*He has had a hard night of drinking and sleeplessness.*] Where Bill-boy? It
890   pourin' down some rain out there. [*Makes his way to the window.*]
TOMMY. What's the matter?
OLDTIMER [*raises the window and starts pulling in the cord, the cord is weightless and he realizes there is nothing on the end of it!*]   No, no, it can't be. Where is it? It's gone! [*Looks out the window.*]
TOMMY. You gonna catch your death. You wringin' wet.
OLDTIMER. Yall take my things in? It was a bag-a loot. A suit and some odds and ends. It was my loot. Yall took it in?
TOMMY. No. [*Realizes his desperation. She calls to* BILL *through the closed bathroom door.*] Did you take in any loot that was outside the window?
900 BILL [*offstage*].   No.
TOMMY. He said "no."
OLDTIMER [*yells out window*].   Thieves, . . . dirty thieves . . . lotta good it'll do you . . .
TOMMY [*leads him to a chair, dries his head with a towel*].   Get outta the wet things. You smell just like a whiskey still. Why don't you take care of yourself. [*Dries off his hands.*]
OLDTIMER. Drinkin' with the boys. Likker was everywhere all night long.
TOMMY. You got to be better than this.
OLDTIMER. Everything I ever put my hand and mind to do, it turn out

---

[12] Paul Lawrence Dunbar (1872–1906), LeRoi Jones (Imamu Amiri Baraka, 1934–), and Margaret Walker (1915–) are prominent black poets.

910   wrong. . . . Nothin' but mistakes . . . When you don' know, you don' know.
I don't know nothin'. I'm ignorant.

TOMMY.   Hush that talk . . . You know lotsa things, everybody does. [*Helps
him remove wet coat.*]

OLDTIMER.   Thanks. How's the trip-tick?

TOMMY.   The what?

OLDTIMER.   *Trip-tick.* That's a paintin'.

TOMMY.   See there, you know more about art than I do. What's a trip-tick?
Have some coffee and explain me a trip-tick.

OLDTIMER [*proud of his knowledge*].   Well, I tell you, . . . a trip-tick is a paintin'
920   that's in three parts . . . but they all belong together to be looked at all at
once. Now . . . this is the first one . . . a little innocent girl . . . [*Unveils
picture.*]

TOMMY.   She's sweet.

OLDTIMER.   And this is "Wine In The Wilderness" . . . The Queen of the
Universe . . . the finest chick in the world.

TOMMY [TOMMY *is thoughtful as he unveils the second picture*].   That's not me.

OLDTIMER.   No, you gonna be this here last one. The worst gal in town. A
messed-up chick that—that—[*He unveils the third canvas and is face to face
with the almost blank canvas, then realizes what he has said. He turns to see the
930   stricken look on* TOMMY'*s face.*]

TOMMY.   The messed-up chick, *that's* why they brought me here, ain't it?
That's why he wanted to paint me! Say it!

OLDTIMER.   No, I'm lyin'. I didn't mean it. It's the society that messed her up.
Awwwwww, Tommy, don't look that-a-way. It's art, . . . it's only art . . . He
couldn't mean you . . . it's art . . . [*The door opens.* CYNTHIA *and* SONNY-MAN
enter.]

SONNY-MAN.   Any body want a ride down . . . down . . . down . . . downtown?
What's wrong? Excuse me . . . [*Starts back out.*]

TOMMY [*blocking the exit to* CYNTHIA *and* SONNY-MAN].   No, come on in. Stay with
940   it . . . "Brother" . . . "Sister." Tell 'em what a trip-tick is, Oldtimer.

CYNTHIA [*very ashamed*].   Oh, no.

TOMMY.   You don't have to tell 'em. They already know. The messed-up
chick! How come you didn't pose for that, my sister? The messed-up chick
lost her home last night, . . . burnt out with no place to go. You and
Sonny-man gave me comfort, you cheered me up and took me in . . . *took
me in!*

CYNTHIA.   Tommy, we didn't know you, we didn't mean . . .

TOMMY.   It's all right! I was lost but now I'm found! Yeah, the blind can see!
[*She dashes behind the screen and puts on her clothing, sweater, skirt etc.*]

950 OLDTIMER [*goes to bathroom door*].   Billy, come out!

SONNY-MAN.   Billy, step out here, please! [BILL *enters shirtless, wearing dungarees.*] Oldtimer let it out 'bout the triptych.

BILL.   The rest of you move on.

TOMMY [*looking out from behind screen*].   No, don't go a step. You brought me
here, see me out!

BILL.   Tommy, let me explain it to you.

TOMMY [*coming out from behind screen*].   I gotta check out my apartment and
my clothes and money. Cynthia, . . . I can't wait for anybody to open the
door or look out for me and all that kinda crap you talk. A bunch-a liars!

960 BILL.   Oldtimer, why you . . .

TOMMY.   Leave him the hell alone. He ain't said nothin' that ain't so!

SONNY-MAN.   Explain to the sister that some mistakes have been made.

BILL.   Mistakes have been made, baby. The mistakes were yesterday, this is today . . .

TOMMY.   Yeah, and I'm Tomorrow, remember? Trouble is I was Tommin' to you, to all of you, . . . "Oh, maybe they gon' like me." . . . I was your fool, thinkin' writers and painters know moren' me, that maybe a little bit of you would rub off on me.

CYNTHIA.   We are wrong. I knew it yesterday. Tommy, I told you not to
970   expect anything out of this . . . arrangement.

BILL.   This is a relationship, not an arrangement.

SONNY-MAN.   Cynthia, I tell you all the time, keep outta other people's business. What the hell you got to do with who's gonna get what outta what? You and Oldtimer, yakkin' and yakkin'. [*To* OLDTIMER.] Man, your mouth gonna kill you.

BILL.   It's me and Tommy. Clear the room.

TOMMY.   Better not, I'll kill him! The "black people" this and the "Afro-American" . . . that . . . You ain't got no use for none-a us. Oldtimer, you their fool too. Till I got here they didn't even know your damn name.
980   There's something inside-a me that says I ain' suppose to let *nobody* play me cheap. Don't care how much they know! [*She sweeps some of the books to the floor.*]

BILL.   Don't you have any forgiveness in you? Would I be beggin' you if I didn't care? Can't you be generous enough . . .

TOMMY.   Nigger, I been too damn generous with you, already. All-a these people know I wasn't down here all night posin' for no pitcher, nigger!

BILL.   Cut that out, Tommy, and you not going anywhere!

TOMMY.   You wanna bet? Nigger!

BILL.   Okay, you called it, baby. I did act like a low, degraded person . . .

990 TOMMY [*combing out her wig with her fingers while holding it*].   Didn't call you no low, degraded person. Nigger! [*To* CYNTHIA *who is handing her a comb.*] "Do you have to wear a wig?" Yes! To soften the blow when yall go upside-a my head with a baseball bat. [*Going back to taunting* BILL *and ignoring* CYNTHIA'S *comb.*] Nigger!

BILL.   That's enough-a that. You right and you're wrong too.

TOMMY.   Ain't a-one-a us you like that's alive and walkin' by you on the street . . . you don't like flesh and blood niggers.

BILL.   Call me that, baby, but don't call yourself. That what you think of yourself?

1000 TOMMY.   If a black somebody is in a history book, or printed on a pitcher, or drawed on a paintin', . . . or if they're a statue, . . . dead, and outta the way, and can't talk back, then you dig 'em and full-a so much-a damn admiration and talk 'bout "our" history. But when you run into us livin' and breathin' ones, with the life's blood still pumpin' through us, . . . then you comin' on 'bout how we ain' never together. You hate us, that's what! *You hate black me!*

BILL [*stung to the heart, confused and saddened by the half truth which applies to himself*].   I never hated you, I never will, no matter what you or any of the rest of you do to *make* me hate you. I won't! Hell, woman, why do you say
1010   that! Why would I hate you??

TOMMY. Maybe I look too much like the mother that gave birth to you. Like the Ma and Pa that worked in the post office to buy you a house and a screen door with a damn duck on it. And you so ungrateful you didn't even like it.

BILL. No, I didn't, baby. I don't like screen doors with ducks on 'em.

TOMMY. You didn't like who was livin' behind them screen doors. Phoney Nigger!

BILL. That's all! Damnit! don't go there no more!

TOMMY. Hit me, so I can tear this place down and scream bloody murder.

1020 BILL [*somewhere between laughter and tears*]. Looka here, baby, I'm willin' to say I'm wrong, even in fronta the room fulla people . . .

TOMMY [*through clenched teeth*]. Nigger.

SONNY-MAN. The sister is upset.

TOMMY. And you stop callin' me "the" sister, . . . if you feelin' so brotherly why don't you say "my" sister? Ain't no we-ness in your talk. "The" Afro-American, "the" black man, there's no we-ness in you. Who you think you are?

SONNY-MAN. I was talkin' in general er . . . *my* sister, 'bout the masses.

TOMMY. There he go again. "The" masses. Tryin' to make out like we pitiful
1030 and you got it made. You the masses your damn self and don't even know it. [*Another angry look at* BILL.] Nigger.

BILL [*pulls dictionary from shelf*]. Let's get this ignorant "nigger" talk squared away. You can stand some education.

TOMMY. You *treat* me like a nigger, that's what. I'd rather be called one than treated that way.

BILL [*questions* TOMMY]. What is a nigger? [*Talks as he is trying to find word.*] A nigger is a low, degraded person, *any* low degraded person. I learned that from my teacher in the fifth grade.

TOMMY. Fifth grade is a liar! Don't pull that dictionary crap on me.

1040 BILL [*pointing to the book*]. Webster's New World Dictionary of The American Language, College Edition.

TOMMY. I don't need to find out what no college white folks say nigger is.

BILL. I'm tellin' you it's a low, degraded person. Listen. [*Reads from the book.*] Nigger, N-i-g-g-e-r, . . . A Negro . . . A member of any dark-skinned people . . . Damn. [*Amazed by dictionary description.*]

SONNY-MAN. Brother Malcolm *said* that's what they meant, . . . nigger is a Negro, Negro is a nigger.

BILL [*slowly finishing his reading*]. A vulgar, offensive term of hostility and contempt. Well, so much for the fifth grade teacher.

1050 SONNY-MAN. No, they do not call low, degraded white folks niggers. Come to think of it, did you ever hear whitey call Hitler a nigger? Now if some whitey digs us, . . . the others might call him a nigger-*lover*, but they don't call him no nigger.

OLDTIMER. No, they don't.

TOMMY [*near tears*]. When they say "nigger," just dry-long-so, they mean educated you and uneducated me. They hate you and call you "nigger," I called you "nigger" but I love you. [*There is dead silence in the room for a split second.*]

SONNY-MAN [*trying to establish peace*]. There you go. There you go.

1060 CYNTHIA [*cautioning* SONNY-MAN]. Now is not the time to talk, darlin'.

BILL. You love me? Tommy, that's the greatest compliment you could . . .

TOMMY [*sorry she said it*]. You must be runnin' a fever, nigger, I ain' said nothin' 'bout lovin' you.

BILL [*in a great mood*]. You did, yes, you did.

TOMMY. Well, you didn't say it to *me*.

BILL. Oh, Tommy, . . .

TOMMY [*cuts him off abruptly*]. And don't you dare say it now. I'm tellin' you, . . . it ain't to be said now. [*Checks through her paper bag to see if she has everything. Starts to put on the wig, changes her mind, holds it to the end of scene.*
1070 *Turns to the others in the room*] Oldtimer, . . . my brothers and my sister.

OLDTIMER. I wish I was a thousand miles away. I'm so sorry. [*He sits at the foot of the model stand.*]

TOMMY. I don't stay mad, it's here today and gone tomorrow. I'm sorry your feelin's got hurt, . . . but when I'm hurt I turn and hurt back. Somewhere, in the middle of last night, I thought the old me was gone, . . . lost forever, and gladly. But today was flippin' time, so back I flipped. Now it's "turn the other cheek" time. If I can go through life other-cheekin' the white folk, . . . guess yall can be other-cheeked too. But I'm going back to the nitty-gritty crowd, where the talk is we-ness and us-ness. I hate to do it but
1080 I have to thank you cause I'm walkin' out with much more than I brought in. [*Goes over and looks at the queen in the "Wine In The Wilderness" painting.*] Tomorrow-Marie had such a lovely yesterday. [BILL *takes her hand, she gently removes it from his grasp.*] Bill, I don't have to wait for anybody's by-your-leave to be a "Wine In The Wilderness" woman. I can be if I wanta, . . . and I *am*. I am. I am. I'm not the one you made up and painted, the very pretty lady who can't talk back, . . . but I'm "Wine In The Wilderness" . . . alive and kickin', me . . . Tomorrow-Marie, cussin' and fightin' and lookin' out for my damn self cause ain' nobody else 'round to do it, dontcha know. And, Cynthia, if my hair is straight, or if it's natural, or if I wear a wig, or
1090 take it off, . . . that's all right; because wigs . . . shoes . . . hats . . . bags . . . and even this . . . [*She picks up the African throw she wore a few moments before . . . fingers it.*] They're just what you call . . . access . . . [*fishing for the word*] . . . like what you wear with your Easter outfit . . .

CYNTHIA. Accessories.

TOMMY. Thank you, my sister. Accessories. Somethin' you add on or take off. The real thing is takin' place on the inside . . . that's where the action is. That's "Wine In The Wilderness," . . . a woman that's a real one and a good one. And yall just better believe I'm it. [*She proceeds to the door.*]

BILL. Tommy. [*She turns. He takes the beautiful queen, "Wine In The Wilderness"*
1100 *from the easel.*] She's not it at all, Tommy. This chick on the canvas, . . . nothin' but accessories, a dream, I drummed up outta the junk room of my mind. [*Places the "queen" to one side.*] You are and . . . [*Points to* OLDTIMER] . . . Edmond Lorenzo Matthews . . . the real beautiful people. . . . Cynthia . . .

CYNTHIA [*bewildered and unbelieving*]. Who? Me?

BILL. Yeah, honey, you and Sonny-man, don't know how beautiful you are. [*Indicates the other side of model stand.*] Sit there.

SONNY-MAN [*places cushions on the floor at the foot of the model stand*]. Just sit here and be my beautiful self. [*To* CYNTHIA]. Turn on, baby, we gonna get
1110 our picture took. [CYNTHIA *smiles.*]

BILL. Now there's Oldtimer, the guy who was here before there were scholarships and grants and stuff like that, the guy they kept outta the schools, the man the factories wouldn't hire, the union wouldn't let him join . . .

SONNY-MAN.   Yeah, yeah, rap to me. Where you goin' with it, man? Rap on.

BILL.   I'm makin' a triptych.

SONNY-MAN.   Make it, man.

BILL [*indicating* CYNTHIA *and* SONNY-MAN].   On the other side, Young Man and Woman, workin' together to do our thing.

TOMMY [*quietly*].   I'm goin' now.

1120   BILL.   But you belong up there in the center, "Wine In The Wilderness" . . . that's who you are. [*Moves the canvas of "the little girl" and places a sketch pad on the easel.*] The nightmare, about all that I've done disappearing before my eyes. It was a good nightmare. I was planning in the dark, all head and no heart. I couldn't see until you came, baby. [*To* CYNTHIA, SONNY-MAN *and* OLDTIMER.] Look at Tomorrow. She came through the biggest riot of all, . . . somethin' called "Slavery," and she's even comin' through the "now" scene, . . . folks laughin' at her, even her own folks laughin' at her. And look how . . . with her head high like she's poppin' her fingers at the world. [*Takes up charcoal pencil and tears old page off sketch pad so he can make*
1130   *a fresh drawing.*] Aw, let me put it down, Tommy. "Wine In The Wilderness," you gotta let me put it down so all the little boys and girls can look up and see you on the wall. And you know what they're gonna say? "Hey, don't she look like somebody we know?" [TOMMY *slowly returns and takes her seat on the stand.* TOMMY *is holding the wig in her lap. Her hands are very graceful looking against the texture of the wig.*] And they'll be right, you're somebody they know. . . . [*He is sketching hastily. There is a sound of thunder and the patter of rain.*] Yeah, roll them hoops and bicycle wheels. [*Music in low. Music up higher as* BILL *continues to sketch.*]

CURTAIN

[1969]

Critical Commentary on *Wine in the Wilderness*

When the curtain rises in Alice Childress's *Wine in the Wilderness*, the first thing we see is a room that is obviously being remodeled. What had once been an ordinary tenement apartment is slowly being transformed into a middle-class residence strongly marked by a consciousness of African-American heritage and culture. The bed is covered with an "African throw." The pieces of sculpture, wall hangings, and paintings are all "obviously black dominated." And the concern with cultural identity is suggested by the sprinkling of artwork by members of the "other darker peoples of the world": "A chinese incense-burner Buddha, an American Indian feathered war helmet, a Mexican serape, a Japanese fan, a West Indian travel poster."

As this setting suggests, the play is more directly concerned with the processes of cultural and personal transformation than with the particular events of the race riot outside—although it too is part of the larger societal change in the relationships between blacks and whites. Throughout the play Childress explores the processes of remodeling—the remodeling of rooms, of lives, of relationships, and of societies. That the transformation of the apartment is only "half finished" suggests (or at least symbolizes) that the parallel transformation within the protagonist, Bill Jameson, is also only half-finished. From his roots in a middle-class black neighborhood on Long Island, he is now well on his way toward becoming a cultured, sophisticated, and somewhat elitist black artist.

For the third part of his triptych, Bill wishes to paint a woman from the dregs of society: "ignorant, unfeminine, coarse, rude . . . vulgar. . . a poor, dumb chick that's had her behind kicked until it's numb." And at first Tommy appears to be just this kind of woman. She arrives on stage "dressed in a mismatched skirt and sweater, wearing a wig that is not comical, but is wiggy looking. . . . She wears sneakers and bobby sox, carries a brown paper sack." She looks a bit like a bag lady, fresh from rummaging in trash cans. In actuality, though, Tommy is far from downtrodden or debased and is indeed farther along in the process of remolding her personal identity than Bill himself. Her pride is such that she now refuses to continue working as anyone's servant, despite the admiration of her previous Park Avenue employers. Instead she prefers a more dignified, but more monotonous, job in a dress factory. And instead of being the victim of the oppressive white majority, as Bill would have her, Tommy has actually been burned out of her rooms by marauding blacks. Her bizarre appearance is a result of dispossession by her own people, and her inconsiderate treatment by Bill, Sonny, and (to some extent) Cynthia is an indication that social prejudice can be as cruelly unfair within the black community as in the larger mixed-race society.

Childress recognizes more clearly than most contemporary writers that social class is at least as powerful a cause of prejudice as race. Thus, she has carefully chosen her characters to represent the range of social classes within the black community. Bill has had a thoroughly middle-class upbringing on Long Island in a tidy home with hedges and crab grass and "an aluminum screen door with a duck on it." Like so many youths of all races, he scorns his parents (drab postal workers) and aspires to a cultivation that they lacked. He surrounds himself with books and paintings, but continues to be plagued by dreams of people "standing in a weird looking art gallery . . . looking and laughing at everything I've ever done." His pose of intellectual superiority is a form of overcompensation for these fears. In his condescending lectures to Tommy about black history, he fails entirely to realize that she too knows something of black history—and indeed knows about the struggle against repression and prejudice far more intimately than he.

Like many intellectuals, Bill and his writer friend Sonny tend to idealize and politicize events without truly considering their human implications. For Bill and Sonny the riot is the beginning of the "The people's revolution." Sonny expects to commemorate it in a novel "nine hundreds pages long," and Bill intends to paint it as something to be "sung and discussed for generations." Indeed the triptych he initially envisions is an overtly intellectual attempt to synthesize the goals of the revolution: it endorses the transformation of black girlhood (all pigtails and innocence) into regal black womanhood (adorned in an African wrap and golden headdress) without tolerating the debasement that Tommy is intended to represent. However, for the rioters themselves (represented in the play by Oldtimer) the riot is merely an opportunity for looting and stealing, for picking up a free bottle of liquor, a suit, a ham, and a salami. Finally, for Tommy the riot is a personal tragedy and a far too typical example of the callous way some human beings treat others. The victims of the riot are mainly members of the black community itself: their grocery stores, restaurants, and shops have been looted and burned; their homes have been damaged or destroyed. She does not hate the rioters themselves, but she does despise their violence, lawlessness, and cruelty.

Childress's play is interesting in part because of its implied comments about revolution, race relations, and the black identity. But it also has very important points to make about the relationships between men and women and the need for a feminist remodeling of society. One of Cynthia's functions in the play is to explain the conventional sociological view of the black "Matriarchal Society" which produces hard, no-nonsense females like Tommy. Tommy's mother had been abandoned by her father, and Tommy herself had dropped out of school early because she got tired of a life in which there was no money for grits or garters. In a world where no one else will look out for her, she has become accustomed to looking out for herself. Having reached age thirty without finding a good man to marry, she is used to opening her own doors, earning her own wages, and speaking her own mind. When Cynthia tells her that she has to "let the black man have his manhood again," Tommy retorts, "I didn't take it from him, how I'm gonna give it back?"

In a very general way Cynthia is correct. Tommy cannot find a man she wants because she is unable, or unwilling, to be the kind of woman such men dream about. Yet the problem is not in Tommy, but in men's dreams, as Bill's initial plan for the triptych indicates. He wants young girls to mold themselves into African queens and not strong, independent women like Tommy or even Cynthia. By the end of the play, he recognizes his error, concluding that his initial portrait of black womanhood was "nothin' but accessories, a dream I drummed up outta the junk room of my mind." The essential movement in the play is Bill's gradual evolution from one dream of black womanhood to another, from an African dream to an American dream that is still emerging.

A Selective Bibliography on *Wine in the Wilderness*

Austin, Gayle. "Alice Childress: Black Woman Playwright as Feminist Critic." *The Southern Quarterly: A Journal of the Arts in the South* 25.3 (1987): 53–62.

Childress, Alice. "A Woman Playwright Speaks Her Mind." *Anthology of the Afro-American in the Theatre: A Critical Approach.* Ed. Lindsay Patterson. Cornwell Heights, PA: Publishers Agency, 1976. 75–79.

Curb, Rosemary. "Alice Childress." *Twentieth-Century American Dramatists.* Vol. 7. *Dictionary of Literary Biography.* Detroit: Gale, 1981. 118–24.

Hey, Samuel A. "Alice Childress's Dramatic Structure." *Black Women Writers (1950–1980): A Critical Evaluation.* Ed. Mari Evans. Garden City, NY: Doubleday, 1984. 117–28.

Holliday, Polly. "I Remember Alice Childress." *The Southern Quarterly: A Journal of the Arts in the South* 25.3 (1987): 63–65.

Killens, John D. "The Literary Genius of Alice Childress." *Black Women Writers (1950–1980): A Critical Evaluation.* Ed. Mari Evans. Garden City, NY: Doubleday, 1984. 129–33.

Peter Shaffer (1926–   )

AMADEUS

THE SET

Amadeus *can and should be played in a variety of settings. What is described in this text is to a large extent based on the exquisite formulation found for the play by the designer John Bury, helped into being by the director, Peter Hall. I was of course in enthusiastic agreement with this formulation, and set it down here as a tribute to exquisite work.*

The set consisted basically of a handsome rectangle of patterned wood—its longest sides leading away from the viewer—set into a stage of ice-blue plastic. This surface shifted beguilingly under various lights played upon it, to show a bluish gray, or azure, or emerald green, and reflected the actors standing upon it. The entire design was undeniably modern, yet it suggested without self-consciousness the age of the Rococo.[1] Costumes and objects were sumptuously of the period—and should always be so wherever the play is produced.

The rectangle largely represented interiors: especially those of Salieri's salon, Mozart's last apartment, assorted reception rooms and opera houses. At the back stood a grand proscenium sporting gilded cherubs blowing huge trumpets, and supporting grand curtains of sky-blue, which could rise and part to reveal an enclosed space almost the width of the area downstage. Into this space superb backdrops were flown, and superb projections thrown, to show the scarlet boxes of theaters, the trees of the Prater, or a huge gilded object composed of Masonic emblems. In it the audience could see an eighteenth-century street at night (cunningly enlarged from the lid of Mozart's own curious snuff-box) or a vast wall of gold mirrors with an immense golden fireplace, representing the encrusted Palace of Schönbrunn. In it also appeared silhouettes of scandal-mongering citizens of Vienna, or the formal figures of the Emperor Joseph II of Austria and his brocaded courtiers. This wonderful upstage space, which was in effect an immense Rococo peep show, will be referred to throughout this text as the Light Box.

* * *

On stage, before the lights are lowered in the theater, four objects are to be seen by the audience. To the left, on the wooden rectangle, stands a small table, bearing a cakestand full of confections. In the center, farther upstage and also on the wood, stands a wheelchair of the eighteenth century, with its back to us. To the right, on the reflecting plastic, stands a beautiful fortepiano in a marquetry case. Above the stage is suspended a large chandelier showing many globes of opaque glass.

All directions will be given from the viewpoint of the audience.

Changes of time and place are indicated throughout by changes of light. In reading the text it must be remembered that the action is wholly continuous. Its fluidity is ensured by the use of servants played by actors in eighteenth-century livery, whose role it is to move the furniture and carry on props with ease and correctness while the action

---

[1] A very elaborate style of architecture and decoration, common in the eighteenth century.

proceeds around them. Through a pleasant paradox of theater their constant coming and going, bearing tables, chairs or cloaks, should render them virtually invisible and certainly unremarkable. This will aid the play to be acted throughout in its proper manner: with the sprung line, gracefulness and energy for which Mozart is so especially celebrated.

CHARACTERS

ANTONIO SALIERI

WOLFGANG AMADEUS MOZART

CONSTANZE WEBER, *wife to Mozart*

JOSEPH II, *Emperor of Austria*

COUNT JOHANN KILIAN VON STRACK,
   Groom of the Imperial Chamber

COUNT FRANZ ORSINI-ROSENBERG,
   Director of the Imperial Opera

BARON GOTTFRIED VAN SWIETEN,
   Prefect of the Imperial Library

TWO "VENTICELLI"— *"Little Winds," purveyors of information, gossip and rumor*

A MAJORDOMO[2]

SALIERI'S VALET *(Silent part)*

SALIERI'S COOK *(Silent part)*

KAPELLMEISTER[3] BONNO *(Silent part)*

KATHERINA CAVALIERI, *Salieri's pupil
   (Silent part)*

CITIZENS OF VIENNA

The VENTICELLI *also play the* TWO
   GALLANTS *at the part in Act One.*

THE CITIZENS OF VIENNA *also play the*
   SERVANTS, *who move furniture and
   bring on props as required.*

The action of the play takes place in Vienna in November 1823, and in recall, the decade 1781–1791.

ACT I

SCENE 1

Vienna

Darkness.

Savage whispers fill the theater. We can distinguish nothing at first from this snakelike hissing save the word SALIERI! *repeated here, there and everywhere around the theater. Also, the barely distinguishable word* ASSASSIN!

The whispers overlap and increase in volume, slashing the air with wicked intensity. The light grows Upstage to reveal the silhouettes of men and women dressed in the top hats and skirts of the early nineteenth century— CITIZENS OF VIENNA, *all crowded together in the Light Box, and uttering their scandal.*

WHISPERERS. *Salieri! . . . Salieri! . . . Salieri!*

[*Upstage, in a wheelchair, with his back to us, sits an old man. We can just see, as the light grows a little brighter, the top of his head, encased in an old red cap, and perhaps the shawl wrapped around his shoulders.*]

WHISPERERS. *Salieri! . . . Salieri! . . . Salieri!*

---

[2] A *majordomo* is the butler or steward in charge of a royal household.
[3] *Kappellmeister* was originally an honorable title given to a conductor.

[*Two middle-aged gentlemen hurry in from either side, also wearing the long cloaks and tall hats of the period. These are the two* Venticelli: *purveyors of fact, rumor and gossip throughout the play. They speak rapidly—in this first appearance extremely rapidly—so that the scene has the air of a fast and dreadful overture.*[4] *Sometimes they speak to each other, sometimes to us—but always with the urgency of men who have ever been first with the news.*]

Venticello 1. I don't believe it.
Venticello 2. I don't believe it.
V.1. I don't believe it.
V.2. I don't believe it.
Whisperers. *Salieri!*

V.1. They say.
V.2. I hear.
10 V.1. I hear.
V.2. They say.
V.1. & V.2. *I don't believe it!*
Whisperers. *Salieri!*

V.1. The whole city is talking.
V.2. You hear it all over.
V.1. The cafés.
V.2. The Opera.
V.1. The Prater.
V.2. The gutter.
20 V.1. They say even Metternich[5] repeats it.
V.2. They say even Beethoven,[6] his old pupil.
V.1. But why now?
V.2. After so long?
V.1. Thirty-two years!
V.1. & V.2. *I don't believe it!*
Whisperers. *SALIERI!*

V.1. They say he shouts it out all day!
V.2. I hear he cries it out all night!
V.1. Stays in his apartments.
30 V.2. Never goes out.
V.1. Not for a year now.
V.2. Longer. Longer.
V.1. Must be seventy.
V.2. Older. Older.
V.1. Antonio Salieri—
V.2. The famous musician—
V.1. Shouting it aloud!
V.2. Crying it aloud!!

---

[4] A musical introduction to a major composition.
[5] Prince Klemens Wenzel Nepomuk Lothar von Metternich (1773–1859) was an Austrian statesman and the most influential diplomat in Europe at the time of the play's action.
[6] Ludwig van Beethoven (1770–1827), the famous German composer.

V.1.   Impossible.
40 V.2.   Incredible.
V.1.   I don't believe it!
V.2.   I don't believe it!
WHISPERERS.   *SALIERI!*

V.1.   I know who *started* the tale!
V.2.   *I* know who started the tale!

[*Two old men—one thin and dry, one very fat—detach themselves from the crowd at the back and walk downstage on either side; Salieri's* VALET *and* PASTRY COOK.]

V.1. [*indicating him*].   The old man's valet!
V.2. [*indicating him*].   The old man's cook!
V.1.   The valet hears him shouting!
V.2.   The cook hears him crying!
50 V.1.   What a story!
V.2.   What a scandal. [*The* VENTICELLI *move quickly upstage, one on either side, and each collects a silent informant.* VENTICELLO ONE *walks down eagerly with the* VALET; VENTICELLO TWO *walks down eagerly with the* COOK.]
V.1. [*to* VALET].   What does he say, your master?
V.2. [*to* COOK].   What *exactly* does he say, the Kapellmeister?
V.1.   Alone in this house—
V.2.   All day and all night—
V.1.   What sins does he shout?
V.2.   The old fellow—
60 V.1.   The recluse—
V.2.   What horrors have you heard?
V.1. & V.2.   *Tell us! Tell us! Tell us at once! What does he cry? What does he cry? What does he cry?*

[VALET AND COOK *gesture toward* SALIERI.]

SALIERI [*in a great cry*].   MOZART!!! [*Silence*]
V.1. [*whispering*].   Mozart!
V.2. [*whispering*].   Mozart!
SALIERI.   *Perdonami, Mozart! Il tuo assassino ti chiede perdono!*[7]
V.1. [*in disbelief*].   Pardon, Mozart!
V.2. [*in disbelief*].   Pardon your assassin!
70 V.1. & V.2.   God preserve us!
SALIERI.   *Pietà, Mozart! . . . Mozart, pietà!*[8]
V.1.   Mercy, Mozart!
V.2.   Mozart have mercy!
V.1.   He speaks in Italian when excited!
V.2.   German when not!
V.1.   *Perdonami, Mozart!*
V.2.   Pardon your assassin!

[*The* VALET *and the* COOK *walk to either side of the stage and stand still. Pause. The* VENTICELLI *cross themselves, deeply shocked.*]

---

[7] "Pardon me, Mozart! Your assassin asks for pardon!"
[8] "Have mercy, Mozart! . . . Mozart, have mercy!

V.1.   There was talk once before, you know.

V.2.   Thirty-two years ago.

80 V.1.   When Mozart was dying.

V.2.   He claimed he'd been poisoned!

V.1.   Some said he accused a man.

V.2.   Some said that man was Salieri!

V.1.   But no one believed it.

V.2.   They *knew* what he died of!

V.1.   Syphilis, surely.

V.2.   Like everybody else. [*Pause.*]

V.1. [*slyly*].   But what if Mozart was right?

V.2.   If he really *was* murdered?

90 V.1.   And by him. Our First Kapellmeister!

V.2.   Antonio Salieri!

V.1.   It can't possibly be true.

V.2.   It's not actually credible.

V.1.   Because *why?*

V.2.   Because why?

V.1. & V.2.   *Why on earth would he do it?*

V.1.   And why confess *now?*

V.2.   After thirty-two years!

Whisperers.   Salieri! [*Pause.*]

100 Salieri.   Mozart! Mozart! Perdonami! . . . Il tuo assasino ti chiede perdono!

[*Pause. They look at him, then at each other.*]

V.1.   What do you think?

V.2.   What do you think?

V.1.   I don't believe it!

V.2.   *I* don't believe it! [*Pause.*]

V.1.   All the same . . .

V.2.   Is it just possible?

V.1. & V.2 [*whispering*].   Did he do it after all?!

Whisperers.   *SALIERI!*

[*The* Venticelli *go off. The* Valet *and the* Cook *remain, on either side of the stage.* Salieri *swivels his wheelchair around and stares at us. We see a man of seventy in an old stained dressing gown. He rises and squints at the audience, as if trying to see it.*]

SCENE II

Salieri's Apartment
November 1823. The small hours

Salieri [*calling to audience*].   Vi saluto! Ombri del Futuro! Antonio Salieri—a

110   vostro servizio![9] [*A clock outside in the street strikes three.*] I can almost see you in your ranks—waiting for your turn to live. Ghosts of the Future! Be visible. I beg you. Be visible. Come to this dusty old room—this time, the smallest hours of dark. November, eighteen hundred and twenty-three—

---

[9] "I salute you! Shades of the Future! Antonio Salieri—at your service!"

and be my confessors! Will you not enter this place and stay with me till dawn? Just till dawn—smeary six o'clock!
WHISPERERS.   *Salieri!* . . . *Salieri!* . . .

[*The curtains slowly descend on the* CITIZENS OF VIENNA. *Faint images of long windows are projected on the silk.*]

SALIERI.   Can you hear them? Vienna is a City of Slander. Everyone tells tales here: even my servants. I keep only two now. [*He indicates them.*] They've been with me ever since I came here, fifty years ago. The keeper of the
120   razor; the maker of the cakes. One keeps me tidy, the other keeps me full. [*To them.*] "Leave me, both of you! Tonight I do not go to bed at all!" [*They react in surprise.*] "Return here tomorrow morning at six precisely—to shave, to feed your capricious master!" [*He smiles at them both and claps his hands in dismissal.*] *Via, Via, via, via! Grazie!*[10] [*They bow, bewildered, and leave the stage. He peers hard at the audience, trying to see it.*] Now, won't you appear? I need you—*desperately!* This is the last hour of my life. Those about to die implore you! . . . What must I do to make you visible? Raise you up in the flesh to be my last, last audience? . . . Does it take an Invocation? That's how it's always done in opera! Ah yes, of course: that's it. An *Invocation.*
130   The only way. [*He rises.*] Let me try to conjure you *now*—Ghosts of the distant Future—so I can see you. [*He gets out of the wheelchair and huddles over to the fortepiano. He stands at the instrument and begins to sing in a high cracked voice, interrupting himself at the end of each sentence with figurations on the keyboard in the manner of a recitativo secco.*[11] *During this, the houselights slowly come up to illuminate the audience.*]
SALIERI [*singing*].

> Ghosts of the Future!
> Shades of time to come!
> So much more unavoidable than those of time gone by!
140 > Appear with what sympathy incarnation may endow you!
> Appear you.
> The yet to be born!
> The yet to hate!
> The yet to *kill!*
> Appear . . . posterity!

[*The light in the audience reaches its maximum. It stays like this during all of the following.*]

SALIERI [*speaking again*].   There. It worked. I can see you! That is the result of proper training. I was taught invocation by Gluck,[12] who was a true master at it. He had to be. In his day, that was what people went to the opera for: the raising of gods, and ghosts. Nowadays, since Rossini[13]

---

[10] "Go. Go, go, go! Thank you!"
[11] In opera, *recitativo secco* is a style of declamatory singing to a bass accompaniment, used to link one aria, duet, or chorus with another.
[12] Christoph Willibald von Gluck (1714–1787) was a German composer whose ideas about opera influenced both Salieri and Mozart.
[13] Gioacchimo Rossini (1792–1868) was an Italian composer, perhaps most famous for his comic opera *The Barber of Seville* (1816) and the *William Tell* overture (1829).

150 became the rage, they prefer to watch the escapades of hairdressers. [*Pause.*] *Scusate.*[14] Invocation is an exhausting business! I need refreshment. [*He sits again in his wheelchair, moves himself over to the cake-stand, selects a cake and eats it.*] It's a little repellant, I admit, but actually, the first sin I have to confess to you is gluttony. Sticky gluttony at that. Infantine, *Italian* gluttony! The truth is that all my life I have never been able to conquer a lust for the sweetmeats of Northern Italy, where I was born. From the ages of three to seventy-three, my entire career has been conducted with the taste of almonds sprinkled with sifted sugar. [*Lustfully.*] Veronese biscuits! Milanese macaroons! Snow dumplings with pistachio sauce! . . . Do not

160 judge me too harshly for this. All men harbor patriotic feelings of some kind. . . . My parents were provincial subjects of the Austrian Empire. A Lombardy merchant and his Lombardy wife. Their notion of place was the tiny town of Legnago—which I could not wait to leave. Their notion of God was a superior Hapsburg emperor, inhabiting a Heaven only slightly farther off than Vienna. All they required of Him was to protect commerce, and keep them forever preserved in mediocrity. My own requirements were very different. [*Pause.*] I wanted *Fame.* Not to deceive you, I wanted to blaze like a comet across the firmament of Europe! Yet only in one especial way. Music! Absolute music! . . . A note of music is either right

170 or wrong *absolutely!* Not even time can alter that: music is God's art. [*Excited by the recollection.*] Already when I was ten a spray of sounded notes would make me dizzy almost to falling! By twelve, I was stumbling about under the poplar trees humming my arias and anthems to the Lord. My one desire was to join all the composers who had celebrated His glory through the long Italian past! . . . Every Sunday I saw Him in church, painted on the flaking wall. I don't mean Christ. The Christs of Lombardy are simpering sillies, with lambkins on their sleeves. No: I mean an old candle-smoked God in a mulberry robe, staring at the world with dealer's eyes. Tradesmen had put him up there. Those eyes made bargains, real

180 and irreversible. "You give me so—I'll give you so! No more. No less!" [*He eats a sweet biscuit in his excitement.*] The night before I left Legnago forever, I went to see Him, and made a bargain with Him myself! I was a sober sixteen, filled with a desperate sense of right. I knelt before the God of Bargains, and I prayed through the moldering plaster with all my soul. [*He kneels.*] "*Signore,* let me be a composer! Grant me sufficient fame to enjoy it. In return, I will live with virtue. I will strive to better the lot of my fellows. And I will honor You with much music all the days of my life!" As I said *Amen,* I saw His eyes flare. [*As "God."*] "*Bene.*[15] Go forth, Antonio. Serve Me and mankind, and you will be blessed!" . . . "*Grazie!*" I called

190 back. "I am Your servant for life!" [*He gets to his feet again.*] The very next day, a family friend suddenly appeared—out of the blue—took me off to Vienna and paid for me to study music! Shortly afterwards I met the Emperor, who favored me. Clearly my bargain had been accepted! [*Pause.*] The same year I left Lombardy, a young prodigy was touring Europe. A miraculous virtuoso aged ten years. Wolfgang Amadeus Mozart. [*Pause. He smiles at the audience.*] And now, gracious ladies! obliging gentlemen! I

---

[14] "Excuse me."
[15] "Good."

present to you—for one performance only—my last composition, entitled
The Death of Mozart; or, Did I Do It? . . . Dedicated to posterity on this, the
last night of my life! [*He bows deeply, undoing as he does so the buttons of his old*
200   *dressing gown. When he straightens himself, divesting himself of this drab outer*
garment and his cap, he is a young man in the prime of life, wearing a sky-blue coat
and the elegant decent clothes of a successful composer of the 1780s. The house
lights go down again on the audience.]

SCENE III

Transformation to the Eighteenth Century

Music sounds softly in the background: a serene piece for strings by Salieri. SER-
VANTS *enter. One takes away the dressing gown and cap; another places on the table*
a wigstand bearing a powdered wig; a third brings on a chair and places it at the left,
upstage.

At the back, the blue curtains rise and part to show the EMPEROR JOSEPH II *and his*
COURT *bathed in golden light, against a golden background of mirrors and an*
immense golden fireplace. His Majesty is seated, holding a rolled paper, listening to
the music. Also listening are COUNT VON STRACK; COUNT ORSINI-ROSENBERG; BARON
VAN SWIETEN; *and an anonymous* PRIEST, *dressed in a soutane. An old wigged* COURT-
IER *enters and takes his place at the keyboard:* KAPELLMEISTER BONNO. SALIERI *takes*
his wig from the stand.

SALIERI [*in a young man's voice: vigorous and confident*].   The place throughout
is Vienna. The year—to begin with—1781. The age still that of the Enlightenment: that clear time before the guillotine fell in France and cut all
our lives in half. I am thirty-one. Already a prolific composer to the
Hapsburg court. I own a respectable house and a respectable wife—Teresa.

[*Enter* TERESA: *a padded, placid lady who seats herself uprightly in the upstage chair.*]

210 SALIERI.   I do not mock her, I assure you. I required only one quality in a
domestic companion—lack of fire. And in that omission Teresa was con-
spicuous. [*Ceremoniously, he puts on his powdered wig.*] I also had a prize
pupil: Katherina Cavalieri.

[KATHERINA *swirls on from the opposite side: a beautiful girl of twenty. The music*
becomes vocal: faintly, we hear a SOPRANO *singing a concert aria.*[16] *Like* TERESA'S,
KATHERINA'S *part is mute, but as she enters she stands by the fortepiano*[17] *and ener-*
getically mimes her rapturous singing. At the keyboard, old BONNO *accompanies her*
appreciatively.]

SALIERI.   She was later to become the best singer of her age. But at that time
she was mainly a bubbling student with merry eyes and a sweet, eatable
mouth. I was very much in love with Katherina—or at least in lust. But
because of my vow to God I was entirely faithful to my wife. I had never

---

[16] An aria is an air or melody for one voice.
[17] A piano.

laid a finger upon the girl—except occasionally to depress her diaphragm
in the way of teaching her to sing. My ambition burned with an unquench-
220 able flame. Its chief goal was the post of First Royal Kappellmeister, then
held by Giuseppe Bonno [*indicating him*], seventy years old, and apparently immortal. [*All on stage, save* SALIERI, *suddenly freeze. He speaks very
directly to the audience.*] You, when you come, will be told that we musicians
of the eighteenth century were no better than servants: the willing slaves
of the well-to-do. This is quite true. It is also quite false. Yes, we were
servants. But we were learned servants! And we used our learning to
celebrate men's average lives.

[*A grander music sounds. The* EMPEROR *remains seated, but the other four men in the
Light Box*—STRACK, ROSENBERG, VAN SWIETEN *and the* PRIEST—*come slowly out onto
the main stage and process imposingly down it, and around it, and up it again to
return to their places. Only the* PRIEST *goes off, as do* TERESA *on her side, and*
KATHERINA *on hers.*]

SALIERI [*over this*].   We took unremarkable men—usual bankers, run-of-the-
mill priests, ordinary soldiers and statesmen and wives—and sacramen-
230 talized their mediocrity. We smoothed their noons with string *divisi!*[18] We
pierced their nights with *chitarrini!*[19] We gave them processions for their
strutting, serenades for their rutting, high horns for their hunting, and
drums for their wars! Trumpets sounded when they entered the world,
and trombones groaned when they left it! The savor of their days remains
behind because of *us*, our music still remembered while their politics are
long forgotten.

[*The* EMPEROR *hands his rolled paper to* STRACK *and goes off. In the Light Box are left
standing, like three icons,* ORSINI-ROSENBERG, *plump and supercilious, aged sixty;*
VON STRACK, *stiff and proper, aged fifty-five;* VAN SWIETEN, *cultivated and serious,
aged fifty. The lights go down on them a little.*]

SALIERI.   Tell me, before you call us servants, who served whom? And who, I
wonder, in your generations, will immortalize *you*?

[*The two* VENTICELLI *come on quickly downstage, from either side. They are now
bewigged also, and are dressed well, in the style of the late eighteenth century. Their
manner is more confidential than before.*]

V.1. [*to* SALIERI].   Sir!
240 V.2. [*to* SALIERI].   Sir!
V.1.   Sir. Sir.
V.2.   Sir. Sir. Sir! [SALIERI *bids them wait for a second.*]
SALIERI.   I was the most successful young musician in the city of musicians.
And now suddenly, without warning—[*They approach him eagerly, from either
side.*]
V.1.   Mozart!
V.2.   Mozart!

---

[18] Musical passages requiring the division of the orchestra into two groups.
[19] Small guitars.

V.1. & V.2. *Mozart has come!*

SALIERI. These are my *Venticelli*. My "Little Winds," as I called them. [*He*
250   *gives each a coin from his pocket.*] The secret of successful living in a large city
is always to know to the minute what is being done behind your back.

V.1.   He's left Salzburg.

V.2.   Means to give concerts.

V.1.   Asking for subscribers.

SALIERI.   I'd known of him for years, of course. Tales of his prowess were told
all over Europe.

V.1.   They say he wrote his first symphony at five.

V.2.   I hear his first concerto at four.

V.1.   A full opera at fourteen!

260 SALIERI [*to them*].   How old is he now?

V.2.   Twenty-five.

SALIERI [*carefully*].   And how long is he remaining?

V.1.   He's not departing.

V.2.   He's here to stay. [*The* VENTICELLI *glide off.*]

SCENE IV

The Palace of Schönbrunn

Lights come up on the three stiff figures of ROSENBERG, STRACK *and* VAN SWIETEN,
standing upstage in the Light Box. The CHAMBERLAIN *hands the paper he has received*
from the EMPEROR *to the* DIRECTOR OF THE OPERA. SALIERI *remains downstage.*

STRACK [*to* ROSENBERG].   You are required to commission a comic opera in
German from Herr Mozart.

SALIERI [*to audience*].   Johann von Strack. Royal Chamberlain. A court official
to his collarbone.

ROSENBERG [*loftily*].   Why in German? Italian is the only possible language for
270   opera!

SALIERI.   Count Orsini-Rosenberg, Director of the Opera. Benevolent to all
things Italian—especially myself.

STRACK [*stiffly*].   The idea of a national opera is dear to His Majesty's heart.
He desires to hear pieces in good plain German.

VAN SWIETEN.   Yes, but why *comic*? It is not the function of music to be funny.

SALIERI.   Baron van Swieten. Prefect of the Imperial Library. Ardent Freemason. Yet to find *anything* funny. Known, for his enthusiasm for old-
fashioned music, as "Lord Fugue."

VAN SWIETEN.   I heard last week a remarkable *serious* opera from Mozart:
280   *Idomeneo, King of Crete.*

ROSENBERG.   I heard that too. A young fellow trying to impress beyond his
abilities. Too much spice. Too many notes.

STRACK [*firmly, to* ROSENBERG].   Nevertheless, kindly convey the commission to
him today.

ROSENBERG [*taking the paper reluctantly*].   I believe we are going to have trouble with this young man. [ROSENBERG *leaves the Light Box and strolls down the*
stage to SALIERI]. He was a child prodigy. That always spells trouble. His
father is Leopold Mozart, a bad-tempered Salzburg musician who dragged

the boy endlessly around Europe, making him play the keyboard blind-
290 folded, with one finger, and that sort of thing. [*To* SALIERI.] All prodigies
are hateful—*non è vero, Compositore?*[20]
SALIERI.   *Divengono sempre sterili con gli anni.*[21]
ROSENBERG.   *Precisamente. Precisamente.*[22]
STRACK [*calling suspiciously*].   What are you saying?
ROSENBERG [*airily*].   Nothing, Herr Chamberlain! ... *Niente, Signor Pom-
poso! ...*[23] [*He strolls on out.* STRACK *strides off, irritated.* VAN SWIETEN *now comes
downstage.*]
VAN SWIETEN.   We meet tomorrow, I believe, on your committee to devise
pensions for old musicians.
300 SALIERI [*deferentially*].   It's most gracious of you to attend, Baron.
VAN SWIETEN.   You're a worthy man, Salieri. You should join our Brother-
hood of Masons. We would welcome you warmly.
SALIERI.   I would be honored, Baron!
VAN SWIETEN.   If you wished, I could arrange initiation into my lodge.
SALIERI.   That would be more than my due.
VAN SWIETEN.   Nonsense. We embrace men of talent of all conditions. I may
invite young Mozart also—dependent on the impression he makes.
SALIERI [*bowing*].   Of course, Baron.

[VAN SWIETEN *goes out.*]

SALIERI [*to audience*].   Honor indeed. In those days almost every man of
310 influence in Vienna was a Mason, and the Baron's lodge by far the most
fashionable. As for young Mozart, I confess I was alarmed by his coming.
Not by the commission of a comic opera, even though I myself was then
attempting one called *The Chimney Sweep*. No, what worried me were reports about the man himself. He was praised altogether too much.

[*The* VENTICELLI *hurry in from either side.*]

V.1.   Such gaiety of spirit!
V.2.   Such ease of manner!
V.1.   Such natural charm!
SALIERI [*to the* VENTICELLI].   Really? Where does he live?
V.1.   Peter Platz.
320 V.2.   Number eleven.
V.1.   The landlady is Madame Weber.
V.2.   A real bitch.
V.1.   Takes in male lodgers, and has a tribe of daughters.
V.2.   Mozart is after one of them.
V.1.   Constanze.
V.2.   Flighty little piece.
V.1.   Her mother's pushing marriage.
V.2.   His *father* isn't!

---

[20] "Isn't that true, Composer?"
[21] "Always becoming impotent with age."
[22] "Precisely. Precisely."
[23] "Nothing, Signor Pompous!"

V.1.   Daddy is worried sick!
330 V.2.   Writes him every day from Salzburg!
SALIERI [to them].   I want to meet him. What houses does he visit?
V.1.   He'll be at the Baroness Waldstädten's tomorrow night.
SALIERI.   Grazie.
V.2.   Some of his music is to be played.
SALIERI [to both].   Restiamo in contatto.[24]
V.1. & V.2.   Certamente, Signore![25] [They go off.]
SALIERI [to audience].   So to the Baroness Waldstädten's I went. That night
changed my life.

SCENE V

The Library of the Baroness Waldstädten

In the Light Box, two elegantly curtained windows surrounded by handsome subdued wallpaper.
TWO SERVANTS bring on a large table loaded with cakes and desserts. Two more
carry on a grand high-backed wing chair, which they place ceremoniously downstage
at the left.

SALIERI [to audience].   I entered the library to take first a little refreshment.
340   My generous hostess always put out the most delicious confections in that
room whenever she knew I was coming. Dolci, caramelli, and most especially a miraculous crema al mascarpone—which is simply cream cheese
mixed with granulated sugar and suffused with rum—that was totally
irresistible! [He takes a little bowl of it from the cake-stand and sits in the wing
chair, facing out front. Thus seated, he is invisible to anyone entering from upstage.] I had just sat down in a high-backed chair to consume this paradisal
dish—unobservable, as it happened, to anyone who might come in.

[Offstage, noises are heard.]

CONSTANZE [off].   Squeak! Squeak! Squeak! [CONSTANZE runs on from upstage: a
pretty girl in her early twenties, full of high spirits. At this second she is pretending
350   to be a mouse. She runs across the stage in her gay party dress, and hides under the
fortepiano.
Suddenly a small, pallid, large-eyed man in a showy wig and a showy set of
clothes runs in after her and freezes—center—as a cat would freeze, hunting a
mouse. This is WOLFGANG AMADEUS MOZART.
As we get to know him through his next scenes, we discover several things about
him: he is an extremely restless man, his hands and feet in almost continuous
motion; his voice is light and high; and he is possessed of an unforgettable giggle—
piercing and infantile.]
MOZART.   Miaouw!
360 CONSTANZE [betraying where she is].   Squeak!

---

[24] "Stay in contact."
[25] "Certainly, Signore!"

MOZART.   Miaouw! . . . Miaouw! . . . Miaouw! [*The composer drops on all fours and, wrinkling his face, begins spitting and stalking his prey. The mouse—giggling with excitement—breaks her cover and dashes across the floor. The cat pursues. Almost at the chair where* SALIERI *sits concealed, the mouse turns at bay. The cat stalks her—nearer and nearer—in its knee breeches and elaborate coat.*] I'm going to pounce-bounce! I'm going to scrunch-munch! I'm going to chew-poo my little mouse-wouse! I'm going to tear her to bits with my paws-claws!

CONSTANZE.   No!

370 MOZART.   Paws-claws—paws-claws—paws-claws. *Ohh!* [*He falls on her. She screams.*]

SALIERI [*to audience*].   Before I could rise, it had become difficult to do so.

MOZART.   I'm going to bite you in half with my fangs-wangs! My little Stanzerl-wanzerl-banzerl! [*She laughs delightedly, lying prone beneath him.*] You're trembling! . . . I think you're frightened of puss-wuss! . . . I think you're scared to death! [*Intimately.*] I think you're going to shit yourself! [*She squeals, but is not really shocked. He emits a high-pitched giggle.*] In a moment it's going to be on the floor!

CONSTANZE.   Sssh! Someone'll hear you! [*He imitates the noise of a fart.*] Stop it

380 Wolferl! Ssh!

MOZART.   Here it comes now! I can hear it *coming!* . . . Oh, what a melancholy note! Something's dropping from your boat! [*Another fart noise, slower.* CONSTANZE *shrieks with amusement.*]

CONSTANZE.   Stop it now! It's stupid! Really *stupid!*

[SALIERI *sits appalled.*]

MOZART.   Hey—hey—what's "Trazom"?

CONSTANZE.   What?

MOZART.   T-r-a-z-o-m. What's that mean?

CONSTANZE.   How should *I* know?

MOZART.   It's Mozart spelled backwards—shit-wit! If you ever married me,

390 you'd be Constanze Trazom.

CONSTANZE.   No, I wouldn't.

MOZART.   Yes, you would. Because I'd want everything backwards once I was married. I'd want to lick my wife's arse instead of her face.

CONSTANZE.   You're not going to lick anything at this rate. Your father's never going to give his consent to us. [*The sense of fun deserts him instantly.*]

MOZART.   And who cares about his consent?

CONSTANZE.   *You* do. You care very much. You wouldn't do it without it.

MOZART.   Wouldn't I?

400 CONSTANZE.   No, you wouldn't. Because you're too scared of him. I know what he says about me. [*Solemn voice.*] "If you marry that dreadful girl, you'll end up lying on straw with beggars for children!"

MOZART [*impulsively*].   Marry me!

CONSTANZE.   Don't be silly.

MOZART.   Marry me!

CONSTANZE.   Are you serious?

MOZART [*defiantly*].   Yes! . . . Answer me this minute: yes or no! Say yes, then

I can go home, climb into bed, shit over the mattress and shout, "I *did* it!" [*He rolls on top of her delightedly, uttering his high whinneying giggle. The* 410   Majordomo *of the house stalks in, upstage.*]

Majordomo [*imperviously*].   Her Ladyship is ready to commence.

Mozart.   Ah! . . . Yes! . . . Good! [*He picks himself up, embarrassed, and helps* Constanze *to rise. With an attempt at dignity.*] Come, my dear. The music waits!

Constanze [*suppressing giggles*].   Oh, by all means—Herr Trazom! [*He takes her arm. They prance off together, followed by the disapproving* Majordomo. Salieri *sits shaken.*]

Salieri [*to audience*].   And then, right away, the concert began. I heard it through the door—some serenade[26]—at first only vaguely, too horrified 420   to attend. But presently the sound insisted—a solemn Adagio[27] in E flat.

[*The Adagio from the Serenade for thirteen wind instruments (K. 361) begins to sound. Quietly and quite slowly, seated in the wing chair,* Salieri *speaks over the music.*]

Salieri.   It started simply enough: just a pulse in the lowest registers—bassoons and basset horns—like a rusty squeezebox. It would have been comic except for the slowness, which gave it instead a sort of serenity. And then suddenly, high above it, sounded a single note on the oboe. [*We hear it.*] It hung there unwavering, piercing me through, till breath could hold it no longer, and a clarinet withdrew it out of me, and sweetened it into a phrase of such delight it had me trembling. The light flickered in the room. My eyes clouded! [*With ever-increasing emotion and vigor.*] The squeezebox groaned louder, and over it the higher instruments wailed 430   and warbled, throwing lines of sound around me—long lines of pain around and through me. Ah, the pain! Pain as I had never known it. I called up to my sharp old God, *"What is this? . . . What?!"* But the squeezebox went on and on, and the pain cut deeper into my shaking head, until suddenly I was running—[*He bolts out of the chair and runs across the stage in a fever, to a corner, down right. Behind him in the Light Box, the library fades into a street scene at night: small houses under a rent sky. The music continues, fainter, underneath.*] dashing through the side door, stumbling downstairs into the street, into the cold night, gasping for life. [*Calling up in agony.*] *"What?! What is this? Tell me, Signore!* What is this *pain?* What is this *need* in the 440   sound? Forever unfillable, yet fulfilling him who hears it, utterly. Is it *Your* need? Can it be Yours? . . ." [*Pause.*] Dimly the music sounded from the salon above. Dimly the stars shone on the empty street. I was suddenly frightened. It seemed to me that I had heard a voice of God—and that it issued from a creature whose own voice I had also heard—and it was the voice of an obscene child!

[*Light change. The street scene fades.*]

---

[26] From the Italian meaning *serene* or *out of doors*, a serenade is a piece of music appropriately played (or imagined as played) by a lover beneath his lady's window.

[27] From Italian meaning *slowly*, an adagio is a movement played at a slow tempo.

SCENE VI

Salieri's Apartment

It remains dark.

SALIERI.   I ran home and buried my fear in work. More pupils—till there were thirty and forty. More committees to help musicians. More motets[28] and anthems to God's glory. And at night I prayed for just one thing. [*He kneels desperately.*] "Let your voice enter *me!* Let *me* conduct you! . . . *Let*
450   me!" [*Pause. He rises.*] As for Mozart, I avoided meeting him—and sent out my Little Winds for whatever scores of his could be found.

[*The* VENTICELLI *come in with manuscripts.* SALIERI *sits at the fortepiano, and they show him the music alternately, as* SERVANTS *unobtrusively remove the Waldstädten table and wing chair.*]

V.1.   Six fortepiano sonatas[29] composed in Munich.

V.2.   Two in Mannheim.

V.1.   A Parisian symphony.

SALIERI [*to audience*].   Clever. They were all clever. But yet they seemed to me completely empty!

V.1.   A Divertimento[30] in D.

V.2.   A Cassazione[31] in G.

V.1.   A Grand Litany[32] in E flat.

460 SALIERI [*to audience*].   The same. Conventional. Even boring. The productions of a precocious youngster—Leopold Mozart's swanky son—nothing more. That Serenade was obviously an exception in his work: the sort of accident which might visit any composer on a lucky day! [*The* VENTICELLI *go off with the music.*] Had I in fact been simply taken by surprise that the filthy creature could write music at all? . . . Suddenly I felt immensely cheered! I would seek him out and welcome him to Vienna!

SCENE VII

The Palace of Schönbrunn

Quick light change. The EMPEROR *is revealed standing in bright light before the gilded mirrors and the fireplace, attended by* CHAMBERLAIN STRACK. *His Majesty is a dapper, cheerful figure, aged forty, largely pleased with himself and the world. Downstage, from opposite sides,* VAN SWIETEN *and* ROSENBERG *hurry on.*

JOSEPH.   Fêtes and fireworks, gentlemen! Mozart is here! He's waiting below! [*All bow.*]

---

[28] Religious polyphonic choruses.

[29] An instrumental composition in three or four movements designed for piano or for other solo instruments, generally with piano accompaniment.

[30] A light instrumental diversion in several movements.

[31] An instrumental composition very like a *divertimento.*

[32] An extended choral composition addressed to God, the Virgin Mary, or the saints.

ALL.   Majesty!

470 JOSEPH.   *Je suis follement impatient!*[33]

SALIERI [*to audience*].   The Emperor Joseph the Second of Austria. Son of
Maria Theresa. Brother of Marie Antoinette. Adorer of music—provided
that it made no demands upon the royal brain. [*To the* EMPEROR, *deferentially.*] Majesty, I have written a little march in Mozart's honor. May I play
it as he comes in?

JOSEPH.   By all means, Court Composer. What a delightful idea! Have you
met him yet?

SALIERI.   Not yet, Majesty.

JOSEPH.   Fêtes and fireworks, what fun! Strack, bring him up at once. [STRACK
480 *goes off. The* EMPEROR *comes onto the stage proper.*] *Mon Dieu,* I wish we could
have a competition! Mozart against some other virtuoso. Two keyboards
in contest. Wouldn't that be fun, Baron?

VAN SWIETEN [*stiffly*].   Not to me, Majesty. In my view, musicians are not
horses to be run against one another. [*Slight pause.*]

JOSEPH.   Ah. Well—there it is. [STRACK *returns.*]

STRACK.   Herr Mozart, Majesty.

JOSEPH.   Ah! Splendid! . . . [*Conspiratorially he signs to* SALIERI, *who moves quickly
to the fortepiano.*] Court Composer—*allons!*[34] [*To* STRACK] Admit him, please.

[*Instantly* SALIERI *sits at the instrument and strikes up his march on the keyboard. At
the same moment* MOZART *struts in, wearing an extremely ornate surcoat, with dress
sword. The* EMPEROR *stands downstage, center, his back to the audience, and as*
MOZART *approaches he signs to him to halt and listen. Bewildered,* MOZART *does so,
becoming aware of* SALIERI *playing his March of Welcome. It is an extremely banal
piece, vaguely—but only vaguely—reminiscent of another march to become very famous later on. All stand frozen in attitudes of listening, until* SALIERI *comes to a finish.
Applause.*]

JOSEPH [*to* SALIERI.] Charming . . . *Comme d'habitude!*[35] [*He turns and extends his
490 hand to be kissed.*] Mozart.

[MOZART *approaches and kneels extravagantly.*]

MOZART.   Majesty! Your Majesty's humble slave! Let me kiss your royal hand
a hundred thousand times! [*He kisses it greedily, over and over, until its owner
withdraws it in embarrassment.*]

JOSEPH.   *Non, non, s'il vous plaît!*[36] A little less enthusiasm, I beg you. Come
sir, *levez-vous!*[37] [*He assists* MOZART *to rise.*] You will not recall it, but the last
time we met, you were also on the floor! My sister remembers it to this day.
This young man—all of six years old, mind you—slipped on the floor at
Schönbrunn—came a nasty purler on his little head. . . . Have I told you
this before?

500 ROSENBERG [*hastily*].   No, Majesty!

---

[33] "I am madly impatient!"
[34] "Let's go!"
[35] "As usual!"
[36] "No, no, if you please!"
[37] "Get up!"

STRACK [*hastily*].   No, Majesty!

SALIERI [*hastily*].   No, Majesty!

JOSEPH.   Well, my sister Antoinette runs forward and picks him up herself. And do you know what he does? Jumps right into her arms—hoopla, just like that!—kisses her on both cheeks and says, "Will you marry me: yes or no?" [*The* COURTIERS *laugh politely.* MOZART *emits his high-pitched giggle. The* EMPEROR *is clearly startled by it.*] I do not mean to embarrass you, Herr Mozart. You know everyone here, surely?

MOZART.   Yes, sire. [*Bowing elaborately. To* ROSENBERG.] Herr Director! [*To* VAN
510   SWIETEN.] Herr Prefect.

VAN SWIETEN [*warmly*].   Delighted to see you again!

JOSEPH.   But not, I think, our esteemed Court Composer! . . . A most serious omission! No one who cares for art can afford not to know Herr Salieri. He wrote that exquisite little March of Welcome for you.

SALIERI.   It was a trifle, Majesty.

JOSEPH.   Nevertheless . . .

MOZART [*to* SALIERI].   I'm overwhelmed, *Signore!*

JOSEPH.   Ideas simply pour out of him—don't they, Strack?

STRACK.   Endlessly, Sire. [*As if tipping him.*] Well done, Salieri.

520 JOSEPH.   Let it be my pleasure then to introduce you. Court Composer Salieri—Herr Mozart of Salzburg.

SALIERI [*sleekly, to* MOZART].   *Finalmente. Che gioia. Che diletto straordinario.*[38] [*He gives him a prim bow and presents the copy of his music to the other composer, who accepts it with a flood of Italian.*]

MOZART.   *Grazie, Signore! Mille milione di benvenuti! Sono commosso! E un onore eccezzionale incontrare! Compositore brillante e famosissimo!*[39] [*He makes an elaborate and showy bow in return.*]

SALIERI [*dryly*].   *Grazie.*

JOSEPH.   Tell me, Mozart, have you received our commission for the opera?

530 MOZART.   Indeed I have, Majesty! I am so grateful I can hardly speak! . . . I swear to you that you will have the best, the most perfect entertainment ever offered a monarch. I've already found a libretto.[40]

ROSENBERG [*startled*].   Have you? I didn't hear of this!

MOZART.   Forgive me, Herr Director, I entirely omitted to tell you.

ROSENBERG.   May I ask why?

MOZART.   It didn't seem very important.

ROSENBERG.   Not important?

MOZART.   Not really, no.

ROSENBERG [*irritated*].   It is important to *me*, Herr Mozart.

540 MOZART [*embarrassed*].   Yes, I see that. Of course.

ROSENBERG.   And who, pray, is it by?

MOZART.   Stephanie.

ROSENBERG.   A most unpleasant man.

MOZART.   But a brilliant writer.

ROSENBERG.   Do you think?

---

[38] "At last, what joy. What extraordinary delight."

[39] "Thank you, Signore! A billion greetings! I am deeply moved! It is an exceptional honor to meet you! A brilliant and most famous composer!"

[40] The book containing the words, or text, of an opera.

MOZART.   The story is really amusing, Majesty. The whole plot is set in a—[*he giggles.*]—in a . . .

JOSEPH [*eagerly*].   Where? Where is it set?

MOZART.   It's—it's rather saucy, Majesty!

550 JOSEPH.   Yes, yes! Where?

MOZART.   Well, it's actually set in a *seraglio.*

JOSEPH.   A what?

MOZART.   A pasha's harem. [*He giggles wildly.*]

ROSENBERG.   And you imagine that is a suitable subject for performance at a national theater?

MOZART [*in a panic*].   Yes! . . . No! . . . Yes, I mean yes, yes I do. Why not? It's very funny, it's amusing. . . . On my honor, Majesty, there's nothing offensive in it. Nothing offensive in the world. It's full of proper German virtues, I swear it!

560 SALIERI [*blandly*].   *Scusate, Signore,*[41] but what are those? Being a foreigner, I'm not sure.

JOSEPH.   You are being *cattivo,*[42] Court Composer.

SALIERI.   Not at all, Majesty.

JOSEPH.   Come then, Mozart. Name us a proper German virtue!

SALIERI.   Love, Sire. I have yet to see that expressed in any opera.

VAN SWIETEN.   Well answered, Mozart.

SALIERI [*smiling*].   *Scusate.* I was under the impression one rarely saw anything *else* expressed in opera.

MOZART.   I mean manly love, *Signore.* Not male sopranos screeching. Or

570 stupid couples rolling their eyes. All that absurd Italian rubbish. [*Pause. Tension.* ROSENBERG *coughs.*] I mean the real thing.

JOSEPH.   And do you know the real thing yourself, Herr Mozart?

MOZART.   Under your pardon, I think I do, Majesty. [*He gives a short high giggle.*]

JOSEPH.   Bravo. When do you think it will be done?

MOZART.   The first act is already finished.

JOSEPH.   But it can't be more than two weeks since you started!

MOZART.   Composing is not hard when you have the right audience to please, Sire.

580 VAN SWIETEN.   A charming reply, Majesty.

JOSEPH.   Indeed, Baron, fêtes and fireworks! I see we are going to have fêtes and fireworks! *Au revoir, Monsieur Mozart. Soyez bienvenu à la court.*[43]

MOZART [*with expert rapidity*].   *Majesté! Je suis comblé d'honneur d'être accepté dans la maison du Père de tous les musiciens! Servir un monarque aussi plein de discernement que votre Majesté, c'est un honneur qui dépasse le sommet de mes dûs!*[44] [*A pause. The* EMPEROR *is taken aback by this flood of French.*]

JOSEPH.   Ah. Well—there it is! I'll leave you gentlemen to get better acquainted.

---

[41] "Excuse me, Signore."

[42] "Naughty."

[43] "Good-bye, Monsieur Mozart. You are welcome to the court."

[44] "Majesty! I am overcome by the honor of being accepted in the home of the father of all musicians! To serve a monarch as full of discernment as your majesty, that is an honor that transcends the summit of my deserts."

SALIERI.   Good day, Majesty.

590 MOZART.   *Votre Majesté.* [*They both bow.* JOSEPH *goes out.*]

ROSENBERG.   Good day to you.

STRACK.   Good day. [*They follow the King.*]

VAN SWIETEN [*warmly shaking his hand*].   Welcome, Mozart. I shall see much more of you. Depend on it!

MOZART.   Thank you. [*He bows. The* BARON *goes.* MOZART *and* SALIERI *are left alone.*]

SALIERI.   *Bene.*

MOZART.   *Bene.*

SALIERI.   I, too, wish you success with your opera.

600 MOZART.   I'll have it. It's going to be superb. I must tell you I have already found the most excellent singer for the leading part.

SALIERI.   Oh? Who is that?

MOZART.   Her name is Cavalieri. Katherina Cavalieri. She's really German, but she thinks it will advance her career if she sports an Italian name.

SALIERI.   She's quite right. It was my idea. She is in fact my prize pupil. Actually, she's a very innocent child. Silly in the way of young singers— but, you know, she's only twenty.

MOZART.   Yes. [*Without emphasis,* MOZART *freezes his movements and* SALIERI *takes one easy step forward to make a fluent aside.*]

610 SALIERI [*to audience*].   I had kept my hands off Katherina. Yes! But I could not bear to think of anyone else's upon her—least of all his!

MOZART [*unfreezing*].   You're a good fellow, Salieri! And that's a jolly little thing you wrote for me.

SALIERI.   It was my pleasure.

MOZART.   Let's see if I can remember it. May I?

SALIERI.   By all means. It's yours.

MOZART.   *Grazie, Signore.* [MOZART *tosses the manuscript onto the lid of the forte-piano, where he cannot see it, sits at the instrument, and plays* SALIERI's *March of Welcome perfectly from memory—at first slowly, recalling it, but on the reprise of*
620 *the tune, very much faster.*] The rest is just the same, isn't it? [*He finishes it with insolent speed.*]

SALIERI.   You have a remarkable memory.

MOZART [*delighted with himself*].   *Grazie ancora, Signore!*[45] [*He plays the opening seven bars again, but this time stops on the interval of the fourth, and sounds it again with displeasure.*] It doesn't really *work*, that fourth, does it? . . . Let's try the third above. . . [*He does so—and smiles happily.*] Ah yes! . . . Good! [*He repeats the new interval, leading up to it smartly with the well-known military-trumpet arpeggio*[46] *which characterizes the celebrated March from* The Marriage of Figaro, *"Non più andrai." Then, using the interval—tentatively, delicately,*
630 *one note at a time, in the treble—he steals into the famous tune itself.*

On and on he plays, improvising happily what is virtually the March we know now, laughing gleefully each time he comes to the amended interval of the third. SALIERI *watches him with an answering smile painted on his face.*

---

[45] "Thank you again, Signore."

[46] In an *arpeggio* the notes of a chord are played rapidly in quick succession instead of all at once.

MOZART's *playing grows more and more exhibitionistic, revealing to the audience the formidable virtuoso he is. The whole time he himself remains totally oblivious of the offense he is giving. Finally, he finishes the march with a series of triumphant flourishes and chords.*
An ominous pause.]

SALIERI.   Scusate. I must go.

640 MOZART.   Really? [*Springing up and indicating the keyboard.*] Why don't *you* try a variation?

SALIERI.   Thank you, but I must attend on the Emperor.

MOZART.   Ah.

SALIERI.   It has been delightful to meet you.

MOZART.   For me too! . . . And thanks for the march! [MOZART *picks up the manuscript from the top of the fortepiano and marches happily offstage. A slight pause.* SALIERI *moves toward the audience. The lights go down around him.*]

SALIERI [*to audience*].   Was it then—so early—that I began to have thoughts of murder? . . . Of course not: at least not in life. In art it was a different

650   matter. I decided I would compose a huge tragic opera: something to astonish the world! And I knew my theme. I would set the legend of Danaius, who for a monstrous crime, was chained to a rock for eternity, his head repeatedly struck by lightning! Wickedly in my head I saw Mozart in that position. . . . In reality, of course, the man was in no danger from me at all. . . . Not yet.

SCENE VIII

The First Performance of The Abduction from the Seraglio

The light changes, and the stage instantly turns into an eighteenth-century theater. The backdrop projection shows a line of softly gleaming chandeliers.

The SERVANTS *bring in chairs and benches. Upon them, facing the audience and regarding it as if watching an opera, sit the* EMPEROR JOSEPH, STRACK, ROSENBERG *and* VAN SWIETEN. *Next to them:* KAPPELLMEISTER BONNO *and* THERESA SALIERI. *A little behind them:* CONSTANZE. *Behind her:* CITIZENS OF VIENNA.

SALIERI.   The first performance of *The Abduction from the Seraglio*. The creature's expression of manly love.

[MOZART *comes on briskly, wearing a gaudy new coat embellished with scarlet ribbons, and a new powdered wig. He struts quickly to the fortepiano, sits at it and mimes conducting.* SALIERI *sits nearby, next to his wife, and watches* MOZART *intently.*]

SALIERI.   He himself contrived to wear for the occasion an even more vulgar coat than usual. As for the music, it matched the coat completely. For my

660   dear pupil Katherina Cavalieri he had written quite simply the showiest Aria I'd ever heard. [*Faintly we hear the whizzing scale passages for soprano which end the aria "Martern aller arten."*] Ten minutes of scales and ornaments, amounting in sum to a vast emptiness. So ridiculous was the piece, in fact—so much what might be demanded by a foolish young soprano— that I knew precisely what Mozart must have demanded in return for it.

[*The final orchestral chords of the aria. Silence. No one moves.*] Although engaged to be married, *he'd had her!* I knew that beyond any doubt. [*Bluntly.*]
The creature had had my darling girl.

[*Loudly we hear the brilliant Turkish finale of* Seraglio. *Great applause from those
watching.* Mozart *jumps to his feet and acknowledges it. The* Emperor *rises—as do
all—and gestures graciously to the "stage" in invitation.* Katherina Cavalieri *runs
on in her costume, all plumes and flounces, to renewed cheering and clapping. She
curtsies to the* Emperor—*is kissed by* Salieri—*presented to his wife—curtsies again to*
Mozart *and, flushed with triumph, moves to one side.*

In the ensuing brief silence, Constanze *rushes down from the back, wildly excited.
She flings herself on* Mozart, *not even noticing the* Emperor.]

Constanze. Oh, well done, lovey! . . . Well done, pussy-wussy! . . . [Mozart
670   *indicates the proximity of His Majesty.*] Oh! . . . 'Scuse me! [*She curtsies in
embarrassment.*]
Mozart. Majesty, may I present my fiancée, Fräulein Weber.
Joseph. *Enchanté, Fräulein.*[47]
Constanze. Your Majesty!
Mozart. Constanze is a singer herself.
Joseph. Indeed?
Constanze [*embarrassed*]. I'm not at all, Majesty. Don't be silly, Wolfgang!
Joseph. So, Mozart—a good effort. Decidedly that. A good effort.
Mozart. Did you really like it, Sire?
680 Joseph. I thought it was most interesting. Yes, indeed. A trifle . . . How shall
one say? [*To* Rosenberg.] How shall one say, Director?
Rosenberg [*subserviently*]. Too many notes, Your Majesty?
Joseph. Very well put. Too many notes.
Mozart. I don't understand.
Joseph. My dear fellow, don't take it too hard. There are in fact only so
many notes the ear can hear in the course of an evening. I think I'm right
in saying that, aren't I, Court Composer?
Salieri [*uncomfortably*]. Well, yes, I would say yes, on the whole, yes, Majesty.
Joseph. There you are. It's clever. It's German. It's quality work. And there
690   are simply too many notes. Do you see?
Mozart. There are just as many notes, Majesty, neither more nor less, as are
required.

[*Pause.*]

Joseph. Ah . . . Well—there it is! [*He goes off abruptly, followed by* Rosenberg
and Strack.]
Mozart [*nervously*]. Is he angry?
Salieri. Not at all. He respects you for your views.
Mozart. I hope so. . . . What did you think yourself, sir? Did you care for
the piece at all?
Salieri. Yes, of course, Mozart—at its best, it is truly charming.
700 Mozart. And at other times?

---

[47] "[I am] enchanted, Fraulein."

SALIERI [*smoothly*].   Well, just occasionally, at other times—in Katherina's aria, for example—it was a little excessive.

MOZART.   Katherina is an excessive girl. In fact, she's insatiable. . . . I mean in regard to vocal ornaments.

SALIERI.   All the same, as my revered teacher the Chevalier Gluck used to say to me, one must avoid music that smells of music.

MOZART.   What does that mean?

SALIERI.   Music which makes one aware too much of the virtuosity of the composer.

710 MOZART.   Gluck is absurd.

SALIERI.   What do you say?

MOZART.   He's talked all his life about modernizing opera, but creates people so lofty they sound as though they shit marble. [CONSTANZE *gives a little scream of shock.*]

CONSTANZE.   Oh, 'scuse me! . . .

MOZART [*breaking out*].   No, but it's too much! . . . Gluck says! Gluck says! Chevalier Gluck! . . . What's a Chevalier? I'm a Chevalier. The Pope made me a Chevalier when I was still wetting my bed.

CONSTANZE.   Wolferl!

720 MOZART.   Anyway, it's ridiculous. Only stupid farts sport titles.

SALIERI [*blandly*].   Such as Court Composer?

MOZART.   What? . . . [*Realizing.*] Ah. Oh. Ha. Ha. Well! . . . My father's right again. He always tells me I should padlock my mouth. . . . Actually, I shouldn't speak at all!

SALIERI [*soothingly*].   Nonsense. I'm just being what the Emperor would call *cattivo.* Won't you introduce me to your charming fiancée?

MOZART.   Oh, of course! Constanze, this is Herr Salieri, the Court Composer. Fräulein Weber.

SALIERI [*bowing*].   Delighted, *cara Fräulein.*[48]

730 CONSTANZE [*bobbing*].   How do you do, Excellency?

SALIERI.   May I ask when you marry?

MOZART [*nervously*].   We have to secure my father's consent. He's an excellent man—a wonderful man—but in some ways a little stubborn.

SALIERI.   Excuse me, but how old are you?

MOZART.   Twenty-six.

SALIERI.   Then your father's consent is scarcely indispensable.

CONSTANZE [*to* MOZART].   You see?

MOZART [*uncomfortably*].   Well, no, it's not *indispensable*—of course not! . . .

SALIERI.   My advice to you is to marry and be happy. You have found—it's

740 quite obvious—*un tesoro raro!*[49]

CONSTANZE.   Ta very much.

SALIERI [*he kisses* CONSTANZE's *hand. She is delighted.*]   Good night to you both.

CONSTANZE.   Good night, Excellency!

MOZART.   Good night, sir. And thank you. . . . Come, Stanzerl. [*They depart delightedly. He watches them go.*]

SALIERI [*to audience*].   As I watched her walk away on the arm of the creature,

---

[48] "Dear Fräulein."

[49] "A rare treasure!"

I felt the lightning thought strike: *"Have her! Her for Katherina!"* . . . Abomination! . . . Never in my life had I entertained a notion so sinful!

[*Light change: the eighteenth century fades.*]

[*The* Venticelli *come on merrily, as if from some celebration. One holds a bottle; the other, a glass.*]

    V.1.   They're married.
750 Salieri [*to them*]. What?
    V.2.   Mozart and Weber—married!
    Salieri.   Really?
    V.1.   His father will be furious!
    V.2.   They didn't even wait for his consent!
    Salieri.   Have they set up house?
    V.1.   Wipplingerstrasse.
    V.2.   Number twelve.
    V.1.   Not bad.
    V.2.   Considering they've no money.
760 Salieri.   Is that really true?
    V.1.   He's wildly extravagant.
    V.2.   Lives way beyond his means.
    Salieri.   But he has pupils.
    V.1.   Only three.
    Salieri [*to them*]. Why so few?
    V.1.   He's embarrassing.
    V.2.   Makes scenes.
    V.1.   Makes enemies.
    V.2.   Even Strack, whom he cultivates.
770 Salieri.   Chamberlain Strack?
    V.1.   Only last night.
    V.2.   At Kapellmeister Bonno's.

SCENE IX

Bonno's Salon

Instant light change. Mozart *comes in with* Strack. *He is high on wine, and holding a glass. The* Venticelli *join the scene, but still talk out of it to Salieri. One of them fills* Mozart's *glass.*

    Mozart.   Seven months in this city and not one job! I'm not to be tried again, is that it?
    Strack.   Of course not.
    Mozart.   I know what goes on, and so do you. Germany is completely in the hands of foreigners. Worthless wops like *Kapellmeister Bonno!*
    Strack.   Please! You're in the man's house!
    Mozart.   Court Composer *Salieri!*
780 Strack.   Hush!
    Mozart.   Did you see his last opera—*The Chimney Sweep?* . . . Did you?
    Strack.   Of course I did.

MOZART.   Dogshit. Dried dogshit.

STRACK [*outraged*].   I beg your pardon!

MOZART [*singing*].   Pom-pom, pom-pom, pom-pom, pom-pom! Tonic and
  dominant, tonic and dominant, from here to resurrection! Not one interesting modulation all night. Salieri is a musical idiot!

STRACK.   Please!

V.1 [*to* SALIERI].   He'd had too much to drink.

790 V.2.   He often has.

MOZART.   Why are Italians so terrified by the slightest complexity in music?
  Show them one chromatic passage and they *faint!* . . . "Oh, how sick! How
  morbid!" [*Falsetto.*] *Morboso!* . . . *Nervoso!* . . . *Ohimè!*[50] . . . No wonder the
  music at this court is so dreary.

STRACK.   Lower your voice.

MOZART.   Lower your breeches! . . . That's just a joke—just a joke!

[*Unobserved by him,* COUNT ROSENBERG *has entered upstage and is suddenly standing
between the* VENTICELLI, *listening. He wears a waistcoat of bright green silk, and an
expression of supercilious interest.* MOZART *sees him. A pause.*]

MOZART [*pleasantly, to* ROSENBERG].   You look like a toad . . . I mean, you're
  goggling like a toad. [*He emits his giggle.*]

ROSENBERG [*blandly*].   You would do best to retire tonight, for your own sake.

800 MOZART.   Salieri has fifty pupils. I have three. How am I to live? I'm a
  married man now! . . . Of course, I realize you don't concern yourself with
  money in these exalted circles. All the same, did you know behind his back
  His Majesty is known as Kaiser Keep-it? [*He giggles wildly.*]

STRACK.   *Mozart!* [*He stops.*]

MOZART.   I shouldn't have said that, should I? . . . Forgive me. It was just a
  joke. Another joke! . . . I can't help myself! . . . We're all friends here,
  aren't we? [STRACK *and* ROSENBERG *glare at him. Then* STRACK *leaves abruptly,
  much offended.*] What's wrong with *him?*

ROSENBERG.   Good night. [*He turns to go.*]

810 MOZART.   No, no, no—please! [*He grabs the* DIRECTOR's *arm.*] Your hand
  please, first!

[*Unwillingly,* ROSENBERG *gives him his hand.* MOZART *kisses it.*]

MOZART [*humbly*].   Give me a post, sir.

ROSENBERG.   That is not in my power, Mozart.

MOZART.   The Princess Elizabeth is looking for an instructor. One word from
  you could secure it for me.

ROSENBERG.   I regret that is solely in the recommendation of Court Composer Salieri. [*He disengages himself.*]

MOZART.   Do you know I am better than any musician in Vienna? . . . Do
  you? [ROSENBERG *leaves.* MOZART *calls after him.*] Foppy-wops—I'm *sick* of
820 them! Foppy-wops? . . . [*Suddenly he giggles to himself, like a child.*] Foppy—
  poppy—snoppy—toppy—hoppy . . . wops! [*He hops offstage.*]

SALIERI [*watching him go*].   Barely one month later, that thought of revenge
  became more than thought.

---

[50] "Morbid . . . High-strung . . . Oh dear!"

SCENE X

The Waldstädten Library

Two simultaneous shouts bring up the lights. Against the handsome wallpaper stand three masked figures: Constanze, *flanked on either side by the* Venticelli. *All three are guests at a party, and are playing a game of forfeits.*

Two Servants *stand frozen, holding the large wing chair between them. Two more hold the big table of sweetmeats.*

V.1.   Forfeit! . . . Forfeit! . . .
V.2.   Forfeit, Stanzerl! You've got to forfeit!
Constanze.   I won't.
V.1.   You have to.
V.2.   It's the game.

[*The* Servants *unfreeze and set down the furniture.* Salieri *moves to the wing chair and sits.*]

Salieri [*to audience*].   Once again—believe it or not—I was in the same con-
830   cealing chair in the Baroness's library [*taking a cup from the little table*] and consuming the same delicious dessert.
V.1.   You lost—now there's the penalty!
Salieri [*to audience*].   A party celebrating the New Year's Eve. I was on my own—my dear spouse, Teresa, visiting her parents in Italy.
Constanze.   Well, *what?* . . . What is it?

[Venticello One *snatches up an old-fashioned round ruler from off the fortepiano.*]

V.1.   I want to measure your calves.
Constanze.   Oooo!
V.1.   Well?
Constanze.   Definitely not. You cheeky bugger!
840   V.1.   Now come on!
V.2.   You've got to let him, Stanzerl. All's fair in love and forfeits.
Constanze.   No, it isn't—so you can both buzz off!
V.1.   If you don't let me, you won't be allowed to play again.
Constanze.   Well, choose something else.
V.1.   I've chosen that! Now get up on the table. Quick, quick! *Allez-oop!* [*Gleefully he shifts the plates of sweetmeats to the fortepiano.*]
Constanze.   Quick, then! . . . Before anyone sees! [*The two masked men lift the shrieking masked girl up onto the table.*]
V.1.   Hold her, Friedrich.
850   Constanze.   I don't have to be held, thank you!
V.2.   Yes, you do—that's part of the penalty. [*He holds her ankles firmly, while* Venticello One *thrusts the ruler under her skirts and measures her legs. Excitedly,* Salieri *reverses his position so that he can kneel in the wing chair and watch.* Constanze *giggles delighted, then becomes outraged—or pretends to be.*]
Constanze.   Stop it! . . . Stop that! That's quite enough of that! [*She bends down and tries to slap him.*]
V.1.   Seventeen inches—knee to ankle!
V.2.   Let me do it! You hold her.

CONSTANZE. That's not fair!

860 V.2. Yes, it is. You lost to me too.

CONSTANZE. It's been done now! Let me *down!*

V.2. Hold her, Karl.

CONSTANZE. No! . . . [VENTICELLO ONE *holds her ankles.* VENTICELLO TWO *thrusts his head entirely under her skirts. She squeals.*] No—stop it . . . *No!* . . .

[*In the middle of this undignified scene,* MOZART *comes rushing on, also masked.*]

MOZART [*outraged*]. Constanze! [*They freeze.* SALIERI *ducks back down and sits hidden in the chair.*] Gentlemen, if you please.

CONSTANZE. It's only a game, Wolferl! . . .

V.1. We meant no harm, 'pon my word.

MOZART [*stiffly*]. Come down off that table, please. [*They hand her down.*]
870 Thank you. We'll see you later.

V.2. Now look, Mozart, don't be pompous—

MOZART. Please excuse us now.

[*They go. The little man is very angry. He tears off his mask.*]

MOZART [*to* CONSTANZE]. Do you realize what you've done?

CONSTANZE. No, what? . . . [*Flustered, she busies herself restoring the plates of sweetmeats to the table.*]

MOZART. Just lost your reputation, that's all! You're now a loose girl.

CONSTANZE. Don't be so stupid. [*She, too, removes her mask.*]

MOZART. You are a married woman, for God's sake!

CONSTANZE. And what of it?

880 MOZART. A young wife does not allow her legs to be handled in public. Couldn't you at least have measured your own ugly legs?

CONSTANZE. *What?*

MOZART [*raising his voice*]. Do you know what you've done? . . . You've shamed me, that's all. *Shamed* me!

CONSTANZE. Oh, don't be so ridiculous!

MOZART. Shamed me—in front of *them!*

CONSTANZE [*suddenly furious*]. *You?* Shamed *you?* . . . That's a laugh! If there's any shame around, lover, it's *mine!*

MOZART. What do you mean?

890 CONSTANZE. You've only had every pupil who ever came to you.

MOZART. That's not true.

CONSTANZE. Every single female pupil!

MOZART. Name them! *Name them!*

CONSTANZE. The Aurnhammer girl! The Rumbeck girl! Katherina Cava-lieri—that sly little whore! *She* wasn't even your pupil—she was Salieri's. Which actually, my dear, may be why he has hundreds and you have none. He doesn't drag them into bed!

MOZART. Of course he doesn't! He can't get it up, that's why! . . . Have you heard his music? That's the sound of someone who *can't get it up!* At least
900 *I* can do *that!*

CONSTANZE. I'm sick of you!

MOZART [*shouting*]. No one ever said I couldn't do *that!*

CONSTANZE [*bursting into tears*]. I don't give a fart! I hate you! I hate you for ever and ever—I hate you! [*A tiny pause. She weeps.*]

MOZART [*helplessly*].   Oh, Stanzerl, don't cry. Please don't cry. . . . I can't bear
it when you cry. I just didn't want you to look cheap in people's eyes, that's
all. Here! [*He snatches up the ruler.*] Beat me. Beat me. . . . I'm your slave.
Stanzi marini. Stanzi marini bini gini. I'll just stand here like a little lamb
and bear your strokes. Here Do it. . . . *Batti.*

910 CONSTANZE.   No.

MOZART.   *Batti, batti. Mio tesoro!*[51]

CONSTANZE.   No!

MOZART.   Stanzerly wanzerly piggy poo!

CONSTANZE.   Stop it.

MOZART.   Stanzy wanzy had a fit. Shit her stays and made them split! [*She
giggles despite herself.*]

CONSTANZE.   Stop it.

MOZART.   When they took away her skirt, Stanzy wanzy ate the dirt!

CONSTANZE.   Stop it now! [*She snatches the ruler and gives him a whack with it. He*
920   *yowls playfully.*]

MOZART.   Oooo! Oooo! Oooo! Do it again! Do it again! I cast myself at your
stinking feet, Madonna! [*He does so. She whacks him some more as he crouches,
but always lightly, scarcely looking at him, divided between tears and laughter.*
MOZART *drums his feet with pleasure.*] Ow! Ow! Ow!

[*And then suddenly* SALIERI, *unable to bear another second, cries out involuntarily.*]

SALIERI.   Ah!!! [*The young couple freezes.* SALIERI, *discovered, hastily converts his
noise of disgust into a yawn, and stretches as if waking up from a nap. He peers
out of the wing chair.*] Good evening.

CONSTANZE [*embarrassed*].   Excellency. . .

MOZART.   How long have you been there?

930 SALIERI.   I was asleep until a second ago. Are you two quarreling?

MOZART.   No, of course not.

CONSTANZE.   Yes, we are. He's been very irritating.

SALIERI [*rising*].   *Caro Herr,*[52] tonight is the time for New Year resolutions.
Irritating lovely ladies cannot surely be one of yours. May I suggest you
bring us each a *sorbetto*[53] from the dining room?

MOZART.   But why don't we all go to the table?

CONSTANZE.   Herr Salieri is quite right. Bring them here—it'll be your punishment.

MOZART.   Stanzi!

940 SALIERI.   Come now, I can keep your wife company. There cannot be a better
peace offering than a *sorbetto* of aniseed.

CONSTANZE.   I prefer tangerine.

SALIERI.   Very well, tangerine. [*Greedily.*] But if you could possibly manage
aniseed for me, I'd be deeply obliged. . . . So the New Year can begin
coolly for all three of us. [*A pause.* MOZART *hesitates—and then bows.*]

MOZART.   I'm honored, *Signore*, of course. And then I'll play you at billiards.
What do you say?

SALIERI.   I'm afraid I don't play.

---

[51] "Beat me, beat me. My treasure!"
[52] "Dear Sir."
[53] Sherbet.

MOZART [*with surprise*]. You don't?

950 CONSTANZE. Wolferl would rather play at billiards than anything. He's very good at it.

MOZART. I'm the best! I may nod occasionally at composing, but at billiards—never!

SALIERI. A virtuoso of the cue.

MOZART. Exactly! It's a virtuoso game! . . . [*He snatches up the ruler and treats it as if it were a cue.*] I think I shall write a Grand Fantasia for Billiard Balls! Trills. Accacciaturas![54] Whole arpeggios in ivory! Then I'll play it myself in public! . . . It'll have to be *me* because none of those Italian charlatans like Clementi will be able to get his fingers round the cue! *Scusate, Signore!* [*He*
960 *gives a swanky flourish of the hand and struts offstage.*]

CONSTANZE. He's a love, really.

SALIERI. And lucky too, in you. You are, if I may say so, an astonishing creature.

CONSTANZE. Me? . . . Ta very much.

SALIERI. On the other hand, your husband does not appear to be so thriving.

CONSTANZE [*seizing her opportunity*]. We're desperate, sir.

SALIERI. What?

CONSTANZE. We've no money and no prospects of any. That's the truth.

SALIERI. I don't understand. He gives many public concerts.

970 CONSTANZE. They don't pay enough. What he needs is pupils. Illustrious pupils. His father calls us spendthrifts, but that's unfair. I manage as well as anyone could. There's simply not enough. Don't tell him I talked to you, please.

SALIERI [*intimately*]. This is solely between us. How can I help?

CONSTANZE. My husband needs security, sir. If only he could find regular employment, everything would be all right. Is there nothing at court?

SALIERI. Not at the moment.

CONSTANZE [*harder*]. The Princess Elizabeth needs a tutor.

SALIERI. Really? I hadn't heard.

980 CONSTANZE. One word from you and the post would be his. Other pupils would follow at once.

SALIERI [*looking off*]. He's coming back.

CONSTANZE. Please . . . please, Excellency. You can't imagine what a difference it would make.

SALIERI. We can't speak of it now.

CONSTANZE. When, then? Oh, please!

SALIERI. Can you come and see me tomorrow? Alone?

CONSTANZE. I can't do that.

SALIERI. I'm a married man.

990 CONSTANZE. All the same.

SALIERI. When does he work?

CONSTANZE. Afternoons.

SALIERI. Then come at three.

---

[54] Often found in combination with arpeggios, *accaciaturas* call for the quick striking and release of a note lower in pitch than that of the primary chord being played—hence, a form of musical embellishment.

CONSTANZE.   I can't possibly!

SALIERI.   Yes or no? . . . In his interests? . . . [*A pause. Constanze hesitates—opens her mouth—then smiles and abruptly runs off. The curtains descend on the Light Box.*]

SALIERI [*to audience*].   So: I'd done it! Spoken aloud! Invited her! . . . What of that vow made in church! Fidelity—virtue—all of that? I couldn't think of
1000   that now!

[SERVANTS *remove the Waldstädten furniture. Others replace it with two small gilded chairs, center, quite close together. Others, again surreptitiously, bring in the old dressing gown and cap which* SALIERI *discarded before Scene 3, placing them on the fortepiano.*]

SCENE XI

Salieri's Apartment

[*On the curtains are thrown projections of long windows.*]

SALIERI.   Next afternoon I waited in a fever. Would she come? I had no idea. And if she did, how would I behave? Was I actually going to seduce a young wife of two months standing? . . . Part of me—much of me—wanted it, badly. *Badly.* Yes, badly was the word! [*The clock strikes three. On the second stroke, the bell sounds. He rises excitedly.*] There she was! On the stroke! She'd come. . . . She'd *come!*

[*Enter from the right the* COOK, *as fat, but forty years younger. He proudly carries a plate piled with brandied chestnuts.* SALIERI *takes them from him nervously, nodding with approval, and sets them on the table.*]

SALIERI [*to the cook*].   Grazie. Grazie tanti. . . . Via, via, via![55]

[*The* COOK *bows as* SALIERI *dismisses him, and goes out the same way, smirking suggestively. The* VALET *comes in from the left—he is also forty years younger—and behind him* CONSTANZE, *wearing a pretty hat and carrying a portfolio.*]

SALIERI.   *Signora!*

CONSTANZE [*curtsying*].   Excellency.

1010 SALIERI.   *Benvenuta.* [*To* VALET *in dismissal.*] *Grazie.* [*The* VALET *goes.*] Well. You have come.

CONSTANZE.   I should not have done. My husband would be frantic if he knew. He's a very jealous man.

SALIERI.   Are you a jealous woman?

CONSTANZE.   Why do you ask?

SALIERI.   It's not a passion I understand. . . . You're looking even prettier than you were last night, if I may say so.

CONSTANZE.   Ta very much! . . . I brought you some manuscripts by Wolfgang. When you see them, you'll understand how right he is for a royal
1020 appointment. Will you look at them, please, while I wait?

---

[55] "Thank you. Thank you so much. . . . Go, go, go!"

SALIERI. You mean now?

CONSTANZE. Yes. I have to take them back with me. He'll miss them otherwise. He doesn't make copies. These are all the originals.

SALIERI. Sit down. Let me offer you something special.

CONSTANZE [*sitting*]. What's that?

SALIERI [*producing the box*]. *Capezzoli di Venere.* Nipples of Venus. Roman chestnuts in brandied sugar.

CONSTANZE. No, thank you.

SALIERI. Do try. My cook made them especially for you.

1030 CONSTANZE. Me?

SALIERI. Yes. They're quite rare.

CONSTANZE. Well then, I'd better, hadn't I? Just one . . . Ta very much. [*She takes one and puts it in her mouth. The taste amazes her.*] Oh! . . . Oh! . . . Oh! . . . They're *delish!*

SALIERI [*lustfully watching her eat*]. Aren't they?

CONSTANZE. Mmmmm!

SALIERI. Have another.

CONSTANZE [*taking two more*]. I couldn't possibly.

[*Carefully he moves round behind her, and seats himself on the chair next to her.*]

SALIERI. I think you're the most generous girl in the world.

1040 CONSTANZE. Generous?

SALIERI. It's my word for you. I thought last night that Constanze is altogether too stiff a name for that girl. I shall rechristen her Generosa. *La Generosa.* Then I'll write a glorious song for her under that title and she'll sing it, just for me.

CONSTANZE [*smiling*]. I am much out of practice, sir.

SALIERI. *La Generosa.* [*He leans a little toward her.*] Don't tell me it's going to prove inaccurate, my name for you.

CONSTANZE [*coolly*]. What name do you give your wife, Excellency?

SALIERI [*equally coolly*]. I'm not an excellency, and I call my wife Signora

1050 Salieri. If I named her anything else, it would be *La Statua.* She is a very upright lady.

CONSTANZE. Is she here now? I'd like to meet her.

SALIERI. Alas, no. At the moment she's visiting her mother in Verona. [*She starts very slightly out of her chair.* SALIERI *gently restrains her.*]

SALIERI. Constanze: tomorrow evening I dine with the Emperor. One word from me recommending your husband as tutor to the Princess Elizabeth, and that invaluable post is his. Believe me, when I speak to His Majesty in matters musical, no one contradicts me.

CONSTANZE. I believe you.

1060 SALIERI. *Bene.* [*Still sitting, he takes his* mouchoir[56] *and delicately wipes her mouth with it.*] Surely service of that sort deserves a little recompense in return?

CONSTANZE. How little? [*Slight pause.*]

SALIERI. The size of a kiss. [*Slight pause.*]

CONSTANZE. Just one? [*Slight pause.*]

---

[56] A napkin or handkerchief.

SALIERI.   If one seems fair to you. [*She looks at him—then kisses him lightly on the mouth. Longer pause.*] Does it? [*She gives him a longer kiss. He makes to touch her with his hand. She breaks off.*]

CONSTANZE.   I fancy that's fairness enough. [*Pause.*]

SALIERI [*carefully*].   A pity . . . It's somewhat small pay, to secure a post every
070   musician in Vienna is hoping for.

CONSTANZE.   What do you mean?

SALIERI.   Is it not clear?

CONSTANZE.   No. Not at all.

SALIERI.   Another pity . . . A thousand pities. [*Pause.*]

CONSTANZE.   I don't believe it. . . . I just don't believe it!

SALIERI.   What?

CONSTANZE.   What you've just said.

SALIERI [*hastily*].   I said nothing. What did I say? [CONSTANZE *gets up and* SALIERI *rises in panic.*]

080   CONSTANZE.   Oh, I'm going! . . . I'm getting out of this!

SALIERI.   Constanze. . . .

CONSTANZE.   Let me pass, please.

SALIERI.   Constanze, listen to me! I'm a clumsy man. You think me sophisticated—I'm not at all. Take a true look. I've no cunning. I live on ink and sweetmeats. I never see women at all. . . . When I met you last night, I envied Mozart from the depths of my soul. Out of that envy came stupid thoughts. For one silly second I dared imagine that, out of the vast store you obviously possess, you might spare me one coin of tenderness your rich husband does not need—and inspire me also. [*Pause. She laughs.*] I
090   amuse.

CONSTANZE.   Mozart was right. You're wicked.

SALIERI.   He said that?

CONSTANZE.   "All wops are performers," he said. "Be very careful with that one." Meaning you. He was being comic, of course.

SALIERI.   Yes. [*Abruptly turns his back on her.*]

CONSTANZE.   But not that comic, actually. I mean, you're acting a pretty obvious role, aren't you, dear? A small-town boy, and all the time as clever as cutlets! . . . [*Mock tender.*] Ah! You are sulking? *Are* you? . . . When Mozart sulks, I smack his botty. He rather likes it. Do you want me to scold
100   you a bit and smack your botty too? [*She hits him lightly with the portfolio. He turns in a fury.*]

SALIERI.   How dare you?! . . . *You silly, common girl!*

[*A dreadful silence.*]

SALIERI [*icily*].   Forgive me. Let us confine our talk to your husband. He is a brilliant keyboard player, no question. However, the Princess Elizabeth also requires a tutor in vocal music. I am not convinced he is the man for that. I would like to look at the pieces you've brought, and decide if he is mature enough. I will study them overnight—and you will study my proposal. Not to be vague, that is the price. [*He extends his hand for the portfolio, and she surrenders it.*] Good afternoon. [*He turns from her and places it on a
110   chair. She lingers—tries to speak—cannot—and goes out quickly.*]

SCENE XII

The Same

[SALIERI *turns in a ferment to the audience.*]

SALIERI.   Fiasco! . . . Fiasco! . . . The sordidness of it! The sheer sweating sordidness! . . . Worse than if I'd actually done it! . . . To be that much in sin and feel so *ridiculous* as well! [*Crying out.*] Nobile, nobile Salieri![57] . . . What had he done to me, this Mozart? Before he came, did I behave like this? Did I? Toy with adultery? Blackmail women? It was all going—slipping—growing rotten . . . Because of *him!* [*He moves upstage in a fever—reaches out to take the portfolio on the chair—but as if fearful of what he might find inside it, he withdraws his hand and sits instead. A pause. He contemplates the music lying there as if it were a great confection he is dying to eat, but dare not.*
1120   *Then suddenly he snatches at it—tears the ribbon—opens the case and stares greedily at the manuscript within.*

Music sounds instantly, faintly, in the theater, as his eye falls on the first page. It is the opening of the Twenty-ninth Symphony, in A major. Over the music, reading it.] She had said that these were his original scores. First and only drafts of the music. Yet they looked like fair copies. They showed no corrections of any kind. It was puzzling—then suddenly alarming. [*He looks up from the manuscript at the audience: the music abruptly stops.*] What was evident was that Mozart was simply transcribing music completely finished in his head. And finished as most music is never finished. [*He resumes*
1130   *looking at the music. Immediately the Sinfonia Concertante for Violin and Viola sounds.*] Displace one note and there would be diminishment. Displace one phrase and the structure would fall. [*He looks up again: the music breaks off.*]

Here again—only now in abundance—were the same sounds I'd heard in the library. [*He resumes reading, and the music also resumes: a ravishing phrase from the slow movement of the Concerto for Flute and Harp.*]

The same crushed harmonies—glancing collisions—agonizing delights. [*He looks up again. The music stops.*] The truth was clear. That Serenade had been no accident. [*Very low, in the theater, a faint thundery sound is heard accumulating, like a distant sea.*] I was staring through the cage of those
1140   miraculous ink strokes at—an Absolute Beauty! [*And out of the thundery roar writhes and rises the clear sound of soprano, singing the Kyrie from the C Minor Mass. The accretion of noise around her voice falls away—it is suddenly clear and bright—then clearer and brighter. The light grows bright: too bright: burning white, then scalding white!* SALIERI *rises in the downpour of it, and in the flood of the music, which is growing ever louder—filling the theater—as the soprano yields to the full chorus, fortissimo,[58] singing its massive counterpoint.[59]*

This is by far the loudest sound the audience has yet heard. SALIERI *staggers toward us, holding the manuscripts in his hand, like a man caught in a tumbling and violent sea. Finally the drums crash in below.* SALIERI *drops the portfolio of*

---

[57] "Noble, noble Salieri!"
[58] Very loud.
[59] Two independent melodies being played simultaneously.

150   manuscripts—*and falls senseless to the ground. At the same second the music
      explodes into a long, echoing, distorted boom, signifying some dreadful annihila-
      tion. The sound remains suspended over the prone figure in a menacing contin-
      uum—no longer music at all. Then it dies away, and there is only silence.*
          The light fades again.
          A long pause.
          Salieri *is quite still, his head by the pile of manuscripts. Finally the clock sounds:
      nine times.* Salieri *stirs as it does. Slowly he raises his head and looks up. And
      now—quietly at first—he addresses his God.*]
      Salieri.   *Capisco!*[60] I know my fate. Now for the first time I feel my emptiness
160   as Adam felt his nakedness. . . . [*Slowly he rises to his feet.*] Tonight at an inn
      somewhere in this city stands a giggling child who can put on paper,
      without actually setting down his billiard cue, casual notes which turn my
      most considered ones into lifeless scratches. *Grazie, Signore!* You gave me
      the desire to serve You—which most men do not have—then saw to it the
      service was shameful in the ears of the server. *Grazie!* You gave me the
      desire to praise You—which most men do not feel—then made me mute.
      Grazie tanti! You put into me perception of the Incomparable—which most
      men never know!—then ensured that I would know myself forever medi-
      ocre. [*His voice gains power.*] Why? . . . What is my fault? . . . Until this day I
170   have pursued virtue with rigor. I have labored long hours to relieve my
      fellow men. I have worked and worked the talent You allowed me. [*Calling
      up.*] *You know how hard I've worked!* Solely that in the end, in the practice
      of the art which alone makes the world comprehensible to me, I might
      hear Your Voice! And now I do hear it—and it says only one name:
      MOZART! . . . Spiteful, sniggering, conceited, infantine Mozart—who has
      never worked one minute to help another man! Shit-talking Mozart, with
      his botty-smacking wife! *Him* You have chosen to be Your sole conduct!
      And *my* only reward—my sublime privilege—is to be the sole man alive in
      this time who shall clearly recognize Your Incarnation! [*Savagely.*] *Grazie e
180   grazie ancora!*[61] [*Pause.*] So be it! From this time we are enemies, You and
      I! I'll not accept it from You—*do you hear?* . . . They say God is not mocked.
      I tell You, *Man* is not mocked! . . . *I* am not mocked! . . . They say the
      spirit bloweth where it listeth: I tell You NO! It must list to virtue or not
      blow at all! [*Yelling.*] *Dio ingiusto*[62]—You are the Enemy! I name Thee
      now—*Nemico Eterno!*[63] And this I swear: To my last breath I shall *block* You
      on earth, as far as I am able! [*He glares up at God. To audience.*] What use,
      after all, is man, if not to teach God His lessons? [*Pause. Suddenly he speaks
      again to us in the voice of an old man. He slips off his powdered wig, crosses to the
      fortepiano and takes from its lid where they lie the old dressing gown and cap which
190   he discarded when he conducted us back to the eighteenth century. He slips these on.
      It is again 1823.*] Before I tell you what happened next—God's answer to
      me—and indeed Constanze's—and all the horrors that followed—let me
      stop. The bladder, being a human appendage, is not something you need

---

[60] "I understand."
[61] "Thank you and thank you again!"
[62] "Unjust God."
[63] "Eternal Enemy!"

concern yourselves with yet. I, being alive, though barely, am at its constant call. It is now one hour before dawn—when I must dismiss us both. When I return, I'll tell you about the war I fought with God through His preferred Creature—Mozart, named *Amadeus*. In the waging of which, of course, the Creature had to be destroyed. [*He bows to the audience with malignant slyness—snatches a pastry from the stand—and leaves the stage, chewing at it voraciously. The manuscripts lie where he spilled them in his fall. The lights in the theater come up as he goes.*]

END OF ACT ONE

ACT II

SCENE I

Salieri's Apartment

[*The lights go down in the theater as* SALIERI *returns.*]

SALIERI. I have been listening to the cats in the courtyard. They are all singing Rossini.[64] It is obvious that cats have declined as badly as composers. Domenico Scarlatti[65] owned one which would actually stroll across the keyboard and pick out passable subjects for fugue.[66] But that was a Spanish cat of the Enlightenment. It appreciated counterpoint. Nowadays all cats appreciate is coloratura.[67] Like the rest of the public. [*He comes downstage and addresses the audience directly.*] This is now the very last hour of my life. You must understand me. Not forgive. I do not seek forgiveness. I was a good man, as the world calls good. What use was it to me? Goodness could not make me a good composer! . . . Was Mozart good? Goodness is nothing in the furnace of art. [*Pause.*] On that dreadful Night of the Manuscripts my life acquired a terrible and thrilling purpose. The blocking of God in one of His purest manifestations. I had the power. God needed Mozart to let Himself into the world. And Mozart needed me to get him worldly advancement. So it would be a battle to the end—and Mozart was the battleground. [*Pause.*] One thing I knew of Him. He was a cunning Enemy. Witness the fact that in blocking Him in the world I was also given the satisfaction of obstructing a disliked human rival. I wonder which of you will refuse that chance if it is offered. [*He regards the audience maliciously and takes off the dressing gown and cap*]. I felt the danger at once, as soon as I'd spoken my challenge. How would He answer? Would He strike me dead for my impiety? Don't laugh. I was not a sophisticate of the salons. I was a small-town Catholic, full of dread! [*He puts on the powdered*

---

[64] Gioacchimo Rossini (1792–1868), a famous Italian composer of operas.
[65] Domenico Scarlatti (1683–1757), an Italian composer and a virtuoso on the harpsichord.
[66] A musical form in which a theme is developed through counterpoint.
[67] Brilliant, rapid runs and trills.

wig again and speaks again in his younger voice. We are back again in the eighteenth century.] The first thing that happened, barely one hour later— [*The doorbell sounds.* CONSTANZE *comes in, followed by a helpless* VALET.] Suddenly Constanze was back. At ten o'clock at night. [*In surprise.*] Signora!

CONSTANZE [*stiffly*]. My husband is at a soiree of Baron van Swieten. A con-
230   cert of Sebastian Bach.[68] He didn't think I would enjoy it.

SALIERI. I see. [*Curtly, to the goggling* VALET.] I'll ring if we require anything. Thank you.

                                      [*The* VALET *goes out. Slight pause.*]

CONSTANZE [*flatly*]. Where do we go, then?

SALIERI. What?

CONSTANZE. Do we do it in here? . . . Why not? [*She sits, still wearing her hat, in one of the little gilded upright chairs. Deliberately she loosens the strings of her bodice, so that one can just see the tops of her breasts, hitches up her silk skirts above the knees, so that one can also just see the flesh above the tops of the stockings, spreads her legs and regards him with an open stare.*]

240 CONSTANZE [*speaking softly*]. Well? . . . Let's get on with it. [*For a second* SALIERI *returns the stare, then looks suddenly away.*]

SALIERI [*stiffly*]. Your manuscripts are there. Please take them and go. Now. At once. [*Pause.*]

CONSTANZE. You shit. [*She jumps up and snatches the portfolio.*]

SALIERI. Via! Don't return!

CONSTANZE. You rotten shit! [*Suddenly she runs at him, trying furiously to hit at his face. He grabs her arms, shakes her violently, and hurls her on the floor.*]

SALIERI. Via!

                                   [*She freezes, staring up at him in hate.*]

SALIERI [*calling to audience*]. You see how it was! I would have liked her—oh,
250   yes, just then more than ever! I wanted nothing petty! . . . My quarrel now wasn't with Mozart—it was *through* him! Through him to God, who loved him so. [*Scornfully.*] Amadeus! . . . Amadeus! . . . [CONSTANZE *picks herself up and runs from the room. Pause. He calms himself, going to the table and selecting a "Nipple of Venus" to eat.*] The next day, when Katherina Cavalieri came for her lesson, I made the same halting speech about "coins of tenderness," and I dubbed the girl *La Generosa.* I regret that my invention in love, as in art, has always been limited. Fortunately, Katherina found it sufficient. She consumed twenty "Nipples of Venus"—kissed me with brandied breath—and slipped easily into my bed. [KATHERINA *comes in languidly, half*
260   *undressed, as if from his bedroom. He embraces her, and helps slyly to adjust her peignoir.*] She remained there as my mistress for many years behind my good wife's back—and I soon erased in sweat the sense of his little body, the Creature's, preceding me. [*The girl gives him a radiant smile, and ambles off.*] So much for my vow of sexual virtue. [*Slight pause.*] The same evening I went to the Palace and resigned from all my committees to help the lot of poor musicians. So much for my vow of social virtue. [*Light change.*]

---

[68] Johann Sebastian Bach (1685–1750), the famous German organist and composer.

Then I went to the Emperor and recommended a man of no talent whatever to instruct the Princess Elizabeth.

SCENE II

The Palace of Schönbrunn

[*The* EMPEROR *stands before the vast fireplace, between the golden mirrors.*]

JOSEPH. Herr Sommer. A dull man, surely? What of Mozart?
1270 SALIERI. Majesty, I cannot with a clear conscience recommend Mozart to teach royalty. One hears too many stories.
JOSEPH. They must be just gossip.
SALIERI. One of them, I regret, relates to a protégée of my own. A very young singer.
JOSEPH. *Charmant!*
SALIERI. Not pleasant, Majesty, but true.
JOSEPH. I see. . . . Let it be Herr Sommer, then. [*He walks down onto the main stage.*] I daresay he can't do much harm. To be frank, no one can do much harm musically to the Princess Elizabeth. [*He strolls away.*]

[MOZART *enters from the other side, downstage. He wears a more natural-looking wig from now on—one indeed intended to represent his own hair of light chestnut, full and gathered at the back with ribbon.*]

1280 SALIERI [*to audience*]. Mozart certainly did not suspect me. The Emperor announced the appointment in his usual way—
JOSEPH [*pausing*]. Well—there it is. [*He goes off.*]
SALIERI. And I commiserated with the loser. [MOZART *turns and stares bleakly out front.* SALIERI *shakes his hand.*]
MOZART [*bitterly*]. It's my own fault. My father always writes I should be more obedient. *Know my place!* . . . He'll send me sixteen lectures when he hears of this! [MOZART *goes slowly up to the fortepiano. Lights lower.*]
SALIERI [*watching him, to audience*]. It was a most serious loss as far as *Mozart* was concerned.

SCENE III

Vienna, and Glimpses of Opera Houses

[*The* VENTICELLI *glide on.*]

1290 V.1. His list of pupils hardly moves.
V.2. Six at most.
V.1. And now a child to keep!
V.2. A boy.
SALIERI. Poor fellow. [*To audience.*] I by contrast prospered. This is the extraordinary truth. If I had expected fury from God, none came. *None!* . . . Instead—incredibly—in '84 and '85 I came to be regarded as infinitely the superior composer. And this despite the fact that these were the two years

in which Mozart wrote his best keyboard concerti[69] and his string quartets.[70]

[*The* VENTICELLI *stand on either side of* SALIERI. MOZART *sits at the fortepiano.*]

1300 V.1.   Haydn[71] calls the quartets unsurpassed.
      SALIERI.   They were, but no one heard them.
      V.2.   Van Swieten calls the concerti sublime.
      SALIERI.   They were, but no one noticed.

[MOZART *plays and conducts from the keyboard. Faintly we hear the Rondo[72] from the Piano Concerto in A major, K. 488.*]

SALIERI [*over this*].   The Viennese greeted each concerto with the squeals of pleasure they usually reserved for a new style of bonnet. Each was played once—then totally forgotten! ... By contrast, my operas were played everywhere and saluted by everyone! I composed a *Semiramide*[73] for Munich.
      V.1.   Rapturously received!
      V.2.   People *faint* with pleasure!

[*In the Light Box is seen the interior of a brilliantly colored opera house, and an audience standing up, applauding vigorously.* SALIERI, *flanked by the* VENTICELLI, *turns upstage and bows to it. The concerts can barely be heard through the din.*]

1310 SALIERI.   I wrote a comic opera for Vienna. *La Grotta di Trofonio.*
      V.1.   The talk of the city!
      V.2.   The cafés are buzzing!

[*Another opera house interior is lit up. Another audience claps vigorously. Again* SALIERI *bows to it.*]

SALIERI [*to audience*].   I finally finished my tragic opera *Danaius*, and produced it in Paris.
      V.1.   Stupendous reception!
      V.2.   The plaudits shake the roof!
      V.1.   Your name sounds throughout the Empire!
      V.2.   Throughout all Europe!

[*Yet another opera house and another excited audience.* SALIERI *bows a third time. Even the* VENTICELLI *now applaud him. The concert stops.* MOZART *rises from the keyboard and, while* SALIERI *speaks, crosses directly through the scene and leaves the stage.*]

SALIERI [*to audience*].   It was incomprehensible. Almost as if I were being
1320 rushed deliberately from triumph to triumph! ... I filled my head with golden opinions—yes, and this house with golden furniture!

---

[69] A musical composition somewhat like a sonata. A concerto is usually written for one solo instrument and an orchestra; it usually has three movements.

[70] A musical composition for four voices or four instruments.

[71] Franz Joseph Haydn (1732–1809), an Austrian composer.

[72] A form often used in the last movement of a sonata in which the principal theme is stated three or more times, separated by musical diversions.

[73] A composition about Semiramis, the legendary founder of Babylon, noted for her beauty, wisdom, and sexual excesses.

SCENE IV

Salieri's Apartment

The stage turns gold.

SERVANTS *come on carrying golden chairs upholstered in golden brocade. They place these all over the wooden floor. The* VALET *appears—a little older—divests* SALIERI *of his sky-blue coat and clothes him instead in a frock coat of gold satin.*

The COOK—*also, of course, a little older—brings in a golden cake-stand piled with more elaborate cakes.*

SALIERI.   My own taste was for plain things—but I *denied* it! The successful lived with gold, and so would I! . . . I grew confident, I grew resplendent. I gave salons and soirees, and worshiped the season round at the altar of sophistication! [*He sits at ease in his salon. The* VENTICELLI *sit with him, one on either side.*]

V.1.   Mozart heard your comedy last night.

V.2.   He spoke of it to the Princess Lichnowsky.

V.1.   He said you should be made to clean up your own mess.

1330 SALIERI [*taking snuff*].   *Really?* What charmers these Salzburgers are!

V.2.   People are outraged by him.

V.1.   He empties drawing rooms. Now Van Swieten is angry with him. [*The* VENTICELLI *laugh maliciously.*]

SALIERI.   Lord Fugue? . . . I thought he was the Baron's little pet.

V.2.   Mozart has asked leave to write an Italian opera.

SALIERI [*to audience*].   *Italian opera! Threat! My kingdom!*

V.1.   And the Baron is scandalized.

SALIERI.   But why? What's the subject?

[VAN SWIETEN *comes on quickly from upstage.*]

VAN SWIETEN.   Figaro! . . . *The Marriage of Figaro!* That disgraceful play of
1340   Beaumarchais![74]

[*At a discreet sign of dismissal from* SALIERI, *the* VENTICELLI *slip away.* VAN SWIETEN *joins* SALIERI, *and sits on one of the gold chairs.*]

VAN SWIETEN [*to* SALIERI].   That's all he can find to waste his talent on: a vulgar farce! Noblemen lusting after chambermaids! Their wives dressing up in stupid disguises anyone could penetrate in a second! . . . When I reproved him, he said I reminded him of his father! . . . I simply cannot imagine why Mozart should want to set that rubbish to music!

[MOZART *enters quickly from upstage, accompanied by* STRACK. *They join* SALIERI *and* VAN SWIETEN.]

MOZART.   Because I want to do a piece about real people, Baron! And I want to set it in a real place! A *boudoir!* Because that to me is the most exciting place on earth! Underclothes on the floor! Sheets still warm from a woman's body! Even a pisspot brimming under the bed!

1350 VAN SWIETEN [*outraged*].   Mozart!

---

[74] Pierre Augustin Caron de Beaumarchais (1732–1799), a French playwright.

MOZART.   I want life, Baron. Not boring legends!

STRACK.   Herr Salieri's recent *Danaius* was a legend, and that did not bore the French.

MOZART.   It is impossible to bore the French—except with real life!

VAN SWIETEN.   I had assumed, now that you had joined our Brotherhood of Masons, you would choose more elevated themes.

MOZART [*impatiently*].   Oh, elevated! Elevated! . . . The only thing a man should elevate is his doodle.

VAN SWIETEN.   You are provoking, sir! Has everything to be a joke with you?

1360 MOZART [*desperate*].   Excuse the language, Baron, but really! . . . How can we go on forever with these gods and heroes!

VAN SWIETEN [*passionately*].   Because they *go* on forever—that's why! They represent the eternal in us. Opera is here to ennoble us, Mozart—you and me just as well as the Emperor. It is an aggrandizing art! It celebrates the eternal man and ignores the ephemeral. The goddess in woman and not the laundress.

STRACK.   Well said, sir. Exactly!

MOZART [*imitating his drawl*].   Oh, well said, yes, well said! Exactly! [*To all of them.*] I don't understand you! You're all up on perches, but it doesn't
1370 hide your arseholes! You don't give a shit about gods and heroes! If you are honest—each one of you—which of you isn't more at home with his hairdresser than Hercules? Or Horatius? [*To* SALIERI.] Or your stupid Danaius, come to that! Or *mine—mine! Idomeneo, King of Crete!* All those anguished antiques! They're all bores! Bores, bores, bores! [*Suddenly he springs up and jumps onto a chair, like an orator. Declaring it.*] All serious operas written this century are boring! [*They turn and look at him in shocked amazement. A pause. He gives his little giggle, and then jumps down again.*] Look at us! Four gaping mouths. What a perfect quartet! I'd love to write it—just this second of time, this *now*, as you are! Herr Cham-
1380 berlain thinking: "Impertinent Mozart. I must speak to the Emperor at once!" Herr Prefect thinking: "Ignorant Mozart. Debasing opera with his vulgarity!" Herr Court Composer thinking: "German Mozart. What can he finally know about music?" And Mozart himself, in the middle, thinking: "I'm just a good fellow. Why do they all disapprove of me? [*Excitedly to* VAN SWIETEN.] That's why opera is important, Baron. Because it's realer than any play! A dramatic poet would have to put all those thoughts down one after another to represent this second of time. The composer can put them all down at once—and still make us hear each one of them. Astonishing device—a vocal quartet! [*More and more excited.*]
1390 I tell you I want to write a finale lasting half an hour! A quartet becoming a quintet becoming a sextet. On and on, wider and wider—all sounds multiplying and rising together—and then together making a sound entirely new! . . . I bet you that's how God hears the world. Millions of sounds ascending at once and mixing in His ear to become an unending music, unimaginable to us! [*To* SALIERI.] That's our job! That's our *job*, we composers: to combine the inner minds of him and him and him, and her and her—the thoughts of chambermaids and Court Composers—and turn the audience into God. [*Pause.* SALIERI *stares at him, fascinated. Embarrassed,* MOZART *sounds a fart noise and giggles.*] I'm sorry. I
1400 talk nonsense all day. It's incurable—ask Stanzerl. [*To* VAN SWIETEN.] My tongue is stupid. My heart isn't.

VAN SWIETEN.   No. You're a good fellow under all your nonsense: I know that.
    He'll make a fine new Brother, won't he, Salieri?
SALIERI.   Better than I, Baron.
VAN SWIETEN.   Just try, my friend, to be more serious with your gifts. [*He
    smiles, presses* MOZART's *hand, and goes.* SALIERI *rises.*]
SALIERI.   *Buona fortuna, Mozart.*[75]
MOZART.   *Grazie, Signore.* [*Rounding on* STRACK.] Stop frowning, Herr Cham-
    berlain. I'm a jackass. It's easy to be friends with a jackass: just shake his
1410   hoof. [*He forms his hand into a hoof. Warily* STRACK *takes it—then springs back
    as* MOZART *brays loudly like a donkey.*] Hee-haw! . . . Tell the Emperor the
    opera's finished.
STRACK.   Finished?
MOZART.   Right here in my noodle. The rest's just scribbling. Goodbye.
STRACK.   Good day to you.
MOZART.   He's going to be proud of me. You'll see! [*He gives his flourish of the
    hand and goes out, delighted with himself.*]
STRACK.   That young man *really is* . . .
SALIERI [*blandly*].   Very lively!
1420 STRACK [*exploding*].   Intolerable! . . . *Intolerable!* [STRACK *freezes in a posture of
    indignation.*]
SALIERI [*to audience*].   How could I stop it? . . . How could I block this opera
    of *Figaro*? . . . Incredible to hear, within six weeks the Creature had fin-
    ished the entire score!

                                                      [ROSENBERG *bustles in.*]

ROSENBERG.   *Figaro* is complete! The first performance will be on May the
    first.
SALIERI.   So soon?
ROSENBERG.   There's no way we can stop it! [*A slight pause.*]
SALIERI [*slyly*].   I have an idea. *Una piccola idea.*[76]
1430 ROSENBERG.   What?
SALIERI.   *Mi ha detto che c'è un balleto nel terzo atto?*[77]
ROSENBERG [*puzzled*].   *Sì.*
STRACK.   What does he say?
SALIERI.   *E dimmi—non è vero che l'Imperatore ha prohibito il balletto nelle sue
    opere?*[78]
ROSENBERG [*realizing*].   *Uno balleto . . . Ah!*
SALIERI.   *Precisamente.*[79]
ROSENBERG.   *Oh, capisco! Ma che meraviglia! Perfetto!* [*He laughs in delight.*]
    Veramente ingegnoso![80]
1440 STRACK [*irritated*].   What is it? What is he suggesting?
SALIERI.   See him at the theater.
ROSENBERG.   Of course. Immediately. I'd forgotten. You are brilliant, Court
    Composer.

---

[75] "Good luck, Mozart."   [76] "One little idea."
[77] "He has told me that there is a ballet in the third act."
[78] "And tell me—is it not true that the Emperor has prohibited ballet in his operas?"
[79] "Precisely."
[80] "Ah, I understand! But how marvelous! Perfect! . . . Truly ingenious!"

SALIERI.   I? . . . I have said nothing. [*He moves away upstage. The light begins to change, dimming down.*]

STRACK [*very cross*].   I must tell you that I resent this extremely. Mozart is right in some things. There is far too much Italian *chittero-chattero* at this court! Now please to inform me at once, what was just said?

ROSENBERG [*lightly*].   *Pazienza,*[81] my dear Chamberlain. *Pazienza.* Just wait
1450   and see!

[*From upstage, SALIERI beckons to STRACK. Baffled and cross, the CHAMBERLAIN joins him. They watch together, unseen. The light dims further.*]

SCENE V

An Unlit Theater

In the background, a projection of lamps glowing faintly in the darkened auditorium. ROSENBERG sits on one of the gold chairs, center. MOZART comes in quickly from the left, wearing another bright coat, and carrying the score of FIGARO. He crosses to the fortepiano.

ROSENBERG.   Mozart! . . . *Mozart!*

MOZART.   Yes, Herr Director.

ROSENBERG [*agreeably*].   A word with you, please. Right away.

MOZART.   Certainly. What is it?

ROSENBERG.   I would like to see your score of *Figaro.*

MOZART.   Oh, yes. Why?

ROSENBERG.   Just bring it here to me. [*Unmoving.*] Into my hand, please.
1460   [*MOZART hands it to him, puzzled. ROSENBERG turns the pages.*] Now tell me: did you not know that His Majesty has expressly forbidden ballet in his operas?

MOZART.   Ballet?

ROSENBERG.   Such as occurs in your third act.

MOZART.   That is not a ballet, Herr Director. That is a dance at Figaro's wedding.

ROSENBERG.   Exactly. A dance.

MOZART [*trying to control himself*].   But the Emperor doesn't mean to prohibit dancing when it's part of the story. He made that law to prevent insertions of stupid ballet like in French operas, and quite right too.

1470 ROSENBERG [*raising his voice*].   It is not for you, Herr Mozart, to interpret the Emperor's edicts. Merely to obey them. [*He seizes the offending pages between his fingers.*]

MOZART.   What are you doing? . . . What are you doing, Excellency?

ROSENBERG.   Taking out what should never have been put in. [*In a terrible silence, ROSENBERG tears out the pages. MOZART watches in disbelief. Upstage, SALIERI and STRACK look on together from the dimness.*] Now sir, perhaps in future you will obey imperial commands. [*He tears out some more pages.*]

MOZART.   But . . . But if all that goes—there'll be a hole right at the climax of the story . . . [*Crying out suddenly.*] Salieri! This is Salieri's idea!

---

[81] "Patience."

1480 ROSENBERG. Don't be absurd.

SALIERI [*to audience*]. How did he think of that?! Nothing I had ever done
could possibly make him think of that on his own. Had God given him the
idea?!

MOZART. It's a conspiracy. I can smell it. I can *smell* it! It's a conspiracy!

ROSENBERG. Control yourself!

MOZART [*howling*]. *But what do you expect me to do?* The first performance is
two days off!

ROSENBERG. Write it over. That's your forte, is it not?—writing at speed.

MOZART. Not when the music's *perfect!* Not when it's absolutely perfect as it
1490 is! . . . [*Wildly.*] I shall appeal to the Emperor! I'll go to him myself. I'll
hold a rehearsal especially for him.

ROSENBERG. The Emperor does not attend rehearsals.

MOZART. He'll attend this one. Make no mistake—he'll come to this one!
Then he'll deal with *you!*

ROSENBERG. This issue is simple. Write your act again today—or withdraw
the opera. That's final. [*Pause. He hands back the mutilated score to its composer.* MOZART *is shaking.*]

MOZART. You shit-pot. [ROSENBERG *turns and walks imperturbably away from
him.*] Woppy, foppy, wet-arsed, Italian-loving, shit-pot!

[*Serenely* ROSENBERG *leaves the stage.*]

1500 MOZART [*screeching after him*]. Count Orsini-Rosenberg! . . . Rosencunt! . . .
Rosenbugger! . . . I'll hold a rehearsal! You'll see. The Emperor will come!
You'll see! You'll see! . . . *You'll see!!* [*He throws down his score in a storm of
hysterical rage.*]

[*Upstage in the dimness,* STRACK *goes out, and* SALIERI *ventures down toward the
shrieking little man.* MOZART *suddenly becomes aware of him. He turns, his hand
shooting out in an involuntary gesture of accusation.*]

MOZART [*to* SALIERI]. I am *forbidden!* . . . I am—But of course you know already.

SALIERI [*quietly*]. Know what? [MOZART *flings away from him.*]

MOZART [*bitterly*]. No matter! [*He makes to go.*]

SALIERI [*always blandly*]. Mozart, permit me. If you wish, I will speak to the
Emperor myself. Ask him to attend a rehearsal.

1510 MOZART [*amazed*]. You wouldn't!

SALIERI. I cannot promise he will come, but I can try.

MOZART [*returning*]. Sir! . . .

SALIERI. Good day. [*He puts up his hand, barring further intimacy.*]

[MOZART *retreats to the fortepiano.*]

SALIERI [*to audience*]. Needless to say, I did nothing whatever in the matter.
Yet—to my total stupefaction—[STRACK *and* ROSENBERG *hurry on downstage.*]
In the middle of the last rehearsal of *Figaro* next day . . . [*The* EMPEROR
JOSEPH *comes on from upstage.*]

JOSEPH [*cheerfully*]. Fêtes and fireworks! Fêtes and fireworks! Gentlemen,
good afternoon!

SCENE VI

The Theater

1520 SALIERI [*to audience*].   Entirely against his usual practice, the Emperor appeared!

[STRACK *and* ROSENBERG *look at each other in consternation.* JOSEPH *seats himself excitedly on one of the gold chairs, facing out front. As with the premiere of* Seraglio *seen in Act I, he watches the audience as if it were the opera.*]

JOSEPH.   I can't wait for this, Mozart, I assure you! *Je prévois des merveilles!*[82]
MOZART [*bowing fervently*].   Majesty!

[*The courtiers sit also:* STRACK *on his right-hand side,* ROSENBERG *on his left.* SALIERI *also sits, near the keyboard.*]

SALIERI [*to audience*].   What did this mean? Was this proof God had finally decided to defend Mozart against me? Was He engaging with me at last?

[MOZART *passes behind* SALIERI.]

MOZART [*earnestly, sotto voce*[83]].   I am so grateful to you, I cannot express—
SALIERI [*aside, to him*].   Hush. Say nothing.

[MOZART *goes on quickly to the fortepiano and sits at it.*]

SALIERI [*to audience*].   One thing about the event seemed more than coincidence. [*Music sounds faintly: the end of the third act of* Figaro, *just before the*
1530   *dance music starts.*] Strangely, His Majesty had arrived at precisely the moment when the dancers would have begun, had not they and their music been entirely cut. [*The music stops abruptly.*] He and all of us watched the action proceed in total silence. [*Flanked by his* COURTIERS, *the* EMPEROR *stares out front, following with his eyes what is obviously a silent pantomime. His face expresses bewilderment.* ROSENBERG *watches his sovereign anxiously. Finally the monarch speaks.*]
JOSEPH.   I don't understand. Is it modern?
MOZART [*jumping up nervously from the keyboard*].   No, Majesty.
JOSEPH.   Then what?
1540 MOZART.   The Herr Director has removed a dance that would have occurred at this point.
JOSEPH [*to* ROSENBERG].   Why was this done?
ROSENBERG.   It's your own regulation, Sire. No ballet in your opera.
MOZART [*nervously*].   Majesty, this is not a ballet! . . . It is part of a wedding feast—entirely necessary for the story.
JOSEPH.   Well, it certainly looks very odd the way it is. I can't say I like it.
MOZART.   Nor do I, Majesty.
JOSEPH.   Do you like it, Rosenberg?
ROSENBERG.   It's not a question of liking, Majesty. Your own law decrees it.

---

[82] "I foresee wonders."   [83] In an undertone.

1550 JOSEPH.   Yes. All the same, this is nonsense. Look at them: they're like wax-
works up there.
ROSENBERG.   Well, not exactly, Majesty.
JOSEPH.   I don't like waxworks.
MOZART.   Nor do I, Majesty.
JOSEPH.   Well, who would? What do you say, Salieri?
SALIERI.   Italians are fond of waxworks, Majesty. [*Pause.*] Our religion is
largely based upon them.
JOSEPH.   You are *cattivo* again, Court Composer.
STRACK [*intervening creamily*].   Your Majesty, Count Rosenberg is very wor-
1560 ried that if this music is put back, it will create the most unfortunate
precedent. One will have thereafter to endure hours of dancing in opera.
JOSEPH.   I think we can guard against that, you know, Chamberlain. I really
think we can guard against hours of dancing. [*To* ROSENBERG.] Please re-
store Herr Mozart's music.
ROSENBERG.   But, Majesty, I must insist—
JOSEPH [*with command*].   You will oblige me, Rosenberg! . . . I wish to hear
Mozart's music. Do you understand me?
ROSENBERG.   Yes Majesty.

[MOZART *explodes with joy, jumps over a chair and throws himself at* JOSEPH's *feet.*]

MOZART.   Oh, God, I thank your Majesty! [*He kisses the* EMPEROR's *hand ex-*
1570 *travagantly, as at their first meeting.*] Oh, thank you—thank you—thank you,
Sire, forever!
JOSEPH [*withdrawing hand*].   Yes, yes—very good. A little less enthusiasm, I
beg you!
MOZART [*abashed*].   Excuse me.

[*The* EMPEROR *rises. All follow suit.*]

JOSEPH.   Well—*there it is!*

SCENE VII

The First Performance of FIGARO

The theater glows with light for the first performance of **Figaro**. COURTIERS *and*
CITIZENS *come in swiftly.*
The EMPEROR *and his* COURT *resume their seats and the others quickly take theirs.
In the front row we note* KATHERINA CAVALIERI, *all plumes and sequins, and* KAPELL-
MEISTER BONNO—*older than ever. Behind them sit* CONSTANZE *and the* VENTICELLI.
*All of them stare out at the audience as if we were the opera they have come to see:
people of fashion down front; poorer people crowded into the Light Box, upstage.*
SALIERI *crosses as he speaks, to where two chairs have been placed side by side apart
from the rest, on the left, to form his box. On the chair upstage sits his good wife,*
TERESA—*more statuesque than ever.*

SALIERI [*to audience*].   And so *Figaro* was produced in spite of all my efforts. I
sat in my box on May the first, 1786, and watched it happen. A conspic-
uous defeat for me. And yet I was strangely excited. [*Faintly we hear Figaro*

singing the tune of "Non più andrai." The stage audience is obviously delighted:
1580   they smile out front as they watch the (invisible) action.] My march! My poor
March of Welcome—now set to enchant the world forever! [*It fades. Applause. The* Emperor *rises, and with him the audience, to denote an intermission.* Joseph *greets* Katherina *and* Bonno. Rosenberg *and* Strack *go to* Salieri's *box.*]

Rosenberg [*to* Salieri]. Almost in your style, that last bit. But more vulgar, of course. Far more obvious than you would ever be.
Strack [*drawling*]. Exactly!

[*A bell rings for the end of the intermission. The* Emperor *returns quickly to his seat. The audience sits. A pause. All look out front, unmoving.*]

Salieri [*raptly and quietly, to audience*]. Trembling, I heard the second act. [*Pause.*] The restored third act. [*Pause.*] The astounding fourth. What shall
1590   I say to you who will one day hear this last act for yourselves? You will—because whatever else shall pass away, this must remain.

[*Faintly we hear the solemn closing ensemble from Act 4 of Figaro, "Ah! Tutti contenti. Saremo così."*]

Salieri [*over this*]. The scene was night in a summer garden. Pinprick stars gleamed down on shaking summerhouses. Plotters glided behind pasteboard hedges. I saw a woman, dressed in her maid's clothes, hear her husband utter the first tender words he has offered her in years, only because he thinks she is someone else. Could one catch a realer moment? And how, except in a net of pure artifice? The disguises of opera had been invented for Mozart. [*He can barely look out at the "stage."*] The final reconciliation melted sight. [*Pause.*] Through my tears I saw the Emperor . . .
1600   yawn.

[Joseph *yawns. The music fades. There is scant applause.* Joseph *rises and the* Courtiers *follow suit.* Mozart *bows.*]

Joseph [*to* Rosenberg: *coolly*]. Most ingenious, Mozart. You are coming along nicely. . . . I do think we must omit encores in future. It really makes things far too long. Make a note, Rosenberg.
Rosenberg. Majesty.

[Mozart *lowers his head, crushed.*]

Joseph. Gentlemen, good night to you. Strack, attend me.

[Joseph *goes out, with* Strack. *Director* Rosenberg *gives* Mozart *one triumphant look and follows.* Salieri *nods to his* Wife, *who leaves with the audience. Only* Constanze *lingers for a second, then she, too, goes. A pause.* Mozart *and* Salieri *are left alone,* Salieri *deeply shaken by the opera,* Mozart *deeply upset by its reception. He sits.*]

Mozart [*low*]. Herr Salieri.
Salieri. Yes?
Mozart. What do you think? Do you think I am coming along nicely? [*A pause.*]

1610 SALIERI [*moved*].   I think the piece is . . . extraordinary. I think it is . . . *mar-velous*. Yes. [*A pause.*]
     MOZART.   I'll tell you what it is. It's the best opera yet written. That's what it is. And only I could have done it. No one else living!

[MOZART *walks away.* SALIERI *turns his head away swiftly, as if he has been slapped. They both freeze. The light changes. The* VENTICELLI *rush on.*]

     V.1.   Rosenberg is furious.
     V.2.   He'll never forgive Mozart.
     V.1.   He'll do anything to get back at him!
     SALIERI [*rising, to audience*].   So it wasn't hard to get the piece canceled. I saw to it through the person of the resentful Director that in the entire year, *Figaro* was played only *nine times!* . . . My defeat finally turned into a vic-
1620   tory. And God's response to my challenge remained as inscrutable as ever. . . Was He taking any notice of me *at all?* . . .

[MOZART *breaks his freeze and comes downstage.*]

     MOZART.   *Withdrawn!* Absolutely no plans for its revival!
     SALIERI.   I commiserate with you, my friend. But if the public does not like one's work, one has to accept the fact gracefully. [*Aside, to audience.*] And certainly they didn't.
     V.1. [*complaining*].   It's too complicated!
     V.2. [*complaining*].   Too tiresome!
     V.1.   All those morbid harmonies!
     V.2.   And never a good bang at the end of songs, so you know when to clap!

[*The* VENTICELLI *go off.*]

1630 SALIERI [*to audience*].   Obviously I would not need to plot too hard against his operas in future. I must concentrate on the man. I decided to see him as much as possible: to learn everything I could of his weaknesses.

SCENE VIII

The Waldstädten Library

[SERVANTS *again bring on the wing chair.*]

     MOZART.   I'll go to England! England loves music. That's the answer!
     SALIERI [*to audience*].   We were yet again in the library of the Baroness Wald-städten—that room fated to be the scene of ghastly encounters between us. Again, too, the compensating *crema al mascarpone.* [*He sits in the chair and eats greedily.*]
     MOZART.   I was there when I was a boy: they absolutely adored me. I had more kisses than you've had cakes! . . . When I was a child people loved
1640   me.
     SALIERI.   Perhaps they will again. Why don't you go to London and try?
     MOZART.   Because I have a wife and child and no money. I wrote to Papa to take the boy off my hands just for a few months so I could go—and he refused! . . . He's a bitter man, of course. After he'd finished showing me

off around Europe he never went anywhere himself. He just stayed up in Salzburg year after year, kissing the ring of the fartbishop and lecturing me! . . . [*Confidentially.*] The real thing is, you see, he's jealous. Under everything he's jealous of *me!* He'll never forgive me for being cleverer than he is. [*He leans excitedly over* SALIERI's *chair like a naughty child.*] I'll tell

1650   you a secret. Leopold Mozart is just a jealous, dried-up old turd. . . . And I actually detest him. [*He giggles guiltily. The* VENTICELLI *appear quickly, and address* SALIERI, *as* MOZART *freezes.*]

V.1. [*solemnly*].   Leopold Mozart—

V.2. [*solemnly*].   Leopold Mozart—

V.1. & V.2.   Leopold Mozart is dead! [*They go off.* MOZART *recoils. A long pause.*]

SALIERI.   Do not despair. Death is inevitable, my friend.

MOZART [*desperately*].   How will I go now?

SALIERI.   What do you mean?

1660   MOZART.   In the world. There's no one else. No one who understands the wickedness around. *I can't see it!* . . . He watched for me all my life—and I betrayed him.

SALIERI.   No!

MOZART.   I talked against him.

SALIERI.   *No!*

MOZART [*distressed*].   I married where he begged me not. I left him alone. I danced and played billiards and fooled about, and he sat by himself night after night in an empty house, and no woman to care for him. . . . *Oh, God!*

[SALIERI *rises in concern.*]

SALIERI.   Wolfgang. My dear Wolfgang. Don't accuse yourself! . . . Lean upon

1670   me, if you care to. . . . Lean upon me! [SALIERI *opens his arms in a wide gesture of paternal benevolence.* MOZART *approaches him and is almost tempted to surrender to the embrace. But at the last moment he avoids it and breaks away down front, to fall on his knees.*]

MOZART.   *Papa!*

SALIERI.   So rose the Ghost Father in *Don Giovanni!*

SCENE IX

The two grim chords which open the overture to Don Giovanni *sound through the theater.* MOZART *seems to quail under them, as he stares out front. On the backdrop in the Light Box appears the silhouette of a giant black figure, in cloak and tricorne hat. It extends its arms, menacingly and engulfingly, toward its begetter.*

SALIERI [*to audience*].   A father more accusing than any in opera. So rose the figure of a Guilty Libertine cast into Hell. I looked on astounded as from his ordinary life he made his art. We were both ordinary men, he and I. Yet from the ordinary he created Legends—and I from Legends created

1680   only the ordinary! [*He stands over the kneeling and agonized* MOZART.] Could I not have stopped my war? Shown him some pity? . . . Oh, yes, my friends, at any time—if He above had shown me *one drop of it!* Every day I sat to work I *prayed*—I still prayed, you understand!

[*We hear the exquisite strains of the terzetto*[84] "*Soave il Vento*" *from* Così Fan Tutte.]

SALIERI [*calling upward*].   "Make this one good in my ears! Just this one! ONE!" [*To audience.*] But would He, ever? . . . I heard my music calmed in convention, not one breath of spirit to lift it off the shallows. And I heard *his*—month after month [*the music grows louder*]—the spirit singing through it, unstoppable, to my ears alone! [*To God, in anguish.*] Grant this to me! Grant this to me! . . . [*As "God."*] "No, no, no: I do not need you, Salieri. 1690   I have Mozart! Better for you to be silent!" *Hahahahahaha!* [*The music cuts off.*] The Creature's dreadful giggle was the laughter of God. . . . I had to end it! But how? [*He regards the audience with an icy stare.*] There was only one way. *Starvation.* Reduce the man to destitution. Starve out the God!

SCENE X

Vienna and the Palace of Schönbrunn

[MOZART *rises, still clutching his stomach.*]

SALIERI [*to* MOZART].   How do you fare today?
MOZART.   Badly. I have no money, and no prospect of any.
SALIERI.   It would not be too hard, surely.

[*Lights up on the Palace of Schönbrunn. The* EMPEROR *stands in the Light Box, in his golden space.*]

JOSEPH.   We must find him a post.
1700 SALIERI [*to audience*].   One danger! The Emperor. [SALIERI *goes upstage to* JO-
      SEPH.] There's nothing available, Majesty.
JOSEPH.   There's Chamber Composer, now that Gluck is dead.
SALIERI [*shocked*].   Mozart to follow Gluck?
JOSEPH.   I won't have him say I drove him away. You know what a tongue he has.
SALIERI.   Then grant him Gluck's post, Majesty, but not his salary. That would be wrong.
JOSEPH.   Gluck got two thousand florins a year. What should Mozart get?
SALIERI.   Two hundred. Light payment, yes, but for light duties.
1710 JOSEPH.   Perfectly fair. I'm obliged to you, Court Composer.
SALIERI [*bowing*].   Majesty. [*To audience.*] And so easily done. Like many men obsessed with being thought generous, Joseph the Second was quintessentially stingy.

[MOZART *kneels to the* EMPEROR.]

JOSEPH.   Herr Mozart, *vous nous faites honneur!*[85] [*Lights down on* JOSEPH, *but he stays where he is in the Light Box.* MOZART *and* SALIERI *come downstage.*]
MOZART.   It's a damned insult. Not enough to keep a mouse in cheese for a week!

---

[84] A *terzetto* is a composition for three voices.   [85] "Herr Mozart, you do us an honor!"

SALIERI. Regard it as a token, *caro Herr*.

MOZART. When I was young they gave me snuffboxes. Now it's tokens! And
1720   for what? Pom-pom for fireworks! Twang-twang for contredanzes![86]

SALIERI. I'm sorry it's made you angry. I'd not have suggested it if I'd known
you'd be distressed.

MOZART. You suggested it?

SALIERI. I regret I was not able to do more.

MOZART. Oh . . . forgive me! You're a good man! I see that now! You're a
truly kind man—and I'm a monstrous fool! [*He grasps* SALIERI's *hand.*]

SALIERI. No, please . . .

MOZART. You make me ashamed. . . . You excellent man!

SALIERI. No, no, no, no, no—*s'il vous plaît*. A little less enthusiasm, I beg you!

[MOZART *laughs delightedly at this imitation of the* EMPEROR. SALIERI *joins in.* MOZART
suddenly doubles over in pain. He groans shortly.]

1730 SALIERI. *Wolfgang?* What is it?

MOZART. Nothing. . . . I get cramps sometimes in my stomach. Quite painful. . . .

SALIERI. I'm sorry.

MOZART. Excuse me. . . . It's nothing really.

SALIERI. I will see you soon again?

MOZART. Of course.

SALIERI. Why not visit me?

MOZART. I will. . . . I promise!

SALIERI. *Bene.*

1740 MOZART. *Bene.*

SALIERI. My friend. My new friend!

[MOZART *giggles with pleasure and goes off. A pause.*]

SALIERI [*to audience*]. And I had him. . . . Now, if ever, was the moment for
God to crush me. I waited—and do you know what happened? I had just
ruined Mozart's career at court. God rewarded me by granting my dearest
wish!

[*The* VENTICELLI *come on.*]

V.1. Kappellmeister Bonno.

V.2. Kapellmeister Bonno.

V.1. & V.2. *Kapellmeister Bonno is dead!*

[SALIERI *opens his mouth in surprise.*]

V.1. You are appointed—

1750 V.2. By royal decree—

V.1. To fill his place.

[*Lights full up on the* EMPEROR, *at the back. He is flanked by* STRACK *and* ORSINI-
ROSENBERG, *standing like icons, as at their first appearance.*]

---

[86] A musical piece based on the English country dance, in which couples face each other in
two lines.

JOSEPH [*formally, as* SALIERI *turns and bows to him*]. First Royal and Imperial Kapellmeister to our court.

[*The* VENTICELLI *applaud.*]

V.1. Bravo.
V.2. Bravo.
ROSENBERG. *Evviva*, Salieri![87]
STRACK. Well done, Salieri!
JOSEPH [*warmly*]. Dear Salieri. There it is! [*The lights go down on Schönbrunn. In the dark, the* EMPEROR *and his* COURT *leave the stage for the last time.* SALIERI *turns round, alarmed.*]

1760

SALIERI [*to audience*]. I was now truly alarmed. How long would I go unpunished?
V.1. Mozart looks appalling.
V.2. It must be galling, of course.
V.1. I hear he's dosing himself constantly with medicine.
SALIERI. For what?
V.2. Envy, I imagine.

SCENE XI

The Prater

Fresh green trees appear on the backdrop. The light changes to yellow, turning the blue surround into a rich verdant green.

MOZART and CONSTANZE enter arm in arm. She is palpably pregnant and wears a poor coat and bonnet. His clothes are poorer, too, and his manner is hectic. SALIERI *promenades with the* VENTICELLI.

SALIERI. I met him next in the Prater.
MOZART [*to* SALIERI]. Congratulations, sir!
1770 SALIERI. I thank you. And to you both! [*To audience.*] Clearly there was a change for the worse. His eyes gleamed, oddly, like a dog's when the light catches. [*To* MOZART.] I hear you are not well, my friend. [*He acknowledges* CONSTANZE, *who curtsies to him.*]
MOZART. I'm not. My pains stay with me.
SALIERI. How wretched. What can they be?
MOZART. Also, I sleep badly. . . . I have . . . bad dreams.
CONSTANZE [*warningly*]. Wolferl!
SALIERI. Dreams?
MOZART. Always the same one: A figure comes to me, wrapped in gray,
1780 doing this. [*Beckoning slowly.*] It has no face—like a mask! What can it mean, do you think?
SALIERI. Surely you do not believe in dreams?
MOZART. No, of course not—really!

---

[87] "Long live, Salieri!"

SALIERI.   Surely *you* do not, Madame?

CONSTANZE.   I never dream, sir. Things are unpleasant enough to me, awake.

[SALIERI *bows.*]

MOZART.   It's all fancy, of course!

CONSTANZE [*coldly*].   If Wolfgang had proper work, he might dream less, First Kapellmeister.

MOZART [*embarrassed, taking her arm*].   Stanzi, please! . . . Excuse us, sir. . . .
1790   Come, dearest. We are well enough, thank you. [*Husband and wife continue their walk, and halt at the side of the stage. The light grows less sunny.* CONSTANZE *helps* WOLFGANG *off with his coat. He is revealed as wearing a Masonic apron.* CONSTANZE *leaves the stage.*]

V.1.   He's growing freakish.

V.2.   No question.

V.1.   Gray figures with no faces!

SALIERI [*looking after him*].   His circumstances make him anxious, I fancy.

V.1.   They've moved house again.

V.2.   To the Rauhensteingasse. Number 970.

1800 V.1.   They must be desperate.

V.2.   It's a real slum.

SALIERI.   Does he earn any money at all, apart from his post?

V.1.   Nothing whatever.

V.2.   I hear he's starting to beg.

V.1.   They say he's written letters to twenty brother Masons.

SALIERI.   Really?

V.2.   And they're giving him money.

SALIERI [*to audience*].   Of course! They *would!* . . . I had *forgotten* the Masons! *Naturally* they would relieve him—how *stupid* of me! . . . There could be no
1810   finally starving him with the Masons there to help! As long as he asked they would keep supplying his wants! . . . How could I stop it? And quickly! . . .

V.1.   Lord Fugue is most displeased with him!

SALIERI.   *Is* he?

SCENE XII

A Masonic Lodge

A huge golden emblem, descends, encrusted with Masonic symbols.
Enter VAN SWIETEN. *He, too, is wearing the ritual apron over his sober clothes. The two men clasp hands in fraternal greeting.*

VAN SWIETEN [*gravely*].   This is not good, Brother. The lodge was not created for you to beg from.

MOZART.   What else can I do?

VAN SWIETEN.   Give concerts, as you used to do.

MOZART.   I have no subscribers left, Baron. I am no longer fashionable.

1820 VAN SWIETEN.   I am not surprised! You write tasteless comedies which give offense. I warned you, often enough.

MOZART [*humbly*].   You did. I admit it.

VAN SWIETEN.   I will send you some fugues of Bach tomorrow. You can arrange those for my Sunday concert. You shall have a small fee.

MOZART.   Thank you, Baron.

[VAN SWIETEN *nods and goes out.* SALIERI *steps forward. He, too, wears the Masonic apron.*]

MOZART [*shouting after* VAN SWIETEN].   I cannot live by arranging Bach!

SALIERI [*sarcastically*].   A generous fellow.

MOZART.   All the same, I'll have to do it. If he were to turn the lodge against me, I'd be finished. My brother Masons virtually keep me now.

1830 SALIERI.   Wolfgang, it's embarrassing, I know—but you must allow me to relieve you also.

MOZART.   No!

SALIERI.   If it is the duty of a Mason to help—how much more of a friend.

MOZART.   Not another word! I would never take money from you. That friendship is worth all the gold in the world. Please—no more of that!

SALIERI.   You overwhelm me.

MOZART.   I'll manage: you'll see! Things are looking up already. I've had a marvelous proposal from Schikaneder. He's a new member of this lodge.

SALIERI.   Schikaneder? The actor?

1840 MOZART.   Yes. He owns a theater in the suburbs.

SALIERI.   Well, more of a music hall, surely?

MOZART.   Yes. . . . He wants me to write him a vaudeville—something for ordinary German people. Isn't that a wonderful idea? . . . He's offered me half the receipts when we open.

SALIERI.   Nothing in advance?

MOZART.   He said he couldn't afford anything. I know it's not much of an offer. But a popular piece about brotherly love could celebrate everything we believe as Mason!

SALIERI.   It certainly could! . . . Why don't you put the Masons *into* it?

1850 MOZART.   Into an opera? . . . I couldn't. [SALIERI *laughs, to indicate that he was simply making a joke.*] All the same—what an idea!

SALIERI [*earnestly*].   Our rituals are secret, Wolfgang.

MOZART.   I needn't copy them exactly. I could adapt them a little.

SALIERI.   Well. . . . It would certainly be in a great cause.

MOZART.   Brotherly love!

SALIERI.   Brotherly love!

[*They both turn and look solemnly at the great golden emblem hanging at the back.*]

SALIERI [*warmly*].   Take courage, Wolfgang. It's a glorious idea.

MOZART.   It is, isn't it? It *really is!*

SALIERI.   Of course say nothing till it's done.

1860 MOZART.   Not a word.

SALIERI [*making a sign: closed fist*].   Secret!

MOZART [*making a similar sign*].   Secret!

SALIERI.   Good.

[*He steps out of the scene downstage.*]

SALIERI [*to audience*]. And if that didn't finish him off with the Masons—nothing would!

[*The gold emblem withdraws. We hear the merry dance of Monostatos and the hypnotized slaves from The Magic Flute: "Das Klinget, so heimlich, Das Klinget so schön!" To the tinkling of the glockenspiel*[88] *SERVANTS bring in a long plain table loaded with manuscripts and bottles. It also bears a plain upturned stool. They place this in the wooden area head-on to the audience. At the same time CONSTANZE appears wearily from the back, and enters the apartment: the Rauhensteingasse.*

    Simultaneously upstage left, two other SERVANTS have placed the little gilded table bearing a loaded cake-stand and three of the gilded chairs from Salieri's resplendent salon. We now have in view the two contrasting apartments.

    As soon as the emblem withdraws, the VENTICELLI appear to SALIERI.]

SCENE XIII

Mozart's Apartment; Salieri's Apartment

V.1.   Mozart is delighted with himself?
V.2.   He's writing a secret opera!
V.1. [*crossly*].   And won't tell anyone its theme.
V.2.   It's really too tiresome. [*The VENTICELLI go off.*]
1870 SALIERI.   He told me. He told me everything! . . . Initiation ceremonies. Ceremonies with blindfolds. All rituals copied from the Masons! . . . He sat at home preparing his own destruction. A home where life grew daily more grim.

[*He goes upstage and sits on one of his gilded chairs, devouring a cake. MOZART also sits at his table, wrapped in a blanket, and starts to write music. Opposite him CONSTANZE sits on a stool, wrapped in a shawl.*]

CONSTANZE.   I'm cold . . . I'm cold all day. . . . Hardly surprising since we have no firewood.
MOZART.   Papa was right. We end exactly as he said. Beggars.
CONSTANZE.   It's all his fault.
MOZART.   Papa's?
CONSTANZE.   He kept you a baby all your life.
1880 MOZART.   I don't understand. . . . You always loved Papa.
CONSTANZE.   *I* did?
MOZART.   You adored him. You told me so often. [*Slight pause.*]
CONSTANZE [*flatly*].   I hated him.
MOZART.   What?
CONSTANZE.   And he hated *me*.
MOZART.   That's absurd. He loved us both very much. You're being extremely silly now.
CONSTANZE.   Am I?
MOZART [*airily*].   Yes you are: little-wife-of-my-heart!

---

[88] A percussion instrument similar to a xylophone.

1890 CONSTANZE.   Do you want to know what I really thought of your father? . . .
Do you remember the fire we had last night, because it was so cold you
couldn't even get the ink wet? You said "What a blaze," remember? "What
a blaze!" All those old papers going up? Well, my dear, those old papers
were just all your father's letters, that's all—every one he wrote since the
day we married.

MOZART.   *What?*

CONSTANZE.   Every one! All the letters about what a ninny I am—what a bad
housekeeper I am! Every one!

MOZART.   Stanzi!

1900 CONSTANZE.   Shit on him! . . . *Shit on him!*

MOZART.   *You bitch!*

CONSTANZE [*savagely*].   At least it kept us warm! What else will do that? Perhaps we should dance! You love to dance, Wolferl—let's dance! Dance to
keep warm! [*Grandly.*] Write me a contredanze, Mozart! It's your job to
write dances, isn't it? [*Hysterical, she snatches up his manuscripts from the table
and scatters them over the floor—pulling up her skirts and dancing roughly round
the room like a demented peasant, to the tune of "Non Più Andrai"!*]

CONSTANZE [*singing savagely*].   *Non più andrai, farfallone amoroso—notte e giorno
d'intorno girando!*[89]

1910 MOZART [*shrieking*].   Stop it! Stop it! [*He rises and tries to seize her.*] Stanzi-
marini! Marini-bini! Don't *please!* . . . Please—please I beg you! . . . Look.
There's a kiss! Where's it coming from? Right out of that corner! There's
another one—all wet, all sloppy wet, coming straight to you! Kiss—kiss—
kiss—kiss! [*She pushes him roughly away.*]

CONSTANZE.   Get off! [*A long pause.*]

MOZART.   I'm frightened, Stanzi. . . . Something awful's happening to me.

CONSTANZE [*quietly*].   I can't bear it. I can't bear much more of this.

MOZART [*absorbed in himself*].   The Figure's like this now—[*beckoning more
urgently*]—Here. Come here. Here . . . Its face still hidden. Always hidden.

1920 CONSTANZE [*crying out*].   Stop it, for God's sake! Stop it! . . . Stop! . . . It's me
who's frightened. . . . *Me!* . . . You frighten me. . . . If you go on like this
I'll leave you. I swear it.

MOZART [*shocked*].   Stanzi!

CONSTANZE.   I mean it . . . I do. . . . [*She puts her hand to her stomach, as if in
pain.*]

MOZART.   I'm sorry. . . . Oh God, I'm sorry . . . I'm sorry, I'm sorry, I'm
sorry! . . . Come here to me, little-wife-of-my-heart! Come . . . Come . . .
[*He kneels and coaxes her to him. She comes half-reluctantly, half-willingly.*] Who
am I? . . . Quick: tell me. Hold me and tell who I am. Who?—come on.

1930 CONSTANZE.   Pussy-wussy.

MOZART.   Who else?

CONSTANZE.   Miaowy-powy.

MOZART.   And you're squeaky-peeky. And Stanzi-manzi. And Bini-gini! [*She
surrenders.*]

CONSTANZE.   Wolfi-polfi!

MOZART.   Poopy-peepee! [*They giggle.*]

---

[89] "You will no longer go on, adventurous lover, night and day spinning round."

CONSTANZE.   Now don't be stupid.
MOZART [*insistent: like a child*].   Come on—do it. Do it. . . . Let's do it. "Poppy."

[*They play a private game, gradually doing it faster, on their knees.*]

CONSTANZE.   Poppy.
1940 MOZART [*changing it*].   Pappy.
CONSTANZE [*copying*].   Pappy.
MOZART.   Pappa.
CONSTANZE.   Pappa.
MOZART.   Pappa-pappa!
CONSTANZE.   Pappa-pappa!
MOZART.   Pappa-pappa-pappa-pappa!
CONSTANZE.   Pappa-pappa-pappa-pappa!

[*They rub noses.*]

TOGETHER.   Pappa-pappa-pappa-pappa! Pappa-pappa-pappa-pappa!
CONSTANZE.   *Ah!* [*She suddenly cries out in distress, and clutches her stomach.*]
1950 MOZART.   Stanzi! . . . Stanzi, what is it?

[*The* VENTICELLI *hurry in.*]

SALIERI.   And suddenly she was delivered! A boy!
V.2.   Poor little imp.
V.1.   To be born to that couple.
V.2.   In that room.
V.1.   With that money.
V.2.   And the Father a baby himself.

[*During the above,* CONSTANZE *has slowly risen, and divested herself of her stuffed apron—thereby ceasing to be pregnant. Now she turns sorrowfully and walks slowly upstage and off it.* MOZART *follows her for a few steps, alarmed. He halts.*]

V.1.   And now I hear—
V.2.   Now I hear—
V.1.   Something more has happened.
1960 V.2.   Even stranger.

[MOZART *picks up a bottle, then moves swiftly into Salieri's room.*]

MOZART.   *She's gone!*
SALIERI.   What do you mean?

[*The* VENTICELLI *slip away.*]

MOZART.   Constanze's gone away. Just for a while, she says. She's taken the baby and gone to Baden. To the spa. It'll cost us the last money we had.
SALIERI.   But *why?*
MOZART.   She's right to go. It's my fault. She thinks I'm mad.
SALIERI.   Surely not?
MOZART.   Perhaps I am. I think I am. Last night I saw the Figure again—the Figure in my dreams.
1970 SALIERI.   Wolfgang—

MOZART.   It stood before my table, its face still gray, still masked. But this
time it spoke to me. "Wolfgang Mozart—you must write now a Requiem
Mass. Take up your pen and begin!"
SALIERI.   A Requiem?
MOZART.   I asked "Who has died? Who is this Requiem for?" It turned and
left the room.
SALIERI.   Oh, this is morbid fancy, my friend!
MOZART.   It had the force of real things! . . . To tell the truth—I do not know
whether it happened in my head or out of it. . . . No wonder Stanzi has
1980   gone. I frightened her away. . . . And now she'll miss the vaudeville.
SALIERI.   You mean it's finished? So soon?
MOZART.   Oh yes—music is easy: it's marriage that's hard!
SALIERI.   I long to see it.
MOZART.   Would you come, truly? The theater isn't grand. No one from
court will be there.
SALIERI.   Do you think that matters to me? I would travel anywhere for a
work by you! . . . I am no substitute for your little wife—but I know some-
one who could be! [*He gets up.* MOZART *rises also.*]
MOZART.   Who?
1990 SALIERI.   I'll tell you what—I'll bring Katherina! She'll cheer you up!
MOZART.   Katherina!
SALIERI.   As I remember it, you quite enjoyed her company!

[MOZART *laughs heartily.* CAVALIERI *enters, now fatter and wearing an elaborate
plumed hat. She curtsies to* MOZART *and takes his arm.*]

MOZART [*bowing*].   *Signora!*
SALIERI [*to audience*].   And so to the opera we went—a strange band of three!
[*The other two freeze.*] The First Kappellmeister—sleek as a cat. His mistress—now fat and feathered like the great song-bird she'd become. And
demented Mozart—drunk on the cheap wine which was now his constant
habit. [*They unfreeze.*] We went out into the suburbs—to a crowded music
hall—in a slum!

SCENE XIV

The Theater by the Weiden

*Two benches are brought in and placed down front. Sudden noise. A crowd of working-
class Germans swarms in from the back: a chattering mass of humanity through which
the three have to push their way to the front. The long table is pushed horizontally, and
the rowdy audience piles on top of it, smoking pipes and chewing sausages. Unobserved,* BARON VAN SWIETEN *comes in also, and stands at the back.*

2000 MOZART.   You must be indulgent now! It's my first piece of this kind!

[*The three sit on the front bench:* MOZART *sick and emaciated;* CAVALIERI *blousy and
bedizened;* SALIERI *as elegant as ever.*]

SALIERI.   We sat as he wished us to, among ordinary Germans! The smell of
sweat and sausage was almost annihilating!

[CAVALIERI *presses a* mouchoir *to her sensitive nose.*]

SALIERI [*to* MOZART].   This is so exciting!

MOZART [*happily*].   Do you think so?

SALIERI [*looking about him*].   Oh yes! This is exactly the audience we should be writing for! Not the dreary court. . . . As always—*you* show the way!

[*The audience freezes.*]

SALIERI [*to us*].   As always, he did. My pungent neighbors *rolled* on their benches at the jokes—[*They unfreeze, briefly, to demonstrate this mirth.*] And I alone, in their midst, heard—*The Magic Flute.* [*They freeze again. The great*
2010   *hymn at the end of Act 2 is heard:* "Heil sei euch Geweihten."] He had put the Masons into it right enough. Oh yes—but how? He had turned them into an order of Eternal Priests. I heard voices calling out of ancient temples. I saw a vast sun rise on a timeless land, where animals danced and children floated, and by its rays all the poisons we feed each other drawn up and burnt away! [*A great sun does indeed rise inside the Light Box, and standing in it the gigantic silhouette of a priestly figure extending its arms to the world in universal greeting.*] And in this sun—behold—I saw his *father!* No more an accusing figure but forgiving!—the highest priest of the Order—his hand extended to the world in love! Wolfgang feared Leopold no longer: a final
2020   legend had been made! . . . Oh, the sound—the sound of that new-found peace in him—mocking my undiminishing pain! *There* was the Magic Flute—there beside me! [*He points to* MOZART. *Applause from all.* MOZART *jumps up excitedly onto the bench and acknowledges it with arms flung out. He turns, a bottle in his hand, his eyes staring, and all freeze again.*] Mozart the flute and God the relentless player! How long could the Creature stand it—so frail, so palpably mortal? And what was this I was tasting suddenly? Could it be pity? . . . *Never!*

VAN SWIETEN [*calling out*].   Mozart! [VAN SWIETEN *pushes his way to the front through the crowd of dispersing* CITIZENS. *He is outraged.*]

2030   MOZART [*turning joyfully to meet him*].   Baron! You here! How wonderful of you to come!

SALIERI [*to audience*].   I had of course suggested it.

VAN SWIETEN [*with cold fury*].   What have you done?

MOZART.   Excellency?

VAN SWIETEN.   You have put our rituals into a vulgar show!

MOZART.   No, sir—

VAN SWIETEN.   They are plain for all to see! And to laugh at! You have betrayed the Order.

MOZART [*in horror*].   No!

2040   SALIERI.   Baron, a word with you—

VAN SWIETEN.   Don't speak for him, Salieri! [*To* MOZART, *with frozen contempt.*] You were ever a cruel vulgarian we hoped to mend. Stupid, hopeless task! Now you are a betrayer as well. I shall never forgive you. And depend upon it—I shall ensure that no Freemason or person of distinction will do so in Vienna so long as I have life!

SALIERI.   Baron, please, I must speak!

VAN SWIETEN.   No, sir! Leave, alone. [*To* MOZART.] I did not look for this reward, Mozart. Never speak to me.

[*He goes out.* CAVALIERI, *embarrassed, goes out another way. The lights change. The benches are taken off.* SALIERI *watches* MOZART, *who stands as one dead.*]

SCENE XV

SALIERI.   Wolfgang? . . . [MOZART *shakes his head sharply—and walks away from
2050   him, upstage, desolate and stunned.*] Wolfgang—all is not lost.

[MOZART *enters his apartment, and freezes.*]

SALIERI [*to audience*].   But of course it was! Now he was ruined. Broken and
shunned by all men of influence. He did not even get his half receipts
from the opera.

[*The* VENTICELLI *come in.*]

V.1.   Schikaneder pays him nothing.
V.2.   Schikaneder cheats him.
V.1.   Gives him enough for liquor.
V.2.   And keeps all the rest.
SALIERI.   I couldn't have managed it better myself. [MOZART *takes up a blanket
and muffles himself in it. Then he sits at his work-table, down front, staring out at
2060   the audience, quite still, the blanket almost over his face.*] And then silence. No
word came from him at all. Why? . . . I waited each day. Nothing. *Why?* . . .
[*To the* VENTICELLI *brusquely.*] *What does he do?*

[MOZART *writes.*]

V.1.   He sits at his window.
V.2.   All day and all night.
V.1.   Writing—
V.2.   Writing—like a man possessed.

[MOZART *springs to his feet, and freezes.*]

V.1.   Springs up every moment!
V.2.   Stares wildly at the street!
V.1.   Expecting something—
2070   V.2.   Someone—
V.1. & V.2.   *We can't imagine what!*
SALIERI [*to audience*].   *I* could! [*He also springs up excitedly, dismissing the* VEN-
TICELLI. MOZART *and* SALIERI *now both stand staring out front.*] Who did he look
for? A Figure in gray, masked and sorrowing, come to take him away. I
knew what he was doing, alone in that slum! He was writing his Requiem
Mass—*for himself!* . . . And now I confess the wickedest thing I did to him.
[*His* VALET *brings him the clothes which he describes, and he puts them on, turning
his back to us to don the hat—to which is attached a mask.*] My friends—there
is no blasphemy a man will not commit, compelled to such a war as mine!
2080   I got me a cloak of gray. Yes. And a mask of gray—Yes! [*He turns around:
he is masked.*] And appeared myself to the demented Creature as—the
Messenger of God! . . . I confess that in November, 1791, I—Antonio
Salieri, then as now First Kapellmeister to the Empire—walked empty
Vienna in the freezing moonlight for seven nights on end! That precisely
as the clocks of the city struck one I would halt beneath Mozart's window—
and become his more terrible clock. [*The clock strikes one.* SALIERI, *without
moving from the left side of the stage, raises his arms: his fingers show seven days.*

Mozart *rises—fascinated and appalled—and stands equally rigid on the right side, looking out.*] Every night I showed him one day less—then stalked
2090 away. Every night the face he showed me at the glass was more crazed at each visitation. Finally—with no days left to him—horror! I arrived as usual. Halted. And instead of fingers, reached up, beseechingly as the Figure of his dreams! [*Urging.*] "Come!—Come!—Come! . . . " [*He beckons to* Mozart, *insidiously.*] He stood swaying, as if he would faint off into death. But suddenly—incredibly—he realized all his little strength, and in a clear voice called down to me the words out of his opera, *Don Giovanni,* inviting the statue to dinner.
Mozart [*pushing open the "window"*]. *O statua gentilissima, venite a cena!*[90] [*He beckons in his turn.*]
2100 Salieri. For a long moment, one terrified man looked at another. Then— unbelievably—I found myself nodding, just as in the opera. Starting to move across the street! [*The rising and falling scale passage from the Overture to* Don Giovanni *sounds darkly, looped in sinister repetition. To this hollow music* Salieri *marches slowly upstage.*] Pushing down the latch of his door—tramping up the stairs with stone feet. There was no stopping it. *I was in his dream!*

[Mozart *stands terrified by his table.* Salieri *throws open the door. An instant light change.*]

SCENE XVI

Mozart's Apartment

[Salieri *stands still, staring impassively downstage.* Mozart *addresses him in awe.*]

Mozart. It's not finished! . . . Not nearly! . . . Forgive me. Time was I could write a Mass in a week! . . . Give me one month more, and it'll be done: I swear it! . . . He'll grant me that, surely? God can't want it unfinished! . . .
2110 Look—look, see what I've done. [*He snatches up the pages from the table and brings them eagerly to the* Figure.] Here's the Kyrie—that's finished! Take that to Him—He'll see it's not unworthy! . . . [*Unwillingly* Salieri *moves across the room, takes the pages, and sits behind the table in* Mozart's *chair, staring out front.*] Grant me time, I beg you! If you do, I swear I'll write a real piece of music. I know I've boasted I've written hundreds, but it's not true. I've written nothing finally good! [Salieri *looks at the pages. Immediately we hear the somber opening of the Requiem Mass. Over this* Mozart *speaks.*] Oh, it began so well, my life. Once the world was so full, so happy! . . . All the journeys—all the carriages—all the rooms of smiles! Everyone smiled at
2120 me once—the king at Schönbrunn; the princess at Versailles—they lit my way with candles to the clavier—my father bowing, bowing, bowing with such joy! . . . "Chevalier Mozart, my miraculous son!" . . . Why has it all gone? . . . Why? . . . Was I so bad? So wicked? . . . Answer for Him and tell me!

---

[90] "O most kind statue, come to dinner."

[*Deliberately* SALIERI *tears the paper into halves. The music stops instantly. Silence.*]

MOZART [*fearfully*].   Why? . . . Is it not good?
SALIERI [*stiffly*].   It is good. Yes. It is good.

[*He tears off a corner of the music paper, elevates it in the manner of the Communion Service, places it on his tongue and eats it.*]

SALIERI [*in pain*].   I eat what God gives me. Dose after dose. For all of life. His poison. We are both poisoned, Amadeus. I with you: you with me. [*In horror,* MOZART *moves slowly behind him, placing his hand over* SALIERI's *mouth—*
2130   *then, still from behind, slowly removes the mask and hat.* SALIERI *stares at us.*] Ecco mi.[91] Antonio Salieri. Ten years of my hate have poisoned you to death.

[MOZART *falls to his knees, by the table.*]

MOZART.   Oh God!
SALIERI [*contemptuously*].   *God?!* . . . God will not help you! God *does* not help!
MOZART.   Oh God! . . . Oh God! . . . Oh God!
SALIERI.   God does not love you, Amadeus! God does not love! He can only *use!* . . . He cares nothing for whom He uses: nothing for whom He denies! . . . You are no use to Him anymore. You're too weak—too sick! He has finished with you! All you can do now is *die!*
MOZART.   Ah! [*With a groan,* MOZART *crawls quickly through the trestle of the table,*
2140   *like an animal finding a burrow—or a child a safe place of concealment.* SALIERI *kneels by the table, calling in at his victim in desperation.*]
SALIERI.   Die, Amadeus! Die, I beg you, die! . . . Leave me alone, *ti imploro!*[92] Leave me alone at last! Leave me alone! [*He beats on the table in his despair.*] Alone! Alone! Alone! Alone!
MOZART [*crying out at the top of his lungs*].   PAPAAAAA!

[*He freezes—his mouth open in the act of screaming—his head staring out from under the table, a gargoyle of fear.* SALIERI *rises in horror. Silence. Very slowly,* MOZART *crawls out from under the table. He stares upward. He sits. He smiles.*]

MOZART [*in a childish voice*].   Papa! [*Silence.*] Papa . . . Papa . . . [*He extends his arms; imploringly. He speaks as a very young boy.*] Take me, Papa. Take me. Put down your arms and I'll hop into them. Just as we used to do it! . . . Hop-hop-hop-hop-UP! [*He jumps up onto the table.* SALIERI *watches in horror.*]
2150   Hold me close to you, Papa. Let's sing our little kissing song together. Do you remember? . . . [*He sings in an infantine voice.*] Oragna figata fa! Marina gamina fa![93]
SALIERI [*quietly*].   Reduce the man: reduce the God. Behold my vow fulfilled. The profoundest voice in the world reduced to a nursery tune. [*He leaves the room, slowly, as* MOZART *resumes his singing.*]
MOZART.   Oragna figata fa! Marina gamina fa! [*As* SALIERI *withdraws,* CONSTANZE *appears from the back of the stage, her bonnet in her hand. She has returned from Baden. She comes downstage toward her husband, and finds him there on the table singing in an obviously childish treble.*] Oragna figata fa! Marina gamina fa. Fa!

---

[91] "Behold me."
[92] "I implore you."
[93] Evidently incomprehensible baby talk.

2160   *Fa!* [*He kisses the air, several times. Finally he becomes aware of his wife standing beside him.*]

MOZART [*uncertainly*]. Stanzi?

CONSTANZE. Wolfi? . . .

MOZART [*in relief*]. Stanzi!

CONSTANZE [*with great tenderness*]. Wolfi—my love! Little husband of my heart! [*He virtually falls off the table into her arms.*]

MOZART. Oh! [*He clings to her in overwhelming pleasure. She helps him gently to move around the table to the chair behind it, facing out front.*]

CONSTANZE. Oh, my dear one—come with me. Come on . . . Come on now.
2170   There . . . There . . . [MOZART *sits weakly.*]

MOZART [*like a child still, and most earnestly*]. Salieri . . . Salieri has killed me.

CONSTANZE. Yes, my dear. [*Practically, she busies herself clearing the table of its candle, its bottle and its inkwell.*]

MOZART. He has! . . . He told me so! . . .

CONSTANZE. Yes, yes: I'm sure. [*She finds two pillows and places them at the left-hand head of the table.*]

MOZART [*petulantly*]. He did. He did! . . .

CONSTANZE. Hush now, lovey. [*She helps her dying husband onto the table, now his bed. He lies down, and she covers him with her shawl.*] I'm back to take care
2180   of you. I'm sorry I went away. I'm here now, for always!

MOZART. Salieri . . . Salieri . . . Salieri . . . Salieri! [*He starts to weep.*]

CONSTANZE. Oh lovey, be silent now. No one has hurt you. You'll get better soon, I promise. Can you hear me? [*Faintly the Lacrimosa of the Requiem Mass begins to sound.* MOZART *rises to hear it—leaning against his wife's shoulder. His hand begins feebly to beat out drum measures from the music. During the whole of the following it is evident that he is composing the Mass in his head, and does not hear his wife at all.*] You've got to get well, Wolfi—because we need you. Karl and baby Franz as well. There's only three of us, lovey: we don't cost much.
    Just don't leave us—we wouldn't know what to do without you. And you
2190   wouldn't know much either, up in Heaven, without us. You soppy thing. You can't even cut up your own meat without help! . . . I'm not clever, lovey. It can't have been easy living with a goose. But I've looked after you, you must admit that. And I've given you fun too—quite a lot really! . . . Are you listening? [*The drum strokes get slower, and stop.*] Know one thing. It was the best day of my life when you married me. And as long as I live I'll be the most honored woman in the world. . . . *Can you hear me?* [*She becomes aware that* MOZART *is dead. She opens her mouth in a silent scream, raising her arm in a rigid gesture of grief. The great chord of the "Amen" does not resolve itself, but lingers on in intense reverberation.*

2200   CITIZENS *of Vienna come in, dressed in black, from the right.* CONSTANZE *kneels and freezes in grief, as* SERVANTS *come in and stand at each of the four corners of the table on which the dead body lies.* VAN SWIETEN *also comes in.*]

SALIERI [*hard*]. The Death Certificate said kidney failure, hastened by exposure to cold. Generous Lord Fugue paid for a pauper's funeral. Twenty other corpses. An unmarked limepit.

[VAN SWIETEN *approaches* CONSTANZE.]

VAN SWIETEN. What little I can spare, you shall have for the children. There's no need to waste it on vain show.

[*The* SERVANTS *lift the table and bear it, with its burden, upstage center, to the Light Box. The* CITIZENS *follow it.*]

SALIERI.   What did I feel? Relief, of course: I confess it. And pity too, for the man I helped to destroy. I felt the pity God can never feel. I weakened
2210   God's flute to thinness. God blew—as He must—without cease. The flute split in the mouth of His insatiable need.

[*The* CITIZENS *kneel. In dead silence the* SERVANTS *throw* MOZART'*s body off the table into space at the back of the stage.*
    All depart save SALIERI *and* CONSTANZE. *She unfreezes and starts assiduously collecting the manuscripts scattered over the floor.*
    SALIERI *now speaks with an increasingly aging voice: a voice poisoned more and more by his own bitterness.*]

SALIERI.   As for Constanze, in the fullness of time she married again—a Danish diplomat as dull as a clock—and retired to Salzburg, birthplace of the Composer, to become the pious Keeper of his Shrine! [CONSTANZE *rises, wrapping her shawl about her, and clasping manuscripts to her bosom.*]
CONSTANZE [*reverentially*].   A sweeter-tongued man never lived! In ten years of blissful marriage I never heard him utter a single coarse or conceited word. The purity of his life is reflected absolutely in the purity of his music! . . . [*More briskly.*] In selling his manuscripts I charge by the ink. So
2220   many notes, so many schillings. That seems to me the simplest way. [*She leaves the stage, a pillar of rectitude.*]

SCENE XVII

SALIERI.   One amazing fact emerged. Mozart did not *imagine* that masked Figure who said "Take up your pen and write a Requiem." It was *real!* . . . A certain bizarre nobleman called Count Walsegg had a longing to be thought a composer. He actually sent his steward in disguise to Mozart to commission the piece—secretly, so that he could pass it off as his own work. And this he even did! After Mozart's death it was actually performed as Count Walsegg's Requiem. . . . And I conducted it. [*He smiles at the audience.*] Naturally I did. In those days I presided over all great musical
2230   occasions. [*He divests himself of his cloak.*] I even conducted the salvos of cannon in Beethoven's dreadful *Battle Symphony*. The experience left me almost as deaf as *he* was! [*The* CITIZENS *bow and kiss their hands to him.*] I remained in Vienna—City of Musicians—reverenced by all. And slowly I understood the nature of God's punishment! . . . What had I begged for in that church as a boy? Was it not *fame!* . . . Fame for excellence? . . . Well now I had fame! I was to become—quite simply—the most famous musician in Europe! [*All the* CITIZENS *fall on their knees before him, clapping their hands silently, and relentlessly extending their arms upward and upward almost obliterating him.*] I was to be bricked up in fame! Embalmed in fame! Buried
2240   in fame—but for work I knew to be *absolutely worthless!* This was my sentence: I must endure thirty years of being called "Distinguished" by people incapable of distinguishing! . . . And finally—His masterstroke! When my nose had been rubbed in fame to vomiting—it would all be taken away

from me. Every scrap. [*The* Citizens *rise, and all walk away indifferently upstage, past him, and on into the Light Box, and off the stage.*] I must survive to see myself become extinct! [*A* Servant *hands him his old stained dressing gown and cap.*] When they trundled me out in a carriage to get my last award, a man on the curb said, "Isn't that one of the generals from Waterloo?" [*The last movement of the "Jupiter" Symphony begins to sound, grow-*
2250 *ing ever louder.*] Mozart's music sounded louder and louder through the world! And mine faded completely, till no one played it at all!

[*The Mozart symphony wells to a huge crescendo, seeming to drown* Salieri. *He sinks to his knees under the weight of it, and finally claps his hands to his aching ears, to shut it out. The deafening music snaps off. The curtain descends in a rush. A clock strikes six.*]

SCENE XVIII

Salieri's Apartment: November 1823

A Servant *comes in quickly with the wheelchair.* Salieri *speaks again in the voice of an old man.*

Salieri [*to audience*].   Dawn has come. I must release you—and myself. One moment's violence and it's done. You see, I cannot accept this. I did not live on earth to be His joke for eternity. I *will* be remembered! *I will be remembered!*—if not in fame, then infamy. One moment more and I win my battle with Him. Watch and see! . . . All this month I've been shouting about murder. "Have mercy, Mozart! Pardon your Assassin! . . . And now my last move. A false confession—short and convincing! [*He pulls it out of his pocket.*] How I really did murder Mozart—with arsenic—out of envy!
2260 And how I cannot live another day under the knowledge! By tonight they'll hear out there how I died—and they'll believe it's true! . . . Let them forget me then. For the rest of time whenever men say Mozart with love, they will say Salieri with loathing! . . . *I am going to be immortal after all!* And He is powerless to prevent it. [*To God.*] So, *Signore*—see now if man is mocked!

[*The* Valet *comes in with a tray, bearing a bowl of hot shaving water, soap and a razor. He sets this on the table.* Salieri *hands him the confession.*]

Salieri [*to* Valet].   Good morning. Lay this on the desk in the cabinet. Append your name to it in witness that this is my hand. *Via—subito!*[94] [*The man takes the paper and goes, bewildered, upstage right.* Salieri *picks up the razor, and rises. He addresses the audience most simply and directly.*]
2270 Salieri.   *Amici cari.*[95] I was born a pair of ears and nothing else. It is only through hearing music that I know God exists. Only through writing music that I could worship. . . . All around me men seek liberty for mankind. I sought only slavery for myself. To be owned—ordered—exhausted by an *Absolute.* Music. This was denied me, and with it all meaning. [*He*

---

94 "Go—quickly!"   95 "Dear friends."

opens the razor.] Now I go to become a ghost myself. I will stand in the shadows when you come here to this earth in your turns. And when you feel the dreadful bite of your failures—and hear the taunting of unachievable, uncaring God—I will whisper my name to you: "Salieri: Patron Saint of Mediocrities!" And in the depth of your downcastness you can pray to
2280   me. And I will forgive you. *Vi saluto.*[96]

[*He cuts his throat, and falls backwards into the wheelchair. The* COOK—*who has just come in, carrying a plate of fresh buns for breakfast, sees this and screams. The* VALET *rushes in at the same time from the other side. Together they pull the wheelchair, with its slumped body, backward upstage, and anchor it in the center. The* VENTICELLI *appear again, in the costume of 1823.*]

SCENE XIX

V.1.   Beethoven's Conversation Book, November 1823. Visitors write the news for the deaf man. [*He hands a book to* VENTICELLO TWO.]
V.2. [*reading*].   "Salieri has cut his throat—but is still alive!"

[SALIERI *stirs and comes to life, looking about him bewilderedly. The* VALET *and the* COOK *depart. He stares out front at us astounded.*]

V.1.   Beethoven's Conversation Book, 1824. Visitors write the news for the deaf man. [*He hands another book to* VENTICELLO TWO.]
V.2. [READING].   "Salieri is quite deranged. He keeps claiming that he is guilty of Mozart's death, and made away with him by poison."

[*The light narrows into a bright cone, beating on* SALIERI.]

V.1.   *The German Musical Times, May 25th, 1825.* [*He hands a newspaper to* VENTICELLO TWO.]
2290   V.2. [*reading*].   "Our worthy Salieri cannot die. In the frenzy of his imagination he is even said to accuse himself of complicity in Mozart's early death. A rambling of the mind believed in truth by no one but the deluded old man himself."

[*The music stops.* SALIERI *stares ahead in pain.*]

V.1.   I don't believe it.
V.2.   I don't believe it.
V.1.   I don't believe it.
V.2.   I don't believe it.
V.1. & V.2.   *No one believes it in the world!*

[*They go off. The light dims a little.* SALIERI *stirs—rises, and looks out far into the darkness of the theater.*]

SALIERI.   Mediocrities everywhere—now and to come—I absolve you all.
2300   Amen!

---

[96] "I salute you."

[He extends his arms upward and outward to embrace the assembled audience in a wide gesture of benediction—finally folding his arms high across his own breast in a gesture of self-satisfaction.

The light fades completely. The last four chords of the Masonic Funeral Music of AMADEUS MOZART *sound throughout the theater.]*

END OF PLAY

[1979]

Critical Commentary on *Amadeus*

Just as *Amadeus* was the biggest theatrical hit in London in 1979, so too it was the biggest hit in Washington and then in New York in 1980 and 1981— eventually capturing five Tony Awards including one for best drama. Furthermore, the film adaptation was just as successful, winning eight Oscars in 1984 including best film, best actor, best set design, best musical score and best adaptation of a play for film. Although some reviewers initially criticized the play for its theatrics, most have given it resounding praise. This praise has even continued in scholarly studies, with a recent study by Huber and Zapf concluding that "there is a degree of thematic and structural complexity to *Amadeus* which makes it, beyond its sensational popularity, a dramatic masterpiece in its own right."

While Shaffer has been careful to disclaim any intention of achieving complete historical accuracy in recounting Mozart's life, he has nonetheless stayed close to the facts. Shaffer gives us a remarkably full and accurate portrait of Mozart, who composed, almost effortlessly, music of almost ethereal beauty and yet who remained "an obscene child" until his death at age thirty-five. As the play indicates, Mozart was one of the most phenomenal of child prodigies and one of the most prolific of adult composers. He was an able musician at age three and at eight he was already writing music that conductor Neville Marriner calls "as good as Haydn at the age of 40." By the time of his death, Mozart had written over 600 pieces of music, including 23 operas, 20 masses, 49 symphonies, 27 piano concerti, and 52 sonatas. And yet one contemporary of Mozart's describes how she watched him perform brilliant spontaneous improvisations on an aria from *Figaro* only to jump up a moment later and begin "to leap over table and chairs, meowing like a cat, and turning somersaults like an unruly boy."

Mozart's fondness for obscene verbal improvisations is also well documented. For example, in November of 1777 he wrote his father:

> I Johannes Chrisostomus Amadeus Wolfgangus Sigismundus Mozart confess that the day before yesterday and yesterday (and often at other times) I did not return home until twelve o'clock at night and that from ten o'clock until the above-mentioned hour I was at Cannabich's in the presence and *en compagnie* of Cannabich, his wife, and daughter, Messieurs Schatzmeister, Raam, and Lang, and that I frequently rhymed away, not with difficulty but with the greatest of ease, and rhymed sheer filth, namely, about shit . . . and did so with thoughts, words, and—not with acts.

Many of the other events in the play also have a basis in fact, including the persistent rumors that Salieri had actually poisoned Mozart. Thus, one reason for studying *Amadeus* is for the information it gives and the curiosity it evokes about one of the supreme musical geniuses of all time.

The play also has a bearing on the history of ideas. Although Mozart was one of the most distinguished composers of the Age of Reason, he was also writing at a time when the Romantic revolution was in its infancy. The play, Salieri tells us, is set in

> Vienna. The year—to begin with—1781. The age still that of the Enlightenment: that clear time before the guillotine fell in France and cut all our lives in half. (I, 3)

Part of Mozart's difficulty in Vienna was that he quickly came to rebel against the musical establishment of the neoclassical age. Mozart resisted the notion that musicians should be mere servants in livery within a nobleman's household. Furthermore, he refused to be bound by the conventions of classical composing. Throughout the play his work is criticized by Rosenberg, Strack, and the Emperor because of its chromatic embellishment—"too many notes," they all agree. And finally, Mozart insisted that opera should reflect real life and not classical gods and goddesses. "Which of you," Mozart asks, "isn't more at home with his hairdresser than Hercules?" His expressed goal in opera was "to do a piece about real people. . . . And I want to set it in a real place! A *boudoir!* Because that to me is the most exciting place on earth! Underclothes on the floor! Sheets still warm from a woman's body! Even a pisspot brimming under the bed! . . . I want life, Baron. Not boring legends!" (II, 4).

Paradoxically, however, Mozart was also able to create music of pure classical beauty. His haughty response to the criticism offered by the Emperor is that his music contains "just as many notes, Majesty, neither more nor less, as are required" (I, 8). Even the insanely jealous Salieri recognizes that in his best music Mozart does indeed achieve neoclassical perfection: "Displace one note and there would be diminishment. Displace one phrase and the structure would fall" (I, 12).

Ultimately, however, it is as a work of literature that *Amadeus* must find justification. Happily, critics and reviewers have been quick to point out that the play explores a number of significant and thought-provoking themes. Among them are the frequent hostility of "the establishment" to creative geniuses, the poisonous effects of envy, the definition of success, and the relationship between man and God. All of these themes are interesting and worthy of classroom discussion, but the most interesting of them all may involve Salieri's relationship with God.

In part, Salieri tells this story to himself in an effort to understand the nature of God, testing at every opportunity for evidence of God's existence. At first he believes that he has evidence for that existence when he becomes a successful composer soon after making a pact with the tradesman God of his village. Then he believes himself mocked by God when the sublime music of undeserving Mozart convinces him of the worthlessness of all that he has composed in the service of God. In the remainder of the play he tries to block God and discovers to his astonishment that if God exists at all, he is "unachievable, uncaring": "God does not love! He can only *use!* . . . He cares nothing for those whom he denies" (II, 16).

This question of the nature of God is perhaps the central issue in the play—at least for Shaffer, who has said, "I have never actually been able to buy anything of official religion—and [yet] . . . to me a life without a sense of the divine is perfectly meaningless." This dilemma is at the heart of *Amadeus* as it is of *Equus*. In both plays human beings get the kind of God that they construct for themselves—and deserve. Let us step back for a moment from Salieri's perceptions and consider the kind of God he believes in.

In Act I, Scene 2, Salieri makes a deal with "the God of Bargains," a God who seems to say, "You give me so—I'll give you so! No more. No less!" And the exact terms of the bargain Salieri drives are:

Signore, let me be a composer! Grant me sufficient fame to enjoy it. In return, I will live with virtue. I will strive to better the lot of my fellows. And I will honor You with much music all the days of my life!

Note that Salieri does not ask to be a "great" or even a "good" composer. He asks merely to be a composer and to enjoy "sufficient fame." Whether by the grace of God or by dint of his own efforts, he soon finds his wishes fulfilled. When Mozart, a greater composer, comes along, Salieri has no reason to reject the God he has served. Indeed, the terms of the "bargain" oblige him to strive to better Mozart's lot. Instead, he rejects his pact, vows eternal defiance of God, and attempts to do everything in his power to destroy Mozart.

In essence, what Salieri does is renounce the values that have guided his entire life and brought him such success as he has achieved. Given Salieri's values and his concept of God, there is nothing unjust about Mozart's genius. Envy alone makes Salieri pronounce this an injustice and envy alone makes him begin to live a life that is untrue to his own deepest values. And whether it is through the justice of God or through the moral effects of his own actions, Salieri suffers horribly for his betrayal. Instead of learning from Mozart (as Haydn did) and growing into a better composer, Salieri poisons his own mind by wasting on malicious schemes an energy that could have been better spent in helping his fellow man and honoring God with music.

When one doesn't grow, one dies. And Salieri's terrible fate is to live on after his death, "to be bricked up in fame! Embalmed in fame! Buried in fame—But for work I knew to be *absolutely worthless*" (II, 17). Furthermore, he lives on to discover himself not just a failure as a composer, but even a failure as a rebel against God. His schemes against Mozart invariably fail or even drive Mozart to greater creativity during his life. And his attempts to silence Mozart's music fail even more miserably: "Mozart's music sounded louder and louder through the world! And mine faded completely, till no one played it at all" (II, 17).

A Selective Bibliography on *Amadeus*

Arens, Katherine. "Mozart: A Case Study in Logocentric Repression." *Comparative Literature Studies* 23.2 (1986): 141–69.

Bidney, Martin. "Thinking about God and Mozart: The Salieris of Puskin and Peter Shaffer." *Slavic and East European Journal* 30.2 (1986): 183–95.

Conroy, Peter V., Jr. "*Amadeus* on Stage and Screen." *Post Script: Essays in Film and the Humanities* 9.1–2 (1989–1990): 25–37.

Cooke, Virginia and Malcolm Page, eds. *File on Shaffer.* London: Methuen, 1987.

Gelatt, Roland. "Peter Shaffer's *Amadeus:* A Controversial Hit." *Saturday Review* Nov. 1980: 11–14.

Gianakaris, C. J. "Drama into Film: The Shaffer Situation." *Modern Drama* 28 (1985): 83–98.

———. "A Playwright Looks at Mozart: Peter Shaffer's *Amadeus.*" *Comparative Drama* 15 (1981): 37–53.

———. "Shaffer's Revisions in *Amadeus.*" *Theatre Journal* 35 (1983): 88–101.

Gillespie, Michael. "Peter Shaffer: 'To Make Whatever God There Is.' " *Claudel Studies* 9.2 (1982): 61–70.

Hinden, Michael. "Trying to Like Shaffer." *Comparative Drama* 19 (1986): 14–29.

———. "When Playwrights Talk to God: Peter Shaffer and the Legacy of O'Neill." *Comparative Drama* 15 (1982): 49–63.

Huber, Werner and Hubert Zapf. "On the Structure of Peter Shaffer's *Amadeus.*" *Modern Drama* 27 (1984): 299–313.

Klein, Dennis A. "*Amadeus:* The Third Part of Peter Shaffer's Dramatic Trilogy." *Modern Language Studies* 13 (1983): 31–38.

———. *Peter Shaffer.* Boston: Twayne, 1979.

Larson, Janet Karsten. "*Amadeus:* Shaffer's Hollow Men." *The Christian Century* 20 (1981): 578–83.

Lounsberry, Barbara. "Peter Shaffer's *Amadeus* and *Shrivings:* God-Hunting Continued." *Theatre Annual* 39 (1984): 15–33

Mikels, Frank and James Rurak. "Finishing Salieri: Another Act to *Amadeus.*" *Soundings* 67 (1984): 42–54.

Plunka, Gene A. *Peter Shaffer: Roles, Rites, and Rituals in the Theatre.* Rutherford, N.J.: Farleigh Dickinson UP, 1988, 172–96.

Sullivan, William J. "Peter Shaffer's *Amadeus:* The Making and Un-Making of the Fathers." *American Imago* 45.1 (1988): 45–60.

Taylor, John Russell. *Peter Shaffer.* Ed. Ian Scott-Kilvert. Harlow, Eng.: Longman, 1974.

Townsend, Martha A. "*Amadeus* as Dramatic Monologue." *Literature/Film Quarterly* 14.4 (1986): 214–19.

Wootton, Carol. "Literary Portraits of Mozart." *Mosaic* 18.4 (1985): 77–84.

Sam Shepard (1943–)
TRUE WEST

CHARACTERS

AUSTIN, *early thirties, light blue sports shirt, light tan cardigan sweater, clean blue jeans, white tennis shoes*

LEE, *his older brother, early forties, filthy white t-shirt, tattered brown overcoat covered with dust, dark blue baggy suit pants from the Salvation Army, pink suede belt, pointed black forties dress shoes scuffed up, holes in the soles, no socks, no hat, long pronounced sideburns, "Gene Vincent" hairdo, two days' growth of beard, bad teeth*

SAUL KIMMER, *late forties, Hollywood producer, pink and white flower print sports shirt, white sports coat with matching polyester slacks, black and white loafers*

MOM, *early sixties, mother of the brothers, small woman, conservative white skirt and matching jacket, red shoulder bag, two pieces of matching red luggage*

SCENE: *All nine scenes take place on the same set; a kitchen and adjoining alcove of an older home in a Southern California suburb, about 40 miles east of Los Angeles. The kitchen takes up most of the playing area to stage left. The kitchen consists of a sink, upstage center, surrounded by counter space, a wall telephone, cupboards, and a small window just above it bordered by neat yellow curtains. Stage left of sink is a stove. Stage right, a refrigerator. The alcove adjoins the kitchen to stage right. There is no wall division or door to the alcove. It is open and easily accessible from the kitchen and defined only by the objects in it: a small round glass breakfast table mounted on white iron legs, two matching white iron chairs set across from each other. The two exterior walls of the alcove which prescribe a corner in the upstage right are composed of many small windows, beginning from a solid wall about three feet high and extending to the ceiling. The windows look out to bushes and citrus trees. The alcove is filled with all sorts of house plants in various pots, mostly Boston ferns hanging in planters at different levels. The floor of the alcove is composed of green synthetic grass.*

    All entrances and exits are made stage left from the kitchen. There is no door. The actors simply go off and come onto the playing area.

NOTE ON SET AND COSTUME: *The set should be constructed realistically with no attempt to distort its dimensions, shapes, objects, or colors. No objects should be introduced which might draw special attention to themselves other than the props demanded by the script. If a stylistic "concept" is grafted onto the set design it will only serve to confuse the evolution of the characters' situation, which is the most important focus of the play.*

Likewise, the costumes should be exactly representative of who the characters are and not added onto for the sake of making a point to the audience.

NOTE ON SOUND: *The Coyote of Southern California has a distinct yapping, dog-like bark, similar to a Hyena. This yapping grows more intense and maniacal as the pack grows in numbers, which is usually the case when they lure and kill pets from suburban yards. The sense of growing frenzy in the pack should be felt in the background, particularly in Scenes VII and VIII. In any case, these Coyotes never make the long, mournful, solitary howl of the Hollywood stereotype.*
   The sound of Crickets can speak for itself.
   These sounds should also be treated realistically even though they sometimes grow in volume and numbers.

ACT I

SCENE I

Night. Sound of crickets in dark. Candlelight appears in alcove, illuminating AUSTIN, *seated at glass table hunched over a writing notebook, pen in hand, cigarette burning in ashtray, cup of coffee, typewriter on table, stacks of paper, candle burning on table.*
   Soft moonlight fills kitchen illuminating LEE, *beer in hand, six-pack on counter behind him. He's leaning against the sink, mildly drunk; takes a slug of beer.*

LEE.   So, Mom took off for Alaska, huh?
AUSTIN.   Yeah.
LEE.   Sorta' left you in charge.
AUSTIN.   Well, she knew I was coming down here so she offered me the place.
LEE.   You keepin' the plants watered?
AUSTIN.   Yeah.
LEE.   Keepin' the sink clean? She don't like even a single tea leaf in the sink ya' know.
AUSTIN [*trying to concentrate on writing*].   Yeah, I know.

[*Pause.*]

10 LEE.   She gonna' be up there a long time?
AUSTIN.   I don't know.
LEE.   Kinda' nice for you, huh? Whole place to yourself.
AUSTIN.   Yeah, it's great.
LEE.   Ya' got crickets anyway. Tons a' crickets out there. [*Looks around kitchen.*] Ya' got groceries? Coffee?
AUSTIN [*looking up from writing*].   What?
LEE.   You got coffee?
AUSTIN.   Yeah.
LEE.   At's good. [*Short pause.*] Real coffee? From the bean?
20 AUSTIN.   Yeah. You want some?
LEE.   Naw. I brought some uh— [*Motions to beer.*]
AUSTIN.   Help yourself to whatever's— [*Motions to refrigerator.*]
LEE.   I will. Don't worry about me. I'm not the one to worry about. I mean I can uh— [*Pause.*] You always work by candlelight?

AUSTIN.   No—uh—Not always.

LEE.   Just sometimes?

AUSTIN [*puts pen down, rubs his eyes*].   Yeah. Sometimes it's soothing.

LEE.   Isn't that what the old guys did?

AUSTIN.   What old guys?

30 LEE.   The Forefathers. You know.

AUSTIN.   Forefathers?

LEE.   Isn't that what they did? Candlelight burning into the night? Cabins in the wilderness.

AUSTIN [*rubs hand through his hair*].   I suppose.

LEE.   I'm not botherin' you am I? I mean I don't wanna break into yer uh—concentration or nothin'.

AUSTIN.   No, it's all right.

LEE.   That's good. I mean I realize that yer line a' work demands a lota' concentration.

40 AUSTIN.   It's okay.

LEE.   You probably think that I'm not fully able to comprehend somethin' like that, huh?

AUSTIN.   Like what?

LEE.   That stuff yer doin'. That art. You know. Whatever you call it.

AUSTIN.   It's just a little research.

LEE.   You may not know it but I did a little art myself once.

AUSTIN.   You did?

LEE.   Yeah! I did some a' that. I fooled around with it. No future in it.

AUSTIN.   What'd you do?

50 LEE.   Never mind what I did! Just never mind about that. [*Pause.*] It was ahead of its time.

[*Pause.*]

AUSTIN.   So, you went out to see the old man, huh?

LEE.   Yeah, I seen him.

AUSTIN.   How's he doing?

LEE.   Same. He's doin' just about the same.

AUSTIN.   I was down there too, you know.

LEE.   What d'ya' want, an award? You want some kinda' medal? You were down there. He told me all about you.

AUSTIN.   What'd he say?

60 LEE.   He told me. Don't worry.

[*Pause.*]

AUSTIN.   Well—

LEE.   You don't have to say nothin'.

AUSTIN.   I wasn't.

LEE.   Yeah, you were gonna' make somethin' up. Somethin' brilliant.

[*Pause.*]

AUSTIN.   You going to be down here very long, Lee?

LEE.   Might be. Depends on a few things.

AUSTIN.   You got some friends down here?

LEE [*laughs*].   I know a few people. Yeah.

AUSTIN. Well, you can stay here as long as I'm here.

70 LEE. I don't need your permission do I?

AUSTIN. No.

LEE. I mean she's my mother too, right?

AUSTIN. Right.

LEE. She might've just as easily asked me to take care of her place as you.

AUSTIN. That's right.

LEE. I mean I know how to water plants.

[*Long pause.*]

AUSTIN. So you don't know how long you'll be staying then?

LEE. Depends mostly on houses, ya' know.

AUSTIN. Houses?

80 LEE. Yeah. Houses. Electric devices. Stuff like that. I gotta' make a little tour first.

[*Short pause.*]

AUSTIN. Lee, why don't you just try another neighborhood, all right?

LEE [*laughs*]. What'sa' matter with this neighborhood? This is a great neighborhood. Lush. Good class a' people. Not many dogs.

AUSTIN. Well, our uh—Our mother just happens to live here. That's all.

LEE. Nobody's gonna' know. All they know is somethin's missing. That's all. She'll never even hear about it. Nobody's gonna' know.

AUSTIN. You're going to get picked up if you start walking around here at night.

90 LEE. Me? I'm gonna' git picked up? What about you? You stick out like a sore thumb. Look at you. You think yer regular lookin'?

AUSTIN. I've got too much to deal with here to be worrying about—

LEE. Yer not gonna' have to worry about me! I've been doin' all right without you. I haven't been anywhere near you for five years! Now isn't that true?

AUSTIN. Yeah.

LEE. So you don't have to worry about me. I'm a free agent.

AUSTIN. All right.

LEE. Now all I wanna' do is borrow yer car.

AUSTIN. No!

100 LEE. Just fer a day. One day.

AUSTIN. No!

LEE. I won't take it outside a twenty mile radius. I promise ya'. You can check the speedometer.

AUSTIN. You're not borrowing my car! That's all there is to it.

[*Pause.*]

LEE. Then I'll just take the damn thing.

AUSTIN. Lee, look—I don't want any trouble, all right?

LEE. That's a dumb line. That is a dumb fuckin' line. You git paid fer dreamin' up a line like that?

AUSTIN. Look, I can give you some money if you need money.

[LEE *suddenly lunges at* AUSTIN, *grabs him violently by the shirt and shakes him with tremendous power.*]

110 Lee.   Don't you say that to me! Don't you ever say that to me! [*Just as suddenly he turns him loose, pushes him away and backs off.*] You may be able to git away with that with the Old Man. Git him tanked up for a week! Buy him off with yer Hollywood blood money, but not me! I can git my own money my own way. Big money!

Austin.   I was just making an offer.

Lee.   Yeah, well keep it to yourself! [*Long pause*]. Those are the most monotonous fuckin' crickets I ever heard in my life.

Austin.   I kinda' like the sound.

Lee.   Yeah. Supposed to be able to tell the temperature by the number a'
120 pulses. You believe that?

Austin.   The temperature?

Lee.   Yeah. The air. How hot it is.

Austin.   How do you do that?

Lee.   I don't know. Some woman told me that. She was a Botanist. So I believed her.

Austin.   Where'd you meet her?

Lee.   What?

Austin.   The woman Botanist?

Lee.   I met her on the desert. I been spendin' a lota' time on the desert.
130 Austin.   What were you doing out there?

Lee [*pause, stares in space*].   I forgit. Had me a Pit Bull there for a while but I lost him.

Austin.   Pit Bull?

Lee.   Fightin' dog. Damn I made some good money off that little dog. Real good money.

[*Pause.*]

Austin.   You could come up north with me, you know.

Lee.   What's up there?

Austin.   My family.

Lee.   Oh, that's right, you got the wife and kiddies now don't ya'. The house,
140 the car, the whole slam. That's right.

Austin.   You could spend a couple days. See how you like it. I've got an extra room.

Lee.   Too cold up there.

[*Pause.*]

Austin.   You want to sleep for a while?

Lee [*pause, stares at* Austin].   I don't sleep.

[*Lights to black.*]

SCENE II

Morning. Austin *is watering plants with a vaporizer,* Lee *sits at glass table in alcove drinking beer.*

Lee.   I never realized the old lady was so security-minded.

Austin.   How do you mean?

Lee.   Made a little tour this morning. She's got locks on everything. Locks and double-locks and chain locks and— What's she got that's so valuable?

150 AUSTIN. Antiques I guess. I don't know.

LEE. Antiques? Brought everything with her from the old place, huh. Just the same crap we always had around. Plates and spoons.

AUSTIN. I guess they have personal value to her.

LEE. Personal value. Yeah. Just a lota' junk. Most of it's phony anyway. Idaho decals. Now who in the hell wants to eat offa' plate with the State of Idaho starin' ya' in the face. Every time ya' take a bite ya' get to see a little bit more.

AUSTIN. Well it must mean something to her or she wouldn't save it.

LEE. Yeah, well personally I don't wann' be invaded by Idaho when I'm eatin'. When I'm eatin' I'm home. Ya' know what I'm sayin'? I'm not driftin',

160 I'm home. I don't need my thoughts swept off to Idaho. I don't need that!

[*Pause.*]

AUSTIN. Did you go out last night?

LEE. Why?

AUSTIN. I thought I heard you go out.

LEE. Yeah, I went out. What about it?

AUSTIN. Just wondered.

LEE. Damn coyotes kept me awake.

AUSTIN. Oh yeah, I heard them. They must've killed somebody's dog or something.

LEE. Yappin' their fools head off. They don't yap like that on the desert.

170 They howl. These are city coyotes here.

AUSTIN. Well, you don't sleep anyway do you?

[*Pause,* LEE *stares at him.*]

LEE: You're pretty smart aren't ya?

AUSTIN. How do you mean?

LEE. I mean you never had any more on the ball than I did. But here you are gettin' invited into prominent people's houses. Sittin' around talkin' like you know somethin'.

AUSTIN. They're not so prominent.

LEE. They're a helluva' lot more prominent than the houses I get invited into.

180 AUSTIN. Well you invite yourself.

LEE. That's right. I do. In fact I probably got a wider range a' choices than you do, come to think of it.

AUSTIN. I wouldn't doubt it.

LEE. In fact I been inside some pretty classy places in my time. And I never even went to an Ivy League school either.

AUSTIN. You want some breakfast or something?

LEE. Breakfast?

AUSTIN. Yeah. Don't you eat breakfast?

LEE. Look, don't worry about me pal. I can take care a' myself. You just go

190 ahead as though I wasn't even here, all right?

[AUSTIN *goes into kitchen, makes coffee.*]

AUSTIN. Where'd you walk to last night?

[*Pause.*]

Lee.   I went up in the foothills there. Up in the San Gabriels.[1] Heat was
 drivin' me crazy.

Austin.   Well, wasn't it hot out on the desert?

Lee.   Different kinda' heat. Out there it's clean. Cools off at night. There's
 a nice little breeze.

Austin.   Where were you, the Mojave?[2]

Lee.   Yeah. The Mojave. That's right.

Austin.   I haven't been out there in years.

200 Lee.   Out past Needles[3] there.

Austin.   Oh yeah.

Lee.   Up here it's different. This country's real different.

Austin.   Well, it's been built up.

Lee.   Built up? Wiped out is more like it. I don't even hardly recognize it.

Austin.   Yeah. Foothills are the same though, aren't they?

Lee.   Pretty much. It's funny goin' up in there. The smells and everything.
 Used to catch snakes up there, remember?

Austin.   You caught snakes.

Lee.   Yeah. And you'd pretend you were Geronimo[4] or some damn thing.
210 You used to go right out to lunch.

Austin.   I enjoyed my imagination.

Lee.   That what you call it? Looks like yer still enjoyin' it.

Austin.   So you just wandered around up there, huh?

Lee.   Yeah. With a purpose.

Austin.   See any houses?

                   [Pause.]

Lee.   Couple. Couple a' real nice ones. One of 'em didn't even have a dog.
 Walked right up and stuck my head in the window. Not a peep. Just a
 sweet kinda' suburban silence.

Austin.   What kind of a place was it?

220 Lee.   Like a paradise. Kinda' place that sorta' kills ya' inside. Warm yellow
 lights. Mexican tile all around. Copper pots hangin' over the stove. Ya'
 know like they got in the magazines. Blonde people movin' in and outa'
 the rooms, talkin' to each other. *[Pause.]* Kinda' place you wish you sorta'
 grew up in, ya' know.

Austin.   That's the kind of place you wish you'd grown up in?

Lee.   Yeah, why not?

Austin.   I thought you hated that kind of stuff.

Lee.   Yeah, well you never knew too much about me did ya'?

                   [Pause.]

Austin.   Why'd you go out to the desert in the first place?

230 Lee.   I was on my way to see the old man.

---

[1] The San Gabriel mountains are located just to the north of greater Los Angeles.

[2] The Mojave Desert, located northeast of Los Angeles, receives about six inches of rain per
year with summer temperatures of over 120°F.

[3] Needles is a town east–northeast of Los Angeles on the California–Arizona border.

[4] Geronimo (1829–1909) was a chief of the Apache Indians who led his people in ten years
of war against the white settlers in Arizona.

AUSTIN.   You mean you just passed through there?
LEE.   Yeah. That's right. Three months of passin' through.
AUSTIN.   Three months?
LEE.   Somethin' like that. Maybe more. Why?
AUSTIN.   You lived on the Mojave for three months?
LEE.   Yeah. What'sa' matter with that?
AUSTIN.   By yourself?
LEE.   Mostly. Had a couple a' visitors. Had that dog for a while.
AUSTIN.   Didn't you miss people?
240 LEE *[laughs]*.   People?
AUSTIN.   Yeah. I mean I go crazy if I have to spend three nights in a motel
     by myself.
LEE.   Yer not in a motel now.
AUSTIN.   No, I know. But sometimes I have to stay in motels.
LEE.   Well, they got people in motels don't they?
AUSTIN.   Strangers.
LEE.   Yer friendly aren't ya'? Aren't you the friendly type?

                                                                         [Pause.]

AUSTIN.   I'm going to have somebody coming by here later, Lee.
LEE.   Ah! Lady friend?
250 AUSTIN.   No, a producer.
LEE.   Aha! What's he produce?
AUSTIN.   Film. Movies. You know.
LEE.   Oh, movies. Motion Pictures! A Big Wig huh?
AUSTIN.   Yeah.
LEE.   What's he comin' by here for?
AUSTIN.   We have to talk about a project.
LEE.   Whadya' mean, "a project"? What's "a project"?
AUSTIN.   A script.
LEE.   Oh. That's what yer doin' with all these papers?
260 AUSTIN.   Yeah.
LEE.   Well, what's the project about?
AUSTIN.   We're uh—it's a period piece.
LEE.   What's "a period piece"?
AUSTIN.   Look, it doesn't matter. The main thing is we need to discuss this
     alone. I mean—
LEE.   Oh, I get it. You want me outa' the picture.
AUSTIN.   Not exactly. I just need to be alone with him for a couple of hours.
     So we can talk.
LEE.   Yer afraid I'll embarrass ya' huh?
270 AUSTIN.   I'm not afraid you'll embarrass me!
LEE.   Well, I tell ya' what—Why don't you just gimme the keys to yer car and
     I'll be back here around six o'clock or so. That give ya' enough time?
AUSTIN.   I'm not loaning you my car, Lee.
LEE.   You want me to just git lost huh? Take a hike? Is that it? Pound the
     pavement for a few hours while you bullshit yer way into a million bucks.
AUSTIN.   Look, it's going to be hard enough for me to face this character on
     my own without—
LEE.   You don't know this guy?

AUSTIN.   No I don't know— He's a producer. I mean I've been meeting with
280   him for months but you never get to know a producer.
LEE.   Yer tryin' to hustle him? Is that it?
AUSTIN.   I'm not trying to hustle him! I'm trying to work out a deal! It's not
easy.
LEE.   What kinda' deal?
AUSTIN.   Convince him it's a worthwhile story.
LEE.   He's not convinced? How come he's comin' over here if he's not con-
vinced? I'll convince him for ya'.
AUSTIN.   You don't understand the way things work down here.
LEE.   How do things work down here?

[*Pause.*]

290   AUSTIN.   Look, if I loan you my car will you have it back here by six?
LEE.   On the button. With a full tank a' gas.
AUSTIN [*digging in his pocket for keys*].   Forget about the gas.
LEE.   Hey, these days gas is gold, old buddy. [AUSTIN *hands the keys to* LEE.]
You remember that car I used to loan you?
AUSTIN.   Yeah.
LEE.   Forty Ford. Flathead.
AUSTIN.   Yeah.
LEE.   Sucker hauled ass didn't it?
AUSTIN.   Lee, it's not that I don't want to loan you my car—
300   LEE.   You are loanin' me yer car.

[LEE *gives* AUSTIN *a pat on the shoulder, pause.*]

AUSTIN.   I know. I just wish—
LEE.   What? You wish what?
AUSTIN.   I don't know. I wish I wasn't—I wish I didn't have to be doing
business down here. I'd like to just spend some time with you.
LEE.   I thought it was "Art" you were doin'.

[LEE *moves across kitchen toward exit, tosses keys in his hand.*]

AUSTIN.   Try to get it back here by six, okay?
LEE.   No sweat. Hey, ya' know, if that uh—story of yours doesn't go over with
the guy—tell him I got a couple a' "projects" he might be interested in.
Real commercial. Full a' suspense. True-to-life stuff.

[LEE *exits*, AUSTIN *stares after* LEE *then turns, goes to papers at table, leafs through
pages, lights fade to black.*]

SCENE III

Afternoon. Alcove, SAUL KIMMER *and* AUSTIN *seated across from each other at table.*

310   SAUL.   Well, to tell you the truth Austin, I have never felt so confident about
a project in quite a long time.
AUSTIN.   Well, that's good to hear, Saul.
SAUL.   I am absolutely convinced we can get this thing off the ground. I

mean we'll have to make a sale to television and that means getting a
major star. Somebody bankable. But I think we can do it. I really do.
AUSTIN.   Don't you think we need a first draft before we approach a star?
SAUL.   No, no, not at all. I don't think it's necessary. Maybe a brief synopsis.
I don't want you to touch the typewriter until we have some seed money.
AUSTIN.   That's fine with me.
320 SAUL.   I mean it's a great story. Just the story alone. You've really managed
to capture something this time.
AUSTIN.   I'm glad you like it, Saul.

[LEE *enters abruptly into kitchen carrying a stolen television set, short pause*.]

LEE.   Aw shit, I'm sorry about that. I am really sorry Austin.
AUSTIN [*standing*].   That's all right.
LEE [*moving toward them*].   I mean I thought it was way past six already. You
said to have it back here by six.
AUSTIN.   We were just finishing up. [*To Saul.*] This is my, uh—brother, Lee.
SAUL [*standing*].   Oh, I'm very happy to meet you.

[LEE *sets T.V. on sink counter, shakes hands with* SAUL.]

LEE.   I can't tell ya' how happy I am to meet you sir.
330 SAUL.   Saul Kimmer.
LEE.   Mr. Kipper.
SAUL.   Kimmer.
AUSTIN.   Lee's been living out on the desert and he just uh—
SAUL.   Oh, that's terrific! [*To* LEE.] Palm Springs?
LEE.   Yeah. Yeah, right. Right around in that area. Near uh—Bob Hope
Drive there.
SAUL.   Oh I love it out there. I just love it. The air is wonderful.
LEE.   Yeah. Sure is. Healthy.
SAUL.   And the golf. I don't know if you play golf, but the golf is just about
340 the best.
LEE.   I play a lota' golf.
SAUL.   Is that right?
LEE.   Yeah. In fact I was hoping I'd run into somebody out here who played
a little golf. I've been lookin' for a partner.
SAUL.   Well, I uh—
AUSTIN.   Lee's just down for a visit while our mother's in Alaska.
SAUL.   Oh, your mother's in Alaska?
AUSTIN.   Yes. She went up there on a little vacation. This is her place.
SAUL.   I see. Well isn't that something. Alaska.
350 LEE.   What kinda' handicap do ya' have, Mr. Kimmer?
SAUL.   Oh I'm just a Sunday duffer really. You know.
LEE.   That's good 'cause I haven't swung a club in months.
SAUL.   Well we ought to get together sometime and have a little game.
Austin, do you play?

[SAUL *mimes a Johnny Carson golf swing for* AUSTIN.]

AUSTIN.   No. I don't uh—I've watched it on T.V.
LEE [*to* SAUL].   How 'bout tomorrow morning? Bright and early. We could
get out there and put in eighteen holes before breakfast.

SAUL. Well, I've got uh—I have several appointments—

LEE. No, I mean real early. Crack a'dawn. While the dew's still thick on the
360   fairway.

SAUL. Sounds really great.

LEE. Austin could be our caddie.

SAUL. Now that's an idea. [*Laughs.*]

AUSTIN. I don't know the first thing about golf.

LEE. There's nothin' to it. Isn't that right, Saul? He'd pick it up in fifteen
       minutes.

SAUL. Sure. Doesn't take long. 'Course you have to play for years to find
       your true form. [*Chuckles.*]

LEE [*to* AUSTIN]. We'll give ya' a quick run-down on the club faces. The irons,
370   the woods. Show ya' a couple pointers on the basic swing. Might even let
       ya' hit the ball a couple times. Whadya' think, Saul?

SAUL. Why not. I think it'd be great. I haven't had any exercise in weeks.

LEE. 'At's the spirit! We'll have a little orange juice right afterwards.

[*Pause.*]

SAUL. Orange juice?

LEE. Yeah! Vitamin C! Nothin' like a shot a' orange juice after a round a'
       golf. Hot shower. Snappin' towels at each other's privates. Real sense a'
       fraternity.

SAUL [*smiles at* AUSTIN]. Well, you make it sound very inviting, I must say. It
       really does sound great.

380 LEE. Then it's a date.

SAUL. Well, I'll call the country club and see if I can arrange something.

LEE. Great! Boy, I sure am sorry that I busted in on ya' all in the middle of
       yer meeting.

SAUL. Oh that's quite all right. We were just about finished anyway.

LEE. I can wait out in the other room if you want.

SAUL. No really—

LEE. Just got Austin's color T.V. back from the shop. I can watch a little
       amateur boxing now.

[LEE *and* AUSTIN *exchange looks.*]

SAUL. Oh—Yes.

390 LEE. You don't fool around in Television, do you Saul?

SAUL. Uh—I have in the past. Produced some T.V. Specials. Network stuff.
       But it's mainly features now.

LEE. That's where the big money is, huh?

SAUL. Yes. That's right.

AUSTIN. Why don't I call you tomorrow, Saul and we'll get together. We can
       have lunch or something.

SAUL. That'd be terrific.

LEE. Right after the golf.

[*Pause.*]

SAUL. What?

400 LEE. You can have lunch right after the golf.

SAUL. Oh, right.

LEE. Austin was tellin' me that yer interested in stories.

SAUL. Well, we develop certain projects that we feel have commercial potential.

LEE. What kinda' stuff do ya' go in for?

SAUL. Oh, the usual. You know. Good love interest. Lots of action. [*Chuckles
at* AUSTIN.]

LEE. Westerns?

SAUL. Sometimes.

410 AUSTIN. I'll give you a ring, Saul.

[AUSTIN *tries to move* SAUL *across the kitchen but* LEE *blocks their way.*]

LEE. I got a Western that'd knock yer lights out.

SAUL. Oh really?

LEE. Yeah. Contemporary Western. Based on a true story. 'Course I'm not
a writer like my brother here. I'm not a man of the pen.

SAUL. Well—

LEE. I mean I can tell ya' a story off the tongue but I can't put it down on
paper. That don't make any difference though does it?

SAUL. No, not really.

LEE. I mean plenty a' guys have stories don't they? True-life stories. Musta'
420 been a lota' movies made from real life.

SAUL. Yes. I suppose so.

LEE. I haven't seen a good Western since "Lonely Are the Brave." You
remember that movie?

SAUL. No, I'm afraid I—

LEE. Kirk Douglas. Helluva' movie. You remember that movie, Austin?

AUSTIN. Yes.

LEE [*to* SAUL]. The man dies for the love of a horse.

SAUL. Is that right.

LEE. Yeah. Ya' hear the horse screamin' at the end of it. Rain's comin'
430 down. Horse is screamin'. Then there's a shot. BLAM! Just a single shot
like that. Then nothin' but the sound of rain. And Kirk Douglas is ridin'
in the ambulance. Ridin' away from the scene of the accident. And when
he hears that shot he knows that his horse has died. He knows. And you
see his eyes. And his eyes die. Right inside his face. And then his eyes
close. And you know that he's died too. You know that Kirk Douglas has
died from the death of his horse.

SAUL [*eyes* AUSTIN *nervously*]. Well, it sounds like a great movie. I'm sorry I
missed it.

LEE. Yeah, you shouldn't a' missed that one.

440 SAUL. I'll have to try to catch it some time. Arrange a screening or something. Well, Austin, I'll have to hit the freeway before rush hour.

AUSTIN [*ushers him toward exit*]. It's good seeing you, Saul.

[AUSTIN *and* SAUL *shake hands.*]

LEE. So ya' think there's room for a real Western these days? A true-to-life
Western?

SAUL. Well, I don't see why not. Why don't you uh—tell the story to Austin
and have him write a little outline.

LEE. You'd take a look at it then?

SAUL. Yes. Sure. I'll give it a read-through. Always eager for new material. [*Smiles at* AUSTIN].

450 LEE. That's great! You'd really read it then huh?

SAUL. It would just be my opinion of course.

LEE. That's all I want. Just an opinion. I happen to think it has a lota' possibilities.

SAUL. Well, it was great meeting you and I'll—

[SAUL *and* LEE *shake.*]

LEE. I'll call you tomorrow about the golf.

SAUL. Oh. Yes, right.

LEE. Austin's got your number, right?

SAUL. Yes.

LEE. So long Saul. [*Gives* SAUL *a pat on the back.*]

[SAUL *exits,* AUSTIN *turns to* LEE, *looks at T.V. then back to* LEE.]

460 AUSTIN. Give me the keys.

[AUSTIN *extends his hand toward* LEE, LEE *doesn't move, just stares at* AUSTIN, *smiles, lights to black.*]

SCENE IV

Night. Coyotes in distance, fade, sound of typewriter in dark, crickets, candlelight in alcove, dim light in kitchen, lights reveal AUSTIN *at glass table typing,* LEE *sits across from him, foot on table, drinking beer and whiskey, the T.V. is still on sink counter,* AUSTIN *types for a while, then stops.*

LEE. All right, now read it back to me.

AUSTIN. I'm not reading it back to you, Lee. You can read it when we're finished. I can't spend all night on this.

LEE. You got better things to do?

AUSTIN. Let's just go ahead. Now what happens when he leaves Texas?

LEE. Is he ready to leave Texas yet? I didn't know we were that far along. He's not ready to leave Texas.

AUSTIN. He's right at the border.

LEE [*sitting up*]. No, see, this is one a' the crucial parts. Right here. [*Taps*
470 *paper with beer can.*] We can't rush through this. He's not right at the border. He's a good fifty miles from the border. A lot can happen in fifty miles.

AUSTIN. It's only an outline. We're not writing an entire script now.

LEE. Well ya' can't leave things out even if it is an outline. It's one a' the most important parts. Ya' can't go leavin' it out.

AUSTIN. Okay, okay. Let's just—get it done.

LEE. All right. Now. He's in the truck and he's got his horse trailer and his horse.

AUSTIN. We've already established that.

480 LEE. And he sees this other guy comin' up behind him in another truck. And that truck is pullin' a gooseneck.

AUSTIN. What's a gooseneck?

LEE. Cattle trailer. You know the kind with a gooseneck, goes right down in the bed a' the pick-up.

AUSTIN. Oh. All right. [*Types.*]

LEE. It's important.

AUSTIN. Okay. I got it.

LEE. All these details are important.

[AUSTIN *types as they talk.*]

AUSTIN. I've got it.

490 LEE. And this other guy's got his horse all saddled up in the back a' the gooseneck.

AUSTIN. Right.

LEE. So both these guys have got their horses right along with 'em, see.

AUSTIN. I understand.

LEE. Then this first guy suddenly realizes two things.

AUSTIN. The guy in front?

LEE. Right. The guy in front realizes two things almost at the same time. Simultaneous.

AUSTIN. What were the two things?

500 LEE. Number one, he realizes that the guy behind him is the husband of the woman he's been—

[LEE *makes gesture of screwing by pumping his arm.*]

AUSTIN [*sees* LEE's *gesture.*] Oh. Yeah.

LEE. And number two, he realizes he's in the middle of Tornado Country.

AUSTIN. What's "Tornado Country"?

LEE. Panhandle.

AUSTIN. Panhandle?

LEE. Sweetwater. Around in that area. Nothin'. Nowhere. And number three—

AUSTIN. I thought there was only two.

510 LEE. There's three. There's a third unforeseen realization.

AUSTIN. And what's that?

LEE. That he's runnin' outa' gas.

AUSTIN [*stops typing*]. Come on, Lee.

[AUSTIN *gets up, moves to kitchen, gets a glass of water.*]

LEE. Whadya' mean, "come on"? That's what it is. Write it down! He's runnin' outa' gas.

AUSTIN. It's too—

LEE. What? It's too what? It's too real! That's what ya' mean isn't it? It's too much like real life!

AUSTIN. It's not like real life! It's not enough like real life. Things don't
520 happen like that.

LEE. What! Men don't fuck other men's women?

AUSTIN. Yes. But they don't end up chasing each other across the Panhandle. Through "Tornado Country."

LEE. They do in this movie!
AUSTIN. And they don't have horses conveniently along with them when
they run out gas! And they don't run out of gas either!
LEE. These guys run outa' gas! This is my story and one a' these guys runs
outa' gas!
AUSTIN. It's just a dumb excuse to get them into a chase scene. It's contrived.
530 LEE. It is a chase scene! It's already a chase scene. They been chasin' each
other fer days.
AUSTIN. So now they're supposed to abandon their trucks, climb on their
horses and chase each other into the mountains?
LEE [*standing suddenly*]. There aren't any mountains in the Panhandle! It's
flat!

[LEE *turns violently toward windows in alcove and throws beer can at them.*]

LEE. Goddamn these crickets! [*Yells at crickets.*] Shut up out there! [*Pause,
turns back toward table.*] This place is like a fuckin' rest home here. How're
you supposed to think!
AUSTIN. You wanna' take a break?
540 LEE. No, I don't wanna' take a break! I wanna' get this done! This is my last
chance to get this done.
AUSTIN [*moves back into alcove*]. All right. Take it easy.
LEE. I'm gonna' be leavin' this area. I don't have time to mess around here.
AUSTIN. Where are you going?
LEE. Never mind where I'm goin'! That's got nothin' to do with you. I just
gotta' get this done. I'm not like you. Hangin' around bein' a parasite offa'
other fools. I gotta' do this thing and get out.

[*Pause.*]

AUSTIN. A parasite? Me?
LEE. Yeah, you!
550 AUSTIN. After you break into people's houses and take their televisions?
LEE. They don't need their televisions! I'm doin' them a service.
AUSTIN. Give me back my keys, Lee.
LEE. Not until you write this thing! You're gonna' write this outline thing
for me or that car's gonna' wind up in Arizona with a different paint job.
AUSTIN. You think you can force me to write this? I was doing you a favor.
LEE. Git off yer high horse will ya'! Favor! Big favor. Handin' down favors
from the mountain top.
AUSTIN. Let's just write it, okay? Let's sit down and not get upset and see if
we can just get through this.

[AUSTIN *sits at typewriter.*]

[*Long pause.*]

560 LEE. Yer not gonna' even show it to him, are ya'?
AUSTIN. What?
LEE. This outline. You got no intention of showin' it to him. Yer just doin'
this 'cause yer afraid a' me.

AUSTIN.   You can show it to him yourself.

LEE.   I will, boy! I'm gonna' read it to him on the golf course.

AUSTIN.   And I'm not afraid of you either.

LEE.   Then how come yer doin' it?

AUSTIN [*pause*].   So I can get my keys back.

[*Pause as* LEE *takes keys out of his pocket slowly and throws them on table, long pause,* AUSTIN *stares at keys.*]

LEE.   There. Now you got yer keys back.

[AUSTIN *looks up at* LEE *but doesn't take keys.*]

570 LEE.   Go ahead. There's yer keys. [AUSTIN *slowly takes keys off table and puts them back in his own pocket.*] Now what're you gonna' do? Kick me out?

AUSTIN.   I'm not going to kick you out, Lee.

LEE.   You couldn't kick me out, boy.

AUSTIN.   I know.

LEE.   So you can't even consider that one. [*Pause.*] You could call the police. That'd be the obvious thing.

AUSTIN.   You're my brother.

LEE.   That don't mean a thing. You go down to the L.A. Police Department there and ask them what kinda' people kill each other the most. What do
580 you think they'd say?

AUSTIN.   Who said anything about killing?

LEE.   Family people. Brothers. Brothers-in-law. Cousins. Real American-type people. They kill each other in the heat mostly. In the Smog-Alerts. In the Brush Fire Season. Right about this time a' year.

AUSTIN.   This isn't the same.

LEE.   Oh no? What makes it different?

AUSTIN.   We're not insane. We're not driven to acts of violence like that. Not over a dumb movie script. Now sit down.

[*Long pause,* LEE *considers which way to go with it.*]

LEE.   Maybe not. [*He sits back down at table across from* AUSTIN.] Maybe you're
590 right. Maybe we're too intelligent, huh? [*Pause.*] We got our heads on our shoulders. One of us has even got a Ivy League diploma. Now that means somethin' don't it? Doesn't that mean somethin'?

AUSTIN.   Look, I'll write this thing for you, Lee. I don't mind writing it. I just don't want to get all worked up about it. It's not worth it. Now, come on. Let's just get through it, okay?

LEE.   Nah. I think there's easier money. Lotsa' places I could pick up thousands. Maybe millions. I don't need this shit. I could go up to Sacramento Valley and steal me a diesel. Ten thousand a week dismantling one a' those suckers. Ten thousand a week!

[LEE *opens another beer, puts his foot back up on table.*]

600 AUSTIN.   No, really, look, I'll write it out for you. I think it's a great idea.

LEE.   Nah, you got yer own work to do. I don't wanna' interfere with yer life.

Austin.   I mean it'd be really fantastic if you could sell this. Turn it into a movie. I mean it.

[Pause.]

Lee.   Ya' think so huh?

Austin.   Absolutely. You could really turn your life around, you know. Change things.

Lee.   I could get me a house maybe.

Austin.   Sure you could get a house. You could get a whole ranch if you wanted to.

610 Lee *[laughs].*   A ranch? I could get a ranch?

Austin.   'Course you could. You know what a screenplay sells for these days?

Lee.   No. What's it sell for?

Austin.   A lot. A whole lot of money.

Lee.   Thousands?

Austin.   Yeah. Thousands.

Lee.   Millions?

Austin.   Well—

Lee.   We could get the old man outa' hock then.

Austin.   Maybe.

620 Lee.   Maybe? Whadya' mean, maybe?

Austin.   I mean it might take more than money.

Lee.   You were just tellin' me it'd change my whole life around. Why wouldn't it change his?

Austin.   He's different.

Lee.   Oh, he's of a different ilk huh?

Austin.   He's not gonna' change. Let's leave the old man out of it.

Lee.   That's right. He's not gonna' change but I will. I'll just turn myself right inside out. I could be just like you then, huh? Sittin' around dreamin' stuff up. Gettin' paid to dream. Ridin' back and forth on the freeway just
630 dreamin' my fool head off.

Austin.   It's not all that easy.

Lee.   It's not, huh?

Austin.   No. There's a lot of work involved.

Lee.   What's the toughest part? Deciding whether to jog or play tennis?

[Long pause.]

Austin.   Well, look. You can stay here—do whatever you want to. Borrow the car. Come in and out. Doesn't matter to me. It's not my house. I'll help you write this thing or—not. Just let me know what you want. You tell me.

Lee.   Oh. So now suddenly you're at my service. Is that it?

640 Austin.   What do you want to do Lee?

[Long pause, Lee stares at him then turns and dreams at windows.]

Lee: I tell ya' what I'd do if I still had that dog. Ya' wanna' know what I'd do?

Austin.   What?

LEE. Head to Ventura.[5] 'Cook up a little match. God that little dog could bear down. Lota' money in dog fightin'. Big money.

[*Pause.*]

AUSTIN. Why don't we try to see this through, Lee. Just for the hell of it. Maybe you've really got something here. What do you think?

[*Pause,* LEE *considers.*]

LEE. Maybe so. No harm in tryin' I guess. You think it's such a hot idea. Besides, I always wondered what'd be like to be you.

650 AUSTIN. You did?

LEE. Yeah, sure. I used to picture you walkin' around some campus with yer arms fulla' books. Blondes chasin' after ya'.

AUSTIN. Blondes? That's funny.

LEE. What's funny about it?

AUSTIN. Because I always used to picture you somewhere.

LEE. Where'd you picture me?

AUSTIN. Oh, I don't know. Different places. Adventures. You were always on some adventure.

LEE. Yeah.

660 AUSTIN. And I used to say to myself, "Lee's got the right idea. He's out there in the world and here I am. What am I doing?"

LEE. Well you were settin' yourself up for somethin'.

AUSTIN. I guess.

LEE. We better get started on this thing then.

AUSTIN. Okay.

[AUSTIN *sits up at typewriter, puts new paper in.*]

LEE. Oh. Can I get the keys back before I forget? [AUSTIN *hesitates.*] You said I could borrow the car if I wanted, right? Isn't that what you said?

AUSTIN. Yeah. Right.

[AUSTIN *takes keys out of his pocket, sets them on table,* LEE *takes keys slowly, plays with them in his hand.*]

LEE. I could get a ranch, huh?

670 AUSTIN. Yeah. We have to write it first though.

LEE. Okay. Let's write it. [*Lights start dimming slowly to end of scene as* AUSTIN *types,* LEE *speaks.*] So they take off after each other straight into an endless black prairie. The sun is just comin' down and they can feel the night on their backs. What they don't know is that each one of 'em is afraid, see. Each one separately thinks that he's the only one that's afraid. And they keep ridin' like that straight into the night. Not knowing. And the one who's chasin' doesn't know where the other one is taking him. And the one who's being chased doesn't know where he's going.

[*Lights to black, typing stops in the dark, crickets fade.*]

---

[5] Ventura is a beach community about fifty miles northwest of Los Angeles.

ACT II

SCENE V

Morning. LEE *at the table in alcove with a set of golf clubs in a fancy leather bag,* AUSTIN *at sink washing a few dishes.*

AUSTIN.   He really liked it, huh?

680 LEE.   He wouldn't a' gave me these clubs if he didn't like it.

AUSTIN.   He gave you the clubs?

LEE.   Yeah. I told ya' he gave me the clubs. The bag too.

AUSTIN.   I thought he just loaned them to you.

LEE.   He said it was part a' the advance. A little gift like. Gesture of his good faith.

AUSTIN.   He's giving you an advance?

LEE.   Now what's so amazing about that? I told ya' it was a good story. You even said it was a good story.

AUSTIN.   Well that is really incredible Lee. You know how many guys spend
690   their whole lives down here trying to break into this business? Just trying to get in the door?

LEE [*pulling clubs out of bag, testing them*].   I got no idea. How many?

[*Pause.*]

AUSTIN.   How much of an advance is he giving you?

LEE.   Plenty. We were talkin' big money out there. Ninth hole is where I sealed the deal.

AUSTIN.   He made a firm commitment?

LEE.   Absolutely.

AUSTIN.   Well, I know Saul and he doesn't fool around when he says he likes something.

700 LEE.   I thought you said you didn't know him.

AUSTIN.   Well, I'm familiar with his tastes.

LEE.   I let him get two up on me goin' into the back nine. He was sure he had me cold. You shoulda' seen his face when I pulled out the old pitching wedge and plopped it pin-high, two feet from the cup. He 'bout shit his pants. "Where'd a guy like you ever learn how to play golf like that?," he says.

[LEE *laughs,* AUSTIN *stares at him.*]

AUSTIN.   'Course there's no contract yet. Nothing's final until it's on paper.

LEE.   It's final, all right. There's no way he's gonna' back out of it now. We gambled for it.

710 AUSTIN.   Saul, gambled?

LEE.   Yeah, sure. I mean he liked the outline already so he wasn't risking that much. I just guaranteed it with my short game.

[*Pause.*]

AUSTIN.   Well, we should celebrate or something. I think Mom left a bottle of champagne in the refrigerator. We should have a little toast.

[AUSTIN *gets glasses from cupboard, goes to refrigerator, pulls out bottle of champagne.*]

LEE.   You shouldn't oughta' take her champagne, Austin. She's gonna' miss that.

AUSTIN.   Oh, she's not going to mind. She'd be glad we put it to good use. I'll get her another bottle. Besides, it's perfect for the occasion.

[*Pause.*]

LEE.   Yer gonna' get a nice fee fer writin' the script a' course. Straight fee.

[AUSTIN *stops, stares at* LEE, *puts glasses and bottle on table, pause.*]

720 AUSTIN: I'm writing the script?

LEE.   That's what he said. Said we couldn't hire a better screenwriter in the whole town.

AUSTIN.   But I'm already working on a script. I've got my own project. I don't have time to write two scripts.

LEE.   No, he said he was gonna' drop that other one.

[*Pause.*]

AUSTIN.   What? You mean mine? He's going to drop mine and do yours instead?

LEE [*smiles*].   Now look, Austin, it's jest beginner's luck ya' know. I mean I sank a fifty foot putt for this deal. No hard feelings. [AUSTIN *goes to phone*
730   *on wall, grabs it, starts dialing.*] He's not gonna' be in, Austin. Told me he wouldn't be in 'till late this afternoon.

AUSTIN [*stays on phone, dialing, listens*].   I can't believe this. I just can't believe it. Are you sure he said that? Why would he drop mine?

LEE.   That's what he told me.

AUSTIN.   He can't do that without telling me first. Without talking to me at least. He wouldn't just make a decision like that without talking to me!

LEE.   Well I was kinda' surprised myself. But he was real enthusiastic about my story.

[AUSTIN *hangs up phone violently, paces.*]

AUSTIN.   What'd he say! Tell me everything he said!
740 LEE.   I been tellin' ya'! He said he liked the story a whole lot. It was the first authentic Western to come along in a decade.

AUSTIN.   He liked that story! Your story?

LEE.   Yeah! What's so surprisin' about that?

AUSTIN.   It's stupid! It's the dumbest story I ever heard in my life.

LEE.   Hey, hold on! That's my story yer talkin' about!

AUSTIN.   It's a bullshit story! It's idiotic. Two lamebrains chasing each other across Texas! Are you kidding? Who do you think's going to see a film like that?

LEE.   It's not a film! It's a movie. There's a big difference. That's somethin'
750   Saul told me.

AUSTIN.   Oh he did, huh?

Lee. Yeah, he said, "In this business we make movies, American movies. Leave the films to the French."

Austin. So you got real intimate with old Saul huh? He started pouring forth his vast knowledge of Cinema.

Lee. I think he liked me a lot, to tell ya' the truth. I think he felt I was somebody he could confide in.

Austin. What'd you do, beat him up or something?

Lee [*stands fast*]. Hey, I've about had it with the insults buddy! You think yer
760   the only one in the brain department here? Yer the only one that can sit around and cook things up? There's other people got ideas too, ya' know!

Austin. You must've done something. Threatened him or something. Now what'd you do Lee?

Lee. I convinced him!

[Lee *makes sudden menacing lunge toward* Austin, *wielding golf club above his head, stops himself, frozen moment, long pause,* Lee *lowers club.*]

Austin. Oh, Jesus. You didn't hurt him did you? [*Long silence,* Lee *sits back down at the table.*] Lee! Did you hurt him?

Lee. I didn't do nothin' to him! He liked my story. Pure and simple. He said it was the best story he's come across in a long, long time.

Austin. That's what he told me about my story! That's the same thing he
770   said to me.

Lee. Well, he musta' been lyin'. He musta' been lyin' to one of us anyway.

Austin. You can't come into this town and start pushing people around. They're gonna' put you away!

Lee. I never pushed anybody around! I beat him fair and square. [*Pause.*] They can't touch me anyway. They can't put a finger on me. I'm gone. I can come in through the window and go out through the door. They never knew what hit 'em. You, yer stuck. Yer the one that's stuck. Not me. So don't be warnin' me what to do in this town.

[*Pause,* Austin *crosses to table, sits at typewriter, rests.*]

Austin. Lee, come on, level with me will you? It doesn't make any sense that
780   suddenly he'd throw my idea out the window. I've been talking to him for months. I've got too much at stake. Everything's riding on this project.

Lee. What's yer idea?

Austin. It's just a simple love story.

Lee. What kinda' love story?

Austin [*stands, crosses into kitchen*]. I'm not telling you!

Lee. Ha! 'Fraid I'll steal it huh? Competition's gettin' kinda' close to home isn't it?

Austin. Where did Saul say he was going?

Lee. He was gonna' take my story to a couple studios.

790 Austin. That's *my* outline you know! I wrote that outline! You've got no right to be peddling it around.

Lee. You weren't ready to take credit for it last night.

Austin. Give me my keys!

Lee. What?

AUSTIN. The keys! I want my keys back!

LEE. Where you goin'?

AUSTIN. Just give me my keys! I gotta' take a drive. I gotta' get out of here for a while.

LEE. Where you gonna' go, Austin?

800 AUSTIN [*pause*]. I might just drive out to the desert for a while. I gotta think.

LEE. You can think here just as good. This is the perfect set-up for thinkin'. We got some writin' to do here, boy. Now let's just have us a little toast. Relax. We're partners now.

[LEE *pops the cork of the champagne bottle, pours two drinks as the lights fade to black.*]

SCENE VI

Afternoon. LEE *and* SAUL *in kitchen,* AUSTIN *in alcove.*

LEE. Now you tell him. You tell him, Mr. Kipper.

SAUL. Kimmer.

LEE. Kimmer. You tell him what you told me. He don't believe me.

AUSTIN. I don't want to hear it.

SAUL. It's really not a big issue, Austin. I was simply amazed by your brother's story and—

810 AUSTIN. Amazed? You lost a bet! You gambled with my material!

SAUL. That's really beside the point, Austin. I'm ready to go all the way with your brother's story. I think it has a great deal of merit.

AUSTIN. I don't want to hear about it, okay? Go tell it to the executives! Tell it to somebody who's going to turn it into a package deal or something. A T.V. series. Don't tell it to me.

SAUL. But I want to continue with your project too, Austin. It's not as though we can't do both. We're big enough for that aren't we?

AUSTIN. "We"? *I* can't do both! I don't know about "we."

LEE [*to* SAUL]. See, what'd I tell ya'. He's totally unsympathetic.

820 SAUL. Austin, there's no point in our going to another screenwriter for this. It just doesn't make sense. You're brothers. You know each other. There's a familiarity with the material that just wouldn't be possible otherwise.

AUSTIN. There's no familiarity with the material! None! I don't know what "Tornado Country" is. I don't know what a "gooseneck" is. And I don't want to know! [*Pointing to* LEE.] He's a hustler! He's a bigger hustler than you are! If you can't see that, then—

LEE [*to* AUSTIN]. Hey, now hold on. I didn't have to bring this bone back to you, boy. I persuaded Saul here that you were the right man for the job. You don't have to go throwin' up favors in my face.

830 AUSTIN. Favors! I'm the one who wrote the fuckin' outline! You can't even spell.

SAUL [*to* AUSTIN]. Your brother told me about the situation with your father.

[*Pause.*]

AUSTIN. What? [*Looks at* LEE.]

SAUL. That's right. Now we have a clear-cut deal here, Austin. We have big studio money standing behind this thing. Just on the basis of your outline.

Austin [*to* Saul]. What'd he tell you about my father?

Saul. Well—that he's destitute. He needs money.

Lee. That's right. He does.

[Austin *shakes his head, stares at them both.*]

Austin [*to* Lee]. And this little assignment is supposed to go toward the old
840   man? A charity project? Is that what this is? Did you cook this up on the
ninth green too?

Saul. It's a big slice, Austin.

Austin [*to* Lee]. I gave him money! I already gave him money. You know
that. He drank it all up!

Lee. This is a different deal here.

Saul. We can set up a trust for your father. A large sum of money. It can be
doled out to him in parcels so he can't misuse it.

Austin. Yeah, and who's doing the doling?

Saul. Your brother volunteered.

[Austin *laughs.*]

850 Lee. That's right. I'll make sure he uses it for groceries.

Austin [*to* Saul]. I'm not doing this script! I'm not writing this crap for you
or anybody else. You can't blackmail me into it. You can't threaten me into
it. There's no way I'm doing it. So just give it up. Both of you.

[*Long pause.*]

Saul. Well, that's it then. I mean this is an easy three hundred grand. Just
for a first draft. It's incredible, Austin. We've got three different studios all
trying to cut each other's throats to get this material. In one morning.
That's how hot it is.

Austin. Yeah, well you can afford to give me a percentage of the outline
then. And you better get the genius here an agent before he gets burned.

860 Lee. Saul's gonna' be my agent. Isn't that right, Saul?

Saul. That's right. [*To* Austin.] Your brother has really got something,
Austin. I've been around too long not to recognize it. Raw talent.

Austin. He's got a lota' balls is what he's got. He's taking you right down the
river.

Saul. Three hundred thousand, Austin. Just for a first draft. Now you've
never been offered that kind of money before.

Austin. I'm not writing it.

[*Pause.*]

Saul. I see. Well—

Lee. We'll just go to another writer then. Right, Saul? Just hire us somebody
870   with some enthusiasm. Somebody who can recognize the value of a good
story.

Saul. I'm sorry about this, Austin.

Austin. Yeah.

Saul. I mean I was hoping we could continue both things but now I don't
see how it's possible.

AUSTIN.   So you're dropping my idea altogether. Is that it? Just trade horses in midstream? After all these months of meetings.
SAUL.   I wish there was another way.
AUSTIN.   I've got everything riding on this, Saul. You know that. It's my only
880   shot. If this falls through—
SAUL.   I have to go with what my instincts tell me—
AUSTIN.   Your instincts!
SAUL.   My gut reaction.
AUSTIN.   You lost! That's your gut reaction. You lost a gamble. Now you're trying to tell me you like his story? How could you possibly fall for that story? It's as phony as Hoppalong Cassidy.[6] What do you see in it? I'm curious.
SAUL.   It has the ring of truth, Austin.
AUSTIN [*laughs*].   Truth?
890 LEE.   It is true.
SAUL.   Something about the real West.
AUSTIN.   Why? Because it's got horses? Because it's got grown men acting like little boys?
SAUL.   Something about the land. Your brother is speaking from experience.
AUSTIN.   So am I!
SAUL.   But nobody's interested in love these days, Austin. Let's face it.
LEE.   That's right.
AUSTIN [*to* SAUL].   He's been camped out on the desert for three months.
900   Talking to cactus. What's he know about what people wanna' see on the screen! I drive on the freeway every day. I swallow the smog. I watch the news in color. I shop in the Safeway. I'm the one who's in touch! Not him!
SAUL.   I have to go now, Austin.

[SAUL *starts to leave.*]

AUSTIN.   There's no such thing as the West anymore! It's a dead issue! It's dried up, Saul, and so are you.

[SAUL *stops and turns to* AUSTIN.]

SAUL.   Maybe you're right. But I have to take the gamble, don't I?
AUSTIN.   You're a fool to do this, Saul.
SAUL.   I've always gone on my hunches. Always. And I've never been wrong.
910   [*To* LEE]. I'll talk to you tomorrow, Lee.
LEE.   All right, Mr. Kimmer.
SAUL.   Maybe we could have some lunch.
LEE.   Fine with me. [*Smiles at* AUSTIN.]
SAUL.   I'll give you a ring.

[SAUL *exits, lights to black as brothers look at each other from a distance.*]

---

[6] The character of Hoppalong Cassidy was created by William Boyd in a series of low-budget films during the 1930s and 1940s. In the early 1950s the televised *Hoppalong Cassidy* show was a hit on NBC.

SCENE VII

Night. Coyotes, crickets, sound of typewriter in dark, candlelight up on LEE *at type-writer struggling to type with one finger system,* AUSTIN *sits sprawled out on kitchen floor with whiskey bottle, drunk.*

AUSTIN [*singing, from floor*].

"Red sails in the sunset
Way out on the blue
Please carry my loved one
Home safely to me

Red sails in the sunset—"

920 LEE [*slams fist on table*].   Hey! Knock it off will ya'! I'm tryin' to concentrate
here.
AUSTIN [*laughs*].   You're tryin' to concentrate?
LEE.   Yeah. That's right.
AUSTIN.   Now you're tryin' to concentrate.
LEE.   Between you, the coyotes and the crickets a thought don't have much
of a chance.
AUSTIN.   "Between me, the coyotes and the crickets." What a great title.
LEE.   I don't need a title! I need a thought.
AUSTIN [*laughs*].   A thought! Here's a thought for ya'—
930 LEE.   I'm not askin' fer yer thoughts! I got my own. I can do this thing on my
own.
AUSTIN.   You're going to write an entire script on your own?
LEE.   That's right.

[*Pause.*]

AUSTIN.   Here's a thought. Saul Kimmer—
LEE.   Shut up will ya'!
AUSTIN.   He thinks we're the same person.
LEE.   Don't get cute.
AUSTIN.   He does! He's lost his mind. Poor old Saul. [*Giggles.*] Thinks we're
one and the same.
940 LEE.   Why don't you ease up on that champagne.
AUSTIN [*holding up bottle*].   This isn't champagne any more. We went through
the champagne a long time ago. This is serious stuff. The days of cham-
pagne are long gone.
LEE.   Well, go outside and drink it.
AUSTIN.   I'm enjoying your company, Lee. For the first time since your arrival I am finally enjoying your company. And now you want me to go
outside and drink alone?
LEE.   That's right.

[LEE *reads through paper in typewriter, makes an erasure.*]

AUSTIN.   You think you'll make more progress if you're alone? You might
950 drive yourself crazy.
LEE.   I could have this thing done in a night if I had a little silence.
AUSTIN.   Well you'd still have the crickets to contend with. The coyotes. The

sounds of the Police Helicopters above the neighborhood. Slashing their searchlights down through the streets. Hunting for the likes of you.

LEE.   I'm a screenwriter now! I'm legitimate.

AUSTIN [*laughing*].   A screenwriter!

LEE.   That's right. I'm on salary. That's more'n I can say for you. I got an advance coming.

AUSTIN.   This is true. This is very true. An advance. [*Pause*]. Well, maybe I
960   oughta' go out and try my hand at your trade. Since you're doing so good at mine.

LEE.   Ha!

[LEE *attempts to type some more but gets the ribbon tangled up, starts trying to re-thread it as they continue talking.*]

AUSTIN.   Well why not? You don't think I've got what it takes to sneak into people's houses and steal their T.V.s?

LEE.   You couldn't steal a toaster without losin' yer lunch.

[AUSTIN *stands with a struggle, supports himself by the sink.*]

AUSTIN.   You don't think I could sneak into somebody's house and steal a toaster?

LEE.   Go take a shower or somethin' will ya!

[LEE *gets more tangled up with the typewriter ribbon, pulling it out of the machine as though it was fishing line.*]

AUSTIN.   You really don't think I could steal a crumby toaster? How much
970   you wanna' bet I can't steal a toaster! How much? Go ahead! You're a gambler aren't you? Tell me how much yer willing to put on the line. Some part of your big advance? Oh, you haven't got that yet have you. I forgot.

LEE.   All right. I'll bet you your car that you can't steal a toaster without gettin' busted.

AUSTIN.   You already got my car!

LEE.   Okay, your house then.

AUSTIN.   What're you gonna' give me! I'm not talkin' about my house and my car, I'm talkin' about what are you gonna' give me. You don't have nothin' to give me.

980 LEE.   I'll give you—shared screen credit. How 'bout that? I'll have it put in the contract that this was written by the both of us.

AUSTIN.   I don't want my name on that piece of shit! I want something of value. You got anything of value? You got any tidbits from the desert? Any Rattlesnake bones? I'm not a greedy man. Any little personal treasure will suffice.

LEE.   I'm gonna' just kick yer ass out in a minute.

AUSTIN.   Oh, so now you're gonna' kick me out! Now I'm the intruder. I'm the one who's invading your precious privacy.

LEE.   I'm trying to do some screenwriting here!!

[LEE *stands, picks up typewriter, slams it down hard on table, pause, silence except for crickets.*]

990 AUSTIN.   Well, you got everything you need. You got plenty a' coffee? Groceries. You got a car. A contract. [*Pause.*] Might need a new typewriter

ribbon but other than that you're pretty well fixed. I'll just leave ya' alone
for a while.

> [AUSTIN *tries to steady himself to leave,* LEE *makes a move toward him.*]

LEE. Where you goin'?
AUSTIN. Don't worry about me. I'm not the one to worry about.

> [AUSTIN *weaves toward exit, stops.*]

LEE. What're you gonna' do? Just go wander out into the night?
AUSTIN. I'm gonna' make a little tour.
LEE. Why don't ya' just go to bed for Christ's sake. Yer makin' me sick.
AUSTIN. I can take care a' myself. Don't worry about me.

[AUSTIN *weaves badly in another attempt to exit, he crashes to the floor,* LEE *goes to him but remains standing.*]

1000 LEE. You want me to call your wife for ya' or something?
AUSTIN [*from floor*]. My wife?
LEE. Yeah. I mean maybe she can help ya' out. Talk to ya' or something'.
AUSTIN [*struggles to stand again*]. She's five hundred miles away. North. North
of here. Up in the North country where things are calm. I don't need any
help. I'm gonna' go outside and I'm gonna' steal a toaster. I'm gonna'
steal some other stuff too. I might even commit bigger crimes. Bigger than
you ever dreamed of. Crimes beyond the imagination!

> [AUSTIN *manages to get himself vertical, tries to head for exit again.*]

LEE. Just hang on a minute, Austin.
AUSTIN. Why? What for? You don't need my help, right? You got a handle
1010   on the project. Besides, I'm lookin' forward to the smell of the night. The
bushes. Orange blossoms. Dust in the driveways. Rain bird sprinklers.
Lights in people's houses. You're right about the lights, Lee. Everybody
else is livin' the life. Indoors. Safe. This is a Paradise down here. You know
that? We're livin' in a Paradise. We've forgotten about that.
LEE. You sound just like the old man now.
AUSTIN. Yeah, well we all sound alike when we're sloshed. We just sorta'
echo each other.
LEE. Maybe if we could work on this together we could bring him back out
here. Get him settled down some place.

[AUSTIN *turns violently toward* LEE, *takes a swing at him, misses and crashes to the floor again,* LEE *stays standing.*]

1020 AUSTIN. I don't want him out here! I've had it with him! I went all the way
out there! I went out of my way. I gave him money and all he did was play
Al Jolson[7] records and spit at me! I gave him money!

> [*Pause.*]

LEE. Just help me a little with the characters, all right? You know how to do
it, Austin.

---

[7] Al Jolson (1888–1950), a comedian and singer, was born in Russia as Asa Yoelson, but
became famous in the United States for his song-and-dance routines in blackface.

AUSTIN [*on floor, laughs*].   The characters!

LEE.   Yeah. You know. The way they talk and stuff. I can hear it in my head but I can't get it down on paper.

AUSTIN.   What characters?

LEE.   The guys. The guys in the story.

1030 AUSTIN.   Those aren't characters.

LEE.   Whatever you call 'em then. I need to write somethin' out.

AUSTIN.   Those are illusions of characters.

LEE.   I don't give a damn what ya' call 'em! You know what I'm talkin' about!

AUSTIN.   Those are fantasies of a long lost boyhood.

LEE.   I gotta' write somethin' out on paper!!

[*Pause.*]

AUSTIN.   What for? Saul's gonna' get you a fancy screenwriter isn't he?

LEE.   I wanna' do it myself!

AUSTIN.   Then do it! Yer on your own now, old buddy. You bulldogged yer way into contention. Now you gotta' carry it through.

1040 LEE.   I will but I need some advice. Just a couple a' things. Come on, Austin. Just help me get 'em talkin' right. It won't take much.

AUSTIN.   Oh, now you're having a little doubt huh? What happened? The pressure's on, boy. This is it. You gotta' come up with it now. You don't come up with a winner on your first time out they just cut your head off. They don't give you a second chance ya' know.

LEE.   I got a good story! I know it's a good story. I just need a little help is all.

AUSTIN.   Not from me. Not from yer little old brother. I'm retired.

LEE.   You could save this thing for me, Austin. I'd give ya' half the money.

1050 I would. I only need half anyway. With this kinda' money I could be a long time down the road. I'd never bother ya' again. I promise. You'd never even see me again.

AUSTIN [*still on floor*].   You'd disappear?

LEE.   I would for sure.

AUSTIN.   Where would you disappear to?

LEE.   That don't matter. I got plenty a' places.

AUSTIN.   Nobody can disappear. The old man tried that. Look where it got him. He lost his teeth.

LEE.   He never had any money.

1060 AUSTIN.   I don't mean that. I mean his teeth! His real teeth. First he lost his real teeth, then he lost his false teeth. You never knew that did ya'? He never confided in you.

LEE.   Nah, I never knew that.

AUSTIN.   You wanna' drink? [AUSTIN *offers bottle to* LEE, LEE *takes it, sits down on kitchen floor with* AUSTIN, *they share the bottle.*] Yeah, he lost his real teeth one at a time. Woke up every morning with another tooth lying on the mattress. Finally, he decides he's gotta' get 'em all pulled out but he doesn't have any money. Middle of Arizona with no money and no insurance and every morning another tooth is lying on the mattress. [*Takes a drink.*] So

1070 what does he do?

LEE.   I dunno'. I never knew about that.

AUSTIN.   He begs the government. G.I. Bill or some damn thing. Some

pension plan he remembers in the back of his head. And they send him
out the money.

LEE.   They did?

> [*They keep trading the bottle between them, taking drinks.*]

AUSTIN.   Yeah. They send him the money but it's not enough money. Costs
a lot to have all yer teeth yanked. They charge by the individual tooth, ya'
know. I mean one tooth isn't equal to another tooth. Some are more
expensive. Like the big ones in the back—

080   LEE.   So what happened?

AUSTIN.   So he locates a Mexican dentist in Juarez who'll do the whole thing
for a song. And he takes off hitchhiking to the border.

LEE.   Hitchhiking?

AUSTIN.   Yeah. So how long you think it takes him to get to the border? A
man his age.

LEE.   I dunno.

AUSTIN.   Eight days it takes him. Eight days in the rain and the sun and every
day he's droppin' teeth on the blacktop and nobody'll pick him up 'cause
his mouth's full a' blood. [*Pause, they drink.*] So finally he stumbles into the

090   dentist. Dentist takes all his money and all his teeth. And there he is, in
Mexico, with his gums sewed up and his pockets empty.

> [*Long silence,* AUSTIN *drinks.*]

LEE.   That's it?

AUSTIN.   Then I go out to see him, see. I go out there and I take him out for
a nice Chinese dinner. But he doesn't eat. All he wants to do is drink
Martinis outa' plastic cups. And he takes his teeth out and lays 'em on the
table 'cause he can't stand the feel of 'em. And we ask the waitress for one
a' those doggie bags to take the Chop Suey home in. So he drops his teeth
in the doggie bag along with the Chop Suey. And then we go out to hit all
the bars up and down the highway. Says he wants to introduce me to all his

1100   buddies. And in one a' those bars, in one a' those bars up and down the
highway, he left that doggie bag with his teeth laying in the Chop Suey.

LEE.   You never found it?

AUSTIN.   We went back but we never did find it. [*Pause.*] Now that's a true
story. True to life.

> [*They drink as lights fade to black.*]

SCENE VIII

*Very early morning, between night and day. No crickets, coyotes yapping feverishly in
distance before light comes up, a small fire blazes up in the dark from alcove area,
sound of* LEE *smashing typewriter with a golf club, lights coming up,* LEE *seen
smashing typewriter methodically then dropping pages of his script into a burning bowl
set on the floor of alcove, flames leap up,* AUSTIN *has a whole bunch of stolen toasters
lined up on the sink counter along with* LEE's *stolen T.V., the toasters are of a wide
variety of models, mostly chrome,* AUSTIN *goes up and down the line of toasters,*

breathing on them and polishing them with a dish towel, both men are drunk, empty whiskey bottles and beer cans litter floor of kitchen, they share a half empty bottle on one of the chairs in the alcove, LEE *keeps periodically taking deliberate ax-chops at the typewriter using a nine-iron as* AUSTIN *speaks, all of their mother's house plants are dead and drooping.*

AUSTIN [*polishing toasters*].   There's gonna' be a general lack of toast in the neighborhood this morning. Many, many unhappy, bewildered breakfast faces. I guess it's best not to even think of the victims. Not to even entertain it. Is that the right psychology?

LEE [*pauses*].   What?

1110 AUSTIN.   Is that the correct criminal psychology? Not to think of the victims?

LEE.   What victims?

[LEE *takes another swipe at typewriter with nine-iron, adds pages to the fire.*]

AUSTIN.   The victims of crime. Of breaking and entering. I mean is it a prerequisite for a criminal not to have a conscience?

LEE.   Ask a criminal. [*Pause,* LEE *stares at* AUSTIN.] What're you gonna' do with all those toasters? That's the dumbest thing I ever saw in my life.

AUSTIN.   I've got hundreds of dollars worth of household appliances here. You may not realize that.

LEE.   Yeah, and how many hundreds of dollars did you walk right past?

AUSTIN.   It was toasters you challenged me to. Only toasters. I ignored every
1120   other temptation.

LEE.   I never challenged you! That's no challenge. Anybody can steal a toaster.

[LEE *smashes typewriter again.*]

AUSTIN.   You don't have to take it out on my typewriter ya' know. It's not the machine's fault that you can't write. It's a sin to do that to a good machine.

LEE.   A sin?

AUSTIN.   When you consider all the writers who never even had a machine. Who would have given an eyeball for a good typewriter. Any typewriter.

[LEE *smashes typewriter again.*]

AUSTIN [*polishing toasters*].   All the ones who wrote on matchbook covers. Paper bags. Toilet paper. Who had their writing destroyed by their jailers.
1130   Who persisted beyond all odds. Those writers would find it hard to understand your actions.

[LEE *comes down on typewriter with one final crushing blow of the nine-iron then collapses in one of the chairs, takes a drink from bottle, pause.*]

AUSTIN [*after pause*].   Not to mention demolishing a perfectly good golf club. What about all the struggling golfers? What about Lee Trevino? What do you think he would've said when he was batting balls around with broomsticks at the age of nine. Impoverished.

[*Pause.*]

LEE.   What time is it anyway?

AUSTIN.   No idea. Time stands still when you're havin' fun.

LEE.　Is it too late to call a woman? You know any women?

AUSTIN.　I'm a married man.

140 LEE.　I mean a local woman.

[AUSTIN *looks out at light through window above sink.*]

AUSTIN.　It's either too late or too early. You're the nature enthusiast. Can't you tell the time by the light in the sky? Orient yourself around the North Star or something?

LEE.　I can't tell anything.

AUSTIN.　Maybe you need a little breakfast. Some toast! How 'bout some toast?

[AUSTIN *goes to cupboard, pulls out loaf of bread and starts dropping slices into every toaster,* LEE *stays sitting, drinks, watches* AUSTIN.]

LEE.　I don't need toast. I need a woman.

AUSTIN.　A woman isn't the answer. Never was.

LEE.　I'm not talkin' about permanent. I'm talkin' about temporary.

150 AUSTIN [*putting toast in toasters*].　We'll just test the merits of these little demons. See which brands have a tendency to burn. See which one can produce a perfectly golden piece of fluffy toast.

LEE.　How much gas you got in yer car?

AUSTIN.　I haven't driven my car for days now. So I haven't had an opportunity to look at the gas gauge.

LEE.　Take a guess. You think there's enough to get me to Bakersfield?[8]

AUSTIN.　Bakersfield? What's in Bakersfield?

LEE.　Just never mind what's in Bakersfield! You think there's enough goddamn gas in the car!

160 AUSTIN.　Sure.

LEE.　Sure. You could care less, right. Let me run outa' gas on the Grapevine. You could give a shit.

AUSTIN.　I'd say there was enough gas to get you just about anywhere, Lee. With your determination and guts.

LEE.　What the hell time is it anyway?

[LEE *pulls out his wallet, starts going through dozens of small pieces of paper with phone numbers written on them, drops some on the floor, drops others in the fire.*]

AUSTIN.　Very early. This is the time of morning when the coyotes kill people's cocker spaniels. Did you hear them? That's what they were doing out there. Luring innocent pets away from their homes.

LEE [*searching through his papers*].　What's the area code for Bakersfield? You 1170　know?

AUSTIN.　You could always call the operator.

LEE.　I can't stand that voice they give ya'.

AUSTIN.　What voice?

LEE.　That voice that warns you that if you'd only tried harder to find the number in the phone book you wouldn't have to be calling the operator to begin with.

---

[8] Bakersfield is an inland city about one hundred miles north and slightly east of Los Angeles.

[LEE *gets up, holding a slip of paper from his wallet, stumbles toward phone on wall, yanks receiver, starts dialing.*]

AUSTIN.   Well I don't understand why you'd want to talk to anybody else anyway. I mean you can talk to me. I'm your brother.

LEE [*dialing*].   I wanna' talk to a woman. I haven't heard a woman's voice in
1180   a long time.

AUSTIN.   Not since the Botanist?

LEE.   What?

AUSTIN.   Nothing. [*Starts singing as he tends toast.*]

> "Red sails in the sunset
> Way out on the blue
> Please carry my loved one
> Home safely to me"

LEE.   Hey, knock it off will ya'! This is long distance here.

AUSTIN.   Bakersfield?

1190 LEE.   Yeah, Bakersfield. It's Kern County.

AUSTIN.   Well, what County are *we* in?

LEE.   You better get yourself a 7-Up, boy.

AUSTIN.   One County's as good as another.

[AUSTIN *hums "Red Sails" softly as* LEE *talks on phone.*]

LEE [*to phone*].   Yeah, operator look—first off I wanna' know the area code for Bakersfield. Right. Bakersfield! Okay. Good. Now I wanna' know if you can help me track somebody down. [*Pause.*] No, no I mean a phone number. Just a phone number. Okay. [*Holds a piece of paper up and reads it.*] Okay, the name is Melly Ferguson. Melly. [*Pause.*] I dunno'. Melly. Maybe. Yeah. Maybe Melanie. Yeah. Melanie Ferguson. Okay. [*Pause.*] What? I
1200   can't hear ya' so good. Sounds like yer under the ocean. [*Pause.*] You got ten Melanie Fergusons? How could that be? Ten Melanie Fergusons in Bakersfield? Well gimme all of 'em then. [*Pause.*] What d'ya' mean? Gimmie all ten Melanie Fergusons! That's right. Just a second. [*To* AUSTIN.] Gimme a pen.

AUSTIN.   I don't have a pen.

LEE.   Gimme a pencil then!

AUSTIN.   I don't have a pencil.

LEE [*to phone*].   Just a second, operator. [*To* AUSTIN.] Yer a writer and ya' don't have a pen or a pencil!

1210 AUSTIN.   I'm not a writer. You're a writer.

LEE.   I'm on the phone here! Get me a pen or a pencil.

AUSTIN.   I gotta' watch the toast.

LEE [*to phone*].   Hang on a second, operator.

[LEE *lets the phone drop then starts pulling all the drawers in the kitchen out on the floor and dumping the contents, searching for a pencil,* AUSTIN *watches him casually.*]

LEE [*crashing through drawers, throwing contents around kitchen*].   This is the last time I try to live with people, boy! I can't believe it. Here I am! Here I am again in a desperate situation! This would never happen out on the desert.

I would never be in this kinda' situation out on the desert. Isn't there a pen or a pencil in this house! Who lives in this house anyway!

AUSTIN.   Our mother.

1220 LEE.   How come she don't have a pen or a pencil! She's a social person isn't she? Doesn't she have to make shopping lists? She's gotta' have a pencil. [*Finds a pencil.*] Aaha! [*He rushes back to phone, picks up receiver.*] All right operator. Operator? Hey! Operator! Goddamnit!

[LEE *rips the phone off the wall and throws it down, goes back to chair and falls into it, drinks, long pause.*]

AUSTIN.   She hung up?

LEE.   Yeah, she hung up. I knew she was gonna' hang up. I could hear it in her voice.

[LEE *starts going through his slips of paper again.*]

AUSTIN.   Well, you're probably better off staying here with me anyway. I'll take care of you.

LEE.   I don't need takin' care of! Not by you anyway.

1230 AUSTIN.   Toast is almost ready.

[AUSTIN *starts buttering all the toast as it pops up.*]

LEE.   I don't want any toast!

[*Long pause.*]

AUSTIN.   You gotta' eat something. Can't just drink. How long have we been drinking, anyway?

LEE [*looking through slips of paper.*]   Maybe it was Fresno. What's the area code for Fresno? How could I have lost that number! She was beautiful.

[*Pause.*]

AUSTIN.   Why don't you just forget about that, Lee. Forget about the woman.

LEE.   She had green eyes. You know what green eyes do to me?

AUSTIN.   I know but you're not gonna' get it on with her now anyway. It's dawn already. She's in Bakersfield for Christ's sake.

[*Long pause,* LEE *considers the situation.*]

1240 LEE.   Yeah. [*Looks at windows.*] It's dawn?

AUSTIN.   Let's just have some toast and—

LEE.   What is this bullshit with the toast anyway! You make it sound like salvation or something. I don't want any goddamn toast! How many times I gotta' tell ya'! [LEE *gets up, crosses upstage to windows in alcove, looks out,* AUSTIN *butters toast.*]

AUSTIN.   Well it is like salvation sort of. I mean the smell. I love the smell of toast. And the sun's coming up. It makes me feel like anything's possible. Ya' know?

LEE [*back to* AUSTIN, *facing windows upstage.*]   So go to church why don't ya'.

1250 AUSTIN.   Like a beginning. I love beginnings.

LEE.   Oh yeah. I've always been kinda' partial to endings myself.

AUSTIN.   What if I come with you, Lee?

LEE [*pause as* LEE *turns toward* AUSTIN].   What?

AUSTIN.   What if I come with you out to the desert?

LEE.   Are you kiddin'?

AUSTIN.   No. I'd just like to see what it's like.

LEE.   You wouldn't last a day out there pal.

AUSTIN.   That's what you said about the toasters. You said I couldn't steal a toaster either.

1260   LEE.   A toaster's got nothin' to do with the desert.

AUSTIN.   I could make it, Lee. I'm not that helpless. I can cook.

LEE.   Cook?

AUSTIN.   I can.

LEE.   So what! You can cook. Toast.

AUSTIN.   I can make fires. I know how to get fresh water from condensation.

[AUSTIN *stacks buttered toast up in a tall stack on plate.*]

[LEE *slams table.*]

LEE.   It's not somethin' you learn out of a Boy Scout handbook!

AUSTIN.   Well how do you learn it then! How're you supposed to learn it!

[*Pause.*]

LEE.   Ya' just learn it, that's all. Ya' learn it 'cause ya' have to learn it. You don't *have* to learn it.

1270   AUSTIN.   You could teach me.

LEE [*stands*].   What're you, crazy or somethin'? You went to college. Here, you are down here, rollin' in bucks. Floatin' up and down in elevators. And you wanna' learn how to live on the desert!

AUSTIN.   I do, Lee. I really do. There's nothin' down here for me. There never was. When we were kids here it was different. There was a life here then. But now—I keep comin' down here thinkin' it's the fifties or somethin'. I keep finding myself getting off the freeway at familiar landmarks that turn out to be unfamiliar. On the way to appointments. Wandering down streets I thought I recognized that turn out to be replicas of streets

1280   I remember. Streets I misremember. Streets I can't tell if I lived on or saw in a postcard. Fields that don't even exist anymore.

LEE.   There's no point cryin' about that now.

AUSTIN.   There's nothin' real down here, Lee! Least of all me!

LEE.   Well I can't save you from that!

AUSTIN.   You can let me come with you.

LEE.   No dice, pal.

AUSTIN.   You could let me come with you, Lee!

LEE.   Hey, do you actually think I chose to live out in the middle a' nowhere? Do ya'? Ya' think it's some kinda' philosophical decision I took or some-

1290   thin'? I'm livin' out there 'cause I can't make it here! And yer bitchin' to me about all yer success!

AUSTIN.   I'd cash it all in in a second. That's the truth.

LEE [*pause, shakes his head*].   I can't believe this.

AUSTIN.   Let me go with you.

LEE.   Stop sayin' that will ya'! Yer worse than a dog.

[AUSTIN *offers out the plate of neatly stacked toast to* LEE.]

AUSTIN.   You want some toast?

[LEE *suddenly explodes and knocks the plate out of* AUSTIN's *hand, toast goes flying, long frozen moment where it appears* LEE *might go all the way this time when* AUSTIN *breaks it by slowly lowering himself to his knees and begins gathering the scattered toast from the floor and stacking it back on the plate,* LEE *begins to circle* AUSTIN *in a slow, predatory way, crushing pieces of toast in his wake, no words for a while,* AUSTIN *keeps gathering toast, even the crushed pieces.*]

LEE.   Tell ya' what I'll do, little brother. I might just consider makin' you a deal. Little trade. [AUSTIN *continues gathering toast as* LEE *circles him through this.*] You write me up this screenplay thing just like I tell ya'. I mean you
1300   can use all yer usual tricks and stuff. Yer fancy language. Yer artistic hocus pocus. But ya' gotta' write everything like I say. Every move. Every time they run outa' gas, they run outa' gas. Every they wanna' jump on a horse, they do just that. If they wanna' stay in Texas, by God they'll stay in Texas! [*Keeps circling.*] And you finish the whole thing up for me. Top to bottom. And you put my name on it. And I own all the rights. And every dime goes in my pocket. You do all that and I'll sure enough take ya' with me to the desert. [LEE *stops, pause, looks down at* AUSTIN.] How's that sound?

[*Pause as* AUSTIN *stands slowly holding plate of demolished toast, their faces are very close, pause.*]

AUSTIN.   It's a deal.

[LEE *stares straight into* AUSTIN's *eyes, then he slowly takes a piece of toast off the plate, raises it to his mouth and takes a huge crushing bite never taking his eyes off* AUSTIN's, *as* LEE *crunches into the toast the lights black out.*]

SCENE IX

Mid-day. No sound, blazing heat, the stage is ravaged; bottles, toasters, smashed typewriter, ripped out telephone, etc. All the debris from previous scene is now starkly visible in intense yellow light, the effect should be like a desert junkyard at high noon, the coolness of the preceding scenes is totally obliterated. AUSTIN *is seated at table in alcove, shirt open, pouring with sweat, hunched over a writing notebook, scribbling notes desperately with a ballpoint pen.* LEE *with no shirt, beer in hand, sweat pouring down his chest, is walking a slow circle around the table, picking his way through the objects, sometimes kicking them aside.*

LEE [*as he walks*].   All right, read it back to me. Read it back to me!
1310 AUSTIN [*scribbling at top speed*].   Just a second.
LEE.   Come on, come on! Just read what ya' got.
AUSTIN.   I can't keep up! It's not the same as if I had a typewriter.
LEE.   Just read what we got so far. Forget about the rest.
AUSTIN.   All right. Let's see—okay—[*Wipes sweat from his face, reads as* LEE *circles.*] Luke says uh—

LEE. Luke?

AUSTIN. Yeah.

LEE. His name's Luke? All right, all right—we can change the names later. What's he say? Come on, come on.

1320 AUSTIN. He says uh—[*Reading.*] "I told ya' you were a fool to follow me in here. I know this prairie like the back a' my hand."

LEE. No, no, no! That's not what I said. I never said that.

AUSTIN. That's what I wrote.

LEE. It's not what I said. I never said "like the back a' my hand." That's stupid. That's one a' those—whadya' call it? Whadya' call that?

AUSTIN. What?

LEE. Whadya' call it when somethin's been said a thousand times before. Whadya' call that?

AUSTIN. Um—a cliché?

1330 LEE. Yeah. That's right. Cliché. That's what that is. A cliché. "The back a' my hand." That's stupid.

AUSTIN. That's what you said.

LEE. I never said that! And even if I did, that's where yer supposed to come in. That's where yer supposed to change it to somethin' better.

AUSTIN. Well how am I supposed to do that and write down what you say at the same time?

LEE. Ya' just do, that's all! You hear a stupid line you change it. That's yer job.

AUSTIN. All right. [*Makes more notes.*]

1340 LEE. What're you changin' it to?

AUSTIN. I'm not changing it. I'm just trying to catch up.

LEE. Well change it! We gotta' change that, we can't leave that in there like that. ". . . the back a' my hand." That's dumb.

AUSTIN [*stops writing, sits back*]. All right.

LEE [*pacing*]. So what'll we change it to?

AUSTIN. Um—How 'bout—"I'm on intimate terms with this prairie."

LEE [*to himself considering line as he walks*]. "I'm on intimate terms with this prairie." Intimate terms, intimate terms. Intimate—that means like uh—sexual right?

1350 AUSTIN. Well—yeah—or—

LEE. He's on sexual terms with the prairie? How dya' figure that?

AUSTIN. Well it doesn't necessarily have to mean sexual.

LEE. What's it mean then?

AUSTIN. It means uh—close—personal—

LEE. All right. How's it sound? Put it into the uh—the line there. Read it back. Let's see how it sounds. [*To himself.*] "Intimate terms."

AUSTIN [*scribbles in notebook*]. Okay. It'd go something like this: [*Reads.*] "I told ya' you were a fool to follow me in here. I'm on intimate terms with this prairie."

1360 LEE. That's good. I like that. That's real good.

AUSTIN. You do?

LEE. Yeah. Don't you?

AUSTIN. Sure.

LEE. Sounds original now. "Intimate terms." That's good. Okay. Now we're cookin'! That has a real ring to it.

[Austin *makes more notes,* Lee *walks around, pours beer on his arms and rubs it over his chest feeling good about the new progress, as he does this* Mom *enters unobtrusively down left with her luggage, she stops and stares at the scene still holding luggage as the two men continue, unaware of her presence,* Austin *absorbed in his writing,* Lee *cooling himself off with beer.*]

Lee [*continues*]. "He's on intimate terms with this prairie." Sounds real mysterious and kinda' threatening at the same time.

Austin [*writing rapidly*]. Good.

Lee. Now—[Lee *turns and suddenly sees* Mom, *he stares at her for a while, she*
1370   *stares back,* Austin *keeps writing feverishly, not noticing,* Lee *walks slowly over to*
Mom *and takes a closer look, long pause.*]

Lee. Mom?

[Austin *looks up suddenly from his writing, sees* Mom, *stands quickly, long pause,*
Mom *surveys the damage.*]

Austin. Mom. What're you doing back?
Mom. I'm back.
Lee. Here, lemme take those for ya.

[Lee *sets beer on counter than takes both her bags but doesn't know where to set them
down in the sea of junk so he just keeps holding them.*]

Austin. I wasn't expecting you back so soon. I thought uh— How was
   Alaska?
Mom. Fine.
Lee. See any igloos?
1380   Mom. No. Just glaciers.
Austin. Cold huh?
Mom. What?
Austin. It must've been cold up there?
Mom. Not really.
Lee. Musta' been colder than this here. I mean we're havin' a real scorcher
   here.
Mom. Oh? [*She looks at damage.*]
Lee. Yeah. Must be in the hundreds.
Austin. You wanna' take your coat off, Mom?
1390   Mom. No. [*Pause, she surveys space.*] What happened in here?
Austin. Oh um— Me and Lee were just sort of celebrating and uh—
Mom. Celebrating?
Austin. Yeah. Uh— Lee sold a screenplay. A story, I mean.
Mom. Lee did?
Austin. Yeah.
Mom. Not you?
Austin. No. Him.
Mom [*to* Lee]. You sold a screenplay?
Lee. Yeah. That's right. We're just sorta' finishing it up right now. That's
1400   what we're doing here.
Austin. Me and Lee are going out to the desert to live.
Mom. You and Lee?

AUSTIN.   Yeah. I'm taking off with Lee.

MOM [*she looks back and forth at each of them, pause*].   You gonna go live with your father?

AUSTIN.   No. We're going to a different desert Mom.

MOM.   I see. Well, you'll probably wind up on the same desert sooner or later. What're all these toasters doing here?

AUSTIN.   Well—we had kind of a contest.

1410 MOM.   Contest?

LEE.   Yeah.

AUSTIN.   Lee won.

MOM.   Did you win a lot of money, Lee?

LEE.   Well not yet. It's comin' in any day now.

MOM [*to* LEE].   What happened to your shirt?

LEE.   Oh. I was sweatin' like a pig and I took it off.

[AUSTIN *grabs* LEE'*s shirt off the table and tosses it to him,* LEE *sets down suitcases and puts his shirt on.*]

MOM.   Well it's one hell of a mess in here isn't it?

AUSTIN.   Yeah, I'll clean it up for you, Mom. I just didn't know you were coming back so soon.

1420 MOM.   I didn't either.

AUSTIN.   What happened?

MOM.   Nothing. I just started missing all my plants.

[*She notices dead plants.*]

AUSTIN.   Oh.

MOM.   Oh, they're all dead aren't they. [*She crosses toward them, examines them closely.*] You didn't get a chance to water I guess.

AUSTIN.   I was doing it and then Lee came and—

LEE.   Yeah I just distracted him a whole lot here, Mom. It's not his fault.

[*Pause, as* MOM *stares at plants.*]

MOM.   Oh well, one less thing to take care of I guess. [*Turns toward brothers.*] Oh, that reminds me— You boys will probably never guess who's in town.

1430   Try and guess.

[*Long pause, brothers stare at her.*]

AUSTIN.   Whadya' mean, Mom?

MOM.   Take a guess. Somebody very important has come to town. I read it, coming down on the Greyhound.

LEE.   Somebody very important?

MOM.   See if you can guess. You'll never guess.

AUSTIN.   Mom—we're trying to uh—[*Points to writing pad.*]

MOM.   Picasso. [*pause*] Picasso's in town. Isn't that incredible? Right now.

[*Pause.*]

AUSTIN.   Picasso's dead, Mom.

MOM.   No, he's not dead. He's visiting the museum. I read it on the bus. We

1440   have to go down there and see him.

AUSTIN. Mom—

MOM. This is the chance of a lifetime. Can you imagine? We could all go down and meet him. All three of us.

LEE. Uh— I don't think I'm really up fer meetin' anybody right now. I'm uh— What's his name?

MOM. Picasso! Picasso! You've never heard of Picasso? Austin, you've heard of Picasso.

AUSTIN. Mom, we're not going to have time.

MOM. It won't take long. We'll just hop in the car and go down there. An opportunity like this doesn't come along every day.

AUSTIN. We're gonna' be leavin' here, Mom!

[*Pause.*]

MOM. Oh.

LEE. Yeah.

[*Pause.*]

MOM. You're both leaving?

LEE [*looks at* AUSTIN]. Well we were thinkin' about that before but now I—

AUSTIN. No, we are! We're both leaving. We've got it all planned.

MOM [*to* AUSTIN]. Well you can't leave. You have a family.

AUSTIN. I'm leaving. I'm getting out of here.

LEE [*to* MOM]. I don't really think Austin's cut out for the desert do you?

MOM. No. He's not.

AUSTIN. I'm going with you, Lee!

MOM. He's too thin.

LEE. Yeah, he'd just burn up out there.

AUSTIN [*to* LEE]. We just gotta' finish this screenplay and then we're gonna' take off. That's the plan. That's what you said. Come on, let's get back to work, Lee.

LEE. I can't work under these conditions here. It's too hot.

AUSTIN. Then we'll do it on the desert.

LEE. Don't be tellin' me what we're gonna do!

MOM. Don't shout in the house.

LEE. We're just gonna' have to postpone the whole deal.

AUSTIN. I can't postpone it! It's gone past postponing! I'm doing everything you said. I'm writing down exactly what you tell me.

LEE. Yeah, but you were right all along see. It is a dumb story. "Two lame-brains chasin' each other across Texas." That's what you said, right?

AUSTIN. I never said that.

[LEE *sneers in* AUSTIN'*s face then turns to* MOM.]

LEE. I'm gonna' just borrow some a' your antiques, Mom. You don't mind do ya'? Just a few plates and things. Silverware.

[LEE *starts going through all the cupboards in kitchen pulling out plates and stacking them on counter as* MOM *and* AUSTIN *watch.*]

MOM. You don't have any utensils on the desert?

LEE. Nah, I'm fresh out.

AUSTIN [*to* LEE]. What're you doing?

MOM. Well some of those are very old. Bone china.

LEE. I'm tired of eatin' outa' my bare hands, ya' know. It's not civilized.

AUSTIN [*to* LEE]. What're you doing? We made a deal!

MOM. Couldn't you borrow the plastic ones instead? I have plenty of plastic ones.

LEE [*as he stacks plates*]. It's not the same. Plastic's not the same at all. What I need is somethin' authentic. Somethin' to keep me in touch. It's easy to get outa' touch out there. Don't worry I'll get em' back to ya'.

[AUSTIN *rushes up to* LEE, *grabs him by shoulders.*]

1490 AUSTIN. You can't just drop the whole thing, Lee!

[LEE *turns, pushes* AUSTIN *in the chest knocking him backwards into the alcove,* MOM *watches numbly,* LEE *returns to collecting the plates, silverware, etc.*]

MOM. You boys shouldn't fight in the house. Go outside and fight.

LEE. I'm not fightin'. I'm leavin'.

MOM. There's been enough damage done already.

LEE [*his back to* AUSTIN *and* MOM, *stacking dishes on counter*]. I'm clearin' outa' here once and for all. All this town does is drive a man insane. Look what it's done to Austin there. I'm not lettin' that happen to me. Sell myself down the river. No sir. I'd rather be a hundred miles from nowhere than let that happen to me.

[*During this* AUSTIN *has picked up the ripped-out phone from the floor and wrapped the cord tightly around both his hands, he lunges at* LEE *whose back is still to him, wraps the cord around* LEE's *neck, plants a foot in* LEE's *back and pulls back on the cord, tightening it,* LEE *chokes desperately, can't speak and can't reach* AUSTIN *with his arms,* AUSTIN *keeps applying pressure on* LEE's *back with his foot, bending him into the sink,* MOM *watches.*]

AUSTIN [*tightening cord*]. You're not goin' anywhere! You're not takin' any-
1500   thing with you. You're not takin' my car! You're not takin' the dishes! You're not takin' anything! You're stayin' right here!

MOM. You'll have to stop fighting in the house. There's plenty of room outside to fight. You've got the whole outdoors to fight in.

[LEE *tries to tear himself away, he crashes across the stage like an enraged bull dragging* AUSTIN *with him, he snorts and bellows but* AUSTIN *hangs on and manages to keep clear of* LEE's *attempts to grab him, they crash into the table, to the floor,* LEE *is face down thrashing wildly and choking,* AUSTIN *pulls cord tighter, stands with one foot planted on* LEE's *back and the cord stretched taut.*]

AUSTIN [*holding cord.*] Gimme back my keys, Lee! Take the keys out! Take 'em out!

[LEE *desperately tries to dig in his pockets, searching for the car keys,* MOM *moves closer.*]

MOM [*calmly to* AUSTIN]. You're not killing him are you?

AUSTIN. I don't know. I don't know if I'm killing him. I'm stopping him. That's all. I'm just stopping him.

[LEE *thrashes but* AUSTIN *is relentless.*]

MOM. You oughta' let him breathe a little bit.

1510 AUSTIN. Throw the keys out, Lee! [LEE *finally gets keys out and throws them on floor but out of* AUSTIN's *reach,* AUSTIN *keeps pressure on cord, pulling* LEE's *neck back,* LEE *gets one hand to the cord but can't relieve the pressure.*] Reach me those keys would ya', Mom.

MOM [*not moving*]. Why are you doing this to him?

AUSTIN. Reach me the keys!

MOM. Not until you stop choking him.

AUSTIN. I can't stop choking him! He'll kill me if I stop choking him!

MOM. He won't kill you. He's your brother.

AUSTIN. Just get me the keys would ya'!

[*Pause.* MOM *picks keys up off floor, hands them to* AUSTIN.]

1520 AUSTIN [*to* MOM]. Thanks.

MOM. Will you let him go now?

AUSTIN. I don't know. He's not gonna' let me get outa' here.

MOM. Well you can't kill him.

AUSTIN. I can kill him! I can easily kill him. Right now. Right here. All I gotta' do is just tighten up. See? [*He tightens cord,* LEE *thrashes wildly,* AUSTIN *releases pressure a little, maintaining control.*] Ya' see that?

MOM. That's a savage thing to do.

AUSTIN. Yeah well don't tell me I can't kill him because I can. I can just twist. I can just keep twisting. [AUSTIN *twists the cord tighter,* LEE *weakens, his*
1530 *breathing changes to a short rasp.*]

MOM. Austin!

[AUSTIN *relieves pressure,* LEE *breathes easier but* AUSTIN *keeps him under control.*]

AUSTIN [*eyes on* LEE, *holding cord*]. I'm goin' to the desert. There's nothing stopping me. I'm going by myself to the desert.

[MOM *moving toward her luggage.*]

MOM. Well, I'm going to go check into a motel. I can't stand this anymore.

AUSTIN. Don't go yet!

[MOM *pauses.*]

MOM. I can't stay here. This is worse than being homeless.

AUSTIN. I'll get everything fixed up for you, Mom. I promise. Just stay for a while.

MOM [*picking up luggage*]. You're going to the desert.

1540 AUSTIN. Just wait!

[LEE *thrashes,* AUSTIN *subdues him,* MOM *watches holding luggage, pause.*]

MOM. It was the worst feeling being up there. In Alaska. Staring out a

window. I never felt so desperate before. That's why when I saw that article
on Picasso I thought—
AUSTIN.   Stay here, Mom. This is where you live.

[*She looks around the stage.*]

MOM.   I don't recognize it at all.

[*She exits with luggage,* AUSTIN *makes a move toward her but* LEE *starts to struggle
and* AUSTIN *subdues him again with cord, pause.*]

AUSTIN [*holding cord*].   Lee? I'll make ya' a deal. You let me get outa' here.
Just let me get to my car. All right, Lee? Gimme a little headstart and I'll
turn you loose. Just gimme a little headstart. All right?

[LEE *makes no response,* AUSTIN *slowly releases tension on cord, still nothing from*
LEE.]

AUSTIN.   Lee?

[LEE *is motionless,* AUSTIN *very slowly begins to stand, still keeping a tenuous hold on
the cord and his eyes riveted to* LEE *for any sign of movement,* AUSTIN *slowly drops the
cord and stands, he stares down at* LEE *who appears to be dead.*]

1550   AUSTIN [*whispers*].   Lee?

[*Pause.* AUSTIN *considers, looks toward exit, back to* LEE, *then makes a small movement as if to leave. Instantly* LEE *is on his feet and moves toward exit, blocking*
AUSTIN's *escape. They square off to each other, keeping a distance between them.
Pause, a single coyote heard in distance, lights fade softly into moonlight, the figures
of the brothers now appear to be caught in a vast desert-like landscape, they are very
still but watchful for the next move, lights go slowly to black as the after-image of the
brothers pulses in the dark, coyote fades.*]

[1980]

Critical Commentary on *True West*[1]

The author of more than forty plays since 1964, Sam Shepard is surely
America's most prolific playwright. Writing rapidly, in a way that seems to
carve through soft tissues toward some quivering nerve, Shepard has produced a series of plays that dissect the American psyche. This is particularly
true of *True West*, a play that announces in its title a concern with the heartland of the American dream.
    True West explores a variety of American myths ranging from the mythic
West of cowboys and Indians to the western promise of easy gold and Hollywood glory. But perhaps the play's central myth is to be found in the

---

[1] This commentary is adapted and condensed from an essay by Jeffrey D. Hoeper entitled
"Cain, Caananites, and Philistines in Sam Shepard's *True West*" in the special issue of *Modern
Drama* on Sam Shepard (March 1993).

concept of the West as Edenic Paradise. As in Genesis, the action takes place to the east of Eden. Shepard sets his play "in a Southern California suburb, about 40 miles east of Los Angeles." Lee describes the suburban homes as being "like a Paradise" and Austin subsequently comments, "This is Paradise down here. . . . We're living' in a Paradise."

In its tantalizing hints about Paradise and in its focus on the mortal conflict between two brothers, Shepard's plot echoes the story of Cain and Abel. One interpretation of that story is that it was part of an effort by the invading Hebrews to discredit the matriarchal worship of the indigenous Canaanites. At the beginning of *True West* there are in fact hints of conflict between patriarchal and matriarchal values. The play is set in the mother's home. Her neighborhood is like Paradise. In a decor appropriate to the mother-goddess of many names (Ishtar, Isis, Astarte, Anath, Aphrodite), her home is filled with vegetation. Boston ferns hang in planters and synthetic grass carpets the floor. Her name is given as "mother" or "Mom," nothing more.

In coming down from the north to write a romantic screenplay, Austin may be said to be acting in the service of love (or Aphrodite) and his wages will be used to support his wife and children. Like Cain, Austin is associated with vegetation; in his mother's absence, he has vowed to tend her flourishing house plants. The first lines in Scene I underscore that duty, and Scene 2 opens with Austin "*watering plants with a vaporizer.*"

In contrast, Lee treks up from the desert, like the nomadic Hebrews at the end of their exodus and the beginning of their conquest of Canaan. Somewhere in that vast desert Lee has communed with the "old man"—the father, whom Austin in his prosperity has abandoned. Lee is Austin's sinister opposite, an outcast who prefers the company of the snakes in the desert to that of other men. A virtual illiterate, he makes his living by theft. Yet like Abel, Lee is associated with the sacrifice of animals. In Scene I he brags to Austin: "Had me a Pit Bull there for a while but I lost him . . . Fightin' dog. Damn I made some good money off that little dog. Real good money."

In Genesis blood sacrifice is required by the patriarchal deity Yahweh, and in *True West* Lee is clearly allied with the masculine and violent values of this deity. Throughout much of the play, any references to the father, who is (like the mother) left unnamed, prompt in Lee a vague sense of pride, while in Austin such references provoke an outbreak of hostility or guilt. Thus, in the play, as in Genesis, the patriarchal and matriarchal systems clash.

In America, however, the only god that truly counts is Success, and Austin is initially that deity's favored child. The agent of Success is a Hollywood producer named Saul Kimmer, who has promised Austin a lucrative movie contract for the love story Austin is writing. Later, Lee offers Saul a Western about a man's confrontation with his wife's lover and involving a bizarre chase on horseback across the Texas panhandle. Clichéd as the story is, it holds out the promise of a bloody duel at the end, the blood offering that Abel presented to the Old Testament's Yahweh. As one might predict, the god of Hollywood eventually rejects Austin's comparatively wholesome love story and offers a contract for that of Lee. In his anticipation of prosperity, Lee arranges to have "a big slice" of his profits (perhaps a tithe?) turned over to the father.

In the second half of the play, Austin becomes more and more embittered and increasingly similar to his evil brother. Having achieved nothing by his service to women, Austin neglects the rites of the goddess. He lets his mother's plants go unwatered, forgets about returning to his wife and children, and begs Lee to take him into the desert. Meanwhile Lee, the creature of the desert and the patriarch, begs for Austin's creative assistance. Eventually, however, Lee too loses his optimism about his story when he hears about Austin's last encounter with their father. Lee is disillusioned and depressed by Austin's description of their patriarch as a toothless, drunken beggar staggering from one bar to another and searching for the doggy bag of Chop Suey that contains his false teeth.

Scene VIII opens upon a tableau of defeatism and desolation, framed by the mother's "dead and drooping" house plants. Both brothers have lost faith in themselves and in the values that had allowed them to define themselves. Austin has transformed himself into a pale imitation of Lee by stealing toasters instead of T.V.'s. Meanwhile Lee has become an even more frustrated writer than Austin had been in Scene I. He stands before us smashing a golf club into Austin's typewriter with the regularity and impassivity of a metronome. For both brothers Hollywood has proven to be no Paradise.

The final scene presents a parody of matriarchal religion to balance the dismissal of the patriarchy in Scene VII. First, we see the comic ineptitude of both brothers as writers. They argue over the clichéd line, "I know this prairie like the back a' my hand"—eventually changing it to "I'm on intimate terms with this prairie" even though they are aware of the sexual connotation of the words "intimate terms." Is it too fanciful to see in this sentence a parody of matriarchal religion, with its emphasis on the planting of seed in the soil of the Mother Earth? Perhaps. But then Mom arrives like a *deus ex machina* at the very moment that Lee repeats, " 'He's on intimate terms with this prairie.' Sounds real mysterious and kinda' threatening at the same time." Yet if Mom is Mother Earth amid her wilted plants, hasn't she become trivial, irrelevant, comic, and a little mad?

Mom says she has come back from Alaska because she "just started missing all [her] plants." The greatest power of the goddess was the ability to bring the dead back to life. Although the plants remain dead in *True West*, Mom does announce a resurrection of sorts. She claims that "Picasso's in town. Isn't that incredible?" When Austin points out that Picasso is dead, she merely reiterates, "No, he's not dead. He's visiting the museum. We have to go down there and see him. . . . This is the chance of a lifetime."

With the patriarch rendered toothless and the matriarch demented, both brothers seem lost. The play concludes with Lee and Austin warily circling each other "in a vast desert-like landscape" while a single coyote yaps for the kill.

True West is, of course, Shepard's attempt to synthesize the characteristics of the "true West"—a West that is represented neither by the love story of Austin, nor by the implausible chase sequence of Lee, but rather by the play itself in which good is warped until it is indistinguishable from evil and craftsmanship of any kind is scorned in the pursuit of popularity. Later, in *A Lie of the Mind* Shepard will begin toying with a synthesis of the masculine and feminine into what Beth calls a "woman-man." In *True West*, however, mothers and fathers, as well as matriarchy and patriarchy, are equally irrelevant to modern life. The modern West is a place guided by false materialistic gods who misjudge the efforts of humans and set them at each others' throats. *True West* is truly Sam Shepard's most forceful and frightening indictment of America.

A Selective Bibliography on *True West*

Auerbach, Doris. *Shepard, Kopit, and the Off Broadway Theater.* Boston: Twayne, 1982.

Berger, Pamela. *The Goddess Obscured: Transformation of the Grain Protector from Goddess to Saint.* Boston: Beacon Press, 1985.

Demastes, William W. *Beyond Naturalism: A New Realism in American Theatre.* New York: Greenwood, 1988. 97–121.

DeRose, David J. *Sam Shepard.* New York: Twayne, 1992.

Dugdale, John. *File on Shepard.* London: Methuen, 1989.

Hart, Lynda. *Sam Shepard's Metaphorical Stages.* New York: Greenwood, 1987. 87–99.

King, Kimball. *Sam Shepard: A Casebook.* New York: Garland, 1988.

Kleb, William. "Sam Shepard's True West." *Theatre* 12 (1980): 65–71.

Mottram, Ron. *Inner Landscapes: The Theater of Sam Shepard.* Columbia: U of Missouri P, 1984.

Orbison, Tucker. "Mythic Levels in Shepard's *True West.*" *Modern Drama* 27 (Dec. 1984): 506–19.

Orr, John. *Tragicomedy and Contemporary Culture: Play and Performance from Beckett to Shepard.* Ann Arbor: U of Michigan P, 1991.

Oumano, Ellen. *Sam Shepard: The Life and Work of an American Dreamer.* New York: St. Martin's, 1986.

Patraka, Vivian M. and Mark Siegel. *Sam Shepard.* Boise, Idaho: Boise State U, 1985.

Podol, Peter L. "Dimensions of Violence in the Theater of Sam Shepard: *True West* and *Fool for Love.*" *Essays in Theatre* 7.2 (1989): 149–58.

Ramsey, Allen. "The True West of Shepard's *True West:* The Strategy of Hyperrealism." *Publications of the Arkansas Philological Association* 15.2 (1989): 63–73.

Shepard, Sam. "Language, Visualization and the Inner Library." *American Dreams: The Imagination of Sam Shepard.* Ed. Bonnie Marranca. New York: Performing Arts Journal, 1981. 214–19.

Shewey, Don. *Sam Shepard: The Life, the Loves, Behind the Legend of a True American Original.* New York: Dell, 1985.

Smith, Molly. "Beckettian Symbolic Structure in Sam Shepard's *True West*: A Jungian Reading." *Journal of Evolutionary Psychology* 10 (1989): 328–34.

Stone, Merlin. *When God Was a Woman.* New York: Harcourt, 1976.

Riemer, James D. "Integrating the Psyche of the American Male: Conflicting Ideals of Manhood in Sam Shepard's *True West.*" *University of Dayton Review* 18.2 (1986–1987): 41–7.

Tager, Michael. "Sam Shepard's Pastoral Dilemmas." *Studies in the Humanities* 14 (1987): 116–26.

Beth Henley (1952–   )
AM I BLUE?

CHARACTERS

JOHN POLK, *seventeen*
ASHBE, *sixteen*
HILDA, *a waitress, thirty-five*

STREET PEOPLE: BARKER, WHORE,
BUM, CLAREECE

SCENE: *A bar, the street, the living room of a run-down apartment.*
TIME: *Fall 1968*

The scene opens on a street in the New Orleans French Quarter on a rainy, blue bourbon night. Various people—a WHORE, BUM, STREET BARKER, CLAREECE—*appear and disappear along the street. The scene then focuses on a bar where a piano is heard from the back room playing softly and indistinctly "Am I Blue?" The lights go up on* JOHN POLK, *who sits alone at a table. He is seventeen, a bit overweight and awkward. He wears nice clothes, perhaps a navy sweater with large white monograms. His navy raincoat is slung over an empty chair. While drinking* JOHN POLK *concentrates on the red and black card that he holds in his hand. As soon as the scene is established,* ASHBE *enters from the street. She is sixteen, wears a flowered plastic raincoat, a white plastic rain cap, red galoshes, a butterfly barrette, and jeweled cat-eye glasses. She is carrying a bag full of stolen goods. Her hair is very curly.* ASHBE *makes her way cautiously to* JOHN POLK's *table. As he sees her coming, he puts the card into his pocket. She sits in the empty chair and pulls his raincoat over her head.*

ASHBE.   Excuse me . . . do you mind if I sit here please?
JOHN POLK [*looks up at her—then down into his glass*].   What are you doing hiding under my raincoat? You're getting it all wet.
ASHBE.   Well, I'm very sorry, but after all it is a raincoat. [*He tries to pull off coat*]. It was rude of me I know, but look I just don't want them to recognize me.
JOHN POLK [*looking about*].   Who to recognize you?
ASHBE.   Well, I stole these two ash trays from the Screw Inn, ya know right down the street. [*She pulls out two glass commercial ash trays from her white plastic bag.*] Anyway, I'm scared the manager saw me. They'll be after me I'm afraid.
JOHN POLK.   Well, they should be. Look, do you mind giving me back my raincoat? I don't want to be found protecting any thief.
ASHBE [*coming out from under coat*].   Thief—would you call Robin Hood a thief?
JOHN POLK.   Christ.

10

1427

ASHBE [*back under coat*].　No, you wouldn't. He was valiant—all the time stealing from the rich and giving to the poor.

JOHN POLK.　But your case isn't exactly the same, is it? You're stealing from
20　some crummy little bar and keeping the ash trays for yourself. Now give me back my coat.

ASHBE [*throws coat at him*].　Sure, take your old coat. I suppose I should have explained—about Miss Marcey. [*Silence.*] Miss Marcey, this cute old lady with a little hump in her back. I always see her in her sun hat and blue print dress. Miss Marcey lives in the apartment building next to ours. I leave all the stolen goods, as gifts on her front steps.

JOHN POLK.　Are you one of those kleptomaniacs? [*He starts checking his wallet.*]

ASHBE.　You mean when people all the time steal and they can't help it?
30　JOHN POLK.　Yeah.

ASHBE.　Oh, no. I'm not a bit careless. Take my job tonight, my very first night job, if you want to know. Anyway, I've been planning it for two months, trying to decipher which bar most deserved to be stolen from. I finally decided on the Screw Inn. Mainly because of the way they're so mean to Mr. Groves. He works at the magazine rack at Diver's Drugstore and is really very sweet, but he has a drinking problem. I don't think that's fair to be mean to people simply because they have a drinking problem— and, well, anyway, you see I'm not just stealing for personal gain. I mean, I don't even smoke.

40　JOHN POLK.　Yeah, well, most infants don't, but then again, most infants don't hang around bars.

ASHBE.　I don't see why not, Toulouse-Latrec[1] did.

JOHN POLK.　They'd throw me out.

ASHBE.　Oh, they throw me out too, but I don't accept defeat. [*Slowly moves into him.*] Why it's the very same with my pickpocketing.

[JOHN POLK *sneers, turns away.*]

ASHBE.　It's a very hard art to master. Why every time I've done it, I've been caught.

JOHN POLK.　That's all I need, is to have some slum kid tell me how good it is to steal. Everyone knows it's not.

50　ASHBE [*about his drink*].　That looks good. What is it?

JOHN POLK.　Hey, would you mind leaving me alone—I just wanted to be alone.

ASHBE.　Okay. I'm sorry. How about if I'm quiet?

[JOHN POLK *shrugs. He sips drink, looks around, catches her eye, she smiles and sighs.*]

ASHBE.　I was just looking at your pin. What fraternity are you in?

JOHN POLK.　S.A.E.

ASHBE.　Is it a good fraternity?

JOHN POLK.　Sure, it's the greatest.

---

[1] Henri Toulouse-Latrec (1864–1901) was a French painter and graphic artist who was famous for depicting the decadent nightlife in Parisian bars.

ASHBE.   I bet you have lots of friends.

JOHN POLK.   Tons.

60 ASHBE.   Are you serious?

JOHN POLK.   Yes.

ASHBE.   Hmm. Do they have parties and all that?

JOHN POLK.   Yeah, lots of parties, booze, honking horns, it's exactly what you would expect.

ASHBE.   I wouldn't expect anything. Why did you join?

JOHN POLK.   I don't know. Well, my brother . . . I guess it was my brother . . . he told me how great it was, how the fraternity was supposed to get you dates, make you study, solve all your problems.

ASHBE.   Gee, does it?

70 JOHN POLK.   Doesn't help you study.

ASHBE.   How about dates? Do they get you a lot of dates?

JOHN POLK.   Some.

ASHBE.   What were the girls like?

JOHN POLK.   I don't know—they were like girls.

ASHBE.   Did you have a good time?

JOHN POLK.   I had a pretty good time.

ASHBE.   Did you make love to any of them?

JOHN POLK [*to self*].   Oh, Christ . . .

ASHBE.   I'm sorry . . . I just figured that's why you had the appointment with
80 the whore . . . cause you didn't have anyone else . . . to make love to.

JOHN POLK.   How did you know I had the, ah, the appointment?

ASHBE.   I saw you put the red card in your pocket when I came up. Those red cards are pretty familiar around here. The house is only about a block or so away. It's one of the best though, really very plush. Only two murders and a knifing in its whole history. Do you go there often?

JOHN POLK.   Yeah, I like to give myself a treat.

ASHBE.   Who do you have?

JOHN POLK.   What do you mean?

ASHBE.   I mean which girl. [JOHN POLK *gazes into his drink.*] Look, I just
90 thought I might know her is all.

JOHN POLK.   Know her, ah, how would you know her?

ASHBE.   Well, some of the girls from my high school go there to work when they get out.

JOHN POLK.   G.G., her name is G.G.

ASHBE.   G.G. . . . Hmm, well, how does she look?

JOHN POLK.   I don't know.

ASHBE.   Oh, you've never been with her before?

JOHN POLK.   No.

ASHBE [*confidentially*].   Are you one of those kinds that likes a lot of variety?

100 JOHN POLK.   Variety? Sure, I guess I like variety.

ASHBE.   Oh, yes, now I remember.

JOHN POLK.   What?

ASHBE.   G.G., that's just her working name. Her real name is Myrtle Reims, she's Kay Reims' older sister. Kay is in my grade at school.

JOHN POLK.   Myrtle? Her name is Myrtle?

ASHBE.   I never liked the name either.

JOHN POLK.   Myrtle, oh, Christ. Is she pretty?

Ashbe [*matter of fact*].   Pretty, no she's not real pretty.

John Polk.   What does she look like?

110 Ashbe.   Let's see . . . she's, ah, well, Myrtle had acne and there are a few scars
left. It's not bad. I think they sort of give her character. Her hair's red,
only I don't think it's really red. It sort of fizzles out all over her head.
She's got a pretty good figure . . . big top . . . but the rest of her is kind of
skinny.

John Polk.   I wonder if she has a good personality.

Ashbe.   Well, she was a senior when I was a freshman; so I never really knew
her. I remember she used to paint her finger nails lots of different colors
. . . pink, orange, purple. I don't know, but she kind of scares me. About
the only time I ever saw her true personality was around a year ago. I was

120 over at Kay's making a health poster for school. Anyway, Myrtle comes
busting in, screaming about how she can't find her spangled bra anywhere. Kay and I just sat on the floor cutting pictures of food out of
magazines while she was storming about slamming drawers and swearing.
Finally, she found it. It was pretty garish—red with black and gold se-
quined G's on each cup. That's how I remember the name—G.G.

[*As* Ashbe *illustrates the placement of the G's she spots* Hilda, *the waitress, approaching.* Ashbe *pulls the raincoat over her head and hides on the floor.* Hilda *enters
through the beaded curtains spilling her tray.* Hilda *is a woman of few words.*]

Hilda.   Shit, damn curtain. Nuther drink?

John Polk.   Mam?

Hilda [*points to drink*].   Vodka coke?

John Polk.   No, thank you. I'm not quite finished yet.

130 Hilda.   Napkin's clean.

[Ashbe *pulls her bag off the table.* Hilda *looks at* Ashbe *then to* John Polk. *She walks
around the table, as* Ashbe *is crawling along the floor to escape.* Ashbe *runs into*
Hilda's *toes.*]

Ashbe.   Are those real gold?

Hilda.   You again. Out.

Ashbe.   She wants me to leave. Why should a paying customer leave? [*Back
to* Hilda.] Now I'll have a mint julep and easy on the mint.

Hilda.   This pre-teen with you?

John Polk.   Well, I . . . No . . . I . . .

Hilda.   I.D.'s

Ashbe.   Certainly, I always try to cooperate with the management.

Hilda [*looking at* John Polk's *I.D.*]   I.D., 11-12-50. Date: 11-11-68.

140 John Polk.   Yes, but . . . well, 11-12 is less than two hours away.

Hilda.   Back in two hours.

Ashbe.   I seem to have left my identification in my gold lamé bag.

Hilda.   Well, boo-hoo. [*Motions for* Ashbe *to leave with a minimum of effort. She
goes back to table.*] No tip.

Ashbe.   You didn't tip her?

John Polk.   I figured the drinks were so expensive . . . I just didn't . . .

Hilda.   No tip!

John Polk.   Look, Miss, I'm sorry. [*Going through his pockets.*] Here would
you like a . . . nickel . . . wait, wait, here's a quarter.

150 HILDA.   Just move ass, sonny. You too, Barbie.
ASHBE.   Ugh, I hate public rudeness. I'm sure I'll refrain from ever coming here again.
HILDA.   Think I'll go in the back room and cry.

[ASHBE *and* JOHN POLK *exit.* HILDA *picks up tray and exits through the curtain, tripping again.*]

HILDA.   Shit, Damn curtain.

[ASHBE *and* JOHN POLK *are now standing outside under the awning of the bar.*]

ASHBE.   Gee, I didn't know it was your birthday tomorrow. Happy birthday! Don't be mad. I thought you were at least twenty or twenty-one, really.
JOHN POLK.   It's o.k. Forget it.

[*As they begin walking, various blues are heard coming from the near-by bars.*]

ASHBE.   It's raining.
JOHN POLK.   I know.
160 ASHBE.   Are you going over to the house now?
JOHN POLK.   No, not till twelve.
ASHBE.   Yeah, the red and black cards—they mean all night. Midnight till morning.

[*At this point a street barker beckons the couple into his establishment. Perhaps he is accompanied by a whore.*]

BARKER.   Hey mister, bring your baby on in, buy her a few drinks, maybe tonight ya get lucky.
ASHBE.   Keep walking.
JOHN POLK.   What's wrong with the place?
ASHBE.   The drinks are watery rot gut, and the show girls are boys . . .
BARKER.   Up yours, punk!
170 JOHN POLK [*who has now sat down on a street bench*].   Look, just tell me where a cheap bar is. I've got to stay drunk, but I just don't have much money left.
ASHBE.   Yikes, there aren't too many cheap bars around here, and a lot of them check I.D.'s.
JOHN POLK.   Well, do you know of any that don't?
ASHBE.   No, not for sure.
JOHN POLK.   Oh, God, I need to get drunk.
ASHBE.   Aren't you?
JOHN POLK.   Some, but I'm losing ground fast.

[*By this time a bum who has been traveling drunkenly down the street falls near the couple and begins throwing up.*]

180 ASHBE.   Oh, I know! You can come to my apartment. It's just down the block. We keep one bottle of rum around. I'll serve you a grand drink, three or four if you like.
JOHN POLK [*fretfully*].   No, thanks.
ASHBE.   But look, we're getting all wet.
JOHN POLK.   Sober too, wet and sober.

ASHBE.   Oh, come on! Rain's blurring my glasses.

JOHN POLK.   Well, how about your parents? What would they say?

ASHBE.   Daddy's out of town and Mama lives in Atlanta; so I'm sure they
won't mind. I think we have some cute, little marshmallows. [*Pulling on*
190   *him.*] Won't you really come?

JOHN POLK.   You've probably got some gang of muggers waiting to kill me.
Oh, all right . . . what the hell, let's go.

ASHBE.   Hurrah! Come on. It's this way. [*She starts across the stage, stops, and
picks up an old hat.*] Hey, look at this hat. Isn't it something! Here, wear it
to keep off the rain.

JOHN POLK [*throwing hat back onto street.*]   No, thanks, you don't know who's
worn it before.

ASHBE [*picking hat back up*].   That makes it all the more exciting. Maybe it was
a butcher who slaughtered his wife or a silver pirate with a black bird on
200   his throat. Who do you guess?

JOHN POLK.   I don't know. Anyway what's the good of guessing? I mean you'll
never really know.

ASHBE [*trying the hat on*].   Yeah, probably not.

[*At this point* ASHBE *and* JOHN POLK *reach the front door.*]

ASHBE.   Here we are.

[ASHBE *begins fumbling for her key.* CLAREECE, *a teeny-bopper, walks up to* JOHN
POLK.]

CLAREECE.   Hey, man, got any spare change?

JOHN POLK [*looking through his pockets*].   Let me see . . . I . . .

ASHBE [*Coming up between them, giving* CLAREECE *a shove*].   Beat it, Clareece.
He's my company.

CLAREECE [*walks away and sneers.*]   Oh, shove it, Frizzels.

210   ASHBE.   A lot of jerks live around here. Come on in.

[*She opens the door. Lights go up on the living room of a run-down apartment in a
run-down apartment house. Besides being merely run-down the room is a malicious
pig sty with colors, paper hats, paper dolls, masks, torn up stuffed animals, dead
flowers and leaves, dress-up clothes, etc., thrown all about.*]

ASHBE.   My bones are cold. Do you want a towel to dry off?

JOHN POLK.   Yes, thank you.

ASHBE [*she picks up a towel off the floor and tosses it to him*].   Here. [*He begins
drying off, as she takes off her rain things; then she begins raking things off the
sofa.*] Please do sit down. [*He sits.*] I'm sorry the place is disheveled, but my
father's been out of town. I always try to pick up and all before he gets in.
Of course, he's pretty used to messes. My mother never was too good at
keeping things clean.

JOHN POLK.   When's he coming back?

220   ASHBE.   Sunday, I believe. Oh, I've been meaning to say . . .

JOHN POLK.   What?

ASHBE.   My name's Ashbe Williams.

JOHN POLK.   Ashbe?

ASHBE.   Yeah, Ashbe.

JOHN POLK.   My name's John Polk Richards.

ASHBE. John Polk? They call you John Polk?

JOHN POLK. It's family.

ASHBE [*putting on socks*]. These are my favorite socks, the red furry ones.
Well, here's some books and magazines to look at while I fix you some-

230 thing to drink. What do you want in your rum?

JOHN POLK. Coke's fine.

ASHBE. I'll see if we have any. I think I'll take some hot Kool-Aid myself.

[*She exits to the kitchen.*]

JOHN POLK. Hot Kool-Aid?

ASHBE. It's just Kool-Aid that's been heated, like hot chocolate or hot tea.

JOHN POLK. Sounds great.

ASHBE. Well, I'm used to it. You get so much for your dime, it makes it worth
your while. I don't buy presweetened, of course, it's better to sugar your
own.

JOHN POLK. I remember once I threw up a lot of grape Kool-Aid when I was

240 a kid. I've hated it ever since. Hey, would you check on the time?

ASHBE [*she enters carrying a tray with several bottles of food coloring, a bottle of rum,
and a huge glass*]. I'm sorry we don't have Coke. I wonder if rum and
Kool-Aid is good? Oh, we don't have a clock either.

[*She pours a large amount of rum into the large glass.*]

JOHN POLK. I'll just have it with water then.

ASHBE [*she finds an almost empty glass of water somewhere in the room and dumps it
in with the rum*]. Would you like food coloring in the water? It makes a
drink all the more aesthetic. Of course, some people don't care for aesthetics.

JOHN POLK. No, thank you, just plain water.

250 ASHBE. Are you sure? The taste is entirely the same. I put it in all my water.

JOHN POLK. Well . . .

ASHBE. What color do you want?

JOHN POLK. I don't know.

ASHBE. What's your favorite color?

JOHN POLK. Blue, I guess.

[*She puts a few blue drops into the glass. As she has nothing to stir with, she blows into
the glass turning the water blue.*]

JOHN POLK. Thanks.

ASHBE [*exits. She screams from the kitchen*]. Come on, say come on, cat, eat your
fresh, good milk.

JOHN POLK. You have a cat?

260 ASHBE [*off*]. No.

JOHN POLK. Oh.

ASHBE [*she enters carrying a tray with a cup of hot Kool-Aid and Cheerios and colored
marshmallows*]. Here are some Cheerios and some cute, little, colored
marshmallows to eat with your drink.

JOHN POLK. Thanks.

ASHBE. I one time smashed all the big white marshmallows in the plastic bag
at the grocery store.

JOHN POLK. Why did you do that?

ASHBE.   I was angry. Do you like ceramics?
270 JOHN POLK.   Yes.
ASHBE.   My mother makes them. It's sort of her hobby. She is very talented.
JOHN POLK.   My mother never does anything. Well, I guess she can shuffle
the bridge deck okay.
ASHBE.   Actually, my mother is a dancer. She teaches at a school in Atlanta.
She's really very talented.
JOHN POLK [indicates ceramics].   She must be to do all these.
ASHBE.   Well, Madeline, my older sister, did the blue one. Madeline gets to
live with Mama.
JOHN POLK.   And you live with your father.
280 ASHBE.   Yeah, but I get to go visit them sometimes.
JOHN POLK.   You do ceramics too?
ASHBE.   No, I never learned . . . but I have this great potholder set. [Gets up
to show him.] See, I make lots of multicolored potholders and send them to
Mama and Madeline. I also make paper hats. [Gets material to show him.] I
guess they're more creative, but making potholders is more relaxing.
Here would you like to make a hat?
JOHN POLK.   I don't know, I'm a little drunk.
ASHBE.   It's not hard a bit. [Hands him material.] Just draw a real pretty design
on the paper. It really doesn't have to be pretty, just whatever you want.
290 JOHN POLK.   It's kind of you to give my creative drives such freedom.
ASHBE.   Ha, ha, ha. I'll work on my potholder set a bit.
JOHN POLK.   What time is it? I've really got to check on the time.
ASHBE.   I know. I'll call the operator.

[She goes to the phone.]

JOHN POLK.   How do you get along without a clock?
ASHBE.   Well, I've been late for school a lot. Daddy has a watch. It's 11:03.
JOHN POLK.   I've got a while yet. [ASHBE twirls back to her chair, drops, and sighs.]
Are you a dancer, too?
ASHBE [delighted].   I can't dance a bit, really. I practice a lot is all, at home in
the afternoon. I imagine you go to a lot of dances.
300 JOHN POLK.   Not really, I'm a terrible dancer. I usually get bored or drunk.
ASHBE.   You probably drink too much.
JOHN POLK.   No, it's just since I've come to college. All you do there is drink
more beer and write more papers.
ASHBE.   What are you studying for to be?
JOHN POLK.   I don't know.
ASHBE.   Why don't you become a rancher?
JOHN POLK.   Dad wants me to help run his soybean farm.
ASHBE.   Soybean farm. Yikes, that's really something. Where is it?
JOHN POLK.   Well, I live in the Delta, Hollybluff, Mississippi. Anyway, Dad
310 feels I should go to business school first; you know, so I'll become, well,
management-minded. Pass the blue.
ASHBE.   Is that what you really want to do?
JOHN POLK.   I don't know. It would probably be as good as anything else I
could do. Dad makes good money. He can take vacations whenever he
wants. Sure it'll be a ball.

ASHBE. I'd hate to have to be management-minded. [JOHN POLK *shrugs.*] I
don't mean to hurt your feelings, but I would really hate to be a management mind. [*She starts walking on her knees, twisting her fists in front of her eyes,
and making clicking sounds as a management mind would make.*]

320 JOHN POLK. Cut it out. Just forget it. The farm could burn down, and I
wouldn't even have to think about it.

ASHBE [*after a pause*]. Well, what do you want to talk about?

JOHN POLK. I don't know.

ASHBE. When was the last dance you went to?

JOHN POLK. Dances. That's a great subject. Let's see, oh, I don't really
remember—it was probably some blind date. God, I hate dates.

ASHBE. Why?

JOHN POLK. Well, they always say that they don't want popcorn, and they
wind up eating all of yours.

330 ASHBE. You mean, you hate dates just because they eat your popcorn? Don't
you think that's kind of stingy?

JOHN POLK. It's the principle of the thing. Why can't they just say, yes, I'd
like some popcorn when you ask them. But, no, they're always so damn
coy.

ASHBE. I'd tell my date if I wanted popcorn. I'm not that immature.

JOHN POLK. Anyway, it's not only the popcorn. It's a lot of little things. I've
finished coloring. What do I do now?

ASHBE. Now you have to fold it. Here . . . like this. [*She explains the process
with relish.*] Say, that's really something.

340 JOHN POLK. It's kind of funny looking. [*Putting the hat on.*] Yeah, I like it, but
you could never wear it anywhere.

ASHBE. Well, like what anyway?

JOHN POLK. Huh?

ASHBE. The things dates do to you that you don't like, the little things.

JOHN POLK. Oh, well, just the way, they wear those false eyelashes and put
their hand on your knee when you're trying to parallel park, and keep on
giggling and going off to the bathroom with their girl friends. It's obvious
they don't want to go out with me. They just want to go out so that they can
wear their new clothes and won't have to sit on their ass in the dormitory.

350 They never want to go out with me. I can never even talk to them.

ASHBE. Well, you can talk to me, and I'm a girl.

JOHN POLK. Well, I'm really kind of drunk, and you're a stranger . . . well, I
probably wouldn't be able to talk to you tomorrow. That makes a difference.

ASHBE. Maybe it does. [*A bit of a pause and then extremely pleased by the idea she
says:*] You know we're alike because I don't like dances either.

JOHN POLK. I thought you said you practiced . . . in the afternoons.

ASHBE. Well, I like dancing. I just don't like dances. At least not like . . . well,
not like the one our school was having tonight . . . they're so corny.

360 JOHN POLK. Yeah, most dances are.

ASHBE. All they serve is potato chips and fruit punch, and then this stupid
baby band plays and everybody dances around thinking they're so hot. I
frankly wouldn't dance there. I would prefer to wait till I am invited to an
exclusive ball. It doesn't really matter which ball, just one where they have
huge, golden chandeliers and silver fountains, and serve delicacies of all

sorts and bubble blue champagne. I'll arrive in a pink silk cape [*laughing*]. I want to dance in pink!

JOHN POLK.   You're mixed up. You're probably one of those people that live in a fantasy world.

370 ASHBE.   I do not. I accept reality as well as anyone. Anyway you can talk to me, remember. I know what you mean by the kind of girls it's hard to talk to. There are girls a lot that way in the small clique at my school. Really tacky and mean. They expect everyone to be as stylish as they are, and they won't even speak to you in the hall. I don't mind if they don't speak to me, but I really love the orphans, and it hurts my feelings when they are so mean to them.

JOHN POLK.   What do you mean—they're mean to the "orpheens?" [*Giggles to himself at the wordplay.*]

ASHBE.   Oh, well, they sometimes snicker at the orphans' dresses. The or-
380 phans usually have hand-me-down, drab, ugly dresses. Once Shelly Max-well wouldn't let Glinda borrow her pencil, even though she had two. It hurt her feelings.

JOHN POLK.   Are you best friends with these orphans?

ASHBE.   I hardly know them at all. They're really shy. I just like them a lot. They're the reason I put spells on the girls in the clique.

JOHN POLK.   Spells, what do you mean, witch spells?

ASHBE.   Witch spells? Not really, mostly just voodoo.

JOHN POLK.   Are you kidding? Do you really do voodoo?

ASHBE.   Sure, here I'll show you my doll. [*Goes to get doll, comes back with straw
390 voodoo doll. Her air as she returns is one of frightening mystery.*] I know a lot about the subject. Cora, she used to wash dishes in the Moonlight Cafe, told me all about voodoo. She's a real expert on the subject, went to all the meetings and everything. Once she caused a man's throat to rot away and turn almost totally black. She's moved to Chicago now.

JOHN POLK.   It doesn't really work. Does it?

ASHBE.   Well, not always. The thing about voodoo is that both parties have to believe in it for it to work.

JOHN POLK.   Do the girls in school believe in it?

ASHBE.   Not really, I don't think. That's where my main problem comes in.
400 I have to make the clique believe in it, yet I have to be very subtle. Mainly, I give reports in English class or Speech.

JOHN POLK.   Reports?

ASHBE.   On voodoo.

JOHN POLK.   That's really kind of sick, you know.

ASHBE.   Not really. I don't cast spells that'll do any real harm. Mainly, just the kind of thing to make them think . . . to keep them on their toes. [*Blue-drink intoxication begins to take over and* JOHN POLK *begins laughing.*] What's so funny?

JOHN POLK.   Nothing. I was just thinking what a mean little person you are.
410 ASHBE.   Mean! I'm not mean a bit.

JOHN POLK.   Yes, you are mean . . . [*picking up color*] . . . and green too.

ASHBE.   Green?

JOHN POLK.   Yes, green with envy of those other girls; so you play all those mean little tricks.

ASHBE.   Envious of those other girls, that stupid, close-minded little clique!

JOHN POLK.   Green as this marshmallow. [*Eats marshmallow.*]

ASHBE.   You think I want to be in some group . . . a sheep like you? A little sheep like you that does everything when he's supposed to do it!

JOHN POLK.   Me a sheep . . . I do what I want!

420 ASHBE.   Ha! I've known you for an hour and already I see you for the sheep you are!

JOHN POLK.   Don't take your green meanness out on me.

ASHBE.   Not only are you a sheep, you are a NORMAL sheep. Give me back my colors! [*Begins snatching colors away.*]

JOHN POLK [*pushing colors at her*].   Green and mean! Green and mean! Green and mean!

ASHBE [*throwing marshmallows at him*].   That's the reason you're in a fraternity and the reason you're going to manage your mind. And dates . . . you go out on dates merely because it's expected of you even though you have a

430 terrible time. That's the reason you go to the whorehouse to prove you're a normal man. Well, you're much too normal for me.

JOHN POLK.   Infant bitch. You think you're really cute.

ASHBE.   That really wasn't food coloring in your drink, it was poison! [*She laughs, he picks up his coat to go, and she stops throwing marshmallows at him.*] Are you going? I was only kidding. For Christ sake, it wasn't really poison. Come on, don't go. Can't you take a little friendly criticism?

JOHN POLK.   Look, did you have to bother me tonight? I had enough problems without . . .

[*Phone rings. Both look at phone, it rings for the third time. He stands undecided.*]

ASHBE.   Look, wait, we'll make it up. [*She goes to answer phone.*] Hello . . .

440 Daddy. How are you? . . . I'm fine . . . Dad, you sound funny . . . What? . . . Come on, Daddy, you know she's not here. [*Pause.*] Look, I told you I wouldn't call anymore. You've got her number in Atlanta. [*Pause, as she sinks to the floor.*] Why have you started again? . . . Don't say that. I can tell it. I can. Hey, I have to go to bed now, I don't want to talk anymore, okay? [*Hangs up phone, then softly to self.*] Goddamnit.

JOHN POLK [*he has heard the conversation and is taking off his coat*].   Hey, Ashbe . . . [*She looks at him blankly, her mind far away.*] You want to talk?

ASHBE.   No. [*Slight pause.*] Why don't you look at my shell collection? I have this special shell collection. [*She shows him collection.*]

450 JOHN POLK.   They're beautiful, I've never seen colors like this. [ASHBE *is silent, he continues to himself.*] I used to go to Biloxi[2] a lot when I was a kid . . . One time my brother and I, we camped out on the beach. The sky was purple. I remember it was really purple. We ate pork and beans out of a can. I'd always kinda wanted to do that. Every night for about a week after I got home, I dreamt about these waves foaming over my head and face. It was funny. Did you find these shells or buy them?

ASHBE.   Some I found, some I bought. I've been trying to decipher their meaning. Here, listen, do you hear that?

JOHN POLK.   Yes.

460 ASHBE.   That's the sound of the sea. [*She listens.*] I'm pretty sure it's the soul

---

[2] Biloxi, Mississippi, is located on the Gulf of Mexico about 100 miles east of New Orleans.

of the sea. Just imagine when I decipher the language. I'll know all the secrets of the world.

JOHN POLK.   Yeah, probably you will. [*Looking into the shell.*] You know, you were right.

ASHBE.   What do you mean?

JOHN POLK.   About me, you were right. I am a sheep, a normal one. I've been trying to get out of it, but now I'm as big a sheep as ever.

ASHBE.   Oh, it doesn't matter. You're company. It was rude of me to say.

JOHN POLK.   No, because it was true. I really didn't want to go into a frater-
470   nity, I didn't even want to go to college, and I sure as hell don't want to go back to Hollybluff and work the soybean farm till I'm eighty.

ASHBE.   I still say you could work on a ranch.

JOHN POLK.   I don't know. I wanted to be a minister or something good, but I don't even know if I believe in God.

ASHBE.   Yeah.

JOHN POLK.   I never used to worry about being a failure. Now I think about it all the time. It's just I need to do something that's . . . fulfilling.

ASHBE.   Fulfilling, yes, I see what you mean. Well, how about college? Isn't it fulfilling? I mean, you take all those wonderful classes, and you have all
480   your very good friends.

JOHN POLK.   Friends, yeah, I have some friends.

ASHBE.   What do you mean?

JOHN POLK.   Nothing . . . well, I do mean something. What the hell, let me try to explain. You see it was my "friends," the fraternity guys that set me up with G.G., excuse me, Myrtle, as a gift for my eighteenth birthday.

ASHBE.   You mean, you didn't want the appointment?

JOHN POLK.   No, I didn't want it. Hey, ah, were did my blue drink go?

ASHBE [*as she hands him the drink*].   They probably thought you really wanted to go.

490 JOHN POLK.   Yeah, I'm sure they gave a damn what I wanted. They never even asked me. Hell, I would have told them a handkerchief, a pair of argyle socks, but, no, they have to get me a whore just because it's a cool-ass thing to do. They make me sick. I couldn't even stay at the party they gave. All the sweaty T-shirts, and moron sex stories . . . I just couldn't take it.

ASHBE.   Is that why you were at the Blue Angel so early?

JOHN POLK.   Yeah, I needed to get drunk, but not with them. They're such creeps.

ASHBE.   Gosh, so you really don't want to go to Myrtle's?

500 JOHN POLK.   No, I guess not.

ASHBE.   Then are you going?

JOHN POLK [*pause*].   Yes.

ASHBE.   That's wrong. You shouldn't go just to please them.

JOHN POLK.   Oh, that's not the point anymore, maybe at first it was, but it's not anymore. Now I have to go for myself . . . to prove to myself that I'm not afraid.

ASHBE.   Afraid? [*Slowly, as she begins to grasp his meaning.*] You mean, you've never slept with a girl before?

JOHN POLK.   Well, I've never been in love.

510 ASHBE [*in amazement*].   You're a virgin?

JOHN POLK.   Oh, God.

ASHBE.   No, don't feel bad, I am too.

JOHN POLK.   I thought I should be in love . . .

ASHBE.   Well, you're certainly not in love with Myrtle. I mean, you haven't even met her.

JOHN POLK.   I know, but, God, I thought maybe I'd never fall in love. What then? You should experience everything . . . shouldn't you? Oh, what's it matter, everything's so screwed.

ASHBE.   Screwed? Yeah, I guess it is. I mean, I always thought it would be fun

520   to have a lot of friends who gave parties and go to dances all dressed up. Like the dance tonight . . . it might have been fun.

JOHN POLK.   Well, why didn't you go?

ASHBE.   I don't know. I'm not sure it would have been fun. Anyway, you can't go . . . alone.

JOHN POLK.   Oh, you need a date?

ASHBE.   Yeah, or something.

JOHN POLK.   Say, Ashbe, ya wanna dance here?

ASHBE.   No, I think we'd better discuss your dilemma.

JOHN POLK.   What dilemma?

530 ASHBE.   Myrtle. It doesn't seem right you should . . .

JOHN POLK.   Let's forget Myrtle for now. I've got a while yet. Here have some more of this blue-moon drink.

ASHBE.   You're only trying to escape through artificial means.

JOHN POLK.   Yeah, you got it. Now come on. Would you like to dance? Hey, you said you liked to dance.

ASHBE.   You're being ridiculous.

JOHN POLK [*winking at her*].   Dance?

ASHBE.   John Polk, I just thought . . .

JOHN POLK.   Hmm?

540 ASHBE.   How to solve your problem . . .

JOHN POLK.   Well . . .

ASHBE.   Make love to me!

JOHN POLK.   What?

ASHBE.   It all seems logical to me. It would prove you weren't scared, and you wouldn't be doing it just to impress others.

JOHN POLK.   Look, I . . . I mean, I hardly know you . . .

ASHBE.   But we've talked. It's better this way, really. I won't be so apt to point out your mistakes.

JOHN POLK.   I'd feel great, stripping a twelve-year-old of her virginity . . .

550 ASHBE.   I'm sixteen! Anyway, I'd be stripping you of yours just as well. I'll go put on some Tiger Claw perfume. [*She runs out.*]

JOHN POLK.   Hey, come back! Tiger Claw perfume, Christ.

ASHBE [*entering*].   I think one should have different scents for different moods.

JOHN POLK.   Hey, stop spraying that! You know I'm not going to . . . well, you'd get neurotic, or pregnant, or some damn thing. Stop spraying, will you!

ASHBE.   Pregnant? You really think I could get pregnant?

JOHN POLK.   Sure, it'd be a delightful possibility.

560 ASHBE.   It really wouldn't be bad. Maybe I would get to go to Tokyo for an
abortion. I've never been to the Orient.

JOHN POLK.   Sure getting cut on is always a real treat.

ASHBE.   Anyway, I might just want to have my dear baby. I could move to
Atlanta with Mama and Madeline. It'd be wonderful fun. Why I could take
him to the supermarket, put him in one of those little baby seats to stroll
him about. I'd buy peach baby food and feed it to him with a tiny golden
spoon. Why I could take colored pictures of him and send them to you
through the mail. Come on. . . . [*Starts putting pillows onto the couch.*] Well,
I guess you should kiss me for a start. It's only etiquette, everyone begins

570 with it.

JOHN POLK.   I don't think I could even kiss you with a clear conscience. I
mean, you're so small with those little cat-eye glasses and curly hair . . . I
couldn't even kiss you.

ASHBE.   You couldn't even kiss me? I can't help it if I have to wear glasses. I
got the prettiest ones I could find.

JOHN POLK.   Your glasses are fine. Let's forget it, okay?

ASHBE.   I know, my lips are too purple, but if I eat carrots, the dye'll come off
and they'll be orange.

JOHN POLK.   I didn't say anything about your lips being too purple.

580 ASHBE.   Well, what is it? You're just plain chicken, I suppose . . .

JOHN POLK.   Sure, right, I'm chicken, totally chicken. Let's forget it. I don't
know how, but, somehow, this is probably all my fault.

ASHBE.   You're darn right it's all your fault! I want to have my dear baby or
at least get to Japan. I'm so sick of school I could smash every marshmallow in sight! [*She starts smashing.*] Go on to your skinny pimple whore. I
hope the skinny whore laughs in your face, which she probably will because you have an easy face to laugh in.

JOHN POLK.   You're absolutely right, she'll probably hoot and howl her damn
fizzle red head off. Maybe you can wait outside the door and hear her, give

590 you lots of pleasure, you sadistic, little thief.

ASHBE.   Thief! Was Robin Hood . . . Oh, what's wrong with this world? I just
wasn't made for it, is all. I've probably been put in the wrong world, I can
see that now.

JOHN POLK.   You're fine in this world.

ASHBE.   Sure, everyone just views me as an undesirable lump.

JOHN POLK.   Who?

ASHBE.   You, for one.

JOHN POLK [*pause*].   You mean because I wouldn't make love to you?

ASHBE.   It seems clear to me.

600 JOHN POLK.   But you're wrong, you know.

ASHBE [*to self, softly*].   Don't pity me.

JOHN POLK.   The reason I wouldn't wasn't that . . . it's just that . . . well, I like
you too much to.

ASHBE.   You like me?

JOHN POLK.   Undesirable lump, Jesus. Your cheeks they're . . . they're . . .

ASHBE.   My cheeks? They're what?

JOHN POLK.   They're rosy.

ASHBE.   My cheeks are rosy?

JOHN POLK.   Yeah, your cheeks, they're really rosy.
610 ASHBE.   Well, they're natural, you know. Say would you like to dance?
JOHN POLK.   Yes.
ASHBE.   I'll turn on the radio. [*She turns on radio. Ethel Waters is heard singing "Honey in the Honeycomb." ASHBE begins snapping her fingers.*] Yikes, let's jazz it out.

[*They dance.*]

JOHN POLK.   Hey, I'm not good or anything . . .
ASHBE.   John Polk.
JOHN POLK.   Yeah?
ASHBE.   Baby, I think you dance fine!

[*They dance on, laughing, saying what they want till end of song. Then a radio announcer comes on and says the 12:00 news will be in five minutes. Billie Holiday or Terry Pierce, begins singing, "Am I Blue?"*]

JOHN POLK: Dance?
620 ASHBE.   News in five minutes.
JOHN POLK.   Yeah.
ASHBE.   That means five minutes till midnight.
JOHN POLK.   Yeah, I know.
ASHBE.   Then you're not . . .
JOHN POLK.   Ashbe, I've never danced all night. Wouldn't it be something to . . . to dance all night and watch the rats come out of the gutter?
ASHBE.   Rats?
JOHN POLK.   Don't they come out at night? I hear New Orleans has lots of rats.
630 ASHBE.   Yeah, Yeah, it's got lots of rats.
JOHN POLK.   Then let's dance all night and wait for them to come out.
ASHBE.   All right . . . but, how about our feet?
JOHN POLK.   Feet?
ASHBE.   They'll hurt.
JOHN POLK.   Yeah.
ASHBE [*smiling*].Okay, then let's dance.

[*He takes her hand, and they dance as lights black out and the music soars and continues to play.*]

END

[1982]

Critical Commentary on *Am I Blue?*

Beth Henley's *Am I Blue?* is a play that depends for its effect upon the clash of opposites. The two principal characters, John Polk and Ashbe, seem at first to be diametric opposites. John Polk comes from a prosperous farming family, attends college, joins a fraternity, and seems to accept all of the values of the middle class. He is uneasy about prostitution, he opposes theft, and he plans to major in management. In contrast, Ashbe is the impoverished child of divorced inner-city residents. She has little interest in education, except to improve her skills at picking pockets. And she has values that are anything but conventional, deeming prostitution nothing more than a disagreeable after-school job and theft a laudable means of spreading wealth. While at first seeming to have little in common, John Polk and Ashbe eventually learn that they share a similar sense of alienation: both are loners and, in an era of rampant sexuality, both are virgins.

Part of the play's effect derives from its setting in the French Quarter of New Orleans, arguably the sleaze capital of the nation. Henley confronts us with the incongruity of historically and culturally important buildings that house bars and brothels, outcasts and derelicts. Henley makes this point visually by opening with a street scene, spottily peopled with the ordinary drifters—"a *WHORE, BUM, STREET BARKER, CLAREECE.*" Only after having established this setting does she narrow the focus to John Polk, seated alone at a bar and waiting for his appointment in the brothel. After the brief scene at the bar, we are taken into the street again on our way to Ashbe's apartment. Young, virginal Ashbe confronts the sordidness of her environment with a surprising matter-of-factness. When the street barker tries to entice John Polk and Ashbe into his seedy establishment, Ashbe intervenes to warn John Polk, "Keep walking. . . . The drinks are watery rot gut, and the show girls are boys." As soon as they leave the barker, who sends a dispirited "Up yours punk!" after Ashbe, they nearly stumble over a drunk vomiting in the gutter. All of this, of course, is an incongruous prelude to the sensitive and innocent courtship that will gradually unfold in Ashbe's apartment.

Like Shaw, Henley develops humor through incongruity and irony. What you expect is rarely what you get. John Polk's appointment, for example, is with a girl named G.G.—a name that rings appropriately erotic variations on Gigi and g-string. It turns out, however, that G.G. is actually Myrtle Reims, the older sister of a girl in Ashbe's class. Myrtle's face is pock-marked from acne, her hair is frizzy, and her figure, as described by Ashbe, is somewhat unbalanced ("big top . . . but the rest of her is kind of skinny"). After hearing this description, John Polk is left hoping that she has "a good personality."

The key image in the play is suggested by its title. "Am I Blue?" Most directly, the allusion refers to the title of the popular blues tune playing in the background of the Blue Angel bar as the curtain rises. But John Polk's mood is also obviously blue, and we initially wonder why. As the play unfolds we rapidly discover that he is depressed *because* of his appointment with the prostitute. His friends believe that he should become a "man" on his eighteenth birthday, and John Polk is too conforming a member of his fraternity to rebel openly against them. But that is only part of the reason for John Polk's depression. He is attending college not because he wants to do so, but because his father wants him to become more "management-minded" before he returns to help run the soybean farm. At the mere thought of this bland future, John Polk asks Ashbe to "Pass the blue." Fortunately he learns from Ashbe about a different kind of blue: a whimsical, gay blue, adding color to a life that might otherwise seem too penuriously deprived. She adds food coloring to water as an inexpensive little treat to herself and serves Cheerios and colored marshmallows to her company. As John Polk sits in Ashbe's apartment coloring his paper hat, he slowly begins to discover that he likes Ashbe, in part because she is unlike the college girls who go out with him only "so that they can wear their new clothes and won't have to sit on their ass in the dormitory."

Perhaps the most extraordinary irony in this play full of ironies is the one that confronts John Polk at the play's climax. He thinks he should be in love with a woman before having sex with her, but he is desperately afraid that he never will fall in love. Having reached the conclusion that he does not wish to have sex with Myrtle Reims because he doesn't know her at all, he now discovers that he is unwilling to have sex with Ashbe because he likes her too well. At five minutes to midnight he teeters on the brink of two abysses. If he leaves the apartment, he fears he will have to put his manhood to the test with G.G., but if he stays in the apartment, he may have to sleep with Ashbe. In a last-ditch attempt to avoid both sordid failings, John Polk hits upon a touchingly romantic alternative. This self-confessed "terrible dancer" invites Ashbe "to dance all night and watch the rats come out of the gutter." As he "takes her hand" and "the music soars," we can scarcely help believing that we are seeing the commencement of a love as rare as a blue moon.

✖ ✖ ✖ ✖ ✖ ✖ ✖ ✖

Glossary

Abbreviations. Common abbreviations encountered in literary study include the following:

anon. anonymous
app. appendix
art., arts. article(s)
b. born
biblio. bibliography, bibliographer
bk., bks. book(s)
bull. bulletin
ca. (or c.) "about," used to indicate an approximate date. For example: ca. 1776.
ch., chs. chapter(s)
d. died
ed., eds. editor(s) or edited by
e.g. *exempli gratia* "for example." Set off by commas.
esp. especially
et al. *et alii* "and others"
etc. *et cetera* "and so forth"
ex., exs. example(s)
f. ff. page or pages following a specific reference. For example: p. 12f.
fig., figs. figure(s)
front. frontispiece
ibid. *ibidem* "in the same place." That is, the title cited in the immediately preceding note.
i.e. *id est* "that is." Preceded and followed by a comma.
illus. illustrator, illustrated by, illustration(s)
intro., introd. introduction, introduced by
jour. journal
l., ll line(s)
loc. cit. *loco citato* "in the place (or passage) cited"
ms, mss manuscript. Capitalized and followed by a period when referring to a specific manuscript.
n., nn. note(s)
n.d. no date. For example, on the title page of a book.
no., nos. number(s)

1445

n.p.   no place of publication cited

p. pp.   page(s)

par., pars.   paragraph(s)

passim   "here and there throughout the work." For example: p. 23 et passim.

pref.   preface

pseud.   pseudonym

pt., pts.   part(s)

pub., pubs.   published by, publication(s)

rev.   revised or revised by; reviewed or reviewed by

rpt.   reprint or reprinted

sc.   scene

sic   "thus." Placed in square brackets [*sic*] to indicate that there is an error in the quoted passage and that the passage in question has been quoted accurately.

tr., trans.   translator or translated by

vol., vols.   volume(s)

Abridgment.   A condensed or shortened version of a work.

Abstract.   The opposite of *concrete;* used to describe a word or group of words representing attitudes, generalities, ideas, or qualities that cannot be perceived directly through the senses. Language is best seen as forming a continuous ladder ranging from earthily concrete at its base to airily abstract at its top. On this ladder the word *insect* is relatively abstract while *spittle bug* is quite concrete.

Absurd, Theater of the.   A type of modern drama (often associated with Edward Albee, Samuel Beckett, Jean Genet, Eugene Ionesco, Arthur Kopit, and Harold Pinter) that attempts to convey the playwright's vision of an absurd, frustrating, illogical, and essentially meaningless human condition by ignoring or distorting the usual conventions of plot, characterization, structure, setting, and dialogue. While drawing philosophically upon existentialism, the absurdist playwrights often use the techniques of surrealism and expressionism.

Act (p. 9).   A major division of a play; sometimes subdivided into a number of separate *scenes.*

Action.   The events or incidents that take place within a literary work which, taken together, provide the plot. See *plot.*

Adaptation.   The recasting of a work from one medium of art to another (as, for example, when a play is made into a film).

Affective Fallacy (p. 63).   According to New Critics, the mistake of confusing what the text is with what the text does. The term was used by William K. Wimsatt in particular to refer to the practice of interpreting texts according to their effects on readers. The designation of this practice as a fallacy or interpretive error has been contested recently, especially by *reader-response criticism.* See also *New Criticism, formalism, intentional fallacy.*

Agon.   A Greek word for "contest." The part of a Greek play (particularly *Old Comedy*) in which two characters, each aided and supported by half the *chorus,* argue with one another.

Agonist.   A participant in the *agon,* a major character in a play or (by extension) a novel. Hence, a *protagonist* is a primary character; an *antagonist* is an opposing major character; and a *deuteragonist* is a secondary, or minor, character.

Allegory.   A type of narrative that attempts to reinforce its thesis by making its characters (and sometimes its events and setting, as well) represent specific ideas or qualities outside the text. In *Everyman*, for example, the various characters (Everyman, Fellowship, Good Deeds, etc.) are both human beings in conflict and representations of the qualities indicated by their names. The story explores both the unique events of Everyman's journey toward death and a set of generalizations about every human death. See *fable, parable,* and *symbol.*

Allusion. A reference, generally brief, to a person, place, thing, or event with which the reader or audience is presumably familiar. Allusion is a device which allows a writer to compress a great deal of meaning into a very few words. Allusions "work" to the extent they are recognized and understood; when they are not they tend to confuse.

Ambiguity. The use of a word or phrase in such a way as to give it two or more meanings. Example: "Nowadays we are all so hard up that the only pleasant things to pay are compliments. They're the only things we can pay" (Oscar Wilde, from *Lady Windemere's Fan,* 1892).

Ambivalence. The existence of two mutually opposed or contradictory feelings about a given issue, idea, person, or object. You feel ambivalent, for example, when you wish to celebrate St. Patrick's Day with plenty of green beer, but you also wish to pass your accounting test the next morning.

Anachronism. A person or thing that is chronologically out of place. For example, in *The Second Shepherds' Play* a number of references to Christ precede the birth of Christ at the end of the play.

Anagnorisis. The scene of recognition or discovery that leads to a reversal. The term was first used by Aristotle in his discussion of *tragedy.*

Analogy. A comparison, usually imaginative, of two essentially unlike things which nonetheless share one or more common features. Writers use analogies as a method of exploring familiar subjects in new and fresh ways or as a method of exploring difficult ideas by comparing them to things known and familiar.

Analysis. An attempt to study one element or part of a literary work. See *criticism.*

Anecdote. A brief, unadorned story about a particular person or incident.

Anthropological criticism (pp. 69–70). An approach to literary study which emphasizes human origins, development, customs, and beliefs. See also *myth criticism.*

Angst. A German word for "anxiety" or "anguish." The term is often applied to the plight of characters in existential literature. See *existentialism.*

Angry Young Men. A group of British playwrights and novelists of the 1950s and 1960s noted for their rejection of bourgeois values and their heated attacks on the established social system. The most notable play from this coterie was Osborne's *Look Back in Anger.*

Annotation. The explanatory note (or notes) that an author or editor supplies for a given text.

Antagonist (p. 46). The rival or opponent against whom the major character (the *protagonist* or *hero*) is contending.

Antecedent events. Events that have taken place before the plot of the play begins, but which are somehow important to that plot.

Anticlimax. A sudden transition from the important (or serious) to the trivial (or ludicrous). We speak of something being anticlimactic when it occurs after the *crisis* (or *climax*) of the plot has been reached.

Antihero. A *protagonist* whose distinctive qualities are directly opposite to, or incompatible with, those associated with the traditional hero. Such an opposition by no means implies that the character is evil or villainous but often tends to reflect the author's belief that modern life no longer tolerates or produces individuals capable of genuine heroism in its classic sense. Examples: Lysistrata in the famous play by Aristophanes (B.C. 411) and Mozart in Peter Shaffer's *Amadeus* (1979).

Aphorism. A short, pithy saying, usually by a known author. Example: "Only the brave deserve the fair." W. S. Gilbert, *Iolanthe* (1882).

Apollonian. A term similar in meaning to classicism and implying the qualities of reason, clarity, and morality that were characteristics of the Greek god Apollo. The term was first used by Friedrich Nietzsche in *The Birth of Tragedy.* See the opposite term, *Dionysian.*

Apology. In literature a term meaning a justification or a defense.

Apostrophe. A figure of speech in which a person (usually not present) or a personified quality or object is addressed as if present.

Apron Stage. A stage that projects out into the audience. In traditional theaters the apron is that part of the stage in front of the *proscenium* arch.

Apothegm. A pithy, witty saying. E.g., Iago's definition of jealousy in *Othello:* "It is the green-eyed monster, which doth mock / The meat it feeds on."

Archaism. An obsolete word or phrase.

Archetype. Used in literary analysis to describe certain basic and recurrent patterns of plot, character, or theme that symbolize universal human experiences and transcend history and individuals; associated with *myth criticism* and the ideas of psychologist Carl Jung. See also *symbol.*

Arena Stage/Arena Theater (p. 33). A theater with seating surrounding, or nearly surrounding, the stage. See *theater in the round.*

Argument. A summary statement of the content or thesis of a literary work.

Aristotelian Criticism. A form of criticism that claims to draw its principles from the philosophical methods of Aristotle in the *Poetics;* associated with *formalist criticism.*

Aside (p. 25). A dramatic convention in which the lines addressed by a character to the audience are presumed to go unheard by the other characters. Example: "IAGO [*aside*]. O, you are well tuned now! / But I'll set down the pegs that make this music / As honest as I am" (Shakespeare, *Othello*, 1604, II.i).

Atmosphere. The mood or feeling that pervades a literary work.

Avant-garde. New, innovative, or experimental art; a work whose subject matter, style, or form places it at the forefront of a literary or artistic trend or movement. Off-Broadway theater—that is, plays presented outside New York's Broadway entertainment district—are frequently experimental or avant-garde.

Bad Quartos. A term for a number of inaccurate or garbled early editions of Shakespeare's plays.

Bathos. Literature in which an excessive striving for the dignity of pathos or tragedy produces a ludicrous insincerity.

Belle-Lettres. Highly artistic literature; as an adjective, spelled *belletristic.*

Bibliography. A list of books, articles, and other references on a particular subject.

Blank verse. Lines of unrhymed iambic pentameter as, for example, in Shakespeare's *Othello* (1604).

Black Humor. Humor which is the product of a morbid, alienated, or pessimistic view of the world. Black humor is often associated with the *theater of the absurd.* Black humor is exemplified in the folk expression, "Been down so long it looks like up to me."

Blocking. The pattern of the actor's position and movement on the stage. Sometimes this pattern is made an explicit part of the playwright's script.

Bombast. Language that is inflated, extravagant, verbose, and insincere.

Bourgeois Tragedy. See *domestic tragedy*.

Bowdlerize. To gut a piece of writing in the interest of morality or decorum. The word originated in 1818 when Thomas Bowdler (1754–1825), an Englishman, published a sanitized version of Shakespeare's plays.

Box Set. A realistic stage setting consisting of a room with a ceiling and three walls. The fourth (imaginary) wall exists between the actors and the audience.

Burlesque. A form of humor that ridicules persons, attitudes, actions, or things by means of distortion and exaggeration. Burlesque of a particular literary work or style is referred to as *parody. Caricature,* on the other hand, creates humor by distorting or exaggerating an individuals' prominent physical features; see also *satire*. Tom Stoppard's *The Real Inspector Hound* (1968), for example, burlesques the conventions of theatrical murder mysteries.

Buskin. A high, thick-soled boot worn to increase stature by Greek tragic actors.

Caricature. Humor or ridicule created by the distortion of a character's physical features. Political cartoonists often create caricatures of the dignitaries they lampoon. See *burlesque*.

Caesura. A pause or break occurring near the middle of a line of verse, customarily marked by a double slash in scansion. Example:

If I quench thee, // thou flaming minister,
I can thy former light restore,
Should I repent me.

(William Shakespeare, *Othello*, IV, ii)

Canon. In contemporary criticism the *canon* is the unspecified, but generally accepted list of established masterpieces. Traditionally, the term refers to the books of the Bible that are accepted as holy.

Caroline. The period in English literature coinciding with the reign of Charles I (1625–1649). A period of decline in drama after the great achievements of *Elizabethan* and *Jacobean* drama. The best-known Caroline playwrights are Philip Massinger, John Ford, and James Shirley.

Catastrophe. A form of *conclusion* (or *denouement*), usually tragic in its outcome.

Catharsis (p. 54). A term used by Aristotle to describe the psychological feeling of relief and release (the purgation of such emotions as pity and fear) experienced by the audience through their exposure to tragedy. See *classical tragedy*.

Chance and Coincidence. *Chance* refers to events or "happenings" within a plot that occur without sufficient preparation; *coincidence* to the accidental occurrence of two (or more) events that have a certain correspondence.

Character (pp. 46–48). An individual within a play.

Characterization. The process by which an author creates, develops, and presents a character.

Chorus (pp. 21–23). In Greek drama the chorus was a group of singers and dancers who sometimes served as actors to comment on or interpret the significance of the action.

Chronicle Play. A form of Elizabethan drama that drew its subject matter from history, particularly the *Chronicles* (1577) of Raphael Holinshed and various continuations by his imitators. Shakespeare's histories are good examples of chronicle plays.

Chronological. A pattern of organization or presentation that introduces events or things in their normal time sequence.

Classical Tragedy (p. 53–54; 184–189). Refers to Greek and Roman tragedies or plays written imitating their subjects or conventions.

Cliché. A trite, worn-out expression that has lost its original vitality and freshness. Examples: "sharp as a tack," "dumb as a doorknob," "boring as a bump on a log."

Climax. See *crisis*.

Cloak and Dagger. A type of play or novel dealing with espionage and intrigue.

Cloak and Sword. A type of play or novel containing swashbuckling action, gallant heroes, and plots filled with intrigue and adventure. Alexander Dumas' *The Count of Monte Cristo* (1844–45) is a good example.

Closet Drama (p. 14). A drama written to be read rather than staged and acted. Examples: *Samson Agonistes* (1672) by Milton, *Cain* (1821) by Byron, and *Prometheus Unbound* (1819) by Shelley.

Clown. A comic character of rustic origins. Example: the profanely punning clown in Act III, Scene I of *Othello* (1604).

Coherence. A principle that insists that the various parts of a literary work be related to one another in a clear and logical manner.

Coincidence. See *chance and coincidence*.

Comedy (pp. 55–57). Any play designed primarily to amuse. The term is usually reserved for plays whose tone is lighthearted and humorous, that are amusing, and that have a happy ending. See *comedy of humours, comedy of manners, farce, new comedy, old comedy, romantic comedy*.

Comedy of Humours. A type of comedy derived from the medieval physiological theory of the "four humours," the four identifiable elements believed to determine and control individual temperament and personality. When these humours became imbalanced the result was a lopsided, eccentric personality whose actions became a fit subject for comedy. Examples: *Every Man In His Humour* (1598) and *Every Man Out of His Humour* (1599) by Ben Jonson.

Comedy of Manners: A type of realistic, often satiric, comedy concerned with the behavior of men and women who violate the manners, norms, and conventions of polite, sophisticated upper-class society. Also referred to as drawing room comedy. Examples: *She Stoops to Conquer* (1773) by Goldsmith, *The School for Scandal* (1777) by Sheridan, and *The Importance of Being Earnest* (1895) by Wilde.

Comedy of Morals. A type of comedy that exposes and ridicules moral posturing. Example: Moliére's *Tartuffe* (1667).

Comedy of Situation. A type of comedy whose chief interest lies in the ingenuity and twists and turns of the plot. Example: Shakespeare's *The Comedy of Errors* (1590).

Comic Relief. A comic scene introduced into an otherwise serious or tragic play, usually to relieve, if only momentarily, the tension of the plot. It often heightens, by contrast, the emotional intensity of the work. Example: the clown scene in Shakespeare's *Othello* (III,i).

Commedia Dell'arte. An early Italian form of improvised comedy that draws much of its humor from the buffoonery of stock characters (the harlequin or the pantaloon). It is most significant for its influence upon the comedies of Shakespeare and Molière.

Complication. That part of a plot in which the conflict is developed and intensified; sometimes referred to as the *rising action*.

Conclusion. See *resolution*.

Concordance. An alphabetical index of the words used in a given text or in the work of a given author.

Concrete. Opposite of *abstract.* Language referring directly to what we see, hear, touch, taste, or smell is concrete. Most literature uses concrete language and expresses even abstract concepts concretely through images and metaphors.

Confidant/Confidante (p. 46). The individual, often a minor character, to whom a major character reveals or "confesses" his or her most private thoughts and feelings. Playwrights use the confidant as a device to communicate necessary information to the reader and audience. Emilia, for example, is Desdemona's confidante in *Othello.*

Conflict. The struggle or encounter within the plot of two opposing forces that serves to create reader or audience interest and suspense.

Consistency. The internal coherence of the various parts and the tone of a literary work.

Convention. Any literary device, technique, style, or form, or any aspect of subject matter, characterization, or theme that has become recognized and accepted by authors and audiences through repeated use. By convention, for example, the open stage in the Greek theater could represent any public locale and by convention the male characters in Greek comedies were equipped with enormous artificial phalluses.

Corpus Christi Plays. See *mystery plays.*

Counterplot. See *subplot.*

Couplet. A single pair of rhymed lines. Couplets were frequently used in Renaissance drama, particularly in comedies such as Shakespeare's *A Midsummer Night's Dream* (1595).

Coup de Théâtre. French for "stroke of theater"—i.e., a striking effect.

Crisis (pp. 43–44). That point during the plot when the action reaches its turning point; also called the *climax;* see *anticlimax.*

Critic. An individual who evaluates and passes judgment on the quality and worth of a literary work. The critic who writes about contemporary works is also known as a reviewer and tends to be much maligned by authors. In this context Richard Le Gallienne has said that "a critic is a man created to praise greater men than himself, but he is never able to find them."

Criticism. The description, analysis, interpretation, or evaluation of a literary work of art; see also *deconstruction, historical criticism, new criticism, textual criticism, theoretical criticism,* and *practical criticism.*

Critique. A critical examination of a work of art.

Curtain Line. A line or lines that come just before the curtain falls ending a scene or act. Especially good examples occur in Ibsen's *Hedda Gabler* (1890).

Curtain Raiser. A brief play performed as a prelude to a more substantial work.

Cruelty, Theater of. A theory about theater formulated by Antonin Artaud in the 1930s. Artaud wished to give modern theater the power of early religious ritual by using shocking or horrifying events to underscore the basic cruelty of life. Jean Genet, Peter Weiss, and Peter Shaffer are important playwrights influenced by Artaud's ideas.

Deconstruction (pp. 70–72). Began as a reaction against structuralism's attempt to uncover fixed laws for the way humans make meaning through signs. Rejects the idea that texts can ever be completely understood and emphasizes the way language and structure reveal contingency and variability. Focuses on ruptures, small inconsistencies in texts, and claims that these indicate that texts are simultaneously contradicting the very meanings they seem to create. Major texts include Derrida's

Of Grammatology (tr. 1976) and *Writing and Difference* (tr. 1978); Paul de Man's *Allegories of Reading* (1979) and *Blindness and Insight* (1981); and Jonathan Culler's *On Deconstruction* (1981). See also *structuralism, semiotics, poststructuralism.*

Decorum.   The idea, derived from classical theory and thus at times approaching the status of doctrine, that all the elements of a literary work (i.e., setting, character, action, style) must be appropriately related to one another.

Denouement.   From the French word meaning "unknotting" or "untying." A term sometimes used for the final resolution of the conflict or complications of the plot.

Deus ex Machina.   "God from the machine." Derived from a practice in Greek drama whereby an impersonation of a god was mechanically lowered onto the stage to intervene in and solve the issues of the play. Commonly used today to describe any apparently contrived or improbable device used by an author to resolve the difficulties of plot. The intervention of the King at the end of *Tartuffe* can, in this sense, be said to illustrate the use of *deus ex machina.*

Dialogue (pp. 35–41).   The conversation that goes on between or among characters in a literary work.

Diction.   The author's choice of words (vocabulary). The artistic arrangement of those words constitutes *style.*

Didactic.   Literature designed more to teach a lesson or instruct the reader or audience than to present an experience objectively. In a didactic work *theme* is generally the most important element.

Différance.   A French word coined by critical theorist Jacques Derrida to combine the concepts of difference, deference, and deferral. See *deconstruction.*

Digression.   The insertion into a work of material that is not closely related to its main subject.

Dionysian.   A term similar in meaning to Romanticism and implying the qualities of emotionalism, irrationality, and inspiration that were associated with the Greek god Dionysus. See the opposite term, *Apollonian.*

Discovery.   A sudden exposure of facts in a tragedy, precipitating the reversal of fortune of the protagonist. In *Oedipus* the discovery occurs when Oedipus finally learns his parentage and thus that he has married his own mother and slain his father.

Distance.   The degree of detachment achieved by the reader and audience from the people and events of a literary work.

Domestic Tragedy.   A type of tragedy (originating in the eighteenth century as a reflection of its growing middle-class society) in which an ordinary middle-class (or lower-class) protagonist suffers ordinary (although by no means insignificant) disasters; also called *bourgeois tragedy.*

Double Entendre.   A form of pun in which one of the two meanings is risqué or sexually suggestive.

Downstage.   See *upstage.*

Drama Criticism.   Useful bibliographies include *Drama Criticism: A Checklist of Interpretation Since 1940 of English and American Plays* (Denver: Alan Swallow, 1966); *Drama Criticism: A Checklist of Interpretation Since 1940 of Classical and Continental Plays* (Chicago: Alan Swallow, 1971); Stanley J. Wells ed., *English Drama* (excluding *Shakespeare*): *Select Bibliographical Guides* (London: Oxford Univ. Press, 1975); Charles A. Carpenter ed., *Modern British Drama* (Arlington Heights, Ill.: AHM Press, 1979); Edward H. Mikhail ed., *English Drama, 1900–1950: A Guide to Information Sources* (Detroit: Gale Research, 1972); Irving Adelman and Rita Dworkin, eds., *Modern Drama: A Checklist of Critical Literature on 20th Century Plays* (Metuchen,

N.J.: Scarecrow Press, 1967); Edward Mikhail ed., *Contemporary British Drama, 1950–1976: An Annotated Critical Bibliography* (Totowa, N.J.: Rowman, 1976); Helen H. Palmer, ed., *European Drama Criticism, 1900–1975* (Hamden, Conn.: Shoe String Press, 1977). See also the annual bibliography in the quarterly journal *Modern Drama* and the *MLA International Bibliography of Books and Articles on the Modern Languages and Literature* (New York: Modern Language Association).

Drama Reviews. For reviews of American plays see the annual volumes of *New York Theatre Critics' Reviews* (New York: Critics' Theatre Reviews) and *New York Times Theatre Reviews, 1870–1980*, 20 vols. (New York: Arno Press, 1980).

Dramatic Irony. See *irony*.

Dramatis Personae. A play's cast of characters.

Drawing Room Comedy. A light *comedy of manners* featuring upper-class characters, so-named because of the frequent setting of the action in aristocratic drawing rooms. Oscar Wilde's *The Importance of Being Earnest* (1895) is a good example.

Dumb Show. A pantomime occurring commonly in an Elizabethan play. See *pantomime*.

Dynamic and Static Characters. A dynamic character is one who develops or changes in the course of the plot; a static character, by contrast, is one who does not.

Edwardian Drama. A drama produced between the death of Queen Victoria in 1901 and the beginning of World War I in 1914. Named for King Edward VII who occupied the throne from 1901 to 1910. Major playwrights include George Bernard Shaw, James Barrie, John Galsworthy, W. B. Yeats, and John M. Synge.

Effect. The total impression or impact of a work upon the reader or audience.

Ego (p. 65). Freud's term for the "I," that part of ourselves which is conscious, rational, and orderly. See also *psychoanalytic criticism, id, superego, Oedipal conflict, unconscious*.

Electra Complex. In psychology, the excessive love of a daughter for her father. The name derives from the Greek mythological character Electra, who avenged the death of her father by helping her brother Orestes to kill their mother Clytemnestra and her lover Aegisthus. See *Oedipus conflict*.

Elizabethan Drama. Drama written during the reign of Elizabeth I of England, 1558–1603. Major playwrights include William Shakespeare and Christopher Marlowe.

Empathy. The state of entering into and actually participating in the emotional, mental, or physical life of an object, person, or literary character.

Emphasis. The weight or stress that an author gives to one or more of the elements of the work.

Entr'acte. The interval between two acts of a play, especially when enlivened by music or dance.

Epigraph. A quotation prefacing a literary work, often containing a clue to the author's intention.

Epilogue. The final, concluding section of a play, offered in summation, to point a lesson or moral, or to thank the audience (reader) for its indulgence; see *prologue*.

Episodic plot (p. 46). A plot that develops through a chronological series of episodes (or incidents), often separated by lengthy periods of time. See *unfolding plot*.

Evaluation. A judgment about the particular merits or success of a given work.

Evidence. The facts, examples, or arguments given in support of a writer's assertion or thesis. Literary analysis invariably requires the amassing of evidence from the work itself.

Existentialism. A philosophy formulated during and after World War II and associated most frequently with the Frenchman Jean Paul Sartre (1905–1980). It posits a meaningless, absurd, and alienating world in which a person must deliberately create his or her own meaning and affirmation through personal choices. Typical existentialist works are Sartre's plays *The Flies* (1943) and *No Exit* (1947), along with Albert Camus's novel *The Stranger* (1942).

Explication. A detailed (often word-by-word and line-by-line) attempt to explain the entire meaning of a literary work. From the Latin word meaning "unfolding."

Exposition (p. 42). The part of the play that provides necessary background information.

Expressionism. A movement in revolt against realism that attempts to objectify inner experience by using nonrealistic techniques. The movement first achieved importance in the plays of August Strindberg, particularly in *A Dream Play* (1902). Expressionism also exerted an influence on Luigi Pirandello, Frederico Garcia Lorca, Arthur Miller, and Tennessee Williams.

Falling Action (pp. 44–45). The part of a dramatic plot that follows the *crisis* (or *climax*) and precedes the *resolution* (or *denouement*).

Farce. A type of comedy which achieves its effect through ridiculous and exaggerated situations, broad, often crude, verbal humor, and various kinds of buffoonery and physical horseplay. There are strong elements of farce in both Aristophanes's *Lysistrata* (411 B.C.) and in Anton Chekhov's *The Cherry Orchard* (1904).

Feminist Criticism (pp. 74–75). Literary criticism written from the perspective of women, reflecting female attitudes, concerns, and values. Feminist criticism is concerned both with how the meaning of a literary work is affected when read from a woman's perspective and how female characters and women in general are treated within the work. This literary movement grows out of (and is part of) the feminist movement which since the late 1960s has attempted to improve equal rights and equal opportunities for women by identifying and removing the political, social, and psychological obstacles that prevent them from achieving their full possibilities as human beings. Major texts include Elaine Showalter, *A Literature of Their Own* (1977) and *The New Feminist Criticism* (1985); Judith Fetterley, *The Resistant Reader* (1978); and Sandra M. Gilbert and Susan Gubar's *The Madwoman in the Attic* (1979).

Figurative Language. Language used imaginatively and nonliterally. Figurative language is composed of such figures of speech (or tropes) as *metaphor, simile, personification, metonymy, synecdoche, apostrophe, hyperbole, symbol, irony,* and *paradox.*

Fin de Siècle. "End of the century," usually applied to the 1890s, a period noted for rapid social change, estheticism, and decadence.

Flashback. The interruption of the plot in order to present an earlier scene; a method of *exposition.*

Flat Character. See *character.*

Foil (p. 46). A character who provides a direct contrast to another character.

Foreshadowing. A device by means of which the author hints at something to follow.

Foreword. A short introductory statement designed to orient the reader to the work that follows. It is often written by someone other than the author.

Formalism (pp. 62–64). Method of analyzing literature which emphasizes intrinsic elements of a literary work, including language, structure, and repetition of images and symbols which occur within a text. See also *New Criticism.*

Fourth Wall. The invisible wall that separates the audience from the action in plays using the *box set.*

Freudian Interpretation. See *psychological/psychoanalytical criticism.*

Freytag's Triangle. A way of describing (and diagramming) the standard plot structure of *exposition, complication, crisis, falling action,* and *resolution.* This structure for a five-act play was analyzed by Gustav Freytag in his *Technik des Dramas* (1863).

Fustian. Bombastic, pretentious speech.

Genre. A form, class, or type of literary work. Drama is a genre of literature; *tragedy* and *comedy* are genres of drama.

Gloss. An explanation of a difficult word or passage, often by means of a footnote.

Hamartia. The error or frailty that leads to the destruction of a tragic hero. See *tragic flaw.*

Harlequin. A conventional *clown* or buffoon in *commedia dell'arte,* usually masked and dressed in parti-colored tights. A *harlequinade* is a play or skit in which the harlequin stars.

Hermeneutics. The science of interpretation.

Hero/Heroine. The central character of the play; also often referred to as the *protagonist.*

High Comedy/Low Comedy. Any type of highly verbal comedy in which the appeal is mainly intellectual and sophisticated, often with a basic seriousness of purpose, is high comedy (e.g., a *comedy of manners*). Low comedy, by contrast, is not intellectual and often lacks serious purpose (e.g., a *farce*).

High Style/Low Style (pp. 40–41). *High style* is a formal and elevated literary style rich in poetic devices. *Low style* is casual and conversational in tone and sometimes ungrammatical and colloquial.

Historical Criticism (pp. 66–69). Interpretive approach which sees the meaning of a literary work as embedded in its historical context. Often looks at author's biographies and historical accounts of period during which a play was written or produced in order to interpret a play's meaning. See also *New Historicism.*

History Play. See *chronicle play.*

Holograph. A manuscript written in the author's own handwriting.

Hubris. The excessive pride, arrogance, or self-confidence that results in the defeat or downfall of the hero; see *tragic flaw.*

Hyperbole. A figure of speech that achieves emphasis and heightened effect (either serious or comic) through deliberate exaggeration.

Id (p. 64–65). Freud's term for the unconscious, irrational part of ourselves which desires pleasure and avoids pain. See also *psychoanalytic criticism, ego, superego, Oedipal conflict, unconscious.*

Imagery. Most commonly refers to visual pictures produced verbally through literal or figurative language, although it is often defined more broadly to include sensory experience other than the visual.

Incongruity. A word, phrase, or idea that is out of keeping, inconsistent, or inappropriate in its context. There is considerable incongruity, for example, in Tom

Stoppard's *The Real Inspector Hound* (1968) when the inspector shows up wearing inflatable pontoon boots and a flashing miner's helmet at a scene where no crime has been discovered, reported, or presumably even perpetrated.

In Medias Res (p. 42).   Latin for a narrative that begins "in the middle of things."

Intentional Fallacy (p. 63).   According to New Critics, the mistake of confusing what is actually in a text with what an author intended to put there. The term was used by William K. Wimsatt in particular to refer to the practice of interpreting texts according to the author's express or implied intentions. The designation of this practice as a fallacy or interpretive error has been contested recently, especially by reader-response criticism. See also *New Criticism, formalism, affective fallacy.*

Interlude.   From the Latin meaning "between the play," the interlude developed in the late fifteenth and early sixteenth centuries as a type of brief stage entertainment produced between the acts of a longer play or between courses of a feast.

Intrigue.   A scheme that one character devises to entrap another, thus providing impetus for the plot.

Irony.   Refers to some contrast or discrepancy between appearance and reality. Irony takes a number of special forms: in *verbal irony* there is a contrast between what is literally said and what is actually meant; in *dramatic irony* the state of affairs known to the audience (or reader) is the reverse of what its participants suppose it to be; in *situational irony* a set of circumstances turns out to be the reverse of what is expected or appropriate.

Jacobean Drama.   Plays written and produced during the reign of James I of England, 1603–1625 ("Jacobus" is Latin for "James"). Major playwrights include William Shakespeare, Ben Jonson, the collaborators Francis Beaumont and John Fletcher, John Webster, Philip Massinger, and Thomas Middleton.

Juxtaposition.   A form of implied comparison or contrast created by placing two items side by side.

Kabuki Plays.   Popular and highly theatrical Japanese plays combining dance, musical theater, and stage spectacle. The acting is formal and stylized instead of realistic.

Leitmotif.   A word, phrase, or theme that recurs in literature.

Linguistic Competence (p. 71).   Noam Chomsky's claim that the study of language can yield principles that guide us to the right or correct way to read a literary text. See also *structuralism, deconstruction.*

Literal.   Accurate, exact, and concrete language, i.e., nonfigurative language; see *figurative language.*

Locale.   See *setting.*

Low Comedy.   See *high comedy/low comedy.*

Malapropism.   A comic misuse of words, from the Latin meaning "ill-suited to the purpose." The term derives from Mrs. Malaprop, a character in Richard Brinsley Sheridan's comedy *The Rivals* (1775), whose garbled exhortations are often quite funny. At one point, for example, she argues that an educated young lady must speak correctly and "be mistress of orthodoxy, that she might not mis-spell and mis-pronounce words so shamefully as girls usually do; and likewise that she might reprehend the true meaning of what she is saying."

Manners. The prevailing code of social conduct or behavior. See *comedy of manners*.

Masque. An elaborate form of court entertainment—a mixture of drama, music, song, and dance—developed in Renaissance Italy and transported to England during Elizabethan times. The speaking characters, who were often courtiers, wore masks. *Comus* (1634) by John Milton is probably the most important masque in English literature.

Melpomene. The Greek Muse or goddess of tragedy.

Melodrama. In its original Greek sense, a "melodrama" meant a play with music (*melos* means "song"). But by the mid-nineteenth century the term had become synonymous with a highly conventionalized type of sensationalistic play pitting stereotypic hero and villain against one another in a series of suspense-ridden, emotion-charged, and violence-filled scenes. The term *melodramatic* is used generally to describe sensational, emotional, and action-oriented writing.

Metaphor. A figure of speech in which two unlike objects are implicitly compared without the use of like or as; see also *simile*.

Metonymy. A figure of speech in which the name for an object or idea is applied to another with which it is closely associated or of which it is a part.

Minor Plot. See *subplot*.

Miracle Play. A medieval religious play concerned with the life and martyrdom of a saint.

Mixed Metaphor. Two or more metaphors combined together in such a way as to be incongruous, illogical, or even ludicrous. Example: That rat cheats on his honey with every vixen in the neighborhood.

Modern. A term applied to works written in the twentieth century. In the sense that it connotes new, the term modern often implies a break with tradition and a rejection of past ideas, values, assumptions, and techniques.

Modern Drama. A period in the history of drama that is usually said to have begun with the first performance of Henrik Ibsen's *A Doll's House* in 1879. Modern drama rejected the romanticized heroes and poetic style of prior drama and made use instead of everyday characters and ordinary prose. From an initial emphasis on *realism* and *naturalism,* modern drama quickly evolved in the more experimental direction of *expressionism.*

Monologue. An extended speech delivered by a single speaker, alone or in the presence of others. In a general sense, *asides, dramatic monologues,* and *soliloquies* are all types of monologues. When the monologue serves to reveal a character's internal thoughts and feelings, it is sometimes referred to as an *interior monologue.* A good example is Othello's speech at the beginning of Act V, Scene ii, in which he reflects on the incipient murder of Desdemona.

Mood. See *atmosphere*.

Morality Play. A form of allegorical medieval drama in which personified virtues and vices struggle for the human soul. *Everyman* (c. 1470) is the most famous morality play.

Motif. An idea, theme, character, situation, or element that recurs in literature or folklore; see *archetype, convention, stock character, stock situation.* For example, one may discuss the revenge motif in *Othello* (1604).

Motive. The cause that moves a character to act.

Multicultural Criticism (pp. 72–76). Term which loosely links a number of approaches to literature, including focuses on gender, race, social class, ethnicity, and sexual orientation.

Mystery Play. A medieval religious play based on stories from the Old and New

Testament to which the author often added comic scenes of his own. Also referred to as Corpus Christi plays because they were frequently performed on Corpus Christi day (the first Thursday after Trinity Sunday). The plays eventually came to be sponsored by the various trade guilds and were staged on movable wagons which could be drawn to various locations in large towns such as York, Chester, Coventry, and Wakefield. Cycles of forty or more mystery plays covered the complete Biblical history from the creation through the resurrection. The *Second Shepherds' Play* (c. 1400) is one of the best of the mystery plays.

Myth. Broadly, any idea or belief to which a number of people subscribe.

Myth Criticism (pp. 69–70). Approach to literature which tries to explain why symbols and patterns of imagery create universal responses in readers. See also *archetype, anthropological criticism.*

Narrative. A series of unified events; see *plot* and *action.*

Narrative Sequence. The order in which events are recounted.

Naturalism. A post-Darwinian movement of the late nineteenth century that tried to apply the "laws" of scientific determinism to fiction and drama. Naturalists believed that art should reflect a deterministic universe in which man is a biological creature controlled by his environment and heredity.

Neoclassical Drama. Plays written and produced between 1660, the year that Charles II regained the English throne, and 1798, the year that Wordsworth and Coleridge published *Lyrical Ballads* that announced the arrival of Romanticism. Playwrights in this period often sought formal perfection by writing in rhymed couplets and abiding by the *three unities.*

New Comedy. A type of comedy of manners, featuring stock characters and conventional plots, which in the fourth and third centuries B.C. replaced the Old Comedy of Aristophanes. See *Old Comedy.*

New Criticism. The term New Criticism refers to a type or "school" of criticism that seeks to analyze and study a literary work as autonomous, without reference to the author's intention, the impact or effect on the reader, the historical or cultural period in which the work was written (see *historical criticism*), or the validity of the ideas that may be extrapolated from it. Its method is based on the close reading and analysis of the verbal elements of the text, although its leading exponents and practitioners (academic critics such as John Crowe Ransom, I. A. Richards, Cleanth Brooks, Robert Penn Warren, Allen Tate, R. P. Blackmur, Yvor Winters, and Kenneth Burke) often disagree on just how this analysis is to be undertaken. The term originates from the title of John Crowe Ransom's book *The New Criticism* (1941) and is "new" in the sense that it constituted a deliberate break with the older subjective and impressionistic theories of art that allowed extrinsic rather than solely intrinsic considerations to influence the evaluation of art.

New Historicism (pp. 67–69). Recent development in literary criticism which claims that the meaning of a literary work is deeply embedded in history. Does not maintain strict boundaries between history and literature. Sees history as never objective or neutral but always a selective account of human experience. Explores the complicated relationships between the perspectives of the writer, critic, and reader. See also *historical criticism.*

Noh Plays. A formal and lofty form of Japanese drama written between 1300 and 1600.

Nom de Plume. French meaning "pen name."

Obligatory Scene (p. 43). A scene whose circumstances are so fully anticipated by the audience as the plot develops that the playwright is "obliged" to provide it.

Oedipus Conflict (p. 65). Fifth stage in Sigmund Freud's scheme of psychosexual development. Encountered by both boys and girls, during which sexual desire for the parent of the opposite sex leads to desire to kill the same-sex parent, thus placing the child in conflict with taboos against incest and patricide or matricide. See also *psychoanalytic criticism, ego, id, superego, unconscious.*

Old Comedy (p. 56). Greek comedies of the fifth century B.C. (represented by Aristophanes), which combined religious ceremony with satire and farce. See *New Comedy.*

Opéra Bouffe. A French term for a light comic opera.

Operetta. A comic opera or musical comedy.

Organization. The overall plan or design which shapes the work.

Pantomime. Silent acting: a form of drama that is acted without speech by means of facial expressions, gestures, and bodily movement.

Paradox. A self-contradictory and absurd statement that turns out to be, in some sense at least, actually true and valid.

Paraphrase. A restatement, using different words, of the essential idea or argument of a piece or passage of writing.

Parody. See *burlesque.*

Passion Play. A play dealing with events in the life of Christ prior to the resurrection. See *Mystery play.*

Pathos. The quality in a literary work that evokes a feeling of pity, tenderness, and sympathy from the reader or audience. Overdone or misused pathos becomes mere sentimentality. There is considerable pathos, for example, in the undeserving death of Desdemona in Shakespeare's *Othello* (1604).

Peripeteia. The unexpected reversal of fortune or circumstances, as for example when the messenger expects to cheer Oedipus by revealing that Polybus and Merope were not really his parents but actually convinces Oedipus that he has murdered his father and married his mother.

Personification. A figure of speech in which an idea or thing is given human attributes or feelings or is spoken of as if it were human and alive.

Pièce Bien Faite. See *well-made play.*

Plot (pp. 41–46). The patterned arrangement of the events in a narrative or play. See also *exposition, complication, crisis, falling action, anticlimax,* and *resolution.*

Poetic Justice. The expectation that by the end of a literary work the wicked will be punished and the virtuous rewarded.

Poetic License. Used to describe (and justify) literary experimentation: a writer's deliberate departure from the conventions of form and language—and at times even the departure from logic and fact.

Point of Attack. The point in the play at which the main action of the plot begins.

Polemic. A work vigorously setting forth the author's point of view, usually on a controversial subject.

Post-Modern. A term used to describe contemporary writing (roughly since 1965) that is experimental in nature.

Poststructuralism (pp. 70–72). Initiated by deconstruction but including many other recent approaches to literature, poststructuralism may be best understood as a broad-based critique of structuralism and its claim that by systematically studying language, scholars could uncover fixed laws for the way humans make meaning through signs. Influenced by political approaches to literature, poststructuralists deny that texts reflect finite, stable meanings. See also *deconstruction, structuralism*.

Practical Criticism.   See *theoretical criticism and practical criticism*.

Preface.   The author's or editor's introduction, in which the writer states his or her purposes and assumptions and makes any acknowledgments.

Primary and Secondary Sources.   Primary sources are the original documents; secondary sources are those that comment on or analyze those original documents.

Private Theaters.   The smaller indoor theaters of the English Renaissance—for example, Blackfriars, The Inns of Court, or the Court. Private theaters attracted a higher class of audience than the *public theaters* and presented *masques* and performances by troupes of child actors as well as more typical Renaissance plays.

Problem Play.   A play that explores a controversial social issue of its day. *Ghosts* (1881), by Henrik Ibsen, is a good example since it explores the implications of wide-spread syphilis in the sexually hypocritical Victorian age. See also *thesis play*.

Prologue.   A prefatory statement or speech beginning a play, preparing the audience for what is to follow; see *epilogue* and *preface*.

Prompt Book.   A copy of a play containing stage directions and other details needed to stage the work.

Proscenium (p. 21).   In modern stagecraft the proscenium is the forward part of the stage between the curtain and orchestra. The arch from which the curtain hangs is the proscenium arch. The area in front of the proscenium is sometimes also referred to as the *apron*.

Protagonist (p. 46).   The chief character of literary work. Also commonly referred to as the hero or heroine; see *antagonist*.

Psychological/Psychoanalytical Criticism.   The use of a psychological or psycho-analytic theory to interpret a writer's work or to understand the personality of the writer. Interpretations based on the theories of Sigmund Freud (1856–1939) are called Freudian and tend to focus on subconscious conflicts—particularly those involving Freud's hypothesis that children develop through oral, anal, Oedipal, and phallic stages. Freud's interpretation of the Oedipal conflict in *The Interpretation of Dreams* (1900) is particularly famous. The psychoanalytic theories of Freud's disciple Carl Jung (1875–1961) are also popular among critics. Jung postulated that human beings share a "collective unconscious" of common *myths* and *archetypes*. See also *id, ego, superego, Oedipus conflict, unconscious*.

Public Theaters (pp. 25–28).   The large, open-air theaters of the English Renaissance such as the Fortune and the Globe. See *private theaters*.

Pun.   A play on words, involving words with similar or identical sounds but with different meanings.

Purpose.   The author's basic reason for writing; the goal or object which the author sets out to achieve.

Raisonneur.   (French for "reasoner.") A character in a play, usually someone who is detached from the main action and is not a central figure, who personifies reason and objectivity. Like the confidant or the chorus, the raisonneur often serves to express the questions in the audience's mind and to deliver the judgments of the author. In Molière's *Tartuffe* (1667), Cléante serves as a raisonneur.

Reader-Response Criticism.   Approach to literature which analyzes the meaning readers make of texts. Rather than seeing the reader as the passive recipient of the text, reader-response criticism emphasizes the reader's construction of textual meaning. Stanley Fish, who founded this critical method in the early 1970's, claimed critics should not view a literary text as an object (what the text is), but as a process (what the text does).

Reader's Theater. A form of theater where the players read from a script.

Realism. The nineteenth-century literary movement that reacted to romanticism by insisting on a faithful, objective presentation of the details of everyday life.

Recognition Scene (p. 186). The moment in a dramatic work in which one of the characters makes an important (and often decisive) discovery that determines his or her subsequent course of action.

Rejoinder. A reply to a reply; a comeback.

Repartee. A witty or ingenious reply. Here, for example, is a brief bit of repartee (involving both a *riposte* and a *rejoinder*) between the playwright Ben Jonson (1572–1637) and one John Sylvester, who challenged him to match his impromptu rhymes. Sylvester began,

> I, John Sylvester,
> Lay with your sister.

To this, Jonson promptly replied,

> And I, Ben Jonson,
> Slept with your wife.

When Sylvester objected that Jonson's endwords did not rhyme, Jonson replied, "Ah yes, but they are true!"

Renaissance. The period in England beginning about 1500 (with the end of the middle ages) and ending with the establishment of the Commonwealth by Oliver Cromwell in 1649. The Renaissance in England, which took much of its direction from the Renaissance that swept Italy a century before, was characterized by a new interest in humanistic learning, which flowered in the plays of Marlowe, Shakespeare, and Jonson.

Resolution (pp. 44–45). The final section of the plot in which the major conflict, issue, or problem is resolved; also referred to as the *conclusion* or *denouement.*

Restoration Drama. Plays written or produced during the period in English literature that begins with the restoration of the monarchy under Charles II and the end of the Commonwealth in 1660 and ends about 1700. Theaters closed under Cromwell and the Puritans reopened. Major dramatists include John Dryden, William Congreve, and William Wycherley.

Revenge Tragedy. A type of tragedy (popularized in Elizabethan England by Thomas Kyd's *The Spanish Tragedy,* 1592) that turns on the motive or revenge, revels in violence, horror, and other forms of sensationalism, and typically has a bloody ending. Shakespeare's *Hamlet* (1604) is probably the most famous example of a revenge tragedy.

Reversal. The protagonist's change of fortune.

Review. A critical appraisal of a play, book, or film, or performance published in a periodical.

Revue. A loose series of musical skits and songs, often satirizing contemporary events.

Rhetorical Question. A question to which no response or reply is expected, because only one answer is possible.

Riposte. A rapid, biting reply. See *repartee.*

Rising Action. See *complication.*

Romantic Comedy. A type of comedy which turns on the adventures and misadventures of lovers and ends happily.

Sarcasm. A type of verbal irony delivered in a derisive, caustic, and bitter manner to belittle or ridicule the subject.

Satire. A type of writing that holds up persons, ideas, or things to varying degrees of amusement, ridicule, or contempt in order, presumably, to improve, correct, or bring about some desirable change.

Satyr Play. An ancient Greek play of comic relief that followed an author's trilogy of tragedies. Euripides' *Cyclops* is the only complete example of a satyr play.

Scenario. The brief outline of the plot of a dramatic work, providing the key details of scenes, situations, and characters.

Scene (p. 9). A self-contained segment of a dramatic work; also used as a synonym for setting; see *act*.

Semiotics (p. 70). An attempt to make the study of language scientific. Associated with the theories of Ferdinand de Saussure. See also *structuralism, signifier, signified, sign*.

Sentimentality. The presence of emotion or feeling that seems excessive or unjustified in terms of the circumstances; see *pathos*.

Setting. The time and place in which the action of the play occurs; physical setting alone is often referred to as the locale.

Sign (p. 70). In semiotics, the sign is the unit of language composed of both the signifier (the unit of language such as a word) and the signified (what the unit of language stands for). Like words, signs are arbitrary and not meaningful in themselves; they acquire meaning only through their relation to other signs and to the system of signs we call language. See also *semiotics, structuralism*.

Signified (p. 70). In semiotics, what the sign refers to. See also *signifier, semiotics, structuralism, sign*.

Signifier (p. 70). In semiotics, the unit of language itself, such as a word, as distinguished from what it refers to. See also *sign, signified, semiotics, structuralism*.

Simile. A figure of speech in which two essentially dissimilar objects are expressly compared with one another by the use of like or as; see *metaphor*.

Situation. Either the basic set of circumstances in which a group of characters find themselves at some point during the plot; or the set of circumstances in effect at the beginning of the plot before the action begins.

Situational Irony. See *irony*.

Slapstick. Low comedy characterized by physical action, horseplay, and practical jokes.

Soliloquy. A dramatic convention in which a character, alone on stage (*solus*), speaks aloud and thus shares his or her thoughts with the audience. See *aside* and *monologue*. Iago's soliloquy at the end of Act I, Scene iii, in *Othello* (1604) is a good example.

Static Character. See *dynamic and static characters*.

Stock Character. Characters who appear so frequently in literature that they are easily recognizable as types: e.g., the rich uncle, the female confidante, the wise if loquacious counsellor.

Stock Situation. A situation or incident that occurs so frequently in literature as to become at once familiar: e.g., the family feud, the missing heir, the love triangle, the case of mistaken identity.

Strong Curtain. A powerful ("strong") conclusion to an act of a play. Henrik Ibsen's *Hedda Gabler* (1890) provides several examples of strong curtain lines.

Structuralism (p. 70). Theoretical system which focuses on the structure of language rather than on the stories language conveys. Seemed to promise that by making the study of language scientific, scholars could uncover fixed laws for the way humans make meaning through signs. See also *deconstruction, semiotics, sign, signified, signifier, linguistic competence, poststructuralism.*

Structure. The overall pattern, design, or organization of a literary work.

Style. The author's characteristic manner of expression; style includes the author's diction, syntax, sentence patterns, punctuation, and spelling, as well as the use made of such devices as sound, rhythm, imagery, and figurative language.

Subplot. The subplot (also called the *minor plot, underplot,* or *counterplot*) is a secondary action or complication within a dramatic work that often serves to reinforce or contrast the main plot.

Superego (p.65). Freud's term for that part of the psyche which mediates between the id and the ego. Superego seems to stand outside the ego, helping us make moral judgments even when such run counter to our own interests. Represents the composite voice of moral authority acquired through culture. See also *psychoanalytic criticism, id, ego, Oedipal conflict, unconscious.*

Suspense. The psychological tension or anxiety resulting from the reader's or audience's uncertainty of just how a situation or conflict is likely to end.

Swashbuckler. A type of literary work containing gallant heroes, beautiful maidens, and plenty of sword fights.

Symbol. Literally, something that stands for something else. In literature, any word, object, action, or character that embodies and evokes a range of additional meaning and significance. See also *allegory.*

Synopsis. A summary or resume of a piece or writing.

Textual Criticism. The kind of scholarship that attempts to establish through reconstruction the "correct" and authoritative text of a literary work as its author originally wrote it. The standard introduction to the theory and practice of textual criticism is James Thorpe's *Principles of Textual Criticism* (1972).

Thalia. The Greek Muse or goddess of comedy.

Theater in the Round. Plays presented on a stage which is surrounded by the audience. See *arena stage/arena theatre.*

Theme. The controlling idea or meaning of a work of art.

Theoretical Criticism and Practical Criticism. Theoretical criticism is concerned with identifying and establishing the general, underlying principles of art; practical criticism (or applied criticism) concerns itself with the study and analysis of specific individual works.

Thesis. The assertion or proposition that unifies and controls the entire work.

Thesis Play. A play that deals with a specific problem and advocates a "thesis" in the form of a solution; also called a *problem play.*

Three Unities. Three rules or absolutes of sixteenth and seventeenth century Italian and French drama, broadly adapted from Aristotle's *Poetics:* The Unity of Time, which limits a play to a single day; the Unity of Place, which limits a play's setting to a single location; and the Unity of Action, which limits a play to a single story line.

Tone. The author's attitude toward the subject or audience.

Tour de Force. A feat of skill and ingenuity.

Tragedy (pp. 53–55; 184–189). Broadly, any serious dramatic work in which the protagonist suffers a major reversal of fortune, often leading to his or her downfall, destruction, and/or death; see *classical tragedy, domestic tragedy, revenge tragedy, tragicomedy.*

Tragicomedy. A type of drama (most often associated with Elizabeth and Jacobean drama) that mixes the conventions of tragedy and comedy and in which the protagonist, although subject to a series of crises (often including the threat of death), manages to escape to celebrate a happy (and frequently highly contrived) ending. Shakespeare's *Cymbeline* (ca. 1608) and John Dryden's *Love Triumphant* (1693) are examples of the genre.

Tragic Flaw (p. 54). The principal defect in character or judgment that leads to the downfall of the tragic hero. In Greek tragedy this flaw is often *hubris,* the hero's excessive pride or self-confidence. The hubris of Oedipus, for example, leads him to ignore well-intentioned warnings by Tiresias, Creon, Jocasta, and the Herdsman in his effort to discover the murderer of King Laius.

Tragic Hero (pp. 54–55). The name sometimes given to the protagonist or a tragedy, if he or she has the qualities of greatness. Thus Oedipus is both a protagonist and a tragic hero, while Willy Loman in Arthur Miller's *Death of a Salesman* (1949) is only the former.

Travesty. A work that is made humorous by a ridiculous treatment of a serious subject.

Type Character. See *stock character.*

Unconscious (p. 65). Part of the mind not accessible to conscious thought. Desires which are taboo or forbidden by the ego and superego are repressed into the unconscious, where they exert powerful influence over human actions. See also *psychoanalytic criticism, id, ego, superego, Oedipal conflict.*

Understatement. A figure of speech in which what is literally said falls considerably short of the seriousness of what is being discussed.

Unfolding Plot (p. 46). A tightly knit plot in which the action unfolds or develops over a short period of time, often a single day. See *episodic plot.*

Unity. The quality of a work of art in which every element or part clearly and effectively relates to the accomplishment of a complete and independent whole. Unity in a literary work requires the presence of some central organizing principle to which all the parts are necessarily related, making the work an organic whole. See also *three unities.*

Upstage (p. 26). *Upstage* is a stage direction that refers to the back half of the stage; *downstage* refers to the front half of the stage, the part nearest to the audience. Thus, in theater jargon, an actor who moves farther back on the stage during dialogue is *upstaging* the other actors by forcing them to face away from the audience while speaking. The term *upstaging* now refers to any showy or theatrical behavior that denies due attention to the other actors.

Variorum Edition. An edition of a work that contains all the possible variant readings of the text together with notes and commentary.

Vaudeville. A lively variety show of song, dance, and comedy. Nowadays *vaudeville* is usually associated with the variety shows that toured America during the early decades of the twentieth century.

Verbal Irony. See *irony.*

Verisimilitude. The quality of being lifelike or true to actuality.

Victorian Period. The literary period coinciding with the long reign of England's Queen Victoria, 1837–1901. Although not a major period in the history of drama, important *fin de siècle* playwrights include Oscar Wilde, William Butler Yeats, George Bernard Shaw, Arthur Pinero, and Lady Gregory.

Well-Made Play (*Pièce Bien Faite*) (p. 46). A type of play, written according to formula, characterized by a tightly structured, suspenseful plot that turns on a secret; quickly rising action; and a series of reversals, inevitably leading to a climactic scene that reveals the secret and allows the hero to triumph.

⊠ ⊠ ⊠ ⊠ ⊠ ⊠ ⊠ ⊠

Acknowledgments

AESCHYLUS. *Agamemnon* from *Aeschylus: The Oresteia,* translated by Douglas Young. Copyright © 1974 by the University of Oklahoma Press. Reprinted by permission of the University of Oklahoma Press.

ARISTOPHANES. *Lysistrata* from *Lysistrata* by Aristophanes, translated by Douglass Parker. Translation copyright © 1964 by William Arrowsmith. Used by permission of New American Library, a division of Penguin Books USA Inc.

SAMUEL BECKETT. *All That Fall* from *Krapp's Last Tape and Other Dramatic Pieces* by Samuel Beckett. Reprinted by permission of Grove Press, Inc. Copyright © 1958 by Grove Press, Inc.

ANTON CHEKHOV. *The Cherry Orchard* from *Anton Chekhov: Four Plays*, translated by David Magarshack. Copyright © 1969 by David Magarshack. Reprinted by permission of Hill & Wang, a division of Farrar, Straus & Giroux, Inc.

ALICE CHILDRESS. *Wine in the Wilderness* by Alice Childress. Copyright © 1969 by Alice Childress. The reprinting of *Wine in the Wilderness* included in this volume is reprinted by permission of the author and Dramatists Play Service, Inc. The amateur performance rights in this play are controlled exclusively by Dramatists Play Service, Inc., 440 Park Avenue South, New York, NY 10016. No amateur performance of the play may be given without obtaining in advance the written permission of Dramatists Play Service, Inc., and paying the requisite fee. Inquiries regarding all other rights should be addressed to the author's agent, Flora Roberts Agency, 157 West 57th Street, New York, NY 10019.

EURIPIDES. *Hippolytus*, translated by David Greene, from *The Complete Greek Tragedies III*. Copyright © 1942, 1955 by The University of Chicago. Reprinted by permission of the publisher, The University of Chicago Press.

SUSAN GLASPELL. *Trifles.* Reprinted by permission of Dodd, Mead & Company, Inc. from *Plays* by Susan Glaspell. Copyright 1920 by Dodd, Mead & Company, Inc. Copyright renewed 1948 by Susan Glaspell.

LORRAINE HANSBERRY. *A Raisin in the Sun* from *A Raisin in the Sun* by Lorraine Hansberry. Copyright © 1958 by Robert Nemiroff, as an unpublished work. Copyright © 1959, 1966, 1984 by Robert Nemiroff. Reprinted by permission of Random House, Inc.

BETH HENLEY. *Am I Blue?* Copyright 1982 by Beth Henley. CAUTION: Professionals and amateurs are hereby warned that *Am I Blue?* is subject to